Collins
Spanish
Dictionary

HarperCollins Publishers
Westerhill Road
Bishopbriggs
Glasgow
G64 2QT
Great Britain

First edition 2007

Reprint 10 9 8 7 6 5 4 3 2 1 0

© HarperCollins Publishers 2007

ISBN 978-0-00-779339-6

Collins® is a registered trademark of
HarperCollins Publishers Limited

www.collins.co.uk

A catalogue record for this book is
available from the British Library

Designed by Mark Thomson

Typeset by Thomas Callan

Printed in Great Britain by
Clays Ltd, St Ives plc

Acknowledgements
We would like to thank those authors and
publishers who kindly gave permission for
copyright material to be used in the Collins
Word Web. We would also like to thank
Times Newspapers Ltd for providing
valuable data.

ÍNDICE

CONTENTS

William Collins' dream of knowledge for all began with the publication of his first book in 1819. A self-educated mill worker, he not only enriched millions of lives, but also founded a flourishing publishing house. Today, staying true to this spirit, Collins books are packed with inspiration, innovation, and practical expertise. They place you at the centre of a world of possibility and give you exactly what you need to explore it.

Language is the key to this exploration, and at the heart of Collins Dictionaries is language as it is really used. New words, phrases, and meanings spring up every day, and all of them are captured and analysed by the Collins Word Web. Constantly updated, and with over 2.5 billion entries, this living language resource is unique to our dictionaries.

Words are tools for life. And a Collins Dictionary makes them work for you.

Collins. Do more

INTRODUCCIÓN

Estamos muy satisfechos de que hayas decidido comprar este diccionario y esperamos que lo disfrutes y que te sirva de gran ayuda ya sea en el colegio, en el trabajo, en tus vacaciones o en casa.

INTRODUCTION

We are delighted that you have decided to buy this Spanish dictionary and hope you will enjoy and benefit from using it at school, at home, on holiday or at work.

ABREVIATURAS

ABBREVIATIONS

abreviatura	*ab(b)r*	abbreviation
adjetivo, locución adjetiva	*adj*	adjective, adjectival phrase
administración	*Admin*	administration
adverbio, locución adverbial	*adv*	adverb, adverbial phrase
agricultura	*Agr*	agriculture
anatomía	*Anat*	anatomy
Argentina	*Arg*	Argentina
arquitectura	*Arq, Arch*	architecture
el automóvil	*Aut(o)*	the motor car and motoring
aviación, viajes aéreos	*Aviac, Aviat*	flying, air travel
biología	*Bio(l)*	biology
botánica, flores	*Bot*	botany
inglés británico	BRIT	British English
Centroamérica	CAM	Central America
química	*Chem*	chemistry
comercio, finanzas, banca	*Com(m)*	commerce, finance, banking
informática	*Comput*	computing
conjunción	*conj*	conjunction
construcción	*Constr*	building
compuesto	*cpd*	compound element
Cono Sur	CS	Southern Cone
cocina	*Culin*	cookery
economía	*Econ*	economics
eletricidad, electrónica	*Elec*	electricity, electronics
enseñanza, sistema escolar y universitario	*Escol*	schooling, schools and universities
España	ESP	Spain
especialmente	*esp*	especially
exclamación, interjección	*excl*	exclamation, interjection
femenino	*f*	feminine
lengua familiar (! vulgar)	*fam(!)*	colloquial usage (! particularly offensive)
ferrocarril	*Ferro*	railways
uso figurado	*fig*	figurative use
fotografía	*Foto*	photography
(verbo inglés) del cual la partícula es inseparable	*fus*	(phrasal verb) where the particle is inseparable
generalmente	*gen*	generally
geografía, geología	*Geo*	geography, geology
geometría	*Geom*	geometry
historia	*Hist*	history
uso familiar (! vulgar)	*inf(!)*	colloquial usage (! particularly offensive)
infinitivo	*infin*	infinitive
informática	*Inform*	computing
invariable	*inv*	invariable
irregular	*irreg*	irregular
lo jurídico	*Jur*	law
América Latina	LAM	Latin America
gramática, lingüística	*Ling*	grammar, linguistics

ABREVIATURAS

ABBREVIATIONS

masculino	*m*	masculine
matemáticas	*Mat(h)*	mathematics
masculino/femenino	*m/f*	masculine/feminine
medicina	*Med*	medicine
México	MÉX, MEX	Mexico
lo militar, ejército	*Mil*	military matters
música	*Mús, Mus*	music
substantivo, nombre	*n*	noun
navegación, náutica	*Náut, Naut*	sailing, navigation
sustantivo numérico	*num*	numeral noun
complemento	*obj*	(grammatical) object
	o.s.	oneself
peyorativo	*pey, pej*	derogatory, pejorative
fotografía	*Phot*	photography
fisiología	*Physiol*	physiology
plural	*pl*	plural
política	*Pol*	politics
participio de pasado	*pp*	past participle
preposición	*prep*	preposition
pronombre	*pron*	pronoun
psicología, psiquiatría	*Psico, Psych*	psychology, psychiatry
tiempo pasado	*pt*	past tense
química	*Quím*	chemistry
ferrocarril	*Rail*	railways
religión	*Rel*	religion
Río de la Plata	RPL	River Plate
	sb	somebody
Cono Sur	SC	Southern Cone
enseñanza, sistema escolar y universitario	*Scol*	schooling, schools and universities
singular	*sg*	singular
España	SP	Spain
	sth	something
sujeto	*su(b)j*	(grammatical) subject
subjuntivo	*subjun*	subjunctive
tauromaquia	*Taur*	bullfighting
también	*tb*	also
técnica, tecnología	*Tec(h)*	technical term, technology
telecomunicaciones	*Telec, Tel*	telecommunications
imprenta, tipografía	*Tip, Typ*	typography, printing
televisión	*TV*	television
universidad	*Univ*	university
inglés norteamericano	US	American English
verbo	*vb*	verb
verbo intransitivo	*vi*	intransitive verb
verbo pronominal	*vr*	reflexive verb
verbo transitivo	*vt*	transitive verb
zoología	*Zool*	zoology
marca registrada	®	registered trademark
indica un equivalente cultural	≈	introduces a cultural equivalent

SPANISH PRONUNCIATION

VOWELS

a	[a]	pata	not as long as *a* in far. When followed by a consonant in the same syllable (i.e. in a closed syllable), as in *a*mante, the *a* is short, as in b*a*t
e	[e]	me	like *e* in th*e*y. In a closed syllable, as in g*e*nte, the *e* is short as in p*e*t
i	[i]	pino	as in m*ea*n or mach*i*ne
o	[o]	lo	as in l*o*cal. In a closed syllable, as in c*o*ntrol, the *o* is short as in c*o*t
u	[u]	lunes	as in r*u*le. It is silent after q, and in *gue, gui*, unless marked *güe, güi* e.g. antig*üe*dad, when it is pronounced like *w* in *w*olf

SEMIVOWELS

i, y	[j]	bien hielo yunta	pronounced like *y* in *y*es
u	[w]	huevo fuento antigüedad	unstressed *u* between consonant and vowel is pronounced like *w* in *w*ell. See notes on *u* above.

DIPHTHONGS

ai, ay	[ai]	baile	as *i* in r*i*de
au	[au]	auto	as *ou* in sh*ou*t
ei, ey	[ei]	buey	as *ey* in gr*ey*
eu	[eu]	deuda	both elements pronounced independently [e] + [u]
oi, oy	[oi]	hoy	as *oy* in t*oy*

CONSONANTS

b	[b,β]	boda bomba labor	see notes on *v* below
c	[k]	caja	*c* before *a, o, u* is pronounced as in *c*at
ce, ci	[θe,θi]	cero cielo	*c* before *e* or *i* is pronounced as in *th*in
ch	[tʃ]	chiste	*ch* is pronounced as *ch* in *ch*air
d	[d,ð]	danés ciudad	at the beginning of a phrase or after *l* or *n*, *d* is pronounced as in English. In any other position it is pronounced like *th* in *th*e

g	[g, ɣ]	**g**afas	*g* before *a*, *o* or *u* is pronounced as in
		pa**g**a	*g*ap, if at the beginning of a phrase or after *n*. In other positions the sound is softened
ge, gi	[xe, xi]	**g**ente	*g* before *e* or *i* is pronounced similar
		girar	to *ch* in Scottish lo*ch*
h		**h**aber	*h* is always silent in Spanish
j	[x]	**j**ugar	*j* is pronounced similar to *ch* in Scottish lo*ch*
ll	[ʎ]	ta**ll**e	*ll* is pronounced like the *y* in *y*et or the *lli* in mi*lli*on
ñ	[ʃ]	ni**ñ**o	*ñ* is pronounced like the *ni* in o*ni*on
q	[k]	**q**ue	*q* is pronounced as *k* in king
r, rr	[r, rr]	qui**t**ar	*r* is always pronounced in Spanish,
		ga**rr**a	unlike the silent *r* in dancer. *rr* is trilled, like a Scottish *r*
s	[s]	quizá**s**	*s* is usually pronounced as in pa**s**s,
		i**s**la	but before *b*, *d*, *g*, *l*, *m* or *n* it is pronounced as in ro**s**e
v	[b, β]	**v**ía	*v* is pronounced something like *b*. At the beginning of a phrase or after *m* or *n* it is pronounced as *b* in *b*oy. In any other position the sound is softened
z	[θ]	tena**z**	*z* is pronounced as *th* in *th*in

f, k, l, m, n, p, t and x are pronounced as in English.

STRESS
The rules of stress in Spanish are as follows:

(a)   when a word ends in a vowel or in *n* or *s*, the second last syllable is stressed:
pat*a*ta, pat*a*tas; c*o*me, c*o*men
(b)   when a word ends in a consonant other than *n* or *s*, the stress falls on the last syllable:
par*ed*, hab*lar*
(c)   when the rules set out in (a) and (b) are not applied, an acute accent appears over the stressed vowel:
com*ún*, geograf*ía*, ingl*és*

In the phonetic transcription, the symbol [¹] precedes the syllable on which the stress falls.

LA PRONUNCIACIÓN INGLESA

VOCALES

	Ejemplo inglés	Explicación
[ɑː]	father	Entre a de padre y o de noche
[ʌ]	but, come	a muy breve
[æ]	man, cat	Con los labios en la posición de e en pena y luego se pronuncia el sonido a parecido a la a de carro
[ə]	father, ago	Vocal neutra parecida a una e u o casi muda
[əː]	bird, heard	Entre e abierta y o cerrada, sonido alargado
[ɛ]	get, bed	Como en perro
[ɪ]	it, big	Más breve que en si
[iː]	tea, see	Como en fino
[ɔ]	hot, wash	Como en torre
[ɔː]	saw, all	Como en por
[u]	put, book	Sonido breve, más cerrado que burro
[uː]	too, you	Sonido largo, como en uno

DIPTONGOS

	Ejemplo inglés	Explicación
[aɪ]	fly, high	Como en fraile
[au]	how, house	Como en pausa
[ɛə]	there, bear	Casi como en vea, pero el sonido a se mezcla con el indistinto [ə]
[eɪ]	day, obey	e cerrada seguida por una i débil
[ɪə]	here, hear	Como en manía, mezclándose el sonido a con el indistinto [ə]
[əu]	go, note	[ə] seguido por una breve u
[əɪ]	boy, oil	Como en voy
[uə]	poor, sure	u bastante larga más el sonido indistinto [ə]

CONSONANTES

	Ejemplo inglés	Explicación
[b]	**b**ig, lo**bb**y	Como en tum**b**an
[d]	men**d**ed	Como en con**d**e, an**d**ar
[g]	**g**o, **g**et, bi**g**	Como en **g**rande, **g**ol
[dʒ]	**g**in, ju**dg**e	Como en la **ll** andaluza y en Generalitat (*catalán*)
[ŋ]	si**ng**	Como en ví**n**culo
[h]	**h**ouse, **h**e	Como la jota hispanoamericana
[j]	**y**oung, **y**es	Como en **y**a
[k]	**c**ome, mo**ck**	Como en **c**aña, Es**c**ocia
[r]	**r**ed, t**r**ead	Se pronuncia con la punta de la lengua hacia atrás y sin hacerla vibrar
[s]	**s**and, ye**s**	Como en ca**s**a, **s**esión
[z]	ro**s**e, **z**ebra	Como en de**s**de, mi**s**mo
[ʃ]	**sh**e, ma**ch**ine	Como en **ch**ambre (*francés*), ro**x**o (*portugués*)
[tʃ]	**ch**in, ri**ch**	Como en **ch**ocolate
[v]	**v**alley	Como *f*, pero se retiran los dientes superiores vibrándolos contra el labio inferior
[w]	**w**ater, **wh**ich	Como la *u* de h**u**evo, p**u**ede
[ʒ]	vi**s**ion	Como en journal (*francés*)
[θ]	**th**ink, my**th**	Como en re**c**eta, **z**apato
[ð]	**th**is, **th**e	Como en habla**d**o, verda**d**

f, l, m, n, p, t y x iguales que en español.

El signo [*] indica que la r final escrita apenas se pronuncia en inglés británico cuando la palabra siguiente empieza con vocal. El signo ['] indica la sílaba acentuada.

SPANISH VERB TABLES

1 Gerund 2 Imperative 3 Present 4 Preterite 5 Future 6 Present
subjunctive 7 Imperfect subjunctive 8 Past participle 9 Imperfect

Etc indicates that the irregular root is used for all persons of the tense,
e.g. **oír**: 6 oiga, oigas, oigamos, oigáis, oigan

agradecer 3 agradezco **6** agradezca
etc

aprobar 2 aprueba **3** apruebo,
apruebas, aprueba, aprueban
6 apruebe, apruebes, apruebe,
aprueben

atravesar 2 atraviesa **3** atravieso,
atraviesas, atraviesa, atraviesan
6 atraviese, atravieses,
atraviese, atraviesen

caber 3 quepo **4** cupe, cupiste,
cupo, cupimos, cupisteis,
cupieron **5** cabré *etc* **6** quepa *etc*
7 cupiera *etc*

caer 1 cayendo **3** caigo **4** cayó,
cayeron **6** caiga *etc* **7** cayera *etc*

cerrar 2 cierra **3** cierro, cierras,
cierra, cierran **6** cierre, cierres,
cierre, cierren

COMER 1 comiendo **2** come,
comed **3** como, comes, come,
comemos, coméis, comen
4 comí, comiste, comió,
comimos, comisteis, comieron
5 comeré, comerás, comerá,
comeremos, comeréis,
comerán **6** coma, comas, coma,
comamos, comáis, coman
7 comiera, comieras, comiera,
comiéramos, comierais,
comieran **8** comido **9** comía,
comías, comía, comíamos,
comíais, comían

conocer 3 conozco **6** conozca *etc*

contar 2 cuenta **3** cuento,
cuentas, cuenta, cuentan

6 cuente, cuentes, cuente,
cuenten

dar 3 doy **4** di, diste, dio, dimos,
disteis, dieron **7** diera *etc*

decir 2 di **3** digo **4** dije, dijiste,
dijo, dijimos, dijisteis, dijeron
5 diré *etc* **6** diga *etc* **7** dijera *etc*
8 dicho

despertar 2 despierta
3 despierto, despiertas,
despierta, despiertan
6 despierte, despiertes,
despierte, despierten

divertir 1 divirtiendo **2** divierte
3 divierto, diviertes, divierte,
divierten **4** divirtió, divirtieron
6 divierta, diviertas, divierta,
divirtamos, divirtáis, diviertan
7 divirtiera *etc*

dormir 1 durmiendo **2** duerme
3 duermo, duermes, duerme,
duermen **4** durmió, durmieron
6 duerma, duermas, duerma,
durmamos, durmáis, duerman
7 durmiera *etc*

empezar 2 empieza **3** empiezo,
empiezas, empieza, empiezan
4 empecé **6** empiece, empieces,
empiece, empecemos,
empecéis, empiecen

entender 2 entiende **3** entiendo,
entiendes, entiende, entienden
6 entienda, entiendas,
entienda, entiendan

ESTAR 2 está **3** estoy, estás, está,
están **4** estuve, estuviste,

estuvo, estuvimos, estuvisteis, estuvieron 6 esté, estés, esté, estén 7 estuviera *etc*

HABER 3 he, has, ha, hemos, han 4 hube, hubiste, hubo, hubimos, hubisteis, hubieron 5 habré *etc* 6 haya *etc* 7 hubiera *etc*

HABLAR 1 hablando 2 habla, hablad 3 hablo, hablas, habla, hablamos, habláis, hablan 4 hablé, hablaste, habló, hablamos, hablasteis, hablaron 5 hablaré, hablarás, hablará, hablaremos, hablaréis, hablarán 6 hable, hables, hable, hablemos, habléis, hablen 7 hablara, hablaras, hablara, habláramos, hablarais, hablaran 8 hablado 9 hablaba, hablabas, hablaba, hablábamos, hablabais, hablaban

hacer 2 haz 3 hago 4 hice, hiciste, hizo, hicimos, hicisteis, hicieron 5 haré *etc* 6 haga *etc* 7 hiciera *etc* 8 hecho

instruir 1 instruyendo 2 instruye 3 instruyo, instruyes, instruye, instruyen 4 instruyó, instruyeron 6 instruya *etc* 7 instruyera *etc*

ir 1 yendo 2 ve 3 voy, vas, va, vamos, vais, van 4 fui, fuiste, fue, fuimos, fuisteis, fueron 6 vaya, vayas, vaya, vayamos, vayáis, vayan 7 fuera *etc* 9 iba, ibas, iba, íbamos, ibais, iban

jugar 2 juega 3 juego, juegas, juega, juegan 4 jugué 6 juegue *etc*

leer 1 leyendo 4 leyó, leyeron 7 leyera *etc*

morir 1 muriendo 2 muere 3 muero, mueres, muere, mueren 4 murió, murieron

6 muera, mueras, muera, muramos, muráis, mueran 7 muriera *etc* 8 muerto

mover 2 mueve 3 muevo, mueves, mueve, mueven 6 mueva, muevas, mueva, muevan

negar 2 niega 3 niego, niegas, niega, niegan 4 negué 6 niegue, niegues, niegue, neguemos, neguéis, nieguen

ofrecer 3 ofrezco 6 ofrezca *etc*

oír 1 oyendo 2 oye 3 oigo, oyes, oye, oyen 4 oyó, oyeron 6 oiga *etc* 7 oyera *etc*

oler 2 huele 3 huelo, hueles, huele, huelen 6 huela, huelas, huela, huelan

parecer 3 parezco 6 parezca *etc*

pedir 1 pidiendo 2 pide 3 pido, pides, pide, piden 4 pidió, pidieron 6 pida *etc* 7 pidiera *etc*

pensar 2 piensa 3 pienso, piensas, piensa, piensan 6 piense, pienses, piense, piensen

perder 2 pierde 3 pierdo, pierdes, pierde, pierden 6 pierda, pierdas, pierda, pierdan

poder 1 pudiendo 2 puede 3 puedo, puedes, puede, pueden 4 pude, pudiste, pudo, pudimos, pudisteis, pudieron 5 podré *etc* 6 pueda, puedas, pueda, puedan 7 pudiera *etc*

poner 2 pon 3 pongo 4 puse, pusiste, puso, pusimos, pusisteis, pusieron 5 pondré *etc* 6 ponga *etc* 7 pusiera *etc* 8 puesto

preferir 1 prefiriendo 2 prefiere 3 prefiero, prefieres, prefiere, prefieren 4 prefirió, prefirieron 6 prefiera, prefieras, prefiera, prefiramos, prefiráis, prefieran 7 prefiriera *etc*

querer 2 quiere 3 quiero, quieres, quiere, quieren 4 quise, quisiste, quiso, quisimos, quisisteis, quisieron 5 querré *etc* 6 quiera, quieras, quiera, quieran 7 quisiera *etc*

reír 2 ríe 3 río, ríes, ríe, ríen 4 reí, rieron 6 ría, rías, ría, riamos, riáis, rían 7 riera *etc*

repetir 1 repitiendo 2 repite 3 repito, repites, repite, repiten 4 repitió, repitieron 6 repita *etc* 7 repitiera *etc*

rogar 2 ruega 3 ruego, ruegas, ruega, ruegan 4 rogué 6 ruegue, ruegues, ruegue, roguemos, roguéis, rueguen

saber 3 sé 4 supe, supiste, supo, supimos, supisteis, supieron 5 sabré *etc* 6 sepa *etc* 7 supiera *etc*

salir 2 sal 3 salgo 5 saldré *etc* 6 salga *etc*

seguir 1 siguiendo 2 sigue 3 sigo, sigues, sigue, siguen 4 siguió, siguieron 6 siga *etc* 7 siguiera *etc*

sentar 2 sienta 3 siento, sientas, sienta, sientan 6 siente, sientes, siente, sienten

sentir 1 sintiendo 2 siente 3 siento, sientes, siente, sienten 4 sintió, sintieron 6 sienta, sientas, sienta, sintamos, sintáis, sientan 7 sintiera *etc*

SER 2 sé 3 soy, eres, es, somos, sois, son 4 fui, fuiste, fue, fuimos, fuisteis, fueron 6 sea *etc* 7 fuera *etc* 9 era, eras, era, éramos, erais, eran

servir 1 sirviendo 2 sirve 3 sirvo, sirves, sirve, sirven 4 sirvió, sirvieron 6 sirva *etc* 7 sirviera *etc*

soñar 2 sueña 3 sueño, sueñas, sueña, sueñan 6 sueñe, sueñes, sueñe, sueñen

tener 2 ten 3 tengo, tienes, tiene, tienen 4 tuve, tuviste, tuvo, tuvimos, tuvisteis, tuvieron 5 tendré *etc* 6 tenga *etc* 7 tuviera *etc*

traer 1 trayendo 3 traigo 4 traje, trajiste, trajo, trajimos, trajisteis, trajeron 6 traiga *etc* 7 trajera *etc*

valer 2 vale 3 valgo 5 valdré *etc* 6 valga *etc*

venir 2 ven 3 vengo, vienes, viene, vienen 4 vine, viniste, vino, vinimos, vinisteis, vinieron 5 vendré *etc* 6 venga *etc* 7 viniera *etc*

ver 3 veo 6 vea *etc* 8 visto 9 veía *etc*

vestir 1 vistiendo 2 viste 3 visto, vistes, viste, visten 4 vistió, vistieron 6 vista *etc* 7 vistiera *etc*

VIVIR 1 viviendo 2 vive, vivid 3 vivo, vives, vive, vivimos, vivís, viven 4 viví, viviste, vivió, vivimos, vivisteis, vivieron 5 viviré, vivirás, vivirá, viviremos, viviréis, vivirán 6 viva, vivas, viva, vivamos, viváis, vivan 7 viviera, vivieras, viviera, viviéramos, vivierais, vivieran 8 vivido 9 vivía, vivías, vivía, vivíamos, vivías, vivían

volver 2 vuelve 3 vuelvo, vuelves, vuelve, vuelven 6 vuelva, vuelvas, vuelva, vuelvan 8 vuelto

VERBOS IRREGULARES EN INGLÉS

PRESENTE	PASADO	PARTICIPIO	PRESENTE	PASADO	PARTICIPIO
arise	arose	arisen	fall	fell	fallen
awake	awoke	awoken	feed	fed	fed
be (am, is, are; being)	was, were	been	feel	felt	felt
			fight	fought	fought
bear	bore	born(e)	find	found	found
beat	beat	beaten	flee	fled	fled
become	became	become	fling	flung	flung
begin	began	begun	fly	flew	flown
bend	bent	bent	forbid	forbad(e)	forbidden
bet	bet, betted	bet, betted	forecast	forecast	forecast
			forget	forgot	forgotten
bid (at auction, cards)	bid	bid	forgive	forgave	forgiven
			forsake	forsook	forsaken
bid (say)	bade	bidden	freeze	froze	frozen
bind	bound	bound	get	got	got, (us) gotten
bite	bit	bitten			
bleed	bled	bled	give	gave	given
blow	blew	blown	go (goes)	went	gone
break	broke	broken	grind	ground	ground
breed	bred	bred	grow	grew	grown
bring	brought	brought	hang	hung	hung
build	built	built	hang (suspend) (execute)	hanged	hanged
burn	burnt, burned	burnt, burned	have	had	had
burst	burst	burst	hear	heard	heard
buy	bought	bought	hide	hid	hidden
can	could	(been able)	hit	hit	hit
cast	cast	cast	hold	held	held
catch	caught	caught	hurt	hurt	hurt
choose	chose	chosen	keep	kept	kept
cling	clung	clung	kneel	knelt, kneeled	knelt, kneeled
come	came	come			
cost (be valued at)	cost	cost	know	knew	known
			lay	laid	laid
cost (work out price of)	costed	costed	lead	led	led
			lean	leant, leaned	leant, leaned
creep	crept	crept			
cut	cut	cut	leap	leapt, leaped	leapt, leaped
deal	dealt	dealt			
dig	dug	dug	learn	learnt, learned	learnt, learned
do (does)	did	done			
draw	drew	drawn	leave	left	left
dream	dreamed, dreamt	dreamed, dreamt	lend	lent	lent
			let	let	let
drink	drank	drunk	lie (lying)	lay	lain
drive	drove	driven	light	lit, lighted	lit, lighted
dwell	dwelt	dwelt			
eat	ate	eaten	lose	lost	lost

XV

PRESENTE	PASADO	PARTICIPIO	PRESENTE	PASADO	PARTICIPIO
make	made	made	speed	sped,	sped,
may	might	–		speeded	speeded
mean	meant	meant	spell	spelt,	spelt,
meet	met	met		spelled	spelled
mistake	mistook	mistaken	spend	spent	spent
mow	mowed	mown,	spill	spilt,	spilt,
		mowed		spilled	spilled
must	(had to)	(had to)	spin	spun	spun
pay	paid	paid	spit	spat	spat
put	put	put	spoil	spoiled,	spoiled,
quit	quit,	quit,		spoilt	spoilt
	quitted	quitted	spread	spread	spread
read	read	read	spring	sprang	sprung
rid	rid	rid	stand	stood	stood
ride	rode	ridden	steal	stole	stolen
ring	rang	rung	stick	stuck	stuck
rise	rose	risen	sting	stung	stung
run	ran	run	stink	stank	stunk
saw	sawed	sawed,	stride	strode	stridden
		sawn	strike	struck	struck
say	said	said	strive	strove	striven
see	saw	seen	swear	swore	sworn
seek	sought	sought	sweep	swept	swept
sell	sold	sold	swell	swelled	swollen,
send	sent	sent			swelled
set	set	set	swim	swam	swum
sew	sewed	sewn	swing	swung	swung
shake	shook	shaken	take	took	taken
shear	sheared	shorn,	teach	taught	taught
		sheared	tear	tore	torn
shed	shed	shed	tell	told	told
shine	shone	shone	think	thought	thought
shoot	shot	shot	throw	threw	thrown
show	showed	shown	thrust	thrust	thrust
shrink	shrank	shrunk	tread	trod	trodden
shut	shut	shut	wake	woke,	woken,
sing	sang	sung		waked	waked
sink	sank	sunk	wear	wore	worn
sit	sat	sat	weave (on	wove	woven
slay	slew	slain	loom)		
sleep	slept	slept	weave (wind)	weaved	weaved
slide	slid	slid	wed	wedded,	wedded,
sling	slung	slung		wed	wed
slit	slit	slit	weep	wept	wept
smell	smelt,	smelt,	win	won	won
	smelled	smelled	wind	wound	wound
sow	sowed	sown,	wring	wrung	wrung
		sowed	write	wrote	written
speak	spoke	spoken			

ESPAÑOL – INGLÉS

SPANISH – ENGLISH

Aa

a (*a+el = al*) *prep* **1** (*dirección*) to; **fueron a Madrid/ Grecia** they went to Madrid/Greece; **me voy a casa** I'm going home; **gira a la derecha** turn right

2 (*posición*): **estar a la mesa** to be at table; **al lado de** next to, beside; **está a la derecha/ izquierda** it's on the right/left; *ver tb* **puerta**

3 (*distancia*): **está a 15 km de aquí** it's 15 kms from here

4 (*tiempo*): **a las 10/a medianoche** at 10/ midnight; **¿a qué hora?** (at) what time?; **a la mañana siguiente** the following morning; **a los pocos días** after a few days; **estamos a 9 de julio** it's the 9th of July; **a los 24 años** at the age of 24; **ocho horas al día** eight hours a day; **al año/a la semana** a year/week later

5 (*manera*): **a la francesa** the French way; **a caballo** on horseback; **a oscuras** in the dark; **a rayas** striped; **lo echaron a patadas** they kicked him out

6 (*medio, instrumento*): **a lápiz** in pencil; **a mano** by hand; **cocina a gas** gas stove

7 (*cantidades*): **a 2 euros la docena** 2 euros (for) a dozen; **a más de 50 kms por hora** at more than 50 kms per hour; **poco a poco** little by little

8 (*complemento directo*): **vi al policía** I saw the policeman

9 (*otros complementos de persona*): **se lo di a él** I gave it to him; **se lo compré a él** I bought it from him

10 (*tras ciertos verbos*): **voy a verlo** I'm going to see him; **empezó a trabajar** he started working *o* to work; **sabe a queso** it tastes of cheese; **¿a qué viene eso?** what's the meaning of this?

11 (*+infin*): **al verla, la reconocí inmediatamente** when I saw her I recognized her at once; **el camino a recorrer** the distance we (*etc*) have to travel; **¡a callar!** keep quiet!; **¡a comer!** let's eat!

12 (*a+que*): **¡a que llueve!** I bet it's going to rain!; **¿a que sí va a venir?** he IS coming, isn't he?; **¿a que no lo haces? — ¡a que sí!** bet you don't do it! — yes, I WILL!

abad, esa *nm/f* abbot (abbess)

abadía *nf* abbey

abajo *adv* (*situación*) (down) below, underneath; (*en mueble*) bottom; (*en edificio*) downstairs; (*dirección*) down, downwards; **no parece tan alta desde ~** it doesn't seem so high from below; **el estante de ~** the bottom shelf; **la parte de ~ del contenedor** the bottom of the container; **el piso de ~** the downstairs flat; **el ~ firmante** the undersigned; **más ~** lower *o* further down; **cuesta/río ~** downhill/downstream; **ir calle ~** to go down the street; **de arriba ~** from top to bottom; **¡~ el gobierno!** *excl* down with the government!; **~ de** *prep* (*LAm*) below, under; **~ de la camisa** under the shirt

abalanzarse *vr*: **~ sobre** *o* **contra** to throw o.s. at

abalorios *nmpl* trinkets

abanderado *nm* standard bearer

abandonado, -a *adj* (*en mal estado*) derelict; (*desatendido*) abandoned; (*desierto*) deserted; (*descuidado*) neglected

abandonar *vt* to leave; (*persona*) to abandon, desert; (*cosa*) to abandon, leave behind; (*descuidar*) to neglect; (*renunciar a*) to give up; (*Inform*) to quit; **abandonarse** *vr*: **~se a** to abandon o.s. to; **~se al alcohol** to take to drink

abandono *nm* (*acto*) desertion, abandonment; (*estado*) abandon, neglect; (*renuncia*) withdrawal, retirement; **ganar por ~** to win by default

abanicar *vt* to fan

abanico *nm* fan; (*Náut*) derrick; **en ~** fan-shaped

abaratar *vt* to lower the price of ▷ *vi*: **abaratarse** *vr* to go *o* come down in price

abarcar *vt* to include, embrace; (*contener*) to comprise; (*LAm*) to monopolize; **quien mucho abarca poco aprieta** don't bite off more than you can chew

abarrotado, -a *adj* packed; **~ de** packed *o* bursting with

abarrotes *nmpl* (*LAm*) groceries, provisions

abastecer *vt*: **~ (de)** to supply (with)

abastecimiento *nm* supply

abasto *nm* supply; (*abundancia*) abundance; **no dar ~ a algo** not to be able to cope with sth

abatido, -a *adj* dejected, downcast; **estar muy ~** to be very depressed

abatimiento *nm* (*depresión*) dejection, depression

abatir *vt* (*muro*) to demolish; (*pájaro*) to shoot *o* bring down; (*fig*) to depress; **abatirse** *vr* to get depressed; **~se sobre** to swoop *o* pounce on

abdicación *nf* abdication

abdicar vi to abdicate; ~ **en algn** to abdicate in favour of sb

abdomen nm abdomen

abdominal adj abdominal ▷ nm: ~**es** (Deporte) sit-ups; (Anat) abdominals, stomach muscles

abecedario nm alphabet

abedul nm birch

abeja nf bee

abejorro nm bumblebee

aberración nf aberration

abertura nf = **apertura**

abertzale adj, nm/f Basque nationalist

abeto nm fir

abierto, -a pp de **abrir** ▷ adj (puerta, ojos, tienda) open; (gas, grifo) on; (carácter, persona) frank

abigarrado, -a adj multicoloured; (fig) motley

abismal adj (fig) vast, enormous

abismo nm abyss; **de sus ideas a las mías hay un ~** our views are worlds apart

abjurar vt to abjure, forswear ▷ vi: ~ **de** to abjure, forswear

ablandar vt to soften up; (conmover) to touch; (Culin) to tenderize ▷ vi: **ablandarse** vr to get softer

abnegación nf self-denial

abnegado, -a adj self-sacrificing

abocado, -a adj: **verse ~ al desastre** to be heading for disaster

abochornar vt to embarrass; **abochornarse** vr to get flustered; (Bot) to wilt; ~**se de** to get embarrassed about

abofetear vt to slap (in the face)

abogacía nf (profesión) legal profession; (ejercicio) practice of the law

abogado, -a nm/f (letrado) lawyer; (asesor) counsel; (en tribunal) barrister, attorney (US); ~ **defensor** defence lawyer o attorney (US); ~ **del diablo** devil's advocate

abogar vi: ~ **por** to plead for; (fig) to advocate

abolengo nm ancestry, lineage

abolición nf abolition

abolir vt to abolish; (cancelar) to cancel

abolladura nf dent

abollar vt to dent

abominable adj abominable

abominación nf abomination

abonado, -a adj (deuda) paid(-up) ▷ nm/f subscriber

abonar vt to pay; (deuda) to settle; (terreno) to fertilize; (idea) to endorse; **abonarse** vr to subscribe; ~ **dinero en una cuenta** to pay money into an account, credit money to an account

abono nm (pago) payment; (fertilizante) fertilizer; (a revista) subscription

abordar vt (barco) to board; (asunto) to broach; (individuo) to approach

aborigen nm/f aborigine

aborrecer vt to hate, loathe

abortar vi (perder el feto) to have a miscarriage; (deliberadamente) to have an abortion

aborto nm (accidental) miscarriage; (provocado) abortion

abotagado, -a adj swollen

abotonar vt to button (up), do up

abovedado, -a adj vaulted, domed

abrasar vt to burn (up); (Agr) to dry up, parch

abrazadera nf bracket

abrazar vt to embrace, hug; **abrazarse** vr to embrace, hug each other

abrazo nm embrace, hug; **un ~** (en carta) with best wishes

abrebotellas nm inv bottle opener

abrecartas nm inv letter opener

abrelatas nm inv tin (Brit) o can (US) opener

abreviar vt to abbreviate; (texto) to abridge ▷ vi: **bueno, para ~** well, to cut a long story short

abreviatura nf abbreviation

abridor nm (de botellas) bottle opener; (de latas) tin (Brit) o can (US) opener

abrigar vt (proteger) to shelter; (suj: ropa) to keep warm; (fig) to cherish; **abrigarse** vr to take shelter, protect o.s.; (con ropa) to cover (o.s.) up; ¡**abrígate bien!** wrap up well!

abrigo nm (prenda) coat, overcoat; (lugar protegido) shelter; **al ~ de** in the shelter of

abril nm April

abrillantar vt (pulir) to polish; (fig) to enhance

abrir vt (puerta, ojos) to open (up); (camino) to open up; (candidatura) to head ▷ vi to open; **abrirse** vr (puerta, ojos) to open (up); (pasillo, desfiladero) to open out; (cielo) to clear; ~ **un negocio** to start up a business; ~ **el apetito a algn** to whet sb's appetite; **en un ~ y cerrar de ojos** in the twinkling of an eye; ~**se paso** to find o force a way through

abrochar vt (con botones) to button (up); (con broche, cordones) to do up; **abrocharse** vr: ~**se los zapatos** to tie one's shoelaces

abrumar vt to overwhelm; (sobrecargar) to weigh down

abrupto, -a adj abrupt; (empinado) steep

absceso nm abscess

absentismo nm (de obreros) absenteeism

absolución nf (Rel) absolution; (Jur) acquittal

absoluto, -a adj absolute; (total) utter, complete; **en ~** adv not at all

absolver vt to absolve; (Jur) to pardon; (: acusado) to acquit

absorbente adj absorbent; (interesante) absorbing, interesting; (exigente) demanding

absorber vt to absorb; (embeber) to soak up; **absorberse** vr to become absorbed

absorción nf absorption; (Com) takeover

absorto, -a pp de **absorber** ▷ adj absorbed, engrossed

abstemio, -a adj teetotal

abstención nf abstention

abstenerse vr: ~ **(de)** to abstain o refrain (from)

abstinencia nf abstinence; (ayuno) fasting

abstracción nf abstraction

abstracto, -a adj abstract; **en ~** in the abstract

abstraer vt to abstract; **abstraerse** vr to be o become absorbed

abstraído, -a *adj* absent-minded
absuelto *pp de* **absolver**
absurdo, -a *adj* absurd; **lo ~ es que ...** the ridiculous thing is that ... ▷ *nm* absurdity
abuchear *vt* to boo
abuela *nf* grandmother; **¡cuéntaselo a tu ~!** (*fam!*) do you think I was born yesterday? (*fam*); **no tener/necesitar ~** (*fam*) to be full of o.s./blow one's own trumpet
abuelo *nm* grandfather; (*antepasado*) ancestor; **abuelos** *nmpl* grandparents
abulia *nf* lethargy
abúlico, -a *adj* lethargic
abultado, -a *adj* bulky
abultar *vt* (*agrandar*) to enlarge; (*aumentar*) to increase; (*fig*) to exaggerate ▷ *vi* to be bulky
abundancia *nf*: **una ~ de** plenty of; **en ~** in abundance
abundante *adj* abundant, plentiful
abundar *vi* to abound, be plentiful; **~ en una opinión** to share an opinion
aburguesarse *vr* to become middle-class
aburrido, -a *adj* (*hastiado*) bored; (*que aburre*) boring
aburrimiento *nm* boredom, tedium
aburrir *vt* to bore; **aburrirse** *vr* to be bored, get bored; **~se como una ostra** to be bored stiff
abusar *vi*: **puedes beber, pero sin ~** you can drink as long as you don't overdo it; **~ de** to abuse; **abusó de nuestra hospitalidad** he abused our hospitality; **no conviene ~ del aceite en las comidas** you shouldn't use too much oil in food; **~ de la confianza de algn** to take advantage of sb
abusivo, -a *adj* (*precio*) exorbitant
abuso *nm* abuse; **~ de confianza** betrayal of trust
abyecto, -a *adj* wretched, abject
a/c *abr* (= *al cuidado de*) c/o; (= *a cuenta*) on account
acá *adv* (*lugar*) here; **pasearse de ~ para allá** to walk up and down; **¡vente para ~!** come over here!; **¿de cuándo ~?** since when?
acabado, -a *adj* finished, complete; (*perfecto*) perfect; (*agotado*) worn out; (*fig*) masterly ▷ *nm* finish
acabar *vt* (*llevar a su fin*) to finish, complete; (*consumir*) to use up; (*rematar*) to finish off ▷ *vi* to finish, end; (*morir*) to die; **acabarse** *vr* to finish, stop; (*terminarse*) to be over; (*agotarse*) to run out; **~ mal** to come to a sticky end; **~ con un problema** to put an end to a problem; **hemos acabado con todas las provisiones** we've finished all our provisions; **esto ~á conmigo** this will be the end of me; **acababa de entrar cuando sonó el teléfono** I had just come in when the phone rang; **~ haciendo** *o* **por hacer algo** to end up (by) doing sth; **¡se acabó!** (*¡basta!*) that's enough!; (*se terminó*) it's all over!; **se me acabó el tabaco** I ran out of cigarettes
acabóse *nm*: **esto es el ~** this is the limit
acacia *nf* acacia
academia *nf* academy; (*Escol*) private school
académico, -a *adj* academic

acaecer *vi* to happen, occur
acallar *vt* (*silenciar*) to silence; (*calmar*) to pacify
acalorado, -a *adj* (*discusión*) heated
acalorarse *vr* (*fig*) to get heated
acampada *nf*: **ir de ~** to go camping
acampanado, -a *adj* flared
acampar *vi* to camp
acanalar *vt* to groove; (*ondular*) to corrugate
acantilado *nm* cliff
acaparar *vt* (*monopolizar*) to monopolize; (*acumular*) to hoard
acariciar *vt* to caress; (*esperanza*) to cherish
acarrear *vt* to transport; (*fig*) to cause, result in; **le acarreó muchos disgustos** it brought him lots of problems
acaso *adv* perhaps, maybe ▷ *nm* chance; **¿~ es mi culpa?** (*LAm fam*) what makes you think it's my fault?; **(por) si ~** (just) in case
acatamiento *nm* respect; (*de la ley*) observance
acatar *vt* to respect; (*ley*) to obey, observe
acatarrarse *vr* to catch a cold
acaudalado, -a *adj* well-off
acaudillar *vt* to lead, command
acceder *vi* to accede, agree; **~ a** (*Inform*) to access
accesible *adj* accessible; **~ a** open to
acceso *nm* access, entry; (*camino*) access road; (*Med*) attack, fit; (*de cólera*) fit; (*Pol*) accession; (*Inform*) access; **~ aleatorio/directo/secuencial** *o* **en serie** (*Inform*) random/direct/sequential *o* serial access; **de ~ múltiple** multi-access
accesorio, -a *adj* accessory ▷ *nm* accessory; **accesorios** *nmpl* (*Auto*) accessories, extras; (*Teat*) props
accidentado, -a *adj* (*terreno*) uneven; (*montañoso*) hilly; (*azaroso*) eventful ▷ *nm/f* accident victim
accidental *adj* accidental; (*empleo*) temporary
accidentarse *vr* to have an accident
accidente *nm* accident; **por ~** by chance; **accidentes** *nmpl* unevenness *sg*, roughness *sg*
acción *nf* action; (*acto*) action, act; (*Teat*) plot; (*Com*) share; (*Jur*) action, lawsuit; **capital en acciones** share capital; **~ liberada/ordinaria/preferente** fully-paid/ordinary/preference share
accionar *vt* to work, operate; (*Inform*) to drive
accionista *nm/f* shareholder
acebo *nm* (*hojas*) holly; (*árbol*) holly tree
acechanza *nf* = **acecho**
acechar *vt* to spy on; (*aguardar*) to lie in wait for
acecho *nm*: **estar al ~ (de)** to lie in wait (for)
aceite *nm* oil; **~ de hígado de bacalao** cod-liver oil; **~ de oliva** olive oil
aceitera *nf* oil bottle
aceitoso, -a *adj* oily
aceituna *nf* olive
acelerador *nm* accelerator
acelerar *vt* to accelerate; **acelerarse** *vr* to hurry
acelga *nf* chard, beet
acento *nm* accent; (*acentuación*) stress; **~ cerrado** strong *o* thick accent
acentuar *vt* (*palabra*) to accent, stress; (*enfatizar*) to accentuate; (*Inform*) to highlight

acepción *nf* meaning
aceptación *nf* acceptance; (*aprobación*) approval
aceptar *vt* to accept
acequia *nf* irrigation ditch
acera *nf* pavement (Brit), sidewalk (US)
acerado, -a *adj* steel; (*afilado*) sharp; (*fig: duro*) steely; (: *mordaz*) biting
acerbo, -a *adj* bitter; (*fig*) harsh
acerca; ~ **de** *prep* about, concerning
acercar *vt* to bring *o* move nearer; **acercarse** *vr* to approach, come near; **acerca tu silla** bring your chair over here; **¿me acercas los alicates?** could you pass me the pliers?; **¿acerco más la cama a la ventana?** shall I put the bed nearer the window?; **nos ~on al aeropuerto** they gave us a lift to the airport; **me acerqué a la ventana** I went over to the window; **acércate a la tienda** go over to the shop; **ya se acerca la Navidad** Christmas is getting near
acerico *nm* pincushion
acero *nm* steel; ~ **inoxidable** stainless steel
acérrimo, -a *adj* (*partidario*) staunch; (*enemigo*) bitter
acertado, -a *adj* correct; (*apropiado*) apt; (*sensato*) sensible
acertar *vt* (*blanco*) to hit; (*pregunta, respuesta, solución*) to get right; (*adivinar*) to guess ▷ *vi* to get it right, be right; **si aciertas cuántos caramelos hay, te los regalo todos** If you guess how many sweets there are, I'll give you them all; **creo que hemos acertado con estas cortinas** I think these curtains were a good choice; **acerté en el blanco** I hit the target; ~ **a** to manage to; ~ **con** to happen *o* hit on
acertijo *nm* riddle, puzzle
acervo *nm* heap; ~ **común** undivided estate
achacar *vt* to attribute
achacoso, -a *adj* sickly
achaque *nm* ailment
achicar *vt* to reduce; (*humillar*) to humiliate; (*Náut*) to bale out; **~se** (*ropa*) to shrink; (*fig*) to humble o.s
achicharrar *vt* to scorch, burn
achicoria *nf* chicory
aciago, -a *adj* ill-fated, fateful
acicalar *vt* to polish; (*adornar*) to bedeck; **acicalarse** *vr* to get dressed up
acicate *nm* spur; (*fig*) incentive
acidez *nf* acidity
ácido, -a *adj* sour, acid ▷ *nm* acid; (*fam: droga*) LSD
acierto *nm* success; (*buen paso*) wise move; (*solución*) solution; (*habilidad*) skill, ability; (*al adivinar*) good guess; **fue un ~ suyo** it was a sensible choice on his part
aclamación *nf* acclamation; (*aplausos*) applause
aclamar *vt* (*proclamar*) to acclaim; (*aplaudir*) to applaud
aclaración *nf* clarification, explanation
aclarar *vt* (*duda, asunto*) to clear up, clarify; (*ropa*) to rinse ▷ *vi* to clear up; **aclararse** *vr*: **¡aclárate!** what are you on about?; **con tantos números no me aclaro** there are so many numbers that

I can't get it straight; **~se la garganta** to clear one's throat; **hasta que no se aclare este asunto** until this business is cleared up
aclaratorio, -a *adj* explanatory
aclimatación *nf* acclimatization
aclimatar *vt* to acclimatize; **aclimatarse** *vr* to become *o* get acclimatized; **~se a algo** to get used to sth
acné *nm* acne
acobardar *vt* to daunt, intimidate; **acobardarse** *vr* (*atemorizarse*) to be intimidated; (*echarse atrás*): **~se (ante)** to shrink back (from)
acodarse *vr*: ~ **en** to lean on
acogedor, a *adj* welcoming; (*hospitalario*) hospitable
acoger *vt* (*recibir*) to welcome; (*abrigar*) to shelter; **acogerse** *vr*: **~se a** (*pretexto*) to take refuge in; (*ley*) to resort to; **la ciudad acoge todos los años a miles de visitantes** the city receives thousands of visitors every year; **me acogieron muy bien en Estados Unidos** I was made very welcome in the United States; **lo acogieron en un asilo de ancianos** he was taken into an old people's home
acogida *nf* reception
acolchar *vt* to pad; (*fig*) to cushion
acometer *vt* to attack; (*emprender*) to undertake
acometida *nf* attack, assault
acomodado, -a *adj* (*persona*) well-to-do
acomodador, a *nm/f* usher(ette)
acomodar *vt* to adjust; (*alojar*) to accommodate; **acomodarse** *vr* to conform; (*instalarse*) to install o.s.; (*adaptarse*) to adapt o.s.; **¡acomódese a su gusto!** make yourself comfortable!
acomodaticio, -a *adj* (*pey*) accommodating, obliging; (*manejable*) pliable
acompañante, -a *nm/f* companion
acompañar *vt* (*a un sitio*) to accompany, come/go with; (*hacer compañía*) to stay with; (*documentos*) to enclose; **¿quieres que te acompañe?** do you want me to come with you?; **me pidió que la ~a a la estación** she asked me to go to the station with her; **¿quieres que te acompañe a casa?** would you like me to see you home?; **me acompañó hasta que llegó el autobús** he stayed with me until the bus arrived; ~ **a algn a la puerta** to see sb to the door *o* out; **lo acompaño en el sentimiento** please accept my condolences
acomplejar *vt* to give a complex to; **acomplejarse** *vr*: **~se (con)** to get a complex (about)
acondicionar *vt* to get ready, prepare; (*pelo*) to condition
acongojar *vt* to distress, grieve
aconsejar *vt* to advise, counsel; **aconsejarse** *vr*: **~se con** *o* **de** to consult
acontecer *vi* to happen, occur
acontecimiento *nm* event
acopio *nm* store, stock
acoplamiento *nm* coupling, joint
acoplar *vt* to fit; (*Elec*) to connect; (*vagones*) to

couple

acorazado, -a *adj* armour-plated, armoured ▷ *nm* battleship

acordar *vt* (*asunto, precio*) to agree on; **acordarse** *vr* to remember; **acordamos un precio y unas condiciones** we agreed on a price and terms; **~ hacer algo** to agree to do something; **ahora mismo no me acuerdo** right now I can't remember; **¿te acuerdas de mí?** do you remember me?; **acuérdate de echar la llave a la puerta** remember to lock the door; **~se de haber hecho algo** to remember doing something; **me acuerdo de habértelo preguntado ya antes** I remember asking you before

acorde *adj* (*Mus*) harmonious; **~ con** (*medidas etc*) in keeping with ▷ *nm* chord

acordeón *nm* accordion

acordonado, -a *adj* (*calle*) cordoned-off

acorralar *vt* to round up, corral; (*fig*) to intimidate

acortar *vt* to shorten; (*duración*) to cut short; (*cantidad*) to reduce; **acortarse** *vr* to become shorter

acosar *vt* to pursue relentlessly; (*fig*) to hound, pester; **~ a algn a preguntas** to pester sb with questions

acoso *nm* relentless pursuit; (*fig*) hounding; **~ sexual** sexual harassment

acostar *vt* (*en cama*) to put to bed; (*en suelo*) to lay down; (*barco*) to bring alongside; **acostarse** *vr* (*irse a dormir*) to go to bed; (*echarse*) to lie down

acostumbrado, -a *adj* (*habitual*) usual; **estar ~ a (hacer) algo** to be used to (doing) sth

acostumbrar *vt*: **~ a algn a algo** to get sb used to sth ▷ *vi*: **~ (a hacer algo)** to be in the habit (of doing sth); **acostumbrarse** *vr*: **~se a** to get used to

acotación *nf* (*apunte*) marginal note; (*Geo*) elevation mark; (*de límite*) boundary mark; (*Teat*) stage direction

ácrata *adj, nm/f* anarchist

acre *adj* (*sabor*) sharp, bitter; (*olor*) acrid; (*fig*) biting ▷ *nm* acre

acrecentar *vt* to increase, augment

acreditar *vt* (*garantizar*) to vouch for, guarantee; (*autorizar*) to authorize; (*dar prueba de*) to prove; (*Com: abonar*) to credit; (*embajador*) to accredit; **acreditarse** *vr* to become famous; (*demostrar valía*) to prove one's worth; **~se de** to get a reputation for

acreedor, a *adj*: **~ a** worthy of ▷ *nm/f* creditor; **~ común/diferido/con garantía** (*Com*) unsecured/deferred/secured creditor

acribillar *vt*: **~ a balazos** to riddle with bullets

acróbata *nm/f* acrobat

acta *nf* certificate; (*de comisión*) minutes *pl*, record; **~ de nacimiento/de matrimonio** birth/marriage certificate; **~ notarial** affidavit; **levantar ~** (*Jur*) to make a formal statement *o* deposition

actitud *nf* attitude; (*postura*) posture; **adoptar**

una ~ firme to take a firm stand

activar *vt* to activate; (*acelerar*) to speed up

actividad *nf* activity; **estar en plena ~** to be in full swing

activo, -a *adj* active; (*vivo*) lively ▷ *nm* (*Com*) assets *pl*; **~ y pasivo** assets and liabilities; **~ circulante/fijo/inmaterial/invisible** (*Com*) current/fixed/intangible/invisible assets; **~ realizable** liquid assets; **~s congelados** *o* **bloqueados** frozen assets; **estar en ~** (*Mil*) to be on active service

acto *nm* act, action; (*ceremonia*) ceremony; (*Teat*) act; **en el ~** immediately; **hacer ~ de presencia** (*asistir*) to attend (formally)

actor *nm* actor; (*Jur*) plaintiff

actriz *nf* actress

actuación *nf* action; (*comportamiento*) conduct, behaviour; (*Jur*) proceedings *pl*; (*desempeño*) performance

actual *adj* present(-day), current; **el 6 del ~** the 6th of this month; **en el momento ~** at the present time; **uno de los mejores pintores del arte ~** one of the greatest painters of today

actualidad *nf* present; **actualidades** *nfpl* news *sg*; **en la ~** nowadays, at present; **ser de gran ~** to be current

actualizar *vt* to update, modernize

actualmente *adv* (*en este momento*) currently, at present; (*hoy día*) nowadays

actuar *vi* (*obrar*) to work, operate; (*actor*) to act, perform ▷ *vt* to work, operate; **~ de** to act as

acuarela *nf* watercolour

acuario *nm* aquarium; **A~** (*Astro*) Aquarius

acuartelar *vt* (*Mil: alojar*) to quarter

acuático, -a *adj* aquatic

acuchillar *vt* (*Tec*) to plane (down), smooth

acuciar *vt* to urge on

acuclillarse *vr* to crouch down

acudir *vi* (*a lugar, reunión*) to attend, turn up; **el perro acude cuando lo llamo** the dog comes when I call; **~ a** to turn to; **~ a una cita** to keep an appointment; **~ a una llamada** to answer a call; **no tener a quién ~** to have nobody to turn to; **acudió a un amigo en busca de consejo** he went to a friend for advice; **acudieron en su ayuda** they went to her aid

acuerdo *nm* agreement; (*Pol*) resolution; **¡de ~!** all right!; **de ~ con** (*persona*) in agreement with; (*acción, documento*) in accordance with; **estar de ~ con algn** to agree with sb; **de común ~** by common consent; **tomar un ~** (*Pol*) to pass a resolution; **llegar a un ~** to reach an agreement; **ponerse de ~** to agree; **al final no nos pusimos de ~** in the end we couldn't agree; **nos pusimos de ~ para darle una sorpresa** we agreed to give him a surprise

acumular *vt* to accumulate, collect

acuñar *vt* (*moneda*) to mint; (*frase*) to coin

acuoso, -a *adj* watery

acupuntura *nf* acupuncture

acurrucarse *vr* to crouch; (*ovillarse*) to curl up

acusación *nf* accusation

acusar vt to accuse; (*revelar*) to reveal; (*denunciar*) to denounce; (*emoción*) to show; ~ **recibo** to acknowledge receipt; **su rostro acusó extrañeza** his face registered surprise; **acusarse** vr: **~se (de)** to confess (to)

acuse nm: ~ **de recibo** acknowledgement of receipt

acústico, -a adj acoustic ▷ nf (*de una sala etc*) acoustics pl; (*ciencia*) acoustics sg

adagio nm adage; (*Mus*) adagio

adaptación nf adaptation

adaptador nm (*Elec*) adapter

adaptar vt to adapt; (*acomodar*) to fit; (*convertir*): ~ **(para)** to convert (to)

adecuado, -a adj (*apto*) suitable; (*oportuno*) appropriate; **el hombre ~ para el puesto** the right man for the job

adecuar vt (*adaptar*) to adapt; (*hacer apto*) to make suitable

a. de J.C. abr (= *antes de Jesucristo*) B.C.

adelantado, -a adj advanced; (*reloj*) fast; **pagar por ~** to pay in advance

adelantamiento nm advance, advancement; (*Auto*) overtaking

adelantar vt (*mover hacia adelante*) to move forward; (*avanzar*) to advance ▷ vi (*ir por delante*) to go ahead; (*progresar*) to improve; (*a un coche*) to overtake; **adelantarse** vr (*tomar la delantera*) to go forward, advance; **tuvimos que ~ la boda** we had to bring the wedding forward; **hay que ~ los relojes una hora** we have to put the clocks forward an hour; **así no adelantas nada** you won't get anywhere that way; **tu reloj adelanta** your watch gains; **~se a algn** to get ahead of sb; **se nos adelantó la competencia** the competition got ahead of us; **~se a los deseos de algn** to anticipate sb's wishes

adelante adv forward(s) ▷ excl come in!; **se inclinó hacia ~** she leant forward; **el pueblo está más ~** the village is further on; **de ahora en ~** from now on; **más ~** later on; (*más allá*) further on; **hay que seguir ~** we must go on; ~ **de** (*LAm*) in front of; **se sentó ~ de mí** he sat in front of me

adelanto nm advance; (*mejora*) improvement; (*progreso*) progress; (*dinero*) advance; **los ~s de la ciencia** the advances of science

adelgazar vt to thin (down); (*afilar*) to taper ▷ vi to get thin; (*con régimen*) to slim down, lose weight

ademán nm gesture; **ademanes** nmpl manners; **en ~ de** as if to

además adv (*también*) as well, also, besides; (*por otra parte*) moreover; ~ **de** besides, in addition to

adentrarse vr: ~ **en** to go into, get inside; (*penetrar*) to penetrate (into)

adentro adv inside, in; **mar ~** out at sea; **tierra ~** inland ▷ nm: **dijo para sus ~s** he said to himself

adepto, -a nm/f supporter

aderezar vt (*ensalada*) to dress; (*comida*) to season

aderezo nm dressing

adeudar vt to owe; **adeudarse** vr to run into

debt; ~ **una suma en una cuenta** to debit an account with a sum

adherirse vr: ~ **a** to adhere to; (*fig*) to follow

adhesión nf adhesion; (*fig*) adherence

adicción nf addiction

adición nf addition

adicionar vt to add

adicto, -a adj: ~ **a** (*droga etc*) addicted to; (*dedicado*) devoted to ▷ nm/f supporter, follower; (*toxicómano etc*) addict

adiestrar vt to train, teach; (*conducir*) to guide, lead; **adiestrarse** vr to practise; (*enseñarse*) to train o.s.

adinerado, -a adj wealthy

adiós excl (*para despedirse*) goodbye!, cheerio!; (*al pasar*) hello!

aditivo nm additive

adivinanza nf riddle

adivinar vt (*profetizar*) to prophesy; (*conjeturar*) to guess

adivino, -a nm/f fortune-teller

adj. abr (= *adjunto*) encl

adjetivo nm adjective

adjudicación nf award; (*Com*) adjudication

adjudicar vt to award; **adjudicarse** vr: **~se algo** to appropriate sth

adjuntar vt to attach, enclose

adjunto, -a adj attached, enclosed ▷ nm/f assistant

administración nf administration; (*dirección*) management; ~ **pública** civil service; **A~ de Correos** General Post Office

administrador, a nm/f (*de bienes*) administrator; (*de empresa*) manager(ess)

administrar vt to administer

administrativo, -a adj administrative

admirable adj admirable

admiración nf admiration; (*asombro*) wonder; (*Ling*) exclamation mark

admirar vt to admire; (*extrañar*) to surprise; **admirarse** vr to be surprised; **se admiró de saberlo** he was amazed to hear it; **no es de ~ que ...** it's not surprising that ...

admisible adj admissible

admisión nf admission; (*reconocimiento*) acceptance

admitir vt (*reconocer*) to admit; (*aceptar*) to accept; **admite que estabas equivocado** admit you were wrong; **la máquina no admite monedas** the machine doesn't accept coins; **espero que me admitan en la universidad** I hope I'll get a place at university; **aquí no admiten perros** dogs aren't allowed in here; **esto no admite demora** this must be dealt with immediately; **no admite dudas** there's no room for doubt

admonición nf warning

ADN nm abr (= *acido desoxirribonucleico*) DNA

adobar vt (*preparar*) to prepare; (*cocinar*) to season

adobe nm adobe, sun-dried brick

adoctrinar vt to indoctrinate

adolecer vi: ~ **de** to suffer from

adolescente nm/f adolescent, teenager ▷ adj

adolescent, teenage

adonde *adv* (to) where

adónde *adv* = **dónde**

adopción *nf* adoption

adoptar *vt* to adopt

adoptivo, -a *adj* (*padres*) adoptive; (*hijo*) adopted

adoquín *nm* paving stone

adorar *vt* to adore

adormecer *vt* to put to sleep; **adormecerse** *vr* to become sleepy; (*dormirse*) to fall asleep

adornar *vt* to adorn

adorno *nm* adornment; (*decoración*) decoration

adosado, -a *adj* (*casa*) semi-detached

adquirir *vt* (*conseguir*) to acquire; (*comprar*) to purchase; **~ conocimientos de algo** to acquire a knowledge of something; **~ una vivienda** to purchase a property; **lo podrá ~ en tiendas especializadas** you'll be able to get it from specialist shops; **~ velocidad** to gain speed; **~ fama** to achieve fame; **~ importancia** to become important

adquisición *nf* acquisition; (*compra*) purchase

adrede *adv* on purpose

adscribir *vt* to appoint; **estuvo adscrito al servicio de ...** he was attached to ...

adscrito *pp de* **adscribir**

ADSL *nm* ADSL; **línea ~** ADSL line

aduana *nf* customs *pl*; (*impuesto*) (customs) duty

aduanero, -a *adj* customs *cpd* ▷ *nm/f* customs officer

aducir *vt* to adduce; (*dar como prueba*) to offer as proof

adueñarse *vr*: **~ de** to take possession of

adulación *nf* flattery

adular *vt* to flatter

adulterar *vt* to adulterate ▷ *vi* to commit adultery

adulterio *nm* adultery

adúltero, -a *adj* adulterous ▷ *nm/f* adulterer/ adulteress

adulto, -a *adj, nm/f* adult

adusto, -a *adj* stern; (*austero*) austere

advenedizo, -a *nm/f* upstart

advenimiento *nm* arrival; (*al trono*) accession

adverbio *nm* adverb

adversario, -a *nm/f* adversary

adversidad *nf* adversity; (*contratiempo*) setback

adverso, -a *adj* adverse; (*suerte*) bad

advertencia *nf* warning; (*prefacio*) preface, foreword

advertir *vt* (*avisar*): **~ a algn de** to warn sb about o of; (*observar*) to notice; **ya te advertí que no intervinieras** I warned you not to get involved; **no advertí nada extraño en su comportamiento** I didn't notice anything strange about his behaviour

Adviento *nm* Advent

adyacente *adj* adjacent

aéreo, -a *adj* aerial; (*tráfico*) air *cpd*

aerobic *nm* aerobics *sg*

aerodinámico, -a *adj* aerodynamic

aeromodelismo *nm* model aircraft making,

aeromodelling

aeromozo, -a *nm/f* (*LAm*) flight attendant, air steward(ess)

aeronáutico, -a *adj* aeronautical

aeronave *nm* spaceship

aeroplano *nm* aeroplane

aeropuerto *nm* airport

aerosol *nm* aerosol, spray

afabilidad *nf* affability, pleasantness

afable *adj* affable, pleasant

afamado, -a *adj* famous

afán *nm* hard work; (*deseo*) desire; **con ~** keenly

afanar *vt* to harass; (*fam*) to pinch; **afanarse** *vr*: **~se por** to strive to

afanoso, -a *adj* (*trabajo*) hard; (*trabajador*) industrious

afear *vt* to disfigure

afección *nf* affection; (*Med*) disease

afectación *nf* affectation

afectado, -a *adj* affected

afectar *vt* to affect, have an effect on; (*LAm: dañar*) to hurt; **por lo que afecta a esto** as far as this is concerned

afectísimo, -a *adj* affectionate; **suyo ~** yours truly

afectivo, -a *adj* affective

afecto, -a *adj*: **~ a** fond of; (*Jur*) subject to ▷ *nm* affection; **tenerle ~ a algn** to be fond of sb

afectuoso, -a *adj* affectionate

afeitar *vt* to shave; **afeitarse** *vr* to shave

afeminado, -a *adj* effeminate

aferrar *vt* to moor; (*fig*) to grasp ▷ *vi* to moor; **aferrarse** *vr* (*agarrarse*) to cling on; **~se a un principio** to stick to a principle; **~se a una esperanza** to cling to a hope

Afganistán *nm* Afghanistan

afianzamiento *nm* (*Tec*) strengthening; (*Fin*) security

afianzar *vt* to strengthen, secure; **afianzarse** *vr* to steady o.s.; (*establecerse*) to become established

afiche *nm* (*LAm*) poster

afición *nf*: **~ a** fondness o liking for; **la ~** the fans *pl*; **pinto por ~** I paint as a hobby

aficionado, -a *adj* amateur ▷ *nm/f* (*de equipo*) fan; (*no profesional*) amateur

aficionar *vt*: **~ a algn a algo** to make sb like sth; **aficionarse** *vr*: **~se a algo** to grow fond of sth

afilado, -a *adj* sharp

afilar *vt* to sharpen; **afilarse** *vr* (*cara*) to grow thin

afiliarse *vr* to affiliate

afín *adj* (*parecido*) similar; (*conexo*) related

afinar *vt* (*Tec*) to refine; (*Mus*) to tune ▷ *vi* to play/ sing in tune

afincarse *vr* to settle

afinidad *nf* affinity; (*parentesco*) relationship

afirmación *nf* affirmation

afirmar *vt* to affirm, state; (*sostener*) to strengthen; **afirmarse** *vr* (*recuperar el equilibrio*) to steady o.s.; **~se en lo dicho** to stand by what one has said

afirmativo, -a *adj* affirmative

aflicción nf affliction; (dolor) grief
afligir vt to afflict; (apenar) to distress; **afligirse** vr: ~**se (por** o **con** o **de)** to grieve (about o at); **no te aflijas tanto** you must not let it affect you like this
aflojar vt to slacken; (desatar) to loosen, undo; (relajar) to relax ▷ vi (amainar) to drop; (bajar) to go down; **aflojarse** vr to relax
aflorar vi (Geo, fig) to come to the surface, emerge
afluente adj flowing ▷ nm (Geo) tributary
afluir vi to flow
afmo., -a. abr (= afectísimo) Yours
afónico, -a adj: **estar** ~ to have lost one's voice
aforo nm (Tec) gauging; (de teatro etc) capacity; **el teatro tiene un** ~ **de 2.000 personas** the theatre can seat 2,000
afortunado, -a adj fortunate, lucky
afrancesado, -a adj francophile; (pey) Frenchified
afrenta nf affront, insult; (deshonra) dishonour (Brit), dishonor (US), shame
África nf Africa; ~ **del Sur** South Africa
africano, -a adj, nm/f African
afrontar vt (poner cara a cara) to bring face to face
after (pl -**s**) nm, **afterhours** nm inv after-hours club
afuera adv out, outside; **por** ~ on the outside; **afueras** nfpl outskirts
agachar vt to bend, bow; **agacharse** vr to stoop, bend
agalla nf (Zool) gill; **tener** ~**s** (fam) to have guts
agarrado, -a adj mean, stingy
agarrar vt to grasp, grab; (LAm) to take, catch ▷ vi (planta) to take root; **agarrarse** vr to hold on (tightly); **agarró al niño por el hombro** he grabbed the child by the shoulder; **agarra bien la sartén** hold the frying pan firmly; **ya han agarrado al ladrón** they've already caught the thief; **he agarrado un buen resfriado** I've caught an awful cold; **agarré otro pedazo de pastel** (LAm) I took another piece of cake; **agarró y se fue** (esp CS fam) he upped and went; **agárrate a la barandilla** hold on to the rail; **agarrársela con algn** (LAm) to pick on sb
agarrotar vt (lío) to tie tightly; (persona) to squeeze tightly; (reo) to garrotte; **agarrotarse** vr (motor) to seize up; (Med) to stiffen
agasajar vt to treat well
agencia nf agency; ~ **de créditos/publicidad/viajes** credit/advertising/travel agency; ~ **inmobiliaria** estate agent's (office) (Brit), real estate office (US); ~ **matrimonial** marriage bureau
agenciar vt to bring about; **agenciarse** vr to look after o.s.; ~**se algo** to get hold of sth
agenda nf diary; ~ **electrónica** PDA; ~ **telefónica** telephone directory
agente nm agent; (de policía) policeman; ~ **femenino** policewoman; ~ **acreditado** (Com) accredited agent; ~ **de bolsa** stockbroker; ~ **inmobiliario** estate agent (Brit), realtor (US); ~

de negocios (Com) business agent; ~ **de seguros** insurance broker; ~ **de viajes** travel agent; ~**s sociales** social partners
ágil adj agile, nimble
agilidad nf agility, nimbleness
agilizar vt to speed up
agitación nf (de mano) waving; (de líquido) shaking, stirring; (de personas) agitation
agitar vt (mano, bandera) to wave; (líquido) to shake, stir; (fig) to stir up, excite; **agitarse** vr to get excited; (inquietarse) to get worried o upset
aglomeración nf: ~ **de tráfico/gente** traffic jam/mass of people
aglomerar vt, **aglomerarse** vr to crowd together
agnóstico, -a adj, nm/f agnostic
agobiar vt to weigh down; (oprimir) to oppress; (cargar) to burden; **sentirse agobiado por** to be overwhelmed by
agolparse vr to crowd together
agonía nf death throes pl; (fig) agony, anguish
agonizante adj dying
agonizar vi (tb: **estar agonizando**) to be dying
agosto nm August; (fig) harvest; **hacer su** ~ to make one's pile
agotado, -a adj (persona) exhausted; (acabado) finished; (Com) sold out; (: libros) out of print; (pila) flat
agotador, a adj exhausting
agotamiento nm exhaustion
agotar vt to exhaust; (consumir) to drain; (recursos) to use up, deplete; **agotarse** vr to be exhausted; (acabarse) to run out; (libro) to go out of print
agraciado, -a adj (atractivo) attractive; (en sorteo etc) lucky
agraciar vt (Jur) to pardon; (con premio) to reward; (hacer más atractivo) to make more attractive
agradable adj pleasant, nice
agradar vt, vi to please; **agradarse** vr to like each other
agradecer vt to thank; (favor etc) to be grateful for; **le** ~**ía me enviara ...** I would be grateful if you would send me ...; **agradecerse** vr: ¡**se agradece!** much obliged!
agradecido, -a adj grateful; ¡**muy** ~! thanks a lot!
agradecimiento nm gratitude
agrado nm: **ser de tu** etc ~ to be to your etc liking
agrandar vt to enlarge; (fig) to exaggerate; **agrandarse** vr to get bigger
agrario, -a adj agrarian, land cpd; (política) agricultural, farming cpd
agravante adj aggravating ▷ nf complication; **con la** ~ **de que ...** with the further difficulty that ...
agravar vt (pesar sobre) to make heavier; (irritar) to aggravate; **agravarse** vr to worsen, get worse
agraviar vt to offend; (ser injusto con) to wrong; **agraviarse** vr to take offence
agravio nm (ofensa) offence; (daño) wrong; (Jur) grievance
agredir vt to attack

agregado *nm* aggregate; (*persona*) attaché; (*profesor*) assistant professor

agregar *vt* to gather; (*añadir*) to add; (*persona*) to appoint

agresión *nf* aggression; (*ataque*) attack

agresivo, -a *adj* aggressive

agriar *vt* (*fig*) to (turn) sour; **agriarse** *vr* to turn sour

agrícola *adj* farming *cpd*, agricultural

agricultor, a *nm/f* farmer

agricultura *nf* agriculture, farming

agridulce *adj* bittersweet; (*Culin*) sweet and sour

agrietarse *vr* to crack; (*la piel*) to chap

agrimensor, a *nm/f* surveyor

agrio, -a *adj* bitter

agronomía *nf* agronomy, agriculture

agropecuario, -a *adj* farming *cpd*, agricultural

agrupación *nf* group; (*acto*) grouping

agrupar *vt* to group; (*Inform*) to block; **agruparse** *vr* (*Pol*) to form a group; (*juntarse*) to gather

agua *nf* water; (*Arq*) slope of a roof; **aguas** *nfpl* (*de joya*) water *sg*, sparkle *sg*; (*Med*) water *sg*, urine *sg*; (*Náut*) waters; **~s abajo/arriba** downstream/upstream; **~ bendita/destilada/potable** holy/distilled/drinking water; **~ caliente** hot water; **~ corriente** running water; **~ de colonia** eau de cologne; **~ mineral (con/sin gas)** (fizzy/non-fizzy) mineral water; **~s jurisdiccionales** territorial waters; **~s mayores** excrement *sg*; **~ pasada no mueve molino** it's no use crying over spilt milk; **estar con el ~ al cuello** to be up to one's neck; **venir como ~ de mayo** to be a godsend

aguacate *nm* avocado (pear)

aguacero *nm* (heavy) shower, downpour

aguado, -a *adj* watery, watered down ▷ *nf* (*Agr*) watering place; (*Náut*) water supply; (*Arte*) watercolour

aguafiestas *nm/f inv* spoilsport

aguafuerte *nf* etching

aguanieve *nf* sleet

aguantar *vt* (*tolerar*) to bear, put up with; (*soportar*) to take; (*sostener*) to hold up ▷ *vi* to last; **aguantarse** *vr* to restrain o.s.; **últimamente estás que no hay quien te aguante** you've been unbearable lately; **no aguanto la ópera** I can't stand opera; **la estantería no va a ~ el peso** the shelf won't take the weight; **aguántame el martillo un momento** can you hold the hammer for me for a moment?; **aguanta la respiración** hold your breath; **no pude ~ la risa** I couldn't help laughing; **este abrigo ya no aguanta otro invierno** this coat won't last another winter; **¡no aguanto más!** I can't take any more!; **¿puedes ~te hasta que lleguemos a casa?** can you hold out until we get home?; **si no puede venir, que se aguante** If he can't come, he'll just have to lump it

aguante *nm* (*paciencia*) patience; (*resistencia*) endurance; (*Deporte*) stamina

aguar *vt* to water down; (*fig*): **~ la fiesta a algn** to spoil sb's fun

aguardar *vt* to wait for

aguardiente *nm* brandy, liquor

aguarrás *nm* turpentine

agudeza *nf* sharpness; (*ingenio*) wit

agudizar *vt* to sharpen; (*crisis*) to make worse; **agudizarse** *vr* to worsen, deteriorate

agudo, -a *adj* sharp; (*voz*) high-pitched, piercing; (*dolor, enfermedad*) acute

agüero *nm*: **buen/mal ~** good/bad omen; **ser de buen ~** to augur well; **pájaro de mal ~** bird of ill omen

aguijón *nm* sting; (*fig*) spur

águila *nf* eagle; (*fig*) genius

aguileño, -a *adj* (*nariz*) aquiline; (*rostro*) sharp-featured

aguinaldo *nm* Christmas box

aguja *nf* needle; (*de reloj*) hand; (*Arq*) spire; (*Tec*) firing-pin; **agujas** *nfpl* (*Zool*) ribs; (*Ferro*) points

agujerear *vt* to make holes in; (*penetrar*) to pierce

agujero *nm* hole; (*Com*) deficit

agujetas *nfpl* stitch *sg*; (*rigidez*) stiffness *sg*; (*Méx: cordones*) shoelaces

aguzar *vt* to sharpen; (*fig*) to incite; **~ el oído** to prick up one's ears

ahí *adv* there; (*más lejos*) over there; **~ llega** here he comes; **~ está el problema** that's the problem; **~ arriba** up there; **lo tienes ~ mismo** you've got it right there; **¡hasta ~ hemos llegado!** so it has come to this!; **¡~ va!** (*objeto*) here it comes!; (*persona*) there he goes!; **~ donde le ve** as sure as he's standing there; **por ~** (*dirección*) that way; (*en algún lugar*) somewhere; (*aproximadamente*) thereabouts; **tú busca por ~** you look over there; **nos iremos por ~ a celebrarlo** we'll go out somewhere to celebrate; **¿las tijeras? andarán por ~** the scissors? they must be somewhere around; **200 o por ~** 200 or thereabouts; **de ~ que** so that, with the result that

ahijado, -a *nm/f* godson/daughter

ahínco *nm* earnestness; **con ~** eagerly

ahogar *vt* (*en agua*) to drown; (*por asfixia*) to suffocate, smother; **ahogarse** *vr* (*en agua*) to drown; (*por asfixia*) to suffocate; **~ el fuego** to put out the fire; **se ahogó en el río** he drowned in the river; **se ~on por falta de aire** they suffocated for lack of air; **me ahogo subiendo las cuestas** I get breathless going uphill

ahogo *nm* (*Med*) breathlessness; (*fig*) distress; (*problema económico*) financial difficulty

ahondar *vt* to deepen, make deeper; (*fig*) to go deeply into ▷ *vi*: **~ en** to go deeply into

ahora *adv* (*en este momento*) now; (*hace poco*) a moment ago, just now; (*dentro de poco*) in a moment; **~ mismo** right now; **~ voy** I'm coming; **de ~ en adelante** from now on; **por ~** for the moment; **~ bien** now then; **hasta ~** so far; **¡hasta ~!** (*despedida*) see you shortly!; **~ bien** however

ahorcar *vt* to hang; **ahorcarse** *vr* to hang o.s.

ahorita, ahoritita *adv* (*esp LAm: fam*) right now

ahorrar *vt* (*dinero*) to save; (*esfuerzos*) to save,

avoid; **ahorrarse** *vr*: **~se molestias** to save o.s. trouble

ahorro *nm* (*acto*) saving; (*frugalidad*) thrift; **ahorros** *nmpl* savings

ahuecar *vt* to hollow (out); (*voz*) to deepen ▷ *vi*: **¡ahueca!** (*fam*) beat it! (*fam*); **ahuecarse** *vr* to give o.s. airs

ahumar *vt* to smoke, cure; (*llenar de humo*) to fill with smoke ▷ *vi* to smoke; **ahumarse** *vr* to fill with smoke

ahuyentar *vt* to drive off, frighten off; (*fig*) to dispel

airado, -a *adj* angry

airar *vt* to anger; **airarse** *vr* to get angry

aire *nm* air; (*viento*) wind; (*corriente*) draught; (*Mus*) tune; **aires** *nmpl*: **darse ~s** to give o.s. airs; **al ~ libre** in the open air; **~ acondicionado** air conditioning; **tener ~ de** to look like; **estar de buen/mal ~** to be in a good/bad mood; **estar en el ~** (*Radio*) to be on the air; (*fig*) to be up in the air

airear *vt* to ventilate; (*fig: asunto*) to air; **airearse** *vr* to take the air

airoso, -a *adj* graceful

aislado, -a *adj* (*remoto*) isolated; (*incomunicado*) cut off; (*Elec*) insulated

aislar *vt* to isolate; (*Elec*) to insulate; **aislarse** *vr* to cut o.s. off

ajar *vt* to spoil; (*fig*) to abuse; **ajarse** *vr* to get crumpled; (*fig: piel*) to get wrinkled

ajardinado, -a *adj* landscaped

ajedrez *nm* chess

ajeno, -a *adj* (*que pertenece a otro*) somebody else's; **~ a** foreign to; **~ de** free from, devoid of; **por razones ajenas a nuestra voluntad** for reasons beyond our control

ajetreado, -a *adj* busy

ajetreo *nm* bustle

ají *nm* (*CS: pimiento picante*) chil(l)i; (*: pimiento dulce*) pepper; (*And: salsa*) chil(l)i sauce

ajo *nm* garlic; **~ porro** *o* **puerro** leek; **(tieso) como un ~** (*fam*) snobbish; **estar en el ~** to be mixed up in it

ajuar *nm* household furnishings *pl*; (*de novia*) trousseau; (*de niño*) layette

ajustado, -a *adj* (*tornillo*) tight; (*cálculo*) right; (*ropa*) tight(-fitting); (*Deporte: resultado*) close

ajustar *vt* (*adaptar*) to adjust; (*encajar*) to fit; (*Tec*) to engage; (*Tip*) to make up; (*apretar*) to tighten; (*concertar*) to agree (on) ▷ *vi* to fit; **ajustarse** *vr*: **~se a** (*coincidir*) to fit in with; (*adaptarse*) to keep to; **hay que ~ los frenos** the brakes need adjusting; **ajusté bien todas las tuercas** I tightened up all the nuts; **~ a algn las cuentas** to give sb a piece of one's mind; **esta puerta no ajusta bien** this door doesn't fit very well; **tu versión no se ajusta a la realidad** your version doesn't fit in with the facts; **nos ~emos al presupuesto** we'll keep to the budget; **tendremos que ~nos al horario previsto** we'll have to fit in with the programme

ajuste *nm* adjustment; (*Costura*) fitting; (*acuerdo*) compromise; (*de cuenta*) settlement; (*Inform*)

patch

al = **a+el**; *ver* **a**

ala *nf* wing; (*de sombrero*) brim; (*futbolista*) winger; **~ delta** hang-glider; **andar con el ~ caída** to be downcast; **cortar las ~s a algn** to clip sb's wings; **dar ~s a algn** to encourage sb

alabanza *nf* praise

alabar *vt* to praise

alacena *nf* cupboard (*Brit*), closet (*US*)

alacrán *nm* scorpion

alado, -a *adj* winged

alambique *nm* still

alambrada *nf*, **alambrado** *nm* wire fence; (*red*) wire netting

alambre *nm* wire; **~ de púas** barbed wire

alameda *nf* (*plantío*) poplar grove; (*lugar de paseo*) avenue, boulevard

álamo *nm* poplar; **~ temblón** aspen

alarde *nm* show, display; **hacer ~ de** to boast of

alargador *nm* extension cable *o* lead

alargar *vt* to lengthen, extend; (*paso*) to hasten; (*brazo*) to stretch out; (*cuerda*) to pay out; (*conversación*) to spin out; **alargarse** *vr* to get longer

alarido *nm* shriek

alarma *nf* alarm; **voz de ~** warning note; **dar la ~** to raise the alarm

alarmante *adj* alarming

alarmar *vt* to alarm; **alarmarse** *vr* to get alarmed

alba *nf* dawn

albacea *nm/f* executor/executrix

albahaca *nf* (*Bot*) basil

Albania *nf* Albania

albañil *nm* bricklayer; (*cantero*) mason

albarán *nm* (*Com*) invoice

albaricoque *nm* apricot

albedrío *nm*: **libre ~** free will

alberca *nf* reservoir; (*CAm, Méx*) swimming pool

albergar *vt* to shelter; (*esperanza*) to cherish; **albergarse** *vr* (*refugiarse*) to shelter; (*alojarse*) to lodge

albergue *nm* shelter, refuge; **~ de juventud** youth hostel

albóndiga *nf* meatball

albornoz *nm* bathrobe

alborotar *vi* to make a row ▷ *vt* to agitate, stir up; **alborotarse** *vr* to get excited; (*mar*) to get rough

alboroto *nm* row, uproar

alborozar *vt* to gladden; **alborozarse** *vr* to rejoice, be overjoyed

alborozo *nm* joy

albricias *nfpl*: **¡~!** good news!

álbum (*pl* **~s** *o* **-es**) *nm* album

albumen *nm* egg white, albumen

alcachofa *nf* (*globe*) artichoke; (*Tip*) golf ball; (*de ducha*) shower head

alcalde, -esa *nm/f* mayor(ess)

alcaldía *nf* mayoralty; (*lugar*) mayor's office

alcance *nm* (*de arma, cohete, onda*) range; (*de ley, reforma*) scope; (*de problema*) scale; (*Com*) adverse balance, deficit; **de gran ~** (*Mil*) long-range; (*fig*) far-reaching; **al ~ de la mano** within arm's reach; **tienen la victoria al ~ de la mano** victory is within their reach; **estar al/ fuera del ~ de algn** to be within/beyond one's reach; (*fig*) to be within one's powers/over one's head; **está al ~ de todos** it's within everybody's reach; **se desconoce el ~ de la catástrofe** the scale of the disaster isn't yet known

alcancía *nf* money box

alcantarilla *nf* (*de aguas residuales*) sewer; (*en la calle*) gutter

alcanzar *vt* (*con la mano, el pie*) to reach; (*autobús*) to catch; (*objetivo*) to achieve; (*bala*) to hit, strike ▷ *vi* (*ser suficiente*) to be enough; **alcánzame la sal, por favor** pass the salt please; **~ a alguien** to catch up (with) sb; **~ algo a algn** to hand sth to sb; **¿me alcanzas las tijeras?** could you pass me the scissors?; **~ un acuerdo** to reach an agreement; **~ la fama** to find fame; **con dos botellas ~á para todos** two bottles will be enough for all of us; **~ a hacer algo** to manage to do sth

alcaparra *nf* (*Bot*) caper

alcatraz *nm* gannet

alcaucil *nf* (*RP*) artichoke

alcayata *nf* hook

alcázar *nm* fortress; (*Náut*) quarter-deck

alcoba *nf* bedroom

alcohol *nm* alcohol; **no bebe ~** he doesn't drink (alcohol)

alcoholemia *nf* blood alcohol level; **prueba de la ~** breath test

alcohólico, -a *adj, nm/f* alcoholic

alcoholímetro *nm* Breathalyser®, drunkometer (US)

alcoholismo *nm* alcoholism

alcornoque *nm* cork tree; (*fam*) idiot

alcurnia *nf* lineage

aldaba *nf* (door) knocker

aldea *nf* village

aldeano, -a *adj* village *cpd* ▷ *nm/f* villager

ale *excl* come on!, let's go!

aleación *nf* alloy

aleatorio, -a *adj* random, contingent; **acceso ~** (*Inform*) random access

aleccionar *vt* to instruct; (*adiestrar*) to train

alegación *nf* allegation

alegar *vt* (*dificultad etc*) to plead; (*Jur*) to allege ▷ *vi* (*LAm*) to argue; **~ que ...** to give as an excuse that ...

alegato *nm* (*Jur*) allegation; (*escrito*) indictment; (*declaración*) statement; (*LAm*) argument

alegoría *nf* allegory

alegrar *vt* (*causar alegría*) to cheer (up); (*fuego*) to poke; (*fiesta*) to liven up; **alegrarse** *vr* (*fam*) to get merry *o* tight; **~se de** to be glad about

alegre *adj* happy, cheerful; (*fam*) merry, tight; (*licencioso*) risqué, blue

alegría *nf* happiness; **~ vital** joie de vivre

alejamiento *nm* removal; (*distancia*) remoteness

alejar *vt* to move away; (*fig*) to estrange; **alejarse**

vr to move away; **alejémonos un poco más** let's move a bit further away; **no te alejes de mi lado** stay by me; **aléjate un poco del fuego** move a bit further away from the fire; **el barco se iba alejando de la costa** the boat was getting further and further away from the coast

aleluya *nm* (*canto*) hallelujah

alemán, -ana *adj, nm/f* German ▷ *nm* (*lengua*) German

Alemania *nf* Germany; **~ Occidental/Oriental** West/East Germany

alentador, a *adj* encouraging

alentar *vt* to encourage

alergia *nf* allergy

alero *nm* (*de tejado*) eaves *pl*; (*de foca, Deporte*) flipper; (*Auto*) mudguard

alerta *adj inv, nm* alert

aleta *nf* (*de pez*) fin; (*de ave*) wing; (*de coche*) mudguard

aletargar *vt* (*adormecer*) to make drowsy; (*entumecer*) to make numb; **aletargarse** *vr* (*adormecerse*) to grow drowsy; (*entumecerse*) to become numb

aletear *vi* to flutter; (*ave*) to flap its wings; (*individuo*) to wave one's arms

alevín *nm* fry, young fish

alevosía *nf* treachery

alfabeto *nm* alphabet

alfalfa *nf* alfalfa, lucerne

alfarería *nf* (*artesanía*) pottery; (*tienda*) pottery shop

alfarero *nm* potter

alféizar *nm* windowsill

alférez *nm* (*Mil*) second lieutenant; (*Náut*) ensign

alfil *nm* (*Ajedrez*) bishop

alfiler *nm* pin; (*broche*) clip; (*pinza*) clothes peg (*Brit*) *o* pin (*US*); **~ de gancho** (*CS*) safety pin; **prendido con ~es** shaky

alfiletero *nm* needle case

alfombra *nf* carpet; (*más pequeña*) rug

alfombrar *vt* to carpet

alfombrilla *nf* rug, mat; (*Inform*) mouse mat *o* pad

alforja *nf* saddlebag

algarabía *nf* (*fam*) gibberish; (*griterío*) hullabaloo

algarroba *nf* carob

algarrobo *nm* carob tree

algas *nfpl* seaweed *sg*

algazara *nf* din, uproar

álgebra *nf* algebra

álgido, -a *adj* icy; (*momento etc*) crucial, decisive

algo *pron* (*en frases afirmativas*) something; (*en frases interrogativas*) anything ▷ *adv* somewhat, rather; **~ se está quemando** something is burning; **¿has visto ~ que te gustara?** have you seen anything you liked?; **¿quieres ~ de comer?** would you like something to eat?; **por ~ será** there must be some reason for it; **~ así como** a bit like; **o ~ así** or something of the sort; **es ~ difícil** it's rather awkward

algodón *nm* cotton; (*planta*) cotton plant; **~ de azúcar** candy floss (*Brit*), cotton candy (*US*); **~ hidrófilo** cotton wool (*Brit*), absorbent cotton

(US)

algodonero, -a adj cotton cpd ▷ nm/f cotton grower ▷ nm cotton plant

alguacil nm bailiff; (Taur) mounted official

alguien pron (en frases afirmativas) someone, somebody; (en frases interrogativas) anyone, anybody

alguno, -a adj (delante de nm **algún**) some; (en preguntas) any; (después de n): **no tiene talento ~** he has no talent, he hasn't any talent ▷ pron (alguien) someone, somebody; **algún día iré** I'll go there some day; **me quedan algunas esperanzas de aprobar** I've still got some hope of passing; **algún que otro libro** some book or other; **algún día iré** I'll go one o some day; **sin interés ~** without the slightest interest; **~ que otro** an occasional one; **he leído algún que otro libro sobre el tema** I've read the odd book on the subject; **¿compraste algún cuadro?** did you buy any pictures?; **¿quieres alguna cosa más?** was there anything else?; **~s piensan** some (people) think; **~ de ellos** one of them

alhaja nf jewel; (tesoro) precious object, treasure

alhelí nm wallflower, stock

aliado, -a adj allied

alianza nf (Pol etc) alliance; (anillo) wedding ring

aliar vt to ally; **aliarse** vr to form an alliance

alias adv alias

alicatar vt to tile

alicate(s) nm(pl) pliers pl; **alicate(s) de uñas** nail clippers

aliciente nm incentive; (atracción) attraction

alienación nf alienation

aliento nm breath; (respiración) breathing; **sin ~** breathless; **de un ~** in one breath; (fig) in one go

aligerar vt to lighten; (reducir) to shorten; (aliviar) to alleviate; (mitigar) to ease

alijo nm (Náut) unloading; (contrabando) smuggled goods

alimaña nf pest

alimentación nf (comida) food; (acción) feeding; (tienda) grocer's (shop); **~ continua** (en fotocopiadora etc) stream feed

alimentador nm: **~ de papel** sheet-feeder

alimentar vt to feed; (nutrir) to nourish; **alimentarse** vr: **~se (de)** to feed (on)

alimenticio, -a adj food cpd; (nutritivo) nourishing, nutritious

alimento nm food; (nutrición) nourishment; **alimentos** nmpl (Jur) alimony sg

alineación nf alignment; (Deporte) line-up

alinear vt to align; (Tip) to justify; **alinearse** vr to line up; **~se en** to fall in with

aliñar vt (Culin) to dress

aliño nm (Culin) dressing

alisar vt to smooth

aliso nm alder

alistar vt to recruit; **alistarse** vr to enlist; (inscribirse) to enrol; (LAm: prepararse) to get ready

aliviar vt (carga) to lighten; (persona) to relieve; (dolor) to relieve, alleviate

alivio nm alleviation, relief; **~ de luto** half-mourning

aljibe nm cistern

allá adv (lugar) there; (por ahí) over there; (tiempo) then; **~ abajo** down there; **más ~ further** on; **más ~ de** beyond; **¡~ tú!** that's your problem!

allanamiento nm (LAm Policía) raid, search; **~ de morada** housebreaking

allanar vt to flatten, level (out); (igualar) to smooth (out); (fig) to subdue; (Jur) to burgle, break into; (LAm Policía) to raid, search; **allanarse** vr to fall down; **~se a** to submit to, accept

allegado, -a adj near, close ▷ nm/f relation

allí adv there; **~ mismo** right there; **por ~** (en ese lugar) over there; (por ese camino) that way

alma nf soul; (persona) person; (Tec) core; **se le cayó el ~ a los pies** he became very disheartened; **entregar el ~** to pass away; **estar con el ~ en la boca** to be scared to death; **lo siento en el ~** I am truly sorry; **tener el ~ en un hilo** to have one's heart in one's mouth; **estar como ~ en pena** to suffer; **ir como ~ que lleva el diablo** to go at breakneck speed

almacén nm (depósito) warehouse, store; (Mil) magazine; (LAm: tienda de comestibles) grocer's shop, foodstore, grocery store (US); **(grandes) almacenes** nmpl department store sg; **~ depositario** (Com) depository

almacenaje nm storage; **~ secundario** (Inform) backing storage

almacenar vt to store, put in storage; (Inform) to store; (proveerse) to stock up with

almanaque nm almanac

almeja nf clam

almendra nf almond

almendro nm almond tree

almíbar nm syrup

almidón nm starch

almidonar vt to starch

almirantazgo nm admiralty

almirante nm admiral

almirez nm mortar

almizcle nm musk

almohada nf pillow; (funda) pillowcase

almohadilla nf cushion; (Tec) pad; (LAm) pincushion

almohadón nm large pillow

almorranas nfpl piles, haemorrhoids (Brit), hemorrhoids (US)

almorzar vt: **~ una tortilla** to have an omelette for lunch ▷ vi to (have) lunch

almuerzo nm lunch

alocado, -a adj crazy

alojamiento nm lodging(s) (pl); (viviendas) housing

alojar vt to lodge; **alojarse** vr: **~se en** to stay at; (bala) to lodge in

alondra nf lark, skylark

alpaca nf alpaca

alpargata nf espadrille

Alpes nmpl: **los ~** the Alps

alpinismo nm mountaineering, climbing

alpinista nm/f mountaineer, climber
alpino, -a adj alpine
alpiste nm (semillas) birdseed; (CAm fam: dinero) dough; (fam: alcohol) booze
alquilar vt (suj: propietario: inmuebles) to let, rent (out); (: coche) to hire out; (: TV) to rent (out); (suj: alquilador: inmuebles, TV) to rent; (: coche) to hire; **"se alquila casa"** "house to let (Brit) o to rent (US) "
alquimia nf alchemy
alquitrán nm tar
alrededor adv around, about; **alrededores** nmpl surroundings; **~ de** prep around, about; **mirar a su ~** to look (round) about one
alta nf (certificate of) discharge; **dar a algn de ~** to discharge sb; **darse de ~** (Mil) to join, enrol; (Deporte) to declare o.s. fit
altanería nf haughtiness, arrogance
altanero, -a adj haughty, arrogant
altar nm altar
altavoz nm loudspeaker; (amplificador) amplifier
alteración nf alteration; (alboroto) disturbance; **~ del orden público** breach of the peace
alterar vt (plan) to alter; (orden público) to disturb; **alterarse** vr (persona) to get upset
altercado nm argument
alternar vt to alternate ▷ vi: **alternarse** vr to alternate; (turnar) to take turns; **~ con** to mix with
alternativo, -a adj alternative; (alterno) alternating ▷ nf alternative; (elección) choice; **alternativas** nfpl ups and downs; **tomar la alternativa** (Taur) to become a fully-qualified bullfighter
alterno, -a adj (Bot, Mat) alternate; (Elec) alternating
alteza nf (tratamiento) highness
altibajos nmpl ups and downs
altiplanicie nf, **altiplano** nm high plateau
altisonante adj high-flown, high-sounding
altitud nf altitude, height; **a una ~ de** at a height of
altivo, -a adj haughty, arrogant
alto, -a adj (monte, techo) high; (persona, edificio) tall; (música, voz) loud; (ideales) high, lofty; (Geo, clase) upper ▷ nm (parada) halt; (Mus) alto; (Geo) hill; (LAm) pile ▷ adv (estar, subir) high; (hablar) loud, loudly; **¡~!** excl halt!; **en alta mar** on the high seas; **en voz alta** in a loud voice; **a altas horas de la noche** in the middle of the night; **alta fidelidad** hi-fi; **la pared tiene 2 metros de ~** the wall is 2 metres high; **hacer un ~ to** stop; **en lo ~ de** at the top of; **pasar algo por ~** to overlook sth; **~s y bajos** ups and downs; **el ~ el fuego** ceasefire; **celebraron la victoria por todo lo ~** they celebrated the victory in style; **poner la radio más ~** to turn the radio up; **¡más ~, por favor!** louder, please!
altoparlante nm (LAm) loudspeaker
altruismo nm altruism
altura nf height; (Náut) depth; (Geo) latitude; **la pared tiene 1.80 de ~** the wall is 1 metre 80 (cm)

high; **a esta ~ del año** at this time of the year; **estar a la ~ de las circunstancias** to rise to the occasion; **ha sido un partido de gran ~** it has been a terrific match
alubia nf French bean, kidney bean
alucinación nf hallucination
alucinante adj (fam: estupendo) great, super
alucinar vi to hallucinate ▷ vt to deceive; (fascinar) to fascinate
alud nm avalanche; (fig) flood
aludir vi: **~ a** to allude to; **darse por aludido** to take the hint; **no te des por aludido** don't take it personally
alumbrado nm lighting
alumbramiento nm lighting; (Med) childbirth, delivery
alumbrar vt to light (up) ▷ vi (iluminar) to give light; (Med) to give birth
aluminio nm aluminium (Brit), aluminum (US)
alumno, -a nm/f pupil, student
alusión nf allusion
alusivo, -a adj allusive
aluvión nm (Geo) alluvium; (fig) flood; **~ de improperios** torrent of abuse
alza nf rise; (Mil) sight; **~s fijas/graduables** fixed/adjustable sights; **al o en ~** (precio) rising; **jugar al ~** to speculate on a rising o bull market; **cotizarse o estar en ~** to be rising
alzamiento nm (aumento) rise, increase; (acción) lifting, raising; (mejor postura) higher bid; (rebelión) rising; (Com) fraudulent bankruptcy
alzar vt (objeto, persona) to lift (up); (brazo, copa, monumento, muro, precio) to raise; (cuello de abrigo) to turn up; (Agr) to gather in; (Tip) to gather; **alzarse** vr (levantarse) to rise; (rebelarse) to revolt; (Com) to go fraudulently bankrupt; (Jur) to appeal; **~ la voz** to raise one's voice; **~ la mirada** o **los ojos** to look up; **se alzó el telón** the curtain rose; **en la plaza se alzaba la iglesia** the church stood in the square; **~se en armas** to take up arms; **~se con el premio** to carry off the prize
ama nf lady of the house; (dueña) owner; (institutriz) governess; (madre adoptiva) foster mother; **~ de casa** housewife; **~ de cría** o de **leche** wet-nurse; **~ de llaves** housekeeper
amabilidad nf kindness; (simpatía) niceness
amable adj kind, nice; **¡muy ~!** thanks very much
amaestrado, -a adj (animal) trained; (en circo etc) performing
amaestrar vt to train
amagar vt, vi to threaten
amago nm threat; (gesto) threatening gesture; (Med) symptom
amainar vt (Náut) to lower, take in; (fig) to calm ▷ vi: **amainarse** vr to drop, die down; **el viento amaina** the wind is dropping
amalgama nf amalgam
amalgamar vt to amalgamate; (combinar) to combine, mix
amamantar vt to suckle, nurse
amanecer vi to dawn; (fig) to appear, begin to

show ▷ *nm* dawn; **el niño amaneció con fiebre** the child woke up with a fever

amanerado, -a *adj* affected

amansar *vt* to tame; (*persona*) to subdue; **amansarse** *vr* (*persona*) to calm down

amante *adj*: ~ **de** fond of ▷ *nm/f* lover

amapola *nf* poppy

amar *vt* to love

amargado, -a *adj* bitter, embittered

amargar *vt* to make bitter; (*fig*) to embitter; **amargarse** *vr* to become embittered

amargo, -a *adj* bitter

amargura *nf* = **amargor**

amarillento, -a *adj* yellowish; (*tez*) sallow

amarillo, -a *adj*, *nm* yellow

amarra *nf* (*Náut*) mooring line; **amarras** *nfpl* (*fig*) protection *sg*; **tener buenas ~s** to have good connections; **soltar ~s** to set off

amarrar *vt* (*Náut*) to moor; (*sujetar*) to tie up

amartillar *vt* (*fusil*) to cock

amasar *vt* to knead; (*mezclar*) to mix, prepare; (*confeccionar*) to concoct

amasijo *nm* (*acción*) kneading; (*fig*) hotchpotch

amateur *nm/f* amateur

amatista *nf* amethyst

amazona *nf* horsewoman

ambages *nmpl*: **sin ~** in plain language

ámbar *nm* amber

ambición *nf* ambition

ambicionar *vt* to aspire to

ambicioso, -a *adj* ambitious

ambidextro, -a *adj* ambidextrous

ambientación *nf* (*Cine, Lit etc*) setting; (*Radio etc*) sound effects *pl*

ambientador *nm* air freshener

ambiente *nm* (*tb fig*) atmosphere; (*LAm*) room; **se respiraba un ~ tenso** there was a tense atmosphere; **había mucho ~ en la plaza de toros** there was a great atmosphere in the bullring; **había un ~ muy cargado en la habitación** it was very stuffy in the room; **necesito cambiar de ~** I need a change of scene; **el medio ~** the environment

ambigüedad *nf* ambiguity

ambiguo, -a *adj* ambiguous

ámbito *nm* (*campo*) field; (*fig*) scope

ambos, -as *adj pl, pron pl* both

ambulancia *nf* ambulance

ambulante *adj* travelling, itinerant; (*biblioteca*) mobile

ambulatorio *nm* state health-service clinic

ameba *nf* amoeba

amedrentar *vt* to scare

amén *excl* amen; ~ **de** *prep* besides, in addition to; **en un decir ~** in the twinkling of an eye; **decir ~ a todo** to have no mind of one's own

amenaza *nf* threat

amenazar *vt* to threaten ▷ *vi*: ~ **con hacer algo** to threaten to do sth

amenidad *nf* pleasantness

ameno, -a *adj* pleasant

América *nf* (*continente*) America, the Americas;

(*EEUU*) America; (*Hispanoamérica*) Latin *o* South America; ~ **del Norte/del Sur** North/South America; ~ **Central/Latina** Central/Latin America

americana *nf* coat, jacket; *ver tb* **americano**

americano, -a *adj, nm/f* (*de EE.UU.*) American; (*latinoamericano*) Latin *o* South American; *ver tb* **americana**

amerindio, -a *adj, nm/f* Amerindian, American Indian

amerizar *vi* (*Aviat*) to land (on the sea)

ametralladora *nf* machine gun

amianto *nm* asbestos

amigable *adj* friendly

amígdala *nf* tonsil

amigo, -a *adj* friendly ▷ *nm/f* friend; (*amante*) lover; ~ **de lo ajeno** thief; ~ **por carta** penfriend; **hacerse ~s** to become friends; **ser ~ de** to like, be fond of; **ser muy ~s** to be close friends

amilanar *vt* to scare; **amilanarse** *vr* to get scared

aminorar *vt* to diminish; (*reducir*) to reduce; ~ **la marcha** to slow down

amistad *nf* friendship; **amistades** *nfpl* friends

amistoso, -a *adj* friendly

amnesia *nf* amnesia

amnistía *nf* amnesty

amo *nm* owner; (*jefe*) boss

amodorrarse *vr* to get sleepy

amoldar *vt* to mould; (*adaptar*) to adapt

amonestación *nf* warning; **amonestaciones** *nfpl* marriage banns

amonestar *vt* (*advertir*) to warn; (*publicar las amonestaciones*) to publish the banns of

amoniaco *nm* ammonia

amontonar *vt* to collect, pile up; **amontonarse** *vr* (*gente*) to crowd together; (*acumularse*) to pile up; (*datos*) to accumulate; (*desastres*) to come one on top of another

amor *nm* love; (*amante*) lover; **hacer el ~** to make love; ~ **propio** self-respect; **por (el) ~ de Dios** for God's sake; **estar al ~ de la lumbre** to be close to the fire

amoratado, -a *adj* purple, blue with cold; (*con cardenales*) bruised

amordazar *vt* to muzzle; (*fig*) to gag

amorfo, -a *adj* amorphous, shapeless

amorío *nm* (*fam*) love affair

amoroso, -a *adj* affectionate, loving

amortajar *vt* (*fig*) to shroud

amortiguador *nm* shock absorber; (*parachoques*) bumper; (*silenciador*) silencer; **amortiguadores** *nmpl* (*Auto*) suspension *sg*

amortiguar *vt* to deaden; (*ruido*) to muffle; (*color*) to soften

amortización *nf* (*de bono*) redemption; (*de préstamo*) repayment; (*Com*) capital allowance

amotinar *vt* to stir up, incite (to riot); **amotinarse** *vr* to mutiny

amparar *vt* to protect; **ampararse** *vr* to seek protection; (*de la lluvia etc*) to shelter

amparo *nm* help, protection; **al ~ de** under the

protection of

amperio nm ampère, amp

ampliación nf enlargement; (extensión) extension

ampliar vt (foto) to enlarge; (espacio, plazo) to extend

amplificación nf enlargement

amplificador nm amplifier

amplificar vt to amplify

amplio, -a adj spacious; (falda etc) full; (extenso) extensive; (ancho) wide

amplitud nf (de sala) spaciousness; (de conocimientos) extent; ~ **de miras** broadmindedness; **de gran** ~ far-reaching

ampolla nf blister; (Med) ampoule

ampuloso, -a adj bombastic, pompous

amputar vt to cut off, amputate

amueblar vt to furnish

amuleto nm (lucky) charm

amurallar vt to wall up o in

anacronismo nm anachronism

ánade nm duck

anagrama nm anagram

anales nmpl annals

analfabetismo nm illiteracy

analfabeto, -a adj, nm/f illiterate

analgésico nm painkiller, analgesic

análisis nm inv analysis; ~ **de costos-beneficios** cost-benefit analysis; ~ **de mercados** market research; ~ **de sangre** blood test

analista nm/f (gen) analyst; (Pol, Historia) chronicler; ~ **de sistemas** (Inform) systems analyst

analizar vt to analyse

analogía nf analogy; **por** ~ **con** on the analogy of

analógico, -a adj analogue

análogo, -a adj analogous, similar

ananá(s) nm pineapple

anaquel nm shelf

anarquía nf anarchy

anarquismo nm anarchism

anarquista nm/f anarchist

anatomía nf anatomy

anca nf rump, haunch; **ancas** nfpl (fam) behind sg; **llevar a algn en ~s** to carry sb behind one

ancestral adj (costumbre) age-old

ancho, -a adj (camino, puente) wide; (calle, sonrisa) broad; (chaqueta, pantalón) loose; (falda) full; (fig) liberal ▷ nm width; (Ferro) gauge; **es ~ de espaldas** he's broad-shouldered; **le gusta llevar ropa ancha** he likes to wear loose clothing; **me está ~ el vestido** the dress is too big for me; **le viene muy ~ el cargo** (fig) the job is too much for him; **ponerse ~** to get conceited; **quedarse tan ~** to go on as if nothing had happened; **estar a sus anchas** to be at one's ease

anchoa nf anchovy

anchura nf width; (extensión) wideness

anciano, -a adj old, aged ▷ nm/f old man/woman ▷ nm elder

ancla nf anchor; **levar ~s** to weigh anchor

ancladero nm anchorage

anclar vi to (drop) anchor

andador nf baby-walker sg

andadura nf gait; (de caballo) pace

Andalucía nf Andalusia

andaluz, a adj, nm/f Andalusian

andamio nm, **andamiaje** nm scaffold(ing)

andar vi (ir a pie) to walk; (dirigirse) to go, travel; (funcionar) to go, work ▷ vt to go, cover, travel ▷ nm walk, gait; **andarse** vr (irse) to go away o off; **iremos andando a la estación** we'll walk to the station; ~ **a pie/a caballo/en bicicleta** to go on foot/on horseback/by bicycle; **anda en o por los 40** he's about 40; **¿en qué andas?** what are you up to?; **¿qué tal andas?** how are you?; **andamos mal de dinero/tiempo** we're short of money/time; **anda por aquí** it's round here somewhere; **anda por los cuarenta** he's about forty; **siempre andan a gritos** they're always shouting; **no andes en los cajones** stop rummaging around in those drawers; **¡anda!** (sorpresa) go on!; ~ **haciendo algo** to be doing sth; **ando buscando un socio** I'm looking for a partner; **este reloj anda muy bien** this watch goes very well; **anduvimos varios kilómetros** we walked several kilometres; **todo se ~á** all in good time; **~se por las ramas** to beat about the bush; **no ~se con rodeos** to call a spade a spade; **ándate con cuidado** take care

andariego, -a adj fond of travelling

andén nm (Ferro) platform; (Náut) quayside; (CAm, Col: acera) pavement (Brit), sidewalk (US)

Andes nmpl: **los ~** the Andes

Andorra nf Andorra

andrajo nm rag

andrajoso, -a adj ragged

andurriales nmpl out-of-the-way place sg, the sticks; **en esos ~** in that godforsaken spot

anécdota nf anecdote, story

anegar vt to flood; (ahogar) to drown; **anegarse** vr to drown; (hundirse) to sink

anejo, -a adj attached ▷ nm (Arq) annexe

anemia nf anaemia

anestesia nf anaesthetic; ~ **general/local** general/local anaesthetic

anestesiar vt to anaesthetize (Brit), anesthetize (US)

anexar vt to annex; (documento) to attach; (Inform) to append

anexión nf, **anexionamiento** nm annexation

anexionar vt to annex; **anexionarse** vr: **~se un país** to annex a country

anexo, -a adj attached ▷ nm annexe

anfetamina nf amphetamine

anfibio, -a adj amphibious ▷ nm amphibian

anfiteatro nm amphitheatre; (Teat) dress circle

anfitrión, -ona nm/f host(ess)

ángel nm angel; ~ **de la guarda** guardian angel; **tener ~** to have charm

angélico, -a, angelical adj angelic(al)

angina nf (Med): ~ **de pecho** angina; **tener ~s** to have a throat infection

anglicano, -a *adj, nm/f* Anglican
anglicismo *nm* anglicism
anglosajón, -ona *adj, nm/f* Anglo-Saxon
angosto, -a *adj* narrow
anguila *nf* eel; **anguilas** *nfpl* slipway *sg*
angula *nf* elver, baby eel
ángulo *nm* angle; (*esquina*) corner; (*curva*) bend
angustia *nf* anguish
angustiar *vt* to distress, grieve; **angustiarse** *vr* to be distressed
anhelante *adj* eager; (*deseoso*) longing
anhelar *vt* (*con impaciencia*) to be eager for; (*con ilusión*) to long for, desire ▷ *vi* to pant, gasp
anhelo *nm* desire
anhídrido *nm*: ~ **carbónico** carbon dioxide
anidar *vt* (*acoger*) to take in, shelter ▷ *vi* to nest; (*fig*) to make one's home
anilla *nf* ring; (**las**) ~**s** (*Deporte*) the rings
anillo *nm* ring; ~ **de boda** wedding ring; ~ **de compromiso** engagement ring; **venir como** ~ **al dedo** to suit to a tee
ánima *nf* soul; **las** ~**s** the Angelus (bell) *sg*
animación *nf* liveliness; (*vitalidad*) life; (*actividad*) bustle
animado, -a *adj* (*vivo*) lively; (*vivaz*) animated; (*concurrido*) bustling; (*alegre*) in high spirits; **dibujos** ~**s** cartoon *sg*
animador, a *nm/f* (*TV*) host(ess); *ver tb* **animadora**
animadora *nf* (*Deporte*) cheerleader; *ver tb* **animador**
animadversión *nf* ill-will, antagonism
animal *adj* animal; (*fig*) stupid ▷ *nm* animal; (*fig*) fool; (*bestia*) brute
animar *vt* (*alegrar*) to liven up, brighten up, cheer up; (*alentar*) to encourage; (*estimular*) to stimulate; (*Bio*) to animate, give life to; **animarse** *vr* (*alegrarse*) to cheer up; (*decidirse*) to make up one's mind; **lo ha pasado muy mal y necesita que la animen** she has had a rough time and needs cheering up; **estuvimos animando al equipo** we were cheering the team on; **sus chistes** ~**on la fiesta** his jokes livened up the party; ~ **a alguien a que haga algo** to encourage somebody to do something; **yo la animé a presentarse al concurso** I encouraged her to take part in the competition; **¡vamos, anímate hombre!** come on, cheer up mate!; ~**se a hacer algo** to make up one's mind to do something
ánimo *nm* soul, mind; (*valentía*) courage ▷ *excl* cheer up!; **cobrar** ~ to take heart; **dar** ~(**s**) **a** to encourage
animoso, -a *adj* brave; (*vivo*) lively
aniquilar *vt* to annihilate, destroy
anís *nm* (*grano*) aniseed; (*licor*) anisette
aniversario *nm* anniversary
anoche *adv* last night; **antes de** ~ the night before last
anochecer *vi* to get dark ▷ *nm* nightfall, dark; **al** ~ at nightfall
anodino, -a *adj* dull, anodyne

anomalía *nf* anomaly
anonadado, -a *adj* stunned
anonimato *nm* anonymity
anónimo, -a *adj* anonymous; (*Com*) limited ▷ *nm* (*carta*) anonymous letter; (: *maliciosa*) poison-pen letter
anorak (*pl* -**s**) *nm* anorak
anorexia *nf* anorexia
anormal *adj* abnormal
anotación *nf* note
anotar *vt* (*dato, número*) to take a note of; (*texto*) to annotate ▷ *vi* (*Deporte*) to score; **Jones anotó 34 puntos** Jones scored 34 points
anquilosamiento *nm* (*fig*) paralysis, stagnation
ansia *nf* anxiety; (*añoranza*) yearning
ansiar *vt* to long for
ansiedad *nf* anxiety
ansioso, -a *adj* anxious; (*anhelante*) eager; ~ **de** o **por algo** greedy for sth
antagónico, -a *adj* antagonistic; (*opuesto*) contrasting
antagonista *nm/f* antagonist
antaño *adv* long ago
Antártico *nm*: **el (océano)** ~ the Antarctic (Ocean)
ante *prep* before, in the presence of; (*encarado con*) faced with ▷ *nm* suede; ~ **todo** above all
anteanoche *adv* the night before last
anteayer *adv* the day before yesterday
antebrazo *nm* forearm
antecedente *adj* previous ▷ *nm*: ~**s** *nmpl* (*profesionales*) background *sg*; ~**s penales** criminal record; **no tener** ~**s** to have a clean record; **estar en** ~**s** to be well-informed; **poner a algn en** ~**s** to put sb in the picture
anteceder *vt* to precede, go before
antecesor, a *nm/f* predecessor
antedicho, -a *adj* aforementioned
antelación *nf*: **con** ~ in advance
antemano: **de** ~ *adv* beforehand, in advance
antena *nf* (*de hormiga*) antenna; (*de televisión etc*) aerial
anteojo *nm* eyeglass; **anteojos** *nmpl* (*esp LAm*) glasses, spectacles
antepasados *nmpl* ancestors
anteponer *vt* to place in front; (*fig*) to prefer
anteproyecto *nm* preliminary sketch; (*fig*) blueprint; (*Pol*): ~ **de ley** draft bill
anterior *adj* preceding, previous
anterioridad *nf*: **con** ~ prior to, before
antes *adv* (*con anteriordad*) before; (*anteriormente*) sooner; (*primero*) first; (*hace tiempo*) previously, once; (*más bien*) rather ▷ *conj*: ~ (**de**) **que** before; **la noche** ~ the night before; **mucho/poco** ~ long/shortly before; **dos días** ~ two days before o previously; ~ **no había tanto desempleo** there didn't use to be so much unemployment; ~ **de** before; **el supermercado está** ~ **del semáforo** the supermarket is just before the lights; ~ **de la cena** before dinner; ~ **de ir al teatro** before going to the theatre; ~ **de que te vayas** before you go; **tomo el avión** ~ **que el barco** I take

the plane rather than the boat; **~ que verlo prefiero esperar aquí** I'd rather stay here than see him; **~ muerto que esclavo** better dead than enslaved; **~ bien** (but) rather; **cuanto ~, lo ~ posible** as soon as possible; **cuanto ~ mejor** the sooner the better; **~ de nada** first and foremost

antesala *nf* anteroom
antiaéreo, -a *adj* anti-aircraft
antibalas *adj inv*: **chaleco ~** bulletproof jacket
antibiótico *nm* antibiotic
anticiclón *nm* (*Meteorología*) anti-cyclone
anticipación *nf* anticipation; **con 10 minutos de ~** 10 minutes early
anticipado, -a *adj* (in) advance; **por ~** in advance
anticipar *vt* to anticipate; (*adelantar*) to bring forward; (*Com*) to advance; **anticiparse** *vr*: **~se a su época** to be ahead of one's time
anticipo *nm* (*Com*) advance; *ver tb* **anticipación**
anticonceptivo, -a *adj, nm* contraceptive; **métodos ~s** contraceptive devices
anticongelante *nm* antifreeze
anticuado, -a *adj* out-of-date, old-fashioned; (*desusado*) obsolete
anticuario *nm* antique dealer
anticuerpo *nm* (*Med*) antibody
antidepresivo *nm* antidepressant
antidoping *adj inv* anti-drug
antídoto *nm* antidote
antiestético, -a *adj* unsightly
antifaz *nm* mask; (*velo*) veil
antiglobalización *nf* anti-globalization; **manifestantes ~** anti-globalization protesters
antigualla *nf* antique; (*reliquia*) relic; **antiguallas** *nfpl* old things
antiguamente *adv* formerly; (*hace mucho tiempo*) long ago
antigüedad *nf* antiquity; (*artículo*) antique; (*rango*) seniority
antiguo, -a *adj* (*objeto, mueble*) old; (*historia, muralla*) ancient; (*anterior*) former; **el ~ Egipto** ancient Egypt; **un coche ~** a vintage car; **el ~ secretario general del partido** the former general secretary of the party; **a la antigua** in the old-fashioned way
antillano, -a *adj, nm/f* West Indian
Antillas *nfpl*: **las ~** the West Indies, the Antilles; **el mar de las ~** the Caribbean Sea
antílope *nm* antelope
antinatural *adj* unnatural
antipatía *nf* antipathy, dislike
antipático, -a *adj* disagreeable, unpleasant
antirrobo *adj inv*: (*dispositivo*) **~** (*para casas etc*) burglar alarm; (*para coches*) car alarm
antisemita *adj* anti-Semitic ▷ *nm/f* anti-Semite
antiséptico, -a *adj, nm* antiseptic
antítesis *nf inv* antithesis
antojadizo, -a *adj* capricious
antojarse *vr* (*desear*): **se me antoja comprarlo** I have a mind to buy it; (*pensar*): **se me antoja que** I have a feeling that
antojo *nm* caprice, whim; (*rosa*) birthmark;

(*lunar*) mole; **hacer a su ~** to do as one pleases
antología *nf* anthology
antonomasia *nf*: **por ~** par excellence
antorcha *nf* torch
antro *nm* cavern; **~ de corrupción** (*fig*) den of iniquity
antropófago, -a *adj, nm/f* cannibal
antropología *nf* anthropology
antropólogo, -a *nm/f* anthropologist
anual *adj* annual
anualidad *nf* annuity, annual payment; **~ vitalicia** life annuity
anuario *nm* yearbook
anudar *vt* to knot, tie; (*unir*) to join; **anudarse** *vr* to get tied up; **se me anudó la voz** I got a lump in my throat
anulación *nf* (*de contrato*) annulment, cancellation; (*de ley*) repeal
anular *vt* to annul, cancel; (*suscripción*) to cancel; (*ley*) to repeal ▷ *nm* ring finger
anunciación *nf* announcement; **A~** (*Rel*) Annunciation
anunciante *nm/f* (*Com*) advertiser
anunciar *vt* to announce; (*proclamar*) to proclaim; (*Com*) to advertise
anuncio *nm* announcement; (*señal*) sign; (*Com*) advertisement; (*cartel*) poster; (*Teat*) bill; **~s por palabras** classified ads
anzuelo *nm* hook; (*para pescar*) fish hook; **picar el ~** to swallow the bait
añadido *nm* addition
añadidura *nf* addition, extra; **por ~** besides, in addition
añadir *vt* to add
añejo, -a *adj* old; (*vino*) vintage; (*jamón*) well-cured
añicos *nmpl*: **hacer ~** to smash, shatter; **hacerse ~** to smash, shatter
añil *nm* (*Bot, color*) indigo
año *nm* year; **¡Feliz A~ Nuevo!** Happy New Year!; **tener 15 ~s** to be 15 (years old); **los ~s 80** the eighties; **~ bisiesto/escolar** leap/school year; **~ fiscal** fiscal o tax year; **estar de buen ~** to look well-fed; **en el ~ de la nana** in the year dot; **el ~ que viene** next year
añoranza *nf* nostalgia; (*anhelo*) longing
añorar *vt* to long for
apabullar *vt* (*lit: fig*) to crush
apacentar *vt* to pasture, graze
apacible *adj* gentle, mild
apaciguar *vt* to pacify, calm (down)
apadrinar *vt* to sponsor, support; (*Rel*) to act as godfather to
apagado, -a *adj* (*volcán*) extinct; (*color*) dull; (*voz*) quiet; (*sonido*) muted, muffled; (*persona: apático*) listless; **estar ~** (*fuego, luz*) to be out; (*radio, TV etc*) to be off
apagar *vt* to put out; (*color*) to tone down; (*sonido*) to silence, muffle; (*sed*) to quench; (*Inform*) to toggle off; **apagarse** *vr* (*luz, fuego*) to go out; (*sonido*) to die away; (*pasión*) to wither; **~ el sistema** (*Inform*) to close o shut down

apagón nm blackout, power cut
apaisado, -a adj (papel) landscape cpd
apalabrar vt to agree to; (obrero) to engage
apalear vt to beat, thrash; (Agr) to winnow
apañado, -a adj (mañoso) resourceful; (arreglado) tidy; (útil) handy
apañar vt to pick up; (asir) to take hold of, grasp; (reparar) to mend, patch up; **apañarse** vr to manage, get by; **yo me (las) apaño muy bien** I manage o get by very well on my own
aparador nm sideboard; (escaparate) shop window
aparato nm apparatus; (máquina) machine; (electrodoméstico) appliance; (boato) ostentation; (Inform) device; **~ de facsímil** facsimile (machine), fax; **~ respiratorio** respiratory system; **~s de mando** (Aviat etc) controls
aparatoso, -a adj showy, ostentatious
aparcamiento nm car park (Brit), parking lot (US)
aparcar vt, vi to park
aparear vt (objetos) to pair, match; (animales) to mate; **aparearse** vr (animales) to mate
aparecer vi, **aparecerse** vr to appear; **apareció borracho** he turned up drunk
aparejado, -a adj fit, suitable; **ir ~ con** to go hand in hand with; **llevar** o **traer ~** to involve
aparejador, a nm/f (Arq) quantity surveyor
aparejo nm preparation; (de caballo) harness; (Náut) rigging; (de poleas) block and tackle
aparentar vt (edad) to look; **~ tristeza** to look sad
aparente adj apparent; (adecuado) suitable
aparición nf appearance; (de libro) publication; (de fantasma) spectre
apariencia nf (outward) appearance; **en ~** outwardly, seemingly
apartado, -a adj separate; (lejano) remote ▷ nm (tipográfico) paragraph; **~ (de correos)** post office box
apartamento nm apartment, flat (Brit)
apartamiento nm separation; (aislamiento) remoteness
apartar vt (alejar) to move away; (separar) to separate; (quitar) to remove; (Mineralogía) to extract; **apartarse** vr (separarse) to separate, part; (irse) to move away; (mantenerse aparte) to keep away; **lo ~on del equipo** they removed him from the team; **aparta todas las sillas** move all the chairs out of the way; **hay que ~ algo del sueldo para las vacaciones** you'll have to set aside some of your pay for the holidays; **¡apártate!** stand aside!; **apártense de la puerta** stand back from the door
aparte adv (separadamente) separately; (además) besides ▷ prep: **~ de** apart from ▷ nm (Teat) aside; (tipográfico) new paragraph; **"punto y ~"** "new paragraph"
apasionado, -a adj passionate; (pey) biassed, prejudiced ▷ nm/f admirer
apasionante adj exciting
apasionar vt to arouse passion in; **apasionarse** vr to get excited; **le apasiona el fútbol** she's crazy about football

apatía nf apathy
apático, -a adj apathetic
apátrida adj stateless
Apdo. nm abr (= Apartado (de Correos)) P.O. Box
apeadero nm halt, stopping place
apearse vr (jinete) to dismount; (bajarse) to get down o out; (de coche) to get out, alight; **no ~ del burro** to refuse to climb down
apechugar vi: **~ con algo** to face up to sth
apedrear vt to stone
apegarse vr: **~ a** to become attached to
apego nm attachment, devotion
apelación nf appeal
apelar vi to appeal; **~ a** (fig) to resort to
apellidar vt to call, name; **apellidarse** vr: **se apellida Pérez** her (sur)name's Pérez
apellido nm surname
apenar vt to grieve, trouble; (LAm: avergonzar) to embarrass; **apenarse** vr to grieve; (LAm) to be embarrassed
apenas adv (casi) hardly, scarcely; (casi nunca) hardly ever; (con números) barely ▷ conj as soon as; **no tenemos ~ nada de comer** we've got hardly anything to eat; **~ podía levantarse** he could hardly stand up; **~ voy al cine** I hardly ever go to the cinema; **hace ~ 10 minutos que hablé con ella** I spoke to her barely 10 minutes ago; **terminé en ~ dos horas** it only took me two hours to finish; **~ me vio, se puso a llorar** as soon as he saw me he began to cry
apéndice nm appendix
apendicitis nf appendicitis
aperitivo nm (bebida) aperitif; (comida) appetizer
apertura nf (gen) opening; (Pol) openness, liberalization; (Teat etc) beginning; **~ de un juicio hipotecario** (Com) foreclosure
apesadumbrar vt to grieve, sadden; **apesadumbrarse** vr to distress o.s.
apestar vt to infect ▷ vi: **~ (a)** to stink (of)
apetecer vt: **¿te apetece una tortilla?** do you fancy an omelette?
apetecible adj desirable; (comida) tempting
apetito nm appetite
apetitoso, -a adj (gustoso) appetizing; (fig) tempting
apiadarse vr: **~ de** to take pity on
ápice nm apex; (fig) whit, iota; **ni un ~** not a whit; **no ceder un ~** not to budge an inch
apilar vt to pile o heap up; **apilarse** vr to pile up
apiñar vt to crowd; **apiñarse** vr to crowd o press together
apio nm celery
apisonadora nf (máquina) steamroller
aplacar vt to placate; **aplacarse** vr to calm down
aplanar vt to smooth, level; (allanar) to roll flat, flatten; **aplanarse** vr (edificio) to collapse; (persona) to get discouraged
aplastar vt to squash (flat); (fig) to crush
aplatanarse vr to get lethargic
aplaudir vt to applaud
aplauso nm applause; (fig) approval, acclaim
aplazamiento nm postponement

aplazar vt to postpone, defer

aplicación nf application; (esfuerzo) effort; **aplicaciones de gestión** business applications

aplicado, -a adj diligent, hard-working

aplicar vt (colocar, untar) to apply; (poner en vigor) to put into effect; (esfuerzos) to devote; **aplicarse** vr to apply o.s.; **apliquese sobre la zona afectada** apply to the affected area; **no se ~on las normas** the rules weren't enforced

aplique nm wall light o lamp

aplomo nm aplomb, self-assurance

apocado, -a adj timid

apocamiento nm timidity; (depresión) depression

apocarse vr to feel small o humiliated

apócope nf apocopation; **gran es ~ de grande** "gran" is the shortened form of "grande"

apodar vt to nickname

apoderado nm agent, representative

apoderar vt to authorize, empower; (Jur) to grant (a) power of attorney to; **apoderarse** vr: **~se de** to take possession of

apodo nm nickname

apogeo nm peak, summit

apolillarse vr to get moth-eaten

apología nf eulogy; (defensa) defence

apoltronarse vr to get lazy

apoplejía nf apoplexy, stroke

apoquinar vt (fam) to cough up, fork out

aporrear vt to beat (up)

aportar vt to contribute ▷ vi to reach port

aposentar vt to lodge, put up

aposento nm lodging; (habitación) room

apósito nm (Med) dressing

aposta adv on purpose

apostar vt (dinero) to bet, stake; (tropas) to station, post ▷ vi (jugarse) to bet; (situarse) to position o.s.; **~ por algo** to bet on something; **¿qué te apuestas a que...?** what's the betting that...?

a posteriori adv at a later date o stage; (Lógica) a posteriori

apostilla nf note, comment

apóstol nm apostle

apóstrofo nm apostrophe

apoyar vt to lean, rest; (fig) to support, back; **apoyarse** vr: **~se en** to lean on

apoyo nm support, backing

apreciable adj considerable; (fig) esteemed

apreciación nf appreciation; (Com) valuation

apreciar vt to evaluate, assess; (Com) to appreciate, value ▷ vi (Econ) to appreciate

aprecio nm valuation, estimate; (fig) appreciation

aprehender vt to apprehend, detain; (ver) to see, observe

aprehensión nf detention, capture

apremiante adj urgent, pressing

apremiar vt to compel, force ▷ vi to be urgent, press

apremio nm urgency; **~ de pago** demand note

aprender vt, vi to learn; **aprenderse** vr: **~se algo** to learn sth (off) by heart; **~ a conducir** to learn to drive

aprendiz, a nm/f apprentice; (principiante) learner, trainee; **~ de comercio** business trainee

aprendizaje nm apprenticeship

aprensión nm apprehension, fear

aprensivo, -a adj apprehensive

apresar vt to seize; (capturar) to capture

aprestar vt to prepare, get ready; (Tec) to prime, size; **aprestarse** vr to get ready

apresurado, -a adj hurried, hasty

apresuramiento nm hurry, haste

apresurar vt to hurry, accelerate; **apresurarse** vr to hurry, make haste; **me apresuré a sugerir que ...** I hastily suggested that ...

apretado, -a adj tight; (escritura) cramped

apretar vt (con la mano) to squeeze; (con un dedo) press; (juntando) to press together, pack; (mano) to clasp; (dientes) to grit; (Tec) to tighten ▷ vi (zapatos, ropa) to be too tight; (calor) to become oppressive; **apretarse** vr to crowd together; **aprieta este botón** press this button; **~ el gatillo** to press the trigger; **la apretó contra su pecho** he clasped her to his bosom; **aprieta bien los tornillos** tighten up the screws; **~ la mano a algn** to shake sb's hand; **~ el paso** to quicken one's step; **me aprietan los zapatos** my shoes are too tight; **apretaos un poco para que me siente yo también** move up a bit so I can sit down too; **~se el cinturón** to tighten one's belt

apretón nm squeeze; **~ de manos** handshake

aprieto nm squeeze; (dificultad) difficulty, jam; **estar en un ~** to be in a jam; **ayudar a algn a salir de un ~** to help sb out of trouble

a priori adv beforehand; (Lógica) a priori

aprisa adv quickly, hurriedly

aprisionar vt to imprison

aprobación nf approval

aprobado nm (nota) pass mark

aprobar vt to approve (of); (examen, materia) to pass ▷ vi to pass

apropiación nf appropriation

apropiado, -a adj appropriate

apropiarse vr: **~ de** to appropriate

aprovechado, -a adj industrious, hardworking; (económico) thrifty; (pey) unscrupulous

aprovechamiento nm use, exploitation

aprovechar vt (hacer uso de) to use; (oferta, oportunidad) to take advantage of; (experiencia) to profit from ▷ vi to progress; **aprovecharse** vr: **~se de** to make use of; (pey) to take advantage of, exploit; **~é los ratos libres para estudiar** I'll use the free time to study; **no aprovecha el tiempo** he doesn't make good use of his time; **mi madre aprovecha toda la comida que le sobra** my mother makes good use of any leftovers; **aprovecho la ocasión para decirles...** I'd like to take this opportunity to tell you...; **~é ahora que estoy solo para llamarlo** I'll call him now while I'm on my own; **¡que aproveche!** enjoy your meal!; **me aproveché de la situación** I took advantage of the situation; **todos se aprovechan del pobre chico** everyone

takes advantage of the poor boy
aproximación nf approximation; (de lotería) consolation prize
aproximado, -a adj approximate
aproximar vt to bring nearer; **aproximarse** vr to come near, approach
aptitud nf aptitude; (capacidad) ability; ~ **para los negocios** business sense
apto, -a adj (apropiado) fit, suitable; (hábil) capable; ~**/no ~ para menores** (Cine) suitable/unsuitable for children
apuesto, -a adj neat, elegant ▷ nf bet, wager
apuntador nm prompter
apuntalar vt to prop up
apuntar vt (anotar) to make a note of; (sugerir) to point out; (señalar: con arma) to aim at; (con dedo) to point at o to; (Teat) to prompt; **apuntarse** vr (Escol) to enrol; (Deporte: tanto, victoria) to score; **apúntalo o se te olvidará** write it down or you'll forget; **apunta mis datos** can you take a note of my details?; ~ **una cantidad en la cuenta de algn** to charge a sum to sb's account; **apuntó el arma hacia nosotros** he pointed the gun at us; **me apuntó con el dedo** he pointed at me; ~**se en un curso** to enrol on a course; **me he apuntado para el viaje a Marruecos** I've put my name down for the trip to Morocco; **¡yo me apunto!** count me in!
apunte nm note; (Teat: voz) prompt; (: texto) prompt book
apuñalar vt to stab
apurado, -a adj needy; (difícil) difficult; (peligroso) dangerous; (LAm) hurried, rushed; **estar en una situación apurada** to be in a tight spot; **estar ~** to be in a hurry
apurar vt (agotar) to drain; (recursos) to use up; (molestar) to annoy; **apurarse** vr (preocuparse) to worry; (esp LAm: darse prisa) to hurry
apuro nm (aprieto) fix, jam*; (vergüenza) embarrassment; (LAm: prisa) haste, urgency; **el dinero de la herencia los sacó del ~** the money they inherited got them out of the fix; **pasé muchos ~s para salir del agua** I had a lot of trouble getting out of the water; **estar en ~s** to be in trouble; **me da mucho ~ no llevar ningún regalo** I feel very embarrassed about not taking a present
aquejado, -a adj: ~ **de** (Med) afflicted by
aquel, aquella, aquellos, -as adj that; (pl) those
aquél, aquélla, aquéllos, -as pron that (one); (pl) those (ones)
aquello pron that, that business
aquí adv (lugar) here; (tiempo) now; ~ **arriba** up here; ~ **mismo** right here; ~ **yace** here lies; **de ~ a siete días** a week from now
aquietar vt to quieten (down), calm (down)
ara nf (altar) altar; **en ~s de** for the sake of
árabe adj Arab, Arabian, Arabic ▷ nm/f Arab ▷ nm (Ling) Arabic
Arabia nf Arabia; ~ **Saudí** o **Saudita** Saudi Arabia
arado nm plough

aragonés, -esa adj, nm/f Aragonese ▷ nm (Ling) Aragonese
arancel nm tariff, duty; ~ **de aduanas** (customs) duty
arandela nf (Tec) washer; (chorrera) frill
araña nf (Zool) spider; (lámpara) chandelier
arañar vt to scratch
arañazo nm scratch
arar vt to plough, till
arbitraje nm arbitration
arbitrar vt to arbitrate in; (recursos) to bring together; (Deporte) to referee ▷ vi to arbitrate
arbitrariedad nf arbitrariness; (acto) arbitrary act
arbitrario, -a adj arbitrary
arbitrio nm free will; (Jur) adjudication, decision; **dejar al ~ de algn** to leave to sb's discretion
árbitro nm arbitrator; (Deporte) referee; (Tenis) umpire
árbol nm (Bot) tree; (Náut) mast; (Tec) axle, shaft
arbolado, -a adj wooded; (camino) tree-lined ▷ nm woodland
arboladura nf rigging
arbolar vt to hoist, raise
arboleda nf grove, plantation
arbusto nm bush, shrub
arca nf chest, box; **A~ de la Alianza** Ark of the Covenant; **A~ de Noé** Noah's Ark
arcada nf arcade; (de puente) arch, span; **arcadas** nfpl retching sg
arcaico, -a adj archaic
arce nm maple tree
arcén nm (de autopista) hard shoulder; (de carretera) verge
archipiélago nm archipelago
archivador nm filing cabinet; ~ **colgante** suspension file
archivar vt to file (away); (Inform) to archive
archivo nm archive(s) (pl); (Inform) file, archive; **A~ Nacional** Public Record Office; ~**s policíacos** police files; **nombre de** ~ (Inform) filename; ~ **adjunto** (Inform) attachment; ~ **de seguridad** (Inform) backup file
arcilla nf clay
arco nm arch; (Mat) arc; (Mil, Mus) bow; (AM Deporte) goal; ~ **iris** rainbow
arder vi to burn; ~ **sin llama** to smoulder; **está que arde** he's fuming
ardid nm ruse
ardiente adj ardent
ardilla nf squirrel
ardor nm (calor) heat, warmth; (fig) ardour; ~ **de estómago** heartburn
ardoroso, -a adj passionate
arduo, -a adj arduous
área nf area; (Deporte) penalty area; ~ **de excedentes** (Inform) overflow area
arena nf sand; (de una lucha) arena
arenal nm (arena movediza) quicksand
arengar vt to harangue
arenisca nf sandstone; (cascajo) grit
arenoso, -a adj sandy

arenque *nm* herring
argamasa *nf* mortar, plaster
Argel *n* Algiers
Argelia *nf* Algeria
argelino, -a *adj, nm/f* Algerian
Argentina *nf*: **(la)** ~ the Argentine, Argentina
argentino, -a *adj* Argentinian; (*de plata*) silvery ▷ *nm/f* Argentinian
argolla *nf* (large) ring; (*LAm: de matrimonio*) wedding ring
argot *nm* (*pl* -**s**) slang
argucia *nf* subtlety, sophistry
argüir *vt* to deduce; (*discutir*) to argue; (*indicar*) to indicate, imply; (*censurar*) to reproach ▷ *vi* to argue
argumentación *nf* (line of) argument
argumentar *vt, vi* to argue
argumento *nm* argument; (*razonamiento*) reasoning; (*de novela etc*) plot; (*Cine, TV*) storyline
aria *nf* aria
aridez *nf* aridity, dryness
árido, -a *adj* arid, dry; **áridos** *nmpl* dry goods
Aries *nm* Aries
ariete *nm* battering ram
ario, -a *adj* Aryan
arisco, -a *adj* surly; (*insociable*) unsociable
aristocracia *nf* aristocracy
aristócrata *nm/f* aristocrat
aritmética *nf* arithmetic
arma *nf* arm; **armas** *nfpl* arms; ~ **blanca** blade, knife; (*espada*) sword; ~ **de fuego** firearm; ~**s cortas** small arms; **rendir las** ~**s** to lay down one's arms; **ser de** ~**s tomar** to be somebody to be reckoned with
armadillo *nm* armadillo
armado, -a *adj* armed; (*Tec*) reinforced
armador *nm* (*Náut*) shipowner
armadura *nf* (*Mil*) armour; (*Tec*) framework; (*Zool*) skeleton; (*Física*) armature
armamento *nm* armament; (*Náut*) fitting-out
armar *vt* (*Mil*) to arm; (*máquina, mueble*) to assemble; (*navío*) to fit out; **armarse** *vr* (*Mil*) to arm o.s.; ~**io viene desmontado y luego tú lo armas** the cupboard comes in pieces and you assemble it; **no armes tanto ruido** don't make so much noise; **si no lo aceptan voy a** ~ **un escándalo** if they don't agree I'm going to make a fuss; ~**la**, ~ **un lío** to start a row; **me armé un lío** I got into a muddle; ~**se de valor** to summon up one's courage; ~**se de paciencia** to be patient; **se armó la gorda** all hell broke loose
armario *nm* wardrobe; **salir del** ~ to come out (of the closet)
armatoste *nm* (*mueble*) monstrosity; (*máquina*) contraption
armazón *nf* o *m* body, chassis; (*de mueble etc*) frame; (*Arq*) skeleton
armiño *nm* stoat; (*piel*) ermine
armisticio *nm* armistice
armonía *nf* harmony
armónica *nf* harmonica
armonioso, -a *adj* harmonious

armonizar *vt* to harmonize; (*diferencias*) to reconcile ▷ *vi* to harmonize; ~ **con** (*fig*) to be in keeping with; (*colores*) to tone in with
arnés *nm* armour; **arneses** *nmpl* harness *sg*
aro *nm* ring; (*tejo*) quoit; (*LAm: pendiente*) earring; **entrar por el** ~ to give in
aroma *nm* aroma
aromaterapia *nf* aromatherapy
aromático, -a *adj* aromatic
arpa *nf* harp
arpía *nf* (*fig*) shrew
arpillera *nf* sacking, sackcloth
arpón *nm* harpoon
arquear *vt* to arch, bend; **arquearse** *vr* to arch, bend
arqueo *nm* (*gen*) arching; (*Náut*) tonnage
arqueología *nf* archaeology
arqueólogo, -a *nm/f* archaeologist
arquero *nm* archer, bowman; (*AM Deporte*) goalkeeper
arquetipo *nm* archetype
arquitecto, -a *nm/f* architect; ~ **paisajista** o **de jardines** landscape gardener
arquitectura *nf* architecture
arrabal *nm* suburb; **arrabales** *nmpl* outskirts
arraigado, -a *adj* deep-rooted; (*fig*) established
arraigar *vt* to establish ▷ *vi*: **arraigarse** *vr* to take root; (*persona*) to settle
arrancar *vt* (*clavo, espina*) to pull out, extract; (*planta*) to pull up; (*cartel, etiqueta, esparadrapo*) to pull off; (*pedazo*) to tear off; (*hoja, página*) to tear out; (*suspiro*) to heave; (*arrebatar*) to snatch (away); (*fig*) to extract; (*Auto*) to start; (*Inform*) to boot ▷ *vi* (*Auto, máquina*) to start; (*ponerse en marcha*) to get going; ~ **de** (*costumbre, idea*) to stem from; (*carretera*) to start from; **le arranqué una espina del dedo** I pulled a thorn out of his finger; **estaba arrancando las malas hierbas** I was pulling up weeds; **el viento arrancó varios árboles** several trees were uprooted by the wind; ~ **algo de raíz** to pull something up by the roots; **me arranqué la tirita** I pulled off the sticking plaster; **arrancó una hoja del cuaderno** he tore a page out of the exercise book; **me lo** ~**on de las manos** they snatched it from me; ~ **información a algn** to extract information from sb; **arranca y vámonos** start the engine and let's get going
arranque *nm* sudden start; (*Auto*) start; (*fig*) fit, outburst
arras *nfpl* pledge *sg*, security *sg*
arrasar *vt* (*aplanar*) to level, flatten; (*destruir*) to demolish
arrastrado, -a *adj* poor, wretched
arrastrar *vt* to drag (along); (*fig*) to drag down, degrade; (*suj: agua, viento*) to carry away ▷ *vi* to drag, trail on the ground; **arrastrarse** *vr* to crawl; (*fig*) to grovel; **llevar algo arrastrado** to drag sth along
arrastre *nm* drag, dragging; (*Deporte*) crawl; **estar para el** ~ (*fig*) to have had it; ~ **de papel por fricción/por tracción** (*en máquina impresora*)

friction/tractor feed

arre *excl* gee up!

arrear *vt* to drive on, urge on ▷ *vi* to hurry along

arrebatado, -a *adj* rash, impetuous; (*repentino*) sudden, hasty

arrebatar *vt* to snatch (away), seize; (*fig*) to captivate; **arrebatarse** *vr* to get carried away, get excited

arrebato *nm* fit of rage, fury; (*éxtasis*) rapture; **en un ~ de cólera** in an outburst of anger

arrecife *nm* reef

arredrar *vt* (*hacer retirarse*) to drive back; **arredrarse** *vr* (*apartarse*) to draw back; **~se ante algo** to shrink away from sth

arreglado, -a *adj* (*ordenado*) neat, orderly; (*moderado*) moderate, reasonable

arreglar *vt* (*reparar*) to fix, repair; (*poner orden*) to tidy up; (*problema*) to solve; **arreglarse** *vr* (*vestirse*) to get ready; (*llegar a un acuerdo*) to reach an understanding; (*manejarse*) to manage; (*solucionarse*) to work out; **están arreglando las aceras** the pavements are being repaired; **este verano hemos arreglado la cocina** this summer we did up the kitchen; **si tienes algún problema, él te lo arregla** if you have any problems, he'll sort them out for you; **deja tu cuarto arreglado antes de salir** leave your room tidy before going out; **se arregló para salir** she got ready to go out; **~se el pelo** to do one's hair; **¿qué tal te arreglas sin coche?** how are you managing without a car?; **arreglárselas para hacer algo** to manage to do something; **siempre se las arregla para no pagar** he always manages not to pay; **ya verás como todo se arregla** it'll all work out, you'll see

arreglo *nm* settlement; (*orden*) order; (*acuerdo*) agreement; (*Mus*) arrangement, setting; (*Inform*) array; **con ~ a** in accordance with; **llegar a un ~** to reach a compromise

arrellanarse *vr* to sprawl; **~ en el asiento** to lie back in one's chair

arremangar *vt* to roll up, turn up; **arremangarse** *vr* to roll up one's sleeves

arremeter *vt* to attack, assault; **~ contra algn** to attack sb

arrendador, a *nm/f* landlord/lady

arrendamiento *nm* letting; (*el alquilar*) hiring; (*contrato*) lease; (*alquiler*) rent

arrendar *vt* (*propietario*) to let, lease; (*inquilino*) to rent; (*coche*) to hire

arrendatario, -a *nm/f* tenant

arreos *nmpl* harness *sg*, trappings

arrepentido, -a *nm/f* (*Pol*) reformed terrorist

arrepentimiento *nm* regret, repentance

arrepentirse *vr* to repent; **~ de (haber hecho) algo** to regret (doing) sth

arrestar *vt* to arrest; (*encarcelar*) to imprison

arresto *nm* arrest; (*Mil*) detention; (*audacia*) boldness, daring; **~ domiciliario** house arrest

arriar *vt* (*velas*) to haul down; (*bandera*) to lower, strike; (*un cable*) to pay out

arriba *adv* **1** (*posición*) above; **los platos están ~** the plates are above; **visto desde ~ parece más pequeño** seen from above it looks smaller; **~ del todo** at the very top, right on top; **~ están los dormitorios** the bedrooms are upstairs; **lo ~ mencionado** the aforementioned; **aquí/allí ~** up here/there; **está hasta ~ de trabajo** (*fam*) he's up to his eyes in work (*fam*)

2 (*dirección*) up, upwards; **más ~** higher o further up; **calle ~** up the street

3: **de ~ abajo** from top to bottom; **mirar a algn de ~ abajo** to look sb up and down

4: **para ~, de 30 euros para ~** from 30 euros up(wards); **de la cintura (para) ~** from the waist up

▷ *adj*: **de ~, el piso de ~** the upstairs flat; **la parte de ~** the top o upper part; **la parte de ~ del biquini** the bikini top

▷ *prep*: **~ de** (*LAm*) on top of; **lo dejé ~ del refrigerador** I left it on top of the fridge; **viven en el departamento ~ del mío** they live in the flat above mine; **~ de 200 dólares** more than 200 dollars

▷ *excl*: **¡~! up!; ¡manos ~!** hands up!; **¡~ España!** long live Spain!

arribar *vi* to put into port; (*esp LAm: llegar*) to arrive

arribista *nm/f* parvenu(e), upstart

arriendo *nm* = **arrendamiento**

arriero *nm* muleteer

arriesgado, -a *adj* (*peligroso*) risky; (*audaz*) bold, daring

arriesgar *vt* to risk; (*poner en peligro*) to endanger; **arriesgarse** *vr* to take a risk

arrimar *vt* (*acercar*) to bring close; (*poner de lado*) to set aside; **arrimarse** *vr* to come close o closer; **~se a** to lean on; (*fig*) to keep company with; (*buscar ayuda*) to seek the protection of; **arrímate a mí** cuddle up to me

arrinconar *vt* to put into a corner; (*fig*) to put on one side; (*abandonar*) to push aside

arrobado, -a *adj* entranced, enchanted

arrodillarse *vr* to kneel (down)

arrogancia *nf* arrogance

arrogante *adj* arrogant

arrojar *vt* to throw, hurl; (*humo*) to emit, give out; (*Com*) to yield, produce; **arrojarse** *vr* to throw o hurl o.s.

arrojo *nm* daring

arrollador, a *adj* crushing, overwhelming

arrollar *vt* (*enrollar*) to roll up; (*suj: inundación*) to wash away; (*Auto*) to run over; (*Deporte*) to crush

arropar *vt* to cover (up), wrap up; **arroparse** *vr* to wrap o.s. up

arrostrar *vt* to face (up to); **arrostrarse** *vr*: **~se con algn** to face up to sb

arroyo *nm* stream; (*de la calle*) gutter; **poner a algn en el ~** to turn sb onto the streets

arroz *nm* rice; **~ con leche** rice pudding

arrozal *nm* paddy field

arruga *nf* fold; (*de cara*) wrinkle; (*de vestido*) crease

arrugar *vt* (*cara*) to wrinkle; (*ropa*) to crease;

arrugarse vr (*cara*) to get wrinkled; (*ropa*) to get creased

arruinar vt to ruin, wreck; **arruinarse** vr to be ruined

arrullar vi to coo ▷ vt to lull to sleep

arrumaco nm (*caricia*) caress; (*halago*) piece of flattery

arsenal nm naval dockyard; (*Mil*) arsenal

arsénico nm arsenic

arte nm (*gen m en sg y siempre f en pl*) art; (*maña*) skill, guile; **por ~ de magia** (as if) by magic; **no tener ~ ni parte en algo** to have nothing whatsoever to do with sth; **artes** nfpl arts; **Bellas A~s** Fine Art sg; **~s y oficios** arts and crafts

artefacto nm appliance; (*Arqueología*) artefact

arteria nf artery

arterial adj arterial; (*presión*) blood cpd

arterio(e)sclerosis nf inv hardening of the arteries, arteriosclerosis

artesanía nf craftsmanship; (*artículos*) handicrafts pl

artesano, -a nm/f artisan, craftsman/woman

ártico, -a adj Arctic ▷ nm: **el (océano) Á~** the Arctic (Ocean)

articulación nf articulation; (*Med, Tec*) joint

articulado, -a adj articulated

articular vt (*lenguaje*) to articulate; (*máquina, mecanismo*) to connect

artículo nm article; (*cosa*) thing, article; (*TV*) feature, report; **~ de fondo** leader, editorial; **artículos** nmpl goods; **~s de marca** (*Com*) proprietary goods

artífice nm artist, craftsman; (*fig*) architect

artificial adj artificial

artificio nm art, skill; (*artesanía*) craftsmanship; (*astucia*) cunning

artillería nf artillery

artillero nm artilleryman, gunner

artilugio nm gadget

artimaña nf trap, snare; (*astucia*) cunning

artista nm/f (*pintor*) artist, painter; (*Teat*) artist, artiste

artístico, -a adj artistic

artritis nf arthritis

arveja nm (*LAm*) pea

arzobispo nm archbishop

as nm ace; **as del fútbol** star player

asa nf handle

asado nm roast (meat); (*LAm: barbacoa*) barbecue

asador nm (*varilla*) spit; (*aparato*) spit roaster

asadura(s) nf(pl) entrails pl, offal sg; (*Culin*) chitterlings pl

asalariado, -a adj paid, wage-earning, salaried ▷ nm/f wage earner

asaltador, a, asaltante nm/f assailant

asaltar vt to attack, assault; (*fig*) to assail

asalto nm attack, assault; (*Deporte*) round

asamblea nf assembly; (*reunión*) meeting

asar vt to roast; **~ al horno/a la parrilla** to bake/grill; **asarse** vr (*fig*): **me aso de calor** I'm roasting; **aquí se asa uno vivo** it's boiling hot here

asbesto nm asbestos

ascendencia nf ancestry; **de ~ francesa** of French origin

ascender vi (*subir*) to ascend, rise; (*ser promovido*) to gain promotion ▷ vt to promote; **~ a** to amount to

ascendiente nm influence ▷ nm/f ancestor

ascensión nf ascent; **la A~** the Ascension

ascenso nm ascent; (*promoción*) promotion

ascensor nm lift (*Brit*), elevator (*US*)

ascético, -a adj ascetic

asco nm: **el ajo me da ~** I hate o loathe garlic; **hacer ~s de algo** to turn up one's nose at sth; **estar hecho un ~** to be filthy; **poner a algn de ~** to call sb all sorts of names o every name under the sun; **¡qué ~!** how revolting o disgusting!

ascua nf ember; **arrimar el ~ a su sardina** to look after number one; **estar en ~s** to be on tenterhooks

aseado, -a adj (*limpio*) clean; (*arreglado*) tidy; (*pulcro*) smart

asear vt (*lavar*) to wash; (*ordenar*) to tidy (up)

asediar vt (*Mil*) to besiege, lay siege to; (*fig*) to chase, pester

asedio nm siege; (*Com*) run

asegurado, a adj insured

asegurador, -a nm/f insurer

asegurar vt (*consolidar*) to secure, fasten; (*afirmar*) to assure, affirm; (*dar garantía de*) to guarantee; (*hacer un seguro*) to insure; **asegurarse** vr (*cerciorarse*) to make sure; (*hacerse un seguro*) to insure o.s.; **asegura bien la cuerda** fasten the rope securely; **te aseguro que es verdad** I assure you it's true; **no he sido yo, te lo aseguro** it wasn't me, I assure you; **ella asegura que no lo conoce** she says that she doesn't know him; **hemos asegurado la casa** we've insured the house; **asegúrate de que los grifos están cerrados** make sure the taps are turned off

asemejarse vr to be alike; **~ a** to be like, resemble

asentado, -a adj established, settled

asentar vt (*sentar*) to seat, sit down; (*poner*) to place, establish; (*alisar*) to level, smooth down o out; (*anotar*) to note down ▷ vi to be suitable, suit

asentir vi to assent, agree

aseo nm cleanliness; **aseos** nmpl toilet sg (*Brit*), restroom sg (*US*), cloakroom sg

aséptico, -a adj germ-free, free from infection

asequible adj (*precio*) reasonable; (*meta*) attainable; (*persona*) approachable

aserradero nm sawmill

aserrar vt to saw

asesinar vt to murder; (*Pol*) to assassinate

asesinato nm (*gen*) murder; (*de personaje público*) assassination

asesino, -a nm/f murderer, killer; (*Pol*) assassin

asesor, a nm/f adviser, consultant; (*Com*) assessor, consultant; **~ administrativo** management consultant

asesorar vt (*Jur*) to advise, give legal advice to;

(*Com*) to act as consultant to; **asesorarse** *vr*: ~**se con** *o* **de** to take advice from, consult

asesoría *nf* (*cargo*) consultancy; (*oficina*) consultant's office

asestar *vt* (*golpe*) to deal; (*arma*) to aim; (*tiro*) to fire

asfalto *nm* asphalt

asfixia *nf* asphyxia, suffocation

asfixiar *vt* to asphyxiate, suffocate

así *adv* (*de esta manera*) in this way, like this; (*de esa manera*) in that way, like that; (*aunque*) although; (*tan pronto como*) as soon as; ~ **que** so; **se hace** ~ you do it like this; ¿**ves aquel abrigo? quiero algo** ~ do you see that coat? I'd like something like that; **un tomate** ~ **de grande** a tomato this big; **no me gusta,** ~ **que lo tiraré** I don't like it, so I'll throw it away; ~ **como** as well as; ~ **y todo** even so; **¡**~ **sea!** so be it!; ~ **es la vida** such is life, that's life; ¿**te gusta?** — ~, ~ do you like it? — so-so; ¿**no es** ~? isn't that so?; **diez euros o** ~ ten euros or thereabouts; **y** ~ **sucesivamente** and so on

Asia *nf* Asia

asiático, -a *adj, nm/f* Asian, Asiatic

asidero *nm* handle

asiduidad *nf* assiduousness

asiduo, -a *adj* assiduous; (*frecuente*) frequent ▷ *nm/f* regular (customer)

asiento *nm* (*mueble*) seat, chair; (*de coche, en tribunal etc*) seat; (*localidad*) seat, place; (*fundamento*) site; ~ **delantero/trasero** front/back seat

asignación *nf* (*atribución*) assignment; (*reparto*) allocation; (*Com*) allowance; ~ **(semanal)** pocket money; ~ **de presupuesto** budget appropriation

asignar *vt* to assign, allocate

asignatura *nf* subject; (*curso*) course; ~ **pendiente** (*fig*) matter pending

asilado, -a *nm/f* refugee

asilo *nm* (*refugio*) asylum, refuge; (*establecimiento*) home, institution; ~ **político** political asylum

asimilación *nf* assimilation

asimilar *vt* to assimilate

asimismo *adv* in the same way, likewise

asir *vt* to seize, grasp; **asirse** *vr* to take hold; ~**se a** *o* **de** to seize

asistencia *nf* presence; (*Teat*) audience; (*Med*) attendance; (*ayuda*) assistance; ~ **social** social *o* welfare work

asistenta *nf* daily help; *ver tb* **asistente**

asistente, -a *nm/f* assistant ▷ *nm* (*Mil*) orderly; **los** ~**s** those present; ~ **social** social worker; *ver tb* **asistenta**

asistido, -a *adj* (*Auto: dirección*) power-assisted; ~ **por ordenador** computer-assisted

asistir *vt* to assist, help ▷ *vi*: ~ **a** to attend, be present at

asma *nf* asthma

asno *nm* donkey; (*fig*) ass

asociación *nf* association; (*Com*) partnership

asociado, -a *adj* associate ▷ *nm/f* associate; (*Com*) partner

asociar *vt* to associate; **asociarse** *vr* to become partners

asolar *vt* to destroy

asomar *vt* to show, stick out ▷ *vi* to appear; **asomarse** *vr* (*objeto*) to appear, show up; (*persona*) to show up; **te asoma el pañuelo por el bolsillo** your handkerchief's sticking out of your pocket; **no asomes la cabeza por la ventanilla** don't lean out of the window; **me asomé a la terraza a ver quién gritaba** I went out onto the balcony to see who was shouting; **asómate a la ventana** look out of the window

asombrar *vt* to amaze, astonish; **asombrarse** *vr*: ~**se (de)** (*sorprenderse*) to be amazed (at); (*asustarse*) to be frightened (at)

asombro *nm* amazement, astonishment

asombroso, -a *adj* amazing, astonishing

asomo *nm* hint, sign; **ni por** ~ by no means

aspa *nf* (*cruz*) cross; (*de molino*) sail; **en** ~ X-shaped

aspaviento *nm* exaggerated display of feeling; (*fam*) fuss

aspecto *nm* (*apariencia*) look, appearance; (*fig*) aspect; **bajo ese** ~ from that point of view

aspereza *nf* roughness; (*de fruta*) sharpness; (*de carácter*) surliness

áspero, -a *adj* (*tela, voz*) rough; (*tono*) sharp; (*clima*) harsh

aspersión *nf* sprinkling; (*Agr*) spraying

aspersor *nm* sprinkler

aspiración *nf* breath, inhalation; (*Mus*) short pause; **aspiraciones** *nfpl* aspirations

aspiradora *nf* vacuum cleaner, Hoover®

aspirante *nm/f* (*candidato*) candidate; (*Deporte*) contender

aspirar *vt* to breathe in ▷ *vi*: ~ **a** to aspire to

aspirina *nf* aspirin

asquear *vt* to sicken ▷ *vi* to be sickening; **asquearse** *vr* to feel disgusted

asqueroso, -a *adj* disgusting, sickening

asta *nf* (*lanza*) lance; (*arpón*) spear; (*mango*) shaft, handle; (*Zool*) horn; **a media** ~ at half mast

asterisco *nm* asterisk

asteroide *nm* asteroid

astigmatismo *nm* astigmatism

astilla *nf* splinter; (*pedacito*) chip; **astillas** *nfpl* firewood *sg*

astillero *nm* shipyard

astringente *adj, nm* astringent

astro *nm* star

astrología *nf* astrology

astrólogo, -a *nm/f* astrologer

astronauta *nm/f* astronaut

astronave *nm* spaceship

astronomía *nf* astronomy

astronómico, -a *adj* (*tb fig*) astronomical

astrónomo, -a *nm/f* astronomer

astucia *nf* astuteness; (*destreza*) clever trick

astuto, -a *adj* astute; (*taimado*) cunning

asueto *nm* holiday; (*tiempo libre*) time off; **día de** ~ day off; **tarde de** ~ (*trabajo*) afternoon off; (*Escol*) half-holiday

asumir *vt* (*carga, deber*) to assume; **ya he asumido**

que no voy a ganar I've already accepted that I'm not going to win; **asumo toda la responsabilidad** I take full responsibility; **no estoy dispuesta a ~ ese riesgo** I'm not prepared to take that risk

asunción *nf* assumption

asunto *nm* (*tema*) matter, subject; (*negocio*) business; **¡eso es ~ mío!** that's my business!; **~s exteriores** foreign affairs; **~s a tratar** agenda *sg*

asustar *vt* to frighten; **asustarse** *vr* to be/ become frightened

atacar *vt* to attack

atadura *nf* bond, tie

atajar *vt* (*gen*) to stop; (*ruta de fuga*) to cut off; (*discurso*) to interrupt ▷ *vi* to take a short cut

atajo *nm* short cut; (*Deporte*) tackle

atañer *vi*: **~ a** to concern; **en lo que atañe a eso** with regard to that

ataque *nm* attack; **~ cardíaco** heart attack

atar *vt* to tie, tie up; **~ la lengua a algn** (*fig*) to silence sb

atardecer *vi* to get dark ▷ *nm* evening; (*crepúsculo*) dusk

atareado, -a *adj* busy

atascar *vt* to clog up; (*obstruir*) to jam; (*fig*) to hinder; **atascarse** *vr* to stall; (*cañería*) to get blocked up; (*fig*) to get bogged down; (*en discurso*) to dry up

atasco *nm* obstruction; (*Auto*) traffic jam

ataúd *nm* coffin

ataviar *vt* to deck, array; **ataviarse** *vr* to dress up

atavío *nm* attire, dress; **atavíos** *nmpl* finery *sg*

atemorizar *vt* to frighten, scare; **atemorizarse** *vr* to get frightened *o* scared

Atenas *nf* Athens

atención *nf* (*cuidado*) attention; (*bondad*) kindness; **hay que poner más ~** you should pay more attention; **escucha con ~** listen carefully; **me llamó la ~ lo grande que era la casa** I was struck by how big the house was; **el director del colegio le llamó la ~** the headmaster gave him a talking-to; **estás llamando la ~ con ese sombrero** you're attracting attention in that hat; **¡~!** (be) careful!, look out!; **en ~ a esto** in view of this

atender *vt* (*persona: en bar, tienda*) to serve; (*en banco, oficina*) to attend to; (*en hospital*) to look after; (*Tec*) to service; (*ruego*) to comply with; (*asunto*) to deal with ▷ *vi* to pay attention; **~ a** (*asistir*) to attend to; (*escuchar*) to pay attention to; (*detalles*) to take care of; **¿le atienden?** are you being served?; **tengo que ~ a dos clientes** I've got a couple of clients to attend to; **~ a los enfermos** to look after the sick; **~ los consejos de alguien** to listen to somebody's advice; **todos en clase atendían al profesor** everyone in the class was paying attention to the teacher; **la recepcionista atiende al teléfono** the receptionist answers the telephone

atenerse *vr*: **~ a** to abide by, adhere to

atentado *nm* crime, illegal act; (*asalto*) assault; (*terrorista*) attack; **~ contra la vida de algn** attempt on sb's life; **~ golpista** (*Pol*) attempted coup

atentamente *adv*: **Le saluda ~** Yours sincerely, Yours faithfully

atentar *vi*: **~ a** *o* **contra** to commit an outrage against

atento, -a *adj* attentive, observant; (*cortés*) polite, thoughtful; **su atenta (carta)** (*Com*) your letter

atenuante *adj*: **circunstancias ~s** extenuating *o* mitigating circumstances ▷ *nfpl*: **~s** extenuating *o* mitigating circumstances

atenuar *vt* to attenuate; (*disminuir*) to lessen, minimize

ateo, -a *adj* atheistic ▷ *nm/f* atheist

aterciopelado, -a *adj* velvety

aterido, -a *adj*: **~ de frío** frozen stiff

aterrador, a *adj* frightening

aterrar *vt* (*asustar*) to frighten; (*aterrorizar*) to terrify; **aterrarse** *vr* (*estar asustado*) to be frightened; (*estar aterrorizado*) to be terrified

aterrizaje *nm* landing; **~ forzoso** forced landing

aterrizar *vi* to land

aterrorizar *vt* to terrify

atesorar *vt* to hoard, store up

atestado, -a *adj* packed ▷ *nm* (*Jur*) affidavit

atestar *vt* to pack, stuff; (*Jur*) to attest, testify to

atestiguar *vt* to testify to, bear witness to

atiborrar *vt* to fill, stuff; **atiborrarse** *vr* to stuff o.s.

ático *nm* attic; **~ de lujo** penthouse flat

atildar *vt* to criticize; (*Tip*) to put a tilde over; **atildarse** *vr* to spruce o.s. up

atinado, -a *adj* correct; (*sensato*) sensible

atinar *vi* (*acertar*) to be right; **~ con** *o* **en** (*solución*) to hit upon; **~ a hacer** to manage to do

atípico, -a *adj* atypical

atisbar *vt* to spy on; (*echar ojeada*) to peep at

atizar *vt* to poke; (*horno etc*) to stoke; (*fig*) to stir up, rouse

atlántico, -a *adj* Atlantic ▷ *nm*: **el (océano) A~** the Atlantic (Ocean)

atlas *nm inv* atlas

atleta *nm/f* athlete

atlético, -a *adj* athletic

atletismo *nm* athletics *sg*

atmósfera *nf* atmosphere

atmosférico, -a *adj* atmospheric

atole *nm* (*CAm, Méx*) cornflour drink

atolladero *nm*: **estar en un ~** to be in a jam

atollarse *vr* to get stuck; (*fig*) to get into a jam

atolondrado, -a *adj* scatterbrained

atolondramiento *nm* bewilderment; (*insensatez*) silliness

atómico, -a *adj* atomic

atomizador *nm* atomizer

átomo *nm* atom

atónito, -a *adj* astonished, amazed

atontado, -a *adj* stunned; (*bobo*) silly, daft

atontar *vt* to stun; **atontarse** *vr* to become confused

atormentar *vt* to torture; (*molestar*) to torment; (*acosar*) to plague, harass

atornillar vt to screw on o down
atosigar vt to harass
atracador, a nm/f robber
atracar vt (Náut) to moor; (robar) to hold up, rob
▷ vi to moor; **atracarse** vr (hartarse) to stuff o.s
atracción nf attraction
atraco nm holdup, robbery
atracón nm: **darse** o **pegarse un ~ (de)** (fam) to
pig out (on)
atractivo, -a adj attractive ▷ nm attraction;
(belleza) attractiveness
atraer vt to attract; **dejarse ~ por** to be tempted
by
atragantarse vr: **~ (con algo)** to choke (on sth);
se me ha atragantado el inglés/el chico ese I
don't take to English/that boy
atrancar vt (con tranca, barra) to bar, bolt
atrapar vt (atrapar) to trap; (resfriado etc) to catch
atrás adv (movimiento) back(wards); (lugar)
behind; (tiempo) previously ▷ prep (LAm): **~ de**
behind; **ir hacia ~** to go back(wards); **estar ~** to
be behind o at the back
atrasado, -a adj slow; (pago) overdue, late; (país)
backward
atrasar vi to be slow; **atrasarse** vr to remain
behind; (llegar tarde) to arrive late
atraso nm (retraso) delay; (de país) backwardness;
atrasos nmpl arrears
atravesado, -a adj: **un tronco ~ en la carretera**
a tree trunk lying across the road
atravesar vt (cruzar) to cross (over); (traspasar)
to pierce; (período) to go through; (poner al través)
to lay o put across; **atravesarse** vr to come in
between; (intervenir) to interfere
atrayente adj attractive
atreverse vr to dare; (insolentarse) to be insolent
atrevido, -a adj (valiente) daring; (insolente)
insolent
atrevimiento nm (valentía) daring; (insolencia)
insolence
atribución nf (Lit) attribution; **atribuciones** nfpl
(Pol) functions; (Admin) responsibilities
atribuir vt to attribute; (funciones) to confer
atributo nm attribute
atril nm lectern; (Mus) music stand
atrincherarse vr (Mil) to dig (o.s.) in; **~ en** (fig) to
hide behind
atrocidad nf atrocity, outrage
atrofiarse vr (tb fig) to atrophy
atropellar vt (dar un golpe a) to knock over o down;
(empujar) to push (aside); (Auto) to run over o
down; (agraviar) to insult; **atropellarse** vr to act
hastily
atropello nm (Auto) accident; (empujón) push;
(agravio) wrong; (atrocidad) outrage
atroz adj atrocious, awful
A.T.S. nm/f abr (= Ayudante Técnico Sanitario) nurse
atto., -a. abr (= atento, a) Yours faithfully
atuendo nm attire
atún nm tuna, tunny
aturdir vt to stun; (suj: ruido) to deafen; (fig) to
dumbfound, bewilder

atusar vt (cortar) to trim; (alisar) to smooth
(down)
audacia nf boldness, audacity
audaz adj bold, audacious
audible adj audible
audición nf hearing; (Teat) audition; **~**
radiofónica radio concert
audiencia nf audience; (Jur) high court; (Pol): **~**
pública public inquiry
audífono nm hearing aid
audiovisual adj audio-visual
auditivo, -a adj hearing cpd; (conducto, nervio)
auditory
auditor nm (Jur) judge-advocate; (Com) auditor
auditoría nf audit; (profesión) auditing
auditorio nm audience; (sala) auditorium
auge nm boom; (clímax) climax; (Econ) expansion;
estar en ~ to thrive
augurar vt to predict; (presagiar) to portend
augurio nm omen
aula nf classroom
aullar vi to howl, yell
aullido nm howl, yell
aumentar vt to increase; (precios) to put up;
(producción) to step up; (con microscopio, anteojos) to
magnify ▷ vi: **aumentarse** vr to increase, be on
the increase
aumento nm increase
aun adv even
aún adv (todavía) still, yet; (incluso) even
aunque conj although, though, even though;
(hipotético) even if
aúpa excl up!, come on!; (fam): **una función de ~**
a slap-up do; **una paliza de ~** a good hiding
aureola nf halo
auricular nm earpiece, receiver; **auriculares**
nmpl headphones
aurora nf dawn; **~ boreal(is)** northern lights pl
auscultar vt (Med: pecho) to listen to, sound
ausencia nf absence
ausentarse vr to go away; (por poco tiempo) to go
out
ausente adj absent ▷ nm/f (Escol) absentee; (Jur)
missing person
auspicios nmpl auspices; (protección) protection sg
austeridad nf austerity
austero, -a adj austere
austral adj southern ▷ nm monetary unit of
Argentina (1985-1991)
Australia nf Australia
australiano, -a adj, nm/f Australian
Austria nf Austria
austríaco, -a, austriaco a adj, nm/f Austrian
auténtico adj authentic
autentificar vt to authenticate
auto nm (coche) car; (Jur) edict, decree; (: orden)
writ; **autos** nmpl (Jur) proceedings; (: acta) court
record sg; **~ de comparecencia** summons,
subpoena; **~ de ejecución** writ of execution
autoadhesivo, -a adj self-adhesive; (sobre) self-
sealing
autobiografía nf autobiography

autobronceador, a adj self-tanning
autobús nm bus (Brit), (passenger) bus (US)
autocar nm coach; ~ **de línea** intercity coach
autóctono, -a adj native, indigenous
autodefensa nf self-defence
autodeterminación nf self-determination
autoescuela nf driving school
autogestión nf self-management
autógrafo nm autograph
automación nf = **automatización**
autómata nm automaton
automáticamente adv automatically
automático, -a adj automatic ▷ nm press stud
automatización nf: ~ **de fábricas** factory
automation; ~ **de oficinas** office automation
automotor, -triz adj self-propelled ▷ nm diesel
train
automóvil nm (motor) car (Brit), automobile (US)
automovilismo nm (Deporte) (sports) car racing
automovilista nm/f motorist, driver
automovilístico, -a adj (industria) car cpd
autonomía nf autonomy; (Esp Pol) autonomy,
self-government; (: comunidad) autonomous
region
autonómico, -a adj (Esp Pol) relating to
autonomy, autonomous; **gobierno** ~
autonomous government
autónomo, -a adj autonomous; (Inform) stand-
alone, offline
autopsia nf autopsy
autor, a nm/f author; **los ~es del atentado** those
responsible for the attack
autoridad nf authority; ~ **local** local authority
autoritario, -a adj authoritarian
autorización nf authorization
autorizado, -a adj authorized; (aprobado)
approved
autorizar vt (dar facultad a) to authorize; (permitir)
to approve
autorretrato nm self-portrait
autoservicio nm self-service shop o store;
(restaurante) self-service restaurant
autostop nm hitch-hiking; **hacer** ~ to hitch-
hike
autostopista nm/f hitch-hiker
autosuficiencia nf self-sufficiency
autosuficiente adj self-sufficient; (pey) smug
autosugestión nf autosuggestion
autovía nf ≈ dual carriageway (Brit), separated
highway (US)
auxiliar vt to help ▷ nm/f assistant
auxilio nm assistance, help; **primeros ~s** first
aid sg
Av abr (= Avenida) Av(e)
aval nm guarantee; (persona) guarantor
avalancha nf avalanche
avalar vt (Com etc) to underwrite; (fig) to endorse
avance nm advance; (pago) advance payment;
(Cine) trailer
avanzado, -a adj advanced; **de edad avanzada**,
~ **de edad** elderly
avanzar vt, vi to advance

avaricia nf avarice, greed
avaricioso, -a adj avaricious, greedy
avaro, -a adj miserly, mean ▷ nm/f miser
avasallar vt to subdue, subjugate
Avda abr (= Avenida) Av(e)
AVE nm abr (= Alta Velocidad Española) ≈ Bullet train
ave nf bird; ~ **de rapiña** bird of prey
avecinarse vr (tormenta, fig) to approach, be on
the way
avellana nf hazelnut
avellano nm hazel tree
avemaría nm Hail Mary, Ave Maria
avena nf oats pl
avenida nf (calle) avenue
avenir vt to reconcile; **avenirse** vr to come to an
agreement, reach a compromise
aventajado, -a adj outstanding
aventajar vt (sobrepasar) to surpass, outstrip
aventura nf adventure; ~ **sentimental** love
affair
aventurado, -a adj risky
aventurero, -a adj adventurous
avergonzar vt (causar vergüenza) to shame;
(desconcertar) to embarrass; **avergonzarse** vr
(sentir vergüenza) to be ashamed; (sentirse violento)
to be embarrassed
avería nf (Tec) breakdown, fault
averiado, -a adj broken-down
averiar vt to break; **averiarse** vr to break down
averiguación nf investigation; (determinación)
ascertainment
averiguar vt to investigate; (descubrir) to find out,
ascertain
aversión nf aversion, dislike; **cobrar** ~ **a** to take a
strong dislike to
avestruz nm ostrich
aviación nf aviation; (fuerzas aéreas) air force
aviador, a nm/f aviator, airman/woman
aviar vt to prepare, get ready
avícola adj poultry cpd
avicultura nf poultry farming
avidez nf avidity, eagerness
ávido, -a adj avid, eager
avinagrado, -a adj sour, acid
avinagrarse vr to go o turn sour
avío nm preparation; **avíos** nmpl gear sg, kit sg
avión nm aeroplane; (ave) martin; ~ **de reacción**
jet (plane); **por** ~ (Correos) by air mail
avioneta nf light aircraft
avisar vt (advertir) to warn, notify; (informar) to
tell; (aconsejar) to advise, counsel
aviso nm warning; (noticia) notice; (Com) demand
note; (Inform) prompt; ~ **escrito** notice in
writing; **sin previo** ~ without warning; **estar**
sobre ~ to be on the look-out
avispa nf wasp
avispado, -a adj sharp, clever
avispero nm wasp's nest
avispón nm hornet
avistar vt to sight, spot
avituallar vt to supply with food
avivar vt to strengthen, intensify; **avivarse** vr to

revive, acquire new life

axila *nf* armpit

axioma *nm* axiom

ay *excl* (*dolor*) ow!, ouch!; (*aflicción*) oh!, oh dear!; ¡**ay de mí!** poor me!

aya *nf* governess; (*niñera*) nanny

ayer *adv, nm* yesterday; **antes de ~** the day before yesterday; **~ por la tarde** yesterday afternoon/evening

ayo *nm* tutor

ayuda *nf* help, assistance; (*Med*) enema ▷ *nm* page; **~ humanitaria** humanitarian aid

ayudante, -a *nm/f* assistant, helper; (*Escol*) assistant; (*Mil*) adjutant

ayudar *vt* to help, assist

ayunar *vi* to fast

ayunas *nfpl*: **estar en ~** (*no haber comido*) to be fasting; (*ignorar*) to be in the dark

ayuno *nm* fasting

ayuntamiento *nm* (*consejo*) town/city council; (*edificio*) town/city hall; (*cópula*) sexual intercourse

azabache *nm* jet

azada *nf* hoe

azafata *nf* air hostess (*Brit*) o stewardess

azafrán *nm* saffron

azahar *nm* orange/lemon blossom

azalea *nf* azalea

azar *nm* (*casualidad*) chance, fate; (*desgracia*) misfortune, accident; **por ~** by chance; **al ~** at random

azogue *nm* mercury

azoramiento *nm* alarm; (*confusión*) confusion

azorar *vt* to alarm; **azorarse** *vr* to get alarmed

Azores *nfpl*: **las (Islas) ~** the Azores

azotar *vt* to whip, beat; (*pegar*) to spank

azote *nm* (*látigo*) whip; (*latigazo*) lash, stroke; (*en las nalgas*) spank; (*calamidad*) calamity

azotea *nf* (flat) roof

azteca *adj, nm/f* Aztec

azúcar *nm* sugar

azucarado, -a *adj* sugary, sweet

azucarero, -a *adj* sugar *cpd* ▷ *nm* sugar bowl

azucena *nf* white lily

azufre *nm* sulphur

azul *adj, nm* blue; **~ celeste/marino** sky/navy blue

azulejo *nm* tile

azuzar *vt* to incite, egg on

Bb

baba *nf* spittle, saliva; **se le caía la ~** (*fig*) he was thrilled to bits

babear *vi* (*echar saliva*) to slobber; (*niño*) to dribble; (*fig*) to drool, slaver

babel *nm o f* bedlam

babero *nm* bib

babor *nm* port (side); **a ~** to port

baboso, -a *adj* slobbering; (*Zool*) slimy; (*LAm*) silly ▷ *nm/f* (*LAm*) fool

babucha *nf* slipper

baca *nf* (*Auto*) luggage *o* roof rack

bacalao *nm* cod(fish)

bache *nm* pothole, rut; (*fig*) bad patch

bachillerato *nm* 2 year secondary school course

bacteria *nf* bacterium, germ

bacteriológico, -a *adj* bacteriological; **guerra bacteriológica** germ warfare

báculo *nm* stick, staff; (*fig*) support

bádminton *nm* badminton

baf(f)le *nm* (*Elec*) speaker

bagaje *nm* baggage; (*fig*) background

bagatela *nf* trinket, trifle

Bahama *nfpl* **las (Islas) ~, las ~s** the Bahamas

bahía *nf* bay

bailar *vt, vi* to dance

bailarín, -ina *nm/f* dancer; (*de ballet*) ballet dancer

baile *nm* dance; (*formal*) ball

baja *nf* (*de precio, temperatura*) drop, fall; (*Econ*) slump; (*Mil*) casualty; **dar de ~** (*soldado*) to discharge; (*empleado*) to dismiss, sack; **darse de ~** (*retirarse*) to drop out; (*Med*) to go sick; (*dimitir*) to resign; **se dieron de ~ en el club** they left the club; **estar de ~** to be on sick leave; **estar a la ~** (*Bolsa*) to be dropping *o* falling; **jugar a la ~** (*Econ*) to speculate on a fall in prices; *ver tb* **bajo**

bajada *nf* descent; (*camino*) slope; (*de aguas*) ebb

bajamar *nf* low tide

bajar *vi* (*persona*) to go *o* come down; (*temperatura, precios*) to drop, fall ▷ *vt* (*cabeza*) to bow; (*escalera*) to go *o* come down; (*radio*) to turn down; (*precio, voz*) to lower; (*llevar abajo*) to take down; (*traer abajo*) to bring down; (*acercar*) to get down; **bajarse** *vr*: **~se de** (*coche*) to get out of; (*autobús, tren, avion*) to get off; (*árbol, escalera, silla*) to get down from; **baja y ayúdame** come down and help me; **bajó la escalera muy despacio** he

went down the stairs very slowly; **han bajado los precios** prices have come down; **los coches han bajado de precio** cars have come down in price; **¿has bajado la basura?** have you taken the rubbish down?; **¿me bajas el abrigo? hace frío aquí fuera** could you bring my coat down, it's cold out here; **¿me bajas la maleta del armario?** could you get me the suitcase down from the wardrobe?; **¿bajo la persiana?** shall I put the blind down?; **¡baja la voz, que no estoy sordo!** keep your voice down, I'm not deaf!; **baja la radio que no oigo nada** turn the radio down, I can't hear a thing; **~le los humos a algn** (*fig*) to cut sb down to size; **se bajó del autobús antes que yo** he got off the bus before me; **¡bájate del coche!** get out of the car!; **¡bájate de ahí!** get down from there!; **~se algo de Internet** to download sth from the Internet

bajeza *nf* baseness; (*acto*) vile deed

bajo, -a *adj* (*persona*) small, short; (*mueble, número, precio, nivel, temperatura*) low; (*terreno*) low(-lying); (*sonido*) faint, soft, low; (*voz, tono*) deep; (*metal*) base ▷ *adv* (*hablar*) softly, quietly; (*volar*) low ▷ *prep* under, below, underneath ▷ *nm* (*Mus*) bass; **es muy ~** he's very short; **una silla muy baja** a very low chair; **la temporada baja** the low season; **viven en la planta baja** they live on the ground floor; **¡habla ~!** speak quietly!; **~ el título de...** under the title of...; **llevaba un libro ~ el brazo** she was carrying a book under her arm; **~ tierra** underground; **~ la lluvia** in the rain; *ver tb* **baja**

bajón *nm* fall, drop

bakalao *nm* (*Mus*) rave music

bala *nf* bullet; **~ de goma** plastic bullet

baladí *adj* trivial

balance *nm* (*Com*) balance; (: *libro*) balance sheet; (: *cuenta general*) stocktaking; **~ de comprobación** trial balance; **~ consolidado** consolidated balance sheet; **hacer ~** to take stock

balancear *vt* to balance ▷ *vi*: **balancearse** *vr* to swing (to and fro); (*vacilar*) to hesitate

balanceo *nm* swinging

balanza *nf* scales *pl*, balance; **~ comercial** balance of trade; **~ de pagos/de poder(es)** balance of payments/of power

balar *vi* to bleat
balaustrada *nf* balustrade; (*pasamanos*) banister
balazo *nm* (*tiro*) shot; (*herida*) bullet wound
balbucear *vi*,*vt* to stammer, stutter
balbuceo *nm* stammering, stuttering
balbucir *vi*,*vt* to stammer, stutter
balcánico, -a *adj* Balkan
balcón *nm* balcony
baldar *vt* to cripple; (*agotar*) to exhaust
balde *nm* (*esp LAm*) bucket, pail; **de ~** *adv* (for) free, for nothing; **en ~** *adv* in vain
baldío, -a *adj* uncultivated; (*terreno*) waste; (*inútil*) vain ▷ *nm* wasteland
baldosa *nf* (*azulejo*) floor tile; (*grande*) flagstone
baldosín *nm* wall tile
Baleares *nfpl*: **las (Islas) ~** the Balearics, the Balearic Islands
balido *nm* bleat, bleating
balín *nm* pellet; **balines** *nmpl* buckshot *sg*
balística *nf* ballistics *pl*
baliza *nf* (*Aviat*) beacon; (*Náut*) buoy
ballena *nf* whale
ballesta *nf* crossbow; (*Auto*) spring
ballet (*pl* **-s**) *nm* ballet
balneario, -a *adj*: **estación balnearia** (bathing) resort ▷ *nm* spa, health resort
balón *nm* ball
baloncesto *nm* basketball
balonmano *nm* handball
balonvolea *nm* volleyball
balsa *nf* raft; (*Bot*) balsa wood
bálsamo *nm* balsam, balm
baluarte *nm* bastion, bulwark
bambolearse *vr* to swing, sway; (*silla*) to wobble
bamboleo *nm* (*de péndulo*) swinging; (*de silla, mesa*) wobbling
bambú *nm* bamboo
banana *nf* (*LAm*) banana
banano *nm* (*LAm*) banana tree
banca *nf* (*asiento*) bench; (*Com*) banking
bancario, -a *adj* banking *cpd*, bank *cpd*; **giro ~** bank draft
bancarrota *nf* bankruptcy; **declararse en** *o* **hacer ~** to go bankrupt
banco *nm* bench; (*Escol*) desk; (*Com*) bank; (*Geo*) stratum; **~ comercial** *o* **mercantil** commercial bank; **~ por acciones** joint-stock bank; **~ de crédito/de ahorros** credit/savings bank; **~ de arena** sandbank; **~ de datos** (*Inform*) data bank; **~ de hielo** iceberg
banda *nf* (*franja*) band; (*de tela*) sash; (*cinta*) ribbon; (*de delincuentes*) gang; (*Mus: grupo*) band; (*de metales*) brass band; (*Náut*) side, edge; **la B~ Oriental** Uruguay; **el jugador estaba fuera de ~** the player was offside; **cerrarse en ~** to stand firm; **~ ancha** broadband; **~ sonora** soundtrack; **~ transportadora** conveyor belt
bandada *nf* (*de pájaros*) flock; (*de peces*) shoal
bandazo *nm*: **dar ~s** (*coche*) to veer from side to side
bandeja *nf* tray; **~ de entrada/salida** in-tray/out-tray

bandera *nf* (*de tela*) flag; (*estandarte*) banner; (*Inform*) marker, flag; **izar la ~** to hoist the flag
banderilla *nf* banderilla; (*tapa*) savoury appetizer (*served on a cocktail stick*)
banderín *nm* pennant, small flag
banderola *nf* (*Mil*) pennant
bandido *nm* bandit
bando *nm* (*edicto*) edict, proclamation; (*facción*) faction; **pasar al otro ~** to change sides; **los ~s** (*Rel*) the banns
bandolera *nf*: **bolsa de ~** shoulder bag
bandolero *nm* bandit, brigand
banquero *nm* banker
banqueta *nf* stool; (*Méx: acera*) pavement (*Brit*), sidewalk (*US*)
banquete *nm* banquet; (*para convidados*) formal dinner; **~ de boda** wedding breakfast
banquillo *nm* (*Jur*) dock, prisoner's bench; (*banco*) bench; (*para los pies*) footstool
bañador *nm* swimming costume (*Brit*), bathing suit (*US*)
bañar *vt* (*niño*) to bath, bathe; (*objeto*) to dip; (*de barniz*) to coat; **bañarse** *vr* (*en el mar*) to bathe, swim; (*en la bañera*) to have a bath
bañero, -a *nm/f* lifeguard, bath(tub)
bañista *nm/f* bather
baño *nm* (*en bañera*) bath; (*en río, mar*) dip, swim; (*cuarto*) bathroom; (*bañera*) bath(tub); (*capa*) coating; **ir a tomar los ~s** to take the waters
baptista *nm/f* Baptist
baqueta *nf* (*Mus*) drumstick
bar *nm* bar
barahúnda *nf* uproar, hubbub
baraja *nf* pack (of cards)
barajar *vt* (*naipes*) to shuffle; (*fig*) to jumble up
baranda, barandilla *nf* rail, railing
baratija *nf* trinket; (*fig*) trifle; **baratijas** *nfpl* (*Com*) cheap goods
baratillo *nm* (*tienda*) junkshop; (*subasta*) bargain sale; (*conjunto de cosas*) second-hand goods *pl*
barato, -a *adj* cheap ▷ *adv* cheap, cheaply
baraúnda *nf* = **barahúnda**
barba *nf* (*mentón*) chin; (*pelo*) beard; **tener ~** to be unshaven; **hacer algo en las ~s de algn** to do sth under sb's very nose; **reírse en las ~s de algn** to laugh in sb's face
barbacoa *nf* (*parrilla*) barbecue; (*carne*) barbecued meat
barbaridad *nf* barbarity; (*acto*) barbarism; (*atrocidad*) outrage; **una ~ de** (*fam*) loads of; **¡qué ~!** (*fam*) how awful!; **cuesta una ~** (*fam*) it costs a fortune
barbarie *nf*, **barbarismo** *nm* barbarism; (*crueldad*) barbarity
bárbaro, -a *adj* barbarous, cruel; (*grosero*) rough, uncouth ▷ *nm/f* barbarian ▷ *adv*: **lo pasamos ~** (*fam*) we had a great time; **¡qué ~!** (*fam*) how marvellous!; **un éxito ~** (*fam*) a terrific success; **es un tipo ~** (*fam*) he's a great bloke
barbecho *nm* fallow land
barbero *nm* barber, hairdresser
barbilla *nf* chin, tip of the chin

barbitúrico *nm* barbiturate

barbo *nm*: ~ **de mar** red mullet

barbudo, -a *adj* bearded

barca *nf* (small) boat; ~ **pesquera** fishing boat; ~ **de pasaje** ferry

barcaza *nf* barge; ~ **de desembarco** landing craft

Barcelona *nf* Barcelona

barcelonés, -esa *adj* of *o* from Barcelona ▷ *nm/f* native *o* inhabitant of Barcelona

barco *nm* boat; (*buque*) ship; (*Com etc*) vessel; ~ **de carga** cargo boat; ~ **de guerra** warship; ~ **de vela** sailing ship; **ir en** ~ to go by boat

baremo *nm* scale; (*tabla de cuentas*) ready reckoner

barítono *nm* baritone

barman *nm* barman

Barna. *abr* = **Barcelona**

barniz *nm* varnish; (*en la loza*) glaze; (*fig*) veneer

barnizar *vt* to varnish; (*loza*) to glaze

barómetro *nm* barometer

barón *nm* baron

baronesa *nf* baroness

barquero *nm* boatman

barquillo *nm* cone, cornet

barra *nf* bar, rod; (*Jur*) rail; (: *banquillo*) dock; (*de un bar, café*) bar; (*de pan*) French loaf; (*palanca*) lever; ~ **de carmín** *o* **de labios** lipstick; ~ **de espaciado** (*Inform*) space bar; ~ **inversa** backslash; ~ **libre** free bar; **no pararse en** ~**s** to stick *o* stop at nothing

barraca *nf* hut, cabin; (*en Valencia*) thatched farmhouse; (*en feria*) booth

barranca *nf* ravine, gully

barranco *nm* ravine; (*fig*) difficulty

barrena *nf* drill

barrenar *vt* to drill (through), bore

barrendero, -a *nm/f* street-sweeper

barreno *nm* large drill

barrer *vt* to sweep; (*quitar*) to sweep away; (*Mil, Náut*) to sweep, rake (with gunfire) ▷ *vi* to sweep up

barrera *nf* barrier; (*Mil*) barricade; (*Ferro*) crossing gate; **poner** ~**s a** to hinder; ~ **arancelaria** (*Com*) tariff barrier; ~ **comercial** (*Com*) trade barrier

barriada *nf* quarter, district

barricada *nf* barricade

barrida *nf*, **barrido** *nm* sweep, sweeping

barriga *nf* belly; (*panza*) paunch; (*vientre*) guts *pl*; **echar** ~ to get middle-age spread

barrigón, -ona, barrigudo, -a *adj* potbellied

barril *nm* barrel, cask; **cerveza de** ~ draught beer

barrio *nm* (*vecindad*) area, neighborhood (*US*); (*en las afueras*) suburb; ~**s bajos** poor quarter *sg*; ~ **chino** red-light district

barro *nm* (*lodo*) mud; (*objetos*) earthenware; (*Med*) pimple

barroco, -a *adj* Baroque; (*fig*) elaborate ▷ *nm* Baroque

barrote *nm* (*de ventana etc*) bar

barruntar *vt* (*conjeturar*) to guess; (*presentir*) to suspect

barrunto *nm* (*conjetura*) guess; (*sospecha*) suspicion

bartola; a la ~ *adv*: **tirarse a la** ~ to take it easy, be lazy

bártulos *nmpl* things, belongings

barullo *nm* row, uproar

basar *vt* to base; **basarse** *vr*: ~**se en** to be based on

basca *nf* nausea

báscula *nf* (*platform*) scales *pl*; ~ **biestable** (*Inform*) flip-flop, toggle

base *nf* (*soporte*) base; (*fundamento*) basis; **la** ~ **de la columna** the base of the column; **el esfuerzo es la** ~ **del éxito** effort is the basis for success; **las** ~**s del concurso** the rules of the competition; **a** ~ **de** by means of; **lo consiguió a** ~ **de mucho trabajo** she managed it by dint of hard work; **un plato a** ~ **de verduras** a vegetable dish; **a** ~ **de bien** in abundance; ~ **de conocimiento** knowledge base; ~ **de datos** database; ~ **militar** military base

básico, -a *adj* basic

basílica *nf* basilica

basket, básquet *nm* basketball

bastante *adj* **1** (*suficiente*) enough; ~ **dinero** enough *o* sufficient money; ~**s libros** enough books; **¿hay** ~**?** is there enough?

2 (*valor intensivo*) quite a lot of; ~ **gente** quite a lot of people; **tener** ~ **calor** to be rather hot; **hace** ~ **tiempo que ocurrió** it happened quite *o* rather a long time ago

▷ *adv* quite a lot; ~ **bueno/malo** quite good/rather bad; **sus padres ganan** ~ their parents earn quite a lot; **me gusta** ~ I like it quite a lot; **voy a tardar** ~ I'm going to be a while *o* quite some time; ~ **rico** pretty rich; **(lo)** ~ **inteligente (como) para hacer algo** clever enough to do sth

bastar *vi* to be enough *o* sufficient; **bastarse** *vr* to be self-sufficient; **con eso basta** that's enough; **nos basta saber que...** it is enough for us to know that...; ~ **para** to be enough to; **¡basta!** (that's) enough!; **¡basta ya de tonterías!** that's enough of your nonsense!; **yo me basto solo** I can manage on my own

bastardilla *nf* italics *pl*

bastardo, -a *adj*, *nm/f* bastard

bastidor *nm* frame; (*de coche*) chassis; (*Arte*) stretcher; (*Teat*) wing; **entre** ~**es** behind the scenes

basto, -a *adj* coarse, rough ▷ *nmpl*: ~**s** (*Naipes*) one of the suits in the Spanish card deck

bastón *nm* stick, staff; (*para pasear*) walking stick; ~ **de mando** baton

bastoncillo *nm* (*tb*: **bastoncillo de algodón**) cotton bud

basura *nf* rubbish, refuse (*Brit*), garbage (*US*) ▷ *adj*: **comida/televisión** ~ junk food/TV

basurero *nm* (*hombre*) dustman (*Brit*), garbage collector *o* man (*US*); (*lugar*) rubbish dump; (*cubo*) (rubbish) bin (*Brit*), trash can (*US*)

bata *nf* (*gen*) dressing gown; (*cubretodo*) smock, overall; (*Med, Tec etc*) lab(oratory) coat

batalla *nf* battle; **de ~** for everyday use

batallar *vi* to fight

batallón *nm* battalion

batata *nf* (*LAm: Culin*) sweet potato

bate *nm* (*Deporte*) bat

bateador *nm* (*Deporte*) batter, batsman

batería *nf* battery; (*Mus*) drums *pl*; (*Teat*) footlights *pl*; **~ de cocina** kitchen utensils *pl*

batida *nf* (*And, CS*) (police) raid

batido, -a *adj* (*camino*) beaten, well-trodden ▷ *nm* (*Culin*) batter; **~ (de leche)** milk shake

batidora *nf* beater, mixer; **~ eléctrica** food mixer, blender

batir *vt* to beat, strike; (*vencer*) to beat, defeat; (*revolver*) to beat, mix; (*pelo*) to back-comb; **batirse** *vr* to fight; **~ palmas** to clap, applaud

baturro, -a *nm/f* Aragonese peasant

batuta *nf* baton; **llevar la ~** (*fig*) to be the boss

baúl *nm* (*arca*) trunk; (*CS Auto*) boot (*Brit*), trunk (*US*)

bautismo *nm* baptism, christening

bautizar *vt* to baptize, christen; (*fam: diluir*) to water down; (*dar apodo*) to dub

bautizo *nm* baptism, christening

bayeta *nf* (*trapo*) floorcloth; (*LAm: pañal*) nappy (*Brit*), diaper (*US*)

bayo, -a *adj* bay

bayoneta *nf* bayonet

baza *nf* trick; **meter ~** to butt in; **sentada esta ~...** this point being established...; **jugar la última ~** to play one's last card

bazar *nm* bazaar

bazo *nm* spleen

bazofia *nf* pigswill (*Brit*), hogwash (*US*); (*libro etc*) trash

BCE *nm abr* (= *Banco Central Europeo*) ECB

beatificar *vt* to beatify

beato, -a *adj* blessed; (*piadoso*) pious

bebe (*RP*) (*pl* **-s**), **bebé** (*pl* **bebés**) *nm* baby

bebedero, -a *nm* (*para animales*) drinking trough

bebedor, a *adj* hard-drinking

bebé-probeta (*pl* **bebés-probeta**) *nm/f* test-tube baby

beber *vt, vi* to drink; **~ a sorbos/tragos** to sip/gulp; **se lo bebió todo** he drank it all up

bebido, -a *adj* drunk ▷ *nf* drink

beca *nf* grant, scholarship

becado, -a *nm/f*, **becario, a** *nm/f* scholarship holder

bechamel *nf* = **besamel**

bedel *nm* porter, janitor

beduino, -a *adj, nm/f* Bedouin

befarse *vr*: **~ de algo** to scoff at sth

beige, beis *adj, nm* beige

béisbol *nm* baseball

beldad *nf* beauty

Belén *nm* Bethlehem; **belén** (*de Navidad*) nativity scene, crib

belga *adj, nm/f* Belgian

Bélgica *nf* Belgium

Belice *nm* Belize

bélico, -a *adj* (*actitud*) warlike

belicoso, -a *adj* (*guerrero*) warlike; (*agresivo*) aggressive, bellicose

beligerante *adj* belligerent

bellaco, -a *adj* sly, cunning ▷ *nm* villain, rogue

bellaquería *nf* (*acción*) dirty trick; (*calidad*) wickedness

belleza *nf* beauty

bello, -a *adj* beautiful, lovely; **Bellas Artes** Fine Art *sg*

bellota *nf* acorn

bemol *nm* (*Mus*) flat; **esto tiene ~es** (*fam*) this is a tough one

bencina *nf* (*Chi*) petrol (*Brit*), gas (*US*)

bendecir *vt* to bless; **~ la mesa** to say grace

bendición *nf* blessing

bendito, -a *pp de* **bendecir** ▷ *adj* (*santo*) blessed; (*agua*) holy; (*afortunado*) lucky; (*feliz*) happy; (*sencillo*) simple ▷ *nm/f* simple soul; **¡~ sea Dios!** thank goodness!; **es un ~** he's sweet; **dormir como un ~** to sleep like a log

benedictino, -a *adj, nm* Benedictine

beneficencia *nf* charity

beneficiar *vt* to benefit, be of benefit to; **beneficiarse** *vr* (*obtener provecho*) to benefit; **~se de algo** to benefit from sth

beneficiario, -a *nm/f* beneficiary; (*de cheque*) payee

beneficio *nm* (*bien*) benefit, advantage; (*Com*) profit, gain; **sacar ~ de algo** to benefit from something; **a ~ de** in aid of; **un concierto a ~ de las víctimas del terremoto** a concert in aid of the earthquake victims; **en ~ propio** to one's own advantage; **concederle a algn el ~ de la duda** to give sb the benefit of the doubt; **obtuvieron un ~ de dos millones de euros** they made a profit of two million euros; **no han tenido ~s este año** they didn't make any profit this year; **~ bruto/neto** gross/net profit; **~ por acción** earnings *pl* per share; *ver tb* **margen**

beneficioso, -a *adj* beneficial

benéfico, -a *adj* charitable; **sociedad benéfica** charity (organization)

beneplácito *nm* approval, consent

benevolencia *nf* benevolence, kindness

benévolo, -a *adj* benevolent, kind

benigno, -a *adj* kind; (*suave*) mild; (*Med: tumor*) benign, non-malignant

beodo, -a *adj* drunk ▷ *nm/f* drunkard

berberecho *nm* cockle

berenjena *nf* aubergine (*Brit*), eggplant (*US*)

Berlín *nm* Berlin

berlinés, -esa *adj* of o from Berlin ▷ *nm/f* Berliner

bermejo, -a *adj* red

bermudas *nfpl* Bermuda shorts

berrear *vi* to bellow, low

berrido *nm* bellow(ing)

berrinche *nm* (*fam*) temper, tantrum

berro *nm* watercress

berza *nf* cabbage; **~ lombarda** red cabbage

besamel, besamela *nf* (*Culin*) white sauce, bechamel sauce

besar vt to kiss; (fig: tocar) to graze; **besarse** vr to kiss (one another)

beso nm kiss

bestia nf beast, animal; (fig) idiot; ~ **de carga** beast of burden; ¡~! you idiot!; ¡**no seas** ~! (bruto) don't be such a brute!; (idiota) don't be such an idiot!

bestial adj bestial; (fam) terrific

bestialidad nf bestiality; (fam) stupidity

besugo nm sea bream; (fam) idiot

besuquear vt to cover with kisses; **besuquearse** vr to kiss and cuddle

betún nm shoe polish; (Química) bitumen, asphalt

biberón nm feeding bottle

Biblia nf Bible

bibliografía nf bibliography

biblioteca nf library; (estantes) bookcase, bookshelves pl; ~ **de consulta** reference library

bibliotecario, -a nm/f librarian

bicarbonato nm bicarbonate

bíceps nm inv biceps

bicho nm (animal) small animal; (sabandija) bug, insect; (Taur) bull; ~ **raro** (fam) queer fish

bici nf (fam) bike

bicicleta nf bicycle, cycle; ~ **estática/de montaña** exercise/mountain bike

bidé nm bidet

bien nm **1** (bienestar) good; **te lo digo por tu** ~ I'm telling you for your own good; **el** ~ **y el mal** good and evil

2 (posesión): ~**es** goods; ~**es de consumo/equipo** consumer/capital goods; ~**es inmuebles** o **raíces/**~**es muebles** real estate sg/personal property sg

▷ adv **1** (de manera satisfactoria, correcta etc) well; **trabaja/come** ~ she works/eats well; **contestó** ~ he answered correctly; **me siento** ~ I feel fine; **no me siento (muy)** ~ I don't feel very well; **¿te encuentras** ~? are you all right?; **sabe** ~ it tastes good; **huele** ~ it smells nice o good; **lo pasamos muy** ~ we had a very good time; **hiciste** ~ **en decírselo** you were right to tell him

2 (valor intensivo) very; **un cuarto** ~ **caliente** a nice warm room; ~ **de veces** lots of times; ~ **se ve que** ... it's quite clear that ...

3: **estar** ~: **estoy muy** ~ **aquí** I feel very happy here; **¿estás** ~? are you OK?; **se está** ~ **aquí** it's nice here; **te está** ~ **la falda** (ser la talla) the skirt fits you; (sentar) the skirt suits you; **el libro está muy** ~ the book is really good; **está** ~ **que vengan** it's all right for them to come; **¡está** ~! lo haré oh all right, I'll do it; **¡ya está** ~! that's enough!; **ya está** ~ **de quejas** that's quite enough complaining

4 (de buena gana): **yo** ~ **que iría pero** ... I'd gladly go but ...

▷ excl: **¡~!** (aprobación) O.K!; **¡muy** ~! well done!; **¡qué** ~! excellent!; ~, **gracias, ¿y usted?** fine thanks, and you?

▷ adj inv: **niño** ~ rich kid; **gente** ~ posh people

▷ conj **1**: ~ ... ~: ~ **en coche** ~ **en tren** either by car or by train

2: **no** ~ (esp LAm): **no** ~ **llegue te llamaré** as soon as I arrive I'll call you

3: **si** ~ even though; ver tb **más**

bienal adj biennial

bienaventurado, -a adj (feliz) happy; (afortunado) fortunate; (Rel) blessed

bienestar nm well-being; **estado de** ~ welfare state

bienhechor, a adj beneficent ▷ nm/f benefactor/ benefactress

bienvenido, -a adj welcome ▷ excl welcome! ▷ nf welcome; **dar la bienvenida a algn** to welcome sb

bies nm: **falda al** ~ bias-cut skirt; **cortar al** ~ to cut on the bias

bife nm (CS) steak

bifocal adj bifocal

bifurcación nf fork; (Ferro, Inform) branch

bifurcarse vr to fork

bigamia nf bigamy

bígamo, -a adj bigamous ▷ nm/f bigamist

bigote nm (tb: **bigotes**) moustache

bigotudo, -a adj with a big moustache

bikini nm bikini; (Culin) toasted cheese and ham sandwich

bilateral adj bilateral

bilingüe adj bilingual

billar nm billiards sg; (lugar) billiard hall; (salón recreativo) amusement arcade; ~ **americano** pool

billete nm ticket; (de banco) banknote (Brit), bill (US); (carta) note; ~ **sencillo**, ~ **de ida solamente/**~ **de ida y vuelta** single (Brit) o one-way (US) ticket/return (Brit) o round-trip (US) ticket; **sacar (un)** ~ to get a ticket; **un** ~ **de 5 libras** a five-pound note

billetera nf, **billetero** nm wallet

billón nm trillion

bimensual adj bimonthly

bimotor adj twin-engined ▷ nm twin-engined plane

bingo nm (juego) bingo; (sala) bingo hall

binóculo nm pince-nez

binomio nm (Mat) binomial

biodegradable adj biodegradable

biodiversidad nf biodiversity

biografía nf biography

biográfico, -a adj biographical

biógrafo, -a nm/f biographer

biología nf biology

biológico, -a adj biological; (cultivo, producto) organic; **guerra biológica** biological warfare

biólogo, -a nm/f biologist

biombo nm (folding) screen

biopsia nf biopsy

biosfera nf biosphere

biquini nm = **bikini**

birlar vt (fam) to pinch

Birmania nf Burma

birria nf (fam): **ser una** ~ to be rubbish; **ir hecho una** ~ to be o look a sight

bis excl encore! ▷ nm encore ▷ adv (dos veces) twice;

viven en el 27 ~ they live at 27a
bisabuelo, -a *nm/f* great-grandfather/mother;
 bisabuelos *nmpl* great-grandparents
bisagra *nf* hinge
bisbisar, bisbisear *vt* to mutter, mumble
bisexual *adj, nm/f* bisexual
bisiesto *adj*: **año ~** leap year
bisnieto, -a *nm/f* great-grandson/daughter;
 bisnietos *nmpl* great-grandchildren
bisonte *nm* bison
bistec, bisté *nm* steak
bisturí *nm* scalpel
bisutería *nf* imitation *o* costume jewellery
bit *nm* (*Inform*) bit; **~ de parada** stop bit; **~ de
 paridad** parity bit
bitácora *nf*: **cuaderno de ~** logbook, ship's log
bizco, -a *adj* cross-eyed
bizcocho *nm* (*Culin*) sponge cake
biznieto, -a *nm/f* = **bisnieto**
bizquear *vi* to squint
blanca *nf* (*Mus*) minim; **estar sin ~** to be broke;
 ver tb **blanco**
blanco, -a *adj* white ▷ *nm/f* white man/woman,
 white ▷ *nm* (*color*) white; (*en texto*) blank; (*Mil*,
 objetivo) target; **me gusta el ~** I like white;
 cheque en ~ blank cheque; **votar en ~** to return
 a blank ballot paper; **dejar algo en ~** to leave
 something blank; **cuando iba a responder me
 quedé en ~** just as I was about to reply my mind
 went blank; **noche en ~** sleepless night; **ser el ~
 de las burlas** to be the butt of jokes; **dar en el ~**
 to hit the target; *ver tb* **blanca**
blancura *nf* whiteness
blandir *vt* to brandish
blando, -a *adj* soft; (*tierno*) tender, gentle;
 (*carácter*) mild; (*fam*) cowardly ▷ *nm/f* (*Pol etc*)
 soft-liner
blandura *nf* (*de cama*) softness; (*de carne*)
 tenderness
blanquear *vt* to whiten; (*fachada*) to whitewash;
 (*paño*) to bleach; (*dinero*) to launder ▷ *vi* to turn
 white
blanquecino, -a *adj* whitish
blanqueo *nm* (*de pared*) whitewashing; (*de dinero*)
 laundering
blasfemar *vi* to blaspheme; (*fig*) to curse
blasfemia *nf* blasphemy
blasón *nm* coat of arms; (*fig*) honour
blasonar *vt* to emblazon ▷ *vi* to boast, brag
bledo *nm*: **(no) me importa un ~** I couldn't care
 less
blindado, -a *adj* (*Mil*) armour-plated; (*antibalas*)
 bulletproof; **coche** *o* (*LAm*) **carro ~** armoured
 car; **puertas blindadas** security doors
blindaje *nm* armour, armour-plating
bloc (*pl* **-s**) *nm* writing pad; (*Escol*) jotter; **~ de
 dibujos** sketch pad
bloque *nm* (*tb Inform*) block; (*Pol*) bloc; **~ de
 cilindros** cylinder block
bloquear *vt* (*Náut etc*) to blockade; (*aislar*) to cut
 off; (*Com, Econ*) to freeze; **fondos bloqueados**
 frozen assets

bloqueo *nm* blockade; (*Com*) freezing, blocking
blusa *nf* blouse
boa *nf* boa
boato *nm* show, ostentation
bobada *nf* foolish action (*o* statement); **decir ~s**
 to talk nonsense
bobería *nf* = **bobada**
bobina *nf* (*Tec*) bobbin; (*Foto*) spool; (*Elec*) coil,
 winding
bobo, -a *adj* (*tonto*) daft, silly; (*cándido*) naïve
 ▷ *nm/f* fool, idiot ▷ *nm* (*Teat*) clown, funny man
boca *nf* mouth; (*de crustáceo*) pincer; (*de cañón*)
 muzzle; (*entrada*) mouth, entrance; (*Inform*) slot;
 bocas *nfpl* (*de río*) mouth *sg*; **~ abajo/arriba** face
 down/up; **a ~ jarro** point-blank; **se me hace
 la ~ agua** my mouth is watering; **todo salió a
 pedir de ~** it all turned out perfectly; **en ~ de**
 (*esp LAm*) according to; **la cosa anda de ~ en
 ~** the story is going the rounds; **¡cállate la ~!**
 (*fam*) shut up!; **quedarse con la ~ abierta** to be
 dumbfounded; **no abrir la ~** to keep quiet; **~ del
 estómago** pit of the stomach; **~ de metro** tube
 (*Brit*) *o* subway (*US*) entrance
bocacalle *nf* (entrance to a) street; **la primera ~**
 the first turning *o* street
bocadillo *nm* sandwich
bocado *nm* mouthful, bite; (*de caballo*) bridle; **~
 de Adán** Adam's apple
bocajarro: **a ~** *adv* (*Mil*) at point-blank range;
 decir algo a ~ to say sth bluntly
bocanada *nf* (*de vino*) mouthful, swallow; (*de aire*)
 gust, puff
bocata *nm* (*fam*) sandwich
bocazas *nm/f inv* (*fam*) bigmouth
boceto *nm* sketch, outline
bocha *nf* bowl; **bochas** *nfpl* bowls *sg*
bochinche *nm* (*fam*) uproar
bochorno *nm* (*vergüenza*) embarrassment; (*calor*):
 hace ~ it's very muggy
bochornoso, -a *adj* (*caluroso*) muggy;
 (*avergonzante*) embarrassing
bocina *nf* (*Mus*) trumpet; (*Auto*) horn; (*para hablar*)
 megaphone; **tocar la ~** (*Auto*) to sound *o* blow
 one's horn
boda *nf* (*tb*: **bodas**) wedding, marriage; (*fiesta*)
 wedding reception; **~s de plata/de oro** silver/
 golden wedding *sg*
bodega *nf* (*de vino*) (wine) cellar; (*bar*) bar;
 (*restaurante*) restaurant; (*depósito*) storeroom; (*de
 barco*) hold
bodegón *nm* (*Arte*) still life
B.O.E. *nm abr* = **Boletín Oficial del Estado**
bofe *nm* (*tb*: **bofes**: *de res*) lights *pl*; **echar los ~s** to
 slave (away)
bofetada *nf* slap (in the face); **dar de ~s a algn**
 to punch sb
bofetón *nm* = **bofetada**
boga *nf*: **en ~** in vogue
bogar *vi* (*remar*) to row; (*navegar*) to sail
bogavante *nm* (*Náut*) stroke, first rower; (*Zool*)
 lobster
Bogotá *n* Bogota

bogotano, -a adj of o from Bogota ▷ nm/f native o inhabitant of Bogota
bohemio, -a adj, nm/f Bohemian
boicot (pl -s) nm boycott
boicotear vt to boycott
boicoteo nm boycott
boina nf beret
bola nf ball; (canica) marble; (Naipes) (grand) slam; (betún: And) shoe polish; (mentira) tale, story; **bolas** nfpl (LAm) bolas; ~ **de billar** billiard ball; ~ **de nieve** snowball
bolchevique adj, nm/f Bolshevik
boleadoras nfpl (LAm) bolas sg
bolera nf skittle o bowling alley
bolero nm (Mús) bolero; (Méx) shoeshine boy
boleta nf (LAm: billete) ticket; (: recibo) receipt; (: para votar) ballot; (: de multa) ticket
boletería nf (LAm) ticket office
boletín nm bulletin; (periódico) journal, review; ~ **escolar** (Esp) school report; ~ **de noticias** news bulletin; ~ **de pedido** application form; ~ **de precios** price list; ~ **de prensa** press release
boleto nm (esp LAm) ticket; ~ **de apuestas** betting slip
boli nm Biro®
boliche nm (bola) jack; (juego) bowls sg; (lugar) bowling alley; (CS: tienda) small grocery store
bólido nm meteorite; (Auto) racing car
bolígrafo nm ball-point pen, biro®
bolívar nm monetary unit of Venezuela
Bolivia nf Bolivia
boliviano, -a adj, nm/f Bolivian
bollo nm (de pan) roll; (dulce) scone; (bulto) bump, lump; (abolladura) dent; **bollos** nmpl (LAm) troubles
bolo nm skittle; (píldora) (large) pill; **(juego de) ~s** skittles sg
bolsa nf (saco) bag; (Méx: de mujer) handbag; (bolsillo) pocket; (Anat) cavity, sac; (Com) stock exchange; (Minería) pocket; ~ **de agua caliente** hot water bottle; ~ **de aire** air pocket; ~ **de (la) basura** bin-liner; ~ **de dormir** (LAm) sleeping bag; ~ **de papel** paper bag; ~ **de plástico** plastic (o carrier) bag; **"B~ de la propiedad"** "Property Mart"; ~ **de trabajo** employment bureau; **jugar a la ~** to play the market
bolsillo nm pocket; **de ~** pocket cpd; **meterse a algn en el ~** to get sb eating out of one's hand
bolsista nm/f stockbroker
bolso nm (bolsa) bag; (de mujer) handbag
boludo, -a (RP fam!) adj stupid ▷ nm/f prat (!)
bomba nf (Mil) bomb; (Tec) pump; (CAm, Perú: borrachera) drunkenness ▷ adj (fam): **noticia ~** bombshell ▷ adv (fam): **pasarlo ~** to have a great time; ~ **atómica/de humo/de retardo** atomic/smoke/time bomb; ~ **de gasolina** petrol pump; ~ **de incendios** fire engine
bombachas nfpl (Andes, CS: de gaucho) baggy trousers; (CS: ropa interior) underwear
bombardear vt to bombard; (Mil) to bomb
bombardeo nm (con artillería) bombardment; (desde el aire) bombing

bombardero nm bomber
bombear vt (agua) to pump (out o up); (Mil) to bomb; (Fútbol) to lob; **bombearse** vr to warp
bombero nm fireman; **(cuerpo de) ~s** fire brigade
bombilla nf, **bombillo** nm (CAm) (light) bulb
bombín nm bowler hat
bombita nf (RP) (light) bulb
bombo nm (Mus) bass drum; (Tec) drum; (fam) exaggerated praise; **hacer algo a ~ y platillo** to make a great song and dance about sth; **tengo la cabeza hecha un ~** I've got a splitting headache
bombón nm chocolate; (belleza) gem
bombona nf: ~ **de butano** gas cylinder
bonachón, -ona adj good-natured
bonaerense adj of o from Buenos Aires ▷ nm/f native o inhabitant of Buenos Aires
bonanza nf (Náut) fair weather; (fig) bonanza; (Minería) rich pocket o vein
bondad nf goodness, kindness; **tenga la ~ de** (please) be good enough to
bondadoso, -a adj good, kind
bonito, -a adj (lindo) pretty; (agradable) nice ▷ adv (LAm fam) well ▷ nm (atún) tuna (fish)
bono nm voucher; (Fin) bond; ~ **de billetes de metro** booklet of metro tickets; ~ **del Tesoro** treasury bill
bonobús nm (Esp) bus pass
Bono Loto, bonoloto nm o f (Esp) state-run weekly lottery
boom (pl -s) nm boom
boquear vi to gasp
boquerón nm (pez) (kind of) anchovy; (agujero) large hole
boquete nm gap, hole
boquiabierto, -a adj open-mouthed (in astonishment); **quedar ~** to be left aghast
boquilla nf (de riego) nozzle; (de cigarro) cigarette holder; (Mus) mouthpiece
borbotón nm: **salir a borbotones** to gush out
borda nf (Náut) gunwale; **echar o tirar algo por la ~** to throw sth overboard
bordado nm embroidery
bordar vt to embroider
borde nm edge, border; (de camino etc) side; (en la costura) hem; **al ~ de** (fig) on the verge o brink of; **ser ~** (Esp fam) to be a pain in the neck
bordear vt to border
bordillo nm kerb (Brit), curb (US)
bordo nm (Náut) side; **a ~** on board
borla nf (gen) tassel; (de gorro) pompon
borrachera nf (ebriedad) drunkenness; (orgía) spree, binge
borracho, -a adj drunk ▷ nm/f (que bebe mucho) drunkard, drunk; (temporalmente) drunk, drunk man/woman ▷ nm (Culin) cake soaked in liqueur or spirit
borrador nm (escritura) first draft, rough sketch; (cuaderno) scribbling pad; (goma) rubber (Brit), eraser; (Com) daybook; (para pizarra) duster; **hacer un nuevo ~ de** (Com) to redraft

borrar vt (con goma, borrador) to erase, rub out; (tachar) to delete; (cinta, disquete) to wipe; (Inform: archivo) to delete, erase; (Pol etc: eliminar) to deal with; **borrarse** vr (desaparecer: inscripción, recuerdo) to fade; **~se de** (lista) to take one's name off; (asociación, club) to leave; **borra la palabra completa** rub out the whole word; **borra la pizarra** clean the blackboard

borrasca nf (Meteorología) depression

borrico, -a nm donkey; (fig) stupid man ▷ nf she-donkey; (fig) stupid woman

borrón nm (mancha) stain; **~ y cuenta nueva** let bygones be bygones

borroso, -a adj vague, unclear; (escritura) illegible; (escrito) smudgy; (Foto) blurred

Bosnia nf Bosnia

bosnio, -a adj, nm/f Bosnian

bosque nm wood; (grande) forest

bosquejar vt to sketch

bosquejo nm sketch

bostezar vi to yawn

bostezo nm yawn

bota nf (calzado) boot; (de vino) leather wine bottle; **ponerse las ~s** (fam) to strike it rich

botana nf (Méx) snack

botánica nf botany; ver tb **botánico**

botánico, -a adj botanical ▷ nm/f botanist; ver tb **botánica**

botar vt to throw, hurl; (Náut) to launch; (esp LAm fam) to throw out ▷ vi to bounce

bote nm (salto: de persona) jump; (de pelota) bounce; (envase: de bebidas) can; (de pintura) tin; (embarcación) boat; **dar o pegar un ~** to jump; **dar ~s** (Auto etc) to bump; **de ~ en ~** packed, jammed full; **a ~ pronto** (Esp) off the top of one's head; **~ de la basura** (Méx) dustbin (Brit), trashcan (US); **~ salvavidas** lifeboat

botella nf bottle; **~ de vino** (contenido) bottle of wine; (recipiente) wine bottle

botellín nm small bottle

botellón nm (Esp: fam) outdoor drinking session (involving groups of young people)

botica nf chemist's (shop) (Brit), pharmacy

boticario, -a nm/f chemist (Brit), pharmacist

botijo nm (earthenware) jug; (tren) excursion train

botín nm (calzado) half boot; (polaina) spat; (Mil) booty; (de ladrón) loot

botiquín nm (armario) medicine chest; (portátil) first-aid kit

botón nm button; (Bot) bud; (de florete) tip; **~ de arranque** (Auto etc) starter; **~ de oro** buttercup; **pulsar el ~** to press the button

botones nm inv bellboy, bellhop (US)

bóveda nf (Arq) vault

boxeador nm boxer

boxear vi to box

boxeo nm boxing

boya nf (Náut) buoy; (flotador) float

boyante adj (Náut) buoyant; (feliz) buoyant; (próspero) prosperous

bozal nm (de caballo) halter; (de perro) muzzle

bracear vi (agitar los brazos) to wave one's arms

bracero nm labourer; (en el campo) farmhand

braga nf (cuerda) sling, rope; (de bebé) nappy, diaper (US); **bragas** nfpl (de mujer) panties

bragueta nf fly (Brit), flies pl (Brit), zipper (US)

braille nm braille

bramar vi to bellow, roar

bramido nm bellow, roar

brasa nf live o hot coal; **carne a la ~** grilled meat

brasero nm (de carbón) brazier; (Méx: hornillo) small stove

Brasil nm: (el) ~ Brazil

brasileño, -a adj, nm/f Brazilian

bravata nf boast

braveza nf (valor) bravery; (ferocidad) ferocity

bravío, -a adj wild; (feroz) fierce

bravo, -a adj (valiente) brave; (bueno) fine, splendid; (feroz) ferocious; (salvaje) wild; (mar etc) rough, stormy; (Culin) hot, spicy ▷ excl bravo!

bravura nf (valentía) bravery; (ferocidad) ferocity

braza nf fathom; **nadar a ~** to swim (the) breast-stroke

brazada nf stroke

brazalete nm (pulsera) bracelet; (banda) armband

brazo nm arm; (Zool) foreleg; (Bot) limb, branch; **~ derecho** (fig) right-hand man; **a ~ partido** hand-to-hand; **cogidos etc del ~** arm in arm; **no dar su ~ a torcer** not to give way easily; **huelga de ~s caídos** sit-down strike

brea nf pitch, tar

brebaje nm potion

brecha nf breach; (hoyo vacío) gap, opening

brega nf (lucha) struggle; (trabajo) hard work

breva nf (Bot) early fig; (puro) flat cigar; **¡no caerá esa ~!** no such luck!

breve adj short, brief; **en ~** (pronto) shortly; (en pocas palabras) in short ▷ nf (Mus) breve

brevedad nf brevity, shortness; **con o a la mayor ~** as soon as possible

brezal nm moor(land), heath

brezo nm heather

bribón, -ona adj idle, lazy ▷ nm/f (vagabundo) vagabond; (pícaro) rascal, rogue

bricolaje nm do-it-yourself, DIY

brida nf bridle, rein; (Tec) clamp; **a toda ~** at top speed

bridge nm (Naipes) bridge

brigada nf (unidad) brigade; (trabajadores) squad, gang ▷ nm warrant officer

brillante adj (pelo, muebles, metal) shiny; (joya, agua) sparkling; (color, luz) bright; (futuro, carrera, representación, victoria) brilliant ▷ nm diamond; **blanco ~** brilliant white

brillar vi (pelo, muebles, metal) to shine; (joya, agua) to sparkle; (persona) to shine; **hoy brilla el sol** the sun is shining today; **¡cómo brilla esa bombilla!** that bulb is so bright!; **siempre brilló en todo lo que hizo** he always shone at everything he did; **~ por su ausencia** to be conspicuous by one's absence

brillo nm (de pelo, muebles, metal) shine; (de joya, agua) sparkle; (brillantez: de persona) brilliance;

(de representación) splendour; **la pantalla tiene mucho ~** the screen is too bright; **sacar ~ a algo** to polish sth

brincar vi to skip about, hop about, jump about; **está que brinca** he's hopping mad

brinco nm jump, leap; **a ~s** by fits and starts; **de un ~** at one bound

brindar vi: **~ a** o **por** to drink (a toast) to ▷ vt to offer, present; **le brinda la ocasión de** it offers o affords him the opportunity to; **brindarse** vr: **~se a hacer algo** to offer to do sth

brindis nm inv toast; (Taur) (ceremony of) dedication

brío nm spirit, dash

brioso, -a adj spirited, dashing

brisa nf breeze

británico, -a adj British ▷ nm/f Briton, British person; **los ~s** the British

brizna nf (hebra) strand, thread; (de hierba) blade; (trozo) piece

broca nf (Costura) bobbin; (Tec) drill bit; (clavo) tack

brocal nm rim

brocha nf (large) paintbrush; **~ de afeitar** shaving brush; **pintor de ~ gorda** painter and decorator; (fig) poor painter

broche nm brooch

broma nf joke; (inocentada) practical joke; **en ~** in fun, as a joke; **gastar una ~ a algn** to play a joke on sb; **tomar algo a ~** to take sth as a joke

bromear vi to joke

bromista adj fond of joking ▷ nm/f joker, wag

bronca nf row; (regañada) ticking-off; **armar una ~** to kick up a fuss; **echar una ~ a algn** to tell sb off

bronce nm bronze; (latón) brass

bronceado, -a adj bronze cpd; (por el sol) tanned ▷ nm (sun)tan; (Tec) bronzing

bronceador nm suntan lotion

broncearse vr to get a suntan

bronco, -a adj (manera) rude, surly; (voz) harsh

bronquios nmpl bronchial tubes

bronquitis nf inv bronchitis

brotar vt (tierra) to produce ▷ vi (Bot) to sprout; (aguas) to gush (forth); (lágrimas) to well up; (Med) to break out

brote nm (Bot) shoot; (Med, fig) outbreak

bruces; **de ~** adv: **caer** o **dar de ~** to fall headlong, fall flat

bruja nf witch

brujería nf witchcraft

brujo nm wizard, magician

brújula nf compass

bruma nf mist

brumoso, -a adj misty

bruñido nm polish

bruñir vt to polish

brusco, -a adj (súbito) sudden; (áspero) brusque

Bruselas nf Brussels

brutal adj brutal

brutalidad nf brutality

bruto, -a adj (idiota) stupid; (bestial) brutish; (peso) gross ▷ nm brute; **a la bruta, a lo ~** roughly; **en ~** raw, unworked

Bs.As. abr = **Buenos Aires**

bucal adj oral; **por vía ~** orally

bucear vi to dive ▷ vt to explore

buceo nm diving; (fig) investigation

bucle nm curl; (Inform) loop

budismo nm Buddhism

budista adj, nm/f Buddhist

buen adj ver **bueno**

buenamente adv (fácilmente) easily; (voluntariamente) willingly

buenaventura nf (suerte) good luck; (adivinación) fortune; **decir** o **echar la ~ a algn** to tell sb's fortune

bueno, -a (antes de nmsg: **buen** adj 1 (excelente) good; (Med) well; **es un libro ~, es un buen libro** it's a good book; **hace ~, hace buen tiempo** the weather is fine, it is fine; **es buena persona** he's a good sort; **el ~ de Paco** good old Paco; **fue muy ~ conmigo** he was very nice o kind to me; **ya está ~** he's fine now

2 (apropiado): **ser ~ para** to be good for; **creo que vamos por buen camino** I think we're on the right track

3 (irónico): **le di un buen rapapolvo** I gave him a good o real ticking off; **¡buen conductor estás hecho!** some driver o a fine driver you are!; **¡estaría ~ que ...!** a fine thing it would be if ...!

4 (atractivo, sabroso): **está ~ este bizcocho** this sponge is delicious; **Julio está muy ~** (fam) Julio is a bit of alright (fam)

5 (grande) good, big; **un buen número de ...** a good number of ...; **un buen trozo de ...** a nice big piece of ...

6 (en saludos): **¡buen día!, ** (LAm) **¡~s días!** (good) morning!; **¡buenas (tardes)!** good afternoon!; (más tarde) good evening!; **¡buenas noches!** good night!; **¡buenas!** (por la mañana) good morning!; (por la tarde) good afternoon!; (más tarde) good evening!

7 (otras locuciones): **estar de buenas** to be in a good mood; **por las buenas** o **por las malas** by hook or by crook; **irás por las buenas** o **por las malas** you'll go whether you like it or not; **de buenas a primeras** all of a sudden ▷ excl: **¡~!** all right!; **~, ¿y qué?** well, so what?; **~, lo que pasa es que ...** well, the thing is ...; **pero ¡~!** well, I like that!; **~, pues ...** right, (then) ...

Buenos Aires nm Buenos Aires

buey nm ox

búfalo nm buffalo

bufanda nf scarf

bufar vi to snort

bufete nm lawyer's office; **establecer su ~** to set up in legal practice

buffer nm (Inform) buffer

bufón nm clown

buhardilla nf attic

búho nm owl; (fig) hermit, recluse

buhonero nm pedlar

buitre nm vulture

bujía *nf* (*vela*) candle; (*Elec*) candle (power); (*Auto*) spark plug
bula *nf* (*papal*) bull
bulbo *nm* (*Bot*) bulb
bulevar *nm* boulevard
Bulgaria *nf* Bulgaria
búlgaro, -a *adj, nm/f* Bulgarian
bulimia *nf* bulimia
bulla *nf* (*ruido*) uproar; (*de gente*) crowd; **armar** *o* **meter** ~ to kick up a row
bullicio *nm* (*ruido*) uproar; (*movimiento*) bustle
bullir *vi* (*hervir*) to boil; (*burbujear*) to bubble; (*mover*) to move, stir; (*insectos*) to swarm; ~ **de** (*fig*) to teem *o* seethe with
bulto *nm* (*silueta*) shape; (*paquete*) package; (*de equipaje*) piece of luggage; (*fardo*) bundle; (*Med*) swelling, lump; (*estatua*) bust, statue; **hacer** ~ to take up space; (*iró*) to make up the numbers; **escurrir el** ~ to make o.s. scarce; (*fig*) to dodge the issue
buñuelo *nm* ≈ doughnut, ≈ donut (US)
BUP *nm abr* (*Esp, Escol*: = *Bachillerato Unificado y Polivalente*) *secondary education for 14-17 age group*
buque *nm* ship, vessel; ~ **de guerra** warship; ~ **mercante** merchant ship; ~ **de vela** sailing ship
burbuja *nf* bubble; **hacer** ~**s** to bubble; (*gaseosa*) to fizz
burbujear *vi* to bubble
burdel *nm* brothel
burdo, -a *adj* coarse, rough
burgués, -esa *adj* middle-class, bourgeois; **pequeño** ~ lower middle-class; (*Pol, pey*) petty bourgeois
burguesía *nf* middle class, bourgeoisie
burla *nf* (*mofa*) gibe; (*broma*) joke; (*engaño*) trick; **hacer** ~ **de** to make fun of
burladero *nm* (*bullfighter's*) refuge
burlador, a *adj* mocking ▷ *nm/f* mocker; (*bromista*) joker ▷ *nm* (*libertino*) seducer
burlar *vt* (*engañar*) to deceive; (*seducir*) to seduce ▷ *vi*: **burlarse** *vr* to joke; ~**se de** to make fun of
burlesco, -a *adj* burlesque
burlón, -ona *adj* mocking
burocracia *nf* bureaucracy
burócrata *nm/f* bureaucrat
buromática *nf* office automation
burrada *nf* stupid act; **decir** ~**s** to talk nonsense
burro, -a *nm/f* (*Zool*) donkey; (*fig*) ass, idiot ▷ *adj* stupid; **caerse del** ~ to realise one's mistake; **no ver tres en un** ~ to be as blind as a bat
bursátil *adj* stock-exchange *cpd*
bus *nm* bus
busca *nf* search, hunt ▷ *nm* bleeper, pager; **en** ~ **de** in search of
buscador *nm* (*Internet*) search engine
buscar *vt* to look for; (*beneficio*) to seek; (*enemigo*) to seek out; (*provocar*) to provoke; (*Inform*) to search ▷ *vi* to look, search, seek; **¿estás buscando las gafas?** are you looking for your glasses?; **estoy buscando trabajo** I'm looking for work; **te voy a** ~ **a la estación** I'll come and get you at the station; **ven a** ~**me a la oficina** come and pick me up at the office; **voy a** ~ **un taxi** I'm going to get a taxi; ~ **una palabra en el diccionario** to look up a word in the dictionary; **"~ y reemplazar"** (*Inform*) "search and replace"; **se busca secretaria** secretary wanted; ~**le tres pies al gato** to split hairs; **se la buscó** he asked for it
buscona *nf* whore
búsqueda *nf* = **busca**
busto *nm* (*Anat, Arte*) bust
butaca *nf* armchair; (*de cine, teatro*) stall, seat
butano *nm* butane (gas); **bombona de** ~ gas cylinder
buzo *nm* diver; (*LAm: chandal*) tracksuit
buzón *nm* (*gen*) letter box; (*en la calle*) pillar box (Brit); (*Telec*) mailbox; **echar al** ~ to post; ~ **de voz** voice mail
buzonear *vt* to leaflet

Cc

C. _abr_ (= _centígrado_) C.; (= _compañía_) Co

c. _abr_ (= _capítulo_) ch

C/ _abr_ (= _calle_) St, Rd

c.a. _abr_ (= _corriente alterna_) A.C

cabal _adj_ (_exacto_) exact; (_correcto_) right, proper; (_acabado_) finished, complete; **cabales** _nmpl_: **estar en sus ~es** to be in one's right mind

cábala _nf_ (_Rel_) cab(b)ala; (_fig_) cabal, intrigue; **cábalas** _nfpl_ guess _sg_, supposition _sg_

cabalgadura _nf_ mount, horse

cabalgar _vt, vi_ to ride

cabalgata _nf_ procession

caballa _nf_ mackerel

caballeresco, -a _adj_ noble, chivalrous

caballería _nf_ mount; (_Mil_) cavalry

caballeriza _nf_ stable

caballerizo _nm_ groom, stableman

caballero _nm_ gentleman; (_de la orden de caballería_) knight; (_trato directo_) sir; **"C~s"** "Gents"

caballerosidad _nf_ chivalry

caballete _nm_ (_Agr_) ridge; (_Arte_) easel

caballito _nm_ (_caballo pequeño_) small horse, pony; (_juguete_) rocking horse; **caballitos** _nmpl_ merry-go-round _sg_; **~ de mar** seahorse; **~ del diablo** dragonfly

caballo _nm_ horse; (_Ajedrez_) knight; (_Naipes_) ≈ queen; **~ de vapor** _o_ **de fuerza** horsepower; **es su ~ de batalla** it's his hobby-horse; **~ blanco** (_Com_) backer

cabaña _nf_ (_casita_) hut, cabin

cabaré, cabaret (_pl_ **cabarets**) _nm_ cabaret

cabecear _vi_ to nod

cabecera _nf_ (_gen_) head; (_de distrito_) chief town; (_de cama_) headboard; (_Imprenta_) headline

cabecilla _nm_ ringleader

cabellera _nf_ (head of) hair; (_de cometa_) tail

cabello _nm_ (_tb_: **cabellos**) hair _sg_

cabelludo _adj ver_ **cuero**

caber _vi_ (_entrar_) to fit, go; **tu guitarra no cabe en mi armario** your guitar won't fit in my cupboard; **no cabe por la puerta** it won't go through the door; **caben 3 más** there's room for 3 more; **eso no me cabe en la cabeza** I don't understand it; **cabe la posibilidad de que llame** he might call; **cabe preguntar si…** one might ask whether…; **cabe que venga más tarde** he may come later; **no está mal dentro**

de lo que cabe it's not bad, considering

cabestrillo _nm_ sling

cabestro _nm_ halter

cabeza _nf_ head; (_Pol_) chief, leader ▷ _nm/f:_ **~ rapada** skinhead; **se tiró de ~ al agua** he dived headfirst into the water; **pagamos diez euros por ~** we paid ten euros each _o_ a head; **al oírlos volví la ~** when I heard them I looked round; **estar mal de la ~** to be crazy (_fam_), be off one's head (_Brit_) (_fam_); **estar a la ~ de la clasificación** to be at the top of the league; **sentar la ~** to settle down; **~ de lectura/escritura** read/write head; **~ impresora** _o_ **de impresión** printhead

cabezada _nf_ (_golpe_) butt; **dar una ~** to nod off

cabezazo _nm_ (_golpe_) headbutt; (_Fútbol_) header

cabezón, -ona _adj_ with a big head; (_vino_) heady; (_obstinado_) obstinate, stubborn

cabezota _adj inv_ obstinate, stubborn

cabida _nf_ space; **dar ~ a** to make room for; **tener ~ para** to have room for

cabildo _nm_ (_de iglesia_) chapter; (_Pol_) town council

cabina _nf_ (_de camión_) cabin; **~ telefónica** (tele)phone box (_Brit_) _o_ booth

cabizbajo, -a _adj_ crestfallen, dejected

cable _nm_ cable; (_de aparato_) lead; **~ aéreo** (_Elec_) overhead cable; **conectar con ~** (_Inform_) to hardwire

cabo _nm_ (_de objeto_) end, extremity; (_Mil_) corporal; (_Náut_) rope, cable; (_Geo_) cape; (_Tec_) thread; **al ~ de 3 días** after 3 days; **de ~ a rabo** _o_ **~ from beginning to end**; (_leer un libro_) from cover to cover; **llevar a ~** to carry out; **atar ~s** to tie up the loose ends; **C~ de Buena Esperanza** Cape of Good Hope; **C~ de Hornos** Cape Horn; **las Islas de C~ Verde** the Cape Verde Islands

cabra _nf_ goat; **estar como una ~** (_fam_) to be nuts

cabrear _vt_ to annoy; **cabrearse** _vr_ to fly off the handle

cabrío, -a _adj_ goatish; **macho ~** (he-)goat, billy goat

cabriola _nf_ caper

cabritilla _nf_ kid, kidskin

cabrito _nm_ kid

cabrón _nm_ (_fig: fam!_) bastard (!)

cabronada _nf_ (_fam!_): **hacer una ~ a algn** to be a bastard to sb

caca _nf_ (_palabra de niños_) pooh ▷ _excl:_ **no toques,**

¡~! don't touch, it's dirty!
cacahuate nm (Méx) peanut
cacahuete nm (Esp) peanut
cacao nm cocoa; (Bot) cacao
cacarear vi (persona) to boast; (gallina) to cackle
cacería nf hunt
cacerola nf pan, saucepan
cachalote nm sperm whale
cacharro nm (vasija) (earthenware) pot; (cerámica)
piece of pottery; (fam) useless object; **cacharros**
nmpl pots and pans
cachear vt to search, frisk
cachemir nm cashmere
cacheo nm searching, frisking
cachete nm (Anat) cheek; (bofetada) slap (in the
face)
cachimba nf, **cachimbo** nm (LAm) pipe
cachiporra nf truncheon
cachivache nm piece of junk; **cachivaches** nmpl
trash sg, junk sg
cacho nm (small) bit; (LAm: cuerno) horn
cachondearse vr: ~ **de algn** to tease sb
cachondeo nm (fam) farce, joke; (guasa) laugh
cachondo, -a adj (Zool) on heat; (persona) randy,
sexy; (gracioso) funny
cachorro, -a nm/f (de perro) pup, puppy; (de león)
cub
cacique nm chief, local ruler; (Pol) local party
boss; (fig) despot
caco nm pickpocket
cacto nm, **cactus** nm inv cactus
cada adj inv (referido a uno en particular) each; (referido
al conjunto) every; ~ **libro es de un color** each
book is a different colour; **le di un caramelo
a ~ niño** I gave a sweet to each child; ~ **día
dice una cosa diferente** she says something
different every day; **viene a verme ~ día** he
comes to see me every day; **pagamos doce
euros ~ uno** we paid twelve euros each; ~ **uno
tiene sus propios problemas** everyone has
their own problems; ~ **diez kilómetros** every
ten kilometres; ~ **vez que la veo** every time I see
her; ~ **dos días** every other day; **uno de ~ diez**
one out of every ten; **viene ~ vez más gente**
more and more people are coming; **viene ~
vez menos** he comes less and less often; ~ **vez
hace más frío** it's getting colder and colder; ¿~
cuánto vas al dentista? how often do you go to
the dentist?; ver tb **dos**
cadalso nm/f scaffold
cadáver nm (dead) body, corpse
cadena nf chain; (TV) channel; **reacción en
~** chain reaction; **trabajo en ~** assembly line
work; ~ **midi/mini** (Mus) midi/mini system;
~ **perpetua** (Jur) life imprisonment; ~ **de
caracteres** (Inform) character string
cadencia nf cadence, rhythm
cadera nf hip
cadete nm cadet
caducar vi to expire
caducidad nf: **fecha de ~** expiry date; (de comida)
sell-by date

caduco, -a adj (idea etc) outdated, outmoded; **de
hoja caduca** deciduous
caer vi to fall; (premio) to go; (sitio) to be, lie; (pago)
to fall due; **caerse** vr to fall (down); **me hice
daño al ~** I fell and hurt myself; **el avión cayó
al mar** the plane came down in the sea; **me cae
bien/mal** I like/don't like him; **su cumpleaños
cae en viernes** her birthday falls on a Friday;
~ **enfermo** to fall ill; **dejar ~** to drop; **estar al
~ (acontecimiento)** to be due to happen; (persona)
to be about to arrive; **¡no caigo!** I don't get it!;
al ~ la noche at nightfall; **tropecé y me caí** I
tripped and fell; **el niño se cayó de la cama**
the child fell out of bed; **se cayó por la ventana**
he fell out of the window; **no te vayas a ~ del
caballo** be careful not to fall off the horse; **el
edificio se está cayendo** the building is falling
down; **se me ha caído el guante** I've dropped
my glove; ver tb **cuenta**
café (pl -s) nm (bebida, planta) coffee; (lugar) café
▷ adj (color) brown; ~ **con leche** white coffee; ~
solo, ~ negro (LAm) (small) black coffee
cafeína nf caffeine(e)
cafetal nm coffee plantation
cafetera nf coffee pot; ver **cafetero**
cafetería nf cafe
cafetero, -a adj coffee cpd; **ser muy ~** to be a
coffee addict
cagalera nf (fam!): **tener ~** to have the runs
cagar (fam!) vt to shit (!); (fig) to bungle, mess up
▷ vi to have a shit (!); **cagarse** vr: **¡me cago en
diez** etc! Christ! (!)
caída nf (al suelo) fall; (de nivel, precio, temperatura)
fall, drop; (de gobierno, imperio) fall, collapse;
sufrir una ~ to have a fall; **la ~ del imperio**
the fall o collapse of the empire; **a la ~ del sol**
at sunset; **a la ~ de la tarde** in the evening; ver
tb **caído**
caído, -a adj fallen; (Inform) down; ~ **del cielo** out
of the blue; ver tb **caída**
caimán nm alligator
caja nf box; (ataúd) coffin, casket (US); (de vino,
champán) case; (de cervezas, refrescos) crate; (para
reloj) case; (de ascensor) shaft; (Com) cashbox;
(Econ) fund; (donde se hacen los pagos) cash desk; (en
supermercado) checkout, till; (Tip) case; **ingresar
en ~** to be paid in; **una ~ de zapatos** a shoe
box; ~ **de ahorros** savings bank; ~ **de cambios**
gearbox; ~ **fuerte, ~ de caudales** safe, strongbox
cajero, -a nm/f cashier; (en banco) (bank) teller
▷ nm: ~ **automático** cash dispenser, automatic
telling machine, A.T.M
cajetilla nf (de cigarrillos) packet
cajón nm big box; (de mueble) drawer
cajuela nf (Méx) boot (Brit), trunk (US)
cal nf lime; **cerrar algo a ~ y canto** to shut sth
firmly
cala nf (Geo) cove, inlet; (de barco) hold
calabacín nm (Bot) baby marrow, courgette,
zucchini (US)
calabacita nm (LAm Bot) baby marrow, courgette,
zucchini (US)

calabaza nf (Bot) pumpkin; **dar ~s a** (candidato) to fail

calabozo nm (cárcel) prison; (celda) cell

calado, -a adj (prenda) lace cpd ▷ nm (Tec) fretwork; (Náut) draught ▷ nf (de cigarrillo) puff; **estar ~ (hasta los huesos)** to be soaked (to the skin)

calamar nm squid

calambre nm (tb: **calambres**) cramp

calamidad nf calamity, disaster; (persona): **es una ~** he's a dead loss

calamina nf calamine

calaña nf model, pattern; (fig) nature, stamp

calar vt (mojar) to soak, drench; (penetrar) to pierce, penetrate; (vela, red) to lower; **calarse** vr (líquido) to soak through; (Auto) to stall; **la lluvia me caló hasta los huesos** I got soaked to the skin in the rain; **la lluvia ha calado la chaqueta** the rain has soaked right through the jacket; **nos ha calado** he's rumbled us; **a ésos los tengo muy calados** I've got them thoroughly sized up; **la lluvia se cala por el tejado** the rain is coming through the roof; **se le caló el coche** he stalled the car; **~se las gafas** to stick one's glasses on; **~se el sombrero** to pull one's hat down

calavera nf skull

calcañal, calcañar nm heel

calcar vt (reproducir) to trace; (imitar) to copy

calceta nf (knee-length) stocking; **hacer ~** to knit

calcetín nm sock

calcinar vt to burn, blacken

calcio nm calcium

calco nm tracing

calcomanía nf transfer

calculador, a adj calculating ▷ nf calculator

calcular vt (Mat) to calculate; **calcula la raíz cuadrada de...** work out o calculate the square root of...; **calculé lo que nos costaría** I calculated what it would cost us; **calculo que nos llevará unos tres días** I reckon that it will take us around three days

cálculo nm calculation; (Med) (gall)stone; (Mat) calculus; **~ de costo** costing; **~ diferencial** differential calculus; **obrar con mucho ~** to act cautiously

caldear vt to warm (up), heat (up); (metales) to weld

caldera nf boiler

calderilla nf (moneda) small change

caldero nm small boiler

caldo nm stock; (consomé) consommé; **~ de cultivo** (Bio) culture medium; **poner a ~ a algn** to tear sb off a strip; **los ~s jerezanos** sherries

caldoso, -a adj (guisado) juicy; (sopa) thin

calefacción nf heating; **~ central** central heating

caleidoscopio nm kaleidoscope

calendario nm calendar

calentador nm heater

calentamiento nm (Deporte) warm-up

calentar vt (comida) to heat (up), warm up; (fam: excitar) to turn on; (LAm: enfurecer) to anger; **calentarse** vr (comida) to heat up; (habitación, persona, motor) warm up; (fig: discusión, debate) to get heated; **¿quieres que te caliente la leche?** do you want me to heat up the milk for you?; **deja que se caliente el motor** let the engine warm up

calentura nf (Med) fever, (high) temperature; (de boca) mouth sore

calenturiento, -a adj (mente) overactive

calesita nf (RP) merry-go-round, roundabout (Brit)

calibrar vt to gauge, measure

calibre nm (de cañón) calibre, bore; (diámetro) diameter; (fig) calibre

calidad nf quality; **de ~** quality cpd; **~ de borrador** (Inform) draft quality; **~ de carta** o **de correspondencia** (Inform) letter quality; **~ texto** (Inform) text quality; **~ de vida** quality of life; **en ~ de** in the capacity of

cálido, -a adj hot; (fig) warm

caliente adj (no frío) warm; (que quema) hot; (fig) fiery; (disputa) heated; (fam: cachondo) randy

califa nm caliph

calificación nf qualification; (de alumno) grade, mark; **~ de sobresaliente** first-class mark

calificar vt to qualify; (alumno) to grade, mark; **~ de** to describe as

caligrafía nf calligraphy

calima nf mist

cáliz nm (Bot) calyx; (Rel) chalice

caliza nf limestone

callado, -a adj quiet, silent

callar vt (dato, información) to keep back; (asunto delicado) to keep quiet about, say nothing about; (persona, oposición) to silence ▷ vi: **callarse** vr (no hablar) to keep quiet, be silent; (dejar de hablar) to stop talking; **calla, que no me dejas concentrarme** be quiet, I can't concentrate; **prefirió ~se** he preferred to keep quiet; **al entrar el profesor todos se ~on** when the teacher came in, everyone stopped talking; **¡cállate!, ¡cállese!** shut up!; **¡cállate la boca!** shut your mouth!

calle nf street; (Deporte) lane; **~ arriba/abajo** up/down the street; **~ de sentido único** one-way street; **poner a algn (de patitas) en la ~** to kick sb out

calleja nf alley, narrow street

callejear vi to wander (about) the streets

callejero, -a adj street cpd ▷ nm street map

callejón nm alley, passage; (Geo) narrow pass; **~ sin salida** cul-de-sac; (fig) blind alley

callejuela nf side-street, alley

callista nm/f chiropodist

callo nm callus; (en el pie) corn; **callos** nmpl (Culin) tripe sg

callosidad nf (de pie) corn; (de mano) callus

calloso, -a adj horny, rough

calma nf calm; (pachorra) slowness; (Com, Econ) calm, lull; **~ chicha** dead calm; **¡~!, ¡con ~!** take it easy!

calmante adj soothing ▷ nm sedative, tranquillizer

calmar vt to calm, calm down; (dolor) to relieve ▷ vi: **calmarse** vr (tempestad) to abate; (mente etc) to become calm

calmoso, -a adj calm, quiet

calor nm heat; (calor agradable) warmth; **entrar en ~** to get warm; **tener ~** to be o feel hot

caloría nf calorie

calorífero, -a adj heat-producing, heat-giving ▷ nm heating system

calumnia nf slander; (por escrito) libel

calumnioso, -a adj (difamatorio) slanderous; (en prensa) libellous

caluroso, -a adj hot; (sin exceso) warm; (fig) enthusiastic

calva nf bald patch; (en bosque) clearing

calvario nm stations pl of the cross; (fig) cross, heavy burden

calvicie nf baldness

calvo, -a adj bald; (terreno) bare, barren; (tejido) threadbare ▷ nm bald man

calza nf wedge, chock

calzado, -a adj shod ▷ nm footwear ▷ nf roadway, highway

calzador nm shoehorn

calzar vt (zapatos etc) to wear; (un mueble) to put a wedge under; (Tec: rueda etc) to scotch; **calzarse** vr: **~se los zapatos** to put on one's shoes; **¿qué (número) calza?** what size do you take?

calzón nm (tb: **calzones**) shorts pl; (LAm: de hombre) pants pl; (: de mujer) panties pl

calzoncillos nmpl underpants

cama nf bed; (Geo) stratum; **~ individual/de matrimonio** single/double bed; **guardar ~** to be ill in bed

camada nf litter; (de personas) gang, band

camafeo nm cameo

camaleón nm chameleon

cámara nf (Pol etc) chamber; (habitación) room; (sala) hall; (Cine) cine camera; (fotográfica) camera; **~ de aire** inner tube; **~ alta/baja** upper/lower house; **~ de comercio** chamber of commerce; **~ digital** digital camera; **~ de gas** gas chamber; **~ de video** video camera; **a ~ lenta** in slow motion

camarada nm comrade, companion

camarero, -a nm waiter ▷ nf (en restaurante) waitress; (en casa, hotel) maid

camarilla nf (clan) clique; (Pol) lobby

camarín nm (Teat) dressing room

camarón nm shrimp

camarote nm (Náut) cabin

cambiable adj (variable) changeable, variable; (intercambiable) interchangeable

cambiante adj variable

cambiar vt (dinero, pieza, sábanas, fecha) to change; (intercambiar) to exchange, swap; (trasladar) to shift, move ▷ vi to change; **cambiarse** vr (de sitio) to move; (de ropa) to change; **quiero ~ este abrigo por uno más grande** I want to change this coat for a larger size; **~ sellos** to exchange stamps, swap stamps; **te cambio mi bolígrafo por tu goma** I'll swap my ballpoint for your rubber; **me gusta el tuyo, te lo cambio** I like yours, let's swap; **no has cambiado nada** you haven't changed a bit; **tenemos que ~ de tren en París** we have to change trains in Paris; **han cambiado de coche** they have changed car; **~ de color** to change colour; **~ de idea/de ropa** to change one's mind/clothes; **voy a ~me (de ropa)** I'm going to get changed; **~se de sitio** to move; **~se de casa** to move house

cambiazo nm: **dar el ~ a algn** to swindle sb

cambio nm (de dinero, temperatura, planes) change; (intercambio) exchange; (de lugar) shift, move; (Com) rate of exchange; (dinero suelto) small change; **un ~ brusco de temperatura** a sudden change in temperature; **~ de impresiones** exchange of views; **¿tiene ~ de cien?** have you got change of a hundred?; **¿te han dado bien el ~?** have they given you the right change?; **necesito ~ para el autobús** I need some change for the bus; **¿a cómo está el ~?** what's the exchange rate?; **me lo regaló a ~ del favor que le hice** he gave it to me in return for the favour I did him; **a mí me encanta y a él, en ~, le fastidia** I really like her, but he finds her irritating; **~ a término** (Com) forward exchange; **~ de divisas** (Com) foreign exchange; **~ de línea** (Inform) line feed; **~ de página** (Inform) form feed; **~ de velocidades** gear lever; **~ de vía** points pl

cambista nm (, Com) exchange broker

camelar vt (con mujer) to flirt with; (persuadir) to cajole

camelia nf camellia

camello nm camel; (fam: traficante) pusher

camelo nm: **me huele a ~** it smells fishy

camerino nm (Teat) dressing room

camilla nf (Med) stretcher

caminante nm/f traveller

caminar vi (marchar) to walk, go; (viajar) to travel, journey ▷ vt (recorrer) to cover, travel

caminata nf long walk

camino nm way, road; (sendero) track; **a medio ~** halfway (there); **en el ~** on the way, en route; **~ de** on the way to; **~ particular** private road; **~ vecinal** country road; **C~s, Canales y Puertos** (Univ) Civil Engineering; **ir por buen ~** (fig) to be on the right track

camión nm lorry, truck (US); (CAm, Méx: autobús) bus; **~ de bomberos** fire engine

camionero nm lorry o truck (US) driver, trucker (esp US)

camioneta nf van, transit®, light truck

camisa nf shirt; (Bot) skin; **~ de dormir** nightdress; **~ de fuerza** straitjacket

camiseta nf tee-shirt; (ropa interior) vest; (de deportista) top

camisón nm nightdress, nightgown

camorra nf: **armar ~** to kick up a row; **buscar ~** to look for trouble

camorrista nm/f thug

camote *nm* (*Méx Culin*) sweet potato
campal *adj*: **batalla ~** pitched battle
campamento *nm* camp
campana *nf* bell
campanada *nf* peal
campanario *nm* belfry
campanilla *nf* (*campana*) small bell
campaña *nf* (*Mil, Pol*) campaign; **hacer ~ (en pro de/contra)** to campaign (for/against); **~ de venta** sales campaign
campechano, -a *adj* open
campeón, -ona *nm/f* champion
campeonato *nm* championship
campesino, -a *adj* country *cpd*, rural; (*gente*) peasant *cpd* ▷ *nm/f* countryman/woman; (*agricultor*) farmer
campestre *adj* country *cpd*, rural
camping *nm* camping; (*lugar*) campsite; **ir de** *o* **hacer ~** to go camping
campiña *nf* countryside
campo *nm* (*fuera de la ciudad*) country, countryside; (*Agr, Elec, Inform*) field; (*de fútbol*) pitch; (*de golf*) course; (*Mil*) camp; **~ de batalla** battlefield; **~ de minas** minefield; **~ petrolífero** oilfield; **~ visual** field of vision; **~ de concentración/ de internación/de trabajo** concentration/ internment/labour camp
camposanto *nm* cemetery
campus *nm inv* (*Univ*) campus
camuflaje *nm* camouflage
camuflar *vt* to camouflage
cana *nf* (*tb*: **canas**) white *o* grey hair; **tener ~s** to be going grey; *ver tb* **cano**
Canadá *nm* Canada
canadiense *adj, nm/f* Canadian ▷ *nf* fur-lined jacket
canal *nm* canal; (*Geo*) channel, strait; (*de televisión*) channel; (*de tejado*) gutter; **C~ de la Mancha** English Channel; **C~ de Panamá** Panama Canal
canalizar *vt* to channel
canalla *nf* rabble, mob ▷ *nm* swine
canalón *nm* (*conducto vertical*) drainpipe; (*del tejado*) gutter
canapé (*pl* **-s**) *nm* sofa, settee; (*Culin*) canapé
Canarias *nfpl*: **las (Islas) ~** the Canaries, the Canary Isles
canario, -a *adj* of *o* from the Canary Isles ▷ *nm/f* native *o* inhabitant of the Canary Isles ▷ *nm* (*Zool*) canary
canasta *nf* (round) basket
canastilla *nf* small basket; (*de niño*) layette
canasto *nm* large basket
cancela *nf* (wrought-iron) gate
cancelación *nf* cancellation
cancelar *vt* to cancel; (*una deuda*) to write off
cáncer *nm* (*Med*) cancer; **C~** (*Astro*) Cancer
cancerígeno, -a *adj* carcinogenic
cancha *nf* (*de baloncesto, tenis etc*) court; (*LAm: de fútbol etc*) pitch
canciller *nm* chancellor; **C~** (*LAm*) Foreign Minister, ≈ Foreign Secretary (*Brit*)

canción *nf* song; **~ de cuna** lullaby
cancionero *nm* song book
candado *nm* padlock
candela *nf* candle
candelero *nm* (*para vela*) candlestick; (*de aceite*) oil lamp
candente *adj* red-hot; (*tema*) burning
candidato, -a *nm/f* candidate; (*para puesto*) applicant
candidez *nf* (*sencillez*) simplicity; (*simpleza*) naiveté
cándido, -a *adj* (*inocente*) naive
candil *nm* oil lamp
candilejas *nfpl* (*Teat*) footlights
candor *nm* (*sinceridad*) frankness; (*inocencia*) innocence
canela *nf* cinnamon
canelones *nmpl* cannelloni
cangrejo *nm* crab
canguro *nm* (*Zool*) kangaroo; (*de niños*) baby-sitter; **hacer de ~** to baby-sit
caníbal *adj, nm/f* cannibal
canica *nf* marble
canijo, -a *adj* frail, sickly
canilla *nf* (*espinilla*) shinbone; (*RP: grifo*) tap (*Brit*), faucet (*US*)
canino, -a *adj* canine ▷ *nm* canine (tooth)
canjear *vt* to exchange; (*trocar*) to swap
cano, -a *adj* grey-haired, white-haired; *ver tb* **cana**
canoa *nf* canoe
canon *nm* canon; (*pensión*) rent; (*Com*) tax
canónico, -a *adj*: **derecho ~** canon law
canónigo *nm* canon
canonizar *vt* to canonize
canoso, -a *adj* (*pelo*) grey (*Brit*), gray (*US*); (*persona*) grey-haired
cansado, -a *adj* (*agotado*) tired, weary; (*agotador*) tiring; (*tedioso*) tedious, boring; **estoy ~ de hacerlo** I'm sick of doing it
cansancio *nm* tiredness, fatigue
cansar *vt* (*fatigar*) to tire, tire out; (*aburrir*) to bore; (*fastidiar*) to bother; **cansarse** *vr* to tire, get tired; (*aburrirse*) to get bored
cantábrico, -a *adj* Cantabrian; **Mar C~** Bay of Biscay; **(Montes) C~s, Cordillera Cantábrica** Cantabrian Mountains
cantante *adj* singing ▷ *nm/f* singer
cantar *vt* to sing ▷ *vi* to sing; (*insecto*) to chirp; (*rechinar*) to squeak; (*fam: criminal*) to squeal ▷ *nm* (*acción*) singing; (*canción*) song; (*poema*) poem; **~ a algn las cuarenta** to tell sb a few home truths; **~ a dos voces** to sing a duet
cántara *nf* large pitcher
cántaro *nm* pitcher, jug
cantautor, a *nm/f* singer-songwriter
cante *nm*: **~ jondo** flamenco singing
cantera *nf* quarry
cantidad *nf* quantity, amount; (*Econ*) sum ▷ *adv* (*fam*) a lot; **~ alzada** lump sum; **~ de** lots of
cantilena *nf* = **cantinela**
cantimplora *nf* (*frasco*) water bottle, canteen

cantina *nf* canteen; (*de estación*) buffet; (*esp LAm*) bar

cantinela *nf* ballad, song

canto *nm* singing; (*canción*) song; (*borde*) edge, rim; (*de un cuchillo*) back; ~ **rodado** boulder

cantor, a *nm/f* singer

canturrear *vi* to sing softly

canutas *nfpl*: **pasarlas** ~ (*fam*) to have a rough time (of it)

canuto *nm* (*tubo*) small tube; (*fam: droga*) joint

caña *nf* (*Bot: tallo*) stem, stalk; (*carrizo*) reed; (*vaso*) tumbler; (*de cerveza*) glass of beer; (*Anat*) shinbone; (*LAm: aguardiente*) cane liquor; ~ **de azúcar** sugar cane; ~ **de pescar** fishing rod

cañada *nf* (*entre dos montañas*) gully, ravine; (*camino*) cattle track

cáñamo *nm* (*Bot*) hemp

cañería *nf* piping; (*tubo*) pipe

caño *nm* (*tubo*) tube, pipe; (*de aguas servidas*) sewer; (*Mus*) pipe; (*Náut*) navigation channel; (*de fuente*) jet

cañón *nm* (*Mil*) cannon; (*de fusil*) barrel; (*Geo*) canyon, gorge

cañonera *nf* (*tb:* **lancha cañonera**) gunboat

caoba *nf* mahogany

caos *nm* chaos

caótico, -a *adj* chaotic

cap. *abr* (= *capítulo*) ch

capa *nf* cloak, cape; (*Culin*) coating; (*Geo*) layer, stratum; (*de pintura*) coat; **de ~ y espada** cloak-and-dagger; **so ~ de** under the pretext of; ~ **de ozono** ozone layer; ~**s sociales** social groups

capacidad *nf* (*medida*) capacity; (*aptitud*) capacity, ability; **una sala con** ~ **para 900** a hall seating 900; ~ **adquisitiva** purchasing power

capacitación *nf* training

capacitar *vt*: ~ **a algn para algo** to qualify sb for sth; (*Tec*) to train sb for sth

capar *vt* to castrate, geld

caparazón *nm* (*Zool*) shell

capataz *nm* foreman, chargehand

capaz *adj* able, capable; **es** ~ **de olvidarse el pasaporte** he's quite capable of forgetting his passport; **por ella sería** ~ **de cualquier cosa** he would do anything for her; **es** ~ **que venga mañana** (*CS*) he'll probably come tomorrow

capcioso, -a *adj* wily, deceitful; **pregunta capciosa** trick question

capea *nf* (*Taur*) bullfight with young bulls

capear *vt* (*dificultades*) to dodge; ~ **el temporal** to weather the storm

capellán *nm* chaplain; (*sacerdote*) priest

caperuza *nf* hood; (*de bolígrafo*) cap

capicúa *nf* reversible number, e.g. 1441

capilar *adj* hair *cpd*

capilla *nf* chapel

capital *adj* capital ▷ *nm* (*Com*) capital ▷ *nf* (*de nación*) capital (city); (*tb:* **capital de provincia**) provincial capital, ≈ county town; ~ **activo/en acciones** working/share o equity capital; ~ **arriesgado** venture capital; ~ **autorizado** o **social** authorised capital; ~ **emitido** issued capital; ~ **improductivo** idle money; ~ **invertido** o **utilizado** capital employed; ~ **pagado** paid-up capital; ~ **de riesgo** risk capital; ~ **social** equity o share capital; **inversión de ~es** capital investment

capitalismo *nm* capitalism

capitalista *adj, nm/f* capitalist

capitalizar *vt* to capitalize

capitán *nm* captain; (*fig*) leader

capitanear *vt* to captain

capitolio *nm* capitol

capitulación *nf* (*rendición*) capitulation, surrender; (*acuerdo*) agreement, pact; **capitulaciones matrimoniales** marriage contract *sg*

capitular *vi* to come to terms, make an agreement; (*Mil*) to surrender

capítulo *nm* chapter

capo *nm* drugs baron

capó *nm* (*Auto*) bonnet (*Brit*), hood (*US*)

capón *nm* capon

caporal *nm* chief, leader

capota *nf* (*de mujer*) bonnet; (*Auto*) hood (*Brit*), top (*US*)

capote *nm* (*abrigo: de militar*) greatcoat; (*de torero*) cloak

capricho *nm* whim, caprice

caprichoso, -a *adj* capricious

Capricornio *nm* Capricorn

cápsula *nf* capsule; ~ **espacial** space capsule

captar *vt* (*comprender*) to understand; (*Radio*) to pick up; (*atención, apoyo*) to attract

captura *nf* capture; (*Jur*) arrest

capturar *vt* to capture; (*Jur*) to arrest; (*datos*) to input

capucha *nf* hood, cowl

capullo *nm* (*Zool*) cocoon; (*Bot*) bud; (*fam!*) berk (*Brit*), jerk (*US*)

caqui *nm* khaki

cara *nf* (*Anat, de moneda*) face; (*de disco, papel*) side; (*fam: descaro*) cheek, nerve; **mirar a algn a la** ~ to look sb in the face; ~ **a** ~ face to face; **tienes mala** ~ you don't look well; **tenía** ~ **de pocos amigos** he looked very unfriendly; **no pongas esa** ~ don't look like that; **se sentó (de)** ~ **a la pared** he sat down facing the wall; **actúan a escondidas y nunca dan la** ~ they do things in secret and never face the consequences; **echar algo en** ~ **a algn** to reproach sb for sth; **plantar** ~ **a algn** to confront sb; **un folio escrito por las dos ~s** a sheet written on both sides; **¿~ o cruz?** heads or tails?; **lo echamos a** ~ **o cruz** we tossed for it; **¡qué ~ (más dura)!** what a cheek!

carabina *nf* carbine, rifle; (*persona*) chaperone

Caracas *nm* Caracas

caracol *nm* (*Zool*) snail; (*concha*) (sea)shell; **escalera de** ~ spiral staircase

caracolear *vi* (*caballo*) to prance about

carácter (*pl* **caracteres**) *nm* (*personalidad, índole*) nature; (*Inform, Tip*) character; **tiene el** ~ **de su padre** he has his father's nature; **tener buen** ~ to be good-natured; **tener mal** ~ to be bad-

tempered; **la chica tiene mucho ~** the girl has
a strong personality; **una visita de ~ oficial**
an official visit, a visit of an official nature; **~
de cambio de página** form feed character; **~
libre** (*Inform*) wildcard character; **escribir
en caracteres de imprenta** to write in block
letters

característico, -a *adj* characteristic ⊳ *nf*
characteristic

caracterizar *vt* (*distinguir*) to characterize, typify;
(*honrar*) to confer a distinction on

caradura *nm/f* cheeky person; **es un ~** he's got
a nerve

carajillo *nm* black coffee with brandy

carajo *nm* (*esp LAm fam!*): **¡~!** shit! (!); **¡qué ~!** what
the hell!; **me importa un ~** I don't give a damn

caramba *excl* well!, good gracious!

carámbano *nm* icicle

caramelo *nm* (*dulce*) sweet; (*azúcar fundido*)
caramel

carantoñas *nfpl*: **hacer ~ a algn** to (try to) butter
sb up

caraqueño, -a *adj* of o from Caracas ⊳ *nm/f*
native o inhabitant of Caracas

carátula *nf* (*máscara*) mask; (*Teat*): **la ~** the stage

caravana *nf* caravan; (*fig*) group; (*de autos*)
tailback

carbón *nm* coal; **~ de leña** charcoal; **papel ~**
carbon paper

carboncillo *nm* (*Arte*) charcoal

carbonilla *nf* coal dust

carbonizar *vt* to carbonize; (*quemar*) to char;
quedar carbonizado (*Elec*) to be electrocuted

carbono *nm* carbon

carburador *nm* carburettor

carburante *nm* fuel

carca *adj, nm/f inv* reactionary

carcajada *nf* (loud) laugh, guffaw

carcajearse *vr* to roar with laughter

cárcel *nf* prison; (*Tec*) clamp

carcelero, -a *adj* prison *cpd* ⊳ *nm/f* warder

carcoma *nf* woodworm

carcomer *vt* to bore into, eat into; (*fig*) to
undermine; **carcomerse** *vr* to become worm-
eaten; (*fig*) to decay

carcomido, -a *adj* worm-eaten; (*fig*) rotten

cardar *vt* (*Tec*) to card, comb

cardenal *nm* (*Rel*) cardinal; (*Med*) bruise

cárdeno, -a *adj* purple; (*lívido*) livid

cardíaco, -a, cardíaco, a *adj* cardiac; (*ataque*)
heart *cpd*

cardinal *adj* cardinal

cardo *nm* thistle

carear *vt* to bring face to face; (*comparar*) to
compare; **carearse** *vr* to come face to face, meet

carecer *vi*: **~ de** to lack, be in need of

carencia *nf* lack; (*escasez*) shortage; (*Med*)
deficiency

carente *adj*: **~ de** lacking in, devoid of

carestía *nf* (*escasez*) scarcity, shortage; (*Com*) high
cost; **época de ~** period of shortage

careta *nf* mask

carga *nf* (*cargamento: de barco, avión*) cargo; (*de
tren*) freight; (*de camión*) load; (*de escopeta, obús*)
charge; (*de bolígrafo, pluma, encendedor*) refill; (*de
batería, pilas*) charge; (*peso*) load; (*impuesto*) tax,
duty; (*Inform*) loading; (*obligación, responsabilidad*)
duty, obligation; **"~ y descarga"** loading and
unloading; **la ~ fiscal** the tax burden; **no
quiero ser una ~ para ellos** I don't want to be
a burden to them; **volver a la ~** to return to the
charge, return to the attack; **~ aérea** (*Com*) air
cargo; **~ máxima** maximum load; **~ útil** (*Com*)
payload

cargado, -a *adj* loaded; (*Elec*) live; (*café, té*)
strong; (*cielo*) overcast

cargamento *nm* (*acción*) loading; (*mercancías*)
load, cargo

cargar *vt* to load; (*bolígrafo, pluma, encendedor*) to
fill; (*batería, pilas*) to charge; (*impuesto*) to impose;
cargarse *vr* (*fam: romper*) to break; (*fam: matar*) to
bump off*; (*Elec*) to become charged; **cárguelo
en mi cuenta** charge it to my account; **tuve
que ~ con todo** I had to take responsibility for
everything; **te vas a ~ el vídeo** you're going to
break the video; **se ~on al presidente de un
tiro** they shot the president

cargo *nm* (*puesto*) post; (*Com*) charge, debit; (*Jur*)
charge; **un ~ de mucha responsabilidad** a
very responsible post; **desempeñar un ~** to fill
an office; **altos ~s** high-ranking officials; **una
cantidad en ~ a algn** a sum chargeable to sb;
está a ~ de la contabilidad he's in charge of
keeping the books; **hacerse ~ de** to take charge
of o responsibility for

carguero *nm* freighter, cargo boat; (*avión*) freight
plane

Caribe *nm*: **el ~** the Caribbean

caribeño, -a *adj* Caribbean

caricatura *nf* caricature

caricia *nf* caress; (*a animal*) pat, stroke

caridad *nf* charity

caries *nf inv* (*Med*) tooth decay

cariño *nm* affection, love; (*caricia*) caress; (*en
carta*) love ...

cariñoso, -a *adj* affectionate

carisma *nm* charisma

carismático, -a *adj* charismatic

caritativo, -a *adj* charitable

cariz *nm*: **tener o tomar buen/mal ~** to look
good/bad

carmesí *adj, nm* crimson

carmín *nm* (*color*) carmine; **~ (de labios)** lipstick

carnal *adj* carnal; **primo ~** first cousin

carnaval *nm* carnival

carne *nf* (*Culin*) meat; (*Anat*) flesh; **no como ~**
I don't eat meat; **~ de cerdo/de cordero/de
ternera/de vaca** pork/lamb/veal/beef; **~ picada**
mince; **ser de ~ y hueso** to be only human; **~ de
cañón** cannon fodder; **~ de gallina** (*fig*) goose
pimples, goose bumps, gooseflesh

carné *nm* = **carnet**

carnero *nm* sheep, ram; (*carne*) mutton

carnet (*pl* **-s**) *nm*: **~ de conducir** driving licence;

~ **de identidad** identity card

carnicería nf butcher's (shop); (fig: matanza) carnage, slaughter

carnicero, -a adj carnivorous ▷ nm/f (tb fig) butcher ▷ nm carnivore

carnívoro, -a adj carnivorous ▷ nm carnivore

carnoso, -a adj beefy, fat

caro, -a adj dear; (Com) dear, expensive ▷ adv dear, dearly; **vender** ~ **lo** sell at a high price

carpa nf (pez) carp; (de circo) big top; (LAm: de camping) tent

carpeta nf folder, file

carpintería nf carpentry

carpintero nm carpenter; **pájaro** ~ woodpecker

carraspear vi to clear one's throat

carraspera nf hoarseness

carrera nf (acción) run(ning); (espacio recorrido) run; (certamen) race; (trayecto) course; (profesión) career; (Escol, Univ) course; (de taxi) ride; (en medias) ladder; **a la** ~ at (full) speed; **caballo de** ~**(s)** racehorse; ~ **de armamentos** arms race

carreta nf wagon, cart

carrete nm reel, spool; (Tec) coil

carretera nf (main) road, highway; ~ **nacional** ≈ A road (Brit), state highway (US); ~ **de circunvalación** ring road

carretilla nf trolley; (Agr) (wheel)barrow

carril nm furrow; (de autopista) lane; (Ferro) rail

carril-bici nm cycle lane, bikeway (US)

carrillo nm (Anat) cheek; (Tec) pulley

carro nm (carreta) cart; (en aeropuerto, supermercado) trolley; (LAm: coche) car; (de máquina de escribir) carriage; ~ **de combate** tank; ~ **blindado** armoured car

carrocería nf body, bodywork no pl (Brit)

carroña nf carrion no pl

carroza nf (vehículo) coach ▷ nm/f (fam) old fogey

carruaje nm carriage

carrusel nm merry-go-round, roundabout (Brit)

carta nf letter; (Culin) menu; (naipe) card; (mapa) map; (Jur) document; ~ **de crédito** credit card; ~ **de crédito documentaria** (Com) documentary letter of credit; ~ **de crédito irrevocable** (Com) irrevocable letter of credit; ~ **certificada/ urgente** registered/special delivery letter; ~ **marítima** chart; ~ **de pedido** (Com) order; ~ **verde** (Auto) green card; ~ **de vinos** wine list; **echar una** ~ **al correo** to post a letter; **echar las** ~**s a algn** to tell sb's fortune

cartabón nm set square

cartearse vr to correspond

cartel nm (anuncio) poster, placard; (Escol) wall chart; (Com) cartel

cartelera nf hoarding, billboard; (en periódico etc) listings pl, entertainments guide; **"en** ~**"** "showing"

cartera nf (de bolsillo) wallet; (de colegial, cobrador) satchel; (LAm: de señora) handbag (Brit), purse (US); (para documentos) briefcase; **ministro sin** ~ (Pol) minister without portfolio; **ocupa la** ~ **de Agricultura** he is Minister of Agriculture; ~ **de pedidos** (Com) order book; **efectos en** ~ (Econ)

holdings

carterista nm/f pickpocket

cartero nm postman

cartilla nf (Escol) primer, first reading book; ~ **de ahorros** bank book

cartografía nf cartography

cartón nm cardboard

cartucho nm (Mil) cartridge; (bolsita) paper cone; ~ **de datos** (Inform) data cartridge

cartulina nf fine cardboard, card

casa nf house; (hogar) home; (edificio) building; (Com) firm, company; ~ **consistorial** town hall; ~ **de huéspedes** ≈ guest house; ~ **rural** (de alquiler) holiday cottage; (pensión) rural B & B; ~ **de socorro** first aid post; ~ **de citas** (fam) brothel; **ir a** ~ to go home; **salir de** ~ to go out; (para siempre) to leave home; **echar la** ~ **por la ventana** (gastar) to spare no expense

casadero, -a adj marriageable

casado, -a a married ▷ nm/f married man/woman

casamiento nm marriage, wedding

casar vt to marry; (Jur) to quash, annul; **casarse** vr to marry, get married; ~**se por lo civil** to have a civil wedding, get married in a registry office (Brit)

cascabel nm (small) bell; (Zool) rattlesnake

cascada nf waterfall

cascanueces nm inv: **un** ~ a pair of nutcrackers

cascar vt to split; (nuez) to crack ▷ vi to chatter; **cascarse** vr to crack, split, break (open)

cáscara nf (de huevo, fruta seca) shell; (de fruta) skin; (de limón) peel, rind

casco nm (de bombero, soldado) helmet; (cráneo) skull; (Náut: de barco) hull; (Zool: de caballo) hoof; (botella) empty bottle; (de ciudad): **el** ~ **antiguo** the old part; **el** ~ **urbano** the town centre; **los** ~**s azules** the UN peace-keeping force, the blue berets

cascote nm piece of rubble; **cascotes** nmpl rubble sg

caserío nm hamlet, group of houses; (casa) country house

casero, -a adj: **ser muy** ~ (persona) to be homeloving; **"comida casera"** "home cooking" ▷ nm/f (propietario) landlord/lady; (Com) house agent

caseta nf hut; (para bañista) cubicle; (de feria) stall

casete nm o f cassette; ~ **digital** digital audio tape, DAT

casi adv (generalmente en oraciones afirmativas) almost, nearly; (generalmente en oraciones negativas) hardly; ~ **te caes** you almost o nearly fell; **son** ~ **las cinco** it's almost o nearly five o'clock; ~ **no comí** I hardly ate; **no queda** ~ **nada en la nevera** there's hardly anything left in the fridge; ~ **nadie estuvo de acuerdo** hardly anybody agreed; ~ **nunca se equivoca** he hardly ever makes a mistake; ~ **nada** next to nothing

casilla nf (casita) hut, cabin; (Teat) box office; (para cartas) pigeonhole; (Ajedrez) square; **C~ postal** o **de Correo(s)** (LAm) P.O. Box; **sacar a**

algn de sus ~s to drive sb round the bend (*fam*), make sb lose his temper
casillero *nm* (set of) pigeonholes
casino *nm* club; (*de juego*) casino
caso *nm* case; **en ~s así es preferible callarse** in such cases it's better to keep quiet; **en ese ~** in that case; **en todo ~** in any case; **el ~ Hess** the Hess affair, the Hess case; **en ~ afirmativo** if so, if it should be so; **en ~ negativo** if not, if it should not be so; **en ~ de que llueva, iremos en autobús** if it rains, we'll go by bus; **el ~ es que no me queda dinero** the thing is, I haven't got any money left; **no le hagas ~** don't take any notice of him; **hazle ~, que ella tiene más experiencia** listen to her, she has more experience; **hacer ~ omiso de** to ignore; **hacer** *o* **venir al ~** to be relevant; **en el mejor/peor de los ~s** at best/worst; **en último ~** as a last resort; **pongamos por ~ que...** let's suppose that...
caspa *nf* dandruff
casquillo *nm* (*de bombilla*) fitting; (*de bala*) cartridge case
cassette *nf o m* = **casete**
casta *nf* caste; (*raza*) breed; (*linaje*) lineage
castaña *nf* chestnut; (*fam: golpe*) punch; *ver* **castaño**
castañetear *vi* (*dientes*) to chatter
castaño, -a *adj* chestnut(-coloured), brown ▷ *nm* chestnut tree; **~ de Indias** horse chestnut tree; *ver tb* **castaña**
castañuelas *nfpl* castanets
castellano, -a *adj* Castilian; (*fam*) Spanish ▷ *nm/f* Castilian; (*fam*) Spaniard ▷ *nm* (*Ling*) Castilian, Spanish
castidad *nf* chastity, purity
castigar *vt* (*niño, delincuente*) to punish; (*Deporte*) to penalize; **mi padre me castigó por contestarle** my father punished me for answering him back
castigo *nm* (*de niño, delincuente*) punishment; (*Deporte*) penalty; **como ~** as punishment
Castilla *nf* Castile
castillo *nm* castle
castizo, -a *adj* (*Ling*) pure; (*de buena casta*) purebred, pedigree; (*auténtico*) genuine
casto, -a *adj* chaste, pure
castor *nm* beaver
castrar *vt* to castrate; (*gato*) to doctor; (*Bot*) to prune
castrense *adj* army *cpd*, military
casual *adj* chance, accidental
casualidad *nf* (*accidente*) chance; (*coincidencia*) coincidence; **nos encontramos por ~** we met by chance; **¿tienes por ~ una pluma?** do you have a pen, by any chance?, do you happen to have a pen?; **¡qué ~!** what a coincidence!; **da la ~ que nacimos el mismo día** it so happens that we were born on the same day
cataclismo *nm* cataclysm
catador *nm* taster
catalán, -ana *adj, nm/f* Catalan ▷ *nm* (*Ling*) Catalan

catalejo *nm* telescope
catalizador *nm* catalyst; (*Auto*) catalytic converter
catalogar *vt* to catalogue; **~ (de)** (*fig*) to classify as
catálogo *nm* catalogue
Cataluña *nf* Catalonia
cataplasma *nf* (*Med*) poultice
catapulta *nf* catapult
catar *vt* to taste, sample
catarata *nf* (*Geo*) (water)fall; (*Med*) cataract
catarro *nm* catarrh; (*constipado*) cold
catarsis *nf* catharsis
catastro *nm* property register
catástrofe *nf* catastrophe
catear *vt* (*fam*) to flunk
catecismo *nm* catechism
cátedra *nf* (*Univ*) chair, professorship; (*Escol*) principal teacher's post; **sentar ~ sobre un argumento** to take one's stand on an argument
catedral *nf* cathedral
catedrático, -a *nm/f* professor; (*Escol*) principal teacher
categoría *nf* (*sección*) category; (*rango*) rank; **cada grupo está dividido en tres ~s** each group is divided into three categories; **tiene ~ de ministro** he has the rank of minister; **un puesto de poca ~** a low-ranking position; **de segunda ~** second-rate; **un hotel de primera ~** a first-class hotel; **es un hombre de cierta ~** he's a man of some standing
categórico, -a *adj* categorical
catequesis *nf* catechism lessons
cateto, -a *nm/f* yokel
catolicismo *nm* Catholicism
católico, -a *adj, nm/f* Catholic
catorce *num* fourteen
catre *nm* camp bed (*Brit*), cot (*US*); (*fam*) pit
cauce *nm* (*de río*) riverbed; (*fig*) channel
caucho *nm* rubber; (*LAm: llanta*) tyre
caución *nf* bail
caudal *nm* (*de río*) volume, flow; (*fortuna*) wealth; (*abundancia*) abundance
caudaloso, -a *adj* (*río*) large; (*persona*) wealthy, rich
caudillo *nm* leader, chief
causa *nf* cause; (*razón*) reason; (*Jur*) lawsuit, case; **a** *o* **por ~ de** because of, on account of
causar *vt* to cause; **la lluvia causó muchos daños** the rain caused a lot of damage; **su visita me causó mucha alegría** his visit made me very happy; **Rosa me causó buena impresión** Rosa made a good impression on me
cautela *nf* caution, cautiousness
cauteloso, -a *adj* cautious, wary
cautivar *vt* to capture; (*fig*) to captivate
cautiverio *nm*, **cautividad** *nf* captivity
cautivo, -a *adj, nm/f* captive
cauto, -a *adj* cautious, careful
cava *nf* (*bodega*) (wine) cellar ▷ *nm* (*vino*) champagne-type wine
cavar *vt* to dig; (*Agr*) to dig over

caverna nf cave, cavern
caviar nm caviar(e)
cavidad nf cavity
cavilar vt to ponder
cayado nm (de pastor) crook; (de obispo) crozier
caza nf (acción: gen) hunting; (: con fusil) shooting; (una caza) hunt, chase; (animales) game; **coto de ~** hunting estate ▷ nm (Aviat) fighter
cazador, a nm/f hunter (huntress); ver tb **cazadora**
cazadora nf jacket; ver tb **cazador**
cazar vt to hunt; (perseguir) to chase; (prender) to catch; **~las al vuelo** to be pretty sharp
cazo nm saucepan
cazuela nf (vasija) pan; (guisado) casserole
CC.OO. nfpl abr = **Comisiones Obreras**
cebada nf barley
cebar vt (animal) to fatten (up); (anzuelo) to bait; (Mil, Tec) to prime; **cebarse** vr: **~se en** to vent one's fury on, take it out on
cebo nm (para animales) feed, food; (para peces, fig) bait; (de arma) charge
cebolla nf onion
cebolleta nf spring onion
cebra nf zebra; **paso de ~** zebra crossing
cecear vi to lisp
ceceo nm lisp
cedazo nm sieve
ceder vt (entregar) to hand over; (renunciar a) to give up, part with ▷ vi (renunciar) to give in, yield; (disminuir) to diminish, decline; (romperse) to give way; (viento) to drop; (fiebre etc) to abate; **"ceda el paso"** (Auto) "give way"
cedro nm cedar
cédula nf certificate, document; **~ de identidad** (LAm) identity card; **~ en blanco** blank cheque
CEE nf abr (= Comunidad Económica Europea) EEC
cegar vt to blind; (tubería etc) to block up, stop up ▷ vi to go blind; **cegarse** vr to be blinded; (de) by
ceguera nf blindness
ceja nf eyebrow; **~s pobladas** bushy eyebrows; **arquear las ~s** to raise one's eyebrows; **fruncir las ~s** to frown
cejar vi (fig) to back down; **no ~** to keep it up, stick at it
celada nf ambush, trap
celador, a nm/f (de edificio) watchman; (de museo etc) attendant; (de cárcel) warder
celda nf cell
celebración nf celebration
celebrar vt (cumpleaños, navidad) to celebrate; (reunión, elecciones) to hold; (misa) to say; **la fiesta de San José no se celebra aquí** Saint Joseph's Day is not celebrated here; **celebro que hayas aprobado** I'm delighted that you have passed
célebre adj celebrated, renowned
celebridad nf (fama) fame; (persona) celebrity
celeste adj sky-blue; (cuerpo etc) heavenly ▷ nm sky blue
celestial adj celestial, heavenly
celibato nm celibacy
célibe adj, nm/f celibate

celo nm zeal; (Rel) fervour; (pey) envy; **celos** nmpl jealousy sg; **dar ~s a algn** to make sb jealous; **tener ~s de algn** to be jealous of sb; **en ~** (animales) on heat
celofán nm Cellophane®
celoso, -a adj (envidioso) jealous; (trabajador) zealous; (desconfiado) suspicious
celta adj Celtic ▷ nm/f Celt
célula nf cell
celulitis nf (enfermedad) cellulitis; (grasa) cellulite
celuloide nm celluloid
celulosa nf cellulose
cementerio nm cemetery, graveyard; **~ de coches** scrapyard
cemento nm cement; (hormigón) concrete; (LAm: cola) glue
cena nf evening meal, dinner
cenagal nm bog, quagmire
cenar vt to have for dinner ▷ vi to have dinner, dine
cenicero nm ashtray
cenit nm zenith
ceniza nf ash, ashes pl
censar vt to take a census of
censo nm census; **~ electoral** electoral roll
censura nf (Pol) censorship; (moral) censure, criticism
censurar vt (idea) to censure; (cortar: película) to censor
centella nf spark
centellear vi (metal) to gleam; (estrella) to twinkle; (fig) to sparkle
centelleo nm (de metal) gleam; (de estrella) twinkle; (de diamante) sparkle
centena nf hundred
centenar nm hundred
centenario, -a adj one hundred years old ▷ nm centenary
centeno nm rye
centésimo, -a adj, nm hundredth
centígrado adj centigrade
centímetro nm centimetre (Brit), centimeter (US)
céntimo, -a adj hundredth ▷ nm cent
centinela nm sentry, guard
centollo, -a nm/f large (o spider) crab
central adj central ▷ nf head office; (Tec) plant; (Telec) exchange; **~ nuclear** nuclear power station
centralita nf (Telec) switchboard
centralización nf centralization
centralizar vt to centralize
centrar vt to centre
céntrico, -a adj central
centrifugar vt (ropa) to spin-dry
centrífugo, -a adj centrifugal
centrista adj centre cpd
centro nm centre; **ser del ~** (Pol) to be a moderate; **~ de acogida (para niños)** children's home; **~ de beneficios** (Com) profit centre; **~ cívico** community centre; **~ comercial** shopping centre; **~ de computación** computer centre; **~ (de determinación) de costos**

(*Com*) cost centre; ~ **delantero** (*Deporte*) centre forward; ~ **docente** teaching institution; ~ **juvenil** youth club; ~ **de llamadas** call centre; ~ **social** community centre

centroamericano, -a *adj, nm/f* Central American

ceñido, -a *adj* tight

ceñir *vt* (*rodear*) to encircle, surround; (*ajustar*) to fit (tightly); (*apretar*) to tighten; **ceñirse** *vr*: **~se algo** to put sth on; **~se al asunto** to stick to the matter in hand

ceño *nm* frown, scowl; **fruncir el ~** to frown, knit one's brow

CEOE *nf abr* (= *Confederación Española de Organizaciones Empresariales*) ≈ CBI (*Brit*)

cepillar *vt* to brush; (*madera*) to plane (down)

cepillo *nm* brush; (*para madera*) plane; (*Rel*) poorbox, alms box

cepo *nm* (*de caza*) trap

cera *nf* wax; **~ de abejas** beeswax

cerámica *nf* pottery; (*arte*) ceramics *sg*

cerca *nf* (*valla*) fence ▷ *adv* near, nearby, close; **el colegio está muy ~** the school is very near; **por aquí ~** nearby; **quería verlo de ~** I wanted to see it close up; **~ de la iglesia** near the church; **son ~ de las seis** it's nearly six o'clock; **~ de dos horas** nearly two hours; **hay ~ de ocho toneladas** there are about eight tons

cercanía *nf* nearness, closeness; **cercanías** *nfpl* outskirts, suburbs; **tren de ~s** commuter *o* local train

cercano, -a *adj* close, near; (*pueblo etc*) nearby; **C~Oriente** Near East

cercar *vt* to fence in; (*rodear*) to surround

cerciorar *vt* (*asegurar*) to assure; **cerciorarse** *vr* (*descubrir*) to find out; (*de*) about; (*asegurarse*) to make sure; (*de*) of

cerco *nm* (*Agr*) enclosure; (*LAm*) fence; (*Mil*) siege

cerda *nf* (*de cepillo*) bristle; (*Zool*) sow

cerdada *nf* (*fam*): **hacer una ~ a algn** to play a dirty trick on sb

cerdo *nm* pig; **carne de ~** pork

cereal *nm* cereal; **cereales** *nmpl* cereals, grain *sg*

cerebral *adj* (*tb fig*) cerebral; (*tumor*) brain *cpd*

cerebro *nm* brain; (*fig*) brains *pl*; **ser un ~** (*fig*) to be brilliant

ceremonia *nf* ceremony; **reunión de ~** formal meeting; **hablar sin ~** to speak plainly

ceremonial *adj, nm* ceremonial

ceremonioso, -a *adj* ceremonious; (*cumplido*) formal

cereza *nf* cherry

cerilla *nf*, **cerillo** *nm* (*CAm, Méx*) match

cerner *vt* to sift, sieve; **cernerse** *vr* to hover

cero *nm* nothing, zero; (*Deporte*) nil; **8 grados bajo ~** 8 degrees below zero; **a partir de ~** from scratch

cerrado, -a *adj* closed, shut; (*con llave*) locked; (*tiempo*) cloudy, overcast; (*curva*) sharp; (*acento*) thick, broad; **a puerta cerrada** (*Jur*) in camera

cerradura *nf* (*acción*) closing; (*mecanismo*) lock

cerrajero, -a *nm/f* locksmith

cerrar *vt* (*puerta, maleta, ojos, boca*) to close, shut;

(*paso, carretera*) to close; (*grifo*) to turn off; (*trato, cuenta, negocio*) to close ▷ *vi* to close, shut;
cerrarse *vr* (*puerta, maleta, boca*) to close, shut; (*herida*) to heal; **cerró el libro** he closed the book; **no puedo ~ la maleta** I can't shut this suitcase; **cerré la puerta con llave** I locked the door; **~ el sistema** (*Inform*) to close *o* shut down the system; **no cierran al mediodía** they don't close for lunch; **la puerta cierra mal** the door doesn't close *o* shut properly; **la puerta se cerró de golpe** the door slammed shut; **se me cierran los ojos** I can't keep my eyes open

cerro *nm* hill; **andar por los ~s de Úbeda** to wander from the point, digress

cerrojo *nm* (*herramienta*) bolt; (*de puerta*) latch

certamen *nm* competition, contest

certero, -a *adj* (*gen*) accurate

certeza, certidumbre *nf* certainty

certificado, -a *adj* certified; (*Correos*) registered ▷ *nm* certificate

certificar *vt* (*asegurar, atestar*) to certify

cervatillo *nm* fawn

cervecería *nf* (*fábrica*) brewery; (*taberna*) public house

cerveza *nf* beer; **~ de barril** draught beer

cervical *adj* cervical

cesación *nf* cessation, suspension

cesante *adj* redundant; (*LAm*) unemployed; (*ministro*) outgoing; (*diplomático*) recalled ▷ *nm/f* redundant worker

cesar *vi* to cease, stop; (*de un trabajo*) to leave ▷ *vt* (*en el trabajo*) to dismiss; (*alto cargo*) to remove from office

cesárea *nf* Caesarean (section)

cese *nm* (*de trabajo*) dismissal; (*de pago*) suspension

césped *nm* grass, lawn

cesta *nf* basket

cesto *nm* (large) basket, hamper

cetro *nm* sceptre

CFC *nm abr* (= *clorofluorocarbono*) CFC

cfr *abr* (= *confróntese, compárese*) cf

Ch, ch *nf former letter in the Spanish alphabet*

chabacano, -a *adj* vulgar, coarse ▷ *nm* (*Méx: árbol*) apricot tree; (: *fruta*) apricot

chabola *nf* shack; **chabolas** *nfpl* shanty town *sg*

chacal *nm* jackal

chacha *nf* (*fam*) maid

cháchara *nf* chatter; **estar de ~** to chatter away

chacra *nf* (*And, CS*) smallholding

chafar *vt* (*aplastar*) to crush, flatten; (*arruinar*) to ruin

chal *nm* shawl

chalado, -a *adj* (*fam*) crazy

chalé (*pl* **-s**) *nm* = **chalet**

chaleco *nm* waistcoat, vest (*US*); **~ antibala** bulletproof vest; **~ salvavidas** life jacket

chalet (*pl* **-s**) *nm* villa, ≈ detached house; **~ adosado** semi-detached house

chalupa *nf* launch, boat

chamaco, -a *nm/f* (*Méx: niño*) kid

champán *nm*, **champaña** *nm* champagne

champiñón *nm* mushroom
champú (*pl* **-es** *o* **-s**) *nm* shampoo
chamuscar *vt* to scorch, sear, singe
chance *nm* (*a veces* *nf*) (*LAm*) chance, opportunity
chancho, -a *nm/f* (*LAm*) pig
chanchullo *nm* (*fam*) fiddle, wangle
chandal *nm* tracksuit; **~ (de tactel)** shellsuit
chantaje *nm* blackmail; **hacer ~ a algn** to
   blackmail sb
chapa *nf* (*de metal*) plate, sheet; (*de madera*) board,
   panel; (*de botella*) bottle top; (*insignia*) (lapel)
   badge; (*LAm: Auto*): ~ **de matrícula** number (*Brit*)
   o license (*US*) plate; (*LAm: cerradura*) lock; **de 3 ~s**
   (*madera*) 3-ply
chaparrón *nm* downpour, cloudburst
chapotear *vt* to sponge down ▷ *vi* (*fam*) to splash
   about
chapucero, -a *adj* rough, crude ▷ *nm/f* bungler
chapurr(e)ar *vt* (*idioma*) to speak badly
chapuza *nf* botched job
chapuzón *nm*: **darse un ~** to go for a dip
chaqué *nm* morning coat
chaqueta *nf* jacket; **cambiar la ~** (*fig*) to change
   sides
chaquetón *nm* three-quarter-length coat
charca *nf* pond, pool
charco *nm* pool, puddle
charcutería *nf* (*tienda*) *shop selling chiefly pork meat
   products*; (*productos*) cooked pork meats *pl*
charla *nf* talk, chat; (*conferencia*) lecture
charlar *vi* to talk, chat
charlatán, -ana *nm/f* chatterbox; (*estafador*)
   trickster
charol *nm* varnish; (*cuero*) patent leather
chárter *adj inv*: **vuelo ~** charter flight
chascarrillo *nm* (*fam*) funny story
chasco *nm* (*broma*) trick, joke; (*desengaño*)
   disappointment
chasis *nm inv* (*Auto*) chassis; (*Foto*) plateholder
chasquear *vt* (*látigo*) to crack; (*lengua*) to click
chasquido *nm* (*de lengua*) click; (*de látigo*) crack
chat *nm* (*Internet*) chat room
chatarra *nf* scrap (metal)
chato, -a *adj* flat; (*nariz*) snub ▷ *nm* wine
   tumbler; **beber unos ~s** to have a few drinks
chaucha *nf* (*RP*) green bean
chaval, a *nm/f* kid (*fam*), lad/lass
checo, -a *adj, nm/f* Czech ▷ *nm* (*Ling*) Czech
cheque *nm* cheque (*Brit*), check (*US*); **~ abierto/
   en blanco/cruzado** open/blank/crossed cheque;
   ~ al portador cheque payable to bearer; **~
   caducado** stale cheque; **~ de viajero** traveller's
   cheque
chequeo *nm* (*Med*) check-up; (*Auto*) service
chequera *nf* (*LAm*) chequebook (*Brit*), checkbook
   (*US*)
chicano, -a *adj, nm/f* chicano, Mexican-American
chícharo *nm* (*Méx*) pea
chicharrón *nm* (pork) crackling
chichón *nm* bump, lump
chicle *nm* chewing gum
chico, -a *adj* small, little ▷ *nm/f* child; (*muchacho*)

boy; (*muchacha*) girl
chiflado, -a *adj* (*fam*) crazy, round the bend ▷ *nm/
   f* nutcase
chiflar *vt* to hiss, boo ▷ *vi* (*esp LAm*) to whistle
chilango, -a *adj* (*Méx*) of/from Mexico City ▷ *nm/f*
   (*Méx*) native/inhabitant of Mexico City
Chile *nm* Chile
chile *nm* chilli, pepper
chileno, -a *adj, nm/f* Chilean
chillar *vi* (*persona*) to yell, scream; (*animal salvaje*)
   to howl; (*cerdo*) to squeal
chillido *nm* (*de persona*) yell, scream; (*de animal*)
   howl
chillón, -ona *adj* (*niño*) noisy; (*color*) loud, gaudy
chimenea *nf* chimney; (*hogar*) fireplace
China *nf*: **(la) ~** China
china *nf* pebble
chinche *nf* bug; (*Tec*) drawing pin (*Brit*),
   thumbtack (*US*) ▷ *nm/f* nuisance, pest
chincheta *nf* drawing pin (*Brit*), thumbtack (*US*)
chingar *vt* (*Méx fam!*) to fuck (*!*), screw (*!*);
   chingarse *vr* (*Méx: emborracharse*) to get pissed
   (*Brit*), get plastered; (*: fracasar*) to fail
chino, -a *adj, nm/f* Chinese ▷ *nm* (*Ling*) Chinese;
   (*Culin*) chinois, conical strainer
chipirón *nm* squid
Chipre *nf* Cyprus
chipriota, chipriote *adj* Cypriot, Cyprian ▷ *nm/f*
   Cypriot
chiquillo, -a *nm/f* kid (*fam*), youngster, child
chiquito, -a *adj* very small, tiny ▷ *nm/f* kid (*fam*)
chiringuito *nm* refreshment stall *o* stand
chiripa *nf* fluke; **por ~** by chance
chirriar *vi* (*goznes*) to creak, squeak; (*pájaros*) to
   chirp, sing
chirrido *nm* creak(ing), squeak(ing); (*de pájaro*)
   chirp(ing)
chis *excl* sh!
chisme *nm* (*habladurías*) piece of gossip; (*fam*:
   objeto) thingummyjig
chismoso, -a *adj* gossiping ▷ *nm/f* gossip
chispa *nf* spark; (*fig*) sparkle; (*ingenio*) wit; (*fam*)
   drunkenness
chispeante *adj* (*tb fig*) sparkling
chispear *vi* to spark; (*lloviznar*) to drizzle
chisporrotear *vi* (*fuego*) to throw out sparks;
   (*leña*) to crackle; (*aceite*) to hiss, splutter
chiste *nm* joke, funny story; **~ verde** blue joke
chistera *nf* top hat
chistoso, -a *adj* (*gracioso*) funny, amusing;
   (*bromista*) witty
chivatazo *nm* (*fam*) tip-off; **dar el ~** to inform
chivo, -a *nm/f* (billy/nanny-)goat; **~ expiatorio**
   scapegoat
chocante *adj* startling; (*extraño*) odd; (*ofensivo*)
   shocking
chocar *vi* (*vehículos*) to collide, crash ▷ *vt*
   (*sorprender*) to surprise; **los trenes ~on de frente**
   the trains crashed head-on; **el coche chocó
   contra un árbol** the car hit a tree; **¡chócala!**
   (*fam*) put it there!; **me choqué contra una
   farola** I bumped into a lamppost; **me choca**

que no sepas nada I'm surprised that you don't know anything about it
chochear vi to dodder, be senile
chocho, -a adj doddering, senile; (fig) soft, doting
choclo nm (CS: planta) maize (Brit), corn (US); (mazorca) corncob; (granos) sweetcorn
chocolate adj chocolate ▷ nm chocolate; (fam) dope, marijuana
chófer, (esp LAm) **chofer** nm driver
chollo nm (fam) bargain, snip
choque nm (impacto) impact; (golpe) jolt; (Auto) crash; (fig) conflict
chorizo nm hard pork sausage; (ladrón) crook
chorrada nf (fam): **¡es una ~!** that's crap! (!); **decir ~s** to talk crap (!)
chorrear vt to pour ▷ vi to gush (out), spout (out); (gotear) to drip, trickle
chorro nm jet; (caudalito) dribble, trickle; (fig) stream; **salir a ~s** to gush forth; **con propulsión a ~** jet-propelled
choza nf hut, shack
chubasco nm squall
chubasquero nm oilskins pl
chuchería nf trinket
chuleta nf chop, cutlet; (Escol etc: fam) crib
chulo, -a adj (encantador) charming; (aire) proud; (pey) fresh; (fam: estupendo) great, fantastic ▷ nm (pícaro) rascal; (madrileño) working-class Madrilenian; (rufián: tb: **chulo de putas**) pimp
chungo, -a (fam) adj lousy ▷ nf: **estar de chunga** to be in a merry mood
chupa nf (fam) jacket
chupado, -a adj (delgado) skinny, gaunt; **está ~** (fam) it's simple, it's dead easy
chupar vt (caramelo, biberón, chupete) to suck; (absorber) to absorb; **chuparse** vr to suck; **el bebé se chupaba el dedo** the baby was sucking his thumb; **para ~se los dedos** (fam) mouthwatering; **¡chúpate esa!** (fam) put that in your pipe and smoke it!
chupete nm dummy (Brit), pacifier (US)
chupetón nm suck
churrasco nm (filete a la parrilla) barbecued meat; (CS: filete) steak
churrería nf stall or shop which sells "churros"
churretón nm stain
churro, -a adj coarse ▷ nm (Culin) (type of) fritter; (chapuza) botch, mess
chusco, -a adj funny
chusma nf rabble, mob
chutar vi (Deporte) to shoot (at goal); **esto va que chuta** it's going fine
Cía abr (= compañía) Co
cianuro nm cyanide
cibercafé nm cybercafe
cibernauta nmf cybernaut
cibernética nf cybernetics sg
cicatriz nf scar
cicatrizar vt to heal; **cicatrizarse** vr to heal (up), form a scar
ciclismo nm cycling

ciclista nm/f cyclist
ciclo nm cycle
ciclomotor nm moped
ciclón nm cyclone
cicloturismo nm touring by bicycle
ciego, -a etc vb ver **cegar** ▷ adj blind ▷ nm/f blind man/woman; **a ciegas** blindly; **me puse ciega de mariscos** (fam) I stuffed myself with seafood
cielo nm sky; (Rel) heaven; (Arq: tb: **cielo raso**) ceiling; **¡~s!** good heavens!; **ver el ~ abierto** to see one's chance
ciempiés nm inv centipede
cien num ver **ciento**
ciénaga nf marsh, swamp
ciencia nf science; **ciencias** nfpl science sg; **saber algo a ~ cierta** to know sth for certain
ciencia-ficción nf science fiction
científico, -a adj scientific ▷ nm/f scientist
ciento, cien num a o one hundred; **pagar al 10 por ~** to pay at 10 per cent
cierne nm: **en ~** in blossom; **en ~(s)** (fig) in its infancy
cierre nm (acción: gen) closing, shutting; (con llave) locking; (: de empresa, hospital, emisora) closing-down; (de pulsera, bolso) clasp; **precios de ~** (Bolsa) closing prices; **~ centralizado** central locking; **~ de cremallera** zip (fastener); **~ del sistema** (Inform) system shutdown
cierto, -a adj (verdadero) true; (alguno) certain; **no, eso no es ~** no, that's not true; **¿no es ~?** isn't that so?; **estar en lo ~** to be right; **lo ~ es que...** the fact is that...; **estar en lo ~** to be right; **cierta persona que yo conozco** a certain person that I know; **día de mayo** one day in may; **por ~** by the way
ciervo nm (Zool) deer; (: macho) stag
cierzo nm north wind
cifra nf number, figure; (cantidad) number, quantity; (secreta) code; **~ global** lump sum; **~ de negocios** (Com) turnover; **en ~s redondas** in round figures; **~ de referencia** (Com) bench mark; **~ de ventas** (Com) sales figures
cifrar vt to code, write in code; (resumir) to abridge; (calcular) to reckon
cigala nf Norway lobster
cigarra nf cicada
cigarrillo nm cigarette
cigarro nm cigarette; (puro) cigar
cigüeña nf stork
cilíndrico, -a adj cylindrical
cilindro nm cylinder
cima nf (de montaña) top, peak; (de árbol) top; (fig) height
címbalo nm cymbal
cimbrear vt to brandish; **cimbrearse** vr to sway
cimentar vt to lay the foundations of; (fig: reforzar) to strengthen; (: fundar) to found
cimiento nm foundation
cinc nm zinc
cincel nm chisel
cincelar vt to chisel
cinco num five; (fecha) fifth; **las ~** five o'clock; **no**

estar en sus ~ (*fam*) to be off one's rocker
cincuenta *num* fifty
cine *nm* cinema; **el ~ mudo** silent films *pl*; **hacer ~** to make films
cineasta *nm/f* (*director de cine*) film-maker *o* director
cinematográfico, -a *adj* cine-, film *cpd*
cínico, -a *adj* cynical; (*descarado*) shameless ▷ *nm/f* cynic
cinismo *nm* cynicism
cinta *nf* band, strip; (*de tela*) ribbon; (*película*) reel; (*de máquina de escribir*) ribbon; (*métrica*) tape measure; (*magnetofónica*) tape; **~ adhesiva** adhesive tape; **~ aislante** insulating tape; **~ de carbón** carbon ribbon; **~ magnética** (*Inform*) magnetic tape; **~ métrica** tape measure; **~ de múltiples impactos** (*en impresora*) multistrike ribbon; **~ de tela** (*para máquina de escribir*) fabric ribbon; **~ transportadora** conveyor belt
cinto *nm* belt, girdle
cintura *nf* waist; (*medida*) waistline
cinturón *nm* belt; (*fig*) belt, zone; **~ salvavidas** lifebelt; **~ de seguridad** safety belt
ciprés *nm* cypress (tree)
circo *nm* circus
circuito *nm* circuit; (*Deporte*) lap; **TV por ~ cerrado** closed-circuit TV; **~ experimental** (*Inform*) breadboard; **~ impreso** printed circuit; **~ lógico** (*Inform*) logical circuit
circulación *nf* circulation; (*Auto*) traffic; **"cerrado a la ~ rodada"** "closed to vehicles"
circular *adj*, *nf* circular ▷ *vt* to circulate ▷ *vi* to circulate; (*dinero*) to be in circulation; (*Auto*) to drive; (*autobús*) to run
círculo *nm* circle; (*centro*) clubhouse; (*Pol*) political group
circuncidar *vt* to circumcise
circundar *vt* to surround
circunferencia *nf* circumference
circunscribir *vt* to circumscribe; **circunscribirse** *vr* to be limited
circunscripción *nf* division; (*Pol*) constituency
circunspecto, -a *adj* circumspect, cautious
circunstancia *nf* circumstance; **~s agravantes/extenuantes** aggravating/extenuating circumstances; **estar a la altura de las ~s** to rise to the occasion
circunvalación *nf*: **carretera de ~** ring road
cirio *nm* (wax) candle
cirrosis *nf* cirrhosis (of the liver)
ciruela *nf* plum; **~ pasa** prune
cirugía *nf* surgery; **~ estética** *o* **plástica** plastic surgery
cirujano *nm* surgeon
cisne *nm* swan; **canto de ~** swan song
cisterna *nf* cistern, tank
cita *nf* (*con profesional*) appointment; (*con amante*) date; (*textual*) quotation; **acudir/faltar a una ~** to turn up for/miss an appointment; **aquí se han dado ~ los mejores atletas** the best athletes are gathered here; **no llegues tarde a la ~ con**

tu novio don't be late for the date with your boyfriend; **una ~ de Quevedo** a quotation from Quevedo
citación *nf* (*Jur*) summons *sg*
citar *vt* to make an appointment with, arrange to meet; (*Jur*) to summons; (*un autor, texto*) to quote; **citarse** *vr*: **~se con algn** to arrange to meet sb; **se ~on en el cine** they arranged to meet at the cinema
citología *nf* smear test
cítrico, -a *adj* citric ▷ *nm*: **~s** citrus fruits
ciudad *nf* town; (*capital de país etc*) city; **~ universitaria** university campus; **C~ del Cabo** Cape Town; **la C~ Condal** Barcelona
ciudadanía *nf* citizenship
ciudadano, -a *adj* civic ▷ *nm/f* citizen
cívico, -a *adj* civic; (*fig*) public-spirited
civil *adj* civil ▷ *nm* (*guardia*) policeman
civilización *nf* civilization
civilizar *vt* to civilize
civismo *nm* public spirit
cizaña *nf* (*fig*) discord; **sembrar ~** to sow discord
cl. *abr* (= *centilitro*) cl
clamar *vt* to clamour for, cry out for ▷ *vi* to cry out, clamour
clamor *nm* (*grito*) cry, shout; (*fig*) clamour, protest
clan *nm* clan; (*de gángsters*) gang
clandestino, -a *adj* clandestine; (*Pol*) underground
clara *nf* (*de huevo*) eggwhite; *ver tb* **claro**
claraboya *nf* skylight
clarear *vi* (*el día*) to dawn; (*el cielo*) to clear up, brighten up; **clarearse** *vr* to be transparent
clarete *nm* rosé (wine)
claridad *nf* (*del día*) brightness; (*de estilo*) clarity
clarificar *vt* to clarify
clarín *nm* bugle
clarinete *nm* clarinet
clarividencia *nf* clairvoyance; (*fig*) far-sightedness
claro, -a *adj* (*agua*) clear, transparent; (*día, luz*) bright; (*color, cuarto*) light; (*sonido, voz*) clear; (*explicación, idea, lenguaje*) clear; (*poco espeso*) thin; (*obvio*) clear, evident ▷ *nm* (*en bosque*) clearing ▷ *adv* clearly ▷ *excl* of course!; **una camisa azul ~** a light blue shirt; **lo quiero mañana, ¿está ~?** I want it tomorrow, is that clear?; **está ~ que esconden algo** it's obvious that they are hiding something; **no tengo muy ~ lo que quiero hacer** I'm not very sure about what I want to do; **lo oí muy ~** I heard it very clearly; **quiero que me hables ~** I want you to be frank with me; **no he sacado nada en ~ de la reunión** I'm none the wiser after that meeting; **¿te oyó? — ¡~ que me oyó!** did he hear you? — of course he heard me!; *ver tb* **clara**
clase *nf* (*tipo*) kind, sort; (*grupo social*) class; (*en tren, avión*) class; (*Escol, Univ*: *lección, grupo*) class; (: *aula*) classroom; **había juguetes de todas ~s** there were all kinds *o* all sorts of toys; **~ alta/media/obrera** upper/middle/working class; **~ económica/turista** economy/tourist

class; **primera ~** first class; **a las diez tengo ~ de física** at ten o'clock I have a physics class; **somos veinte en mi ~** there are twenty people in my class; **no hay nadie en la ~** there's no one in the classroom; **dar ~s** to teach; **hoy no hay ~** there's no school today; **~s de conducir** driving lessons; **~s particulares** private classes
clásico, -a *adj* classical; *(fig)* classic
clasificación *nf* classification; *(Deporte)* league (table); *(Com)* ratings *pl*
clasificar *vt* to classify; *(Inform)* to sort; **clasificarse** *vr (Deporte: en torneo)* to qualify
claudia *nf* greengage
claudicar *vi (fig)* to back down
claustro *nm* cloister; *(Univ)* staff; *(junta)* senate
claustrofobia *nf* claustrophobia
cláusula *nf* clause; **~ de exclusión** *(Com)* exclusion clause
clausura *nf* closing, closure
clausurar *vt (congreso etc)* to close, bring to a close; *(Pol etc)* to adjourn; *(cerrar)* to close (down)
clavar *vt (clavo, punta)* to hammer in; *(tablas)* to nail; **~ una punta en algo** to hammer a nail into something; **las tablas están mal clavadas** the boards aren't properly nailed down; **le clavó un cuchillo en el cuello** he stuck a knife in his throat; **me he clavado una espina en el dedo** I got a thorn in my finger; **aquí te clavan** *(fam)* you get ripped off in this place; **se clavó el cuchillo en el pecho** he thrust the knife into his chest
clave *nf* key; *(Mus)* clef ▷ *adj inv* key *cpd*; **~ de acceso** password; **~ de búsqueda** *(Inform)* search key; **~ de clasificación** *(Inform)* sort key
clavel *nm* carnation
clavícula *nf* collar bone
clavija *nf* peg, pin; *(Mus)* peg; *(Elec)* plug
clavo *nm (de metal)* nail; *(Bot)* clove; **dar en el ~** *(fig)* to hit the nail on the head
claxon *(pl -s)* *nm* horn; **tocar el ~** to sound one's horn
clemencia *nf* mercy, clemency
cleptómano, -a *nm/f* kleptomaniac
clerical *adj* clerical
clérigo *nm* priest, clergyman
clero *nm* clergy
clicar *vi (Inform)* to click; **clica en el icono** click on the icon; **~ dos veces** to double-click
cliché *nm* cliché; *(Tip)* stencil; *(Foto)* negative
cliente, -a *nm/f* client, customer
clientela *nf* clientele, customers *pl*; *(Com)* goodwill; *(Med)* patients *pl*
clima *nm* climate
climatizado, -a *adj* air-conditioned
clímax *nm inv* climax
clínico, -a *adj* clinical ▷ *nf* clinic; *(particular)* private hospital
clip *(pl -s)* *nm* paper clip
clítoris *nm inv* clitoris
cloaca *nf* sewer, drain
clonación *nf* cloning
clorhídrico, -a *adj* hydrochloric

cloro *nm* chlorine
clorofila *nf* chlorophyl(l)
club *(pl -s o -es)* *nm* club; **~ de jóvenes** youth club
cm *abr (= centímetro)* cm
C.N.T. *nf abr (Esp: = Confederación Nacional de Trabajo)* Anarchist Union Confederation; *(LAm)* = **Confederación Nacional de Trabajadores**
coacción *nf* coercion, compulsion
coaccionar *vt* to coerce, compel
coagular *vt*, **coagularse** *vr (sangre)* to clot; *(leche)* to curdle
coágulo *nm* clot
coalición *nf* coalition
coartada *nf* alibi
coartar *vt* to limit, restrict
coba *nf*: **dar ~ a algn** to soft-soap sb
cobarde *adj* cowardly ▷ *nm/f* coward
cobardía *nf* cowardice
cobaya *nf* guinea pig
cobertizo *nm* shelter
cobertor *nm* bedspread
cobertura *nf* cover; *(Com)* coverage; **~ de dividendo** *(Com)* dividend cover; **estar fuera de ~** to be out of range; **no tengo ~** I'm out of range
cobija *nf (CAm, Méx)* blanket
cobijar *vt (cubrir)* to cover; *(abrigar)* to shelter; **cobijarse** *vr* to take shelter
cobijo *nm* shelter
cobra *nf* cobra
cobrador, a *nm/f (de autobús)* conductor/conductress; *(de impuestos, gas)* collector
cobrar *vt (precio)* to charge; *(cheque)* to cash; *(sueldo)* to get; *(deuda)* to collect ▷ *vi* to get one's wages; **cobrarse** *vr*: **me cobró 50 euros por la reparación** he charged me 50 euros for the repair; **¿me cobra los cafés?** how much do I owe for the coffees?; **cuando cobre el sueldo de este mes** when I get my wages this month; **¿cuánto cobras al año?** how much do you get o earn a year?; **cantidades por ~** sums due; **¡cóbrese, por favor!** can I pay, please?; **el accidente se cobró la vida de 50 personas** the accident took the life of 50 people
cobre *nm* copper; *(LAm fam)* cent; **cobres** *nmpl* brass instruments
cobro *nm (de cheque)* cashing; *(pago)* payment; **presentar al ~** to cash; *ver tb* **llamada**
Coca-Cola® *nf* Coca-Cola®
cocaína *nf* cocaine
cocción *nf (Culin)* cooking; *(el hervir)* boiling
cocear *vi* to kick
cocer *vt, vi* to cook; *(en agua)* to boil; *(en horno)* to bake
coche *nm (Auto)* car, automobile (US); *(de tren, de caballos)* coach, carriage; *(para niños)* pram (Brit), baby carriage (US); **~ de bomberos** fire engine; **~ celular** Black Maria, prison van; **~ (comedor)** *(Ferro)* (dining) car; **~ fúnebre** hearse
coche-bomba *(pl coches-bomba)* *nm* car bomb
coche-cama *(pl coches-cama)* *nm (Ferro)* sleeping car, sleeper
cochera *nf* garage; *(de autobuses, trenes)* depot

coche-restaurante (pl **coches-restaurante**) nm (Ferro) dining-car, diner

cochino, -a adj filthy, dirty ▷ nm/f pig

cocido, -a adj boiled; (fam) plastered ▷ nm stew

cociente nm quotient

cocina nf kitchen; (aparato) cooker, stove; (acto) cookery; ~ **casera** home cooking; ~ **eléctrica** electric cooker; ~ **francesa** French cuisine; ~ **de gas** gas cooker

cocinar vt, vi to cook

cocinero, -a nm/f cook

coco nm coconut; (fantasma) bogeyman; (fam: cabeza) nut; **comer el ~ a algn** (fam) to brainwash sb

cocodrilo nm crocodile

cocotero nm coconut palm

cóctel nm (bebida) cocktail; (reunión) cocktail party; ~ **Molotov** Molotov cocktail, petrol bomb

codazo nm: **dar un ~ a algn** to nudge sb

codear vi to elbow, jostle; **codearse** vr: ~**se con** to rub shoulders with

codicia nf greed; (fig) lust

codiciar vt to covet

codicioso, -a adj covetous

codificar vt (mensaje) to (en)code; (leyes) to codify

código nm code; ~ **de barras** (Com) bar code; ~ **binario** binary code; ~ **de caracteres** (Inform) character code; ~ **de (la) circulación** highway code; ~ **civil** common law; ~ **de control** (Inform) control code; ~ **máquina** (Inform) machine code; ~ **militar** military law; ~ **de operación** (Inform) operational o machine code; ~ **penal** penal code; ~ **de práctica** code of practice

codillo nm (Zool) knee; (Tec) elbow

codo nm (Anat, de tubo) elbow; (Zool) knee; **hablar por los ~s** to talk nineteen to the dozen

codorniz nf quail

coerción nf coercion

coetáneo, -a nm/f: ~**s** contemporaries

coexistir vi to coexist

cofradía nf brotherhood, fraternity

cofre nm (baúl) trunk; (de joyas) box; (LAm Auto) bonnet (Brit), hood (US)

coger vt (Esp: tomar) to take; (flor, fruto) to pick; (algo caído) to pick up; (entrada, billete) to get; (persona, pez, prisionero) to catch; (tomar prestado) to borrow; (atropellar) to knock down, run over; (RP, Méx, Ven fam!) to fuck (!), screw (!); **cogerse** vr (el dedo) to catch; **coge el que más te guste** take the one which you like best; **coja la primera calle a la derecha** take the first street on the right; **voy a ~ el autobús** I'm going to get the bus; ~ **a algn de la mano** to take sb by the hand; **coge al niño, que está llorando** pick up the baby, he's crying; **¿te puedo ~ el bolígrafo?** can I borrow your pen?; **¡coge la pelota!** catch the ball!; **la cogieron robando** they caught her stealing; ~ **un resfriado** to catch a cold; ~**se a algo** to get hold of sth; **se cogió el dedo con la puerta** he caught his finger in the door

cogollo nm (de lechuga) heart; (fig) core, nucleus

cogorza nf (fam): **agarrar una ~** to get smashed

cogote nm back o nape of the neck

cohabitar vi to live together, cohabit

cohecho nm (acción) bribery; (soborno) bribe

coherencia nf coherence

coherente adj coherent

cohesión nm cohesion

cohete nm rocket

cohibido, -a adj (Psico) inhibited; (tímido) shy; **sentirse ~** to feel embarrassed

cohibir vt to restrain, restrict; **cohibirse** vr to feel inhibited

coima nf (And, CS fam) bribe

coincidencia nf coincidence

coincidir vi (personas: en idea, opinión) to coincide, agree; (: en un lugar) to coincide; (sucesos, fechas) to clash; (informes, resultados, versiones) to agree, coincide; **todos coinciden en que...** everyone agrees that...; **coincidimos en el tren** we happened to meet on the train; **el problema es que esas fechas coinciden con mi viaje** the problem is, those dates clash with my trip; **las huellas dactilares coinciden** the fingerprints match

coito nm intercourse, coitus

cojear vi (persona) to limp, hobble; (mueble) to wobble, rock

cojera nf lameness; (andar cojo) limp

cojín nm cushion

cojinete nm small cushion, pad; (Tec) (ball) bearing

cojo, -a adj (que no puede andar) lame, crippled; (mueble) wobbly ▷ nm/f lame person, cripple

cojón nm (fam!) ball (!), testicle; **¡cojones!** shit! (!)

cojonudo, -a adj (Esp fam) great, fantastic

col nf cabbage; ~**es de Bruselas** Brussels sprouts

cola nf tail; (de gente) queue; (lugar) end, last place; (para pegar) glue, gum; (de vestido) train; **hacer ~** to queue (up)

colaboración nf (gen) collaboration; (en periódico) contribution

colaborador, a nm/f (en actividad) collaborator; (en periódico) contributor

colaborar vi to collaborate

colado, -a adj (metal) cast ▷ nf: **hacer la colada** to do the washing

colador nm (de té) strainer; (para verduras etc) colander

colapsar vt (tráfico etc) to bring to a standstill

colapso nm collapse; ~ **nervioso** nervous breakdown

colar vt (verduras, té) to strain off; (metal) to cast; **colarse** vr (saltarse la cola) to jump the queue; (sin pagar) to get in without paying; (en lugar prohibido) to sneak in; **nos colamos en el cine** we sneaked into the cinema without paying; ~**se en una fiesta** to gatecrash; **¡a mí no me la cuelas!** (fam) don't give me any of that! (fam)

colateral nm collateral

colcha nf bedspread

colchón nm mattress; ~ **inflable** inflatable mattress

colchoneta nf (en gimnasio) mattress; ~

hinchable airbed
colear vi (perro) to wag its tail
colección nf collection
coleccionar vt to collect
coleccionista nm/f collector
colecta nf collection
colectivo, -a adj collective, joint ▷ nm (Arg: autobús) bus; (And: taxi) collective taxi
colector nm collector; (sumidero) sewer
colega nm/f colleague
colegiado, -a adj (profesional) registered ▷ nm/f referee
colegial, a adj (Escol etc) school cpd, college cpd ▷ nm/f schoolboy/girl
colegio nm college; (escuela) school; (de abogados etc) association; **~ de internos** boarding school; **ir al ~** to go to school
colegir vt (juntar) to collect, gather; (deducir) to infer, conclude
cólera nf (ira) anger; **montar en ~** to get angry ▷ nm (Med) cholera
colérico, -a adj angry, furious
colesterol nm cholesterol
coleta nf pigtail
coletilla nf (en carta) postscript; (en conversación) filler phrase
colgante adj hanging; ver **puente** ▷ nm (joya) pendant
colgar vt (cuadro, diploma, abrigo) to hang (up); (ropa lavada) to hang out; (criminal) to hang; (teléfono, auricular) to put down ▷ vi to hang; (al teléfono) to hang up; **colgamos un cuadro en la pared** we hung a picture on the wall; **¡no dejes la chaqueta en la silla, cuélgala!** don't leave your jacket on the chair, hang it up!; **le ~on al amanecer** he was hanged at dawn; **me colgó el teléfono** he hung up on me; **¡cuelga, por favor, que quiero hacer una llamada!** hang up, please, I want to use the phone!; **no cuelgue, por favor** please hold
cólico nm colic
coliflor nf cauliflower
colilla nf cigarette end, butt
colina nf hill
colindante adj adjacent, neighbouring
colindar vi to adjoin, be adjacent
colisión nf collision; **~ de frente** head-on crash
collar nm necklace; (de perro) collar
colmado, -a adj full ▷ nm grocer's (shop) (Brit), grocery store (US)
colmar vt to fill to the brim; (fig) to fulfil, realize
colmena nf beehive
colmillo nm (diente) eye tooth; (de elefante) tusk; (de perro) fang
colmo nm height, summit; **para ~ de desgracias** to cap it all; **¡eso es ya el ~!** that's beyond a joke!
colocación nf (acto) placing; (empleo) job, position; (situación) place, position; (Com) placement
colocar vt (poner) to place, put; (ordenar) to arrange; **colocarse** vr (ubicarse) to place o.s.; (conseguir trabajo) to get a job; (fam: con alcohol) to get plastered; (: con droga) to get high; **colocamos la mesa en medio del comedor** we put the table in the middle of the dining room; **he colocado los libros por temas** I've arranged the books by subject; **¡colocaos en fila!** get into a line!; **el equipo se ha colocado en quinto lugar** the team are now in fifth place; **ha colocado a su hermano como camarero en su bar** he got his brother a job as a waiter in his bar; **se ha colocado como o de enfermera** she's got a job as a nurse
Colombia nf Colombia
colombiano, -a adj, nm/f Colombian
colonia nf colony; (de casas) housing estate; (agua de colonia) cologne; **~ escolar** summer camp (for schoolchildren)
colonización nf colonization
colonizador, a adj colonizing ▷ nm/f colonist, settler
colonizar vt to colonize
colono nm (Pol) colonist, settler; (Agr) tenant farmer
coloquial adj colloquial
coloquio nm conversation; (congreso) conference; (Inform) handshake
color nm colour; **¿de qué ~ son?** what colour are they?; **un vestido de ~ azul** a blue dress; **persona de ~** coloured person; **una televisión en ~** a colour television; **a todo ~** in full colour; **verlo todo ~ de rosa** to see everything through rose-coloured spectacles; **le salieron los ~es** she blushed
colorado, -a adj (rojo) red; (LAm: chiste) rude, blue; **ponerse ~** to blush
colorante nm colouring (matter)
colorar vt to colour; (teñir) to dye
colorear vt to colour
colorete nm blusher
colorido nm colour(ing)
coloso nm colossus
columna nf column; (pilar) pillar; (apoyo) support; **~ blindada** (Mil) armoured column; **~ vertebral** spine, spinal column
columpiar vt, **columpiarse** vr to swing
columpio nm swing
colza nf rape; **aceite de ~** rapeseed oil
coma nf comma ▷ nm (Med) coma
comadre nf (madrina) godmother; (vecina) neighbour; (chismosa) gossip
comadrear vi (esp LAm) to gossip
comadrona nf midwife
comandancia nf command
comandante nm commandant; (grado) major
comandar vt to command
comarca nf region
comba nf (curva) curve; (en viga) warp; (cuerda) skipping rope; **saltar a la ~** to skip
combar vt to bend, curve
combate nm fight; (fig) battle; **fuera de ~** out of action
combatiente nm combatant
combatir vt to fight, combat

combi *nm* fridge-freezer

combinación *nf* combination; (*Química*) compound; (*bebida*) cocktail; (*plan*) scheme, setup; (*prenda*) slip

combinar *vt* to combine; (*colores*) to match

combustible *nm* fuel

combustión *nf* combustion

comedia *nf* comedy; (*Teat*) play, drama; (*fig*) farce

comediante *nm/f* (comic) actor/actress

comedido, -a *adj* moderate

comedor, a *nm/f* (*persona*) glutton ▷ *nm* (*habitación*) dining room; (*restaurante*) restaurant; (*cantina*) canteen

comensal *nm/f* fellow guest/diner

comentar *vt* to comment on; (*fam*) to discuss; **comentó que...** he made the comment that...

comentario *nm* comment, remark; (*Lit*) commentary; **comentarios** *nmpl* gossip *sg*; **dar lugar a ~s** to cause gossip

comentarista *nm/f* commentator

comenzar *vt, vi* to begin, start, commence; **~ a hacer algo** to begin o start doing o to do sth

comer *vt* (*alimentos*) to eat; (*Damas, Ajedrez*) to take, capture ▷ *vi* (*ingerir alimentos*) to eat; (*Esp: almorzar*) to have lunch; (*Lam: cenar*) to have dinner; **comerse** *vr* to eat up; **¿quieres ~ algo?** do you want something to eat?; **me comí una manzana** I had an apple; **comimos paella** we had paella for lunch; **~ el coco a algn** (*fam*) to brainwash sb; **¿qué hay para ~?** what is there for lunch?; **¡a ~!** food's ready!; **le estaba dando de ~ a su hijo** she was feeding her son; **se lo comió todo** he ate it all up; **no te comas el coco por eso** (*fam*) don't worry too much about it

comercial *adj* commercial; (*relativo al negocio*) business *cpd*

comerciante *nm/f* trader, merchant; (*tendero*) shopkeeper; **~ exclusivo** (*Com*) sole trader

comerciar *vi* to trade, do business

comercio *nm* commerce, trade; (*negocio*) business; (*grandes empresas*) big business; (*fig*) dealings *pl*; **~ autorizado** (*Com*) licensed trade; **~ electrónico** e-commerce; **~ exterior** foreign trade

comestible *adj* eatable, edible ▷ *nm*: **~s** food *sg*, foodstuffs; (*Com*) groceries

cometa *nm* comet ▷ *nf* kite

cometer *vt* to commit

cometido *nm* (*misión*) task, assignment; (*deber*) commitment

comezón *nf* itch, itching

cómic (*pl* **-s**) *nm* comic

comicios *nmpl* elections; (*voto*) voting *sg*

cómico, -a *adj* (*divertido*) comic; (*absurdo*) comical ▷ *nm/f* comedian; (*de teatro*) (comic) actor/actress

comida *nf* (*alimento*) food; (*almuerzo, cena*) meal; (*de mediodía*) lunch; (*LAm: por la noche*) dinner

comidilla *nf*: **ser la ~ de la ciudad** to be the talk of the town

comienzo *nm* beginning, start; **dar ~ a un acto** to begin a ceremony; **~ del archivo** (*Inform*) top-of-file

comillas *nfpl* quotation marks

comilón, -ona *adj* greedy ▷ *nf* (*fam*) blow-out

comino *nm* cumin (seed); **no me importa un ~** I don't give a damn

comisaría *nf* police station, precinct (US); (*Mil*) commissariat

comisario *nm* (*Mil etc*) commissary ▷ *nmf* (*Pol*) commissar

comisión *nf* (*Com: pago*) commission, rake-off (*fam*); (: *junta*) board; (*encargo*) assignment; **~ mixta/permanente** joint/standing committee; **Comisiones Obreras** (*Esp*) *formerly* Communist Union Confederation

comité (*pl* **-s**) *nm* committee; **~ de empresa** works council

comitiva *nf* suite, retinue

como *adv* (*igual que*) like, as; (*en calidad de*) as; (*aproximadamente*) about ▷ *conj* (*ya que, puesto que*) as, since; (*si: +subjun*) if; **tienen un perro ~ el nuestro** they've got a dog like ours; **se portó ~ un imbécil** he behaved like an idiot; **juega ~ yo** he plays like I do; **sabe ~ a cebolla** it tastes a bit like onion; **hazlo ~ te dijo ella** do it like o the way she told you; **tan ... ~ as ... as**; **lo usé ~ cuchara** I used it as a spoon; **lo dice ~ juez** he says it (in his capacity) as judge; **vino ~ a las dos** he came at about o around two; **~ ella no llegaba, me fui** as she didn't arrive, I left; **~ lo vuelvas a hacer se lo digo a tu madre** if you do it again I'll tell your mother; **~ no lo haga hoy ...** unless he does it today ..., if he doesn't do it today ...; **~ si** (*+subjun*) as if

cómo *adv* how? ▷ *excl* what?, I beg your pardon? ▷ *nm*: **el ~ y el porqué** the whys and wherefores; **¿~ está Ud?** how are you?; **¿~ no?** why not?; **¡~ no!** (*esp LAm*) of course!; **¿~ son?** what are they like?

cómoda *nf* chest of drawers

comodidad *nf* comfort; **venga a su ~** come at your convenience

comodín *nm* joker; (*Inform*) wild card; **símbolo ~** wild-card character

cómodo, -a *adj* comfortable; (*práctico, de fácil uso*) convenient

comodón, -ona *adj* comfort-loving ▷ *nm/f*: **ser un(a) ~** to like one's home comforts

compacto, -a *adj* compact

compadecer *vt* to pity, be sorry for; **compadecerse** *vr*: **~se de** to pity, be sorry for

compadre *nm* (*padrino*) godfather; (*esp LAm: amigo*) friend, pal

compaginar *vt*: **~ A con B** to bring A into line with B; **compaginarse** *vr*: **~se con** to tally with, square with

compañerismo *nm* comradeship

compañero, -a *nm/f* companion; (*novio*) boyfriend/girlfriend; **~ de clase** classmate

compañía *nf* company; **~ afiliada** associated company; **~ concesionaria** franchiser; **~ (no) cotizable** (un)listed company; **~ inversionista** investment trust; **hacer ~ a algn** to keep sb company

comparación *nf* comparison; **en ~ con** in comparison with

comparar *vt* to compare

comparativo, -a *adj* comparative

comparecer *vi* to appear (in court)

comparsa *nm/f* extra

compartimento, compartimiento *nm* (*Ferro*) compartment; (*de mueble, cajón*) section; ~ **estanco** (*fig*) watertight compartment

compartir *vt* to divide (up), share (out)

compás *nm* (*Mus*) beat, rhythm; (*Mat*) compasses *pl*; (*Náut etc*) compass; **al ~** in time

compasión *nf* compassion, pity

compasivo, -a *adj* compassionate

compatibilidad *nf* (*tb Inform*) compatibility

compatible *adj* compatible

compatriota *nm/f* compatriot, fellow countryman/woman

compendiar *vt* to summarize; (*libro*) to abridge

compendio *nm* (*resumen*) summary; (*abreviación*) abridgement

compenetrarse *vr* (*fig*): ~ **(muy) bien** to get on (very) well together

compensación *nf* compensation; (*Jur*) damages *pl*; (*Com*) clearing

compensar *vt* (*económicamente*) to compensate; (*algo escaso, pérdida*) to make up for; **el gobierno ~á a los agricultores por la mala cosecha** the government will compensate farmers for the bad harvest; **le ~on con 100 dólares por los cristales rotos** they gave him 100 dollars' compensation for the broken windows; **intentan ~ la falta de medios con imaginación** what they lack in resources they try to make up for in imagination; **no sé si compensa** I don't know if it's worth it; **no compensa viajar tan lejos por tan poco tiempo** it's not worth travelling that far for such a short time

competencia *nf* (*incumbencia*) domain, field; (*Com*) receipt; (*Jur, habilidad*) competence; (*rivalidad*) competition

competente *adj* (*Jur, persona*) competent; (*conveniente*) suitable

competición *nf* competition

competir *vi* to compete

competitivo, -a *adj* competitive

compilar *vt* to compile

compinche *nm/f* (*fam*) crony

complacencia *nf* (*placer*) pleasure; (*satisfacción*) satisfaction; (*buena voluntad*) willingness

complacer *vt* to please; **complacerse** *vr* to be pleased

complaciente *adj* kind, obliging, helpful

complejo, -a *adj, nm* complex

complementario, -a *adj* complementary

complemento *nm* (*de moda, diseño*) accessory; (*Ling*) complement

completar *vt* to complete

completo, -a *adj* (*lleno*) full; (*total*) complete; **los hoteles estaban ~s** the hotels were full; **las obras completas de Lorca** the complete

works of Lorca; **fue un ~ fracaso** it was a complete *o* total *o* utter failure; **me olvidé por ~** I completely forgot

complexión *nf* constitution

complicación *nf* complication

complicado, -a *adj* complicated; **estar ~ en** to be involved in

complicar *vt* to complicate

cómplice *nm/f* accomplice

complot (*pl* **-s**) *nm* plot; (*conspiración*) conspiracy

componente *adj, nm* component

componer *vt* to make up, put together; (*Mus, Lit, Imprenta*) to compose; (*algo roto*) to mend, repair; (*adornar*) to adorn; (*arreglar*) to arrange; (*reconciliar*) to reconcile; **componerse** *vr*: ~**se de** to consist of; **componérselas para hacer algo** to manage to do sth

comportamiento *nm* behaviour, conduct

comportarse *vr* to behave

composición *nf* composition

compositor, a *nm/f* composer

compostura *nf* (*reparación*) mending, repair; (*composición*) composition; (*acuerdo*) agreement; (*actitud*) composure

compra *nf* purchase; **compras** *nfpl* purchases, shopping *sg*; **hacer la ~/ir de ~s** to do the/go shopping; ~ **a granel** (*Com*) bulk buying; ~ **proteccionista** (*Com*) support buying

comprador, a *nm/f* buyer, purchaser

comprar *vt* to buy, purchase; ~ **deudas** (*Com*) to factor

comprender *vt* to understand; (*incluir*) to comprise, include

comprensible *adj* understandable

comprensión *nf* understanding; (*totalidad*) comprehensiveness

comprensivo, -a *adj* comprehensive; (*actitud*) understanding

compresa *nf* compress; ~ **higiénica** sanitary towel (*Brit*) *o* napkin (*US*)

comprimido, -a *adj* compressed ▷ *nm* (*Med*) pill, tablet; **en caracteres ~s** (*Tip*) condensed

comprimir *vt* to compress; (*fig*) to control; (*Inform*) to pack

comprobante *nm* proof; (*Com*) voucher; ~ **(de pago)** receipt

comprobar *vt* to check; (*probar*) to prove; (*Tec*) to check, test

comprometer *vt* (*poner en peligro*) to endanger; (*poner en entredicho*) to compromise; **comprometerse** *vr* (*involucrarse*) to get involved; **aquellas cartas le comprometieron** those letters compromised him; **me he comprometido a ayudarlos** I have promised to help them; **no quiero ~me por si después no puedo ir** I don't want to commit myself in case I can't go

compromiso *nm* (*obligación*) obligation; (*cita*) engagement, date; (*cometido*) commitment; (*convenio*) agreement; (*dificultad*) awkward situation; **libre de ~** (*Com*) without obligation

compuesto, -a *pp de* **componer** ▷ *adj*: ~ **de**

composed of, made up of ▷ *nm* compound; (*Med*) preparation

compungido, -a *adj* remorseful

computador *nm*, **computadora** *nf* computer; ~ **central** mainframe computer; ~ **especializado** dedicated computer; ~ **personal** personal computer

cómputo *nm* calculation, computation

comulgar *vi* to receive communion

común *adj* (*frontera, característica, objetivo*) common; **un apellido muy** ~ a very common surname; **no tenemos nada en** ~ we have nothing in common; **hicimos el trabajo en** ~ we did the work between us; **las zonas de uso** ~ the communal areas; **por lo** ~ generally; **fuera de lo** ~ out of the ordinary

comunicación *nf* communication; (*informe*) report

comunicado *nm* announcement; ~ **de prensa** press release

comunicar *vt* (*decisión, resultado*) to announce; (*habitaciones*) to connect ▷ *vi* (*teléfono*) to be engaged; **comunicarse** *vr* (*personas*) to communicate; (*habitaciones*) to be connected; **le encargaron que ~ a la noticia** he was given the task of announcing the news; ~ **algo a algn** to inform sb of sth; **cuando le ~on la noticia** when they told her the news; **está comunicando** (*teléfono*) the line's engaged (*Brit*) o busy (*US*); **le cuesta ~se con los demás** he finds it hard to communicate with others; **los dos despachos se comunican** the two offices are connected

comunicativo, -a *adj* communicative

comunidad *nf* community; ~ **autónoma** autonomous region; ~ **de vecinos** residents' association; **C~ Económica Europea (CEE)** European Economic Community (EEC)

comunión *nf* communion

comunismo *nm* communism

comunista *adj, nm/f* communist

comunitario, -a *adj* (*de la CE*) Community *cpd*, EC *cpd*

con *prep* **1** (*compañía*) with; **vivo ~ mis padres** I live with my parents; **¿~ quién vas a ir?** who are you going with?

2 (*adición*): **pan ~ mantequilla** bread and butter; **vodka ~ naranja** vodka and orange; **café ~ leche** white coffee; **once ~ siete** eleven point seven

3 (*medio*): ~ **su ayuda** with his help; **lo he escrito ~ bolígrafo** I wrote it in pen; **comer ~ cuchara** to eat with a spoon; ~ **estudiar un poco apruebas** with a bit of studying you should pass; **¡chócala!** (*fam*)

4 (*modo*): ~ **habilidad** skilfully; ~ **cuidado** carefully; ~ **llegar a las seis estará bien** if you come by six it will be fine

5 (*como complemento personal*): **¿~ quién hablas?** who are you speaking to?; **se ha casado ~ Jesús** she's married Jesús, she's got married to Jesús

6 (*con características, estados*): **estoy ~ catarro** I've got a cold; **murió ~ sesenta años** she died at the age of sixty

7 (*a pesar de*): ~ **todo, merece nuestros respetos** all the same o even so, he deserves our respect

8 (*enfático*): **¡~ las ganas que tenía de ir!** and I really wanted to go (too)!

9: **para ~, es muy bueno para ~ los niños** he's very good with (the) children; **amable para ~ todos** kind to everyone

10: ~ **que, será suficiente ~ que le escribas** it will be enough if you write to her

conato *nm* attempt; ~ **de robo** attempted robbery

concebir *vt* to conceive; (*imaginar*) to imagine ▷ *vi* to conceive

conceder *vt* to concede

concejal, a *nm/f* town councillor

concejo *nm* council

concentración *nf* concentration

concentrar *vt*, **concentrarse** *vr* to concentrate

concéntrico, -a *adj* concentric

concepción *nf* conception

concepto *nm* concept; **por ~ de** as, by way of; **tener buen ~ de algn** to think highly of sb; **bajo ningún** ~ under no circumstances

concertar *vt* (*Mus*) to harmonize; (*acordar: precio*) to agree; (: *tratado*) to conclude; (*trato*) to arrange, fix up; (*combinar: esfuerzos*) to coordinate; (*reconciliar: personas*) to reconcile ▷ *vi* to harmonize, be in tune

concesión *nf* concession; (*Com: fabricación*) licence

concesionario, -a *nm/f* (*Com*) (licensed) dealer, agent, concessionaire; (: *de venta*) franchisee; (: *de transportes etc*) contractor

concha *nf* shell

conchabarse *vr*: ~ **contra** to gang up on

conciencia *nf* (*moral*) conscience; (*conocimiento*) awareness; **tener la ~ tranquila** to have a clear conscience; **le remuerde la ~** his conscience is pricking him; **libertad de ~** freedom of conscience; **lo han estudiado a ~** they've studied it thoroughly; **tener/tomar ~ de** to be/become aware of

concienciar *vt* to make aware; **concienciarse** *vr* to become aware

concienzudo, -a *adj* conscientious

concierto *nm* concert; (*obra*) concerto

conciliar *vt* to reconcile ▷ *adj* (*Rel*) of a council; ~ **el sueño** to get to sleep

concilio *nm* council

conciso, -a *adj* concise

conciudadano, -a *nm/f* fellow citizen

concluir *vt* (*acabar*) to conclude; (*inferir*) to infer, deduce ▷ *vi*: **concluirse** *vr* to conclude; **todo ha concluido** it's all over

conclusión *nf* conclusion; **llegar a la ~ de que ...** to come to the conclusion that ...

concluyente *adj* (*prueba, información*) conclusive

concordar *vt* to reconcile ▷ *vi* to agree, tally

concordia *nf* harmony

concretar *vt* (*precisar*) to specify; (*fecha, cita*) to fix, set; (*resumir*) to sum up; ~ **los términos del**

acuerdo to specify the terms of the agreement; **el portavoz no quiso ~ más datos** the spokesman declined to be more specific; **en la reunión no concretamos nada** we didn't settle on anything specific at the meeting, nothing specific came out of the meeting

concreto, -a adj (específico) specific; (definitivo) definite ▷ nm (LAm: cemento) concrete; **por poner un ejemplo ~** to take a specific example; **este modelo en ~** this particular model; **no hablo de personas concretas** I don't mean anyone in particular; **en ~ había siete** there were seven to be exact; **todavía no hay fechas concretas** there are no definite dates yet; **todavía no hemos decidido nada en ~** we still haven't decided anything definite

concurrencia nf turnout

concurrido, -a a (calle) busy; (local: reunión) crowded

concurrir vi (juntarse: ríos) to meet, come together; (: personas) to gather, meet

concursante nm competitor

concursar vi to compete

concurso nm (de público) crowd; (Escol, Deporte, competición) competition; (Com) invitation to tender; (examen) open competition; (TV etc) quiz; (ayuda) help, cooperation

condal adj: **la ciudad ~** Barcelona

conde nm count

condecoración nf (Mil) medal, decoration

condecorar vt to decorate

condena nf sentence; **cumplir una ~** to serve a sentence

condenación nf condemnation; (Rel) damnation

condenar vt to condemn; (Jur) to convict; **condenarse** vr (Jur) to confess (one's guilt); (Rel) to be damned

condensar vt to condense

condesa nf countess

condescender vi to acquiesce, comply

condición nf (requisito) condition; (manera de ser) nature; (status social) social background; **sí, pero con dos condiciones...** all right, but with two conditions...; **a ~ de que apruebes** on condition that you pass; **condiciones de trabajo/de vida** working/living conditions; **las condiciones del contrato** the terms of the contract; **el piso está en muy malas condiciones** the flat is in a very bad condition; **no está en condiciones de viajar** he's not fit to travel

condicional adj conditional

condicionar vt (acondicionar) to condition; **~ algo a algo** to make sth conditional o dependent on sth

condimento nm seasoning

condolerse vr to sympathize

condón nm condom

conducir vt to take, convey; (Elec etc) to carry; (Auto) to drive; (negocio) to manage ▷ vi to drive; (fig) to lead; **conducirse** vr to behave

conducta nf conduct, behaviour

conducto nm pipe, tube; (fig) channel; (Elec)

lead; **por ~ de** through

conductor, a adj leading, guiding ▷ nm (Física) conductor; (de vehículo) driver

conectado, -a adj (Elec) connected, plugged in; (Inform) on-line

conectar vt (cables, tubos) to connect (up); (televisión, lavadora) to switch on; (dos ciudades) to link; **esta autovía ~á Granada con Almería** this dual carriageway will link Granada and o to Almería; **conectamos con nuestro corresponsal en Londres** and now it's over to our correspondent in London, and now we're going over to our correspondent in London; **le cuesta ~ con la gente** he has trouble relating to people; **~se a Internet** to get connected to the Internet

conejillo nm: **~ de Indias** guinea pig

conejo nm rabbit

conexión nf connection; (Inform) logging in (on)

confección nf (preparación) preparation, making-up; (industria) clothing industry; (producto) article; **de ~** (ropa) off-the-peg

confeccionar vt to make (up)

confederación nf confederation

conferencia nf conference; (lección) lecture; (Telec) call; **~ de cobro revertido** (Telec) reversed-charge (Brit) o collect (US) call; **~ cumbre** summit (conference)

conferir vt to award

confesar vt (admitir) to confess, admit; (error) to acknowledge; (crimen) to own up to

confesión nf confession

confesionario nm confessional

confeti nm confetti

confiado, -a adj (crédulo) trusting; (seguro) confident; (presumido) conceited, vain

confianza nf (fe) trust, confidence; (familiaridad) intimacy, familiarity; **confianzas** nfpl liberties; **han puesto toda su ~ en él** they have put all their trust in him; **tengo ~ en ti** I trust you; **no me inspira ~** he doesn't inspire me with confidence; **no tiene ~ en sí mismo** he has no self-confidence; **un empleado de ~** a trusted employee; **se lo dije porque tenemos mucha ~** I told her about it because we're very close; **los alumnos se toman demasiadas ~s con él** the students take too many liberties with him

confiar vi (fiarse) to trust; **confiarse** vr (fiarse en exceso) to be over-confident; **no confío en ella** I don't trust her; **confiaba en que su familia lo ayudaría** he was confident that his family would help him; **no hay que ~se demasiado** you mustn't be over-confident

confidencia nf confidence

confidencial adj confidential

confidente nm/f confidant/e; (policial) informer

configurar vt to shape, form

confín nm limit; **confines** nmpl confines, limits

confinar vi to confine; (desterrar) to banish

confirmación nf confirmation; (Rel) Confirmation

confirmar vt to confirm; (Jur etc) to corroborate;

la **excepción confirma la regla** the exception proves the rule

confiscar vt to confiscate

confite nm sweet (Brit), candy (US)

confitería nf confectionery; (tienda) confectioner's (shop)

confitura nf jam

conflictivo, -a adj (asunto, propuesta) controversial; (país, situación) troubled

conflicto nm conflict; (fig) clash; (: dificultad): **estar en un ~** to be in a jam; **~ laboral** labour dispute

confluir vi (ríos etc) to meet; (gente) to gather

conformar vt (dar forma a) to shape, fashion; (constituir) to make up; **conformarse** vr (resignarse) to resign o.s.; **seis de los ocho cuentos que conforman este libro** six of the eight stories that make up this book; **tengo que ~me con lo que tengo** I have to be satisfied with what I've got; **se conforman con poco** they're easily satisfied; **tendrás que ~te con uno más barato** you'll have to make do with a cheaper one

conforme adj (satisfecho) satisfied; (de acuerdo) agreed, in agreement ▷ adv (según) as ▷ prep: **~ a** according to; **no se quedó muy ~ con esa explicación** he wasn't very satisfied with that explanation; **¿estáis todos ~s?** do you all agree?; **no estoy ~ con ella en eso** I don't agree with her on that; **lo hice ~ me dijiste** I did it as you told me to; **~ entraban, se iban sentando** as they came in, they sat down; **serán juzgados ~ a las leyes españolas** they will be tried according to Spanish law

conformidad nf (semejanza) similarity; (acuerdo) agreement; (resignación) resignation; **de/en ~ con** in accordance with; **dar su ~** to consent

conformista nm/f conformist

confort (pl **-s**) nm comfort

confortable adj comfortable

confortar vt to comfort

confraternizar vi to fraternize

confrontar vt to confront; (dos personas) to bring face to face; (cotejar) to compare ▷ vi to border

confundir vt (equivocar) to mistake; (ofuscar) to confuse; **confundirse** vr (equivocarse) to make a mistake; **confundí la sal con el azúcar** I mistook the salt for the sugar; **la confundí con su hermana gemela** I got her mixed up with her twin sister, I mistook her for her twin sister; **en este planteamiento se están confundiendo causa y efecto** this approach confuses cause and effect; **su explicación me confundió todavía más** his explanation confused me even more; **¡vaya! ¡me he confundido!** oh! I've made a mistake!; **me confundí de piso** I got the wrong flat

confusión nf confusion

confuso, -a adj (gen) confused; (recuerdo) hazy; (estilo) obscure

congelado, -a adj frozen ▷ nmpl: **~s** frozen food sg o foods

congelador nm freezer, deep freeze

congelar vt to freeze; **congelarse** vr (sangre, grasa) to congeal

congénere nm/f: **sus ~s** his peers

congeniar vi to get on (Brit) o along (US) (well)

congestión nf congestion

congestionar vt to congest; **congestionarse** vr to become congested; **se le congestionó la cara** his face became flushed

congoja nf distress, grief

congraciarse vr to ingratiate o.s.

congratular vt to congratulate

congregación nf congregation

congregar vt, **congregarse** vr to gather together

congresista nm/f delegate, congressman/woman

congreso nm congress; **C~ de los Diputados** (Esp Pol) ≈ House of Commons (Brit), House of Representatives (US)

conífera nf conifer

conjetura nf guess; (Com) guesstimate

conjeturar vt to guess

conjugación nf conjugation

conjugar vt to combine, fit together; (Ling) to conjugate

conjunción nf conjunction

conjuntivitis nf conjunctivitis

conjunto, -a adj joint, united ▷ nm whole; (Mus) band; (vestido) ensemble; (Inform) set; **en ~** as a whole; **~ integrado de programas** (Inform) integrated software suite

conjurar vt (Rel) to exorcise; (peligro) to ward off ▷ vi to plot

conmemoración nf commemoration

conmemorar vt to commemorate

conmigo pron with me

conminar vt to threaten

conmoción nf shock; (Pol) disturbance; (fig) upheaval; **~ cerebral** (Med) concussion

conmovedor, a adj touching, moving; (emocionante) exciting

conmover vt to shake, disturb; (fig) to move; **conmoverse** vr (fig) to be moved

conmutador nm switch; (LAm Telec) switchboard

connotación nf connotation

cono nm cone; **C~ Sur** Southern Cone

conocedor, a adj expert, knowledgeable ▷ nm/f expert, connoisseur

conocer vt (persona: saber quién es) to know; (: por primera vez) to meet; (: reconocer) to recognize; (método, resultado) to know about; (país, ciudad) to visit; **conocerse** vr (reflexivo) to know o.s.; (recíproco) to (get to) know each other; **conozco a todos sus hermanos** I know all his brothers; **la conocí en una fiesta** I met her at a party; **te he conocido por el modo de andar** I recognized o knew you from the way you walk; **me encantaría ~ China** I would love to visit China; **nos conocemos desde el colegio** we know each other from school; **¿dónde os conocisteis?** where did you first meet?; **se conoce que se lo**

han contado apparently he's been told about it, it seems that he's been told about it

conocido, -a adj (well-)known ▷ nm/f acquaintance

conocimiento nm (saber) knowledge; (Med) consciousness; (sentido común) common sense; **conocimientos** nmpl knowledge sg; **un ~ profundo del tema** a thorough knowledge of the subject; **tengo algunos ~s musicales** I have some knowledge of music; **hablar con ~ de causa** to speak from experience; **perder el ~** to lose consciousness; **estuvo sin ~ durante unos minutos** he was unconscious for a few minutes; **los niños no tienen ~** children have no common sense

conque conj and so, so then

conquista nf conquest

conquistador, a adj conquering ▷ nm conqueror

conquistar vt (Mil) to conquer; (puesto, simpatía) to win; (enamorar) to win the heart of

consagrar vt (Rel) to consecrate; (fig) to devote

consciente adj conscious; **ser** o **estar ~ de** to be aware of

consecución nf acquisition; (de fin) attainment

consecuencia nf consequence, outcome; (firmeza) consistency; **de ~** of importance

consecuente adj consistent

consecutivo, -a adj consecutive

conseguir vt (trabajo, dinero, entrada) to get; (visado, permiso, beca) to get, obtain; (premio) to win; (resultado) to obtain; (meta, objetivo) to achieve; (acuerdo) to reach; **él me consiguió el trabajo** he got me the job; **consiguió las mejores notas de la clase** she achieved the best results in the class; **nuestro equipo consiguió el triunfo** our team won; **después de muchos intentos, al final lo consiguió** after many attempts, he finally succeeded; **~ hacer algo** to manage to do sth; **~ que algn haga algo** to get sb to do sth

consejería nf (Pol) ministry (in a regional government)

consejero, -a nm/f adviser, consultant; (Pol) minister (in a regional government); (Com) director; (en comisión) member

consejo nm advice; (Pol) council; (Com) board; **un ~ a** piece of advice; **~ de administración** board of directors; **~ de guerra** court-martial; **C~ de Europa** Council of Europe

consenso nm consensus

consentimiento nm consent

consentir vt (permitir, tolerar) to consent to; (mimar) to pamper, spoil ▷ vi to agree, consent; **~ que algn haga algo** to allow sb to do sth

conserje nm caretaker; (portero) porter

conserva nf: **en ~** (alimentos) tinned (Brit), canned; **~s** tinned o canned foods

conservación nf conservation; (de alimentos, vida) preservation

conservador, a adj (Pol) conservative ▷ nm/f conservative

conservante nm preservative

conservar vt (calor) to retain, conserve; (alimentos, tradición, costumbre) to preserve; (amistades) to maintain; **conservarse** vr (tradición, costumbre, ruinas) to survive; **el frío conserva los alimentos** the cold preserves food; **todavía conservamos el piso de Madrid** we are still keeping on the flat in Madrid; **aún conservo varias cartas suyas** I still have several of his letters; **conservo un recuerdo magnífico de esas vacaciones** I have wonderful memories of that holiday; **los alimentos se conservan mejor en la nevera** food keeps better in a fridge; **consérvese en lugar seco y fresco** store in a cool dry place; **~ la calma** to keep calm; **¡qué bien se conserva!** he looks very well for his age!, he's very well-preserved (fam); **Enrique se conserva joven** Enrique looks good for his age

conservas nfpl: **~ (alimenticias)** tinned (Brit) o canned goods

conservatorio nm (Mus) conservatoire; (LAm) greenhouse

considerable adj considerable

consideración nf (respeto) consideration; (reflexión) consideration; **eso sería una falta de ~ hacia nuestros invitados** that would be showing a lack of consideration towards our guests; **¡qué falta de ~!** how inconsiderate!; **tener** o **tomar algo en ~** to take sth into consideration; **de ~** important; **De mi** o **nuestra (mayor) ~** (LAm) Dear Sir(s) o Madam

considerado, -a adj (atento) considerate; (respetado) respected

considerar vt (gen) to consider; (meditar) to think about; (tener en cuenta) to take into account

consigna nf (orden) order, instruction; (para equipajes) left-luggage office (Brit), checkroom (US)

consigo pron (con él) with him; (con ella) with her; (con usted) with you; (con uno mismo) with you; (con ellos, ellas) with them

consiguiente adj consequent; **por ~** and so, therefore, consequently

consistente adj consistent; (sólido) solid, firm; (válido) sound; **~ en** consisting of

consistir vi: **~ en: el menú consiste en tres platos** the menu consists of three courses; **¿en qué consiste el trabajo?** what does the job involve?; **su misión consiste en aclarar el problema** her task is to clarify the problem; **el secreto** o **truco consiste en añadir un poco de vino** the secret lies in adding a little wine; **¿en qué consiste para ti la democracia?** what does democracy mean for you?

consola nf console, control panel; (mueble) console table; **~ de juegos** games console; **~ de mando** (Inform) control console; **~ de visualización** visual display console

consolación nf consolation

consolar vt to console

consolidar vt to consolidate

consomé (pl **-s**) nm consommé, clear soup

consonante adj consonant, harmonious ▷ nf

consonant
consorcio nm (Com) consortium, syndicate
conspiración nf conspiracy
conspirador, a nm/f conspirator
conspirar vi to conspire
constancia nf (gen) constancy; (certeza) certainty; **dejar ~ de algo** to put sth on record
constante adj, nf constant
constar vi (evidenciarse) to be clear o evident; **~ (en)** to appear (in); **~ de** to consist of; **hacer ~** to put on record; **me consta que ...** I have evidence that ...; **que conste que lo hice por ti** believe me, I did it for your own good
constatar vt (controlar) to check; (observar) to note
constelación nf constellation
consternación nf consternation
constipado, -a adj: **estar ~** to have a cold ▷ nm cold
constiparse vr to catch a cold
constitución nf constitution; **Día de la C~** (Esp) Constitution Day (6th December)
constitucional adj constitutional
constituir vt (comité, asamblea) to set up, constitute; (empresa) to set up; (representar) to represent, constitute; **constituirse** vr (empresa, sociedad) to be set up; **constituyeron una comisión de investigación** a committee of inquiry was set up o constituted; **la pesca constituye la principal riqueza de la región** fishing represents o constitutes the region's main source of wealth; **¿en qué fecha se constituyó la sociedad?** when was the company set up?
constitutivo, -a adj constitutive, constituent
constituyente adj constituent
constreñir vt (obligar) to compel, oblige; (restringir) to restrict
construcción nf construction, building
constructivo, -a adj constructive
constructor, a nm/f builder
construir vt to build, construct
consuelo nm consolation, solace
cónsul nm consul
consulado nm (sede) consulate; (cargo) consulship
consulta nf consultation; (Med: consultorio) consulting room; (Inform) enquiry; **horas de ~** surgery hours; **obra de ~** reference book
consultar vt to consult; **~ un archivo** (Inform) to interrogate a file
consultorio nm (Med) surgery
consumar vt to complete, carry out; (crimen) to commit; (sentencia) to carry out
consumición nf consumption; (bebida) drink; (comida) food; **~ mínima** cover charge
consumidor, a nm/f consumer
consumir vt (comida, bebida, droga) to consume; (gasolina, energía) to use, consume ▷ vi (en un bar: comer) to eat; (: beber) to drink; (gastar) to consume; **consumirse** vr (líquido) to boil away; (salsa) to reduce; (vela, cigarro) to burn down; (anciano, enfermo) to waste away; **consúmase**

inmediatamente después de abierto consume immediately after opening; **sólo consumo alimentos frescos** I only eat fresh food; **en casa no consumimos leche de cabra** we don't drink goat's milk at home; **no pueden sentarse aquí si no van a ~ nada** you can't sit here if you're not going to have anything to eat or drink; **~ preferentemente antes de ...** best before ...; **el mercado nos impulsa a ~ sin parar** the market encourages us to consume constantly
consumismo nm (Com) consumerism
consumo nm consumption; **bienes de ~** consumer goods
contabilidad nf accounting, book-keeping; (profesión) accountancy; (Com): **~ analítica** variable costing; **~ de costos** cost accounting; **~ de doble partida** double-entry book-keeping; **~ de gestión** management accounting; **~ por partida simple** single-entry book-keeping
contabilizar vt to enter in the accounts
contable nm/f bookkeeper; (licenciado) accountant; **~ de costos** (Com) cost accountant
contactar vi: **~ con algn** to contact sb
contacto nm contact; **lentes de ~** contact lenses; **estar en ~ con** to be in touch with
contado, -a adj: **~s** (escasos) numbered, scarce, few ▷ nm: **al ~** for cash; **pagar al ~** to pay (in) cash; **precio al ~** cash price
contador nm (aparato) meter; (LAm: contable) accountant
contagiar vt (enfermedad) to pass on, transmit; (persona) to infect; **contagiarse** vr to become infected
contagio nm infection
contagioso, -a adj infectious; (fig) catching
contaminación nf (gen) contamination; (del ambiente etc) pollution
contaminar vt (gen) to contaminate; (aire, agua) to pollute; (fig) to taint
contante adj: **dinero ~ (y sonante)** hard cash
contar vt (páginas, dinero, objetos) to count; (anécdota, historia) to tell ▷ vi (calcular) to count; (relatar) to tell; (importar, valer) to count; **contarse** vr (incluirse, figurar) to be counted, figure; **cuenta cuántos alumnos hay en la clase** count how many pupils there are in the class; **lo cuento entre mis amigos** I count him among my friends; **sus seguidores se cuentan por miles** he has thousands of supporters; **seis en total, sin ~me a mí** six altogether, not counting me; **sabe ~ hasta diez** he can count to ten; **cuéntame lo que pasó** tell me what happened; **¿y a mí qué me cuentas?** so what?; **el último gol no cuenta** the last goal doesn't count; **no cuentes con mi ayuda** don't count on my help; **tienes que ~ con el mal estado de la carretera** you have to take into account o remember the bad state of the road; **cuenta conmigo para la cena** count me in for dinner; **el polideportivo cuenta con una piscina olímpica** the sports centre has o boasts an Olympic-size swimming pool; **¿qué te cuentas?** (fam) how's things?

contemplación *nf* contemplation; **no andarse con contemplaciones** not to stand on ceremony

contemplar *vt* to contemplate; (*mirar*) to look at

contemporáneo, -a *adj, nm/f* contemporary

contendiente *nm/f* contestant

contenedor *nm* container; (*de escombros*) skip; ~ **de (la) basura** wheelie-bin (Brit); ~ **de vidrio** bottle bank

contener *vt* to contain, hold; (*risa etc*) to hold back, contain; **contenerse** *vr* to control *o* restrain o.s

contenido, -a *adj* (*moderado*) restrained; (*risa etc*) suppressed ▷ *nm* contents *pl*, content

contentar *vt* (*satisfacer*) to satisfy; (*complacer*) to please; (*Com*) to endorse; **contentarse** *vr* to be satisfied

contento, -a *adj* contented, content; (*alegre*) pleased; (*feliz*) happy

contestación *nf* answer, reply; ~ **a la demanda** (*Jur*) defence plea

contestador *nm*: ~ **automático** answering machine

contestar *vt* to answer (back), reply; (*Jur*) to corroborate, confirm

contestatario, -a *adj* anti-establishment, nonconformist

contexto *nm* context

contienda *nf* contest, struggle

contigo *pron* with you

contiguo, -a *adj* (*de al lado*) next; (*vecino*) adjacent, adjoining

continental *adj* continental

continente *adj, nm* continent

contingencia *nf* contingency; (*riesgo*) risk; (*posibilidad*) eventuality

contingente *adj* contingent ▷ *nm* contingent; (*Com*) quota

continuación *nf* continuation; **a** ~ then, next

continuamente *adv* (*sin interrupción*) continuously; (*a todas horas*) constantly

continuar *vt* to continue, go on with ▷ *vi* to continue, go on; ~**emos la clase mañana** we will go on with *o* continue the lesson tomorrow; **si continúa así habrá que llevarlo al hospital** if he goes on *o* continues like this, he'll have to be taken to hospital; **la puerta continúa cerrada** the door is still shut

continuidad *nf* continuity

continuo, -a *adj* (*sin interrupción*) continuous, constant; (*acción perseverante*) continual

contorno *nm* outline; (*Geo*) contour; **contornos** *nmpl* neighbourhood *sg*, surrounding area *sg*

contorsión *nf* contortion

contra *prep* against ▷ *nm* (*inconveniente*) disadvantage, drawback ▷ *nf*: **la C~ (nicaragüense)** the Contras *pl*; **no tengo nada** ~ **ti** I have nothing against you; **¿quién está en** ~? who is against?; **estoy en** ~ **de la subida de los impuestos** I'm against an increase in taxes; **apoyó la bici** ~ **la pared** he leaned the bike against the wall; **se chocó** ~ **la valla** he crashed into the fence; **unas pastillas** ~ **el mareo** some (anti-)travel sickness pills; **la fama también tiene sus** ~**s** fame also has its disadvantages *o* drawbacks; *ver tb* **pro**

contraataque *nm* counterattack

contrabajo *nm* double bass

contrabandista *nm/f* smuggler

contrabando *nm* (*acción*) smuggling; (*mercancías*) contraband; ~ **de armas** gun-running

contracción *nf* contraction

contrachapado *nm* plywood

contracorriente *nf* cross-current

contradecir *vt* to contradict

contradicción *nf* contradiction; **espíritu de** ~ contrariness

contradictorio, -a *adj* contradictory

contraer *vt* to contract; (*hábito*) to acquire; (*limitar*) to restrict; **contraerse** *vr* to contract; (*limitarse*) to limit o.s.

contraespionage *nm* counter-espionage

contrafuerte *nm* (*Arq*) buttress

contragolpe *nm* backlash

contraluz *nf* (*Foto etc*) back lighting; **a** ~ against the light

contramaestre *nm* foreman

contraofensiva *nf* counteroffensive

contrapartida *nf* (*Com*) balancing entry; **como** ~ **(de)** in return (for), as *o* in compensation (for)

contrapelo; **a** ~ *adv* the wrong way

contrapesar *vt* to counterbalance; (*fig*) to offset

contrapeso *nm* counterweight; (*fig*) counterbalance; (*Com*) makeweight

contraportada *nf* (*de revista*) back page

contraproducente *adj* counterproductive

contrariar *vt* (*oponerse*) to oppose; (*poner obstáculo*) to impede; (*enfadar*) to vex

contrariedad *nf* (*oposición*) opposition; (*obstáculo*) obstacle, setback; (*disgusto*) vexation, annoyance

contrario, -a *adj* (*partido, equipo*) opposing; (*lado, efecto, significado, sexo*) opposite ▷ *nm/f* (*adversario*) enemy, adversary; (*Deporte*) opponent; **se pasó al bando** ~ he went over to the other *o* opposing side; **los dos coches viajaban en dirección contraria** the two cars were travelling in opposite directions; **soy** ~ **al aborto** I am opposed to *o* against abortion; **ella opina lo** ~ she thinks the opposite; **se puso el jersey al** ~ he put his jumper on inside out; **al** ~, **me gusta mucho** on the contrary, I like it a lot; —**¿te aburres?** —**¡que va, al** ~!" "are you bored?" —"no way, quite the opposite!"; **de lo** ~, **tendré que castigarte** otherwise, I will have to punish you; **los inviernos, por el** ~, **son muy fríos** the winters, on the other hand *o* on the contrary, are very cold

contrarreloj *nf* (*tb*: **prueba contrarreloj**) time trial

contrarrestar *vt* to counteract

contrasentido *nm* contradiction; **es un** ~ **que él ... ** it doesn't make sense for him to ...

contraseña *nf* countersign; (*frase*) password

contrastar *vt* to resist ▷ *vi* to contrast

contraste *nm* contrast

contrata *nf* (*Jur*) written contract; (*empleo*) hiring

contratar *vt* (*firmar un acuerdo para*) to contract for; (*empleados, obreros*) to hire, engage; (*Deporte*) to sign up; **contratarse** *vr* to sign on

contratiempo *nm* (*revés*) setback; (*accidente*) mishap; **a ~** (*Mus*) off-beat

contratista *nm/f* contractor

contrato *nm* contract; **~ de compraventa** contract of sale; **~ a precio fijo** fixed-price contract; **~ a término** forward contract; **~ de trabajo** contract of employment *o* service

contravenir *vi*: **~ a** to contravene, violate

contraventana *nf* shutter

contribución *nf* (*municipal etc*) tax; (*ayuda*) contribution; **exento de contribuciones** tax-free

contribuir *vt, vi* to contribute; (*Com*) to pay (in taxes)

contribuyente *nm/f* (*Com*) taxpayer; (*que ayuda*) contributor

contrincante *nm* opponent, rival

control *nm* control; (*inspección*) inspection, check; (*Com*): **~ de calidad** quality control; **~ de cambios** exchange control; **~ de costos** cost control; **~ de créditos** credit control; **~ de existencias** stock control; **~ de precios** price control

controlador, a *nm/f* controller; **~ aéreo** air-traffic controller

controlar *vt* (*situación, emoción, vehículo, inflación*) to control; **los bomberos consiguieron ~ el fuego** the firefighters managed to bring the fire under control; **inspectores para ~ el proceso electoral** observers to monitor the electoral process; **deberías ~ tu peso** you should watch your weight; **no controlo muy bien ese tema** (*fam*) I'm not very hot on that subject (*fam*); **tuve que ~me para no pegarle** I had to control myself, otherwise I would have hit him

controversia *nf* controversy

contundente *adj* (*prueba*) conclusive; (*fig*: *argumento*) convincing; **instrumento ~** blunt instrument

contusión *nf* bruise

convalecencia *nf* convalescence

convalecer *vi* to convalesce, get better

convaleciente *adj, nm/f* convalescent

convalidar *vt* (*título*) to recognize

convencer *vt*: **~ a algn (de algo)** to convince sb (of sth), persuade sb (of sth); **~ a algn (de *o* para hacer algo)** to persuade sb (to do sth); **me convencieron de su inocencia** they convinced *o* persuaded me he was innocent; **me han convencido de *o* para que los vote** they persuaded me to vote for them; **no me convence nada la idea** I'm not convinced by the idea

convencimiento *nm* (*acción*) convincing; (*persuasión*) persuasion; (*certidumbre*) conviction; **tener el ~ de que ...** to be convinced that ...

convención *nf* convention

convencional *adj* conventional

conveniencia *nf* suitability; (*conformidad*) agreement; (*utilidad, provecho*) usefulness; **conveniencias** *nfpl* conventions; (*Com*) property *sg*; **ser de la ~ de algn** to suit sb

conveniente *adj* suitable; (*útil*) useful; (*correcto*) fit, proper; (*aconsejable*) advisable

convenio *nm* agreement, treaty; **~ de nivel crítico** threshold agreement

convenir *vt* (*hora, lugar, precio*) to agree (on) ▷ *vi* (*ser oportuno*) to suit, be suitable; **~ en algo** to agree on sth; **~ en hacer algo** to agree to do sth; **el método que más le convenga** the method that suits you best; **conviene recordar que ...** it should be remembered that ...; **"sueldo a ~"** "salary to be agreed"

convento *nm* monastery; (*de monjas*) convent

convergencia *nf* convergence

converger, convergir *vi* to converge; **sus esfuerzos convergen a un fin común** their efforts are directed towards the same objective

conversación *nf* conversation

conversar *vi* to talk, converse

conversión *nf* conversion

convertir *vt* to convert; (*transformar*) to transform, turn; (*Com*) to (ex)change; **convertirse** *vr* (*Rel*) to convert

convexo, -a *adj* convex

convicción *nf* conviction

convicto, -a *adj* convicted; (*condenado*) condemned

convidado, -a *nm/f* guest

convidar *vt* to invite

convincente *adj* convincing

convite *nm* invitation; (*banquete*) banquet

convivencia *nf* coexistence, living together

convivir *vi* to live together; (*Pol*) to coexist

convocar *vt* to summon, call (together)

convocatoria *nf* summons *sg*; (*anuncio*) notice of meeting; (*Escol*) examination session

convulsión *nf* convulsion; (*Pol etc*) upheaval

conyugal *adj* conjugal; **vida ~** married life

cónyuge *nm/f* spouse, partner

coñac (*pl* **-s**) *nm* cognac, brandy

coñazo *nm* (*fam*) pain; **dar el ~** to be a real pain

coño (*fam!*) *nm* cunt (!); (*LAm pey*) Spaniard ▷ *excl* (*enfado*) shit (!); (*sorpresa*) bloody hell (!); **¡qué ~!** what a pain in the arse (!)

cool *adj* (*fam*) cool

cooperación *nf* cooperation

cooperar *vi* to cooperate

cooperativo, -a *adj* cooperative ▷ *nf* cooperative

coordinador, a *nm/f* coordinator; *ver tb* **coordinadora**

coordinadora *nf* coordinating committee; *ver tb* **coordinador**

coordinar *vt* to coordinate

copa *nf* (*tb Deporte*) cup; (*vaso*) glass; (*de árbol*) top; (*de sombrero*) crown; **copas** *nfpl* (*Naipes*) one of the suits in the Spanish card deck; (**tomar una**) **~** (to have a) drink; **ir de ~s** to go out for a drink

copar *vt* (*puestos*) to monopolize

copia nf copy; (Arte) replica; (Com etc) duplicate; (Inform): ~ **impresa** hard copy; ~ **de respaldo** o **de seguridad** backup copy; **hacer ~ de seguridad** to back up; ~ **de trabajo** working copy; ~ **vaciada** dump

copiar vt to copy; ~ **al pie de la letra** to copy word for word

copiloto nm (Aviat) co-pilot; (Auto) co-driver

copioso, -a adj copious, plentiful

copla nf verse; (canción) (popular) song

copo nm: ~**s de maíz** cornflakes; ~ **de nieve** snowflake

copropietarios nmpl (Com) joint owners

coqueta adj flirtatious, coquettish ⊳ nf (mujer) flirt

coquetear vi to flirt

coraje nm courage; (ánimo) spirit; (ira) anger

coral adj choral ⊳ nf choir ⊳ nm (Zool) coral

coraza nf (armadura) armour; (blindaje) armour-plating

corazón nm heart; (Bot) core; **corazones** nmpl (Naipes) hearts; **de buen ~** kind-hearted; **de todo** ~ wholeheartedly; **estar mal del ~** to have heart trouble

corazonada nf impulse; (presentimiento) presentiment, hunch

corbata nf tie

corchea nf quaver

corchete nm catch, clasp; **corchetes** nmpl (Tip) square brackets

corcho nm cork; (Pesca) float

cordel nm cord, line

cordero nm lamb; (piel) lambskin

cordial adj cordial ⊳ nm cordial, tonic

cordialidad nf warmth, cordiality

cordillera nf range (of mountains)

cordón nm (cuerda) cord, string; (de zapatos) lace; (Elec) flex, wire (US); (Mil etc) cordon

cordura nf (Med) sanity; (fig) good sense

coreografía nf choreography

córner (pl -s) nm corner (kick)

corneta nf bugle

cornisa nf cornice

coro nm chorus; (conjunto de cantores) choir

corona nf crown; (de flores) garland

coronación nf coronation

coronar vt to crown

coronel nm colonel

coronilla nf (Anat) crown (of the head); **estar hasta la ~ (de)** to be utterly fed up (with)

corporación nf corporation

corporal adj corporal, bodily

corporativo, -a adj corporate

corpulento, -a adj (persona) well-built

corral nm (patio) farmyard; (Agr: de aves) poultry yard; (redil) pen

correa nf strap; (cinturón) belt; (de perro) lead, leash; ~ **transportadora** conveyor belt

corrección nf correction; (reprensión) rebuke; (cortesía) good manners; (Inform): ~ **por líneas** line editing; ~ **en pantalla** screen editing; ~ **(de pruebas)** (Tip) proofreading

correccional nm reformatory

correcto, -a adj correct; (persona) well-mannered

corrector, a nm/f: ~ **de pruebas** proofreader

corredizo, -a adj (puerta etc) sliding; (nudo) running

corredor, a adj running; (rápido) fast ⊳ nm/f (Deporte) runner ⊳ nm (pasillo) corridor; (balcón corrido) gallery; (Com) agent, broker; (pasillo) corridor, passage; ~ **de bienes raíces** real-estate broker; ~ **de bolsa** stockbroker; ~ **de seguros** insurance broker

corregir vt (error) to correct; (amonestar, reprender) to rebuke, reprimand; **corregirse** vr to reform

correo nm post, mail; (persona) courier; **Correos** nmpl Post Office sg; ~ **aéreo** airmail; ~ **basura** (por carta) junk mail; (por Internet) spam; ~ **certificado** registered mail; ~ **electrónico** e-mail, electronic mail; ~ **urgente** special delivery; ~ **de voz** voice mail; **a vuelta de ~** by return (of post); ~ **web** webmail

correr vi (ir rápido: persona, animal) to run; (: vehículo, conductor) to go fast; (darse prisa) to hurry; (fluir: líquido) to run, flow; (: aire) to flow; (: grifo, fuente) to run; (rumor) to go round ⊳ vt (recorrer: distancia) to run; (objeto) to move along; (silla) to move; (cortinas) to draw; **correrse** vr (desplazarse: objeto, persona) to move; (colores, maquillaje, tinta) to run; (fam!: tener orgasmo) to come; **tuve que ~ para alcanzar el autobús** I had to run to catch the bus; **corre que llegamos tarde** hurry or we'll be late; **subió las escaleras corriendo** he ran up the stairs; **no corras que te equivocarás** don't rush or you'll make a mistake; ~ **con los gastos** to pay the expenses; **eso corre de mi cuenta** I'll take care of that; **corre un poco la silla para allá** move the chair that way a little; **corrió el pestillo** she bolted the door; **no quería ~ la misma suerte de su amigo** he didn't want to suffer o undergo the same fate as his friend; **no corréis peligro** you're not in (any) danger; **córrete un poco hacia la izquierda** move a bit to the left; ver tb **riesgo**

correspondencia nf correspondence; (Ferro) connection; (reciprocidad) return; ~ **directa** (Com) direct mail

corresponder vi: **me pagó lo que me correspondía** he paid me my share; **estas fotos corresponden a otro álbum** these photos belong to another album; **los dos cadáveres corresponden a los dos secuestrados** the two bodies are those of the two kidnap victims; **no me corresponde a mí hacerlo** it's not for me to do it; **ella lo amaba, pero él no le correspondía** she loved him but he did not return her love; **esa forma de actuar no corresponde con sus principios** such behaviour is not in keeping with his principles; **"a quien corresponda"** "to whom it may concern"

correspondiente adj corresponding; (respectivo) respective

corresponsal nm/f (newspaper) correspondent;

(*Com*) agent

corrido, -a *adj* (*avergonzado*) abashed; (*fluido*) fluent ▷ *nf* run, dash; (*de toros*) bullfight; **de ~** fluently; **3 noches corridas** 3 nights running; **un kilo ~ a** good kilo

corriente *adj* (*agua*) running; (*dinero, cuenta*) current; (*frecuente: error, apellido*) common; (*habitual*) usual, customary; (*no especial*) ordinary; (*actual: mes, año*) current ▷ *nf* (*de fluido*) current; (*de aire*) draught, draft (*US*); (*Elec*) current; (*tendencia: ideológica*) tendency; (*: artística*) trend; **Pérez es un apellido muy ~** Pérez is a very common surname; **es un caso poco ~** it's an unusual case; **no es nada especial, es sólo un anillo ~** it's nothing special, it's just an ordinary ring; **aquí hay mucha ~** it's very draughty here; **estar al ~ de algo** to know (about sth); **tengo que ponerle al ~ de lo que ha pasado** I have to let him know what has happened; **~ de aire** draught, draft (*US*); **~ eléctrica** electric current

corrillo *nm* ring, circle (of people); (*fig*) clique

corro *nm* ring, circle (of people); (*baile*) ring-a-ring-a-roses; **la gente hizo ~** the people formed a ring

corroborar *vt* to corroborate

corroer *vt* (*tb fig*) to corrode, eat away; (*Geo*) to erode

corromper *vt* (*madera*) to rot; (*fig*) to corrupt

corrosivo, -a *adj* corrosive

corrupción *nf* rot, decay; (*fig*) corruption

corrupto, -a *adj* corrupt

corsé *nm* corset

cortacésped *nm* lawn mower

cortado, -a *adj* (*con cuchillo*) cut; (*leche*) sour; (*confuso*) confused; (*desconcertado*) embarrassed; (*tímido*) shy ▷ *nm* white coffee (with a little milk)

cortar *vt* (*carne, pastel, pan, pelo*) to cut; (*agua, teléfono*) to cut off; (*calle, carretera: cerrar*) to close; (*: bloquear*) to block ▷ *vi* (*tijeras, cuchillo*) to cut; (*LAm Telec*) to hang up; **cortarse** *vr* (*con cuchillo*) to cut o.s.; (*luz*) to go off, go out; (*leche, natillas, mayonesa*) to curdle; (*avergonzarse*) to become embarrassed; **corta la manzana por la mitad** cut the apple in half; **~ algo en rebanadas** to slice sth; **~ algo en trozos** to chop sth; **han cortado el gas** the gas has been cut off; **~ por lo sano** to settle things once and for all; **ha cortado con su novia** he's broken up with o finished with his girlfriend; **te vas a ~** you're going to cut yourself; **me corté el dedo con un cristal** I cut my finger on a piece of broken glass; **~se las uñas** to cut one's nails; **~se el pelo** to have one's hair cut; **de repente se cortó la comunicación** suddenly we were cut off; **no te cortes** don't be shy

cortauñas *nm inv* nail clippers *pl*

corte *nm* (*incisión, herida*) cut; (*Costura: diseño*) cut; (*interrupción*) cut ▷ *nf* (*de la monarquía*) (royal) court; **~ de pelo** cut, haircut; **tenía un ~ en la frente** he had a cut on his forehead; **me he hecho un ~ en el dedo** I've cut my finger; **un traje de ~ muy moderno** a suit with a very modern cut; **~ y confección** dressmaking; **me da ~ pedírselo** I'm embarrassed to ask him for it; **¡qué ~ le di!** I left him with no comeback!; **~ de corriente** o **luz** power cut; **~ de carretera** (*para obras, accidente*) road closure; (*: como protesta*) roadblock; **C~ Internacional de Justicia** International Court of Justice; **las C~s** the Spanish Parliament *sg*; **hacer la ~ a** to woo, court

cortedad *nf* shortness; (*fig*) bashfulness, timidity

cortejar *vt* to court

cortejo *nm* entourage; **~ fúnebre** funeral procession, cortège

cortés *adj* courteous, polite

cortesía *nf* courtesy

corteza *nf* (*de árbol*) bark; (*de pan*) crust; (*de fruta*) peel, skin; (*de queso*) rind

cortijo *nm* farmhouse

cortina *nf* curtain; **~ de humo** smoke screen

corto, -a *adj* (*longitud, distancia*) short; (*período, visita, reunión*) short, brief; (*tímido*) shy; (*torpe*) dim (*fam*), thick (*fam*) ▷ *nm* (*Cine*) short, short film, short movie (*US*); **Susana tiene el pelo ~** Susana has short hair; **un relato ~** a short story; **las mangas me están cortas** the sleeves are too short for me; **la película se me hizo muy corta** the film was over very quickly; **dos niñas de corta edad** two very young girls; **costará 50 euros, y seguro que me quedo ~** it will cost 50 euros, and I'm probably underestimating; **estar ~ de fondos** to be short of funds; **~ de luces** not very bright; **~ de oído** hard of hearing; **~ de vista** short-sighted

cortocircuito *nm* short-circuit

cortometraje *nm* (*Cine*) short

corvo, -a *adj* curved; (*nariz*) hooked ▷ *nf* back of knee

cosa *nf* thing; (*asunto*) affair; **eso es ~ mía** that's my business; **es poca ~** it's not important; **¡qué ~ más rara!** how strange; **~ de** about; **en ~ de 10 minutos** in about 10 minutes

coscorrón *nm* bump on the head

cosecha *nf* (*Agr*) harvest; (*acto*) harvesting; (*de vino*) vintage; (*producción*) yield

cosechar *vt* to harvest, gather (in)

coser *vt* to sew; (*Med*) to stitch (up)

cosmético, -a *adj, nm* cosmetic ▷ *nf* cosmetics *pl*

cosmos *nm* cosmos

cosquillas *nfpl*: **hacer ~** to tickle; **tener ~** to be ticklish

costa *nf* (*Geo*) coast; **C~ Brava** Costa Brava; **C~ Cantábrica** Cantabrian Coast; **C~ de Marfil** Ivory Coast; **C~ del Sol** Costa del Sol; **a ~ (de)** (*Com*) at cost; **a ~ de** at the expense of; **a toda ~** at any price

costado *nm* side; **de ~** (*dormir*) on one's side; **español por los 4 ~s** Spanish through and through

costal *nm* sack

costar *vt* (*dinero*) to cost; **me costó 25 euros** it cost me 25 euros; **¿cuánto cuesta?** how much does it cost?; **~ trabajo: las matemáticas le**

cuestan mucho trabajo he finds maths very difficult; **¿te ha costado trabajo encontrar la casa?** did you have trouble finding the house?; **me cuesta hablarle** I find it hard to talk to him; **ese error te ~á el puesto** that mistake will cost you your job o will lose you your job

Costa Rica nf Costa Rica

costarricense, costarriqueño, -a adj, nm/f Costa Rican

coste nm (Com): **~ promedio** average cost; **~s fijos** fixed costs; ver tb **costo**

costear vt to pay for; (Com etc) to finance; (Náut) to sail along the coast of; **costearse** vr (negocio) to pay for itself, cover its costs

costero adj coastal, coast cpd

costilla nf rib; (Culin) cutlet

costo nm cost, price; **~ directo** direct cost; **~ de expedición** shipping charges; **~ de sustitución** replacement cost; **~ unitario** unit cost; **~ de la vida** cost of living; ver tb **coste**

costoso, -a adj costly, expensive

costra nf (corteza) crust; (Med) scab

costumbre nf custom, habit; **como de ~** as usual

costura nf sewing, needlework; (confección) dressmaking; (zurcido) seam

costurera nf dressmaker

costurero nm sewing box o case

cota nf (Geo) height above sea level; (fig) height

cotarro nm: **dirigir el ~** (fam) to rule the roost

cotejar vt to compare

cotidiano, -a adj daily, day to day

cotilla nf busybody, gossip

cotillear vi to gossip

cotilleo nm gossip(ing)

cotización nf (Com) quotation, price; (de club) dues pl

cotizar vt (Com) to quote, price; **cotizarse** vr (fig) to be highly prized; **~se a** to sell at, fetch; (Bolsa) to stand at, be quoted at

coto nm (terreno cercado) enclosure; (de caza) reserve; (Com) price-fixing agreement; **poner ~ a** to put a stop to

cotorra nf (Zool: loro) parrot; (fam: persona) windbag

COU nm abr (Esp: = Curso de Orientación Universitario) one year course leading to final school leaving certificate and university entrance examinations

coyote nm coyote, prairie wolf

coyuntura nf (Anat) joint; (fig) juncture, occasion; **esperar una ~ favorable** to await a favourable moment

coz nf kick

cráneo nm skull, cranium

cráter nm crater

creación nf creation

creador, a adj creative ▷ nm/f creator

crear vt (obra, objeto, empleo) to create; (comité, negocio, asociación) to set up; (condiciones, clima, ambiente) to create; (problemas) to cause, create; (Inform: archivo) to create; **la nicotina crea adicción** nicotine is addictive; **no quiero ~me problemas** I don't want to create problems for

myself; **~se enemigos** to make enemies

creativo, -a adj creative

crecer vi (animal, planta, cabello, ciudad) to grow; (gasto, precio) to increase, rise; (cantidad, producción, sentimiento) to grow; (inflación) to rise; (desempleo) to increase, grow, rise; **¡cómo has crecido!** haven't you grown!; **crecí en Sevilla** I grew up in Seville; **~ en importancia** to grow in importance

creces; **con ~** adv amply, fully

crecido, -a adj (persona, planta) full-grown; (cantidad) large ▷ nf (de río) spate, flood

creciente adj growing; (cantidad) increasing; (luna) crescent ▷ nm crescent

crecimiento nm growth; (aumento) increase; (Com) rise

credenciales nfpl credentials

crédito nm credit; **a ~** on credit; **dar ~ a** to believe (in); **~ al consumidor** consumer credit; **~ rotativo o renovable** revolving credit

credo nm creed

crédulo, -a adj credulous

creencia nf belief

creer vi (pensar) to think, believe ▷ vt (considerar cierto) to believe; (pensar) to think; **creerse** vr (considerar cierto) to believe; (pensar) to think; (considerarse) to think; **es de Madrid, según creo** I think o believe she's from Madrid; **no creo** I don't think so; **~ en algo/algn** to believe in sth/sb; **creen en Dios** they believe in God; **nadie me cree** nobody believes me; **no creo que pueda ir** I don't think I'll be able to go; **no (me) creo lo que dijo** I don't believe what she said; **creo que sí** I think so; **creo que no** I don't think so; **no lo creía capaz de hacerlo** I didn't think him capable of doing it; **¿de dónde te crees que sacan el dinero?** where do you think they get the money?; **se cree muy listo** he thinks he's pretty clever

creíble adj credible, believable

creído, -a adj (engreído) conceited

crema adj inv cream (coloured) ▷ nf cream; (natillas) custard; **la ~ de la sociedad** the cream of society

cremallera nf zip (fastener) (Brit), zipper (US)

crematorio nm crematorium (Brit), crematory (US)

crepitar vi (fuego) to crackle

crepúsculo nm twilight, dusk

crespo, -a adj (pelo) curly

crespón nm crêpe

cresta nf (Geo, Zool) crest

cretino, -a adj cretinous ▷ nm/f cretin

creyente nm/f believer

cría nf (de animales) rearing, breeding; (animal) young; ver tb **crío**

criada nf ver **criado**

criadero nm nursery; (Zool) breeding place

criado, -a nm servant ▷ nf servant, maid

criador nm breeder

crianza nf rearing, breeding; (fig) breeding; (Med) lactation

criar vt (amamantar) to suckle, feed; (educar) to bring up; (producir) to grow, produce; (animales) to breed; **criarse** vr to grow (up); ~ **cuervos** to nourish a viper in one's bosom; **Dios los cría y ellos se juntan** birds of a feather flock together

criatura nf creature; (niño) baby, (small) child

criba nf sieve

cribar vt to sieve

crimen nm crime; ~ **pasional** crime of passion

criminal adj, nm/f criminal

crin nf (tb: **crines**) mane

crío, -a nm/f (fam: chico) kid; ver tb **cría**

cripta nf crypt

crisis nf inv crisis; ~ **nerviosa** nervous breakdown

crisma nf: **romperle la ~ a algn** (fam) to knock sb's block off

crispación nf tension

crispar vt (músculo) to cause to contract; (nervios) to set on edge

cristal nm crystal; (de ventana) glass, pane; (lente) lens; **de ~** glass cpd; ~ **ahumado/tallado** smoked/cut glass

cristalino, -a adj crystalline; (fig) clear ▷ nm lens of the eye

cristalizar vt, vi to crystallize

cristiandad nf, **cristianismo** nm Christianity

cristiano, -a adj, nm/f Christian; **hablar en ~** to speak proper Spanish; (fig) to speak clearly

Cristo nm (dios) Christ; (crucifijo) crucifix

criterio nm criterion; (juicio) judgement; (enfoque) attitude, approach; (punto de vista) view, opinion; ~ **de clasificación** (Inform) sort criterion

criticar vt to criticize

crítico, -a adj critical ▷ nm critic ▷ nf criticism; (Teat etc) review, notice; **la crítica** the critics pl

Croacia nf Croatia

croar vi to croak

croata adj, nm/f Croat(ian) ▷ nm (Ling) Croat(ian)

croissan(t) nm croissant

crol nm crawl

cromo nm chrome; (Tip) coloured print

cromosoma nm chromosome

crónico, -a adj chronic ▷ nf chronicle, account; (de periódico) feature, article

cronología nf chronology

cronológico, -a adj chronological

cronometrar vt to time

cronómetro nm (Deporte) stopwatch; (Tec etc) chronometer

croqueta nf croquette, rissole

cruce nm crossing; (de carreteras) crossroads; (Auto etc) junction, intersection; (Bio: proceso) crossbreeding; **luces de ~** dipped headlights

crucero nm (Náut: barco) cruise ship; (: viaje) cruise

crucial adj crucial

crucificar vt to crucify; (fig) to torment

crucifijo nm crucifix

crucigrama nm crossword (puzzle)

crudo, -a adj raw; (no maduro) unripe; (petróleo) crude; (rudo, cruel) cruel; (agua) hard; (clima etc) harsh ▷ nm crude (oil)

cruel adj cruel

crueldad nf cruelty

crujido nm (de madera etc) creak

crujiente adj (galleta etc) crunchy

crujir vi (madera etc) to creak; (dedos) to crack; (dientes) to grind; (nieve, arena) to crunch

cruz nf cross; (de moneda) tails sg; (fig) burden; ~ **gamada** swastika; **C~ Roja** Red Cross

cruzado, -a adj crossed ▷ nm crusader ▷ nf crusade

cruzar vt (calle, río, frontera, puente) to cross; (palabras) to exchange ▷ vi (peatón) to cross; **cruzarse** vr (líneas) to cross, intersect; (caminos) to cross; (personas, vehículos) to pass each other; ~ **los dedos/las piernas** to cross one's fingers/legs; ~**on el lago a nado** they swam across the lake; ~**se con algn en la calle** to pass sb in the street; ~**se de brazos** (lit) to fold one's arms; (fig) not to do anything

cuaderno nm notebook; (de escuela) exercise book; (Náut) logbook

cuadra nf (caballeriza) stable; (LAm) (city) block

cuadrado, -a adj square ▷ nm (Mat) square

cuadrar vt to square; (Tip) to justify ▷ vi: ~ **con** (cuenta) to square with, tally with; **cuadrarse** vr (soldado) to stand to attention; ~ **por la derecha/izquierda** to right-/left-justify

cuadriculado, -a adj: **papel** ~ squared o graph paper

cuadrilátero nm (Deporte) boxing ring; (Geom) quadrilateral

cuadrilla nf (de amigos) party, group; (de ladrones) gang; (de obreros) team

cuadro nm (cuadrado) square; (Pintura: original) painting; (: reproducción) picture; (Teat) scene; (de bicicleta, ventana) frame; (Deporte) team; **un mantel a ~s** a checked tablecloth; **un ~ de Picasso** a painting by Picasso; **¿quién pintó ese ~?** who did that painting?; **hay varios ~s en la pared** there are several pictures on the wall; ~ **de mandos** control panel; ~ **sinóptico** chart, table, diagram

cuádruplo, -a, cuádruple adj quadruple

cuajar vt (leche) to curdle; (sangre) to congeal; (adornar) to adorn; (Culin) to set ▷ vi (nieve) to settle; (fig) to become set, become established; (idea) to be received, be acceptable; **cuajarse** vr (leche) to curdle; (sangre) to congeal; (llenarse) to fill up

cuajo nm: **arrancar algo de ~** to tear sth out by its roots

cual pron (referido a persona: sujeto) who; (: objeto) whom; (referido a una cosa) which ▷ adv (como) like, as; **el primo del ~ te estuve hablando** the cousin who I was speaking to you about; **la ventana desde la ~ nos observaban** the window from which they were watching us; **se ofendió, lo ~ es comprensible** he took offence, which is understandable; **Juan se puso enfermo, con lo ~ tuve que hacerlo yo solo** Juan fell ill, with the result that I had to do it alone; **cada ~ puede hacer lo que crea conveniente** everyone may do what they think fit; **son a ~ más gandul** each is as idle as the other; **sea ~ sea la razón** whatever the reason may be; **frágil ~ mariposa** as delicate as a butterfly

cuál *pron interrogativo* what; (*entre varios*) which (one), what; **no sé ~ es la solución** I don't know what the solution is; **¿~ te gusta más?** which one do you like best?

cualesquier(a) *pl de* **cualquier(a)**

cualidad *nf* quality

cualquiera, cualquier (*pl* **cualesquier(a)**) *adj* any; **en cualquier ciudad española** in any Spanish town; **puedes usar un bolígrafo ~** you can use any pen; **no es un empleo ~** it's not just any job ▷ *pron* (*referido a más de dos personas*) anybody, anyone; (*referido a dos personas o cosas*) either (of them); (*referido a más de dos cosas*) any one; **~ puede hacer eso** anyone can do that; **me da igual, ~** it doesn't matter, any one; **en ~ de las habitaciones** in any one of the rooms; **~ que elijas** whichever one you choose; **en cualquier momento** any time; **en cualquier parte** anywhere; **¿cuál de los dos prefieres? — ~** which of the two do you prefer? — either

cuando *conj* **1** (*temporal: en momento concreto*) when; (*en cualquier momento*) whenever; **~ vienen a vernos** when they come to see us; **lo haré ~ tenga tiempo** I'll do it when I have time; **ven ~ quieras** come when(ever) you like
2 (*condicional, causal*) if; **~ él lo dice, será verdad** if he says so, it must be true
▷ *adv* when; **en abril es ~ más casos hay** April is when there are most cases, it's in April that there are most cases; **de ~ en ~, de vez en ~** from time to time, now and again, every so often; **~ más** at (the) most; **~ menos** at least
▷ *prep*: **~ niño yo era muy travieso** as a child *o* when I was a child I was very naughty; **eso fue ~ la guerra** that was during the war

cuándo *adv* when; **¿~ te va mejor?** when does it suit you?; **no sabe ~ ocurrió** he doesn't know when it happened; **¿desde ~?** how long?; **¿hasta ~ vamos a aguantar esta injusticia?** how long are we going to put up with this injustice?; **¿para ~ estará listo el proyecto?** when will the project be ready (by)?

cuantía *nf* (*alcance*) extent; (*importancia*) importance

cuantioso, -a *adj* substantial

cuanto, -a *adj* **1** (*cantidad*): **le daremos ~s ejemplares necesite** we'll give him as many copies as *o* all the copies he needs; **unos ~s** (*no muchos*) a few; (*bastantes*) quite a few; **~s hombres la ven** all the men who see her
2 (*en correlaciones: +más*): **~ más vino bebas peor te sentirás** the more wine you drink the worse you'll feel; (*+menos*): **cuantas menos personas haya mejor** the fewer people the better
▷ *pron* **1** (*cantidad*): **tiene (todo) ~ desea** he's got everything he wants; **tome ~/~s quiera** take as much/many as you want; **unos ~s** (*no muchos*) a few; (*bastantes*) quite a few; **lo sabíamos unos**

~s, pero la mayoría no a few of us knew, but most people didn't
2 (*en correlaciones*): **~s más, mejor** the more the merrier; **~s menos seamos, mejor** the fewer of us there are the better; **~ más gana menos gasta** the more he earns the less he spends
▷ *conj, adv* **1**: **~ más lo pienso menos lo entiendo** the more I think about it, the less I understand it
2: **en ~**: **en ~ llegue** as soon as I arrive; **en ~ a mí** as for me; *ver tb* **antes**

cuánto, -a *adj* **1** (*interrogativo: en singular*) how much?; (*: en plural*) how many?; **¿~ dinero?** how much money?; **¿~ tiempo?** how long?; **¿cuántas sillas?** how many chairs?; **no sabe ~s cuadros hay** he doesn't know how many paintings there are
2 (*exclamativo*) what a lot of; **¡cuánta gente!** what a lot of people!
▷ *pron, adv* **1** (*interrogativo: en singular*) how much?; (*: en plural*) how many?; **¿~ cuesta?** how much does it cost?; **no sé ~ es** I don't know how much it is; **¿a ~ están las peras?** how much are (the) pears?; **¿~ hay de aquí a Bilbao?** how far is it from here to Bilbao?; **¿a ~ estamos?** what's the date?; **Señor no sé ~s** Mr. So-and-So
2 (*exclamativo*): **¡~ me alegro!** I'm so glad!; **¡~ has tardado!** you've been ages!, you took ages!

cuarenta *num* forty

cuarentena *nf* (*Med etc*) quarantine; (*conjunto*) forty(-odd)

cuaresma *nf* Lent

cuarta *nf* (*Mat*) quarter, fourth; (*palmo*) span; *ver tb* **cuarto**

cuartear *vt* to quarter; (*dividir*) to divide up; **cuartearse** *vr* to crack, split

cuartel *nm* (*de ciudad*) quarter, district; (*Mil*) barracks *pl*; **~ general** headquarters *pl*

cuarteto *nm* quartet

cuartilla *nf* (*hoja*) sheet (of paper); **cuartillas** *nfpl* (*Tip*) copy *sg*

cuarto, -a *adj* fourth ▷ *n* (*habitación*) room; (*Mat*) quarter, fourth; **vivo en el ~ piso** I live on the fourth floor; **los niños jugaban en su ~** the children were playing in their room; **~ de baño** bathroom; **~ de estar** living room; **he leído un ~ del libro** I've read a quarter of the book; **~ de kilo** quarter kilo; **~ de hora** quarter (of an) hour; **son las once y ~** It's a quarter past eleven; **a las diez menos ~** at a quarter to ten; **es un ~ para las diez** (*Lam*) it's a quarter to ten; **no tener un ~** to be broke (*fam*); **~s de final** quarter finals; *ver tb* **cuarta**

cuarzo *nm* quartz

cuatrimestre *nm* four-month period

cuatro *num* four; **las ~** four o'clock; **el ~ de octubre** (on) the fourth of October; *ver tb* **seis**

cuatrocientos, -as *num* four hundred

Cuba *nf* Cuba

cuba *nf* cask, barrel; **estar como una ~** (*fam*) to be sloshed

cubano, -a *adj, nm/f* Cuban

cúbico, -a adj cubic

cubierto, -a pp de **cubrir** ▷ adj covered; (cielo) overcast ▷ nm cover; (en la mesa) place ▷ nf cover, covering; (neumático) tyre; (Náut) deck; **cubiertos** nmpl cutlery sg; **a ~ de** covered with o in; **precio del ~** cover charge

cubil nm den

cubilete nm (en juegos) cup

cubito nm: **~ de hielo** ice cube

cubo nm cube; (balde) bucket, tub; (Tec) drum; **~ de (la) basura** dustbin

cubrecama nm bedspread

cubrir vt (rostro, superficie, objeto) to cover; (ruta, distancia) to cover; (hueco, vacante, plaza) to fill; (agujero) to fill in; (gastos, déficit, préstamo) to cover; (necesidades, demanda) to meet; (Prensa: suceso) to cover; **cubrirse** vr (cielo) to become overcast; **habían cubierto el suelo de papeles** they had covered the floor with papers; **el agua casi me cubría** I was almost out of my depth; **son capaces de ~ grandes distancias** they can cover great distances; **las mujeres se cubren la cara con un velo** the women cover their face with a veil

cucaracha nf cockroach

cuchara nf spoon; (Tec) scoop

cucharada nf spoonful; **~ colmada** heaped spoonful

cucharadita nf teaspoonful

cucharilla nf teaspoon

cucharita nf teaspoon

cucharón nm ladle

cuchichear vi to whisper

cuchilla nf (large) knife; (de arma blanca) blade; **~ de afeitar** razor blade; **pasar a ~** to put to the sword

cuchillada nf (golpe) stab; (herida) knife o stab wound

cuchillo nm knife

cuchitril nm hovel; (habitación etc) pigsty

cuclillas nfpl: **en ~** squatting

cuco, -a adj pretty; (astuto) sharp ▷ nm cuckoo

cucurucho nm paper cone, cornet

cuello nm (Anat) neck; (de vestido, camisa) collar

cuenca nf (Anat) eye socket; (Geo: valle) bowl, deep valley; (: fluvial) basin

cuenco nm (earthenware) bowl

cuenta nf (cálculo) count, counting; (en café, restaurante) bill; (Com) account; (de collar) bead; (fig) account; **a fin de ~s** in the end; **en resumidas ~s** in short; **caer en la ~** to catch on; **dar ~ a algn de sus actos** to account to sb for one's actions; **darse ~ de** to realize; **tener en ~** to bear in mind; **echar ~s** to take stock; **~ atrás** countdown; **abonar una cantidad en ~ a algn** to credit a sum to sb's account; **ajustar** o **liquidar una ~** to settle an account; **pasar la ~** to send the bill; **~ corriente/de ahorros/a plazo (fijo)** current/savings/deposit account; **~ de asignación** appropriation account; **~ de caja** cash account; **~ de capital** capital account; **~ de correo** (Internet) e-mail account; **~ de crédito** credit o loan account; **~ de gastos e ingresos** income and expenditure account; **~ por cobrar** account receivable; **~ por pagar** account payable

cuentakilómetros nm inv (de distancias) ≈ milometer, clock; (velocímetro) speedometer

cuento nm story; (Lit) short story; **~ de hadas** fairy story; **es el ~ de nunca acabar** it's an endless business; **eso no viene a ~** that's irrelevant

cuerda nf rope; (hilo) string; (de reloj) spring; (Mus: de violín etc) string; (Mat) chord; (Anat) cord; **~ floja** tightrope; **~s vocales** vocal cords; **dar ~ a un reloj** to wind up a clock

cuerdo, -a adj sane; (prudente) wise, sensible

cuerno nm (Zool: gen) horn; (: de ciervo) antler; **poner los ~s a** (fam) to cuckold; **saber a ~ quemado** to leave a nasty taste

cuero nm (Zool) skin, hide; (Tec) leather; **en ~s** stark naked; **~ cabelludo** scalp

cuerpo nm (Anat) body; (cadáver) corpse; (parte principal) main part; (objeto) body, object; **el ~ humano** the human body; **el ~ de bomberos** the fire brigade; **~ diplomático** diplomatic corps; **~ extraño** foreign body; **tomar ~** to take shape; **luchar ~ a ~** to fight hand-to-hand

cuervo nm (Zool) raven, crow; ver **criar**

cuestión nf (asunto) matter, question; (pregunta) question; **quedan algunas cuestiones por resolver** there are still a few matters o questions to be resolved; **eso es otra ~** that's another matter; **poner algo en ~** to call sth into question, raise doubts about sth; **llegaron en ~ de minutos** they arrived in a matter of minutes

cuestionario nm questionnaire

cueva nf cave

cuidado nm (atención) care; **pone mucho ~ en su trabajo** he takes great care over his work; **deben lavarse con ~** they should be washed with care; **conducía con ~** he was driving carefully; **debes tener mucho ~ al cruzar la calle** you must be very careful crossing the street; **¡~!** careful!; **Carlos está al ~ de los niños** Carlos looks after the children; **eso me tiene sin ~** I'm not worried about that

cuidadoso, -a adj careful; (preocupado) anxious

cuidar vt (libros, plantas, niño, salud) look after, take care of; (enfermo) to care for; (detalles, ortografía) to pay attention to ▷ vi: **~ de algn/algo** to take care of sb/sth, look after sb/sth; **cuidarse** vr (de sí mismo) to look after o.s.; **ella cuida de los niños** she looks after the children; **cuide de que no pase nadie** make sure nobody gets in; **tienes que ~te** make sure you look after yourself; **¡cuídate!** take care!

culata nf (de fusil) butt

culebra nf snake; **~ de cascabel** rattlesnake

culebrón nm (fam) soap (opera)

culinario, -a adj culinary, cooking cpd

culminación nf culmination

culminar vi to culminate

culo *nm* (*fam: asentaderas*) bottom, backside, bum (*Brit*); (: *ano*) arse(hole) (*Brit!*), ass(hole) (*US!*); (*de vaso*) bottom

culpa *nf* fault; (*Jur*) guilt; **culpas** *nfpl* sins; **por ~ de** through, because of; **tener la ~ (de)** to be to blame (for)

culpabilidad *nf* guilt

culpable *adj* guilty ▷ *nm/f* culprit; **confesarse ~** to plead guilty; **declarar ~ a algn** to find sb guilty

culpar *vt* to blame; (*acusar*) to accuse

cultivar *vt* to cultivate; (*cosecha*) to raise; (*talento*) to develop

cultivo *nm* (*acto*) cultivation; (*plantas*) crop; (*Bio*) culture

culto, -a *adj* (*cultivado*) cultivated; (*que tiene cultura*) cultured, educated ▷ *nm* (*veneración*) worship; (*religión*) cult; (*Pol etc*) cult

cultura *nf* culture

cultural *adj* cultural

culturismo *nm* body-building

cumbre *nf* summit, top; (*fig*) top, height; **conferencia (en la) ~** summit (conference)

cumpleaños *nm inv* birthday

cumplido, -a *adj* complete, perfect; (*abundante*) plentiful; (*cortés*) courteous ▷ *nm* compliment; **visita de ~** courtesy call

cumplidor, a *adj* reliable

cumplimentar *vt* to congratulate; (*órdenes*) to carry out

cumplimiento *nm* (*de un deber*) fulfilment, execution, performance; (*acabamiento*) completion; (*Com*) expiry, end

cumplir *vt* (*amenaza*) to carry out; (*promesa*) to keep; (*objetivo, sueño*) to achieve; (*ambición*) to fulfil, fulfill (*US*), achieve; (*papel*) to play; (*ley, norma, sentencia*) to observe, obey; (*orden*) to carry out, obey; (*condición, requisito*) to comply with, fulfil, fulfill (*US*), meet; (*condena, pena*) to serve; (*servicio militar*) to do, complete ▷ *vi* (*pago*) to fall due; (*plazo*) to expire; **cumplirse** *vr* (*plazo*) to expire; (*plan, proyecto*) to be implemented; (*deseo, sueño, vaticinio*) to come true; **hoy cumple dieciocho años** he is eighteen today; **¡que cumplas muchos más!** many happy returns!; **~ con** (*deber*) to carry out, fulfil; (*ley*) to observe, obey

cúmulo *nm* (*montón*) heap; (*nube*) cumulus

cuna *nf* cradle, cot; **canción de ~** lullaby

cundir *vi* (*noticia, rumor, pánico*) to spread; (*rendir*) to go a long way

cuneta *nf* ditch

cuña *nf* (*Tec*) wedge; (*Com*) advertising spot; (*Med*) bedpan; **tener ~s** to have influence

cuñado, -a *nm/f* brother/sister-in-law

cuota *nf* (*parte proporcional*) share; (*cotización*) fee,

dues *pl*; **~ inicial** (*Com*) down payment

cupo *nm* quota, share; (*Com*): **~ de importación** import quota; **~ de ventas** sales quota

cupón *nm* coupon; **~ de la ONCE** *o* **de los ciegos** ONCE lottery ticket

cúpula *nf* (*Arq*) dome

cura *nf* (*curación*) cure; (*método curativo*) treatment ▷ *nm* priest; **~ de emergencia** emergency treatment

curación *nf* cure; (*acción*) curing

curandero, -a *nm/f* healer

curar *vt* (*Med: herida*) to treat, dress; (: *enfermo*) to cure; (*Culin*) to cure, salt; (*cuero*) to tan ▷ *vi*: **curarse** *vr* to get well, recover

curiosear *vt* to glance at, look over ▷ *vi* to look round, wander round; (*explorar*) to poke about

curiosidad *nf* curiosity

curioso, -a *adj* curious; (*aseado*) neat ▷ *nm/f* bystander, onlooker; **¡qué ~!** how odd!

curita *nf* (*LAm*) (sticking) plaster, Band-Aid® (*US*)

currante *nm/f* (*fam*) worker

currar *vi* (*fam*), **currelar** *vi* (*fam*) to work

currículo *nm*, **currículum** *nm* curriculum vitae

curro *nm* (*fam*) work, job

cursar *vt* (*Escol*) to study

cursi *adj* (*fam*) pretentious; (: *amanerado*) affected

cursilada *nf*: **¡qué ~!** how tacky!

cursillo *nm* short course

cursiva *nf* italics *pl*

curso *nm* (*dirección*) course; (*fig*) progress; (*Escol*) school year; (*Univ*) academic year; **en ~** (*año*) current; (*proceso*) going on, under way; **moneda de ~ legal** legal tender

cursor *nm* (*Inform*) cursor; (*Tec*) slide

curtido, -a *adj* (*cara etc*) weather-beaten; (*fig: persona*) experienced

curtir *vt* (*piel*) to tan; (*fig*) to harden

curvo, -a *adj* (*gen*) curved; (*torcido*) bent ▷ *nf* (*gen*) curve, bend; **curva de rentabilidad** (*Com*) break-even chart

cúspide *nf* (*Geo*) summit, peak; (*fig*) top, pinnacle

custodia *nf* (*cuidado*) safekeeping; (*Jur*) custody

custodiar *vt* (*conservar*) to keep, take care of; (*vigilar*) to guard

custodio *nm* guardian, keeper

cutáneo, -a *adj* skin *cpd*

cutícula *nf* cuticle

cutis *nm inv* skin, complexion

cutre *adj* (*fam: lugar*) grotty; (: *persona*) naff

cuyo, -a *pron* (*de quien*) whose; (*de que*) whose, of which; **la señora en cuya casa me hospedé** the lady in whose house I stayed; **el asunto ~s detalles conoces** the affair the details of which you know; **por ~ motivo** for which reason

C.V. *abr* (= *caballos de vapor*) H.P.; (= *Curriculum Vitae*) C.V.

Dd

D. *abr* = **Don**

dádiva *nf* (*donación*) donation; (*regalo*) gift

dadivoso, -a *adj* generous

dado, -a *pp de* **dar** ▷ *nm* die; **dados** *nmpl* dice ▷ *adj:* **en un momento** ~ at a certain point; **ser** ~ **a (hacer algo)** to be very fond of (doing sth); ~ **que** *conj* given that

daltónico, -a *adj* colour-blind

dama *nf* (*gen*) lady; (*Ajedrez*) queen; **damas** *nfpl* draughts; **primera** ~ (*Teat*) leading lady; (*Pol*) president's wife, first lady (*US*); ~ **de honor** (*de reina*) lady-in-waiting; (*de novia*) bridesmaid

damasco *nm* (*tela*) damask; (*And, CS: árbol*) apricot tree; (: *fruta*) apricot

damnificar *vt* to harm; (*persona*) to injure

danés, -esa *adj* Danish ▷ *nm/f* Dane ▷ *nm* (*Ling*) Danish

danza *nf* (*gen*) dancing; (*una danza*) dance

danzar *vt, vi* to dance

dañar *vt* (*objeto*) to damage; (*persona*) to hurt; (*estropear*) to spoil; **dañarse** *vr* (*objeto*) to get damaged

dañino, -a *adj* harmful

daño *nm* (*a un objeto*) damage; (*a una persona*) harm, injury; **~s y perjuicios** (*Jur*) damages; **hacer** ~ **a** to damage; (*persona*) to hurt, injure; **hacerse** ~ to hurt o.s.

dar *vt* **1** (*entregar*) to give; ~ **algo a algn** to give sb sth *o* sth to sb; **le dio un bocadillo a su hijo** he gave his son a sandwich, he gave a sandwich to his son; **se lo di a Teresa** I gave it to Teresa; **deme 2 kilos** 2 kilos please; ~ **de beber a algn** to give sb a drink

2 (*producir: intereses*) to yield; (*fruta*) to produce

3 (*con sustantivos de acción: película*) to show; (*obra de teatro*) to put on; (*fiesta*) to have; ~ **una patada a algn/algo** to kick sb/sth, give sb/sth a kick; ~ **un susto a algn** to give sb a fright; *ver tb* **gracia**; **aseo** *y otros sustantivos*

4 (*con sensaciones*): **da gusto escucharle** it's a pleasure to listen to him; **me dio mucha alegría verla** I was very pleased to see her; **me da pena/asco** it frightens/sickens me; **el ejercicio me da hambre** exercise makes me hungry; **me da lo mismo** it's all the same to me; **¿qué más te da?** what does it matter to you?; *ver tb* **igual**

5 (*considerar*): ~ **algo por descontado/entendido** to take sth for granted/as read; ~ **algo por concluido** to consider sth finished; **lo dieron por desaparecido** they gave him up as lost

6 (*hora*): **el reloj dio las 6** the clock struck 6 (o'clock)

7: **¡y dale!** (*¡otra vez!*) not again!; **estar/seguir dale que dale** *o* **dale que te pego** *o* (*LAm*) **dale y dale** to go/keep on and on ▷ *vi* **1**: ~ **a** (*habitación*) to overlook, look on to; (*accionar: botón etc*) to press, hit; **mi ventana da al jardín** my window looks out onto the garden

2: ~ **con**: **dimos con él dos horas más tarde** we came across him two hours later; **al final di con la solución** I eventually came up with the answer

3: ~ **en** (*blanco, suelo*) to hit; **el sol me da en la cara** the sun is shining (right) in my face

4: ~ **de sí** (*zapatos etc*) to stretch, give

5: ~ **para** to be enough for; **nuestro presupuesto no da para más** our budget's really tight

6: ~ **por**: **le ha dado por estudiar música** now he's into studying music

7: ~ **que hablar** to set people talking; **una película que da que pensar** a thought-provoking film

darse *vr* **1**: **~se un baño** to have a bath; **~se un golpe** to hit o.s.

2: **~se por vencido** to give up; **con eso me doy por satisfecho** I'd settle for that

3 (*ocurrir*): **se han dado muchos casos** there have been a lot of cases

4: **~se a**: **se ha dado a la bebida** he's taken to drinking

5: **se me dan bien/mal las ciencias** I'm good/bad at science

6: **dárselas de**: **se las da de experto** he fancies himself *o* poses as an expert

dardo *nm* dart

dársena *nf* (*Naut*) dock

datar *vi*: ~ **de** to date from

dátil *nm* date

dato *nm* fact, piece of information; (*Mat*) datum; **datos** *nmpl* (*Inform*) data; **~s de entrada/salida** input/output data; **~s personales** personal details

dcha. *abr* (= *derecha*) r.h.

d. de J. C. *abr* (= *después de Jesucristo*) A.D.

de *prep* (*de+el = del*) **1** (*posesión, pertenencia*) of; **la casa de Isabel/mis padres** Isabel's/my parents' house; **es de ellos/ella** it's theirs/hers; **un libro de Unamuno** a book by Unamuno

2 (*origen, distancia, con números*) from; **soy de Gijón** I'm from Gijón; **de 8 a 20** from 8 to 20; **5 metros de largo** 5 metres long; **salir del cine** to go out of o leave the cinema; **de 2 en 2** by 2, 2 at a time; **9 de cada 10** 9 out of every 10

3 (*con valor descriptivo*) **una copa de vino** a glass of wine; **una silla de madera** a wooden chair; **un anillo de oro** a gold ring; **la mesa de la cocina** the kitchen table; **un viaje de dos días** a two-day journey; **un billete de 50 euros** a 50-euro note; **un niño de tres años** a three-year-old (child); **una máquina de coser** a sewing machine; **la ciudad de Madrid** (the city of) Madrid; **el tonto de Juan** that idiot Juan; **ir vestido de gris** to be dressed in grey; **la niña del vestido azul** the girl in the blue dress; **la chica del pelo largo** the girl with long hair; **trabaja de profesora** she works as a teacher; **de lado** sideways; **de atrás/delante** rear/front

4 (*hora, tiempo*): **a las 8 de la mañana** at 8 o'clock in the morning; **de día/noche** by day/night; **de hoy en ocho días** a week from now; **de niño era gordo** as a child he was fat

5 (*en comparaciones*) than; **más/menos de cien personas** more/less than a hundred people; **es más difícil de lo que creía** it's more difficult than I thought it would be; **menos/más de lo pensado** less/more than expected; **el más caro de la tienda** the most expensive in the shop

6 (*causa*): **del calor** from the heat; **de puro tonto** out of sheer stupidity

7 (*tema*) about; **¿sabes algo de él?** do you know anything about him?; **clases de inglés** English classes; **un libro de física** a physics book

8 (*adj+de+infin*): **fácil de entender** easy to understand

9 (*oraciones pasivas*): **fue respetado de todos** he was loved by all

10 (*condicional: +infin*) if; **de ser posible** if possible; **de no terminarlo hoy** if I etc don't finish it today

deambular *vi* to stroll, wander

debajo *adv* underneath; **~ de** below, under; **por ~ de** beneath

debate *nm* debate

debatir *vt* to debate; **debatirse** *vr* to struggle

deber *nm* duty; **deberes** *nmpl* (*Escol*) homework *sg* ▷ *vt* to owe ▷ *vi*: **debe (de)** (*obligación*) it must, it should; (*suposición*) it must; **deberse** *vr*: **~se a** to be owing o due to; **sólo cumplí mi ~,** I simply did my duty; **¿qué o cuánto le debo?** how much is it?; **debo intentar verla** I must try to see her; **no debes preocuparte** you mustn't worry; **~ía dejar de fumar** I should stop smoking; **no ~ías haberla dejado sola** you shouldn't have left her alone; **como debe ser** as it should be; **debe de**

ser canadiense he must be Canadian; **no debe de tener mucho dinero** he can't have much money; **el retraso se debió a una huelga** the delay was due to a strike

debido, -a *adj* proper, due; **~ a** due to, because of; **en debida forma** duly

débil *adj* weak; (*persona: físicamente*) feeble; (*salud*) poor; (*voz, ruido*) faint; (*luz*) dim

debilidad *nf* (*de fuerzas, carácter*) weakness; (*de esfuerzo*) feebleness; (*de luz*) dimness; **tener ~ por algn** to have a soft spot for sb

debilitar *vt* to weaken; **debilitarse** *vr* to grow weak

debutar *vi* to make one's debut

década *nf* decade

decadencia *nf* (*estado*) decadence; (*proceso*) decline, decay

decaer *vi* (*declinar*) to decline; (*debilitarse*) to weaken; (*salud*) to fail; (*negocio*) to fall off

decaído, -a *adj*: **estar ~** (*persona*) to be down

decaimiento *nm* (*declinación*) decline; (*desaliento*) discouragement; (*Med: depresión*) depression

decano, -a *nm/f* (*Univ etc*) dean; (*de grupo*) senior member

decapitar *vt* to behead

decena *nf*: **una ~** ten

decencia *nf* (*modestia*) modesty; (*honestidad*) respectability

decente *adj* (*correcto*) proper; (*honesto*) respectable

decepción *nf* disappointment

decepcionar *vt* to disappoint

decidir *vt* to decide ▷ *vi* to decide; **decidirse** *vr*: **~se a** to make up one's mind to; **~ el futuro de algo** to decide the future of sth; **tú decides** you decide; **¡decídete!** make up your mind!; **¿qué fue lo que al final te decidió?** what finally made up your mind?; **~se a hacer algo** to decide to do sth; **~se por algo** to decide on sth

decimal *adj, nm* decimal

décimo, -a *num* tenth ▷ *nf* (*Mat*) tenth; **tiene unas ~as de fiebre** he has a slight temperature

decimoctavo, -a *num* eighteenth

decimocuarto, -a *num* fourteenth

decimonoveno, -a *num* nineteenth

decimoquinto, -a *num* fifteenth

decimoséptimo, -a *num* seventeenth

decimosexto, -a *num* sixteenth

decimotercero, -a *num* thirteenth

decir *nm* saying ▷ *vt* (*expresar*) to say; (*contar*) to tell; (*hablar*) to speak; (*indicar*) to show; (*fam: nombrar*) to call; **decirse** *vr*: **se dice** it is said, they say; **es un ~** it's a manner of speaking; **¿qué dijo?** what did he say?; **¿cómo se dice "casa" en inglés?** how do you say "casa" in English?; **~ para o entre sí** to say to o.s.; **~ por ~** to talk for talking's sake; **querer ~** to mean; **es ~** that is to say, namely; **ni que ~ tiene que ...** it goes without saying that ...; **como quien dice** so to speak; **¡quién lo diría!** would you believe it!; **~ a alguien que haga algo** to tell somebody to do sth; **le dije que fuera más tarde** I told her to go later; **¡no me digas!** really?; **el qué dirán**

gossip; **¡diga!, ¡dígame!** (*en tienda etc*) can I help you?; (*Telec*) hello?; **no sé lo que quiere ~ esto** I don't know what this means

decisión *nf* decision; (*firmeza*) decisiveness; (*voluntad*) determination

decisivo, -a *adj* decisive

declamar *vt, vi* to declaim; (*versos etc*) to recite

declaración *nf* (*manifestación*) statement; (*explicación*) explanation; (*Jur: testimonio*) evidence; **~ de derechos** (*Pol*) bill of rights; **~ de impuestos** (*Com*) tax return; **~ de ingresos** o **de la renta** income tax return; **~ jurada** affidavit; **falsa ~** (*Jur*) misrepresentation

declarar *vt* to declare; (*Econ*) to declare ▷ *vi* to declare; (*Jur*) to testify; **declararse** *vr* (*persona*) to declare o.s.; (*guerra, incendio*) to break out; **¿algo que ~?** anything to declare?; **declaró que apoyaría el proyecto** she declared her support for the project; **~ culpable/inocente a algn** to find sb guilty/not guilty; **~ en un juicio** to give evidence at a trial; **se declaró partidario de hacerlo** he declared himself in favour of doing it; **~se culpable/inocente** to plead guilty/not guilty; **~se a algn** to declare one's love to sb

declinar *vt* (*gen, Ling*) to decline; (*Jur*) to reject ▷ *vi* (*el día*) to draw to a close

declive *nm* (*cuesta*) slope; (*inclinación*) incline; (*fig*) decline; (*Com: tb:* **declive económico**) slump

decolorarse *vr* to become discoloured

decomiso *nm* seizure

decoración *nf* decoration; (*Teat*) scenery, set; **~ de escaparates** window dressing

decorado *nm* (*Cine, Teat*) scenery, set

decorar *vt* to decorate

decorativo, -a *adj* ornamental, decorative

decoro *nm* (*respeto*) respect; (*dignidad*) decency; (*recato*) propriety

decoroso, -a *adj* (*decente*) decent; (*modesto*) modest; (*digno*) proper

decrecer *vi* to decrease, diminish; (*nivel de agua*) to go down; (*días*) to draw in

decrépito, -a *adj* decrepit

decretar *vt* to decree

decreto *nm* decree; (*Pol*) act

decreto-ley (*pl* **decretos-leyes**) *nm* decree

dedal *nm* thimble

dedicación *nf* dedication; **con ~ exclusiva** o **plena** full-time

dedicar *vt* (*libro*) to dedicate; (*tiempo, dinero*) to devote; **dedicarse** *vr*: **~se a** to devote o.s. to; (*hacer algo*) doing sth; (*carrera, estudio*) to go in for, take up; **¿a qué se dedica usted?** what do you do (for a living)?

dedicatoria *nf* (*de libro*) dedication

dedo *nm* (*de la mano*) finger; (*del pie*) toe; (*de vino etc*) drop; **~ pulgar** thumb; **~ índice** index finger; **~ mayor** o **cordial** middle finger; **~ anular** ring finger; **~ meñique** little finger; **contar con los ~s** to count on one's fingers; **comerse los ~s** to get very impatient; **entrar a ~** to get a job by pulling strings; **hacer ~** (*fam*) to hitch (a lift); **poner el ~ en la llaga** to put one's finger on it; **no tiene dos ~s de frente** he's pretty dim

deducción *nf* deduction

deducir *vt* (*concluir*) to deduce, infer; (*Com*) to deduct

defecto *nm* defect, flaw; (*de cara*) imperfection; **~ de pronunciación** speech defect; **por ~** (*Inform*) default; **~ latente** (*Com*) latent defect

defectuoso, -a *adj* defective, faulty

defender *vt* to defend; (*ideas*) to uphold; (*causa*) to champion; (*amigos*) to stand up for; **defenderse** *vr* to defend o.s.; **~se bien** to give a good account of o.s.; **me defiendo en inglés** (*fig*) I can get by in English

defensa *nf* defence; (*Naut*) fender ▷ *nm* (*Deporte*) back; **en ~ propia** in self-defence

defensivo, -a *adj* defensive ▷ *nf*: **a la defensiva** on the defensive

defensor, -a *adj* defending ▷ *nm/f* (*abogado defensor*) defending counsel; (*protector*) protector; **~ del pueblo** (*Esp*) ≈ ombudsman

deferente *adj* deferential

deficiencia *nf* deficiency

deficiente *adj* (*defectuoso*) defective; **~ en** lacking o deficient in ▷ *nm/f*: **ser un ~ mental** to be mentally handicapped

déficit, déficits *nm* (*Com*) deficit; (*fig*) lack, shortage; **~ presupuestario** budget deficit

deficitario, -a *adj* (*Com*) in deficit; (*empresa*) loss-making

definición *nf* definition; (*Inform: de pantalla*) resolution

definir *vt* (*determinar*) to determine, establish; (*decidir, Inform*) to define; (*aclarar*) to clarify

definitivo, -a *adj* (*edición, texto*) definitive; (*fecha*) definite; **en definitiva** definitively; (*en conclusión*) finally; (*en resumen*) in short

deforestación *nf* deforestation

deformación *nf* (*alteración*) deformation; (*Radio etc*) distortion

deformar *vt* (*gen*) to deform; **deformarse** *vr* to become deformed

deforme *adj* (*sin forma*) deformed; (*feo*) ugly; (*mal hecho*) misshapen

defraudar *vt* (*decepcionar*) to disappoint; (*estafar*) to defraud; **~ impuestos** to evade tax

defunción *nf* decease, demise

degeneración *nf* (*de las células*) degeneration; (*moral*) degeneracy

degenerar *vi* to degenerate; (*empeorar*) to get worse

degollar *vt* to slaughter

degradar *vt* to debase, degrade; (*Inform: datos*) to corrupt; **degradarse** *vr* to demean o.s.

degustación *nf* sampling, tasting

deificar *vt* (*persona*) to deify

dejadez *nf* (*negligencia*) neglect; (*descuido*) untidiness, carelessness

dejado, -a *adj* (*desaliñado*) slovenly; (*negligente*) careless; (*indolente*) lazy

dejar *vt* (*gen*) to leave; (*permitir*) to allow, let; (*prestar*) to lend; (*familia*) to abandon; (*actividad,* *empleo*) to give up ▷ *vi*: ~ **de** to stop; **dejarse** *vr* (*abandonarse*) to let o.s. go; **he dejado las llaves en la mesa** I've left the keys on the table; **su novio la ha dejado** her fiancé has left her; **dejó todo su dinero a sus hijos** he left all his money to his children; **te dejo en tu casa** I'll drop you off at your place; **déjame tranquilo** leave me alone; **deja mucho que desear** it leaves a lot to be desired; **mis padres no me dejan salir de noche** my parents won't let me go out at night; **le dejé mi libro de matemáticas** I lent him my maths book, he borrowed my maths book; **dejó el esquí después del accidente** he gave up skiing after the accident; **¡déjalo ya!** don't worry about it!; ~ **a un lado** to leave *o* set aside; ~ **caer** to drop; ~ **entrar/salir** to let in/out; ~ **pasar** to let through; **no puedo ~ de fumar** I can't give up smoking; **no dejes de visitarles** don't fail to visit them; **no dejes de comprar un billete** make sure you buy a ticket; **se dejó el bolso en un taxi** she left her bag in a taxi; ~**se persuadir** to allow o.s. to *o* let o.s. be persuaded; ~**se barba** to grow a beard; ~**se el pelo largo** to grow one's hair long; **¡déjate de tonterías!** stop messing about!

dejo *nm* (*Ling*) accent

del = **de**+**el**; *ver* **de**

delantal *nm* apron

delante *adv* in front; (*enfrente*) opposite; (*adelante*) ahead ▷ *prep*: ~ **de** in front of, before; **la parte de** ~ the front part; **estando otros** ~ with others present

delantero, -a *adj* front; (*patas de animal*) fore ▷ *nm* (*Deporte*) forward ▷ *nf* (*de vestido, casa etc*) front part; (*Teat*) front row; (*Deporte*) forward line; **llevar la delantera (a algn)** to be ahead (of sb)

delatar *vt* to inform on *o* against, betray; **los delató a la policía** he reported them to the police

delator, -a *nm/f* informer

delegación *nf* (*acción, delegados*) delegation; (*Com: oficina*) district office, branch; ~ **de poderes** (*Pol*) devolution

delegado, -a *nm/f* delegate; (*Com*) agent

delegar *vt* to delegate

deletrear *vt* (*tb fig*) to spell (out)

deleznable *adj* (*frágil*) fragile; (*fig: malo*) poor; (*excusa*) feeble

delfín *nm* dolphin

delgadez *nf* thinness, slimness

delgado, -a *adj* thin; (*persona*) slim, thin; (*tierra*) poor; (*tela etc*) light, delicate ▷ *adv*: **hilar (muy)** ~ (*fig*) to split hairs

deliberación *nf* deliberation

deliberar *vt* to debate, discuss ▷ *vi* to deliberate

delicadeza *nf* delicacy; (*refinamiento, sutileza*) refinement

delicado, -a *adj* delicate; (*sensible*) sensitive; (*rasgos*) dainty; (*gusto*) refined; (*situación: difícil*) tricky; (: *violento*) embarrassing; (*punto, tema*) sore; (*persona: difícil de contentar*) hard to please; (: *sensible*) touchy, hypersensitive; (: *atento*) considerate

delicia *nf* delight

delicioso, -a *adj* (*gracioso*) delightful; (*exquisito*) delicious

delimitar *vt* to delimit

delincuencia *nf*: ~ **juvenil** juvenile delinquency; **cifras de la** ~ crime rate

delincuente *nm/f* delinquent; (*criminal*) criminal; ~ **sin antecedentes** first offender; ~ **habitual** hardened criminal

delineante *nm/f* draughtsman

delinear *vt* to delineate; (*dibujo*) to draw; (*contornos, fig*) to outline; ~ **un proyecto** to outline a project

delinquir *vi* to commit an offence

delirante *adj* delirious

delirar *vi* to be delirious, rave; (*fig: desatinar*) to talk nonsense

delirio *nm* (*Med*) delirium; (*palabras insensatas*) ravings *pl*; ~ **de grandeza** megalomania; ~ **de persecución** persecution mania; **con** ~ (*fam*) madly; **¡fue el ~!** (*fam*) it was great!

delito *nm* (*gen*) crime; (*infracción*) offence

delta *nm* delta

demacrado, -a *adj* emaciated

demagogia *nf* demagogy, demagoguery

demagogo *nm* demagogue

demanda *nf* (*pedido, Com*) demand; (*petición*) request; (*pregunta*) inquiry; (*reivindicación*) claim; (*Jur*) action, lawsuit; (*Teat*) call; (*Elec*) load; ~ **de pago** demand for payment; **escribir en** ~ **de ayuda** to write asking for help; **entablar** ~ (*Jur*) to sue; **presentar** ~ **de divorcio** to sue for divorce; ~ **final** final demand; ~ **indirecta** derived demand; ~ **de mercado** market demand

demandante *nm/f* claimant; (*Jur*) plaintiff

demandar *vt* (*gen*) to demand; (*Jur*) to sue, file a lawsuit against, start proceedings against; ~ **a algn por calumnia/daños y perjuicios** to sue sb for libel/damages

demarcación *nf* (*de terreno*) demarcation

demás *adj*: **los** ~ **niños** the other children, the remaining children ▷ *pron*: **los/las** ~ the others, the rest (of them); **lo** ~ the rest (of it); **por** ~ moreover; (*en vano*) in vain; **y** ~ etcetera

demasía *nf* (*exceso*) excess, surplus; **comer en** ~ to eat to excess

demasiado, -a *adj*: ~ **vino** too much wine ▷ *adv* (*antes de adj, adv*) too; ~**s libros** too many books; **¡es ~!** it's too much!; **es ~ pesado para levantarlo** it is too heavy to lift; ~ **bien lo sé** I know it only too well; **hace ~ calor** it's too hot; **hace ~ tiempo** it was too long ago

demencia *nf* (*locura*) madness

demente *adj* mad, insane ▷ *nm/f* lunatic

democracia *nf* democracy

demócrata *nm/f* democrat

democrático, -a *adj* democratic

demoler *vt* to demolish; (*edificio*) to pull down

demolición *nf* demolition

demonio *nm* devil, demon; **¡~s!** hell!; **¿cómo ~s?** how the hell?; **¿qué ~s será?** what the devil can it be?; **¿dónde ~s lo habré dejado?** where the devil can I have left it?; **tener el ~ en el cuerpo** (*no parar*) to be always on the go

demora *nf* delay

demorar *vt* (*retardar*) to delay, hold back; (*dilatar*) to hold up ▷ *vi* to linger, stay on; **demorarse** *vr* to linger, stay on; (*retrasarse*) to take a long time; **~se en hacer algo** (*esp LAm*) to take time doing sth

demostración *nf* (*gen, Mat*) demonstration; (*de cariño, fuerza*) show; (*de teorema*) proof; (*de amistad*) gesture; (*de cólera, gimnasia*) display; **~ comercial** commercial exhibition

demostrar *vt* (*probar*) to prove; (*mostrar*) to show; (*manifestar*) to demonstrate

demostrativo, -a *adj* demonstrative

demudado, -a *adj* (*rostro*) pale; (*fig*) upset; **tener el rostro ~** to look pale

denegar *vt* (*rechazar*) to refuse; (*negar*) to deny; (*Jur*) to reject

denigrar *vt* (*desacreditar*) to denigrate; (*injuriar*) to insult

denominación *nf* (*acto*) naming; (*clase*) denomination

denominador *nm*: **~ común** common denominator

denotar *vt* (*indicar*) to indicate, denote

densidad *nf* (*Física*) density; (*fig*) thickness; **~ de caracteres** (*Inform*) pitch

denso, -a *adj* (*apretado*) solid; (*espeso, pastoso*) thick; (*fig*) heavy

dentadura *nf* (set of) teeth *pl*; **~ postiza** false teeth *pl*

dental *adj* dental

dentera *nf* (*sensación desgradable*) the shivers *pl*

dentífrico, -a *adj* dental, tooth *cpd* ▷ *nm* toothpaste; **pasta dentífrica** toothpaste

dentista *nm/f* dentist

dentro *adv* inside ▷ *prep*: **~ de** in, inside, within; **allí ~** in there; **mirar por ~** to look inside; **~ de lo posible** as far as possible; **~ de todo** all in all; **~ de tres meses** within three months

denuncia *nf* (*delación*) denunciation; (*acusación*) accusation; (*de accidente*) report; **hacer** *o* **poner una ~** to report an incident to the police

denunciar *vt* to report; (*delatar*) to inform on *o* against

departamento *nm* (*sección administrativa*) department, section; (*LAm: piso*) flat (*Brit*), apartment (*US*); (*distrito*) department, province; **~ de envíos** (*Com*) dispatch department; **~ de máquinas** (*Naut*) engine room

departir *vi* to talk, converse

dependencia *nf* dependence; (*Pol*) dependency; (*Com*) office, section; (*sucursal*) branch office; (*Arq: cuarto*) room; **dependencias** *nfpl* outbuildings

depender *vi*: **~ de** to depend on; (*contar con*) to rely on; (*autoridad*) to be under, be answerable to; **depende** it (all) depends; **no depende de mí** it's not up to me

dependienta *nf* saleswoman, shop assistant

dependiente *adj* dependent ▷ *nm* salesman, shop assistant

depilar *vt* (*con cera: piernas*) to wax; (*cejas*) to pluck

depilatorio, -a *adj* depilatory ▷ *nm* hair remover

deplorable *adj* deplorable

deplorar *vt* to deplore

deponer *vt* (*armas*) to lay down; (*rey*) to depose; (*gobernante*) to oust; (*ministro*) to remove from office ▷ *vi* (*Jur*) to give evidence; (*declarar*) to make a statement

deportar *vt* to deport

deporte *nm* sport

deportista *adj* sports *cpd* ▷ *nm/f* sportsman(woman)

deportivo, -a *adj* (*club, periódico*) sports *cpd* ▷ *nm* sports car

depositante *nm/f* depositor

depositar *vt* (*dinero*) to deposit; (*mercaderías*) to put away, store; **depositarse** *vr* to settle; **~ la confianza en algn** to place one's trust in sb

depositario, -a *nm/f* trustee; **~ judicial** official receiver

depósito *nm* (*gen*) deposit; (*de mercaderías*) warehouse, store; (*de animales, coches*) pound; (*de agua, gasolina etc*) tank; (*en retrete*) cistern; **~ afianzado** bonded warehouse; **~ bancario** bank deposit; **~ de cadáveres** mortuary; **~ de maderas** timber yard; **~ de suministro** feeder bin

depravar *vt* to deprave, corrupt; **depravarse** *vr* to become depraved

depreciar *vt* to depreciate, reduce the value of; **depreciarse** *vr* to depreciate, lose value

depredador, a (*Zool*) *adj* predatory ▷ *nm* predator

depresión *nf* (*gen, Med*) depression; (*hueco*) hollow; (*en horizonte, camino*) dip; (*merma*) drop; (*Econ*) slump, recession; **~ nerviosa** nervous breakdown

deprimido, -a *adj* depressed

deprimir *vt* to depress; **deprimirse** *vr* (*persona*) to become depressed

deprisa *adv* ver **prisa**

depuración *nf* purification; (*Pol*) purge; (*Inform*) debugging

depuradora *nf* (*de agua*) water-treatment plant; (*tb*: **depuradora de aguas residuales**) sewage farm

depurar *vt* to purify; (*purgar*) to purge; (*Inform*) to debug

derecha *nf, nf* right(-hand) side; **la(s) ~(s)** (*pl*) (*Pol*) the Right; **de ~s** (*Pol*) right-wing; **a la ~** (*situación*) on the right; (*dirección*) to the right; **a ~s** rightly, correctly; *ver tb* **derecho**

derecho, -a *adj* (*mano, ojo*) right; (*lado*) right-hand ▷ *nm* (*privilegio*) right; (*título*) claim, title; (*leyes*) law ▷ *adv* straight, directly; **derechos** *nmpl* (*de un sindicato*) dues; (*profesionales*) fees; (*impuestos*) taxes; (*de autor*) royalties; **me duele el ojo ~** I've got a pain in my right eye; **a mano derecha** on the right-hand side; **¡ponte ~!** stand up straight!; **"reservados todos los ~s"** "all rights reserved"; **¡no hay ~!** it's not fair!; **tener**

~ a hacer algo to have the right to do sth; **no tienes ~ a decir eso** you have no right to say that; **estudio ~** I'm studying law; **Facultad de D~** Faculty of Law; **ponte la camiseta del ~** put your T-shirt on the right way out; **~ a voto** voting right; **~s civiles** civil rights; **~s humanos** human rights; **~s de muelle** (Com) dock dues; **~s de patente** patent rights; **~ de propiedad literaria** copyright; **~ de retención** (Com) lien; **~ de timbre** (Com) stamp duty; **~ de votar** right to vote; **~s portuarios** (Com) harbour dues; **vino ~ hacia mí** he came straight towards me; **siga ~** carry straight on; ver tb **derecha**

deriva nf: **ir** o **estar a la ~** to drift, be adrift

derivado, -a adj derived ▷ nm (Ling) derivative; (Industria, Química) by-product

derivar vt to derive; (desviar) to direct ▷ vi: **derivarse** vr to derive, be derived; **~(se) de** (consecuencia) to spring from

dermoprotector, a adj protective

derramamiento nm (dispersión) spilling; (fig) squandering; **~ de sangre** bloodshed

derramar vt to spill; (verter) to pour out; (esparcir) to scatter; **derramarse** vr to pour out; **~ lágrimas** to weep

derrame nm (de líquido) spilling; (de sangre) shedding; (de tubo etc) overflow; (pérdida) leakage; (Med) discharge; (declive) slope; **~ cerebral** brain haemorrhage; **~ sinovial** water on the knee

derrapar vi to skid

derredor adv: **al** o **en ~ de** around, about

derretido, -a adj melted; (metal) molten; **estar ~ por algn** (fig) to be crazy about sb

derretir vt (gen) to melt; (nieve) to thaw; (fig) to squander; **derretirse** vr to melt

derribar vt to knock down; (construcción) to demolish; (persona, gobierno, político) to bring down

derrocar vt (gobierno) to bring down, overthrow; (ministro) to oust

derrochar vt (dinero, recursos) to squander; (energía, salud) to be bursting with o full of

derroche nm (despilfarro) waste, squandering; (exceso) extravagance; **con un ~ de buen gusto** with a fine display of good taste

derrota nf (Naut) course; (Mil) defeat, rout; **sufrir una grave ~** (fig) to suffer a grave setback

derrotar vt (gen) to defeat

derrotero nm (rumbo) course; **tomar otro ~** (fig) to adopt a different course

derruir vt to demolish, tear down

derrumbar vt to throw down; (despeñar) to fling o hurl down; (volcar) to upset; **derrumbarse** vr (hundirse) to collapse; (: techo) to fall in, cave in; (fig: esperanzas) to collapse

desabotonar vt to unbutton, undo ▷ vi (flores) to blossom; **desabotonarse** vr to come undone

desabrido, -a adj (comida) insipid, tasteless; (persona: soso) dull; (: antipático) rude, surly; (respuesta) sharp; (tiempo) unpleasant

desabrochar vt (botones, broches) to undo, unfasten; **desabrocharse** vr (ropa etc) to come undone

desacato nm (falta de respeto) disrespect; (Jur) contempt

desacertado, -a adj (equivocado) mistaken; (inoportuno) unwise

desacierto nm (error) mistake, error; (dicho) unfortunate remark

desaconsejado, -a adj ill-advised

desaconsejar vt: **~ algo a algn** to advise sb against sth

desacorde adj (Mus) discordant; (fig: opiniones) conflicting; **estar ~ con algo** to disagree with sth

desacreditar vt (desprestigiar) to discredit, bring into disrepute; (denigrar) to run down

desacuerdo nm (conflicto) disagreement, discord; (error) error, blunder; **en ~** out of keeping

desafiar vt (retar) to challenge; (enfrentarse a) to defy

desafilado, -a adj blunt

desafinado, -a adj: **estar ~** to be out of tune

desafinar vi to be out of tune; **desafinarse** vr to go out of tune

desafío nm (reto) challenge; (combate) duel; (resistencia) defiance

desaforado, -a adj (grito) ear-splitting; (comportamiento) outrageous

desafortunadamente adv unfortunately

desafortunado, -a adj (desgraciado) unfortunate, unlucky

desagradable adj (fastidioso, enojoso) unpleasant; (irritante) disagreeable; **ser ~ con algn** to be rude to sb

desagradar vi (disgustar) to displease; (molestar) to bother

desagradecido, -a adj ungrateful

desagrado nm (disgusto) displeasure; (contrariedad) dissatisfaction; **con ~** unwillingly

desagraviar vt to make amends to

desagravio nm (satisfacción) amends; (compensación) compensation

desagüe nm (de un líquido) drainage; (cañería: tb: **tubo de desagüe**) drainpipe; (salida) outlet, drain

desaguisado, -a adj illegal ▷ nm outrage

desahogado, -a adj (holgado) comfortable; (espacioso) roomy

desahogar vt (aliviar) to ease, relieve; (ira) to vent; **desahogarse** vr (distenderse) to relax; (desfogarse) to let off steam (fam); (confesarse) to confess, get sth off one's chest (fam)

desahogo nm (alivio) relief; (comodidad) comfort, ease; **vivir con ~** to be comfortably off

desahuciar vt (enfermo) to give up hope for; (inquilino) to evict

desahucio nm eviction

desairar vt (menospreciar) to slight, snub; (cosa) to disregard; (Com) to default on

desaire nm (menosprecio) slight; (falta de garbo) unattractiveness; **dar** o **hacer un ~ a algn** to offend sb; **¿me va usted a hacer ese ~?** I won't take no for an answer!

desajustar vt (*desarreglar*) to disarrange; (*desconcertar*) to throw off balance; (*fig: planes*) to upset; **desajustarse** vr to get out of order; (*aflojarse*) to loosen

desajuste nm (*de máquina*) disorder; (*avería*) breakdown; (*situación*) imbalance; (*desacuerdo*) disagreement

desalentador, -a adj discouraging

desalentar vt (*desanimar*) to discourage; **desalentarse** vr to get discouraged

desaliento nm discouragement; (*abatimiento*) depression

desaliño nm (*descuido*) slovenliness; (*negligencia*) carelessness

desalmado, -a adj (*cruel*) cruel, heartless

desalojar vt (*gen*) to remove, expel; (*expulsar, echar*) to eject; (*abandonar*) to move out of ▷ vi to move out; **la policía desalojó el local** the police cleared people out of the place

desamarrar vt to untie; (*Naut*) to cast off

desamor nm (*frialdad*) indifference; (*odio*) dislike

desamparado, -a adj (*persona*) helpless; (*lugar: expuesto*) exposed; (: *desierto*) deserted

desamparar vt (*abandonar*) to desert, abandon; (*Jur*) to leave defenceless; (*barco*) to abandon

desandar vt: ~ **lo andado** o **el camino** to retrace one's steps

desangrar vt to bleed; (*fig: persona*) to bleed dry; (*lago*) to drain; **desangrarse** vr to lose a lot of blood; (*morir*) to bleed to death

desanimado, -a adj (*persona*) downhearted; (*espectáculo, fiesta*) dull

desanimar vt (*desalentar*) to discourage; (*deprimir*) to depress; **desanimarse** vr to lose heart

desapacible adj unpleasant

desaparecer vi to disappear; (*el sol, la luz*) to vanish; (*desaparecer de vista*) to drop out of sight; (*efectos, señales*) to wear off ▷ vt (*esp LAm Pol*) to cause to disappear

desaparecido, -a adj missing; (*especie*) extinct ▷ nm/f (*LAm Pol*) kidnapped o missing person

desaparición nf disappearance; (*de especie etc*) extinction

desapasionado, -a adj dispassionate, impartial

desapego nm (*frialdad*) coolness; (*distancia*) detachment

desapercibido, -a adj unnoticed; (*desprevenido*) unprepared; **pasar** ~ to go unnoticed

desaprensivo, -a adj unscrupulous

desaprobar vt (*reprobar*) to disapprove of; (*condenar*) to condemn; (*no consentir*) to reject

desaprovechado, -a adj (*oportunidad, tiempo*) wasted; (*estudiante*) slack

desaprovechar vt to waste; (*talento*) not to use to the full ▷ vi (*perder terreno*) to lose ground

desarmar vt (*Mil, fig*) to disarm; (*Tec*) to take apart, dismantle

desarme nm disarmament

desarraigar vt to uproot; (*fig: costumbre*) to root out; (: *persona*) to banish

desarraigo nm uprooting

desarreglado, -a adj (*desordenado*) disorderly, untidy; (*hábitos*) irregular

desarreglar vt to mess up; (*desordenar*) to disarrange; (*trastocar*) to upset, disturb

desarreglo nm (*de casa, persona*) untidiness; (*desorden*) disorder; (*Tec*) trouble; (*Med*) upset; **viven en el mayor** ~ they live in complete chaos

desarrollar vt (*gen*) to develop; (*extender*) to unfold; (*teoría*) to explain; **desarrollarse** vr to develop; (*extenderse*) to open (out); (*película*) to develop; (*fig*) to grow; (*tener lugar*) to take place; **aquí desarrollan un trabajo muy importante** they carry on very important work here; **la acción se desarrolla en Roma** (*Cine etc*) the scene is set in Rome

desarrollo nm development; (*de acontecimientos*) unfolding; (*de industria, mercado*) expansion, growth; **país en vías de** ~ developing country; **la industria está en pleno** ~ industry is expanding steadily

desarticular vt (*huesos*) to dislocate, put out of joint; (*objeto*) to take apart; (*grupo terrorista etc*) to break up

desaseo nm (*suciedad*) dirtiness; (*desarreglo*) untidiness

desasir vt to loosen; **desasirse** vr to extricate o.s.; ~**se de** to let go, give up

desasosegar vt (*inquietar*) to disturb, make uneasy; **desasosegarse** vr to become uneasy

desasosiego nm (*intranquilidad*) uneasiness, restlessness; (*ansiedad*) anxiety; (*Pol etc*) unrest

desastrado, -a adj (*desaliñado*) shabby; (*sucio*) dirty

desastre nm disaster; **¡qué ~!** how awful!; **la función fue un** ~ the show was a shambles

desastroso, -a adj disastrous

desatado, -a adj (*desligado*) untied; (*violento*) violent, wild

desatar vt (*nudo*) to untie; (*paquete*) to undo; (*perro, odio*) to unleash; (*misterio*) to solve; (*separar*) to detach; **desatarse** vr (*zapatos*) to come untied; (*tormenta*) to break; (*perder control de sí*) to lose self-control; ~**se en injurias** to pour out a stream of insults

desatascar vt (*cañería*) to unblock, clear; (*carro*) to pull out of the mud; ~ **a algn** (*fig*) to get sb out of a jam

desatender vt (*no prestar atención a*) to disregard; (*abandonar*) to neglect

desatento, -a adj (*distraído*) inattentive; (*descortés*) discourteous

desatinado, -a adj foolish, silly

desatino nm (*idiotez*) foolishness, folly; (*error*) blunder; **desatinos** nmpl nonsense sg; **¡qué ~!** how silly!, what rubbish!

desatornillar vt to unscrew

desatrancar vt (*puerta*) to unbolt; (*cañería*) to unblock

desautorizado, -a adj unauthorized

desautorizar vt (*oficial*) to deprive of authority; (*informe*) to deny

desavenencia nf (*desacuerdo*) disagreement; (*discrepancia*) quarrel

desaventajado, -a adj (inferior) inferior; (poco ventajoso) disadvantageous

desayunar vi: **desayunarse** vr to have breakfast ▷ vt to have for breakfast; **~ con café** to have coffee for breakfast; **~ con algo** (fig) to get the first news of sth

desayuno nm breakfast

desazón nf (angustia) anxiety; (Med) discomfort; (fig) annoyance

desazonar vt (fig) to annoy, upset; **desazonarse** vr (enojarse) to be annoyed; (preocuparse) to worry, be anxious

desbandarse vr (Mil) to disband; (fig) to flee in disorder

desbarajuste nm confusion, disorder; **¡qué ~!** what a mess!

desbaratar vt (gen) to mess up; (plan) to spoil; (deshacer, destruir) to ruin ▷ vi to talk nonsense; **desbaratarse** vr (máquina) to break down; (persona: irritarse) to fly off the handle (fam)

desbloquear vt (negociaciones, tráfico) to get going again; (Com: cuenta) to unfreeze

desbocado, -a adj (caballo) runaway; (herramienta) worn

desbordar vt (sobrepasar) to go beyond; (exceder) to exceed; **desbordarse** vr (contenedor, río) to overflow; (entusiasmo) to erupt; (persona: exaltarse) to get carried away; **esto desborda mi tolerancia** this is more than I can tolerate; **~se de alegría** to be bursting with happiness

descabalgar vi to dismount

descabellado, -a adj (disparatado) wild, crazy; (insensato) preposterous

descabellar vt to ruffle; (Taur: toro) to give the coup de grace to

descafeinado, -a adj decaffeinated ▷ nm decaffeinated coffee, de-caff

descalabro nm blow; (desgracia) misfortune

descalificación nf disqualification; **descalificaciones** nfpl discrediting sg

descalificar vt to disqualify; (desacreditar) to discredit

descalzar vt (zapato) to take off

descalzo, -a adj barefoot(ed); (fig) destitute; **estar (con los pies) ~(s)** to be barefooted

descambiar vt to exchange

descaminado, -a adj (equivocado) on the wrong road; (fig) misguided; **en eso no anda usted muy ~** you're not far wrong there

descampado nm open space, piece of empty ground; **comer al ~** to eat in the open air

descansado, -a adj (gen) rested; (que tranquiliza) restful

descansar vt (gen) to rest; (apoyar): **~ (sobre)** to lean (on) ▷ vi to rest, have a rest; (echarse) to lie down; (cadáver, restos) to lie; **¡que usted descanse!** sleep well!; **~ en** (argumento) to be based on

descansillo nm (de escalera) landing

descanso nm (reposo) rest; (alivio) relief; (pausa) break; (Deporte) interval, half time; **día de ~** day off; **~ de enfermedad/maternidad** sick/maternity leave; **tomarse unos días de ~** to take a few days' leave o rest

descapotable nm (tb: **coche descapotable**) convertible

descarado, -a adj (sinvergüenza) shameless; (insolente) cheeky

descarga nf (Arq, Elec, Mil) discharge; (Naut) unloading

descargar vt (camión, mercancías) to unload; (golpe) to let fly; (arma) to fire; (Elec) to discharge; (conciencia) to relieve; (Com) to take up; (persona: de una obligación) to release; (de una deuda) to free; (Jur) to clear ▷ vi (río): **~ (en)** to flow (into); **descargarse** vr (persona) to unburden o.s.; (batería) to run down; **me ayudó a ~ los muebles de la camioneta** he helped me unload the furniture from the van; **descarga su mal humor sobre mí** he takes his bad moods out on me; **se ha descargado la batería** the battery has run down; **~se de algo** to get rid of sth; **~se algo de Internet** to download sth from the Internet

descargo nm (de obligación) release; (Com: recibo) receipt; (: de deuda) discharge; (Jur) evidence; **~ de una acusación** acquittal on a charge

descarnado, -a adj scrawny; (fig) bare; (estilo) straightforward

descaro nm nerve

descarriar vt (descaminar) to misdirect; (fig) to lead astray; **descarriarse** vr (perderse) to lose one's way; (separarse) to stray; (pervertirse) to err, go astray

descarrilamiento nm (de tren) derailment

descarrilar vi to be derailed

descartar vt (rechazar) to reject; (eliminar) to rule out; **descartarse** vr (Naipes) to discard; **~se de** to shirk

descascarillado, -a adj (paredes) peeling

descendencia nf (origen) origin, descent; (hijos) offspring; **morir sin dejar ~** to die without issue

descender vt (bajar: escalera) to go down ▷ vi to descend; (temperatura, nivel) to fall, drop; (líquido) to run; (cortina etc) to hang; (fuerzas, persona) to fail, get weak; **~ de** to be descended from

descendiente nm/f descendant

descenso nm descent; (de temperatura) drop; (de producción) downturn; (de calidad) decline; (Minería) collapse; (bajada) slope; (fig: decadencia) decline; (de empleado etc) demotion

descifrar vt (escritura) to decipher; (mensaje) to decode; (problema) to puzzle out; (misterio) to solve

descodificador nm decoder

descodificar vt to decode

descolgar vt (bajar) to take down; (desde una posición alta) to lower; (de una pared etc) to unhook; (teléfono) to pick up; **descolgarse** vr to let o.s. down; **~se por** (bajar escurriéndose) to slip down; (pared) to climb down; **dejó el teléfono descolgado** he left the phone off the hook

descollar vi (sobresalir) to stand out; (montaña etc) to rise; **la obra que más descuella de las suyas**

his most outstanding work

descolorido, -a adj (color, tela) faded; (pálido) pale; (fig: estilo) colourless

descompaginar vt (desordenar) to disarrange, mess up

descompasado, -a adj (sin proporción) out of all proportion; (excesivo) excessive; (hora) unearthly

descomponer vt (gen, Ling, Mat) to break down; (desordenar) to disarrange, disturb; (materia orgánica) to rot, decompose; (Tec) to put out of order; (facciones) to distort; (estómago etc) to upset; (: planes) to mess up; (persona: molestar) to upset; (irritar) to annoy; **descomponerse** vr (corromperse) to rot, decompose; (estómago) to get upset; (el tiempo) to change (for the worse); (Tec) to break down

descomposición nf (gen) breakdown; (de fruta etc) decomposition; (putrefacción) rotting; (de cara) distortion; ~ **de vientre** (Med) stomach upset, diarrhoea

descompostura nf (Tec) breakdown; (desorganización) disorganization; (desorden) untidiness

descompuesto, -a pp de **descomponer** ▷ adj (corrompido) decomposed; (roto) broken (down)

descomunal adj (enorme) huge; (fam: excelente) fantastic

desconcertado, -a adj disconcerted, bewildered

desconcertar vt (confundir) to baffle; (incomodar) to upset, put out; (orden) to disturb; **desconcertarse** vr (turbarse) to be upset; (confundirse) to be bewildered

desconchado, -a adj (pintura) peeling

desconcierto nm (gen) disorder; (desorientación) uncertainty; (inquietud) uneasiness; (confusión) bewilderment

desconectar vt to disconnect; (desenchufar) to unplug; (radio, televisión) to switch off; (Inform) to toggle off

desconfianza nf distrust

desconfiar vi to be distrustful; ~ **de** (sospechar) to mistrust, suspect; (no tener confianza en) to have no faith o confidence in; **desconfío de ello** I doubt it; **desconfíe de las imitaciones** (Com) beware of imitations

descongelar vt (nevera) to defrost; (comida) to thaw; (Auto) to de-ice; (Com, Pol) to unfreeze

descongestionar vt (cabeza, tráfico) to clear; (calle, ciudad) to relieve congestion in; (fig: despejar) to clear

desconocer vt (ignorar) not to know, be ignorant of; (no aceptar) to deny; (repudiar) to disown

desconocido, -a adj unknown; (que no se conoce) unfamiliar; (no reconocido) unrecognized ▷ nm/f stranger; (recién llegado) newcomer; **está** ~ he is hardly recognizable

desconocimiento nm (falta de conocimientos) ignorance; (repudio) disregard

desconsiderado, -a adj inconsiderate; (insensible) thoughtless

desconsolar vt to distress; **desconsolarse** vr to despair

desconsuelo nm (tristeza) distress; (desesperación) despair

descontado, -a adj: **por** ~ of course; **dar por** ~ **(que)** to take it for granted (that)

descontar vt (deducir) to take away, deduct; (rebajar) to discount

descontento, -a adj dissatisfied ▷ nm dissatisfaction, discontent

descontrol nm (fam) lack of control

descontrolarse vr (persona) to lose control

desconvocar vt to call off

descorazonar vt to discourage, dishearten; **descorazonarse** vr to get discouraged, lose heart

descorchar vt to uncork, open

descorrer vt (cortina, cerrojo) to draw back; (velo) to remove

descortés adj (mal educado) discourteous; (grosero) rude

descoser vt to unstitch; **descoserse** vr to come apart (at the seams); (fam: descubrir un secreto) to blurt out a secret; ~**se de risa** to split one's sides laughing

descosido, -a adj (costura) unstitched; (desordenado) disjointed ▷ nm: **como un** ~ (obrar) wildly; (beber, comer) to excess; (estudiar) like mad

descrédito nm discredit; **caer en** ~ to fall into disrepute; **ir en** ~ **de** to be to the discredit of

descreído, -a adj (incrédulo) incredulous; (falto de fe) unbelieving

descremado, -a adj skimmed

describir vt to describe

descripción nf description

descrito pp de **describir**

descuartizar vt (animal) to carve up, cut up; (fig: hacer pedazos) to tear apart

descubierto, -a pp de **descubrir** ▷ adj uncovered, bare; (persona) bare-headed; (cielo) clear; (coche) open; (campo) treeless ▷ nm (lugar) open space; (Com: en el presupuesto) shortage; (: bancario) overdraft; **al** ~ in the open; **poner al** ~ to lay bare; **quedar al** ~ to be exposed; **estar en** ~ to be overdrawn

descubrimiento nm (hallazgo) discovery; (de criminal, fraude) detection; (revelación) revelation; (de secreto etc) disclosure; (de estatua etc) unveiling

descubrir vt (encontrar) to discover, find; (petróleo) to strike; (inaugurar) to unveil; (vislumbrar) to detect; (enterarse de: causa, solución) to find out; (revelar: secreto) to reveal; (crimen) to bring to light, show; (naipes) to lay down; (quitar la tapa de) to uncover; (cacerola) to take the lid off; (divisar) to see, make out; (delatar) to give away, betray; **descubrirse** vr to reveal o.s.; (quitarse sombrero) to take off one's hat; (confesar) to confess; (fig: salir a la luz) to come out o to light; **Colón descubrió América en 1492** Columbus discovered America in 1492; **¡me has descubierto!** you've found me out!; **hemos descubierto sus motivos** we've found out o discovered what his motives are; **descúbrase el brazo** pull up your sleeve, please

descuento nm discount; ~ **del 3%** 3% off; **con** ~

at a discount; ~ **por pago al contado** (Com) cash discount; ~ **por volumen de compras** (Com) volume discount

descuidado, -a adj (sin cuidado) careless; (desordenado) untidy; (olvidadizo) forgetful; (dejado) neglected; (desprevenido) unprepared

descuidar vt (dejar) to neglect; (olvidar) to overlook ▷ vi: **descuidarse** vr (distraerse) to be careless; (estar desaliñado) to let o.s. go; (desprevenirse) to drop one's guard; **¡descuida!** don't worry!

descuido nm (dejadez) carelessness; (olvido) negligence; (acto) oversight; **al** ~ casually; (sin cuidado) carelessly; **al menor** ~ if my etc attention wanders for a minute; **con** ~ thoughtlessly; **por** ~ by an oversight

desde prep 1 (procedencia) from; ~ **Burgos hasta mi casa hay 30 km** it's 30 kms from Burgos to my house; **la llamaré** ~ **la oficina** I'll ring her from the office; ~ **lejos** from a distance
2 (posición): **hablaba** ~ **el balcón** she was speaking from the balcony
3 (tiempo: +adv, n): ~ **ahora** from now on; ~ **entonces/la boda** since then/the wedding; **la conozco** ~ **niño** I've known her since I was a child
4 (tiempo: +vb: con momento concreto) since; (con período de tiempo) for; **nos conocemos** ~ **1978/~ hace 20 años** we've known each other since 1978/for 20 years; **no lo veo** ~ **1983/~ hace 5 años** I haven't seen him since 1983/for 5 years; **¿~ cuándo vives aquí?** how long have you lived here?
5 (gama): ~ **los más lujosos hasta los más económicos** from the most luxurious to the most reasonably priced
6: ~ **luego (que no)** of course (not)
▷ conj: ~ **que:** ~ **que recuerde** for as long as I can remember; ~ **que llegó no ha salido** he hasn't been out since he arrived

desdecir vi: ~ **de** (no merecer) to be unworthy of; (no corresponder) to clash with; **desdecirse** vr: ~**se de** to go back on

desdén nm scorn

desdeñar vt (despreciar) to scorn

desdicha nf (desgracia) misfortune; (infelicidad) unhappiness

desdichado, -a adj (sin suerte) unlucky; (infeliz) unhappy; (día) ill-fated ▷ nm/f (pobre desgraciado) poor devil

desdoblar vt (extender) to spread out; (desplegar) to unfold

desear vt to want, desire, wish for; **¿qué desea la señora?** (en tienda) what can I do for you, madam?; **te deseo mucha suerte** I wish you lots of luck; **dejar mucho que** ~ to leave a lot to be desired; **estoy deseando que esto termine** I'm longing for this to finish

desecar vt, **desecarse** vr to dry up

desechar vt (basura) to throw out o away; (ideas) to reject, discard; (miedo) to cast aside; (plan) to drop

desecho nm (desprecio) contempt; (lo peor) dregs pl; **desechos** nmpl rubbish sg, waste sg; **de** ~ (hierro) scrap; (producto) waste; (ropa) cast-off

desembalar vt to unpack

desembarazado, -a adj (libre) clear, free; (desenvuelto) free and easy

desembarazar vt (desocupar) to clear; (desenredar) to free; **desembarazarse** vr: ~**se de** to free o.s. of, get rid of

desembarcar vt (personas) to land; (mercancías etc) to unload ▷ vi: **desembarcarse** vr (de barco, avión) to disembark

desembocadura nf (de río) mouth; (de calle) opening

desembocar vi: ~ **en** to flow into; (fig) to result in

desembolso nm payment

desembragar vt (Tec) to disengage; (embrague) to release ▷ vi (Auto) to declutch

desembrollar vt (madeja) to unravel; (asunto, malentendido) to sort out

desempatar vi to break a tie; **volvieron a jugar para** ~ they held a play-off

desempate nm (Fútbol) play-off; (Tenis) tie-break(er)

desempeñar vt (cargo) to hold; (papel) to play; (deber, función) to perform, carry out; (lo empeñado) to redeem; **desempeñarse** vr to get out of debt; ~ **un papel** (fig) to play (a role)

desempeño nm occupation; (de lo empeñado) redeeming; **de mucho** ~ very capable

desempleado, -a adj unemployed, out of work ▷ nm/f unemployed person

desempleo nm unemployment

desempolvar vt (muebles etc) to dust; (lo olvidado) to revive

desencadenar vt to unchain; (ira) to unleash; (provocar) to cause, set off; **desencadenarse** vr to break loose; (tormenta) to burst; (guerra) to break out; **se desencadenó una lucha violenta** a violent struggle ensued

desencajar vt (hueso) to put out of joint; (mandíbula) to dislocate; (mecanismo, pieza) to disconnect, disengage

desencanto nm disillusionment, disenchantment

desenchufar vt to unplug, disconnect

desenfadado, -a adj (desenvuelto) uninhibited; (descarado) forward; (en el vestir) casual

desenfado nm (libertad) freedom; (comportamiento) free and easy manner; (descaro) forwardness; (desenvoltura) self-confidence

desenfocado, -a adj (Foto) out of focus

desenfrenado, -a adj (descontrolado) uncontrolled; (inmoderado) unbridled

desenfreno nm (vicio) wildness; (falta de control) lack of self-control; (de pasiones) unleashing

desenganchar vt (gen) to unhook; (Ferro) to uncouple; (Tec) to disengage

desengañar vt to disillusion; (abrir los ojos a) to open the eyes of; **desengañarse** vr to become disillusioned; **¡desengáñate!** don't you believe it!

desengaño nm disillusionment; (decepción) disappointment; **sufrir un ~ amoroso** to be disappointed in love

desenlace nm outcome; (Lit) ending

desenmarañar vt (fig) to unravel

desenmascarar vt to unmask, expose

desenredar vt to resolve

desentenderse vr: **~ de** to pretend not to know about; (apartarse) to have nothing to do with

desenterrar vt to exhume; (tesoro, fig) to unearth, dig up

desentonar vi (Mus) to sing (o play) out of tune; (no encajar) to be out of place; (color) to clash

desentrañar vt (misterio) to unravel

desentumecer vt (pierna etc) to stretch; (Deporte) to loosen up

desenvoltura nf (libertad, gracia) ease; (descaro) free and easy manner; (al hablar) fluency

desenvolver vt (paquete) to unwrap; (fig) to develop; **desenvolverse** vr (desarrollarse) to unfold, develop; (suceder) to go off; (prosperar) to prosper; (arreglárselas) to cope

deseo nm desire, wish; **~ de saber** thirst for knowledge; **buen ~** good intentions pl; **arder en ~s de algo** to yearn for sth

deseoso, -a adj: **estar ~ de hacer** to be anxious to do

desequilibrado, -a adj unbalanced ▷ nm/f unbalanced person; **~ mental** mentally disturbed person

desertar vt (Jur: derecho de apelación) to forfeit ▷ vi to desert; **~ de sus deberes** to neglect one's duties

desértico, -a adj desert cpd; (vacío) deserted

desertor, a nm/f deserter

desesperación nf desperation, despair; (irritación) fury; **es una ~** it's maddening; **es una ~ tener que ...** it's infuriating to have to ...

desesperado, -a adj (persona: sin esperanza) desperate; (caso, situación) hopeless; (esfuerzo) furious ▷ nm: **como un ~** like mad ▷ nf: **hacer algo a la desesperada** to do sth as a last resort o in desperation

desesperar vt to drive to despair; (exasperar) to drive to distraction ▷ vi: **~ de** to despair of; **desesperarse** vr to despair, lose hope

desestabilizar vt to destabilize

desestimar vt (menospreciar) to have a low opinion of; (rechazar) to reject

desfachatez nf (insolencia) impudence; (descaro) rudeness

desfalco nm embezzlement

desfallecer vi (perder las fuerzas) to become weak; (desvanecerse) to faint

desfasado, -a adj (anticuado) old-fashioned; (Tec) out of phase

desfase nm (diferencia) gap

desfavorable adj unfavourable

desfigurar vt (cara) to disfigure; (cuerpo) to deform; (cuadro, monumento) to deface; (Foto) to blur; (sentido) to twist; (suceso) to misrepresent

desfiladero nm gorge, defile

desfilar vi to parade; **~on ante el general** they marched past the general

desfile nm procession; (Mil) parade; **~ de modelos** fashion show

desfogar vt (fig) to vent ▷ vi (Naut: tormenta) to burst; **desfogarse** vr (fig) to let off steam

desgajar vt (arrancar) to tear off; (romper) to break off; (naranja) to split into segments; **desgajarse** vr to come off

desgana nf (falta de apetito) loss of appetite; (renuencia) unwillingness; **hacer algo a ~** to do sth unwillingly

desganado, -a adj: **estar ~** (sin apetito) to have no appetite; (sin entusiasmo) to have lost interest

desgarrador, a adj heartrending

desgarrar vt to tear (up); (fig) to shatter

desgarro nm (en tela) tear; (aflicción) grief; (descaro) impudence

desgastar vt (deteriorar) to wear away o down; (estropear) to spoil; **desgastarse** vr to get worn out

desgaste nm wear (and tear); (de roca) erosion; (de cuerda) fraying; (de metal) corrosion; **~ económico** drain on one's resources

desglosar vt to detach

desgracia nf misfortune; (accidente) accident; (vergüenza) disgrace; (contratiempo) setback; **por ~** unfortunately; **en el accidente no hay que lamentar ~s personales** there were no casualties in the accident; **caer en ~** to fall from grace; **tener la ~ de** to be unlucky enough to

desgraciado, -a adj (sin suerte) unlucky, unfortunate; (miserable) wretched; (infeliz) miserable ▷ nm/f (malo) swine; (infeliz) poor creature; **¡esa radio desgraciada!** (esp LAm) that lousy radio!

desgravación nf (Com): **~ de impuestos** tax relief; **~ personal** personal allowance

desgravar vt (producto) to reduce the tax o duty on

desgreñado, -a adj dishevelled

desguace nm (de coches) scrapping; (lugar) scrapyard

desguazar vt (coche) to scrap

deshabitado, -a adj uninhabited

deshacer vt (lo hecho) to undo, unmake; (maleta) to unpack; (paquete) to unwrap; (nudo) to untie; (costura) to unpick; (cama) to strip; (Tec) to take apart; (enemigo) to defeat; (diluir) to melt; (acuerdo, contrato) to break; (intriga) to solve; (proyectos) to spoil; **deshacerse** vr (desatarse) to come undone; (estropearse) to be spoiled; (descomponerse) to fall to pieces; (disolverse) to melt; (despedazarse) to come apart o undone; (Com) to dump, unload; **~se de algo** to get rid of sth; **~se en** (cumplidos, elogios) to be lavish with; **~se en lágrimas** to burst into tears; **~se por algo** to be crazy about sth

deshecho, -a pp de **deshacer** ▷ adj (lazo, nudo) undone; (roto) smashed; (despedazado) in pieces; (cama) unmade; (Med: persona) weak, emaciated; (: salud) broken; **estoy ~** I'm shattered

deshelar vt (cañería) to thaw; (congelador) to defrost

desheredar vt to disinherit

deshidratar vt to dehydrate

deshielo nm thaw

deshinchar vt (neumático) to let down; (herida etc) to reduce (the swelling of); **deshincharse** vr (neumático) to go flat; (hinchazón) to go down

deshonesto, -a adj (no honrado) dishonest; (indecente) indecent

deshonra nf (deshonor) dishonour; (vergüenza) shame

deshonrar vt to dishonour

deshora: a ~ adv at the wrong time; (llegar) unexpectedly; (acostarse) at some unearthly hour

deshuesar vt (carne) to bone; (fruta) to stone

desierto, -a adj (casa, calle, negocio) deserted; (paisaje) bleak ▷ nm desert

designar vt (nombrar) to designate; (indicar) to fix

designio nm plan; **con el ~ de** with the intention of

desigual adj (lucha) unequal; (diferente) different; (terreno) uneven; (tratamiento) unfair; (cambiadizo: tiempo) changeable; (: carácter) unpredictable

desigualdad nf (Econ, Pol) inequality; (de carácter, tiempo) unpredictability; (de escritura) unevenness; (de terreno) roughness

desilusión nf disillusionment; (decepción) disappointment

desilusionar vt to disillusion; (decepcionar) to disappoint; **desilusionarse** vr to become disillusioned

desinfectar vt to disinfect

desinflar vt to deflate; **desinflarse** vr (neumático) to go down o flat

desintegración nf disintegration; **~ nuclear** nuclear fission

desinterés nm (objetividad) disinterestedness; (altruismo) unselfishness

desistir vi (renunciar) to stop, desist; **~ de** (empresa) to give up; (derecho) to waive

desleal adj (infiel) disloyal; (Com: competencia) unfair

deslealtad nf disloyalty

desleír vt (líquido) to dilute; (sólido) to dissolve

deslenguado, -a adj (grosero) foul-mouthed

desligar vt (desatar) to untie, undo; (separar) to separate; **desligarse** vr (de un compromiso) to extricate o.s.

desliz nm (fig) lapse; **~ de lengua** slip of the tongue; **cometer un ~** to slip up

deslizar vt to slip, slide; **deslizarse** vr (escurrirse: persona) to slip, slide; (: coche) to skid; (aguas mansas) to flow gently; (error) to creep in; (tiempo) to pass; (persona: irse) to slip away; **~se en un cuarto** to slip into a room

deslucido, -a adj dull; (torpe) awkward, graceless; (deslustrado) tarnished; (fracasado) unsuccessful; **quedar ~** to make a poor impression

deslucir vt (deslustrar) to tarnish; (estropear) to spoil, ruin; (persona) to discredit; **la lluvia deslució el acto** the rain ruined the ceremony

deslumbrar vt (con la luz) to dazzle; (cegar) to

blind; (impresionar) to dazzle; (dejar perplejo a) to puzzle, confuse

desmadrarse vr (fam) to run wild

desmadre nm (fam: desorganización) chaos; (: jaleo) commotion

desmán nm (exceso) outrage; (abuso de poder) abuse

desmandarse vr (portarse mal) to behave badly; (excederse) to get out of hand; (caballo) to bolt

desmano: a ~ adv: **me coge** o **pilla a ~** it's out of my way

desmantelar vt (deshacer) to dismantle; (casa) to strip; (organización) to disband; (Mil) to raze; (andamio) to take down; (Naut) to unrig

desmaquillador nm make-up remover

desmaquillarse vr to take off one's make-up

desmarcarse vr: **~ de** (Deporte) to get clear of; (fig) to distance o.s. from

desmayado, -a adj (sin sentido) unconscious; (carácter) dull; (débil) faint, weak; (color) pale

desmayar vi to lose heart; **desmayarse** vr (Med) to faint

desmayo nm (Med: acto) faint; (estado) unconsciousness; (depresión) dejection; (de voz) faltering; **sufrir un ~** to have a fainting fit

desmedido, -a adj excessive; (ambición) boundless

desmejorar vt (dañar) to impair, spoil; (Med) to weaken

desmembrar vt (Med) to dismember; (fig) to separate

desmemoriado, -a adj forgetful, absent-minded

desmentir vt (contradecir) to contradict; (refutar) to deny; (rumor) to scotch ▷ vi: **~ de** to refute; **desmentirse** vr to contradict o.s.

desmenuzar vt (deshacer) to crumble; (carne) to chop; (examinar) to examine closely

desmerecer vt to be unworthy of ▷ vi (deteriorarse) to deteriorate

desmesurado, -a adj (desmedido) disproportionate; (enorme) enormous; (ambición) boundless; (descarado) insolent

desmontable adj (que se quita) detachable; (en compartimientos) sectional; (que se puede plegar etc) collapsible

desmontar vt (deshacer) to dismantle; (motor) to strip down; (máquina) to take apart; (escopeta) to uncock; (tienda de campaña) to take down; (tierra) to level; (quitar los árboles a) to clear; (jinete) to throw ▷ vi to dismount

desmoralizar vt to demoralize

desmoronar vt to wear away, erode; **desmoronarse** vr (edificio, dique) to fall into disrepair; (economía) to decline

desnatado, -a adj (leche) skimmed; (yogur) low-fat

desnivel nm (de terreno) unevenness; (Pol) inequality; (diferencia) difference

desnudar vt (desvestir) to undress; (despojar) to strip; **desnudarse** vr (desvestirse) to get undressed

desnudez nf (de persona) nudity; (fig) bareness

desnudo, -a adj (cuerpo) naked; (árbol, brazo) bare;

(*paisaje*) flat; (*estilo*) unadorned; (*verdad*) plain
▷ *nm/f* nude; ~ **de** devoid *o* bereft of; **la retrató
al** ~ he painted her in the nude; **poner al** ~ to
lay bare

desnutrición *nf* malnutrition

desnutrido, -a *adj* undernourished

desobedecer *vt, vi* to disobey

desobediencia *nf* disobedience

desocupado, -a *adj* at leisure; (*desempleado*)
unemployed; (*deshabitado*) empty, vacant

desocupar *vt* to vacate; **desocuparse** *vr* (*quedar
libre*) to be free; **se ha desocupado aquella
mesa** that table's free now

desodorante *nm* deodorant

desolación *nf* (*de lugar*) desolation; (*fig*) grief

desolar *vt* to ruin, lay waste

desorbitado, -a *adj* (*excesivo*) excessive; (*precio*)
exorbitant; **con los ojos ~s** pop-eyed

desorden *nm* confusion; (*de casa, cuarto*) mess;
(*político*) disorder; **desórdenes** *nmpl* (*alborotos*)
disturbances; (*excesos*) excesses; **en ~** (*gente*) in
confusion

desordenado, -a *adj* (*habitación, persona*) untidy;
(*objetos revueltos*) in a mess, jumbled; (*conducta*)
disorderly

desorganizar *vt* to disorganize

desorientar *vt* (*extraviar*) to mislead; (*confundir,
desconcertar*) to confuse; **desorientarse** *vr*
(*perderse*) to lose one's way

desovar *vi* (*peces*) to spawn; (*insectos*) to lay eggs

despabilado, -a *adj* (*despierto*) wide-awake; (*fig*)
alert, sharp

despabilar *vt* (*despertar*) to wake up; (*fig: persona*)
to liven up; (*trabajo*) to get through quickly ▷ *vi*:
despabilarse *vr* to wake up; (*fig*) to get a move
on

despachar *vt* (*vender: carne, género*) to sell, deal
in; (*billete*) to issue; (*Com: cliente*) to attend to;
(*asunto*) to do, complete; (*resolver: problema*) to
settle; (*correspondencia*) to deal with; (*fam: comida*)
to polish off; (: *bebida*) to knock back; (*enviar*)
to send, dispatch; (*mandar ir*) to send away ▷ *vi*
(*decidirse*) to get things settled; (*apresurarse*) to
hurry up; **despacharse** *vr* (*acabar*) to finish
off; (*apresurarse*) to hurry up; **me despachó un
dependiente muy educado** I was served by a
very polite sales assistant; **me despachó sin
ninguna explicación** he dismissed me without
any explanation; **¿quién despacha?** is anybody
serving?; **está despachando con el jefe** he's
busy with *o* in with the boss, he's talking to the
boss; **~se de algo** to get rid of sth; **~se a gusto
con algn** to tell sb exactly what one thinks

despacho *nm* (*oficina*) office; (: *en una casa*) study;
(*de paquetes*) dispatch; (*Com: venta*) sale (of goods);
(*comunicación*) message; ~ **de billetes** *o* **boletos**
(*LAm*) booking office; ~ **de localidades** box
office; **géneros sin** ~ unsaleable goods; **tener
buen** ~ to find a ready sale

despacio *adv* (*lentamente*) slowly; (*esp LAm: en voz
baja*) softly; **¡~!** take it easy!

desparpajo *nm* (*desenvoltura*) self-confidence;

(*pey*) nerve

desparramar *vt* (*esparcir*) to scatter; (*líquido*) to
spill

despavorido, -a *adj* terrified

despecho *nm* spite; **a ~ de** in spite of; **por ~** out
of (sheer) spite

despectivo, -a *adj* (*despreciativo*) derogatory;
(*Ling*) pejorative

despedazar *vt* to tear to pieces

despedida *nf* (*adiós*) goodbye, farewell; (*antes
de viaje*) send-off; (*en carta*) closing formula; (*de
obrero*) sacking; (*Inform*) logout; **cena/función
de** ~ farewell dinner/performance; **regalo de**
~ parting gift; ~ **de soltero/soltera** stag/hen
party

despedir *vt* (*visita*) to see off, show out; (*empleado*)
to dismiss; (*inquilino*) to evict; (*objeto*) to hurl;
(*olor etc*) to give out *o* off; **despedirse** *vr* (*dejar un
empleo*) to give up one's job; (*Inform*) to log out *o*
off; **~se de** to say goodbye to; **se despidieron**
they said goodbye to each other

despegar *vt* to unstick; (*sobre*) to open ▷ *vi* (*avión*)
to take off; (*cohete*) to blast off; **despegarse** *vr*
to come loose, come unstuck; **sin ~ los labios**
without uttering a word

despego *nm* detachment

despegue *nm* takeoff; (*de cohete*) blast-off

despeinado, -a *adj* dishevelled, unkempt

despeinar *vt* (*pelo*) to ruffle; **¡me has
despeinado entera!** you've completely ruined
my hairdo!

despejado, -a *adj* (*lugar*) clear, free; (*cielo*) clear;
(*persona*) wide-awake, bright

despejar *vt* (*gen*) to clear; (*misterio*) to clarify, clear
up; (*Mat: incógnita*) to find ▷ *vi* (*el tiempo*) to clear;
despejarse *vr* (*tiempo, cielo*) to clear (up); (*misterio*)
to become clearer; (*cabeza*) to clear; **¡despejen!**
(*moverse*) move along!; (*salirse*) everybody out!

despellejar *vt* (*animal*) to skin; (*criticar*) to
criticize unmercifully; (*fam: arruinar*) to fleece

despenalizar *vt* to decriminalize

despensa *nf* (*armario*) larder; (*Naut*) storeroom;
(*provisión de comestibles*) stock of food

despeñadero *nm* (*Geo*) cliff, precipice

despeñar *vt* (*arrojar*) to fling down; **despeñarse**
vr to fling o.s. down; (*caer*) to fall headlong

desperdicio *nm* (*despilfarro*) squandering; (*residuo*)
waste; **desperdicios** *nmpl* (*basura*) rubbish *sg*,
refuse *sg*, garbage *sg* (US); (*residuos*) waste *sg*; **~s
de cocina** kitchen scraps; **el libro no tiene** ~
the book is excellent from beginning to end

desperezarse *vr* to stretch

desperfecto *nm* (*deterioro*) slight damage;
(*defecto*) flaw, imperfection

despertador *nm* alarm clock; ~ **de viaje**
travelling clock

despertar *vt* (*persona*) to wake up; (*recuerdos*) to
revive; (*esperanzas*) to raise; (*sentimiento*) to arouse
▷ *vi*: **despertarse** *vr* to awaken, wake up ▷ *nm*
awakening; **~se a la realidad** to wake up to
reality

despiadado, -a *adj* (*ataque*) merciless; (*persona*)

heartless

despido nm dismissal, sacking; **~ improcedente** o **injustificado** wrongful dismissal; **~ injusto** unfair dismissal; **~ libre** right to hire and fire; **~ voluntario** voluntary redundancy

despierto adj awake; (fig) sharp, alert

despilfarrar vt (gen) to waste; (dinero) to squander

despilfarro nm (derroche) squandering; (lujo desmedido) extravagance

despistado, -a adj (distraído) vague, absent-minded; (poco práctico) unpractical; (confuso) confused; (desorientado) off the track ▷ nm/f (persona distraída) scatterbrain, absent-minded person

despistar vt to throw off the track o scent; (fig) to mislead, confuse; **despistarse** vr to take the wrong road; (fig) to become confused

despiste nm (Auto etc) swerve; (error) slip; (distracción) absent-mindedness; **tiene un terrible ~** he's terribly absent-minded

desplazamiento nm displacement; (viaje) journey; (de opinión, votos) shift, swing; (Inform) scrolling; **~ hacia arriba/abajo** (Inform) scroll up/down

desplazar vt (gen) to move; (Física, Naut, Tec) to displace; (tropas) to transfer; (suplantar) to take the place of; (Inform) to scroll; **desplazarse** vr (persona, vehículo) to travel, go; (objeto) to move, shift; (votos, opinión) to shift, swing

desplegar vt (tela, papel) to unfold, open out; (bandera) to unfurl; (alas) to spread; (Mil) to deploy; (manifestar) to display

despliegue nm unfolding, opening; deployment, display

desplomarse vr (edificio, gobierno, persona) to collapse; (derrumbarse) to topple over; (precios) to slump; **se ha desplomado el techo** the ceiling has fallen in

desplumar vt (ave) to pluck; (fam: estafar) to fleece

despoblado, -a adj (sin habitantes) uninhabited; (con pocos habitantes) depopulated; (con insuficientes habitantes) underpopulated ▷ nm deserted spot

despojar vt (bienes) to strip; (de su cargo) to divest; **despojarse** vr (desnudarse) to undress; **~se de** (ropa, hojas) to shed; (poderes) to relinquish

despojo nm (acto) plundering; (objetos) plunder, loot; **despojos** nmpl (de ave, res) offal sg

desposado, -a adj, nm/f newly-wed

desposar vt (pareja) to marry; **desposarse** vr (casarse) to marry, get married

desposeer vt (despojar) to dispossess; **~ a algn de su autoridad** to strip sb of his authority

déspota nm/f despot

despotismo nm despotism

despotricar vi: **~ contra** to moan o complain about

despreciar vt (desdeñar) to despise, scorn; (afrentar) to slight

desprecio nm (desdén) scorn, contempt; (desaire) slight

desprender vt (soltar) to loosen; (separar) to separate; (desatar) to unfasten; (olor) to give off; **desprenderse** vr (botón: caerse) to fall off; (: abrirse) to unfasten; (olor, perfume) to be given off; **~se de** to follow from; **~se de algo** (ceder) to give sth up; (desembarazarse) to get rid of sth; **se desprende que** it transpires that

desprendimiento nm (gen) loosening; (generosidad) disinterestedness; (indiferencia) detachment; (de tierra, rocas) landslide

despreocupado, -a adj (sin preocupación) unworried, unconcerned; (tranquilo) nonchalant; (en el vestir) casual; (negligente) careless

despreocuparse vr to be carefree; (dejar de inquietarse) to stop worrying; (ser indiferente) to be unconcerned; **~ de** to have no interest in

desprestigiar vt (criticar) to run down, disparage; (desacreditar) to discredit

desprevenido, -a adj (no preparado) unprepared, unready; **coger** (Esp) o **agarrar** (LAm) **a algn ~** to catch sb unawares

desproporcionado, -a adj disproportionate, out of proportion

desprovisto, -a adj: **~ de** devoid of; **estar ~ de** to lack

después adv afterwards, later; (desde entonces) since (then); (próximo paso) next; **poco ~** soon after; **un año ~** a year later; **~ se debatió el tema** next the matter was discussed ▷ prep: **~ de** (tiempo) after, since; (orden) next (to); **~ de comer** after lunch; **~ de corregido el texto** after the text had been corrected; **~ de esa fecha** (pasado) since that date; (futuro) from o after that date; **~ de todo** after all; **~ de verlo** after seeing it, after I etc saw it; **mi nombre está ~ del tuyo** my name comes next to yours ▷ conj: **~ (de) que** after; **~ (de) que lo escribí** after o since I wrote it, after writing it

desquite nm (satisfacción) satisfaction; (venganza) revenge

destacado, -a adj outstanding

destacar vt (Arte: hacer resaltar) to make stand out; (subrayar) to emphasize, point up; (Mil) to detach, detail; (Inform) to highlight ▷ vi: **destacarse** vr (resaltarse) to stand out; (persona) to be outstanding o exceptional; **quiero ~ que...** I wish to emphasize that...; **~(se) contra** o **en** o **sobre** to stand out o be outlined against

destajo nm: **a ~** (por pieza) by the job; (con afán) eagerly; **trabajar a ~** to do piecework; (fig) to work one's fingers to the bone

destapar vt (botella) to open; (cacerola) to take the lid off; (descubrir) to uncover; **destaparse** vr (descubrirse) to get uncovered; (revelarse) to reveal one's true character

destartalado, -a adj (desordenado) untidy; (casa etc: grande) rambling; (: ruinoso) tumbledown

destello nm (de diamante) sparkle; (de metal) glint; (de estrella) twinkle; (de faro) signal light; **no tiene un ~ de verdad** there's not a grain of truth in it

destemplado, -a adj (Mus) out of tune; (voz) harsh; (Med) out of sorts; (Meteorología) unpleasant, nasty

desteñir *vt* to fade ▷ *vi*: **desteñirse** *vr* to fade;
  esta tela no destiñe this fabric will not run
desternillarse *vr*: ~ **de risa** to split one's sides
  laughing
desterrar *vt* (*exilar*) to exile; (*fig*) to banish,
  dismiss
destetar *vt* to wean
destiempo; **a** ~ *adv* at the wrong time
destierro *nm* exile; **vivir en el** ~ to live in exile
destilar *vt* to distil; (*pus, sangre*) to ooze; (*fig*:
  rebosar) to exude; (: *revelar*) to reveal ▷ *vi* (*gotear*)
  to drip
destilería *nf* distillery; ~ **de petróleo** oil refinery
destinar *vt* (*funcionario*) to appoint, assign;
  (*fondos*) to set aside; **es un libro destinado a**
  los niños it is a book (intended *o* meant) for
  children; **una carta que viene destinada a**
  usted, a letter addressed to you
destinatario, -a *nm/f* addressee; (*Com*) payee
destino *nm* (*suerte*) destiny; (*de viajero*)
  destination; (*función*) use; (*puesto*) post,
  placement; ~ **público** public appointment;
  salir con ~ a to leave for; **con ~ a Londres** (*avión,
  barco*) (bound) for London; (*carta*) to London
destituir *vt* (*despedir*) to dismiss; (: *ministro,
  funcionario*) to remove from office
destornillador *nm* screwdriver
destornillar *vt* to unscrew; **destornillarse** *vr*
  (*tornillo*) to become unscrewed
destreza *nf* (*habilidad*) skill; (*maña*) dexterity
destrozar *vt* (*romper*) to smash, break (up);
  (*estropear*) to ruin; (*nervios*) to shatter; ~ **a algn en**
  una discusión to crush sb in an argument
destrozo *nm* (*acción*) destruction; (*desastre*)
  smashing; **destrozos** *nmpl* (*pedazos*) pieces;
  (*daños*) havoc *sg*
destrucción *nf* destruction
destruir *vt* to destroy; (*casa*) to demolish;
  (*equilibrio*) to upset; (*proyecto*) to spoil; (*esperanzas*)
  to dash; (*argumento*) to demolish
desuso *nm* disuse; **caer en** ~ to fall into disuse,
  become obsolete; **una expresión caída en** ~ an
  obsolete expression
desvalido, -a *adj* (*desprotegido*) destitute; (*sin
  fuerzas*) helpless; **niños ~s** waifs and strays
desvalijar *vt* (*persona*) to rob; (*casa, tienda*) to
  burgle; (*coche*) to break into
desván *nm* attic
desvanecer *vt* (*disipar*) to dispel; (*recuerdo, temor*)
  to banish; (*borrar*) to blur; **desvanecerse** *vr*
  (*humo etc*) to vanish, disappear; (*duda*) to be
  dispelled; (*color*) to fade; (*recuerdo, sonido*) to fade
  away; (*Med*) to pass out
desvanecimiento *nm* (*desaparición*)
  disappearance; (*de dudas*) dispelling; (*de colores*)
  fading; (*evaporación*) evaporation; (*Med*) fainting
  fit
desvariar *vi* (*enfermo*) to be delirious; (*delirar*) to
  talk nonsense
desvarío *nm* delirium; (*desatino*) absurdity;
  desvaríos *nmpl* ravings
desvelar *vt* to keep awake; **desvelarse** *vr* (*no
  poder dormir*) to stay awake; (*vigilar*) to be vigilant *o*
  watchful; ~ **se por algo** (*inquietarse*) to be anxious
  about sth; (*poner gran cuidado*) to take great care
  over sth
desvencijado, -a *adj* (*silla*) rickety; (*máquina*)
  broken-down
desventaja *nf* disadvantage; (*inconveniente*)
  drawback
desventura *nf* misfortune
desvergonzado, -a *adj* (*sin vergüenza*) shameless;
  (*descarado*) insolent ▷ *nm/f* shameless person
desvergüenza *nf* (*descaro*) shamelessness;
  (*insolencia*) impudence; (*mala conducta*) effrontery;
  esto es una ~ this is disgraceful; **¡qué ~!** what
  a nerve!
desvestir *vt*, **desvestirse** *vr* to undress
desviación *nf* deviation; (*Auto: rodeo*) diversion,
  detour; (: *carretera de circunvalación*) ring road (Brit),
  circular route (US); ~ **de la circulación** traffic
  diversion; **es una ~ de sus principios** it is a
  departure from his usual principles
desviar *vt* to turn aside; (*balón, flecha, golpe*) to
  deflect; (*pregunta*) to parry; (*ojos*) to avert, turn
  away; (*río*) to alter the course of; (*navío*) to divert,
  re-route; (*conversación*) to sidetrack; **desviarse** *vr*
  (*apartarse del camino*) to turn aside; (: *barco*) to go
  off course; (*Auto: dar un rodeo*) to make a detour;
  ~ **se de un tema** to get away from the point
desvío *nm* (*desviación*) detour, diversion; (*fig*)
  indifference
desvirgar *vt* to deflower
desvirtuar *vt* (*estropear*) to spoil; (*argumento,
  razonamiento*) to detract from; (*efecto*) to
  counteract; (*sentido*) to distort; **desvirtuarse** *vr*
  to spoil
desvitalizar *vt* (*nervio*) to numb
desvivirse *vr*: ~ **por** to long for, crave for; ~ **por**
  los amigos to do anything for one's friends
detallar *vt* to detail; (*asunto por asunto*) to itemize
detalle *nm* detail; (*fig*) gesture, token; **al** ~ in
  detail; (*Com*) retail *cpd*; **comercio al** ~ retail
  trade; **vender al** ~ to sell retail; **no pierde** ~ he
  doesn't miss a trick; **me observaba sin perder**
  ~ he watched my every move; **tiene muchos ~s**
  she is very considerate
detallista *nm/f* retailer ▷ *adj* (*meticuloso*)
  meticulous; **comercio** ~ retail trade
detectar *vt* to detect
detective *nm/f* detective; ~ **privado** private
  detective
detector *nm* (*Naut, Tec etc*) detector; ~ **de**
  mentiras/de minas lie/mine detector
detener *vt* (*gen*) to stop; (*Jur: arrestar*) to arrest;
  (: *encarcelar*) to detain; (*objeto*) to keep; (*retrasar*) to
  hold up, delay; (*aliento*) to hold; **detenerse** *vr* to
  stop; ~ **se en** (*demorarse*) to delay over, linger over
detenidamente *adv* (*minuciosamente*) carefully;
  (*extensamente*) at great length
detenido, -a *adj* (*arrestado*) under arrest;
  (*minucioso*) detailed; (*examen*) thorough; (*tímido*)
  timid ▷ *nm/f* person under arrest, prisoner
detenimiento *nm* care; **con** ~ thoroughly

detergente *adj, nm* detergent
deteriorar *vt* to spoil, damage; **deteriorarse** *vr* to deteriorate
deterioro *nm* deterioration
determinación *nf* (*empeño*) determination; (*decisión*) decision; (*de fecha, precio*) settling, fixing
determinado, -a *adj* (*preciso*) fixed, set; (*Ling: artículo*) definite; (*persona: resuelto*) determined; **un día ~** on a certain day; **no hay ningún tema ~** there is no particular theme
determinar *vt* (*plazo*) to fix; (*precio*) to settle; (*daños, impuestos*) to assess; (*pleito*) to decide; (*causar*) to cause; **determinarse** *vr* to decide; **el reglamento determina que ...** the rule lays it down o states that ...; **aquello determinó la caída del gobierno** that brought about the fall of the government; **esto le determinó** this decided him
detestar *vt* to detest
detonación *nf* detonation; (*sonido*) explosion
detonante *nm* (*fig*) trigger
detonar *vi* to detonate
detractor, a *adj* disparaging ▷ *nm/f* detractor
detrás *adv* behind; (*atrás*) at the back ▷ *prep*: **~ de** behind; **por ~ de algn** (*fig*) behind sb's back; **salir de ~** to come out from behind; **por ~** behind
detrimento *nm*: **en ~ de** to the detriment of
deuda *nf* (*condición*) indebtedness, debt; (*cantidad*) debt; **~ a largo plazo** long-term debt; **~ exterior/pública** foreign/national debt; **~ incobrable o morosa** bad debt; **~s activas/ pasivas** assets/liabilities; **contraer ~s** to get into debt
deudor, a *nm/f* debtor; **~ hipotecario** mortgager; **~ moroso** slow payer
devaluación *nf* devaluation
devaluar *vt* to devalue
devastar *vt* (*destruir*) to devastate
devengar *vt* (*salario: ganar*) to earn; (*: tener que cobrar*) to be due; (*intereses*) to bring in, accrue, earn
devoción *nf* devotion; (*afición*) strong attachment
devolución *nf* (*reenvío*) return, sending back; (*reembolso*) repayment; (*Jur*) devolution
devolver *vt* (*lo extraviado, prestado: al dueño*) to give back; (*a su sitio*) to put back; (*carta al correo*) to send back; (*Com: compra, prenda*) to bring/take back; (*dinero*) to repay, refund; (*visita, la palabra*) to return; (*salud, vista*) to restore; (*fam: vomitar*) to throw up ▷ *vi* (*fam*) to be sick; **devolverse** *vr* (*LAm*) to return; **¿me puedes ~ la cinta que te presté?** could you give me back the tape I lent you?; **me devolvieron mal el cambio** they gave me the wrong change; **te ~é el favor cuando pueda** I'll return the favour when I can; **devolví la falda porque me iba pequeña** I took the skirt back as it was too small for me; **devolvió toda la cena** he threw up his dinner; **~ mal por bien** to return ill for good; **~ la pelota a algn** to give sb tit for tat

devorar *vt* to devour; (*comer ávidamente*) to gobble up; (*fig: fortuna*) to run through; **todo lo devoró el fuego** the fire consumed everything; **le devoran los celos** he is consumed with jealousy
devoto, -a *adj* (*Rel: persona*) devout; (*: obra*) devotional; (*amigo*) **~ (de algn)** devoted (to sb) ▷ *nm/f* admirer; **los ~s** (*Rel*) the faithful; **su muy ~ servant** your devoted servant
di *vb ver* **dar**; **decir**
día *nm* day; **~ de asueto** day off; **D~ de Reyes** Epiphany (*6 January*); **~ feriado** (*LAm*) o **de fiesta** o **festivo** (public) holiday; **~ hábil/inhábil** working/non-working day; **~ laborable** working day; **~ domingo, ~ lunes** (*LAm*) Sunday, Monday; **~ lectivo** teaching day; **~ libre** day off; **¿qué ~ es?** what's the date?; **estar/poner al ~** to be/keep up to date; **el ~ de hoy/de mañana** today/tomorrow; **el ~ menos pensado** when you least expect it; **al ~ siguiente** on the following day; **todos los ~s** every day; **un ~ sí y otro no** every other day; **vivir al ~** to live from hand to mouth; **de ~** during the day, by day; **es de ~** it's daylight; **del ~** (*estilos*) fashionable; (*menú*) today's; **pan del ~** fresh bread; **de un ~ para otro** any day now; **en pleno ~** in full daylight; **en su ~** in due time; **¡buenos ~s!** good morning!; **¡hasta otro ~!** so long!
diabetes *nf* diabetes *sg*
diabético, -a *adj, nm/f* diabetic
diablo *nm* (*tb fig*) devil; **pobre ~** poor devil; **hace un frío de todos los ~s** it's hellishly cold
diablura *nf* prank; (*travesura*) mischief
diadema *nf* (*para el pelo*) Alice band, headband; (*joya*) tiara
diafragma *nm* diaphragm
diagnosis *nf inv*, **diagnóstico** *nm* diagnosis
diagnosticar *vt* to diagnose
diagonal *adj* diagonal ▷ *nf* (*Geom*) diagonal; **en ~** diagonally
diagrama *nm* diagram; **~ de barras** (*Com*) bar chart; **~ de dispersión** (*Com*) scatter diagram; **~ de flujo** (*Inform*) flowchart
dial *nm* dial
dialecto *nm* dialect
dialogar *vt* to write in dialogue form ▷ *vi* (*conversar*) to have a conversation; **~ con** (*Pol*) to hold talks with
diálogo *nm* dialogue
diamante *nm* diamond
diámetro *nm* diameter; **~ de giro** (*Auto*) turning circle; **faros de gran ~** wide-angle headlights
diana *nf* (*Mil*) reveille; (*de blanco*) centre, bull's-eye
diapositiva *nf* (*Foto*) slide, transparency
diario, -a *adj* daily ▷ *nm* (*periódico*) newspaper; (*libro diario*) diary; (*: Com*) daybook; (*Com: gastos*) daily expenses; **~ de navegación** (*Naut*) logbook; **~ hablado** (*Radio*) news (bulletin); **~ de sesiones** parliamentary report; **a ~** daily; **de** o **para ~** everyday
diarrea *nf* diarrhoea
dibujante *nm/f* (*de bosquejos*) sketcher; (*de dibujos*

animados) cartoonist; (*de moda*) designer; ~ **de publicidad** commercial artist

dibujar *vt* to draw, sketch; **dibujarse** *vr* (*emoción*) to show; ~**se contra** to be outlined against

dibujo *nm* drawing; (*Tec*) design; (*en papel, tela*) pattern; (*en periódico*) cartoon; (*fig*) description; ~**s animados** cartoons; ~ **del natural** drawing from life

diccionario *nm* dictionary

dicho, -a *pp de* **decir** ▷ *adj* (*susodicho*) aforementioned ▷ *nm* saying; (*proverbio*) proverb; (*ocurrencia*) bright remark ▷ *nf* (*buena suerte*) good luck; **mejor** ~ rather; ~ **y hecho** no sooner said than done

dichoso, -a *adj* (*feliz*) happy; (*afortunado*) lucky; ¡aquel ~ **coche!** (*fam*) that blessed car!

diciembre *nm* December

dictado *nm* dictation; **escribir al** ~ to take dictation; **los ~s de la conciencia** (*fig*) the dictates of conscience

dictador *nm* dictator

dictadura *nf* dictatorship

dictamen *nm* (*opinión*) opinion; (*informe*) report; ~ **contable** auditor's report; ~ **facultativo** (*Med*) medical report

dictar *vt* (*carta*) to dictate; (*Jur: sentencia*) to pass; (*decreto*) to issue; (*LAm: clase*) to give; (: *conferencia*) to deliver

didáctico, -a *adj* didactic; (*material*) teaching *cpd*; (*juguete*) educational

diecinueve *num* nineteen; (*fecha*) nineteenth; *ver tb* **seis**

dieciocho *num* eighteen; (*fecha*) eighteenth; *ver tb* **seis**

dieciséis *num* sixteen; (*fecha*) sixteenth; *ver tb* **seis**

diecisiete *num* seventeen; (*fecha*) seventeenth; *ver tb* **seis**

diente *nm* (*Anat, Tec*) tooth; (*Zool*) fang; (: *de elefante*) tusk; (*de ajo*) clove; ~ **de león** dandelion; ~**s postizos** false teeth; **enseñar los ~s** (*fig*) to show one's claws; **hablar entre ~s** to mutter, mumble; **hincar el** ~ **en** (*comida*) to bite into

diesel *adj*: **motor** ~ diesel engine

diestro, -a *adj* (*derecho*) right; (*hábil*) skilful; (: *con las manos*) handy ▷ *nm* (*Taur*) matador ▷ *nf* right hand; **a** ~ **y siniestro** (*sin método*) wildly

dieta *nf* diet; **dietas** *nfpl* expenses; **estar a** ~ to be on a diet

dietética *nf* dietetics *sg*; *ver tb* **dietético**

dietético, -a *adj* dietetic ▷ *nm/f* dietician; *ver tb* **dietética**

diez *num* ten; (*fecha*) tenth; **hacer las** ~ **de últimas** (*Naipes*) to sweep the board; *ver tb* **seis**

diezmar *vt* to decimate

difamación *nf* (*al hablar*) slander; (*al escribir*) libel

difamar *vt* (*Jur: hablando*) to slander; (: *por escrito*) to libel

diferencia *nf* difference; **a** ~ **de** unlike; **hacer** ~ **entre** to make a distinction between; ~ **salarial** (*Com*) wage differential

diferenciar *vt* to differentiate between ▷ *vi* to

differ; **diferenciarse** *vr* to differ, be different; (*distinguirse*) to distinguish o.s.

diferente *adj* different

diferido *nm*: **en** ~ (*TV etc*) recorded

diferir *vt* to defer

difícil *adj* difficult; (*tiempos, vida*) hard; (*situación*) delicate; **es un hombre** ~ he's a difficult man to get on with

dificultad *nf* difficulty; (*problema*) trouble; (*objeción*) objection

dificultar *vt* (*complicar*) to complicate, make difficult; (*estorbar*) to obstruct; **las restricciones dificultan el comercio** the restrictions hinder trade

difundir *vt* (*calor, luz*) to diffuse; (*Radio*) to broadcast; **difundirse** *vr* to spread (out); ~ **una noticia** to spread a piece of news

difunto, a *adj* dead, deceased ▷ *nm/f*: **el** ~ the deceased

difusión *nf* (*de calor, luz*) diffusion; (*de noticia, teoría*) dissemination; (*de programa*) broadcasting; (*programa*) broadcast

difuso, -a *adj* (*luz*) diffused; (*conocimientos*) widespread; (*estilo, explicación*) wordy

digerir *vt* to digest; (*fig*) to absorb; (*reflexionar sobre*) to think over

digestión *nf* digestion; **corte de** ~ indigestion

digestivo, -a *adj* digestive ▷ *nm* (*bebida*) liqueur, digestif

digital *adj* (*Inform*) digital; (*dactilar*) finger *cpd* ▷ *nf* (*Bot*) foxglove; (*droga*) digitalis

dignarse *vr* to deign to

dignidad *nf* dignity; (*honra*) honour; (*rango*) rank; (*persona*) dignitary; **herir la** ~ **de algn** to hurt sb's pride

digno, -a *adj* worthy; (*persona: honesto*) honourable; ~ **de elogio** praiseworthy; ~ **de mención** worth mentioning; **es** ~ **de verse** it is worth seeing; **poco** ~ unworthy

dilapidar *vt* to squander, waste

dilatado, -a *adj* dilated; (*período*) long drawn-out; (*extenso*) extensive

dilatar *vt* (*gen*) to dilate; (*prolongar*) to prolong; (*aplazar*) to delay; **dilatarse** *vr* (*pupila etc*) to dilate; (*agua*) to expand

dilema *nm* dilemma

diligencia *nf* diligence; (*rapidez*) speed; (*ocupación*) errand, job; (*carruaje*) stagecoach; **diligencias** *nfpl* (*Jur*) formalities; ~**s judiciales** judicial proceedings; ~**s previas** inquest *sg*

diligente *adj* diligent; **poco** ~ slack

diluir *vt* to dilute; (*aguar, fig*) to water down

diluvio *nm* deluge, flood; **un** ~ **de cartas** (*fig*) a flood of letters

dimensión *nf* dimension; **dimensiones** *nfpl* size *sg*; **tomar las dimensiones de** to take the measurements of

diminutivo *nm* diminutive

diminuto, -a *adj* tiny, diminutive

dimisión *nf* resignation

dimitir *vt* (*cargo*) to give up; (*despedir*) to sack ▷ *vi* to resign

Dinamarca *nf* Denmark
dinámico, -a *adj* dynamic ▷ *nf* dynamics *sg*
dinamita *nf* dynamite
dinamo, dínamo *nf (nm en LAm)* dynamo
dinastía *nf* dynasty
dineral *nm* fortune
dinero *nm* money; *(dinero en circulación)* currency;
~ **caro** *(Com)* dear money; ~ **contante (y
sonante)** hard cash; ~ **de curso legal** legal
tender; ~ **efectivo** cash, ready cash; **es hombre
de** ~ he is a man of means; **andar mal de** ~ to be
short of money; **ganar** ~ **a espuertas** to make
money hand over fist
dinosaurio *nm* dinosaur
diócesis *nf inv* diocese
Dios *nm* God; ~ **mediante** God willing; **a** ~
gracias thank heaven; **a la buena de** ~ any old
how; **una de** ~ **es Cristo** an almighty row; ~ **los
cría y ellos se juntan** birds of a feather flock
together; **como** ~ **manda** as is proper; **¡~ mío!**
(oh) my God!; **¡por ~!** for God's sake!; **¡válgame ~!**
bless my soul!
dios *nm* god
diosa *nf* goddess
diploma *nm* diploma
diplomacia *nf* diplomacy; *(fig)* tact
diplomado, -a *adj* qualified ▷ *nm/f* holder of a
diploma; *(Univ)* graduate
diplomático, -a *adj (cuerpo)* diplomatic; *(que tiene
tacto)* tactful ▷ *nm/f* diplomat
diptongo *nm* diphthong
diputación *nf* deputation; ~ **permanente** *(Pol)*
standing committee; ~ **provincial** ≈ county
council
diputado, -a *nm/f* delegate; *(Pol)* ≈ member of
parliament *(Brit)*, ≈ representative *(US)*
dique *nm* dyke; *(rompeolas)* breakwater; ~ **de
contención** dam
dirección *nf* direction; *(fig: tendencia)* trend;
(señas, tb Inform) address; *(Auto)* steering; *(gerencia)*
management; *(de periódico)* editorship; *(en
escuela)* headship; *(Pol)* leadership; *(junta)* board
of directors; *(despacho)* director's/manager's/
headmaster's/editor's office; ~ **absoluta**
(Inform) absolute address; ~ **administrativa**
office management; ~ **asistida** power-assisted
steering; **D~ General de Seguridad/Turismo**
State Security/Tourist Office; ~ **relativa** *(Inform)*
relative address; ~ **única** *o* **prohibida** one-way;
tomar la ~ **de una empresa** to take over the
running of a company
directiva *nf (norma)* directive; *(tb: **junta
directiva**)* board of directors; *ver tb* **directivo**
directivo, -a *adj (junta)* managing; *(función)*
administrative ▷ *nm/f (Com)* manager; *ver tb*
directiva
directo, -a *adj* direct; *(línea)* straight; *(inmediato)*
immediate; *(tren)* through; *(TV)* live; **en** ~
(Inform) on line; **transmitir en** ~ to broadcast
live
director, a *adj* leading ▷ *nm/f* director; *(Escol)*
head (teacher) *(Brit)*, principal *(US)*; *(gerente)*
manager(ess); *(de compañía)* president; *(jefe)*
head; *(Prensa)* editor; *(de prisión)* governor; *(Mus)*
conductor; ~ **adjunto** assistant manager; ~
de cine film director; ~ **comercial** marketing
manager; ~ **ejecutivo** executive director; ~ **de
empresa** company director; ~ **general** general
manager; ~ **gerente** managing director; ~ **de
sucursal** branch manager
dirigente *adj* leading ▷ *nm/f (Pol)* leader; **los ~s
del partido** the party leaders
dirigir *vt (esfuerzos, comentario, mirada, tráfico)* to
direct; *(acusación)* to level; *(carta)* to address; *(obra
de teatro, película)* to direct; *(orquesta)* to conduct;
(comercio, empresa) to manage; *(expedición)* to lead;
(sublevación) to head; *(periódico)* to edit; *(tesis)* to
supervise; **dirigirse** *vr:* ~**se a** to go towards,
make one's way towards; *(hablar con)* to speak
to; **se dirigió a la terminal del aeropuerto**
he made his way to the airport terminal; ~**se
a algn solicitando algo** to apply to sb for sth;
"diríjase a …" "apply to …"; **el Rey se dirigió
a la nación** the King addressed the nation; **me
dirijo a ustedes para pedirles información
sobre cursos de idiomas** I am writing to you to
ask you for information about language courses;
¿a quién va dirigida la carta? who is the letter
addressed to?; **este anuncio va dirigido a los
niños** this advertisement is aimed at children;
no ~ la palabra a algn not to speak to sb
discernir *vt* to discern ▷ *vi* to distinguish
disciplina *nf* discipline
discípulo, -a *nm/f* disciple; *(seguidor)* follower;
(Escol) pupil
Discman® *nm* Discman®
disco *nm* disc *(Brit)*, disk *(US)*; *(Deporte)* discus;
(Telec) dial; *(Auto: semáforo)* light; *(Mus)* record;
(Inform) disk; ~ **de arranque** boot disk; ~
compacto compact disc; ~ **de densidad
sencilla/doble** single/double density disk; ~
de larga duración long-playing record (LP); ~
flexible *o* **floppy** floppy disk; ~ **de freno** brake
disc; ~ **maestro** master disk; ~ **de reserva**
backup disk; ~ **rígido** hard disk; ~ **de una cara/
dos caras** single-/double-sided disk; ~ **virtual**
ramdisk
discográfico, -a *adj* record *cpd*; **casa
discográfica** record company; **sello** ~ label
disconforme *adj* differing; **estar** ~ **(con)** to be in
disagreement (with)
discontinuo, -a *adj* discontinuous; *(Auto: línea)*
broken
discordia *nf* discord
discoteca *nf* disco(theque)
discreción *nf* discretion; *(reserva)* prudence; **¡a ~!**
(Mil) stand easy!; **añadir azúcar a** ~ *(Culin)* add
sugar to taste; **comer a** ~ to eat as much as one
wishes
discrecional *adj (facultativo)* discretionary;
parada ~ request stop
discrepancia *nf (diferencia)* discrepancy;
(desacuerdo) disagreement
discrepar *vi* to disagree

discreto, -a *adj* (*diplomático*) discreet; (*sensato*) sensible; (*reservado*) quiet; (*sobrio*) sober; (*mediano*) fair, fairly good; **le daremos un plazo** ~ we'll allow him a reasonable time

discriminación *nf* discrimination

discriminar *vt* to discriminate against; (*diferenciar*) to discriminate between

disculpa *nf* excuse; (*pedir perdón*) apology; **pedir ~s a/por** to apologize to/for

disculpar *vt* to excuse, pardon; **disculparse** *vr* (*dispensarse*) to excuse o.s.; (*pedir disculpas*) to apologize

discurrir *vt* to contrive, think up ▷ *vi* (*pensar, reflexionar*) to think, meditate; (*recorrer*) to roam, wander; (*río*) to flow; (*el tiempo*) to pass, flow by

discurso *nm* speech; ~ **de clausura** closing speech; **pronunciar un** ~ to make a speech

discusión *nf* (*diálogo*) discussion; (*riña*) argument; **tener una** ~ to have an argument

discutible *adj* debatable; **de mérito** ~ of dubious worth

discutir *vt* (*debatir*) to discuss; (*pelear*) to argue about; (*contradecir*) to argue against ▷ *vi* to discuss; (*disputar*) to argue; ~ **de política** to argue about politics; **¡no discutas!** don't argue!

disecar *vt* (*para conservar: animal*) to stuff; (: *planta*) to dry

diseminar *vt* to disseminate, spread

disentir *vi* to dissent, disagree

diseñador, a *nm/f* designer

diseñar *vt* to design

diseño *nm* (*Tec*) design; (*Arte*) drawing; (*Costura*) pattern; **de ~ italiano** Italian-designed; ~ **asistido por ordenador** computer-assisted design, CAD

disfraz *nm* (*máscara*) disguise; (*traje*) fancy dress; (*excusa*) pretext; **bajo el** ~ **de** under the cloak of

disfrazar *vt* to disguise; **disfrazarse** *vr* to dress (o.s.) up; **~se de** to disguise o.s. as

disfrutar *vt* to enjoy ▷ *vi* to enjoy o.s.; **¡que disfrutes!** have a good time; ~ **de** to enjoy, possess; ~ **de buena salud** to enjoy good health

disgregar *vt* (*desintegrar*) to disintegrate; (*manifestantes*) to disperse; **disgregarse** *vr* to disintegrate, break up

disgustar *vt* (*sentar mal*) to upset; (*no gustar*) to displease; (*contrariar, enojar*) to annoy; **disgustarse** *vr* (*enfadarse*) to be annoyed; (*dos amigos*) to fall out; **estaba muy disgustado con el asunto** he was very upset about the affair

disgusto *nm* (*repugnancia*) disgust; (*contrariedad*) annoyance; (*desagrado*) displeasure; (*tristeza*) grief; (*riña*) quarrel; (*avería*) misfortune; **hacer algo a** ~ to do sth unwillingly; **matar a algn a ~s** to drive sb to distraction

disidente *nm* dissident

disimular *vt* (*ocultar*) to hide, conceal ▷ *vi* to dissemble

disipar *vt* (*duda, temor*) to dispel; (*esperanza*) to destroy; (*fortuna*) to squander; **disiparse** *vr* (*nubes*) to vanish; (*dudas*) to be dispelled; (*indisciplinarse*) to dissipate

dislexia *nf* dyslexia

dislocar *vt* (*gen*) to dislocate; (*tobillo*) to sprain

disminución *nf* diminution

disminuido, -a *nm/f*: ~ **mental/físico** mentally/physically-handicapped person

disminuir *vt* (*en número, cantidad*) to decrease, diminish; (*en coste, peligro*) to lessen; (*temperatura*) to lower; (*gastos, raciones*) to cut down, reduce; (*dolor*) to relieve; (*autoridad, prestigio*) to weaken; (*entusiasmo*) to damp ▷ *vi* (*precios, temperatura*) to drop, fall; (*velocidad*) to slacken; (*población*) to decrease; (*beneficios, número*) to fall off; (*memoria, vista*) to fail; **hemos conseguido ~ los gastos** we've managed to bring down *o* cut down *o* reduce the costs; **una forma de ~ las posibilidades de contagio** a way of reducing the risk of contagion; **ha disminuido el número de accidentes** the number of accidents has fallen

disolución *nf* (*acto*) dissolution; (*Química*) solution; (*Com*) liquidation; (*moral*) dissoluteness

disolvente *nm* solvent, thinner

disolver (*gen*) to dissolve; (*manifestación*) to break up; **disolverse** *vr* to dissolve; (*Com*) to go into liquidation

dispar *adj* (*distinto*) different; (*irregular*) uneven

disparar *vt, vi* to shoot, fire; **dispararse** *vr* (*arma de fuego*) to go off; (*persona: marcharse*) to rush off; (*caballo*) to bolt; (*enojarse*) to lose control

disparatado, -a *adj* crazy

disparate *nm* (*tontería*) foolish remark; (*error*) blunder; **decir ~s** to talk nonsense; **¡qué ~!** how absurd!; **costar un** ~ to cost a hell of a lot

disparo *nm* shot; (*acto*) firing; **disparos** *nmpl* shooting *sg*, (exchange of) shots (*sg*); ~ **inicial** (*de cohete*) blast-off

dispensar *vt* to dispense; (*ayuda*) to give; (*honores*) to grant; (*disculpar*) to excuse; **¡usted dispense!** I beg your pardon!; ~ **a algn de hacer algo** to excuse sb from doing sth

dispersar *vt* to disperse; (*manifestación*) to break up; **dispersarse** *vr* to scatter

disperso, -a *adj* scattered

disponer *vt* (*dictaminar: ley*) to provide; (*juez, general*) to order; (*colocar*) to arrange; (*ordenar*) to put in order; (*preparar*) to prepare, get ready ▷ *vi*: ~ **de** to have, own; **disponerse** *vr*: **~se para** to prepare to, prepare for; **la ley dispone que ...** the law provides that ...; **el juez dispuso su puesta en libertad** the judge ordered his release; **dispusieron las sillas en un círculo** they arranged the chairs in a circle; **disponéis de diez minutos para leer las preguntas** you have ten minutes to read the questions; **no puede ~ de esos bienes** she cannot dispose of those properties; **me disponía a salir cuando sonó el teléfono** I was getting ready to go out when the phone rang

disponible *adj* available; (*tiempo*) spare; (*dinero*) on hand

disposición *nf* arrangement, disposition;

(*de casa, Inform*) layout; (*ley*) order; (*cláusula*) provision; (*aptitud*) aptitude; **~ de ánimo** attitude of mind; **última ~** last will and testament; **a la ~ de** at the disposal of; **a su ~** at your service

dispositivo *nm* device, mechanism; **~ de alimentación** hopper; **~ de almacenaje** storage device; **~ periférico** peripheral (device); **~ de seguridad** safety catch; (*fig*) security measure

dispuesto, -a *pp de* **disponer** ▷ *adj* (*arreglado*) arranged; (*preparado*) disposed; (*persona: dinámico*) bright; **estar ~/poco ~ a hacer algo** to be inclined/reluctant to do sth

disputa *nf* (*discusión*) dispute, argument; (*controversia*) controversy

disputar *vt* (*discutir*) to dispute, question; (*contender*) to contend for ▷ *vi* to argue

disquete *nm* (*Inform*) diskette, floppy disk

disquetera *nf* disk drive

distancia *nf* distance; (*de tiempo*) interval; **~ de parada** braking distance; **~ del suelo** (*Auto etc*) height off the ground; **a gran** *o* **a larga ~** long-distance; **mantenerse a ~** to keep one's distance; (*fig*) to remain aloof; **guardar las ~s** to keep one's distance

distanciar *vt* to space out; **distanciarse** *vr* to become estranged

distante *adj* distant

distar *vi*: **dista 5 kms de aquí** it is 5 kms from here; **¿dista mucho?** is it far?; **dista mucho de la verdad** it's very far from the truth

distensión *nf* distension; (*Pol*) détente; **~ muscular** (*Med*) muscular strain

distinción *nf* distinction; (*elegancia*) elegance; (*honor*) honour; **a ~ de** unlike; **sin ~** indiscriminately; **sin ~ de edades** irrespective of age

distinguido, -a *adj* distinguished; (*famoso*) prominent, well-known; (*elegante*) elegant

distinguir *vt* (*diferenciar*) to distinguish; (*divisar*) to make out; (*caracterizar*) to mark out; **distinguirse** *vr* to be distinguished; (*destacarse*) to distinguish o.s.; **resulta difícil ~ el macho de la hembra** it's difficult to distinguish the male from the female; **no distingue entre el rojo y el verde** he can't tell the difference between red and green; **no sé ~ entre un coche u otro** I can't tell one car from another; **se parecen tanto que no los distingo** they're so alike that I can't tell them apart; **no pude ~la entre tanta gente** I couldn't make her out amongst so many people; **a lo lejos no se distingue** it's not visible from a distance; **se distinguía por su elegancia en el vestir** he was famous *o* known for dressing stylishly; **no le gusta ~se de los demás** he doesn't like to stand out

distintivo, -a *adj* distinctive; (*signo*) distinguishing ▷ *nm* (*de policía etc*) badge; (*fig*) characteristic

distinto, -a *adj* different; (*claro*) clear; **~s** several, various

distorsión *nf* (*Anat*) twisting; (*Radio etc*) distortion

distorsionar *vt, vi* to distort

distracción *nf* distraction; (*pasatiempo*) hobby, pastime; (*olvido*) absent-mindedness, distraction

distraer *vt* (*atención*) to distract; (*entretener*) to amuse; (*fondos: Econ*) to embezzle ▷ *vi* to be relaxing; **distraerse** *vr* (*despistarse*) to allow one's attention to wander; (*entretenerse*) to amuse o.s.; **no me distraigas, que tengo trabajo** don't distract me. I've got work to do; **~ a algn de su pensamiento** to divert sb from his train of thought; **les pondré un vídeo para ~los** I'll put a video on to keep them entertained *o* amused; **me distrae mucho escuchar música** I really enjoy listening to music; **ir de pesca distrae** fishing is relaxing; **me distraje un momento y me pasé de parada** I let my mind wander for a minute and missed my stop

distraído, -a *adj* (*gen*) absent-minded; (*desatento*) inattentive; (*entretenido*) amusing ▷ *nm*: **hacerse el ~** to pretend not to notice; **con aire ~** idly; **me miró distraída** she gave me a casual glance

distribuidor, a *nm/f* (*persona: gen*) distributor; (: *Correos*) sorter; (: *Com*) dealer; **su ~ habitual** your regular dealer

distribuir *vt* to distribute; (*prospectos*) to hand out; (*cartas*) to deliver; (*trabajo*) to allocate; (*premios*) to award; (*dividendos*) to pay; (*peso*) to distribute; (*Arq*) to plan

distrito *nm* (*sector, territorio*) region; (*barrio*) district; **~ electoral** constituency; **~ postal** postal district

disturbio *nm* disturbance; (*desorden*) riot; **los ~s** the troubles

disuadir *vt* to dissuade

disuelto *pp de* **disolver**

disyuntiva *nf* (*dilema*) dilemma

DIU *nm abr* (= *dispositivo intrauterino*) I.U.D.

diurno, -a *adj* day *cpd*, diurnal

divagar *vi* (*desviarse*) to digress

diván *nm* divan

divergencia *nf* divergence

diversidad *nf* diversity, variety

diversificar *vt* to diversify

diversión *nf* (*entretenimiento*) fun, entertainment; (*actividad*) hobby, pastime

diverso, -a *adj* diverse; (*diferente*) different ▷ *nm*: **~s** (*Com*) sundries; **~s libros** several books

divertido, -a *adj* (*chiste*) amusing, funny; (*fiesta etc*) enjoyable; (*película, libro*) entertaining; **está ~** (*irónico*) this is going to be fun

divertir *vt* (*entretener, recrear*) to amuse, entertain; **divertirse** *vr* (*pasarlo bien*) to have a good time; (*distraerse*) to amuse o.s.

dividendo *nm* (*Com*): **~s** *nmpl* dividends; **~s por acción** earnings per share; **~ definitivo** final dividend

dividir *vt* (*gen: tb Mat*) to divide; (*separar*) to separate; (*distribuir*) to distribute, share out; **dividirse** *vr* (*repartirse*) to divide; (*separarse*) to split; **el libro está dividido en dos partes**

the book is divided into two parts; **dividió sus tierras entre sus tres hijas** he divided his land between his three daughters; **divide cuatro entre** *o* **por dos** divide four by two; **divide y vencerás** divide and conquer; **nos dividimos el trabajo entre los tres** we divided the work between the three of us; **se dividieron el dinero de la lotería** they shared the lottery money; **el grupo se dividió** the band split up

divino, -a *adj* divine; *(fig)* lovely

divisa *nf (emblema, moneda)* emblem, badge; **divisas** *nfpl* currency *sg*; *(Com)* foreign exchange *sg*; **control de ~s** exchange control; **~ de reserva** reserve currency

divisar *vt* to make out, distinguish

división *nf* division; *(de partido)* split; *(de país)* partition

divorciado, -a *adj* divorced; *(opinión)* split ▷ *nm/f* divorcé(e)

divorciar *vt* to divorce; **divorciarse** *vr* to get divorced

divorcio *nm* divorce; *(fig)* split

divulgar *vt (desparramar)* to spread; *(popularizar)* to popularize; *(hacer circular)* to divulge, circulate; **divulgarse** *vr (secreto)* to leak out; *(rumor)* to get about

DNI *nm abr (Esp)* = **Documento Nacional de Identidad**

Dña. *abr* = **Doña**

do *nm (Mús)* C

dobladillo *nm (de vestido)* hem; *(de pantalón: vuelta)* turn-up *(Brit)*, cuff *(US)*

doblaje *nm (Cine)* dubbing

doblar *vt* to double; *(papel)* to fold; *(caño)* to bend; *(la esquina)* to turn, go round; *(película)* to dub ▷ *vi* to turn; *(campana)* to toll; **doblarse** *vr (plegarse)* to fold (up), crease; *(encorvarse)* to bend

doble *adj (gen)* double; *(de dos aspectos)* dual; *(cuerda)* thick; *(ambiguo)* two-faced ▷ *nm* double ▷ *nm/f (Teat)* double, stand-in; **dobles** *nmpl (Deporte)* doubles *sg*; **~ página** double-page spread; **con ~ sentido** with a double meaning; **una habitación ~** a double room; **~ cara** *(Inform)* double-sided; **~ densidad** double density; **~ espacio** double spacing; **el ~** twice the quantity *o* as much; **su sueldo es el ~ del mío** his salary is twice as much as mine; **comes el ~ que yo** you eat twice as much as I do; **trabaja el ~ que tú** he works twice as hard as you do; **~ o nada** double or quits; **jugar un partido de ~s** to play doubles

doblegar *vt* to fold, crease; **doblegarse** *vr* to yield

doblez *nm (pliegue)* fold, hem ▷ *nf (falsedad)* duplicity

doce *num* twelve; *(fecha)* twelfth; **las ~** twelve o'clock; *ver tb* **seis**

docena *nf* dozen; **por ~s** by the dozen

docente *adj*: **centro/personal ~** teaching institution/staff

dócil *adj (pasivo)* docile; *(manso)* gentle; *(obediente)* obedient

doctor, a *nm/f* doctor; **~ en filosofía** Doctor of Philosophy

doctorado *nm* doctorate

doctrina *nf* doctrine, teaching

documentación *nf* documentation; *(de identidad etc)* papers *pl*

documental *adj, nm* documentary

documentar *vt* to document; **documentarse** *vr* to gather information

documento *nm (certificado)* document; *(Jur)* exhibit; **documentos** *nmpl* papers; **~ adjunto** *(Inform)* attachment; **~ justificativo** voucher; **D~ Nacional de Identidad** national identity card

dogma *nm* dogma

dogmático, -a *adj* dogmatic

dólar *nm* dollar

doler *vt, vi* to hurt; *(fig)* to grieve; **dolerse** *vr (de su situación)* to grieve, feel sorry; *(de las desgracias ajenas)* to sympathize; *(quejarse)* to complain; **me duele el brazo** my arm hurts; **no me duele el dinero** I don't mind about the money; **¡ahí le duele!** you've put your finger on it!

dolor *nm* pain; *(fig)* grief, sorrow; **~ de cabeza** headache; **~ de estómago** stomach ache; **~ de oídos** earache; **~ sordo** dull ache

dolorido, -a *adj (Med)* sore; **la parte dolorida** the part which hurts

doloroso, -a *adj (Med)* painful; *(fig)* distressing

domar *vt* to tame

domesticar *vt* to tame

doméstico, -a *adj* domestic ▷ *nm/f* servant; **economía doméstica** home economy; **gastos ~s** household expenses

domiciliación *nf*: **~ de pagos** *(Com)* standing order, direct debit

domiciliar *vt* to domicile; **domiciliarse** *vr* to take up (one's) residence

domicilio *nm* home; **~ particular** private residence; **~ social** *(Com)* head office, registered office; **servicio a ~** delivery service; **sin ~ fijo** of no fixed abode

dominante *adj* dominant; *(person)* domineering

dominar *vt (gen)* to dominate; *(países)* to rule over; *(adversario)* to overpower; *(caballo, nervios, emoción)* to control; *(incendio, epidemia)* to bring under control; *(idiomas)* to be fluent in ▷ *vi* to dominate, prevail; **dominarse** *vr* to control o.s.

domingo *nm* Sunday; **D~ de Ramos** Palm Sunday; **D~ de Resurrección** Easter Sunday; *ver tb* **sábado**

dominguero, -a *adj* Sunday *cpd*

dominical *adj* Sunday *cpd*; **periódico ~** Sunday newspaper

dominicano, -a *adj, nm/f* Dominican

dominio *nm (tierras)* domain; *(Pol)* dominion; *(autoridad)* power, authority; *(supremacía)* supremacy; *(de las pasiones)* grip, hold; *(de idioma)* command; **ser del ~ público** to be widely known

don *nm (talento)* gift; **D~ Juan Gómez** Mr Juan Gómez, Juan Gómez Esq. *(Brit)*; **tener ~ de gentes** to know how to handle people; **~**

de lenguas gift for languages; **~ de mando** (qualities of) leadership; **~ de palabra** gift of the gab

donación *nf* donation

donaire *nm* charm

donante *nm/f* donor; **~ de sangre** blood donor

donar *vt* to donate

doncella *nf* (*criada*) maid

donde *adv* where ▷ *prep*: **el coche está allí ~ la farola** the car is over there by the lamppost *o* where the lamppost is; **por ~** through which; **a ~** to where, to which; **en ~** where, in which; **la casa ~ nací** the house where I was born; **la nota está ~ la dejaste** the note's where you left it; **podemos salir a cenar ~ quieras** we can go out for dinner wherever you like; **es a ~ vamos nosotros** that's where we're going; *ver tb* **adonde**

dónde *adv interrogativo* where?; **¿a ~ vas?** where are you going (to)?; **¿de ~ vienes?** where have you come from?; **¿en ~?** where?; **¿por ~?** where?, whereabouts?; **¿por ~ se va al estadio?** how do you get to the stadium?

dondequiera *adv* anywhere ▷ *conj*: **~ que** wherever; **por ~** everywhere, all over the place

doña *nf*: **D~ Carmen Gómez** Mrs Carmen Gómez

dopar *vt* to dope, drug

doping *nm* doping, drugging

dorado, -a *adj* (*color*) golden; (*Tec*) gilt

dorar *vt* (*Tec*) to gild; (*Culin*) to brown, cook lightly; **~ la píldora** to sweeten the pill

dormir *vt*: **~ la siesta por la tarde** to have an afternoon nap ▷ *vi* to sleep; **dormirse** *vr* (*persona, brazo, pierna*) to fall asleep; **~la** (*fam*) to sleep it off; **~ la mona** (*fam*) to sleep off a hangover; **~ como un lirón** *o* **tronco** to sleep like a log; **~ a pierna suelta** to sleep soundly

dormitar *vi* to doze

dormitorio *nm* bedroom; **~ común** dormitory

dorsal *adj* dorsal ▷ *nm* (*Deporte*) number

dorso *nm* back; **escribir algo al ~** to write sth on the back; **"vease al ~"** "see other side", "please turn over"

dos *num* two; (*fecha*) second; **los ~** the two of them, both of them; **cada ~ por tres** every five minutes; **de ~ en ~** in twos; **estamos a ~** (*Tenis*) the score is deuce; *ver tb* **seis**

doscientos, -as *num* two hundred

dosis *nf inv* dose, dosage

dossier *nm* dossier, file

dotado, -a *adj* gifted; **~ de** (*persona*) endowed with; (*máquina*) equipped with

dotar *vt* to endow; (*Tec*) to fit; (*barco*) to man; (*oficina*) to staff

dote *nf* (*de novia*) dowry; **dotes** *nfpl* (*talentos*) gifts

dragón *nm* dragon

drama *nm* drama; (*obra*) play

dramático, -a *adj* dramatic ▷ *nm/f* dramatist; (*actor*) actor; **obra dramática** play

dramaturgo, -a *nm/f* dramatist, playwright

drástico, -a *adj* drastic

droga *nf* drug; (*Deporte*) dope; **el problema de la ~** the drug problem

drogadicto, -a *nm/f* drug addict

drogar *vt* to drug; (*Deporte*) to dope; **drogarse** *vr* to take drugs

drogodependencia *nf* drug addiction

droguería *nf* ≈ hardware shop (*Brit*) *o* store (*US*)

dromedario *nm* dromedary

ducha *nf* (*baño*) shower; (*Med*) douche

ducharse *vr* to take a shower

duda *nf* (*incertidumbre*) doubt; (*pregunta*) query, question; **sin ~** no doubt, doubtless; **sin ~ alguna** without a doubt; **¡sin ~!** of course!; **no cabe ~** there is no doubt about it; **no le quepa ~** make no mistake about it; **no quiero poner en ~ su conducta** I don't want to call his behaviour into question; **sacar a algn de la ~** to settle sb's doubts; **tengo mis ~s** I have my doubts; **tengo una ~** I have a query; **¿alguna ~?** any questions?

dudar *vt* to doubt ▷ *vi* to doubt, have doubts; **~ acerca de algo** to be uncertain about sth; **dudó en comprarlo** he hesitated to buy it; **dudan que sea verdad** they doubt whether *o* if it's true

dudoso, -a *adj* (*incierto*) hesitant; (*sospechoso*) doubtful; (*conducta*) dubious

duelo *nm* (*combate*) duel; (*luto*) mourning; **batirse en ~** to fight a duel

duende *nm* imp, goblin; **tiene ~** he's got real soul

dueño, -a *nm/f* (*propietario*) owner; (*de pensión, taberna*) landlord(-lady); (*de casa, perro*) master (mistress); (*empresario*) employer; **ser ~ de sí mismo** to have self-control; (*libre*) to be one's own boss; **eres ~ de hacer como te parezca** you're free to do as you think fit; **hacerse ~ de una situación** to take command of a situation

dulce *adj* sweet; (*carácter, clima*) gentle, mild ▷ *adv* gently, softly ▷ *nm* sweet

dulzón, -ona *adj* (*alimento*) sickly-sweet, too sweet; (*canción etc*) gooey

dulzura *nf* sweetness; (*ternura*) gentleness

duna *nf* dune

dúo *nm* duet, duo

duodécimo, -a *adj* twelfth

dúplex *nm inv* (*piso*) flat on two floors; (*Telec*) link-up; (*Inform*): **~ integral** full duplex

duplicar *vt* (*hacer el doble de*) to duplicate; (*cantidad*) to double; **duplicarse** *vr* to double

duque *nm* duke

duquesa *nf* duchess

duración *nf* duration, length; (*de máquina*) life; **~ media de la vida** average life expectancy; **de larga ~** (*enfermedad*) lengthy; (*pila*) long-life; (*disco*) long-playing; **de poca ~** short

duradero, -a *adj* (*tela*) hard-wearing; (*fe, paz*) lasting

durante *adv* during; **~ toda la noche** all night long; **habló ~ una hora** he spoke for an hour

durar *vi* (*permanecer*) to last; (*recuerdo*) to remain; (*ropa*) to wear (well)

durazno *nm* (*LAm: fruta*) peach; (*: árbol*) peach tree

durex *nm* (*LAm: tira adhesiva*) Sellotape® (*Brit*), Scotch tape® (*US*)

dureza *nf* (*cualidad*) hardness; (*de carácter*) toughness

durmiente *adj* sleeping ▷ *nm/f* sleeper

duro, -a *adj* hard; (*carácter*) tough; (*pan*) stale; (*cuello, puerta*) stiff; (*clima, luz*) harsh ▷ *adv* hard ▷ *nm* (*moneda Hist*) five peseta coin; **el sector ~ del partido** the hardliners in the party; **ser ~ con algn** to be tough with *o* hard on sb; **~ de mollera** (*torpe*) dense; **~ de oído** hard of hearing; **trabajar ~** to work hard; **estar sin un ~** to be broke

DVD *nm abr* (= *disco de vídeo digital*) DVD

Ee

E, e *nf* (*letra*) E, e; **E de Enrique** E for Edward (*Brit*) o Easy (*US*)

E *abr* (= *este*) E

e *conj* (*delante de* i- e -hi *pero no* hie-) and; *ver tb* **y**

ebanista *nm/f* cabinetmaker

ébano *nm* ebony

ebrio, -a *adj* drunk

ebullición *nf* boiling; **punto de ~** boiling point

eccema *nm* (*Med*) eczema

echar *vt* (*lanzar*) to throw; (*agua, vino*) to pour (out); (*Culin*) to put in, add; (*dientes*) to cut; (*discurso*) to give; (*hojas*) to sprout; (*carta*) to post; (*reprimenda*) to deal out; (*cuenta*) to make up; (*freno*) to put on; (*expulsar: gen*) to throw out; (: *empleado*) to fire, sack; (: *alumno*) to expel ▷ *vi*: **~ a correr/llorar** to break into a run/burst into tears; **echarse** *vr* to lie down; **échame las llaves** throw me the keys over; **eché la carta en el buzón** I posted the letter; **tengo que ~ gasolina** I need to get petrol; **¿has echado sal a la sopa?** have you put salt in the soup?; **la chimenea echa humo** smoke is coming out of the chimney; **~ abajo** (*gobierno*) to overthrow; (*edificio*) to demolish; **~ la buenaventura a algn** to tell sb's fortune; **~ la culpa a** to lay the blame on; **~ de menos** to miss; **me eché en el sofá y me quedé dormido** I lay down on the sofa and fell asleep; **los niños se ~on al agua** the children jumped into the water; **~se atrás** to throw o.s. back(wards); (*fig*) to go back on what one has said; **~se crema** to put on cream; **~se una novia** to get o.s. a girlfriend; **~se una siestecita** to have a nap; **~se a reír** to burst out laughing

eclesiástico, -a *adj* ecclesiastical; (*autoridades etc*) church *cpd* ▷ *nm* clergyman

eclipsar *vt* to eclipse; (*fig*) to outshine, overshadow

eclipse *nm* eclipse

eco *nm* echo; **encontrar un ~ en** to produce a response from; **hacerse ~ de una opinión** to echo an opinion; **tener ~** to catch on

ecografía *nf* ultrasound

ecología *nf* ecology

ecológico, -a *adj* ecological; (*producto, método*) environmentally-friendly; (*agricultura*) organic

ecologista *adj* environmental, conservation *cpd*

▷ *nm/f* environmentalist

economato *nm* cooperative store

economía *nf* (*sistema*) economy; (*cualidad*) thrift; **~ dirigida** planned economy; **~ doméstica** housekeeping; **~ de mercado** market economy; **~ mixta** mixed economy; **~ sumergida** black economy; **hacer ~s** to economize; **~s de escala** economies of scale

económico, -a *adj* (*barato*) cheap, economical; (*persona*) thrifty; (*Com: año etc*) financial; (: *situación*) economic

economista *nm/f* economist

ecosistema *nm* ecosystem

ecu *nm* ecu

ecuación *nf* equation

ecuador *nm* equator; **(el) E~** Ecuador

ecuánime *adj* (*carácter*) level-headed; (*estado*) calm

ecuatoriano, -a *adj, nm/f* Ecuador(i)an

ecuestre *adj* equestrian

eczema *nm* = **eccema**

edad *nf* age; **¿qué ~ tienes?** how old are you?; **tiene ocho años de ~** he is eight (years old); **de ~ corta** young; **ser de ~ mediana/avanzada** to be middle-aged/getting on; **ser mayor de ~** to be of age; **llegar a mayor ~** to come of age; **ser menor de ~** to be under age; **la E~ Media** the Middle Ages; **la E~ de Oro** the Golden Age

edición *nf* (*acto*) publication; (*ejemplar*) edition; **"al cerrar la ~"** (*Tip*) "stop press"

edicto *nm* edict, proclamation

edificar *vt* (*Arq*) to build

edificio *nm* building; (*fig*) edifice, structure

Edimburgo *nm* Edinburgh

editar *vt* (*publicar*) to publish; (*preparar textos, tb Inform*) to edit

editor, a *nm/f* (*que publica*) publisher; (*redactor*) editor ▷ *adj*: **casa ~a** publishing company

editorial *adj* editorial ▷ *nm* leading article, editorial ▷ *nf* (*tb*: **casa editorial**) publishers

edredón *nm* eiderdown, quilt; **~ nórdico** continental quilt, duvet

educación *nf* education; (*crianza*) upbringing; (*modales*) (good) manners *pl*; (*formación*) training; **sin ~** ill-mannered; **¡qué falta de ~!** how rude!

educado, -a *adj* well-mannered; **mal ~** ill-mannered

educar vt to educate; (*criar*) to bring up; (*voz*) to train

educativo, -a adj educational; (*política*) education cpd

EE.UU. nmpl abr (= *Estados Unidos*) USA

efectista adj sensationalist

efectivamente adv (*como respuesta*) exactly, precisely; (*verdaderamente*) really; (*de hecho*) in fact

efectivo, -a adj effective; (*real*) actual, real ▷ nm: **pagar en ~** to pay (in) cash; **hacer ~ un cheque** to cash a cheque

efecto nm (*consecuencia*) effect, result; (*objetivo*) purpose, end; **efectos** nmpl (*personales*) effects; (*bienes*) goods; (*Com*) assets; (*Econ*) bills, securities; **hacer o surtir ~** to have the desired effect; **hacer ~** (*impresionar*) to make an impression; (*tener consecuencias*) to take effect; **la aspirina enseguida me hizo ~** the aspirin took effect on me immediately; **devolvió la pelota con ~** he put some spin on the ball; **una bomba de ~ retardado** a delayed-action bomb; **llevar algo a ~** to carry sth out; **en ~** in fact; (*como respuesta*) exactly, indeed; **~ invernadero** greenhouse effect; **~s a cobrar** bills receivable; **~s de consumo** consumer goods; **~s especiales** special effects; **~s personales** personal effects; **~s secundarios** (*Med*) side effects; (*Com*) spin-off effects; **~s sonoros** sound effects

efectuar vt to carry out; (*viaje*) to make

eficacia nf (*de persona*) efficiency; (*de medicamento etc*) effectiveness

eficaz adj (*persona*) efficient; (*acción*) effective

eficiente adj efficient

efusivo, -a adj effusive; **mis más efusivas gracias** my warmest thanks

EGB nf abr (*Esp Escol*: = *Educación General Básica*) *primary education for 6-14 year olds*

egipcio, -a adj, nm/f Egyptian

Egipto nm Egypt

egoísmo nm egoism

egoísta adj egoistical, selfish ▷ nm/f egoist

egregio, -a adj eminent, distinguished

Eire nm Eire

ej. abr (= *ejemplo*) ex.

eje nm (*Geo, Mat*) axis; (*Pol, fig*) axis, main line; (*de rueda*) axle; (*de máquina*) shaft, spindle

ejecución nf execution; (*cumplimiento*) fulfilment; (*actuación*) performance; (*Jur: embargo de deudor*) attachment

ejecutar vt to execute, carry out; (*matar*) to execute; (*cumplir*) to fulfil; (*Mus*) to perform; (*Jur: embargar*) to attach, distrain; (*deseos*) to fulfil; (*Inform*) to run

ejecutivo, -a adj, nm/f executive; **el (poder) ~** the Executive (Power)

ejemplar adj exemplary ▷ nm example; (*Zool*) specimen; (*de libro*) copy; (*de periódico*) number, issue; **~ de regalo** complimentary copy; **sin ~** unprecedented

ejemplo nm example; (*caso*) instance; **por ~** for example; **dar ~** to set an example

ejercer vt to exercise; (*funciones*) to perform;

(*negocio*) to manage; (*influencia*) to exert; (*un oficio*) to practise; (*poder*) to wield ▷ vi: **- de** to practise as

ejercicio nm exercise; (*Mil*) drill; (*Com*) fiscal o financial year; (*período*) tenure; **~ acrobático** (*Aviat*) stunt; **~ comercial** business year; **~s espirituales** (*Rel*) retreat sg; **hacer ~** to take exercise

ejercitar vt to exercise; (*Mil*) to drill

ejército nm army; **E~ del Aire/de Tierra** Air Force/Army; **~ de ocupación** army of occupation; **~ permanente** standing army; **entrar en el ~** to join the army, join up

ejote nm (*CAm, Méx*) green bean

el (*f* la, *pl* los, las, *neutro* lo) art def 1 (*con un objeto definido o único*) the; **el libro/la mesa/los estudiantes/las flores** the book/table/students/flowers; **el sol** the sun

2 (*con sustantivos abstractos, generales o propios: no se traduce*): **el amor/la juventud** love/youth; **me gusta el fútbol** I like football; **no me gusta el pescado** I don't like fish; **está en la cama** she's in bed; **el Conde Drácula** Count Dracula; **ha llamado el Sr. Sendra** Mr. Sendra called

3 (*posesión o con partes del cuerpo: se traduce a menudo por adj posesivo*): **romperse el brazo** to break one's arm; **levantó la mano** he put his hand up; **se puso el sombrero** she put her hat on

4 (*valor descriptivo*): **tener la boca grande/los ojos azules** to have a big mouth/blue eyes

5 (*con días*) on; **me iré el viernes** I'll leave on Friday; **los domingos suelo ir a nadar** on Sundays I generally go swimming; **el lunes que viene** next Monday

6 (*lo + adj*): **lo difícil/caro es...** what is difficult/expensive is...; (*cuán*): **no se da cuenta de lo pesado que es** he doesn't realize how boring he is

▷ *pron demos* **1**: **mi libro y el de usted** my book and yours; **las de Pepe son mejores** Pepe's are better; **no la(s) blanca(s) sino la(s) gris(es)** not the white one(s) but the grey one(s)

2: **lo de: lo de ayer** what happened yesterday; **lo de las facturas** that business about the invoices

▷ *pron relativo*: **el que** etc **1** (*indef*): **el (los) que quiera(n) que se vaya(n)** anyone who wants to can leave; **llévese el/la que más le guste** take the one you like best

2 (*def*): **el que compré ayer** the one I bought yesterday; **los que se van** those who leave

3: **lo que: lo que pienso yo/más me gusta** what I think/like most

▷ *conj*: **el que: el que lo diga** the fact that he says so; **el que sea tan vago me molesta** his being so lazy bothers me

▷ *excl*: **¡el susto que me diste!** what a fright you gave me!

▷ *pron personal* **1** (*persona: m*) him; (: *f*) her; (: *pl*) them; **lo/las veo** I can see him/them; **la del sombrero rojo** the one with the red hat; **yo fui el que lo encontró** I was the one who found it

2 (*animal, cosa: sg*) it; (: *pl*) them; **lo (o la) veo** I can

see it; **los** (*o* **las**) **veo** I can see them
3: **lo** (*como sustituto de frase*): **no lo sabía** I didn't
know; **ya lo entiendo** I understand now; *ver tb*
lo; **las**; **les**
él *pron* (*persona*) he; (*cosa*) it; (*después de prep*: *persona*)
him; (: *cosa*) it; **mis libros y los de él** my books
and his
elaboración *nf* (*producción*) manufacture; **~ de
presupuestos** (*Com*) budgeting
elaborar *vt* (*producto*) to make, manufacture;
(*preparar*) to prepare; (*madera, metal etc*) to work;
(*proyecto etc*) to work on *o* out
elasticidad *nf* elasticity
elástico, -a *adj* elastic; (*flexible*) flexible ▷ *nm*
elastic; (*gomita*) elastic band
elección *nf* election; (*selección*) choice, selection;
elecciones parciales by-election *sg*; **elecciones
generales** general election *sg*
electorado *nm* electorate, voters *pl*
electoral *adj* electoral
electricidad *nf* electricity
electricista *nm/f* electrician
eléctrico, -a *adj* electric, electrical
electrificar *vt* to electrify
electrizar *vt* (*Ferro, fig*) to electrify
electro... *pref* electro...
electrocardiograma *nm* electrocardiogram
electrocución *nf* electrocution
electrocutar *vt* to electrocute
electrodo *nm* electrode
electrodomésticos *nmpl* (electrical) household
appliances; (*Com*) white goods
electroimán *nm* electromagnet
electromagnético, -a *adj* electromagnetic
electrón *nm* electron
electrónico, -a *adj* electronic ▷ *nf* electronics
sg; **proceso ~ de datos** (*Inform*) electronic data
processing
electrotecnia *nf* electrical engineering
electrotécnico, -a *nm/f* electrical engineer
elefante *nm* elephant
elegancia *nf* elegance, grace; (*estilo*) stylishness
elegante *adj* elegant, graceful; (*traje etc*) smart,
fashionable; (*decoración*) tasteful
elegía *nf* elegy
elegir *vt* (*escoger*) to choose, select; (*optar*) to opt
for; (*presidente*) to elect
elemental *adj* (*claro, obvio*) elementary;
(*fundamental*) elemental, fundamental
elemento *nm* element; (*fig*) ingredient; (*LAm*)
person, individual; (*tipo raro*) odd person; (*de
pila*) cell; **elementos** *nmpl* elements, rudiments;
estar en su ~ to be in one's element; **vino a
verle un ~** someone came to see you
elepé *nm* LP
elevación *nf* elevation; (*acto*) raising, lifting; (*de
precios*) rise; (*Geo etc*) height, altitude
elevador *nm* (*LAm*) lift, elevator (US)
elevar *vt* (*subir: nivel*) to raise, lift (up); (*precio*) to
put up; (*producción*) to step up; (*presentar: informe,
recurso*) to present; **elevarse** *vr* (*precios*) to go up;
(*edificio*) to rise; **la cantidad se eleva a ...** the

total amounts to ...; **el número de muertos se
eleva a 35** the death toll is 35; **el lugar donde se
elevaba la torre** the place where the tower rose
eliminar *vt* to eliminate, remove; (*olor, persona*) to
get rid of; (*Deporte*) to eliminate, knock out
eliminatoria *nf* heat, preliminary (round)
elite *nf*, **élite** *nf* elite, élite
elitista *adj* elitist
elixir *nm* elixir; (*tb*: **elixir bucal**) mouthwash
ella *pron* (*persona*) she; (*cosa*) it; (*después de prep*:
persona) her; (: *cosa*) it; **de ~** hers
ellas *pron ver* **ellos**
ello *pron neutro* it; **es por ~ que ...** that's why ...
ellos, -as *pron personal pl* they; (*después de prep*)
them; **~ todavía no lo saben** they don't know
yet; **yo me iré con ellas** I'll leave with them;
somos mejores que ~ we're better than them;
~ mismos themselves; **me lo dijeron ellas
mismos** they told me themselves; **de ~** theirs;
el coche era de ~ the car was theirs
elocuencia *nf* eloquence
elocuente *adj* eloquent; (*fig*) significant; **un
dato ~** a fact which speaks for itself
elogiar *vt* to praise, eulogize
elogio *nm* praise; **queda por encima de todo ~**
it's beyond praise; **hacer ~ de** to sing the praises
of
elote *nm* (*CAm, Méx: mazorca*) corn on the cob;
(: *granos*) sweetcorn
eludir *vt* (*evitar*) to avoid, evade; (*escapar*) to
escape, elude
e-mail *nm* (*gen*) e-mail; (*dirección*) e-mail address;
mandar un ~ a algn to e-mail sb, send sb an
e-mail
emanar *vi*: **~ de** to emanate from, come from;
(*derivar de*) to originate in
emancipar *vt* to emancipate; **emanciparse** *vr* to
become emancipated, free o.s.
embadurnar *vt* to smear
embajada *nf* embassy
embajador, a *nm/f* ambassador (ambassadress)
embalar *vt* (*envolver*) to parcel, wrap (up); (*envasar*)
to package ▷ *vi* to sprint
embalsamar *vt* to embalm
embalse *nm* (*presa*) dam; (*lago*) reservoir
embarazada *adj f* pregnant ▷ *nf* pregnant
woman
embarazar *vt* to obstruct, hamper;
embarazarse *vr* (*aturdirse*) to become
embarrassed; (*confundirse*) to get into a mess
embarazo *nm* (*de mujer*) pregnancy; (*impedimento*)
obstacle, obstruction; (*timidez*) embarrassment
embarazoso, -a *adj* (*molesto*) awkward; (*violento*)
embarrassing
embarcación *nf* (*barco*) boat, craft; (*acto*)
embarkation; **~ de arrastre** trawler; **~ de
cabotaje** coasting vessel
embarcadero *nm* pier, landing stage
embarcar *vt* (*cargamento*) to ship, stow; (*persona*)
to embark, put on board; (*fig*): **~ a algn en una
empresa** to involve sb in an undertaking;
embarcarse *vr* to embark, go on board;

(*marinero*) to sign on; (*LAm: en tren etc*) to get on, get in

embargar vt (*frenar*) to restrain; (*sentidos*) to overpower; (*Jur*) to seize, impound

embargo nm (*Jur*) seizure; (*Com etc*) embargo; **sin ~** still, however, nonetheless

embarque nm shipment, loading

embaucar vt to trick, fool

embeber vt (*absorber*) to absorb, soak up; (*empapar*) to saturate ▷ vi to shrink; **embeberse** vr: **~se en un libro** to be engrossed o absorbed in a book

embellecer vt to embellish, beautify

embestida nf attack, onslaught; (*carga*) charge

embestir vt (*atacar*) to attack, assault; (*toro*) to charge ▷ vi to attack

emblema nm emblem

embobado, -a adj (*atontado*) stunned, bewildered

émbolo nm (*Auto*) piston

embolsar vt to pocket, put in one's pocket

emborrachar vt to make drunk; **emborracharse** vr to get drunk

emboscada nf (*celada*) ambush

embotar vt to blunt, dull; **embotarse** vr (*adormecerse*) to go numb

embotellamiento nm (*Auto*) traffic jam

embotellar vt to bottle; **embotellarse** vr (*circulación*) to get into a jam

embragar vt (*Auto, Tec*) to engage; (*partes*) to connect ▷ vi to let in the clutch

embrague nm (*tb*: **pedal de embrague**) clutch

embriagar vt (*emborrachar*) to make drunk; (*alegrar*) to delight; **embriagarse** vr (*emborracharse*) to get drunk

embriaguez nf (*borrachera*) drunkenness

embrión nm embryo

embrollar vt (*asunto*) to confuse, complicate; (*persona*) to involve, embroil; **embrollarse** vr (*confundirse*) to get into a muddle o mess

embrollo nm (*enredo*) muddle, confusion; (*aprieto*) fix, jam

embromar vt (*burlarse de*) to tease, make fun of; (*LAm fam: molestar*) to annoy

embrujado, -a adj (*persona*) bewitched; **casa embrujada** haunted house

embrujo nm (*de mirada etc*) charm, magic

embrutecer vt (*atontar*) to stupefy; **embrutecerse** vr to be stupefied

embudo nm funnel

embuste nm trick; (*mentira*) lie; (*hum*) fib

embustero, -a adj lying, deceitful ▷ nm/f (*tramposo*) cheat; (*mentiroso*) liar; (*hum*) fibber

embutido nm (*Culin*) sausage; (*Tec*) inlay

embutir vt to insert; (*Tec*) to inlay; (*llenar*) to pack tight, cram

emergencia nf emergency; (*surgimiento*) emergence

emerger vi to emerge, appear

emigración nf emigration; (*de pájaros*) migration

emigrante adj, nm/f emigrant

emigrar vi (*personas*) to emigrate; (*pájaros*) to migrate

eminencia nf eminence; (*en títulos*): **Su E~** His Eminence; **Vuestra E~** Your Eminence

eminente adj eminent, distinguished; (*elevado*) high

emisario nm emissary

emisión nf (*acto*) emission; (*Com etc*) issue; (*Radio, TV: acto*) broadcasting; (*: programa*) broadcast, programme, program (*US*); **~ de acciones** (*Com*) share issue; **~ gratuita de acciones** (*Com*) rights issue; **~ de valores** (*Com*) flotation

emisor, a nm transmitter ▷ nf radio o broadcasting station

emitir vt (*olor etc*) to emit, give off; (*moneda etc*) to issue; (*opinión*) to express; (*voto*) to cast; (*señal*) to send out; (*Radio*) to broadcast; **~ una señal sonora** to beep

emoción nf emotion; (*excitación*) excitement; (*sentimiento*) feeling; **¡qué ~!** how exciting!; (*irónico*) what a thrill!

emocionado, -a adj deeply moved, stirred

emocionante adj (*excitante*) exciting, thrilling

emocionar vt (*excitar*) to excite, thrill; (*conmover*) to move, touch; (*impresionar*) to impress; **emocionarse** vr to get excited

emoticón nm smiley, emoticon

emotivo, -a adj emotional

empacar vt (*gen*) to pack; (*en caja*) to bale, crate

empacho nm (*Med*) indigestion; (*fig*) embarrassment

empadronarse vr (*Pol: como elector*) to register

empalagoso, -a adj cloying; (*fig*) tiresome

empalmar vt to join, connect ▷ vi (*dos caminos*) to meet, join

empalme nm joint, connection; (*de vías*) junction; (*de trenes*) connection

empanada nf pie, pasty

empantanarse vr to get swamped; (*fig*) to get bogged down

empañarse vr (*nublarse*) to get misty, steam up

empapar vt (*mojar*) to soak, saturate; (*absorber*) to soak up, absorb; **empaparse** vr: **~se de** to soak up

empapelar vt (*paredes*) to paper

empaquetar vt to pack, parcel up; (*Com*) to package

emparedado nm sandwich

empastar vt (*embadurnar*) to paste; (*diente*) to fill

empaste nm (*de diente*) filling

empatar vi to draw, tie

empate nm draw, tie; **un ~ a cero** a no-score draw

empedernido, -a adj hard, heartless; (*fijado*) hardened, inveterate; **un fumador ~** a heavy smoker

empedrado, -a adj paved ▷ nm paving

empedrar vt to pave

empeine nm (*de pie, zapato*) instep

empellón nm push, shove; **abrirse paso a empellones** to push o shove one's way past o through

empeñado, -a adj (*persona*) determined; (*objeto*) pawned

empeñar vt (objeto) to pawn, pledge; (persona) to compel; **empeñarse** vr (obligarse) to bind o.s., pledge o.s.; (endeudarse) to get into debt; **~se en hacer** to be set on doing, be determined to do

empeño nm (determinación) determination; (cosa prendada) pledge; **casa de ~s** pawnshop; **con ~** insistently; (con celo) eagerly; **tener ~ en hacer algo** to be bent on doing sth

empeorar vt to make worse, worsen ▷ vi to get worse, deteriorate

empequeñecer vt to dwarf; (fig) to belittle

emperador nm emperor

emperatriz nf empress

empezar vt, vi to begin, start; **empezó a llover** it started to rain; **bueno, para ~** well, to start with

empinar vt to raise; (botella) to tip up; **empinarse** vr (persona) to stand on tiptoe; (animal) to rear up; (camino) to climb steeply; **~ el codo** to booze (fam)

empírico, -a adj empirical

emplaste, emplasto nm (Med) plaster

emplazamiento nm site, location; (Jur) summons sg

emplazar vt (ubicar) to site, place, locate; (Jur) to summon; (convocar) to summon

empleado, -a nm/f (gen) employee; (de banco etc) clerk; **~ público** civil servant

emplear vt (usar) to use, employ; (dar trabajo a) to employ; **emplearse** vr (conseguir trabajo) to be employed; (ocuparse) to occupy o.s.; **~ mal el tiempo** to waste time; **¡te está bien empleado!** it serves you right!

empleo nm (puesto) job; (puestos: colectivamente) employment; (uso) use, employment; **"modo de ~"** "instructions for use"

empobrecer vt to impoverish; **empobrecerse** vr to become poor o impoverished

empollar vt to incubate; (Escol fam) to swot (up) ▷ vi (gallina) to brood; (Escol fam) to swot

empollón, -ona nm/f (Escol fam) swot

emporio nm emporium, trading centre; (AM: gran almacén) department store

empotrado, -a adj (armario etc) built-in

emprendedor, a adj enterprising

emprender vt to undertake; (empezar) to begin, embark on; (acometer) to tackle, take on; **~ marcha a** to set out for

empresa nf enterprise; (Com: sociedad) firm, company; (: negocio) business; (esp Teat) management; **~ filial** (Com) affiliated company; **~ matriz** (Com) parent company

empresariales nfpl business studies

empresario, -a nm/f (Com) businessman(-woman), entrepreneur; (Tec) manager; (Mus: de ópera etc) impresario; **~ de pompas fúnebres** undertaker (Brit), mortician (US)

empréstito nm (public) loan; (Com) loan capital

empujar vt to push, shove

empuje nm thrust; (presión) pressure; (fig) vigour, drive

empujón nm push, shove; **abrirse paso a empujones** to shove one's way through

empuñar vt (asir) to grasp, take (firm) hold of; **~ las armas** (fig) to take up arms

emular vt to emulate; (rivalizar) to rival

emulsión nf emulsion

en prep **1** (posición: dentro) in; (: sobre) on; (de forma menos precisa) at; **está en el cajón** it's in the drawer; **en Argentina/Madrid** in Argentina/Madrid; **está en el hospital** she's in hospital; **en el periódico** in the paper; **las llaves están en la mesa** the keys are on the table; **está en el suelo/quinto piso** it's on the floor/the fifth floor; **la librería está en la calle Pelayo** the bookshop is on Pelayo street; **en el colegio/la oficina** at school/the office; **en casa** at home; **te veo en el cine** see you at the cinema; **vivía en el número 17** I was living at number 17

2 (dirección) into; **entró en el aula** she went into the classroom; **meter algo en el bolso** to put sth into one's bag; **ir de puerta en puerta** to go from door to door; **me metí en la cama a las diez** I got into bed at ten o'clock

3 (tiempo: periodo largo) in; (día concreto) on; **en 1605/3 semanas/invierno** in 1605/3 weeks/winter; **en (el mes de) enero** in (the month of) January; **en aquella ocasión/época** on that occasion/at that time; **mi cumpleaños cae en viernes** my birthday falls on a Friday; **en Navidades** at Christmas

4 (manera, material, ocupación) in; **escrito en inglés** written in English; **en espiral/círculo** in a spiral/circle; **una inscripción en oro** a gold inscription; **trabaja en la construcción** he works in the building industry; **en serio** seriously

5 (precio) for; **lo vendió en 20 dólares** he sold it for 20 dollars

6 (medio de transporte) by; **en avión/autobús** by plane/bus

7 (diferencia) by; **reducir/aumentar en una tercera parte/un 20 por ciento** to reduce/increase by a third/20 per cent

8 (tema) on; **experto en la materia** expert on the subject; **han cobrado demasiado en dietas** they've charged too much to expenses; **se le va la mitad del sueldo en comida** half his salary goes on food

9 (adj + en + infin): **lento en reaccionar** slow to react; **ser el primero en llegar** to be the first to arrive

enajenación nf, **enajenamiento** nm alienation; (fig: distracción) absent-mindedness; (: embelesamiento) rapture, trance; **~ mental** mental derangement

enajenar vt to alienate; (fig) to carry away

enamorado, -a adj in love ▷ nm/f lover; **estar ~ (de)** to be in love (with)

enamorar vt to win the love of; **enamorarse** vr: **~se (de)** to fall in love (with)

enano, -a adj tiny, dwarf ▷ nm/f dwarf; (pey) runt

enardecer vt (pasiones) to fire, inflame; (persona) to fill with enthusiasm; **enardecerse** vr to get excited; **~se por** to get enthusiastic about

encabezamiento nm (de carta) heading; (Com) billhead, letterhead; (de periódico) headline; (preámbulo) foreword, preface; ~ **normal** (Tip etc) running head

encabezar vt (movimiento, revolución) to lead, head; (lista) to head; (carta) to put a heading to; (libro) to entitle

encadenar vt to chain (together); (poner grilletes a) to shackle

encajar vt (ajustar): ~ **en** to fit (into); (meter a la fuerza) to push in; (máquina etc) to house; (partes) to join; (derrota) to take; (fam: golpe) to give, deal ▷ vi to fit (well); (fig: corresponder a) to match; **encajarse** vr: **~se en un sillón** to squeeze into an armchair; **las piezas no encajan** the pieces don't fit; **sabe ~ bien las críticas** he can take criticism; **ha encajado muy bien la muerte de su madre** she's coped very well with her mother's death; **su versión no encaja con la nuestra** his version doesn't tally with ours

encaje nm (labor) lace

encalar vt (pared) to whitewash

encallar vi (Naut) to run aground

encaminar vt to direct, send; **encaminarse** vr: **~se a** to set out for; **~ por** (expedición etc) to route via

encandilar vt to dazzle; (persona) to daze, bewilder

encantado, -a adj delighted; **¡~!** how do you do!, pleased to meet you

encantador, a adj charming, lovely ▷ nm/f magician, enchanter (enchantress)

encantar vt to charm, delight; (cautivar) to fascinate; (hechizar) to bewitch, cast a spell on

encanto nm (magia) spell, charm; (fig) charm, delight; (expresión de ternura) sweetheart; **como por ~** as if by magic

encarcelar vt to imprison, jail

encarecer vt to put up the price of ▷ vi: **encarecerse** vr to get dearer

encarecimiento nm price increase

encargado, -a adj in charge ▷ nm/f agent, representative; (responsable) person in charge

encargar vt (pedir) to ask; (Com) to order; (recomendar) to urge, recommend ▷ vi: **~ de algo a algn** to put sb in charge of sth; **encargarse** vr: **~se de** to look after, take charge of; **le encargó que le recogiera los documentos** she asked him to fetch the documents for her; **encargamos dos pizzas** we ordered two pizzas; **yo me ~é de avisar a los demás** I'll take care of letting the others know; **no te preocupes, ya me encargo yo de él** don't worry, I'll take care of him o I'll deal with him; **estoy encargada de vender las entradas** I'm in charge of selling the tickets

encargo nm (pedido) assignment, job; (responsabilidad) responsibility; (recomendación) recommendation; (Com) order

encariñarse vr: **~ con** to grow fond of, get attached to

encarnación nf incarnation, embodiment

encarnizado, -a adj (lucha) bloody, fierce

encarrilar vt (tren) to put back on the rails; (fig) to correct, put on the right track

encasillar vt (Teat) to typecast; (clasificar: pey) to pigeonhole

encasquetar vt (sombrero) to pull down o on; **encasquetarse** vr: **~se el sombrero** to pull one's hat down o on; **~ algo a algn** to offload sth onto sb

encauzar vt to channel; (fig) to direct

encendedor nm lighter

encender vt (con fuego) to light; (incendiar) to set fire to; (luz, radio) to put on, switch on; (Inform) to toggle on, switch on; (avivar: pasiones etc) to inflame; (despertar: entusiasmo) to arouse; (odio) to awaken; **encenderse** vr to catch fire; (excitarse) to get excited; (de cólera) to flare up; (el rostro) to blush

encendido, -a adj alight; (aparato) (switched) on; (mejillas) glowing; (cara: por el vino etc) flushed; (mirada) passionate ▷ nm (Auto) ignition; (de faroles) lighting

encerado, -a adj (suelo) waxed, polished ▷ nm (Escol) blackboard; (hule) oilcloth

encerar vt (suelo) to wax, polish

encerrar vt (confinar) to shut in o up; (con llave) to lock in o up; (comprender, incluir) to include, contain; **encerrarse** vr to shut o lock o.s. up o in

encestar vi to score a basket

encharcar vt to swamp, flood; **encharcarse** vr to become flooded

enchilada nf (CAm, Méx) stuffed flour tortilla

enchufar vt (Elec) to plug in; (Tec) to connect, fit together; (Com) to merge

enchufe nm (Elec: clavija) plug; (: toma) socket; (de dos tubos) joint, connection; (fam: influencia) contact, connection; (puesto) cushy job; **~ de clavija** jack plug; **tiene un ~ en el ministerio** he can pull strings at the ministry

encía nf (Anat) gum

enciclopedia nf encyclopaedia

encierro nm shutting in o up; (calabozo) prison; (Agr) pen; (Taur) penning

encima adv (sobre: con contacto) on; (sin contacto) above, over; (además) besides; **~ de** (sobre: con contacto) on, on top of; (sin contacto) above, over; (además de) besides, on top of; **por ~ de** over; **pon el cenicero ahí ~** put the ashtray on there; **¿llevas dinero ~?** have you (got) any money on you?; **se me vino ~** it took me by surprise; **lo leí por ~** I glanced at it; **ponlo ~ de la mesa** put it on the table; **mi maleta está ~ del armario** my case is on top of the wardrobe; **los helicópteros volaban por ~ de nuestras cabezas** the helicopters were flying above our heads; **tuve que saltar por ~ de la mesa** I had to jump over the table; **las temperaturas han subido por ~ de lo normal** temperatures have been above average; **¡y ~ no te da ni las gracias!** and on top of it he doesn't even thank you!

encina nf (holm) oak

encinta adj f pregnant

enclave *nm* enclave
enclenque *adj* weak, sickly
encoger *vt* (*gen*) to shrink, contract; (*fig: asustar*) to scare; (*: desanimar*) to discourage; **encogerse** *vr* to shrink, contract; (*fig*) to cringe; **~se de hombros** to shrug one's shoulders
encolar *vt* (*engomar*) to glue, paste; (*pegar*) to stick down
encolerizar *vt* to anger, provoke; **encolerizarse** *vr* to get angry
encomendar *vt* to entrust, commend; **encomendarse** *vr*: **~se a** to put one's trust in
encomiar *vt* to praise, pay tribute to
encomienda *nf* (*encargo*) charge, commission; (*elogio*) tribute; (*LAm*) parcel, package; **~ postal** (*LAm*) parcel post
encono *nm* (*rencor*) rancour, spite
encontrado, -a *adj* (*contrario*) contrary, conflicting; (*hostil*) hostile
encontrar *vt* (*algo perdido, oculto*) to find; (*persona*) to meet, run into; **encontrarse** *vr* (*reunirse: personas*) to meet (each other); (*casualmente*) to bump into each other; (*estar situado: edificio, exposición*) to be (situated); (*persona*) to find o.s., be; (*entrar en conflicto*) to crash, collide; **no encuentro las llaves** I can't find the keys; **mi hermano ha encontrado trabajo** my brother has found a job; **no sé lo que le encuentran** I don't know what they see in her; **lo encuentro un poco arrogante** I find him a bit arrogant; **¿cómo encuentras la sopa?** what do you think of the soup?; **nos encontramos en el cine** we met at the cinema; **~se con** to meet; **me encontré con Manolo en la calle** I bumped into Manolo in the street; **me encontré con que no tenía gasolina** I found I was out of petrol; **~se bien (de salud)** to feel well; **ahora se encuentra mejor** now she's feeling better; **no se encuentra aquí en este momento** he's not in at the moment
encorvar *vt* to curve; (*inclinar*) to bend (down); **encorvarse** *vr* to bend down, bend over
encrespar *vt* (*cabellos*) to curl; (*fig*) to anger, irritate; **encresparse** *vr* (*el mar*) to get rough; (*fig*) to get cross o irritated
encrucijada *nf* crossroads *sg*; (*empalme*) junction
encuadernación *nf* binding; (*taller*) binder's
encuadernador, a *nm/f* bookbinder
encuadrar *vt* (*retrato*) to frame; (*ajustar*) to fit, insert; (*encerrar*) to contain
encubrir *vt* (*ocultar*) to hide, conceal; (*criminal*) to harbour, shelter; (*ayudar*) to be an accomplice in
encuentro *nm* (*de personas*) meeting; (*Auto etc*) collision, crash; (*Deporte*) match, game; (*Mil*) encounter
encuesta *nf* inquiry, investigation; (*sondeo*) public opinion poll; **~ judicial** post-mortem
encumbrado, -a *adj* eminent, distinguished
encumbrar *vt* (*persona*) to exalt; **encumbrarse** *vr* (*fig*) to become conceited
endeble *adj* (*argumento, excusa, persona*) weak
endémico, -a *adj* endemic

endemoniado, -a *adj* possessed (of the devil); (*travieso*) devilish
enderezar *vt* (*poner derecho*) to straighten (out); (*: verticalmente*) to set upright; (*fig*) to straighten o sort out; (*dirigir*) to direct; **enderezarse** *vr* (*persona sentada*) to sit up straight
endeudarse *vr* to get into debt
endiablado, -a *adj* devilish, diabolical; (*hum*) mischievous
endibia *nf* endive
endilgar *vt* (*fam*): **~ algo a algn** to lumber sb with sth; **~ un sermón a algn** to give sb a lecture
endiñar *vt*: **~ algo a algn** to land sth on sb
endomingarse *vr* to dress up, put on one's best clothes
endosar *vt* (*cheque etc*) to endorse
endulzar *vt* to sweeten; (*suavizar*) to soften
endurecer *vt* to harden; **endurecerse** *vr* to harden, grow hard
endurecido, -a *adj* (*duro*) hard; (*fig*) hardy, tough; **estar ~ a algo** to be hardened o used to sth
enemigo, -a *adj* enemy, hostile ▷ *nm/f* enemy; **ser ~ de** (*persona*) to dislike; (*tendencia*) to be inimical to
enemistad *nf* enmity
enemistar *vt* to make enemies of, cause a rift between; **enemistarse** *vr* to become enemies; (*amigos*) to fall out
energía *nf* (*vigor*) energy, drive; (*Tec, Elec*) energy, power; **~ atómica/eléctrica/eólica** atomic/ electric/wind power
enérgico, -a *adj* (*gen*) energetic; (*ataque*) vigorous; (*ejercicio*) strenuous; (*medida*) bold; (*voz, modales*) forceful
energúmeno, -a *nm/f* madman(woman); **ponerse como un ~ con algn** to get furious with sb
enero *nm* January
enésimo, -a *adj* (*Mat*) nth; **por enésima vez** (*fig*) for the umpteenth time
enfadado, -a *adj* angry, annoyed
enfadar *vt* to anger, annoy; **enfadarse** *vr* to get angry o annoyed
enfado *nm* (*enojo*) anger, annoyance; (*disgusto*) trouble, bother
énfasis *nm* emphasis, stress; **poner ~ en** to stress
enfático, -a *adj* emphatic
enfermar *vt* to make ill ▷ *vi* to fall ill, be taken ill; **su actitud me enferma** his attitude makes me sick; **~ del corazón** to develop heart trouble
enfermedad *nf* illness, disease; **pegar una ~ a algn** to give sb a disease
enfermera *nf ver* **enfermero**
enfermería *nf* infirmary; (*de colegio etc*) sick bay
enfermero, -a *nm* (male) nurse ▷ *nf* nurse; **enfermera jefa** matron
enfermizo, -a *adj* (*persona*) sickly, unhealthy; (*fig*) unhealthy
enfermo, -a *adj* ill, sick ▷ *nm/f* invalid, sick person; (*en hospital*) patient
enflaquecer *vt* (*adelgazar*) to make thin; (*debilitar*) to weaken

enfocar vt (foto etc) to focus; (problema etc) to consider, look at

enfoque nm focus; (acto) focusing; (óptica) approach

enfrascarse vr: **~ en un libro** to bury o.s. in a book

enfrentamiento nm confrontation

enfrentar vt (peligro) to face (up to), confront; (oponer) to bring face to face; **enfrentarse** vr (dos personas) to face o confront each other; (Deporte: dos equipos) to meet; **~se a** o **con** to face up to, confront

enfrente adv opposite; **~ de** prep opposite, facing; **la casa de ~** the house opposite, the house across the street

enfriamiento nm chilling, refrigeration; (Med) cold, chill

enfriar vt (alimentos) to cool, chill; (algo caliente) to cool down; (habitación) to air, freshen; (entusiasmo) to dampen; **enfriarse** vr to cool down; (Med) to catch a chill; (amistad) to cool

enfurecer vt to enrage, madden; **enfurecerse** vr to become furious, fly into a rage; (mar) to get rough

engalanar vt (adornar) to adorn; (ciudad) to decorate; **engalanarse** vr to get dressed up

enganchar vt to hook; (ropa) to hang up; (dos vagones) to hitch up; (Tec) to couple, connect; (Mil) to recruit; (fam: atraer: persona) to rope into; **engancharse** vr (Mil) to enlist, join up; **~se (a)** (drogas) to get hooked (on)

enganche nm hook; (Tec) coupling, connection; (acto) hooking (up); (Mil) recruitment, enlistment; (Méx: depósito) deposit

engañar vt to deceive; (estafar) to cheat, swindle ▷ vi: **las apariencias engañan** appearances are deceptive; **engañarse** vr (equivocarse) to be wrong; (asimismo) to deceive o kid o.s.; **engaña a su mujer** he's unfaithful to o cheats on his wife

engaño nm deceit; (estafa) trick, swindle; (error) mistake, misunderstanding; (ilusión) delusion

engañoso, -a adj (tramposo) crooked; (mentiroso) dishonest, deceitful; (aspecto) deceptive; (consejo) misleading

engarzar vt (joya) to set, mount; (fig) to link, connect

engatusar vt (fam) to coax

engendrar vt to breed; (procrear) to beget; (fig) to cause, produce

engendro nm (Bio) foetus; (fig) monstrosity; (idea) brainchild

englobar vt (comprender) to include, comprise; (incluir) to lump together

engomar vt to glue, stick

engordar vt to fatten ▷ vi to get fat, put on weight

engorroso, -a adj bothersome, trying

engranaje nm (Auto) gear; (juego) gears pl

engrandecer vt to enlarge, magnify; (alabar) to praise, speak highly of; (exagerar) to exaggerate

engrasar vt (Tec: poner grasa) to grease; (: lubricar) to lubricate, oil; (manchar) to make greasy

engreído, -a adj vain, conceited

engrosar vt (ensanchar) to enlarge; (aumentar) to increase; (hinchar) to swell

enhebrar vt to thread

enhorabuena excl congratulations

enigma nm enigma; (problema) puzzle; (misterio) mystery

enjabonar vt to soap; (barba) to lather; (fam: adular) to soft-soap; (: regañar) to tick off

enjambre nm swarm

enjaular vt to (put in a) cage; (fam) to jail, lock up

enjuagar vt (ropa) to rinse (out)

enjuague nm (Med) mouthwash; (de ropa) rinse, rinsing

enjugar vt to wipe (off); (lágrimas) to dry; (déficit) to wipe out

enjuiciar vt (Jur: procesar) to prosecute, try; (fig) to judge

enjuto, -a adj dry, dried up; (fig) lean, skinny

enlace nm link, connection; (relación) relationship; (tb: **enlace matrimonial**) marriage; (de trenes) connection; **~ de datos** data link; **~ sindical** shop steward; **~ telefónico** telephone link-up

enlazar vt (unir con lazos) to bind together; (atar) to tie; (conectar) to link, connect; (LAm) to lasso

enlodar vt to cover in mud; (fig: manchar) to stain; (: rebajar) to debase

enloquecer vt to drive mad ▷ vi: **enloquecerse** vr to go mad

enlutado, -a adj (persona) in mourning

enmarañar vt (enredar) to tangle up, entangle; (complicar) to complicate; (confundir) to confuse; **enmarañarse** vr (enredarse) to become entangled; (confundirse) to get confused

enmarcar vt (cuadro) to frame; (fig) to provide a setting for

enmascarar vt to mask; (intenciones) to disguise; **enmascararse** vr to put on a mask

enmendar vt to emend, correct; (constitución etc) to amend; (comportamiento) to reform; **enmendarse** vr to reform, mend one's ways

enmienda nf correction; amendment; reform

enmohecerse vr (metal) to rust, go rusty; (muro, plantas) to go mouldy

enmudecer vt to silence ▷ vi: **enmudecerse** vr (perder el habla) to fall silent; (guardar silencio) to remain silent; (por miedo) to be struck dumb

ennegrecer vt (poner negro) to blacken; (oscurecer) to darken; **ennegrecerse** vr to turn black; (oscurecerse) to get dark, darken

ennoblecer vt to ennoble

enojadizo, -a adj irritable, short-tempered

enojar (esp LAm) vt (encolerizar) to anger; (disgustar) to annoy, upset; **enojarse** vr (ponerse furioso) to get angry; (molestarse) to get annoyed

enojo nm (esp LAm: cólera) anger; (irritación) annoyance; **enojos** nmpl trials, problems

enojoso, -a adj annoying

enorgullecerse vr to be proud; **~ de** to pride o.s. on, be proud of

enorme adj enormous, huge; (fig) monstrous

enormidad *nf* hugeness, immensity
enraizar *vi* to take root
enrarecido, -a *adj* rarefied
enredadera *nf* (*Bot*) creeper, climbing plant
enredar *vt* (*cables, hilos etc*) to tangle (up), entangle; (*situación*) to complicate, confuse; (*meter cizaña*) to sow discord among o between; (*implicar*) to embroil, implicate; **enredarse** *vr* to get entangled, get tangled (up); (*situación*) to get complicated; (*persona*) to get embroiled
enredo *nm* (*maraña*) tangle; (*confusión*) mix-up, confusion; (*intriga*) intrigue; (*apuro*) jam; (*amorío*) love affair
enrevesado, -a *adj* (*asunto*) complicated, involved
enriquecer *vt* to make rich; (*fig*) to enrich; **enriquecerse** *vr* to get rich
enrojecer *vt* to redden ▷ *vi*: **enrojecerse** *vr* (*persona*) to blush
enrolar *vt* (*Mil*) to enlist; (*reclutar*) to recruit; **enrolarse** *vr* (*Mil*) to join up; (*afiliarse*) to enrol, sign on
enrollar *vt* to roll (up), wind (up); **enrollarse** *vr*: **~se con algn** to get involved with sb
enroscar *vt* (*torcer, doblar*) to twist; (*arrollar*) to coil (round), wind; (*tornillo, rosca*) to screw in; **enroscarse** *vr* to coil, wind
ensalada *nf* salad; (*lío*) mix-up
ensaladilla *nf* (*tb*: **ensaladilla rusa**) ≈ Russian salad
ensalzar *vt* (*alabar*) to praise, extol; (*exaltar*) to exalt
ensambladura *nf*, **ensamblaje** *nm* assembly; (*Tec*) joint
ensamblar *vt* (*montar*) to assemble; (*madera etc*) to join
ensanchar *vt* (*hacer más ancho*) to widen; (*agrandar*) to enlarge, expand; (*Costura*) to let out; **ensancharse** *vr* to get wider, expand; (*pey*) to give o.s. airs
ensanche *nm* (*de calle*) widening; (*de negocio*) expansion
ensangrentar *vt* to stain with blood
ensañarse *vr*: **~ con** to treat brutally
ensartar *vt* (*gen*) to string (together); (*carne*) to spit, skewer
ensayar *vt* to test, try (out); (*Teat*) to rehearse
ensayista *nm/f* essayist
ensayo *nm* test, trial; (*Química*) experiment; (*Teat*) rehearsal; (*Deporte*) try; (*Escol, Literatura*) essay; **pedido de ~** (*Com*) trial order; **~ general** (*Teat*) dress rehearsal; (*Mus*) full rehearsal
enseguida *adv* at once, right away; **~ termino** I've nearly finished, I shan't be long now
ensenada *nf* inlet, cove
enseñanza *nf* (*educación*) education; (*acción*) teaching; (*doctrina*) teaching, doctrine; **~ primaria/secundaria/superior** primary/secondary/higher education
enseñar *vt* (*educar*) to teach; (*instruir*) to teach, instruct; (*mostrar, señalar*) to show
enseres *nmpl* belongings

ensillar *vt* to saddle (up)
ensimismarse *vr* (*abstraerse*) to become lost in thought; (*estar absorto*) to be lost in thought; (*LAm*) to become conceited
ensordecer *vt* to deafen ▷ *vi* to go deaf
ensortijado, -a *adj* (*pelo*) curly
ensuciar *vt* (*manchar*) to dirty, soil; (*fig*) to defile; **ensuciarse** *vr* (*mancharse*) to get dirty; (*niño*) to dirty (o wet) o.s.
ensueño *nm* (*sueño*) dream, fantasy; (*ilusión*) illusion; (*soñando despierto*) daydream; **de ~** dream-like
entablado *nm* (*piso*) floorboards *pl*; (*armazón*) boarding
entablar *vt* (*recubrir*) to board (up); (*Ajedrez, Damas*) to set up; (*conversación*) to strike up; (*Jur*) to file ▷ *vi* to draw
entablillar *vt* (*Med*) to (put in a) splint
entallado, -a *adj* waisted
entallar *vt* (*traje*) to tailor ▷ *vi*: **el traje entalla bien** the suit fits well
ente *nm* (*organización*) body, organization; (*compañía*) company; (*fam: persona*) odd character; (*ser*) being; **~ público** (*Esp*) state(-owned) body
entender *nm*: **a mi ~** in my opinion ▷ *vt* (*comprender*) to understand; (*darse cuenta*) to realize; (*creer*) to think, believe; (*querer decir*) to mean ▷ *vi* to understand; **entenderse** *vr* (*texto, mensaje*) to be understood; (*2 personas: llevarse bien*) to get on together; (*ponerse de acuerdo*) to agree, reach an agreement; (*comunicarse*) to communicate; **no entiendo el francés** I don't understand French; **¿lo entiendes?** do you understand?; **¿entiendes lo que quiero decir?** do you know what I mean?; **creo que lo he entendido mal** I think I've misunderstood; **¿entiendes?** (do you) understand?; **~ de** to know all about; **mi primo entiende algo/mucho de coches** my cousin knows a little/a lot about cars; **~ en** to deal with, have to do with; **dar a ~ que ...** to lead to believe that ...; **dio a ~ que no le gustaba** he implied that he didn't like it; **~se mal** to get on badly; **se entienden por gestos** they communicate through sign language
entendido, -a *adj* (*comprendido*) understood; (*hábil*) skilled; (*inteligente*) knowledgeable ▷ *nm/f* (*experto*) expert ▷ *excl* agreed!
entendimiento *nm* (*comprensión*) understanding; (*inteligencia*) mind, intellect; (*juicio*) judgement
enterado, -a *adj* well-informed; **estar ~ de** to know about, be aware of; **no darse por ~** to pretend not to understand
enteramente *adv* entirely, completely
enterarse *vr* (*comprender*) to understand; **~ (de)** (*averiguar*) to find out (about); (*notar*) to notice; **no me hables en francés que no me entero** don't talk to me in French – I won't understand; **ya me voy enterando** I'm beginning to understand; **me enteré por Manolo** I found out from Manolo; **entérate bien de todos los detalles** make sure you find out about all the details; **¡que no se entere mamá de esto!** mum

mustn't find out about this!; **se enteraron del accidente por la tele** they heard about the accident on the TV; **me sacaron una muela y ni me enteré** they took out a tooth and I didn't notice a thing; **para que te enteres ...** (*fam*) for your information ...

entereza *nf* (*totalidad*) entirety; (*fig: de carácter*) strength of mind; (*honradez*) integrity

enternecer *vt* (*ablandar*) to soften; (*apiadar*) to touch, move; **enternecerse** *vr* to be touched, be moved

entero, -a *adj* (*total*) whole, entire; (*fig: recto*) honest; (: *firme*) firm, resolute ▷ *nm* (*Mat*) integer; (*Com: punto*) point; **las acciones han subido dos ~s** the shares have gone up two points

enterrador *nm* gravedigger

enterrar *vt* to bury; (*fig*) to forget

entibiar *vt* (*enfriar*) to cool; (*calentar*) to warm; **entibiarse** *vr* (*fig*) to cool

entidad *nf* (*empresa*) firm, company; (*organismo*) body; (*sociedad*) society; (*Filosofía*) entity

entierro *nm* (*acción*) burial; (*funeral*) funeral

entomología *nf* entomology

entonación *nf* (*Ling*) intonation; (*fig*) conceit

entonar *vt* (*canción*) to intone; (*colores*) to tone; (*Med*) to tone up ▷ *vi* to be in tune; **entonarse** *vr* (*engreírse*) to give o.s. airs

entonces *adv* then, at that time; **desde ~** since then; **en aquel ~** at that time; (*pues*) **~** and so; **el ~ embajador de España** the then Spanish ambassador

entornar *vt* (*puerta, ventana*) to half close, leave ajar; (*los ojos*) to screw up

entorno *nm* setting, environment; **~ de redes** (*Inform*) network environment

entorpecer *vt* (*entendimiento*) to dull; (*impedir*) to obstruct, hinder; (*tránsito*) to slow down, delay

entrada *nf* (*acción*) entry, access; (*lugar de acceso*) entrance, way in; (*principio*) beginning; (*billete*) ticket; (*Com*) receipts *pl*, takings *pl*; (*Culin*) entrée; (*Teat: público*) house, audience; (*Inform*) input; (*Deporte*) tackle; (*Econ*): **~s** *nfpl* income *sg*; **"~ libre"** "admission free"; **"prohibida la ~"** "no entry"; **nos vemos en la ~** I'll see you at the entrance; **la ~ de España en la Comunidad Europea** Spain's entry into the European Community; **la ~ de la primavera** the beginning of spring; **de ~** right away; **le hizo una ~ al portero** he tackled the goalkeeper; **pagamos una ~ de 20.000 euros** we paid a deposit of 20,000 euros; **tiene ~s** to have a receding hairline; **~ de aire** (*Tec*) air intake *o* inlet; **~ de datos vocal** (*Inform*) voice input; **~s brutas** gross receipts; **~s y salidas** (*Com*) income and expenditure; *ver tb* **entrado**

entrado, -a *adj*: **~ en años** elderly; **(una vez) ~ el verano** in the summer(time), when summer comes; *ver tb* **entrada**

entrante *adj* next, coming; (*Pol*) incoming ▷ *nm* inlet; (*Culin*) starter; **mes/año ~** next month/year

entraña *nf* (*fig: centro*) heart, core; (*raíz*) root; **entrañas** *nfpl* (*Anat*) entrails; (*fig*) heart *sg*

entrañable *adj* (*persona, lugar*) dear; (*relación*) close; (*acto*) intimate

entrañar *vt* to entail

entrar *vi* (*meterse*) to go *o* come in, enter; (*caber*) to fit; (*estar incluido*) to be included; (*comenzar*): **~ diciendo** to begin by saying ▷ *vt* (*introducir*) to bring in; (*persona*) to show in; (*Inform*) to input; **abrí la puerta y entré** I opened the door and went in; **¿se puede? — sí, entra** may I? — yes, come in; **¡éntrale!, ¡éntrele!** (*Méx*) come in!; **entré en** *o* a (*LAm*) **la casa** I went into the house; **~on en mi cuarto mientras yo dormía** they came into my room while I was asleep; **Pedro entra a trabajar a las 8** Pedro starts work at 8 o'clock; **le ~on ganas de reír** she wanted to laugh; **de repente le entró sueño** he suddenly felt sleepy; **me ha entrado hambre al verte comer** watching you eat made me hungry; **estos zapatos no me entran** these shoes don't fit me; **la maleta no entra en el maletero** the case won't fit in the boot; **el vino no entra en el precio** the wine is not included in the price; **las matemáticas no le entran** (*fam*) he can't get the hang of maths (*fam*)

entre *prep* (*en medio de: dos*) between; (*varios*) among(st); (*al dividir*) by; (*a través de*) through; **lo terminamos ~ los dos** between the two of us we finished it; **vendrá ~ las diez y las once** he'll be coming between ten and eleven; **había un baúl ~ las maletas** there was a trunk in among the cases; **las mujeres hablaban ~ sí** the women were talking among themselves; **le compraremos un regalo ~ todos** we'll buy her a present between all of us; **15 dividido ~ 3 es 5** 15 divided by 3 is 5; **se abrieron paso ~ la multitud** they forced their way through the crowd; **~ una cosa y otra** what with one thing and another; *ver tb* **entretanto**

entreabrir *vt* to half-open, open halfway

entrecejo *nm*: **fruncir el ~** to frown

entrecortado, -a *adj* (*respiración*) laboured, difficult; (*habla*) faltering

entredicho *nm* (*Jur*) injunction; **poner en ~** to cast doubt on; **estar en ~** to be in doubt

entrega *nf* (*de mercancías*) delivery; (*de premios*) presentation; (*de novela etc*) instalment; **"~ a domicilio"** "door-to-door delivery service"

entregar *vt* (*dar: en mano*) to hand (over); (*carta, pedido*) deliver; (*deberes, trabajo*) to hand in; (*premio*) to present; **entregarse** *vr* (*rendirse*) to surrender, give in, submit; **~se a** (*dedicarse*) to devote o.s. to; **el cartero entregó el paquete** the postman delivered the parcel; **Marta entregó el examen** Marta handed her exam paper in; **el director le entregó la medalla** the director presented him with the medal; **a ~** (*Com*) to be supplied; **el ladrón se entregó a la policía** the thief gave himself up

entrelazar *vt* to entwine

entremeses *nmpl* hors d'œuvres

entremeter *vt* to insert, put in; **entremeterse** *vr* to meddle, interfere

entremezclar *vt*: **entremezclarse** *vr* to intermingle

entrenador, a *nm/f* trainer, coach

entrenamiento *nm* training

entrenar *vt* (*Deporte*) to train; (*caballo*) to exercise ▷ *vi*: **entrenarse** *vr* to train

entrepierna *nf* (*tb*: **entrepiernas**) crotch, crutch

entresacar *vt* to pick out, select

entresuelo *nm* mezzanine, entresol; (*Teat*) dress o first circle

entretanto *adv* meanwhile, meantime

entretejer *vt* to interweave

entretener *vt* (*divertir*) to entertain, amuse; (*detener*) to hold up, delay; (*mantener*) to maintain; **entretenerse** *vr* (*divertirse*) to amuse o.s.; (*retrasarse*) to delay, linger; **no le entretengo más** I won't keep you any longer

entretenido, -a *adj* entertaining, amusing

entretenimiento *nm* entertainment, amusement; (*mantenimiento*) upkeep, maintenance

entretiempo *nm*: **ropa de ~** *clothes for spring and autumn*

entrever *vt* to glimpse, catch a glimpse of

entrevista *nf* interview

entrevistar *vt* to interview; **entrevistarse** *vr*: **~se con** to have an interview with, see; **el ministro se entrevistó con el Rey ayer** the minister had an audience with the King yesterday

entristecer *vt* to sadden, grieve; **entristecerse** *vr* to grow sad

entrometerse *vr*: **~ (en)** to interfere (in o with)

entroncar *vi* to be connected o related

entumecer *vt* to numb, benumb; **entumecerse** *vr* (*por el frío*) to go o become numb

entumecido, -a *adj* numb, stiff

enturbiar *vt* (*el agua*) to make cloudy; (*fig*) to confuse; **enturbiarse** *vr* (*oscurecerse*) to become cloudy; (*fig*) to get confused, become obscure

entusiasmar *vt* to excite, fill with enthusiasm; (*gustar mucho*) to delight; **entusiasmarse** *vr*: **~se con** o **por** to get enthusiastic o excited about

entusiasmo *nm* enthusiasm; (*excitación*) excitement

entusiasta *adj* enthusiastic ▷ *nm/f* enthusiast

enumerar *vt* to enumerate

enunciación *nf*, **enunciado** *nm* enunciation; (*declaración*) declaration, statement

envainar *vt* to sheathe

envalentonar *vt* to give courage to; **envalentonarse** *vr* (*pey: jactarse*) to boast, brag

envanecer *vt* to make conceited; **envanecerse** *vr* to grow conceited

envasar *vt* (*empaquetar*) to pack, wrap; (*enfrascar*) to bottle; (*enlatar*) to can; (*embolsar*) to pocket

envase *nm* (*empaquetado*) packaging, wrapping; (*embotellado*) bottling; (*enlatado*) canning; (*recipiente*) container; (*paquete*) package; (*botella*) bottle; (*lata*) tin (*Brit*), can

envejecer *vt* to make old, age ▷ *vi*: **envejecerse** *vr* (*volverse viejo*) to grow old; (*parecer viejo*) to age

envenenar *vt* to poison; (*fig*) to embitter

envergadura *nf* (*expansión*) expanse; (*Naut*) breadth; (*fig*) scope; **un programa de gran ~** a wide-ranging programme

envés *nm* (*de tela*) back, wrong side

enviar *vt* to send; **~ un mensaje a algn** (*por móvil*) to text sb, send sb a text message

enviciar *vt* to corrupt ▷ *vi* (*trabajo etc*) to be addictive; **enviciarse** *vr*: **~se (con** o **en)** to get addicted (to)

envidia *nf* envy; **tener ~ a** to envy, be jealous of

envidiar *vt* (*desear*) to envy; (*tener celos de*) to be jealous of

envío *nm* (*acción*) sending; (*de mercancías*) consignment; (*de dinero*) remittance; (*en barco*) shipment; **gastos de ~** postage and packing; **~ contra reembolso** COD shipment

enviudar *vi* to be widowed

envoltura *nf* (*cobertura*) cover; (*embalaje*) wrapper, wrapping

envolver *vt* to wrap (up); (*cubrir*) to cover; (*enemigo*) to surround; (*implicar*) to involve, implicate

enyesar *vt* (*pared*) to plaster; (*Med*) to put in plaster

enzarzarse *vr*: **~ en algo** to get mixed up in sth

epicentro *nm* epicentre

épico, -a *adj* epic ▷ *nf* epic (poetry)

epidemia *nf* epidemic

epidermis *nf* epidermis

epilepsia *nf* epilepsy

epiléptico, -a *adj*, *nm/f* epileptic

epílogo *nm* epilogue

episodio *nm* episode; (*suceso*) incident

epístola *nf* epistle

epíteto *nm* epithet

época *nf* period, time; (*temporada*) season; (*Historia*) age, epoch; **hacer ~** to be epoch-making

equidad *nf* equity, fairness

equilibrar *vt* to balance

equilibrio *nm* balance, equilibrium; **~ político** balance of power

equilibrista *nm/f* (*funámbulo*) tightrope walker; (*acróbata*) acrobat

equipaje *nm* luggage (Brit), baggage (US); (*avíos*) equipment, kit; **~ de mano** hand luggage; **hacer el ~** to pack

equipar *vt* (*proveer*) to equip

equiparar *vt* (*igualar*) to put on the same level; (*comparar*): **~ (con)** to compare (with); **equipararse** *vr*: **~se con** to be on a level with

equipo *nm* (*conjunto de cosas*) equipment; (*Deporte, grupo*) team; (*de obreros*) shift; (*de máquinas*) plant; (*turbinas etc*) set; **~ de caza** hunting gear; **~ físico** (*Inform*) hardware; **~ médico** medical team; **~ de música** music centre

equis *nf* (the letter) X

equitación *nf* (*acto*) riding; (*arte*) horsemanship

equitativo, -a *adj* equitable, fair

equivalente *adj, nm* equivalent
equivaler *vi*: ~ **a** to be equivalent o equal to; (*en rango*) to rank as
equivocación *nf* mistake, error; (*malentendido*) misunderstanding
equivocado, -a *adj* wrong, mistaken
equivocarse *vr* to be wrong, make a mistake; ~ **de camino** to take the wrong road
equívoco, -a *adj* (*dudoso*) suspect; (*ambiguo*) ambiguous ▷ *nm* ambiguity; (*malentendido*) misunderstanding
era *nf* era, age; (*Agr*) threshing floor
erario *nm* exchequer, treasury
erección *nf* erection
erguir *vt* to raise, lift; (*poner derecho*) to straighten; **erguirse** *vr* to straighten up
erigir *vt* to erect, build; **erigirse** *vr*: ~**se en** to set o.s. up as
erizado, -a *adj* bristly
erizarse *vr* (*pelo: de perro*) to bristle; (*: de persona*) to stand on end
erizo *nm* hedgehog; ~ **de mar** sea urchin
ermita *nf* hermitage
ermitaño, -a *nm/f* hermit
erosión *nf* erosion
erosionar *vt* to erode
erótico, -a *adj* erotic
erotismo *nm* eroticism
erradicar *vt* to eradicate
errante *adj* wandering, errant
errar *vi* (*vagar*) to wander, roam; (*equivocarse*) to be mistaken ▷ *vt*: ~ **el camino** to take the wrong road; ~ **el tiro** to miss
errata *nf* misprint
erróneo, -a *adj* (*equivocado*) wrong, mistaken; (*falso*) false, untrue
error *nm* mistake, error; (*Inform*) bug; ~ **de imprenta** misprint; ~ **de lectura/escritura** (*Inform*) read/write error; ~ **sintáctico** syntax error; ~ **judicial** miscarriage of justice
eructar *vt* to belch, burp
eructo *nm* belch
erudito, -a *adj* erudite, learned ▷ *nm/f* scholar; **los ~s en esta materia** the experts in this field
erupción *nf* eruption; (*Med*) rash; (*de violencia*) outbreak; (*de ira*) outburst
esa, esas *adj demostrativo ver* **ese**
ésa, ésas *pron ver* **ése**
esbelto, -a *adj* slim, slender
esbozo *nm* sketch, outline
escabeche *nm* brine; (*de aceitunas etc*) pickle; **en ~** pickled
escabroso, -a *adj* (*accidentado*) rough, uneven; (*fig*) tough, difficult; (*: atrevido*) risqué
escabullirse *vr* to slip away; (*largarse*) to clear out
escacharrar *vt* (*fam*) to break; **escacharrarse** *vr* to get broken
escafandra *nf* (*buzo*) diving suit; (*escafandra espacial*) spacesuit
escala *nf* (*proporción, Mus*) scale; (*de mano*) ladder; (*Aviat*) stopover; (*de colores etc*) range; ~ **de tiempo** time scale; ~ **de sueldos** salary scale;

una investigación a ~ nacional a nationwide inquiry; **reproducir según ~** to reproduce to scale; **hacer ~ en** to stop off o over at
escalafón *nm* (*escala de salarios*) salary scale, wage scale
escalar *vt* to climb, scale ▷ *vi* (*Mil, Pol*) to escalate
escalera *nf* stairs *pl*, staircase; (*escala*) ladder; (*Naipes*) run; (*de camión*) tailboard; ~ **mecánica** escalator; ~ **de caracol** spiral staircase; ~ **de incendios** fire escape
escalerilla *nf* (*de avión*) steps *pl*
escalfar *vt* (*huevos*) to poach
escalinata *nf* staircase
escalofriante *adj* chilling
escalofrío *nm* (*Med*) chill; **escalofríos** *nmpl* (*fig*) shivers
escalón *nm* step, stair; (*de escalera*) rung; (*fig: paso*) step; (*al éxito*) ladder
escalope *nm* (*Culin*) escalope
escama *nf* (*de pez, serpiente*) scale; (*de jabón*) flake; (*fig*) resentment
escamar *vt* (*pez*) to scale; (*producir recelo*) to make wary
escamotear *vt* (*fam: robar*) to lift, swipe; (*hacer desaparecer*) to make disappear
escampar *vb impersonal* to stop raining
escanciar *vt* (*vino*) to pour (out)
escandalizar *vt* to scandalize, shock; **escandalizarse** *vr* to be shocked; (*ofenderse*) to be offended
escándalo *nm* scandal; (*alboroto, tumulto*) row, uproar; **armar un ~** to make a scene; **¡es un ~!** it's outrageous!
escandaloso, -a *adj* scandalous, shocking; (*risa*) hearty; (*niño*) noisy
escandinavo, -a *adj, nm/f* Scandinavian
escaneo *nm* scanning
escáner *nm* (*aparato*) scanner; (*imagen*) scan
escaño *nm* bench; (*Pol*) seat
escapar *vi* (*gen*) to escape, run away; **escaparse** *vr* (*preso*) to escape, get away; (*ciclista*) to break away; (*agua, gas, noticias*) to leak (out); **conseguí ~ de la fiesta** I managed to escape from the party; **dejó ~ un suspiro** he let out a sigh; **no quiero dejar ~ esta oportunidad** I don't want to let this opportunity slip; **el ladrón se escapó de la cárcel** the thief escaped from prison; **el calor se escapa por esta rendija** the heat escapes through this grill; **se me escapó un eructo** I let out a burp; **se me escapa su nombre** his name escapes me; **no se me escapa que...** I am perfectly aware that...
escaparate *nm* shop window; (*Com*) showcase
escape *nm* (*huida*) escape; (*de agua, gas*) leak; (*de motor*) exhaust; **salir a ~** to rush out
escaquearse *vr* (*fam*) to duck out
escarabajo *nm* beetle
escaramuza *nf* skirmish; (*fig*) brush
escarbar *vt* (*gallina*) to scratch; (*fig*) to inquire into, investigate
escarceos *nmpl*: **en sus ~ con la política** in his occasional forays into politics; ~ **amorosos**

flirtations

escarcha *nf* frost

escarlata *adj inv* scarlet

escarlatina *nf* scarlet fever

escarmentar *vt* to punish severely ▷ *vi* to learn one's lesson; **¡para que escarmientes!** that'll teach you!

escarmiento *nm* (*ejemplo*) lesson; (*castigo*) punishment

escarnio *nm* mockery; (*injuria*) insult

escarola *nf* (*Bot*) endive

escarpado, -a *adj* (*pendiente*) sheer, steep; (*rocas*) craggy

escasear *vi* to be scarce

escasez *nf* (*falta*) shortage, scarcity; (*pobreza*) poverty; **vivir con** ~ to live on the breadline

escaso, -a *adj* (*poco*) scarce; (*raro*) rare; (*ralo*) thin, sparse; (*limitado*) limited; (*recursos*) scanty; (*público*) sparse; (*posibilidad*) slim; (*visibilidad*) poor

escatimar *vt* (*limitar*) to skimp (on), be sparing with; **no** ~ **esfuerzos (para)** to spare no effort (to)

escayola *nf* plaster

escayolar *vt* to put in plaster

escena *nf* scene; (*decorado*) scenery; (*escenario*) stage; **poner en** ~ to put on

escenario *nm* (*Teat*) stage; (*Cine*) set; (*fig*) scene; **el** ~ **del crimen** the scene of the crime; **el** ~ **político** the political scene

escenografía *nf* set o stage design

escepticismo *nm* scepticism

escéptico, -a *adj* sceptical ▷ *nm/f* sceptic

escisión *nf* (*Med*) excision; (*fig, Pol*) split; ~ **nuclear** nuclear fission

esclarecer *vt* (*iluminar*) to light up, illuminate; (*misterio, problema*) to shed light on

esclavitud *nf* slavery

esclavizar *vt* to enslave

esclavo, -a *nm/f* slave

esclusa *nf* (*de canal*) lock; (*compuerta*) floodgate

escoba *nf* broom; **pasar la** ~ to sweep up

escobilla *nf* brush

escocer *vi* to burn, sting; **escocerse** *vr* to chafe, get chafed

escocés, -esa *adj* Scottish; (*whisky*) Scotch ▷ *nm/f* Scotsman(woman), Scot ▷ *nm* (*Ling*) Scots *sg*; **tela escocesa** tartan

Escocia *nf* Scotland

escoger *vt* to choose, pick, select

escogido, -a *adj* chosen, selected; (*calidad*) choice, select; (*persona*): **ser muy** ~ to be very fussy

escolar *adj* school *cpd* ▷ *nm/f* schoolboy(-girl), pupil

escollo *nm* (*arrecife*) reef, rock; (*fig*) pitfall

escolta *nf* escort

escoltar *vt* to escort; (*proteger*) to guard

escombros *nmpl* (*basura*) rubbish *sg*; (*restos*) debris *sg*

esconder *vt* to hide, conceal; **esconderse** *vr* to hide

escondidas *nfpl* (*LAm*) hide-and-seek *sg*; **a** ~

secretly; **hacer algo a** ~ **de algn** to do sth behind sb's back

escondite *nm* hiding place; (*juego*) hide-and-seek

escondrijo *nm* hiding place, hideout

escopeta *nf* shotgun; ~ **de aire comprimido** air gun

escoria *nf* (*desecho mineral*) slag; (*fig*) scum, dregs *pl*

Escorpio *nm* (*Astro*) Scorpio

escorpión *nm* scorpion

escotado, -a *adj* low-cut

escote *nm* (*de vestido*) low neck; **pagar a** ~ to share the expenses

escotilla *nf* (*Naut*) hatchway

escozor *nm* (*dolor*) sting(ing)

escribano, -a, escribiente *nm/f* clerk; (*secretario judicial*) court o lawyer's clerk

escribir *vt, vi* to write; ~ **a máquina** to type; **¿cómo se escribe?** how do you spell it?

escrito, -a *pp de* **escribir** ▷ *adj* written, in writing; (*examen*) written ▷ *nm* (*documento*) document; (*manuscrito*) text, manuscript; **por** ~ in writing

escritor, a *nm/f* writer

escritorio *nm* desk; (*oficina*) office

escritura *nf* (*acción*) writing; (*caligrafía*) (hand)writing; (*Jur: documento*) deed; (*Com*) indenture; ~ **de propiedad** title deed; **Sagrada E~** (Holy) Scripture; ~ **social** articles *pl* of association

escrúpulo *nm* scruple; (*minuciosidad*) scrupulousness

escrupuloso, -a *adj* scrupulous

escrutar *vt* to scrutinize, examine; (*votos*) to count

escrutinio *nm* (*examen atento*) scrutiny; (*Pol: recuento de votos*) count(ing)

escuadra *nf* (*Tec*) square; (*Mil etc*) squad; (*Naut*) squadron; (*de coches etc*) fleet

escuadrilla *nf* (*de aviones*) squadron

escuadrón *nm* squadron

escuálido, -a *adj* skinny, scraggy; (*sucio*) squalid

escucha *nf* (*acción*) listening ▷ *nm* (*Telec: sistema*) monitor; (*oyente*) listener; **estar a la** ~ to listen in; **estar de** ~ to spy; ~**s telefónicas** (phone)tapping *sg*

escuchar *vt* to listen to; (*consejo*) to heed; (*esp LAm*: *oír*) to hear ▷ *vi* to listen; **escucharse** *vr*: **se escucha muy mal** (*Telec*) it's a very bad line

escudarse *vr*: ~ **en** (*fig*) to hide behind

escudilla *nf* bowl, basin

escudo *nm* shield; ~ **de armas** coat of arms

escudriñar *vt* (*examinar*) to investigate, scrutinize; (*mirar de lejos*) to scan

escuela *nf* (*tb fig*) school; **hoy no tengo que ir a la** ~ I don't have to go to school today; **gente de la vieja** ~ people of the old school; ~ **de párvulos** kindergarten; ~ **normal** teacher training college; **la** ~ **primaria** primary school; ~ **técnica superior** *university offering 5-year courses in engineering and technical subjects*; ~ **universitaria**

university offering 3-year diploma courses

escueto, -a *adj* plain; *(estilo)* simple; *(explicación)* concise

escuincle *nm (Méx fam)* kid

esculpir *vt* to sculpt; *(grabar)* to engrave; *(tallar)* to carve

escultor, a *nm/f* sculptor

escultura *nf* sculpture

escupidera *nf* spittoon

escupir *vt* to spit (out) ▷ *vi* to spit

escupitajo *nm (fam)* gob of spit

escurreplatos *nm inv* plate rack

escurridizo, -a *adj* slippery

escurrir *vt (ropa)* to wring out; *(verduras, platos)* to drain ▷ *vi (los líquidos)* to drip; **escurrirse** *vr (secarse)* to drain; *(resbalarse)* to slip, slide; *(escaparse)* to slip away

ese *nf* (the letter) S; **hacer ~s** *(carretera)* to zigzag; *(borracho)* to reel about

ése, ésa, ésos, ésas *pron (sg)* that (one); *(pl)* those (ones); **~ ... éste ...** the former ... the latter ...; **¡no me vengas con ésas!** don't give me any more of that nonsense!

esencia *nf* essence

esencial *adj* essential; *(principal)* chief; **lo ~** the main thing

esfera *nf* sphere; *(de reloj)* face; **~ de acción** scope; **~ terrestre** globe

esférico, -a *adj* spherical

esforzado, -a *adj (enérgico)* energetic, vigorous

esforzarse *vr* to exert o.s., make an effort

esfuerzo *nm* effort; **sin ~** effortlessly

esfumarse *vr (apoyo, esperanzas)* to fade away; *(persona)* to vanish

esgrima *nf* fencing

esgrimir *vt (arma)* to brandish; *(argumento)* to use ▷ *vi* to fence

esguince *nm (Med)* sprain

eslabón *nm* link; **~ perdido** *(Bio, fig)* missing link

eslálom *nm* slalom

eslavo, -a *adj* Slav, Slavonic ▷ *nm/f* Slav ▷ *nm (Ling)* Slavonic

eslogan *nm (pl ~s)*; **slogan**

esmaltar *vt* to enamel

esmalte *nm* enamel; **~ de uñas** nail varnish *o* polish

esmerado, -a *adj* careful, neat

esmeralda *nf* emerald

esmerarse *vr (aplicarse)* to take great pains, exercise great care; *(afanarse)* to work hard; *(hacer lo mejor)* to do one's best

esmero *nm* (great) care

esnob *adj inv (persona)* snobbish; *(coche etc)* posh ▷ *nm/f* snob

esnobismo *nm* snobbery

eso *pron* that, that thing *o* matter; **~ de su coche** that business about his car; **~ de ir al cine** all that about going to the cinema; **a ~ de las cinco** at about five o'clock; **en ~** thereupon, at that point; **por ~** therefore; **~ es** that's it; **nada de ~** far from it; **¡~ sí que es vida!** now this is really living!; **por ~ te lo dije** that's why I told you; **y ~**

que llovía in spite of the fact it was raining

esófago *nm (Anat)* oesophagus

esos *adj demostrativo ver* **ese**

ésos *pron ver* **ése**

esotérico, -a *adj* esoteric

espabilado, -a *adj* quick-witted

espachurrar *vt* to squash; **espachurrarse** *vr* to get squashed

espacial *adj (del espacio)* space *cpd*

espaciar *vt* to space (out)

espacio *nm* space; *(Mus)* interval; *(Radio, TV)* programme, program *(US)*; **el ~** space; **ocupar mucho ~** to take up a lot of room; **a dos ~s, a doble ~** *(Tip)* double-spaced; **por ~ de** during, for

espacioso, -a *adj* spacious, roomy

espada *nf* sword ▷ *nm* swordsman; *(Taur)* matador; **espadas** *nfpl (Naipes)* one of the suits in the Spanish card deck; **estar entre la ~ y la pared** to be between the devil and the deep blue sea

espaguetis *nmpl* spaghetti *sg*

espalda *nf (gen)* back; *(Natación)* backstroke; **~s** *nfpl (hombros)* shoulders; **a ~s de algn** behind sb's back; **estar de ~s** to have one's back turned; **tenderse de ~s** to lie (down) on one's back; **volver la ~ a algn** to cold-shoulder sb

espaldilla *nf* shoulder blade

espantadizo, -a *adj* timid, easily frightened

espantajo *nm*, **espantapájaros** *nm inv* scarecrow

espantar *vt (asustar)* to frighten, scare; *(ahuyentar)* to frighten off; *(asombrar)* to horrify, appal; **espantarse** *vr (asustarse)* to get frightened *o* scared; *(horrorizarse)* to be appalled

espanto *nm (susto)* fright; *(terror)* terror; *(asombro)* astonishment; **¡qué ~!** how awful!

espantoso, -a *adj* frightening, terrifying; *(ruido)* dreadful

España *nf* Spain

español, a *adj* Spanish ▷ *nm/f* Spaniard ▷ *nm (Ling)* Spanish

esparadrapo *nm* (sticking) plaster, Band-Aid® *(US)*

esparcimiento *nm (dispersión)* spreading; *(derramamiento)* scattering; *(fig)* cheerfulness

esparcir *vt* to spread, scatter; **esparcirse** *vr (repartirse)* to spread (out), scatter; *(divertirse)* to enjoy o.s.

espárrago *nm (tb: espárragos)* asparagus; **estar hecho un ~** to be as thin as a rake; **¡vete a freír ~s!** *(fam)* go to hell!

esparto *nm* esparto (grass)

espasmo *nm* spasm

espátula *nf (Med)* spatula; *(Arte)* palette knife; *(Culin)* fish slice

especia *nf* spice

especial *adj* special ▷ *nm* special; **fue un día muy ~** it was a very special day; **no me gusta ninguno en ~** I don't like any of them particularly; **¿desea ver a alguien en ~?** is there anybody you particularly want to see?; **un ~ informativo sobre las elecciones** a news special on the elections

especialidad *nf* speciality, specialty (US); (*Escol: ramo*) specialism

especialista *nm/f* specialist; (*Cine*) stuntman(-woman)

especializado, -a *adj* specialized; (*obrero*) skilled

especialmente *adv* (*sobre todo*) particularly, especially; (*para un fin concreto*) specially

especie *nf* (*Bio*) species; (*clase*) kind, sort; **pagar en ~** to pay in kind

especificar *vt* to specify

específico, -a *adj* specific

espécimen (*pl* **especímenes**) *nm* specimen

espectáculo *nm* (*gen*) spectacle; (*Teat etc*) show; (*función*) performance; **dar un ~** to make a scene

espectador, a *nm/f* spectator; (*de incidente*) onlooker; **los ~es** (*Teat*) the audience *sg*

espectro *nm* ghost; (*fig*) spectre

especulación *nf* speculation; **~ bursátil** speculation on the Stock Market

especular *vt, vi* to speculate

espejismo *nm* mirage

espejo *nm* mirror; (*fig*) model; **~ retrovisor** rearview mirror; **mirarse al ~** to look (at o.s.) in the mirror

espeleología *nf* potholing

espeluznante *adj* horrifying, hair-raising

espera *nf* (*pausa, intervalo*) wait; (*Jur: plazo*) respite; **en ~ de** waiting for; (*con expectativa*) expecting; **en ~ de su contestación** awaiting your reply

esperanza *nf* hope; **no tengo ~s de aprobar** I have no hope of passing; **eres su última ~** you're his last hope; **no pierdas las ~s** don't give up hope; **hay pocas ~s de que venga** there is little prospect of his coming; **tener la ~ puesta en...** to pin one's hopes on

esperanzar *vt* to give hope to

esperar *vt* (*aguardar*) to wait for; (*tener expectativa de*) to expect; (*desear*) to hope for ▷ *vi* (*con paciencia*) to wait; (*con expectativa*) to expect; (*con esperanza*) to hope; **esperarse** *vr* to expect; **estaba esperando el tren** I was waiting for the train; **no me esperéis** don't wait for me; **fuimos a ~la a la estación** we went to the station to meet her; **espera un momento, por favor** wait a moment, please; **llegaron antes de lo que yo esperaba** they arrived sooner than I expected; **llamará cuando menos lo esperes** he'll call when you're least expecting it; **no esperes que venga a ayudarte** don't expect him to come and help you; **me espera un largo día de trabajo** I've got a long day of work ahead of me; **~ un bebé** to be expecting (a baby); **espero que no sea nada grave** I hope it isn't anything serious; **¿vendrás a la fiesta?** — **espero que sí** are you coming to the party? — I hope so; **¿crees que Carmen se enfadará?** — **espero que no** do you think Carmen will be angry? — I hope not; **era de ~ que no viniera** he was bound not to come; **hacer ~ a algn** to keep sb waiting; **como podía ~se** as was to be expected

esperma *nf* sperm

espermatozoide *nm* spermatozoid

espesar *vt* to thicken; **espesarse** *vr* to thicken, get thicker

espeso, -a *adj* thick; (*bosque*) dense; (*nieve*) deep; (*sucio*) dirty

espesor *nm* thickness; (*de nieve*) depth

espía *nm/f* spy

espiar *vt* (*observar*) to spy on ▷ *vi*: **~ para** to spy for

espiga *nf* (*Bot: de trigo etc*) ear; (*: de flores*) spike

espina *nf* thorn; (*de pez*) bone; **~ dorsal** (*Anat*) spine; **me da mala ~** I don't like the look of it

espinaca *nf* (*tb*: **espinacas**) spinach

espinazo *nm* spine, backbone

espinilla *nf* (*Anat: tibia*) shin(bone); (*: en la piel*) blackhead

espino *nm* hawthorn

espinoso, -a *adj* (*planta*) thorny, prickly; (*fig*) bony; (*problema*) knotty

espionaje *nm* spying, espionage

espiral *adj, nf* spiral; **la ~ inflacionista** the inflationary spiral

espirar *vt, vi* to breathe out, exhale

espiritista *adj, nm/f* spiritualist

espíritu *nm* spirit; (*mente*) mind; (*inteligencia*) intelligence; (*Rel*) spirit, soul; **E~ Santo** Holy Ghost; **con ~ amplio** with an open mind

espiritual *adj* spiritual

espita *nf* tap (Brit), faucet (US)

espléndido, -a *adj* (*magnífico*) magnificent, splendid; (*generoso*) generous, lavish

esplendor *nm* splendour

espolear *vt* to spur on

espoleta *nf* (*de bomba*) fuse

espolvorear *vt* to dust, sprinkle

esponja *nf* sponge; (*fig*) sponger

esponjoso, -a *adj* spongy

espontaneidad *nf* spontaneity

espontáneo, -a *adj* spontaneous; (*improvisado*) impromptu; (*persona*) natural

esporádico, -a *adj* sporadic

esposa *nf ver* **esposo**

esposar *vt* to handcuff

esposo, -a *nm* husband ▷ *nf* wife; **esposas** *nfpl* handcuffs

espuela *nf* spur; (*fam: trago*) one for the road

espuma *nf* foam; (*de cerveza*) froth, head; (*de jabón*) lather; (*de olas*) surf

espumadera *nf* skimmer

espumoso, -a *adj* frothy, foamy; (*vino*) sparkling

esqueje *nm* (*Bot*) cutting

esquela *nf*: **~ mortuoria** announcement of death

esquelético, -a *adj* (*fam*) skinny

esqueleto *nm* skeleton; (*lo esencial*) bare bones (of a matter); **en ~** unfinished

esquema *nm* (*diagrama*) diagram; (*dibujo*) plan; (*plan*) scheme; (*Filosofía*) schema

esquemático, -a *adj* schematic; **un resumen ~** a brief outline

esquí (*pl* **-s**) *nm* (*objeto*) ski; (*deporte*) skiing; **~ acuático** water-skiing; **hacer ~** to go skiing

esquiar *vi* to ski

esquilar vt to shear

esquimal adj, nm/f Eskimo

esquina nf corner; **doblar la ~** to turn the corner

esquinazo nm: **dar ~ a algn** to give sb the slip

esquirol nm blackleg

esquivar vt to avoid; (evadir) to dodge, elude

esquivo, -a adj (altanero) aloof; (desdeñoso) scornful, disdainful

esta adj demostrativo ver **este**

ésta pron ver **éste**

estabilidad nf stability

estabilizar vt to stabilize; (fijar) to make steady; (precios) to peg; **estabilizarse** vr to become stable

estable adj stable

establecer vt to establish; (fundar) to set up; (colonos) to settle; (récord) to set (up); **establecerse** vr to establish o.s.; (echar raíces) to settle (down); (Com) to start up

establecimiento nm establishment; (fundación) institution; (de negocio) start-up; (de colonias) settlement; (local) establishment; **~ comercial** business house

establo nm (Agr) stall; (: esp LAm) barn

estaca nf stake, post; (de tienda de campaña) peg

estacada nf (cerca) fence, fencing; (palenque) stockade; **dejar a algn en la ~** to leave sb in the lurch

estación nf station; (del año) season; **~ de autobuses/ferrocarril** bus/railway station; **~ balnearia** seaside resort; **~ de servicio** service station; **~ terminal** terminus; **~ de trabajo** (Com) work station; **~ transmisora** transmitter; **~ de visualización** display unit

estacionamiento nm (Auto) parking; (Mil) stationing

estacionar vt (Auto) to park; (Mil) to station

estacionario, -a adj stationary; (Com: mercado) slack

estadio nm (fase) stage, phase; (Deporte) stadium

estadista nm (Pol) statesman; (Estadística) statistician

estadística nf (una estadística) figure, statistic; (ciencia) statistics sg

estado nm (Pol: condición) state; **~ civil** marital status; **~ de cuenta(s)** bank statement, statement of accounts; **~ de excepción** (Pol) state of emergency; **~ financiero** (Com) financial statement; **~ mayor** (Mil) staff; **~ de pérdidas y ganancias** (Com) profit and loss statement, operating statement; **E~s Unidos (EE.UU.)** United States (of America) (USA); **estar en ~ (de buena esperanza)** to be pregnant

estadounidense adj United States cpd, American ▷ nm/f United States citizen, American

estafa nf swindle, trick; (Com etc) racket

estafar vt to swindle, defraud

estafeta nf (oficina de correos) post office; **~ diplomática** diplomatic bag

estallar vi to burst; (bomba) to explode, go off; (volcán) to erupt; (vidrio) to shatter; (látigo) to crack; (epidemia, guerra, rebelión) to break out; **~ en llanto** to burst into tears

estallido nm explosion; (de látigo, trueno) crack; (fig) outbreak

Estambul nm Istanbul

estampa nf (impresión, imprenta) print, engraving; (imagen, figura: de persona) appearance

estampado, -a adj printed ▷ nm (impresión: acción) printing; (: efecto) print; (marca) stamping

estampar vt (imprimir) to print; (marcar) to stamp; (metal) to engrave; (poner sello en) to stamp; (fig) to stamp, imprint

estampida nf stampede

estampido nm bang, report

estampilla nf (sello de goma) (rubber) stamp; (LAm) (postage) stamp

estancado, -a adj (agua) stagnant

estancar vt (aguas) to hold up, hold back; (Com) to monopolize; (fig) to block, hold up; **estancarse** vr to stagnate

estancia nf (permanencia) stay; (sala) room; (LAm) farm, ranch

estanciero nm (LAm) farmer, rancher

estanco, -a adj watertight ▷ nm tobacconist's (shop)

estándar adj, nm standard

estandarizar vt to standardize

estandarte nm banner, standard

estanque nm (lago) pool, pond; (Agr) reservoir

estanquero, -a nm/f tobacconist

estante nm (armario) rack, stand; (biblioteca) bookcase; (anaquel) shelf; (LAm) prop

estantería nf shelving, shelves pl

estaño nm tin

estar vi **1** (situación) to be; **está en la plaza** it's in the square; **¿dónde estabas?** where were you?; **¿está Mónica?** is Mónica there?; **estamos a 30 km de Almería** we're 30 kms from Almería; **sólo ~é un fin de semana** I'll only stay for a weekend

2 (+ adj o adv: estado) to be; (aspecto) to look; **¿cómo estás?** how are you?; **estoy muy cansada** I'm very tired; **¿estás casado o soltero?** are you married or single?; **~ enfermo** to be ill; **¡qué guapa estás esta noche!** you look really pretty tonight!; **el sofá ~á mejor al lado de la ventana** the sofa will look better next to the window; **ese vestido te está muy bien** that dress looks very good on you; **está muy elegante** he's looking very smart

3 (+ gerundio o participio) to be; **estoy leyendo** I'm reading; **estaba sentada en la arena** she was sitting on the sand; **la radio está rota** the radio's broken

4 (uso pasivo): **está condenado a muerte** he's been condemned to death; **está envasado en ...** it's packed in ...

5: **~ a**: **¿a cuántos estamos?** what's the date today?; **estamos a 3 de mayo** it's the 3rd of May; **¿a cuánto está el kilo de naranjas?** what price are oranges per kilo?; **las manzanas están a dos euros** apples are (selling at) two euros; **estamos a 25 grados** it's 25 degrees today

6 (locuciones): **¿estamos?** (¿de acuerdo?) okay?;

(¿listo?) ready?; **¡ya está bien!** that's enough!;
¿está la comida? is dinner ready?; **¡ya está!**
(LAm): **¡ya estuvo!** that's it!

7: ~ **con**: **está con gripe** he's got (the) flu
8: ~ **de**: ~ **de vacaciones/viaje** to be on holiday/
away o on a trip; **está de camarero** he's
working as a waiter

9: ~ **para**: **está para salir** he's about to leave;
no estoy para bromas I'm not in the mood for
jokes

10: ~ **por** (propuesta) to be in favour of; (persona)
to support, side with; **está todavía por limpiar**
it still has to be cleaned; **¡estoy por dejarlo!** I
think I'm going to leave this!

11 (+que): **está que rabia** (fam) he's hopping
mad (fam); **estoy que me caigo de sueño** I'm
terribly sleepy, I can't keep my eyes open

12: ~ **sin**: ~ **sin dinero** to have no money; **está
sin terminar** it isn't finished yet

estarse vr: **se estuvo en la cama toda la tarde**
he stayed in bed all afternoon; **¡estáte quieto!**
stop fidgeting!

estárter nm (Auto) choke

estas adj demostrativo ver **este**

éstas pron ver **éste**

estatal adj state cpd

estático, -a adj static

estatua nf statue

estatura nf stature, height

estatus nm inv status

estatuto nm (Jur) statute; (de ciudad) bye-law;
(de comité) rule; **~s sociales** (Com) articles of
association

este¹ adj (lado) east; (dirección) easterly ▷ nm east;
el ~ del país the east of the country; **en el ~ de
España** in the East of Spain; **los países del E~**
the Eastern bloc countries; **en la parte del ~** in
the eastern part; **vientos del ~** easterly winds

este², **esta**, **estos**, **estas** adj demostrativo (sg)
this; (pl) these; (LAm: como muletilla) er, um

éste, **ésta**, **éstos**, **éstas** pron (sg) this (one);
(pl) these (ones); **ése … ~ …** the former … the
latter …

estela nf wake, wash; (fig) trail

estelar adj (Astro) stellar; (Teat) star cpd

estenografía nf shorthand

estepa nf (Geo) steppe

estera nf (alfombra) mat; (tejido) matting

estéreo adj inv, nm stereo

estereotipo nm stereotype

estéril adj sterile, barren; (fig) vain, futile

esterilizar vt to sterilize

esterlina adj: **libra ~** pound sterling

estético, -a adj aesthetic ▷ nf aesthetics sg

estiércol nm dung, manure

estigma nm stigma

estilarse vr (estar de moda) to be in fashion; (usarse)
to be used

estilo nm style; (Tec) stylus; (Natación) stroke; ~
de vida lifestyle; **al ~ de** in the style of; **algo por
el ~** something along those lines

estima nf esteem, respect

estimación nf (evaluación) estimation; (aprecio,
afecto) esteem, regard

estimado, -a adj esteemed; **"E~ Señor"** "Dear
Sir"

estimar vt (evaluar) to estimate; (valorar) to value;
(apreciar) to esteem, respect; (pensar, considerar) to
think, reckon

estimulante adj stimulating ▷ nm stimulant

estimular vt to stimulate; (excitar) to excite;
(animar) to encourage

estímulo nm stimulus; (ánimo) encouragement;
(Inform) prompt

estío nm summer

estipulación nf stipulation, condition

estipular vt to stipulate

estirado, -a adj (tenso) (stretched o drawn) tight;
(fig: persona) stiff, pompous; (engreído) stuck-up

estirar vt to stretch; (dinero, suma etc) to stretch
out; (cuello) to crane; (dinero) to eke out; (discurso)
to spin out; **estirarse** vr to stretch; ~ **la pata**
(fam) to kick the bucket

estirón nm pull, tug; (crecimiento) spurt, sudden
growth; **dar un ~** (niño) to shoot up

estirpe nf stock, lineage

estival adj summer cpd

esto pron this, this thing o matter; (como muletilla)
er, um; ~ **de la boda** this business about the
wedding; **en ~** at this o that point; **por ~** for this
reason

Estocolmo nm Stockholm

estofa nf: **de baja ~** poor-quality

estofado nm stew

estofar vt (bordar) to quilt; (Culin) to stew

estómago nm stomach; **tener ~** to be thickskinned

estorbar vt to hinder, obstruct; (fig) to bother,
disturb ▷ vi to be in the way

estorbo nm (molestia) bother, nuisance; (obstáculo)
hindrance, obstacle

estornudar vi to sneeze

estornudo nm sneeze

estos adj demostrativo ver **este**

éstos pron ver **éste**

estrado nm (tarima) platform; (Mus) bandstand;
estrados nmpl law courts

estrafalario, -a adj odd, eccentric; (desarreglado)
slovenly, sloppy

estrago nm ruin, destruction; **hacer ~s en** to
wreak havoc among

estragón nm (Culin) tarragon

estrambótico, -a adj odd, eccentric

estrangulador, -a nm/f strangler ▷ nm (Tec)
throttle; (Auto) choke

estrangulamiento nm (Auto) bottleneck

estrangular vt (persona) to strangle; (Med) to
strangulate

estraperlo nm black market

estratagema nf (Mil) stratagem; (astucia)
cunning

estrategia nf strategy

estratégico, -a adj strategic

estratificar vt to stratify

estrato nm stratum, layer

estrechar vt (reducir) to narrow; (vestido) to take in; (persona) to hug, embrace; **estrecharse** vr (reducirse) to narrow, grow narrow; (2 personas) to embrace; **~ la mano** to shake hands

estrechez nf narrowness; (de ropa) tightness; (intimidad) intimacy; (Com) want o shortage of money; **estrecheces** nfpl financial difficulties

estrecho, -a adj narrow; (apretado) tight; (íntimo) close, intimate; (miserable) mean ▷ nm strait; **~ de miras** narrow-minded; **E~ de Gibraltar** Straits of Gibraltar

estrella nf star; **~ fugaz** shooting star; **~ de mar** starfish; **tener (buena)/mala ~** to be lucky/ unlucky

estrellado, -a adj (forma) star-shaped; (cielo) starry; (huevos) fried

estrellar vt (hacer añicos) to smash (to pieces); (huevos) to fry; **estrellarse** vr to smash; (chocarse) to crash; (fracasar) to fail

estremecer vt to shake; **estremecerse** vr to shake, tremble; **~ de** (horror) to shudder with; (frío) to shiver with

estremecimiento nm (temblor) trembling, shaking

estrenar vt (vestido) to wear for the first time; (casa) to move into; (película, obra de teatro) to present for the first time; **estrenarse** vr (persona) to make one's début; (película) to have its première; (Teat) to open

estreno nm (primer uso) first use; (Cine etc) première

estreñido, -a adj constipated

estreñimiento nm constipation

estreñir vt to constipate

estrépito nm noise, racket; (fig) fuss

estrepitoso, -a adj noisy; (fiesta) rowdy

estrés nm stress

estría nf groove; **~s (en el cutis)** stretchmarks

estribación nf (Geo) spur; **estribaciones** nfpl foothills

estribar vi: **~ en** to rest on, be supported by; **la dificultad estriba en el texto** the difficulty lies in the text

estribillo nm (Literatura) refrain; (Mus) chorus

estribo nm (de jinete) stirrup; (de coche, tren) step; (de puente) support; (Geo) spur; **perder los ~s** to fly off the handle

estribor nm (Naut) starboard

estricnina nf strychnine

estricto, -a adj (riguroso) strict; (severo) severe

estridente adj (color) loud; (voz) raucous

estrofa nf verse

estropajo nm scourer

estropeado, -a adj: **está ~** it's not working

estropear vt (dañar: mecanismo) to damage; (máquina) to break; (arruinar) to spoil; **estropearse** vr (objeto) to get damaged; (coche) to break down; (la piel etc) to be ruined; **ese detergente me estropeó la ropa** that detergent ruined my clothes; **la lluvia nos estropeó las vacaciones** the rain ruined our holidays; **se nos ha estropeado la tele** the TV's broken; **se me estropeó el coche en la autopista** my car broke down on the motorway; **la fruta se está estropeando con este calor** the fruit's going off in this heat

estructura nf structure

estruendo nm (ruido) racket, din; (fig: alboroto) uproar, turmoil

estrujar vt (apretar) to squeeze; (aplastar) to crush; (fig) to drain, bleed

estuario nm estuary

estuche nm box, case

estudiante nm/f student

estudiantil adj inv student cpd

estudiar vt (aprender) to learn; (cursar) to study; (propuesta) to think about o over ▷ vi to study; **ayer no salí porque tenía que ~ para el examen** I didn't go out yesterday because I had to study for the exam; **~ para abogado** to study to become a lawyer

estudio nm study; (encuesta) research; (proyecto) plan; (piso) studio flat; (Cine, Arte, Radio) studio; **estudios** nmpl studies; (erudición) learning sg; **cursar o hacer ~s** to study; **~ de casos prácticos** case study; **~ de desplazamientos y tiempos** (Com) time and motion study; **~s de motivación** motivational research sg; **~ del trabajo** (Com) work study; **~ de viabilidad** (Com) feasibility study

estudioso, -a adj studious

estufa nf heater, fire

estupefaciente adj, nm narcotic

estupefacto, -a adj speechless, thunderstruck

estupendamente adv (fam): **estoy ~** I feel great; **le salió ~** he did it very well

estupendo, -a adj wonderful, terrific; (fam) great; **¡~!** that's great!, fantastic!

estupidez nf (torpeza) stupidity; (acto) stupid thing (to do); **fue una ~ mía** that was a silly thing for me to do o say

estúpido, -a adj stupid, silly

estupor nm stupor; (fig) astonishment, amazement

estupro nm rape

esvástica nf swastika

ETA nf abr (Pol: = Euskadi Ta Askatasuna) ETA

etapa nf (de viaje) stage; (Deporte) leg; (parada) stopping place; (fig) stage, phase; **por ~s** gradually, in stages

etarra adj ETA cpd ▷ nm/f member of ETA

etc. abr (= etcétera) etc

etcétera adv etcetera

eternidad nf eternity

eternizarse vr: **~ en hacer algo** to take ages to do sth

eterno, -a adj eternal, everlasting; (despectivo) never-ending

ético, -a adj ethical ▷ nf ethics

etiqueta nf (modales) etiquette; (rótulo) label, tag; **de ~** formal

etnia nf ethnic group

étnico, -a adj ethnic

Eucaristía *nf* Eucharist
eufemismo *nm* euphemism
euforia *nf* euphoria
eunuco *nm* eunuch
euro *sm* (*moneda*) euro
eurodiputado, -a *nm/f* Euro MP, MEP
Europa *nf* Europe
europeo, -a *adj, nm/f* European
Euskadi *nm* the Basque Provinces *pl*
euskera, eusquera *nm* (*Ling*) Basque
eutanasia *nf* euthanasia
evacuación *nf* evacuation
evacuar *vt* to evacuate
evadir *vt* to evade, avoid; **evadirse** *vr* to escape
evaluación *nf* evaluation, assessment
evaluar *vt* to evaluate, assess
evangélico, -a *adj* evangelical
evangelio *nm* gospel
evaporar *vt* to evaporate; **evaporarse** *vr* to vanish
evasión *nf* escape, flight; (*fig*) evasion; **~ fiscal** *o* **tributaria** tax evasion
evasivo, -a *adj* evasive, non-committal ▷ *nf* (*pretexto*) excuse; **contestar con evasivas** to avoid giving a straight answer
evento *nm* event; (*eventualidad*) eventuality
eventual *adj* possible, conditional (upon circumstances); (*trabajador*) casual, temporary
evidencia *nf* evidence, proof; **poner en ~** to make clear; **ponerse en ~** (*persona*) to show o.s. up
evidenciar *vt* (*hacer patente*) to make evident; (*probar*) to prove, show; **evidenciarse** *vr* to be evident
evidente *adj* obvious, clear, evident
evitar *vt* (*evadir*) to avoid; (*impedir*) to prevent; (*peligro*) to escape; (*molestia*) to save; (*tentación*) to shun; **si puedo ~lo** if I can help it
evocar *vt* to evoke, call forth
evolución *nf* (*desarrollo*) evolution, development; (*cambio*) change; (*Mil*) manoeuvre
evolucionar *vi* to evolve; (*Mil, Aviat*) to manoeuvre
ex *adj* ex-; **el ex ministro** the former minister, the ex-minister
exacerbar *vt* to irritate, annoy
exactamente *adv* exactly
exactitud *nf* exactness; (*precisión*) accuracy; (*puntualidad*) punctuality
exacto, -a *adj* (*número, copia, descripción*) exact; (*cálculo, medida, respuesta*) accurate; **¡~!** exactly!; **eso no es del todo ~** that's not quite right; **para ser ~** to be precise
exageración *nf* exaggeration
exagerar *vt* to exaggerate; (*exceder*) to overdo
exaltado, -a *adj* (*apasionado*) over-excited, worked up; (*exagerado*) extreme; (*fanático*) hot-headed; (*discurso*) impassioned ▷ *nm/f* (*fanático*) hothead; (*Pol*) extremist
exaltar *vt* to exalt, glorify; **exaltarse** *vr* (*excitarse*) to get excited *o* worked up
examen *nm* examination; (*de problema*)

consideration; **~ de** (*encuesta*) inquiry into; **~ de ingreso** entrance examination; **~ de conducir** driving test; **~ eliminatorio** qualifying examination
examinar *vt* to examine; (*poner a prueba*) to test; (*inspeccionar*) to inspect; **examinarse** *vr* to be examined, take an examination
exasperar *vt* to exasperate; **exasperarse** *vr* to get exasperated, lose patience
excavador, a *nm/f* (*persona*) excavator; *ver tb* **excavadora**
excavadora *nf* (*Tec*) digger; *ver tb* **excavador**
excavar *vt* to excavate, dig (out)
excedencia *nf* (*Mil*) leave; (*Escol*) sabbatical
excedente *adj, nm* excess, surplus
exceder *vt* to exceed, surpass; **excederse** *vr* (*extralimitarse*) to go too far; (*sobrepasarse*) to excel o.s.
excelencia *nf* excellence; **E~** Excellency; **por ~** par excellence
excelente *adj* excellent
excelso, -a *adj* lofty, sublime
excentricidad *nf* eccentricity
excéntrico, -a *adj, nm/f* eccentric
excepción *nf* exception; **la ~ confirma la regla** the exception proves the rule
excepcional *adj* exceptional
excepto *adv* excepting, except (for)
exceptuar *vt* to except, exclude
excesivo, -a *adj* excessive
exceso *nm* excess; (*Com*) surplus; **~ de equipaje/ peso** excess luggage/weight; **~ de velocidad** speeding; **en** *o* **por ~** excessively
excitación *nf* (*sensación*) excitement; (*acción*) excitation
excitado, -a *adj* excited; (*emociones*) aroused
excitar *vt* to excite; (*incitar*) to urge; (*emoción*) to stir up; (*esperanzas*) to raise; (*pasión*) to arouse; **excitarse** *vr* to get excited
exclamación *nf* exclamation
exclamar *vi* to exclaim; **exclamarse** *vr*: **~se (contra)** to complain (about)
excluir *vt* to exclude; (*dejar fuera*) to shut out; (*solución*) to reject; (*posibilidad*) to rule out
exclusión *nf* exclusion
exclusiva *nf* (*Prensa*) exclusive, scoop; (*Com*) sole right *o* agency
exclusivo, -a *adj* exclusive; **derecho ~** sole *o* exclusive right
excomulgar *vt* (*Rel*) to excommunicate
excomunión *nf* excommunication
excremento *nm* excrement
excursión *nf* excursion, outing; **ir de ~** to go (off) on a trip
excursionista *nm/f* (*turista*) sightseer
excusa *nf* excuse; (*disculpa*) apology; **presentar sus ~s** to excuse o.s.
excusar *vt* to excuse; (*evitar*) to avoid, prevent; **excusarse** *vr* (*disculparse*) to apologize
exento, -a *pp de* **eximir** ▷ *adj* exempt
exequias *nfpl* funeral rites
exfoliar *vt* to exfoliate

exhalar *vt* to exhale, breathe out; (*olor etc*) to give off; (*suspiro*) to breathe, heave

exhaustivo, -a *adj* exhaustive

exhausto, -a *adj* exhausted, worn-out

exhibición *nf* exhibition; (*demostración*) display, show; (*de película*) showing; (*de equipo*) performance

exhibir *vt* (*cuadros*) to exhibit; (*artículos*) to display; (*pasaporte*) to show; (*película*) to screen; (*mostrar con orgullo*) to show off; **exhibirse** *vr* (*mostrarse en público*) to show o.s. off; (*fam: indecentemente*) to expose o.s.

exhortación *nf* exhortation

exhortar *vt*: ~ **a** to exhort to

exigencia *nf* demand, requirement

exigente *adj* demanding; (*profesor*) strict; **ser ~ con algn** to be hard on sb

exigir *vt* (*gen*) to demand, require; (*impuestos*) to exact, levy; ~ **el pago** to demand payment

exiliado, -a *adj* exiled, in exile ▷ *nm/f* exile

exilio *nm* exile

eximio, -a *adj* (*eminente*) distinguished, eminent

eximir *vt* to exempt

existencia *nf* existence; **existencias** *nfpl* stock *sg*; ~ **de mercancías** (*Com*) stock-in-trade; **tener en ~** to have in stock; **amargar la ~ a algn** to make sb's life a misery

existir *vi* to exist, be

éxito *nm* (*buen resultado*) success; (*Mus, Teat*) hit; ~ **editorial** bestseller; ~ **rotundo** smash hit; **tener ~** to be successful

éxodo *nm* exodus; **el ~ rural** the drift from the land

exonerar *vt* to exonerate; ~ **de una obligación** to free from an obligation

exorcizar *vt* to exorcize

exótico, -a *adj* exotic

expandir *vt* to expand; (*Com*) to expand, enlarge; **expandirse** *vr* to expand, spread

expansión *nf* expansion; (*recreo*) relaxation; **la ~ económica** economic growth; **economía en ~** expanding economy

expansionarse *vr* (*dilatarse*) to expand; (*recrearse*) to relax

expansivo, -a *adj* expansive; (*efusivo*) communicative

expatriarse *vr* to emigrate; (*Pol*) to go into exile

expectativa *nf* (*espera*) expectation; (*perspectiva*) prospect; ~ **de vida** life expectancy; **estar a la ~** to wait and see (what will happen)

expedición *nf* (*excursión*) expedition; **gastos de ~** shipping charges

expediente *nm* expedient; (*Jur: procedimento*) action, proceedings *pl*; (: *papeles*) dossier, file, record; ~ **judicial** court proceedings *pl*; ~ **académico** (student's) record

expedir *vt* (*despachar*) to send, forward; (*pasaporte*) to issue; (*cheque*) to make out

expedito, -a *adj* (*libre*) clear, free

expendedor, a *nm/f* (*vendedor*) dealer; (*Teat*) ticket agent ▷ *nm* (*aparato*) (vending) machine; ~ **de cigarrillos** cigarette machine

expendeduría *nf* (*estanco*) tobacconist's (shop) (Brit), cigar store (US)

expensas *nfpl* (*Jur*) costs; **a ~ de** at the expense of

experiencia *nf* experience

experimentado, -a *adj* experienced

experimentar *vt* (*en laboratorio*) to experiment with; (*probar*) to test, try out; (*notar, observar*) to experience; (*deterioro, pérdida*) to suffer; (*aumento*) to show; (*sensación*) to feel

experimento *nm* experiment

experto, -a *adj* expert ▷ *nm/f* expert

expiar *vt* to atone for

expirar *vi* to expire

explayarse *vr* (*en discurso*) to speak at length; ~ **con algn** to confide in sb

explicación *nf* explanation

explicar *vt* to explain; (*teoría*) to expound; (*Univ*) to lecture in; **explicarse** *vr* to explain (o.s.); **no me lo explico** I can't understand it

explícito, -a *adj* explicit

explorador, a *nm/f* (*pionero*) explorer; (*Mil*) scout ▷ *nm* (*Med*) probe; (*radar*) (radar) scanner

explorar *vt* to explore; (*Med*) to probe; (*radar*) to scan

explosión *nf* explosion

explosivo, -a *adj* explosive

explotación *nf* exploitation; (*de planta etc*) running; (*de mina*) working; (*de recurso*) development; ~ **minera** mine; **gastos de ~** operating costs

explotar *vt* to exploit; (*planta*) to run, operate; (*mina*) to work ▷ *vi* (*bomba etc*) to explode, go off

exponer *vt* to expose; (*cuadro*) to display; (*vida*) to risk; (*idea*) to explain; (*teoría*) to expound; (*hechos*) to set out; **exponerse** *vr*: ~**se a (hacer) algo** to run the risk of (doing) sth

exportación *nf* (*acción*) export; (*mercancías*) exports *pl*

exportar *vt* to export

exposición *nf* (*gen*) exposure; (*de arte*) show, exhibition; (*Com*) display; (*feria*) show, fair; (*explicación*) explanation; (*de teoría*) exposition; (*narración*) account, statement

exprés *adj inv* (*café*) espresso ▷ *nm* (*Ferro*) express (train)

expresar *vt* to express; (*redactar*) to phrase, put; (*emoción*) to show; **expresarse** *vr* to express o.s.; (*dato*) to be stated; **como abajo se expresa** as stated below

expresión *nf* expression; ~ **familiar** colloquialism

expreso, -a *adj* (*explícito*) express; (*claro*) specific, clear; (*tren*) fast ▷ *nm* (*Ferro*) fast train ▷ *adv*: **mandar ~** to send by express (delivery)

exprimidor *nm* (lemon) squeezer

exprimir *vt* (*fruta*) to squeeze; (*zumo*) to squeeze out

ex profeso *adv* expressly

expropiar *vt* to expropriate

expuesto, -a *pp de* **exponer** ▷ *adj* exposed; (*cuadro etc*) on show, on display; **según lo ~ arriba** according to what has been stated above

expulsar vt (echar) to eject, throw out; (alumno) to expel; (despedir) to sack, fire; (Deporte) to send off
expulsión nf (de gases, persona) expulsion; (en deportes) sending-off
exquisito, -a adj exquisite; (comida) delicious; (afectado) affected
éxtasis nm (tb droga) ecstasy
extender vt (mapa, tela) to spread (out), open (out); (mantequilla, pintura) to spread; (plazo) to extend; (certificado) to issue; (cheque, recibo) to make out; (documento) to draw up; **extenderse** vr (en el espacio: terreno) to stretch (out), spread (out); (en el suelo: persona) to stretch out; (en el tiempo) to extend, last; (costumbre, epidemia) to spread; **extendí la toalla sobre la arena** I spread the towel out on the sand; **~ los brazos** to stretch one's arms out; **delante de nosotros se extendía el océano** the ocean lay spread out before us; **~se sobre un tema** to enlarge on a subject; **el fuego se extendió rápidamente** the fire spread quickly
extendido, -a adj (abierto) spread out, open; (brazos) outstretched; (costumbre etc) widespread
extensión nf (de terreno, mar) expanse, stretch; (Mus) range; (de conocimientos) extent; (de programa) scope; (de tiempo) length, duration; (Telec) extension; **en toda la ~ de la palabra** in every sense of the word; **de ~** (Inform) add-on
extenso, -a adj extensive
extenuar vt (debilitar) to weaken
exterior adj (de fuera) external; (afuera) outside, exterior; (apariencia) outward; (deuda, relaciones) foreign ▷ nm exterior, outside; (aspecto) outward appearance; (Deporte) wing(er); (países extranjeros) abroad; **asuntos ~es** foreign affairs; **al ~** outwardly, on the outside; **en el ~** abroad; **noticias del ~** foreign o overseas news
exteriorizar vt (emociones) to show, reveal
exterminar vt to exterminate
exterminio nm extermination
externo, -a adj (exterior) external, outside; (superficial) outward ▷ nm/f day pupil
extinguir vt (fuego) to extinguish, put out; (raza, población) to wipe out; **extinguirse** vr (fuego) to go out; (Bio) to die out, become extinct
extinto, -a adj extinct
extintor nm (fire) extinguisher
extra adj inv (tiempo) extra; (vino) vintage; (chocolate) good-quality; (gasolina) high-octane ▷ nm/f extra ▷ nm (bono) bonus; (periódico) special edition

extracción nf extraction; (en lotería) draw; (de carbón) mining
extracto nm extract
extractor nm (tb: **extractor de humos**) extractor fan
extraer vt to extract, take out
extralimitarse vr to go too far
extranjero, -a adj foreign ▷ nm/f foreigner ▷ nm foreign lands pl; **en el ~** abroad
extrañar vt (sorprender) to find strange o odd; (echar de menos) to miss; **extrañarse** vr (sorprenderse) to be amazed, be surprised; (distanciarse) to become estranged, grow apart; **me extraña** I'm surprised
extrañeza nf (rareza) strangeness, oddness; (asombro) amazement, surprise
extraño, -a adj (extranjero) foreign; (raro, sorprendente) strange, odd
extraordinario, -a adj extraordinary; (edición, número) special ▷ nm (de periódico) special edition; **horas extraordinarias** overtime sg
extrarradio nm suburbs pl
extravagancia nf oddness; (de aspecto, ropa) outlandishness; (rareza) peculiarity; **extravagancias** nfpl (tonterías) nonsense sg
extravagante adj (excéntrico) eccentric; (estrafalario) outlandish
extraviado, -a adj lost, missing
extraviar vt to mislead, misdirect; (perder) to lose, misplace; **extraviarse** vr to lose one's way, get lost; (objeto) to go missing, be mislaid
extravío nm loss; (fig) misconduct
extremar vt to carry to extremes; **extremarse** vr to do one's utmost, make every effort
extremaunción nf extreme unction, last rites pl
extremidad nf (punta) extremity; (fila) edge; **extremidades** nfpl (Anat) extremities
extremista adj, nm/f extremist
extremo, -a adj (de mayor grado) extreme; (más alejado) furthest; (último) last ▷ nm (final) end; (situación) extreme; **la extrema derecha** (Pol) the far right; **~ derecho/izquierdo** (Deporte) outside right/left; **E~ Oriente** Far East; **en último ~** as a last resort; **pasar de un ~ a otro** (fig) to go from one extreme to the other; **con ~** in the extreme
extrovertido, -a adj extrovert, outgoing ▷ nm/f extrovert
exuberancia nf exuberance
exuberante adj exuberant; (fig) luxuriant, lush
eyaculación nf ejaculation
eyacular vt, vi to ejaculate

Ff

fa *nm* (*Mus*) F

f.a.b. *abr* (= *franco a bordo*) f.o.b.

fabada *nf* bean and sausage stew

fábrica *nf* factory; **~ de moneda** mint; **marca de ~** trademark; **precio de ~** factory price

fabricación *nf* (*manufactura*) manufacture; (*producción*) production; **de ~ casera** home-made; **de ~ nacional** home produced; **~ en serie** mass production

fabricante *nm/f* manufacturer

fabricar *vt* (*manufacturar*) to manufacture, make; (*construir*) to build; (*cuento*) to fabricate, devise; **~ en serie** to mass-produce

fábula *nf* (*cuento*) fable; (*chisme*) rumour; (*mentira*) fib

fabuloso, -a *adj* fabulous, fantastic

facción *nf* (*Pol*) faction; **facciones** *nfpl* (*del rostro*) features

faceta *nf* facet

facha (*fam*) *nm/f* fascist, right-wing extremist ▷ *nf* (*aspecto*) look; (*cara*) face; **¡qué ~ tienes!** you look a sight!

fachada *nf* (*Arq*) façade, front; (*Tip*) title page; (*fig*) façade, outward show

facial *adj* facial

fácil *adj* (*simple*) easy; (*sencillo*) simple, straightforward; (*probable*) likely; (*respuesta*) facile; **~ de usar** (*Inform*) user-friendly

facilidad *nf* (*capacidad*) ease; (*sencillez*) simplicity; (*de palabra*) fluency; **facilidades** *nfpl* facilities; **"~es de pago"** (*Com*) "credit facilities", "payment terms"

facilitar *vt* (*hacer fácil*) to make easy; (*proporcionar*) to provide; (*documento*) to issue; **le agradecería me ~a ...** I would be grateful if you could let me have ...

fácilmente *adv* easily

facsímil *nm* (*documento*) facsimile

factible *adj* feasible

factor *nm* factor; (*Com*) agent; (*Ferro*) freight clerk

factura *nf* (*cuenta*) bill; (*nota de pago*) invoice; (*hechura*) manufacture; **presentar ~ a** to invoice

facturar *vt* (*Com*) to invoice, charge for; (*Aviat*) to check in; (*equipaje*) to register, check (*US*)

facultad *nf* (*aptitud, Escol etc*) faculty; (*poder*) power

facultativo, -a *adj* optional; (*de un oficio*) professional; **prescripción facultativa** medical prescription

faena *nf* (*trabajo*) work; (*quehacer*) task, job; **~s domésticas** housework *sg*

fagot *nm* (*Mus*) bassoon

faisán *nm* pheasant

faja *nf* (*para la cintura*) sash; (*de mujer*) corset; (*de tierra*) strip

fajo *nm* (*de papeles*) bundle; (*de billetes*) role, wad

falange *nf*: **la F~** (*Pol*) the Falange

falda *nf* (*prenda de vestir*) skirt; (*Geo*) foothill; **~ escocesa** kilt

falla *nf* (*defecto*) fault, flaw

fallar *vt* (*Jur*) to pronounce sentence on; (*Naipes*) to trump ▷ *vi* (*memoria*) to fail; (*plan*) to go wrong; (*motor*) to miss; **~ a algn** to let sb down

fallecer *vi* to pass away, die

fallecimiento *nm* decease, demise

fallido, -a *adj* vain; (*intento*) frustrated, unsuccessful; (*esperanza*) disappointed

fallo *nm* (*Jur*) verdict, ruling; (*decisión*) decision; (*de jurado*) findings; (*fracaso*) failure; (*Deporte*) miss; (*Inform*) bug

falo *nm* phallus

falsear *vt* to falsify; (*firma etc*) to forge ▷ *vi* (*Mus*) to be out of tune

falsedad *nf* falseness; (*hipocresía*) hypocrisy; (*mentira*) falsehood

falsificar *vt* (*firma etc*) to forge; (*voto etc*) to rig; (*moneda*) to counterfeit

falso, -a *adj* false; (*erróneo*) wrong, mistaken; (*firma, documento*) forged; (*documento, moneda etc*) fake; **en ~** falsely; **dar un paso en ~** to trip; (*fig*) to take a false step

falta *nf* (*defecto*) fault, flaw; (*privación*) lack, want; (*carencia*) shortage; (*por no asistir*) absence; (*equivocación*) mistake; (*Jur*) offence; (*Fútbol*) foul; (*Tenis*) fault; **la ~ de dinero** lack of money; **tiene cinco ~s de asistencia** he has been absent five times; **ha sido ~** it was a foul; **por ~ de** through o for lack of; **echar en ~** to miss; **me hace ~ un ordenador** I need a computer; **hacer ~ hacer algo** to be necessary to do sth; **no hace ~ que vengáis** you don't need to come; **sin ~** without fail; **~ de ortografía** spelling mistake; **~ de respeto** disrespect

faltar vi (no estar) to be missing; (escasear) to be lacking, be wanting; (necesitar) not to have enough; **faltan varios libros del estante** there are several books missing from the shelf; **no podemos irnos, falta Manolo** we can't go, Manolo isn't here yet; **¿falta algo?** is anything missing?; **falta mucho todavía** there's plenty of time yet; **¿falta mucho?** is there long to go?; **¿te falta mucho?** will you be long?; **a la sopa le falta sal** there isn't enough salt in the soup; **faltan 2 horas para llegar** there are 2 hours to go till arrival; ~ **(al respeto) a algn** to be disrespectful to sb; ~ **a una cita** to miss an appointment; ~ **al colegio** to miss school; ~ **a una promesa** to break a promise, go back on one's word; ~ **a la verdad** to lie; **¡no faltaba más!** that's the last straw!

falto, -a adj (desposeído) deficient, lacking; (necesitado) poor, wretched; **estar ~ de** to be short of

fama nf (renombre) fame; (reputación) reputation

famélico, -a adj starving

familia nf family; ~ **política** in-laws pl

familiar adj (relativo a la familia) family cpd; (conocido, informal) familiar; (estilo) informal; (Ling) colloquial ▷ nm/f relative, relation

familiaridad nf familiarity; (informalidad) homeliness

familiarizarse vr: ~ **con** to familiarize o.s. with

famoso, -a adj (renombrado) famous

fan (pl **-s**) nm fan

fanático, -a adj fanatical ▷ nm/f fanatic; (Cine, Deporte etc) fan

fanatismo nm fanaticism

fanfarrón, -ona adj boastful; (pey) showy

fanfarronear vi to boast

fango nm mud

fangoso, -a adj muddy

fantasía nf fantasy, imagination; (Mus) fantasia; (capricho) whim; **joyas de ~** imitation jewellery sg

fantasma nm (espectro) ghost, apparition; (presumido) show-off

fantástico, -a adj (irreal, fam) fantastic

fanzine nm fanzine

faquir nm fakir

faraón nm Pharaoh

faraónico, -a adj Pharaonic; (fig) grandiose

faringe nf pharynx

faringitis nf pharyngitis

farmacéutico, -a adj pharmaceutical ▷ nm/f chemist (Brit), pharmacist

farmacia nf (ciencia) pharmacy; (tienda) chemist's (shop) (Brit), pharmacy, drugstore (US); ~ **de turno** duty chemist

fármaco nm medicine, drug

faro nm (Naut: torre) lighthouse; (señal) beacon; (Auto) headlamp; **~s antiniebla** fog lamps; **~s delanteros/traseros** headlights/rear lights

farol nm (luz) lantern, lamp; (Ferro) headlamp; (poste) lamppost; **echarse un ~** (fam) to show off

farola nf street lamp (Brit) o light (US), lamppost

farsa nf (gen) farce

farsante nm/f fraud, fake

fascículo nm (gen) part, instalment (Brit), installment (US)

fascinar vt to fascinate; (encantar) to captivate

fascismo nm fascism

fascista adj, nm/f fascist

fase nf phase

fashion adj (fam) trendy

fastidiar vt (disgustar) to annoy, bother; (estropear) to spoil; **fastidiarse** vr (disgustarse) to get annoyed o cross; **¡no fastidies!** you're joking!; **¡que se fastidie!** (fam) he'll just have to put up with it!

fastidio nm (disgusto) annoyance

fastidioso, -a adj (molesto) annoying

fastuoso, -a adj (espléndido) magnificent; (banquete etc) lavish

fatal adj (gen) fatal; (desgraciado) ill-fated; (fam: malo, pésimo) awful ▷ adv terribly; **lo pasó ~** he had a terrible time (of it)

fatalidad nf (destino) fate; (mala suerte) misfortune

fatiga nf (cansancio) fatigue, weariness; **fatigas** nfpl hardships

fatigar vt to tire, weary; **fatigarse** vr to get tired

fatigoso, -a adj (cansador) tiring

fatuo, -a adj (vano) fatuous; (presuntuoso) conceited

fauces nfpl (Anat) gullet sg; (fam) jaws

fauna nf fauna

favor nm (ayuda) favour (Brit), favor (US); (protección) protection; **haga el ~ de hablar más bajo** would you be kind enough to lower your voice?; **por ~** please; **¿puedes hacerme un ~?** can you do me a favour?; **gracias al ~ del rey** thanks to the king's protection; **a ~ in** favo(u)r; **45 votos a ~** 45 votes in favour; **estar a ~ de algo** to be in favour of sth

favorable adj favourable (Brit), favorable (US); (condiciones etc) advantageous

favorecer vt to favour (Brit), favor (US); (amparar) to help; (vestido etc) to become, flatter; **este peinado le favorece** this hairstyle suits him

favorito, -a adj, nm/f favourite (Brit), favorite (US)

fax nm inv fax; **mandar por ~** to fax

faz nf face; **la ~ de la tierra** the face of the earth

fe nf (Rel) faith; (confianza) belief; (documento) certificate; **de buena fe** (Jur) bona fide; **prestar fe a** to believe, credit; **actuar con buena/mala fe** to act in good/bad faith; **dar fe de** to bear witness to; **fe de erratas** errata

fealdad nf ugliness

febrero nm February

febril adj feverish; (movido) hectic

fecha nf date; ~ **límite** o **tope** closing o last date; ~ **límite de venta** (de alimentos) sell-by date; ~ **de caducidad** (de alimentos) sell-by date; (de contrato) expiry date; **en ~ próxima** soon; **hasta la ~** to date, so far; ~ **de vencimiento** (Com) due date; ~ **de vigencia** (Com) effective date

fechar vt to date

fechoría nf misdeed

fecundar *vt* (*generar*) to fertilize, make fertile
fecundo, -a *adj* (*fértil*) fertile; (*fig*) prolific; (*productivo*) productive
federación *nf* federation
federal *adj* federal
felicidad *nf* (*satisfacción, contento*) happiness; **felicidades** *nfpl* congratulations
felicitación *nf* (*tarjeta*) greetings card; **felicitaciones** *nfpl* (*enhorabuena*) congratulations; **~ navideña** *o* **de Navidad** Christmas Greetings
felicitar *vt* to congratulate
feligrés, -esa *nm/f* parishioner
felino, -a *adj* cat-like; (*Zool*) feline ▷ *nm* feline
feliz *adj* (*contento*) happy; (*afortunado*) lucky
felpudo *nm* doormat
femenino, -a *adj* feminine; (*Zool etc*) female ▷ *nm* (*Ling*) feminine
feminista *adj, nm/f* feminist
fenomenal *adj* phenomenal; (*fam*) great, terrific
fenómeno *nm* phenomenon; (*fig*) freak, accident ▷ *adv*: **lo pasamos ~** we had a great time ▷ *excl* great!, marvellous!
feo, -a *adj* (*gen*) ugly; (*desagradable*) bad, nasty ▷ *nm* insult; **hacer un ~ a algn** to offend sb; **más ~ que Picio** as ugly as sin
féretro *nm* (*ataúd*) coffin; (*sarcófago*) bier
feria *nf* (*gen*) fair; (*LAm: mercado*) market; (*descanso*) holiday, rest day; (*CAm, Méx: cambio*) small change; **~ comercial** trade fair; **~ de muestras** trade show
feriado, -a *adj* (*LAm*): **día ~** public holiday ▷ *nm* public holiday
fermentar *vi* to ferment
ferocidad *nf* fierceness, ferocity
feroz *adj* (*cruel*) cruel; (*salvaje*) fierce
férreo, -a *adj* iron *cpd*; (*Tec*) ferrous; (*fig*) (of) iron
ferretería *nf* (*tienda*) ironmonger's (shop) (*Brit*), hardware store
ferrocarril *nm* railway, railroad (*US*); **~ de vía estrecha/única** narrow-gauge/single-track railway *o* line
ferroviario, -a *adj* rail *cpd*, railway *cpd* (*Brit*), railroad *cpd* (*US*) ▷ *nm*: **~s** railway (*Brit*) *o* railroad (*US*) workers
fértil *adj* (*productivo*) fertile; (*rico*) rich
fertilidad *nf* (*gen*) fertility; (*productividad*) fruitfulness
fertilizante *nm* fertilizer
fertilizar *vt* to fertilize
ferviente *adj* fervent
fervor *nm* fervour (*Brit*), fervor (*US*)
fervoroso, -a *adj* fervent
festejar *vt* (*agasajar*) to wine and dine, fête; (*galantear*) to court; (*celebrar*) to celebrate
festejo *nm* (*diversión*) entertainment; (*galanteo*) courtship; (*fiesta*) celebration
festín *nm* feast, banquet
festival *nm* festival
festividad *nf* festivity
festivo, -a *adj* (*de fiesta*) festive; (*fig*) witty; (*Cine, Lit*) humorous; **día ~** holiday
fétido, -a *adj* (*hediondo*) foul-smelling

feto *nm* foetus; (*fam*) monster
fiable *adj* (*persona*) trustworthy; (*máquina*) reliable
fiaca *nf* (*CS: fam: pereza*) laziness
fiador, a *nm/f* (*Jur*) surety, guarantor; (*Com*) backer; **salir ~ por algn** to stand bail for sb
fiambre *adj* (*Culin*) served cold ▷ *nm* (*Culin*) cold meat (*Brit*), cold cut (*US*); (*fam*) corpse, stiff
fianza *nf* surety; (*Jur*): **libertad bajo ~** release on bail
fiar *vt* (*salir garante de*) to guarantee; (*Jur*) to stand bail *o* bond (*US*) for; (*vender a crédito*) to sell on credit; (*secreto*) to confide ▷ *vi*: **~ (de)** to trust (in); **ser de ~** to be trustworthy; **fiarse** *vr*: **~se de** to trust (in), rely on
fibra *nf* fibre (*Brit*), fiber (*US*); (*fig*) vigour (*Brit*), vigor (*US*); **~ óptica** (*Inform*) optical fibre (*Brit*) *o* fiber (*US*)
ficción *nf* fiction
ficha *nf* (*Telec*) token; (*en juegos*) counter, marker; (*en casino*) chip; (*Com, Econ*) tally, check (*US*); (*Inform*) file; (*tarjeta*) (index) card; (*Elec*) plug; (*en hotel*) registration form; **~ policíaca** police dossier
fichar *vt* (*archivar*) to file, index; (*Deporte*) to sign (up) ▷ *vi* (*deportista*) to sign (up); (*obrero*) to clock in *o* on; **estar fichado** to have a record
fichero *nm* card index; (*archivo*) filing cabinet; (*Com*) box file; (*Inform*) file, archive; (*de policía*) criminal records; **~ activo** (*Inform*) active file; **~ archivado** (*Inform*) archived file; **~ indexado** (*Inform*) index file; **~ de reserva** (*Inform*) backup file; **~ de tarjetas** card index; **nombre de ~** filename
ficticio, -a *adj* (*imaginario*) fictitious; (*falso*) fabricated
fidelidad *nf* (*lealtad*) fidelity, loyalty; (*exactitud: de dato etc*) accuracy; **alta ~** high fidelity, hi-fi
fideos *nmpl* (*pasta fina*) noodles; (*RP: pasta en general*) pasta
fiebre *nf* (*Med*) fever; (*fig*) fever, excitement; **~ amarilla/del heno** yellow/hay fever; **~ palúdica** malaria; **tener ~** to have a temperature
fiel *adj* (*leal*) faithful, loyal; (*fiable*) reliable; (*exacto*) accurate ▷ *nm* (*aguja*) needle, pointer; **los ~es** the faithful
fieltro *nm* felt
fiera *nf* (*animal feroz*) wild animal *o* beast; (*fig*) dragon; *ver tb* **fiero**
fiero, -a *adj* (*cruel*) cruel; (*feroz*) fierce; (*duro*) harsh ▷ *nm/f* (*fig*) fiend; *ver tb* **fiera**
fiesta *nf* party; (*de pueblo*) festival; **la ~ nacional** bullfighting; **(día de) ~** (public) holiday; **mañana es ~** it's a holiday tomorrow; **~ de guardar** (*Rel*) day of obligation
figura *nf* (*gen*) figure; (*forma, imagen*) shape, form; (*Naipes*) face card
figurado, -a *adj* figurative
figurante *nm/f* (*Teat*) walk-on part; (*Cine*) extra
figurar *vt* (*representar*) to represent; (*fingir*) to feign ▷ *vi* to figure; **figurarse** *vr* (*imaginarse*) to imagine; (*suponer*) to suppose; **ya me lo figuraba** I thought as much

fijador *nm* (*Foto etc*) fixative; (*de pelo*) gel

fijar *vt* (*asegurar: poste, plancha, foto*) to fix; (*cartel*) to post, put up, stick (on); (*pelo*) to set; (*estampilla*) to affix; (*fig*) to settle (on), decide; **fijarse** *vr*: **-se en** to notice; **¿dónde han fijado su residencia?** where have they taken up residence?; **tienes que - la fecha** you must fix the date; **según lo fija la ley** as the law states o stipulates; **no me fijé en la ropa que llevaba** I didn't notice what she was wearing; **tienes que -te más en lo que haces** you must pay more attention to what you're doing; **¡fíjate en esos dos!** just look at those two!; **¡fíjate!** just imagine!; **¿te fijas?** see what I mean?

fijo, -a *adj* (*gen*) fixed; (*firme*) firm; (*permanente*) permanent; (*trabajo*) steady; (*color*) fast ▷ *adv*: **mirar -** to stare

fila *nf* row; (*Mil*) rank; (*cadena*) line; (*Mil*) rank; (*en marcha*) file; **- india** single file; **ponerse en -** to line up, get into line; **primera -** front row

filántropo, -a *nm/f* philanthropist

filatelia *nf* philately, stamp collecting

filete *nm* (*de carne*) fillet steak; (*de cerdo*) tenderloin; (*pescado*) fillet; (*Mec: rosca*) thread

filial *adj* filial ▷ *nf* subsidiary; (*sucursal*) branch

Filipinas *nfpl*: **las (Islas) -** the Philippines

filipino, -a *adj, nm/f* Philippine

film (*pl* **-s**) *nm* = **filme**

filmar *vt* to film, shoot

filme *nm* film, movie (US)

filo *nm* (*gen*) edge; **sacar - a** to sharpen; **al - del medio día** at about midday; **de doble -** double-edged

filología *nf* philology

filón *nm* (*Minería*) vein, lode; (*fig*) gold mine

filosofía *nf* philosophy

filósofo, -a *nm/f* philosopher

filtrar *vt, vi* to filter, strain; (*información*) to leak; **filtrarse** *vr* to filter; (*fig: dinero*) to dwindle

filtro *nm* (*Tec, utensilio*) filter

fin *nm* (*final*) end; (*objetivo*) purpose; **el - de una época** the end of an era; **el - de año** New Year's Eve; **al - llegaron a un acuerdo** they finally reached an agreement; **a - de** in order to; **por - finally**; **¡por - hemos llegado!** we've got here at last!; **a - de cuentas** at the end of the day; **al - y al cabo** after all; **en -** (*resumiendo*) in short; **¡en -!** (*resignación*) oh, well!; **sin -** endless(ly); **- de archivo** (*Inform*) end-of-file; **- de semana** weekend

final *adj* final ▷ *nm* end, conclusion ▷ *nf* (*Deporte*) final

finalidad *nf* finality; (*propósito*) purpose, aim

finalista *nm/f* finalist

finalizar *vt* to end, finish ▷ *vi* to end, come to an end; **- la sesión** (*Inform*) to log out o off

financiar *vt* to finance

financiero, -a *adj* financial ▷ *nm/f* financier

finanzas *nfpl* finances

finca *nf* country estate

finde *nm abr* (*fam: fin de semana*) weekend

fingir *vt* (*simular*) to simulate, feign; (*pretextar*) to sham, fake ▷ *vi* (*aparentar*) to pretend; **fingirse** *vr*: **-se dormido** to pretend to be asleep

finlandés, -esa *adj* Finnish ▷ *nm/f* Finn ▷ *nm* (*Ling*) Finnish

Finlandia *nf* Finland

fino, -a *adj* fine; (*delgado*) slender; (*de buenas maneras*) polite, refined; (*inteligente*) shrewd; (*punta*) sharp; (*gusto*) discriminating; (*oído*) sharp; (*jerez*) fino, dry ▷ *nm* (*jerez*) dry sherry

firma *nf* signature; (*Com*) firm, company

firmamento *nm* firmament

firmante *adj, nm/f* signatory; **los abajo -s** the undersigned

firmar *vt* to sign; **- un contrato** (*Com: colocarse*) to sign on; **firmado y sellado** signed and sealed

firme *adj* firm; (*estable*) stable; (*sólido*) solid; (*constante*) steady; (*decidido*) resolute; (*duro*) hard; **¡-s!** (*Mil*) attention!; **oferta en -** (*Com*) firm offer ▷ *nm* road (surface)

firmemente *adv* firmly

firmeza *nf* firmness; (*constancia*) steadiness; (*solidez*) solidity

fiscal *adj* fiscal ▷ *nm* (*Jur*) ≈ Crown Prosecutor, Procurator Fiscal (*Escocia*), district attorney (US)

fisco *nm* (*hacienda*) treasury, exchequer; **declarar algo al -** to declare sth for tax purposes

fisgar *vt* to pry into

fisgón, -ona *adj* nosey

física *nf* physics *sg; ver tb* **físico**

físico, -a *adj* physical ▷ *nm* physique; (*aspecto*) appearance, looks *pl* ▷ *nm/f* physicist; *ver tb* **física**

fisioterapia *nf* physiotherapy

flác(c)ido, -a *adj* flabby

flaco, -a *adj* (*muy delgado*) skinny, thin; (*débil*) weak, feeble

flagrante *adj* flagrant

flamante *adj* (*fam*) brilliant; (*nuevo*) brand-new

flamenco, -a *adj* (*de Flandes*) Flemish; (*baile, música*) gipsy ▷ *nm/f* Fleming; **los -s** the Flemish ▷ *nm* (*Ling*) Flemish; (*baile, música*) flamenco; (*Zool*) flamingo

flan *nm* creme caramel

flaquear *vi* (*debilitarse*) to weaken; (*persona*) to slack

flaqueza *nf* (*delgadez*) thinness, leanness; (*fig*) weakness

flash (*pl* **-es**) *nm* (*Foto*) flash

flauta (*Mus*) *nf* flute ▷ *nm/f* flautist, flute player; **¡la gran -!** (*CS*) my God!; **hijo de la gran -** (*CS fam!*) bastard (!), son of a bitch (US) (!)

flecha *nf* arrow

flechazo *nm* (*acción*) bowshot; (*fam*): **fue un -** it was love at first sight

fleco *nm* fringe

flema *nm* phlegm

flemón *nm* (*Med*) gumboil

flequillo *nm* (*de pelo*) fringe

flete *nm* (*carga*) freight; (*alquiler*) charter; (*precio*) freightage; **- debido** (*Com*) freight forward; **- sobre compras** (*Com*) freight inward

flexible *adj* flexible; (*individuo*) compliant

flexión *nf* (*Deporte*) bend; (*: en el suelo*) press-up

flexo nm adjustable table lamp

flipper nm pinball machine

flojear vi (piernas: al andar) to give way; (alumno) to do badly; (cosecha, mercado) to be poor

flojera nf (LAm) laziness; **me da ~** I can't be bothered

flojo, -a adj (gen) loose; (sin fuerzas) limp; (débil) weak; (viento) light; (bebida) weak; (trabajo) poor; (actitud) slack; (precio) low; (Com: mercado) dull, slack; (LAm) lazy

flor nf flower; (piropo) compliment; **la ~ y nata de la sociedad** (fig) the cream of society; **en la ~ de la vida** in the prime of life; **a ~ de** on the surface of

flora nf flora

florecer vi (Bot) to flower, bloom; (fig) to flourish

floreciente adj (Bot) in flower, flowering; (fig) thriving

florero nm vase

florista nm/f florist

floristería nf florist's (shop)

flota nf fleet

flotador nm (gen) float; (para nadar) rubber ring; (de cisterna) ballcock

flotar vi to float

flote nm: **a ~** afloat; **ponerse a ~** (fig) to get back on one's feet

fluctuar vi (oscilar) to fluctuate

fluidez nf fluidity; (fig) fluency

fluido, -a adj fluid; (lenguaje) fluent; (estilo) smooth ▷ nm (líquido) fluid

fluir vi to flow

flujo nm flow; (Pol) swing; (Naut) rising tide; **~ y reflujo** ebb and flow; **~ de sangre** flow of blood; **~ positivo/negativo de efectivo** (Com) positive/negative cash flow

flúor nm fluorine; (en dentífrico) fluoride

fluorescente adj fluorescent ▷ nm (tb: **tubo fluorescente**) fluorescent tube

fluvial adj fluvial, river cpd

FMI nm abr (= Fondo Monetario Internacional) IMF

foca nf seal

foco nm focus; (centro) focal point; (fuente) source; (de incendio) seat; (Elec) floodlight; (Teat) spotlight; (And, Méx: bombilla) (light) bulb, light

fofo, -a adj (esponjoso) soft, spongy; (músculo) flabby

fogón nm (de cocina) ring, burner

fogoso, -a adj spirited

fólder nm (LAm) folder

folio nm folio; (hoja) leaf

folklore nm folklore

folklórico, -a adj traditional

follaje nm foliage

follar vt, vi (fam!) to fuck (!)

folleto nm pamphlet; (Com) brochure; (prospecto) leaflet; (Escol etc) handout

follón nm (fam: lío) mess; (: conmoción) fuss, rumpus, shindy; **armar un ~** to kick up a fuss; **se armó un ~** there was a hell of a row

fomentar vt (Med) to foment; (fig: promover) to promote, foster; (odio etc) to stir up

fomento nm (fig: ayuda) fostering; (promoción) promotion

fonda nf ≈ guest house

fondo nm (de caja, cazuela: lo profundo) bottom; (lo hondo) depth; (de coche, sala, armario) back; (de pasillo, calle) end; (Arte etc) background; (reserva) fund; (fig: carácter) nature; **fondos** nmpl (Com) funds, resources; **en el ~ del mar** at the bottom of the sea; **¿cuanto mide de ~?** how deep is it?; **un corredor de ~** a long-distance runner; **una investigación a ~** a thorough investigation; **estudiar una materia a ~** to study a subject in depth; **tener buen ~** to be good-natured; **en el ~ es una buena persona** deep down, she's a good person; **recaudar ~s** to raise funds; **~ de amortización** (Com) sinking fund; **~ de escritorio** (Inform) wallpaper; **F~ Monetario Internacional** International Monetary Fund

fonética nf phonetics sg

fono nm (CS) telephone (number)

fontanería nf plumbing

fontanero nm plumber

footing nm jogging; **hacer ~** to jog

forastero, -a nm/f stranger

forcejear vi (luchar) to struggle

fórceps nm inv forceps

forense adj forensic ▷ nm/f pathologist

forestal adj forest cpd

forjar vt to forge; (formar) to form

forma nf (figura) form, shape; (modelo) mould, pattern; (Med) fitness; (manera) way; **me gusta la ~ de esa mesa** I like the shape of that table; **en ~ de pera** pear-shaped; **me miraba de una ~ extraña** she was looking at me in a strange way; **¡vaya ~ de tratar a la gente!** what a way to treat people!; **es mi ~ de ser** that's just the way I am; **estar en ~** to be fit; **guardar las ~s** to keep up appearances; **de ~ que ...** so that ...; **de todas ~s** in any case; **~ de pago** (Com) method of payment

formación nf (gen) formation; (enseñanza) training; **~ profesional** vocational training; **~ fuera del trabajo** off-the-job training; **en el trabajo** o **sobre la práctica** on-the-job training

formal adj (gen) formal; (fig: persona) serious; (: de fiar) reliable; (conducta) steady

formalidad nf (formalismo) formality; (seriedad) seriousness; (fiabilidad) reliability

formalizar vt (Jur) to formalize; (plan) to draw up; (situación) to put in order, regularize; **formalizarse** vr (situación) to be put in order, be regularized

formar vt (componer) to form, shape; (constituir) to make up, constitute; (Escol) to train, educate ▷ vi (Mil) to fall in; (Deporte) to line up; **formarse** vr (crearse) to form, take form; (desarrollarse) to develop; (Escol) to be trained o educated; **quieren ~ una orquesta** they want to start an orchestra; **~ gobierno** to form a government; **España forma parte de la Comunidad Europea** Spain is part of the European Community; **el comité está formado por cinco miembros** the committee is made up of five members; **se formó una cola enorme en la puerta** a huge queue formed at the door; **te has formado una idea equivocada de mí** you've formed the wrong idea about me

formatear vt (Inform) to format

formato nm (Inform): **sin ~** (disco, texto) unformatted; **~ de registro** record format

formica® nf Formica®

formidable adj (temible) formidable; (asombroso) tremendous

fórmula nf formula

formular vt (queja) to lodge; (petición) to draw up; (pregunta) to pose, formulate; (idea) to formulate

formulario nm form; **~ de solicitud/de pedido** (Com) application/order form; **llenar un ~** to fill in a form

fornido, -a adj well-built

foro nm (gen) forum; (Jur) court

forrar vt (abrigo) to line; (libro) to cover; (coche) to upholster; **forrarse** vr (fam) to line one's pockets

forro nm (de cuaderno) cover; (costura) lining; (de sillón) upholstery; **~ polar** fleece

fortalecer vt to strengthen; **fortalecerse** vr to fortify o.s.; (opinión etc) to become stronger

fortaleza nf (Mil) fortress, stronghold; (fuerza) strength; (determinación) resolution

fortuito, -a adj accidental, chance cpd

fortuna nf (suerte) fortune, (good) luck; (riqueza) fortune, wealth

forzar vt (puerta) to force (open); (compeler) to compel; (violar) to rape; (ojos etc) to strain

forzoso, -a adj necessary; (inevitable) inescapable; (obligatorio) compulsory

fosa nf (sepultura) grave; (en tierra) pit; (Med) cavity; **~s nasales** nostrils

fosforescente adj phosphorescent

fósforo nm (Química) phosphorus; (esp LAm: cerilla) match

fósil adj fossil, fossilized ▷ nm fossil

foso nm ditch; (Teat) pit; (Auto): **~ de reconocimiento** inspection pit

foto nf photo, snap(shot); **sacar una ~** to take a photo o picture

fotocopia nf photocopy

fotocopiadora nf photocopier

fotocopiar vt to photocopy

fotogénico, -a adj photogenic

fotografía nf (arte) photography; (una fotografía) photograph

fotografiar vt to photograph

fotógrafo, -a nm/f photographer

fotomatón nm (cabina) photo booth

fotonovela nf photo-story

frac (pl **-s** o o **fraques**) nm dress coat, tails

fracasar vi (gen) to fail; (plan etc) to fall through

fracaso nm (desgracia, revés) failure; (de negociaciones etc) collapse, breakdown

fracción nf fraction; (Pol) faction, splinter group

fraccionamiento nm (Méx) housing estate

fractura nf fracture, break

fragancia nf (olor) fragrance, perfume

fraganti: **in ~** adv: **coger a algn in ~** to catch sb red-handed

fragata nf frigate

frágil adj (débil) fragile; (Com) breakable; (fig) frail, delicate

fragmento nm fragment; (pedazo) piece; (de discurso) excerpt; (de canción) snatch

fragua nf forge

fraguar vt to forge; (fig) to concoct ▷ vi to harden

fraile nm (Rel) friar; (: monje) monk

frambuesa nf raspberry

francés, -esa adj French ▷ nm/f Frenchman(woman) ▷ nm (Ling) French

Francia nf France

franco, -a adj (cándido) frank, open; (Com: exento) free ▷ nm (moneda) franc; **~ de derechos** duty-free; **~ al costado del buque** (Com) free alongside ship; **~ puesto sobre vagón** (Com) free on rail; **~ a bordo** free on board

francotirador, a nm/f sniper

franela nf flannel

franja nf fringe; (de uniforme) stripe; (de tierra etc) strip

franquear vt (camino) to clear; (carta, paquete postal) to frank, stamp; (obstáculo) to overcome; (Com etc) to free, exempt

franqueo nm postage

franqueza nf (candor) frankness

franquismo nm: **el ~** (sistema) the Franco system; (período) the Franco years

franquista adj pro-Franco ▷ nm/f supporter of Franco

frasco nm bottle, flask; **~ al vacío** (vacuum) flask

frase nf sentence; (locución) phrase, expression; **~ hecha** set phrase; (despectivo) cliché

fraternal adj brotherly, fraternal

fraude nm (cualidad) dishonesty; (acto) fraud, swindle

fraudulento, -a adj fraudulent

frazada nf (LAm) blanket

frecuencia nf frequency; **con ~** frequently, often; **~ de red** (Inform) mains frequency; **~ del reloj** (Inform) clock speed; **~ telefónica** voice frequency

frecuentar vt (lugar) to frequent; (persona) to see frequently o often; **~ la buena sociedad** to mix in high society

frecuente adj frequent; (costumbre) common; (vicio) rife

fregadero nm (kitchen) sink

fregar vt (frotar) to scrub; (platos) to wash (up); (LAm: fastidiar) to annoy

fregona nf (utensilio) mop; (pey: sirvienta) skivvy

freidora nf deep-fat fryer

freír vt to fry

frenar vt to brake; (fig) to check

frenazo nm: **dar un ~** to brake sharply

frenesí nm frenzy

frenético, -a adj frantic; **ponerse ~** to lose one's head

freno nm (Tec, Auto) brake; (de cabalgadura) bit; (fig) check

frente nm (Arq, Mil, Pol) front; (de objeto) front

part ▷ *nf* forehead, brow; **un ~ frío** a cold front; **un ~ común** a united front; **~ de batalla** battle front; **hacer ~ común con algn** to make common cause with sb; **estaba al ~ de la editorial** he was in charge of the publishing house; **~ a** (*delante*) in front of; (*en situación opuesta a*) opposite; **una casa ~ al mar** a house facing the sea; **~ al hotel hay un banco** there's a bank opposite the hotel; **~ a ~** face to face; **los coches chocaron de ~** the cars collided head on; **viene un coche de ~** there's a car coming straight for us; **hacer ~ a algo** to face up to something

fresa *nf* (*Esp: fruta*) strawberry; (*de dentista*) drill

fresco, -a *adj* (*nuevo*) fresh; (*huevo*) newly-laid; (*frío*) cool; (*descarado*) cheeky, bad-mannered ▷ *nm* (*aire*) fresh air; (*Arte*) fresco; (*CAm: bebida*) fruit juice *o* drink ▷ *nm/f* (*fam*) shameless person; (*persona insolente*) impudent person; **tomar el ~** to get some fresh air; **¡qué ~!** what a cheek!

frescura *nf* freshness; (*descaro*) cheek, nerve; (*calma*) calmness

frialdad *nf* (*gen*) coldness; (*indiferencia*) indifference

fricción *nf* (*gen*) friction; (*acto*) rub(bing); (*Med*) massage; (*Pol, fig etc*) friction, trouble

frigidez *nf* frigidity

frigorífico, -a *adj* refrigerating ▷ *nm* refrigerator; (*camión*) freezer lorry *o* truck (US); **instalación frigorífica** cold-storage plant

frijol, frijol *nm* (*LAm*) bean

frío, -a *adj* cold; (*fig: indiferente*) unmoved, indifferent; (*poco entusiasta*) chilly ▷ *nm* (*baja temperatura*) cold(ness); (*indiferencia*) indifference; **tengo las manos frías** my hands are cold; **estuvo muy ~ conmigo** he was very cold towards me; **tengo mucho ~** I'm very cold; **¡qué ~!** how cold it is!

frito, -a *pp de* **freír** ▷ *adj* fried ▷ *nm* fry; **me trae ~ ese hombre** I'm sick and tired of that man

frívolo, -a *adj* frivolous

frontal *nm*: **choque ~** head-on collision

frontera *nf* frontier; (*línea divisoria*) border; (*zona*) frontier area

fronterizo, -a *adj* frontier *cpd*; (*contiguo*) bordering

frontón *nm* (*Deporte: cancha*) pelota court; (*: juego*) pelota

frotar *vt* to rub; (*fósforo*) to strike; **frotarse** *vr*: **~se las manos** to rub one's hands

fructífero, -a *adj* productive, fruitful

frugal *adj* frugal

fruncir *vt* (*Costura*) to gather; (*ceño*) to frown; (*labios*) to purse

frustración *nf* frustration

frustrar *vt* to frustrate; **frustrarse** *vr* to be frustrated; (*plan etc*) to fail

fruta *nf* fruit

frutería *nf* fruit shop

frutero, -a *adj* fruit *cpd* ▷ *nm/f* fruiterer ▷ *nm* fruit dish *o* bowl

frutilla *nf* (*CS*) strawberry

fruto *nm* (*Bot*) fruit; (*fig: resultado*) result, outcome; **~s secos** ≈ nuts and raisins

fuego *nm* (*gen*) fire; (*Culin: gas*) burner, ring; (*Mil*) fire; (*fig: pasión*) fire, passion; **~s artificiales** *o* **de artificio** fireworks; **~ amigo** friendly fire; **prender ~ a** to set fire to; **a ~ lento** on a low flame *o* gas; **¡alto el ~!** cease fire!; **estar entre dos ~s** to be in the crossfire; **¿tienes ~?** have you (got) a light?

fuente *nf* fountain; (*manantial, fig*) spring; (*origen*) source; (*plato*) large dish; **~ de alimentación** (*Inform*) power supply; **de ~ desconocida/fidedigna** from an unknown/reliable source

fuera *adv* (*en el exterior*) out(side); (*en otra parte*) away; (*excepto*) except, save ▷ *prep*: **~ de** (*en el exterior de*) outside; (*además de*) besides; **¡estamos aquí ~!** we are out here!; **hoy vamos a cenar ~** we're going out for dinner tonight; **los niños estaban jugando ~** the children were playing outside; **por ~ es blanco** it is white on the outside; **la parte de ~** the outside part, the outer part; **mis padres llevan varios días ~** my parents have been away for several days; **el equipo de ~** the away team; **estar ~** (*en el extranjero*) to be abroad; **~ de mi casa** outside my house; **~ del alcance de algn** out of reach of sb; **~ de combate** out of action; (*Boxeo*) knocked out; **~ de sí** beside o.s.; **el enfermo está ~ de peligro** the patient is out of danger; **¡~ de aquí!** get out (of here)!; *ver tb* **serie**

fuero *nm* (*carta municipal*) municipal charter; (*leyes locales*) local *o* regional law code; (*privilegio*) privilege; (*autoridad*) jurisdiction; (*fig*): **en mi** *etc* **~ interno** ... in my *etc* heart of hearts ..., deep down ...

fuerte *adj* (*persona, material, olor, carácter, viento*) strong; (*golpe*) hard; (*ruido, voz*) loud; (*comida*) rich; (*lluvia*) heavy; (*calor, dolor*) intense ▷ *adv* (*jugar, trabajar, golpear*) hard; (*hablar*) loud(ly) ▷ *nm* (*Mil*) fort, strongpoint; (*fig*): **el canto no es mi ~** singing is not my strong point; **¡eso es un poco ~!** that's a bit much!; **"un beso muy ~"** "lots of love"; **no le pegues tan ~** don't hit him so hard; **agárrate ~** hold on tight; **hablaba ~** he was talking loudly

fuerza *nf* (*resistencia: de persona*) strength; (*de argumento*) force; (*Tec, Elec*) power; (*violencia*) violence; (*Mil: tb*: **fuerzas**) forces *pl*; **tener mucha ~** to be very strong; **un viento de ~ 6** a force 6 wind; **recurrir a la ~** to resort to force; **a ~ de** (*dint of*) by; **sólo lo conseguirás a ~ de practicar** you'll only manage it by practising; **a la ~, por ~** of necessity; **hacer algo a la ~** to be forced to do sth; **tiene que venir por aquí a la ~** he has to come, he has no choice; **no te lo comas a la ~** don't force yourself to eat it; **con ~ legal** (*Com*) legally binding; **~ bruta** brute force; **~ de arrastre** (*Tec*) pulling power; **~ de brazos** manpower; **la ~ de la gravedad** the force of gravity; **~ de Orden Público (F.O.P.)** police (forces); **~ de voluntad** willpower; **tiene mucha ~ de voluntad** he has a lot of willpower;

~ **mayor** force majeure; ~ **vital** vitality; **no le quedaban ~s** he had no strength left; **cobrar ~s** to recover one's strength; **tener ~s para** to have the strength to; ~**s armadas (FF.AA.)** armed forces

fuga *nf* (*huida*) flight, escape; (*de enamorados*) elopement; (*de gas etc*) leak; ~ **de cerebros** (*fig*) brain drain

fugarse *vr* to flee, escape

fugaz *adj* fleeting

fugitivo, -a *adj* fugitive, fleeing ▷ *nm/f* fugitive

fulano, -a *nm/f* so-and-so, what's-his-name

fulgor *nm* brilliance

fulminante *adj* (*pólvora*) fulminating; (*fig: mirada*) withering; (*Med*) fulminant; (*fam*) terrific, tremendous

fulminar *vt*: **caer fulminado por un rayo** to be struck down by lightning; ~ **a algn con la mirada** to look daggers at sb

fumador, a *nm/f* smoker; **no ~** non-smoker

fumar *vt, vi* to smoke; **fumarse** *vr* (*disipar*) to squander; ~ **en pipa** to smoke a pipe

fumigar *vt* to fumigate

funámbulo, -a, funambulista *nm/f* tightrope walker

función *nf* (*de máquina, organismo*) function; (*de persona, institución*) role; (*Mat, Ling*) function; (*Teat etc*) performance; **los insectos desempeñan una ~ muy importante** insects perform a very useful function; **la ~ de la policía en la sociedad** the role of the police in society; **entrar en funciones** to take up one's duties; **el ministro en funciones** the acting minister; **en ~ de** according to; **los niños van a representar una ~ en el colegio** the children are putting on a show at school; ~ **de tarde/de noche** matinée/evening performance

funcional *adj* functional

funcionamiento *nm* functioning; (*Tec*) working; **en ~** (*Com*) on stream; **entrar en ~** to come into operation

funcionar *vi* (*gen*) to function; (*máquina*) to work; **"no funciona"** "out of order"

funcionario, -a *nm/f* official; (*público*) civil servant

funda *nf* (*gen*) cover; (*de almohada*) pillowcase; ~ **protectora del disco** (*Inform*) disk-jacket

fundación *nf* foundation

fundamental *adj* fundamental, basic

fundamentalismo *nm* fundamentalism

fundamentalista *adj, nm/f* fundamentalist

fundamentar *vt* (*poner base*) to lay the foundations of; (*establecer*) to found; (*fig*) to base

fundamento *nm* (*base*) foundation; (*razón*) grounds *pl*; **eso carece de ~** that is groundless

fundar *vt* to found; (*crear*) to set up; (*fig: basar*): ~ **(en)** to base *o* found (on); **fundarse** *vr*: ~**se en** to be founded on

fundición *nf* (*acción*) smelting; (*fábrica*) foundry; (*Tip*) fount (*Brit*), font

fundir *vt* to melt; (*para extraer metal*) to smelt, melt down; (*dando forma*) to cast; (*Com*) to merge; (*estatua*) to cast; **fundirse** *vr* (*colores etc*) to merge, blend; (*unirse*) to fuse together; (*plomo, nieve, queso*) to melt; (*Elec: fusible, bombilla*) to blow; ~ **los plomos** to blow the fuses; ~ **el oro en lingotes** to cast the gold in ingots; **la nieve se está fundiendo** the snow's melting; **se han fundido los fusibles** the fuses have blown

fúnebre *adj* funeral *cpd*, funereal

funeral *nm* funeral

funeraria *nf* undertaker's (*Brit*), mortician's (*US*)

funesto, -a *adj* ill-fated; (*desastroso*) fatal

furgón *nm* wagon

furgoneta *nf* (*Auto, Com*) (transit) van (*Brit*), pickup (truck) (*US*)

furia *nf* (*ira*) fury; (*violencia*) violence

furibundo, -a *adj* furious

furioso, -a *adj* (*iracundo*) furious; (*violento*) violent

furor *nm* (*cólera*) rage; (*pasión*) frenzy, passion; **hacer ~** to be a sensation

furtivo, -a *adj* furtive ▷ *nm* poacher

furúnculo *nm* (*Med*) boil

fusible *nm* fuse

fusil *nm* rifle

fusilar *vt* to shoot

fusión *nf* (*gen*) melting; (*unión*) fusion; (*Com*) merger, amalgamation

fusta *nf* (*látigo*) riding crop

fútbol *nm* football (*Brit*), soccer (*esp US*)

futbolín *nm* table football

futbolista *nm/f* footballer

fútil *adj* trifling

futilidad, futileza *nf* triviality

futón *nm* futon

futuro, -a *adj* future ▷ *nm* future; (*Ling*) future tense; **futuros** *nmpl* (*Com*) futures

Gg

gabacho, -a *adj* Pyrenean; (*fam*) Frenchified
▷ *nm/f* Pyrenean villager; (*fam*) Frenchy

gabán *nm* overcoat

gabardina *nf* (*tela*) gabardine; (*prenda*) raincoat

gabinete *nm* (*Pol*) cabinet; (*estudio*) study; (*de abogados etc*) office; **~ de consulta/de lectura** consulting/reading room

gaceta *nf* gazette

gafar *vt* (*fam: traer mala suerte*) to put a jinx on

gafas *nfpl* glasses; **~ oscuras** dark glasses; **~ de sol** sunglasses

gafe *adj*: **ser ~** to be jinxed ▷ *nm* (*fam*) jinx

gaita *nf* flute; (*gaita gallega*) bagpipes *pl*; (*dificultad*) bother; (*cosa engorrosa*) tough job

gajes *nmpl* (*salario*) pay *sg*; **los ~ del oficio** occupational hazards; **~ y emolumentos** perquisites

gajo *nm* (*gen*) bunch; (*de árbol*) bough; (*de naranja*) segment

gala *nf* full dress; (*fig: lo mejor*) cream, flower; **galas** *nfpl* finery *sg*; **estar de ~** to be in one's best clothes; **hacer ~ de** to display, show off; **tener algo a ~** to be proud of sth

galán *nm* lover, gallant; (*hombre atractivo*) ladies' man; (*Teat*): **primer ~** leading man

galante *adj* gallant; (*atento*) charming; (*cortés*) polite

galantear *vt* (*hacer la corte a*) to court, woo

galantería *nf* (*caballerosidad*) gallantry; (*cumplido*) politeness; (*piropo*) compliment

galápago *nm* (*Zool*) freshwater tortoise

galardón *nm* award, prize

galardonar *vt* (*premiar*) to reward; (*una obra*) to award a prize for

galaxia *nf* galaxy

galera *nf* (*nave*) galley; (*carro*) wagon; (*Med*) hospital ward; (*Tip*) galley

galería *nf* (*gen*) gallery; (*balcón*) veranda(h); (*de casa*) corridor; (*fam: público*) audience; **~ secreta** secret passage

Gales *nm*: **(el País de) ~** Wales

galés, -esa *adj* Welsh ▷ *nm/f* Welshman(-woman) ▷ *nm* (*Ling*) Welsh

galgo, -a *nm/f* greyhound

Galicia *nf* Galicia

galimatías *nm inv* (*asunto*) rigmarole; (*lenguaje*) gibberish, nonsense

gallardía *nf* (*galantería*) dash; (*gracia*) gracefulness; (*valor*) bravery; (*elegancia*) elegance; (*nobleza*) nobleness

gallego, -a *adj* Galician; (*LAm fam*) Spanish ▷ *nm/f* Galician; (*LAm fam*) Spaniard ▷ *nm* (*Ling*) Galician

galleta *nf* biscuit; (*fam: bofetada*) whack, slap

gallina *nf* hen ▷ *nm* (*fam*) coward; **~ ciega** blind man's buff; **~ llueca** broody hen

gallinero *nm* (*criadero*) henhouse; (*Teat*) gods *sg*, top gallery; (*voces*) hubbub

gallo *nm* cock, rooster; (*Mus*) false *o* wrong note; (*cambio de voz*) break in the voice; **en menos que canta un ~** in an instant

galón *nm* (*Costura*) braid; (*Mil*) stripe; (*medida*) gallon

galopante *adj* galloping

galopar *vi* to gallop

gama *nf* (*Mus*) scale; (*fig*) range; (*Zool*) doe

gamba *nf* prawn

gamberrada *nf* act of hooliganism

gamberro, -a *nm/f* hooligan, lout

gamuza *nf* (*animal*) chamois; (*bayeta*) duster; (*LAm: piel*) suede

gana *nf* (*deseo*) desire, wish; (*apetito*) appetite; (*voluntad*) will; **me dan ~s de ir** I feel like going, I want to go; **tener ~s de hacer algo** to feel like doing sth; **tengo ~s de ir al cine** I feel like going to the cinema; **tengo ~s de que llegue el sábado** I'm looking forward to Saturday; **hazlo como te dé la ~** do it however you like; **no me da la (real) ~** I don't (damned well) want to; **son ~s de molestar** they're just trying to be awkward; **hacer algo de buena/mala ~** to do sth willingly/reluctantly

ganadería *nf* (*ganado*) livestock; (*ganado vacuno*) cattle *pl*; (*cría, comercio*) cattle raising

ganadero, -a *adj* stock *cpd* ▷ *nm* stockman

ganado *nm* livestock; **~ caballar/cabrío** horses *pl*/goats *pl*; **~ lanar** *u* **ovejuno** sheep *pl*; **~ porcino/vacuno** pigs *pl*/cattle *pl*

ganador, -a *adj* winning ▷ *nm/f* winner; (*Econ*) earner

ganancia *nf* (*lo ganado*) gain; (*aumento*) increase; (*beneficio*) profit; **ganancias** *nfpl* (*ingresos*) earnings; (*beneficios*) profit *sg*, winnings; **~s y pérdidas** profit and loss; **~ bruta/líquida** gross/

net profit; **~s de capital** capital gains; **sacar ~ de** to draw profit from

ganar vt (dinero) to earn; (premio, guerra, partido) to win; (tiempo, peso, terreno) to gain; (alcanzar) to reach; (a contrincante) to beat; (Mil: objetivo) to take; (apoyo) to gain, win ▷ vi (Deporte) to win; **ganarse** vr (obtener) to win, earn; (merecerse) to deserve; **gana un buen sueldo** he earns a good wage; **ganamos al Olimpic tres a cero** we beat Olimpic three-nil; **con eso no ganas nada** you won't achieve anything by doing that; **salir ganando** to do well; **salí ganando con la venta del coche** I did well out of the sale of the car; **~se la confianza de algn** to win sb's trust; **se lo ha ganado** he deserves it; **~se la vida** to earn one's living

ganchillo nm (para croché) crochet hook; (arte) crochet work

gancho nm (gen) hook; (colgador) hanger; (pey: revendedor) tout; (fam: atractivo) sex appeal; (Boxeo: golpe) hook

gandul, -a adj, nm/f good-for-nothing

ganga nf (cosa) bargain; (buena situación) cushy job

gangrena nf gangrene

gansada nf (fam) stupid thing (to do)

ganso, -a nm/f (Zool) gander (goose); (fam) idiot

ganzúa nf skeleton key ▷ nm/f burglar

garabatear vt to scribble, scrawl

garabato nm (gancho) hook; (garfio) grappling iron; (escritura) scrawl, scribble; (fam) sex appeal

garaje nm garage

garante adj responsible ▷ nm/f guarantor

garantía nf guarantee; (seguridad) pledge; (compromiso) undertaking; (Jur: caución) warranty; **de máxima ~** absolutely guaranteed; **~ de trabajo** job security

garantizar vt (hacerse responsable de) to vouch for; (asegurar) to guarantee

garbanzo nm chickpea

garbo nm grace, elegance; (aire) jauntiness; (de mujer) glamour; **andar con ~** to walk gracefully

garete nm: **irse al ~** to go to the dogs

garfio nm grappling iron; (gancho) hook; (Alpinismo) climbing iron

garganta nf (interna) throat; (externa, de botella) neck; (Geo: barranco) ravine; (desfiladero) narrow pass

gargantilla nf necklace

gárgara nf gargle, gargling; **hacer ~s** to gargle; **¡vete a hacer ~s!** (fam) go to blazes!

garita nf cabin, hut; (Mil) sentry box; (puesto de vigilancia) lookout post

garito nm (lugar) gaming house o den

garra nf (de gato, Tec) claw; (de ave) talon; (fam) hand, paw; (fig: de canción etc) bite; **caer en las ~s de algn** to fall into sb's clutches

garrafa nf carafe, decanter

garrapata nf (Zool) tick

garrote nm (palo) stick; (porra) club, cudgel; (suplicio) garrotte

garza nf heron

gas nm gas; (vapores) fumes pl; **¿no hueles a ~?**

can you smell gas?; **~es lacrimógenos** tear gas sg; **el niño tiene muchos ~es** the baby's got a lot of wind; **agua mineral sin ~** still mineral water; **pasó una moto a todo ~** a motorbike shot past at full speed; **~es de escape** exhaust (fumes)

gasa nf gauze; (de pañal) nappy liner

gaseoso, -a adj gassy, fizzy ▷ nf lemonade, pop (fam)

gasoil, gasóleo nm diesel (oil)

gasolina nf petrol, gas(oline) (US); **~ sin plomo** unleaded petrol

gasolinera nf petrol (Brit) o gas (US) station

gastado, -a adj (ropa) worn out; (usado: frase etc) trite

gastar vt (dinero, tiempo) to spend; (gasolina, electricidad) to use (up), consume; (desperdiciar) to waste; (llevar puesto) to wear; **gastarse** vr (desgastarse) to wear out; (terminarse) to run out; (estropearse) to waste; **Javier gasta mucho en ropa** Javier spends a lot of money on clothes; **gastamos mucha agua** we use a lot of water; **gasté una caja entera de cerillas** I used up a whole box of matches; **¿qué número gastas?** what size (shoe) do you take?; **~ bromas** to crack jokes; **le gastamos una broma a Juan** we played a joke on Juan; **se me han gastado las suelas** the soles of my shoes have worn out; **se han gastado las pilas** the batteries have run out

gasto nm (desembolso) expenditure, spending; (cantidad gastada) outlay, expense; (consumo, uso) use; (desgaste) waste; **gastos** nmpl (desembolsos) expenses; (cargos) charges, costs; **~ corriente** (Com) revenue expenditure; **~ fijo** (Com) fixed charge; **~s bancarios** bank charges; **~s corrientes** running expenses; **~s de distribución** (Com) distribution costs; **~s generales** overheads; **~s de mantenimiento** maintenance expenses; **~s operacionales** operating costs; **~s de tramitación** (Com) handling charge sg; **~s vencidos** (Com) accrued charges; **cubrir ~s** to cover expenses; **meterse en ~s** to incur expense

gastronomía nf gastronomy

gata nf (Zool) she-cat; **andar a ~s** to go on all fours

gatear vi to go on all fours

gatillo nm (de arma de fuego) trigger; (de dentista) forceps

gato nm (Zool) cat; (Tec) jack; **~ de Angora** Angora cat; **~ montés** wildcat; **dar a algn ~ por liebre** to take sb in; **aquí hay ~ encerrado** there's something fishy here

gaucho nm gaucho, South American cowboy

gaveta nf drawer

gaviota nf seagull

gay adj, nm gay, homosexual

gazapo nm young rabbit

gazpacho nm gazpacho

gel nm gel

gelatina nf jelly; (polvos etc) gelatine

gema nf gem

gemelo, -a *adj, nm/f* twin; **gemelos** *nmpl* (*de camisa*) cufflinks; **~s de campo** field glasses, binoculars; **~s de teatro** opera glasses

gemido *nm* (*quejido*) moan, groan; (*lamento*) wail, howl

Géminis *nm* (*Astro*) Gemini

gemir *vi* (*quejarse*) to moan, groan; (*animal*) to whine; (*viento*) to howl

gen *nm* gene

generación *nf* generation; **primera/segunda/ tercera/cuarta ~** (*Inform*) first/second/third/ fourth generation

general *adj* (*no particular*) general; (*común*) common; (*pey: corriente*) rife; (*frecuente*) usual ▷ *nm* general; **medicina ~** general medicine; **en ~** in general; **en ~ las clases son interesantes** in general the classes are interesting; **por lo ~** generally; **por lo ~ me acuesto temprano** I generally go to bed early; **~ de brigada/de división** brigadier-/major-general

Generalitat *nf* regional government of Catalonia; **~ Valenciana** regional government of Valencia

generalizar *vt* to generalize; **generalizarse** *vr* to become generalized, spread; (*difundirse*) to become widely known

generalmente *adv* generally

generar *vt* to generate

género *nm* (*clase*) kind, sort; (*tipo*) type; (*Bio*) genus; (*Ling*) gender; (*Com*) material; **géneros** *nmpl* (*productos*) goods; **~ humano** human race; **~ chico** (*zarzuela*) Spanish operetta; **~s de punto** knitwear *sg*

generosidad *nf* generosity

generoso, -a *adj* generous

genético, -a *adj* genetic ▷ *nf* genetics *sg*

genial *adj* inspired; (*idea*) brilliant; (*afable*) genial

genio *nm* (*carácter*) nature, disposition; (*humor*) temper; (*facultad creadora*) genius; **mal ~** bad temper; **~ vivo** quick o hot temper; **de mal ~** bad-tempered

genital *adj* genital ▷ *nm:* **~es** genitals, genital organs

gente *nf* (*personas*) people *pl*; (*nación*) nation; (*parientes*) relatives *pl*; **había poca ~ en la sala** there were few people in the room; **la ~ está cansada de promesas** people are tired of promises; **la ~ de la calle** the people in the street; **es buena ~** (*fam: esp LAm*) he's a good sort; **una ~ como usted** (*LAm*) a person like you; **~ bien/baja** posh/lower-class people *pl*; **~ menuda** (*niños*) children *pl*

gentil *adj* (*amable*) kind; (*elegante*) graceful; (*Rel*) gentile

gentileza *nf* (*encanto*) charm; (*cortesía*) courtesy; **por ~ de** by courtesy of

gentío *nm* crowd, throng

genuino, -a *adj* genuine

geografía *nf* geography

geográfico, -a *adj* geographic(al)

geología *nf* geology

geometría *nf* geometry

geranio *nm* (*Bot*) geranium

gerencia *nf* management; (*cargo*) post of manager; (*oficina*) manager's office

gerente *nm/f* (*supervisor*) manager; (*jefe*) director

geriatría *nf* (*Med*) geriatrics *sg*

geriátrico, -a *adj* geriatric

germen *nm* germ

germinar *vi* to germinate; (*brotar*) to sprout

gerundio *nm* (*Ling*) gerund

gestación *nf* gestation

gesticulación *nf* (*ademán*) gesticulation; (*mueca*) grimace

gesticular *vi* (*con ademanes*) to gesture; (*con muecas*) to make faces

gestión *nf* management; (*diligencia, acción*) negotiation; **hacer las gestiones preliminares** to do the groundwork; **~ de cartera** (*Com*) portfolio management; **~ financiera** (*Com*) financial management; **~ interna** (*Inform*) housekeeping; **~ de personal** personnel management; **~ de riesgos** (*Com*) risk management

gestionar *vt* (*lograr*) to try to arrange; (*llevar*) to manage

gesto *nm* (*mueca*) grimace; (*ademán*) gesture; **hacer ~s** to make faces

gestoría *nf* agency undertaking business with government departments, insurance companies etc

Gibraltar *nm* Gibraltar

gibraltareño, -a *adj* of o from Gibraltar ▷ *nm/f* native o inhabitant of Gibraltar

gigante *adj, nm/f* giant

gilipollas (*fam*) *adj inv* daft ▷ *nm/f* berk

gilipollez *nf* (*fam*): **es una ~** that's a load of crap (!); **decir gilipolleces** to talk crap (!)

gimnasia *nf* gymnastics *pl*; **confundir la ~ con la magnesia** to get things mixed up

gimnasio *nm* gym(nasium)

gimnasta *nm/f* gymnast

gimotear *vi* to whine, whimper; (*lloriquear*) to snivel

ginebra *nf* gin

ginecología *nf* gyn(a)ecology

ginecólogo, -a *nm/f* gyn(a)ecologist

gira *nf* tour, trip

girar *vt* (*dar la vuelta a*) to turn (around); (*: rápidamente*) to spin; (*cantidad*) to draw; (*letra de cambio*) to issue ▷ *vi* (*dar un giro*) to turn (round); (*dar vueltas*) to rotate; (*rápido*) to spin; **giré la cabeza para ver quién era** I turned my head to see who it was; **al llegar al semáforo gira a la derecha** when you get to the lights turn right; **la Tierra gira alrededor de su eje** the Earth rotates on its axis; **la Luna gira alrededor de la Tierra** the moon revolves around the Earth; **la conversación giraba en torno a las elecciones** the conversation centred on the election; **~ en descubierto** to overdraw

giratorio, -a *adj* (*gen*) revolving; (*puente*) swing *cpd*; (*silla*) swivel *cpd*

giro *nm* (*movimiento*) turn, revolution; (*Ling*) expression; (*Com*) draft; (*de sucesos*) trend, course; **~ bancario** money order, bank giro; **~**

de existencias (*Com*) stock turnover; **~ postal** postal order; **~ a la vista** (*Com*) sight draft

gis *nm* (*Méx*) chalk

gitano, -a *adj, nm/f* gypsy

glacial *adj* icy, freezing

glaciar *nm* glacier

glándula *nf* (*Anat, Bot*) gland

global *adj* (*en conjunto*) global; (*completo*) total; (*investigación*) full; (*suma*) lump *cpd*

globo *nm* (*esfera*) globe, sphere; (*aerostato, juguete*) balloon

glóbulo *nm* globule; (*Anat*) corpuscle; **~ blanco/ rojo** white/red corpuscle

gloria *nf* glory; (*fig*) delight; (*delicia*) bliss

glorieta *nf* (*de jardín*) bower, arbour, arbor (*US*); (*Auto*) roundabout (*Brit*), traffic circle (*US*); (*plaza redonda*) circus; (*cruce*) junction

glorificar *vt* (*enaltecer*) to glorify, praise

glorioso, -a *adj* glorious

glosa *nf* comment; (*explicación*) gloss

glosar *vt* (*comentar*) to comment on

glosario *nm* glossary

glotón, -ona *adj* gluttonous, greedy ▷ *nm/f* glutton

gobernación *nf* government, governing; (*Pol*) Provincial Governor's office; **Ministro de la G~** Minister of the Interior, Home Secretary (*Brit*)

gobernador, -a *adj* governing ▷ *nm/f* governor

gobernante *adj* governing ▷ *nm* ruler, governor ▷ *nf* (*en hotel etc*) housekeeper

gobernar *vt* (*dirigir*) to guide, direct; (*Pol*) to rule, govern ▷ *vi* to govern; (*Naut*) to steer; **~ mal** to misgovern

gobierno *nm* (*Pol*) government; (*gestión*) management; (*dirección*) guidance, direction; (*Naut*) steering; (*puesto*) governorship

goce *nm* enjoyment

gol *nm* goal

golf *nm* golf

golfa *nf* (*fam: prostituta*) slut, whore, hooker (*US*); *ver tb* **golfo**

golfo, -a *nm/f* (*pilluelo*) street urchin; (*vago*) tramp; (*gorrón*) loafer; (*gamberro*) lout ▷ *nm* (*Geo*) gulf; *ver tb* **golfa**

golondrina *nf* swallow

golosina *nf* titbit; (*dulce*) sweet

goloso, -a *adj* sweet-toothed; (*fam: glotón*) greedy

golpe *nm* blow; (*con puño*) punch; (*con mano*) smack; (*de remo*) stroke; (*Fútbol*) kick; (*Tenis etc*) hit, shot; (*en puerta*) knock; (*mala suerte*) misfortune; (*fam: atraco*) job, heist (*US*); (*fig: choque*) clash; **de un ~** with one blow; **me he dado un ~ en el codo** I banged my elbow; **se dio un ~ contra la pared** he hit the wall; **el coche de atrás nos dio un ~** the car behind ran into us; **oímos un ~ a la puerta** we heard a knock at the door; **de ~** suddenly; **de ~ decidió dejar el trabajo** he suddenly decided to give up work; **cerrar una puerta de ~** to slam a door; **no dar ~** to be bone idle; **~ (de estado)** coup (d'état); **~ de gracia** coup de grâce (*tb fig*); **~ de fortuna/ maestro** stroke of luck/genius

golpear *vt, vi* to strike, knock; (*asestar*) to beat; (*de puño*) to punch; (*golpetear*) to tap; (*mesa*) to bang

golpista *adj*: **intentona ~** coup attempt ▷ *nm/f* participant in a coup (d'état)

goma *nf* (*caucho*) rubber; (*elástico*) elastic; (*tira*) rubber o elastic (*Brit*) band; (*fam: preservativo*) condom; (*droga*) hashish; (*explosivo*) plastic explosive; **~ (de borrar)** eraser, rubber (*Brit*); **~ de mascar** chewing gum; **~ de pegar** gum, glue

gomina *nf* hair gel

gordo, -a *adj* (*gen*) fat; (*persona*) plump; (*agua*) hard; (*fam*) enormous ▷ *nm/f* fat man o woman; **el (premio) ~** (*en lotería*) first prize; **¡~!** (*fam*) fatty!

gordura *nf* fat; (*corpulencia*) fatness, stoutness

gorila *nm* gorilla; (*fam*) tough, thug; (*guardaespaldas*) bodyguard

gorjear *vi* to twitter, chirp

gorra *nf* (*gen*) cap; (*de niño*) bonnet; (*militar*) bearskin; **~ de montar/de paño/de punto/de visera** riding/cloth/knitted/peaked cap; **andar** o **ir** o **vivir de ~** to sponge, scrounge; **entrar de ~** (*fam*) to gatecrash

gorrión *nm* sparrow

gorro *nm* cap; (*de niño, mujer*) bonnet; **estoy hasta el ~** I am fed up

gorrón, -ona *nm* pebble; (*Tec*) pivot ▷ *nm/f* scrounger

gorronear *vi* (*fam*) to sponge, scrounge

gota *nf* (*gen*) drop; (*de pintura*) blob; (*de sudor*) bead; (*Med*) gout; **~ a ~** drop by drop; **caer a ~s** to drip

gotear *vi* to drip; (*escurrir*) to trickle; (*salirse*) to leak; (*cirio*) to gutter; (*lloviznar*) to drizzle

gotera *nf* leak

gótico, -a *adj* Gothic

gozar *vi* to enjoy o.s.; **~ de** (*disfrutar*) to enjoy; (*poseer*) to possess; **~ de buena salud** to enjoy good health

gozne *nm* hinge

gozo *nm* (*alegría*) joy; (*placer*) pleasure; **¡mi ~ en un pozo!** that's torn it!, just my luck!

grabación *nf* recording

grabado, -a *adj* (*Mus*) recorded; (*en cinta*) taped, on tape ▷ *nm* print, engraving; **~ al agua fuerte** etching; **~ al aguatinta** aquatint; **~ en cobre** copperplate; **~ en madera** woodcut; **~ rupestre** rock carving

grabador, -a *nm/f* engraver; *ver tb* **grabadora**

grabadora *nf* tape-recorder; **~ de cassettes** cassette recorder; *ver tb* **grabador**

grabar *vt* to engrave; (*discos, cintas*) to record; (*impresionar*) to impress

gracia *nf* (*humor*) humour, wit; (*chiste*) joke; (*encanto*) grace, gracefulness; (*Rel*) grace; **gracias** *nfpl* thank you, thanks; **tener ~** to be funny; **sus chistes tienen mucha ~** his jokes are very funny; **¡qué ~!** how funny!; (*irónico*) what a nerve!; **no me hace ~** (*broma*) it's not funny; (*plan*) I'm not too keen; **no me hace ~ tener que salir con este tiempo** I'm not too pleased about having to go out in this weather; **¡muchas ~s!** thanks very much!; **muchas ~s por adelantado** thanking you in advance; **dar**

las ~s a algn por algo to thank sb for sth; **vino a darme las ~s por las flores** he came to thank me for the flowers; **ni siquiera me dio las ~s** he didn't even say thank you; **~s a** thanks to; **~s a él me encuentro con vida** thanks to him I'm still alive

gracioso, -a adj (garboso) graceful; (chistoso) funny; (cómico) comical; (agudo) witty; (título) gracious ▷ nm/f (Teat) comic character, fool; **su graciosa Majestad** His/Her Gracious Majesty

grada nf (de escalera) step; (de anfiteatro) tier, row; **gradas** nfpl (de estadio) terraces

gradación nf gradation; (serie) graded series

gradería nf (gradas) (flight of) steps pl; (de anfiteatro) tiers pl, rows pl; **~ cubierta** covered stand

grado nm (gen) degree; (etapa) stage, step; (nivel) rate; (de parentesco) degree; (de aceite, vino) grade; (Univ) degree; (Ling) degree of comparison; (Mil) rank; **estaban a diez ~s bajo cero** it was ten degrees below zero; **quemaduras de primer ~** first-degree burns; **en sumo ~, en ~ superlativo** in the highest degree; **de buen ~** willingly

graduación nf (acto) gradation; (clasificación) rating; (del alcohol) proof, strength; (Escol) graduation; (Mil) rank; **de alta ~** high-ranking

gradual adj gradual

graduar vt (gen) to graduate; (medir) to gauge; (Tec) to calibrate; (Univ) to confer a degree on; (Mil) to commission; **graduarse** vr to graduate; **~se la vista** to have one's eyes tested

gráfico, -a adj graphic; (fig: vívido) vivid, lively ▷ nm diagram ▷ nf graph; **~ de barras** (Com) bar chart; **~ de sectores** o **de tarta** (Com) pie chart; **gráficos** nmpl (tb Inform) graphics; **~s empresariales** (Com) business graphics

grajo nm rook

Gral. abr (Mil: = General) Gen.

gramática nf grammar; ver tb **gramático**

gramático, -a nm/f (persona) grammarian; ver tb **gramática**

gramo nm gramme (Brit), gram (US)

gran adj ver **grande**

grana nf (Bot) seedling; (color) scarlet; **ponerse como la ~** to go as red as a beetroot

granada nf pomegranate; (Mil) grenade; **~ de mano** hand grenade; **~ de metralla** shrapnel shell

granate adj inv maroon ▷ nm garnet; (color) maroon

Gran Bretaña nf Great Britain

grande, gran adj (de tamaño) big, large; (de cantidad) large; (alto) tall; (en importancia, grado) great; (impresionante) grand ▷ nm grandee; **viven en una casa muy ~** they live in a very big house; **¿cómo es de ~?** how big is it?, what size is it?; **la camisa me está ~** the shirt is too big for me; **unos ~s almacenes** a department store; **un gran número de visitantes** a large number of visitors; **~s sumas de dinero** large sums of money; **un gran pintor** a great painter; **es una ventaja muy ~** it's a great advantage; **pasarlo**

en ~ to have a great time

grandeza nf greatness; (tamaño) bigness; (esplendidez) grandness; (nobleza) nobility

grandioso, -a adj magnificent, grand

granel nm (montón) heap; **a ~** (Com) in bulk

granero nm granary, barn

granito nm (Agr) small grain; (roca) granite

granizado nm iced drink; **~ de café** iced coffee

granizar vi to hail

granizo nm hail

granja nf (gen) farm; **~ avícola** chicken o poultry farm

granjear vt (cobrar) to earn; (ganar) to win; (avanzar) to gain; **granjearse** vr (amistad etc) to gain for o.s.

granjero, -a nm/f farmer

grano nm grain; (semilla) seed; (baya) berry; (Med) pimple, spot; (partícula) particle; (punto) speck; **granos** nmpl cereals; **~ de café** coffee bean; **ir al ~** to get to the point

granuja nm rogue; (golfillo) urchin

grapa nf staple; (Tec) clamp; (sujetador) clip, fastener; (Arq) cramp

grapadora nf stapler

grasa nf ver **graso**

grasiento, -a adj greasy; (de aceite) oily; (mugriento) filthy

graso, -a adj fatty; (aceitoso) greasy, oily ▷ nf (gen) grease; (de cocina) fat, lard; (sebo) suet; (mugre) filth; (Auto) oil; (lubricante) grease; **grasa de ballena** blubber; **grasa de pescado** fish oil

gratificación nf (propina) tip; (aguinaldo) gratuity; (bono) bonus; (recompensa) reward

gratificar vt (dar propina) to tip; (premiar) to reward; **"se ~á"** "a reward is offered"

gratinar vt to cook au gratin

gratis adv free, for nothing

gratitud nf gratitude

grato, -a adj (agradable) pleasant, agreeable; (bienvenido) welcome; **nos es ~ informarle que ...** we are pleased to inform you that ...

gratuito, -a adj (gratis) free; (sin razón) gratuitous; (acusación) unfounded

grava nf (guijos) gravel; (piedra molida) crushed stone; (en carreteras) road metal

gravamen nm (carga) burden; (impuesto) tax; **libre de ~** (Econ) free from encumbrances

gravar vt to burden; (Com) to tax; (Econ) to assess for tax; **~ con impuestos** to burden with taxes

grave adj heavy; (fig, Med) grave, serious; (importante) important; (herida) severe; (Mus) low, deep; (Ling: acento) grave; **estar ~** to be seriously ill

gravedad nf gravity; (fig) seriousness; (grandeza) importance; (dignidad) dignity; (Mus) depth

gravilla nf gravel

gravitar vi to gravitate; **~ sobre** to rest on

gravoso, -a adj (pesado) burdensome; (costoso) costly

graznar vi (cuervo) to squawk; (pato) to quack; (hablar ronco) to croak

Grecia nf Greece

gremio *nm* (*asociación*) professional association, guild

greña *nf* (*cabellos*) shock of hair; (*maraña*) tangle; **andar a la ~** to bicker, squabble

gresca *nf* uproar; (*trifulca*) row

griego, -a *adj* Greek, Grecian ▷ *nm/f* Greek ▷ *nm* (*Ling*) Greek

grieta *nf* crack; (*hendidura*) chink; (*quiebra*) crevice; (*Med*) chap; (*Pol*) rift

grifo *nm* tap (*Brit*), faucet (*US*); (*Perú*) petrol (*Brit*) o gas (*US*) station

grilletes *nmpl* fetters, shackles

grillo *nm* (*Zool*) cricket; (*Bot*) shoot; **grillos** *nmpl* shackles, irons

gripe *nf* flu, influenza

gris *adj* grey

gritar *vt, vi* to shout, yell; **¡no grites!** stop shouting!

grito *nm* shout, yell; (*de horror*) scream; **a ~ pelado** at the top of one's voice; **poner el ~ en el cielo** to scream blue murder; **es el último ~** (*de moda*) it's all the rage

grosella *nf* (red)currant; **~ negra** blackcurrant

grosería *nf* (*actitud*) rudeness; (*comentario*) vulgar comment; (*palabrota*) swearword

grosero, -a *adj* (*poco cortés*) rude, bad-mannered; (*ordinario*) vulgar, crude

grosor *nm* thickness

grotesco, -a *adj* grotesque; (*absurdo*) bizarre

grúa *nf* (*Tec*) crane; (*de petróleo*) derrick; **~ corrediza** o **móvil/de pescante/puente/de torre** travelling/jib/overhead/tower crane

grueso, -a *adj* thick; (*persona*) stout; (*calidad*) coarse ▷ *nm* bulk; (*espesor*) thickness; (*densidad*) density; (*de gente*) main body, mass; **el ~ de** the bulk of

grulla *nf* (*Zool*) crane

grumo *nm* (*coágulo*) clot, lump; (*masa*) dollop

gruñido *nm* grunt, growl; (*fig*) grumble

gruñir *vi* (*animal*) to grunt, growl; (*fam*) to grumble

grupa *nf* (*Zool*) rump

grupo *nm* group; (*Tec*) unit, set; (*de árboles*) cluster; **~ sanguíneo** blood group

gruta *nf* grotto

guacamole *nm* guacamole

guadaña *nf* scythe

guagua *nf* (*Cuba, Canarias*) bus; (*And: bebé*) baby; **tener ~** (*And*) to have a baby

guajolote *nm* (*Méx*) turkey

guante *nm* glove; **se ajusta como un ~** it fits like a glove; **echar el ~ a algn** to catch hold of sb; (*fig: policía*) to catch sb

guapo, -a *adj* good-looking; (*mujer*) pretty, attractive; (*hombre*) handsome; (*elegante*) smart ▷ *nm* lover, gallant; (*LAm fam*) tough guy, bully

guarda *nm/f* (*persona*) warden, keeper ▷ *nf* (*acto*) guarding; (*custodia*) custody; (*Tip*) flyleaf, endpaper; **~ forestal** game warden

guardabarros *nm inv* mudguard (*Brit*), fender (*US*)

guardabosques *nm inv* gamekeeper

guardacostas *nm inv* coastguard vessel

guardador, -a *adj* protective; (*tacaño*) mean, stingy ▷ *nm/f* guardian, protector

guardaespaldas *nm/f inv* bodyguard

guardameta *nm* goalkeeper

guardapolvo *nm* dust cover; (*prenda de vestir*) overalls *pl*

guardar *vt* (*gen*) to keep; (*recoger*) to put away; (*dinero*) to save; (*ley*) to observe; (*rencor*) to bear, harbour; (*Inform: archivo*) to save; **guardarse** *vr* (*preservarse*) to protect o.s.; **guarda el recibo** keep the receipt; **los niños ~on los juguetes** the children put away their toys; **guardé los documentos en el cajón** I put the documents away in the drawer; **Raúl se guardó el pañuelo en el bolsillo** Raúl put the handkerchief in his pocket; **~ las apariencias** to keep up appearances; **guardársela a algn** to have it in for sb; **~se de algo** (*evitar*) to avoid sth; (*abstenerse*) to refrain from sth; **~se de hacer algo** to be careful not to do sth

guardarropa *nm* (*armario*) wardrobe; (*en establecimiento público*) cloakroom

guardería *nf* nursery

guardia *nf* (*Mil*) guard; (*cuidado*) care, custody ▷ *nm/f* guard; (*policía*) policeman(woman); **estar de ~** to be on guard; **montar ~** to mount guard; **~ municipal** o **urbana** municipal police; **la G~ Civil** the Civil Guard; **un ~ civil** a Civil Guard(sman); **un(a) ~ nacional** a policeman(-woman); **~ urbano** traffic policeman

guardián, -ana *nm/f* (*gen*) guardian, keeper

guarecer *vt* (*proteger*) to protect; (*abrigar*) to shelter; **guarecerse** *vr* to take refuge

guarida *nf* (*de animal*) den, lair; (*de persona*) haunt, hideout; (*refugio*) refuge

guarnecer *vt* (*equipar*) to provide; (*adornar*) to adorn; (*Tec*) to reinforce

guarnición *nf* (*de vestimenta*) trimming; (*de piedra*) mount; (*Culin*) garnish; (*arneses*) harness; (*Mil*) garrison

guarrada (*fam*) *nf* (*cosa sucia*) dirty mess; (*acto o dicho obsceno*) obscenity; **hacer una ~ a algn** to do the dirty on sb

guarrería *nf* = **guarrada**

guarro, -a *nm/f* (*fam*) pig; (*fig*) dirty o slovenly person

guasa *nf* joke; **con** o **de ~** jokingly, in fun

guasón, -ona *adj* witty; (*bromista*) joking ▷ *nm/f* (*bromista*) joker; (*ocurrente*) wit

Guatemala *nf* Guatemala

guay *adj* (*fam*) super, great

gubernamental, gubernativo, -a *adj* governmental

güero, -a *adj* (*rubio*) blond(e)

guerra *nf* war; (*arte*) warfare; (*pelea*) struggle; **~ atómica/bacteriológica/nuclear/de guerrillas** atomic/germ/nuclear/guerrilla warfare; **Primera/Segunda G~ Mundial** First/Second World War; **~ de precios** (*Com*) price war; **~ civil/fría** civil/cold war; **~ a muerte** fight to the death; **de ~** military, war *cpd*; **estar en ~** to be at war; **dar ~** to be annoying

guerrear *vi* to wage war

guerrero, -a *adj* fighting; (*carácter*) warlike ▷ *nm/f* warrior

guerrilla *nf* guerrilla warfare; (*tropas*) guerrilla band *o* group

guerrillero, -a *nm/f* guerrilla (fighter); (*contra invasor*) partisan

gueto *nm* ghetto

guía *nm/f* (*persona*) guide ▷ *nf* (*libro*) guidebook; (*manual*) handbook; (*Inform*) prompt; **~ de ferrocarriles** railway timetable; **~ telefónica** telephone directory; **~ del turista/del viajero** tourist/traveller's guide

guiar *vt* to guide, direct; (*dirigir*) to lead; (*orientar*) to advise; (*Auto*) to steer; **guiarse** *vr*: **~se por** to be guided by

guijarro *nm* pebble

guillotina *nf* guillotine

guinda *nf* morello cherry; (*licor*) cherry liqueur

guindilla *nf* chil(l)i pepper

guiñapo *nm* (*harapo*) rag; (*persona*) rogue

guiñar *vi* to wink

guiño *nm* (*parpadeo*) wink; (*muecas*) grimace; **hacer ~s a** (*enamorados*) to make eyes at

guión *nm* (*Ling*) hyphen, dash; (*esquema*) summary, outline; (*Cine*) script

guionista *nm/f* scriptwriter

guiri *nm/f* (*fam, pey*) foreigner

guirnalda *nf* garland

guisa *nf*: **a ~ de** as, like

guisado *nm* stew

guisante *nm* pea

guisar *vt, vi* to cook; (*fig*) to arrange

guiso *nm* cooked dish

guitarra *nf* guitar

guitarrista *nm/f* guitarist

gula *nf* gluttony, greed

gusano *nm* maggot, worm; (*de mariposa, polilla*) caterpillar; (*fig*) worm; (*ser despreciable*) creep; **~ de seda** silk-worm

gustar *vt* to taste, sample ▷ *vi*: **me gustan las uvas** I like grapes; **le gusta nadar** she likes *o* enjoys swimming; **me gustó como hablaba** I liked the way he spoke; **me ~ía conocerla** I would like to meet her; **me gusta su hermana** I fancy his sister; **le gusta más llevar pantalones** she prefers to wear trousers; **~ de algo** to like *o* enjoy sth; **¿gusta usted?** would you like some?; **como usted guste** as you wish

gusto *nm* (*sentido, sabor*) taste; (*agrado*) liking; (*placer*) pleasure; **tiene un ~ amargo** it has a bitter taste; **tener buen ~** to have good taste; **sobre ~s no hay nada escrito** there's no accounting for tastes; **no tiene ~ para vestirse** he has no taste in clothes; **me he decorado la habitación a mi ~** I've decorated the room to my taste; **de buen/mal ~** in good/bad taste; **un comentario de mal ~** a tasteless remark; **tomar ~ a** to take a liking to; **sentirse a ~** to feel at ease; **¡mucho *o* tanto ~ (en conocerle)!** how do you do?, pleased to meet you; **el ~ es mío** the pleasure is mine; **¡con mucho ~!** with pleasure!

gustoso, -a *adj* (*sabroso*) tasty; (*agradable*) pleasant; (*con voluntad*) willing, glad; **lo hizo ~** he did it gladly

gutural *adj* guttural

Hh

haba *nf* bean; **son ~s contadas** it goes without saying; **en todas partes cuecen ~s** it's the same (story) the whole world over

Habana *nf*: **la ~** Havana

habano *nm* Havana cigar

haber *vb aux* **1** (*tiempos compuestos*) to have; **he/hemos comido** I've/we've eaten; **había comido** I'd eaten; **se ha sentado** she's sat down; **antes/después de ~lo visto** before seeing/after seeing *o* having seen it; **si lo hubiera sabido, habría ido** if I had known, I would have gone

2 (*obligación*): **¡~lo dicho antes!** you should have said so before!; **¿habráse visto (cosa igual)?** have you ever seen anything like it?

3 (*obligación*): **~ de: he de hacerlo** I must do it; **ha de llegar mañana** it should arrive tomorrow

▷ *vb impers* **1** (*existencia: sg*) there is; (: *pl*) there are; **hay un hermano/dos hermanos** there is one brother/there are two brothers; **hay una iglesia en la esquina** there's a church on the corner; **hubo una guerra** there was a war; **no hay quien te entienda** there's no understanding you; **¿cuánto hay de aquí a Sucre?** how far is it from here to Sucre?; **habrá unos 4 grados** it must be about 4 degrees; **hay treinta alumnos en mi clase** there are thirty pupils in my class; **¿hay entradas?** are there any tickets?

2 (*obligación*): **hay que hacer algo** something must be done; **hay que ser respetuoso** you must be respectful; **hay que apuntarlo para acordarse** you have to write it down to remember; **¡habrá que decírselo!** we'll have to tell him!

3: **¡hay que ver!** well I never!

4: **¡no hay de** *o* **por** (*LAm*) **qué!** don't mention it!, not at all!

5: **¿qué hay?** (*¿qué pasa?*) what's up?, what's the matter?; (*¿qué tal?*) how's it going?; **¿qué hubo?** (*And, Méx: fam*) how are things?

haberse *vr*: **habérselas con algn** to have it out with sb

▷ *vt*: **he aquí unas sugerencias** here are some suggestions; **todos los inventos habidos y por ~** all inventions present and future; **en el encuentro habido ayer** in yesterday's game

▷ *nm* (*en cuenta*) credit side

haberes *nmpl* assets; **¿cuánto tengo en el ~?** how much do I have in my account?; **tiene varias novelas en su ~** he has several novels to his credit

habichuela *nf* kidney bean

hábil *adj* (*listo*) clever, smart; (*capaz*) fit, capable; (*experto*) expert; **día ~** working day

habilidad *nf* (*gen*) skill, ability; (*inteligencia*) cleverness; (*destreza*) expertness, expertise; (*Jur*) competence; **~ (para)** fitness (for); **tener ~ manual** to be clever with one's hands

habilitar *vt* to qualify; (*autorizar*) to authorize; (*capacitar*) to enable; (*dar instrumentos*) to equip; (*financiar*) to finance

hábilmente *adv* skilfully, expertly

habitación *nf* (*cuarto*) room; (*casa*) dwelling, abode; (*Bio: morada*) habitat; **~ sencilla** *o* **individual** single room; **~ doble** *o* **de matrimonio** double room

habitante *nm/f* inhabitant

habitar *vt* (*residir en*) to inhabit; (*ocupar*) to occupy

▷ *vi* to live

hábitat (*pl* **-s**) *nm* habitat

hábito *nm* habit; **tener el ~ de hacer algo** to be in the habit of doing sth

habitual *adj* habitual

habituar *vt* to accustom; **habituarse** *vr*: **~se a** to get used to

habla *nf* (*capacidad de hablar*) speech; (*idioma*) language; (*dialecto*) dialect; **perder el ~** to become speechless; **de ~ francesa** French-speaking; **estar al ~** to be in contact; (*Telec*) to be on the line; **¡González al ~!** (*Telec*) Gonzalez speaking!

hablador, a *adj* talkative ▷ *nm/f* chatterbox

habladuría *nf* rumour; **habladurías** *nfpl* gossip *sg*

hablante *adj* speaking ▷ *nm/f* speaker

hablar *vi* to talk, speak ▷ *vt* to speak; **hablarse** *vr* to speak to each other; **~ alto/bajo/claro** to speak loudly/quietly/plainly *o* bluntly; **estuvimos hablando toda la tarde** we were talking all afternoon; **~ con algn** to speak to sb; **¿has hablado ya con el profesor?** have you spoken to the teacher yet?; **necesito ~ contigo** I need to talk to you; **~ de algo** to talk about something; **acabamos de ~ del premio** we were just talking about the prize; **¡hable!,**

¡**puede ~**! (*al teléfono*) you're through!; **¿quién habla**? (*al teléfono*) who's calling?; **de eso ni ~** no way, that's not on; **¿hablas español?** do you speak Spanish?; **"se habla inglés"** "English spoken here"; **no se hablan** they are not on speaking terms

hacedor, a *nm/f* maker

hacendado, -a *adj* property-owning ▷ *nm* (*terrateniente*) large landowner

hacendoso, -a *adj* industrious, hard-working

hacer *vt* **1** (*fabricar, producir, conseguir*) to make; (*construir*) to build; **~ una película/un ruido** to make a film/noise; **el guisado lo hice yo** I made *o* cooked the stew; **~ amigos** to make friends **2** (*realizar*) to do; **estoy haciendo los deberes** I'm doing my homework; **~ la colada** to do the washing; **~ la comida** to do the cooking; **¿qué haces?** what are you doing?; **¿qué hace tu padre?** what does your father do?; **se hace con huevos y leche** it's made out of eggs and milk; **eso no se hace** that's not done; **¡eso está hecho!** you've got it!; **~ el tonto/indio** to act the fool/clown; **~ el malo** *o* **el papel del malo** (*Teat*) to play the villain **3** (*estudios, algunos deportes*) to do; **~ español/económicas** to do *o* study Spanish/economics; **~ yoga/gimnasia** to do yoga/go to the gym **4** (*transformar, incidir en*): **esto lo hará más difícil** this will make it more difficult; **salir te hará sentir mejor** going out will make you feel better; **te hace más joven** it makes you look younger **5** (*cálculo*) to make; **2 y 2 hacen 4** 2 and 2 make 4; **éste hace 100** this one makes 100 **6** (+ *subjun*): **esto hará que ganemos** this will make us win; **harás que no quiera venir** you'll stop him wanting to come **7** (*como sustituto de vb*) to do; **él bebió y yo hice lo mismo** he drank and I did likewise **8**: **no hace más que criticar** all he does is criticize

▷ *vb semi-aux: hacer + infin* **1** (*directo*): **~ a algn ~ algo** to make sb do sth; **les hice venir** I made *o* had them come; **~ trabajar a los demás** to get others to work **2** (*por intermedio de otros*): **~ ~ algo** to have sth done; **hicieron pintar la fachada del colegio** they had the front of the school painted; **~ reparar algo** to get sth repaired

▷ *vi* **1**: **haz como que no lo sabes** act as if you don't know; **hiciste bien en decírmelo** you were right to tell me **2** (*ser apropiado*): **si os hace** if it's alright with you **3**: **~ de**: **~ de madre para algn** to be like a mother to sb; (*Teat*): **~ de Otelo** to play Othello; **la tabla hace de mesa** the board does as a table ▷ *vb impers* **1** (*Meteorología*) to be; **hace calor/frío** it's hot/cold; **hizo dos grados bajo cero** it was two degrees below zero; *ver tb* **bueno; sol; tiempo 2** (*tiempo*): **hace 3 años** 3 years ago; **hace un mes que voy/no voy** I've been going/I haven't been for a month; **no lo veo desde hace mucho**

I haven't seen him for a long time; **ha estado aquí hasta hace poco** he was here a few minutes ago **3**: **¿cómo has hecho para llegar tan rápido?** how did you manage to get here so quickly?

hacerse *vr* **1** (*volverse*) to become; **se hicieron amigos** they became friends; **quiere ~se famoso** he wants to become famous; **~se viejo** to get *o* grow old; **se hace tarde** it's getting late **2**: **~se algo, me hice un traje** I got a suit made **3** (*acostumbrarse*): **~se a** to get used to; **~se a la idea** to get used to the idea **4** (*obtener*): **~se de** *o* **con algo** to get hold of sth **5** (*fingirse*): **~se el sordo/sueco** to turn a deaf ear/pretend not to notice

hacha *nf* axe; (*antorcha*) torch

hachazo *nm* axe blow

hachís *nm* hashish

hacia *prep* (*en dirección de, actitud*) towards; (*cerca de*) near; **~ arriba/abajo** up(wards)/down(wards); **~ mediodía** about noon

hacienda *nf* (*propiedad*) property; (*finca*) farm; (*LAm*) ranch; **~ pública** public finance; (**Ministerio de**) **H~** Exchequer (*Brit*), Treasury Department (*US*)

hada *nf* fairy; **~ madrina** fairy godmother

Haití *nm* Haiti

halagar *vt* (*lisonjear*) to flatter

halago *nm* (*adulación*) flattery

halagüeño, -a *adj* flattering

halcón *nm* falcon, hawk

hálito *nm* breath

hallar *vt* (*gen*) to find; (*descubrir*) to discover; **hallarse** *vr* to be (situated); (*encontrarse*) to find o.s.; **se halla fuera del país** he's out of the country; **no se halla** he feels out of place

hallazgo *nm* discovery; (*cosa*) find

halógeno, a *adj*: **faro ~** halogen lamp

halterofilia *nf* weightlifting

hamaca *nf* hammock

hambre *nf* hunger; (*carencia*) famine; (*inanición*) starvation; (*fig*) longing; **tener ~** to be hungry

hambriento, -a *adj* hungry, starving ▷ *nm/f* starving person; **los ~s** the hungry; **~ de** hungry *o* longing for

hambruna *nf* famine

hamburguesa *nf* hamburger, burger

hampón *nm* thug

haragán, -ana *adj, nm/f* good-for-nothing

harapiento, -a *adj* tattered, in rags

harapo *nm* rag

harina *nf* flour; **eso es ~ de otro costal** that's another kettle of fish

hartar *vt* (*atiborrar*): **~ a algn a** *o* **de** to fill sb full of; (*cansar*): **me harta tanta televisión** I get tired of watching so much television; **hartarse** *vr*: **~se de** (*comida*) to gorge o.s. on; (*cansarse de*) to get fed up with; **¡me estás hartando!** you're getting on my nerves!; **me harté de pasteles** I stuffed myself with cakes (*col*); **me harté de estudiar** I got fed up with studying

hartazgo *nm* surfeit, glut

harto, -a *adj* (*lleno*) full; (*cansado*) fed up; (*mucho: LAm*) a lot of ▷ *adv* (*muy*) very; (*bastante: LAm*) enough; **estar ~ de algo/algn** to be fed up with sth/sb; **estábamos ~s de repetirlo** we were fed up with repeating it; **¡estoy ~ de decírtelo!** I'm sick and tired of telling you (so)!; **¡me tienes ~!** I'm fed up with you!; **había harta comida** there was a lot of food; **es un idioma ~ difícil** It's a very difficult language; **tenemos ~ que estudiar** we've got a lot to study

hartura *nf* (*exceso*) surfeit; (*abundancia*) abundance; (*satisfacción*) satisfaction

hasta *adv* even ▷ *prep* (*alcanzando a*) as far as, up/down to; (*de tiempo: a tal hora*) till, until; (: *antes de*) before ▷ *conj*: **~ que** until; **estudia ~ cuando está de vacaciones** he even studies when he's on holiday; **~ en Valencia hiela a veces** even in Valencia it freezes sometimes; **desde aquí se ve ~ el pueblo vecino** from here you can see as far as the next town; **caminamos ~ la puerta** we walked up to the door; **está abierto ~ las cuatro** It's open till four o'clock; **¿~ cuándo?** how long?; **¿~ cuándo te quedas?** — **~ la semana que viene** how long are you staying? — till next week; **~ luego** *o* **ahora/el sábado** see you soon/on Saturday; **~ ahora no ha llamado nadie** no one has called up to now; **~ la fecha** (up) to date; **~ nueva orden** until further notice; **espera aquí ~ que te llamen** wait here until you're called

hastiar *vt* (*gen*) to weary; (*aburrir*) to bore; **hastiarse** *vr*: **~se de** to get fed up with

hastío *nm* (*cansancio*) weariness; (*aburrimiento*) boredom

hatillo *nm* belongings *pl*, kit; (*montón*) bundle, heap

Haya *nf*: **la ~** The Hague

haz *vb ver* **hacer** ▷ *nm* bundle, bunch; (*rayo: de luz*) beam ▷ *nf*: **~ de la tierra** face of the earth

hazaña *nf* feat, exploit; **sería una ~** it would be a great achievement

hazmerreír *nm inv* laughing stock

he *adv*: **he aquí** here is, here are; **he aquí por qué ...** that is why ...

hebilla *nf* buckle, clasp

hebra *nf* thread; (*Bot: fibra*) fibre, grain

hebreo, -a *adj, nm/f* Hebrew ▷ *nm* (*Ling*) Hebrew

hechicero, -a *nm/f* sorcerer (sorceress)

hechizar *vt* to cast a spell on, bewitch

hechizo *nm* witchcraft, magic; (*acto de magia*) spell, charm

hecho, -a *pp de* **hacer** ▷ *adj* made; (*maduro*) mature; (*Costura*) ready-to-wear ▷ *nm* (*gen*) deed, act; (*dato*) fact; (*cuestión*) matter; (*suceso*) event ▷ *excl* agreed!, done!; **¿de qué está ~?** what's it made of?; **~ a medida** made-to-measure; **~ a mano** handmade; **~ a máquina** machine-made; **un hombre ~ y derecho** a fully grown man; **me gusta la carne bien hecha** I like my meat well done; **un filete poco ~** a rare steak; **¡bien ~!** well done!; **a lo ~, pecho** it's no use crying over spilt milk; **el ~ de que...** the fact that...; **el ~ es que...** the fact is that...; **un ~ histórico** an

historic event; **de ~** in fact, as a matter of fact; **de ~, yo no sé nada de eso** in fact, I don't know anything about that

hechura *nf* making, creation; (*producto*) product; (*forma*) form, shape; (*de persona*) build; (*Tec*) craftsmanship

hectárea *nf* hectare

heder *vi* to stink, smell; (*fig*) to be unbearable

hediondo, -a *adj* stinking

hedor *nm* stench

hegemonía *nf* hegemony

helada *nf* frost

heladera *nf* (*CS: refrigerador*) refrigerator

heladería *nf* ice-cream stall (*o* parlour)

helado, -a *adj* frozen; (*glacial*) icy; (*fig*) chilly, cold ▷ *nm* ice-cream; **dejar ~ a algn** to dumbfound sb

helar *vt* to freeze, ice (up); (*dejar atónito*) to amaze; (*desalentar*) to discourage ▷ *vi*: **helarse** *vr* to freeze; (*Aviat, Ferro etc*) to ice (up), freeze up; (*líquido*) to set

helecho *nm* bracken, fern

hélice *nf* spiral; (*Tec*) propeller; (*Mat*) helix

helicóptero *nm* helicopter

helio *nm* helium

hematoma *nm* bruise

hembra *nf* (*Bot, Zool*) female; (*mujer*) woman; (*Tec*) nut; **un elefante ~** a she-elephant

hemiciclo *nm*: **el ~** (*Pol*) the floor

hemisferio *nm* hemisphere

hemorragia *nf* haemorrhage (*Brit*), hemorrhage (*US*)

hemorroides *nfpl* haemorrhoids (*Brit*), hemorrhoids (*US*)

hendidura *nf* crack, split; (*Geo*) fissure

heno *nm* hay

hepatitis *nf inv* hepatitis

herbicida *nm* weedkiller

herbívoro, -a *adj* herbivorous

herboristería *nf* herbalist's shop

heredad *nf* landed property; (*granja*) farm

heredar *vt* to inherit

heredero, -a *nm/f* heir(ess); **~ del trono** heir to the throne

hereditario, -a *adj* hereditary

hereje *nm/f* heretic

herencia *nf* inheritance; (*fig*) heritage; (*Bio*) heredity

herida *nf* wound, injury; *ver tb* **herido**

herido, -a *adj* injured, wounded; (*fig*) offended ▷ *nm/f* casualty; *ver tb* **herida**

herir *vt* to wound, injure; (*fig*) to offend; (*conmover*) to touch, move

hermana *nf ver* **hermano**

hermanastro, -a *nm/f* stepbrother(sister)

hermandad *nf* brotherhood; (*de mujeres*) sisterhood; (*sindicato etc*) association

hermano, -a *adj* similar ▷ *nm* brother ▷ *nf* sister; **~ gemelo** twin brother; **~/a político/a** brother-/sister-in-law; **~ primo** first cousin

hermético, -a *adj* hermetic; (*fig*) watertight

hermoso, -a *adj* beautiful, lovely; (*estupendo*) splendid; (*guapo*) handsome

hermosura *nf* beauty; *(de hombre)* handsomeness
hernia *nf* hernia, rupture; ~ **discal** slipped disc
herniarse *vr* to rupture o.s.; *(fig)* to break one's back
héroe *nm* hero
heroína *nf (mujer)* heroine; *(droga)* heroin
heroinómano, -a *nm/f* heroin addict
heroísmo *nm* heroism
herradura *nf* horseshoe
herramienta *nf* tool
herrería *nf* smithy; *(Tec)* forge
herrero *nm* blacksmith
herrumbre *nf* rust
hervidero *nm (fig)* swarm; *(Pol etc)* hotbed
hervir *vi* to boil; *(burbujear)* to bubble; *(fig)*: ~ **de** to teem with; ~ **a fuego lento** to simmer
hervor *nm* boiling; *(fig)* ardour, fervour
heterosexual *adj, nm/f* heterosexual
híbrido, -a *adj* hybrid
hidratante *adj*: **crema** ~ moisturizing cream, moisturizer
hidratar *vt* to moisturize
hidrato *nm* hydrate; ~ **de carbono** carbohydrate
hidráulico, -a *adj* hydraulic ▷ *nf* hydraulics *sg*
hidro... *pref* hydro..., water-...
hidroeléctrico, -a *adj* hydroelectric
hidrofobia *nf* hydrophobia, rabies
hidrógeno *nm* hydrogen
hiedra *nf* ivy
hiel *nf* gall, bile; *(fig)* bitterness
hielo *nm (gen)* ice; *(escarcha)* frost; *(fig)* coldness, reserve; **romper el** ~ *(fig)* to break the ice
hiena *nf (Zool)* hyena
hierba *nf (pasto)* grass; *(Culin, Med: planta)* herb; **mala** ~ weed; *(fig)* evil influence
hierbabuena *nf* mint
hierro *nm (metal)* iron; *(objeto)* iron object; ~ **acanalado** corrugated iron; ~ **colado** *o* **fundido** cast iron; **de** ~ iron *cpd*
hígado *nm* liver; **hígados** *nmpl (fig)* guts; **echar los ~s** to wear o.s. out
higiene *nf* hygiene
higiénico, -a *adj* hygienic
higo *nm* fig; ~ **seco** dried fig; ~ **chumbo** prickly pear; **de ~s a brevas** once in a blue moon
higuera *nf* fig tree
hijastro, -a *nm/f* stepson(daughter)
hijo, -a *nm/f* son (daughter), child; *(uso vocativo)* dear; **hijos** *nmpl* children, sons and daughters; **sin ~s** childless; **~/hija político/a** son-/daughter-in-law; ~ **pródigo** prodigal son; ~ **de papá/mamá** daddy's/mummy's boy; ~ **de puta** *(fam!)* bastard *(!)*, son of a bitch *(!)*; **cada ~ de vecino** any Tom, Dick or Harry
hilar *vt* to spin; *(fig)* to reason, infer; ~ **delgado** to split hairs
hilera *nf* row, file
hilo *nm* thread; *(Bot)* fibre; *(lino)* linen; *(de metal)* wire; *(de agua)* trickle, thin stream; *(de luz)* beam, ray; *(de conversación)* thread, theme; *(de pensamientos)* train; ~ **dental** dental floss; **colgar de un** ~ *(fig)* to hang by a thread; **traje de** ~ linen suit
hilvanar *vt (Costura)* to tack *(Brit)*, baste *(US)*; *(fig)* to do hurriedly
himno *nm* hymn; ~ **nacional** national anthem
hincapié *nm*: **hacer** ~ **en** to emphasize, stress
hincar *vt* to drive (in), thrust (in); *(diente)* to sink; **hincarse** *vr*: **~se de rodillas** *(esp LAm)* to kneel down
hincha *nm/f (fam: Deporte)* fan
hinchado, -a *adj (gen)* swollen; *(persona)* pompous ▷ *nf (group of)* supporters *o* fans
hinchar *vt (gen)* to swell; *(inflar)* to blow up, inflate; *(fig)* to exaggerate; **hincharse** *vr (inflarse)* to swell up; *(fam: llenarse)* to stuff o.s.; *(fig)* to get conceited; **~se de reír** to have a good laugh
hinchazón *nf (Med)* swelling; *(protuberancia)* bump, lump; *(altivez)* arrogance
hindú *adj, nm/f* Hindu
hinojo *nm* fennel
hipermercado *nm* hypermarket, superstore
hipertensión *nf* high blood pressure, hypertension
hípico, -a *adj* horse *cpd*, equine; **club** ~ riding club
hipnosis *nf inv* hypnosis
hipnotismo *nm* hypnotism
hipnotizar *vt* to hypnotize
hipo *nm* hiccups *pl*; **quitar el** ~ **a algn** to cure sb's hiccups
hipocresía *nf* hypocrisy
hipócrita *adj* hypocritical ▷ *nm/f* hypocrite
hipódromo *nm* racetrack
hipopótamo *nm* hippopotamus
hipoteca *nf* mortgage; **redimir una** ~ to pay off a mortgage
hipotecar *vt* to mortgage; *(fig)* to jeopardize
hipótesis *nf inv* hypothesis; **es una** ~ **(nada más)** that's just a theory
hiriente *adj* offensive, wounding
hispánico, -a *adj* Hispanic, Spanish
hispano, -a *adj* Hispanic, Spanish, Hispano- ▷ *nm/f* Spaniard
Hispanoamérica *nf* Spanish *o* Latin America
hispanoamericano, -a *adj, nm/f* Spanish *o* Latin American
histeria *nf* hysteria
histérico, -a *adj* hysterical
historia *nf (ciencia)* history; *(cuento)* story, tale; **historias** *nfpl (chismes)* gossip *sg*; **la ~ de España** Spanish history; **pasar a la** ~ to go down in history; **la misma ~ de siempre** the same old story; **dejarse de ~s** to come to the point
historiador, a *nm/f* historian
historial *nm* record; *(profesional)* curriculum vitae, c.v., résumé *(US)*; *(Med)* case history
histórico, -a *adj* historical; *(fig)* historic
historieta *nf* tale, anecdote; *(de dibujos)* comic strip
hito *nm (fig)* landmark; *(objetivo)* goal, target; *(fig)* milestone
hocico *nm* snout; *(fig)* grimace
hockey *nm* hockey; ~ **sobre hielo** ice hockey

hogar nm fireplace, hearth; (casa) home; (vida familiar) home life

hogareño, -a adj home cpd; (persona) home-loving

hoguera nf (gen) bonfire; (para herejes) stake

hoja nf (gen) leaf; (de flor) petal; (de hierba) blade; (de papel) sheet; (página) page; (formulario) form; (de puerta) leaf; ~ **de afeitar** razor blade; ~ **de cálculo electrónica** spreadsheet; ~ **de trabajo** (Inform) worksheet; **de ~ ancha** broad-leaved; **de ~ caduca/perenne** deciduous/evergreen

hojalata nf tin(plate)

hojaldre nm (Culin) puff pastry

hojear vt to leaf through, turn the pages of

hola excl hello!

Holanda nf Holland

holandés, -esa adj Dutch ▷ nm/f Dutchman(-woman); **los holandeses** the Dutch ▷ nm (Ling) Dutch

holgado, -a adj loose, baggy; (rico) well-to-do

holgar vi (descansar) to rest; (sobrar) to be superfluous; **huelga decir que** it goes without saying that

holgazán, -ana adj idle, lazy ▷ nm/f loafer

holgura nf looseness, bagginess; (Tec) play, free movement; (vida) comfortable living, luxury

hollín nm soot

hombre nm man; (raza humana): **el ~** man(kind) ▷ excl: **¡sí ~!** (claro) of course!; (para énfasis) man, old chap; ~ **de negocios** businessman; ~~**rana** frogman; ~ **de bien** o **pro** honest man; ~ **de confianza** right-hand man; ~ **de estado** statesman; **el ~ medio** the average man

hombrera nf shoulder strap

hombro nm shoulder; **arrimar el ~** to lend a hand; **encogerse de ~s** to shrug one's shoulders

hombruno, -a adj mannish

homenaje nm (gen) homage; (tributo) tribute; **un partido ~** a benefit match

homeopatía nf hom(o)eopathy

homeopático, -a adj hom(o)eopathic

homicida adj homicidal ▷ nm/f murderer

homicidio nm murder, homicide; (involuntario) manslaughter

homologar vt (Com) to standardize; (Escol) to officially approve; (Deporte) to officially recognize; (sueldos) to equalize

homólogo, -a nm/f counterpart, opposite number

homosexual adj, nm/f homosexual

hondo, -a adj deep; **lo ~** the depth(s) (pl), the bottom; **con ~ pesar** with deep regret

hondonada nf hollow, depression; (cañón) ravine; (Geo) lowland

hondura nf depth, profundity

Honduras nf Honduras

hondureño, -a adj, nm/f Honduran

honestidad nf (sinceridad) honesty; (honradez) honour

honesto, -a adj (sincero) honest; (honrado) honourable

hongo nm (Bot: gen) fungus; (: comestible) mushroom; (: venenoso) toadstool; (sombrero) bowler (hat) (Brit), derby (US); ~**s del pie** footrot sg, athlete's foot sg

honor nm (gen) honour (Brit), honor (US); (gloria) glory; ~ **profesional** professional etiquette; **en ~ a la verdad** to be fair

honorable adj honourable (Brit), honorable (US)

honorario, -a adj honorary ▷ nm: ~**s** fees

honra nf (gen) honour; (renombre) good name; ~**s fúnebres** funeral rites; **tener algo a mucha ~** to be proud of sth

honradez nf honesty; (de persona) integrity

honrado, -a adj honest, upright

honrar vt to honour; **honrarse** vr: ~**se con algo/ de hacer algo** to be honoured by sth/to do sth

honroso, -a adj (honrado) honourable; (respetado) respectable

hora nf (60 minutos) hour; (tiempo) time; (cita) appointment; **el viaje dura una ~** the journey lasts an hour; **media ~** half an hour; **dar la ~** to strike the hour; **en mis ~s libres** in my spare time; **¿qué ~ es?** what time is it?, what's the time?; **¿tienes ~?** have you got the time?; **¿a qué ~ llega?** what time is he arriving?; **llegar a la ~** to arrive on time; **a la ~ de comer/del recreo** at lunchtime/at playtime; **a primera ~ (de la mañana)** first thing (in the morning); **a última ~** at the last moment; **"última ~"** "stop press"; **noticias de última ~** last-minute news; **a altas ~s** in the small hours; **a la ~ en punto** on the dot; **¡a buena ~!** about time, too!; **en mala ~** unluckily; **poner el reloj en ~** to set one's watch; **después de inglés tenemos una ~ libre** after English we have a free period; **tengo ~ para el dentista** I've got an appointment at the dentist's; **no ver la ~ de** to look forward to; **¡ya era ~!** and about time too!; ~**s de oficina/de trabajo** office/working hours; ~**s de visita** visiting times; ~**s extras** o **extraordinarias** overtime sg; ~**s punta** rush hours

horadar vt to drill, bore

horario, -a adj hourly, hour cpd ▷ nm timetable; ~ **comercial** business hours

horca nf gallows sg; (Agr) pitchfork

horcajadas: a ~ adv astride

horchata nf cold drink made from tiger nuts and water, tiger nut milk

horda nf horde

horizontal adj horizontal

horizonte nm horizon

horma nf mould; ~ **(de calzado)** last; ~ **de sombrero** hat block

hormiga nf ant; **hormigas** nfpl (Med) pins and needles

hormigón nm concrete; ~ **armado/pretensado** reinforced/prestressed concrete

hormigueo nm (comezón) itch; (fig) uneasiness

hormiguero nm (Zool) ant's nest; **era un ~** it was swarming with people

hormona nf hormone

hornada nf batch of loaves (etc)

hornillo nm (cocina) portable stove

horno nm (Culin) oven; (Tec) furnace; (para cerámica) kiln; ~ **microondas** microwave (oven); **alto** ~ blast furnace; ~ **crematorio** crematorium

horóscopo nm horoscope

horquilla nf hairpin; (Agr) pitchfork

horrendo, -a adj horrendous, frightful

horrible adj horrible, dreadful

horripilante adj hair-raising, horrifying

horror nm horror, dread; (atrocidad) atrocity; **¡qué ~!** (fam) how awful!; **estudia ~es** he studies a hell of a lot

horrorizar vt to horrify, frighten; **horrorizarse** vr to be horrified

horroroso, -a adj horrifying, ghastly

hortaliza nf vegetable

hortelano, -a nm/f (market) gardener

hortera adj (fam) vulgar, tacky

horterada nf (fam): **es una ~** it's really tacky

hortofrutícola adj fruit and vegetable cpd

hosco, -a adj dark; (persona) sullen, gloomy

hospedar vt to put up; **hospedarse** vr: ~**se (con/ en)** to stay o lodge (with/at)

hospital nm hospital

hospitalario, -a adj (acogedor) hospitable

hospitalidad nf hospitality

hospitalizar vt to send o take to hospital, hospitalize

hostal nm small hotel

hostelería nf hotel business o trade

hostia nf (Rel) host, consecrated wafer; (fam: golpe) whack, punch ▷ excl: **¡~(s)!** (fam!) damn!

hostigar vt to whip; (fig) to harass, pester

hostil adj hostile

hostilidad nf hostility

hotel nm hotel

hotelero, -a adj hotel cpd ▷ nm/f hotelier

hoy adv (este día) today; (en la actualidad) nowadays ▷ nm present time; ~ **(en) día** nowadays; **el día de ~, ~ día** (LAm) this very day; ~ **por ~** right now; **de ~ en ocho días** a week today; **de ~ en adelante** from now on

hoyo nm hole, pit; (tumba) grave; (Golf) hole; (Med) pockmark

hoyuelo nm dimple

hoz nf sickle

huacal nm (And, Méx) wooden box

hucha nf money box

hueco, -a adj (vacío) hollow, empty; (resonante) booming; (sonido) resonant; (persona) conceited; (estilo) pompous ▷ nm hollow, cavity; (agujero) hole; (de escalera) well; (de ascensor) shaft; (vacante) vacancy; ~ **de la mano** hollow of the hand

huelga nf strike; **declararse en ~** to go on strike, come out on strike; ~ **general** general strike; ~ **de hambre** hunger strike; ~ **oficial** official strike

huelguista nm/f striker

huella nf (acto de pisar, pisada) tread(ing); (marca del paso) footprint, footstep; (: de animal, máquina) track; ~ **digital** fingerprint; **sin dejar ~** without leaving a trace

huérfano, -a adj orphan(ed); (fig) unprotected ▷ nm/f orphan

huerta nf market garden (Brit), truck farm (US); (de Murcia, Valencia) irrigated region

huerto nm kitchen garden; (de árboles frutales) orchard

hueso nm (Anat) bone; (de fruta) stone, pit (US); **sin ~** (carne) boned; **estar en los ~s** to be nothing but skin and bone; **ser un ~** (profesor) to be terribly strict; **un ~ duro de roer** a hard nut to crack

huésped, a nm/f (invitado) guest; (habitante) resident; (anfitrión) host(ess)

huesudo, -a adj bony, big-boned

huevas nfpl eggs, roe sg; (CS: fam!) balls (!)

huevera nf eggcup

huevo nm egg; (fam!) ball (!), testicle; ~ **duro/ escalfado/estrellado** o **frito/pasado por agua** hard-boiled/poached/fried/soft-boiled egg; ~**s revueltos** scrambled eggs; **me costó un ~** (fam!) it was hard work; **tener ~s** (fam!) to have guts

huida nf escape, flight; ~ **de capitales** (Com) flight of capital

huidizo, -a adj (tímido) shy; (pasajero) fleeting

huir vi to flee, escape ▷ vt to avoid; **huirse** vr to escape; **huyeron del país** they fled the country; **huyó de la cárcel** he escaped from prison; **salir huyendo** to run away; **¡no me huyas!** don't try to avoid me!

hule nm (encerado) oilskin; (esp LAm) rubber

humanidad nf (género humano) man(kind); (cualidad) humanity; (fam: gordura) corpulence

humanitario, -a adj humanitarian; (benévolo) humane

humano, -a adj (gen) human; (humanitario) humane ▷ nm human; **ser ~** human being

humareda nf cloud of smoke

humedad nf (del clima) humidity; (de pared etc) dampness; **a prueba de ~** damp-proof

humedecer vt to moisten, wet; **humedecerse** vr to get wet

húmedo, -a adj (mojado) damp, wet; (tiempo etc) humid

humildad nf humility, humbleness

humilde adj humble, modest; (clase etc) low, modest

humillación nf humiliation

humillante adj humiliating

humillar vt to humiliate; **humillarse** vr to humble o.s., grovel

humo nm (de fuego) smoke; (gas nocivo) fumes pl; (vapor) steam, vapour; **humos** nmpl (fig) conceit sg; **irse todo en ~** (fig) to vanish without trace; **bajar los ~s a algn** to take sb down a peg or two

humor nm (disposición) mood, temper; (lo que divierte) humour; **de buen/mal ~** in a good/bad mood

humorismo nm humour

humorista nm/f comic

humorístico, -a adj funny, humorous

hundimiento nm (gen) sinking; (colapso) collapse

hundir vt to sink; (edificio, plan) to ruin, destroy; **hundirse** vr to sink, collapse; (fig: arruinarse) to be ruined; (*desaparecer*) to disappear; **se hundió la economía** the economy collapsed; **se hundieron los precios** prices slumped

húngaro, -a *adj, nm/f* Hungarian ▷ *nm* (*Ling*) Hungarian, Magyar

Hungría *nf* Hungary

huracán *nm* hurricane

huraño, -a *adj* shy; (*antisocial*) unsociable

hurgar *vt* to poke, jab; (*remover*) to stir (up); **hurgarse** *vr:* ~**se** (**las narices**) to pick one's nose

hurón *nm* (*Zool*) ferret

hurtadillas; a ~ *adv* stealthily, on the sly

hurtar *vt* to steal; **hurtarse** *vr* to hide, keep out of the way

hurto *nm* theft, stealing; (*lo robado*) (piece of) stolen property, loot

husmear *vt* (*oler*) to sniff out, scent; (*fam*) to pry into ▷ *vi* to smell bad

huso *nm* (*Tec*) spindle; (*de torno*) drum

huy *excl* (*dolor*) ow!, ouch!; (*sorpresa*) well!; (*alivio*) phew!; ¡~, **perdona!** oops, sorry!

Ii

ibérico, -a *adj* Iberian; **la Península ibérica** the Iberian Peninsula

iberoamericano, -a *adj, nm/f* Latin American

íbice *nm* ibex

Ibiza *nf* Ibiza

iceberg *nm* iceberg

icono *nm* (*tb Inform*) icon

iconoclasta *adj* iconoclastic ▷ *nm/f* iconoclast

ictericia *nf* jaundice

I+D *abr* (= *Investigación y Desarrollo*) R&D

ida *nf* going, departure; **~ y vuelta** round trip, return; **~s y venidas** comings and goings

idea *nf* (*gen*) idea; (*impresión*) opinion; (*propósito*) intention; **¡qué buena ~!** what a good idea!; **~ genial** brilliant idea; **ya me voy haciendo a la ~** I'm beginning to get used to the idea; **no tengo ni (la menor) ~** I haven't the faintest idea, I haven't a clue; **he cambiado de ~** I've changed my mind; **a mala ~** out of spite

ideal *adj, nm* ideal

idealista *adj* idealistic ▷ *nm/f* idealist

idealizar *vt* to idealize

idear *vt* to think up; (*aparato*) to invent; (*viaje*) to plan

ídem *pron* ditto

idéntico, -a *adj* identical

identidad *nf* identity; **~ corporativa** corporate identity *o* image

identificación *nf* identification

identificar *vt* to identify; **identificarse** *vr*: **~se con** to identify with

ideología *nf* ideology

idilio *nm* love affair

idioma *nm* language

idiota *adj* idiotic ▷ *nm/f* idiot

idiotez *nf* idiocy

idolatrar *vt* (*fig*) to idolize

ídolo *nm* (*tb fig*) idol

idóneo, -a *adj* suitable

iglesia *nf* church; **~ parroquial** parish church; **¡con la ~ hemos topado!** now we're really up against it!

iglú *nm* igloo; (*contenedor*) bottle bank

ignominia *nf* ignominy

ignorancia *nf* ignorance; **por ~** through ignorance

ignorante *adj* ignorant, uninformed ▷ *nm/f* ignoramus

ignorar *vt* not to know, be ignorant of; (*no hacer caso a*) to ignore; **ignoramos su paradero** we don't know his whereabouts

igual *adj* (*idéntico*) equal; (*similar*) like, similar; (*mismo*) (the) same; (*constante*) constant; (*temperatura*) even ▷ *adv* (*de la misma forma*) the same; (*quizás*) maybe; (*de todas formas*) anyway ▷ *nm/f* equal; **se dividieron el dinero en partes ~es** they divided the money into equal shares; **X es ~ a Y** X is equal to Y; **todas las casas son ~es** all the houses are the same; **es ~ a su madre** (*físicamente*) she looks just like her mother; (*en la personalidad*) she's just like her mother; **~ que** the same as; **tengo una falda ~ que la tuya** I've got a skirt just like yours; **es ~ hoy que mañana** today or tomorrow, it doesn't matter; **ir ~es** to be even; **van quince ~es** it's fifteen all; **me da *o* es ~** I don't care, it makes no difference; **no tener ~** to be unrivalled; **se visten ~** they dress the same; **~ no lo saben todavía** maybe they don't know yet; **no hizo nada pero la castigaron ~** she didn't do anything but they punished her anyway; **al ~ que** like, just like

igualada *nf* equalizer

igualar *vt* (*gen*) to equalize, make equal; (*terreno*) to make even; (*Com*) to agree upon; **igualarse** *vr* (*platos de balanza*) to balance out; **~se (a)** (*equivaler*) to be equal (to)

igualdad *nf* equality; (*similaridad*) sameness; (*uniformidad*) uniformity; **en ~ de condiciones** on an equal basis

igualmente *adv* equally; (*también*) also, likewise ▷ *excl* the same to you!

ikurriña *nf* Basque flag

ilegal *adj* illegal

ilegítimo, -a *adj* illegitimate

ileso, -a *adj* unhurt, unharmed

ilícito, -a *adj* illicit

ilimitado, -a *adj* unlimited

ilógico, -a *adj* illogical

iluminación *nf* illumination; (*alumbrado*) lighting; (*fig*) enlightenment

iluminar *vt* to illuminate, light (up); (*fig*) to enlighten

ilusión *nf* illusion; (*quimera*) delusion; (*esperanza*) hope; (*emoción*) excitement, thrill; **hacerse**

ilusiones to build up one's hopes; **no te hagas ilusiones** don't build up your hopes o get too excited

ilusionado, -a *adj* excited

ilusionar *vt*: ~ **a algn** *(falsamente)* to build up sb's hopes; **ilusionarse** *vr (falsamente)* to build up one's hopes; *(entusiasmarse)* to get excited; **me ilusiona mucho el viaje** I'm really excited about the trip

ilusionista *nm/f* conjurer

iluso, -a *adj* gullible, easily deceived ▷ *nm/f* dreamer, visionary

ilusorio, -a *adj (de ilusión)* illusory, deceptive; *(esperanza)* vain

ilustración *nf* illustration; *(saber)* learning, erudition; **la I~** the Enlightenment

ilustrado, -a *adj (libro)* illustrated; *(persona)* learned

ilustrar *vt* to illustrate; *(instruir)* to instruct; *(explicar)* to explain, make clear; **ilustrarse** *vr* to acquire knowledge

ilustre *adj* famous, illustrious

imagen *nf (gen)* image; *(dibujo, TV)* picture; *(Rel)* statue; **han decidido cambiar de** ~ they've decided to change their image; **ser la viva ~ de alguien** to be the spitting image of sb; **a su ~** in one's own image

imaginación *nf* imagination; *(fig)* fancy; **ni por ~** on no account; **no se me pasó por la ~ que ...** it never even occurred to me that ...

imaginar *vt (gen)* to imagine; *(idear)* to think up; *(suponer)* to suppose; **imaginarse** *vr* to imagine; **¡imagínate!** just imagine!, just fancy!; **no te imaginas lo mal que me sentí** you can't imagine how bad I felt; **me imagino que seguirá en Madrid** I imagine that he's still in Madrid; **imagínese que ...** suppose that ...; **me imagino que sí** I should think so; **me imagino que no** I shouldn't think so

imaginario, -a *adj* imaginary

imaginativo, -a *adj* imaginative ▷ *nf* imagination

imán *nm* magnet

imbécil *nm/f* imbecile, idiot

imbuir *vi* to imbue

imitación *nf* imitation; *(parodia)* mimicry; **a ~ de** in imitation of; **desconfíe de las imitaciones** *(Com)* beware of copies o imitations

imitar *vt* to imitate; *(parodiar, remedar)* to mimic, ape; *(copiar)* to follow

impaciencia *nf* impatience

impaciente *adj* impatient; *(nervioso)* anxious

impacto *nm* impact; *(esp LAm: fig)* shock

impar *adj* odd ▷ *nm* odd number

imparcial *adj* impartial, fair

imparcialidad *nf* impartiality, fairness

impartir *vt* to impart, give

impasible *adj* impassive

impávido, -a *adj* fearless, intrepid

impecable *adj* impeccable

impedimento *nm* impediment, obstacle

impedir *vt (obstruir)* to impede, obstruct; *(estorbar)* to prevent; ~ **el tráfico** to block the traffic

impeler *vt* to drive, propel; *(fig)* to impel

impenetrable *adj* impenetrable; *(fig)* incomprehensible

imperar *vi (reinar)* to rule, reign; *(fig)* to prevail, reign; *(precio)* to be current

imperativo, -a *adj (persona)* imperious; *(urgente, Ling)* imperative

imperceptible *adj* imperceptible

imperdible *nm* safety pin

imperdonable *adj* unforgivable, inexcusable

imperfección *nf* imperfection; *(falla)* flaw, fault

imperfecto, -a *adj* faulty, imperfect ▷ *nm (Ling)* imperfect tense

imperial *adj* imperial

imperialismo *nm* imperialism

imperio *nm* empire; *(autoridad)* rule, authority; *(fig)* pride, haughtiness; **vale un ~** *(fig)* it's worth a fortune

imperioso, -a *adj* imperious; *(urgente)* urgent; *(imperativo)* imperative

impermeable *adj (a prueba de agua)* waterproof ▷ *nm* raincoat, mac *(Brit)*

impersonal *adj* impersonal

impertérrito, -a *adj* undaunted

impertinencia *nf* impertinence

impertinente *adj* impertinent

imperturbable *adj* imperturbable; *(sereno)* unruffled; *(impasible)* impassive

ímpetu *nm (impulso)* impetus, impulse; *(impetuosidad)* impetuosity; *(violencia)* violence

impetuoso, -a *adj* impetuous; *(río)* rushing; *(acto)* hasty

impío, -a *adj* impious, ungodly; *(cruel)* cruel, pitiless

implacable *adj* implacable, relentless

implantar *vt (costumbre)* to introduce; *(Bio)* to implant; **implantarse** *vr* to be introduced

implicar *vt* to involve; *(entrañar)* to imply; **esto no implica que ...** this does not mean that ...

implícito, -a *adj (tácito)* implicit; *(sobreentendido)* implied

implorar *vt* to beg, implore

imponente *adj (impresionante)* impressive, imposing; *(solemne)* grand ▷ *nm/f (Com)* depositor

imponer *vt (gen)* to impose; *(tarea)* to set; *(exigir)* to exact; *(miedo)* to inspire; *(Com)* to deposit; **imponerse** *vr (hacerse obedecer)* to assert o.s.; *(vencer)* to triumph; *(prevalecer)* to prevail; *(costumbre)* to grow up; **le impusieron una multa de 100 euros** they imposed a 100-euro fine on him; **~se un deber** to assume a duty

imponible *adj (Com)* taxable, subject to tax; *(importación)* dutiable, subject to duty; **no ~** tax-free, tax-exempt *(US)*

impopular *adj* unpopular

importación *nf (acto)* importing; *(mercancías)* imports *pl*

importancia *nf* importance; *(valor)* value, significance; *(extensión)* size, magnitude; **no dar ~ a** to consider unimportant; *(fig)* to make light

of; **no tiene ~** it's nothing
importante *adj* important; (*acontecimiento,
cambio*) significant; (*cantidad, retraso*)
considerable
importar *vi* (*tener importancia*) to matter; (*molestar*)
to mind ▷ *vt* (*del extranjero*) to import; (*costar*) to
amount to; **no importa** it doesn't matter; **no
importa, podemos hacerlo mañana** never
mind, we can do it tomorrow; **no importa
lo que piensen los demás** it doesn't matter
what other people think; **¿le importa que
fume?** do you mind if I smoke?; **¿te importa
prestármelo?** would you mind lending it to
me?; **¿qué importa?** what difference does
it make?; **¿y a ti qué te importa?** what's it
to you?; **me importa un bledo** I don't give a
damn; **no le importa** he doesn't care, it doesn't
bother him
importe *nm* (*cantidad*) amount; (*valor*) value
importunar *vt* to bother, pester
imposibilidad *nf* impossibility; **mi ~ para
hacerlo** my inability to do it
imposibilitar *vt* to make impossible, prevent
imposible *adj* impossible; (*insoportable*)
unbearable, intolerable; **es ~** it's out of the
question; **es ~ de predecir** it's impossible to
forecast *o* predict
imposición *nf* imposition; (*Com*) tax; (*inversión*)
deposit; **efectuar una ~** to make a deposit
impostor, a *nm/f* impostor
impotencia *nf* impotence
impotente *adj* impotent
impracticable *adj* (*irrealizable*) impracticable;
(*intransitable*) impassable
imprecar *vi* to curse
impreciso, -a *adj* imprecise, vague
impregnar *vt* to impregnate; (*fig*) to pervade;
impregnarse *vr* to become impregnated
imprenta *nf* (*acto*) printing; (*aparato*) press; (*casa*)
printer's; (*letra*) print
imprescindible *adj* essential, vital
impresión *nf* impression; (*Imprenta*) printing;
(*edición*) edition; (*Foto*) print; (*marca*) imprint; **~
digital** fingerprint
impresionable *adj* (*sensible*) impressionable
impresionante *adj* impressive; (*tremendo*)
tremendous; (*maravilloso*) great, marvellous
impresionar *vt* (*conmover*) to move; (*afectar*) to
impress, strike; (*película fotográfica*) to expose;
impresionarse *vr* to be impressed; (*conmoverse*)
to be moved
impreso, -a *pp de* **imprimir** ▷ *adj* printed ▷ *nm*
printed paper/book *etc*; **impresos** *nmpl* printed
matter *sg*; **~ de solicitud** application form
impresora *nf* (*Inform*) printer; **~ de chorro de
tinta** ink-jet printer; **~ (por) láser** laser printer;
~ de línea line printer; **~ de matriz (de agujas)**
dot-matrix printer; **~ de rueda** *o* **de margarita**
daisy-wheel printer
imprevisto, -a *adj* unforeseen; (*inesperado*)
unexpected ▷ *nm*: **~s** (*dinero*) incidentals,
unforeseen expenses

imprimir *vt* to stamp; (*textos*) to print; (*Inform*) to
output, print out
improbable *adj* improbable; (*inverosímil*) unlikely
improcedente *adj* inappropriate; (*Jur*)
inadmissible
improductivo, -a *adj* unproductive
improperio *nm* insult; **improperios** *nmpl* abuse
sg
impropiedad *nf* impropriety (of language)
impropio, -a *adj* improper; (*inadecuado*)
inappropriate
improvisación *nf* improvization
improvisado, -a *adj* improvised, impromptu
improvisar *vt* to improvise; (*comida*) to rustle up
▷ *vi* to improvise; (*Mus*) to extemporize; (*Teat
etc*) to ad-lib
improviso *adv*: **de ~** unexpectedly, suddenly;
(*Mus etc*) impromptu
imprudencia *nf* imprudence; (*indiscreción*)
indiscretion; (*descuido*) carelessness
imprudente *adj* (*irreflexivo*) imprudent; (*indiscreto*)
indiscreet
impúdico, -a *adj* shameless; (*lujurioso*) lecherous
impudor *nm* shamelessness; (*lujuria*) lechery
impuesto, -a *pp de* **imponer** ▷ *adj* imposed ▷ *nm*
tax; (*derecho*) duty; **anterior al ~** pre-tax; **sujeto
a ~** taxable; **~ de lujo** luxury tax; **~ de plusvalía**
capital gains tax; **~ sobre la propiedad** property
tax; **~ sobre la renta** income tax; **~ sobre la
renta de las personas físicas (IRPF)** personal
income tax; **~ sobre la riqueza** wealth tax; **~ de
transferencia de capital** capital transfer tax;
~ de venta sales tax; **~ sobre el valor añadido
(IVA)** value added tax (VAT)
impugnar *vt* to oppose, contest; (*refutar*) to
refute, impugn
impulsar *vt* to promote
impulsivo, -a *adj* impulsive
impulso *nm* impulse; (*fuerza, empuje*) thrust,
drive; (*fig: sentimiento*) urge, impulse; **a ~s del
miedo** driven on by fear
impune *adj* unpunished
impureza *nf* impurity; (*fig*) lewdness
impuro, -a *adj* impure
imputar *vt*: **~ a** to attribute to, to impute to
inacabable *adj* (*infinito*) endless; (*interminable*)
interminable
inaccesible *adj* inaccessible; (*fig: precio*) beyond
one's reach, prohibitive; (*individuo*) aloof
inacción *nf* inactivity
inaceptable *adj* unacceptable
inactividad *nf* inactivity; (*Com*) dullness
inactivo, -a *adj* inactive; (*Com*) dull; (*población*)
non-working
inadaptación *nf* maladjustment
inadecuado, -a *adj* (*insuficiente*) inadequate;
(*inapto*) unsuitable
inadmisible *adj* inadmissible
inadvertido, -a *adj* (*no visto*) unnoticed
inagotable *adj* inexhaustible
inaguantable *adj* unbearable
inalámbrico, -a *adj* cordless

inalterable *adj* immutable, unchangeable
inanición *nf* starvation
inanimado, -a *adj* inanimate
inapreciable *adj* invaluable
inaudito, -a *adj* unheard-of
inauguración *nf* inauguration; *(de exposición)* opening
inaugurar *vt (edificio)* to inaugurate; *(exposición)* to open
inca *nm/f* Inca
incaico, -a *adj* Inca
incalculable *adj* incalculable
incandescente *adj* incandescent
incansable *adj* tireless, untiring
incapacidad *nf* incapacity; *(incompetencia)* incompetence; ~ **física/mental** physical/mental disability
incapacitar *vt (inhabilitar)* to incapacitate, handicap; *(descalificar)* to disqualify
incapaz *adj* incapable; **es ~ de estarse callado** he is incapable of keeping quiet; **hoy soy ~ de concentrarme** I can't concentrate today
incautación *nf* seizure, confiscation
incautarse *vr*: ~ **de** to seize, confiscate
incauto, -a *adj (imprudente)* incautious, unwary
incendiar *vt* to set fire to; *(fig)* to inflame; **incendiarse** *vr* to catch fire
incendiario, -a *adj* incendiary ▷ *nm/f* fire-raiser, arsonist
incendio *nm* fire; ~ **intencionado** arson
incentivo *nm* incentive
incertidumbre *nf (inseguridad)* uncertainty; *(duda)* doubt
incesante *adj* incessant
incesto *nm* incest
incidencia *nf (Mat)* incidence; *(fig)* effect
incidente *nm* incident
incidir *vi*: ~ **en** *(influir)* to influence; *(afectar)* to affect; ~ **en un error** to be mistaken
incienso *nm* incense
incierto, -a *adj* uncertain
incineración *nf* incineration; *(de cadáveres)* cremation
incinerar *vt (basuras)* to burn; *(cadáver)* to cremate
incipiente *adj* incipient
incisión *nf* incision
incisivo, -a *adj* sharp, cutting; *(fig)* incisive
incitar *vt* to incite, rouse
incivil *adj* rude, uncivil
inclemencia *nf (severidad)* harshness, severity; *(del tiempo)* inclemency
inclinación *nf (gen)* inclination; *(de tierras)* slope, incline; *(de cabeza)* nod, bow; *(fig)* leaning, bent
inclinado, -a *adj (objeto)* leaning; *(superficie)* sloping
inclinar *vt* to incline; *(cabeza)* to nod, bow; **inclinarse** *vr* to lean, slope; *(en reverencia)* to bow; *(encorvarse)* to stoop; ~**se a** *(parecerse)* to take after, resemble; ~**se ante** to bow down to; **me inclino a pensar que ...** I'm inclined to think that ...
incluir *vt* to include; *(incorporar)* to incorporate; *(meter)* to enclose; **todo incluido** *(Com)* inclusive, all-in

inclusive *adv* inclusive ▷ *prep* including
incluso, -a *adj* included ▷ *adv* inclusively; *(hasta)* even
incógnita *nf (fig)* mystery
incógnito; de ~ *adv* incognito
incoherente *adj* incoherent
incoloro, -a *adj* colourless
incólume *adj* safe; *(indemne)* unhurt, unharmed
incomodar *vt* to inconvenience; *(molestar)* to bother, trouble; *(fastidiar)* to annoy; **incomodarse** *vr* to put o.s. out; *(fastidiarse)* to get annoyed; **no se incomode** don't bother
incomodidad *nf* inconvenience; *(fastidio, enojo)* annoyance; *(de vivienda)* discomfort
incómodo, -a *adj (no confortable)* uncomfortable; *(molesto)* annoying; *(inconveniente)* inconvenient; **sentirse ~** to feel ill at ease
incomparable *adj* incomparable
incompatible *adj* incompatible
incompetencia *nf* incompetence
incompetente *adj* incompetent
incompleto, -a *adj* incomplete, unfinished
incomprendido, -a *adj* misunderstood
incomprensible *adj* incomprehensible
incomunicado, -a *adj (aislado)* cut off, isolated; *(confinado)* in solitary confinement
inconcebible *adj* inconceivable
inconcluso, -a *adj (inacabado)* unfinished
incondicional *adj* unconditional; *(apoyo)* wholehearted; *(partidario)* staunch
inconexo, -a *adj* unconnected; *(desunido)* disconnected; *(incoherente)* incoherent
inconformista *adj, nm/f* nonconformist
inconfundible *adj* unmistakable
incongruente *adj* incongruous
inconmensurable *adj* immeasurable, vast
inconsciencia *nf* unconsciousness; *(fig)* thoughtlessness
inconsciente *adj (desvanecido)* unconscious; *(irresponsable)* thoughtless; *(ignorante)* unaware; *(involuntario)* unwitting
inconsecuente *adj* inconsistent
inconsiderado, -a *adj* inconsiderate
inconsistente *adj* inconsistent; *(Culin)* lumpy; *(endeble)* weak; *(tela)* flimsy
inconstancia *nf* inconstancy; *(de tiempo)* changeability; *(capricho)* fickleness
inconstante *adj (equipo, sistema)* inconstant; *(tiempo)* changeable; *(persona)* fickle
incontable *adj* countless, innumerable
incontestable *adj* unanswerable; *(innegable)* undeniable
incontinencia *nf* incontinence
inconveniencia *nf* unsuitability, inappropriateness; *(falta de cortesía)* impoliteness
inconveniente *adj* unsuitable ▷ *nm* obstacle; *(desventaja)* disadvantage; **el ~ es que ...** the trouble is that ...; **no hay ~ en o para hacer eso** there is no objection to doing that; **no tengo ~** I don't mind
incordiar *vt (fam)* to hassle

incorporación *nf* incorporation; *(fig)* inclusion
incorporar *vt* to incorporate; *(abarcar)* to embody; *(Culin)* to mix; **incorporarse** *vr* to sit up; **~se a** to join
incorrección *nf* incorrectness, inaccuracy; *(descortesía)* bad-mannered behaviour
incorrecto, -a *adj* incorrect, wrong; *(comportamiento)* bad-mannered
incorregible *adj* incorrigible
incredulidad *nf* incredulity; *(escepticismo)* scepticism
incrédulo, -a *adj* *(desconfiado)* incredulous, unbelieving; *(escéptico)* sceptical
increíble *adj* incredible
incremento *nm* increment; *(aumento)* rise, increase; **~ de precio** rise in price
increpar *vt* to reprimand
incruento, -a *adj* bloodless
incrustar *vt* to incrust; *(piedras: en joya)* to inlay; *(fig)* to graft; *(Tec)* to set
incubar *vt* to incubate; *(fig)* to hatch
inculcar *vt* to inculcate
inculpar *vt*: **~ de** *(acusar)* to accuse of; *(achacar, atribuir)* to charge with, blame for
inculto, -a *adj* *(persona)* uneducated, uncultured; *(fig: grosero)* uncouth ▷ *nm/f* ignoramus
incumplimiento *nm* non-fulfilment; *(Com)* repudiation; **~ de contrato** breach of contract; **por ~** by default
incurable *adj* *(enfermedad)* incurable; *(paciente)* incurably ill
incurrir *vi*: **~ en** to incur; *(crimen)* to commit; **~ en un error** to make a mistake
indagación *nf* investigation; *(búsqueda)* search; *(Jur)* inquest
indagar *vt* *(investigar)* to investigate; *(registrar)* to search; *(averiguar)* to ascertain
indecencia *nf* indecency; *(dicho)* obscenity
indecente *adj* indecent, improper; *(lascivo)* obscene
indecible *adj* unspeakable; *(indescriptible)* indescribable
indeciso, -a *adj* *(por decidir)* undecided; *(vacilante)* hesitant
indefenso, -a *adj* defenceless
indefinido, -a *adj* indefinite; *(vago)* vague, undefined
indeleble *adj* indelible
indemne *adj* *(objeto)* undamaged; *(persona)* unharmed, unhurt
indemnizar *vt* to indemnify; *(compensar)* to compensate
independencia *nf* independence
independiente *adj* *(libre)* independent; *(autónomo)* self-sufficient; *(Inform)* stand-alone
indeseable *adj, nm/f* undesirable
indeterminado, -a *adj* *(tb Ling)* indefinite; *(desconocido)* indeterminate
India *nf*: **la ~** India
indicación *nf* indication; *(dato)* piece of information; *(señal)* sign; *(sugerencia)* suggestion, hint; **indicaciones** *nfpl* *(Com)* instructions

indicado, -a *adj* *(apto)* right, appropriate
indicador *nm* indicator; *(Tec)* gauge, meter; *(aguja)* hand, pointer; *(de carretera)* roadsign; **~ de encendido** *(Inform)* power-on indicator
indicar *vt* *(mostrar)* to indicate, show; *(termómetro etc)* to read, register; *(señalar)* to point to; *(aconsejar)* to advise; **todo indica que...** everything indicates that...; **¿puede ~me dónde hay una gasolinera?** please can you tell where there's a petrol station?; **el médico me indicó que no fumara** the doctor advised me not to smoke
indicativo, -a *adj* indicative ▷ *nm* *(Radio)* call sign; **~ de nacionalidad** *(Auto)* national identification plate
índice *nm* index; *(catálogo)* catalogue; *(Anat)* index finger, forefinger; **~ del coste de (la) vida** cost-of-living index; **~ de crédito** credit rating; **~ de materias** table of contents; **~ de natalidad** birth rate; **~ de precios al por menor (IPM)** *(Com)* retail price index (RPI)
indicio *nm* indication, sign; *(en pesquisa etc)* clue; *(Inform)* marker, mark
indiferencia *nf* indifference; *(apatía)* apathy
indiferente *adj* indifferent; **parece ~ al cariño** she seems indifferent to affection; **es ~ que viva en Glasgow o Edimburgo** it makes no difference whether he lives in Glasgow or Edinburgh; **me es ~** it makes no difference to me; **me es ~ hacerlo hoy o mañana** I don't mind whether I do it today or tomorrow
indígena *adj* indigenous, native ▷ *nm/f* native
indigencia *nf* poverty, need
indigestión *nf* indigestion
indigesto, -a *adj* undigested; *(indigerible)* indigestible; *(fig)* turgid
indignación *nf* indignation
indignar *vt* to anger, make indignant; **indignarse** *vr*: **~se por** to get indignant about
indigno, -a *adj* *(despreciable)* low, contemptible; *(inmerecido)* unworthy
indio, -a *adj, nm/f* Indian
indirecto, -a *adj* indirect ▷ *nf* insinuation, innuendo; *(sugerencia)* hint
indiscreción *nf* *(imprudencia)* indiscretion; *(irreflexión)* tactlessness; *(acto)* gaffe, faux pas; **..., si no es ~** ..., if I may say so
indiscreto, -a *adj* indiscreet
indiscriminado, -a *adj* indiscriminate
indiscutible *adj* indisputable, unquestionable
indispensable *adj* indispensable
indisponer *vt* to spoil, upset; *(salud)* to make ill; **indisponerse** *vr* to fall ill; **~se con algn** to fall out with sb
indisposición *nf* indisposition; *(desgana)* unwillingness
indistinto, -a *adj* indistinct; *(vago)* vague
individual *adj* individual; *(habitación)* single ▷ *nm* *(Deporte)* singles *sg*
individuo, -a *adj* individual ▷ *nm* individual
índole *nf* *(naturaleza)* nature; *(clase)* sort, kind
indolencia *nf* indolence, laziness

indomable *adj* (*animal*) untameable; (*espíritu*) indomitable

indómito, -a *adj* indomitable

inducir *vt* to induce; (*inferir*) to infer; (*persuadir*) to persuade; **~ a algn en el error** to mislead sb

indudable *adj* undoubted; (*incuestionable*) unquestionable; **es ~ que** ... there is no doubt that ...

indulgencia *nf* indulgence; (*Jur etc*) leniency; **proceder sin ~ contra** to proceed ruthlessly against

indultar *vt* (*perdonar*) to pardon, reprieve; (*librar de pago*) to exempt

indulto *nm* (*perdón*) pardon; (*exención*) exemption

industria *nf* industry; (*habilidad*) skill; **~ agropecuaria** farming and fishing; **~ pesada** heavy industry; **~ petrolífera** oil industry

industrial *adj* industrial ▷ *nm* industrialist

industrializar *vt* to industrialize; **industrializarse** *vr* to become industrialized

inédito, -a *adj* (*libro*) unpublished; (*nuevo*) unheard-of

inefable *adj* ineffable, indescribable

ineficaz *adj* (*inútil*) ineffective; (*ineficiente*) inefficient

ineludible *adj* inescapable, unavoidable

ineptitud *nf* ineptitude, incompetence

inepto, -a *adj* inept, incompetent

inequívoco, -a *adj* unequivocal; (*inconfundible*) unmistakable

inercia *nf* inertia; (*pasividad*) passivity

inerme *adj* (*sin armas*) unarmed; (*indefenso*) defenceless

inerte *adj* inert; (*inmóvil*) motionless

inescrutable *adj* inscrutable

inesperado, -a *adj* unexpected, unforeseen

inestable *adj* unstable

inestimable *adj* inestimable; **de valor ~** invaluable

inevitable *adj* inevitable

inexactitud *nf* inaccuracy

inexacto, -a *adj* inaccurate; (*falso*) untrue

inexorable *adj* inexorable

inexperto, -a *adj* (*novato*) inexperienced

infalible *adj* infallible; (*indefectible*) certain, sure; (*plan*) foolproof

infame *adj* infamous

infamia *nf* infamy; (*deshonra*) disgrace

infancia *nf* infancy, childhood; **jardín de ~** nursery school

infante *nm* (*hijo del rey*) infante, prince

infantería *nf* infantry

infantil *adj* child's, children's; (*pueril, aniñado*) infantile; (*cándido*) childlike

infarto *nm* (*tb:* **infarto de miocardio**) heart attack

infatigable *adj* tireless, untiring

infección *nf* infection

infeccioso, -a *adj* infectious

infectar *vt* to infect; **infectarse** *vr:* **~se (de)** (*tb fig*) to become infected (with)

infeliz *adj* (*desgraciado*) unhappy, wretched; (*inocente*) gullible ▷ *nm/f* (*desgraciado*) wretch;

(*inocentón*) simpleton

inferior *adj* inferior; (*situación, Mat*) lower ▷ *nm/f* inferior, subordinate; **cualquier número ~ a 9** any number less than o under o below 9; **una cantidad ~** a lesser quantity

inferioridad *nf* inferiority; **estar en ~ de condiciones** to be at a disadvantage

inferir *vt* (*deducir*) to infer, deduce; (*causar*) to cause

infernal *adj* infernal

infestar *vt* to infest

infidelidad *nf* (*gen*) infidelity, unfaithfulness

infiel *adj* unfaithful, disloyal; (*falso*) inaccurate ▷ *nm/f* infidel, unbeliever

infierno *nm* hell; **¡vete al ~!** go to hell; **está en el quinto ~** it's at the back of beyond

infiltrar *vt* to infiltrate; **infiltrarse** *vr* to infiltrate, filter; (*líquidos*) to percolate

ínfimo, -a *adj* (*vil*) vile, mean; (*más bajo*) lowest; (*peor*) worst; (*miserable*) wretched

infinidad *nf* infinity; (*abundancia*) great quantity; **~ de** vast numbers of; **~ de veces** countless times

infinitivo *nm* infinitive

infinito, -a *adj* infinite; (*fig*) boundless ▷ *adv* infinitely ▷ *nm* infinite; (*Mat*) infinity; **hasta lo ~** ad infinitum

inflación *nf* (*hinchazón*) swelling; (*monetaria*) inflation; (*fig*) conceit

inflacionario, -a *adj* inflationary

inflamar *vt* to set on fire; (*Med, fig*) to inflame; **inflamarse** *vr* (*encenderse*) to catch fire; (*hincharse*) to become inflamed

inflar *vt* (*hinchar*) to inflate, blow up; (*fig*) to exaggerate; **inflarse** *vr* to swell (up); (*fig*) to get conceited

inflexible *adj* inflexible; (*fig*) unbending

infligir *vt* to inflict

influencia *nf* influence

influenciar *vt* to influence

influir *vt* to influence ▷ *vi* to have influence, carry weight; **~ en o sobre** to influence, affect; (*contribuir a*) to have a hand in

influjo *nm* influence; **~ de capitales** (*Econ etc*) capital influx

influyente *adj* influential

información *nf* information; (*noticias*) news *sg*; (*informe*) report; (*Inform: datos*) data; (*Jur*) inquiry; **I-** (*oficina*) Information; (*Telec*) Directory Enquiries (*Brit*), Directory Assistance (*US*); (*mostrador*) Information Desk; **una ~** a piece of information; **abrir una ~** (*Jur*) to begin proceedings; **~ deportiva** (*en periódico*) sports section

informal *adj* (*gen*) informal

informante *nm/f* informant

informar *vt* (*gen*) to inform; (*revelar*) to reveal, make known ▷ *vi* (*denunciar*) to inform; (*dar cuenta de*) to report on; (*Jur*) to plead; **informarse** *vr* to find out; **nos ~on que venía con retraso** they informed us that it was going to be late; **nos han informado mal** we've been misinformed; **¿me podría ~ sobre los cursos**

de inglés? could you give me some information about English courses?; **~se de** to inquire into

informática *nf* ver **informático**

informático, -a *adj* computer *cpd* ▷ *nf* (*ciencia*) computing; (*asignatura*) computer science *o* studies; **~ de gestión** commercial computing

informativo, -a *adj* (*libro*) informative; (*folleto*) information *cpd*; (*Radio, TV*) news *cpd* ▷ *nm* (*Radio, TV*) news programme

informe *adj* shapeless ▷ *nm* report; (*dictamen*) statement; (*Mil*) briefing; (*Jur*) plea; **informes** *nmpl* information *sg*; (*datos*) data; **~ anual** annual report; **~ del juez** summing-up

infortunio *nm* misfortune

infracción *nf* infraction, infringement; (*Auto*) offence

in fraganti *adv*: **pillar a algn ~** to catch sb red-handed

infranqueable *adj* impassable; (*fig*) insurmountable

infravalorar *vt* to undervalue; (*Fin*) to underestimate

infringir *vt* to infringe, contravene

infructuoso, -a *adj* fruitless, unsuccessful

infundado, -a *adj* groundless, unfounded

infundir *vt* to infuse, instil; **~ ánimo a algn** to encourage sb; **~ miedo a algn** to intimidate sb

infusión *nf* infusion; **~ de manzanilla** camomile tea

ingeniar *vt* to think up, devise; **ingeniarse** *vr* to manage; **ingeniárselas para** to manage to

ingeniería *nf* engineering; **~ genética** genetic engineering; **~ de sistemas** (*Inform*) systems engineering

ingeniero, -a *nm/f* engineer; **~ de sonido** sound engineer; **~ de caminos** civil engineer

ingenio *nm* (*talento*) talent; (*agudeza*) wit; (*habilidad*) ingenuity, inventiveness; (*Tec*): **~ azucarero** sugar refinery

ingenioso, -a *adj* ingenious, clever; (*divertido*) witty

ingenuidad *nf* ingenuousness; (*sencillez*) simplicity

ingenuo, -a *adj* ingenuous

ingerir *vt* to ingest; (*tragar*) to swallow; (*consumir*) to consume

Inglaterra *nf* England

ingle *nf* groin

inglés, -esa *adj* English ▷ *nm/f* Englishman(-woman) ▷ *nm* (*Ling*) English; **los ingleses** the English

ingratitud *nf* ingratitude

ingrato, -a *adj* ungrateful; (*tarea*) thankless

ingrediente *nm* ingredient; **ingredientes** *nmpl* (*CS: tapas*) titbits

ingresar *vt* (*dinero*) to deposit, pay in ▷ *vi* to come *o* go in; **~ un cheque en una cuenta** to pay a cheque into an account; **~ en** (*club*) to join; (*Mil, Escol*) to enrol in; **~ en el hospital** to go into hospital; **~ a** (*esp LAm*) to enter

ingreso *nm* (*entrada*) entry; (: *en hospital etc*) admission; (*Mil, Escol*) enrolment; (*depósito*)

deposit; **ingresos** *nmpl* (*dinero*) income *sg*; (: *Com*) takings *pl*; **el ~ de España en la OTAN** Spain's entry into NATO; **tras su ~ en la Academia** after he joined the Academy, after his admission to the Academy; **examen de ~** (*Univ*) entrance examination; **hacer un ~** to make a deposit, pay in some money; **tiene unos ~s muy bajos** he has a very low income; **~s brutos** gross receipts; **~s exentos de impuestos** non-taxable income *sg*

inhabilitar *vt* (*Pol, Med*): **~ a algn (para hacer algo)** to disqualify sb (from doing sth)

inhabitable *adj* uninhabitable

inhalar *vt* to inhale

inherente *adj* inherent

inhibir *vt* to inhibit; (*Rel*) to restrain; **inhibirse** *vr* to keep out

inhumano, -a *adj* inhuman

INI *nm abr* = **Instituto Nacional de Industria**

inicial *adj, nf* initial

iniciar *vt* (*persona*) to initiate; (*empezar*) to begin, commence; (*conversación*) to start up; **~ a algn en un secreto** to let sb into a secret; **~ la sesión** (*Inform*) to log in *o* on

iniciativa *nf* initiative; (*liderazgo*) leadership; **la ~ privada** private enterprise

inicio *nm* start, beginning

inicuo, -a *adj* iniquitous

ininterrumpido, -a *adj* uninterrupted; (*proceso*) continuous; (*progreso*) steady

injerencia *nf* interference

injertar *vt* to graft

injerto *nm* graft; **~ de piel** skin graft

injuria *nf* (*insulto*) insult; (*Jur*) slander; **injurias** *nfpl* abuse *sg*

injuriar *vt* to insult

injurioso, -a *adj* offensive, insulting

injusticia *nf* injustice, unfairness; **con ~** unjustly

injusto, -a *adj* unjust, unfair

inmadurez *nf* immaturity

inmaduro, -a *adj* immature; (*fruta*) unripe

inmediaciones *nfpl* neighbourhood *sg*, environs

inmediato, -a *adj* immediate; (*contiguo*) adjoining; (*rápido*) prompt; (*próximo*) neighbouring, next; **de ~** (*esp LAm*) immediately

inmejorable *adj* unsurpassable; (*precio*) unbeatable

inmenso, -a *adj* immense, huge

inmerecido, -a *adj* undeserved

inmigración *nf* immigration

inmigrante *adj, nm/f* immigrant

inminente *adj* imminent, impending

inmiscuirse *vr* to interfere, meddle

inmobiliario, -a *adj* real-estate *cpd*, property *cpd* ▷ *nf* estate agency

inmolar *vt* to immolate, sacrifice

inmoral *adj* immoral

inmortal *adj* immortal

inmortalizar *vt* to immortalize

inmóvil *adj* immobile

inmovilizar *vt* to immobilize; (*paralizar*) to

paralyse; **inmovilizarse** *vr*: **se le inmovilizó la pierna** her leg was paralysed

inmueble *adj*: **bienes ~s** real estate *sg*, landed property *sg* ▷ *nm* property

inmundicia *nf* filth

inmundo, -a *adj* filthy

inmune *adj* (*Med*) immune

inmunidad *nf* immunity; (*fisco*) exemption; **~ diplomática/parlamentaria** diplomatic/parliamentary immunity

inmunitario, -a *adj*: **sistema ~** immune system

inmunización *nf* immunization

inmunizar *vt* to immunize

inmutable *adj* immutable; **permaneció ~** he didn't flinch

inmutarse *vr*: **siguió sin ~** he carried on unperturbed

innato, -a *adj* innate

innecesario, -a *adj* unnecessary

innoble *adj* ignoble

innovación *nf* innovation

innovar *vt* to introduce

inocencia *nf* innocence

inocentada *nf* practical joke

inocente *adj* (*ingenuo*) naive, innocent; (*no culpable*) innocent; (*sin malicia*) harmless ▷ *nm/f* simpleton; **día de los (Santos) I~s** ≈ April Fool's Day

inodoro, -a *adj* odourless ▷ *nm* toilet (*Brit*), lavatory (*Brit*), washroom (*US*)

inofensivo, -a *adj* inoffensive

inolvidable *adj* unforgettable

inoperante *adj* ineffective

inopinado, -a *adj* unexpected

inoportuno, -a *adj* untimely; (*molesto*) inconvenient; (*inapropiado*) inappropriate

inoxidable *adj* stainless; **acero ~** stainless steel

inquebrantable *adj* unbreakable; (*fig*) unshakeable

inquietar *vt* to worry, trouble; **inquietarse** *vr* to worry, get upset

inquieto, -a *adj* anxious, worried; **estar ~ por** to be worried about

inquietud *nf* anxiety, worry

inquilino, -a *nm/f* tenant; (*Com*) lessee

inquirir *vt* to enquire into, investigate

insaciable *adj* insatiable

insalubre *adj* unhealthy; (*condiciones*) insanitary

inscribir *vt* (*gen*) to inscribe; (*en lista*) to put; (*en censo*) to register; **inscribirse** *vr* to register; (*Escol etc*) to enrol

inscripción *nf* inscription; (*Escol etc*) enrolment; (*en censo*) registration

insecticida *nm* insecticide

insecto *nm* insect

inseguridad *nf* insecurity

inseguro, -a *adj* insecure; (*inconstante*) unsteady; (*incierto*) uncertain

inseminación *nf*: **~ artificial** artificial insemination (A.I.)

insensato, -a *adj* foolish, stupid

insensibilidad *nf* (*gen*) insensitivity; (*dureza de corazón*) callousness

insensible *adj* (*gen*) insensitive; (*movimiento*) imperceptible; (*sin sensación*) numb

inseparable *adj* inseparable

insertar *vt* to insert

inservible *adj* useless

insidioso, -a *adj* insidious

insignia *nf* (*señal distintiva*) badge; (*estandarte*) flag

insignificante *adj* insignificant

insinuar *vt* to insinuate, imply; **insinuarse** *vr*: **~se con algn** to ingratiate o.s. with sb

insípido, -a *adj* insipid

insistencia *nf* insistence

insistir *vi* to insist; **~ en algo** to insist on sth; (*enfatizar*) to stress sth

in situ *adv* on the spot, in situ

insociable *adj* unsociable

insolación *nf* (*Med*) sunstroke

insolencia *nf* insolence

insolente *adj* insolent

insólito, -a *adj* unusual

insoluble *adj* insoluble

insolvencia *nf* insolvency

insomnio *nm* insomnia

insondable *adj* bottomless

insonorizado, -a *adj* (*cuarto etc*) soundproof

insoportable *adj* unbearable

insospechado, -a *adj* (*inesperado*) unexpected

inspección *nf* inspection, check; **I~** inspectorate; **~ técnica (de vehículos)** ≈ MOT (test) (*Brit*)

inspeccionar *vt* (*examinar*) to inspect, examine; (*controlar*) to check; (*Inform*) to peek

inspector, a *nm/f* inspector

inspiración *nf* inspiration

inspirar *vt* to inspire; (*Med*) to inhale; **inspirarse** *vr*: **~se en** to be inspired by

instalación *nf* (*equipo*) fittings *pl*, equipment; **~ eléctrica** wiring

instalar *vt* (*establecer*) to install; (*erguir*) to set up, erect; **instalarse** *vr*: **~se en** (*casa, oficina*) to settle into; (*ciudad, país*) to settle in; **instaló una alarma en el coche** he installed an alarm in the car; **aquí van a ~ unas oficinas** they're going to set up offices here; **decidieron ~se en el centro** they decided to settle in the town centre

instancia *nf* (*solicitud*) application; (*ruego*) request; (*Jur*) petition; **a ~ de** at the request of; **en última ~** in the last resort

instantáneo, -a *adj* instantaneous ▷ *nf* snap(shot); **café ~** instant coffee

instante *nm* instant, moment; **en un ~** in a flash

instar *vt* to press, urge

instaurar *vt* (*establecer*) to establish, set up

instigar *vt* to instigate

instinto *nm* instinct; **por ~** instinctively

institución *nf* institution, establishment; **~ benéfica** charitable foundation

instituir *vt* to establish; (*fundar*) to found

instituto *nm* (*gen*) institute; **I~ Nacional de Enseñanza** (*Esp*) ≈ comprehensive (*Brit*) o high (*US*) school; **I~ Nacional de Industria (INI)** (*Esp Com*) ≈ National Enterprise Board (*Brit*)

institutriz *nf* governess
instrucción *nf* instruction; (*enseñanza*) education, teaching; (*Jur*) proceedings *pl*; (*Mil*) training; (*Deporte*) coaching; (*conocimientos*) knowledge; (*Inform*) statement; **instrucciones para el uso** directions for use; **instrucciones de funcionamiento** operating instructions
instructivo, -a *adj* instructive
instruir *vt* (*gen*) to instruct; (*enseñar*) to teach, educate; (*Jur: proceso*) to prepare, draw up; (*Mil*) to train; **instruirse** *vr* to learn, teach o.s.; **~ a algn en algo** to instruct sb in sth, train sb in sth; **la experiencia instruye mucho** experience is a great teacher
instrumento *nm* (*gen, Mus*) instrument; (*herramienta*) tool, implement; (*Com*) indenture; (*Jur*) legal document; **~ de percusión/cuerda/viento** percussion/string(ed)/wind instrument
insubordinarse *vr* to rebel
insuficiencia *nf* (*carencia*) lack; (*inadecuación*) inadequacy; **~ cardíaca/renal** heart/kidney failure
insuficiente *adj* (*gen*) insufficient; (*Escol: nota*) unsatisfactory
insufrible *adj* insufferable
insular *adj* insular
insulina *nf* insulin
insultar *vt* to insult
insulto *nm* insult
insumisión *nf* *refusal to do military service or community service*
insumiso, -a *adj* (*rebelde*) rebellious ▷ *nm/f* (*Pol*) *person who refuses to do military service or community service*
insuperable *adj* (*excelente*) unsurpassable; (*problema etc*) insurmountable
insurgente *adj, nm/f* insurgent
insurrección *nf* insurrection, rebellion
intachable *adj* irreproachable
intacto, -a *adj* (*sin tocar*) untouched; (*entero*) intact
integral *adj* integral; (*completo*) complete; (*Tec*) built-in; **pan ~** wholemeal bread
integrar *vt* to make up, compose; (*Mat, fig*) to integrate; **integrarse** *vr*: **~se en** (*grupo*) to fit into, integrate into; (*conjunto, entorno*) to blend with; (*asociación, conjunto*) to join; **no le costó nada ~se en la clase** he had no difficulty fitting *o* integrating into the class
integridad *nf* wholeness; (*carácter, tb Inform*) integrity; **en su ~** completely
integrismo *nm* fundamentalism
integrista *adj, nm/f* fundamentalist
íntegro, -a *adj* whole, entire; (*texto*) uncut, unabridged; (*honrado*) honest
intelectual *adj, nm/f* intellectual
inteligencia *nf* intelligence; (*ingenio*) ability; **~ artificial** artificial intelligence
inteligente *adj* intelligent
inteligible *adj* intelligible
intemperie *nf*: **a la ~** outdoors, in the open air
intempestivo, -a *adj* untimely

intención *nf* (*gen*) intention, purpose; **con segundas intenciones** maliciously; **con ~** deliberately
intencionado, -a *adj* deliberate; **bien ~** well-meaning; **mal ~** ill-disposed, hostile
intensidad *nf* (*gen*) intensity; (*Elec, Tec*) strength; (*de recuerdo*) vividness; **llover con ~** to rain hard
intensivo, -a *adj* intensive; **curso ~** crash course
intenso, -a *adj* intense; (*impresión*) vivid; (*sentimiento*) profound, deep
intentar *vt* (*probar*) to try, attempt; **¿por qué no lo intentas otra vez?** why don't you try again?; **~ hacer algo** to try to do sth; **intente no fumar** try not to smoke; **con ~lo nada se pierde** there's no harm in trying
intento *nm* (*intención*) intention, purpose; (*tentativa*) attempt
interactivo, -a *adj* interactive; (*Inform*): **computación interactiva** interactive computing
intercalar *vt* to insert; (*Inform: archivos, texto*) to merge
intercambio *nm* (*canje*) exchange; (*trueque*) swap
interceder *vi* to intercede
interceptar *vt* to intercept, cut off; (*Auto*) to hold up
intercesión *nf* intercession
interés *nm* (*gen, Com*) interest; (*importancia*) concern; (*parte*) share, part; (*pey*) self-interest; **tienes que poner más ~ en tus estudios** you must take more of an interest in your studies; **tener ~ en hacer algo** to be keen to do sth; **tengo mucho ~ en visitar tu país** I'm very keen to visit your country; **con un ~ del 9%** at an interest of 9%; **dar a ~** to lend at interest; **tener ~ en** (*Com*) to hold a share in; **todo lo hace por ~** everything he does is out of self-interest; **~ compuesto** compound interest; **~ simple** simple interest; **intereses acumulados** accrued interest *sg*; **intereses creados** vested interests
interesado, -a *adj* interested; (*prejuiciado*) prejudiced; (*pey*) mercenary, self-seeking ▷ *nm/f* person concerned; (*firmante*) the undersigned
interesante *adj* interesting
interesar *vt* to interest, be of interest to ▷ *vi* (*despertar interés*) to interest, be of interest; (*importar*) to be important; **interesarse** *vr*: **~se en** *o* **por** to take an interest in; **eso es algo que siempre me ha interesado** that's something that has always interested me; **¿te interesa la política?** are you interested in politics?; **no me interesan los toros** bullfighting does not appeal to me
interface, interfase *nm* (*Inform*) interface; **~ hombre/máquina/por menús** man/machine/menu interface
interfaz *nm* = **interface**
interferencia *nf* interference
interferir *vt* to interfere with; (*Telec*) to jam ▷ *vi* to interfere
interfono *nm* intercom

interino, -a adj temporary; (empleado etc)
provisional ▷ nm/f temporary holder of a post;
(Med) locum; (Escol) supply teacher; (Teat) stand-
in
interior adj inner, inside; (Com) domestic,
internal ▷ nm interior, inside; (fig) soul, mind;
(Deporte) inside forward; **Ministerio del I~**
= Home Office (Brit), Ministry of the Interior;
dije para mi ~ I said to myself
interjección nf interjection
interlocutor, -a nm/f speaker; (al teléfono) person
at the other end (of the line); **mi ~** the person I
was speaking to
intermediario, -a adj (mediador) mediating ▷ nm/
f intermediary, go-between; (mediador) mediator
intermedio, -a adj intermediate; (tiempo)
intervening ▷ nm interval; (Pol) recess
interminable adj endless, interminable
intermitente adj intermittent ▷ nm (Auto)
indicator
internacional adj international
internado nm boarding school
internar vt to intern; (en un manicomio) to commit;
internarse vr (penetrar) to penetrate; **~se en** to go
into o right inside; **~se en un estudio** to study a
subject in depth
internauta nmf Internet user
Internet nm o nf Internet
interno, -a adj internal, interior; (Pol etc)
domestic ▷ nm/f (alumno) boarder
interponer vt to interpose, put in; **interponerse**
vr to intervene
interpretación nf interpretation; (Mus, Teat)
performance; **mala ~** misinterpretation
interpretar vt to interpret
intérprete nm/f (Ling) interpreter, translator;
(Mus, Teat) performer, artist(e)
interrogación nf interrogation; (Ling: tb: **signo
de interrogación**) question mark; (Telec) polling
interrogante adj questioning ▷ nm question
mark; (fig) question mark, query
interrogar vt to interrogate, question
interrumpir vt to interrupt; (vacaciones) to cut
short; (servicio) to cut off; (tráfico) to block
interrupción nf interruption
interruptor nm (Elec) switch
intersección nf intersection; (Auto) junction
interurbano, -a adj inter city; (Telec) long-
distance
intervalo nm interval; (descanso) break; **a ~s** at
intervals, every now and then
intervención nf supervision; (Com) audit(ing);
(Med) operation; (Telec) tapping; (participación)
intervention; **~ quirúrgica** surgical operation;
la política de no ~ the policy of non-
intervention
intervenir vt (controlar) to control, supervise;
(Com) to audit; (Med) to operate on; (Telec) to tap
▷ vi (participar) to take part, participate; (mediar)
to intervene
interventor, a nm/f inspector; (Com) auditor
interviú nf interview

intestino nm intestine
intimar vt to intimate, announce; (mandar) to
order ▷ vi: **intimarse** vr to become friendly
intimidad nf intimacy; (familiaridad) familiarity;
(vida privada) private life; (Jur) privacy
íntimo, -a adj intimate; (pensamientos)
innermost; (vida) personal, private; **una boda
íntima** a quiet wedding
intolerable adj intolerable, unbearable
intolerancia nf intolerance
intoxicación nf poisoning; **~ alimenticia** food
poisoning
intranet nf intranet
intranquilizarse vr to get worried o anxious
intranquilo, -a adj worried
intransigente adj intransigent
intransitable adj impassable
intransitivo, -a adj intransitive
intrepidez nf courage, bravery
intrépido, -a adj intrepid, fearless
intriga nf intrigue; (plan) plot
intrigar vt, vi to intrigue
intrincado, -a adj intricate
intrínseco, -a adj intrinsic
introducción nf introduction; (de libro) foreword;
(Inform) input
introducir vt (gen) to introduce; (moneda) to
insert; (Inform) to input, enter; **esperan ~ un
nuevo sistema de trabajo** they're hoping to
bring in o introduce new working methods; **han
introducido cambios en el horario** they've
made o introduced changes to the timetable;
introdujo la moneda en la ranura he inserted
the coin in the slot
intromisión nf interference, meddling
introvertido, -a adj, nm/f introvert
intruso, -a adj intrusive ▷ nm/f intruder
intuición nf intuition
intuir vt to know by intuition, intuit
inundación nf flood(ing)
inundar vt to flood; (fig) to swamp, inundate
inusitado, -a adj unusual
inútil adj useless; (esfuerzo) vain, fruitless
inutilidad nf uselessness
inutilizar vt to make unusable, put out of action;
(incapacitar) to disable; **inutilizarse** vr to become
useless
invadir vt to invade
invalidar vt to invalidate
inválido, -a adj invalid; (Jur) null and void ▷ nm/f
invalid
invariable adj invariable
invasión nf invasion
invasor, a adj invading ▷ nm/f invader
invencible adj invincible; (timidez, miedo)
unsurmountable
invención nf invention
inventar vt to invent
inventario nm inventory; (Com) stocktaking
inventiva nf inventiveness
invento nm invention; (fig) brainchild; (pey)
silly idea

inventor, a *nm/f* inventor
invernadero *nm* greenhouse
invernar *vi* (*Zool*) to hibernate
inverosímil *adj* implausible
inversión *nf* (*Com*) investment; ~ **de capitales** capital investment; **inversiones extranjeras** foreign investment *sg*
inverso, a *adj* inverse, opposite; **en el orden** ~ in reverse order; **a la inversa** inversely, the other way round
inversor, -a *nm/f* (*Com*) investor
invertebrado, -a *adj, nm* invertebrate
invertir *vt* (*Com*) to invest; (*volcar*) to turn upside down; (*tiempo etc*) to spend
investigación *nf* investigation; (*indagación*) inquiry; (*Univ*) research; ~ **y desarrollo** (*Com*) research and development (R & D); ~ **de los medios de publicidad** media research; ~ **del mercado** market research
investigar *vt* to investigate; (*estudiar*) to do research into
investir *vt*: ~ **a algn con algo** to confer sth on sb; **fue investido Doctor Honoris Causa** he was awarded an honorary doctorate
invicto, -a *adj* unconquered
invidente *adj* sightless ▷ *nm/f* blind person; **los ~s** the sightless
invierno *nm* winter
invisible *adj* invisible; **exportaciones/importaciones ~s** invisible exports/imports
invitación *nf* invitation
invitado, -a *nm/f* guest
invitar *vt* to invite; (*incitar*) to entice; ~ **a algn a hacer algo** to invite sb to do sth; ~ **a algo** to pay for sth; **nos invitó a cenar fuera** she took us out for dinner; **invito yo** it's on me
in vitro *adv* in vitro
invocar *vt* to invoke, call on; (*Inform*) to call
involucrar *vt*: ~ **algo en un discurso** to bring sth irrelevant into a discussion; ~ **a algn en algo** to involve sb in sth; **involucrarse** *vr* (*interesarse*) to get involved
involuntario, -a *adj* involuntary; (*ofensa etc*) unintentional
inyección *nf* injection
inyectar *vt* to inject
ión *nm* ion
IPC *nm abr* (*Esp*: = *índice de precios al consumo*) CPI
ir *vi* **1** (*acudir, marchar*) to go; **anoche fuimos al cine** we went to the cinema last night; **voy a la calle** I'm going out; **¿a qué colegio vas?** what school do you go to?; **ir de vacaciones** to go on holiday; **ir de pesca** to go fishing; **ir caminando** to walk; **fui en tren** I went *o* travelled by train; **ir en coche/en bicicleta** to drive/cycle; **¡(ahora) voy!** (I'm just) coming!
2: **ir (a) por** to go and get; **voy a por el paraguas** I'll go and get the umbrella; **ha ido a por el médico** she has gone to get the doctor
3 (*progresar: persona, cosa*) to go; **el trabajo va muy bien** work is going very well; **¿cómo te va?** how are things going?; **me va muy bien** I'm getting

on very well; **le fue fatal** it went awfully badly for him
4 (*funcionar*): **el coche no va muy bien** the car isn't running very well
5 (*sentar*): **me va estupendamente** (*ropa, color*) it suits me really well; (*medicamento*) it works really well for me; **ir bien con algo** to go well with sth
6 (*aspecto*): **iba muy bien vestido** he was very well dressed; **ir con zapatos negros** to wear black shoes
7 (*locuciones*): **¿vino?** — **¡qué va!** did he come? — of course not!; **vamos, no llores** come on, don't cry; **¡vaya coche!** (*admiración*) what a car!, that's some car!; (*desprecio*) that's a terrible car!; **¡vaya! ¿qué haces tú por aquí?** well, what a surprise! what are you doing here?; **¡que le vaya bien!** (*adiós*) take care!
8: **no vaya a ser**: **tienes que correr, no vaya a ser que pierdas el tren** you'll have to run so as not to miss the train
9: **no me** *etc* **va ni me viene** I *etc* don't care
▷ *vb aux* **1**: **ir a**: **voy/iba a hacerlo hoy** I am/was going to do it today
2 (+*gerundio*): **iba anocheciendo** it was getting dark; **todo se me iba aclarando** everything was gradually becoming clearer to me; **como iba diciendo** as I was saying
3 (+*pp = pasivo*): **van vendidos 300 ejemplares** 300 copies have been sold so far
irse *vr* **1**: **¿por dónde se va al zoológico?** which is the way to the zoo?
2 (*marcharse*) to leave; **ya se habrán ido** they must already have left *o* gone; **vete a hacer los deberes** go and do your homework; **¡vámonos!** (*LAm*): **¡nos fuimos!** let's go!; **¡vete!** go away!; **¡vete a saber!** your guess is as good as mine!, who knows!
ira *nf* anger, rage
iracundo, -a *adj* irascible
Irak *nm* = **Iraq**
Irán *nm* Iran
iraní *adj, nm/f* Iranian
Iraq *nm* Iraq
iraquí *adj, nm/f* Iraqi
irascible *adj* irascible
iris *nm inv* (*arco iris*) rainbow; (*Anat*) iris
Irlanda *nf* Ireland; ~ **del Norte** Northern Ireland, Ulster
irlandés, -esa *adj* Irish ▷ *nm/f* Irishman(-woman) ▷ *nm* (*Ling*) Gaelic, Irish; **los irlandeses** *npl* the Irish
ironía *nf* irony
irónico, -a *adj* ironic(al)
IRPF *nm abr* (*Esp*) = **impuesto sobre la renta de las personas físicas**
irracional *adj* irrational
irreal *adj* unreal
irrecuperable *adj* irrecoverable, irretrievable
irreflexión *nf* thoughtlessness; (*ímpetu*) rashness
irregular *adj* irregular; (*situación*) abnormal, anomalous; **margen izquierdo/derecho** ~ (*texto*) ragged left/right (margin)

irregularidad *nf* irregularity
irremediable *adj* irremediable; (*vicio*) incurable
irreprochable *adj* irreproachable
irresistible *adj* irresistible
irresoluto, -a *adj* irresolute, hesitant; (*sin resolver*) unresolved
irrespetuoso, -a *adj* disrespectful
irresponsable *adj* irresponsible
irreversible *adj* irreversible
irrevocable *adj* irrevocable
irrigar *vt* to irrigate
irrisorio, -a *adj* derisory, ridiculous; (*precio*) bargain *cpd*
irritación *nf* irritation
irritar *vt* to irritate, annoy; **irritarse** *vr* to get angry, lose one's temper
irrupción *nf* irruption; (*invasión*) invasion
IRTP *nm abr* (*Esp*: = *impuesto sobre el rendimiento del trabajo personal*) ≈ PAYE
isla *nf* (*Geo*) island; **I-s Británicas** British Isles; **I-s Filipinas/Malvinas/Canarias** Philippines/Falklands/Canaries
islámico, -a *adj* Islamic

islandés, -esa *adj* Icelandic ▷ *nm/f* Icelander ▷ *nm* (*Ling*) Icelandic
Islandia *nf* Iceland
isleño, -a *adj* island *cpd* ▷ *nm/f* islander
isotónico, -a *adj* isotonic
Israel *nm* Israel
israelí *adj, nm/f* Israeli
istmo *nm* isthmus; **el I- de Panamá** the Isthmus of Panama
Italia *nf* Italy
italiano, -a *adj, nm/f* Italian ▷ *nm* (*Ling*) Italian
itinerario *nm* itinerary, route
ITV *nf abr* (= *Inspección Técnica de Vehículos*) ≈ MOT (test) (*Brit*)
IVA *nm abr* (*Esp Com*: = *Impuesto sobre el Valor Añadido*) VAT
izar *vt* to hoist
izquierda *nf* left; (*Pol*) left (wing); **a la ~** on the left; **es un cero a la ~** (*fam*) he is a nonentity; **conducción por la ~** left-hand drive
izquierdista *adj* leftist, left-wing ▷ *nm/f* left-winger, leftist
izquierdo, -a *adj* left; *ver tb* **izquierda**

Jj

jabalí *nm* wild boar

jabalina *nf* javelin

jabón *nm* soap; (*fam: adulación*) flattery; **~ de afeitar** shaving soap; **~ de tocador** toilet soap; **dar ~ a algn** to soft-soap sb

jabonar *vt* to soap

jaca *nf* pony

jacinto *nm* hyacinth

jactarse *vr*: **~ (de)** to boast *o* brag (about *o* of)

jadear *vi* to pant, gasp for breath

jadeo *nm* panting, gasping

jaguar *nm* jaguar

jalapeño *nm* (*Méx*) jalapeño pepper

jalbegue *nm* (*pintura*) whitewash

jalea *nf* jelly

jaleo *nm* racket, uproar; **armar un ~** to kick up a racket

jalón *nm* (*LAm*) tug

Jamaica *nf* Jamaica

jamás *adv* never, not ... ever; (*interrogativo*) ever; **¿se vio tal cosa?** did you ever see such a thing?

jamón *nm* ham; **~ dulce/serrano** boiled/cured ham

Japón *nm*: **el ~** Japan

japonés, -esa *adj*, *nm/f* Japanese ▷ *nm* (*Ling*) Japanese

jaque *nm*: **~ mate** checkmate

jaqueca *nf* (very bad) headache, migraine

jarabe *nm* syrup; **~ para la tos** cough syrup *o* mixture

jarcia *nf* (*Naut*) ropes *pl*, rigging

jardín *nm* garden; **~ botánico** botanical garden; **~ de (la) infancia** (*Esp*) *o* **de niños** (*LAm*) *o* **infantil** (*LAm*) kindergarten, nursery school

jardinería *nf* gardening

jardinero, -a *nm/f* gardener

jarra *nf* jar; (*jarro*) jug; (*de leche*) churn; (*de cerveza*) mug; **de** *o* **en ~s** with arms akimbo

jarro *nm* jug

jarrón *nm* vase; (*Arqueología*) urn

jaula *nf* cage; (*embalaje*) crate

jauría *nf* pack of hounds

J.C. *abr* = **Jesucristo**

jeep® (*pl* **-s**) *nm* Jeep®

jefa *nf ver* **jefe**

jefatura *nf* (*liderazgo*) leadership; (*sede*) central office; **J~ de la aviación civil** ≈ Civil Aviation Authority; **~ de policía** police headquarters *sg*

jefe, -a *nm/f* (*gen*) chief, head; (*patrón*) boss; (*Pol*) leader; (*Com*) manager(ess), **~ de camareros** head waiter; **~ de cocina** chef; **~ ejecutivo** (*Com*) chief executive; **~ de estación** stationmaster; **~ de estado** head of state; **~ de oficina** (*Com*) office manager; **~ de producción** (*Com*) production manager; **~ supremo** commander-in-chief; **ser el ~** (*fig*) to be the boss

jengibre *nm* ginger

jeque *nm* sheik(h)

jerarquía *nf* (*orden*) hierarchy; (*rango*) rank

jerárquico, -a *adj* hierarchic(al)

jerez *nm* sherry; **J~ de la Frontera** Jerez

jerga *nf* (*tela*) coarse cloth; (*lenguaje*) jargon; **~ informática** computer jargon

jerigonza *nf* (*jerga*) jargon, slang; (*galimatías*) nonsense, gibberish

jeringa *nf* syringe; (*LAm*) annoyance, bother; **~ de engrase** grease gun

jeringar *vt* to annoy, bother

jeringuilla *nf* hypodermic (syringe)

jeroglífico *nm* hieroglyphic

jersey (*pl* **-s**) *nm* jersey, pullover, jumper

Jerusalén *n* Jerusalem

Jesucristo *nm* Jesus Christ

jesuita *adj*, *nm* Jesuit

Jesús *nm* Jesus; **¡~!** good heavens!; (*al estornudar*) bless you!

jet (*pl* **-s**) *nm* jet (plane) ▷ *nf*: **la ~** the jet set

jeta *nf* (*Zool*) snout; (*fam: cara*) mug; **¡que ~ tienes!** (*fam: insolencia*) you've got a nerve!

jilguero *nm* goldfinch

jinete, -a *nm/f* horseman(-woman)

jirafa *nf* giraffe

jirón *nm* rag, shred

jitomate *nm* (*Méx*) tomato

jocoso, -a *adj* humorous, jocular

joder (*fam!*) *vt* to fuck (*!*), screw (*!*); (*fig: fastidiar*) to piss off (*!*), bug; **joderse** *vr* (*fracasar*) to fail; **¡~!** damn it!; **se jodió todo** everything was ruined

jornada *nf* (*viaje de un día*) day's journey; (*camino o viaje entero*) journey; (*día de trabajo*) working day; **~ de 8 horas** 8-hour day; (**trabajar a**) **~ partida** (to work a) split shift

jornal *nm* (day's) wage

jornalero, -a *nm/f* (day) labourer

joroba *nf* hump
jorobado, -a *adj* hunchbacked ▷ *nm/f* hunchback
jota *nf* letter J; (*danza*) Aragonese dance; (*fam*) jot, iota; **no saber ni ~** to have no idea
joven *adj* young ▷ *nm* young man, youth ▷ *nf* young woman, girl
jovial *adj* cheerful, jolly
jovialidad *nf* cheerfulness, jolliness
joya *nf* jewel, gem; (*fig: persona*) gem; **~s de fantasía** imitation jewellery *sg*
joyería *nf* (*joyas*) jewellery; (*tienda*) jeweller's (shop)
joyero *nm* (*persona*) jeweller; (*caja*) jewel case
juanete *nm* (*del pie*) bunion
jubilación *nf* (*retiro*) retirement
jubilado, -a *adj* retired ▷ *nm/f* retired person, pensioner (*Brit*), senior citizen
jubilar *vt* to pension off, retire; (*fam*) to discard; **jubilarse** *vr* to retire
júbilo *nm* joy, rejoicing
jubiloso, -a *adj* jubilant
judía *nf* (*Culin*) bean; **~ blanca** haricot bean; **~ verde** French o string bean; *ver tb* **judío**
judicial *adj* judicial
judío, -a *adj* Jewish ▷ *nmf* Jew, Jewess o Jewish woman; *ver tb* **judía**
juego *nm* (*gen*) play; (*pasatiempo, partido*) game; (*en casino*) gambling; (*deporte*) sport; (*conjunto*) set; **las cortinas hacen ~ con el sofá** the curtains go with the sofa; **~ limpio/sucio** fair/foul o dirty play; **~ de azar** game of chance; **~s de cartas** card games; **~s de mesa** board games; **J~s Olímpicos** Olympic Games; **fuera de ~** (*Deporte: persona*) offside; (: *pelota*) out of play; **~ de café** coffee set; **~ de caracteres** (*Inform*) font; **~ de herramientas** tool set
juerga *nf* binge; (*fiesta*) party; **ir de ~** to go out on a binge
jueves *nm inv* Thursday
juez *nm/f* (*f tb:* **jueza**) judge; (*Tenis*) umpire; **~ de línea** linesman; **~ de paz** justice of the peace; **~ de salida** starter
jugada *nf* play; **buena ~** good move (o shot o stroke) *etc*
jugador, a *nm/f* player; (*en casino*) gambler
jugar *vt* (*por diversión*) to play; (*en casino*) to gamble; (*apostar*) to bet ▷ *vi* (*por diversión*) to play; (*en casino*) to gamble; (*Com*) to speculate; **jugarse** *vr* to gamble (away); **¿jugamos una partida de dominó?** shall we have a game of dominoes?; **¿quién juega?** whose move is it?; **~ al fútbol** to play football; **~ a la lotería** to do the lottery; **¡me la han jugado!** (*fam*) I've been had!; **~se el todo por el todo** to stake one's all, go for bust
juglar *nm* minstrel
jugo *nm* (*Bot, de fruta*) juice; (*fig*) essence, substance; **~ de naranja** (*LAm*) orange juice
jugoso, -a *adj* juicy; (*fig*) substantial, important
juguete *nm* toy
juguetear *vi* to play
juguetería *nf* toyshop

juguetón, -ona *adj* playful
juicio *nm* judgement; (*sana razón*) sanity, reason; (*opinión*) opinion; (*Jur: proceso*) trial; **estar fuera de ~** to be out of one's mind; **a mi ~** in my opinion
juicioso, -a *adj* wise, sensible
julio *nm* July
junco *nm* rush, reed
jungla *nf* jungle
junio *nm* June
junta *nf* (*asamblea*) meeting, assembly; (*comité, consejo*) board, council, committee; (*Mil, Pol*) junta; (*articulación*) joint; **~ constitutiva** (*Com*) statutory meeting; **~ directiva** (*Com*) board of management; **~ general extraordinaria** (*Com*) extraordinary general meeting; *ver tb* **junto**
juntar *vt* (*unir*) to put together; (*personas*) to gather together; (*dinero*) to collect; **juntarse** *vr* (*unirse*) to join, meet; (*arrimarse*) to move closer; (*reunirse: personas*) to meet up; **vamos a ~ los pupitres** let's put the desks together; **consiguieron ~ a mil personas** they managed to gather together one thousand people; **si os juntáis más cabremos todos** if you move closer together we'll all fit in; **nos juntamos los domingos para comer** we meet up for dinner on Sundays; **~se con algn** to join sb
junto, -a *adj* (*unido*) united; (*anexo*) near, close; (*contiguo, próximo*) next, adjacent; **juntos** *adj pl* together ▷ *adv:* **todo ~** all at once ▷ *prep:* **~ a** by, next to; **~ con** together with; **apenas hablamos cuando estamos ~s** we hardly talk when we're together; **los muebles están demasiado ~s** the furniture is too close together; **ocurrió todo ~** it happened all at once; **mi apellido se escribe todo ~** my surname is all in one word; **hay una mesa ~ a la ventana** there's a table by the window; **~ con el vídeo viene un libro de regalo** you get a free book together with the video; *ver tb* **junta**
jurado *nm* (*Jur: individuo*) juror; (: *grupo*) jury; (*de concurso: individuo*) member of a panel; (: *grupo*) panel (of judges)
juramento *nm* oath; (*maldición*) oath, curse; **bajo ~** on oath; **prestar ~** to take the oath; **tomar ~ a** to swear in, administer the oath to
jurar *vt, vi* to swear; **~ en falso** to commit perjury; **jurárselas a algn** to have it in for sb
jurídico, -a *adj* legal, juridical
jurisdicción *nf* (*poder, autoridad*) jurisdiction; (*territorio*) district
jurisprudencia *nf* jurisprudence
jurista *nm/f* jurist
justamente *adv* justly, fairly; (*precisamente*) just, exactly
justicia *nf* justice; (*equidad*) fairness, justice; **de ~** deservedly
justiciero, -a *adj* just, righteous
justificación *nf* justification; **~ automática** (*Inform*) automatic justification
justificante *nm* voucher; **~ médico** sick note
justificar *vt* (*tb Tip*) to justify; (*probar*) to verify

justo, -a adj (equitativo) fair, just; (preciso) right, exact; (ajustado) tight ▷ adv (precisamente) just; (apenas a tiempo) just in time; **tuvo un juicio ~** he had a fair trial; **apareció en el momento ~** he appeared at the right time; **tengo el dinero ~ para el billete** I have just enough money for the ticket; **¡~!** that's it!, correct!; **me están muy ~s estos pantalones** these trousers are tight on me; **el supermercado está ~ al doblar la esquina** the supermarket is just round the corner; **la vi ~ cuando entrábamos** I saw her just as we came in; **me dio un puñetazo ~ en la nariz** he punched me right on the nose.; **llegaste muy ~** you just made it; **vivir muy ~** to be hard up

juvenil adj youthful

juventud nf (adolescencia) youth; (jóvenes) young people pl

juzgado nm tribunal; (Jur) court

juzgar vt to judge; **a ~ por ...** to judge by ..., judging by ...; **~ mal** to misjudge; **júzguelo usted mismo** see for yourself

Kk

karaoke *nm* karaoke
kárate, karate *nm* karate
kg. *abr* (= *kilogramo(s)*) kg.
kilo *nm* kilo
kilogramo *nm* kilogramme (*Brit*), kilogram (*US*)
kilometraje *nm* distance in kilometres,
  ≈ mileage

kilómetro *nm* kilometre (*Brit*), kilometer (*US*)
kilovatio *nm* kilowatt
kiosco *nm* = quiosco
kiwi *nm* kiwi (fruit)
km *abr* (= *kilómetro(s)*) km
kv *abr* (= *kilovatio*) kw

Ll

la *artículo definido fsg* the ▷ *pron* her; *(referido a usted)* you; *(referido a una cosa)* it ▷ *nm (Mus)* A; **está en la cárcel** he's in jail; **me ha manchado la chaqueta** I got my jacket dirty; **la del sombrero rojo** the woman/girl/one in the red hat; *ver tb* **el**

laberinto *nm* labyrinth

labia *nf* fluency; *(pey)* glibness; **tener mucha ~** to have the gift of the gab

labial *adj* labial

labio *nm* lip; *(de botella, etc)* edge, rim; **~ inferior/superior** lower/upper lip

labor *nf (trabajo)* work; *(Agr)* farm work; *(tarea)* job, task; *(Costura)* needlework, sewing; *(punto)* knitting; **~ de equipo** teamwork; **~ de ganchillo** crochet

laborable *adj (Agr)* workable; **día ~** working day

laboral *adj (accidente, conflictividad)* industrial; *(jornada)* working; *(derecho, relaciones)* labour *cpd*

laboralista *adj*: **abogado ~** labour lawyer

laborar *vi* to work

laboratorio *nm* laboratory

laborioso, -a *adj (persona)* hard-working; *(trabajo)* tough

laborista *(Brit Pol) adj*: **Partido L~** Labour Party ▷ *nm/f* Labour Party member o supporter

labrado, -a *adj* worked; *(madera)* carved; *(metal)* wrought ▷ *nm (Agr)* cultivated field

labrador, a *nm/f* farmer

labranza *nf (Agr)* cultivation

labrar *vt (campo)* to work; *(madera etc)* to carve; *(porvenir, ruina)* to cause, bring about

labriego, -a *nm/f* peasant

laca *nf (de pelo)* hairspray; *(esmalte)* lacquer; **~ de uñas** nail varnish

lacayo *nm* lackey

lacerar *vt* to lacerate

lacio, -a *adj (pelo)* straight

lacónico, -a *adj* laconic

lacra *nf (defecto)* blemish; **~ social** social disgrace

lacrar *vt (cerrar)* to seal (with sealing wax)

lacre *nm* sealing wax

lacrimoso, -a *adj* tearful

lactancia *nf* breast-feeding

lactar *vt, vi* to suckle, breast-feed

lácteo, -a *adj*: **productos ~s** dairy products

ladear *vt* to tip, tilt ▷ *vi* to tilt; **ladearse** *vr* to lean; *(Deporte)* to swerve; *(Aviat)* to bank, turn

ladera *nf* slope

ladino, -a *adj* cunning

lado *nm (gen)* side; *(Mil)* flank; **~ izquierdo** left(-hand) side; **~ a ~** side by side; **por todos ~s** on all sides, all round *(Brit)*; **hacerse a un ~** to stand aside; **poner de ~** to put on its side; **poner a un ~** to put aside; **por un ~ ..., por otro ~ ...** on the one hand ..., on the other (hand) ...; **mi casa está aquí al ~** my house is right nearby; **Felipe se sentó a mi ~** Felipe sat beside me; **al ~ de** next to, beside

ladrar *vi* to bark

ladrido *nm* bark, barking

ladrillo *nm* brick; *(azulejo)* tile

ladrón, -ona *nm/f* thief

lagar *nm (wine/oil)* press

lagartija *nf (small)* lizard, wall lizard

lagarto *nm (Zool)* lizard; *(LAm)* alligator

lago *nm* lake

lágrima *nf* tear

lagrimal *nm (inner)* corner of the eye

laguna *nf (lago)* lagoon; *(en escrito, conocimientos)* gap

laico, -a *adj* lay ▷ *nm/f* layman(-woman)

lamentable *adj* lamentable, regrettable; *(miserable)* pitiful

lamentar *vt (sentir)* to regret; *(deplorar)* to lament; **lamentarse** *vr* to lament; **lo lamento mucho** I'm very sorry

lamento *nm* lament

lamer *vt* to lick

lámina *nf (plancha delgada)* sheet; *(para estampar)* plate; *(grabado)* engraving

laminar *vt (en libro)* to laminate; *(Tec)* to roll

lámpara *nf* lamp; **~ de alcohol/gas** spirit/gas lamp; **~ de pie** standard lamp

lamparón *nm (Med)* scrofula; *(mancha)* (large) grease spot

lampiño, -a *adj (sin pelo)* hairless

lana *nf (tejido)* wool; *(tela)* woollen *(Brit) o* woolen *(US)* cloth; *(LAm fam: dinero)* dough; **(hecho) de ~** wool *cpd*

lance *nm (golpe)* stroke; *(suceso)* event, incident

lancha *nf* launch; **~ motora** motorboat; **~ neumática** rubber dinghy; **~ de pesca** fishing boat; **~ salvavidas/torpedera** lifeboat/torpedo boat

lanero, -a adj wool cpd
langosta nf (insecto) locust; (crustáceo) lobster; (de río) crayfish
langostino nm prawn; (de agua dulce) crayfish
languidecer vi to languish
languidez nf languor
lánguido, -a adj (gen) languid; (sin energía) listless
lanilla nf nap; (tela) thin flannel cloth
lanudo, -a adj woolly, fleecy
lanza nf (arma) lance, spear; **medir ~s** to cross swords
lanzadera nf shuttle
lanzado, -a adj (atrevido) forward; (decidido) determined; **ir ~** (rápido) to fly along
lanzamiento nm (gen) throwing; (Naut, Com) launch, launching; **~ de pesos** putting the shot
lanzar vt (gen) to throw; (con violencia) to fling; (Deporte: pelota) to bowl; (US) to pitch; (Naut, Com) to launch; (Jur) to evict; (grito) to give, utter; **lanzarse** vr to throw o.s.; (fig) to take the plunge; **lanzó una piedra al río** he threw a stone into the river; **los niños se ~on a la piscine** the children dived into the swimming pool; **~se a** (fig) to embark upon
lapa nf limpet
La Paz nf La Paz
lapicero nm pencil; (LAm) propelling (Brit) o mechanical (US) pencil; (bolígrafo) Biro®
lápida nf stone; **~ conmemorativa** memorial stone; **~ mortuoria** headstone
lapidar vt to stone; (Tec) to polish, lap
lapidario, -a adj, nm lapidary
lápiz nm pencil; **~ de color** coloured pencil; **~ de labios** lipstick; **~ luminoso** u **óptico** light pen
lapón, -ona adj Lapp ⊳ nm/f Laplander, Lapp ⊳ nm (Ling) Lapp
Laponia nf Lapland
lapso nm lapse; (error) error; **~ de tiempo** interval of time
lapsus nm inv error, mistake
larga nf: **me dio ~s con una promesa** she put me off with a promise; **a la ~** in the long run; ver tb **largo**
largar vt (soltar) to release; (aflojar) to loosen; (lanzar) to launch; (fam) to let fly; (velas) to unfurl; (CS) to throw; **largarse** vr (fam) to beat it; **~se a** (CS) to start to
largo, -a adj (pasillo, falda, conferencia) long; (tiempo) lengthy; (persona: alto) tall; (: fig) generous ⊳ nm length; (Mus) largo; **dos años ~s** two long years; **a ~ plazo** in the long term; **tiene 9 metros de ~** it is 9 metres long; **a lo ~** (posición) lengthways; **a lo ~ de** (camino, espacio) along; (tiempo) all through, throughout; **¡~ de aquí!** (fam) clear off!; ver tb **larga**
largometraje nm full-length film, feature film
largura nf length
laringe nf larynx
laringitis nf laryngitis
larva nf larva
las artículo definido fpl the ⊳ pron (a ellas) them; (a ustedes) you; **me duelen ~ muelas** my teeth

hurt; **~ que cantan** the ones/women/girls who sing; **~ vi por la calle** I saw them in the street; **~ acompañaré hasta la puerta** I'll see you out; ver tb **el**
lasaña nf lasagne, lasagna
lascivo, -a adj lewd
láser nm laser
lástima nf (pena) pity; **es una ~ que** it's a pity that; **¡qué ~!** what a pity!; **estar hecho una ~** to be a sorry sight; **dar ~** to be pitiful
lastimar vt (herir) to wound; (ofender) to offend; **lastimarse** vr to hurt o.s.
lastimero, -a adj pitiful, pathetic
lastre nm (Tec, Naut) ballast; (fig) dead weight
lata nf (metal) tin; (envase) tin, can; **en ~** tinned; (fam) nuisance; **dar la ~** to be a nuisance; **ser una ~** to be a pain (fam)
latente adj latent
lateral adj side, lateral ⊳ nm (Teat) wings pl
latido nm (del corazón) beat; (de herida) throb(bing)
latifundio nm large estate
latifundista nm/f owner of a large estate
latigazo nm (golpe) lash; (sonido) crack; (fig: regañada) dressing-down
látigo nm whip
latín nm Latin; **saber (mucho) ~** (fam) to be pretty sharp
latino, -a adj Latin
Latinoamérica nf Latin America
latinoamericano, -a adj, nm/f Latin American
latir vi (corazón, pulso) to beat
latitud nf (Geo) latitude; (fig) breadth, extent
latón nm brass
latoso, -a adj (molesto) annoying; (aburrido) boring
laúd nm lute
laurel nm (Bot) laurel; (Culin) bay; **una hoja de ~** a bay leaf
lava nf lava
lavabo nm (recipiente) washbasin; (servicio) lavatory (Brit), toilet (Brit), washroom (US)
lavadero nm laundry
lavado nm washing; (de ropa) wash, laundry; (Arte) wash; **~ de cerebro** brainwashing
lavadora nf washing machine
lavanda nf lavender
lavandería nf laundry; **~ automática** launderette
lavaplatos nm inv dishwasher
lavar vt (limpiar) to wash; (borrar) to wipe away; **lavarse** vr to wash o.s.; **~se las manos** to wash one's hands; (fig) to wash one's hands of it; **~ y marcar** (pelo) to shampoo and set; **~ en seco** to dry-clean
lavavajillas nm inv dishwasher
laxante nm laxative
lazada nf bow
lazarillo nm: **perro de ~** guide dog
lazo nm knot; (lazada) bow; (para animales) lasso; (trampa) snare; (vínculo) tie; **~ corredizo** slipknot
le pron (indirecto: a él, a ella) to him (o her o it); (: a usted) to you; (directo) him; (: en relación a usted) you; **le mandé una carta** I sent him a letter, I

sent a letter to him; **¿le pongo algo de beber?** can I get you something to drink?

leal *adj* loyal

lealtad *nf* loyalty

lebrel *nm* greyhound

lección *nf* lesson; **dar lecciones** to teach, give lessons; **dar una ~ a** algn (*fig*) to teach sb a lesson; **~ práctica** object lesson

leche *nf* milk; (*fam!*) semen, spunk (!); **estar de mala ~** (*fam*) to be in a foul mood; **tener mala ~** (*fam*) to be a nasty piece of work; **dar una ~ a** algn (*fam*) to belt sb; **~ condensada/desnatada/en polvo** condensed/skimmed/powdered milk; **~ de magnesia** milk of magnesia

lechera *nf* (*recipiente*) milk pan; (*para servir*) milk churn; *ver tb* **lechero**

lechería *nf* dairy

lechero, -a *adj* milk *cpd* ▷ *nm/f* milkman/milkmaid; *ver tb* **lechera**

lecho *nm* (*cama, de río*) bed; (*Geo*) layer; **~ mortuorio** deathbed

lechón *nm* sucking (*Brit*) *o* suckling (*US*) pig

lechoso, -a *adj* milky

lechuga *nf* lettuce

lechuza *nf* (*barn*) owl

lectivo, -a *adj* (*horas*) teaching *cpd*; **año** *o* **curso ~** (*Escol*) school year; (*Univ*) academic year

lector, a *nm/f* reader; (*Escol, Univ*) (*conversation*) assistant ▷ *nm*: **~ óptico de caracteres** (*Inform*) optical character reader; *ver tb* **lectora**

lectora *nf* (*tb*: **lectora de fichas**: *Inform*) card reader; *ver tb* **lector**

lectura *nf* reading; **~ de marcas sensibles** (*Inform*) mark sensing

leer *vt* to read; **~ entre líneas** to read between the lines

legado *nm* (*herencia*) legacy; (*don*) bequest; (*enviado*) legate

legajo *nm* file, bundle (of papers)

legal *adj* legal, lawful; (*persona*) trustworthy

legalidad *nf* legality

legalizar *vt* to legalize; (*documento*) to authenticate

legaña *nf* sleep (*in eyes*)

legar *vt* to bequeath, leave

legendario, -a *adj* legendary

legión *nf* legion

legionario, -a *adj* legionary ▷ *nm* legionnaire

legislación *nf* legislation; (*leyes*) laws *pl*

legislar *vt* to legislate

legislativo, -a *adj*: (**elecciones**) **legislativas** ≈ general election

legislatura *nf* (*Pol*) period of office

legitimar *vt* to legitimize

legítimo, -a *adj* (*genuino*) authentic; (*legal*) legitimate, rightful

lego, -a *adj* (*Rel*) secular; (*ignorante*) ignorant ▷ *nm* layman

legua *nf* league; **se ve** (*o* **nota**) **a la ~** you can tell (it) a mile off

legumbres *nfpl* pulses

leído, -a *adj* well-read

lejanía *nf* distance

lejano, -a *adj* (*en el espacio*) far-off; (*en el tiempo*) distant; (*fig*) remote; **L~ Oriente** Far East

lejía *nf* bleach

lejos *adv* far (away); **~ de** *prep* far from; **no está ~ de aquí** it's not far from here; **¿está ~?** is it far?; **está muy ~** it's a long way (away); **a lo ~** in the distance; **de** *o* **desde ~** from a distance

lelo, -a *adj* silly ▷ *nm/f* idiot

lema *nm* motto; (*Pol*) slogan

lencería *nf* (*ropa interior*) lingerie; (*telas*) linen, drapery

lengua *nf* tongue; **dar a la ~** to chatter; **morderse la ~** to hold one's tongue; **sacar la ~ a** algn (*fig*) to cock a snook at sb; **~ de tierra** (*Geo*) spit *o* tongue of land; **~ materna** mother tongue

lenguado *nm* sole

lenguaje *nm* (*medio de comunicación*) language; (*forma de hablar*) (mode of) speech; **en ~ llano** ≈ in plain English; **~ comercial** business language; **~ de programación** (*Inform*) programming language; **~ de alto nivel** *o* **ensamblador/máquina** (*Inform*) high-level/machine language; **~ original** source language; **~ periodístico** journalese

lengüeta *nf* (*Anat*) epiglottis; (*de zapatos, Mus*) tongue

lente *nf* lens; (*lupa*) magnifying glass; **lentes** *nmpl* glasses; **~s de contacto** contact lenses; **~s progresivas** varifocal lenses

lenteja *nf* lentil

lentejuela *nf* sequin

lentilla *nf* contact lens

lentitud *nf* slowness; **con ~** *adv* slowly

lento, -a *adj* slow ▷ *adv* slowly; **vas un poco ~** you're going a bit slowly

leña *nf* firewood; **dar ~ a** algn to thrash sb; **echar ~ al fuego** (*fig*) to add fuel to the flames

leñador, a *nm/f* woodcutter

leño *nm* (*trozo de árbol*) log; (*madera*) timber; (*fig*) blockhead

Leo *nm* (*Astro*) Leo

león *nm* lion; **~ marino** sea lion

leonino, -a *adj* leonine

leopardo *nm* leopard

leotardos *nmpl* tights

lepra *nf* leprosy

leproso, -a *nm/f* leper

lerdo, -a *adj* (*lento*) slow; (*patoso*) clumsy

les *pron* (*indirecto*) to them; (: *a ustedes*) to you; (*directo*) them; (: *en relación a ustedes*) you; **~ mandé una carta** I sent them a letter, I sent a letter to them; **~ abrí la puerta** I opened the door for them

lesbiana *nf* lesbian

lesión *nf* wound, lesion; (*Deporte*) injury

lesionado, -a *adj* injured ▷ *nm/f* injured person

lesionar *vt* (*dañar*) to hurt; (*herir*) to wound; **lesionarse** *vr* to get hurt

letal *adj* lethal

letanía *nf* (*Rel*) litany; (*retahíla*) long list

letargo *nm* lethargy

letra nf letter; (escritura) handwriting; (Com)
letter, bill, draft; (Mus) lyrics pl; **letras** nfpl (Univ)
arts; **tiene muy buena ~** his handwriting is
very poor; **escribir cuatro ~s a algn** to drop
a line to sb; **lo tomó al pie de la ~** he took
it literally; **~ bancaria** (Com) bank draft; **~
bastardilla/cursiva** italics pl; **~ de cambio** bill
of exchange; **~ de imprenta** print; **~ de patente**
(Com) letters patent pl; **~ inicial** initial letter; **~
mayúscula/minúscula** capital/small letter; **~
negrilla** bold type

letrado, -a adj learned; (fam) pedantic ▷ nm/f
lawyer

letrero nm (cartel) sign; (etiqueta) label

letrina nf latrine

leucemia nf leukaemia

leucocito nm white blood cell, leucocyte

levadizo, -a adj: **puente ~** drawbridge

levadura nf yeast, leaven; **~ de cerveza** brewer's
yeast

levantamiento nm (de objeto) raising, lifting;
(rebelión) revolt, rising; (Geo) survey; **~ de pesos**
weightlifting

levantar vt (gen) to raise; (del suelo) to pick
up; (hacia arriba) to lift (up); (plan) to make,
draw up; (mesa) to clear; (campamento) to
strike; **levantarse** vr to get up; (enderezarse)
to straighten up; (rebelarse) to rebel; (niebla) to
lift; (viento) to rise; **~ el ánimo** to cheer up; **se
levanta la sesión** the meeting is adjourned; **~se
(de la cama)** to get up, get out of bed

levante nm east; (viento) east wind; **el L~** region of
Spain extending from Castellón to Murcia

levar vi to weigh anchor

leve adj light; (fig) trivial; (mínimo) slight

levedad nf lightness; (fig) levity

levita nf frock coat

léxico, -a adj lexical ▷ nm (vocabulario)
vocabulary; (Ling) lexicon

ley nf (gen) law; (metal) standard; **decreto-~**
decree law; **según la ~** in accordance with the
law, by law, in law; **de buena ~** (fig) genuine

leyenda nf legend; (Tip) inscription

liar vt (atar) to tie (up); (unir) to bind; (envolver) to
wrap (up); (enredar) to confuse; (cigarrillo) to roll;
liarse vr (fam) to get involved; (confundirse) to get
mixed up; **me estoy liando, empezaré otra
vez** I'm getting muddled up, I'll start again; **nos
liamos a hablar** we got talking; **~se a palos** to
get involved in a fight

Líbano nm: **el ~** the Lebanon

libar vt to suck

libelo nm satire, lampoon; (Jur) petition

libélula nf dragonfly

liberación nf liberation; (de la cárcel) release

liberal adj, nm/f liberal

liberalidad nf liberality, generosity

liberar vt to liberate

libertad nf liberty, freedom; **estar en ~** to be free;
poner a algn en ~ to set sb free; **~ condicional**
probation; **~ bajo palabra** parole; **~ bajo fianza**
bail; **~ de asociación/de culto/de palabra/de**

prensa freedom of association/of worship/of
speech/of the press

libertar vt (preso) to set free; (de una obligación) to
release; (eximir) to exempt

libertinaje nm licentiousness

libertino, -a adj permissive ▷ nm/f permissive
person

libidinoso, -a adj lustful; (viejo) lecherous

líbido nf libido

libra nf pound, Libra; **~ esterlina** pound sterling;
L~ (Astro)

librador, a nm/f drawer

libramiento nm rescue; (Com) delivery

librar vt (de peligro) to save; (de impuestos) to
exempt; (batalla) to wage, fight; (cheque) to make
out; (Jur) to exempt; **librarse** vr: **~se de** to escape
from, free o.s. from; **de buena nos hemos
librado** we're well out of that

libre adj (gen) free; (lugar) unoccupied; (tiempo)
spare; (asiento) vacant; **¿estás ~?** are you free?; **al
aire ~** in the open air; **tiro ~** free kick; **los 100
metros ~s** the 100 metres freestyle (race); (Com):
~ a bordo free on board; **~ de franqueo** post-
free; **~ de impuestos** free of tax

librería nf (tienda) bookshop; (estante) bookcase; **~
de ocasión** secondhand bookshop

librero, -a nm/f bookseller

libreta nf (cuaderno) notebook; (pan) one-pound
loaf; **~ de ahorros** savings book

libro nm book; **~ de actas** minute book; **~ de
bolsillo** paperback; **~ de cabecera** bedside
book; **~ de caja** (Com) cashbook; **~ de caja
auxiliar** (Com) petty cash book; **~ de cheques**
cheque (Brit) o check (US) book; **~ de cocina**
cookery book (Brit), cookbook (US); **~ de
consulta/cuentas** reference/account book; **~
de cuentos** storybook; **~ de entradas y salidas**
(Com) daybook; **~ de honor** visitors' book; **~ de
reclamaciones** complaints book; **~ de texto**
textbook; **~ diario** journal; **~ electrónico** e-
book; **~ mayor** (Com) general ledger

Lic. abr = **Licenciado, a**

licencia nf (gen) licence; (permiso) permission;
~ de armas/caza gun/game licence; **~ de
exportación** (Com) export licence; **~ de obras**
planning permission; **~ poética** poetic licence

licenciado, -a adj licensed ▷ nm/f graduate; **L~
en Filosofía y Letras** = Bachelor of Arts

licenciar vt (empleado) to dismiss; (soldado) to
discharge; (estudiante) to confer a degree upon;
(permitir) to permit, allow; **licenciarse** vr: **~se en
letras** to get an arts degree

licencioso, -a adj licentious

liceo nm (esp LAm) (high) school

licitar vt to bid for ▷ vi to bid

lícito, -a adj (legal) lawful; (justo) fair, just;
(permisible) permissible

licor nm (de hierbas, frutas, etc) liqueur; (alcohol)
spirits pl (Brit), liquor (US)

licra® nf Lycra®

licuadora nf blender

licuar vt to liquidize

lid *nf* combat; *(fig)* controversy

líder *nm/f* leader

liderato *nm*, **liderazgo** *nm* leadership

lidia *nf* bullfighting; *(una lidia)* bullfight; **toros de ~** fighting bulls

lidiar *vt, vi* to fight

liebre *nf* hare; **dar gato por ~** to con

lienzo *nm* linen; *(Arte)* canvas; *(Arq)* wall

liga *nf* *(de medias)* garter, suspender; *(Deporte)* league; *(LAm: gomita)* rubber band

ligadura *nf* bond, tie; *(Med, Mús)* ligature

ligamento *nm* *(Anat)* ligament; *(atadura)* tie; *(unión)* bond

ligar *vt* *(atar)* to tie; *(unir)* to join; *(Med)* to bind up; *(Mus)* to slur; *(fam)* to get off with, pick up ▷ *vi* to mix, blend; *(fam)* to get off with sb; *(2 personas)* to get off with one another; **ligarse** *vr* *(fig)* to commit o.s.; **~ con** *(fam)* to get off with, pick up; **~se a algn** to get off with o pick up sb

ligereza *nf* *(poco peso)* lightness; *(rapidez)* swiftness; *(agilidad)* agility; *(superficialidad)* flippancy

ligero, -a *adj* *(de peso)* light; *(tela)* thin; *(rápido)* swift, quick; *(ágil)* agile, nimble; *(de importancia)* slight; *(de carácter)* flippant, superficial ▷ *adv* quickly, swiftly; **a la ligera** superficially; **juzgar a la ligera** to jump to conclusions

light *adj inv* *(cigarrillo)* low-tar; *(comida)* diet *cpd*

ligue *nm/f* boyfriend (girlfriend) ▷ *nm* *(persona)* pick-up

liguero *nm* suspender *(Brit)* o garter *(US)* belt

lija *nf* *(Zool)* dogfish; **(papel de) ~** sandpaper

lijar *vt* to sand

lila *adj inv, nf* lilac ▷ *nm* *(fam)* twit

lima *nf* file; *(Bot)* lime; **comer como una ~** to eat like a horse; **~ de uñas** nail file

limar *vt* to file; *(alisar)* to smooth over; *(fig)* to polish up

limbo *nm* *(Rel)* limbo; **estar en el ~** to be on another planet

limitación *nf* limitation, limit; **~ de velocidad** speed limit

limitar *vt* to limit; *(reducir)* to reduce, cut down ▷ *vi*: **~ con** to border on; **limitarse** *vr*: **~se a** to limit o confine o.s. to

límite *nm* *(gen)* limit; *(fin)* end; *(frontera)* border; **como ~** at (the) most; *(fecha)* at the latest; **no tener ~s** to know no bounds; **~ de crédito** *(Com)* credit limit; **~ de página** *(Inform)* page break; **~ de velocidad** speed limit

limítrofe *adj* bordering, neighbouring

limón *nm* lemon ▷ *adj*: **amarillo ~** lemon-yellow

limonada *nf* lemonade

limonero *nm* lemon tree

limosna *nf* alms *pl*; **pedir ~** to beg; **vivir de ~** to live on charity

limpiabotas *nm/f inv* bootblack *(Brit)*, shoeshine boy(-girl)

limpiaparabrisas *nm inv* windscreen *(Brit)* o windshield *(US)* wiper

limpiar *vt* *(gen)* to clean; *(con trapo)* to wipe; *(quitar)* to wipe away; *(zapatos)* to shine, polish; *(fig)* to clean up; *(: purificar)* to cleanse, purify; *(Mil)* to mop up; **~ en seco** to dry-clean

limpieza *nf* *(acto)* cleaning; *(: de las calles)* cleansing; *(: de zapatos)* polishing; *(Policía)* clean-up; *(estado)* cleanliness; *(habilidad)* skill; *(fig: pureza)* purity; **operación de ~** *(Mil)* mopping-up operation; **~ en seco** dry cleaning; **~ étnica** ethnic cleansing

limpio, -a *adj* clean; *(moralmente)* pure; *(ordenado)* tidy; *(despejado)* clear; *(Com)* clear, net; *(fam)* honest ▷ *adv*: **jugar ~** to play fair; **pasar a ~** to make a fair copy; **sacar algo en ~** to get benefit from sth; **~ de** free from

linaje *nm* lineage, family

linaza *nf* linseed; **aceite de ~** linseed oil

lince *nm* lynx; **ser un ~** *(fig: observador)* to be very observant; *(: astuto)* to be shrewd

linchar *vt* to lynch

lindar *vi* to adjoin; **~ con** to border on; *(Arq)* to abut on

linde *nm o nf* boundary

lindero, -a *adj* adjoining ▷ *nm* boundary

lindo, -a *adj* pretty, lovely ▷ *adv* *(esp LAm: fam)* nicely, very well; **canta muy ~** *(LAm)* he sings beautifully; **se divertían de lo ~** they enjoyed themselves enormously

línea *nf* *(gen, moral, Pol, etc)* line; *(talle)* figure; **la ~ de 1995** *(moda)* the 1995 look; **en ~** *(Inform)* on line; **fuera de ~** off line; **~ aérea** airline; **~ de alto el fuego** ceasefire line; **~ de estado** status line; **~ de formato** format line; **~ de fuego** firing line; **~ de meta** goal line; *(de carrera)* finishing line; **~ de montaje** assembly line; **~ dura** *(Pol)* hard line; **~ recta** straight line

lingote *nm* ingot

lingüista *nm/f* linguist

lingüística *nf* linguistics *sg*

linimento *nm* liniment

lino *nm* linen; *(Bot)* flax

linóleo *nm* lino, linoleum

linterna *nf* *(farol)* lantern, lamp; **~ eléctrica** o **a pilas** torch *(Brit)*, flashlight *(US)*

lío *nm* *(fardo)* bundle; *(desorden)* muddle, mess; *(fam: follón)* fuss; *(: relación amorosa)* affair; **hacerse un ~** to get muddled up; **armar un ~** to make a fuss; **meterse en un ~** to get into a jam; **tener un ~ con algn** to be having an affair with sb

lipotimia *nf* blackout

liquen *nm* lichen

liquidación *nf* liquidation; *(de cuenta)* settlement; **venta de ~** clearance sale

liquidar *vt* *(Química)* to liquefy; *(Com)* to liquidate; *(deudas)* to pay off; *(empresa)* to wind up; **~ a algn** to bump sb off, rub sb out *(fam)*

liquidez *nf* liquidity

líquido, -a *adj* liquid; *(ganancia)* net ▷ *nm* liquid; *(Com: efectivo)* ready cash o money; *(: ganancia)* net amount o profit; **~ imponible** net taxable income

lira *nf* *(Mus)* lyre; *(moneda)* lira

lírico, -a *adj* lyrical

lirio *nm* (*Bot*) iris
lirón *nm* (*Zool*) dormouse; (*fig*) sleepyhead
Lisboa *nf* Lisbon
lisiado, -a *adj* injured ▷ *nm/f* cripple
lisiar *vt* to maim; **lisiarse** *vr* to injure o.s.
liso, -a *adj* (*terreno*) flat; (*cabello*) straight;
(*superficie*) even; (*tela*) plain; **lisa y llanamente**
in plain language, plainly
lisonja *nf* flattery
lisonjear *vt* to flatter; (*fig*) to please
lisonjero, -a *adj* flattering; (*agradable*) gratifying,
pleasing ▷ *nm/f* flatterer
lista *nf* list; (*de alumnos*) school register; (*de libros*)
catalogue; (*de platos*) menu; (*de precios*) price list;
pasar ~ to call the roll; (*Escol*) to call the register;
tela a ~s striped material; **~ de correos** poste
restante; **~ de direcciones** mailing list; **~ de**
espera waiting list; **~ electoral** electoral roll
listado, -a *adj* striped ▷ *nm* (*Com, Inform*) listing;
~ paginado (*Inform*) paged listing
listo, -a *adj* (*perspicaz*) smart, clever; (*preparado*)
ready; **pasarse de ~** to be too clever by half;
¿estás ~? are you ready?; **~ para usar** ready-to-
use
listón *nm* (*de tela*) ribbon; (*de madera, metal*) strip
litera *nf* (*en barco, tren*) berth; (*en dormitorio*) bunk,
bunk bed
literal *adj* literal
literario, -a *adj* literary
literato, -a *nm/f* writer
literatura *nf* literature
litigar *vt* to fight ▷ *vi* (*Jur*) to go to law; (*fig*) to
dispute, argue
litigio *nm* (*Jur*) lawsuit; (*fig*): **en ~ con** in dispute
with
litografía *nf* (*técnica*) lithography; (*grabado*)
lithograph
litoral *adj* coastal ▷ *nm* coast, seaboard
litro *nm* litre, liter (*US*)
liviano, -a *adj* (*persona*) fickle; (*cosa, objeto*) trivial;
(*LAm*) light
lívido, -a *adj* livid
llaga *nf* wound
llama *nf* flame; (*fig*) passion; (*Zool*) llama; **en ~s**
burning, ablaze
llamada *nf* call; (*a la puerta*) knock; (*: al timbre*)
ring; **hacer una ~ de teléfono** to make a phone
call; **~ a cobro revertido** reverse-charge call;
~ al orden call to order; **~ a pie de página**
reference note; **~ a procedimiento** (*Inform*)
procedure call; **~ interurbana** trunk call
llamamiento *nm* call; **hacer un ~ a algn para**
que haga algo to appeal to sb to do sth
llamar *vt* (*avisar*) to call; (*convocar*) to summon;
(*invocar*) to invoke; (*atraer con gesto*) to beckon;
(*atención*) to attract; (*Mil*) to call up; (*Telec: tb*:
llamar por teléfono) to call, ring up, telephone
▷ *vi* (*por teléfono*) to phone; (*a la puerta*) to knock
(*o ring*); (*por señas*) to beckon; **llamarse** *vr* to be
called, be named; **no me llama la atención**
(*fam*) I don't fancy it; **¿quién llama?** (*Telec*) who's
calling?, who's that?; **¿cómo se llama usted?**
what's your name?
llamarada *nf* (*llamas*) blaze; (*rubor*) flush; (*fig*)
flare-up
llamativo, -a *adj* (*ropa, plumas*) showy; (*color*) loud
llamear *vi* to blaze
llano, -a *adj* (*superficie*) flat; (*persona*)
straightforward; (*estilo*) clear ▷ *nm* plain, flat
ground
llanta *nf* (*wheel*) rim; (*LAm: neumático*) tyre;
(*: cámara*) (inner) tube
llanto *nm* weeping; (*fig*) lamentation; (*canción*)
dirge, lament
llanura *nf* (*lisura*) flatness, smoothness; (*Geo*)
plain
llave *nf* key; (*de gas, agua*) tap (*Brit*), faucet (*US*);
(*Mecánica*) spanner; (*de la luz*) switch; (*Mus*)
key; **echar ~ a** to lock up; **~ de contacto** (*Auto*)
ignition key; **~ de paso** stopcock; **~ inglesa**
monkey wrench; **~ maestra** master key
llavero *nm* keyring
llavín *nm* latchkey
llegada *nf* arrival
llegar *vi* (*a un lugar*) to arrive; (*bastar*) to be
enough; **~ a** (*alcanzar*) to reach; (*conseguir*) to
manage to, succeed in; **llegarse** *vr*: **~se a** to
approach; **no ha llegado todavía** she hasn't
arrived yet; **no llegues tarde** don't be late; **esta**
cuerda no llega this rope isn't long enough; **~**
a las manos to come to blows; **~ a las manos de**
to come into the hands of; **~ a saber** to find out;
~ a ser famoso/el jefe to become famous/the
boss
llenar *vt* (*recipiente*) to fill; (*superficie*) to cover;
(*espacio, tiempo*) to fill, take up; (*formulario*) to fill
in *o* out; **llenarse** *vr* to fill (up); **~se de** (*fam*) to
stuff o.s. with
lleno, -a *adj* (*completo*) full; (*repleto*) full up ▷ *nm*
(*abundancia*) abundance; (*Teat*) full house; **dar de**
~ contra un muro to hit a wall head-on
llevadero, -a *adj* bearable, tolerable
llevar *vt* (*gen*) to take; (*ropa*) to wear; (*cargar*) to
carry; (*quitar*) to take away; (*en coche*) to drive;
(*transportar*) to transport; (*ruta*) to follow, keep
to; (*traer: dinero*) to carry; (*camino etc*): **~ a** to lead
to; (*Mat*) to carry; (*aguantar*) to bear; (*negocio*)
to run; **llevarse** *vr* to carry off, take away;
nos llevó a cenar fuera she took us out for a
meal; **llevo las de perder** I'm likely to lose;
no las lleva todas consigo he's not all there;
llevamos dos días aquí we have been here for
two days; **él me lleva 2 años** he's 2 years older
than me; **~ adelante** (*fig*) to carry forward; **~ la**
ventaja to be winning *o* in the lead; **~ los libros**
(*Com*) to keep the books; **~se a uno por delante**
(*atropellar*) to run sb over; **~se bien** to get on well
(together)
llorar *vt* to cry, weep ▷ *vi* to cry, weep; (*ojos*) to
water; **~ de risa** to cry with laughter; **~ a moco**
tendido to sob one's heart out
lloriquear *vi* to snivel, whimper
lloro *nm* crying, weeping
llorón, -ona *adj* tearful ▷ *nm/f* cry-baby

lloroso, -a *adj* (*gen*) weeping, tearful; (*triste*) sad, sorrowful

llover *vi* to rain; **~ a cántaros** *o* **a cubos** *o* **a mares** to rain cats and dogs, pour (down); **ser una cosa llovida del cielo** to be a godsend; **llueve sobre mojado** it never rains but it pours

llovizna *nf* drizzle

lloviznar *vi* to drizzle

lluvia *nf* rain; (*cantidad caída*) rainfall; (*fig: de balas etc*) hail, shower; **día de ~** rainy day; **una ~ de regalos** a shower of gifts; **~ radioactiva** radioactive fallout

lluvioso, -a *adj* rainy

lo *artículo definido neutro*: **lo peor fue que ...** the worst thing was that ...; **no me gusta lo picante** I don't like spicy things; **lo mío son las matemáticas** maths is my thing; **dame lo mío** give me what is mine; **lo de** that matter of; **lo que** that, that which; **toma lo que quieras** take what(ever) you want; **lo que sea** whatever ▷ *pron* (*en relación a una persona*) him; (*en relación a una cosa*) it; **lo han despedido** he's been sacked; **no lo sabía** I didn't know; *ver tb* **el**

loa *nf* praise

loable *adj* praiseworthy

loar *vt* to praise

lobato *nm* (*Zool*) wolf cub

lobo *nm* wolf; **~ de mar** (*fig*) sea dog; **~ marino** seal

lóbrego, -a *adj* dark; (*fig*) gloomy

lóbulo *nm* lobe

local *adj* local ▷ *nm* place, site; (*oficinas*) premises *pl*

localidad *nf* (*población*) town; (*lugar*) location; (*Teat*) seat, ticket

localizar *vt* (*ubicar*) to locate, find; (*encontrar*) to find, track down; (*restringir*) to localize; (*situar*) to place

loción *nf* lotion, wash

loco, -a *adj* mad; (*fig*) wild, mad ▷ *nm/f* lunatic, madman(-woman); **estar ~ de alegría** to be overjoyed *o* over the moon; **ando ~ con el examen** the exam is driving me crazy; **a lo ~** without rhyme or reason; **~ de atar** *o* **de remate** *o* **rematado** raving mad

locomoción *nf* locomotion

locomotora *nf* engine, locomotive

locuaz *adj* loquacious, talkative

locución *nf* expression

locura *nf* madness; (*acto*) crazy act

locutor, a *nm/f* (*Radio*) announcer; (*comentarista*) commentator; (*TV*) newscaster, newsreader

locutorio *nm* (*Telec*) telephone box *o* booth

lodo *nm* mud

lógico, -a *adj* logical; (*correcto*) natural; (*razonable*) reasonable ▷ *nm* logician ▷ *nf* logic; **es ~ que ...** it stands to reason that ...; **ser de una lógica aplastante** to be as clear as day

logístico, -a *adj* logistical ▷ *nf* logistics *pl*

logotipo *nm* logo

logrado, -a *adj* accomplished

lograr *vt* (*obtener*) to get, obtain; (*conseguir*) to achieve, attain; **~ hacer** to manage to do; **~ que algn venga** to manage to get sb to come; **~ acceso a** (*Inform*) to access

logro *nm* achievement, success; (*Com*) profit

LOGSE *nf abr* (= *Ley Orgánica de Ordenación General del Sistema Educativo*) *educational reform act*

loma *nf* hillock, low ridge

lombriz *nf* (earth)worm

lomo *nm* (*de animal*) back; (*Culin: de cerdo*) pork loin; (*: de vaca*) rib steak; (*de libro*) spine

lona *nf* canvas

loncha *nf* = **lonja**

lonche *nm* (*Perú: merienda*) tea

lonchería *nf* (*LAm*) snack bar, diner (US)

Londres *nm* London

longaniza *nf* longpork sausage

longevidad *nf* longevity

longitud *nf* length; (*Geo*) longitude; **tener 3 metros de ~** to be 3 metres long; **salto de ~** long jump; **~ de onda** wavelength

longitudinal *adj* longitudinal

lonja *nf* slice; (*de tocino*) rasher; (*Com*) market, exchange; **~ de pescado** fish market

loro *nm* parrot

los *artículo definido mpl* the ▷ *pron* them; (*en relación a ustedes*) you; **mis libros y ~ de usted** my books and yours; **me duelen ~ pies** my feet hurt; **solo viene ~ lunes** he only comes on Mondays; *ver tb* **el**

losa *nf* stone; **~ sepulcral** gravestone

lote *nm* portion, share; (*Com*) lot; (*Inform*) batch

lotería *nf* lottery; (*juego*) lotto; **le tocó la ~** he won a big prize in the lottery; (*fig*) he struck lucky; **~ nacional** national lottery; **~ primitiva** (*Esp*) *type of state-run lottery*

loza *nf* crockery; **~ fina** china

lozanía *nf* (*lujo*) freshness

lozano, -a *adj* luxuriant; (*animado*) lively

lubricante *adj, nm* lubricant

lubricar, lubrificar *vt* to lubricate

lucero *nm* (*Astro*) bright star; (*fig*) brilliance; **~ de la tarde/del alba** evening/morning star

luces *nfpl de* **luz**

lucha *nf* fight, struggle; **~ de clases** class struggle; **~ libre** wrestling

luchar *vi* to fight

lucidez *nf* lucidity

lúcido, -a *adj* lucid

luciérnaga *nf* glow-worm

lucimiento *nm* (*brillo*) brilliance; (*éxito*) success

lucir *vt* to illuminate, light (up); (*ostentar*) to show off ▷ *vi* (*brillar*) to shine; (*LAm: parecer*) to look, seem; **la casa luce limpia** the house looks clean; **lucirse** *vr* (*irónico*) to make a fool of o.s.; (*presumir*) to show off

lucro *nm* profit, gain; **~s y daños** (*Com*) profit and loss *sg*

lúdico, -a *adj* playful; (*actividad*) recreational

ludopatía *nf* addiction to gambling

luego *adv* (*después*) next; (*más tarde*) later, afterwards; (*LAm fam: en seguida*) at once, immediately; **¡hasta ~!** see you later!, so long!;

¿y ~? what next?; **desde ~** of course
lugar nm (gen) place; (sitio) spot; (pueblo) village, town; **en primer ~** in the first place, firstly; **hacer ~** to make room; **fuera de ~** out of place; **tener ~** to take place; **no hay ~ para preocupaciones** there is no cause for concern; **yo en su ~** if I were him; **en ~ de** instead of; **dar ~ a** to give rise to; **~ común** commonplace
lugareño, -a adj village cpd ▷ nm/f villager
lugarteniente nm deputy
lúgubre adj mournful
lujo nm luxury; (fig) profusion, abundance; **de ~** luxury antes de s, de luxe
lujoso, -a adj luxurious
lujuria nf lust
lumbago nm lumbago
lumbre nf (luz) light; (fuego) fire; **cerca de la ~** near the fire, at the fireside; **¿tienes ~?** (para cigarro) have you got a light?
lumbrera nf luminary; (fig) leading light
luminoso, -a adj luminous, shining; (idea) bright, brilliant
luna nf moon; (vidrio: escaparate) plate glass; (de un espejo) glass; (de gafas) lens; (fig) crescent; **estar en la ~** to have one's head in the clouds; **~ creciente/llena/menguante/nueva** crescent/full/waning/new moon; **~ de miel** honeymoon
lunar adj lunar ▷ nm (Anat) mole; **tela a ~es**

spotted material
lunes nm inv Monday
lupa nf magnifying glass
lustrabotas nm/f (LAm) bootblack
lustrar vt (esp LAm: mueble) to polish; (zapatos) to shine
lustre nm polish; (fig) lustre; **dar ~ a** to polish
lustroso, -a adj shining
luterano, -a adj Lutheran
luto nm mourning; (congoja) grief, sorrow; **llevar el o vestirse de ~** to be in mourning
Luxemburgo nm Luxembourg
luz (pl **luces**) nf (tb fig) light; (fam) electricity; **dar** (Esp) o **encender** (Esp) o **prender** (LAm)/**apagar la ~** to switch the light on/off; **les cortaron la ~** their (electricity) supply was cut off; **a la ~ de** in the light of; **a todas luces** by any reckoning; **hacer la ~ sobre** to shed light on; **dar a ~ un niño** to give birth to a child; **sacar a la ~** to bring to light; **tener pocas luces** to be dim o stupid; **el Siglo de las Luces** the Age of Enlightenment; **traje de luces** bullfighter's costume; **~ de cruce** (Auto) dipped headlight; **~ de freno** brake light; **~ de la luna** moonlight; **~ del sol** sunlight; **luces de tráfico** traffic lights; **~ eléctrica/intermitente/roja/trasera** electric/flashing/red/rear light

Mm

m. *abr* (= *metro(s)*) m; (= *minuto(s)*) min., m;
(= *masculino*) m., masc
macarra *nm* (*fam*) thug
macarrones *nmpl* macaroni *sg*
macedonia *nf*: ~ **de frutas** fruit salad
macerar *vt* (*Culin*) to soak, macerate; **macerarse**
vr to soak, soften
maceta *nf* (*vacía*) flowerpot; (*con planta*) plant
machacar *vt* to crush, pound; (*moler*) to grind
(up); (*aplastar*) to mash ▷ *vi* (*insistir*) to go on,
keep on
machete *nm* machete, (large) knife
machismo *nm* (*de sociedad*) sexism; (*de hombre*)
male chauvinism
machista *adj, nm* sexist
macho *adj* male; (*fig*) virile ▷ *nm* male; (*fig*) he-
man, tough guy (US); (*Tec: perno*) pin, peg; (*Elec*)
pin, plug; (*Costura*) hook
macizo, -a *adj* (*grande*) massive; (*fuerte, sólido*)
solid ▷ *nm* mass, chunk; (*Geo*) massif
macramé *nm* macramé
mácula *nf* stain, blemish
madeja *nf* (*de lana*) skein, hank
madera *nf* wood; (*fig*) nature, character;
(: *aptitud*) aptitude; **una ~** a piece of wood; **tiene
buena ~** he's made of solid stuff; **tiene ~ de
futbolista** he's got the makings of a footballer;
~ contrachapada o **laminada** plywood
madero *nm* beam; (*fig*) ship
madrastra *nf* stepmother
madre *adj* mother *cpd*; (*LAm*) tremendous ▷ *nf*
mother; (*de vino etc*) dregs *pl*; **sin ~** motherless; **¡~
mía!** oh dear!; **¡tu ~!** (*fam!*) fuck off! (!); **salirse
de ~** (*río*) to burst its banks; (*persona*) to lose
all self-control; **~ adoptiva/soltera** foster/
unmarried mother; **la M~ Patria** the Mother
Country; **~ política** mother-in-law
madreperla *nf* mother-of-pearl
madreselva *nf* honeysuckle
Madrid *n* Madrid
madriguera *nf* burrow
madrileño, -a *adj* o from Madrid ▷ *nm/f* native
o inhabitant of Madrid
madrina *nf* godmother; (*Arq*) prop, shore; (*Tec*)
brace; **~ de boda** maid of honour
madrugada *nf* early morning, small hours;
(*alba*) dawn, daybreak; **a las 4 de la ~** at 4 o'clock

in the morning
madrugador, a *adj* early-rising
madrugar *vi* to get up early; (*fig*) to get a head
start
madurar *vt, vi* (*fruta*) to ripen; (*fig*) to mature
madurez *nf* ripeness; (*fig*) maturity
maduro, -a *adj* ripe; (*fig*) mature; **poco ~** unripe
maestra *nf ver* **maestro**
maestría *nf* mastery; (*habilidad*) skill, expertise;
(*LAm*) Master's Degree
maestro, -a *adj* masterly; (*perito*) skilled, expert;
(*principal*) main; (*educado*) trained ▷ *nm/f* master/
mistress; (*docente*) teacher ▷ *nm* (*autoridad*)
authority; (*Mus*) maestro; (*obrero*) skilled
workman; **~ albañil** master mason; **~ de obras**
foreman
mafia *nf* mafia; **la M~** the Mafia
magia *nf* magic
mágico, -a *adj* (*de magia*) magic; (*sobrenatural,
encantador*) magical ▷ *nm/f* magician
magisterio *nm* (*enseñanza*) teaching; (*profesión*)
teaching profession; (*maestros*) teachers *pl*
magistrado *nm* magistrate; **Primer M~** (*LAm*)
President, Prime Minister
magistral *adj* magisterial; (*fig*) masterly
magnánimo, -a *adj* magnanimous
magnate *nm* magnate, tycoon; **~ de la prensa**
press baron
magnético, -a *adj* magnetic
magnetismo *nm* magnetism
magnetizar *vt* to magnetize
magnetófon, magnetófono *nm* tape recorder
magnetofónico, -a *adj*: **cinta magnetofónica**
recording tape
magnífico, -a *adj* splendid, magnificent
magnitud *nf* magnitude
mago, -a *nm/f* magician, wizard; **los Reyes M~s**
the Magi, the Three Wise Men
magro, -a *adj* (*persona*) thin, lean; (*carne*) lean
magullar *vt* (*amoratar*) to bruise; (*dañar*) to
damage; (*fam: golpear*) to bash, beat
mahometano, -a *adj* Mohammedan
mahonesa *nf* = **mayonesa**
maíz *nm* (*planta*) maize (Brit), corn (US); (*para
comer*) sweet corn
majadero, -a *adj* silly, stupid
majestad *nf* majesty; **Su M~** His/Her Majesty;

(Vuestra) M~ Your Majesty
majestuoso, -a *adj* majestic
majo, -a *adj* nice; (*guapo*) attractive, good-looking; (*elegante*) smart
mal *adv* badly; (*equivocadamente*) wrongly; (*con dificultad*) with difficulty ▷ *adj* = **malo, a** ▷ *nm* evil; (*desgracia*) misfortune; (*daño*) harm, damage; (*conj*): **~ que le pese** whether he likes it or not; **no hay ~ que por bien no venga** every cloud has a silver lining; **~ de ojo** evil eye; **me entendió ~** he misunderstood me; **hablar ~ de algn** to speak ill of sb; **huele ~** it smells bad; **ir de ~ en peor** to go from bad to worse; **oigo/veo ~** I can't hear/see very well; **si ~ no recuerdo** if my memory serves me right; **¡menos ~!** just as well!; **~ que bien** rightly or wrongly
malabarismo *nm* juggling
malabarista *nm/f* juggler
malaconsejado, -a *adj* ill-advised
malaria *nf* malaria
malcriado, -a *adj* (*consentido*) spoiled
maldad *nf* evil, wickedness
maldecir *vt* to curse ▷ *vi*: **~ de** to speak ill of
maldición *nf* curse; **¡~!** curse it!, damn!
maldito, -a *adj* (*condenado*) damned; (*perverso*) wicked; **¡maldita sea!** damn it!; **no le hace ~ (el) caso** he doesn't take a blind bit of notice ▷ *nm*: **el ~** the devil
maleante *adj* wicked ▷ *nm/f* criminal, crook
malecón *nm* pier, jetty
maledicencia *nf* slander, scandal
maleducado, -a *adj* bad-mannered, rude
maleficio *nm* curse, spell
malentendido *nm* misunderstanding
malestar *nm* (*gen*) discomfort; (*enfermedad*) indisposition; (*fig: inquietud*) uneasiness; (*Pol*) unrest; **siento un ~ en el estómago** my stomach is upset
maleta *nf* case, suitcase; (*Auto*) boot (*Brit*), trunk (*US*); **hacer la ~** to pack
maletera *nf* (*And Auto*) boot (*Brit*), trunk (*US*)
maletero *nm* (*Auto*) boot (*Brit*), trunk (*US*); (*persona*) porter
maletín *nm* small case, bag; (*portafolio*) briefcase
malévolo, -a *adj* malicious, spiteful
maleza *nf* (*malas hierbas*) weeds *pl*; (*arbustos*) thicket
malgastar *vt* (*tiempo, dinero*) to waste; (*recursos*) to squander; (*salud*) to ruin
malhechor, a *nm/f* delinquent; (*criminal*) criminal
malherido, -a *adj* badly injured
malhumorado, -a *adj* bad-tempered
malicia *nf* (*maldad*) wickedness; (*astucia*) slyness, guile; (*mala intención*) malice, spite; (*carácter travieso*) mischievousness
malicioso, -a *adj* (*malvado*) wicked, evil; (*pícaro*) sly, crafty; (*malicioso*) malicious, spiteful
maligno, -a *adj* (*malvado*) evil; (*dañino*) pernicious, harmful; (*malévolo*) malicious; (*Med*) malignant ▷ *nm*: **el ~** the devil

malla *nf* (*de una red*) mesh; (*red*) network; (*CS: de baño*) swimsuit; (*de ballet, gimnasia*) leotard; **mallas** *nfpl* tights; **~ de alambre** wire mesh
Mallorca *nf* Majorca
malo, -a *adj* (**mal** *before a masculine noun*: *gen*) bad; (*calidad*) poor; (*carne, pescado*) off; (*travieso*) naughty; (*enfermo*) ill ▷ *nm/f* villain ▷ *nm* (*Cine fam*) bad guy; **un mal día** a bad day; **este programa es muy ~** this is a very bad programme; **soy muy mala para las matemáticas** I'm very bad at maths; **esta carne está mala** this meat's off; **¿por qué eres tan ~?** why are you so naughty?; **estar ~** to be ill; **se puso ~ después de comer** he started to feel ill after lunch; **lo ~ es que ...** the trouble is that ...; **andar a malas con algn** to be on bad terms with sb; **estar de malas** to be in a bad mood
malograr *vt* (*tranquilidad, objeto*) to spoil; (*plan*) to upset; (*ocasión*) to waste; **malograrse** *vr* (*plan etc*) to fail, come to grief; (*persona*) to die before one's time
malparado, -a *adj*: **salir ~** to come off badly
malpensado, -a *adj* evil-minded
malsano, -a *adj* unhealthy
Malta *nf* Malta
malta *nf* malt
malteada *nf* (*LAm*) milk shake
maltratar *vt* to ill-treat, mistreat
maltrecho, -a *adj* battered, damaged
malva *nf* mallow; **~ loca** hollyhock; **(de color de) ~** mauve
malvado, -a *adj* evil, villainous
malvavisco *nm* marshmallow
malversar *vt* to embezzle, misappropriate
Malvinas *nfpl*: **Islas ~** Falkland Islands
mama (*pl* **mamás**) *nf* (*de animal*) teat; (*de mujer*) breast
mamá *nf* (*fam*) mum, mummy
mamar *vt* (*pecho*) to suck; (*fig*) to absorb, assimilate ▷ *vi* to suck; **dar de ~** to (breast-)feed; (*animal*) to suckle
mamarracho *nm* sight, mess
mambo *nm* (*Mus*) mambo
mamífero, -a *adj* mammalian, mammal *cpd* ▷ *nm* mammal
mamón, -ona *adj* small, baby *cpd* ▷ *nm/f* small baby; (*fam!*) wanker (!)
mampara *nf* (*entre habitaciones*) partition; (*biombo*) screen
mampostería *nf* masonry
mamut *nm* mammoth
manada *nf* (*Zool*) herd; (: *de leones*) pride; (: *de lobos*) pack; **llegaron en ~s** (*fam*) they came in droves
Managua *n* Managua
manantial *nm* (*origen de agua*) spring; (*fuente*) fountain; (*fig*) source
manar *vt* to run with, flow with ▷ *vi* to run, flow; (*abundar*) to abound
mancha *nf* stain, mark; (*de tinta*) blot; (*de vegetación*) patch; (*imperfección*) stain, blemish, blot; (*boceto*) sketch, outline; **la M~** La Mancha

manchar vt to stain, mark; (Zool) to patch; (ensuciar) to soil, dirty; **mancharse** vr to get dirty; (fig) to dirty one's hands

manchego, -a adj of o from La Mancha ▷ nm/f native o inhabitant of La Mancha

mancilla nf stain, blemish

manco, -a adj (con un brazo) one-armed; (con una mano) one-handed; (fig) defective, faulty; **no ser ~** to be useful o active

mancomunar vt to unite, bring together; (recursos) to pool; (Jur) to make jointly responsible

mancomunidad nf union, association; (comunidad) community; (Jur) joint responsibility

mandado nm (orden) order; (recado) commission, errand

mandamiento nm (orden) order, command; (Rel) commandment; **~ judicial** warrant

mandar vt (ordenar) to order; (dirigir) to lead, command; (país) to rule over; (enviar) to send; (pedir) to order, ask for ▷ vi to be in charge; (pey) to be bossy; **mandarse** vr: **~se mudar** (LAm fam) to go away, clear off; **el sargento le mandó barrer el patio** the sergeant ordered him to sweep the yard; **nos mandó callar** he told us to be quiet; **~ hacer un traje** to have a suit made; **~ a arreglar algo** (LAm) to have something repaired; **se lo ~emos por correo** we'll post it to you; **~ a algn a paseo** o **a la porra** to tell sb to go to hell; **el médico me mandó un jarabe** the doctor gave me a prescription for cough mixture; **~ llamar a alguien** (LAm) to send for someone; **aquí mando yo** I'm the boss here; **¿mande?** pardon?, excuse me? (US)

mandarín nm petty bureaucrat

mandarina nf (fruta) tangerine, mandarin (orange)

mandatario, -a nm/f (representante) agent; **primer ~** (esp LAm) head of state

mandato nm (orden) order; (Pol: período) term of office; (: territorio) mandate; (Inform) command; **~ judicial** (search) warrant

mandíbula nf jaw

mandil nm (delantal) apron

mando nm (Mil) command; (de país) rule; (el primer lugar) lead; (Pol) term of office; (Tec) control; **al ~ de** in charge of; **tomar el ~** to take the lead; **los altos ~s** the high command sg; **~ a distancia/ por botón** remote/push-button control; **~ a la izquierda** left-hand drive

mandolina nf mandolin(e)

mandón, -ona adj bossy, domineering

manejable adj manageable; (fácil de usar) handy

manejar vt (máquina) to work, operate; (caballo etc) to handle; (casa, empresa) to run, manage; (LAm Auto) to drive ▷ vi (LAm Auto) to drive; **manejarse** vr (comportarse) to act, behave; (arreglárselas) to manage; **"~ con cuidado"** "handle with care"

manejo nm (de máquina) handling; (de casa, empresa) running; (de coche) driving; (de idioma) command; (facilidad de trato) ease, confidence; **tengo un buen ~ del francés** I have a good command of French; **manejos** nmpl intrigues

manera nf way, manner, fashion; (Arte, Literatura etc: estilo) manner, style; **maneras** nfpl (modales) manners; **lo hice a mi ~** I did it my way; **su ~ de ser** (comportamiento) the way he is; (aire) his manner; **no hay ~ de persuadirle** there's no way of convincing him; **de mala ~** (fam) badly, unwillingly; **de ninguna ~** no way, by no means; **a mi ~ de ver** in my view; **de ~ que** (así que) so; (para que) so that; **no has hecho los deberes, de ~ que no hay tele** you haven't done your homework so there's no TV; **lo puse de ~ que pudieran verlo** I put it so that they could see it; **de otra ~** otherwise; **en gran ~** to a large extent; **sobre ~** exceedingly; **de todas ~s** anyway; **de todas ~s no habría podido ir** I wouldn't have been able to go anyway

manga nf (de camisa) sleeve; (de riego) hose; **de ~ corta/larga** short-/long-sleeved; **estar ~ por hombro** (desorden) to be topsy-turvy; **tener ~ ancha** to be easy-going

mangar vt (fam: birlar) to pinch, nick, swipe; (mendigar) to beg

mango nm (asa) handle; (Bot) mango; **~ de escoba** broomstick

mangonear vt to boss about ▷ vi to be bossy

manguera nf (de riego) hose; (tubo) pipe; **~ de incendios** fire hose

maní (pl **-es** o **manises**) (LAm: cacahuete) peanut; (: planta) groundnut plant

manía nf (Med) mania; (fig: costumbre) habit; (disgusto) dislike; (malicia) spite; **tiene ~s** she's a bit fussy; **tiene la ~ de repetir todo lo que digo** he has an irritating habit of repeating everything I say; **tener ~ a algn** to dislike sb; **el profesor me tiene ~** the teacher has it in for me

maníaco, -a adj maniac(al) ▷ nm/f maniac

maniatar vt to tie the hands of

maniático, -a adj maniac(al); (loco) crazy; (tiquismiquis) fussy ▷ nm/f maniac

manicomio nm mental hospital (Brit), insane asylum (US)

manicura nf manicure; ver tb **manicuro**

manicuro, -a nm/f manicurist; ver tb **manicura**

manifestación nf (declaración) statement, declaration; (demostración) show, display; (Pol) demonstration

manifestante nm/f demonstrator

manifestar vt to show, manifest; (declarar) to state, declare; **manifestarse** vr to show, become apparent; (Pol: desfilar) to demonstrate; (: reunirse) to hold a mass meeting

manifiesto adj clear, manifest ▷ nm manifesto; (Anat, Naut) manifest; **poner algo de ~** (aclarar) to make sth clear; (revelar) to reveal sth; **quedar ~** to be plain o clear

manija nf handle

manillar nm handlebars pl

maniobra nf (acción) manoevring; (manejo) handling; (fig: movimiento) manoevre, move; (: estratagema) trick, stratagem; **maniobras** nfpl manoevres

maniobrar *vt* to manoeuvre; (*manejar*) to handle
▷ *vi* to manoeuvre
manipulación *nf* manipulation; (*Com*) handling
manipular *vt* to manipulate; (*manejar*) to handle
maniquí *nm/f* model ▷ *nm* dummy
manirroto, -a *adj* lavish, extravagant ▷ *nm/f*
spendthrift
manitas *adj inv* good with one's hands ▷ *nm/f inv*:
ser un ~ to be very good with one's hands
manivela *nf* crank
manjar *nm* (tasty) dish
mano¹ *nf* (*Anat*) hand; (*Zool*) foot, paw; (*de pintura*)
coat; (*serie*) lot, series; **a ~ derecha/izquierda**
on (*o* to) the right(-hand side)/left(-hand side);
a ~ by hand; **hecho a ~** handmade; **a ~s llenas**
lavishly, generously; **de primera/segunda ~**
(at) first/second hand; **robo a ~ armada** armed
robbery; **Pedro es mi ~ derecha** Pedro is my
right-hand man; **darse la(s) ~(s)** to shake
hands; **echar una ~** to lend a hand; **echar una**
~ a to lay hands on; **echar ~ de** to make use of;
estrechar la ~ a algn to shake sb's hand; **traer**
o **llevar algo entre ~s** to deal *o* be busy with sth;
está en tus ~s it's up to you; **se le fue la ~** his
hand slipped; (*fig*) he went too far; **¡~s a la obra!**
to work!; **~ de obra** labour, manpower; **~ de**
santo sure remedy
mano² *nm* (*Méx fam*) friend, mate (*Brit*)
manojo *nm* handful, bunch; **~ de llaves** bunch
of keys
manopla *nf* (*paño*) flannel; **manoplas** *nfpl*
mittens
manoseado, -a *adj* well-worn
manosear *vt* (*tocar*) to handle, touch; (*desordenar*)
to mess up, rumple; (*insistir en*) to overwork;
(*acariciar*) to caress, fondle; (*pey: persona*) to feel *o*
touch up
manotazo *nm* slap, smack
mansalva: **a ~** *adv* indiscriminately
mansedumbre *nf* (*de persona*) gentleness,
meekness; (*de animal*) tameness
mansión *nf* mansion
manso, -a *adj* (*persona*) gentle, mild; (*animal*)
tame
manta *nf* blanket; (*And, Méx*) poncho
manteca *nf* (*grasa*) fat; (*RP*) butter; **~ de maní/**
cacao peanut/cocoa butter; **~ de cerdo** lard
mantecado *nm* traditional Christmas cake
mantel *nm* tablecloth
mantener *vt* (*soportar*) to support, maintain;
(*alimentar*) to sustain; (*conservar*) to keep; (*Tec*)
to maintain, service; **mantenerse** *vr* (*seguir de*
pie) to be still standing; (*no ceder*) to hold one's
ground; (*subsistir*) to sustain o.s., keep going; **~**
algo en equilibrio to keep sth balanced; **les**
mantendremos informados we'll keep you
informed; **mantiene a su familia** he supports
his family; **~ la calma** to keep calm; **~ una**
conversación to have a conversation; **~se a**
distancia to keep one's distance; **~se en forma**
to keep fit; **~se firme** to hold one's ground
mantenimiento *nm* (*conservación*) maintenance;

(*sustento*) support
mantequilla *nf* butter
mantilla *nf* mantilla; **mantillas** *nfpl* baby
clothes; **estar en ~s** (*persona*) to be terribly
innocent; (*proyecto*) to be in its infancy
manto *nm* (*capa*) cloak; (*de ceremonia*) robe, gown
mantón *nm* shawl
manual *adj* manual ▷ *nm* manual, handbook;
habilidad ~ manual skill
manubrio *nm* (*LAm Auto*) steering wheel
manufactura *nf* manufacture; (*fábrica*) factory
manufacturado, -a *adj* manufactured
manuscrito, -a *adj* handwritten ▷ *nm*
manuscript
manutención *nf* maintenance; (*sustento*)
support
manzana *nf* apple; (*Arq*) block; **~ de la discordia**
(*fig*) bone of contention
manzanilla *nf* (*planta*) camomile; (*infusión*)
camomile tea; (*vino*) manzanilla
manzano *nm* apple tree
maña *nf* (*gen*) skill, dexterity; (*pey*) guile;
(*costumbre*) habit; (*truco*) trick, knack; **con ~**
craftily
mañana *adv* tomorrow ▷ *nm* future ▷ *nf*
morning; **de** *o* **por la ~** in the morning; **¡hasta**
~! see you tomorrow!; **pasado ~** the day after
tomorrow; **~ por la ~** tomorrow morning
mañanero, -a *adj* early-rising
maño, -a *adj* Aragonese ▷ *nm/f* native *o*
inhabitant of Aragon
mañoso, -a *adj* (*hábil*) skilful; (*astuto*) smart,
clever
mapa *nm* map
maqueta *nf* (*scale*) model
maquillaje *nm* (*cosmético*) make-up; (*acto*)
making up
maquillar *vt* to make up; **maquillarse** *vr* to put
on (some) make-up
máquina *nf* machine; (*de tren*) locomotive,
engine; (*Foto*) camera; (*LAm: coche*) car; (*fig*)
machinery; (*: proyecto*) plan, project; **escrito a ~**
typewritten; **a toda ~** at full speed; **~ de escribir**
typewriter; **~ de coser/franqueo/lavar** sewing/
franking/washing machine; **~ de facsímil**
facsimile (machine), fax; **~ tragaperras** fruit
machine; (*Com*) slot machine
maquinación *nf* machination, plot
maquinal *adj* (*fig*) mechanical, automatic
maquinaria *nf* (*máquinas*) machinery;
(*mecanismo*) mechanism, works *pl*
maquinilla *nf* small machine; (*torno*) winch; **~**
de afeitar razor; **~ eléctrica** electric razor
maquinista *nm* (*Ferro*) engine driver (*Brit*),
engineer (*US*); (*Tec*) operator; (*Naut*) engineer
mar *nm* sea; **~ adentro** *o* **afuera** out at sea; **en**
alta ~ on the high seas; **por ~** by sea *o* boat;
hacerse a la ~ to put to sea; **a ~es** in abundance;
un ~ de lots of; **es la ~ de guapa** she is ever
so pretty; **el M~ Báltico/del Norte/Muerto/**
Negro/Rojo the Baltic/North/Dead/Black/Red
Sea; **~ de fondo** groundswell; **~ llena** high tide

maraca *nf* maraca
maraña *nf* (*maleza*) thicket; (*confusión*) tangle
maravilla *nf* marvel, wonder; (*Bot*) marigold;
hacer ~s to work wonders; **a (las mil) ~s**
wonderfully well
maravillar *vt* to astonish, amaze; **maravillarse**
vr to be astonished, be amazed
maravilloso, -a *adj* wonderful, marvellous
marca *nf* mark; (*sello*) stamp; (*Com*) make,
brand; (*de ganado*) brand; (: *acto*) branding; (*Naut*)
seamark; (: *boya*) marker; (*Deporte*) record; ~
de fábrica trademark; ~ **propia** own brand; ~
registrada registered trademark
marcado, -a *adj* marked, strong
marcador *nm* marker; (*rotulador*) marker
(pen); (*de libro*) bookmark; (*Deporte*) scoreboard;
(: *persona*) scorer
marcapasos *nm inv* pacemaker
marcar *vt* (*ropa, objetos personales*) to mark; (*número
de teléfono*) to dial; (*gol*) to score; (*números*) to
record, keep a tally of; (*pelo*) to set; (*ganado*) to
brand; (*termómetro*) to read, register; (: *tarea*)
to assign; (*Com*) to put a price on ▷ *vi* (*Deporte*)
to score; (*Telec*) to dial; **¿qué precio marca la
etiqueta?** what's the price (marked) on the
label?; **este reloj marca la hora exacta** this
watch keeps the right time; **mi reloj marca las
2** it's 2 o'clock by my watch, my watch says two
o'clock; **una vida marcada por el sufrimiento**
a life marked by suffering; ~ **el compás** (*Mus*) to
keep time; ~ **el paso** (*Mil*) to mark time
marcha *nf* (*partida*) departure; (*Mil, Mus*) march;
(*Deporte*) walk; (*Tec*) running, working; (*Auto*)
gear; (*velocidad*) speed; (*fig*) progress; (*dirección*)
course; **¡en ~!** (*Mil*) forward march!; (*fig*) let's
go!; **estar en ~** (*motor*) to be running; (*proyecto*)
to be underway; **no te subas nunca a un tren
en ~** never get onto a moving train; **poner en
~** to put into gear; **ponerse en ~** to start, get
going; **cambiar de ~** to change gear; **dar ~ atrás**
to reverse, put into reverse; **"~ moderada"**
(*Auto*) "drive slowly"; **a toda ~** at full speed; **a ~s
forzadas** (*fig*) with all speed; **hacer algo sobre
la ~** to do sth as you *etc* go along; **que tiene** o **de
mucha ~** (*fam*) very lively; **salir de ~** (*fam*) to go
out on the town
marchar *vi* (*ir*) to go; (*funcionar*) to work, go; (*fig*)
to go, proceed; **marcharse** *vr* to go (away), leave;
todo marcha bien everything is going well
marchitar *vt* to wither, dry up; **marchitarse** *vr*
(*Bot*) to wither; (*fig*) to fade away
marchito, -a *adj* withered, faded; (*fig*) in decline
marchoso, -a *adj* (*fam*: *animado*) lively; (: *moderno*)
modern
marcial *adj* martial, military
marciano, -a *adj* Martian, of o from Mars
marco *nm* frame; (*Deporte*) goalposts *pl*; (*moneda*)
mark; (*fig*) setting; (*contexto*) framework; ~ **de
chimenea** mantelpiece
marea *nf* tide; (*llovizna*) drizzle; ~ **alta/baja** high/
low tide; ~ **negra** oil slick
marear *vt* (*fig*: *irritar*) to annoy, upset; (*Med*): ~

a algn to make sb feel sick; **marearse** *vr* (*tener
náuseas*) to feel sick; (*desvanecerse*) to feel faint;
(*aturdirse*) to feel dizzy; (*fam*: *emborracharse*) to get
tipsy
maremoto *nm* tidal wave
mareo *nm* (*náusea*) sick feeling; (*aturdimiento*)
dizziness; (*fam*: *lata*) nuisance
marfil *nm* ivory
margarina *nf* margarine
margarita *nf* (*Bot*) daisy; (**rueda**) ~ (*en máquina
impresora*) daisy wheel
margen *nm* margin, space ▷ *nf* (*de río*) bank; (*de
camino*) side; **escribe las notas al ~** write your
notes in the margin; **dejar a algn al ~** to leave
sb out (in the cold); **mantenerse al ~** to keep out
(of things); **al ~ de lo que digas** despite what
you say; **dar ~ para** to give an opportunity for; ~
comercial mark-up; ~ **de beneficio** o **ganancia**
profit margin; ~ **de confianza** credibility gap
marginal *adj* (*tema, error*) minor; (*grupo*) fringe *cpd*;
(*anotación*) marginal
marginar *vt* to exclude
maría *nf* (*fam*: *mujer*) housewife
mariachi *nm* (*música*) mariachi music; (*grupo*)
mariachi band; (*persona*) mariachi player
marica *nm* (*fam*) sissy; (*homosexual*) queer
maricón *nm* (*fam*) queer
marido *nm* husband
marihuana *nf* marijuana, cannabis
marimacho *nf* (*fam*) mannish woman
marina *nf* navy; ~ **mercante** merchant navy
marinero, -a *adj* sea *cpd*; (*barco*) seaworthy ▷ *nm*
sailor, seaman
marino, -a *adj* sea *cpd*, marine ▷ *nm* sailor;
~ **de agua dulce/de cubierta/de primera**
landlubber/deckhand/able seaman
marioneta *nf* puppet
mariposa *nf* butterfly
mariquita *nm* (*fam*) sissy; (*homosexual*) queer ▷ *nf*
(*Zool*) ladybird (*Brit*), ladybug (*US*)
marisco *nm* (*tb*: **mariscos**) shellfish, seafood
marisma *nf* marsh, swamp
marítimo, -a *adj* sea *cpd*, maritime
marmita *nf* pot
mármol *nm* marble
marqués, -esa *nm/f* marquis (marchioness)
marranada *nf* (*fam*): **es una ~** that's disgusting;
hacer una ~ a algn to do the dirty on sb
marrano, -a *adj* filthy, dirty ▷ *nm* (*Zool*) pig;
(*malo*) swine; (*sucio*) dirty pig
marrón *adj* brown
marroquí *adj*, *nm/f* Moroccan ▷ *nm* Morocco
(leather)
Marruecos *nm* Morocco
martes *nm inv* Tuesday; ~ **de carnaval** Shrove
Tuesday
martillar, martillear *vt* to hammer
martillo *nm* hammer; (*de presidente de asamblea,
comité*) gavel; ~ **neumático** pneumatic drill
(*Brit*), jackhammer (*US*)
mártir *nm/f* martyr
martirio *nm* martyrdom; (*fig*) torture, torment

maruja *nf* (*fam*) = **maría**

marxismo *nm* Marxism

marxista *adj*, *nm/f* Marxist

marzo *nm* March

mas *conj* but

más *adj*, *adv* **1**: ~ **(que, de)** (*compar*) ...+ er (than), more (than); ~ **grande/inteligente** bigger/more intelligent; **este bolígrafo es ~ caro que el mío** this pen's more expensive than mine; **trabaja ~ (que yo)** he works more (than me); **corre ~ rápido que yo** he runs faster than I do; ~ **de 6** more than 6; ~ **de lo que yo creía** more than I thought; **es ~ de medianoche** it's after midnight; **durar ~** to last longer; *ver tb* **cada**
2 (*superl*): **el ~** the most, ...+ est; **el ~ grande/inteligente (de)** the biggest/most intelligent (in); **el bolígrafo ~ barato** the cheapest pen; **el niño ~ pequeño** the youngest child
3 (*uso negativo*): **no tengo ~ dinero** I haven't got any more money; **no viene ~ por aquí** he doesn't come round here any more; **no sé ~** I don't know any more, that's all I know
4 (*adicional*): **un kilómetro ~** one more kilometre; **no le veo ~ solución que ...** I see no other solution than to ...; **¿algo ~?** anything else?; **¿quién ~?** anybody else?
5 (+ *adj*: *valor intensivo*): **¡qué perro ~ sucio!** what a filthy dog!; **¡es ~ tonto!** he's so stupid!
6 (*locuciones*): ~ **o menos** more or less; **los ~** most people; **es ~** in fact, furthermore; ~ **bien** rather; **¡qué ~ da!** what does it matter!; *ver tb* **no**
7: **por ~**: **por ~ que lo intento** no matter how much *o* hard I try; **por ~ que quisiera ayudar** much as I should like to help
8: **de ~**: **veo que aquí estoy de ~** I can see I'm not needed here; **tenemos uno de ~** we've got one extra
9 (*LAm*): **no ~** only, just; **ayer no ~** just yesterday ▷ *prep*: **2 ~ 2 son 4** 2 and *o* plus 2 are 4 ▷ *nm inv*: **este trabajo tiene sus ~ y sus menos** this job's got its good points and its bad points

masa *nf* (*mezcla*) dough; (*volumen*) volume, mass; (*Física*) mass; **en ~** en masse; **las ~s** (*Pol*) the masses

masacre *nf* massacre

masaje *nm* massage; **dar ~ a** to massage

mascar *vt*, *vi* to chew; (*fig*) to mumble, mutter

máscara *nf* (*tb Inform*) mask ▷ *nm/f* masked person; ~ **antigás** gas mask

mascarada *nf* masquerade

mascarilla *nf* mask; (*vaciado*) deathmask; (*de maquillaje*) face pack

mascota *nf* mascot

masculino, -a *adj* masculine; (*Bio*) male ▷ *nm* (*Ling*) masculine

mascullar *vt* to mumble, mutter

masificación *nf* overcrowding

masilla *nf* putty

masivo, -a *adj* (*en masa*) mass

masón *nm* (free)mason

masoquista *adj* masochistic ▷ *nm/f* masochist

mastectomía *nf* mastectomy

máster (*pl* **masters**) *nm* postgraduate degree

masticar *vt* to chew; (*fig*) to ponder over

mástil *nm* (*de navío*) mast; (*de guitarra*) neck

mastín *nm* mastiff

masturbación *nf* masturbation

masturbarse *vr* to masturbate

mata *nf* (*arbusto*) bush, shrub; (*de hierbas*) tuft; (*campo*) field; (*manojo*) tuft, blade; **matas** *nfpl* scrub *sg*; ~ **de pelo** mop of hair; **a salto de ~** (*día a día*) from day to day; (*al azar*) haphazardly

matadero *nm* slaughterhouse, abattoir

matador, a *adj* killing ▷ *nm/f* killer ▷ *nm* (*Taur*) matador, bullfighter

matamoscas *nm inv* (*palo*) fly swat

matanza *nf* slaughter

matar *vt* to kill; ~ **el tiempo** to kill time ▷ *vi* to kill; **el jefe me va a ~** the boss will kill me; ~ **el hambre** to stave off hunger; ~ **a algn a disgustos** to make sb's life a misery; ~ **las callando** to go about things slyly; **matarse** *vr* (*suicidarse*) to kill o.s., commit suicide; (*morir*) to be *o* get killed; (*gastarse*) to wear o.s. out; ~**se trabajando** to kill o.s. with work; ~**se por hacer algo** to struggle to do sth

matasellos *nm inv* postmark

mate *adj* (*sin brillo: color*) dull, matt ▷ *nm* (*en ajedrez*) (check)mate; (*LAm: hierba*) maté; (: *vasija*) gourd

matemáticas *nfpl* mathematics *sg*

matemático, -a *adj* mathematical ▷ *nm/f* mathematician

materia *nf* (*gen*) matter; (*Tec*) material; (*Escol*) subject; **en ~ de** on the subject of; (*en cuanto a*) as regards; **entrar en ~** to get down to business; ~ **prima** raw material

material *adj* material; (*dolor*) physical; (*real*) real; (*literal*) literal ▷ *nm* material; (*Tec*) equipment; ~ **de construcción** building material; ~**es de derribo** rubble *sg*

materialismo *nm* materialism

materialista *adj* materialist(ic)

materialmente *adv* materially; (*fig*) absolutely

maternal *adj* motherly, maternal

maternidad *nf* motherhood, maternity

materno, -a *adj* maternal; (*lengua*) mother *cpd*

matinal *adj* morning *cpd*

matiz *nm* shade; (*de sentido*) shade, nuance; (*de ironía*) touch

matizar *vt* (*variar*) to vary; (*Arte*) to blend; ~ **de** to tinge with

matón *nm* bully

matorral *nm* thicket

matraca *nf* rattle; (*fam*) nuisance

matrícula *nf* (*registro*) register; (*Escol: inscripción*) registration; (*Auto*) registration number; (: *placa*) number plate

matricular *vt* to register, enrol

matrimonial *adj* matrimonial

matrimonio *nm* (*pareja*) (married) couple; (*acto*) marriage; **contraer ~ (con)** to marry; ~ **civil/clandestino** civil/secret marriage

matriz *nf* (*Anat*) womb; (*Tec*) mould; (*Mat*) matrix; **casa ~** (*Com*) head office

matrona *nf* (*mujer de edad*) matron
maullar *vi* to mew, miaow
mausoleo *nm* mausoleum
maxilar *nm* jaw(bone)
máxima *nf* maxim; *ver tb* **máximo**
máxime *adv* especially
máximo, -a *adj* maximum; (*más alto*) highest; (*más grande*) greatest ▷ *nm* maximum; **~ jefe** *o* **líder** (*LAm*) President, leader; **como ~** at most; **al ~** to the utmost; *ver tb* **máxima**
maxisingle *nm* twelve-inch (single)
maya *adj* Mayan ▷ *nm/f* Maya(n)
mayo *nm* May
mayonesa *nf* mayonnaise
mayor *adj* (*principal*) main, chief; (*adulto*) grown-up, adult; (*Jur*) of age; (*de edad avanzada*) elderly; (*Mus*) major ▷ *compar* (*de tamaño*) bigger; (: *de edad*) older ▷ *superl* (*de tamaño*) biggest; (*tb fig*) greatest; (: *de edad*) oldest ▷ *nm* (*adulto*) adult; (*Mil*) major; **nuestros hijos ya son ~es** our children are grown-up now; **la gente ~** the elderly; **mi casa es ~ que la suya** my house is bigger than his; **Paco es ~ que Nacho** Paco is older than Nacho; **es tres años ~ que yo** he is three years older than me; **el hermano ~** (*de dos*) the older *o* elder brother; (*de más de dos*) the oldest *o* eldest brother; **Emilio es el ~ de los dos** Emilio is the older *o* elder of the two; **Juan es el ~ de todos** Juan is the oldest *o* eldest ▷ *adv*: **al por ~** wholesale; **~ de edad** adult; *ver tb* **mayores**
mayoral *nm* foreman
mayordomo *nm* butler
mayores *nmpl* grown-ups; **llegar a ~** (*fig*) to get out of hand
mayoría *nf* majority, greater part; **en la ~ de los casos** in most cases; **en su ~** on the whole
mayorista *nm/f* wholesaler
mayoritario, -a *adj* majority *cpd*; **gobierno ~** majority government
mayúsculo, -a *adj* (*fig*) big, tremendous ▷ *nf* capital (letter); **mayúsculas** *nfpl* capitals; (*Tip*) upper case *sg*
mazapán *nm* marzipan
mazo *nm* (*martillo*) mallet; (*de mortero*) pestle; (*de flores*) bunch; (*Deporte*) bat
me *pron* (*directo*) me; (*indirecto*) (to) me; (*reflexivo*) (to) myself; **me quiere** he loves me; **¡dámelo!** give it to me!; **me lo compró** (*de mí*) he bought it from me; (*para mí*) he bought it for me; **me duelen los pies** my feet hurt; **me puse el abrigo** I put my coat on
meandro *nm* meander
mear (*fam*) *vt* to piss on (!) ▷ *vi* to pee, piss (!), have a piss (!); **mearse** *vr* to wet o.s.
mecánica *nf* (*estudio*) mechanics *sg*; (*mecanismo*) mechanism; *ver tb* **mecánico**
mecánico, -a *adj* mechanical; (*repetitivo*) repetitive ▷ *nm/f* mechanic; *ver tb* **mecánica**
mecanismo *nm* mechanism; (*engranaje*) gear
mecanografía *nf* typewriting
mecanógrafo, -a *nm/f* (*copy*) typist
mecate *nm* (*CAm, Méx*) rope

mecer *vt* (*cuna*) to rock; **mecerse** *vr* to rock; (*rama*) to sway
mecha *nf* (*de vela*) wick; (*de bomba*) fuse; **a toda ~** at full speed; **ponerse ~s** to streak one's hair
mechero *nm* (cigarette) lighter
mechón *nm* (*gen*) tuft; (*manojo*) bundle; (*de pelo*) lock
medalla *nf* medal
media *nf* (*prenda de vestir*) stocking; (*LAm*) sock; (*promedio*) average; **medias** *nfpl* tights; **lo dejó a ~s** he left it half-done; **ir a ~s** to go fifty-fifty; *ver tb* **medio**
mediación *nf* mediation; **por ~ de** through
mediado, -a *adj* half-full; (*trabajo*) half-completed; **a ~s de** in the middle of, halfway through
mediana *nf* (*Aut*) central reservation, median (*US*); *ver tb* **mediano**
mediano, -a *adj* (*regular*) medium, average; (*mediocre*) mediocre; **(de tamaño) ~** medium-sized; *ver tb* **mediana**
medianoche *nf* midnight
mediante *adv* by (means of), through
mediar *vi* (*tiempo*) to elapse; (*interceder*) to mediate, intervene; (*existir*) to exist; **media el hecho de que ...** there is the fact that ...
medicación *nf* medication, treatment
medicamento *nm* medicine, drug
medicina *nf* medicine
medicinal *adj* medicinal
medición *nf* measurement
médico, -a *adj* medical ▷ *nm/f* doctor; **~ de cabecera** family doctor; **~ pediatra** paediatrician; **~ residente** house physician, intern (*US*)
medida *nf* measure; (*medición*) measurement; (*de camisa, zapato etc*) size, fitting; (*moderación*) moderation, prudence; **~s de seguridad** security measures; **tomar ~s** to take measures, take steps; **tomar ~s contra la inflación** to take measures against inflation; **un traje a la ~** a made-to-measure suit; **el sastre le tomó las ~s** the tailor took his measurements; **con ~** with restraint; **sin ~** immoderately; **en cierta/gran ~** up to a point/to a great extent; **a ~ de** in proportion to; (*de acuerdo con*) in keeping with; **a ~ que ...** (at the same time) as ...; **saludaba a los invitados a ~ que iban llegando** he greeted the guests as they arrived; **~ de cuello** collar size
medieval *adj* medieval
medio, -a *adj* half (a); (*punto*) mid, middle; (*promedio*) average ▷ *adv* half-; (*esp LAm: un tanto*) rather, quite ▷ *nm* (*centro*) middle, centre; (*método*) means, way; (*ambiente*) environment; **media hora** half an hour; **~ litro** half a litre; **las tres y media** half past three; **M~ Oriente** Middle East; **a ~ camino** halfway (there); **~ dormido** half asleep; **~ enojado** (*esp LAm*) rather annoyed; **a ~ terminar** half finished; **en ~** in the middle; (*entre*) in between; **por ~ de** by (means of), through; **en los ~s financieros** in financial circles; **encontrarse en su ~** to be in

one's element; ~ **ambiente** environment; ~
circulante (*Com*) money supply; *ver tb* **media**;
medios

medioambiental *adj* environmental

mediocre *adj* middling, average; (*pey*) mediocre

mediodía *nm* midday, noon

medios *nmpl* means, resources; **los ~ de
comunicación** the media

medir *vt* (*gen*) to measure ▷ *vi* to measure;
medirse *vr* (*moderarse*) to be moderate, act with
restraint; **¿cuánto mides? — mido 1,50 m** how
tall are you? — I am 1.50 m tall

meditabundo, -a *adj* pensive

meditar *vt* to ponder, think over, meditate
on; (*planear*) to think out ▷ *vi* to ponder, think,
meditate

mediterráneo, -a *adj* Mediterranean ▷ *nm:* **el
(mar) M~** the Mediterranean (Sea)

médula *nf* (*Anat*) marrow; (*Bot*) pith; **hasta la ~**
(*fig*) to the core; **~ espinal** spinal cord

medusa *nf* (*Esp*) jellyfish

megafonía *nf* PA, public address system

megáfono *nm* megaphone

megalómano, -a *nm/f* megalomaniac

mejicano, -a *adj, nm/f* Mexican

Méjico *nm* Mexico

mejilla *nf* cheek

mejillón *nm* mussel

mejor *adj, adv* (*compar*) better; (*superl*) best; **éste
es ~ que el otro** this one is better than the other
one; **es el ~ de los dos** he's the better of the two;
mi ~ amiga my best friend; **el ~ de la clase** the
best in the class; **es el ~ de todos** he's the best of
all; **lo ~** the best thing; **lo ~ de la vida** the prime
of life; **la conozco ~ que tú** I know her better
than you do; **a lo ~** probably; (*quizá*) maybe; **~
dicho** rather; **tanto ~** so much the better; **~ nos
vamos** we had better go

mejora *nf*, **mejoramiento** *nm* improvement

mejorar *vt* to improve, make better ▷ *vi:*
mejorarse *vr* to improve, get better; (*Com*) to do
well, prosper; **los negocios mejoran** business is
picking up; **~ a** to be better than

mejunje *nm* (*pey*) concoction

melancolía *nf* melancholy

melancólico, -a *adj* (*triste*) sad, melancholy;
(*soñador*) dreamy

melena *nf* (*de persona*) long hair; (*Zool*) mane

mellizo, -a *adj, nm/f* twin

melocotón *nm* (*Esp*) peach

melodía *nf* melody; (*tonada*) tune

melodrama *nm* melodrama

melodramático, -a *adj* melodramatic

melón *nm* melon

meloso, -a *adj* honeyed, sweet; (*empalagoso*)
sickly, cloying; (*voz*) sweet; (*zalamero*) smooth

membrana *nf* membrane

membrete *nm* letterhead; **papel con ~** headed
notepaper

membrillo *nm* quince; **carne de ~** quince jelly

memorable *adj* memorable

memorándum *nm* (*libro*) notebook; (*comunicación*)
memorandum

memoria *nf* (*tb Inform*) memory; (*artículo*)
(learned) paper; **memorias** *nfpl* (*Lit*) memoirs;
tener mala ~ to have a bad memory; **aprender
algo de ~** to learn sth by heart; **venir a la ~**
to come to mind; **~ anual** annual report; **~
auxiliar** backing storage; **~ de acceso aleatorio**
random access memory, RAM; **~ fija** read-only
memory, ROM

memorizar *vt* to memorize

menaje *nm* (*muebles*) furniture; (*utensilios
domésticos*) household equipment; **~ de cocina**
kitchenware

mención *nf* mention; **digno de ~** noteworthy;
hacer ~ de to mention

mencionar *vt* to mention; (*nombrar*) to name;
sin ~ ... let alone ...

mendigar *vt* to beg (for)

mendigo, -a *nm/f* beggar

mendrugo *nm* crust

menear *vt* to move; (*cola*) to wag; (*cadera*) to
swing; (*fig*) to handle; **menearse** *vr* to shake;
(*balancearse*) to sway; (*moverse*) to move; (*fig*) to get
a move on

menester *nm* (*necesidad*) necessity; **es ~ hacer
algo** it is necessary to do sth, sth must be done;
menesteres *nmpl* (*deberes*) duties

menestra *nf:* **~ de verduras** vegetable stew

menguante *adj* decreasing, diminishing; (*luna*)
waning; (*marea*) ebb *cpd*

menguar *vt* to lessen, diminish; (*fig*) to discredit
▷ *vi* to diminish, decrease; (*fig*) to decline

menopausia *nf* menopause

menor *adj* (*más pequeño: compar*) smaller; (*número*)
less, lesser; (: *superl*) smallest; (*número*) least; (*más
joven: compar*) younger; (: *superl*) youngest; (*Mus*)
minor ▷ *adv:* **al por ~** retail ▷ *nm/f* (*joven*) young
person, juvenile; **mi casa es ~ que la suya** my
house is smaller than hers; **es tres años ~ que
yo** he's three years younger than me; **Manuel
es ~ que Pepe** Manuel is younger than Pepe; **el
hermano ~** (*de dos*) the younger brother; (*de más
de dos*) the youngest brother; **Emilio es el ~ de
los dos** Emilio is the younger of the two; **ella
es la ~ de todas** she is the youngest of all; **no
tengo la ~ idea** I haven't the faintest idea; **~ de
edad** under age; **un ~ de edad** a minor; **los ~es**
the under-18s

Menorca *nf* Minorca

menos *adj* **1** (*compar: con sustantivos incontables*)
less; (*con sustantivos contables*) fewer; **con ~
entusiasmo** with less enthusiasm; **~ harina**
less flour; **~ gente** fewer people; **~ que** fewer
than; **A tiene ~ ventajas que B** A has fewer
advantages than B; *ver tb* **cada**

2 (*superl: con sustantivos incontables*) least; (*con
sustantivos contables*) fewest; **es el que ~ culpa
tiene** he is the least to blame; **el método que
lleva ~ tiempo** the method which takes the
least time; **donde ~ problemas hay** where
there are fewest problems; **el examen con
~ errores** the exam paper with the fewest

mistakes

▷ adv **1** (comparativo) less; **Fernando está ~ cansado** Fernando is less tired; **ahora salgo ~** I go out less these days; **~ aún** even less; **este me gusta ~ aún** I like this one even less; **~ de** (con sustantivos incontables) less than; (con sustantivos contables) fewer than; **~ de 5** less than 5; **~ de lo que piensas** less than you think; **~ de 50 cajas** fewer than 50 boxes; **~ que** less than; **me gusta ~ que el otro** I like it less than the other one; **lo hizo ~ cuidadosamente que ayer** he did it less carefully than yesterday

2 (superlativo) least; **su película ~ innovadora** his least innovative film; **es el ~ listo (de su clase)** he's the least bright (in his class); **de todas ellas es la que ~ me agrada** out of all of them she's the one I like least; **fue el que ~ trabajó** he was the one who worked the least hard

3 (locuciones): **no quiero verlo y ~ visitarlo** I don't want to see him let alone visit him; **al ~** o **por lo ~ at** (the very) least; **si al ~** if only; **eso es lo de ~** that's the least of it; **es lo ~ que puedo hacer** it's the least I can do; **lo ~ posible** as little as possible; **tenemos 7 (de) ~** we're 7 short; **¡~ mal!** thank goodness!; **¡~ mal que habéis venido!** thank goodness you've come!

▷ prep except; (con cifras) minus; **todos ~ él** everyone except (for) him; **¡todo ~ eso!** anything but that!; **5 ~ 2** 5 minus 2; **las 7 ~ 20** (hora) 20 to 7

▷ conj **a ~ que** unless ...; **a ~ que venga mañana** unless he comes tomorrow

menoscabar vt (estropear) to damage, harm; (fig) to discredit

menospreciar vt to underrate, undervalue; (despreciar) to scorn, despise

mensaje nm message; **~ de error** (Inform) error message; **~ de texto** text message

mensajero, -a nm/f messenger

menstruación nf menstruation

menstruar vi to menstruate

mensual adj monthly; **500 dólares ~es** 500 dollars a month

mensualidad nf (salario) monthly salary; (Com) monthly payment o instalment

menta nf mint

mental adj mental

mentalidad nf mentality, way of thinking

mentalizar vt (sensibilizar) to make aware; (convencer) to convince; (preparar mentalmente) to psych up; **mentalizarse** vr (concienciarse) to become aware; (prepararse mentalmente) to get psyched up; **~se de que ...** (convencerse) to get it into one's head that ...

mentar vt to mention, name; **~ la madre a algn** to swear at sb

mente nf mind; (inteligencia) intelligence; **no tengo en ~ hacer eso** it is not my intention to do that

mentecato, -a adj silly, stupid ▷ nm/f fool, idiot

mentir vi to lie; **¡miento!** sorry, I'm wrong!

mentira nf (cosa dicha) lie; (acto) lying; (invención)

fiction; **una ~ como una casa** a whopping great lie (fam); **parece ~ que ...** it seems incredible that ..., I can't believe that ...; **~ piadosa** white lie

mentiroso, -a adj lying; (falso) deceptive ▷ nm/f liar

menú nm (tb Inform) menu; (en restaurante) set meal; **guiado por ~** (Inform) menu-driven; **menu del día** set meal

menudo, -a adj (pequeño) small, tiny; (sin importancia) petty, insignificant; **¡~ negocio!** (fam) some deal!; **a ~** often, frequently

meñique nm little finger

meollo nm (fig) essence, core

mercado nm market; **M~ Común** Common Market; **~ de demanda** seller's market; **~ de oferta** buyer's market; **~ de productos básicos** commodity market; **~ de valores** stock market; **~ en baja** falling market; **~ exterior/interior** overseas/home market; **~ laboral/libre** labour/ free market; **~ nacional/objetivo** home/target market

mercancía nf commodity; **mercancías** nfpl goods, merchandise sg; **~s en depósito/ perecederas** bonded/perishable goods

mercantil adj mercantile, commercial

mercenario, -a adj, nm mercenary

mercería nf (artículos) haberdashery (Brit), notions pl (US); (tienda) haberdasher's shop (Brit), drapery (Brit), notions store (US)

mercurio nm mercury

merecer vt to deserve, merit ▷ vi to be deserving, be worthy; **merece la pena** it's worthwhile

merecido, -a adj (well) deserved; **llevarse su ~** to get one's deserts

merendar vt to have for tea ▷ vi to have tea; (en el campo) to have a picnic

merengue nm meringue

meridiano nm (Astro, Geo) meridian; **la explicación es de una claridad meridiana** the explanation is as clear as day

merienda nf (light) tea, afternoon snack; (de campo) picnic; **~ de negros** free-for-all

mérito nm merit; (valor) worth, value; **hacer ~s** to make a good impression; **restar ~ a** to detract from

merluza nf hake; **coger una ~** (fam) to get sozzled (fam)

merma nf decrease; (pérdida) wastage

mermar vt to reduce, lessen ▷ vi to decrease, dwindle

mermelada nf jam; **~ de naranja** marmalade

mero, -a adj mere, simple; (CAm, Méx fam) real ▷ adv (LAm) just, right ▷ nm (Zool) grouper; **el ~ ~** (CAm, Méx fam) the boss

merodear vi (Mil) to maraud; (de noche) to prowl (about); (curiosear) to snoop around

mes nm month; (salario) month's pay; **el ~ corriente** this o the current month

mesa nf table; (de trabajo) desk; (Com) counter; (en mitin) platform; (Geo) plateau; (Arq) landing; **poner/quitar la ~** to lay/clear the table; **~ de**

noche/operaciones/tijera bedside/operating/ folding table; **~ digitalizadora** (*Inform*) graph pad; **~ directiva** board; **~ redonda** (*reunión*) round table; **~ y cama** bed and board
mesero, -a *nm/f* (*LAm*) waiter/waitress
meseta *nf* (*Geo*) meseta, tableland; (*Arq*) landing
mesilla, mesita *nf*: **~ de noche** bedside table
mesón *nm* inn
mestizo, -a *adj* half-caste, of mixed race; (*Zool*) crossbred ▷ *nm/f* half-caste
mesura *nf* (*calma*) calm; (*moderación*) moderation, restraint; (*cortesía*) courtesy
meta *nf* goal; (*de carrera*) finish; (*fig*) goal, aim, objective
metabolismo *nm* metabolism
metáfora *nf* metaphor
metal *nm* (*materia*) metal; (*Mus*) brass
metálico, -a *adj* metallic; (*de metal*) metal ▷ *nm* (*dinero contante*) cash
metalurgia *nf* metallurgy
metedura *nf*: **~ de pata** (*fam*) blunder
meteorito *nm* meteorite
meteoro *nm* meteor
meteorología *nf* meteorology
meter *vt* (*colocar*) to put, place; (*introducir*) to put in, insert; (*involucrar*) to involve; (*causar*) to make; (*Deporte*) to score; (*Auto: marcha*) to go into; **meterse** *vr*: **~se en** (*entrar*) to go into, enter; (*entrometerse*) to interfere in, meddle in; **¿dónde has metido las llaves?** where have you put the keys?; **metió la mano en el bolsillo** she put her hand in(to) her pocket; **~ dinero en el banco** to put money in the bank; **~ a algn en la cárcel** to put sb in prison; **él me metió en el negocio** he got me involved in the business; **~ ruido** to make a noise; **~ miedo a algn** to scare o frighten sb; **~ prisa a algn** to hurry sb; **¡no me metas prisa!** don't rush me!; **~ un gol** to score a goal; **a todo ~** (*fam*) as fast as possible; **está lloviendo a todo ~** it's pelting with rain, it's pelting down; **se metió en la cueva** he went into the cave; **~se en líos** to get into trouble; **~se en política** to go into politics; **no te metas donde no te llaman** don't poke your nose in where it doesn't belong; **~se a** to start; **~se a escritor** to become a writer; **~se con algn** to provoke sb, pick a quarrel with sb
meticuloso, -a *adj* meticulous, thorough
metódico, -a *adj* methodical
metodismo *nm* Methodism
método *nm* method
metodología *nf* methodology
metralla *nf* shrapnel
metralleta *nf* sub-machine-gun
métrico, -a *adj* metric ▷ *nf* metrics *pl*; **cinta métrica** tape measure
metro *nm* metre; (*tren: tb:* **metropolitano**) underground (*Brit*), subway (*US*); (*cinta*) tape measure; **~ cuadrado/cúbico** square/cubic metre
metrópoli, metrópolis *nf* (*ciudad*) metropolis; (*colonial*) mother country

México *nm* (*LAm*) Mexico; **Ciudad de ~** Mexico City
mezcla *nf* mixture; (*fig*) blend
mezclar *vt* (*revolver*) to mix (up); (*armonizar*) to blend; (*combinar*) to merge; **mezclarse** *vr* to mix, mingle; **hay que ~ el azúcar y la harina** you need to mix the sugar and the flour; **~se en algo** to get mixed up in something
mezquino, -a *adj* (*cicatero*) mean ▷ *nm/f* (*avaro*) mean person; (*miserable*) petty individual
mezquita *nf* mosque
mg. *abr* (= *miligramo(s)*) mg.
mi *adj posesivo* my ▷ *nm* (*Mus*) E
mí *pron* me, myself; **¿y a mí qué?** so what?
miaja *nf* crumb; **ni una ~** (*fig*) not the least little bit
miau *nm* miaow
michelín *nm* (*fam*) spare tyre
micro *nm* (*Radio*) mike, microphone; (*LAm: pequeño*) minibus; (: *grande*) coach, bus
microbio *nm* microbe
microbús *nm* minibus
microfilm (*pl* **-s**) *nm* microfilm
micrófono *nm* microphone
microonda *nf* microwave; (**horno**) **~s** microwave (oven)
microscópico, -a *adj* microscopic
microscopio *nm* microscope
miedo *nm* fear; (*nerviosismo*) apprehension, nervousness; **¡qué ~!** (*fam*) how awful!; **me da ~** it scares me; **meter ~ a** to scare, frighten; **tener ~** to be afraid; **de ~** wonderful, marvellous; **hace un frío de ~** (*fam*) it's terribly cold
miedoso, -a *adj* fearful, timid
miel *nf* honey; **no hay ~ sin hiel** there's no rose without a thorn
miembro *nm* limb; (*socio*) member; (*de institución*) fellow; **~ viril** penis
mientes *nfpl*: **no parar ~ en** to pay no attention to; **traer a las ~** to recall
mientras *conj* while; (*duración*) as long as ▷ *adv* meanwhile; **~ (que)** whereas; **~ tanto** meanwhile; **~ más tiene, más quiere** the more he has, the more he wants
miércoles *nm inv* Wednesday; **~ de ceniza** Ash Wednesday
mierda *nf* (*fam!*) shit (!), crap (!); (*fig*) filth, dirt; **¡vete a la ~!** go to hell!
miga *nf* crumb; (*fig: meollo*) essence; **hacer buenas ~s** (*fam*) to get on well; **esto tiene su ~** there's more to this than meets the eye
migaja *nf*: **una ~ de** (*un poquito*) a little; **migajas** *nfpl* crumbs; (*pey*) left-overs
migración *nf* migration
migratorio, -a *adj* migratory
mil *num* a o one thousand; **dos ~ libras** two thousand pounds
milagro *nm* miracle; **hacer ~s** (*fig*) to work wonders
milagroso, -a *adj* miraculous
milésimo, -a *num* thousandth
mili *nf*: **hacer la ~** (*fam*) to do one's military

service

milicia *nf* (*Mil*) militia; (*servicio militar*) military service

miligramo *nm* milligram

milímetro *nm* millimetre (*Brit*), millimeter (*US*)

militante *adj* militant

militar *adj* military ▷ *nm* soldier f ▷ *vi* to serve in the army; (*fig*) to militate, fight

militarismo *nm* militarism

milla *nf* mile; **~ marina** nautical mile

millar *num* thousand; **a ~es** in thousands

millón *num* million

millonario, -a *nm/f* millionaire

mimar *vt* to spoil, pamper

mimbre *nm* wicker; **de ~** wicker *cpd*, wickerwork

mímica *nf* (*para comunicarse*) sign language; (*imitación*) mimicry

mimo *nm* (*caricia*) caress; (*de niño*) spoiling; (*Teat*) mime; (: *actor*) mime artist

mina *nf* mine; (*pozo*) shaft; (*de lápiz*) lead refill; **~ de carbón** coalmine

minar *vt* to mine; (*fig*) to undermine

mineral *adj* mineral ▷ *nm* (*Geo*) mineral; (*mena*) ore

minero, -a *adj* mining *cpd* ▷ *nm/f* miner

miniatura *adj inv, nf* miniature

minicadena *nf* (*Mus*) mini hi-fi

MiniDisc® *nm* MiniDisc

minifalda *nf* miniskirt

minifundio *nm* smallholding, small farm

minimizar *vt* to minimize

mínimo, -a *adj* (*muy pequeño*) minimum; (*insignificante*) minimal ▷ *nm* minimum; **precio/salario ~** minimum price/wage; **no tienes ni la más mínima idea** you haven't the faintest idea; **lo ~ que pueden hacer** the least they can do; **un ~ de 20 euros** a minimum of 20 euros; **como ~ podrías haber llamado** you could at least have called

minino, -a *nm/f* (*fam*) puss, pussy

ministerio *nm* ministry (*Brit*), department (*US*); **M~ de Asuntos Exteriores** Foreign Office (*Brit*), State Department (*US*); **M~ de Comercio e Industria** Department of Trade and Industry; **M~ de Hacienda** Treasury (*Brit*), Treasury Department (*US*); **M~ del Interior** ≈ Home Office (*Brit*), Ministry of the Interior

ministro, -a *nm/f* minister, secretary (*esp US*); **M~ de Hacienda** Chancellor of the Exchequer, Secretary of the Treasury (*US*); **M~ del Interior** ≈ Home Secretary (*Brit*), Secretary of the Interior (*US*)

minoría *nf* minority

minorista *nm* retailer

minucioso, -a *adj* thorough, meticulous; (*prolijo*) very detailed

minúsculo, -a *adj* tiny, minute ▷ *nf* small letter; **minúsculas** *nfpl* (*Tip*) lower case *sg*

minusválido, -a *adj* (*physically*) handicapped *o* disabled ▷ *nm/f* disabled person

minuta *nf* (*de comida*) menu; (*de abogado etc*) fee

minutero *nm* minute hand

minuto *nm* minute

mío, -a *adj, pron*: **el ~** mine; **un amigo ~** a friend of mine; **lo ~** what is mine; **los ~s** my people, my relations

miope *adj* short-sighted

miopía *nf* near- *o* short-sightedness

mira *nf* (*de arma*) sight(s) *pl*; (*fig*) aim, intention; **de amplias/estrechas ~s** broad-/narrow-minded

mirada *nf* (*acto*) look, glance; (*expresión*) look, expression; **con una ~ de odio** with a look of hatred; **echar una ~ a algo** to have a look at sth; **¿has tenido tiempo de echarle una ~ a mi informe?** have you had time to have a look at my report?; **levantar/bajar la ~** to look up/down; **resistir la ~ de algn** to stare sb out; **~ de soslayo** sidelong glance; **~ fija** stare, gaze; **~ perdida** distant look

mirado, -a *adj* (*sensato*) sensible; (*considerado*) considerate; **bien/mal ~** well/not well thought of

mirador *nm* viewpoint, vantage point

mirar *vt* (*gen*) to look at; (*observar*) to watch; (*considerar*) to consider, think over; (*vigilar, cuidar*) to watch, look after ▷ *vi* to look; (*Arq*) to face; **mirarse** *vr* (*dos personas*) to look at each other; **mira esta foto** look at this photo; **¡mira! un ratón** look! a mouse; **~ algo/a algn de reojo** *o* **de través** to look askance at sth/sb; **~ algo/a algn por encima del hombro** to look down on sth/sb; **~ algo/a algn fijamente** to stare *o* gaze at sth/sb; **~ bien a algn** to think highly of sb; **~ mal a algn** to have a poor opinion of sb; **mira a ver si está ahí** look and see if he is there; **~ por la ventana** to look out of the window; **~ por algn** to look after sb; **¡mira que es tonto!** what an idiot!; **se ~on asombrados** they looked at each other in amazement; **~se a los ojos** to look into each other's eyes; **~se al espejo** to look at o.s. in the mirror

mirilla *nf* (*agujero*) spyhole, peephole

mirlo *nm* blackbird

misa *nf* mass; **como en ~** in dead silence; **estos datos van a ~** (*fig*) these facts are utterly trustworthy; **~ del gallo** midnight mass (*on Christmas Eve*); **~ de difuntos** requiem mass

miserable *adj* (*avaro*) mean, stingy; (*nimio*) miserable, paltry; (*lugar*) squalid; (*fam*) vile, despicable ▷ *nm/f* (*malvado*) rogue

miseria *nf* misery; (*pobreza*) poverty; (*tacañería*) meanness, stinginess; (*condiciones*) squalor; **una ~ a** pittance

misericordia *nf* (*compasión*) compassion, pity; (*perdón*) forgiveness, mercy

misil *nm* missile

misión *nf* mission; (*tarea*) job, duty; (*Pol*) assignment; **misiones** *nfpl* (*Rel*) overseas missions

misionero, -a *nm/f* missionary

mismo, -a *adj* (*semejante*) same; (*después de pronombre*) -self; (*dando énfasis*) very ▷ *adv*: **ahora ~** right now ▷ *pron*: **lo ~** the same ▷ *conj*: **lo ~ que**

just like, just as; **el ~ traje** the same suit; **vivo en su misma calle** I live in the same street as him; **vino el ~ ministro** the minister himself came; **yo ~ lo vi** I saw it myself; **lo hizo por sí ~ he** did it by himself; **en ese ~ momento** at that very moment; **hoy ~ le escribiré** I'll write to him today; **mañana ~ te llamo** I'll call you tomorrow; **nos podemos encontrar aquí ~** we can meet right here; **enfrente ~ del colegio** right opposite the school; **yo tomaré lo ~** I'll have the same; **por lo ~** for the same reason; **da lo ~** it's all the same; **no ha llamado pero lo ~ viene** he hasn't phoned but he may well come; **estamos en las mismas** we're no further forward

misterio *nm* mystery; *(lo secreto)* secrecy
misterioso, -a *adj* mysterious; *(inexplicable)* puzzling
mitad *nf (medio)* half; *(centro)* middle; **~ (y) ~** half-and-half; *(fig)* yes and no; **a ~ de precio** (at) half-price; **en o a ~ del camino** halfway along the road; **cortar por la ~** to cut through the middle
mitigar *vt* to mitigate; *(dolor)* to relieve; *(sed)* to quench; *(ira)* to appease; *(preocupación)* to allay; *(soledad)* to alleviate
mitin *nm (esp Pol)* meeting
mito *nm* myth
mitología *nf* mythology
mixto, -a *adj* mixed; *(comité)* joint
ml. *abr* (= *mililitro*) ml
mm. *abr* (= *milímetro*) mm
mobiliario *nm* furniture
mocasín *nm* moccasin
mochila *nf* rucksack *(Brit)*, backpack
moción *nf (Pol)* motion; **~ compuesta** *(Pol)* composite motion
moco *nm* mucus; **limpiarse los ~s** to blow one's nose; **no es ~ de pavo** it's no trifle
moda *nf* fashion; *(estilo)* style; **de o a la ~** in fashion, fashionable; **pasado de ~** out of fashion; **vestido a la última ~** trendily dressed
modal *adj* modal ▷ *nm:* **modales** *nmpl* manners
modalidad *nf (clase)* kind, variety; *(manera)* way; *(Inform)* mode; **~ de texto** *(Inform)* text mode
modelar *vt* to model
modelo *adj inv* model ▷ *nm/f* model ▷ *nm (patrón)* pattern; *(norma)* standard
módem *nm (Inform)* modem
moderado, -a *adj* moderate
moderar *vt* to moderate; *(violencia)* to restrain, control; *(velocidad)* to reduce; **moderarse** *vr* to restrain o.s., control o.s.
modernizar *vt* to modernize; *(Inform)* to upgrade
moderno, -a *adj* modern; *(actual)* present-day; *(equipo, técnica)* up-to-date
modestia *nf* modesty
modesto, -a *adj* modest
módico, -a *adj* moderate, reasonable
modificar *vt* to modify
modismo *nm* idiom
modisto, -a *nm/f* dressmaker
modo *nm (manera, forma)* way, manner; *(Inform,*

Mus) mode; *(Ling)* mood; **modos** *nmpl (modales)* manners; **le gusta hacerlo todo a su ~** she likes to do everything her own way; **de este ~** in this way; **de un ~ u otro** (in) one way or another; **de ningún ~** in no way; **de todos ~s** anyway; **no puedo ir al cine, y de todos ~s ya he visto la película** I can't go to the cinema, and anyway I've already seen the film; **a ~ de** like; **de ~ que** *(así que)* so; *(para que)* so that; **no has hecho los deberes, de ~ que no puedes salir** you haven't done your homework so you can't go out; **mueve la tele de ~ que todos la podamos ver** move the TV so that we can all see it; **"~ de empleo"** "instructions for use"; **~ de gobierno** form of government; **buenos/malos ~s** good/bad manners
modorra *nf* drowsiness
módulo *nm* module; *(de mueble)* unit
mogollón *(fam) nm:* **~ de discos** *etc* loads of records *etc* ▷ *adv:* **un ~** a hell of a lot
moho *nm (Bot)* mould, mildew; *(en metal)* rust
mohoso, -a *adj (alimento)* mouldy; *(metal)* rusty
mojado, -a *adj* wet; *(húmedo)* damp; *(empapado)* drenched
mojar *vt* to wet; *(humedecer)* to damp(en), moisten; *(calar)* to soak; **mojarse** *vr* to get wet; **~ el pan en el café** to dip o dunk one's bread in one's coffee
mojón *nm (hito)* landmark; *(en un camino)* signpost; *(mojón kilométrico)* milestone
moldavo, -a *adj, nm/f* Moldavian, Moldovan
molde *nm* mould; *(vaciado)* cast; *(de costura)* pattern; *(fig)* model
moldear *vt* to mould; *(en yeso etc)* to cast
mole *nf* mass, bulk; *(edificio)* pile; *(Méx: salsa)* thick chili sauce often containing chocolate
molécula *nf* molecule
moler *vt* to grind, crush; *(pulverizar)* to pound; *(trigo etc)* to mill; *(cansar)* to tire out, exhaust; **~ a algn a palos** to give sb a beating
molestar *vt (causar molestia)* to bother; *(fastidiar)* to annoy; *(incomodar)* to inconvenience, put out; *(perturbar)* to trouble, upset ▷ *vi* to be a nuisance; **molestarse** *vr (incomodarse)* to go to a lot of trouble; *(ofenderse)* to take offence; *(tomarse la molestia)* to bother; **¿te molesta la radio?** is the radio bothering you?; **¿le molesta el ruido?** do you mind the noise?; **no me molestes, que estoy trabajando** don't disturb me, I'm working; **siento ~le** I'm sorry to trouble you; **se molestó por algo que dije** she got upset because of something I said; **~se en hacer algo** to bother to do sth
molestia *nf* bother, trouble; *(incomodidad)* inconvenience; *(Med)* discomfort; **no es ninguna ~** it's no trouble at all
molesto, -a *adj (que molesta)* annoying; *(incómodo)* inconvenient; *(inquieto)* uncomfortable, ill at ease; *(enfadado)* annoyed; **¡qué ruido tan ~!** what an irritating noise!; **es muy ~ para mí** it's very inconvenient for me; **estar ~** *(Med)* to be in some discomfort; **estar ~ con algn** to be cross with sb

molido, -a adj (machacado) ground; (pulverizado) powdered; **estar ~** (fig) to be exhausted o dead beat

molinillo nm hand mill; **~ de café** coffee grinder; **~ de carne** mincer

molino nm (edificio) mill; (máquina) grinder

molusco nm mollusc

momentáneo, -a adj momentary

momento nm (gen) moment; (Tec) momentum; **espera un ~** wait a moment; **en un ~** in a moment; **en ese ~** at that moment, just then; **en este ~** at the moment; **de un ~ a otro** any moment now; **por el ~, de ~** for the moment, for the time being; **llegó el ~ de irnos** the time came for us to go

momia nf mummy

mona nf: **dormir la ~** to sleep it off; ver tb **mono**

monaguillo nm altar boy

monarca nm/f monarch, ruler

monarquía nf monarchy

monárquico, -a nm/f royalist, monarchist

monasterio nm monastery

mondadientes nm inv toothpick

mondar vt (limpiar) to clean; (pelar) to peel; **mondarse** vr: **~se de risa** (fam) to split one's sides laughing

moneda nf (tipo de dinero) currency, money; (pieza) coin; **una ~ de dos euros** a two-euro coin; **es ~ corriente** (fig) it's common knowledge; **~ de curso legal** legal tender; **~ extranjera** foreign exchange; **~ única** single currency

monedero nm purse

monetario, -a adj monetary, financial

mongólico, -a adj, nm/f Mongol

monigote nm (dibujo) doodle; (de papel) cut-out figure; (pey) wimp

monitor nm (Inform) monitor; **~ en color** colour monitor; **~ verde** green screen

monja nf nun

monje nm monk

mono, -a adj (bonito) lovely, pretty; (gracioso) nice, charming, cold turkey; **una chica muy mona** a very pretty girl ▷ nm/f monkey, ape ▷ nm dungarees pl; (de trabajo) overalls pl; (fam: de droga) ver tb **mona**

monóculo nm monocle

monografía nf monograph

monomando nm (tb: **grifo monomando**) mixer tap

monoparental adj: **familia ~** single-parent family

monopatín nm skateboard

monopolio nm monopoly; **~ total** absolute monopoly

monopolizar vt to monopolize

monotonía nf (de sonido) monotone; (de actividad) monotony

monótono, -a adj monotonous

monstruo nm monster ▷ adj inv fantastic

monstruoso, -a adj monstrous

monta nf total, sum; **de poca ~** unimportant, of little account

montacargas nm inv service lift (Brit), freight elevator (US)

montaje nm assembly; (organización) fitting up; (Teat) décor; (Cine) montage

montaña nf (monte) mountain; (sierra) mountains pl, mountainous area; (LAm: selva) forest; **~ rusa** roller coaster

montañero, -a adj mountain cpd ▷ nm/f mountaineer, climber

montañés, -esa adj (de montaña) mountain cpd; (de Santander) of o from the Santander region ▷ nm/f (de montaña) highlander; (de Santander) native o inhabitant of the Santander region

montañismo nm mountaineering, climbing

montañoso, -a adj mountainous

montar vt (subir a) to mount, get on; (caballo etc) to ride; (Tec) to assemble, put together; (negocio) to set up; (colocar) to lift on to; (Cine: película) to edit; (Teat: obra) to stage, put on; (Culin: batir) to whip, beat ▷ vi (ir a caballo) to ride; (subirse a caballo) to mount, get on; (sobresalir) to overlap; **~ una tienda** to put up a tent; **~ un número** o **pollo** (fam) to make a scene; **~ a caballo** to ride a horse; **~ en bici** to ride a bike; **~ en cólera** to get angry; **llegó corriendo y se montó en el autobús** he came running up and got on the bus; **tanto monta** it makes no odds

montaraz adj mountain cpd, highland cpd; (pey) uncivilized

monte nm (montaña) mountain; (bosque) woodland; (área sin cultivar) wild area, wild country; **~ alto** forest; **~ bajo** scrub(land); **~ de piedad** pawnshop

monto nm total, amount

montón nm heap, pile; **un ~ de** (fig) heaps of, lots of; **a montones** by the score, galore

monumental adj (tb fig) monumental; **zona ~** area of historical interest

monumento nm monument; (de conmemoración) memorial

monzón nm monsoon

moño nm (de pelo) bun; **estar hasta el ~** (fam) to be fed up to the back teeth

moqueta nf fitted carpet

mora nf (Bot) mulberry; (zarzamora) blackberry; (Com): **en ~** in arrears

morado, -a adj purple, violet ▷ nm bruise ▷ nf (casa) dwelling, abode; **pasarlas moradas** to have a tough time of it

moral adj moral ▷ nf (ética) ethics pl; (moralidad) morals pl, morality; (ánimo) morale; **tener baja la ~** to be in low spirits

moraleja nf moral

moralidad nf morals pl, morality

moralizar vt to moralize

moratón nm bruise

morbo nm (fam) morbid pleasure

morboso, -a adj morbid

morcilla nf blood sausage, ≈ black pudding (Brit)

mordaz adj (crítica) biting, scathing

mordaza nf (para la boca) gag; (Tec) clamp

morder vt to bite; (mordisquear) to nibble; (fig:

consumir) to eat away, eat into ▷ *vi*: **morderse** *vr* to bite; **está que muerde** he's hopping mad; **~se la lengua** to hold one's tongue

mordisco *nm* bite

moreno, -a *adj* (*color*) (dark) brown; (*de tez*) dark; (*de pelo moreno*) dark-haired; (*negro*) black ▷ *nm/f* (*de tez*) dark-skinned man/woman; (*de pelo*) dark-haired man/woman

morfina *nf* morphine

moribundo, -a *adj* dying ▷ *nm/f* dying person

morir *vi* (*ser vivo*) to die; (*fuego*) to die down; (*luz*) to go out; **morirse** *vr* to die; (*fig*) to be dying; (*Ferro etc: vías*) to end; (*calle*) to come out; **murió de cáncer** he died of cancer; **~ de frío/hambre** to die of cold/starve to death; **fue muerto a tiros/en un accidente** he was shot (dead)/was killed in an accident; **me muero de ganas de ir a nadar** I'm dying to go for a swim; **¡me muero de hambre!** I'm starving!; **~se de vergüenza** to die of shame; **~se por algo** to be dying for sth; **~se por algn** to be crazy about sb

mormón, -ona *nm/f* Mormon

moro, -a *adj* Moorish ▷ *nm/f* Moor; **¡hay ~s en la costa!** watch out!

moroso, -a *adj* (*lento*) slow ▷ *nm* (*Com*) bad debtor, defaulter; **deudor ~** (*Com*) slow payer

morral *nm* haversack

morriña *nf* homesickness; **tener ~** to be homesick

morro *nm* (*Zool*) snout, nose; (*Auto, Aviat*) nose; (*fam: labio*) (thick) lip; **beber a ~** to drink from the bottle; **caer de ~** to nosedive; **estar de ~s (con algn)** to be in a bad mood (with sb); **tener ~** to have a nerve

morsa *nf* walrus

morse *nm* Morse (code)

mortadela *nf* mortadella, bologna sausage

mortaja *nf* shroud; (*Tec*) mortise; (*LAm*) cigarette paper

mortal *adj* mortal; (*golpe*) deadly

mortalidad, mortandad *nf* mortality

mortero *nm* mortar

mortífero, -a *adj* deadly, lethal

mortificar *vt* to mortify; (*atormentar*) to torment

mosaico *nm* mosaic

mosca *nf* fly; **estar ~** (*desconfiar*) to smell a rat; **tener la ~ en** *o* **detrás de la oreja** to be wary; **por si las ~s** just in case

Moscú *nm* Moscow

mosquear (*fam*) *vt* (*hacer sospechar*) to make suspicious, (*fastidiar*) to annoy; **mosquearse** *vr* (*enfadarse*) to get annoyed; (*ofenderse*) to take offence

mosquita *nf*: **parece una ~ muerta** he looks as though butter wouldn't melt in his mouth

mosquitero *nm* mosquito net

mosquito *nm* mosquito

mostaza *nf* mustard

mosto *nm* *unfermented grape juice*

mostrador *nm* (*de tienda*) counter; (*de café*) bar

mostrar *vt* to show; (*exhibir*) to display, exhibit; (*explicar*) to explain; **mostrarse** *vr*: **~se amable**

to be kind; **no se muestra muy inteligente** he doesn't seem (to be) very intelligent; **~ en pantalla** (*Inform*) to display

mota *nf* speck, tiny piece; (*en diseño*) dot

mote *nm* (*apodo*) nickname

motín *nm* (*del pueblo*) revolt, rising; (*del ejército*) mutiny

motivación *nf* motivation

motivar *vt* (*causar*) to cause, motivate; (*explicar*) to explain, justify

motivo *nm* motive, reason; (*Arte, Mus*) motif; **con ~ de** (*debido a*) because of; (*en ocasión de*) on the occasion of; (*con el fin de*) in order to; **sin ~** for no reason at all

moto *nf*, **motocicleta** *nf* motorbike (*Brit*), motorcycle

motor, a *adj* (*Tec*) motive; (*Anat*) motor ▷ *nm* motor, engine; **~ a chorro** jet engine; **~ de explosión** internal combustion engine; **~ de reacción** jet engine; *ver tb* **motora**

motora *nf* motorboat; *ver tb* **motor**

motorista *nm/f* (*motociclista*) motorcyclist; (*: esp LAm: automovilista*) motorist

motosierra *nf* mechanical saw

motriz *adj*: **fuerza ~** motive power; (*fig*) driving force

movedizo, -a *adj* (*inseguro*) unsteady; (*fig*) unsettled, changeable; (*persona*) fickle

mover *vt* (*gen*) to move; (*cambiar de lugar*) to shift; (*cabeza: para negar*) to shake; (*: para asentir*) to nod; (*accionar*) to drive; (*fig*) to cause, provoke; **moverse** *vr* to move; (*mar*) to get rough; (*viento*) to rise; (*fig: apurarse*) to get a move on; (*: transformarse*) to be on the move; **¡no te muevas!** don't move!

movido, -a *adj* (*Foto*) blurred; (*persona: activo*) active; (*mar*) rough; (*día*) hectic ▷ *nf* move; **la movida madrileña** the Madrid scene

móvil *adj* mobile; (*pieza de máquina*) moving; (*mueble*) movable ▷ *nm* (*motivo*) motive; (*teléfono*) mobile

movilidad *nf* mobility

movilizar *vt* to mobilize

movimiento *nm* (*gen, Lit, Pol*) movement; (*Tec*) motion; (*actividad*) activity; (*Mus*) tempo; **~ hacia arriba/hacia abajo** upward/downward movement; **el M~** (*Pol*) the Falangist Movement; **~ de mercancías** (*Com*) turnover, volume of business; **~ obrero** workers' movement; **~ sindical** trade union movement; **~ sísmico** earth tremor

mozo, -a *adj* (*joven*) young; (*soltero*) single, unmarried ▷ *nm/f* (*joven*) youth, young man(-girl); (*camarero*) waiter; (*camarera*) waitress; **~ de estación** porter

MP3 *nm* MP3; **reproductor (de) ~** MP3 player

muchacho, -a *nm/f* (*niño*) boy/girl; (*criado*) servant/servant *o* maid

muchedumbre *nf* crowd

mucho, -a *adj* **1** (*con contables*) lots of, a lot of, many; (*con incontables*) a lot of, much; **~ dinero** a lot of money; **no tenemos ~ tiempo** we haven't

got much time; **hace ~ calor** it's very hot; **tengo ~ frío** I'm very cold; **tengo mucha hambre/sed** I'm very hungry/thirsty; **muchas amigas** lots *o* a lot of *o* many friends; **¿conoces a mucha gente?** do you know many people?
2 (*sg: fam*): **ésta es mucha casa para él** this house is much too big for him; **había ~ borracho** there were a lot *o* lots of drunks
▷ *pron* (*con contables*) a lot, many; (*con incontables*) a lot, much; **tengo ~ que hacer** I've got a lot to do; **no tengo ~ que hacer** I haven't got much to do; **~s dicen que ...** a lot of people say that ...; **¿cuántos había? — ~s** how many were there? — a lot; **¿hay manzanas? — sí, pero no muchas** are there any apples? — yes, but not many; **¿vinieron ~s?** did many people come?; **~s dicen que...** many people say that...; *ver tb* **tener**
▷ *adv* **1** (*cantidad*) a lot, very much; **me gusta ~** I like it a lot *o* very much; **come ~** he eats a lot; **~ más/menos** much *o* a lot more/less; **lo siento ~** I'm very sorry; **trabaja ~** he works hard; **me molesta ~** it really annoys me; **no tardes ~** don't be long
2 (*respuesta*) very; **¿estás cansado? — ¡~!** are you tired? — very!
3 (*locuciones*): **como ~** at (the) most; **como ~ leo un libro al mes** at most I read one book a month; **el mejor con ~** by far the best; **¡ni ~ menos!** far from it!; **no es rico ni ~ menos** he's far from being rich
4: por ~ que no matter how much, however much; **por ~ que lo quieras no debes mimarlo** no matter how much you love him, you shouldn't spoil him

muda *nf* (*de ropa*) change of clothing; (*Zool*) moult; (*de serpiente*) slough

mudanza *nf* (*cambio*) change; (*de casa*) move; **estar de ~** to be moving

mudar *vt* to change; (*Zool*) to shed ▷ *vi* to change; **mudarse** *vr* (*la ropa*) to change; **~se de casa** to move house

mudo, -a *adj* dumb; (*película*) silent; (*Ling: letra*) mute; (*: consonante*) voiceless; **quedarse ~ (de)** (*fig*) to be speechless with; **quedarse ~ de asombro** to be speechless

mueble *nm* piece of furniture; **muebles** *nmpl* furniture *sg*

mueca *nf* face, grimace; **hacer ~s a** to make faces at

muégano *nm* (*Méx*) toffee

muela *nf* (*diente*) tooth; (*: de atrás*) molar; (*de molino*) millstone; (*de afilar*) grindstone; **~ del juicio** wisdom tooth

muelle *adj* (*blando*) soft; (*fig*) soft, easy ▷ *nm* spring; (*Naut*) wharf; (*malecón*) jetty

muermo *nm* (*fam*) wimp

muerte *nf* death; (*homicidio*) murder; **dar ~ a** to kill; **de mala ~** (*fam*) lousy, rotten; **es la ~** (*fam*) it's deadly boring

muerto, -a *pp de* **morir** ▷ *adj* (*sin vida*) dead; (*color*) dull ▷ *nm/f* dead man(-woman); (*difunto*) deceased; (*cadáver*) corpse; **estar ~ de cansancio**

to be dead tired; **los ~s** the dead; **hubo tres ~s** three people were killed; **cargar con el ~** (*fam*) to carry the can; **echar el ~ a algn** to pass the buck; **hacer el ~** (*en agua*) to float

muesca *nf* nick

muestra *nf* (*señal*) indication, sign; (*demostración*) demonstration; (*prueba*) proof; (*estadística*) sample; (*modelo*) model, pattern; (*testimonio*) token; **dar ~s de** to show signs of; **~ al azar** (*Com*) random sample

muestreo *nm* sample, sampling

mugir *vi* (*vaca*) to moo

mugre *nf* dirt, filth, muck

mugriento, -a *adj* dirty, filthy, mucky

mujer *nf* woman; (*esposa*) wife

mujeriego *nm* womaniser

mula *nf* mule

mulato, -a *adj, nm/f* mulatto

muleta *nf* (*para andar*) crutch; (*Taur*) *stick with red cape attached*

mullido, -a *adj* (*cama*) soft; (*hierba*) soft, springy

multa *nf* fine; **echar** *o* **poner una ~ a** to fine

multar *vt* to fine; (*Deporte*) to penalize

multicine *nm* multiscreen cinema

multicolor *adj* multicoloured

multicopista *nm* duplicator

multimillonario, -a *adj* (*contrato*) multimillion pound *o* dollar *cpd* ▷ *nm/f* multimillionaire/ -millionairess

multinacional *adj, nf* multinational

múltiple *adj* multiple; (*pl*) many, numerous; **de tarea/usuario ~** (*Inform*) multi-tasking/-user

multiplicar *vt* (*Mat*) to multiply; (*fig*) to increase; **multiplicarse** *vr* (*Bio*) to multiply; (*fig*) to be everywhere at once

múltiplo *adj, nm* multiple

multitud *nf* (*muchedumbre*) crowd; **~ de** lots of

mundano, -a *adj* worldly; (*de moda*) fashionable

mundial *adj* world-wide, universal; (*guerra, récord*) world *cpd*

mundo *nm* world; (*ámbito*) world, circle; **el otro ~** the next world; **el ~ del espectáculo** show business; **todo el ~** everybody; **el ~ es un pañuelo** it's a small world; **no es nada del otro ~** it's nothing special; **se le cayó el ~ (encima)** his world fell apart; **tener ~** to be experienced

munición *nf* (*Mil: provisiones*) stores *pl*, supplies *pl*; (*: de armas*) ammunition

municipal *adj* (*elección*) municipal; (*concejo*) town *cpd*, local; (*piscina etc*) public ▷ *nm* (*guardia*) policeman

municipio *nm* (*ayuntamiento*) town council, corporation; (*territorio administrativo*) town, municipality

muñeca *nf* (*Anat*) wrist; (*juguete*) doll

muñeco *nm* (*figura*) figure; (*marioneta*) puppet; (*fig*) puppet, pawn; (*niño*) pretty little boy; **~ de nieve** snowman

muñequera *nf* wristband

mural *adj* mural, wall *cpd* ▷ *nm* mural

muralla *nf* (*city*) wall(s) *pl*

murciélago *nm* bat

murmullo nm murmur(ing); (*cuchicheo*) whispering; (*de arroyo*) murmur, rippling; (*de hojas, viento*) rustle, rustling; (*ruido confuso*) hum(ming)

murmuración nf gossip; (*críticas*) backbiting

murmurar vi to murmur, whisper; (*criticar*) to criticize; (*cotillear*) to gossip

muro nm wall; ~ **de contención** retaining wall

mus nm card game

muscular adj muscular

músculo nm muscle

musculoso, -a adj muscular

museo nm museum, gallery; ~ **de arte** o **pintura** art gallery; ~ **de cera** waxworks pl

musgo nm moss

música nf music; **irse con la ~ a otra parte** to clear off; ver tb **músico**

musical adj, nm musical

músico, -a adj musical ▷ nm/f musician; ver tb **música**

musitar vt, vi to mutter, mumble

muslo nm thigh; (*de pollo*) leg, drumstick

mustio, -a adj (*persona*) depressed, gloomy; (*planta*) faded, withered

musulmán, -ana nm/f Moslem, Muslim

mutación nf (*Bio*) mutation; (: *cambio*) (sudden) change

mutilar vt to mutilate; (*a una persona*) to maim

mutismo nm silence

mutuamente adv mutually

mutuo, -a adj mutual

muy adv (*mucho*) very; (*demasiado*) too; ~ **bien** (*perfecto*) very well; (*de acuerdo*) all right; ~ **de noche** very late at night; **eso es ~ de él** that's just like him; **eso es ~ español** that's typically Spanish; **M~ Señor mío** Dear Sir

Nn

N, n *nf* (*letra*) N, n; **N de Navarra** N for Nellie (*Brit*) o Nan (*US*)

n/ *abr* = **nuestro, a**

nabo *nm* turnip

nácar *nm* mother-of-pearl

nacer *vi* (*persona, animal*) to be born; (*de un huevo*) to hatch; (*vegetal*) to sprout; (*río*) to rise; (*fig*) to begin, originate, have its origins; **nació para poeta** he was born to be a poet; **nadie nace enseñado** we all have to learn; **nació una sospecha en su mente** a suspicion formed in her mind

nacido, -a *adj* born; **recién ~** newborn

naciente *adj* new, emerging; (*sol*) rising

nacimiento *nm* (*de persona, animal*) birth; (*fig*) birth, origin; (*de Navidad*) Nativity; (*de río*) source; **ciego de ~** blind from birth

nación *nf* (*país*) nation; (*pueblo*) people; **Naciones Unidas** United Nations

nacional *adj* national; (*Com, Econ*) domestic, home *antes de n*

nacionalidad *nf* nationality; (*Esp Pol*) autonomous region

nacionalismo *nm* nationalism

nacionalista *adj, nm/f* nationalist

nacionalizar *vt* to nationalize; **nacionalizarse** *vr* (*persona*) to become naturalized

nada *pron* (*con verbo afirmativo*) nothing; (*con verbo negativo*) anything ▷ *adv* not at all, in no way ▷ *nf* nothingness; **no dijo ~ (más)** he said nothing (else), he didn't say anything (else); **no quiero ~ más** I don't want anything; **quiero uno ~ más** I only want one, that's all; **encendió la tele ~ más llegar** he turned on the TV as soon as he came in; **¡gracias! — de ~** thanks! — don't mention it; **~ de eso** nothing of the kind; **no sabe ~ de español** he knows no Spanish at all; **no me dio ~ de** he gave me absolutely nothing; **fue una mentirijilla de ~** it was only a little white lie; **antes de ~** right away; **se lo advertí, pero como si ~** I warned him but he paid no attention; **no ha sido ~** it's nothing; **esto no me gusta ~** I don't like this at all; **no está ~ triste** he isn't sad at all; **la ~** the void

nadador, a *nm/f* swimmer

nadar *vi* to swim; **~ en la abundancia** (*fig*) to be rolling in money

nadie *pron* (*con verbo afirmativo*) nobody, no-one; (*con verbo negativo*) anybody, anyone; **~ habló** nobody spoke; **no había ~** there was nobody there, there wasn't anybody there; **es un don ~** he's a nobody o nonentity

nado; a ~ *adv*: **pasar a ~** to swim across

nafta *nf* (*RP*) petrol (*Brit*), gas(oline) (*US*)

naguas *nfpl* (*Méx fam*) petticoat

náhuatl *adj* Nahuatl ▷ *nm/f* Nahuatl Indian ▷ *nm* (*Ling*) Nahuatl language

naipe *nm* (*playing*) card; **naipes** *nmpl* cards

nalgas *nfpl* buttocks

nana *nf* lullaby

napias *nfpl* (*fam*) conk *sg*

naranja *adj inv, nf* orange; **media ~** (*fam*) better half; **¡~s de la China!** nonsense!

naranjada *nf* orangeade

naranjo *nm* orange tree

narcisista *adj* narcissistic

narciso *nm* narcissus

narcótico, -a *adj, nm* narcotic

narcotizar *vt* to drug

narcotráfico *nm* narcotics o drug trafficking

nardo *nm* lily

narigón, -ona, narigudo, a *adj* big-nosed

nariz *nf* nose; **narices** *nfpl* nostrils; **¡narices!** (*fam*) rubbish!; **delante de las narices de algn** under one's (very) nose; **estar hasta las narices** to be completely fed up; **meter las narices en algo** to poke one's nose into sth

narración *nf* narration

narrador, a *nm/f* narrator

narrar *vt* to narrate, recount

narrativa *nf* narrative, story; *ver tb* **narrativo**

narrativo, -a *adj* narrative; *ver tb* **narrativa**

nata *nf* cream (*tb fig*); (*en leche hervida etc*) skin; **~ batida** whipped cream

natación *nf* swimming

natal *adj* natal; (*país*) native; **ciudad ~** home town

natalidad *nf* birth rate

natillas *nfpl* (*egg*) custard *sg*

natividad *nf* nativity

nativo, -a *adj, nm/f* native

nato, -a *adj* born; **un músico ~** a born musician

natural *adj* natural; (*fruta etc*) fresh ▷ *nm/f* native ▷ *nm* disposition, temperament; **buen ~** good

nature; **fruta al ~** fruit in its own juice
naturaleza nf nature; (género) nature, kind; **~ muerta** still life
naturalidad nf naturalness
naturalización nf naturalization
naturalizarse vr to become naturalized
naturalmente adv naturally; **¡~!** of course!
naturista adj (Med) naturopathic ▷ nm/f naturopath
naufragar vi (barco) to sink; (gente) to be shipwrecked; (fig) to fail
naufragio nm shipwreck
náufrago, -a nm/f castaway, shipwrecked person
náusea nf nausea; **me da ~s** it makes me feel sick
nauseabundo, -a adj nauseating, sickening
náutica nf navigation, seamanship; ver tb **náutico**
náutico, -a adj nautical; **club ~** sailing o yacht club; ver tb **náutica**
navaja nf (cortaplumas) clasp knife (Brit), penknife; **~ (de afeitar)** razor
navajazo nm (herida) gash; (acto) slash
naval adj (Mil) naval; **construcción ~** shipbuilding; **sector ~** shipbuilding industry
Navarra nf Navarre
nave nf (barco) ship, vessel; (Arq) nave; **~ espacial** spaceship; **quemar las ~s** to burn one's boats
navegación nf navigation; (viaje) sea journey; **~ aérea** air traffic; **~ costera** coastal shipping; **~ fluvial** river navigation
navegante nm/f navigator
navegar vi (barco) to sail; (avión) to fly ▷ vt (barco) to sail; (avión) to fly; (dirigir el rumbo de) to navigate; **~ por Internet** to surf the Net
Navidad nf Christmas; **Navidades** nfpl Christmas time sg; **día de ~** Christmas Day; **por ~s** at Christmas (time); **¡Felices ~es!** Merry Christmas
navideño, -a adj Christmas antes de n
navío nm ship
nazi adj, nm/f Nazi
nazismo nm Nazism
NE abr (= nor(d)este) NE
neblina nf mist
nebulosa nf nebula; ver tb **nebuloso**
nebuloso, -a adj (con neblina) misty; (indefinido) nebulous, vague; ver tb **nebulosa**
necedad nf foolishness; (una necedad) foolish act
necesario, -a adj necessary; **no estudié más de lo ~** I didn't study any more than necessary; **ya tengo el dinero ~ para el billete** I've now got the money I need for the ticket; **llamaré al médico si fuera ~** I'll call the doctor if necessary o if need be; **no es ~ que vengas** you don't need to come
neceser nm toilet bag; **~ de belleza** vanity case
necesidad nf need; (obligación) necessity; (miseria) poverty, need; **no hay ~ de hacerlo** there is no need to do it; **comer bien es una ~, no un lujo** eating well is a necessity, not a luxury; **en caso de ~** in case of need o emergency; **pasar ~es** to

suffer hardship; **hacer sus ~es** to relieve o.s.
necesitado, -a adj needy, poor; **~ de** in need of
necesitar vt to need, require; **necesíto que me ayudes** I need you to help me; **"necesítase coche"** (en anuncios) "car wanted" ▷ vi: **~ de** to have need of
necio, -a adj foolish ▷ nm/f fool
necrología nf obituary
necrópolis nf inv cemetery
néctar nm nectar
nectarina nf nectarine
nefasto, -a adj ill-fated, unlucky
negación nf negation; (Ling) negative; (rechazo) refusal, denial
negado, -a adj: **~ para** inept at, unfitted for
negar vt (renegar, rechazar) to refuse; (prohibir) to refuse, deny; (desmentir) to deny; **~ con la cabeza** to shake one's head; **negarse** vr: **~se a hacer algo** to refuse to do sth
negativa nf (gen) negative; (rechazo) refusal, denial; **~ rotunda** flat refusal; ver tb **negativo**
negativo, -a adj negative ▷ nm (Foto) negative; (Mat) minus; ver tb **negativa**
negligencia nf negligence
negligente adj negligent
negociable adj (Com) negotiable
negociación nf negotiation
negociado nm department, section
negociante nm/f businessman(-woman)
negociar vt, vi to negotiate; **~ en** to deal in, trade in
negocio nm (Com) business; (asunto) affair, business; (operación comercial) deal, transaction; (LAm) shop, store; (lugar) place of business; **hemos montado un ~** we set up a business; **hacer ~** to do business; **hacer un buen ~** to pull off a profitable deal; **¡mal ~!** it looks bad!; **~ autorizado** licensed trade; **~ sucio** shady deal; **los ~s** business sg; **el mundo de los ~s** the business world; **hombre de ~s** businessman
negra nf (Mus) crotchet; ver tb **negro**
negro, -a adj black; (suerte) awful, atrocious; (humor etc) sad; (lúgubre) gloomy; **estoy ~ con esto** I'm getting desperate about it; **~ como la boca del lobo** pitch-black; **ponerse ~** (fam) to get cross ▷ nm (color) black ▷ nm/f black person, black man/woman; ver tb **negra**
negrura nf blackness
nene, -a nm/f baby, small child
nenúfar nm water lily
neologismo nm neologism
neón nm neon
neoyorquino, -a adj New York antes de n ▷ nm/f New Yorker
nepotismo nm nepotism
nervio nm (Anat) nerve; (fig) vigour; (Tec) rib; **crispar los ~s a algn, poner los ~s de punta a algn, poner de los ~s a algn** to get on sb's nerves
nerviosismo nm nervousness, nerves pl
nervioso, -a adj nervous; (sensible) nervy, highly-strung; (impaciente) restless; **¡no te pongas ~!** take it easy!; **¡me pone nerviosa!** he gets on my

nerves!

neto, -a *adj* (*Com*) net; (*claro*) clear

neumático, -a *adj* pneumatic ▷ *nm* (*Esp*) tyre (*Brit*), tire (*US*); ~ **de recambio** *o* **repuesto** spare tyre

neumonía *nf* pneumonia; ~ **asiática** SARS

neura (*fam*) *nm/f* (*persona*) neurotic ▷ *nf* (*obsesión*) obsession

neurálgico, -a *adj* neuralgic; (*fig: centro*) nerve *antes de n*

neurastenia *nf* neurasthenia; (*fig*) excitability

neurólogo, -a *nm/f* neurologist

neurona *nf* neuron

neutral *adj* neutral

neutralizar *vt* to neutralize

neutro, -a *adj* (*Bio, Ling*) neuter

neutrón *nm* neutron

nevada *nf* snowstorm; (*caída de nieve*) snowfall

nevado, -a *adj* snow-covered; (*montaña*) snow-capped; (*fig*) snowy, snow-white

nevar *vi* to snow

nevera *nf* (*Esp*) refrigerator, fridge, icebox (*US*)

nevisca *nf* flurry of snow

nexo *nm* link, connection

ni *conj* (*precedido de negación*) or; (*como distributivo*) nor, neither; (*como enfático*) even; **no bebe ni fuma** he doesn't drink or smoke; **ella no fue, ni yo tampoco** she didn't go and went and neither did I; **no vendieron ni un solo disco** they didn't sell one single record; **ni ... ni** neither ... nor; **ni el uno ni el otro** neither one nor the other; **no compré ni uno ni otro** I didn't buy either of them; **ni que** not even if; **¡ni hablar!** no way!, out of the question!; **¡ni muerto le vuelvo a saludar!** say hello to her again? No chance *o* no way!; **ni siquiera** not even; **ni siquiera me saludó** he didn't even say hello

Nicaragua *nf* Nicaragua

nicaragüense *adj, nm/f* Nicaraguan

nicho *nm* niche

nicotina *nf* nicotine

nido *nm* nest; (*fig*) hiding place; ~ **de ladrones** den of thieves

niebla *nf* fog; (*neblina*) mist; **hay ~** it is foggy

nieto, -a *nm/f* grandson (granddaughter); **nietos** *nmpl* grandchildren

nieve *nf* snow; (*LAm*) ice cream; **copo de ~** snowflake

N.I.F. *nm abr* (= *Número de Identificación Fiscal*) ID number used for tax purposes

Nilo *nm*: **el (Río) ~** the Nile

nimiedad *nf* triviality; (*una nimiedad*) trifle, tiny detail

nimio, -a *adj* trivial, insignificant

ninfa *nf* nymph

ninfómana *nf* nymphomaniac

ninguno, -a *adj* (*delante de nmsg* **ningún**: *con verbo afirmativo*) no; (*con verbo negativo*) any ▷ *pron* (*nadie*) nobody, no-one; (*ni uno: de dos*) neither; (*de varios*) none, not one; **no tengo ningún interés en ir** I have no interest in going; **no voy a ninguna parte** I'm not going anywhere; **de ninguna**

manera by no means, not at all; **a ninguna de las dos les gusta el café** neither of them likes coffee; **no me queda ~** I have none left

niña *nf ver* **niño**

niñera *nf* nursemaid, nanny

niñería *nf* childish act

niñez *nf* childhood

niño, -a *adj* (*joven*) young; (*inmaduro*) immature ▷ *nm* (*chico*) boy, child ▷ *nf* girl, child; (*Anat*) pupil; **los ~s** the children; **de ~** as a child; **ser el ~ mimado de algn** to be sb's pet; **ser la niña de los ojos de algn** to be the apple of sb's eye; ~ **bien** rich kid; ~ **de pecho** babe-in-arms; ~ **expósito** foundling; ~ **prodigio** child prodigy

nipón, -ona *adj, nm/f* Japanese; **los nipones** the Japanese

níquel *nm* nickel

niquelar *vt* (*Tec*) to nickel-plate

níspero *nm* medlar

nitidez *nf* (*claridad*) clarity; (*de atmósfera*) brightness; (*de imagen*) sharpness

nítido, -a *adj* bright; (*imagen*) clear, sharp

nitrato *nm* nitrate

nitrógeno *nm* nitrogen

nitroglicerina *nf* nitroglycerine

nivel *nm* (*Geo*) level; (*norma determinada*) level, standard; (*altura*) height; **a 900m sobre el ~ del mar** at 900m above sea level; **quieren mejorar el ~ de la educación** they are trying to raise the standard of education; **al ~ de** on a level with, at the same height as; (*fig*) on a par with; ~ **de aceite** oil level; ~ **de aire** spirit level; ~ **de vida** standard of living

nivelar *vt* to level out; (*fig*) to even up; (*Com*) to balance

NN. UU. *nfpl abr* (= *Naciones Unidas*) UN *sg*

NO *abr* (= *noroeste*) NW

no *adv* (*uso independiente*) no; (*con verbo*) not; **no bien** as soon as ▷ *nm* no; **¿te gusta? — no mucho** do you like it? — not really; **no tengo nada** I don't have anything, I have nothing; **¿no lo sabes?** don't you know?; **no es el mío** it's not mine; **ahora no** not now; **esto es tuyo, ¿no?** this is yours, isn't it?; **creo que no** I don't think so; **¿puedo salir esta noche? — ¡que no!** can I go out tonight? — I said no!; **¡a que no lo sabes!** I bet you don't know!; **¡cómo no!** of course!; **no bien termine, lo entregaré** as soon as I finish I'll hand it over; **pacto de no agresión** non-aggression pact; **los países no alineados** the non-aligned countries; **la no intervención** non-intervention; **los no fumadores** non-smokers; **el no va más** the ultimate

noble *adj, nm/f* noble; **los ~s** the nobility *sg*

nobleza *nf* nobility

noche *nf* (*parte del día*) night; (*al atardecer*) evening; (*fig*) darkness; **pasó la ~ sin dormir** he had a sleepless night; **esta ~** tonight; **se hace de ~** it's getting dark; **(en) toda la ~** all night; **de ~**, **por la ~** at night; **estudia por la ~** he studies at night; **era de ~ cuando llegamos a casa** it was night-time when we got back home; **no**

me gusta conducir de ~ I don't like driving at night; **el sábado por la ~** on Saturday night; **ayer por la ~** last night; **hacer ~ en un sitio** to spend the night in a place

Nochebuena *nf* Christmas Eve

Nochevieja *nf* New Year's Eve

noción *nf* notion; **nociones** *nfpl* elements, rudiments

nocivo, -a *adj* harmful

noctámbulo, -a *nm/f* sleepwalker

nocturno, -a *adj* night *antes de n*; (*de la tarde*) evening *antes de n*; (*animal*) nocturnal ▷ *nm* nocturne

nodriza *nf* wet nurse; **buque** *o* **nave ~** supply ship

nogal *nm* walnut tree; (*madera*) walnut

nómada *adj* nomadic ▷ *nm/f* nomad

nombramiento *nm* naming; (*para un empleo*) appointment; (*Pol etc*) nomination; (*Mil*) commission

nombrar *vt* (*gen: mencionar*) to mention; (*designar*) to appoint, nominate; (*Mil*) to commission

nombre *nm* name; (*sustantivo*) noun; (*fama*) renown; **~ y apellidos** name in full; **su conducta no tiene ~** his behaviour is utterly despicable; **en ~ de** in the name of, on behalf of; **sin ~** nameless; (*pey*) unspeakable; **~ común/propio** common/ proper noun; **~ de pila/de soltera** Christian/ maiden name; **~ de fichero** (*Inform*) filename

nomenclatura *nf* nomenclature

nomeolvides *nm inv* forget-me-not

nómina *nf* (*lista*) list; (*hoja de pago*) pay slip; (*Com: tb*: **nóminas**) payroll

nominal *adj* nominal; (*valor*) face *antes de n*; (*Ling*) noun *antes de n*

nominar *vt* to nominate

nominativo, -a *adj* (*Ling*) nominative; (*Com*): **un cheque ~ a X** a cheque made out to X

non *adj* odd, uneven ▷ *nm* odd number; **pares y ~es** odds and evens

nono, -a *num* ninth

nopal *nm* prickly pear

nordeste *adj* north-east, north-eastern, north-easterly ▷ *nm* north-east; (*viento*) north-east wind, north-easterly

nórdico, -a *adj* (*del norte*) northern, northerly; (*escandinavo*) Nordic, Norse ▷ *nm/f* northerner; (*escandinavo*) Norseman/woman

noreste *adj, nm* = **nordeste**

noria *nf* (*Agr*) waterwheel; (*de feria*) big (*Brit*) *o* Ferris (*US*) wheel

norma *nf* (*regla*) rule; (*patrón*) pattern; (*método*) standard, norm

normal *adj* (*corriente*) normal; (*habitual*) usual, natural; (*Tec*) standard; **Escuela N~** teacher training college; **gasolina ~** two-star petrol

normalidad *nf* normality; **restablecer la ~** to restore order

normalizar *vt* (*reglamentar*) to normalize; (*Com, Tec*) to standardize; **normalizarse** *vr* to return to normal

normalmente *adv* (*con normalidad*) normally; (*habitualmente*) usually

normando, -a *adj, nm/f* Norman

normativo, -a *adj*: **es ~ en todos los coches nuevos** it is standard in all new cars ▷ *nf* regulations *pl*

noroeste *adj* north-west, north-western, north-westerly ▷ *nm* north-west; (*viento*) north-west wind, north-westerly

norte *adj* north, northern, northerly ▷ *nm* north; (*fig*) guide

norteamericano, -a *adj, nm/f* (North) American

Noruega *nf* Norway

noruego, -a *adj, nm/f* Norwegian ▷ *nm* (*Ling*) Norwegian

nos *pron* (*directo*) us; (*indirecto*) (to) us; (*reflexivo*) (to) ourselves; (*recíproco*) (to) each other; **~ levantamos a las 7** we get up at 7; **~ dolían los pies** our feet were hurting; **~ pusimos los abrigos** we put our coats on

nosotros, -as *pron* (*sujeto*) we; (*después de prep*) us; **~ (mismos)** ourselves

nostalgia *nf* nostalgia, homesickness

nota *nf* note; (*Escol*) mark; (*Com*) account; **tomar ~s** to take notes; **~ a pie de página** footnote; **~ de aviso** advice note; **~ de crédito/débito** credit/debit note; **~ de gastos** expenses claim; **~s de sociedad** gossip column

notable *adj* noteworthy, notable; (*Escol etc*) outstanding ▷ *nm/f* notable

notar *vt* (*darse cuenta de*) to notice, note; (*percibir*) to feel; (*ver*) to see; **notarse** *vr* to be obvious; **notó que lo seguían** he noticed they were following him; **con este abrigo no noto el frío** I don't feel the cold with this coat on; **se nota que has estudiado mucho este trimestre** you can tell that you've studied a lot this term

notarial *adj* (*estilo*) legal; **acta ~** affidavit

notario *nm* notary; (*abogado*) solicitor

noticia *nf* (*información*) piece of news; (*TV etc*) news item; **las ~s** the news *sg*; **las ~s de las nueve** the nine o'clock news; **según nuestras ~s** according to our information; **tener ~s de algn** to hear from sb

noticiario *nm* (*Cine*) newsreel; (*TV*) news bulletin

noticiero *nm* newspaper, gazette; (*LAm: tb*: **noticiero telediario**) news bulletin

notificación *nf* notification

notificar *vt* to notify, inform

notoriedad *nf* fame, renown

notorio, -a *adj* (*público*) well-known; (*evidente*) obvious

novato, -a *adj* inexperienced ▷ *nm/f* beginner, novice

novecientos, -as *num* nine hundred

novedad *nf* (*calidad de nuevo*) newness, novelty; (*cambio*) change, (new) development; (*sorpresa*) surprise; (*noticia*) piece of news; **novedades** *nfpl* (*noticia*) latest (news) *sg*

novedoso, -a *adj* novel

novel *adj* new; (*inexperto*) inexperienced ▷ *nm/f* beginner

novela *nf* novel; **~ policíaca** detective story

novelero, -a *adj* highly imaginative
novelesco, -a *adj* fictional; (*romántico*) romantic; (*fantástico*) fantastic
novelista *nm/f* novelist
noveno, -a *num* ninth
noventa *num* ninety
novia *nf ver* **novio**
noviazgo *nm* engagement
novicio, -a *nm/f* novice
noviembre *nm* November
novilla *nf* heifer
novillada *nf* (*Taur*) bullfight with young bulls
novillero *nm* (novice) bullfighter
novillo *nm* young bull, bullock; **hacer ~s** (*fam*) to play truant (*Brit*) o hooky (*US*)
novio, -a *nm/f* boyfriend/girlfriend; (*prometido*) fiancé/fiancée; (*recién casado*) bridegroom/bride; **los ~s** the newly-weds
N. S. *abr* = **Nuestro Señor**
nubarrón *nm* storm cloud
nube *nf* cloud; (*Med: ocular*) cloud, film; (*fig*) mass; **una ~ de críticas** a storm of criticism; **los precios están por las ~s** prices are sky-high; **estar en las ~s** to be away with the fairies
nublado, -a *adj* cloudy ▷ *nm* storm cloud
nublar *vt* (*oscurecer*) to darken; (*confundir*) to cloud; **nublarse** *vr* to cloud over
nuca *nf* nape of the neck
nuclear *adj* nuclear
núcleo *nm* (*centro*) core; (*Física*) nucleus; **~ urbano** town
nudillo *nm* knuckle
nudista *adj, nm/f* nudist
nudo *nm* knot; (*unión*) bond; (*de problema*) crux; (*Ferro*) junction; (*fig*) lump; **con un ~ en la garganta** with a lump in one's throat; **~ corredizo** slipknot
nudoso, -a *adj* knotty; (*tronco*) gnarled; (*bastón*) knobbly
nuera *nf* daughter-in-law
nuestro, -a *adj posesivo* our ▷ *pron* ours; **~ padre** our father; **un amigo ~** a friend of ours; **es el ~** it's ours; **los ~s** our people; (*Deporte*) our o the local team o side
nueva *nf* piece of news; *ver tb* **nuevo**
nuevamente *adv* (*otra vez*) again; (*de nuevo*) anew
Nueva York *nf* New York
Nueva Zeland(i)a *nf* New Zealand

nueve *num* nine
nuevo, -a *adj* (*gen*) new; **¿qué hay de ~?** (*fam*) what's new?; **de ~** again; *ver tb* **nueva**
nuez (*pl* **nueces**) *nf* (*del nogal*) walnut; (*fruto seco*) nut; **~ de Adán** Adam's apple; **~ moscada** nutmeg
nulidad *nf* (*incapacidad*) incompetence; (*abolición*) nullity; (*individuo*) nonentity; **es una ~** he's a dead loss
nulo, -a *adj* (*inepto, torpe*) useless; (*inválido*) (null and) void; (*Deporte*) drawn, tied
núm. *abr* (= *número*) no
numeración *nf* (*cifras*) numbers *pl*; (*arábiga, romana etc*) numerals *pl*; **~ de línea** (*Inform*) line numbering
numerador *nm* (*Mat*) numerator
numeral *nm* numeral
numerar *vt* to number; **numerarse** *vr* (*Mil etc*) to number off
numérico, -a *adj* numerical
número *nm* (*gen*) number; (*de camisa, zapato*) size; (*ejemplar: de diario*) number, issue; (*Teat etc*) turn, act, number; **sin ~** numberless, unnumbered; **montar un ~** to make a scene; **~ atrasado** back number; **~ binario** (*Inform*) binary number; **~ de matrícula/de teléfono** registration/telephone number; **~ de serie** (*Com*) serial number; **~ personal de identificación** (*Inform etc*) personal identification number
numeroso, -a *adj* numerous; **familia numerosa** large family
numerus *nm*: **~ clausus** (*Univ*) restricted o selective entry
nunca *adv* (*jamás*) never; (*con verbo negativo*) ever; **~ lo pensé** I never thought it; **no viene ~** he never comes; **~ más** never again
nuncio *nm* (*Rel*) nuncio
nupcial *adj* wedding *antes de n*
nupcias *nfpl* wedding *sg*, nuptials
nutria *nf* otter
nutrición *nf* nutrition
nutrido, -a *adj* (*alimentado*) nourished; (*fig: grande*) large; (*abundante*) abundant; **mal ~** undernourished; **~ de** full of
nutrir *vt* to feed, nourish; (*fig*) to feed, strengthen
nutritivo, -a *adj* nourishing, nutritious
nylon *nm* nylon

ñato, -a *adj* (*LAm*) snub-nosed
ñoñería, ñoñez *nf* insipidness

ñoño, -a *adj* (*soso*) insipid; (*persona: débil*) spineless

Oo

O, o nf (letra) O, o; **O de Oviedo** O for Oliver (Brit)
o Oboe (US)

o [o] conj or; **o ... o** either ... or; **o sea** that is

o/ nm (Com: = orden) o

oasis nm inv oasis

obcecarse vr to be obstinate; **~ en hacer algo** to
insist on doing sth

obedecer vt to obey; **~ a** (Med etc) to yield to; (fig):
~ a ..., ~ al hecho de que ... to be due to ..., arise
from ...

obediencia nf obedience

obediente adj obedient

obertura nf overture

obesidad nf obesity

obeso, -a adj obese

obispo nm bishop

objeción nf objection; **hacer una ~, poner
objeciones** to raise objections, object

objetar vt, vi to object

objetivo, -a adj objective ▷ nm objective; (fig)
aim; (Foto) lens

objeto nm (cosa) object; (fin) aim

objetor, a nm/f objector; **~ de conciencia**
conscientious objector

oblicuo, -a adj oblique; (mirada) sidelong

obligación nf obligation; (Com) bond, debenture

obligar vt to force; **obligarse** vr: **~se a** to commit
o.s. to

obligatorio, -a adj compulsory, obligatory

oboe nm (instrumento) oboe; (músico) oboist

obra nf (creación) work; (pieza creada) piece of
work; (Constr) building site; (libro) book; (Mus)
work, opus; **"~s** (en edificio) "building work
in progress", "construction in progress"; (en
carretera) "roadworks in progress"; **"página
en ~s"** (Internet) "site under construction"; **~s
son amores y no buenas razones** actions
speak louder than words; **por ~ de** thanks
to (the efforts of); **una ~ de arte** a work
of art; **~ benéfica** charity; **~s completas**
complete works; **~ de teatro** play; **~ maestra**
masterpiece; **~s públicas** public works

obrar vt to work; (tener efecto) to have an effect
on ▷ vi to act, behave; (tener efecto) to have an
effect; **la carta obra en su poder** the letter is in
his/her possession

obrero, -a adj working; (movimiento) labour antes

de n; **clase obrera** working class ▷ nm/f (gen)
worker; (sin oficio) labourer

obscenidad nf obscenity

obsceno, -a adj obscene

obsequiar vt (ofrecer) to present; (agasajar) to
make a fuss of, lavish attention on

obsequio nm (regalo) gift; (cortesía) courtesy,
attention

obsequioso, -a adj attentive

observación nf observation; (comentario) remark;
(objeción) objection

observador, a adj observant ▷ nm/f observer

observancia nf observance

observar vt (mirar) to observe; (notar) to notice;
(comentar) to remark; (leyes) to observe, respect;
(reglas) to abide by

observatorio nm observatory; **~ del tiempo**
weather station

obsesión nf obsession

obsesionar vt to obsess

obseso, -a nm/f (sexual) sex maniac

obsoleto, -a adj obsolete

obstaculizar vt (dificultar) to hinder, hamper

obstáculo nm (gen) obstacle; (impedimento)
hindrance, drawback

obstante; no ~ adv (sin embargo) nevertheless; (de
todos modos) all the same prep in spite of

obstetra nm/f obstetrician

obstetricia nf obstetrics sg

obstinado, -a adj (gen) obstinate; (terco) stubborn

obstinarse vr to dig one's heels in; **~ en** to
persist in

obstrucción nf obstruction

obstruir vt to obstruct; (bloquear) to block;
(estorbar) to hinder

obtener vt (trabajo, apoyo, satisfacción, información) to
obtain; (independencia, control, derechos) to gain

obturador nm (Foto) shutter

obtuso, -a adj (filo) blunt; (Mat, fig) obtuse

obviar vt to obviate, remove

obvio, -a adj obvious

oca nf goose; (tb: **juego de la oca**) ≈ snakes and
ladders

ocasión nf (oportunidad) opportunity, chance;
(momento) occasion, time; **en algunas ocasiones**
sometimes; **aprovechar la ~** to seize one's
opportunity; **libro de ~** secondhand book; **con ~**

de on the occasion of
ocasionar vt to cause
ocaso nm sunset; (fig) decline
occidental adj western ▷ nm/f westerner ▷ nm west
occidente nm west; **el O~** the West
O.C.D.E. nf abr (= Organización para la Cooperación y el Desarrollo Económico) OECD
océano nm ocean; **el ~ Índico** the Indian Ocean
ochenta num eighty
ocho num eight; (fecha) eighth; **~ días** a week
ochocientos, -as num eight hundred
ocio nm (tiempo) leisure; (pey) idleness; **"guía del ~"** "what's on"
ociosidad nf idleness
ocioso, -a adj (inactivo) idle; (inútil) useless
octanaje nm: **de alto ~** high octane
octano nm octane
octavilla nf leaflet, pamphlet
octavo, -a num eighth
octogenario, -a adj, nm/f octogenarian
octubre nm October
ocular adj ocular, eye antes de n; **testigo ~** eyewitness
oculista nm/f oculist
ocultar vt (esconder) to hide; (callar) to conceal; (disfrazar) to screen; **ocultarse** vr to hide (o.s.); **~se a la vista** to keep out of sight
oculto, -a adj hidden; (fig) secret
ocupación nf occupation; (tenencia) occupancy
ocupado, -a adj (persona) busy; (sitio) occupied, taken; (línea, teléfono) engaged; **¿está ocupada esa silla?** is that seat taken?
ocupar vt (territorio, espacio) to occupy; (puesto) to hold; (persona) to engage; (obreros) to employ; (confiscar) to seize; **ocuparse** vr: **~se de o en** (dedicarse a) to concern o.s. with; (cuidar) to look after; **el edificio ocupa todo el solar** the building occupies the whole site; **los espectadores ~on sus asientos** the spectators took their seats; **ocupa casi todo mi tiempo** it takes up almost all my time; **~se de lo suyo** to mind one's own business; **ahora sus hijos se ocupan de la empresa** his sons look after the business now; **me ~é de ello mañana** I'll deal with it tomorrow
ocurrencia nf (agudeza) witticism; (ocasión) occurrence; **¡qué ~!** him and his crazy ideas!
ocurrir vi to happen; **¿qué ocurre?** what's going on?; **¿qué te ocurre?** what's the matter?; **ocurrirse** vr: **se me ocurrió que ...** it occurred to me that ...; **¿se te ocurre algo?** can you think of o come up with anything?
odiar vt to hate
odio nm (gen) hate, hatred
odioso, -a adj (gen) hateful; (malo) nasty
odisea nf odyssey
odontólogo, -a nm/f dentist, dental surgeon
O.E.A. nf abr (= Organización de Estados Americanos) O.A.S
oeste nm west; **una película del ~** a western
ofender vt (agraviar) to offend; (insultar) to insult;

ofenderse vr to take offence
ofensa nf (ataque) offence; (desaire) slight
ofensiva nf offensive
ofensivo, -a adj (insultante) insulting; (Mil) offensive
oferta nf (ofrecimiento) offer; (propuesta) proposal; (para contrato) bid, tender; **la ~ y la demanda** supply and demand; **artículos en ~** goods on offer; **~s de empleo** (en periódicos) situations vacant column; **~ excedentaria** (Com) excess supply; **~ monetaria** money supply; **~ pública de adquisición (OPA)** (Com) takeover bid
offset nm offset
oficial adj official ▷ nm official; (Mil) officer
oficina nf office; **~ de colocación** employment agency; **~ de información** information bureau; **~ de objetos perdidos** lost property office (Brit), lost-and-found department (US); **~ de turismo** tourist office
oficinista nm/f clerk; **los ~s** white-collar workers
oficio nm (profesión) profession; (puesto) post; (Rel) service; (función) function; (comunicado) official letter; **ser del ~** to be an old hand; **tener mucho ~** to have a lot of experience; **de ~** officially; **~ de difuntos** funeral service
oficioso, -a adj (pey) officious; (no oficial) unofficial, informal
ofimática nf office automation
ofrecer vt (dar) to offer; (proponer) to propose; **ofrecerse** vr (persona) to offer o.s., volunteer; (situación) to present itself; **le ofrecimos nuestra ayuda** we offered to help; **me ofrecí de guía** I offered myself as a guide; **~se para hacer algo** to offer to do something; **¿qué se le ofrece?, ¿se le ofrece algo?** what can I do for you?
ofrecimiento nm offer, offering
ofrendar vt to offer, contribute
oftalmólogo, -a nm/f ophthalmologist
ofuscación nf, **ofuscamiento** nm (fig) bewilderment
ofuscar vt (confundir) to bewilder; (cegar) to dazzle, blind
oída nf: **de ~s** by hearsay
oído nm (Anat, Mus) ear; (sentido) hearing; **apenas pude dar crédito a mis ~s** I could scarcely believe my ears; **de ~** by ear; **hacer ~s sordos a** to turn a deaf ear to; **~ interno** inner ear
oír vt (gen) to hear; (esp LAm: escuchar) to listen to; **¡oye!** (sorpresa) I say!, say! (US); **¡oiga!** (para llamar la atención) excuse me!; **~ misa** to attend mass; **como quien oye llover** without paying (the slightest) attention
ojal nm buttonhole
ojalá excl if only (it were so)!, some hope! ▷ conj if only...!, would that...!; **~ que venga hoy** I hope he comes today; **¡~ pudiera!** I wish I could!
ojeada nf glance; **echar una ~ a** to take a quick look at
ojera nf: **tener ~s** to have bags under one's eyes
ojeriza nf ill-will; **tener ~ a** to have a grudge against, have it in for

ojeroso, -a *adj* haggard
ojo *nm* eye; *(de puente)* span; *(de cerradura)* keyhole
▷ *excl* careful!; **tener ~ para** to have an eye for; **~ por ~** an eye for an eye; **en un abrir y cerrar de ~s** in the twinkling of an eye; **a ~s vistas** openly; *(crecer etc)* before one's (very) eyes; **a ~ (de buen cubero)** roughly; **~s que no ven, corazón que no siente** out of sight, out of mind; **ser el ~ derecho de algn** *(fig)* to be the apple of sb's eye; **~s saltones** bulging *o* goggle eyes; **~ de buey** porthole
ojota *nf* (CS) flip-flop *(Brit)*, thong *(US)*
okupa *nm/f (fam)* squatter
ola *nf* wave; **~ de calor/frío** heatwave/cold spell; **la nueva ~** the latest fashion; *(Cine, Mus)* (the) new wave
olé *excl* bravo!, olé!
oleada *nf (fig)* wave
oleaje *nm* swell
óleo *nm* oil
oleoducto *nm* (oil) pipeline
oler *vt (gen)* to smell; *(inquirir)* to pry into; *(fig: sospechar)* to sniff out ▷ *vi* to smell; **~ a** to smell of; **huele mal** it smells bad, it stinks
olfatear *vt* to smell; *(fig: sospechar)* to sniff out; *(inquirir)* to pry into
olfato *nm* sense of smell
oligarquía *nf* oligarchy
olimpiada *nf*: **la ~ o las ~s** the Olympics
olímpicamente *adv*: **pasar ~ de algo** to totally ignore sth
olímpico, -a *adj* Olympian; *(Deporte)* Olympic
oliva *nf (aceituna)* olive; **aceite de ~** olive oil
olivo *nm* olive tree
olla *nf* pan; *(para hervir agua)* kettle; *(comida)* stew; **~ a presión** pressure cooker
olmo *nm* elm (tree)
olor *nm* smell
oloroso, -a *adj* scented
olote *nm* (CAm, Méx) corncob
olvidadizo, -a *adj* forgetful
olvidar *vt* to forget; *(omitir)* to omit; *(abandonar)* to leave behind; **olvidé las llaves encima de la mesa** I left the keys on top of the table; **olvidarse** *vr (fig)* to forget o.s.; **se me olvidó** I forgot
olvido *nm (abandono)* oblivion; *(acto)* oversight; *(descuido)* slip; **caer en el ~** to fall into oblivion
ombligo *nm* navel
ominoso, -a *adj* ominous
omisión *nf (abstención)* omission; *(descuido)* neglect
omiso, -a *adj*: **hacer caso ~ de** to ignore, pass over
omitir *vt* to leave *o* miss out, omit
omnipotente *adj* omnipotent
omnívoro, -a *adj* omnivorous
omoplato, omóplato *nm* shoulder-blade
OMS *nf abr* (= *Organización Mundial de la Salud*) WHO
once *num* eleven ▷ *nm* (LAm): **onces** *nfpl* tea break *sg*
onda *nf* wave; **~ corta/larga/media** short/

long/medium wave; **~s acústicas/hertzianas** acoustic/Hertzian waves; **~ sonora** sound wave
ondear *vi* to wave; *(tener ondas)* to be wavy; *(agua)* to ripple; **ondearse** *vr* to swing, sway
ondulación *nf* undulation
ondulado, -a *adj* wavy
ondulante *adj* undulating
ondular *vt (el pelo)* to wave ▷ *vi*: **ondularse** *vr* to undulate
oneroso, -a *adj* onerous
ONG *nf abr* (= *organización no gubernamental*) NGO
ONU *nf abr ver* **Organización de las Naciones Unidas**
OPA *nf abr* (= *oferta pública de adquisición*) takeover bid
opaco, -a *adj* opaque; *(fig)* dull
ópalo *nm* opal
opción *nf (gen)* option; *(derecho)* right, option; **no hay ~** there is no alternative
opcional *adj* optional
ópera *nf* opera; **~ bufa o cómica** comic opera
operación *nf (gen)* operation; *(Com)* transaction, deal; **operaciones accesorias** *(Inform)* housekeeping; **~ a plazo** *(Com)* forward transaction; **operaciones a término** *(Com)* futures
operador, a *nm/f* operator; *(Cine: de proyección)* projectionist; (: *de rodaje*) cameraman
operante *adj* operating
operar *vt (producir)* to produce, bring about; *(Med)* to operate on ▷ *vi (Com)* to operate, deal; **operarse** *vr* to occur; *(Med)* to have an operation; **se han operado grandes cambios** great changes have been made *o* have taken place
opereta *nf* operetta
opinar *vt (estimar)* to think ▷ *vi (enjuiciar)* to give one's opinion; **~ bien de** to think well of, have a good opinion of
opinión *nf (creencia)* belief; *(criterio)* opinion; **la ~ pública** public opinion
opio *nm* opium
oponente *nm/f* opponent
oponer *vt (resistencia)* to put up, offer; *(negativa)* to raise; **~ A a B** to set A against B; **oponerse** *vr (objetar)* to object; *(estar frente a frente)* to be opposed; *(dos personas)* to oppose each other; **me opongo a pensar que ...** I refuse to believe *o* think that ...
oporto *nm* port
oportunidad *nf (ocasión)* opportunity; *(posibilidad)* chance
oportunismo *nm* opportunism
oportunista *nm/f* opportunist ▷ *adj (infección)* opportunistic
oportuno, -a *adj (en su tiempo)* opportune, timely; *(respuesta)* suitable; **en el momento ~** at the right moment
oposición *nf* opposition; **oposiciones** *nfpl* public examinations; **ganar un puesto por oposiciones** to win a post by public competitive examination; **hacer oposiciones a, presentarse a unas oposiciones a** to sit a

competitive examination for

opositar *vi* to sit a public entrance examination

opositor, -a *nm/f* (*Admin*) candidate to a public examination; (*adversario*) opponent

opresión *nf* oppression

opresivo, -a *adj* oppressive

opresor, a *nm/f* oppressor

oprimir *vt* (*apretar*) to squeeze; (*pulsar*) to press; (*fig*) to oppress

oprobio *nm* (*infamia*) ignominy; (*descrédito*) shame

optar *vi* (*elegir*) to choose; ~ **a o por** to opt for

optativo, -a *adj* optional

óptica *nf* optics *sg*; (*fig*) viewpoint; *ver tb* **óptico**

óptico, -a *adj* optic(al) ▷ *nm/f* optician; *ver tb* **óptica**

optimismo *nm* optimism

optimista *nm/f* optimist

óptimo, -a *adj* (*el mejor*) very best

opuesto, -a *pp de* **oponer** ▷ *adj* (*contrario*) opposite; (*antagónico*) opposing

opulencia *nf* opulence

opulento, -a *adj* opulent

oración *nf* (*Rel*) prayer; (*Ling*) sentence

oráculo *nm* oracle

orador, a *nm/f* orator; (*conferenciante*) speaker

oral *adj* oral; **por vía ~** (*Med*) orally

órale *excl* (*Méx*: *¡vamos!*) come on!; (*¡oiga!*) hey!

orangután *nm* orang-utan

orar *vi* (*Rel*) to pray

oratoria *nf* oratory

órbita *nf* orbit; (*Anat*: *ocular*) (eye-)socket

orden *nm* order; ~ **público** public order, law and order; **del ~ de** about; **de primer ~** first-rate; **por ~ alfabético** in alphabetical order; **en ~ de prioridad** in order of priority ▷ *nf* order; ~ **bancaria** banker's order; ~ **de compra** (*Com*) purchase order; ~ **del día** (*plan de trabajo*) agenda; **a la ~ de usted** at your service; **hasta nueva ~** till further notice; **dar la ~ de hacer algo** to give the order to do sth

ordenado, -a *adj* (*metódico*) methodical; (*arreglado*) orderly

ordenador *nm* computer; ~ **central** mainframe computer; ~ **de gestión** business computer; ~ **de sobremesa** desktop computer; ~ **portátil** laptop (computer)

ordenamiento *nm* legislation

ordenanza *nf* ordinance; ~**s municipales** by-laws ▷ *nm* (*Com etc*) messenger; (*Mil*) orderly; (*bedel*) porter

ordenar *vt* (*mandar*) to order; (*poner orden*) to put in order, arrange; **ordenarse** *vr* (*Rel*) to be ordained

ordeñar *vt* to milk

ordinario, -a *adj* (*común*) ordinary, usual; (*vulgar*) vulgar, common

orégano *nm* oregano

oreja *nf* ear; (*Mecánica*) lug, flange

orfanato *nm*, **orfanatorio** *nm* orphanage

orfandad *nf* orphanhood

orfebrería *nf* gold/silver work

orgánico, -a *adj* organic

organigrama *nm* flow chart; (*de organización*) organization chart

organismo *nm* (*Bio*) organism; (*Pol*) organization; **O~ Internacional para la Energía Atómica** International Atomic Energy Agency

organista *nm/f* organist

organización *nf* organization; **O~ de las Naciones Unidas (ONU)** United Nations Organization; **O~ del Tratado del Atlántico Norte (OTAN)** North Atlantic Treaty Organization (NATO)

organizar *vt* to organize

órgano *nm* organ

orgasmo *nm* orgasm

orgía *nf* orgy

orgullo *nm* (*satisfacción, altanería*) pride; (*respeto a uno mismo*) self-respect

orgulloso, -a *adj* (*satisfecho*) proud; (*altanero*) haughty

orientación *nf* (*posición*) position; (*dirección*) direction; ~ **profesional** occupational guidance

oriental *adj* oriental; (*región etc*) eastern ▷ *nm/f* oriental

orientar *vt* (*situar*) to orientate; (*señalar*) to point; (*dirigir*) to direct; (*guiar*) to guide; **orientarse** *vr* to get one's bearings; (*decidirse*) to decide on a course of action

oriente *nm* east; **el O~** the East, the Orient; **Cercano/Medio/Lejano O~** Near/Middle/Far East

origen *nm* origin; (*nacimiento*) lineage, birth; **dar ~ a** to cause, give rise to

original *adj* (*nuevo*) original; (*extraño*) odd, strange ▷ *nm* original; (*Tip*) manuscript; (*Tec*) master (copy)

originalidad *nf* originality

originar *vt* to originate; **originarse** *vr* to originate

originario, -a *adj* (*nativo*) native; (*primordial*) original; **país ~** country of origin; **ser ~ de** to originate from

orilla *nf* (*borde*) border; (*de río*) bank; (*de bosque, tela*) edge; (*del mar*) shore; **a ~s de** on the banks of

orín *nm* rush

orina *nf* urine

orinal *nm* (chamber) pot

orinar *vi* to urinate; **orinarse** *vr* to wet o.s.

orines *nmpl* urine *sg*

oriundo, -a *adj*: ~ **de** native of

ornar *vt* to adorn

ornitología *nf* ornithology, bird watching

oro *nm* gold; ~ **en barras** gold ingots; **de ~** gold, golden; **hacerse de ~** to make a fortune; **no es ~ todo lo que reluce** all that glitters is not gold; *ver tb* **oros**

oropel *nm* tinsel

oros *nmpl* (*Naipes*) one of the suits in the Spanish card deck

orquesta *nf* orchestra; ~ **de cámara/sinfónica** chamber/symphony orchestra; ~ **de jazz** jazz band

orquestar *vt* to orchestrate

orquídea *nf* orchid

ortiga *nf* nettle

ortodoncia *nf* orthodontics *sg*

ortodoxo, -a *adj* orthodox

ortografía *nf* spelling

ortopedia *nf* orthop(a)edics *sg*

ortopédico, -a *adj* orthop(a)edic

oruga *nf* caterpillar

orzuelo *nm* (*Med*) stye

os *pron* (*gen*) you; (*a vosotros*) (to) you; (*reflexivo*) (to) yourselves; (*mutuo*) (to) each other; **vosotros os laváis** you wash yourselves; **no hace falta que os quitéis los abrigos** you don't need to take your cotas off; **¡callaos!** (*fam*) shut up!

osa *nf* (she-)bear; **O~ Mayor/Menor** Great/Little Bear, Ursa Major/Minor

osadía *nf* daring; (*descaro*) impudence

osar *vi* to dare

oscilación *nf* (*movimiento*) oscillation; (*fluctuación*) fluctuation; (*de columpio*) swinging, movement to and fro

oscilar *vi* (*péndulo*) to oscillate; (*precio, temperatura*) to fluctuate

oscurecer *vt* to darken ▷ *vi* to grow dark; **oscurecerse** *vr* to grow *o* get dark

oscuridad *nf* (*tinieblas*) darkness; (*anonimato*) obscurity

oscuro, -a *adj* dark; (*fig*) obscure; (*indefinido*) confused; (*cielo*) overcast, cloudy; (*futuro etc*) uncertain; **a oscuras** in the dark

óseo, -a *adj* (*Med etc*) bone *antes de n*

oso *nm* bear; **hacer el ~** to play the fool; **~ blanco/gris/pardo** polar/grizzly/brown bear; **~ de peluche** teddy bear; **~ hormiguero** anteater

ostensible *adj* obvious

ostentación *nf* (*gen*) ostentation; (*acto*) display

ostentar *vt* (*gen*) to show; (*pey*) to flaunt, show off; (*poseer*) to have, possess

ostentoso, -a *adj* ostentatious, showy

ostra *nf* oyster ▷ *excl*: **¡~s!** (*fam*) sugar!

OTAN *nf abr ver* **Organización del Tratado del Atlántico Norte**

otear *vt* to observe

otitis *nf* earache

otoñal *adj* autumnal

otoño *nm* autumn, fall (*US*)

otorgamiento *nm* conferring, granting; (*Jur*) execution

otorgar *vt* (*conceder*) to concede; (*dar*) to grant; (*poderes*) to confer; (*premio*) to award

otorrinolaringólogo, -a *nm/f* (*Med*: *tb*: **otorrino**) ear, nose and throat specialist

otro, -a *adj* **1** (*distinto*: *sg*) another; (: *pl*) other; **otra cosa/persona** something/someone else; **con ~s amigos** with other *o* different friends; **tengo ~s planes** I have other plans; **a la otra semana** the following week; **a/en otra parte** elsewhere, somewhere else

2 (*adicional*): **tráigame ~ café (más), por favor** can I have another coffee please; **¿hay alguna otra manera de hacerlo?** is there any other way of doing it?; **~s tres libros** another three books; **recibió una decena de telegramas y otras tantas llamadas** he got about ten telegrams and as many calls; **~s 10 días más** another 10 days; **otra vez** again

▷ *pron* **1** (*distinto*: *sg*) another one; **el ~** the other one; (los) **~s** (the) others; **no quiero éste, quiero el ~** I don't want this one, I want the other one; **de ~** somebody else's; **que lo haga ~** let somebody else do it; **ni uno ni ~** neither one nor the other

2 (*adicional*) another one; **¡otra!** (*Mus*) more!

3 (*recíproco*): **se odian (la) una a (la) otra** they hate each other *o* one another; **están enamorados el uno del ~** they're in love with each other *o* one another

4: **~ tanto**: **comer ~ tanto** to eat the same *o* as much again

ovación *nf* ovation

oval, ovalado, a *adj* oval

óvalo *nm* oval

ovario *nm* ovary

oveja *nf* sheep; **~ negra** (*fig*) black sheep (of the family)

overol *nm* (*LAm*) overalls *pl*

ovillo *nm* (*de lana*) ball; (*fig*) tangle; **hacerse un ~** to curl up (into a ball)

OVNI *nm abr* (= *objeto volante no identificado*) UFO

ovulación *nf* ovulation

óvulo *nm* ovum

oxidación *nf* rusting

oxidar *vt* to rust; **oxidarse** *vr* to go rusty; (*Tec*) to oxidize

óxido *nm* oxide

oxigenado, -a *adj* (*Química*) oxygenated; (*pelo*) bleached

oxígeno *nm* oxygen

oyente *nm/f* (*Radio*) listener; (*Escol*) unregistered *o* occasional student

Pp

P, p *nf* (*letra*) P, p; **P de París** P for Peter
pabellón *nm* bell tent; (*Arq*) pavilion; (*de hospital etc*) block, section; (*bandera*) flag; **~ de conveniencia** (*Com*) flag of convenience; **~ de la oreja** outer ear
pábilo *nm* wick
pacer *vi* to graze
pachanguero, -a *adj* (*pey: música*) noisy and catchy
paciencia *nf* patience; **¡~!** be patient!; **perder la ~** to lose one's temper; **¡~ y barajar!** don't give up!
paciente *adj, nm/f* patient
pacificación *nf* pacification
pacificar *vt* to pacify; (*tranquilizar*) to calm
pacífico, -a *adj* peaceful; (*persona*) peace-loving; (*existencia*) pacific; **el (Océano) P~** the Pacific (Ocean)
pacifismo *nm* pacifism
pacifista *nm/f* pacifist
pack *nm* (*de yogures, latas*) pack; (*de vacaciones*) package
pacotilla *nf* trash; **de ~** second-rate
pactar *vt* to agree to, agree on ▷ *vi* to come to an agreement
pacto *nm* (*tratado*) pact; (*acuerdo*) agreement
padecer *vt* (*sufrir*) to suffer; (*soportar*) to endure, put up with; (*ser víctima de*) to be a victim of ▷ *vi*: **~ de** to suffer from; **padece del corazón** he has heart trouble
padecimiento *nm* suffering
pádel *nm* paddle tennis
padrastro *nm* stepfather
padre *adj* (*fam*): **un éxito ~** a tremendous success ▷ *nm* father; **padres** *nmpl* parents; **~ espiritual** confessor; **P~ Nuestro** Lord's Prayer; **~ político** father-in-law; **¡tu ~!** (*fam!*) up yours! (*!*)
padrino *nm* godfather; (*fig*) sponsor, patron; **padrinos** *nmpl* godparents; **~ de boda** best man
padrón *nm* (*censo*) census, roll; (*de socios*) register
paella *nf* paella, *dish of rice with meat, shellfish etc*
paga *nf* (*dinero pagado*) payment; (*sueldo*) pay, wages *pl*
pagadero, -a *adj* payable; **~ a la entrega/a plazos** payable on delivery/in instalments
pagano, -a *adj, nm/f* pagan, heathen
pagar *vt* (*facturas, impuestos*) to pay; (*compra, producto, crimen*) to pay for; (*deuda*) to pay (off); (*favor*) to repay ▷ *vi* to pay; **pagarse** *vr*: **~se con algo** to be content with sth; **no han pagado el alquiler** they haven't paid the rent; **se puede ~ con tarjeta de crédito** you can pay by credit card; **tengo que ~ las entradas** I have to pay for the tickets; **me pagan muy poco** I get paid very little; **¡me las ~ás!** I'll get you for this!
pagaré *nm* I.O.U.
página *nf* page; **~ de inicio** (*Inform*) home page; **~s amarillas** Yellow Pages®
pago *nm* (*dinero*) payment; (*fig*) return; **en ~ de** in return for; **~ anticipado/a cuenta/a la entrega/en especie/inicial** advance payment/ payment on account/cash on delivery/payment in kind/down payment; **~ a título gracioso** ex gratia payment
país *nm* (*gen*) country; (*región*) land; **los Países Bajos** the Low Countries; **el P~ Vasco** the Basque Country
paisaje *nm* landscape; (*vista*) scenery
paisano, -a *adj* of the same country ▷ *nm/f* (*compatriota*) fellow countryman(-woman); **vestir de ~** (*soldado*) to be in civilian clothes; (*guardia*) to be in plain clothes
paja *nf* straw; (*fig*) trash, rubbish; (*en libro, ensayo*) padding, waffle; **riñeron por un quítame allá esas ~s** they quarrelled over a trifle
pajar *nm* hay loft
pajarita *nf* bow tie
pájaro *nm* bird; (*fam: astuto*) clever fellow; **tener la cabeza llena de ~s** to be featherbrained
pajita *nf* (drinking) straw
pala *nf* (*de mango largo*) spade; (*de mango corto*) shovel; (*raqueta etc*) bat; (*de tenis*) racquet; (*Culin*) slice; **~ matamoscas** fly swat
palabra *nf* (*vocablo, promesa*) word; (*facultad*) (power of) speech; (*derecho de hablar*) right to speak; **un título de dos ~s** a two-word title; **sin decir ~** without a word; **no encuentro ~s para expresarme** words fail me; **comerse las ~s** to mumble; **quedarse con la ~ en la boca** to stop short; **tomar la ~** (*en reunión, comité etc*) to speak, take the floor; **pedir la ~** to ask to be allowed to speak; **tener la ~** to have the floor; **faltar a su ~** to go back on one's word; **cumplió su ~** he was true to his word; **~ de honor** word of honour

palabrería nf hot air
palabrota nf swearword
palacio nm palace; (mansión) mansion, large house; ~ **de justicia** courthouse; ~ **municipal** town/city hall
paladar nm palate
paladear vt to taste
palanca nf lever; (fig) pull, influence; ~ **de cambio** (Auto) gear lever, gearshift (US); ~ **de control** (Inform) joystick; ~ **de freno** (Auto) brake lever
palangana nf washbasin
palco nm box
Palestina nf Palestine
palestino, -a adj, nm/f Palestinian
palestra nf: **salir** o **saltar a la** ~ to come into the spotlight
paleta nf (Constr) trowel; (Arte) palette; (Anat) shoulder blade; (LAm) ice lolly; ver tb **paleto**
paleto, -a nm/f yokel, hick (US); ver tb **paleta**
paliar vt (mitigar) to mitigate; (disfrazar) to conceal
paliativo nm palliative
palidecer vi to turn pale
palidez nf paleness
pálido, -a adj pale
palillo nm small stick; (para dientes) toothpick; ~**s (chinos)** chopsticks; **estar hecho un** ~ to be as thin as a rake
palio nm canopy
paliza nf beating, thrashing; **dar** o **propinar** (fam) **una** ~ **a algn** to give sb a thrashing; **sus clases son una** ~ (fam) his classes are a real pain (fam)
palma nf (Anat) palm; (árbol) palm tree; **batir** o **dar** ~**s** to clap, applaud; **llevarse la** ~ to triumph, win
palmada nf slap; **palmadas** nfpl clapping sg, applause sg
palmar vi (tb: **palmarla**) to die, kick the bucket
palmarés nm (lista) list of winners; (historial) track record
palmear vi to clap
palmo nm (medida) span; (fig) small amount; ~ **a** ~ inch by inch
palmotear vi to clap, applaud
palmoteo nm clapping, applause
palo nm stick; (poste) post, pole; (mango) handle, shaft; (golpe) blow, hit; (de golf) club; (de béisbol) bat; (Naut) mast; (Naipes) suit; **vermut a** ~ **seco** straight vermouth; **de tal** ~ **tal astilla** like father like son
paloma nf (gen) pigeon; (gen) dove; ~ **de la paz** dove of peace; ~ **mensajera** carrier o homing pigeon
palomilla nf moth; (Tec: tuerca) wing nut; (soporte) bracket
palomitas nfpl popcorn sg
palpar vt to touch, feel
palpitación nf palpitation
palpitante adj palpitating; (fig) burning
palpitar vi to palpitate; (latir) to beat
palta nf (CS) avocado

palúdico, -a adj marshy
paludismo nm malaria
pamela nf sun hat
pampa nf (LAm) pampa(s), prairie
pan nm bread; **un(a barra de)** ~ a loaf of bread; ~ **de molde** sliced loaf; ~ **integral** wholemeal bread; ~ **rallado** breadcrumbs pl; **eso es** ~ **comido** it's a cinch; **llamar al** ~ ~ **y al vino vino** to call a spade a spade
pana nf corduroy
panadería nf baker's (shop)
panadero, -a nm/f baker
Panamá nm Panama
panameño, -a adj Panamanian
pancarta nf placard, banner
páncreas nm pancreas
panda nm panda ▷ nf gang
pandereta nf tambourine
pandilla nf set, group; (de criminales) gang; (pey) clique
panel nm panel; ~ **acústico** acoustic screen
panfleto nm (Pol etc) pamphlet; (sátira) lampoon
pánico nm panic
panificadora nf bakery
panorama nm panorama; (vista) view
pantalla nf (de cine) screen; (de lámpara) lampshade; (Inform) screen, display; **servir de** ~ **a** to be a blind for; ~ **de ayuda** help screen; ~ **de cristal líquido** liquid crystal display; ~ **plana** plane screen; ~ **táctil** touch-sensitive screen
pantalón nm, **pantalones** nmpl trousers pl, pants pl (US); **pantalones vaqueros** jeans pl
pantano nm (ciénaga) marsh, swamp; (depósito de agua) reservoir; (fig) jam, fix, difficulty
pantera nf panther
pantis nmpl tights
pantomima nf pantomime
pantorrilla nf calf (of the leg)
pantufla nf slipper
panty nm = **pantis**
panza nf belly, paunch
panzón, -ona, panzudo, -a adj fat, potbellied
pañal nm nappy, diaper (US); **estar todavía en** ~**es** (persona) to be still wet behind the ears; (ciencia, técnica) to be in its infancy
pañería nf (artículos) drapery; (tienda) draper's (shop), dry-goods store (US)
paño nm (tela) cloth; (pedazo de tela) (piece of) cloth; (trapo) duster, rag; ~**s calientes** (fig) half-measures; **no andarse con** ~**s calientes** to pull no punches; ~ **de cocina** dishcloth; ~ **higiénico** sanitary towel; ~**s menores** underwear
pañuelo nm handkerchief, hanky (fam); (para la cabeza) (head)scarf
papa nf (LAm) potato ▷ nm: **el P**~ the Pope
papá nm (pl -**s**) (fam) dad, daddy, pop (US); **papás** nmpl parents; **niño de** ~ Hooray Henry (fam)
papada nf double chin
papagayo nm parrot
papalote nm (CAm, Méx: cometa) kite
papanatas nm inv (fam) sucker, simpleton
paparrucha nf (tontería) piece of nonsense

papaya *nf* papaya

papear *vt, vi (fam)* to eat

papel *nm (gen)* paper; *(folio)* sheet of paper; *(Teat)* part, role; **papeles** *nmpl* identification papers; ~ **carbón** carbon paper; ~ **contínuo** *(Inform)* continuous stationery; ~ **de aluminio** tinfoil; ~ **de calco/de cartas** tracing paper/stationery; ~ **de envolver/de regalo** brown paper/wrapping paper; ~ **del Estado** *o* **de pagos al Estado** government bonds *pl*; ~ **de lija** sandpaper; ~ **higiénico** toilet paper; ~ **moneda** paper money; ~ **pintado** wallpaper; ~ **plegado (en abanico** *o* **en acordeón)** fanfold paper; ~ **secante** blotting paper; ~ **térmico** thermal paper

papeleo *nm* red tape

papelera *nf (en oficina)* wastepaper bin; *(en la calle)* litter bin; ~ **de reciclaje** wastebasket

papelería *nf (tienda)* stationer's (shop)

papeleta *nf (de rifa)* raffle ticket; *(pedazo de papel)* slip *o* bit of paper; *(Pol)* ballot paper; *(Escol)* report; ¡**vaya** ~! this is a tough one!

paperas *nfpl* mumps *sg*

papilla *nf (de bebé)* baby food; *(pey)* mush; **estar hecho** ~ to be dog-tired

paquete *nm (envase)* packet; *(bulto)* parcel; *(LAm fam)* nuisance, bore; *(Inform)* package *(of software)*; *(de vacaciones)* package tour; **un** ~ **de tabaco** a packet of cigarettes; ~**s postales** parcel post *sg*; ~ **de aplicaciones** *(Inform)* applications package; ~ **integrado** *(Inform)* integrated package; ~ **de gestión integrado** combined management suite

par *adj (igual)* like, equal; *(Mat)* even ▷ *nm* equal; *(de guantes)* pair; *(de veces)* couple; *(título)* peer; *(Golf, Com)* par ▷ *nf* par; ~**es o nones** odds or evens; **abrir de** ~ **en** ~ to open wide; **a la** ~ par; **sobre/bajo la** ~ above/below par

para *prep (destino, finalidad)* for; *(con verbos en infinitivo)* to; **es** ~ **ti** it's for you; **decir** ~ **sí** to say to o.s.; *¿*~ **qué lo quieres?** what do you want it for?; **lo recordaré** ~ **siempre** I'll remember it forever; **lo tendré** ~ **mañana** I'll have it for tomorrow; ~ **entonces ya era tarde** it was already too late by then; **ir** ~ **casa** to go home, head for home; ~ **profesor es muy tonto** he's very stupid for a teacher; *¿*~ **quién es usted** ~ **gritar así?** who are you to shout like that?; **tengo bastante** ~ **vivir** I have enough to live on; ~ **que te acuerdes de mí** so that you remember me; ~ **ruidosos, los españoles** for noisy people, there's nobody like the Spaniards; **son cinco** ~ **las ocho** *(LAm)* it's five to eight

parabién *nm* congratulations *pl*

parábola *nf* parable; *(Mat)* parabola

parabólica *nf (tb:* **antena parabólica)** satellite dish

parabrisas *nm inv* windscreen, windshield *(US)*

paracaídas *nm inv* parachute

paracaidista *nm/f* parachutist; *(Mil)* paratrooper

parachoques *nm inv (Aut)* bumper, fender *(US)*; *(Mec)* shock absorber

parada *nf (gen)* stop; *(acto)* stopping; *(de industria)* shutdown, stoppage; *(lugar)* stopping-place; **hicimos una** ~ **corta para descansar** we made a short stop to rest; ~ **cardíaca** cardiac arrest; ~ **de autobús** bus stop; ~ **de taxis** taxi rank; ~ **discrecional** request stop; ~ **en seco** sudden stop; *ver tb* **parado**

paradero *nm* stopping-place; *(situación)* whereabouts

parado, -a *adj (quieto: persona)* motionless, standing still; *(: coche)* stopped; *(fábrica)* closed, at a standstill; *(: sin empleo)* unemployed, idle; *(confuso)* confused; *(LAm: de pie)* standing (up); **no te quedes ahí** ~ don't just stand there; **hace seis meses que está parada** she's been unemployed for six months; **los** ~**s** the unemployed; **estuve toda la mañana** ~ *(LAm)* I was standing all morning; **salir bien** ~ to come off well; *ver tb* **parada**

paradoja *nf* paradox

parador *nm (luxury)* hotel

paráfrasis *nf inv* paraphrase

paraguas *nm inv* umbrella

Paraguay *nm*: **el** ~ Paraguay

paraguayo, -a *adj, nm/f* Paraguayan

paraíso *nm* paradise, heaven; ~ **fiscal** *(Com)* tax haven

paraje *nm* place, spot

paralelo, -a *adj, nm* parallel; **en** ~ *(Elec, Inform)* (in) parallel

parálisis *nf inv* paralysis; ~ **cerebral** cerebral palsy; ~ **progresiva** creeping paralysis

paralítico, -a *adj, nm/f* paralytic

paralizar *vt* to paralyse; **paralizarse** *vr* to become paralysed; *(fig)* to come to a standstill

paramilitar *adj* paramilitary

páramo *nm* bleak plateau

parangón *nm*: **sin** ~ incomparable

paranoia *nf* paranoia

paranoico, -a *adj, nm/f* paranoid

paranormal *adj* paranormal

parapléjico, -a *adj, nm/f* paraplegic

parar *vt (persona, máquina, coche)* to stop; *(progreso)* to check, halt; *(golpe)* to ward off ▷ *vi (detenerse)* to stop; *(hospedarse)* to stay; **pararse** *vr (detenerse)* to stop; *(LAm: ponerse de pie)* to stand up; **el autobús para enfrente** the bus stops opposite; **paramos a poner gasolina** we stopped to get some petrol; **no** ~ **de hacer algo** to keep on doing sth; **ha parado de llover** it has stopped raining; **hablar sin** ~ to talk non-stop; **van a ir a** ~ **a la comisaría** they're going to end up in the police station; **no sabemos donde irá a** ~ **todo esto** we don't know where all this is going to end; ~**se a hacer algo** to stop to do sth; **el reloj se ha parado** the clock has stopped; **se me paró el coche en la autopista** the engine cut out while I was on the motorway; ~**se en algo** *(prestar atención)* to pay attention to sth

pararrayos *nm inv* lightning conductor

parásito, -a *nm/f* parasite

parcela *nf* plot, piece of ground, smallholding

parche *nm* patch

parchís nm ludo
parcial adj (pago) part-; (eclipse) partial; (juez) prejudiced, biased
parcialidad nf (prejuicio) prejudice, bias
parco, -a adj (frugal) sparing; (moderado) moderate
pardillo, -a adj (pey) provincial ▷ nm/f (pey) country bumpkin ▷ nm (Zool) linnet
pardo, -a adj (color) brown
parear vt (juntar, hacer par) to match, put together; (calcetines) to put into pairs; (Bio) to mate, pair
parecer nm (opinión) opinion, view; (aspecto) looks pl ▷ vi (aparentar: físicamente) to look; (en comportamiento, etc) to seem; (asemejarse) to look like, seem like; (opinar) to think; **parecerse** vr to look alike, resemble each other; **al ~** apparently; **parece más joven** he looks younger; **parece una modelo** she looks like a model; **parece muy simpática** she seems very nice; **parece mentira que ya haya pasado tanto tiempo** I can't believe it has been so long; **¿qué te pareció la película?** what did you think of the film?; **me parece bien que los multen** I think it's right that they should be fined; **si te parece bien** if that's all right with you; **me parece que sí** I think so; **me parece que no** I don't think so; **~se a** to look like, resemble; **María y Ana se parecen mucho** María and Ana look very much alike; **te pareces mucho a tu madre** you look very very much like your mother
parecido, -a adj similar ▷ nm similarity, likeness, resemblance; **~ a** like, similar to; **bien ~** good-looking, nice-looking
pared nf wall; **subirse por las ~es** (fam) to go up the wall; **~ divisoria/medianera** dividing/party wall
pareja nf (dos) pair; (de personas) couple; (el otro: de un par) other one (of a pair); (: persona) partner; (de Guardias) Civil Guard patrol; ver tb **parejo**
parejo, -a adj (igual) equal; (liso) smooth, even; ver tb **pareja**
parentela nf relations pl
parentesco nm relationship
paréntesis nm inv parenthesis; (digresión) digression; (en escrito) bracket
parida nf: **~ mental** (fam) dumb idea
paridad nf (Econ) parity
pariente, -a nm/f relative, relation
parir vt to give birth to ▷ vi (mujer) to give birth, have a baby; (yegua) to foal; (vaca) to calve
París nm Paris
paritario, -a adj equal
parking nm car park, parking lot (US)
parlamentar vi (negociar) to parley
parlamentario, -a adj parliamentary ▷ nm/f member of parliament
parlamento nm (Pol) parliament; (Jur) speech
parlanchín, -ina adj loose-tongued, indiscreet ▷ nm/f chatterbox
parlar vi to chatter (away)
parlotear vi to chatter, prattle
paro nm (huelga) stoppage (of work), strike; (desempleo) unemployment; **hay ~ en la industria** work in the industry is at a standstill; **subsidio de ~** unemployment benefit; **~ cardiaco** cardiac arrest; **~ del sistema** (Inform) system shutdown
parodia nf parody
parodiar vt to parody
parpadear vi (ojo /jmr/) to blink; (luz) to flicker
párpado nm eyelid
parque nm park; **~ de atracciones/de bomberos/zoológico** amusement park/fire station/zoo
parqué, parquet nm parquet
parquímetro nm parking meter
parra nf grapevine
párrafo nm paragraph; **echar un ~** (fam) to have a chat
parranda nf (fam) spree, binge
parrilla nf (Culin) grill; (LAm Auto) roof-rack; **~ (de salida)** (Auto) starting grid; **carne a la ~** grilled meat
parrillada nf barbecue
párroco nm parish priest
parroquia nf parish; (iglesia) parish church; (Com) clientele, customers pl
parroquiano, -a nm/f (feligrés) parishioner; (cliente) client, customer
parte nm message; (informe) report ▷ nf (porción) part; (al repartir) share; (lado, cara) side; (Jur) party; **dar ~ a algn** to report to sb; **~ meteorológico** weather forecast; **¿de qué ~ de Inglaterra eres?** what part of England are you from?; **la mayor ~ de los españoles** most Spaniards; **mi ~ de la herencia** my share of the inheritance; **estoy de tu ~** I'm on your side; **llamo de ~ de Juan** I'm calling on behalf of Juan; **¿de ~ de quién?** (Telec) who is speaking?; **yo por mi ~** I for my part; **de algún tiempo a esta ~** for some time past; **tomar ~** to take part; **formar ~ de** to form a part of; (persona) to be a member of; **en alguna ~ de Europa** somewhere in Europe; **en cualquier ~** anywhere; **por todas ~s** everywhere; **por ahí no se va a ninguna ~** that leads nowhere; (fig) this is getting us nowhere; **en gran ~** to a large extent; **por una ~ ..., por otra ...** on the one hand ..., on the other hand ...
partera nf midwife
partición nf division, sharing-out; (Pol) partition
participación nf (acto) participation, taking part; (parte) share; (Com) share, stock (US); (de lotería) (share in a) lottery ticket; (aviso) notice, notification; **~ en los beneficios** profit-sharing; **~ minoritaria** minority interest
participante nm/f participant
participar vt to notify, inform ▷ vi to take part, participate; **~ en una empresa** (Com) to invest in an enterprise; **le participo que ...** I have to tell you that ...
partícipe nm/f participant; **hacer ~ a algn de algo** to inform sb of sth
particular adj (especial) particular, special; (individual, personal) private, personal ▷ nm (punto,

asunto) particular, point; (*individuo*) individual; **tiene coche** ~ he has a car of his own; **en** ~ in particular; **no dijo mucho sobre el** ~ he didn't say much about the matter

particularizar *vt* to distinguish; (*especificar*) to specify; (*detallar*) to give details about

partida *nf* (*salida*) departure; (*Com*) entry, item; (*juego*) game; (*grupo, bando*) band, group; **mala** ~ dirty trick; **echar una** ~ to have a game; ~ **de nacimiento/matrimonio/defunción** birth/marriage/death certificate

partidario, -a *adj* partisan ▷ *nm/f* (*Deporte*) supporter; (*Pol*) partisan

partido *nm* (*Pol*) party; (*encuentro*) game, match; (*apoyo*) support; **sacar** ~ **de** to profit from, benefit from; **tomar** ~ to take sides; ~ **amistoso** (*Deporte*) friendly (game); ~ **de fútbol** football match

partir *vt* (*romper: tarta, sandía*) to cut; (*nuez, almendra*) to crack; (*rama, tableta de chocolate*) to break off; (*rebanada*) to cut (off); (*dividir*) to split, divide; (*compartir, distribuir*) to share (out), distribute; (*vi: ponerse en camino*) to set off, set out; (*comenzar*) to start (off o out); **partirse** *vr* to crack o split o break (in two *etc*); **a** ~ **de** (starting) from; **a** ~ **de enero** from January; **a** ~ **de ahora** from now on; ~**se de risa** to split one's sides (laughing)

partitura *nf* score

parto *nm* birth, delivery; (*fig*) product, creation; **estar de** ~ to be in labour

pasa *nf* raisin; ~ **de Corinto/de Esmirna** currant/sultana

pasable *adj* passable

pasada *nf* passing, passage; (*acción de pulir*) rub, polish; **una mala** ~ a dirty trick; **de** ~ in passing, incidentally; *ver tb* **pasado**

pasadizo *nm* (*pasillo*) passage, corridor; (*callejuela*) alley

pasado, -a *adj* past; (*malo: comida, fruta*) bad; (*muy cocido*) overdone; (*anticuado*) out of date ▷ *nm* past; (*Ling*) past (tense); ~ **mañana** the day after tomorrow; **el mes** ~ last month; ~ **dos días** after two days; **lo** ~, ~ let bygones be bygones; ~ **de moda** old-fashioned; **huevo** ~ **por agua** boiled egg; **estar** ~ **de vueltas** o **de rosca** (*grifo, tuerca*) to be worn; *ver tb* **pasada**

pasador *nm* (*de cerrojo*) bolt; (*de pelo*) pin, grip, slide; (*de corbata*) tiepin; **pasadores** *nmpl* (*Perú: cordones*) shoelaces

pasaje *nm* (*gen*) passage; (*pago de viaje*) fare; (*los pasajeros*) passengers *pl*; (*lugar de paso*) passageway

pasajero, -a *adj* passing; (*ave*) migratory ▷ *nm/f* passenger; (*viajero*) traveller

pasamanos *nm inv* rail, handrail; (*de escalera*) banister

pasamontañas *nm inv* balaclava (helmet)

pasaporte *nm* passport

pasar *vt* (*dar*) to pass; (*tiempo*) to spend; (*dificultades*) to suffer, endure; (*noticia*) to give, pass on; (*película*) to show; (*persona*) to take, conduct; (*río*) to cross; (*barrera*) to pass through;

(*falta*) to overlook, tolerate; (*contrincante*) to surpass, do better than; (*coche*) to overtake; (*contrabando*) to smuggle (in/out); (*enfermedad*) to give, infect with ▷ *vi* (*cruzar*) to go past; (*transcurrir*) to go; (*terminarse*) to be over; (*ocurrir*) to happen; **pasarse** *vr* (*efectos*) to pass, be over; (*flores*) to fade; (*comida*) to go bad, go off; (*fig*) to overdo it, go too far o over the top; **cuando termines pásasela a Isabel** when you've finished pass it on to Isabel; **un momento, te paso con Pedro** just a moment, I'll put you on to Pedro; **me pasé el fin de semana estudiando** I spent the weekend studying; ~**lo bien/bomba** o **de maravilla** to have a good/great time; ~**lo mal** to have a bad time; **están pasando hambre** they are starving; ~ **algo a máquina** to type something; **¿qué pasa?** (*¿cuál es el problema?*) what's the matter?; (*¿qué está ocurriendo?*) what's happening?; **pase lo que pase** come what may; **¡cómo pasa el tiempo!** time just flies!; **ya ha pasado una hora** it's been an hour already; **¡pase!** come in!; **nos hicieron** ~ they showed us in; **cuando muera, la empresa** ~**á al hijo** when he dies the company will go to his son; **¡paso de todo!** (*col*) I couldn't care less! (*col*); ~ **por** (*atravesar*) to go through; ~ **por una crisis** to go through a crisis; **se hace** ~ **por médico** he passes himself off as a doctor; ~ **por alto** to skip; ~**se al enemigo** to go over to the enemy; ~**se de moda** to go out of fashion; **no se le pasa nada** nothing escapes him, he misses nothing; ~**se de la raya** to go too far; **¡no te pases!** don't try me!; **se me pasó** I forgot; **se me pasó el turno** I missed my turn; **ya se te** ~**á** you'll get over it

pasarela *nf* (*puente*) footbridge; (*en barco*) gangway; (*de modelos*) catwalk

pasatiempo *nm* pastime, hobby; (*distracción*) amusement

Pascua, pascua *nf*: ~ (**de Resurrección**) Easter; ~ **de Navidad** Christmas; **Pascuas** *nfpl* Christmas time *sg*; **¡felices** ~**s!** Merry Christmas; **de** ~**s a Ramos** once in a blue moon; **hacer la** ~ **a** (*fam*) to annoy, bug

pase *nm* pass; (*Cine*) performance, showing; (*Com*) permit; (*Jur*) licence

pasear *vt* to take for a walk; (*perro*) to walk; (*exhibir*) to parade, show off ▷ *vi*: **pasearse** *vr* to walk, go for a walk; ~ **en coche** to go for a drive

paseo *nm* (*avenida*) avenue; (*distancia corta*) short walk; **dar un** ~ to go for a walk; **mandar a algn a** ~ to tell sb to go to blazes; **¡vete a** ~**!** get lost!; ~ **marítimo** promenade

pasillo *nm* passage, corridor

pasión *nf* passion

pasional *adj* passionate; **crimen** ~ crime of passion

pasivo, -a *adj* passive; (*inactivo*) inactive ▷ *nm* (*Com*) liabilities *pl*, debts *pl*; (*de cuenta*) debit side; ~ **circulante** current liabilities

pasma *nf* (*fam*) cops *pl*

pasmar *vt* (*asombrar*) to amaze, astonish; **pasmarse** *vr* to be amazed o astonished

pasmo *nm* amazement, astonishment; (*fig*) wonder, marvel

pasmoso, -a *adj* amazing, astonishing

paso, -a *adj* dried ▷ *nm* (*al andar, de baile*) step; (*modo de andar*) walk; (*huella*) footprint; (*rapidez*) speed, pace, rate; (*camino accesible*) way through, passage; (*cruce*) crossing; (*pasaje*) passing, passage; (*Rel*) pass; (*estrecho*) strait; (*fig*) step, measure; (*apuro*) difficulty; **dio un ~ para atrás** he took a step backwards; **~ a ~** step by step; **vive a un ~ de aquí** he lives right near here; **la policía le abría ~** the police made way for him; **están de ~ por Barcelona** they're just passing through Barcelona; **"prohibido el ~"** "no entry"; **"ceda el ~"** "give way"; **salir al ~ de** *o* **a** to waylay; **salir del ~** to get out of trouble; **dar un ~ en falso** to trip; (*fig*) to take a false step; **~ atrás** step backwards; (*fig*) backward step; **~ de cebra** zebra crossing; **~ de peatones** pedestrian crossing; **~ elevado** flyover; **~ subterráneo** subway, underpass (US)

pasota *adj, nm/f* (*fam*) ≈ dropout; **ser un (tipo) ~** to be a bit of a dropout; (*ser indiferente*) not to care about anything

pasta *nf* (*gen*) paste; (*Culin: masa*) dough; (: *de bizcochos etc*) pastry; (*fam*) money, dough; (*encuadernación*) hardback; (*fideos, espaguetis etc*) noodles, spaghetti *sg etc*; **~ de dientes** *o* **dentífrica** toothpaste; **~ de madera** wood pulp; **pastas** *nfpl* (*bizcochos*) pastries, small cakes

pastar *vi* to graze

pastel *nm* (*dulce*) cake; (*de carne*) pie; (*Arte*) pastel; (*fig*) plot; **pasteles** *nmpl* pastry *sg*, confectionery *sg*

pastelería *nf* cake shop, pastry shop

pasteurizado, -a *adj* pasteurized

pastilla *nf* (*de jabón, chocolate*) cake, bar; (*píldora*) tablet, pill

pasto *nm* (*hierba*) grass; (*lugar*) pasture, field; (*fig*) food, nourishment

pastor, a *nm/f* shepherd(ess) ▷ *nm* clergyman, pastor; (*Zool*) sheepdog; **~ alemán** Alsatian

pata *nf* (*pierna*) leg; (*pie*) foot; (*de muebles*) leg; **~s arriba** upside down; **a cuatro ~s** on all fours; **meter la ~** to put one's foot in it; **tener buena/mala ~** to be lucky/unlucky; **~ de cabra** (*Tec*) crowbar; **~s de gallo** crow's feet; *ver tb* **pato**

patada *nf* kick; **a ~s** in abundance; (*trato*) roughly; **echar a algn a ~s** to kick sb out

patalear *vi* to stamp one's feet

patata *nf* potato; **~s fritas** (*de sartén*) chips, French fries; **de paquete** crisps; **ni ~** (*fam*) nothing at all; **no entendió ni ~** he didn't understand a single word

paté *nm* pâté

patear *vt* (*pisar*) to stamp on, trample (on); (*pegar con el pie*) to kick ▷ *vi* to stamp (with rage), stamp one's foot

patentar *vt* to patent

patente *adj* obvious, evident; (*Com*) patent ▷ *nf* patent

patera *nf* boat

paternal *adj* fatherly, paternal

paterno, -a *adj* paternal

patético, -a *adj* pathetic, moving

patilla *nf* (*de gafas*) arm; (*de pelo*) sideburn

patín *nm* skate; (*de tobogán*) runner; **~ de hielo** ice skate; **~ de ruedas** roller skate

patinaje *nm* skating

patinar *vi* to skate; (*resbalarse*) to skid, slip; (*fam*) to slip up, blunder

patio *nm* (*de casa*) patio, courtyard; **~ de recreo** playground

pato, -a *nm/f* duck; **pagar el ~** (*fam*) to take the blame, carry the can; *ver tb* **pata**

patológico, -a *adj* pathological

patoso, -a *adj* awkward, clumsy

patraña *nf* story, fib

patria *nf* native land, mother country; **~ chica** home town

patrimonio *nm* inheritance; (*fig*) heritage; (*Com*) net worth

patriota *nm* patriot *f*

patriótico, -a *adj* patriotic

patriotismo *nm* patriotism

patrocinador, a *nm/f* sponsor

patrocinar *vt* to sponsor; (*apoyar*) to back, support

patrocinio *nm* (*ayuda económica*) sponsorship; (*respaldo*) backing, support

patrón, -ona *nm/f* (*jefe*) boss, chief, master (mistress); (*propietario*) landlord(-lady); (*Rel*) patron saint ▷ *nm* (*Costura*) pattern; (*Tec*) standard; **~ oro** gold standard

patronal *adj*: **clase ~** management; **cierre ~** lockout

patronato *nm* sponsorship; (*acto*) patronage; (*Com*) employers' association; (*fundación*) trust; **el ~ de turismo** the tourist board

patrulla *nf* patrol

pausa *nf* pause; (*intervalo*) break; (*interrupción*) interruption; (*Tec: en videograbadora*) hold; **con ~** slowly

pausado, -a *adj* slow, deliberate

pauta *nf* line, guideline

pavimento *nm* (*Arq*) flooring; (*de carretera*) road surface

pavo *nm* turkey; (*necio*) silly thing, idiot; **¡no seas ~!** don't be silly!; **~ real** peacock

pavor *nm* dread, terror

payaso, -a *nm/f* clown

payo, -a *adj, nm/f* non-gipsy

paz *nf* peace; (*tranquilidad*) peacefulness, tranquillity; **¡haya ~!** stop it!; **dejar a algn en ~** to leave sb alone *o* in peace; **hacer las paces** to make peace; (*fig*) to make up

PC *nm* PC, personal computer

P.D. *abr* (= *posdata*) P.S.

peaje *nm* toll; **autopista de ~** toll motorway, turnpike (US)

peatón *nm* pedestrian; **paso de peatones** pedestrian crossing, crosswalk (US)

peca *nf* freckle

pecado nm sin
pecador, a adj sinful ▷ nm/f sinner
pecaminoso, -a adj sinful
pecar vi (Rel) to sin; (fig): ~ **de generoso** to be too generous
pecera nf goldfish bowl
pecho nm (Anat) chest; (de mujer) breast(s) pl, bosom; **dar el** ~ **a** to breast-feed; **tomar algo a** ~ to take sth to heart; **no le cabía en el** ~ he was bursting with happiness
pechuga nf breast (of chicken etc)
pecoso, -a adj freckled
peculiar adj special, peculiar; (característico) typical, characteristic
peculiaridad nf peculiarity
pedagogía nf education
pedal nm pedal; ~ **de embrague** clutch (pedal); ~ **de freno** footbrake
pedalear vi to pedal
pedante adj pedantic ▷ nm/f pedant
pedantería nf pedantry
pedazo nm piece, bit; **hacer ~s** (jarrón) to smash; (carta) to tear up; **hacerse ~s** to smash, shatter; **un ~ de pan** a scrap of bread; (fig) a terribly nice person
pedernal nm flint
pedestal nm base; **tener/poner a algn en un** ~ to put sb on a pedestal
pediatra nm/f paediatrician (Brit), pediatrician (US)
pedicuro, -a nm/f chiropodist (Brit), podiatrist (US)
pedido nm (Com: encargo) order; (petición) request; **~s en cartera** (Com) backlog sg
pedigrí nm pedigree
pedir vt (dinero, libro, consejo, etc) to ask for; (canción) to request; (comida, Com) to order; (precio) to ask; (necesitar) to need, demand, require ▷ vi to ask; **le pedí dinero a mi padre** I asked my father for some money; **¿te puedo ~ un favor?** can I ask you a favour?; **le pedí disculpas** I apologized to him; **tuve que ~ dinero prestado** I had to borrow money; **pedí los folletos por teléfono** I ordered the brochures over the phone; ~ **peras al olmo** to ask for the impossible; **¿cuánto pide por el coche?** how much is he asking for the car?
pedo (fam) adj inv: **estar** ~ to be pissed (!) ▷ nm fart (!)
pedrada nf throw of a stone; (golpe) blow from a stone
pega nf (dificultad) snag; **de** ~ false, dud; **poner ~s** to raise objections
pegadizo, -a adj (canción etc) catchy
pegajoso, -a adj sticky, adhesive
pegamento nm glue
pegar vt (unir: papel, sellos) to stick (on); (con cola) to glue; (cartel) to post, stick up; (coser) to sew (on); (partes) to join, fix together; (Inform) to paste; (Med) to give, infect with; (golpear) to hit; (golpe) to give, deal ▷ vi (adherirse) to stick, adhere; (ir juntos: colores) to match, go together; (quemar:

el sol) to strike hot, burn; (fig): ~ **en** to touch; **pegarse** vr (gen) to stick; (dos personas) to hit each other, fight; ~ **un grito** to let out a yell; ~ **un salto** to jump (with fright); ~ **fuego** to catch fire; ~ **un tiro a algn** to shoot sb; **¡qué susto me has pegado!** what a fright you gave me!; **~le a algo** to be a great one for sth; **~se un tiro** to shoot o.s.; **no pega** that doesn't seem right; **ese sombrero no pega con el abrigo** that hat doesn't go with the coat
pegatina nf (Pol etc) sticker
pego nm (Esp): **dar el** ~ to look like the real thing
pegote nm (fig) patch, ugly mend; **tirarse ~s** (fam) to come on strong
peinado nm (en peluquería) hairdo; (estilo) hair style
peinar vt to comb sb's hair; (con un cierto estilo) to style; **peinarse** vr to comb one's hair
peine nm comb
peineta nf ornamental comb
p.ej. abr (= por ejemplo) e.g.
Pekín n Beijing, Peking
pelado, -a adj (cabeza) shorn; (fruta) peeled; (campo, fig) bare; (fam: sin dinero) broke
pelaje nm (Zool) fur, coat; (fig) appearance
pelambre nm long hair, mop
pelar vt (fruta, patatas) to peel; (cortar el pelo a) to cut the hair of; (quitar la piel: animal) to skin; (ave) to pluck; (habas etc) to shell; **pelarse** vr (la piel) to peel off; **hace un frío que pela** it's bitterly cold; **corre que se las pela** (fam) he runs like nobody's business
peldaño nm (escalón) step; (de escalera de mano) rung
pelea nf (lucha) fight; (discusión) quarrel, row
peleado, -a adj: **estar** ~ **(con algn)** to have fallen out (with sb)
pelear vi to fight; **pelearse** vr to fight; (reñir) to fall out, quarrel
peletería nf furrier's, fur shop
peliagudo, -a adj tricky
pelícano nm pelican
película nf (Cine) film, movie (US); (cobertura ligera) film, thin covering; (Foto) roll o reel of film; **de** ~ (fam) astonishing, out of this world; ~ **de dibujos (animados)** cartoon film; ~ **muda** silent film
peligrar vi to be in danger
peligro nm danger; (riesgo) risk; **correr** ~ **de** to be in danger of; **con** ~ **de la vida** at the risk of one's life; **"~ de muerte"** "danger"
peligroso, -a adj dangerous; (arriesgado) risky
pelirrojo, -a adj red-haired, red-headed
pellejo nm (de animal) skin, hide; **salvar el** ~ to save one's skin
pellizcar vt to pinch, nip
pellizco nm pinch
pelma, pelmazo, -a nm/f (fam) pest
pelo nm (cabellos) hair; (de barba, bigote) whisker; (de animal: piel) fur, coat; (de perro etc) hair, coat; (de ave) down; (de tejido) nap; (Tec) fibre; **a** ~ bareheaded; (desnudo) naked; **al** ~ just right;

venir al ~ to be exactly what one needs; **por los ~s** by the skin of one's teeth; **escaparse por un ~** to have a close shave; **se me pusieron los ~s de punta** my hair stood on end; **no tener ~s en la lengua** to be outspoken, not mince words; **tomar el ~ a algn** to pull sb's leg

pelón, -ona *adj* hairless, bald

pelota *nf* ball; *(fam: cabeza)* nut *(fam)*; **en ~(s)** stark naked; **~ vasca** pelota; **devolver la ~ a algn** *(fig)* to turn the tables on sb; **hacer la ~ (a algn)** to creep (to sb)

pelotera *nf (fam)* barney

pelotón *nm (Mil)* squad, detachment

peluca *nf* wig

peluche *nm:* **muñeco de ~** soft toy

peludo, -a *adj* hairy, shaggy

peluquería *nf* hairdresser's; *(para hombres)* barber's (shop)

peluquero, -a *nm/f (de mujeres, hombres)* hairdresser; *(de hombres sólo)* barber

pelusa *nf (Bot)* down; *(Costura)* fluff

pelvis *nf* pelvis

pena *nf (congoja)* grief, sadness; *(dificultad)* trouble; *(dolor)* pain; *(LAm: vergüenza)* shame; *(Jur)* sentence; *(Deporte)* penalty; **¡qué ~!** what a shame o pity!; **es una ~ que no puedas venir** it's a shame you can't come; **me da ~ tener que marcharme** I'm so sad to have to go away; **vale la ~** it's worth it; **no vale la ~ gastarse tanto dinero** it's not worth spending so much money; **¿no te da ~ hacerlo?** *(LAm)* aren't you embarrassed doing that?; **a duras ~s** with great difficulty; **so ~ de** on pain of; **~ capital** capital punishment; **~ de muerte** death penalty; **~ pecuniaria** fine

penal *adj* penal ▷ *nm (cárcel)* prison; *(LAm Dep)* penalty

penalidad *nf (problema, dificultad)* trouble, hardship; *(Jur)* penalty, punishment

penalizar *vt* to penalize

penalti, penalty *nm (Deporte)* penalty

penar *vt* to penalize; *(castigar)* to punish ▷ *vi* to suffer

pendiente *adj* pending, unsettled ▷ *nm* earring ▷ *nf* hill, slope; **tener una asignatura ~** to have to resit a subject

péndulo *nm* pendulum

pene *nm* penis

penetración *nf (acto)* penetration; *(agudeza)* sharpness, insight

penetrante *adj (herida)* deep; *(persona, arma)* sharp; *(sonido)* penetrating, piercing; *(mirada)* searching; *(viento, ironía)* biting

penetrar *vt* to penetrate, pierce; *(entender)* to grasp ▷ *vi* to penetrate, go in; *(líquido)* to soak in; *(emoción)* to pierce

penicilina *nf* penicillin

península *nf* península; **P~ Ibérica** Iberian Península

peninsular *adj* peninsular

penique *nm* penny; **peniques** *nmpl* pence

penitencia *nf (remordimiento)* penitence; *(castigo)* penance; **en ~** as a penance

penitenciaría *nf* prison, penitentiary

penitenciario, -a *adj* prison *antes de n*

penoso, -a *adj* laborious, difficult

pensador, a *nm/f* thinker

pensamiento *nm (gen)* thought; *(mente)* mind; *(idea)* idea; *(Bot)* pansy; **no se le pasó por el ~ it** never occurred to him

pensar *vt (tener pensamientos)* to think; *(considerar)* to think over, think out; *(proponerse)* to intend, plan, propose; *(imaginarse)* to think up, invent ▷ *vi* to think ▷ *vr:* **pensarse: piénsatelo** think it over; **¿qué piensas de Manolo?** what do you think of Manolo?; **¿qué piensas del aborto?** what do you think about abortion?; **tengo que ~lo** I'll have to think about it; **pensándolo bien ...** on second thoughts ...; **¡ni ~lo!** *(col)* no way! *(col)*; **~ en** to think of o about; *(anhelar)* to aim at, aspire to; **sólo piensa en pasarlo bien** all he thinks about is having a good time; **dar que ~ a algn** to make sb think

pensativo, -a *adj* thoughtful, pensive

pensión *nf (casa)* ≈ guest house; *(dinero)* pension; *(cama y comida)* board and lodging; **~ de jubilación** retirement pension; **~ completa** full board; **media ~** half board

pensionista *nm/f (jubilado)* (old-age) pensioner; *(el que vive en una pensión)* lodger; *(Escol)* boarder

penúltimo, -a *adj* penultimate, second last

penumbra *nf* half-light, semi-darkness

penuria *nf* shortage, want

peña *nf (roca)* rock; *(acantilado)* cliff, crag; *(grupo)* group, circle; *(Deporte)* supporters' club

peñasco *nm* large rock, boulder

peñón *nm* crag; **el P~** the Rock (of Gibraltar)

peón *nm* labourer; *(LAm)* farm labourer, farmhand; *(Tec)* spindle, shaft; *(Ajedrez)* pawn

peonza *nf* spinning top

peor *adj, adv (comparativo)* worse; *(superlativo)* worst; **su caso es ~ que el nuestro** his case is worse than ours; **mis notas son malas pero las tuyas son ~es** my marks are bad but yours are worse; **el ~ día de mi vida** the worst day of my life; **sacó la ~ nota de toda la clase** he got the worst mark in the whole class; **y lo ~ es que ...** and the worst thing is that ...; **hoy me siento ~** I feel worse today; **de mal en ~** from bad to worse; **tanto ~** so much the worse; **el restaurante donde ~ se come** the restaurant with the worst food

pepinillo *nm* gherkin

pepino *nm* cucumber; **(no) me importa un ~** I don't care two hoots

pepita *nf (Bot)* pip; *(Minería)* nugget

pequeñez *nf* smallness, littleness; *(trivialidad)* trifle, triviality

pequeño, -a *adj* small, little; *(cifra)* small, low; *(problema)* slight; *(bajo)* short; **mi hermana pequeña** my younger sister; **~ burgués** lower middle-class

pera *adj inv* classy ▷ *nf* pear; **niño ~** spoiled upper-class brat; **eso es pedir ~s al olmo** that's asking the impossible

peral *nm* pear tree

percance *nm* setback, misfortune

per cápita *adj*: **renta** ~ per capita income

percatarse *vr*: ~ **de** to notice, take note of

percepción *nf* (*vista*) perception; (*idea*) notion, idea; (*Com*) collection

perceptible *adj* perceptible, noticeable; (*Com*) payable, receivable

percha *nf* (*en la pared*) peg; (*de pie*) coat stand; (*en armario*) coat hanger; (*de ave*) perch

percibir *vt* to perceive, notice; (*ver*) to see; (*peligro etc*) to sense; (*Com*) to earn, receive, get

percusión *nf* percussion

perdedor, a *adj* losing ▷ *nm/f* loser

perder *nm*: **tener buen** ~ to be a good loser ▷ *vt* (*llaves, carnet, partido, etc*) to lose; (*tiempo, palabras*) to waste; (*oportunidad*) to lose, miss; (*tren, avión*) to miss ▷ *vi* to lose; **perderse** *vr* (*extraviarse*) to get lost; (*desaparecer*) to disappear, be lost to view; (*arruinarse*) to be ruined; (*película, concierto*) to miss; **perdimos dos a cero** we lost two nil; **está intentando** ~ **peso** he's trying to lose weight; **he perdido la costumbre** I have got out of the habit; ~ **el conocimiento** to lose consciousness; **¡me estás haciendo** ~ **el tiempo!** you're wasting my time!; **¡no te lo pierdas!** don't miss it!; **Ana es la que saldrá perdiendo** Ana is the one who will lose out; **echar a** ~ (*comida*) to spoil, ruin; (*oportunidad*) to waste; **has echado a** ~ **la sorpresa** you've ruined the surprise; **se le perdieron las llaves** he lost his keys

perdición *nf* perdition; (*fig*) ruin

pérdida *nf* loss; (*de tiempo*) waste; (*Com*) net loss; **pérdidas** *nfpl* (*Com*) losses; **¡no tiene** ~! you can't go wrong!

perdido, -a *adj* lost; **estar** ~ **por** to be crazy about; **es un caso** ~ he is a hopeless case

perdigón *nm* pellet

perdiz *nf* partridge

perdón *nm* (*disculpa*) forgiveness; (*Jur*) pardon; **¡~!** (*disculpándose*) sorry!; (*llamando la atención*) excuse me!; **le pedí** ~ I apologized to him; **con** ~ if I may, if you don't mind

perdonar *vt* (*disculpar*) to pardon, forgive; (*excusar*) to exempt, excuse ▷ *vi* to pardon, forgive; **¿me perdonas?** do you forgive me?; **no me perdona que me haya olvidado de su cumpleaños** he hasn't forgiven me for forgetting his birthday; **¡perdona! ¿tienes hora?** excuse me, do you have the time?; **¡perdona! ¿te he hecho daño?** I'm so sorry, did I hurt you?; **¡perdone (usted)!** sorry!; **perdone, pero me parece que ...** excuse me, but I think ...

perdurable *adj* lasting; (*eterno*) everlasting

perdurar *vi* (*resistir*) to last, endure; (*seguir existiendo*) to stand, still exist

perecedero, -a *adj* perishable

perecer *vi* to perish, die

peregrinación *nf* (*Rel*) pilgrimage

peregrino, -a *adj* (*extraño*) strange; (*singular*) rare ▷ *nm/f* pilgrim

perejil *nm* parsley

perenne *adj* everlasting, perennial

perentorio, -a *adj* (*urgente*) urgent; (*terminante*) peremptory; (*inamovible*) set, fixed

pereza *nf* (*flojera*) laziness; (*lentitud*) sloth, slowness

perezoso, -a *adj* lazy

perfección *nf* perfection; **a la** ~ to perfection

perfeccionar *vt* to perfect; (*acabar*) to complete, finish

perfecto, -a *adj* perfect ▷ *nm* (*Ling*) perfect (tense)

perfidia *nf* perfidy, treachery

perfil *nm* (*parte lateral*) profile; (*silueta*) silhouette, outline; (*Tec*) (cross) section; **ponerse de** ~ to stand side on; ~ **del cliente** (*Com*) customer profile

perfilado, -a *adj* (*bien formado*) well-shaped; (*largo: cara*) long

perfilar *vt* (*trazar*) to outline; (*dar carácter a*) to shape, give character to; **perfilarse** *vr* to be silhouetted (*en* against); **el proyecto se va perfilando** the project is taking shape

perforación *nf* perforation; (*con taladro*) drilling

perforadora *nf* drill; ~ **de fichas** card-punch

perforar *vt* to perforate; (*agujero*) to drill, bore; (*papel*) to punch a hole in ▷ *vi* to drill, bore

perfume *nm* perfume, scent

pericia *nf* skill, expertise

periferia *nf* periphery; (*de ciudad*) outskirts *pl*

periférico, -a *adj* peripheral ▷ *nm* (*Inform*) peripheral; (*LAm: Auto*) ring road; **barrio** ~ outlying district

perilla *nf* goatee

perímetro *nm* perimeter

periódico, -a *adj* periodic(al) ▷ *nm* (news)paper; ~ **del domingo** Sunday (news)paper

periodismo *nm* journalism

periodista *nm/f* journalist

periodo, período *nm* period; **un** ~ **de tres meses** a three-month period; ~ **contable** (*Com*) accounting period

peripecias *nfpl* adventures

perito, -a *adj* (*experto*) expert; (*diestro*) skilled, skilful ▷ *nm/f* (*experto*) expert; (*técnico*) technician

perjudicar *vt* (*gen*) to damage, harm; (*fig*) to prejudice

perjudicial *adj* damaging, harmful

perjuicio *nm* damage, harm; **en/sin** ~ **de** to the detriment of/without prejudice to

perjurar *vi* to commit perjury

perla *nf* pearl; **me viene de** ~**s** it suits me fine

permanecer *vi* (*quedarse*) to stay, remain; (*seguir*) to continue to be

permanencia *nf* (*duración*) permanence; (*estancia*) stay

permanente *adj* (*que queda*) permanent; (*constante*) constant; (*comisión etc*) standing ▷ *nf* perm; **hacerse una** ~ to have one's hair permed

permisible *adj* permissible, allowable

permiso *nm* permission; (*licencia*) permit, licence

(*Brit*), license (*US*); **con ~** excuse me; **estar de ~** (*Mil*) to be on leave; **~ de conducir** *o* **conductor** driving licence (*Brit*), driver's license (*US*); **~ de exportación/importación** export/import licence; **~ de trabajo** work permit; **~ por asuntos familiares** compassionate leave

permitir *vt* to permit, allow; **permitirse** *vr*: **~se algo** to allow o.s. sth; **no nos permiten fumar en la oficina** we're not allowed to smoke in the office; **me permito recordarle que ...** may I remind you that ...; **¿me permite?** may I?; **si el tiempo lo permite** weather permitting; **no me puedo ~ ese lujo** I can't afford that

pernicioso, -a *adj* (*maligno, Med*) pernicious

perno *nm* bolt

pero *conj* but; (*aún*) yet ▷ *nm* (*defecto*) flaw, defect; (*reparo*) objection; **¡no hay ~ que valga!** there are no buts about it

perol *nm*, **perola** *nf* pan

perpendicular *adj* perpendicular; **el camino es ~ al río** the road is at right angles to the river

perpetrar *vt* to perpetrate

perpetuar *vt* to perpetuate

perpetuo, -a *adj* perpetual; **cadena perpetua** life sentence

perplejo, -a *adj* perplexed, bewildered

perra *nf* bitch; (*fam: dinero*) money; (*: manía*) mania, crazy idea; (*: rabieta*) tantrum; **estar sin una ~** to be flat broke

perrera *nf* kennel

perro *nm* dog; **"~ peligroso"** "beware of the dog"; **tiempo de ~s** filthy weather; **ser ~ viejo** to be an old hand; **~ que ladra no muerde** his bark is worse than his bite; **~ caliente** hot dog

persa *adj*, *nm/f* Persian ▷ *nm* (*Ling*) Persian

persecución *nf* pursuit, hunt, chase; (*Rel, Pol*) persecution

perseguir *vt* to pursue, hunt; (*cortejar*) to chase after; (*molestar*) to pester, annoy; (*Rel, Pol*) to persecute; (*Jur*) to prosecute

perseverante *adj* persevering, persistent

perseverar *vi* to persevere, persist; **~ en** to persevere in, persist with

persiana *nf* (*Venetian*) blind

persignarse *vr* to cross o.s.

persistente *adj* persistent

persistir *vi* to persist

persona *nf* person; **10 ~s** 10 people; **tercera ~** third party; (*Ling*) third person; **en ~** in person, in the flesh; **por ~** a head; **es buena ~** he's a good sort

personaje *nm* important person, celebrity; (*Teat*) character

personal *adj* (*particular*) personal; (*para una persona*) single, for one person ▷ *nm* (*plantilla*) personnel, staff; (*Naut*) crew; (*fam: gente*) people

personalidad *nf* personality; (*Jur*) status

personalizar *vt* to personalize ▷ *vi* (*al hablar*) to name names

personarse *vr* to appear in person; **~ en** to present o.s. at, report to

personificar *vt* to personify

perspectiva *nf* perspective; (*vista, panorama*) view, panorama; (*posibilidad futura*) outlook, prospect; **tener algo en ~** to have sth in view

perspicacia *nf* discernment, perspicacity

perspicaz *adj* shrewd

persuadir *vt* (*gen*) to persuade; (*convencer*) to convince; **persuadirse** *vr* to become convinced

persuasión *nf* (*acto*) persuasion; (*convicción*) conviction

persuasivo, -a *adj* (*vendedor, carácter*) persuasive; (*argumento*) convincing

pertenecer *vi*: **~ a** to belong to; (*fig*) to concern

perteneciente *adj*: **~ a** belonging to

pertenencia *nf* ownership; **pertenencias** *nfpl* possessions, property *sg*

pértiga *nf* pole; **salto de ~** pole vault

pertinaz *adj* (*persistente*) persistent; (*terco*) obstinate

pertinente *adj* relevant, pertinent; (*apropiado*) appropriate; **~ a** concerning, relevant to

perturbación *nf* (*Pol*) disturbance; (*Med*) upset, disturbance; **~ del orden público** breach of the peace

perturbador, a *adj* (*que perturba*) perturbing, disturbing; (*subversivo*) subversive

perturbar *vt* (*el orden*) to disturb; (*Med*) to upset, disturb; (*mentalmente*) to perturb

Perú *nm*: **el ~** Peru

peruano, -a *adj*, *nm/f* Peruvian

perversión *nf* perversion

perverso, -a *adj* perverse; (*depravado*) depraved

pervertido, -a *adj* perverted ▷ *nm/f* pervert

pervertir *vt* to pervert, corrupt

pesa *nf* weight; **hacer ~s** to do weight training

pesadez *nf* (*calidad de pesado*) heaviness; (*lentitud*) slowness; (*aburrimiento*) tediousness; **es una ~ tener que ...** it's a bind having to ...

pesadilla *nf* nightmare, bad dream; (*fig*) worry, obsession

pesado, -a *adj* (*gen*) heavy; (*lento*) slow; (*difícil, duro*) tough, hard; (*aburrido*) tedious, boring; (*bochornoso*) sultry ▷ *nm/f* bore; **tener el estómago ~** to feel bloated; **¡no seas ~!** don't be a pain in the neck! (*fam*)

pesadumbre *nf* grief, sorrow

pésame *nm* expression of condolence, message of sympathy; **dar el ~** to express one's condolences

pesar *nm* (*arrepentimiento*) regret; (*pena*) grief, sorrow ▷ *vt* to weigh; (*fig*) to weigh heavily on; (*afligir*) to grieve ▷ *vi* (*tener peso*) to weigh; (*ser pesado*) to weigh a lot, be heavy; (*fig: opinión*) to carry weight; **pese a** *prep* in spite of; **el paquete pesaba 2 kilos** the package weighed 2 kilos; **sobre ella pesan muchas obligaciones** many obligations bear heavily on her; **esta maleta pesa mucho** this suitcase is very heavy; **¡no pesa nada!** it's not heavy at all!; **no me pesa haberlo hecho** I'm not sorry I did it; **a ~ de (que)** in spite of, despite; **a ~ del mal tiempo** in spite of the bad weather; **a ~ de que la quiero** even though I love her; **pese a las dificultades**

in spite of the difficulties

pesca *nf* (*acto*) fishing; (*cantidad de pescado*) catch; **ir de ~** to go fishing; **~ de altura/de bajura** deep sea/coastal fishing

pescadería *nf* fish shop, fishmonger's

pescadilla *nf* whiting

pescado *nm* fish

pescador, a *nm/f* fisherman(-woman)

pescar *vt* (*coger*) to catch; (*tratar de coger*) to fish for; (*fam: lograr*) to get hold of, land; (*conseguir: trabajo*) to manage to get; (*sorprender*) to catch unawares ▷ *vi* to fish, go fishing

pescuezo *nm* neck

pesebre *nm* manger

pesimismo *nm* pessimism

pesimista *adj* pessimistic ▷ *nm/f* pessimist

pésimo, -a *adj* abominable, vile

peso *nm* weight; (*balanza*) scales *pl*; (*LAm Com*) monetary unit; (*moneda*) peso; (*Deporte*) shot; **de poco ~** light(weight); **levantamiento de ~s** weightlifting; **vender al ~** to sell by weight; **argumento de ~** weighty argument; **eso cae por su propio ~** that goes without saying; **~ bruto/neto** gross/net weight; **~ mosca/pesado** fly-/heavyweight

pesquero, -a *adj* fishing *antes de n*

pesquisa *nf* inquiry, investigation

pestaña *nf* (*Anat*) eyelash; (*borde*) rim

pestañear *vi* to blink

peste *nf* plague; (*fig*) nuisance; (*mal olor*) stink, stench; **echar ~s** to swear, fume; **~ negra** Black Death

pesticida *nm* pesticide

pestilencia *nf* (*mal olor*) stink, stench

pestillo *nm* (*de puerta, ventana*) bolt; (*de cerradura*) latch; (*cerrojo*) catch

petaca *nf* (*de cigarrillos*) cigarette case; (*de pipa*) tobacco pouch; (*Méx: maleta*) suitcase

pétalo *nm* petal

petanca *nf* *a game in which metal bowls are thrown at a target bowl*

petardo *nm* firework, firecracker

petición *nf* (*pedido*) request, plea; (*memorial*) petition; (*Jur*) plea; **a ~ de** at the request of; **~ de aumento de salarios** wage demand *o* claim

petrificar *vt* to petrify

petróleo *nm* oil, petroleum

petrolero, -a *adj* petroleum *antes de n* ▷ *nm* (*Com*) oil man; (*buque*) (oil) tanker

peyorativo, -a *adj* pejorative

pez *nm* fish; **estar como el ~ en el agua** to feel completely at home; **~ de colores** goldfish; **~ espada** swordfish

pezón *nm* (*de animal*) teat; (*de persona*) nipple

pezuña *nf* hoof

piadoso, -a *adj* (*devoto*) pious, devout; (*misericordioso*) kind, merciful

pianista *nm/f* pianist

piano *nm* piano; **~ de cola** grand piano

piar *vi* to cheep

PIB *nm abr* (*Esp Com*: = *Producto Interior Bruto*) GDP

pibe, -a *nm/f* (*RP*) boy (girl), kid, child

picadero *nm* riding school

picadillo *nm* mince, minced meat

picado, -a *adj* pricked, punctured; (*mar*) choppy; (*diente*) bad; (*tabaco*) cut; (*enfadado*) cross

picador *nm* (*Taur*) picador; (*minero*) faceworker

picadora *nf* mincer

picadura *nf* (*pinchazo*) puncture; (*de abeja, avispa*) sting; (*de mosquito, serpiente*) bite; (*tabaco picado*) cut tobacco

picana (*LAm*) *nf* (*Agr*) cattle prod; (*Pol: para tortura*) electric prod

picante *adj* (*comida, sabor*) hot; (*comentario*) racy, spicy

picaporte *nm* (*tirador*) door handle; (*pestillo*) latch

picar *vt* (*agujerear, perforar*) to prick, puncture; (*billete*) to punch, clip; (*abeja, avispa*) to sting; (*mosquito, serpiente*) to bite; (*persona*) to nibble (at); (*incitar*) to incite, goad; (*irritar*) to annoy, bother; (*quemar: lengua*) to burn, sting ▷ *vi* (*pez*) to bite, take the bait; (*el sol*) to burn, scorch; (*abeja, Med*) to sting; (*mosquito*) to bite; **picarse** *vr* (*agriarse*) to turn sour, go off; (*mar*) to get choppy; (*ofenderse*) to take offence; **me pican los ojos** my eyes sting; **me pica el brazo** my arm itches

picardía *nf* villainy; (*astucia*) slyness, craftiness; **una ~** (*acto malvado*) dirty trick; (*palabra soez*) rude/bad word *o* expression

pícaro, -a *adj* (*malicioso*) villainous; (*travieso*) mischievous ▷ *nm* (*astuto*) sly sort; (*sinvergüenza*) rascal, scoundrel

pichón, -ona *nm/f* (*de paloma*) young pigeon; (*apelativo*) darling, dearest

pico *nm* (*de ave*) beak; (*punta afilada*) peak, sharp point; (*Tec*) pick, pickaxe; (*Geo*) peak, summit; **no abrir el ~** to keep quiet; **y ~** and a bit; **son las 3 y ~** it's just after 3; **tiene 50 libros y ~** he has 50-odd books; **me costó un ~** it cost me quite a bit; **cuello de ~** V-neck; **~ parásito** (*Elec*) spike

picor *nm* itch; (*ardor*) sting(ing feeling)

picotear *vt* to peck ▷ *vi* to nibble, pick

picudo, -a *adj* pointed, with a point

pie (*pl* **-s**) *nm* (*gen, Mat*) foot; (*de cama, página, escalera*) foot, bottom; (*Teat*) cue; **~s planos** flat feet; **ir a ~** to go on foot, walk; **estar de ~** to be standing (up); **ponerse de ~** to stand up; **al ~ de la letra** (*citar*) literally, verbatim; (*copiar*) exactly, word for word; **de ~s a cabeza** from head to foot; **en ~ de guerra** on a war footing; **sin ~s ni cabeza** pointless, absurd; **dar ~ a** to give cause for; **no dar ~ con bola** to be no good at anything; **saber de qué ~ cojea algn** to know sb's weak spots

piedad *nf* (*lástima*) pity, compassion; (*clemencia*) mercy; (*devoción*) piety, devotion; **tener ~ de** to have mercy on

piedra *nf* stone; (*roca*) rock; (*de mechero*) flint; (*Meteorología*) hailstone; **primera ~** foundation stone; **~ arenisca/caliza** sand-/limestone; **~ de afilar** grindstone

piel *nf* (*Anat*) skin; (*Zool*) skin, hide; (*de oso*) fur; (*cuero*) leather; (*Bot*) skin, peel ▷ *nm/f*: **~ roja** redskin

pienso *nm* (*Agr*) feed

piercing *nm* piercing

pierna *nf* leg; **en ~s** bare-legged

pieza *nf* (*trozo, parte*) piece; (*esp LAm: habitación*) room; (*Mus*) piece, composition; (*Teat*) work, play; **quedarse de una ~** to be dumbfounded; **~ de recambio** *o* **repuesto** spare (part), extra (*US*); **~ de ropa** article of clothing

pigmento *nm* pigment

pigmeo, -a *adj, nm/f* pigmy

pijama *nm* pyjamas *pl*

pijo, -a *nm/f* (*fam*) upper-class twit

pila *nf* (*Elec*) battery; (*montón*) heap, pile; (*de fuente*) sink; (*tb:* **pila bautismal***: Rel*) font; **nombre de ~** Christian *o* first name; **tengo una ~ de cosas que hacer** (*fam*) I have heaps *o* stacks of things to do; **~ de discos** (*Inform*) disk pack

pilar *nm* (*de techo*) pillar; (*de puente*) pier; (*fig*) prop, mainstay

píldora *nf* pill; **la ~ (anticonceptiva)** the pill; **tragarse la ~** to be taken in

pileta *nf* basin, bowl; (*RP: de cocina*) sink; (*: piscina*) swimming pool

pillaje *nm* pillage, plunder

pillar *vt* (*fam: coger*) to catch; (*: agarrar*) to grasp, seize; (*: entender*) to grasp, catch on to; (*atropellar*) to run over; **~ un resfriado** (*fam*) to catch a cold; **la pilló una moto** she was hit by a motorbike

pillo, -a *adj* villainous; (*astuto*) sly, crafty ⊳ *nm/f* rascal, rogue, scoundrel

pilotar *vt* (*avión*) to pilot; (*barco*) to steer

piloto *nm* (*de avión*) pilot; (*de coche*) driver; (*Auto*) rear light, tail light ⊳ *adj inv*: **planta ~** pilot plant; **luz ~** side light

pimentón *nm* (*polvo*) paprika

pimienta *nf* pepper

pimiento *nm* pepper

pin (*pl* -**s**) *nm* badge

pinacoteca *nf* art gallery

pinar *nm* pinewood

pincel *nm* paintbrush

pinchadiscos *nm/f inv* disc jockey, DJ

pinchar *vt* (*perforar*) to prick, pierce; (*neumático*) to puncture; (*incitar*) to prod ⊳ *vi* (*Mus fam*) to be a DJ; (*Inform*) to click; **pincharse** *vr* (*con droga*) to inject o.s.; (*neumático*) to burst, puncture; **el clavo pinchó la pelota** the nail burst the ball; **me ~on en el brazo** they gave me an injection in the arm; **no ~ ni cortar** (*fam*) to cut no ice; **me pinché con un alfiler** I pricked myself on a pin; **se me pinchó una rueda** I had a puncture; **tener un neumático pinchado** to have a puncture *o* a flat tyre

pinchazo *nm* (*perforación*) prick; (*de llanta*) puncture, flat (*US*)

pincho *nm* point; (*aguijón*) spike; (*Culin*) savoury (snack); **~ moruno** shish kebab; **~ de tortilla** small slice of omelette

ping-pong *nm* table tennis

pingüino *nm* penguin

pinitos *nmpl*: **hacer sus primeros ~** to take one's first steps

pino *nm* pine (tree); **vivir en el quinto ~** to live at the back of beyond

pinta *nf* spot; (*gota*) spot, drop; (*aspecto*) appearance, look(s) *pl*; (*medida*) pint; **tener buena ~** to look good, look well; **por la ~** by the look of it

pintado, -a *adj* spotted; (*de muchos colores*) colourful ⊳ *nf* piece of political graffiti; **pintadas** *nfpl* political graffiti *sg*; **me sienta** *o* **viene que ni ~** it suits me a treat

pintar *vt* (*con pintura, óleo*) to paint; (*con lápices de colores*) to colour in ⊳ *vi* to paint; (*fam*) to count, be important; **pintarse** *vr* to put on make-up; **quiero ~ la habitación de azul** I want to paint the room blue; **me gusta ~** I like painting; **este boli no pinta** this pen doesn't write; **no pinta nada** (*fam*) he has no say; **nunca me pinto** I never wear makeup; **~se los labios** to put on lipstick; **~se las uñas** to paint one's nails; **pintárselas solo para hacer algo** to manage to do sth by o.s.

pintor, a *nm/f* painter; **~ de brocha gorda** house painter; (*fig*) bad painter

pintoresco, -a *adj* picturesque

pintura *nf* painting; **~ a la acuarela** watercolour; **~ al óleo** oil painting; **~ rupestre** cave painting

pinza *nf* (*Zool*) claw; (*para colgar ropa*) clothes peg, clothespin (*US*); (*Tec*) pincers *pl*; **pinzas** *nfpl* (*para depilar*) tweezers

piña *nf* (*del pino*) pine cone; (*tropical*) pineapple; (*fig*) group

piñón *nm* (*Bot*) pine nut; (*Tec*) pinion

pío, -a *adj* (*devoto*) pious, devout; (*misericordioso*) merciful ⊳ *nm*: **no decir ni ~** not to breathe a word

piojo *nm* louse

pionero, -a *adj* pioneering ⊳ *nm/f* pioneer

pipa *nf* pipe; (*Bot*) seed, pip

pipí *nm* (*fam*): **hacer ~** to have a wee(-wee)

pique *nm* (*resentimiento*) pique, resentment; (*rivalidad*) rivalry, competition; **irse a ~** to sink; (*familia*) to be ruined; **tener un ~ con algn** to have a grudge against sb

piqueta *nf* pick(axe)

piquete *nm* (*agujerito*) small hole; (*Mil*) squad, party; (*de obreros*) picket; **~ secundario** secondary picket

pirado, -a *adj* (*fam*) round the bend

piragua *nf* canoe

piragüismo *nm* (*Deporte*) canoeing

pirámide *nf* pyramid

piraña *nf* piranha

pirarse *vr*: **~(las)** (*largarse*) to beat it (*fam*); (*Escol*) to cut class

pirata *adj*: **edición/disco ~** pirate edition/bootleg record ⊳ *nm* pirate; **~ informático** hacker

Pirineo(s) *nm(pl)* Pyrenees *pl*

pirómano, -a *nm/f* (*Psico*) pyromaniac; (*Jur*) arsonist

piropo *nm* compliment, (piece of) flattery; **echar ~s a** to make flirtatious remarks to

pirueta *nf* pirouette

pis *nm* (*fam*) pee; **hacer ~** to have a pee

pisada *nf* (*paso*) footstep; (*huella*) footprint

pisar *vt* (*caminar sobre*) to walk on, tread on; (*apretar con el pie*) to press; (*fig*) to trample on, walk all over ▷ *vi* to tread, step, walk; **~ el acelerador** to step on the accelerator; **~ fuerte** (*fig*) to act determinedly

piscifactoría *nf* fish farm

piscina *nf* swimming pool

Piscis *nm* (*Astro*) Pisces

piso *nm* (*suelo: de edificio*) floor; (*LAm*) ground; (*vivienda*) flat, apartment; **primer ~** (*Esp*) first *o* second (*US*) floor; (*LAm*) ground *o* first (*US*) floor

pisotear *vt* to trample (on *o* underfoot); (*fig: humillar*) to trample on

pisotón *nm* (*con el pie*) stamp

pista *nf* track, trail; (*indicio*) clue; (*Inform*) track; **estar sobre la ~ de algn** to be on sb's trail; **~ de aterrizaje** runway; **~ de auditoría** (*Com*) audit trail; **~ de baile** dance floor; **~ de hielo** ice rink; **~ de tenis** tennis court

pisto *nm* (*Culin*) ratatouille; **darse ~** (*fam*) to show off

pistola *nf* pistol; (*Tec*) spray-gun

pistolera *nf* holster; *ver tb* **pistolero**

pistolero, -a *nm/f* gunman, gangster; *ver tb* **pistolera**

pistón *nm* (*Tec*) piston; (*Mus*) key

pitar *vt* (*hacer sonar*) to blow; (*partido*) to referee; (*rechiflar*) to whistle at, boo; (*actor, obra*) to hiss ▷ *vi* to whistle; (*Auto*) to sound *o* toot one's horn; (*LAm*) to smoke; **salir pitando** (*fam*) to beat it

pitido *nm* whistle; (*sonido agudo*) beep; (*sonido corto*) pip

pitillera *nf* cigarette case

pitillo *nm* cigarette

pito *nm* whistle; (*de coche*) horn; (*cigarrillo*) cigarette; (*fam: de marihuana*) joint; (*fam!*) prick (!); **me importa un ~** I don't care two hoots

pitón *nm* (*Zool*) python

pitonisa *nf* fortune-teller

pitorreo *nm* joke, laugh; **estar de ~** to be in a joking mood

pizarra *nf* (*piedra*) slate; (*para escribir*) blackboard

pizca *nf* pinch, spot; **ni ~** not a bit

pizza *nf* pizza

placa *nf* plate; (*Med*) dental plate; (*distintivo*) badge; **~ de matrícula** number plate; **~ madre** (*Inform*) mother board

placaje *nm* tackle

placenta *nf* placenta; (*tras el parto*) afterbirth

placentero, -a *adj* pleasant, agreeable

placer *nm* pleasure; **a ~** at one's pleasure

plácido, -a *adj* placid

plaga *nf* pest; (*Med*) plague; (*fig*) swarm

plagar *vt* to infest, plague; (*llenar*) to fill; **plagado de** riddled with; **han plagado la ciudad de carteles** they have plastered the town with posters

plagiar *vt* to plagiarize; (*LAm*) to kidnap

plagio *nm* plagiarism; (*LAm*) kidnap

plan *nm* (*esquema, proyecto*) plan; (*idea, intento*) idea, intention; **tener ~** (*fam*) to have a date; **tener un ~** (*fam*) to have an affair; **en ~ de cachondeo** for a laugh; **en ~ económico** (*fam*) on the cheap; **vamos en ~ de turismo** we're going as tourists; **si te pones en ese ~ ...** if that's your attitude ...; **~ de estudios** curriculum, syllabus; **~ de incentivos** (*Com*) incentive scheme

plana *nf* sheet of paper, page; (*Tec*) trowel; **en primera ~** on the front page; **~ mayor** staff; *ver tb* **plano**

plancha *nf* (*para planchar*) iron; (*rótulo*) plate, sheet; (*Naut*) gangway; (*Culin*) grill; **pescado a la ~** grilled fish

planchado, -a *adj* (*ropa*) ironed; (*traje*) pressed ▷ *nm* ironing

planchar *vt* to iron ▷ *vi* to do the ironing

planeador *nm* glider

planear *vt* to plan ▷ *vi* to glide

planeta *nm* planet

planicie *nf* plain

planificación *nf* planning; **diagrama de ~** (*Com*) planner; **~ corporativa** (*Com*) corporate planning; **~ familiar** family planning

plano, -a *adj* flat, level, even; (*liso*) smooth ▷ *nm* (*Mat, Tec, Aviat*) plane; (*Foto*) shot; (*Arq*) plan; (*Geo*) map; (*de ciudad*) map, street plan; **primer ~** close-up; **caer de ~** to fall flat; **rechazar algo de ~** to turn sth down flat; **le daba el sol de ~** (*fig*) the sun shone directly on it; *ver tb* **plana**

planta *nf* (*Bot, Tec*) plant; (*Anat*) sole of the foot, foot; **~ baja** ground floor

plantación *nf* (*Agr*) plantation; (*acto*) planting

plantar *vt* (*Bot*) to plant; (*colocar*) to put in; (*levantar*) to erect, set up; **plantarse** *vr*: **~se en** (*mantenerse firme*) to stick to; (*llegar*) to get to; **~ a algn en la calle** to throw sb out; **lo plantó delante del altar** she left him standing at the altar; **dejar plantado a algn** (*fam*) to stand sb up; **35, y me planto** 35, and there I stop; **se plantó en su decisión** she stuck to her decision; **en tres horas se plantó en Sevilla** he got to Seville in 3 hours

plantear *vt* (*problema: Mat*) to pose; (*causar*) to create; (*dificultad*) to raise; **plantearse** *vr* to think about; **nos ha planteado muchos problemas** it has created a lot of problems for us; **se lo ~é al jefe** I'll bring it up with the boss; **incluso me planteé dejar los estudios** I even thought of giving up my studies

plantilla *nf* (*de zapato*) insole; (*personal*) personnel; **ser de ~** to be on the staff

plantón *nm* (*Mil*) guard, sentry; (*fam*) long wait; **dar (un) ~ a algn** to stand sb up

plañir *vi* to mourn

plasma *nm* plasma

plástico, -a *adj* plastic ▷ *nf* (art of) sculpture, modelling ▷ *nm* plastic

plastilina *nf* Plasticine®

plata *nf* (*metal*) silver; (*objetos de plata*) silverware; (*LAm*) cash, dough (*fam*); **hablar en ~** to speak bluntly *o* frankly

plataforma *nf* platform; ~ **de lanzamiento/
perforación** launch(ing) pad/drilling rig; ~
petrolífera oil rig

plátano *nm* (*fruta*) banana; (*árbol*) plane tree

platea *nf* (*Teat*) pit

plateado, -a *adj* silver; (*Tec*) silver-plated

plática *nf* (*CAm, Méx*) talk, chat; (*Rel*) sermon

platicar *vi* (*CAm, Méx*) to talk, chat

platillo *nm* (*de taza*) saucer; (*de limosnas*) collecting
bowl; **platillos** *nmpl* cymbals; **pasar el ~** to pass
the hat round; ~ **volador** o **volante** flying saucer

platina *nf* (*Mus*) tape deck

platino *nm* platinum; **platinos** *nmpl* (*Auto*)
(contact) points

plato *nm* (*utensilio*) plate, dish; (*parte de comida*)
course; (*guiso*) dish; **pagar los ~s rotos** (*fam*) to
carry the can (*fam*); ~ **frutero/sopero** fruit/soup
dish

plató *nm* set

platónico, -a *adj* platonic

playa *nf* beach; (*costa*) seaside; ~ **de
estacionamiento** (*CS, Perú*) car park

playera *nf* (*LAm: camiseta*) T-shirt; **playeras** *nfpl*
canvas shoes; (*Tenis*) tennis shoes; *ver tb* **playero**

playero, -a *adj* beach *antes de n*; *ver tb* **playera**

plaza *nf* square; (*mercado*) market(place); (*sitio*)
room, space; (*en vehículo*) seat, place; (*colocación*)
post, job; **hacer la ~** to do the daily shopping;
reservar una ~ to reserve a seat; **el hotel tiene
100 ~s** the hotel has 100 beds; ~ **de abastos** food
market; ~ **de toros** bullring; ~ **mayor** main
square

plazo *nm* (*lapso de tiempo*) time, period, term;
(*fecha de vencimiento*) expiry date; (*pago parcial*)
instalment; **a corto/largo ~** short-/long-term;
comprar a ~s to buy on hire purchase, pay for in
instalments; **nos dan un ~ de 8 días** they allow
us a week

plazoleta, plazuela *nf* small square

pleamar *nf* high tide

plebe *nf*: **la ~** the common people *pl*, the masses
pl; (*pey*) the plebs *pl*

plebeyo, -a *adj* plebeian; (*pey*) coarse, common

plebiscito *nm* plebiscite

plegable *adj* folding

plegar *vt* (*doblar*) to fold, bend; (*Costura*) to pleat;
plegarse *vr* to yield, submit

pleito *nm* (*Jur*) lawsuit, case; (*fig*) dispute, feud;
pleitos *nmpl* litigation *sg*; **entablar un ~** to
bring an action o a lawsuit; **poner un ~ a algn**
to sue sb

plenilunio *nm* full moon

plenitud *nf* plenitude, fullness; (*abundancia*)
abundance

pleno, -a *adj* full; (*completo*) complete ⊳ *nm*
plenary; **en ~ día** in broad daylight; **en ~ verano**
at the height of summer; **en plena cara** full
in the face; **en ~** as a whole; (*por unanimidad*)
unanimously

pletina *nf* (*Mus*) tape deck

pliego *nm* (*hoja*) sheet (of paper); (*carta*) sealed
letter/document; ~ **de condiciones** details *pl*,
specifications *pl*

pliegue *nm* fold, crease; (*de vestido*) pleat

plisado *nm* pleating

plomero *nm* (*LAm*) plumber

plomo *nm* (*metal*) lead; (*Elec*) fuse; **caer a ~** to fall
heavily o flat

pluma *nf* (*Zool*) feather; ~ **estilográfica**, ~ **fuente**
(*LAm*) fountain pen

plumero *nm* (*quitapolvos*) feather duster; **se te ve
el ~** I know what you're up to

plumón *nm* (*Chi*) felt-tip pen

plural *adj* plural ⊳ *nm*: **en ~** in the plural

pluralidad *nf* plurality

pluriempleo *nm* moonlighting

plus *nm* bonus

plusvalía *nf* (*mayor valor*) appreciation, added
value; (*Com*) goodwill

plutocracia *nf* plutocracy

PNB *nm abr* (*Esp Com*: = *producto nacional bruto*) GNP

población *nf* population; (*pueblo, ciudad*) town,
city; ~ **activa** working population

poblado, -a *adj* inhabited; (*barba*) thick; (*cejas*)
bushy ⊳ *nm* (*aldea*) village; (*pueblo*) (small) town;
~ **de** (*lleno de*) filled with; **densamente ~** densely
populated

poblador, a *nm/f* settler, colonist

poblar *vt* (*colonizar*) to colonize; (*fundar*) to found;
(*habitar*) to inhabit; **poblarse** *vr*: **~se de** to fill up
with; (*irse cubriendo*) to become covered with

pobre *adj* poor ⊳ *nm/f* poor person; (*mendigo*)
beggar; **los ~s** the poor; **¡~!** poor thing!; ~ **diablo**
(*fig*) poor wretch o devil

pobreza *nf* poverty

pocilga *nf* pigsty

pocillo *nm* (*LAm*) coffee cup

pócima, poción *nf* potion; (*brebaje*) concoction,
nasty drink

poco, -a *adj* **1** (*sg*) little, not much; **de ~ interés**
of little interest, not very interesting; **hay poca
leche** there isn't much milk; **poca cosa** not
much

2 (*pl*) few, not many; **tiene ~s amigos** he hasn't
got many friends

⊳ *pron*: **un ~** a bit, a little; **unos ~s** a few; **es un
~ aburrido** it's a bit boring; **tomé un ~ de vino**
I had a bit of o a little wine; **me llevé unos ~s** I
took a few with me

⊳ *adv* **1** (*poca cantidad*) little, not much; **cuesta
~** it doesn't cost much; ~ **más o menos** more
or less

2 (+ *adj, pp: para negar algo*): ~ **amable/inteligente**
not very nice/intelligent; **sus libros son ~
conocidos aquí** his books are not very well
known here

3: **por ~** nearly; **por ~ me caigo** I almost fell

4 (*tiempo*): ~ **después** soon after that; **dentro
de ~** shortly; **hace ~** a short time ago, not long
ago; **a ~ de haberse casado** shortly after getting
married

5: ~ **a ~** little by little

6 (*CAm, Méx*): **¿a ~ no está divino?** isn't it just
divine?

7 (*LAm*): **de a ~** gradually

podar *vt* to prune

poder *vi* **1** (*capacidad*) can, be able to; **yo puedo ayudarte** I can help you; **no puedo hacerlo** I can't do it, I'm unable to do it; **creo que mañana no voy a ~ ir** I don't think I'll be able to go tomorrow; **¡no puedo más!** I've had enough!; **no pude menos que dejarlo** I couldn't help but leave it; **es tonto a más no ~** he's as stupid as they come

2 (*permiso*) can, may, be allowed to; **¿se puede?** may I?; **puedes irte ahora** you may go now; **no se puede fumar** smoking is not allowed; **¿puedo usar su teléfono?** can I use your phone?

3 (*posibilidad*) may, might, could; **puede llegar mañana** he may o might arrive tomorrow; **pudiste haberte hecho daño** you might o could have hurt yourself; **¡me lo podías haber dicho!** you could have told me!

4: **puede (ser)** perhaps; **puede que lo sepa Tomás** Tomás may o might know; **¡no puede ser!** that can't be true!

5: **~ con, ¿puedes con la maleta?** can you manage the case?; **no puedo con tanto trabajo** I can't cope with so much work; **no puedo con este crío** this kid's too much for me

6: **él me puede** (*fam*) he's stronger than me ▷ *nm* power; **el ~** the Government; **detentar** *u* **ocupar** o **estar en el ~** to be in power o office; **estar** *u* **obrar en ~ de** to be in the hands o possession of; **casarse por ~(es)** to get married by proxy; **~ adquisitivo** purchasing power; **~ ejecutivo** executive power

poderoso, -a *adj* powerful

podio *nm* podium

podólogo, -a *nm/f* chiropodist (*Brit*), podiatrist (*US*)

podrido, -a *adj* rotten, bad; (*fig*) rotten, corrupt

podrir = **pudrir**

poema *nm* poem

poesía *nf* poetry

poeta *nm* poet

poético, -a *adj* poetic(al)

poetisa *nf* (woman) poet

póker *nm* poker

polaco, -a *adj* Polish ▷ *nm/f* Pole ▷ *nm* (*Ling*) Polish

polar *adj* polar

polaridad *nf* polarity

polea *nf* pulley

polémica *nf* controversy

polémico, -a *adj* polemic(al)

polen *nm* pollen

poleo *nm* pennyroyal

policía *nm/f* policeman(-woman) ▷ *nf* police

policíaco, -a *adj* police *antes de n*; **novela policíaca** detective story

polideportivo *nm* sports centre

poliéster *nm* polyester

polietileno *nm* polythene (*Brit*), polyethylene (*US*)

poligamia *nf* polygamy

polígono *nm* (*Mat*) polygon; (*solar*) building lot; (*zona*) area; (*unidad vecina*) housing estate; **~ industrial** industrial estate

polígrafo *nm* polygraph

polilla *nf* moth

polio *nf* polio

politécnico *nm* polytechnic

política *nf* politics *sg*; (*económica, agraria*) policy; **~ exterior/de ingresos y precios** foreign/prices and incomes policy; *ver tb* **político**

politicastro *nm* (*pey*) politician, politico

político, -a *adj* political; (*discreto*) tactful; (*pariente*) in-law ▷ *nm/f* politician; **padre ~** father-in-law; *ver tb* **política**

póliza *nf* certificate, voucher; (*impuesto*) tax o fiscal stamp; **~ de seguro(s)** insurance policy

polizón *nm* (*Aviat, Naut*) stowaway

pollera *nf* (*criadero*) hencoop; (*And, CS*) skirt, overskirt

pollería *nf* poulterer's (shop)

pollo *nm* chicken; (*joven*) young man; (*señorito*) playboy; **~ asado** roast chicken

polo *nm* (*Geo, Elec*) pole; (*helado*) ice lolly; (*Deporte*) polo; (*suéter*) polo-neck; **esto es el ~ opuesto de lo que dijo antes** this is the exact opposite of what he said before; **P~ Norte/Sur** North/South Pole

Polonia *nf* Poland

poltrona *nf* reclining chair, easy chair

polución *nf* pollution; **~ ambiental** environmental pollution

polvera *nf* powder compact

polvo *nm* dust; (*Química, Culin, Med*) powder; **en ~** powdered; **~ de talco** talcum powder; **estar hecho ~** to be worn out o exhausted; **hacer algo ~** to smash sth; **hacer ~ a algn** to shatter sb; **echar un ~** (*fam!*) to screw (!); *ver tb* **polvos**

pólvora *nf* gunpowder; (*fuegos artificiales*) fireworks *pl*; **propagarse como la ~** (*noticia*) to spread like wildfire

polvoriento, -a *adj* (*superficie*) dusty; (*sustancia*) powdery

polvos *nmpl* powder *sg*

pomada *nf* pomade

pomelo *nm* grapefruit

pómez *nf*: **piedra ~** pumice stone

pomo *nm* handle

pompa *nf* (*burbuja*) bubble; (*esplendor*) pomp, splendour; **~s fúnebres** funeral *sg*

pomposo, -a *adj* splendid, magnificent; (*pey*) pompous

pómulo *nm* cheekbone

ponche *nm* punch

poncho *nm* (*LAm*) poncho, cape

ponderar *vt* (*considerar*) to weigh up, consider; (*elogiar*) to praise highly, speak in praise of

poner *vt* **1** (*colocar*) to put; (*ropa*) to put on; (*telegrama*) to send; (*interés*) to show; **¿dónde pongo mis cosas?** where shall I put my things?; **~ la mesa** to set the table; **~ algo a secar** to put sth (out) to dry; **¡no pongas esa cara!** don't look at me like that!

2 (*dar: obra de teatro*) to put on; (*: película*) to show; **¿qué ponen en el Excelsior?** what's on at the Excelsior?; **¿ponen alguna película esta noche?** is there a film on tonight?

3 (*radio, TV*) to switch *o* turn on; **¿pongo música?** shall I put some music on?; **pon el radiador** put the heater on; **pon la radio más alta** turn the radio up

4 (*instalar: tienda, negocio*) to open; (*gas etc*) to put in, install; **queremos ~ la calefacción central** we want to put in *o* install central heating

5 (*suponer*): **pongamos que ...** let's suppose that ...

6 (*Telec*): **póngame con el Sr. López** can you put me through to Mr. Lopez?

7 (*estar escrito*) to say; **¿qué pone aquí?** what does it say here?

8: **~ de: lo han puesto de director general** they've appointed him general manager

9 (+*adj*) to make; **me estás poniendo nerviosa** you're making me nervous

10 (*dar nombre*): **al niño le pusieron Diego** they called their son Diego

▷ *vi* (*gallina*) to lay

ponerse *vr* **1** (*situarse*): **se puso a mi lado** he came and stood beside me; **se ponía debajo de la ventana** he used to stand under the window; **tú ponte en esa silla** you go and sit on that chair; **~se delante** to get in the way

2 (*Telec*): **ahora mismo se pone** he's just coming

3 (*ropa, cosméticos*) to put on; **me puse el abrigo** I put on my coat; **¿por qué no te pones el vestido nuevo?** why don't you put on *o* wear your new dress?; **no sé qué ~me** I don't know what to wear

4 (*sol*) to set

5 (+*adj*) to get, become, turn; **~se enfermo/gordo/triste** to get ill/fat/sad; **se puso muy serio** he got very serious; **¡qué guapa te has puesto!** you look beautiful!; **después de lavarla la tela se puso azul** after washing it the material turned blue; **¡no te pongas así!** don't be like that!; **~se cómodo** to make o.s. comfortable

6: **~se a hacer algo** to start doing sth; **se puso a llorar** he started to cry; **tienes que ~te a estudiar** you must get down to studying

7: **~se a bien con algn** to make it up with sb; **~se a mal con algn** to get on the wrong side of sb

8 (*LAm*): **se me pone que ...** it seems to me that ..., I think that ...

poniente *nm* west

pontificado *nm* papacy, pontificate

pontífice *nm* pope, pontiff; **el Sumo P~** His Holiness the Pope

pontón *nm* pontoon

ponzoña *nf* poison, venom

pop *adj inv, nm* (*Mus*) pop

popa *nf* stern; **a ~** astern, abaft; **de ~ a proa** fore and aft

popular *adj* (*tradicional, exitoso*) popular; (*del pueblo*) of the people

popularidad *nf* popularity

por *prep* **1** (*objetivo*) for; **hazlo ~ mí** do it for my sake

2 (+*infin*): **~ no llegar tarde** so as not to arrive late; **~ citar unos ejemplos** to give a few examples; **me castigaron ~ mentir** I was punished for lying

3 (*causa*) for; **~ escasez de fondos** through *o* for lack of funds; **no es ~ eso** that's not the reason

4 (*tiempo*): **~ la mañana/noche** in the morning/at night; **se queda ~ una semana** she's staying (for) a week

5 (*lugar*): **caminar ~ la calle** to walk along the street; **~ allí** over there; **tenemos que ir ~ ahí** we have to go that way; **¿~ dónde?** which way?; **viajar ~ el mundo** to travel around the world; **~ todo el país** throughout the country

6 (*cambio, precio*): **te doy uno nuevo ~ el que tienes** I'll give you a new one (in return) for the one you've got; **lo vendí ~ 15 dólares** I sold it for 15 dollars

7 (*valor distributivo*): **diez euros ~ hora/cabeza** ten euros an *o* per hour/a *o* per head; **10 ~ ciento** 10 per cent; **80 (km) ~ hora** 80 (km) an *o* per hour

8 (*modo, medio*) by; **~ correo/avión** by post/air; **día ~ día** day by day; **me agarró ~ el brazo** he grabbed me by the arm; **~ escrito** in writing

9 (*a través de*) through; **pasamos ~ Valencia** we went through Valencia; **ir a Guayaquil ~ Quito** to go to Guayaquil via Quito; **entrar ~ la entrada principal** to go in through the main entrance; **la conozco ~ mi hermano** I know her through my brother

10 (*agente*) by; **hecho ~ él** done by him; **fueron apresados ~ la policía** they were captured by the police; **dirigido ~ ...** directed by ...

11 (*Mat*): **2 ~ 2 son 4** 2 by 2 is 4

12 (*en lugar de*): **vino él ~ su jefe** he came instead of his boss

13: **~ mí ...** as far as I'm concerned ...

14 (*evidencia*): **~ lo que dicen** judging by *o* from what they say

15: **estar/quedar ~ hacer** to be still *o* remain to be done

16: **~ (muy) difícil que sea** however hard it is *o* may be; **~ más que lo intente** no matter how *o* however hard I try

17: **¿~ qué?** why?; **¿~?** (*fam*) why (do you ask)?; **¿~ qué no vienes conmigo?** why don't you come with me?

porcelana *nf* porcelain; (*china*) china

porcentaje *nm* percentage; **~ de actividad** (*Inform*) hit rate

porción *nf* (*parte*) portion, share; (*cantidad*) quantity, amount

pordiosero, -a *nm/f* beggar

porfía *nf* persistence; (*terquedad*) obstinacy

porfiado, -a *adj* (*insistente*) persistent; (*obstinado*) stubborn, obstinate

porfiar *vi* to persist, insist; (*disputar*) to argue

stubbornly
pormenor *nm* detail, particular
porno *adj inv* porno ▷ *nm* porn
pornografía *nf* pornography
poro *nm* pore
poroso, -a *adj* porous
poroto *nm* (*And, CS Culin*) bean
porque *conj* (*a causa de*) because; (*ya que*) since; ~ **sí**
because I feel like it
porqué *nm* reason, cause
porquería *nf* (*suciedad*) filth, muck, dirt; (*acción*)
dirty trick; (*objeto*) small thing, trifle; (*fig*)
rubbish
porra *nf* (*arma*) stick, club; (*cachiporra*) truncheon;
¡~s! oh heck!; ¡vete a la ~! go to heck!
porrazo *nm* (*golpe*) blow; (*caída*) bump
porro *nm* joint
porrón *nm* *glass wine jar with a long spout*
portaaviones *nm inv* aircraft carrier
portada *nf* (*Tip*) title page; (: *de revista*) cover
portador, a *nm/f* carrier, bearer; (*Com*) bearer,
payee; (*Med*) carrier
portaequipajes *nm inv* boot (*Brit*), trunk (*US*);
(*baca*) luggage rack
portafolio(s) *nm* (*LAm*) briefcase; **portafolio(s)**
de inversiones (*Com*) investment portfolio
portal *nm* (*entrada*) vestibule, hall; (*pórtico*) porch,
doorway; (*puerta de entrada*) main door; (*Deporte*)
goal; **portales** *nmpl* arcade *sg*
portamaletas *nm inv* roof rack
portar *vt* to carry, bear; **portarse** *vr* to behave,
conduct o.s.; **se portó muy bien conmigo** he
treated me very well; **~se mal** to misbehave
portátil *adj* portable
portaviones *nm inv* aircraft carrier
portavoz *nm/f* spokesman(-woman)
portazo *nm*: **dar un ~** to slam the door
porte *nm* (*Com*) transport; (*precio*) transport
charges *pl*; (*Correos*) postage; **~ debido** (*Com*)
carriage forward; **~ pagado** (*Com*) carriage paid,
post-paid
portento *nm* marvel, wonder
portentoso, -a *adj* marvellous, extraordinary
porteño, -a *adj* of *o* from Buenos Aires ▷ *nm/f*
native *o* inhabitant of Buenos Aires
portería *nf* (*oficina*) porter's office; (*gol*) goal
portero, -a *nm/f* porter; (*conserje*) caretaker;
(*Deporte*) goalkeeper
pórtico *nm* (*porche*) portico, porch; (*fig*) gateway;
(*arcada*) arcade
portilla *nf*, **portillo** *nm* gate
portorriqueño, -a *adj, nm/f* Puerto Rican
Portugal *nm* Portugal
portugués, -esa *adj, nm/f* Portuguese ▷ *nm* (*Ling*)
Portuguese
porvenir *nm* future
pos: **en ~ de** *prep* after, in pursuit of
posada *nf* (*refugio*) shelter, lodging; (*mesón*) guest
house; **dar ~ a** to give shelter to, take in
posaderas *nfpl* backside *sg*, buttocks
posar *vt* (*en el suelo*) to lay down, put down; (*la*
mano) to place, put gently ▷ *vi* to sit, pose;

posarse *vr* to settle; (*pájaro*) to perch; (*avión*) to
land, come down
posdata *nf* postscript
pose *nf* (*Arte, afectación*) pose
poseedor, a *nm/f* owner, possessor; (*de récord,*
puesto) holder
poseer *vt* to have, possess, own; (*ventaja*) to
enjoy; (*récord, puesto*) to hold
poseído, -a *adj* possessed; **estar muy ~ de** to be
very vain about
posesión *nf* possession; **tomar ~ (de)** to take
over
posesivo, -a *adj* possessive
posgrado *nm* = **postgrado**
posibilidad *nf* possibility; (*oportunidad*) chance
posibilitar *vt* to make possible, permit; (*hacer*
factible) to make feasible
posible *adj* (*realizable*) possible; (*factible*) feasible
▷ *nm*: **posibles** (*medios*) means; (*bienes*) funds,
assets; **un ~ candidato** a possible candidate;
hacer todo lo ~ to do everything possible; **es ~**
que ganen they might win; **de ser ~** if possible;
en o dentro de lo ~ as far as possible; **lo antes ~**
as soon as possible
posición *nf* (*gen*) position; (*rango social*) status
positivo, -a *adj* positive ▷ *nf* (*Foto*) print
poso *nm* sediment
posoperatorio, -a *adj, nm* = **postoperatorio**
posponer *vt* to postpone
posta *nf* (*de caballos*) relay, team; **a ~** on purpose,
deliberately
postal *adj* postal ▷ *nf* postcard
poste *nm* (*de telégrafos*) post, pole; (*columna*) pillar
póster (*pl* **posters**) *nm* poster
postergar *vt* (*esp LAm*) to put off, postpone, delay
posteridad *nf* posterity
posterior *adj* back, rear; (*siguiente*) following,
subsequent; **ser ~ a** to be later than
posterioridad *nf*: **con ~** later, subsequently
postgrado *nm*: **curso de ~** postgraduate course
postizo, -a *adj* false, artificial; (*sonrisa*) false,
phoney ▷ *nm* hairpiece
postoperatorio, -a *adj* postoperative ▷ *nm*
postoperative period
postor, a *nm/f* bidder; **mejor ~** highest bidder
postrado, -a *adj* prostrate
postre *nm* sweet, dessert ▷ *nf*: **a la ~** in the end,
when all is said and done; **para ~** (*fam*) to crown
it all; **llegar para los ~s** (*fig*) to come too late
postrero, -a *adj* (*delante de nmsg*: **postrer**) last
postulado *nm* postulate
póstumo, -a *adj* posthumous
postura *nf* (*del cuerpo*) posture, position; (*fig*)
attitude, position
potable *adj* drinkable
potaje *nm* thick vegetable soup
pote *nm* pot, jar
potencia *nf* power; (*capacidad*) capacity; (*en*
caballos) horsepower; **en ~** potential, in the
making; **las grandes ~s** the great powers
potencial *adj, nm* potential
potenciar *vt* (*promover*) to promote; (*fortalecer*) to

boost

potente *adj* powerful

potro *nm* (*Zool*) colt; (*Deporte*) vaulting horse

pozo *nm* well; (*de río*) deep pool; (*de mina*) shaft; **ser un ~ de ciencia** (*fig*) to be deeply learned; **~ negro** cesspool

práctica *nf* practice; (*método*) method; (*arte, capacidad*) skill; **en la ~** in practice; *ver tb* **práctico**

practicable *adj* practicable; (*camino*) passable, usable

prácticamente *adv* practically

practicante *nm/f* (*Med: enfermero*) nurse; (*el que practica algo*) practitioner ▷ *adj* practising

practicar *vt* to practise; (*deporte*) to go in for, play; (*ejecutar*) to carry out, perform

práctico, -a *adj* (*gen: persona, ejercicio*) practical; (*conveniente*) handy; *ver tb* **práctica**

pradera *nf* meadow; (*de Canadá*) prairie

prado *nm* (*campo*) meadow, field; (*pastizal*) pasture; (*LAm*) lawn

Praga *nf* Prague

pragmático, -a *adj* pragmatic

preámbulo *nm* preamble, introduction; **decir algo sin ~s** to say sth without beating about the bush

precalentamiento *nm* (*Deporte*) warm-up

precario, -a *adj* precarious

precaución *nf* (*medida preventiva*) preventive measure, precaution; (*prudencia*) caution, wariness

precaver *vt* to guard against; (*impedir*) to forestall; **precaverse** *vr*: **~se de** *o* **contra algo** to (be on one's) guard against sth

precavido, -a *adj* cautious, wary

precedencia *nf* precedence; (*prioridad*) priority; (*superioridad*) greater importance, superiority

precedente *adj* preceding; (*anterior*) former ▷ *nm* precedent; **establecer** *o* **sentar un ~** to establish *o* set a precedent; **sin ~(s)** unprecedented

preceder *vt, vi* to precede, go/come before

precepto *nm* precept

preciado, -a *adj* (*estimado*) esteemed, valuable

preciar *vt* to esteem, value; **preciarse** *vr* to boast; **~se de** to pride o.s. on

precintar *vt* (*local*) to seal off; (*producto*) to seal

precinto *nm* (*Com: tb*: **precinto de garantía**) seal

precio *nm* (*de mercado*) price; (*costo*) cost; (*valor*) value, worth; (*de viaje*) fare; **~ al contado** cash price; **~ al detalle** *o* **al por menor** retail price; **~ al detallista** trade price; **~ de coste** *o* **de cobertura** cost price; **~ de entrega inmediata** spot price; **~ de oferta** offer price; **~ de oportunidad** bargain price; **~ de salida** upset price; **no tener ~** (*fig*) to be priceless; **"no importa ~"** "cost no object"

preciosidad *nf* (*encanto*) charm; (*cosa bonita*) beautiful thing; **es una ~** it's lovely, it's really beautiful

precioso, -a *adj* (*bonito*) lovely, beautiful; (*valioso*) precious

precipicio *nm* cliff, precipice; (*fig*) abyss

precipitación *nf* (*prisa*) haste; (*lluvia*) rainfall; (*Química*) precipitation

precipitado, -a *adj* hasty, rash; (*salida*) hasty, sudden ▷ *nm* (*Química*) precipitate

precipitar *vt* (*arrojar*) to hurl, throw; (*apresurar*) to hasten; (*acelerar*) to speed up, accelerate; (*Química*) to precipitate; **precipitarse** *vr* (*arrojarse*) to throw o.s.; (*apresurarse*) to rush; (*actuar sin pensar*) to act rashly; **~se hacia** to rush towards

precisamente *adv* precisely; (*justo*) precisely, exactly, just; **~ por eso** for that very reason; **~ fue él quien lo dijo** as a matter of fact he said it; **no es eso ~** it's not really that

precisar *vt* (*necesitar*) to need, require; (*fijar*) to determine exactly, fix; (*especificar*) to specify; (*señalar*) to pinpoint

precisión *nf* (*exactitud*) precision

preciso, -a *adj* (*exacto*) precise; (*necesario*) necessary, essential; (*estilo, lenguaje*) concise; **es ~ que lo hagas** you must do it

preconcebido, -a *adj* preconceived

precoz *adj* (*persona*) precocious; (*calvicie*) premature

precursor, a *nm/f* precursor

predecesor, a *nm/f* predecessor

predecir *vt* to predict, foretell, forecast

predestinado, -a *adj* predestined

predeterminar *vt* to predetermine

predicado *nm* predicate

predicador, a *nm/f* preacher

predicar *vt, vi* to preach

predicción *nf* prediction; (*pronóstico*) forecast; **~ del tiempo** weather forecast(ing)

predilecto, -a *adj* favourite

predisponer *vt* to predispose; (*pey*) to prejudice

predisposición *nf* (*tendencia*) predisposition, inclination; (*prejuicio*) prejudice, bias; (*Med*) tendency

predominante *adj* predominant; (*preponderante*) prevailing; (*interés*) controlling

predominar *vt* to dominate ▷ *vi* to predominate; (*prevalecer*) to prevail

predominio *nm* (*dominio*) predominance; (*mayor frecuencia*) prevalence

preescolar *adj* preschool

prefabricado, -a *adj* prefabricated

prefacio *nm* preface

preferencia *nf* preference; **de ~** preferably, for preference; **localidad de ~** reserved seat

preferible *adj* preferable

preferir *vt* to prefer

prefijo *nm* prefix

pregonar *vt* to proclaim, announce; (*mercancía*) to hawk

pregunta *nf* question; **hacer una ~** to ask a question; **~ capciosa** catch question; **~s frecuentes** frequently asked questions, FAQs

preguntar *vt* to ask; (*cuestionar*) to question ▷ *vi* to ask; **preguntarse** *vr* to wonder; **~ por algn** to ask for sb; **~ por la salud de algn** to ask after sb's health

preguntón, -ona *adj* inquisitive

prehistórico, -a adj prehistoric
prejuicio nm prejudgement; (preconcepción)
preconception; (pey) prejudice, bias
preliminar adj, nm preliminary
preludio nm (Mus, fig) prelude
premamá adj: vestido ~ maternity dress
prematrimonial adj: relaciones ~es premarital
sex
prematuro, -a adj premature
premeditación nf premeditation
premeditar vt to premeditate
premiar vt to reward; (en un concurso) to give a
prize to
premio nm (recompensa) reward; (trofeo) prize;
(Com) premium; ~ gordo first prize
premisa nf premise
premonición nf premonition
premura nf (prisa) haste, urgency
prenatal adj antenatal, prenatal
prenda nf (de ropa) garment, article of clothing;
(garantía) pledge; (fam) darling!; dejar algo en ~
to pawn sth; no soltar ~ to give nothing away;
(fig) not to say a word; prendas nfpl talents, gifts
prendar vt to captivate, enchant; ~se de algo to
fall in love with sth
prendedor nm brooch
prender vt (captar) to catch, capture; (detener) to
arrest; (coser) to pin, attach; (sujetar) to fasten;
(LAm) to switch on ▷ vi to catch; (arraigar) to take
root; prenderse vr (encenderse) to catch fire
prendido, -a adj (LAm: luz etc) on
prensa nf press; la P~ the press; tener mala
~ to have o get a bad press; la ~ nacional the
national press
prensar vt to press
preñado, -a adj (mujer) pregnant; ~ de pregnant
with, full of
preocupación nf worry, concern; (ansiedad)
anxiety
preocupado, -a adj (por algo) worried, concerned;
(ansioso) anxious
preocupar vt to worry; preocuparse vr to worry;
~se de algo (hacerse cargo de algo) to take care of
sth; ~se por algo to worry about sth
preparación nf (acto) preparation; (estado)
preparedness, readiness; (entrenamiento) training
preparado, -a adj (dispuesto) prepared; (Culin)
ready (to serve) ▷ nm (Med) preparation; ¡~s,
listos, ya! ready, steady, go!
preparar vt (disponer) to prepare, get ready; (Culin)
to cook; (Tec: tratar) to prepare, process, treat;
(entrenar) to teach, train; prepararse vr (persona)
to prepare for; (problema, tormenta) to be brewing;
no he preparado el discurso I haven't prepared
my speech; mi madre está preparando la
cena my mother is cooking dinner; ~se a o para
hacer algo to prepare o get ready to do sth
preparativo, -a adj preparatory, preliminary
▷ nm: ~s nmpl preparations
preposición nf preposition
prepotencia nf abuse of power; (Pol) high-
handedness; (soberbia) arrogance

prepotente adj (Pol) high-handed; (soberbio)
arrogant
prerrogativa nf prerogative, privilege
presa nf (cosa apresada) catch; (víctima) victim; (de
animal) prey; (pantano) dam; hacer ~ en to clutch
(on to), seize; ser ~ de (fig) to be a prey to
presagiar vt to forebode
presagio nm omen
prescindir vi: ~ de (privarse de) to do without,
go without; (descartar) to dispense with; no
podemos ~ de él we can't manage without him
prescribir vt to prescribe
prescripción nf prescription; ~ facultativa
medical prescription
presencia nf presence; en ~ de in the presence of
presencial adj: testigo ~ eyewitness
presenciar vt to be present at; (asistir a) to attend;
(ver) to see, witness
presentación nf presentation; (introducción)
introduction
presentador, a nm/f (de programa) presenter; (de
noticias) newsreader
presentar vt (entregar) to hand in, present;
(mostrar) to show, produce; (renuncia) to tender;
(moción) to propose; (a una persona) to introduce;
presentarse vr (llegar inesperadamente) to appear,
turn up; (ofrecerse: como candidato) to run, stand;
(aparecer) to show, appear; (solicitar empleo) to
apply; he presentado mi proyecto ante
la comisión I've presented my plan to the
committee; presentó la dimisión he handed
in his resignation; me presentó a sus padres
he introduced me to his parents; ~ algo al cobro
(Com) to present sth for payment; se presentó
en mi casa a las doce de la noche he turned up
at my house at twelve o'clock at night; antes de
nada, me voy a ~ first of all, let me introduce
myself; ~se a un examen to sit an exam; ~se a
la policía to report to the police
presente adj present ▷ nm present; (Ling)
present (tense); (regalo) gift; la carta ~, la ~ this
letter; no estaba ~ en la reunión she was not
present at the meeting; ¡~! present!; hacer ~ to
state, declare; tener algo ~ to remember sth,
bear sth in mind; hasta el ~ up to the present;
los ~s those present
presentimiento nm premonition, presentiment
presentir vt to have a premonition of
preservación nf protection, preservation
preservar vt to protect, preserve
preservativo nm condom
presidencia nf presidency; (de comité)
chairmanship; ocupar la ~ to preside, be in o
take the chair
presidente nm/f (de país, asociación) president;
(de comité, reunión) chairman(-woman); (en
parlamento) speaker; (Jur) presiding magistrate
presidiario nm convict
presidio nm prison, penitentiary
presidir vt (dirigir) to preside at, preside over;
(: comité) to take the chair at; (dominar) to
dominate, rule ▷ vi (en ceremonia) to preside; (en

reunión) to take the chair

presión *nf* pressure; **a** ~ under pressure; ~ **arterial** *o* **sanguínea** blood pressure

presionar *vt* to press; (*botón*) to push, press; (*fig*) to press, put pressure on ▷ *vi:* ~ **para** *o* **por** to press for

preso, -a *adj:* **estar ~ de terror** *o* **pánico** to be panic-stricken ▷ *nm/f* prisoner; **tomar** *o* **llevar ~ a algn** to arrest sb, take sb prisoner

prestación *nf* (*aportación*) lending; (*Inform*) capability; (*servicio*) service; (*subsidio*) benefit; **prestaciones** *nfpl* (*Auto*) performance features; ~ **de juramento** oath-taking; ~ **personal** obligatory service; **P~ Social Sustitutoria** *community service for conscientious objectors*

prestado, -a *adj* on loan; **dar algo** ~ to lend sth; **pedir** ~ to borrow

prestamista *nm/f* moneylender

préstamo *nm* loan; ~ **con garantía** loan against collateral; ~ **hipotecario** mortgage

prestar *vt* to lend, loan; (*atención*) to pay; (*ayuda*) to give; (*servicio*) to do, render; (*juramento*) to take, swear; **prestarse** *vr* (*ofrecerse*) to offer *o* volunteer

presteza *nf* speed, promptness

prestigio *nm* prestige; (*reputación*) face; (*renombre*) good name

prestigioso, -a *adj* (*honorable*) prestigious; (*famoso, renombrado*) renowned, famous

presto, -a *adj* (*rápido*) quick, prompt; (*dispuesto*) ready ▷ *adv* at once, right away

presumido, -a *adj* conceited

presumir *vt* to presume ▷ *vi* (*darse aires*) to be conceited; **según cabe** ~ as may be presumed, presumably; ~ **de listo** to think o.s. very smart

presunción *nf* presumption; (*sospecha*) suspicion; (*vanidad*) conceit

presunto, -a *adj* (*supuesto*) supposed, presumed; (*así llamado*) so-called

presuntuoso, -a *adj* conceited, presumptuous

presuponer *vt* to presuppose

presupuesto *pp de* **presuponer** ▷ *nm* (*Finanzas*) budget; (*estimación: de costo*) estimate; **asignación de** ~ (*Com*) budget appropriation

presuroso, -a *adj* (*rápido*) quick, speedy; (*que tiene prisa*) hasty

pretencioso, -a *adj* pretentious

pretender *vt* (*intentar*) to try to, seek to; (*reivindicar*) to claim; (*buscar*) to seek, try for; (*cortejar*) to woo, court; ~ **que** to expect that; **¿qué pretende usted?** what are you after?

pretendiente *nm/f* (*candidato*) candidate, applicant; (*amante*) suitor

pretensión *nf* (*aspiración*) aspiration; (*reivindicación*) claim; (*orgullo*) pretension

pretexto *nm* pretext; (*excusa*) excuse; **so ~ de** under pretext of

prevalecer *vi* to prevail

prevención *nf* prevention; ~ **de incendios** fire prevention; **medidas de prevención** preventive measure

prevenido, -a *adj* prepared, ready; (*cauteloso*) cautious; **estar** ~ (*preparado*) to be ready; **ser** ~

(*cuidadoso*) to be cautious; **hombre ~ vale por dos** forewarned is forearmed

prevenir *vt* (*impedir*) to prevent; (*prever*) to foresee, anticipate; (*predisponer*) to prejudice, bias; (*avisar*) to warn; (*preparar*) to prepare, get ready; **prevenirse** *vr* to get ready, prepare; ~**se contra** to take precautions against

preventivo, -a *adj* preventive, precautionary

prever *vt* to foresee; (*anticipar*) to anticipate

previo, -a *adj* (*anterior*) previous, prior ▷ *prep:* ~ **acuerdo con los otros** subject to the agreement of the others; ~ **pago de los derechos** on payment of the fees

previsión *nf* (*perspicacia*) foresight; (*predicción*) forecast; (*prudencia*) caution; ~ **de ventas** (*Com*) sales forecast

previsor, a *adj* (*precavido*) far-sighted; (*prudente*) thoughtful

previsto *pp de* **prever**

prima *nf* (*Com*) bonus; (*de seguro*) premium; (*a la exportación*) subsidy; *ver tb* **primo**

primacía *nf* primacy

primaria *nf* primary education

primario, -a *adj* primary

primavera *nf* (*estación*) spring; (*período*) springtime

primera *nf* (*Auto*) first gear; (*Ferro*) first class; **de** ~ (*fam*) first-class, first-rate; **de buenas a ~s** suddenly; *ver tb* **primero**

primero, -a *adj* (*delante de nmsg*): **primer** (*numeral*) first; (*principal*) prime; (*anterior*) former ▷ *adv* (*orden*) first; (*más bien*) sooner, rather ▷ *nm* first floor; **el primer día** the first day; **en primer lugar, veamos los datos** firstly, let's look at the facts; **lo ~ es la salud** the most important thing is your health; **primer ministro** prime minister; **primera dama** (*Teat*) leading lady; *ver tb* **primera**

primicia *nf* (*Prensa*) scoop; **primicias** *nfpl* (*tb fig*) first fruits

primitiva *nf:* (**Lotería**) **P~** weekly state-run lottery; *ver tb* **primitivo**

primitivo, -a *adj* (*antiguo*) primitive; (*original*) original; (*Com: acción*) ordinary; *ver tb* **primitiva**

primo, -a *adj* (*Mat*) prime ▷ *nm/f* cousin; (*fam*) fool, dupe; **materias primas** raw materials; **hacer el** ~ to be taken for a ride; ~ **hermano** first cousin; *ver tb* **prima**

primogénito, -a *adj* first-born

primor *nm* (*cuidado*) care; **es un** ~ it's lovely

primordial *adj* basic, fundamental

primoroso, -a *adj* exquisite, fine

princesa *nf* princess

principal *adj* principal, main; (*más destacado*) foremost; (*piso*) first, second (US); (*Inform*) foreground ▷ *nm* (*jefe*) chief, principal

príncipe *nm* prince; **P~ de Asturias** *King's son and heir to the Spanish throne*; ~ **de gales** (*tela*) check; ~ **heredero** crown prince

principiante *nm/f* beginner; (*novato*) novice

principio *nm* (*comienzo*) beginning, start; (*origen*) origin; (*moral*) principle; **a ~s de** at the beginning of; **desde el ~** from the first; **en un ~** at first

pringar vt (Culin: pan) to dip; (ensuciar) to dirty; **~ a algn en un asunto** (fam) to involve sb in a matter; **pringarse** vr to get splashed o soiled

pringoso, -a adj greasy; (pegajoso) sticky

pringue nm (grasa) grease, fat, dripping

prioridad nf priority; (Auto) right of way

prisa nf (apresuramiento) hurry, haste; (rapidez) speed; (urgencia) (sense of) urgency; **correr ~** to be urgent; **darse ~** to hurry up; **estar de o tener ~** to be in a hurry

prisión nf (cárcel) prison; (período de cárcel) imprisonment

prisionero, -a nm/f prisoner

prismáticos nmpl binoculars

privación nf deprivation; (falta) want, privation; **privaciones** nfpl hardships, privations

privado, -a adj (particular) private; (Pol: favorito) favourite (Brit), favorite (US); **en ~** privately, in private; **"~ y confidencial"** "private and confidential"

privar vt to deprive; **privarse** vr: **~se de** (abstenerse de) to deprive o.s. of; (renunciar a) to give up

privativo, -a adj exclusive

privatizar vt to privatize

privilegiado, -a adj privileged; (memoria) very good ▷ nm/f (afortunado) privileged person

privilegiar vt to grant a privilege to; (favorecer) to favour

privilegio nm privilege; (concesión) concession

pro nm o nf profit, advantage ▷ prep: **asociación ~ ciegos** association for the blind ▷ pref: **~-soviético/americano** pro-Soviet/-American; **en ~ de** on behalf of, for; **los ~s y los contras** the pros and cons

proa nf (Naut) bow, prow

probabilidad nf probability, likelihood; (oportunidad, posibilidad) chance, prospect

probable adj probable, likely; **es ~ que** (+ subjun) it is probable o likely that; **es ~ que no venga** he probably won't come

probador nm (persona) taster (of wine etc); (en una tienda) fitting room

probar vt (demostrar) to prove; (someter a prueba) to test, try out; (ropa) to try on; (comida) to taste ▷ vi to try; **probarse** vr: **~se un traje** to try on a suit

probeta nf test tube

problema nm problem

procedencia nf (principio) source, origin; (lugar de salida) point of departure

procedente adj (razonable) reasonable; (conforme a derecho) proper, fitting; **~ de** coming from, originating in

proceder vi (avanzar) to proceed; (actuar) to act; (ser correcto) to be right (and proper), be fitting ▷ nm (comportamiento) behaviour, conduct; **no procede obrar así** it is not right to act like that; **~ de** to come from, originate in

procedimiento nm procedure; (proceso) process; (método) means, method; (trámite) proceedings pl

procesado, -a nm/f accused (person)

procesador nm: **~ de textos** (Inform) word processor

procesar vt to try, put on trial; (Inform) to process

procesión nf procession

proceso nm process; (Jur) trial; (lapso) course (of time); (Inform): **~ (automático) de datos** (automatic) data processing; **~ no prioritario** background process; **~ por pasadas** batch processing

proclamar vt to proclaim

procreación nf procreation

procrear vt, vi to procreate

procurador, a nm/f attorney, solicitor

procurar vt (intentar) to try, endeavour; (conseguir) to get, obtain

prodigar vt to lavish; **prodigarse** vr: **~se en** to be lavish with

prodigio nm prodigy; (milagro) wonder, marvel; **niño ~** child prodigy

prodigioso, -a adj prodigious, marvellous

pródigo, -a adj (rico) rich, productive; **hijo ~** prodigal son

producción nf production; (suma de productos) output; (producto) product; **~ en serie** mass production

producir vt (Com, Cine) to produce; (causar) to cause, bring about; (impresión) to give; (interés) to bear; **producirse** vr (suceder) to come about, happen; (hacerse) to be produced, be made; (estallar) to break out; **no producimos lo suficiente** we are not producing enough; **puede ~ efectos secundarios** it can cause side-effects; **le produjo una gran tristeza** it caused her much sadness; **¿cómo se produjo el accidente?** how did the accident happen?; **se produjo una explosión** there was an explosion

productividad nf productivity

productivo, -a adj productive; (provechoso) profitable

producto nm (resultado) product; (producción) production; **~ alimenticio** foodstuff; **~ (nacional) bruto** gross (national) product; **~ interior bruto** gross domestic product

productor, a adj productive, producing ▷ nm/f producer

proeza nf exploit, feat

profanar vt to desecrate, profane

profano, -a adj profane ▷ nm/f (inexperto) layman(-woman); **soy ~ en música** I don't know anything about music

profecía nf prophecy

proferir vt (palabra, sonido) to utter; (injuria) to hurl, let fly

profesar vt (declarar) to profess; (practicar) to practise

profesión nf profession; **abogado de ~, de ~ abogado** a lawyer by profession

profesional adj professional

profesor, a nm/f teacher; (instructor) instructor; **~ de universidad** lecturer; **~ adjunto** assistant lecturer, associate professor (US)

profesorado nm (profesión) teaching profession;

(*cuerpo*) teaching staff, faculty (US); (*cargo*) professorship

profeta *nm/f* prophet

profetizar *vt, vi* to prophesy

prófugo, -a *nm/f* fugitive; (*desertor*) deserter

profundidad *nf* depth; **tener una ~ de 30 cm** to be 30 cm deep

profundizar *vt* (*fig*) to go deeply into, study in depth

profundo, -a *adj* deep; (*misterio, pensador*) profound; **poco ~** shallow

profusión *nf* (*abundancia*) profusion; (*prodigalidad*) wealth

progenitor *nm* ancestor; **progenitores** *nmpl* (*fam*) parents

programa *nm* programme; (*Inform*) program; **~ de estudios** curriculum, syllabus; **~ corrector ortográfico** (*Inform*) spelling checker

programación *nf* (*Inform*) programming; **~ estructurada** structured programming

programador, a *nm/f* (computer) programmer; **~ de aplicaciones** applications programmer

programar *vt* (*Inform*) to programme

progre *adj* (*fam*) trendy

progresar *vi* to progress, make progress

progresión *nf*: **~ geométrica/aritmética** geometric/arithmetic progression

progresista *adj, nm/f* progressive

progresivo, -a *adj* progressive; (*gradual*) gradual; (*continuo*) continuous

progreso *nm* (*tb*: **progresos**) progress; **hacer ~s** to progress, advance

prohibición *nf* prohibition, ban; **levantar la ~ de** to remove the ban on

prohibir *vt* to prohibit, ban; **han prohibido las armas de fuego** firearms have been banned; **le prohibieron la entrada en el edificio** he was banned from entering the building; **queda terminantemente prohibido** it is strictly forbidden; **te prohíbo que toques mi ordenador** I won't allow you to touch my computer; **"prohibido fumar"** "no smoking"

prójimo, -a *nm* fellow man ▷ *nm/f* (*vecino*) neighbour

proletariado *nm* proletariat

proletario, -a *adj, nm/f* proletarian

proliferación *nf* proliferation; **~ de armas nucleares** spread of nuclear arms

proliferar *vi* to proliferate

prolífico, -a *adj* prolific

prolijo, -a *adj* long-winded, tedious; (*LAm*) neat

prólogo *nm* prologue; (*preámbulo*) preface, introduction

prolongación *nf* extension

prolongado, -a *adj* (*largo*) long; (*alargado*) lengthy

prolongar *vt* (*gen*) to extend; (*en el tiempo*) to prolong; (*calle, tubo*) to make longer, extend; **prolongarse** *vr* (*alargarse*) to extend, go on

promedio *nm* (*media*) average; (*punto medio*) middle, mid-point

promesa *nf* promise; **faltar a una ~** to break a promise ▷ *adj inv*: **jugador ~** promising player

prometer *vt* to promise ▷ *vi* to show promise; **prometerse** *vr* (*dos personas*) to get engaged

prometido, -a *adj* (*ayuda, favor*) promised; (*persona*) engaged ▷ *nm/f* fiancé (fiancée)

prominente *adj* prominent

promiscuo, -a *adj* promiscuous

promoción *nf* promotion; (*año*) class, year; **~ de ventas** sales promotion o drive; **~ por correspondencia directa** (*Com*) direct mailshot

promocionar *vt* (*Com: dar publicidad*) to promote

promontorio *nm* promontory

promotor *nm* promoter; (*instigador*) instigator

promover *vt* to promote; (*causar*) to cause; (*juicio*) to bring; (*motín*) to instigate, stir up

promulgar *vt* to promulgate; (*fig*) to proclaim

pronombre *nm* pronoun

pronosticar *vt* to predict, foretell, forecast

pronóstico *nm* prediction, forecast; (*profecía*) omen; (*Med: diagnóstico*) prognosis; **de ~ leve** slight, not serious; **~ del tiempo** weather forecast

pronto, -a *adj* (*rápido*) prompt, quick; (*preparado*) ready ▷ *adv* quickly, promptly; (*en seguida*) at once, right away; (*dentro de poco*) soon; (*temprano*) early ▷ *nm* urge, sudden feeling; **al ~** at first; **de ~** suddenly; **¡hasta ~!** see you soon!; **lo más ~ posible** as soon as possible; **por lo ~** meanwhile, for the present; **tan ~ como** as soon as; **tener ~s de enojo** to be quick-tempered

pronunciación *nf* pronunciation

pronunciar *vt* to pronounce; (*discurso*) to make, deliver; (*Jur: sentencia*) to pass, pronounce; **pronunciarse** *vr* to revolt, rise, rebel; (*declararse*) to declare o.s.; **~se sobre** to pronounce on

propagación *nf* propagation; (*difusión*) spread(ing)

propaganda *nf* (*política*) propaganda; (*comercial*) advertising; **hacer ~ de** (*Com*) to advertise

propagar *vt* to propagate; (*difundir*) to spread, disseminate; **propagarse** *vr* (*Bio*) to propagate; (*fig*) to spread

propano *nm* propane

propasarse *vr* (*excederse*) to go too far; (*sexualmente*) to take liberties

propensión *nf* inclination, propensity

propenso, -a *adj*: **~ a** prone o inclined to; **ser ~ a hacer algo** to be inclined o have a tendency to do sth

propiamente *adv* properly; (*realmente*) really, exactly; **~ dicho** real, true

propicio, -a *adj* favourable, propitious

propiedad *nf* (*cosa poseída*) property; (*posesión*) possession, ownership; (*conveniencia*) suitability; **~ particular** private property; **~ pública** (*Com*) public ownership; **ceder algo a algn en ~** to transfer to sb the full rights over sth

propietario, -a *nm/f* owner, proprietor

propina *nf* tip; **dar algo de ~** to give something extra

propio, -a *adj* (*de propiedad*) own, of one's own; (*característico*) characteristic, typical; (*conveniente*) proper; (*mismo*) selfsame, very; **¿tienes casa**

propia? do you have a house of your own?; **eso es muy ~ de él** that's just like him; **tiene un olor muy ~** it has a smell of its own; **eso es muy ~ de los países mediterráneos** that's very typical of the Mediterranean countries; **el ~ ministro** the minister himself; **un nombre ~** a proper noun

proponer vt (idea, sugerencia) to suggest, propose; (teoría, plan) put forward; (candidato) to propose, nominate; (problema) to pose; **proponerse** vr to propose, plan, intend; **nos propuso pagar la cena a medias** he suggested that we should share the cost of the meal; **lo propusieron para alcalde** he was nominated for mayor; **se ha propuesto adelgazar** he's decided to lose some weight; **te has propuesto hacerme perder el tren** you set out deliberately to make me miss the train

proporción nf proportion; (Mat) ratio; (razón, porcentaje) rate; **en ~ con** in proportion to; **proporciones** nfpl dimensions; (fig) size sg

proporcionado, -a adj proportionate; (regular) medium, middling; (justo) just right; **bien ~** well-proportioned

proporcional adj proportional; **~ a** proportional to

proporcionar vt (dar) to give, supply, provide; **esto le proporciona una renta anual de ...** this brings him in a yearly income of ...

proposición nf proposition; (propuesta) proposal

propósito nm purpose ▷ adv: **a ~** (adrede) on purpose, deliberately; (por cierto) by the way; **¿cuál es el ~ de su visita?** what is the purpose of your visit?; **lo hizo a ~** he did it deliberately; **a ~, ya tengo los billetes** by the way, I've got the tickets; **buenos ~s** good intentions; **a ~ de** about, with regard to

propuesto, -a pp de **proponer** ▷ nf proposal

propugnar vt to uphold

propulsar vt to drive, propel; (fig) to promote, encourage

propulsión nf propulsion; **~ a chorro** o **por reacción** jet propulsion

prórroga nf (gen) extension; (Jur) stay; (Com) deferment

prorrogar vt (período) to extend; (decisión) to defer, postpone

prorrumpir vi to burst forth, break out; **~ en gritos** to start shouting; **~ en lágrimas** to burst into tears

prosa nf prose

prosaico, -a adj prosaic, dull

proscripción nf (prohibición) ban, prohibition (frm); (destierro) banishment; (de partido) proscription

proscrito, -a pp de **proscribir** ▷ adj (prohibido) banned; (desterrado) outlawed ▷ nm/f (exilado) exile; (bandido) outlaw

prosecución nf continuation; (persecución) pursuit

proseguir vt to continue, carry on, proceed with; (investigación, estudio) to pursue ▷ vi to continue, go on

prospección nf exploration; (del petróleo, del oro) prospecting

prospecto nm prospectus; (folleto) leaflet, sheet of instructions

prosperar vi to prosper, thrive, flourish

prosperidad nf prosperity; (éxito) success

próspero, -a adj prosperous, thriving, flourishing; (que tiene éxito) successful

prostíbulo nm brothel

prostitución nf prostitution

prostituir vt to prostitute; **prostituirse** vr to prostitute o.s., become a prostitute

prostituta nf prostitute

protagonista nm/f protagonist; (Lit: personaje) main character, hero(ine)

protagonizar vt to head, take the chief role in

protección nf protection

protector, a adj protective, protecting; (tono) patronizing ▷ nm/f protector; (bienhechor) patron; (de la tradición) guardian

proteger vt to protect; **~ contra grabación** o **contra escritura** (Inform) to write-protect

protegido, -a nm/f protégé (protégée)

proteína nf protein

prótesis nf (Med) prosthesis

protesta nf protest; (declaración) protestation

protestante adj Protestant

protestar vt to protest, declare; (fe) to protest ▷ vi to protest; (objetar) to object; **cheque protestado por falta de fondos** cheque referred to drawer

protocolo nm protocol; **sin ~s** (formalismo) informal(ly), without formalities

protón nm proton

prototipo nm prototype; (ideal) model

protuberancia nf protuberance

prov. abr (= provincia) prov

provecho nm advantage, benefit; (Finanzas) profit; **¡buen ~!** bon appétit!; **en ~ de** to the benefit of; **sacar ~ de** to benefit from, profit by

proveer vt to provide, supply; (preparar) to provide, get ready; (vacante) to fill; (negocio) to transact, dispatch ▷ vi: **~ a** to provide for; **proveerse** vr: **~se de** to provide o.s. with

provenir vi: **~ de** to come from, stem from

proverbio nm proverb

providencia nf providence; (previsión) foresight; **providencias** nfpl measures, steps

provincia nf province; (Esp: Admin) ≈ county, ≈ region (Scot); **una ciudad de ~(s)** a country town

provinciano, -a adj provincial; (del campo) country antes de n

provisión nf provision; (abastecimiento) provision, supply; (medida) measure, step

provisional adj provisional

provocación nf provocation

provocar vt to provoke; (alentar) to tempt, invite; (causar) to bring about, lead to; (promover) to promote; (estimular) to rouse, stir, stimulate; (protesta, explosión) to cause, spark off; (LAm): **¿te**

provoca un café? would you like a coffee?
provocativo, -a *adj* provocative
próximamente *adv* shortly, soon
proximidad *nf* closeness, proximity
próximo, -a *adj* near, close; *(vecino)*
neighbouring; *(el que viene)* next; **en fecha
próxima** at an early date; **el mes ~** next month
proyectar *vt (objeto)* to hurl, throw; *(luz)* to cast,
shed; *(Cine)* to screen, show; *(hacer planes)* to plan
proyectil *nm* projectile, missile; **~ (tele)dirigido**
guided missile
proyecto *nm* plan; *(idea)* project; *(estimación de
costo)* detailed estimate; **tener algo en ~** to be
planning sth; **~ de ley** *(Pol)* bill
proyector *nm (Cine)* projector
prudencia *nf (sabiduría)* wisdom, prudence;
(cautela) care
prudente *adj* sensible, wise, prudent; *(cauteloso)*
careful
prueba *nf (demostración)* proof; *(comprobación)* test;
(muestra) sample; *(de ropa)* fitting; *(Deporte)* event;
eso es la ~ de que lo hizo él that is the proof
that he did it; **¿tiene usted ~ de ello?** can you
prove it?, do you have proof?; **el fiscal presentó
nuevas ~s** the prosecutor presented new
evidence; **a ~** on trial; *(Com)* on approval; **a ~ de**
proof against; **a ~ de agua/fuego** waterproof/
fireproof; **a ~ de balas** bullet-proof; **el médico
me hizo más ~s** the doctor did some more tests;
poner *o* **someter algo a ~** to put sth to the test;
~ de capacitación *(Com)* proficiency test; **~ de
fuego** *(fig)* acid test; **~ de vallas** hurdles; **~s
nucleares** nuclear tests
prurito *nm* itch; *(de bebé)* nappy rash; *(anhelo)*
urge
psicoanálisis *nm* psychoanalysis
psicología *nf* psychology
psicológico, -a *adj* psychological
psicólogo, -a *nm/f* psychologist
psicópata *nm/f* psychopath
psicosis *nf inv* psychosis
psicosomático, -a *adj* psychosomatic
psiquiatra *nm/f* psychiatrist
psiquiátrico, -a *adj* psychiatric ▷ *nm* mental
hospital
psíquico, -a *adj* psychic(al)
PSOE *nm abr* = **Partido Socialista Obrero Español**
PSS *nf abr* (= *Prestación Social Sustitutoria*) *community
service for conscientious objectors*
púa *nf* sharp point; *(para guitarra)* plectrum;
alambre de ~s barbed wire
pub *nm* bar
pubertad *nf* puberty
publicación *nf* publication
publicar *vt (editar)* to publish; *(hacer público)* to
publicize; *(divulgar)* to make public, divulge
publicidad *nf* publicity; *(Com)* advertising; **dar
~ a** to publicize, give publicity to; **~ en el punto
de venta** point-of-sale advertising; **~ gráfica**
display advertising
publicitario, -a *adj* publicity *antes de n*;
advertising *antes de n*; **campaña publicitaria**
advertising campaign
público, -a *adj* public ▷ *nm* public; *(Teat etc)*
audience; *(Deporte)* spectators *pl*, crowd; *(en
restaurantes etc)* clients *pl*; **hacer ~** to publish;
(difundir) to disclose; **el gran ~** the general
public; **~ objetivo** *(Com)* target audience
puchero *nm (Culin: olla)* cooking pot; *(: guiso)* stew;
hacer ~s to pout
púdico, -a *adj* modest; *(pudibundo)* bashful
pudiente *adj (opulento)* wealthy; *(poderoso)*
powerful
pudor *nm* modesty; *(vergüenza)* (sense of) shame
pudrir *vt* to rot; *(fam)* to upset, annoy; **pudrirse** *vr*
to rot, decay; *(fig)* to rot, languish
pueblo *nm* people; *(nación)* nation; *(aldea)* village;
(plebe) common people; *(población pequeña)* small
town, country town
puente *nm (gen)* bridge; *(Naut: tb:* **puente de
mando)** bridge; *(: cubierta)* deck; **hacer ~** *(fam)* to
take a long weekend; **~ aéreo** airlift; **~ colgante**
suspension bridge; **~ levadizo** drawbridge
puenting *nm* bungee jumping
puerco, -a *adj (sucio)* dirty, filthy; *(obsceno)*
disgusting ▷ *nm/f* pig (sow)
pueril *adj* childish
puerro *nm* leek
puerta *nf (de casa, coche)* door; *(de jardín)* gate;
(portal) doorway; *(fig)* gateway; **llaman a la ~**
somebody's at the door; **un coche de cuatro
~s** a four-door car; **me acompañó a la ~** she
saw me out; **a ~ cerrada** behind closed doors;
tomar la ~ *(fam)* to leave; **un saque de ~** *(Deporte)*
a goal kick; **~ corredera/giratoria** sliding/
swing *o* revolving door; **~ principal/trasera** *o*
de servicio front/back door; **~ de embarque**
boarding gate
puerto *nm (tb Inform)* port; *(de mar)* seaport; *(paso)*
pass; *(fig)* haven, refuge; **llegar a ~** *(fig)* to get
over a difficulty
Puerto Rico *nm* Puerto Rico
puertorriqueño, -a *adj, nm/f* Puerto Rican
pues *adv (entonces)* then; *(¡entonces!)* well, well
then; *(así que)* so ▷ *conj (porque)* since; **~ ... no sé**
well ... I don't know
puesta *nf (apuesta)* bet, stake; **~ en escena**
staging; **~ en marcha** starting; **~ del sol** sunset;
~ a cero *(Inform)* reset; *ver tb* **puesto**
puesto, -a *pp de* **poner** ▷ *adj* dressed ▷ *nm (lugar,
posición)* place; *(trabajo)* post, job; *(Mil)* post; *(Com)*
stall; *(quiosco)* kiosk ▷ *conj:* **~ que** since, as; **~
de mercado** market stall; **~ de policía** police
station; **~ de socorro** first aid post; *ver tb* **puesta**
pugna *nf* battle, conflict
pugnar *vi (luchar)* to struggle, fight; *(pelear)* to
fight
pujar *vt (precio)* to raise, push up ▷ *vi (en licitación)*
to bid, bid up; *(fig: esforzarse)* to struggle, strain
pulcro, -a *adj* neat, tidy
pulga *nf* flea; **tener malas ~s** to be short-
tempered
pulgada *nf* inch
pulgar *nm* thumb

pulir vt to polish; (alisar) to smooth; (fig) to polish up, touch up

pulla nf cutting remark

pulmón nm lung; **a pleno ~** (respirar) deeply; (gritar) at the top of one's voice; **~ de acero** iron lung

pulmonía nf pneumonia

pulpa nf pulp; (de fruta) flesh, soft part

pulpería nf (CS) small grocery store

púlpito nm pulpit

pulpo nm octopus

pulque nm alcoholic drink brewed from the juice of the agave plant

pulquería nm (Méx) bar (serving pulque)

pulsación nf beat, pulsation; (Anat) throb(bing); (en máquina de escribir) tap; (de pianista, mecanógrafo) touch; **~ (de una tecla)** (Inform) keystroke; **~ doble** (Inform) strikeover

pulsador nm button, push button

pulsar vt (tecla) to touch, tap; (Mus) to play; (botón) to press, push ▷ vi to pulsate; (latir) to beat, throb

pulsera nf bracelet; **reloj de ~** wristwatch

pulso nm (Med) pulse; **hacer algo a ~** to do sth unaided o by one's own efforts

pulverizador nm spray, spray gun

pulverizar vt to pulverize; (líquido) to spray

puna nf (And Med) mountain sickness

punición nf punishment

punitivo, -a adj punitive

punki adj, nm/f punk

punta adj inv: **la hora ~** the rush hour ▷ nf (de bolígrafo, cuchillo, lápiz) point; (de dedo, lengua) tip; (extremo) end; (promontorio) headland; (Costura) corner; (Tec) small nail; (fig) touch, trace; **sácale ~ al lápiz** sharpen your pencil; **a ~ de pistola** at gunpoint; **vivo en la otra ~ del pueblo** I live at the other end of the town; **de ~ a ~** from one end to the other; **estar de ~** to be edgy; **ir de ~ en blanco** to be all dressed up to the nines; **tener algo en la ~ de la lengua** to have sth on the tip of one's tongue; **se le pusieron los pelos de ~** her hair stood on end

puntada nf (Costura) stitch

puntal nm prop, support

puntapié (pl **-s**) nm kick; **echar a algn a ~s** to kick sb out

puntear vt to tick, mark; (Mus) to pluck

puntería nf (de arma) aim, aiming; (destreza) marksmanship

puntero, -a adj leading ▷ nm (señal, Inform) pointer; (dirigente) leader

puntiagudo, -a adj sharp, pointed

puntilla nf (Tec) tack, braid; (Costura) lace edging; **(andar) de ~s** (to walk) on tiptoe

punto nm (gen) point; (señal diminuta) spot, dot; (sobre la i) dot; (lugar) spot, place; (momento) point, moment; (en un examen) mark; (tema) item; (Costura, Med) stitch; (Inform: al imprimir) pitch; (: en pantalla) pixel; **a ~** ready; **ése es un ~ importante** that's an important point; **desde ese ~ de vista** from that point of view; **estar a ~**

de to be on the point of o about to; **estábamos a ~ de salir cuando llamaste** we were about to go out when you phoned; **estuve a ~ de perder el tren** I very nearly missed the train; **llegar a ~ to** come just at the right moment; **al ~** at once; **en ~** on the dot; **a la una en ~** at one o'clock sharp; **estar en su ~** (Culin) to be done to a turn; **hasta cierto ~** to some extent; **hacer ~** to knit; **poner un motor a ~** to tune an engine; **dos ~s** colon; **~ acápite** (LAm) full stop, new paragraph; **~s a tratar** matters to be discussed, agenda sg; **~ de partida/de congelación/de fusión** starting/ freezing/melting point; **~ de interrogación** question mark; **~ de equilibrio/de pedido** (Com) breakeven/reorder point; **~ inicial o de partida** (Inform) home; **~ de referencia/de venta** (Com) benchmark point/point-of-sale; **~ final** full stop; **~ muerto** dead centre; (Auto) neutral (gear); **~s suspensivos** suspension points; **~ y aparte** full stop, new paragraph; **~ y coma** semicolon; **~ y seguido** full stop, new sentence

puntocom nf inv, adj inv dotcom

puntuación nf punctuation; (puntos: en examen) mark(s) pl; (: Deporte) score

puntual adj (a tiempo) punctual; (cálculo) exact, accurate; (informe) reliable

puntualidad nf (en una cita) punctuality; (precisión) exactness, accuracy; (fiabilidad) reliability

puntualizar vt to fix, specify

puntuar vt (Ling, Tip) to punctuate; (examen) to mark ▷ vi (Deporte) to score, count

punzada nf (puntura) prick; (Med) stitch; (dolor) twinge (of pain)

punzante adj (dolor) shooting, sharp; (herramienta) sharp; (comentario) biting

punzar vt to prick, pierce ▷ vi to shoot, stab

puñado nm handful (tb fig); **a ~s** by handfuls

puñal nm dagger

puñalada nf stab

puñetazo nm punch

puño nm (Anat) fist; (cantidad) fistful, handful; (Costura) cuff; (de herramienta) handle; **como un ~** (verdad) obvious; **de ~ y letra del poeta** in the poet's own handwriting

pupila nf (Anat) pupil

pupitre nm desk

puré (pl **-s**) nm puree; (sopa) (thick) soup; **~ de patatas** mashed potatoes; **estar hecho ~** (fig) to be knackered

pureza nf purity

purga nf purge

purgante adj, nm purgative

purgar vt to purge; (Pol: depurar) to purge, liquidate; **purgarse** vr (Med) to take a purge

purgatorio nm purgatory

purificar vt to purify; (refinar) to refine

puritano, -a adj (actitud) puritanical; (iglesia, tradición) puritan ▷ nm/f puritan

puro, -a adj pure; (depurado) unadulterated; (oro) solid; (cielo) clear; (verdad) simple, plain ▷ nm cigar ▷ adv: **de ~ cansado** out of sheer tiredness;

por pura casualidad by sheer chance
púrpura *nf* purple
purpúreo, -a *adj* purple
pus *nm* pus
pústula *nf* pimple, sore
puta *nf* whore, prostitute
putada *nf* (*fam!*): **hacer una ~ a algn** to play a dirty trick on sb; **¡qué ~!** what a pain in the arse! (*!*)
putrefacción *nf* rotting, putrefaction
pútrido, -a *adj* rotten
puzzle *nm* jigsaw puzzle
PVP *abr* (*Esp*: = *Precio Venta al Público*) ≈ RRP
PYME *nf abr* (= *Pequeña y Mediana Empresa*) SME

Qq

que *conj* **1** (*con oración subordinada: muchas veces no se traduce*) that; **dijo ~ vendría** he said (that) he would come; **dile ~ me llame** ask him to call me; *ver tb* **el**
2 (*en oración independiente*): **¡~ entre!** send him in!; **¡~ se mejore tu padre!** I hope your father gets better; **¡~ te mejores!** get well soon!; **¡~ lo haga él!** he can do it!; (*orden*) get him to do it!
3 (*enfático*): **¿me quieres? — ¡~ sí!** do you love me? — of course!; **te digo ~ sí** I'm telling you
4 (*consecutivo: muchas veces no se traduce*) that; **es tan grande ~ no lo puedo levantar** it's so big (that) I can't lift it
5 (*comparaciones*) than; **yo ~ tú/él** if I were you/him; *ver tb* **más**; **menos**
6 (*valor disyuntivo*): **~ le guste o no** whether he likes it or not; **~ venga o ~ no venga** whether he comes or not
7 (*causa*): **no puedo, ~ tengo ~ quedarme en casa** I can't, I've got to stay in; **suéltame, ~ voy a gritar** let go or I'll scream
8: **siguió toca ~ toca** he kept on playing; **estuvieron habla ~ te habla toda la noche** they talked and talked all night
▷ *pron* **1** (*referido a cosas*) that, which; (*+prep*) which; **el sombrero ~ te compraste** the hat (that o which) you bought; **la cama en ~ dormí** the bed (that o which) I slept in; **el día (en) ~ ella nació** the day (when) she was born
2 (*referido a personas: suj*) that, who; (: *objeto*) that, whom; **el amigo ~ me acompañó al museo** the friend that o who went to the museum with me; **la chica ~ conocí** the girl (that o whom) I met
qué *adj* (*interrogativo*) what?, which?; (*exclamativo*) what! ▷ *pron* what?; ▷ *adv* (*exclamativo*) how!; **¿~ fecha es hoy?** what's today's date?; **¿~ edad tienes?** how old are you?; **¡~ día más espléndido!** what a glorious day!; **¿de ~ me hablas?** what are you saying to me?; **¿~ tal?** how are you?, how are things?; **¿~ hay (de nuevo)?** what's new?; **¿~ más?** anything else?; **no lo he hecho. ¿Y ~?** (*col*) I haven't done it. So what?; **¡~ divertido/asco!** how funny/revolting!

quebrada *nf* ravine; *ver tb* **quebrado**
quebradero *nm*: **~ de cabeza** headache, worry
quebradizo, -a *adj* fragile; (*persona*) frail
quebrado, -a *adj* (*roto*) broken; (*terreno*) rough, uneven ▷ *nm/f* bankrupt ▷ *nm* (*Mat*) fraction; **~ rehabilitado** discharged bankrupt; *ver tb* **quebrada**
quebrantar *vt* (*infringir*) to violate, transgress; **quebrantarse** *vr* (*persona*) to fail in health
quebranto *nm* damage, harm; (*decaimiento*) exhaustion; (*dolor*) grief, pain
quebrar *vt* to break, smash ▷ *vi* to go bankrupt; **quebrarse** *vr* to break, get broken; (*Med*) to be ruptured
quedar *vi* (*permanecer*) to stay, remain; (*encontrarse*) to be; (*restar*) to be left; **quedarse** *vr* (*permanecer*) to remain, stay (behind); **no queda ninguno** there are none left; **me quedan diez euros** I've got ten euros left; **nos quedan 12 km para llegar al pueblo** there are still 12 km before we get to the village; **eso queda muy lejos** that's a long way (away); **~ ciego/mudo** to be left blind/dumb; **por no ~ mal** in order to do the right thing; **no te queda bien ese vestido** that dress doesn't suit you; **~ por hacer** to be still to be done; **~ en** (*acordar*) to agree on/to; (*acabar siendo*) to end up as; **~se atrás** to fall behind; **~se sordo** to go deaf; **quédate con el cambio** keep the change; **~se con algn** (*fam*) to swindle sb; **~se en nada** to come to nothing o nought; **~se sin** to run out of
quedo, -a *adj* still ▷ *adv* softly, gently
quehacer *nm* task, job; **~es (domésticos)** household chores
queja *nf* complaint
quejarse *vr* (*enfermo*) to moan, groan; (*protestar*) to complain; **~ de que ...** to complain (about the fact) that ...
quejido *nm* moan
quejoso, -a *adj* complaining
quemado, -a *adj* burnt; (*irritado*) annoyed
quemadura *nf* burn, scald; (*de sol*) sunburn
quemar *vt* to burn; (*fig: malgastar*) to burn up, squander; (*Com: precios*) to slash, cut; (*fastidiar*) to annoy, bug ▷ *vi* to be burning hot; **quemarse** *vr* (*consumirse*) to burn (up); (*del sol*) to get sunburnt
quemarropa; **a ~** *adv* point-blank
quemazón *nf* burn; (*calor*) intense heat; (*sensación*) itch
querella *nf* (*Jur*) charge; (*disputa*) dispute
querellarse *vr* to file a complaint

querer vt 1 (*desear*) to want; **quiero más dinero** I want more money; **quisiera** o **querría un té** I'd like a tea; **quiero ayudar/que vayas** I want to help/you to go; **lo hizo sin ~** he didn't mean to do it; **como usted quiera** as you wish, as you please; **ven cuando quieras** come when you like; **no quiero** I don't want to; **le pedí que me dejara ir pero no quiso** I asked him to let me go but he refused

2 (*preguntas: para pedir u ofrecer algo*): **¿quiere abrir la ventana?** could you open the window?; **¿quieres echarme una mano?** can you give me a hand?; **¿quiere un café?** would you like some coffee?

3 (*amar*) to love; (*tener cariño a*) to be fond of; **quiere mucho a sus hijos** he's very fond of his children; **en la oficina lo quieren mucho** he's well liked at the office

4 (*requerir*): **esta planta quiere más luz** this plant needs more light

5: **~ decir** to mean; **¿qué quieres decir?** what do you mean?

querido, -a adj dear ▷ nm/f darling; (*amante*) lover; **nuestra querida patria** our beloved country

quesería nf dairy; (*fábrica*) cheese factory

queso nm cheese; **dárselas con ~ a algn** (*fam*) to take sb in; **~ rallado** grated cheese; **~ crema** cream cheese

quicio nm hinge; **estar fuera de ~** to be beside o.s.; **sacar a algn de ~** to drive sb up the wall

quiebra nf break, split; (*Com*) bankruptcy; (*Econ*) slump

quiebro nm (*del cuerpo*) swerve

quien pron relativo (*suj*) who; (*complemento*) whom; (*indefinido*): **~ dice eso es tonto** whoever says that is a fool; **hay ~ piensa que** there are those who think that; **no hay ~ lo haga** no-one will do it; **~ más, ~ menos, tiene sus problemas** everybody has problems

quién pron interrogativo who; (*complemento*) whom; **¿~ es?** who is it?, who's there?; (*Telec*) who's calling?

quienquiera (*pl* **quienesquiera**) pron whoever

quieto, -a adj still; (*carácter*) placid; **¡estáte ~!** keep still!

quietud nf stillness

quijada nf jaw, jawbone

quilate nm carat

quilla nf keel

quimera nf (*sueño*) pipe dream

quimérico, -a adj fantastic

química nf chemistry; *ver tb* **quimico**

químico, -a adj chemical ▷ nm/f chemist; *ver tb* **quimica**

quimioterapia nf chemotherapy

quince num fifteen; **~ días** a fortnight

quinceañero, -a adj fifteen-year-old; (*adolescente*) teenage ▷ nm/f fifteen-year-old; (*adolescente*) teenager

quincena nf fortnight; (*pago*) fortnightly pay

quincenal adj fortnightly

quiniela nf football pools *pl*; **quinielas** *nfpl* pools coupon *sg*

quinientos, -as num five hundred

quinina nf quinine

quinqui nm delinquent

quinteto nm quintet

quinto, -a adj fifth ▷ nm (*Mil*) conscript, draftee ▷ nf country house; (*Mil*) call-up, draft

quiosco nm (*de música*) bandstand; (*de periódicos*) news stand (*also selling sweets, cigarettes etc*)

quirófano nm operating theatre

quirúrgico, -a adj surgical

quisquilloso adj (*susceptible*) touchy; (*meticuloso*) pernickety

quiste nm cyst

quitaesmalte(s) nm nail polish remover

quitamanchas nm inv stain remover

quitanieves nm inv snowplough (Brit), snowplow (US)

quitar vt (*retirar*) to remove, take away; (*para no estorbar*) to get off; (*ropa*) to take off; (*dolor*) to relieve; (*vida*) to take; (*valor*) to reduce; (*hurtar*) to remove, steal ▷ vi: **¡quita de ahí!** get away!; **quitarse** vr (*apartarse*) to withdraw; (*mancha*) to come off o out; (*ropa*) to take off; **tardaron dos días en ~ los escombros** it took two days to remove the rubble; **este producto quita todo tipo de manchas** this product removes all types of stains; **su hermana le quitó la pelota** his sister took the ball away from him; **me han quitado la cartera** I've had my wallet stolen; **me quita mucho tiempo** it takes up a lot of my time; **el café me quita el sueño** coffee stops me sleeping; **~ de en medio algo** to get sth out of the way; **¡quítate de en medio!** get out of the way!; **~ de en medio a algn** to get rid of sb; **se quitó el sombrero** he took off his hat; **~se algo de encima** to get rid of sth; **~se del tabaco** to give up smoking

quite nm (*en esgrima*) parry; (*evasión*) dodge; **estar al ~** to be ready to go to sb's aid

Quito n Quito

quizá(s) adv perhaps, maybe

Rr

rabadilla *nf* base of the spine
rábano *nm* radish; **me importa un ~** I don't give two hoots
rabia *nf* (*Med*) rabies *sg*; (*fig: ira*) fury, rage; **¡qué ~!** isn't it infuriating!; **me da ~** it maddens me; **tener ~ a algn** to have a grudge against sb
rabiar *vi* (*tener rabia*) to have rabies; (*estar furioso*) to be furious; **~ por algo** to long for sth
rabieta *nf* tantrum, fit of temper
rabino *nm* rabbi
rabioso, -a *adj* rabid; (*fig*) furious
rabo *nm* tail
racha *nf* gust of wind; (*serie*) string, series; **buena/mala ~** spell of good/bad luck
racial *adj* racial, race *cpd*
racimo *nm* bunch
raciocinio *nm* reason; (*razonamiento*) reasoning
ración *nf* portion; **raciones** *nfpl* rations
racional *adj* (*razonable*) reasonable; (*lógico*) rational
racionalizar *vt* to rationalize; (*Com*) to streamline
racionar *vt* to ration (out)
racismo *nm* racialism, racism
racista *adj, nm/f* racist
radar *nm* radar
radiactividad *nf* radioactivity
radiactivo, -a *adj* radioactive
radiador *nm* radiator
radiante *adj* radiant
radical *adj, nm/f* radical ▷ *nm* (*Ling*) root; (*Mat*) square-root sign
radicar *vi* to take root; **~ en** to lie *o* consist in; **radicarse** *vr* to establish o.s., put down (one's) roots
radio *nf* radio; (*aparato*) radio (set) ▷ *nm* (*Mat*) radius; (*LAm*) radio; (*Química*) radium; **~ de acción** extent of one's authority, sphere of influence
radioaficionado, -a *nm/f* radio ham
radiocasete *nm* radiocassette (player)
radiodifusión *nf* broadcasting
radioemisora *nf* transmitter, radio station
radiografía *nf* X-ray
radionovela *nf* radio series
radiotaxi *nm* radio taxi
radioterapia *nf* radiotherapy

radioyente *nm/f* listener
ráfaga *nf* gust; (*de luz*) flash; (*de tiros*) burst
raído, -a *adj* (*ropa*) threadbare; (*persona*) shabby
raigambre *nf* (*Bot*) roots *pl*; (*fig*) tradition
raíz (*pl* **raíces**) *nf* root; **a ~ de** as a result of; (*después de*) immediately after; **~ cuadrada** square root
raja *nf* (*hendidura*) slit, split; (*grieta*) crack; (*de melón etc*) slice
rajar *vt* to split; (*fam*) to slash; **rajarse** *vr* to split, crack; **~se de** to back out of
rajatabla: a ~ *adv* (*estrictamente*) strictly, to the letter
rallador *nm* grater
rallar *vt* to grate
ralo, -a *adj* thin, sparse
rama *nf* bough, branch; **andarse por las ~s** (*fig: fam*) to beat about the bush
ramaje *nm* branches *pl*, foliage
ramal *nm* (*de cuerda*) strand; (*Ferro*) branch line; (*Auto*) branch (road)
rambla *nf* (*avenida*) avenue
ramera *nf* whore, hooker (*US*)
ramificación *nf* ramification
ramificarse *vr* to branch out
ramillete *nm* bouquet; (*fig*) select group
ramo *nm* branch, twig; (*sección*) department, section; (*sector*) field, sector
rampa *nf* ramp
ramplón, -ona *adj* uncouth, coarse
rana *nf* frog; **salto de ~** leapfrog; **cuando las ~s críen pelos** when pigs fly
ranchero *nm* (*Méx*) rancher; (*pequeño propietario*) smallholder
rancho *nm* (*Mil*) food; (*LAm: grande*) ranch; (: *pequeño*) small farm
rancio, -a *adj* (*comestibles*) stale, rancid; (*vino*) aged, mellow; (*fig*) ancient
rango *nm* rank; (*prestigio*) standing
ranura *nf* groove; (*de teléfono etc*) slot; **~ de expansión** (*Inform*) expansion slot
rap *nm* (*Mus*) rap
rapar *vt* to shave; (*los cabellos*) to crop
rapaz *adj* (*Zool*) predatory ▷ *nm/f*; (*f tb* **~a**) young boy/girl
rape *nm* quick shave; (*pez*) angler (fish); **al ~** cropped

rapé *nm* snuff

rapidez *nf* speed, rapidity

rápido, -a *adj* fast, quick ▷ *adv* quickly ▷ *nm* (*Ferro*) express; **rápidos** *nmpl* rapids

rapiña *nm* robbery; **ave de ~** bird of prey

rap(p)el *nm* (*Deporte*) abseiling

raptar *vt* to kidnap

rapto *nm* kidnapping; (*impulso*) sudden impulse; (*éxtasis*) ecstasy, rapture

raqueta *nf* racquet

raquítico, -a *adj* stunted; (*fig*) poor, inadequate

raquitismo *nm* rickets *sg*

rareza *nf* rarity; (*fig*) eccentricity

raro, -a *adj* (*poco común*) rare; (*extraño*) odd, strange; (*excepcional*) remarkable; **¡qué ~!** how (very) odd!; **¡qué cosa más rara!** how strange!

ras *nm*: **a ~ de** level with; **a ~ de tierra** at ground level

rasar *vt* to level

rascacielos *nm inv* skyscraper

rascar *vt* (*con las uñas etc*) to scratch; (*raspar*) to scrape; **rascarse** *vr* to scratch (o.s.)

rasgar *vt* to tear, rip (up)

rasgo *nm* (*con pluma*) stroke; **rasgos** *nmpl* features, characteristics; **a grandes ~s** in outline, broadly

rasguñar *vt* to scratch; (*bosquejar*) to sketch

rasguño *nm* scratch

raso, -a *adj* (*liso*) flat, level; (*a baja altura*) very low ▷ *nm* (*tejido*) satin; (*campo llano*) flat country; **cielo ~** clear sky; **al ~** in the open

raspado *nm* (*Med*) scrape; (*CAm, Méx, Col: bebida*) water ice, sherbet (*US*)

raspadura *nf* (*acto*) scrape, scraping; (*marca*) scratch; **raspaduras** *nfpl* scrapings

raspar *vt* to scrape; (*arañar*) to scratch; (*limar*) to file ▷ *vi* (*manos*) to be rough; (*vino*) to be sharp, have a rough taste

rastra *nf*: **a ~s** by dragging; (*fig*) unwillingly

rastreador *nm* tracker; **~ de minas** minesweeper

rastrear *vt* (*seguir*) to track; (*minas*) to sweep

rastrero, -a *adj* (*Bot, Zool*) creeping; (*fig*) despicable, mean

rastrillar *vt* to rake

rastrillo *nm* rake; (*Méx*) safety razor

rastro *nm* (*Agr*) rake; (*pista*) track, trail; (*vestigio*) trace; (*mercado*) fleamarket; **el R~** *the Madrid fleamarket*; **perder el ~** to lose the scent; **desaparecer sin ~** to vanish without trace

rastrojo *nm* stubble

rasurador *nm*, (*CAm, Méx*) **rasuradora** *nf* electric shaver *o* razor

rasurarse *vr* to shave

rata *nf* rat

ratear *vt* (*robar*) to steal

ratero, -a *adj* light-fingered ▷ *nm/f* pickpocket; (*Méx: de casas*) burglar

ratificar *vt* to ratify

rato *nm* while, short time; **después de un ~** after a while; **estaba aquí hace un ~** he was here a few minutes ago; **hay para ~** there's still a long way to go; **tengo para ~ con esta redacción** I've got a way to go yet with this essay; **pasar el ~** to kill time; **pasar un buen/mal ~** to have a good/rough time; **a ~s** from time to time; **al poco ~** shortly after, soon afterwards; **~s libres** *o* **de ocio** leisure *sg*, spare *o* free time *sg*

ratón *nm* (*tb Inform*) mouse

ratonera *nf* mousetrap

raudal *nm* torrent; **a ~es** in abundance; **entrar a ~es** to pour in

raya *nf* line; (*en tela*) stripe; (*Tip*) hyphen; (*de pelo*) parting; (*límite*) boundary; (*pez*) ray; **a ~s** striped; **pasarse de la ~** to overstep the mark, go too far; **tener a ~** to keep in check

rayar *vt* (*arañar*) to scratch; (*subrayar*) to underline ▷ *vi*: **~ en** *o* **con** to border on; **al ~ el alba** at first light

rayo *nm* (*del sol*) ray, beam; (*de luz*) shaft; (*en una tormenta*) (flash of) lightning; **~ solar** *o* **de sol** sunbeam; **~s infrarrojos** infrared rays; **~s X** X-rays; **como un ~** like a shot; **la noticia cayó como un ~** the news was a bombshell; **pasar como un ~** to flash past

raza *nf* race; (*de animal*) breed; **de pura ~** (*caballo*) thoroughbred; (*perro etc*) pedigree; **~ humana** human race

razón *nf* (*motivo, entendimiento*) reason; (*justicia*) right, justice; (*razonamiento*) reasoning; (*proporción*) rate; (*Mat*) ratio; **¿cuál era la ~ de su visita?** what was the reason for his visit?; **la ~ por la que lo hizo** the reason why he did it; **tener/no tener ~** to be right/wrong; **perder la ~** to go out of one's mind; **al final me dio la ~** in the end he agreed that I was right; **dar ~ de** to give an account of, report on; **"~: en la portería"** "inquiries to the caretaker"; **a ~ de 10 cada día** at the rate of 10 a day; **en ~ de** with regard to; **~ de ser** raison d'être; **~ directa/inversa** direct/inverse proportion

razonable *adj* reasonable; (*justo, moderado*) fair

razonamiento *nm* (*juicio*) judgement; (*argumento*) reasoning

razonar *vt, vi* to reason, argue

RDSI *nf abr* (= *Red Digital de Servicios Integrados*) ISDN

re *nm* (*Mus*) D

reacción *nf* reaction; **avión a ~** jet plane; **~ en cadena** chain reaction

reaccionar *vi* to react

reaccionario, -a *adj* reactionary

reacio, -a *adj* stubborn; **ser** *o* **estar ~ a** to be opposed to

reactivar *vt* to reactivate; **reactivarse** *vr* (*economía*) to be on the upturn

reactor *nm* reactor; (*avión*) jet plane; **~ nuclear** nuclear reactor

readaptación *nf*: **~ profesional** industrial retraining

readmitir *vt* to readmit

reajuste *nm* readjustment; **~ de plantilla** rationalization; **~ salarial** wage increase

real *adj* real; (*del rey, fig*) royal; (*espléndido*) grand ▷ *nm* (*de feria*) fairground

realce nm (Tec) embossing; (lustre, fig) splendour (Brit), splendor (US); (Arte) highlight; **poner de ~ to** emphasize

real-decreto (pl **reales-decretos**) nm royal decree

realidad nf reality; (verdad) truth; **en ~** in fact; **~ virtual** virtual reality

realismo nm realism

realista nm/f realist

realización nf fulfilment, realization; (Com) selling up (Brit), conversion into money (US); **~ de plusvalías** profit-taking

realizador, a nm/f (TV etc) producer

realizar vt (objetivo) to achieve; (plan) to carry out; (viaje) to make, undertake; (Com) to realize; **realizarse** vr to come about, come true; **~se como persona** to fulfil one's aims in life

realmente adv really

realojar vt to rehouse

realquilar vt to sublet

realzar vt (Tec) to raise; (embellecer) to enhance; (acentuar) to highlight

reanimar vt to revive; (alentar) to encourage; **reanimarse** vr to revive

reanudar vt (renovar) to renew; (historia, viaje) to resume

reaparición nf reappearance; (vuelta) return

rearme nm rearmament

reavivar vt (persona) to revive; (fig) to rekindle

rebaja nf reduction, lowering; (Com) discount; "**grandes ~s**" "big reductions", "sale"

rebajar vt (bajar) to lower; (reducir) to reduce; (precio) to cut; (disminuir) to lessen; (humillar) to humble; **rebajarse** vr: **~se a hacer algo** to lower o.s. to do sth; **me han rebajado diez euros** they took ten euros off the price for me; **han rebajado los abrigos** coats have been reduced; **cada fin de temporada rebajan los precios** prices are reduced at the end of every season; **yo no me ~ía a hablar con él** I wouldn't lower myself to speak to him

rebanada nf slice

rebañar vt to scrape clean

rebaño nm herd; (de ovejas) flock

rebasar vt (tb: **rebasar de**) to exceed; (Auto) to overtake

rebatir vt to refute; (rebajar) to reduce; (ataque) to repel

rebeca nf cardigan

rebelarse vr to rebel, revolt

rebelde adj rebellious; (niño) unruly ▷ nm/f rebel; **ser ~ a** to be in revolt against, rebel against

rebeldía nf rebelliousness; (desobediencia) disobedience; (Jur) default

rebelión nf rebellion

reblandecer vt to soften

rebobinar vt to rewind

rebosante adj: **~ de** (fig) brimming o overflowing with

rebosar vi to overflow; (abundar) to abound, be plentiful; **~ de salud** to be bursting o brimming with health

rebotar vt to bounce; (rechazar) to repel

rebote nm rebound; **de ~** on the rebound

rebozado, -a adj (Culin) fried in batter o breadcrumbs o flour

rebozar vt to wrap up; (Culin) to fry in batter etc

rebuscado, -a adj affected

rebuscar vi (en bolsillo, cajón) to fish; (en habitación) to search high and low

rebuznar vi to bray

recabar vt (obtener) to manage to get; **~ fondos** to collect money

recado nm message; **dejar/tomar un ~** (Telec) to leave/take a message

recaer vi to relapse; **~ en** to fall to o on; (criminal etc) to fall back into, relapse into; (premio) to go to

recaída nf relapse

recalcar vt (fig) to stress, emphasize

recalcitrante adj recalcitrant

recalentamiento nm: **~ global** global warming

recalentar vt (comida) to warm up, reheat; (demasiado) to overheat; **recalentarse** vr to overheat, get too hot

recámara nf side room; (CAm, Méx) bedroom

recambio nm spare; (de pluma) refill; **piezas de ~** spares

recapacitar vi to reflect

recapitular vt to recap

recargable adj (batería, pila) rechargeable; (mechero, pluma) refillable

recargado, -a adj overloaded; (exagerado) over-elaborate

recargar vt to overload; (batería) to recharge; (mechero, pluma) to refill

recargo nm surcharge; (aumento) increase

recatado, -a adj (modesto) modest, demure; (prudente) cautious

recato nm (modestia) modesty, demureness; (cautela) caution

recauchutado, -a adj remould cpd

recaudación nf (acción) collection; (cantidad) takings pl; (en deporte) gate; (oficina) tax office

recaudador, a nm/f tax collector

recaudar vt to collect

recelar vt: **~ que** (sospechar) to suspect that; (temer) to fear that ▷ vi: **~(se) de** to distrust

recelo nm distrust, suspicion

receloso, -a adj distrustful, suspicious

recepción nf reception; (acto de recibir) receipt

recepcionista nm/f receptionist

receptáculo nm receptacle

receptivo, -a adj receptive

receptor, a nm/f recipient ▷ nm (Telec) receiver; **descolgar el ~** to pick up the receiver

recesión nf (Com) recession

receta nf (Culin) recipe; (Med) prescription

recetar vt to prescribe

rechazar vt to repel, drive back; (idea) to reject; (oferta) to turn down

rechazo nm (de fusil) recoil; (rebote) rebound; (negación) rebuff

rechifla nf hissing, booing; (fig) derision

rechinar vi to creak; (dientes) to grind; (máquina)

to clank, clatter; (*metal seco*) to grate; (*motor*) to hum

rechistar *vi*: **sin ~** without complaint

rechoncho, -a *adj* (*fam*) stocky, thickset (*Brit*), heavy-set (*US*)

rechupete; **de ~** *adj* (*comida*) delicious

recibidor *nm* entrance hall

recibimiento *nm* reception, welcome

recibir *vt* (*mensaje, premio, sugerencia*) to receive; (*persona: dar la bienvenida*) to welcome; (*salir al encuentro de*) to go and meet ▷ *vi* to entertain; **recibirse** *vr* (*LAm*): **~se de** to qualify as; **no he recibido tu carta** I haven't received your letter; **recibí muchos regalos** I got a lot of presents; **reciba un saludo de ...** yours sincerely ...; **vinieron a ~nos al aeropuerto** they came and met us at the airport; **el director me recibió en su despacho** the manager saw me in his office

recibo *nm* receipt; **acusar ~ de** to acknowledge receipt of

reciclable *adj* recyclable

reciclaje *nm* recycling; (*de trabajadores*) retraining; **cursos de ~** refresher courses

reciclar *vt* to recycle; (*trabajador*) to retrain

recién *adv* recently, newly; (*CAm, Méx*) just, recently; **~ casado** newly-wed; **el ~ llegado** the newcomer; **el ~ nacido** the newborn child; **~ a las seis** only at six o'clock

reciente *adj* recent; (*fresco*) fresh

recientemente *adv* recently

recinto *nm* (*zona*) area, place; (*lugar cerrado*) enclosure

recio, -a *adj* (*fuerte*) strong, tough; (*voz*) loud ▷ *adv* (*soplar, golpear*) hard; (*cantar*) loud(ly)

recipiente *nm* (*objeto*) container, receptacle; (*persona*) recipient

reciprocidad *nf* reciprocity

recíproco, -a *adj* reciprocal

recital *nm* (*Mus*) recital; (*Lit*) reading

recitar *vt* to recite

reclamación *nf* claim, demand; (*queja*) complaint; **~ salarial** pay claim

reclamar *vt* to claim, demand ▷ *vi*: **~ contra** to complain about; **~ a algn en justicia** to take sb to court

reclamo *nm* (*anuncio*) advertisement; (*tentación*) attraction

reclinar *vt* to recline, lean; **reclinarse** *vr* to lean back

recluir *vt* to intern, confine

reclusión *nf* (*prisión*) prison; (*refugio*) seclusion; **~ perpetua** life imprisonment

recluta *nm/f* recruit ▷ *nf* recruitment

reclutamiento *nm* recruitment

recobrar *vt* (*recuperar*) to recover; (*rescatar*) to get back; (*ciudad*) to recapture; (*tiempo*) to make up (for); **recobrarse** *vr* to recover

recochineo *nm* (*fam*) mickey-taking

recodo *nm* (*de río, camino*) bend

recoger *vt* (*recolectar*) to collect; (*levantar*) to pick up; (*juntar*) to gather; (*pasar a buscar*) to come for, get; (*dar asilo*) to give shelter to; (*cosecha*) to

harvest; **recogerse** *vr* (*retirarse*) to retire; (*faldas*) to gather up; (*mangas*) to roll up; **¿a qué hora recogen el correo?** what time do they collect the mail?; **a las diez recogen la basura** the rubbish gets collected at ten o'clock; **recógelo todo antes de marcharte** clear up everything before you leave; **~ la mesa** to clear the table; **~ fruta** to pick fruit; **recogí el papel del suelo** I picked the paper up off the floor; **me recogieron en la estación** they picked me up at the station; **~se el pelo** to put one's hair up

recogida *nf* (*Correos*) collection; (*Agr*) harvest; **~ de datos** (*Inform*) data capture; *ver tb* **recogido**

recogido, -a *adj* (*lugar*) quiet, secluded; (*pequeño*) small; *ver tb* **recogida**

recolección *nf* (*Agr*) harvesting; (*colecta*) collection

recomendación *nf* (*sugerencia*) suggestion, recommendation; (*referencia*) reference; **carta de ~ para** letter of introduction to

recomendar *vt* to suggest, recommend; (*confiar*) to entrust

recompensa *nf* reward, recompense; (*compensación*): **~ (de una pérdida)** compensation (for a loss); **como** *o* **en ~ por** in return for

recompensar *vt* to reward, recompense

recomponer *vt* to mend; (*Inform: texto*) to reformat

reconciliación *nf* reconciliation

reconciliar *vt* to reconcile; **reconciliarse** *vr* to become reconciled

recóndito, -a *adj* (*lugar*) hidden, secret

reconfortar *vt* to comfort

reconocer *vt* to recognize; **~ los hechos** to face the facts

reconocido, -a *adj* recognized; (*agradecido*) grateful

reconocimiento *nm* recognition; (*registro*) search; (*inspección*) examination; (*gratitud*) gratitude; (*confesión*) admission; **~ de la voz** (*Inform*) speech recognition; **~ médico** checkup; **~ óptico de caracteres** (*Inform*) optical character recognition

reconquista *nf* reconquest

reconstituyente *nm* tonic

reconstruir *vt* to reconstruct

reconversión *nf* restructuring, reorganization; (*tb*: **reconversión industrial**) rationalization

recopilación *nf* (*resumen*) summary; (*compilación*) compilation

recopilar *vt* to compile

récord *adj inv* record; **cifras ~** record figures ▷ *nm* (*pl* **records** *o* **-s**) record; **batir el ~** to break the record

recordar *vt* (*acordarse de*) to remember, recall; (*traer a la memoria*) to remind ▷ *vi* to remember; **no recuerdo dónde lo puse** I can't remember where I put it; **esto recuerda aquella escena de la película** this recalls that scene in the film; **recuérdale que me debe 5 dólares** remind him that he owes me 5 dollars; **que yo recuerde** as far as I can remember; **creo ~, si mal no**

recuerdo if my memory serves me right; **me recuerda a su padre** he reminds me of his father; **el paisaje me recuerda a Escocia** the scenery reminds me of Scotland

recordatorio *nm* (*de bautizo, comunión*) commemorative card; (*de fallecimiento*) in memoriam card

recorrer *vt* (*país*) to cross, travel through; (*distancia*) to cover

recorrido *nm* run, journey; **tren de largo ~** main-line *o* inter-city (*Brit*) train

recortado, -a *adj* uneven, irregular

recortar *vt* (*papel*) to cut out; (*el pelo*) to trim; (*dibujar*) to draw in outline; **recortarse** *vr* to stand out, be silhouetted

recorte *nm* (*de papel*) cutting; (*de telas, chapas*) trimming; **~ presupuestario** budget cut; **~ salarial** wage cut

recostado, -a *adj* leaning; **estar ~** to be lying down

recostar *vt* to lean; **recostarse** *vr* to lie down

recoveco *nm* (*de camino, río etc*) bend; (*en casa*) cubbyhole

recreación *nf* recreation

recrear *vt* (*entretener*) to entertain; (*volver a crear*) to recreate

recreativo, -a *adj* recreational

recreo *nm* recreation; (*Escol*) break, playtime

recriminar *vt* to reproach ▷ *vi* to recriminate; **recriminarse** *vr* to reproach each other

recrudecer *vt, vi*, **recrudecerse** *vr* to worsen

recta *nf* straight line; (*Atletismo*) straight; **~ final** *o* **de llegada** home straight; *ver tb* **recto**

rectangular *adj* rectangular

rectángulo, -a *adj* rectangular ▷ *nm* rectangle

rectificar *vt* to rectify; (*volverse recto*) to straighten ▷ *vi* to correct o.s.

rectitud *nf* straightness; (*fig*) rectitude

recto, -a *adj* straight; (*persona*) honest, upright; (*estricto*) strict; (*juez*) fair; (*juicio*) sound ▷ *nm* rectum; **en el sentido ~ de la palabra** in the proper sense of the word; *ver tb* **recta**

rector, a *adj* governing ▷ *nm/f* head, chief; (*Escol*) rector, president (*US*)

recuadro *nm* box; (*Tip*) inset

recubrir *vt* to cover

recuento *nm* inventory; **hacer el ~ de** to count *o* reckon up

recuerdo *nm* souvenir; **recuerdos** *nmpl* memories; **¡~s a tu madre!** give my regards to your mother!; **"R~ de Mallorca"** "a present from Majorca"; **contar los ~s** to reminisce

recular *vi* to back down

recuperable *adj* recoverable

recuperación *nf* recovery; **~ de datos** (*Inform*) data retrieval

recuperar *vt* (*tener otra vez*) to get back, recover; (*tiempo, clase perdida*) to make up; (*Inform*) to retrieve; **recuperarse** *vr* to recuperate; **tardé unos minutos en ~ el aliento** it took me a few minutes to get my breath back; **~ fuerzas** to get one's strength back; **~ el tiempo perdido** to

make up for lost time; **~se de** (*gripe, resfriado*) to get over; (*operación, infarto*) to recover from

recurrir *vi* (*Jur*) to appeal; **~ a** to resort to; (*persona*) to turn to

recurso *nm* resort; (*medio*) means *pl*, resource; (*Jur*) appeal; **como último ~** as a last resort; **~s económicos** economic resources; **~s naturales** natural resources

recusar *vt* to reject, refuse

red *nf* net, mesh; (*Ferro, Inform*) network; (*Elec, de agua*) mains, supply system; (*de tiendas*) chain; (*trampa*) trap; **~ de transmisión** (*Inform*) data network; **~ local** (*Inform*) local area network

redacción *nf* (*acción*) writing; (*Escol*) essay, composition; (*personal editorial*) editorial staff

redactar *vt* to draw up, draft; (*periódico, Inform*) to edit

redactor, a *nm/f* writer; (*en periódico*) editor

redada *nf* (*Pesca*) cast, throw; (*fig*) catch; **~ policial** police raid, round-up

redención *nf* redemption

redentor, a *adj* redeeming ▷ *nm/f* (*Com*) redeemer

redescubrir *vt* to rediscover

redicho, -a *adj* affected

redil *nm* sheepfold

redimir *vt* to redeem; (*rehén*) to ransom

rédito *nm* interest, yield

redoblar *vt* to redouble ▷ *vi* (*tambor*) to play a roll on the drums

redomado, -a *adj* (*astuto*) sly, crafty; (*perfecto*) utter

redonda *nf*: **a la ~** around, round about; **en muchas millas a la ~** for many miles around

redondear *vt* to round, round off; (*cifra*) to round up

redondel *nm* circle

redondo, -a *adj* (*circular*) round; (*completo*) complete; **rehusar en ~** to give a flat refusal

reducción *nf* reduction; **~ del activo** (*Com*) divestment; **~ de precios** (*Com*) price-cutting

reducido, -a *adj* reduced; (*limitado*) limited; (*pequeño*) small; **quedar ~ a** to be reduced to

reducir *vt* (*rebajar: producción, condena, fotografía*) to reduce; (*gastos, impuestos*) to cut; (*someter*) to bring under control; **reducirse** *vr* to diminish; (*Mat*): **reduzca la velocidad** reduce speed; **van a ~ personal** they're going to cut staff; **~ las millas a kilómetros** to convert miles into kilometres; **~se a** (*fig*) to come *o* boil down to

reducto *nm* redoubt

redundancia *nf* redundancy

reedición *nf* reissue

reeditar *vt* to reissue

reelección *nf* re-election

reelegir *vt* to re-elect

reembolsar *vt* (*persona*) to reimburse; (*dinero*) to repay, pay back; (*depósito*) to refund

reembolso *nm* (*de gastos*) reimbursement; (*de inversión, compra*) refund; **enviar algo contra ~** to send sth cash on delivery; **contra ~ del flete** freight forward; **~ fiscal** tax rebate

reemplazar vt to replace
reemplazo nm replacement; **de ~** (Mil) reserve
reencuentro nm reunion
reengancharse vr (Mil) to re-enlist
reestreno nm rerun
reestructurar vt to restructure
referencia nf reference; **con ~ a** with reference to; **hacer ~ a** to refer o allude to; **~ comercial** (Com) trade reference
referéndum (pl **-s**) nm referendum
referente adj: **~ a** concerning, relating to
referir vt (contar) to tell, recount; (relacionar) to refer, relate; **referirse** vr: **~se a** to refer to; **por lo que se refiere a eso** as for that, as regards that; **~ al lector a un apéndice** to refer the reader to an appendix; **~ a** (Com) to convert into
refilón; **de ~** adv obliquely; **mirar a algn de ~** to look out of the corner of one's eye at sb
refinado, -a adj refined
refinamiento nm refinement; **~ por pasos** (Inform) stepwise refinement
refinar vt to refine
refinería nf refinery
reflejar vt to reflect; **reflejarse** vr to be reflected
reflejo, -a adj reflected; (movimiento) reflex ▷ nm reflection; (Anat) reflex; (en el pelo): **~s** nmpl highlights; **tiene el pelo castaño con ~s rubios** she has chestnut hair with blond streaks
reflexión nf reflection
reflexionar vt to reflect on ▷ vi to reflect; (detenerse) to pause (to think); **¡reflexione!** you think it over!
reflexivo, -a adj thoughtful; (Ling) reflexive
reflujo nm ebb
reforma nf reform; (Arq etc) repair; **~ agraria** agrarian reform
reformar vt to reform; (modificar) to change, alter; (texto) to revise; (Arq) to repair; **reformarse** vr to mend one's ways
reformatorio nm reformatory; **~ de menores** remand home
reformista adj, nm/f reformist
reforzar vt to strengthen; (Arq) to reinforce; (fig) to encourage
refractario, -a adj (Tec) heat-resistant; **ser ~ a una reforma** to resist o be opposed to a reform
refrán nm proverb, saying
refregar vt to scrub
refrenar vt to check, restrain
refrendar vt (firma) to endorse, countersign; (ley) to approve
refrescante adj refreshing, cooling
refrescar vt to refresh ▷ vi to cool down; **refrescarse** vr to get cooler; (tomar aire fresco) to go out for a breath of fresh air; (beber) to have a drink
refresco nm soft drink, cool drink; **"~s"** "refreshments"
refriega nf scuffle, brawl
refrigeración nf refrigeration; (de casa) air-conditioning
refrigerador nm, (And) **refrigeradora** nf refrigerator, icebox (US)
refrigerar vt (en nevera) to refrigerate; (con aire acondicionado) to air-condition
refrito nm (Culin): **un ~ de cebolla y tomate** sautéed onions and tomatoes; **un ~** (fig) a rehash
refuerzo nm reinforcement; (Tec) support
refugiado, -a nm/f refugee
refugiarse vr to take refuge, shelter
refugio nm refuge; (protección) shelter; (Auto) street o traffic island; **~ alpino** o **de montaña** mountain hut; **~ subterráneo** (Mil) underground shelter
refulgir vi to shine, be dazzling
refunfuñar vi to grunt, growl; (quejarse) to grumble
refutar vt to refute
regadera nf watering can; (LAm) shower; **estar como una ~** (fam) to be as mad as a hatter
regadío nm irrigated land
regalado, -a adj comfortable, luxurious; (gratis) free, for nothing; **lo tuvo ~** it was handed to him on a plate
regalar vt (dar) to give (as a present); (entregar) to give away; **regalarse** vr to treat o.s. to; **¿qué te ~on para tu cumpleaños?** what did you get for your birthday?
regalía nf privilege, prerogative; (Com) bonus; (de autor) royalty
regaliz nm liquorice
regalo nm (obsequio) gift, present; (gusto) pleasure; (comodidad) comfort
regañadientes: **a ~** adv reluctantly
regañar vt to scold ▷ vi to grumble; (dos personas) to fall out, quarrel
regañón, -ona adj nagging
regar vt to water, irrigate; (fig) to scatter, sprinkle
regatear vt (Com) to bargain over; (escatimar) to be mean with ▷ vi to bargain, haggle; (Deporte) to dribble; **no ~ esfuerzo** to spare no effort
regateo nm bargaining; (Deporte) dribbling; (con el cuerpo) swerve, dodge
regazo nm lap
regencia nf regency
regeneración nf regeneration
regenerar vt to regenerate
regentar vt to direct, manage; (puesto) to hold in an acting capacity; (negocio) to be in charge of
regente, -a adj (príncipe) regent; (director) managing ▷ nm (Com) manager; (Pol) regent
régimen (pl **regímenes**) nm regime; (reinado) rule; (de adelgazamiento) diet; (reglas) (set of) rules pl; (manera de vivir) lifestyle; **estar a ~** to be on a diet
regimiento nm regiment
regio, -a adj royal, regal; (fig: suntuoso) splendid; (CS fam) great, terrific
región nf region; (área) area
regional adj regional
regir vt to govern, rule; (dirigir) to manage, run; (Econ, Jur, Ling) to govern ▷ vi to apply, be in force
registrador nm registrar, recorder
registrar vt (buscar) to search; (en cajón) to look

through; (*inspeccionar*) to inspect; (*anotar*)
to register, record; (*Inform, Mus*) to record;
registrarse *vr* to register; (*ocurrir*) to happen
registro *nm* (*acto*) registration; (*Mus, libro*)
register; (*lista*) list, record; (*Inform*) record;
(*inspección*) inspection, search; ~ **civil** registry
office; ~ **de la propiedad** land registry (office); ~
electoral voting register
regla *nf* (*ley*) rule, regulation; (*de medir*) ruler,
rule; (*menstruación*) period; (*norma científica*) law,
principle; **no hay ~ sin excepción** every rule has
its exception
reglamentación *nf* (*acto*) regulation; (*lista*)
rules *pl*
reglamentar *vt* to regulate
reglamentario, -a *adj* statutory; **en la forma
reglamentaria** in the properly established way
reglamento *nm* rules *pl*, regulations *pl*
reglar *vt* (*acciones*) to regulate; **reglarse** *vr*: ~**se
por** to be guided by
regocijarse *vr*: ~ **de** *o* **por** to rejoice at, be glad
about
regocijo *nm* joy, happiness
regodearse *vr* to be glad, be delighted; (*pey*): ~
con *o* **en** to gloat over
regodeo *nm* delight; (*pey*) perverse pleasure
regresar *vi* to come/go back, return; **regresarse**
vr (*LAm*) to return
regresivo, -a *adj* backward; (*fig*) regressive
regreso *nm* return; **estar de ~** to be back, be
home
reguero *nm* (*de sangre*) trickle; (*de humo*) trail
regulación *nf* regulation; (*Tec*) adjustment;
(*control*) control; ~ **de empleo** redundancies *pl*; ~
del tráfico traffic control
regulador *nm* (*Tec*) regulator; (*de radio etc*) knob,
control
regular *adj* regular; (*normal*) normal, usual;
(*común*) ordinary; (*organizado*) regular, orderly;
(*mediano*) average; (*fam*) not bad, so-so ▷ *adv*:
estar ~ to be so-so *o* alright ▷ *vt* (*controlar*) to
control, regulate; (*Tec*) to adjust; **por lo ~** as a
rule
regularidad *nf* regularity; **con ~** regularly
regularizar *vt* to regularize
regusto *nm* aftertaste
rehabilitación *nf* rehabilitation; (*Arq*)
restoration
rehabilitar *vt* to rehabilitate; (*Arq*) to restore;
(*reintegrar*) to reinstate
rehacer *vt* (*reparar*) to mend, repair; (*volver a hacer*)
to redo, repeat; **rehacerse** *vr* (*Med*) to recover
rehén *nm/f* hostage
rehogar *vt* to sauté, toss in oil
rehuir *vt* to avoid, shun
rehusar *vt, vi* to refuse
reina *nf* queen
reinado *nm* reign
reinante *adj* (*fig*) prevailing
reinar *vi* to reign; (*fig: prevalecer*) to prevail, be
general
reincidir *vi* to relapse; (*criminal*) to repeat an

offence
reincorporarse *vr*: ~ **a** to rejoin
reino *nm* kingdom; **el R~ Unido** the United
Kingdom
reinserción *nf* rehabilitation
reinsertar *vt* to rehabilitate
reintegrar *vt* (*reconstituir*) to reconstruct; (*persona*)
to reinstate; (*dinero*) to refund, pay back;
reintegrarse *vr*: ~**se a** to return to
reír *vi*, **reírse** *vr* to laugh; ~**se de** to laugh at
reiterado, -a *adj* repeated
reiterar *vt* to reiterate; (*repetir*) to repeat
reivindicación *nf* (*demanda*) claim, demand;
(*justificación*) vindication
reivindicar *vt* to claim
reja *nf* (*de ventana*) grille, bars *pl*; (*en la calle*)
grating
rejilla *nf* grating, grille; (*en muebles*) wickerwork;
(*de ventilación*) vent; (*de coche etc*) luggage rack
rejuvenecer *vt, vi* to rejuvenate
relación *nf* (*unión*) relation, relationship;
(*conexión*) link; (*Mat*) ratio; (*lista*) list; (*narración*)
account; **la ~ entre el tabaco y el cáncer**
the link between smoking and cancer; **las
relaciones entre empresarios y trabajadores**
the relationship between employers and
workers; **tener relaciones con alguien** to
have a relationship with somebody; **estar en**
o **tener buenas relaciones con** to be on good
terms with; **con ~ a, en ~ con** in relation to;
relaciones carnales/sexuales sexual relations;
relaciones comerciales business connections;
relaciones empresariales/humanas
industrial/human relations; **relaciones
laborales/públicas** labour/public relations
relacionar *vt* to relate, connect; **relacionarse** *vr*
to be connected *o* linked
relajación *nf* relaxation
relajado, -a *adj* (*disoluto*) loose; (*cómodo*) relaxed;
(*Med*) ruptured
relajar *vt*, **relajarse** *vr* to relax
relamerse *vr* to lick one's lips
relamido, -a *adj* (*pulcro*) overdressed; (*afectado*)
affected
relámpago *nm* flash of lightning ▷ *adj inv*
lightning *cpd*; **como un ~** as quick as lightning,
in a flash; **visita/huelga ~** lightning visit/strike
relampaguear *vi* to flash
relanzar *vt* to relaunch
relatar *vt* to tell, relate
relatividad *nf* relativity
relativo, -a *adj* relative; **en lo ~ a** concerning
relato *nm* (*narración*) story, tale
relax *nm* rest; **"R~"** (*en anuncio*) "Personal
services"
relegar *vt* to relegate; ~ **algo al olvido** to banish
sth from one's mind
relevante *adj* eminent, outstanding
relevar *vt* (*sustituir*) to relieve; **relevarse** *vr* to
relay; ~ **a algn de un cargo** to relieve sb of his
post
relevo *nm* relief; **carrera de ~s** relay race; **coger**

o **tomar el ~** to take over, stand in; **~ con cinta** (*Inform*) tape relay

relieve *nm* (*Arte, Tec*) relief; (*fig*) prominence, importance; **bajo ~** bas-relief; **un personaje de ~** an important man; **dar ~ a** to highlight

religión *nf* religion

religioso, -a *adj* religious ▷ *nm/f* monk/nun

relinchar *vi* to neigh

relincho *nm* neigh; (*acto*) neighing

reliquia *nf* relic; **~ de familia** heirloom

rellano *nm* (*Arq*) landing

rellenar *vt* (*llenar*) to fill up; (*Culin*) to stuff; (*Costura*) to pad; (*formulario etc*) to fill in *o* out

relleno, -a *adj* full up; (*Culin*) stuffed ▷ *nm* (*Culin*) stuffing; (*de tapicería*) padding

reloj *nm* clock; **como un ~** like clockwork; **contra (el) ~** against the clock; **~ de pie** grandfather clock; **~ de pulsera** wristwatch; **~ de sol** sundial; **~ despertador** alarm (clock)

relojero, -a *nm/f* (*de relojes de pared*) clockmaker; (*de relojes de pulsera*) watchmaker

reluciente *adj* brilliant, shining

relucir *vi* to shine; (*fig*) to excel; **sacar algo a ~** to show sth off

relumbrar *vi* to dazzle, shine brilliantly

remachar *vt* to rivet; (*fig*) to hammer home, drive home

remache *nm* rivet

remanente *nm* remainder; (*Com*) balance; (*de producto*) surplus

remangarse *vr* to roll one's sleeves up

remanso *nm* pool

remar *vi* to row

rematado, -a *adj* complete, utter; **es un loco ~** he's a raving lunatic

rematar *vt* to finish off; (*animal*) to put out of its misery; (*Com*) to sell off cheap ▷ *vi* to end, finish off; (*Deporte*) to shoot

remate *nm* end, finish; (*punta*) tip; (*Deporte*) shot; (*Arq*) top; (*Com*) auction sale; **de** *o* **para ~** to crown it all (*Brit*), to top it off

remediar *vt* (*gen*) to remedy; (*subsanar*) to make good, repair; (*evitar*) to avoid; **sin poder ~lo** without being able to prevent it

remedio *nm* remedy; (*Jur*) recourse, remedy; **poner ~ a** to correct, stop; **no tener más ~** to have no alternative; **¡qué ~!** there's no other way; **como último ~** as a last resort; **sin ~** inevitable; (*Med*) hopeless

remedo *nm* imitation; (*pey*) parody

remendar *vt* to repair; (*con parche*) to patch; (*fig*) to correct

remesa *nf* remittance; (*Com*) shipment

remiendo *nm* mend; (*con parche*) patch; (*cosido*) darn; (*fig*) correction

remilgado, -a *adj* prim; (*afectado*) affected

remilgo *nm* primness; (*afectación*) affectation

reminiscencia *nf* reminiscence

remiso, -a *adj* remiss

remite *nm* (*en sobre*) name and address of sender

remitente *nm/f* (*Correos*) sender

remitir *vt* to remit, send ▷ *vi* to slacken

remo *nm* (*de barco*) oar; (*Deporte*) rowing; **cruzar un río a ~** to row across a river

remojar *vt* to steep, soak; (*galleta etc*) to dip, dunk; (*fam*) to celebrate with a drink

remojo *nm* steeping, soaking; (*por la lluvia*) drenching, soaking; **dejar la ropa en ~** to leave clothes to soak

remolacha *nf* beet, beetroot (*Brit*)

remolcador *nm* (*Naut*) tug; (*Auto*) breakdown lorry

remolcar *vt* to tow

remolino *nm* eddy; (*de agua*) whirlpool; (*de viento*) whirlwind; (*de gente*) crowd

remolque *nm* tow, towing; (*cuerda*) towrope; **llevar a ~** to tow

remontar *vt* to mend; (*obstáculo*) to negotiate, get over; **remontarse** *vr* to soar; **~se a** (*Com*) to amount to; (*en tiempo*) to go back to, date from; **~ el vuelo** to soar

remorder *vt* to distress, disturb

remordimiento *nm* remorse

remoto, -a *adj* remote

remover *vt* to stir; (*tierra*) to turn over; (*objetos*) to move round

remozar *vt* (*Arq*) to refurbish; (*fig*) to brighten *o* polish up

remuneración *nf* remuneration

remunerar *vt* to remunerate; (*premiar*) to reward

renacer *vi* to be reborn; (*fig*) to revive

renacimiento *nm* rebirth; **el R~** the Renaissance

renacuajo *nm* (*Zool*) tadpole

renal *adj* renal, kidney *cpd*

rencilla *nf* quarrel; **rencillas** *nfpl* bickering *sg*

rencor *nm* (*resentimiento*) ill feeling, resentment; **guardar ~ a** to bear a grudge against

rencoroso, -a *adj* spiteful

rendición *nf* surrender

rendido, -a *adj* (*sumiso*) submissive; (*agotado*) worn-out, exhausted; (*enamorado*) devoted

rendija *nf* (*hendidura*) crack; (*abertura*) aperture; (*fig*) rift, split; (*Jur*) loophole

rendimiento *nm* (*producción*) output; (*Com*) yield, profit(s) (*pl*); (*Tec, Com*) efficiency; **~ de capital** (*Com*) return on capital

rendir *vt* (*vencer*) to defeat; (*producir*) to produce; (*dar beneficio*) to yield; (*agotar*) to exhaust ▷ *vi* to pay; (*Com*) to yield, produce; **rendirse** *vr* (*someterse*) to surrender; (*ceder*) to yield; (*cansarse*) to wear o.s. out; **~ homenaje** *o* **culto a** to pay homage to; **el negocio no rinde** the business doesn't pay

renegado, -a *adj*, *nm/f* renegade

renegar *vt* (*negar*) to deny vigorously ▷ *vi* (*blasfemar*) to blaspheme; **~ de** (*renunciar*) to renounce; (*quejarse*) to complain about

RENFE *nf abr* (*Esp*) = **Red Nacional de Ferrocarriles Españoles**

renglón *nm* (*línea*) line; (*Com*) item, article; **a ~ seguido** immediately after

renombrado, -a *adj* renowned

renombre *nm* renown

renovable *adj* renewable

renovación *nf* (*de contrato*) renewal; (*Arq*) renovation

renovar *vt* to renew; (*Arq*) to renovate; (*sala*) to redecorate

renta *nf* (*ingresos*) income; (*beneficio*) profit; (*alquiler*) rent; **política de ~s** incomes policy; **vivir de sus ~s** to live on one's private income; **~ gravable** *o* **imponible** taxable income; **~ nacional (bruta)** (gross) national income; **~ no salarial** unearned income; **~ sobre el terreno** (*Com*) ground rent; **~ vitalicia** annuity

rentabilizar *vt* to make profitable

rentable *adj* profitable; **no ~** unprofitable

rentar *vt* to produce, yield; (*LAm*) to rent

renuencia *nf* reluctance

renuncia *nf* resignation

renunciar *vt* to renounce, give up ▷ *vi* to resign; **~ a hacer algo** to give up doing sth

reñido, -a *adj* (*batalla*) bitter, hard-fought; **estar ~ con algn** to be on bad terms with sb; **está ~ con su familia** he has fallen out with his family

reñir *vt* (*regañar*) to scold ▷ *vi* (*estar peleado*) to quarrel, fall out; (*combatir*) to fight

reo *nm/f* culprit, offender; (*Jur*) accused

reojo; de ~ *adv* out of the corner of one's eye

reparación *nf* (*acto*) mending, repairing; (*Tec*) repair; (*fig*) amends, reparation; **"reparaciones en el acto"** "repairs while you wait"

reparar *vt* to repair; (*fig*) to make amends for; (*suerte*) to retrieve; (*observar*) to observe ▷ *vi*: **~ en** (*darse cuenta de*) to notice; (*poner atención en*) to pay attention to; **sin ~ en (los) gastos** regardless of the cost

reparo *nm* (*advertencia*) observation; (*duda*) doubt; (*dificultad*) difficulty; (*escrúpulo*) scruple, qualm; **no tuvo ~ en hacerlo** he did not hesitate to do it; **poner ~s (a)** to raise objections (to); (*criticar*) to criticize

repartición *nf* distribution; (*división*) division

repartidor, a *nm/f* distributor; **~ de leche** milkman

repartir *vt* to distribute, share out; (*Com, Correos*) to deliver; (*Mil*) to partition; (*libros*) to give out; (*comida*) to serve out; (*Naipes*) to deal

reparto *nm* distribution; (*Com, Correos*) delivery; (*Teat, Cine*) cast; (*CAm, Méx: urbanización*) housing estate (*Brit*), real estate development (*US*); **"~ a domicilio"** "home delivery service"

repasar *vt* (*Escol*) to revise; (*Mecánica*) to check, overhaul; (*Costura*) to mend

repaso *nm* revision; (*Mecánica*) overhaul, checkup; (*Costura*) mending; **curso de ~** refresher course

repatriar *vt* to repatriate; **repatriarse** *vr* to return home

repelente *adj* repellent, repulsive

repeler *vt* to repel; (*idea, oferta*) to reject

repente *nm* sudden movement; (*fig*) impulse; **de ~** suddenly; **~ de ira** fit of anger

repentino, -a *adj* sudden; (*imprevisto*) unexpected

repercusión *nf* repercussion; **de amplia** *o* **ancha ~** far-reaching

repercutir *vi* (*objeto*) to rebound; (*sonido*) to echo; **~ en** (*fig*) to have repercussions *o* effects on

repertorio *nm* list; (*Teat*) repertoire

repesca *nf* (*Escol fam*) resit

repetición *nf* repetition

repetir *vt* to repeat; (*plato*) to have a second helping of; (*Teat*) to give as an encore, sing *etc* again ▷ *vi* to repeat; (*sabor*) to come back; **repetirse** *vr* (*persona*) to repeat o.s.; (*suceso*) to recur

repicar *vi* (*campanas*) to ring (out)

repipi *adj* la-di-da ▷ *nf*: **es una ~** she's a little madam

repique *nm* pealing, ringing

repiqueteo *nm* pealing; (*de tambor*) drumming

repisa *nf* ledge, shelf; **~ de chimenea** mantelpiece; **~ de ventana** windowsill

replantear *vt* (*cuestión pública*) to readdress; (*problema personal*) to reconsider; (*en reunión*) to raise again; **replantearse** *vr*: **~se algo** to reconsider sth

replegarse *vr* to fall back, retreat

repleto, -a *adj* replete, full up; **~ de** filled *o* crammed with

réplica *nf* answer; (*Arte*) replica; **derecho de ~** right of *o* to reply

replicar *vi* to answer; (*objetar*) to argue, answer back

repliegue *nm* (*Mil*) withdrawal

repoblación *nf* repopulation; (*de río*) restocking; **~ forestal** reforestation

repoblar *vt* (*con personas*) to repopulate; (*con peces*) to restock; (*con árboles*) to reforest

repollo *nm* cabbage

reponer *vt* to replace, put back; (*máquina*) to re-set; (*Teat*) to revive; **reponerse** *vr* to recover; **~ que** to reply that

reportaje *nm* report, article; **~ gráfico** illustrated report

reportero, -a *nm/f* reporter; **~ gráfico/a** news photographer

reposacabezas *nm inv* headrest

reposado, -a *adj* (*descansado*) restful; (*tranquilo*) calm

reposar *vi* (*persona*) to rest, repose; (*restos mortales*) to lie, rest

reposición *nf* replacement; (*Cine*) second showing; (*Teat*) revival

reposo *nm* rest

repostar *vt* to replenish; (*Auto*) to fill up (with petrol *o* gasoline)

repostería *nf* (*arte*) confectionery, pastry-making; (*tienda*) confectioner's (shop)

repostero, -a *nm/f* confectioner

reprender *vt* to reprimand; (*niño*) to scold

represa *nf* dam; (*lago artificial*) lake, pool

represalia *nf* reprisal; **tomar ~s** to take reprisals, retaliate

representación *nf* representation; (*Teat*) performance; **en ~ de** representing; **por ~** by proxy; **~ visual** (*Inform*) display

representante *nm/f* (*Pol, Com*) representative;

(*Teat*) performer

representar *vt* (*país, organización*) to represent; (*significar*) to mean; (*aparentar*) to look; (*Teat: obra*) to perform; (*papel*) to play; **representarse** *vr* to imagine; **la representaba su abogado** her lawyer was representing her; **tal acto ~ía la guerra** such an act would mean war; **tiene cuarenta años pero no los representa** he's forty but he doesn't look it; **los niños van a ~ una obra de teatro** the children are going to put on a play

representativo, -a *adj* representative

represión *nf* repression

represivo, -a *adj* repressive

reprimenda *nf* reprimand, rebuke

reprimir *vt* to repress; **reprimirse** *vr*: **~se de hacer algo** to stop o.s. from doing sth

reprobar *vt* to censure, reprove

réprobo, -a *nm/f* reprobate

reprochar *vt* to reproach; (*censurar*) to condemn, censure

reproche *nm* reproach

reproducción *nf* reproduction

reproducir *vt* to reproduce; **reproducirse** *vr* to breed; (*situación*) to recur

reproductor, a *adj* reproductive ▷ *nm*: **~ de discos compactos** CD player

reptil *nm* reptile

república *nf* republic; **R~ Dominicana** Dominican Republic

republicano, -a *adj, nm/f* republican

repudiar *vt* to repudiate; (*fe*) to renounce

repudio *nm* repudiation

repuesto *pp de* **reponer** ▷ *nm* (*pieza de recambio*) spare (part); (*abastecimiento*) supply; **rueda de ~** spare wheel; **y llevamos otro de ~** and we have another as a spare *o* in reserve

repugnancia *nf* repugnance

repugnante *adj* repugnant, repulsive

repugnar *vt* to disgust ▷ *vi* to be disgusting

repujar *vt* to emboss

repulsa *nf* rebuff

repulsión *nf* repulsion, aversion

repulsivo, -a *adj* repulsive

reputación *nf* reputation

reputar *vt* to consider, deem

requemado, -a *adj* (*quemado*) scorched; (*bronceado*) tanned

requerimiento *nm* request; (*demanda*) demand; (*Jur*) summons

requerir *vt* (*pedir*) to ask, request; (*exigir*) to require; (*ordenar*) to call for; (*llamar*) to send for, summon

requesón *nm* cottage cheese

réquiem *nm* requiem

requisa *nf* (*inspección*) survey, inspection; (*Mil*) requisition

requisar *vt* (*Mil*) to requisition; (*confiscar*) to seize, confiscate

requisito *nm* requirement, requisite; **~ previo** prerequisite; **tener los ~s para un cargo** to have the essential qualifications for a post

res *nf* beast, animal

resabio *nm* (*maña*) vice, bad habit; (*dejo*) (unpleasant) aftertaste

resaca *nf* (*en el mar*) undertow, undercurrent; (*fig*) backlash; (*fam*) hangover

resaltar *vi* to project, stick out; (*fig*) to stand out

resarcir *vt* to compensate; (*pagar*) to repay; **resarcirse** *vr* to make up for; **~ a algn de una pérdida** to compensate sb for a loss; **~ a algn de una cantidad** to repay sb a sum

resbaladizo, -a *adj* slippery

resbalar *vi*, **resbalarse** *vr* to slip, slide; (*fig*) to slip (up); **le resbalaban las lágrimas por las mejillas** tears were trickling down his cheeks

resbalón *nm* (*acción*) slip; (*deslizamiento*) slide; (*fig*) slip

rescatar *vt* (*salvar*) to save, rescue; (*objeto*) to get back, recover; (*cautivos*) to ransom

rescate *nm* (*de persona*) rescue; (*de objeto*) recovery; **pagar un ~** to pay a ransom

rescindir *vt* (*contrato*) to annul, rescind

rescisión *nf* cancellation

rescoldo *nm* embers *pl*

resecar *vt* to dry off, dry thoroughly; (*Med*) to cut out, remove; **resecarse** *vr* to dry up

reseco, -a *adj* very dry; (*fig*) skinny

resentido, -a *adj* resentful ▷ *nm/f*: **es un ~** he's bitter

resentimiento *nm* resentment, bitterness

resentirse *vr* (*debilitarse: persona*) to suffer; **~ con** to resent; **~ de** (*sufrir las consecuencias de*) to feel the effects of

reseña *nf* (*cuenta*) account; (*informe*) report; (*Lit*) review

reseñar *vt* to describe; (*Lit*) to review

reserva *nf* reserve; (*de hotel, duda*) reservation; (*secreto*) confidence; **a ~ de que ...** unless ...; **con toda ~** in strictest confidence; **de ~** spare; **tener algo de ~** to have sth in reserve; **~ de caja** *o* **en efectivo** (*Com*) cash reserves; **~ de indios** Indian reservation; **~s del Estado** (*Com*) government stock; **~s en oro** (*Com*) gold reserves; **~ natural** nature reserve

reservado, -a *adj* reserved; (*retraído*) cold, distant ▷ *nm* private room; (*Ferro*) reserved compartment

reservar *vt* (*guardar*) to keep; (*Ferro, Teat etc*) to reserve, book; **reservarse** *vr* to save o.s.; (*callar*) to keep to o.s.; **~ con exceso** to overbook

resfriado *nm* cold

resfriarse *vr* to cool off; (*Med*) to catch (a) cold

resguardar *vt* to protect, shield; **resguardarse** *vr*: **~se de** to guard against

resguardo *nm* defence, shield; (*vale*) voucher; (*recibo*) receipt, slip

residencia *nf* residence; (*Univ*) hall of residence; **~ para ancianos** *o* **jubilados** rest home

residencial *adj* residential ▷ *nf* (*urbanización*) housing estate (Brit), real estate development (US)

residente *adj, nm/f* resident

residir *vi* to reside, live; **~ en** (*estar en*) to reside *o* lie in; (*consistir en*) to consist of

residuo *nm* residue; **~s atmosféricos** *o* **radiactivos** fallout *sg*

resignación *nf* resignation

resina *nf* resin

resistencia *nf* (*dureza*) endurance, strength; (*oposición, Elec*) resistance; **la R~** (*Mil*) the Resistance

resistente *adj* strong, hardy; (*Tec*) resistant; **~ al calor** heat-resistant

resistir *vt* (*soportar*) to bear; (*oponerse a*) to resist, oppose; (*aguantar*) to put up with; **no puedo ~ este frío** I can't bear *o* stand this cold ▷ *vi* to resist; (*aguantar*) to last, endure; **resistirse** *vr*: **~se a** to refuse to, resist; **me resisto a creerlo** I refuse to believe it; **se le resiste la química** chemistry escapes her

resollar *vi* to breathe noisily, wheeze

resolución *nf* resolution; (*decisión*) decision; (*moción*) motion; **tomar una ~** to take a decision; **~ judicial** legal ruling

resoluto, -a *adj* resolute

resolver *vt* (*resolver*) to resolve; (*solucionar*) to solve, resolve; (*decidir*) to decide, settle; **resolverse** *vr* to make up one's mind

resonancia *nf* (*del sonido*) resonance; (*repercusión*) repercussion; (*fig*) wide effect, impact

resonante *adj* resonant, resounding; (*fig*) tremendous

resonar *vi* to ring, echo

resoplar *vi* to snort; (*por cansancio*) to puff

resoplido *nm* heavy breathing

resorte *nm* spring; (*fig*) lever

respaldar *vt* to back (up), support; (*Inform*) to back up; **respaldarse** *vr* to lean back; **~se con** *o* **en** (*fig*) to take one's stand on

respaldo *nm* (*de sillón*) back; (*fig*) support, backing

respectivo, -a *adj* respective; **en lo ~ a** with regard to

respecto *nm*: **al ~** on this matter; **con ~ a, ~ de** with regard to, in relation to

respetable *adj* respectable

respetar *vt* to respect

respeto *nm* respect; (*acatamiento*) deference; **respetos** *nmpl* respects; **por ~ a** out of consideration for; **presentar sus ~s a** to pay one's respects to

respetuoso, -a *adj* respectful

respingo *nm* start, jump

respiración *nf* breathing; (*Med*) respiration; (*ventilación*) ventilation

respirar *vt, vi* to breathe; **no dejar ~ a algn** to keep on at sb; **estuvo escuchándolo sin ~** he listened to him in complete silence

respiratorio, -a *adj* respiratory

respiro *nm* breathing; (*fig: descanso*) respite, rest; (*Com*) period of grace

resplandecer *vi* to shine

resplandeciente *adj* shining

resplandor *nm* brilliance, brightness; (*del fuego*) blaze

responder *vt* to answer ▷ *vi* (*contestar*) to answer; (*reaccionar*) to respond; (*pey*) to answer back; (*corresponder*) to correspond; **~ a** (*situación etc*) to respond to; **no me respondió** he didn't answer (me), he didn't reply; **respondió que habían salido con unos amigos** he replied that they had gone out with some friends; **~ a una pregunta** to answer a question; **no han respondido a mi carta** they haven't replied to my letter; **no responde al tratamiento** he's not responding to the treatment; **~ a una descripción** to fit a description; **~ al nombre de ...** to go by the name of ...

respondón, -ona *adj* cheeky

responsabilidad *nf* responsibility; **bajo mi ~** on my authority; **~ ilimitada** (*Com*) unlimited liability

responsabilizarse *vr* to make o.s. responsible, take charge

responsable *adj* responsible; **la persona ~** the person in charge; **hacerse ~ de algo** to assume responsibility for sth

respuesta *nf* answer, reply; (*reacción*) response

resquebrajar *vt*, **resquebrajarse** *vr* to crack, split

resquemor *nm* resentment

resquicio *nm* (*hendidura*) crack

resta *nf* (*Mat*) subtraction

restablecer *vt* to re-establish, restore; **restablecerse** *vr* to recover

restallar *vi* to crack

restante *adj* remaining; **lo ~** the remainder; **los ~s** the rest, those left (over)

restar *vt* (*Mat*) to subtract; (*descontar*) to deduct; (*fig*) to take away ▷ *vi* to remain, be left

restauración *nf* restoration

restaurante *nm* restaurant

restaurar *vt* to restore

restitución *nf* return, restitution

restituir *vt* (*devolver*) to return, give back; (*rehabilitar*) to restore

resto *nm* (*residuo*) rest, remainder; (*apuesta*) stake; **restos** *nmpl* remains; (*Culin*) leftovers, scraps; **~s mortales** mortal remains

restregar *vt* to scrub, rub

restricción *nf* restriction; **sin ~ de** without restrictions on *o* as to; **hablar sin restricciones** to talk freely

restrictivo, -a *adj* restrictive

restringir *vt* to restrict, limit

resucitar *vt, vi* to resuscitate, revive

resuello *nm* (*aliento*) breath

resuelto, -a *pp de* **resolver** ▷ *adj* resolute, determined; **estar ~ a algo** to be set on sth; **estar ~ a hacer algo** to be determined to do sth

resultado *nm* result; (*conclusión*) outcome; **resultados** *nmpl* (*Inform*) output *sg*; **dar ~** to produce results

resultante *adj* resulting, resultant

resultar *vi* (*ser*) to be; (*llegar a ser*) to turn out to be; (*salir bien*) to turn out well; (*seguir*) to ensue; (*funcionar*) to work; **resultó muy divertido** it turned out to be great fun; **me resulta difícil**

hacerlo it's difficult for me to do it; **me resultó violento decírselo** I found it embarrassing to tell him; **el conductor resultó muerto** the driver was killed; **resulta que ...** (*en consecuencia*) it follows that ...; (*parece que*) it seems that ...; **al final resultó que él tenía razón** in the end it turned out that he was right; **no resultó** it didn't work *o* come off; **~ a** (*Com*) to amount to; **~ de** to stem from; **~ en** to result in, produce

resumen *nm* summary, résumé; **en ~** in short

resumir *vt* to sum up; (*condensar*) to summarize; (*cortar*) to abridge, cut down; **resumirse** *vr*: **la situación se resume en pocas palabras** the situation can be summed up in a few words

resurgir *vi* (*reaparecer*) to reappear

resurrección *nf* resurrection

retablo *nm* altarpiece

retaguardia *nf* rearguard

retahíla *nf* series, string; (*de injurias*) volley, stream

retal *nm* remnant

retar *vt* (*gen*) to challenge; (*desafiar*) to defy, dare

retardar *vt* (*demorar*) to delay; (*hacer más lento*) to slow down; (*retener*) to hold back

retardo *nm* delay

retazo *nm* snippet (*Brit*), fragment

retener *vt* (*guardar*) to retain, keep; (*intereses*) to withhold

reticente *adj* reluctant; **se mostró ~ a aceptar** he was reluctant to accept

retina *nf* retina

retintín *nm* jangle, jingle; **decir algo con ~** to say sth sarcastically

retirada *nf* (*Mil*) retreat; (*de dinero*) withdrawal; (*de embajador*) recall; **batirse en ~** to retreat

retirado, -a *adj* (*lugar*) remote; (*vida*) quiet; (*jubilado*) retired

retirar *vt* (*quitar*) to take away; (*apartar*) to withdraw; (*la mano*) to draw back; (*dinero*) to take out; (*acusación, palabra*) to withdraw; (*jubilar*) to retire, pension off; **retirarse** *vr* (*apartarse*) to move back, move away; (*Mil*) to retreat, withdraw; (*jubilarse*) to retire; (*acostarse*) to retire, go to bed; **la camarera retiró las copas** the waitress took the glasses away; **le han retirado el permiso de conducir** he's had his driving licence taken away; **fui a ~ dinero de la cuenta** I went to withdraw some money from my account; **mi padre se retira el año que viene** my father will be retiring next year

retiro *nm* retreat; (*jubilación, tb Deporte*) retirement; (*pago*) pension; (*lugar*) quiet place

reto *nm* dare, challenge

retocar *vt* to touch up, retouch

retoño *nm* sprout, shoot; (*fig*) offspring, child

retoque *nm* retouching

retorcer *vt* to turn, twist; (*argumento*) to turn, twist; (*manos, lavado*) to wring; **retorcerse** *vr* to become twisted; (*persona*) to writhe; **~se de dolor** to writhe in *o* squirm with pain

retorcido, -a *adj* (*tb fig*) twisted

retorcimiento *nm* twist, twisting; (*fig*)

deviousness

retórico, -a *adj* rhetorical; (*pey*) affected, windy ▷ *nf* rhetoric; (*pey*) affectedness

retornable *adj* returnable

retornar *vt* to return, give back ▷ *vi* to return, go/come back

retorno *nm* return; **~ del carro** (*Inform, Tip*) carriage return; **~ del carro automático** (*Inform*) wordwrap, word wraparound

retortijón *nm* twist, twisting; **~ de tripas** stomach cramp

retozar *vi* (*juguetear*) to frolic, romp; (*saltar*) to gambol

retozón, -ona *adj* playful

retracción *nf* retraction

retractarse *vr* to retract; **me retracto** I take that back

retraerse *vr* to retreat, withdraw

retraído, -a *adj* shy, retiring

retraimiento *nm* (*aislamiento*) retirement; (*timidez*) shyness

retransmisión *nf* repeat (broadcast)

retransmitir *vt* (*mensaje*) to relay; (*TV etc*) to repeat, retransmit; (: *en vivo*) to broadcast live

retrasado, -a *adj* late; (*Med*) mentally retarded; (*país etc*) backward, underdeveloped; **estar ~** (*reloj*) to be slow; (*persona, industria*) to be *o* lag behind

retrasar *vt* (*reunión, viaje*) to postpone, put off; (*salida*) to delay; (*enfermedad, crecimiento*) to slow down; (*reloj*) to put back ▷ *vi*: **tu reloj retrasa** your watch is slow; **retrasarse** *vr* (*persona, avión*) to be late; (*producción*) to fall (away); (*quedarse atrás*) to lag behind; **~on la boda al día quince** they postponed the wedding until the fifteenth; **a las tres hay que ~ los relojes una hora** at three o'clock the clocks have to be put back one hour; **el tren de las nueve se retrasó** the nine o'clock train was late

retraso *nm* (*demora*) delay; (*lentitud*) slowness; (*tardanza*) lateness; (*atraso*) backwardness; **retrasos** *nmpl* (*Com*) arrears; (*deudas*) deficit *sg*, debts; **llegar con ~** to arrive late; **llegar con 25 minutos de ~** to be 25 minutes late; **llevo un ~ de 6 semanas** I'm 6 weeks behind (with my work *etc*); **~ mental** mental deficiency

retratar *vt* (*Arte*) to paint the portrait of; (*fotografiar*) to photograph; (*fig*) to depict, describe; **retratarse** *vr* (*en pintura*) to have one's portrait painted; (*en foto*) to have one's photograph taken

retrato *nm* portrait; (*Foto*) photograph; (*descripción*) portrayal, depiction; (*fig*) likeness; **ser el vivo ~** to be the spitting image of

retrato-robot (*pl* **retratos-robot**) *nm* Identikit® picture

retreta *nf* retreat

retrete *nm* toilet

retribución *nf* (*recompensa*) reward; (*pago*) pay, payment

retribuir *vt* (*recompensar*) to reward; (*pagar*) to pay

retroactivo, -a *adj* retroactive, retrospective;

dar efecto ~ a un pago to backdate a payment

retroceder vi (echarse atrás) to move back(wards); (fig) to back down; **no ~ to** stand firm; **la policía hizo ~ a la multitud** the police forced the crowd back

retroceso nm backward movement; (Med) relapse; (Com) recession, depression; (fig) backing down

retrógrado, -a adj retrograde, retrogressive; (Pol) reactionary

retropropulsión nf jet propulsion

retrospectivo, -a adj retrospective; **mirada retrospectiva** backward glance

retrovisor nm rear-view mirror

retumbar vi to echo, resound; (continuamente) to reverberate

reuma nm rheumatism

reumatismo nm rheumatism

reunificar vt to reunify

reunión nf (asamblea) meeting; (fiesta) party; **~ en la cumbre** summit meeting; **~ de ventas** (Com) sales meeting

reunir vt (juntar) to reunite, join (together); (recoger) to gather (together); (personas) to bring o get together; (cualidades) to combine; **reunirse** vr (personas: en asamblea) to meet, gather; **reunió a sus amigos para discutirlo** he got his friends together to talk it over

revalidar vt (ratificar) to confirm, ratify

revalorar vt to revalue, reassess

revalor(iz)ación nf revaluation; (Econ) reassessment

revancha nf revenge; (Deporte) return match; (Boxeo) return fight

revelación nf revelation

revelado nm developing

revelar vt to reveal; (secreto) to disclose; (mostrar) to show; (Foto) to develop

reventa nf resale; (especulación) speculation; (de entradas) touting

reventar vt to burst, explode; (molestar) to annoy, rile ▷ vi: **reventarse** vr (estallar) to burst, explode; **me revienta tener que ponérmelo** I hate having to wear it; **~ de** (fig) to be bursting with; **~ por** to be bursting to

reventón nm (Auto) blow-out (Brit), flat (US)

reverberación nf reverberation

reverberar vi (luz) to play, be reflected; (superficie) to shimmer; (nieve) to glare; (sonido) to reverberate

reverencia nf reverence; (inclinación) bow

reverenciar vt to revere

reverendo, -a adj reverend; (fam) big, awful; **un ~ imbécil** an awful idiot

reverente adj reverent

reversible adj reversible

reverso nm (parte posterior) back, other side; (de moneda) reverse

revertir vi to revert; **~ en beneficio de** to be to the advantage of; **~ en perjuicio de** to be to the detriment of

revés nm (dorso) back; (parte equivocada) wrong side; (golpe: tb Tenis) backhand; (desgracia) setback, reverse; **los reveses de la fortuna** the blows of fate; **al ~** the other way round; (de arriba abajo) upside down; (ropa: de dentro afuera) inside out; (de delante atrás) back to front; **el dibujo está al ~** the picture's upside down; **llevaba el jersey al ~** I had my jumper on back to front; **volver al o del ~** to turn round; (ropa) to turn inside out; **y al ~** and vice versa

revestir vt (poner) to put on; (cubrir) to cover, coat; (cualidad) to have, possess; **revestirse** vr (Rel) to put on one's vestments; (ponerse) to put on; **~se con o de** to arm o.s. with; **el acto revestía gran solemnidad** the ceremony had great dignity

revisar vt (examinar) to check; (texto etc) to revise; (Jur) to review

revisión nf revision; **~ aduanera** customs inspection; **~ de cuentas** audit

revisor, a nm/f inspector; (Ferro) ticket collector; **~ de cuentas** auditor

revista nf magazine, review; (sección) section, page; (Teat) revue; (inspección) inspection; **~ literaria** literary review; **~ de libros** book reviews (page); **pasar ~ a** to review, inspect

revivir vt (recordar) to revive memories of ▷ vi to revive

revocación nf repeal

revocar vt (decisión) to revoke; (Arq) to plaster

revolcar vt to knock down, send flying; **revolcarse** vr to roll about

revolotear vi to flutter

revoltijo nm mess, jumble

revoltoso, -a adj (travieso) naughty, unruly

revolución nf revolution

revolucionar vt to revolutionize

revolucionario, -a adj, nm/f revolutionary

revolver vt (desordenar) to disturb, mess up; (agitar) to shake; (líquido) to stir; (mover) to move about; (Pol) to stir up ▷ vi: **~ en** to go through, rummage (about) in; **revolverse** vr (en cama) to toss and turn; (Meteorología) to break, turn stormy; **~se contra** to turn on o against; **han revuelto toda la casa** they've turned the whole house upside down

revólver nm revolver

revuelo nm fluttering; (fig) commotion; **armar o levantar un gran ~** to cause a great stir

revuelta nf (motín) revolt; (agitación) commotion; ver tb **revuelto**

revuelto, -a pp de **revolver** ▷ adj (mezclado) mixed-up, in disorder; (mar) rough; (tiempo) unsettled; **todo estaba ~** everything was in disorder o was topsy-turvy; ver tb **revuelta**

revulsivo nm: **servir de ~** to have a salutary effect

rey nm king; **los R~es** the King and Queen

reyerta nf quarrel, brawl

rezagado, -a adj: **quedar ~** to be left behind ▷ nm/f straggler

rezagar vt (dejar atrás) to leave behind; (retrasar) to delay, postpone; **rezagarse** vr (atrasarse) to fall behind

rezar vi to pray; ~ **con** (fam) to concern, have to do with

rezo nm prayer

rezongar vi to grumble; (murmurar) to mutter; (refunfuñar) to growl

rezumar vt to ooze ▷ vi to leak; **rezumarse** vr to leak out

ría nf estuary

riachuelo nm stream

riada nf flood

ribera nf (de río) bank; (área) riverside

ribete nm (de vestido) border; (fig) addition

ribetear vt to edge, border

ricino nm: **aceite de** ~ castor oil

rico, -a adj (adinerado) rich, wealthy; (lujoso) luxurious; (comida) delicious; (niño) lovely, cute ▷ nm/f rich person; **nuevo** ~ nouveau riche

rictus nm (mueca) sneer, grin; ~ **de amargura** bitter smile

ridiculez nf absurdity

ridiculizar vt to ridicule

ridículo, -a adj ridiculous; **hacer el** ~ to make a fool of o.s.; **poner a algn en** ~ to make a fool of sb; **ponerse en** ~ to make a fool o laughing-stock of o.s.

riego nm (aspersión) watering; (irrigación) irrigation

riel nm rail

rienda nf rein; (fig) restraint, moderating influence; **dar** ~ **suelta a** to give free rein to; **llevar las** ~**s** to be in charge

riesgo nm risk; **seguro** o **contra todo** ~ comprehensive insurance; ~ **para la salud** health hazard; **correr el** ~ **de** to run the risk of

rifa nf raffle

rifar vt to raffle

rifle nm rifle

rigidez nf (de objeto, pierna) rigidity, stiffness; (de comportamiento) strictness

rígido, -a adj rigid, stiff; (moralmente) strict, inflexible; (cara) wooden, expressionless

rigor nm strictness, rigour; (dureza) toughness; (inclemencia) harshness; (meticulosidad) accuracy; **el** ~ **del verano** the hottest part of the summer; **con todo** ~ **científico** with scientific precision; **de** ~ de rigueur, essential; **después de los saludos de** ~ after the inevitable greetings

riguroso, -a adj rigorous; (Meteorología) harsh; (severo) severe

rimar vi to rhyme

rimbombante adj (fig) pompous

rímel, rímmel nm mascara

rincón nm corner (inside)

ring nm (Boxeo) ring

rinoceronte nm rhinoceros

riña nf (disputa) argument; (pelea) brawl

riñón nm kidney; **me costó un** ~ (fam) it cost me an arm and a leg; **tener riñones** to have guts

río nm river; (fig) torrent, stream; ~ **abajo/arriba** downstream/upstream; **cuando el** ~ **suena, agua lleva** there's no smoke without fire

rioplatense adj of o from the River Plate region

▷ nm/f native o inhabitant of the River Plate region

riqueza nf wealth, riches pl; (cualidad) richness

risa nf laughter; (una risa) laugh; **¡qué** ~! what a laugh!; **caerse** o **morirse de** ~ to split one's sides laughing, die laughing; **tomar algo a** ~ to laugh sth off

risco nm crag, cliff

risible adj ludicrous, laughable

risotada nf guffaw, loud laugh

ristra nf string

risueño, -a adj (sonriente) smiling; (contento) cheerful

ritmo nm rhythm; **a** ~ **lento** slowly; **trabajar a** ~ **lento** to go slow

rito nm rite

ritual adj, nm ritual

rival adj, nm/f rival

rivalidad nf rivalry, competition

rivalizar vi: ~ **con** to rival, compete with

rizado, -a adj (pelo) curly; (superficie) ridged; (terreno) undulating; (mar) choppy ▷ nm curls pl

rizar vt to curl; **rizarse** vr (el pelo) to curl; (agua) to ripple; (el mar) to become choppy

rizo nm (en pelo) curl; (en agua) ripple

RNE nf abr = **Radio Nacional de España**

robar vt to rob; (objeto) to steal; (casa etc) to break into; (Naipes) to draw; (atención) to steal, capture; (paciencia) to exhaust

roble nm oak

robledal, robledo nm oakwood

robo nm robbery, theft; (objeto robado) stolen article o goods pl; **¡esto es un** ~! this is daylight robbery!

robot (pl -**s**) adj, nm robot ▷ nm (tb: **robot de cocina**) food processor

robustecer vt to strengthen

robusto, -a adj robust, strong

roca nf rock; **la R**~ the Rock (of Gibraltar)

roce nm rub, rubbing; (caricia) brush; (Tec) friction; (en la piel) graze; **tener** ~ **con** to have a brush with

rociar vt to sprinkle, spray

rocín nm nag, hack

rocío nm dew

rock nm (Mus) rock

rockero, -a adj rock cpd ▷ nm/f rocker

rocoso, -a adj rocky

rodado, -a adj (con ruedas) wheeled

rodaja nf (raja) slice

rodaje nm (Cine) shooting, filming; (Auto): **en** ~ running in

rodamiento nm (Auto) tread

rodar vt (vehículo) to wheel (along); (viajar por) to travel (over) ▷ vi to roll; (coche) to go, run; (Cine) to shoot, film; (persona) to move about (from place to place), drift; **echarlo todo a** ~ (fig) to mess it all up

rodear vt to surround ▷ vi to go round; **rodearse** vr: ~**se de amigos** to surround o.s. with friends

rodeo nm (ruta indirecta) long way round, roundabout way; (desvío) detour; (evasión) evasion; (*LAm*) rodeo; **dejarse de ~s** to talk straight; **hablar sin ~s** to come to the point, speak plainly

rodilla *nf* knee; **de ~s** kneeling

rodillo *nm* roller; (*Culin*) rolling-pin; (*en máquina de escribir, impresora*) platen

rododendro *nm* rhododendron

roedor, a *adj* gnawing ▷ *nm* rodent

roer *vt* (*masticar*) to gnaw; (*corroer, fig*) to corrode

rogar *vt* (*pedir*) to beg, ask for ▷ *vi* (*suplicar*) to beg, plead; **~ que** (+*subjun*) to ask to ...; **ruegue a este señor que nos deje en paz** please ask this gentleman to leave us alone; **"se ruega no fumar"** "please do not smoke"; **no se hace de ~** he doesn't have to be asked twice

rojizo, -a *adj* reddish

rojo, -a *adj* red ▷ *nm* red (colour); (*Pol*) red; **ponerse ~** to turn red, blush; **al ~ vivo** red-hot

rol *nm* list, roll; (*esp LAm: papel*) role

rollizo, -a *adj* (*objeto*) cylindrical; (*persona*) plump

rollo *adj inv* (*fam*) boring, tedious ▷ *nm* roll; (*de cuerda*) coil; (*de madera*) log; (*fam*) bore; (*discurso*) boring speech; **¡qué ~!** what a carry-on!; **la conferencia fue un ~** the lecture was a big drag

Roma *nf* Rome; **por todas partes se va a ~** all roads lead to Rome

romance *nm* (*Ling*) Romance language; (*Lit*) ballad; **hablar en ~** to speak plainly

románico, -a *adj, nm* Romanesque

romano, -a *adj* Roman, of Rome ▷ *nm/f* Roman

romanticismo *nm* romanticism

romántico, -a *adj* romantic

rombo *nm* (*Geom*) rhombus; (*diseño*) diamond; (*Tip*) lozenge

romería *nf* (*Rel*) pilgrimage; (*excursión*) trip, outing

romero, -a *nm/f* pilgrim ▷ *nm* rosemary

romo, -a *adj* blunt; (*fig*) dull

rompecabezas *nm inv* riddle, puzzle; (*juego*) jigsaw (puzzle)

rompehielos *nm inv* icebreaker

rompeolas *nm inv* breakwater

romper *vt* (*cristal, objeto, pierna: estropear, partir*) to break; (*hacer pedazos*) to smash; (*papel, tela etc*) to tear, rip; (*relaciones*) to break off ▷ *vi* (*olas*) to break; (*sol, diente*) to break through; **romperse** *vr* (*pierna*) to break; (*cristal, objeto*) to break, smash; (*papel, tela*) to tear, rip; **rompí la foto** I tore up the photo; **rompió la carta a pedazos** he tore the letter up; **~ un contrato** to break a contract; **~ a** to start (suddenly) to; **~ a llorar** to burst into tears; **~ con algn** to fall out with sb; **ha roto con el novio** she has broken up with her boyfriend; **me rompí el brazo** I broke my arm; **se ha roto una taza** a cup has got broken; **se me han roto los pantalones** I've torn my trousers

rompimiento *nm* (*acto*) breaking; (*fig*) break; (*quiebra*) crack; **~ de relaciones** breaking off of relations

ron *nm* rum

roncar *vi* (*al dormir*) to snore; (*animal*) to roar

roncha *nf* (*cardenal*) bruise; (*hinchazón*) swelling

ronco, -a *adj* (*afónico*) hoarse; (*áspero*) raucous

ronda *nf* (*de bebidas etc*) round; (*patrulla*) patrol; (*de naipes*) hand, game; **ir de ~** to do one's round

rondar *vt* to patrol; (*a una persona*) to hang round; (*molestar*) to harass; (*a una chica*) to court ▷ *vi* to patrol; (*fig*) to prowl round; (*Mus*) to go serenading

ronquido *nm* snore, snoring

ronronear *vi* to purr

ronroneo *nm* purr

roña *nf* (*en veterinaria*) mange; (*mugre*) dirt, grime; (*óxido*) rust

roñica *nm/f* (*fam*) skinflint

roñoso, -a *adj* (*mugriento*) filthy; (*tacaño*) mean

ropa *nf* clothes *pl*, clothing; **~ de cama** bed linen; **~ interior** underwear; **~ lavada** *o* **para lavar** washing; **~ planchada** ironing; **~ sucia** dirty clothes *pl*, washing; **~ usada** secondhand clothes

ropaje *nm* gown, robes *pl*

ropero *nm* linen cupboard; (*guardarropa*) wardrobe

rosa *adj inv* pink ▷ *nf* rose; (*Anat*) red birthmark; **estar como una ~** to feel as fresh as a daisy; **(color) de ~** pink; **la ~ de los vientos** the compass

rosado, -a *adj* pink ▷ *nm* rosé

rosal *nm* rosebush

rosario *nm* (*Rel*) rosary; (*fig: serie*) string; **rezar el ~** to say the rosary

rosca *nf* (*de tornillo*) thread; (*de humo*) coil, spiral; (*pan, postre*) ring-shaped roll/pastry; **hacer la ~ a algn** (*fam*) to suck up to sb; **pasarse de ~** (*fig*) to go too far

rosetón *nm* rosette; (*Arq*) rose window

rosquilla *nf* small ring-shaped cake; (*de humo*) ring

rostro *nm* (*cara*) face; (*fig*) cheek

rotación *nf* rotation; **~ de cultivos** crop rotation

rotativo, -a *adj* rotary ▷ *nm* newspaper

roto, -a *pp de* **romper** ▷ *adj* broken; (*en pedazos*) smashed; (*tela, papel*) torn; (*vida*) shattered ▷ *nm* (*en vestido*) hole, tear

rótula *nf* kneecap; (*Tec*) ball-and-socket joint

rotulador *nm* felt-tip pen

rotular *vt* (*carta, documento*) to head, entitle; (*objeto*) to label

rótulo *nm* (*título*) heading, title; (*etiqueta*) label; (*letrero*) sign

rotundo, -a *adj* round; (*enfático*) emphatic

rotura *nf* (*rompimiento*) breaking; (*Med*) fracture

roturar *vt* to plough

roulote *nf* caravan (*Brit*), trailer (*US*)

rozadura *nf* abrasion, graze

rozar *vt* (*frotar*) to rub; (*ensuciar*) to dirty; (*Med*) to graze; (*tocar ligeramente*) to shave, skim; (*fig*) to touch *o* border on; **rozarse** *vr* to rub (together); **~se con** (*fam*) to rub shoulders with

Rte. *abr* = **remite, remitente**

RTVE *nf abr* (*TV*) = **Radiotelevisión Española**

rubí *nm* ruby; (*de reloj*) jewel

rubio, -a *adj* fair-haired, blond(e) ▷ *nm/f* blond/ blonde; **tabaco ~** Virginia tobacco; **(cerveza)**

rubia lager
rubor nm (sonrojo) blush; (timidez) bashfulness
ruboroso, -a adj blushing
rúbrica nf (título) title, heading; (de la firma) flourish; **bajo la ~ de** under the heading of
rubricar vt (firmar) to sign with a flourish; (concluir) to sign and seal
rudeza nf (tosquedad) coarseness; (sencillez) simplicity
rudimentario, -a adj rudimentary, basic
rudo, -a adj (sin pulir) unpolished; (grosero) coarse; (violento) violent; (sencillo) simple
rueda nf (de vehículo) wheel; (círculo) ring, circle; (rodaja) slice, round; (en impresora etc) sprocket; **~ delantera/trasera/de repuesto** front/back/spare wheel; **~ de prensa** press conference; **~ impresora** (Inform) print wheel
ruedo nm (contorno) edge, border; (de vestido) hem; (círculo) circle; (Taur) arena, bullring; (esterilla) (round) mat
ruego nm request; **a ~ de** at the request of; **"~s y preguntas"** "question and answer session"
rufián nm scoundrel
rugby nm rugby
rugido nm roar
rugir vi (león) to roar; (toro) to bellow; (estómago) to rumble
rugoso, -a adj (arrugado) wrinkled; (áspero) rough; (desigual) ridged
ruido nm noise; (sonido) sound; (alboroto) racket, row; (escándalo) commotion, rumpus; **~ de fondo** background noise; **hacer o meter ~ to** cause a stir
ruidoso, -a adj noisy, loud; (fig) sensational
ruin adj contemptible, mean
ruina nf ruin; (colapso) collapse; (de persona) ruin, downfall; **estar hecho una ~** to be a wreck; **la empresa le llevó a la ~** the venture ruined him (financially)

ruindad nf (cualidad) lowness, meanness; (acto) low o mean act
ruinoso, -a adj ruinous; (destartalado) dilapidated, tumbledown; (Com) disastrous
ruiseñor nm nightingale
ruleta nf roulette
rulo nm (para el pelo) curler
rulot(e) nf caravan (Brit), trailer (US)
Rumanía nf Rumania
rumano, -a adj, nm/f Rumanian
rumba nf rumba
rumbo nm (ruta) route, direction; (ángulo de dirección) course, bearing; (fig) course of events; **con ~ a** in the direction of; **ir con ~ a** to be heading for; (Naut) to be bound for
rumboso, -a adj (generoso) generous
rumiante nm ruminant
rumiar vt to chew; (fig) to chew over ▷ vi to chew the cud
rumor nm (murmuración) murmur, buzz; (ruido sordo) low sound
runrún nm (de voces) murmur, sound of voices; (de una máquina) whirr; (fig) rumour
rupestre adj rock cpd; **pintura ~** cave painting
ruptura nf (de contrato) breach; (de relaciones) breaking-off; (disputa) split; **~ matrimonial** breakdown of a marriage
rural adj rural
Rusia nf Russia
ruso, -a adj, nm/f Russian ▷ nm (Ling) Russian
rústica nf: **libro en ~** paperback (book); ver tb **rústico**
rústico, -a adj rustic; (ordinario) coarse, uncouth ▷ nm/f yokel; ver tb **rústica**
ruta nf route
rutina nf routine; **por ~** as a matter of course; **~ diaria** daily routine
rutinario, -a adj routine

Ss

S, s *nf* (*letra*) S, s; **S de Salamanca** S for Sugar
S *abr* = **san**; (= *santo, a*) St.; (= *Sur*) S
s. *abr* (= *siglo*) c.; (= *siguiente*) foll.
S.ª *abr* (= *Sierra*) Mts
S.A. *abr* (= *Sociedad Anónima*) Ltd., Inc. (US); (= *Su Alteza*) H.H.
sábado *nm* Saturday; (*de los judíos*) Sabbath; **una semana a partir del ~** a week on Saturday; **un ~ sí y otro no, cada dos ~s** every other Saturday; **S~ Santo** Holy Saturday
sábana *nf* sheet; **se le pegan las ~s** he can't get up in the morning
sabandija *nf* (*bicho*) bug; (*fig*) louse
sabañón *nm* chilblain
sabelotodo *nm/f inv* know-all
saber *vt* (*tener conocimiento de*) to know; (*llegar a conocer*) to find out, learn; (*tener capacidad de*) to know how to ▷ *vi:* **hacer ~** to inform, let know ▷ *nm* knowledge, learning; **saberse** *vr:* **se sabe la lista de memoria** he knows the list off by heart; **no lo sé** I don't know; **¡y yo que sé!** how should I know?; **¿sabes conducir/nadar?** can you drive/swim?; **¿sabes francés?** do you o can you speak French?; **~ algo de memoria** to know sth by heart; **no se sabe** nobody knows; **lo dudo, pero nunca se sabe** I doubt it, but you never know; **que yo sepa** as far as I know; **a ~** namely; **vete** o **anda a ~** your guess is as good as mine, who knows!; **¿sabe?** (*fam*) you know (what I mean)?; **~ a** to taste of, taste like; **sabe a pescado** it tastes of fish; **se sabe que ...** it is known that ...
sabiduría *nf* (*conocimientos*) wisdom; (*instrucción*) learning; **~ popular** folklore
sabiendas; a ~ *adv* knowingly; **a ~ de que ...** knowing full well that ...
sabio, -a *adj* (*docto*) learned; (*prudente*) wise, sensible
sable *nm* sabre
sabor *nm* taste, flavour; (*fig*) flavour; **sin ~** flavourless
saborear *vt* to taste, savour; (*fig*) to relish
sabotaje *nm* sabotage
saboteador, a *nm/f* saboteur
sabotear *vt* to sabotage
sabroso, -a *adj* tasty; (*fig fam*) racy, salty
sacacorchos *nm inv* corkscrew

sacapuntas *nm inv* pencil sharpener
sacar *vt* (*de bolso, cajón*) to take out; (*fig: extraer*) to get (out); (*quitar*) to remove, get out; (*hacer salir*) to bring out; (*de cuenta bancaria*) to draw out, withdraw; (*obtener: legado etc*) to get, show; (*conclusión*) to draw; (*publicar: novela*) to publish, bring out; (*disco*) to release; (*obra*) to make; (*Tenis*) to serve; (*Fútbol*) to put into play; **voy a ~ dinero del cajero** I'm going to take some money out of the machine; **~ la basura** to take the rubbish out; **~ la lengua a algn** to stick one's tongue out at sb; **~ a pasear al perro** to take the dog out for a walk; **yo ~é las entradas** I'll get the tickets; **~ adelante** (*niño*) to bring up; (*proyecto, negocio*) to conclude; **~ una foto (a algn)** to take a photo (of sb); **~ buenas/malas notas** to get good/bad marks; **~ a algn a bailar** to get sb up for a dance; **~ a algn de sí** to infuriate sb; **se sacó las llaves del bolsillo** he took the keys out of his pocket; **~se el carnet de conducir** to pass one's driving test; **~se el título de abogado** to qualify as a lawyer
sacarina *nf* saccharin(e)
sacerdote *nm* priest
saciar *vt* (*hartar*) to satiate; (*fig*) to satisfy; **saciarse** *vr* (*fig*) to be satisfied
saco *nm* bag; (*grande*) sack; (*contenido*) bagful; (*LAm: chaqueta*) jacket; **~ de dormir** sleeping bag
sacramento *nm* sacrament
sacrificar *vt* to sacrifice; (*animal*) to slaughter; (*para evitar sufrimiento*) to put to sleep; **sacrificarse** *vr* to sacrifice o.s.
sacrificio *nm* sacrifice
sacrilegio *nm* sacrilege
sacrílego, -a *adj* sacrilegious
sacristán *nm* verger
sacristía *nf* sacristy
sacro, -a *adj* sacred
sacudida *nf* (*agitación*) shake, shaking; (*sacudimiento*) jolt, bump; (*fig*) violent change; (*Pol etc*) upheaval; **~ eléctrica** electric shock
sacudir *vt* to shake; (*golpear*) to hit; (*ala*) to flap; (*alfombra*) to beat; **~ a algn** (*fam*) to belt sb
sádico, -a *adj* sadistic ▷ *nm/f* sadist
sadismo *nm* sadism
sadomasoquismo *nm* sadomasochism
sadomasoquista *adj* sadomasochistic ▷ *nm/f*

sadomasochist

saeta nf (flecha) arrow; (Mus) sacred song in flamenco style

safari nm safari

sagacidad nf shrewdness, cleverness

sagaz adj shrewd, clever

Sagitario nm (Astro) Sagittarius

sagrado, -a adj sacred, holy

Sáhara nm: **el ~** the Sahara (desert)

sal nf salt; (gracia) wit; (encanto) charm; **~es de baño** bath salts; **~ gorda** o **de cocina** kitchen o cooking salt

sala nf (cuarto grande) large room; (sala de estar) living room; (Teat) house, auditorium; (de hospital) ward; **~ de apelación** court; **~ de conferencias** lecture hall; **~ de embarque** departure lounge; **~ de espera/estar** waiting/living room; **~ de fiestas** function room; **~ de juntas** (Com) boardroom

salado, -a adj salty; (fig) witty, amusing; **agua salada** salt water

salar vt to salt, add salt to

salarial adj (aumento, revisión) wage cpd, salary cpd, pay cpd

salario nm wage, pay

salchicha nf (pork) sausage

salchichón nm (salami-type) sausage

saldar vt to pay; (vender) to sell off; (fig) to settle, resolve

saldo nm (pago) settlement; (de una cuenta) balance; (lo restante) remnant(s) (pl), remainder; (liquidación) sale; (de móvil) credit; (Com): **~ anterior** balance brought forward; **~ acreedor/deudor** o **pasivo** credit/debit balance; **~ final** final balance; **no me queda ~ en el móvil** I haven't any credit left on my mobile

salero nm salt cellar; (ingenio) wit; (encanto) charm

salida nf (lugar de escape) exit; (pasillo) way out; (acto) leaving, going out; (de tren, Aviat) departure; (Com, Tec) output, production; (fig) way out; (resultado) outcome; (Com: oportunidad) opening; (Geo, válvula) outlet; (ocurrencia) joke; **calle sin ~** cul-de-sac; **a la ~ del teatro** after the theatre; **dar la ~** (Deporte) to give the starting signal; **no hay ~** there's no way out of it; **no tenemos otra ~** we have no option; **tener ~s** to be witty; **~ de emergencia** emergency exit; **~ de incendios** fire escape; **~ del sol** sunrise

salido, -a adj (fam) randy

saliente adj (Arq) projecting; (sol) rising; (fig) outstanding

salir vi 1 (marcharse: persona) to come o go out; (tren, avión) to leave; **¿vas a ~ esta noche?** are you going out tonight?; **salió de la cocina** he came out of the kitchen; **salimos de Madrid a las 8** we left Madrid at 8 (o'clock); **salió corriendo (del cuarto)** he ran out (of the room); **¡sal de ahí ahora mismo!** get out of there right now!; **~ de un apuro** to get out of a jam

2 (aparecer: pelo) to grow; (: diente) to come through; (: disco, libro) to come out; (planta, número de lotería;) to come up; **~ a la superficie** to come to the surface; **anoche salió en la tele** she appeared o was on TV last night; **salió en todos los periódicos** it was in all the papers; **le salió un trabajo** he got a job; **nos levantamos antes de que saliera el sol** we got up before the sun came out

3 (resultar): **la muchacha nos salió muy trabajadora** the girl turned out to be a very hard worker; **la comida te ha salido exquisita** the food was delicious; **sale muy caro** it's very expensive; **la entrevista que hice me salió bien/mal** the interview I did turned out o went well/badly; **espero que todo salga bien** I hope everything works out all right; **nos salió a 15 euros cada uno** it worked out at 15 euros each; **no salen las cuentas** it doesn't work out o add up; **he intentado resolver el problema pero no me sale** I've tried to solve the problem but I can't do it; **~ ganando** to come out on top; **~ perdiendo** to lose out

4 (empezar: Deporte) to start; (: Naipes) to lead

5: **~ con algn** to go out with sb; **está saliendo con un compañero de clase** she's going out with one of her classmates

6: **~ adelante, no sé como haré para ~ adelante** I don't know how I'll get by

salirse vr 1 (líquido: rebosar) to overflow; (filtrarse) to leak; **se ha salido la leche** the milk's boiled over

2 (soltarse: animal) to escape; **se ha salido el enchufe** the plug has come out

3 (desviarse): **~se de la carretera** to leave o go off the road; **~se de lo normal** to be unusual; **~se del tema** to get off the point

4: **~se con la suya** to get one's own way

saliva nf saliva

salmo nm psalm

salmón nm salmon

salmuera nf brine

salón nm (de casa) living-room, lounge; (muebles) lounge suite; **~ de baile** dance hall; **~ de belleza** beauty parlour; **~ de sesiones** assembly hall

salpicadero nm (Auto) dashboard

salpicar vt (de barro, pintura) to splash; (rociar) to sprinkle, spatter; (esparcir) to scatter

salsa nf sauce; (con carne asada) gravy; (fig) spice; (Mús) salsa; **estar en su ~** (fam) to be in one's element; **~ mayonesa** mayonnaise

saltamontes nm inv grasshopper

saltar vt (obstáculo) to jump (over), leap (over); (párrafo) to skip, miss out ▷ vi (persona, animal) to jump, leap; (al agua) to dive; (pelota) to bounce; (al aire) to fly up; (quebrarse) to break; (fig) to explode, blow up; (botón) to come off; (tapón de corcho) to pop out; **saltarse** vr (omitir) to skip, miss; **el caballo saltó la valla** the horse jumped over the wall; **hacer ~ algo por los aires** to blow sth up; **salta a la vista** it's obvious; **nos saltamos el desayuno** we skipped breakfast; **te has saltado una página** you've skipped a page; **~se un semáforo en rojo** to go through a red

light; **~se todas las reglas** to break all the rules
saltear vt (Culin) to sauté
saltimbanqui nm/f acrobat
salto nm (bote) jump, leap; (al agua) dive; **dar un
~** to jump; **a ~s** by jumping; **~ con pértiga** pole
vault; **~ de agua** waterfall; (Inform): **~ de altura**
high jump; **~ de cama** negligee; **~ de línea** line
feed; **~ de línea automático** wordwrap; **~ de
longitud** long jump; **~ de página** formfeed; **~
de trampolín** springboard diving; **~ mortal**
somersault
saltón, -ona adj (ojos) bulging, popping; (dientes)
protruding
salubre adj healthy, salubrious
salud nf health; **estar bien/mal de ~** to be
in good/poor health; **¡(a su) ~!** cheers!, good
health!; **beber a la ~ de** to drink (to) the health
of
saludable adj (de buena salud) healthy; (provechoso)
good, beneficial
saludar vt to greet; (Mil) to salute; **ir a ~ a algn**
to drop in to see sb; **salude de mi parte a X** give
my regards to X; **le saluda atentamente** (en
carta) yours faithfully
saludo nm greeting; **~s** (en carta) best wishes,
regards; **un ~ afectuoso o cordial** yours
sincerely
salva nf (Mil) salvo; **una ~ de aplausos**
thunderous applause
salvación nf salvation; (rescate) rescue
salvado nm bran
salvador nm rescuer, saviour; **el S~** (Rel) the
Saviour; **El S~** (país) El Salvador; **San S~** San
Salvador
salvadoreño, -a adj, nm/f Salvadoran,
Salvadorian
salvaguardar vt to safeguard
salvajada nf savage deed, atrocity
salvaje adj wild; (tribu) savage
salvajismo nm savagery
salvamento nm (acción) rescue; (de naufragio)
salvage; **~ y socorrismo** life-saving
salvapantallas nm inv screen saver
salvar vt (rescatar) to save, rescue; (resolver) to
overcome, resolve; (cubrir distancias) to cover,
travel; (hacer excepción) to except, exclude; (un
barco) to salvage; **salvarse** vr to save o.s., escape
salvavidas adj inv: **bote/chaleco/cinturón ~**
lifeboat/lifejacket/lifebelt
salvia nf sage
salvo, -a adj safe ▷ prep except (for), save; **~ error
u omisión** (Com) errors and omissions excepted;
a ~ out of danger; **~ que** unless
salvoconducto nm safe-conduct
samba nf samba
san nm (apócope) de **santo** saint; **~ Juan** St. John
sanar vt (herida) to heal; (persona) to cure ▷ vi
(persona) to get well, recover; (herida) to heal
sanatorio nm sanatorium
sanción nf sanction
sancionar vt to sanction
sandalia nf sandal

sandez nf (cualidad) foolishness; (acción) stupid
thing; **decir sandeces** to talk nonsense
sandía nf watermelon
sandinista adj, nm/f Sandinist(a)
sandwich (pl **-s** o **-es**) nm sandwich
saneamiento nm sanitation
sanear vt to drain; (indemnizar) to compensate;
(Econ) to reorganize
sangrar vt, vi to bleed; (texto) to indent
sangre nf blood; **~ fría** sangfroid; **a ~ fría** in cold
blood
sangría nf (Med) bleeding; (Culin) sangria,
sweetened drink of red wine with fruit, ≈ fruit cup
sangriento, -a adj bloody
sanguijuela nf (Zool, fig) leech
sanguinario, -a adj bloodthirsty
sanguíneo, -a adj blood cpd
sanidad nf sanitation; (calidad de sano) health,
healthiness; **~ pública** public health
(department)
sanitario, -a adj sanitary; (de la salud) health cpd
▷ nm: **~s** nmpl toilets (Brit), restroom sg (US)
sano, -a adj healthy; **~ y salvo** safe and sound
Santiago nm: **~ (de Chile)** Santiago
santiamén nm: **en un ~** in no time at all
santidad nf holiness, sanctity
santificar vt to sanctify, make holy
santiguarse vr to make the sign of the cross
santo, -a adj holy; (fig) wonderful, miraculous
▷ nm/f saint ▷ nm saint's day; **hacer su santa
voluntad** to do as one jolly well pleases; **¿a ~ de
qué ...?** why on earth ...?; **se le fue el ~ al cielo**
he forgot what he was about to say; **~ y seña**
password
santuario nm sanctuary, shrine
saña nf rage, fury
sapo nm toad
saque nm (Tenis) service, serve; (Fútbol) throw-in;
~ inicial kick-off; **~ de esquina** corner (kick);
tener buen ~ to eat heartily
saquear vt (Mil) to sack; (robar) to loot, plunder;
(fig) to ransack
saqueo nm (Mil) sacking; (robo) looting,
plundering
sarampión nm measles sg
sarcasmo nm sarcasm
sarcástico, -a adj sarcastic
sarcófago nm sarcophagus
sardina nf sardine
sardónico, -a adj sardonic; (irónico) ironical,
sarcastic
sargento nm sergeant
sarmiento nm vine shoot
sarna nf itch; (Med) scabies
sarpullido nm (Med) rash
sarro nm deposit; (en dientes) tartar
sartén nf frying pan; **tener la ~ por el mango** to
rule the roost
sastre nm tailor
sastrería nf (arte) tailoring; (tienda) tailor's
(shop)
Satanás nm Satan

satélite *nm* satellite

sátira *nf* satire

satisfacción *nf* satisfaction

satisfacer *vt* to satisfy; (*gastos*) to meet; (*deuda*) to pay; (*Com: letra de cambio*) to honour (Brit), honor (US); (*pérdida*) to make good; **satisfacerse** *vr* to satisfy o.s., be satisfied; (*vengarse*) to take revenge

satisfecho, -a *pp de* **satisfacer** ▷ *adj* satisfied; (*contento*) content(ed), happy; (*tb*: **satisfecho de sí mismo**) self-satisfied, smug

saturación *nf* saturation; **llegar a la ~** to reach saturation point

saturar *vt* to saturate; **saturarse** *vr* (*mercado, aeropuerto*) to reach saturation point; **¡estoy saturado de tanta televisión!** I can't take any more television!

sauce *nm* willow; **~ llorón** weeping willow

saudí *adj, nm/f* Saudi

sauna *nf* sauna

savia *nf* sap

saxo *nm* sax

saxofón *nm* saxophone

sazonado, -a *adj* (*fruta*) ripe; (*Culin*) flavoured, seasoned

sazonar *vt* to ripen; (*Culin*) to flavour, season

SE *abr* (= *sudeste*) SE

se *pron* **1** (*reflexivo: sg: m*) himself; (*: f*) herself; (*: pl*) themselves; (*: cosa*) itself; (*: de Vd*) yourself; (*: de Vds*) yourselves; (*indefinido*) oneself; **se mira en el espejo** he/she looks at himself/herself in the mirror; **¡siéntese!** sit down!; **se durmió** he fell asleep; **se está preparando** she's getting (herself) ready; **Margarita se estaba preparando para salir** Margarita was getting herself ready to go out; **la calefacción se apaga sola** the heating turns itself off automatically; **¿se ha hecho usted daño?** have you hurt yourself?, *para usos léxicos del pron ver el vb en cuestión, p.ej* **arrepentirse**

2 (*como complemento indirecto*) to him; (*:*) to her; (*:*) to them; (*:*) to it; (*:*) to you; **se lo dije ayer** (*a usted*) I told you yesterday; **se compró un sombrero** she bought herself a hat; **se rompió la pierna** he broke his leg; **cortarse el pelo** to get one's hair cut; (*uno mismo*) to cut one's hair; **se comió un pastel** he ate a cake

3 (*uso recíproco*) each other, one another; **se miraron (el uno al otro)** they looked at each other *o* one another; **se dieron un beso** they gave each other a kiss

4 (*en oraciones pasivas*): **se han vendido muchos libros** a lot of books have been sold

5 (*impers*): **se dice que** people say that, it is said that; **allí se come muy bien** the food there is very good, you can eat very well there; **se cree que el tabaco produce cáncer** it is believed that smoking causes cancer; **"se vende"** "for sale"

sebo *nm* fat, grease

seca *nf* dry season; **habrá pan a ~s** there will be just bread; **decir algo a ~s** to say sth curtly; *ver*

tb **seco**

secador *nm*: **~ para el pelo** hairdryer

secadora *nf* tumble dryer; **~ centrífuga** spin-dryer

secano *nm* (*Agr: tb*: **tierra de secano**) dry land *o* region; **cultivo de ~** dry farming

secar *vt* to dry; (*superficie*) to wipe dry; (*frente, suelo*) to mop; (*líquido*) to mop up; (*tinta*) to blot; **secarse** *vr* to dry (off); (*río, planta*) to dry up

sección *nf* section; (*Com*) department; **~ deportiva** (*en periódico*) sports page(s)

seco, -a *adj* dry; (*fruta*) dried; (*persona: magro*) thin, skinny; (*carácter*) cold; (*antipático*) disagreeable; (*respuesta*) sharp, curt; **parar en ~** to stop dead; *ver tb* **seca**

secretaría *nf* (*oficina*) secretary's office; (*Pol*) secretariat

secretario, -a *nm/f* secretary; **~ adjunto** (*Com*) assistant secretary

secreto, -a *adj* secret ▷ *nm* secret; (*calidad*) secrecy

secta *nf* sect

sectario, -a *adj* sectarian

sector *nm* sector (*tb Inform*); (*de opinión*) section; (*fig: campo*) area, field; **~ privado/público** (*Com, Econ*) private/public sector

secuela *nf* consequence

secuencia *nf* sequence

secuestrar *vt* to kidnap; (*avión*) to hijack; (*bienes*) to seize, confiscate

secuestro *nm* (*de persona*) kidnapping; (*de avión*) hijack; (*de cargamento*) seizure, confiscation

secular *adj* secular

secundar *vt* to second, support

secundaria *nf* secondary education

secundario, -a *adj* secondary; (*carretera*) side *cpd*; (*Inform*) background *cpd*

sed *nf* thirst; (*fig*) thirst, craving; **tener ~** to be thirsty

seda *nf* silk; **~ dental** dental floss

sedal *nm* fishing line

sedante *nm* sedative

sede *nf* (*de gobierno*) seat; (*de compañía*) headquarters *pl*, head office; **Santa S~** Holy See

sedentario, -a *adj* sedentary

sediento, -a *adj* thirsty

sedimentar *vt* to deposit; **sedimentarse** *vr* to settle

sedimento *nm* sediment

sedoso, -a *adj* silky, silken

seducción *nf* seduction

seducir *vt* to seduce; (*sobornar*) to bribe; (*cautivar*) to charm, fascinate; (*atraer*) to attract

seductor, a *adj* (*sexualmente*) seductive; (*cautivador*) charming; (*atractivo*) attractive ▷ *nm/f* seducer

segadora-trilladora *nf* combine harvester

segar *vt* (*mies*) to reap, cut; (*hierba*) to mow, cut; (*esperanzas*) to ruin

seglar *adj* secular, lay

segregación *nf* segregation; **~ racial** racial segregation

segregar *vt* to segregate, separate
seguido, -a *adj* (*continuo*) continuous, unbroken; (*recto*) straight ▷ *adv* (*directo*) straight (on); (*después*) after; (*LAm: a menudo*) often; **5 días ~s** 5 days running, 5 days in a row; **en seguida** at once, right away; **en seguida termino** I've nearly finished, I shan't be long now
seguimiento *nm* chase, pursuit; (*continuación*) continuation
seguir *vt* (*persona, coche, instrucciones*) to follow; (*ocurrir después*) to follow on, come after; (*proseguir*) to continue; (*perseguir*) to chase, pursue; (*indicio, pista*) to follow up ▷ *vi* (*continuar*) to continue, carry o go on; (*acontecimiento*) to follow; **seguirse** *vr* to follow; **¡sigue, por favor!** carry on, please!; **siguió hablando con nosotros** he carried on speaking to us; **el ascensor sigue estropeado** the lift's still not working; **sigo sin comprender** I still don't understand; **sigue lloviendo** it's still raining; **~ adelante** to go ahead; **¡siga!** (*LAm: pase*) come in!
según *prep* according to ▷ *adv*: **~ (y conforme)** it all depends ▷ *conj* as; **~ esté el tiempo** depending on the weather; **~ me consta** as far as I know; **está ~ lo dejaste** it is just as you left it
segunda *nf* (*sentido*) second meaning; *ver tb* **segundo**
segundo, -a *adj* second; (*en discurso*) secondly ▷ *nm* (*gen, medida de tiempo*) second; (*piso*) second floor; **~ (de a bordo)** (*Naut*) first mate; **segunda (clase)** (*Ferro*) second class; **segunda (marcha)** (*Auto*) second (gear); **de segunda mano** second hand; *ver tb* **segunda**
seguramente *adv* (*probablemente*) probably, surely; (*con certeza*) for sure, with certainty; **¿lo va a comprar?** — **~** is he going to buy it? — I should think so
seguridad *nf* safety; (*del estado, de casa etc*) security; (*certidumbre*) certainty; (*confianza*) confidence; (*estabilidad*) stability; **~ contra incendios** fire precautions *pl*; **~ en sí mismo** (self-)confidence; **~ social** social security
seguro, -a *adj* (*convencido, confirmado: persona, resultado*) sure, certain; (*datos etc*) reliable; (*fecha*) firm; (*libre de peligro*) safe; (*bien defendido, firme*) secure; (*fiel*) trustworthy ▷ *adv* for sure, certainly ▷ *nm* (*dispositivo*) safety device; (*de cerradura*) tumbler; (*de arma*) safety catch; (*Com*) insurance; (*CAm, Méx: imperdible*) safety pin; **estoy segura de que ganaremos** I'm sure we'll win; **está muy ~ de sí mismo** he's very sure of himself; **aquí estaremos ~s** we'll be safe here; **todavía no lo ha dicho** ~ he still hasn't said for sure; **~ contra accidentes/incendios** fire/ accident insurance; **~ contra terceros/a todo riesgo** third party/comprehensive insurance; **~ de enfermedad** ≈ National Insurance; **~ de vida** life insurance; **~ dotal con beneficios** with-profits endowment assurance; **~ marítimo** marine insurance; **~ mixto** endowment assurance; **~ temporal** term insurance

seis *num* six; **~ mil** six thousand; **tiene ~ años** she is six (years old); **unos ~** about six; **hoy es día ~** today is the sixth
seiscientos, -as *num* six hundred
seísmo *nm* tremor, earthquake
selección *nf* selection; **~ nacional** (*Deporte*) national team
seleccionar *vt* to pick, choose, select
selectividad *nf* (*Univ*) entrance examination
selecto, -a *adj* select, choice; (*escogido*) selected
sellar *vt* (*documento oficial*) to seal; (*pasaporte, visado*) to stamp; (*marcar*) to brand; (*pacto, labios*) to seal
sello *nm* stamp; (*precinto*) seal; (*fig: tb*: **sello distintivo**) hallmark; **~ fiscal** revenue stamp; **~s de prima** (*Com*) trading stamps
selva *nf* (*bosque*) forest, woods *pl*; (*jungla*) jungle; **la S~ Negra** the Black Forest
semáforo *nm* (*Auto*) traffic lights *pl*; (*Ferro*) signal
semana *nf* week; **entre ~** during the week; **~ inglesa** 5-day (working) week; **~ laboral** working week; **S~ Santa** Holy Week
semanal *adj* weekly
semblante *nm* face; (*fig*) look
sembrar *vt* to sow; (*objetos*) to sprinkle, scatter about; (*noticias etc*) to spread
semejante *adj* (*parecido*) similar; (*tal*) such ▷ *nm* fellow man, fellow creature; **~s** alike, similar; **son muy ~s** they are very much alike; **nunca hizo cosa ~** he never did such a o any such thing
semejanza *nf* similarity, resemblance; **a ~ de** like, as
semejar *vi* to seem like, resemble; **semejarse** *vr* to look alike, be similar
semen *nm* semen
semental *nm* (*macho*) stud
semestral *adj* half-yearly, bi-annual
semicírculo *nm* semicircle
semiconsciente *adj* semiconscious
semidesnatado, -a *adj* semi-skimmed
semifinal *nf* semifinal
semiinconsciente *adj* semiconscious
semilla *nf* seed
seminario *nm* (*Rel*) seminary; (*Escol*) seminar
sémola *nf* semolina
sempiterno, -a *adj* everlasting
Sena *nm*: **el ~** the (river) Seine
senado *nm* senate
senador, a *nm/f* senator
sencillez *nf* simplicity; (*de persona*) naturalness
sencillo, -a *adj* simple; (*carácter*) natural, unaffected; (*billete*) single ▷ *nm* (*disco*) single; (*LAm*) small change
senda *nf*, **sendero** *nm* path, track; **Sendero Luminoso** the Shining Path (guerrilla movement)
senderismo *nm* trekking
sendos, -as *adj pl*: **les dio ~ golpes** he hit both of them
senil *adj* senile
seno *nm* (*Anat*) bosom, bust; (*fig*) bosom; **senos** *nmpl* breasts; **~ materno** womb
sensación *nf* sensation; (*sentido*) sense;

(*sentimiento*) feeling; **causar** *o* **hacer ~** to cause a sensation

sensacional *adj* sensational

sensatez *nf* common sense

sensato, -a *adj* sensible

sensibilidad *nf* sensitivity; (*para el arte*) feel

sensibilizar *vt*: **~ a la población/opinión pública** to raise public awareness

sensible *adj* sensitive; (*apreciable*) perceptible, appreciable; (*pérdida*) considerable

sensiblero, -a *adj* sentimental, slushy

sensitivo, -a, sensorial *adj* sense *cpd*

sensual *adj* sensual

sentada *nf* sitting; (*Pol*) sit-in, sit-down protest; **de una ~** at one sitting; *ver tb* **sentado**

sentado, -a *adj* (*establecido*) settled; (*carácter*) sensible; **dar por ~** to take for granted, assume; **dejar algo ~** to establish sth firmly; **estar ~** to sit, be sitting (down); *ver tb* **sentada**

sentar *vt* to sit, seat; (*fig*) to establish ▷ *vi* (*vestido*) to suit; (*alimento*): **~ bien/mal a** to agree/disagree with; **sentarse** *vr* (*persona*) to sit, sit down; **¡siéntese!** (do) sit down, take a seat

sentencia *nf* (*máxima*) maxim, saying; (*Jur*) sentence; (*Inform*) statement; **~ de muerte** death sentence

sentenciar *vt* to sentence

sentido, -a *adj* (*pérdida*) regrettable; (*carácter*) sensitive ▷ *nm* (*capacidad de sentir*) sense; (*sentimiento*) feeling; (*significado*) sense, meaning; (*dirección*) direction; **mi más ~ pésame** my deepest sympathy; **no tiene ~ del ritmo** he has no sense of rhythm; **palabras con doble ~** words with a double meaning; **en el buen ~ de la palabra** in the best sense of the word; **sin ~** meaningless; **tener ~** to make sense; **en algún ~** in some respects; **una calle de ~ único** a one-way street; **en el ~ de las agujas del reloj** clockwise; **~ del humor** sense of humour; **~ común** common sense

sentimental *adj* sentimental; **vida ~** love life

sentimiento *nm* (*emoción*) feeling, emotion; (*sentido*) sense; (*pesar*) regret, sorrow

sentir *nm* opinion, judgement ▷ *vt* (*notar*) to feel; (*percibir*) to perceive, sense; (*esp LAm*: *oír*) to hear; (*lamentar*) to regret, be sorry for; (*música etc*) to have a feeling for ▷ *vi* to feel; (*lamentarse*) to feel sorry; **sentirse** *vr* to feel; **sentí un dolor en la pierna** I felt a pain in my leg; **no la sentí entrar** I didn't hear her come in; **lo siento mucho** I'm very sorry; **siento llegar tarde** I'm sorry I'm late; **~se mejor/mal** to feel better/ill; **no me siento nada bien** I don't feel at all well; **~se como en su casa** to feel at home

seña *nf* sign; (*Mil*) password; **señas** *nfpl* address *sg*; **~s personales** personal description *sg*; **por más ~s** moreover; **dar ~s de** to show signs of

señal *nf* (*indicador*) sign; (*síntoma*) symptom; (*indicio*) indication; (*Ferro, Telec*) signal; (*marca*) mark; (*Com*) deposit; (*Inform*) marker, mark; **en ~ de** as a token of, as a sign of; **dar ~es de** to show signs of; **yo daré la ~** I'll give the signal;

les hice una ~ para que se fueran I signalled to them to go; **dimos una ~ de 50 euros** we paid a deposit of 50 euros; **~ de auxilio/de peligro** distress/danger signal; **~ de llamada** ringing tone; **~ de tráfico** road sign; **~ indicadora** signpost; **~ para marcar** dialling tone (*Brit*), dial tone (*US*)

señalar *vt* to mark; (*indicar*) to point out, indicate; (*significar*) to denote; (*referirse a*) to allude to; (*fijar*) to fix, settle

señalizar *vt* (*Auto*) to put up road signs on; (*Ferro*) to put signals on; (*Auto*: *ruta*): **está bien señalizada** it's well signposted

señor, a *adj* (*fam*) lordly ▷ *nm* (*hombre*) man; (*caballero*) gentleman; (*dueño*) owner, master; (*fórmula de tratamiento: antes de nombre propio*) Mr; (*: hablando directamente*) sir; **los ~es González** Mr and Mrs González; **S~ Don Jacinto Benavente** (*en sobre*) Mr J. Benavente, J. Benavente Esq.; **S~ Director ...** (*de periódico*) Dear Sir ...; **~ juez** my lord, your worship (*US*); **~ Presidente** Mr Chairman *o* President; **Muy ~ mío** Dear Sir; **Muy ~es nuestros** Dear Sirs; **Nuestro S~** (*Rel*) Our Lord; *ver tb* **señora**

señora *nf* (*dama*) lady; (*fórmula de tratamiento: antes de nombre propio*) Mrs, Ms; (*: hablando directamente*) madam; (*esposa*) wife; **¿está la ~?** is the lady of the house in?; **la ~ de Smith** Mrs Smith; **Nuestra S~** (*Rel*) Our Lady; *ver tb* **señor**

señorita *nf* (*gen*) Miss, Ms; (*mujer joven*) young lady; (*maestra*) schoolteacher

señorito *nm* young gentleman; (*lenguaje de criados*) master; (*pey*) toff

señuelo *nm* decoy

separación *nf* separation; (*división*) division; (*distancia*) gap, distance; **~ de bienes** division of property

separado, -a *adj* separate; (*Tec*) detached; **vive ~ de su mujer** he is separated from his wife; **por ~** separately

separar *vt* (*apartar*) to separate; (*silla: de la mesa*) to move away; (*Tec: pieza*) to detach; (*persona: de un cargo*) to remove, dismiss; (*dividir*) to divide; **separarse** *vr* (*parte*) to come away; (*partes*) to come apart; (*persona*) to leave, go away; (*matrimonio*) to separate; (*novios, grupo*) to split up; **se ha separado de su mujer** he has left his wife

separatismo *nm* (*Pol*) separatism

sepia *nf* cuttlefish

septentrional *adj* north *cpd*, northern

septiembre *nm* September

séptimo, -a *adj, nm* seventh

sepulcral *adj* sepulchral; (*fig*) gloomy, dismal

sepulcro *nm* tomb, grave, sepulchre

sepultar *vt* to bury; (*en accidente*) to trap; **quedaban sepultados en la caverna** they were trapped in the cave

sepultura *nf* (*acto*) burial; (*tumba*) grave, tomb; **dar ~ a** to bury; **recibir ~** to be buried

sepulturero, -a *nm/f* gravedigger

sequedad *nf* dryness; (*fig*) brusqueness, curtness

sequía *nf* drought

séquito nm (de rey etc) retinue; (Pol) followers pl
ser vi **1** (descripción, identidad) to be; **es muy alta** she's very tall; **es médico** he's a doctor; **soy Ana** (al teléfono) it's Ana; **¡es cierto!** that's right!
2: ~ **de** (origen) to be from; (material) to be made of; (propiedad): **es de Joaquín** it's Joaquín's, it belongs to Joaquín; **¿de dónde eres?** where are you from?; **su familia es de Cuzco** his family is from Cuzco; **es de piedra** it's made of stone
3 (horas, fechas, números): **es la una** it's one o'clock; **son las seis y media** it's half-past six; **es uno de junio** it's the first of June; **era de noche** it was night; **somos/son seis** there are six of us/them; **2 y 2 son 4** 2 and 2 are o make 4
4 (suceso): **¿qué ha sido eso?** what was that?; **la fiesta es en mi casa** the party's at my house; **¿qué ~á de mí?** what will become of me?; **"érase una vez ..."** "once upon a time ..."
5 (en oraciones pasivas): **ha sido descubierto ya** it's already been discovered; **fue construido en 1960** it was built in 1960
6: **es de esperar que ...** it is to be hoped o I etc hope that ...
7 (locuciones con sub): **o sea** that is to say; **o sea, que no vienes** so you're not coming; **sea él sea su hermana** either him or his sister; **tengo que irme, no sea que mis hijos estén esperándome** I have to go in case my children are waiting for me
8: **a** o **de no** ~ **por él ...** but for him ...
9: **a no** ~ **que, a no** ~ **que tenga uno ya** unless he's got one already
▷ nm being; ~ **humano** human being; ~ **vivo** living creature
Serbia nf Serbia
serbio, -a adj Serbian ▷ nm/f Serb
serenarse vr (persona) to calm down; (mar) to grow calm; (tiempo) to clear up
serenidad nf calmness
sereno, -a adj (persona) calm, unruffled; (tiempo) fine, settled; (ambiente) calm, peaceful ▷ nm night watchman
serial nm serial
serie nf series; (cadena) sequence, succession; (TV etc) serial; (de inyecciones) course; **fuera de** ~ out of order; (fig) special, out of the ordinary; **fabricación en** ~ mass production; (Inform): **interface/impresora en** ~ serial interface/printer
seriedad nf seriousness; (formalidad) reliability; (de crisis) gravity, seriousness
serigrafía nf silk screen printing
serio, -a adj (no alegre) serious; (de confianza) reliable, dependable; (grave) serious, grave; **poco** ~ (actitud) undignified; (carácter) unreliable; **en** ~ seriously
sermón nm (Rel) sermon
seropositivo, -a adj HIV-positive
serpentear vi (gusano, pez) to wriggle; (camino, río) to wind, snake
serpentina nf streamer
serpiente nf snake; ~ **boa** boa constrictor; ~ **de**

cascabel rattlesnake
serranía nf mountainous area
serrano, -a adj highland cpd, hill cpd ▷ nm/f highlander
serrar vt to saw
serrín nm sawdust
serrucho nm handsaw
servicio nm (atención) service; (Culin etc) set; **servicios** nmpl toilet(s) (pl); ~ **incluido** (en hotel etc) service charge included; **estar al** ~ **de algn** to be in the service of; **estar de** ~ to be on duty; **al** ~, **Costa** (Tenis) Costa to serve; **está en el** ~ he's in the toilet; ~ **aduanero** o **de aduana** customs service; ~ **a domicilio** home delivery service; ~ **de caballeros** gents'; ~ **de señoras** ladies'; ~ **militar** national service; ~ **público** (Com) public utility
servidor, a nm/f servant; **su seguro** ~ **(s.s.s.)** yours faithfully; **un** ~ (el que habla o escribe) your humble servant ▷ nm (Inform) server
servidumbre nf (sujeción) servitude; (criados) servants pl, staff
servil adj servile
servilleta nf serviette, napkin
servir vt (comida, bebida) to serve; (atender) to serve; (Tenis etc) to serve ▷ vi (echar comida) to serve; (camarero) to serve, wait; (tener utilidad) to be of use, be useful; **servirse** vr to serve o help o.s.; **la cena está servida** dinner is served; ~ **vino a algn** to pour out wine for sb; **¿en qué puedo ~le?** how can I help you?; **¿para qué sirve esto?** what's this for?; **esta radio aún sirve** this radio still works; **no sirve para nada** it's no use at all; ~ **de guía** to act o serve as a guide; **sírvete más** have some more!; ~**se de algo** to make use of sth, use sth; **sírvase pasar** please come in
sesenta num sixty
sesgo nm slant; (fig) slant, twist
sesión nf (Pol) session, sitting; (Cine) showing; (Teat) performance; **abrir/levantar la** ~ to open/close o adjourn the meeting; **la segunda** ~ the second house
seso nm brain; (fig) intelligence; **sesos** nmpl (Culin) brains; **devanarse los ~s** to rack one's brains
sesudo, -a adj sensible, wise
set (pl -s) nm (Tenis) set
seta nf mushroom; ~ **venenosa** toadstool
setecientos, -as num seven hundred
setenta num seventy
seudo... pref pseudo...
seudónimo nm pseudonym
severidad nf severity
severo, -a adj severe; (disciplina) strict; (frío) bitter
Sevilla nf Seville
sevillano, -a adj o of from Seville ▷ nm/f native o inhabitant of Seville
sexo nm sex; **el** ~ **femenino/masculino** the female/male sex
sexto, -a num sixth; **Juan S~** John the Sixth
sexual adj sexual; **vida** ~ sex life
sexualidad nf sexuality

si *conj* (*condicional*) if; (*en pregunta indirecta*) if, whether ▷ *nm* (*Mus*) B; **¿y si llueve?** and what if it rains?; **si ... si ...** whether ... or ...; **¡si fuera verdad!** if only it were true!; **¿sabes si hemos cobrado ya?** do you know if we've been paid yet?; **me pregunto si ...** I wonder if *o* whether ...; **no sé si ir o (si) no** I don't know whether to go or not; **por si viene** in case he comes; **si no** (*condicional*) if not; (*advertencia*) otherwise; **avisadme si no podéis venir** let me know if you can't come; **ponte crema; si no, te quemarás** put some cream on, otherwise you'll get sunburned

sí *adv* yes ▷ *nm* consent ▷ *pron* (*uso impersonal*) oneself; (*sg: m*) himself; (: *f*) herself; (: *de cosa*) itself; (: *de usted*) yourself; (*pl*) themselves; (: *de ustedes*) yourselves; (: *recíproco: entre dos*) each other; (*entre varios*) among themselves; **él no quiere pero yo sí** he doesn't want to but I do; **ella sí vendrá** she will certainly come, she is sure to come; **claro que sí** of course; **creo que sí** I think so; **porque sí** (*porque es así*) because that's the way it is; (*porque lo digo yo*) because I say so; **¡sí que lo es!** I'll say it is!; **¡eso sí que no!** never; **se ríe de sí misma** she laughs at herself; **la pregunta en sí** *o* **de por sí no era difícil** the question itself wasn't difficult; **la Tierra gira sobre sí misma** the Earth turns on its own axis; **cambiaron una mirada entre sí** they gave each other a look; **hablaban entre sí** they were talking among themselves

siamés, -esa *adj*, *nm/f* Siamese

sibarita *adj* sybaritic ▷ *nm/f* sybarite

sicario *nm* hired killer

SIDA, sida *nm abr* (= *síndrome de inmunodeficiencia adquirida*) AIDS

siderúrgico, -a *adj* iron and steel *cpd*

sidra *nf* cider

siembra *nf* sowing

siempre *adv* always; (*todo el tiempo*) all the time; (*LAm: así y todo*) still ▷ *conj*: **~ que ...** (+ *indic*) whenever ...; (+ *subjun*) provided that ...; **es lo de ~** it's the same old story; **como ~** as usual; **para ~** forever; **~ me voy mañana** (*LAm*) I'm still leaving tomorrow

sien *nf* (*Anat*) temple

sierra *nf* (*Tec*) saw; (*Geo*) mountain range; **S~ Leona** Sierra Leone

siervo, -a *nm/f* slave

siesta *nf* siesta, nap; **dormir la** *o* **echarse una** *o* **tomar una ~** to have an afternoon nap *o* a doze

siete *num* seven ▷ *excl* (*CS fam*): **¡la gran ~!** wow!, hell!; **hijo de la gran ~** (*fam!*) bastard (!), son of a bitch (*US!*)

sífilis *nf* syphilis

sifón *nm* syphon; **whisky con ~** whisky and soda

sigilo *nm* secrecy; (*discreción*) discretion

sigla *nf* initial, abbreviation

siglo *nm* century; (*fig*) age; **S~ de las Luces** Age of Enlightenment; **S~ de Oro** Golden Age

significación *nf* significance

significado *nm* significance; (*de palabra etc*) meaning

significar *vt* to mean, signify; (*notificar*) to make known, express

significativo, -a *adj* significant

signo *nm* sign; **~ de admiración** *o* **exclamación** exclamation mark; **~ de interrogación** question mark; **~ más/ menos** plus/minus sign; **~s de puntuación** punctuation marks; **~ igual** equals sign

siguiente *adj* next

silbar *vt*, *vi* to whistle; (*silbato*) to blow; (*Teat etc*) to hiss

silbato *nm* (*instrumento*) whistle

silbido *nm* whistle, whistling; (*abucheo*) hiss

silenciador *nm* silencer

silenciar *vt* (*persona*) to silence; (*escándalo*) to hush up

silencio *nm* silence, quiet; **en el ~ más absoluto** in dead silence; **guardar ~** to keep silent

silencioso, -a *adj* silent, quiet

silicio *nm* silicon

silla *nf* (*asiento*) chair; (*tb*: **silla de montar**) saddle; **~ de ruedas** wheelchair

sillín *nm* saddle, seat

sillón *nm* armchair, easy chair

silueta *nf* silhouette; (*de edificio*) outline; (*figura*) figure

silvestre *adj* (*Bot*) wild; (*fig*) rustic, rural

simbólico, -a *adj* symbolic(al)

simbolizar *vt* to symbolize

símbolo *nm* symbol; **~ gráfico** (*Inform*) icon

simetría *nf* symmetry

simétrico, -a *adj* symmetrical

simiente *nf* seed

similar *adj* similar

simio *nm* ape

simpatía *nf* (*afecto*) affection; (*amabilidad*) kindness; (*de ambiente*) friendliness; (*de persona, lugar*) charm, attractiveness; (*solidaridad*) mutual support, solidarity; **tener ~ a** to like; **la conocida ~ andaluza** that well-known Andalusian charm

simpático, -a *adj* nice, pleasant; (*bondadoso*) kind; **no le hemos caído muy ~s** she didn't much take to us

simpatizante *nm/f* sympathizer

simpatizar *vi*: **~ con** to get on well with

simple *adj* simple; (*elemental*) simple, easy; (*mero*) mere; (*puro*) pure, sheer ▷ *nm/f* simpleton; **un ~ soldado** an ordinary soldier

simpleza *nf* simpleness; (*necedad*) silly thing

simplicidad *nf* simplicity

simplificar *vt* to simplify

simposio *nm* symposium

simulacro *nm* (*apariencia*) semblance; (*fingimiento*) sham

simular *vt* to simulate; (*fingir*) to feign, sham

simultáneo, -a *adj* simultaneous

sin *prep* without ▷ *conj*: **~ que** (+ *subjun*) without; **iba en moto ~ casco** he was riding a motorbike without a helmet; **me he quedado ~ cerillas** I've run out of matches; **me quedé ~ habla** I

was speechless; **la gente ~ hogar** the homeless;
salió ~ hacer ruido she went out without
making a noise; **~ verlo yo** without my seeing
it; **~ decir nada** without a word; **platos ~ lavar**
unwashed *o* dirty dishes; **la ropa está ~ lavar**
the clothes are unwashed; **~ que lo sepa él**
without his knowing; *ver tb* **embargo**

sinagoga *nf* synagogue

sinceridad *nf* sincerity

sincero, -a *adj* sincere; *(persona)* genuine;
(opinión) frank; *(felicitaciones)* heartfelt

sincronizar *vt* to synchronize

sindical *adj* union *cpd*, trade-union *cpd*

sindicalista *adj* trade-union *cpd* ▷ *nm/f* trade
unionist

sindicato *nm* *(de trabajadores)* trade(s) *o* labor (US)
union; *(de negociantes)* syndicate

síndrome *nm* syndrome; **~ de abstinencia**
withdrawal symptoms; **~ de la clase turista**
economy-class syndrome

sine qua non *adj:* **condición ~** sine qua non

sinfín *nm:* **un ~ de** a great many, no end of

sinfonía *nf* symphony

sinfónico, -a *adj* *(música)* symphonic; **orquesta
sinfónica** symphony orchestra

singular *adj* singular; *(fig)* outstanding,
exceptional; *(pey)* peculiar, odd ▷ *nm* *(Ling)*
singular; **en ~** in the singular

singularidad *nf* singularity, peculiarity

singularizar *vt* to single out; **singularizarse** *vr*
to distinguish o.s., stand out

siniestro, -a *adj* left; *(fig)* sinister ▷ *nm* *(accidente)*
accident; *(desastre)* natural disaster

sinnúmero *nm* = **sinfín**

sino *nm* fate, destiny ▷ *conj* but, save; **no son 8 ~
9** there are not 8 but 9

sinónimo, -a *adj* synonymous ▷ *nm* synonym

sintaxis *nf* syntax

síntesis *nf inv* synthesis

sintético, -a *adj* synthetic

sintetizar *vt* to synthesize

síntoma *nm* symptom

sintomático, -a *adj* symptomatic

sintonía *nf* *(Radio)* tuning; *(melodía)* signature
tune

sintonizar *vt* *(Radio)* to tune (in) to, pick up

sinvergüenza *nm/f* rogue, scoundrel

sionismo *nm* Zionism

siquiera *conj* even if, even though ▷ *adv* *(esp LAm)*
at least; **ni ~** not even; **~ bebe algo** at least drink
something

sirena *nf* siren, mermaid; *(bocina)* siren, hooter

Siria *nf* Syria

sirio, -a *adj*, *nm/f* Syrian

sirviente, -a *nm/f* servant

sisear *vt, vi* to hiss

sísmico, -a *adj:* **movimiento ~** earthquake

sismógrafo *nm* seismograph

sistema *nm* system; *(método)* method; **~ binario**
(Inform) binary system; **~ de alerta inmediata**
early-warning system; **~ de facturación** *(Com)*
invoicing system; **~ de fondo fijo** *(Com)* imprest

system; **~ de lógica compartida** *(Inform)* shared
logic system; **~ experto** expert system; **~
impositivo** *o* **tributario** taxation, tax system;
sistema métrico metric system; **~ operativo
(en disco)** *(Inform)* (disk-based) operating
system; **~ pedagógico** educational system

sistemático, -a *adj* systematic

sitiar *vt* to besiege, lay siege to

sitio *nm* *(lugar)* place; *(espacio)* room; *(Mil)* siege;
¿hay ~? is there any room?; **hay ~ de sobra**
there's plenty of room; **~ web** *(Internet)* website

situación *nf* situation, position; *(estatus)*
position, standing

situado, -a *adj* situated, placed; **estar ~** *(Com)* to
be financially secure

situar *vt* to place, put; *(edificio)* to locate, situate

slip *(pl -s)* *nm* pants *pl*, briefs *pl*

SME *nm abr* (= *Sistema Monetario Europeo*) EMS;
(mecanismo de cambios del) **~** ERM

smoking *(pl -s)* *nm* dinner jacket (Brit), tuxedo
(US)

SMS *nm* *(mensaje)* text (message), SMS (message)

snob; = **esnob**

SO *abr* (= *suroeste*) SW

so *excl* whoa! ▷ *prep* under; **¡so burro!** you idiot!

sobaco *nm* armpit

sobar *vt* *(tela)* to finger; *(ropa)* to rumple, mess
up; *(músculos)* to rub, massage

soberanía *nf* sovereignty

soberano, -a *adj* sovereign; *(fig)* supreme ▷ *nm/f*
sovereign; **los ~s** the king and queen

soberbia *nf* *(orgullo)* pride; *(altanería)*
haughtiness, arrogance; *(magnificencia)*
magnificence; *ver tb* **soberbio**

soberbio, -a *adj* *(orgulloso)* proud; *(altivo)* haughty,
arrogant; *(fig)* magnificent, superb; *ver tb*
soberbia

sobornar *vt* to bribe

soborno *nm* *(cantidad de dinero)* bribe; *(delito)*
bribery

sobra *nf* excess, surplus; **sobras** *nfpl* left-overs,
scraps; **de ~** surplus, extra; **lo sé de ~** I'm only
too aware of it; **tengo de ~** I've more than
enough

sobrado, -a *adj* *(más que suficiente)* more than
enough; *(superfluo)* excessive ▷ *adv* too,
exceedingly; **sobradas veces** repeatedly

sobrante *adj* remaining, extra ▷ *nm* surplus,
remainder

sobrar *vt* to exceed, surpass ▷ *vi* *(tener de más)* to
be more than enough; *(quedar)* to remain, be left
(over)

sobrasada *nf* = sausage spread

sobre *prep* *(gen)* on; *(encima)* on (top of); *(sin
contacto con la superficie)* over, above; *(más que)* more
than; *(además)* in addition to, besides; *(alrededor
de)* about; *(porcentaje)* in, out of; *(acerca de)* about,
on ▷ *nm* envelope; **dejó el dinero ~ la mesa**
he left the money on the table; **un préstamo ~
una propiedad** a loan on a property; **~ las seis**
at about six o'clock; **3 ~ 100** 3 in a 100, 3 out of
every 100; **información ~ vuelos** information

about flights; **un libro ~ Tirso** a book about Tirso; **~ todo** above all; **~ de ventanilla** window envelope

sobrecama *nf* bedspread

sobrecargar *vt* (*camión*) to overload; (*Com*) to surcharge

sobrecoger *vt* (*sobresaltar*) to startle; (*asustar*) to scare; **sobrecogerse** *vr* (*sobresaltarse*) to be startled; (*asustarse*) to get scared; (*quedar impresionado*): **~se (de)** to be overawed (by)

sobredosis *nf inv* overdose

sobre(e)ntender *vt* to understand; (*adivinar*) to deduce, infer; **se sobre(e)ntiende que ...** it is implied that ...

sobrehumano, -a *adj* superhuman

sobrellevar *vt* (*fig*) to bear, endure

sobremesa *nf* (*después de comer*) sitting on after a meal; (*Inform*) desktop; **conversación de ~** table talk

sobrenatural *adj* supernatural

sobrenombre *nm* nickname

sobrepasar *vt* to exceed, surpass

sobreponer *vt* (*poner encima*) to put on top; (*añadir*) to add; **sobreponerse** *vr*: **~se a** to overcome

sobresaliente *adj* projecting; (*fig*) outstanding, excellent; (*Univ etc*) first class ▷ *nm* (*Univ etc*) first class (mark), distinction

sobresalir *vi* to project, jut out; (*fig*) to stand out, excel

sobresaltar *vt* (*asustar*) to scare, frighten; (*sobrecoger*) to startle

sobresalto *nm* (*movimiento*) start; (*susto*) scare; (*turbación*) sudden shock

sobretodo *nm* overcoat

sobrevenir *vi* (*ocurrir*) to happen (unexpectedly); (*resultar*) to follow, ensue

sobreviviente *adj* surviving ▷ *nm/f* survivor

sobrevivir *vi* to survive; (*persona*) to outlive

sobrevolar *vt* to fly over

sobriedad *nf* sobriety, soberness; (*moderación*) moderation, restraint

sobrino, -a *nm/f* nephew/niece

sobrio, -a *adj* (*moderado*) moderate, restrained

socarrón, -ona *adj* sarcastic, ironic(al)

socavar *vt* to undermine; (*excavar*) to dig underneath o below

socavón *nm* (*en mina*) gallery; (*hueco*) hollow; (*en la calle*) hole

sociable *adj* (*persona*) sociable, friendly; (*animal*) social

social *adj* social; (*Com*) company *cpd*

socialdemócrata *adj* social-democratic ▷ *nm/f* social democrat

socialista *adj, nm/f* socialist

socializar *vt* to socialize

sociedad *nf* society; (*Com*) company; **~ de ahorro y préstamo** savings and loan society; **~ anónima (S.A.)** limited company (Ltd) (*Brit*), incorporated company (Inc) (*US*); **~ comanditaria** (*Com*) co-ownership; **~ conjunta** (*Com*) joint venture; **~ de beneficiencia** friendly society (*Brit*), benefit association (*US*); **~ de**

cartera investment trust; **~ inmobiliaria** building society (*Brit*), savings and loan (society) (*US*); **~ de responsabilidad limitada** (*Com*) private limited company

socio, -a *nm/f* (*miembro*) member; (*Com*) partner; **~ activo** active partner; **~ capitalista** o **comanditario** sleeping o silent (*US*) partner

sociología *nf* sociology

sociólogo, -a *nm/f* sociologist

socorrer *vt* to help

socorrismo *nm* life-saving

socorrista *nm/f* first aider; (*en piscina, playa*) lifeguard

socorro *nm* (*ayuda*) help, aid; (*Mil*) relief; ¡~! help!

soda *nf* (*sosa*) soda; (*bebida*) soda (water)

sódico, -a *adj* sodium *cpd*

sofá *nm* sofa, settee

sofá-cama *nm* studio couch, sofa bed

sofisticación *nf* sophistication

sofisticado, -a *adj* sophisticated

sofocar *vt* to suffocate; (*apagar*) to smother, put out; **sofocarse** *vr* to suffocate; (*fig*) to blush, feel embarrassed

sofoco *nm* (*ahogo*) suffocation; (*azoro*) embarrassment

sofreír *vt* to fry lightly

soga *nf* rope

soja *nf* soya

sojuzgar *vt* to subdue, rule despotically

sol *nm* sun; (*luz*) sunshine, sunlight; (*Mus*) G; **hace ~** it is sunny; **tomar el ~** to sunbathe; **~ naciente/poniente** rising/setting sun

solamente *adv* only, just

solapa *nf* (*de chaqueta*) lapel; (*de libro*) jacket

solapado, -a *adj* sly, underhand

solar *adj* solar, sun *cpd* ▷ *nm* (*terreno*) plot (of ground); (*local*) undeveloped site

solaz *nm* recreation, relaxation

solazar *vt* (*divertir*) to amuse; **solazarse** *vr* to enjoy o.s., relax

soldado *nm* soldier; **~ raso** private

soldador *nm* soldering iron; (*persona*) welder

soldar *vt* to solder, weld; (*unir*) to join, unite

soleado, -a *adj* sunny

soledad *nf* solitude; (*estado infeliz*) loneliness

solemne *adj* solemn; (*tontería*) utter; (*error*) complete

solemnidad *nf* solemnity

soler *vi* to be in the habit of, be accustomed to; **suele salir a las ocho** she usually goes out at 8 o'clock; **solíamos ir todos los años** we used to go every year

solfeo *nm* singing of scales; **ir a clases de ~** to take singing lessons

solicitar *vt* (*permiso*) to ask for, seek; (*puesto*) to apply for; (*votos*) to canvass for; (*atención*) to attract; (*persona*) to pursue, chase after

solícito, -a *adj* (*diligente*) diligent; (*cuidadoso*) careful

solicitud *nf* (*calidad*) great care; (*petición*) request; (*a un puesto*) application

solidaridad *nf* solidarity; **por ~ con** (*Pol etc*) out of *o* in solidarity with

solidario, -a *adj* (*participación*) joint, common; (*compromiso*) mutually binding; **mostrarse ~ con** to declare one's solidarity with

solidarizarse *vr*: **~ con algn** to support sb, sympathize with sb

solidez *nf* solidity

sólido, -a *adj* solid; (*Tec*) solidly made; (*bien construido*) well built

soliloquio *nm* soliloquy

solista *nm/f* soloist

solitaria *nf* tapeworm; *ver tb* **solitario**

solitario, -a *adj* (*persona*) lonely, solitary; (*lugar*) lonely, desolate ▷ *nm/f* (*reclusa*) recluse; (*en la sociedad*) loner ▷ *nm* solitaire; *ver tb* **solitaria**

sollozar *vi* to sob

sollozo *nm* sob

solo, -a *adj* (*único*) single, sole; (*sin compañía*) alone; (*solitario*) lonely; (*Mus*) solo; **hay una sola dificultad** there is just one difficulty; **a solas** alone, by o.s.

sólo *adv* only, just; (*exclusivamente*) solely; **tan ~** only just

solomillo *nm* sirloin

solsticio *nm* solstice

soltar *vt* (*dejar ir*) to let go of; (*dejar caer*) to drop; (*desprender*) to unfasten, loosen; (*liberar*) to release, set free; (*amarras*) to cast off; (*Auto: freno etc*) to release; (*suspiro*) to heave; (*risa etc*) to let out; **soltarse** *vr* (*desanudarse*) to come undone; (*desprenderse*) to come off; (*adquirir destreza*) to become expert; (*en idioma*) to become fluent; **suelta la cerilla o te quemarás** let go of the match or you'll burn yourself; **¡suéltame!** let me go!; **han soltado a los rehenes** they've released the hostages; **solté un suspiro de alivio** I let out a sigh of relief

soltero, -a *adj* single, unmarried ▷ *nm* bachelor ▷ *nf* single woman, spinster

solterón *nm* confirmed bachelor

soltura *nf* looseness, slackness; (*de los miembros*) agility, ease of movement; (*en el hablar*) fluency, ease

soluble *adj* (*Química*) soluble; (*problema*) solvable; **~ en agua** soluble in water

solución *nf* solution; **~ de continuidad** break in continuity

solucionar *vt* (*problema*) to solve; (*asunto*) to settle, resolve

solventar *vt* (*pagar*) to settle, pay; (*resolver*) to resolve

solvente *adj* solvent, free of debt

sombra *nf* shadow; (*como protección*) shade; **sombras** *nfpl* darkness *sg*, shadows; **sin ~ de duda** without a shadow of doubt; **tener buena/ mala ~** (*suerte*) to be lucky/unlucky; (*carácter*) to be likeable/disagreeable

sombrero *nm* hat; **~ de copa** *o* **de pelo** (*LAm*) top hat; **~ hongo** bowler (hat), derby (*US*)

sombrilla *nf* parasol, sunshade

sombrío, -a *adj* (*oscuro*) shady; (*fig*) sombre, sad; (*persona*) gloomy

somero, -a *adj* superficial

someter *vt* (*país*) to conquer; (*persona*) to subject to one's will; (*informe*) to present, submit; **someterse** *vr* to give in, yield, submit; **~se a una operación** to undergo an operation

somier (*pl* **-s**) *nm* spring mattress

somnífero *nm* sleeping pill *o* tablet

somnolencia *nf* sleepiness, drowsiness

son *nm* sound; **en ~ de broma** as a joke

sonajero *nm* (baby's) rattle

sonambulismo *nm* sleepwalking

sonámbulo, -a *nm/f* sleepwalker

sonar *vt* (*campana*) to ring; (*trompeta, sirena*) to blow ▷ *vi* (*parecer por el sonido*) to sound; (*hacer ruido*) to make a noise; (*Ling*) to be sounded, be pronounced; (*campana, timbre, teléfono*) to ring; (*despertador*) to go off; (*reloj*) to strike, chime; (*ser conocido*) to sound familiar; **sonarse** *vr*: **~se (la nariz)** to blow one's nose; **sonabas un poco triste por teléfono** you sounded a bit sad on the phone; **escríbelo tal y como suena** write it down just the way it sounds; **me suena ese nombre** that name rings a bell *o* sounds familiar

sonda *nf* (*Náut*) sounding; (*Téc*) bore, drill; (*Méd*) probe

sondear *vt* (*Náut*) to sound; (*Téc*) to bore (into), drill; (*Med*) to probe; (*fig*) to sound out

sondeo *nm* (*Náut*) sounding; (*Téc*) boring, drilling; (*encuesta*) poll, survey; **~ de la opinión pública** public opinion poll

sónico, -a *adj* sonic, sound *cpd*

sonido *nm* sound

sonoro, -a *adj* sonorous; (*resonante*) loud, resonant; (*Ling*) voiced; **efectos ~s** sound effects

sonreír *vi*, **sonreírse** *vr* to smile

sonriente *adj* smiling

sonrisa *nf* smile

sonrojar *vt*: **~ a algn** to make sb blush; **sonrojarse** *vr*: **~se (de)** to blush (at)

sonrojo *nm* blush

sonsacar *vt* to wheedle, coax; **~ (información) a algn** to pump sb for information

soñador, a *nm/f* dreamer

soñar *vt*, *vi* to dream; **~ con** to dream about *o* of; **soñé contigo anoche** I dreamed about you last night

soñoliento, -a *adj* sleepy, drowsy

sopa *nf* soup; **~ de fideos** noodle soup

sopera *nf* soup tureen; *ver tb* **sopero**

sopero, -a *adj* (*plato, cuchara*) soup *cpd* ▷ *nm* soup plate; *ver tb* **sopera**

sopesar *vt* to try the weight of; (*fig*) to weigh up

soplar *vt* (*polvo*) to blow away, blow off; (*inflar*) to blow up; (*vela*) to blow out; (*ayudar a recordar*) to prompt; (*birlar*) to nick; (*delatar*) to split on ▷ *vi* to blow; (*delatar*) to squeal; (*beber*) to booze, bend the elbow

soplo *nm* blow, puff; (*de viento*) puff, gust

soplón, -ona *nm/f* (*fam: chismoso*) telltale; (*: de policía*) informer, grass

sopor *nm* drowsiness

soporífero, -a *adj* sleep-inducing; *(fig)* soporific
▷ *nm* sleeping pill

soportable *adj* bearable

soportal *nm* porch; **soportales** *nmpl* arcade *sg*

soportar *vt* to bear, carry; *(fig)* to stand, bear, put
up with

soporte *nm* support; *(fig)* pillar, support; *(Inform)*
medium; **~ de entrada/salida** input/output
medium

soprano *nf* soprano

sor *nf*: **S~ María** Sister Mary

sorber *vt* *(chupar)* to sip; *(inhalar)* to sniff, inhale;
(absorber) to soak up, absorb

sorbete *nm* sherbet

sorbo *nm* *(trago)* gulp, swallow; *(chupada)* sip;
beber a ~s to sip

sordera *nf* deafness

sórdido, -a *adj* dirty, squalid

sordo, -a *adj* *(persona)* deaf; *(ruido)* dull; *(Ling)*
voiceless ▷ *nm/f* deaf person; **quedarse ~** to go
deaf

sordomudo, -a *adj* deaf and dumb ▷ *nm/f* deaf-
mute

sorna *nf* *(malicia)* slyness; *(tono burlón)* sarcastic
tone

soroche *nm* *(LAm And, CS)* mountain sickness

sorprendente *adj* surprising

sorprender *vt* to surprise; *(asombrar)* to amaze;
(sobresaltar) to startle; *(coger desprevenido)* to catch
unawares; **sorprenderse** *vr*: **~se (de)** to be
surprised o amazed (at)

sorpresa *nf* surprise

sortear *vt* to draw lots for; *(rifar)* to raffle;
(dificultad) to dodge, avoid

sorteo *nm* *(en lotería)* draw; *(rifa)* raffle

sortija *nf* *(anillo)* ring; *(rizo)* ringlet, curl

sosegado, -a *adj* quiet, calm

sosegar *vt* to quieten, calm; *(el ánimo)* to reassure
▷ *vi* to rest

sosiego *nm* quiet(ness), calm(ness)

soslayar *vt* *(preguntas)* to get round

soslayo; **de ~** *adv* obliquely, sideways; **mirar de
~** to look out of the corner of one's eye (at)

soso, -a *adj* *(Culin)* tasteless; *(fig)* dull,
uninteresting

sospecha *nf* suspicion

sospechar *vt* to suspect ▷ *vi*: **~ de** to be
suspicious of

sospechoso, -a *adj* suspicious; *(testimonio,
opinión)* suspect ▷ *nm/f* suspect

sostén *nm* *(apoyo)* support; *(sujetador)* bra;
(alimentación) sustenance, food

sostener *vt* *(sujetar)* to support; *(mantener)* to
keep up, maintain; *(alimentar)* to sustain, keep
going; *(opinión, promesa)* to stand by; **sostenerse**
vr *(mantenerse en pie)* to stand; *(seguir)* to continue,
remain; **está sostenido por cuatro columnas**
it is supported by four columns; **sostuvieron
la caja entre los dos** they held the box between
the two of them; **la sombrilla no se sostiene
con el viento** the sunshade won't stay up in
the wind

sostenido, -a *adj* continuous, sustained;
(prolongado) prolonged; *(Mus)* sharp ▷ *nm (Mus)*
sharp

sota *nf (Naipes)* ≈ jack

sotana *nf (Rel)* cassock

sótano *nm* basement

soviético, -a *adj*, *nm/f* Soviet; **los ~s** the Soviets,
the Russians

spot *(pl* **-s)** *nm (publicitario)* ad

squash *nm (Deporte)* squash

Sr. *abr (= Señor)* Mr

Sra. *abr (= Señora)* Mrs

S.R.C. *abr (= se ruega contestación)* R.S.V.P.

Sres., Srs. *abr (= Señores)* Messrs

Srta. *abr = **Señorita**

Sta. *abr (= Santa)* St; *(= Señorita)* Miss

stand *(pl* **-s)** *nm (Com)* stand

status *nm inv* status

statu(s) quo *nm* status quo

Sto. *abr (= Santo)* St.

stop *(pl* **-s)** *nm (Auto)* stop sign

su *pron (de él)* his; *(de ella)* her; *(de una cosa)* its; *(de
ellos, ellas)* their; *(de usted, ustedes)* your

suave *adj* gentle; *(superficie)* smooth; *(trabajo)*
easy; *(música, voz)* soft, sweet; *(clima, sabor)* mild

suavidad *nf* gentleness; *(de superficie)*
smoothness; *(de música)* softness, sweetness

suavizante *nm* conditioner

suavizar *vt* to soften; *(quitar la aspereza)* to smooth
(out); *(pendiente)* to ease; *(colores)* to tone down;
(carácter) to mellow; *(dureza)* to temper

subalimentado, -a *adj* undernourished

subasta *nf* auction; **poner en** o **sacar a pública
~** to put up for public auction; **~ a la rebaja**
Dutch auction

subastar *vt* to auction (off)

subcampeón, -ona *nm/f* runner-up

subconsciente *adj* subconscious

subdesarrollado, -a *adj* underdeveloped

subdesarrollo *nm* underdevelopment

subdirector, a *nm/f* assistant o deputy manager

súbdito, -a *nm/f* subject

subdividir *vt* to subdivide

subestimar *vt* to underestimate, underrate

subida *nf (de montaña etc)* ascent, climb; *(de precio)*
rise, increase; *(pendiente)* slope, hill

subido, -a *adj (color)* bright, strong; *(precio)* high

subir *vt (levantar)* to lift up, raise; *(cuesta, calle)* to
go up; *(montaña)* to climb; *(precio)* to raise, put
up; *(empleado etc)* to promote ▷ *vi* to go/come
up; *(a un coche)* to get in(to); *(a un autobús, tren)* to
get on(to); *(precio, fiebre)* to go up; *(en el empleo)*
to be promoted; *(río, marea)* to rise; **subirse** *vr*
(engreírse) to get conceited; **~se a** *(coche)* to get
in(to); *(bicicleta)* to get on(to); *(autobús, tren, avión)*
to get on; **sube los brazos** raise your arms;
subimos la cuesta we went up the hill; **los
taxistas han subido sus tarifas** taxi drivers
have put their fares up; **sube la radio, que no
se oye** turn the radio up, I can't hear it; **sube,
que te voy a enseñar unos discos** come up, I've
got some records to show you; **~se a un árbol** to

climb a tree
súbito, -a *adj* (*repentino*) sudden; (*imprevisto*) unexpected
subjetivo, -a *adj* subjective
subjuntivo *nm* subjunctive (mood)
sublevación *nf* revolt, rising
sublevar *vt* to rouse to revolt; **sublevarse** *vr* to revolt, rise
sublime *adj* sublime
subliminal *adj* subliminal
submarinista *nm/f* underwater explorer
submarino, -a *adj* underwater ▷ *nm* submarine
subnormal *adj* subnormal ▷ *nm/f* subnormal person
subordinado, -a *adj, nm/f* subordinate
subrayar *vt* to underline; (*recalcar*) to underline, emphasize
subrepticio, -a *adj* surreptitious
subsanar *vt* (*reparar*) to make good; (*perdonar*) to excuse; (*sobreponerse a*) to overcome
subscribir *vt* = **suscribir**
subsidiariedad *nf* (*Pol*) subsidiarity
subsidiario, -a *adj* subsidiary
subsidio *nm* (*ayuda*) aid, financial help; (*subvención*) subsidy, grant; (*de enfermedad, paro etc*) benefit, allowance
subsistencia *nf* subsistence
subsistir *vi* to subsist; (*vivir*) to live; (*sobrevivir*) to survive, endure
subterráneo, -a *adj* underground, subterranean ▷ *nm* underpass, underground passage; (*CS*) underground railway, subway (US)
subtítulo *nm* subtitle, subheading
suburbano, -a *adj* suburban
suburbio *nm* (*barrio*) slum quarter; (*afueras*) suburbs *pl*
subvención *nf* subsidy, subvention, grant; **~ estatal** state subsidy *o* support; **~ para la inversión** (*Com*) investment grant
subvencionar *vt* to subsidize
subversión *nf* subversion
subversivo, -a *adj* subversive
subyugar *vt* (*país*) to subjugate, subdue; (*enemigo*) to overpower; (*voluntad*) to dominate
succión *nf* suction
sucedáneo, -a *adj* substitute ▷ *nm* substitute (food)
suceder *vi* to happen; **~ a** (*seguir*) to succeed, follow; **lo que sucede es que ...** the fact is that ...; **~ en el trono** to succeed to the throne
sucesión *nf* succession; (*serie*) sequence, series; (*hijos*) issue, offspring
sucesivamente *adv*: **y así ~** and so on
sucesivo, -a *adj* successive, following; **en lo ~** in future, from now on
suceso *nm* (*hecho*) event, happening; (*incidente*) incident
suciedad *nf* (*estado*) dirtiness; (*mugre*) dirt, filth
sucinto, -a *adj* (*conciso*) succinct, concise
sucio, -a *adj* dirty; (*mugriento*) grimy; (*manchado*) grubby; (*borroso*) smudged; (*conciencia*) bad; (*conducta*) vile; (*táctica*) dirty, unfair

Sucre *n* Sucre
suculento, -a *adj* (*sabroso*) tasty; (*jugoso*) succulent
sucumbir *vi* to succumb
sucursal *nf* branch (office); (*filial*) subsidiary
Sudáfrica *nf* South Africa
Sudamérica *nf* South America
sudamericano, -a *adj, nm/f* South American
sudar *vt, vi* to sweat; (*Bot*) to ooze, give out *o* off
sudeste *adj* south-east(ern); (*rumbo, viento*) south-easterly ▷ *nm* south-east; (*viento*) south-east wind
sudoeste *adj* south-west(ern); (*rumbo, viento*) south-westerly ▷ *nm* south-west; (*viento*) south-west wind
sudor *nm* sweat
Suecia *nf* Sweden
sueco, -a *adj* Swedish ▷ *nm/f* Swede ▷ *nm* (*Ling*) Swedish; **hacerse el ~** to pretend not to hear *o* understand
suegro, -a *nm/f* father-/mother-in-law; **los ~s** one's in-laws
suela *nf* (*de zapato*) sole
sueldo *nm* pay, wage(s) (*pl*)
suelo *nm* (*tierra*) ground; (*de casa*) floor
suelto, -a *adj* loose; (*libre*) free; (*separado*) detached; (*ágil*) quick, agile; (*que corre*) fluent, flowing ▷ *nm* (*loose*) change, small change; **está muy ~ en inglés** he is very good at *o* fluent in English
sueño *nm* sleep; (*somnolencia*) sleepiness, drowsiness; (*lo soñado, fig*) dream; **~ pesado** *o* **profundo** deep *o* heavy sleep; **tener ~** to be sleepy
suero *nm* (*Med*) serum; (*de leche*) whey
suerte *nf* (*fortuna*) luck; (*azar*) chance; (*destino*) fate, destiny; (*condición*) lot; (*género*) sort, kind; **¡que tengas ~!** good luck!; **tuvo ~** she was lucky; **¡qué ~!** how lucky!; **por ~** luckily; **lo echaron a ~s** they drew lots *o* tossed up for it; **de otra ~** otherwise, if not; **de ~ que ...** so that ..., in such a way that ...
suéter (*pl* **-s**) *nm* sweater
suficiente *adj* enough, sufficient
sufragar *vt* (*ayudar*) to help; (*gastos*) to meet; (*proyecto*) to pay for
sufragio *nm* (*voto*) vote; (*derecho de voto*) suffrage
sufrido, -a *adj* (*de carácter fuerte*) tough; (*paciente*) long-suffering; (*tela*) hard-wearing; (*color*) that does not show the dirt; (*marido*) complaisant
sufrimiento *nm* suffering
sufrir *vt* (*padecer*) to suffer; (*soportar*) to bear, stand, put up with ▷ *vi* to suffer
sugerencia *nf* suggestion
sugerir *vt* to suggest; (*sutilmente*) to hint; (*idea*) to prompt
sugestión *nf* suggestion; (*sutil*) hint; (*poder*) hypnotic power
sugestionar *vt* to influence
sugestivo, -a *adj* stimulating; (*atractivo*) attractive; (*fascinante*) fascinating
suicida *adj* suicidal ▷ *nm/f* suicidal person;

(*muerto*) suicide, person who has committed suicide

suicidarse *vr* to commit suicide, kill o.s.

suicidio *nm* suicide

Suiza *nf* Switzerland

suizo, -a *adj, nm/f* Swiss ▷ *nm* sugared bun

sujeción *nf* subjection

sujetador *nm* fastener, clip; (*prenda femenina*) bra, brassiere

sujetar *vt* (*sostener*) to hold; (*fijar*) to fasten; (*detener*) to hold down; (*fig*) to subject, subjugate; (*pelo etc*) to keep o hold in place; (*papeles*) to fasten together; **sujetarse** *vr*: **~se a algo** to hold on to sth; **sujétame estos libros un momento** hold these books for me a moment

sujeto, -a *adj* fastened, secure ▷ *nm* (*Ling*) subject; (*individuo*) individual; (*fam: tipo*) character; **~ a** subject to

suma *nf* (*cantidad*) total, sum; (*de dinero*) sum; (*acto*) adding (up), addition; **en ~** in short; **~ y sigue** (*Com*) carry forward

sumamente *adv* extremely, exceedingly

sumar *vt* to add (up); (*reunir*) to collect, gather ▷ *vi* to add up

sumario, -a *adj* brief, concise ▷ *nm* summary

sumergir *vt* to submerge; (*hundir*) to sink; (*bañar*) to immerse, dip; **sumergirse** *vr* (*hundirse*) to sink beneath the surface

sumidero *nm* drain, sewer; (*Tec*) sump

suministrar *vt* to supply, provide

suministro *nm* supply; (*acto*) supplying, providing

sumir *vt* to sink, submerge; (*fig*) to plunge; **sumirse** *vr* (*objeto*) to sink; **~se en el estudio** to become absorbed in one's studies

sumisión *nf* (*acto*) submission; (*calidad*) submissiveness, docility

sumiso, -a *adj* submissive, docile

sumo, -a *adj* great, extreme; (*mayor*) highest, supreme ▷ *nm* sumo (wrestling); **a lo ~** at most

suntuoso, -a *adj* sumptuous, magnificent; (*lujoso*) lavish

supeditar *vt* to subordinate; (*sojuzgar*) to subdue; (*oprimir*) to oppress; **supeditarse** *vr*: **~se a** to subject o.s. to

super... *pref* super..., over...

súper *adj* (*fam*) super, great

superación *nf* (*tb*: **superación personal**) self-improvement

superar *vt* (*sobreponerse a*) to overcome; (*rebasar*) to surpass, do better than; (*pasar*) to go beyond; (*marca, récord*) to break; (*etapa: dejar atrás*) to get past; **superarse** *vr* to excel o.s.

superávit (*pl* **-s**) *nm* surplus

superficial *adj* superficial; (*medida*) surface *cpd*

superficie *nf* surface; (*área*) area; **grandes ~s** (*Com*) superstores

superfluo, -a *adj* superfluous

superintendente *nm/f* supervisor, superintendent

superior, -a *adj* (*piso, clase*) upper; (*temperatura, número, nivel*) higher; (*mejor: calidad, producto*) superior, better ▷ *nm/f* superior

superioridad *nf* superiority

superlativo, -a *adj, nm* superlative

supermercado *nm* supermarket

superponer *vt* (*Inform*) to overstrike

supersónico, -a *adj* supersonic

superstición *nf* superstition

supersticioso, -a *adj* superstitious

supervisar *vt* to supervise; (*Com*) to superintend

supervisor, a *nm/f* supervisor

supervivencia *nf* survival

superviviente *adj* surviving ▷ *nm/f* survivor

suplantar *vt* (*persona*) to supplant; (*hacerse pasar por otro*) to take the place of

suplementario, -a *adj* supplementary

suplemento *nm* supplement

suplente *adj* substitute; (*disponible*) reserve ▷ *nm/f* substitute

supletorio, -a *adj* supplementary; (*adicional*) extra ▷ *nm* supplement; **mesa supletoria** spare table

súplica *nf* request; (*Rel*) supplication; (*Jur: instancia*) petition; **súplicas** *nfpl* entreaties

suplicar *vt* (*cosa*) to beg (for), plead for; (*persona*) to beg, plead with; (*Jur*) to appeal to, petition

suplicio *nm* torture; (*tormento*) torment; (*emoción*) anguish; (*experiencia penosa*) ordeal

suplir *vt* (*compensar*) to make good, make up for; (*reemplazar*) to replace, substitute ▷ *vi*: **~ a** to take the place of, substitute for

suponer *vt* (*imaginar: indicando expectación*) to suppose; (*indicando decepción*) to think; (*significar*) to mean; (*conllevar*) to involve; **supongo que vendrá** I suppose she'll come; **supongo que sí** I suppose so; **suponíamos que no vendrías** we didn't think you would be coming; **te suponía más alto** I thought you'd be taller; **era de ~ que** ... it was to be expected that ...

suposición *nf* supposition

supositorio *nm* suppository

supremacía *nf* supremacy

supremo, -a *adj* supreme

supresión *nf* suppression; (*de derecho*) abolition; (*de dificultad*) removal; (*de palabra etc*) deletion; (*de restricción*) cancellation, lifting

suprimir *vt* to suppress; (*derecho, costumbre*) to abolish; (*dificultad*) to remove; (*palabra etc, Inform*) to delete; (*restricción*) to cancel, lift

supuesto, -a *pp de* **suponer** ▷ *adj* (*hipotético*) supposed; (*falso*) false ▷ *nm* assumption, hypothesis ▷ *conj*: **~ que** since; **dar por ~ algo** to take sth for granted; **por ~** of course

supurar *vi* to fester, suppurate

sur *adj* southern; (*rumbo*) southerly ▷ *nm* south; (*viento*) south wind

surcar *vt* to plough; (*superficie*) to cut, score

surco *nm* (*en metal, disco*) groove; (*Agr*) furrow

sureste = **sudeste**

surf *nm* surfing

surgir *vi* to arise, emerge; (*dificultad*) to come up, crop up

suroeste = **sudoeste**

surtido, -a *adj* mixed, assorted ▷ *nm* (*selección*) selection, assortment; (*abastecimiento*) supply, stock

surtidor *nm* (*chorro*) jet, spout; (*fuente*) fountain; ~ **de gasolina** petrol (*Brit*) o gas (*US*) pump

surtir *vt* to supply, provide; (*efecto*) to have, produce ▷ *vi* to spout, spurt; **surtirse** *vr*: ~**se de** to provide o.s. with

susceptible *adj* susceptible; (*sensible*) sensitive; ~ **de** capable of

suscitar *vt* to cause, provoke; (*discusión*) to start; (*duda, problema*) to raise; (*interés, sospechas*) to arouse

suscribir *vt* (*firmar*) to sign; (*respaldar*) to subscribe to, endorse; (*Com: acciones*) to take out an option on; **suscribirse** *vr* to subscribe; ~ **a algn a una revista** to take out a subscription to a journal for sb

suscripción *nf* subscription

susodicho, -a *adj* above-mentioned

suspender *vt* (*objeto*) to hang (up), suspend; (*trabajo*) to stop, suspend; (*Escol*) to fail

suspense *nm* suspense

suspensión *nf* suspension; (*fig*) stoppage, suspension; (*Jur*) stay; ~ **de fuego** o **de hostilidades** ceasefire, cessation of hostilities; ~ **de pagos** suspension of payments

suspenso, -a *adj* hanging, suspended; (*Escol*) failed ▷ *nm* (*Escol*) fail(ure); **quedar** o **estar en** ~ to be pending

suspicacia *nf* suspicion, mistrust

suspicaz *adj* suspicious, distrustful

suspirar *vi* to sigh

suspiro *nm* sigh

sustancia *nf* substance; ~ **gris** (*Anat*) grey matter; **sin** ~ lacking in substance, shallow

sustancial *adj* substantial

sustancioso, -a *adj* substantial; (*discurso*) solid

sustantivo, -a *adj* substantive; (*Ling*) substantival, noun *cpd* ▷ *nm* noun, substantive

sustentar *vt* (*alimentar*) to sustain, nourish; (*objeto*) to hold up, support; (*idea, teoría*) to maintain, uphold; (*fig*) to sustain, keep going

sustento *nm* support; (*alimento*) sustenance, food

sustituir *vt* to substitute, replace

sustituto, -a *nm/f* substitute, replacement

susto *nm* fright, scare; **dar un** ~ **a algn** to give sb a fright; **darse** o **pegarse un** ~ (*fam*) to get a fright

sustraer *vt* to remove, take away; (*Mat*) to subtract

sustrato *nm* substratum

susurrar *vi* to whisper

susurro *nm* whisper

sutil *adj* (*aroma*) subtle; (*tenue*) thin; (*hilo, hebra*) fine; (*olor*) delicate; (*brisa*) gentle; (*diferencia*) fine, subtle; (*inteligencia*) sharp, keen

sutileza *nf* subtlety; (*delgadez*) thinness; (*delicadeza*) delicacy; (*agudeza*) keenness

suturar *vt* to suture; (*coser con puntos*) to stitch

suyo, -a *adj* (*con artículo o después del verbo ser: de él*) his; (: *de ella*) hers; (: *de ellos, ellas*) theirs; (: *de usted, ustedes*) yours; (*después de un nombre: de él*) of his; (: *de ella*) of hers; (: *de ellos, ellas*) of theirs; (: *de usted, ustedes*) of yours; **lo** ~ (what is) his; (*su parte*) his share, what he deserves; **los ~s** (*su familia*) one's family o relations; (*sus partidarios*) one's own people o supporters; ~ **afectísimo** (*en carta*) yours faithfully o sincerely; **de** ~ in itself; **eso es muy** ~ that's just like him; **hacer de las suyas** to get up to one's old tricks; **ir a la suya, ir a lo** ~ to go one's own way; **salirse con la suya** to get one's way

Tt

Tabacalera *nf* Spanish state tobacco monopoly
tabaco *nm* tobacco; (*fam*) cigarettes *pl*
tábano *nm* horsefly
taberna *nf* bar
tabernero, -a *nm/f* (*encargado*) publican; (*camarero*) barman/barmaid
tabique *nm* (*pared*) thin wall; (*separando habitaciones*) partition
tabla *nf* (*de madera*) plank; (*estante*) shelf; (*de anuncios*) board; (*lista, catálogo*) list; (*mostrador*) counter; (*de vestido*) pleat; (*Arte*) panel; **tablas** *nfpl* (*Taur, Teat*) boards; **hacer ~s** to draw
tablado *nm* (*plataforma*) platform; (*suelo*) plank floor; (*Teat*) stage
tablao *nm* (*tb:* **tablao flamenco**) flamenco show
tablero *nm* (*de madera*) plank, board; (*pizarra*) blackboard; (*de ajedrez, damas*) board; (*Auto*) dashboard
tableta *nf* (*Med*) tablet; (*de chocolate*) bar
tablón *nm* (*de suelo*) plank; (*de techo*) beam; (*de anuncios*) notice board
tabú *nm* taboo
tabular *vt* to tabulate; (*Inform*) to tab
taburete *nm* stool
tacaño, -a *adj* (*avaro*) mean; (*astuto*) crafty
tacha *nf* (*defecto*) flaw, defect; (*Tec*) stud; **poner ~ a** to find fault with; **sin ~** flawless
tachar *vt* (*borrar*) to cross out; (*corregir*) to correct; (*criticar*) to criticize; **~ de** to accuse of
tacho *nm* (*CS: cubo*) bucket; (*: olla*) pan; **~ de la basura** (*CS*) dustbin (*Brit*), trashcan (*US*)
tácito, -a *adj* tacit; (*acuerdo*) unspoken; (*Ling*) understood; (*ley*) unwritten
taciturno, -a *adj* (*callado*) silent; (*malhumorado*) sullen
taco *nm* (*Billar*) cue; (*libro de billetes*) book; (*manojo de billetes*) wad; (*CS*) heel; (*tarugo*) peg; (*fam: bocado*) snack; (*: palabrota*) swear word; (*: trago de vino*) swig; (*Méx*) filled tortilla; **armarse o hacerse un ~** to get into a mess
tacón *nm* heel; **de ~ alto** high-heeled
taconear *vi* (*dar golpecitos*) to tap with one's heels; (*Mil etc*) to click one's heels
taconeo *nm* (heel) tapping *o* clicking
táctico, -a *adj* tactical ▷ *nf* tactics *pl*
tacto *nm* touch; (*acción*) touching; (*fig*) tact
tafetán *nm* taffeta; **tafetanes** *nmpl* (*fam*) frills; **~ adhesivo** *o* **inglés** sticking plaster
tafilete *nm* morocco leather
tahona *nf* (*panadería*) bakery; (*molino*) flourmill
tahur *nm* gambler; (*pey*) cheat
taimado, -a *adj* (*astuto*) sly; (*resentido*) sullen
taita *nm* dad, daddy
tajada *nf* slice; (*fam*) rake-off; **sacar ~** to get one's share
tajante *adj* sharp; (*negativa*) emphatic; **es una persona ~** he's an emphatic person
tajar *vt* to cut, slice
tajo *nm* (*corte*) cut; (*filo*) cutting edge; (*Geo*) cleft
tal *adj* such ▷ *pron*: **hablábamos de que si ~ de si cual** we were talking about this, that and the other ▷ *adv*: **~ como: lo dejé ~ como estaba** I left it just as it was; **~ cual: es ~ cual ella siempre deseó** it's just as she had always wanted ▷ *conj*: **con ~ (de) que** as long as, provided (that); **¡en el aeropuerto había ~ confusión!** there was such confusion at the airport!; **en el pueblo no existía ~ persona** there was no such person in the village; **un ~ García** a man called García; **~ vez** perhaps; **y como ~, tiene que pagar matrícula** and as such, he has to pay the fees; **ella sigue ~ cual** she hasn't changed; **hola, ¿qué ~?** hi, how are things?; **¿qué ~ si lo compramos?** how about buying it?; **con ~ de que regreséis antes de las once** as long as you get back before eleven
taladradora *nf* drill; **~ neumática** pneumatic drill
taladrar *vt* to drill; (*fig: suj: ruido*) to pierce
taladro *nm* (*gen*) drill; (*hoyo*) drill hole; **~ neumático** pneumatic drill
talante *nm* (*humor*) mood; (*voluntad*) will, willingness
talar *vt* to fell, cut down; (*fig*) to devastate
talco *nm* (*polvos*) talcum powder; (*Mineralogía*) talc
talega *nf* sack
talego *nm* sack; **tener ~** (*fam*) to have money
talento *nm* talent; (*capacidad*) ability; (*don*) gift
Talgo *nm abr* (*Ferro:* = *tren articulado ligero Goicoechea-Oriol*) high-speed train
talismán *nm* talisman
talla *nf* (*estatura, fig, Med*) height, stature; (*de ropa*) size, fitting; (*palo*) measuring rod; (*Arte: de madera*) carving; (*de piedra*) sculpture

tallado, -a adj carved ▷ nm (de madera) carving; (de piedra) sculpture

tallar vt (trabajar) to work, carve; (grabar) to engrave; (medir) to measure; (repartir) to deal ▷ vi to deal

tallarín nm noodle

talle nm (Anat) waist; (medida) size; (física) build; (: de mujer) figure; (fig) appearance; **de ~ esbelto** with a slim figure

taller nm (Tec) workshop; (fábrica) factory; (Auto) garage; (de artista) studio

tallo nm (de planta) stem; (de hierba) blade; (brote) shoot; (col) cabbage; (Culin) candied peel

talón nm (gen) heel; (Com) counterfoil; (Tec) rim; **~ de Aquiles** Achilles heel

talonario nm (de cheques) cheque book; (de billetes) book of tickets; (de recibos) receipt book

tamal nm tamale, crushed maize and minced meat stew, wrapped in maize husks

tamaño, -a adj (tan grande) such a big; (tan pequeño) such a small ▷ nm size; **de ~ natural** full-size; **¿qué ~ tiene?** what size is it?

tamarindo nm tamarind

tambalearse vr (persona) to stagger; (mueble) to wobble; (vehículo) to sway

también adv also, too, as well; **canta flamenco y ~ baila** he sings flamenco and he also dances, he sings flamenco and dances too o as well; **¿usted ~?** you too?, you as well?; **estoy cansado — yo ~** I'm tired — so am I o me too

tambor nm drum; (Anat) eardrum; **~ del freno** brake drum; **~ magnético** (Inform) magnetic drum

tamiz nm sieve

tamizar vt to sieve

tampoco adv nor, neither; **yo ~ lo compré** I didn't buy it either

tampón nm plug; (Med) tampon

tan adv so; **~ es así que** so much so that; **¡qué cosa ~ rara!** how strange!; **no es una idea ~ buena** it is not such a good idea

tanate nm (CAm, Méx: cesto) basket

tanatorio nm (privado) funeral home o parlour; (público) mortuary

tanda nf (gen) series; (de inyecciones) course; (juego) set; (turno) shift; (grupo) gang

tanga nm (bikini) tanga; (ropa interior) tanga briefs

tangente nf tangent; **salirse por la ~** to go off at a tangent

Tánger n Tangier

tangible adj tangible

tango nm tango

tanque nm (gen) tank; (Aut, Náut) tanker

tanqueta nf (Mil) small tank, armoured vehicle

tantear vt (calcular) to reckon (up); (medir) to take the measure of; (probar) to test, try out; (tomar la medida: persona) to take the measurements of; (considerar) to weigh up ▷ vi (Deporte) to score

tanteo nm (cálculo aproximado) (rough) calculation; (prueba) test, trial; (Deporte) scoring; (adivinanzas) guesswork; **al ~** by trial and error

tanto, -a adj, pron (en singular) so much, as much; (en plural) so many, as many ▷ adv (referido a cantidad) so much, as much; (referido a tiempo) so long, as long ▷ nm (suma) so much, certain amount; (Deporte: punto) point; (: gol) goal; **ahora no bebo tanta leche** I don't drink so much milk now; **¡tengo tantas cosas que hacer hoy!** I have so many things to do today!; **no recibe tantas llamadas como yo** he doesn't get as many calls as I do; **¡~ gusto!** how do you do?; **cada uno paga ~** each one pays so much; **gano ~ como tú** I earn as much as you; **no necesitamos tantas** we don't need so many; **treinta y ~s** thirty-odd; **estuvieron fuera hasta las tantas** they stayed out until all hours; **es uno de ~s** it's one of many; **~ tú como yo** both you and I; **~ más ... cuanto que** it's all the more ... because ...; **~ mejor/peor** so much the better/the worse; **~ si viene como si va** whether he comes or whether he goes; **~ es así que ...** so much so that ...; **me he vuelto ronco de o con ~ hablar** I have become hoarse with so much talking; **entre ~** meanwhile; **no es para ~** it's not as bad as that; **por (lo) ~** therefore; **estar al ~ de los acontecimientos** to be fully abreast of events; **es un ~ difícil** it's a bit awkward; **~ por ciento** percentage

tapa nf (de caja, olla) lid; (de botella) top; (de libro) cover; (de comida) snack

tapadera nf lid, cover

tapar vt (cubrir) to cover; (recipiente, cazuela) to put the lid on; (cara) to cover up, hide; (en cama) to wrap up; (LAm: diente) to fill; **taparse** vr (con ropa) to wrap o.s. up; **la tapé con una manta** I covered her with a blanket; **tapa la olla** put the lid on the pan; **me estás tapando el sol** you're keeping the sun off me; **tápate bien que hace frío** wrap up well as it's cold

tapete nm table cover; **estar sobre el ~** (fig) to be under discussion

tapia nf (garden) wall

tapiar vt to wall in

tapicería nf tapestry; (para muebles) upholstery; (tienda) upholsterer's (shop)

tapiz nm (alfombra) carpet; (tela tejida) tapestry

tapizar vt (pared) to wallpaper; (suelo) to carpet; (muebles) to upholster

tapón nm (corcho) stopper; (Tec) plug; (Med) tampon; **~ de rosca** o **de tuerca** screw-top

taquigrafía nf shorthand

taquígrafo, -a nm/f shorthand writer

taquilla nf (de estación etc) booking office; (de teatro) box office; (suma recogida) takings pl; (archivador) filing cabinet

taquillero, -a adj: **función taquillera** box office success ▷ nm/f ticket clerk

taquimecanografía nf shorthand and typing

tara nf (defecto) defect; (Com) tare

tarántula nf tarantula

tararear vi to hum

tardanza nf (demora) delay; (lentitud) slowness

tardar vi (tomar tiempo) to take a long time; (llegar tarde) to be late; (demorar) to delay; **¿tarda**

mucho el tren? does the train take long?; **a
más ~** at the (very) latest; **~ en hacer algo** to be
slow o take a long time to do sth; **no tardes en
venir** come soon, come before long
tarde *adv* *(hora)* late; *(fuera de tiempo)* too late
▷ *nf* *(de día)* afternoon; *(de noche)* evening; **~ o
temprano** sooner or later; **de ~ en ~** from time
to time; **¡buenas ~s!** *(de día)* good afternoon!;
(de noche) good evening!; **a** o **por la ~** in the
afternoon; in the evening
tardío, -a *adj* *(retrasado)* late; *(lento)* slow (to
arrive)
tardo, -a *adj* *(lento)* slow; *(torpe)* dull; **~ de oído**
hard of hearing
tarea *nf* task; **tareas** *nfpl* *(Escol)* homework *sg*
tarifa *nf* *(lista de precios)* price list; *(Com)* tariff;
~ a destajo piece rate; **~ básica** basic rate; **~
completa** all-in cost; **~ doble** double time
tarima *nf* platform
tarjeta *nf* card; **~ comercial** *(Com)* calling card; **~
de crédito/de Navidad** credit/Christmas card; **~
de circuitos** *(Inform)* circuit board; **~ de cliente**
loyalty card; **~ dinero** cash card; **~ de gráficos/
de sonido/de vídeo** *(Inform)* graphics/sound/
video card; **~ postal** postcard
tarot *nm* tarot
tarro *nm* jar, pot
tarta *nf* *(pastel)* cake; *(torta)* tart
tartamudear *vi* to stutter, stammer
tartamudo, -a *adj* stuttering, stammering
▷ *nm/f* stutterer, stammerer
tártaro *adj, nm* Tartar ▷ *nm* *(Química)* tartar
tasa *nf* *(precio)* (fixed) price, rate; *(valoración)*
valuation; *(medida, norma)* measure, standard;
de ~ cero *(Com)* zero-rated; **~ básica** *(Com)*
basic rate; **~ de cambio** exchange rate; **~ de
crecimiento** growth rate; **~ de interés/de
nacimiento** rate of interest/birth rate; **~
de rendimiento** *(Com)*: **~s universitarias**
university fees, rate of return
tasación *nf* assessment, valuation; *(fig)*
appraisal
tasador, a *nm/f* valuer; *(Com: de impuestos)*
assessor
tasar *vt* *(arreglar el precio)* to fix a price for; *(valorar)*
to value, assess; *(limitar)* to limit
tasca *nf* *(fam)* pub
tata *nf* *(LAm fam)* dad, daddy, pop *(US)*
tatarabuelo, -a *nm/f* great-great-grandfather/
mother; **los ~s** one's great-great-grandparents
tatuaje *nm* *(dibujo)* tattoo; *(acto)* tattooing
tatuar *vt* to tattoo
taurino, -a *adj* bullfighting *cpd*
Tauro *nm* Taurus
tauromaquia *nf* (art of) bullfighting
taxi *nm* taxi
taxista *nm/f* taxi driver
taza *nf* cup; *(de retrete)* bowl; **~ para café** coffee
cup
tazón *nm* mug, large cup
te *pron* *(complemento de objeto)* you; *(complemento
indirecto)* (to) you; *(reflexivo)* (to) yourself; **¿te**

duele mucho el brazo? does your arm hurt
a lot?; **te equivocas** you're wrong; **¡cálmate!**
calm yourself!
té *(pl* **tés)** *nm* tea
tea *nf* *(antorcha)* torch
teatral *adj* theatre *cpd*; *(fig)* theatrical
teatro *nm* theatre; *(Literatura)* plays *pl*, drama; **el
~ cinema** the theatre, acting; **~ de aficionados/
de variedades** amateur/variety theatre,
vaudeville theater *(US)*; **hacer un ~** *(fig)* to make
a fuss
tebeo *nm* children's comic
techo *nm* *(externo)* roof; *(interno)* ceiling
tecla *nf* *(Inform, Mus, Tip)* key; *(Inform)*: **~ de
anulación/de borrar** cancel/delete key; **~ de
control/de edición** control/edit key; **~s de
control direccional del cursor** cursor control
keys; **~ de retorno/de tabulación** return/tab
key; **~ del cursor** cursor key; **~ con flecha** arrow
key; **~ programable** user-defined key
teclado *nm* keyboard *(tb Inform)*; **~ numérico**
(Inform) numeric keypad
teclear *vi* to strum; *(fam)* to drum ▷ *vt* *(Inform)* to
key (in), type in, keyboard
tecleo *nm* *(Mús: sonido)* strumming; *(: forma de
tocar)* fingering; *(fam)* drumming
técnico, -a *adj* technical ▷ *nm* technician;
(experto) expert ▷ *nf* *(procedimientos)* technique;
(arte, oficio) craft
tecnicolor *nm* Technicolor®
tecnócrata *nm/f* technocrat
tecnología *nf* technology; **~ de estado
sólido** *(Inform)* solid-state technology; **~ de la
información** information technology
tecnológico, -a *adj* technological
tecolote *nm* *(CAm, Méx: búho)* owl
tedio *nm* *(aburrimiento)* boredom; *(apatía)* apathy;
(fastidio) depression
tedioso, -a *adj* *(aburrido)* boring; *(cansado)*
wearisome, tedious
teja *nf* *(azulejo)* tile; *(Bot)* lime (tree)
tejado *nm* *(tiled)* roof
tejano, -a *adj, nm/f* Texan ▷ *nmpl*: **~s** *(vaqueros)*
jeans
tejemaneje *nm* *(actividad)* bustle; *(lío)* fuss, to-do;
(intriga) intrigue
tejer *vt* to weave; *(tela de araña)* to spin; *(LAm)* to
knit; *(fig)* to fabricate ▷ *vi*: **~ y destejer** to chop
and change
tejido *nm* fabric; *(estofa, tela)* (knitted) material;
(Anat) tissue; *(textura)* texture
tela *nf* *(material)* material; *(de fruta, en líquido)* skin;
(del ojo) film; **hay ~ para rato** there's lots to talk
about; **poner en ~ de juicio** to (call in) question;
~ de araña cobweb, spider's web
telar *nm* *(máquina)* loom; *(de teatro)* gridiron;
telares *nmpl* textile mill *sg*
telaraña *nf* cobweb, spider's web
tele *nf* *(fam)* TV
telecomunicación *nf* telecommunication
teleconferencia *nf* *(reunión)* teleconference;
(sistema) teleconferencing

telecontrol nm remote control
telediario nm television news
teledifusión nf (television) broadcast
teledirigido, -a adj remote-controlled
teléf. abr (= teléfono) tel
teleférico nm (tren) cable-railway; (en estación de esquí) ski-lift
telefonear vi to telephone
telefónico, -a adj telephone cpd ▷ nf: **Telefónica** (Esp) Spanish national telephone company, ≈ British Telecom
telefonista nm/f telephonist
teléfono nm (tele)phone; **está hablando por ~** he's on the phone; **~ móvil** (Esp) o **celular** (LAm) mobile phone
telegrafía nf telegraphy
telégrafo nm telegraph; (fam: persona) telegraph boy
telegrama nm telegram
teleimpresor nm teleprinter
telenovela nf soap (opera)
teleobjetivo nm telephoto lens
telepatía nf telepathy
telepático, -a adj telepathic
telescópico, -a adj telescopic
telescopio nm telescope
telesilla nm chairlift
telespectador, a nm/f viewer
telesquí nm ski-lift
teletex(to) nm teletext
teletipo nm teletype(writer)
teletrabajo nm teleworking
televentas nfpl telesales
televidente nm/f viewer
televisar vt to televise
televisión nf television; **~ en color/por satélite** colour/satellite television; **~ digital** digital television
televisor nm television set
télex nm telex; **máquina ~** telex (machine); **enviar por ~** to telex
telón nm curtain; **~ de acero** (Pol) iron curtain; **~ de boca/seguridad** front/safety curtain; **~ de fondo** backcloth, background
telonero, -a nm/f support act; **los ~s** (Mús) the support band
tema nm (asunto) subject, topic; (Mús) theme; **~s de actualidad** current affairs
temario nm (Escol) set of topics; (de una conferencia) agenda
temático, -a adj thematic ▷ nf subject matter
temblar vi to shake, tremble; (de frío) to shiver
tembleque adj shaking ▷ nm shaking
temblón, -ona adj shaking
temblor nm trembling; (de tierra) earthquake
tembloroso, -a adj trembling
temer vt to fear ▷ vi to be afraid; **temo que Juan llegue tarde** I am afraid Juan may be late
temerario, -a adj (imprudente) rash; (descuidado) reckless; (arbitrario) hasty
temeridad nf (imprudencia) rashness; (audacia) boldness

temeroso, -a adj (miedoso) fearful; (que inspira temor) frightful
temible adj fearsome
temor nm (miedo) fear; (duda) suspicion
témpano nm (Mús) kettledrum; **~ de hielo** ice floe
temperamento nm temperament; **tener ~** to be temperamental
temperatura nf temperature
tempestad nf storm; **~ en un vaso de agua** (fig) storm in a teacup
tempestuoso, -a adj stormy
templado, -a adj (moderado) moderate; (: en el comer) frugal; (: en el beber) abstemious; (agua) lukewarm; (clima) mild; (Mús) in tune, well-tuned
templanza nf moderation; (en el beber) abstemiousness; (del clima) mildness
templar vt (moderar) to moderate; (furia) to restrain; (calor) to reduce; (solución) to dilute; (afinar) to tune (up); (acero) to temper ▷ vi to moderate; **templarse** vr to be restrained
temple nm (humor) mood; (coraje) courage; (ajuste) tempering; (afinación) tuning; (pintura) tempera
templo nm (iglesia) church; (pagano etc) temple; **~ metodista** Methodist chapel
temporada nf time, period; (estación, Deporte) season; **en plena ~** at the height of the season
temporal adj (no permanente) temporary; (Rel) temporal ▷ nm storm
tempranero, -a adj (Bot) early; (persona) early-rising
temprano, -a adj early ▷ adv early; (demasiado pronto) too soon, too early
tenacidad nf (gen) tenacity; (dureza) toughness; (terquedad) stubbornness
tenacillas nfpl (gen) tongs; (para el pelo) curling tongs; (Med) forceps
tenaz adj (material) tough; (persona) tenacious; (pegajoso) sticky; (terco) stubborn
tenaza(s) nf(pl) (Med) forceps; (Tec) pliers; (Zool) pincers
tendedero nm (para ropa) drying-place; (cuerda) clothes line
tendencia nf tendency; (proceso) trend; **tener ~ a** to tend o have a tendency to; **~ imperante** prevailing tendency; **~ del mercado** run of the market
tendencioso, -a adj tendentious
tender vt (extender) to spread out; (ropa) to hang out; (vía férrea, cable) to lay; (cuerda) to stretch; (trampa) to set ▷ vi to tend; **tenderse** vr to lie down; **~ la cama/la mesa** (LAm) to make the bed/lay the table
tenderete nm (puesto) stall; (carretilla) barrow; (exposición) display of goods
tendero, -a nm/f shopkeeper
tendido, -a adj (acostado) lying down, flat; (colgado) hanging ▷ nm (ropa) washing; (Taur) front rows pl of seats; (colocación) laying; (Arq) enyesado) coat of plaster; **a galope ~** flat out
tendón nm tendon

tenebroso, -a adj (oscuro) dark; (fig) gloomy; (siniestro) sinister

tenedor nm (Culin) fork; (poseedor) holder; ~ **de acciones** shareholder; ~ **de libros** book-keeper; ~ **de póliza** policyholder

teneduría nf keeping; ~ **de libros** book-keeping

tenencia nf (de casa) tenancy; (de oficio) tenure; (de propiedad) possession; ~ **asegurada** security of tenure; ~ **ilícita de armas** illegal possession of weapons

tener vt **1** (poseer) to have, have got (esp Brit); **¿tienes dinero?** do you have any money?, have you got any money?; **¿tienes un boli?** do you have a pen?, have you got a pen?; **va a ~ un niño** she's going to have a baby; **¡ten (o tenga)!, ¡aquí tienes (o tiene)!** here you are!
2 (con edad, medidas) to be; **tiene 7 años** she's 7 (years old); **tiene 15 cm de largo** it's 15 cm long
3 (con sensaciones, sentimientos): ~ **sed/hambre/frío/calor** to be thirsty/hungry/cold/hot; ~ **celos** to be jealous; ~ **cariño a algn** to be fond of sb
4: ~ **cuidado** to be careful; ~ **razón** to be right; ~ **suerte** to be lucky
5 (considerar): ~ **en mucho a algn** to think very highly of sb
6 (+ pp, + adj, + gerundio): **tengo terminada ya la mitad del trabajo** I've done half the work already; **tenía el sombrero puesto** he had his hat on; **tenía pensado llamarte** I had been thinking of phoning you; **nos tiene hartos** we're fed up with him; **me ha tenido tres horas esperando** he kept me waiting three hours
7: ~ **que hacer algo** to have to do sth; **tengo que acabar este trabajo hoy** I have to finish this job today; **no tienes por qué ir** there's no reason why you should go
8 (locuciones): **eso no tiene nada que ver** that's got nothing to do with it; **¿conque ésas tenemos?** so it's like that, then?; **no las tengo todas conmigo** I'm a bit unsure (about it); **lo tiene difícil** he'll have a hard job
tenerse vr **1**: ~**se en pie** to stand up
2: ~**se por** to think o.s.; **se tiene por un gran cantante** he thinks himself a great singer

tenia nf tapeworm

teniente nm lieutenant; ~ **coronel** lieutenant colonel

tenis nm tennis; ~ **de mesa** table tennis

tenista nm/f tennis player

tenor nm (Mús) tenor; **a ~ de** on the lines of

tensar vt to tauten; (arco) to draw

tensión nf tension; (Tec) stress; (Med): **tener la ~ alta** to have high blood pressure; ~ **arterial** blood pressure; ~ **nerviosa** nervous strain

tenso, -a adj tense; (relaciones) strained

tentación nf temptation

tentáculo nm tentacle

tentador, a adj tempting ▷ nm/f tempter/temptress

tentar vt (tocar) to touch, feel; (seducir) to tempt;

(atraer) to attract; (probar) to try (out); (Med) to probe; ~ **hacer algo** to try to do sth

tentativa nf attempt; ~ **de asesinato** attempted murder

tentempié nm (fam) snack

tenue adj (delgado) thin, slender; (alambre) fine; (insustancial) tenuous; (sonido) faint; (neblina) light; (lazo, vínculo) slight

teñir vt to dye; (fig) to tinge; ~**se el pelo** to dye one's hair

teología nf theology

teorema nm theorem

teoría nf theory; **en ~** in theory

teóricamente adv theoretically

teórico, -a adj theoretic(al) ▷ nm/f theoretician, theorist

teorizar vi to theorize

tequila nm o f tequila

terapéutica nf therapeutics sg; ver tb **terapéutico**

terapéutico adj therapeutic(al); ver tb **terapéutica**

terapia nf therapy; ~ **laboral** occupational therapy

tercer adj ver **tercero**

tercermundista adj Third World cpd

tercero, -a adj third; (delante de nmsg): **tercer** nm (árbitro) mediator; (Jur) third party

terceto nm trio

terciado, -a adj slanting; **azúcar ~** brown sugar

terciar vt (Mat) to divide into three; (inclinarse) to slope; (llevar) to wear across one's chest ▷ vi (participar) to take part; (hacer de árbitro) to mediate; **terciarse** vr to arise

terciario, -a adj tertiary

tercio nm third

terciopelo nm velvet

terco, -a adj obstinate, stubborn; (material) tough

tergal® nm Terylene®

tergiversar vt to distort ▷ vi to prevaricate

termal adj thermal

termas nfpl hot springs

térmico, -a adj thermic, thermal, heat cpd

terminación nf (final) end; (conclusión) conclusion, ending

terminal adj terminal ▷ nm (Elec, Inform) terminal ▷ nf (Aviat, Ferro) terminal; ~ **conversacional** interactive terminal; ~ **de pantalla** visual display unit

terminante adj (final) final, definitive; (tajante) categorical

terminar vt (libro, trabajo) to finish ▷ vi (curso, año, película) to end, come to an end; **terminarse** vr (curso, año, película) to end, come to an end; (comida, existencias) to run out; **¿has terminado?** have you finished?; **cuando terminó de hablar** when he finished talking; **esto acabará en tragedia** this will end in tragedy; ~ **por hacer algo** to end up (by) doing sth; ~**on peleándose** they ended up fighting; **se nos ha terminado el café** we've run out of coffee

término nm (fin) end, conclusion; (palabra) term;

(de un contrato) term; **al ~ de la entrevista** at
the end of the interview; **poner ~ a algo** to put
an end to sth; **un ~ médico** a medical term;
en otros ~s in other words; **por ~ medio** on
average; **en último ~** (a fin de cuentas) in the last
analysis; (como último recurso) as a last resort
terminología nf terminology
termita nf termite
termo nm Thermos® (flask)
termodinámico, -a adj thermodynamic ▷ nf
thermodynamics sg
termómetro nm thermometer
termonuclear adj thermonuclear
termostato nm thermostat
ternera nf (carne) veal; ver tb **ternero**
ternero, -a nm/f (animal) calf; ver tb **ternera**
terno nm (traje) three-piece suit; (conjunto) set of
three
ternura nf (trato) tenderness; (palabra)
endearment; (cariño) fondness
terquedad nf obstinacy; (dureza) harshness
terrado nm terrace
terraplén nm (Agr) terrace; (Ferro) embankment;
(Mil) rampart; (cuesta) slope
terráqueo, -a adj: **globo ~** globe
terrateniente nm landowner
terraza nf (balcón) balcony; (azotea) flat roof; (Agr)
terrace
terremoto nm earthquake
terrenal adj earthly
terreno nm (extensión de tierra) land; (para cultivar)
plot, field; (para construir) plot of land; (suelo) soil;
(fig: de investigación, estudio) field; **una granja con
mucho ~** a farm with a lot of land; **~s plantados
de naranjos** fields planted with orange
trees; **en el ~ de la informática** in the field of
computing science; **ceder/perder ~** to give/lose
ground; **preparar el ~ (a/para algo)** (fig) to pave
the way (for sth); **~ de juego** pitch
terrestre adj terrestrial; (ruta) land cpd
terrible adj (espantoso) terrible; (aterrador)
dreadful; (tremendo) awful
territorial adj territorial
territorio nm territory; **~ bajo mandato**
mandated territory
terrón nm (de azúcar) lump; (de tierra) clod, lump;
terrones nmpl land sg
terror nm terror
terrorífico, -a adj terrifying
terrorismo nm terrorism
terrorista adj, nm/f terrorist
terroso, -a adj earthy
terruño nm (pedazo) clod; (parcela) plot; (fig) native
soil; **apego al ~** attachment to one's native soil
terso, -a adj (liso) smooth; (pulido) polished; (fig:
estilo) flowing
tersura nf smoothness; (brillo) shine
tertulia nf (reunión informal) social gathering;
(grupo) group, circle; (sala) clubroom; **~ literaria**
literary circle
tesina nf dissertation
tesis nf inv thesis

tesón nm (firmeza) firmness; (tenacidad) tenacity
tesorero, -a nm/f treasurer
tesoro nm treasure; **T~ público** (Pol) Exchequer
test (pl **-s**) nm test
testaferro nm figurehead
testamentaría nf execution of a will
testamentario, -a adj testamentary ▷ nm/f
executor/executrix
testamento nm will
testar vi to make a will
testarudo, -a adj stubborn
testículo nm testicle
testificar vt to testify; (fig) to attest ▷ vi to give
evidence
testigo nm/f witness; **poner a algn por ~** to cite
sb as a witness; **~ de cargo/descargo** witness
for the prosecution/defence; **~ ocular** eye
witness
testimonial adj (prueba) testimonial; (gesto)
token
testimoniar vt to testify to; (fig) to show
testimonio nm testimony; **en ~ de** as a token
o mark of; **falso ~** perjured evidence, false
witness
teta nf (de biberón) teat; (Anat) nipple; (fam) breast;
(fam!) tit (!)
tétanos nm tetanus
tetera nf teapot; (para hervir agua) kettle
tetilla nf (Anat) nipple; (de biberón) teat
tétrico, -a adj gloomy, dismal
textil adj textile
texto nm text
textual adj textual; **palabras ~es** exact words
textura nf (de tejido) texture; (de mineral) structure
tez nf (cutis) complexion; (color) colouring
ti pron you; (reflexivo) yourself
tía nf (pariente) aunt; (mujer cualquiera) girl, bird
(col)
tibieza nf (temperatura) tepidness; (fig) coolness
tibio, -a adj lukewarm, tepid
tiburón nm shark
tic nm (ruido) click; (de reloj) tick; **~ nervioso** (Med)
nervous tic
tictac nm (de reloj) tick tock
tiempo nm (cronológico) time; (meteorológico)
weather; (Ling) tense; **no tengo ~** I don't have
time; **hace mucho ~ que no la veo** I haven't
seen her for a long time; **¿cuánto ~ hace que
vives aquí?** how long have you been living
here?; **hace ~ que lo compré** I bought it some
time ago; **al poco ~** soon after; **no llegaremos
a ~** we won't get there in time; **al mismo ~** at
the same time; **a su debido ~** in due course;
cada cierto ~ every so often; **deberías llegar
con ~** you should arrive in good time; **con el
~ eventually; **hacer ~** to while away the time;
metieron el gol durante el segundo ~ they
scored the goal during the second half; **trabajar
a ~ parcial/completo** to work part time/full
time; **motor de 2 ~s** two-stroke engine; **en mis
~s** in my time; **en los buenos ~s** in the good
old days; **hace buen/mal ~** the weather is fine/

bad; **~ compartido** (*Inform*) time sharing; **~ de ejecución** (*Inform*) run time; **~ libre** spare time; *ver tb* **perder**

tienda *nf* shop; (*más grande*) store; (*Náut*) awning; **~ de campaña** tent

tienta *nf* (*Med*) probe; (*fig*) tact; **andar a ~s** to grope one's way along

tiento *nm* (*tacto*) touch; (*precaución*) wariness; (*pulso*) steady hand; (*Zool*) feeler, tentacle

tierno, -a *adj* (*blando, dulce*) tender; (*fresco*) fresh

tierra *nf* (*planeta, arena*) earth; (*para macetas, plantas*) soil; (*terreno*) land; (*suelo*) ground; (*país, región*) land; (*Elec*) earth, ground (*US*); **la T~** the Earth; **trabajan la ~** they work the land; **viajar por ~** to travel by land; **~ adentro** inland; **caer a ~** to fall down; **no es de estas ~s** he's not from these parts; **echar algo por ~** to ruin something; **echar ~ a un asunto** to hush an affair up; **~ natal** native land; **(la) T~ Santa** the Holy Land

tieso, -a *adj* (*rígido*) rigid; (*duro*) stiff; (*fig: testarudo*) stubborn; (*fam: orgulloso*) conceited ▷ *adv* strongly

tiesto *nm* flowerpot

tifoidea *nf* typhoid

tifón *nm* (*huracán*) typhoon; (*de mar*) tidal wave

tifus *nm* typhus

tigre *nm* tiger; (*LAm*) jaguar

tijera *nf* (*Zool*) claw; **de ~** folding; **tijeras** *nfpl* scissors; (*para plantas*) shears; **unas ~s** a pair of scissors

tijeretear *vt* to snip ▷ *vi* (*fig*) to meddle

tildar *vt*: **~ de** to brand as

tilde *nf* (*defecto*) defect; (*trivialidad*) triviality; (*Tip*) tilde

tilín *nm* tinkle

tilo *nm* lime tree

timar *vt* (*robar*) to steal; (*estafar*) to swindle; (*persona*) to con; **timarse** *vr* (*fam*) to make eyes; (*con algn*) at sb

timbal *nm* small drum

timbrar *vt* to stamp; (*sellar*) to seal; (*carta*) to postmark

timbre *nm* (*sello*) stamp; (*campanilla*) bell; (*tono*) timbre; (*Com*) stamp duty

timidez *nf* shyness

tímido, -a *adj* shy, timid

timo *nm* swindle; **dar un ~ a algn** to swindle sb

timón *nm* helm, rudder; (*LAm*) steering wheel; **coger el ~** (*fig*) to take charge

timonel *nm* helmsman

tímpano *nm* (*Anat*) eardrum; (*Mús*) small drum

tina *nf* tub; (*LAm: baño*) bath(tub)

tinaja *nf* large earthen jar

tinglado *nm* (*cobertizo*) shed; (*fig: truco*) trick; (*intriga*) intrigue; **armar un ~** to lay a plot

tinieblas *nfpl* darkness *sg*; (*sombras*) shadows; **estamos en ~ sobre sus proyectos** (*fig*) we are in the dark about his plans

tino *nm* (*habilidad*) skill; (*Mil*) marksmanship; (*juicio*) insight; (*moderación*) moderation; **sin ~** immoderately; **coger el ~** to get the feel *o* hang of it

tinta *nf* ink; (*Tec*) dye; (*Arte*) colour; **tintas** *nfpl* (*fig*) shades; **~ china** Indian ink; **medias ~s** (*fig*) half measures; **saber algo de buena ~** to have sth on good authority

tinte *nm* (*acto*) dyeing; (*fig*) tinge; (*barniz*) veneer

tintero *nm* inkwell; **se le quedó en el ~** he clean forgot about it

tintinear *vt* to tinkle

tinto, -a *adj* (*teñido*) dyed; (*manchado*) stained ▷ *nm* red wine

tintorería *nf* dry cleaner's

tintura *nf* (*acto*) dyeing; (*Química*) dye; (*farmacéutico*) tincture

tío *nm* (*pariente*) uncle; (*fam: individuo*) bloke, chap, guy (*US*)

tiovivo *nm* roundabout

típico, -a *adj* typical; (*pintoresco*) picturesque

tiple *nm* soprano (voice) ▷ *nf* soprano

tipo *nm* (*clase*) type, kind; (*norma*) norm; (*patrón*) pattern; (*fam: hombre*) fellow, bloke, guy (*US*); (*Anat*) build; (*: de mujer*) figure; (*Imprenta*) type; **dos ~s sospechosos** two suspicious characters; **~ a término** (*Com*) forward rate; **~ base** (*Com*) base rate; **~ bancario** bank rate; **~ de datos** (*Inform*) data type; **~ de descuento/interés** discount/interest rate; **~ de interés vigente** (*Com*) standard rate; **~ de letra** (*Inform, Tip*) typeface

tipografía *nf* (*tipo*) printing; (*lugar*) printing press

tipográfico, -a *adj* printing

tipógrafo, -a *nm/f* printer

tíque(t) (*pl* **tíque(t)s**) *nm* ticket; (*en tienda*) cash slip

tiquismiquis *nm* fussy person ▷ *nmpl* (*querellas*) squabbling *sg*; (*escrúpulos*) silly scruples

tira *nf* strip; (*fig*) abundance ▷ *nm*: **~ y afloja** give and take; (*cautela*) caution; **la ~ de ...** (*fam*) lots of ...

tirabuzón *nm* corkscrew; (*rizo*) curl

tirada *nf* (*acto*) cast, throw; (*distancia*) distance; (*serie*) series; (*Tip*) printing, edition; **de una ~** at one go

tiradero *nm* (*Méx*) rubbish dump

tirado, -a *adj* (*barato*) dirt-cheap; (*fam: fácil*) very easy; **está ~** (*fam*) it's a cinch

tirador, a *nm/f* (*persona*) shooter ▷ *nm* (*mango*) handle; (*Elec*) flex; **~ certero** sniper

tiralíneas *nm inv* ruling-pen

tiranía *nf* tyranny

tiránico, -a *adj* tyrannical

tiranizar *vt* (*pueblo, empleado*) to tyrannize

tirano, -a *adj* tyrannical ▷ *nm/f* tyrant

tirante *adj* (*cuerda*) tight, taut; (*relaciones*) strained ▷ *nm* (*Arq*) brace; (*Tec*) stay; (*correa*) shoulder strap; **tirantes** *nmpl* braces, suspenders (*US*)

tirantez *nf* tightness; (*fig*) tension

tirar *vt* (*arrojar: piedra, pelota*) to throw; (*: bomba*) to drop; (*: desechos, desperdicios, dinero*) to throw away; (*derribar: edificio*) to pull down; (*: muro, pared*) to knock down ▷ *vi* (*disparar*) to shoot; (*dar tirón*) to

pull; (fam: ir) to go; (Deporte) to shoot; **tirarse**
vr (arrojarse) to throw o.s.; **~ algo a la basura** to
throw something out; **la moto la tiró al suelo**
the motorbike knocked her over; **~ algo abajo**
to bring sth down, destroy sth; **tire usted**
adelante go straight on; **~ a la derecha** to turn
o go right; **tira más a su padre** he takes more
after his father; **~ de algo** to pull sth; **vamos**
tirando we're getting by; **se tiró al suelo** he
threw himself to the ground; **~se al agua** to
plunge into the water; **~se de cabeza** to dive in
head first; **~se en el sofá** to lie down on the sofa;
se tiró toda la mañana estudiando (fam) he
spent the whole morning studying

tirita nf (sticking) plaster, bandaid (US)

tiritar vi to shiver

tiro nm (disparo) shot; (de balón) shot; (Tenis, Golf)
drive; **oímos un ~** we heard a shot; **se pegó un**
~ he shot himself; **le salió el ~ por la culata** it
backfired on him; **no lo haría ni a ~s** I wouldn't
do it for love nor money; **andar de ~s largos** to
be all dressed up; **al ~** (LAm) at once; **de a ~** (Méx
fam) completely; **~ al blanco** target practice; **~**
libre (Fútbol) free kick

tiroides nm inv thyroid

tirón nm (sacudida) pull, tug; **de un ~** in one go;
dar un ~ a to pull at, tug at

tiroteo nm exchange of shots, shooting;
(escaramuza) skirmish

tísico, -a adj, nm/f consumptive

tisis nf consumption, tuberculosis

titánico, -a adj titanic

títere nm puppet; **no dejar ~ con cabeza** to turn
everything upside-down

titilar vi (luz, estrella) to twinkle; (párpado) to
flutter

titiritero, -a nm/f (acróbata) acrobat; (malabarista)
juggler

titubeante adj (inestable) shaky, tottering;
(farfullante) stammering; (dudoso) hesitant

titubear vi to stagger; (tartamudear) to stammer;
(vacilar) to hesitate

titubeo nm (tartamudeo) stammering; (vacilación)
hesitation

titulado, -a adj (libro) entitled; (persona) titled

titular adj titular ▷ nm/f (de pasaporte) holder ▷ nm
headline ▷ vt to title; **titularse** vr to be entitled

título nm (gen) title; (certificado) professional
qualification; (universitario) university
degree; (Com) bond; (fig) right; **títulos** nmpl
qualifications; **a ~ de** by way of; (en calidad de) in
the capacity of; **a ~ de curiosidad** as a matter of
interest; **~s convertibles de interés fijo** (Com)
convertible loan stock sg; **~ de propiedad** title
deed

tiza nf chalk; **una ~** a piece of chalk

tiznar vt to blacken; (manchar) to smudge, stain;
(fig) to tarnish

tizón, tizo nm brand; (fig) stain

TLC nm abr (= Tratado de Libre Comercio) NAFTA

toalla nf towel

tobillo nm ankle

tobogán nm chute, slide

toca nf headdress

tocadiscos nm inv record player

tocado, -a adj (fruta etc) rotten ▷ nm headdress;
estar ~ de la cabeza (fam) to be weak in the head

tocador nm (mueble) dressing table; (cuarto)
boudoir; (neceser) toilet case; (fam) ladies' room

tocante: **~ a** prep with regard to; **en lo ~ a** as for,
so far as concerns

tocar vt (con la mano) to touch; (instrumento, canción)
to play; (timbre, campana) to ring; (bocina) to blow;
(tema, asunto) to touch on, refer to ▷ vi (a la puerta)
to knock (on o at the door); **tocarse** vr (recíproco)
to touch each other; (cubrirse la cabeza) to cover
one's head; **~ algo a algn**: **te toca fregar los**
platos It's your turn to do the dishes; **¿a quién**
le toca? whose turn is it?; **toca el violín** he
plays the violin; **le tocó la lotería** he won the
lottery

tocateja (fam): **a ~** adv in readies

tocayo, -a nm/f namesake

tocino nm (bacon) fat; **~ de panceta** bacon

todavía adv (incluso) even; (aún) still, yet; **~ más**
yet o still more; **~ no** not yet; **~ en 1970** as late as
1970; **está lloviendo ~** it's still raining

todo, -a adj **1** (sg: en su totalidad) all, whole; (cada
uno) every; **toda la carne** all the meat; **toda**
la noche all night, the whole night; **~ el libro**
the whole book; **toda una botella** a whole
bottle; **~ lo contrario** quite the opposite; **a**
toda velocidad at full speed; **por ~ el país**
throughout the whole country; **~ el mundo lo**
sabe everybody knows; **es ~ un hombre** he's
every inch a man; **soy ~ oídos** I'm all ears

2 (pl: en sentido general) all; (cada uno) every; **~s los**
libros all the books; **~s los que quieran salir**
all those who want to leave; **~s vosotros** all of
you; **todas las noches** every night; **pararon a**
~s los coches que pasaban they stopped every
car that went by

▷ pron **1** (sg) everything, all; (pl) everyone,
everybody; **lo sabemos ~** we know everything;
~s querían más tiempo everybody o everyone
wanted more time; **nos marchamos ~s** all of
us left

2 (en locs): **a pesar de ~** even so, in spite of
everything; **con ~, él me sigue gustando**
even so I still like him; **le llamaron de ~** they
called him all the names under the sun; **no me**
agrada del ~ I don't entirely like it; **arriba del**
~ at the very top; **corriendo y ~, no llegaron a**
tiempo even though they ran, they still didn't
arrive in time

▷ adv (completamente) all; **está toda sucia** she's
all dirty; **vaya ~ seguido** keep straight on o
ahead

▷ nm: **como un ~** as a whole; **~ a cien** ≈ pound
store (Brit), ≈ dollar store (US)

todopoderoso, -a adj all powerful; (Rel)
almighty

todoterreno nm (tb: **vehículo todoterreno**) four-
by-four

toga nf toga; (Escol) gown
Tokio n Tokyo
toldo nm (para el sol) sunshade; (en tienda) marquee; (fig) pride
tole nm (fam) commotion
tolerancia nf tolerance
tolerante adj tolerant; (fig) open-minded
tolerar vt to tolerate; (resistir) to endure
toma nf (gen) taking; (Med) dose; (Elec: tb: **toma de corriente**) socket; (Mec) inlet; ~ **de posesión** (por presidente) taking up office; ~ **de tierra** (Aviat) landing
tomar vt (tren, foto, decisión) to take; (café, bocadillo) to have; (actitud) to adopt; (aspecto) to take on; (notas, apuntes) to take ▷ vi (tener) to take; (LAm: beber) to drink; **tomarse** vr to take; ¿**qué quieres ~?** what are you going to have?; **de postre tomé un helado** I had an ice cream for dessert; ~ **nota de algo** to note something down; ~ **asiento** to sit down; ~ **el aire** to get some fresh air; ~ **cariño a algn** to become fond of sb; ~ **a algn por loco** to think sb mad; **~la con algn** to pick a quarrel with sb; **toma y daca** give and take; **~(se) algo a bien/a mal** to take sth well/badly; **~(se) algo en serio** to take sth seriously; **se tomó la molestia de acompañarnos** he took the trouble to accompany us; **~se por** to consider o.s. to be; ver tb **pelo; sol**
tomate nm tomato
tomatera nf tomato plant
tomavistas nm inv movie camera
tomillo nm thyme
tomo nm volume
ton abr = **tonelada** ▷ nm = **sin ton ni son** without rhyme or reason
tonada nf tune
tonalidad nf tone
tonel nm barrel
tonelada nf ton; ~ **métrica** metric ton
tonelaje nm tonnage
tonelero nm cooper
tongo nm (Deporte) fix
tónica nf (Mús) tonic; (fig) keynote
tónico, -a adj tonic ▷ nm (Med) tonic
tonificar vt to tone up
tono nm (de voz, sonido) tone; (de color) shade; **lo dijo en ~ cariñoso** he said it in an affectionate tone; **un ~ un poco más oscuro** a slightly darker shade; **fuera de ~** inappropriate; **darse ~** to put on airs; **estar a ~ con** to be in tune with
tontería nf (estupidez) foolishness; (una tontería) silly thing; **tonterías** nfpl rubbish sg, nonsense sg
tonto, -a adj (persona: necio) stupid; (: ingenuo) silly; (error) silly ▷ nm/f fool; **hacer el ~** (hacer payasadas) to act the fool; **hacerse el ~** to act dumb; **a tontas y a locas** anyhow
topacio nm topaz
topar vt (tropezar) to bump into; (encontrar) to find, come across; (cabra etc) to butt ▷ vi: ~ **contra** o **en** to run into; ~ **con** to run up against; **toparse** vr: **~se con algn** to bump into sb

tope adj maximum ▷ nm (fin) end; (límite) limit; (Ferro) buffer; (Auto) bumper; **fecha ~** closing date; **precio ~** top price; **sueldo ~** maximum salary; **al ~** end to end; ~ **de tabulación** tab stop
tópico, -a adj topical; (Med) local ▷ nm platitude, cliché; **de uso ~** for external application
topo nm (Zool) mole; (fig) blunderer
topografía nf topography
topógrafo, -a nm/f topographer; (agrimensor) surveyor
toque nm touch; (Mús) beat; (de campana) ring, chime; (Mil) bugle call; (fig) crux; **dar un ~ a** to test; **dar el último ~ a** to put the final touch to; ~ **de queda** curfew
toquetear vt to handle; (fam!) to touch up
toquilla nf (chal) shawl
torax nm inv thorax
torbellino nm whirlwind; (fig) whirl
torcedura nf twist; (Med) sprain
torcer vt to twist; (la esquina) to turn; (Med) to sprain; (cuerda) to plait; (ropa, manos) to wring; (persona) to corrupt; (sentido) to distort ▷ vi (cambiar de dirección) to turn; **torcerse** vr to twist; (doblar) to bend; (desviarse) to go astray; (fracasar) to go wrong; **~se un pie** to twist one's foot; ~ **el gesto** to scowl; **el coche torció a la derecha** the car turned right
torcido, -a adj twisted; (fig) crooked ▷ nm curl
tordo, -a adj dappled ▷ nm thrush
torear vt (fig: evadir) to dodge; (toro) to fight ▷ vi to fight bulls
toreo nm bullfighting
torero, -a nm/f bullfighter
tormenta nf storm; (fig: confusión) turmoil
tormento nm torture; (fig) anguish
tornar vt (devolver) to return, give back; (transformar) to transform ▷ vi to go back; **tornarse** vr (ponerse) to become; (volver) to return
tornasolado, -a adj (brillante) iridescent; (reluciente) shimmering
torneo nm tournament
tornillo nm screw; **apretar los ~s a algn** to apply pressure on sb; **le falta un ~** (fam) he's got a screw loose
torniquete nm (puerta) turnstile; (Med) tourniquet
torno nm (Tec: grúa) winch; (: de carpintero) lathe; (tambor) drum; **en ~ (a)** round, about; ~ **de banco** vice, vise (US)
toro nm bull; (fam) he-man; **los ~s** bullfighting sg
toronja nf grapefruit
torpe adj (poco hábil) clumsy, awkward; (movimiento) sluggish; (necio) dim; (lento) slow; (indecente) crude; (no honrado) dishonest
torpedo nm torpedo
torpeza nf (falta de agilidad) clumsiness; (lentitud) slowness; (rigidez) stiffness; (error) mistake; (crudeza) obscenity
torre nf tower; (de petróleo) derrick; (de electricidad) pylon; (Ajedrez) rook; (Aviat, Mil, Náut) turret
torrefacto, -a adj: **café ~** high roast coffee

torrente nm torrent

tórrido, -a adj torrid

torrija nf fried bread; **~s** French toast sg

torsión nf twisting

torso nm torso

torta nf cake; (fam) slap; **no entendió ni ~** he didn't understand a word of it; **~ de huevos** (LAm) omelette

tortazo nm (bofetada) slap; (de coche) crash

tortícolis nm inv stiff neck

tortilla nf (de huevos) omelette; (de maíz) maize pancake, tortilla; **cambiar** o **volver la ~ a algn** to turn the tables on sb; **~ francesa/española** plain/potato omelette

tórtola nf turtledove

tortuga nf tortoise; **~ marina** turtle

tortuoso, -a adj winding

tortura nf torture

torturar vt to torture

tos nf inv cough; **~ ferina** whooping cough

tosco, -a adj coarse

toser vi to cough; **no hay quien le tosa** he's in a class by himself

tostada nf tan; (pan) piece of toast; **tostadas** nfpl toast sg

tostado, -a adj toasted; (por el sol) dark brown; (piel) tanned

tostador nm toaster

tostar vt (pan) to toast; (café) to roast; (al sol) to tan; **tostarse** vr to get brown

tostón nm: **ser un ~** to be a drag

total adj total ▷ adv in short; (al fin y al cabo) when all is said and done ▷ nm total; **en ~** in all; **~ que** to cut a long story short; **~ de comprobación** (Inform) hash total; **~ debe/haber** (Com) debit/ assets total

totalidad nf whole

totalitario, -a adj totalitarian

totalmente adv totally

tóxico, -a adj toxic ▷ nm poison

toxicómano, -a adj addicted to drugs ▷ nm/f drug addict

toxina nf toxin

tozudo, -a adj obstinate

traba nf bond, tie; **poner ~s a** to restrain

trabajador, a nm/f worker ▷ adj hard-working

trabajar vt, vi to work; **no trabajes tanto** don't work so hard; **¿en qué trabajas?** what's your job?; **trabajo de camarero** I work as a waiter; **~ jornada completa** to work full-time; **~ media jornada** to work part-time; **¡a ~!** let's get to work!

trabajo nm (empleo) job; (actividad) work; (Escol: redacción) essay; (esfuerzo) effort; **tengo mucho ~** I have a lot of work; **me puedes llamar al ~** you can call me at work; **estar sin ~** to be unemployed; **el ~ de la casa** the housework; **le han ofrecido un ~ en el banco** he's been offered a job in the bank; **quedarse sin ~** to find oneself out of work; **~ en equipo** teamwork; ver tb **costar**

trabajoso, -a adj hard; (Med) pale

trabalenguas nm inv tongue twister

trabar vt (juntar) to join, unite; (agarrar) to seize; (amistad) to strike up; **trabarse** vr to become entangled; (reñir) to squabble; **se le traba la lengua** he gets tongue-tied

tracción nf traction; **~ delantera/trasera** front-wheel/rear-wheel drive

tractor nm tractor

tradición nf tradition

tradicional adj traditional

traducción nf translation; **~ asistida por ordenador** computer-assisted translation

traducir vt to translate; **traducirse** vr: **~se en** (fig) to entail, result in

traductor, a nm/f translator

traer vt (transportar) to bring; (llevar puesto) to wear; (incluir) to carry; (fig: causar) to cause; **traerse** vr: **traérselas: es un problema que se las trae** it's a difficult problem; **he traído el paraguas por si acaso** I've brought the umbrella just in case; **traía (puesto) un vestido nuevo** she was wearing a new dress; **el periódico trae un artículo sobre la Reina** the newspaper carries an article on the Queen

traficar vi to trade; **~ con** (pey) to deal illegally in

tráfico nm (Com) trade; (Auto) traffic

tragaluz nm skylight

tragamonedas nm inv, **tragaperras** nm inv slot machine

tragar vt to swallow; (devorar) to devour, bolt down; **tragarse** vr to swallow; (tierra) to absorb, soak up; **no lo puedo ~** (persona) I can't stand him

tragedia nf tragedy

trágico, -a adj tragic

trago nm (de líquido) drink; (comido de golpe) gulp; (fam: de bebida) swig; (desgracia) blow; **~ amargo** (fig) hard time

traición nf treachery; (Jur) treason; (acto) act of treachery

traicionar vt to betray

traicionero, -a: = **traidor, a**

traidor, a adj treacherous ▷ nm/f traitor

trailer (pl **-s**) nm trailer

traje nm (gen) dress; (de hombre) suit; (traje típico) costume; (fig) garb; **~ de baño** swimsuit; **~ de luces** bullfighter's costume; **~ hecho a la medida** made-to-measure suit

trajín nm haulage; (fam: movimiento) bustle; **trajines** nmpl goings-on

trajinar vt (llevar) to carry, transport ▷ vi (moverse) to bustle about; (viajar) to travel around

trama nf (fig) link; (: intriga) plot; (de tejido) weft

tramar vt to plot; (Tec) to weave; **algo se está tramando** (fig) there's something going on

tramitar vt (asunto) to transact; (negociar) to negotiate; (manejar) to handle

trámite nm (paso) step; (Jur) transaction; **trámites** nmpl (burocracia) paperwork sg, procedures; (Jur) proceedings

tramo nm (de tierra) plot; (de escalera) flight; (de vía) section

tramoya nf (Teat) piece of stage machinery; (fig) trick

tramoyista nm/f scene shifter; (fig) trickster

trampa nf trap; (en el suelo) trapdoor; (prestidigitación) conjuring trick; (engaño) trick; (fam) fiddle; **caer en la ~** to fall into the trap; **hacer ~s** to cheat

trampolín nm trampoline; (de piscina etc) diving board

tramposo, -a adj crooked, cheating ▷ nm/f crook, cheat

tranca nf (palo) stick; (viga) beam; (de puerta, ventana) bar; (borrachera) binge; **a ~s y barrancas** with great difficulty

trancar vt to bar ▷ vi to stride along

trance nm (momento difícil) difficult moment; (situación crítica) critical situation; (estado de hipnosis) trance; **estar en ~ de muerte** to be at death's door

tranco nm stride

tranquilamente adv (sin preocupaciones: leer, trabajar) peacefully; (sin enfadarse: hablar, discutir) calmly

tranquilidad nf (calma) calmness, stillness; (paz) peacefulness

tranquilizante nm tranquillizer

tranquilizar vt (calmar) to calm (down); (asegurar) to reassure

tranquilo, -a adj (calmado) calm; (apacible) peaceful; (mar) calm; (mente) untroubled

transacción nf transaction

transatlántico, -a adj transatlantic ▷ nm (ocean) liner

transbordador nm ferry

transbordar vt to transfer; **transbordarse** vr to change

transbordo nm transfer; **hacer ~** to change (trains)

transcender vt = **trascender**

transcribir vt to transcribe

transcurrir vi (tiempo) to pass; (hecho) to take place

transcurso nm passing, lapse; **en el ~ de 8 días** in the course of a week

transeúnte adj transient ▷ nm/f passer-by

transexual adj, nm/f transsexual

transferencia nf transference; (Com) transfer; **~ bancaria** banker's order; **~ de crédito** (Com) credit transfer; **~ electrónica de fondos** (Com) electronic funds transfer

transferir vt to transfer; (aplazar) to postpone

transformación nf transformation

transformador nm transformer

transformar vt to transform; (convertir) to convert

tránsfuga nm/f (Mil) deserter; (Pol) turncoat

transfusión nf (tb: **transfusión de sangre**) (blood) transfusion

transgénico, -a adj genetically modified, GM

transgredir vt to transgress

transición nf transition; **período de ~** transitional period

transido, -a adj overcome; **~ de angustia** beset with anxiety; **~ de dolor** racked with pain

transigir vi to compromise; (ceder) to make concessions

transistor nm transistor

transitar vi to go (from place to place)

transitivo, -a adj transitive

tránsito nm transit; (Auto) traffic; (parada) stop; **horas de máximo ~** rush hours; **"se prohíbe el ~"** "no thoroughfare"; **los pasajeros en ~ para Moscú** transfer passengers to Moscow

transitorio, -a adj transitory

transmisión nf (Radio, TV) transmission, broadcast(ing); (transferencia) transfer; **~ de datos (en paralelo/en serie)** (Inform) (parallel/serial) data transfer o transmission; **~ en circuito** hookup; **~ en directo/exterior** live/outside broadcast; **plena/media ~ bidireccional** (Inform) full/half duplex

transmitir vt to transmit; (Radio, TV) to broadcast; (enfermedad) to give, pass on

transparencia nf transparency; (claridad) clearness, clarity; (foto) slide

transparentar vt to reveal ▷ vi to be transparent

transparente adj transparent; (aire) clear; (ligero) diaphanous ▷ nm curtain

transpirar vi to perspire; (fig) to transpire

transponer vt to transpose; (cambiar de sitio) to move about ▷ vi (desaparecer) to disappear; (ir más allá) to go beyond; **transponerse** vr to change places; (ocultarse) to hide; (sol) to go down

transportar vt to transport; (llevar) to carry

transporte nm transport; (Com) haulage; **Ministerio de T~s** Ministry of Transport

transversal adj transverse, cross ▷ nf (tb: **calle transversal**) cross street

tranvía nm tram, streetcar (US)

trapecio nm trapeze

trapecista nm/f trapeze artist

trapero, -a nm/f ragman

trapicheos nmpl (fam) schemes, fiddles

trapo nm (tela) rag; (de cocina) cloth; **trapos** nmpl (fam: de mujer) clothes, dresses; **a todo ~** under full sail; **soltar el ~** (llorar) to burst into tears

tráquea nf trachea, windpipe

traqueteo nm (crujido) crack; (golpeteo) rattling

tras prep (detrás) behind; (después) after; **~ de** besides; **día ~ día** day after day; **uno ~ otro** one after the other

trascendencia nf (importancia) importance; (en filosofía) transcendence

trascendental adj (importante) important; (Fil) transcendental

trascender vi (oler) to smell; (noticias) to come out, leak out; (sucesos, sentimientos) to spread, have a wide effect; **~ a** (afectar) to reach, have an effect on; **en su novela todo trasciende a romanticismo** everything in his novel smacks of romanticism

trasegar vt (mover) to move about; (vino) to decant

trasero, -a adj back, rear ▷ nm (Anat) bottom;

traseros *nmpl* ancestors
trasfondo *nm* background
trasgredir *vt* to contravene
trashumante *adj* migrating
trasladar *vt* to move; *(persona)* to transfer; *(postergar)* to postpone; *(copiar)* to copy; *(interpretar)* to interpret; **trasladarse** *vr (irse)* to go; *(mudarse)* to move; **~se a otro puesto** to move to a new job
traslado *nm* move; *(mudanza)* move, removal; *(de persona)* transfer; *(copia)* copy; **~ de bloque** *(Inform)* block move, cut-and-paste
traslucir *vt* to show; **traslucirse** *vr* to be translucent
trasluz *nm* reflected light; **al ~** against o up to the light
trasnochado, -a *adj* dated
trasnochador, a *adj* given to staying up late ▷ *nm/f (fig)* night bird
trasnochar *vi (acostarse tarde)* to stay up late; *(no dormir)* to have a sleepless night; *(pasar la noche)* to stay the night
traspasar *vt (bala)* to pierce, go through; *(propiedad)* to sell, transfer; *(calle)* to cross over; *(límites)* to go beyond; *(ley)* to break; **"traspaso negocio"** "business for sale"
traspaso *nm* transfer; *(fig)* anguish
traspié *(pl* **-s**) *nm (caída)* stumble; *(tropezón)* trip; *(fig)* blunder
trasplantar *vt* to transplant
trasplante *nm* transplant
traspuesto, -a *adj:* **quedarse ~** to doze off
trastada *nf (fam)* prank
trastazo *nm (fam)* bump; **darse un ~** *(persona)* to bump o.s.; *(en coche)* to have a bump
traste *nm (Mús)* fret; **dar al ~ con algo** to ruin sth; **ir al ~** to fall through
trastero *nm* lumber room
trastienda *nf* backshop
trasto *nm (mueble)* piece of furniture; *(pey: cosa)* piece of junk; *(: persona)* dead loss; **trastos** *nmpl (Teat)* scenery *sg*; **tirar los ~s a la cabeza** to have a blazing row
trastocar *vt (papeles)* to mix up
trastornado, -a *adj (loco)* mad; *(agitado)* crazy
trastornar *vt* to overturn, upset; *(fig: ideas)* to confuse; *(: nervios)* to shatter; *(: persona)* to drive crazy; **trastornarse** *vr (plan)* to fall through
trastorno *nm (acto)* overturning; *(confusión)* confusion; *(Pol)* disturbance, upheaval; *(Med)* upset; **~ estomacal** stomach upset; **~ mental** mental disorder, breakdown
trasvase *nm (de río)* diversion
tratable *adj* friendly
tratado *nm (Pol)* treaty; *(Com)* agreement; *(Literatura)* treatise
tratamiento *nm* treatment; *(Tec)* processing; *(de problema)* handling; **~ de datos** *(Inform)* data processing; **~ de gráficos** *(Inform)* graphics; **~ de márgenes** margin settings; **~ de textos** *(Inform)* word processing; **~ por lotes** *(Inform)* batch processing

tratar *vt (persona, animal, libro)* to treat; *(tema, asunto, cuestión)* deal with; *(enfermo, enfermedad)* to treat; *(Quim: sustancia)* to treat; *(Inform)* to process; *(dirigirse a: persona)* to address ▷ *vi:* **~ de** *(hablar sobre)* to deal with, be about; *(intentar)* to try to; **~ con** *(tener relación con)* to deal with; **tratarse** *vr (reflexivo)* to treat o.s.; *(recíproco)* to treat each other; **su novio la trata muy mal** her boyfriend treats her very badly; **~emos este tema en la reunión** we'll deal with this subject in the meeting; **lo tratamos de tú** we address him as tú; **la película trata de un adolescente en Nueva York** the film is about a teenager in New York; **~é de llegar pronto** I'll try to arrive early; **¿de qué se trata?** what's it about?
trato *nm* dealings *pl*; *(relaciones)* relationship; *(comportamiento)* manner; *(Com, Jur)* agreement, contract; *(título)* (form of) address; **de ~ agradable** pleasant; **lo tratamos de tú** easy to get on with; **~ equitativo** fair deal; **¡~ hecho!** it's a deal!; **malos ~s** ill-treatment *sg*
trauma *nm* trauma
través *nm:* **al ~** across, crossways; **a ~ de** across; *(sobre)* over; *(por)* through; **de ~** across; *(de lado)* sideways
travesaño *nm (Arq)* crossbeam; *(Deporte)* crossbar
travesía *nf (calle)* cross-street; *(Náut)* crossing
travesti *nm/f* transvestite
travesura *nf (broma)* prank; *(ingenio)* wit
traviesa *nf (crossing)*; *(Arq)* crossbeam; *(Ferro)* sleeper; *ver tb* **travieso**
travieso, -a *adj (niño)* naughty; *(adulto)* restless; *(ingenioso)* witty; *ver tb* **traviesa**
trayecto *nm (ruta)* road, way; *(viaje)* journey; *(tramo)* stretch; *(curso)* course; **final del ~** end of the line
trayectoria *nf* trajectory; *(desarrollo)* development, path; **la ~ actual del partido** the party's present line
traza *nf (Arq)* plan, design; *(aspecto)* looks *pl*; *(señal)* sign; *(engaño)* trick; *(habilidad)* skill; *(Inform)* trace
trazado, -a *adj:* **bien ~** shapely, well-formed ▷ *nm (Arq)* plan, design; *(fig)* outline; *(de carretera etc)* line, route
trazar *vt (Arq)* to plan; *(Arte)* to sketch; *(fig)* to trace; *(itinerario)* to plot; *(plan)* to follow
trazo *nm (línea)* line; *(bosquejo)* sketch; **trazos** *nmpl (de cara)* lines, features
trébol *nm (Bot)* clover; **tréboles** *nmpl (Naipes)* clubs
trece *num* thirteen; **estar en sus ~** to stand firm
trecho *nm (distancia)* distance; *(de tiempo)* while; *(fam)* piece; **de ~ en ~** at intervals
tregua *nf (Mil)* truce; *(fig)* lull; **sin ~** without respite
treinta *num* thirty
tremendo, -a *adj (terrible)* terrible; *(imponente: cosa)* imposing; *(fam: fabuloso)* tremendous; *(divertido)* entertaining
trémulo, -a *adj* quivering; *(luz)* flickering
tren *nm (Ferro)* train; **~ de aterrizaje**

undercarriage; ~ **directo/expreso/(de) mercancías/de pasajeros/suplementario** through/fast/goods o freight/passenger/relief train; ~ **de vida** way of life

trenca nf duffel coat

trenza nf (de pelo) plait

trenzar vt (el pelo) to plait ▷ vi (en baile) to weave in and out; **trenzarse** vr (LAm) to become involved

trepar vt, vi to climb; (Tec) to drill

trepidar vi to shake, vibrate

tres num three; (fecha) third; **las** ~ three o'clock

trescientos, -as num three hundred

tresillo nm three-piece suite; (Mús) triplet

treta nf (Com etc) gimmick; (fig) trick

triangular adj triangular

triángulo nm triangle

tribal adj tribal

tribu nf tribe

tribuna nf (plataforma) platform; (Deporte) stand; (fig) public speaking; ~ **de la prensa** press box; ~ **del acusado** (Jur) dock; ~ **del jurado** jury box

tribunal nm (en juicio) court; (comisión, fig) tribunal; (Escol: examinadores) board of examiners; **T~ de Justicia de las Comunidades Europeas** European Court of Justice; **T~ Supremo** High Court, Supreme Court (US); ~ **popular** jury

tributar vt to pay; (las gracias) to give; (cariño) to show

tributo nm (Com) tax

triciclo nm tricycle

tricotar vi to knit

trifulca nf (fam) row, shindy

trigal nm wheat field

trigo nm wheat; **trigos** nmpl wheat field(s) (pl)

trigueño, -a adj (pelo) corn-coloured; (piel) olive-skinned

trillado, -a adj threshed; (fig) trite, hackneyed

trilladora nf threshing machine

trillar vt (Agr) to thresh; (fig) to frequent

trimestral adj quarterly; (Escol) termly

trimestre nm (Escol) term; (Com) quarter, financial period; (: pago) quarterly payment

trinar vi (Mús) to trill; (ave) to sing, warble; **está que trina** he's hopping mad

trincar vt (atar) to tie up; (Náut) to lash; (agarrar) to pinion

trinchar vt to carve

trinchera nf (fosa) trench; (para vía) cutting; (impermeable) trench-coat

trineo nm sledge

trinidad nf trio; (Rel): **la T~** the Trinity

trino nm trill

trío nm trio

tripa nf (Anat) intestine; (fig: fam) belly; **tripas** nfpl (Anat) insides; (Culin) tripe sg; **tener mucha** ~ to be fat; **me duelen las ~s** I have a stomach ache

triple adj triple; (tres veces) threefold

triplicado, -a adj: **por** ~ in triplicate

triplicar vt to treble

triplo adj = **triple**

trípode nm tripod

tripulación nf crew

tripulante nm/f crewman/woman

tripular vt (barco) to man; (Auto) to drive

triquiñuela nf trick

tris nm crack; **en un** ~ in an instant; **estar en un** ~ **de hacer algo** to be within an inch of doing sth

triste adj (afligido) sad; (sombrío) melancholy, gloomy; (desolado) desolate; (lamentable) sorry, miserable; **no queda sino un** ~ **penique** there's just one miserable penny left

tristeza nf (aflicción) sadness; (melancolía) melancholy; (de lugar) desolation; (pena) misery

triturar vt (moler) to grind; (mascar) to chew; (documentos) to shred

triunfal adj triumphant; (arco) triumphal

triunfar vi (tener éxito) to triumph; (ganar) to win; (Naipes) to be trumps; **triunfan corazones** hearts are trumps; ~ **en la vida** to succeed in life

triunfo nm triumph; (Naipes) trump

trivial adj trivial

trivializar vt to minimize, play down

triza nf bit, piece; **hacer algo ~s** to smash sth to bits; (papel) to tear sth to shreds

trocar vt (Com) to exchange; (confundir) to confuse; **trocarse** vr (confundirse) to get mixed up; (transformarse): ~**se (en)** to change (into)

trocear vt to cut up

trocha nf (sendero) by-path; (atajo) shortcut

troche; a ~ y moche adv helter-skelter, pell-mell

trofeo nm trophy

trola nf (fam) fib

tromba nf whirlwind; ~ **de agua** cloudburst

trombón nm trombone

trombosis nf inv thrombosis

trompa nf (Mús) horn; (de elefante) trunk; (trompo) humming top; (hocico) snout; (Anat) tube, duct ▷ nm (Mús) horn player; ~ **de Falopio** Fallopian tube; **cogerse una** ~ (fam) to get tight

trompada nf, **trompazo** nm (choque) bump, bang; (puñetazo) punch

trompeta nf trumpet; (clarín) bugle ▷ nm/f trumpeter

trompetilla nf ear trumpet

trompicón; a trompicones adv in fits and starts

trompo nm spinning top

trompón nm bump

tronar vt (CAm, Méx) to shoot, execute ▷ vi to thunder; (fig) to rage; (fam) to go broke

tronchar vt (árbol) to chop down; (fig: vida) to cut short; (esperanza) to shatter; (persona) to tire out; **troncharse** vr to fall down; ~**se de risa** to split one's sides with laughter

tronco nm (de árbol, Anat) trunk; (de planta) stem; **estar hecho un** ~ to be sound asleep

trono nm throne

tropa nf (Mil) troop; (soldados) soldiers pl; (soldados rasos) ranks pl; (gentío) mob

tropel nm (muchedumbre) crowd; (prisa) rush; (montón) throng; **acudir** etc **en** ~ to come etc in a mad rush

tropelía *nm* outrage

tropezar *vi* to trip, stumble; (*fig*) to slip up; **tropezarse** *vr* (*dos personas*) to run into each other; ~ **con** (*encontrar*) to run into; (*topar con*) to bump into

tropezón *nm* trip; (*fig*) blunder; (*traspié*): **dar un** ~ to trip

tropical *adj* tropical

trópico *nm* tropic

tropiezo *nm* (*error*) slip, blunder; (*desgracia*) misfortune; (*revés*) setback; (*obstáculo*) snag; (*discusión*) quarrel

trotamundos *nm inv* globetrotter

trotar *vi* to trot; (*viajar*) to travel about

trote *nm* trot; (*fam*) travelling; **de mucho** ~ hard-wearing

trozo *nm* bit, piece; (*Literatura, Mús*) passage; **a ~s** in bits

trucha *nf* (*pez*) trout; (*Tec*) crane

truco *nm* (*habilidad*) knack; (*engaño*) trick; (*Cine*) trick effect *o* photography; ~ **publicitario** advertising gimmick

trueno *nm* (*gen*) thunder; (*estampido*) boom; (*de arma*) bang

trueque *nm* exchange; (*Com*) barter

trufa *nf* (*Bot*) truffle; (*fig: fam*) fib

truhán, -ana *nm/f* rogue

truncar *vt* (*cortar*) to truncate; (*vida etc*) to cut short; (*desarrollo*) to stunt

tu *adj* your

tú *pron* you

tubérculo *nm* (*Bot*) tuber

tuberculosis *nf inv* tuberculosis

tubería *nf* pipes *pl*, piping; (*conducto*) pipeline

tubo *nm* tube, pipe; ~ **de desagüe** drainpipe; ~ **de ensayo** test-tube; ~ **de escape** exhaust (pipe); ~ **digestivo** alimentary canal

tuerca *nf* (*Tec*) nut

tuerto, -a *adj* blind in one eye ▷ *nm/f* one-eyed person; **a tuertas** upside-down

tuétano *nm* (*Anat: médula*) marrow; (*Bot*) pith; **hasta los ~s** through and through, utterly

tufo *nm* vapour; (*fig: pey*) stench

tugurio *nm* slum

tul *nm* tulle

tulipán *nm* tulip

tullido, -a *adj* crippled; (*cansado*) exhausted

tumba *nf* tomb; **ser (como) una** ~ to keep one's mouth shut

tumbar *vt* to knock down; (*doblar*) to knock over; (*fam: suj: olor*) to overpower ▷ *vi* to fall down; **tumbarse** *vr* (*echarse*) to lie down; (*extenderse*) to stretch out

tumbo *nm* (*caída*) fall; (*de vehículo*) jolt

tumbona *nf* lounger

tumor *nm* tumour

tumulto *nm* turmoil; (*Pol: motín*) riot

tuna *nf* (*Mús*) student music group; *ver tb* **tuno**

tunante *adj* rascally ▷ *nm* rogue, villain; **¡~!** you villain!

tunda *nf* (*de tela*) shearing; (*de golpes*) beating

túnel *nm* tunnel

Túnez *nm* Tunis

tuno, -a *nm/f* (*fam*) rogue ▷ *nm* (*Mús*) member of a "tuna"; *ver tb* **tuna**

tuntún: al ~ *adv* thoughtlessly

tupé *nm* quiff

tupido, -a *adj* (*denso*) dense; (*fig: torpe*) dim; (*tela*) close-woven

turba *nf* (*combustible*) turf; (*muchedumbre*) crowd

turbación *nf* (*molestia*) disturbance; (*preocupación*) worry

turbado, -a *adj* (*molesto*) disturbed; (*preocupado*) worried

turbante *nm* turban

turbar *vt* (*molestar*) to disturb; (*incomodar*) to upset; **turbarse** *vr* to be disturbed

turbina *nf* turbine

turbio, -a *adj* (*agua etc*) cloudy; (*vista*) dim, blurred; (*tema*) unclear, confused; (*negocio*) shady ▷ *adv* indistinctly

turbo *adj inv* turbo(-charged) ▷ *nm* (*tb coche*) turbo

turbulencia *nf* turbulence; (*fig*) restlessness

turbulento, -a *adj* turbulent; (*fig: intranquilo*) restless; (: *ruidoso*) noisy

turco, -a *adj* Turkish ▷ *nm/f* Turk ▷ *nm* (*Ling*) Turkish

turismo *nm* tourism; (*coche*) saloon car; **hacer** ~ to go travelling (abroad)

turista *nm/f* tourist; (*de vacaciones*) holidaymaker (*Brit*), vacationer (*US*)

turístico, -a *adj* tourist *cpd*

turnar *vi*, **turnarse** *vr* to take (it in) turns

turno *nm* (*oportunidad, orden de prioridad*) opportunity; (*Deporte etc*) turn; **es su** ~ it's his turn (next); ~ **de día/de noche** day/night shift

turquesa *nf* turquoise

Turquía *nf* Turkey

turrón *nm* kind of nougat traditionally eaten at Christmas

tute *nm* (*Naipes*) card game; **darse un** ~ to break one's back

tutear *vt* to address as familiar "tú"; **tutearse** *vr* to be on familiar terms

tutela *nf* (*legal*) guardianship; (*instrucción*) guidance; **estar bajo la** ~ **de** (*fig*) to be under the protection of

tutelar *adj* tutelary ▷ *vt* to protect

tutor, a *nm/f* (*legal*) guardian; (*Escol*) tutor; ~ **de curso** form master/mistress

tuyo, -a *adj* yours, of yours ▷ *pron* yours; **los ~s** (*fam*) your relations, your family

TVE *nf abr* = **Televisión Española**

Uu

u *conj* or

ubicar *vt (esp LAm)* to place, situate; *(: fig)* to install in a post; *(: encontrar)* to find; **ubicarse** *vr* to be situated, be located

ubre *nf* udder

Ud(s) *abr* = **usted(es)**

UE *nf abr* (= *Unión Europea*) EU

UEFA *nf abr* (= *Unión de Asociaciones de Fútbol Europeo*) UEFA

UEO *nf abr* (= *Unión Europea Occidental*) WEU

ufanarse *vr* to boast; **~ de** to pride o.s. on

ufano, -a *adj (arrogante)* arrogant; *(presumido)* conceited

UGT *nf abr ver* **Unión General de Trabajadores**

ujier *nm* usher; *(portero)* doorkeeper

úlcera *nf* ulcer

ulcerar *vt* to make sore; **ulcerarse** *vr* to ulcerate

ulpo *nm (Chi, Perú)* sweet drink made with roasted flour

ulterior *adj (más allá)* farther, further; *(subsecuente, siguiente)* subsequent

últimamente *adv (recientemente)* lately, recently; *(finalmente)* finally; *(como último recurso)* as a last resort

ultimar *vt* to finish; *(finalizar)* to finalize; *(LAm: rematar)* to finish off, murder

ultimátum *nm (pl -s)* ultimatum

último, -a *adj (en el tiempo)* last, latest; *(en el espacio: más bajo)* bottom; *(: más alto)* top; **la última vez que hablé con ella** the last time I spoke to her; **a última hora decidió acompañarme** he decided to come with me at the last minute; **llegar en ~ lugar** to arrive last; **no llego al ~ estante** I can't reach the top shelf; **nos sentamos en la última fila** we sat in the back row; **la última moda** the latest fashion; **en las últimas** on one's last legs; **por ~** finally

ultra *adj* ultra ▷ *nm/f* extreme right-winger

ultracongelar *vt* to deep-freeze

ultraderecha *nf* extreme right (wing)

ultrajar *vt (escandalizar)* to outrage; *(insultar)* to insult, abuse

ultraje *nm (atrocidad)* outrage; *(injuria)* insult

ultraligero *nm* microlight *(Brit)*, microlite *(US)*

ultramar *nm*: **de** *o* **en ~** abroad, overseas; **los países de ~** the overseas countries

ultramarino, -a *adj* overseas, foreign ▷ *nmpl*: **~s** groceries; **tienda de ~s** grocer's (shop)

ultranza; **a ~** *adv* to the death; *(a toda costa)* at all costs; *(completo)* outright; *(Pol etc)* out-and-out, extreme; **un nacionalista a ~** a rabid nationalist

ultrasónico, -a *adj* ultrasonic

ultratumba *nf*: **la vida de ~** the next life; **una voz de ~** a ghostly voice

ultravioleta *adj inv* ultraviolet

ulular *vi* to howl; *(búho)* to hoot

umbilical *adj*: **cordón ~** umbilical cord

umbral *nm (gen)* threshold; **~ de rentabilidad** *(Com)* break-even point

UME *nf abr* (= *Unión Monetaria y Económica*) EMU

un, una *art indef (sg)* a; *(antes de vocal)* an; *(pl)* some; **una mujer/naranja** a woman/an orange; **hay unos regalos para ti** there are some presents for you; **hay unas cervezas en la nevera** there are some beers in the fridge; **tiene unas uñas muy largas** he has very long nails; **me he comprado unos zapatos de tacón** I have bought a pair of high-heels
▷ *adj* **1** *(numeral)* one; **un coche rojo y dos verdes** one red car and two green ones; *ver tb* **uno 2** *(enfático)*: **¡hace un frío!** it's so cold!; **¡tiene una casa!** he's got some house!

una *nf* one; **es la ~** it's one o'clock

unánime *adj* unanimous

unanimidad *nf* unanimity; **por ~** unanimously

unción *nf* anointing

undécimo, -a *adj, nm/f* eleventh

UNED *nf abr (Esp Univ*: = *Universidad Nacional de Enseñanza a Distancia)* ≈ Open University *(Brit)*

ungir *vt* to rub with ointment; *(Rel)* to anoint

ungüento *nm* ointment; *(fig)* salve, balm

únicamente *adv* solely; *(solamente)* only

único, -a *adj* only; *(solo)* sole, single; *(sin par)* unique; **hijo ~** only child

unidad *nf* unity; *(Tec)* unit; **~ móvil** *(TV)* mobile unit; *(Inform)*: **~ central** system unit, central processing unit; **~ de control** control unit; **~ de disco** disk drive; **~ de entrada/salida** input/output device; **~ de presentación visual** *o* **de visualización** visual display unit; **~ procesadora central** central processing unit; **~ periférica** peripheral device

unido, -a *adj* joined, linked; *(fig)* united

unifamiliar *adj*: **vivienda ~** single-family home

unificar *vt* to unite, unify
uniformar *vt* to make uniform; (*Tec*) to standardize
uniforme *adj* uniform, equal; (*superficie*) even ▷ *nm* uniform
uniformidad *nf* uniformity; (*llaneza*) levelness, evenness
unilateral *adj* unilateral
unión *nf* (*gen*) union; (*acto*) uniting, joining; (*calidad*) unity; (*Tec*) joint; (*fig*) closeness, togetherness; **punto de ~** (*Tec*) junction; **en ~ con** (together) with, accompanied by; **~ aduanera** customs union; **U~ Europea** European Union; **U~ General de Trabajadores (UGT)** (*Esp*) *Socialist Union Confederation*; **la U~ Soviética** the Soviet Union
unir *vt* (*ciudades*) to link; (*empresas, bancos*) to merge; (*personas*) to unite, bring together; **unirse** *vr* (*personas, grupos*) to join together, unite; (*empresas, bancos*) to merge; **este pasaje une los dos edificios** this passage links the two buildings; **unió los dos extremos con una cuerda** he joined the two ends with some string; **los unió en matrimonio** he united them in marriage; **la enfermedad de la madre ha unido a los hijos** the mother's illness has brought the children together; **les une una fuerte simpatía** they are bound by (a) strong affection; **~se en matrimonio** to marry
unisex *adj inv* unisex
unísono *nm*: **al ~** in unison
universal *adj* universal; (*mundial*) world *cpd*; **historia ~** world history
universidad *nf* university; **~ laboral** polytechnic, poly
universitario, -a *adj* university *cpd* ▷ *nm/f* (*profesor*) lecturer; (*estudiante*) (university) student
universo *nm* universe
uno, -a *adj* **1** (*numeral*) one; **Dios es ~** God is one; **~s pocos** a few; **~s cien dólares** about a hundred dollars; *ver tb* **un**
2 (*enfático*): **¡había una de gente!** there were so many people!
▷ *pron* **1** (*numeral*) one; **quiero ~ solo** I only want one; **~ de ellos** one of them; **una de dos** either one or the other; **¡no doy una hoy!** (*fam*) I can't do anything right today!; *ver tb* **cada**
2 (*alguien*) somebody, someone; **conozco a ~ que se te parece** I know somebody *o* someone who looks like you; **~s querían quedarse** some (people) wanted to stay
3 (*impersonal*) one; **~ nunca sabe qué hacer** one never knows what to do; **~ mismo** oneself
4: **~s ... otros ...** some ... others; **una y otra son muy agradables** they're both very nice; **(los) ~(s) a (los) otro(s)** each other, one another; **~ tras otro** one after the other
▷ *num* (number) one; **el día ~** the first
untar *vt* (*gen*) to rub; (*engrasar*) to grease, oil; (*Med*) to rub (with ointment); (*fig*) to bribe; **untarse** *vr* (*fig*) to be crooked; **~ el pan con**

mantequilla to spread butter on one's bread
uña *nf* (*Anat*) nail; (*del pie*) toenail; (*garra*) claw; (*casco*) hoof; (*arrancaclavos*) claw; **ser ~ y carne** to be as thick as thieves; **enseñar** *o* **mostrar** *o* **sacar las ~s** to show one's claws
uperizado, -a *adj*: **leche uperizada** UHT milk
uralita® *nf* corrugated asbestos cement
uranio *nm* uranium
urbanidad *nf* courtesy, politeness
urbanismo *nm* town planning
urbanización *nf* (*colonia, barrio*) estate, housing scheme
urbanizar *vt* to develop
urbano, -a *adj* (*de ciudad*) urban, town *cpd*; (*cortés*) courteous, polite
urbe *nf* large city, metropolis
urdimbre *nf* (*de tejido*) warp; (*intriga*) intrigue
urdir *vt* to warp; (*fig*) to plot, contrive
urgencia *nf* urgency; (*prisa*) haste, rush; **salida de ~** emergency exit; **servicios de ~** emergency services
urgente *adj* urgent; (*insistente*) insistent; **carta ~** registered (*Brit*) *o* special delivery (*US*) letter
urgir *vi* to be urgent; **me urge** I'm in a hurry for it; **me urge terminarlo** I must finish it as soon as I can
urinario, -a *adj* urinary ▷ *nm* urinal, public lavatory, comfort station (*US*)
urna *nf* urn; (*Pol*) ballot box; **acudir a las ~s** (*fig: persona*) to (go and) vote; (*: gobierno*) to go to the country
urología *nf* urology
urraca *nf* magpie
URSS *nf abr* (= *Unión de Repúblicas Socialistas Soviéticas*) USSR
Uruguay *nm*: **El ~** Uruguay
uruguayo, -a *adj, nm/f* Uruguayan
usado, -a *adj* (*gen*) used; (*ropa etc*) worn; **muy ~** worn out
usanza *nf* custom, usage
usar *vt* to use; (*ropa*) to wear ▷ *vi*: **~ de** to make use of; **usarse** *vr* to be used; (*ropa*) to be worn *o* in fashion
uso *nm* use; (*Mecánica etc*) wear; (*costumbre*) usage, custom; (*moda*) fashion; **al ~** in keeping with custom; **al ~ de** in the style of; **de ~ externo** (*Med*) for external application; **estar en el ~ de la palabra** to be speaking, have the floor; **~ y desgaste** (*Com*) wear and tear
usted *pron* (*sg: abr*): **Ud** *o*, **Vd** (formal) you *sg*; **~es** (*pl: abr*): **Uds** *o*, **Vds** (formal) you *pl*; (*LAm formal y fam*) you *pl*
usual *adj* usual
usuario, -a *nm/f* user; **~ final** (*Com*) end user
usufructo *nm* use; **~ vitalicio (de)** life interest (in)
usura *nf* usury
usurero, -a *nm/f* usurer
usurpar *vt* to usurp
utensilio *nm* tool; (*Culin*) utensil
útero *nm* uterus, womb
útil *adj* useful; (*servible*) usable, serviceable; **día ~**

working day, weekday; **es muy ~ tenerlo aquí cerca** it's very handy having it here close by
▷ *nm* tool
utilidad *nf* usefulness, utility; (*Com*) profit; **~es líquidas** net profit *sg*
utilizar *vt* to use, utilize; (*explotar*) to harness

utopía *nf* Utopia
utópico, -a *adj* Utopian
uva *nf* grape; **estar de mala ~** to be in a bad mood; **~ de Corinto** currant; **~ pasa** raisin
UVI *nf abr* (*Esp Med*: = *unidad de vigilancia intensiva*) ICU

Vv

v. *abr* (= *voltio*) v.; (= *véase*) v.; (= *verso*) v.

vaca *nf* (*animal*) cow; (*carne*) beef; (*cuero*) cowhide; **~s flacas/gordas** (*fig*) bad/good times

vacaciones *nfpl* holiday(s); **estar/irse o marcharse de ~** to be/go (away) on holiday

vacante *adj* vacant, empty ▷ *nf* vacancy

vaciar *vt* to empty (out); (*ahuecar*) to hollow out; (*moldear*) to cast; (*Inform*) to dump ▷ *vi* (*río*): **~ (en)** to flow (into); **vaciarse** *vr* to empty; (*fig*) to blab, spill the beans

vaciedad *nf* emptiness

vacilación *nf* hesitation

vacilante *adj* unsteady; (*habla*) faltering; (*luz*) flickering; (*fig*) hesitant

vacilar *vi* (*dudar*) to hesitate, waver; (*al andar*) to stagger, stumble; (*memoria*) to fail; (*esp LAm*: *divertirse*) to have a great time

vacilón *nm* (*esp LAm*): **estar o ir de ~** to have a great time

vacío, -a *adj* empty; (*puesto*) vacant; (*desocupado*) idle; (*vano*) vain; (*charla etc*) light, superficial ▷ *nm* emptiness; (*Física*) vacuum; (*espacio*) (empty) space; **hacer el ~ a algn** to send sb to Coventry

vacuna *nf* vaccine

vacunar *vt* to vaccinate; **vacunarse** *vr* to get vaccinated

vacuno, -a *adj* bovine

vacuo, -a *adj* empty

vadear *vt* (*río*) to ford; (*problema*) to overcome; (*persona*) to sound out

vado *nm* ford; (*solución*) solution; (*descanso*) respite

vagabundo, -a *adj* wandering; (*pey*) vagrant ▷ *nm/f* (*errante*) wanderer; (*vago*) tramp, bum (US)

vagamente *adv* vaguely

vagancia *nf* vagrancy

vagar *vi* to wander; (*pasear*) to saunter up and down; (*no hacer nada*) to idle ▷ *nm* leisure

vagina *nf* vagina

vago, -a *adj* vague; (*perezoso*) lazy; (*ambulante*) wandering ▷ *nm/f* (*vagabundo*) tramp, bum (US); (*perezoso*) lazybones *sg*, idler

vagón *nm* (*de pasajeros*) carriage; (*de mercancías*) wagon; **~ cama/restaurante** sleeping/dining car

vaguear *vi* to laze around

vaguedad *nf* vagueness

vaho *nm* (*vapor*) vapour, steam; (*olor*) smell; (*respiración*) breath; **vahos** *nmpl* (*Med*) inhalation *sg*

vaina *nf* sheath ▷ *nm* (*LAm*) nuisance

vainilla *nf* vanilla

vainita *nf* (*Col, Ven*) green o French bean

vaivén *nm* to-and-fro movement; (*de tránsito*) coming and going; **vaivenes** *nmpl* (*fig*) ups and downs

vajilla *nf* crockery, dishes *pl*; (*juego*) service; **~ de porcelana** chinaware

vale *nm* voucher; (*recibo*) receipt; (*pagaré*) I.O.U.; **~ de compra** voucher; **~ de regalo** gift voucher o token

valedero, -a *adj* valid

valenciano, -a *adj, nm/f* Valencian ▷ *nm* (*Ling*) Valencian

valentía *nf* courage, bravery; (*pey*) boastfulness; (*acción*) heroic deed

valentón, -ona *adj* blustering

valer *vt* (*costar*) to cost; (*tener valor*) to be worth; (*Mat*) to equal ▷ *vi* (*ser útil*) to be useful; (*fam*: *estar permitido*) to be allowed; (: *ser justo*) to be fair; **valerse** *vr* to defend o.s.; **¿cuánto vale?** how much does it cost?; **el terreno vale más que la casa** the land is worth more than the house; **este cuchillo no vale para nada** this knife is useless; **yo no valdría para enfermera** I'd make a hopeless nurse; **¡eso no vale!** that's not fair!; **¿vale?** O.K.?; **más vale que nos vayamos** we'd better go; **~ la pena** to be worthwhile; **más vale tarde que nunca** better late than never; **no puede ~se por sí mismo** he can't look after himself; **~se de** to make use of, take advantage of

valía *nf* worth; **de gran ~** (*objeto*) very valuable

validar *vt* to validate; (*Pol*) to ratify

validez *nf* validity; **dar ~ a** to validate

válido, -a *adj* valid

valiente *adj* brave, valiant; (*audaz*) bold; (*pey*) boastful; (*con ironía*) fine, wonderful ▷ *nm/f* brave man/woman

valija *nf* case; (*RP*) suitcase; (*Correos*) mailbag; **~ diplomática** diplomatic bag

valioso, -a *adj* valuable; (*rico*) wealthy

valla *nf* fence; (*Deporte*) hurdle; (*fig*) barrier; **~**

publicitaria billboard
vallar vt to fence in
valle nm valley, vale
valor nm (de moneda, joya) value; (valentía) courage; (importancia) importance; (fam: descaro) nerve, cheek (fam); **una pulsera de gran ~** an extremely valuable bracelet; **sin ~** worthless; **objetos de ~** valuables; **armarse de ~** to pluck up courage; **tuvo el ~ de pedírmelo** (fam) he had the cheek to ask me for it (fam); **dar ~ a algo** to attach importance to sth; **quitar ~ a algo** to minimize the importance of sth; **~ adquisitivo** purchasing power; **~ comercial** o **de mercado** market value; **~ de rescate/de sustitución** surrender/replacement value; **~ neto** net worth; **~ sentimental** sentimental value; ver tb **valores**
valoración nf valuation
valorar vt to value; (tasar) to price; (fig) to assess
valores nmpl (Com) securities; **~ en cartera** o **habidos** investments
vals nm waltz
válvula nf valve
vampiresa nf (Cine) vamp, femme fatale
vampiro, -a nm/f vampire
vanagloriarse vr to boast
vandalismo nm vandalism
vándalo, -a nm/f vandal
vanguardia nf vanguard; **de ~** (Arte) avant-garde; **estar en** o **ir a la ~ de** (fig) to be in the forefront of
vanguardista adj avant-garde
vanidad nf vanity; (inutilidad) futility; (irrealidad) unreality
vanidoso, -a adj vain, conceited
vano, -a adj (irreal) unreal; (irracional) unreasonable; (inútil) vain, useless; (persona) vain, conceited; (frívolo) frivolous
vapor nm vapour; (vaho) steam; (de gas) fumes pl; **vapores** nmpl (Med) hysterics; **al ~** (Culin) steamed
vaporizador nm (de perfume etc) spray
vaporizar vt to vaporize; (perfume) to spray
vaporoso, -a adj vaporous; (vahoso) steamy; (tela) light, airy
vapulear vt to thrash; (fig) to slate
vaquero, -a adj cattle cpd ▷ nm cowboy; **vaqueros** nmpl jeans
vaquilla nf heifer
vara nf stick, pole; (Tec) rod
variable adj, nf variable (tb Inform)
variación nf variation; **sin ~** unchanged
variado, -a adj varied; (dulces, galletas) assorted; **entremeses ~s** a selection of starters
variante adj variant ▷ nf (alternativa) alternative; (Auto) bypass
variar vt (cambiar) to change; (poner variedad) to vary; (modificar) to modify; (cambiar de posición) to switch around ▷ vi to vary; **~ de** to differ from; **~ de opinión** to change one's mind; **para ~** just for a change
varicela nf chicken pox
varices nfpl varicose veins

variedad nf variety
varilla nf stick; (Bot) twig; (Tec) rod; (de rueda) spoke
vario, -a adj (variado) varied; (multicolor) motley; (cambiable) changeable; **~s** various, several
variopinto, -a adj diverse; **un público ~** a mixed audience
varita nf: **~ mágica** magic wand
varón nm male, man
varonil adj manly
Varsovia nf Warsaw
vasco, -a, vascongado, -a adj, nm/f Basque ▷ nm (Ling) Basque
vascongadas nfpl: **las V~** the Basque Country sg o Provinces
vascuence nm (Ling) Basque
vasectomía nf vasectomy
vaselina nf Vaseline®
vasija nf (earthenware) vessel
vaso nm glass, tumbler; (Anat) vessel; (cantidad) glass(ful); **~ de vino** glass of wine; **~ para vino** wineglass
vástago nm (Bot) shoot; (Tec) rod; (fig) offspring
vasto, -a adj vast, huge
Vaticano nm: **el ~** the Vatican; **la Ciudad del ~** the Vatican City
vaticinio nm prophecy
vatio nm (Elec) watt
Vd(s) abr = **usted(es)**
vecindad nf, **vecindario** nm neighbourhood; (habitantes) residents pl
vecino, -a adj neighbouring ▷ nm/f neighbour; (residente) resident; **somos ~s** we live next door to one another
vector nm vector
veda nf prohibition; (temporada) close season
vedado nm preserve
vedar vt (prohibir) to ban, prohibit; (idea, plan) to veto; (impedir) to stop, prevent
vega nf fertile plain o valley
vegetación nf vegetation
vegetal adj, nm vegetable
vegetar vi to vegetate
vegetariano, -a adj, nm/f vegetarian
vegetativo, -a adj vegetative
vehemencia nf (insistencia) vehemence; (pasión) passion; (fervor) fervour; (violencia) violence
vehemente adj vehement
vehículo nm vehicle; (Med) carrier; **~ de servicio público** public service vehicle; **~ espacial** spacecraft
veinte num twenty; (orden, fecha) twentieth; **el siglo ~** the twentieth century
vejación nf vexation; (humillación) humiliation
vejar vt (irritar) to annoy, vex; (humillar) to humiliate
vejatorio, -a adj humiliating, degrading
vejez nf old age
vejiga nf (Anat) bladder
vela nf (de cera) candle; (Náut) sail; (Mil) sentry duty; (fam) snot; **a toda ~** (Náut) under full sail; **estar a dos ~s** (fam) to be skint; **pasar la noche**

en ~ to have a sleepless night
velada nf soirée; ver tb **velado**
velado, -a adj veiled; (sonido) muffled; (Foto) blurred; ver tb **velada**
velador nm watchman; (candelero) candlestick; (LAm) bedside table
velar vt (vigilar) to keep watch over; (cubrir) to veil ▷ vi to stay awake; **~ por** to watch over, look after
velatorio nm (funeral) wake
veleidad nf (ligereza) fickleness; (capricho) whim
velero nm (Náut) sailing ship; (Aviat) glider
veleta nm/f fickle person ▷ nf weather vane
veliz nm (Méx) suitcase
vello nm down, fuzz
velo nm veil; **~ del paladar** (Anat) soft palate
velocidad nf speed; (Tec) rate, pace, velocity; (Mecánica, Auto) gear; **¿a qué ~?** how fast?; **de alta ~** high-speed; **cobrar ~** to pick up o gather speed; **meter la segunda ~** to change into second gear; **~ máxima de impresión** (Inform) maximum print speed
velocímetro nm speedometer
veloz adj fast, swift
vena nf vein; (fig) vein, disposition; (Geo) seam, vein
venado nm deer; (Culin) venison
vencedor, a adj victorious ▷ nm/f victor, winner
vencer vt (enemigo) to defeat; (rival) to defeat, beat; (tentación) to overcome; (miedo, obstáculo) to overcome, surmount ▷ vi (jugador, partido político) to win; (pago) to fall due; (plazo, documento) to expire; **por fin lo venció el sueño** sleep finally overcame him; **dejarse ~** to yield, give in; **el pasaporte me vence mañana** my passport expires tomorrow
vencido, -a adj (derrotado) defeated, beaten; (Com) payable, due ▷ adv: **pagar ~** to pay in arrears; **le pagan por meses ~s** he is paid at the end of the month; **darse por ~** to give up
vencimiento nm collapse; (Com: de plazo) expiration; **a su ~** when it falls due
venda nf bandage
vendaje nm bandage, dressing
vendar vt to bandage; **~ los ojos** to blindfold
vendaval nm (viento) gale; (huracán) hurricane
vendedor, a nm/f seller; **~ ambulante** hawker, pedlar (Brit), peddler (US)
vender vt to sell; (comerciar) to market; (traicionar) to sell out, betray; **~ al contado/al por mayor/al por menor/a plazos** to sell for cash/wholesale/retail/on credit; **"se vende"** "for sale"; **"véndese coche"** "car for sale"; **~ al descubierto** to sell short
vendimia nf grape harvest; **la ~ de 1973** the 1973 vintage
vendimiar vi to pick grapes
veneno nm poison, venom
venenoso, -a adj poisonous
venerable adj venerable
venerar vt (reconocer) to venerate; (adorar) to worship
venéreo, -a adj venereal

venezolano, -a adj, nm/f Venezuelan
Venezuela nf Venezuela
venganza nf vengeance, revenge
vengar vt to avenge; **vengarse** vr to take revenge
vengativo, -a adj (persona) vindictive
venia nf (perdón) pardon; (permiso) consent; **con su ~** by your leave
venial adj venial
venida nf (llegada) arrival; (regreso) return; (fig) rashness
venidero, -a adj coming, future; **en lo ~** in (the) future
venir vi (a un lugar) to come; (noticia, comentario, foto) to be; **venirse** vr: **~se abajo** to collapse; **vino en taxi** he came by taxi; **¡ven acá!** come (over) here!; **enseguida vengo** I'll be back in a minute; **¡venga!** (Esp) come on!; **el año que viene** next year; **esta palabra no viene en el diccionario** this word isn't in the dictionary; **viene en varios colores** it comes in several colours; **¿te viene bien el sábado?** is Saturday alright for you?; **este jersey no me viene bien** this jumper doesn't fit me; **mañana me viene mal** tomorrow isn't good for me; **~ a menos** (persona) to lose status; (empresa) to go downhill
venta nf (Com) sale; (posada) inn; **estar de o en ~** to be (up) for sale o on the market; **~ a plazos** hire purchase; **~s a término** forward sales; **~ al contado/al por mayor/al por menor** o **al detalle** cash sale/wholesale/retail; **~ a domicilio** door-to-door selling; **~s brutas** gross sales; **~ de liquidación** clearance sale
ventaja nf advantage; **llevar la ~** (en carrera) to be leading o ahead
ventajoso, -a adj advantageous
ventana nf (tb Inform) window; **~ de guillotina/galería** sash/bay window; **~ de la nariz** nostril
ventanilla nf (de taquilla) window
ventilación nf ventilation; (corriente) draught; (fig) airing
ventilador nm ventilator; (eléctrico) fan
ventilar vt to ventilate; (poner a secar) to put out to dry; (fig) to air, discuss
ventisca nf blizzard
ventisquero nm snowdrift
ventosidad nf flatulence
ventoso, -a adj windy ▷ nf (Zool) sucker; (instrumento) suction pad
ventrílocuo, -a nm/f ventriloquist
ventura nf (felicidad) happiness; (buena suerte) luck; (destino) fortune; **a la (buena) ~** at random
venturoso, -a adj happy; (afortunado) lucky, fortunate
ver vi to see ▷ vt (percibir) to see; (tele, programa) to watch; **verse** vr (encontrarse) to meet; (hallarse: en una situación) to find o.s., be; **¿ves? ya te lo dije** see? I told you so; **a ~ ...** let's see ...; **no tener nada que ~ con algn/algo** to have nothing to do with sb/sth; **a mi modo de ~** as I see it; **eso está por ~** that remains to be seen; **¡cuánto tiempo sin ~te!** I haven't seen you for ages!; **no he visto esa película** I haven't seen that film; **¡no la**

puedo ~! I can't stand her!; **por lo que veo ...** apparently ...; **¡viera(n)** o **hubiera(n) visto qué casa!** (LAm fam) if only you'd seen the house!, what a house!; **ya se ve que ...** it is obvious that ...; **merece ~se** it's worth seeing; **¡habráse visto!** did you ever! (fam); **quedamos en ~nos en la estación** we arranged to meet at the station; **¡luego nos vemos!** see you later!

vera nf edge, verge; (de río) bank; **a la ~ de** near, next to

veracidad nf truthfulness

veranear vi to spend the summer

veraneo nm: **estar de ~** to be away on (one's summer) holiday; **lugar de ~** holiday resort

veraniego, -a adj summer cpd

verano nm summer

veras nfpl truth sg; **de ~** really, truly; **esto va de ~** this is serious

veraz adj truthful

verbal adj verbal; (mensaje etc) oral

verbena nf street party

verbo nm verb

verboso, -a adj verbose

verdad nf truth; **les dije la ~** I told them the truth; **la ~ es que no tengo ganas** I don't really feel like it; **¡es ~!** it's true!; **es bonito, ¿~?** it's pretty, isn't it?; **no te gusta, ¿~?** you don't like it, do you?; **de ~: de ~ que yo no dije eso** I didn't say that, honestly; **no era un policía de ~** he wasn't a real policeman

verdadero, -a adj (veraz) true, truthful; (fiable) reliable; (fig) real

verde adj green; (fruta etc) green, unripe; (chiste etc) blue, smutty, dirty; **viejo ~** dirty old man; **poner ~ a algn** to give sb a dressing-down ⊳ nm green

verdear, verdecer vi to turn green

verdor nm (lo verde) greenness; (Bot) verdure; (fig) youthful vigour

verdugo nm executioner; (Bot) shoot; (cardenal) weal

verdulero, -a nm/f greengrocer

verdura nf greenness; **verduras** nfpl (Culin) greens

vereda nf path; (CS: acera) pavement, sidewalk (US); **meter a algn en ~** to bring sb into line

veredicto nm verdict

vergel nm lush garden

vergonzoso, -a adj shameful; (tímido) timid, bashful

vergüenza nf shame, sense of shame; (timidez) bashfulness; (pudor) modesty; **tener ~** to be ashamed; **me da ~ decírselo** I feel too shy o it embarrasses me to tell him; **¡qué ~!** (de situación) what a disgrace!; (a persona) shame on you!

verídico, -a adj true, truthful

verificar vt to check; (corroborar) to verify (tb Inform); (testamento) to prove; (llevar a cabo) to carry out; **verificarse** vr to occur, happen; (mitin etc) to be held; (profecía etc) to come o prove true

verja nf iron gate; (cerca) railing(s) (pl); (rejado) grating

vermut (pl **-s**) nm vermouth ⊳ nf (esp LAm) matinée

verosímil adj likely, probable; (relato) credible

verruga nf wart

versado, -a adj: **~ en** versed in

versátil adj versatile

versión nf version; (traducción) translation

verso nm (estilo) verse; **un ~** a line of poetry; **~ libre/suelto** free/blank verse

vértebra nf vertebra

vertebrado, -a adj, nm/f vertebrate

vertebral adj vertebral; **columna ~** spine

verter vt (vaciar) to empty, pour (out); (tirar) to dump ⊳ vi to flow

vertical adj vertical; (postura, piano etc) upright ⊳ nf vertical

vértice nm vertex, apex

vertiente nf slope

vertiginoso, -a adj giddy, dizzy

vértigo nm vertigo; (mareo) dizziness; (actividad) intense activity; **de ~** (fam: velocidad) giddy; (: ruido) tremendous; (: talento) fantastic

vesícula nf blister; **~ biliar** gall bladder

vespa® nf (motor) scooter

vespertino, -a adj evening cpd

vespino® nm o f ≈ moped

vestíbulo nm hall; (de teatro) foyer

vestido nm (ropa) clothes pl, clothing; (de mujer) dress, frock

vestigio nm (trazo) trace; (señal) sign; **vestigios** nmpl remains

vestimenta nf clothing

vestir vt (a otra persona) to dress; (llevar puesto: ropa) to wear ⊳ vi to dress; **vestirse** vr to get dressed, dress o.s.; **estaba vistiendo a los niños** I was dressing the children; **vestía pantalones vaqueros y una camiseta** he was wearing jeans and a T-shirt; **~ bien** to dress well; **viste de negro** he dresses in black; **se está vistiendo** he's getting dressed; **se vistió de princesa** she dressed up as a princess

vestuario nm clothes pl, wardrobe; (Teat: para actores) dressing room; (: para público) cloakroom; (Deporte) changing room

veta nf (vena) vein, seam; (raya) streak; (de madera) grain

vetar vt to veto

veterano, -a adj, nm/f veteran

veterinaria nf veterinary science; ver tb **veterinario**

veterinario, -a nm/f vet(erinary surgeon); ver tb **veterinaria**

veto nm veto

vetusto, -a adj ancient

vez nf (pl **veces**) (momento) time; (turno) turn; **la próxima ~** next time; **¿cuántas veces al año?** how many times a year?; **¿la has visto alguna ~?** have you ever seen her?; **a la ~ (que)** at the same time (as); **una ~** once; **la veo una ~ a la semana** I see her once a week; **dos veces** twice; **a veces** sometimes; **cada ~ más** more and more; **cada ~ menos** less and less; **de ~ en cuando**

from time to time; **de una (sola)** ~ in one go; **de una ~ para siempre** once and for all; **en ~ de** instead of; **otra** ~ again; **una y otra** ~ again and again; **pocas veces** seldom; **7 veces 9** 7 times 9; **érase una** ~ once upon a time (there was); **hacer las veces de** to stand in for; **tal** ~ perhaps
vía nf (calle) road; (ruta) track, route; (Ferro) line; (fig) way; (Anat) passage, tube; **el tren está en la ~ 8** the train is (standing) at platform 8; **por ~ oral** orally; **por ~ judicial** by legal means; **por ~ oficial** through official channels; **por ~ de** by way of; **en ~s de** in the process of; **un país en ~s de desarrollo** a developing country; **~ aérea** airway; **V~ Láctea** Milky Way; **~ pública** public highway o thoroughfare; **~ única** one-way street ▷ prep via, by way of
viable adj (Com) viable; (plan etc) feasible
viaducto nm viaduct
viajante nm commercial traveller, traveling salesman (US)
viajar vi to travel, journey
viaje nm (de ida y vuelta) trip; (trayecto) journey; (Náut) voyage; (Com: carga) load; **los ~s** travel sg; **estar de** ~ to be on a journey; **~ de ida y vuelta** round trip; **~ de novios** honeymoon
viajero, -a adj travelling (Brit), traveling (US); (Zool) migratory ▷ nm/f (quien viaja) traveller; (pasajero) passenger
vial adj road cpd, traffic cpd
víbora nf viper
vibración nf vibration
vibrador nm vibrator
vibrante adj vibrant, vibrating
vibrar vt to vibrate ▷ vi to vibrate; (pulsar) to throb, beat, pulsate
vicario nm curate
vicegerente nm/f assistant manager
vicepresidente nm/f vice president; (de comité etc) vice-chairman
viceversa adv vice versa
viciado, -a adj (corrompido) corrupt; (contaminado) foul, contaminated
viciar vt (pervertir) to pervert; (adulterar) to adulterate; (falsificar) to falsify; (Jur) to nullify; (estropear) to spoil; (sentido) to twist; **viciarse** vr to become corrupted; (aire, agua) to be(come) polluted
vicio nm (libertinaje) vice; (mala costumbre) bad habit; (mimo) spoiling; (alabeo) warp, warping; **de** o **por** ~ out of sheer habit
vicioso, -a adj (muy malo) vicious; (corrompido) depraved; (mimado) spoiled ▷ nm/f depraved person; (adicto) addict
vicisitud nf vicissitude
víctima nf victim; (de accidente etc) casualty
victoria nf victory
victorioso, -a adj victorious
vicuña nf vicuna
vid nf vine
vida nf life; (duración) lifetime; (modo de vivir) way of life; **¡~!, ¡~ mía!** (saludo cariñoso) my love!; **de por** ~ for life; **de ~ airada** o **libre** loose-living;

en la/mi ~ never; **estar con** ~ to be still alive; **ganarse la** ~ to earn one's living; **¡esto es ~!** this is the life!; **le va la ~ en esto** his life depends on it
vidente nm/f (adivino) clairvoyant; (no ciego) sighted person
vídeo nm video; (aparato) video (recorder); **cinta de** ~ videotape; **película de** ~ videofilm; **grabar en** ~ to record, (video)tape; **~ compuesto/inverso** (Inform) composite/reverse video
videocámara nf video camera; (pequeña) camcorder
videocassette nm video cassette
videoclip nm (music) video
videoclub nm video shop
videojuego nm video game
videotex(o) nm Videotex®
vidriera nf (ventana) stained-glass window; (LAm: de tienda) shop window; (puerta) glass door; ver tb **vidriero**
vidriero, -a nm/f glazier; ver tb **vidriera**
vidrio nm glass; (LAm) window; **~ cilindrado/inastillable** plate/splinter-proof glass
vidrioso, -a adj glassy; (frágil) fragile, brittle; (resbaladizo) slippery
viejo, -a adj old ▷ nm/f old man/woman; **mi ~/vieja** (fam) my old man/woman; **hacerse** o **ponerse** ~ to grow o get old
Viena nf Vienna
vienés, -esa adj, nm/f Viennese
viento nm wind; **ir ~ en popa** to go splendidly; (negocio) to prosper; **contra ~ y marea** at all costs
vientre nm belly; (matriz) womb; **vientres** nmpl bowels; **hacer de** ~ to have a movement of the bowels
viernes nm inv Friday; **V~ Santo** Good Friday
Vietnam nm: **el** ~ Vietnam
vietnamita adj, nm/f Vietnamese
viga nf beam, rafter; (de metal) girder
vigencia nf validity; (de contrato etc) term, life; **estar/entrar en** ~ to be in/come into effect o force
vigente adj valid, in force; (imperante) prevailing
vigésimo, -a num twentieth
vigía nm look-out ▷ nf (atalaya) watchtower; (acción) watching
vigilancia nf vigilance
vigilante adj vigilant ▷ nm caretaker; (en cárcel) warder; (en almacén) shopwalker (Brit), floorwalker (US); **~ jurado** security guard (licensed to carry a gun); **~ nocturno** night watchman
vigilar vt to watch over; (cuidar) to look after, keep an eye on ▷ vi to be vigilant; (hacer guardia) to keep watch
vigilia nf wakefulness; (Rel) fast; **comer de** ~ to fast
vigor nm vigour, vitality; **en** ~ in force; **entrar/poner en** ~ to take/put into effect
vigoroso, -a adj vigorous
VIH nm abr (= virus de inmunodeficiencia humana) HIV
vil adj vile, low
vileza nf vileness; (acto) base deed

vilipendiar vt to vilify, revile
villa nf (pueblo) small town; (municipalidad) municipality; **la V~** (Esp) Madrid; **~ miseria** shanty town
villancico nm (Christmas) carol
villorrio nm one-horse town, dump; (LAm: barrio pobre) shanty town
vilo: en ~ adv in the air, suspended; (fig) on tenterhooks, in suspense; **estar** o **quedar en ~** to be left in suspense
vinagre nm vinegar
vinagrera nf vinegar bottle; **vinagreras** nfpl cruet stand sg
vinagreta nf French dressing
vincha nf (And, CS) hairband
vinculación nf (lazo) link, bond; (acción) linking
vincular vt to link, bind
vínculo nm link, bond
vinicultura nf wine growing
vino nm wine; **~ de solera/seco/tinto** vintage/dry/red wine; **~ de Jerez** sherry; **~ de Oporto** port (wine)
viña nf, **viñedo** nm vineyard
viñeta nf (en historieta) cartoon
viola nf viola
violación nf violation; (Jur) offence, infringement; (estupro): **~ (sexual)** rape; **~ de contrato** (Com) breach of contract
violar vt to violate; (Jur) to infringe; (cometer estupro) to rape
violencia nf (fuerza) violence, force; (situación comprometida) embarrassment; (acto injusto) unjust act
violentar vt to force; (casa) to break into; (agredir) to assault; (violar) to violate
violento, -a adj violent; (furioso) furious; (situación) embarrassing; (acto) forced, unnatural; (difícil) awkward; **me es muy ~** it goes against the grain with me
violeta nf violet
violín nm violin
violón nm double bass
viraje nm turn; (de vehículo) swerve; (de carretera) bend; (fig) change of direction
virar vi (hacer girar) to turn; (bruscamente) to swerve; (cambiar de dirección) to change direction
virgen adj virgin; (cinta) blank ▷ nm/f virgin; **la Santísima V~** (Rel) the Blessed Virgin
virginidad nf virginity
Virgo nm Virgo
viril adj virile
virilidad nf virility
virtual adj (real) virtual; (en potencia) potential
virtud nf virtue; **en ~ de** by virtue of
virtuoso, -a adj virtuous ▷ nm/f virtuoso
viruela nf smallpox; **viruelas** nfpl pockmarks; **~s locas** chickenpox sg
virulento, -a adj virulent
virus nm inv virus
visa nf, (LAm) **visado** nm visa; **~ de permanencia** residence permit
víscera nf internal organ; **vísceras** nfpl entrails

visceral adj (odio) deep-rooted; **reacción ~** gut reaction
viscoso, -a adj viscous
visera nf visor
visibilidad nf visibility
visible adj visible; (fig) obvious; **exportaciones/importaciones ~s** (Com) visible exports/imports
visillo nm lace curtain
visión nf (Anat) vision, (eye)sight; (fantasía) vision, fantasy; (panorama) view; **ver visiones** to see o be seeing things
visionario, -a adj (que prevé) visionary; (alucinado) deluded ▷ nm/f visionary; (chalado) lunatic
visita nf call, visit; (persona) visitor; **horas/tarjeta de ~** visiting hours/card; **hacer una ~** to pay a visit; **ir de ~** to go visiting; **~ de cortesía/de cumplido/de despedida** courtesy/formal/farewell visit
visitar vt to visit, call on; (inspeccionar) to inspect
vislumbrar vt to glimpse, catch a glimpse of
vislumbre nf glimpse; (centelleo) gleam; (idea vaga) glimmer
viso nm (de metal) glint, gleam; (de tela) sheen; (aspecto) appearance; **hay un ~ de verdad en esto** there is an element of truth in this
visón nm mink
visor nm (Foto) viewfinder
víspera nf eve, day before; **la ~** o **en ~s de** on the eve of
vista nf (sentido) (eye)sight; (perspicacia) vision; (panorama) view; (Jur) hearing; **perder la ~** to lose one's sight; **conocer a alguien de ~** to know someone by sight; **fijar** o **clavar la ~ en algn/algo** to stare at sb/sth; **a primera ~** at first glance; **¡hasta la ~!** see you!; **hacer la ~ gorda** to turn a blind eye; **volver la ~** to look back; **está a la ~ que ...** it's obvious that ...; **perder algo de ~** to lose sight of sth; **a la ~** (Com) at sight; **a la ~ de sus informes** at the light of his reports; **en ~ de ...** in view of ...; **en ~ de que ...** in view of the fact that ...; **con ~s a una solución del problema** with a view to solving the problem; ver tb **visto**
vistazo nm glance; **dar** o **echar un ~ a** to glance at
visto, -a adj seen; (considerado) considered ▷ nm: **~ bueno** approval; **por lo ~** evidently; **está ~ que** it's clear that; **está bien/mal** it's acceptable/unacceptable; **está muy ~** it is very common; **estaba ~** it had to be; **~ que** conj since, considering that; **"~ bueno"** "approved"; **dar el ~ bueno a algo** to give sth the go-ahead
vistoso, -a adj colourful; (alegre) gay; (pey) gaudy
visual adj visual
vital adj life cpd, living cpd; (fig) vital; (persona) lively, vivacious
vitalicio, -a adj for life
vitalidad nf vitality
vitamina nf vitamin
viticultor, a nm/f vine grower
viticultura nf vine growing
vitorear vt to cheer, acclaim
vítores nmpl cheers

vítreo, -a *adj* vitreous

vitrina *nf* glass case; (*en casa*) display cabinet; (*LAm*) shop window

vituperio *nm* (*condena*) condemnation; (*censura*) censure; (*insulto*) insult

viudedad *nf* widowhood

viudo, -a *adj* widowed ▷ *nm/f* widow/widower

viva *excl* hurrah! ▷ *nm* cheer; **¡~ el rey!** long live the King!

vivacidad *nf* (*vigor*) vigour; (*vida*) vivacity

vivaracho, -a *adj* jaunty, lively; (*ojos*) bright, twinkling

vivaz *adj* (*que dura*) enduring; (*vigoroso*) vigorous; (*vivo*) lively

vivencia *nf* experience

víveres *nmpl* provisions

vivero *nm* (*Horticultura*) nursery; (*para peces*) fishpond; (: *Com*) fish farm

vivienda *nf* (*alojamiento*) housing; (*morada*) dwelling; **~s protegidas** o **sociales** council housing *sg* (*Brit*), public housing *sg* (*US*)

viviente *adj* living

vivir *vi* to live ▷ *vt* (*experimentar*) to live o go through ▷ *nm* life, way of life; **¿dónde vives?** where do you live?; **viven juntos** they live together; **¿todavía vive?** is he still alive?; **~ de**: **viven de su pensión** they live on his pension

vivo, -a *adj* living, live, alive; (*fig*) vivid; (*movimiento*) quick; (*color*) bright; (*protesta etc*) strong; (*astuto*) smart, clever; **en ~** (*TV etc*) live; **llegar a lo ~** to cut to the quick; *ver tb* **viva**

V.O. *abr* = **versión original**

vocablo *nm* (*palabra*) word; (*término*) term

vocabulario *nm* vocabulary, word list

vocación *nf* vocation

vocacional *nf* (*LAm*) ≈ technical college

vocal *adj* vocal ▷ *nm/f* member (of a committee etc) ▷ *nm* non-executive director ▷ *nf* vowel

vocalizar *vt* to vocalize

vocear *vt* (*para vender*) to cry; (*aclamar*) to acclaim; (*fig*) to proclaim ▷ *vi* to yell

vocerío *nm* shouting; (*escándalo*) hullabaloo

vocero, -a *nm/f* (*LAm*) spokesman/woman

vociferar *vt* to shout; (*jactarse*) to proclaim boastfully ▷ *vi* to yell

vodka *nm* vodka

vol *abr* = **volumen**

volador, a *adj* flying

volandas: en ~ *adv* in o through the air; (*fig*) swiftly

volante *adj* flying ▷ *nm* (*de máquina, coche*) steering wheel; (*de reloj*) balance; (*nota*) note; **ir al ~** to be at the wheel, be driving

volar *vt* (*demoler*) to blow up, demolish ▷ *vi* to fly; (*fig: correr*) to rush, hurry; (*fam: desaparecer*) to disappear; **voy volando** I must dash; **¡cómo vuela el tiempo!** how time flies!

volátil *adj* volatile; (*fig*) changeable

volcán *nm* volcano

volcánico, -a *adj* volcanic

volcar *vt* to upset, overturn; (*tumbar, derribar*) to knock over; (*vaciar*) to empty out ▷ *vi* to

overturn; **volcarse** *vr* to tip over; (*barco*) to capsize

voleibol *nm* volleyball

volqué, volquemos *etc vb ver* **volcar**

volquete *nm* dumper, dump truck (*US*)

voltaje *nm* voltage

voltear *vt* to turn over; (*volcar*) to knock over; (*doblar*) to peal ▷ *vi* to roll over; **voltearse** *vr* (*LAm*) to turn round; **~ a hacer algo** (*LAm*) to do sth again

voltereta *nf* somersault; **~ lateral** cartwheel; **~ sobre las manos** handspring

voltio *nm* volt

voluble *adj* fickle

volumen *nm* volume; **bajar el ~** to turn down the volume; **poner la radio a todo ~** to turn the radio up full; **~ de negocios** turnover; **~ monetario** money supply

voluminoso, -a *adj* voluminous; (*enorme*) massive

voluntad *nf* will, willpower; (*deseo*) desire, wish; (*afecto*) fondness; **a ~** at will; (*cantidad*) as much as one likes; **buena ~** goodwill; **mala ~** ill will, malice; **por causas ajenas a mi ~** for reasons beyond my control

voluntario, -a *adj* voluntary ▷ *nm/f* volunteer

voluntarioso, -a *adj* headstrong

voluptuoso, -a *adj* voluptuous

volver *vi* (*ir de vuelta*) to go back; (*venir de vuelta*) to come back ▷ *vt* (*colcha, cabeza, esquina*) to turn; (*manga*) to roll up; (*poner boca abajo*) to turn over, turn upside down; (*poner lo de dentro afuera*) to turn inside out; (*poner lo de atrás adelante*) to turn back to front, turn (the other way) round; **volverse** *vr* (*girarse*) to turn round; (*llegar a ser*) to become; **~ a hacer algo** to do sth again; **he vuelto a equivocarme** I've made a mistake again; **~ en sí** to come to o round, regain consciousness; **~ loco a algn** to drive sb mad; **me volvió la espalda** he turned away from me; **~ la vista atrás** to look back; **se ha vuelto muy cariñoso** he's become very affectionate; **~se loco** to go mad

vomitar *vt, vi* to vomit

vómito *nm* (*acto*) vomiting; (*resultado*) vomit

voracidad *nf* voracity

voraz *adj* voracious; (*fig*) fierce

vórtice *nm* whirlpool; (*de aire*) whirlwind

vos *pron* (*CAm, CS*) you

vosotros, -as *pron* you *pl*; (*reflexivo*) yourselves; **entre ~** among yourselves

votación *nf* (*acto*) voting; (*voto*) vote; **someter algo a ~** to put sth to the vote; **~ a mano alzada** show of hands

votar *vt* (*Pol: partido etc*) to vote for; (*proyecto: aprobar*) to pass; (*Rel*) to vow ▷ *vi* to vote

voto *nm* vote; (*promesa*) vow; (*maldición*) oath, curse; **votos** *nmpl* (good) wishes; **dar su ~** to cast one's vote; **~ de bloque/de grupo** block/card vote; **~ de censura/de (des)confianza/de gracias** vote of censure/(no) confidence/thanks

voy *vb ver* **ir**

voz *nf* voice; (*grito*) shout; (*chisme*) rumour; (*Ling*:

palabra) word; (: *del verbo*) voice; **dar voces** to shout, yell; **a media ~** in a low voice; **en ~ alta** aloud; **de viva ~** verbally; **a ~ en cuello** *o* **en grito** at the top of one's voice; **llamar a algn a voces** to shout to sb; **llevar la ~ cantante** (*fig*) to be the boss; **tener la ~ tomada** to be hoarse; **tener ~ y voto** to have the right to speak; **~ de mando** command

vuelco *nm* spill, overturning; (*fig*) collapse; **mi corazón dio un ~** my heart missed a beat

vuelo *nm* flight; (*encaje*) lace, frill; (*de falda etc*) loose part; (*fig*) importance; **de altos ~s** (*fig*: *plan*) grandiose; (: *persona*) ambitious; **alzar el ~** to take flight; (*fig*) to dash off; **coger al ~** to catch in flight; **~ en picado** dive; **~ libre** hang-gliding; **~ regular** scheduled flight; **falda de mucho ~** full *o* wide skirt

vuelta *nf* (*giro*) turn; (*regreso*) return; (*paseo: a pie*) stroll; (: *en coche*) drive; (*curva*) bend; (*en circuito*) lap; (*cambio*) change; **el coche dio la ~** the car turned round; **dar la ~ al mundo** to go round the world; **dimos una ~ de campana** we overturned completely; **dar ~s a una idea** to turn over an idea (in one's mind); **vive a la**

~ de la esquina he lives round the corner; **iré a verte a la ~** (*Esp*) I'll come and see you when I get back; **estar de ~** to be back; **un billete de ida y ~** a return ticket; **a ~ de correo** by return of post; **dar una ~** (*a pie*) to go for a walk; (*en coche*) to go for a drive; **~ a empezar** back to square one; **poner a algn de ~ y media** to heap abuse on sb; **no tiene ~ de hoja** there's no alternative; **~ ciclista** cycle race

vuelto *pp de* **volver** ▷ *nm* (*LAm*: *moneda*) change

vuestro, -a *adj* your; (*después de n*) of yours ▷ *pron*: **el ~/la vuestra/los ~s/las vuestras** yours; **lo ~** (what is) yours; **un amigo ~** a friend of yours; **una idea vuestra** an idea of yours

vulgar *adj* (*ordinario*) vulgar; (*común*) common

vulgaridad *nf* commonness; (*acto*) vulgarity; (*expresión*) coarse expression; **vulgaridades** *nfpl* banalities

vulgarizar *vt* to popularize

vulgo *nm* common people

vulnerable *adj* vulnerable

vulnerar *vt* to harm, damage; (*derechos*) to interfere with; (*Jur*, *Com*) to violate

vulva *nf* vulva

walkie-talkie *nm* walkie-talkie
walkman® *nm* Walkman®
wáter *nm* lavatory
waterpolo *nm* waterpolo
web *nm* o *nf* (*página*) web page; (*red*) (World Wide) Web

webcam *nf* webcam
webmaster *nm/f* webmaster
web site *nm* website
whisky *nm* whisky
windsurf *nm* windsurfing

Xx

xenofobia *nf* xenophobia
xenófobo, -a *adj* xenophobic ▷ *nm/f* xenophobe

xerografía *nf* xerography
xilófono *nm* xylophone

Yy

y *conj* and; **Andrés y su novia** Andrés and his girlfriend; **yo quiero una ensalada, ¿y tú?** I'd like a salad, what about you?; **¿y eso?** why?, how so?; **¡y yo!** me too!; **¿y qué?** so what?; **son las tres y cinco** it's five minutes past three; **y bueno ...** well ...; *ver tb* **e**

ya [ja] *adv* (*gen*) already; (*ahora*) now; (*en seguida*) at once; (*pronto*) soon ▷ *excl* all right!; (*por supuesto*) of course! ▷ *conj* (*ahora que*) now that; **ya no** not any more, no longer; **ya lo sé** I know; **ya dice que sí, ya dice que no** first he says yes, then he says no; **¡ya, ya!** yes, yes!; (*con impaciencia*) all right!, O.K.!; **¡ya voy!** (*enfático: no se suele traducir*) coming!; **ya que** since

yacer *vi* to lie

yacimiento *nm* bed, deposit; **~ petrolífero** oilfield

yagual *nm* padded ring (*for carrying loads on the head*)

yanqui *adj* Yankee ▷ *nm/f* Yank, Yankee

yate *nm* yacht

yedra *nf* ivy

yegua *nf* mare

yema *nf* (*del huevo*) yoke; (*Bot*) leaf bud; **~ del dedo** fingertip

yermo, -a *adj* barren; (*de gente*) uninhabited ▷ *nm* waste land

yerno *nm* son-in-law

yerto, -a *adj* stiff

yesca *nf* tinder

yeso *nm* (*Geo*) gypsum; (*Arq*) plaster

yo *pron personal* I; **soy yo** it's me, it is I; **yo que tú/usted** if I were you

yodo *nm* iodine

yoga *nm* yoga

yogur(t) *nm* yogurt

yuca *nm* (*comestible*) manioc root, cassava; (*ornamental*) yucca

yudo *nm* judo

yugo *nm* yoke

Yugoslavia *nf* Yugoslavia

yugular *adj* jugular

yunque *nm* anvil

yunta *nf* yoke

yuntero *nm* ploughman

yute *nm* jute

yuxtaponer *vt* to juxtapose

yuxtaposición *nf* juxtaposition

Zz

zafar vt (soltar) to untie; (superficie) to clear; **zafarse** vr (escaparse) to escape; (ocultarse) to hide o.s. away; (Tec) to slip off; **~se de** (persona) to get away from

zafio, -a adj coarse

zafiro nm sapphire

zaga nf rear; **a la ~** behind, in the rear

zagal nm boy, lad

zaguán nm hallway

zaherir vt (criticar) to criticize; (fig: herir) to wound

zaino, -a adj (color de caballo) chestnut; (pérfido) treacherous; (animal) vicious

zalamería nf flattery

zalamero, -a adj flattering; (relamido) suave

zamarra nf (piel) sheepskin; (chaqueta) sheepskin jacket

zambullirse vr to dive; (ocultarse) to hide o.s.

zampar vt (esconder) to hide o put away (hurriedly); (comer) to gobble; (arrojar) to hurl ▷ vi to eat voraciously; **zamparse** vr (chocar) to bump; (fig) to gatecrash

zanahoria nf carrot

zancada nf stride

zancadilla nf trip; (fig) stratagem; **echar** o **poner la ~ a algn** to trip sb up

zanco nm stilt

zancudo, -a adj long-legged ▷ nm (LAm) mosquito

zángano nm (insecto) drone; (holgazán) idler, slacker

zanja nf (fosa) ditch; (tumba) grave

zanjar vt (fosa) to ditch, trench; (problema) to surmount; (conflicto) to resolve

zapallito nm (CS) baby marrow, courgette, zucchini (US)

zapallo nm (CS, Perú) pumpkin

zapata nf half-boot; (Mecánica) shoe

zapatear vt (tocar) to tap with one's foot; (patear) to kick; (fam) to ill-treat ▷ vi to tap with one's feet

zapatería nf (oficio) shoemaking; (tienda) shoe-shop; (fábrica) shoe factory

zapatero, -a nm/f shoemaker; **~ remendón** cobbler

zapatilla nf slipper; (Tec) washer; (de deporte) training shoe

zapato nm shoe

zapping nm channel-hopping; **hacer ~** to channel-hop

zar nm tsar, czar

zarandear vt to sieve; (fam) to shake vigorously

zarpa nf (garra) claw, paw; **echar la ~ a** to claw at; (fam) to grab

zarpar vi to weigh anchor

zarpazo nm: **dar un ~** to claw

zarza nf (Bot) bramble

zarzal nm (matorral) bramble patch

zarzamora nf blackberry

zarzuela nf Spanish light opera; **la Z~** home of the Spanish Royal Family

zigzag adj zigzag

zigzaguear vi to zigzag

zinc nm zinc

zócalo nm (Arq) plinth, base; (de pared) skirting board

zoco nm (Arab) market, souk

zodíaco nm zodiac; **signo del ~** star sign

zona nf zone; **~ de fomento** o **de desarrollo** development area; **~ del dólar** (Com) dollar area; **~ fronteriza** border area

zoología nf zoology

zoológico, -a adj zoological ▷ nm (tb: **parque zoológico**) zoo

zoólogo, -a nm/f zoologist

zopenco, -a (fam) adj dull, stupid ▷ nm/f clot, nitwit

zopilote nm (LAm) buzzard

zoquete nm (de madera) block; (de pan) crust; (persona: fam) blockhead

zorra nf (fam) whore, tart, hooker (US); ver tb **zorro**

zorro, -a adj crafty ▷ nm/f fox/vixen; ver tb **zorra**

zozobra nf (fig) anxiety

zozobrar vi (hundirse) to capsize; (fig) to fail

zueco nm clog

zumbar vt (burlar) to tease; (golpear) to hit ▷ vi to buzz; (fam) to be very close; **zumbarse** vr: **~se de** to tease; **me zumban los oídos** I have a buzzing o ringing in my ears

zumbido nm buzzing; (fam) punch; **~ de oídos** buzzing o ringing in the ears

zumo nm juice; **~ de naranja** (fresh) orange juice

zurcir *vt* (*coser*) to darn; (*fig*) to put together; **¡que las zurzan!*** to blazes with them!*

zurdo, -a *adj* (*mano*) left; (*persona*) left-handed

zurrar *vt* (*Tec*) to dress; (*fam: pegar duro*) to wallop; (: *aplastar*) to flatten; (: *criticar*) to criticize harshly

zurrón *nm* pouch

zutano, -a *nm/f* so-and-so

ENGLISH – SPANISH

INGLÉS – ESPAÑOL

Aa

A, a [eɪ] *n* (*letter*) A, a; (*Scol: mark*) ≈ sobresaliente; (*Mus*): **A** la; **A for Andrew**, (*US*) **A for Able** A de Antonio; **A road** *n* (*Brit Aut*) ≈ carretera nacional; **A shares** *npl* (*Brit Stock Exchange*) acciones de clase A

a [ə] *indef art* (*before vowel or silent h:* **an an**) **1** un(a); **a book** un libro; **an apple** una manzana; **she's a nurse** (ella) es enfermera; **I haven't got a car** no tengo coche
2 (*instead of the number "one"*) un(a); **a year ago** hace un año; **a hundred/thousand pounds** cien/mil libras
3 (*in expressing ratios, prices etc*): **3 a day/week** 3 al día/a la semana; **10 km an hour** 10 km por hora; **£5 a person** 5 libras por persona; **30p a kilo** 30p el kilo; **3 times a month** 3 veces al mes

AA *n abbr* (*Brit*: = *Automobile Association*) ≈ RACE (*Esp*); = **Alcoholics Anonymous**; (*US*: = *Associate in/of Arts*) título universitario; (= *anti-aircraft*) A.A.

AAA *n abbr* (= *American Automobile Association*) ≈ RACE (*Esp*) [ˈθriːˈeɪz] (*Brit*: = *Amateur Athletics Association*) asociación de atletismo amateur

aback [əˈbæk] *adv*: **to be taken ~** quedar(se) desconcertado

abandon [əˈbændən] *vt* abandonar; (*renounce*) renunciar a ▷ *n* abandono; (*wild behaviour*): **with ~ con** desenfreno; **to ~ ship** abandonar el barco

abate [əˈbeɪt] *vi* moderarse; (*lessen*) disminuir; (*calm down*) calmarse

abattoir [ˈæbətwɑːʳ] *n* (*Brit*) matadero

abbey [ˈæbɪ] *n* abadía

abbot [ˈæbət] *n* abad

abbreviate [əˈbriːvieɪt] *vt* abreviar

abbreviation [əbriːvɪˈeɪʃən] *n* (*short form*) abreviatura; (*act*) abreviación

ABC *n abbr* (= *American Broadcasting Company*) cadena de televisión

abdicate [ˈæbdɪkeɪt] *vt, vi* abdicar

abdication [æbdɪˈkeɪʃən] *n* abdicación

abdomen [ˈæbdəmən] *n* abdomen

abduct [æbˈdʌkt] *vt* raptar, secuestrar

abductor [æbˈdʌktəʳ] *n* raptor(a), secuestrador(a)

abduction [æbˈdʌkʃən] *n* rapto, secuestro

aberration [æbəˈreɪʃən] *n* aberración; **in a moment of mental ~** en un momento de enajenación mental

abet [əˈbɛt] *vt see* **aid**

abeyance [əˈbeɪəns] *n*: **in ~** (*law*) en desuso; (*matter*) en suspenso

abide [əˈbaɪd] *vt*: **I can't ~ it/him** no lo/le puedo ver *or* aguantar; **to ~ by** *vt fus* atenerse a

abiding [əˈbaɪdɪŋ] *adj* (*memory etc*) perdurable

ability [əˈbɪlɪtɪ] *n* habilidad, capacidad; (*talent*) talento; **to the best of my ~** lo mejor que pueda *etc*

abject [ˈæbdʒɛkt] *adj* (*poverty*) sórdido; (*apology*) rastrero; (*coward*) vil

ablaze [əˈbleɪz] *adj* en llamas, ardiendo

able [ˈeɪbl] *adj* capaz; (*skilled*) hábil; **to be ~ to do sth** poder hacer algo; **will you be ~ to come on Saturday?** ¿puedes venir el sábado?; **he won't be ~ to resist it** no será capaz de *or* podrá resistirlo

able-bodied [ˈeɪblˈbɔdɪd] *adj* sano; **~ seaman** marinero de primera

ably [ˈeɪblɪ] *adv* hábilmente

abnormal [æbˈnɔːməl] *adj* anormal

aboard [əˈbɔːd] *adv* a bordo ▷ *prep* a bordo de; **~ the train** en el tren

abode [əˈbəud] *n* (*old*) morada; (*Law*) domicilio; **of no fixed ~** sin domicilio fijo

abolish [əˈbɔlɪʃ] *vt* suprimir, abolir

abolition [æbəuˈlɪʃən] *n* supresión, abolición

aborigine [æbəˈrɪdʒɪnɪ] *n* aborigen

abort [əˈbɔːt] *vt* abortar; (*Comput*) interrumpir ▷ *vi* (*Comput*) interrumpir el programa

abortion [əˈbɔːʃən] *n* aborto (provocado); **to have an ~** abortar

abortive [əˈbɔːtɪv] *adj* fracasado

abound [əˈbaund] *vi*: **to ~ (in *or* with)** abundar (de *or* en)

about [əˈbaut] *adv* **1** (*approximately*) más o menos, aproximadamente; **~ a hundred/thousand** *etc* unos(unas) *or* como cien/mil *etc*; **it takes ~ 10 hours** se tarda unas *or* más o menos 10 horas; **at ~ 2 o'clock** sobre las dos; **I've just ~ finished** casi he terminado
2 (*referring to place*) por todas partes; **to leave things lying ~** dejar las cosas (tiradas) por ahí; **to run ~** correr por todas partes; **to walk ~** pasearse, ir y venir; **is Paul ~?** ¿está por aquí Paul?; **it's the other way ~** es al revés
3: **to be ~ to do sth** estar a punto de hacer algo; **I**

was ~ **to go out** estaba a punto de salir; **I'm not ~ to do all that for nothing** no pienso hacer todo eso para nada
▷ *prep* **1** (*relating to*) de, sobre, acerca de; **a book ~ London** un libro sobre *or* acerca de Londres; **what is it ~?** (*book, film*) ¿de qué se trata?; **we talked ~ it** hablamos de eso *or* ello; **I don't know anything ~ it** no sé nada sobre eso; **I'm phoning you ~ tomorrow's meeting** te llamo por lo de la reunión de mañana; **what** *or* **how ~ going to the cinema?** ¿qué tal si vamos al cine?; **what ~ me?** ¿y yo?
2 (*referring to place*) por; **to walk ~ the town** caminar por la ciudad
about face, about turn *n* (*Mil*) media vuelta; (*fig*) cambio radical
above [ə'bʌv] *adv* encima, por encima, arriba
▷ *prep* encima de; **mentioned ~** susodicho; **~ all** sobre todo; **he's not ~ a bit of blackmail** es capaz hasta de hacer chantaje
above board *adj* legítimo
abrasive [ə'breɪzɪv] *adj* abrasivo
abreast [ə'brɛst] *adv* uno al lado de otro; **to keep ~ of** mantenerse al corriente de
abridge [ə'brɪdʒ] *vt* abreviar
abroad [ə'brɔːd] *adv* (*be*) en el extranjero; (*go*) al extranjero; **there is a rumour ~ that ...** corre el rumor de que ...
abrupt [ə'brʌpt] *adj* (*sudden: departure*) repentino; (*manner*) brusco
abruptly [ə'brʌptlɪ] *adv* (*leave*) repentinamente; (*speak*) bruscamente
abscess ['æbsɪs] *n* absceso
abscond [əb'skɔnd] *vi* fugarse
absence ['æbsəns] *n* ausencia; **in the ~ of** (*person*) en ausencia de; (*thing*) a falta de
absent ['æbsənt] *adj* ausente; **~ without leave (AWOL)** ausente sin permiso
absentee [æbsən'tiː] *n* ausente
absent-minded [æbsənt'maɪndɪd] *adj* distraído
absolute ['æbsəluːt] *adj* absoluto; **~ monopoly** monopolio total
absolutely [æbsə'luːtlɪ] *adv* totalmente; **oh yes, ~!** ¡claro *or* por supuesto que sí!
absolution [æbsə'luːʃən] *n* (*Rel*) absolución
absolve [əb'zɔlv] *vt*: **to ~ sb (from)** absolver a algn (de)
absorb [əb'zɔːb] *vt* absorber; **to be ~ed in a book** estar enfrascado en un libro
absorbent cotton *n* (*US*) algodón hidrófilo
absorption [əb'zɔːpʃən] *n* absorción
abstain [əb'steɪn] *vi*: **to ~ (from)** abstenerse (de)
abstention [əb'stɛnʃən] *n* abstención
abstract ['æbstrækt] *adj* abstracto
absurd [əb'səːd] *adj* absurdo
ABTA ['æbtə] *n abbr* = **Association of British Travel Agents**
abundance [ə'bʌndəns] *n* abundancia
abundant [ə'bʌndənt] *adj* abundante
abuse *n* (*insults*) insultos, improperios; (*misuse*) abuso ▷ *vt* (*ill-treat*) maltratar; (*take advantage of*) abusar de; **open to ~** sujeto al abuso

abusive [ə'bjuːsɪv] *adj* ofensivo
abysmal [ə'bɪzməl] *adj* pésimo
abyss [ə'bɪs] *n* abismo
AC *abbr* (= *alternating current*) corriente alterna ▷ *n abbr* (*US*) = **athletic club**
academic [ækə'dɛmɪk] *adj* académico, universitario; (*pej: issue*) puramente teórico ▷ *n* estudioso(-a); (*lecturer*) profesor(a) universitario(-a); **~ year** (*Univ*) año académico
academy [ə'kædəmɪ] *n* (*learned body*) academia; (*school*) instituto, colegio; **~ of music** conservatorio
accelerate [æk'sɛləreɪt] *vt* acelerar ▷ *vi* acelerarse
acceleration [æksɛlə'reɪʃən] *n* aceleración
accelerator [æk'sɛləreɪtəʳ] *n* (*Brit*) acelerador
accent ['æksɛnt] *n* acento
accentuate [æk'sɛntjueɪt] *vt* (*syllable*) acentuar; (*need, difference etc*) recalcar, subrayar
accept [ək'sɛpt] *vt* aceptar; (*approve*) aprobar; (*concede*) admitir; **she ~ed the offer** aceptó la oferta; **to ~ responsibility for sth** asumir la responsabilidad de algo; **this telephone ~s 10 pence coins only** este teléfono sólo admite monedas de 10 peniques
acceptable [ək'sɛptəbl] *adj* aceptable, admisible
acceptance [ək'sɛptəns] *n* aceptación; aprobación; **to meet with general ~** recibir la aprobación general
access ['æksɛs] *n* acceso ▷ *vt* (*Comput*) acceder a; **the burglars gained ~ through a window** los ladrones lograron entrar por una ventana; **to have ~ to** tener acceso a
accessible [æk'sɛsəbl] *adj* accesible
accessory [æk'sɛsərɪ] *n* accesorio; **toilet accessories** artículos de tocador
accident ['æksɪdənt] *n* accidente; (*chance*) casualidad; **by ~** (*unintentionally*) sin querer; (*by coincidence*) por casualidad; **~s at work** accidentes de trabajo; **to meet with** *or* **to have an ~** tener *or* sufrir un accidente
accidental [æksɪ'dɛntl] *adj* accidental, fortuito
accidentally [æksɪ'dɛntəlɪ] *adv* sin querer; por casualidad
accident-prone ['æksɪdənt'prəun] *adj* propenso a los accidentes
acclaim [ə'kleɪm] *vt* aclamar, aplaudir ▷ *n* aclamación, aplausos
acclimatize [ə'klaɪmətaɪz], (*US*) **acclimate** [ə'klaɪmət] *vt*: **to become ~d** aclimatarse
accommodate [ə'kɔmədeɪt] *vt* alojar, hospedar; (*oblige, help*) complacer; **this car ~s 4 people comfortably** en este coche caben 4 personas cómodamente
accommodating [ə'kɔmədeɪtɪŋ] *adj* servicial, complaciente
accommodation *n*, (*US*) **accommodations** *npl* [əkɔmə'deɪʃən(z)] alojamiento; **"~ to let"** "se alquilan habitaciones"; **seating ~** asientos
accompany [ə'kʌmpənɪ] *vt* acompañar
accomplice [ə'kʌmplɪs] *n* cómplice
accomplish [ə'kʌmplɪʃ] *vt* (*finish*) acabar; (*aim*)

realizar; (*task*) llevar a cabo

accomplished [ə'kʌmplɪʃt] *adj* experto, hábil

accomplishment [ə'kʌmplɪʃmənt] *n* (*ending*) conclusión; (*bringing about*) realización; (*skill*) talento

accord [ə'kɔːd] *n* acuerdo ▷ *vt* conceder; **of his own ~** espontáneamente; **with one ~** de *or* por común acuerdo

accordance [ə'kɔːdəns] *n*: **in ~ with** de acuerdo con

according [ə'kɔːdɪŋ]: **~ to** *prep* según; (*in accordance with*) conforme a; **it went ~ to plan** salió según lo previsto

accordingly [ə'kɔːdɪŋlɪ] *adv* (*thus*) por consiguiente

accordion [ə'kɔːdɪən] *n* acordeón

accost [ə'kɔst] *vt* abordar, dirigirse a

account [ə'kaunt] *n* (*Comm*) cuenta, factura; (*report*) informe; **accounts** *npl* (*Comm*) cuentas; **to do the ~s** llevar la contabilidad; **a bank ~** una cuenta bancaria; **"~ payee only"** "únicamente en cuenta del beneficiario"; **your ~ is still outstanding** su cuenta está todavía pendiente; **on ~** a crédito; **to buy sth on ~** comprar algo a crédito; **to keep an ~ of** llevar la cuenta de; **of little ~** de poca importancia; **on no ~** bajo ningún concepto; **on ~ of** a causa de, por motivo de; **to take into ~, take ~ of** tener en cuenta; **to bring sb to ~ for sth/for having done sth** pedirle cuentas a algn por algo/por haber hecho algo; **by all ~s** a decir de todos

▷ **account for** *vt fus* (*explain*) explicar; **that ~s for it** ésa es la razón; **all the children were ~ed for** no faltaba ningún niño

accountability [əkauntə'bɪlɪtɪ] *n* responsabilidad

accountable [ə'kauntəbl] *adj*: **~ (for)** responsable (de)

accountancy [ə'kauntənsɪ] *n* contabilidad

accountant [ə'kauntənt] *n* contable, contador(a) (*LAm*)

account number *n* (*at bank etc*) número de cuenta

accumulate [ə'kjuːmjuleɪt] *vt* acumular ▷ *vi* acumularse

accumulation [əkjuːmju'leɪʃən] *n* acumulación

accuracy ['ækjurəsɪ] *n* exactitud, precisión

accurate ['ækjurɪt] *adj* (*number*) exacto; (*answer*) acertado; (*shot*) certero

accurately ['ækjurɪtlɪ] *adv* (*count, shoot, answer*) con precisión

accusation [ækjuˈzeɪʃən] *n* acusación

accuse [ə'kjuːz] *vt* acusar; (*blame*) echar la culpa a

accused [ə'kjuːzd] *n* acusado(-a)

accuser [ə'kjuːzəʳ] *n* acusador(a)

accustom [ə'kʌstəm] *vt* acostumbrar; **to ~ o.s. to sth** acostumbrarse a algo

accustomed [ə'kʌstəmd] *adj*: **~ to** acostumbrado a

AC/DC *abbr* = **alternating current/direct current**

ace [eɪs] *n* as

ache [eɪk] *n* dolor ▷ *vi* doler; (*yearn*): **to ~ to do sth** ansiar hacer algo; **I've got (a) stomach ~** tengo dolor de estómago, me duele el estómago; **my head ~s** me duele la cabeza

achieve [ə'tʃiːv] *vt* (*reach*) alcanzar; (*realize*) realizar; (*victory, success*) lograr, conseguir

achievement [ə'tʃiːvmənt] *n* (*completion*) realización; (*success*) éxito

Achilles heel [ə'kɪliːz-] *n* talón de Aquiles

acid ['æsɪd] *adj* ácido; (*bitter*) agrio ▷ *n* ácido

acid rain *n* lluvia ácida

acid test *n* (*fig*) prueba de fuego

acknowledge [ək'nɔlɪdʒ] *vt* (*letter: also*: **acknowledge receipt of**) acusar recibo de; (*fact*) reconocer

acknowledgement [ək'nɔlɪdʒmənt] *n* acuse de recibo; reconocimiento; **~s** (*in book*) agradecimientos

acne ['æknɪ] *n* acné

acorn ['eɪkɔːn] *n* bellota

acoustic [ə'kuːstɪk] *adj* acústico

acoustics [ə'kuːstɪks] *n, npl* acústica

acquaint [ə'kweɪnt] *vt*: **to ~ sb with sth** (*inform*) poner a algn al corriente de algo; **to be ~ed with** (*person*) conocer; (*fact*) estar al corriente de

acquaintance [ə'kweɪntəns] *n* conocimiento; (*person*) conocido(-a); **to make sb's ~** conocer a algn

acquiesce [ækwɪ'ɛs] *vi* (*agree*): **to ~ (in)** consentir (en), conformarse (con)

acquire [ə'kwaɪəʳ] *vt* adquirir

acquisition [ækwɪ'zɪʃən] *n* adquisición

acquit [ə'kwɪt] *vt* absolver, exculpar; **to ~ o.s. well** defenderse bien

acquittal [ə'kwɪtl] *n* absolución, exculpación

acre ['eɪkəʳ] *n* acre

acrid ['ækrɪd] *adj* (*smell*) acre; (*fig*) mordaz, sarcástico

acrobat ['ækrəbæt] *n* acróbata

acrobatic [ækrə'bætɪk] *adj* acrobático

acrobatics [ækrə'bætɪks] *npl* acrobacias

acronym ['ækrənɪm] *n* siglas

across [ə'krɔs] *prep* (*on the other side of*) al otro lado de; (*crosswise*) a través de ▷ *adv* de un lado a otro, de una parte a otra; a través, al través; **he lives ~ the river** vive al otro lado del río; **an expedition ~ the Sahara** una expedición a través del Sahara; **the shop ~ the road** la tienda en la acera de enfrente; **to run/swim ~** atravesar corriendo/nadando; **~ from** enfrente de; **it's ~ from the church** está enfrente de la iglesia; **he sat down ~ from her** se sentó frente a ella; **the lake is 12 km ~** el lago tiene 12 km de ancho; **to get sth ~ to sb** (*fig*) hacer comprender algo a algn

acrylic [ə'krɪlɪk] *adj* acrílico

act [ækt] *n* acto, acción; (*Theat*) acto; (*in music-hall etc*) número; (*Law*) decreto, ley ▷ *vi* (*behave*) comportarse; (*Theat*) actuar; (*pretend*) fingir; (*take action*) tomar medidas ▷ *vt* (*part*) hacer, representar; **~ of God** fuerza mayor; **it's only an ~** es cuento; **to catch sb in the ~** coger a algn in fraganti *or* con las manos en la masa; **in the first ~** (*Theat*) en el primer acto; **an A~ of Parliament** una ley parlamentaria; **to ~ as** actuar *or* hacer de; **she ~s as his interpreter** ella le hace de intérprete; **~ing in my capacity as chairman, I ...** en mi calidad de presidente, yo ...; **it ~s as a deterrent** sirve para disuadir; **he ~s really well** actúa muy bien; **he's only ~ing** está fingiendo nada más; **to ~ (the part of) Hamlet** hacer el papel de Hamlet

▶ **act on** *vt*: **to ~ on sth** actuar *or* obrar sobre algo

▶ **act out** *vt* (*event*) representar; (*fantasies*) realizar

acting ['æktɪŋ] *adj* suplente ▷ *n*: **to do some ~** hacer algo de teatro; **he is the ~ manager** es el gerente en funciones

action ['ækʃən] *n* acción; (*Mil*) intervención; (*Law*) proceso, demanda; **the film was full of ~** era una película con mucha acción; **to put a plan into ~** poner un plan en acción *or* en marcha; **killed in ~** (*Mil*) muerto en acto de servicio *or* en combate; **out of ~** (*person*) fuera de combate; (*thing*) averiado, descompuesto; **to take ~** tomar medidas; **to take firm ~ against** tomar severas medidas contra; **to take no ~** no hacer nada; **to bring an ~ against sb** (*Law*) entablar *or* presentar demanda contra algn; **~s speak louder than words** dicho sin hecho no trae provecho

action replay *n* (*TV*) repetición

activate ['æktɪveɪt] *vt* activar

active ['æktɪv] *adj* activo, enérgico; (*volcano*) en actividad; **to play an ~ part in** colaborar activamente en; **~ file** (*Comput*) fichero activo

actively ['æktɪvlɪ] *adv* (*participate*) activamente; (*discourage, dislike*) enérgicamente

activity [æk'tɪvɪtɪ] *n* actividad

actor ['æktər] *n* actor

actress ['æktrɪs] *n* actriz

actual ['æktjuəl] *adj* verdadero, real

actually ['æktjuəlɪ] *adv* (*really*) realmente, en realidad; (*in fact*) de hecho; **did it ~ happen?** ¿ocurrió realmente?; **I was so bored I ~ fell asleep!** ¡me aburría tanto que de hecho me quedé dormido!; **you only pay for the electricity you ~ use** sólo pagas la electricidad que consumes; **Fiona's awful, isn't she? —~, I quite like her** Fiona es una antipática, ¿verdad? — pues a mí me cae bien; **~, I don't know him at all** la verdad es que no lo conozco de nada

acumen ['ækjumən] *n* perspicacia; **business ~** talento para los negocios

acupuncture ['ækjupʌŋktʃər] *n* acupuntura

acute [ə'kju:t] *adj* agudo

acutely [ə'kju:tlɪ] *adv* profundamente, extremadamente

AD *adv abbr* (= *Anno Domini*) A.C. ▷ *n abbr* (*US Mil*) *see* **active duty**

ad [æd] *n abbr* = **advertisement**

Adam ['ædəm] *n* Adán; **~'s apple** *n* nuez (de la garganta)

adamant ['ædəmənt] *adj* firme, inflexible

adapt [ə'dæpt] *vt* adaptar; (*reconcile*) acomodar ▷ *vi*: **to ~ (to)** adaptarse (a), ajustarse (a)

adaptability [ədæptə'bɪlɪtɪ] *n* (*of person, device etc*) adaptabilidad

adaptable [ə'dæptəbl] *adj* (*device*) adaptable; (*person*) acomodadizo, que se adapta

adaptation [ædæp'teɪʃən] *n* adaptación

adapter, adaptor [ə'dæptər] *n* (*Elec*) adaptador

add [æd] *vt* añadir, agregar (*esp LAm*); (*figures: also*: **add up**) sumar ▷ *vi*: **to ~ to** (*increase*) aumentar, acrecentar

▶ **add on** *vt* añadir

▶ **add up** *vt* (*figures*) sumar ▷ *vi* (*fig*): **it doesn't ~ up** no tiene sentido; **it doesn't ~ up to much** es poca cosa, no tiene gran *or* mucha importancia

addendum [ə'dɛndəm] *n* ad(d)enda

adder ['ædər] *n* víbora

addict ['ædɪkt] *n* (*to drugs etc*) adicto(-a); (*enthusiast*) aficionado(-a), entusiasta; **heroin ~** heroinómano(-a)

addicted [ə'dɪktɪd] *adj*: **to be ~ to** ser adicto a; ser aficionado a

addiction [ə'dɪkʃən] *n* (*dependence*) hábito morboso; (*enthusiasm*) afición

addictive [ə'dɪktɪv] *adj* que causa adicción

addition [ə'dɪʃən] *n* (*adding up*) adición; (*thing added*) añadidura, añadido; **in ~** además, por añadidura; **in ~ to** además de

additional [ə'dɪʃənl] *adj* adicional

additive ['ædɪtɪv] *n* aditivo

address [ə'drɛs] *n* dirección, señas; (*speech*) discurso; (*Comput*) dirección ▷ *vt* (*letter*) dirigir; (*speak to*) dirigirse a, dirigir la palabra a; **form of ~** tratamiento; **absolute/relative ~** (*Comput*) dirección absoluta/relativa; **to ~ o.s. to sth** (*issue, problem*) abordar

address book *n* agenda (de direcciones)

addressee [ædrɛ'si:] *n* destinatario(-a)

adenoids ['ædɪnɔɪdz] *npl* vegetaciones (adenoideas)

adept ['ædɛpt] *adj*: **~ at** experto *or* ducho en

adequate ['ædɪkwɪt] *adj* (*satisfactory*) adecuado; (*enough*) suficiente; **to feel ~ to a task** sentirse con fuerzas para una tarea

adequately ['ædɪkwɪtlɪ] *adv* adecuadamente

adhere [əd'hɪər] *vi*: **to ~ to** adherirse a; (*fig: abide by*) observar

adhesive [əd'hi:zɪv] *adj, n* adhesivo

adhesive tape *n* (*Brit*) cinta adhesiva; (*US Med*) esparadrapo

ad hoc [æd'hɔk] *adj* (*decision*) ad hoc; (*committee*) formado con fines específicos ▷ *adv* ad hoc

adjacent [ə'dʒeɪsənt] *adj*: **~ to** contiguo a, inmediato a

adjective ['ædʒɛktɪv] *n* adjetivo

adjoining [ə'dʒɔɪnɪŋ] *adj* contiguo, vecino

adjourn [ə'dʒə:n] *vt* aplazar; (*session*) suspender, levantar; (*US: end*) terminar ▷ *vi* suspenderse; **the meeting has been ~ed till next week** se ha levantado la sesión hasta la semana que viene; **they ~ed to the pub** (*col*) se trasladaron al bar

adjournment [ə'dʒə:nmənt] *n* (*period*)

suspensión; (*postponement*) aplazamiento
adjudicate [ə'dʒu:dɪkeɪt] *vi* sentenciar ▷ *vt*
(*contest*) hacer de árbitro en, juzgar; (*claim*)
decidir
adjust [ə'dʒʌst] *vt* (*change*) modificar; (*arrange*)
arreglar; (*machine*) ajustar ▷ *vi*: **to ~ (to)**
adaptarse (a)
adjustable [ə'dʒʌstəbl] *adj* ajustable
adjustment [ə'dʒʌstmənt] *n* modificación;
arreglo; (*of prices, wages*) ajuste
ad-lib [æd'lɪb] *vt,vi* improvisar ▷ *adv*: **ad lib** a
voluntad, a discreción
admin ['ædmɪn] *n abbr* (*col*) = **administration**
administer [əd'mɪnɪstə^r] *vt* proporcionar;
(*justice*) administrar
administration [ædmɪnɪ'streɪʃən] *n*
administración; (*government*) gobierno; **the A~**
(*US*) la Administración
administrative [əd'mɪnɪstrətɪv] *adj*
administrativo
administrator [əd'mɪnɪstreɪtə^r] *n*
administrador(a)
admirable ['ædmərəbl] *adj* admirable
admiral ['ædmərəl] *n* almirante
Admiralty ['ædmərəltɪ] *n* (*Brit*) Ministerio de
Marina, Almirantazgo
admiration [ædmə'reɪʃən] *n* admiración
admire [əd'maɪə^r] *vt* admirar
admirer [əd'maɪərə^r] *n* admirador(a); (*suitor*)
pretendiente
admiring [əd'maɪrɪŋ] *adj* (*expression*) de
admiración
admissible [əd'mɪsəbl] *adj* admisible
admission [əd'mɪʃən] *n* (*to exhibition, nightclub*)
entrada; (*enrolment*) ingreso; (*confession*)
confesión; **"~ free"** "entrada gratis *or* libre"; **by
his own ~** él mismo reconoce que
admit [əd'mɪt] *vt* dejar entrar, dar entrada a;
(*permit*) admitir; (*acknowledge*) reconocer; **"this
ticket ~s 2"** "entrada para 2 personas"; **children
not ~ted** se prohíbe la entrada a (los) menores
de edad; **I must ~ that** ... debo reconocer que ...
▸ **admit of** *vt fus* admitir, permitir
▸ **admit to** *vt fus* confesarse culpable de
admittance [əd'mɪtəns] *n* entrada; **"no ~"** "se
prohíbe la entrada", "prohibida la entrada"
admittedly [əd'mɪtədlɪ] *adv* de acuerdo que
admonish [əd'mɒnɪʃ] *vt* amonestar; (*advise*)
aconsejar
ad nauseam [æd'nɔːsɪæm] *adv* hasta la saciedad
ado [ə'duː] *n*: **without (any) more ~** sin más (ni
más)
adolescence [ædəu'lɛsns] *n* adolescencia
adolescent [ædəu'lɛsnt] *adj,n* adolescente
adopt [ə'dɒpt] *vt* adoptar
adopted [ə'dɒptɪd] *adj* adoptivo
adoption [ə'dɒpʃən] *n* adopción
adorable [ə'dɔːrəbl] *adj* adorable
adore [ə'dɔː^r] *vt* adorar
adoring [ə'dɔːrɪŋ] *adj*: **to his ~ public** a un
público que le adora *or* le adoraba *etc*
adorn [ə'dɔːn] *vt* adornar

adrenalin [ə'drɛnəlɪn] *n* adrenalina
Adriatic [eɪdrɪ'ætɪk] *n*: **the ~ (Sea)** el (Mar)
Adriático
adrift [ə'drɪft] *adv* a la deriva; **to come ~** (*boat*) ir
a la deriva, soltarse; (*wire, rope etc*) soltarse
ADSL *n abbr* (= *asymmetric digital subscriber line*) ADSL
adult ['ædʌlt] *n* adulto(-a) ▷ *adj*: **~ education**
educación para adultos
adultery [ə'dʌltərɪ] *n* adulterio
advance [əd'vɑːns] *n* adelanto, progreso; (*money*)
anticipo; (*Mil*) avance ▷ *vt* avanzar, adelantar;
(*money*) anticipar ▷ *vi* avanzar, adelantarse; **in ~**
por adelantado; (*book*) con antelación; **to make
~s to sb** (*gen*) ponerse en contacto con algn;
(*amorously*) insinuarse a algn
advanced *adj* avanzado; (*Scol: studies*)
adelantado; **~ in years** entrado en años
advantage [əd'vɑːntɪdʒ] *n* (*also Tennis*) ventaja;
to take ~ of aprovecharse de; **it's to our ~** es
ventajoso para nosotros
advantageous [ædvən'teɪdʒəs] *adj* ventajoso,
provechoso
advent ['ædvənt] *n* advenimiento; **A~** Adviento
adventure [əd'vɛntʃə^r] *n* aventura
adventure playground *n* parque infantil
adventurous [əd'vɛntʃərəs] *adj* aventurero;
(*bold*) arriesgado
adverb ['ædvəːb] *n* adverbio
adversary ['ædvəsərɪ] *n* adversario, contrario
adverse ['ædvəːs] *adj* adverso, contrario; **~ to**
adverso a
adversity [əd'vəːsɪtɪ] *n* infortunio
advert ['ædvəːt] *n abbr* (*Brit*) = **advertisement**
advertise ['ædvətaɪz] *vi* hacer propaganda; (*in
newspaper etc*) poner un anuncio, anunciarse; **to
~ for** (*staff*) buscar por medio de anuncios ▷ *vt*
anunciar
advertisement [əd'vəːtɪsmənt] *n* (*Comm*)
anuncio
advertiser ['ædvətaɪzə^r] *n* anunciante
advertising ['ædvətaɪzɪŋ] *n* publicidad,
propaganda; anuncios
advertising agency *n* agencia de publicidad
advice [əd'vaɪs] *n* consejo, consejos; (*notification*)
aviso; **a piece of ~** un consejo; **to take legal ~**
consultar a un abogado; **to ask (sb) for ~** pedir
consejo (a algn)
advisable [əd'vaɪzəbl] *adj* aconsejable,
conveniente
advise [əd'vaɪz] *vt* aconsejar; **to ~ sb of sth**
(*inform*) informar a algn de algo; **to ~ sb against
sth/doing sth** desaconsejar algo a algn/
aconsejar a algn que no haga algo; **you will be
well/ill ~d to go** deberías/no deberías ir
advisedly [əd'vaɪzɪdlɪ] *adv* (*deliberately*)
deliberadamente
adviser [əd'vaɪzə^r] *n* consejero(-a); (*business
adviser*) asesor(a)
advisory [ad'vaɪzərɪ] *adj* consultivo; **in an ~
capacity** como asesor
advocate *vt* (*argue for*) abogar por; (*give support to*)
ser partidario de ▷ *n* abogado(-a)

aerial ['ɛərɪəl] n antena ▷ adj aéreo
aerobatics [ɛərəʊˈbætɪks] npl acrobacia aérea
aerobics [ɛəˈrəʊbɪks] nsg aerobic, aerobismo (LAm)
aeroplane ['ɛərəpleɪn] n (Brit) avión
aerosol ['ɛərəsɔl] n aerosol
aesthetic [iːsˈθɛtɪk] adj estético
afar [əˈfɑːʳ] adv lejos; **from ~** desde lejos
affair [əˈfɛəʳ] n asunto; (also: **love affair**) aventura amorosa; **~s** (business) asuntos; **the Watergate ~** el asunto (de) Watergate
affect [əˈfɛkt] vt afectar, influir en; (move) conmover
affected [əˈfɛktɪd] adj afectado
affection [əˈfɛkʃən] n afecto, cariño
affectionate [əˈfɛkʃənɪt] adj afectuoso, cariñoso
affinity [əˈfɪnɪtɪ] n afinidad
affirm [əˈfəːm] vt afirmar
affirmative [əˈfəːmətɪv] adj afirmativo
afflict [əˈflɪkt] vt afligir
affluence ['æfluəns] n opulencia, riqueza
affluent ['æfluənt] adj adinerado, acaudalado; **the ~ society** la sociedad opulenta
afford [əˈfɔːd] vt poder permitirse; (provide) proporcionar; **can we ~ a car?** ¿podemos permitirnos el gasto de comprar un coche?
affordable [əˈfɔːdəbl] adj asequible
Afghanistan [æfˈgænɪstæn] n Afganistán
afield [əˈfiːld] adv: **far ~** muy lejos
afloat [əˈfləʊt] adv (floating) a flote; (at sea) en el mar
afoot [əˈfʊt] adv: **there is something ~** algo se está tramando
afraid [əˈfreɪd] adj: **to be ~ of** (person) tener miedo a; (thing) tener miedo de; **to be ~ to** tener miedo de, temer; **I am ~ that** me temo que; **I'm ~ so** ¡me temo que sí!, ¡lo siento, pero es así!; **I'm ~ not** me temo que no
afresh [əˈfrɛʃ] adv de nuevo, otra vez
Africa ['æfrɪkə] n África
African ['æfrɪkən] adj, n africano(-a)
Afro-American ['æfrəʊəˈmɛrɪkən] adj, n afroamericano(-a)
aft [ɑːft] adv (be) en popa; (go) a popa
after ['ɑːftəʳ] prep (time) después de; (place, order) detrás de, tras ▷ adv después ▷ conj después (de) que; **~ the match** después del partido; **~ dinner** después de cenar or comer; **the day ~ tomorrow** pasado mañana; **quarter ~ 2** (US) las 2 y cuarto; **he ran ~ me** corrió detrás de mí; **what/who are you ~?** ¿qué/a quién buscas?; **the police are ~ him** la policía le está buscando; **to ask ~ sb** preguntar por algn; **~ all** después de todo, al fin y al cabo; **~ you!** ¡Vd primero!; **soon ~** poco después; **~ watching the television I went to bed** después de ver la televisión me fui a la cama; **I met her ~ she had left the company** la conocí después de que dejó la empresa; **I'll help you ~ we've finished this** te ayudaré después de que terminemos esto
afterbirth ['ɑːftəbəːθ] n placenta
after-effects ['ɑːftərɪfɛkts] npl secuelas, efectos

afterlife ['ɑːftəlaɪf] n vida después de la muerte
aftermath ['ɑːftəmɑːθ] n consecuencias, resultados
afternoon [ɑːftəˈnuːn] n tarde; **good ~!** ¡buenas tardes!
afters ['ɑːftəz] n (col: dessert) postre
after-sales service [ɑːftəˈseɪlz-] n (Brit Comm: for car, washing machine etc) servicio de asistencia pos-venta
after-shave (lotion) ['ɑːftəʃeɪv-] n loción para después del afeitado, aftershave
aftertaste ['ɑːftəteɪst] n regusto
afterthought ['ɑːftəθɔːt] n ocurrencia (tardía)
afterwards ['ɑːftəwədz] adv después, más tarde
again [əˈgɛn] adv otra vez, de nuevo; **try it ~** inténtalo otra vez or de nuevo; **to do sth ~** volver a hacer algo; **I'd like to hear it ~** me gustaría escucharlo otra vez, me gustaría volver a escucharlo; **I won't tell you ~!** ¡no te lo vuelvo a repetir!; **can you tell me ~?** ¿me lo puedes repetir?; **not...~** no...más; **I won't go there ~** no volveré más por allí; **~ and ~** una y otra vez; **now and ~** de vez en cuando; **never ~** nunca más
against [əˈgɛnst] prep (opposed to) en contra de; (close to) contra, junto a; **I'm ~ nuclear testing** estoy en contra de las pruebas nucleares; **they turned him ~ us** le pusieron en contra nuestra; **he leant ~ the wall** se apoyó contra la pared; **(as) ~** frente a
age [eɪdʒ] n edad; (old age) vejez; (period) época ▷ vi envejecer ▷ vt envejecer; **what ~ is he?** ¿qué edad or cuántos años tiene?; **he is 20 years of ~** tiene 20 años; **at the ~ of 16** a los 16 años; **under ~** menor de edad; **to come of ~** llegar a la mayoría de edad; **it's been ~s since I saw you, I haven't seen you for ~s** hace siglos que no te veo
aged [eɪdʒd] adj: **~ 10** de 10 años de edad ▷ npl ['eɪdʒɪd]: **the ~** los ancianos
age group n: **to be in the same ~** tener la misma edad; **the 40 to 50 ~** las personas de 40 a 50 años
ageing ['eɪdʒɪŋ] adj que envejece; (pej) en declive ▷ n envejecimiento
age limit n límite de edad, edad tope
agency ['eɪdʒənsɪ] n agencia; **through or by the ~ of** por medio de
agenda [əˈdʒɛndə] n orden del día; **on the ~** (Comm) en el orden del día
agent ['eɪdʒənt] n (gen) agente; (representative) representante delegado(-a)
aggravate ['ægrəveɪt] vt agravar; (annoy) irritar, exasperar
aggravating ['ægrəveɪtɪŋ] adj irritante, molesto
aggravation [ægrəˈveɪʃən] n agravamiento
aggregate ['ægrɪgeɪt] n conjunto
aggression [əˈgrɛʃən] n agresión
aggressive [əˈgrɛsɪv] adj agresivo; (vigorous) enérgico
aggressor [əˈgrɛsəʳ] n agresor(a)
aggrieved [əˈgriːvd] adj ofendido, agraviado
aggro ['ægrəʊ] n (col: physical violence) bronca; (bad feeling) mal rollo; (hassle) rollo, movida

aghast [ə'gɑ:st] *adj* horrorizado

agile ['ædʒaɪl] *adj* ágil

agility [ə'dʒɪlɪtɪ] *n* agilidad

agitate ['ædʒɪteɪt] *vt* (*shake*) agitar; (*trouble*) inquietar; **to ~ for** hacer campaña en pro de *or* en favor de

agitated ['ædʒɪteɪtɪd] *adj* agitado

AGM *n abbr* = **annual general meeting**

agnostic [æg'nɒstɪk] *adj, n* agnóstico(-a)

ago [ə'gəʊ] *adv*: **2 days ~** hace 2 días; **not long ~** hace poco; **how long ~?** ¿hace cuánto tiempo?; **how long ~ did it happen?** ¿cuánto hace que ocurrió?; **as long ~ as 1960** ya en 1960

agog [ə'gɒg] *adj* (*anxious*) ansioso; (*excited*): (**all**) ~ (**for**) (todo) emocionado (por)

agonize ['ægənaɪz] *vi*: **to ~ (over)** atormentarse (por)

agonized ['ægənaɪzd] *adj* angustioso

agonizing ['ægənaɪzɪŋ] *adj* (*pain*) atroz; (*suspense*) angustioso

agony ['ægənɪ] *n* (*pain*) dolor atroz; (*distress*) angustia; **to be in ~** retorcerse de dolor

agony aunt *n* (*Brit col*) consejera sentimental

agree [ə'gri:] *vt* (*price*) acordar, quedar en ▷ *vi* (*statements etc*) coincidir, concordar; (*people*) estar de acuerdo; **I don't ~!** ¡no estoy de acuerdo!; **I ~ with Carol** estoy de acuerdo con Carol; **to ~ to do sth** (*when someone requests*) aceptar hacer algo; (*arrange*) acordar hacer algo; **he ~d to go with her** aceptó acompañarla; **they ~d to meet again next week** acordaron volver a reunirse la semana próxima; **to ~ to sth** consentir en algo; **to ~ that** (*admit*) reconocer que; **I ~ it's difficult** reconozco que es difícil; **it was ~d that ...** se acordó que ...; **garlic doesn't ~ with me** el ajo no me sienta bien

agreeable [ə'gri:əbl] *adj* agradable; (*person*) simpático; (*willing*) de acuerdo, conforme

agreed [ə'gri:d] *adj* (*time, place*) convenido

agreement [ə'gri:mənt] *n* acuerdo; (*Comm*) contrato; **in ~** de acuerdo, conforme; **by mutual ~** de común acuerdo

agricultural [ægrɪ'kʌltʃərəl] *adj* agrícola

agriculture ['ægrɪkʌltʃəʳ] *n* agricultura

aground [ə'graʊnd] *adv*: **to run ~** encallar, embarrancar

ahead [ə'hɛd] *adv* delante; **she looked straight ~** miró hacia delante; **go right** *or* **straight ~** siga adelante; **to plan ~** hacer planes con antelación; **the Spanish are 5 points ~** los españoles llevan 5 puntos de ventaja; **go ~!** **help yourself!** ¡venga! ¡sírvete!; **~ of** delante de; (*fig: schedule etc*) antes de; **~ of time** antes de la hora; **to be ~ of sb** (*fig*) llevar ventaja *or* la delantera a algn; **they were (right) ~ of us** iban (justo) delante de nosotros

aid [eɪd] *n* ayuda, auxilio ▷ *vt* ayudar, auxiliar; **in ~ of** a beneficio de; **with the ~ of** con la ayuda de; **to ~ and abet** (*Law*) ser cómplice

aide [eɪd] *n* (*Pol*) ayudante

AIDS [eɪdz] *n abbr* (= *acquired immune* (or *immuno-*) *deficiency syndrome*) SIDA, sida

ailing ['eɪlɪŋ] *adj* (*person, economy*) enfermizo

ailment ['eɪlmənt] *n* enfermedad, achaque

aim [eɪm] *vt* (*gun*) apuntar; (*missile, remark*) dirigir; (*blow*) asestar ▷ *vi* (*also*: **take aim**) apuntar ▷ *n* puntería; (*objective*) propósito, meta; **to ~ at** (*objective*) aspirar a, pretender; **to ~ to do** tener como objetivo hacer, aspirar a hacer

aimless ['eɪmlɪs] *adj* sin propósito, sin objeto

ain't [eɪnt] (*col*) = **am not; aren't; isn't**

air [ɛəʳ] *n* aire; (*appearance*) aspecto ▷ *vt* (*room*) ventilar; (*clothes, bed, grievances, ideas*) airear; (*views*) hacer público; **to get some fresh ~** tomar un poco el aire; **to throw sth into the ~** (*ball etc*) lanzar algo al aire; **by ~** (*travel*) en avión; **to be on the ~** (*Radio, TV: programme*) estarse emitiendo; (: *station*) estar emitiendo

airbag ['ɛəbæg] *n* airbag

air bed *n* (*Brit*) colcheta inflable *or* neumática

airborne ['ɛəbɔ:n] *adj* (*in the air*) en el aire; (*Mil*) aerotransportado; **as soon as the plane was ~** tan pronto como el avión estuvo en el aire

air-conditioned ['ɛəkən'dɪʃənd] *adj* climatizado

air conditioning [-kən'dɪʃənɪŋ] *n* aire acondicionado

aircraft ['ɛəkrɑ:ft] *n* (*pl inv*) avión

aircraft carrier *n* porta(a)viones

airfield ['ɛəfi:ld] *n* campo de aviación

Air Force *n* fuerzas aéreas, aviación

air freshener *n* ambientador

air gun *n* escopeta de aire comprimido

air hostess (*Brit*) *n* azafata, aeromoza (*LAm*)

air letter *n* (*Brit*) carta aérea

airlift ['ɛəlɪft] *n* puente aéreo

airline ['ɛəlaɪn] *n* línea aérea

airliner ['ɛəlaɪnəʳ] *n* avión de pasajeros

airmail ['ɛəmeɪl] *n*: **by ~** por avión

airplane ['ɛəpleɪn] *n* (*US*) avión

air pocket *n* bolsa de aire

airport ['ɛəpɔ:t] *n* aeropuerto

air rage *n* *conducta agresiva de pasajeros a bordo de un avión*

air raid *n* ataque aéreo

air rifle *n* escopeta de aire comprimido

airsick ['ɛəsɪk] *adj*: **to be ~** marearse (en avión)

airspeed ['ɛəspi:d] *n* velocidad de vuelo

air terminal *n* terminal

airtight ['ɛətaɪt] *adj* hermético

air time *n* (*Radio, TV*) tiempo en antena

air traffic control *n* control de tráfico aéreo

air traffic controller *n* controlador(a) aéreo(-a)

airway ['ɛəweɪ] *n* (*Aviat*) vía aérea; (*Anat*) vía respiratoria

airy ['ɛərɪ] *adj* (*room*) bien ventilado; (*manners*) despreocupado

aisle [aɪl] *n* (*of church*) nave lateral; (*of theatre, plane*) pasillo

ajar [ə'dʒɑ:ʳ] *adj* entreabierto

akin [ə'kɪn] *adj*: **~ to** semejante a

alarm [ə'lɑ:m] *n* alarma; (*anxiety*) inquietud ▷ *vt* asustar, alarmar

alarm clock *n* despertador

alarmed [ə'lɑ:md] *adj* (*person*) alarmado, asustado; (*house, car etc*) con alarma

alarming [ə'lɑːmɪŋ] *adj* alarmante
alas [ə'læs] *adv* desgraciadamente ▷ *excl* ¡ay!
Albania [æl'beɪnɪə] *n* Albania
albatross ['ælbətrɔs] *n* albatros
albeit [ɔːl'biːɪt] *conj* (*although*) aunque
album ['ælbəm] *n* álbum; (*L.P.*) elepé
alcohol ['ælkəhɔl] *n* alcohol
alcohol-free *adj* sin alcohol
alcoholic [ælkə'hɔlɪk] *adj*, *n* alcohólico(-a)
alcoholism ['ælkəhɔlɪzəm] *n* alcoholismo
alcove ['ælkəuv] *n* nicho, hueco
ale [eɪl] *n* cerveza
alert [ə'ləːt] *adj* alerta; (*sharp*) despierto, despabilado ▷ *n* alerta, alarma ▷ *vt* poner sobre aviso; **to ~ sb (to sth)** poner sobre aviso *or* alertar a algn (de algo); **to ~ sb to the dangers of sth** poner sobre aviso *or* alertar a algn de los peligros de algo; **to be on the ~** estar alerta *or* sobre aviso
algebra ['ældʒɪbrə] *n* álgebra
Algeria [æl'dʒɪərɪə] *n* Argelia
Algerian [æl'dʒɪərɪən] *adj*, *n* argelino(-a)
alias ['eɪlɪəs] *adv* alias, conocido por ▷ *n* alias
alibi ['ælɪbaɪ] *n* coartada
alien ['eɪlɪən] *n* (*foreigner*) extranjero(-a) ▷ *adj*: **~ to** ajeno a
alienate ['eɪlɪəneɪt] *vt* enajenar, alejar
alight [ə'laɪt] *adj* ardiendo ▷ *vi* apearse, bajar
align [ə'laɪn] *vt* alinear
alignment [ə'laɪnmənt] *n* alineación; **the desks are out of ~** los pupitres no están bien alineados
alike [ə'laɪk] *adj* semejantes, iguales ▷ *adv* igualmente, del mismo modo; **to look ~** parecerse
alimony ['ælɪmənɪ] *n* (*Law*) pensión alimenticia
alive [ə'laɪv] *adj* (*gen*) vivo; (*lively*) activo
alkali ['ælkəlaɪ] *n* álcali
all [ɔːl] *adj* (*sg*) todo(-a); (*pl*) todos(-as); **~ day** todo el día; **~ night** toda la noche; **~ men** todos los hombres; **~ 5 came** vinieron los 5; **~ the books** todos los libros; **~ the time** todo el tiempo; **she talks ~ the time** no para de hablar; **~ his life** toda su vida; **for ~ their efforts** a pesar de todos sus esfuerzos
▷ *pron* **1** todo; **that's ~ I can remember** eso es todo lo que recuerdo; **I ate it ~, I ate ~ of it** me lo comí todo; **~ of them** todos (ellos); **~ of us went** fuimos todos; **~ the boys went** fueron todos los chicos; **is that ~?** ¿eso es todo?, ¿algo más?; (*in shop*) ¿algo más?, ¿alguna cosa más?
2 (*in phrases*): **above ~** sobre todo; por encima de todo; **after ~** después de todo; **at ~, anything at ~** lo que sea; **not at ~** (*in answer to question*) en absoluto; (*in answer to thanks*) ¡de nada!, ¡no hay de qué!; **I'm not at ~ tired** no estoy nada cansado(-a); **anything at ~ will do** cualquier cosa viene bien; **~ in ~** a fin de cuentas
▷ *adv*: **~ alone** completamente solo(-a); **to be/feel ~ in** estar rendido; **it's not as hard as ~ that** no es tan difícil como lo pintas; **~ the more/the better** tanto más/mejor; **~ but** casi; **the score is 2 ~** están empatados a 2
all-around ['ɔːlə'raund] *adj* (*US*) = **all-round**

allay [ə'leɪ] *vt* (*fears*) aquietar; (*pain*) aliviar
allegation [ælɪ'geɪʃən] *n* alegato
allege [ə'ledʒ] *vt* pretender; **he is ~d to have said ...** se afirma que él dijo ...
alleged [ə'ledʒd] *adj* supuesto, presunto
allegedly [ə'ledʒɪdlɪ] *adv* supuestamente, según se afirma
allegiance [ə'liːdʒəns] *n* lealtad
allegory ['ælɪɡərɪ] *n* alegoría
allergic [ə'ləːdʒɪk] *adj*: **~ to** alérgico a
allergy ['ælədʒɪ] *n* alergia
alleviate [ə'liːvɪeɪt] *vt* aliviar
alley ['ælɪ] *n* (*street*) callejuela; (*in garden*) paseo
alleyway ['ælɪweɪ] *n* callejón
alliance [ə'laɪəns] *n* alianza
allied ['ælaɪd] *adj* aliado; (*related*) relacionado
alligator ['ælɪɡeɪtə*] *n* caimán
all-in ['ɔːlɪn] *adj* (*Brit: also adv: charge*) todo incluido
all-in wrestling *n* lucha libre
alliteration [əlɪtə'reɪʃən] *n* aliteración
all-night ['ɔːl'naɪt] *adj* (*café*) abierto toda la noche; (*party*) que dura toda la noche
allocate ['æləkeɪt] *vt* (*share out*) repartir; (*devote*) asignar
allocation [ælə'keɪʃən] *n* (*of money*) ración, cuota; (*distribution*) reparto
allot [ə'lɔt] *vt* asignar; **in the ~ted time** en el tiempo asignado
allotment [ə'lɔtmənt] *n* porción; (*garden*) parcela
all-out ['ɔːlaut] *adj* (*effort etc*) supremo ▷ *adv*: **all out** con todas las fuerzas, a fondo
allow [ə'lau] *vt* (*permit*) permitir, dejar; (*a claim*) admitir; (*sum to spend, time estimated*) dejar; (*concede*): **to ~ that** reconocer que; **to ~ sb to do sth** permitir *or* dejar a algn hacer algo; **his mother ~ed him to go out** su madre le dejó salir; **he is ~ed to ...** se le permite ...; **smoking is not ~ed** está prohibido fumar, se prohíbe fumar; **we must ~ 3 days for the journey** debemos dejar 3 días para el viaje
▷ **allow for** *vt fus* tener en cuenta
allowance [ə'lauəns] *n* concesión; (*payment*) subvención, pensión; (*discount*) descuento, rebaja; **to make ~s for** (*person*) disculpar a; (*thing: take into account*) tener en cuenta
alloy ['ælɔɪ] *n* aleación
all right *adv* (*feel, work*) bien; (*as answer*) ¡de acuerdo!, ¡está bien!
all-round ['ɔːl'raund] *adj* completo; (*view*) amplio
all-rounder ['ɔːl'raundə*] *n*: **to be a good ~** ser una persona que hace de todo
all-time ['ɔːl'taɪm] *adj* (*record*) de todos los tiempos
allude [ə'luːd] *vi*: **to ~ to** aludir a
alluring [ə'ljuərɪŋ] *adj* seductor(a), atractivo
allusion [ə'luːʒən] *n* referencia, alusión
ally *n* aliado(-a) ▷ *vt*: **to ~ o.s. with** aliarse con
almighty [ɔːl'maɪtɪ] *adj* todopoderoso
almond ['ɑːmənd] *n* (*fruit*) almendra; (*tree*) almendro
almost ['ɔːlməust] *adv* casi; **he ~ fell** casi *or* por poco se cae

alms [ɑ:mz] *npl* limosna

aloft [ə'lɒft] *adv* arriba

alone [ə'ləun] *adj* solo ▷ *adv* sólo, solamente; **to leave sb** ~ dejar a algn en paz; **to leave sth** ~ no tocar algo; **let** ~ ... y mucho menos, y no digamos ...

along [ə'lɒŋ] *prep* a lo largo de, por ▷ *adv*: **is he coming** ~ **with us?** ¿viene con nosotros?; **Chris was walking** ~ **the beach** Chris paseaba por la playa; **there were bars all** ~ **the street** había bares a lo largo de toda la calle; **he was limping** ~ iba cojeando; ~ **with** junto con; **all** ~ (*all the time*) desde el principio; **he was lying to me all** ~ me había mentido desde el principio

alongside [ə'lɒŋ'saɪd] *prep* al lado de ▷ *adv* (*Naut*) de costado; **we brought our boat** ~ atracamos nuestro barco

aloof [ə'lu:f] *adj* distante ▷ *adv*: **to stand** ~ mantenerse a distancia

aloud [ə'laud] *adv* en voz alta

alphabet ['ælfəbet] *n* alfabeto

alphabetical [ælfə'betɪkəl] *adj* alfabético; **in** ~ **order** por orden alfabético

alpine ['ælpaɪn] *adj* alpino, alpestre

Alps [ælps] *npl*: **the** ~ los Alpes

already [ɔ:l'redɪ] *adv* ya

alright ['ɔ:l'raɪt] *adv* (*Brit*) = **all right**

Alsatian [æl'seɪʃən] *n* (*dog*) pastor alemán

also ['ɔ:lsəu] *adv* también, además

altar ['ɔltə'] *n* altar

alter ['ɔltə'] *vt* cambiar, modificar ▷ *vi* cambiarse, modificarse

alteration [ɔltə'reɪʃən] *n* cambio, modificación; **alterations** *npl* (*Arch*) reformas; (*Sewing*) arreglos; **timetable subject to** ~ el horario puede cambiar

altercation [ɔltə'keɪʃən] *n* altercado

alternate *adj* alterno ▷ *vi*: **to** ~ (**with**) alternar (con); **on** ~ **days** en días alternos

alternately [ɔl'tə:nɪtlɪ] *adv* alternativamente, por turno

alternating ['ɔltəneɪtɪŋ] *adj* (*current*) alterno

alternative [ɔl'tə:nətɪv] *adj* alternativo ▷ *n* alternativa

alternatively [ɔl'tə:nətɪvlɪ] *adv*: ~ **one could** ... por otra parte se podría...

alternative medicine *n* medicina alternativa

alternator ['ɔltəneɪtə'] *n* (*Aut*) alternador

although [ɔ:l'ðəu] *conj* aunque, si bien

altitude ['æltɪtju:d] *n* altitud, altura

alto ['æltəu] *n* (*female*) contralto; (*male*) alto

altogether [ɔ:ltə'geðə'] *adv* completamente, del todo; (*on the whole, in all*) en total, en conjunto; **how much is that** ~? ¿cuánto es todo *or* en total?

altruism ['æltruɪzəm] *n* altruismo

aluminium [ælju'mɪnɪəm], (*US*) **aluminum** [ə'lu:mɪnəm] *n* aluminio

always ['ɔ:lweɪz] *adv* siempre

Alzheimer's ['æltshaɪməz] (*also*: **Alzheimer's disease**) enfermedad de Alzheimer

AM *abbr* (= *amplitude modulation*) A.M.; (*Pol*: = *Assembly Member*) parlamentario(-a)

am [æm] *vb see* **be**

amalgamate [ə'mælgəmeɪt] *vi* amalgamarse ▷ *vt* amalgamar

amateur ['æmətə'] *n* aficionado(-a), amateur; ~ **dramatics** dramas presentados por aficionados, representación de aficionados

amateurish ['æmətərɪʃ] *adj* (*pej*) torpe, inexperto

amaze [ə'meɪz] *vt* asombrar, pasmar; **to be** ~**d (at)** asombrarse (de)

amazement [ə'meɪzmənt] *n* asombro, sorpresa; **to my** ~ para mi sorpresa

amazing [ə'meɪzɪŋ] *adj* extraordinario, asombroso; (*bargain, offer*) increíble

ambassador [æm'bæsədə'] *n* embajador(a)

amber ['æmbə'] *n* ámbar; **at** ~ (*Brit Aut*) en amarillo

ambiguity [æmbɪ'gjuɪtɪ] *n* ambigüedad; (*of meaning*) doble sentido

ambiguous [æm'bɪgjuəs] *adj* ambiguo

ambition [æm'bɪʃən] *n* ambición; **to achieve one's** ~ realizar su ambición

ambitious [æm'bɪʃəs] *adj* ambicioso; (*plan*) grandioso

amble ['æmbl] *vi* (*gen: also*: **amble along**) deambular, andar sin prisa

ambulance ['æmbjuləns] *n* ambulancia

ambush ['æmbuʃ] *n* emboscada ▷ *vt* tender una emboscada a; (*fig*) coger (*Esp*) *or* agarrar (*LAm*) por sorpresa

amenable [ə'mi:nəbl] *adj*: ~ **to** (*advice etc*) sensible a

amend [ə'mend] *vt* (*law, text*) enmendar; **to make** ~**s** (*apologize*) enmendarlo, dar cumplida satisfacción

amendment [ə'mendmənt] *n* enmienda

amenities [ə'mi:nɪtɪz] *npl* comodidades

amenity [ə'mi:nɪtɪ] *n* servicio

America [ə'merɪkə] *n* América (del Norte)

American [ə'merɪkən] *adj*, *n* (norte)americano(-a), estadounidense

amiable ['eɪmɪəbl] *adj* (*kind*) amable, simpático

amicable ['æmɪkəbl] *adj* amistoso, amigable

amid(st) [ə'mɪd(st)] *prep* entre, en medio de

amiss [ə'mɪs] *adv*: **to take sth** ~ tomar algo a mal; **there's something** ~ pasa algo

ammonia [ə'məunɪə] *n* amoníaco

ammunition [æmju'nɪʃən] *n* municiones; (*fig*) argumentos

amnesia [æm'ni:zɪə] *n* amnesia

amnesty ['æmnɪstɪ] *n* amnistía; **to grant an** ~ **to** amnistiar (a); **A**~ **International** Amnistía Internacional

amok [ə'mɒk] *adv*: **to run** ~ enloquecerse, desbocarse

among(st) [ə'mʌŋ(st)] *prep* entre, en medio de

amorous ['æmərəs] *adj* cariñoso

amount [ə'maunt] *n* (*gen*) cantidad; (*of bill etc*) suma, importe ▷ *vi*: **to** ~ **to** (*total*) sumar; (*be the same as*) equivaler a, significar; **this** ~**s to a refusal** esto equivale a una negativa; **the total** ~ (*of money*) la suma total

amp(ère) ['æmp(εə')] *n* amperio; **a 13 amp plug**

un enchufe de 13 amperios

amphetamine [æm'fɛtəmiːn] n anfetamina

amphibian [æm'fɪbɪən] n anfibio

ample ['æmpl] adj (spacious) amplio; (abundant) abundante; **to have ~ time** tener tiempo de sobra

amplifier ['æmplɪfaɪəʳ] n amplificador

amplify ['æmplɪfaɪ] vt amplificar, aumentar; (explain) explicar

amply ['æmplɪ] adv ampliamente

amputate ['æmpjuteɪt] vt amputar

amuse [ə'mjuːz] vt divertir; (distract) distraer, entretener; **to ~ o.s. with sth/by doing sth** distraerse con algo/haciendo algo; **he was ~d at the joke** el divirtió el chiste

amusement [ə'mjuːzmənt] n diversión; (pastime) pasatiempo; (laughter) risa; **much to my ~** con gran regocijo mío

amusement arcade n salón de juegos

amusement park n parque de atracciones

amusing [ə'mjuːzɪŋ] adj divertido

an [æn, ən, n] indef art see **a**

anaemia [ə'niːmɪə] n anemia

anaemic [ə'niːmɪk] adj anémico; (fig) flojo

anaesthetic [ænɪs'θetɪk] n anestesia; **local/ general ~** anestesia local/general

anaesthetist [æ'niːsθɪtɪst] n anestesista

anagram ['ænəgræm] n anagrama

anal ['eɪnl] adj anal

analogous [ə'næləgəs] adj: **~ to** or **with** análogo a

analog(ue) ['ænəlɔg] adj (computer, watch) analógico

analogy [ə'nælədʒɪ] n analogía; **to draw an ~ between** señalar la analogía entre

analyse ['ænəlaɪz] vt (Brit) analizar

analysis [ə'næləsɪs] (pl **analyses**) n análisis

analyst ['ænəlɪst] n (political analyst) analista; (psychoanalyst) psicoanalista

analytic(al) [ænə'lɪtɪk(əl)] adj analítico

analyze ['ænəlaɪz] vt (US) = **analyse**

anarchic [æ'nɑːkɪk] adj anárquico

anarchist ['ænəkɪst] adj, n anarquista

anarchy ['ænəkɪ] n anarquía, desorden

anathema [ə'næθɪmə] n: **that is ~ to him** eso es pecado para él

anatomy [ə'nætəmɪ] n anatomía

ancestor ['ænsɪstəʳ] n antepasado

ancestry ['ænsɪstrɪ] n ascendencia, abolengo

anchor ['æŋkəʳ] n ancla, áncora ▷ vi (also: **to drop anchor**) anclar, echar el ancla ▷ vt (fig) sujetar, afianzar; **to weigh ~** levar anclas

anchor man, anchor woman n (Radio, TV) presentador(a)

anchovy ['æntʃəvɪ] n anchoa

ancient ['eɪnʃənt] adj antiguo; **~ monument** monumento histórico

ancillary [æn'sɪlərɪ] adj (worker, staff) auxiliar

and [ænd] conj y; (before i, hi) e; **~ so on** etcétera; **try ~ come** procure or intente venir; **two hundred ~ fifty** doscientos cincuenta; **better ~ better** cada vez mejor; **he talked ~ talked** no paraba de hablar; **bread ~ butter** pan con mantequilla

Andalusia [ændə'luːzɪə] n Andalucía

Andean ['ændɪən] adj andino(-a); **~ high plateau** altiplanicie, altiplano (LAm)

Andes ['ændiːz] npl: **the ~** los Andes

anecdote ['ænɪkdəut] n anécdota

anemia [ə'niːmɪə] n (US) = **anaemia**

anemic [ə'niːmɪk] adj (US) = **anaemic**

anesthetic [ænɪs'θetɪk] adj, n (US) = **anaesthetic**

anesthetist [æ'niːsθɪtɪst] n (US) = **anaesthetist**

anew [ə'njuː] adv de nuevo, otra vez

angel ['eɪndʒəl] n ángel

angel dust n polvo de ángel

anger ['æŋgəʳ] n ira, cólera, enojo (LAm) ▷ vt enojar, enfurecer

angina [æn'dʒaɪnə] n angina (del pecho)

angle ['æŋgl] n ángulo; **from their ~** desde su punto de vista

angler ['æŋgləʳ] n pescador(a) (de caña)

Anglican ['æŋglɪkən] adj, n anglicano(-a)

angling ['æŋglɪŋ] n pesca con caña

Anglo- ['æŋgləu] pref anglo...

angrily ['æŋgrɪlɪ] adv enojado, enfadado

angry ['æŋgrɪ] adj enfadado, enojado (esp LAm); **to be ~ with sb/at sth** estar enfadado con algn/ por algo; **to get ~** enfadarse, enojarse (esp LAm)

anguish ['æŋgwɪʃ] n (physical) tormentos; (mental) angustia

anguished ['æŋgwɪʃt] adj angustioso

angular ['æŋgjuləʳ] adj (shape) angular; (features) anguloso

animal ['ænɪməl] adj, n animal

animal rights [-raɪts] npl derechos de los animales

animate vt (enliven) animar; (encourage) estimular, alentar ▷ adj vivo, animado

animated ['ænɪmeɪtɪd] adj vivo, animado

animation [ænɪ'meɪʃən] n animación

animosity [ænɪ'mɔsɪtɪ] n animosidad, rencor

aniseed ['ænɪsiːd] n anís

ankle ['æŋkl] n tobillo

ankle sock n calcetín

annex n (Brit: also: **annexe**: building) edificio anexo ▷ vt (territory) anexar

annihilate [ə'naɪəleɪt] vt aniquilar

annihilation [ənaɪə'leɪʃən] n aniquilación

anniversary [ænɪ'vəːsərɪ] n aniversario

announce [ə'nauns] vt (gen) anunciar; (inform) comunicar; **he ~d that he wasn't going** declaró que no iba

announcement [ə'naunsmənt] n (gen) anuncio; (declaration) declaración; **I'd like to make an ~** quisiera anunciar algo

announcer [ə'naunsəʳ] n (Radio, TV) locutor(a)

annoy [ə'nɔɪ] vt molestar, fastidiar, fregar (LAm), embromar (LAm); **to be ~ed (at sth/with sb)** estar enfadado or molesto (por algo/con algn); **don't get ~ed!** ¡no se enfade!

annoyance [ə'nɔɪəns] n enojo; (thing) molestia

annoying [ə'nɔɪɪŋ] adj molesto, fastidioso, fregado (LAm), embromado (LAm); (person) pesado

annual ['ænjuəl] adj anual ▷ n (Bot) anual; (book)

anuario
annual general meeting (AGM) n junta general anual
annually ['ænjuəlı] adv anualmente, cada año
annual report n informe or memoria anual
annul [ə'nʌl] vt anular; (law) revocar
annum ['ænəm] n see **per annum**
anomaly [ə'nɒmǝlı] n anomalía
anon. [ə'nɒn] abbr = **anonymous**
anonymity [ænə'nımıtı] n anonimato
anonymous [ə'nɒnıməs] adj anónimo; **to remain** ~ quedar en el anonimato
anorak ['ænəræk] n anorak
anorexia [ænə'rɛksıə] n (Med) anorexia
anorexic [ænə'rɛksık] adj, n anoréxico(-a)
another [ə'nʌðə'] adj otro ▷ pron otro; ~ **book** otro libro; **have you got ~ skirt?** ¿tienes otra falda?; ~ **beer?** ¿(quieres) otra cerveza?; ~ **2 km** 2 km más; **in ~ 5 years** en 5 años más; **help yourself to ~** sírvete otro; see also **one**
answer ['ɑ:nsə'] n (to question) respuesta, contestación; (to problem) solución ▷ vi contestar, responder ▷ vt (reply to: person, question) contestar a, responder a; (letter) contestar a; (solve: problem) resolver; **in ~ to your letter** contestando or en contestación a su carta; **to ~ the phone** contestar el teléfono; **to ~ the bell** or **the door** abrir la puerta
▶ **answer back** vi replicar; **don't ~ back!** ¡no seas respondón!
▶ **answer for** vt fus responder de or por
▶ **answer to** vt fus (description) corresponder a
answerable ['ɑ:nsərəbl] adj: ~ **to sb for sth** responsable ante algn de algo
answering machine ['ɑ:nsərıŋ-] n contestador automático
ant [ænt] n hormiga
antagonism [æn'tægənızəm] n antagonismo
antagonistic [æntægə'nıstık] adj antagónico; (opposed) contrario, opuesto
antagonize [æn'tægənaız] vt provocar la enemistad de
Antarctic [ænt'ɑ:ktık] adj antártico ▷ n: **the ~** el Antártico
Antarctica [æn'tɑ:ktıkə] n Antártida
Antarctic Circle n Círculo Polar Antártico
Antarctic Ocean n Océano Antártico
antelope ['æntıləup] n antílope
antenatal [æntı'neıtl] adj prenatal
antenna [æn'tɛnə] (pl -**e**) [-ni:] n antena
anthem ['ænθəm] n: **national ~** himno nacional
anthology [æn'θɒlədʒı] n antología
anthropologist [ænθrə'pɒlədʒıst] n antropólogo(-a)
anthropology [ænθrə'pɒlədʒı] n antropología
anti-aircraft ['æntı'ɛəkrɑ:ft] adj antiaéreo
antibiotic [æntıbaı'ɒtık] adj, n antibiótico
antibody ['æntıbɒdı] n anticuerpo
anticipate [æn'tısıpeıt] vt (foresee) prever; (expect) esperar, contar con; (forestall) anticiparse a, adelantarse a; **this is worse than I ~d** esto es peor de lo que esperaba; **as ~d** según se esperaba

anticipation [æntısı'peıʃən] n previsión; esperanza; anticipación
anticlimax [æntı'klaımæks] n decepción
anticlockwise [æntı'klɒkwaız] adv en dirección contraria a la de las agujas del reloj
antics ['æntıks] npl payasadas
antidepressant [ˌæntıdı'presnt] n antidepresivo
antidote ['æntıdəut] n antídoto
antifreeze ['æntıfri:z] n anticongelante
anti-globalization [ˌæntıgləubəlaı'zeıʃən] n antiglobalización
antihistamine [æntı'hıstəmi:n] n antihistamínico
antiperspirant ['æntıpə:spırənt] n antitranspirante
antiquated ['æntıkweıtıd] adj anticuado
antique [æn'ti:k] n antigüedad ▷ adj antiguo
antique dealer n anticuario(-a)
antique shop n tienda de antigüedades
anti-Semitism [æntı'sɛmıtızəm] n antisemitismo
antiseptic [æntı'sɛptık] adj, n antiséptico
antisocial [æntı'səuʃəl] adj antisocial
antlers ['æntləz] npl cornamenta
anvil ['ænvıl] n yunque
anxiety [æŋ'zaıətı] n (worry) inquietud; (eagerness) ansia, anhelo
anxious ['æŋkʃəs] adj (worried) inquieto; (keen) deseoso; **I'm very ~ about you** me tienes muy preocupado
any ['ɛnı] adj **1** (in questions etc) algún/alguna; **have got you ~ butter/children?** ¿tienes mantequilla/hijos?; **if there are ~ tickets left** si quedan billetes, si queda algún billete
2 (with negative): **I haven't got ~ money/books** no tengo dinero/libros
3 (no matter which) cualquier; ~ **excuse will do** valdrá or servirá cualquier excusa; **choose ~ book you like** escoge el libro que quieras; ~ **teacher you ask will tell you** cualquier profesor al que preguntes te lo dirá
4 (in phrases): **in ~ case** de todas formas, en cualquier caso; ~ **day now** cualquier día (de estos); **at ~ moment** en cualquier momento, de un momento a otro; **at ~ rate** en todo caso; ~ **time, come (at) ~ time** ven cuando quieras; **he might come (at) ~ time** podría llegar de un momento a otro
▷ pron **1** (in questions etc) alguno(-a); **have you got ~?** ¿tienes alguno/a?; **can ~ of you sing?** ¿sabe cantar alguno de vosotros/ustedes?
2 (with negative) ninguno(-a); **I haven't got ~ (of them)** no tengo ninguno
3 (no matter which one(s)): **take ~ of those books (you like)** toma el libro que quieras de ésos
▷ adv **1** (in questions etc): **do you want ~ more soup/sandwiches?** ¿quieres más sopa/bocadillos?; **are you feeling ~ better?** ¿te sientes algo mejor?
2 (with negative): **I can't hear him ~ more** ya no le oigo; **don't wait ~ longer** no esperes más
anybody ['ɛnıbɒdı] pron (in affirmative sentences)

cualquiera, cualquier persona; (*in interrogative sentences*) alguien; (*in negative sentences*) nadie; ~ **can learn to swim** cualquiera puede aprender a nadar; **has ~ got a pen?** ¿tiene alguien un bolígrafo?; **I can't see** ~ no veo a nadie

anyhow ['ɛnɪhaʊ] *adv* de todos modos, de todas maneras; (*carelessly*) de cualquier manera; (*haphazardly*) de cualquier modo; **I shall go** ~ iré de todas maneras

anyone ['ɛnɪwʌn] = **anybody**

anyplace ['ɛnɪpleɪs] *adv* (*US*) = **anywhere**

anything ['ɛnɪθɪŋ] *pron* (*in affirmative sentences*) cualquier cosa; (*in interrogative sentences*) algo; (*in negative sentences*) nada; (*everything*) todo; ~ **could happen** puede pasar cualquier cosa; **it can cost ~ between £15 and £20** puede costar entre 15 y 20 libras; **do you need ~?** ¿necesitas algo?; **would you like ~ to eat?** ¿quieres algo de comer?; ~ **else?** ¿algo más?; **I can't hear ~** no oigo nada

anytime ['ɛnɪtaɪm] *adv* (*at any moment*) en cualquier momento, de un momento a otro; (*whenever*) no importa cuándo, cuando quiera

anyway ['ɛnɪweɪ] *adv* de todas maneras; de cualquier modo

anywhere ['ɛnɪwɛəʳ] *adv* (*in affirmative sentences*) en cualquier sitio; a cualquier sitio; (*in interrogative sentences*) en algún sitio; a algún sitio; (*in negative sentences*) en ningún sitio; a ningún sitio; **you can buy stamps almost** ~ se pueden comprar sellos casi en cualquier sitio; ~ **in the world** en cualquier parte del mundo; **you can sit ~ you like** siéntate donde quieras; **have you seen my coat ~?** ¿has visto mi abrigo en algún sitio?; **are we going ~?** ¿vamos a algún sitio?; **I don't see him ~** no le veo en ningún sitio; **I can't go ~** no puedo ir a ningún sitio

apart [ə'pɑːt] *adv* aparte, separadamente; **10 miles ~** separados por 10 millas; **to take ~** desmontar; ~ **from** *prep* aparte de

apartheid [ə'pɑːteɪt] *n* apartheid

apartment [ə'pɑːtmənt] *n* (*US*) piso (*Esp*), departamento (*LAm*), apartamento; (*room*) cuarto

apartment block *or* **building** (*US*) bloque *m* de pisos

apathetic [æpə'θɛtɪk] *adj* apático, indiferente

apathy ['æpəθɪ] *n* apatía, indiferencia

ape [eɪp] *n* mono ▷ *vt* imitar, remedar

aperitif [ə'pɛrɪtiːf] *n* aperitivo

aperture ['æpətʃjʊəʳ] *n* rendija, resquicio; (*Phot*) abertura

apex ['eɪpɛks] *n* ápice; (*fig*) cumbre

aphorism ['æfərɪzəm] *n* aforismo

aphrodisiac [æfrəʊ'dɪzɪæk] *adj, n* afrodisíaco

apiece [ə'piːs] *adv* cada uno

apologetic [əpɔlə'dʒɛtɪk] *adj* (*look, remark*) de disculpa

apologize [ə'pɔlədʒaɪz] *vi*: **to ~ (for sth to sb)** disculparse (con algn por algo)

apology [ə'pɔlədʒɪ] *n* disculpa, excusa; **please accept my apologies** le ruego me disculpe

apostle [ə'pɔsl] *n* apóstol

apostrophe [ə'pɔstrəfɪ] *n* apóstrofo

appal [ə'pɔːl] *vt* horrorizar, espantar

appalling [ə'pɔːlɪŋ] *adj* espantoso; (*awful*) pésimo; **she's an ~ cook** es una cocinera malísima

apparatus [æpə'reɪtəs] *n* aparato; (*in gymnasium*) aparatos

apparel [ə'pærl] *n* (*US*) indumentaria

apparent [ə'pærənt] *adj* aparente; (*obvious*) manifiesto, evidente; **it is ~ that** está claro que

apparently [ə'pærəntlɪ] *adv* por lo visto, al parecer, dizque (*LAm*)

appeal [ə'piːl] *vi* hacer un llamamiento; (*Law*) apelar ▷ *n* (*request*) llamamiento, llamado (*LAm*); (*plea*) súplica; (*Law*) apelación; (*charm*) atractivo, encanto; **to ~ for** (*call publicly for*) hacer un llamamiento a; (*request*) solicitar; **to ~ to** (*person*) rogar a, suplicar a; (*thing*) atraer, interesar; **to ~ to sb for mercy** rogarle misericordia a algn; **it doesn't ~ to me** no me atrae, no me llama la atención; **they have launched an ~ for unity** han hecho un llamamiento a la unidad; **right of ~** (*Law*) derecho de apelación

appealing [ə'piːlɪŋ] *adj* (*nice*) atractivo; (*touching*) conmovedor(a), emocionante

appear [ə'pɪəʳ] *vi* aparecer, presentarse; (*Law*) comparecer; (*publication*) salir (a luz), publicarse; (*seem*) parecer; **the bus ~ed around the corner** el autobús apareció por la esquina; **to ~ on TV** salir en la tele; **she ~ed to be asleep** parecía estar dormida; **it would ~ that** parecería que

appearance [ə'pɪərəns] *n* aparición; (*look, aspect*) apariencia, aspecto; **to keep up ~s** salvar las apariencias; **to all ~s** al parecer

appease [ə'piːz] *vt* (*pacify*) apaciguar; (*satisfy*) satisfacer

appendicitis [əpɛndɪ'saɪtɪs] *n* apendicitis

appendix [ə'pɛndɪks] (*pl* **appendices**) *n* apéndice; **to have one's ~ out** operarse de apendicitis

appetite ['æpɪtaɪt] *n* apetito; (*fig*) deseo, anhelo; **that walk has given me an ~** ese paseo me ha abierto el apetito

appetizer ['æpɪtaɪzəʳ] *n* (*drink*) aperitivo; (*food*) tapas (*Esp*)

applaud [ə'plɔːd] *vt, vi* aplaudir

applause [ə'plɔːz] *n* aplausos

apple ['æpl] *n* manzana

apple tree *n* manzano

appliance [ə'plaɪəns] *n* aparato; **electrical ~s** electrodomésticos

applicable [ə'plɪkəbl] *adj* aplicable, pertinente; **the law is ~ from January** la ley es aplicable *or* se pone en vigor a partir de enero; **to be ~ to** referirse a

applicant ['æplɪkənt] *n* candidato(-a); solicitante

application [æplɪ'keɪʃən] *n* aplicación; (*for a job, a grant etc*) solicitud

application form *n* solicitud

applied [ə'plaɪd] *adj* (*science, art*) aplicado

apply [ə'plaɪ] vt: **to ~ (to)** aplicar (a); (fig) emplear (para) ▷ vi: **to ~ to** (ask) dirigirse a; (be suitable for) ser aplicable a; (be relevant to) tener que ver con; **this rule doesn't ~ to us** esta norma no nos afecta; **to ~ for** (permit, grant, job) solicitar; **to ~ the brakes** echar el freno; **to ~ o.s. to** aplicarse a, dedicarse a

appoint [ə'pɔɪnt] vt (to post) nombrar; (date, place) fijar, señalar

appointment [ə'pɔɪntmənt] n (engagement) cita; (date) compromiso; (act) nombramiento; (post) puesto; **to make an ~ (with)** (doctor) pedir hora (con); (friend) citarse (con); **"~s (vacant)"** "ofertas de trabajo"; **by ~** mediante cita

apportion [ə'pɔːʃən] vt repartir

appraisal [ə'preɪzl] n evaluación

appreciably [ə'priːʃəblɪ] adv sensiblemente, de manera apreciable

appreciate [ə'priːʃɪeɪt] vt (like) apreciar, tener en mucho; (be grateful for) agradecer; (be aware of) comprender ▷ vi (Comm) aumentar en valor; **I ~d your help** agradecí tu ayuda

appreciation [əpriːʃɪ'eɪʃən] n aprecio; reconocimiento, agradecimiento; aumento en valor

appreciative [ə'priːʃɪətɪv] adj agradecido

apprehend [æprɪ'hend] vt percibir; (arrest) detener

apprehension [æprɪ'henʃən] n (fear) aprensión

apprehensive [æprɪ'hensɪv] adj aprensivo

apprentice [ə'prentɪs] n aprendiz(a) ▷ vt: **to be ~d to** estar de aprendiz con

apprenticeship [ə'prentɪsʃɪp] n aprendizaje; **to serve one's ~** hacer el aprendizaje

approach [ə'prəutʃ] vi acercarse ▷ vt acercarse a; (be approximate to) aproximarse a; (ask, apply to) dirigirse a; (problem) abordar ▷ n acercamiento; aproximación; (access) acceso; (proposal) proposición; (to problem etc) enfoque; **to ~ sb about sth** hablar con algn sobre algo

approachable [ə'prəutʃəbl] adj (person) abordable; (place) accesible

appropriate adj apropiado, conveniente ▷ vt (take) apropiarse de; (allot): **to ~ sth for** destinar algo a; **~ for** or **to** apropiado para; **it would not be ~ for me to comment** no estaría bien or sería pertinente que yo diera mi opinión

approval [ə'pruːvəl] n aprobación, visto bueno; **on ~** (Comm) a prueba; **to meet with sb's ~** obtener la aprobación de algn

approve [ə'pruːv] vt aprobar
▷ **approve of** vt fus aprobar

approved school n (Brit) correccional

approx. abbr (= approximately) aprox

approximate [ə'prɔksɪmɪt] adj aproximado

approximately [ə'prɔksɪmɪtlɪ] adv aproximadamente, más o menos

approximation [əprɔksɪ'meɪʃən] n aproximación

apr n abbr (= annual percentage rate) tasa de interés anual

apricot ['eɪprɪkɔt] n albaricoque, damasco (And,

CS), chabacano (Méx)

April ['eɪprəl] n abril; **~ Fools' Day** n ≈ día de los (Santos) Inocentes

apron ['eɪprən] n delantal; (Aviat) pista

apt [æpt] adj (to the point) acertado, oportuno; (appropriate) apropiado; **~ to do** (likely) propenso a hacer

aptitude ['æptɪtjuːd] n aptitud, capacidad

aquarium [ə'kwɛərɪəm] n acuario

Aquarius [ə'kwɛərɪəs] n Acuario

Arab ['ærəb] adj, n árabe

Arabia [ə'reɪbɪə] n Arabia

Arabian [ə'reɪbɪən] adj árabe, arábigo

Arabian Desert n Desierto de Arabia

Arabian Sea n Mar de Omán

Arabic ['ærəbɪk] adj (language, manuscripts) árabe, arábigo ▷ n árabe; **~ numerals** numeración arábiga

arable ['ærəbl] adj cultivable

Aragon ['ærəgən] n Aragón

arbitrary ['ɑːbɪtrərɪ] adj arbitrario

arbitration [ɑːbɪ'treɪʃən] n arbitraje; **the dispute went to ~** el conflicto laboral fue sometido al arbitraje

arbitrator ['ɑːbɪtreɪtəʳ] n árbitro

arc [ɑːk] n arco

arcade [ɑː'keɪd] n (Arch) arcada; (round a square) soportales; (shopping arcade) galería comercial

arch [ɑːtʃ] n arco; (vault) bóveda; (of foot) empeine ▷ vt arquear

archaeological [ɑːkɪə'lɔdʒɪkl] adj arqueológico

archaeologist [ɑːkɪ'ɔlədʒɪst] n arqueólogo(-a)

archaeology [ɑːkɪ'ɔlədʒɪ] n arqueología

archaic [ɑː'keɪɪk] adj arcaico

archbishop [ɑːtʃ'bɪʃəp] n arzobispo

archenemy ['ɑːtʃɛnəmɪ] n enemigo jurado

archeology etc [ɑːkɪ'ɔlədʒɪ] (US) see **archaeology** etc

archery ['ɑːtʃərɪ] n tiro al arco

architect ['ɑːkɪtɛkt] n arquitecto(-a)

architecture ['ɑːkɪtɛktʃəʳ] n arquitectura

archive ['ɑːkaɪv] n (also Comput) archivo

archives ['ɑːkaɪvz] npl archivo

Arctic ['ɑːktɪk] adj ártico ▷ n: **the ~** el Ártico

Arctic Circle n Círculo Polar Ártico

Arctic Ocean n Océano (Glacial) Ártico

ardent ['ɑːdənt] adj (desire) ardiente; (supporter, lover) apasionado

are [ɑːʳ] vb see **be**

area ['ɛərɪə] n área; (Math etc) superficie, extensión; (zone) región, zona; **the London ~** la zona de Londres

area code n (US Tel) prefijo

arena [ə'riːnə] n arena; (of circus) pista; (for bullfight) plaza, ruedo

aren't [ɑːnt] = **are not**

Argentina [ɑːdʒən'tiːnə] n Argentina

Argentinian [ɑːdʒən'tɪnɪən] adj, n argentino(-a)

arguable ['ɑːgjuəbl] adj: **it is ~ whether ...** es dudoso que

arguably ['ɑːgjuəblɪ] adv: **it is ~ ...** es discutiblemente ...

argue ['ɑːgjuː] vt (*debate: case, matter*) mantener, argüir ▷ vi (*quarrel*) discutir; (*reason*) razonar, argumentar; **to ~ that** sostener que; **to ~ about sth (with sb)** pelearse (con algn) por algo

argument ['ɑːgjumənt] n (*reasons*) argumento; (*quarrel*) discusión; (*debate*) debate; **~ for/against** argumento en pro/contra de

argumentative [ɑːgju'mɛntətɪv] adj discutidor(a)

Aries ['ɛərɪz] n Aries

arise [ə'raɪz] (*pt* **arose**, *pp* **-n**) [ə'rɪzn] vi (*rise up*) levantarse, alzarse; (*emerge*) surgir, presentarse; **to ~ from** derivar de; **should the need ~** si fuera necesario

aristocracy [ærɪs'tɔkrəsɪ] n aristocracia

aristocrat ['ærɪstəkræt] n aristócrata

aristocratic [ərɪstə'krætɪk] adj aristocrático

arithmetic [ə'rɪθmətɪk] n aritmética

Ark [ɑːk] n: **Noah's ~** el Arca de Noé

arm [ɑːm] n (*Anat*) brazo ▷ vt armar; **~ in ~** cogidos del brazo; *see also* **arms**

armaments ['ɑːməmənts] npl (*weapons*) armamentos

armchair ['ɑːmtʃɛər] n sillón, butaca

armed [ɑːmd] adj armado; **the ~ forces** las fuerzas armadas

armed robbery n robo a mano armada

Armenia [ɑː'miːnɪə] n Armenia

armour, (*US*) **armor** ['ɑːmər] n armadura

armo(u)red car n coche *or* carro (*LAm*) blindado

armpit ['ɑːmpɪt] n sobaco, axila

armrest ['ɑːmrɛst] n reposabrazos, brazo

arms [ɑːmz] npl (*weapons*) armas; (*Heraldry*) escudo

arms control n control de armamentos

army ['ɑːmɪ] n ejército

aroma [ə'rəumə] n aroma, fragancia

aromatherapy [ərəumə'θɛrəpɪ] n aromaterapia

arose [ə'rəuz] pt of **arise**

around [ə'raund] adv alrededor; (*in the area*) a la redonda ▷ prep alrededor de; **to look ~** echar una mirada alrededor; **we walked ~ for a while** paseamos por ahí durante un rato; **she wore a scarf ~ her neck** llevaba una bufanda alrededor del cuello; **she ignored the people ~ her** ignoró a la gente que estaba a su alrededor; **it costs ~ £100** cuesta alrededor de 100 libras; **shall we meet at ~ 8 o'clock?** ¿quedamos sobre las 8?; **I've been walking ~ the town** he estado paseando por la ciudad; **is there a chemist's ~ here?** ¿hay alguna farmacia por aquí?

arousal [ə'rauzəl] n (*sexual*) excitación; (*of feelings, interest*) despertar

arouse [ə'rauz] vt despertar

arrange [ə'reɪndʒ] vt arreglar, ordenar; (*party, event*) organizar; (*appointment*) concertar ▷ vi: **we have ~d for a taxi to pick you up** hemos organizado todo para que le recoja un taxi; **to ~ to do sth** quedar en hacer algo; **it was ~d that ... se** quedó en que ...

arrangement [ə'reɪndʒmənt] n arreglo; (*agreement*) acuerdo; **arrangements** npl (*plans*)

planes, medidas; (*preparations*) preparativos; **I'll make ~s for you to be met** haré los preparativos para que le estén esperando; **to come to an ~ (with sb)** llegar a un acuerdo (con algn); **by ~** a convenir

arrant ['ærənt] adj: **~ nonsense** una verdadera tontería

array [ə'reɪ] n (*Comput*) matriz; **~ of** (*things*) serie o colección de; (*people*) conjunto de

arrears [ə'rɪəz] npl atrasos; **in ~** (*Comm*) en mora; **to be in ~ with one's rent** estar retrasado en el pago del alquiler

arrest [ə'rɛst] vt detener; (*sb's attention*) llamar ▷ n detención; **under ~** detenido

arrival [ə'raɪvəl] n llegada, arribo (*LAm*); **new ~** recién llegado(-a)

arrive [ə'raɪv] vi llegar, arribar (*LAm*)

arrogance ['ærəgəns] n arrogancia, prepotencia (*LAm*)

arrogant ['ærəgənt] adj arrogante, prepotente (*LAm*)

arrow ['ærəu] n flecha

arse [ɑːs] n (*Brit col!*) culo, trasero

arsenal ['ɑːsɪnl] n arsenal

arsenic ['ɑːsnɪk] n arsénico

arson ['ɑːsn] n incendio provocado

art [ɑːt] n arte; (*skill*) destreza; (*technique*) técnica; **Arts** npl (*Scol*) Letras; **work of ~** obra de arte

artefact ['ɑːtɪfækt] n artefacto

artery ['ɑːtərɪ] n (*Med: road etc*) arteria

artful ['ɑːtful] adj (*cunning: person, trick*) mañoso

art gallery n pinacoteca, museo de pintura; (*Comm*) galería de arte

arthritis [ɑː'θraɪtɪs] n artritis

artichoke ['ɑːtɪtʃəuk] n alcachofa, alcaucil (*RP*); **Jerusalem ~** aguaturma

article ['ɑːtɪkl] n artículo, objeto, cosa; (*in newspaper*) artículo; (*Brit Law: training*): **~s** npl contrato de aprendizaje; **~s of clothing** prendas de vestir

articulate adj (*speech*) claro; (*person*) que se expresa bien ▷ vi articular

articulated lorry n (*Brit*) trailer

artificial [ɑːtɪ'fɪʃəl] adj artificial; (*teeth etc*) postizo

artificial insemination n inseminación artificial

artificial respiration n respiración artificial

artillery [ɑː'tɪlərɪ] n artillería

artisan ['ɑːtɪzæn] n artesano(-a)

artist ['ɑːtɪst] n artista; (*Mus*) intérprete

artistic [ɑː'tɪstɪk] adj artístico

artistry ['ɑːtɪstrɪ] n arte, habilidad (*artística*)

art school n escuela de bellas artes

artwork ['ɑːtwəːk] n material gráfico

as [æz] conj **1** (*referring to time: while*) mientras; (*: when*) cuando; **she wept as she told her story** lloraba mientras contaba lo que le ocurrió; **as the years go by** a medida que pasan los años, con el paso de los años; **he came in as I was leaving** entró cuando me marchaba; **as from tomorrow** a partir de *or* desde mañana

2 (*in comparisons*): **as big as** tan grande como; **twice as big as** el doble de grande que; **as much money/many books as** tanto dinero/tantos libros como; **as soon as** en cuanto, no bien (*LAm*) **3** (*since, because*) como, ya que; **as I don't speak German I can't understand him** como no hablo alemán no le entiendo, no le entiendo ya que no hablo alemán **4** (*although*): **much as I like them, ...** aunque me gustan, ... **5** (*referring to manner, way*): **do as you wish** haz lo que quieras; **as she said** como dijo; **he gave it to me as a present** me lo dio de regalo; **it's on the left as you go in** según se entra, a la izquierda **6** (*concerning*): **as for** *or* **to that** por *or* en lo que respecta a eso **7**: **as if** *or* **though** como si; **he looked as if** *or* **as though he was ill** parecía como si estuviera enfermo, tenía aspecto de enfermo; **she acted as if** *or* **as though she hadn't seen me** hizo como si no me hubiese visto; *see also* **long**; **such**; **well** ▷ *prep* (*in the capacity of*): **he works as a barman** trabaja de barman; **as chairman of the company, he ...** como presidente de la compañía, ...

asbestos [æz'bestəs] *n* asbesto, amianto
ascend [ə'sɛnd] *vt* subir, ascender
ascendancy [ə'sɛndənsɪ] *n* ascendiente, dominio
ascent [ə'sɛnt] *n* subida; (*slope*) cuesta, pendiente; (*of plane*) ascenso
ascertain [æsə'teɪn] *vt* averiguar
ascetic [ə'sɛtɪk] *adj* ascético
ASCII ['æski:] *n abbr* (= *American Standard Code for Information Interchange*) ASCII
ascribe [ə'skraɪb] *vt*: **to ~ sth to** atribuir algo a
ash [æʃ] *n* ceniza; (*tree*) fresno
ashamed [ə'feɪmd] *adj* avergonzado; **to be ~ of** avergonzarse de
ashen ['æʃn] *adj* pálido
ashore [ə'ʃɔːʳ] *adv* en tierra
ashtray ['æʃtreɪ] *n* cenicero
Ash Wednesday *n* miércoles de ceniza
Asia ['eɪʃə] *n* Asia
Asian ['eɪʃən], **Asiatic** [eɪsɪ'ætɪk] *adj, n* asiático(-a)
aside [ə'saɪd] *adv* a un lado ▷ *n* aparte; **~ from** *prep* (*as well as*) aparte *or* además de
ask [ɑːsk] *vt* (*question*) preguntar; (*demand*) pedir; (*invite*) invitar ▷ *vi*: **to ~ about sth** preguntar acerca de algo; **"have you finished?" she ~ed** "¿has terminado?" preguntó; **to ~ sb sth** preguntar algo a algn; **to ~ sb to do sth** pedir a algn que haga algo; **she ~ed him to do the shopping** le pidió que hiciera la compra; **to ~ sb about sth** preguntar algo a algn; **to ~ (sb) a question** hacer una pregunta (a algn); **to ~ sb the time** preguntar la hora a algn; **have you ~ed Matthew to the party?** ¿has invitado a Matthew a la fiesta?; **Peter ~ed her out** Peter

le pidió que saliera con él; **to ~ sb out to dinner** invitar a cenar a algn
▸ **ask after** *vt fus* preguntar por
▸ **ask for** *vt fus* pedir; **he ~ed for a cup of tea** pidió una taza de té; **it's just ~ing for trouble** *or* **for it** es buscarse problemas
askance [ə'skɑːns] *adv*: **to look ~ at sb** mirar con recelo a algn
asking price *n* (*Comm*) precio inicial
asleep [ə'sliːp] *adj* dormido; **to fall ~** dormirse, quedarse dormido
asparagus [əs'pærəgəs] *n* espárragos
aspect ['æspɛkt] *n* aspecto, apariencia; (*direction in which a building etc faces*) orientación
aspersions [əs'pə:ʃənz] *npl*: **to cast ~ on** difamar a, calumniar a
asphyxiate [æs'fɪksɪeɪt] *vt* asfixiar
asphyxiation [aesfɪksɪ'eɪʃən] *n* asfixia
aspirate *vt* aspirar ▷ *adj* aspirado
aspirations [æspə'reɪʃənz] *npl* aspiraciones; (*ambition*) ambición
aspire [əs'paɪəʳ] *vi*: **to ~ to** aspirar a, ambicionar
aspirin ['æsprɪn] *n* aspirina
aspiring [əs'paɪərɪŋ] *adj*: **an ~ actor** un aspirante a actor
ass [æs] *n* asno, burro; (*col*) imbécil; (*US col!*) culo, trasero
assailant [ə'seɪlənt] *n* agresor(a)
assassin [ə'sæsɪn] *n* asesino(-a)
assassinate [ə'sæsɪneɪt] *vt* asesinar
assassination [əsæsɪ'neɪʃən] *n* asesinato
assault [ə'sɔːlt] *n* (*gen: attack*) asalto, agresión ▷ *vt* asaltar, agredir; (*sexually*) violar
assemble [ə'sɛmbl] *vt* reunir, juntar; (*Tech*) montar ▷ *vi* reunirse, juntarse
assembly [ə'sɛmblɪ] *n* (*meeting*) reunión, asamblea; (*construction*) montaje
assembly line *n* cadena de montaje
Assembly Member *n* (*in Wales*) miembro *mf* de la Asamblea Nacional (de Gales)
assent [ə'sɛnt] *n* asentimiento, aprobación ▷ *vi* consentir, asentir; **to ~ (to sth)** consentir (en algo)
assert [ə'sə:t] *vt* afirmar; (*insist on*) hacer valer; **to ~ o.s.** imponerse
assertion [ə'sə:ʃən] *n* afirmación
assertive [ə'sə:tɪv] *adj* enérgico, agresivo, perentorio
assess [ə'sɛs] *vt* valorar, calcular; (*tax, damages*) fijar; (*property etc: for tax*) gravar
assessment [ə'sɛsmənt] *n* valoración; gravamen; (*judgment*): **~ (of)** juicio (sobre)
assessor [ə'sɛsəʳ] *n* asesor(a); (*of tax*) tasador(a)
asset ['æsɛt] *n* posesión; (*quality*) ventaja; **assets** *npl* (*funds*) activo, fondos
assiduous [ə'sɪdjuəs] *adj* asiduo
assign [ə'saɪn] *vt* (*date*) fijar; (*task*) asignar; (*resources*) destinar; (*property*) traspasar
assignment [ə'saɪnmənt] *n* asignación; (*task*) tarea
assimilate [ə'sɪmɪleɪt] *vt* asimilar
assimilation [əsɪmɪ'leɪʃən] *n* asimilación

assist [ə'sɪst] vt ayudar

assistance [ə'sɪstəns] n ayuda, auxilio

assistant [ə'sɪstənt] n ayudante; (Brit: also: **shop assistant**) dependiente(-a)

associate adj asociado ▷ n socio(-a), colega; (in crime) cómplice; (member) miembro(-a) ▷ vt asociar; (ideas) relacionar ▷ vi: **to ~ with sb** tratar con algn; **~ director** subdirector(a); **~d company** compañía afiliada

association [əsəusɪ'eɪʃən] n asociación; (Comm) sociedad; **in ~ with** en asociación con

assorted [ə'sɔːtɪd] adj surtido, variado; **in ~ sizes** en distintos tamaños

assortment [ə'sɔːtmənt] n surtido

Asst. abbr = **Assistant**

assume [ə'sjuːm] vt (suppose) suponer; (responsibilities etc) asumir; (attitude, name) adoptar, tomar

assumed name n nombre falso

assumption [ə'sʌmpʃən] n (supposition) suposición, presunción; (act) asunción; **on the ~ that** suponiendo que

assurance [ə'ʃuərəns] n garantía, promesa; (confidence) confianza, aplomo; (Brit: insurance) seguro; **I can give you no ~s** no puedo hacerle ninguna promesa

assure [ə'ʃuəʳ] vt asegurar

assured [ə'ʃuəd] adj seguro

asterisk ['æstərɪsk] n asterisco

asteroid ['æstərɔɪd] n asteroide

asthma ['æsmə] n asma

astonish [ə'stɒnɪʃ] vt asombrar, pasmar

astonishing [ə'stɒnɪʃɪŋ] adj asombroso, pasmoso; **I find it ~ that ...** me asombra or pasma que ...

astonishment [ə'stɒnɪʃmənt] n asombro, sorpresa; **to my ~** con gran sorpresa mía

astound [ə'staund] vt asombrar, pasmar

astounding [ə'staundɪŋ] adj asombroso

astray [ə'streɪ] adv: **to go ~** extraviarse; **to lead ~** llevar por mal camino; **to go ~ in one's calculations** equivocarse en sus cálculos

astride [ə'straɪd] prep a caballo or horcajadas sobre

astrologer [əs'trɒlədʒəʳ] n astrólogo(-a)

astrology [əs'trɒlədʒɪ] n astrología

astronaut ['æstrənɔːt] n astronauta

astronomer [əs'trɒnəməʳ] n astrónomo(-a)

astronomical [æstrə'nɒmɪkəl] adj astronómico

astronomy [aes'trɒnəmɪ] n astronomía

astute [əs'tjuːt] adj astuto

asylum [ə'saɪləm] n (refuge) asilo; (hospital) manicomio; **to seek political ~** pedir asilo político

at [æt] prep **1** (referring to position) en; (direction) a; **at the top** en lo alto; **at home/school** en casa/la escuela; **at work/the office** en el trabajo/la oficina; **to look at sth/sb** mirar algo/a algn
2 (referring to time): **at 4 o'clock** a las 4; **at night** por la noche; **at Christmas** en Navidad; **at times** a veces
3 (referring to rates, speed etc): **at £1 a kilo** a una

libra el kilo; **2 at a time** de 2 en 2; **at 50 km/h** a 50 km/h
4 (referring to manner): **at a stroke** de un golpe; **at peace** en paz
5 (referring to activity): **to be at work** estar trabajando; **to play at cowboys** jugar a los vaqueros; **to be good at sth** ser bueno en algo
6 (referring to cause): **shocked/surprised/annoyed at sth** asombrado/sorprendido/fastidiado por algo; **I went at his suggestion** fui a instancias suyas

ate [ɛt, eɪt] pt of **eat**

atheism ['eɪθɪɪzəm] n ateísmo

atheist ['eɪθɪɪst] n ateo(-a)

Athens ['æθɪnz] n Atenas

athlete ['æθliːt] n atleta

athletic [æθ'lɛtɪk] adj atlético

athletics [æθ'lɛtɪks] n atletismo

Atlantic [ət'læntɪk] adj atlántico ▷ n: **the ~ (Ocean)** el (Océano) Atlántico

atlas ['ætləs] n atlas

atmosphere ['ætməsfɪəʳ] n (air) atmósfera; (fig) ambiente

atom ['ætəm] n átomo

atomic [ə'tɒmɪk] adj atómico

atom(ic) bomb n bomba atómica

atomizer ['ætəmaɪzəʳ] n atomizador

atone [ə'təun] vi: **to ~ for** expiar

A to Z® n guía alfabética; (map) callejero

atrocious [ə'trəuʃəs] adj atroz; (fig) horrible, infame

atrocity [ə'trɒsɪtɪ] n atrocidad

attach [ə'tætʃ] vt sujetar; (stick) pegar; (document, letter) adjuntar; **the ~ed letter** la carta adjunta; **to be ~ed to sb/sth** (like) tener cariño a algn/algo

attaché [ə'tæʃeɪ] n agregado(-a)

attaché case n (Brit) maletín

attachment [ə'tætʃmənt] n (tool) accesorio; (Comput) archivo o documento adjunto; (love): **~ (to)** apego (a), cariño (a)

attack [ə'tæk] vt (Mil) atacar; (criminal) agredir, asaltar; (task etc) emprender ▷ n ataque, asalto; (on sb's life) atentado; **heart ~** infarto (de miocardio)

attacker [ə'tækəʳ] n agresor(a), asaltante

attain [ə'teɪn] vt (also: **attain to**) alcanzar; (achieve) lograr, conseguir

attainments [ə'teɪnmənts] npl (skill) talento

attempt [ə'tɛmpt] n tentativa, intento; (attack) atentado ▷ vt intentar, tratar de; **he made no ~ to help** ni siquiera intentó ayudar; **to ~ to do sth** intentar hacer algo; **I ~ed to write a song** intenté escribir una canción

attempted [ə'tɛmptɪd] adj: **~ murder/burglary/suicide** tentativa or intento de asesinato/robo/suicidio

attend [ə'tɛnd] vt asistir a; (patient) atender ▷ **attend to** vt fus (needs, affairs etc) ocuparse de; (speech etc) prestar atención a; (customer) atender a

attendance [ə'tɛndəns] n asistencia, presencia; (people present) concurrencia

attendant [əˈtɛndənt] n sirviente(-a), mozo(-a); (Theat) acomodador(a) ▷ adj concomitante

attention [əˈtɛnʃən] n atención ▷ excl (Mil) ¡firme(s)!; **for the ~ of…** (Admin) a la atención de…; **it has come to my ~ that …** me he enterado de que …

attentive [əˈtɛntɪv] adj atento; (polite) cortés

attest [əˈtɛst] vi: **to ~ to** dar fe de

attic [ˈætɪk] n desván, altillo (LAm), entretecho (LAm)

attitude [ˈætɪtjuːd] n (gen) actitud; (disposition) disposición

attorney [əˈtəːnɪ] n (US: lawyer) abogado(-a); (having proxy) apoderado

Attorney General n (Brit) ≈ Presidente del Consejo del Poder Judicial (Esp); (US) ≈ ministro de justicia

attract [əˈtrækt] vt atraer; (attention) llamar

attraction [əˈtrækʃən] n (gen) encanto, atractivo; (Physics, towards sth) atracción

attractive [əˈtræktɪv] adj atractivo

attribute n atributo ▷ vt: **to ~ sth to** atribuir algo a; (accuse) achacar algo a

attrition [əˈtrɪʃən] n: **war of ~** guerra de agotamiento or desgaste

atypical [eɪˈtɪpɪkl] adj atípico

aubergine [ˈəubəʒiːn] n (Brit) berenjena

auburn [ˈɔːbən] adj color castaño rojizo

auction [ˈɔːkʃən] n (also: **sale by auction**) subasta ▷ vt subastar

auctioneer [ɔːkʃəˈnɪər] n subastador(a)

audacious [ɔːˈdeɪʃəs] adj (bold) audaz, osado; (impudent) atrevido, descarado

audacity [ɔːˈdæsɪtɪ] n audacia, atrevimiento; (pej) descaro

audible [ˈɔːdɪbl] adj audible, que se puede oír

audience [ˈɔːdɪəns] n auditorio; (gathering) público; (interview) audiencia

audio-typist [ˈɔːdɪəuˈtaɪpɪst] n mecanógrafo(-a) de dictáfono

audiovisual [ɔːdɪəuˈvɪzjuəl] adj audiovisual

audiovisual aid n ayuda or medio audiovisual

audit [ˈɔːdɪt] vt revisar, intervenir

audition [ɔːˈdɪʃən] n audición ▷ vi: **to ~ for the part of** hacer una audición para el papel de

auditor [ˈɔːdɪtər] n interventor(a), censor(a) de cuentas

auditorium [ɔːdɪˈtɔːrɪəm] n auditorio

augur [ˈɔːgər] vi: **it ~s well** es de buen agüero

August [ˈɔːgəst] n agosto

aunt [ɑːnt] n tía

auntie, aunty [ˈɑːntɪ] n diminutive of **aunt**

au pair [ˈəuˈpɛər] n (also: **au pair girl**) chica au pair

auspicious [ɔːsˈpɪʃəs] adj propicio, de buen augurio

austere [ɔsˈtɪər] adj austero; (manner) adusto

austerity [ɔˈstɛrɪtɪ] n austeridad

Australasia [ɔːstrəˈleɪzɪə] n Australasia

Australia [ɔsˈtreɪlɪə] n Australia

Australian [ɔsˈtreɪlɪən] adj, n australiano(-a)

Austria [ˈɔstrɪə] n Austria

Austrian [ˈɔstrɪən] adj, n austríaco(-a)

authentic [ɔːˈθɛntɪk] adj auténtico

authenticity [ɔːθɛnˈtɪsɪtɪ] n autenticidad

author [ˈɔːθər] n autor(a)

authoritarian [ɔːθɔrɪˈtɛərɪən] adj autoritario

authoritative [ɔːˈθɔrɪtətɪv] adj autorizado; (manner) autoritario

authority [ɔːˈθɔrɪtɪ] n autoridad; **the authorities** npl las autoridades; **to have ~ to do sth** tener autoridad para hacer algo

authorization [ɔːθəraɪˈzeɪʃən] n autorización

authorize [ˈɔːθəraɪz] vt autorizar

auto [ˈɔːtəu] n (US) coche, carro (LAm), auto (CS), automóvil

autobiography [ɔːtəbaɪˈɔgrəfɪ] n autobiografía

autograph [ˈɔːtəgrɑːf] n autógrafo ▷ vt firmar; (photo etc) dedicar

automated [ˈɔːtəmeɪtɪd] adj automatizado

automatic [ɔːtəˈmætɪk] adj automático ▷ n (gun) pistola automática; (washing machine) lavadora

automatically [ɔːtəˈmætɪklɪ] adv automáticamente

automation [ɔːtəˈmeɪʃən] n automatización

automobile [ˈɔːtəməbiːl] n (US) coche, carro (LAm), automóvil

autonomous [ɔːˈtɔnəməs] adj autónomo

autonomy [ɔːˈtɔnəmɪ] n autonomía

autopsy [ˈɔːtɔpsɪ] n autopsia

autumn [ˈɔːtəm] n otoño

auxiliary [ɔːgˈzɪlɪərɪ] adj auxiliar

Av. abbr (= avenue) Av., Avda.

avail [əˈveɪl] vt: **to ~ o.s.** of aprovechar(se) de, valerse de ▷ n: **to no ~** en vano, sin resultado

availability [əveɪləˈbɪlɪtɪ] n disponibilidad

available [əˈveɪləbl] adj disponible; (obtainable) asequible; **according to the ~ information …** de acuerdo con la información disponible …; **free brochures are ~ on request** disponemos de folletos gratuitos para quien los solicite; **to make sth ~ to sb** poner algo a la disposición de algn; **is the manager ~?** ¿está libre el gerente?

avalanche [ˈævəlɑːnʃ] n alud, avalancha

Ave. abbr (= avenue) Av., Avda.

avenge [əˈvɛndʒ] vt vengar

avenue [ˈævənjuː] n avenida; (fig) camino, vía

average [ˈævərɪdʒ] n promedio, media ▷ adj (mean) medio; (ordinary) regular, corriente ▷ vt calcular el promedio de; **on ~** por término medio ▶ **average out** vi: **to ~ out at** salir a un promedio de

averse [əˈvəːs] adj: **to be ~ to sth/doing** sentir aversión or antipatía por algo/por hacer

aversion [əˈvəːʃən] n aversión, repugnancia

avert [əˈvəːt] vt prevenir; (blow) desviar; (one's eyes) apartar

aviary [ˈeɪvɪərɪ] n pajarera

aviation [eɪvɪˈeɪʃən] n aviación

avid [ˈævɪd] adj ávido, ansioso

avocado [ævəˈkɑːdəu] n (Brit: also: **avocado pear**) aguacate, palta (CS)

avoid [əˈvɔɪd] vt evitar, eludir

avoidable [əˈvɔɪdəbl] adj evitable, eludible

await [əˈweɪt] vt esperar, aguardar; **long ~ed**

largamente esperado

awake [ə'weɪk] (pt **awoke**, pp **awoken** or **-d**) adj despierto ▷ vt despertar ▷ vi despertarse; **to be ~** estar despierto

awakening [ə'weɪknɪŋ] n despertar

award [ə'wɔːd] n (prize) premio; (medal) condecoración; (Law) fallo, sentencia; (act) concesión ▷ vt (prize) otorgar, conceder; (Law: damages) adjudicar

aware [ə'wɛəʳ] adj consciente; (awake) despierto; (informed) enterado; **to become ~ of** darse cuenta de, enterarse de; **I am fully ~ that ...** sé muy bien que ...

awareness [ə'wɛənɪs] n conciencia, conocimiento

awash [ə'wɒʃ] adj inundado

away [ə'weɪ] adv fuera; **to be ~** estar fuera; **he was ~ on a business trip** estaba fuera en viaje de negocios; **he's ~ for a week** estará ausente una semana; **he's ~ in Barcelona** está en Barcelona; **it's 2 kilometres ~** está a 2 kilómetros (de distancia); **the coast is 2 hours ~ by car** la costa está a 2 horas en coche; **the holiday was 2 weeks ~** faltaban 2 semanas para las vacaciones; **far ~** lejos; **~ from** lejos de; **~ from family and friends** lejos de la familia y los amigos; **it's 30 miles ~ from town** está a 30 millas de la ciudad; **go ~!** ¡vete!; **to take ~** llevar(se); **to work/pedal ~** seguir trabajando/pedaleando; **he was still working ~ in the library** seguía trabajando sin parar en la biblioteca; **to fade ~** desvanecerse; (sound) apagarse

away game n (Sport) partido de fuera

awe [ɔː] n respeto, temor reverencial

awe-inspiring ['ɔːɪnspaɪərɪŋ], **awesome** ['ɔːsəm] adj imponente, pasmoso

awful ['ɔːfəl] adj terrible; **an ~ lot of** (people, cars, dogs) la mar de, muchísimos

awfully ['ɔːflɪ] adv (very) terriblemente

awhile [ə'waɪl] adv (durante) un rato, algún tiempo

awkward ['ɔːkwəd] adj (clumsy) desmañado, torpe; (shape, situation) incómodo; (difficult: question) difícil; (problem) complicado

awning ['ɔːnɪŋ] n (of shop) toldo; (of window etc) marquesina

awoke [ə'wəuk], **awoken** [ə'wəukən] pt, pp of **awake**

awry [ə'raɪ] adv: **to be ~** estar descolocado or atravesado; **to go ~** salir mal, fracasar

axe, (US) **ax** [æks] n hacha ▷ vt (employee) despedir; (project etc) cortar; (jobs) reducir; **to have an ~ to grind** (fig) tener un interés creado or algún fin interesado

axes ['æksiːz] npl of **axis**

axis ['æksɪs] (pl **axes**) n eje

axle ['æksl] n eje, árbol

ay(e) [aɪ] excl (yes) sí; **the ~s** los que votan a favor

Azerbaijan [æzəbaɪ'dʒɑːn] n Azerbaiyán

Aztec ['æztɛk] adj, n azteca

Bb

B, b [biː] n (letter) B, b; (Scol: mark) N; (Mus) si; **B for Benjamin**, (US) **B for Baker** B de Barcelona; **B road** (Brit Aut) ≈ carretera secundaria

BA n abbr = **British Academy**; (Scol) = **Bachelor of Arts**; see also **Bachelor's Degree**

babble ['bæbl] vi farfullar

baboon [bə'buːn] n mandril

baby ['beɪbɪ] n bebé

baby carriage n (US) cochecito

baby-sit ['beɪbɪsɪt] vi hacer de canguro

baby-sitter ['beɪbɪsɪtər] n canguro

bachelor ['bætʃələr] n soltero; **B~ of Arts/ Science (BA/BSc)** licenciado(-a) en Filosofía y Letras/Ciencias

back [bæk] n (of person) espalda; (of animal) lomo; (of hand, page) dorso; (as opposed to front) parte de atrás; (of room) fondo; (of chair) respaldo; (Football) defensa; **to have one's ~ to the wall** (fig) estar entre la espada y la pared; **to break the ~ of a job** hacer lo más difícil de un trabajo; **on the ~ of the cheque** al dorso del cheque; **at the ~ of the house** en la parte de atrás de la casa; **at the ~ of the class** al fondo de la clase; **at the ~ of my mind was the thought that ...** en el fondo tenía la idea de que ...; **~ to front** al revés ▷ vt (candidate: also: **back up**) respaldar, apoyar; (horse: at races) apostar por; (car) dar marcha atrás a or con; **the union is ~ing his claim for compensation** el sindicato respalda su demanda de compensación ▷ vi (car etc) dar marcha atrás; **she ~ed into the parking space** aparcó dando marcha atrás ▷ adj (in compounds) de atrás; **~ garden/room** jardín/habitación de atrás; **the ~ door** la puerta de atrás; **~ seats/ wheels** (Aut) asientos/ruedas traseros(-as); **~ payments** pagos con efecto retroactivo; **~ rent** renta atrasada; **to take a ~ seat** (fig) pasar a segundo plano ▷ adv (not forward) (hacia) atrás; **he's ~** (returned) ha vuelto; **when will you be ~?** ¿cuándo volverá?; **what time did you get ~?** ¿a qué hora volviste?; **he ran ~** volvió corriendo; **we went there by bus and walked ~** fuimos allí en autobús y volvimos a pie; **throw the ball ~** devuelve la pelota; **can I have it ~?** ¿me lo devuelve?; **to call sb ~** (Telec: call again) volver a llamar a algn; (: return call) devolver la llamada a; **I'll call ~ later** volveré a llamar más tarde; **~ and forth** de acá para allá; **as far ~ as the 13th century** ya en el siglo XIII

▸ **back down** vi echarse atrás

▸ **back out** vi (of promise) echarse atrás

▸ **back on to** vt fus: **the house ~s on to the golf course** por atrás la casa da al campo de golf

▸ **back up** vt (support: person) apoyar, respaldar; (: theory) defender; (car) dar marcha atrás a; (Comput) hacer una copia de reserva de; **she complained, and her colleagues ~ed her up** presentó una queja y sus colegas la respaldaron

backache ['bækeɪk] n dolor de espalda

backbencher ['bæk'bentʃər] n (Brit) diputado sin cargo oficial en el gobierno o la oposición

backbone ['bækbəun] n columna vertebral; **the ~ of the organization** el pilar de la organización

backcloth ['bækklɔθ] n telón de fondo

backdate [bæk'deɪt] vt (letter) poner fecha atrasada a; **~d pay rise** aumento de sueldo con efecto retroactivo

backdrop ['bækdrɔp] n = **backcloth**

backer ['bækər] n partidario(-a); (Comm) promotor(a)

backfire [bæk'faɪər] vi (Aut) petardear; (plans) fallar, salir mal

background ['bækgraund] n fondo; (of events) antecedentes; (basic knowledge) bases; (experience) conocimientos, educación ▷ cpd (noise, music) de fondo; (Comput) secundario; **~ reading** lectura de preparación; **family ~** origen, antecedentes familiares

backhand ['bækhænd] n (Tennis: also: **backhand stroke**) revés

backhanded ['bæk'hændɪd] adj (fig) ambiguo, equívoco

backhander ['bæk'hændər] n (Brit: bribe) soborno

backing ['bækɪŋ] n (fig) apoyo, respaldo; (Comm) respaldo financiero; (Mus) acompañamiento

backlash ['bæklæʃ] n reacción (en contra)

backlog ['bæklɔg] n: **~ of work** trabajo atrasado

back number n (of magazine etc) número atrasado

backpack ['bækpæk] n mochila

backpacker ['bækpækər] n mochilero(-a)

back pay n atrasos

backpedal ['bækpedl] vi (fig) volverse/echarse atrás

backseat driver ['bæksiːt-] n *pasajero que se empeña en aconsejar al conductor*
backside ['bæksaɪd] n (col) trasero
backstage [bæk'steɪdʒ] adv *entre bastidores*
backstroke ['bækstrəʊk] n espalda
backtrack ['bæktræk] vi (fig) = **backpedal**
backup ['bækʌp] adj (train, plane) suplementario; (Comput: disk, file) de reserva ▷ n (support) apoyo; (also: **backup file**) copia de reserva; (US: congestion) embotellamiento, retención
backward ['bækwəd] adj (movement) hacia atrás; (person, country) atrasado; (shy) tímido
backwards ['bækwədz] adv (move, go) hacia atrás; (read a list) al revés; (fall) de espaldas; **to know sth ~** or (US) **~ and forwards** (col) saberse algo al dedillo
backwater ['bækwɔːtəʳ] n (fig) lugar atrasado or apartado
backyard [bæk'jɑːd] n patio trasero
bacon ['beɪkən] n tocino, bacon, beicon
bacteria [bæk'tɪərɪə] npl bacterias
bad [bæd] adj malo; (serious) grave; (meat, food) podrido, pasado; **to be in a ~ mood** estar de mal humor; **to be ~ at sth** ser malo para algo; **I'm really ~ at maths** soy muy malo para las matemáticas; **a ~ accident** un accidente grave; **to go ~** (food) pasarse, echarse a perder; **to have a ~ time of it** pasarlo mal; **I feel ~ about it** (guilty) me siento culpable; **how are you? — not ~** ¿cómo estás? — bien; **that's not ~ at all** no está nada mal; **~ language** las palabrotas; **~ debt** (Comm) cuenta incobrable; **in ~ faith** de mala fe
baddie, baddy ['bædɪ] n (col: Cine etc) malo(-a)
bade [bæd, beɪd] pt of **bid**
badge [bædʒ] n insignia; (metal badge) chapa; (of policeman) placa; (stick-on) pegatina
badger ['bædʒəʳ] n tejón
badly ['bædlɪ] adv (work, dress etc) mal; **~ wounded** gravemente herido; **he needs it ~** le hace mucha falta; **to be ~ off** (for money) andar mal de dinero; **things are going ~** las cosas van muy mal
bad-mannered ['bæd'mænəd] adj mal educado
badminton ['bædmɪntən] n bádminton
bad-tempered ['bæd'tɛmpəd] adj de mal genio or carácter; (temporary) de mal humor
baffle ['bæfl] vt desconcertar, confundir
baffling ['bæflɪŋ] adj incomprensible
bag [bæg] n bolsa; (handbag) bolso; (satchel) mochila; (case) maleta; (of hunter) caza ▷ vt (col: take) coger (Esp), agarrar (LAm), pescar; **~s of** (col: lots of) un montón de; **to pack one's ~s** hacer las maletas
baggage ['bægɪdʒ] n equipaje
baggy ['bægɪ] adj (trousers) ancho, holgado
bag lady n (col) mujer sin hogar cargada de bolsas
bagpipes ['bægpaɪps] npl gaita
Bahamas [bə'hɑːməz] npl: **the ~** las (Islas) Bahama
bail [beɪl] n fianza ▷ vt (prisoner: also: **grant bail to**) poner en libertad bajo fianza; (boat: also: **bail out**) achicar; **on ~** (prisoner) bajo fianza; **to be**

released on ~ ser puesto en libertad bajo fianza; **to ~ sb out** pagar la fianza de algn; see also **bale**
bailiff ['beɪlɪf] n alguacil
bait [beɪt] n cebo ▷ vt poner el cebo en
bake [beɪk] vt cocer (al horno) ▷ vi (cook) cocerse; (be hot) hacer un calor terrible
baked beans npl judías en salsa de tomate
baker ['beɪkəʳ] n panadero(-a)
baker's dozen n docena del fraile
bakery ['beɪkərɪ] n (for bread) panadería; (for cakes) pastelería
baking ['beɪkɪŋ] n (act) cocción; (batch) hornada
baking powder n levadura (en polvo)
balaclava [bælə'klɑːvə] n (also: **balaclava helmet**) pasamontañas
balance ['bæləns] n equilibrio; (Comm: sum) balance; (remainder) resto; (scales) balanza ▷ vt equilibrar; (budget) nivelar; (account) saldar; (compensate) compensar; **~ of trade/payments** balanza de comercio/pagos; **~ carried forward** balance pasado a cuenta nueva; **~ brought forward** saldo de hoja anterior; **to ~ the books** hacer el balance
balanced ['bælənst] adj (personality, diet) equilibrado
balance sheet n balance
balcony ['bælkənɪ] n (open) balcón; (closed) galería
bald [bɔːld] adj calvo; (tyre) liso
baldness ['bɔːldnɪs] n calvicie
bale [beɪl] n (Agr) paca, fardo
▶ **bale out** vi (of a plane) lanzarse en paracaídas ▷ vt (Naut) achicar; **to ~ sb out of a difficulty** sacar a algn de un apuro
Balearic Islands [bælɪ'ærɪk-] npl: **the ~** las (Islas) Baleares
balk [bɔːk] vi: **to ~ (at)** resistirse (a); (horse) plantarse (ante)
ball [bɔːl] n (sphere) bola; (football) balón; (for tennis, golf etc) pelota; (dance) baile; **to be on the ~** (fig: competent) ser un enterado; (: alert) estar al tanto; **to play ~ (with sb)** jugar a la pelota (con algn); (fig) cooperar (con algn); **to start the ~ rolling** (fig) empezar; **the ~ is in your court** (fig) le toca a usted
ballad ['bæləd] n balada, romance
ballast ['bæləst] n lastre
ball bearing n cojinete de bolas
ballerina [bælə'riːnə] n bailarina
ballet ['bæleɪ] n ballet
ballet dancer n bailarín(-ina) (de ballet)
balloon [bə'luːn] n globo; (in comic strip) bocadillo ▷ vi dispararse
ballot ['bælət] n votación
ballot box n urna (electoral)
ballot paper n papeleta
ballpark ['bɔːlpɑːk] n (US) estadio de béisbol
ball-point pen ['bɔːlpɔɪnt-] n bolígrafo
ballroom ['bɔːlrʊm] n salón de baile
balm [bɑːm] n (also fig) bálsamo
balmy ['bɑːmɪ] adj (breeze, air) suave
bamboo [bæm'buː] n bambú

ban [bæn] *n* prohibición ▷ *vt* prohibir; *(exclude)* excluir; **he was ~ned from driving** le retiraron el carnet de conducir

banal [bə'nɑːl] *adj* banal, vulgar

banana [bə'nɑːnə] *n* plátano, banana *(LAm)*

band [bænd] *n (group)* banda; *(gang)* pandilla; *(strip)* faja, tira; *(at a dance)* orquesta; *(Mil)* banda; *(rock band)* grupo
  ▶ **band together** *vi* juntarse, asociarse

bandage ['bændɪdʒ] *n* venda, vendaje ▷ *vt* vendar

Band-Aid® ['bændeɪd] *n (US)* tirita *(Esp)*, curita *(LAm)*

bandit ['bændɪt] *n* bandido; **one-armed ~** máquina tragaperras

bandwagon ['bændwægən] *n*: **to jump on the ~** *(fig)* subirse al carro

bandy ['bændɪ] *vt (jokes, insults)* intercambiar

bandy-legged ['bændɪ'legd] *adj* patizambo

bang [bæŋ] *n* estallido; *(of door)* portazo; *(blow)* golpe ▷ *vt* golpear ▷ *vi* estallar ▷ *adv*: **to be ~ on time** *(col)* llegar en punto; **to ~ the door** dar un portazo; **to ~ into sth** chocar con algo, golpearse contra algo; *see also* **bangs**

banger ['bæŋəʳ] *n (Brit: car: also:* **old banger**) armatoste, cacharro; *(Brit col: sausage)* salchicha; *(firework)* petardo

Bangladesh [bæŋglə'dɛʃ] *n* Bangladesh

bangle ['bæŋgl] *n* brazalete, ajorca

bangs [bæŋz] *npl (US)* flequillo

banish ['bænɪʃ] *vt* desterrar

banister(s) ['bænɪstə(z)] *n(pl)* barandilla, pasamanos

banjo ['bændʒəʊ] *(pl* **-es** *or* **-s**) *n* banjo

bank [bæŋk] *n (Comm)* banco; *(of river, lake)* ribera, orilla; *(of earth)* terraplén ▷ *vi (Aviat)* ladearse; *(Comm)*: **to ~ with** tener la cuenta en
  ▶ **bank on** *vt fus* contar con; **I was ~ing on your coming today** contaba con que vendrías hoy; **I wouldn't ~ on it** yo no me confiaría demasiado

bank account *n* cuenta bancaria

bank balance *n* saldo

bank card *n* = **banker's card**

bank charges *npl* comisión

bank draft *n* letra de cambio

banker ['bæŋkəʳ] *n* banquero; **~'s card** *(Brit)* tarjeta bancaria; **~'s order** orden bancaria

bank giro *n* giro bancario

bank holiday *n (Brit)* día festivo *or* de fiesta

banking ['bæŋkɪŋ] *n* banca

bank loan *n* préstamo bancario

bank manager *n* director(a) (de sucursal) de banco

banknote ['bæŋknəʊt] *n* billete de banco

bank rate *n* tipo de interés bancario

bankrupt ['bæŋkrʌpt] *n* quebrado(-a) ▷ *adj* quebrado, insolvente; **to go ~** quebrar, hacer bancarrota; **to be ~** estar en quiebra

bankruptcy ['bæŋkrʌptsɪ] *n* quiebra, bancarrota

bank statement *n* extracto de cuenta

banned substance *n* sustancia prohibida

banner ['bænəʳ] *n* bandera; *(in demonstration)* pancarta

banns [bænz] *npl* amonestaciones

banquet ['bæŋkwɪt] *n* banquete

banter ['bæntəʳ] *n* guasa, bromas

baptism ['bæptɪzəm] *n* bautismo; *(act)* bautizo

baptize [bæp'taɪz] *vt* bautizar

bar [bɑːʳ] *n* barra; *(on door)* tranca; *(of window, cage)* reja; *(of soap)* pastilla; *(fig: hindrance)* obstáculo; *(prohibition)* prohibición; *(pub)* bar, cantina *(esp LAm)*; *(counter: in pub)* barra, mostrador; *(Mus)* barra ▷ *vt (road)* obstruir; *(window, door)* atrancar; *(person)* excluir; *(activity)* prohibir; **behind ~s** entre rejas; **the B~** *(Law: profession)* la abogacía; *(: people)* el cuerpo de abogados; **~ none** sin excepción

barbarian [bɑː'bɛərɪən] *n* bárbaro(-a)

barbaric [bɑː'bærɪk] *adj* bárbaro

barbarity [bɑː'bærɪtɪ] *n* barbaridad

barbecue ['bɑːbɪkjuː] *n* barbacoa, asado *(LAm)*

barbed wire ['bɑːbd-] *n* alambre de espino

barber ['bɑːbəʳ] *n* peluquero, barbero

Barcelona [bɑːsɪ'ləʊnə] *n* Barcelona

bar chart *n* gráfico de barras

bar code *n* código de barras

bare [bɛəʳ] *adj* desnudo; *(head)* descubierto ▷ *vt* desnudar; **to ~ one's teeth** enseñar los dientes

bareback ['bɛəbæk] *adv* a pelo

barefaced ['bɛəfeɪst] *adj* descarado

barefoot ['bɛəfut] *adj, adv* descalzo

barely ['bɛəlɪ] *adv* apenas

bargain ['bɑːgɪn] *n* pacto; *(transaction)* negocio; *(good buy)* ganga ▷ *vi* negociar; *(haggle)* regatear; **into the ~** además, por añadidura
  ▶ **bargain for** *vt fus (col)*: **he got more than he ~ed for** le resultó peor de lo que esperaba

bargaining position *n*: **to be in a strong/weak ~** estar/no estar en una posición de fuerza para negociar

barge [bɑːdʒ] *n* barcaza
  ▶ **barge in** *vi* irrumpir; *(in conversation)* entrometerse
  ▶ **barge into** *vt fus* dar contra

baritone ['bærɪtəʊn] *n* barítono

barium meal ['bɛərɪəm-] *n (Med)* sulfato de bario

bark [bɑːk] *n (of tree)* corteza; *(of dog)* ladrido ▷ *vi* ladrar

barley ['bɑːlɪ] *n* cebada

barley sugar *n* azúcar cande

barmaid ['bɑːmeɪd] *n* camarera

barman ['bɑːmən] *n* camarero, barman

barmy ['bɑːmɪ] *adj (col)* chiflado, chalado

barn [bɑːn] *n* granero; *(for animals)* cuadra

barnacle ['bɑːnəkl] *n* percebe

barometer [bə'rɒmɪtəʳ] *n* barómetro

baron ['bærən] *n* barón; *(fig)* magnate; **the press ~s** los magnates de la prensa

baroness ['bærənɪs] *n* baronesa

baroque [bə'rɒk] *adj* barroco

barrack ['bærək] *vt (Brit)* abuchear

barracking ['bærəkɪŋ] *n*: **to give sb a ~** *(Brit)* abuchear a algn

barracks ['bærəks] npl cuartel
barrage ['bærɑːʒ] n (Mil) cortina de fuego; (dam) presa; (fig: of criticism etc) lluvia, aluvión; **a ~ of questions** una lluvia de preguntas
barrel ['bærəl] n barril; (of wine) tonel, cuba; (of gun) cañón
barren ['bærən] adj estéril
barricade [bærɪ'keɪd] n barricada ▷ vt cerrar con barricadas
barrier ['bærɪəʳ] n barrera; (crash barrier) barrera
barrier cream n crema protectora
barring ['bɑːrɪŋ] prep excepto, salvo
barrister ['bærɪstəʳ] n (Brit) abogado(-a)
barrow ['bærəu] n (cart) carretilla
bartender ['bɑːtɛndəʳ] n (US) camarero, barman
barter ['bɑːtəʳ] vt: **to ~ sth for sth** trocar algo por algo
base [beɪs] n base ▷ vt: **to ~ sth on** basar or fundar algo en ▷ adj bajo, infame; **to ~ at** (troops) estacionar en; **I'm ~d in London** (work) trabajo en Londres
baseball ['beɪsbɔːl] n béisbol
baseline ['beɪslaɪn] n (Tennis) línea de fondo
basement ['beɪsmənt] n sótano
bases ['beɪsiːz] npl of basis ['beɪsɪz] ▷ npl of base
bash [bæʃ] n: **I'll have a ~ (at it)** lo intentaré ▷ vt (col) golpear
  ▶ **bash up** vt (col: car) destrozar; (: person) aporrear, vapulear
bashful ['bæʃful] adj tímido, vergonzoso
basic ['beɪsɪk] adj (salary etc) básico; (elementary: principles) fundamental
basically ['beɪsɪklɪ] adv fundamentalmente, en el fondo
basil ['bæzl] n albahaca
basin ['beɪsn] n (vessel) cuenco, tazón; (Geo) cuenca; (also: washbasin) palangana, jofaina; (in bathroom) lavabo
basis ['beɪsɪs] (pl -ses) [-siːz] n base; **on the ~ of what you've said** en base a lo que has dicho
bask [bɑːsk] vi: **to ~ in the sun** tomar el sol
basket ['bɑːskɪt] n cesta, cesto
basketball ['bɑːskɪtbɔːl] n baloncesto
Basque [bæsk] adj, n vasco(-a)
Basque Country n Euskadi, País Vasco
bass [beɪs] n (Mus) bajo
bassoon [bə'suːn] n fagot
bastard ['bɑːstəd] n bastardo(-a); (col!) cabrón, hijo de puta (!)
bat [bæt] n (Zool) murciélago; (for ball games) palo; (for cricket, baseball) bate; (Brit: for table tennis) pala; **he didn't ~ an eyelid** ni pestañeó, ni se inmutó
batch [bætʃ] n lote, remesa; (of bread) hornada
bated ['beɪtɪd] adj: **with ~ breath** sin respirar
bath [bɑːθ, pl bɑːðz] n (action) baño; (bathtub) bañera, tina (esp LAm) ▷ vt bañar; **to have a ~** bañarse, darse un baño; see also **baths**
bathe [beɪð] vi bañarse; (US) darse un baño, bañarse ▷ vt (wound etc) lavar; (US) bañar, dar un baño a

bather ['beɪðəʳ] n bañista
bathing ['beɪðɪŋ] n baño
bathing cap n gorro de baño
bathing costume, (US) **bathing suit** n traje de baño, bañador (Esp), malla (CS)
bathing trunks npl traje de baño, bañador (Esp), malla (CS)
bathrobe ['bɑːrəub] n albornoz
bathroom ['bɑːθrum] n (cuarto de) baño
baths [bɑːðz] npl piscina
bath towel n toalla de baño
bathtub ['bɑːθtʌb] n bañera
baton ['bætən] n (Mus) batuta
battalion [bə'tælɪən] n batallón
batter ['bætəʳ] vt maltratar; (wind, rain) azotar ▷ n batido
battered ['bætəd] adj (hat, pan) estropeado
battery ['bætərɪ] n batería; (of torch) pila
battery charger n cargador de baterías
battery farming n cría intensiva
battle ['bætl] n batalla; (fig) lucha ▷ vi luchar; **that's half the ~** (col) ya hay medio camino andado; **to fight a losing ~** (fig) luchar por una causa perdida
battlefield ['bætlfiːld] n campo de batalla
battleship ['bætlʃɪp] n acorazado
batty ['bætɪ] adj (col: person) chiflado; (: idea) de chiflado
bauble ['bɔːbl] n chuchería
bawdy ['bɔːdɪ] adj indecente; (joke) verde
bawl [bɔːl] vi chillar, gritar
bay [beɪ] n (Geo) bahía; (for parking) parking, estacionamiento; (loading bay) patio de carga; (Bot) laurel ▷ vi aullar; **to hold sb at ~** mantener a algn a raya
bay leaf n (hoja de) laurel
bayonet ['beɪənɪt] n bayoneta
bay window n ventana salediza
bazaar [bə'zɑːʳ] n bazar
bazooka [bə'zuːkə] n bazuca
BB n abbr (Brit: = Boys' Brigade) organización juvenil para chicos
B. & B. n abbr = **bed and breakfast**
BBC n abbr (= British Broadcasting Corporation) BBC
BC adj abbr (= before Christ) a. de J.C. ▷ abbr (Canada) = **British Columbia**
be [biː] (pt **was, were**, pp **been**) aux vb **1** (with present participle: forming continuous tenses): **what are you doing?** ¿qué estás haciendo?, ¿qué haces?; **they're coming tomorrow** vienen mañana; **I've been waiting for you for hours** llevo horas esperándote
  2 (with pp: forming passives): ser (but often replaced by active or reflexive constructions); **to be murdered** ser asesinado; **the box had been opened** habían abierto la caja; **the thief was nowhere to be seen** no se veía al ladrón por ninguna parte
  3 (in tag questions): **it was fun, wasn't it?** fue divertido, ¿no? or ¿verdad?; **he's good-looking, isn't he?** es guapo, ¿no te parece?; **she's back again, is she?** entonces, ¿ha vuelto?
  4 (+to +infin): **the house is to be sold** (necessity)

hay que vender la casa; (*future*) van a vender la casa; **he's not to open it** no tiene que abrirlo; **he was to have come yesterday** debía de haber venido ayer; **am I to understand that ...?** ¿debo entender que ...?

▷ *vb +complement* **1** (*with n or num complement*) ser; **he's a doctor** es médico; **2 and 2 are 4** 2 y 2 son 4 **2** (*with adj complement: expressing permanent or inherent quality*) ser; (*: expressing state seen as temporary or reversible*) estar; **I'm English** soy inglés(-esa); **she's tall/pretty** es alta/bonita; **he's young** es joven; **be careful/good/quiet** ten cuidado/pórtate bien/cállate; **I'm tired** estoy cansado(-a); **I'm warm** tengo calor; **it's dirty** está sucio(-a) **3** (*of health*) estar; **how are you?** ¿cómo estás?; **he's very ill** está muy enfermo; **I'm better now** ya estoy mejor **4** (*of age*) tener; **how old are you?** ¿cuántos años tienes?; **I'm 16 (years old)** tengo 16 años **5** (*cost*) costar; ser; **how much was the meal?** ¿cuánto fue *or* costó la comida?; **that'll be £5.75, please** son £5.75, por favor; **this shirt is £17** esta camisa cuesta £17

▷ *vi* **1** (*exist, occur etc*) existir, haber; **the best singer that ever was** el mejor cantante que existió jamás; **is there a God?** ¿hay un Dios?, ¿existe Dios?; **be that as it may** sea como sea; **so be it** así sea **2** (*referring to place*) estar; **I won't be here tomorrow** no estaré aquí mañana **3** (*referring to movement*): **where have you been?** ¿dónde has estado?

▷ *impers vb* **1** (*referring to time*): **it's 5 o'clock** son las 5; **it's the 28th of April** estamos a 28 de abril **2** (*referring to distance*): **it's 10 km to the village** el pueblo está a 10 km **3** (*referring to the weather*): **it's too hot/cold** hace demasiado calor/frío; **it's windy today** hace viento hoy **4** (*emphatic*): **it's me** soy yo; **it was Maria who paid the bill** fue María la que pagó la cuenta

beach [biːtʃ] *n* playa ▷ *vt* varar

beacon ['biːkən] *n* (*lighthouse*) faro; (*marker*) guía; (*radio beacon*) radiofaro

bead [biːd] *n* cuenta, abalorio; (*of dew, sweat*) gota; **beads** *npl* (*necklace*) collar

beak [biːk] *n* pico

beaker ['biːkəʳ] *n* vaso

beam [biːm] *n* (*Arch*) viga; (*of light*) rayo, haz de luz; (*Radio*) rayo ▷ *vi* brillar; (*smile*) sonreír; **to drive on full** *or* **main ~** conducir con las luces largas

bean [biːn] *n* judía, fríjol/frijol (*esp LAm*), poroto (*And, CS*); **runner/broad ~** habichuela/haba; **coffee ~** grano de café

beanpole ['biːnpəul] *n* (*col*) espárrago

beansprouts ['biːnsprauts] *npl* brotes de soja

bear [bɛəʳ] *n* oso; (*Stock Exchange*) bajista ▷ *vb* (*pt* **bore**, *pp* **borne**) ▷ *vt* (*weight etc*) llevar; (*cost*) pagar; (*responsibility*) tener; (*traces, signs*) mostrar; (*produce: fruit*) dar; (*Comm: interest*) devengar;

(*endure*) soportar, aguantar; (*stand up to*) resistir a; (*children*) tener, dar a luz ▷ *vi*: **to ~ right/left** torcer a la derecha/izquierda; **I can't ~ him** no le puedo ver, no lo soporto; **I can't ~ it!** ¡no lo aguanto!; **to bring pressure to ~ on sb** ejercer presión sobre algn

▶ **bear on** *vt fus* tener que ver con, referirse a

▶ **bear out** *vt fus* (*suspicions*) corroborar, confirmar; (*person*) confirmar lo dicho por

▶ **bear up** *vi* (*cheer up*) animarse; (*withstand*) resistir; **he bore up well under the strain** resistió bien la presión

▶ **bear with** *vt fus* (*sb's moods, temper*) tener paciencia con; **if you would ~ with me for a moment...** tenga la bondad de esperar un momento...

beard [bɪəd] *n* barba

bearded ['bɪədɪd] *adj* con barba

bearer ['bɛərəʳ] *n* (*of news, cheque*) portador(a); (*of passport*) titular

bearing ['bɛərɪŋ] *n* porte; (*connection*) relación; **(ball) bearings** *npl* cojinetes a bolas; **to take a ~** marcarse; **to find one's ~s** orientarse

beast [biːst] *n* bestia; (*col*) bruto, salvaje

beastly ['biːstlɪ] *adj* bestial; (*awful*) horrible

beat [biːt] *n* (*of heart*) latido; (*Mus*) ritmo, compás; (*of policeman*) ronda ▷ *vb* (*pt* **-**, *pp* **-en**) ▷ *vt* (*hit*) golpear; (*eggs*) batir; (*defeat*) ganar a; (*better*) sobrepasar; (*drum*) tocar; (*rhythm*) marcar ▷ *vi* (*heart*) latir; **off the ~en track** aislado; **to ~ it** (*col*) largarse; **we ~ them three-nil** les ganamos tres a cero; **that ~s everything!** (*col*) ¡eso es el colmo!; **to ~ on a door** dar golpes en una puerta; **to ~ about the bush** andarse con rodeos

▶ **beat down** *vt* (*door*) derribar a golpes; (*price*) conseguir rebajar, regatear; (*seller*) hacer rebajar el precio ▷ *vi* (*rain*) llover a cántaros; (*sun*) caer de plomo

▶ **beat off** *vt* rechazar

▶ **beat up** *vt* (*col: person*) dar una paliza a

beating ['biːtɪŋ] *n* paliza, golpiza (*LAm*); **to take a ~** recibir una paliza

beautiful ['bjuːtɪful] *adj* hermoso, bello, lindo (*esp LAm*)

beautifully ['bjuːtɪfəlɪ] *adv* de maravilla

beauty ['bjuːtɪ] *n* belleza, hermosura; (*concept, person*) belleza; **the ~ of it is that ...** lo mejor de esto es que ...

beauty salon *n* salón de belleza

beauty sleep *n*: **to get one's ~** no perder horas de sueño

beauty spot *n* lunar postizo; (*Brit: Tourism*) lugar pintoresco

beaver ['biːvəʳ] *n* castor

became [bɪ'keɪm] *pt of* **become**

because [bɪ'kɔz] *conj* porque; **~ of** *prep* debido a, a causa de

beck [bɛk] *n*: **to be at the ~ and call of** estar a disposición de

beckon ['bɛkən] *vt* (*also*: **beckon to**) llamar con señas

become [bɪ'kʌm] (*irreg: like* **come**) *vi* (+ *noun*)

hacerse, llegar a ser; (+ *adj*) ponerse, volverse
▷ *vt* (*suit*) favorecer, sentar bien a; **to ~ a doctor**
hacerse médico; **to ~ fat** engordar; **to ~ angry**
enfadarse; **it became known that ...** se
descubrió que ...

becoming [bɪ'kʌmɪŋ] *adj* (*behaviour*) decoroso;
(*clothes*) favorecedor(a)

bed [bed] *n* cama; (*of flowers*) macizo; (*of sea,*
lake) fondo; (*of coal, clay*) capa; **to go to ~**
acostarse

▶ **bed down** *vi* acostarse, irse a la cama

bed and breakfast (B & B) *n* ≈ pensión

bedclothes ['bedkləuðz] *npl* ropa de cama

bedding ['bedɪŋ] *n* ropa de cama

bedraggled [bɪ'dræɡld] *adj* desastrado

bedridden ['bedrɪdn] *adj* postrado (en cama)

bedroom ['bedrum] *n* dormitorio, alcoba

bed settee *n* sofá-cama

bedside ['bedsaɪd] *n*: **at sb's ~** a la cabecera de
algn

bedsit(ter) ['bedsɪt(əʳ)] *n* (*Brit*) estudio

bedspread ['bedspred] *n* cubrecama, colcha

bedtime ['bedtaɪm] *n* hora de acostarse; **it's ~** es
hora de acostarse *or* de irse a la cama

bee [biː] *n* abeja; **to have a ~ in one's bonnet**
(about sth) tener una idea fija (de algo)

beech [biːtʃ] *n* haya

beef [biːf] *n* carne de vaca; **roast ~** rosbif

▶ **beef up** *vt* (*col*) reforzar

beefburger ['biːfbəːɡəʳ] *n* hamburguesa

beefeater ['biːfiːtəʳ] *n* *alabardero de la Torre de*
Londres

beehive ['biːhaɪv] *n* colmena

beeline ['biːlaɪn] *n*: **to make a ~ for** ir derecho a

been [biːn] *pp of* **be**

beeper ['biːpəʳ] *n* (*of doctor etc*) busca

beer [bɪəʳ] *n* cerveza

beer belly *n* (*col*) barriga (*de bebedor de cerveza*)

beet [biːt] *n* (*US*) remolacha

beetle ['biːtl] *n* escarabajo

beetroot ['biːtruːt] *n* (*Brit*) remolacha

before [bɪ'fɔːʳ] *prep* (*of time*) antes de; (*of space*)
delante de ▷ *conj* antes (de) que ▷ *adv* (*time*)
antes; (*space*) delante, adelante; **~ Tuesday**
antes del martes; **~ going** antes de marcharse;
I'll phone ~ I leave llamaré antes de salir; **~ she**
goes antes de que se vaya; **the week ~** la semana
anterior; **I've seen this film ~** esta película ya
la he visto; **I've never seen it ~** no lo he visto
nunca

beforehand [bɪ'fɔːhænd] *adv* de antemano, con
anticipación

befriend [bɪ'frend] *vt* ofrecer amistad a

beg [beɡ] *vi* pedir limosna, mendigar ▷ *vt*
pedir, rogar; (*entreat*) suplicar; **I ~ your pardon**
(*apologising*) perdóneme; (*not hearing*) ¿perdón?

began [bɪ'ɡæn] *pt of* **begin**

beggar ['beɡəʳ] *n* mendigo(-a)

begin [bɪ'ɡɪn] (*pt* **began**, *pp* **begun**) [bɪ'ɡæn,
bɪ'ɡʌn] *vt, vi* empezar, comenzar; **to ~ doing**
or **to do sth** empezar a hacer algo; **I can't ~**
to thank you no encuentro palabras para

agradecerle; **to ~ with, I'd like to know ...** en
primer lugar, quisiera saber ...; **~ning from**
Monday a partir del lunes

beginner [bɪ'ɡɪnəʳ] *n* principiante

beginning [bɪ'ɡɪnɪŋ] *n* principio, comienzo;
right from the ~ desde el principio

begun [bɪ'ɡʌn] *pp of* **begin**

behalf [bɪ'hɑːf] *n*: **on ~ of** (*US*): **in ~ of** en nombre
de; (*for benefit of*) por

behave [bɪ'heɪv] *vi* (*person*) portarse,
comportarse; (*thing*) funcionar; (*well: also:*
behave o.s) portarse bien

behaviour, (*US*) **behavior** [bɪ'heɪvjəʳ] *n*
comportamiento, conducta

behead [bɪ'hed] *vt* decapitar

beheld [bɪ'held] *pt, pp of* **behold**

behind [bɪ'haɪnd] *prep* detrás de ▷ *adv* detrás,
por detrás, atrás ▷ *n* trasero; **~ the television**
detrás de la televisión; **~ the scenes** (*fig*) entre
bastidores; **we're ~ them in technology** (*fig*)
nos dejan atrás en tecnología; **to leave sth ~**
olvidar *or* dejarse algo; **to be ~ (schedule)** ir
retrasado; **to be ~ with sth** estar atrasado en
algo; **to be ~ with payments (on sth)** estar
atrasado en el pago (de algo); **I'm ~ with my**
work voy atrasado con mi trabajo

behold [bɪ'həuld] (*irreg: like* **hold**) *vt* contemplar

beige [beɪʒ] *adj* (*color*) beige

being ['biːɪŋ] *n* ser; **to come into ~** nacer,
aparecer

Beirut [beɪ'ruːt] *n* Beirut

Belarus [belə'rus] *n* Bielorrusia

belated [bɪ'leɪtɪd] *adj* atrasado, tardío

belch [beltʃ] *vi* eructar ▷ *vt* (*also:* **belch out:** *smoke*
etc) vomitar, arrojar

belfry ['belfrɪ] *n* campanario

Belgian ['beldʒən] *adj, n* belga

Belgium ['beldʒəm] *n* Bélgica

belie [bɪ'laɪ] *vt* (*give false impression of*) desmentir,
contradecir

belief [bɪ'liːf] *n* (*opinion*) opinión; (*trust, faith*)
fe; (*acceptance as true*) creencia; **it's beyond ~** es
increíble; **in the ~ that** creyendo que

believable [bɪ'liːvəbl] *adj* creíble

believe [bɪ'liːv] *vt, vi* creer; **I don't ~ you** no te
creo; **I don't ~ it!** ¡no me lo creo!; **to ~ that** creer
que; **he is ~d to be abroad** se cree que está
en el extranjero; **to ~ in** (*God, ghosts*) creer en;
(*method*) ser partidario de; **do you ~ in ghosts?**
¿crees en los fantasmas?; **I don't ~ in corporal**
punishment no soy partidario del castigo
corporal

believer [bɪ'liːvəʳ] *n* (*in idea, activity*) partidario(-a)
(*Rel*) creyente, fiel

belittle [bɪ'lɪtl] *vt* despreciar

Belize [be'liːz] *n* Belice

bell [bel] *n* campana; (*small*) campanilla; (*on door*)
timbre; (*animal's*) cencerro; (*on toy etc*) cascabel;
that rings a ~ (*fig*) eso me suena

belligerent [bɪ'lɪdʒərənt] *adj* (*at war*) beligerante,
(*fig*) agresivo

bellow ['beləu] *vi* bramar; (*person*) rugir ▷ *vt*

(orders) gritar

elly ['bɛlɪ] n barriga, panza

ellyful ['bɛlɪful] n: **to have had a ~ of ...** (col) estar más que harto de ...

elong [bɪ'lɔŋ] vi: **to ~ to** pertenecer a; (club etc) ser socio de; **this book ~s here** este libro va aquí

elongings [bɪ'lɔŋɪŋz] npl: **personal ~** pertenencias

elorussia [bɛləʊ'rʌʃə] n Bielorrusia

eloved [bɪ'lʌvɪd] adj, n querido(-a), amado(-a)

elow [bɪ'ləʊ] prep bajo, debajo de ▷ adv abajo, (por) debajo; **see ~** véase más abajo

elt [bɛlt] n cinturón; (Tech) correa, cinta ▷ vt (thrash) golpear con correa; **industrial ~** cinturón industrial

▶ **belt out** vt (song) cantar a voz en grito or a grito pelado

▶ **belt up** vi (Aut) ponerse el cinturón de seguridad; (fig, col) cerrar el pico

eltway ['bɛltweɪ] n (US Aut) carretera de circunvalación

emused [bɪ'mju:zd] adj perplejo

ench [bɛntʃ] n banco; **the B~** (Law) el tribunal; (people) la judicatura

end [bɛnd] vb (pt, pp **bent**) ▷ vt doblar; (body, head) inclinar ▷ vi inclinarse; (road) curvarse ▷ n (Brit: in road, river) recodo; (in pipe) codo; see also **bends**

▶ **bend down** vi inclinarse, doblarse

▶ **bend over** vi inclinarse

ends [bɛndz] npl (Med) apoplejía por cambios bruscos de presión

eneath [bɪ'ni:θ] prep bajo, debajo de; (unworthy of) indigno de ▷ adv abajo, (por) debajo

enefactor ['bɛnɪfæktə'] n bienhechor

eneficial [bɛnɪ'fɪʃəl] adj: **~ to** beneficioso para

eneficiary [bɛnɪ'fɪʃərɪ] n (Law) beneficiario(-a)

enefit ['bɛnɪfɪt] n beneficio, provecho; (allowance of money) subsidio ▷ vt beneficiar ▷ vi: **he'll ~ from it** le sacará provecho; **unemployment ~** subsidio de desempleo

enelux ['bɛnɪlʌks] n Benelux

enevolent [bɪ'nɛvələnt] adj benévolo

enign [bɪ'naɪn] adj (person, Med) benigno; (smile) afable

ent [bɛnt] pt, pp of **bend** ▷ n inclinación ▷ adj (wire, pipe) doblado, torcido; **to be ~ on** estar empeñado en

equest [bɪ'kwɛst] n legado

ereaved [bɪ'ri:vd] adj afligido ▷ n: **the ~** los afligidos

ereavement [bɪ'ri:vmənt] n aflicción

eret ['bɛreɪ] n boina

erk [bə:k] n (Brit col) capullo(-a) (!)

erlin [bə:'lɪn] n Berlín; **East/West ~** Berlín del Este/Oeste

erm [bə:m] n (US Aut) arcén

erry ['bɛrɪ] n baya

erserk [bə'sə:k] adj: **to go ~** perder los estribos

erth [bə:θ] n (in bed) litera; (cabin) camarote; (for ship) amarradero ▷ vi atracar, amarrar; **to give sb a wide ~** (fig) evitar encontrarse con algn

beseech [bɪ'si:tʃ] (pt, pp **besought**) vt suplicar

beset [bɪ'sɛt] (pt, pp-) vt (person) acosar ▷ adj: **a policy ~ with dangers** una política rodeada de peligros

beside [bɪ'saɪd] prep junto a, al lado de; (compared with) comparado con; **to be ~ o.s. with anger** estar fuera de sí; **that's ~ the point** eso no tiene nada que ver con el asunto

besides [bɪ'saɪdz] adv además ▷ prep (as well as) además de; (except) excepto

besiege [bɪ'si:dʒ] vt (town) sitiar; (fig) asediar

best [bɛst] adj (el/la) mejor ▷ adv (lo) mejor; **he's the ~ player in the team** es el mejor jugador del equipo; **Janet's the ~ at maths** Janet es la mejor en matemáticas; **Emma sings ~** Emma es la que canta mejor; **the ~ part of** (most of) la mayor parte de; **at ~** en el mejor de los casos; **to make the ~ of sth** sacar el mejor partido de algo; **you'll just have to make the ~ of it** tendrás que arreglártelas con lo que hay; **to do one's ~** hacer todo lo posible; **it's not perfect, but I did my ~** no es perfecto, pero he hecho todo lo posible; **that's the ~ I can do** no puedo hacer más; **to the ~ of my knowledge** que yo sepa; **to the ~ of my ability** como mejor puedo; **the ~ thing to do is ...** lo mejor (que se puede hacer) es ...; **he's not exactly patient at the ~ of times** no es que tenga mucha paciencia precisamente

best man n padrino de boda

bestow [bɪ'stəʊ] vt otorgar; (honour, praise) dispensar; **to ~ sth on sb** conceder or dar algo a algn

bestseller ['bɛst'sɛlə'] n éxito de ventas, best-seller

bet [bɛt] n apuesta ▷ vt, vi (pt, pp- or -**ted**) apostar; **to ~ (on)** apostar (a); **it's a safe ~** (fig) es cosa segura

betray [bɪ'treɪ] vt traicionar; (inform on) delatar

betrayal [bɪ'treɪəl] n traición

better ['bɛtə'] adj mejor ▷ adv mejor ▷ vt mejorar; (record etc) superar ▷ n: **to get the ~ of sb** quedar por encima de algn; **a change for the ~** una mejora; **this one's ~ than that one** este es mejor que aquél; **are you feeling ~ now?** ¿te sientes mejor ahora?; **that's ~!** ¡eso es!; **~ still** mejor todavía; **to get ~** (improve) mejorar; (from illness) reponerse, mejorarse; **I hope the weather gets ~ soon** espero que el tiempo mejore pronto; **I hope you get ~ soon** espero que te mejores pronto; **they are ~ off than we are** están mejor de dinero que nosotros; **you had ~ do it** más vale que lo hagas; **I had ~ go** tengo que irme; **he thought ~ of it** cambió de parecer

betting ['bɛtɪŋ] n juego, apuestas

betting shop n (Brit) casa de apuestas

between [bɪ'twi:n] prep entre ▷ adv (also: **in between**: time) mientras tanto; (: place) en medio; **the road ~ here and London** la carretera de aquí a Londres; **we only had 5 ~ us** teníamos sólo 5 entre todos

beverage ['bɛvərɪdʒ] n bebida

beware [bɪˈwɛəʳ] *vi*: **to ~ (of)** tener cuidado (con) ▷ *excl* ¡cuidado!

bewildered [bɪˈwɪldəd] *adj* aturdido, perplejo

bewildering [bɪˈwɪldərɪŋ] *adj* desconcertante

beyond [bɪˈjɔnd] *prep* más allá de; (*exceeding*) además de, fuera de; (*above*) superior a ▷ *adv* más allá, más lejos; **~ doubt** fuera de toda duda; **~ repair** irreparable

bhp *n abbr* (= *brake horsepower*) potencia al freno

bias [ˈbaɪəs] *n* (*prejudice*) prejuicio; (*preference*) predisposición

bias(s)ed [ˈbaɪəst] *adj* parcial; **to be bias(s)ed against** tener perjuicios contra

biathlon [baɪˈæθlən] *n* biatlón

bib [bɪb] *n* babero

Bible [ˈbaɪbl] *n* Biblia

bibliography [bɪblɪˈɔgrəfɪ] *n* bibliografía

bicarbonate of soda [baɪˈkɑːbənɪt-] *n* bicarbonato de soda

biceps [ˈbaɪsɛps] *n* bíceps

bicker [ˈbɪkəʳ] *vi* reñir

bicycle [ˈbaɪsɪkl] *n* bicicleta

bicycle pump *n* bomba de bicicleta

bid [bɪd] *n* (*at auction*) oferta, puja, postura; (*attempt*) tentativa, conato ▷ *vi* (*pt, pp* **-**) hacer una oferta ▷ *vt* (*pt* **bade**, *pp* **-den**) [bæd, ˈbɪdn] mandar, ordenar; **to ~ sb good day** dar a algn los buenos días

bidder [ˈbɪdəʳ] *n*: **the highest ~** el mejor postor

bidding [ˈbɪdɪŋ] *n* (*at auction*) ofertas, puja; (*order*) orden, mandato

bide [baɪd] *vt*: **to ~ one's time** esperar el momento adecuado

bidet [ˈbiːdeɪ] *n* bidet

bifocals [baɪˈfəuklz] *npl* gafas *or* anteojos (*LAm*) bifocales

big [bɪg] *adj* grande; **~ business** gran negocio; **to do things in a ~ way** hacer las cosas en grande; **my ~ brother** mi hermano mayor; **~ deal!** ¡vaya cosa!

bigamy [ˈbɪgəmɪ] *n* bigamia

biggish [ˈbɪgɪʃ] *adj* más bien grande; (*man*) más bien alto

bigheaded [ˈbɪgˈhɛdɪd] *adj* engreído

bigot [ˈbɪgət] *n* fanático(-a), intolerante

bigoted [ˈbɪgətɪd] *adj* fanático, intolerante

bigotry [ˈbɪgətrɪ] *n* fanatismo, intolerancia

big toe *n* dedo gordo (del pie)

big top *n* (*circus*) circo; (*main tent*) carpa principal

big wheel *n* (*at fair*) noria

bike [baɪk] *n* bici

bike lane *n* carril-bici

bikini [bɪˈkiːnɪ] *n* bikini

bilateral [baɪˈlætərl] *adj* (*agreement*) bilateral

bilingual [baɪˈlɪŋgwəl] *adj* bilingüe

bill [bɪl] *n* (*gen*) cuenta; (*invoice*) factura; (*Pol*) proyecto de ley; (*US: banknote*) billete; (*of bird*) pico; (*notice*) cartel; (*Theat*) programa ▷ *vt* extender *or* pasar la factura a; **may I have the ~ please?** ¿puede traerme la cuenta, por favor?; **~ of exchange** letra de cambio; **~ of lading** conocimiento de embarque; **~ of sale** escritura de venta; **"post no ~s"** "prohibido fijar carteles

billboard [ˈbɪlbɔːd] *n* (*US*) valla publicitaria

billet [ˈbɪlɪt] *n* alojamiento ▷ *vt*: **to ~ sb (on sb)** alojar a algn (con algn)

billfold [ˈbɪlfəuld] *n* (*US*) cartera

billiards [ˈbɪljədz] *n* billar

billion [ˈbɪljən] *n* (*thousand million*) mil millones; (*Brit: million million*) billón

bimbo [ˈbɪmbəu] *n* (*col*) tía buena sin seso

bin [bɪn] *n* (*gen*) cubo *or* tacho (*CS*) *or* bote (*Méx*) de la basura; **litter~** *n* (*Brit*) papelera

binary [ˈbaɪnərɪ] *adj* (*Math*) binario; **~ code** código binario; **~ system** sistema binario

bind [baɪnd] (*pt, pp* **bound**) *vt* atar, liar; (*wound*) vendar; (*book*) encuadernar; (*oblige*) obligar

▶ **bind over** *vt* (*Law*) obligar por vía legal

▶ **bind up** *vt* (*wound*) vendar; **to be bound up in** (*work, research etc*) estar absorto en; **to be bound up with** (*person*) estar estrechamente ligado a

binder [ˈbaɪndəʳ] *n* (*file*) archivador

binding [ˈbaɪndɪŋ] *adj* (*contract*) vinculante

binge [bɪndʒ] *n* borrachera, juerga; **to go on a ~** ir de juerga

bingo [ˈbɪŋgəu] *n* bingo

bin-liner [ˈbɪnlaɪnəʳ] *n* bolsa de la basura

binoculars [bɪˈnɔkjuləz] *npl* prismáticos, gemelos

biochemistry [baɪəˈkɛmɪstrɪ] *n* bioquímica

biodegradable [ˈbaɪəudɪˈgreɪdəbl] *adj* biodegradable

biodiversity [ˈbaɪəudaɪˈvəːsɪtɪ] *n* biodiversidad

biofuel [ˈbaɪəufjuəl] *n* biocarburante

biographer [baɪˈɔgrəfəʳ] *n* biógrafo(-a)

biographical [baɪəˈgræfɪkəl] *adj* biográfico

biography [baɪˈɔgrəfɪ] *n* biografía

biological [baɪəˈlɔdʒɪkəl] *adj* biológico

biological clock *n* reloj biológico

biologist [baɪˈɔlədʒɪst] *n* biólogo(-a)

biology [baɪˈɔlədʒɪ] *n* biología

biopic [ˈbaɪəupɪk] *n* filme biográfico

biopsy [ˈbaɪɔpsɪ] *n* biopsia

biosphere [ˈbaɪəsfɪəʳ] *n* biosfera

bioterrorism [ˈbaɪəuˈtɛrərɪzəm] *n* bioterrorismo

birch [bəːtʃ] *n* abedul; (*cane*) vara

bird [bəːd] *n* ave, pájaro; (*Brit col: girl*) chica

birdcage [ˈbəːdkeɪdʒ] *n* jaula

bird of prey *n* ave de presa

bird's-eye view [ˈbəːdzaɪ-] *n* vista de pájaro

bird watcher *n* ornitólogo(-a)

Biro® [ˈbaɪrəu] *n* bolígrafo

birth [bəːθ] *n* nacimiento; (*Med*) parto; **to give ~ to** parir, dar a luz a; (*fig*) dar origen a

birth certificate *n* partida de nacimiento

birth control *n* control de natalidad; (*methods*) métodos anticonceptivos

birthday [ˈbəːθdeɪ] *n* cumpleaños

birthplace [ˈbəːθpleɪs] *n* lugar de nacimiento

birth rate *n* (tasa de) natalidad

Biscay [ˈbɪskeɪ] *n*: **the Bay of ~** el Mar Cantábrico, el golfo de Vizcaya

biscuit [ˈbɪskɪt] *n* (*Brit*) galleta

bisect [baɪˈsɛkt] *vt* (*also Math*) bisecar

bisexual ['baɪˈsɛksjʊəl] *adj, n* bisexual
bishop ['bɪʃəp] *n* obispo; (*Chess*) alfil
bistro ['biːstrəʊ] *n* café-bar
bit [bɪt] *pt of* **bite** ▷ *n* trozo, pedazo, pedacito; (*Comput*) bit; (*for horse*) freno, bocado; **would you like another ~?** ¿quieres otro trozo?; **a ~ of cake** un trozo de pastel; **a ~ of music** un poco de música; **it's a ~ of a nuisance** es un poco fastidioso; **a ~ mad** algo loco; **wait a ~!** ¡espera un poco!; **~ by ~** poco a poco; **to do one's ~** aportar su granito de arena; **to come to ~s** (*break*) hacerse pedazos; **to fall to ~s** caerse a pedazos; **to take sth to ~s** desmontar algo; **bring all your ~s and pieces** trae todas tus cosas
bitch [bɪtʃ] *n* (*dog*) perra; (*col!*) zorra (!)
bite [baɪt] *vt, vi* (*pt* **bit**, *pp* **bitten**) (*person, dog*) morder; (*insect etc*) picar ▷ *n* (*wound: of dog, snake etc*) mordedura; (*of insect*) picadura; (*mouthful*) bocado; **to ~ one's nails** morderse las uñas; **I got bitten by mosquitoes** me picaron los mosquitos; **let's have a ~ (to eat)** comamos algo
bitten ['bɪtn] *pp of* **bite**
bitter ['bɪtər] *adj* amargo; (*wind, criticism*) cortante, penetrante; (*icy: weather*) glacial; (*battle*) encarnizado ▷ *n* (*Brit: beer*) cerveza típica británica a base de lúpulos
bitterness ['bɪtənɪs] *n* amargura; (*anger*) rencor
bizarre [bɪˈzɑːr] *adj* raro, estrafalario
blab [blæb] *vi* cantar ▷ *vt* (*also:* **blab out**) soltar, contar
black [blæk] *adj* (*colour*) negro; (*dark*) oscuro ▷ *n* (*colour*) color negro; (*person*): **B~** negro(-a) ▷ *vt* (*shoes*) lustrar; (*Brit Industry*) boicotear; **to give sb a ~ eye** ponerle a algn el ojo morado; **~ coffee** café solo; **~ and white** (*TV, photo*) blanco y negro; **there it is in ~ and white** (*fig*) ahí está bien claro; **to be in the ~** (*in credit*) tener saldo positivo; **~ and blue** *adj* amoratado; **she's ~** es negra
  ▶ **black out** *vi* (*faint*) desmayarse
blackberry ['blækbəri] *n* zarzamora
blackbird ['blækbəːd] *n* mirlo
blackboard ['blækbɔːd] *n* pizarra
black box *n* (*Aviat*) caja negra
blackcurrant ['blækˈkʌrənt] *n* grosella negra
black economy *n* economía sumergida
blacken ['blækən] *vt* ennegrecer; (*fig*) denigrar
black hole *n* (*Astro*) agujero negro
black ice *n* hielo invisible en la carretera
blackleg ['blæklɛg] *n* (*Brit*) esquirol
blacklist ['blæklɪst] *n* lista negra ▷ *vt* poner en la lista negra
blackmail ['blækmeɪl] *n* chantaje ▷ *vt* chantajear
black market *n* mercado negro, estraperlo
blackout ['blækaʊt] *n* (*TV, Elec*) apagón; (*fainting*) desmayo, pérdida de conocimiento
black pepper *n* pimienta negra
Black Sea *n*: **the ~** el Mar Negro
black sheep *n* oveja negra
blacksmith ['blæksmɪθ] *n* herrero

black spot *n* (*Aut*) punto negro
bladder ['blædər] *n* vejiga
blade [bleɪd] *n* hoja; (*cutting edge*) filo; **a ~ of grass** una brizna de hierba
blame [bleɪm] *n* culpa ▷ *vt*: **to ~ sb for sth** echar a algn la culpa de algo; **to be to ~ (for)** tener la culpa (de); **I'm not to ~** yo no tengo la culpa; **and I don't ~ him** y lo comprendo perfectamente
blameless ['bleɪmlɪs] *adj* (*person*) inocente
bland [blænd] *adj* suave; (*taste*) soso
blank [blæŋk] *adj* en blanco; (*shot*) de fogueo; (*look*) sin expresión ▷ *n* blanco, espacio en blanco; cartucho de fogueo; **to draw a ~** (*fig*) no conseguir nada
blank cheque, (*US*) **blank check** *n* cheque en blanco
blanket ['blæŋkɪt] *n* manta, frazada (*LAm*), cobija (*LAm*) ▷ *adj* (*statement, agreement*) comprensivo, general; **to give ~ cover** (*insurance policy*) dar póliza a todo riesgo
blare [blɛər] *vi* (*brass band, horns, radio*) resonar
blasphemous ['blæsfɪməs] *adj* blasfemo
blasphemy ['blæsfɪmɪ] *n* blasfemia
blast [blɑːst] *n* (*of wind*) ráfaga, soplo; (*of whistle*) toque; (*of explosive*) carga explosiva; (*force*) choque ▷ *vt* (*blow up*) volar; (*blow open*) abrir con carga explosiva ▷ *excl* (*Brit col*) ¡maldito sea!; (**at**) **full ~** (*also fig*) a toda marcha
  ▶ **blast off** *vi* (*spacecraft etc*) despegar
blast-off ['blɑːstɔf] *n* (*Space*) lanzamiento
blatant ['bleɪtənt] *adj* descarado
blaze [bleɪz] *n* (*fire*) fuego; (*flames*) llamarada; (*glow: of fire, sun etc*) resplandor; (*fig*) arranque ▷ *vi* (*fire*) arder con llamaradas; (*fig*) brillar ▷ *vt*: **to ~ a trail** (*fig*) abrir (un) camino; **in a ~ of publicity** bajo los focos de la publicidad
blazer ['bleɪzər] *n* chaqueta de uniforme de colegial o de socio de club
bleach [bliːtʃ] *n* (*also:* **household bleach**) lejía ▷ *vt* (*linen*) blanquear
bleached [bliːtʃt] *adj* (*hair*) de colorado; (*clothes*) blanqueado
bleachers ['bliːtʃəz] *npl* (*US Sport*) gradas
bleak [bliːk] *adj* (*countryside*) desierto; (*landscape*) desolado, desierto; (*weather*) desapacible; (*smile*) triste; (*prospect, future*) poco prometedor(a)
bleary-eyed ['blɪərɪˈaɪd] *adj*: **to be ~** tener ojos de cansado
bleat [bliːt] *vi* balar
bleed [bliːd] (*pt, pp* **bled**) *vt* sangrar; (*brakes, radiator*) desaguar ▷ *vi* sangrar
bleep [bliːp] *n* pitido ▷ *vi* pitar ▷ *vt* llamar por el busca
bleeper ['bliːpər] *n* (*of doctor etc*) busca
blemish ['blɛmɪʃ] *n* mancha, tacha
blend [blɛnd] *n* mezcla ▷ *vt* mezclar ▷ *vi* (*colours etc*) combinarse, mezclarse
blender ['blɛndər] *n* (*Culin*) batidora
bless [blɛs] (*pt, pp* **-ed** *or* **blest**) *vt* bendecir
blessed ['blɛsɪd] *adj* (*Rel: holy*) santo, bendito; (*: happy*) dichoso; **every ~ day** cada santo día

blessing ['blɛsɪŋ] n bendición; (advantage) beneficio, ventaja; **to count one's ~s** agradecer lo que se tiene; **it was a ~ in disguise** no hay mal que por bien no venga

blew [blu:] pt of **blow**

blight [blaɪt] vt (hopes etc) frustrar, arruinar

blimey ['blaɪmɪ] excl (Brit col) ¡caray!

blind [blaɪnd] adj ciego ▷ n (for window) persiana ▷ vt cegar; (dazzle) deslumbrar

blind alley n callejón sin salida

blind corner n (Brit) esquina or curva sin visibilidad

blind date n cita a ciegas

blindfold ['blaɪndfəuld] n venda ▷ adj, adv con los ojos vendados ▷ vt vendar los ojos a

blinding ['blaɪndɪŋ] adj (flash, light) cegador; (pain) intenso

blindingly ['blaɪndɪŋlɪ] adv: **it's ~ obvious** salta a la vista

blindly ['blaɪndlɪ] adv a ciegas, ciegamente

blindness ['blaɪndnɪs] n ceguera

blind spot n (Aut) ángulo muerto; **to have a ~ about sth** estar ciego para algo

blink [blɪŋk] vi parpadear, pestañear; (light) oscilar; **to be on the ~** (col) estar estropeado

blinkers ['blɪŋkəz] npl (esp Brit) anteojeras

blip [blɪp] n señal luminosa; (on graph) pequeña desviación; (fig) pequeña anomalía

bliss [blɪs] n felicidad

blissful ['blɪsful] adj dichoso; **in ~ ignorance** feliz en la ignorancia

blister ['blɪstə^r] n (on skin, paint) ampolla ▷ vi ampollarse

blistering ['blɪstərɪŋ] adj (heat) abrasador(a)

blithely ['blaɪðlɪ] adv alegremente, despreocupadamente

blizzard ['blɪzəd] n ventisca

bloated ['bləutɪd] adj hinchado

blob [blɔb] n (drop) gota; (stain, spot) mancha

block [blɔk] n bloque (also Comput); (in pipes) obstáculo; (of buildings) manzana ▷ vt (gen) obstruir, cerrar; (progress) estorbar; (Comput) agrupar; **~ of flats** (Brit) bloque de pisos; **mental ~ amnesia** temporal; **~ and tackle** (Tech) aparejo de polea; **3 ~s from here** a 3 manzanas or cuadras (LAm) de aquí
▶ **block up** vt tapar, obstruir; (pipe) atascar

blockade [blɔ'keɪd] n bloqueo ▷ vt bloquear

blockage ['blɔkɪdʒ] n estorbo, obstrucción

block booking n reserva en grupo

blockbuster ['blɔkbʌstə^r] n (book) best-seller; (film) éxito de público

block capitals npl mayúsculas

block letters npl letras de molde

bloke [bləuk] n (Brit col) tipo, tío

blond(e) [blɔnd] adj, n rubio(-a)

blood [blʌd] n sangre; **new ~** (fig) gente nueva

blood bank n banco de sangre

blood count n recuento de glóbulos rojos y blancos

blood donor n donante de sangre

blood group n grupo sanguíneo

bloodhound ['blʌdhaund] n sabueso

blood poisoning n septicemia de la sangre

blood pressure n tensión sanguínea; **to have high/low ~** tener la tensión alta/baja

bloodshed ['blʌdʃed] n baño de sangre

bloodshot ['blʌdʃɔt] adj inyectado en sangre

bloodstream ['blʌdstri:m] n corriente sanguínea

blood test n análisis de sangre

bloodthirsty ['blʌdθə:stɪ] adj sanguinario

blood transfusion n transfusión de sangre

blood type n grupo sanguíneo

blood vessel n vaso sanguíneo

bloody ['blʌdɪ] adj sangriento; (Brit col!): **this ~...** este condenado or puñetero or fregado (LAm) ... (!) ▷ adv (Brit col!): **~ strong/good** terriblemente fuerte/bueno

bloody-minded ['blʌdɪ'maɪndɪd] adj (Brit col) cor malas pulgas

bloom [blu:m] n floración; **in ~** en flor ▷ vi florecer

blossom ['blɔsəm] n flor ▷ vi florecer; (fig) desarrollarse; **to ~ into** (fig) convertirse en

blot [blɔt] n borrón ▷ vt (dry) secar; (stain) manchar; **to ~ out** vt (view) tapar; (memories) borrar; **to be a ~ on the landscape** estropear el paisaje; **to ~ one's copy book** (fig) manchar su reputación

blotchy ['blɔtʃɪ] adj (complexion) lleno de mancha

blotting paper ['blɔtɪŋ-] n papel secante

blouse [blauz] n blusa

blow [bləu] n golpe (pt **blew**, pp **-n**) [blu:, bləun] ▷ vi soplar; (fuse) fundirse ▷ vt (glass) soplar; (fuse) quemar; (instrument) tocar; **to come to ~s** llegar a golpes; **a cold wind was ~ing** soplaba un viento frío; **he blew on his fingers** se sopló los dedos; **they were one-all when the whistle blew** iban uno a uno cuando sonó el pito; **to ~ one's nose** sonarse la nariz
▶ **blow away** vt llevarse, arrancar
▶ **blow down** vt derribar
▶ **blow off** vt arrebatar
▶ **blow out** vt apagar ▷ vi apagarse; (tyre) reventar; **~ out the candles!** ¡apaga las velas!
▶ **blow over** vi amainar
▶ **blow up** vi estallar ▷ vt volar; (tyre) inflar; (Phot) ampliar; **they blew up a plane** volaron un avión; **we've ~n up the balloons** hemos inflado los globos

blow-dry ['bləudraɪ] n secado con secador de mano ▷ vt secar con secador de mano

blowlamp ['bləulæmp] n (Brit) soplete, lámpara de soldar

blow-out ['bləuaut] n (of tyre) pinchazo; (col: big meal) banquete, festín

blowtorch ['bləutɔ:tʃ] n = **blowlamp**

blue [blu:] adj azul; **~ film** película porno; **~ joke** chiste verde; **out of the ~ a ~ moon** de higos a brevas; **to come out of the ~** (fig) ser completamente inesperado; see also **blues**

bluebell ['blu:bɛl] n campanilla, campánula azu

bluebottle ['blu:bɔtl] n moscarda, mosca azul

lueprint ['blu:prɪnt] n proyecto; ~ **(for)** (fig) anteproyecto (de)

lues [blu:z] npl: **the** ~ (Mus) el blues; **to have the** ~ estar triste

luff [blʌf] vi tirarse un farol, farolear ▷ n bluff, farol; (Geo) precipicio, despeñadero; **to call sb's** ~ coger a algn en un renuncio

lunder ['blʌndə^r] n patinazo, metedura de pata ▷ vi cometer un error, meter la pata; **to** ~ **into sb/sth** tropezar con algn/algo

lunt [blʌnt] adj (knife) desafilado; (person) franco, directo ▷ vt embotar, desafilar; **this pencil is** ~ este lápiz está despuntado; ~ **instrument** (Law) instrumento contundente

lur [blə:^r] n aspecto borroso ▷ vt (vision) enturbiar; (memory) empañar

lurb [blə:b] n propaganda

lurred [blə:d] adj borroso

lurt [blə:t]: **to** ~ **out** vt (say) descolgarse con, dejar escapar

lush [blʌʃ] vi ruborizarse, ponerse colorado ▷ n rubor

lusher ['blʌʃə^r] n colorete

lustery ['blʌstərɪ] adj (weather) tempestuoso, tormentoso

MA n abbr = **British Medical Association**

O n abbr (col: = body odour) olor a sudor; (US = **box office**

oar [bɔ:^r] n verraco, cerdo

oard [bɔ:d] n tabla, tablero; (on wall) tablón; (for chess etc) tablero; (committee) junta, consejo; (in firm) mesa or junta directiva; (Naut, Aviat): **on** ~ a bordo ▷ vt (ship) embarcarse en; (train) subir a; **full** ~ (Brit) pensión completa; **half** ~ (Brit) media pensión; ~ **and lodging** alojamiento y comida; **to go by the** ~ (fig) irse por la borda; **above** ~ (fig) sin tapujos; **across the** ~ (fig: adv) en todos los niveles; (: adj) general

▶ **board up** vt (door) tapar, cegar

oarder ['bɔ:də^r] n huésped(a); (Scol) interno(-a)

oard game n juego de tablero

oarding card ['bɔ:dɪŋ-] n (Brit: Aviat, Naut) tarjeta de embarque

oarding house ['bɔ:dɪŋ-] n casa de huéspedes

oarding party ['bɔ:dɪŋ-] n brigada de inspección

oarding pass ['bɔ:dɪŋ-] n (US) = **boarding card**

oarding school ['bɔ:dɪŋ-] n internado

oard meeting n reunión de la junta directiva

oard room n sala de juntas

oast [bəust] vi: **to** ~ **(about** or **of)** alardear (de) ▷ vt ostentar ▷ n alarde, baladronada

oat [bəut] n barco, buque; (small) barca, bote; **to go by** ~ ir en barco

oater ['bəutə^r] n (hat) canotié

oat people npl refugiados que huyen en barca

ob [bɔb] vi (boat, cork on water: also: **bob up and down**) menearse, balancearse ▷ n (Brit col) = **shilling**

▶ **bob up** vi (re)aparecer de repente

obby ['bɔbɪ] n (Brit col) poli

obsleigh ['bɔbsleɪ] n bob, trineo de competición

bode [bəud] vi: **to** ~ **well/ill (for)** ser de buen/mal agüero (para)

bodily ['bɔdɪlɪ] adj (comfort, needs) corporal; (pain) corpóreo ▷ adv (in person) en persona; (carry) corporalmente; (lift) en peso

body ['bɔdɪ] n cuerpo; (corpse) cadáver; (of car) caja, carrocería; (also: **body stocking**) body; (fig: organization) organización; (: public body) organismo; (: quantity) masa; (: of speech, document) parte principal; **the human** ~ el cuerpo humano; **ruling** ~ directiva; **in a** ~ todos juntos, en masa

body blow n (fig) palo

body-building ['bɔdɪ'bɪldɪŋ] n culturismo

bodyguard ['bɔdɪgɑ:d] n guardaespaldas

body language n lenguaje gestual

body search n cacheo; **to carry out a** ~ **on sb** registrar a algn; **to submit to** or **undergo a** ~ ser registrado

bodywork ['bɔdɪwə:k] n carrocería

bog [bɔg] n pantano, ciénaga ▷ vt: **to get** ~**ged down** (fig) empantanarse, atascarse

boggle ['bɔgl] vi: **the mind** ~**s!** ¡no puedo creerlo!

bogus ['bəugəs] adj falso, fraudulento; (person) fingido

boil [bɔɪl] vt cocer; (eggs) pasar por agua ▷ vi hervir ▷ n (Med) furúnculo, divieso; **to bring to the** ~ calentar hasta que hierva; **to come to the** (Brit) or **a** (US) ~ comenzar a hervir; ~**ed egg** huevo pasado por agua; ~**ed potatoes** patatas or papas (LAm) cocidas

▶ **boil down** vi (fig): **to** ~ **down to** reducirse a

▶ **boil over** vi (liquid) rebosar; (anger, resentment) llegar al colmo

boiler ['bɔɪlə^r] n caldera

boiler suit n (Brit) mono, overol (LAm)

boiling ['bɔɪlɪŋ] adj: **I'm** ~ **(hot)** (col) estoy asado

boiling point n punto de ebullición

boil-in-the-bag [bɔɪlɪnðə'bæg] adj: ~ **meals** platos que se cuecen en su misma bolsa

boisterous ['bɔɪstərəs] adj (noisy) bullicioso; (excitable) exuberante; (crowd) tumultuoso

bold [bəuld] adj (brave) valiente, audaz; (pej) descarado; (outline) grueso; (colour) vivo; ~ **type** (Typ) negrita

Bolivia [bə'lɪvɪə] n Bolivia

Bolivian [bə'lɪvɪən] adj, n boliviano(-a)

bollard ['bɔləd] n (Brit Aut) poste

bolshy ['bɔlʃɪ] adj (Brit col) protestón(-ona); **to be in a** ~ **mood** tener el día protestón

bolster ['bəulstə^r] n travesero, cabezal

▶ **bolster up** vt reforzar; (fig) alentar

bolt [bəult] n (lock) cerrojo; (with nut) perno, tornillo ▷ adv: ~ **upright** rígido, erguido ▷ vt (door) echar el cerrojo a; (food) engullir ▷ vi fugarse; (horse) desbocarse

bomb [bɔm] n bomba ▷ vt bombardear

bombard [bɔm'bɑ:d] vt bombardear; (fig) asediar

bombardment [bɔm'bɑ:dmənt] n bombardeo

bombastic [bɔm'bæstɪk] adj rimbombante; (person) pomposo

bomb disposal n desactivación de explosivos

bomb disposal expert n artificiero(-a)
bomber ['bɒmə'] n (Aviat) bombardero; (terrorist) persona que pone bombas
bombing ['bɒmɪŋ] n bombardeo
bomb scare n amenaza de bomba
bombshell ['bɒmʃɛl] n obús, granada; (fig) bomba
bomb site n lugar donde estalló una bomba
bona fide ['bəunə'faɪdɪ] adj genuino, auténtico
bonanza [bə'nænzə] n bonanza
bond [bɒnd] n (binding promise) fianza; (Finance) bono; (link) vínculo, lazo; **in ~** (Comm) en depósito bajo fianza
bondage ['bɒndɪdʒ] n esclavitud
bone [bəun] n hueso; (of fish) espina ▷ vt deshuesar; quitar las espinas a; **~ of contention** manzana de la discordia
bone idle adj gandul
bone marrow n médula; **~ transplant** transplante de médula
bonfire ['bɒnfaɪə'] n hoguera, fogata
bonkers ['bɒŋkəz] adj (Brit col) majareta
bonnet ['bɒnɪt] n gorra; (of car) capó
bonus ['bəunəs] n (at Christmas etc) paga extraordinaria; (merit award) sobrepaga, prima
bony ['bəunɪ] adj (arm, face, Med: tissue) huesudo; (meat) lleno de huesos; (fish) lleno de espinas; (thin: person) flaco, delgado
boo [buː] vt abuchear
booby trap ['buːbɪ-] n (Mil etc) trampa explosiva
book [buk] n libro; (notebook) libreta; (of stamps etc) librillo; **~s** (Comm) cuentas, contabilidad ▷ vt (ticket, seat, room) reservar; (driver) fichar; (Football) amonestar; **to keep the ~s** llevar las cuentas or los libros; **by the ~** según las reglas; **to throw the ~ at sb** echar un rapapolvo a algn; **we haven't ~ed** no hemos hecho reserva
  ▶ **book in** vi (at hotel) registrarse
  ▶ **book up** vt: **all seats are ~ed up** todas las plazas están reservadas; **the hotel is ~ed up** el hotel está lleno
bookcase ['bukkeɪs] n librería, estante para libros
booking office ['bukɪŋ-] n (Brit: Rail) despacho de billetes or boletos (LAm); (: Theat) taquilla, boletería (LAm)
book-keeping ['buk'kiːpɪŋ] n contabilidad
booklet ['buklɪt] n folleto
bookmaker ['bukmeɪkə'] n corredor de apuestas
bookseller ['buksɛlə'] n librero(-a)
bookshelf ['bukʃɛlf] n estante
bookshop ['bukʃɒp] n librería
bookstall ['bukstɔːl] n quiosco de libros
book store n = **bookshop**
book token n vale para libros
boom [buːm] n (noise) trueno, estampido; (in prices etc) alza rápida; (Econ) boom, auge ▷ vi (cannon) hacer gran estruendo, retumbar; (Econ) estar en alza
boomerang ['buːməræŋ] n bumerang (also fig) ▷ vi: **to ~ on sb** (fig) ser contraproducente para algn

boon [buːn] n favor, beneficio
boost [buːst] n estímulo, empuje ▷ vt estimular, empujar; (increase: sales, production) aumentar; **to give a ~ to** (morale) levantar; **it gave a ~ to his confidence** le dio confianza en sí mismo
booster ['buːstə'] n (Med) reinyección; (TV) repetidor; (Elec) elevador de tensión; (also: **booster rocket**) cohete
boot [buːt] n bota; (ankle boot) botín, borceguí; (Brit: of car) maleta, maletero, cajuela (Méx), baúl (CS) ▷ vt dar un puntapié a; (Comput) arrancar; **to ~** (in addition) además, por añadidura; **to give sb the ~** (col) despedir a algn, poner a algn en la calle
booth [buːð] n (at fair) barraca; (telephone booth, voting booth) cabina
booty ['buːtɪ] n botín
booze [buːz] (col) n bebida ▷ vi emborracharse
border ['bɔːdə'] n borde, margen; (of a country) frontera ▷ adj fronterizo; **the B~s** región fronteriza entre Escocia e Inglaterra
  ▶ **border on** vt fus lindar con; (fig) rayar en
borderline ['bɔːdəlaɪn] n (fig) frontera
bore [bɔː'] pt of **bear** ▷ vt (hole) taladrar; (person) aburrir ▷ n (person) pelmazo, pesado; (of gun) calibre
bored [bɔːd] adj aburrido; **he's ~ to tears** or **to death** or **stiff** está aburrido como una ostra, está muerto de aburrimiento
boredom ['bɔːdəm] n aburrimiento
boring ['bɔːrɪŋ] adj aburrido, pesado
born [bɔːn] adj: **to be ~** nacer; **I was ~ in 1960** nací en 1960
born-again [bɔːnə'gɛn] adj: **~ Christian** evangelista
borne [bɔːn] pp of **bear**
borough ['bʌrə] n municipio
borrow ['bɔrəu] vt: **to ~ sth (from sb)** tomar algo prestado (a algn); **may I ~ your car?** ¿me prestas tu coche?
borrower ['bɔrəuə'] n prestatario(-a)
borstal ['bɔːstl] n (Brit) reformatorio (de menores)
Bosnia ['bɒznɪə] n Bosnia
Bosnia-Herzegovina, Bosnia-Hercegovina ['bɒːsnɪəhɜːzə'gəuviːnə] n Bosnia-Herzegovina
bosom ['buzəm] n pecho; (fig) seno; **~ friend** n amigo(-a) íntimo(-a) or del alma
boss [bɒs] n jefe(-a); (employer) patrón(-ona); (political etc) cacique ▷ vt (also: **boss about** or **around**) mangonear; **stop ~ing everyone about!** ¡deja de dar órdenes or de mangonear a todos!
bossy ['bɒsɪ] adj mandón(-ona)
bosun ['bəusn] n contramaestre
botanist ['bɒtənɪst] n botanista
botany ['bɒtənɪ] n botánica
botch [bɒtʃ] vt (also: **botch up**) arruinar, estropea
both [bəuθ] adj, pron ambos(-as), los/las dos ▷ adv **~ A and B** tanto A como B; **~ of us went, we ~ went** fuimos los dos, ambos fuimos; **~ of them play the piano, they ~ play the piano** los dos

tocan el piano; **~ (of) your answers are wrong** tus respuestas están las dos mal; **he has houses in ~ France and in Spain** tiene casas tanto en Francia como en España; **~ Emma and Jane went** fueron Emma y Jane

bother ['bɔðə^r] *vt* (*worry*) preocupar; (*disturb*) molestar, fastidiar, fregar (*LAm*), embromar (*LAm*) ▷ *vi* (*also:* **bother o.s.**) molestarse ▷ *n:* **what a ~!** ¡qué lata! ▷ *excl* ¡maldita sea!, ¡caramba!; **what's ~ing you?** ¿qué es lo que te preocupa?; **I'm sorry to ~ you** perdona que te moleste; **please don't ~** no te molestes; **to ~ doing, ~ to do** tomarse la molestia de hacer; **he didn't ~ to tell me about it** ni se tomó la molestia de decírmelo

▶ **bottle up** *vt* (*fig*) contener, reprimir

bottle bank *n* contenedor de vidrio, iglú

bottleneck ['bɔtlnɛk] *n* embotellamiento

bottle-opener ['bɔtləupnə^r] *n* abrebotellas

bottom ['bɔtəm] *n* (*of box, sea*) fondo; (*buttocks*) trasero, culo; (*of page, mountain, tree*) pie; (*of list*) final ▷ *adj* (*lowest*) más bajo; (*last*) último; **to get to the ~ of sth** (*fig*) llegar al fondo de algo

bottomless ['bɔtəmlɪs] *adj* sin fondo, insondable

bottom line *n:* **the ~** lo fundamental; **the ~ is he has to go** el caso es que tenemos que despedirle

botulism ['bɔtjulɪzəm] *n* botulismo

bough [bau] *n* rama

bought [bɔːt] *pt, pp of* **buy**

boulder ['bəuldə^r] *n* canto rodado

bounce [bauns] *vi* (*ball*) (re)botar; (*cheque*) ser rechazado ▷ *vt* hacer (re)botar ▷ *n* (*rebound*) (re)bote; **he's got plenty of ~** (*fig*) tiene mucha energía

bouncer ['baunsə^r] *n* (*col*) forzudo, gorila

bouncy castle® ['baunsɪ-] *n* castillo inflable

bound [baund] *pt, pp of* **bind** ▷ *n* (*leap*) salto; (*gen pl: limit*) límite ▷ *vi* (*leap*) saltar ▷ *adj:* **~ by** rodeado de; **to be ~ to do sth** (*obliged*) tener el deber de hacer algo; **he's ~ to come** es seguro que vendrá; **"out of ~s to the public"** "prohibido el paso"; **~ for** con destino a

boundary ['baundrɪ] *n* límite, lindero

boundless ['baundlɪs] *adj* ilimitado

bouquet ['bukeɪ] *n* (*of flowers*) ramo, ramillete; (*of wine*) aroma

bourbon ['buəbən] *n* (*US: also:* **bourbon whiskey**) whisky americano, bourbon

bourgeois ['buəʒwɑː] *adj, n* burgués(-esa)

bout [baut] *n* (*of malaria etc*) ataque; (*Boxing etc*) combate, encuentro

boutique [buːˈtiːk] *n* boutique, tienda de ropa

bow¹ *n* [bəu] (*knot*) lazo; (*weapon, Mus*) arco

bow² [bau] (*of the head*) reverencia; (*Naut: also:* **bows**) proa ▷ *vi* inclinarse, hacer una reverencia; (*yield*): **to ~ to** *or* **before** ceder ante, someterse a; **to ~ to the inevitable** resignarse

a lo inevitable

bowels ['bauəlz] *npl* intestinos, vientre

bowl [bəul] *n* tazón, cuenco; (*for washing*) palangana, jofaina; (*ball*) bola; (*US: stadium*) estadio ▷ *vi* (*Cricket*) arrojar la pelota; *see also* **bowls**

bow-legged ['bəuˈlɛgɪd] *adj* estevado

bowler ['bəulə^r] *n* (*Cricket*) lanzador (de la pelota); (*Brit: also:* **bowler hat**) hongo, bombín

bowling ['bəulɪŋ] *n* (*game*) bolos, bochas

bowling alley *n* bolera

bowling green *n* pista para bochas

bowls [bəulz] *n* juego de los bolos, bochas

bow tie ['bəu-] *n* corbata de lazo, pajarita

box [bɔks] *n* (*also:* **cardboard box**) caja, cajón; (*for jewels*) estuche; (*for money*) cofre; (*crate*) cofre, arca; (*Theat*) palco ▷ *vt* encajonar ▷ *vi* (*Sport*) boxear

boxer ['bɔksə^r] *n* (*person*) boxeador; (*dog*) bóxer

boxing ['bɔksɪŋ] *n* (*Sport*) boxeo, box (*LAm*)

Boxing Day *n* (*Brit*) día de San Esteban

boxing gloves *npl* guantes de boxeo

boxing ring *n* ring, cuadrilátero

box number *n* (*for advertisements*) apartado

box office *n* taquilla, boletería (*LAm*)

boxroom ['bɔksrum] *n* trastero

boy [bɔɪ] *n* (*young*) niño; (*older*) muchacho

boycott ['bɔɪkɔt] *n* boicot ▷ *vt* boicotear

boyfriend ['bɔɪfrɛnd] *n* novio

boyish ['bɔɪɪʃ] *adj* de muchacho, inmaduro

boy scout *n* boy scout

BR *abbr* = **British Rail**

bra [brɑː] *n* sostén, sujetador, corpiño (*LAm*)

brace [breɪs] *n* refuerzo, abrazadera; (*Brit: on teeth*) corrector; (*tool*) berbiquí ▷ *vt* asegurar, reforzar; **to ~ o.s. (for)** (*fig*) prepararse (para); *see also* **braces**

bracelet ['breɪslɪt] *n* pulsera, brazalete, pulso (*LAm*)

braces ['breɪsɪz] *npl* (*Brit*) tirantes, suspensores (*LAm*); (*US: on teeth*) corrector

bracing ['breɪsɪŋ] *adj* vigorizante, tónico

bracket ['brækɪt] *n* (*Tech*) soporte, puntal; (*group*) clase, categoría; (*also:* **brace bracket**) soporte, abrazadera; (*also:* **round bracket**) paréntesis; (*gen*): **square ~** corchete ▷ *vt* (*fig: also:* **bracket together**) agrupar; **income ~** nivel económico; **in ~s** entre paréntesis

brag [bræg] *vi* jactarse

braid [breɪd] *n* (*trimming*) galón; (*of hair*) trenza

Braille [breɪl] *n* Braille

brain [breɪn] *n* cerebro; **brains** *npl* sesos; **she's got ~s** es muy lista

brainchild ['breɪnʃaɪld] *n* invención

braindead ['breɪndɛd] *adj* (*Med*) clínicamente muerto; (*col*) subnormal, tarado

brainwash ['breɪnwɔʃ] *vt* lavar el cerebro a

brainwave ['breɪnweɪv] *n* idea luminosa *or* genial, inspiración

brainy ['breɪnɪ] *adj* muy listo *or* inteligente

braise [breɪz] *vt* cocer a fuego lento

brake [breɪk] *n* (*on vehicle*) freno ▷ *vt, vi* frenar

brake fluid n líquido de frenos
brake light n luz de frenado
bran [bræn] n salvado
branch [brɑːntʃ] n rama; (fig) ramo; (Comm)
sucursal ▷ vi ramificarse; (fig) extenderse
▶ **branch out** vi ramificarse
brand [brænd] n marca; (iron) hierro de marcar
▷ vt (cattle) marcar con hierro candente
brand-new ['brænd'njuː] adj flamante,
completamente nuevo
brandy ['brændɪ] n coñac, brandy
brash [bræʃ] adj (rough) tosco; (cheeky) descarado
brass [brɑːs] n latón; **the ~** (Mus) los cobres
brass band n banda de metal
brassière ['bræsɪəʳ] n sostén, sujetador
brass tacks npl: **to get down to ~** ir al grano
brat [bræt] n (pej) mocoso(-a)
bravado [brə'vɑːdəu] n fanfarronería
brave [breɪv] adj valiente, valeroso ▷ n guerrero
indio ▷ vt (challenge) desafiar; (resist) aguantar
bravery ['breɪvərɪ] n valor, valentía
bravo [brɑːˈvəu] excl ¡bravo!, ¡olé!
brawl [brɔːl] n pendencia, reyerta ▷ vi pelearse
bray [breɪ] n rebuzno ▷ vi rebuznar
brazen ['breɪzn] adj descarado, cínico ▷ vt: **to ~ it
out** echarle cara al asunto
brazier ['breɪzɪəʳ] n brasero
Brazil [brə'zɪl] n (el) Brasil
Brazilian [brə'zɪlɪən] adj, n brasileño(-a)
breach [briːtʃ] vt abrir brecha en ▷ n (gap)
brecha; (estrangement) ruptura; (breaking): ~
of confidence abuso de confianza; **~ of
contract** infracción de contrato; **~ of the peace**
perturbación del órden público; **in ~ of** por
incumplimiento o infracción de
bread [brɛd] n pan; (col: money) pasta, lana (LAm);
~ and butter n pan con mantequilla; (fig) pan
(de cada día) ▷ adj común y corriente; **to earn
one's daily ~** ganarse el pan; **to know which
side one's ~ is buttered (on)** saber dónde
aprieta el zapato
breadbin ['brɛdbɪn] n panera
breadbox ['brɛdbɔks] n (US) panera
breadcrumbs ['brɛdkrʌmz] npl migajas; (Culin)
pan rallado
breadline ['brɛdlaɪn] n: **on the ~** en la miseria
breadth [brɛtθ] n anchura; (fig) amplitud
breadwinner ['brɛdwɪnəʳ] n sostén de la familia
break [breɪk] vb (pt **broke**, pp **broken**) ▷ vt (gen)
romper; (promise) no cumplir; (fall) amortiguar;
(journey) interrumpir; (law) violar, infringir;
(record) batir; (news) comunicar ▷ vi romperse,
quebrarse; (storm) estallar; (weather) cambiar ▷ n
(gap) abertura; (crack) grieta; (fracture) fractura;
(in relations) ruptura; (rest) descanso; (time)
intervalo; (: at school) (período de) recreo; (holiday)
vacaciones; (chance) oportunidad; (escape)
evasión, fuga; **careful, you'll ~ something!**
¡cuidado, que vas a romper algo!; **I broke my
leg** me rompí la pierna; **careful, it'll ~!** ¡ten
cuidado, que se va a romper!; **to ~ with sb** (fig)
romper con algn; **to ~ even** cubrir los gastos; **to**

~ free or **loose** escaparse; **lucky ~** (col) chiripa,
racha de buena suerte; **to have** or **take a ~** (few
minutes) descansar; **without a ~** sin descanso or
descansar; **the Christmas ~** las vacaciones de
Navidad; **give me a ~!** ¡déjame en paz!
▶ **break down** vt (door etc) echar abajo, derribar;
(resistance) vencer, acabar con; (figures, data)
analizar, descomponer; (undermine) acabar
con ▷ vi (machine) estropearse; (Aut) averiarse,
descomponerse (LAm); (person) romper a llorar;
(Med) sufrir un colapso; (health) quebrantarse;
(talks) fracasar; **the car broke down** el coche
se averió
▶ **break in** vt (horse etc) domar ▷ vi (burglar) forzar
una entrada; **the thief had broken in through
a window** el ladrón había entrado por una
ventana
▶ **break into** vt fus (house) entrar en; **thieves
broke into the house** los ladrones entraron en
la casa
▶ **break off** vi (speaker) pararse, detenerse;
(branch) partir; (come free) desprenderse ▷ vt
(talks) suspender; (engagement) romper
▶ **break open** vt (door etc) abrir por la fuerza,
forzar
▶ **break out** vi (war) estallar; (fire, fighting)
desencadenarse; (prisoner) escaparse; **to ~ out
in spots** salir a algn granos; **he broke out in a
rash** le salió un sarpullido
▶ **break through** vi: **the sun broke through**
asomó el sol ▷ vt fus (defences, barrier, crowd) abrirse
paso por
▶ **break up** vi (partnership) disolverse; (friends)
romper; (crowd) dispersarse ▷ vt (rocks, ice
etc) partir; (crowd) disolver; **more and more
marriages ~ up** cada día fracasan más
matrimonios; **Richard and Marie have
broken up** Richard y Marie han roto; **we ~ up
next Wednesday** (Scol) el miércoles que viene
empezamos las vacaciones; **police broke
up the demonstration** la policía disolvió la
demostración; **to ~ up a fight** poner fin a una
pelea
breakable ['breɪkəbl] adj quebradizo ▷ n: **~s**
cosas frágiles
breakage ['breɪkɪdʒ] n rotura; **to pay for ~s**
pagar por los objetos rotos
breakdown ['breɪkdaun] n (Aut) avería; (in
communications) interrupción; (Med: also: **nervous
breakdown**) colapso, crisis nerviosa; (of figures)
desglose
breakdown van n (Brit) (camión) grúa
breaker ['breɪkəʳ] n rompiente, ola grande
breakfast ['brɛkfəst] n desayuno
break-in ['breɪkɪn] n robo con allanamiento de
morada
breaking and entering ['breɪkɪŋənd'ɛntərɪŋ] n
(Law) violación de domicilio, allanamiento de
morada
breaking point ['breɪkɪŋ-] n punto de ruptura
breakthrough ['breɪkθruː] n ruptura; (fig)
avance, adelanto

break-up ['breɪkʌp] n (of partnership, marriage) disolución

breakwater ['breɪkwɔ:təʳ] n rompeolas

breast [brɛst] n (of woman) pecho, seno; (chest) pecho; (of bird) pechuga

breast-feed ['brɛstfi:d] vt, vi (irreg: like **feed**) amamantar, dar el pecho

breaststroke ['brɛststrəuk] n braza de pecho

breath [brɛθ] n aliento, respiración; **out of ~** sin aliento, sofocado; **to go out for a ~ of air** salir a tomar el fresco

Breathalyser® ['brɛθəlaɪzəʳ] n (Brit) alcoholímetro; **~ test** n prueba de alcoholemia

breathe [bri:ð] vt, vi respirar; (noisily) resollar; **I won't ~ a word about it** no diré ni una palabra de ello

▸ **breathe in** vt, vi aspirar

▸ **breathe out** vt, vi espirar

breather ['bri:ðəʳ] n respiro, descanso

breathing ['bri:ðɪŋ] n respiración

breathing space n (fig) respiro, pausa

breathless ['brɛθlɪs] adj sin aliento, jadeante; (with excitement) pasmado

breathtaking ['brɛθteɪkɪŋ] adj imponente, pasmoso

breath test n prueba de la alcoholemia

breed [bri:d] vb (pt, pp **bred**) [brɛd] ▷ vt criar; (fig: hate, suspicion) crear, engendrar ▷ vi reproducirse, procrear ▷ n raza, casta

breeding ['bri:dɪŋ] n (of person) educación

breeze [bri:z] n brisa

breezy ['bri:zɪ] adj de mucho viento, ventoso; (person) despreocupado

brevity ['brɛvɪtɪ] n brevedad

brew [bru:] vt (tea) hacer; (beer) elaborar; (plot) tramar ▷ vi hacerse; elaborarse; tramarse; (storm) amenazar

brewer ['bru:əʳ] n cervecero, fabricante de cerveza

brewery ['bru:ərɪ] n fábrica de cerveza

briar ['braɪəʳ] n (thorny bush) zarza; (wild rose) escaramujo, rosa silvestre

bribe [braɪb] n soborno ▷ vt sobornar, cohechar; **to ~ sb to do sth** sobornar a algn para que haga algo

bribery ['braɪbərɪ] n soborno, cohecho

brick [brɪk] n ladrillo

bricklayer ['brɪkleɪəʳ] n albañil

bridal ['braɪdl] adj nupcial

bride [braɪd] n novia

bridegroom ['braɪdgru:m] n novio

bridesmaid ['braɪdzmeɪd] n dama de honor

bridge [brɪdʒ] n puente; (Naut) puente de mando; (of nose) caballete; (Cards) bridge ▷ vt (river) tender un puente sobre

bridle ['braɪdl] n brida, freno ▷ vt poner la brida a; (fig) reprimir, refrenar ▷ vi (in anger etc) picarse

bridle path n camino de herradura

brief [bri:f] adj breve, corto ▷ n (Law) escrito ▷ vt (inform) informar; (instruct) dar instrucciones a; **in ~ ...** en resumen ...; **to ~ sb (about sth)** informar a algn (sobre algo)

briefcase ['bri:fkeɪs] n cartera, portafolio(s) (LAm)

briefly adv (smile, glance) brevemente; (explain, say) brevemente, en pocas palabras

briefs [bri:fs] npl (for men) calzoncillos; (for women) bragas (Esp), calzones (LAm), bombachas (CS)

brigade [brɪ'geɪd] n (Mil) brigada

bright [braɪt] adj claro; (room) luminoso; (day) de sol; (person: clever) listo, inteligente; (: lively) alegre, animado; (colour) vivo; **to look on the ~ side** mirar el lado bueno

brighten ['braɪtn] (also: **brighten up**) vt (room) hacer más alegre ▷ vi (weather) despejarse; (person) animarse, alegrarse

brill [brɪl] adj (Brit col) guay

brilliance ['brɪljəns] n brillo, brillantez; (fig: of person) inteligencia

brilliant ['brɪljənt] adj (light, idea, person, success) brillante; (clever) genial

brim [brɪm] n borde; (of hat) ala

brine [braɪn] n (Culin) salmuera

bring [brɪŋ] (pt, pp **brought**) vt (thing) traer; (person) llevar; **~ warm clothes** trae ropa de abrigo; **can I ~ a friend?** ¿puedo traer a un amigo?; **to ~ sth to an end** terminar con algo; **I can't ~ myself to sack him** no soy capaz de echarle

▸ **bring about** vt ocasionar, producir

▸ **bring back** vt volver a traer; (return) devolver; **that song ~s back memories** esa canción me trae recuerdos

▸ **bring down** vt bajar; (price) rebajar

▸ **bring forward** vt adelantar; (Bookkeeping) sumar y seguir; **the meeting was brought forward** la reunión se adelantó

▸ **bring in** vt (harvest) recoger; (person) hacer entrar or pasar; (object) traer; (Pol: bill, law) presentar; (Law: verdict) pronunciar; (produce: income) producir, rendir

▸ **bring off** vt (task, plan) lograr, conseguir; (deal) cerrar

▸ **bring out** vt (object) sacar; (new product) sacar; (book) publicar

▸ **bring round** vt (unconscious person) hacer volver en sí; (convince) convencer

▸ **bring up** vt (person) educar, criar; (carry up) subir; (question) sacar a colación; (food: vomit) devolver, vomitar; **she brought up 5 children on her own** crió a 5 hijos ella sola

brink [brɪŋk] n borde; **on the ~ of doing sth** a punto de hacer algo; **she was on the ~ of tears** estaba al borde de las lágrimas

brisk [brɪsk] adj (walk) enérgico, vigoroso; (speedy) rápido; (wind) fresco; (trade) activo, animado; (abrupt) brusco; **business is ~** el negocio va bien or a paso activo

bristle ['brɪsl] n cerda ▷ vi erizarse

Britain ['brɪtən] n (also: **Great Britain**) Gran Bretaña

British ['brɪtɪʃ] adj británico; **the British** npl los británicos; **the British Isles** npl las Islas Británicas

British Rail (BR) *n* ≈ RENFE *f* (*Esp*)
British Summer Time *n hora de verano británica*
Briton ['brɪtən] *n* británico(-a)
brittle ['brɪtl] *adj* quebradizo, frágil
broach [brəʊtʃ] *vt* (*subject*) abordar
broad [brɔːd] *adj* ancho, amplio; (*accent*) cerrado
  ▷ *n* (*US col*) tía; **in ~ daylight** en pleno día; **the ~ outlines** las líneas generales
broadband ['brɔːdbænd] *n* banda ancha
broadcast ['brɔːdkɑːst] *n* emisión ▷ *vt, vi* (*pt, pp* -) (*Radio*) emitir; (*TV*) transmitir
broadcaster ['brɔːdkɑːstə'] *n* locutor(a)
broadcasting ['brɔːdkɑːstɪŋ] *n* radiodifusión, difusión
broaden ['brɔːdn] *vt* ensanchar ▷ *vi* ensancharse
broadly ['brɔːdlɪ] *adv* en general
broad-minded ['brɔːd'maɪndɪd] *adj* tolerante, liberal
broadsheet ['brɔːdʃiːt] *n* (*Brit*) periódico de gran formato (*no sensacionalista*); *see also* **quality press**
broccoli ['brɔkəlɪ] *n* brécol, bróculi
brochure ['brəʊʃjʊə'] *n* folleto
brogue [brəʊg] *n* (*accent*) acento regional; (*shoe*) (*tipo de*) zapato de cuero grueso
broil [brɔɪl] *vt* (*US*) asar a la parrilla
broke [brəʊk] *pt of* **break** ▷ *adj* (*col*) pelado, sin una perra; **to go ~** quebrar
broken ['brəʊkən] *pp of* **break** ▷ *adj* (*stick*) roto; (*fig: marriage*) deshecho; (: *promise, vow*) violado; **~ leg** pierna rota; **in ~ English** en un inglés chapurreado
broken-down ['brəʊkn'daʊn] *adj* (*car*) averiado; (*machine*) estropeado; (*house*) destartalado
broken-hearted ['brəʊkn'hɑːtɪd] *adj* con el corazón destrozado
broker ['brəʊkə'] *n* corredor(a) de bolsa
brolly ['brɔlɪ] *n* (*Brit col*) paraguas
bronchitis [brɔŋ'kaɪtɪs] *n* bronquitis
bronze [brɔnz] *n* bronce
brooch [brəʊtʃ] *n* broche
brood [bruːd] *n* camada, cría; (*children*) progenie ▷ *vi* (*hen*) empollar; **to ~ over** dar vueltas a, rumiar
broom [brum] *n* escoba; (*Bot*) retama
broomstick ['brumstɪk] *n* palo de escoba
Bros. *abbr* (*Comm:* = *Brothers*) Hnos
broth [brɔθ] *n* caldo
brothel ['brɔθl] *n* burdel
brother ['brʌðə'] *n* hermano
brotherhood ['brʌðəhud] *n* hermandad
brother-in-law ['brʌðərɪn'lɔː] *n* cuñado
brought [brɔːt] *pt, pp of* **bring**
brow [braʊ] *n* (*forehead*) frente; (*of hill*) cumbre
brown [braʊn] *adj* marrón; (*hair, eyes*) castaño; (*tanned*) moreno ▷ *n* (*colour*) marrón ▷ *vt* (*tan*) poner moreno; (*Culin*) dorar; **to go ~** (*person*) ponerse moreno; (*leaves*) dorarse
brown bread *n* pan integral
brownie ['braʊnɪ] *n* niña exploradora
brown paper *n* papel de estraza
brown sugar *n* azúcar moreno
browse [braʊz] *vi* (*animal*) pacer; (*among books*)

hojear libros; **to ~ through a book** hojear un libro
browser ['braʊzə'] *n* (*Comput*) navegador
bruise [bruːz] *n* (*on person*) cardenal, hematoma ▷ *vt* (*leg etc*) magullar; (*fig: feelings*) herir
brunch [brʌntʃ] *n* desayuno-almuerzo
brunette [bruː'net] *n* morena, morocha (*LAm*)
brunt [brʌnt] *n*: **to bear the ~ of** llevar el peso de
brush [brʌʃ] *n* cepillo, escobilla (*LAm*); (*large*) escoba; (*for painting, shaving etc*) brocha; (*artist's*) pincel; (*Bot*) maleza ▷ *vt* cepillar; (*also*: **brush past, brush against**) rozar al pasar; **to have a ~ with the police** tener un roce con la policía
  ▶ **brush aside** *vt* rechazar, no hacer caso a
  ▶ **brush up** *vt* (*knowledge*) repasar, refrescar
brushwood ['brʌʃwud] *n* (*bushes*) maleza; (*sticks*) leña
Brussels ['brʌslz] *n* Bruselas
Brussels sprout *n* col de Bruselas
brutal ['bruːtl] *adj* brutal
brutality [bruː'tælɪtɪ] *n* brutalidad
brute [bruːt] *n* bruto; (*person*) bestia ▷ *adj*: **by ~ force** por la fuerza bruta
BSc *abbr* = **Bachelor of Science**; *see also* **Bachelor's Degree**
bubble ['bʌbl] *n* burbuja; (*in paint*) ampolla ▷ *vi* burbujear, borbotar
bubble bath *n* espuma para el baño
bubble gum *n* chicle
bubbly ['bʌblɪ] *adj* (*person*) vivaracho; (*liquid*) con burbujas ▷ *n* (*col*) champán
buck [bʌk] *n* macho; (*US col*) dólar ▷ *vi* corcovear; **to pass the ~ (to sb)** echar (a algn) el muerto
  ▶ **buck up** *vi* (*cheer up*) animarse, cobrar ánimo ▷ *vt*: **to ~ one's ideas up** poner más empeño
bucket ['bʌkɪt] *n* cubo, balde (*esp LAm*) ▷ *vi*: **the rain is ~ing (down)** (*col*) está lloviendo a cántaros
Buckingham Palace ['bʌkɪŋəm-] *n* el Palacio de Buckingham
buckle ['bʌkl] *n* hebilla ▷ *vt* abrochar con hebilla ▷ *vi* torcerse, combarse
  ▶ **buckle down** *vi* poner empeño
bud [bʌd] *n* brote, yema; (*of flower*) capullo ▷ *vi* brotar, echar brotes
Buddhism ['budɪzm] *n* Budismo
budding ['bʌdɪŋ] *adj* en ciernes, en embrión
buddy ['bʌdɪ] *n* (*US*) compañero, compinche
budge [bʌdʒ] *vt* mover; (*fig*) hacer ceder ▷ *vi* moverse
budgerigar ['bʌdʒərɪgɑ:'] *n* periquito
budget ['bʌdʒɪt] *n* presupuesto ▷ *vi*: **to ~ for sth** presupuestar algo; **I'm on a tight ~** no puedo gastar mucho; **she works out her ~ every month** planea su presupuesto todos los meses
budgie ['bʌdʒɪ] *n* = **budgerigar**
buff [bʌf] *adj* (*colour*) color de ante ▷ *n* (*enthusiast*) entusiasta
buffalo ['bʌfələʊ] (*pl* - *or* -**es**) *n* (*Brit*) búfalo; (*US*: *bison*) bisonte
buffer ['bʌfə'] *n* amortiguador; (*Comput*) memoria intermedia, buffer

buffer zone *n* zona (que sirve de) colchón
buffet *n* ['bufeɪ] (*Brit: bar*) bar, cafetería; (*food*)
buffet ▷ *vt* ['bʌfɪt] (*strike*) abofetear; (*wind etc*)
golpear
buffet car *n* (*Brit Rail*) coche-restaurante
bug [bʌg] *n* (*insect*) chinche; (: *gen*) bicho,
sabandija; (*germ*) microbio, bacilo; (*spy device*)
micrófono oculto; (*Comput*) fallo, error ▷ *vt*
(*annoy*) fastidiar; (*room*) poner un micrófono
oculto en; (*phone*) pinchar; **I've got the travel
~ (*fig*)** me encanta viajar; **it really ~s me** me
fastidia *or* molesta mucho
bugle ['bjuːgl] *n* corneta, clarín
build [bɪld] *n* (*of person*) talle, tipo ▷ *vt* (*pt, pp* **built**)
[bɪlt] construir, edificar
  ▶ **build on** *vt fus* (*fig*) basar en
  ▶ **build up** *vt* (*Med*) fortalecer; (*stocks*) acumular;
  (*establish: business*) fomentar, desarrollar;
  (: *reputation*) crear(se); (*increase: production*)
  aumentar ▷ *vi* acumularse; **he has built up a
huge collection of stamps** ha ido acumulando
una gran colección de sellos; **don't ~ your
hopes up too soon** no te hagas demasiadas
ilusiones; **our debts are ~ing up** nuestras
deudas se están acumulando
builder ['bɪldə'] *n* constructor(a); (*contractor*)
contratista
building ['bɪldɪŋ] *n* (*act*) construcción; (*habitation,
offices*) edificio
building site *n* solar (*Esp*), obra (*LAm*)
building society *n* (*Brit*) sociedad de préstamo
inmobiliario
build-up ['bɪldʌp] *n* (*publicity*): **to give sb/sth a
good ~** hacer mucha propaganda de algn/algo
built [bɪlt] *pt, pp of* **build**
built-in ['bɪlt'ɪn] *adj* (*cupboard*) empotrado;
(*device*) interior, incorporado; **~ obsolescence**
caducidad programada
built-up ['bɪlt'ʌp] *adj* (*area*) urbanizado
bulb [bʌlb] *n* (*Bot*) bulbo; (*Elec*) bombilla,
bombillo (*CAm*), foco (*And, Méx*), bombita (*RP*)
Bulgaria [bʌl'gɛərɪə] *n* Bulgaria
bulge [bʌldʒ] *n* bombeo, pandeo; (*in birth rate,
sales*) alza, aumento ▷ *vi* bombearse, pandearse;
(*pocket etc*) hacer bulto
bulimia [bə'lɪmɪə] *n* bulimia
bulk [bʌlk] *n* (*mass*) bulto, volumen; (*major part*)
grueso; **in ~** (*Comm*) a granel; **the ~ of** la mayor
parte de; **to buy in ~** comprar en grandes
cantidades
bulky ['bʌlkɪ] *adj* voluminoso, abultado
bull [bul] *n* toro; (*Stock Exchange*) alcista de bolsa;
(*Rel*) bula
bulldog ['buldɔg] *n* dogo
bulldoze ['buldəuz] *vt* mover con excavadora;
I was ~d into doing it (*fig col*) me obligaron a
hacerlo
bulldozer ['buldəuzə'] *n* buldozer, excavadora
bullet ['bulɪt] *n* bala; **~ wound** balazo
bulletin ['bulɪtɪn] *n* comunicado, parte; (*journal*)
boletín
bulletin board *n* (*US*) tablón de anuncios;

(*Comput*) tablero de noticias
bulletproof ['bulɪtpruːf] *adj* a prueba de balas; **~
vest** chaleco anti-balas
bullfight ['bulfaɪt] *n* corrida de toros
bullfighter ['bulfaɪtə'] *n* torero
bullfighting ['bulfaɪtɪŋ] *n* los toros, el toreo; (*art
of bullfighting*) tauromaquia
bullion ['buljən] *n* oro *or* plata en barras
bullock ['bulək] *n* novillo
bullring ['bulrɪŋ] *n* plaza de toros
bull's-eye ['bulzaɪ] *n* blanco, diana
bullshit ['bulʃɪt] (*col!*) *excl* chorradas ▷ *n*
chorradas ▷ *vi* decir chorradas ▷ *vt*: **to ~ sb**
quedarse con algn
bully ['bulɪ] *n* valentón, matón ▷ *vt* intimidar,
tiranizar
bum [bʌm] *n* (*Brit: col: backside*) culo; (: *tramp*)
vagabundo; (*col: esp US: idler*) holgazán(-ana),
flojo(-a)
bumblebee ['bʌmblbiː] *n* abejorro
bump [bʌmp] *n* (*blow*) tope, choque; (*jolt*)
sacudida; (*noise*) choque, topetón; (*on road etc*)
bache; (*on head*) chichón ▷ *vt* (*strike*) chocar
contra, topetar ▷ *vi* dar sacudidas
  ▶ **bump into** *vt fus* chocar contra, tropezar
  con; (*person*) topar con; (*col: meet*) tropezar con,
  toparse con
bumper ['bʌmpə'] *n* (*Brit*) parachoques ▷ *adj*: **~
crop/harvest** cosecha abundante
bumper cars *npl* (*US*) autos *or* coches de choque
bumpy ['bʌmpɪ] *adj* (*road*) lleno de baches;
(*journey, flight*) agitado
bun [bʌn] *n* (*Brit: cake*) pastel; (*US: bread*) bollo; (*of
hair*) moño
bunch [bʌntʃ] *n* (*of flowers*) ramo; (*of keys*) manojo;
(*of bananas*) piña; (*of people*) grupo; (*pej*) pandilla
bundle ['bʌndl] *n* (*gen*) bulto, fardo; (*of sticks*)
haz; (*of papers*) legajo ▷ *vt* (*also*: **bundle up**) atar,
envolver; **to ~ sth/sb into** meter algo/a algn
precipitadamente en
bung [bʌŋ] *n* tapón, bitoque ▷ *vt* (*throw: also*:
bung into) arrojar; (*also*: **bung up**: *pipe, hole*)
tapar; **my nose is ~ed up** (*col*) tengo la nariz
atascada *or* taponada
bungalow ['bʌŋgələu] *n* bungalow, chalé
bungee jumping ['bʌndʒiː'dʒʌmpɪŋ] *n*
puenting, banyi
bungle ['bʌŋgl] *vt* chapucear
bunion ['bʌnjən] *n* juanete
bunk [bʌŋk] *n* litera; **~ beds** *npl* literas
bunker ['bʌŋkə'] *n* (*coal store*) carbonera; (*Mil*)
refugio; (*Golf*) bunker
bunk off *vi*: **to ~ school** (*Brit col*) pirarse las clases;
I'll ~ at 3 this afternoon me voy a pirar a las 3
esta tarde
bunny ['bʌnɪ] *n* (*also*: **bunny rabbit**) conejito
bunting ['bʌntɪŋ] *n* empavesada, banderas
buoy [bɔɪ] *n* boya
  ▶ **buoy up** *vt* mantener a flote; (*fig*) animar
buoyant ['bɔɪənt] *adj* (*carefree*) boyante,
optimista; (*Comm: market, prices etc*) sostenido
BUPA ['buːpə] *n abbr* (= *British United Provident*

Association) seguro médico privado

burden ['bəːdn] *n* carga ▷ *vt* cargar; **to be a ~ to sb** ser una carga para algn

bureau ['bjuərəu] (*pl* -**x**) *n* (*Brit: writing desk*) escritorio, buró; (*US: chest of drawers*) cómoda; (*office*) oficina, agencia

bureaucracy [bjuə'rɔkrəsɪ] *n* burocracia

bureaucrat ['bjuərəkræt] *n* burócrata

bureaucratic [bjuərə'krætɪk] *adj* burocrático

burger ['bəːgəʳ] *n* hamburguesa

burglar ['bəːgləʳ] *n* ladrón(-ona)

burglar alarm *n* alarma contra robo

burglarize ['bəːgləraɪz] *vt* (*US*) robar (con allanamiento)

burglary ['bəːglərɪ] *n* robo con allanamiento *or* fractura, robo de una casa

burgle ['bəːgl] *vt* robar (con allanamiento)

Burgundy ['bəːgəndɪ] *n* Borgoña

burial ['bɛrɪəl] *n* entierro

burly ['bəːlɪ] *adj* fornido, membrudo

Burma ['bəːmə] *n* Birmania; *see also* **Myanmar**

burn [bəːn] *vb* (*pt, pp* -**ed** *or* -**t**) ▷ *vt* quemar; (*house*) incendiar ▷ *vi* quemarse, arder; incendiarse; (*sting*) escocer ▷ *n* (*Med*) quemadura; **the cigarette ~t a hole in her dress** se ha quemado el vestido con el cigarrillo; **I've ~t myself!** ¡me he quemado!

  ▶ **burn down** *vt* incendiar

  ▶ **burn out** *vt* (*writer etc*): **to ~ o.s. out** agotarse

burner ['bəːnəʳ] *n* (*gas*) quemador

burning ['bəːnɪŋ] *adj* ardiente; (*building, forest*) en llamas

burp [bəːp] (*col*) *n* eructo ▷ *vi* eructar

burrow ['bʌrəu] *n* madriguera ▷ *vt* hacer una madriguera

bursary ['bəːsərɪ] *n* (*Brit*) beca

burst [bəːst] *vb* (*pt, pp* -) ▷ *vt* (*balloon, pipe*) reventar; (*banks etc*) romper ▷ *vi* reventarse; romperse; (*tyre*) pincharse; (*bomb*) estallar ▷ *n* (*explosion*) estallido; (*also*: **burst pipe**) reventón; **the river has ~ its banks** el río se ha desbordado; **the balloon ~** el globo se reventó; **to ~ into flames** estallar en llamas; **to ~ out laughing** soltar la carcajada; **to ~ into tears** deshacerse en lágrimas; **to be ~ing with** reventar de; **to ~ open** *vi* abrirse de golpe; **a ~ of energy** una explosión de energía; **a ~ of applause** una salva de aplausos; **a ~ of speed** una escapada

  ▶ **burst into** *vt fus* (*room etc*) irrumpir en

bury ['bɛrɪ] *vt* enterrar; (*body*) enterrar, sepultar; **to ~ the hatchet** enterrar el hacha (de guerra), echar pelillos a la mar

bus [bʌs] *n* (*local*) autobús, camión (*CAm, Méx*); colectivo (*Arg*), guagua (*Cuba, Canarias*); (*long-distance*) autobús, autocar (*Esp*), micro (*Arg*)

bus boy *n* (*US*) ayudante de camarero

bush [buʃ] *n* arbusto; (*scrub land*) monte bajo; **to beat about the ~** andar(se) con rodeos

bushed [buʃt] *adj* (*col*) molido

bush fire *n* incendio en el monte

bushy ['buʃɪ] *adj* (*beard, eyebrows*) poblado; (*hair*)

espeso; (*fur*) tupido

busily ['bɪzɪlɪ] *adv* afanosamente

business ['bɪznɪs] *n* (*matter, affair*) asunto; (*trading*) comercio, negocios; (*firm*) empresa, casa; (*occupation*) oficio; **it's none of my ~** no es asunto mío; **it's my ~ to ...** me toca *or* corresponde ...; **to be away on ~** estar en viaje de negocios; **I'm here on ~** estoy aquí por mi trabajo; **to do ~ with sb** hacer negocios con algn; **he's got his own ~** tiene su propio negocio; **he's in the insurance ~** se dedica a los seguros; **he means ~** habla en serio

business card *n* tarjeta de visita

businesslike ['bɪznɪslaɪk] *adj* (*company*) serio; (*person*) eficiente

businessman ['bɪznɪsmən] *n* hombre de negocios

business trip *n* viaje de negocios

businesswoman ['bɪznɪswumən] *n* mujer de negocios

busker ['bʌskəʳ] *n* (*Brit*) músico(-a) ambulante

bus route *n* recorrido del autobús

bus station *n* estación *or* terminal de autobuses

bus-stop ['bʌsstɔp] *n* parada de autobús, paradero (*LAm*)

bust [bʌst] *n* (*Anat*) pecho ▷ *adj* (*col: broken*) roto, estropeado ▷ *vt* (*col: Police: arrest*) detener; **to go ~** quebrar

bustle ['bʌsl] *n* bullicio, movimiento ▷ *vi* menearse, apresurarse

bustling ['bʌslɪŋ] *adj* (*town*) animado, bullicioso

bust-up ['bʌstʌp] *n* (*col*) riña

busy ['bɪzɪ] *adj* ocupado, atareado; (*shop, street*) concurrido, animado ▷ *vt*: **to ~ o.s. with** ocuparse en; **he's a ~ man** (*normally*) es un hombre muy ocupado; (*temporarily*) está muy ocupado; **the line's ~** (*esp US*) está comunicando

busybody ['bɪzɪbɔdɪ] *n* entrometido(-a)

busy signal *n* (*US Tel*) señal de comunicado

but [bʌt] *conj* **1** pero; **he's not very bright, ~ he's hard-working** no es muy inteligente, pero es trabajador

2 (*in direct contradiction*) sino; **he's not English ~ French** no es inglés sino francés; **he didn't sing ~ he shouted** no cantó sino que gritó

3 (*showing disagreement, surprise etc*): **~ that's far too expensive!** ¡pero eso es carísimo!; **~ it does work!** ¡(pero) sí que funciona!

▷ *prep* (*apart from, except*) menos, salvo; **they won all ~ two of their matches** ganaron todos los partidos menos dos; **we've had nothing ~ trouble** no hemos tenido más que problemas; **no-one ~ him can do it** nadie más que él puede hacerlo; **the last ~ one** el penúltimo; **who ~ a lunatic would do such a thing?** ¡sólo un loco haría una cosa así!; **~ for you/your help** si no fuera por ti/tu ayuda; **anything ~ that** cualquier cosa menos eso

▷ *adv* (*just, only*): **she's ~ a child** no es más que una niña; **had I ~ known** si lo hubiera sabido; **I can ~ try** al menos lo puedo intentar; **it's all ~ finished** está casi acabado

butch [butʃ] *adj* (*pej: woman*) machirula, marimacho; (*col: man*) muy macho

butcher ['butʃəʳ] *n* carnicero(-a) ▷ *vt* hacer una carnicería con; (*cattle etc for meat*) matar; **~'s (shop)** carnicería

butler ['bʌtləʳ] *n* mayordomo

butt [bʌt] *n* (*cask*) tonel; (*for rain*) tina; (*thick end*) cabo, extremo; (*of gun*) culata; (*of cigarette*) colilla; (*Brit fig: target*) blanco; (*US col: backside*) culo ▷ *vt* dar cabezadas contra, topetar
 ▸ **butt in** *vi* (*interrupt*) interrumpir

butter ['bʌtəʳ] *n* mantequilla, manteca (*LAm*) ▷ *vt* untar con mantequilla

buttercup ['bʌtəkʌp] *n* ranúnculo

butterfly ['bʌtəflaɪ] *n* mariposa; (*Swimming: also:* **butterfly stroke**) (braza de) mariposa

buttocks ['bʌtəks] *npl* nalgas

button ['bʌtn] *n* botón ▷ *vt* (*also:* **button up**) abotonar, abrochar ▷ *vi* abrocharse

buttress ['bʌtrɪs] *n* contrafuerte; (*fig*) apoyo, sostén

buxom ['bʌksəm] *adj* (*woman*) frescachona, rolliza

buy [baɪ] *vb* (*pt, pp* **bought**) ▷ *vt* comprar ▷ *n* compra; **to ~ sb sth** comprarle algo a algn; **he bought me an ice cream** me compró un helado; **to ~ sb a drink** invitar a algn a una copa; **to ~ sth from sb** comprarle algo a algn; **I bought a watch from him** le compré un reloj; **a good/bad ~** una buena/mala compra
 ▸ **buy back** *vt* volver a comprar
 ▸ **buy in** *vt* proveerse *or* abastecerse de
 ▸ **buy into** *vt fus* comprar acciones en
 ▸ **buy off** *vt* (*col: bribe*) sobornar
 ▸ **buy out** *vt* (*partner*) comprar la parte de

buyer ['baɪəʳ] *n* comprador(a); **~'s market** mercado favorable al comprador

buy-out ['baɪaut] *n* (*Comm*) adquisición de (la totalidad de) las acciones

buzz [bʌz] *n* zumbido; (*col: phone call*) llamada (telefónica) ▷ *vt* (*call on intercom*) llamar; (*with buzzer*) hacer sonar; (*Aviat: plane, building*) pasar rozando ▷ *vi* zumbar; **my head is ~ing** me zumba la cabeza
 ▸ **buzz off** *vi* (*Brit col*) largarse

buzzer ['bʌzəʳ] *n* timbre

buzz word *n* palabra que está de moda

by [baɪ] *prep* **1** (*referring to cause, agent*) por; de; **abandoned by his mother** abandonado por su madre; **surrounded by enemies** rodeado de enemigos; **a painting by Picasso** un cuadro de Picasso

2 (*referring to method, manner, means*): **by bus/car/train** en autobús/coche/tren; **to pay by cheque** pagar con cheque(s); **by moonlight/candlelight** a la luz de la luna/una vela; **by saving hard, he ...** ahorrando, ...

3 (*via, through*) por; **we came by Dover** vinimos por Dover

4 (*close to, past*): **the house by the river** la casa junto al río; **she rushed by me** pasó a mi lado como una exhalación; **I go by the post office every day** paso por delante de Correos todos los días

5 (*time: not later than*) para; (*: during*): **by daylight** de día; **by 4 o'clock** para las 4; **by this time tomorrow** mañana a estas horas; **by the time I got here it was too late** cuando llegué ya era demasiado tarde; **it'll be ready by the time you get back** estará listo para cuando regreses

6 (*amount*): **by the metre/kilo** por metro/kilo; **paid by the hour** pagado por hora

7 (*Math, measure*): **to divide/multiply by 3** dividir/multiplicar por 3; **a room 3 metres by 4** una habitación de 3 metros por 4; **it's broader by a metre** es un metro más ancho; **the bus missed me by inches** no me pilló el autobús por un pelo

8 (*according to*) según, de acuerdo con; **it's 3 o'clock by my watch** según mi reloj, son las 3; **it's all right by me** por mí, está bien

9: **(all) by oneself** *etc* todo solo; **he did it (all) by himself** lo hizo él solo; **he was standing (all) by himself in a corner** estaba de pie solo en un rincón

10: **by the way** a propósito, por cierto; **this wasn't my idea, by the way** pues, no fue idea mía
 ▷ *adv* **1** *see* **go**; **pass** *etc*
 2: **by and by** finalmente; **they'll come back by and by** acabarán volviendo; **by and large** en líneas generales, en general

bye(-bye) ['baɪ'baɪ] *excl* adiós, hasta luego, chao (*esp LAm*)

by(e)-law ['baɪlɔ:] *n* ordenanza municipal

by-election ['baɪɪlɛkʃən] *n* (*Brit*) elección parcial

Byelorussia [bjɛləu'rʌʃə] *n* Bielorrusia

bygone ['baɪɡɔn] *adj* pasado, del pasado ▷ *n*: **let ~s be ~s** lo pasado, pasado está

bypass ['baɪpɑ:s] *n* carretera de, circunvalación; (*Med*) (operación de) by-pass ▷ *vt* evitar

by-product ['baɪprɔdʌkt] *n* subproducto, derivado

bystander ['baɪstændəʳ] *n* espectador(a)

byte [baɪt] *n* (*Comput*) byte, octeto

byword ['baɪwə:d] *n*: **to be a ~ for** ser sinónimo de

by-your-leave ['baɪjɔ:'li:v] *n*: **without so much as a ~** sin decir nada, sin dar ningún tipo de explicación

Cc

C, c [siː] n (letter) C, c; (Mus): **C** do; **C for Charlie** C de Carmen

C n (= Celsius, Centigrade) C

c abbr (= century) S.; (= circa) hacia; (US etc) = **cent(s)**

CA n abbr = **Central America**; (Brit) = **chartered accountant**; (US) = **California**

CAA n abbr (Brit: = Civil Aviation Authority) organismo de control y desarrollo de la aviación civil

cab [kæb] n taxi; (of truck) cabina

cabaret ['kæbəreɪ] n cabaret

cabbage ['kæbɪdʒ] n col, berza

cabbie, cabby ['kæbɪ] n (col) taxista

cabin ['kæbɪn] n cabaña; (on ship) camarote

cabin cruiser n yate de motor

cabinet ['kæbɪnɪt] n (Pol) consejo de ministros; (furniture) armario; (also: **display cabinet**) vitrina

cable ['keɪbl] n cable ▷ vt cablegrafiar

cable-car ['keɪblkɑːʳ] n teleférico

cable television n televisión por cable

cache [kæʃ] n (of drugs) alijo; (of arms) zulo

cackle ['kækl] vi cacarear

cactus ['kæktəs] (pl **cacti**) n cacto

caddie, caddy ['kædɪ] n (Golf) cadi

cadet [kə'dɛt] n (Mil) cadete; **police ~** cadete de policía

cadge [kædʒ] vt gorronear

Caesarean, (US) Cesarean [siː'zɛərɪən] adj: **~ (section)** cesárea

café ['kæfeɪ] n café

cafeteria [kæfɪ'tɪərɪə] n cafetería (con autoservicio para comer)

caffein(e) ['kæfiːn] n cafeína

cage [keɪdʒ] n jaula ▷ vt enjaular

cagey ['keɪdʒɪ] adj (col) cauteloso, reservado

cagoule [kə'guːl] n canguro

cahoots [kə'huːts] n: **to be in ~ (with sb)** estar conchabado (con algn)

cajole [kə'dʒəʊl] vt engatusar

cake [keɪk] n pastel; (of soap) pastilla; **he wants to have his ~ and eat it** (fig) quiere estar en misa y repicando; **it's a piece of ~** (col) es pan comido

caked [keɪkt] adj: **~ with** cubierto de

calamity [kə'læmɪtɪ] n calamidad

calcium ['kælsɪəm] n calcio

calculate ['kælkjuleɪt] vt (estimate: chances, effect) calcular

▸ **calculate on** vt fus: **to ~ on sth/on doing sth** contar con algo/con hacer algo

calculation [kælkju'leɪʃən] n cálculo, cómputo

calculator ['kælkjuleɪtəʳ] n calculadora

calculus ['kælkjuləs] n cálculo

calendar ['kæləndəʳ] n calendario; **~ month/ year** n mes/año civil

calf [kɑːf] (pl **calves**) [kɑːf, kɑːvz] n (of cow) ternero, becerro; (of other animals) cría; (also: **calfskin**) piel de becerro; (Anat) pantorrilla, canilla (LAm)

caliber ['kælɪbəʳ] n (US) = **calibre**

calibre, (US) caliber ['kælɪbəʳ] n calibre

call [kɔːl] vt (gen, also Tel) llamar; (announce: flight) anunciar; (meeting, strike) convocar ▷ vi (shout) llamar; (telephone) llamar (por teléfono), telefonear; (visit: also: **call in, call round**) hacer una visita ▷ n (shout, Tel) llamada, llamado (LAm); (of bird) reclamo; (appeal) llamamiento, llamado (LAm); (summons: for flight etc) llamada; (fig: lure) llamada; **we ~ed the police** llamamos a la policía; **to be ~ed** (person, object) llamarse; **he's ~ed Fluffy** se llama Fluffy; **what's she ~ed?** ¿cómo se llama?; **to ~ sb names** poner verde a algn; **let's ~ it a day** (col) ¡dejémoslo!, ¡ya está bien!; **I'll tell him you ~ed** le diré que has llamado; **who is ~ing?** ¿de parte de quién?; **London ~ing** (Radio) aquí Londres; **to be on ~** (nurse, doctor etc) estar de guardia; **please give me a ~ at 7** despiérteme or llámeme a las 7, por favor; **long-distance ~** conferencia (interurbana); **to make a ~** llamar por teléfono; **port of ~** puerto de escala; **to pay a ~ on sb** pasarse a ver a algn; **there's not much ~ for these items** estos artículos no tienen mucha demanda

▸ **call at** vt fus (ship) hacer escala en; (train) parar en

▸ **call back** vi (return) volver; (Tel) volver a llamar; **can I ~ you back?** ¿puedo llamarte más tarde?

▸ **call for** vt fus (demand) pedir, exigir; (fetch) venir por; **shall I ~ for you at seven thirty?** ¿paso a recogerte a las siete y media?; **this job ~s for strong nerves** este trabajo requiere nervios de acero; **this ~s for a drink!** ¡esto hay que celebrarlo!

▸ **call in** vt (doctor, expert, police) llamar

▸ **call off** vt suspender; **the match was ~ed off**

el partido se suspendió; **the strike was ~ed off** se desconvocó la huelga

► **call on** vt fus (visit) ir a ver; (turn to) acudir a

► **call out** vi gritar ▷ vt (doctor) llamar; (police, troops) hacer intervenir

► **call up** vt (Brit: Mil) llamar a filas

callbox ['kɔːlbɒks] n (Brit) cabina telefónica

call centre n (Brit: Telec) centro de llamadas, central de llamadas

caller ['kɔːləʳ] n visita; (Tel) usuario(-a); **hold the line, ~!** ¡no cuelgue!

call girl n prostituta

call-in ['kɔːlɪn] n (US) programa de línea abierta al público

calling ['kɔːlɪŋ] n vocación; (profession) profesión

calling card n tarjeta de visita

callous ['kæləs] adj insensible, cruel

calm [kɑːm] adj tranquilo; (sea) tranquilo, en calma ▷ n calma, tranquilidad ▷ vt calmar, tranquilizar

► **calm down** vi calmarse, tranquilizarse ▷ vt calmar, tranquilizar

calmly ['kɑːmlɪ] adv tranquilamente, con calma

calmness ['kɑːmnɪs] n calma

Calor gas® ['kælə'-] n butano

calorie ['kælərɪ] n caloría; **low-~ product** producto bajo en calorías

calves [kɑːvz] npl of **calf**

camber ['kæmbəʳ] n (of road) combadura

Cambodia [kæm'bəudjə] n Camboya

camcorder ['kæmkɔːdəʳ] n videocámara

came [keɪm] pt of **come**

camel ['kæməl] n camello

camera ['kæmərə] n cámara or máquina fotográfica; (Cine, TV) cámara; (movie camera) cámara, tomavistas; **in ~** a puerta cerrada

cameraman ['kæmərəmən] n cámara

camouflage ['kæməflɑːʒ] n camuflaje ▷ vt camuflar

camp [kæmp] n campo, campamento ▷ vi acampar ▷ adj afectado, afeminado; **to go ~ing** ir de or hacer camping

campaign [kæm'peɪn] n (Mil, Pol etc) campaña ▷ vi: **to ~ (for/against)** hacer campaña (a favor de/en contra de)

campbed ['kæmpbɛd] n (Brit) cama plegable

camper ['kæmpəʳ] n campista; (vehicle) caravana

camping ['kæmpɪŋ] n camping

campsite ['kæmpsaɪt] n camping

campus ['kæmpəs] n campus

can [kæn] aux vb see next headword, n (of oil, water) bidón; (tin) lata, bote ▷ vt enlatar; (preserve) conservar en lata; **a ~ of beer** una lata or un bote de cerveza; **to carry the ~** (col) pagar el pato

can (negative **-not, -'t**, conditional and pt **could**) aux vb

1 (be able to) poder; **you ~ do it if you try** puedes hacerlo si lo intentas; **I ~'t see you** (not translated) no te veo; **~ you hear me?** (not translated) ¿me oyes?

2 (know how to) saber; **I ~ swim/play tennis/ drive** sé nadar/jugar al tenis/conducir; **~ you speak French?** ¿hablas or sabes hablar francés?

3 (may) poder; **~ I use your phone?** ¿me dejas or puedo usar tu teléfono?; **could I have a word with you?** ¿podría hablar contigo un momento?

4 (expressing disbelief, puzzlement etc): **it ~'t be true!** ¡no puede ser (verdad)!; **what CAN he want?** ¿qué querrá?

5 (expressing possibility, suggestion etc): **he could be in the library** podría estar en la biblioteca; **she could have been delayed** puede que se haya retrasado

6 (expressing occasional state): **she ~ be very annoying** a veces te pone negro; **it ~ get very cold here** aquí puede llegar a hacer mucho frío

Canada ['kænədə] n Canadá

Canadian [kə'neɪdɪən] adj, n canadiense

canal [kə'næl] n canal

canary [kə'nɛərɪ] n canario

Canary Islands, Canaries [kə'nɛərɪz] npl las (Islas) Canarias

cancel ['kænsəl] vt cancelar; (train) suprimir; (appointment, cheque) anular; (cross out) tachar

► **cancel out** vt (Math) anular; (fig) contrarrestar; **they ~ each other out** se anulan mutuamente

cancellation [kænsə'leɪʃən] n cancelación; supresión

cancer ['kænsəʳ] n cáncer; **C~** (Astro) Cáncer

candid ['kændɪd] adj franco, abierto

candidate ['kændɪdeɪt] n candidato(-a)

candle ['kændl] n vela; (in church) cirio

candlelight ['kændllaɪt] n: **by ~** a la luz de una vela

candlestick ['kændlstɪk] n (also: **candle holder**: single) candelero; (: low) palmatoria; (bigger, ornate) candelabro

candour, (US) **candor** ['kændəʳ] n franqueza

candy ['kændɪ] n azúcar cande; (US) caramelo ▷ vt (fruit) escarchar

candy-floss ['kændɪflɒs] n (Brit) algodón (azucarado)

cane [keɪn] n (Bot) caña; (for baskets, chairs etc) mimbre; (stick) vara, palmeta; (for walking) bastón ▷ vt (Brit Scol) castigar (con palmeta); **~ liquor** caña

canister ['kænɪstəʳ] n bote

cannabis ['kænəbɪs] n canabis

canned [kænd] adj en lata, de lata; (col: music) grabado; (: drunk) mamado

cannibal ['kænɪbəl] n caníbal, antropófago(-a)

cannon ['kænən] (pl ~ or **-s**) n cañón

cannot ['kænɔt] = **can not**

canoe [kə'nuː] n canoa; (Sport) piragua

canoeing [kə'nuːɪŋ] n (Sport) piragüismo

canon ['kænən] n (clergyman) canónigo; (standard) canon

canonize ['kænənaɪz] vt canonizar

can opener n abrelatas

canopy ['kænəpɪ] n dosel, toldo

can't [kænt] = **can not**

cantankerous [kæn'tæŋkərəs] adj arisco, malhumorado

canteen [kæn'tiːn] n (eating place) comedor; (Brit:

of cutlery) juego

canter ['kæntər] *n* medio galope ▷ *vi* ir a medio galope

canvas ['kænvəs] *n* (*material*) lona; (*painting*) lienzo; (*Naut*) velamen; **under ~** (*camping*) en tienda de campaña

canvass ['kænvəs] *vt* (*Pol: district*) hacer campaña (puerta a puerta) en; (: *person*) hacer campaña (puerta a puerta) a favor de; (*Comm: district*) sondear el mercado en; (: *citizens, opinions*) sondear

canyon ['kænjən] *n* cañón

cap [kæp] *n* (*hat*) gorra; (*for swimming*) gorro; (*of pen*) capuchón; (*of bottle*) tapón; (: *metal*) chapa; (*contraceptive*) diafragma ▷ *vt* (*outdo*) superar; (*Brit Sport*) seleccionar (para el equipo nacional); **and to ~ it all, he ...** y para colmo, él ...

capability [keɪpə'bɪlɪtɪ] *n* capacidad

capable ['keɪpəbl] *adj* capaz

capacity [kə'pæsɪtɪ] *n* capacidad; (*position*) calidad; **filled to ~** lleno a reventar; **this work is beyond my ~** este trabajo es superior a mí; **in an advisory ~** como asesor

cape [keɪp] *n* capa; (*Geo*) cabo

caper ['keɪpər] *n* (*Culin: also*: **capers**) alcaparra; (*prank*) travesura

capital ['kæpɪtl] *n* (*also*: **capital city**) capital; (*money*) capital; (*also*: **capital letter**) mayúscula

capital gains tax *n* impuesto sobre la plusvalía

capitalism ['kæpɪtəlɪzəm] *n* capitalismo

capitalist ['kæpɪtəlɪst] *adj, n* capitalista

capitalize ['kæpɪtəlaɪz] *vt* (*Comm: provide with capital*) capitalizar
  ▸ **capitalize on** *vt fus* (*fig*) sacar provecho de, aprovechar

capital punishment *n* pena de muerte

Capitol ['kæpɪtl] *n*: **the ~** el Capitolio

capitulate [kə'pɪtjuleɪt] *vi* capitular, rendirse

Capricorn ['kæprɪkɔːn] *n* Capricornio

caps [kæps] *abbr* (= *capital letters*) may

capsize [kæp'saɪz] *vt* volcar, hacer zozobrar ▷ *vi* volcarse, zozobrar

capsule ['kæpsjuːl] *n* cápsula

Capt. *abbr* = **Captain**

captain ['kæptɪn] *n* capitán ▷ *vt* capitanear, ser el capitán de

caption ['kæpʃən] *n* (*heading*) título; (*to picture*) leyenda, pie

captivate ['kæptɪveɪt] *vt* cautivar, encantar

captive ['kæptɪv] *adj, n* cautivo(-a)

captivity [kæp'tɪvɪtɪ] *n* cautiverio

captor ['kæptər] *n* captor(a)

capture ['kæptʃər] *vt* capturar; (*place*) tomar; (*attention*) captar, llamar ▷ *n* captura; toma; (*data capture*) formulación de datos

car [kɑːr] *n* coche, carro (*LAm*), automóvil, auto (*CS*); (*US Rail*) vagón; **by ~** en coche

carafe [kə'ræf] *n* garrafa

caramel ['kærəməl] *n* caramelo

carat ['kærət] *n* quilate; **18-~ gold** oro de 18 quilates

caravan ['kærəvæn] *n* (*Brit*) caravana, remolque;

(of camels) caravana

caravan site *n* (*Brit*) camping para caravanas

carbohydrates [kɑːbəu'haɪdreɪts] *npl* (*foods*) hidratos de carbono

car bomb *n* coche-bomba

carbon ['kɑːbən] *n* carbono

carbon copy *n* copia al carbón

carbon dioxide *n* dióxido de carbono, anhídrido carbónico

carbon monoxide *n* monóxido de carbono

carbon paper *n* papel carbón

car boot sale *n* mercadillo (*de objetos usados expuestos en el maletero del coche*)

carburettor, (*US*) **carburetor** [kɑːbju'retər] *n* carburador

card [kɑːd] *n* (*thin cardboard*) cartulina; (*playing card*) carta, naipe; (*visiting card, greetings card etc*) tarjeta; (*index card*) ficha; **membership ~** carnet; **to play ~s** jugar a las cartas *or* los naipes

cardboard ['kɑːdbɔːd] *n* cartón, cartulina

cardboard city *n* zona de marginados sin hogar (*que se refugian entre cartones*)

card game *n* juego de naipes *or* cartas

cardiac ['kɑːdɪæk] *adj* cardíaco

cardigan ['kɑːdɪgən] *n* chaqueta (de punto), rebeca

cardinal ['kɑːdɪnl] *adj* cardinal ▷ *n* cardenal

cardinal number *n* número cardinal

card index *n* fichero

cardphone ['kɑːdfəun] *n* cabina que funciona con tarjetas telefónicas

care [keər] *n* cuidado; (*worry*) preocupación; (*charge*) cargo, custodia ▷ *vi*: **to ~ about** preocuparse por; **~ of** (*c/o*) en casa de, al cuidado de; (*on letter*) para (entregar a); **in sb's ~** a cargo de algn; **the child has been taken into ~** pusieron al niño bajo custodia del gobierno; **"handle with ~"** "¡frágil!"; **take ~!** (*be careful!*) ¡ten cuidado!; **take ~!** (*look after yourself!*) ¡cuídate!; **to take ~ to** cuidarse de, tener cuidado de; **to take ~ of** *vt* cuidar; (*details, arrangements*) encargarse de; **I take ~ of the children on Saturdays** yo cuido a los niños los sábados; **I don't ~** no me importa; **I couldn't ~ less** me trae sin cuidado; **who ~s?** ¿y a quién le importa?
  ▸ **care for** *vt fus* (*look after*) cuidar; (*like*): **he wanted me to know he still ~d for me** quería que supiera que todavía se preocupaba por mí; **I don't ~ for coffee** no me gusta el café

career [kə'rɪər] *n* carrera (profesional); (*occupation*) profesión ▷ *vi* (*also*: **career along**) correr a toda velocidad

carefree ['keəfriː] *adj* despreocupado

careful ['keəful] *adj* cuidadoso; (*cautious*) cauteloso; **(be) ~!** ¡ten cuidado!; **he's very ~ with his money** mira mucho el dinero; (*pej*) es muy tacaño

carefully ['keəfəlɪ] *adv* con cuidado, cuidadosamente

careless ['keəlɪs] *adj* descuidado; (*heedless*) poco atento

carelessness ['kɛəlɪsnɪs] n descuido, falta de atención

carer ['kɛərər] (Brit) n persona que cuida de enfermos, ancianos o disminuidos

caress [kə'rɛs] n caricia ▷ vt acariciar

caretaker ['kɛəteɪkər] n portero(-a), conserje

car-ferry ['kɑːfɛrɪ] n transbordador para coches

cargo ['kɑːgəu] (pl -es) n cargamento, carga

car hire n alquiler de coches

Caribbean [kærɪ'biːən] adj caribe, caribeño; **the ~ (Sea)** el (Mar) Caribe

caricature ['kærɪkətjuər] n caricatura

caring ['kɛərɪŋ] adj humanitario

carnal ['kɑːnl] adj carnal

carnation [kɑː'neɪʃən] n clavel

carnival ['kɑːnɪvəl] n carnaval; (US) parque de atracciones

carnivore ['kɑːnɪvɔːr] n carnívoro(-a)

carnivorous [kɑː'nɪvrəs] adj carnívoro

carol ['kærəl] n: **(Christmas)** ~ villancico

carp [kɑːp] n (fish) carpa
  ▶ **carp at** or **about** vt fus sacar faltas de

car park n (Brit) aparcamiento, parking, playa de estacionamiento (LAm)

carpenter ['kɑːpɪntər] n carpintero

carpentry ['kɑːpɪntrɪ] n carpintería

carpet ['kɑːpɪt] n alfombra ▷ vt alfombrar; **fitted ~** moqueta

carpet bombing n bombardeo de arrasamiento

carpet slippers npl zapatillas

carpet sweeper [-'swiːpər] n cepillo mecánico

car phone n teléfono de coche

carriage ['kærɪdʒ] n coche; (Brit Rail) vagón; (for goods) transporte; (of typewriter) carro; (bearing) porte; **~ forward** porte debido; **~ free** franco de porte; **~ paid** porte pagado; **~ inwards/outwards** gastos de transporte a cargo del comprador/vendedor

carriageway ['kærɪdʒweɪ] n (Brit: part of road) calzada; **dual ~** autovía

carrier ['kærɪər] n transportista; (company) empresa de transportes; (Med) portador(a)

carrier bag n (Brit) bolsa de papel or plástico

carrot ['kærət] n zanahoria

carry ['kærɪ] vt (person) llevar; (transport) transportar; (a motion, bill) aprobar; (involve: responsibilities etc) entrañar, conllevar; (Comm: stock) tener en existencia; (interest) llevar; (Math: figure) llevarse ▷ vi (sound) oírse; **I'll ~ your bag** te llevo la bolsa; **to get carried away** (fig) entusiasmarse; **this loan carries 10% interest** este empréstito devenga un interés del 10%
  ▶ **carry forward** vt (Math, Comm) pasar a la página/columna siguiente
  ▶ **carry on** vi (continue) seguir, continuar; (fam: complain) montar el número ▷ vt seguir, continuar; **she carried on talking** siguió hablando; **~ on!** ¡sigue!
  ▶ **carry out** vt (orders) cumplir; (investigation) llevar a cabo, realizar

carrycot ['kærɪkɔt] n (Brit) cuna portátil, capazo

carry-on ['kærɪ'ɔn] n (col) follón

cart [kɑːt] n carro, carreta ▷ vt cargar con

carton ['kɑːtən] n caja (de cartón); (of cigarettes) cartón

cartoon [kɑː'tuːn] n (Press) chiste; (comic strip) historieta, tira cómica; (film) dibujos animados

cartoonist [kɑː'tuːnɪst] n humorista gráfico

cartridge ['kɑːtrɪdʒ] n cartucho

cartwheel ['kɑːtwiːl] n: **to turn a ~** dar una voltereta lateral

carve [kɑːv] vt (meat) trinchar; (wood) tallar; (stone) cincelar, esculpir; (on tree) grabar
  ▶ **carve up** vt dividir, repartir; (meat) trinchar

carving ['kɑːvɪŋ] n (in wood etc) escultura, talla

carving knife n trinchante

car wash n túnel de lavado

case [keɪs] n (container) caja; (situation, Med) caso; (for jewels etc) estuche; (Law) causa, proceso; (Brit: also: **suitcase**) maleta; **I've packed my ~** he hecho mi maleta; **lower/upper ~** (Typ) caja baja/alta; **in ~ it rains** por si llueve; **in ~ of** en caso de; **in any ~** en todo caso; **in some ~s** en algunos casos; **just in ~** por si acaso; **to have a good ~** tener buenas razones; **there's a strong ~ for reform** hay razones sólidas para exigir una reforma

cash [kæʃ] n (dinero) efectivo; (col: money) dinero ▷ vt cobrar, hacer efectivo; **to pay (in) ~** pagar al contado; **~ on delivery (COD)** entrega contra reembolso; **~ with order** paga al hacer el pedido; **to be short of ~** estar pelado, estar sin blanca
  ▶ **cash in** vt (insurance policy etc) cobrar ▷ vi: **to ~ in on sth** sacar partido or aprovecharse de algo

cash and carry n cash and carry, autoservicio mayorista

cashbook ['kæʃbuk] n libro de caja

cash card n (Brit) tarjeta de(l) cajero (automático)

cash desk n (Brit) caja

cash dispenser n (Brit) cajero automático

cashew [kæ'ʃuː] n (also: **cashew nut**) anacardo

cash flow n flujo de fondos, cash-flow, movimiento de efectivo

cashier [kæ'ʃɪər] n cajero(-a) ▷ vt (Mil) destituir, expulsar

cashmere ['kæʃmɪər] n cachemir, cachemira

cash register n caja

casing ['keɪsɪŋ] n revestimiento

casino [kə'siːnəu] n casino

casket ['kɑːskɪt] n cofre, estuche; (US: coffin) ataúd

casserole ['kæsərəul] n (food, pot) cazuela

cassette [kæ'sɛt] n cas(s)et(t)e

cassette player, cassette recorder n cas(s)et(t)e

cast [kɑːst] vb (pt, pp ~) ▷ vt (throw) echar, arrojar, lanzar; (skin) mudar, perder; (metal) fundir; (Theat): **to ~ sb as Othello** dar a algn el papel de Otelo ▷ n (Theat) reparto; (mould) forma, molde; (also: **plaster cast**) vaciado; **to ~ loose** soltar; **to ~ one's vote** votar
  ▶ **cast aside** vt (reject) descartar, desechar
  ▶ **cast away** vt desechar

▶ **cast down** vt derribar

▶ **cast off** vi (Naut) soltar amarras; (Knitting) cerrar los puntos ▷ vt (Knitting) cerrar; **to ~ sb off** abandonar a algn, desentenderse de algn

▶ **cast on** vt (Knitting) montar

castaway ['kɑːstəwəɪ] n náufrago(-a)

caster sugar ['kɑːstəʳ-] n (Brit) azúcar en polvo

Castile [kæs'tiːl] n Castilla

Castilian [kæs'tɪlɪən] adj, n castellano(-a) ▷ n (Ling) castellano

casting vote ['kɑːstɪŋ-] n (Brit) voto decisivo

cast iron n hierro fundido or colado ▷ adj (fig: alibi) irrebatible; (will) férreo

castle ['kɑːsl] n castillo; (Chess) torre

castor ['kɑːstəʳ] n (wheel) ruedecilla

castor oil n aceite de ricino

castrate [kæs'treɪt] vt castrar

casual ['kæʒjul] adj (by chance) fortuito; (irregular: work etc) eventual, temporero; (unconcerned) despreocupado; (informal: clothes) de sport

casually ['kæʒjulɪ] adv por casualidad; de manera despreocupada

casualty ['kæʒjultɪ] (Brit) n víctima, herido; (dead) muerto; (Mil) baja; **heavy casualties** numerosas bajas

casualty ward n urgencias

cat [kæt] n gato

Catalan ['kætəlæn] adj, n catalán(-ana)

catalogue, (US) **catalog** ['kætəlɔg] n catálogo ▷ vt catalogar

Catalonia [kætə'ləunɪə] n Cataluña

catalyst ['kætəlɪst] n catalizador

catalytic converter [kætə'lɪtɪkkən'vəːtəʳ] n catalizador

catapult ['kætəpʌlt] n tirachinas

cataract ['kætərækt] n (Med) cataratas

catarrh [kə'tɑːʳ] n catarro

catastrophe [kə'tæstrəfɪ] n catástrofe

catch [kætʃ] vb (pt, pp **caught**) ▷ vt coger (Esp), agarrar (LAm); (train, bus) coger (Esp), tomar (LAm); (arrest) atrapar, coger (Esp); (grasp) asir; (breath) recobrar; (person: by surprise) pillar; (attract: attention) captar; (Med) contagiarse de; (also: **catch up**) alcanzar ▷ vi (fire) encenderse; (in branches etc) engancharse ▷ n (fish etc) captura; (act of catching) cogida; (trick) trampa; (of lock) pestillo; **my cat ~es birds** mi gato caza pájaros; **he caught her arm** la agarró del brazo; **he caught her stealing** la pilló robando; **I didn't ~ his name** no me enteré de su nombre; **to ~ a cold** resfriarse; **to ~ fire** prenderse; (house) incendiarse; **to ~ sight of** divisar

▶ **catch on** vi (understand) caer en la cuenta; (grow popular) tener éxito, cuajar

▶ **catch out** vt (fig: with trick question) hundir

▶ **catch up** vt: **she caught me up** me alcanzó ▷ vi (fig) ponerse al día; **I've got to ~ up on my work** tengo que ponerme al día con el trabajo

catching ['kætʃɪŋ] adj (Med) contagioso

catchment area ['kætʃmənt-] n (Brit) zona de captación

catch phrase n frase de moda

catchy ['kætʃɪ] adj (tune) pegadizo

categoric(al) [kætɪ'gɔrɪk(əl)] adj categórico, terminante

category ['kætɪgərɪ] n categoría

cater ['keɪtəʳ] vi: **to ~ for** (Brit) abastecer a; (needs) atender a; (consumers) proveer a

caterer ['keɪtərəʳ] n abastecedor(a), proveedor(a)

catering ['keɪtərɪŋ] n (trade) hostelería

caterpillar ['kætəpɪləʳ] n oruga

caterpillar track n rodado de oruga

cat flap n gatera

cathedral [kə'θiːdrəl] n catedral

catholic ['kæθəlɪk] adj católico; **C~** adj, n (Rel) católico(-a)

cat's-eye ['kætsaɪ] n (Brit Aut) catafaro

cattle ['kætl] npl ganado

catty ['kætɪ] adj malicioso

catwalk ['kætwɔːk] n pasarela

caucus ['kɔːkəs] n (Pol: local committee) comité local; (: US: to elect candidates) comité electoral; (: group) camarilla política

caught [kɔːt] pt, pp of **catch**

cauliflower ['kɒlɪflauəʳ] n coliflor

cause [kɔːz] n causa; (reason) motivo, razón ▷ vt causar; (provoke) provocar; **to ~ sb to do sth** hacer que algn haga algo

caution ['kɔːʃən] n cautela, prudencia; (warning) advertencia, amonestación ▷ vt amonestar

cautious ['kɔːʃəs] adj cauteloso, prudente, precavido

cavalry ['kævəlrɪ] n caballería

cave [keɪv] n cueva, caverna ▷ vi: **to go caving** ir en una expedición espeleológica

▶ **cave in** vi (roof etc) derrumbarse, hundirse

caveman ['keɪvmæn] n cavernícola

caviar(e) ['kævɪɑːʳ] n caviar

cavity ['kævɪtɪ] n hueco, cavidad

cavort [kə'vɔːt] vi hacer cabrioladas

CB n abbr (= Citizens' Band (Radio)) frecuencias de radio usadas para la comunicación privada; (Brit: = Companion of (the Order of) the Bath) título de nobleza

CBE n abbr (= Companion of (the Order of) the British Empire) título de nobleza

CBI n abbr (= Confederation of British Industry) ≈ C. E.O.E. (Esp)

CBS n abbr (US: = Columbia Broadcasting System) cadena de radio y televisión

cc abbr (= cubic centimetres) cc, cm³; (on letter etc) = **carbon copy**

CCTV n abbr = **closed-circuit television**

CD n abbr (= compact disc) CD; **CD player** reproductor de compact disc

CD-ROM n abbr (= compact disc read-only memory) CD-ROM; ~ **drive** (lector de) CD-ROM

cease [siːs] vt cesar

ceasefire ['siːsfaɪəʳ] n alto el fuego

ceaseless ['siːslɪs] adj incesante

cedar ['siːdəʳ] n cedro

ceilidh ['keɪlɪ] n baile con música y danzas tradicionales escocesas o irlandesas

ceiling ['siːlɪŋ] n techo; (fig: upper limit) límite, tope

celebrate ['sɛlɪbreɪt] vt celebrar; (have a party) festejar ▷ vi: **let's ~!** ¡vamos a celebrarlo!
celebrated ['sɛlɪbreɪtɪd] adj célebre
celebration [sɛlɪ'breɪʃən] n celebración, festejo
celebrity [sɪ'lɛbrɪtɪ] n celebridad
celery ['sɛlərɪ] n apio
celibacy ['sɛlɪbəsɪ] n celibato
cell [sɛl] n celda; (Biol) célula; (Elec) elemento
cellar ['sɛlə'] n sótano; (for wine) bodega
cello ['tʃɛləʊ] n violoncelo
cellophane ['sɛləfeɪn] n celofán
cellphone ['sɛlfəʊn] n teléfono celular
cellular ['sɛljulə'] adj celular
Celsius ['sɛlsɪəs] adj centígrado
Celt [kɛlt, sɛlt] n celta
Celtic ['kɛltɪk, 'sɛltɪk] adj celta, céltico ▷ n (Ling) celta
cement [sə'mɛnt] n cemento ▷ vt cementar; (fig) cimentar
cement mixer n hormigonera
cemetery ['sɛmɪtrɪ] n cementerio
cenotaph ['sɛnətɑːf] n cenotafio
censor ['sɛnsə'] n censor(a) ▷ vt (cut) censurar
censorship ['sɛnsəʃɪp] n censura
censure ['sɛnʃə'] vt censurar
census ['sɛnsəs] n censo
cent [sɛnt] n (US: unit of dollar) centavo; (unit of euro) céntimo; see also **per**
centenary [sɛn'tiːnərɪ], **centennial** [sɛn'tɛnɪəl] (US) n centenario
center ['sɛntə'] n (US) = **centre**
centigrade ['sɛntɪgreɪd] adj centígrado
centimetre, (US) **centimeter** ['sɛntɪmiːtə'] n centímetro
centipede ['sɛntɪpiːd] n ciempiés
central ['sɛntrəl] adj central; (house etc) céntrico
Central America n Centroamérica
Central American adj, n centroamericano(-a)
central heating n calefacción central
central reservation n (Brit Aut) mediana
centre, (US) **center** ['sɛntə'] n centro ▷ vt centrar; **to ~ (on)** (concentrate) concentrar (en)
centre-forward ['sɛntə'fɔːwəd] n (Sport) delantero centro
centre-half ['sɛntə'hɑːf] n (Sport) medio centro
centre-stage n: **to take ~** pasar a primer plano
century ['sɛntjurɪ] n siglo; **20th ~** siglo veinte; **in the twentieth ~** en el siglo veinte
CEO n abbr (US) = **chief executive officer**
ceramic [sɪ'ræmɪk] adj de cerámica
cereal ['siːrɪəl] n cereal
ceremony ['sɛrɪmənɪ] n ceremonia; **to stand on ~** hacer ceremonias, andarse con cumplidos
cert [sə:t] n (Brit col): **it's a dead ~** ¡es cosa segura!
certain ['sə:tən] adj seguro; (correct) cierto; (particular) cierto; **for ~** a ciencia cierta
certainly ['sə:tənlɪ] adv desde luego, por supuesto
certainty ['sə:təntɪ] n certeza, certidumbre, seguridad
certificate [sə'tɪfɪkɪt] n certificado
certified ['sə:tɪfaɪd] adj: **~ mail** (US) correo

certificado
certified public accountant (CPA) n (US) contable diplomado(-a) (Esp), contador(a) público(-a) (LAm)
certify ['sə:tɪfaɪ] vt certificar
cervical ['sə:vɪkl] adj: **~ cancer** cáncer cervical; **~ smear** citología
cervix ['sə:vɪks] n cerviz, cuello del útero
Cesarean [sɪ'zɛərɪən] adj, n (US) = **Caesarean**
cessation [sə'seɪʃən] n cese, suspensión
CET n abbr (= Central European Time) hora de Europa central
cf. abbr (= compare) cfr
CFC n abbr (= chlorofluorocarbon) CFC
ch. abbr (= chapter) cap
chafe [tʃeɪf] vt (rub) rozar; (irritate) irritar; **to ~ (against)** (fig) irritarse or enojarse (con)
chain [tʃeɪn] n cadena ▷ vt (also: **chain up**) encadenar
chain reaction n reacción en cadena
chain-smoke ['tʃeɪnsməʊk] vi fumar un cigarrillo tras otro
chain store n tienda de una cadena, ≈ grandes almacenes
chair [tʃɛə'] n silla; (armchair) sillón; (of university) cátedra ▷ vt (meeting) presidir; **the ~** (US: electric chair) la silla eléctrica; **please take a ~** siéntese or tome asiento, por favor
chairlift ['tʃɛəlɪft] n telesilla
chairman ['tʃɛəmən] n presidente
chairperson ['tʃɛəpə:sn] n presidente(-a)
chairwoman ['tʃɛəwumən] n presidenta
chalet ['ʃæleɪ] n chalet (de madera)
chalice ['tʃælɪs] n cáliz
chalk [tʃɔːk] n (Geo) creta; (for writing) tiza, gis (LAm)
▶ **chalk up** vt apuntar; (fig: success, victory) apuntarse
challenge ['tʃælɪndʒ] n desafío, reto ▷ vt desafiar, retar; (statement, right) poner en duda; **to ~ sb to do sth** retar a algn a que haga algo
challenger ['tʃælɪndʒə'] n (Sport) contrincante
challenging ['tʃælɪndʒɪŋ] adj que supone un reto; (tone) de desafío
chamber ['tʃeɪmbə'] n cámara, sala; **~ of commerce** cámara de comercio
chambermaid ['tʃeɪmbəmeɪd] n camarera
chamber music n música de cámara
champagne [ʃæm'peɪn] n champaña, champán
champers ['ʃæmpəz] nsg (col) champán
champion ['tʃæmpɪən] n campeón(-ona); (of cause) defensor(a), paladín ▷ vt defender, apoyar
championship ['tʃæmpɪənʃɪp] n campeonato
chance [tʃɑːns] n (coincidence) casualidad; (luck) suerte; (fate) azar; (opportunity) ocasión, oportunidad, chance (LAm); (likelihood) posibilidad; (risk) riesgo ▷ vt arriesgar, probar ▷ adj fortuito, casual; **by ~** por casualidad; **it's the ~ of a lifetime for her** es la oportunidad de su vida; **I'll write when I get the ~** te escribiré cuando tenga un momento; **the team's ~s of winning are very good** el equipo tiene muchas

posibilidades de ganar; **the ~s are that ...** lo más probable es que ...; **no ~!** ¡ni en broma!; **to take a ~** arriesgarse; **to ~ it** arriesgarse; **to ~ to do sth** (*happen*) hacer algo por casualidad
▸ **chance (up)on** *vt fus* tropezar(se) con

chancellor [ˈtʃɑːnsələʳ] *n* canciller; **C~ of the Exchequer** (*Brit*) Ministro de Economía y Hacienda; *see also* **Downing Street**

chancy [ˈtʃɑːnsɪ] *adj* (*col*) arriesgado

chandelier [ʃændəˈlɪəʳ] *n* araña (de luces)

change [tʃeɪndʒ] *vt* cambiar; (*clothes*) cambiarse de; (*transform*) transformar ▷ *vi* cambiar(se); (*change trains*) hacer transbordo; (*be transformed*): **to ~ into** transformarse en ▷ *n* cambio; (*alteration*) modificación; (*coins*) suelto; (*money returned*) vuelta, vuelto (*LAm*); **I'd like to ~ £50** quisiera cambiar 50 libras; **he wants to ~ his job** quiere cambiar de trabajo; **I'm going to ~ my shoes** voy a cambiarme de zapatos; **to ~ one's mind** cambiar de opinión *or* idea; **to ~ gear** (*Brit Aut*) cambiar de marcha; **to get ~d** cambiarse; **she ~d into an old skirt** se puso una falda vieja; **there's been a ~ of plan** ha habido un cambio de planes; **a ~ of clothes** una muda; **for a ~** para variar; **can you give me ~ for £1?** ¿tiene cambio de una libra?; **keep the ~** quédese con la vuelta

changeable [ˈtʃeɪndʒəbl] *adj* (*weather*) cambiable; (*person*) variable

change machine *n* máquina de cambio

changeover [ˈtʃeɪndʒəʊvəʳ] *n* (*to new system*) cambio

changing [ˈtʃeɪndʒɪŋ] *adj* cambiante

changing room *n* (*Brit*) vestuario

channel [ˈtʃænl] *n* (*TV*) canal; (*of river*) cauce; (*of sea*) estrecho; (*groove, fig: medium*) conducto, medio ▷ *vt* (*river etc*) encauzar; **to ~ into** (*fig: interest, energies*) encauzar a, dirigir a; **the (English) C~** el Canal (de la Mancha); **the C~ Islands** las Islas Anglonormandas; **~s of communication** canales de comunicación; **green/red ~** pasillo verde/rojo

Channel Tunnel *n*: **the ~** el túnel del Canal de la Mancha, el Eurotúnel

chant [tʃɑːnt] *n* canto; (*of crowd*) gritos ▷ *vt* cantar; **the demonstrators ~ed their disapproval** los manifestantes corearon su desaprobación

chaos [ˈkeɪɔs] *n* caos

chap [tʃæp] *n* (*Brit col: man*) tío, tipo; **old ~** amigo (mío)

chapel [ˈtʃæpəl] *n* capilla

chaplain [ˈtʃæplɪn] *n* capellán

chapped [tʃæpt] *adj* agrietado

chapter [ˈtʃæptəʳ] *n* capítulo

char [tʃɑːʳ] *vt* (*burn*) carbonizar, chamuscar ▷ *n* (*Brit*) = **charlady**

character [ˈkærɪktəʳ] *n* carácter, naturaleza, índole; (*in novel, film*) personaje; (*role*) papel; (*individuality, Comput*) carácter; **a person of good ~** una persona de buena reputación

characteristic [kærɪktəˈrɪstɪk] *adj* característico

▷ *n* característica

characterize [ˈkærɪktəraɪz] *vt* caracterizar

charcoal [ˈtʃɑːkəʊl] *n* carbón vegetal; (*Art*) carboncillo

charge [tʃɑːdʒ] *n* carga; (*Law*) cargo, acusación; (*cost*) precio, coste; (*responsibility*) cargo; (*task*) encargo ▷ *vt* (*Law*): **to ~ (with)** acusar (de); (*gun, battery, Mil: enemy*) cargar; (*price*) pedir; (*customer*) cobrar; (*person: with task*) encargar ▷ *vi* (*rush*) precipitarse; (*make pay*) cobrar; **charges** *npl*: **bank ~s** comisiones bancarias; **to reverse the ~s** (*Brit Tel*) llamar a cobro revertido; **is there a ~ for delivery?** ¿cobran por el envío?; **extra ~** recargo, suplemento; **free of ~** gratis; **to take ~ of** hacerse cargo de, encargarse de; **to be in ~ of** estar encargado de; **she was in ~ of the group** ella era la responsable del grupo; **how much do you ~?** ¿cuánto cobra usted?; **to ~ an expense (up) to sb's account** cargar algo a cuenta de algn; **~ it to my account** póngalo *or* cárguelo a mi cuenta

charge card *n* tarjeta de cuenta

chargehand [ˈtʃɑːdʒhænd] *n* capataz

chariot [ˈtʃærɪət] *n* carro

charisma [kæˈrɪzmə] *n* carisma

charitable [ˈtʃærɪtəbl] *adj* caritativo

charity [ˈtʃærɪtɪ] *n* (*gen*) caridad; (*organization*) organización benéfica

charm [tʃɑːm] *n* encanto, atractivo; (*spell*) hechizo; (*object*) amuleto ▷ *vt* encantar; hechizar

charming [ˈtʃɑːmɪŋ] *adj* encantador(a); (*person*) simpático

chart [tʃɑːt] *n* (*table*) cuadro; (*graph*) gráfica; (*map*) carta de navegación; (*weather chart*) mapa meteorológico ▷ *vt* (*course*) trazar; (*sales, progress*) hacer una gráfica de; **to be in the ~s** (*record, pop group*) estar en la lista de éxitos

charter [ˈtʃɑːtəʳ] *vt* (*bus*) alquilar; (*plane, ship*) fletar ▷ *n* (*document*) estatuto, carta; **on ~** en alquiler, alquilado

chartered accountant (CA) *n* (*Brit*) contable diplomado(-a) (*Esp*), contador(a) público(-a) (*LAm*)

charter flight *n* vuelo chárter

chase [tʃeɪs] *vt* (*pursue*) perseguir; (*hunt*) cazar ▷ *n* persecución; caza; **to ~ after** correr tras
▸ **chase up** *vt* (*information*) tratar de conseguir; **to ~ sb up about sth** recordar algo a algn

chasm [ˈkæzəm] *n* abismo

chassis [ˈʃæsɪ] *n* chasis

chaste [tʃeɪst] *adj* casto

chastity [ˈtʃæstɪtɪ] *n* castidad

chat [tʃæt] *vi* (*also*: **have a chat**) charlar ▷ *n* charla
▸ **chat up** *vt* (*col: girl*) ligar con, enrollarse con

chatline [ˈtʃætlaɪn] *n* (*Brit*) línea (telefónica) múltiple, party line

chat room *n* (*Internet*) chat

chat show *n* (*Brit*) programa de entrevistas

chatter [ˈtʃætəʳ] *vi* (*person*) charlar; (*teeth*) castañetear ▷ *n* (*of birds*) parloteo; (*of people*)

charla, cháchara
chatterbox ['tʃætəbɔks] n parlanchín(-ina)
chattering classes ['tʃætərɪŋ'klɑːsɪz] npl: **the ~** (col: pej) los intelectualillos
chatty ['tʃætɪ] adj (style) informal; (person) hablador(a)
chauffeur ['ʃəufər] n chófer
chauvinist ['ʃəuvɪnɪst] n (male chauvinist) machista; (nationalist) chovinista, patriotero(-a)
cheap [tʃiːp] adj barato; (joke) de mal gusto, chabacano; (poor quality) malo; (reduced: ticket) económico; (: fare) barato ▷ adv barato
cheaply ['tʃiːplɪ] adv barato, a bajo precio
cheat [tʃiːt] vi hacer trampa; (in exam) copiar ▷ vt estafar, timar ▷ n trampa; estafa; (person) tramposo(-a); **he's been ~ing on his wife** ha estado engañando a su esposa
check [tʃɛk] vt comprobar; (halt) frenar; (restrain) refrenar, restringir ▷ vi: **to ~ with sb** consultar con algn; (official etc) informarse por ▷ n (inspection) control, inspección; (curb) freno; (bill) nota, cuenta; (US) = **cheque**; (pattern: gen pl) cuadro ▷ adj (also: **checked**: pattern, cloth) a cuadros; **I'll ~ with the driver what time the bus leaves** le preguntaré al conductor a qué hora sale el autobús; **a security ~** un control de seguridad; **to keep a ~ on sth/sb** controlar algo/a algn
  ▸ **check in** vi (in hotel) registrarse; (at airport) facturar ▷ vt (luggage) facturar
  ▸ **check out** vt (investigate: story) comprobar; (: person) informarse sobre ▷ vi (of hotel) dejar el hotel
  ▸ **check up** vi: **to ~ up on sth** comprobar algo; **to ~ up on sb** investigar a algn
checkbook ['tʃɛkbuk] n (US) = **chequebook**
checkered ['tʃɛkəd] adj (US) = **chequered**
checkers ['tʃɛkəz] n (US) damas
check-in ['tʃɛkɪn] n (also: **check-in desk**: at airport) mostrador de facturación
checking account ['tʃɛkɪŋ-] n (US) cuenta corriente
checkmate ['tʃɛkmeɪt] n jaque mate
checkout ['tʃɛkaut] n (in supermarket) caja
checkpoint ['tʃɛkpɔɪnt] n (punto de) control, retén (LAm)
checkroom ['tʃɛkrum] n (US) consigna
checkup ['tʃɛkʌp] n (Med) reconocimiento general; (of machine) revisión
cheek [tʃiːk] n (Brit) mejilla; (impudence) descaro
cheekbone ['tʃiːkbəun] n pómulo
cheeky ['tʃiːkɪ] adj (Brit) fresco, descarado
cheep [tʃiːp] n (of bird) pío ▷ vi piar
cheer [tʃɪər] vt vitorear, ovacionar; (gladden) alegrar, animar ▷ vi dar vivas ▷ n viva; **cheers** npl vítores; **~s!** ¡salud!
  ▸ **cheer on** vt (person etc) animar con aplausos or gritos
  ▸ **cheer up** vi animarse ▷ vt alegrar, animar
cheerful ['tʃɪəful] adj alegre
cheerio [tʃɪərɪ'əu] excl (Brit) ¡hasta luego!
cheerleader ['tʃɪəliːdər] n animador(a)

cheese [tʃiːz] n queso
cheeseboard ['tʃiːzbɔːd] n tabla de quesos
cheeseburger ['tʃiːzbəːgər] n hamburguesa con queso
cheesecake ['tʃiːzkeɪk] n pastel de queso
cheetah ['tʃiːtə] n guepardo
chef [ʃɛf] n jefe(-a) de cocina
chemical ['kɛmɪkəl] adj químico ▷ n producto químico
chemist ['kɛmɪst] n (Brit: pharmacist) farmacéutico(-a); (scientist) químico(-a); **~'s (shop)** n (Brit) farmacia
chemistry ['kɛmɪstrɪ] n química
chemotherapy [kiːməu'θɛrəpɪ] n qᵘⁱmioterapia
cheque [tʃɛk], (US) **check** [tʃɛk] n (Brit) cheque; **to pay by ~** pagar con cheque
chequebook, (US) **checkbook** ['tʃɛkbuk] n talonario (de cheques), chequera (LAm)
cheque card n (Brit) tarjeta de identificación bancaria
chequered, (US) **checkered** ['tʃɛkəd] adj (fig) accidentado; (pattern) de cuadros
cherish ['tʃɛrɪʃ] vt (love) querer, apreciar; (protect) cuidar; (hope etc) abrigar
cherry ['tʃɛrɪ] n cereza
chess [tʃɛs] n ajedrez
chessboard ['tʃɛsbɔːd] n tablero (de ajedrez)
chest [tʃɛst] n (Anat) pecho; (box) cofre; **to get sth off one's ~** (col) desahogarse; **~ of drawers** n cómoda
chestnut ['tʃɛsnʌt] n castaña; (also: **chestnut tree**) castaño; (colour) castaño ▷ adj (color) castaño
chesty ['tʃɛstɪ] adj (cough) de bronquios, de pecho
chew [tʃuː] vt mascar, masticar
chewing gum ['tʃuːɪŋ-] n chicle
chic [ʃiːk] adj elegante
Chicano [tʃɪ'kɑːnəu] adj, n chicano(-a)
chick [tʃɪk] n pollito, polluelo; (US col) chica
chicken ['tʃɪkɪn] n gallina, pollo; (food) pollo; (col: coward) gallina
  ▸ **chicken out** vi (col) rajarse; **to ~ out of doing sth** rajarse y no hacer algo
chickenpox ['tʃɪkɪnpɔks] n varicela
chicory ['tʃɪkərɪ] n (for coffee) achicoria; (salad) escarola
chief [tʃiːf] n jefe(-a) ▷ adj principal, máximo (esp LAm); **C~ of Staff** (Mil) Jefe del Estado mayor
chief executive, (US) **chief executive officer** n director general
chiefly ['tʃiːflɪ] adv principalmente
chiffon ['ʃɪfɔn] n gasa
chilblain ['tʃɪlbleɪn] n sabañón
child [tʃaɪld] (pl **-ren**) n niño(-a); (offspring) hijo(-a)
child benefit n (Brit) subsidio por cada hijo pequeño
childbirth ['tʃaɪldbəːθ] n parto
childhood ['tʃaɪldhud] n niñez, infancia
childish ['tʃaɪldɪʃ] adj pueril, infantil
childlike ['tʃaɪldlaɪk] adj de niño, infantil
child minder n (Brit) niñera, madre de día
child prodigy n niño(-a) prodigio
children ['tʃɪldrən] npl of **child**

children's home n centro de acogida para niños

Chile ['tʃɪlɪ] n Chile

Chilean ['tʃɪlɪən] adj, n chileno(-a)

chill [tʃɪl] n frío; (Med) resfriado ▷ adj frío ▷ vt enfriar; (Culin) refrigerar
▶ **chill out** vi (esp US col) tranquilizarse

chil(l)i ['tʃɪlɪ] n (Brit) chile, ají (LAm)

chilling ['tʃɪlɪŋ] adj escalofriante

chilly ['tʃɪlɪ] adj frío

chime [tʃaɪm] n repique, campanada ▷ vi repicar, sonar

chimney ['tʃɪmnɪ] n chimenea

chimney sweep n deshollinador

chimpanzee [tʃɪmpæn'ziː] n chimpancé

chin [tʃɪn] n mentón, barbilla

China ['tʃaɪnə] n China

china ['tʃaɪnə] n porcelana; (crockery) loza

Chinese [tʃaɪ'niːz] adj chino ▷ n (pl inv) chino(-a); (Ling) chino

chink [tʃɪŋk] n (opening) rendija, hendedura; (noise) tintineo

chinwag ['tʃɪnwæg] n (Brit col): **to have a ~** echar una parrafada

chip [tʃɪp] n (gen pl: Culin: Brit) patata or (LAm) papa frita; (: US: also: **potato chip**) patata or (LAm) papa frita; (of wood) astilla; (stone) lasca; (in gambling) ficha; (Comput) chip ▷ vt (cup, plate) desconchar; **when the ~s are down** (fig) a la hora de la verdad
▶ **chip in** vi (col: interrupt) interrumpir, meterse; (: contribute) contribuir

chiropodist [kɪ'rɔpədɪst] n (Brit) podólogo(-a)

chirp [tʃəːp] vi gorjear; (cricket) cantar ▷ n (of cricket) canto

chisel ['tʃɪzl] n (for wood) escoplo; (for stone) cincel

chit [tʃɪt] n nota

chitchat ['tʃɪttʃæt] n chismes, habladurías

chivalry ['ʃɪvəlrɪ] n caballerosidad

chives [tʃaɪvz] npl cebollinos

chlorine ['klɔːriːn] n cloro

chock-a-block ['tʃɔkə'blɔk], **chock-full** [tʃɔk'fʊl] adj atestado

chocolate ['tʃɔklɪt] n chocolate

choice [tʃɔɪs] n elección; (preference) preferencia ▷ adj escogido; **I did it by** or **from ~** lo hice de buena gana; **a wide ~** un gran surtido, una gran variedad

choir ['kwaɪər] n coro

choirboy ['kwaɪəbɔɪ] n niño de coro

choke [tʃəuk] vi ahogarse; (on food) atragantarse ▷ vt ahogar; (block) atascar ▷ n (Aut) estárter

cholera ['kɔlərə] n cólera

cholesterol [kə'lɛstərəl] n colesterol

choose [tʃuːz] (pt **chose**, pp **chosen**) vt escoger, elegir; (team) seleccionar; **to ~ between** elegir or escoger entre; **to ~ from** escoger entre

choosy ['tʃuːzɪ] adj remilgado

chop [tʃɔp] vt (wood) cortar, talar; (Culin: also: **chop up**) picar ▷ n tajo, golpe cortante; (Culin) chuleta; **chops** npl (jaws) boca; **to get the ~** (col: project) ser suprimido; (: person: be sacked) ser despedido

chopper ['tʃɔpər] n (helicopter) helicóptero

choppy ['tʃɔpɪ] adj (sea) picado, agitado

chopsticks ['tʃɔpstɪks] npl palillos

chord [kɔːd] n (Mus) acorde

chore [tʃɔːr] n faena, tarea; (routine task) trabajo rutinario

choreographer [kɔrɪ'ɔgrəfər] n coreógrafo(-a)

choreography [kɔrɪ'ɔgrəfɪ] n coreografía

chortle ['tʃɔːtl] vi reírse satisfecho

chorus ['kɔːrəs] n coro; (refrain) estribillo

chose [tʃəuz] pt of **choose**

chosen ['tʃəuzn] pp of **choose**

Christ [kraɪst] n Cristo

christen ['krɪsn] vt bautizar

christening ['krɪsnɪŋ] n bautizo

Christian ['krɪstɪən] adj, n cristiano(-a)

Christianity [krɪstɪ'ænɪtɪ] n cristianismo

Christian name n nombre de pila

Christmas ['krɪsməs] n Navidad; **Merry ~!** ¡Felices Navidades!, ¡Felices Pascuas!

Christmas card n crismas, tarjeta de Navidad

Christmas Day n día de Navidad

Christmas Eve n Nochebuena

Christmas tree n árbol de Navidad

chrome [krəum] n = **chromium plating**

chromium ['krəumɪəm] n cromo; (also: **chromium plating**) cromado

chromosome ['krəuməsəum] n cromosoma

chronic ['krɔnɪk] adj crónico; (fig: liar, smoker) empedernido

chronicle ['krɔnɪkl] n crónica

chronological [krɔnə'lɔdʒɪkəl] adj cronológico

chrysanthemum [krɪ'sænθəməm] n crisantemo

chubby ['tʃʌbɪ] adj rechoncho

chuck [tʃʌk] vt tirar; **to ~ (up** or **in)** vt (Brit) dejar, mandar a paseo

chuckle ['tʃʌkl] vi reírse entre dientes

chuffed [tʃʌft] adj (col): **to be ~ (about sth)** estar encantado (con algo)

chug [tʃʌg] vi (also: **chug along**: train) ir despacio; (: fig) ir tirando

chum [tʃʌm] n amiguete(-a), coleguilla

chunk [tʃʌŋk] n pedazo, trozo

Chunnel [tʃʌnl] n = **Channel Tunnel**

church [tʃəːtʃ] n iglesia; **the C~ of England** la Iglesia Anglicana

churchyard ['tʃəːtʃjɑːd] n cementerio, camposanto

churn [tʃəːn] n (for butter) mantequera; (for milk) lechera
▶ **churn out** vt producir en serie

chute [ʃuːt] n (also: **rubbish chute**) vertedero; (Brit: children's slide) tobogán

chutney ['tʃʌtnɪ] n salsa picante de frutas y especias

CIA n abbr (US: = Central Intelligence Agency) CIA, Agencia Central de Inteligencia

CID n abbr (Brit: = Criminal Investigation Department) ≈ B.I.C. (Esp)

cider ['saɪdər] n sidra

cigar [sɪ'gɑːr] n puro

cigarette [sɪgə'rɛt] n cigarrillo, pitillo

cigarette case n pitillera
cigarette end n (Brit) colilla
Cinderella [sɪndə'rɛlə] n Cenicienta
cinders ['sɪndəz] npl cenizas
cine-camera ['sɪnɪ'kæmərə] n (Brit) cámara cinematográfica
cinema ['sɪnəmə] n cine
cinnamon ['sɪnəmən] n canela
circle ['sɜːkl] n círculo; (in theatre) anfiteatro ▷ vi dar vueltas ▷ vt (surround) rodear, cercar; (move round) dar la vuelta a
circuit ['sɜːkɪt] n circuito; (track) pista; (lap) vuelta
circuitous [sə'kjuɪtəs] adj indirecto
circular ['sɜːkjulər] adj circular ▷ n circular; (as advertisement) panfleto
circulate ['sɜːkjuleɪt] vi circular; (person: socially) alternar, circular ▷ vt poner en circulación
circulation [sɜːkju'leɪʃən] n circulación; (of newspaper etc) tirada
circumcise ['sɜːkəmsaɪz] vt circuncidar
circumference [sə'kʌmfərəns] n circunferencia
circumstances ['sɜːkəmstənsɪz] npl circunstancias; (financial condition) situación económica; **in the ~** en or dadas las circunstancias; **under no ~** de ninguna manera, bajo ningún concepto
circumvent ['sɜːkəmvɛnt] vt (rule etc) burlar
circus ['sɜːkəs] n circo; (also: **Circus**: in place names) Plaza
cirrhosis [sɪ'rəusɪs] n (also: **cirrhosis of the liver**) cirrosis
CIS n abbr (= Commonwealth of Independent States) CEI
cissy ['sɪsɪ] n = **sissy**
cistern ['sɪstən] n tanque, depósito; (in toilet) cisterna
citation [saɪ'teɪʃən] n cita; (Law) citación; (Mil) mención
citizen ['sɪtɪzn] n (Pol) ciudadano(-a); (of city) habitante
Citizens' Advice Bureau n (Brit) organización voluntaria británica que aconseja especialmente en temas legales o financieros
citizenship ['sɪtɪznʃɪp] n ciudadanía
citric ['sɪtrɪk] adj: **~ acid** ácido cítrico
citrus fruits ['sɪtrəs-] npl cítricos
city ['sɪtɪ] n ciudad; **the C~** centro financiero de Londres
city centre n centro de la ciudad
City Hall n (US) ayuntamiento
City Technology College n (Brit) ≈ Centro de formación profesional
civic ['sɪvɪk] adj cívico; (authorities) municipal
civic centre n (Brit) centro de administración municipal
civil ['sɪvɪl] adj civil; (polite) atento, cortés; (well-bred) educado
civil defence n protección civil
civil engineer n ingeniero(-a) de caminos
civil engineering n ingeniería de caminos
civilian [sɪ'vɪlɪən] adj civil; (clothes) de paisano ▷ n civil

civilization [sɪvɪlaɪ'zeɪʃən] n civilización
civilized ['sɪvɪlaɪzd] adj civilizado
civil law n derecho civil
civil liberties npl libertades civiles
civil rights npl derechos civiles
civil servant n funcionario(-a) (del Estado)
Civil Service n administración pública
civil war n guerra civil
civvies ['sɪvɪz] npl: **in ~** (col) de paisano
clad [klæd] adj: **~ (in)** vestido (de)
claim [kleɪm] vt reclamar; (rights etc) reivindicar; (assert) asegurar ▷ vi (for insurance) presentar reclamación ▷ n (for expenses) reclamación; (of right) reivindicación; (Law) demanda; (assertion) afirmación; **he ~s he found the money** asegura haber encontrado el dinero; **she's ~ing unemployment benefit** cobra subsidio de desempleo; **we ~ed on our insurance** reclamamos al seguro; **to make a ~** (on insurance) reclamar al seguro; **to put in a ~ for sth** (expenses) presentar una solicitud de algo
claimant ['kleɪmənt] n (Admin, Law) demandante
clairvoyant [klɛə'vɔɪənt] n clarividente
clam [klæm] n almeja
▶ **clam up** vi (col) cerrar el pico
clamber ['klæmbər] vi trepar
clammy ['klæmɪ] adj (cold) frío y húmedo; (sticky) pegajoso
clamour, (US) **clamor** ['klæmər] n (noise) clamor; (protest) protesta ▷ vi: **to ~ for sth** clamar por algo, pedir algo a voces
clamp [klæmp] n abrazadera; (laboratory clamp) grapa; (Brit: wheel clamp) cepo ▷ vt (Brit) afianzar (con abrazadera)
▶ **clamp down on** vt fus (government, police) poner coto a
clampdown ['klæmpdaun] n restricción; **there has been a ~ on terrorism** se ha puesto coto al terrorismo
clan [klæn] n clan
clang [klæŋ] n estruendo ▷ vi sonar con estruendo
clanger [klæŋər] n: **to drop a ~** (Brit col) meter la pata
clap [klæp] vi aplaudir ▷ vt (hands) batir ▷ n (of hands) palmada; **to ~ one's hands** dar palmadas, batir las palmas; **a ~ of thunder** un trueno
clapping ['klæpɪŋ] n aplausos
claptrap ['klæptræp] n (col) gilipolleces
claret ['klærət] n burdeos
clarification [klærɪfɪ'keɪʃən] n aclaración
clarify ['klærɪfaɪ] vt aclarar
clarinet [klærɪ'nɛt] n clarinete
clarity ['klærɪtɪ] n claridad
clash [klæʃ] n estruendo; (fig) choque ▷ vi enfrentarse; (personalities, interests) oponerse, chocar; (colours) desentonar; (dates, events) coincidir
clasp [klɑːsp] n broche; (on jewels) cierre ▷ vt abrochar; (hand) apretar; (embrace) abrazar
class [klɑːs] n (gen) clase; (group, category) clase, categoría ▷ cpd de clase ▷ vt clasificar; **we're in**

the same ~ estamos en la misma clase; **I go to dancing ~es** voy a clases de baile; **it's in a ~ of its own** no tiene par

classic ['klæsɪk] *adj* clásico ▷ *n* (*work*) obra clásica, clásico; **classics** *npl* (*Univ*) clásicas

classical ['klæsɪkəl] *adj* clásico; ~ **music** música clásica

classification [klæsɪfɪ'keɪʃən] *n* clasificación

classified ['klæsɪfaɪd] *adj* (*information*) reservado

classified advertisement *n* anuncio por palabras

classify ['klæsɪfaɪ] *vt* clasificar

classmate ['klɑ:smeɪt] *n* compañero(-a) de clase

classroom ['klɑ:srʊm] *n* aula

clatter ['klætəʳ] *n* ruido, estruendo; (*of hooves*) trápala ▷ *vi* hacer ruido *or* estruendo

clause [klɔ:z] *n* cláusula; (*Ling*) oración

claustrophobia [klɔ:strə'fəʊbɪə] *n* claustrofobia

claustrophobic [klɔ:strə'fəʊbɪk] *adj* claustrofóbico; **I feel ~** me entra claustrofobia

claw [klɔ:] *n* (*of cat*) uña; (*of bird of prey*) garra; (*of lobster*) pinza; (*Tech*) garfio ▷ *vi*: **to ~ at** arañar; (*tear*) desgarrar

clay [kleɪ] *n* arcilla

clean [kli:n] *adj* limpio; (*copy*) en limpio; (*lines*) bien definido ▷ *vt* limpiar ▷ *adv*: **he ~ forgot** lo olvidó por completo; **to come ~** (*col: admit guilt*) confesarlo todo; **to have a ~ driving licence** tener el carnet de conducir sin sanciones; **to ~ one's teeth** lavarse los dientes
▸ **clean off** *vt* limpiar
▸ **clean out** *vt* limpiar (a fondo)
▸ **clean up** *vt* limpiar, asear ▷ *vi* (*fig: make profit*): **to ~ up on** sacar provecho de

clean-cut ['kli:n'kʌt] *adj* bien definido; (*outline*) nítido; (*person*) de buen parecer

cleaner ['kli:nəʳ] *n* encargado(-a) de la limpieza; (*also*: **dry cleaner**) tintorero(-a)

cleaning ['kli:nɪŋ] *n* limpieza

cleanliness ['klɛnlɪnɪs] *n* limpieza

cleanse [klɛnz] *vt* limpiar

cleanser ['klɛnzəʳ] *n* detergente; (*cosmetic*) loción *or* crema limpiadora

clean-shaven ['kli:n'ʃeɪvn] *adj* bien afeitado

cleansing department ['klɛnzɪŋ-] *n* (*Brit*) servicio municipal de limpieza

clean sweep *n*: **to make a ~** (*Sport*) arrasar, barrer

clear [klɪəʳ] *adj* claro; (*road, way*) libre; (*profit*) neto; (*majority*) absoluto ▷ *vt* (*area, road*) despejar; (*Law: suspect*) absolver; (*obstacle*) salvar, saltar por encima de; (*debt*) liquidar; (*cheque*) aceptar; (*site, woodland*) desmontar ▷ *vi* (*fog etc*) despejarse ▷ *n*: **to be in the ~** (*out of debt*) estar libre de deudas; (*out of suspicion*) estar fuera de toda sospecha; (*out of danger*) estar fuera de peligro ▷ *adv*: **to stand ~ of sth** mantenerse apartado de algo; **it's ~ you don't believe me** está claro que no me crees; **to make o.s. ~** explicarse claramente; **have I made myself ~?** ¿me explico?; **to make it ~ to sb that ...** hacer entender a algn que ...; **a ~ day** (*not cloudy*) un día despejado; **I have a ~ day tomorrow** mañana tengo el día libre; **it**

comes in a ~ plastic bottle viene en una botella de plástico transparente; **to keep ~ of sth/sb** evitar algo/a algn; **to ~ a profit of ...** sacar una ganancia de ...; **to ~ the table** recoger *or* quitar la mesa
▸ **clear off** *vi* (*Brit col: leave*) marcharse, mandarse mudar (*LAm*)
▸ **clear up** *vt* (*room, books, toys*) ordenar; (*mystery*) aclarar, resolver ▷ *vi*: **I think it's going to ~ up** (*weather*) creo que va a despejar

clearance ['klɪərəns] *n* (*removal*) despeje; (*permission*) acreditación

clear-cut ['klɪə'kʌt] *adj* bien definido, claro

clearing ['klɪərɪŋ] *n* (*in wood*) claro

clearing bank *n* (*Brit*) banco central

clearly ['klɪəlɪ] *adv* claramente

clearway ['klɪəweɪ] *n* (*Brit*) carretera en la que no se puede estacionar

clef [klɛf] *n* (*Mus*) clave

cleft [klɛft] *n* (*in rock*) grieta, hendedura

clemency ['klɛmənsɪ] *n* clemencia

clench [klɛntʃ] *vt* apretar, cerrar

clergy ['klə:dʒɪ] *n* clero

clergyman ['klə:dʒɪmən] *n* clérigo

clerical ['klɛrɪkəl] *adj* de oficina; (*Rel*) clerical; (*error*) de copia

clerk [klɑ:k, (*US*) klə:k] *n* oficinista; (*US*) dependiente(-a), vendedor(a); **C~ of the Court** secretario(-a) de juzgado

clever ['klɛvəʳ] *adj* (*mentally*) inteligente, listo; (*skilful*) hábil; (*device, arrangement*) ingenioso

clew [klu:] *n* (*US*) = **clue**

cliché ['kli:ʃeɪ] *n* cliché, frase hecha

click [klɪk] *vt* (*tongue*) chasquear ▷ *vi* (*Comput*) hacer clic; **to ~ one's heels** taconear

client ['klaɪənt] *n* cliente

clientele [kli:ā:n'tɛl] *n* clientela

cliff [klɪf] *n* acantilado

climate ['klaɪmɪt] *n* clima; (*fig*) clima, ambiente

climax ['klaɪmæks] *n* punto culminante; (*of play etc*) clímax; (*sexual climax*) orgasmo

climb [klaɪm] *vi* subir, trepar; (*plane*) elevarse, remontar el vuelo ▷ *vt* (*stairs*) subir; (*tree*) trepar a; (*mountain*) escalar ▷ *n* subida, ascenso; **to ~ over a wall** saltar una tapia
▸ **climb down** *vi* (*fig*) volverse atrás

climbdown ['klaɪmdaʊn] *n* vuelta atrás

climber ['klaɪməʳ] *n* escalador(a)

climbing ['klaɪmɪŋ] *n* escalada

clinch [klɪntʃ] *vt* (*deal*) cerrar; (*argument*) rematar

cling [klɪŋ] (*pt, pp* **clung**) *vi*: **to ~ (to)** agarrarse (a); (*clothes*) pegarse (a)

clingfilm ['klɪŋfɪlm] *n* plástico adherente

clinic ['klɪnɪk] *n* clínica

clinical ['klɪnɪkl] *adj* clínico; (*fig*) frío, impasible

clink [klɪŋk] *vi* tintinear

clip [klɪp] *n* (*for hair*) horquilla; (*also*: **paper clip**) sujetapapeles, clip; (*clamp*) grapa ▷ *vt* (*cut*) cortar; (*hedge*) podar; (*also*: **clip together**) unir

clippers ['klɪpəz] *npl* (*for gardening*) tijeras de podar; (*for hair*) maquinilla; (*for nails*) cortaúñas

clipping ['klɪpɪŋ] *n* (*from newspaper*) recorte

clique [kliːk] *n* camarilla
cloak [kləuk] *n* capa, manto ▷ *vt* (*fig*) encubrir, disimular
cloakroom ['kləukrum] *n* guardarropa; (*Brit*: WC) lavabo, aseos, baño (*esp LAm*)
clock [klɔk] *n* reloj; (*in taxi*) taxímetro; **to work against the ~** trabajar contra reloj; **around the ~** las veinticuatro horas; **to sleep round the ~** dormir un día entero; **30,000 on the ~** (*Aut*) treinta mil millas en el cuentakilómetros
▸ **clock in, clock on** *vi* fichar, picar
▸ **clock off, clock out** *vi* fichar *or* picar la salida
▸ **clock up** *vt* hacer
clockwise ['klɔkwaɪz] *adv* en el sentido de las agujas del reloj
clockwork ['klɔkwəːk] *n* aparato de relojería
▷ *adj* (*toy, train*) de cuerda
clog [klɔg] *n* zueco, chanclo ▷ *vt* atascar ▷ *vi* atascarse
cloister ['klɔɪstəʳ] *n* claustro
clone [kləun] *n* clon
close *adj* (*near*): **~ (to)** cerca (de); (*relation*) cercano; (*friend*) íntimo; (*print, weave*) tupido, compacto; (*connection*) estrecho; (*examination*) detallado, minucioso; (*contest*) reñido; (*weather*) bochornoso; (*atmosphere*) sofocante; (*room*) mal ventilado ▷ *adv* cerca ▷ *vt* cerrar; (*end*) concluir, terminar ▷ *vi* (*shop etc*) cerrar; (*end*) concluir(se), terminar(se) ▷ *n* (*end*) fin, final; **the shops are very ~** las tiendas están muy cerca; **come ~r** acércate más; **at ~ quarters** de cerca; **~ by, ~ at hand** *adj, adv* muy cerca; **~ to** *prep* cerca de; **how ~ is Edinburgh to Glasgow?** ¿qué distancia hay de Edimburgo a Glasgow?; **she was ~ to tears** estaba a punto de llorar; **I'm very ~ to my sister** estoy muy unida a mi hermana; **to have a ~ shave** (*fig*) escaparse por un pelo; **it's ~ this afternoon** hace bochorno esta tarde; **the doors ~ automatically** las puertas se cierran automáticamente; **to bring sth to a ~** terminar algo
▸ **close down** *vi* cerrar definitivamente
▸ **close in** *vi* (*hunters*) acercarse rodeando; (*evening, night*) caer; (*fog*) cerrarse; **to ~ in on sb** rodear *or* cercar a algn; **the days are closing in** los días son cada vez más cortos
▸ **close off** *vt* (*area*) cerrar al tráfico *or* al público
closed [kləuzd] *adj* (*shop etc*) cerrado
closed-circuit ['kləuzd'səːkɪt] *adj*: **~ television** televisión por circuito cerrado
closed shop *n* empresa en la que todo el personal está afiliado a un sindicato
close-knit ['kləus'nɪt] *adj* (*fig*) muy unido
closely ['kləuslɪ] *adv* (*study*) con detalle; (*listen*) con atención; (*watch: person, events*) de cerca; **we are ~ related** somos parientes cercanos; **a ~ guarded secret** un secreto rigurosamente guardado
close season [kləuz-] *n* (*Football*) temporada de descanso; (*Hunting*) veda
closet ['klɔzɪt] *n* (*cupboard*) armario, placar(d) (*LAm*)

close-up ['kləusʌp] *n* primer plano
closing time *n* hora de cierre
closure ['kləuʒəʳ] *n* cierre
clot [klɔt] *n* (*gen: also*: **blood clot**) embolia; (*Brit col: idiot*) imbécil ▷ *vi* (*blood*) coagularse
cloth [klɔθ] *n* (*material*) tela, paño; (*table cloth*) mantel; (*rag*) trapo
clothe [kləuð] *vt* vestir; (*fig*) revestir
clothes [kləuðz] *npl* ropa; **to put one's ~ on** vestirse, ponerse la ropa; **to take one's ~ off** desvestirse, desnudarse
clothes brush *n* cepillo (para la ropa)
clothes line *n* cuerda (para tender la ropa)
clothes peg, (US) **clothes pin** *n* pinza
clothing ['kləuðɪŋ] *n* = **clothes**
cloud [klaud] *n* nube; (*storm cloud*) nubarrón ▷ *vt* (*liquid*) enturbiar; **every ~ has a silver lining** no hay mal que por bien no venga; **to ~ the issue** empañar el problema
▸ **cloud over** *vi* (*also fig*) nublarse
cloudburst ['klaudbəːst] *n* chaparrón
cloudy ['klaudɪ] *adj* nublado; (*liquid*) turbio
clout [klaut] *n* (*fig*) influencia, peso ▷ *vt* dar un tortazo a
clove [kləuv] *n* clavo; **~ of garlic** diente de ajo
clover ['kləuvəʳ] *n* trébol
clown [klaun] *n* payaso ▷ *vi* (*also*: **clown about, clown around**) hacer el payaso
cloying ['klɔɪɪŋ] *adj* (*taste*) empalagoso
club [klʌb] *n* (*society*) club; (*weapon*) porra, cachiporra; (*also*: **golf club**) palo ▷ *vt* aporrear ▷ *vi*: **to ~ together** (*join forces*) unir fuerzas; **clubs** *npl* (*Cards*) tréboles
club car *n* (*US Rail*) coche salón
club class *n* (*Aviat*) clase preferente
clubhouse ['klʌbhaus] *n* local social, sobre todo en clubs deportivos
club soda *n* (*US*) soda
cluck [klʌk] *vi* cloquear
clue [kluː] *n* pista; (*in crosswords*) indicación; **I haven't a ~** no tengo ni idea
clump [klʌmp] *n* (*of trees*) grupo
clumsy ['klʌmzɪ] *adj* (*person*) torpe; (*tool*) difícil de manejar
clung [klʌŋ] *pt, pp of* **cling**
cluster ['klʌstəʳ] *n* grupo; (*Bot*) racimo ▷ *vi* agruparse, apiñarse
clutch [klʌtʃ] *n* (*Aut*) embrague; (*pedal*) (pedal de) embrague ▷ *vt* agarrar; **to fall into sb's ~es** caer en las garras de algn
clutter ['klʌtəʳ] *vt* (*also*: **clutter up**) atestar, llenar desordenadamente ▷ *n* desorden, confusión
cm *abbr* (= *centimetre*) cm
CND *n abbr* (= *Campaign for Nuclear Disarmament*) plataforma pro desarme nuclear
Co. *abbr* = **county; company**
c/o *abbr* (= *care of*) c/a, a/c
coach [kəutʃ] *n* (*Brit*: *bus*) autocar (*Esp*), autobús; (*horse-drawn*) coche; (*ceremonial*) carroza; (*of train*) vagón, coche; (*Sport*) entrenador(a), instructor(a) ▷ *vt* (*Sport*) entrenar; (*student*) preparar, enseñar
coach trip *n* (*Brit*) excursión en autocar

coal [kəul] n carbón
coal face n (Brit) frente de carbón
coalfield ['kəulfiːld] n yacimiento de carbón
coalition [kəuə'lɪʃən] n coalición
coal man n carbonero
coalmine ['kəulmaɪn] n mina de carbón
coarse [kɔːs] adj basto, burdo; (vulgar) grosero, ordinario
coast [kəust] n costa, litoral ▷ vi (Aut) ir en punto muerto
coastal ['kəustl] adj costero
coastguard ['kəustgɑːd] n guardacostas
coastline ['kəustlaɪn] n litoral
coat [kəut] n (jacket) chaqueta, saco (LAm); (overcoat) abrigo; (of animal) pelo, lana; (of paint) mano, capa ▷ vt cubrir, revestir
coat hanger n percha, gancha (LAm)
coating ['kəutɪŋ] n capa, baño
coat of arms n escudo de armas
coax [kəuks] vt engatusar
cob [kɔb] n see **corn**
cobbler ['kɔblə^r] n zapatero (remendón)
cobbles ['kɔblz], **cobblestones** ['kɔblstəunz] npl adoquines
cobweb ['kɔbwɛb] n telaraña
cocaine [kə'keɪn] n cocaína
cock [kɔk] n (rooster) gallo; (male bird) macho ▷ vt (gun) amartillar
cockerel ['kɔkərl] n gallito, gallo joven
cock-eyed ['kɔkaɪd] adj bizco; (fig: crooked) torcido; (: idea) disparatado
cockle ['kɔkl] n berberecho
cockney ['kɔknɪ] n habitante de ciertos barrios de Londres
cockpit ['kɔkpɪt] n (in aircraft) cabina
cockroach ['kɔkrəutʃ] n cucaracha
cocktail ['kɔkteɪl] n combinado, cóctel; **prawn ~** cóctel de gambas
cocktail cabinet n mueble-bar
cocktail party n cóctel
cocky ['kɔkɪ] adj farruco, flamenco
cocoa ['kəukəu] n cacao; (drink) chocolate
coconut ['kəukənʌt] n coco
cod [kɔd] n bacalao
COD abbr see **cash on delivery**; (US) see **collect on delivery**
code [kəud] n código; (cipher) clave; (Tel) prefijo; **~ of behaviour** código de conducta; **~ of practice** código profesional
codger [kɔdʒə^r] n (Brit col): **an old ~** un abuelo
cod-liver oil ['kɔdlɪvə^r-] n aceite de hígado de bacalao
coercion [kəu'əːʃən] n coacción
coffee ['kɔfɪ] n café; **white ~** (US): **~ with cream** café con leche
coffee bar n (Brit) cafetería
coffee bean n grano de café
coffee break n descanso (para tomar café)
coffeepot ['kɔfɪpɔt] n cafetera
coffee table n mesita baja
coffin ['kɔfɪn] n ataúd
cog [kɔg] n diente

cogent ['kəudʒənt] adj lógico, convincente
cognac ['kɔnjæk] n coñac
coherent [kəu'hɪərənt] adj coherente
coil [kɔɪl] n rollo; (of rope) vuelta; (of smoke) espiral; (Aut, Elec) bobina, carrete; (contraceptive) DIU ▷ vt enrollar
coin [kɔɪn] n moneda ▷ vt acuñar; (word) inventar, acuñar
coinage ['kɔɪnɪdʒ] n moneda
coin-box ['kɔɪnbɔks] n (Brit) caja recaudadora
coincide [kəuɪn'saɪd] vi coincidir
coincidence [kəu'ɪnsɪdəns] n casualidad, coincidencia
Coke® [kəuk] n Coca Cola®
coke [kəuk] n (coal) coque
colander ['kɔləndə^r] n escurridor
cold [kəuld] adj frío ▷ n frío; (Med) resfriado; **it's ~** hace frío; **to be ~** tener frío, resfriarse, acatarrarse; **in ~ blood** a sangre fría; **the room's getting ~** está empezando a hacer frío en la habitación; **to give sb the ~ shoulder** tratar a algn con frialdad; **to catch a ~** coger un catarro
cold sore n calentura, herpes labial
cold sweat n: **to be in a ~ (about sth)** tener sudores fríos (por algo)
cold turkey n (col) mono
Cold War n: **the ~** la guerra fría
coleslaw ['kəulslɔː] n ensalada de col con zanahoria
colic ['kɔlɪk] n cólico
colicky ['kɔlɪkɪ] adj: **to be ~** tener un cólico
collaborate [kə'læbəreɪt] vi colaborar
collaboration [kəlæbə'reɪʃən] n colaboración; (Pol) colaboracionismo
collapse [kə'læps] vi (gen) hundirse, derrumbarse; (Med) sufrir un colapso ▷ n (gen) hundimiento; (Med) colapso; (of government) caída; (of plans, scheme) fracaso; (of business) ruina
collapsible [kə'læpsəbl] adj plegable
collar ['kɔlə^r] n (of coat, shirt) cuello; (for dog, Tech) collar ▷ vt (col: person) agarrar; (: object) birlar
collarbone ['kɔləbəun] n clavícula
collateral [kɔ'lætərəl] n (Comm) garantía subsidiaria
colleague ['kɔliːg] n colega, compañero(-a)
collect [kə'lɛkt] vt reunir; (as a hobby) coleccionar; (Brit: call and pick up) recoger; (wages) cobrar; (debts) recaudar; (donations, subscriptions) colectar ▷ vi (crowd) reunirse ▷ adv: **to call ~** (US Tel) llamar a cobro revertido; **to ~ one's thoughts** reponerse, recobrar el dominio de sí mismo; **~ on delivery (COD)** (US) entrega contra reembolso
collection [kə'lɛkʃən] n colección; (of fares, wages) cobro; (of post) recogida
collective [kə'lɛktɪv] adj colectivo
collector [kə'lɛktə^r] n coleccionista; (of taxes etc) recaudador(a); **~'s item** or **piece** pieza de coleccionista
college ['kɔlɪdʒ] n colegio; (of technology, agriculture etc) escuela
collide [kə'laɪd] vi chocar

collie ['kɔlɪ] n (dog) collie, perro pastor escocés
colliery ['kɔlɪərɪ] n (Brit) mina de carbón
collision [kə'lɪʒən] n choque, colisión; **to be on a ~ course** (also fig) ir rumbo al desastre
colloquial [kə'ləukwɪəl] adj coloquial
cologne [kə'ləun] n (also: **eau de cologne**) (agua de) colonia
Colombia [kə'lɔmbɪə] n Colombia
Colombian [kə'lɔmbɪən] adj, n colombiano(-a)
colon ['kəulən] n (sign) dos puntos; (Med) colon
colonel ['kə:nl] n coronel
colonial [kə'ləunɪəl] adj colonial
colonize ['kɔlənaɪz] vt colonizar
colony ['kɔlənɪ] n colonia
color etc ['kʌləʳ] (US) = **colour**
colossal [kə'lɔsl] adj colosal
colour, (US) **color** ['kʌləʳ] n color ▷ vt colorear, pintar; (dye) teñir ▷ vi (blush) sonrojarse; **colours** npl (of party, club) colores
colo(u)r bar n segregación racial
colo(u)r-blind ['kʌləblaɪnd] adj daltónico
colo(u)red ['kʌləd] adj de color; (photo) en color; (of race) de color
colo(u)r film n película en color
colo(u)rful ['kʌləful] adj lleno de color; (person) pintoresco
colo(u)ring ['kʌlərɪŋ] n colorido, color; (substance) colorante
colo(u)rless ['kʌləlɪs] adj incoloro, sin color
colo(u)r scheme n combinación de colores
colour supplement n (Brit Press) suplemento semanal or dominical
colo(u)r television n televisión en color
colt [kəult] n potro
column ['kɔləm] n columna; (fashion column, sports column etc) sección, columna; **the editorial ~** el editorial
columnist ['kɔləmnɪst] n columnista
coma ['kəumə] n coma
comb [kəum] n peine; (ornamental) peineta ▷ vt (hair) peinar; (area) registrar a fondo, peinar
combat ['kɔmbæt] n combate ▷ vt combatir
combination [kɔmbɪ'neɪʃən] n (gen) combinación
combine vt combinar; (qualities) reunir ▷ vi combinarse ▷ n (Econ) cartel; **a ~d effort** un esfuerzo conjunto
combine (harvester) ['kɔmbaɪn ('hɑːvɪstəʳ)] n cosechadora
come [kʌm] (pt **came**, pp **-**) vi **1** (movement towards) venir; **to ~ running** venir corriendo; **~ with me** ven conmigo; **~ and see us soon** ven a vernos pronto
2 (arrive) llegar; **he's ~ here to work** ha venido aquí para trabajar; **to ~ home** volver a casa; **the letter came this morning** la carta llegó esta mañana; **we've just ~ from Seville** acabamos de llegar de Sevilla; **(I'm) coming!** ¡(ya) voy!
3 (reach): **to ~ to** llegar a; **the bill came to £40** la cuenta ascendía a cuarenta libras
4 (occur): **an idea came to me** se me ocurrió una idea; **if it ~s to it** llegado el caso

5 (be, become): **to ~ loose/undone** etc aflojarse/ desabrocharse, desatarse etc; **I've ~ to like him** ha llegado a gustarme
▸ **come about** vi suceder, ocurrir
▸ **come across** vt fus (person) encontrarse con; (thing) encontrar ▷ vi: **to ~ across well/badly** causar buena/mala impresión; **she ~s across as a nice girl** da la impresión de ser una chica simpática
▸ **come away** vi (leave) marcharse; (become detached) desprenderse
▸ **come back** vi (return) volver; (reply): **can I ~ back to you on that one?** volvamos sobre ese punto
▸ **come by** vt fus (acquire) conseguir
▸ **come down** vi (price) bajar; (building) derrumbarse; ser derribado
▸ **come forward** vi presentarse
▸ **come from** vt fus (place, source) ser de; **where do you ~ from?** ¿de dónde eres?
▸ **come in** vi (visitor) entrar; (train, report) llegar; (fashion) ponerse de moda; (on deal etc) entrar
▸ **come in for** vt fus (criticism etc) recibir
▸ **come into** vt fus (money) heredar; (be involved) tener que ver con; **to ~ into fashion** ponerse de moda
▸ **come off** vi (button) soltarse, desprenderse; (attempt) salir bien
▸ **come on** vi (pupil, work, project) marchar; (lights) encenderse; (electricity) volver; **~ on!** (expressing encouragement, urging haste) ¡vamos!; (expressing disbelief) ¡venga ya!
▸ **come out** vi (fact) salir a la luz; (book, sun) salir; (stain) quitarse; **we came out of the cinema at 10** salimos del cine a las 10; **to ~ out (on strike)** declararse en huelga; **none of my photos came out** no salió ninguna de mis fotos; **to ~ out for/ against** declararse a favor/en contra de
▸ **come over** vt fus: **I don't know what's ~ over him!** ¡no sé lo que le pasa!
▸ **come round** vi (after faint, operation) volver en sí
▸ **come through** vi (survive) sobrevivir; (telephone call): **the call came through** recibimos la llamada
▸ **come to** vi (wake) volver en sí; (total) sumar; **how much does it ~ to?** ¿cuánto es en total?, ¿a cuánto asciende?
▸ **come under** vt fus (heading) entrar dentro de; (influence) estar bajo
▸ **come up** vi (sun) salir; (problem) surgir; (event) aproximarse; (in conversation) mencionarse; **~ up here!** ¡sube aquí!
▸ **come up against** vt fus (resistance etc) tropezar con
▸ **come up to** vt fus llegar hasta; **she came up to me and kissed me** se me acercó y me besó; **the film didn't ~ up to our expectations** la película no fue tan buena como esperábamos
▸ **come up with** vt fus (idea) sugerir; (money) conseguir
▸ **come upon** vt fus (find) dar con
comeback ['kʌmbæk] n (reaction) reacción;

(response) réplica; **to make a ~** *(Theat)* volver a las tablas
comedian [kə'miːdɪən] *n* humorista
comedienne [kəmiːdɪ'ɛn] *n* humorista
comedy ['kɔmɪdɪ] *n* comedia
comet ['kɔmɪt] *n* cometa
comeuppance [kʌm'ʌpəns] *n*: **to get one's ~** llevar su merecido
comfort ['kʌmfət] *n* comodidad, confort; *(wellbeing)* bienestar; *(solace)* consuelo; *(relief)* alivio ▷ *vt* consolar; *see also* **comforts**
comfortable ['kʌmfətəbl] *adj* cómodo; *(income)* adecuado; *(majority)* suficiente; **I don't feel very ~ about it** la cosa me tiene algo preocupado
comfortably ['kʌmfətəblɪ] *adv* *(sit)* cómodamente; *(live)* holgadamente
comforts ['kʌmfəts] *npl* comodidades
comfort station *n* *(US)* servicios
comic ['kɔmɪk] *adj* *(also:* **comical)** cómico, gracioso ▷ *n* *(magazine)* tebeo; *(for adults)* cómic
comic strip *n* tira cómica
coming ['kʌmɪŋ] *n* venida, llegada ▷ *adj* que viene; *(next)* próximo; *(future)* venidero; **~(s) and going(s)** *n(pl)* ir y venir, ajetreo; **in the ~ weeks** en las próximas semanas
comma ['kɔmə] *n* coma
command [kə'mɑːnd] *n* orden, mandato; *(Mil: authority)* mando; *(mastery)* dominio; *(Comput)* orden, comando ▷ *vt* *(troops)* mandar; *(give orders to)* mandar, ordenar; *(be able to get)* disponer de; *(deserve)* merecer; **to have at one's ~** *(money, resources etc)* disponer de; **to have/take ~ of** estar al/asumir el mando de
commandeer [kɔmən'dɪə'] *vt* requisar
commander [kə'mɑːndə'] *n* *(Mil)* comandante, jefe(-a)
commandment [kə'mɑːndmənt] *n* *(Rel)* mandamiento
commando [kə'mɑːndəu] *n* comando
commemorate [kə'mɛməreit] *vt* conmemorar
commemoration [kəmɛmə'reɪʃən] *n* conmemoración
commemorative [kə'mɛmərətɪv] *adj* conmemorativo
commence [kə'mɛns] *vt, vi* comenzar
commend [kə'mɛnd] *vt* *(praise)* elogiar, alabar; *(recommend)* recomendar; *(entrust)* encomendar
commensurate [kə'mɛnʃərɪt] *adj*: **~ with** en proporción a
comment ['kɔment] *n* comentario ▷ *vt*: **to ~ that** comentar *or* observar que ▷ *vi*: **to ~ (on)** comentar, hacer comentarios (sobre); **"no ~"** "no tengo nada que decir", "sin comentarios"
commentary ['kɔmentərɪ] *n* comentario
commentator ['kɔmenteɪtə'] *n* comentarista
commerce ['kɔmə:s] *n* comercio
commercial [kə'mə:ʃəl] *adj* comercial ▷ *n* *(TV)* anuncio
commercial break *n* intermedio para publicidad
commercialism [kə'mə:ʃəlɪzəm] *n* comercialismo

commercial television *n* televisión comercial
commiserate [kə'mɪzəreit] *vi*: **to ~ with** compadecerse de, condolerse de
commission [kə'mɪʃən] *n* *(committee, fee, order for work of art etc)* comisión; *(act)* perpetración ▷ *vt* *(Mil)* nombrar; *(work of art)* encargar; **out of ~** *(machine)* fuera de servicio; **~ of inquiry** comisión investigadora; **I get 10% ~** me dan el diez por ciento de comisión; **to ~ sb to do sth** encargar a algn que haga algo; **to ~ sth from sb** *(painting etc)* encargar algo a algn
commissionaire [kəmɪʃə'nɛə'] *n* *(Brit)* portero, conserje
commissioner [kə'mɪʃənə'] *n* comisario; *(Police)* comisario de policía
commit [kə'mɪt] *vt* *(act)* cometer; *(to sb's care)* entregar; **to ~ o.s. (to do)** comprometerse (a hacer); **to ~ suicide** suicidarse; **to ~ sb for trial** remitir a algn al tribunal
commitment [kə'mɪtmənt] *n* compromiso
committed [kə'mɪtɪd] *adj* *(writer, politician etc)* comprometido
committee [kə'mɪtɪ] *n* comité; **to be on a ~** ser miembro(-a) de un comité
commodity [kə'mɔdɪtɪ] *n* mercancía
common ['kɔmən] *adj* *(gen)* común; *(pej)* ordinario ▷ *n* campo comunal; **in ~** en común; **we've got a lot in ~** tenemos mucho en común; **in ~ use** de uso corriente
common cold *n*: **the ~** el resfriado
common denominator *n* común denominador
commoner ['kɔmənə'] *n* plebeyo(-a)
common land *n* campo comunal, ejido
common law *n* ley consuetudinaria
common-law ['kɔmənlɔ:] *adj*: **~ wife** esposa de hecho
commonly ['kɔmənlɪ] *adv* comúnmente
Common Market *n* Mercado Común
commonplace ['kɔmənpleɪs] *adj* corriente
commonroom ['kɔmənrum] *n* sala de reunión
Commons ['kɔmənz] *npl* *(Brit Pol)*: **the ~** (la Cámara de) los Comunes
common sense *n* sentido común
Commonwealth ['kɔmənwɛlθ] *n*: **the ~** la Comunidad (Británica) de Naciones, la Commonwealth
commotion [kə'məuʃən] *n* tumulto, confusión
communal ['kɔmju:nl] *adj* comunal; *(kitchen)* común
commune *n* *(group)* comuna ▷ *vi*: **to ~ with** comunicarse con
communicate [kə'mju:nɪkeit] *vt* comunicar ▷ *vi*: **to ~ (with)** comunicarse (con)
communication [kəmju:nɪ'keɪʃən] *n* comunicación
communication cord *n* *(Brit)* timbre de alarma
communion [kə'mju:nɪən] *n* *(also:* **Holy Communion)** comunión
communiqué [kə'mju:nɪkeɪ] *n* comunicado, parte
communism ['kɔmjunɪzəm] *n* comunismo
communist ['kɔmjunɪst] *adj, n* comunista

community [kəˈmjuːnɪtɪ] *n* comunidad; (*large group*) colectividad; (*local*) vecindario

community centre *n* centro social

community chest *n* (US) fondo social

commutation ticket [kɔmjuˈteɪʃən-] *n* (US) billete de abono

commute [kəˈmjuːt] *vi* viajar a diario de casa al trabajo ▷ *vt* conmutar

commuter [kəˈmjuːtəʳ] *n* persona que viaja a diario de casa al trabajo

compact *adj* compacto; (*style*) conciso; (*packed*) apretado ▷ *n* (*pact*) pacto; (*also:* **powder compact**) polvera

compact disc [ˈkɔmpækt-] *n* compact disc, disco compacto

compact disc player [ˈkɔmpækt-] *n* lector *or* reproductor de discos compactos

companion [kəmˈpænɪən] *n* compañero(-a)

companionship [kəmˈpænjənʃɪp] *n* compañerismo

company [ˈkʌmpənɪ] *n* (*gen*) compañía; (*Comm*) empresa, compañía; **to keep sb ~** acompañar a algn; **Smith and C~** Smith y Compañía

company secretary *n* (*Brit*) administrador(a) de empresa

comparative [kəmˈpærətɪv] *adj* (*freedom, luxury, cost*) relativo; (*study, linguistics*) comparado

comparatively [kəmˈpærətɪvlɪ] *adv* (*relatively*) relativamente

compare [kəmˈpɛəʳ] *vt* comparar ▷ *vi:* **to ~ (with)** poder compararse (con); **~d with** *or* **to** comparado con *or* a; **how do the prices ~?** ¿cómo son los precios en comparación?

comparison [kəmˈpærɪsn] *n* comparación; **in ~ (with)** en comparación (con)

compartment [kəmˈpɑːtmənt] *n* compartim(i)ento; (*Rail*) departamento, compartimento

compass [ˈkʌmpəs] *n* brújula; **compasses** *npl* compás; **within the ~ of** al alcance de

compassion [kəmˈpæʃən] *n* compasión

compassionate [kəmˈpæʃənɪt] *adj* compasivo; **on ~ grounds** por compasión

compassionate leave *n* permiso por asuntos familiares

compatible [kəmˈpætɪbl] *adj* compatible

compel [kəmˈpɛl] *vt* obligar

compelling [kəmˈpɛlɪŋ] *adj* (*fig: argument*) convincente

compensate [ˈkɔmpənseɪt] *vt* compensar ▷ *vi:* **to ~ for** compensar

compensation [kɔmpənˈseɪʃən] *n* (*for loss*) indemnización

compère [ˈkɔmpɛəʳ] *n* (*Brit*) presentador(a)

compete [kəmˈpiːt] *vi* (*take part*) competir; (*vie with*) competir, hacer la competencia

competent [ˈkɔmpɪtənt] *adj* competente, capaz

competition [kɔmpɪˈtɪʃən] *n* (*contest*) concurso; (*Sport*) competición; (*Econ, rivalry*) competencia; **in ~ with** en competencia con

competitive [kəmˈpɛtɪtɪv] *adj* (*Econ, Sport*) competitivo; (*spirit*) competidor(a), de

competencia; (*selection*) por concurso

competitor [kəmˈpɛtɪtəʳ] *n* (*rival*) competidor(a); (*participant*) concursante

compile [kəmˈpaɪl] *vt* recopilar

complacency [kəmˈpleɪsnsɪ] *n* autosatisfacción

complacent [kəmˈpleɪsənt] *adj* autocomplaciente

complain [kəmˈpleɪn] *vi* (*gen*) quejarse; (*Comm*) reclamar

complaint [kəmˈpleɪnt] *n* (*gen*) queja; (*Comm*) reclamación; (*Law*) demanda, querella; (*Med*) enfermedad

complement *n* [ˈkɔmplɪmənt] complemento; (*esp ship's crew*) dotación ▷ *vt* [ˈkɔmplɪmɛnt] (*enhance*) complementar

complementary [kɔmplɪˈmɛntərɪ] *adj* complementario

complete [kəmˈpliːt] *adj* (*full: set*) completo; (*finished*) acabado ▷ *vt* (*fulfil*) completar; (*finish*) acabar; (*form*) rellenar; **it's a ~ disaster** es un desastre total; **it comes ~ with instructions** viene con sus correspondientes instrucciones

completely [kəmˈpliːtlɪ] *adv* completamente

completion [kəmˈpliːʃən] *n* (*gen*) conclusión, terminación; **to be nearing ~** estar a punto de terminarse; **on ~ of contract** cuando se realice el contrato

complex [ˈkɔmplɛks] *adj* complejo ▷ *n* (*gen*) complejo

complexion [kəmˈplɛkʃən] *n* (*of face*) tez, cutis; (*fig*) aspecto

complexity [kəmˈplɛksɪtɪ] *n* complejidad

compliance [kəmˈplaɪəns] *n* (*submission*) sumisión; (*agreement*) conformidad; **in ~ with** de acuerdo con

complicate [ˈkɔmplɪkeɪt] *vt* complicar

complicated [ˈkɔmplɪkeɪtɪd] *adj* complicado

complication [kɔmplɪˈkeɪʃən] *n* complicación

compliment *n* [ˈkɔmplɪmənt] *n* (*formal*) cumplido; (*flirtation*) piropo ▷ *vt* felicitar; **compliments** *npl* saludos; **to pay sb a ~** (*formal*) hacer cumplidos a algn; (*flirt*) piropear, echar piropos a algn; **to ~ sb (on sth/on doing sth)** felicitar a algn (por algo/por haber hecho algo)

complimentary [kɔmplɪˈmɛntərɪ] *adj* elogioso; (*copy*) de regalo; **~ ticket** invitación

comply [kəmˈplaɪ] *vi:* **to ~ with** acatar

component [kəmˈpəunənt] *adj* componente ▷ *n* (*Tech*) pieza, componente

compose [kəmˈpəuz] *vt* componer; **to be ~d of** componerse de, constar de; **to ~ o.s.** tranquilizarse

composed [kəmˈpəuzd] *adj* sosegado

composer [kəmˈpəuzəʳ] *n* (*Mus*) compositor(a)

composition [kɔmpəˈzɪʃən] *n* composición

compost [ˈkɔmpɔst] *n* abono

composure [kəmˈpəuʒəʳ] *n* serenidad, calma

compound *n* (*Chem*) compuesto; (*Ling*) término compuesto; (*enclosure*) recinto ▷ *adj* (*gen*) compuesto; (*fracture*) complicado ▷ *vt* (*fig: problem, difficulty*) agravar

comprehend [kɔmprɪˈhɛnd] *vt* comprender

comprehension [kɔmprɪ'hɛnʃən] *n*
comprensión

comprehensive [kɔmprɪ'hɛnsɪv] *adj* (*broad*)
extenso; (*general*) de conjunto; ~ **(school)** (*Brit*)
▷ *n* centro estatal de enseñanza secundaria, ≈ Instituto
Nacional de Bachillerato (*Esp*)

comprehensive insurance policy *n* seguro a
todo riesgo

compress *vt* comprimir ▷ *n* (*Med*) compresa

comprise [kəm'praɪz] *vt* (*also:* **be comprised of**)
comprender, constar de

compromise ['kɔmprəmaɪz] *n* solución
intermedia; (*agreement*) arreglo ▷ *vt*
comprometer ▷ *vi* transigir, transar (*LAm*) ▷ *cpd*
(*decision, solution*) de término medio

compulsion [kəm'pʌlʃən] *n* obligación; **under ~**
a la fuerza, por obligación

compulsive [kəm'pʌlsɪv] *adj* compulsivo

compulsory [kəm'pʌlsərɪ] *adj* obligatorio

computer [kəm'pjuːtəʳ] *n* ordenador,
computador, computadora

computer game *n* juego de ordenador

computerize [kəm'pjuːtəraɪz] *vt* (*data*)
computerizar; (*system*) informatizar

computer literate *adj*: **to be ~** tener
conocimientos de informática a nivel de usuario

computer programmer *n* programador(a)

computer programming *n* programación

computer science *n* informática

computing [kəm'pjuːtɪŋ] *n* (*activity*) informática

comrade ['kɔmrɪd] *n* compañero(-a)

con [kɔn] *vt* timar, estafar ▷ *n* timo, estafa; **to ~
sb into doing sth** (*col*) engañar a algn para que
haga algo

conceal [kən'siːl] *vt* ocultar; (*thoughts etc*)
disimular

concede [kən'siːd] *vt* reconocer; (*game*) darse
por vencido en; (*territory*) ceder ▷ *vi* darse por
vencido

conceit [kən'siːt] *n* orgullo, presunción

conceited [kən'siːtɪd] *adj* orgulloso

conceivable [kən'siːvəbl] *adj* concebible; **it is ~
that ...** es posible que ...

conceive [kən'siːv] *vt, vi* concebir; **to ~ of sth/of
doing sth** imaginar algo/imaginarse haciendo
algo

concentrate ['kɔnsəntreɪt] *vi* concentrarse ▷ *vt*
concentrar

concentration [kɔnsən'treɪʃən] *n* concentración

concentration camp *n* campo de concentración

concept ['kɔnsɛpt] *n* concepto

conception [kən'sɛpʃən] *n* (*idea*) concepto, idea;
(*Biol*) concepción

concern [kən'səːn] *n* (*anxiety*) preocupación;
(*matter*) asunto; (*Comm*) empresa ▷ *vt* (*relate to*)
tener que ver con; (*affect*) atañer, concernir;
(*worry*) preocupar; **it's of no ~ to me** me tiene sin
cuidado; **to be ~ed** (*about*) preocuparse (por);
to be ~ed with tratar de; **"to whom it may ~"** "a
quien corresponda"; **the department ~ed** (*under
discussion*) el departamento en cuestión; (*relevant*)
el departamento competente; **it's a stressful**

situation for everyone ~ed es una situación
estresante para todos los involucrados; **as far
as I am ~ed** en cuanto a mí, por lo que a mí se
refiere; **as far as the new project is ~ed** en lo
que respecta al nuevo proyecto

concerning [kən'səːnɪŋ] *prep* sobre, acerca de

concert ['kɔnsət] *n* concierto

concerted [kən'səːtəd] *adj* (*efforts etc*) concertado

concert hall *n* sala de conciertos

concerto [kən'tʃəːtəu] *n* concierto

concession [kən'sɛʃən] *n* concesión; (*price
concession*) descuento; **tax ~** privilegio fiscal

conciliation [kənsɪlɪ'eɪʃən] *n* conciliación

concise [kən'saɪs] *adj* conciso

conclude [kən'kluːd] *vt* (*finish*) concluir; (*treaty
etc*) firmar; (*agreement*) llegar a; (*decide*): **to ~ that
...** llegar a la conclusión de que ... ▷ *vi* (*events*)
concluir, terminar

concluding [kən'kluːdɪŋ] *adj* (*remarks etc*) final

conclusion [kən'kluːʒən] *n* conclusión; **to come
to the ~ that** llegar a la conclusión de que

conclusive [kən'kluːsɪv] *adj* decisivo,
concluyente

concoct [kən'kɔkt] *vt* (*food, drink*) preparar; (*story*)
inventar; (*plot*) tramar

concoction [kən'kɔkʃən] *n* (*food*) mezcla; (*drink*)
brebaje

concourse ['kɔŋkɔːs] *n* (*hall*) vestíbulo

concrete ['kɔnkriːt] *n* hormigón ▷ *adj* concreto

concur [kən'kəːʳ] *vi* estar de acuerdo

concurrently [kən'kʌntlɪ] *adv* al mismo tiempo

concussion [kən'kʌʃən] *n* conmoción cerebral

condemn [kən'dɛm] *vt* condenar

condensation [kɔndɛn'seɪʃən] *n* condensación

condense [kən'dɛns] *vi* condensarse ▷ *vt*
condensar; (*text*) abreviar

condensed milk *n* leche condensada

condescending [kɔndɪ'sɛndɪŋ] *adj* superior

condition [kən'dɪʃən] *n* condición; (*of health*)
estado; (*disease*) enfermedad ▷ *vt* condicionar;
on ~ that a condición (de) que; **I'll do it, on
one ~** lo haré, con una condición; **weather ~s**
condiciones atmosféricas; **in good/poor ~** en
buenas/malas condiciones, en buen/mal estado;
~s of sale condiciones de venta; **she has a heart
~** tiene una afección cardíaca

conditional [kən'dɪʃənl] *adj* condicional

conditioner [kən'dɪʃənəʳ] *n* (*for hair*) suavizante,
acondicionador

condo ['kɔndəu] *n* (*US col*) = **condominium**

condolences [kən'dəulənsɪz] *npl* pésame

condom ['kɔndəm] *n* condón

condominium [kɔndə'mɪnɪəm] *n* (*US: building*)
bloque de pisos *or* apartamentos (*propiedad de
quienes lo habitan*), condominio (*LAm*); (*: apartment*)
piso *or* apartamento (en propiedad), condominio
(*LAm*)

condone [kən'dəun] *vt* condonar

conducive [kən'djuːsɪv] *adj*: **~ to** conducente a

conduct *n* conducta, comportamiento ▷ *vt* (*lead*)
conducir; (*manage*) llevar, dirigir; (*Mus*) dirigir
▷ *vi* (*Mus*) llevar la batuta; **to ~ o.s.** comportarse

conducted tour n (Brit) visita con guía

conductor [kən'dʌktəʳ] n (of orchestra) director(a); (US: on train) revisor(a); (on bus) cobrador; (Elec) conductor

conductress [kən'dʌktrɪs] n (on bus) cobradora

cone [kəun] n cono; (pine cone) piña; (for ice cream) cucurucho

confectioner [kən'fɛkʃənəʳ] n (of cakes) pastelero(-a); (of sweets) confitero(-a); ~'s (shop) n pastelería; confitería

confectionery [kən'fɛkʃənrɪ] n pasteles; dulces

confer [kən'fəːʳ] vt: ~ (on) otorgar (a) ▷ vi conferenciar; **to ~ (with sb about sth)** consultar (con algn sobre algo)

conference ['kɔnfərns] n (meeting) reunión; (convention) congreso; **to be in ~** estar en una reunión

confess [kən'fɛs] vt confesar ▷ vi confesar; (Rel) confesarse

confession [kən'fɛʃən] n confesión

confessional [kən'fɛʃənl] n confesionario

confessor [kən'fɛsəʳ] n confesor

confetti [kən'fɛtɪ] n confeti

confide [kən'faɪd] vi: **to ~ in** confiar en

confidence ['kɔnfɪdns] n (gen: also: **self-confidence**) confianza; (secret) confidencia; **in ~** (speak, write) en confianza; **to have (every) ~ that** estar seguro or confiado de que; **motion of no ~** moción de censura; **to tell sb sth in strict ~** decir algo a algn de manera confidencial

confidence trick n timo

confident ['kɔnfɪdənt] adj seguro de sí mismo

confidential [kɔnfɪ'dɛnʃəl] adj confidencial; (secretary) de confianza

confidentiality [kɔnfɪdɛnʃɪ'ælɪtɪ] n confidencialidad

confine [kən'faɪn] vt (limit) limitar; (shut up) encerrar; **to ~ o.s. to doing sth** limitarse a hacer algo

confined [kən'faɪnd] adj (space) reducido

confinement [kən'faɪnmənt] n (prison) reclusión; (Med) parto; **in solitary ~** incomunicado

confines ['kɔnfaɪnz] npl confines

confirm [kən'fəːm] vt confirmar

confirmation [kɔnfə'meɪʃən] n confirmación

confirmed [kən'fəːmd] adj empedernido

confiscate ['kɔnfɪskeɪt] vt confiscar

conflict n conflicto ▷ vi (opinions) estar reñido; (reports, evidence) contradecirse

conflicting [kən'flɪktɪŋ] adj (reports, evidence, opinions) contradictorio

conform [kən'fɔːm] vi: **to ~ to** (laws) someterse a; (usages, mores) amoldarse a; (standards) ajustarse a

confound [kən'faund] vt confundir; (amaze) pasmar

confront [kən'frʌnt] vt (problems) hacer frente a; (enemy, danger) enfrentarse con

confrontation [kɔnfrən'teɪʃən] n enfrentamiento, confrontación

confuse [kən'fjuːz] vt (perplex) desconcertar; (mix up) confundir

confused [kən'fjuːzd] adj confuso; (person) desconcertado; **to get ~** desconcertarse; (muddled up) hacerse un lío

confusing [kən'fjuːzɪŋ] adj confuso

confusion [kən'fjuːʒən] n confusión

congeal [kən'dʒiːl] vi coagularse

congenial [kən'dʒiːnɪəl] adj agradable

congested [kən'dʒɛstɪd] adj (gen) atestado; (telephone lines) saturado

congestion [kən'dʒɛstʃən] n congestión

congestion charge(s) n(pl) (Aut) tasa por congestión

conglomerate [kən'glɔmərət] n (Comm, Geo) conglomerado

congratulate [kən'grætjuleɪt] vt felicitar

congratulations [kəngrætju'leɪʃənz] npl: ~ **(on)** felicitaciones (por); **~!** ¡enhorabuena!, ¡felicidades!

congregate ['kɔngrɪgeɪt] vi congregarse

congregation [kɔngrɪ'geɪʃən] n (Rel) fieles

congress ['kɔngrɛs] n congreso; (US Pol): **C~** el Congreso (de los Estados Unidos)

congressman ['kɔngrɛsmən] n (US) diputado, miembro del Congreso

conifer ['kɔnɪfəʳ] n conífera

conjecture [kən'dʒɛktʃəʳ] n conjetura

conjugate ['kɔndʒugeɪt] vt conjugar

conjunction [kən'dʒʌŋkʃən] n conjunción; **in ~ with** junto con

conjunctivitis [kəndʒʌŋktɪ'vaɪtɪs] n conjuntivitis

conjure ['kʌndʒəʳ] vi hacer juegos de manos
▶ **conjure up** vt (ghost, spirit) hacer aparecer; (memories) evocar

conjurer ['kʌndʒərəʳ] n ilusionista

conk out [kɔŋk-] vi (col) estropearse, fastidiarse, descomponerse (LAm)

con man n timador

connect [kə'nɛkt] vt juntar, unir; (Elec) conectar; (pipes) empalmar; (fig) relacionar, asociar ▷ vi: **to ~ with** (train) enlazar con; **to be ~ed with** (associated) estar relacionado con; (related) estar emparentado con; **I am trying to ~ you** (Tel) estoy intentando ponerle al habla

connection [kə'nɛkʃən] n juntura, unión; (Elec) conexión; (Tech) empalme; (Rail) enlace; (Tel) comunicación; (fig) relación; **what is the ~ between them?** ¿qué relación hay entre ellos?; **in ~ with** con respecto a, en relación a; **she has many business ~s** tiene muchos contactos profesionales; **to miss/make a ~** perder/coger el enlace

connive [kə'naɪv] vi: **to ~ at** hacer la vista gorda a

connotation [kɔnə'teɪʃən] n connotación

conquer ['kɔŋkəʳ] vt (territory) conquistar; (enemy, feelings) vencer

conquest ['kɔŋkwɛst] n conquista

cons [kɔnz] npl see **convenience**; **pro**

conscience ['kɔnʃəns] n conciencia; **in all ~** en conciencia

conscientious [kɔnʃɪ'ɛnʃəs] adj concienzudo; (objection) de conciencia

conscious ['kɔnʃəs] adj consciente; (deliberate: insult, error) premeditado, intencionado; **to become ~ of sth/that** darse cuenta de algo/de que

consciousness ['kɔnʃəsnɪs] n conciencia; (Med) conocimiento

conscript ['kɔnskrɪpt] n (Brit) recluta

conscription [kən'skrɪpʃən] n servicio militar (obligatorio)

consecrate ['kɔnsɪkreɪt] vt consagrar

consecutive [kən'sɛkjutɪv] adj consecutivo; **on 3 ~ occasions** en 3 ocasiones consecutivas

consensus [kən'sɛnsəs] n consenso; **the ~ of opinion** el consenso general

consent [kən'sɛnt] n consentimiento ▷ vi: **to ~ to** consentir en; **by common ~** de común acuerdo

consenting adults [kən'sɛntɪŋ-] npl adultos con capacidad de consentir

consequence ['kɔnsɪkwəns] n consecuencia; **in ~** por consiguiente

consequently ['kɔnsɪkwəntlɪ] adv por consiguiente

conservation [kɔnsə'veɪʃən] n conservación; (of nature) conservación, protección

conservationist [kɔnsə'veɪʃnɪst] n conservacionista

conservative [kən'sə:vətɪv] adj conservador(a); (cautious) moderado; **C~** adj, n (Brit Pol) conservador(a); **the C~ Party** el partido conservador (británico)

conservatory [kən'sə:vətrɪ] n (greenhouse) invernadero

conserve [kən'sə:v] vt conservar ▷ n conserva

consider [kən'sɪdəʳ] vt considerar; (take into account) tomar en cuenta; (study) estudiar, examinar; **~ how much you owe him** considera lo que le debes; **to ~ doing sth** pensar en (la posibilidad de) hacer algo; **would you ~ buying it?** ¿te interesa comprarlo?; **he is ~ed to be the best** se le considera el mejor; **all things ~ed** pensándolo bien; **~ yourself lucky!** ¡date por satisfecho!

considerable [kən'sɪdərəbl] adj considerable

considerably [kən'sɪdərəblɪ] adv bastante, considerablemente

considerate [kən'sɪdərɪt] adj considerado

consideration [kənsɪdə'reɪʃən] n consideración; (reward) retribución; **to be under ~** estar estudiándose; **my first ~ is my family** mi primera consideración es mi familia

considered [kən'sɪdəd] adj: **it's my ~ opinion that …** depués de haber reflexionado mucho, pienso que …

considering [kən'sɪdərɪŋ] prep: **~ (that)** teniendo en cuenta (que)

consign [kən'saɪn] vt consignar

consignment [kɔn'saɪnmənt] n envío

consist [kən'sɪst] vi: **to ~ of** consistir en

consistency [kən'sɪstənsɪ] n (of person etc) consecuencia, coherencia; (thickness) consistencia

consistent [kən'sɪstənt] adj (person, argument) consecuente, coherente; (results) constante

consolation [kɔnsə'leɪʃən] n consuelo

console vt consolar ▷ n (control panel) consola

consolidate [kən'sɔlɪdeɪt] vt consolidar

consonant ['kɔnsənənt] n consonante

consortium [kən'sɔ:tɪəm] n consorcio

conspicuous [kən'spɪkjuəs] adj (visible) visible; (garish etc) llamativo; (outstanding) notable; **to make o.s. ~** llamar la atención

conspiracy [kən'spɪrəsɪ] n conjura, complot

constable ['kʌnstəbl] n (Brit) agente (de policía); **chief ~** ≈ jefe de policía

constabulary [kən'stæbjulərɪ] n (Brit) ≈ policía

constant ['kɔnstənt] adj (gen) constante; (loyal) leal, fiel

constantly ['kɔnstəntlɪ] adv constantemente

constellation [kɔnstə'leɪʃən] n constelación

consternation [kɔnstə'neɪʃən] n consternación

constipated ['kɔnstɪpeɪtəd] adj estreñido

constipation [kɔnstɪ'peɪʃən] n estreñimiento

constituency [kən'stɪtjuənsɪ] n (Pol) distrito electoral; (people) electorado

constituent [kən'stɪtjuənt] n (Pol) elector(a); (part) componente

constitute ['kɔnstɪtju:t] vt constituir

constitution [kɔnstɪ'tju:ʃən] n constitución

constitutional [kɔnstɪ'tju:ʃənl] adj constitucional; **~ monarchy** monarquía constitucional

constraint [kən'streɪnt] n (force) fuerza; (limit) restricción; (restraint) reserva; (embarrassment) cohibición

construct [kən'strʌkt] vt construir

construction [kən'strʌkʃən] n construcción; (fig: interpretation) interpretación; **under ~** en construcción

constructive [kən'strʌktɪv] adj constructivo

construe [kən'stru:] vt interpretar

consul ['kɔnsl] n cónsul

consulate ['kɔnsjulɪt] n consulado

consult [kən'sʌlt] vt, vi consultar; **to ~ sb (about sth)** consultar a algn (sobre algo)

consultancy [kən'sʌltənsɪ] n (Comm) consultoría; (Med) puesto de especialista

consultant [kən'sʌltənt] n (Brit Med) especialista; (other specialist) asesor(a), consultor(a)

consultation [kɔnsəl'teɪʃən] n consulta; **in ~ with** en consulta con

consulting room n (Brit) consulta, consultorio

consume [kən'sju:m] vt (eat) comerse; (drink) beberse; (fire etc, Comm) consumir

consumer [kən'sju:məʳ] n (of electricity, gas etc) consumidor(a)

consumer goods npl bienes de consumo

consumer society n sociedad de consumo

consumer watchdog n organización protectora del consumidor

consummate ['kɔnsʌmeɪt] vt consumar

consumption [kən'sʌmpʃən] n consumo; (Med) tisis; **not fit for human ~** no apto para el consumo humano

cont. *abbr* (= *continued*) sigue

contact ['kɒntækt] *n* contacto; (*person: pej*) enchufe ▷ *vt* ponerse en contacto con; **~ lenses** *npl* lentes de contacto; **to be in ~ with sb/sth** estar en contacto con algn/algo; **business ~s** relaciones comerciales

contagious [kən'teɪdʒəs] *adj* contagioso

contain [kən'teɪn] *vt* contener; **to ~ o.s.** contenerse

container [kən'teɪnər] *n* recipiente; (*for shipping etc*) contenedor

container ship *n* buque contenedor, portacontenedores

contaminate [kən'tæmɪneɪt] *vt* contaminar

contamination [kəntæmɪ'neɪʃən] *n* contaminación

cont'd *abbr* (= *continued*) sigue

contemplate ['kɒntəmpleɪt] *vt* (*gen*) contemplar; (*reflect upon*) considerar; (*intend*) pensar

contemplation [kɒntəm'pleɪʃən] *n* contemplación

contemporary [kən'tɛmpərəri] *adj, n* (*of the same age*) contemporáneo(-a)

contempt [kən'tɛmpt] *n* desprecio; **~ of court** (*Law*) desacato (a los tribunales *or* a la justicia)

contemptuous [kən'tɛmptjuəs] *adj* desdeñoso

contend [kən'tɛnd] *vt* (*argue*) afirmar ▷ *vi* (*struggle*) luchar; **he has a lot to ~ with** tiene que hacer frente a muchos problemas

contender [kən'tɛndər] *n* (*Sport*) contendiente

content *adj* (*happy*) contento; (*satisfied*) satisfecho ▷ *vt* contentar; satisfacer ▷ *n* contenido; **contents** *npl* contenido; (**table of**) índice de materias; (*in magazine*) sumario; **to be ~ with** conformarse con; **to ~ o.s. with sth/with doing sth** conformarse con algo/con hacer algo

contented [kən'tɛntɪd] *adj* contento; satisfecho

contention [kən'tɛnʃən] *n* discusión; (*belief*) argumento; **bone of ~** manzana de la discordia

contentious [kən'tɛnʃəs] *adj* discutible

contentment [kən'tɛntmənt] *n* satisfacción

contest *n* contienda; (*competition*) concurso ▷ *vt* (*dispute*) impugnar; (*Law*) disputar, litigar; (*Pol: election, seat*) presentarse como candidato(-a) a

contestant [kən'tɛstənt] *n* concursante; (*in fight*) contendiente

context ['kɒntɛkst] *n* contexto; **in/out of ~** en/ fuera de contexto

continent ['kɒntɪnənt] *n* continente; **the C~** (*Brit*) el continente europeo, Europa; **on the C~** en el continente europeo, en Europa

continental [kɒntɪ'nɛntl] *adj* continental; (*Brit: European*) europeo

continental breakfast *n* desayuno estilo europeo

continental quilt *n* (*Brit*) edredón

contingency [kən'tɪndʒənsɪ] *n* contingencia

contingent [kən'tɪndʒənt] *n* (*group*) representación

continual [kən'tɪnjuəl] *adj* continuo

continuation [kəntɪnju'eɪʃən] *n* prolongación;

(*after interruption*) reanudación; (*story, episode*) continuación

continue [kən'tɪnjuː] *vi, vt* seguir, continuar; **~d on page 10** sigue en la página 10

continuing education [kən'tɪnjuɪŋ-] *n* educación continua de adultos

continuity [kɒntɪ'njuɪtɪ] *n* (*also Cine*) continuidad

continuous [kən'tɪnjuəs] *adj* continuo; **~ performance** (*Cine*) sesión continua; **~ stationery** papel continuo

contort [kən'tɔːt] *vt* retorcer

contour ['kɒntuər] *n* contorno; (*also:* **contour line**) curva de nivel

contraband ['kɒntrəbænd] *n* contrabando ▷ *adj* de contrabando

contraception [kɒntrə'sɛpʃən] *n* contracepción

contraceptive [kɒntrə'sɛptɪv] *adj, n* anticonceptivo

contract *n* contrato ▷ *cpd* (*price, date*) contratado, de contrato; (*work*) bajo contrato ▷ *vi* (*Comm*): **to ~ to do sth** comprometerse por contrato a hacer algo; (*become smaller*) contraerse, encogerse ▷ *vt* contraer; **to be under ~ to do sth** estar bajo contrato para hacer algo; **~ of employment** *or* **of service** contrato de trabajo

  ▶ **contract in** *vi* tomar parte

  ▶ **contract out** *vi*: **to ~ out (of)** optar por no tomar parte (en); **to ~ out of a pension scheme** dejar de cotizar en un plan de jubilación

contraction [kən'trækʃən] *n* contracción

contractor [kən'træktər] *n* contratista

contractual [kən'træktjuəl] *adj* contractual

contradict [kɒntrə'dɪkt] *vt* (*declare to be wrong*) desmentir; (*be contrary to*) contradecir

contradiction [kɒntrə'dɪkʃən] *n* contradicción; **to be in ~ with** contradecir

contradictory [kɒntrə'dɪktərɪ] *adj* (*statements*) contradictorio; **to be ~ to** contradecir

contralto [kən'træltəu] *n* contralto

contraption [kən'træpʃən] *n* (*pej*) artilugio

contrary ['kɒntrərɪ] *adj* (*opposite, different*) contrario [kən'trɛərɪ] (*perverse*) terco ▷ *n*: **on the ~** al contrario; **unless you hear to the ~** a no ser que le digan lo contrario; **~ to what we thought** al contrario de lo que pensábamos

contrast *n* contraste ▷ *vt* contrastar; **in ~ to** *or* **with** a diferencia de

contravene [kɒntrə'viːn] *vt* contravenir

contravention [kɒntrə'vɛnʃən] *n*: **~ (of)** contravención (de)

contribute [kən'trɪbjuːt] *vi* contribuir ▷ *vt*: **to ~ to** (*gen*) contribuir a; (*newspaper*) colaborar en; (*discussion*) intervenir en

contribution [kɒntrɪ'bjuːʃən] *n* (*money*) contribución; (*to debate*) intervención; (*to journal*) colaboración

contributor [kən'trɪbjutər] *n* (*to newspaper*) colaborador(a)

contrive [kən'traɪv] *vt* (*invent*) idear ▷ *vi*: **to ~ to do** lograr hacer; (*try*) procurar hacer

control [kən'trəul] *vt* controlar; (*traffic*

etc) dirigir; (*machinery*) manejar; (*temper*) dominar; (*disease, fire*) dominar, controlar ▷ *n* (*command*) control; (*of car*) conducción; (*check*) freno; **controls** *npl* (*of machine*) mandos; **to ~ o.s.** controlarse, dominarse; **owing to circumstances beyond our ~** debido a circunstancias ajenas a nuestra voluntad; **everything is under ~** todo está bajo control; **he always seems to be in ~** parece que siempre está en control de la situación; **she was in complete ~ of the situation** tenía la situación totalmente controlada; **she can't keep ~ of the class** no sabe controlar a la clase; **the car went out of ~** el coche se descontroló; **that boy is out of ~** ese muchacho está fuera de control

control panel *n* (*on aircraft, ship, TV etc*) tablero de instrumentos

control room *n* (*Naut, Mil*) sala de mandos; (*Radio, TV*) sala de control

control tower *n* (*Aviat*) torre de control

controversial [kɔntrə'və:ʃl] *adj* polémico

controversy ['kɔntrəvə:sɪ] *n* polémica

convalesce [kɔnvə'lɛs] *vi* convalecer

convector [kən'vɛktər] *n* calentador de convección

convene [kən'vi:n] *vt* (*meeting*) convocar ▷ *vi* reunirse

convenience [kən'vi:nɪəns] *n* (*comfort*) comodidad; (*advantage*) ventaja; **at your earliest ~** (*Comm*) tan pronto como le sea posible; **all modern ~s** (*Brit*): **all mod cons** todo confort

convenient [kən'vi:nɪənt] *adj* (*useful*) útil; (*place*) conveniente; (*time*) oportuno; **if it is ~ for you** si le viene bien

convent ['kɔnvənt] *n* convento

convention [kən'vɛnʃən] *n* convención; (*meeting*) asamblea

conventional [kən'vɛnʃənl] *adj* convencional

conversant [kən'və:snt] *adj*: **to be ~ with** estar familiarizado con

conversation [kɔnvə'seɪʃən] *n* conversación

converse *n* inversa ▷ *vi* conversar; **to ~ (with sb about sth)** conversar *or* platicar (*LAm*) (con algn de algo)

conversely [kɔn'və:slɪ] *adv* a la inversa

conversion [kən'və:ʃən] *n* conversión; (*house conversion*) reforma, remodelación

convert *vt* (*Rel, Comm*) convertir; (*alter*) transformar ▷ *n* converso(-a)

convertible [kən'və:təbl] *adj* convertible ▷ *n* descapotable; **~ loan stock** obligaciones convertibles

convey [kən'veɪ] *vt* transportar; (*thanks*) comunicar; (*idea*) expresar

conveyancing [kən'veɪənsɪŋ] *n* (*Law*) preparación de escrituras de traspaso

conveyor belt [kən'veɪər-] *n* cinta transportadora

convict *vt* (*gen*) condenar; (*find guilty*) declarar culpable a ▷ *n* presidiario(-a)

conviction [kən'vɪkʃən] *n* condena; (*belief*) creencia, convicción

convince [kən'vɪns] *vt* convencer; **to ~ sb (of sth/that)** convencer a algn (de algo/de que)

convinced [kən'vɪnst] *adj*: **~ of/that** convencido de/de que

convincing [kən'vɪnsɪŋ] *adj* convincente

convoluted ['kɔnvəlu:tɪd] *adj* (*argument etc*) enrevesado; (*shape*) enrollado, enroscado

convoy ['kɔnvɔɪ] *n* convoy

convulse [kən'vʌls] *vt* convulsionar; **to be ~d with laughter** dislocarse de risa

convulsion [kən'vʌlʃən] *n* convulsión

coo [ku:] *vi* arrullar

cook [kuk] *vt* cocinar; (*stew etc*) guisar; (*meal*) preparar ▷ *vi* hacerse; (*person*) cocinar ▷ *n* cocinero(-a)

▸ **cook up** *vt* (*col: excuse, story*) inventar

cookbook ['kukbuk] *n* libro de cocina

cooker ['kukər] *n* cocina

cookery ['kukərɪ] *n* cocina

cookery book *n* (*Brit*) = **cookbook**

cookie ['kukɪ] *n* (*US*) galleta

cooking ['kukɪŋ] *n* cocina ▷ *cpd* (*apples*) para cocinar; (*utensils, salt, foil*) de cocina

cool [ku:l] *adj* fresco; (*not hot*) tibio; (*not afraid*) tranquilo; (*unfriendly*) frío; (*fam: trendy*) cool ▷ *vt* enfriar ▷ *vi* enfriarse; **it is ~** (*weather*) hace fresco; **to keep sth ~ or in a ~ place** conservar algo fresco *or* en un sitio fresco

▸ **cool down** *vi* enfriarse; (*fig: person, situation*) calmarse

coolant ['ku:lənt] *n* refrigerante

coop [ku:p] *n* gallinero ▷ *vt*: **to ~ up** (*fig*) encerrar

co-op ['kəuɔp] *n abbr* (= **Cooperative (Society)**) cooperativa

cooperate [kəu'ɔpəreɪt] *vi* cooperar, colaborar; **will he ~?** ¿querrá cooperar?

cooperation [kəuɔpə'reɪʃən] *n* cooperación, colaboración

cooperative [kəu'ɔpərətɪv] *adj* cooperativo; (*person*) dispuesto a colaborar ▷ *n* cooperativa

coordinate *vt* coordinar ▷ *n* (*Math*) coordenada; **coordinates** *npl* (*clothes*) coordinados

coordination [kəuɔ:dɪ'neɪʃən] *n* coordinación

co-ownership [kəu'əunəʃɪp] *n* co-propiedad

cop [kɔp] *n* (*col*) poli

cope [kəup] *vi*: **to ~ with** poder con; (*problem*) hacer frente a

copier ['kɔpɪər] *n* (*photocopier*) (foto)copiadora

copper ['kɔpər] *n* (*metal*) cobre; (*col: policeman*) poli; **coppers** *npl* (*small change*) calderilla

copy ['kɔpɪ] *n* copia; (*of book*) ejemplar; (*of magazine*) número; (*material: for printing*) original ▷ *vt* copiar (*also Comput*); (*imitate*) copiar, imitar; **to make good ~** (*fig*) ser una noticia de interés; **rough ~** borrador; **fair ~** copia en limpio

▸ **copy out** *vt* copiar

copycat ['kɔpɪkæt] *n* (*pej*) imitador(a)

copyright ['kɔpɪraɪt] *n* derechos de autor

coral ['kɔrəl] *n* coral

coral reef *n* arrecife (de coral)

cord [kɔ:d] *n* cuerda; (*Elec*) cable; (*fabric*) pana; **cords** *npl* (*trousers*) pantalones de pana

cordial ['kɔːdɪəl] adj cordial ▷ n cordial
cordless ['kɔːdlɪs] adj sin hilos
cordon ['kɔːdn] n cordón
 ▶ **cordon off** vt acordonar
corduroy ['kɔːdərɔɪ] n pana
core [kɔːʳ] n (of earth, nuclear reactor) centro, núcleo; (of fruit) corazón; (of problem etc) esencia, meollo ▷ vt quitar el corazón de
cork [kɔːk] n corcho; (tree) alcornoque
corkscrew ['kɔːkskruː] n sacacorchos
corn [kɔːn] n (Brit: wheat) trigo; (US: maize) maíz, elote (CAm, Méx), choclo (CS); (on foot) callo; ~ **on the cob** (Culin) maíz en la mazorca, elote (CAm, Méx)
corned beef ['kɔːnd-] n carne de vaca acecinada
corner ['kɔːnəʳ] n (outside) esquina; (inside) rincón; (in road) curva; (Football) córner, saque de esquina ▷ vt (trap) arrinconar; (Comm) acaparar ▷ vi (in car) tomar las curvas; **to cut ~s** atajar
cornerstone ['kɔːnəstəun] n piedra angular
cornet ['kɔːnɪt] n (Mus) corneta; (Brit: of ice cream) cucurucho
cornflakes ['kɔːnfleɪks] npl copos de maíz, cornflakes
cornflour ['kɔːnflauəʳ] n (Brit) harina de maíz
Cornwall ['kɔːnwəl] n Cornualles
corny ['kɔːnɪ] adj (col) gastado
coronary ['kɔrənərɪ] n: ~ **(thrombosis)** infarto
coronation [kɔrə'neɪʃən] n coronación
coroner ['kɔrənəʳ] n juez de instrucción
corporal ['kɔːpərl] n cabo ▷ adj: ~ **punishment** castigo corporal
corporate ['kɔːpərɪt] adj corporativo
corporate hospitality n obsequios a los clientes por cortesía de la empresa
corporation [kɔːpə'reɪʃən] n (of town) ayuntamiento; (Comm) corporación
corps [kɔːʳ] (pl ~) [kɔːz] n cuerpo; **press ~** gabinete de prensa
corpse [kɔːps] n cadáver
correct [kə'rɛkt] adj correcto; (accurate) exacto ▷ vt corregir; **you are ~** tiene razón
correction [kə'rɛkʃən] n rectificación; (erasure) tachadura
correlation [kɔrɪ'leɪʃən] n correlación
correspond [kɔrɪs'pɔnd] vi (write) escribirse; (be equal to) corresponder
correspondence [kɔrɪs'pɔndəns] n correspondencia
correspondence course n curso por correspondencia
correspondent [kɔrɪs'pɔndənt] n corresponsal
corresponding [kɔrɪs'pɔndɪŋ] adj correspondiente
corridor ['kɔrɪdɔːʳ] n pasillo
corroborate [kə'rɔbəreɪt] vt corroborar
corrode [kə'rəud] vt corroer ▷ vi corroerse
corrosion [kə'rəuʒən] n corrosión
corrugated ['kɔrəgeɪtɪd] adj ondulado
corrugated iron n chapa ondulada
corrupt [kə'rʌpt] adj corrompido; (person) corrupto ▷ vt corromper; (bribe) sobornar;

(data) degradar; ~ **practices** (dishonesty, bribery) corrupción
corruption [kə'rʌpʃən] n corrupción; (of data) alteración
corset ['kɔːsɪt] n faja; (old-style) corsé
Corsica ['kɔːsɪkə] n Córcega
cortège [kɔː'teɪʒ] n cortejo, comitiva
cortisone ['kɔːtɪzəun] n cortisona
cosh [kɔʃ] n (Brit) cachiporra
cosmetic [kɔz'mɛtɪk] n cosmético ▷ adj (also fig) cosmético; (surgery) estético
cosmic ['kɔzmɪk] adj cósmico
cosmos ['kɔzmɔs] n cosmos
cosset ['kɔsɪt] vt mimar
cost [kɔst] n (gen) coste, costo; (price) precio; **costs** npl (Law) costas ▷ vt (pt, pp ~) costar; (estimate price of) preparar el presupuesto de; **the ~ of living** el coste or costo de la vida; **at all ~s** a toda costa; **at the ~ of his health** a costa de su salud; **to my ~** a mis expensas; **how much does it ~?** ¿cuánto cuesta?, ¿cuánto vale?; **what will it ~ to have it repaired?** ¿cuánto costará repararlo?; **it ~ me a great deal of effort** me costó mucho esfuerzo
co-star ['kəustaːʳ] n coprotagonista
Costa Rica ['kɔstə'riːkə] n Costa Rica
Costa Rican ['kɔstə'riːkən] adj, n costarriqueño(-a), costarricense
cost-effective [kɔstɪ'fɛktɪv] adj (Comm) rentable
costly ['kɔstlɪ] adj (expensive) costoso
cost-of-living [kɔstəv'lɪvɪŋ] adj: ~ **allowance** n plus de carestía de vida; ~ **index** n índice del coste de vida
cost price n (Brit) precio de coste
costume ['kɔstjuːm] n traje; (Brit: also: **swimming costume**) traje de baño
costume jewellery n bisutería
cosy, (US) **cozy** ['kəuzɪ] adj cómodo, a gusto; (room, atmosphere) acogedor(a)
cot [kɔt] n (Brit: child's) cuna; (US: folding bed) cama plegable
cot death n (Brit) muerte en la cuna
Cotswolds ['kɔtswəuldz] npl región de colinas del suroeste inglés
cottage ['kɔtɪdʒ] n casita de campo
cottage cheese n requesón
cottage industry n industria artesanal
cotton ['kɔtn] n algodón; (Brit: thread) hilo
 ▶ **cotton on** vi (col): **to ~ on (to sth)** caer en la cuenta (de algo)
cotton candy n (US) algodón (azucarado)
cotton wool n (Brit) algodón (hidrófilo)
couch [kautʃ] n sofá; (in doctor's surgery) camilla
couchette [kuː'ʃɛt] n litera
couch potato n (col) persona comodona que no se mueve en todo el día
cough [kɔf] vi toser ▷ n tos
 ▶ **cough up** vt escupir
cough drop n pastilla para la tos
could [kud] pt of **can**
couldn't ['kudnt] = **could not**
council ['kaunsl] n consejo; **city or town ~**

ayuntamiento; **C~ of Europe** Consejo de Europa
council estate n (Brit) barriada de viviendas
sociales de alquiler
council house n (Brit) vivienda social de alquiler
councillor ['kaunslə^r] n concejal
council tax n (Brit) contribución municipal
(dependiente del valor de la vivienda)
counsel ['kaunsl] n (advice) consejo; (lawyer)
abogado(-a) ▷ vt aconsejar; **~ for the defence/
the prosecution** abogado(-a) defensor(a)/fiscal;
to ~ sth/sb to do sth aconsejar algo/a algn que
haga algo
counsellor, (US) **counselor** ['kaunslə^r] n
consejero(-a); (US Law) abogado(-a)
count [kaunt] vt (gen) contar; (include) incluir
▷ vt contar ▷ n cuenta; (of votes) escrutinio;
(nobleman) conde; (sum) total, suma; **to ~
the cost of** calcular el coste de; **not ~ing
the children** niños aparte; **10 ~ing him** 10
incluyéndolo a él, 10 con él; **~ yourself lucky**
date por satisfecho; **that doesn't ~!** ¡eso no vale!;
to ~ (up) to 10 contar hasta 10; **it ~s for very
little** cuenta poco; **at the last ~** en el último
recuento; **to keep/lose ~ of sth** llevar/perder la
cuenta de algo
  ▶ **count on** vt fus contar con; **I wouldn't ~ on it!**
  ¡no contaría con ello!; **to ~ on doing sth** contar
  con hacer algo
  ▶ **count up** vt contar
countdown ['kauntdaun] n cuenta atrás
countenance ['kauntɪnəns] n semblante, rostro
▷ vt (tolerate) aprobar, consentir
counter ['kauntə^r] n (in shop) mostrador; (position:
in post office, bank) ventanilla; (in games) ficha;
(Tech) contador ▷ vt contrarrestar; (blow) parar;
(attack) contestar a ▷ adv: **~ to** contrario a; **to
buy under the ~** (fig) comprar de estraperlo or
bajo mano; **to ~ sth with sth/by doing sth**
contestar algo con algo/haciendo algo
counteract ['kauntər'ækt] vt contrarrestar
counterattack ['kauntərə'tæk] n contraataque
▷ vi contraatacar
counterfeit ['kauntəfɪt] n falsificación ▷ vt
falsificar ▷ adj falso, falsificado
counterfoil ['kauntəfɔɪl] n (Brit) matriz, talón
countermand ['kauntəmɑːnd] vt revocar
counterpart ['kauntəpɑːt] n (of person)
homólogo(-a)
countersign ['kauntəsaɪn] vt ratificar, refrendar
countess ['kauntɪs] n condesa
countless ['kauntlɪs] adj innumerable
country ['kʌntrɪ] n país; (native land) patria; (as
opposed to town) campo; (region) región, tierra;
in the ~ en el campo; **mountainous ~** región
montañosa
country and western (music) n música
country
country dancing n (Brit) baile regional
country house n (Brit) casa de campo
countryman ['kʌntrɪmən] n (national)
compatriota; (rural) hombre del campo
countryside ['kʌntrɪsaɪd] n campo

countrywide ['kʌntrɪ'waɪd] adj nacional ▷ adv
por todo el país
county ['kauntɪ] n condado; see also **district
council**
county council n (Brit) ≈ diputación provincial
coup [kuː] (pl **~s**) [kuːz] n golpe; (triumph) éxito;
(also: **coup d'état**) golpe de estado
couple ['kʌpl] n (of things) par; (of people) pareja;
(married couple) matrimonio ▷ vt (ideas, names)
unir, juntar; (machinery) acoplar; **a ~ of** un par de
coupon ['kuːpɔn] n cupón; (pools coupon) boleto
(de quiniela)
courage ['kʌrɪdʒ] n valor, valentía
courageous [kə'reɪdʒəs] adj valiente
courgette [kuə'ʒɛt] n (Brit) calabacín, zapallito
(CS), calabacita (Méx)
courier ['kurɪə^r] n mensajero(-a); (diplomatic)
correo; (for tourists) guía (de turismo)
course [kɔːs] n (of river, Scol) curso; (of ship) rumbo;
(fig: of action) proceder; (Golf) campo; (part of meal)
plato; **of ~** adv desde luego, naturalmente; **of ~!**
¡claro!, ¡cómo no! (LAm); **do you love me? — of ~
I do!** ¿me quieres? — ¡por supuesto que sí!; **(no)
of ~ not!** ¡claro que no!, ¡por supuesto que no!; **in
due ~** a su debido tiempo; **in the ~ of the next
few days** durante los próximos días; **it changed
the ~ of history** cambió el curso de la historia;
to go on a ~ hacer un curso; **we have no other ~
but to ...** no tenemos más remedio que ...; **there
are 2 ~s (of action) open to us** se nos ofrecen
dos posibilidades; **the best ~ (of action) would
be to ...** lo mejor sería ...; **~ of treatment** (Med)
tratamiento; **main ~** plato principal; **first ~**
primer plato; **a three-~ meal** una comida de
tres platos
court [kɔːt] n (royal) corte; (Law: institution)
tribunal; (building) juzgado; (Tennis) pista,
cancha ▷ vt (woman) cortejar; (fig: favour,
popularity) solicitar, buscar; (: death, disaster,
danger etc) buscar ▷ vi: **they've been ~ing for 3
years** llevan 3 años de relaciones; **to take sb
to ~** demandar a algn; **~ of appeal** tribunal de
apelación
courteous ['kəːtɪəs] adj cortés
courtesy ['kəːtəsɪ] n cortesía; **by ~ of** (por)
cortesía de
court-house ['kɔːthaus] n (US) palacio de
justicia
courtier ['kɔːtɪə^r] n cortesano
court martial ['kɔːt'mɑːʃəl] (pl **courts martial**)
n consejo de guerra ▷ vt someter a consejo de
guerra
courtroom ['kɔːtrum] n sala de justicia
courtyard ['kɔːtjɑːd] n patio
cousin ['kʌzn] n primo(-a); **first ~** primo(-a)
carnal
cove [kəuv] n cala, ensenada
covenant ['kʌvənənt] n convenio ▷ vt: **to ~ £20
per year to a charity** concertar el pago de veinte
libras anuales a una sociedad benéfica
cover ['kʌvə^r] vt cubrir; (with lid) tapar; (chairs
etc) revestir; (distance) cubrir, recorrer; (include)

abarcar; (*protect*) abrigar; (*issues*) tratar ▷ *n*
cubierta; (*lid*) tapa; (*for chair etc*) funda; (*envelope*)
sobre; (*of magazine*) portada; (*shelter*) abrigo; (*Brit:
insurance*) cobertura; **covers** *npl* (*of bed*) cobertor;
my face was ~ed in *or* **with mosquito bites**
tenía la cara cubierta de picaduras de mosquito;
our insurance didn't ~ it nuestro seguro
no lo cubría; **to take ~** (*shelter*) protegerse,
resguardarse; **under ~** (*indoors*) bajo techo;
under ~ of darkness al amparo de la oscuridad;
under separate ~ (*Comm*) por separado; **£10 will
~ everything** con diez libras cubriremos todos
los gastos
  ▶ **cover up** *vt* (*child, object*) cubrir, tapar; (*fig:
hide: truth, facts*) ocultar ▷ *vi*: **to ~ up for sb** (*fig*)
encubrir a algn
coverage ['kʌvərɪdʒ] *n* alcance; (*in media*)
reportaje; (*Insurance*) cobertura
cover charge *n* precio del cubierto
covering ['kʌvərɪŋ] *n* cubierta, envoltura
covering letter, (*US*) **cover letter** *n* carta de
explicación
cover note *n* (*Insurance*) póliza provisional
covert ['kəuvət] *adj* (*secret*) secreto, encubierto;
(*dissembled*) furtivo
cover-up ['kʌvərʌp] *n* encubrimiento
covet ['kʌvɪt] *vt* codiciar
cow [kau] *n* vaca ▷ *vt* intimidar
coward ['kauəd] *n* cobarde
cowardice ['kauədɪs] *n* cobardía
cowardly ['kauədlɪ] *adj* cobarde
cowboy ['kaubɔɪ] *n* vaquero
cower ['kauəʳ] *vi* encogerse (de miedo)
coy [kɔɪ] *adj* tímido
cozy ['kəuzɪ] *adj* (*US*) = **cosy**
CPA *n abbr* (*US*) = **certified public accountant**
CPI *n abbr* (= *Consumer Price Index*) IPC
CPU *n abbr* = **central processing unit**
crab [kræb] *n* cangrejo
crab apple *n* manzana silvestre
crack [kræk] *n* (*in wall, skin, ground, wood*) grieta;
(*in pottery, glass*) raja; (*noise*) crujido; (*: of whip*)
chasquido; (*joke*) chiste; (*col: drug*) crack;
(*attempt*): **to have a ~ at sth** intentar algo ▷ *vt*
(*wall, skin, ground, wood*) agrietar; (*pottery, glass*)
rajar; (*nut, egg*) cascar; (*safe*) forzar; (*whip etc*)
chasquear; (*knuckles*) crujir; (*joke*) contar; (*solve:
case*) resolver; (*code*) descifrar ▷ *vi* (*wall, skin,
ground, wood*) agrietarse; (*pottery, glass*) rajarse
▷ *adj* (*athlete*) de primera clase; **he opened the
door a ~** abrió la puerta un poquito; **he ~ed his
head on the pavement** se dio con la cabeza en
la acera; **to ~ jokes** (*col*) bromear; **I think we've
~ed it!** ¡creo que lo hemos resuelto!
  ▶ **crack down on** *vt fus* adoptar medidas severas
contra
  ▶ **crack up** *vi* (*col: have nervous breakdown*) sufrir
una crisis nerviosa; (*burst out laughing*) troncharse
de risa
cracker ['krækəʳ] *n* (*biscuit*) galleta salada,
cráquer; (*Christmas cracker*) sorpresa (navideña)
crackle ['krækl] *vi* crepitar

crackpot ['krækpɔt] (*col*) *n* pirado(-a) ▷ *adj* de
pirado
cradle ['kreɪdl] *n* cuna ▷ *vt* (*child*) mecer, acunar;
(*object*) abrazar
craft [krɑːft] *n* (*skill*) arte; (*trade*) oficio; (*cunning*)
astucia; (*boat*) embarcación
craftsman ['krɑːftsmən] *n* artesano
craftsmanship ['krɑːftsmənʃɪp] *n* artesanía
crafty ['krɑːftɪ] *adj* astuto
crag [kræg] *n* peñasco
cram [kræm] *vt* (*fill*): **to ~ sth with** llenar algo (a
reventar) de; (*put*): **to ~ sth into** meter algo a la
fuerza en ▷ *vi* (*for exams*) empollar
cramp [kræmp] *n* (*Med*) calambre; (*Tech*) grapa
▷ *vt* (*limit*) poner trabas a
cramped [kræmpt] *adj* apretado; (*room*)
minúsculo
cranberry ['krænbərɪ] *n* arándano
crane [kreɪn] *n* (*Tech*) grúa; (*bird*) grulla ▷ *vt, vi*:
to ~ forward, to ~ one's neck estirar el cuello
crank [kræŋk] *n* manivela; (*person*) chiflado(-a)
crankshaft ['kræŋkʃɑːft] *n* cigüeñal
cranky ['kræŋkɪ] *adj* (*eccentric*) maniático; (*bad-
tempered*) de mal genio
cranny ['krænɪ] *n see* **nook**
crash [kræʃ] *n* (*noise*) estrépito; (*of cars, plane*)
accidente; (*of business*) quiebra; (*Stock Exchange*)
crac ▷ *vt* (*plane*) estrellar ▷ *vi* (*plane*) estrellarse;
(*two cars*) chocar; (*fall noisily*) caer con estrépito;
he ~ed the car into a wall estrelló el coche
contra una pared o tapia
crash barrier *n* (*Aut*) barrera de protección
crash course *n* curso acelerado
crash helmet *n* casco (protector)
crash landing *n* aterrizaje forzoso
crass [kræs] *adj* grosero, maleducado
crate [kreɪt] *n* caja, cajón de embalaje; (*col*)
armatoste
crater ['kreɪtəʳ] *n* cráter
cravat(e) [krə'væt] *n* pañuelo
crave [kreɪv] *vt, vi*: **to ~ (for)** ansiar, anhelar
crawl [krɔːl] *vi* (*drag o.s.*) arrastrarse; (*child*) andar
a gatas, gatear; (*vehicle*) avanzar (lentamente);
(*col*): **to ~ to sb** dar coba a algn, hacerle la pelota
a algn ▷ *n* (*Swimming*) crol
crawler lane [krɔː'lə-] *n* (*Brit Aut*) carril para
tráfico lento
crayfish ['kreɪfɪʃ] *n* (*pl inv: freshwater*) cangrejo (de
río); (*saltwater*) cigala
crayon ['kreɪən] *n* lápiz de color
craze [kreɪz] *n* manía; (*fashion*) moda
crazy ['kreɪzɪ] *adj* (*person*) loco; (*idea*) disparatado;
to go ~ volverse loco; **to be ~ about sb/sth** (*col*)
estar loco por algn/algo
creak [kriːk] *vi* crujir; (*hinge etc*) chirriar, rechinar
cream [kriːm] *n* (*of milk*) nata, crema; (*lotion*)
crema; (*fig*) flor y nata ▷ *adj* (*colour*) color crema;
whipped ~ nata batida
  ▶ **cream off** *vt* (*fig: best talents, part of profits*)
separar lo mejor de
cream cake *n* pastel de nata
cream cheese *n* queso fresco cremoso

creamy ['kri:mɪ] *adj* cremoso

crease [kri:s] *n (fold)* pliegue; *(in trousers)* raya; *(wrinkle)* arruga ▷ *vt (fold)* doblar, plegar; *(wrinkle)* arrugar ▷ *vi (wrinkle up)* arrugarse

create [kri:'eɪt] *vt (also Comput)* crear; *(impression)* dar; *(fuss, noise)* hacer

creation [kri:'eɪʃən] *n* creación

creative [kri:'eɪtɪv] *adj* creativo

creativity [kri:eɪ'tɪvɪtɪ] *n* creatividad

creature ['kri:tʃəʳ] *n (living thing)* criatura; *(animal)* animal; *(insect)* bicho

creature comforts *npl* comodidades materiales

crèche, creche [krɛʃ] *n (Brit)* guardería (infantil)

credence ['kri:dəns] *n*: **to lend** *or* **give ~ to** creer en, dar crédito a

credentials [krɪ'dɛnʃlz] *npl* credenciales; *(letters of reference)* referencias

credibility [krɛdɪ'bɪlɪtɪ] *n* credibilidad

credible ['krɛdɪbl] *adj* creíble; *(witness, source)* fidedigno

credit ['krɛdɪt] *n (gen)* crédito; *(merit)* honor, mérito ▷ *vt (Comm)* abonar; *(believe)* creer, dar crédito a ▷ *adj* crediticio; **to be in ~** *(person, bank account)* tener saldo a favor; **on ~** a crédito; *(col)* al fiado; **he's a ~ to his family** hace honor a su familia; **to ~ sb with** *(fig)* reconocer a algn el mérito de; *see also* **credits**

credit card *n* tarjeta de crédito

credit note *n (Brit)* nota de crédito

creditor ['krɛdɪtəʳ] *n* acreedor(a)

credits ['krɛdɪts] *npl (Cine)* títulos *or* rótulos de crédito, créditos

creed [kri:d] *n* credo

creek [kri:k] *n* cala, ensenada; *(US)* riachuelo

creep [kri:p] *(pt, pp* **crept)** [krɛpt] *vi (animal)* deslizarse; *(plant)* trepar; **to ~ up on sb** acercarse sigilosamente a algn; *(fig: old age etc)* acercarse ▷ *n (col)*: **he's a ~** ¡qué lameculos es!; **it gives me the ~s** me da escalofríos

creeper ['kri:pəʳ] *n* enredadera

creepy ['kri:pɪ] *adj (frightening)* horripilante

cremate [krɪ'meɪt] *vt* incinerar

cremation [krɪ'meɪʃən] *n* incineración, cremación

crematorium [krɛmə'tɔ:rɪəm] *(pl* **crematoria)** [krɛmə'tɔ:rɪə] *n* crematorio

creosote ['krɪəsəʊt] *n* creosota

crêpe [kreɪp] *n (fabric)* crespón; *(also:* **crêpe rubber)** crep(é)

crêpe bandage *n (Brit)* venda elástica

crêpe paper *n* papel crep(é)

crept [krɛpt] *pt, pp of* **creep**

crescent ['krɛsnt] *n* media luna; *(street)* calle *(en forma de semicírculo)*

cress [krɛs] *n* berro

crest [krɛst] *n (of bird)* cresta; *(of hill)* cima, cumbre; *(of helmet)* cimera; *(of coat of arms)* blasón

crestfallen ['krɛstfɔ:lən] *adj* alicaído

crevice ['krɛvɪs] *n* grieta, hendedura

crew [kru:] *n (of ship etc)* tripulación; *(Cine etc)* equipo; *(gang)* pandilla, banda; *(Mil)* dotación

crew-cut ['kru:kʌt] *n* corte al rape

crew-neck ['kru:nɛk] *n* cuello de caja

crib [krɪb] *n* pesebre ▷ *vt (col)* plagiar; *(Brit Scol)* copiar

crick [krɪk] *n*: **~ in the neck** tortícolis

cricket ['krɪkɪt] *n (insect)* grillo; *(game)* críquet

crime [kraɪm] *n* crimen; *(less serious)* delito

criminal ['krɪmɪnl] *n* criminal, delincuente ▷ *adj* criminal; *(law)* penal

Criminal Investigation Department (CID) *n* ≈ Brigada de Investigación Criminal *(Esp)*

crimson ['krɪmzn] *adj* carmesí

cringe [krɪndʒ] *vi* encogerse

crinkle ['krɪŋkl] *vt* arrugar

cripple ['krɪpl] *n* lisiado(-a), cojo(-a) ▷ *vt* lisiar, mutilar; *(ship, plane)* inutilizar; *(production, exports)* paralizar; **~d with arthritis** paralizado por la artritis

crisis ['kraɪsɪs] *(pl* **crises)** ['kraɪsi:z] *n* crisis

crisp [krɪsp] *adj* fresco; *(toast, snow)* crujiente; *(manner)* seco

crisps [krɪsps] *npl (Brit)* patatas fritas

crisscross ['krɪskrɔs] *adj* entrelazado, entrecruzado ▷ *vt* entrecruzar(se)

criterion [kraɪ'tɪərɪən] *(pl* **criteria)** [kraɪ'tɪərɪə] *n* criterio

critic ['krɪtɪk] *n* crítico(-a)

critical ['krɪtɪkl] *adj (gen)* crítico; *(illness)* grave; **to be ~ of sb/sth** criticar a algn/algo

critically ['krɪtɪklɪ] *adv (speak etc)* en tono crítico; *(ill)* gravemente

criticism ['krɪtɪsɪzm] *n* crítica

criticize ['krɪtɪsaɪz] *vt* criticar

croak [krəʊk] *vi (frog)* croar; *(raven)* graznar ▷ *n (of raven)* graznido

Croat ['krəʊæt] *adj, n* = **Croatian**

Croatia [krəʊ'eɪʃə] *n* Croacia

Croatian [krəʊ'eɪʃən] *adj, n* croata

crochet ['krəʊʃeɪ] *n* ganchillo

crockery ['krɔkərɪ] *n (plates, cups etc)* loza, vajilla

crocodile ['krɔkədaɪl] *n* cocodrilo

crocus ['krəʊkəs] *n* azafrán

croft [krɔft] *n* granja pequeña

croissant ['krwas] *n* croissant, medialuna *(esp LAm)*

crony ['krəʊnɪ] *n* compinche

crook [kruk] *n (fam)* ladrón(-ona); *(of shepherd)* cayado; *(of arm)* pliegue

crooked ['krukɪd] *adj* torcido; *(path)* tortuoso; *(fam)* sucio

crop [krɔp] *n (produce)* cultivo; *(amount produced)* cosecha; *(riding crop)* látigo de montar; *(of bird)* buche ▷ *vt* cortar, recortar; *(animals: grass)* pacer
  ▸ **crop up** *vi* surgir, presentarse

croquet ['krəʊkeɪ] *n* croquet

cross [krɔs] *n* cruz ▷ *vt (street etc)* cruzar, atravesar; *(thwart: person)* contrariar ▷ *vi*: **the boat ~es from Santander to Plymouth** el barco hace la travesía de Santander a Plymouth ▷ *adj* enfadado, enojado *(esp LAm)*; **it's a ~ between geography and sociology** es una mezcla de geografía y sociología; **to ~ one's legs** cruzar las piernas; **to ~ o.s.** santiguarse; **it ~ed**

my mind that ... se me ocurrió que ...; **they've got their lines ~ed** (*fig*) hay un malentendido entre ellos; **to be/get ~ with sb (about sth)** estar enfadado/enfadarse con algn (por algo); **it makes me ~ when that happens** me da mucha rabia que pase eso
▶ **cross out** *vt* tachar
▶ **cross over** *vi* cruzar
crossbar ['krɔsbɑːʳ] *n* travesaño; (*of bicycle*) barra
crossbow ['krɔsbəu] *n* ballesta
cross-Channel ferry ['krɔs'tʃænl-] *n* transbordador que cruza el Canal de la Mancha
cross-country (race) ['krɔs'kʌntrɪ-] *n* carrera a campo traviesa, cross
cross-dressing [krɔs'dresɪŋ] *n* travestismo
cross-examination ['krɔsɪgzæmɪ'neɪʃən] *n* interrogatorio
cross-examine ['krɔsɪg'zæmɪn] *vt* interrogar
cross-eyed ['krɔsaɪd] *adj* bizco
crossfire ['krɔsfaɪəʳ] *n* fuego cruzado
crossing ['krɔsɪŋ] *n* (*road*) cruce; (*rail*) paso a nivel; (*sea passage*) travesía; (*Brit: also:* **pedestrian crossing**) paso de peatones
crossing guard *n* (*US*) *persona encargada de ayudar a los niños a cruzar la calle*
crossing point *n* paso; (*at border*) paso fronterizo
cross purposes *npl:* **to be at ~ with sb** tener un malentendido con algn
cross-question ['krɔs'kwɛstʃən] *vt* interrogar
cross-reference ['krɔs'rɛfrəns] *n* remisión
crossroads ['krɔsrəudz] *nsg* cruce; (*fig*) encrucijada
cross section *n* corte transversal; (*of population*) muestra (representativa)
crosswalk ['krɔswɔːk] *n* (*US*) paso de peatones
crosswind ['krɔswɪnd] *n* viento de costado
crossword ['krɔswəːd] *n* crucigrama
crotch [krɔtʃ] *n* (*of garment*) entrepierna
crotchet ['krɔtʃɪt] *n* (*Brit Mus*) negra
crouch [krautʃ] *vi* agacharse
crow [krəu] *n* (*bird*) cuervo; (*of cock*) canto, cacareo ▷ *vi* (*cock*) cantar; (*fig*) jactarse
crowbar ['krəubɑːʳ] *n* palanca
crowd [kraud] *n* muchedumbre; (*Sport*) público; (*common herd*) vulgo ▷ *vt* (*gather*) amontonar; (*fill*) llenar ▷ *vi* (*gather*) reunirse; (*pile up*) amontonarse; **~s of people** gran cantidad de gente
crowded ['kraudɪd] *adj* (*full*) atestado; (*well-attended*) concurrido
crown [kraun] *n* corona; (*of head*) coronilla; (*of hat*) copa; (*of hill*) cumbre ▷ *vt* (*also tooth*) coronar; **and to ~ it all ...** (*fig*) y para colmo or remate ...
crown court *n* (*Law*) tribunal superior
crown jewels *npl* joyas reales
crown prince *n* príncipe heredero
crow's feet ['krəuzfiːt] *npl* patas de gallo
crucial ['kruːʃl] *adj* crucial, decisivo; **his approval is ~ to the success of the project** su aprobación es crucial para el éxito del proyecto
crucifix ['kruːsɪfɪks] *n* crucifijo

crucifixion [kruːsɪ'fɪkʃən] *n* crucifixión
crucify ['kruːsɪfaɪ] *vt* crucificar; (*fig*) martirizar
crude [kruːd] *adj* (*materials*) bruto; (*fig: basic*) tosco; (: *vulgar*) ordinario
crude (oil) *n* (petróleo) crudo
cruel ['kruəl] *adj* cruel
cruelty ['kruəltɪ] *n* crueldad
cruise [kruːz] *n* crucero ▷ *vi* (*ship*) navegar; (*holidaymakers*) hacer un crucero; (*car*) ir a velocidad constante
cruiser ['kruːzəʳ] *n* crucero
crumb [krʌm] *n* miga, migaja
crumble ['krʌmbl] *vt* desmenuzar ▷ *vi* (*gen*) desmenuzarse; (*building*) desmoronarse
crumbly ['krʌmblɪ] *adj* desmenuzable
crumpet ['krʌmpɪt] *n* ≈ bollo para tostar
crumple ['krʌmpl] *vt* (*paper*) estrujar; (*material*) arrugar
crunch [krʌntʃ] *vt* (*with teeth*) ronzar; (*underfoot*) hacer crujir ▷ *n* (*fig*) hora de la verdad
crunchy ['krʌntʃɪ] *adj* crujiente
crusade [kruː'seɪd] *n* cruzada ▷ *vi:* **to ~ for/against** (*fig*) hacer una campaña en pro de/en contra de
crush [krʌʃ] *n* (*crowd*) aglomeración ▷ *vt* (*gen*) aplastar; (*paper*) estrujar; (*cloth*) arrugar; (*grind, break up: garlic, ice*) picar; (*fruit*) exprimir; (*grapes*) exprimir, prensar; **to have a ~ on sb** estar enamorado de algn
crushing ['krʌʃɪŋ] *adj* aplastante; (*burden*) agobiante
crust [krʌst] *n* corteza
crutch [krʌtʃ] *n* (*Med*) muleta; (*support*) apoyo
crux [krʌks] *n:* **the ~** lo esencial, el quid
cry [kraɪ] *vi* llorar; (*shout: also:* **cry out**) gritar ▷ *n* grito; (*howl*) aullido; (*weep*): **she had a good ~** lloró a lágrima viva; **what are you ~ing about?** ¿por qué lloras?; **to ~ for help** pedir socorro a voces; **"it isn't true", he cried** "no es cierto", gritó; **it's a far ~ from ...** (*fig*) dista mucho de ...
▶ **cry off** *vi* (*withdraw*) retirarse; (*back out*) rajarse
cryptic ['krɪptɪk] *adj* enigmático
crystal ['krɪstl] *n* cristal
crystal-clear ['krɪstl'klɪəʳ] *adj* claro como el agua; (*fig*) cristalino
CS gas *n* (*Brit*) gas lacrimógeno
cub [kʌb] *n* cachorro; (*also:* **cub scout**) niño explorador
Cuba ['kjuːbə] *n* Cuba
Cuban ['kjuːbən] *adj, n* cubano(-a)
cubbyhole ['kʌbɪhəul] *n* cuchitril
cube [kjuːb] *n* cubo; (*of sugar*) terrón ▷ *vt* (*Math*) elevar al cubo
cubic ['kjuːbɪk] *adj* cúbico; **~ capacity** (*Aut*) capacidad cúbica
cubicle ['kjuːbɪkl] *n* (*at pool*) caseta; (*for bed*) cubículo
cuckoo ['kuku:] *n* cuco
cuckoo clock *n* reloj de cuco
cucumber ['kjuːkʌmbəʳ] *n* pepino
cuddle ['kʌdl] *vt* abrazar ▷ *vi* abrazarse
cue [kjuː] *n* (*snooker cue*) taco; (*Theat etc*) entrada

cuff [kʌf] n (Brit: of shirt, coat etc) puño; (US: of trousers) vuelta; (blow) bofetada ▷ vt bofetear; **off the ~** adv improvisado

cufflinks ['kʌflɪŋks] npl gemelos

cul-de-sac ['kʌldəsæk] n (Brit) callejón sin salida

cull [kʌl] vt (select) entresacar; (kill selectively: animals) matar selectivamente ▷ n matanza selectiva; **seal ~** matanza selectiva de focas

culminate ['kʌlmɪneɪt] vi: **to ~ in** culminar en

culmination [kʌlmɪ'neɪʃən] n culminación, colmo

culottes [ku:'lɔts] npl falda pantalón

culprit ['kʌlprɪt] n culpable

cult [kʌlt] n culto; **a ~ figure** un ídolo

cultivate ['kʌltɪveɪt] vt (also fig) cultivar

cultivation [kʌltɪ'veɪʃən] n cultivo; (fig) cultura

cultural ['kʌltʃərəl] adj cultural

culture ['kʌltʃəʳ] n (also fig) cultura

cultured ['kʌltʃəd] adj culto

cumbersome ['kʌmbəsəm] adj voluminoso

cunning ['kʌnɪŋ] n astucia ▷ adj astuto; (clever: device, idea) ingenioso

cup [kʌp] n taza; (prize, event) copa; **a ~ of tea** una taza de té

cupboard ['kʌbəd] n armario, placar(d) (LAm)

cuppa ['kʌpə] n (Brit col) (taza de) té

cup-tie ['kʌptaɪ] n (Brit) partido de copa

curate ['kjuərɪt] n coadjutor

curator [kjuə'reɪtəʳ] n director(a)

curb [kəːb] vt refrenar; (powers, spending) limitar ▷ n freno; (US: kerb) bordillo

curdle ['kəːdl] vi cuajarse

cure [kjuəʳ] vt curar ▷ n cura, curación; **to be ~d of sth** curarse de algo; **to take a ~** tomar un remedio

curfew ['kəːfjuː] n toque de queda

curio ['kjuərɪəu] n curiosidad

curiosity [kjuərɪ'ɔsɪtɪ] n curiosidad

curious ['kjuərɪəs] adj curioso; **I'm ~ about him** me intriga

curl [kəːl] n rizo; (of smoke etc) espiral, voluta ▷ vt (hair) rizar; (paper) arrollar; (lip) fruncir ▷ vi rizarse; arrollarse
  ▶ **curl up** vi arrollarse; (person) hacerse un ovillo; (fam) morirse de risa

curler ['kəːləʳ] n bigudí

curly ['kəːlɪ] adj rizado

currant ['kʌrnt] n pasa; (black, red) grosella

currency ['kʌrnsɪ] n moneda; **to gain ~** (fig) difundirse

current ['kʌrnt] n corriente ▷ adj actual; **direct/ alternating ~** corriente directa/alterna; **the ~ issue of a magazine** el último número de una revista; **in ~ use** de uso corriente

current account n (Brit) cuenta corriente

current affairs npl (noticias de) actualidad

currently ['kʌrntlɪ] adv actualmente

curriculum [kə'rɪkjuləm, -lə] (pl **-s** or **curricula**) n plan de estudios

curriculum vitae (CV) [-'viːtaɪ] n currículum m (vitae)

curry ['kʌrɪ] n curry ▷ vt: **to ~ favour with** buscar el favor de

curse [kəːs] vi echar pestes ▷ vt maldecir ▷ n maldición; (swearword) palabrota

cursor ['kəːsəʳ] n (Comput) cursor

cursory ['kəːsərɪ] adj rápido, superficial

curt [kəːt] adj seco

curtail [kəː'teɪl] vt (cut short) acortar; (restrict) restringir

curtain ['kəːtn] n cortina; (Theat) telón; **to draw the ~s** (together) cerrar las cortinas; (apart) abrir las cortinas

curts(e)y ['kəːtsɪ] n reverencia ▷ vi hacer una reverencia

curve [kəːv] n curva ▷ vt, vi torcer

cushion ['kuʃən] n cojín; (Snooker) banda ▷ vt (seat) acolchar; (shock) amortiguar

cushy ['kuʃɪ] adj (col): **a ~ job** un chollo; **to have a ~ time** tener la vida arreglada

custard ['kʌstəd] n (for pouring) natillas

custodial sentence [kʌs'təudɪəl-] n (Brit) pena de prisión

custody ['kʌstədɪ] n custodia; **to take sb into ~** detener a algn; **in the ~ of** al cuidado or cargo de

custom ['kʌstəm] n costumbre; (Comm) clientela; see also **customs**

customary ['kʌstəmərɪ] adj acostumbrado; **it is ~ to do ...** es la costumbre hacer ...

customer ['kʌstəməʳ] n cliente; **he's an awkward ~** (col) es un tipo difícil

customized ['kʌstəmaɪzd] adj (car etc) hecho a encargo

custom-made ['kʌstəm'meɪd] adj hecho a la medida

customs ['kʌstəmz] npl aduana; **to go through (the) ~** pasar la aduana

customs officer n aduanero(-a), funcionario(-a) de aduanas

cut [kʌt] vb (pt, pp **-**) ▷ vt cortar; (price) rebajar; (reduce) reducir; (record) grabar; (col: avoid: class, lecture) fumarse ▷ vi cortar; (intersect) cruzarse ▷ n corte; (in skin) corte, cortadura; (with sword) tajo; (of knife) cuchillada; (in salary etc) recorte; (slice of meat) tajada; **to ~ one's finger** cortarse un dedo; **I ~ my foot on a piece of glass** me corté el pie con un cristal; **to ~ oneself** cortarse; **to ~ sth open** (vegetable, package) abrir algo; **to get one's hair ~** cortarse el pelo; **to ~ and paste** (Comput) cortar y pegar; **to ~ sb dead** (Brit fig) negarle el saludo or cortarle (LAm) a algn; **it ~s both ways** (fig) tiene doble filo; **to ~ a tooth** echar un diente; **power ~** (Brit) apagón; **price ~** rebaja
  ▶ **cut back** vt (plants) podar; (production, expenditure) reducir
  ▶ **cut down** vt (tree) cortar, talar; (consumption, expenses) reducir; **I'm ~ting down on coffee and cigarettes** estoy intentando tomar menos café y fumar menos; **to ~ sb down to size** (fig) bajarle los humos a algn
  ▶ **cut in** vi: **to ~ in on** (interrupt: conversation) interrumpir; (Aut) cerrar el paso a
  ▶ **cut off** vt cortar; (fig) aislar; (troops) cercar;

the electricity has been ~ off han cortado la electricidad; **we've been ~ off** (Tel) se ha cortado la comunicación

▶ **cut out** vt (article, picture) recortar; (delete) suprimir; **she's not ~ out to be a poet** no tiene madera de poeta; **~ it out!** ¡basta ya!

▶ **cut up** vt cortar (en pedazos); (chop: food) trinchar, cortar

cutback ['kʌtbæk] n reducción

cute [kjuːt] adj lindo, mono; (shrewd) listo

cuticle ['kjuːtɪkl] n cutícula

cutlery ['kʌtlərɪ] n (Brit) cubiertos

cutlet ['kʌtlɪt] n chuleta

cutout ['kʌtaut] n (shape) recortable

cut-price ['kʌt'praɪs], (US) **cut-rate** ['kʌt'reɪt] adj a precio reducido

cutthroat ['kʌtθrəut] n asesino(-a) ▷ adj feroz; **~ competition** competencia encarnizada or despiadada

cutting ['kʌtɪŋ] adj (gen) cortante; (remark) mordaz ▷ n (Brit: from newspaper) recorte; (: Rail) desmonte; (Cine) montaje

cutting edge n (of knife) filo; (fig) vanguardia; **a country on** or **at the ~ of space technology** un país puntero en tecnología del espacio

CV n abbr see **curriculum vitae**

cwt. abbr = **hundredweight(s)**

cyanide ['saɪənaɪd] n cianuro

cybercafé ['saɪbəkæfeɪ] n cibercafé

cyberspace ['saɪbəspeɪs] n ciberespacio

cyberterrorism ['saɪbətɛrərɪzəm] n ciberterrorismo

cycle ['saɪkl] n ciclo; (bicycle) bicicleta ▷ vi ir en bicicleta

cycle lane, cycle path n (Brit) carril-bici

cycling ['saɪklɪŋ] n ciclismo

cyclist ['saɪklɪst] n ciclista

cyclone ['saɪkləun] n ciclón

cygnet ['sɪgnɪt] n pollo de cisne

cylinder ['sɪlɪndəʳ] n cilindro

cylinder-head gasket n junta de culata

cymbals ['sɪmblz] npl platillos, címbalos

cynic ['sɪnɪk] n cínico(-a)

cynical ['sɪnɪkl] adj cínico

cynicism ['sɪnɪsɪzəm] n cinismo

Cypriot ['sɪprɪət] adj, n chipriota

Cyprus ['saɪprəs] n Chipre

cyst [sɪst] n quiste

cystitis [sɪs'taɪtɪs] n cistitis

czar [zɑːʳ] n zar

Czech [tʃɛk] adj checo ▷ n checo(-a); (Ling) checo; **the ~ Republic** la República Checa

Dd

D, d [di:] *n* (*letter*) D, d; (*Mus*): **D** re; **D for David**,
(US) **D for Dog** D de Dolores
D *abbr* (*US Pol*) = **democrat(ic)**
DA *n abbr* (*US*) = **district attorney**
dab [dæb] *vt*: **to ~ ointment onto a wound**
aplicar pomada sobre una herida; **to ~ with
paint** dar unos toques de pintura ▷ *n* (*light stroke*)
toque; (*small amount*) pizca
dabble ['dæbl] *vi*: **to ~ in** hacer por afición
dad [dæd], **daddy** ['dædɪ] *n* papá
daddy-long-legs [dædɪ'lɒŋlegz] *n* típula
daffodil ['dæfədɪl] *n* narciso
daft [dɑ:ft] *adj* chiflado
dagger ['dægə^r] *n* puñal, daga; **to look ~s at sb**
fulminar a algn con la mirada
daily ['deɪlɪ] *adj* diario, cotidiano ▷ *n* (*paper*)
diario; (*domestic help*) asistenta ▷ *adv* todos los
días, cada día; **twice ~** dos veces al día
dainty ['deɪntɪ] *adj* delicado
dairy ['dɛərɪ] *n* (*shop*) lechería; (*on farm*) vaquería
▷ *adj* (*cow etc*) lechero
dairy produce *n* productos lácteos
dais ['deɪɪs] *n* estrado
daisy ['deɪzɪ] *n* margarita
dale [deɪl] *n* valle
dally ['dælɪ] *vi* entretenerse
dam [dæm] *n* presa; (*reservoir*) embalse ▷ *vt*
embalsar
damage ['dæmɪdʒ] *n* daño; (*fig*) perjuicio; (*to
machine*) avería ▷ *vt* dañar; perjudicar; averiar; **~
to property** daños materiales
damages ['dæmɪdʒɪz] *npl* (*Law*) daños y
perjuicios; **to pay £5000 in ~** pagar 5000 libras
por daños y perjuicios
damaging ['dæmɪdʒɪŋ] *adj*: **~ (to)** perjudicial (a)
dame [deɪm] *n* (*title*) dama; (*US col*) tía; (*Theat*)
vieja; *see also* **pantomime**
damn [dæm] *vt* condenar; (*curse*) maldecir ▷ *n*
(*col*): **I don't give a ~** me importa un pito ▷ *adj*
(*col: also:* **damned**) maldito, fregado (*LAm*); **~ (it)!**
¡maldito sea!
damnation [dæm'neɪʃən] *n* (*Rel*) condenación
▷ *excl* (*col*) ¡maldición!, ¡maldito sea!
damning ['dæmɪŋ] *adj* (*evidence*) irrecusable
damp [dæmp] *adj* húmedo, mojado ▷ *n*
humedad ▷ *vt* (*also:* **dampen**: *cloth, rag*) mojar;
(*enthusiasm*) enfriar

damper ['dæmpə^r] *n* (*Mus*) sordina; (*of fire*)
regulador de tiro; **to put a ~ on things** ser un
jarro de agua fría
dampness ['dæmpnɪs] *n* humedad
damson ['dæmzən] *n* ciruela damascena
dance [dɑ:ns] *n* baile ▷ *vi* bailar; **to ~ about**
saltar
dance hall *n* salón de baile
dancer ['dɑ:nsə^r] *n* bailador(a); (*professional*)
bailarín(-ina)
dancing ['dɑ:nsɪŋ] *n* baile
dandelion ['dændɪlaɪən] *n* diente de león
dandruff ['dændrəf] *n* caspa
Dane [deɪn] *n* danés(-esa)
danger ['deɪndʒə^r] *n* peligro; (*risk*) riesgo; **~!** (*on
sign*) ¡peligro!; **to be in ~ of** correr riesgo de; **out
of ~** fuera de peligro
danger list *n* (*Med*): **to be on the ~** estar grave
dangerous ['deɪndʒərəs] *adj* peligroso
dangle ['dæŋgl] *vt* colgar ▷ *vi* pender, estar
colgado
Danish ['deɪnɪʃ] *adj* danés(-esa) ▷ *n* (*Ling*) danés
dapper ['dæpə^r] *adj* pulcro, apuesto
dare [dɛə^r] *vt*: **to ~ sb to do sth** retar *or* desafiar a
algn a hacer algo ▷ *vi*: **to ~ (to do sth)** atreverse
(a hacer algo); **I ~ you!** ¡a que no te atreves!; **I ~
say** (*I suppose*) puede ser, a lo mejor; **I ~ say that
...** no me sorprendería que ...; **I ~n't tell him**
no me atrevo a decírselo; **how ~ you!** ¡cómo te
atreves!; **don't you ~!** ¡ni se te ocurra!
daredevil ['dɛədevl] *n* temerario(-a), atrevido(-a)
daring ['dɛərɪŋ] *adj* (*person*) osado; (*plan, escape*)
atrevido ▷ *n* atrevimiento, osadía
dark [dɑ:k] *adj* oscuro; (*hair, complexion*) moreno;
(*fig: cheerless*) triste, sombrío ▷ *n* (*gen*) oscuridad;
(*night*) tinieblas; **~ chocolate** chocolate amargo;
it is/is getting ~ es de noche/está oscureciendo;
in the ~ about (*fig*) ignorante de; **after ~**
después del anochecer
darken ['dɑ:kn] *vt* oscurecer; (*colour*) hacer más
oscuro ▷ *vi* oscurecerse; (*cloud over*) nublarse
dark glasses *npl* gafas oscuras
dark horse *n* (*fig*) incógnita
darkness ['dɑ:knɪs] *n* (*in room*) oscuridad; (*night*)
tinieblas
darkroom ['dɑ:krum] *n* cuarto oscuro
darling ['dɑ:lɪŋ] *adj, n* querido(-a)

darn [dɑːn] vt zurcir
dart [dɑːt] n dardo; (in sewing) pinza ▷ vi
precipitarse; **to ~ away/along** salir/marchar
disparado
dartboard ['dɑːtbɔːd] n diana
darts [dɑːts] n dardos
dash [dæʃ] n (small quantity: of liquid) gota, chorrito;
(of solid) pizca; (sign) guión; (: long) raya ▷ vt
(break) romper, estrellar; (hopes) defraudar ▷ vi
precipitarse, ir de prisa; **a ~ of soda** un poco or
chorrito de sifón or soda
▶ **dash away, dash off** vi marcharse
apresuradamente
dashboard ['dæʃbɔːd] n (Aut) salpicadero
dashing ['dæʃɪŋ] adj gallardo
data ['deɪtə] npl datos
database ['deɪtəbeɪs] n base de datos
data processing n proceso or procesamiento de
datos
date [deɪt] n (day) fecha; (with friend) cita; (person)
pareja; (fruit) dátil ▷ vt (letter, document) fechar;
(col: girl etc) salir con; **what's the ~ today?** ¿a qué
estamos hoy?, ¿qué fecha es hoy?; **~ of birth**
fecha de nacimiento; **closing ~** fecha tope;
expiry ~ (of food, medicine) fecha de caducidad;
(of visa, contract) fecha de vencimiento; **to ~** adv
hasta la fecha; **out of ~** (unfashionable) pasado
de moda; (technology, idea) anticuado; (document)
caducado; **my passport's out of ~** tengo el
pasaporte caducado; **up to ~** (technology, attitudes)
moderno; (updated) puesto al día; **to bring up to
~** (correspondence, information) poner al día; (method)
actualizar; **to bring sb up to ~** poner a algn
al corriente; **he's got a ~ with his girlfriend**
ha quedado con su novia; **to make a ~ with sb**
quedar con algn; **a letter ~d 5 July** una carta
fechada el 5 de julio
dated ['deɪtɪd] adj anticuado
daub [dɔːb] vt embadurnar
daughter ['dɔːtəʳ] n hija
daughter-in-law ['dɔːtərɪnlɔː] n nuera, hija
política
daunting ['dɔːntɪŋ] adj desalentador(-a)
dawdle ['dɔːdl] vi (waste time) perder el tiempo;
(go slowly) andar muy despacio; **to ~ over one's
work** trabajar muy despacio
dawn [dɔːn] n alba, amanecer ▷ vi amanecer;
(fig): **it ~ed on him that ...** cayó en la cuenta
de que ...; **at ~** al amanecer; **from ~ to dusk** de
sol a sol
day [deɪ] n día; (working day) jornada; **during
the ~** por el día; **it's a lovely ~** hace un día
precioso; **the ~ before** el día anterior; **the ~
after, the following ~** el día siguiente; **the ~
after tomorrow** pasado mañana; **the ~ before
yesterday** anteayer, antes de ayer; **all ~ (long)**
todo el día; **any ~ now** cualquier día de éstos;
by ~ de día; **~ by ~** día a día; **every ~** todos los
días; **(on) the ~ that ...** el día que ...; **to work
an 8-hour ~** trabajar 8 horas diarias or al día; **he
works 8 hours a ~** trabaja 8 horas al día; **paid
by the ~** pagado por día; **a ~ off** un día libre;

one of these ~s un día de éstos; **these ~s, in
the present ~** hoy en día; **(back) in those ~s**
en aquellos tiempos; **that'll be the ~, when he
offers to pay!** ¡él nos invitará cuando las ranas
crien pelo!
daybreak ['deɪbreɪk] n amanecer
day-care centre ['deɪkɛə-] n centro de día; (for
children) guardería infantil
daydream ['deɪdriːm] n ensueño ▷ vi soñar
despierto
daylight ['deɪlaɪt] n luz (del día)
daylight robbery n: **it's ~!** (fig, col) ¡es un robo
descarado!
Daylight Saving Time n (US) hora de verano
day return (ticket) n (Brit) billete de ida y vuelta
(en un día)
daytime ['deɪtaɪm] n día
day-to-day ['deɪtə'deɪ] adj cotidiano, diario;
(expenses) diario; **on a ~ basis** día por día
day trip n excursión (de un día)
day tripper n excursionista
daze [deɪz] vt (stun) aturdir ▷ n: **in a ~** aturdido
dazed [deɪzd] adj aturdido
dazzle ['dæzl] vt deslumbrar
dazzling ['dæzlɪŋ] adj (light, smile) deslumbrante;
(colour) fuerte
DC abbr (Elec) = **direct current**; (US) = **District of
Columbia**
D/D abbr = **direct debit**
D-day ['diːdeɪ] n (fig) día clave
DEA n abbr (US: = Drug Enforcement Administration)
brigada especial dedicada a la lucha contra el tráfico de
estupefacientes
dead [dɛd] adj muerto; (limb) dormido; (battery)
agotado ▷ adv (completely) totalmente; (exactly)
justo; **she was ~** estaba muerta; **he was ~ on
arrival** ingresó cadáver; **to shoot sb ~** matar a
algn a tiros; **it was ~ easy** fue facilísimo; **you're
~ right!** ¡tienes toda la razón!; **~ tired** muerto
(de cansancio); **to stop ~** parar en seco; **~ centre**
justo en el centro; **~ on time** a la hora exacta;
the line has gone ~ (Tel) se ha cortado la línea;
the ~ npl los muertos
dead beat adj: **to be ~** (col) estar hecho polvo
deaden ['dɛdn] vt (blow, sound) amortiguar; (pain)
calmar, aliviar
dead end n callejón sin salida
dead-end ['dɛdɛnd] adj: **a ~ job** un trabajo sin
porvenir
dead heat n (Sport) empate
deadline ['dɛdlaɪn] n fecha tope; **to work to a ~**
trabajar con una fecha tope
deadlock ['dɛdlɔk] n punto muerto
dead loss n (col): **to be a ~** (person) ser un inútil;
(thing) ser una birria
deadly ['dɛdlɪ] adj mortal, fatal; **~ dull**
aburridísimo
deadpan ['dɛdpæn] adj sin expresión
Dead Sea n: **the ~** el Mar Muerto
deaf [dɛf] adj sordo; **to turn a ~ ear to sth** hacer
oídos sordos a algo
deaf-and-dumb ['dɛfən'dʌm] adj (person)

sordomudo; (*alphabet*) para sordomudos
deafen ['dɛfn] *vt* ensordecer
deafening ['dɛfnɪŋ] *adj* ensordecedor(a)
deaf-mute ['dɛfmjuːt] *n* sordomudo(-a)
deafness ['dɛfnɪs] *n* sordera
deal [diːl] *n* (*agreement*) trato; (*business*) negocio, transacción; (*Cards*) reparto ▷ *vb* (*pt, pp* -**t**) ▷ *vt* (*cards, blow*) dar ▷ *vi* (*in cards*) dar, repartir; **it's a ~!** (*col*) ¡trato hecho!, ¡de acuerdo!; **to do** *or* **make a ~ with sb** hacer un trato con algn; **it's a good ~** es un buen trato; **he got a bad/fair ~ from them** le trataron mal/bien; **a great ~ (of effort/money)** mucho (esfuerzo/dinero); **big ~!** ¡vaya cosa!; **it's no big ~** no pasa nada; **it's your ~** te toca dar
▷ **deal in** *vt fus* tratar en, comerciar en
▷ **deal with** *vt fus* (*people*) tratar con; (*problem*) ocuparse de; (*subject*) tratar de
dealer ['diːlə^r] *n* comerciante; (*Cards*) mano
dealership ['diːləʃɪp] *n* concesionario
dealings ['diːlɪŋz] *npl* (*Comm*) transacciones; (*relations*) relaciones
dealt [dɛlt] *pt, pp of* **deal**
dean [diːn] *n* (*Rel*) deán; (*Scol*) decano(-a)
dear [dɪə^r] *adj* querido; (*expensive*) caro ▷ *n*: **my ~** querido(-a); **~ me!** ¡Dios mío!; **D~ Sir/Madam** (*in letter*) Muy señor mío, Estimado señor/Estimada señora, De mi/nuestra (mayor) consideración (*esp LAm*); **D~ Mr/Mrs X** Estimado(-a) señor(a) X
dearly ['dɪəlɪ] *adv* (*love*) mucho; (*pay*) caro
dearth [dəːθ] *n* (*of food, resources, money*) escasez
death [dɛθ] *n* muerte
deathbed ['dɛθbɛd] *n* lecho de muerte
death certificate *n* partida de defunción
deathly ['dɛθlɪ] *adj* mortal; (*silence*) profundo
death penalty *n* pena de muerte
death rate *n* tasa de mortalidad
death row *n*: **to be on ~** (*US*) estar condenado a muerte
death sentence *n* condena a muerte
death squad *n* escuadrón de la muerte
deathtrap ['dɛθtræp] *n* lugar (*or* vehículo *etc*) muy peligroso
debacle [deɪ'bɑːkl] *n* desastre, catástrofe
debar [dɪ'bɑː^r] *vt*: **to ~ sb from doing** prohibir a algn hacer
debase [dɪ'beɪs] *vt* degradar
debatable [dɪ'beɪtəbl] *adj* discutible; **it is ~ whether ...** es discutible si ...
debate [dɪ'beɪt] *n* debate ▷ *vt* discutir
debauchery [dɪ'bɔːtʃərɪ] *n* libertinaje
debenture [dɪ'bɛntʃə^r] *n* (*Comm*) bono, obligación
debilitating [dɪ'bɪlɪteɪtɪŋ] *adj* (*illness etc*) debilitante
debit ['dɛbɪt] *n* debe ▷ *vt*: **to ~ a sum to sb** *or* **to sb's account** cargar una suma en cuenta a algn
debrief [diː'briːf] *vt* hacer dar parte
debriefing [diː'briːfɪŋ] *n* relación (de un informe)
debris ['dɛbriː] *n* escombros
debt [dɛt] *n* deuda; **to be in ~** tener deudas; **~s of £5000** deudas de cinco mil libras; **bad ~** deuda incobrable
debt collector *n* cobrador(a) de deudas
debtor ['dɛtə^r] *n* deudor(a)
debug ['diː'bʌg] *vt* (*Comput*) depurar
debunk [diː'bʌŋk] *vt* (*col: theory*) desprestigiar, desacreditar; (*: claim*) desacreditar; (*: person, institution*) desenmascarar
début ['deɪbjuː] *n* presentación
decade ['dɛkeɪd] *n* década, decenio
decadence ['dɛkədəns] *n* decadencia
decadent ['dɛkədənt] *adj* decadente
de-caff ['diː'kæf] *n* (*col*) descafeinado
decaffeinated [dɪ'kæfɪneɪtɪd] *adj* descafeinado
decanter [dɪ'kæntə^r] *n* jarra, decantador
decathlon [dɪ'kæθlən] *n* decatlón
decay [dɪ'keɪ] *n* (*fig*) decadencia; (*of building*) desmoronamiento; (*of tooth*) caries ▷ *vi* (*rot*) pudrirse; (*fig*) decaer
deceased [dɪ'siːst] *adj* difunto
deceit [dɪ'siːt] *n* engaño
deceitful [dɪ'siːtful] *adj* engañoso
deceive [dɪ'siːv] *vt* engañar
December [dɪ'sɛmbə^r] *n* diciembre
decency ['diːsənsɪ] *n* decencia
decent ['diːsənt] *adj* (*proper*) decente; (*person*) amable, bueno
deception [dɪ'sɛpʃən] *n* engaño
deceptive [dɪ'sɛptɪv] *adj* engañoso
decibel ['dɛsɪbɛl] *n* decibel(io)
decide [dɪ'saɪd] *vt* (*person*) decidir; (*question, argument*) resolver ▷ *vi* decidir, decidirse; **haven't you ~d yet?** ¿aún no te has decidido?; **to ~ to do sth/that...** decidir hacer algo/que...; **I ~d not to go** decidí no ir; **to ~ against doing sth** decidir en contra de hacer algo
▷ **decide on** *vt fus*: **to ~ on sth** decidirse por algo; **to ~ on doing sth** decidir hacer algo
decided [dɪ'saɪdɪd] *adj* (*resolute*) decidido; (*clear, definite*) indudable
decidedly [dɪ'saɪdɪdlɪ] *adv* decididamente
deciduous [dɪ'sɪdjuəs] *adj* de hoja caduca
decimal ['dɛsɪməl] *adj* decimal ▷ *n* decimal; **to 3 ~ places** con 3 cifras decimales
decimal point *n* coma decimal
decipher [dɪ'saɪfə^r] *vt* descifrar
decision [dɪ'sɪʒən] *n* decisión; **to make a ~** tomar una decisión
decisive [dɪ'saɪsɪv] *adj* (*influence*) decisivo; (*manner, person*) decidido; (*reply*) tajante
deck [dɛk] *n* (*Naut*) cubierta; (*of bus*) piso; (*of cards*) baraja; **cassette ~** platina; **to go up on ~** subir a (la) cubierta; **below ~** en la bodega
deckchair ['dɛktʃɛə^r] *n* tumbona
declaration [dɛklə'reɪʃən] *n* declaración
declare [dɪ'klɛə^r] *vt* (*gen*) declarar
decline [dɪ'klaɪn] *n* decaimiento, decadencia; (*lessening*) disminución ▷ *vt* rehusar ▷ *vi* decaer; disminuir; **~ in living standards** disminución del nivel de vida; **to ~ to do sth** rehusar hacer algo
decoder [diː'kəʊdə^r] *n* (*Comput, TV*) de(s)codificador

decompose [di:kəm'pəuz] *vi* descomponerse
decomposition [di:kɔmpə'zɪʃən] *n* descomposición
decompression [di:kəm'preʃən] *n* descompresión
decongestant [di:kən'dʒɛstənt] *n* descongestionante
decontaminate [di:kən'tæmɪneɪt] *vt* descontaminar
décor ['deɪkɔ:ʳ] *n* decoración; *(Theat)* decorado
decorate ['dɛkəreɪt] *vt (paint)* pintar; *(paper)* empapelar; *(adorn)*: **to ~ (with)** adornar (de), decorar (de)
decoration [dɛkə'reɪʃən] *n* adorno; *(act)* decoración; *(medal)* condecoración
decorator ['dɛkəreɪtəʳ] *n (workman)* pintor decorador
decoy ['di:kɔɪ] *n* señuelo; **police ~** trampa *or* señuelo policial
decrease *n* disminución ▷ *vt* disminuir, reducir ▷ *vi* reducirse; **to be on the ~** ir disminuyendo
decree [dɪ'kri:] *n* decreto ▷ *vt*: **to ~ (that)** decretar (que); **~ absolute/nisi** sentencia absoluta/provisional de divorcio
decrepit [dɪ'krɛpɪt] *adj (person)* decrépito; *(building)* ruinoso
dedicate ['dɛdɪkeɪt] *vt* dedicar
dedicated ['dɛdɪkeɪtɪd] *adj* dedicado; *(Comput)* especializado
dedication [dɛdɪ'keɪʃən] *n (devotion)* dedicación; *(in book)* dedicatoria
deduce [dɪ'dju:s] *vt* deducir
deduct [dɪ'dʌkt] *vt* restar; *(from wage etc)* descontar, deducir
deduction [dɪ'dʌkʃən] *n (amount deducted)* descuento; *(conclusion)* deducción, conclusión
deed [di:d] *n* hecho, acto; *(feat)* hazaña; *(Law)* escritura; **~ of covenant** escritura de contrato
deem [di:m] *vt (formal)* juzgar, considerar; **to ~ it wise to do** considerar prudente hacer
deep [di:p] *adj* profundo; *(voice, sound)* grave; *(breath)* profundo ▷ *adv*: **the spectators stood 20 ~** los espectadores se formaron de 20 en fondo; **a ~ layer of snow** una espesa capa de nieve; **the ~ end** *(of swimming pool)* lo hondo; **he's got a ~ voice** tiene la voz grave; **to take a ~ breath** respirar hondo; **he thrust his hand ~ into his pocket** metió la mano hasta el fondo del bolsillo; **to be 4 metres ~** tener 4 metros de profundidad; **a hole 4 metres ~** un agujero de 4 metros de profundidad; **how ~ is the lake?** ¿qué profundidad tiene el lago?; **to be ~ in debt** estar hasta el cuello de deudas
deepen ['di:pn] *vt* ahondar, profundizar ▷ *vi (darkness)* intensificarse
deep-freeze ['di:p'fri:z] *n* arcón congelador
deep-fry ['di:p'fraɪ] *vt* freír en aceite abundante
deeply ['di:plɪ] *adv (breathe)* profundamente, a pleno pulmón; *(interested, moved, grateful)* profundamente, hondamente; **to regret sth ~** sentir algo profundamente
deep-rooted ['di:p'ru:tɪd] *adj (prejudice, habit)*

profundamente arraigado; *(affection)* profundo
deep-sea ['di:p'si:] *adj*: **~ diver** buzo; **~ diving** buceo de altura
deep-seated ['di:p'si:tɪd] *adj (beliefs)* (profundamente) arraigado
deep-vein thrombosis *n* trombosa venosa profunda
deer [dɪəʳ] *n, pl inv* ciervo
deface [dɪ'feɪs] *vt* desfigurar, mutilar
defamation [dɛfə'meɪʃən] *n* difamación
default [dɪ'fɔ:lt] *vi* faltar al pago; *(Sport)* no presentarse, no comparecer ▷ *n (Comput)* defecto; **by ~** *(Law)* en rebeldía; *(Sport)* por incomparecencia; **to ~ on a debt** dejar de pagar una deuda
defeat [dɪ'fi:t] *n* derrota ▷ *vt* derrotar, vencer; *(fig: efforts)* frustrar
defecate ['dɛfəkeɪt] *vi* defecar
defect *n* defecto ▷ *vi*: **to ~ to the enemy** pasarse al enemigo; **physical ~** defecto físico; **mental ~** deficiencia mental
defective [dɪ'fɛktɪv] *adj (gen)* defectuoso; *(person)* anormal
defector [dɪ'fɛktə] *n* tránsfuga
defence, *(US)* **defense** [dɪ'fɛns] *n* defensa; **the Ministry of D~** el Ministerio de Defensa; **witness for the ~** testigo de descargo
defenceless [dɪ'fɛnslɪs] *adj* indefenso
defend [dɪ'fɛnd] *vt* defender; *(decision, action)* defender; *(opinion)* mantener
defendant [dɪ'fɛndənt] *n* acusado(-a); *(in civil case)* demandado(-a)
defender [dɪ'fɛndəʳ] *n* defensor(a)
defense [dɪ'fɛns] *n (US)* = **defence**
defensive [dɪ'fɛnsɪv] *adj* defensivo ▷ *n* defensiva; **on the ~** a la defensiva
defer [dɪ'fə:ʳ] *vt (postpone)* aplazar; **to ~ to** diferir a; *(submit)*: **to ~ to sb/sb's opinion** someterse a algn/a la opinión de algn
deference ['dɛfərəns] *n* deferencia, respeto; **out of** *or* **in ~ to** por respeto a
defiance [dɪ'faɪəns] *n* desafío; **in ~ of** en contra de
defiant [dɪ'faɪənt] *adj (insolent)* insolente; *(challenging)* retador(a)
deficiency [dɪ'fɪʃənsɪ] *n (lack)* falta; *(Comm)* déficit; *(defect)* defecto
deficient [dɪ'fɪʃənt] *adj (lacking)* insuficiente; *(incomplete)* incompleto; *(defective)* defectuoso; *(mentally)* anormal; **~ in** deficiente en
deficit ['dɛfɪsɪt] *n* déficit
defile [dɪ'faɪl] *vt* manchar; *(violate)* violar
define [dɪ'faɪn] *vt (Comput)* definir
definite ['dɛfɪnɪt] *adj (fixed)* determinado; *(clear, obvious)* claro; **he was ~ about it** no dejó lugar a dudas (sobre ello)
definitely ['dɛfɪnɪtlɪ] *adv*: **he's ~ mad** no cabe duda de que está loco
definition [dɛfɪ'nɪʃən] *n* definición
deflate [di:'fleɪt] *vt (gen)* desinflar; *(pompous person)* quitar *or* rebajar los humos a; *(Econ)* deflacionar

deflect [dɪ'flɛkt] vt desviar
deform [dɪ'fɔːm] vt deformar
deformed [dɪ'fɔːmd] adj deformado
deformity [dɪ'fɔːmɪtɪ] n deformación
defraud [dɪ'frɔːd] vt estafar; **to ~ sb of sth** estafar algo a algn
defrost [diː'frɔst] vt (frozen food, fridge) descongelar
defroster [diː'frɔstəʳ] n (US) eliminador de vaho
deft [dɛft] adj diestro, hábil
defunct [dɪ'fʌŋkt] adj difunto; (organization etc) ya desaparecido
defuse [diː'fjuːz] vt desarmar; (situation) calmar, apaciguar
defy [dɪ'faɪ] vt (resist) oponerse a; (challenge) desafiar; (order) contravenir
degenerate vi degenerar ▷ adj degenerado
degradation [dɛgrə'deɪʃən] n degradación
degree [dɪ'griː] n grado; (Scol) título; **10 ~s below freezing** 10 grados bajo cero; **to have a ~ in maths** ser licenciado(-a) en matemáticas; **by ~s** (gradually) poco a poco, por etapas; **to some ~**, **to a certain ~** hasta cierto punto; **a considerable ~ of risk** un gran índice de riesgo
dehydrated [diːhaɪ'dreɪtɪd] adj deshidratado; (milk) en polvo
dehydration [diːhaɪ'dreɪʃən] n deshidratación
de-ice [diː'aɪs] vt (windscreen) deshelar
de-icer [diː'aɪsəʳ] n descongelador
deign [deɪn] vi: **to ~ to do** dignarse hacer
deity ['diːɪtɪ] n deidad, divinidad
déjà vu [deɪʒaː'vuː] n: **I had a sense of ~** sentía como si ya lo hubiera vivido
dejected [dɪ'dʒɛktɪd] adj abatido, desanimado
dejection [dɪ'dʒɛkʃən] n abatimiento
delay [dɪ'leɪ] vt demorar, aplazar; (person) entretener; (train) retrasar; (payment) aplazar ▷ vi tardar ▷ n demora, retraso; **without ~** en seguida, sin tardar
delectable [dɪ'lɛktəbl] adj (person) encantador(a); (food) delicioso
delegate n delegado(-a) ▷ vt delegar; **to ~ sth to sb/sb to do sth** delegar algo en algn/en algn para hacer algo
delegation [dɛlɪ'geɪʃən] n (of work etc) delegación
delete [dɪ'liːt] vt suprimir, tachar; (Comput) suprimir, borrar
deli ['dɛlɪ] n = **delicatessen**
deliberate adj (intentional) intencionado; (slow) pausado, lento ▷ vi deliberar
deliberately [dɪ'lɪbərɪtlɪ] adv (on purpose) a propósito; (slowly) pausadamente
deliberation [dɪlɪbə'reɪʃən] n (consideration) reflexión; (discussion) deliberación, discusión
delicacy ['dɛlɪkəsɪ] n delicadeza; (choice food) manjar
delicate ['dɛlɪkɪt] adj (gen) delicado; (fragile) frágil
delicatessen [dɛlɪkə'tɛsn] n tienda especializada en comida exótica
delicious [dɪ'lɪʃəs] adj delicioso, rico
delight [dɪ'laɪt] n (feeling) placer, deleite; (object) encanto, delicia ▷ vt encantar, deleitar; **to take ~ in** deleitarse en

delighted [dɪ'laɪtɪd] adj: **~ (at or with/to do)** encantado (con/de hacer); **to be ~ that** estar encantado de que; **I'd be ~** con mucho or todo gusto
delightful [dɪ'laɪtful] adj encantador(a), delicioso
delinquent [dɪ'lɪŋkwənt] adj, n delincuente
delirious [dɪ'lɪrɪəs] adj (Med: fig) delirante; **to be ~** delirar, desvariar
deliver [dɪ'lɪvəʳ] vt (distribute) repartir; (hand over) entregar; (message) comunicar; (speech) pronunciar; (blow) lanzar, dar; (Med) asistir al parto de
delivery [dɪ'lɪvərɪ] n reparto; entrega; (of speaker) modo de expresarse; (Med) parto, alumbramiento; **to take ~ of** recibir
delude [dɪ'luːd] vt engañar
deluge ['dɛljuːdʒ] n diluvio ▷ vt (fig): **to ~ (with)** inundar (de)
delusion [dɪ'luːʒən] n ilusión, engaño
delve [dɛlv] vi: **to ~ into** hurgar en
Dem. abbr (US Pol) = **democrat(ic)**
demand [dɪ'mɑːnd] vt (gen) exigir; (rights) reclamar; (need) requerir ▷ n (gen) exigencia; (claim) reclamación; (Econ) demanda; **to ~ sth (from or of sb)** exigir algo (a algn); **I ~ an explanation** exijo una explicación; **her children make great ~s on her time** sus hijos absorben gran parte de su tiempo; **to be in ~** ser muy solicitado; **on ~** a solicitud
demanding [dɪ'mɑːndɪŋ] adj (boss) exigente; (work) absorbente
demean [dɪ'miːn] vt: **to ~ o.s** rebajarse
demeanour, (US) **demeanor** [dɪ'miːnəʳ] n porte, conducta, comportamiento
demented [dɪ'mɛntɪd] adj demente
demilitarize [diː'mɪlɪtəraɪz] vt desmilitarizar; **~d zone** zona desmilitarizada
demise [dɪ'maɪz] n (death) fallecimiento
demister [diː'mɪstəʳ] n (Aut) eliminador de vaho
demo ['dɛməu] n abbr (col: = demonstration) manifestación
democracy [dɪ'mɔkrəsɪ] n democracia
democrat ['dɛməkræt] n demócrata
democratic [dɛmə'krætɪk] adj democrático; **the D~ Party** el partido demócrata (estadounidense)
demography [dɪ'mɔgrəfɪ] n demografía
demolish [dɪ'mɔlɪʃ] vt derribar, demoler
demolition [dɛmə'lɪʃən] n derribo, demolición
demonstrate ['dɛmənstreɪt] vt demostrar ▷ vi manifestarse; **to ~ (for/against)** manifestarse (a favor de/en contra de)
demonstration [dɛmən'streɪʃən] n (Pol) manifestación; (proof) prueba, demostración; **to hold a ~** (Pol) hacer una manifestación
demonstrator ['dɛmənstreɪtəʳ] n (Pol) manifestante
demote [dɪ'məut] vt degradar
demotion [dɪ'məuʃən] n degradación; (Comm) descenso
demure [dɪ'mjuəʳ] adj recatado
den [dɛn] n (of animal) guarida; (study) estudio

denatured alcohol [di:'neɪtʃəd-] n (US) alcohol desnaturalizado

denial [dɪ'naɪəl] n (refusal) negativa; (of report etc) denegación

denim ['dɛnɪm] n tela vaquera; see also **denims**

denims ['dɛnɪms] npl vaqueros

Denmark ['dɛnmɑ:k] n Dinamarca

denomination [dɪnɒmɪ'neɪʃən] n valor; (Rel) confesión

denominator [dɪ'nɒmɪneɪtəʳ] n denominador

denote [dɪ'nəʊt] vt indicar, significar

denounce [dɪ'naʊns] vt denunciar

dense [dɛns] adj (thick) espeso; (foliage etc) tupido; (stupid) torpe

densely ['dɛnslɪ] adv: ~ **populated** con una alta densidad de población

density ['dɛnsɪtɪ] n densidad; **single/double- ~ disk** n disco de densidad sencilla/de doble densidad

dent [dɛnt] n abolladura ▷ vt (also: **make a dent in**) abollar

dental ['dɛntl] adj dental

dental floss [-'flɔs] n seda dental

dental surgeon n odontólogo(-a)

dentist ['dɛntɪst] n dentista; ~'**s surgery** (Brit) consultorio dental

dentistry ['dɛntɪstrɪ] n odontología

dentures ['dɛntʃəz] npl dentadura (postiza)

denunciation [dɪnʌnsɪ'eɪʃən] n denuncia, denunciación

deny [dɪ'naɪ] vt negar; (charge) rechazar; (report) desmentir; **to ~ o.s.** privarse (de); **he denies having said it** niega haberlo dicho

deodorant [di:'əʊdərənt] n desodorante

depart [dɪ'pɑ:t] vi irse, marcharse; (train) salir; **to ~ from** (fig: differ from) apartarse de

departed [dɪ'pɑ:tɪd] adj (bygone: days, glory) pasado; (dead) difunto ▷ n: **the (dear) ~** el/la/los/ las difunto/a/os/as

department [dɪ'pɑ:tmənt] n (Comm) sección; (Scol) departamento; (Pol) ministerio; **that's not my ~** (fig) no tiene que ver conmigo; **D~ of State** (US) Ministerio de Asuntos Exteriores

department store n gran almacén

departure [dɪ'pɑ:tʃəʳ] n partida, ida; (of train) salida; **a new ~** un nuevo rumbo

departure lounge n (at airport) sala de embarque

depend [dɪ'pɛnd] vi: **to ~ (up)on** (be dependent upon) depender de; (rely on) contar con; **it ~s** depende, según; ~**ing on the result** según el resultado

dependable [dɪ'pɛndəbl] adj (person) formal, serio

dependant [dɪ'pɛndənt] n dependiente

dependence [dɪ'pɛndəns] n dependencia

dependent [dɪ'pɛndənt] adj: **to be ~ (on)** depender (de) ▷ n = **dependant**

depict [dɪ'pɪkt] vt (in picture) pintar; (describe) representar

depleted [dɪ'pli:tɪd] adj reducido

deplorable [dɪ'plɔ:rəbl] adj deplorable

deploy [dɪ'plɔɪ] vt desplegar

deport [dɪ'pɔ:t] vt deportar

deportation [di:pɔ:'teɪʃən] n deportación

deportee [di:pɔ:'ti:] n deportado(-a)

deposit [dɪ'pɔzɪt] n depósito; (Chem) sedimento; (of ore, oil) yacimiento ▷ vt (gen) depositar; **to put down a ~ of £50** dejar un depósito de 50 libras

deposit account n (Brit) cuenta de ahorros

depot ['dɛpəʊ] n (storehouse) depósito; (for vehicles) parque

depraved [dɪ'preɪvd] adj depravado, vicioso

depravity [dɪ'prævɪtɪ] n depravación, vicio

depreciation [dɪpri:ʃɪ'eɪʃən] n depreciación

depress [dɪ'prɛs] vt deprimir; (press down) apretar

depressant [dɪ'prɛsnt] n (Med) calmante, sedante

depressed [dɪ'prɛst] adj deprimido; (Comm: market, economy) deprimido; (area) deprimido (económicamente); **to get ~** deprimirse

depressing [dɪ'prɛsɪŋ] adj deprimente

depression [dɪ'prɛʃən] n depresión; **the economy is in a state of ~** la economía está deprimida

deprivation [dɛprɪ'veɪʃən] n privación; (loss) pérdida

deprive [dɪ'praɪv] vt: **to ~ sb of** privar a algn de

deprived [dɪ'praɪvd] adj necesitado

dept. abbr (= department) dto

depth [dɛpθ] n profundidad; **at a ~ of 3 metres** a 3 metros de profundidad; **to be out of one's ~** (swimmer) perder pie; (fig) estar perdido; **to study sth in ~** estudiar algo a fondo; **in the ~s of** en lo más hondo de

deputize ['dɛpjʊtaɪz] vi: **to ~ for sb** sustituir a algn

deputy ['dɛpjʊtɪ] adj: ~ **head** subdirector(a) ▷ n sustituto(-a), suplente; (Pol) diputado(-a); (agent) representante

derail [dɪ'reɪl] vt: **to be ~ed** descarrilarse

deranged [dɪ'reɪndʒd] adj trastornado

derby ['də:bɪ] n (US) hongo

deregulation [di:rɛgjʊ'leɪʃən] n desreglamentación

derelict ['dɛrɪlɪkt] adj abandonado

derision [dɪ'rɪʒən] n irrisión, mofas

derisory [dɪ'raɪzərɪ] adj (sum) irrisorio; (laughter, person) burlón(-ona), irónico

derivative [dɪ'rɪvətɪv] n derivado ▷ adj (work) poco original

derive [dɪ'raɪv] vt derivar ▷ vi: **to ~ from** derivarse de

dermatitis [də:mə'taɪtɪs] n dermatitis

derogatory [dɪ'rɒgətərɪ] adj despectivo

derv [də:v] n (Brit) gasoil

descend [dɪ'sɛnd] vt, vi descender, bajar; **to ~ from** descender de; **in ~ing order of importance** de mayor a menor importancia ▶ **descend on** vt fus (enemy, angry person) caer sobre; (misfortune) sobrevenir; (fig: gloom, silence) invadir; **visitors ~ed (up)on us** las visitas nos invadieron

descendant [dɪ'sɛndənt] n descendiente

descent [dɪ'sɛnt] n descenso; (Geo) pendiente,

declive; (*origin*) descendencia

describe [dɪs'kraɪb] *vt* describir

description [dɪs'krɪpʃən] *n* descripción; (*sort*) clase, género; **of every ~** de toda clase

descriptive [dɪs'krɪptɪv] *adj* descriptivo

desecrate ['desɪkreɪt] *vt* profanar

desert *n* desierto ▷ *vt* abandonar, desamparar ▷ *vi* (*Mil*) desertar; *see also* **deserts**

deserter [dɪ'zə:tə^r] *n* desertor(-a)

desertion [dɪ'zə:ʃən] *n* deserción

desert island *n* isla desierta

deserts [dɪ'zə:ts] *npl*: **to get one's just ~** llevarse su merecido

deserve [dɪ'zə:v] *vt* merecer, ser digno de, ameritar (*LAm*)

deserving [dɪ'zə:vɪŋ] *adj* (*person*) digno; (*action, cause*) meritorio

design [dɪ'zaɪn] *n* (*of dress, car, Educ*) diseño; (*sketch*) bosquejo; (*pattern*) dibujo ▷ *vt* (*gen*) diseñar; **a ~ fault** un fallo en el diseño; **fashion ~** diseño de modas; **industrial ~** diseño industrial; **a geometric ~** un dibujo geométrico; **to do sth by ~** hacer algo a propósito; **to have ~s on sb** tener la(s) mira(s) puesta(s) en algn; **to be ~ed for sb/sth** (*perfect*) estar hecho para algn/algo

designate *vt* (*appoint*) nombrar; (*destine*) designar ▷ *adj* designado

designer [dɪ'zaɪnə^r] *n* diseñador(a); (*fashion designer*) modisto(-a)

desirable [dɪ'zaɪərəbl] *adj* (*proper*) deseable; (*attractive*) atractivo; **it is ~ that** es conveniente que

desire [dɪ'zaɪə^r] *n* deseo ▷ *vt* desear; **to ~ sth/to do sth/that** desear algo/hacer algo/que

desk [desk] *n* (*in office*) escritorio; (*for pupil*) pupitre; (*in hotel, at airport*) recepción; (*Brit: in shop, restaurant*) caja

desktop computer ['desktɔp-] *n* ordenador de sobremesa

desktop publishing ['desktɔp-] *n* autoedición

desolate ['desəlɪt] *adj* (*place*) desierto; (*person*) afligido

desolation [desə'leɪʃən] *n* (*of place*) desolación; (*of person*) aflicción

despair [dɪs'peə^r] *n* desesperación ▷ *vi*: **to ~ of** desesperar de; **in ~** desesperado

despatch [dɪs'pætʃ] *n, vt* = **dispatch**

desperate ['despərɪt] *adj* desesperado; (*fugitive*) peligroso; (*measures*) extremo; **we are getting ~** estamos al borde de la desesperación

desperately ['despərɪtlɪ] *adv* desesperadamente; (*very*) terriblemente, gravemente; **~ ill** gravemente enfermo

desperation [despə'reɪʃən] *n* desesperación; **in ~** desesperado

despicable [dɪs'pɪkəbl] *adj* vil, despreciable

despise [dɪs'paɪz] *vt* despreciar

despite [dɪs'paɪt] *prep* a pesar de, pese a

despondent [dɪs'pɔndənt] *adj* deprimido, abatido

dessert [dɪ'zə:t] *n* postre

dessertspoon [dɪ'zə:tspu:n] *n* cuchara (de postre)

destination [destɪ'neɪʃən] *n* destino

destine ['destɪn] *vt* destinar

destined ['destɪnd] *adj*: **~ for London** con destino a Londres

destiny ['destɪnɪ] *n* destino

destitute ['destɪtju:t] *adj* desamparado, indigente

destitution [destɪ'tju:ʃən] *n* indigencia, miseria

destroy [dɪs'trɔɪ] *vt* destruir; (*finish*) acabar con

destroyer [dɪs'trɔɪə^r] *n* (*Naut*) destructor

destruction [dɪs'trʌkʃən] *n* destrucción; (*fig*) ruina

destructive [dɪs'trʌktɪv] *adj* destructivo, destructor(a)

detach [dɪ'tætʃ] *vt* separar; (*unstick*) despegar

detached [dɪ'tætʃt] *adj* (*attitude*) objetivo, imparcial

detached house *n* chalé, chalet

detachment [dɪ'tætʃmənt] *n* separación; (*Mil*) destacamento; (*fig*) objetividad, imparcialidad

detail ['di:teɪl] *n* detalle; (*Mil*) destacamento ▷ *vt* detallar; (*Mil*) destacar; **in ~** detalladamente; **to go into ~(s)** entrar en detalles

detailed ['di:teɪld] *adj* detallado

detain [dɪ'teɪn] *vt* retener; (*in captivity*) detener

detainee [di:teɪ'ni:] *n* detenido(-a)

detect [dɪ'tekt] *vt* (*discover*) descubrir; (*Med, Police*) identificar; (*Mil, Radar, Tech*) detectar; (*notice*) percibir

detection [dɪ'tekʃən] *n* descubrimiento; identificación; **crime ~** investigación; **to escape ~** (*criminal*) escaparse sin ser descubierto; (*mistake*) pasar inadvertido

detective [dɪ'tektɪv] *n* detective

detective story *n* novela policíaca

detector [dɪ'tektə^r] *n* detector

detention [dɪ'tenʃən] *n* detención, arresto

deter [dɪ'tə:^{r}] *vt* (*dissuade*) disuadir; (*prevent*) impedir; **to ~ sb from doing sth** disuadir a algn de que haga algo

detergent [dɪ'tə:dʒənt] *n* detergente

deteriorate [dɪ'tɪərɪəreɪt] *vi* deteriorarse

determination [dɪtə:mɪ'neɪʃən] *n* resolución

determine [dɪ'tə:mɪn] *vt* determinar; **to ~ to do sth** decidir hacer algo

determined [dɪ'tə:mɪnd] *adj*: **to be ~ to do sth** estar decidido *or* resuelto a hacer algo; **a ~ effort** un esfuerzo enérgico

deterrent [dɪ'terənt] *n* fuerza de disuasión; **to act as a ~** servir para prevenir

detest [dɪ'test] *vt* aborrecer

detonate ['detəneɪt] *vi* estallar ▷ *vt* hacer detonar

detonator ['detəneɪtə^r] *n* detonador, fulminante

detour ['di:tuə^r] *n* (*gen, US Aut: diversion*) desvío ▷ *vt* (*US: traffic*) desviar; **to make a ~** dar un rodeo

detract [dɪ'trækt] *vt*: **to ~ from** quitar mérito a, restar valor a

detractor [dɪ'træktə^r] *n* detractor(a)

detriment ['detrɪmənt] *n*: **to the ~ of** en

perjuicio de; **without ~ to** sin detrimento de, sin perjuicio para

detrimental [dɛtrɪˈmɛntl] *adj* perjudicial

deuce [djuːs] *n* (*Tennis*) cuarenta iguales

devaluation [dɪvæljuˈeɪʃən] *n* devaluación

devalue [dɪˈvæljuː] *vt* devaluar

devastate [ˈdɛvəsteɪt] *vt* devastar; **he was ~d by the news** las noticias le dejaron desolado

devastating [ˈdɛvəsteɪtɪŋ] *adj* devastador(-a); (*fig*) arrollador(-a)

devastation [dɛvəsˈteɪʃən] *n* devastación, ruina

develop [dɪˈvɛləp] *vt* desarrollar; (*Phot*) revelar; (*disease*) contraer; (*habit*) adquirir ▷ *vi* desarrollarse; (*advance*) progresar; **I ~ed his original idea** yo desarrollé su idea original; **this land is to be ~ed** se va a construir en este terreno; **to ~ a taste for sth** tomar gusto a algo; **to ~ into** transformarse *or* convertirse en

developer [dɪˈvɛləpəʳ] *n* (*property developer*) promotor(a)

developing country *n* país en (vías de) desarrollo

development [dɪˈvɛləpmənt] *n* desarrollo; (*advance*) progreso; (*of affair, case*) desenvolvimiento; (*of land*) urbanización

deviant [ˈdiːvɪənt] *adj* anómalo, pervertido

deviate [ˈdiːvɪeɪt] *vi*: **to ~ (from)** desviarse (de)

device [dɪˈvaɪs] *n* (*scheme*) estratagema, recurso; (*apparatus*) aparato, mecanismo; (*explosive device*) artefacto explosivo

devil [ˈdɛvl] *n* diablo, demonio

devil's advocate *n*: **to play (the) devil's advocate** hacer de abogado del diablo

devious [ˈdiːvɪəs] *adj* intricado, enrevesado; (*person*) taimado

devise [dɪˈvaɪz] *vt* idear, inventar

devoid [dɪˈvɔɪd] *adj*: **~ of** desprovisto de

devolution [diːvəˈluːʃən] *n* (*Pol*) descentralización

devote [dɪˈvəut] *vt*: **to ~ sth to** dedicar algo a

devoted [dɪˈvəutɪd] *adj* (*loyal*) leal, fiel; **the book is ~ to politics** el libro trata de política

devotee [dɛvəuˈtiː] *n* devoto(-a)

devotion [dɪˈvəuʃən] *n* dedicación; (*Rel*) devoción

devour [dɪˈvauəʳ] *vt* devorar

devout [dɪˈvaut] *adj* devoto

dew [djuː] *n* rocío

dexterity [dɛksˈtɛrɪtɪ] *n* destreza

diabetes [daɪəˈbiːtiːz] *n* diabetes

diabetic [daɪəˈbɛtɪk] *n* diabético(-a) ▷ *adj* diabético; (*chocolate, jam*) para diabéticos

diabolical [daɪəˈbɔlɪkəl] *adj* diabólico; (*col: dreadful*) horrendo, horroroso

diagnose [ˈdaɪəgnəuz] *vt* diagnosticar

diagnosis [daɪəgˈnəusɪs] (*pl* **diagnoses**) *n* diagnóstico

diagonal [daɪˈægənl] *adj* diagonal ▷ *n* diagonal

diagram [ˈdaɪəgræm] *n* diagrama, esquema

dial [ˈdaɪəl] *n* esfera; (*of radio*) dial; (*tuner*) sintonizador; (*of phone*) disco ▷ *vt* (*number*) marcar, discar (*LAm*); **to ~ a wrong number**

equivocarse de número; **can I ~ London direct?** ¿puedo marcar un número de Londres directamente?

dial code *n* (*US*) prefijo

dialect [ˈdaɪəlɛkt] *n* dialecto

dialling code [ˈdaɪəlɪŋ-] *n* (*Brit*) prefijo

dialling tone [ˈdaɪəlɪŋ-] *n* (*Brit*) señal *or* tono de marcar

dialogue, (*US*) **dialog** [ˈdaɪəlɔg] *n* diálogo

dial tone *n* (*US*) señal *or* tono de marcar

dialysis [daɪˈælɪsɪs] *n* diálisis

diameter [daɪˈæmɪtəʳ] *n* diámetro

diamond [ˈdaɪəmənd] *n* diamante; **diamonds** *npl* (*Cards*) diamantes

diaper [ˈdaɪəpəʳ] *n* (*US*) pañal

diaphragm [ˈdaɪəfræm] *n* diafragma

diarrhoea, (*US*) **diarrhea** [daɪəˈriːə] *n* diarrea

diary [ˈdaɪərɪ] *n* (*daily account*) diario; (*book*) agenda; **to keep a ~** escribir un diario

dice [daɪs] *n* (*pl inv*) dados ▷ *vt* (*Culin*) cortar en cuadritos

Dictaphone® [ˈdɪktəfəun] *n* dictáfono®

dictate *vt* dictar ▷ *n* dictado

▶ **dictate to** *vt fus* (*person*) dar órdenes a; **I won't be ~d to** no recibo órdenes de nadie

dictation [dɪkˈteɪʃən] *n* (*to secretary etc*) dictado; **at ~ speed** para tomar al dictado

dictator [dɪkˈteɪtəʳ] *n* dictador

dictatorship [dɪkˈteɪtəʃɪp] *n* dictadura

diction [ˈdɪkʃən] *n* dicción

dictionary [ˈdɪkʃənrɪ] *n* diccionario

did [dɪd] *pt of* **do**

didactic [daɪˈdæktɪk] *adj* didáctico

diddle [ˈdɪdl] *vt* (*col*) estafar, timar

didn't [ˈdɪdənt] = **did not**

die [daɪ] *vi* morir; **to ~ of** *or* **from** morirse de; **he ~d last year** murió el año pasado; **he's dying** se está muriendo; **I nearly ~d (laughing)!** ¡me moría de la risa!; **to be dying for sth/to do sth** morirse por algo/de ganas de hacer algo

▶ **die away** *vi* (*sound, light*) desvanecerse

▶ **die down** *vi* (*gen*) apagarse; (*wind*) amainar

▶ **die out** *vi* desaparecer, extinguirse

diehard [ˈdaɪhɑːd] *n* intransigente

diesel [ˈdiːzl] *n* diesel

diesel engine *n* motor diesel

diesel fuel, diesel oil *n* gas-oil

diet [ˈdaɪət] *n* dieta; (*restricted food*) régimen ▷ *vi* (*also*: **be on a diet**) estar a dieta, hacer régimen; **to live on a ~ of** alimentarse de

dietician [daɪəˈtɪʃən] *n* dietista

differ [ˈdɪfəʳ] *vi* (*be different*) ser distinto, diferenciarse; (*disagree*) discrepar

difference [ˈdɪfrəns] *n* diferencia; (*quarrel*) desacuerdo; **it makes no ~ to me** me da igual *or* lo mismo; **to settle one's ~s** arreglarse

different [ˈdɪfrənt] *adj* diferente, distinto

differentiate [dɪfəˈrɛnʃɪeɪt] *vt* distinguir ▷ *vi* diferenciarse; **to ~ between** distinguir entre

difficult [ˈdɪfɪkəlt] *adj* difícil; **~ to understand** difícil de entender

difficulty [ˈdɪfɪkəltɪ] *n* dificultad; **to have**

difficulties with (*police, landlord etc*) tener problemas con; **to be in ~** estar en apuros
diffident ['dɪfɪdənt] *adj* tímido
dig [dɪg] *vt* (*pt, pp* **dug**) (*hole: with tool*) cavar; (: *with hands, paws*) escarbar; (*ground*) remover; (*coal*) extraer; (*nails etc*) clavar ▷ *vi* cavar ▷ *n* (*prod*) empujón; (*archaeological*) excavación; (*remark*) indirecta; **the dog dug a hole in the sand** el perro escarbó un agujero en la arena; **to ~ one's nails into sth** clavar las uñas en algo; **dad's out ~ging the garden** papá está fuera cavando en el jardín; **to ~ into one's pockets for sth** hurgar en el bolsillo buscando algo; **I had to ~ into my savings** tuve que echar mano de mis ahorros; *see also* **digs**
▶ **dig in** *vi* (*col: eat*) hincar los dientes ▷ *vt* (*compost*) añadir al suelo; (*knife, claw*) clavar; **to ~ o.s. in** (*Mil*) atrincherarse; **to ~ in one's heels** (*fig*) mantenerse en sus trece
▶ **dig out** *vt* (*hole*) excavar; (*survivors, car from snow*) sacar
▶ **dig up** *vt* desenterrar; (*plant*) desarraigar; **the cat's dug up my plants** el gato me ha arrancado las plantas
digest *vt* (*food*) digerir; (*facts*) asimilar ▷ *n* resumen
digestion [dɪ'dʒɛstʃən] *n* digestión
digit ['dɪdʒɪt] *n* (*number*) dígito; (*finger*) dedo
digital ['dɪdʒɪtl] *adj* digital
digital camera *n* cámara digital
digital TV *n* televisión digital
dignified ['dɪgnɪfaɪd] *adj* grave, solemne; (*action*) decoroso
dignitary ['dɪgnɪtərɪ] *n* dignatario(-a)
dignity ['dɪgnɪtɪ] *n* dignidad
digress [daɪ'grɛs] *vi*: **to ~ from** apartarse de
digression [daɪ'grɛʃən] *n* digresión
digs [dɪgz] *npl* (*Brit: col*) pensión, alojamiento
dilapidated [dɪ'læpɪdeɪtɪd] *adj* desmoronado, ruinoso
dilate [daɪ'leɪt] *vt* dilatar ▷ *vi* dilatarse
dilemma [daɪ'lɛmə] *n* dilema; **to be in a ~** estar en un dilema
diligence ['dɪlɪdʒəns] *n* diligencia
diligent ['dɪlɪdʒənt] *adj* diligente
dilute [daɪ'lu:t] *vt* diluir
dim [dɪm] *adj* (*light*) débil; (*sight*) turbio; (*outline*) borroso; (*stupid*) lerdo; (*room*) oscuro ▷ *vt* (*light*) bajar; **to take a ~ view of sth** tener una pobre opinión de algo
dime [daɪm] *n* (*US*) *moneda de diez centavos*
dimension [dɪ'mɛnʃən] *n* dimensión
dimensions [dɪ'mɛnʃənz] *npl* dimensiones
diminish [dɪ'mɪnɪʃ] *vt, vi* disminuir
diminished [dɪ'mɪnɪʃt] *adj*: **~ responsibility** (*Law*) responsabilidad disminuida
diminutive [dɪ'mɪnjutɪv] *adj* diminuto ▷ *n* (*Ling*) diminutivo
dimmer ['dɪmər] *n* (*also*: **dimmer switch**) regulador (de intensidad); (*US Aut*) interruptor
dimple ['dɪmpl] *n* hoyuelo
din [dɪn] *n* estruendo, estrépito ▷ *vt*: **to ~ sth**

into sb (*col*) meter algo en la cabeza a algn
dine [daɪn] *vi* cenar
diner ['daɪnər] *n* (*person: in restaurant*) comensal; (*Brit Rail*) = **dining car**; (*US*) restaurante económico
dinghy ['dɪŋgɪ] *n* bote; (*also*: **rubber dinghy**) lancha (neumática)
dingy ['dɪndʒɪ] *adj* (*room*) sombrío; (*dirty*) sucio; (*dull*) deslucido
dining car ['daɪnɪŋ-] *n* (*Brit*) coche-restaurante
dining room ['daɪnɪŋ-] *n* comedor
dinner ['dɪnər] *n* (*evening meal*) cena, comida (*LAm*); (*lunch*) comida; (*public*) cena, banquete; **~'s ready!** ¡la cena está servida!
dinner jacket *n* smoking
dinner party *n* cena
dinner time *n* hora de cenar *or* comer
dinosaur ['daɪnəsɔːr] *n* dinosaurio
dint [dɪnt] *n*: **by ~ of (doing) sth** a fuerza de (hacer) algo
diocese ['daɪəsɪs] *n* diócesis
dioxide [daɪ'ɔksaɪd] *n* bióxido; **carbon ~** bióxido de carbono
Dip. *abbr* (*Brit*) = **diploma**
dip [dɪp] *n* (*slope*) pendiente; (*in sea*) chapuzón ▷ *vt* (*in water*) mojar; (*ladle etc*) meter; (*Brit Aut*): **to ~ one's lights** poner la luz de cruce ▷ *vi* inclinarse hacia abajo
diphtheria [dɪf'θɪərɪə] *n* difteria
diphthong ['dɪfθɔŋ] *n* diptongo
diploma [dɪ'pləumə] *n* diploma
diplomacy [dɪ'pləuməsɪ] *n* diplomacia
diplomat ['dɪpləmæt] *n* diplomático(-a)
diplomatic [dɪplə'mætɪk] *adj* diplomático; **to break off ~ relations** romper las relaciones diplomáticas
diplomatic immunity *n* inmunidad diplomática
dipstick ['dɪpstɪk] *n* (*Aut*) varilla de nivel (del aceite)
dipswitch ['dɪpswɪtʃ] *n* (*Brit Aut*) interruptor
dire [daɪər] *adj* calamitoso
direct [daɪ'rɛkt] *adj* (*gen*) directo; (*manner, person*) franco ▷ *vt* dirigir; **the most ~ route** el camino más directo; **you can't fly to Manchester ~ from Seville** no hay vuelos directos a Manchester desde Sevilla; **he's the ~ opposite** es exactamente el contrario; **to make a ~ hit** dar en el blanco; **can you ~ me to...?** ¿puede indicarme dónde está...?; **to ~ sb to do sth** mandar a algn hacer algo
direct current *n* corriente continua
direct debit *n* domiciliación bancaria de recibos; **to pay by ~** domiciliar el pago
direct dialling *n* servicio automático de llamadas
direction [dɪ'rɛkʃən] *n* dirección; **directions** *npl* (*advice*) órdenes, instrucciones; (*to a place*) señas; **~s for use** modo de empleo; **to ask for ~s** preguntar el camino; **sense of ~** sentido de la orientación; **in the ~ of** hacia, en dirección a
directive [daɪ'rɛktɪv] *n* orden, instrucción; **a**

government ~ una orden del gobierno

directly [dɪˈrɛktlɪ] *adv* (*in straight line*) directamente; (*at once*) en seguida

directness [dɪˈrɛktnɪs] *n* (*of person, speech*) franqueza

director [dɪˈrɛktəʳ] *n* director(a); **managing ~** director(a) gerente

Director of Public Prosecutions *n* ≈ fiscal general del Estado

directory [dɪˈrɛktərɪ] *n* (*Tel*) guía (telefónica); (*street directory*) callejero; (*trade directory*) directorio de comercio; (*Comput*) directorio

directory enquiries, (*US*) **directory assistance** *n* (*service*) (servicio de) información

dirt [dəːt] *n* suciedad

dirt-cheap [ˈdəːtˈtʃiːp] *adj* baratísimo

dirty [ˈdəːtɪ] *adj* sucio; (*joke*) verde, colorado (*LAm*) ▷ *vt* ensuciar; (*stain*) manchar

disability [dɪsəˈbɪlɪtɪ] *n* incapacidad

disabled [dɪsˈeɪbld] *adj* minusválido

disadvantage [dɪsədˈvɑːntɪdʒ] *n* desventaja, inconveniente

disagree [dɪsəˈɡriː] *vi* (*differ*) discrepar; **to ~ (with)** no estar de acuerdo (con); **I ~ with you** no estoy de acuerdo contigo

disagreeable [dɪsəˈɡriəbl] *adj* desagradable

disagreement [dɪsəˈɡriːmənt] *n* (*gen*) desacuerdo; (*quarrel*) riña; **to have a ~ with sb** estar en desacuerdo con algn

disallow [ˈdɪsəˈlau] *vt* (*goal*) anular; (*claim*) rechazar

disappear [dɪsəˈpɪəʳ] *vi* desaparecer

disappearance [dɪsəˈpɪərəns] *n* desaparición

disappoint [dɪsəˈpɔɪnt] *vt* decepcionar; (*hopes*) defraudar

disappointed [dɪsəˈpɔɪntɪd] *adj* decepcionado

disappointing [dɪsəˈpɔɪntɪŋ] *adj* decepcionante

disappointment [dɪsəˈpɔɪntmənt] *n* decepción

disapproval [dɪsəˈpruːvəl] *n* desaprobación

disapprove [dɪsəˈpruːv] *vi*: **to ~ of** desaprobar

disarmament [dɪsˈɑːməmənt] *n* desarme

disarray [dɪsəˈreɪ] *n*: **in ~** (*troops*) desorganizado; (*thoughts*) confuso; (*hair, clothes*) desarreglado; **to throw into ~** provocar el caos

disaster [dɪˈzɑːstəʳ] *n* desastre

disastrous [dɪˈzɑːstrəs] *adj* desastroso

disband [dɪsˈbænd] *vt* disolver ▷ *vi* desbandarse

disbelief [dɪsbəˈliːf] *n* incredulidad; **in ~** con incredulidad

disc [dɪsk] *n* disco; (*Comput*) = **disk**

discard [dɪsˈkɑːd] *vt* (*old things*) tirar; (*fig*) descartar

discern [dɪˈsəːn] *vt* percibir, discernir; (*understand*) comprender

discerning [dɪˈsəːnɪŋ] *adj* perspicaz

discharge *vt* (*task, duty*) cumplir; (*ship etc*) descargar; (*patient*) dar de alta; (*employee*) despedir; (*soldier*) licenciar; (*defendant*) poner en libertad; (*settle: debt*) saldar ▷ *n* (*Elec*) descarga; (*vaginal discharge*) emisión vaginal; (*dismissal*) despedida; (*of duty*) desempeño; (*of debt*) pago, descargo; (*of gas, chemicals*) escape; **~d bankrupt**

quebrado/a rehabilitado/a

disciple [dɪˈsaɪpl] *n* discípulo(-a)

discipline [ˈdɪsɪplɪn] *n* disciplina ▷ *vt* disciplinar; **to ~ o.s. to do sth** obligarse a hacer algo

disc jockey, (DJ) *n*, pinchadiscos

disclaim [dɪsˈkleɪm] *vt* negar tener

disclaimer [dɪsˈkleɪməʳ] *n* rectificación; **to issue a ~** hacer una rectificación

disclose [dɪsˈkləuz] *vt* revelar

disclosure [dɪsˈkləuʒəʳ] *n* revelación

disco [ˈdɪskəu] *n abbr* = **discothèque**

discolo(u)red [dɪsˈkʌləd] *adj* descolorido

discomfort [dɪsˈkʌmfət] *n* incomodidad; (*unease*) inquietud; (*physical*) malestar

disconcert [dɪskənˈsəːt] *vt* desconcertar

disconnect [dɪskəˈnɛkt] *vt* (*gen*) separar; (*Elec etc*) desconectar; (*supply*) cortar (el suministro) a

disconsolate [dɪsˈkɔnsəlɪt] *adj* desconsolado

discontent [dɪskənˈtɛnt] *n* descontento

discontented [dɪskənˈtɛntɪd] *adj* descontento

discontinue [dɪskənˈtɪnjuː] *vt* interrumpir; (*payments*) suspender

discord [ˈdɪskɔːd] *n* discordia; (*Mus*) disonancia

discordant [dɪsˈkɔːdənt] *adj* disonante

discothèque [ˈdɪskəutɛk] *n* discoteca

discount *n* descuento ▷ *vt* descontar; (*report etc*) descartar; **at a ~** con descuento; **~ for cash** descuento por pago en efectivo; **to give sb a ~ on sth** hacer un descuento a algn en algo

discourage [dɪsˈkʌrɪdʒ] *vt* desalentar; (*oppose*) oponerse a; (*dissuade, deter*) desanimar, disuadir

discouraging [dɪsˈkʌrɪdʒɪŋ] *adj* desalentador(a)

discourteous [dɪsˈkəːtɪəs] *adj* descortés

discover [dɪsˈkʌvəʳ] *vt* descubrir

discovery [dɪsˈkʌvərɪ] *n* descubrimiento

discredit [dɪsˈkrɛdɪt] *vt* desacreditar

discreet [dɪˈskriːt] *adj* (*tactful*) discreto; (*careful*) circunspecto, prudente

discrepancy [dɪˈskrɛpənsɪ] *n* (*difference*) diferencia; (*disagreement*) discrepancia

discretion [dɪˈskrɛʃən] *n* (*tact*) discreción; (*care*) prudencia, circunspección; **use your own ~** haz lo que creas oportuno

discriminate [dɪˈskrɪmɪneɪt] *vi*: **to ~ between** distinguir entre; **to ~ against** discriminar contra

discriminating [dɪˈskrɪmɪneɪtɪŋ] *adj* entendido

discrimination [dɪskrɪmɪˈneɪʃən] *n* (*discernment*) perspicacia; (*bias*) discriminación; **racial/sexual ~** discriminación racial/sexual

discus [ˈdɪskəs] *n* disco

discuss [dɪˈskʌs] *vt* (*gen*) discutir; (*a theme*) tratar

discussion [dɪˈskʌʃən] *n* discusión; **under ~** en discusión

disdain [dɪsˈdeɪn] *n* desdén ▷ *vt* desdeñar

disease [dɪˈziːz] *n* enfermedad

diseased [dɪˈziːzd] *adj* enfermo

disembark [dɪsɪmˈbɑːk] *vt, vi* desembarcar

disengage [dɪsɪnˈɡeɪdʒ] *vt* soltar; **to ~ the clutch** (*Aut*) desembragar

disentangle [dɪsɪnˈtæŋɡl] *vt* desenredar

disfigure [dɪsˈfɪɡəʳ] vt desfigurar
disgrace [dɪsˈɡreɪs] n ignominia; (downfall) caída; (shame) vergüenza, escándalo ▷ vt deshonrar
disgraceful [dɪsˈɡreɪsful] adj vergonzoso; (behaviour) escandaloso
disgruntled [dɪsˈɡrʌntld] adj disgustado, descontento
disguise [dɪsˈɡaɪz] n disfraz ▷ vt disfrazar; (voice) disimular; (feelings etc) ocultar; **in ~** disfrazado; **to ~ o.s. as** disfrazarse de; **there's no disguising the fact that ...** no puede ocultarse el hecho de que ...
disgust [dɪsˈɡʌst] n repugnancia ▷ vt repugnar, dar asco a
disgusting [dɪsˈɡʌstɪŋ] adj repugnante, asqueroso
dish [dɪʃ] n (gen) plato; **to do** or **wash the ~es** fregar los platos
▶ **dish out** vt (money, exam papers) repartir; (food) servir; (advice) dar
▶ **dish up** vt servir
dishcloth [ˈdɪʃklɔθ] n paño de cocina, bayeta
dishearten [dɪsˈhɑːtn] vt desalentar
dishevelled, (US) **disheveled** [dɪˈʃevəld] adj (hair) despeinado; (clothes, appearance) desarreglado
dishonest [dɪsˈɔnɪst] adj (person) poco honrado, tramposo; (means) fraudulento
dishonesty [dɪsˈɔnɪstɪ] n falta de honradez
dishonour, (US) **dishonor** [dɪsˈɔnəʳ] n deshonra
dishono(u)rable [dɪsˈɔnərəbl] adj deshonroso
dishtowel [ˈdɪʃtauəl] n (US) trapo de fregar
dishwasher [ˈdɪʃwɔʃəʳ] n lavaplatos; (person) friegaplatos
dishy [ˈdɪʃɪ] adj (Brit col) buenón(-ona)
disillusion [dɪsɪˈluːʒən] vt desilusionar; **to become ~ed (with)** quedar desilusionado (con)
disincentive [dɪsɪnˈsentɪv] n freno; **to act as a ~ (to)** actuar de freno (a); **to be a ~ to** ser un freno a
disinfect [dɪsɪnˈfekt] vt desinfectar
disinfectant [dɪsɪnˈfektənt] n desinfectante
disinformation [dɪsɪnfəˈmeɪʃən] n desinformación
disintegrate [dɪsˈɪntɪɡreɪt] vi disgregarse, desintegrarse
disinterested [dɪsˈɪntrəstɪd] adj desinteresado
disjointed [dɪsˈdʒɔɪntɪd] adj inconexo
disk [dɪsk] n (Comput) disco, disquete; **single-/double-sided ~** disco de una cara/dos caras
disk drive n disc drive
diskette [dɪsˈket] n diskette, disquete, disco flexible
disk operating system (DOS) n sistema m operativo de discos
dislike [dɪsˈlaɪk] n antipatía, aversión ▷ vt tener antipatía a; **to take a ~ to sb/sth** cogerle or (LAm) agarrarle antipatía a algn/algo; **I ~ the idea** no me gusta la idea
dislocate [ˈdɪsləkeɪt] vt dislocar; **he ~d his shoulder** se dislocó el hombro
dislodge [dɪsˈlɔdʒ] vt sacar; (enemy) desalojar

disloyal [dɪsˈlɔɪəl] adj desleal
dismal [ˈdɪzml] adj (dark) sombrío; (depressing) triste; (very bad) fatal
dismantle [dɪsˈmæntl] vt desmontar, desarmar
dismay [dɪsˈmeɪ] n consternación ▷ vt consternar; **much to my ~** para gran consternación mía
dismiss [dɪsˈmɪs] vt (worker) despedir; (official) destituir; (idea, Law) rechazar; (possibility) descartar ▷ vi (Mil) romper filas
dismissal [dɪsˈmɪsl] n despedida; destitución
dismount [dɪsˈmaunt] vi apearse; (rider) desmontar
disobedience [dɪsəˈbiːdɪəns] n desobediencia
disobedient [dɪsəˈbiːdɪənt] adj desobediente
disobey [dɪsəˈbeɪ] vt desobedecer; (rule) infringir
disorder [dɪsˈɔːdəʳ] n desorden; (rioting) disturbio; (Med) trastorno; (disease) enfermedad; **civil ~** desorden civil
disorderly [dɪsˈɔːdəlɪ] adj (untidy) desordenado; (meeting) alborotado; **~ conduct** (Law) conducta escandalosa
disorganized [dɪsˈɔːɡənaɪzd] adj desorganizado
disorientated [dɪsˈɔːrɪenteɪtəd] adj desorientado
disown [dɪsˈəun] vt renegar de
disparaging [dɪsˈpærɪdʒɪŋ] adj despreciativo; **to be ~ about sth/sb** menospreciar algo/a algn
dispassionate [dɪsˈpæʃənɪt] adj (unbiased) imparcial; (unemotional) desapasionado
dispatch [dɪsˈpætʃ] vt enviar; (kill) despachar; (deal with: business) despachar ▷ n (sending) envío; (speed) prontitud; (Press) informe; (Mil) parte
dispel [dɪsˈpel] vt disipar, dispersar
dispense [dɪsˈpens] vt dispensar, repartir; (medicine) preparar
▶ **dispense with** vt fus (make unnecessary) prescindir de
dispenser [dɪsˈpensəʳ] n (container) distribuidor automático
dispensing chemist [dɪsˈpensɪŋ-] n (Brit) farmacia
disperse [dɪsˈpəːs] vt dispersar ▷ vi dispersarse
dispirited [dɪˈspɪrɪtɪd] adj desanimado, desalentado
displace [dɪsˈpleɪs] vt (person) desplazar; (replace) reemplazar
display [dɪsˈpleɪ] n (exhibition) exposición; (Comput) visualización; (Mil) desfile; (of feeling) manifestación; (pej) aparato, pompa ▷ vt exponer; manifestar; (ostentatiously) lucir; **on ~** (exhibits) expuesto, exhibido; (goods) en el escaparate
displease [dɪsˈpliːz] vt (offend) ofender; (annoy) fastidiar; **~d with** disgustado con
displeasure [dɪsˈpleʒəʳ] n disgusto
disposable [dɪsˈpəuzəbl] adj (not reusable) desechable; **~ personal income** ingresos personales disponibles
disposable nappy n pañal desechable
disposal [dɪsˈpəuzl] n (sale) venta; (of house) traspaso; (by giving away) donación; (arrangement) colocación; (of rubbish) destrucción; **at one's ~**

a la disposición de algn; **to put sth at sb's ~**
poner algo a disposición de algn
disposed [dɪs'pəuzd] *adj*: **~ to do** dispuesto a
hacer
dispose of [dɪs'pəuz] *vt fus* (*time, money*) disponer
de; (*unwanted goods*) deshacerse de; (*Comm: sell*)
traspasar, vender; (*throw away*) tirar
disposition [dɪspə'zɪʃən] *n* disposición;
(*temperament*) carácter
disproportionate [dɪsprə'pɔːʃənət] *adj*
desproporcionado
disprove [dɪs'pruːv] *vt* refutar
dispute [dɪs'pjuːt] *n* disputa; (*verbal*) discusión;
(*also*: **industrial dispute**) conflicto (laboral) ▷ *vt*
(*argue*) disputar; (*question*) cuestionar; **to be in**
or **under ~** (*matter*) discutirse; (*territory*) estar en
disputa; (*Jur*) estar en litigio
disqualification [dɪskwɔlɪfɪ'keɪʃən]
n inhabilitación; (*Sport, from driving*)
descalificación
disqualify [dɪs'kwɔlɪfaɪ] *vt* (*Sport*) desclasificar;
to ~ sb for sth/from doing sth incapacitar a
algn para algo/para hacer algo
disquiet [dɪs'kwaɪət] *n* preocupación, inquietud
disregard [dɪsrɪ'gɑːd] *vt* desatender; (*ignore*) no
hacer caso de ▷ *n* (*indifference: to feelings, danger,
money*): **~ (for)** indiferencia (a); **~ (of)** (*non-
observance: of law, rules*) violación (de)
disrepair [dɪsrɪ'pɛəʳ] *n*: **to fall into ~** (*building*)
desmoronarse; (*street*) deteriorarse
disreputable [dɪs'rɛpjutəbl] *adj* (*person, area*) de
mala fama; (*behaviour*) vergonzoso
disrespectful [dɪsrɪ'spɛktful] *adj* irrespetuoso
disrupt [dɪs'rʌpt] *vt* (*meeting, public transport,
conversation*) interrumpir; (*plans*) desbaratar,
alternar, trastornar
disruption [dɪs'rʌpʃən] *n* trastorno;
desbaratamiento; interrupción
disruptive [dɪs'rʌptɪv] *adj* (*influence*) disruptivo;
(*strike action*) perjudicial
dissatisfaction [dɪssætɪs'fækʃən] *n* disgusto,
descontento
dissatisfied [dɪs'sætɪsfaɪd] *adj* insatisfecho
dissect [dɪ'sɛkt] *vt* (*also fig*) disecar
disseminate [dɪ'sɛmɪneɪt] *vt* divulgar, difundir
dissent [dɪ'sɛnt] *n* disensión
dissertation [dɪsə'teɪʃən] *n* (*Univ*) tesina; *see also*
master's degree
disservice [dɪs'sə:vɪs] *n*: **to do sb a ~** perjudicar
a algn
dissimilar [dɪ'sɪmɪləʳ] *adj* distinto
dissipate ['dɪsɪpeɪt] *vt* disipar; (*waste*)
desperdiciar
dissolute ['dɪsəluːt] *adj* disoluto
dissolve [dɪ'zɔlv] *vt* (*gen, Comm*) disolver ▷ *vi*
disolverse
dissuade [dɪ'sweɪd] *vt*: **to ~ sb (from)** disuadir
a algn (de)
distance ['dɪstns] *n* distancia; **in the ~** a lo lejos;
what ~ is it to London? ¿qué distancia hay de
aquí a Londres?; **it's within walking ~** se puede
ir andando

distant ['dɪstnt] *adj* lejano; (*manner*) reservado,
frío
distaste [dɪs'teɪst] *n* repugnancia
distasteful [dɪs'teɪstful] *adj* repugnante,
desagradable
distemper [dɪs'tɛmpəʳ] *n* (*of dogs*) moquillo
distended [dɪ'stɛndɪd] *adj* (*stomach*) hinchado
distil, (*US*) **distill** [dɪs'tɪl] *vt* destilar
distillery [dɪs'tɪlərɪ] *n* destilería
distinct [dɪs'tɪŋkt] *adj* (*different*) distinto; (*clear*)
claro; (*unmistakeable*) inequívoco; **as ~ from** a
diferencia de
distinction [dɪs'tɪŋkʃən] *n* distinción; (*in
exam*) sobresaliente; **a writer of ~** un escritor
destacado; **to draw a ~ between** hacer una
distinción entre
distinctive [dɪs'tɪŋktɪv] *adj* distintivo
distinctly [dɪs'tɪŋktlɪ] *adv* claramente
distinguish [dɪs'tɪŋgwɪʃ] *vt* distinguir ▷ *vi*: **to ~
(between)** distinguir (entre)
distinguished [dɪs'tɪŋgwɪʃt] *adj* (*eminent*)
distinguido; (*career*) eminente; (*refined*)
distinguido, de categoría
distinguishing [dɪs'tɪŋgwɪʃɪŋ] *adj* (*feature*)
distintivo
distort [dɪs'tɔːt] *vt* torcer, retorcer; (*account, news*)
desvirtuar, deformar
distortion [dɪs'tɔːʃən] *n* deformación; (*of sound*)
distorsión; (*of truth etc*) tergiversación; (*of facts*)
falseamiento
distract [dɪs'trækt] *vt* distraer
distracted [dɪs'træktɪd] *adj* distraído
distraction [dɪs'trækʃən] *n* distracción;
(*confusion*) aturdimiento; (*amusement*) diversión;
to drive sb to ~ (*distress, anxiety*) volver loco a algn
distraught [dɪs'trɔːt] *adj* turbado, enloquecido
distress [dɪs'trɛs] *n* (*anguish*) angustia; (*want*)
miseria; (*pain*) dolor; (*danger*) peligro ▷ *vt* afligir;
(*pain*) doler; **in ~** (*ship etc*) en peligro
distressing [dɪs'trɛsɪŋ] *adj* angustioso; doloroso
distribute [dɪs'trɪbjuːt] *vt* (*gen*) distribuir; (*share
out*) repartir
distribution [dɪstrɪ'bjuːʃən] *n* distribución
distributor [dɪs'trɪbjutəʳ] *n* (*Aut*) distribuidor;
(*Comm*) distribuidora
district ['dɪstrɪkt] *n* (*of country*) zona, región; (*of
town*) barrio; (*Admin*) distrito
district attorney *n* (US) fiscal
district council *n* ≈ municipio
district nurse *n* (*Brit*) enfermera que atiende a
pacientes a domicilio
distrust [dɪs'trʌst] *n* desconfianza ▷ *vt*
desconfiar de
disturb [dɪs'tə:b] *vt* (*person: bother, interrupt*)
molestar; (*meeting*) interrumpir; (*disorganize*)
desordenar; **sorry to ~ you** perdone la molestia
disturbance [dɪs'tə:bəns] *n* (*political etc*)
disturbio; (*violence*) alboroto; (*of mind*) trastorno;
to cause a ~ causar alboroto; **~ of the peace**
alteración del orden público
disturbed [dɪs'tə:bd] *adj* (*worried, upset*)
preocupado, angustiado; **to be emotionally/**

mentally ~ tener problemas emocionales/ser un trastornado mental

disturbing [dɪs'tə:bɪŋ] *adj* inquietante, perturbador(a)

disuse [dɪs'ju:s] *n*: **to fall into ~** caer en desuso

disused [dɪs'ju:zd] *adj* abandonado

ditch [dɪtʃ] *n* zanja; (*irrigation ditch*) acequia ▷ *vt* (*col*) deshacerse de

dither ['dɪðə'] *vi* vacilar

ditto ['dɪtəu] *adv* ídem, lo mismo

dive [daɪv] *n* (*from board*) salto; (*underwater*) buceo; (*of submarine*) inmersión; (*Aviat*) picada ▷ *vi* saltar; bucear; sumergirse; picar

diver ['daɪvə'] *n* (*Sport*) saltador(a); (*underwater*) buzo

diverse [daɪ'və:s] *adj* diversos(-as), varios(-as)

diversification [daɪvə:sɪfɪ'keɪʃən] *n* diversificación

diversion [daɪ'və:ʃən] *n* (*Brit Aut*) desviación, desvío; (*distraction, Mil*) diversión

diversity [daɪ'və:sɪtɪ] *n* diversidad

divert [daɪ'və:t] *vt* (*Brit: train, plane, traffic*) desviar; (*amuse*) divertir

divide [dɪ'vaɪd] *vt* dividir; (*separate*) separar ▷ *vi* dividirse; (*road*) bifurcarse; **to ~ (between, among)** repartir *or* dividir (entre); **40 ~d by 5** 40 dividido por 5
  ▶ **divide out** *vt*: **to ~ out (between, among)** (*sweets, tasks etc*) repartir (entre)

divided [dɪ'vaɪdɪd] *adj* (*country, couple*) dividido, separado; (*opinions*) en desacuerdo

divided highway *n* (*US*) carretera de doble calzada

dividend ['dɪvɪdɛnd] *n* dividendo; (*fig*) beneficio

divine [dɪ'vaɪn] *adj* divino ▷ *vt* (*future*) vaticinar; (*truth*) alumbrar; (*water, metal*) descubrir, detectar

diving ['daɪvɪŋ] *n* (*Sport*) salto; (*underwater*) buceo

diving board *n* trampolín

divinity [dɪ'vɪnɪtɪ] *n* divinidad; (*Scol*) teología

division [dɪ'vɪʒən] *n* (*also Brit Football*) división; (*sharing out*) repartimiento; (*Brit Pol*) votación; **~ of labour** división del trabajo

divisive [dɪ'vaɪsɪv] *adj* divisivo

divorce [dɪ'vɔ:s] *n* divorcio ▷ *vt* divorciarse de

divorced [dɪ'vɔ:st] *adj* divorciado

divorcee [dɪvɔ:'si:] *n* divorciado(-a)

divot ['dɪvət] *n* (*Golf*) chuleta

divulge [daɪ'vʌldʒ] *vt* divulgar, revelar

dizziness ['dɪzɪnɪs] *n* vértigo

dizzy ['dɪzɪ] *adj* (*person*) mareado; (*height*) vertiginoso; **to feel ~** marearse; **I feel ~** estoy mareado

DJ *n abbr see* **disc jockey**

DNA *n abbr* (= *deoxyribonucleic acid*) ADN

do [du:] (*pt* **did**, *pp* **done**) *n* **1** (*col: party etc*): **we're having a little do on Saturday** damos una fiestecita el sábado; **it was rather a grand do** fue una fiesta a lo grande
2: **the dos and don'ts** lo que se debe y no se debe hacer
  ▷ *aux vb* (*in negative constructions: not translated*): **I don't understand** no entiendo; **you didn't tell me anything** no me dijiste nada
2 (*to form questions: not translated*): **do you speak English?** ¿habla (usted) inglés?; **didn't you know?** ¿no lo sabías?; **what do you think?** ¿qué opinas?; **do you like reading?** ¿te gusta leer?
3 (*for emphasis, in polite expressions*): **people do make mistakes sometimes** a veces sí se cometen errores; **she does seem rather late** a mí también me parece que se ha retrasado; **do sit down/help yourself** siéntate/sírvete por favor; **do take care!** ¡ten cuidado! ¿eh?; **I DO wish I could ...** ojalá (que) pudiera ...; **but I DO like it** pero, sí (que) me gusta
4 (*used to avoid repeating vb*): **she sings better than I do** canta mejor que yo; **do you agree? — yes, I do/no, I don't** ¿estás de acuerdo? — sí/no; **she lives in Glasgow — so do I** vive en Glasgow — yo también; **he didn't like it and neither did we** no le gustó y a nosotros tampoco; **who made this mess? — I did** ¿quién hizo esta chapuza? — yo; **he asked me to help him and I did** me pidió que le ayudara y lo hice
5 (*in question tags*): **you like him, don't you?** te gusta, ¿verdad? *or* ¿no?; **I don't know him, do I?** creo que no le conozco; **he laughed, didn't he?** se rió ¿no?; **it doesn't matter, does it?** no importa, ¿verdad?
  ▷ *vt* (*gen, carry out, perform etc*) hacer; **what are you doing tonight?** ¿qué haces esta noche?; **what can I do for you?** (*in shop*) ¿en qué puedo servirle?; **what does he do (for a living)?** ¿a qué se dedica?; **I'll do all I can** haré todo lo que pueda; **what have you done with my slippers?** ¿qué has hecho con mis zapatillas?; **to do the washing-up/cooking** fregar los platos/cocinar; **to do one's teeth/hair/nails** lavarse los dientes/arreglarse el pelo/arreglarse las uñas
2 (*Aut etc*): **the car was doing 70** el coche iba a 70; **he can do 100 in that car** puede ir a 100 en ese coche; **we've done 200 km already** ya hemos hecho 200 km
3 (*visit: city, museum*) visitar
4 (*cook*): **I'll have a steak...well done please** un filete bien hecho, por favor
5 (*study*) hacer; **I want to do physics at university** quiero hacer física en la universidad
  ▷ *vi* **1** (*act, behave*) hacer; **do as I do** haz como yo
2 (*get on, fare*): **he's doing well/badly at school** va bien/mal en la escuela; **the firm is doing well** la empresa anda *or* va bien; **how are you doing?** ¿qué tal?; **how do you do?** mucho gusto
3 (*suit*): **will it do?** ¿sirve?, ¿está *or* va bien?; **it doesn't do to upset her** cuidado con ofenderla
4 (*be sufficient*) bastar; **it's not very good, but it'll do** no es muy bueno, pero valdrá; **will £10 do?** ¿será bastante con 10 libras?, ¿valdrá con 10 libras?; **that'll do** así está bien; **that'll do!** (*in annoyance*) ¡ya está bien!, ¡basta ya!; **to make do (with)** arreglárselas (con)
  ▶ **do away with** *vt fus* (*person, disease*) eliminar; (*abolish: law etc*) abolir; (*withdraw*) retirar
  ▶ **do out of** *vt fus*: **to do sb out of sth, he did her

out of a job le quitó el trabajo

▸ **do up** *vt* (*laces*) atar; (*dress, shirt*) abrochar; (*renovate: room, house*) renovar; **do your coat up** abróchate el abrigo; **do your zip!** ¡súbete la cremallera!; **do up your shoes!** ¡átate los zapatos!

▸ **do with** *vt fus* (*need*): **I could do with a drink/some help** no me vendría mal un trago/un poco de ayuda; **to have to do with** (*be connected with*) tener que ver con; **what has it got to do with you?** ¿qué tiene que ver contigo?

▸ **do without** *vi*: **if you're late for dinner then you'll do without** si llegas tarde tendrás que quedarte sin cenar ▷ *vt fus* pasar sin; **I can do without a car** puedo pasar sin coche

DOA *abbr* = **dead on arrival**

doc [dɔk] *n* (*col*) médico(-a)

dock [dɔk] *n* (*Naut: wharf*) dársena, muelle; (*Law*) banquillo (de los acusados) ▷ *vi* (*enter dock*) atracar (en el muelle) ▷ *vt* (*pay etc*) descontar; **docks** *npl* muelles, puerto

docker ['dɔkər] *n* trabajador portuario, estibador

dockyard ['dɔkjɑːd] *n* astillero

doctor ['dɔktər] *n* médico; (*Ph.D. etc*) doctor(a) ▷ *vt* (*fig*) arreglar, falsificar; (*drink etc*) adulterar

doctorate ['dɔktərɪt] *n* doctorado

doctrine ['dɔktrɪn] *n* doctrina

docudrama [dɔkju'drɑːmə] *n* (*TV*) docudrama

document *n* documento ▷ *vt* documentar

documentary [dɔkju'mɛntərɪ] *adj* documental ▷ *n* documental

documentation [dɔkjumɛn'teɪʃən] *n* documentación

doddering ['dɔdərɪŋ] *adj*, **doddery** ['dɔdərɪ] ▷ *adj* vacilante

doddle ['dɔdl] *n*: **it's a ~** (*Brit col*) es pan comido

dodge [dɔdʒ] *n* (*of body*) regate; (*fig*) truco ▷ *vt* (*gen*) evadir; (*blow*) esquivar ▷ *vi* escabullirse; (*Sport*) hacer una finta; **to ~ out of the way** echarse a un lado; **to ~ through the traffic** esquivar el tráfico

dodgems ['dɔdʒəmz] *npl* (*Brit*) autos *or* coches de choque

dodgy ['dɔdʒɪ] *adj* (*col: uncertain*) dudoso; (*shady*) sospechoso; (*risky*) arriesgado

DOE *n abbr* (*Brit*) = **Department of the Environment**; (*US*) = **Department of Energy**

doe [dəu] *n* (*deer*) cierva, gama; (*rabbit*) coneja

does [dʌz] *vb see* **do**

doesn't ['dʌznt] = **does not**

dog [dɔg] *n* perro ▷ *vt* seguir (de cerca); (*fig: memory etc*) perseguir; **to go to the ~s** (*person*) echarse a perder; (*nation etc*) ir a la ruina

dog collar *n* collar de perro; (*fig*) alzacuello(s)

dog-eared ['dɔgɪəd] *adj* sobado; (*page*) con la esquina doblada

dogged ['dɔgɪd] *adj* tenaz, obstinado

doggy ['dɔgɪ] *n* (*col*) perrito

doggy bag *n* bolsa para llevarse las sobras de la comida

dogma ['dɔgmə] *n* dogma

dogmatic [dɔg'mætɪk] *adj* dogmático

dogsbody ['dɔgzbɔdɪ] *n* (*Brit*) burro de carga

doily ['dɔɪlɪ] *n* pañito de adorno

doings ['duɪŋz] *npl* (*events*) sucesos; (*acts*) hechos

do-it-yourself [duːɪtjɔː'sɛlf] *n* bricolaje

doldrums ['dɔldrəmz] *npl*: **to be in the ~** (*person*) estar abatido; (*business*) estar estancado

dole [dəul] *n* (*Brit: payment*) subsidio de paro; **on the ~** parado

▸ **dole out** *vt* repartir

doleful ['dəulful] *adj* triste, lúgubre

doll [dɔl] *n* muñeca

▸ **doll up** *vt*: **to ~ o.s. up** ataviarse

dollar ['dɔlər] *n* dólar

dollop ['dɔləp] *n* buena cucharada

dolly ['dɔlɪ] *n* muñeca

dolphin ['dɔlfɪn] *n* delfín

domain [də'meɪn] *n* (*fig*) campo, competencia; (*land*) dominios

dome [dəum] *n* (*Arch*) cúpula; (*shape*) bóveda

domestic [də'mɛstɪk] *adj* (*animal, duty*) doméstico; (*flight, news, policy*) nacional

domesticated [də'mɛstɪkeɪtɪd] *adj* domesticado; (*person: home-loving*) casero, hogareño

dominant ['dɔmɪnənt] *adj* dominante

dominate ['dɔmɪneɪt] *vt* dominar

domination [dɔmɪ'neɪʃən] *n* dominación

domineering [dɔmɪ'nɪərɪŋ] *adj* dominante

Dominican Republic [də'mɪnɪkən-] *n* República Dominicana

dominion [də'mɪnɪən] *n* dominio

domino ['dɔmɪnəu] (*pl* **-es**) *n* ficha de dominó

dominoes ['dɔmɪnəuz] *n* (*game*) dominó

don [dɔn] *n* (*Brit*) profesor(a) de universidad

donate [də'neɪt] *vt* donar

donation [də'neɪʃən] *n* donativo

done [dʌn] *pp of* **do**

donkey ['dɔŋkɪ] *n* burro

donor ['dəunər] *n* donante

donor card *n* carnet de donante de órganos

don't [dəunt] = **do not**

donut ['dəunʌt] *n* (*US*) = **doughnut**

doodle ['duːdl] *n* garabato ▷ *vi* pintar dibujitos *or* garabatos

doom [duːm] *n* (*fate*) suerte; (*death*) muerte ▷ *vt*: **to be ~ed to failure** estar condenado al fracaso

doomsday ['duːmzdeɪ] *n* día del juicio final

door [dɔːr] *n* puerta; (*of car*) portezuela; (*entry*) entrada; **from ~ to ~** de puerta en puerta

doorbell ['dɔːbɛl] *n* timbre

door handle *n* tirador; (*of car*) manija

doorman ['dɔːmən] *n* (*in hotel*) portero

doormat ['dɔːmæt] *n* felpudo, estera

doorstep ['dɔːstɛp] *n* peldaño; **on your ~** en la puerta de casa; (*fig*) al lado de casa

doorway ['dɔːweɪ] *n* entrada, puerta; **in the ~** en la puerta

dope [dəup] *n* (*col: person*) imbécil; (: *drugs*) drogas ▷ *vt* (*horse etc*) drogar

dopey ['dəupɪ] *adj* atontado

dormant ['dɔːmənt] *adj* inactivo; (*latent*) latente

dormitory ['dɔːmɪtrɪ] *n* (*Brit*) dormitorio; (*US: hall of residence*) residencia, colegio mayor

dormouse ['dɔːmaus] (*pl* **dormice**) *n* lirón

DOS *n abbr* = disk operating system
dose [dəus] *n (of medicine)* dosis; **a ~ of flu**
un ataque de gripe ▷ *vt:* **to ~ o.s. with**
aùtomedicarse con
dosser ['dɔsər] *n (Brit col)* mendigo(-a); *(lazy
person)* vago(-a)
doss house ['dɔs-] *n (Brit)* pensión de mala
muerte
dossier ['dɔsɪeɪ] *n:* ~ **(on)** expediente (sobre)
dot [dɔt] *n* punto ▷ *vt:* **~ted with** salpicado de;
on the ~ en punto
dotcom ['dɔtkɔm] puntocom
dote [dəut]: **to ~ on** *vt fus* adorar, idolatrar
dot-matrix printer [dɔt'meɪtrɪks-] *n* impresora
matricial *or* de matriz
dotted line ['dɔtɪd-] *n* línea de puntos; **to sign
on the ~** firmar
double ['dʌbl] *adj* doble ▷ *adv (twice):* **to cost
~** costar el doble ▷ *n (gen)* doble ▷ *vt* doblar;
(efforts) redoblar ▷ *vi* doblarse; *(have two uses etc):*
to ~ as hacer las veces de; **~ five two six (5526)**
(Telec) cinco cinco dos seis; **spelt with a ~ "s"**
escrito con dos "eses"; **on the ~** *(Brit):* **at the ~**
corriendo
▸ **double back** *vi (person)* volver sobre sus pasos
▸ **double up** *vi (bend over)* doblarse; *(share bedroom)*
compartir
double bass *n* contrabajo
double bed *n* cama matrimonial
double-breasted ['dʌbl'brestɪd] *adj* cruzado
doublecross ['dʌbl'krɔs] *vt (trick)* engañar;
(betray) traicionar
double-click ['dʌbl'klɪk] *vi (Comput)* hacer doble
click
doubledecker ['dʌbl'dekər] *n* autobús de dos
pisos
double glazing *n (Brit)* doble acristalamiento
double room *n* cuarto para dos
double whammy [-'wæmɪ] *n (col)* palo doble
doubly ['dʌblɪ] *adv* doblemente
doubt [daut] *n* duda ▷ *vt* dudar; *(suspect)* dudar
de; **to ~ that** dudar que; **there is no ~ that**
no cabe duda de que; **without (a) ~** sin duda
(alguna); **beyond ~** fuera de duda; **I ~ it very
much** lo dudo mucho
doubtful ['dautful] *adj* dudoso; *(arousing
suspicion: person)* sospechoso; **to be ~ about sth**
tener dudas sobre algo; **I'm a bit ~** no estoy
convencido
doubtless ['dautlɪs] *adv* sin duda
dough [dəu] *n* masa, pasta; *(col: money)* pasta,
lana *(LAm)*
doughnut ['dəunʌt] *n* buñuelo
douse [daus] *vt (drench: with water)* mojar;
(extinguish: flames) apagar
dove [dʌv] *n* paloma
Dover ['dəuvər] *n* Dover
dovetail ['dʌvteɪl] *vi (fig)* encajar
dowdy ['daudɪ] *adj* desaliñado; *(inelegant)* poco
elegante
Dow-Jones average ['daudʒəunz-] *n (US)* índice
Dow-Jones

down [daun] *n (fluff)* pelusa; *(feathers)* plumón,
flojel ▷ *adv (also:* **downwards)** abajo, hacia
abajo; *(on the ground)* por/en tierra ▷ *prep* abajo
▷ *vt (depressed)* deprimido ▷ *vt (col: drink)* beberse,
tragar(se); **~s** *npl (hills)* lomas; **to fall ~** caer;
~ with X! ¡abajo X!; **~ there** allí abajo; **~ here**
aquí abajo; **his office is ~ on the first floor** su
despacho está abajo en el primer piso; **I'll be ~
in a minute** ahora bajo; **he threw ~ his racket**
tiró la raqueta al suelo; **England are two goals
~** Inglaterra está perdiendo por dos tantos; **I've
been ~ with flu** he estado con gripe; **the price
of meat is ~** ha bajado el precio de la carne;
I've got it ~ in my diary lo he apuntado en mi
agenda; **to pay £2 ~** dejar dos libras de depósito;
he went ~ the hill fue cuesta abajo; **they live
just ~ the road** viven más adelante en esta calle;
~ under *(in Australia or New Zealand)* en Australia/
Nueva Zelanda; **to feel ~** estar deprimido; **the
computer's ~** el ordenador no funciona; **to ~
tools** *(fig)* declararse en huelga
down-and-out ['daunəndaut] *n (tramp)*
vagabundo(-a)
down-at-heel ['daunət'hi:l] *adj* venido a menos;
(appearance) desaliñado
downcast ['daunkɑ:st] *adj* abatido
downfall ['daunfɔ:l] *n* caída, ruina
downhearted [daun'hɑ:tɪd] *adj* desanimado
downhill [daun'hɪl] *adv:* **to go ~** ir cuesta abajo;
(business) estar en declive
down payment *n* entrada, pago al contado
downpour ['daunpɔ:r] *n* aguacero
downright ['daunraɪt] *adj (nonsense, lie)*
manifiesto; *(refusal)* terminante
downsize [daun'saɪz] *vt* reducir la plantilla de
Down's syndrome [daunz-] *n* síndrome de
Down
downstairs [daun'steəz] *adv (below)* (en el piso
de) abajo; *(motion)* escaleras abajo; **to come (or
go) ~** bajar la escalera
downstream [daun'stri:m] *adv* aguas *or* río
abajo
down-to-earth [dauntu'ə:θ] *adj* práctico
downtown [daun'taun] *adv* en el centro de la
ciudad
downward ['daunwəd] *adv* hacia abajo ▷ *adj:* **a ~
trend** una tendencia descendente
downward(s) ['daunwəd(z)] *adv* hacia abajo;
face downward(s) *(person)* boca abajo; *(object)*
cara abajo
dowry ['daurɪ] *n* dote
doz. *abbr* = dozen
doze [dəuz] *vi* dormitar
▸ **doze off** *vi* echar una cabezada
dozen ['dʌzn] *n* docena; **a ~ books** una docena de
libros; **~s of** cantidad de; **~s of times** cantidad
de veces; **8op a ~** 80 peniques la docena
DPP *n abbr (Brit)* = **Director of Public
Prosecutions**
Dr, Dr. *abbr (= doctor)* Dr
Dr. *abbr* = **in street names;** = **Drive**
drab [dræb] *adj* gris, monótono

draft [drɑːft] n (first copy: of document, report) borrador; (Comm) giro; (US: call-up) quinta ▷ vt (write roughly) hacer un borrador de; see also **draught**

draftsman etc ['drɑːftsmən] (US) = **draughtsman** etc

drag [dræg] vt arrastrar; (river) dragar, rastrear ▷ vi arrastrarse por el suelo ▷ n (Aviat: resistance) resistencia aerodinámica; (col) lata; (women's clothing): **in ~** travestido
▸ **drag away** vt: **to ~ away (from)** separar a rastras (de)
▸ **drag on** vi ser interminable

dragon ['drægən] n dragón

dragonfly ['drægənflaɪ] n libélula

drain [dreɪn] n desaguadero; (in street) sumidero; (drain cover) rejilla del sumidero ▷ vt (land, marshes) desecar; (Med) drenar; (reservoir) desecar; (fig) agotar ▷ vi escurrirse; **to be a ~ on** consumir, agotar; **to feel ~ed (of energy)** (fig) sentirse agotado

drainage ['dreɪnɪdʒ] n (act) desagüe; (Med, Agr) drenaje; (sewage) alcantarillado

draining board ['dreɪnɪŋ-], (US) **drainboard** ['dreɪnbɔːd] n escurridero, escurridor

drainpipe ['dreɪnpaɪp] n tubo de desagüe

dram [dræm] n (drink) traguito, copita

drama ['drɑːmə] n (art) teatro; (play) drama

dramatic [drə'mætɪk] adj dramático

dramatist ['dræmətɪst] n dramaturgo(-a)

dramatize ['dræmətaɪz] vt (events etc) dramatizar; (adapt: novel: for TV, cinema) adaptar

drank [dræŋk] pt of **drink**

drape [dreɪp] vt cubrir

drapes [dreɪps] npl (US) cortinas

drastic ['dræstɪk] adj (measure, reduction) severo; (change) radical

draught, (US) **draft** [drɑːft] n (of air) corriente de aire; (drink) trago; (Naut) calado; **on ~** (beer) de barril

draught beer n cerveza de barril

draughtboard ['drɑːftbɔːd] (Brit) n tablero de damas

draughts [drɑːfts] n (Brit) juego de damas

draughtsman, (US) **draftsman** ['drɑːftsmən] n proyectista, delineante

draw [drɔː] vb (pt **drew**, pp **-n**) ▷ vt (scene, person) dibujar; (pull) tirar; (take out) sacar; (attract) atraer; (money) retirar; (Sport) empatar ▷ vi (Sport) empatar ▷ n (Sport) empate; (lottery) sorteo; (attraction) atracción; **to ~ a picture** hacer un dibujo; **to ~ a picture of sb** hacer un retrato de algn; **to ~ a line** trazar una línea; **to ~ the curtains** (open) descorrer las cortinas; (close) correr las cortinas; **to ~ a conclusion (from)** sacar una conclusión (de); **to ~ a comparison/distinction (between)** hacer una comparación/distinción (entre); **we drew two all** empatamos a dos; **to ~ near** (approach) acercarse
▸ **draw back** vi: **to ~ back (from)** echarse atrás (de)
▸ **draw in** vi (train) entrar en la estación

▸ **draw on** vt (resources) utilizar, servirse de; (imagination, experience, person) recurrir a
▸ **draw out** vt (lengthen) alargar
▸ **draw up** vi (stop) pararse; **the car drew up in front of the house** el coche se paró delante de la casa ▷ vt (document) redactar; (plan) trazar

drawback ['drɔːbæk] n inconveniente, desventaja

drawbridge ['drɔːbrɪdʒ] n puente levadizo

drawer [drɔːʳ] n cajón; (of cheque) librador(a)

drawing ['drɔːɪŋ] n dibujo

drawing board n tablero (de dibujante)

drawing pin n (Brit) chincheta (Esp), chinche (LAm)

drawing room n salón

drawl [drɔːl] n habla lenta y cansina

drawn [drɔːn] pp of **draw** ▷ adj (haggard: with tiredness) ojeroso; (: with pain) macilento

dread [dred] n pavor, terror ▷ vt temer, tener miedo or pavor a

dreadful ['dredful] adj espantoso; **I feel ~!** (ill) ¡me siento fatal or malísimo!; (ashamed) ¡qué vergüenza!

dream [driːm] n sueño ▷ vt, vi (pt, pp **-ed** or **-t**) [dremt] soñar; **to have a ~ about sb/sth** soñar con algn/algo; **sweet ~s!** ¡que sueñes con los angelitos!
▸ **dream up** vt (reason, excuse) inventar; (plan, idea) idear

dreamy ['driːmɪ] adj (person) soñador(a), distraído; (music) de sueño

dreary ['drɪərɪ] adj monótono, aburrido

dredge [dredʒ] vt dragar
▸ **dredge up** vt sacar con draga; (fig: unpleasant facts) pescar, sacar a luz

dregs [dregz] npl heces

drench [drentʃ] vt empapar; **~ed to the skin** calado hasta los huesos

dress [dres] n vestido; (clothing) ropa ▷ vt vestir; (wound) vendar; (Culin) aliñar; (shop window) decorar, arreglar ▷ vi vestirse; **to ~ o.s., get ~ed** vestirse; **she ~es very well** se viste muy bien
▸ **dress up** vi vestirse de etiqueta; (in fancy dress) disfrazarse

dress circle n (Brit) principal

dresser ['dresəʳ] n (furniture) aparador; (: US) tocador; (Theat) camarero(-a)

dressing ['dresɪŋ] n (Med) vendaje; (Culin) aliño

dressing gown n (Brit) bata

dressing room n (Theat) camarín; (Sport) vestidor

dressing table n tocador

dressmaker ['dresmeɪkəʳ] n modista, costurera

dress rehearsal n ensayo general

drew [druː] pt of **draw**

dribble ['drɪbl] vi gotear, caer gota a gota; (baby) babear ▷ vt (ball) driblar, regatear

dried [draɪd] adj (gen) seco; (fruit) paso; (milk) en polvo

drier ['draɪəʳ] n = **dryer**

drift [drɪft] n (of current etc) velocidad; (of sand) montón; (of snow) ventisquero; (meaning) significado ▷ vi (boat) ir a la deriva; (sand, snow) amontonarse; **to catch sb's ~** cogerle el hilo a algn; **to let things ~** dejar las cosas como están; **to ~ apart** (*friends*) seguir su camino; (*lovers*) disgustarse, romper

driftwood ['drɪftwʊd] *n* madera flotante

drill [drɪl] *n* taladro; (*bit*) broca; (*of dentist*) fresa; (*for mining etc*) perforadora, barrena; (*Mil*) instrucción ▷ *vt* perforar, taladrar; (*soldiers*) ejercitar; (*pupils: in grammar*) hacer ejercicios con ▷ *vi* (*for oil*) perforar

drink [drɪŋk] *n* bebida ▷ *vt, vi* (*pt* **drank**, *pp* **drunk**) beber, tomar (*LAm*); (*imbibe*) beber; tomar una copa *or* un trago; **a ~ of water** un trago de agua; **to invite sb for ~s** invitar a algn a tomar unas copas; **there's food and ~ in the kitchen** hay de comer y de beber en la cocina; **would you like something to ~?** ¿quieres beber *or* tomar algo?

▶ **drink in** *vt* (*person: fresh air*) respirar; (*: story, sight*) beberse

drink-driving [drɪŋk'draɪvɪŋ] *n*: **to be charged with ~** ser acusado de conducir borracho *or* en estado de embriaguez

drinker ['drɪŋkər] *n* bebedor(a)

drinking water *n* agua potable

drip [drɪp] *n* (*act*) goteo; (*one drip*) gota; (*Med*) gota a gota; (*sound: of water etc*) goteo; (*pej*) soso(-a) ▷ *vi* gotear, caer gota a gota

drip-dry ['drɪp'draɪ] *adj* (*shirt*) de lava y pon

dripping ['drɪpɪŋ] *n* (*animal fat*) pringue ▷ *adj*: **~ wet** calado

drive [draɪv] *n* (*for pleasure*) paseo (en coche); (*journey*) viaje (en coche); (*also*: **driveway**) entrada; (*street*) calle; (*energy*) energía, vigor; (*Psych*) impulso; (*Sport*) ataque; (*Comput: also*: **disk drive**) unidad de disco ▷ *vb* (*pt* **drove**, *pp* **-n**) ▷ *vt* (*car*) conducir, manejar (*LAm*); (*transport by car*) llevar en coche; (*nail*) clavar; (*push*) empujar; (*Tech: motor*) impulsar ▷ *vi* (*Aut: at controls*) conducir, manejar (*LAm*); (*: travel for pleasure*) pasearse en coche; (*: go by car*) ir en coche; **to go for a ~** dar una vuelta en coche; **it's 3 hours' ~ from London** es un viaje de 3 horas en coche desde Londres; **he parked his car in the ~** aparcó el coche en el camino de entrada a la casa; **a left-/right-hand ~ car** un coche con el volante a la izquierda/derecha; **front-/rear-wheel ~** tracción delantera/trasera; **hard ~** (*Comput*) disco duro; **sales ~** promoción de ventas; **he ~s a taxi** es taxista; **he ~s a Mercedes** tiene un Mercedes; **my mother ~s me to school** mi madre me lleva al colegio en coche; **to ~ sb home** acercar a algn a su casa en coche; **to ~ sb mad** volverle loco a algn; **to ~ sb to (do) sth** empujar a algn a (hacer) algo; **can you ~?** ¿sabes conducir *or* (*LAm*) manejar?; **to ~ at 50 km an hour** ir a 50 km por hora; **we never ~ into town** nunca vamos en coche al centro; **she drove into a tree** chocó con un muro

▶ **drive at** *vt fus* (*fig: intend, mean*) querer decir, insinuar

▶ **drive on** *vi* seguir adelante ▷ *vt* (*incite, encourage*) empujar

drive-by ['draɪvbaɪ] *n*: **~ shooting** tiroteo desde el coche

drive-in ['draɪvɪn] *adj* (*esp US*): **~ cinema** autocine

drivel ['drɪvl] *n* (*col*) tonterías

driven ['drɪvn] *pp of* **drive**

driver ['draɪvər] *n* conductor(a), chofer (*LAm*); (*of taxi*) taxista

driver's license *n* (*US*) carnet *or* permiso de conducir

driveway ['draɪvweɪ] *n* camino de entrada

driving ['draɪvɪŋ] *n* conducir, manejar (*LAm*) ▷ *adj* (*force*) impulsor(a)

driving instructor *n* instructor(a) de autoescuela

driving lesson *n* clase de conducir

driving licence *n* (*Brit*) carnet *or* permiso de conducir

driving school *n* autoescuela

driving test *n* examen de conducir

drizzle ['drɪzl] *n* llovizna, garúa (*LAm*) ▷ *vi* lloviznar

drone [drəʊn] *vi* (*bee, aircraft, engine*) zumbar; (*also*: **drone on**) murmurar sin interrupción ▷ *n* zumbido; (*male bee*) zángano

drool [druːl] *vi* babear; **to ~ over sb/sth** caérsele la baba por algn/algo

droop [druːp] *vi* (*fig*) decaer, desanimarse

drop [drɒp] *n* (*of water*) gota; (*fall: in price*) bajada; (*: in salary*) disminución ▷ *vt* (*allow to fall*) dejar caer; (*voice, eyes, price*) bajar; (*set down from car*) dejar ▷ *vi* (*price, temperature*) bajar; (*wind*) calmarse, amainar; (*numbers, attendance*) disminuir; **drops** *npl* (*Med*) gotas; **cough ~s** pastillas para la tos; **would you like some milk? — just a ~** ¿quieres leche? — una gota nada más; **a ~ of 10%** una bajada del 10 por ciento; **a ~ in temperature** una bajada de las temperaturas; **the cat ~ped the mouse at my feet** el gato soltó al ratón junto a mis pies; **I ~ped the glass** se me cayó el vaso; **to ~ anchor** echar el ancla; **to ~ sb a line** mandar unas líneas a algn; **I'm going to ~ chemistry** no voy a dar más química

▶ **drop in** *vi* (*col: visit*): **to ~ in (on)** pasar por casa (de)

▶ **drop off** *vi* (*sleep*) dormirse ▷ *vt* (*passenger*) dejar

▶ **drop out** *vi* (*withdraw*) retirarse

dropout ['drɒpaʊt] *n* (*from society*) marginado(-a); (*from university*) estudiante que ha abandonado los estudios

dropper ['drɒpər] *n* (*Med*) cuentagotas

droppings ['drɒpɪŋz] *npl* excremento

dross [drɒs] *n* (*coal, fig*) escoria

drought [draʊt] *n* sequía

drove [drəʊv] *pt of* **drive**

drown [draʊn] *vt* (*also*: **drown out**: *sound*) ahogar ▷ *vi* ahogarse

drowsy ['draʊzɪ] *adj* soñoliento; **to be ~** tener sueño

drudgery ['drʌdʒərɪ] *n* trabajo pesado *or*

monótono

drug [drʌg] n (Med) medicamento, droga; (narcotic) droga ▷ vt drogar; **to be on ~s** drogarse; **he's on ~s** se droga

drug addict n drogadicto(-a)

druggist ['drʌgɪst] n (US) farmacéutico(-a)

drugstore ['drʌgstɔːʳ] n (US) tienda (de comestibles, periódicos y medicamentos)

drug trafficker n narcotraficante

drum [drʌm] n tambor; (large) bombo; (for oil, petrol) bidón ▷ vi tocar el tambor; (with fingers) tamborilear ▷ vt: **to ~ one's fingers on the table** tamborilear con los dedos sobre la mesa; **drums** npl batería

▶ **drum up** vt (enthusiasm, support) movilizar, fomentar

drummer ['drʌməʳ] n (in military band) tambor; (in jazz/pop group) batería

drumstick ['drʌmstɪk] n (Mus) palillo, baqueta; (chicken leg) muslo (de pollo)

drunk [drʌŋk] pp of **drink** ▷ adj borracho ▷ n (also: **drunkard**) borracho(-a); **to get ~** emborracharse

drunken ['drʌŋkən] adj borracho

dry [draɪ] adj seco; (day) sin lluvia; (climate) árido, seco; (humour) agudo; (uninteresting: lecture) aburrido, pesado ▷ vt secar; (tears) enjugarse ▷ vi secarse; **on ~ land** en tierra firme; **to ~ one's hands/hair/eyes** secarse las manos/el pelo/las lágrimas

▶ **dry up** vi (supply, imagination etc) agotarse; (in speech) atascarse

dry-clean ['draɪ'kliːn] vt limpiar or lavar en seco; **"~ only"** (on label) "limpieza or lavado en seco"

dry-cleaner's ['draɪ'kliːnəz] n tintorería

dry-cleaning ['draɪ'kliːnɪŋ] n lavado en seco

dryer ['draɪəʳ] n (for hair) secador; (for clothes) secadora

dryness ['draɪnɪs] n sequedad

dry rot n putrefacción

DTP n abbr = **desktop publishing**

dual ['djuəl] adj doble

dual carriageway n (Brit) ≈ autovía

dual nationality n doble nacionalidad

dual-purpose ['djuəl'pə:pəs] adj de doble uso

dubbed [dʌbd] adj (Cine) doblado

dubious ['dju:bɪəs] adj indeciso; (reputation, company) dudoso; (character) sospechoso; **I'm very ~ about it** tengo mis dudas sobre ello

Dublin ['dʌblɪn] n Dublín

duchess ['dʌtʃɪs] n duquesa

duck [dʌk] n pato ▷ vi agacharse ▷ vt (plunge in water) zambullir

duckling ['dʌklɪŋ] n patito

duct [dʌkt] n conducto, canal

dud [dʌd] n (shell) obús que no estalla; (object, tool): **it's a ~** es una filfa ▷ adj: **~ cheque** (Brit) cheque sin fondos

due [dju:] adj (proper) debido; (fitting) conveniente, oportuno ▷ adv: **~ north** derecho al norte; **dues** npl (for club, union) cuota; (in harbour) derechos; **in ~ course** a su debido tiempo; **~ to** debido a; **to be ~ to** deberse a; **the train is ~ to**

arrive at 8.oo el tren tiene (prevista) la llegada a las 8; **the rent's ~ on the 30th** hay que pagar el alquiler el día 30; **I am ~ 6 days' leave** me deben 6 días de vacaciones; **she is ~ back tomorrow** ella debe volver mañana

duel ['djuəl] n duelo

duet [dju:'ɛt] n dúo

duffel bag ['dʌfl-] n macuto

duffel coat ['dʌfl-] n trenca

dug [dʌg] pt, pp of **dig**

dugout ['dʌgaut] n (canoe) piragua (hecha de un solo tronco); (Sport) banquillo; (Mil) refugio subterráneo

duke [dju:k] n duque

dull [dʌl] adj (light) apagado; (stupid) torpe; (boring) pesado; (sound, pain) sordo; (weather, day) gris ▷ vt (pain, grief) aliviar; (mind, senses) entorpecer

duly ['dju:lɪ] adv debidamente; (on time) a su debido tiempo

dumb [dʌm] adj mudo; (stupid) estúpido; **to be struck ~** (fig) quedar boquiabierto

dumbfounded [dʌm'faundɪd] adj pasmado

dummy ['dʌmɪ] n (tailor's model) maniquí; (Brit: for baby) chupete ▷ adj falso, postizo; **~ run** ensayo

dump [dʌmp] n (heap) montón de basura; (place) basurero, vertedero; (col) tugurio; (Mil) depósito; (Comput) copia vaciada ▷ vt (put down) dejar; (get rid of) deshacerse de; (Comput) vaciar; (Comm: goods) inundar el mercado de; **to be (down) in the ~s** (col) tener murria, estar deprimido

dumpling ['dʌmplɪŋ] n bola de masa hervida

dumpy ['dʌmpɪ] adj regordete(-a)

dunce [dʌns] n zopenco

dune [dju:n] n duna

dung [dʌŋ] n estiércol

dungarees [dʌŋgə'ri:z] npl mono, overol (LAm)

dungeon ['dʌndʒən] n calabozo

duplex ['dju:plɛks] n (US: also: **duplex apartment**) dúplex

duplicate n duplicado; (copy of letter etc) copia ▷ adj (copy) duplicado ▷ vt duplicar; (on machine) multicopiar; **in ~** por duplicado

durable ['djuərəbl] adj duradero

duration [djuə'reɪʃən] n duración

duress [djuə'rɛs] n: **under ~** por coacción

during ['djuərɪŋ] prep durante

dusk [dʌsk] n crepúsculo, anochecer

dust [dʌst] n polvo ▷ vt (furniture) desempolvar; (cake etc): **to ~ with** espolvorear de

▶ **dust off** vt (also fig) desempolvar, quitar el polvo de

dustbin ['dʌstbɪn] n (Brit) cubo de la basura, balde (LAm)

duster ['dʌstəʳ] n paño, trapo; (feather duster) plumero

dust jacket n sobrecubierta

dustman ['dʌstmən] n (Brit) basurero

dustpan ['dʌstpæn] n cogedor

dusty ['dʌstɪ] adj polvoriento

Dutch [dʌtʃ] adj holandés(-esa) ▷ n (Ling) holandés ▷ adv: **to go ~** pagar a escote; **the Dutch** npl los holandeses

Dutchman ['dʌtʃmən], **Dutchwoman** ['dʌtʃwumən] n holandés(-esa)

dutiful ['djuːtɪful] adj (child) obediente; (husband) sumiso; (employee) cumplido

duty ['djuːtɪ] n deber; (tax) derechos de aduana; (Med: in hospital) servicio, guardia; **on** ~ de servicio; (at night etc) de guardia; **off** ~ libre (de servicio); **to make it one's** ~ **to do sth** encargarse de hacer algo sin falta; **to pay** ~ **on sth** pagar los derechos sobre algo

duty-free [djuːtɪ'friː] adj libre de derechos de aduana; ~ **shop** tienda libre de impuestos

duvet ['duːveɪ] n (Brit) edredón (nórdico)

DVD n abbr (= digital versatile or video disc) DVD

DVLA n abbr (Brit: = Driver and Vehicle Licensing Agency) organismo encargado de la expedición de permisos de conducir y matriculación de vehículos

dwarf [dwɔːf] (pl **dwarves**) [dwɔːvz] n enano ▷ vt empequeñecer

dwell [dwɛl] (pt, pp **dwelt**) [dwɛlt] vi morar

▶ **dwell on** vt fus explayarse en

dwelling ['dwɛlɪŋ] n vivienda

dwelt [dwɛlt] pt, pp of **dwell**

dwindle ['dwɪndl] vi menguar, disminuir

dwindling ['dwɪndlɪŋ] adj (strength, interest) menguante; (resources, supplies) en disminución

dye [daɪ] n tinte ▷ vt teñir; **hair** ~ tinte para el pelo

dying ['daɪɪŋ] adj moribundo, agonizante; (moments) final; (words) último

dyke [daɪk] n (Brit) dique; (channel) arroyo, acequia; (causeway) calzada

dynamic [daɪ'næmɪk] adj dinámico

dynamite ['daɪnəmaɪt] n dinamita ▷ vt dinamitar

dynamo ['daɪnəməu] n dinamo

dynasty ['dɪnəstɪ] n dinastía

dysentery ['dɪsɪntrɪ] n disentería

dyslexia [dɪs'lɛksɪə] n dislexia

dyslexic [dɪs'lɛksɪk] adj, n disléxico(-a)

Ee

E, e [i:] *n* (*letter*) E, e; (*Mus*) mi; **E for Edward**, (*US*) **E for Easy** E de Enrique

E *abbr* (= *east*) E ⊳ *n abbr* (= *Ecstasy*) éxtasis

each [i:tʃ] *adj* cada ⊳ *pron* cada uno; **~ day** cada día; **~ house has its own garden** todas las casas tienen jardín; **they have 2 books ~** tienen 2 libros cada uno; **they cost £5 ~** cuestan cinco libras cada uno; **~ of us** cada uno de nosotros; **he gave ~ of us £10** nos dio 10 libras a cada uno; **they hate ~ other** se odian; **we write to ~ other** nos escribimos; **they don't know ~ other** no se conocen

eager ['i:gəʳ] *adj* (*gen*) impaciente; (*hopeful*) ilusionado; (*keen*) entusiasmado; (*pupil*) apasionado; **to be ~ to do sth** estar deseoso de hacer algo; **to be ~ for** ansiar, anhelar

eagle ['i:gl] *n* águila

ear [ɪəʳ] *n* oreja; (*sense of hearing*) oído; (*of corn*) espiga; **up to the ~s in debt** abrumado de deudas

earache ['ɪəreɪk] *n* dolor de oídos

eardrum ['ɪədrʌm] *n* tímpano

earful ['ɪəful] *n*: **to give sb an ~** (*col*) echar una bronca a algn

earl [ə:l] *n* conde

early ['ə:lɪ] *adv* (*gen*) temprano; (*ahead of time*) con tiempo, con anticipación ⊳ *adj* (*gen*) temprano; (*reply*) pronto; (*man*) primitivo; (*first: Christians, settlers*) primero; **I have to get up ~** tengo que levantarme temprano; **~ in the morning/afternoon** a primeras horas de la mañana/tarde; **you're ~!** ¡has llegado temprano *or* pronto!; **I can't come any earlier** no puedo llegar antes; **I came ~ to avoid the heavy traffic** vine pronto para evitar el tráfico denso; **you're five minutes ~** llegas con cinco minutos de adelanto; **to have an ~ night/lunch** acostarse/almorzar temprano; **in the ~** *or* **~ in the spring/19th century** a principios de primavera/del siglo diecinueve; **she's in her ~ forties** tiene poco más de cuarenta años; **at your earliest convenience** (*Comm*) con la mayor brevedad posible

early retirement *n* jubilación anticipada

earmark ['ɪəmɑ:k] *vt*: **to ~ for** reservar para, destinar a

earn [ə:n] *vt* (*gen*) ganar; (*interest*) devengar;

(*praise*) ganarse; **to ~ one's living** ganarse la vida

earnest ['ə:nɪst] *adj* serio, formal ⊳ *n* (*also*: **earnest money**) anticipo, señal; **in ~** *adv* en serio

earnings ['ə:nɪŋz] *npl* (*personal*) ingresos; (*of company etc*) ganancias

earphones ['ɪəfəunz] *npl* auriculares

earplugs ['ɪəplʌgz] *npl* tapones para los oídos

earring ['ɪərɪŋ] *n* pendiente, arete (*LAm*)

earshot ['ɪəʃɔt] *n*: **out of/within ~** fuera del/al alcance del oído

earth [ə:θ] *n* (*gen*) tierra; (*Brit Elec*) toma de tierra ⊳ *vt* (*Brit Elec*) conectar a tierra

earthenware ['ə:θnwɛəʳ] *n* loza (de barro)

earthly ['ə:θlɪ] *adj* terrenal, mundano; **~ paradise** paraíso terrenal; **there is no ~ reason to think …** no existe razón para pensar …

earthquake ['ə:θkweɪk] *n* terremoto

earth-shattering ['ə:θʃætərɪŋ] *adj* trascendental

earthy ['ə:θɪ] *adj* (*simple*) sencillo; (*coarse*) grosero

ease [i:z] *n* facilidad; (*comfort*) comodidad ⊳ *vt* (*task*) facilitar; (*pain*) aliviar; (*loosen*) soltar; (*relieve: pressure, tension*) aflojar; (*weight*) aligerar; (*help pass*): **to ~ sth in/out** meter/sacar algo con cuidado ⊳ *vi* (*situation*) relajarse; **the camera's ~ of use** la facilidad de uso de la cámara; **with ~** con facilidad; **to feel at ~/ill at ~** sentirse a gusto/a disgusto; **at ~!** (*Mil*) ¡descansen!
  ▶ **ease off, ease up** *vi* (*work, business*) aflojar; (*person*) relajarse

easel ['i:zl] *n* caballete

easily ['i:zɪlɪ] *adv* fácilmente

east [i:st] *n* este, oriente ⊳ *adj* del este, oriental ⊳ *adv* al este, hacia el este; **the E~** el Oriente; (*Pol*) el Este

Easter ['i:stəʳ] *n* Pascua (de Resurrección)

Easter egg *n* huevo de Pascua

easterly ['i:stəlɪ] *adj* (*to the east*) al este; (*from the east*) del este

Easter Monday *n* lunes de Pascua

eastern ['i:stən] *adj* del este, oriental; **E~ Europe** Europa del Este; **the E~ bloc** (*Pol*) los países del Este

Easter Sunday *n* Domingo de Resurrección

East Germany *n* (*formerly*) Alemania Oriental *or* del Este

eastward(s) ['i:stwəd(z)] *adv* hacia el este

easy ['i:zɪ] *adj* fácil; (*life*) holgado, cómodo; (*relaxed*) natural ▷ *adv*: **to take it** *or* **things** ~ (*not worry*) no preocuparse; (*go slowly*) tomarlo con calma; (*rest*) descansar; **to be far from** ~ no ser nada fácil; **to be within** ~ **reach of sth** estar muy cerca de algo; **payment on** ~ **terms** (*Comm*) facilidades de pago; **I'm** ~ (*col*) me da igual, no me importa; **easier said than done** del dicho al hecho hay buen trecho; ~ **does it!** ¡despacio!; **go** ~ **on the sugar!** no te pases con el azúcar!

easy chair *n* butaca

easy-going ['i:zɪ'ɡəʊɪŋ] *adj* acomodadizo

eat [i:t] (*pt* **ate**, *pp* **-en**) [eɪt] ['i:tn] *vt* comer
 ▸ **eat away** *vt* (*sea*) desgastar; (*acid*) corroer
 ▸ **eat into**, **eat away at** *vt fus* corroer
 ▸ **eat out** *vi* comer fuera
 ▸ **eat up** *vt* (*meal*) comerse; (*electricity*) consumir mucho

eau de Cologne [əʊdəkə'ləʊn] *n* (agua de) colonia

eaves [i:vz] *npl* alero

eavesdrop ['i:vzdrɔp] *vi*: **to** ~ (**on sb**) escuchar a escondidas (a algn)

ebb [ɛb] *n* reflujo ▷ *vi* bajar; (*fig: also*: **ebb away**) decaer; ~ **and flow** el flujo y reflujo; **to be at a low** ~ (*fig: person*) estar de capa caída

ebony ['ɛbənɪ] *n* ébano

e-book ['i:buk] *n* libro electrónico

e-business ['i:bɪznɪs] *n* (*commerce*) comercio electrónico; (*company*) negocio electrónico *negocio por Internet*

EC *n abbr* (= *European Community*) CE

ECB *n abbr* (= *European Central Bank*) BCE

eccentric [ɪk'sɛntrɪk] *adj*, *n* excéntrico(-a)

ECG *n abbr* (= *electrocardiogram*) E.C.

echo ['ɛkəʊ] (*pl* **-es**) *n* eco ▷ *vt* (*sound*) repetir ▷ *vi* resonar, hacer eco

eclipse [ɪ'klɪps] *n* eclipse ▷ *vt* eclipsar

eco-friendly ['i:kəʊfrɛndlɪ] *adj* ecológico

ecological [i:kə'lɔdʒɪkl] *adj* ecológico

ecologist [ɪ'kɔlədʒɪst] *n* ecologista; (*scientist*) ecólogo(-a)

ecology [ɪ'kɔlədʒɪ] *n* ecología

e-commerce [i:'kɔməːs] *n* comercio electrónico

economic [i:kə'nɔmɪk] *adj* (*profitable: price*) económico; (*business etc*) rentable

economical [i:kə'nɔmɪkl] *adj* económico

economics [i:kə'nɔmɪks] *n* economía ▷ *npl* (*financial aspects*) finanzas

economist [ɪ'kɔnəmɪst] *n* economista

economize [ɪ'kɔnəmaɪz] *vi* economizar

economy [ɪ'kɔnəmɪ] *n* economía; **economies of scale** economías de escala

economy class *n* (*Aviat etc*) clase turista

economy-class syndrome *n* síndrome de la clase turista

economy size *n* tamaño familiar

ecosystem ['i:kəʊsɪstəm] *n* ecosistema

eco-tourism [i:kəʊ'tʊərɪzm] *n* turismo verde *or* ecológico

ecstasy ['ɛkstəsɪ] *n* éxtasis

ecstatic [ɛks'tætɪk] *adj* extático, extasiado

ECT *n abbr* = **electroconvulsive therapy**

ECU, ecu *n abbr* (= *European Currency Unit*) ECU, ecu

Ecuador ['ɛkwədɔːʳ] *n* Ecuador

Ecuador(i)an [ɛkwə'dɔːr(ɪ)ən] *adj*, *n* ecuatoriano(-a)

ecumenical [i:kju'mɛnɪkl] *adj* ecuménico

eczema ['ɛksɪmə] *n* eczema

edge [ɛdʒ] *n* (*of knife etc*) filo; (*of object*) borde; (*of lake etc*) orilla ▷ *vt* (*Sewing*) ribetear ▷ *vi*: **to** ~ **past** pasar con dificultad; **on** ~ (*fig*) = **edgy**; **to** ~ **away from** alejarse poco a poco de; **to** ~ **forward** avanzar poco a poco; **to** ~ **up** subir lentamente

edgeways ['ɛdʒweɪz] *adv*: **he couldn't get a word in** ~ no pudo meter baza

edgy ['ɛdʒɪ] *adj* nervioso, inquieto

edible ['ɛdɪbl] *adj* comestible

edict ['i:dɪkt] *n* edicto

Edinburgh ['ɛdɪnbərə] *n* Edimburgo

edit ['ɛdɪt] *vt* (*be editor of*) dirigir; (*re-write*) redactar; (*cut*) cortar; (*Comput*) editar

edition [ɪ'dɪʃən] *n* (*gen*) edición; (*number printed*) tirada

editor ['ɛdɪtəʳ] *n* (*of newspaper*) director(a); (*of book*) redactor(a); (*film editor*) montador(a)

editorial [ɛdɪ'tɔːrɪəl] *adj* editorial ▷ *n* editorial; ~ **staff** redacción

EDT *n abbr* (*US*: = *Eastern Daylight Time*) hora de verano de Nueva York

educate ['ɛdjukeɪt] *vt* (*gen*) educar; (*instruct*) instruir

education [ɛdju'keɪʃən] *n* educación; (*schooling*) enseñanza; (*Scol: subject etc*) pedagogía; **primary/secondary** ~ enseñanza primaria/secundaria

educational [ɛdju'keɪʃənl] *adj* (*policy etc*) de educación, educativo; (*teaching*) docente; (*instructive*) educativo; ~ **technology** tecnología educacional

EEC *n abbr* (= *European Economic Community*) CEE

eel [i:l] *n* anguila

eerie ['ɪərɪ] *adj* (*sound, experience*) espeluznante

effect [ɪ'fɛkt] *n* efecto ▷ *vt* efectuar; **effects** *npl* (*property*) efectos; **special** ~**s** efectos especiales; **to come into** ~ entrar en vigor; **to take** ~ (*law*) entrar en vigor; (*drug*) surtir efecto; **in** ~ en realidad; **to have an** ~ **on sb/sth** hacerle efecto a algn/afectar algo; **to put into** ~ (*plan*) llevar a la práctica; **his letter is to the** ~ **that...** su carta viene a decir que...; **or words to that** ~ o algo por el estilo

effective [ɪ'fɛktɪv] *adj* (*gen*) eficaz; (*striking: display, outfit*) impresionante; (*real*) efectivo; **to become** ~ (*law*) entrar en vigor; ~ **date** fecha de vigencia

effectively [ɪ'fɛktɪvlɪ] *adv* (*efficiently*) eficazmente; (*strikingly*) de manera impresionante; (*in reality*) en efecto

effectiveness [ɪ'fɛktɪvnɪs] *n* eficacia

effeminate [ɪ'fɛmɪnɪt] *adj* afeminado

effervescent [ɛfə'vɛsnt] *adj* efervescente

efficiency [ɪ'fɪʃənsɪ] *n* (*gen*) eficiencia; (*of machine*) rendimiento

efficient [ɪ'fɪʃənt] *adj* eficiente; (*remedy, product,*

system) eficaz; (*machine, car*) de buen rendimiento
effort ['ɛfət] *n* esfuerzo; **to make an ~ to do** sth hacer un esfuerzo *or* esforzarse para hacer algo
effortless ['ɛfətlɪs] *adj* sin ningún esfuerzo
effusive [ɪ'fju:sɪv] *adj* efusivo
EFL *n abbr* (*Scol*) = **English as a foreign language**
egg [ɛg] *n* huevo; **hard-boiled/soft-boiled/ poached ~** huevo duro *or* (*LAm*) a la copa *or* (*LAm*) tibio/pasado por agua/escalfado; **scrambled ~s** huevos revueltos
▸ **egg on** *vt* incitar
eggcup ['ɛgkʌp] *n* huevera
eggplant ['ɛgplɑ:nt] *n* (*esp US*) berenjena
eggshell ['ɛgʃɛl] *n* cáscara de huevo
egg yolk *n* yema de huevo
ego ['i:gəu] *n* ego
egotism ['ɛgəutɪzəm] *n* egoísmo
egotist ['ɛgəutɪst] *n* egoísta
Egypt ['i:dʒɪpt] *n* Egipto
Egyptian [ɪ'dʒɪpʃən] *adj*, *n* egipcio(-a)
eiderdown ['aɪdədaun] *n* edredón
eight [eɪt] *num* ocho
eighteen [eɪ'ti:n] *num* dieciocho
eighth [eɪtθ] *adj* octavo
eighty ['eɪtɪ] *num* ochenta
Eire ['ɛərə] *n* Eire
either ['aɪðəʳ] *adj* cualquiera de los dos ...; (*both, each*) cada ▷ *pron*: **~ (of them)** cualquiera (de los dos) ▷ *adv* tampoco ▷ *conj*: **~ yes or no** o sí o no; **on ~ side** en ambos lados; **I don't like ~** no me gusta ninguno de los dos; **no, I don't ~** no, yo tampoco
eject [ɪ'dʒɛkt] *vt* echar; (*tenant*) desahuciar ▷ *vi* eyectarse
eke out [i:k-] *vt fus* (*money*) hacer que llegue
EKG *n abbr* (*US*) *see* **electrocardiogram**
elaborate *adj* (*design, pattern*) complicado ▷ *vt* elaborar ▷ *vi* explicarse con muchos detalles
elapse [ɪ'læps] *vi* transcurrir
elastic [ɪ'læstɪk] *adj*, *n* elástico
elastic band *n* (*Brit*) gomita
elated [ɪ'leɪtɪd] *adj*: **to be ~** estar eufórico
elation [ɪ'leɪʃən] *n* euforia
elbow ['ɛlbəu] *n* codo ▷ *vt*: **to ~ one's way through the crowd** abrirse paso a codazos por la muchedumbre
elbow grease *n* (*col*): **to use a bit of** *or* **some ~** menearse
elder ['ɛldəʳ] *adj* mayor ▷ *n* (*tree*) saúco; (*person*) mayor; (*of tribe*) anciano
elderly ['ɛldəlɪ] *adj* de edad, mayor ▷ *npl*: **the ~** la gente mayor, los ancianos
eldest ['ɛldɪst] *adj*, *n* el/la mayor
elect [ɪ'lɛkt] *vt* elegir; (*choose*): **to ~ to do** optar por hacer ▷ *adj*: **the president ~** el presidente electo
election [ɪ'lɛkʃən] *n* elección; **to hold an ~** convocar elecciones
election campaign *n* campaña electoral
electioneering [ɪlɛkʃə'nɪərɪŋ] *n* campaña electoral
elector [ɪ'lɛktəʳ] *n* elector(a)

electoral [ɪ'lɛktərəl] *adj* electoral
electoral college *n* colegio electoral
electoral roll *n* censo electoral
electorate [ɪ'lɛktərɪt] *n* electorado
electric [ɪ'lɛktrɪk] *adj* eléctrico
electrical [ɪ'lɛktrɪkl] *adj* eléctrico
electric blanket *n* manta eléctrica
electric chair *n* silla eléctrica
electric cooker *n* cocina eléctrica
electric current *n* corriente eléctrica
electric fire *n* estufa eléctrica
electrician [ɪlɛk'trɪʃən] *n* electricista
electricity [ɪlɛk'trɪsɪtɪ] *n* electricidad; **to switch on/off the ~** conectar/desconectar la electricidad
electricity board *n* (*Brit*) compañía eléctrica (estatal)
electric light *n* luz eléctrica
electric shock *n* electrochoque
electrify [ɪ'lɛktrɪfaɪ] *vt* (*Rail*) electrificar; (*fig: audience*) electrizar
electrocardiogram (ECG) [ɪ'lɛktrə'kɑ:dɪəgræm] *n* electrocardiograma *m*
electroconvulsive therapy (ECT) [ɪ'lɛktrəkən'vʌlsɪv-] *n* electroterapia
electrocute [ɪ'lɛktrəukju:t] *vt* electrocutar
electrode [ɪ'lɛktrəud] *n* electrodo
electron [ɪ'lɛktrɔn] *n* electrón
electronic [ɪlɛk'trɔnɪk] *adj* electrónico
electronic mail *n* correo electrónico
electronics [ɪlɛk'trɔnɪks] *n* electrónica
elegance ['ɛlɪgəns] *n* elegancia
elegant ['ɛlɪgənt] *adj* elegante
elegy ['ɛlɪdʒɪ] *n* elegía
element ['ɛlɪmənt] *n* (*gen*) elemento; (*of heater, kettle etc*) resistencia
elementary [ɛlɪ'mɛntərɪ] *adj* elemental; (*primitive*) rudimentario; (*school, education*) primario
elementary school *n* (*US*) escuela de enseñanza primaria
elephant ['ɛlɪfənt] *n* elefante
elevate ['ɛlɪveɪt] *vt* (*gen*) elevar; (*in rank*) ascender
elevation [ɛlɪ'veɪʃən] *n* elevación; (*rank*) ascenso; (*height*) altitud
elevator ['ɛlɪveɪtəʳ] *n* (*US*) ascensor (*Esp*), elevador (*LAm*)
eleven [ɪ'lɛvn] *num* once
elevenses [ɪ'lɛvnzɪz] *npl* (*Brit*) ≈ café de media mañana
eleventh [ɪ'lɛvnθ] *adj* undécimo; **at the ~ hour** (*fig*) a última hora
elf [ɛlf] (*pl* **elves**) *n* duende
elicit [ɪ'lɪsɪt] *vt*: **to ~ sth (from sb)** obtener algo (de algn)
eligible ['ɛlɪdʒəbl] *adj* cotizado; **to be ~ for a pension** tener derecho a una pensión
eliminate [ɪ'lɪmɪneɪt] *vt* eliminar; (*score out*) suprimir; (*a suspect, possibility*) descartar
elite [eɪ'li:t] *n* élite
elm [ɛlm] *n* olmo
elocution [ɛlə'kju:ʃən] *n* elocución

elongated ['iːlɒŋgeɪtɪd] *adj* alargado

elope [ɪ'ləup] *vi* fugarse

elopement [ɪ'ləupmənt] *n* fuga

eloquent ['ɛləkwənt] *adj* elocuente

else [ɛls] *adv*: **or ~** si no; **arrive on time, or ~!** ¡llega a tiempo o si no...!; **somebody ~** otra persona; **something ~** otra cosa, algo más; **somewhere ~** en otra parte; **everywhere ~** en los demás sitios; **everyone ~** todos los demás; **everything ~** todo lo demás; **nobody ~** nadie más; **nothing ~** nada más; **nowhere ~** en ningún otro sitio; **I don't know anyone ~ here** aquí no conozco a nadie más; **is there anything ~ I can do?** ¿puedo hacer algo más?; **would you like anything ~?** ¿desea alguna otra cosa?; **I don't want anything ~** no quiero nada más; **I didn't look anywhere ~** no miré en ningún otro sitio; **I'd be happy anywhere ~** estaría contento en cualquier otro sitio; **what ~?** ¿qué más?; **where ~?** ¿dónde más?, ¿en qué otra parte?; **who ~ could do it?** ¿quién más podría hacerlo?; **there was little ~ to do** apenas quedaba otra cosa que hacer

elsewhere [ɛls'wɛəʳ] *adv* (*be*) en otra parte; (*go*) a otra parte

ELT *n abbr* (*Scol*) = **English Language Teaching**

elude [ɪ'luːd] *vt* eludir; (*blow, pursuer*) esquivar

elusive [ɪ'luːsɪv] *adj* escurridizo; (*answer*) difícil de encontrar; **he is very ~** no es fácil encontrarlo

elves [ɛlvz] *npl of* **elf**

emaciated [ɪ'meɪsɪeɪtɪd] *adj* escuálido

e-mail ['iːmeɪl] *n* e-mail, correo electrónico ▷ *vt*: **to ~ sb** mandar un e-mail *or* un correo electrónico a algn

e-mail account *n* cuenta de correo

e-mail address *n* e-mail, dirección electrónica, dirección de Internet

emancipate [ɪ'mænsɪpeɪt] *vt* emancipar

embankment [ɪm'bæŋkmənt] *n* (*of railway*) terraplén; (*riverside*) dique

embargo [ɪm'baːgəu] (*pl* **-es**) *n* prohibición; (*Comm, Naut*) embargo; **to put an ~ on sth** poner un embargo en algo

embark [ɪm'baːk] *vi* embarcarse ▷ *vt* embarcar; **to ~ on** (*journey*) comenzar, iniciar; (*fig*) emprender

embarkation [ɛmbaː'keɪʃən] *n* (*of people*) embarco; (*of goods*) embarque

embarrass [ɪm'bærəs] *vt* avergonzar, dar vergüenza a; (*financially etc*) poner en un aprieto

embarrassed [ɪm'bærəst] *adj* azorado, violento; **I was ~** me dio vergüenza

embarrassing [ɪm'bærəsɪŋ] *adj* (*situation*) violento; (*question*) embarazoso

embarrassment [ɪm'bærəsmənt] *n* vergüenza, azoramiento; (*financial*) apuros

embassy ['ɛmbəsɪ] *n* embajada; **the Spanish E~** la embajada española

embed [ɪm'bɛd] *vt* (*jewel*) empotrar; (*teeth etc*) clavar

embellish [ɪm'bɛlɪʃ] *vt* embellecer; (*fig: story, truth*) adornar

embers ['ɛmbəz] *npl* rescoldo, ascuas

embezzle [ɪm'bɛzl] *vt* desfalcar, malversar

embezzlement [ɪm'bɛzlmənt] *n* desfalco, malversación

embitter [ɪm'bɪtəʳ] *vt* (*person*) amargar

emblem ['ɛmbləm] *n* emblema

embody [ɪm'bɒdɪ] *vt* (*spirit*) encarnar; (*ideas*) expresar

embossed [ɪm'bɒst] *adj* realzado; **~ with ...** con ... en relieve

embrace [ɪm'breɪs] *vt* abrazar, dar un abrazo a; (*include*) abarcar; (*adopt: idea*) adherirse a ▷ *vi* abrazarse ▷ *n* abrazo

embroider [ɪm'brɔɪdəʳ] *vt* bordar; (*fig: story*) adornar, embellecer

embroidery [ɪm'brɔɪdərɪ] *n* bordado

embryo ['ɛmbrɪəu] *n* (*also fig*) embrión

emcee [ɛm'siː] *n* (*US*) presentador(a)

emend [ɪ'mɛnd] *vt* (*text*) enmendar

emerald ['ɛmərəld] *n* esmeralda

emerge [ɪ'məːdʒ] *vi* (*gen*) salir; (*arise*) surgir; **it ~s that** resulta que

emergency [ɪ'məːdʒənsɪ] *n* (*event*) emergencia; (*crisis*) crisis; **in an ~** en caso de urgencia; (**to declare a**) **state of ~** (declarar) estado de emergencia *or* de excepción

emergency cord *n* (*US*) timbre de alarma

emergency exit *n* salida de emergencia

emergency landing *n* aterrizaje forzoso

emergency service *n* servicio de urgencia

emergent [ɪ'məːdʒənt] *adj* (*nation*) recientemente independizado

emery board ['ɛmərɪ-] *n* lima de uñas

emigrant ['ɛmɪgrənt] *n* emigrante

emigrate ['ɛmɪgreɪt] *vi* emigrar

emigration [ɛmɪ'greɪʃən] *n* emigración

émigré ['ɛmɪgreɪ] *n* emigrado(-a)

eminence ['ɛmɪnəns] *n* eminencia; **to gain** *or* **win ~** ganarse fama

eminent ['ɛmɪnənt] *adj* eminente

emission [ɪ'mɪʃən] *n* emisión

emit [ɪ'mɪt] *vt* emitir; (*smell, smoke*) despedir

emotion [ɪ'məuʃən] *n* emoción

emotional [ɪ'məuʃənl] *adj* (*person*) sentimental; (*scene*) conmovedor(a), emocionante

emotive [ɪ'məutɪv] *adj* emotivo

empathy ['ɛmpəθɪ] *n* empatía; **to feel ~ with sb** sentirse identificado con algn

emperor ['ɛmpərəʳ] *n* emperador

emphasis ['ɛmfəsɪs] (*pl* **emphases**) *n* énfasis; **to lay** *or* **place ~ on sth** (*fig*) hacer hincapié en algo; **the ~ is on sport** se da mayor importancia al deporte

emphasize ['ɛmfəsaɪz] *vt* (*word, point*) subrayar, recalcar; (*feature*) hacer resaltar

emphatic [ɛm'fætɪk] *adj* (*condemnation*) enérgico; (*denial*) rotundo

emphatically [ɛm'fætɪklɪ] *adv* con énfasis

empire ['ɛmpaɪəʳ] *n* imperio

employ [ɪm'plɔɪ] *vt* (*give job to*) emplear; (*make use of: thing, method*) emplear, usar; **he's ~ed in a bank** está empleado en un banco

employee [ɪmplɔɪ'iː] n empleado(-a)
employer [ɪm'plɔɪəʳ] n patrón(-ona);
(businessman) empresario(-a)
employment [ɪm'plɔɪmənt] n empleo; **full ~**
pleno empleo; **without ~** sin empleo; **to find ~**
encontrar trabajo; **place of ~** lugar de trabajo
employment agency n agencia de colocaciones
or empleo
empower [ɪm'pauəʳ] vt: **to ~ sb to do sth**
autorizar a algn para hacer algo
empress ['emprɪs] n emperatriz
emptiness ['emptɪnɪs] n vacío
empty ['emptɪ] adj vacío; (street, area) desierto;
(threat) vano ▷ n (bottle) envase ▷ vt vaciar; (place)
dejar vacío ▷ vi vaciarse; (house) quedar(se) vacío
or desocupado; (place) quedar(se) desierto; **to ~
into** (river) desembocar en
empty-handed ['emptɪ'hændɪd] adj con las
manos vacías
EMS n abbr (= European Monetary System) SME
EMU n abbr (= Economic and Monetary Union) UME,
UEM
emulate ['emjuleɪt] vt emular
emulsion [ɪ'mʌlʃən] n emulsión
enable [ɪ'neɪbl] vt: **to ~ sb to do sth** (allow)
permitir a algn hacer algo; (prepare) capacitar a
algn para hacer algo
enact [ɪn'ækt] vt (law) promulgar; (play, scene, role)
representar
enamel [ɪ'næməl] n esmalte
enamoured [ɪ'næməd] adj: **to be ~ of** (person)
estar enamorado de; (activity etc) tener gran
afición a; (idea) aferrarse a
encased [ɪn'keɪst] adj: **~ in** (covered) revestido de
enchant [ɪn'tʃɑːnt] vt encantar
enchanting [ɪn'tʃɑːntɪŋ] adj encantador(a)
encl. abbr (= enclosed) adj.
enclose [ɪn'kləuz] vt (land) cercar; (with letter etc)
adjuntar; (in receptacle): **to ~ (with)** encerrar
(con); **please find ~d** le mandamos adjunto
enclosure [ɪn'kləuʒəʳ] n cercado, recinto; (Comm)
carta adjunta
encompass [ɪn'kʌmpəs] vt abarcar
encore [ɔŋ'kɔːʳ] excl ¡otra!, ¡bis! ▷ n bis
encounter [ɪn'kauntəʳ] n encuentro ▷ vt
encontrar, encontrarse con; (difficulty) tropezar
con
encourage [ɪn'kʌrɪdʒ] vt alentar, animar;
(growth) estimular; **to ~ sb (to do sth)** animar a
algn (a hacer algo)
encouragement [ɪn'kʌrɪdʒmənt] n estímulo;
(of industry) fomento
encroach [ɪn'krəutʃ] vi: **to ~ (up)on** (gen) invadir;
(time) adueñarse de
encyclop(a)edia [ɛnsaɪkləu'piːdɪə] n
enciclopedia
end [ɛnd] n fin, final; (of table) extremo; (of line,
rope etc) cabo; (of pointed object) punta; (of town)
barrio; (of street) final; (Sport) lado ▷ vt (finish)
terminar, acabar; (also: **bring to an end, put an
end to**) acabar con ▷ vi terminar, acabar; **to ~
(with)** terminar (con); **the ~ of the film** el final

de la película; **in the ~** al final; **it turned out
all right in the ~** al final resultó bien; **it is at
an ~** ha llegado a su fin; **to come to an ~** llegar a
su fin; **at the ~ of the century** a fines del siglo;
at the ~ of the day (fig) al fin y al cabo, a fin de
cuentas; **it caused no ~ of trouble** causó la mar
de problemas; **to this ~, with this ~ in view** con
este propósito; **from ~ to ~** de punta a punta; **on
~** (object) de punta, de cabeza; **to stand on ~** (hair)
erizarse, ponerse de punta; **for hours on ~** hora
tras hora
▶ **end up** vi: **to ~ up in** terminar en; (place) ir a
parar a; **to ~ up doing sth** terminar haciendo
algo
endanger [ɪn'deɪndʒəʳ] vt poner en peligro; **an
~ed species** (of animal) una especie en peligro de
extinción
endearing [ɪn'dɪərɪŋ] adj entrañable
endeavour, (US) **endeavor** [ɪn'dɛvəʳ] n esfuerzo;
(attempt) tentativa ▷ vi: **to ~ to do** esforzarse por
hacer; (try) procurar hacer
ending ['endɪŋ] n fin, final; (of book) desenlace;
(Ling) terminación
endive ['endaɪv] n (curly) escarola; (smooth, flat)
endibia
endless ['endlɪs] adj interminable, inacabable;
(possibilities) infinito
endorse [ɪn'dɔːs] vt (cheque) endosar; (approve)
aprobar
endorsement [ɪn'dɔːsmənt] n (approval)
aprobación; (signature) endoso; (Brit: on driving
licence) nota de sanción
endow [ɪn'dau] vt (provide with money) dotar;
(found) fundar; **to be ~ed with** (fig) estar dotado
de
endowment mortgage [ɪn'daumənt-] n
hipoteca dotal
endowment policy [ɪn'daumənt-] n póliza
dotal
endurance [ɪn'djuərəns] n resistencia
endure [ɪn'djuəʳ] vt (bear) aguantar, soportar;
(resist) resistir ▷ vi (last) perdurar; (resist) resistir
enema ['enɪmə] n (Med) enema
enemy ['enəmɪ] adj, n enemigo(-a); **to make an
~ of sb** enemistarse con algn
energetic [enə'dʒetɪk] adj enérgico
energy ['enədʒɪ] n energía
enforce [ɪn'fɔːs] vt (law) hacer cumplir
engage [ɪn'geɪdʒ] vt (attention) captar; (in
conversation) abordar; (worker, lawyer) contratar
▷ vi (Tech) engranar; **to ~ sb in conversation**
entablar conversación con algn; **to ~ the clutch**
embragar; **to ~ in** dedicarse a, ocuparse en
engaged [ɪn'geɪdʒd] adj (Brit: busy, in use) ocupado;
(betrothed) prometido; **to get ~** prometerse; **he is
~ in research** se dedica a la investigación
engaged tone n (Brit Tel) señal de comunicando
engagement [ɪn'geɪdʒmənt] n (appointment)
compromiso, cita; (battle) combate; (to marry)
compromiso; (period) noviazgo; **I have a
previous ~** ya tengo un compromiso
engagement ring n anillo de pedida

engaging [ɪn'ɡeɪdʒɪŋ] adj atractivo, simpático
engender [ɪn'dʒendər] vt engendrar
engine ['endʒɪn] n (Aut) motor; (Rail) locomotora
engine driver n (Brit: of train) maquinista
engineer [endʒɪ'nɪər] n ingeniero(-a); (Brit: for repairs) técnico(-a); (US Rail) maquinista; **civil/ mechanical** ~ ingeniero(-a) de caminos, canales y puertos/industrial
engineering [endʒɪ'nɪərɪŋ] n ingeniería ▷ cpd (works, factory) de componentes mecánicos
England ['ɪŋɡlənd] n Inglaterra
English ['ɪŋɡlɪʃ] adj inglés(-esa) ▷ n (Ling) el inglés; **the English** npl los ingleses
English Channel n: **the** ~ el Canal de la Mancha
Englishman ['ɪŋɡlɪʃmən], **Englishwoman** ['ɪŋɡlɪʃwumən] n inglés(-esa)
English-speaker ['ɪŋɡlɪʃspiːkər] n persona de habla inglesa
English-speaking ['ɪŋɡlɪʃspiːkɪŋ] adj de habla inglesa
engraving [ɪn'ɡreɪvɪŋ] n grabado
engrossed [ɪn'ɡrəust] adj: ~ **in** absorto en
engulf [ɪn'ɡʌlf] vt sumergir, hundir; (fire) devorar
enhance [ɪn'hɑːns] vt (gen) aumentar; (beauty) realzar; (position, reputation) mejorar
enigma [ɪ'nɪɡmə] n enigma
enjoy [ɪn'dʒɔɪ] vt (have: health, fortune) disfrutar de, gozar de; (food) comer con gusto; **I ~ doing...** me gusta hacer...; **to ~ o.s.** divertirse, pasarlo bien
enjoyable [ɪn'dʒɔɪəbl] adj (pleasant) agradable; (amusing) divertido
enjoyment [ɪn'dʒɔɪmənt] n (use) disfrute; (joy) placer
enlarge [ɪn'lɑːdʒ] vt aumentar; (broaden) extender; (Phot) ampliar ▷ vi: **to ~ on** (subject) tratar con más detalles
enlargement [ɪn'lɑːdʒmənt] n (Phot) ampliación
enlighten [ɪn'laɪtn] vt informar, instruir
enlightened [ɪn'laɪtnd] adj iluminado; (tolerant) comprensivo
Enlightenment [ɪn'laɪtnmənt] n (History): **the** ~ la Ilustración, el Siglo de las Luces
enlist [ɪn'lɪst] vt alistar; (support) conseguir ▷ vi alistarse; **~ed man** (US Mil) soldado raso
enmity ['enmɪtɪ] n enemistad
enormity [ɪ'nɔːmɪtɪ] n enormidad
enormous [ɪ'nɔːməs] adj enorme
enough [ɪ'nʌf] adj bastante ▷ pron bastante ▷ adv bastante; ~ **time/books** bastante tiempo/ bastantes libros; **more than ~ time/money** tiempo/dinero más que suficiente; **have you got ~?** ¿tiene usted bastante?; **that's ~, thanks** con eso basta, gracias; **(that's) ~!** ¡basta ya!, ¡ya está bien!; **will 5 be ~?** ¿bastará con 5?; **I've had** ~ estoy harto; **big** ~ bastante or suficientemente grande; **it's not big** ~ no es (lo) suficientemente grande; **he has not worked** ~ no ha trabajado bastante; **he was kind** ~ **to lend me the money** tuvo la bondad or amabilidad de prestarme el dinero; **... which, funnily** ~ ... ... lo que, por

extraño que parezca ...
enquire [ɪn'kwaɪər] vt, vi = **inquire**
enrage [ɪn'reɪdʒ] vt enfurecer
enrich [ɪn'rɪtʃ] vt enriquecer
enrol, (US) **enroll** [ɪn'rəul] vt (member) inscribir; (Scol) matricular ▷ vi inscribirse; (Scol) matricularse
enrol(l)ment [ɪn'rəulmənt] n inscripción; matriculación
en route [ɔn'ruːt] adv durante el viaje; ~ **for/ from/to** camino de/de/a
ensconce [ɪn'skɔns] vt: **to ~ o.s.** instalarse cómodamente, acomodarse
ensue [ɪn'sjuː] vi seguirse; (result) resultar
ensure [ɪn'ʃuər] vt asegurar
entail [ɪn'teɪl] vt (imply) suponer; (result in) acarrear
entangle [ɪn'tæŋɡl] vt (thread etc) enredar, enmarañar; **to become ~d in sth** (fig) enredarse en algo
enter ['entər] vt (room, profession) entrar en; (club) hacerse socio de; (army) alistarse en; (competition) presentarse a; (write down) anotar, apuntar; (Comput) introducir ▷ vi entrar; **he ~ed the room** entró en la habitación; **to ~ sb for a competition** inscribir a algn en un concurso; **~!** (come in) ¡pase!; **to ~ for** vt fus presentarse a; **to ~ into** vt fus (relations) establecer; (plans) formar parte de; (debate) tomar parte en; (negotiations) entablar; (agreement) llegar a, firmar; **to ~ (up)on** vt fus (career) emprender
enterprise ['entəpraɪz] n empresa; (spirit) iniciativa; **free** ~ la libre empresa; **private** ~ la iniciativa privada
enterprising ['entəpraɪzɪŋ] adj emprendedor(a)
entertain [entə'teɪn] vt (amuse) divertir; (receive: guest) recibir (en casa); (idea) abrigar
entertainer [entə'teɪnər] n artista
entertaining [entə'teɪnɪŋ] adj divertido, entretenido ▷ n: **to do a lot of** ~ dar muchas fiestas, tener muchos invitados
entertainment [entə'teɪnmənt] n (amusement) diversión; (show) espectáculo; (party) fiesta
enthralled [ɪn'θrɔːld] adj cautivado
enthralling [ɪn'θrɔːlɪŋ] adj cautivador(a)
enthusiasm [ɪn'θuːzɪæzəm] n entusiasmo
enthusiast [ɪn'θuːzɪæst] n entusiasta
enthusiastic [ɪnθuːzɪ'æstɪk] adj entusiasta; **to be ~ about sb/sth** estar entusiasmado con algn/algo
entice [ɪn'taɪs] vt tentar; (seduce) seducir
entire [ɪn'taɪər] adj entero, todo
entirely [ɪn'taɪəlɪ] adv totalmente
entirety [ɪn'taɪərətɪ] n: **in its** ~ en su totalidad
entitle [ɪn'taɪtl] vt: **to ~ sb to sth** dar a algn derecho a algo
entitled [ɪn'taɪtld] adj (book) titulado; **to be ~ to sth/to do sth** tener derecho a algo/a hacer algo
entity ['entɪtɪ] n entidad
entourage [ɔntu'rɑːʒ] n séquito
entrance n entrada ▷ vt encantar, hechizar; **to gain ~ to** (university etc) ingresar en

entrance examination n (to school) examen de ingreso

entrance fee n entrada

entrance ramp n (US Aut) rampa de acceso

entrant ['entrənt] n (in race, competition) participante; (in exam) candidato(-a)

entrenched [ɛn'trɛntʃd] adj: ~ **interests** intereses creados

entrepreneur [ɔntrəprə'nə:ʳ] n empresario(-a), capitalista

entrust [ɪn'trʌst] vt: **to ~ sth to sb** confiar algo a algn

entry ['entrɪ] n entrada; (permission to enter) acceso; (in register, diary, ship's log) apunte; (in account book, ledger, list) partida; **no ~** prohibido el paso; (Aut) dirección prohibida; **single/double ~ book-keeping** contabilidad simple/por partida doble

entry form n boletín de inscripción

entry phone n (Brit) portero automático

E-number ['i:nʌmbəʳ] n número E

enunciate [ɪ'nʌnsɪeɪt] vt pronunciar; (principle etc) enunciar

envelop [ɪn'vɛləp] vt envolver

envelope ['ɛnvələup] n sobre

enviable ['ɛnvɪəbl] adj envidiable

envious ['ɛnvɪəs] adj envidioso; (look) de envidia

environment [ɪn'vaɪərnmənt] n medio ambiente; (surroundings) entorno; **Department of the E~** ministerio del medio ambiente

environmental [ɪnvaɪərn'mɛntl] adj (medio) ambiental; ~ **studies** (in school etc) ecología

environmentalist [ɪnvaɪərn'mɛntlɪst] n ecologista

environmentally [ɪnvaɪərn'mɛntlɪ] adv: ~ **sound/friendly** ecológico

envisage [ɪn'vɪzɪdʒ] vt (foresee) prever; (imagine) concebir

envoy ['ɛnvɔɪ] n enviado(-a)

envy ['ɛnvɪ] n envidia ▷ vt tener envidia a; **to ~ sb sth** envidiar algo a algn

EPA n abbr (US: = Environmental Protection Agency) Agencia del Medio Ambiente

epic ['ɛpɪk] n epopeya ▷ adj épico

epicentre, (US) **epicenter** ['ɛpɪsɛntəʳ] n epicentro

epidemic [ɛpɪ'dɛmɪk] n epidemia

epilepsy ['ɛpɪlɛpsɪ] n epilepsia

epileptic [ɛpɪ'lɛptɪk] adj, n epiléptico(-a)

epilogue ['ɛpɪlɔg] n epílogo

episode ['ɛpɪsəud] n episodio

epitome [ɪ'pɪtəmɪ] n arquetipo

epitomize [ɪ'pɪtəmaɪz] vt representar

epoch ['i:pɔk] n época

equable ['ɛkwəbl] adj (climate) estable; (character) ecuánime

equal ['i:kwl] adj (gen) igual; (treatment) equitativo ▷ n igual ▷ vt ser igual a; (fig) igualar; **to be ~ to** (task) estar a la altura de; **the E~ Opportunities Commission** (Brit) comisión para la igualdad de la mujer en el trabajo

equality [i:'kwɔlɪtɪ] n igualdad

equalize ['i:kwəlaɪz] vt, vi igualar; (Sport) empatar

equally ['i:kwəlɪ] adv igualmente; (share etc) a partes iguales; **they are ~ clever** son tan listos uno como otro

equanimity [ɛkwə'nɪmɪtɪ] n ecuanimidad

equate [ɪ'kweɪt] vt: **to ~ sth with** equiparar algo con

equation [ɪ'kweɪʒən] n (Math) ecuación

equator [ɪ'kweɪtəʳ] n ecuador

equilibrium [i:kwɪ'lɪbrɪəm] n equilibrio

equip [ɪ'kwɪp] vt (gen) equipar; (person) proveer; ~**ped with** (machinery etc) provisto de; **to be well ~ped** estar bien equipado; **he is well ~ped for the job** está bien preparado para este puesto

equipment [ɪ'kwɪpmənt] n equipo

equities ['ɛkwɪtɪz] npl (Brit Comm) acciones ordinarias

equivalent [ɪ'kwɪvəlnt] adj, n equivalente; **to be ~ to** equivaler a

equivocal [ɪ'kwɪvəkl] adj equívoco

ER abbr (Brit: = Elizabeth Regina) la reina Isabel

era ['ɪərə] n era, época

eradicate [ɪ'rædɪkeɪt] vt erradicar, extirpar

erase [ɪ'reɪz] vt (Comput) borrar

eraser [ɪ'reɪzəʳ] n goma de borrar

erect [ɪ'rɛkt] adj erguido ▷ vt erigir, levantar; (assemble) montar

erection [ɪ'rɛkʃən] n (of building) construcción; (of machinery) montaje; (structure) edificio; (Med) erección

Eritrea [ɛrɪ'treɪə] n Eritrea

ERM n abbr (= Exchange Rate Mechanism) (mecanismo de cambios del) SME

erode [ɪ'rəud] vt (Geo) erosionar; (metal) corroer, desgastar

erosion [ɪ'rəuʒən] n erosión; desgaste

erotic [ɪ'rɔtɪk] adj erótico

err [ə:ʳ] vi errar; (Rel) pecar

errand ['ɛrnd] n recado, mandado; **to run ~s** hacer recados; ~ **of mercy** misión de caridad

erratic [ɪ'rætɪk] adj variable; (results etc) desigual, poco uniforme

error ['ɛrəʳ] n error, equivocación; **typing/spelling ~** error de mecanografía/ortografía; **in ~** por equivocación; ~**s and omissions excepted** salvo error u omisión

erupt [ɪ'rʌpt] vi entrar en erupción; (Med) hacer erupción; (fig) estallar

eruption [ɪ'rʌpʃən] n erupción; (fig: of anger, violence) explosión, estallido

escalate ['ɛskəleɪt] vi extenderse, intensificarse; (costs) aumentar vertiginosamente

escalator ['ɛskəleɪtəʳ] n escalera mecánica

escapade [ɛskə'peɪd] n aventura

escape [ɪ'skeɪp] n (gen) fuga; (Tech) escape; (from duties) escapatoria; (from chase) evasión ▷ vi (gen) escaparse; (flee) huir, evadirse ▷ vt evitar, eludir; (consequences) escapar a; **to ~ from** (place) escaparse de; (person) huir de; (clutches) librarse de; **to ~ to** (another place, freedom, safety) huir a; **to ~ notice** pasar desapercibido

escapism [ɪˈskeɪpɪzəm] n escapismo, evasión
eschew [ɪsˈtʃuː] vt evitar, abstenerse de
escort n acompañante; (Mil) escolta; (Naut) convoy ⊳ vt acompañar; (Mil, Naut) escoltar
Eskimo [ˈɛskɪməu] adj, n esquimal
ESL n abbr (Scol) = **English as a Second Language**
esophagus [iːˈsɔfəgəs] n (US) = **oesophagus**
ESP n abbr = **extrasensory perception**; (Scol: = English for Special Purposes) inglés especializado
esp. abbr = **especially**
especially [ɪˈspɛʃlɪ] adv (gen) especialmente; (above all) sobre todo; (particularly) en especial
espionage [ˈɛspɪənɑːʒ] n espionaje
Esq. abbr (= Esquire) D.
Esquire [ɪˈskwaɪəʳ] n: **J. Brown, ~ Sr.** D. J. Brown
essay [ˈɛseɪ] n (Scol) redacción; (: longer) trabajo
essence [ˈɛsns] n esencia; **in ~** esencialmente; **speed is of the ~** es esencial hacerlo con la mayor prontitud
essential [ɪˈsɛnʃl] adj (necessary) imprescindible; (basic) esencial ⊳ n (often pl) lo esencial; **it is ~ that** es imprescindible que
essentially [ɪˈsɛnʃlɪ] adv esencialmente
EST n abbr (US: = Eastern Standard Time) hora de invierno de Nueva York
establish [ɪˈstæblɪʃ] vt establecer; (fact, identity) comprobar, verificar; (prove) demostrar; (relations) entablar
established [ɪˈstæblɪʃt] adj (business) de buena reputación; (staff) de plantilla
establishment [ɪˈstæblɪʃmənt] n (also business) establecimiento; **the E~** la clase dirigente; **a teaching ~** un centro de enseñanza
estate [ɪˈsteɪt] n (land) finca, hacienda; (property) propiedad; (inheritance) herencia; (Pol) estado; **housing ~** (Brit) urbanización; **industrial ~** polígono industrial
estate agent n (Brit) agente inmobiliario(-a)
estate car n (Brit) ranchera
esteem [ɪˈstiːm] n: **to hold sb in high ~** estimar en mucho a algn ⊳ vt estimar
esthetic [iːsˈθɛtɪk] adj (US) = **aesthetic**
estimate n estimación; (assessment) tasa, cálculo; (Comm) presupuesto ⊳ vt estimar; tasar, calcular; **to give sb an ~ of** presentar a algn un presupuesto de; **at a rough ~** haciendo un cálculo aproximado; **to ~ for** (Comm) hacer un presupuesto de, presupuestar
estimation [ɛstɪˈmeɪʃən] n opinión, juicio; (esteem) aprecio; **in my ~** a mi juicio
Estonia [ɛˈstəunɪə] n Estonia
estranged [ɪˈstreɪndʒd] adj separado
e-tailing [ˈiːteɪlɪŋ] n venta en línea, venta vía o por Internet
et al. abbr (= et alii: and others) et al.
etc abbr (= et cetera) etc.
etching [ˈɛtʃɪŋ] n aguafuerte
eternal [ɪˈtəːnl] adj eterno
eternity [ɪˈtəːnɪtɪ] n eternidad
ethical [ˈɛθɪkl] adj ético; (honest) honrado
ethics [ˈɛθɪks] n ética ⊳ npl moralidad
Ethiopia [iːθɪˈəupɪə] n Etiopía

ethnic [ˈɛθnɪk] adj étnico
ethnic cleansing [-klɛnzɪŋ] n limpieza étnica
ethos [ˈiːθɔs] n (of group) sistema de valores
etiquette [ˈɛtɪkɛt] n etiqueta
EU n abbr (= European Union) UE
Eucharist [ˈjuːkərɪst] n Eucaristía
euphemism [ˈjuːfəmɪzm] n eufemismo
euphoria [juːˈfɔːrɪə] n euforia
Eurasia [juəˈreɪʃə] n Eurasia
Eurasian [juəˈreɪʃən] adj, n eurasiático(-a)
euro [ˈjuərəu] n (currency) euro
Eurocheque [ˈjuərəutʃɛk] n Eurocheque
Euroland [ˈjuərəulænd] n Eurolandia
Europe [ˈjuərəp] n Europa
European [juərəˈpiːən] adj, n europeo(-a)
European Court of Justice n Tribunal de Justicia de las Comunidades Europeas
European Economic Community n Comunidad Económica Europea
Euro-sceptic [juərəuˈskɛptɪk] n euroescéptico(-a)
Eurozone [ˈjuərəuzəun] n eurozona, zona euro
euthanasia [juːθəˈneɪzɪə] n eutanasia
evacuate [ɪˈvækjueɪt] vt evacuar; (place) desocupar
evacuation [ɪvækjuˈeɪʃən] n evacuación
evacuee [ɪvækjuˈiː] n evacuado(-a)
evade [ɪˈveɪd] vt evadir, eludir
evaluate [ɪˈvæljueɪt] vt evaluar; (value) tasar; (evidence) interpretar
evangelist [ɪˈvændʒəlɪst] n evangelista; (preacher) evangelizador(a)
evaporate [ɪˈvæpəreɪt] vi evaporarse; (fig) desvanecerse ⊳ vt evaporar
evaporated milk [ɪˈvæpəreɪtɪd-] n leche evaporada
evaporation [ɪvæpəˈreɪʃən] n evaporación
evasion [ɪˈveɪʒən] n evasión
evasive [ɪˈveɪsɪv] adj evasivo
eve [iːv] n: **on the ~ of** en vísperas de
even [ˈiːvn] adj (level) llano; (smooth) liso; (speed, temperature) uniforme; (number) par; (contest) igualado ⊳ adv hasta, incluso; **an ~ layer of snow** una capa de nieve uniforme; **our score is ~** estamos igualados; **~ he was there** hasta él estaba allí; **~ on Sundays** incluso los domingos; **~ faster** aún más rápido; **~ if, ~ though** aunque, así (LAm); **I'd never do that, ~ if you asked me** nunca haría eso, aunque me lo pidieras; **he's never got any money, ~ though his parents are quite rich** nunca tiene dinero aunque sus padres son bastante ricos; **~ more** aún más; **~ so** aun así; **not ~** ni siquiera; **he didn't ~ say hello** ni siquiera saludó; **to break ~** cubrir los gastos; **to get ~ with sb** ajustar cuentas con algn
▸ **even out** vi nivelarse
▸ **even up** vt igualar; **to ~ things up** nivelar la situación
evening [ˈiːvnɪŋ] n tarde; (dusk) atardecer; (night) noche; **in the ~** por la tarde; **this ~** esta tarde o noche; **tomorrow/yesterday ~** mañana/ayer por la tarde o noche

evening class n clase nocturna
evening dress n (man's) traje de etiqueta; (woman's) traje de noche
event [ɪ'vɛnt] n suceso, acontecimiento; (Sport) prueba; **a sporting ~** un acontecimiento deportivo; **she took part in two ~s at the last Olympic Games** participó en dos pruebas en los últimos Juegos Olímpicos; **in the ~ ...** resultó que ...; **in the ~ of** en caso de; **in the ~ of an accident** en caso de accidente; **during the course of ~s** en el curso de los acontecimientos; **at all ~s, in any ~** en cualquier caso
eventful [ɪ'vɛntful] adj azaroso; (game etc) lleno de emoción
eventual [ɪ'vɛntʃuəl] adj final
eventuality [ɪvɛntʃu'ælɪtɪ] n eventualidad
eventually [ɪ'vɛntʃuəlɪ] adv (finally) por fin; (in time) con el tiempo
ever ['ɛvəʳ] adv (at any time) alguna vez; (at all times) siempre; **did you ~ meet him?** ¿llegaste a conocerle?; **have you ~ been there?** ¿has estado allí alguna vez?; **have you ~ seen it?** ¿lo has visto alguna vez?; **I haven't ~ done that** jamás he hecho eso; **hardly ~** casi nunca; **the best I've ~ seen** el mejor que he visto; **it's the best ~** jamás ha habido mejor; **the coldest night ~** la noche más fría que nunca hemos tenido; **better than ~** mejor que nunca; **for the first time ~** por primera vez; **for ~** (para) siempre; **they lived happily ~ after** vivieron felices; **~ since I met him** desde que le conozco; **I've hated him ~ since** desde entonces lo odio; **it will become ~ more complex** irá siendo cada vez más complicado; **thank you ~ so much** muchísimas gracias; **it's ~ so kind of you** es muy amable de su parte; **yours ~** (in letters) un abrazo de
evergreen ['ɛvəgriːn] n árbol de hoja perenne
everlasting [ɛvə'lɑːstɪŋ] adj eterno, perpetuo
every ['ɛvrɪ] adj **1** (each) cada; **~ pupil** cada alumno; **~ time** cada vez; **~ one of them** (people) todos ellos(-as); (objects) cada uno de ellos(-as); **~ shop in the town was closed** todas las tiendas de la ciudad estaban cerradas
2 (all possible) todo(-a); **I gave you ~ assistance** te di toda la ayuda posible; **I have ~ confidence in him** tiene toda mi confianza; **we wish you ~ success** te deseamos todo el éxito posible
3 (showing recurrence) todo(-a); **~ day/week** todos los días/todas las semanas; **~ other car had been broken into** habían forzado uno de cada dos coches; **she visits me ~ other/third day** me visita cada dos/tres días; **~ now and then, ~ so often** de vez en cuando
everybody ['ɛvrɪbɔdɪ] pron todos, todo el mundo; **~ knows about it** todo el mundo lo sabe; **~ else** todos los demás
everyday ['ɛvrɪdeɪ] adj (daily: use, occurrence, experience) diario, cotidiano; (usual: expression) corriente; (common) vulgar; (routine) rutinario
everyone ['ɛvrɪwʌn] = **everybody**
everything ['ɛvrɪθɪŋ] pron todo; **~ is ready** todo está dispuesto; **he did ~ possible** hizo todo lo posible

everywhere ['ɛvrɪwɛəʳ] adv (be) en todas partes; (go) a o por todas partes; **~ you go you meet...** en todas partes encontrarás...
evict [ɪ'vɪkt] vt desahuciar
eviction [ɪ'vɪkʃən] n desahucio
evidence ['ɛvɪdəns] n (proof) prueba; (of witness) testimonio; (facts) datos, hechos; **to give ~** prestar declaración, dar testimonio
evident ['ɛvɪdənt] adj evidente, manifiesto
evidently ['ɛvɪdəntlɪ] adv (obviously) obviamente, evidentemente; (apparently) por lo visto
evil ['iːvl] adj malo; (influence) funesto; (smell) horrible ▷ n mal
evoke [ɪ'vəuk] vt evocar; (admiration) provocar
evolution [iːvə'luːʃən] n evolución
evolve [ɪ'vɔlv] vt desarrollar ▷ vi evolucionar, desarrollarse
ewe [juː] n oveja
ex- [ɛks] pref (former: husband, president etc) ex-
exact [ɪg'zækt] adj exacto ▷ vt: **to ~ sth (from)** exigir algo (de)
exacting [ɪg'zæktɪŋ] adj exigente; (conditions) arduo
exactly [ɪg'zæktlɪ] adv exactamente; (time) en punto; **~!** ¡exacto!
exaggerate [ɪg'zædʒəreɪt] vt, vi exagerar
exaggeration [ɪgzædʒə'reɪʃən] n exageración
exalted [ɪg'zɔːltɪd] adj (position) elevado; (elated) enardecido
exam [ɪg'zæm] n abbr (Scol) = **examination**
examination [ɪgzæmɪ'neɪʃən] n (gen) examen; (Law) interrogación; (inquiry) investigación; **to take** or **sit an ~** hacer un examen; **the matter is under ~** se está examinando el asunto
examine [ɪg'zæmɪn] vt (gen) examinar; (inspect: machine, premises) inspeccionar; (Scol, Law: person) interrogar; (at customs: luggage, passport) registrar; (Med) hacer un reconocimiento médico de, examinar
examiner [ɪg'zæmɪnəʳ] n examinador(a)
example [ɪg'zɑːmpl] n ejemplo; **for ~** por ejemplo; **to set a good/bad ~** dar buen/mal ejemplo
exasperate [ɪg'zɑːspəreɪt] vt exasperar, irritar; **~d by** or **at** or **with** exasperado por or con
exasperation [ɪgzɑːspə'reɪʃən] n exasperación, irritación
excavate ['ɛkskəveɪt] vt excavar
excavation [ɛkskə'veɪʃən] n excavación
exceed [ɪk'siːd] vt exceder; (number) pasar de; (speed limit) sobrepasar; (limits) rebasar; (powers) excederse en; (hopes) superar
exceedingly [ɪk'siːdɪŋlɪ] adv sumamente, sobremanera
excel [ɪk'sɛl] vi sobresalir; **to ~ o.s** lucirse
excellence ['ɛksələns] n excelencia
Excellency ['ɛksələnsɪ] n: **His ~** Su Excelencia
excellent ['ɛksələnt] adj excelente
except [ɪk'sɛpt] prep (also: **except for, excepting**) excepto, salvo ▷ vt exceptuar, excluir; **~ if/when** excepto si/cuando; **~ that** salvo que

exception [ɪk'sɛpʃən] n excepción; **to take ~ to** ofenderse por; **with the ~ of** a excepción de; **to make an ~** hacer una excepción

exceptional [ɪk'sɛpʃənl] adj excepcional

excerpt ['ɛksəːpt] n extracto

excess [ɪk'sɛs] n exceso; **in ~ of** superior a; *see also* **excesses**

excess baggage n exceso de equipaje

excesses npl excesos

excess fare n suplemento

excessive [ɪk'sɛsɪv] adj excesivo

exchange [ɪks'tʃeɪndʒ] n cambio; *(of prisoners)* canje; *(of ideas)* intercambio; *(also:* **telephone exchange**) central (telefónica) ▷ vt intercambiar; **to ~ (for)** cambiar (por); **in ~ for** a cambio de; **foreign ~** *(Comm)* divisas

exchange rate n tipo de cambio

exchequer [ɪks'tʃɛkər] n: **the ~** *(Brit)* Hacienda

excise ['ɛksaɪz] n impuestos sobre el consumo interior

excite [ɪk'saɪt] vt *(stimulate)* entusiasmar; *(anger)* suscitar, provocar; *(move)* emocionar; **to get ~d** emocionarse

excitement [ɪk'saɪtmənt] n emoción

exciting [ɪk'saɪtɪŋ] adj emocionante

excl. abbr = **excluding; exclusive (of)**

exclaim [ɪk'skleɪm] vi exclamar

exclamation [ɛksklə'meɪʃən] n exclamación

exclamation mark n signo de admiración

exclude [ɪk'skluːd] vt excluir; *(except)* exceptuar

excluding [ɪks'kluːdɪŋ] prep: **~ VAT** IVA no incluido

exclusion [ɪk'skluːʒən] n exclusión; **to the ~ of** con exclusión de

exclusion zone n zona de exclusión

exclusive [ɪk'skluːsɪv] adj exclusivo; *(club, district)* selecto; **~ of tax** excluyendo impuestos; **~ of postage/service** franqueo/servicio no incluido; **from 1st to 13th March ~** del 1 al 13 de marzo exclusive

excommunicate [ɛkskə'mjuːnɪkeɪt] vt excomulgar

excrement ['ɛkskrəmənt] n excremento

excruciating [ɪk'skruːʃɪeɪtɪŋ] adj *(pain)* agudísimo, atroz

excursion [ɪk'skəːʃən] n excursión

excuse n excusa; *(evasion)* pretexto ▷ vt disculpar, perdonar; *(justify)* justificar; **there's no ~ for this** esto no admite disculpa; **to make ~s for sb** presentar disculpas por algn; **to ~ sb from doing sth** dispensar a algn de hacer algo; **to ~ o.s. (for (doing) sth)** pedir disculpas (por (hacer) algo); **~ me!** *(trying to get past)* ¡con permiso!; *(apologizing)* ¡perdone!; *(attracting attention)* ¡oiga (,por favor)!; **if you will ~ me** con su permiso

ex-directory ['ɛksdɪ'rɛktərɪ] adj *(Brit)*: **~ (phone) number** número que no figura en la guía (telefónica)

execute ['ɛksɪkjuːt] vt *(plan)* realizar; *(order)* cumplir; *(person)* ajusticiar, ejecutar

execution [ɛksɪ'kjuːʃən] n realización; cumplimiento; ejecución

executioner [ɛksɪ'kjuːʃənər] n verdugo

executive [ɪg'zɛkjutɪv] n *(Comm)* ejecutivo(-a); *(Pol)* poder ejecutivo ▷ adj ejecutivo; *(car, plane, position)* de ejecutivo; *(offices, suite)* de la dirección; *(secretary)* de dirección

executor [ɪg'zɛkjutər] n albacea, testamentario

exemplary [ɪg'zɛmplərɪ] adj ejemplar

exemplify [ɪg'zɛmplɪfaɪ] vt ejemplificar

exempt [ɪg'zɛmpt] adj: **~ from** exento de ▷ vt: **to ~ sb from** eximir a algn de

exemption [ɪg'zɛmpʃən] n exención; *(immunity)* inmunidad

exercise ['ɛksəsaɪz] n ejercicio ▷ vt ejercer; *(patience etc)* proceder con; *(dog)* sacar de paseo ▷ vi hacer ejercicio

exercise bike n bicicleta estática

exercise book n cuaderno de ejercicios

exert [ɪg'zəːt] vt ejercer; *(strength, force)* emplear; **to ~ o.s.** esforzarse

exertion [ɪg'zəːʃən] n esfuerzo

exhale [ɛks'heɪl] vt despedir, exhalar ▷ vi espirar

exhaust [ɪg'zɔːst] n *(pipe)* (tubo de) escape; *(fumes)* gases de escape ▷ vt agotar; **to ~ o.s.** agotarse

exhausted [ɪg'zɔːstɪd] adj agotado

exhausting [ɪg'zɔːstɪŋ] adj: **an ~ journey/day** un viaje/día agotador

exhaustion [ɪg'zɔːstʃən] n agotamiento; **nervous ~** agotamiento nervioso

exhaustive [ɪg'zɔːstɪv] adj exhaustivo

exhibit [ɪg'zɪbɪt] n *(Art)* obra expuesta; *(Law)* objeto expuesto ▷ vt *(show: emotions)* manifestar; *(: courage, skill)* demostrar; *(paintings)* exponer

exhibition [ɛksɪ'bɪʃən] n exposición

exhilarating [ɪg'zɪləreɪtɪŋ] adj estimulante, tónico

exile ['ɛksaɪl] n exilio; *(person)* exiliado(-a) ▷ vt desterrar, exiliar

exist [ɪg'zɪst] vi existir

existence [ɪg'zɪstəns] n existencia

existing [ɪg'zɪstɪŋ] adj existente, actual

exit ['ɛksɪt] n salida ▷ vi *(Theat)* hacer mutis; *(Comput)* salir (del sistema)

exit poll n encuesta a la salida de los colegios electorales

exit ramp n *(US Aut)* vía de acceso

exodus ['ɛksədəs] n éxodo

exonerate [ɪg'zɒnəreɪt] vt: **to ~ from** exculpar de

exotic [ɪg'zɒtɪk] adj exótico

expand [ɪk'spænd] vt ampliar, extender; *(number)* aumentar ▷ vi *(trade etc)* ampliarse, expandirse; *(gas, metal)* dilatarse; **to ~ on** *(notes, story etc)* ampliar

expanse [ɪk'spæns] n extensión

expansion [ɪk'spænʃən] n ampliación; aumento; *(of trade)* expansión

expect [ɪk'spɛkt] vt *(gen)* esperar; *(count on)* contar con; *(suppose)* suponer ▷ vi: **to be ~ing** estar encinta; **I'm ~ing him for dinner** Lo espero para cenar; **she's ~ing a baby** está esperando un bebé; **I didn't ~ that from him** no me esperaba eso de él; **to ~ to do sth** esperar hacer algo; **they ~ to arrive tomorrow** esperan llegar mañana; **as ~ed** como era de esperar; **I ~ he'll be late** me imagino que or supongo que llegará tarde; **I ~ so** supongo que sí

expectancy [ɪk'spɛktənsɪ] n (anticipation) expectación; **life ~** esperanza de vida

expectant mother [ɪk'spɛktənt-] n futura madre

expectation [ɛkspɛk'teɪʃən] n esperanza, expectativa; **in ~ of** esperando; **against** or **contrary to all ~(s)** en contra de todas las previsiones; **to come up to** or **live up to sb's ~s** resultar tan bueno como se esperaba; **to fall short of sb's ~s** no cumplir las esperanzas de algn, decepcionar a algn

expedient [ɪk'spi:dɪənt] adj conveniente, oportuno ▷ n recurso, expediente

expedition [ɛkspə'dɪʃən] n expedición

expel [ɪk'spɛl] vt expulsar

expend [ɪk'spɛnd] vt gastar; (use up) consumir

expendable [ɪk'spɛndəbl] adj prescindible

expenditure [ɪk'spɛndɪtʃəʳ] n gastos, desembolso; (of time, effort) gasto

expense [ɪk'spɛns] n gasto, gastos; (high cost) coste; **expenses** npl (Comm) gastos; **at the ~ of** a costa de; **to meet the ~ of** hacer frente a los gastos de

expense account n cuenta de gastos (de representación)

expensive [ɪk'spɛnsɪv] adj caro, costoso

experience [ɪk'spɪərɪəns] n experiencia ▷ vt experimentar; (suffer) sufrir; **to learn by** or **from ~** aprender con la experiencia; **I know from personal ~** lo sé por experiencia propria; **a driver with ten years' ~** un conductor con diez años de experiencia; **work ~** experiencia laboral

experienced [ɪk'spɪərɪənst] adj experimentado

experiment [ɪk'spɛrɪmənt] n experimento ▷ vi hacer experimentos, experimentar; **to perform** or **carry out an ~** realizar un experimento; **as an ~** como experimento; **to ~ with a new vaccine** experimentar con una vacuna nueva

expert ['ɛkspə:t] adj experto, perito ▷ n experto(-a), perito(-a) (specialist) especialista; **~ witness** (Law) testigo pericial; **~ in** or **at doing sth** experto or perito en hacer algo; **an ~ on sth** un experto en algo

expertise [ɛkspə:'ti:z] n pericia

expire [ɪk'spaɪəʳ] vi (gen) caducar, vencerse

expiry [ɪk'spaɪərɪ] n caducidad, vencimiento

explain [ɪk'spleɪn] vt explicar; (mystery) aclarar ▶ **explain away** vt justificar

explanation [ɛksplə'neɪʃən] n explicación; aclaración; **to find an ~ for sth** encontrarle una explicación a algo

explanatory [ɪk'splænətrɪ] adj explicativo, aclaratorio

explicit [ɪk'splɪsɪt] adj explícito

explode [ɪk'spləud] vi estallar, explotar; (with anger) reventar ▷ vt hacer explotar; (fig: theory, myth) demoler

exploit n hazaña ▷ vt explotar

exploitation [ɛksplɔɪ'teɪʃən] n explotación

exploratory [ɪk'splɔrətrɪ] adj (fig: talks) exploratorio, preliminar

explore [ɪk'splɔ:ʳ] vt explorar; (fig) examinar, sondear

explorer [ɪk'splɔ:rəʳ] n explorador(a)

explosion [ɪk'spləuʒən] n explosión

explosive [ɪk'spləusɪv] adj, n explosivo

exponent [ɪk'spəunənt] n partidario(-a); (of skill, activity) exponente

export vt exportar ▷ n exportación ▷ cpd de exportación

exporter [ɛk'spɔ:təʳ] n exportador(a)

expose [ɪk'spəuz] vt exponer; (unmask) desenmascarar

exposed [ɪk'spəuzd] adj expuesto; (land, house) desprotegido; (Elec: wire) al aire; (pipe, beam) al descubierto

exposure [ɪk'spəuʒəʳ] n exposición; (Phot: speed) (tiempo de) exposición; (: shot) fotografía; **to die from ~** (Med) morir de frío

exposure meter n fotómetro

express [ɪk'sprɛs] adj (definite) expreso, explícito; (Brit: letter etc) urgente ▷ n (train) rápido ▷ adv (send) por correo extraordinario ▷ vt expresar; (squeeze) exprimir; **to send sth ~** enviar algo por correo urgente; **to ~ o.s.** expresarse

expression [ɪk'sprɛʃən] n expresión

expressive [ɪk'sprɛsɪv] adj expresivo

expressly [ɪk'sprɛslɪ] adv expresamente

expressway [ɪk'sprɛsweɪ] n (US: urban motorway) autopista

expulsion [ɪk'spʌlʃən] n expulsión

exquisite [ɛk'skwɪzɪt] adj exquisito

ext. abbr (Tel) = **extension**

extend [ɪk'stɛnd] vt (visit, street) prolongar; (building) ampliar; (thanks, friendship etc) extender; (Comm: credit) conceder; (deadline) prorrogar ▷ vi (land) extenderse; **the contract ~s to/for …** el contrato se prolonga hasta/por …

extension [ɪk'stɛnʃən] n extensión; (building) ampliación; (Tel: line) extensión; (: telephone) supletorio; (of deadline) prórroga; **~ 3718** extensión 3718

extensive [ɪk'stɛnsɪv] adj (gen) extenso; (damage) importante; (knowledge) amplio

extensively [ɪk'stɛnsɪvlɪ] adv (altered, damaged etc) extensamente; **he's travelled ~** ha viajado por muchos países

extent [ɪk'stɛnt] n (breadth) extensión; (scope: of knowledge, activities) alcance; (degree: of damage, loss) grado; **to some ~** hasta cierto punto; **to a certain ~** hasta cierto punto; **to a large ~** en gran parte; **to the ~ of…** hasta el punto de…; **to such an ~ that…** hasta tal punto que…; **to what ~?** ¿hasta qué punto?; **debts to the ~ of £5000** deudas por la cantidad de 5000 libras

extenuating [ɪk'stɛnjueɪtɪŋ] adj: **~ circumstances** circunstancias atenuantes

exterior [ɛk'stɪərɪəʳ] adj exterior, externo ▷ n exterior

exterminate [ɪk'stə:mɪneɪt] vt exterminar

external [ɛk'stə:nl] adj externo, exterior ▷ n:

the ~s la apariencia exterior; ~ **affairs** asuntos exteriores; **for ~ use only** (*Med*) para uso tópico

extinct [ɪk'stɪŋkt] *adj* (*volcano*) extinguido, apagado; (*animal, race*) extinguido

extinction [ɪk'stɪŋkʃən] *n* extinción

extinguish [ɪk'stɪŋgwɪʃ] *vt* extinguir, apagar

extinguisher [ɪk'stɪŋgwɪʃəʳ] *n* extintor

extol, (*US*) **extoll** [ɪk'stəul] *vt* (*merits, virtues*) ensalzar, alabar; (*person*) alabar, elogiar

extort [ɪk'stɔːt] *vt* sacar a la fuerza; (*confession*) arrancar

extortion [ɪk'stɔːʃən] *n* extorsión

extortionate [ɪk'stɔːʃnət] *adj* excesivo, exorbitante

extra ['ɛkstrə] *adj* adicional ▷ *adv* (*in addition*) más ▷ *n* (*addition*) extra, suplemento; (*Theat*) extra, comparsa; (*newspaper*) edición extraordinaria; **wine will cost ~** el vino se paga aparte; **~ large sizes** tallas extragrandes; *see also* **extras**

extract *vt* sacar; (*tooth*) sacar; (*confession*) arrancar ▷ *n* fragmento; (*Culin*) extracto

extraction [ɪk'strækʃən] *n* extracción; (*origin*) origen

extracurricular [ɛkstrəkə'rɪkjuləʳ] *adj* (*Scol*) extraescolar

extradite ['ɛkstrədaɪt] *vt* extraditar

extradition [ɛkstrə'dɪʃən] *n* extradición

extramarital [ɛkstrə'mærɪtl] *adj* extramatrimonial

extramural [ɛkstrə'mjuərl] *adj* extra-académico

extraneous [ɪk'streɪnɪəs] *adj* extraño, ajeno

extraordinary [ɪk'strɔːdnrɪ] *adj* extraordinario; (*odd*) raro; **the ~ thing is that ...** lo más extraordinario es que ...

extraordinary general meeting *n* junta general extraordinaria

extras *npl* (*additional expense*) extras

extra time *n* (*Football*) prórroga

extravagance [ɪk'strævəgəns] *n* (*excessive spending*) derroche; (*item*) extravagancia

extravagant [ɪk'strævəgənt] *adj* (*wasteful*) derrochador(a); (*taste, gift*) excesivamente caro; (*price*) exorbitante; (*praise*) excesivo

extreme [ɪk'striːm] *adj* extremo; (*poverty etc*)

extremado; (*case*) excepcional ▷ *n* extremo; **the ~ left/right** (*Pol*) la extrema izquierda/derecha; **~s of temperature** temperaturas extremas

extremely [ɪk'striːmlɪ] *adv* sumamente, extremadamente

extremist [ɪk'striːmɪst] *adj, n* extremista

extremity [ɪk'strɛmətɪ] *n* extremidad, punta; (*need*) apuro, necesidad; **extremities** *npl* (*hands and feet*) extremidades

extricate ['ɛkstrɪkeɪt] *vt*: **to ~ o.s. from** librarse de

extrovert ['ɛkstrəvəːt] *n* extrovertido(-a)

exuberance [ɪg'zjuːbərns] *n* exuberancia

exuberant [ɪg'zjuːbərnt] *adj* (*person*) eufórico; (*style*) exuberante

exude [ɪg'zjuːd] *vt* rezumar

eye [aɪ] *n* ojo ▷ *vt* mirar; **I've got green ~s** tengo los ojos verdes; **I couldn't believe my ~s** no daba crédito a lo que veían mis ojos; **to look sb in the ~** mirar a algn a los ojos; **to keep an ~ on sb/sth** vigilar algn/algo; **keep an ~ out for snakes** cuidado por si hay culebras; **as far as the ~ can see** hasta donde alcanza la vista; **with an ~ to doing sth** con vistas *or* miras a hacer algo; **to have an ~ for sth** tener mucha vista *or* buen ojo para algo; **there's more to this than meets the ~** esto tiene su miga

eyeball ['aɪbɔːl] *n* globo ocular

eyebath ['aɪbɑːθ] *n* baño ocular, lavaojos

eyebrow ['aɪbrau] *n* ceja

eyebrow pencil *n* lápiz de cejas

eyedrops ['aɪdrɔps] *npl* gotas para los ojos

eyeful ['aɪful] *n* (*col*): **to get an ~ of sth** ver bien algo

eyelash ['aɪlæʃ] *n* pestaña

eyelid ['aɪlɪd] *n* párpado

eyeliner ['aɪlaɪnəʳ] *n* lápiz de ojos

eye-opener ['aɪəupnəʳ] *n* revelación, gran sorpresa

eyeshadow ['aɪʃædəu] *n* sombra de ojos

eyesight ['aɪsaɪt] *n* vista

eyesore ['aɪsɔːʳ] *n* monstruosidad

eye witness *n* testigo ocular

eyrie ['ɪərɪ] *n* aguilera

Ff

F, f [ɛf] *n* (*letter*) F, f; (*Mus*) fa; **F for Frederick,** (*US*) **F for Fox** F de Francia

FA *n abbr* (*Brit*: = *Football Association*) ≈ AFE (*Esp*)

fable ['feɪbl] *n* fábula

fabric ['fæbrɪk] *n* tejido, tela

fabricate ['fæbrɪkeɪt] *vt* fabricar; (*fig*) inventar

fabrication [fæbrɪ'keɪʃən] *n* fabricación; (*fig*) invención

fabulous ['fæbjuləs] *adj* fabuloso

façade [fə'sɑːd] *n* fachada

face [feɪs] *n* (*Anat*) cara, rostro; (*of clock*) esfera, cara; (*side*) cara; (*surface*) superficie ▷ *vt* (*be facing*) estar frente a; (*confront*) enfrentarse a; **he was red in the ~** tenía la cara colorada; **the north ~ of the mountain** la cara norte de la montaña; **~ down** (*person, card*) boca abajo; **to lose ~** desprestigiarse; **to save ~** salvar las apariencias; **to make** *or* **pull a ~** hacer muecas; **in the ~ of** (*difficulties etc*) en vista de, ante; **on the ~ of it** a primera vista; **~ to ~** cara a cara; **they stood facing each other** estaban de pie el uno frente al otro; **the garden ~s south** el jardín da al sur; **they ~ serious problems** se enfrentan a graves problemas; **to ~ the fact that ...** reconocer que ...; **let's ~ it, we're lost** admitámoslo, estamos perdidos
  ▶ **face up to** *vt fus* afrontar, enfrentarse a; **he refuses to ~ up to his responsibilities** se niega a afrontar sus responsabilidades

face cloth *n* (*Brit*) toallita

face cream *n* crema (de belleza)

face lift *n* lifting, estirado facial

face powder *n* polvos para la cara

facet ['fæsɪt] *n* faceta

facetious [fə'siːʃəs] *adj* chistoso

face value *n* (*of stamp*) valor nominal; **to take sth at ~** (*fig*) tomar algo en sentido literal, aceptar las apariencias de algo

facial ['feɪʃəl] *adj* de la cara ▷ *n* (*also*: **beauty facial**) tratamiento facial, limpieza

facile ['fæsaɪl] *adj* superficial

facilitate [fə'sɪlɪteɪt] *vt* facilitar

facility [fə'sɪlɪtɪ] *n* facilidad; **facilities** *npl* instalaciones; **credit ~** facilidades de crédito

facing ['feɪsɪŋ] *prep* frente a ▷ *adj* de enfrente

facsimile [fæk'sɪmɪlɪ] *n* facsímil(e)

fact [fækt] *n* hecho; **in ~** en realidad; **to know for a ~ that ...** saber a ciencia cierta que ...; **the ~ that you are very busy is of no interest to me** el hecho de que estés muy ocupado no me interesa; **~s and figures** datos y cifras

faction ['fækʃən] *n* facción

factional ['fækʃənl] *adj* (*fighting*) entre distintas facciones

factor ['fæktər] *n* factor; (*Comm*: *person*) agente comisionado(-a) ▷ *vi* (*Comm*) comprar deudas; **safety ~** factor de seguridad

factory ['fæktərɪ] *n* fábrica

factory floor *n* (*workers*) trabajadores, mano de obra directa; (*area*) talleres

factual ['fæktjuəl] *adj* basado en los hechos

faculty ['fækəltɪ] *n* facultad; (*US*: *teaching staff*) personal docente

fad [fæd] *n* novedad, moda

fade [feɪd] *vi* descolorarse, desteñirse; (*sound, hope*) desvanecerse; (*light*) apagarse; (*flower*) marchitarse
  ▶ **fade away** *vi* (*sound*) apagarse
  ▶ **fade in** *vt* (*TV, Cine*) fundir; (*Radio*: *sound*) mezclar ▷ *vi* (*TV, Cine*) fundirse; (*Radio*) oírse por encima
  ▶ **fade out** *vt* (*TV, Cine*) fundir; (*Radio*) apagar, disminuir el volumen de ▷ *vi* (*TV, Cine*) desvanecerse; (*Radio*) apagarse, dejarse de oír

faeces, (*US*) **feces** ['fiːsiːz] *npl* excremento, heces

fag [fæg] *n* (*Brit col*: *cigarette*) pitillo (*Esp*), cigarro; (*US col*: *homosexual*) maricón

fail [feɪl] *vt* (*exam*) suspender; (*subj*: *memory etc*) fallar a ▷ *vi* suspender; (*be unsuccessful*) fracasar; (*strength, brakes, engine*) fallar; **he ~ed his driving test** suspendió el examen de conducir; **to ~ to do sth** (*neglect*) dejar de hacer algo; (*be unable*) no lograr hacer algo; **they ~ed to reach the quarter finals** no lograron alcanzar los cuartos de final; **the bomb ~ed to explode** la bomba no llegó a estallar; **words ~ me!** ¡no sé qué decir!; **the plan ~ed** el plan fracasó; **the lorry's brakes ~ed** al camión le fallaron los frenos; **without ~** sin falta

failing ['feɪlɪŋ] *n* falta, defecto ▷ *prep* a falta de; **~ that** de no ser posible eso

failure ['feɪljər] *n* fracaso; (*person*) fracasado(-a); (*mechanical etc*) fallo; (*in exam*) suspenso; (*of crops*) pérdida, destrucción; **it was a complete ~** fue un fracaso total

faint [feɪnt] adj débil; (smell, breeze, trace) leve; (recollection) vago; (mark) apenas visible ▷ n desmayo ▷ vi desmayarse; **to feel ~** estar mareado, marearse

faintest ['feɪntɪst] adj: **I haven't the ~ idea** no tengo la más remota idea

fair [fɛəʳ] adj justo; (hair, person) rubio; (weather) bueno; (good enough) suficiente; (sizeable) considerable ▷ adv: **to play ~** jugar limpio ▷ n feria; (Brit: funfair) parque de atracciones; **it's not ~!** ¡no es justo!, ¡no hay derecho!; **I paid more than my ~ share** pagué más de lo que me correspondía; **~ play** juego limpio; **~ wear and tear** desgaste natural; **he's got ~ hair** tiene el pelo rubio; **people with ~ skin** la gente con la piel blanca; **I have a ~ chance of winning** tengo bastantes posibilidades de ganar; **~ copy** copia en limpio; **that's a ~ distance** esa es una distancia considerable; **a ~ amount of** bastante; **trade ~** feria de muestras

fair game n: **to be ~** ser blanco legítimo

fairground ['fɛəɡraund] n recinto ferial

fair-haired [fɛə'hɛəd] adj (person) rubio

fairly ['fɛəlɪ] adv (justly) con justicia; (equally) equitativamente; (quite) bastante; **I'm ~ sure** estoy bastante seguro

fairness ['fɛənɪs] n justicia; (impartiality) imparcialidad; **in all ~** a decir verdad

fairy ['fɛərɪ] n hada

fairy tale n cuento de hadas

faith [feɪθ] n fe; (trust) confianza; (sect) religión; **to have ~ in sb/sth** confiar en algn/algo

faithful ['feɪθful] adj fiel

faithfully ['feɪθfulɪ] adv fielmente; **yours ~** (Brit: in letters) le saluda atentamente

fake [feɪk] n (painting etc) falsificación; (person) impostor(a) ▷ adj falso ▷ vt fingir; (painting etc) falsificar

falcon ['fɔːlkən] n halcón

Falkland Islands ['fɔːlklənd-] npl Islas Malvinas

fall [fɔːl] n caída; (US) otoño; (decrease) disminución ▷ vi (pt **fell**, pp **-en**) caer; (accidentally) caerse; (price) bajar; **falls** npl (waterfall) cataratas, salto de agua; **Niagara F~s** las cataratas del Niágara; **she had a nasty ~** tuvo una mala caída; **a ~ of earth** un desprendimiento de tierra; **a ~ of snow** una nevada; **bombs fell on the town** las bombas caían sobre la ciudad; **he tripped and fell** tropezó y se cayó; **the book fell off the shelf** el libro se cayó de la estantería; **to ~ flat on one's face** caerse de bruces; **to ~ flat** (joke, story) no hacer gracia; **to ~ short of sb's expectations** decepcionar a algn; **to ~ in love (with sb/sth)** enamorarse (de algn/algo)

▶ **fall apart** vi romperse; **the book fell apart when he opened it** el libro se rompió cuando lo abrió

▶ **fall back** vi retroceder

▶ **fall back on** vt fus (remedy etc) recurrir a; **to have sth to ~ back on** tener algo a que recurrir

▶ **fall behind** vi quedarse atrás; (fig: with payments) retrasarse

▶ **fall down** vi (person) caerse; (building) derrumbarse; **she's ~en down** se ha caído; **the house is slowly ~ing down** la casa se cae poco a poco

▶ **fall for** vt fus (trick) tragar; (person) enamorarse de; **they fell for it!** ¡se lo tragaron!; **she fell for him immediately** se enamoró de él en el acto

▶ **fall in** vi (roof) hundirse; (Mil) alinearse

▶ **fall in with** vt fus: **to ~ in with sb's plans** acomodarse con los planes de algn

▶ **fall off** vi caerse; (diminish) disminuir

▶ **fall out** vi (friends etc) reñir; (Mil) romper filas; **Sarah's ~en out with her boyfriend** Sarah ha reñido con su novio

▶ **fall over** vi caer(se)

▶ **fall through** vi (plan, project) fracasar

fallacy ['fæləsɪ] n error

fallen ['fɔːlən] pp of **fall**

fallible ['fæləbl] adj falible

fallout ['fɔːlaut] n lluvia radioactiva

fallout shelter n refugio antinuclear

fallow ['fæləu] adj (land, field) en barbecho

false [fɔːls] adj (gen) falso; (teeth etc) postizo; (disloyal) desleal, traidor(a); **under ~ pretences** con engaños

false alarm n falsa alarma

falsehood ['fɔːlshud] n falsedad

falsely ['fɔːlslɪ] adv falsamente

false teeth npl (Brit) dentadura postiza

falsify ['fɔːlsɪfaɪ] vt falsificar

falter ['fɔːltəʳ] vi vacilar

fame [feɪm] n fama

familiar [fə'mɪlɪəʳ] adj familiar; (well-known) conocido; (tone) de confianza; **to be ~ with** (subject) estar enterado de; **to make o.s. ~ with** familiarizarse con; **to be on ~ terms with sb** tener confianza con algn

familiarity [fəmɪlɪ'ærɪtɪ] n familiaridad

familiarize [fə'mɪlɪəraɪz] vt: **to ~ o.s. with** familiarizarse con

family ['fæmɪlɪ] n familia

family credit n (Brit) ≈ ayuda familiar

family man n (home-loving) hombre casero; (having family) padre de familia

family planning n planificación familiar

family tree n árbol genealógico

famine ['fæmɪn] n hambre, hambruna

famished ['fæmɪʃt] adj hambriento; **I'm ~!** (col) ¡estoy muerto de hambre!, ¡tengo un hambre canina!

famous ['feɪməs] adj famoso, célebre

famously ['feɪməslɪ] adv (get on) estupendament

fan [fæn] n abanico; (Elec) ventilador; (person) aficionado(-a); (Sport) hincha; (of pop star) fan ▷ vt abanicar; (fire, quarrel) atizar

▶ **fan out** vi desplegarse

fanatic [fə'nætɪk] n fanático(-a)

fanatical [fə'nætɪkəl] adj fanático

fan belt n correa de ventilador

fanciful ['fænsɪful] adj (gen) fantástico;

(*imaginary*) fantasioso; (*design*) rebuscado

an club n club de fans

ancy ['fænsɪ] n (*whim*) capricho, antojo; (*imagination*) imaginación ▷ adj (*luxury*) de lujo; (*price*) exorbitado ▷ vt (*feel like, want*) tener ganas de; (*imagine*) imaginarse, figurarse; **to take a ~ to sb** tomar cariño a algn; **when the ~ takes him** cuando se le antoja; **it took** *or* **caught my ~** me cayó en gracia; **to ~ that ...** imaginarse que ...; **he fancies her** le gusta (ella) mucho

ancy dress n disfraz

ancy-dress ball ['fænsɪdrɛs-] n baile de disfraces

ang [fæŋ] n colmillo

antasize ['fæntəsaɪz] vi fantasear, hacerse ilusiones

antastic [fæn'tæstɪk] adj fantástico

antasy ['fæntəzɪ] n fantasía

anzine ['fænziːn] n fanzine

FAQs abbr (= *frequently asked questions*) preguntas frecuentes

ar [fɑːʳ] adj (*distant*) lejano ▷ adv lejos; **the ~ left/ right** (Pol) la extrema izquierda/derecha; **at the ~ end of the swimming pool** al otro extremo de la piscina; **is it ~?** ¿está lejos?; **is it ~ to London?** ¿estamos lejos de Londres?, ¿Londres queda lejos?; **how ~ is it to Madrid?** ¿a qué distancia está Madrid?; **how ~ have you got with your work?** ¿hasta dónde has llegado en tu trabajo?; **~ away, ~ off** (a lo) lejos; **go as ~ as the farm** vaya hasta la granja; **as ~ as I know** que yo sepa; **~ from** lejos de; **it's not ~ (from here)** no está lejos (de aquí); **it's ~ from easy** no es nada fácil; **by ~** con mucho; **it's by ~ the best** es con mucho el mejor; **~ better, better by ~** mucho mejor; **so ~** hasta ahora

araway ['fɑːrəweɪ] adj remoto; (*look*) ausente, perdido

arce [fɑːs] n farsa

arcical ['fɑːsɪkəl] adj absurdo

are [fɛəʳ] n (*on trains, buses*) precio (del billete); (*in taxi: cost*) tarifa; (*: passenger*) pasajero; (*food*) comida; **half/full ~** medio billete/billete completo

ar East n: **the ~** el Extremo *or* Lejano Oriente

arewell [fɛə'wɛl] excl, n adiós

arm [fɑːm] n granja, finca, estancia (LAm), chacra (LAm), rancho (LAm) ▷ vt cultivar
▶ **farm out** vt (*work*): **to ~ out (to sb)** mandar hacer fuera (a algn)

armer ['fɑːməʳ] n granjero(-a), estanciero(-a) (LAm)

armhand ['fɑːmhænd] n peón

armhouse ['fɑːmhaus] n granja, casa de hacienda (LAm)

arming ['fɑːmɪŋ] n (*gen*) agricultura; (*tilling*) cultivo; **sheep ~** cría de ovejas

armland ['fɑːmlænd] n tierra de cultivo

arm worker n = **farmhand**

armyard ['fɑːmjɑːd] n corral

ar-reaching [fɑːˈriːtʃɪŋ] adj (*reform, effect*) de gran alcance

fart [fɑːt] (*col!*) n pedo (!) ▷ vi tirarse un pedo (!)

farther ['fɑːðəʳ] adv más lejos, más allá ▷ adj más lejano

farthest ['fɑːðɪst] *superlative of* **far**

fascinate ['fæsɪneɪt] vt fascinar

fascinating ['fæsɪneɪtɪŋ] adj fascinante

fascination [fæsɪ'neɪʃən] n fascinación

fascism ['fæʃɪzəm] n fascismo

fascist ['fæʃɪst] adj, n fascista

fashion ['fæʃən] n moda; (*manner*) manera ▷ vt formar; **in ~** a la moda; **out of ~** pasado de moda; **in the Greek ~** a la griega, al estilo griego; **after a ~** (*finish, manage etc*) en cierto modo

fashionable ['fæʃnəbl] adj de moda; (*writer*) de moda, popular; **it is ~ to do ...** está de moda hacer ...

fashion show n desfile de modelos

fast [fɑːst] adj (*also Phot: film*) rápido; (*dye, colour*) sólido; (*clock*): **to be ~** estar adelantado ▷ adv rápidamente, de prisa; (*stuck, held*) firmemente ▷ n ayuno ▷ vi ayunar; **a ~ car** un coche rápido; **in the ~ lane** (Aut) en el carril de adelantamiento; **~ asleep** profundamente dormido; **my watch is 5 minutes ~** mi reloj está adelantado 5 minutos; **to make a boat ~** amarrar una barca; **as ~ as I** *etc* **can** lo más rápido posible; **they work very ~** trabajan muy rápido

fasten ['fɑːsn] vt asegurar, sujetar; (*coat, belt*) abrochar ▷ vi cerrarse
▶ **fasten (up)on** vt fus (*idea*) aferrarse a

fastener ['fɑːsnəʳ] n cierre; (*Brit: zip*) cremallera

fastening ['fɑːsnɪŋ] n = **fastener**

fast food n comida rápida, platos preparados

fastidious [fæs'tɪdɪəs] adj (*fussy*) delicado; (*demanding*) exigente

fat [fæt] adj gordo; (*meat*) con mucha grasa; (*greasy*) grasiento ▷ n grasa; (*on person*) carnes; (*lard*) manteca; **to live off the ~ of the land** vivir a cuerpo de rey

fatal ['feɪtl] adj (*mistake*) fatal; (*injury*) mortal; (*consequence*) funesto

fatality [fə'tælɪtɪ] n (*death*) víctima mortal

fate [feɪt] n destino, sino

fateful ['feɪtful] adj fatídico

fat-free ['fætfriː] adj sin grasa

father ['fɑːðəʳ] n padre

Father Christmas n Papá Noel

fatherhood ['fɑːðəhud] n paternidad

father-in-law ['fɑːðərɪnlɔː] n suegro

fatherly ['fɑːðəlɪ] adj paternal

fathom ['fæðəm] n braza ▷ vt (*unravel*) desentrañar; (*understand*) explicarse

fatigue [fə'tiːg] n fatiga, cansancio; **metal ~** fatiga del metal

fatten ['fætn] vt, vi engordar; **chocolate is ~ing** el chocolate engorda

fatty ['fætɪ] adj (*food*) graso ▷ n (*fam*) gordito(-a), gordinflón(-ona)

fatuous ['fætjuəs] adj fatuo, necio

faucet ['fɔːsɪt] n (US) grifo, llave, canilla (LAm)

fault [fɔːlt] n (*blame*) culpa; (*defect: in character*)

defecto; (*in manufacture*) desperfecto; (*Geo*) falla
▷ *vt* criticar; **it's my** ~ es culpa mía; **to find** ~
with criticar, poner peros a; **at** ~ culpable
faulty ['fɔ:ltɪ] *adj* defectuoso
fauna ['fɔ:nə] *n* fauna
faux pas ['fəu'pɑ:] *n* desacierto
favour, (*US*) **favor** ['feɪvə'] *n* favor; (*approval*)
aprobación ▷ *vt* (*proposition*) estar a favor de,
aprobar; (*person etc*) preferir; (*assist*) favorecer; **to**
ask a ~ **of** pedir un favor a; **to do sb a** ~ hacer un
favor a algn; **to find** ~ **with sb** (*subj: person*) caerle
bien a algn; (: *suggestion*) tener buena acogida
por parte de algn; **in** ~ **of** a favor de; **to be in** ~ **of**
sth/of doing sth ser partidario *or* estar a favor de
algo/de hacer algo
favo(u)rable ['feɪvərəbl] *adj* favorable
favo(u)rably ['feɪvərəblɪ] *adv* favorablemente
favo(u)rite ['feɪvərɪt] *adj, n* favorito(-a),
preferido(-a)
favo(u)ritism ['feɪvərɪtɪzəm] *n* favoritismo
fawn [fɔ:n] *n* cervato ▷ *adj* (*also:* **fawn-coloured**)
de color cervato, leonado ▷ *vi:* **to** ~ **(up)on** adular
fax [fæks] *n* fax ▷ *vt* mandar *or* enviar por fax
FBI *n abbr* (*US:* = *Federal Bureau of Investigation*) FBI
FE *n abbr* = **further education**
fear [fɪə'] *n* miedo, temor ▷ *vt* temer; **for** ~ **of**
por temor a; **for** ~ **of being criticized** por temor
a ser criticado; ~ **of heights** vértigo; **you have**
nothing to ~ no tienes nada que temer; **to** ~ **for/**
that temer por/que
fearful ['fɪəful] *adj* temeroso; (*awful*) espantoso;
to be ~ **of** (*frightened*) tener miedo de
fearless ['fɪəlɪs] *adj* (*gen*) sin miedo *or* temor;
(*bold*) audaz
feasibility [fi:zə'bɪlɪtɪ] *n* factibilidad, viabilidad
feasible ['fi:zəbl] *adj* factible, viable
feast [fi:st] *n* banquete; (*Rel: also:* **feast day**)
fiesta ▷ *vi* banquetear
feat [fi:t] *n* hazaña
feather ['feðə'] *n* pluma ▷ *vt:* **to** ~ **one's nest** (*fig*)
hacer su agosto, sacar tajada ▷ *cpd* (*mattress, bed,*
pillow) de plumas
feature ['fi:tʃə'] *n* (*gen*) característica; (*Anat*)
rasgo; (*article*) reportaje ▷ *vt* (*film*) presentar
▷ *vi* figurar; **features** *npl* (*of face*) facciones; **a**
(special) ~ **on sth/sb** un reportaje (especial)
sobre algo/algn; **it** ~**d prominently in** ... tuvo
un papel destacado en ...
feature film *n* largometraje
February ['fɛbruərɪ] *n* febrero
feces ['fi:si:z] *npl* (*US*) = **faeces**
Fed *abbr* (*US*) = **federal; federation**
fed [fɛd] *pt, pp of* **feed**
Fed. [fɛd] *n abbr* (*US col*) = **Federal Reserve Board**
federal ['fɛdərəl] *adj* federal
Federal Republic of Germany *n* República
Federal de Alemania
federation [fɛdə'reɪʃən] *n* federación
fed-up [fɛd'ʌp] *adj:* **to be** ~ **(with)** estar harto (de)
fee [fi:] *n* (*professional*) honorarios; (*for examination*)
derechos; (*of school*) matrícula; (*membership fee*)
cuota; (*entrance fee*) entrada; **for a small** ~ por

poco dinero
feeble ['fi:bl] *adj* débil
feed [fi:d] *n* (*gen, of baby*) comida; (*of animal*)
pienso; (*on printer*) dispositivo de alimentación
▷ *vb* (*pp, pt* **fed**) ▷ *vt* (*gen*) alimentar; (*Brit:*
breastfeed) dar el pecho a; (*animal, baby*) dar de
comer a ▷ *vi* (*baby, animal*) comer
▶ **feed back** *vt* (*results*) pasar
▶ **feed in** *vt* (*Comput*) introducir
▶ **feed into** *vt* (*data, information*) suministrar a;
to ~ **sth into a machine** introducir algo en una
máquina
▶ **feed on** *vt fus* alimentarse de
feedback ['fi:dbæk] *n* (*from person*) reacción;
(*Tech*) realimentación, feedback
feeding bottle ['fi:dɪŋ-] *n* (*Brit*) biberón
feel [fi:l] *n* (*sensation*) sensación; (*sense of touch*)
tacto ▷ *vt* (*pt, pp* **felt**) tocar; (*pain*) sentir;
(*think, believe*) creer; **to get the** ~ **of sth** (*fig*)
acostumbrarse a algo; **the doctor felt his**
forehead el médico le tocó la frente; **I was**
~**ing hungry/thirsty/hot/cold** tenía hambre/
sed/calor/frío; **to** ~ **lonely/better/ill** sentirse
solo/mejor/mal; **I don't** ~ **well** no me siento
bien; **I** ~ **fine** me siento bien; **how do you** ~
now? ¿cómo te encuentras ahora?; **it** ~**s soft** es
suave al tacto; **it** ~**s colder out here** se siente
más frío aquí fuera; **to** ~ **like** (*want*) tener ganas
de; **to** ~ **like doing sth** tener ganas de hacer
algo; **I don't** ~ **like going out tonight** no tengo
ganas de salir esta noche; **do you** ~ **like an ice**
cream? ¿te apetece un helado?; **I felt like a fool**
me sentí (un) estúpido; **I** ~ **a failure** me siento
un fracasado; **I'm still** ~**ing my way** (*fig*) todavía
me estoy orientando; **I** ~ **that you ought to do**
it creo que debes hacerlo; **to** ~ **about** *or* **around**
tantear
feeler ['fi:lə'] *n* (*of insect*) antena; **to put out** ~**s**
(*fig*) tantear el terreno
feeling ['fi:lɪŋ] *n* (*physical*) sensación; (*foreboding*)
presentimiento; (*impression*) impresión; (*emotion*)
sentimiento; **what are your** ~**s about the**
matter? ¿qué opinas tú del asunto?; **to hurt**
sb's ~**s** herir los sentimientos de algn; ~**s ran**
high about it causó mucha controversia; **I**
got the ~ **that** ... me dio la impresión de que
...; **there was a general** ~ **that** ... la opinión
general fue que ...
fee-paying school ['fi:peɪŋ-] *n* colegio de pago
feet [fi:t] *npl of* **foot**
feign [feɪn] *vt* fingir
fell [fɛl] *pt of* **fall** ▷ *vt* (*tree*) talar ▷ *adj:* **with one**
~ **blow** con un golpe feroz; **at one** ~ **swoop**
de un solo golpe ▷ *n* (*Brit: mountain*) montaña;
(: *moorland*): **the** ~**s** los páramos
fellow ['fɛləu] *n* tipo, tío (*Esp*); (*of learned society*)
socio(-a); (*Univ*) *miembro de la junta de gobierno de*
un colegio ▷ *cpd:* ~ **students** compañeros(-as) de
curso, condiscípulos(-as)
fellow citizen *n* conciudadano(-a)
fellow countryman *n* compatriota
fellow men *npl* semejantes

fellowship ['fɛləʊʃɪp] n compañerismo; (grant) beca

felony ['fɛlənɪ] n crimen, delito mayor

felt [fɛlt] pt, pp of **feel** ▷ n fieltro

felt-tip pen ['fɛlttɪp-] n rotulador

female ['fiːmeɪl] n (woman) mujer; (Zool) hembra ▷ adj femenino

feminine ['fɛmɪnɪn] adj femenino

feminism ['fɛmɪnɪzəm] n feminismo

feminist ['fɛmɪnɪst] n feminista

fence [fɛns] n valla, cerca; (Racing) valla ▷ vt (also: **fence in**) cercar ▷ vi hacer esgrima; **to sit on the ~** (fig) nadar entre dos aguas
▸ **fence in** vt cercar
▸ **fence off** vt separar con cerca

fencing ['fɛnsɪŋ] n esgrima

fend [fɛnd] vi: **to ~ for o.s.** valerse por sí mismo
▸ **fend off** vt (attack, attacker) rechazar, repeler; (blow) desviar; (awkward question) esquivar

fender ['fɛndə^r] n pantalla; (US Aut) parachoques; (: Rail) trompa

ferment vi fermentar ▷ n (fig) agitación

fern [fəːn] n helecho

ferocious [fəˈrəʊʃəs] adj feroz

ferocity [fəˈrɒsɪtɪ] n ferocidad

ferret ['fɛrɪt] n hurón
▸ **ferret about, ferret around** vi rebuscar
▸ **ferret out** vt (secret, truth) desentrañar

ferry ['fɛrɪ] n (small) barca de pasaje, balsa; (large: also: **ferryboat**) transbordador, ferry ▷ vt transportar; **to ~ sth/sb across** or **over** transportar algo/a algn a la otra orilla; **to ~ sb to and fro** llevar a algn de un lado para otro

fertile ['fəːtaɪl] adj fértil; (Biol) fecundo

fertility [fəˈtɪlɪtɪ] n fertilidad; fecundidad

fertilize ['fəːtɪlaɪz] vt fertilizar; (Biol) fecundar; (Agr) abonar

fertilizer ['fəːtɪlaɪzə^r] n abono, fertilizante

fervent ['fəːvənt] adj ferviente

fester ['fɛstə^r] vi supurar

festival ['fɛstɪvəl] n (Rel) fiesta; (Art, Mus) festival

festive ['fɛstɪv] adj festivo; **the ~ season** (Brit: Christmas) las Navidades

festivities [fɛsˈtɪvɪtɪz] npl festejos

festoon [fɛsˈtuːn] vt: **to ~ with** festonear or engalanar de

fetch [fɛtʃ] vt ir a buscar; (Brit: sell for) venderse por; **how much did it ~?** ¿por cuánto se vendió?
▸ **fetch up** vi ir a parar

fetching ['fɛtʃɪŋ] adj atractivo

fête [feɪt] n fiesta

fetish ['fɛtɪʃ] n fetiche

fetus ['fiːtəs] n (US) = **foetus**

feud [fjuːd] n (hostility) enemistad; (quarrel) disputa; **a family ~** una pelea familiar

feudal ['fjuːdl] adj feudal

fever ['fiːvə^r] n fiebre; **he has a ~** tiene fiebre

feverish ['fiːvərɪʃ] adj febril

few [fjuː] adj (not many) pocos ▷ pron algunos; **he has ~ friends** tiene pocos amigos; **~ people** poca gente; **a ~ (some)** unos; algunos; **he has a ~ friends** tiene algunos amigos; **she was silent for a ~ seconds** se quedó unos segundos callada; **a ~ more days** unos días más; **a good ~, quite a ~ bastantes; quite a ~ people** bastante gente; **in** or **over the next ~ days** en los próximos días; **every ~ weeks** cada 2 o 3 semanas; **a ~ of them** algunos de ellos

fewer ['fjuːə^r] adj menos

fewest ['fjuːɪst] adj los/las menos

fiancé [fɪˈãːŋseɪ] n novio, prometido

fiancée [fɪˈãːŋseɪ] n novia, prometida

fiasco [fɪˈæskəʊ] n fiasco

fib [fɪb] n mentirijilla ▷ vi decir mentirijillas

fibre, (US) **fiber** ['faɪbə^r] n fibra

fibreglass, (US) **fiberglass** ['faɪbəglɑːs] n fibra de vidrio

fickle ['fɪkl] adj inconstante

fiction ['fɪkʃən] n (gen) ficción

fictional ['fɪkʃənl] adj novelesco

fictitious [fɪkˈtɪʃəs] adj ficticio

fiddle ['fɪdl] n (Mus) violín; (cheating) trampa ▷ vt (Brit: accounts) falsificar; **tax ~** evasión fiscal; **to work a ~** hacer trampa
▸ **fiddle with** vt fus juguetear con

fiddler ['fɪdlə^r] n violinista

fiddly ['fɪdlɪ] adj (task) delicado, mañoso; (object) enrevesado

fidelity [fɪˈdɛlɪtɪ] n fidelidad

fidget ['fɪdʒɪt] vi moverse (nerviosamente)

fidgety ['fɪdʒɪtɪ] adj nervioso

field [fiːld] n (gen, Comput) campo; (fig) campo, esfera; (Sport) campo, cancha (LAm); (competitors) competidores ▷ cpd: **to have a ~ day** (fig) ponerse las botas; **to lead the ~** (Sport, Comm) llevar la delantera; **to give sth a year's trial in the ~** (fig) sacar algo al mercado a prueba por un año; **my particular ~** mi especialidad

field hospital n hospital de campaña

field marshal n mariscal

fieldwork ['fiːldwəːk] n (Archaeology, Geo) trabajo de campo

fiend [fiːnd] n demonio

fiendish ['fiːndɪʃ] adj diabólico

fierce [fɪəs] adj feroz; (wind, attack) violento; (heat) intenso; (fighting, enemy) encarnizado

fiery ['faɪərɪ] adj (burning) ardiente; (temperament) apasionado

FIFA ['fiːfə] n abbr (= Fédération Internationale de Football Association) FIFA

fifteen [fɪfˈtiːn] num quince

fifth [fɪfθ] adj quinto

fiftieth ['fɪftɪɪθ] adj quincuagésimo

fifty ['fɪftɪ] num cincuenta; **the fifties** los años cincuenta; **to be in one's fifties** andar por los cincuenta

fifty-fifty ['fɪftɪ'fɪftɪ] adv: **to go ~ with sb** ir a medias con algn ▷ adj: **we have a ~ chance of success** tenemos un cincuenta por ciento de posibilidades de tener éxito

fig [fɪg] n higo

fight [faɪt] n (gen) pelea; (Mil) combate; (struggle) lucha ▷ vb (pt, pp **fought**) ▷ vt luchar contra; (cancer, alcoholism) combatir; (Law): **to ~ a case**

defenderse ▷ vi (brawl) pelear, luchar; (quarrel) pelear; (struggle) luchar; **there was a ~ in the pub** hubo una pelea en el pub; **she had a ~ with her best friend** se peleó con su mejor amiga; **the ~ against cancer** la lucha contra el cáncer; **the doctors tried to ~ the disease** los médicos intentaron combatir la enfermedad; **the fans started ~ing** los hinchas empezaron a pelearse; **the demonstrators fought with the police** los manifestantes lucharon con la policía; **she has fought against racism all her life** ha luchado toda su vida contra el racismo; **to ~ for sth** (fig) luchar por algo
▸ **fight back** vi defenderse; (after illness) recuperarse ▷ vt (tears) contener
▸ **fight down** vt (anger, anxiety, urge) reprimir
▸ **fight off** vt (attack, attacker) rechazar; (disease, sleep, urge) luchar contra
▸ **fight out** vt: **to ~ it out** decidirlo en una pelea
fighter ['faɪtər] n combatiente; (fig) luchador(a); (plane) caza
fighting ['faɪtɪŋ] n (gen) el luchar; (battle) combate; (in streets) disturbios
figment ['fɪgmənt] n: **a ~ of the imagination** un producto de la imaginación
figurative ['fɪgjʊrətɪv] adj (meaning) figurado; (Art) figurativo
figure ['fɪgər] n (Drawing, Geom) figura, dibujo; (number, cipher) cifra; (person, outline) figura; (body shape) línea; (: attractive) tipo ▷ vt (esp US: think, calculate) calcular, imaginarse ▷ vi (appear) figurar; (esp US: make sense) ser lógico; **can you give me the exact ~s?** ¿me puedes dar las cifras exactas?; **Helen saw the ~ of a man on the bridge** Helen vio la silueta de un hombre en el puente; **she's got a good ~** tiene buen tipo; **I have to watch my ~** tengo que mantener la línea; **~ of speech** (Ling) figura retórica; **public ~** personaje; **he's an important political ~** es una importante figura política; **I ~ they'll come** me imagino que vendrán; **that ~!** ¡lógico!
▸ **figure on** vt fus (US) contar con
▸ **figure out** vt (calculate) calcular; (manage to understand) llegar a comprender; **I'll try to ~ out how much it'll cost** intentaré calcular lo que va a costar; **I couldn't ~ out what it meant** no llegué a comprender lo que significaba
figurehead ['fɪgəhed] n (fig) figura decorativa
file [faɪl] n (tool) lima; (for nails) lima de uñas; (dossier) expediente; (folder) carpeta; (in cabinet) archivo; (Comput) fichero ▷ vt limar; (papers) clasificar; (Law: claim) presentar; (store) archivar; **to open/close a ~** (Comput) abrir/cerrar un fichero; **to ~ in/out** vi entrar/salir en fila; **to ~ a suit against sb** entablar pleito contra algn; **to ~ past** desfilar ante
filing ['faɪlɪŋ] n: **to do the ~** llevar los archivos
filing cabinet n fichero, archivo
fill [fɪl] vt llenar; (tooth) empastar; (vacancy) cubrir ▷ n: **to eat one's ~** comer hasta hartarse; **we've already ~ed that vacancy** ya hemos cubierto esa vacante; **~ed with admiration**

(for) lleno de admiración (por)
▸ **fill in** vt rellenar; (details, report) completar; **to ~ sb in on sth** (col) poner a algn al corriente or al día sobre algo
▸ **fill out** vt (form, receipt) rellenar
▸ **fill up** vt llenar (hasta el borde) ▷ vi (Aut) echar gasolina
fillet ['fɪlɪt] n filete
fillet steak n filete de ternera
filling ['fɪlɪŋ] n (Culin) relleno; (for tooth) empaste
filling station n estación de servicio
fillip ['fɪlɪp] n estímulo
film [fɪlm] n película ▷ vt (scene) filmar ▷ vi rodar
film star n estrella de cine
Filofax® ['faɪləʊfæks] n agenda (profesional)
filter ['fɪltər] n filtro ▷ vt filtrar
▸ **filter in, filter through** vi filtrarse
filter lane n (Brit) carril de selección
filter-tipped ['fɪltətɪpt] adj con filtro
filth [fɪlθ] n suciedad
filthy ['fɪlθɪ] adj sucio; (language) obsceno
fin [fɪn] n (gen) aleta
final ['faɪnl] adj (last) final, último; (definitive) definitivo ▷ n (Sport) final; **finals** npl (Scol) exámenes finales; **~ demand** (on invoice etc) último aviso; **~ dividend** dividendo final
finale [fɪ'nɑːlɪ] n final
finalist ['faɪnəlɪst] n (Sport) finalista
finalize ['faɪnəlaɪz] vt ultimar
finally ['faɪnəlɪ] adv (lastly) por último, finalmente; (eventually) por fin; (irrevocably) de modo definitivo; (once and for all) definitivamente
finance [faɪ'næns] n (money, funds) fondos ▷ cpd (page, section, company) financiero ▷ vt financiar; **finances** npl finanzas
financial [faɪ'nænʃəl] adj financiero
financial year n ejercicio (financiero)
find [faɪnd] vt (pt, pp **found**) (gen) encontrar, hallar; (come upon) descubrir ▷ n hallazgo; descubrimiento; **I can't ~ the exit** no encuentro la salida; **to ~ sb guilty** (Law) declarar culpable a algn; **I ~ it easy** me resulta fácil
▸ **find out** vt averiguar; (truth, secret) descubrir ▷ vi: **to ~ out about** enterarse de; **I found out that she had been lying** descubrí or me enteré que había estado mintiendo; **~ out as much as possible about the town** entérate de todo lo que puedas sobre la ciudad
findings ['faɪndɪŋz] npl (Law) veredicto, fallo; (of report) recomendaciones
fine [faɪn] adj (delicate) fino; (beautiful) hermoso ▷ adv (well) bien ▷ n (Law) multa ▷ vt (Law) multar; **she's got very ~ hair** tiene el pelo muy fino; **the weather is ~** hace buen tiempo; **he's a ~ musician** es un músico estupendo; **how are you?** — **I'm ~** ¿qué tal estás? — bien; **I feel ~** me siento bien; **it'll be ready tomorrow** — **that's ~, thanks** mañana estará listo — muy bien, gracias; **you're doing ~** lo estás haciendo muy bien; **to cut it ~** (of time, money) calcular muy justo; **to get a ~ for (doing) sth** recibir una

multa por (hacer) algo; **I got a ~ for driving through a red light** me pusieron una multa por saltarme un semáforo en rojo

fine arts *npl* bellas artes

fine print *n*: **the ~** la letra pequeña *or* menuda

finery ['faɪnərɪ] *n* galas

finger ['fɪŋgə^r] *n* dedo ▷ *vt* (*touch*) manosear; (*Mus*) puntear; **little/index ~** (dedo) meñique/índice

fingernail ['fɪŋgəneɪl] *n* uña

fingerprint ['fɪŋgəprɪnt] *n* huella dactilar ▷ *vt* tomar las huellas dactilares de

fingertip ['fɪŋgətɪp] *n* yema del dedo; **to have sth at one's ~s** saberse algo al dedillo

finicky ['fɪnɪkɪ] *adj* (*fussy*) delicado

finish ['fɪnɪʃ] *n* (*end*) fin; (*Sport*) meta; (*polish etc*) acabado ▷ *vt, vi* acabar, terminar; **to ~ doing sth** acabar de hacer algo; **to ~ first/second/ third** (*Sport*) llegar el primero/segundo/tercero; **I've ~ed with the paper** he terminado con el periódico; **she's ~ed with him** ha roto *or* acabado con él
  ▶ **finish off** *vt* acabar, terminar; (*kill*) rematar
  ▶ **finish up** *vt* acabar, terminar ▷ *vi* ir a parar, terminar

finishing line *n* línea de llegada *or* meta

finishing school *n* colegio para la educación social de señoritas

finite ['faɪnaɪt] *adj* finito

Finland ['fɪnlənd] *n* Finlandia

Finn [fɪn] *n* finlandés(-esa)

Finnish ['fɪnɪʃ] *adj* finlandés(-esa) ▷ *n* (*Ling*) finlandés

fir [fə:^r] *n* abeto

fire ['faɪə^r] *n* fuego; (*accidental, damaging*) incendio ▷ *vt* (*gun*) disparar; (*set fire to*) incendiar; (*excite*) exaltar; (*interest*) despertar; (*dismiss*) despedir ▷ *vi* encenderse; (*Aut: subj: engine*) encender; **electric/ gas ~** estufa eléctrica/de gas; **on ~** ardiendo, en llamas; **to be on ~** estar ardiendo; **to catch ~** prenderse fuego; **to set ~ to sth, set sth on ~** prender fuego a algo; **insured against ~** asegurado contra incendios; **to be/come under ~** estar/caer bajo el fuego enemigo

fire alarm *n* alarma de incendios

firearm ['faɪərɑ:m] *n* arma de fuego

fire brigade, (*US*) **fire department** *n* (cuerpo de) bomberos

fire door *n* puerta contra incendios

fire engine *n* coche de bomberos

fire escape *n* escalera de incendios

fire extinguisher *n* extintor

fireman ['faɪəmən] *n* bombero

fireplace ['faɪəpleɪs] *n* chimenea

fireplug ['faɪəplʌg] *n* (*US*) boca de incendios

fireproof ['faɪəpru:f] *adj* a prueba de fuego; (*material*) incombustible

fireside ['faɪəsaɪd] *n*: **by the ~** al lado de la chimenea

fire station *n* parque de bomberos

firewood ['faɪəwud] *n* leña

fireworks ['faɪəwə:ks] *npl* fuegos artificiales

firing squad *n* pelotón de ejecución

firm [fə:m] *adj* firme; (*offer, decision*) en firme ▷ *n* empresa; **to be ~ with sb** mostrarse firme con algn; **a ~ mattress** un colchón duro; **to be a ~ believer in sth** ser un partidario convencido de algo; **to stand ~ or take a ~ stand on sth** (*fig*) mantenerse firme ante algo

first [fə:st] *adj* primero ▷ *adv* (*before others*) primero; (*when listing reasons etc*) en primer lugar, primeramente ▷ *n* (*person: in race*) primero(-a); (*Aut: also*: **first gear**) primera; **for the ~ time** por primera vez; **in the ~ instance** en primer lugar; **I'll do it ~ thing tomorrow** lo haré mañana a primera hora; **Rachel came ~ in the race** Rachel quedó primera en la carrera; **at ~** al principio; **~ of all** ante todo; **I want to get a job, but ~ I have to pass my exams** quiero conseguir un trabajo, pero antes tengo que aprobar los exámenes; **head ~** de cabeza; **the ~ of January** el uno *or* primero de enero; **she was the ~ to arrive** fue la primera en llegar; **from the (very) ~** desde el principio

first aid *n* primeros auxilios

first aid kit *n* botiquín

first-class ['fə:stklɑ:s] *adj* de primera clase; **~ ticket** (*Rail etc*) billete *or* (*LAm*) boleto de primera clase; **~ mail** correo de primera clase

first-hand [fə:st'hænd] *adj* de primera mano

first lady *n* (*esp US*) primera dama

firstly ['fə:stlɪ] *adv* en primer lugar

first name *n* nombre de pila

first-rate [fə:st'reɪt] *adj* de primera (clase)

first-time buyer [fə:sttaɪm-] *n* persona que compra su primera vivienda

fish [fɪʃ] *n* (*pl inv*) pez; (*food*) pescado ▷ *vt* pescar en ▷ *vi* pescar; **to go ~ing** ir de pesca
  ▶ **fish out** *vt* (*from water, box etc*) sacar

fish-and-chip shop *n* = **chip shop**

fisherman ['fɪʃəmən] *n* pescador

fish farm *n* piscifactoría

fish fingers *npl* (*Brit*) palitos de pescado (empanado)

fishing boat ['fɪʃɪŋ-] *n* barca de pesca

fishing industry *n* industria pesquera

fishing line *n* sedal

fishing net *n* red de pesca

fishing rod *n* caña (de pescar)

fishmonger ['fɪʃmʌŋgə^r] *n* (*Brit*) pescadero(-a)

fishmonger's (shop) *n* (*Brit*) pescadería

fish sticks *npl* (*US*) = **fish fingers**

fishy ['fɪʃɪ] *adj* (*fig*) sospechoso

fist [fɪst] *n* puño

fit [fɪt] *adj* (*Med, Sport*) en (buena) forma; (*proper*) adecuado, apropiado ▷ *vt* (*subj: clothes*) quedar bien a; (*try on: clothes*) probar; (*match: facts*) cuadrar *or* corresponder *or* coincidir con; (: *description*) estar de acuerdo con; (*accommodate*) ajustar, adaptar; (*install*) instalar; (*attach*) poner ▷ *vi* (*clothes*) quedar bien; (*in space, gap*) caber; (*facts*) coincidir ▷ *n* (*Med*) ataque; (*outburst*) arranque; **~ to** apto para; **~ for** apropiado para; **do as you think** *or* **see ~** haz lo que te parezca mejor; **to keep ~** mantenerse en forma; **to be ~ for work** (*after illness*) estar en condiciones para trabajar; **will he be ~ to play next Saturday?** ¿estará en condiciones de jugar el próximo sábado?; **he can't find shirts to ~ him** no encuentra camisas que le queden bien; **your story doesn't ~ the facts** tu historia no se corresponde con los factos; **he ~ted an alarm in his car** instaló una alarma en el coche; **she ~ted a plug to the hair dryer** le puso un enchufe al secador; **the dress doesn't ~ very well** el vestido no le queda muy bien; **it's small enough to ~ into your pocket** es lo bastante pequeño como para que le quepa en el bolsillo; **~ of coughing** acceso de tos; **~ of anger/enthusiasm** arranque de cólera/entusiasmo; **to have** or **suffer a ~** tener un ataque o acceso; **my Mum will have a ~ when she sees the carpet!** (*col*) ¡mi madre se va a poner hecha una furia cuando vea la moqueta!; **this dress is a good ~** este vestido me queda bien; **by ~s and starts** a rachas

▶ **fit in** *vi* encajar ▷ *vt* (*object*) acomodar; (*fig: appointment, visitor*) encontrar un hueco para; **that story doesn't ~ in with what he told us** esa historia no encaja con lo que él nos contó; **to ~ in with sb's plans** acomodarse a los planes de algn; **she ~ted in well at her new school** se adaptó bien al nuevo colegio

▶ **fit out**, (*Brit*) **fit up** *vt* equipar

fitful ['fɪtfʊl] *adj* espasmódico, intermitente

fitment ['fɪtmənt] *n* mueble

fitness ['fɪtnɪs] *n* (*Med*) forma física

fitted carpet ['fɪtɪd-] *n* moqueta

fitted kitchen ['fɪtɪd-] *n* cocina amueblada

fitter ['fɪtəʳ] *n* ajustador(a)

fitting ['fɪtɪŋ] *adj* apropiado ▷ *n* (*of dress*) prueba; *see also* **fittings**

fitting room *n* (*in shop*) probador

fittings ['fɪtɪŋz] *npl* instalaciones

five [faɪv] *num* cinco; **she is ~ (years old)** tiene cinco años (de edad); **it costs ~ pounds** cuesta cinco libras; **it's ~ (o'clock)** son las cinco

fiver ['faɪvəʳ] *n* (*col: Brit*) billete de cinco libras; (*: US*) billete de cinco dólares

fix [fɪks] *vt* (*secure*) fijar, asegurar; (*mend*) arreglar; (*make ready: meal, drink*) preparar ▷ *n*: **to be in a ~** estar en un aprieto; **to ~ sth in one's mind** fijar algo en la memoria; **let's ~ a date for the party** vamos a fijar una fecha para la fiesta; **can you ~ my bike?** ¿me puedes arreglar la bici?; **the fight was a ~** (*col*) la pelea estaba amañada

▶ **fix on** *vt* (*decide on*) fijar

▶ **fix up** *vt* (*arrange: date, meeting*) arreglar; **to ~ sb up with sth** conseguirle algo a algn

fixation [fɪk'seɪʃən] *n* (*Psych, fig*) fijación

fixed [fɪkst] *adj* (*prices etc*) fijo; **how are you ~ for money?** (*col*) ¿qué tal andas de dinero?

fixture ['fɪkstʃəʳ] *n* (*Sport*) encuentro; **fixtures** *npl* instalaciones fijas

fizzle out ['fɪzl-] *vi* apagarse; (*enthusiasm, interest*) decaer; (*plan*) quedar en agua de borrajas

fizzy ['fɪzɪ] *adj* (*drink*) gaseoso

flabbergasted ['flæbəgɑːstɪd] *adj* pasmado

flabby ['flæbɪ] *adj* flojo (de carnes); (*skin*) fofo

flag [flæg] *n* bandera; (*stone*) losa ▷ *vi* decaer; **~ of convenience** pabellón de conveniencia

▶ **flag down** *vt*: **to ~ sb down** hacer señas a algn para que se pare

flagpole ['flægpəʊl] *n* asta de bandera

flagrant ['fleɪgrənt] *adj* flagrante

flagship ['flægʃɪp] *n* buque insignia *or* almirante

flair [fleəʳ] *n* aptitud especial

flak [flæk] *n* (*Mil*) fuego antiaéreo; (*col: criticism*) lluvia de críticas

flake [fleɪk] *n* (*of rust, paint*) desconchón; (*of snow*) copo; (*of soapff*) escama ▷ *vi* (*also:* **flake off**: *paint*) desconcharse; (*skin*) descamarse

flamboyant [flæm'bɔɪənt] *adj* (*dress*) vistoso; (*person*) extravagante

flame [fleɪm] *n* llama; **to burst into ~s** incendiarse; **old ~** (*col*) antiguo amor

flamingo [flə'mɪŋgəʊ] *n* flamenco

flammable ['flæməbl] *adj* inflamable

flan [flæn] *n* (*Brit*) tarta

flank [flæŋk] *n* flanco; (*of person*) costado ▷ *vt* flanquear

flannel ['flænl] *n* (*Brit: also:* **face flannel**) toallita; (*fabric*) franela; **flannels** *npl* pantalones de franela

flap [flæp] *n* (*of pocket, envelope*) solapa; (*of table*) hoja (plegadiza); (*wing movement*) aletazo; (*Aviat*) flap ▷ *vt* (*wings*) batir ▷ *vi* (*sail, flag*) ondear

flare [fleəʳ] *n* llamarada; (*Mil*) bengala; (*in skirt etc*) vuelo

▶ **flare up** *vi* encenderse; (*fig: person*) encolerizarse; (*: revolt*) estallar

flash [flæʃ] *n* relámpago; (*also:* **news flash**) noticias de última hora; (*Phot*) flash; (*US: torch*) linterna ▷ *vt* (*light, headlights*) lanzar destellos con; (*torch*) encender ▷ *vi* destellar; **a ~ of lightning** un relámpago; **in a ~** en un santiamén; **~ of inspiration** ráfaga de inspiración; **a lorry driver ~ed him** un camionero le hizo señales con los faros; **they ~ed a torch in his face** le enfocaron una linterna en la cara; **to ~ sth about** (*fig, col: flaunt*) ostentar algo, presumir con algo; **he ~ed by** or **past** pasó como un rayo

flashbulb ['flæʃbʌlb] *n* bombilla de flash

flash cube *n* cubo de flash

flashlight ['flæʃlaɪt] *n* (*US: torch*) linterna

flashy ['flæʃɪ] *adj* (*pej*) ostentoso

flask [flɑːsk] *n* petaca; (*also:* **vacuum flask**) termo

flat [flæt] *adj* llano; (*smooth*) liso; (*tyre*) desinflado; (*battery*) descargado; (*beer*) sin gas; (*Mus: instrument*) desafinado ▷ *n* (*Brit: apartment*) piso (*Esp*), departamento (*LAm*), apartamento; (*Aut*) pinchazo; (*Mus*) bemol; **a ~ surface** una superficie llana; **~ shoes** zapatos bajos; **I've got a ~ tyre** tengo una rueda desinflada; **(to work) ~ out** (trabajar) a tope; **~ rate of pay** sueldo fijo

flatly ['flætlɪ] *adv* rotundamente, de plano

flatmate ['flætmeɪt] *n* compañero(-a) de piso

flat pack *n*: **it comes in a ~** viene en un paquete plano para su automontaje

flat-screen ['flætskri:n] *adj* de pantalla plana

flatten ['flætn] *vt* (*also*: **flatten out**) allanar; (*smooth out*) alisar; (*house, city*) arrasar

flatter ['flætə^r] *vt* adular, halagar; (*show to advantage*) favorecer

flattering ['flætərɪŋ] *adj* halagador(a); (*clothes etc*) que favorece, favorecedor(a)

flattery ['flætərɪ] *n* adulación

flaunt [flɔ:nt] *vt* ostentar, lucir

flavour, (*US*) **flavor** ['fleɪvə^r] *n* sabor, gusto ▷ *vt* sazonar, condimentar; **strawberry ~ed** con sabor a fresa

flavo(u)ring ['fleɪvərɪŋ] *n* (*in product*) aromatizante

flaw [flɔ:] *n* defecto

flawless ['flɔ:lɪs] *adj* intachable

flax [flæks] *n* lino

flaxen ['flæksən] *adj* muy rubio

flea [fli:] *n* pulga

fleck [flɛk] *n* mota ▷ *vt* (*with blood, mud etc*) salpicar; **brown ~ed with white** marrón con motas blancas

flee [fli:] (*pt, pp* **fled**) [flɛd] *vt* huir de, abandonar ▷ *vi* huir

fleece [fli:s] *n* (*of sheep*) vellón; (*wool*) lana; (*top*) forro polar ▷ *vt* (*col*) desplumar

fleet [fli:t] *n* flota; (*of cars, lorries etc*) parque

fleeting ['fli:tɪŋ] *adj* fugaz

Flemish ['flɛmɪʃ] *adj* flamenco ▷ *n* (*Ling*) flamenco; **the ~** los flamencos

flesh [flɛʃ] *n* carne; (*of fruit*) pulpa; **of ~ and blood** de carne y hueso

flesh wound *n* herida superficial

flew [flu:] *pt of* **fly**

flex [flɛks] *n* cable ▷ *vt* (*muscles*) tensar

flexibility [flɛksɪ'bɪlɪtɪ] *n* flexibilidad

flexible ['flɛksəbl] *adj* (*gen, disk*) flexible; **~ working hours** horario flexible

flexitime ['flɛksɪtaɪm] *n* horario flexible

flick [flɪk] *n* golpecito; (*with finger*) capirotazo; (*Brit: col: film*) película ▷ *vt* dar un golpecito a
▶ **flick off** *vt* quitar con el dedo
▶ **flick through** *vt fus* hojear

flicker ['flɪkə^r] *vi* (*light*) parpadear; (*flame*) vacilar ▷ *n* parpadeo

flier ['flaɪə^r] *n* aviador(a)

flies [flaɪz] *npl of* **fly**

flight [flaɪt] *n* vuelo; (*escape*) huida, fuga; (*also*: **flight of steps**) tramo (de escaleras); **to take ~** huir, darse a la fuga; **to put to ~** ahuyentar; **how long is the ~?** ¿cuánto dura el vuelo?

flight attendant *n* (*US*) auxiliar de vuelo

flight deck *n* (*Aviat*) cabina de mandos

flight path *n* trayectoria de vuelo

flight recorder *n* registrador de vuelo

flimsy ['flɪmzɪ] *adj* (*thin*) muy ligero; (*excuse*) flojo

flinch [flɪntʃ] *vi* encogerse

fling [flɪŋ] *vt* (*pt, pp* **flung**) arrojar ▷ *n* (*love affair*) aventura amorosa

flint [flɪnt] *n* pedernal; (*in lighter*) piedra

flip [flɪp] *vt*: **to ~ a coin** echar a cara o cruz
▶ **flip over** *vt* dar la vuelta a
▶ **flip through** *vt fus* (*book*) hojear; (*records*) ver de pasada

flippant ['flɪpənt] *adj* poco serio

flipper ['flɪpə^r] *n* (*of seal etc, for swimming*) aleta

flirt [flə:t] *vi* coquetear, flirtear ▷ *n* coqueta

flit [flɪt] *vi* revolotear

float [fləut] *n* flotador; (*in procession*) carroza; (*sum of money*) (dinero suelto para) cambio ▷ *vi* (*Comm: currency*) flotar ▷ *vt* (*gen*) hacer flotar; (*company*) lanzar; **to ~ an idea** plantear una idea

flock [flɔk] *n* (*of sheep*) rebaño; (*of birds*) bandada; (*of people*) multitud

flog [flɔg] *vt* azotar; (*col*) vender

flood [flʌd] *n* inundación; (*of words, tears etc*) torrente ▷ *vt* (*also Aut: carburettor*) inundar; **to ~ the market** (*Comm*) inundar el mercado

flooding ['flʌdɪŋ] *n* inundación

floodlight ['flʌdlaɪt] *n* foco ▷ *vt* (*irreg: like* **light**) iluminar con focos

floodwater ['flʌdwɔ:tə^r] *n* aguas (de la inundación)

floor [flɔ:^r] *n* suelo, piso (*LAm*); (*storey*) piso; (*of sea, valley*) fondo; (*dance floor*) pista ▷ *vt* (*fig: baffle*) dejar anonadado; **ground ~** (*US*): **first ~** planta baja; **first ~** (*US*): **second ~** primer piso; **top ~** último piso; **to have the ~** (*speaker*) tener la palabra

floorboard ['flɔ:bɔ:d] *n* tabla

floor show *n* cabaret

flop [flɔp] *n* fracaso ▷ *vi* (*fail*) fracasar

floppy ['flɔpɪ] *adj* flojo ▷ *n* = **floppy disk**

floppy disk *n* (*Comput*) floppy, floppy-disk, disco flexible

flora ['flɔ:rə] *n* flora

floral ['flɔ:rl] *adj* floral; (*dress, wallpaper*) de flores

florid ['flɔrɪd] *adj* (*style*) florido

florist ['flɔrɪst] *n* florista; **~'s (shop)** *n* floristería

flotation [fləu'teɪʃən] *n* (*of shares*) emisión; (*of company*) lanzamiento

flounce [flauns] *n* volante
▶ **flounce in** *vi* entrar con gesto exagerado
▶ **flounce out** *vi* salir con gesto airado

flounder ['flaundə^r] *vi* tropezar ▷ *n* (*Zool*) platija

flour ['flauə^r] *n* harina

flourish ['flʌrɪʃ] *vi* florecer ▷ *n* ademán, movimiento (ostentoso)

flout [flaut] *vt* burlarse de; (*order*) no hacer caso de, hacer caso omiso de

flow [fləu] *n* (*movement*) flujo; (*direction*) curso; (*Elec*) corriente ▷ *vi* correr, fluir

flow chart *n* organigrama

flower ['flauə^r] *n* flor ▷ *vi* florecer; **in ~** en flor

flower bed *n* macizo

flowerpot ['flauəpɔt] *n* tiesto

flowery ['flauərɪ] *adj* florido; (*perfume, pattern*) de flores

flown [fləun] *pp of* **fly**

flu [flu:] *n* gripe

fluctuate ['flʌktjueɪt] *vi* fluctuar

fluency ['flu:ənsɪ] *n* fluidez, soltura

fluent ['flu:ənt] *adj* (*speech*) elocuente; **he speaks**

~ **French, he's ~ in French** domina el francés

fluently ['flu:əntlɪ] *adv* con soltura

fluff [flʌf] *n* pelusa

fluffy ['flʌfɪ] *adj* lanoso

fluid ['flu:ɪd] *adj*, *n* fluido, líquido; (*in diet*) líquido

fluke [flu:k] *n* (*col*) chiripa

flung [flʌŋ] *pt*, *pp* of **fling**

fluoride ['fluəraɪd] *n* fluoruro

fluoride toothpaste *n* pasta de dientes con flúor

flurry ['flʌrɪ] *n* (*of snow*) ventisca; (*haste*) agitación; **~ of activity** frenesí de actividad

flush [flʌʃ] *n* (*on face*) rubor; (*fig: of youth, beauty*) resplandor ▷ *vt* limpiar con agua; (*also*: **flush out**: *game, birds*) levantar; (*fig: criminal*) poner al descubierto ▷ *vi* ruborizarse ▷ *adj*: **~ with** a ras de; **hot ~es** (*Med*) sofocos; **to ~ the toilet** tirar de la cadena (del wáter)

flushed [flʌʃt] *adj* ruborizado

flustered ['flʌstəd] *adj* aturdido

flute [flu:t] *n* flauta travesera

flutter ['flʌtəʳ] *n* (*of wings*) revoloteo, aleteo; (*col: bet*) apuesta ▷ *vi* revolotear; **to be in a ~** estar nervioso

flux [flʌks] *n* flujo; **in a state of ~** cambiando continuamente

fly [flaɪ] *n* (*insect*) mosca; (*on trousers: also*: **flies**) bragueta ▷ *vb* (*pt* **flew**, *pp* **flown**) ▷ *vt* (*plane*) pilotar; (*cargo*) transportar (en avión); (*distance*) recorrer (en avión) ▷ *vi* volar; (*passenger*) ir en avión; (*escape*) evadirse; (*flag*) ondear; **do you ~ often?** ¿viajas mucho en avión?

▶ **fly away** *vi* (*bird, insect*) irse volando

▶ **fly in** *vi* (*person*) llegar en avión; (*plane*) aterrizar; **he flew in from Bilbao** llegó en avión desde Bilbao

▶ **fly off** *vi* irse volando

▶ **fly out** *vi* irse en avión

flying ['flaɪɪŋ] *n* (*activity*) (el) volar ▷ *adj*: **~ visit** visita relámpago; **with ~ colours** con lucimiento

flying picket *n* piquete volante

flying saucer *n* platillo volante

flying squad *n* (*Police*) brigada móvil

flying start *n*: **to get off to a ~** empezar con buen pie

flyover ['flaɪəuvəʳ] *n* (*Brit: bridge*) paso elevado *or* (*LAm*) a desnivel

flysheet ['flaɪʃi:t] *n* (*for tent*) doble techo

flyweight ['flaɪweɪt] *adj* de peso mosca ▷ *n* peso mosca

FM *abbr* (*Brit Mil*) = **field marshal**; (*Radio*: = *frequency modulation*) FM

FO *n abbr* (*Brit*: = *Foreign Office*) ≈ Min. de AA. EE.

foal [fəul] *n* potro

foam [fəum] *n* espuma ▷ *vi* hacer espuma

fob [fɔb] *n* (*also*: **watch fob**) leontina ▷ *vt*: **to ~ sb off with sth** deshacerse de algn con algo

focal ['fəukəl] *adj* focal; **~ point** punto focal; (*fig*) centro de atención

focus ['fəukəs] (*pl* **-es**) *n* foco ▷ *vt* (*field glasses etc*) enfocar ▷ *vi*: **to ~ (on)** enfocar (a); (*issue etc*)

centrarse en; **in/out of ~** enfocado/desenfocado

fodder ['fɔdəʳ] *n* pienso

foe [fəu] *n* enemigo

foetus, (*US*) **fetus** ['fi:təs] *n* feto

fog [fɔg] *n* niebla

foggy ['fɔgɪ] *adj*: **it's ~** hay niebla

fog lamp, (*US*) **fog light** *n* (*Aut*) faro antiniebla

foil [fɔɪl] *vt* frustrar ▷ *n* hoja; (*kitchen foil*) papel (de) aluminio; (*Fencing*) florete

fold [fəuld] *n* (*bend, crease*) pliegue; (*Agr*) redil ▷ *vt* doblar; (*map etc*) plegar; **to ~ one's arms** cruzarse de brazos

▶ **fold up** *vi* plegarse, doblarse; (*business*) quebrar

folder ['fəuldəʳ] *n* (*for papers*) carpeta; (*binder*) carpeta de anillas; (*brochure*) folleto

folding ['fəuldɪŋ] *adj* (*chair, bed*) plegable

foliage ['fəulɪɪdʒ] *n* follaje

folk [fəuk] *npl* gente ▷ *adj* popular, folklórico; **folks** *npl* familia, parientes

folklore ['fəuklɔ:ʳ] *n* folklore

folk music *n* música folk

folk singer *n* cantante de música folk

folk song *n* canción popular *or* folk

follow ['fɔləu] *vt* seguir ▷ *vi* seguir; (*result*) resultar; **he ~ed suit** hizo lo mismo; **to ~ sb's advice** seguir el consejo de algn; **I don't quite ~ you** no te comprendo muy bien; **you go first and I'll ~** ve tú primero y yo te sigo; **to ~ in sb's footsteps** seguir los pasos de algn; **it doesn't ~ that ...** no se deduce que ....

▶ **follow on** *vi* seguir; (*continue*): **to ~ on from** ser la consecuencia lógica de

▶ **follow out** *vt* (*implement: idea, plan*) realizar, llevar a cabo

▶ **follow through** *vt* llevar hasta el fin ▷ *vi* (*Sport*) dar el remate

▶ **follow up** *vt* (*letter, offer*) responder a; (*case*) investigar

follower ['fɔləuəʳ] *n* seguidor(a); (*Pol*) partidario(-a)

following ['fɔləuɪŋ] *adj* siguiente ▷ *n* seguidores

follow-up ['fɔləuʌp] *n* continuación

folly ['fɔlɪ] *n* locura

fond [fɔnd] *adj* (*loving*) cariñoso; **to be ~ of sb** tener cariño a algn; **she's ~ of swimming** tiene afición a la natación, le gusta nadar

fondle ['fɔndl] *vt* acariciar

font [fɔnt] *n* pila bautismal

food [fu:d] *n* comida

food chain *n* cadena alimenticia

food mixer *n* batidora

food poisoning *n* intoxicación alimentaria

food processor *n* robot de cocina

food stamp *n* (*US*) vale para comida

foodstuffs ['fu:dstʌfs] *npl* comestibles

fool [fu:l] *n* tonto(-a); (*Culin*) mousse de frutas ▷ *vt* engañar; **to make a ~ of o.s.** ponerse en ridículo; **you can't ~ me** a mí no me engañas; *see also* **April Fool's Day**

▶ **fool about, fool around** *vi* hacer el tonto

foolhardy ['fu:lhɑ:dɪ] *adj* temerario

foolish ['fu:lɪʃ] *adj* tonto; (*careless*) imprudente

foolproof ['fu:lpru:f] *adj* (*plan etc*) infalible

foot [fut] (*pl* **feet**) *n* (*gen, also of page, stairs etc*) pie; (*measure*) pie (= 30,48 *cm*); (*of animal, table*) pata ▷ *vt* (*bill*) pagar; **my feet are aching** me duelen los pies; **on ~ a** pie; **to find one's feet** acostumbrarse; **to put one's ~ down** (*say no*) plantarse; (*Aut*) pisar el acelerador; **he is 6 ~ tall** mide un metro ochenta

footage ['futɪdʒ] *n* (*Cine*) imágenes

football ['futbɔ:l] *n* balón; (*game: Brit*) fútbol; (: *US*) fútbol americano

footballer ['futbɔ:lə^r] *n* (*Brit*) = **football player**

football match *n* partido de fútbol

football player *n* futbolista, jugador(a) de fútbol

footbrake ['futbreɪk] *n* freno de pie

footbridge ['futbrɪdʒ] *n* pasarela, puente para peatones

foothills ['futhɪlz] *npl* estribaciones

foothold ['futhəuld] *n* pie firme

footing ['futɪŋ] *n* (*fig*) nivel; **to lose one's ~** perder el equilibrio; **on an equal ~** en pie de igualdad

footlights ['futlaɪts] *npl* candilejas

footman ['futmən] *n* lacayo

footnote ['futnəut] *n* nota (de pie de página)

footpath ['futpɑ:θ] *n* sendero

footprint ['futprɪnt] *n* huella, pisada

footsie ['futsɪ] *n*: **to play ~ with sb** (*col*) juguetear con los pies de algn

footstep ['futstɛp] *n* paso

footwear ['futwɛə^r] *n* calzado

for [fɔ:] *prep* **1** (*indicating destination, intention*) para; **the train ~ London** el tren para Londres; (*in announcements*) el tren con destino a Londres; **he left ~ Rome** marchó para Roma; **he went ~ the paper** fue por el periódico; **is this ~ me?** ¿es esto para mí?; **it's time ~ lunch** es la hora de comer **2** (*indicating purpose*) para; **what's it ~?** ¿para qué (es)?; **what's this button ~?** ¿para qué sirve este botón?; **to pray ~ peace** rezar por la paz **3** (*on behalf of, representing*): **the MP ~ Hove** el diputado por Hove; **he works ~ the government/a local firm** trabaja para el gobierno/en una empresa local; **I'll ask him ~ you** se lo pediré por ti; **G ~ George** G de Gerona **4** (*because of*) por esta razón; **~ fear of being criticized** por temor a ser criticado **5** (*with regard to*) para; **it's cold ~ July** hace frío para julio; **he has a gift ~ languages** tiene don de lenguas **6** (*in exchange for*) por; **I sold it ~ £5** lo vendí por 5 libras; **to pay 50 pence ~ a ticket** pagar 50 peniques por un billete **7** (*in favour of*): **are you ~ or against us?** ¿estás con nosotros o contra nosotros?; **I'm all ~ it** estoy totalmente a favor; **vote ~ X** vote (a) X **8** (*referring to distance*): **there are roadworks ~ 5 km** hay obras en 5 km; **we walked ~ miles** caminamos kilómetros y kilómetros **9** (*referring to time*): **he was away ~ 2 years** estuvo fuera (durante) 2 años; **it hasn't rained ~ 3 weeks** no ha llovido durante *or* en 3 semanas; **I**

have known her ~ years la conozco desde hace años; **can you do it ~ tomorrow?** ¿lo podrás hacer para mañana? **10** (*with infinitive clauses*): **it is not ~ me to decide** la decisión no es cosa mía; **it would be best ~ you to leave** sería mejor que te fueras; **there is still time ~ you to do it** todavía te queda tiempo para hacerlo; **~ this to be possible ...** para que esto sea posible ... **11** (*in spite of*) a pesar de; **~ all his complaints** a pesar de sus quejas

▷ *conj* (*since, as: rather formal*) puesto que

forage ['fɔrɪdʒ] *n* forraje

foray ['fɔreɪ] *n* incursión

forbid [fə'bɪd] (*pt* **forbad(e)**, *pp* **-den**) [fə'bæd] [fə'bɪdn] *vt* prohibir; **to ~ sb to do sth** prohibir a algn hacer algo

forbidding [fə'bɪdɪŋ] *adj* (*landscape*) inhóspito; (*severe*) severo

force [fɔ:s] *n* fuerza ▷ *vt* obligar, forzar; **the F~s** *npl* (*Brit*) las Fuerzas Armadas; **UN ~s** las fuerzas de la ONU; **sales ~** (*Comm*) personal de ventas; **a ~ 5 wind** un viento fuerza 5; **to join ~s** unir fuerzas; **in ~** (*law etc*) en vigor; **to ~ sb to do sth** obligar a algn a hacer algo; **to ~ o.s. to do sth** hacer un esfuerzo por hacer algo

▶ **force back** *vt* (*crowd, enemy*) hacer retroceder; (*tears*) reprimir

▶ **force down** *vt* (*food*) tragar con esfuerzo

force-feed ['fɔ:sfi:d] *vt* (*animal, prisoner*) alimentar a la fuerza

forceful ['fɔ:sful] *adj* enérgico

forceps ['fɔ:sɛps] *npl* fórceps

forcibly ['fɔ:səblɪ] *adv* a la fuerza

ford [fɔ:d] *n* vado ▷ *vt* vadear

fore [fɔ:^r] *n*: **to bring to the ~** sacar a la luz pública; **to come to the ~** empezar a destacar

forearm ['fɔ:rɑ:m] *n* antebrazo

foreboding [fɔ:'bəudɪŋ] *n* presentimiento

forecast ['fɔ:kɑ:st] *n* pronóstico ▷ *vt* (*irreg: like* **cast**) pronosticar; **weather ~** previsión meteorológica

forecourt ['fɔ:kɔ:t] *n* (*of garage*) área de entrada

forefathers ['fɔ:fɑ:ðəz] *npl* antepasados

forefinger ['fɔ:fɪŋgə^r] *n* (dedo) índice

forefront ['fɔ:frʌnt] *n*: **in the ~ of** en la vanguardia de

forego [fɔ:'gəu] (*pt* **forewent**, *pp* **-ne**) *vt* = **forgo**

foregone ['fɔ:gɔn] *pp of* **forego** ▷ *adj*: **it's a ~ conclusion** es una conclusión inevitable

foreground ['fɔ:graund] *n* primer plano

forehand ['fɔ:hænd] *n* (*Tennis*) derechazo directo

forehead ['fɔrɪd] *n* frente

foreign ['fɔrɪn] *adj* extranjero; (*trade*) exterior

foreign currency *n* divisas

foreigner ['fɔrɪnə^r] *n* extranjero(-a)

foreign exchange *n* (*system*) cambio de divisas; (*money*) divisas, moneda extranjera

Foreign Minister *n* Ministro(-a) de Asuntos Exteriores, Canciller (*LAm*)

Foreign Office *n* Ministerio de Asuntos Exteriores

Foreign Secretary n (Brit) Ministro(-a) de
Asuntos Exteriores, Canciller (LAm)
foreleg ['fɔːlɛg] n pata delantera
foreman ['fɔːmən] n capataz; (Law: of jury)
presidente
foremost ['fɔːməʊst] adj principal ▷ adv: **first
and ~** ante todo, antes que nada
forename ['fɔːneɪm] n nombre (de pila)
forensic [fə'rɛnsɪk] adj forense; **~ scientist**
forense
foreplay ['fɔːpleɪ] n preámbulos (de estimulación
sexual)
forerunner ['fɔːrʌnər] n precursor(a)
foresee [fɔː'siː] (pt **foresaw**, pp -n) [fɔː'sɔː, fɔː'siːn]
vt prever
foreseeable [fɔː'siːəbl] adj previsible
foreshadow [fɔː'ʃædəʊ] vt prefigurar, anunciar
foresight ['fɔːsaɪt] n previsión
foreskin ['fɔːskɪn] n (Anat) prepucio
forest ['fɔrɪst] n bosque
forestall [fɔː'stɔːl] vt anticiparse a
forestry ['fɔrɪstrɪ] n silvicultura
foretaste ['fɔːteɪst] n anticipo
foretell [fɔː'tɛl] (pt, pp **foretold**) vt predecir,
pronosticar
forever [fə'rɛvər] adv siempre; (for good) para
siempre
forewent [fɔː'wɛnt] pt of **forego**
foreword ['fɔːwəːd] n prefacio
forfeit ['fɔːfɪt] n (in game) prenda ▷ vt perder
(derecho a)
forgave [fə'geɪv] pt of **forgive**
forge [fɔːdʒ] n fragua; (smithy) herrería ▷ vt
(signature: Brit: money) falsificar; (metal) forjar
▶ **forge ahead** vi avanzar mucho
forger ['fɔːdʒər] n falsificador(a)
forgery ['fɔːdʒərɪ] n falsificación
forget [fə'gɛt] (pt **forgot**, pp **forgotten**) vt olvidar,
olvidarse de ▷ vi olvidarse
forgetful [fə'gɛtful] adj olvidadizo
forget-me-not [fə'gɛtmɪnɒt] n nomeolvides
forgive [fə'gɪv] (pt **forgave**, pp -n) [fə'geɪv]
[fə'gɪvn] vt perdonar; **to ~ sb for sth/for doing
sth** perdonar algo a algn/a algn por haber hecho
algo
forgiveness [fə'gɪvnɪs] n perdón
forgo [fɔː'gəʊ] (pt **forwent**, pp -ne) [fɔː'wɛnt]
[fɔː'gɒn] vt (give up) renunciar a; (go without)
privarse de
forgot [fə'gɒt] pt of **forget**
forgotten [fə'gɒtn] pp of **forget**
fork [fɔːk] n (for eating) tenedor; (for gardening)
horca; (of roads) bifurcación; (in tree) horcadura
▷ vi (road) bifurcarse
▶ **fork out** vt (col: pay) soltar
fork-lift truck ['fɔːklɪft-] n máquina elevadora
forlorn [fə'lɔːn] adj (person) triste, melancólico;
(deserted: cottage) abandonado; (desperate: attempt)
desesperado
form [fɔːm] n forma; (Brit Scol) curso; (document)
formulario, planilla (LAm) ▷ vt formar; **in the
~ of** en forma de; **in top ~** en plena forma; **to**

be in good ~ (Sport, fig) estar en plena forma;
I'm against hunting in any ~ estoy en contra
de cualquier forma de caza; **she's in the first
~** está haciendo primero de secundaria; **to fill
in a ~** rellenar un formulario; **to ~ part of sth**
formar parte de algo; **to ~ a circle/a queue**
hacer una curva/una cola
formal ['fɔːml] adj (offer, receipt) por escrito;
(person etc) correcto; (occasion, dinner) ceremonioso;
~ dress traje de vestir; (evening dress) traje de
etiqueta
formalities [fɔː'mælɪtɪz] npl formalidades
formality [fɔː'mælɪtɪ] n ceremonia
formally ['fɔːməlɪ] adv oficialmente
format ['fɔːmæt] n formato ▷ vt (Comput)
formatear
formation [fɔː'meɪʃən] n formación
formative ['fɔːmətɪv] adj (years) de formación
former ['fɔːmər] adj anterior; (earlier) antiguo;
(ex) ex; **the ~ ... the latter ...** aquél ... éste ...;
the ~ president el antiguo or ex presidente;
the ~ Yugoslavia/Soviet Union la antigua or
ex Yugoslavia/Unión Soviética; **a ~ pupil** un
antiguo alumno
formerly ['fɔːməlɪ] adv antiguamente
formidable ['fɔːmɪdəbl] adj formidable
formula ['fɔːmjulə] n fórmula; **F~ One** (Aut)
Fórmula Uno
forsake [fə'seɪk] (pt **forsook**, pp -n) [fə'suk]
[fə'seɪkən] vt (gen) abandonar; (plan) renunciar a
fort [fɔːt] n fuerte; **to hold the ~** (fig) quedarse
a cargo
forte ['fɔːtɪ] n fuerte
forth [fɔːθ] adv: **back and ~** de acá para allá; **and
so ~** y así sucesivamente
forthcoming [fɔːθ'kʌmɪŋ] adj próximo,
venidero; (character) comunicativo
forthright ['fɔːθraɪt] adj franco
forthwith ['fɔːθ'wɪθ] adv en el acto, acto seguido
fortify ['fɔːtɪfaɪ] vt fortalecer
fortitude ['fɔːtɪtjuːd] n fortaleza
fortnight ['fɔːtnaɪt] n (Brit) quincena; **it's a ~
since ...** hace quince días que ...
fortnightly ['fɔːtnaɪtlɪ] adj quincenal ▷ adv
quincenalmente
fortress ['fɔːtrɪs] n fortaleza
fortunate ['fɔːtʃənɪt] adj: **it is ~ that ...** (es una)
suerte que ...
fortunately ['fɔːtʃənɪtlɪ] adv afortunadamente
fortune ['fɔːtʃən] n suerte; (wealth) fortuna; **to
make a ~** hacer un dineral
fortuneteller ['fɔːtʃəntɛlər] n adivino(-a)
forty ['fɔːtɪ] num cuarenta
forum ['fɔːrəm] n (also fig) foro
forward ['fɔːwəd] adj (position) avanzado;
(movement) hacia delante; (front) delantero; (not
shy) atrevido ▷ n (Sport) delantero ▷ vt (letter)
remitir; (career) promocionar; **to look ~** mirar
hacia delante; **to move ~** avanzar; **"please ~"**
"remítase al destinatario"
forward planning n planificación por
anticipado

forward(s) ['fɔ:wəd(z)] adv (hacia) adelante
forwent [fɔ:'wɛnt] pt of **forgo**
fossil ['fɔsl] n fósil; **~ fuel** combustible fósil
foster ['fɔstə'] vt (child) acoger en familia; (idea) fomentar
foster child n hijo(-a) adoptivo(-a)
fought [fɔ:t] pt, pp of **fight**
foul [faul] adj (gen) sucio, puerco; (weather, smell etc) asqueroso ▷ n (Football) falta ▷ vt (dirty) ensuciar; (block) atascar; (entangle: anchor, propeller) atascar, enredarse en; (football player) cometer una falta contra
foul play n (Sport) mala jugada; (Law) muerte violenta
found [faund] pt, pp of **find** ▷ vt (establish) fundar
foundation [faun'deɪʃən] n (act) fundación; (basis) base; (also: **foundation cream**) base de maquillaje
foundations [faun'deɪʃənz] npl (of building) cimientos; **to lay the ~** poner los cimientos
founder ['faundə'] n fundador(a) ▷ vi irse a pique
foundry ['faundrɪ] n fundición
fountain ['fauntɪn] n fuente
fountain pen n (pluma) estilográfica, pluma fuente (LAm)
four [fɔ:'] num cuatro; **on all ~s** a gatas
four-letter word ['fɔ:lɛtə-] n taco
four-poster ['fɔ:'pəustə'] n (also: **four-poster bed**) cama de columnas
foursome ['fɔ:səm] n grupo de cuatro personas
fourteen ['fɔ:'ti:n] num catorce
fourteenth [fɔ:'ti:nθ] adj decimocuarto
fourth [fɔ:θ] adj cuarto ▷ n (Aut: also: **fourth gear**) cuarta (velocidad)
four-wheel drive ['fɔ:wi:l-] n tracción a las cuatro ruedas
fowl [faul] n ave (de corral)
fox [fɔks] n zorro ▷ vt confundir
foyer ['fɔɪeɪ] n vestíbulo
FP n abbr (Brit) = **former pupil**; (US) = **fireplug**
Fr. abbr (Rel: = Father) P.; (= friar) Fr.
fracas ['fræka:] n gresca, refriega
fraction ['frækʃən] n fracción
fracture ['fræktʃə'] n fractura ▷ vt fracturar
fragile ['frædʒaɪl] adj frágil
fragment n fragmento ▷ vt fragmentar ▷ vi fragmentarse
fragrance ['freɪgrəns] n fragancia
fragrant ['freɪgrənt] adj fragante, oloroso
frail [freɪl] adj (fragile) frágil, quebradizo; (weak) delicado
frame [freɪm] n (Tech) armazón; (of picture, door etc) marco; (of spectacles: also: **frames**) montura ▷ vt encuadrar; (picture) enmarcar; (reply) formular; **to ~ sb** (col) inculpar por engaños a algn
frame of mind n estado de ánimo
framework ['freɪmwə:k] n marco
France [frɑ:ns] n Francia
franchise ['fræntʃaɪz] n (Pol) derecho al voto, sufragio; (Comm) licencia, concesión

frank [fræŋk] adj franco ▷ vt (Brit: letter) franquear
frankly ['fræŋklɪ] adv francamente
frankness ['fræŋknɪs] n franqueza
frantic ['fræntɪk] adj (desperate: need, desire) desesperado; (: search) frenético; (: person) desquiciado
fraternity [frə'tə:nɪtɪ] n (club) fraternidad; (US) club de estudiantes; (guild) gremio
fraud [frɔ:d] n fraude; (person) impostor(a)
fraught [frɔ:t] adj (tense) tenso; **~ with** cargado de
fray [freɪ] n combate, lucha, refriega ▷ vi deshilacharse; **tempers were ~ed** el ambiente se ponía tenso
freak [fri:k] n (person) fenómeno; (event) suceso anormal; (col: enthusiast) adicto(-a) ▷ adj (storm, conditions) anormal; **health ~** (col) maniático(-a) en cuestión de salud
  ▶ **freak out** vi (col: on drugs) flipar
freckle ['frɛkl] n peca
free [fri:] adj (person: at liberty) libre; (not fixed) suelto; (without charge) gratuito; (unoccupied) desocupado; (liberal) generoso ▷ vt (prisoner etc) poner en libertad; (jammed object) soltar; **to set ~** (prisoner) liberar; (animal) soltar; **to give sb a ~ hand** dar carta blanca a algn; **~ and easy** despreocupado; **~ of tax** libre de impuestos; **a ~ brochure** un folleto gratuito; **admission ~** entrada libre; **to get sth for ~** obtener algo gratis; **you can get it for ~** se puede conseguir gratis; **is this seat ~?** ¿está libre este asiento?; **are you ~ after school?** ¿estás libre después de clase?
freedom ['fri:dəm] n libertad; **~ of association** libertad de asociación
Freefone® ['fri:fəun] n (Brit) número gratuito
free-for-all ['fri:fərɔ:l] n riña general
free gift n regalo
freehold ['fri:həuld] n propiedad absoluta
free kick n tiro libre
freelance ['fri:lɑ:ns] adj, adv por cuenta propia; **to do ~ work** trabajar por su cuenta
freely ['fri:lɪ] adv libremente; (liberally) generosamente
free-market economy ['fri:'mɑ:kɪt-] n economía de libre mercado
freemason ['fri:meɪsn] n francmasón
freepost ['fri:pəust] n porte pagado
free-range ['fri:reɪndʒ] adj (hen, egg) de granja
free speech n libertad de expresión
free trade n libre comercio
freeway ['fri:weɪ] n (US) autopista
free will n libre albedrío; **of one's own ~** por su propia voluntad
freeze [fri:z] vb (pt **froze**, pp **frozen**) ▷ vi helarse, congelarse ▷ vt helar; (prices, food, salaries) congelar ▷ n helada; congelación
  ▶ **freeze over** vi (lake, river) helarse, congelarse; (window, windscreen) cubrirse de escarcha
  ▶ **freeze up** vi helarse, congelarse
freeze-dried ['fri:zdraɪd] adj liofilizado

freezer ['fri:zə^r] n congelador, congeladora
freezing ['fri:zɪŋ] adj helado
freezing point n punto de congelación; **3 degrees below ~** 3 grados bajo cero
freight [freɪt] n (goods) carga; (money charged) flete; **~ forward** contra reembolso del flete, flete por pagar; **~ inward** flete sobre compras
freight train n tren de mercancías
French [frɛntʃ] adj francés(-esa) ▷ n (Ling) francés; **the French** npl los franceses
French bean n judía verde (Esp), habichuela (LAm), ejote (CAm, Méx), chaucha (RP)
French bread n pan francés
French dressing n (Culin) vinagreta
French fried potatoes, (US) **French fries** npl patatas or (LAm) papas fritas
French loaf n barra de pan
Frenchman ['frɛntʃmən] n francés
French stick n barra de pan
French window n puertaventana
Frenchwoman ['frɛntʃwumən] n francesa
frenzy ['frɛnzɪ] n frenesí
frequency ['fri:kwənsɪ] n frecuencia
frequency modulation (FM) n frecuencia modulada
frequent adj frecuente ▷ vt frecuentar
frequently ['fri:kwəntlɪ] adv frecuentemente, a menudo
fresco ['frɛskəu] n fresco
fresh [frɛʃ] adj (gen) fresco; (new) nuevo; (water) dulce; **to make a ~ start** empezar de nuevo
freshen ['frɛʃən] vi (wind) arreciar; (air) refrescar
  ▸ **freshen up** vi (person) refrescarse
fresher ['frɛʃə^r] n (Brit Scol: col) estudiante de primer año
freshly ['frɛʃlɪ] adv: **~ painted/arrived** recién pintado/llegado
freshman ['frɛʃmən] n (US Scol) = **fresher**
freshness ['frɛʃnɪs] n frescura
freshwater ['frɛʃwɔ:tə^r] adj (fish) de agua dulce
fret [frɛt] vi inquietarse
FRG n abbr (= Federal Republic of Germany) RFA
friar ['fraɪə^r] n fraile; (before name) fray
friction ['frɪkʃən] n fricción
Friday ['fraɪdɪ] n viernes
fridge [frɪdʒ] n (Brit) nevera, frigo, refrigeradora (LAm), heladera (LAm)
fridge-freezer ['frɪdʒ'fri:zə^r] n frigorífico-congelador, combi
fried [fraɪd] pt, pp of **fry** ▷ adj: **~ egg** huevo frito, huevo estrellado
friend [frɛnd] n amigo(-a)
friendly ['frɛndlɪ] adj simpático
friendly fire n fuego amigo, disparos del propio bando
friendship ['frɛndʃɪp] n amistad
frieze [fri:z] n friso
fright [fraɪt] n susto; **to take ~** asustarse
frighten ['fraɪtn] vt asustar
  ▸ **frighten away**, **frighten off** vt (birds, children etc) espantar, ahuyentar
frightened ['fraɪtnd] adj asustado

frightening ['fraɪtnɪŋ] adj: **it's ~** da miedo
frightful ['fraɪtful] adj espantoso, horrible
frigid ['frɪdʒɪd] adj (Med) frígido
frill [frɪl] n volante; **without ~s** (fig) sin adornos
frilly ['frɪlɪ] adj con volantes
fringe [frɪndʒ] n (Brit: of hair) flequillo; (edge: of forest etc) borde, margen
fringe benefits npl ventajas complementarias
Frisbee® ['frɪzbɪ] n frisbee®
frisk [frɪsk] vt cachear, registrar
frisky ['frɪskɪ] adj juguetón(-ona)
fritter ['frɪtə^r] n buñuelo
  ▸ **fritter away** vt desperdiciar
frivolous ['frɪvələs] adj frívolo
frizzy ['frɪzɪ] adj crespo
fro [frəu] see **to**
frock [frɔk] n vestido
frog [frɔg] n rana; **to have a ~ in one's throat** tener carraspera
frogman ['frɔgmən] n hombre-rana
frolic ['frɔlɪk] vi juguetear
from [frɔm] prep **1** (indicating starting place) de, desde; **where do you come ~?**, **where are you ~?** ¿de dónde eres?; **where has he come ~?** ¿de dónde ha venido?; **~ London to Glasgow** de Londres a Glasgow; **to escape ~ sth/sb** escaparse de algo/algn
2 (indicating origin etc) de; **a letter/telephone call ~ my sister** una carta/llamada de mi hermana; **tell him ~ me that ...** dígale de mi parte que ...
3 (indicating time): **~ one o'clock to** or **until** or **till nine** de la una a las nueve, desde la una hasta las nueve; **~ January (on)** a partir de enero; **(as) ~ Friday** a partir del viernes
4 (indicating distance) de; **the hotel is 1 km ~ the beach** el hotel está a 1 km de la playa
5 (indicating price, number etc) de; **prices range ~ £10 to £50** los precios van desde £10 a or hasta £50; **the interest rate was increased ~ 9% to 10%** el tipo de interés fue incrementado de un 9% a un 10%
6 (indicating difference) de; **he can't tell red ~ green** no sabe distinguir el rojo del verde; **to be different ~ sb/sth** ser diferente a algn/algo
7 (because of, on the basis of): **~ what he says** por lo que dice; **weak ~ hunger** debilitado por el hambre

front [frʌnt] n (foremost part) parte delantera; (of house) fachada; (promenade: also: **sea front**) paseo marítimo; (Mil, Pol, Meteorology) frente; (fig: appearances) apariencia ▷ adj (wheel, leg) delantero; (row, line) primero ▷ vi: **to ~ onto sth** dar a algo; **the switch is at the ~ of the vacuum cleaner** el interruptor está en la parte delantera de la aspiradora; **the ~ of the dress** el delantero del vestido; **I was sitting in the ~** (of car) yo iba sentado delante; **at the ~ of the train** al principio del tren; **in ~** delante; **the car in ~** el coche de delante; **in ~ of** delante de; **Irene sits in ~ of me in class** Irene se sienta delante de mí en clase; **the ~ seats of the car** los asientos delanteros del coche; **the ~ door** la puerta principal; **the ~ row** la primera fila

frontage ['frʌntɪdʒ] n (of building) fachada

frontbencher ['frʌnt'bentʃər] n (Brit) see **front bench**

front door n puerta principal

frontier ['frʌntɪər] n frontera

front page n primera plana

front room n (Brit) salón, sala

front-wheel drive ['frʌntwiː-l-] n tracción delantera

frost [frɔst] n (gen) helada; (also: **hoarfrost**) escarcha ▷ vt (US Culin) escarchar

frostbite ['frɔstbaɪt] n congelación

frosted ['frɔstɪd] adj (glass) esmerilado; (esp US: cake) glaseado

frosty ['frɔstɪ] adj (surface) cubierto de escarcha; (welcome etc) glacial

froth [frɔθ] n espuma

frothy ['frɔθɪ] adj espumoso

frown [fraun] vi fruncir el ceño ▷ n: **with a ~** frunciendo el entrecejo

  ▶ **frown on** vt fus desaprobar

froze [frəuz] pt of **freeze**

frozen ['frəuzn] pp of **freeze** ▷ adj (food) congelado; (Comm): **~ assets** activos congelados or bloqueados

frugal ['fruːɡəl] adj (person) frugal

fruit [fruːt] n (pl inv) fruta

fruiterer ['fruːtərər] n frutero(-a); **~'s (shop)** frutería

fruit fly n mosca de la fruta

fruitful ['fruːtful] adj provechoso

fruition [fruːˈɪʃən] n: **to come to ~** realizarse

fruit juice n jugo or (Esp) zumo de fruta

fruitless ['fruːtlɪs] adj (fig) infructuoso, inútil

fruit machine n (Brit) máquina tragaperras

fruit salad n macedonia or (LAm) ensalada de frutas

frustrate [frʌsˈtreɪt] vt frustrar

frustrated [frʌsˈtreɪtɪd] adj frustrado

frustrating [frʌsˈtreɪtɪŋ] adj (job, day) frustrante

frustration [frʌsˈtreɪʃən] n frustración

fry [fraɪ] (pt, pp **fried**) vt freír ▷ n: **small ~** gente menuda

frying pan ['fraɪɪŋ-] n sartén

FT n abbr (Brit: = Financial Times) periódico financiero; **the FT index** el índice de valores del Financial Times

ft. abbr = **foot; feet**

FTSE 100 Index n abbr (= Financial Times Stock Exchange 100 Index) índice bursátil del Financial Times

fuddy-duddy ['fʌdɪdʌdɪ] (pej) n carcamal, carroza ▷ adj chapado a la antigua

fudge [fʌdʒ] n (Culin) caramelo blando ▷ vt (issue, problem) rehuir, esquivar

fuel [fjuəl] n (for heating) combustible; (coal) carbón; (wood) leña; (for engine) carburante ▷ vt (furnace etc) alimentar; (aircraft, ship etc) aprovisionar de combustible

fuel oil n fuel oil

fuel tank n depósito de combustible

fugitive ['fjuːdʒɪtɪv] n (from prison) fugitivo(-a)

fulfil, (US) **fulfill** [fulˈfɪl] vt (function)

desempeñar; (condition) cumplir; (wish, desire) realizar

fulfil(l)ment [fulˈfɪlmənt] n realización; (of promise) cumplimiento

full [ful] adj lleno; (fig) pleno; (complete) completo; (information) detallado; (price) íntegro, sin descuento ▷ adv: **~ well** perfectamente; **the tank's ~** el depósito está lleno; **there was a ~ moon** había luna llena; **we're ~ up for July** estamos completos para julio; **I'm ~ (up)** estoy lleno; **~ employment** pleno empleo; **~ name** nombre completo; **my ~ name is Ian John Marr** mi nombre completo es Ian John Marr; **~ board** la pensión completa; **a ~ two hours** dos horas enteras; **at ~ speed** a toda velocidad; **in ~** (reproduce, quote) íntegramente; **to write sth in ~** escribir algo por extenso; **to pay in ~** pagar la deuda entera

full-length ['fulˈleŋθ] adj (portrait) de cuerpo entero; (film) de largometraje

full moon n luna llena, plenilunio

full-scale ['fulskeɪl] adj (attack, war, search, retreat) en gran escala; (plan, model) de tamaño natural

full stop n punto

full-time ['fultaɪm] adj (work) de tiempo completo ▷ adv: **to work ~** trabajar a tiempo completo

fully ['fulɪ] adv completamente; (at least) al menos

fully-fledged ['fulɪˈfledʒd], (US) **full-fledged** adj (teacher, barrister) diplomado; (bird) con todas sus plumas, capaz de volar; (fig) de pleno derecho

fumble with ['fʌmbl-] vt fus manosear

fume [fjuːm] vi humear, echar humo

fumes [fjuːmz] npl humo, gases

fun [fʌn] n (amusement) diversión; (joy) alegría; **to have ~** divertirse; **for ~** por gusto; **to make ~ of** reírse de

function ['fʌŋkʃən] n función ▷ vi funcionar; **to ~ as** hacer (las veces) de, fungir de (LAm)

functional ['fʌŋkʃənl] adj funcional

fund [fʌnd] n fondo; (reserve) reserva; **funds** npl fondos

fundamental [fʌndəˈmentl] adj fundamental ▷ n: **~s** fundamentos

fundamentalism [fʌndəˈmentəlɪzəm] n fundamentalismo, integrismo

fundamentalist [fʌndəˈmentəlɪst] n fundamentalista, integrista

funding ['fʌndɪŋ] n financiación

fund-raising ['fʌndreɪzɪŋ] n recaudación de fondos

funeral ['fjuːnərəl] n (burial) entierro; (ceremony) funerales

funeral director n director(a) de pompas fúnebres

funeral parlour n (Brit) funeraria

funeral service n misa de cuerpo presente

funfair ['fʌnfɛər] n (Brit) parque de atracciones; (travelling) feria

fungus ['fʌŋɡəs] (pl **fungi**) n hongo

funky ['fʌŋkɪ] adj (music) funky; (col: good) guay

funnel ['fʌnl] n embudo; (of ship) chimenea
funny ['fʌnɪ] adj gracioso, divertido; (strange) curioso, raro
fun run n maratón popular
fur [fəːʳ] n piel; (Brit: on tongue etc) sarro
fur coat n abrigo de pieles
furious ['fjʊərɪəs] adj furioso; (effort, argument) violento; **to be ~ with sb** estar furioso con algn
furlong ['fəːlɔŋ] n octava parte de una milla
furlough ['fəːləʊ] n (US Mil) permiso
furnace ['fəːnɪs] n horno
furnish ['fəːnɪʃ] vt amueblar; (supply) proporcionar; (information) facilitar
furnished ['fəːnɪʃt] adj: **~ flat** or (US) **apartment** piso amueblado
furnishings ['fəːnɪʃɪŋz] npl mobiliario
furniture ['fəːnɪtʃəʳ] n muebles; **piece of ~** mueble
furore [fjʊə'rɔːrɪ] n (protests) escándalo
furrow ['fʌrəʊ] n surco ▷ vt (forehead) arrugar
furry ['fəːrɪ] adj peludo; (toy) de peluche
further ['fəːðəʳ] adj (new) nuevo; (place) más lejano ▷ adv más lejos; (more) más; (moreover) además ▷ vt hacer avanzar; **if you need any ~ information ...** si necesita más información ...; **London is ~ from here than Paris** Londres está más lejos de aquí que París; **I can't walk any ~** no puedo andar más; **how much ~ is it?** ¿a qué distancia queda?; **~ to your letter of ...** (Comm) con referencia a su carta de ...; **to ~ one's interests** fomentar sus intereses
further education n educación postescolar

furthermore [fəːðə'mɔːʳ] adv además
furthest ['fəːðɪst] superlative of **far**
furtive ['fəːtɪv] adj furtivo
fury ['fjʊərɪ] n furia
fuse, (US) **fuze** [fjuːz] n fusible; (for bomb etc) mecha ▷ vt (metal) fundir; (fig) fusionar ▷ vi fundirse; fusionarse; **a ~ has blown** se ha fundido un fusible; (Brit Elec): **to ~ the lights** fundir los plomos
fuse box n caja de fusibles
fuse wire n hilo fusible
fusion ['fjuːʒən] n fusión
fuss [fʌs] n (noise) bulla; (dispute) lío, jaleo; (complaining) protesta ▷ vi preocuparse (por pequeñeces) ▷ vt (person) molestar; **to make a ~** armar jaleo
   ▶ **fuss over** vt fus (person) contemplar, mimar
fusspot ['fʌspɔt] n (col) quisquilloso(-a)
fussy ['fʌsɪ] adj (person) quisquilloso; **I'm not ~** (col) me da igual
fusty ['fʌstɪ] adj (pej) rancio; **to smell ~** oler a cerrado
futile ['fjuːtaɪl] adj vano
futon ['fuːtɔn] n futón
future ['fjuːtʃəʳ] adj (gen) futuro; (coming) venidero ▷ n futuro, porvenir; **in ~** de ahora en adelante
fuze [fjuːz] (US) = **fuse**
fuzzy ['fʌzɪ] adj (Phot) borroso; (hair) muy rizado
fwd. abbr = **forward**
FYI abbr = **for your information**

Gg

G, g [dʒi:] n (letter) G, g; **G** (Mus) sol; **G for George** G de Gerona

G n abbr (Brit Scol: = good) N; (US Cine: = general audience) todos los públicos

G8 n abbr (Pol: = Group of Eight) G8

gab [gæb] n: **to have the gift of the ~** (col) tener mucha labia

gabble ['gæbl] vi hablar atropelladamente; (gossip) cotorrear

gable ['geɪbl] n aguilón

gadget ['gædʒɪt] n aparato

Gaelic ['geɪlɪk] adj, n (Ling) gaélico

gag [gæg] n (on mouth) mordaza; (joke) chiste ⊳ vt (prisoner etc) amordazar ⊳ vi (choke) tener arcadas

gaiety ['geɪɪtɪ] n alegría

gain [geɪn] n ganancia ⊳ vt ganar ⊳ vi (watch) adelantarse; **to ~ by sth** ganar con algo; **to ~ ground** ganar terreno; **to ~ 3 lbs (in weight)** engordar 3 libras
▶ **gain (up)on** vt fus alcanzar

gainfully ['geɪnfʊlɪ] adv: **to be ~ employed** tener un trabajo remunerado

gait [geɪt] n forma de andar, andares

galaxy ['gæləksɪ] n galaxia

gale [geɪl] n (wind) vendaval; **~ force 10** vendaval de fuerza 10

gal(l). abbr = **gallon(s)**

gallant ['gælənt] adj valeroso; (towards ladies) galante

gall bladder n vesícula biliar

gallery ['gælərɪ] n (Theat) galería; (for spectators) tribuna; (also: **art gallery**: state-owned) pinacoteca or museo de arte; (: private) galería de arte

galley ['gælɪ] n (ship's kitchen) cocina; (ship) galera

gallon ['gæln] n galón (= 8 pints; Brit = 4,546 litros; US = 3,785 litros)

gallop ['gæləp] n galope ⊳ vi galopar; **~ing inflation** inflación galopante

gallows ['gæləʊz] n horca

gallstone ['gɔ:lstəʊn] n cálculo biliar

Gallup poll ['gæləp-] n sondeo de opinión

galore [gə'lɔ:r] adv en cantidad, en abundancia

galvanize ['gælvənaɪz] vt (metal) galvanizar; (fig): **to ~ sb into action** mover or impulsar a algn a actuar

Gambia ['gæmbɪə] n Gambia

gambit ['gæmbɪt] n (fig): **opening ~** táctica inicial

gamble ['gæmbl] n (risk) jugada arriesgada; (bet) apuesta ⊳ vt: **to ~ on** apostar a; (fig) confiar en que ⊳ vi jugar; (Comm) especular; **to ~ on the Stock Exchange** jugar a la bolsa

gambler ['gæmblər] n jugador(a)

gambling ['gæmblɪŋ] n juego

game [geɪm] n (gen) juego; (match) partido; (of cards) partida; (Hunting) caza ⊳ adj valiente; (ready): **to be ~ for anything** estar dispuesto a todo; **~s** (Scol) deportes; **big ~** caza mayor

gamekeeper ['geɪmki:pər] n guardabosque

games console [geɪmz-] n consola de juegos

game show n programa concurso, concurso

gammon ['gæmən] n (bacon) tocino ahumado; (ham) jamón ahumado

gamut ['gæmət] n (Mus) gama; **to run the (whole) ~ of emotions** (fig) recorrer toda la gama de emociones

gang [gæŋ] n pandilla; (of criminals etc) banda; (of kids) pandilla; (of colleagues) peña; (of workmen) brigada ⊳ vi: **to ~ up on sb** conchabarse contra algn

gangly ['gæŋglɪ] adj desgarbado

gangrene ['gæŋgri:n] n gangrena

gangster ['gæŋstər] n gángster

gang warfare n guerra entre bandas

gangway ['gæŋweɪ] n (Brit: in theatre, bus etc) pasillo; (on ship) pasarela

gantry ['gæntrɪ] n (for crane, railway signal) pórtico; (for rocket) torre de lanzamiento

gaol [dʒeɪl] n, vt (Brit): **jail**

gap [gæp] n hueco; (in trees, traffic) claro; (in market, records) laguna; (in time) intervalo

gape [geɪp] vi mirar boquiabierto

gaping ['geɪpɪŋ] adj (hole) muy abierto

gap year n año sabático

garage ['gærɑ:ʒ] n garaje

garbage ['gɑ:bɪdʒ] n (US) basura; (nonsense) bobadas; (fig: film, book etc) basura

garbage can n (US) cubo or balde (LAm) or bote (Méx) de la basura

garbage collector n (US) basurero(-a)

garbage truck n (US) camión de la basura

garbled ['gɑ:bld] adj (account, explanation) confuso

garden ['gɑ:dn] n jardín; **gardens** npl (public)

parque, jardines; (*private*) huertos
garden centre *n* centro de jardinería
garden city *n* (*Brit*) ciudad jardín
gardener ['gɑːdnəʳ] *n* jardinero(-a)
gardening ['gɑːdnɪŋ] *n* jardinería
gargle ['gɑːgl] *vi* hacer gárgaras, gargarear (*LAm*)
garish ['gɛərɪʃ] *adj* chillón(-ona)
garland ['gɑːlənd] *n* guirnalda
garlic ['gɑːlɪk] *n* ajo
garment ['gɑːmənt] *n* prenda (de vestir)
garrison ['gærɪsn] *n* guarnición ▷ *vt* guarnecer
garrulous ['gærjuləs] *adj* charlatán(-ana)
garter ['gɑːtəʳ] *n* (*US*) liga
gas [gæs] *n* gas; (*US: gasoline*) gasolina ▷ *vt* asfixiar con gas; **Calor ~®** (*gas*) butano
gas cooker *n* (*Brit*) cocina de gas
gas cylinder *n* bombona de gas
gas fire *n* estufa de gas
gas-fired ['gæsfaɪəd] *adj* de gas
gash [gæʃ] *n* brecha, raja; (*from knife*) cuchillada ▷ *vt* rajar; (*with knife*) acuchillar
gasket ['gæskɪt] *n* (*Aut*) junta
gas mask *n* careta antigás
gas meter *n* contador de gas
gasoline ['gæsəliːn] *n* (*US*) gasolina
gasp [gɑːsp] *n* grito sofocado ▷ *vi* (*pant*) jadear
▶ **gasp out** *vt* (*say*) decir jadeando
gas station *n* (*US*) gasolinera
gassy ['gæsɪ] *adj* con mucho gas
gas tap *n* llave del gas
gastric ['gæstrɪk] *adj* gástrico
gate [geɪt] *n* (*also at airport*) puerta; (*Rail: at level crossing*) barrera; (*metal*) verja
gâteau ['gætəu] (*pl* **-x**) *n* tarta
gatecrash ['geɪtkræʃ] *vt* colarse en
gateway ['geɪtweɪ] *n* puerta
gather ['gæðəʳ] *vt* (*flowers, fruit*) coger (*Esp*), recoger (*LAm*); (*assemble*) reunir; (*pick up*) recoger; (*Sewing*) fruncir; (*understand*) sacar en consecuencia ▷ *vi* (*assemble*) reunirse; (*dust*) acumularse; (*clouds*) cerrarse; **we ~ed enough firewood to last the night** reunimos leña suficiente para toda la noche; **to ~ information** reunir información; **to ~ speed** ganar velocidad; **we ~ed around the fireplace** nos reunimos en torno a la chimenea; **to ~ (from/that)** deducir (por/que); **as far as I can ~** por lo que tengo entendido
gathering ['gæðərɪŋ] *n* reunión, asamblea
gaudy ['gɔːdɪ] *adj* chillón(-ona)
gauge, (*US*) **gage** [geɪdʒ] *n* calibre; (*Rail*) ancho de vía, entrevía; (*instrument*) indicador ▷ *vt* medir; (*fig: sb's capabilities, character*) juzgar, calibrar; **petrol ~** indicador (del nivel) de gasolina; **to ~ the right moment** elegir el momento (oportuno)
gaunt [gɔːnt] *adj* descarnado; (*fig*) adusto
gauntlet ['gɔːntlɪt] *n* (*fig*): **to run the ~ of sth** exponerse a algo; **to throw down the ~** arrojar el guante
gauze [gɔːz] *n* gasa
gave [geɪv] *pt of* **give**

gawk [gɔːk] *vi* mirar pasmado
gay [geɪ] *adj* (*colour, person*) alegre; (*homosexual*) gay
gaze [geɪz] *n* mirada fija ▷ *vi*: **to ~ at sth** mirar algo fijamente
gazump [gə'zʌmp] *vt*, *vi* (*Brit*) echarse atrás en la venta ya acordada de una casa por haber una oferta más alta
GB *abbr* (= *Great Britain*) G.B.
GBH *n abbr* (*Brit Law: col*) = **grievous bodily harm**
GCE *n abbr* (*Brit*: = *General Certificate of Education*) ≈ certificado de bachillerato
GCSE *n abbr* (*Brit*: = *General Certificate of Secondary Education*) ≈ certificado de bachillerato
Gdns. *abbr* (= *gardens*) jdns.
GDP *n abbr* (= *gross domestic product*) PIB
GDR *n abbr* (= *German Democratic Republic*) RDA
gear [gɪəʳ] *n* equipo; (*Tech*) engranaje; (*Aut*) velocidad, marcha ▷ *vt* (*fig: adapt*): **to ~ sth to** adaptar *or* ajustar algo a; **top** *or* (*US*) **high/low ~** cuarta/primera; **in ~** con la marcha metida; **our service is ~ed to meet the needs of the disabled** nuestro servicio va enfocado a responder a las necesidades de los minusválidos
▶ **gear up** *vi* prepararse
gear box *n* caja de cambios
gear lever, (*US*) **gear shift** *n* palanca de cambio
geese [giːs] *npl of* **goose**
gel [dʒɛl] *n* gel
gelignite ['dʒɛlɪgnaɪt] *n* gelignita
gem [dʒɛm] *n* gema, piedra preciosa; (*fig*) joya
Gemini ['dʒɛmɪnaɪ] *n* Géminis
gen [dʒɛn] *n* (*Brit col*): **to give sb the ~ on sth** poner a algn al tanto de algo
Gen. *abbr* (*Mil*: = *General*) Gen., Gral.
gen. *abbr* (= *general*) grl.; = **generally**
gender ['dʒɛndəʳ] *n* género
gene [dʒiːn] *n* gen(e)
general ['dʒɛnərl] *n* general ▷ *adj* general; **in ~** en general; **~ audit** auditoría general; **the ~ public** el gran público
general anaesthetic, (*US*) **general anesthetic** *n* anestesia general
general delivery *n* (*US*) lista de correos
general election *n* elecciones generales
generalization [dʒɛnrəlaɪ'zeɪʃən] *n* generalización
generalize ['dʒɛnrəlaɪz] *vi* generalizar
generally ['dʒɛnrəlɪ] *adv* generalmente, en general
general practitioner *n* médico(-a) de medicina general
general strike *n* huelga general
generate ['dʒɛnəreɪt] *vt* generar
generation [dʒɛnə'reɪʃən] *n* (*of electricity etc*) generación; **first/third/~** (*of computer*) primera/tercera/generación
generator ['dʒɛnəreɪtəʳ] *n* generador
generosity [dʒɛnə'rɔsɪtɪ] *n* generosidad
generous ['dʒɛnərəs] *adj* generoso; (*copious*) abundante
genetic [dʒɪ'nɛtɪk] *adj* genético
genetically modified organism [dʒɪ'nɛtɪkəlɪ-]

n (organismo) transgénico, organismo
genéticamente modificado
genetic engineering *n* ingeniería genética
genetic fingerprinting [-'fɪŋɡəprɪntɪŋ] *n*
identificación genética
genetics [dʒɪ'nɛtɪks] *n* genética
Geneva [dʒɪ'niːvə] *n* Ginebra
genial ['dʒiːnɪəl] *adj* afable
genitals ['dʒɛnɪtlz] *npl* (órganos) genitales
genitive ['dʒɛnɪtɪv] *n* genitivo
genius ['dʒiːnɪəs] *n* genio
genocide ['dʒɛnəusaɪd] *n* genocidio
gent [dʒɛnt] *n abbr* (Brit col) = **gentleman**
genteel [dʒɛn'tiːl] *adj* fino, distinguido
gentle ['dʒɛntl] *adj* (sweet) dulce; (touch etc) ligero,
suave
gentleman ['dʒɛntlmən] *n* señor; (well-bred
man) caballero; **~'s agreement** acuerdo entre
caballeros
gently ['dʒɛntlɪ] *adv* suavemente
gentry ['dʒɛntrɪ] *npl* pequeña nobleza
gents [dʒɛnts] *n* servicios (de caballeros)
genuine ['dʒɛnjuɪn] *adj* auténtico; (person)
sincero
geographic(al) [dʒɪə'ɡræfɪk(l)] *adj* geográfico
geography [dʒɪ'ɔɡrəfɪ] *n* geografía
geological [dʒɪə'lɔdʒɪkl] *adj* geológico
geologist [dʒɪ'ɔlədʒɪst] *n* geólogo(-a)
geology [dʒɪ'ɔlədʒɪ] *n* geología
geometric(al) [dʒɪə'mɛtrɪk(l)] *adj* geométrico
geometry [dʒɪ'ɔmətrɪ] *n* geometría
Geordie ['dʒɔːdɪ] *n* habitante de Tyneside
Georgia ['dʒɔːdʒə] *n* Georgia
geranium [dʒɪ'reɪnjəm] *n* geranio
geriatric [dʒɛrɪ'ætrɪk] *adj*, *n* geriátrico(-a)
germ [dʒəːm] *n* (microbe) microbio, bacteria; (seed,
fig) germen
German ['dʒəːmən] *adj* alemán(-ana) ▷ *n*
alemán(-ana); (Ling) alemán
German Democratic Republic *n* República
Democrática Alemana
germane [dʒəː'meɪn] *adj*: **~ (to)** pertinente (a)
German measles *n* rubeola, rubéola
Germany ['dʒəːmənɪ] *n* Alemania
gesticulate [dʒɛs'tɪkjuleɪt] *vi* gesticular
gesture ['dʒɛstjə*] *n* gesto; **as a ~ of friendship**
en señal de amistad
get [ɡɛt] (*pt, pp* **got**) (US) (*pp* **gotten**) *vi* **1** (become,
be) ponerse, volverse; **to ~ old** envejecer; **to ~
tired** cansarse; **to ~ drunk** emborracharse; **to
~ dirty** ensuciarse; **to ~ ready** prepararse; **to ~
washed** lavarse; **to ~ married** casarse; **when do
I ~ paid?** ¿cuándo me pagan *or* se me paga?; **it's
~ting late** se está haciendo tarde
2 (go): **to ~ to/from** llegar a/de; **to ~ home** llegar
a casa; **he should ~ here soon** debería llegar
pronto; **he got under the fence** pasó por debajo
de la barrera
3 (begin) empezar a; **to ~ to know sb** (llegar a)
conocer a algn; **I'm ~ting to like him** me está
empezando a gustar; **let's ~ going** *or* **started**
¡vamos (a empezar)!

4 (modal aux vb): **you've got to do it** tienes que
hacerlo
▷ *vt* **1**: **to ~ sth done** (finish) hacer algo; (have
done) mandar hacer algo; **I'm ~ting my car
fixed** he mandado arreglar el coche; **to ~ one's
hair cut** cortarse el pelo; **to ~ the car going** *or* **to
go** arrancar el coche; **to ~ sb to do sth** conseguir
or hacer que algn haga algo; **to ~ sth/sb ready**
preparar algo/a algn
2 (obtain: money, permission, results) conseguir; (find:
job, flat) encontrar; (fetch: person, doctor) buscar;
(object) ir a buscar, traer; **quick, ~ help!** ¡rápido,
ve a buscar ayuda!; **he got good exam results**
sacó buenas notas en los exámenes; **to ~ sth for
sb** conseguir algo para algn; **the librarian got
the book for me** el bibliotecario me consiguió
el libro; **~ me Mr Jones, please** (Tel) póngame *or*
(LAm) comuníqueme con el Sr. Jones, por favor;
can I ~ you a drink? ¿quieres algo de beber?
3 (receive: present, letter) recibir; (acquire: reputation)
alcanzar; (: prize) ganar; **what did you ~ for
your birthday?** ¿qué te regalaron por tu
cumpleaños?; **how much did you ~ for the
painting?** ¿cuánto sacaste por el cuadro?
4 (catch) coger, agarrar (LAm); (hit: target etc) dar
en; **to ~ sb by the arm/throat** coger *or* agarrar
a algn por el brazo/cuello; **~ him!** ¡cógelo! (Esp),
¡atrápalo! (LAm); **they've got the thief** han
cogido *or* atrapado al ladrón; **the bullet got him
in the leg** la bala le dio en la pierna
5 (take, move) llevar; **to ~ sth to sb** hacer llegar
algo a algn; **do you think we'll ~ it through
the door?** ¿crees que lo podremos meter por la
puerta?
6 (catch, take: plane, bus etc) coger (Esp),
tomar (LAm); **where do I ~ the train for
Birmingham?** ¿dónde se coge *or* se toma el tren
para Birmingham?
7 (understand) entender; (hear) oír; **I've got it!**
¡ya lo tengo!, ¡eureka!; **I don't ~ your meaning**
no te entiendo; **I don't ~ the joke** no entiendo
el chiste; **I'm sorry, I didn't ~ your name** lo
siento, no me he enterado de tu nombre
8 (have, possess): **to have got** tener; **I've got an
idea** tengo una idea
9 (answer): **I'll ~ it!** (telephone) ¡yo contesto!; (door)
¡ya voy yo!
10 (col: annoy) molestar; (: thrill) chiflar
▶ **get about** *vi* salir mucho; (news) divulgarse
▶ **get across** *vt* (message, meaning) lograr
comunicar ▷ *vi*: **to ~ across to sb** hacer que algn
comprenda
▶ **get along** *vi* (agree) llevarse bien; (depart)
marcharse; (manage) = **get by**
▶ **get at** *vt fus* (attack) meterse con; (reach)
alcanzar; (the truth) descubrir; **what are you
~ting at?** ¿qué insinúas?
▶ **get away** *vi* marcharse; (escape) escaparse;
one of the burglars got away uno de los
ladrones escapó
▶ **get away with** *vt fus* hacer impunemente;
you'll never ~ away with it esto no te lo van a

consentir

▸ **get back** vi (return) volver ▷ vt recuperar; **what time did you ~ back?** ¿a qué hora volvisteis?; **he got his money back** recuperó su dinero

▸ **get back at** vt fus (col): **to ~ back at sb (for sth)** vengarse de algn (por algo)

▸ **get by** vi (pass) (lograr) pasar; (manage) arreglárselas; **I can ~ by in Dutch** me defiendo en holandés

▸ **get down** vi bajar(se) ▷ vt fus bajar ▷ vt bajar; (depress) deprimir; **~ down from there!** ¡baja de ahí!

▸ **get down to** vt fus: **to ~ down to work** ponerse a trabajar (en serio)

▸ **get in** vi entrar; (train) llegar; (arrive home) volver a casa, regresar; (political party) ser elegido; **what time did you ~ in last night?** ¿a qué hora llegaste anoche? ▷ vt (bring in: harvest) recoger; (: coal, shopping, supplies) comprar, traer; (insert) meter

▸ **get into** vt fus entrar en; (vehicle) subir a; **how did you ~ into the house?** ¿cómo entraste en casa?; **she got into the car** subió al coche; **~ into bed!** ¡métete en la cama!; **to ~ into a rage** enfadarse

▸ **get off** vi (from train etc) bajar(se); (depart: person, car) marcharse ▷ vt (remove) quitar; (send off) mandar; (have as leave: day, time) tener libre ▷ vt fus (train, bus) bajar(se) de; **he managed to ~ off early from work** logró salir de trabajar pronto; **to ~ off to a good start** (fig) empezar muy bien or con buen pie; **she got off the train** se bajó del tren

▸ **get on** vi (at exam etc): **how are you ~ting on?** ¿cómo te va?; (agree): **to ~ on (with)** llevarse bien (con); **we got on really well** nos llevábamos muy bien; **he doesn't ~ on with his parents** no se lleva bien con sus padres ▷ vt fus subir(se) a; **she got on the bus** se subió al autobús

▸ **get on to** vt fus (deal with) ocuparse de; (col: contact on phone etc) hablar con

▸ **get out** vi salir; (of vehicle) bajar(se); (news) saberse ▷ vt sacar; **~ out!** ¡sal!; **she got out of the car** se bajó del coche; **she got the map out** sacó el mapa

▸ **get out of** vt fus salir de; (duty etc) escaparse de; (gain from: pleasure, benefit) sacar de

▸ **get over** vt fus (illness) recobrarse de; **he managed to ~ over the problem** logró superar el problema

▸ **get round** vt fus rodear; (fig: person) engatusar a ▷ vi: **to ~ round to doing sth** encontrar tiempo para hacer algo; **I'll ~ round to it eventually** ya encontraré tiempo para hacerlo

▸ **get through** vt fus (finish) acabar ▷ vi (Tel) (lograr) comunicar

▸ **get through to** vt fus (Tel) comunicar con

▸ **get together** vi reunirse ▷ vt reunir, juntar; **could we ~ together this evening?** ¿podemos reunirnos esta tarde?

▸ **get up** vi (rise) levantarse ▷ vt fus subir; **what time do you ~ up?** ¿a qué hora te levantas?; **to**

~ up enthusiasm for sth cobrar entusiasmo por algo

▸ **get up to** vt fus (reach) llegar a; (prank) hacer

getaway ['gɛtəweɪ] n fuga

get-together ['gɛttəgɛðəʳ] n reunión; (party) fiesta

get-up ['gɛtʌp] n (Brit col: outfit) atavío, atuendo

get-well card [gɛt'wɛl-] n tarjeta en la que se desea a un enfermo que se mejore

geyser ['giːzəʳ] n (water heater) calentador de agua; (Geo) géiser

Ghana ['gɑːnə] n Ghana

ghastly ['gɑːstlɪ] adj horrible; (pale) pálido

gherkin ['gəːkɪn] n pepinillo

ghetto ['gɛtəu] n gueto

ghetto blaster [-'blɑːstəʳ] n radiocas(s)et(t)e portátil (de gran tamaño)

ghost [gəust] n fantasma ▷ vt (book) escribir por otro

ghost story n cuento de fantasmas

GI n abbr (US col: = government issue) soldado del ejército norteamericano

giant ['dʒaɪənt] n gigante ▷ adj gigantesco, gigante; **~ (size) packet** paquete (de tamaño gigante or familiar

giant killer n (Sport) matagigantes

gibberish ['dʒɪbərɪʃ] n galimatías

giblets ['dʒɪblɪts] npl menudillos

Gibraltar [dʒɪ'brɔːltəʳ] n Gibraltar

giddy ['gɪdɪ] adj (dizzy) mareado; (height, speed) vertiginoso; **it makes me ~** me marea; **I feel ~** me siento mareado

gift [gɪft] n (gen) regalo; (Comm: also: **free gift**) obsequio; (ability) don; **to have a ~ for sth** tener dotes para algo

gifted ['gɪftɪd] adj dotado

gift token, gift voucher n vale-regalo

gigantic [dʒaɪ'gæntɪk] adj gigantesco

giggle ['gɪgl] vi reírse tontamente ▷ n risilla

gill [dʒɪl] n (measure) = **0.25 pints** (Brit = 0,142 l.; US = 0,118 l.)

gills [gɪlz] npl (of fish) branquias, agallas

gilt [gɪlt] adj, n dorado

gilt-edged ['gɪltɛdʒd] adj (Comm: stocks, securities) de máxima garantía

gimmick ['gɪmɪk] n reclamo; **sales ~** reclamo promocional

gin [dʒɪn] n (liquor) ginebra

ginger ['dʒɪndʒəʳ] n jengibre

ginger ale n ginger ale

ginger beer n refresco de jengibre

gingerbread ['dʒɪndʒəbrɛd] n pan de jengibre

gingerly ['dʒɪndʒəlɪ] adv con pies de plomo

ginseng ['dʒɪnsɛŋ] n ginseng

gipsy ['dʒɪpsɪ] n gitano(-a)

giraffe [dʒɪ'rɑːf] n jirafa

girder ['gəːdəʳ] n viga

girdle ['gəːdl] n (corset) faja ▷ vt ceñir

girl [gəːl] n (small) niña; (young woman) chica, joven, muchacha; **an English ~** una (chica) inglesa

girlfriend ['gəːlfrɛnd] n (of girl) amiga; (of boy)

novia
Girl Guide n exploradora
girlish ['gə:lɪʃ] adj de niña
Girl Scout n (US) = **Girl Guide**
giro ['dʒaɪrəu] n (Brit: bank giro) giro bancario; (post office giro) giro postal
girth [gə:θ] n circunferencia; (of saddle) cincha
gist [dʒɪst] n lo esencial
give [gɪv] (pt **gave**, pp **-n**) [geɪv, 'gɪvn] vt dar; (deliver) entregar; (as gift) regalar ▷ vi (break) romperse; (stretch: fabric) dar de sí; **to ~ sb sth**, **~ sth to sb** dar algo a algn; **he gave me £10** me dio 10 libras; **to ~ sb a present** hacer un regalo a algn; **how much did you ~ for it?** ¿cuánto pagaste por él?; **12 o'clock**, **~ or take a few minutes** más o menos las 12; **~ them my regards** dales recuerdos de mi parte; **I can ~ you 10 minutes** le puedo conceder 10 minutos; **to ~ way** (Brit Aut) ceder el paso; **to ~ way to despair** ceder a la desesperación
▸ **give away** vt (give free) regalar; (betray) traicionar; (disclose) revelar
▸ **give back** vt devolver; **I gave the book back to him** le devolví el libro
▸ **give in** vi ceder ▷ vt entregar; **I ~ in!** ¡me rindo!
▸ **give off** vt despedir
▸ **give out** vt distribuir, repartir ▷ vi (be exhausted: supplies) agotarse; (fail: engine) averiarse; (strength) fallar; **he gave out the exam papers** repartió las hojas de examen
▸ **give up** vi rendirse, darse por vencido ▷ vt renunciar a; **I couldn't do it, so I gave up** no podía hacerlo, así que me di por vencido; **don't ~ up yet!** ¡no te rindas todavía!; **to ~ up smoking** dejar de fumar; **to ~ o.s. up** entregarse
giveaway ['gɪvəweɪ] n (col): **her expression was a ~** su expresión la delataba; **the exam was a ~!** ¡el examen estaba tirado! ▷ cpd: **~ prices** precios de regalo
given ['gɪvn] pp of **give** ▷ adj (fixed: time, amount) determinado ▷ conj: **~ (that)** ... dado (que) ...; **~ the circumstances** ... dadas las circunstancias ...
glacier ['glæsɪər] n glaciar
glad [glæd] adj contento; **to be ~ about sth/that** alegrarse de algo/de que; **I'm ~ you're here** me alegro de que estés aquí; **she's ~ she's done it** está contenta de haberlo hecho; **I was ~ of his help** agradecí su ayuda
gladly ['glædlɪ] adv con mucho gusto
glamorous ['glæmərəs] adj con encanto, atractivo
glamour ['glæmər] n encanto, atractivo
glance [glɑ:ns] n ojeada, mirada ▷ vi: **to ~ at** echar una ojeada a
▸ **glance off** vt fus (bullet) rebotar en
glancing ['glɑ:nsɪŋ] adj (blow) oblicuo
gland [glænd] n glándula
glare [glɛər] n deslumbramiento, brillo ▷ vi deslumbrar; **to ~ at** mirar con odio
glaring ['glɛərɪŋ] adj (mistake) manifiesto
glass [glɑ:s] n vidrio, cristal; (for drinking) vaso;

(: with stem) copa; (also: **looking glass**) espejo
glass ceiling n (fig) techo or barrera invisible (que impide ascender profesionalmente a las mujeres o miembros de minorías étnicas)
glasses ['glɑ:səs] npl gafas, anteojos (LAm)
glasshouse ['glɑ:shaus] n invernadero
glassware ['glɑ:swɛər] n cristalería
Glaswegian [glæs'wi:dʒən] adj de Glasgow ▷ n nativo(-a) or habitante de Glasgow
glaze [gleɪz] vt (window) acristalar; (pottery) vidriar; (Culin) glasear ▷ n barniz; (Culin) glaseado
glazed [gleɪzd] adj (eye) vidrioso; (pottery) vidriado
glazier ['gleɪzɪər] n vidriero(-a)
gleam [gli:m] n destello ▷ vi relucir; **a ~ of hope** un rayo de esperanza
glean [gli:n] vt (gather: information) recoger
glee [gli:] n alegría, regocijo
glen [glɛn] n cañada
glib [glɪb] adj (person) de mucha labia; (comment) fácil
glide [glaɪd] vi deslizarse; (Aviat, bird) planear
glider ['glaɪdər] n (Aviat) planeador
gliding ['glaɪdɪŋ] n (Aviat) vuelo sin motor
glimmer ['glɪmər] n luz tenue
glimpse [glɪmps] n vislumbre ▷ vt vislumbrar, entrever; **to catch a ~ of** vislumbrar
glint [glɪnt] n destello; (in the eye) chispa ▷ vi centellear
glisten ['glɪsn] vi relucir, brillar
glitter ['glɪtər] vi relucir, brillar ▷ n brillo
gloat [gləut] vi: **to ~ over** regodearse con
global ['gləubl] adj (world-wide) mundial; (comprehensive) global
globalization [gləubəlaɪ'zeɪʃən] n globalización, mundialización
global warming [-'wɔ:mɪŋ] n (re)calentamiento global or de la tierra
globe [gləub] n globo, esfera; (model) bola del mundo; globo terráqueo
gloom [glu:m] n penumbra; (sadness) desaliento, melancolía
gloomy ['glu:mɪ] adj (dark) oscuro; (sad) triste; (pessimistic) pesimista; **to feel ~** sentirse pesimista
glorify ['glɔ:rɪfaɪ] vt glorificar
glorious ['glɔ:rɪəs] adj glorioso; (weather, sunshine) espléndido
glory ['glɔ:rɪ] n gloria
gloss [glɔs] n (shine) brillo; (also: **gloss paint**) (pintura) esmalte
▸ **gloss over** vt fus restar importancia a; (omit) pasar por alto
glossary ['glɔsərɪ] n glosario
glossy ['glɔsɪ] adj (hair) brillante; (photograph) con brillo; (magazine) de papel satinado or cuché
glove [glʌv] n guante
glove compartment n (Aut) guantera
glow [gləu] vi (shine) brillar ▷ n brillo
glower ['glauər] vi: **to ~ at** mirar con ceño
glucose ['glu:kəus] n glucosa

glue [glu:] n pegamento, cemento (LAm) ▷ vt pegar

glum [glʌm] adj (mood) abatido; (person, tone) melancólico

glut [glʌt] n superabundancia

glutton ['glʌtn] n glotón(-ona); ~ **for punishment** masoquista

gluttony ['glʌtənɪ] n gula, glotonería

GM adj abbr (= genetically modified) transgénico; **GM foods** alimentos transgénicos

gm abbr (= gram) g

GMO n abbr (= genetically modified organism) (organismo) transgénico, organismo genéticamente modificado, OGM

GMT abbr (= Greenwich Mean Time) GMT

gnarled [nɑ:ld] adj nudoso

gnat [næt] n mosquito

gnaw [nɔ:] vt roer

gnome [nəum] n gnomo

GNP n abbr (= gross national product) PNB

go [gəu] vb (pt **went**, pp **gone**) ▷ vi ir; (travel) viajar; (depart) irse, marcharse; (work) funcionar, marchar; (be sold) venderse; (time) pasar; (become) ponerse; (break etc) estropearse, romperse ▷ n (pl **goes**); **to have a go (at)** probar suerte (con); **to have a go at doing sth** probar a hacer algo; **he had a go at making a cake** probó a hacer una tarta; **to be on the go** no parar; **whose go is it?** ¿a quién le toca?; **it's your go** te toca a ti; **where are you going?** ¿adónde vas?; **I'm going to the cinema tonight** voy al cine esta noche; **to go by car/on foot** ir en coche/a pie; **to go for a walk** ir a dar un paseo; **to go dancing** ir a bailar; **to go looking for sth/sb** ir a buscar algo/a algn; **to go and see sb, go to see sb** ir a ver a algn; **to go round the back** pasar por detrás; **where's Judy? — she's gone** ¿dónde está Judy? — se ha ido; **I'm going now** yo me voy ya; **we went home** nos fuimos a casa; **my voice has gone** he perdido la voz; **the cake is all gone** se acabó la tarta; **the money will go towards our holiday** el dinero es para (ayuda de) nuestras vacaciones; **my car won't go** el coche no funciona; **to make sth go, get sth going** poner algo en marcha; **how did it go?** ¿qué tal salió or resultó?, ¿cómo ha ido?; **the meeting went well** la reunión salió bien; **to go to sleep** dormirse; **I'm going to do it tomorrow** lo voy a hacer mañana; **it's going to be difficult** va a ser difícil; **I'll take whatever is going** acepto lo que haya; **... to go** (US: food) ... para llevar

▸ **go about** vi (rumour) propagarse; (also: **go round**: wander about) andar (de un sitio para otro) ▷ vt fus: **how do I go about this?** ¿cómo me las arreglo para hacer esto?; **to go about one's business** ocuparse de sus asuntos

▸ **go after** vt fus (pursue) perseguir; (job, record etc) andar tras; **quick, go after them!** ¡rápido, persíguelos!

▸ **go against** vt fus (be unfavourable to: results) ir en contra de; (be contrary to: principles) ser contrario a

▸ **go ahead** vi seguir adelante; **we'll go ahead with your suggestion** seguiremos adelante con su propuesta

▸ **go along** vi ir ▷ vt fus bordear; **as you go along** sobre la marcha

▸ **go along with** vt fus (accompany) acompañar; (agree with: idea) estar de acuerdo con

▸ **go around** vi = **go round**

▸ **go away** vi irse, marcharse; **go away!** ¡vete!

▸ **go back** vi volver; **we went back to the same place** volvimos al mismo sitio; **he's gone back home** ha vuelto a casa

▸ **go back on** vt fus (promise) faltar a

▸ **go by** vi (years, time) pasar ▷ vt fus guiarse por; **two policemen went by** pasaron dos policías

▸ **go down** vi (gen) bajar; (ship) hundirse; (sun) ponerse; (balloon) desinflarse ▷ vt fus bajar por; **the price of computers has gone down** ha bajado el precio de los ordenadores; **my airbed's gone down** mi colchoneta se ha desinflado; **that should go down well with him** eso le va a gustar; **she's gone down with (the) flu** ha cogido la gripe; **he went down the stairs** bajó las escaleras

▸ **go for** vt fus (fetch) ir por; (like) gustar; (attack) atacar; **go for it!** ¡adelante!; **I don't go for it much** no me gusta mucho; **suddenly the dog went for me** de pronto el perro me atacó

▸ **go in** vi entrar; **he knocked on the door and went in** llamó a la puerta y entró

▸ **go in for** vt fus (competition) presentarse a

▸ **go into** vt fus entrar en; (investigate) investigar; (embark on) dedicarse a

▸ **go off** vi (leave) irse, marcharse; (food) pasarse; (lights etc) apagarse; (explode) estallar; (event) realizarse ▷ vt fus perder el interés por; **they went off after lunch** se marcharon después de comer; **this milk has gone off** esta leche se ha echado a perder; **all the lights went off** se apagaron todas las luces; **the bomb went off at 10 o'clock** la bomba estalló a las 10; **the gun went off by accident** el arma se disparó accidentalmente; **my alarm goes off at 7** mi despertador suena a las 7; **the party went off well** la fiesta salió bien; **I've gone off that idea** ya no me gusta la idea

▸ **go on** vi (continue) seguir, continuar; (lights) encenderse; (happen) pasar, ocurrir ▷ vt fus (be guided by: evidence etc) partir de; **to go on doing sth** seguir haciendo algo; **he went on reading** siguió leyendo; **go on!** ¡sigue!; (come on) ¡venga!; **go on, tell me what the problem is!** ¡venga, dime cuál es el problema!; **the concert went on until 11 o'clock at night** el concierto duró hasta las 11 de la noche; **what's going on here?** ¿qué pasa aquí?; **there's nothing to go on** no hay nada en que basarse

▸ **go on at** vt fus (nag) dar la lata a; **they're always going on at me** están siempre dándome la lata

▸ **go out** vi salir; (fire, light) apagarse; (ebb: tide) bajar, menguar; **are you going out tonight?** ¿vas a salir esta noche?; **they went out for a**

meal salieron a comer; **to go out with sb** salir con algn; **suddenly the lights went out** de pronto se apagaron las luces

▶ **go over** vi (ship) zozobrar ▷ vt fus (check) revisar; **to go over sth in one's mind** repasar algo mentalmente

▶ **go round** vt (as tourist etc) visitar ▷ vi (circulate: news, rumour) correr; (suffice) bastar; (revolve) girar, dar vueltas; **we want to go round the museum today** hoy queremos visitar el museo; **I love going round the shops** me encanta ir de tiendas; **to go round to sb's house** ir a casa de algn; **we're all going round to Linda's house tonight** esta noche vamos todos a casa de Linda; **to go round (by)** (make a detour) dar la vuelta (por); **there's a rumour going round that ...** corre el rumor de que ...; **there's a bug going round** hay un virus por ahí rondando; **is there enough food to go round?** ¿hay comida suficiente para todos?

▶ **go through** vt fus (town etc) atravesar; (search through) revisar; (perform: ceremony) realizar; (examine: list, book) repasar; **we went through London to get to Brighton** atravesamos Londres para llegar a Brighton; **someone had gone through her things** alguien había registrado sus cosas; **they went through the plan again** repasaron de nuevo el plan; **I know what you're going through** sé por lo que estás pasando

▶ **go through with** vt fus (plan, crime) llevar a cabo; **I couldn't go through with it** no pude llevarlo a cabo

▶ **go together** vi (harmonize: colours) hacer juego; (: people) entenderse; **green and mauve go well together** el verde y el malva hacen juego

▶ **go under** vi (sink: ship, person) hundirse; (fig: business, firm) quebrar

▶ **go up** vi subir ▷ vt fus subir por; **the price has gone up** el precio ha subido; **to go up in flames** estallar en llamas; **she went up the stairs** subió las escaleras

▶ **go with** vt fus pegar con, hacer juego con; **does this blouse go with that skirt?** ¿pega esta blusa con la falda?

▶ **go without** vt fus pasarse sin

goad [gəʊd] vt aguijonear

go-ahead ['gəʊəhɛd] adj emprendedor(a) ▷ n luz verde; **to give sth/sb the ~** dar luz verde a algo/algn

goal [gəʊl] n meta, arco (LAm); (score) gol

goalkeeper ['gəʊlkiːpəʳ] n portero, guardameta, arquero (LAm)

goal post n poste (de la portería)

goat [gəʊt] n cabra

gobble ['gɔbl] vt (also: **gobble down**, **gobble up**) engullir

go-between ['gəʊbɪtwiːn] n intermediario(-a)

goblin ['gɔblɪn] n duende

go-cart ['gəʊkɑːt] n = **go-kart**

god [gɔd] n dios; **G~** Dios

godchild ['gɔdtʃaɪld] n ahijado(-a)

goddamn ['gɔddæm] adj (col: also: **goddamned**) maldito, puñetero ▷ excl: **~!** ¡caguen diez!

goddess ['gɔdɪs] n diosa

godfather ['gɔdfɑːðəʳ] n padrino

god-forsaken ['gɔdfəseɪkən] adj dejado de la mano de Dios

godmother ['gɔdmʌðəʳ] n madrina

godparents ['gɔdpɛərənts] npl: **the ~** los padrinos

godsend ['gɔdsɛnd] n: **to be a ~** venir como llovido del cielo

godson ['gɔdsʌn] n ahijado

goes [gəʊz] vb see **go**

gofer ['gəʊfəʳ] n (col) chico(-a) para todo

goggles ['gɔglz] npl (Aut) gafas, anteojos (LAm); (diver's) gafas submarinas

going ['gəʊɪŋ] n (conditions) cosas ▷ adj: **the ~ rate** la tarifa corriente or en vigor; **it was slow ~** las cosas iban lentas

goings-on ['gəʊɪŋz'ɔn] npl (col) tejemanejes

go-kart ['gəʊkɑːt] n kart

gold [gəʊld] n oro ▷ adj (reserves) de oro

golden ['gəʊldn] adj (made of gold) de oro; (golden in colour) dorado

golden rule n regla de oro

goldfish ['gəʊldfɪʃ] n pez de colores

gold-plated ['gəʊld'pleɪtɪd] adj chapado en oro

goldsmith ['gəʊldsmɪθ] n orfebre

golf [gɔlf] n golf

golf ball n (for game) pelota de golf; (on typewriter) esfera impresora

golf club n club de golf; (stick) palo (de golf)

golf course n campo de golf

golfer ['gɔlfəʳ] n jugador(a) de golf, golfista

golfing ['gɔlfɪŋ] n: **to go ~** jugar al golf

gone [gɔn] pp of **go**

goner ['gɔnəʳ] n (col): **to be a ~** estar en las últimas

gong [gɔŋ] n gong

good [gʊd] adj bueno; (before m sing n) buen; (well-behaved) educado ▷ n bien; **it's a very ~ film** es una película muy buena; **be ~!** ¡sé bueno!; **have a ~ journey!** ¡buen viaje!; **~!** ¡qué bien!; **he's ~ at it** se le da bien; **she's ~ at singing** canta bien; **to be ~ for** servir para; **it's ~ for you** te hace bien; **would you be ~ enough to...?** ¿podría hacerme el favor de...?, ¿sería tan amable de...?; **that's very ~ of you** es usted muy amable; **they were very ~ to me** se portaron muy bien conmigo; **to feel ~** sentirse bien; **it's ~ to see you** me alegro de verte; **a ~ deal (of)** mucho; **a ~ many** muchos; **to make ~** reparar; **it's no ~ complaining** no sirve de nada quejarse; **is this any ~?** (will it do?) ¿sirve esto?; (what's it like?) ¿qué tal es esto?; **it's a ~ thing you were there** menos mal que estabas allí; **for ~** (for ever) para siempre, definitivamente; **one day he left for ~** un día se marchó definitivamente; **~ morning/afternoon!** ¡buenos días/buenas tardes!; **~ evening!** ¡buenas noches!; **~ night!** ¡buenas noches!; **he's up to no ~** está tramando algo; **for the common ~** para el bien común; *see*

also **goods**
goodbye [gud'baɪ] *excl* ¡adiós!; **to say ~ (to)** (*person*) despedirse (de)
Good Friday *n* Viernes Santo
good-looking ['gud'lukɪŋ] *adj* guapo
good-natured ['gud'neɪtʃəd] *adj* (*person*) de buen carácter; (*discussion*) cordial
goodness ['gudnɪs] *n* (*of person*) bondad; **for ~ sake!** ¡por Dios!; **~ gracious!** ¡madre mía!
goods [gudz] *npl* bienes; (*Comm etc*) géneros, mercancías, artículos; **all his ~ and chattels** todos sus bienes
goods train *n* (*Brit*) tren de mercancías
goodwill [gud'wɪl] *n* buena voluntad; (*Comm*) fondo de comercio; (*customer connections*) clientela
goose [guːs] (*pl* **geese**) *n* ganso, oca
gooseberry ['guzbərɪ] *n* grosella espinosa *or* silvestre
gooseflesh ['guːsflɛʃ] *n*, **goosepimples** ['guːspɪmplz] ▷ *npl* carne de gallina
gopher ['gəufə^r] *n* = **gofer**
gore [gɔː^r] *vt* dar una cornada a, cornear ▷ *n* sangre
gorge [gɔːdʒ] *n* garganta ▷ *vr*: **to ~ o.s. (on)** atracarse (de)
gorgeous ['gɔːdʒəs] *adj* precioso; (*weather*) estupendo; (*person*) guapísimo
gorilla [gə'rɪlə] *n* gorila
gorse [gɔːs] *n* tojo
gory ['gɔːrɪ] *adj* sangriento
go-slow ['gəu'sləu] *n* (*Brit*) huelga de celo
gospel ['gɔspl] *n* evangelio
gossip ['gɔsɪp] *n* cotilleo; (*person*) cotilla ▷ *vi* cotillear, comadrear (*LAm*); **a piece of ~** un cotilleo
gossip column *n* ecos de sociedad
got [gɔt] *pt, pp of* **get**
Gothic ['gɔθɪk] *adj* gótico
gotten ['gɔtn] (*US*) *pp of* **get**
gourmet ['guəmeɪ] *n* gastrónomo(-a)
gout [gaut] *n* gota
govern ['gʌvən] *vt* (*gen*) gobernar; (*event, conduct*) regir
governess ['gʌvənɪs] *n* institutriz
government ['gʌvnmənt] *n* gobierno; **local ~** administración municipal
governor ['gʌvənə^r] *n* gobernador(a); (*of jail*) director(a)
Govt. *abbr* (= *Government*) gobno.
gown [gaun] *n* vestido; (*of teacher, Brit: of judge*) toga
GP *n abbr* = **general practitioner**
GPO *n abbr* (*Brit: old*) = **General Post Office**; (*US*) = **Government Printing Office**
gr. *abbr* (*Comm*: = *gross*) bto.
grab [græb] *vt* coger (*Esp*) *or* agarrar; **to ~ at** intentar agarrar
grace [greɪs] *n* (*Rel*) gracia; (*gracefulness*) elegancia, gracia; (*graciousness*) cortesía, gracia ▷ *vt* (*favour*) honrar; (*adorn*) adornar; **5 days' ~** un plazo de 5 días; **to say ~** bendecir la mesa; **his sense of humour is his saving ~** lo que le salva

es su sentido del humor
graceful ['greɪsful] *adj* elegante
gracious ['greɪʃəs] *adj* amable ▷ *excl*: **good ~!** ¡Dios mío!
grade [greɪd] *n* (*quality*) clase, calidad; (*in hierarchy*) grado; (*US Scol*) curso; (: *gradient*) pendiente, cuesta ▷ *vt* clasificar; **to make the ~** (*fig*) dar el nivel; *see also* **high school**
grade crossing *n* (*US*) paso a nivel
grade school *n* (*US*) escuela primaria; *see also* **elementary school**
gradient ['greɪdɪənt] *n* pendiente
gradual ['grædjuəl] *adj* gradual
gradually ['grædjuəlɪ] *adv* gradualmente
graduate *n* licenciado(-a), graduado(-a), egresado(-a) (*LAm*), (*US Scol*) bachiller ▷ *vi* licenciarse, graduarse, recibirse (*LAm*); (*US*) obtener el título de bachillerato
graduation [grædju'eɪʃən] *n* graduación; (*US Scol*) entrega de los títulos de bachillerato
graffiti [grə'fiːtɪ] *npl* pintadas
graft [grɑːft] *n* (*Agr, Med*) injerto; (*bribery*) corrupción ▷ *vt* injertar; **hard ~** (*col*) trabajo duro
grain [greɪn] *n* (*single particle*) grano; (*no pl: cereals*) cereales; (*US: corn*) trigo; (*in wood*) veta
gram [græm] *n* (*US*) gramo
grammar ['græmə^r] *n* gramática
grammar school *n* (*Brit*) ≈ instituto (de segunda enseñanza); (*US*) escuela primaria; *see also* **comprehensive school**
grammatical [grə'mætɪkl] *adj* gramatical
gramme [græm] *n* = **gram**
grand [grænd] *adj* grandioso ▷ *n* (*US: col*) mil dólares
grandchildren ['græntʃɪldrən] *npl* nietos
granddad ['grændæd] *n* yayo, abuelito
granddaughter ['grændɔːtə^r] *n* nieta
grandfather ['grænfɑːðə^r] *n* abuelo
grand jury *n* (*US*) jurado de acusación
grandma ['grænmɑː] *n* yaya, abuelita
grandmother ['grænmʌðə^r] *n* abuela
grandpa ['grænpɑː] *n* = **granddad**
grandparents ['grændpɛərənts] *npl* abuelos
grand piano *n* piano de cola
Grand Prix ['grɑ̃ː'priː] *n* (*Aut*) gran premio, Grand Prix
grandson ['grænsʌn] *n* nieto
grandstand ['grændstænd] *n* (*Sport*) tribuna
grand total *n* suma total, total
granite ['grænɪt] *n* granito
granny ['grænɪ] *n* abuelita, yaya
grant [grɑːnt] *vt* (*concede*) conceder; (*admit*): **to ~ (that)** reconocer (que) ▷ *n* (*Scol*) beca; **to take sth for ~ed** dar algo por sentado
granulated sugar ['grænjuleɪtɪd-] *n* (*Brit*) azúcar granulado
granule ['grænjuːl] *n* gránulo
grape [greɪp] *n* uva; **sour ~s** (*fig*) envidia; **a bunch of ~s** un racimo de uvas
grapefruit ['greɪpfruːt] *n* pomelo, toronja
grapevine ['greɪpvaɪn] *n* vid, parra; **I heard it**

on the ~ (fig) me enteré, me lo contaron

graph [grɑ:f] n gráfica

graphic ['græfɪk] adj gráfico

graphic equalizer n ecualizador gráfico

graphics ['græfɪks] n (art, process) artes gráficas
▷ npl (drawings: Comput) gráficos

grapple ['græpl] vi: **to ~ with a problem**
enfrentarse a un problema

grasp [grɑ:sp] vt agarrar, asir; (understand)
comprender ▷ n (grip) asimiento; (reach) alcance;
(understanding) comprensión; **to have a good ~ of**
(subject) dominar
▸ **grasp at** vt fus (rope etc) tratar de agarrar; (fig:
opportunity) aprovechar

grasping ['grɑ:spɪŋ] adj avaro

grass [grɑ:s] n hierba, grama (LAm); (lawn)
césped; (pasture) pasto; (col: informer) soplón(-ona)

grasshopper ['grɑ:shɔpəʳ] n saltamontes

grass roots adj de base ▷ npl (Pol) bases

grate [greɪt] n parrilla ▷ vi chirriar, rechinar ▷ vt
(Culin) rallar

grateful ['greɪtful] adj agradecido

grater ['greɪtəʳ] n rallador

gratifying ['grætɪfaɪɪŋ] adj gratificante

grating ['greɪtɪŋ] n (iron bars) rejilla ▷ adj (noise)
chirriante

gratitude ['grætɪtju:d] n agradecimiento

gratuitous [grə'tju:ɪtəs] adj gratuito

gratuity [grə'tju:ɪtɪ] n gratificación

grave [greɪv] n tumba ▷ adj serio, grave

gravel ['grævl] n grava

gravestone ['greɪvstəun] n lápida

graveyard ['greɪvjɑ:d] n cementerio,
camposanto

gravity ['grævɪtɪ] n gravedad; (seriousness)
seriedad

gravy ['greɪvɪ] n salsa de carne

gray [greɪ] adj (US) = **grey**

graze [greɪz] vi pacer ▷ vt (touch lightly, scrape)
rozar ▷ n (Med) rozadura

grease [gri:s] n (fat) grasa; (lubricant) lubricante
▷ vt engrasar; **to ~ the skids** (US: fig) engrasar el
mecanismo

greaseproof ['gri:spru:f] adj a prueba de grasa; ~
paper papel encerado

greasy ['gri:sɪ] adj (hands, clothes) grasiento; (road,
surface) resbaladizo

great [greɪt] adj grande; (before n sing) gran; (col)
estupendo, macanudo (LAm); (pain, heat) intenso;
a ~ oak tree un gran roble; **we had a ~ time** nos
lo pasamos muy bien; **they're ~ friends** son
íntimos or muy amigos; **the ~ thing is that ...** lo
bueno es que ...; **it was ~!** ¡fue estupendo!

Great Barrier Reef n Gran Barrera de Coral

Great Britain n Gran Bretaña

greater ['greɪtəʳ] adj mayor; **G~ London** el área
metropolitana de Londres

greatest ['greɪtɪst] adj (el/la) mayor; **a ~ hits
album** un disco de grandes éxitos

great-grandchild [greɪt'grændtʃaɪld] (pl -
children) n bisnieto(-a)

great-grandfather [greɪt'grændfɑ:ðəʳ] n

bisabuelo

great-grandmother [greɪt'grændmʌðəʳ] n
bisabuela

Great Lakes npl: **the ~** los Grandes Lagos

greatly ['greɪtlɪ] adv sumamente, muy

greatness ['greɪtnɪs] n grandeza

Greece [gri:s] n Grecia

greed [gri:d] n (also: **greediness**) codicia; (for
food) gula

greedy ['gri:dɪ] adj codicioso; (for food)
glotón(-ona)

Greek [gri:k] adj griego ▷ n griego(-a); (Ling)
griego; **ancient/modern ~** griego antiguo/
moderno

green [gri:n] adj verde; (inexperienced) novato
▷ n verde; (stretch of grass) césped; (of golf course)
campo, "green"; **greens** npl verduras; **the G~s**
(Pol) los verdes; **the G~ party** (Pol) el partido
verde; **a ~ light** (at traffic lights) un semáforo en
verde; **to have ~ fingers** (fig) tener buena mano
para las plantas; **a dark ~** un verde oscuro

green belt n cinturón verde

green card n (Aut) carta verde

greenery ['gri:nərɪ] n vegetación

greengrocer ['gri:ngrəusəʳ] n (Brit) frutero(-a),
verdulero(-a)

greenhouse ['gri:nhaus] n invernadero

greenhouse effect n: **the ~** el efecto
invernadero

greenhouse gas n gas que produce el efecto
invernadero

greenish ['gri:nɪʃ] adj verdoso

Greenland ['gri:nlənd] n Groenlandia

green light n luz verde

green pepper n pimiento verde

greet [gri:t] vt saludar; (news) recibir

greeting ['gri:tɪŋ] n (gen) saludo; (welcome)
bienvenida; **~s** saludos; **season's ~s** Felices
Pascuas

greeting(s) card n tarjeta de felicitación

gregarious [grə'gɛərɪəs] adj gregario

grenade [grə'neɪd] n (also: **hand grenade**)
granada

grew [gru:] pt of **grow**

grey [greɪ] adj gris; **to go ~** salirle canas

grey-haired [greɪ'hɛəd] adj canoso

greyhound ['greɪhaund] n galgo

grid [grɪd] n rejilla; (Elec) red

gridlock ['grɪdlɔk] n (esp US) retención

grief [gri:f] n dolor, pena; **to come to ~** (plan)
fracasar, ir al traste; (person) acabar mal,
desgraciarse

grievance ['gri:vəns] n (cause for complaint) motivo
de queja, agravio

grieve [gri:v] vi afligirse, acongojarse ▷ vt
afligir, apenar; **to ~ for** llorar por; **to ~ for sb**
(dead person) llorar la pérdida de algn

grievous ['gri:vəs] adj grave; (loss) cruel; **~ bodily
harm** (Law) daños corporales graves

grill [grɪl] n (on cooker) parrilla ▷ vt (Brit) asar a la
parrilla; (question) interrogar; **~ed meat** carne
(asada) a la parrilla or plancha

grille [grɪl] n rejilla
grim [grɪm] adj (place) lúgubre; (person) adusto
grimace [grɪ'meɪs] n mueca ▷ vi hacer muecas
grime [graɪm] n mugre
grin [grɪn] n sonrisa abierta ▷ vi: **to ~ (at)** sonreír abiertamente (a)
grind [graɪnd] (pt, pp **ground**) vt (coffee, pepper etc) moler; (US: meat) picar; (make sharp) afilar; (polish: gem, lens) esmerilar ▷ vi (car gears) rechinar ▷ n: **the daily ~** (col) la rutina diaria; **to ~ one's teeth** hacer rechinar los dientes; **to ~ to a halt** (vehicle) pararse con gran estruendo de frenos; (fig: talks, scheme) interrumpirse; (work, production) paralizarse
grip [grɪp] n (hold) asimiento; (of hands) apretón; (handle) asidero; (of racquet etc) mango; (understanding) comprensión ▷ vt agarrar; **to get to ~s with** enfrentarse con; **to lose one's ~** (fig) perder el control; **he lost his ~ of the situation** la situación se le fue de las manos
gripping ['grɪpɪŋ] adj absorbente
grisly ['grɪzlɪ] adj horripilante, horrible
gristle ['grɪsl] n cartílago
grit [grɪt] n gravilla; (courage) valor ▷ vt (road) poner gravilla en; **I've got a piece of ~ in my eye** tengo una arenilla en el ojo; **to ~ one's teeth** apretar los dientes
groan [grəʊn] n gemido, quejido ▷ vi gemir, quejarse
grocer ['grəʊsəʳ] n tendero (de ultramarinos); **~'s (shop)** n tienda de ultramarinos or (LAm) de abarrotes
groceries ['grəʊsərɪz] npl comestibles
grocery ['grəʊsərɪ] n (shop) tienda de ultramarinos or (LAm) de abarrotes
groin [grɔɪn] n ingle
groom [gruːm] n mozo(-a) de cuadra; (also: **bridegroom**) novio ▷ vt (horse) almohazar; **well-~ed** acicalado
groove [gruːv] n ranura; (of record) surco
grope [grəʊp] vi ir a tientas; **to ~ for** buscar a tientas
gross [grəʊs] adj grueso; (Comm) bruto ▷ vt (Comm) recaudar en bruto
gross domestic product (GDP) n producto interior bruto
grossly ['grəʊslɪ] adv (greatly) enormemente
gross national product (GNP) n producto nacional bruto
grotesque [grə'tɛsk] adj grotesco
grotto ['grɔtəʊ] n gruta
grotty ['grɔtɪ] adj asqueroso
ground [graʊnd] pt, pp of **grind** ▷ n suelo, tierra; (Sport) campo, terreno; (reason: gen pl) motivo, razón; (US Elec: also: **ground wire**) tierra ▷ vt (plane) mantener en tierra; (US Elec) conectar con tierra ▷ vi (ship) varar, encallar ▷ adj (coffee etc) molido; **grounds** npl (of coffee etc) poso; (gardens etc) jardines, parque; **on the ~** en el suelo; **we sat on the ~** nos sentamos en el suelo; **common ~** terreno común; **to gain/lose ~** ganar/perder terreno; **to the ~** al suelo; **below ~** bajo tierra;

he covered a lot of ~ in his lecture abarcó mucho en la clase; **a football ~** un campo de fútbol; **we've got ~s for complaint** tenemos motivos para quejarnos
ground cloth n (US) = **groundsheet**
ground floor n (Brit) planta baja
grounding ['graʊndɪŋ] n (in education) conocimientos básicos
groundless ['graʊndlɪs] adj infundado, sin fundamento
ground rules npl normas básicas
groundsheet ['graʊndʃiːt] (Brit) n tela impermeable
ground staff n personal de tierra
ground swell n mar de fondo; (fig) ola
ground-to-air ['graʊntə'ɛə] adj tierra-aire
ground-to-ground ['graʊntə'graʊnd] adj tierra-tierra
groundwork ['graʊndwəːk] n trabajo preliminar
group [gruːp] n grupo; (Mus: pop group) conjunto, grupo; (vb: also: **group together**) ▷ vt agrupar ▷ vi agruparse
grouse [graʊs] n (pl inv: bird) urogallo ▷ vi (complain) quejarse
grove [grəʊv] n arboleda
grovel ['grɔvl] vi (fig) arrastrarse
grow [grəʊ] (pt **grew**, pp **-n**) vi crecer; (increase) aumentar; (expand) desarrollarse; (become) volverse ▷ vt cultivar; (hair, beard) dejar crecer; **haven't you ~n!** ¡cómo has crecido!; **the number of unemployed has ~n** ha aumentado el número de desempleados; **to ~ rich/weak** enriquecerse/debilitarse; **to ~ tired of waiting** cansarse de esperar; **he grew vegetables in his garden** cultivaba hortalizas en su jardín; **I'm ~ing a beard** me estoy dejando barba; **he grew a moustache** se dejó bigote
▶ **grow apart** vi (fig) alejarse uno del otro
▶ **grow away from** vt fus (fig) alejarse de
▶ **grow on** vt fus: **that painting is ~ing on me** ese cuadro me gusta cada vez más
▶ **grow out of** vt fus (habit) perder; (clothes): **I've ~n out of this shirt** esta camisa se me ha quedado pequeña
▶ **grow up** vi (become adult) hacerse mayor; (spend young life) crecer; **I watched Tim ~ up** vi a Tim hacerse mayor; **we grew up together** crecimos juntos; **oh, ~ up!** ¡no seas niño!
grower ['grəʊəʳ] n (Agr) cultivador(a), productor(a)
growing ['grəʊɪŋ] adj creciente; **~ pains** (also fig) problemas de crecimiento
growl [graʊl] vi gruñir
grown [grəʊn] pp of **grow**
grown-up [grəʊn'ʌp] n adulto(-a), mayor
growth [grəʊθ] n crecimiento, desarrollo; (what has grown) brote; (Med) tumor
grub [grʌb] n gusano; (col: food) comida
grubby ['grʌbɪ] adj sucio, mugriento, mugroso (LAm)
grudge [grʌdʒ] n rencor ▷ vt: **to ~ sb sth** dar

algo a algn de mala gana; **to bear sb a** ~ guardar rencor a algn; **he ~s (giving) the money** da el dinero de mala gana

gruelling, (US) **grueling** ['gruəlɪŋ] *adj* agotador

gruesome ['gru:səm] *adj* horrible

gruff [grʌf] *adj* (*voice*) ronco; (*manner*) brusco

grumble ['grʌmbl] *vi* refunfuñar, quejarse

grumpy ['grʌmpɪ] *adj* gruñón(-ona)

grunt [grʌnt] *vi* gruñir ▷ *n* gruñido

G-string ['dʒi:strɪŋ] *n* tanga

guarantee [gærən'ti:] *n* garantía ▷ *vt* garantizar; **he can't ~ (that) he'll come** no está seguro de poder venir

guard [gɑ:d] *n* guardia; (*person*) guarda; (*Brit Rail*) jefe de tren; (*safety device: on machine*) cubierta de protección; (*protection*) protección; (*fireguard*) pantalla; (*mudguard*) guardabarros ▷ *vt* guardar; **to ~ (against or from)** proteger (de); **to be on one's ~** (*fig*) estar en guardia
  ▶ **guard against** *vi*: **to ~ against doing sth** guardarse de hacer algo

guarded ['gɑ:dɪd] *adj* (*fig*) cauteloso

guardian ['gɑ:dɪən] *n* guardián(-ana); (*of minor*) tutor(a)

guard's van *n* (*Brit Rail*) furgón del jefe de tren

Guatemala [gwɑ:tə'mɑ:lə] *n* Guatemala

Guatemalan [gwɑ:tə'mɑ:lən] *adj*, *n* guatemalteco(-a)

guerrilla [gə'rɪlə] *n* guerrillero(-a)

guess [gɛs] *vi*, *vt* (*gen*) adivinar; (*suppose*) suponer ▷ *n* suposición, conjetura; **I ~ you're right** (*esp US*) supongo que tienes razón; **to keep sb ~ing** mantener a algn a la expectativa; **to take or have a ~** tratar de adivinar; **my ~ is that ...** yo creo que ....

guesswork ['gɛswə:k] *n* conjeturas; **I got the answer by ~** acerté a ojo de buen cubero

guest [gɛst] *n* invitado(-a); (*in hotel*) huésped(a); **be my ~** (*col*) estás en tu casa

guest-house ['gɛsthaus] *n* casa de huéspedes, pensión

guest room *n* cuarto de huéspedes

guff [gʌf] *n* (*col*) bobadas

guffaw [gʌ'fɔ:] *n* carcajada ▷ *vi* reírse a carcajadas

guidance ['gaɪdəns] *n* (*gen*) dirección; (*advice*) consejos; **marriage/vocational ~** orientación matrimonial/profesional

guide [gaɪd] *n* (*person, book, fig*) guía; (*also*: **girl guide**) exploradora ▷ *vt* guiar; **to be ~d by sb/ sth** dejarse guiar por algn/algo

guidebook ['gaɪdbuk] *n* guía

guide dog *n* perro guía

guidelines ['gaɪdlaɪnz] *npl* (*fig*) directrices

guild [gɪld] *n* gremio

guildhall ['gɪldhɔ:l] *n* (*Brit: town hall*) ayuntamiento

guile [gaɪl] *n* astucia

guillotine ['gɪləti:n] *n* guillotina

guilt [gɪlt] *n* culpabilidad

guilty ['gɪltɪ] *adj* culpable; **to feel ~ (about)**

sentirse culpable (de); **to plead ~/not ~** declararse culpable/inocente

guinea ['gɪnɪ] *n* (*Brit: old*) guinea (= *21 chelines: en la actualidad ya no se usa esta moneda*)

guinea pig *n* cobaya; (*fig*) conejillo de Indias

guise [gaɪz] *n*: **in or under the ~ of** bajo la apariencia de

guitar [gɪ'tɑ:ʳ] *n* guitarra

gulf [gʌlf] *n* golfo; (*abyss*) abismo; **the G~** el Golfo (Pérsico)

Gulf States *npl*: **the ~** los países del Golfo

gull [gʌl] *n* gaviota

gullet ['gʌlɪt] *n* esófago

gullible ['gʌlɪbl] *adj* crédulo

gully ['gʌlɪ] *n* barranco

gulp [gʌlp] *vi* tragar saliva ▷ *vt* (*also*: **gulp down**) tragarse ▷ *n* (*of liquid*) trago; (*of food*) bocado; **in or at one ~** de un trago

gum [gʌm] *n* (*Anat*) encía; (*glue*) goma, cemento (*LAm*); (*sweet*) gominola; (*also*: **chewing-gum**) chicle ▷ *vt* pegar con goma
  ▶ **gum up** *vt*: **to ~ up the works** (*col*) entorpecerlo todo

gumboots ['gʌmbu:ts] *npl* (*Brit*) botas de goma

gun [gʌn] *n* (*small*) pistola; (*shotgun*) escopeta; (*rifle*) fusil; (*cannon*) cañón ▷ *vt* (*also*: **gun down**) abatir a tiros; **to stick to one's ~s** (*fig*) mantenerse firme or en sus trece

gunboat ['gʌnbəut] *n* cañonero

gunfire ['gʌnfaɪəʳ] *n* disparos

gunman ['gʌnmən] *n* pistolero

gunpoint ['gʌnpɔɪnt] *n*: **at ~** a mano armada

gunpowder ['gʌnpaudəʳ] *n* pólvora

gunshot ['gʌnʃɔt] *n* disparo

gurgle ['gə:gl] *vi* gorgotear

gush [gʌʃ] *vi* chorrear; (*fig*) deshacerse en efusiones

gust [gʌst] *n* (*of wind*) ráfaga

gusto ['gʌstəu] *n* entusiasmo

gut [gʌt] *n* intestino; (*Mus etc*) cuerda de tripa ▷ *vt* (*poultry, fish*) destripar; (*building*): **the blaze ~ted the entire building** el fuego destruyó el edificio entero

guts [gʌts] *npl* (*courage*) agallas, valor; (*col: innards: of people, animals*) tripas; **to hate sb's ~** odiar a algn (a muerte)

gutted ['gʌtɪd] *adj* (*col: disappointed*): **I was ~** me quedé hecho polvo

gutter ['gʌtəʳ] *n* (*of roof*) canalón; (*in street*) cuneta; **the ~** (*fig*) el arroyo

gutter press *n* (*col*): **the ~** la prensa sensacionalista or amarilla; *see also* **tabloid press**

guy [gaɪ] *n* (*also*: **guyrope**) viento, cuerda; (*col: man*) tío (*Esp*), tipo

Guy Fawkes' Night ['gaɪfɔ:ks-] (*Brit*): **n**

guzzle ['gʌzl] *vi* tragar ▷ *vt* engullir

gym [dʒɪm] *n* (*also*: **gymnasium**) gimnasio; (*also*: **gymnastics**) gimnasia

gymnast ['dʒɪmnæst] *n* gimnasta

gymnastics [dʒɪm'næstɪks] *n* gimnasia

gym shoes *npl* zapatillas de gimnasia

gym slip n (Brit) pichi
gynaecologist, (US) **gynecologist**
 [gaɪnɪˈkɔlədʒɪst] n ginecólogo(-a)

gynaecology, (US) **gynecology** [gaɪnəˈkɔlədʒɪ]
 n ginecología
gypsy [ˈdʒɪpsɪ] n = **gipsy**

Hh

H, h [eɪtʃ] *n* (*letter*) H, h; **H for Harry**, (US) **H for How** H de Historia

haberdashery ['hæbə'dæʃərɪ] *n* (*Brit*) mercería; (US: *men's clothing*) prendas de caballero

habit ['hæbɪt] *n* hábito, costumbre; **to get out of/into the ~ of doing sth** perder la costumbre de/acostumbrarse a hacer algo

habitat ['hæbɪtæt] *n* hábitat

habitual [hə'bɪtjuəl] *adj* acostumbrado, habitual; (*drinker, liar*) empedernido

hack [hæk] *vt* (*cut*) cortar; (*slice*) tajar ▷ *n* corte; (*axe blow*) hachazo; (*pej: writer*) escritor(a) a sueldo; (*old horse*) jamelgo

hacker ['hækə^r] *n* (*Comput*) pirata informático

hackneyed ['hæknɪd] *adj* trillado, gastado

hacksaw ['hæksɔː] *n* sierra para metales

had [hæd] *pt, pp of* **have**

haddock ['hædək] (*pl - or -s*) *n especie de merluza*

hadn't ['hædnt] = **had not**

haematology, (US) **hematology** ['hiːmə'tɔlədʒɪ] *n* hematología

haemophilia, (US) **hemophilia** ['hiːmə'fɪlɪə] *n* hemofilia

haemorrhage, (US) **hemorrhage** ['hɛmərɪdʒ] *n* hemorragia

haemorrhoids, (US) **hemorrhoids** ['hɛmərɔɪdz] *npl* hemorroides, almorranas

hag [hæg] *n* (*ugly*) vieja fea, tarasca; (*nasty*) bruja; (*witch*) hechicera

haggard ['hægəd] *adj* ojeroso

haggis ['hægɪs] *n* (*Scottish*) *asadura de cordero cocida; see also* **Burns' Night**

haggle ['hægl] *vi* (*argue*) discutir; (*bargain*) regatear

haggling ['hæglɪŋ] *n* regateo

Hague [heɪg] *n*: **The ~** La Haya

hail [heɪl] *n* (*weather*) granizo ▷ *vt* saludar; (*call*) llamar a ▷ *vi* granizar; **to ~ (as)** aclamar (como), celebrar (como); **he ~s from Scotland** es natural de Escocia

hailstone ['heɪlstəun] *n* (*piedra de*) granizo

hailstorm ['heɪlstɔːm] *n* granizada

hair [hɛə^r] *n* (*gen*) pelo, cabellos; (*one hair*) pelo, cabello; (*head of hair*) pelo, cabellera; (*on legs etc*) vello; **to do one's ~** arreglarse el pelo; **grey ~** canas

hairbrush ['hɛəbrʌʃ] *n* cepillo (para el pelo)

haircut ['hɛəkʌt] *n* corte de pelo

hairdo ['hɛəduː] *n* peinado

hairdresser ['hɛədrɛsə^r] *n* peluquero(-a); **~'s** peluquería

hair-dryer ['hɛədraɪə^r] *n* secador (de pelo)

hairgrip ['hɛəgrɪp] *n* horquilla

hairnet ['hɛənɛt] *n* redecilla

hairpiece ['hɛəpiːs] *n* trenza postiza

hairpin ['hɛəpɪn] *n* horquilla

hairpin bend, (US) **hairpin curve** *n* curva muy cerrada

hair-raising ['hɛəreɪzɪŋ] *adj* espeluznante

hair spray *n* laca

hairstyle ['hɛəstaɪl] *n* peinado

hairy ['hɛərɪ] *adj* peludo, velludo

hake [heɪk] *n* merluza

half [hɑːf] *n* (*pl* **halves**) [hɑːvz] mitad; (*Sport: of match*) tiempo, parte; (: *of ground*) campo; (*ticket*) billete para niños ▷ *adj* medio ▷ *adv* medio, a medias; **~ of the cake** la mitad de la tarta; **~ an hour** media hora; **~ a kilo** medio kilo; **~ a dozen** media docena; **~ a pound** media libra, ≈ 250 gr.; **two and a ~** dos y media; **to cut sth in ~** cortar algo por la mitad; **to go halves (with sb)** ir a medias (con algn); **one and two halves, please** un billete normal y dos para niños, por favor; **~ past 3** las 3 y media; **a ~ chicken** medio pollo; **~ empty** medio vacío; **~ asleep** medio dormido; **~ closed** medio entreabierto; **they were ~ drunk** estaban medio borrachos

half-baked ['hɑːf'beɪkt] *adj* (*col: idea, scheme*) mal concebido or pensado

half-caste ['hɑːfkɑːst] *n* mestizo(-a)

half-hearted ['hɑːf'hɑːtɪd] *adj* indiferente, poco entusiasta

half-hour [hɑːf'auə^r] *n* media hora

half-mast ['hɑːf'mɑːst] *n*: **at ~** (*flag*) a media asta

halfpenny ['heɪpnɪ] *n* medio penique

half-price ['hɑːf'praɪs] *adj* a mitad de precio

half term *n* (*Brit Scol*) *vacaciones de mediados del trimestre*

half-time [hɑːf'taɪm] *n* descanso

halfway ['hɑːf'weɪ] *adv* a medio camino; **to meet sb ~** (*fig*) llegar a un acuerdo con algn

halfway house *n* centro de readaptación de antiguos presos; (*fig*) solución intermedia

half-wit ['hɑːfwɪt] *n* (*col*) zoquete

hall [hɔːl] *n* (*for concerts*) sala; (*entrance way*) entrada, vestíbulo

hallmark ['hɔːlmɑːk] *n* (*mark*) rasgo distintivo; (*seal*) sello

hallo [hə'ləu] *excl* = **hello**

hall of residence *n* (*Brit*) colegio mayor, residencia universitaria

Hallowe'en [hæləu'iːn] *n* víspera de Todos los Santos

hallucination [həluːsɪ'neɪʃən] *n* alucinación

hallway ['hɔːlweɪ] *n* vestíbulo

halo ['heɪləu] *n* (*of saint*) aureola

halt [hɔːlt] *n* (*stop*) alto, parada; (*Rail*) apeadero ⊳ *vt* parar ⊳ *vi* pararse; (*process*) interrumpirse; **to call a ~ (to sth)** (*fig*) poner fin (a algo)

halve [hɑːv] *vt* partir por la mitad

halves [hɑːvz] *pl of* **half**

ham [hæm] *n* jamón (cocido); (*col: also*: **radio ham**) radioaficionado(-a); (: *also*: **ham actor**) comicastro

hamburger ['hæmbɜːgəʳ] *n* hamburguesa

hamlet ['hæmlɪt] *n* aldea

hammer ['hæməʳ] *n* martillo ⊳ *vt* (*nail*) clavar; **to ~ a point home to sb** remacharle un punto a algn

▶ **hammer out** *vt* (*metal*) forjar a martillo; (*fig: solution, agreement*) elaborar (trabajosamente)

hammock ['hæmək] *n* hamaca

hamper ['hæmpəʳ] *vt* estorbar ⊳ *n* cesto

hamster ['hæmstəʳ] *n* hámster

hand [hænd] *n* mano; (*of clock*) aguja, manecilla; (*writing*) letra; (*worker*) obrero; (*measurement: of horse*) palmo ⊳ *vt* (*give*) dar, pasar; (*deliver*) entregar; **to give sb a ~** echar una mano a algn, ayudar a algn; **can you give me a ~?** ¿me echas una mano?; **to force sb's ~** forzarle la mano a algn; **at ~** a mano; **in ~** entre manos; **we have the matter in ~** tenemos el asunto entre manos; **to have in one's ~** (*knife, victory*) tener en la mano; **to have a free ~** tener carta blanca; **on ~** (*person, services*) a mano, al alcance; **to ~** (*information etc*) a mano; **on the one ~ ..., on the other ~ ...** por una parte ... por otra (parte) ...; **he ~ed me the book** me pasó el libro

▶ **hand down** *vt* pasar, bajar; (*tradition*) transmitir; (*heirloom*) dejar en herencia; (*US: sentence, verdict*) imponer

▶ **hand in** *vt* entregar; **he ~ed in his exam paper** entregó su examen

▶ **hand out** *vt* (*leaflets, advice*) repartir, distribuir; **the teacher ~ed out the books** el profesor repartió los libros

▶ **hand over** *vt* (*deliver*) entregar; (*surrender*) ceder; **she ~ed the keys over to me** me entregó las llaves

▶ **hand round** *vt* (*Brit: papers*) pasar (de mano en mano); (: *chocolates etc*) ofrecer

handbag ['hændbæg] *n* bolso, cartera (*LAm*), bolsa (*Méx*)

hand baggage *n* = **hand luggage**

handbasin ['hændbeɪsn] *n* lavabo

handbook ['hændbuk] *n* manual

handbrake ['hændbreɪk] *n* freno de mano

hand cream *n* crema para las manos

handcuffs ['hændkʌfs] *npl* esposas

handful ['hændful] *n* puñado

handicap ['hændɪkæp] *n* desventaja; (*Sport*) hándicap ⊳ *vt* estorbar

handicapped ['hændɪkæpt] *adj*: **to be mentally ~** ser deficiente mental; **to be physically ~** ser minusválido(-a)

handicraft ['hændɪkrɑːft] *n* artesanía

handiwork ['hændɪwəːk] *n* manualidad(es); (*fig*) obra; **this looks like his ~** (*pej*) es obra de él, parece

handkerchief ['hæŋkətʃɪf] *n* pañuelo

handle ['hændl] *n* (*of door etc*) pomo; (*of cup etc*) asa; (*of knife etc*) mango; (*for winding*) manivela ⊳ *vt* (*touch*) tocar; (*deal with*) encargarse de; (*treat: people*) manejar; **"~ with care"** "(manéjese) con cuidado"; **to fly off the ~** perder los estribos

handlebar(s) ['hændlbɑː(z)] *n(pl)* manillar

hand luggage *n* equipaje de mano

handmade ['hændmeɪd] *adj* hecho a mano

handout ['hændaut] *n* (*distribution*) repartición; (*charity*) limosna; (*leaflet*) folleto, octavilla; (*press handout*) nota

handrail ['hændreɪl] *n* (*on staircase etc*) pasamanos, barandilla

handset ['hændset] *n* (*Tel*) auricular

handshake ['hændʃeɪk] *n* apretón de manos; (*Comput*) coloquio

handsome ['hænsəm] *adj* guapo

hands-on ['hændz'ɔn] *adj* práctico; **she has a very ~ approach** le gusta tomar parte activa; **~ experience** (*Comput*) experiencia práctica

handstand ['hændstænd] *n* voltereta, salto mortal

handwriting ['hændraɪtɪŋ] *n* letra

handwritten ['hændrɪtn] *adj* escrito a mano, manuscrito

handy ['hændɪ] *adj* (*close at hand*) a mano; (*useful: machine, tool etc*) práctico; (*skilful*) hábil, diestro; **to come in ~** venir bien

handyman ['hændɪmæn] *n* manitas

hang [hæŋ] (*pt, pp* **hung**) *vt* colgar; (*head*) bajar; (*criminal*) (*pt, pp* **-ed**) ahorcar ⊳ *vi* colgar ⊳ *n*: **to get the ~ of sth** (*col*) coger el tranquillo a algo; **there was a bulb ~ing from the ceiling** una bombilla colgaba del techo

▶ **hang about** *vi* haraganear

▶ **hang around** *vi* pasar el rato; **on Saturdays we ~ around in the park** los sábados pasamos el rato en el parque

▶ **hang back** *vi* (*hesitate*) vacilar; **to ~ back from doing sth** vacilar en hacer algo

▶ **hang on** *vi* (*wait*) esperar ⊳ *vt fus* (*depend on: decision etc*) depender de; **~ on a minute please** espera un momento, por favor; **to ~ on to** (*keep*) guardar, quedarse con

▶ **hang out** *vt* (*washing*) tender, colgar ⊳ *vi* (*col: live*) vivir; (: *often be found*) moverse; **to ~ out of sth** colgar fuera de algo

▶ **hang together** *vi* (*cohere: argument etc*)

sostenerse
▶ **hang up** vt (coat) colgar ▷ vi (Tel) colgar; **don't ~ up!** ¡no cuelgues!; **to ~ up on sb** colgarle a algn
hangar ['hæŋəʳ] n hangar
hanger ['hæŋəʳ] n percha
hanger-on [hæŋər'ɔn] n parásito
hang-gliding ['hæŋglaɪdɪŋ] n vuelo con ala delta
hanging ['hæŋɪŋ] n (execution) ejecución (en la horca)
hangover ['hæŋəuvəʳ] n (after drinking) resaca
hang-up ['hæŋʌp] n complejo
hanker ['hæŋkəʳ] vi: **to ~ after** (miss) echar de menos; (long for) añorar
hankie, hanky ['hæŋkɪ] n abbr = **handkerchief**
Hansard ['hænsɑːd] n actas oficiales de las sesiones del parlamento británico
haphazard [hæp'hæzəd] adj fortuito
happen ['hæpən] vi suceder, ocurrir; (take place) tener lugar, realizarse; **what's ~ing?** ¿qué pasa?; **as it ~s ...** da la casualidad de que ...; **do you ~ to know if she's at home?** ¿por casualidad sabes si está en casa?
▶ **happen (up)on** vt fus tropezar or dar con
happening ['hæpnɪŋ] n suceso, acontecimiento
happily ['hæpɪlɪ] adv (luckily) afortunadamente; (cheerfully) alegremente
happiness ['hæpɪnɪs] n (contentment) felicidad; (joy) alegría
happy ['hæpɪ] adj feliz; (cheerful) alegre; **to be ~ (with)** estar contento (con); **yes, I'd be ~ to** sí, con mucho gusto; **H~ Christmas/New Year!** ¡Feliz Navidad!/Año Nuevo!; **~ birthday!** ¡felicidades!, ¡feliz cumpleaños!
happy-go-lucky ['hæpɪgəu'lʌkɪ] adj despreocupado
happy hour n hora en la que la bebida es más barata en un bar
harass ['hærəs] vt acosar, hostigar
harassed ['hærəst] adj agobiado, presionado
harassment ['hærəsmənt] n persecución, acoso; (worry) preocupación
harbour, (US) **harbor** ['hɑːbəʳ] n puerto ▷ vt (hope etc) abrigar; (hide) dar abrigo a; (retain: grudge etc) guardar
hard [hɑːd] adj duro; (difficult) difícil; (person) severo ▷ adv (work) mucho, duro; (think) profundamente; **this cheese is very ~** este queso está muy duro; **no ~ feelings!** ¡sin rencor(es)!; **to be ~ of hearing** ser duro de oído; **the exam was very ~** el examen fue muy difícil; **I find it ~ to believe that ...** me cuesta trabajo creer que ...; **to be ~ done by** ser tratado injustamente; **to be ~ on sb** ser muy duro con algn; **to look ~ at sb/sth** clavar los ojos en algn/algo; **to try ~** esforzarse
hardback ['hɑːdbæk] n libro de tapas duras
hard cash n dinero en efectivo
hard copy n (Comput) copia impresa
hard-core ['hɑːd'kɔːʳ] adj (pornography) duro; (supporters) incondicional
hard disk n (Comput) disco duro
harden ['hɑːdn] vt endurecer; (steel) templar;

(fig) curtir; (: determination) fortalecer ▷ vi (substance) endurecerse
hard-headed ['hɑːd'hɛdɪd] adj poco sentimental, realista
hard-hitting ['hɑːd'hɪtɪŋ] adj (speech, article) contundente
hard labour n trabajos forzados
hardly ['hɑːdlɪ] adv (scarcely) apenas; **I can ~ believe it** apenas me lo puedo creer; **that can ~ be true** eso difícilmente puede ser cierto; **~ ever** casi nunca
hard sell n publicidad agresiva
hardship ['hɑːdʃɪp] n (troubles) penas; (financial) apuro
hard shoulder n (Aut) arcén
hard-up [hɑːd'ʌp] adj (col) sin un duro (Esp), sin plata (LAm)
hardware ['hɑːdwɛəʳ] n ferretería; (Comput) hardware
hardware shop n ferretería
hard-wearing [hɑːd'wɛərɪŋ] adj resistente, duradero; (shoes) resistente
hard-won ['hɑːd'wʌn] adj ganado con esfuerzo
hard-working [hɑːd'wəːkɪŋ] adj trabajador(a)
hardy ['hɑːdɪ] adj fuerte; (plant) resistente
hare [hɛəʳ] n liebre
hare-brained ['hɛəbreɪnd] adj atolondrado
harem [hɑː'riːm] n harén
haricot (bean) ['hærɪkəu-] n alubia
hark back [hɑːk-] vi: **to ~ back to** (former days, earlier occasion) recordar
harm [hɑːm] n daño, mal ▷ vt (person) hacer daño a; (health, interests) perjudicar; (thing) dañar; **out of ~'s way** a salvo; **there's no ~ in trying** no se pierde nada con intentar
harmful ['hɑːmful] adj (gen) dañino; (reputation) perjudicial
harmless ['hɑːmlɪs] adj (person) inofensivo; (drug) inocuo
harmonica [hɑː'mɔnɪkə] n armónica
harmonize ['hɑːmənaɪz] vt, vi armonizar
harmony ['hɑːmənɪ] n armonía
harness ['hɑːnɪs] n arreos ▷ vt (horse) enjaezar; (resources) aprovechar
harp [hɑːp] n arpa ▷ vi: **to ~ on (about)** machacar (con)
harpoon [hɑː'puːn] n arpón
harrowing ['hærəuɪŋ] adj angustioso
harsh [hɑːʃ] adj (cruel) duro, cruel; (severe) severo; (words) hosco; (colour) chillón(-ona); (contrast) violento
harvest ['hɑːvɪst] n cosecha; (of grapes) vendimia ▷ vt, vi cosechar
has [hæz] vb see **have**
has-been ['hæzbiːn] n (col: person) persona acabada; (: thing) vieja gloria
hash [hæʃ] n (Culin) picadillo; (fig: mess) lío
hashish ['hæʃɪʃ] n hachís
hasn't ['hæznt] = **has not**
hassle ['hæsl] n (col) lío, rollo ▷ vt incordiar
haste [heɪst] n prisa
hasten ['heɪsn] vt acelerar ▷ vi darse prisa; **I ~ to**

add that... me apresuro a añadir que ...
hastily ['heɪstɪlɪ] *adv* de prisa
hasty ['heɪstɪ] *adj* apresurado
hat [hæt] *n* sombrero
hatch [hætʃ] *n* (*Naut: also:* **hatchway**) escotilla
▷ *vi* salir del cascarón ▷ *vt* incubar; (*fig: scheme, plot*) idear, tramar
hatchback ['hætʃbæk] *n* (*Aut*) tres *or* cinco puertas
hatchet ['hætʃɪt] *n* hacha
hate [heɪt] *vt* odiar, aborrecer ▷ *n* odio; **I ~ to trouble you, but ...** siento *or* lamento molestarle, pero ...
hateful ['heɪtful] *adj* odioso
hatred ['heɪtrɪd] *n* odio
hat trick *n:* **to score a ~** (*Brit Sport*) marcar tres tantos (*or* triunfos) seguidos
haughty ['hɔːtɪ] *adj* altanero, arrogante
haul [hɔːl] *vt* tirar, jalar (*LAm*); (*by lorry*) transportar ▷ *n* (*of fish*) redada; (*of stolen goods etc*) botín
haulage ['hɔːlɪdʒ] *n* (*Brit*) transporte; (*costs*) gastos de transporte
haulier ['hɔːlɪəʳ], (*US*) **hauler** ['hɔːləʳ] *n* transportista
haunch [hɔːntʃ] *n* anca; (*of meat*) pierna
haunt [hɔːnt] *vt* (*ghost*) aparecer en; (*frequent*) frecuentar; (*obsess*) obsesionar ▷ *n* guarida
haunted ['hɔːntɪd] *adj* (*castle etc*) embrujado; (*look*) de angustia
Havana [hə'vɑːnə] *n* La Havana
have [hæv] (*pt, pp* **had**) *aux vb* **1** (*gen*) haber; **to ~ arrived/eaten** haber llegado/comido; **having finished** *or* **when he had finished, he left** cuando hubo acabado, se fue
2 (*in tag questions*): **you've done it, ~n't you?** lo has hecho, ¿verdad? *or* ¿no?
3 (*in short answers and questions*): **I ~n't** no; **so I ~** pues, es verdad; **we ~n't paid — yes we ~!** no hemos pagado — ¡sí que hemos pagado!; **I've been there before, ~ you?** he estado allí antes, ¿y tú?
▷ *modal aux vb* (*be obliged*): **to ~ (got) to do sth** tener que hacer algo; **you ~n't got to tell her, you don't ~ to tell her** no hay que *or* no debes decírselo; **you didn't ~ to tell her** no tenías por qué decírselo
▷ *vt* **1** (*possess*) tener; **he has (got) blue eyes/dark hair** tiene los ojos azules/el pelo negro
2 (*referring to meals etc*): **to ~ breakfast/lunch/dinner** desayunar/comer/cenar; **to ~ a drink/a cigarette** tomar algo/fumar un cigarrillo
3 (*receive*) recibir; (*obtain*) obtener; **may I ~ your address?** ¿puedes darme tu dirección?; **you can ~ it for £5** te lo puedes quedar por 5 libras; **I must ~ it by tomorrow** lo necesito para mañana; **to ~ a baby** tener un niño *or* bebé
4 (*maintain, allow*): **I won't ~ it!** ¡no lo permitiré!; **I won't ~ this nonsense!** ¡no permitiré estas tonterías!; **we can't ~ that** no podemos permitir eso
5: **to ~ sth done** hacer *or* mandar hacer algo; **to ~ one's hair cut** cortarse el pelo; **to ~ sb do sth** hacer que algn haga algo
6 (*experience, suffer*): **to ~ a cold/flu** tener un resfriado/la gripe; **she had her bag stolen** le robaron el bolso; **she had her arm broken** se rompió un brazo; **to ~ an operation** operarse; **he had trouble getting a hotel room** tuvo dificultades para conseguir una habitación de hotel
7 (+*noun*): **to ~ a swim/walk/bath/rest** nadar/dar un paseo/darse un baño/descansar; **let's ~ a look** vamos a ver; **to ~ a meeting/party** celebrar una reunión/una fiesta; **let me ~ a try** déjame intentarlo
▶ **have in** *vt:* **to ~ it in for sb** (*col*) tenerla tomada con algn
▶ **have on** *vt:* **~ you (got) anything on tomorrow?** ¿vas a hacer algo mañana?; **I don't ~** *or* **I ~n't got any money on me** no llevo dinero (encima); **to ~ sb on** (*Brit col*) tomarle el pelo a algn
▶ **have out** *vt:* **to ~ it out with sb** (*settle a problem etc*) dejar las cosas en claro con algn
haven ['heɪvn] *n* puerto; (*fig*) refugio
haven't ['hævnt] = **have not**
havoc ['hævək] *n* estragos; **to play ~ with sth** hacer estragos en algo
hawk [hɔːk] *n* halcón ▷ *vt* (*goods*) pregonar
hay [heɪ] *n* heno
hay fever *n* fiebre del heno
haystack ['heɪstæk] *n* almiar
haywire ['heɪwaɪəʳ] *adj* (*col*): **to go ~** (*person*) volverse loco; (*plan*) irse al garete
hazard ['hæzəd] *n* riesgo; (*danger*) peligro ▷ *vt* (*remark*) aventurar; (*one's life*) arriesgar; **to be a health ~** ser un peligro para la salud; **to ~ a guess** aventurar una respuesta *or* hipótesis
hazard warning lights *npl* (*Aut*) señales de emergencia
haze [heɪz] *n* neblina
hazel ['heɪzl] *n* (*tree*) avellano ▷ *adj* (*eyes*) color de avellano
hazelnut ['heɪzlnʌt] *n* avellana
hazy ['heɪzɪ] *adj* brumoso; (*idea*) vago
h & c *abbr* (*Brit*) = **hot and cold (water)**
he [hiː] *pron* él; **he who...** aquél que..., quien...
head [hɛd] *n* cabeza; (*leader*) jefe(-a); (*of school*) director(a); (*Comput*) cabeza (grabadora) ▷ *vt* (*list*) encabezar; (*group*) capitanear; **mind your ~!** ¡cuidado con la cabeza!; **the wine went to my ~** el vino se me subió a la cabeza; **~ first** de cabeza; **~ over heels** patas arriba; **~ over heels in love** perdidamente enamorado; **on your ~ be it!** ¡allá tú!; **they went over my ~ to the manager** fueron directamente al gerente sin hacerme caso; **it was above** *or* **over their ~s** (*fig*) no alcanzaron a entenderlo; **to come to a ~** (*fig: situation etc*) llegar a un punto crítico; **to have a ~ for business** tener talento para los negocios; **to have no ~ for heights** no resistir las alturas; **I've got no ~ for figures** no se me dan bien los números; **to lose/keep one's ~** perder la

cabeza/mantener la calma; **he lost his ~ and started screaming** perdió la cabeza y empezó a gritar; **to sit at the ~ of the table** sentarse a la cabecera de la mesa; **~s or tails?** ¿cara o cruz?; **a ~ of state** un jefe de Estado; **to ~ the ball** cabecear (el balón)

▸ **head for** *vt fus* dirigirse a; **they ~ed for the church** se dirigieron a la iglesia
▸ **head off** *vt (threat, danger)* evitar

headache ['hɛdeɪk] *n* dolor de cabeza; **to have a ~** tener dolor de cabeza

headband ['hɛdbænd] *n* cinta (para la cabeza), vincha (*LAm*)

headdress ['hɛddrɛs] *n (of bride, Indian)* tocado

header ['hɛdəʳ] *n (Brit col: Football)* cabezazo; *(: fall)* caída de cabeza

headhunt ['hɛdhʌnt] *vt:* **to be ~ed** ser seleccionado por un cazatalentos

heading ['hɛdɪŋ] *n* título

headlamp ['hɛdlæmp] *n (Brit)* = **headlight**

headland ['hɛdlənd] *n* promontorio

headlight ['hɛdlaɪt] *n* faro

headline ['hɛdlaɪn] *n* titular

headlong ['hɛdlɔŋ] *adv (fall)* de cabeza; *(rush)* precipitadamente

headmaster/mistress [hɛd'mɑːstəʳ/mɪstrɪs] *n* director(a) (de escuela)

head office *n* oficina central, central

head-on [hɛd'ɔn] *adj (collision)* de frente

headphones ['hɛdfəunz] *npl* auriculares

headquarters (HQ) ['hɛdkwɔːtəz] *npl* sede central; *(Mil)* cuartel general

head-rest ['hɛdrɛst] *n* reposa-cabezas

headroom ['hɛdrum] *n (in car)* altura interior; *(under bridge)* (límite de) altura

headscarf ['hɛdskɑːf] *n* pañuelo

headstrong ['hɛdstrɔŋ] *adj* testarudo

head waiter *n* maître

headway ['hɛdweɪ] *n:* **to make ~** *(fig)* hacer progresos

headwind ['hɛdwɪnd] *n* viento contrario

heady ['hɛdɪ] *adj (experience, period)* apasionante; *(wine)* fuerte

heal [hiːl] *vt* curar ▷ *vi* cicatrizar

health [hɛlθ] *n* salud

health care *n* asistencia sanitaria

health centre *n* ambulatorio, centro médico

health food(s) *n(pl)* alimentos orgánicos

health hazard *n* riesgo para la salud

Health Service *n (Brit)* servicio de salud pública, ≈ Insalud (*Esp*)

healthy ['hɛlθɪ] *adj (gen)* sano; *(economy, bank balance)* saludable

heap [hiːp] *n* montón ▷ *vt* amontonar; *(plate)* colmar; **~s (of)** *(col: lots)* montones (de); **to ~ favours/praise/gifts** *etc* **on sb** colmar a algn de favores/elogios/regalos *etc*

hear [hɪəʳ] *vt* oír; *(pt, pp ~d)*; *(listen to)* escuchar; *(lecture)* asistir a; *(Law: case)* ver ▷ *vi* oír; **we ~d the dog bark** oímos ladrar al perro; **did you ~ the good news?** ¿te has enterado de la buena noticia?; **I ~d (that) she was ill** me han dicho

que estaba enferma; **she can't ~ very well** no oye bien; **to ~ about** enterarse de; **I've ~d about your new job** me he enterado de que tienes un nuevo trabajo; **I don't want to ~ about it** no quiero oír hablar del tema; **to ~ from sb** tener noticias de algn; **I haven't ~d from him recently** últimamente no tengo noticias de él; **I've never ~d of that book** nunca he oído hablar de ese libro

▸ **hear out** *vt:* **to ~ sb out** dejar que algn termine de hablar

hearing ['hɪərɪŋ] *n (sense)* oído; *(Law)* vista; **to give sb a ~** dar a algn la oportunidad de hablar, escuchar a algn

hearing aid *n* audífono

hearsay ['hɪəseɪ] *n* rumores, habladurías

hearse [həːs] *n* coche fúnebre

heart [hɑːt] *n* corazón; **hearts** *npl (Cards)* corazones; **the ace of ~s** el as de corazones; **to have a weak ~** tener el corazón débil; **at ~** en el fondo; **by ~** *(learn, know)* de memoria; **to set one's ~ on sth/on doing sth** anhelar algo/hacer algo; **I did not have the ~ to tell her** no tuve valor para decírselo; **to take ~** cobrar ánimos; **the ~ of the matter** lo esencial *or* el meollo del asunto

heartache ['hɑːteɪk] *n* angustia

heart attack *n* infarto (de miocardio)

heartbeat ['hɑːtbiːt] *n* latido (del corazón)

heartbreak ['hɑːtbreɪk] *n* angustia, congoja

heartbreaking ['hɑːtbreɪkɪŋ] *adj* desgarrador(a)

heartbroken ['hɑːtbrəukən] *adj:* **she was ~ about it** le partió el corazón

heartburn ['hɑːtbəːn] *n* acedía

heart failure *n (Med)* paro cardíaco

heartfelt ['hɑːtfɛlt] *adj (cordial)* cordial; *(deeply felt)* sincero

hearth [hɑːθ] *n (gen)* hogar; *(fireplace)* chimenea

heartily ['hɑːtɪlɪ] *adv* sinceramente, cordialmente; *(laugh)* a carcajadas; *(eat)* con buen apetito; **to be ~ sick of** estar completamente harto de

heartland ['hɑːtlænd] *n* zona interior *or* central; *(fig)* corazón

heartless ['hɑːtlɪs] *adj* despiadado

heart-to-heart ['hɑːttə'hɑːt] *n (also:* **heart-to-heart talk**) conversación íntima

heart transplant *n* transplante de corazón

hearty ['hɑːtɪ] *adj* cordial

heat [hiːt] *n (gen)* calor; *(Sport: also:* **qualifying heat**) prueba eliminatoria; *(Zool):* **in** *or* **on ~** en celo ▷ *vt* calentar

▸ **heat up** *vi (gen)* calentarse

heated ['hiːtɪd] *adj* caliente; *(fig)* acalorado

heater ['hiːtəʳ] *n* calentador

heath [hiːθ] *n (Brit)* brezal

heather ['hɛðəʳ] *n* brezo

heating ['hiːtɪŋ] *n* calefacción

heatstroke ['hiːtstrəuk] *n* insolación

heatwave ['hiːtweɪv] *n* ola de calor

heave [hiːv] *vt (pull)* tirar; *(push)* empujar con esfuerzo; *(lift)* levantar (con esfuerzo) ▷ *vi*

(*water*) subir y bajar ▷ *n* tirón; empujón; (*effort*)
esfuerzo; (*throw*) echada; **to ~ a sigh** dar *or* echar
un suspiro, suspirar
▶ **heave to** *vi* (*Naut*) ponerse al pairo
heaven ['hɛvn] *n* cielo; (*Rel*) paraíso; **thank
~!** ¡gracias a Dios!; **for ~'s sake!** (*pleading*) ¡por
el amor de Dios!, ¡por lo que más quiera!;
(*protesting*) ¡por Dios!
heavenly ['hɛvnlɪ] *adj* celestial; (*Rel*) divino
heavily ['hɛvɪlɪ] *adv* pesadamente; (*drink, smoke*)
en exceso; (*sleep, sigh*) profundamente
heavy ['hɛvɪ] *adj* pesado; (*work*) duro; (*sea, rain,
meal*) fuerte; (*eater*) comilón(-ona); **to be a ~
drinker** beber mucho
heavy goods vehicle (HGV) *n* (*Brit*) vehículo
pesado
heavyweight ['hɛvɪweɪt] *n* (*Sport*) peso pesado
Hebrew ['hiːbruː] *adj, n* (*Ling*) hebreo
Hebrides ['hɛbrɪdiːz] *npl*: **the ~** las Hébridas
heck [hɛk] *n* (*col*): **why the ~ ...?** ¿por qué porras
...?; **a ~ of a lot of** cantidad de
heckle ['hɛkl] *vt* interrumpir
heckler ['hɛklə^r] *n* el/la que interrumpe a un
orador
hectare ['hɛktaː^r] *n* (*Brit*) hectárea
hectic ['hɛktɪk] *adj* agitado; (*busy*) ocupado
he'd [hiːd] = **he would; he had**
hedge [hɛdʒ] *n* seto ▷ *vt* cercar (con un seto) ▷ *vi*
contestar con evasivas; **as a ~ against inflation**
como protección contra la inflación; **to ~ one's
bets** (*fig*) cubrirse
hedgehog ['hɛdʒhɔg] *n* erizo
heed [hiːd] *vt* (*also*: **take heed of**: *pay attention to*)
hacer caso de; (*bear in mind*) tener en cuenta; **to
pay (no) ~ to, take (no) ~ of** (no) hacer caso a,
(no) tener en cuenta
heedless ['hiːdlɪs] *adj* desatento
heel [hiːl] *n* talón ▷ *vt* (*shoe*) poner tacón a; **to
take to one's ~s** (*col*) poner pies en polvorosa; **to
bring to ~** meter en cintura; *see also* **dig**
hefty ['hɛftɪ] *adj* (*person*) fornido; (*piece*) grande;
(*price*) alto
heifer ['hɛfə^r] *n* novilla, ternera
height [haɪt] *n* (*of person*) talla; (*of building*) altura;
(*high ground*) cerro; (*altitude*) altitud; **what ~ are
you?** ¿cuánto mides?; **of average ~** de estatura
mediana; **to be afraid of ~s** tener miedo a las
alturas; **it's the ~ of fashion** es el último grito
en moda
heighten ['haɪtn] *vt* elevar; (*fig*) aumentar
heir [ɛə^r] *n* heredero
heiress ['ɛərɛs] *n* heredera
heirloom ['ɛəluːm] *n* reliquia de familia
held [hɛld] *pt, pp of* **hold**
helicopter ['hɛlɪkɔptə^r] *n* helicóptero
helium ['hiːlɪəm] *n* helio
hell [hɛl] *n* infierno; **oh ~!** (*col*) ¡demonios!,
¡caramba!
he'll [hiːl] = **he will; he shall**
hellish ['hɛlɪʃ] *adj* infernal; (*col*) horrible
hello [hə'ləu] *excl* ¡hola!; (*surprise*) ¡caramba!; (*Tel*)
¡dígame! (*esp Esp*), ¡aló! (*LAm*), ¡bueno! (*Méx*)

helm [hɛlm] *n* (*Naut*) timón
helmet ['hɛlmɪt] *n* casco
help [hɛlp] *n* ayuda; (*charwoman*) criada,
asistenta ▷ *vt* ayudar; **do you need any ~?**
¿necesitas ayuda?; **with the ~ of** con la ayuda
de; **to be of ~ to sb** servir a algn; **~!** ¡socorro!;
can you ~ me? ¿puedes ayudarme?; **can I ~
you?** (*in shop*) ¿qué desea?; **to ~ sb (to) do sth**
echarle una mano *or* ayudar a algn a hacer algo;
~ yourself sírvete; **he can't ~ it** no lo puede
evitar; **I couldn't ~ laughing** no pude evitar
reírme
helper ['hɛlpə^r] *n* ayudante
helpful ['hɛlpful] *adj* útil; (*person*) servicial
helping ['hɛlpɪŋ] *n* ración
helping hand *n*: **to give sb a ~** echar una mano
a algn
helpless ['hɛlplɪs] *adj* (*incapable*) incapaz;
(*defenceless*) indefenso
helpline ['hɛlplaɪn] *n* teléfono de asistencia al
público
hem [hɛm] *n* dobladillo ▷ *vt* poner *or* coser el
dobladillo a
▶ **hem in** *vt* cercar; **to feel ~med in** (*fig*) sentirse
acosado
hematology [hiːmə'tɔlədʒɪ] *n* (*US*) =
haematology
hemisphere ['hɛmɪsfɪə^r] *n* hemisferio
hemophilia [hiːmə'fɪlɪə] *n* (*US*) = **haemophilia**
hemorrhage ['hɛmərɪdʒ] *n* (*US*) = **haemorrhage**
hemorrhoids ['hɛmərɔɪdz] *npl* (*US*) =
haemorrhoids
hen [hɛn] *n* gallina; (*female bird*) hembra
hence [hɛns] *adv* (*therefore*) por lo tanto; **2 years ~**
de aquí a 2 años
henceforth [hɛns'fɔːθ] *adv* de hoy en adelante
henchman ['hɛntʃmən] *n* (*pej*) secuaz
hepatitis [hɛpə'taɪtɪs] *n* hepatitis
her [həː^r] *pron* (*direct*) la; (*indirect*) le; (*stressed, after
prep*) ella ▷ *adj* su; *see also* **me; my**
herald ['hɛrəld] *n* (*forerunner*) precursor(a) ▷ *vt*
anunciar
heraldry ['hɛrəldrɪ] *n* heráldica
herb [həːb] *n* hierba
herbicide ['həːbɪsaɪd] *n* herbicida
herd [həːd] *n* rebaño; (*of wild animals, swine*) piara
▷ *vt* (*drive, gather: animals*) llevar en manada;
(: *people*) reunir
▶ **herd together** *vt* agrupar, reunir ▷ *vi*
apiñarse, agruparse
here [hɪə^r] *adv* aquí; **I live ~** vivo aquí; **~!** (*present*)
¡presente!; **~ is/are** aquí está/están; **~ are the
books** aquí están los libros; **~'s your coffee** aquí
tienes el café; **have you got my pen? — ~ you
are** ¿tienes mi boli? — aquí tienes; **~ are the
papers you asked for** aquí tienes los papeles
que pediste; **~ she is** aquí está; **come ~!** ¡ven
aquí *or* acá!; **~ and t~** aquí y allá
hereafter [hɪər'ɑːftə^r] *adv* en el futuro ▷ *n*: **the
~** el más allá
hereby [hɪə'baɪ] *adv* (*in letter*) por la presente
hereditary [hɪ'rɛdɪtrɪ] *adj* hereditario

heresy ['hɛrəsɪ] n herejía
heretic ['hɛrətɪk] n hereje
heritage ['hɛrɪtɪdʒ] n (gen) herencia; (fig) patrimonio; **our national ~** nuestro patrimonio nacional
hermit ['hə:mɪt] n ermitaño(-a)
hernia ['hə:nɪə] n hernia
hero ['hɪərəu] (pl **-es**) n héroe; (in book, film) protagonista
heroin ['hɛrəuɪn] n heroína
heroine ['hɛrəuɪn] n heroína; (in book, film) protagonista
heron ['hɛrən] n garza
herring ['hɛrɪŋ] n arenque
hers [hə:z] pron (el) suyo/(la) suya etc; **a friend of ~** un amigo suyo; **this is ~** esto es suyo or de ella; see also **mine**
herself [hə:'sɛlf] pron (reflexive) se; (emphatic) ella misma; (after prep) sí (misma); see also **oneself**
he's [hi:z] = **he is; he has**
hesitant ['hɛzɪtənt] adj indeciso; **to be ~ about doing sth** no decidirse a hacer algo
hesitate ['hɛzɪteɪt] vi dudar, vacilar; **don't ~ to ask (me)** no dudes en pedírmelo
hesitation [hɛzɪ'teɪʃən] n indecisión; **I have no ~ in saying (that) ...** no tengo el menor reparo en afirmar que ...
heterosexual [hɛtərəu'sɛksjuəl] adj, n heterosexual
het up [hɛt'ʌp] adj (col) agitado, nervioso
hew [hju:] vt cortar
hexagon ['hɛksəgən] n hexágono
hey [heɪ] excl ¡oye!, ¡oiga!
heyday ['heɪdeɪ] n: **the ~ of** el apogeo de
HGV n abbr = **heavy goods vehicle**
hi [haɪ] excl ¡hola!
hiatus [haɪ'eɪtəs] n vacío, interrupción; (Ling) hiato
hibernate ['haɪbəneɪt] vi invernar
hibernation [haɪbə'neɪʃən] n hibernación
hiccough, hiccup ['hɪkʌp] vi hipar; **hiccoughs** npl hipo
hid [hɪd] pt of **hide**
hidden ['hɪdn] pp of **hide** ⊳ adj: **there are no ~ extras** no hay suplementos ocultos; **~ agenda** plan encubierto
hide [haɪd] (pt **hid**, pp **hidden**) n (skin) piel ⊳ vt esconder, ocultar; (feelings, truth) encubrir, ocultar ⊳ vi: **to ~ (from sb)** esconderse or ocultarse (de algn)
hide-and-seek ['haɪdən'si:k] n escondite
hideaway ['haɪdəweɪ] n escondite
hideous ['hɪdɪəs] adj horrible
hiding ['haɪdɪŋ] n (beating) paliza; **to be in ~** (concealed) estar escondido
hierarchy ['haɪəra:kɪ] n jerarquía
hi-fi ['haɪfaɪ] abbr = **high fidelity** ⊳ n estéreo, hifi ⊳ adj de alta fidelidad
high [haɪ] adj alto; (speed, number) grande, alto; (price) elevado; (wind) fuerte; (voice) agudo; (col: on drugs) colocado; (: on drink) borracho; (Culin: meat, game) pasado; (: spoilt) estropeado ⊳ adv

alto, a gran altura ⊳ n: **exports have reached a new ~** las exportaciones han alcanzado niveles inusitados; **the gate's too ~** la verja es demasiado alta; **how ~ is the wall?** ¿cómo es de alto el muro?; **it is 20 m ~** tiene 20 m de altura; **~ in the air** en las alturas; **the plane flew ~ over the mountains** el avión volaba alto sobre las montañas; **at ~ speed** a gran velocidad; **it's very ~ in fat** tiene un alto contenido en grasas; **prices are ~er in Germany** los precios están más altos en Alemania; **to pay a ~ price for sth** pagar algo muy caro; **she's got a very ~ voice** tiene la voz muy aguda; **to get ~** (col: on drugs) colocarse
highbrow ['haɪbrau] adj culto
highchair ['haɪtʃɛəʳ] n silla alta (para niños)
High Court n (Law) tribunal supremo
higher ['haɪəʳ] adj (form of life, study etc) superior ⊳ adv más alto
higher education n educación or enseñanza superior
high-flier, high-flyer [haɪ'flaɪəʳ] n ambicioso(-a)
high-handed [haɪ'hændɪd] adj despótico
highjack ['haɪdʒæk] = **hijack**
high jump n (Sport) salto de altura
highlands ['haɪləndz] npl tierras altas; **the H~** (in Scotland) las Tierras Altas de Escocia
highlight ['haɪlaɪt] n (fig: of event) punto culminante ⊳ vt subrayar
highly ['haɪlɪ] adv sumamente; **~ paid** muy bien pagado; **to speak ~ of** hablar muy bien de
highly-strung ['haɪlɪ'strʌŋ] adj muy excitable
highness ['haɪnɪs] n altura; **Her** or **His H~** Su Alteza
high-pitched [haɪ'pɪtʃt] adj agudo
high-rise ['haɪraɪz] n (also: **high-rise block, high-rise building**) torre de pisos
high school n centro de enseñanza secundaria, ≈ Instituto Nacional de Bachillerato (Esp), liceo (LAm)
high season n (Brit) temporada alta
high spirits npl ánimos
high street n (Brit) calle mayor
high tide n marea alta
highway ['haɪweɪ] n carretera; (US) autopista; **the information ~** la autopista de la información
Highway Code n (Brit) código de la circulación
hijack ['haɪdʒæk] vt secuestrar ⊳ n (also: **hijacking**) secuestro
hijacker ['haɪdʒækəʳ] n secuestrador(a)
hike [haɪk] vi (go walking) ir de excursión (a pie); (tramp) caminar ⊳ n caminata; (col: in prices etc) aumento
▸ **hike up** vt (raise) aumentar
hiker ['haɪkəʳ] n excursionista
hilarious [hɪ'lɛərɪəs] adj divertidísimo
hill [hɪl] n colina; (high) montaña; (slope) cuesta
hillside ['hɪlsaɪd] n ladera
hilltop ['hɪltɔp] n cumbre
hilly ['hɪlɪ] adj montañoso; (uneven) accidentado

hilt [hɪlt] *n* (*of sword*) empuñadura; **to the ~** (*fig: support*) incondicionalmente; **to be in debt up to the ~** estar hasta el cuello de deudas

him [hɪm] *pron* (*direct*) le, lo; (*indirect*) le; (*stressed, after prep*) él; *see also* **me**

Himalayas [hɪməˈleɪəz] *npl*: **the ~** el Himalaya

himself [hɪmˈself] *pron* (*reflexive*) se; (*emphatic*) él mismo; (*after prep*) sí (mismo); *see also* **oneself**

hind [haɪnd] *adj* posterior ▷ *n* cierva

hinder [ˈhɪndəʳ] *vt* estorbar, impedir

hindrance [ˈhɪndrəns] *n* estorbo, obstáculo

hindsight [ˈhaɪndsaɪt] *n* percepción tardía *or* retrospectiva; **with the benefit of ~** con la perspectiva del tiempo transcurrido

Hindu [ˈhɪnduː] *n* hindú

hinge [hɪndʒ] *n* bisagra, gozne ▷ *vi* (*fig*): **to ~ on** depender de

hint [hɪnt] *n* indirecta; (*advice*) consejo ▷ *vt*: **to ~ that** insinuar que ▷ *vi*: **to ~ at** aludir a; **to drop a ~** soltar *or* tirar una indirecta; **give me a ~** dame una pista

hip [hɪp] *n* cadera; (*Bot*) escaramujo

hippopotamus [hɪpəˈpɔtəməs] (*pl* **-es** *or* **hippopotami**) *n* hipopótamo

hire [ˈhaɪəʳ] *vt* (*Brit: car, equipment*) alquilar; (*worker*) contratar ▷ *n* alquiler; **for ~** se alquila; (*taxi*) libre; **on ~** de alquiler
▸ **hire out** *vt* alquilar, arrendar

hire(d) car *n* (*Brit*) coche de alquiler

hire purchase, (H.P.) *n* (*Brit*) compra a plazos; **to buy sth on ~** comprar algo a plazos

his [hɪz] *pron* (el) suyo/(la) suya *etc* ▷ *adj* su; **this is ~** esto es suyo *or* de él; *see also* **my**; **mine**

Hispanic [hɪsˈpænɪk] *adj* hispánico

hiss [hɪs] *vi* (*snake*) sisear ▷ *n* siseo; silbido

historian [hɪˈstɔːrɪən] *n* historiador(a)

historic(al) [hɪˈstɔrɪk(l)] *adj* histórico

history [ˈhɪstərɪ] *n* historia; **there's a long ~ of that illness in his family** esa enfermedad corre en su familia

hit [hɪt] *vt* (*pt, pp* **~**) (*strike*) golpear, pegar; (*collide with: car*) chocar contra; (*fig: affect*) afectar ▷ *n* golpe; (*success*) éxito; **he ~ the ball** le pegó a la bola; **Andrew ~ him** Andrew le pegó; **to ~ the target** dar en el blanco; **the car ~ a road sign** el coche chocó con una señal de tráfico; **he was ~ by a car** le pilló un coche; **to ~ the headlines** salir en primera plana; **to ~ the road** (*col*) largarse; **to ~ it off with sb** hacer buenas migas con algn; **Madonna's latest ~** el último éxito de Madonna; **the film was a massive ~** la película fue un éxito enorme
▸ **hit back** *vi* defenderse; (*fig*) devolver golpe por golpe
▸ **hit out at** *vt fus* asestar un golpe a; (*fig*) atacar
▸ **hit (up)on** *vt fus* (*answer*) dar con; (*solution*) hallar, encontrar

hit-and-run driver [ˈhɪtənˈrʌn-] *n* conductor que tras atropellar a algn se da a la fuga

hitch [hɪtʃ] *vt* (*fasten*) atar, amarrar; (*also:* **hitch up**) arremangarse ▷ *n* (*difficulty*) problema, pega; **to ~ a lift** hacer autostop; **technical ~** problema

técnico
▸ **hitch up** *vt* (*horse, cart*) enganchar, uncir

hitch-hike [ˈhɪtʃhaɪk] *vi* hacer autostop

hitch-hiker [ˈhɪtʃhaɪkəʳ] *n* autostopista

hi-tech [ˈhaɪˈtek] *adj* de alta tecnología

hitherto [ˈhɪðəˈtuː] *adv* hasta ahora, hasta aquí

hit list *n* lista negra

hitman [ˈhɪtmæn] *n* asesino a sueldo

HIV *n abbr* (= *human immunodeficiency virus*) VIH; **~- negative** no portador(a) del virus del sida, no seropositivo; **~-positive** portador(a) del virus del sida, seropositivo

hive [haɪv] *n* colmena; **the shop was a ~ of activity** (*fig*) la tienda era una colmena humana
▸ **hive off** *vt* (*col: separate*) separar; (: *privatize*) privatizar

HM *abbr* (= *His* (*or Her*) *Majesty*) S.M.

HMS *abbr* = **His** (*or Her*) **Majesty's Ship**

HMSO *n abbr* (= *His* (*or Her*) *Majesty's Stationery Office*) distribuidor oficial de las publicaciones del gobierno del Reino Unido

HNC *n abbr* (*Brit*: = *Higher National Certificate*) título académico

HND *n abbr* (*Brit*: = *Higher National Diploma*) título académico

hoard [hɔːd] *n* (*treasure*) tesoro; (*stockpile*) provisión ▷ *vt* acumular

hoarding [ˈhɔːdɪŋ] *n* (*for posters*) valla publicitaria

hoarse [hɔːs] *adj* ronco

hoax [həʊks] *n* engaño

hob [hɔb] *n* quemador

hobble [ˈhɔbl] *vi* cojear

hobby [ˈhɔbɪ] *n* pasatiempo, afición

hobby-horse [ˈhɔbɪhɔːs] *n* (*fig*) tema preferido

hobo [ˈhəʊbəʊ] *n* (*US*) vagabundo

hockey [ˈhɔkɪ] *n* hockey

hodge-podge [ˈhɔdʒpɔdʒ] *n* (*US*) = **hotchpotch**

hog [hɔg] *n* cerdo, puerco ▷ *vt* (*fig*) acaparar; **to go the whole ~** echar el todo por el todo

Hogmanay [hɔgməˈneɪ] *n* (*Scottish*) Nochevieja

hoist [hɔɪst] *n* (*crane*) grúa ▷ *vt* levantar, alzar

hold [həʊld] (*pt, pp* **held**) *vt* tener; (*contain*) contener; (*keep back*) retener; (*believe*) sostener; (*take hold of*) coger (*Esp*), agarrar (*LAm*); (*bear: weight*) soportar; (*meeting*) celebrar ▷ *vi* (*remain firm: rope, nail*) resistir; (*be valid*) ser válido; (*stick*) pegarse ▷ *n* (*grasp*) asimiento; (*fig*) dominio; (*Wrestling*) presa; (*Naut*) bodega; **he was ~ing her in his arms** la tenía entre sus brazos; **~ the ladder** sujeta la escalera; **this bottle ~s one litre** esta botella contiene un litro; **~ the line!** (*Tel*) ¡no cuelgue!; **to ~ one's own** (*fig*) defenderse; **to ~ office** (*Pol*) ocupar un cargo; **he ~s the view that ...** opina *or* es su opinión que ...; **to ~ sb responsible for sth** culpar *or* echarle la culpa a algn de algo; **~ it!** ¡espera!; **to ~ firm** *or* **fast** mantenerse firme; **where can I get ~ of ...?** ¿dónde puedo encontrar (a) ...?; **to catch** *or* **get (a) ~ of** agarrarse *or* asirse de
▸ **hold back** *vt* retener; (*secret*) ocultar; **to ~ sb back from doing sth** impedir a algn hacer algo, impedir que algn haga algo

▸ **hold down** *vt* (*person*) sujetar; (*job*) mantener
▸ **hold forth** *vi* perorar
▸ **hold off** *vt* (*enemy*) rechazar ▹ *vi*: **if the rain ~s off** si no llueve
▸ **hold on** *vi* agarrarse bien; (*wait*) esperar; **the cliff was slippery but he managed to ~ on** el acantilado se escurría, pero logró agarrarse; **~ on, I'm coming!** ¡espera que ya voy!; **~ on!** (*on telephone*) ¡no cuelgue!
▸ **hold on to** *vt fus* agarrarse a; (*keep*) guardar
▸ **hold out** *vt* ofrecer ▹ *vi* (*resist*) resistir; **to ~ out against** resistir a, sobrevivir
▸ **hold over** *vt* (*meeting etc*) aplazar
▸ **hold up** *vt* (*raise*) levantar; (*support*) apoyar; (*delay*) retrasar; (: *traffic*) demorar; (*rob: bank*) asaltar, atracar; **he held up his hand** levantó la mano; **we were held up by the traffic** nos retrasamos por culpa del tráfico; **I was held up at the office** me entretuvieron en la oficina
holdall ['həʊldɔːl] *n* (*Brit*) bolsa
holder ['həʊldə^r] *n* (*of ticket, record*) poseedor(a); (*of passport, post, office, title etc*) titular
holding ['həʊldɪŋ] *n* (*share*) participación
holdup ['həʊldʌp] *n* (*robbery*) atraco; (*delay*) retraso; (*Brit: in traffic*) embotellamiento
hole [həʊl] *n* agujero ▹ *vt* agujerear; **~ in the heart** (*Med*) boquete en el corazón; **to pick ~s in** (*fig*) encontrar defectos en; **the ship was ~d** se abrió una vía de agua en el barco
▸ **hole up** *vi* esconderse
holiday ['hɒlədɪ] *n* vacaciones; (*day off*) (día de) fiesta, día festivo *or* feriado (*LAm*); **on ~** de vacaciones; **to be on ~** estar de vacaciones
holiday camp *n* colonia *or* centro vacacional; (*for children*) colonia veraniega infantil
holiday job *n* (*Brit*) trabajo *or* trabajillo extra para las vacaciones
holidaymaker ['hɒlədɪmeɪkə^r] *n* (*Brit*) turista
holiday pay *n* paga de las vacaciones
holiday resort *n* centro turístico
Holland ['hɒlənd] *n* Holanda
holler ['hɒlə^r] *vi* (*col*) gritar, vocear
hollow ['hɒləʊ] *adj* hueco; (*fig*) vacío; (*eyes*) hundido; (*sound*) sordo ▹ *n* (*gen*) hueco; (*in ground*) hoyo ▹ *vt*: **to ~ out** ahuecar
holly ['hɒlɪ] *n* acebo
holocaust ['hɒləkɔːst] *n* holocausto
hologram ['hɒləgræm] *n* holograma
hols [hɒlz] *npl* (*col*): **the ~** las vacaciones
holster ['həʊlstə^r] *n* pistolera
holy ['həʊlɪ] *adj* (*gen*) santo, sagrado; (*water*) bendito; **the H~ Father** el Santo Padre
Holy Communion *n* Sagrada Comunión
Holy Ghost, Holy Spirit *n* Espíritu Santo
homage ['hɒmɪdʒ] *n* homenaje; **to pay ~ to** rendir homenaje a
home [həʊm] *n* casa; (*country*) patria; (*institution*) asilo; (*Comput*) punto inicial *or* de partida ▹ *adj* (*domestic*) casero, de casa; (*Econ, Pol*) nacional; (*Sport: team*) de casa; (: *match, win*) en casa ▹ *adv* (*direction*) a casa; **at ~** en casa; **I'll be ~ at 5 o'clock** estaré en casa a las 5; **to go/come ~**

ir/volver a casa; **to get ~** llegar a casa; **make yourself at ~** ¡estás en tu casa!; **it's near my ~** está cerca de mi casa; **an old people's ~** una residencia de ancianos
▸ **home in on** *vt fus* (*missile*) dirigirse hacia
home address *n* domicilio
home-brew [həʊm'bruː] *n* cerveza *etc* casera
Home Counties *npl* condados que rodean Londres
home economics *n* economía doméstica
home help *n* (*Brit*) trabajador(a) del servicio de atención domiciliaria
homeland ['həʊmlænd] *n* tierra natal
homeless ['həʊmlɪs] *adj* sin hogar, sin casa ▹ *npl*: **the ~** las personas sin hogar
homely ['həʊmlɪ] *adj* (*domestic*) casero; (*simple*) sencillo
home-made [həʊm'meɪd] *adj* hecho en casa
Home Office *n* (*Brit*) Ministerio del Interior
homeopathy *etc* [həʊmɪ'ɒpəθɪ] (*US*) = **homoeopathy** *etc*
home page *n* (*Comput*) página de inicio
home rule *n* autonomía
Home Secretary *n* (*Brit*) Ministro del Interior
homesick ['həʊmsɪk] *adj*: **to be ~** tener morriña *or* nostalgia
home town *n* ciudad natal
home truth *n*: **to tell sb a few ~s** decir cuatro verdades a algn
homeward ['həʊmwəd] *adj* (*trip*) de vuelta
homeward(s) ['həʊmwəd(z)] *adv* hacia casa
homework ['həʊmwɜːk] *n* deberes
homicidal [hɒmɪ'saɪdl] *adj* homicida
homicide ['hɒmɪsaɪd] *n* (*US*) homicidio
homoeopath, (*US*) **homeopath** ['həʊmɪəʊpæθ] *n* homeópata
homoeopathic, (*US*) **homeopathic** [həʊmɪəʊ'pæθɪk] *adj* homeopático
homoeopathy, (*US*) **homeopathy** [həʊmɪ'ɒpəθɪ] *n* homeopatía
homogeneous [hɒmə'dʒiːnɪəs] *adj* homogéneo
homosexual [hɒməʊ'sɛksjʊəl] *adj, n* homosexual
Hon *abbr* (= *honourable, honorary*) *en títulos*
Honduras [hɒn'djʊərəs] *n* Honduras
honest ['ɒnɪst] *adj* honrado; (*sincere*) franco, sincero; **to be quite ~ with you ...** para serte franco ...
honestly ['ɒnɪstlɪ] *adv* honradamente; francamente, de verdad
honesty ['ɒnɪstɪ] *n* honradez
honey ['hʌnɪ] *n* miel; (*US col*) cariño; (: *to strangers*) guapo, linda
honeycomb ['hʌnɪkəʊm] *n* panal; (*fig*) laberinto
honeymoon ['hʌnɪmuːn] *n* luna de miel
honeysuckle ['hʌnɪsʌkl] *n* madreselva
honk [hɒŋk] *vi* (*Aut*) tocar la bocina
honorary ['ɒnərərɪ] *adj* no remunerado; (*duty, title*) honorario
honour, (*US*) **honor** ['ɒnə^r] *vt* honrar ▹ *n* honor, honra; **in ~ of** en honor de; **it's a great ~** es un gran honor
hono(u)rable ['ɒnərəbl] *adj* honrado, honorable

hono(u)rs degree n (Univ) licenciatura superior
honours list n (Brit) lista de distinciones honoríficas
que entrega la reina
Hons. abbr (Univ) = **hono(u)rs degree**
hood [hʊd] n capucha; (Brit Aut) capota; (US Aut)
capó; (US col) matón
hoof [huːf] (pl **-s** or **hooves**) n pezuña
hook [hʊk] n gancho; (on dress) corchete,
broche; (for fishing) anzuelo ▷ vt enganchar; **~s
and eyes** corchetes, macho y hembra; **by ~ or
by crook** por las buenas o por las malas,
cueste lo que cueste; **to be ~ed on** (col) estar
enganchado a
▶ **hook up** vt (Radio, TV) transmitir en cadena
hooligan ['huːlɪɡən] n gamberro
hooliganism ['huːlɪɡənɪzəm] n gamberrismo
hoop [huːp] n aro
hoot [huːt] vi (Brit Aut) tocar la bocina; (siren)
sonar; (owl) ulular ▷ n bocinazo, toque de sirena;
to ~ with laughter morirse de risa
hooter ['huːtər] n (Brit Aut) bocina; (of ship, factory)
sirena
hoover® ['huːvər] (Brit) n aspiradora ▷ vt pasar la
aspiradora por
hooves [huːvz] pl of **hoof**
hop [hɒp] vi saltar, brincar; (on one foot) saltar con
un pie ▷ n salto, brinco; see also **hops**
hope [həʊp] vt, vi esperar ▷ n esperanza; **I ~ so/
not** espero que sí/no
hopeful ['həʊpful] adj (person) optimista;
(situation) prometedor(a); **I'm ~ that she'll
manage to come** confío en que podrá venir
hopefully ['həʊpfulɪ] adv con optimismo, con
esperanza
hopeless ['həʊplɪs] adj desesperado
hops [hɒps] npl lúpulo
horizon [hə'raɪzn] n horizonte
horizontal [hɒrɪ'zɒntl] adj horizontal
hormone ['hɔːməun] n hormona
horn [hɔːn] n cuerno, cacho (LAm); (Mus: also:
French horn) trompa; (Aut) bocina, claxon
hornet ['hɔːnɪt] n avispón
horny ['hɔːnɪ] adj (material) córneo; (hands)
calloso; (US col) cachondo
horoscope ['hɒrəskəʊp] n horóscopo
horrendous [hə'rɛndəs] adj horrendo
horrible ['hɒrɪbl] adj horrible
horrid ['hɒrɪd] adj horrible, horroroso
horrific [hə'rɪfɪk] adj (accident) horroroso; (film)
horripilante
horrify ['hɒrɪfaɪ] vt horrorizar
horror ['hɒrər] n horror
horror film n película de terror or miedo
hors d'œuvre [ɔː'dəːvrə] n entremeses
horse [hɔːs] n caballo
horseback ['hɔːsbæk] n: **on ~** a caballo
horse chestnut n (tree) castaño de Indias
horseman ['hɔːsmən] n jinete
horsepower (hp) ['hɔːspauər] n caballo (de
fuerza), potencia en caballos
horse-racing ['hɔːsreɪsɪŋ] n carreras de caballos
horseradish ['hɔːsrædɪʃ] n rábano picante

horseshoe ['hɔːsʃuː] n herradura
hose [həʊz] n (also: **hosepipe**) manguera
▶ **hose down** vt limpiar con manguera
hospice ['hɒspɪs] n hospicio
hospitable ['hɒspɪtəbl] adj hospitalario
hospital ['hɒspɪtl] n hospital
hospitality [hɒspɪ'tælɪtɪ] n hospitalidad
host [həʊst] n anfitrión; (TV, Radio)
presentador(a); (of inn etc) mesonero; (Rel)
hostia; (large number): **a ~ of** multitud de
hostage ['hɒstɪdʒ] n rehén
hostel ['hɒstl] n hostal; (for students, nurses etc)
residencia; (also: **youth hostel**) albergue juvenil;
(for homeless people) hospicio
hostess ['həʊstɪs] n anfitriona; (Brit: air hostess)
azafata; (in night-club) señorita de compañía
hostile ['hɒstaɪl] adj hostil
hostility [hɒ'stɪlɪtɪ] n hostilidad
hot [hɒt] adj caliente; (weather) caluroso, de
calor; (as opposed to only warm) muy caliente; (spicy)
picante; (fig) ardiente, acalorado; **to be ~** (person)
tener calor; (object) estar caliente; (weather) hacer
calor
▶ **hot up** vi (col: situation) ponerse difícil or
apurado; (: party) animarse ▷ vt (col: pace)
apretar; (: engine) aumentar la potencia de
hotbed ['hɒtbɛd] n (fig) semillero
hotchpotch ['hɒtʃpɒtʃ] n mezcolanza, baturrillo
hot dog n perrito caliente
hotel [həʊ'tɛl] n hotel
hotelier [həʊ'tɛlɪər] n hotelero
hotheaded [hɒt'hɛdɪd] adj exaltado
hothouse ['hɒthaʊs] n invernadero
hot line n (Pol) teléfono rojo, línea directa
hotly ['hɒtlɪ] adv con pasión, apasionadamente
hotplate ['hɒtpleɪt] n (on cooker) hornillo
hot potato n (Brit col) asunto espinoso; **to drop
sth/sb like a ~** no querer saber ya nada de algo/
algn
hot seat n primera fila
hot spot n (trouble spot) punto caliente; (night club
etc) lugar popular
hot-water bottle [hɒt'wɔːtə-] n bolsa de agua
caliente
hot-wire ['hɒtwaɪər] vt (col: car) hacer el puente
en
hound [haʊnd] vt acosar ▷ n perro de caza
hour ['auər] n hora; **she always takes ~s to get
ready** siempre se tira horas para arreglarse;
a quarter of an ~ un cuarto de hora; **half an
~** media hora; **two and a half ~s** dos horas y
media; **at 30 miles an ~** a 30 millas por hora;
lunch ~ la hora del almuerzo or de comer; **to pay
sb by the ~** pagar a algn por horas
hourly ['auəlɪ] adj (de) cada hora; (rate) por hora
▷ adv cada hora
house n casa; (Pol) cámara; (Theat) sala ▷ vt
(person) alojar; (also: **at/to my house**) en/a
mi casa; **the H~** (of Commons/Lords) (Brit)
la Cámara de los Comunes/Lores; **the H~
(of Representatives)** (US) la Cámara de
Representantes; **it's on the ~** (fig) la casa invita

house arrest n arresto domiciliario
houseboat ['hausbəut] n casa flotante
housebound ['hausbaund] adj confinado en casa
housebreaking ['hausbreɪkɪŋ] n allanamiento de morada
housecoat ['hauskəut] n bata
household ['haushəuld] n familia
householder ['haushəuldəʳ] n propietario(-a); (head of house) cabeza de familia
housekeeper ['hauski:pəʳ] n ama de llaves
housekeeping ['hauski:pɪŋ] n (work) trabajos domésticos; (Comput) gestión interna; (also: **housekeeping money**) dinero para gastos domésticos
house plant n planta de interior
house-proud ['hauspraud] adj preocupado por el embellecimiento de la casa
house-warming ['hauswɔ:mɪŋ] n (also: **house-warming party**) fiesta de estreno de una casa
housewife ['hauswaɪf] n ama de casa
housework ['hauswə:k] n faenas (de la casa)
housing ['hauzɪŋ] n (act) alojamiento; (houses) viviendas ▷ cpd (problem, shortage) de (la) vivienda
housing association n asociación de la vivienda
housing benefit n (Brit) subsidio por alojamiento
housing development, (Brit) **housing estate** n urbanización
hovel ['hɔvl] n casucha
hover ['hɔvəʳ] vi flotar (en el aire); (helicopter) cernerse; **to ~ on the brink of disaster** estar al borde mismo del desastre
hovercraft ['hɔvəkrɑ:ft] n aerodeslizador, hovercraft
how [hau] adv cómo; **~ are you?** ¿cómo está usted?, ¿cómo estás?; **~ do you do?** encantado, mucho gusto; **~ far is it to ...?** ¿qué distancia hay de aquí a ...?; **~ long have you been here?** ¿cuánto (tiempo) hace que estás aquí?, ¿cuánto (tiempo) llevas aquí?; **~ long does it take?** ¿cuánto se tarda?; **~ lovely!** ¡qué bonito!; **he told them ~ happy he was** les dijo lo feliz que era; **~ many/much?** ¿cuántos/cuánto?; **~ much is it?** ¿cuánto es?; **~ much sugar do you want?** ¿cuánto azúcar quieres?; **~ old are you?** ¿cuántos años tienes?; **~ is school?** ¿qué tal la escuela?; **~ about a drink?** ¿te gustaría algo de beber?, ¿qué te parece una copa?
however [hau'evəʳ] adv de cualquier manera; (+ adjective) por muy ... que; (in questions) cómo ▷ conj sin embargo, no obstante; **this, ~, isn't true** esto, sin embargo, no es cierto
howl [haul] n aullido ▷ vi aullar
HP n abbr = **hire purchase**
hp abbr = **horsepower**
HQ n abbr = **headquarters**
HR n abbr (US) = **House of Representatives**
HRH abbr (= His (or Her) Royal Highness) S.A.R.
hr(s) abbr (= hour(s)) h.
HTML n abbr (= Hypertext Mark-up Language) HTML
hub [hʌb] n (of wheel) cubo; (fig) centro

hubbub ['hʌbʌb] n barahúnda, barullo
hubcap ['hʌbkæp] n tapacubos
huddle ['hʌdl] vi: **to ~ together** amontonarse
hue [hju:] n color, matiz; **~ and cry** n protesta
huff [hʌf] n: **in a ~** enojado
hug [hʌg] vt abrazar ▷ n abrazo
huge [hju:dʒ] adj enorme
hulk [hʌlk] n (ship) barco viejo; (person, building etc) mole
hull [hʌl] n (of ship) casco
hullo [hə'ləu] excl = **hello**
hum [hʌm] vt tararear, canturrear ▷ vi tararear, canturrear; (insect) zumbar ▷ n (Elec) zumbido; (of traffic, machines) zumbido, ronroneo; (of voices etc) murmullo
human ['hju:mən] adj humano ▷ n (also: **human being**) ser humano
humane [hju:'meɪn] adj humano, humanitario
humanitarian [hju:mænɪ'tɛərɪən] adj humanitario
humanity [hju:'mænɪtɪ] n humanidad
human rights npl derechos humanos
humble ['hʌmbl] adj humilde ▷ vt humillar
humbug ['hʌmbʌg] n patrañas; (Brit: sweet) caramelo de menta
humdrum ['hʌmdrʌm] adj (boring) monótono, aburrido; (routine) rutinario
humid ['hju:mɪd] adj húmedo
humidity [hju:mɪdɪtɪ] n humedad
humiliate [hju:'mɪlɪeɪt] vt humillar
humiliation [hju:mɪlɪ'eɪʃən] n humillación
humility [hju:'mɪlɪtɪ] n humildad
humorous ['hju:mərəs] adj gracioso, divertido
humour, (US) **humor** ['hju:məʳ] n humorismo, sentido del humor; (mood) humor ▷ vt (person) complacer; **sense of ~** sentido del humor; **to be in a good/bad ~** estar de buen/mal humor
hump [hʌmp] n (in ground) montículo; (camel's) giba
hunch [hʌntʃ] n (premonition) presentimiento; **I have a ~ that** tengo la corazonada or el presentimiento de que
hunchback ['hʌntʃbæk] n jorobado(-a)
hunched [hʌntʃt] adj jorobado
hundred ['hʌndrəd] num ciento; (before n) cien; **about a ~ people** unas cien personas, alrededor de cien personas; **~s of** centenares de; **~s of people** centenares de personas; **I'm a ~ per cent sure** estoy completamente seguro
hundredweight ['hʌndrədweɪt] n (Brit) = 50.8 kg; 112 lb; (US) = 45.3 kg; 100 lb
hung [hʌŋ] pt, pp of **hang**
Hungary ['hʌŋgərɪ] n Hungría
hunger ['hʌŋgəʳ] n hambre ▷ vi: **to ~ for** (fig) tener hambre de, anhelar
hungover [hʌŋ'əuvəʳ] adj (col): **to be ~** tener resaca
hungry ['hʌŋgrɪ] adj hambriento; **to be ~** tener hambre; **~ for** (fig) sediento de
hunk [hʌŋk] n (of bread etc) trozo, pedazo
hunt [hʌnt] vt (seek) buscar; (Sport) cazar ▷ vi cazar ▷ n caza, cacería

▶ **hunt down** vt acorralar, seguir la pista a
hunter ['hʌntər] n cazador(a); (horse) caballo de caza
hunting ['hʌntɪŋ] n caza
hurdle ['hə:dl] n (Sport) valla; (fig) obstáculo
hurl [hə:l] vt lanzar, arrojar
hurling ['hə:lɪŋ] n (Sport) juego irlandés semejante al hockey
hurrah [hu'rɑ:], **hurray** [hu'reɪ] excl ¡viva!, ¡hurra!
hurricane ['hʌrɪkən] n huracán
hurried ['hʌrɪd] adj (fast) apresurado; (rushed) hecho de prisa
hurriedly ['hʌrɪdlɪ] adv con prisa, apresuradamente
hurry ['hʌrɪ] n prisa ▷ vb (also: **hurry up**) ▷ vi apresurarse, darse prisa, apurarse (LAm) ▷ vt (person) dar prisa a; (work) apresurar, hacer de prisa; **to be in a** ~ tener prisa, tener apuro (LAm), estar apurado (LAm); **to** ~ **back/home** darse prisa en volver/volver a casa
▶ **hurry along** vi pasar de prisa
▶ **hurry away**, **hurry off** vi irse corriendo
▶ **hurry on** vi: **to** ~ **on to say** apresurarse a decir
▶ **hurry up** vi darse prisa, apurarse (LAm)
hurt [hə:t] (pt, pp ~) vt hacer daño a; (business, interests etc) perjudicar ▷ vi doler ▷ adj lastimado; **I** ~ **my arm** me lastimé el brazo; **where does it** ~? ¿dónde te duele?
hurtful ['hə:tful] adj (remark etc) hiriente, dañino
hurtle ['hə:tl] vi: **to** ~ **past** pasar como un rayo
husband ['hʌzbənd] n marido
hush [hʌʃ] n silencio ▷ vt hacer callar; (cover up) encubrir; ~! ¡chitón!, ¡cállate!
▶ **hush up** vt (fact) encubrir, callar
husk [hʌsk] n (of wheat) cáscara
husky ['hʌskɪ] adj ronco; (burly) fornido ▷ n perro esquimal
hustle ['hʌsl] vt (push) empujar; (hurry) dar prisa a ▷ n bullicio, actividad febril; ~ **and bustle** ajetreo

hut [hʌt] n cabaña; (shed) cobertizo
hutch [hʌtʃ] n conejera
hyacinth ['haɪəsɪnθ] n jacinto
hydrant ['haɪdrənt] n (also: **fire hydrant**) boca de incendios
hydraulic [haɪ'drɔ:lɪk] adj hidráulico
hydroelectric [haɪdrəuɪ'lɛktrɪk] adj hidroeléctrico
hydrofoil ['haɪdrəfɔɪl] n aerodeslizador
hydrogen ['haɪdrədʒən] n hidrógeno
hyena [haɪ'i:nə] n hiena
hygiene ['haɪdʒi:n] n higiene
hygienic [haɪ'dʒi:nɪk] adj higiénico
hymn [hɪm] n himno
hype [haɪp] n (col) bombo
hyperactive [haɪpər'æktɪv] adj hiperactivo
hypermarket ['haɪpəmɑ:kɪt] n hipermercado
hyphen ['haɪfn] n guión
hypnosis [hɪp'nəusɪs] n hipnosis
hypnotic [hɪp'nɔtɪk] adj hipnótico
hypnotism ['hɪpnətɪzəm] n hipnotismo
hypnotist ['hɪpnətɪst] hipnotista
hypnotize ['hɪpnətaɪz] vt hipnotizar
hypochondriac [haɪpəu'kɔndrɪæk] n hipocondríaco(-a)
hypocrisy [hɪ'pɔkrɪsɪ] n hipocresía
hypocrite ['hɪpəkrɪt] n hipócrita
hypocritical [hɪpə'krɪtɪkl] adj hipócrita
hypodermic [haɪpə'də:mɪk] adj hipodérmico ▷ n (syringe) aguja hipodérmica
hypotenuse [haɪ'pɔtɪnju:z] n hipotenusa
hypothermia [haɪpəu'θə:mɪə] n hipotermia
hypothesis [haɪ'pɔθɪsɪs] (pl **hypotheses**) n hipótesis
hypothetical [haɪpə'θɛtɪkl] adj hipotético
hysterectomy [hɪstə'rɛktəmɪ] n histerectomía
hysteria [hɪ'stɪərɪə] n histeria
hysterical [hɪ'stɛrɪkl] adj histérico
hysterics [hɪ'stɛrɪks] npl histeria, histerismo; **to have** ~ ponerse histérico

I i

I, i [aɪ] n (letter) I, i; **I for Isaac**, (US) **I for Item** I de Inés, I de Israel

I [aɪ] pron yo ▷ abbr = **island**; **isle**

IBA n abbr (Brit) = **Independent Broadcasting Authority**; see **ITV**

Iberian [aɪˈbɪərɪən] adj ibero, ibérico

Iberian Peninsula n: **the ~** la Península Ibérica

ice [aɪs] n hielo ▷ vt (cake) alcorzar ▷ vi (also: **ice over, ice up**) helarse; **to keep sth on ~** (fig: plan, project) tener algo en reserva

iceberg [ˈaɪsbəːg] n iceberg; **the tip of the ~** la punta del iceberg

icebox [ˈaɪsbɔks] n (Brit) congelador; (US) nevera, refrigeradora (LAm)

ice bucket n cubo para el hielo

ice cream n helado

ice cube n cubito de hielo

iced [aɪst] adj (drink) con hielo; (cake) escarchado

ice hockey n hockey sobre hielo

Iceland [ˈaɪslənd] n Islandia

Icelandic [aɪsˈlændɪk] adj islandés(-esa) ▷ n (Ling) islandés

ice lolly n (Brit) polo

ice rink n pista de hielo

ice-skating [ˈaɪsskeɪtɪŋ] n patinaje sobre hielo

icicle [ˈaɪsɪkl] n carámbano

icing [ˈaɪsɪŋ] n (Culin) alcorza; (Aviat etc) formación de hielo

icing sugar n (Brit) azúcar glas(eado)

icon [ˈaɪkɔn] n (gen, Comput) icono

ICU n abbr (= intensive care unit) UVI

icy [ˈaɪsɪ] adj (road) helado; (fig) glacial

I'd [aɪd] = **I would; I had**

ID card n (identity card) DNI

idea [aɪˈdɪə] n idea; **good ~!** ¡buena idea!; **to have an ~ that ...** tener la impresión de que ...; **I haven't the least ~** no tengo ni (la más remota) idea

ideal [aɪˈdɪəl] n ideal ▷ adj ideal

idealism [aɪˈdɪəlɪzəm] n idealismo

idealist [aɪˈdɪəlɪst] n idealista

ideally [aɪˈdɪəlɪ] adv perfectamente; **~, the book should have ...** idealmente, el libro debería tener ...

identical [aɪˈdɛntɪkl] adj idéntico

identification [aɪdɛntɪfɪˈkeɪʃən] n identificación; **means of ~** documentos personales

identify [aɪˈdɛntɪfaɪ] vt identificar ▷ vi: **to ~ with** identificarse con

Identikit® [aɪˈdɛntɪkɪt] n: **~ (picture)** retrato-robot

identity [aɪˈdɛntɪtɪ] n identidad

identity card n carnet de identidad, cédula (de identidad) (LAm)

identity parade n identificación de acusados

ideological [aɪdɪəˈlɔdʒɪkəl] adj ideológico

ideology [aɪdɪˈɔlədʒɪ] n ideología

idiom [ˈɪdɪəm] n modismo; (style of speaking) lenguaje

idiomatic [ɪdɪəˈmætɪk] adj idiomático

idiosyncrasy [ɪdɪəuˈsɪŋkrəsɪ] n idiosincrasia

idiot [ˈɪdɪət] n (gen) idiota; (fool) tonto(-a)

idiotic [ɪdɪˈɔtɪk] adj idiota; tonto

idle [ˈaɪdl] adj (lazy) holgazán(-ana); (unemployed) parado, desocupado; (talk) frívolo ▷ vi (machine) funcionar or marchar en vacío; **~ capacity** (Comm) capacidad sin utilizar; **~ money** (Comm) capital improductivo; **~ time** (Comm) tiempo de paro

▶ **idle away** vt: **to ~ away one's time** malgastar or desperdiciar el tiempo

idol [ˈaɪdl] n ídolo

idolize [ˈaɪdəlaɪz] vt idolatrar

if [ɪf] conj si ▷ n: **there are a lot of ifs and buts** hay muchas dudas sin resolver; **you can go if you like** puedes ir si quieres; **he asked me if I had eaten** me preguntó si había comido; **if it's fine we'll go swimming** si hace bueno, iremos a nadar; **if you studied harder you would pass your exams** si estudiaras más aprobarías los exámenes; **I'd be pleased if you could do it** yo estaría contento si pudieras hacerlo; **if I were you I would go to Spain** yo que tú iría a España; **if necessary** si resultase necesario; **if only si** solamente, ojalá; **if only I had more money!** ¡ojalá tuviera más dinero!; **if not** si no; **are you coming? if not, I'll go with Mark** ¿vienes? si no, iré con Mark; **if so** si es así; **are you coming? if so, I'll wait** ¿vienes? si es así te espero; **as if** como si; **even if** aunque, si bien

iffy [ˈɪfɪ] adj (col) dudoso

igloo [ˈɪgluː] n iglú

ignite [ɪgˈnaɪt] vt (set fire to) encender ▷ vi

encenderse
ignition [ɪgˈnɪʃən] *n (Aut)* encendido; **to switch on/off the ~** arrancar/apagar el motor
ignition key *n (Aut)* llave de contacto
ignorance [ˈɪgnərəns] *n* ignorancia; **to keep sb in ~ of sth** ocultarle algo a algn
ignorant [ˈɪgnərənt] *adj* ignorante; **to be ~ of** *(subject)* desconocer; *(events)* ignorar
ignore [ɪgˈnɔːʳ] *vt (person)* no hacer caso de; *(fact)* pasar por alto
ill [ɪl] *adj* enfermo, malo ▷ *n* mal; *(fig)* infortunio ▷ *adv* mal; **to take** *or* **be taken ~** caer *or* ponerse enfermo; **to feel ~ (with)** encontrarse mal (de); **to speak/think ~ of sb** hablar/pensar mal de algn; *see also* **ills**
I'll [aɪl] = **I will; I shall**
ill-advised [ɪlədˈvaɪzd] *adj* poco recomendable; **he was ~ to go** se equivocaba al ir
ill-at-ease [ɪlətˈiːz] *adj* incómodo
illegal [ɪˈliːgl] *adj* ilegal
illegible [ɪˈlɛdʒɪbl] *adj* ilegible
illegitimate [ɪlɪˈdʒɪtɪmət] *adj* ilegítimo
ill-fated [ɪlˈfeɪtɪd] *adj* malogrado
ill feeling *n* rencor
ill health *n* mala salud; **to be in ~** estar mal de salud
illicit [ɪˈlɪsɪt] *adj* ilícito
illiterate [ɪˈlɪtərət] *adj* analfabeto
ill-mannered [ɪlˈmænəd] *adj* mal educado
illness [ˈɪlnɪs] *n* enfermedad
ills [ɪlz] *npl* males
ill-treat [ɪlˈtriːt] *vt* maltratar
illuminate [ɪˈluːmɪneɪt] *vt (room, street)* iluminar, alumbrar; *(subject)* aclarar; **~d sign** letrero luminoso
illumination [ɪluːmɪˈneɪʃən] *n* alumbrado; **illuminations** *npl* luminarias, luces
illusion [ɪˈluːʒən] *n* ilusión; **to be under the ~ that...** estar convencido de que ...
illustrate [ˈɪləstreɪt] *vt* ilustrar
illustration [ɪləˈstreɪʃən] *n (example)* ejemplo, ilustración; *(in book)* lámina, ilustración
illustrious [ɪˈlʌstrɪəs] *adj* ilustre
ill will *n* rencor
I'm [aɪm] = **I am**
image [ˈɪmɪdʒ] *n* imagen
imagery [ˈɪmɪdʒərɪ] *n* imágenes
imaginary [ɪˈmædʒɪnərɪ] *adj* imaginario
imagination [ɪmædʒɪˈneɪʃən] *n* imaginación; *(inventiveness)* inventiva; *(illusion)* fantasía
imaginative [ɪˈmædʒɪnətɪv] *adj* imaginativo
imagine [ɪˈmædʒɪn] *vt* imaginarse; *(suppose)* suponer
imbalance [ɪmˈbæləns] *n* desequilibrio
imbue [ɪmˈbjuː] *vt*: **to ~ sth with** imbuir algo de
IMF *n abbr (= International Monetary Fund)* FMI
imitate [ˈɪmɪteɪt] *vt* imitar
imitation [ɪmɪˈteɪʃən] *n* imitación; *(copy)* copia; *(pej)* remedo
immaculate [ɪˈmækjulət] *adj* limpísimo, inmaculado; *(Rel)* inmaculado
immaterial [ɪməˈtɪərɪəl] *adj* incorpóreo; **it is ~**

whether... no importa si...
immature [ɪməˈtjuəʳ] *adj (person)* inmaduro; *(of one's youth)* joven
immaturity [ɪməˈtjuərɪtɪ] *n* inmadurez
immediate [ɪˈmiːdɪət] *adj* inmediato; *(pressing)* urgente, apremiante; **in the ~ future** en un futuro próximo
immediately [ɪˈmiːdɪətlɪ] *adv (at once)* en seguida; **~ next to** justo al lado de
immense [ɪˈmɛns] *adj* inmenso, enorme
immensely [ɪˈmɛnslɪ] *adv* enormemente
immerse [ɪˈmɜːs] *vt (submerge)* sumergir; **to be ~d in** *(fig)* estar absorto en
immersion heater [ɪˈmɜːʃən-] *n (Brit)* calentador de inmersión
immigrant [ˈɪmɪgrənt] *n* inmigrante
immigrate [ˈɪmɪgreɪt] *vi* inmigrar
immigration [ɪmɪˈgreɪʃən] *n* inmigración
imminent [ˈɪmɪnənt] *adj* inminente
immobilize [ɪˈməubɪlaɪz] *vt* inmovilizar
immoral [ɪˈmɔrl] *adj* inmoral
immorality [ɪmɔˈrælɪtɪ] *n* inmoralidad
immortal [ɪˈmɔːtl] *adj* inmortal
immortality [ɪmɔːˈtælɪtɪ] *n* inmortalidad
immortalize [ɪˈmɔːtlaɪz] *vt* inmortalizar
immune [ɪˈmjuːn] *adj*: **~ (to)** inmune (a)
immune system *n* sistema inmunitario
immunity [ɪˈmjuːnɪtɪ] *n (Med, of diplomat)* inmunidad; *(Comm)* exención
immunization [ɪmjunaɪˈzeɪʃən] *n* inmunización
imp [ɪmp] *n (small devil, also fig: child)* diablillo
impact [ˈɪmpækt] *n (gen)* impacto
impair [ɪmˈpɛəʳ] *vt* perjudicar
impart [ɪmˈpɑːt] *vt* comunicar; *(make known)* participar; *(bestow)* otorgar
impartial [ɪmˈpɑːʃl] *adj* imparcial
impassable [ɪmˈpɑːsəbl] *adj (barrier)* infranqueable; *(road)* intransitable
impassive [ɪmˈpæsɪv] *adj* impasible
impatience [ɪmˈpeɪʃəns] *n* impaciencia
impatient [ɪmˈpeɪʃənt] *adj* impaciente; **to get** *or* **grow ~** impacientarse
impeccable [ɪmˈpɛkəbl] *adj* impecable
impede [ɪmˈpiːd] *vt* estorbar, dificultar
impediment [ɪmˈpɛdɪmənt] *n* obstáculo, estorbo; *(also: speech impediment)* defecto (del habla)
impending [ɪmˈpɛndɪŋ] *adj* inminente
imperative [ɪmˈpɛrətɪv] *adj (tone)* imperioso; *(necessary)* imprescindible ▷ *n (Ling)* imperativo
imperfect [ɪmˈpɜːfɪkt] *adj* imperfecto; *(goods etc)* defectuoso
imperfection [ɪmpəˈfɛkʃən] *n (blemish)* desperfecto; *(fault, flaw)* defecto
imperial [ɪmˈpɪərɪəl] *adj* imperial
imperialism [ɪmˈpɪərɪəlɪzəm] *n* imperialismo
impersonal [ɪmˈpɜːsənl] *adj* impersonal
impersonate [ɪmˈpɜːsəneɪt] *vt* hacerse pasar por
impersonation [ɪmpɜːsəˈneɪʃən] *n* imitación
impertinence [ɪmˈpɜːtɪnəns] *n* impertinencia, insolencia
impertinent [ɪmˈpɜːtɪnənt] *adj* impertinente,

insolente

impervious [ɪm'pə:vɪəs] *adj* impermeable; *(fig)*: ~ **to** insensible a

impetuous [ɪm'pɛtjuəs] *adj* impetuoso

impetus ['ɪmpətəs] *n* ímpetu; *(fig)* impulso

impinge [ɪm'pɪndʒ]: **to** ~ **on** *vt fus (affect)* afectar a

implant [ɪm'plɑ:nt] *vt (Med)* injertar, implantar; *(fig: idea, principle)* inculcar

implausible [ɪm'plɔ:zɪbl] *adj* implausible

implement *n* ['ɪmplɪmənt] instrumento, herramienta ▷ *vt* ['ɪmplɪmɛnt] hacer efectivo; *(carry out)* realizar

implicate ['ɪmplɪkeɪt] *vt (compromise)* comprometer; *(involve)* enredar; **to** ~ **sb in sth** comprometer a algn en algo

implication [ɪmplɪ'keɪʃən] *n* consecuencia; **by** ~ indirectamente

implicit [ɪm'plɪsɪt] *adj (gen)* implícito; *(complete)* absoluto

implicitly [ɪm'plɪsɪtlɪ] *adv* implícitamente

imply [ɪm'plaɪ] *vt (involve)* implicar, suponer; *(hint)* insinuar

impolite [ɪmpə'laɪt] *adj* mal educado

import *vt* importar ▷ *n (Comm)* importación; *(meaning)* significado, sentido ▷ *cpd (duty, licence etc)* de importación

importance [ɪm'pɔ:təns] *n* importancia; **to be of great/little** ~ tener mucha/poca, importancia

important [ɪm'pɔ:tənt] *adj* importante; **it's not** ~ no importa, no tiene importancia; **it is** ~ **that** es importante que

importer [ɪm'pɔ:tər] *n* importador(a)

impose [ɪm'pəuz] *vt* imponer ▷ *vi*: **to** ~ **on sb** abusar de algn

imposing [ɪm'pəuzɪŋ] *adj* imponente, impresionante

imposition [ɪmpə'zɪʃn] *n (of tax etc)* imposición; **to be an** ~ molestar

impossible [ɪm'pɔsɪbl] *adj* imposible; *(person)* insoportable; **it is** ~ **for me to leave now** me es imposible salir ahora

impostor [ɪm'pɔstər] *n* impostor(a)

impotence ['ɪmpətəns] *n* impotencia

impotent ['ɪmpətənt] *adj* impotente

impound [ɪm'paund] *vt* embargar

impoverished [ɪm'pɔvərɪʃt] *adj* necesitado; *(land)* agotado

impractical [ɪm'præktɪkl] *adj (person)* poco práctico

imprecise [ɪmprɪ'saɪs] *adj* impreciso

impregnable [ɪm'prɛgnəbl] *adj* invulnerable; *(castle)* inexpugnable

impress [ɪm'prɛs] *vt* impresionar; *(mark)* estampar ▷ *vi* causar buena impresión; **to** ~ **sth on sb** convencer a algn de la importancia de algo

impression [ɪm'prɛʃən] *n* impresión; *(footprint etc)* huella; *(print run)* edición; **to be under the** ~ **that** tener la idea de que; **to make a good/bad** ~ **on sb** causar buena/mala impresión a algn

impressionist [ɪm'prɛʃənɪst] *n* impresionista

impressive [ɪm'prɛsɪv] *adj* impresionante

imprint ['ɪmprɪnt] *n (Publishing)* pie de imprenta; *(fig)* sello

imprison [ɪm'prɪzn] *vt* encarcelar

imprisonment [ɪm'prɪznmənt] *n* encarcelamiento; *(term of imprisonment)* cárcel; **life** ~ cadena perpetua

improbable [ɪm'prɔbəbl] *adj* improbable, inverosímil

impromptu [ɪm'prɔmptju:] *adj* improvisado ▷ *adv* de improviso

improper [ɪm'prɔpər] *adj (incorrect)* impropio; *(unseemly)* indecoroso; *(indecent)* indecente

improve [ɪm'pru:v] *vt* mejorar; *(foreign language)* perfeccionar ▷ *vi* mejorar

▶ **improve (up)on** *vt fus (offer)* mejorar

improvement [ɪm'pru:vmənt] *n* mejora; perfeccionamiento; **to make ~s to** mejorar

improvise ['ɪmprəvaɪz] *vt, vi* improvisar

imprudent [ɪm'pru:dnt] *adj* imprudente

impudent ['ɪmpjudnt] *adj* descarado, insolente

impulse ['ɪmpʌls] *n* impulso; **to act on** ~ actuar sin reflexionar, dejarse llevar por el impulso

impulsive [ɪm'pʌlsɪv] *adj* irreflexivo, impulsivo

impure [ɪm'pjuər] *adj (adulterated)* adulterado; *(morally)* impuro

impurity [ɪm'pjuərɪtɪ] *n* impureza

in [ɪn] *prep* **1** *(indicating place, position, with place names)* en; **in the house/garden** en (la) casa/el jardín; **in here/there** aquí/ahí or allí dentro; **in London/England** en Londres/Inglaterra; **in town** en el centro (de la ciudad)

2 *(indicating time)* en; **in spring** en (la) primavera; **in 1888/May** en 1888/mayo; **in the afternoon** por la tarde; **at 4 o'clock in the afternoon** a las 4 de la tarde; **I did it in 3 hours/days** lo hice en 3 horas/días; **I'll see you in 2 weeks** *or* **in 2 weeks' time** te veré dentro de 2 semanas; **once in a hundred years** una vez cada cien años

3 *(indicating manner etc)* en; **in a loud/soft voice** en voz alta/baja; **in pencil/ink** a lápiz/bolígrafo; **the boy in the blue shirt** el chico de la camisa azul; **in writing** por escrito; **to pay in dollars** pagar en dólares

4 *(indicating circumstances)*: **in the sun/shade** al sol/a la sombra; **in the rain** bajo la lluvia; **a change in policy** un cambio de política; **a rise in prices** un aumento de precios

5 *(indicating mood, state)*: **in tears** llorando; **in anger/despair** enfadado/desesperado; **to live in luxury** vivir lujosamente

6 *(with ratios, numbers)*: **1 in 10 households, 1 household in 10** una de cada 10 familias; **20 pence in the pound** 20 peniques por libra; **they lined up in twos** se alinearon de dos en dos; **in hundreds** a *or* por centenares

7 *(referring to people, works)* en; entre; **the disease is common in children** la enfermedad es común entre los niños; **in (the works of) Dickens** en (las obras de) Dickens

8 *(indicating profession etc)*: **to be in teaching** dedicarse a la enseñanza

9 (*after superlative*) de; **the best pupil in the class** el (la) mejor alumno(-a) de la clase
10 (*with present participle*): **in saying this** al decir esto
▷ *adv*: **to be in** (*person: at home*) estar en casa; (: *at work*) estar; (*train, ship, plane*) haber llegado; (*in fashion*) estar de moda; **she'll be in later today** llegará más tarde hoy; **to ask sb in** hacer pasar a algn; **to run/limp** *etc* **in** entrar corriendo/cojeando *etc*; **in that** *conj* ya que
▷ *npl*: **the ins and outs** (*of proposal, situation etc*) los detalles
in., ins *abbr* = **inch(es)**
inability [ɪnə'bɪlɪtɪ] *n* incapacidad; **~ to pay** insolvencia en el pago
inaccuracy [ɪn'ækjurəsɪ] *n* inexactitud
inaccurate [ɪn'ækjurət] *adj* inexacto, incorrecto
inadequate [ɪn'ædɪkwət] *adj* (*insufficient*) insuficiente; (*unsuitable*) inadecuado; (*person*) incapaz
inadmissible [ɪnəd'mɪsəbl] *adj* improcedente, inadmisible
inadvertent [ɪnəd'və:tənt] *adj* descuidado, involuntario
inadvertently [ɪnəd'və:tntlɪ] *adv* por descuido
inadvisable [ɪnəd'vaɪzəbl] *adj* poco aconsejable
inane [ɪ'neɪn] *adj* necio, fatuo
inanimate [ɪn'ænɪmət] *adj* inanimado
inapplicable [ɪn'æplɪkəbl] *adj* inaplicable
inappropriate [ɪnə'prəuprɪət] *adj* inadecuado
inarticulate [ɪnɑː'tɪkjulət] *adj* (*person*) incapaz de expresarse; (*speech*) mal pronunciado
inasmuch as [ɪnəz'mʌtʃ-] *adv* en la medida en que
inaugural [ɪ'nɔːgjurəl] *adj* inaugural; (*speech*) de apertura
inaugurate [ɪ'nɔːgjureɪt] *vt* inaugurar; (*president, official*) investir
inauguration [ɪnɔːgju'reɪʃən] *n* inauguración; (*of official*) investidura; (*of event*) ceremonia de apertura
in-between [ɪnbɪ'twiːn] *adj* intermedio
inborn [ɪn'bɔːn] *adj* (*feeling*) innato
inbred [ɪn'bred] *adj* innato; (*family*) consanguíneo
Inc. *abbr* = **incorporated**
Inca ['ɪŋkə] *adj* (*also*: **Incan**) inca, de los incas ▷ *n* inca
incapable [ɪn'keɪpəbl] *adj*: **~ (of doing sth)** incapaz (de hacer algo)
incapacitate [ɪnkə'pæsɪteɪt] *vt*: **to ~ sb** incapacitar a algn
incapacity [ɪnkə'pæsɪtɪ] *n* (*inability*) incapacidad
incarcerate [ɪn'kɑːsəreɪt] *vt* encarcelar
incarnate *adj* en persona ▷ *vt* encarnar
incarnation [ɪnkɑː'neɪʃən] *n* encarnación
incendiary [ɪn'sendɪərɪ] *adj* incendiario ▷ *n* (*bomb*) bomba incendiaria
incense *n* incienso ▷ *vt* (*anger*) indignar, encolerizar
incentive [ɪn'sentɪv] *n* incentivo, estímulo
incessant [ɪn'sesnt] *adj* incesante, continuo

incessantly [ɪn'sesəntlɪ] *adv* constantemente
incest ['ɪnsest] *n* incesto
inch [ɪntʃ] *n* pulgada; **to be within an ~ of** estar a dos dedos de; **he didn't give an ~** no hizo la más mínima concesión; **a few ~es** unas pulgadas
▸ **inch forward** *vi* avanzar palmo a palmo
incidence ['ɪnsɪdns] *n* (*of crime, disease*) incidencia
incident ['ɪnsɪdnt] *n* incidente; (*in book*) episodio
incidental [ɪnsɪ'dentl] *adj* circunstancial, accesorio; (*unplanned*) fortuito; **~ to** relacionado con; **~ expenses** (gastos) imprevistos
incidentally [ɪnsɪ'dentəlɪ] *adv* (*by the way*) por cierto
incident room *n* (*Police*) centro de coordinación
incinerate [ɪn'sɪnəreɪt] *vt* incinerar, quemar
incinerator [ɪn'sɪnəreɪtəʳ] *n* incinerador, incineradora
incision [ɪn'sɪʒən] *n* incisión
incisive [ɪn'saɪsɪv] *adj* (*mind*) penetrante; (*remark etc*) incisivo
incite [ɪn'saɪt] *vt* provocar, incitar
incl. *abbr* = **including; inclusive(of)**
inclination [ɪnklɪ'neɪʃən] *n* (*tendency*) tendencia, inclinación
incline *n* pendiente, cuesta ▷ *vt* (*slope*) inclinar; (*head*) poner de lado ▷ *vi* inclinarse; **to be ~d to** (*tend*) ser propenso a; (*be willing*) estar dispuesto a
include [ɪn'kluːd] *vt* incluir, comprender; (*in letter*) adjuntar; **the tip is/is not ~d** la propina está/no está incluida
including [ɪn'kluːdɪŋ] *prep* incluso, inclusive; **~ tip** propina incluida
inclusion [ɪn'kluːʒən] *n* inclusión
inclusive [ɪn'kluːsɪv] *adj* inclusivo ▷ *adv* inclusive; **~ of tax** incluidos los impuestos; **$50, ~ of all surcharges** 50 dólares, incluidos todos los recargos
incognito [ɪnkɔg'niːtəu] *adv* de incógnito
incoherent [ɪnkəu'hɪərənt] *adj* incoherente
income ['ɪnkʌm] *n* (*personal*) ingresos; (*from property etc*) renta; (*profit*) rédito; **gross/net ~** ingresos brutos/netos; **~ and expenditure account** cuenta de gastos e ingresos
income support *n* (*Brit*) ≈ ayuda familiar
income tax *n* impuesto sobre la renta
incoming ['ɪnkʌmɪŋ] *adj* (*passengers, flight*) de llegada; (*government*) entrante; (*tenant*) nuevo
incompatible [ɪnkəm'pætɪbl] *adj* incompatible
incompetence [ɪn'kɔmpɪtəns] *n* incompetencia
incompetent [ɪn'kɔmpɪtənt] *adj* incompetente
incomplete [ɪnkəm'pliːt] *adj* incompleto; (*unfinished*) sin terminar
incomprehensible [ɪnkɔmprɪ'hensɪbl] *adj* incomprensible
inconceivable [ɪnkən'siːvəbl] *adj* inconcebible
inconclusive [ɪnkən'kluːsɪv] *adj* sin resultado (definitivo); (*argument*) poco convincente
incongruous [ɪn'kɔŋgruəs] *adj* discordante
inconsiderate [ɪnkən'sɪdərət] *adj* desconsiderado; **how ~ of him!** ¡qué falta de consideración (de su parte)!

inconsistency [ɪnkən'sɪstənsɪ] *n*
inconsecuencia; *(of actions etc)* falta de lógica;
(of work) carácter desigual, inconsistencia; *(of
statement etc)* contradicción
inconsistent [ɪnkən'sɪstnt] *adj* inconsecuente; ~
with que no concuerda con
inconspicuous [ɪnkən'spɪkjuəs] *adj* *(discreet)*
discreto; *(person)* que llama poco la atención
incontinent [ɪn'kɔntɪnənt] *adj* incontinente
inconvenience [ɪnkən'viːnjəns] *n* *(gen)*
inconvenientes; *(trouble)* molestia ▷ *vt*
incomodar; **to put sb to** ~ causar mucha
molestia a algn; **don't** ~ **yourself** no se moleste
inconvenient [ɪnkən'viːnjənt] *adj* incómodo,
poco práctico; *(time, place)* inoportuno; **that
time is very** ~ **for me** esa hora me es muy
inconveniente
incorporate [ɪn'kɔːpəreɪt] *vt* incorporar;
(contain) comprender; *(add)* agregar
incorporated [ɪn'kɔːpəreɪtɪd] *adj*: ~ **company**,
(US: *abbr*) **Inc** ≈ Sociedad Anónima (S.A.)
incorrect [ɪnkə'rɛkt] *adj* incorrecto
increase *n* aumento ▷ *vi* aumentar; *(grow)*
crecer; *(price)* subir ▷ *vt* aumentar; **an** ~ **of 5%**
un aumento de 5%; **an** ~ **in road accidents** un
aumento de accidentes de tráfico; **to be on the**
~ ir en aumento; **traffic on motorways has** ~**d**
el tráfico en las autopistas ha aumentado; **to** ~
in size aumentar de tamaño; **they have** ~**d his
salary** le han aumentado el sueldo
increasing [ɪn'kriːsɪŋ] *adj* *(number)* creciente, que
va en aumento
increasingly [ɪn'kriːsɪŋlɪ] *adv* cada vez más
incredible [ɪn'krɛdɪbl] *adj* increíble
incredulous [ɪn'krɛdjuləs] *adj* incrédulo
increment ['ɪnkrɪmənt] *n* aumento,
incremento
incriminate [ɪn'krɪmɪneɪt] *vt* incriminar
incubate ['ɪnkjubeɪt] *vt* *(egg)* incubar, empollar
▷ *vi* *(egg, disease)* incubar
incubation [ɪnkju'beɪʃən] *n* incubación
incubator ['ɪnkjubeɪtəʳ] *n* incubadora
incumbent [ɪn'kʌmbənt] *n* ocupante ▷ *adj*: **it is**
~ **on him to...** le incumbe...
incur [ɪn'kəːʳ] *vt* *(expenses)* incurrir en; *(loss)* sufrir
incurable [ɪn'kjuərəbl] *adj* incurable
indebted [ɪn'dɛtɪd] *adj*: **to be** ~ **to sb** estar
agradecido a algn
indecency [ɪn'diːsnsɪ] *n* indecencia
indecent [ɪn'diːsnt] *adj* indecente
indecent assault *n* *(Brit)* atentado contra el
pudor
indecent exposure *n* exhibicionismo
indecision [ɪndɪ'sɪʒən] *n* indecisión
indecisive [ɪndɪ'saɪsɪv] *adj* indeciso; *(discussion)*
no resuelto, inconcluyente
indeed [ɪn'diːd] *adv* efectivamente, en realidad;
yes ~! ¡claro que sí!
indefinite [ɪn'dɛfɪnɪt] *adj* indefinido; *(uncertain)*
incierto
indefinitely [ɪn'dɛfɪnɪtlɪ] *adv* *(wait)*
indefinidamente

indemnity [ɪn'dɛmnɪtɪ] *n* *(insurance)*
indemnidad; *(compensation)* indemnización
indent [ɪn'dɛnt] *vt* *(text)* sangrar
independence [ɪndɪ'pɛndns] *n* independencia
Independence Day *n* Día de la Independencia
independent [ɪndɪ'pɛndənt] *adj* independiente;
to become ~ independizarse
in-depth ['ɪndɛpθ] *adj* en profundidad, a fondo
index ['ɪndɛks] *n* *(pl* -**es**) *(in book)* índice; *(in library
etc)* catálogo *(pl* **indices**) *(ratio, sign)* exponente
index card *n* ficha
index finger *n* índice
index-linked ['ɪndɛks'lɪŋkt], (US) **indexed**
['ɪndɛkst] *adj* indexado
India ['ɪndɪə] *n* la India
Indian ['ɪndɪən] *adj, n* indio(-a); *(American Indian)*
indio(-a) de América, amerindio(-a); **Red** ~ piel
roja
Indian Ocean *n*: **the** ~ el Océano Índico, el Mar
de las Indias
Indian summer *n* *(fig)* veranillo de San Martín
indicate ['ɪndɪkeɪt] *vt* indicar ▷ *vi* *(Brit Aut)*: **to** ~
left/right indicar a la izquierda/a la derecha
indication [ɪndɪ'keɪʃən] *n* indicio, señal
indicative [ɪn'dɪkətɪv] *adj*: **to be** ~ **of sth** indicar
algo ▷ *n* *(Ling)* indicativo
indicator ['ɪndɪkeɪtəʳ] *n* *(gen)* indicador; *(Aut)*
intermitente, direccional *(LAm)*
indices ['ɪndɪsiːz] *npl of* **index**
indict [ɪn'daɪt] *vt* acusar
indictment [ɪn'daɪtmənt] *n* acusación
indifference [ɪn'dɪfrəns] *n* indiferencia
indifferent [ɪn'dɪfrənt] *adj* indiferente; *(poor)*
regular
indigenous [ɪn'dɪdʒənəs] *adj* indígena
indigestion [ɪndɪ'dʒɛstʃən] *n* indigestión
indignant [ɪn'dɪgnənt] *adj*: **to be** ~ **about sth**
indignarse por algo
indignation [ɪndɪg'neɪʃən] *n* indignación
indignity [ɪn'dɪgnɪtɪ] *n* indignidad
indigo ['ɪndɪgəu] *adj* *(colour)* (de color) añil ▷ *n*
añil
indirect [ɪndɪ'rɛkt] *adj* indirecto
indiscreet [ɪndɪ'skriːt] *adj* indiscreto,
imprudente
indiscriminate [ɪndɪ'skrɪmɪnət] *adj*
indiscriminado
indisputable [ɪndɪ'spjuːtəbl] *adj* incontestable
indistinct [ɪndɪ'stɪŋkt] *adj* indistinto
indistinguishable [ɪndɪ'stɪŋgwɪʃəbl] *adj*
indistinguible
individual [ɪndɪ'vɪdjuəl] *n* individuo ▷ *adj*
individual; *(personal)* personal; *(for/of one only)*
particular
individuality [ɪndɪvɪdju'ælɪtɪ] *n* individualidad
indoctrination [ɪndɔktrɪ'neɪʃən] *n*
adoctrinamiento
Indonesia [ɪndə'niːzɪə] *n* Indonesia
indoor ['ɪndɔːʳ] *adj* *(swimming pool)* cubierto;
(plant) de interior; *(sport)* bajo cubierta
indoors [ɪn'dɔːz] *adv* dentro; *(at home)* en casa
induce [ɪn'djuːs] *vt* inducir, persuadir; *(bring*

about) producir; **to ~ sb to do sth** persuadir a algn a que haga algo

inducement [ɪn'dju:smənt] *n (incentive)* incentivo, aliciente

induction [ɪn'dʌkʃən] *n (Med: of birth)* inducción

indulge [ɪn'dʌldʒ] *vt (whim)* satisfacer; *(person)* complacer; *(child)* mimar ▷ *vi*: **to ~ in** darse el gusto de

indulgence [ɪn'dʌldʒəns] *n* vicio

indulgent [ɪn'dʌldʒənt] *adj* indulgente

industrial [ɪn'dʌstrɪəl] *adj* industrial

industrial action *n* huelga

industrial estate *n (Brit)* polígono *or (LAm)* zona industrial

industrialist [ɪn'dʌstrɪəlɪst] *n* industrial

industrialize [ɪn'dʌstrɪəlaɪz] *vt* industrializar

industrial park *n (US)* = **industrial estate**

industrial relations *npl* relaciones empresariales

industrious [ɪn'dʌstrɪəs] *adj (gen)* trabajador(a); *(student)* aplicado

industry ['ɪndəstrɪ] *n* industria; *(diligence)* aplicación

inebriated [ɪ'ni:brɪeɪtɪd] *adj* borracho

inedible [ɪn'edɪbl] *adj* incomible; *(plant etc)* no comestible

ineffective [ɪnɪ'fektɪv], **ineffectual** [ɪnɪ'fektʃuəl] *adj* ineficaz, inútil

inefficiency [ɪnɪ'fɪʃənsɪ] *n* ineficacia

inefficient [ɪnɪ'fɪʃənt] *adj* ineficaz, ineficiente

ineligible [ɪn'elɪdʒɪbl] *adj* inelegible

inept [ɪ'nept] *adj* incompetente, incapaz

inequality [ɪnɪ'kwɔlɪtɪ] *n* desigualdad

inertia [ɪ'nə:ʃə] *n* inercia; *(laziness)* pereza

inescapable [ɪnɪ'skeɪpəbl] *adj* ineludible, inevitable

inevitable [ɪn'evɪtəbl] *adj* inevitable; *(necessary)* forzoso

inevitably [ɪn'evɪtəblɪ] *adv* inevitablemente; **as ~ happens** ... como siempre pasa ...

inexact [ɪnɪg'zaekt] *adj* inexacto

inexcusable [ɪnɪks'kju:zəbl] *adj* imperdonable

inexhaustible [ɪnɪg'zɔ:stɪbl] *adj* inagotable

inexpensive [ɪnɪk'spensɪv] *adj* económico

inexperience [ɪnɪk'spɪərɪəns] *n* falta de experiencia

inexperienced [ɪnɪk'spɪərɪənst] *adj* inexperto; **to be ~ in sth** no tener experiencia en algo

infallible [ɪn'fælɪbl] *adj* infalible

infamous ['ɪnfəməs] *adj* infame

infancy ['ɪnfənsɪ] *n* infancia

infant ['ɪnfənt] *n* niño(-a)

infantry ['ɪnfəntrɪ] *n* infantería

infant school *n (Brit)* escuela de párvulos; *see also* **primary school**

infatuated [ɪn'fætjueɪtɪd] *adj*: **~ with** *(in love)* loco por; **to become ~ (with sb)** enamoriscarse (de algn), encapricharse (con algn)

infatuation [ɪnfætju'eɪʃən] *n* enamoramiento

infect [ɪn'fekt] *vt (wound)* infectar; *(person)* contagiar; *(fig: pej)* corromper; **~ed with** *(illness)* contagiado de; **to become ~ed** *(wound)*

infectarse

infection [ɪn'fekʃən] *n* infección; *(fig)* contagio

infectious [ɪn'fekʃəs] *adj* contagioso; *(fig)* infeccioso

infer [ɪn'fə:ʳ] *vt* deducir, inferir; **to ~ (from)** inferir (de), deducir (de)

inference ['ɪnfərəns] *n* deducción, inferencia

inferior [ɪn'fɪərɪəʳ] *adj, n* inferior; **to feel ~** sentirse inferior

inferiority [ɪnfɪərɪ'ɔrɪtɪ] *n* inferioridad

inferiority complex *n* complejo de inferioridad

inferno [ɪn'fə:nəu] *n* infierno; *(fig)* hoguera

infertile [ɪn'fə:taɪl] *adj* estéril; *(person)* infecundo

infertility [ɪnfə:'tɪlɪtɪ] *n* esterilidad; infecundidad

infidelity [ɪnfɪ'delɪtɪ] *n* infidelidad

in-fighting ['ɪnfaɪtɪŋ] *n (fig)* lucha(s) interna(s)

infinite ['ɪnfɪnɪt] *adj* infinito; **an ~ amount of money/time** un sinfín de dinero/tiempo

infinitive [ɪn'fɪnɪtɪv] *n* infinitivo

infinity [ɪn'fɪnɪtɪ] *n (Math)* infinito; *(an infinity)* infinidad

infirm [ɪn'fə:m] *adj* enfermizo, débil

infirmary [ɪn'fə:mərɪ] *n* hospital

inflamed [ɪn'fleɪmd] *adj*: **to become ~** inflamarse

inflammable [ɪn'flæməbl] *adj (Brit)* inflamable; *(situation etc)* explosivo

inflammation [ɪnflə'meɪʃən] *n* inflamación

inflatable [ɪn'fleɪtəbl] *adj* inflable

inflate [ɪn'fleɪt] *vt (tyre, balloon)* inflar; *(fig)* hinchar

inflation [ɪn'fleɪʃən] *n (Econ)* inflación

inflationary [ɪn'fleɪʃnərɪ] *adj* inflacionario

inflict [ɪn'flɪkt] *vt*: **to ~ on** infligir en; *(tax etc)* imponer a

influence ['ɪnfluəns] *n* influencia ▷ *vt* influir en, influenciar; **under the ~ of alcohol** en estado de embriaguez

influential [ɪnflu'enʃl] *adj* influyente

influenza [ɪnflu'enzə] *n* gripe

influx ['ɪnflʌks] *n* afluencia

inform [ɪn'fɔ:m] *vt*: **to ~ sb of sth** informar a algn sobre *or* de algo; *(warn)* avisar a algn de algo; *(communicate)* comunicar algo a algn ▷ *vi*: **to ~ on sb** delatar a algn

informal [ɪn'fɔ:ml] *adj (manner, tone)* desenfadado; *(dress, interview, occasion)* informal

informality [ɪnfɔ:'mælɪtɪ] *n* falta de ceremonia; *(intimacy)* intimidad; *(familiarity)* familiaridad; *(ease)* afabilidad

informant [ɪn'fɔ:mənt] *n* informante

information [ɪnfə'meɪʃən] *n* información; *(knowledge)* conocimientos; *(Law)* delación; **a piece of ~** un dato; **for your ~** para su información

information science *n* gestión de la información

information technology (IT) *n* informática

informative [ɪn'fɔ:mətɪv] *adj* informativo

informer [ɪn'fɔ:məʳ] *n* delator(a); *(also:* **police informer)** soplón(-ona)

infra-red [ɪnfrə'rɛd] *adj* infrarrojo
infrastructure ['ɪnfrəstrʌktʃəʳ] *n* (*of system etc*, *Econ*) infraestructura
infringe [ɪn'frɪndʒ] *vt* infringir, violar ▷ *vi*: **to ~ on** invadir
infringement [ɪn'frɪndʒmənt] *n* infracción; (*of rights*) usurpación; (*Sport*) falta
infuriating [ɪn'fjuərɪeɪtɪŋ] *adj*: **I find it ~** me saca de quicio
ingenious [ɪn'dʒiːnjəs] *adj* ingenioso
ingenuity [ɪndʒɪ'njuːɪtɪ] *n* ingeniosidad
ingenuous [ɪn'dʒɛnjuəs] *adj* ingenuo
ingot ['ɪŋgət] *n* lingote, barra
ingrained [ɪn'greɪnd] *adj* arraigado
ingratiate [ɪn'greɪʃɪeɪt] *vt*: **to ~ o.s. with** congraciarse con
ingratitude [ɪn'grætɪtjuːd] *n* ingratitud
ingredient [ɪn'griːdɪənt] *n* ingrediente
ingrowing ['ɪngrəuɪŋ] *adj*: **~ (toe)nail** uña encarnada
inhabit [ɪn'hæbɪt] *vt* vivir en; (*occupy*) ocupar
inhabitant [ɪn'hæbɪtənt] *n* habitante
inhale [ɪn'heɪl] *vt* inhalar ▷ *vi* (*in smoking*) tragar
inhaler [ɪn'heɪləʳ] *n* inhalador
inherent [ɪn'hɪərənt] *adj*: **~ in** or **to** inherente a
inherit [ɪn'hɛrɪt] *vt* heredar
inheritance [ɪn'hɛrɪtəns] *n* herencia; (*fig*) patrimonio
inhibit [ɪn'hɪbɪt] *vt* inhibir, impedir; **to ~ sb from doing sth** impedir a algn hacer algo
inhibited [ɪn'hɪbɪtɪd] *adj* (*person*) cohibido
inhibition [ɪnhɪ'bɪʃən] *n* cohibición
in-house ['ɪnhaus] *adj* dentro de la empresa
inhuman [ɪn'hjuːmən] *adj* inhumano
inhumane [ɪnhjuː'meɪn] *adj* inhumano
inimitable [ɪ'nɪmɪtəbl] *adj* inimitable
initial [ɪ'nɪʃl] *adj* inicial; (*first*) primero ▷ *n* inicial ▷ *vt* firmar con las iniciales; **initials** *npl* iniciales; (*abbreviation*) siglas
initially [ɪ'nɪʃəlɪ] *adv* en un principio
initiate [ɪ'nɪʃɪeɪt] *vt* (*start*) iniciar; **to ~ sb into a secret** iniciar a algn en un secreto; **to ~ proceedings against sb** (*Law*) poner una demanda contra algn
initiation [ɪnɪʃɪ'eɪʃən] *n* (*into secret etc*) iniciación; (*beginning*) comienzo
initiative [ɪ'nɪʃətɪv] *n* iniciativa; **to take the ~** tomar la iniciativa
inject [ɪn'dʒɛkt] *vt* inyectar; (*money, enthusiasm*) aportar
injection [ɪn'dʒɛkʃən] *n* inyección; **to have an ~** ponerse una inyección
injure ['ɪndʒəʳ] *vt* herir; (*hurt*) lastimar; (*fig: reputation etc*) perjudicar; (*feelings*) herir; **to ~ o.s.** hacerse daño, lastimarse
injured ['ɪndʒəd] *adj* (*also fig*) herido; **~ party** (*Law*) parte perjudicada
injury ['ɪndʒərɪ] *n* herida, lesión; (*wrong*) perjuicio, daño; **to escape without ~** salir ileso
injury time *n* (*Sport*) descuento
injustice [ɪn'dʒʌstɪs] *n* injusticia; **you do me an ~** usted es injusto conmigo

ink [ɪŋk] *n* tinta
inkling ['ɪŋklɪŋ] *n* sospecha; (*idea*) idea
inlaid ['ɪnleɪd] *adj* (*wood*) taraceado; (*tiles*) entarimado
inland *adj* interior; (*town*) del interior ▷ *adv* tierra adentro
Inland Revenue *n* (*Brit*) ≈ Hacienda
in-laws ['ɪnlɔːz] *npl* suegros
inlet ['ɪnlɛt] *n* (*Geo*) ensenada, cala; (*Tech*) admisión, entrada
inmate ['ɪnmeɪt] *n* (*in prison*) preso(-a), presidiario(-a); (*in asylum*) internado(-a)
inmost ['ɪnməust] *adj* más íntimo, más secreto
inn [ɪn] *n* posada, mesón; **the I~s of Court**; *see* **barrister**
innate [ɪ'neɪt] *adj* innato
inner ['ɪnəʳ] *adj* interior, interno
inner city *n barrios deprimidos del centro de una ciudad*
innermost ['ɪnəməust] *adj* más íntimo, más secreto
inner tube *n* (*of tyre*) cámara, llanta (*LAm*)
innings ['ɪnɪŋz] *n* (*Cricket*) entrada, turno
innocence ['ɪnəsns] *n* inocencia
innocent ['ɪnəsnt] *adj* inocente
innocuous [ɪ'nɔkjuəs] *adj* inocuo
innovation [ɪnəu'veɪʃən] *n* novedad
innuendo [ɪnju'ɛndəu] (*pl* **-es**) *n* indirecta
innumerable [ɪ'njuːmrəbl] *adj* innumerable
inoculate [ɪ'nɔkjuleɪt] *vt*: **to ~ sb with sth/ against sth** inocular or vacunar a algn con algo/ contra algo
inoculation [ɪnɔkju'leɪʃən] *n* inoculación
inoffensive [ɪnə'fɛnsɪv] *adj* inofensivo
inordinate [ɪ'nɔːdɪnət] *adj* excesivo, desmesurado
inordinately [ɪ'nɔːdɪnətlɪ] *adv* excesivamente, desmesuradamente
in-patient ['ɪnpeɪʃənt] *n* (paciente) interno(-a)
input ['ɪnput] *n* (*Elec*) entrada; (*Comput*) entrada de datos ▷ *vt* (*Comput*) introducir, entrar
inquest ['ɪnkwɛst] *n* (*coroner's*) investigación post-mortem
inquire [ɪn'kwaɪəʳ] *vi* preguntar ▷ *vt*: **to ~ when/ where/whether** preguntar cuándo/dónde/si; **to ~ about** (*person*) preguntar por; (*fact*) informarse de
▶ **inquire into** *vt fus*: **to ~ into sth** investigar or indagar algo
inquiry [ɪn'kwaɪərɪ] *n* pregunta; (*Law*) investigación, pesquisa; (*commission*) comisión investigadora; **to hold an ~ into sth** emprender una investigación sobre algo
inquiry office *n* (*Brit*) oficina de información
inquisition [ɪnkwɪ'zɪʃən] *n* inquisición
inquisitive [ɪn'kwɪzɪtɪv] *adj* (*mind*) inquisitivo; (*person*) fisgón(-ona)
inroad ['ɪnrəud] *n* incursión; (*fig*) invasión; **to make ~s into** (*time*) ocupar parte de; (*savings, supplies*) agotar parte de
insane [ɪn'seɪn] *adj* loco; (*Med*) demente
insanity [ɪn'sænɪtɪ] *n* demencia, locura
inscribe [ɪn'skraɪb] *vt* inscribir; (*book etc*): **to ~**

(**to sb**) dedicar (a algn)

inscription [ɪn'skrɪpʃən] n (gen) inscripción; (in book) dedicatoria

inscrutable [ɪn'skru:təbl] adj inescrutable, insondable

insect ['ɪnsɛkt] n insecto

insecticide [ɪn'sɛktɪsaɪd] n insecticida

insecure [ɪnsɪ'kjuə'] adj inseguro

insecurity [ɪnsɪ'kjuərɪtɪ] n inseguridad

insemination [ɪnsɛmɪ'neɪʃn] n: **artificial ~** inseminación artificial

insensitive [ɪn'sɛnsɪtɪv] adj insensible

inseparable [ɪn'sɛprəbl] adj inseparable; **they were ~ friends** los unía una estrecha amistad

insert vt (into sth) introducir; (Comput) insertar ▷ n encarte

insertion [ɪn'sə:ʃən] n inserción

in-service [ɪn'sə:vɪs] adj (training, course) en el trabajo, a cargo de la empresa

inshore [ɪn'ʃɔ:'] adj: **~ fishing** pesca costera ▷ adv (fish) a lo largo de la costa; (move) hacia la orilla

inside ['ɪn'saɪd] n interior; (lining) forro; (of road: Brit) izquierdo; (: US, Europe etc) derecho ▷ adj interior, interno; (information) confidencial ▷ adv (within) (por) dentro, adentro (esp LAm); (with movement) hacia dentro; (col: in prison) en chirona ▷ prep dentro de; (of time): **~ 10 minutes** en menos de 10 minutos; **insides** npl (col) tripas; **he opened the envelope and read what was ~** abrió el sobre y leyó lo que había dentro; **come ~!** ¡entra!; **let's go ~, it's starting to rain** entremos, está empezando a llover; **~ the house** dentro de la casa; **~ out** adv (turn) al revés; (know) a fondo; **he put his jumper on ~ out** se puso el jersey al revés

inside information n información confidencial

inside lane n (Aut: Brit) carril izquierdo; (: US, Europe etc) carril derecho

insider [ɪn'saɪdə'] n enterado(-a)

insider dealing, insider trading n (Stock Exchange) abuso de información privilegiada

insight ['ɪnsaɪt] n perspicacia, percepción; **to gain** or **get an ~ into sth** comprender algo mejor

insignificant [ɪnsɪg'nɪfɪknt] adj insignificante

insincere [ɪnsɪn'sɪə'] adj poco sincero

insinuate [ɪn'sɪnjueɪt] vt insinuar

insinuation [ɪnsɪnju'eɪʃən] n insinuación

insist [ɪn'sɪst] vi insistir; **to ~ on doing** empeñarse en hacer; **to ~ that** insistir en que; (claim) exigir que

insistence [ɪn'sɪstəns] n insistencia; (stubbornness) empeño

insistent [ɪn'sɪstənt] adj insistente; empeñado

insofar as [ɪnsəu'fɑː-] conj en la medida en que, en tanto que

insole ['ɪnsəul] n plantilla

insolence ['ɪnsələns] n insolencia, descaro

insolent ['ɪnsələnt] adj insolente, descarado

insolvent [ɪn'sɔlvənt] adj insolvente

insomnia [ɪn'sɔmnɪə] n insomnio

insomniac [ɪn'sɔmnɪæk] n insomne

inspect [ɪn'spɛkt] vt inspeccionar, examinar;

(troops) pasar revista a

inspection [ɪn'spɛkʃən] n inspección, examen

inspector [ɪn'spɛktə'] n inspector(a); (Brit: on buses, trains) revisor(a)

inspiration [ɪnspə'reɪʃən] n inspiración

inspire [ɪn'spaɪə'] vt inspirar; **to ~ sb (to do sth)** alentar a algn (a hacer algo)

install [ɪn'stɔ:l] vt instalar

installation [ɪnstə'leɪʃən] n instalación

instalment, (US) **installment** [ɪn'stɔ:lmənt] n plazo; (of story) entrega; (of TV serial etc) capítulo; **in ~s** (pay, receive) a plazos; **to pay in ~s** pagar a plazos or por abonos

instance ['ɪnstəns] n ejemplo, caso; **for ~** por ejemplo; **in the first ~** en primer lugar; **in that ~** en ese caso

instant ['ɪnstənt] n instante, momento ▷ adj inmediato; (coffee) instantáneo

instantly ['ɪnstəntlɪ] adv en seguida, al instante

instead [ɪn'stɛd] adv en cambio; **~ of** en lugar de, en vez de

instep ['ɪnstɛp] n empeine

instigate ['ɪnstɪgeɪt] vt (rebellion, strike, crime) instigar; (new ideas etc) fomentar

instigation [ɪnstɪ'geɪʃən] n instigación; **at sb's ~** a instigación de algn

instil [ɪn'stɪl] vt: **to ~ into** inculcar a

instinct ['ɪnstɪŋkt] n instinto

instinctive [ɪn'stɪŋktɪv] adj instintivo

institute ['ɪnstɪtjuːt] n instituto; (professional body) colegio ▷ vt (begin) iniciar, empezar; (proceedings) entablar

institution [ɪnstɪ'tjuːʃən] n institución; (beginning) iniciación; (Med: home) asilo; (asylum) manicomio; (custom) costumbre arraigada

instruct [ɪn'strʌkt] vt: **to ~ sb in sth** instruir a algn en or sobre algo; **to ~ sb to do sth** dar instrucciones a algn de or mandar a algn hacer algo

instruction [ɪn'strʌkʃən] n (teaching) instrucción; **instructions** npl órdenes; **~s (for use)** modo de empleo

instructor [ɪn'strʌktə'] n instructor(a)

instrument ['ɪnstrəmənt] n instrumento

instrumental [ɪnstrə'mɛntl] adj (Mus) instrumental; **to be ~ in** ser el artífice de; **to be ~ in sth/in doing sth** ser responsable de algo/de hacer algo

instrument panel n tablero (de instrumentos)

insufficient [ɪnsə'fɪʃənt] adj insuficiente

insular ['ɪnsjulə'] adj insular; (outlook) estrecho de miras

insulate ['ɪnsjuleɪt] vt aislar

insulating tape ['ɪnsjuleɪtɪŋ-] n cinta aislante

insulation [ɪnsju'leɪʃən] n aislamiento

insulin ['ɪnsjulɪn] n insulina

insult n insulto; (offence) ofensa ▷ vt insultar, ofender

insurance [ɪn'ʃuərəns] n seguro; **fire/life ~** seguro de incendios/vida; **to take out ~ (against)** hacerse un seguro (contra)

insurance policy n póliza (de seguros)

insure [ɪn'ʃuəʳ] *vt* asegurar; **to ~ sb** *or* **sb's life** hacer un seguro de vida a algn; **to ~ (against)** asegurar (contra); **to be ~d for £5000** tener un seguro de 5000 libras

insured [ɪn'ʃuəd] *n*: **the ~** el (la) asegurado(-a)

insurer [ɪn'ʃuərəʳ] *n* asegurador(a)

intact [ɪn'tækt] *adj* íntegro; *(untouched)* intacto

intake ['ɪnteɪk] *n (Tech)* entrada, toma; (: *pipe*) tubo de admisión; *(of food)* ingestión; *(Brit Scol)*: **an ~ of 200 a year** 200 matriculados al año

integer ['ɪntɪdʒəʳ] *n* (número) entero

integral ['ɪntɪgrəl] *adj (whole)* íntegro; *(part)* integrante

integrate ['ɪntɪgreɪt] *vt* integrar ▷ *vi* integrarse

integrity [ɪn'tɛgrɪtɪ] *n* honradez, rectitud; *(Comput)* integridad

intellect ['ɪntəlɛkt] *n* intelecto

intellectual [ɪntə'lɛktjuəl] *adj, n* intelectual

intelligence [ɪn'tɛlɪdʒəns] *n* inteligencia

intelligence quotient (IQ) *n* coeficiente *m* intelectual

Intelligence Service *n* Servicio de Inteligencia

intelligence test *n* prueba de inteligencia

intelligent [ɪn'tɛlɪdʒənt] *adj* inteligente

intend [ɪn'tɛnd] *vt (gift etc)*: **to ~ sth for** destinar algo a; **to ~ to do sth** tener intención de *or* pensar hacer algo

intended [ɪn'tɛndɪd] *adj (effect)* deseado

intense [ɪn'tɛns] *adj* intenso; **to be ~** *(person)* tomárselo todo muy en serio

intensely [ɪn'tɛnslɪ] *adv* intensamente; *(very)* sumamente

intensify [ɪn'tɛnsɪfaɪ] *vt* intensificar; *(increase)* aumentar

intensity [ɪn'tɛnsɪtɪ] *n (gen)* intensidad

intensive [ɪn'tɛnsɪv] *adj* intensivo

intensive care *n*: **to be in ~** estar bajo cuidados intensivos; **~ unit** *n* unidad de vigilancia intensiva

intent [ɪn'tɛnt] *n* propósito ▷ *adj (absorbed)* absorto; *(attentive)* atento; **to all ~s and purposes** a efectos prácticos; **to be ~ on doing sth** estar resuelto *or* decidido a hacer algo

intention [ɪn'tɛnʃən] *n* intención, propósito

intentional [ɪn'tɛnʃənl] *adj* deliberado

intently [ɪn'tɛntlɪ] *adv* atentamente, fijamente

interact [ɪntər'ækt] *vi (substances)* influirse mutuamente; *(people)* relacionarse

interaction [ɪntər'ækʃən] *n* interacción, acción recíproca

interactive [ɪntər'æktɪv] *adj (Comput)* interactivo

intercept [ɪntə'sɛpt] *vt* interceptar; *(stop)* detener

interception [ɪntə'sɛpʃən] *n* interceptación; detención

interchange *n* intercambio; *(on motorway)* intersección ▷ *vt* intercambiar

interchangeable [ɪntə'tʃeɪndʒəbl] *adj* intercambiable

intercity [ɪntə'sɪtɪ] *adj*: **~ (train)** (tren) intercity

intercom ['ɪntəkɔm] *n* interfono

intercourse ['ɪntəkɔːs] *n (sexual intercourse)* relaciones sexuales, contacto sexual; *(social)* trato

interest ['ɪntrɪst] *n (also Comm)* interés ▷ *vt* interesar; **to show an ~ in sth** mostrar interés en algo; **my main ~ is music** mi mayor afición es la música; **it's in your own ~ to study hard** te conviene estudiar mucho; **compound/simple ~** interés compuesto/simple; **business ~s** negocios; **British ~s in the Middle East** los intereses británicos en el Medio Oriente; **it doesn't ~ me** no me interesa

interested ['ɪntrɪstɪd] *adj* interesado; **to be ~ in** estar interesado en; **I'm very ~ in what you're telling me** estoy muy interesado en lo que me dices; **are you ~ in politics?** ¿te interesa la política?; **to get ~ in** interesarse por

interesting ['ɪntrɪstɪŋ] *adj* interesante

interest rate *n* tipo *(Esp)* or tasa *(LAm)* de interés

interface ['ɪntəfeɪs] *n (Comput)* junción, interface

interfere [ɪntə'fɪəʳ] *vi*: **to ~ in** *(quarrel, other people's business)* entrometerse en; **to ~ with** *(hinder)* estorbar; *(damage)* estropear; *(Radio)* interferir con

interference [ɪntə'fɪərəns] *n (gen)* intromisión; *(Radio, TV)* interferencia

interim ['ɪntərɪm] *adj*: **~ dividend** dividendo parcial ▷ *n*: **in the ~** en el ínterin

interior [ɪn'tɪərɪəʳ] *n, adj, adj* interior

interior decorator, interior designer *n* interiorista, diseñador(a) de interiores

interjection [ɪntə'dʒɛkʃən] *n* interrupción

interlock [ɪntə'lɔk] *vi* entrelazarse; *(wheels etc)* endentarse

interlude ['ɪntəluːd] *n* intervalo; *(rest)* descanso; *(Theat)* intermedio

intermediary [ɪntə'miːdɪərɪ] *n* intermediario(-a)

intermediate [ɪntə'miːdɪət] *adj* intermedio

intermission [ɪntə'mɪʃən] *n (Theat)* intermedio

intermittent [ɪntə'mɪtnt] *adj* intermitente

intern *vt* internar; *(enclose)* encerrar ▷ *n (US)* médico(-a) interno(-a)

internal [ɪn'təːnl] *adj* interno, interior; **~ injuries** heridas *or* lesiones internas

internally [ɪn'təːnəlɪ] *adv* interiormente; **"not to be taken ~"** "uso externo"

Internal Revenue Service (IRS) *n (US)* = Hacienda

international [ɪntə'næʃənl] *adj* internacional; **~ (game)** partido internacional; **~ (player)** jugador(a) internacional

International Monetary Fund (IMF) *n* Fondo Monetario Internacional

internee [ɪntəː'niː] *n* interno(-a), recluso(-a)

Internet ['ɪntənet] *n*: **the ~** (el *or* la) Internet

Internet café *n* cibercafé

Internet Service Provider *n* proveedor de (acceso a) Internet

Internet user *n* internauta

internment [ɪn'təːnmənt] *n* internamiento

interplay ['ɪntəpleɪ] *n* interacción

interpret [ɪn'təːprɪt] *vt* interpretar; *(translate)*

traducir; (*understand*) entender ▷ vi hacer de
intérprete
interpretation [ɪntəːprɪ'teɪʃən] n
interpretación; traducción
interpreter [ɪn'təːprɪtəʳ] n intérprete
interrelated [ɪntərɪ'leɪtɪd] adj interrelacionado
interrogate [ɪn'tɛrəʊgeɪt] vt interrogar
interrogation [ɪntɛrəʊ'geɪʃən] n interrogatorio
interrupt [ɪntə'rʌpt] vt, vi interrumpir
interruption [ɪntə'rʌpʃən] n interrupción
intersect [ɪntə'sɛkt] vt cruzar ▷ vi cruzarse
intersection [ɪntə'sɛkʃən] n intersección; (*of roads*) cruce
intersperse [ɪntə'spəːs] vt: **to ~ with** salpicar de
intertwine [ɪntə'twaɪn] vt entrelazar ▷ vi entrelazarse
interval ['ɪntəvl] n intervalo; (*Brit Theat*) intermedio; (*Sport*) descanso; **at ~s** a ratos, de vez en cuando; **sunny ~s** claros
intervene [ɪntə'viːn] vi intervenir; (*take part*) participar; (*occur*) sobrevenir
intervention [ɪntə'vɛnʃən] n intervención
interview ['ɪntəvjuː] n (*Radio, TV etc*) entrevista ▷ vt entrevistar a
interviewee [ɪntəvjuː'iː] n entrevistado(-a)
interviewer ['ɪntəvjuːəʳ] n entrevistador(a)
intestate [ɪn'tɛsteɪt] adj intestado
intestine [ɪn'tɛstɪn] n: **large/small ~** intestino grueso/delgado
intimacy ['ɪntɪməsɪ] n intimidad; (*relations*) relaciones íntimas
intimate adj íntimo; (*friendship*) estrecho; (*knowledge*) profundo ▷ vt (*announce*) dar a entender
intimidate [ɪn'tɪmɪdeɪt] vt intimidar, amedrentar
intimidation [ɪntɪmɪ'deɪʃən] n intimidación
into ['ɪntuː] prep (*gen*) en; (*towards*) a; (*inside*) hacia el interior de; **I poured the milk ~ a cup** vertí la leche en una taza; **they divided ~ two groups** se dividieron en dos grupos; **I'm going ~ town** voy a la ciudad; **translate it ~ Spanish** tradúcelo al español; **he got ~ the car** subió al coche; **to get ~ bed** meterse a la cama; **to change pounds ~ dollars** cambiar libras por dólares; **to walk ~ a lamppost** tropezar con una farola
intolerable [ɪn'tɔlərəbl] adj intolerable, insoportable
intolerant [ɪn'tɔlərənt] adj: **~ (of)** intolerante (con)
intoxicated [ɪn'tɔksɪkeɪtɪd] adj embriagado
intoxication [ɪntɔksɪ'keɪʃən] n embriaguez
intractable [ɪn'træktəbl] adj (*person*) intratable; (*problem*) irresoluble; (*illness*) incurable
intranet ['ɪntrænet] n intranet
intransitive [ɪn'trænsɪtɪv] adj intransitivo
intravenous [ɪntrə'viːnəs] adj intravenoso
in-tray ['ɪntreɪ] n bandeja de entrada
intrepid [ɪn'trɛpɪd] adj intrépido
intricate ['ɪntrɪkət] adj intrincado; (*plot, problem*) complejo
intrigue [ɪn'triːg] n intriga ▷ vt fascinar ▷ vi

andar en intrigas
intriguing [ɪn'triːgɪŋ] adj fascinante
intrinsic [ɪn'trɪnsɪk] adj intrínseco
introduce [ɪntrə'djuːs] vt introducir, meter; **to ~ sb (to sb)** presentar algn (a algn); **to ~ sb to** (*pastime, technique*) introducir a algn a; **may I ~ ...** permítame presentarle a ...
introduction [ɪntrə'dʌkʃən] n introducción; (*of person*) presentación; **a letter of ~** una carta de recomendación
introductory [ɪntrə'dʌktərɪ] adj introductorio; **an ~ offer** una oferta introductoria; **~ remarks** comentarios preliminares
introvert ['ɪntrəʊvəːt] adj, n introvertido(-a)
intrude [ɪn'truːd] vi (*person*) entrometerse; **to ~ on** estorbar
intruder [ɪn'truːdəʳ] n intruso(-a)
intrusion [ɪn'truːʒən] n invasión
intuition [ɪntjuː'ɪʃən] n intuición
intuitive [ɪn'tjuːɪtɪv] adj intuitivo
inundate ['ɪnʌndeɪt] vt: **to ~ with** inundar de
invade [ɪn'veɪd] vt invadir
invalid n minusválido(-a) ▷ adj (*not valid*) inválido, nulo
invaluable [ɪn'væljuəbl] adj inestimable
invariably [ɪn'vɛərɪəblɪ] adv sin excepción, siempre; **she is ~ late** siempre llega tarde
invasion [ɪn'veɪʒən] n invasión
invent [ɪn'vɛnt] vt inventar
invention [ɪn'vɛnʃən] n invento; (*inventiveness*) inventiva; (*lie*) invención
inventive [ɪn'vɛntɪv] adj inventivo
inventor [ɪn'vɛntəʳ] n inventor(a)
inventory ['ɪnvəntrɪ] n inventario
invert [ɪn'vəːt] vt invertir
inverted commas [ɪn'vəːtɪd] npl (*Brit*) comillas
invest [ɪn'vɛst] vt invertir; (*fig: time, effort*) dedicar ▷ vi invertir; **to ~ sb with sth** conferir algo a algn
investigate [ɪn'vɛstɪgeɪt] vt investigar; (*study*) estudiar, examinar
investigation [ɪnvɛstɪ'geɪʃən] n investigación, pesquisa; examen
investment [ɪn'vɛstmənt] n inversión
investor [ɪn'vɛstəʳ] n inversor(a)
invigilator [ɪn'vɪdʒɪleɪtəʳ] n celador(a)
invigorating [ɪn'vɪgəreɪtɪŋ] adj vigorizante
invisible [ɪn'vɪzɪbl] adj invisible
invitation [ɪnvɪ'teɪʃən] n invitación; **at sb's ~** a invitación de algn; **by ~ only** solamente por invitación
invite [ɪn'vaɪt] vt invitar; (*opinions etc*) solicitar, pedir; (*trouble*) buscarse; **to ~ sb (to do)** invitar a algn (a hacer); **to ~ sb to dinner** invitar a algn a cenar
▸ **invite out** vt invitar a salir
▸ **invite over** vt invitar a casa
inviting [ɪn'vaɪtɪŋ] adj atractivo; (*look*) provocativo; (*food*) apetitoso
invoice ['ɪnvɔɪs] n factura ▷ vt facturar; **to ~ sb for goods** facturar a algn las mercancías
involuntary [ɪn'vɔləntrɪ] adj involuntario

involve [ɪn'vɔlv] *vt* (*entail*) suponer, implicar; **it ~s a lot of work** supone mucho trabajo; **to ~ sb (in)** involucrar a algn (en); **to be/become ~d in sth** estar involucrado/involucrarse en algo; **he wasn't ~d in the robbery** no estuvo implicado en el robo; **she was ~d in politics** estaba metida en política; **to be ~d with sb** tener una relación con algn; **she was ~d with a married man** tenía una relación con un hombre casado; **I don't want to get ~d in the argument** no quiero meterme en la discusión

involved [ɪn'vɔlvd] *adj* complicado

involvement [ɪn'vɔlvmənt] *n* (*gen*) enredo; (*obligation*) compromiso; (*difficulty*) apuro

inward ['ɪnwəd] *adj* (*movement*) interior, interno; (*thought, feeling*) íntimo

inward(s) ['ɪnwəd(z)] *adv* hacia dentro

I/O *abbr* (*Comput:* = input/output) E/S; **~ error** error de E/S

iodine ['aɪəudi:n] *n* yodo

ioniser ['aɪənaɪzə^r] *n* ionizador

iota [aɪ'əutə] *n* (*fig*) jota, ápice

IOU *n abbr* (= I owe you) pagaré

IPA *n abbr* (= International Phonetic Alphabet) AFI

IQ *n abbr* (= intelligence quotient) C.I.

IRA *n abbr* (= Irish Republican Army) IRA; (*US*) = **individual retirement account**

Iran [ɪ'rɑ:n] *n* Irán

Iranian [ɪ'reɪnɪən] *adj, n* iraní

Iraq [ɪ'rɑ:k] *n* Irak

Iraqi [ɪ'rɑ:kɪ] *adj, n* irakí

irate [aɪ'reɪt] *adj* enojado, airado

Ireland ['aɪələnd] *n* Irlanda; **Republic of ~** República de Irlanda

iris ['aɪrɪs] (*pl* **-es**) *n* (*Anat*) iris; (*Bot*) lirio

Irish ['aɪrɪʃ] *adj* irlandés(-esa) ▷ *n* (*Ling*) irlandés; **the ~** *npl* los irlandeses

Irishman ['aɪrɪʃmən] *n* irlandés

Irish Sea *n:* **the ~** el Mar de Irlanda

Irishwoman ['aɪrɪʃwumən] *n* irlandesa

irk [ə:k] *vt* fastidiar

irksome ['ə:ksəm] *adj* fastidioso

IRN *n abbr* (= Independent Radio News) servicio de noticias en las cadenas de radio privadas

iron ['aɪən] *n* hierro; (*for clothes*) plancha ▷ *adj* de hierro ▷ *vt* (*clothes*) planchar; **irons** *npl* (*chains*) grilletes
  ▶ **iron out** *vt* (*crease*) quitar; (*fig*) allanar, resolver

Iron Curtain *n:* **the ~** el Telón de Acero

ironic(al) [aɪ'rɔnɪk(l)] *adj* irónico

ironing ['aɪənɪŋ] *n* (*act*) planchado; (*ironed clothes*) ropa planchada; (*clothes to be ironed*) ropa por planchar

ironing board *n* tabla de planchar

ironmonger ['aɪənmʌŋgə^r] *n* (*Brit*) ferretero(-a); **~'s (shop)** ferretería

irony ['aɪrənɪ] *n* ironía; **the ~ of it is that ...** lo irónico del caso es que ...

irrational [ɪ'ræʃənl] *adj* irracional

irregular [ɪ'regjulə^r] *adj* irregular; (*surface*) desigual

irrelevant [ɪ'reləvənt] *adj* irrelevante; **to be ~** estar fuera de lugar, no venir al caso

irresistible [ɪrɪ'zɪstɪbl] *adj* irresistible

irrespective [ɪrɪ'spɛktɪv]: **~ of** *prep* sin tener en cuenta, no importa

irresponsible [ɪrɪ'spɔnsɪbl] *adj* (*act*) irresponsable; (*person*) poco serio

irreverent [ɪ'revərnt] *adj* irreverente, irrespetuoso

irrevocable [ɪ'revəkəbl] *adj* irrevocable

irrigate ['ɪrɪgeɪt] *vt* regar

irrigation [ɪrɪ'geɪʃən] *n* riego

irritable ['ɪrɪtəbl] *adj* (*person: temperament*) irritable; (*: mood*) de mal humor

irritate ['ɪrɪteɪt] *vt* fastidiar; (*Med*) picar

irritating ['ɪrɪteɪtɪŋ] *adj* fastidioso

irritation [ɪrɪ'teɪʃən] *n* fastidio; picazón, picor

IRS *n abbr* (*US*) = **Internal Revenue Service**

is [ɪz] *vb see* **be**

ISA ['aɪsə] *n abbr* (*Brit: Comm:* = Individual Savings Account) plan de ahorro personal para pequeños inversores con fiscalidad cero

ISBN *n abbr* (= International Standard Book Number) ISBN

ISDN *n abbr* (= Integrated Services Digital Network) RDSI

Islam ['ɪzlɑ:m] *n* Islam

island ['aɪlənd] *n* isla; (*also:* **traffic island**) isleta

islander ['aɪləndə^r] *n* isleño(-a)

isle [aɪl] *n* isla

isn't ['ɪznt] = **is not**

isobar ['aɪsəubɑ:^{r}] *n* isobara

isolate ['aɪsəleɪt] *vt* aislar

isolated ['aɪsəleɪtɪd] *adj* aislado

isolation [aɪsə'leɪʃən] *n* aislamiento

isotope ['aɪsəutəup] *n* isótopo

ISP *n abbr* = **Internet Service Provider**

Israel ['ɪzreɪl] *n* Israel

Israeli [ɪz'reɪlɪ] *adj, n* israelí

issue ['ɪʃju:] *n* cuestión, asunto; (*outcome*) resultado; (*of banknote etc*) emisión; (*of newspaper etc*) número; (*offspring*) sucesión, descendencia ▷ *vt* (*rations, equipment*) distribuir, repartir; (*orders*) dar; (*certificate, passport*) expedir; (*decree*) promulgar; (*magazine*) publicar; (*cheque*) extender; (*banknote, stamp*) emitir ▷ *vi:* **to ~ (from)** derivar (de), brotar (de); **a controversial ~** un tema polémico; **at ~** en cuestión; **to take ~ with sb (over)** disentir con algn (en); **to avoid the ~** andarse con rodeos; **to confuse** *or* **obscure the ~** confundir las cosas; **to make an ~ of sth** dar a algo más importancia de lo necesario; **a back ~** un número atrasado; **to ~ sth to sb**, **~ sb with sth** entregar algo a algn; **the minister ~d a statement yesterday** el ministro hizo pública una declaración ayer

isthmus ['ɪsməs] *n* istmo

IT *n abbr* = **information technology**

it [ɪt] *pron* **1** (*specific: subject: not generally translated*) él (ella); (*: direct object*) lo (la); (*: indirect object*) le; (*after prep*) él (ella); (*abstract concept*) ello; **it's on the table** está en la mesa; **it's expensive** es caro; **I can't find it** no lo (*or* la) encuentro; **give**

it to me dámelo (or dámela); **I spoke to him about it** le hablé del asunto; **what did you learn from it?** ¿qué aprendiste de él (or ella)?; **did you go to it?** (party, concert etc) ¿fuiste?; **I'm against it** estoy en contra de ello **2** (impersonal): **it's raining** llueve, está lloviendo; **it's 6 o'clock** son las 6; **it's the 10th of August** es el 10 de agosto; **how far is it? — it's 10 miles/2 hours on the train** ¿a qué distancia está? — a 10 millas/2 horas en tren; **who is it? — it's me** ¿quién es? — soy yo

Italian [ɪ'tæljən] adj italiano ▷ n italiano(-a); (Ling) italiano

italic [ɪ'tælɪk] adj cursivo; **italics** npl cursiva

Italy ['ɪtəlɪ] n Italia

itch [ɪtʃ] n picazón; (fig) prurito ▷ vi (person) sentir or tener comezón; (part of body) picar; **to be ~ing to do sth** rabiar por or morirse de ganas de hacer algo

itchy ['ɪtʃɪ] adj: **to be ~** picar

it'd ['ɪtd] = **it would; it had**

item ['aɪtəm] n artículo; (on agenda) asunto (a tratar); (in programme) número; (also: **news item**) noticia; **~s of clothing** prendas de vestir

itemize ['aɪtəmaɪz] vt detallar

itemized bill ['aɪtəmaɪzd-] n recibo detallado

itinerary [aɪ'tɪnərərɪ] n itinerario

it'll ['ɪtl] = **it will; it shall**

ITN n abbr = **ITV**

its [ɪts] adj su

it's [ɪts] = **it is; it has**

itself [ɪt'sɛlf] pron (reflexive) sí mismo(-a); (emphatic) él mismo (ella misma)

ITV n abbr (Brit) = **Independent Television**

IUD n abbr (= intra-uterine device) DIU

I've [aɪv] = **I have**

ivory ['aɪvərɪ] n marfil

ivy ['aɪvɪ] n hiedra

Jj

j [dʒeɪ] n (letter) J, j; **J for Jack**, (US) **J for Jig** J
de José

..b [dʒæb] vt (elbow) dar un codazo a; (punch) dar
..n golpe rápido a ▷ vi: **to ~ at** intentar golpear
a ▷ n codazo; golpe (rápido); (Med: col) pinchazo;
to ~ sth into sth clavar algo en algo

.ck [dʒæk] n (Aut) gato; (Bowls) boliche; (Cards)
sota
▶ **jack in** vt (col) dejar
▶ **jack up** vt (Aut) levantar con el gato

.ckal ['dʒækl] n (Zool) chacal

.ckdaw ['dʒækdɔ:] n grajo(-a), chova

.cket ['dʒækɪt] n chaqueta, americana, saco
'LAm); (of boiler etc) camisa; (of book) sobrecubierta

.cket potato n patata asada (con piel)

.ck-in-the-box ['dʒækɪnðəbɔks] n caja
sorpresa, caja de resorte

.ck-knife ['dʒæknaɪf] vi colear

.ck plug n (Elec) enchufe de clavija

.ckpot ['dʒækpɔt] n premio gordo

.cuzzi® [dʒəˈkuːzɪ] n jacuzzi®

.ded ['dʒeɪdɪd] adj (tired) cansado; (fed up)
hastiado

.gged ['dʒægɪd] adj dentado

.il [dʒeɪl] n cárcel ▷ vt encarcelar

.m [dʒæm] n mermelada; (also: **traffic jam**)
atasco, embotellamiento; (difficulty) apuro
▷ vt (passage etc) obstruir; (mechanism, drawer
etc) atascar; (Radio) interferir ▷ vi atascarse,
trabarse; **strawberry ~** la mermelada de fresas;
to get sb out of a ~ sacar a algn del paso or de un
apuro; **to ~ sth into sth** meter algo a la fuerza
en algo; **the window's ~med** la ventana está
atascada; **the telephone lines are ~med** las
líneas están saturadas

.maica [dʒəˈmeɪkə] n Jamaica

.mb [dʒæm] n jamba

.ngle ['dʒæŋgl] vi sonar (de manera)
discordante

.nitor ['dʒænɪtə^r] n (caretaker) portero, conserje

.nuary ['dʒænjuərɪ] n enero

.pan [dʒəˈpæn] n (el) Japón

.panese [dʒæpəˈniːz] adj japonés(-esa) ▷ n (pl
inv) japonés(-esa); (Ling) japonés

.r [dʒɑːr] n (glass: large) jarra; (: small) tarro ▷ vi
(sound) chirriar; (colours) desentonar

.rgon ['dʒɑːgən] n jerga

jaundice ['dʒɔːndɪs] n ictericia

jaundiced ['dʒɔːndɪst] adj (fig: embittered)
amargado; (: disillusioned) desilusionado

javelin ['dʒævlɪn] n jabalina

jaw [dʒɔː] n mandíbula; **jaws** npl (Tech: of vice etc)
mordaza

jay [dʒeɪ] n (Zool) arrendajo

jaywalker ['dʒeɪwɔːkə^r] n peatón(-ona)
imprudente

jazz [dʒæz] n jazz
▶ **jazz up** vt (liven up) animar

JCB® n abbr excavadora

jealous ['dʒeləs] adj (gen) celoso; (envious)
envidioso; **to be ~** tener celos

jealousy ['dʒeləsɪ] n celos; envidia

jeans [dʒiːnz] npl (pantalones) vaqueros or
tejanos, bluejean (LAm)

Jeep® [dʒiːp] n jeep

jeer [dʒɪə^r] vi: **to ~ (at)** (boo) abuchear; (mock)
mofarse (de)

jelly ['dʒelɪ] n gelatina, jalea

jellyfish ['dʒelɪfɪʃ] n medusa

jeopardize ['dʒepədaɪz] vt arriesgar, poner en
peligro

jeopardy ['dʒepədɪ] n: **to be in ~** estar en peligro

jerk [dʒəːk] n (jolt) sacudida; (wrench) tirón; (US
col) imbécil, pendejo(-a) (LAm) ▷ vt dar una
sacudida a; tirar bruscamente de ▷ vi (vehicle) dar
una sacudida

jersey ['dʒəːzɪ] n jersey; (fabric) tejido de punto

Jesus ['dʒiːzəs] n Jesús; **~ Christ** Jesucristo

jet [dʒet] n (of gas, liquid) chorro; (Aviat) avión a
reacción

jet-black ['dʒet'blæk] adj negro como el azabache

jet engine n motor a reacción

jet lag n desorientación por desfase horario

jet-setter ['dʒetsetə^r] n personaje de la jet

jettison ['dʒetɪsn] vt desechar

jetty ['dʒetɪ] n muelle, embarcadero

Jew [dʒuː] n judío

jewel ['dʒuːəl] n joya; (in watch) rubí

jeweller, (US) **jeweler** ['dʒuːələ^r] n joyero(-a); **~'s
(shop)** joyería

jewellery, (US) **jewelry** ['dʒuːəlrɪ] n joyas,
alhajas

Jewess ['dʒuːɪs] n judía

Jewish ['dʒuːɪʃ] adj judío

jibe [dʒaɪb] *n* mofa

jiffy ['dʒɪfɪ] *n* (*col*): **in a ~** en un santiamén

jigsaw ['dʒɪgsɔ:] *n* (*also*: **jigsaw puzzle**) rompecabezas; (*tool*) sierra de vaivén

jilt [dʒɪlt] *vt* dejar plantado a

jingle ['dʒɪŋgl] *n* (*advert*) musiquilla ▷ *vi* tintinear

jinx [dʒɪŋks] *n*: **there's a ~ on it** está gafado

jitters ['dʒɪtəz] *npl* (*col*): **to get the ~** ponerse nervioso

jittery ['dʒɪtərɪ] *adj* (*col*) agitado

job [dʒɔb] *n* trabajo; (*task*) tarea; (*duty*) deber; (*post*) empleo; (*col*: *difficulty*) dificultad; **a part-time/full-time ~** un trabajo a tiempo parcial/ tiempo completo; **that's not my ~** eso no me incumbe or toca a mí; **he's only doing his ~** está cumpliendo nada más; **you've done a good ~** lo has hecho muy bien; **it's a good ~ that...** menos mal que...; **just the ~!** ¡justo lo que necesito!

job centre *n* (*Brit*) oficina de empleo

jobless ['dʒɔblɪs] *adj* sin trabajo ▷ *n*: **the ~** los parados

job satisfaction *n* satisfacción en el trabajo

job security *n* garantía de trabajo

jockey ['dʒɔkɪ] *n* jockey ▷ *vi*: **to ~ for position** maniobrar para sacar delantera

jockstrap ['dʒɔkstræp] *n* suspensorio

jocular ['dʒɔkjuləʳ] *adj* (*humorous*) gracioso; (*merry*) alegre

jog [dʒɔg] *vt* empujar (ligeramente) ▷ *vi* (*run*) hacer footing; **to ~ sb's memory** refrescar la memoria a algn; **to ~ along** (*fig*) ir tirando

jogger ['dʒɔgəʳ] *n* corredor(a)

jogging ['dʒɔgɪŋ] *n* footing

join [dʒɔɪn] *vt* (*things*) unir, juntar; (*become member of*: *club*) hacerse socio de; (*Pol*: *party*) afiliarse a; (*meet*: *people*) reunirse con; (*fig*) unirse a ▷ *vi* (*roads*) empalmar; (*rivers*) confluir ▷ *n* juntura; **will you ~ us for dinner?** ¿quieres cenar con nosotros?; **I'll ~ you later** me reuniré contigo luego; **if you're going for a walk, do you mind if I ~ you?** si vais a dar un paseo, ¿os importa que os acompañe?; **to ~ forces (with)** aliarse (con)
  ▶ **join in** *vi* tomar parte, participar ▷ *vt fus* tomar parte or participar en; **she started singing, and the audience ~ed in** empezó a cantar, y el público se unió a ella
  ▶ **join up** *vi* unirse; (*Mil*) alistarse

joiner ['dʒɔɪnəʳ] *n* carpintero(-a)

joint [dʒɔɪnt] *n* (*Tech*) juntura, unión; (*Anat*) articulación; (*Brit Culin*) pieza de carne (para asar); (*col*: *place*) garito ▷ *adj* (*common*) común; (*combined*) conjunto; (*responsibility*) compartido; (*committee*) mixto

joint account (J/A) *n* (*with bank etc*) cuenta común

joist [dʒɔɪst] *n* viga

joke [dʒəuk] *n* chiste; (*also*: **practical joke**) broma ▷ *vi* bromear; **to play a ~ on** gastar una broma a

joker ['dʒəukəʳ] *n* chistoso(-a), bromista; (*Cards*) comodín

jolly ['dʒɔlɪ] *adj* (*merry*) alegre; (*enjoyable*) divertido ▷ *adv* (*col*) muy, la mar de ▷ *vt*: **to ~ sb along** animar or darle ánimos a algn; **~ good!** ¡estupendo!

jolt [dʒəult] *n* (*shake*) sacudida; (*blow*) golpe; (*shock*) susto ▷ *vt* sacudir

Jordan ['dʒɔ:dən] *n* (*country*) Jordania; (*river*) Jordán

jostle ['dʒɔsl] *vt* dar empujones or empellones a

jot [dʒɔt] *n*: **not one ~** ni pizca, ni un ápice
  ▶ **jot down** *vt* apuntar

jotter ['dʒɔtəʳ] *n* (*Brit*) bloc

journal ['dʒə:nl] *n* (*paper*) periódico; (*magazine*) revista; (*diary*) diario

journalism ['dʒə:nəlɪzəm] *n* periodismo

journalist ['dʒə:nəlɪst] *n* periodista

journey ['dʒə:nɪ] *n* viaje; (*distance covered*) trayecto ▷ *vi* viajar; **return ~** viaje de regreso; **a 5-hour ~** un viaje de 5 horas

joy [dʒɔɪ] *n* alegría

joyful ['dʒɔɪful] *adj* alegre

joyrider ['dʒɔɪraɪdəʳ] *n* persona que se da una vuelta e un coche robado

joystick ['dʒɔɪstɪk] *n* (*Aviat*) palanca de mando; (*Comput*) palanca de control

JP *n abbr see* **Justice of the Peace**

Jr *abbr* = **junior**

jubilant ['dʒu:bɪlnt] *adj* jubiloso

judge [dʒʌdʒ] *n* juez ▷ *vt* juzgar; (*competition*) actuar de or ser juez en; (*estimate*) considerar; (: *weight, size etc*) calcular ▷ *vi*: **judging** or **to ~ by his expression** a juzgar por su expresión; **as far as I can ~** por lo que puedo entender, a mi entender; **I ~d it necessary to inform him** consideré necesario informarle

judg(e)ment ['dʒʌdʒmənt] *n* juicio; (*punishment* sentencia, fallo; **to pass judg(e)ment (on)** (*Law*) pronunciar or dictar sentencia (sobre); (*fig* emitir un juicio crítico or dictaminar (sobre); **ir my judg(e)ment** a mi juicio

judicial [dʒu:'dɪʃl] *adj* judicial

judiciary [dʒu:'dɪʃɪərɪ] *n* poder judicial, magistratura

judo ['dʒu:dəu] *n* judo

jug [dʒʌg] *n* jarro

juggernaut ['dʒʌgənɔ:t] *n* (*Brit*: *huge truck*) camión de carga pesada

juggle ['dʒʌgl] *vi* hacer juegos malabares

juggler ['dʒʌgləʳ] *n* malabarista

juice [dʒu:s] *n* jugo, zumo (*Esp*); (*of meat*) jugo; (*col*: *petrol*): **we've run out of ~** se nos acabó la gasolina

juicy ['dʒu:sɪ] *adj* jugoso

jukebox ['dʒu:kbɔks] *n* máquina de discos

July [dʒu:'laɪ] *n* julio; **the first of ~** el uno or primero de julio; **during ~** en el mes de julio; **ir ~ of next year** en julio del año que viene

jumble ['dʒʌmbl] *n* revoltijo ▷ *vt* (*also*: **jumble together, jumble up**: *mix up*) revolver; (: *disarrange*) mezclar

jumble sale *n* (*Brit*) mercadillo

jumbo (jet) ['dʒʌmbəu-] *n* jumbo

jump [dʒʌmp] *vi* saltar, dar saltos; (*start*)

sobresaltarse; (*increase*) aumentar ▷ vt saltar ▷ n
salto; (*fence*) obstáculo; (*increase*) aumento; **to ~
the queue** (*Brit*) colarse
▶ **jump about** vi dar saltos, brincar
▶ **jump at** vt fus (*fig*) apresurarse a aprovechar;
he ~ed at the offer se apresuró a aceptar la
oferta
▶ **jump down** vi bajar de un salto, saltar a tierra
▶ **jump up** vi levantarse de un salto
jumper ['dʒʌmpəʳ] n (*Brit: pullover*) jersey, suéter;
(*US: pinafore dress*) pichi; (*Sport*) saltador(a)
jump leads, (*US*) **jumper cables** npl cables
puente de batería
jump-start ['dʒʌmpstɑːt] vt (*car*) arrancar
con ayuda de otra batería *or* empujando; (*fig:
economy*) reactivar
jumpy ['dʒʌmpɪ] adj nervioso
Jun. *abbr* = **junior**; (= *June*) jun.
junction ['dʒʌŋkʃən] n (*Brit: of roads*) cruce; (*Rail*)
empalme
juncture ['dʒʌŋktʃəʳ] n: **at this ~** en este
momento, en esta coyuntura
June [dʒuːn] n junio
jungle ['dʒʌŋgl] n selva, jungla
junior ['dʒuːnɪəʳ] adj (*in age*) menor, más joven;
(*competition*) juvenil; (*position*) subalterno ▷ n
menor, joven; **he's ~ to me** es menor que yo
junior school n (*Brit*) escuela primaria; *see also*
primary school
junk [dʒʌŋk] n (*cheap goods*) baratijas; (*lumber*)
trastos viejos; (*rubbish*) basura; (*ship*) junco ▷ vt
(*esp US*) deshacerse de
junk bond n (*Comm*) obligación basura
junket ['dʒʌŋkɪt] n (*Culin*) dulce de leche cuajada
junk food n comida basura *or* de plástico
junkie ['dʒʌŋkɪ] n (*col*) yonqui, heroinómano(-a)
junk mail n propaganda (buzoneada)
junk shop n tienda de objetos usados
Jupiter ['dʒuːpɪtəʳ] n (*Mythology, Astro*) Júpiter
jurisdiction [dʒuərɪs'dɪkʃən] n jurisdicción; **it
falls** *or* **comes within/outside our ~** es/no es de
nuestra competencia

jurisprudence [dʒuərɪs'pruːdəns] n
jurisprudencia
juror ['dʒuərəʳ] n jurado
jury ['dʒuərɪ] n jurado
just [dʒʌst] adj justo ▷ adv (*exactly*) exactamente;
(*only*) sólo, solamente, no más (*LAm*); **he's ~ done
it/left** acaba de hacerlo/irse; **I've ~ seen him**
acabo de verle; **~ right** perfecto; **~ 2 o'clock** las
2 en punto; **she's ~ as clever as you** es tan lista
como tú; **~ as well that...** menos mal que...;
it's ~ as well you didn't go menos mal que
no fuiste; **it's ~ as good (as)** es igual (que), es
tan bueno (como); **~ as he was leaving** en el
momento en que se marchaba; **we were ~ going
money** teníamos el dinero justo; **~ here** aquí
mismo; **he ~ missed** falló por poco; **I did it ~
now** lo acabo de hacer; **not ~ now** ahora no;
I'm rather busy ~ now ahora mismo estoy
bastante ocupada; **it's ~ a suggestion** es sólo
una sugerencia; **~ listen to this** escucha esto
un momento; **~ a minute!** ¡un momento!; **I ~
thought that you would like it** yo pensé que te
gustaría; **~ ask someone the way** simplemente
pregúntale a alguien por dónde se va; **~ about**
casi; **it's ~ about finished** está casi terminado
justice ['dʒʌstɪs] n justicia; **this photo doesn't
do you ~** esta foto no te favorece
Justice of the Peace (JP) n juez de paz; *see also*
Crown Court
justification [dʒʌstɪfɪ'keɪʃən] n justificación
justify ['dʒʌstɪfaɪ] vt justificar; (*text*) alinear,
justificar; **to be justified in doing sth** tener
motivo para *or* razón al hacer algo
jut [dʒʌt] vi (*also:* **jut out**) sobresalir
juvenile ['dʒuːvənaɪl] adj juvenil; (*court*) de
menores ▷ n joven, menor de edad

Kk

K, k [keɪ] *n* (*letter*) K, k; **K for King** K de Kilo

K *abbr* (= *one thousand*) K; **kilobyte**; (*Brit*: = *Knight*) *caballero de un orden*

kamikaze [kæmɪˈkɑːzɪ] *adj* kamikaze

kangaroo [kæŋɡəˈruː] *n* canguro

karaoke [kɑːrəˈəʊkɪ] *n* karaoke

karate [kəˈrɑːtɪ] *n* karate

Kazakhstan [kɑːzɑːkˈstæn] *n* Kazajstán

kebab [kəˈbæb] *n* pincho moruno, brocheta

keel [kiːl] *n* quilla; **on an even ~** (*fig*) en equilibrio
  ▶ **keel over** *vi* (*Naut*) zozobrar, volcarse; (*person*) desplomarse

keen [kiːn] *adj* (*interest, desire*) grande, vivo; (*eye, intelligence*) agudo; (*competition*) intenso; (*edge*) afilado; (*Brit: eager*) entusiasta; **to be ~ to do** or **on doing sth** tener muchas ganas de hacer algo; **to be ~ on sth/sb** interesarse por algo/algn; **I'm not ~ on going** no tengo ganas de ir

keep [kiːp] (*pt, pp* **kept**) *vt* (*retain, preserve*) guardar; (*hold back*) quedarse con; (*shop*) ser propietario de; (*feed: family etc*) mantener; (*promise*) cumplir; (*chickens, bees etc*) criar ▷ *vi* (*food*) conservarse; (*remain*) seguir, continuar ▷ *n* (*of castle*) torreón; (*food etc*) comida, sustento; **you can ~ the watch** puedes quedarte con el reloj; **~ the change** quédese con la vuelta; **to ~ sb from doing sth** impedir a algn hacer algo; **to ~ sth from happening** impedir que algo ocurra; **to ~ sb happy** tener a algn contento; **to ~ sb waiting** hacer esperar a algn; **to ~ a place tidy** mantener un lugar limpio; **to ~ sth to o.s.** no decirle algo a nadie; **to ~ time** (*clock*) mantener la hora exacta; **to ~ an appointment** acudir a una cita; **to ~ a record** or **note of sth** tomar nota de or apuntar algo; **~ straight on** siga recto; **to ~ fit** mantenerse en forma; **~ still!** ¡estáte quieto!; **~ quiet!** ¡cállate!; **to ~ doing sth** (*without stopping*) seguir haciendo algo; (*repeatedly*) no dejar de hacer algo; **to ~ standing** seguir en pie; **she ~s talking** no deja de hablar; **I ~ forgetting my keys** siempre me olvido las llaves; *see also* **keeps**
  ▶ **keep away** *vt*: **to ~ sth/sb away from sb** mantener algo/a algn apartado de algn ▷ *vi*: **to ~ away (from)** mantenerse apartado (de)
  ▶ **keep back** *vt* (*crowd, tears*) contener; (*money*) quedarse con; (*conceal: information*): **to ~ sth back from sb** ocultar algo a algn ▷ *vi* hacerse a un lado
  ▶ **keep down** *vt* (*control: prices, spending*) controlar; (*retain: food*) retener ▷ *vi* seguir agachado, no levantar la cabeza
  ▶ **keep in** *vt* (*invalid, child*) impedir que salga, no dejar salir; (*Scol*) castigar (a quedarse en el colegio) ▷ *vi* (*col*): **to ~ in with sb** mantener la relación con algn
  ▶ **keep off** *vt* (*dog, person*) mantener a distancia ▷ *vi* mantenerse a distancia ▷ *vt fus*: **"~ off the grass"** "prohibido pisar el césped"; **~ your hands off!** ¡no toques!
  ▶ **keep on** *vi* seguir, continuar; **he kept on reading** continuó leyendo; **the car ~s on breaking down** el coche no deja de averiarse
  ▶ **keep out** *vi* (*stay out*) permanecer fuera; **"~ out"** "prohibida la entrada"
  ▶ **keep up** *vt* mantener, conservar ▷ *vi* no rezagarse; (*fig: in comprehension*) seguir (el hilo); **he walks so fast I can't ~ up** camina tan rápido que no puedo seguirle el ritmo; **to ~ up with** (*in pace*) ir al paso de; (*rival*) mantenerse a la altura de; **to ~ up with sb** (*walking, running etc*) seguir el ritmo a algn; (*fig*) seguir a algn

keeper [ˈkiːpə*] *n* guarda

keep-fit [kiːpˈfɪt] *n* gimnasia (de mantenimiento)

keeping [ˈkiːpɪŋ] *n* (*care*) cuidado; **in ~ with** de acuerdo con

keeps [kiːps] *n*: **for ~** (*col*) para siempre

keepsake [ˈkiːpseɪk] *n* recuerdo

keg [kɛɡ] *n* barrilete, barril

kennel [ˈkɛnl] *n* perrera; **kennels** *npl* perrera

kept [kɛpt] *pt, pp of* **keep**

kerb [kəːb] *n* (*Brit*) bordillo

kerb crawler [-krɔːlə*] *n conductor en busca de prostitutas desde su coche*

kernel [ˈkəːnl] *n* (*nut*) fruta; (*fig*) meollo

kerosene [ˈkɛrəsiːn] *n* keroseno

ketchup [ˈkɛtʃəp] *n* salsa de tomate, ketchup

kettle [ˈkɛtl] *n* hervidor

kettle drum *n* (*Mus*) timbal

key [kiː] *n* (*gen*) llave; (*Mus*) tono; (*of piano, typewriter*) tecla; (*on map*) clave ▷ *cpd* (*vital: position, industry etc*) clave ▷ *vt* (*also*: **key in**) teclear

keyboard [ˈkiːbɔːd] *n* teclado ▷ *vt* (*text*) teclear

keyboarder ['ki:bɔːdəʳ] n teclista
keyed up [ki:d-] adj (person) nervioso; **to be (all)**
~ estar nervioso or emocionado
keyhole ['ki:həul] n ojo (de la cerradura)
keyhole surgery n cirugía cerrada or no invasiva
keynote ['ki:nəut] n (Mus) tónica; (fig) idea
fundamental
keypad ['ki:pæd] n teclado numérico
keyring ['ki:rɪŋ] n llavero
kg abbr (= kilogram) kg
khaki ['kɑːkɪ] n caqui
kick [kɪk] vt (person) dar una patada a; (ball) dar
un puntapié a ▷ vi (horse) dar coces ▷ n patada;
puntapié, tiro; (of rifle) culetazo; (col: thrill): **he**
does it for ~**s** lo hace por pura diversión
  ▸ **kick around** vt (idea) dar vueltas a; (person)
tratar a patadas a
  ▸ **kick off** vi (Sport) hacer el saque inicial
kid [kɪd] n (col: child) niño(-a), chiquillo(-a);
(animal) cabrito; (leather) cabritilla ▷ vi (col)
bromear
kid gloves npl: **to treat sb with** ~ andarse con
pies de plomo con algn
kidnap ['kɪdnæp] vt secuestrar
kidnapper ['kɪdnæpəʳ] n secuestrador(a)
kidnapping ['kɪdnæpɪŋ] n secuestro
kidney ['kɪdnɪ] n riñón
kidney bean n judía, alubia
kill [kɪl] vt matar; (murder) asesinar, matar; (fig:
rumour, conversation) acabar con ▷ n matanza; **she**
~**ed her husband** mató a su marido; **he was**
~**ed in a car accident** murió en un accidente de
coche; **to** ~ **o.s.** suicidarse; **he** ~**ed himself** se
suicidó; **to** ~ **time** matar el tiempo
  ▸ **kill off** vt exterminar, terminar con; (fig) echar
por tierra
killer ['kɪləʳ] n asesino(-a)
killer instinct n: **to have the** ~ ir a por todas
killing ['kɪlɪŋ] n (one) asesinato; (several) matanza;
(Comm): **to make a** ~ tener un gran éxito
financiero
killjoy ['kɪldʒɔɪ] n (Brit) aguafiestas
kiln [kɪln] n horno
kilo ['ki:ləu] n (abbr = kilogram(me)) kilo
kilobyte ['kɪləubaɪt] n (Comput) kilobyte,
kiloocteto
kilogram(me) ['kɪləugræm] n kilogramo
kilometre, (US) **kilometer** ['kɪləmi:təʳ] n
kilómetro
kilowatt ['kɪləuwɔt] n kilovatio
kilt [kɪlt] n falda escocesa
kin [kɪn] n parientes
kind [kaɪnd] adj (person, act, word) amable, atento;
(treatment) bueno, cariñoso ▷ n (type) clase,
especie; (species) género; **to be** ~ **to sb** ser amable
con algn; **thank you for being so** ~ gracias por
su amabilidad; **would you be** ~ **enough to ...?**,
would you be so ~ **as to ...?** ¿me hace el favor de
...?; **that's very** ~ **of you** es usted muy amable;
a ~ **of** una especie de, un tipo de; **it's a** ~ **of**
sausage es un tipo de salchicha; **to be two of a**
~ ser tal para cual; **in** ~ en especie

kindergarten ['kɪndəgaːtn] n jardín de infancia
kind-hearted [kaɪnd'haːtɪd] adj bondadoso, de
buen corazón
kindle ['kɪndl] vt encender
kindly ['kaɪndlɪ] adj bondadoso; (gentle) cariñoso
  ▷ adv bondadosamente, amablemente; **will you**
~ ... sería usted tan amable de ...
kindness ['kaɪndnɪs] n bondad, amabilidad
kindred ['kɪndrɪd] n familia, parientes ▷ adj: ~
spirits almas gemelas
kinetic [kɪ'nɛtɪk] adj cinético
king [kɪŋ] n rey
kingdom ['kɪŋdəm] n reino
kingfisher ['kɪŋfɪʃəʳ] n martín pescador
king-size(d) ['kɪŋsaɪz(d)] adj de tamaño gigante;
(cigarette) extra largo
kinky ['kɪŋkɪ] adj (pej) perverso
kiosk ['ki:ɔsk] n quiosco; (Brit Tel) cabina;
newspaper ~ quiosco, kiosco
kipper ['kɪpəʳ] n arenque ahumado
Kirghizia [kəː'gɪzɪə] n Kirguizistán
kiss [kɪs] n beso ▷ vt besar; ~ **of life** (artificial
respiration) respiración artificial; **to** ~ **sb goodbye**
dar un beso de despedida a algn; **to** ~ **(each**
other) besarse
kissogram ['kɪsəgræm] n servicio de felicitaciones
mediante el que se envía a una persona vestida de manera
sugerente para besar a algn
kit [kɪt] n equipo; (set of tools etc) (caja de)
herramientas; (assembly kit) juego de armar; **tool**
~ juego o estuche de herramientas
  ▸ **kit out** vt equipar
kitchen ['kɪtʃɪn] n cocina
kitchen sink n fregadero
kite [kaɪt] n (toy) cometa
kith [kɪθ] n: ~ **and kin** parientes y allegados
kitten ['kɪtn] n gatito(-a)
kitty ['kɪtɪ] n (pool of money) fondo común; (Cards)
bote
kiwi ['ki:wi:] n (col: New Zealander)
neozelandés(-esa); (also: **kiwi fruit**) kiwi
km abbr (= kilometre) km
km/h abbr (= kilometres per hour) km/h
knack [næk] n: **to have the** ~ **of doing sth** tener
facilidad para hacer algo
knackered ['nækəd] adj (col) hecho polvo
knapsack ['næpsæk] n mochila
knead [ni:d] vt amasar
knee [ni:] n rodilla
kneecap [ni:kæp] vt destrozar a tiros la rótula
de ▷ n rótula
kneel [ni:l] (pt, pp knelt) vi (also: **kneel down**)
arrodillarse
knelt [nɛlt] pt, pp of **kneel**
knew [nju:] pt of **know**
knickers ['nɪkəz] npl (Brit) bragas (Esp), calzones
(LAm), bombachas (CS)
knife [naɪf] (pl **knives**) n cuchillo ▷ vt acuchillar;
~, **fork and spoon** cubiertos
knife edge n: **to be on a** ~ estar en la cuerda floja
knight [naɪt] n caballero; (Chess) caballo
knighthood ['naɪthud] n (title): **to get a** ~ recibir

el título de *Sir*

knit [nɪt] *vt* tejer, tricotar; (*brows*) fruncir; (*fig*): **to ~ together** unir, juntar ▷ *vi* hacer punto, tejer, tricotar; (*bones*) soldarse

knitting ['nɪtɪŋ] *n* labor de punto

knitting needle, (US) **knit pin** *n* aguja de hacer punto *or* tejer

knitwear ['nɪtwɛə^r] *n* prendas de punto

knives [naɪvz] *pl of* **knife**

knob [nɔb] *n* (*of door*) pomo; (*of stick*) puño; (*lump*) bulto; (*fig*): **a ~ of butter** (*Brit*) un pedazo de mantequilla

knock [nɔk] *vt* (*strike*) golpear; (*bump into*) chocar contra; (*fig: col*) criticar ▷ *vi* (*at door etc*): **to ~ at/on** llamar a ▷ *n* golpe; (*on door*) llamada; **he ~ed at the door** llamó a la puerta

▶ **knock down** *vt* (*pedestrian*) atropellar; (*price*) rebajar; **she was ~ed down by a car** la atropelló un coche

▶ **knock off** *vi* (*col: finish*) salir del trabajo ▷ *vt* (*col: steal*) birlar; (*strike off*) quitar; (*fig: from price, record*): **to ~ off £10** rebajar en £10

▶ **knock out** *vt* (*stun*) dejar sin sentido; (*Boxing*) poner fuera de combate, dejar K.O.; (*defeat*) eliminar; (*stop*) estropear, dejar fuera de servicio; **they ~ed out the watchman** dejaron al vigilante sin sentido; **they were ~ed out early in the tournament** fueron eliminados al poco de iniciarse el torneo

▶ **knock over** *vt* (*object*) derribar, tirar; (*pedestrian*) atropellar; **she was ~ed over by a car** la atropelló un coche

knockdown ['nɔkdaun] *adj* (*price*) de saldo

knocker ['nɔkə^r] *n* (*on door*) aldaba

knockout ['nɔkaut] *n* (*Boxing*) K.O., knockout

knot [nɔt] *n* (*gen*) nudo ▷ *vt* anudar; **to tie a ~** hacer un nudo

knotty ['nɔtɪ] *adj* (*fig*) complicado

know [nəu] (*pt* **knew**, *pp* **-n**) *vt* (*gen*) saber; (*person, author, place*) conocer ▷ *vi*: **as far as I ~ ...** que yo sepa ...; **yes, I ~** sí, ya lo sé; **I don't ~** no lo sé; **how should I ~?** ¿y yo qué sé?; **you never ~!** ¡nunca se sabe!; **to ~ how to do** saber hacer; **to ~ how to swim** saber nadar; **to ~ about** (*be knowledgeable about*) saber de; (*be aware of*) estar enterado de; **he ~s a lot about cars** sabe mucho

de coches; **I don't ~ much about computers** no sé mucho de ordenadores; **I ~ nothing about it** no sé nada de eso; **do you ~ about the meeting this afternoon?** ¿estás enterado de la reunión de esta tarde?; **to ~ of sb/sth** saber de algn/algo; **I don't ~ any German** no sé nada de alemán; **I didn't ~ (that) your Dad was a policeman** no sabía que tu padre era policía; **I don't ~ him** no lo *or* le conozco; **I ~ Paris well** conozco bien París; **to get to ~ sb** llegar a conocer a algn; **to get to ~ sth** enterarse de algo; **to ~ right from wrong** saber distinguir el bien del mal

know-all ['nəuɔːl] *n* (*Brit pej*) sabelotodo, sabihondo(-a)

know-how ['nəuhau] *n* conocimientos

knowing ['nəuɪŋ] *adj* de complicidad

knowingly ['nəuɪŋlɪ] *adv* (*purposely*) a sabiendas; (*smile, look*) con complicidad

knowledge ['nɔlɪdʒ] *n* (*gen*) conocimiento; (*learning*) saber, conocimientos; **to have no ~ of** no saber nada de; **with my ~** con mis conocimientos, sabiéndolo; **to (the best of) my ~** a mi entender, que yo sepa; **not to my ~** que yo sepa, no; **it is common ~ that ...** es del dominio público que ...; **it has come to my ~ that ...** me he enterado de que ...; **to have a working ~ of Spanish** defenderse con el español

knowledgeable ['nɔlɪdʒəbl] *adj* entendido, erudito

known [nəun] *pp of* **know** ▷ *adj* (*thief, facts*) conocido; (*expert*) reconocido

knuckle ['nʌkl] *n* nudillo

▶ **knuckle down** *vi* (*col*) ponerse a trabajar en serio

▶ **knuckle under** *vi* someterse

KO *n abbr* (= *knockout*) K.O. ▷ *vt* (*knock out*) dejar K.O.

Koran [kɔ'rɑːn] *n* Corán

Korea [kə'rɪə] *n* Corea; **North/South ~** Corea del Norte/Sur

kosher ['kəuʃə^r] *adj* autorizado por la ley judía

Kosovo ['kɔsəvəu] *n* Kosovo

kudos ['kjuːdɔs] *n* gloria, prestigio

Kuwait [ku'weɪt] *n* Kuwait

kW *abbr* (= *kilowatt*) Kv

L, l [ɛl] *n* (*letter*) L, l; **L for Lucy**, (*US*) **L for Love** L de Lorenzo

L *abbr* (*on maps etc*) = **lake**; **large**; (= *left*) izq.; (*Brit Aut: learner*) L

l. *abbr* = **litre**

LA *n abbr* (*US*) = **Los Angeles** ▷ *abbr* (*US*) = **Louisiana**

lab [læb] *n abbr* = **laboratory**

Lab. *abbr* (*Canada*) = **Labrador**

label ['leɪbl] *n* etiqueta; (*brand: of record*) sello (discográfico) ▷ *vt* poner una etiqueta a, etiquetar

labor *etc* ['leɪbəʳ] (*US*) = **labour**

laboratory [ləˈbɔrətərɪ] *n* laboratorio

Labor Day *n* (*US*) día de los trabajadores (*primer lunes de septiembre*)

laborious [ləˈbɔːrɪəs] *adj* penoso

labor union *n* (*US*) sindicato

Labour ['leɪbəʳ] *n* (*Brit Pol: also*: **the Labour Party**) el partido laborista, los laboristas

labour, (*US*) **labor** ['leɪbəʳ] *n* (*task*) trabajo; (*labour force*) mano de obra; (*workers*) trabajadores; (*Med*) (*dolores del*) parto ▷ *vi*: **to ~ (at)** trabajar (en) ▷ *vt* insistir en; **hard ~** trabajos forzados; **the ~ market** el mercado de trabajo; **to be in ~** estar de parto

labo(u)r dispute *n* conflicto laboral

labo(u)red ['leɪbəd] *adj* (*breathing*) fatigoso; (*style*) forzado, pesado

labo(u)rer ['leɪbərəʳ] *n* peón; (*on farm*) peón, obrero; (*day labo(u)rer*) jornalero

labo(u)r force *n* mano de obra

labo(u)r relations *npl* relaciones laborales

labyrinth ['læbɪrɪnθ] *n* laberinto

lace [leɪs] *n* encaje; (*of shoe etc*) cordón, agujeta (*Méx*), pasador (*Perú*) ▷ *vt* (*shoes: also*: **lace up**) atarse; (*drink: fortify with spirits*) echar licor a

laceration [læsəˈreɪʃən] *n* laceración

lack [læk] *n* (*absence*) falta, carencia; (*scarcity*) escasez ▷ *vt* faltarle a algn, carecer de; **through** *or* **for ~ of** por falta de; **to be ~ing** faltar, no haber

lacquer ['lækəʳ] *n* laca; **hair ~** laca para el pelo

lad [læd] *n* muchacho, chico; (*in stable etc*) mozo

ladder ['lædəʳ] *n* escalera (de mano); (*Brit: in tights*) carrera ▷ *vt* (*Brit: tights*) hacer una carrera en

laden ['leɪdn] *adj*: **~ (with)** cargado (de); **fully ~** (*truck, ship*) cargado hasta el tope

ladle ['leɪdl] *n* cucharón

lady ['leɪdɪ] *n* señora; (*distinguished, noble*) dama; **young ~** señorita; **the ladies' (room)** los servicios de señoras

ladybird ['leɪdɪbəːd], (*US*) **ladybug** ['leɪdɪbʌg] *n* mariquita

ladylike ['leɪdɪlaɪk] *adj* fino

Ladyship ['leɪdɪʃɪp] *n*: **your ~** su Señoría

LAFTA *n abbr* (= *Latin American Free Trade Association*) ALALC

lag [læg] *vi* (*also*: **lag behind**) retrasarse, quedarse atrás ▷ *vt* (*pipes*) revestir

lager ['lɑːgəʳ] *n* cerveza (rubia)

lager lout *n* (*Brit col*) gamberro borracho

lagoon [ləˈguːn] *n* laguna

laid [leɪd] *pt, pp of* **lay**

laid-back [leɪdˈbæk] *adj* (*col*) tranquilo, relajado

laid up *adj*: **to be ~** (*person*) tener que guardar cama

lain [leɪn] *pp of* **lie**

lair [lɛəʳ] *n* guarida

laity ['leɪtɪ] *n* laicado

lake [leɪk] *n* lago

Lake District *n* (*Brit*): **the ~** la Región de los Lagos

lamb [læm] *n* cordero; (*meat*) carne de cordero

lamb chop *n* chuleta de cordero

lame [leɪm] *adj* cojo, rengo (*LAm*); (*weak*) débil, poco convincente; **~ duck** (*fig: person*) inútil; (*: firm*) empresa en quiebra

lament [ləˈmɛnt] *n* lamento ▷ *vt* lamentarse de

laminated ['læmɪneɪtɪd] *adj* laminado

lamp [læmp] *n* lámpara

lamppost ['læmppəʊst] *n* (*Brit*) farola

lampshade ['læmpʃeɪd] *n* pantalla

lance [lɑːns] *n* lanza ▷ *vt* (*Med*) abrir con lanceta

land [lænd] *n* tierra; (*country*) país; (*piece of land*) terreno; (*estate*) tierras, finca; (*Agr*) campo ▷ *vi* (*from ship*) desembarcar; (*Aviat*) aterrizar; (*fig: fall*) caer ▷ *vt* (*obtain*) conseguir; (*passengers, goods*) desembarcar; **to own ~** ser dueño de tierras; **we have a lot of ~** tenemos mucha tierra; **to work on the ~** trabajar la tierra; **to ~ on one's feet** caer de pie; (*fig: to be lucky*) salir bien parado

▶**land up** vi: **to ~ up in/at** ir a parar a/en
landfill site ['lændfɪl-] n vertedero
landing ['lændɪŋ] n desembarco; aterrizaje; (of staircase) rellano
landing gear n (Aviat) tren de aterrizaje
landing strip n pista de aterrizaje
landlady ['lændleɪdɪ] n (of boarding house) patrona; (owner) dueña
landlocked ['lændlɔkt] adj cercado de tierra
landlord ['lændlɔːd] n propietario; (of pub etc) patrón
landmark ['lændmɑːk] n lugar conocido; **to be a ~** (fig) hacer época
landowner ['lændəunəʳ] n terrateniente
landscape ['lænskeɪp] n paisaje
landscape gardener n diseñador(a) de paisajes
landslide ['lændslaɪd] n (Geo) corrimiento de tierras; (fig: Pol) victoria arrolladora
lane [leɪn] n (in country) camino; (in town) callejón; (Aut) carril; (in race) calle; (for air or sea traffic) ruta; **shipping ~** ruta marina
language ['læŋgwɪdʒ] n lenguaje; (national tongue) idioma, lengua; **bad ~** palabrotas
language laboratory n laboratorio de idiomas
language studies npl estudios filológicos
languid ['læŋgwɪd] adj lánguido
languish ['læŋgwɪʃ] vi languidecer
lank [læŋk] adj (hair) lacio
lanky ['læŋkɪ] adj larguirucho
lantern ['læntn] n linterna, farol
lap [læp] n (of track) vuelta; (of body): **to sit on sb's ~** sentarse en las rodillas de algn ▷ vt (also: **lap up**) beber a lengüetadas or con la lengua ▷ vi (waves) chapotear
▶**lap up** vt beber a lengüetadas or con la lengua; (fig: compliments, attention) disfrutar; (: lies etc) tragarse
lapdog ['læpdɔg] n perro faldero
lapel [lə'pɛl] n solapa
Lapland ['læplænd] n Laponia
lapse [læps] n (fault) error, fallo; (moral) desliz ▷ vi (expire) caducar; (morally) cometer un desliz; (time) pasar, transcurrir; **to ~ into bad habits** volver a las andadas; **~ of time** lapso, período; **a ~ of memory** un lapsus de memoria
laptop ['læptɔp] n (also: **laptop computer**) (ordenador) portátil
larceny ['lɑːsənɪ] n latrocinio
lard [lɑːd] n manteca (de cerdo)
larder ['lɑːdəʳ] n despensa
large [lɑːdʒ] adj grande ▷ adv: **by and ~** en general, en términos generales; **at ~** (free) en libertad; (generally) en general; **to make ~(r)** hacer mayor or más extenso; **a ~ number of people** una gran cantidad de personas; **on a ~ scale** a gran escala
largely ['lɑːdʒlɪ] adv en gran parte
large-scale ['lɑːdʒ'skeɪl] adj (map, drawing) a gran escala; (reforms) importante
lark [lɑːk] n (bird) alondra; (joke) broma
▶**lark about** vi bromear, hacer el tonto
larva ['lɑːvə] (pl **-e**) n larva

laryngitis [lærɪn'dʒaɪtɪs] n laringitis
larynx ['lærɪŋks] n laringe
lasagne [lə'zænjə] n lasaña
laser ['leɪzəʳ] n láser
laser beam n rayo láser
laser printer n impresora láser
lash [læʃ] n latigazo; (punishment) azote; (also: **eyelash**) pestaña ▷ vt azotar; (tie) atar
▶**lash down** vt sujetar con cuerdas ▷ vi (rain) caer a trombas
▶**lash out** vi (col: spend) gastar a la loca; **to ~ out at** or **against ʒ ⁊** (fig) lanzar invectivas contra algn
lass [læs] n chica
lasso [læ'suː] n lazo ▷ vt coger con lazo
last [lɑːst] adj (gen) último; (final) último, final ▷ adv por último; por última vez; en último lugar ▷ vi (endure) durar; (continue) continuar, seguir; **the ~ time** la última vez; **~ but one** penúltimo; **~ night** anoche; **~ week** la semana pasada; **at ~** por fin; **I've lost my bag — when did you ~ see it?** he perdido el bolso — ¿cuándo lo viste por última vez?; **the team which finished ~** el equipo que quedó en último lugar; **he arrived ~** llegó el último; **it ~s (for) 2 hours** dura 2 horas
last-ditch ['lɑːst'dɪtʃ] adj (attempt) de último recurso, último, desesperado
lasting ['lɑːstɪŋ] adj duradero
lastly ['lɑːstlɪ] adv por último, finalmente
last-minute ['lɑːstmɪnɪt] adj de última hora
latch [lætʃ] n picaporte, pestillo
▶**latch on to** vt fus (cling to: person) pegarse a; (: idea) agarrarse de
late [leɪt] adj (not on time) tarde, atrasado; (towards end of period) tardío; (hour) avanzado; (deceased) difunto ▷ adv tarde; (behind time, schedule) con retraso; **hurry up or you'll be ~!** ¡date prisa o llegarás tarde!; **I'm often ~ for school** a menudo llego tarde al colegio; **to be 10 minutes ~** llegar con 10 minutos de retraso; **to be ~ with** estar atrasado con; **~ delivery** entrega tardía; **in ~ May** hacia fines de mayo; **in the ~ afternoon** al final de la tarde; **in the ~ 18th century** a fines del siglo XVIII; **the ~ Mr Philips** el difunto Sr Philips; **I went to bed ~** me fui a la cama tarde; **to arrive ~** llegar tarde; **to work ~** trabajar hasta tarde; **of ~** últimamente; **~ in life** a una edad avanzada
latecomer ['leɪtkʌməʳ] n recién llegado(-a)
lately ['leɪtlɪ] adv últimamente
latent ['leɪtnt] adj latente; **~ defect** defecto latente
later ['leɪtəʳ] adj (date etc) posterior; (version etc) más reciente ▷ adv más tarde, después; **I'll do it ~** lo haré más tarde; **~ on today** hoy más tarde; **see you ~!** ¡hasta luego!
latest ['leɪtɪst] adj último; **their ~ album** su último álbum; **at the ~** a más tardar; **by 10 o'clock at the ~** a las 10 como muy tarde
latex ['leɪtɛks] n látex
lathe [leɪð] n torno
lather ['lɑːðəʳ] n espuma (de jabón) ▷ vt

enjabonar

Latin ['lætɪn] n latín ▷ adj latino

Latin America n América Latina, Latinoamérica

Latin American adj, n latinoamericano(-a)

Latino [læ'tiːnəu] adj, n latino(-a)

latitude ['lætɪtjuːd] n latitud; (fig: freedom) libertad

latter ['lætəʳ] adj último; (of two) segundo ▷ n: **the ~** el último, éste

latterly ['lætəlɪ] adv últimamente

Latvia ['lætvɪə] n Letonia

laudable ['lɔːdəbl] adj loable

laugh [lɑːf] n risa; (loud) carcajada ▷ vi reírse, reír; reírse a carcajadas; **it was a good ~** fue muy divertido

▶ **laugh at** vt fus reírse de

▶ **laugh off** vt tomar a risa

laughable ['lɑːfəbl] adj ridículo

laughing ['lɑːfɪŋ] adj risueño ▷ n: **it's no ~ matter** no es cosa de risa

laughing stock n: **to be the ~ of the town** ser el hazmerreír de la ciudad

laughter ['lɑːftəʳ] n risa

launch [lɔːntʃ] n (boat) lancha; see also **launching** ▷ vt (ship) botar; (rocket, plan) lanzar

▶ **launch forth** vi: **to ~ forth (into)** lanzarse (a or en), emprender

▶ **launch out** vi = **launch forth**

launching ['lɔːntʃɪŋ] n (of rocket etc) lanzamiento; (inauguration) estreno

Launderette® [lɔːn'drɛt], **Laundromat®** (US) ['lɔːndrəmæt] n lavandería (automática)

laundry ['lɔːndrɪ] n lavandería; (clothes) ropa sucia; **to do the ~** hacer la colada

laureate ['lɔːrɪət] adj see **poet**

laurel ['lɔrl] n laurel; **to rest on one's ~s** dormirse en or sobre los laureles

lava ['lɑːvə] n lava

lavatory ['lævətərɪ] n wáter; **lavatories** npl servicios, aseos, sanitarios (LAm)

lavender ['lævəndəʳ] n lavanda

lavish ['lævɪʃ] adj abundante; (giving freely): **~ with** pródigo en ▷ vt: **to ~ sth on sb** colmar a algn de algo

law [lɔː] n ley; (study) derecho; (of game) regla; **against the ~** contra la ley; **to study ~** estudiar derecho; **to go to ~** recurrir a la justicia

law-abiding ['lɔːəbaɪdɪŋ] adj respetuoso con la ley

law and order n orden público

law court n tribunal (de justicia)

lawful ['lɔːful] adj legítimo, lícito

lawless ['lɔːlɪs] adj (act) ilegal; (person) rebelde; (country) ingobernable

Law Lord n (Brit) miembro de la Cámara de los Lores y del más alto tribunal de apelación

lawn [lɔːn] n césped

lawnmower ['lɔːnməuəʳ] n cortacésped

lawn tennis n tenis sobre hierba

law school n (US) facultad de derecho

lawsuit ['lɔːsuːt] n pleito; **to bring a ~ against** entablar un pleito contra

lawyer ['lɔːjəʳ] n abogado(-a); (for sales, wills etc) notario(-a)

lax [læks] adj (discipline) relajado; (person) negligente

laxative ['læksətɪv] n laxante

lay [leɪ] pt of **lie** ▷ adj laico; (not expert) lego ▷ vt (pt, pp **laid**) (place) colocar; (eggs, table) poner; (trap) tender; **she laid the baby in his cot** puso al bebé en la cuna; **to ~ the facts/one's proposals before sb** presentar los hechos/sus propuestas a algn

▶ **lay aside, lay by** vt dejar a un lado

▶ **lay down** vt (pen etc) dejar; (arms) rendir; (policy) trazar; **to ~ down the law** imponer las normas

▶ **lay in** vt abastecerse de

▶ **lay into** vt fus (col: attack, scold) arremeter contra

▶ **lay off** vt (workers) despedir; **my father's been laid off** han despedido a mi padre

▶ **lay on** vt (water, gas) instalar; (meal, facilities) proporcionar; **they laid on extra buses** proporcionaron más autobuses; **they laid on a special meal** prepararon una comida especial

▶ **lay out** vt (plan) trazar; (display) exponer; (spend) gastar

▶ **lay up** vt (store) guardar; (ship) desarmar; (subj: illness) obligar a guardar cama

layabout ['leɪəbaut] n vago(-a)

lay-by ['leɪbaɪ] n (Brit Aut) apartadero

layer ['leɪəʳ] n capa

layman ['leɪmən] n lego

layout ['leɪaut] n (design) plan, trazado; (disposition) disposición; (Press) composición

laze [leɪz] vi no hacer nada; (pej) holgazanear

lazy ['leɪzɪ] adj perezoso, vago, flojo (LAm)

lb. abbr = **pound** (peso)

LCD n abbr see **liquid crystal display**

lead [liːd] n (front position) delantera; (distance, time ahead) ventaja; (clue) pista; (Elec) cable; (for dog) correa; (Theat) papel principal [lɛd] (metal) plomo; (in pencil) mina ▷ vb (pt, pp **led**) ▷ vt conducir; (life) llevar; (be leader of) dirigir; (Sport) ir en cabeza de; (orchestra: Brit) ser el primer violín en; (: US) dirigir ▷ vi ir primero; **to be in the ~** (Sport) llevar la delantera; (fig) ir a la cabeza; **to take the ~** (Sport) tomar la delantera; (fig) tomar la iniciativa; **"Dogs must be kept on a ~"** "Los perros deben llevarse siempre sujetos con una correa"; **to ~ the way** ir delante; **to ~ sb to believe that ...** hacer creer a algn que ...; **to ~ sb to do sth** llevar a algn a hacer algo; **the street that ~s to the station** la calle que lleva a la estación; **it could ~ to a civil war** podría llevar a una guerra civil

▶ **lead astray** vt llevar por mal camino

▶ **lead away** vt llevar; **the police led the man away** la policía se llevó al hombre

▶ **lead back** vt hacer volver

▶ **lead off** vt llevar ▷ vi (in game) abrir

▶ **lead on** vt (tease) engañar; **to ~ sb on to** (induce) incitar a algn a

▶ **lead to** *vt fus* producir, provocar
▶ **lead up to** *vt fus* conducir a
leaded ['lɛdɪd] *adj*: **~ windows** ventanas emplomadas
leaden ['lɛdn] *adj* (*sky, sea*) plomizo; (*heavy: footsteps*) pesado
leader ['li:dəʳ] *n* jefe(-a), líder; (*of union etc*) dirigente; (*guide*) guía; (*of newspaper*) editorial; **they are ~s in their field** (*fig*) llevan la delantera en su especialidad
leadership ['li:dəʃɪp] *n* dirección; **qualities of ~** iniciativa; **under the ~ of ...** bajo la dirección de ..., al mando de ...
lead-free ['lɛdfri:] *adj* sin plomo
leading ['li:dɪŋ] *adj* (*main*) principal; (*outstanding*) destacado; (*first*) primero; (*front*) delantero; **a ~ question** una pregunta tendenciosa
leading lady *n* (*Theat*) primera actriz
leading light *n* (*fig: person*) figura principal
leading man *n* (*Theat*) primer actor
lead-up ['li:dʌp] *n*: **in the ~ to the election** cuando falta *etc* poco para las elecciones
leaf [li:f] (*pl* **leaves**) *n* hoja; **to turn over a new ~** (*fig*) volver la hoja, hacer borrón y cuenta nueva; **to take a ~ out of sb's book** (*fig*) seguir el ejemplo de algn
▶ **leaf through** *vt fus* (*book*) hojear
leaflet ['li:flɪt] *n* folleto
league [li:g] *n* sociedad; (*Football*) liga; **to be in ~ with** estar confabulado con
league table *n* clasificación
leak [li:k] *n* (*of liquid, gas*) escape, fuga; (*in pipe*) agujero; (*in roof*) gotera; (*fig: of information, in security*) filtración ▷ *vi* (*ship*) hacer agua; (*shoes*) tener un agujero; (*pipe*) tener un escape; (*roof*) tener goteras; (*also*: **leak out**: *liquid, gas*) escaparse, salirse; (*fig: news*) trascender, divulgarse ▷ *vt* (*gen*) dejar escapar; (*fig: information*) filtrar
leakage ['li:kɪdʒ] *n* (*of water, gas etc*) escape, fuga
lean [li:n] *adj* (*thin*) flaco; (*meat*) magro ▷ *vb* (*pt, pp* **-ed** *or* **-t**) ▷ *vt*: **to ~ sth on sth** apoyar algo en algo ▷ *vi* (*slope*) inclinarse; (*rest*): **to ~ against** apoyarse contra; **to ~ on** apoyarse en
▶ **lean back** *vi* inclinarse hacia atrás
▶ **lean forward** *vi* inclinarse hacia adelante
▶ **lean out** *vi*: **to ~ out (of)** asomarse (a)
▶ **lean over** *vi* inclinarse
leaning ['li:nɪŋ] *adj* inclinado ▷ *n*: **~ (towards)** inclinación (hacia); **the L~ Tower of Pisa** la Torre Inclinada de Pisa
leant [lɛnt] *pt, pp of* **lean**
leap [li:p] *n* salto ▷ *vi* (*pt, pp* **-ed** *or* **-t**) [lɛpt] saltar; **to ~ at an offer** apresurarse a aceptar una oferta
▶ **leap up** *vi* (*person*) saltar
leapfrog ['li:pfrɒg] *n* pídola ▷ *vi*: **to ~ over sb/sth** saltar por encima de algn/algo
leapt [lɛpt] *pt, pp of* **leap**
leap year *n* año bisiesto
learn [lə:n] **-ed** *or* **-t**) *pt, pp vt* (*gen*) aprender; (*come to know of*) enterarse de ▷ *vi* aprender; **to ~ how to do sth** aprender a hacer algo; **I'm**

~ing to ski estoy aprendiendo a esquiar; **to ~ about sth** (*Scol*) aprender algo; (*hear*) enterarse or informarse de algo; **to ~ that ...** enterarse or informarse de que ...; **we were sorry to ~ that ...** nos dio tristeza saber que ....
learned ['lə:nɪd] *adj* erudito
learner ['lə:nəʳ] *n* principiante; (*Brit: also:* **learner driver**) conductor(a) en prácticas; *see also* **L-plates**
learning ['lə:nɪŋ] *n* saber, conocimientos
learnt [lə:nt] *pp of* **learn**
lease [li:s] *n* arriendo ▷ *vt* arrendar; **on ~** en arriendo
▶ **lease back** *vt* subarrendar
leash [li:ʃ] *n* correa
least [li:st] *adj* (*slightest*) menor, más pequeño; (*smallest amount of*) mínimo ▷ *adv* menos ▷ *n*: **the ~** lo menos; **I haven't the ~ idea** no tengo la menor idea; **the ~ expensive car** el coche menos caro; **go for the ones with ~ fat** escoge los que tengan menos grasa; **it takes the ~ time** es lo que menos tiempo lleva; **at ~** por lo menos, al menos; **it'll cost at ~ £200** costará por lo menos 200 libras esterlinas; **there was a lot of damage but at ~ nobody was hurt** hubo muchos daños pero al menos nadie resultó herido; **it's very unfair, at ~ that's my opinion** es muy injusto, al menos eso pienso yo; **it's the ~ I can do** es lo menos que puedo hacer; **maths is the subject I like the ~** las matemáticas es la asignatura que menos me gusta; **not in the ~** en absoluto
leather ['lɛðəʳ] *n* cuero ▷ *cpd*: **~ goods** artículos de cuero or piel
leave [li:v] (*pt, pp* **left**) *vt* (*thing*) dejar; (*place*) salir de; (*husband, wife*) abandonar ▷ *vi* irse; (*train*) salir ▷ *n* permiso; **don't ~ your camera in the car** no dejes la cámara en el coche; **to ~ school** (*finish studies*) dejar la escuela or el colegio; **she left home when she was sixteen** se fue de casa a los dieciséis años; **we ~ London at 6 o'clock** salimos de Londres a las 6; **he has left his wife** ha dejado or abandonado a su mujer; **~ it to me!** ¡yo me encargo!; **to ~ sb alone** dejar a algn en paz; **~ me alone!** ¡déjame en paz!; **they left yesterday** se fueron ayer; **the bus ~s at 8** el autobús sale a las 8; **he's already left for the airport** ya se ha marchado al aeropuerto; **to be left** quedar, sobrar; **there's some milk left over** sobra or queda algo de leche; **on ~** de permiso; **my brother is on ~ for a week** mi hermano está de permiso durante una semana; **to take one's ~ of** despedirse de
▶ **leave behind** *vt* (*on purpose*) dejar (atrás); (*accidentally*) olvidar
▶ **leave off** *vt* (*lid*) no poner; (*switch*) no encender; (*col: stop*): **to ~ off doing sth** dejar de hacer algo
▶ **leave on** *vt* (*lid*) dejar puesto; (*light, fire, cooker*) dejar encendido
▶ **leave out** *vt* (*omit*) omitir; (*exclude*) excluir; **he feels left out** se siente excluido
▶ **leave over** *vt* (*postpone*) dejar, aplazar

leave of absence n excedencia
leaves [li:vz] pl of **leaf**
Lebanon ['lɛbənən] n: **the ~** el Líbano
lecherous ['lɛtʃərəs] adj lascivo
lectern ['lɛktə:n] n atril
lecture ['lɛktʃər] n conferencia; (Scol) clase ▷ vi
dar clase(s) ▷ vt (scold) sermonear; (reprove)
echar una reprimenda a; **to give a ~ on** dar una
conferencia sobre
lecture hall n sala de conferencias; (Univ) aula
lecturer ['lɛktʃərər] n conferenciante; (Brit: at
university) profesor(a)
lecture theatre n = **lecture hall**
LED n abbr (= light-emitting diode) LED
led [lɛd] pt, pp of **lead**
ledge [lɛdʒ] n (of window, on wall) repisa, reborde;
(of mountain) saliente
ledger ['lɛdʒər] n libro mayor
lee [li:] n sotavento; **in the ~ of** al abrigo de
leech [li:tʃ] n sanguijuela
leek [li:k] n puerro
leer [lɪər] vi: **to ~ at sb** mirar de manera lasciva
a algn
leeway ['li:weɪ] n (fig): **to have some ~** tener
cierta libertad de acción
left [lɛft] pt, pp of **leave** ▷ adj izquierdo ▷ n
izquierda ▷ adv a la izquierda; **on** or **to the ~** a la
izquierda; **the L~** (Pol) la izquierda
left-handed [lɛft'hændɪd] adj zurdo; **~ scissors**
tijeras zurdas or para zurdos
left-hand side ['lɛfthænd-] n izquierda
left-luggage (office) [lɛft'lʌgɪdʒ(-)] n (Brit)
consigna
left-overs ['lɛftəuvəz] npl sobras
left-wing [lɛft'wɪŋ] adj (Pol) de izquierda(s),
izquierdista
lefty ['lɛftɪ] n (col: Pol) rojillo(-a)
leg [lɛg] n pierna; (of animal, chair) pata; (Culin: of
meat) pierna; (of journey) etapa; **1st/2nd ~** (Sport)
partido de ida/de vuelta; **to pull sb's ~** tomar el
pelo a algn; **to stretch one's ~s** dar una vuelta
legacy ['lɛgəsɪ] n herencia; (fig) herencia, legado
legal ['li:gl] adj (permitted by law) lícito; (of law)
legal; (inquiry etc) jurídico; **to take ~ action** or
proceedings against sb entablar or levantar un
pleito contra algn
legal holiday n (US) fiesta oficial
legality [lɪ'gælɪtɪ] n legalidad
legalize ['li:gəlaɪz] vt legalizar
legally ['li:gəlɪ] adv legalmente; **~ binding** con
fuerza legal
legal tender n moneda de curso legal
legend ['lɛdʒənd] n leyenda
leggings ['lɛgɪŋz] npl mallas, leggins
legible ['lɛdʒəbl] adj legible
legion ['li:dʒən] n legión
legionnaire [li:dʒə'nɛər] n legionario
legislation [lɛdʒɪs'leɪʃən] n legislación; **a piece
of ~** (bill) un proyecto de ley; (act) una ley
legislative ['lɛdʒɪslətɪv] adj legislativo
legislator ['lɛdʒɪsleɪtər] n legislador(a)
legislature ['lɛdʒɪslətʃər] n cuerpo legislativo

legitimacy [lɪ'dʒɪtɪməsɪ] n legitimidad
legitimate adj legítimo ▷ vt legitimar
legitimize [lɪ'dʒɪtɪmaɪz] vt legitimar
legless ['lɛglɪs] adj (Brit col) mamado
leg-room ['lɛgru:m] n espacio para las piernas
leisure ['lɛʒər] n ocio, tiempo libre; **at ~** con
tranquilidad
leisure centre n centro recreativo
leisurely ['lɛʒəlɪ] adj sin prisa; lento
lemon ['lɛmən] n limón
lemonade [lɛmə'neɪd] n (fruit juice) limonada;
(fizzy) gaseosa
lemon tea n té con limón
lend [lɛnd] (pt, pp **lent**) vt: **to ~ sth to sb** prestar
algo a algn
lender ['lɛndər] n prestamista
length [lɛŋθ] n (size) largo, longitud; (section: of
road, pipe) tramo; (: of rope etc) largo; **at ~** (at last)
por fin, finalmente; (lengthily) largamente; **it is
2 metres in ~** tiene 2 metros de largo; **what ~ is
it?** ¿cuánto tiene de largo?; **to fall full ~** caer de
bruces; **to go to any ~(s) to do sth** ser capaz de
hacer cualquier cosa para hacer algo
lengthen ['lɛŋθn] vt alargar ▷ vi alargarse
lengthways ['lɛŋθweɪz] adv a lo largo
lengthy ['lɛŋθɪ] adj largo, extenso; (meeting)
prolongado
lenient ['li:nɪənt] adj indulgente
lens [lɛnz] n (of spectacles) lente; (of camera)
objetivo
Lent [lɛnt] n Cuaresma
lent [lɛnt] pt, pp of **lend**
lentil ['lɛntl] n lenteja
Leo ['li:əu] n Leo
leopard ['lɛpəd] n leopardo
leotard ['li:əta:d] n leotardo
leper ['lɛpər] n leproso(-a)
leprosy ['lɛprəsɪ] n lepra
lesbian ['lɛzbɪən] adj lesbiano ▷ n lesbiana
lesion ['li:ʒən] n (Med) lesión
less [lɛs] adj (in size, degree etc) menor; (in quantity)
menos ▷ pron, adv menos; **~ than half** menos
de la mitad; **~ than £1/a kilo/3 metres** menos
de una libra/un kilo/3 metros; **~ than ever**
menos que nunca; **I've got ~ than you** tengo
menos que tú; **it cost ~ than we thought** costó
menos de lo que pensábamos; **~ 5%** menos el 5
por ciento; **~ and ~** cada vez menos; **the ~ he
works...** cuanto menos trabaja ...
lessen ['lɛsn] vi disminuir, reducirse ▷ vt
disminuir, reducir
lesser ['lɛsər] adj menor; **to a ~ extent** or **degree**
en menor grado
lesson ['lɛsn] n clase; **a maths ~** una clase de
matemáticas; **to give ~s in** dar clases de; **it
taught him a ~** (fig) le sirvió de lección
lest [lɛst] conj: **~ it happen** para que no pase
let [lɛt] (pt, pp **~**) vt (allow) dejar, permitir; (Brit:
lease) alquilar; **to ~ sb do sth** dejar que algn
haga algo; **~ me have a look** déjame ver; **~
me go!** ¡suéltame!; **to ~ sb have sth** dar algo a
algn; **to ~ sb know sth** informar a algn de algo;

we must ~ him know that we are coming to
stay tenemos que informarle de que venimos
a quedarnos; **when can you come to dinner?**
— **I'll ~ you know** ¿cuándo puedes venir a cenar?
— ya te lo diré; **~'s go!** ¡vamos!; **~'s go to the
cinema!** ¿por qué no vamos al cine?; **~'s have
a break!** — yes, **~'s** vamos a descansar un poco
— ¡buena idea!; **~ him come** que venga; **"to ~"**
"se alquila"
▶ **let down** vt (lower) bajar; (dress) alargar; (tyre)
desinflar; (hair) soltar; (disappoint) defraudar; **I
won't ~ you down** no te defraudaré
▶ **let go** vi soltar; (fig) dejarse ir ▷ vt soltar
▶ **let in** vt dejar entrar; (visitor etc) hacer pasar;
they wouldn't ~ me in because I was under 18
no me dejaron entrar porque tenía menos de 18
años; **what have you ~ yourself in for?** ¿en qué
te has metido?
▶ **let off** vt dejar escapar; (firework etc) disparar;
(bomb) accionar; (passenger) dejar, bajar; **to ~ off
steam** (fig, col) desahogarse, desfogarse
▶ **let on** vi: **to ~ on that ...** revelar que ...
▶ **let out** vt dejar salir; (dress) ensanchar; (rent
out) alquilar
▶ **let up** vi disminuir; (rain etc) amainar
lethal ['li:θl] adj (weapon) mortífero; (poison,
wound) mortal
lethargic [lɛˈθɑːdʒɪk] adj aletargado
letter ['lɛtə'] n (of alphabet) letra; (correspondence)
carta; **letters** npl (literature, learning) letras;
small/capital ~ minúscula/mayúscula; **covering ~** carta adjunta
letter bomb n carta-bomba
letterbox ['lɛtəbɔks] n (Brit) buzón
lettering ['lɛtərɪŋ] n letras
letter-opener ['lɛtərəupnə'] n abrecartas
lettuce ['lɛtɪs] n lechuga
let-up ['lɛtʌp] n descanso, tregua
leukaemia, (US) **leukemia** [luːˈkiːmɪə] n
leucemia
level ['lɛvl] adj (flat) llano; (flattened) nivelado;
(uniform) igual ▷ adv a nivel ▷ n nivel ▷ vt
nivelar, allanar; (gun) apuntar; (accusation):
to ~ (against) levantar (contra) ▷ vi (col): **to ~
with sb** ser franco con algn; **a ~ surface** una
superficie llana; **to be ~ with** estar a nivel de;
a ~ spoonful (Culin) una cucharada rasa; **to
draw ~ with** (team) igualar; (runner, car) alcanzar
a; **the ~ of the river is rising** el nivel del río
está subiendo; **"A" ~s** npl (Brit) ≈ Bachillerato
Superior, B.U.P.; **"O" ~s** npl (Brit) ≈ bachillerato
elemental, octavo de Básica; **on the ~** (fig: honest)
en serio; **talks at ministerial ~** charlas a nivel
ministerial
▶ **level off** or **out** vi (prices etc) estabilizarse;
(ground) nivelarse; (aircraft) ponerse en una
trayectoria horizontal
level crossing n (Brit) paso a nivel
level-headed [lɛvlˈhɛdɪd] adj sensato
level playing field n situación de igualdad;
to compete on a ~ competir en igualdad de
condiciones

lever ['liːvə'] n palanca ▷ vt: **to ~ up** levantar con
palanca
leverage ['liːvərɪdʒ] n (fig: influence) influencia
levity ['lɛvɪtɪ] n frivolidad, informalidad
levy ['lɛvɪ] n impuesto ▷ vt exigir, recaudar
lewd [luːd] adj lascivo, obsceno, colorado (LAm)
lexicographer [lɛksɪˈkɔɡrəfə'] n lexicógrafo(-a)
lexicography [lɛksɪˈkɔɡrəfɪ] n lexicografía
LGV n abbr (= Large Goods Vehicle) vehículo pesado
liabilities [laɪəˈbɪlətɪz] npl obligaciones; pasivo
liability [laɪəˈbɪlətɪ] n responsabilidad; (handicap)
desventaja
liable ['laɪəbl] adj (subject): **~ to** sujeto a;
(responsible): **~ for** responsable de; (likely): **~ to do**
propenso a hacer; **to be ~ to a fine** exponerse a
una multa
liaise [liːˈeɪz] vi: **to ~ (with)** colaborar (con); **to ~
with sb** mantener informado a algn
liaison [liːˈeɪzɔn] n (coordination) enlace; (affair)
relación
liar ['laɪə'] n mentiroso(-a)
libel ['laɪbl] n calumnia ▷ vt calumniar
libellous ['laɪbləs] adj difamatorio, calumnioso
liberal ['lɪbərl] adj (gen) liberal; (generous): **~ with**
generoso con ▷ n: **L~** (Pol) liberal
Liberal Democrat n (Brit) demócrata liberal
liberalize ['lɪbərəlaɪz] vt liberalizar
liberate ['lɪbəreɪt] vt liberar
liberation [lɪbəˈreɪʃən] n liberación
liberation theology n teología de la liberación
liberty ['lɪbətɪ] n libertad; **to be at ~ to do** estar
libre para hacer; **to take the ~ of doing sth**
tomarse la libertad de hacer algo
Libra ['liːbrə] n Libra
librarian [laɪˈbrɛərɪən] n bibliotecario(-a)
library ['laɪbrərɪ] n biblioteca
libretto [lɪˈbrɛtəu] n libreto
Libya ['lɪbɪə] n Libia
lice [laɪs] pl of **louse**
licence, (US) **license** ['laɪsns] n licencia; (permit)
permiso; (also: **driving licence**, US: also: **driver's
license**) carnet de conducir; (excessive freedom)
libertad; **import ~** licencia or permiso de
importación; **produced under ~** elaborado bajo
licencia
licence number n (número de) matrícula
licence plate n (placa de) matrícula
license ['laɪsns] n (US) = **licence** ▷ vt autorizar,
dar permiso a; (car) sacar la matrícula de or (LAm)
la patente de
licensed ['laɪsnst] adj (for alcohol) autorizado para
vender bebidas alcohólicas
licensee [laɪsənˈsiː] n (in a pub) concesionario(-a),
dueño(-a) de un bar
lick [lɪk] vt lamer; (col: defeat) dar una paliza a ▷ n
lamedura; **a ~ of paint** una mano de pintura
licorice ['lɪkərɪs] n = **liquorice**
lid [lɪd] n (of box, case) tapa; (of pan) cobertera;
to take the ~ off sth (fig) exponer algo a la luz
pública
lie [laɪ] n mentira ▷ vi mentir (pt **lay**, pp **lain**) [leɪ,
leɪn] (rest) estar echado, estar tumbado; (object:

be situated) estar, encontrarse; **to tell ~s, tell a ~** mentir; **you ~d to me!** ¡me mentiste!; **I lay on the floor** me tumbé en el suelo; **he was lying on the sofa** estaba tumbado en el sofá; **to ~ low** (*fig*) mantenerse a escondidas

▸ **lie about, lie around** *vi* (*things*) estar tirado; (*Brit: people*) estar acostado *or* tumbado

▸ **lie back** *vi* recostarse

▸ **lie down** *vi* echarse, acostarse, tumbarse; **why not go and ~ down for a bit?** ¿por qué no vas a acostarte un rato?; **to be lying down** estar tendido

▸ **lie up** *vi* (*hide*) esconderse

lie detector *n* detector de mentiras

lie-down ['laɪdaun] *n* (*Brit*): **to have a ~** echarse (una siesta)

lie-in ['laɪɪn] *n* (*Brit*): **to have a ~** quedarse en la cama

lieu [luː]: **in ~ of** *prep* en lugar de

lieutenant [lɛfˈtɛnənt] *n* (*Mil*) teniente

life [laɪf] (*pl* **lives**) *n* vida; (*of licence etc*) vigencia; **to be sent to prison for ~** ser condenado a cadena perpetua; **country/city ~** la vida en el campo/en la ciudad; **true to ~** fiel a la realidad; **to paint from ~** pintar del natural; **to put** *or* **breathe new ~ into** (*person*) reanimar; (*project, area etc*) infundir nueva vida a

life assurance *n* (*Brit*) seguro de vida

lifebelt ['laɪfbɛlt] *n* (*Brit*) cinturón salvavidas

lifeboat ['laɪfbəut] *n* lancha de socorro

life-buoy ['laɪfbɔɪ] *n* boya *or* guindola salvavidas

life expectancy *n* esperanza de vida

lifeguard ['laɪfgɑːd] *n* vigilante

life insurance *n* = **life assurance**

life jacket *n* chaleco salvavidas

lifeless ['laɪflɪs] *adj* sin vida; (*dull*) soso

lifelike ['laɪflaɪk] *adj* natural

lifeline ['laɪflaɪn] *n* (*fig*) cordón umbilical

lifelong ['laɪflɔŋ] *adj* de toda la vida

life preserver *n* (*US*) = **lifebelt**

lifer ['laɪfər] *n* (*col*) condenado(-a) a cadena perpetua

life sentence *n* cadena perpetua

life-sized ['laɪfsaɪzd] *adj* de tamaño natural

life span *n* vida

lifestyle ['laɪfstaɪl] *n* estilo de vida

life support system *n* (*Med*) sistema de respiración asistida

lifetime ['laɪftaɪm] *n*: **in his ~** durante su vida; **once in a ~** una vez en la vida; **the chance of a ~** una oportunidad única

lift [lɪft] *vt* levantar; (*copy*) plagiar ▷ *vi* (*fog*) disiparse ▷ *n* (*Brit: elevator*) ascensor (*Esp*), elevador (*LAm*); **to give sb a ~** (*Brit*) llevar a algn en coche

▸ **lift off** *vt* levantar, quitar ▷ *vi* (*rocket, helicopter*) despegar

▸ **lift out** *vt* sacar; (*troops, evacuees etc*) evacuar

▸ **lift up** *vt* levantar

lift-off ['lɪftɔf] *n* despegue

ligament ['lɪgəmənt] *n* ligamento

light [laɪt] *n* luz; (*flame*) lumbre; (*lamp*) luz,

lámpara; (*daylight*) luz del día; (*headlight*) faro; (*rear light*) luz trasera; (*for cigarette etc*): **have you got a ~?** ¿tienes fuego? ▷ *vt* (*pt, pp* **-ed** *or* **lit**) (*candle, cigarette, fire*) encender; (*room*) alumbrar ▷ *adj* (*colour*) claro; (*not heavy, also fig*) ligero, liviano (*LAm*); (*room*) alumbrado ▷ *adv* (*travel*) con poco equipaje; **to turn** *o* **switch the ~ on** encender la luz; **to turn** *o* **switch the ~ off** apagar la luz; **the traffic ~s** el semáforo; **in the ~ of what you have said** ... en vista de *or* a la luz de lo que has dicho ...; **to come to ~** salir a la luz; **to cast** *or* **shed** *or* **throw ~ on** arrojar luz sobre; **to make ~ of sth** (*fig*) no dar importancia a algo; **a ~ blue sweater** un jersey azul claro; **a ~ jacket** una chaqueta ligera; **a ~ meal** una comida ligera

▸ **light up** *vi* (*smoke*) encender un cigarrillo; (*face*) iluminarse ▷ *vt* (*illuminate*) iluminar, alumbrar

light bulb *n* bombilla, bombillo (*CAm*), foco (*And, Méx*), bombita (*RP*)

lighten ['laɪtn] *vi* (*grow light*) clarear ▷ *vt* (*give light to*) iluminar; (*make lighter*) aclarar; (*make less heavy*) aligerar

lighter ['laɪtər] *n* (*also*: **cigarette lighter**) mechero, encendedor (*LAm*)

light-headed [laɪtˈhɛdɪd] *adj* (*dizzy*) mareado; (*excited*) exaltado; (*by nature*) atolondrado

light-hearted [laɪtˈhɑːtɪd] *adj* alegre

lighthouse ['laɪthaus] *n* faro

lighting ['laɪtɪŋ] *n* (*act*) iluminación; (*system*) alumbrado

lightly ['laɪtlɪ] *adv* ligeramente; (*not seriously*) con poca seriedad; **to get off ~** ser castigado con poca severidad

lightness ['laɪtnɪs] *n* claridad; (*in weight*) ligereza

lightning ['laɪtnɪŋ] *n* relámpago, rayo

lightning conductor, (*US*) **lightning rod** *n* pararrayos

light pen *n* lápiz óptico

lightweight ['laɪtweɪt] *adj* (*suit*) ligero ▷ *n* (*Boxing*) peso ligero

light year *n* año luz

like [laɪk] *vt* (*thing*): **I ~ swimming/apples** me gusta nadar/me gustan las manzanas ▷ *prep* como ▷ *adj* parecido, semejante ▷ *n*: **did you ever see the ~ (of it)?** ¿has visto cosa igual?; **his ~s and dislikes** sus gustos y aversiones; **the ~s of him** personas como él; **I ~ him** me cae bien; **I would ~, I'd ~** me gustaría; (*for purchase*) quería; **I'd ~ to go to China** me gustaría ir a China; **I'd ~ this blouse in size 10, please** quería esta blusa en la talla 10, por favor; **would you ~ a coffee?** ¿te apetece un café?; **would you ~ to go for a walk?** ¿quieres ir a dar un paseo?; **if you ~** si quieres; **a city ~ Paris** una ciudad como París; **to be** *or* **look ~ sb/sth** parecerse a algn/algo; **it's a bit ~ salmon** se parece un poco al salmón; **that's just ~ him** es muy de él, es típico de él; **do it ~ this** hazlo así; **something ~ that** algo así *or* por el estilo; **it is nothing ~...** no tiene parecido alguno con...; **what's he ~?** ¿cómo es (él)?; **what does he look ~?** ¿cómo es físicamente?; **what's**

the weather ~? ¿qué tiempo hace?; **I feel ~ a
drink** me apetece algo de beber
likeable ['laɪkəbl] *adj* simpático, agradable
likelihood ['laɪklɪhud] *n* probabilidad; **in all ~**
según todas las probabilidades
likely ['laɪklɪ] *adj* probable, capaz (*LAm*); **that's
not very ~** es poco probable; **he's ~ to leave** es
probable que se vaya; **she's not ~ to come** es
probable que no venga; **not ~!** (*col*) ¡ni hablar!
liken ['laɪkən] *vt*: **to ~ to** comparar con
likeness ['laɪknɪs] *n* (*similarity*) semejanza,
parecido
likewise ['laɪkwaɪz] *adv* igualmente
liking ['laɪkɪŋ] *n*: **~ (for)** (*person*) cariño (a); (*thing*)
afición (a); **to take a ~ to sb** tomar cariño a
algn; **to be to sb's ~** ser del gusto de algn
lilac ['laɪlək] *n* lila ▷ *adj* (*colour*) de color lila
Lilo® ['laɪləu] *n* colchoneta inflable
lily ['lɪlɪ] *n* lirio, azucena
lily of the valley *n* lirio de los valles
limb [lɪm] *n* miembro; (*of tree*) rama; **to be out
on a ~** (*fig*) estar aislado
limber up ['lɪmbə^r-] *vi* (*fig*) entrenarse; (*Sport*)
hacer (ejercicios de) precalentamiento
limbo ['lɪmbəu] *n*: **to be in ~** (*fig*) quedar a la
expectativa
lime [laɪm] *n* (*tree*) limero; (*fruit*) lima; (*Geo*) cal
limelight ['laɪmlaɪt] *n*: **to be in the ~** (*fig*) ser el
centro de atención
limerick ['lɪmərɪk] *n* quintilla humorística
limestone ['laɪmstəun] *n* piedra caliza
limit ['lɪmɪt] *n* límite ▷ *vt* limitar; **weight/speed
~** peso máximo/velocidad máxima; **within ~s**
entre límites
limitation [lɪmɪ'teɪʃən] *n* limitación
limited ['lɪmɪtɪd] *adj* limitado; **to be ~ to**
limitarse a; **~ edition** edición limitada
limited (liability) company (Ltd) *n* (*Brit*)
sociedad anónima (SA)
limousine ['lɪməziːn] *n* limusina
limp [lɪmp] *n*: **to have a ~** tener cojera ▷ *vi* cojear,
renguear (*LAm*) ▷ *adj* flojo
limpet ['lɪmpɪt] *n* lapa
line [laɪn] *n* (*also Comm*) línea; (*straight line*) raya;
(*rope*) cuerda; (*for fishing*) sedal; (*wire*) hilo; (*row,
series*) fila, hilera; (*of writing*) renglón; (*on face*)
arruga; (*speciality*) rama ▷ *vt* (*Sewing*): **to ~ (with)**
forrar (de); **to ~ the streets** ocupar las aceras;
a straight ~ una línea recta; **to draw a ~** trazar
una línea; **a new ~ in cosmetics** una nueva
línea en cosméticos; **a ~ of people** una fila de
gente; **he wrote a few ~s** escribió unas cuantas
líneas; **in ~ with** de acuerdo con; **she's in ~ for
promotion** (*fig*) tiene muchas posibilidades de
que la asciendan; **to bring sth into ~ with sth**
poner algo de acuerdo con algo; **~ of research/
business** campo de investigación/comercio; **to
take the ~ that ...** ser de la opinión que ...; **to
draw the ~ at doing sth** negarse a hacer algo;
no permitir que se haga algo; **on the right ~s**
por buen camino; **hold the ~ please** (*Tel*) no
cuelgue usted, por favor; **it's a very bad ~** (*Tel*)

se oye muy mal; **railway ~** la vía férrea; *see also*
lines
 ▸ **line up** *vi* hacer cola ▷ *vt* alinear, poner en fila;
to have sth ~d up tener algo arreglado
lined [laɪnd] *adj* (*face*) arrugado; (*paper*) rayado;
(*clothes*) forrado
lineman ['laɪnmən] *n* (*US*) técnico de las líneas;
(*Football*) delantero
linen ['lɪnɪn] *n* ropa blanca; (*cloth*) lino
liner ['laɪnə^r] *n* vapor de línea transatlántico;
dustbin ~ bolsa de la basura
lines [laɪnz] *npl* (*Rail*) vía, raíles
linesman ['laɪnzmən] *n* (*Sport*) juez de línea
line-up ['laɪnʌp] *n* alineación
linger ['lɪŋgə^r] *vi* retrasarse, tardar en marcharse;
(*smell, tradition*) persistir
lingerie ['lænʒəriː] *n* ropa interior *or* íntima (de
mujer)
lingo ['lɪŋgəu] (*pl* **-es**) *n* (*pej*) jerga
linguist ['lɪŋgwɪst] *n* lingüista
linguistic [lɪŋ'gwɪstɪk] *adj* lingüístico
linguistics [lɪŋ'gwɪstɪks] *n* lingüística
lining ['laɪnɪŋ] *n* forro; (*Tech*) revestimiento; (*of
brake*) guarnición
link [lɪŋk] *n* (*of chain*) eslabón; (*connection*)
conexión; (*bond*) vínculo, lazo; (*Internet*) link,
enlace ▷ *vt* vincular, unir; **rail ~** línea de
ferrocarril, servicio de trenes
 ▸ **link up** *vt* acoplar ▷ *vi* unirse
lino ['laɪnəu], (*Brit*) **linoleum** [lɪ'nəulɪəm] *n*
linóleo
lion ['laɪən] *n* león
lioness ['laɪənɪs] *n* leona
lip [lɪp] *n* labio; (*of jug*) pico; (*of cup etc*) borde
liposuction ['lɪpəusʌkʃən] *n* liposucción
lipread ['lɪpriːd] *vi* leer los labios
lip salve *n* crema protectora para labios
lip service *n*: **to pay ~ to sth** alabar algo pero sin
hacer nada
lipstick ['lɪpstɪk] *n* lápiz *or* barra de labios,
carmín
liqueur [lɪ'kjuə^r] *n* licor
liquid ['lɪkwɪd] *adj*, *n* líquido
liquidation [lɪkwɪ'deɪʃən] *n* liquidación; **to go
into ~** entrar en liquidación
liquid crystal display (LCD) *n* pantalla de
cristal líquido
liquidize ['lɪkwɪdaɪz] *vt* (*Culin*) licuar
liquidizer ['lɪkwɪdaɪzə^r] *n* (*Culin*) licuadora
liquor ['lɪkə^r] *n* licor, bebidas alcohólicas
liquorice ['lɪkərɪs] *n* regaliz
liquor store *n* (*US*) bodega, *tienda de vinos y bebidas
alcohólicas*
Lisbon ['lɪzbən] *n* Lisboa
lisp [lɪsp] *n* ceceo
list [lɪst] *n* lista; (*of ship*) inclinación ▷ *vt* (*write
down*) hacer una lista de; (*enumerate*) catalogar;
(*Comput*) hacer un listado de ▷ *vi* (*ship*) inclinarse;
shopping ~ lista de las compras; *see also* **lists**
listed building ['lɪstɪd-] *n* (*Archit*) edificio de
interés histórico-artístico
listen ['lɪsn] *vi* escuchar, oír; (*pay attention*)

atender
listener ['lɪsnə^r] n oyente
listeria [lɪs'tɪərɪə] n listeria
listing ['lɪstɪŋ] n (Comput) listado
listless ['lɪstlɪs] adj apático, indiferente
lists [lɪsts] npl (History) liza; **to enter the ~ (against sb/sth)** salir a la palestra (contra algn/algo)
lit [lɪt] pt, pp of **light**
litany ['lɪtənɪ] n letanía
liter ['li:tə^r] n (US) = **litre**
literacy ['lɪtərəsɪ] n capacidad de leer y escribir; **~ campaign** campaña de alfabetización
literal ['lɪtərl] adj literal
literally ['lɪtrəlɪ] adv literalmente
literary ['lɪtərərɪ] adj literario
literate ['lɪtərət] adj que sabe leer y escribir; (fig) culto
literature ['lɪtərɪtʃə^r] n literatura; (brochures etc) folletos
lithe [laɪð] adj ágil
Lithuania [lɪθju'eɪnɪə] n Lituania
litigate ['lɪtɪgeɪt] vi litigar
litigation [lɪtɪ'geɪʃən] n litigio
litmus paper ['lɪtməs-] n papel de tornasol
litre, (US) **liter** ['li:tə^r] n litro
litter ['lɪtə^r] n (rubbish) basura; (paper) papeles (tirados); (young animals) camada, cría
litter bin n (Brit) papelera
littered ['lɪtəd] adj: **~ with** lleno de
little ['lɪtl] adj (small) pequeño, chico (LAm); (not much) poco; (often translated by suffix, eg): **~ house** casita ▷ adv poco; **a ~ girl** una niña pequeña; **~ finger** (dedo) meñique; **a ~** un poco (de); **how much would you like? — just a ~** ¿cuánto quiere? — sólo un poco; **I'm a ~ tired** estoy un poco cansado; **a ~ sugar** un poco de azúcar; **~ by ~** poco a poco; **for a ~ while** (durante) un rato; **with ~ difficulty** sin problema or dificultad; **we've got very ~ time** tenemos muy poco tiempo; **as ~ as possible** lo menos posible
little-known ['lɪtl'nəun] adj poco conocido
liturgy ['lɪtədʒɪ] n liturgia
live vi vivir ▷ vt (a life) llevar; (experience) vivir ▷ adj (animal) vivo; (wire) conectado; (broadcast) en directo; (issue) de actualidad; (unexploded) sin explotar; **to ~ in London** vivir en Londres; **where do you ~?** ¿dónde vives?; **to ~ together** vivir juntos; **a ~ concert** un concierto en vivo
▶ **live down** vt hacer olvidar
▶ **live off** vt fus (land, fish etc) vivir de; (pej: parents etc) vivir a costa de
▶ **live on** vt fus (food) vivir de, alimentarse de; **to ~ on £50 a week** vivir con 50 libras semanales or a la semana
▶ **live out** vi (student) ser externo ▷ vt: **to ~ out one's days** or **life** pasar el resto de la vida
▶ **live up** vt: **to ~ it up** (col) tirarse la gran vida
▶ **live up to** vt fus (fulfil) cumplir con; (justify) justificar
livelihood ['laɪvlɪhud] n sustento
lively ['laɪvlɪ] adj (gen) vivo; (talk) animado; (pace)

rápido; (party, tune) alegre
liven up ['laɪvn-] vt (discussion, evening) animar
liver ['lɪvə^r] n hígado
lives [laɪvz] npl of **life**
livestock ['laɪvstɔk] n ganado
livid ['lɪvɪd] adj lívido; (furious) furioso
living ['lɪvɪŋ] adj (alive) vivo ▷ n: **to earn** or **make a ~** ganarse la vida; **cost of ~** coste de la vida; **in ~ memory** que se recuerde or recuerda
living conditions npl condiciones de vida
living room n sala (de estar), living (LAm)
living standards npl nivel de vida
living wage n sueldo suficiente para vivir
lizard ['lɪzəd] n lagartija
llama ['lɑ:mə] n llama
load [ləud] n (gen) carga; (weight) peso ▷ vt (Comput) cargar; (also: **load up**): **to ~ (with)** cargar (con or de); **a ~ of, ~s of** (fig) (gran) cantidad de, montones de
loaded ['ləudɪd] adj (dice) cargado; (question) intencionado; (col: rich) forrado (de dinero)
loaf [ləuf] (pl **loaves**) n (barra de) pan ▷ vi (also: **loaf about, loaf around**) holgazanear
loan [ləun] n préstamo; (Comm) empréstito ▷ vt prestar; **on ~** (book, painting) prestado; **to raise a ~** (money) procurar un empréstito
loath [ləuθ] adj: **to be ~ to do sth** ser reacio a hacer algo
loathe [ləuð] vt aborrecer; (person) odiar
loaves [ləuvz] pl of **loaf**
lob [lɔb] vt (ball) volear por alto
lobby ['lɔbɪ] n vestíbulo, sala de espera; (Pol: pressure group) grupo de presión ▷ vt presionar
lobbyist ['lɔbɪɪst] n cabildero(-a)
lobe [ləub] n lóbulo
lobster ['lɔbstə^r] n langosta
local ['ləukl] adj local ▷ n (pub) bar; **the locals** npl los vecinos, los del lugar
local anaesthetic n (Med) anestesia local
local authority n municipio, ayuntamiento (Esp)
local call n (Tel) llamada local
local government n gobierno municipal
locality [ləu'kælɪtɪ] n localidad
locate [ləu'keɪt] vt (find) localizar; (situate) situar, ubicar (LAm)
location [ləu'keɪʃən] n situación; **on ~** (Cine) exteriores, fuera del estudio
loch [lɔx] n lago
lock [lɔk] n (of door, box) cerradura, chapa (LAm); (of canal) esclusa; (of hair) mechón ▷ vt (with key) cerrar con llave; (immobilize) inmovilizar ▷ vi (door etc) cerrarse con llave; (wheels) trabarse; **~ stock and barrel** (fig) por completo or entero; **on full ~** (Aut) con el volante girado al máximo
▶ **lock away** vt (valuables) guardar bajo llave; (criminal) encerrar
▶ **lock out** vt: **the workers were ~ed out** los trabajadores tuvieron que enfrentarse con un cierre patronal
▶ **lock up** vi echar la llave
locker ['lɔkə^r] n casillero

locket ['lɔkɪt] n medallón
locksmith ['lɔksmɪθ] n cerrajero(-a)
lock-up ['lɔkʌp] n (prison) cárcel; (cell) jaula; (also: **lock-up garage**) jaula, cochera
locum ['ləukəm] n (Med) (médico(-a)) suplente
locust ['ləukəst] n langosta
lodge [lɔdʒ] n casa del guarda; (porter's) portería; (Freemasonry) logia ▷ vi (person): **to ~ (with)** alojarse (en casa de) ▷ vt (complaint) presentar
lodger ['lɔdʒəʳ] n huésped(a)
lodgings ['lɔdʒɪŋz] npl alojamiento; (house) casa de huéspedes
loft [lɔft] n desván
lofty ['lɔftɪ] adj alto; (haughty) altivo, arrogante; (sentiments, aims) elevado, noble
log [lɔg] n (of wood) leño, tronco; (book) = **logbook** ▷ n abbr (= logarithm) log ▷ vt anotar, registrar
  ▶ **log in, log on** vi (Comput) iniciar la (or una) sesión
  ▶ **log off, log out** vi (Comput) finalizar la sesión
logarithm ['lɔgərɪðəm] n logaritmo
logbook ['lɔgbuk] n (Naut) diario de a bordo; (Aviat) libro de vuelo; (of car) documentación (del coche)
logger ['lɔgəʳ] n leñador(a)
loggerheads ['lɔgəhɛdz] npl: **at ~ (with)** de pique (con)
logic ['lɔdʒɪk] n lógica
logical ['lɔdʒɪkl] adj lógico
login ['lɔgɪn] n login
log jam n: **to break the ~** poner fin al estancamiento
logo ['ləugəu] n logotipo
loin [lɔɪn] n (Culin) lomo, solomillo; (**loins** npl lomos
loiter ['lɔɪtəʳ] vi vagar; (pej) merodear
loll [lɔl] vi (also: **loll about**) repantigarse
lollipop ['lɔlɪpɔp] n pirulí; (iced) polo
lolly ['lɔlɪ] n (col: ice cream) polo; (: lollipop) piruleta; (: money) guita
London ['lʌndən] n Londres
Londoner ['lʌndənəʳ] n londinense
lone [ləun] adj solitario
loneliness ['ləunlɪnɪs] n soledad, aislamiento
lonely ['ləunlɪ] adj solitario, solo
lone parent family n familia monoparental
loner ['ləunəʳ] n solitario(-a)
long [lɔŋ] adj largo ▷ adv mucho tiempo, largamente ▷ vi: **to ~ for sth** anhelar algo; **to ~ to do sth** estar deseando hacer algo ▷ n: **the ~ and the short of it is that ...** (fig) en resumidas cuentas ...; **she's got ~ hair** tiene el pelo largo; **in the ~ run** a la larga; **a ~ time** mucho tiempo; **it takes a ~ time** lleva mucho tiempo; **I've been waiting a ~ time** llevo esperando mucho tiempo; **so** or **as ~ as** mientras, con tal de que; **as ~ as I live** mientras vive; **don't be ~!** ¡no tardes!, ¡vuelve pronto!; **I shan't** o **won't be ~** (in finishing) termino pronto; (in returning) vuelvo pronto; **how ~ is the street?** ¿cuánto tiene la calle de largo?; **how ~ is the lesson?** ¿cuánto dura la clase?;

how ~ have you been here? ¿cuánto tiempo llevas aquí?; **how ~ will it take?** ¿cuánto tiempo llevará?; **the room is 6 metres** ~ la habitación tiene seis metros de largo; **6 months** ~ que dura 6 meses, de 6 meses de duración; **all night** ~ toda la noche; **~ ago** hace mucho (tiempo); **he no ~er comes** ya no viene; ~ **before** mucho antes; **before** ~ (+ future) dentro de poco; (+ past) poco tiempo después; **at ~ last** al fin, por fin
long-distance [lɔŋ'dɪstəns] adj (race) de larga distancia; (call) interurbano
longhand ['lɔŋhænd] n escritura (corriente)
longing ['lɔŋɪŋ] n anhelo, ansia; (nostalgia) nostalgia ▷ adj anhelante
longitude ['lɔŋgɪtjuːd] n longitud
long jump n salto de longitud
long-lost ['lɔŋlɔst] adj desaparecido hace mucho tiempo
long-playing record (LP) ['lɔŋpleɪɪŋ-] n elepé, disco de larga duración
long-range ['lɔŋ'reɪndʒ] adj de gran alcance; (weather forecast) a largo plazo
long-sighted ['lɔŋ'saɪtɪd] adj (Brit) présbita
long-standing ['lɔŋ'stændɪŋ] adj de mucho tiempo
long-suffering [lɔŋ'sʌfərɪŋ] adj sufrido
long-term ['lɔŋtəːm] adj a largo plazo
long wave n onda larga
long-winded [lɔŋ'wɪndɪd] adj prolijo
loo [luː] n (Brit: col) váter
look [luk] vi mirar; (seem) parecer; (face: building etc): **to ~ south/on to the sea** dar al sur/al mar ▷ n mirada; (glance) vistazo; (appearance) aire, aspecto; **looks** npl físico, belleza; **~!** ¡mira!; **to ~ at sth** mirar algo; **to ~ ahead** mirar hacia delante; **it ~s all right to me** a mí me parece que está bien; **she ~s surprised** parece sorprendida; **that cake ~s nice** ese pastel tiene buena pinta; **it ~s about 4 metres long** yo calculo que tiene unos 4 metros de largo; **he ~s like his brother** se parece a su hermano; **what does she ~ like?** ¿cómo es físicamente?; **to have a ~ at sth** echar un vistazo a algo; **to have a ~ for sth** buscar algo; **I don't like the ~ of it** no me gusta nada
  ▶ **look after** vt fus cuidar; **I ~ after my little sister** cuido a mi hermana pequeña
  ▶ **look around** vi echar una mirada alrededor
  ▶ **look at** vt fus mirar; (consider) considerar; **~ at the picture** mira la foto
  ▶ **look back** vi mirar hacia atrás; **to ~ back at sb/sth** mirar hacia atrás algo/a algn; **to ~ back on** (event, period) recordar
  ▶ **look down on** vt fus (fig) despreciar, mirar con desprecio
  ▶ **look for** vt fus buscar; **I'm ~ing for my passport** estoy buscando mi pasaporte
  ▶ **look forward to** vt fus esperar con ilusión; (in letters): **we ~ forward to hearing from you** quedamos a la espera de su respuesta or contestación; **I'm really ~ing forward to**

the holidays estoy deseando que lleguen las vacaciones; **I'm not ~ing forward to it** no tengo ganas de eso, no me hace ilusión; **to ~ forward to doing sth** tener muchas ganas de hacer algo; **I'm ~ing forward to meeting you** tengo muchas ganas de conocerte
▶ **look in** *vi*: **to ~ in on sb** (*visit*) pasar por casa de algn
▶ **look into** *vt fus* investigar
▶ **look on** *vi* mirar (como espectador)
▶ **look out** *vi* (*beware*) tener cuidado; **~ out!** ¡cuidado!
▶ **look out for** *vt fus* (*seek*) buscar; (*await*) esperar; (*beware*) tener cuidado de
▶ **look over** *vt* (*essay*) revisar; (*town, building*) inspeccionar, registrar; (*person*) examinar
▶ **look round** *vi* (*turn*) volver la cabeza, volverse; (*browse: in shop, house etc*) mirar; **I called him and he ~ed round** lo llamé y se volvió; **I'm just ~ing round** sólo estoy mirando; **to ~ round for sth** buscar algo; **I like ~ing round the shops** me gusta ir a ver tiendas
▶ **look through** *vt fus* (*papers, book*) hojear; (*briefly*) echar un vistazo a; (*telescope*) mirar por
▶ **look to** *vt fus* ocuparse de; (*rely on*) contar con
▶ **look up** *vi* mirar hacia arriba; (*improve*) mejorar ▷ *vt* (*word*) buscar; (*friend*) visitar; **if you don't know a word, ~ it up in the dictionary** si no conoces una palabra, búscala en el diccionario
▶ **look up to** *vt fus* admirar
loom [lu:m] *n* telar ▷ *vi* (*threaten*) amenazar
loony ['lu:nɪ] *adj, n* (*col*) loco(-a)
loop [lu:p] *n* lazo; (*bend*) vuelta, recodo; (*Comput*) bucle
loophole ['lu:phəʊl] *n* laguna
loose [lu:s] *adj* (*gen*) suelto; (*not tight*) flojo; (*wobbly etc*) movedizo; (*clothes*) ancho, holgado; (*morals, discipline*) relajado ▷ *vt* (*free*) soltar; (*slacken*) aflojar (*also:* **loose off:** *arrow*) disparar, soltar; **a ~ shirt** una camisa holgada; **a ~ screw** un tornillo flojo; **a ~ connection** (*Elec*) un hilo desempalmado; **to be at a ~ end** or (*US*) **at ~ ends** no saber qué hacer; **to tie up ~ ends** (*fig*) no dejar ningún cabo suelto, atar cabos
loose change *n* cambio, dinero suelto
loose chippings [-'tʃɪpɪŋz] *npl* (*on road*) gravilla suelta
loosely ['lu:slɪ] *adv* libremente, aproximadamente
loosely-knit [-nɪt] *adj* de estructura abierta
loosen ['lu:sn] *vt* (*free*) soltar; (*untie*) desatar; (*slacken*) aflojar
▶ **loosen up** *vi* (*before game*) hacer (ejercicios de) precalentamiento; (*col: relax*) soltarse, relajarse
loot [lu:t] *n* botín ▷ *vt* saquear
looting ['lu:tɪŋ] *n* pillaje
lop-sided ['lɔp'saɪdɪd] *adj* desequilibrado
lord [lɔ:d] *n* señor; **L~ Smith** Lord Smith; **the L~** el Señor; **the (House of) L~s** (*Brit*) la Cámara de los Lores
Lordship ['lɔ:dʃɪp] *n*: **your ~** su Señoría

lore [lɔ:ʳ] *n* saber popular, tradiciones
lorry ['lɔrɪ] *n* (*Brit*) camión
lorry driver *n* camionero(-a)
lose [lu:z] (*pt, pp* **lost**) *vt* perder ▷ *vi* perder, ser vencido; **I've lost my purse** he perdido el monedero; **to ~ (time)** (*clock*) atrasarse; **to ~ no time (in doing sth)** no tardar (en hacer algo); **the team lost 5-2** el equipo perdió por 5-2
▶ **lose out** *vi* salir perdiendo
loser ['lu:zəʳ] *n* perdedor(a); **to be a bad ~** no saber perder
loss [lɔs] *n* pérdida; **heavy ~es** (*Mil*) grandes pérdidas; **to be at a ~** no saber qué hacer; **to be a dead ~** (*col*) ser completamente inútil; **to cut one's ~es** reducir las pérdidas; **to sell sth at a ~** vender algo perdiendo dinero
lost [lɔst] *pt, pp of* **lose** ▷ *adj* perdido; **~ in thought** absorto, ensimismado; **to get ~** (*object*) extraviarse; (*person*) perderse; **I was afraid of getting ~** tenía miedo de perderme
lost and found *n* (*US*) = **lost property**; **lost property office** or **department**
lost cause *n* causa perdida
lost property *n* (*Brit*) objetos perdidos
lost property office or **department** *n* (*Brit*) departamento de objetos perdidos
lot [lɔt] *n* (*at auction*) lote; (*destiny*) suerte; **the ~** el todo, todos(-as); **he took the ~** se lo llevó todo; **that's the ~** eso es todo; **a ~** mucho, bastante; **she talks a ~** habla mucho; **I read a ~** leo bastante; **do you like football? — not a ~** ¿te gusta el fútbol? — no mucho; **a ~ of, ~s of** mucho(s)(-a(s)); **I drink a ~ of coffee** bebo mucho café; **we saw a ~ of interesting things** vimos muchas cosas interesantes; **he's got ~s of friends** tiene muchos amigos; **she's got ~s of self-confidence** tiene mucha confianza en sí misma; **to draw ~s (for sth)** echar suertes (para decidir algo)
lotion ['ləʊʃən] *n* loción
lottery ['lɔtərɪ] *n* lotería
loud [laʊd] *adj* (*voice, sound*) fuerte; (*laugh, shout*) estrepitoso; (*gaudy*) chillón(-ona) ▷ *adv* (*speak etc*) fuerte; **out ~** en voz alta
loudhailer [laʊd'heɪləʳ] *n* (*Brit*) megáfono
loudly ['laʊdlɪ] *adv* (*noisily*) fuerte; (*aloud*) en alta voz
loudspeaker [laʊd'spi:kəʳ] *n* altavoz
lounge [laʊndʒ] *n* salón, sala de estar; (*of hotel*) salón; (*of airport*) sala de embarque ▷ *vi* (*also:* **lounge about, lounge around**) holgazanear, no hacer nada; *see also* **pub**
lounge bar *n* salón
lounge suit *n* (*Brit*) traje de calle
louse [laʊs] *n* (*pl* **lice**) *n* piojo
▶ **louse up** *vt* (*col*) echar a perder
lousy ['laʊzɪ] *adj* (*fig*) vil, asqueroso
lout [laʊt] *n* gamberro(-a)
lovable ['lʌvəbl] *adj* amable, simpático
love [lʌv] *n* amor ▷ *vt* amar, querer; **to send one's ~ to sb** dar sus recuerdos a algn; **give Gloria my ~** dale recuerdos a Gloria de mi parte;

~ from Anne, ~, Anne (*in letter*) con cariño de Anne, un abrazo, Anne; **to be in ~ (with sb)** estar enamorado (de algn); **to make ~** hacer el amor; **for the ~ of** por amor a; **"15 ~ "** (*Tennis*) "15 a cero"; **everybody ~s her** todos la quieren; **I ~ you** te quiero; **I ~ paella** me encanta la paella; **I ~ to read** me encanta leer; **I'd ~ to come** me gustaría muchísimo venir; **would you like to come? — yes, I'd ~ to** ¿te gustaría venir? — sí, me encantaría

love affair *n* aventura sentimental *or* amorosa
loved ones ['lʌvdwʌnz] *npl* seres queridos
love-hate relationship ['lʌvheɪt-] *n* relación de amor y odio
love life *n* vida sentimental
lovely ['lʌvlɪ] *adj* (*delightful*) precioso, encantador(a), lindo (*esp LAm*); (*beautiful*) hermoso, lindo (*esp LAm*); **we had a ~ time** lo pasamos estupendo
lover ['lʌvəʳ] *n* amante; (*amateur*): **a ~ of** un(a) aficionado(-a) *or* un(a) amante de
lovesick ['lʌvsɪk] *adj* enfermo de amor, amartelado
loving ['lʌvɪŋ] *adj* amoroso, cariñoso
low [ləu] *adj, adv* bajo ▷ *n* (*Meteorology*) área de baja presión ▷ *vi* (*cow*) mugir; **~ prices** los bajos precios; **that plane is flying very ~** ese avión vuela muy bajo; **in the ~ season** en temporada baja; **to feel ~** sentirse deprimido; **to turn (down) ~** bajar; **to reach a new** *or* **an all-time ~** llegar a su punto más bajo
low-alcohol [ləu'ælkəhɒl] *adj* bajo en alcohol
low-calorie ['ləu'kæləri] *adj* bajo en calorías
low-cut ['ləukʌt] *adj* (*dress*) escotado
lower ['ləuəʳ] *vt* bajar; (*reduce: price*) reducir, rebajar; (: *resistance*) debilitar; **to ~ o.s. to** (*fig*) rebajarse a ▷ *vi* ['lauəʳ]: **to ~ (at sb)** fulminar (a algn) con la mirada
Lower House *n* (*Pol*): **the ~** la Cámara baja
low-fat ['ləu'fæt] *adj* (*milk, yoghurt*) desnatado; (*diet*) bajo en calorías
lowland ['ləulənd] *n* tierra baja
lowly ['ləulɪ] *adj* humilde
low-tech ['ləutɛk] *adj* de baja tecnología, tradicional
loyal ['lɔɪəl] *adj* leal
loyalist ['lɔɪəlɪst] *n* legitimista
loyalty ['lɔɪəltɪ] *n* lealtad
loyalty card *n* (*Brit*) tarjeta cliente
lozenge ['lɒzɪndʒ] *n* (*Med*) pastilla
LP *n abbr* (= *long-playing record*) elepé
L-plates ['ɛlpleɪts] *npl* (*Brit*) (placas de) la L
Ltd *abbr* (= *limited company*) S.A.
lubricant ['lu:brɪkənt] *n* lubricante
lubricate ['lu:brɪkeɪt] *vt* lubricar, engrasar
lucid ['lu:sɪd] *adj* lúcido
luck [lʌk] *n* suerte; **good/bad ~** buena/mala suerte; **good ~!** ¡(que tengas) suerte!; **to be in ~** estar de suerte; **to be out of ~** tener mala suerte
luckily ['lʌkɪlɪ] *adv* afortunadamente
lucky ['lʌkɪ] *adj* afortunado

lucrative ['lu:krətɪv] *adj* lucrativo
ludicrous ['lu:dɪkrəs] *adj* absurdo
lug [lʌg] *vt* (*drag*) arrastrar
luggage ['lʌgɪdʒ] *n* equipaje
luggage rack *n* (*in train*) rejilla, redecilla; (*on car*) baca, portaequipajes
lukewarm ['lu:kwɔ:m] *adj* tibio, templado
lull [lʌl] *n* tregua ▷ *vt* (*child*) acunar; (*person, fear*) calmar
lullaby ['lʌləbaɪ] *n* nana
lumbago [lʌm'beɪgəu] *n* lumbago
lumber ['lʌmbəʳ] *n* (*junk*) trastos viejos; (*wood*) maderos ▷ *vt* (*Brit col*): **to ~ sb with sth/sb** hacer que algn cargue con algo/algn ▷ *vi* (*also:* **lumber about, lumber along**) moverse pesadamente
lumberjack ['lʌmbədʒæk] *n* maderero
luminous ['lu:mɪnəs] *adj* luminoso
lump [lʌmp] *n* terrón; (*fragment*) trozo; (*in sauce*) grumo; (*in throat*) nudo; (*swelling*) bulto ▷ *vt* (*also:* **lump together**) juntar; (*persons*) poner juntos
lump sum *n* suma global
lumpy ['lʌmpɪ] *adj* (*sauce*) lleno de grumos
lunacy ['lu:nəsɪ] *n* locura
lunar ['lu:nəʳ] *adj* lunar
lunatic ['lu:nətɪk] *adj, n* loco(-a)
lunch [lʌntʃ] *n* almuerzo, comida ▷ *vi* almorzar; **to invite sb to** *or* **for ~** invitar a algn a almorzar
lunch break, lunch hour *n* hora del almuerzo
luncheon ['lʌntʃən] *n* almuerzo
luncheon meat *n* tipo de fiambre
luncheon voucher *n* vale de comida
lunchtime ['lʌntʃtaɪm] *n* hora del almuerzo *or* de comer
lung [lʌŋ] *n* pulmón
lunge [lʌndʒ] *vi* (*also:* **lunge forward**) abalanzarse; **to ~ at** arremeter contra
lurch [lə:tʃ] *vi* dar sacudidas ▷ *n* sacudida; **to leave sb in the ~** dejar a algn plantado
lure [luəʳ] *n* (*bait*) cebo; (*decoy*) señuelo ▷ *vt* convencer con engaños
lurid ['luərɪd] *adj* (*colour*) chillón(-ona); (*account*) sensacional; (*detail*) horripilante
lurk [lə:k] *vi* (*hide*) esconderse; (*wait*) estar al acecho
luscious ['lʌʃəs] *adj* delicioso
lush [lʌʃ] *adj* exuberante
lust [lʌst] *n* lujuria; (*greed*) codicia
▸ **lust after** *vt fus* codiciar
lusty ['lʌstɪ] *adj* robusto, fuerte
lute [lu:t] *n* laúd
Luxembourg ['lʌksəmbə:g] *n* Luxemburgo
luxurious [lʌg'zjuərɪəs] *adj* lujoso
luxury ['lʌkʃərɪ] *n* lujo ▷ *cpd* de lujo
LV *n abbr* (*Brit*) = **luncheon voucher**
LW *abbr* (*Radio*) = **long wave**
Lycra® ['laɪkrə] *n* licra®
lying ['laɪɪŋ] *n* mentiras ▷ *adj* (*statement, story*) falso; (*person*) mentiroso
lyric ['lɪrɪk] *adj* lírico; **lyrics** *npl* (*of song*) letra
lyrical ['lɪrɪkl] *adj* lírico

Mm

M, m [ɛm] n (letter) M, m; **M for Mary**, (US) **M for Mike** M de Madrid

M n abbr = **million(s)**; (= medium) M; (Brit) = **motorway**; **the M8** = la A8

m abbr (= metre) m.; = **mile(s)**

MA n abbr (US) = **Military Academy**; see **Master of Arts** ▷ abbr (US) = **Massachusetts**

mac [mæk] n (Brit) impermeable

macaroni [mækəˈrəʊnɪ] n macarrones

Macedonia [mæsɪˈdəʊnɪə] n Macedonia

machine [məˈʃiːn] n máquina ▷ vt (dress etc) coser a máquina; (Tech) trabajar a máquina

machine gun n ametralladora

machine language n (Comput) lenguaje máquina

machinery [məˈʃiːnərɪ] n maquinaria; (fig) mecanismo

machine translation n traducción automática

machine washable adj lavable a máquina

macho [ˈmætʃəʊ] adj macho

mackerel [ˈmækrl] n (pl inv) caballa

mackintosh [ˈmækɪntɒʃ] n (Brit) impermeable

mad [mæd] adj loco; (idea) disparatado; (angry) furioso, enojado (LAm); **~ (at or with sb)** furioso (con algn); **to be ~ (keen) about** or **on sth** estar loco por algo; **to go ~** volverse loco, enloquecer(se)

madam [ˈmædəm] n señora; **can I help you, ~?** ¿le puedo ayudar, señora?; **M~ Chairman** señora presidenta

mad cow disease n encefalopatía espongiforme bovina

madden [ˈmædn] vt volver loco

made [meɪd] pt, pp of **make**

Madeira [məˈdɪərə] n (Geo) Madeira; (wine) madeira

made-to-measure [ˈmeɪdtəmɛʒəʳ] adj (Brit) hecho a la medida

madhouse [ˈmædhaʊs] n (also fig) manicomio

madly [ˈmædlɪ] adv locamente

madman [ˈmædmən] n loco

madness [ˈmædnɪs] n locura

Madrid [məˈdrɪd] n Madrid

Mafia [ˈmæfɪə] n Mafia

mag [mæg] n abbr (Brit col) = **magazine**

magazine [mægəˈziːn] n revista; (Mil: store) almacén; (of firearm) recámara

maggot [ˈmægət] n gusano

magic [ˈmædʒɪk] n magia ▷ adj mágico

magical [ˈmædʒɪkəl] adj mágico

magician [məˈdʒɪʃən] n mago(-a)

magistrate [ˈmædʒɪstreɪt] n juez (municipal); **M~s' Courts**; see **crown court**

magnesium [mægˈniːzɪəm] n magnesio

magnet [ˈmægnɪt] n imán

magnetic [mægˈnɛtɪk] adj magnético

magnetic tape n cinta magnética

magnificent [mægˈnɪfɪsnt] adj magnífico

magnify [ˈmægnɪfaɪ] vt aumentar; (fig) exagerar

magnifying glass [ˈmægnɪfaɪɪŋ-] n lupa

magnitude [ˈmægnɪtjuːd] n magnitud

magpie [ˈmægpaɪ] n urraca

mahogany [məˈhɒgənɪ] n caoba ▷ cpd de caoba

maid [meɪd] n criada; **old ~** (pej) solterona

maiden [ˈmeɪdn] n doncella ▷ adj (aunt etc) solterona; (speech, voyage) inaugural

maiden name n apellido de soltera

mail [meɪl] n correo; (letters) cartas ▷ vt (post) echar al correo; (send) mandar por correo; **by ~** por correo

mailbox [ˈmeɪlbɒks] n (US: for letters etc; Comput) buzón

mailing list [ˈmeɪlɪŋ-] n lista de direcciones

mail-order [ˈmeɪlɔːdəʳ] n pedido postal; (business) venta por correo ▷ adj: **~ firm** or **house** casa de venta por correo

maim [meɪm] vt mutilar, lisiar

main [meɪn] adj principal, mayor ▷ n (pipe) cañería principal or maestra; (US) red eléctrica; **the ~s** (Brit Elec) la red eléctrica; **in the ~** en general

mainframe [ˈmeɪnfreɪm] n (also: **mainframe computer**) ordenador or computadora central

mainland [ˈmeɪnlənd] n continente

mainly [ˈmeɪnlɪ] adv principalmente, en su mayoría

main road n carretera principal

mainstay [ˈmeɪnsteɪ] n (fig) pilar

mainstream [ˈmeɪnstriːm] n (fig) corriente principal

main street n calle mayor

maintain [meɪnˈteɪn] vt mantener; (affirm) sostener; **to ~ that …** mantener or sostener que …

maintenance ['meɪntənəns] n mantenimiento; (*alimony*) pensión alimenticia

maize [meɪz] n (*Brit*) maíz, choclo (*LAm*)

majestic [mə'dʒestɪk] adj majestuoso

majesty ['mædʒɪstɪ] n majestad

major ['meɪdʒəʳ] n (*Mil*) comandante ▷ adj muy importante; (*Mus*) mayor ▷ vi (*US Univ*): **to ~ in** especializarse en; **a ~ factor** un factor muy importante; **drugs are a ~ problem** la droga es un grave problema; **a ~ operation** (*Med*) una operación or intervención de gran importancia; **in C ~** en do mayor

Majorca [mə'jɔ:kə] n Mallorca

majority [mə'dʒɔrɪtɪ] n mayoría ▷ cpd (*verdict*) mayoritario

make [meɪk] vt (*pt, pp* **made**) hacer; (*manufacture*) hacer, fabricar; (*earn*) ganar; (*cause to be*): **to ~ sb sad** poner triste or entristecer a algn; (*force*): **to ~ sb do sth** hacer a algn a hacer algo; **my mother ~s me eat vegetables** mi madre me hace comer verduras; (*equal*): **2 and 2 ~ 4** 2 y 2 son 4 ▷ n marca; **I'm going to ~ a cake** voy a hacer un pastel; **I'd like to ~ a phone call** quisiera hacer una llamada; **I ~ my bed every morning** me hago la cama cada mañana; **it's well made** está bien hecho; **she's making lunch** está preparando el almuerzo; **to ~ a profit/loss** obtener ganancias/sufrir pérdidas; **to ~ a profit of £500** sacar una ganancia de 500 libras; **to ~ a fool of sb** poner a algn en ridículo; **to ~ sb cry/laugh** hacer llorar/reír a algn; **to ~ it** (*arrive*) llegar; (*achieve sth*) tener éxito; **what time do you ~ it?** ¿qué hora tienes?; **to ~ do with sth** arreglárselas con algo; **I'll ~ do with what I've got** me las arreglaré con lo que tengo; **what ~ is it?** ¿de qué marca es?

▸ **make for** vt fus (*place*) dirigirse a

▸ **make off** vi largarse

▸ **make out** vt (*decipher*) descifrar; (*understand*) entender; (*see*) distinguir; (*write: cheque*) extender; **to ~ out (that)** (*claim, imply*) dar a entender (que); **I can't ~ out the address** no consigo descifrar la dirección; **I can't ~ her out at all** no la entiendo en absoluto; **to ~ a cheque out to sb** hacer un cheque a favor de algn; **they're making out it was my fault** están dando a entender que fue culpa mía; **to ~ out a case for sth** dar buenas razones en favor de algo

▸ **make over** vt (*assign*): **to ~ over (to)** ceder or traspasar (a)

▸ **make up** vt (*invent*) inventar(se); (*parcel*) hacer; (*comprise*) componer ▷ vi reconciliarse; (*with cosmetics*) maquillarse; **he made up the whole story** se inventó toda la historia; **women ~ up 30% of the police force** las mujeres componen el 30% del cuerpo de policía; **to be made up of** estar compuesto de; **she spends hours making herself up** pasa horas maquillándose; **they had a quarrel, but soon made up** riñeron, pero poco después hicieron las paces

▸ **make up for** vt fus compensar

make-believe ['meɪkbɪliːv] n ficción, fantasía

maker ['meɪkəʳ] n fabricante

makeshift ['meɪkʃɪft] adj improvisado

make-up ['meɪkʌp] n maquillaje

make-up remover n desmaquillador

making ['meɪkɪŋ] n (*fig*): **in the ~** en vías de formación; **to have the ~s of** (*person*) tener madera de

malaria [mə'lɛərɪə] n malaria

Malaysia [mə'leɪzɪə] n Malaisia, Malaysia

male [meɪl] n (*Biol, Elec*) macho ▷ adj (*sex, attitude*) masculino; (*child etc*) varón

male chauvinist (pig) n machista

malevolent [mə'levələnt] adj malévolo

malfunction [mæl'fʌŋkʃən] n mal funcionamiento

malice ['mælɪs] n (*ill will*) malicia; (*rancour*) rencor

malicious [mə'lɪʃəs] adj malicioso; rencoroso

malign [mə'laɪn] vt difamar, calumniar ▷ adj maligno

malignant [mə'lɪgnənt] adj (*Med*) maligno

mall [mɔːl] n (*US: also:* **shopping mall**) centro comercial

mallet ['mælɪt] n mazo

malnutrition [mælnju:'trɪʃən] n desnutrición

malpractice [mæl'præktɪs] n negligencia profesional

malt [mɔːlt] n malta

Malta ['mɔːltə] n Malta

mammal ['mæml] n mamífero

mammoth ['mæməθ] n mamut ▷ adj gigantesco

man [mæn] n (*pl* **men**) hombre; (*Chess*) pieza ▷ vt (*Naut*) tripular; (*Mil*) defender; **an old ~** un viejo; **~ and wife** marido y mujer

manage ['mænɪdʒ] vi arreglárselas ▷ vt (*be in charge of*) dirigir; (*person etc*) manejar; **we haven't got much money, but we ~** no tenemos mucho dinero, pero nos las arreglamos; **can you ~ with that suitcase?** ¿puedes con la maleta?; **to ~ to do sth** conseguir hacer algo; **I ~d to pass the exam** conseguí aprobar el examen; **to ~ without sth/sb** poder prescindir de algo/algn; **she ~s a big store** dirige una tienda grande; **he ~s our football team** dirige nuestro equipo de fútbol; **can you ~ a bit more?** (*food*) ¿te pongo un poco más?

manageable ['mænɪdʒəbl] adj manejable

management ['mænɪdʒmənt] n dirección, administración; **"under new ~"** "bajo nueva dirección"

manager ['mænɪdʒəʳ] n director; (*Sport*) entrenador; **sales ~** jefe(-a) de ventas

manageress ['mænɪdʒəres] n directora; (*Sport*) entrenadora

managerial [mænə'dʒɪərɪəl] adj directivo

managing director (MD) ['mænɪdʒɪŋ-] n director(a) m/f general

Mancunian [mæŋ'kju:nɪən] adj de Manchester ▷ n nativo(-a) or habitante de Manchester

mandarin ['mændərɪn] n (*also:* **mandarin orange**) mandarina; (*person*) mandarín

mandate ['mændeɪt] n mandato
mandatory ['mændətərɪ] adj obligatorio
mane [meɪn] n (of horse) crin; (of lion) melena
maneuver [mə'nu:vəʳ] (US) = **manoeuvre**
manfully ['mænfəlɪ] adv resueltamente
mangle ['mæŋgl] vt mutilar, destrozar ▷ n
escurridor
mango ['mæŋgəu] (pl -es) n mango
mangy ['meɪndʒɪ] adj roñoso; (Med) sarnoso
manhandle ['mænhændl] vt maltratar; (move by hand: goods) manipular
manhole ['mænhəul] n boca de acceso
manhood ['mænhud] n edad viril; (manliness) virilidad
man-hour ['mæn'auəʳ] n hora-hombre
manhunt ['mænhʌnt] n caza de hombre
mania ['meɪnɪə] n manía
maniac ['meɪnɪæk] n maníaco(-a); (fig) maniático
manic ['mænɪk] adj (behaviour, activity) frenético
manicure ['mænɪkjuəʳ] n manicura
manicure set n estuche de manicura
manifest ['mænɪfɛst] vt manifestar, mostrar ▷ adj manifiesto ▷ n manifiesto
manifesto [mænɪ'fɛstəu] n manifiesto
manipulate [mə'nɪpjuleɪt] vt manipular
mankind [mæn'kaɪnd] n humanidad, género humano
manly ['mænlɪ] adj varonil
man-made ['mæn'meɪd] adj artificial
manner ['mænəʳ] n manera, modo; (behaviour) conducta, manera de ser; (type) clase; **manners** npl modales, educación; (good) ~s (buena) educación, (buenos) modales; **bad ~s** falta de educación, pocos modales; **all ~ of** toda clase or suerte de
mannerism ['mænərɪzəm] n gesto típico
manoeuvre, (US) **maneuver** [mə'nu:vəʳ] vt, vi maniobrar ▷ n maniobra; **to ~ sb into doing sth** manipular a algn para que haga algo
manor ['mænəʳ] n (also: **manor house**) casa solariega
manpower ['mænpauəʳ] n mano de obra
mansion ['mænʃən] n mansión
manslaughter ['mænslɔ:təʳ] n homicidio involuntario
mantelpiece ['mæntlpi:s] n repisa de la chimenea
manual ['mænjuəl] adj manual ▷ n manual; ~ **worker** obrero, trabajador manual
manufacture [mænju'fæktʃəʳ] vt fabricar ▷ n fabricación
manufacturer [mænju'fæktʃərəʳ] n fabricante
manure [mə'njuəʳ] n estiércol, abono
manuscript ['mænjuskrɪpt] n manuscrito
Manx [mæŋks] adj de la Isla de Man
many ['mɛnɪ] adj muchos(-as) ▷ pron muchos(-as); **he hasn't got ~ friends** no tiene muchos amigos; **were there ~ people at the concert?** — **not ~** ¿había mucha gente en el concierto? — no mucha; **a great ~** muchísimos(-as), un buen número de; **very** ~ **muchos(-as); I haven't got very ~ CDs** no tengo muchos CDs; **too ~** demasiados(-as); **too ~ difficulties** demasiadas dificultades; **16 people? that's too ~** ¿16 personas? son demasiadas; **so ~** tantos(-as); **he told so ~ lies!** ¡dijo tantas mentiras!; **twice as ~** el doble; **how ~?** ¿cuántos(-as)?; **how ~ hours a week do you work?** ¿cuántas horas trabajas a la semana?; ~ **a time** muchas veces
map [mæp] n mapa ▷ vt trazar el mapa de
▶ **map out** vt (fig: career, holiday, essay) proyectar, planear
maple ['meɪpl] n arce, maple (LAm)
mar [mɑ:ʳ] vt estropear
marathon ['mærəθən] n maratón ▷ adj: **a ~ session** una sesión maratoniana
marble ['mɑ:bl] n mármol; (toy) canica
March [mɑ:tʃ] n marzo
march [mɑ:tʃ] vi (Mil) marchar; (fig) caminar con resolución ▷ n marcha; (demonstration) manifestación
mare [mɛəʳ] n yegua
margarine [mɑ:dʒə'ri:n] n margarina
marg(e) [mɑ:dʒ] n abbr = **margarine**
margin ['mɑ:dʒɪn] n margen
marginal ['mɑ:dʒɪnl] adj marginal
marginal seat n (Pol) circunscripción políticamente no definida
marigold ['mærɪgəuld] n caléndula
marijuana [mærɪ'wɑ:nə] n marihuana
marina [mə'ri:nə] n marina
marine [mə'ri:n] adj marino ▷ n soldado de infantería de marina
marital ['mærɪtl] adj matrimonial; ~ **status** estado civil
maritime ['mærɪtaɪm] adj marítimo
marjoram ['mɑ:dʒərəm] n mejorana
mark [mɑ:k] n marca, señal; (imprint) huella; (stain) mancha; (Brit Scol) nota; (currency) marco ▷ vt (make a mark on) marcar; (indicate) señalar; (stain) manchar; (Brit Scol) calificar, corregir; (Sport: player) marcar; **there were red ~s all over his back** tenía manchas rojas por toda la espalda; **you've got a ~ on your shirt** tienes una mancha en la camisa; **I get good ~s for French** saco buenas notas en francés; **punctuation ~s** signos de puntuación; **to be quick off the ~** (fig) ser listo; **up to the ~** (in efficiency) a la altura de las circunstancias; ~ **its position on the map** señala su posición en el mapa; **the teacher hasn't ~ed my homework yet** el maestro no me ha corregido los deberes todavía; **to ~ time** marcar el paso
▶ **mark down** vt (reduce: prices, goods) rebajar
▶ **mark off** vt (tick) indicar, señalar
▶ **mark out** vt trazar
▶ **mark up** vt (price) aumentar
marker ['mɑ:kəʳ] n (sign) marcador; (bookmark) registro
market ['mɑ:kɪt] n mercado ▷ vt (Comm) comercializar; (promote) publicitar; **open ~** mercado libre; **to be on the ~** estar en venta; **to**

play the ~ jugar a la bolsa
market economy n economía de mercado
market garden n (Brit) huerto
marketing ['mɑːkɪtɪŋ] n marketing, mercadotecnia
marketplace ['mɑːkɪtpleɪs] n mercado
market research n (Comm) estudios de mercado
marksman ['mɑːksmən] n tirador
marmalade ['mɑːməleɪd] n mermelada de naranja
maroon [mə'ruːn] vt: **to be ~ed** (shipwrecked) naufragar; (fig) quedar abandonado ▷ adj granate
marquee [mɑː'kiː] n carpa, entoldado
marriage ['mærɪdʒ] n (state) matrimonio; (wedding) boda; (act) casamiento
marriage bureau n agencia matrimonial
marriage certificate n partida de casamiento
marriage of convenience n matrimonio de conveniencia
married ['mærɪd] adj casado; (life, love) conyugal
marrow ['mærəu] n médula; (vegetable) calabacín
marry ['mærɪ] vt casarse con; (subj: father, priest etc) casar ▷ vi (also: **get married**) casarse
Mars [mɑːz] n Marte
marsh [mɑːʃ] n pantano; (salt marsh) marisma
marshal ['mɑːʃl] n (Mil) mariscal; (at sports meeting, demonstration etc) oficial; (US: of police, fire department) jefe(-a) ▷ vt (facts) ordenar; (soldiers) formar
marshy ['mɑːʃɪ] adj pantanoso
martial arts npl artes marciales
martial law n ley marcial
martyr ['mɑːtəʳ] n mártir ▷ vt martirizar
martyrdom ['mɑːtədəm] n martirio
marvel ['mɑːvl] n maravilla, prodigio ▷ vi: **to ~ (at)** maravillarse (de)
marvellous, (US) **marvelous** ['mɑːvləs] adj maravilloso
Marxism ['mɑːksɪzəm] n marxismo
Marxist ['mɑːksɪst] adj, n marxista
marzipan ['mɑːzɪpæn] n mazapán
mascara [mæs'kɑːrə] n rimel
mascot ['mæskət] n mascota
masculine ['mæskjulɪn] adj masculino
mash [mæʃ] n (mix) mezcla; (Culin) puré; (pulp) amasijo
mashed potatoes [mæʃt-] npl puré de patatas or (LAm) papas
mask [mɑːsk] n (also Elec) máscara ▷ vt enmascarar
masochist ['mæsəukɪst] n masoquista
mason ['meɪsn] n (also: **stonemason**) albañil; (also: **freemason**) masón
masonic [mə'sɒnɪk] adj masónico
masonry ['meɪsnrɪ] n masonería; (building) mampostería
masquerade [mæskə'reɪd] n baile de máscaras; (fig) mascarada ▷ vi: **to ~ as** disfrazarse de, hacerse pasar por
mass [mæs] n (people) muchedumbre; (Physics) masa; (Rel) misa; (great quantity) montón ▷ vi

reunirse; (Mil) concentrarse; **the ~es** las masas; **to go to ~** ir a or oír misa
massacre ['mæsəkəʳ] n masacre ▷ vt masacrar
massage ['mæsɑːʒ] n masaje ▷ vt dar masajes or un masaje a
massive ['mæsɪv] adj enorme; (support, intervention) masivo
mass media npl medios de comunicación de masas
mass-production ['mæsprə'dʌkʃən] n fabricación or producción en serie
mast [mɑːst] n (Naut) mástil; (Radio etc) torre, antena
mastectomy [mæs'tektəmɪ] n mastectomía
master ['mɑːstəʳ] n (of servant, animal) amo; (fig: of situation) dueño; (Art, Mus) maestro; (in secondary school) profesor; (title for boys): **M~ X** Señorito X ▷ vt dominar
masterly ['mɑːstəlɪ] adj magistral
mastermind ['mɑːstəmaɪnd] n inteligencia superior ▷ vt dirigir, planear
Master of Arts (MA) n licenciatura superior en Letras; see also **master's degree**
masterpiece ['mɑːstəpiːs] n obra maestra
master plan n plan rector
master's degree n máster
mastery ['mɑːstərɪ] n maestría
masturbate ['mæstəbeɪt] vi masturbarse
masturbation [mæstə'beɪʃən] n masturbación
mat [mæt] n alfombrilla; (also: **doormat**) felpudo ▷ adj = **matt**
match [mætʃ] n cerilla, fósforo, cerillo (CAm, Méx); (game) partido; (fig) igual ▷ vt emparejar; (go well with) hacer juego con; (equal) igualar ▷ vi hacer juego; **a box of ~es** una caja de cerillas; **a football ~** un partido de fútbol; **to be a good ~** hacer buena pareja; **the jacket ~es the trousers** la chaqueta hace juego con los pantalones; **these colours don't ~** estos colores no hacen juego
matchbox ['mætʃbɒks] n caja de cerillas
matching ['mætʃɪŋ] adj que hace juego; **my bedroom has ~ wallpaper and curtains** mi habitación tiene el papel y las cortinas a juego
mate [meɪt] n (workmate) compañero(-a), colega; (col: friend) amigo(-a), compadre (LAm); (animal) macho (hembra); (in merchant navy) primer oficial ▷ vi acoplarse, parearse ▷ vt acoplar, parear
material [mə'tɪərɪəl] n (substance) materia; (equipment) material; (cloth) tela, tejido ▷ adj material; (important) esencial; **materials** npl materiales; (equipment etc) artículos
maternal [mə'təːnl] adj maternal; **~ grandmother** abuela materna
maternity [mə'təːnɪtɪ] n maternidad
maternity dress n vestido premamá
maternity hospital n hospital de maternidad
maternity leave n baja por maternidad
math [mæθ] n abbr (US: = mathematics) matemáticas
mathematical [mæθə'mætɪkl] adj matemático
mathematician [mæθəmə'tɪʃən] n matemático

mathematics [mæθə'mætɪks] n matemáticas
maths [mæθs] n abbr (Brit: = mathematics)
matemáticas
matinée ['mætɪneɪ] n función de la tarde,
vermú(t) (LAm)
mating call n llamada del macho
matrices ['meɪtrɪsi:z] pl of **matrix**
matriculation [mətrɪkju'leɪʃən] n
matriculación, matrícula
matrimonial [mætrɪ'məʊnɪəl] adj matrimonial
matrimony ['mætrɪmənɪ] n matrimonio
matrix ['meɪtrɪks] (pl **matrices**) n matriz
matron ['meɪtrən] n (in hospital) enfermera jefe;
(in school) ama de llaves
matt [mæt] adj mate
matted ['mætɪd] adj enmarañado
matter ['mætər] n cuestión, asunto; (Physics)
sustancia, materia; (content) contenido; (Med:
pus) pus ▷ vi importar; **it's a ~ of life and
death** es un asunto de vida o muerte; **as a ~
of course** por rutina; **as a ~ of fact** de hecho,
en realidad; **printed ~** impresos; **reading ~**
material de lectura, lecturas; **what's the ~?** ¿qué
pasa?; **it doesn't ~** no importa; **shall I phone
today or tomorrow? — whenever, it doesn't
~** ¿telefoneo hoy o mañana? — cuando quieras,
da igual; **it ~s a lot to me** significa mucho para
mí; **no ~ what** pase lo que pase
matter-of-fact ['mætərəv'fækt] adj (style)
prosaico; (person) práctico; (voice) neutro
mattress ['mætrɪs] n colchón
mature [mə'tjuər] adj maduro ▷ vi madurar
mature student n estudiante de más de 21 años
maturity [mə'tjuərɪtɪ] n madurez
maul [mɔ:l] vt magullar
mausoleum [mɔ:sə'lɪəm] n mausoleo
mauve [məʊv] adj de color malva
maverick ['mævrɪk] n (fig) inconformista,
persona independiente
max abbr = **maximum**
maximize ['mæksɪmaɪz] vt (profits etc) llevar al
máximo; (chances) maximizar
maximum ['mæksɪməm] adj máximo ▷ n (pl
maxima) ['mæksɪmə] máximo
May [meɪ] n mayo
may [meɪ] vi (conditional **might**) (indicating
possibility): **he ~ come** puede que venga; (wishes):
~ God bless you! ¡que Dios le bendiga!; (giving/
asking permission): **~ I sit here?** ¿me puedo sentar
aquí?; **it ~ rain** puede que llueva; **are you going
to the party? — I don't know, I ~** ¿vas a ir a la
fiesta? — no sé, a lo mejor
maybe ['meɪbi:] adv quizá(s); **~ not** quizá(s) no
May Day n el primero de Mayo
mayday ['meɪdeɪ] n señal de socorro
mayhem ['meɪhɛm] n caos total
mayonnaise [meɪə'neɪz] n mayonesa
mayor [mɛər] n alcalde
mayoress ['mɛərɛs] n alcaldesa
maze [meɪz] n laberinto
MBE n abbr (Brit: = Member of the Order of the British
Empire) título ceremonial

MC n abbr (= master of ceremonies) e.p.; (US: = Member
of Congress) diputado del Congreso de los Estados Unidos
MD n abbr (= Doctor of Medicine) título universitario;
(Comm) = **managing director**; (= MiniDisc®)
MiniDisc® ▷ abbr (US) = **Maryland**
MD player n MiniDisc®
me [mi:] pron (direct) me; (stressed, after pronoun)
mí; **can you hear me?** ¿me oyes?; **he heard ME!**
me oyó a mí; **it's me** soy yo; **give them to me**
dámelos; **with/without me** conmigo/sin mí;
it's for me es para mí
meadow ['mɛdəʊ] n prado, pradera
meagre, (US) **meager** ['mi:gər] adj escaso, pobre
meal [mi:l] n comida; (flour) harina; **to go out
for a ~** salir a comer
meals on wheels nsg (Brit) servicio de alimentación a
domicilio para necesitados y tercera edad
mealtime ['mi:ltaɪm] n hora de comer
mean [mi:n] adj (with money) tacaño; (unkind)
mezquino, malo; (average) medio; (US: vicious:
animal) resabiado; (: person) malicioso ▷ vt (pt,
pp -t) (signify) querer decir, significar; (intend):
to ~ to do sth pensar hacer algo; **I ~t to help**
pensaba ayudar; **he didn't ~ to do it** lo hizo
sin querer ▷ n medio, término medio; **he's too
~ to buy presents** es demasiado tacaño para
comprar regalos; **you're being ~ to me** estás
siendo mezquino conmigo; **that's a really
~ thing to say!** ¡parece mentira que digas
eso!; **what does "alcalde" ~?** ¿qué significa
"alcalde"?; **I don't know what it ~s** no sé lo que
significa; **that's not what I ~t** eso no es lo que
quería decir; **what do you ~?** ¿qué quiere decir?;
which one did he ~? ¿a cuál se refería?; **do you
~ me?** ¿te refieres a mí?; **do you (really) ~ it?**
¿lo dices en serio?; **he ~s what he says** habla en
serio; **to be ~t for sb/sth** ser para algn/algo; see
also **means**
meander [mɪ'ændər] vi (river) serpentear; (person)
vagar
meaning ['mi:nɪŋ] n significado, sentido
meaningful ['mi:nɪŋful] adj significativo
meaningless ['mi:nɪŋlɪs] adj sin sentido
meanness ['mi:nnɪs] n (with money) tacañería;
(unkindness) maldad, mezquindad
means [mi:nz] npl medio, manera; (resource)
recursos, medios; **by ~ of** mediante, por medio
de; **by all ~!** ¡naturalmente!, ¡claro que sí!
meant [mɛnt] pt, pp of **mean**
meantime ['mi:ntaɪm], **meanwhile** ['mi:nwaɪl]
adv (also: **in the meantime**) mientras tanto
measles ['mi:zlz] n sarampión
measly ['mi:zlɪ] adj (col) miserable
measure ['mɛʒər] vt medir; (person: for clothes etc)
tomar las medidas a ▷ vi medir ▷ n medida;
(also: **tape measure**) cinta métrica; (rule) metro;
a litre ~ una medida de un litro; **some ~ of
success** cierto éxito; **to take ~s to do sth** tomar
medidas para hacer algo
▶ **measure up** vi: **to ~ up (to)** estar a la altura
(de)
measurement ['mɛʒəmənt] n (measure) medida;

(*act*) medición; **to take sb's ~s** tomar las medidas a algn

meat [miːt] *n* carne; **cold ~s** fiambres

meatball ['miːtbɔːl] *n* albóndiga

Mecca ['mɛkə] *n* (*city*) la Meca; (*fig*) meca

mechanic [mɪ'kænɪk] *n* mecánico(-a)

mechanical [mɪ'kænɪkl] *adj* mecánico

mechanics [mə'kænɪks] *n* mecánica ▷ *npl* mecanismo

mechanism ['mɛkənɪzəm] *n* mecanismo

medal ['mɛdl] *n* medalla

medallion [mɪ'dælɪən] *n* medallón

medallist, (US) **medalist** ['mɛdlɪst] *n* (*Sport*) medallista

meddle ['mɛdl] *vi*: **to ~ in** entrometerse en; **to ~ with sth** manosear algo

media ['miːdɪə] *npl* medios de comunicación

media circus *n* excesivo despliegue informativo

mediaeval [mɛdɪ'iːvl] *adj* = **medieval**

median ['miːdɪən] *n* (US: *also*: **median strip**) mediana

mediate ['miːdɪeɪt] *vi* mediar

mediator ['miːdɪeɪtəʳ] *n* mediador(a)

Medicaid ['mɛdɪkeɪd] *n* (US) *programa de ayuda médica*

medical ['mɛdɪkl] *adj* médico ▷ *n* (*also*: **medical examination**) reconocimiento médico

Medicare ['mɛdɪkɛəʳ] *n* (US) *seguro médico del Estado*

medication [mɛdɪ'keɪʃən] *n* (*drugs etc*) medicación

medicine ['mɛdsɪn] *n* medicina; (*drug*) medicamento

medieval, mediaeval [mɛdɪ'iːvl] *adj* medieval

mediocre [miːdɪ'əʊkəʳ] *adj* mediocre

mediocrity [miːdɪ'ɔkrɪtɪ] *n* mediocridad

meditate ['mɛdɪteɪt] *vi* meditar

meditation [mɛdɪ'teɪʃən] *n* meditación

Mediterranean [mɛdɪtə'reɪnɪən] *adj* mediterráneo; **the ~ (Sea)** el (Mar) Mediterráneo

medium ['miːdɪəm] *adj* mediano; (*level, height*) medio ▷ *n* (*pl* **media**) medio (*pl* **-s**) (*person*) médium; **happy ~** punto justo

medium-dry ['miːdɪəm'draɪ] *adj* semiseco

medium wave *n* onda media

medley ['mɛdlɪ] *n* mezcla; (*Mus*) popurrí

meek [miːk] *adj* manso, sumiso

meet [miːt] (*pt, pp* **met**) *vt* encontrar; (*accidentally*) encontrar con; (*by arrangement*) reunirse con; (*for the first time*) conocer; (*go and fetch*) ir a buscar; (*opponent*) enfrentarse con; (*obligations*) cumplir; (*bill, expenses*) pagar, costear ▷ *vi* encontrarse; (*in session*) reunirse; (*join: objects*) unirse; (*get to know*) conocerse ▷ *n* (*Brit Hunting*) cacería; (*US Sport*) encuentro; **I met Paul in town** me encontré con Paul en el centro; **where shall we ~?** ¿dónde quedamos?; **I'm going to ~ my friends at the swimming pool** he quedado con mis amigos en la piscina; **he met Tim at a party** conoció a Tim en una fiesta; **have you met her before?** ¿la conoces?; **pleased to ~ you!** ¡encantado (de conocerle)!, ¡mucho gusto!; **I'll ~ you at the**

station te voy a buscar a la estación; **we met by chance in the supermarket** nos encontramos por casualidad en el supermercado; **the committee met at two o'clock** el comité se reunió a las dos

▸ **meet up** *vi*: **to ~ up with sb** reunirse con algn
▸ **meet with** *vt fus* reunirse con; (*difficulty*) tropezar con

meeting ['miːtɪŋ] *n* (*socially*) encuentro; (*arranged*) cita, compromiso (LAm); (*for work etc*) reunión; (*Pol*) mitin; (*Sport: rally*) encuentro; **their first ~** su primer encuentro; **a business ~** una reunión de trabajo; **to call a ~** convocar una reunión

megabyte ['mɛgə'baɪt] *n* (*Comput*) megabyte, megaocteto

megaphone ['mɛgəfəʊn] *n* megáfono

megawatt ['mɛgəwɔt] *n* megavatio

melancholy ['mɛlənkəlɪ] *n* melancolía ▷ *adj* melancólico

mellow ['mɛləʊ] *adj* (*wine*) añejo; (*sound, colour*) suave; (*fruit*) maduro ▷ *vi* (*person*) madurar

melody ['mɛlədɪ] *n* melodía

melon ['mɛlən] *n* melón

melt [mɛlt] *vi* (*metal*) fundirse; (*snow*) derretirse; (*fig*) ablandarse ▷ *vt* (*also*: **melt down**) fundir; **~ed butter** mantequilla derretida
▸ **melt away** *vi* desvanecerse

meltdown ['mɛltdaʊn] *n* (*in nuclear reactor*) fusión (de un reactor nuclear)

melting pot ['mɛltɪŋ-] *n* (*fig*) crisol; **to be in the ~** estar sobre el tapete

member ['mɛmbəʳ] *n* (*of political party*) miembro; (*of club*) socio(-a); **M~ of Parliament (MP)** (*Brit*) diputado(-a); **M~ of the European Parliament (MEP)** (*Brit*) eurodiputado(-a); **M~ of the House of Representatives (MHR)** (*US*) diputado(-a) del Congreso de los Estados Unidos; **M~ of the Scottish Parliament** (*Brit*) diputado(-a) del Parlamento escocés; **"~s only"** "reservado para los socios"

membership ['mɛmbəʃɪp] *n* (*members*) miembros; socios; (*numbers*) número de miembros *or* socios; **to seek ~ of** pedir el ingreso a

membership card *n* carnet de socio

memento [mə'mɛntəʊ] *n* recuerdo

memo ['mɛməʊ] *n abbr* (= *memorandum*) nota (de servicio)

memoirs ['mɛmwɑːz] *npl* memorias

memorandum [mɛmə'rændəm] **memoranda**) *n* nota (de servicio); (*Pol*) memorándum

memorial [mɪ'mɔːrɪəl] *n* monumento conmemorativo ▷ *adj* conmemorativo

Memorial Day *n* (US) *día de conmemoración de los caídos en la guerra*

memorize ['mɛməraɪz] *vt* aprender de memoria

memory ['mɛmərɪ] *n* memoria; (*recollection*) recuerdo; (*Comput*) memoria; **to have a good/ bad ~** tener buena/mala memoria; **loss of ~** pérdida de memoria

men [mɛn] *pl of* **man**

menace ['mɛnəs] *n* amenaza; (*col: nuisance*) lata ▷ *vt* amenazar; **a public ~** un peligro público

menacing ['mɛnɪsɪŋ] *adj* amenazador(a)
mend [mɛnd] *vt* reparar, arreglar; *(darn)* zurcir
▷ *vi* reponerse ▷ *n (gen)* remiendo; *(darn)* zurcido;
to be on the ~ ir mejorando
mending ['mɛndɪŋ] *n* arreglo, reparación;
(clothes) ropa por remendar
menial ['miːnɪəl] *adj (pej)* bajo, servil
meningitis [mɛnɪn'dʒaɪtɪs] *n* meningitis
menopause ['mɛnəupɔːz] *n* menopausia
men's room *n (US):* **the men's room** el servicio
de caballeros
menstruate ['mɛnstrueɪt] *vi* menstruar
menstruation [mɛnstru'eɪʃən] *n* menstruación
menswear ['mɛnzweəʳ] *n* confección de
caballero
mental ['mɛntl] *adj* mental; **~ illness**
enfermedad mental
mental hospital *n* (hospital) psiquiátrico
mentality [mɛn'tælɪtɪ] *n* mentalidad
mentally ['mɛntlɪ] *adv:* **to be ~ handicapped** ser
un disminuido mental
menthol ['mɛnθɔl] *n* mentol
mention ['mɛnʃən] *n* mención ▷ *vt* mencionar;
(speak of) hablar de; **don't ~ it!** ¡de nada!; **I need
hardly ~ that** ... huelga decir que ...; **not to ~,
without ~ing** sin contar
menu ['mɛnjuː] *n (set menu)* menú; *(printed)* carta;
(Comput) menú
MEP *n abbr* = **Member of the European
Parliament**
mercenary ['mɜːsɪnərɪ] *adj, n* mercenario
merchandise ['mɜːtʃəndaɪz] *n* mercancías
merchant ['mɜːtʃənt] *n* comerciante
merchant bank *n (Brit)* banco comercial
merchant navy, *(US)* **merchant marine** *n*
marina mercante
merciful ['mɜːsɪful] *adj* compasivo
merciless ['mɜːsɪlɪs] *adj* despiadado
mercury ['mɜːkjurɪ] *n* mercurio
mercy ['mɜːsɪ] *n* compasión; *(Rel)* misericordia;
at the ~ of a la merced de
mere [mɪəʳ] *adj* simple, mero
merely ['mɪəlɪ] *adv* simplemente, sólo
merge [mɜːdʒ] *vt (join)* unir; *(mix)* mezclar; *(fuse)*
fundir; *(Comput: files, text)* intercalar ▷ *vi* unirse;
(Comm) fusionarse
merger ['mɜːdʒəʳ] *n (Comm)* fusión
meringue [mə'ræŋ] *n* merengue
merit ['mɛrɪt] *n* mérito ▷ *vt* merecer
mermaid ['mɜːmeɪd] *n* sirena
merry ['mɛrɪ] *adj* alegre; **M~ Christmas!** ¡Felices
Pascuas!
merry-go-round ['mɛrɪɡəuraund] *n* tiovivo
mesh [mɛʃ] *n* malla; *(Tech)* engranaje ▷ *vi (gears)*
engranar; **wire ~** tela metálica
mesmerize ['mɛzməraɪz] *vt* hipnotizar
mess [mɛs] *n* confusión; *(of objects)* revoltijo;
(tangle) lío; *(Mil)* comedor; **to be (in) a ~** *(room)*
estar revuelto; **my hair's a ~, it needs cutting**
tengo el pelo hecho un desastre; tengo que
cortármelo; **to be/get o.s. in a ~** estar/meterse
en un lío; **I'll be in a ~ if I fail the exam** voy a
tener problemas si suspendo el examen
▶ **mess about, mess around** *vi (col)* perder el
tiempo; *(pass the time)* pasar el rato; **I didn't do
much at the weekend, just ~ed about with
some friends** no hice mucho el fin de semana;
estuve ganduleando con unos amigos
▶ **mess about** *or* **around with** *vt fus (col: play with)*
divertirse con; *(: handle)* manosear; **stop ~ing
about with my computer!** ¡deja de toquetear
mi ordenador!
▶ **mess up** *vt (disarrange)* desordenar; *(spoil)*
estropear; *(dirty)* ensuciar; **you've ~ed up my
cassettes!** ¡me has estropeado los casetes!; **I
~ed up my chemistry exam** metí la pata en el
examen de química
message ['mɛsɪdʒ] *n* recado, mensaje; **to get
the ~** *(fig, col)* enterarse
messenger ['mɛsɪndʒəʳ] *n* mensajero(-a)
Messiah [mɪ'saɪə] *n* Mesías
Messrs *abbr (on letters:* = **Messieurs)** Sres.
messy ['mɛsɪ] *adj (dirty)* sucio; *(untidy)*
desordenado; *(confused: situation etc)* confuso
met [mɛt] *pt, pp of* **meet** ▷ *adj abbr* =
meteorological
metal ['mɛtl] *n* metal
metallic [mɛ'tælɪk] *adj* metálico
metaphor ['mɛtəfəʳ] *n* metáfora
mete [miːt]: **to ~ out** *vt fus (punishment)* imponer
meteor ['miːtɪəʳ] *n* meteoro
meteorite ['miːtɪəraɪt] *n* meteorito
meteorological [miːtɪərə'lɔdʒɪkl] *adj*
meteorológico
meteorology [miːtɪə'rɔlədʒɪ] *n* meteorología
meter ['miːtəʳ] *n (instrument)* contador; *(US: unit)*
= **metre** ▷ *vt (US Post)* franquear; **parking ~**
parquímetro
methane ['miːθeɪn] *n* metano
method ['mɛθəd] *n* método; **~ of payment**
método de pago
methodical [mɪ'θɔdɪkl] *adj* metódico
Methodist ['mɛθədɪst] *adj, n* metodista
methodology [mɛθə'dɔlədʒɪ] *n* metodología
meths [mɛθs], **methylated spirit(s)**
['mɛθɪleɪtɪd-] *n (Brit)* alcohol metilado *or*
desnaturalizado
meticulous [mɛ'tɪkjuləs] *adj* meticuloso
metre, *(US)* **meter** ['miːtəʳ] *n* metro
metric ['mɛtrɪk] *adj* métrico; **to go ~** pasar al
sistema métrico
metropolitan [mɛtrə'pɔlɪtən] *adj* metropolitano
mettle ['mɛtl] *n* valor, ánimo
mew [mjuː] *vi (cat)* maullar
mews [mjuːz] *(Brit) n:* **~ cottage** casa acondicionada
en antiguos establos o cocheras; **~ flat** *piso en antiguos
establos o cocheras*
Mexican ['mɛksɪkən] *adj, n* mejicano(-a),
mexicano(-a) *(LAm)*
Mexico ['mɛksɪkəu] *n* Méjico, México *(LAm)*
Mexico City *n* Ciudad de Méjico *or (LAm)* México
mezzanine ['mɛtsəniːn] *n* entresuelo
mg *abbr* (= **milligram)** mg.
Mgr *abbr* (= *Monseigneur, Monsignor)* Mons.

MHz *abbr* (= *megahertz*) MHz

MI5 *n abbr* (Brit: = *Military Intelligence 5*) *servicio de contraespionaje del gobierno británico*

MI6 *n abbr* (Brit: = *Military Intelligence 6*) *servicio de inteligencia del gobierno británico*

MIA *abbr* (= *missing in action*) desaparecido

miaow [mi:'au] *vi* maullar

mice [maɪs] *pl of* **mouse**

mickey ['mɪkɪ] *n*: **to take the ~ out of sb** tomar el pelo a algn

microbe ['maɪkrəub] *n* microbio

microbiology [maɪkrəubaɪ'ɔlədʒɪ] *n* microbiología

microchip ['maɪkrəutʃɪp] *n* microchip, microplaqueta

microcosm ['maɪkrəukɔzəm] *n* microcosmo

microfiche ['maɪkrəufi:ʃ] *n* microficha

microfilm ['maɪkrəufɪlm] *n* microfilm

microlight ['maɪkrəulaɪt] *n* ultraligero

microphone ['maɪkrəfəun] *n* micrófono

microprocessor ['maɪkrəu'prəusɛsəʳ] *n* microprocesador

microscope ['maɪkrəskəup] *n* microscopio; **under the ~** al microscopio

microwave ['maɪkrəuweɪv] *n* (*also*: **microwave oven**) horno microondas

mid [mɪd] *adj*: **in ~ May** a mediados de mayo; **in ~ afternoon** a media tarde; **in ~ air** en el aire; **he's in his ~ thirties** tiene unos treinta y cinco años

midday [mɪd'deɪ] *n* mediodía

middle ['mɪdl] *n* medio, centro; (*waist*) cintura ▷ *adj* de en medio; **the car was in the ~ of the road** el coche estaba en medio de la carretera; **in the ~ of the night** en plena noche; **in the ~ of May** a mediados de mayo; **I woke up in the ~ of the morning** me desperté a media mañana; **I'm in the ~ of reading it** lo estoy leyendo ahora mismo; **she was in the ~ of her exams** estaba en plenos exámenes; **the ~ seat** el asiento del medio

middle-aged [mɪdl'eɪdʒd] *adj* de mediana edad

Middle Ages *npl*: **the ~** la Edad Media

middle class *n*: **the ~(es)** la clase media ▷ *adj* (*also*: **middle-class**) de clase media

Middle East *n* Oriente Medio

middleman ['mɪdlmæn] *n* intermediario

middle name *n* segundo nombre

middle-of-the-road ['mɪdləvðə'rəud] *adj* moderado

middleweight ['mɪdlweɪt] *n* (*Boxing*) peso medio

middling ['mɪdlɪŋ] *adj* mediano

midge [mɪdʒ] *n* mosquito

midget ['mɪdʒɪt] *n* enano(-a)

midi system *n* cadena midi

Midlands ['mɪdləndz] *npl* región central de Inglaterra

midnight ['mɪdnaɪt] *n* medianoche; **at ~** a medianoche

midriff ['mɪdrɪf] *n* diafragma

midst [mɪdst] *n*: **in the ~ of** entre, en medio de

midsummer [mɪd'sʌməʳ] *n*: **a ~ day** un día de pleno verano

midway [mɪd'weɪ] *adj*, *adv*: **~ (between)** a mitad de camino *or* a medio camino (entre)

midweek [mɪd'wi:k] *adv* entre semana

midwife ['mɪdwaɪf] (*pl* **midwives**) ['mɪdwaɪvz] *n* comadrona

midwinter [mɪd'wɪntəʳ] *n*: **in ~** en pleno invierno

might [maɪt] *vb conditional of* **may** ▷ *n* fuerza, poder; **he ~ be there** puede que esté allí, a lo mejor está allí; **the teacher ~ come at any moment** el profesor podría venir en cualquier momento; **she ~ not have understood** puede que no haya entendido; **I ~ as well go** más vale que vaya; **you ~ like to try** podría intentar

mightn't ['maɪtnt] = **might not**

mighty ['maɪtɪ] *adj* fuerte, poderoso

migraine ['mi:greɪn] *n* jaqueca

migrant ['maɪgrənt] *adj* migratorio ▷ *n* (*bird*) ave migratoria; (*worker*) emigrante

migrate [maɪ'greɪt] *vi* emigrar

mike [maɪk] *n abbr* (= *microphone*) micro

mild [maɪld] *adj* (*person*) apacible; (*climate*) templado; (*slight*) ligero; (*taste*) suave; (*illness*) leve

mildly ['maɪldlɪ] *adv* ligeramente; suavemente; **to put it ~** por no decir algo peor

mile [maɪl] *n* milla; **to do 20 ~s per gallon** hacer 20 millas por galón

mileage ['maɪlɪdʒ] *n* número de millas; (*Aut*) kilometraje

mileometer [maɪ'lɔmɪtəʳ] *n* (Brit) = **milometer**

milestone ['maɪlstəun] *n* mojón; (*fig*) hito

militant ['mɪlɪtnt] *adj*, *n* militante

military ['mɪlɪtərɪ] *adj* militar

military service *n* servicio militar

militate ['mɪlɪteɪt] *vi*: **to ~ against** militar en contra de

militia [mɪ'lɪʃə] *n* milicia

milk [mɪlk] *n* leche ▷ *vt* (*cow*) ordeñar; (*fig*) chupar

milk chocolate *n* chocolate con leche

milkman ['mɪlkmən] *n* lechero, repartidor de la leche

milk shake *n* batido, malteada (*LAm*)

milky ['mɪlkɪ] *adj* lechoso

Milky Way *n* Vía Láctea

mill [mɪl] *n* (*windmill etc*) molino; (*coffee mill*) molinillo; (*factory*) fábrica; (*spinning mill*) hilandería ▷ *vt* moler ▷ *vi* (*also*: **mill about**) arremolinarse

miller ['mɪləʳ] *n* molinero

milligram(me) ['mɪlɪgraem] *n* miligramo

millimetre, (US) **millimeter** ['mɪlɪmi:təʳ] *n* milímetro

millinery ['mɪlɪnərɪ] *n* sombrerería

million ['mɪljən] *n* millón; **a ~ times** un millón de veces

millionaire [mɪljə'nɛəʳ] *n* millonario(-a)

milometer [maɪ'lɔmɪtəʳ] *n* (Brit) cuentakilómetros

mime [maɪm] *n* mímica; (*actor*) mimo(-a) ▷ *vt* remedar ▷ *vi* actuar de mimo

mimic ['mɪmɪk] *n* imitador(a) ▷ *adj* mímico ▷ *vt* remedar, imitar

min. *abbr* (= *minute(s)*) m.; = **minimum**

mince [mɪns] *vt* picar ▷ *vi* (*in walking*) andar con pasos menudos ▷ *n* (*Brit Culin*) carne picada, picadillo

mincemeat ['mɪnsmiːt] *n* conserva de fruta picada

mince pie *n* pastelillo relleno de fruta picada

mincer ['mɪnsə'] *n* picadora de carne

mind [maɪnd] *n* (*gen*) mente; (*contrasted with matter*) espíritu ▷ *vt* (*attend to, look after*) ocuparse de, cuidar; (*be careful of*) tener cuidado con; (*object to*): **I don't ~ the noise** no me molesta el ruido; **it is on my ~** me preocupa; **to my ~** a mi parecer or juicio; **to change one's ~** cambiar de idea or de parecer; **he's changed his ~** ha cambiado de idea; **to bring** or **call sth to ~** recordar algo; **to have sth/sb in ~** tener algo/a algn en mente; **what have you got in ~?** ¿qué tienes en mente?; **to be out of one's ~** haber perdido el juicio; **are you out of your ~?** ¿estás loco?; **to bear sth in ~** tomar or tener algo en cuenta; **to make up one's ~** decidirse; **I haven't made up my ~ yet** no me he decidido todavía; **it went right out of my ~** se me fue por completo (de la cabeza); **to be in two ~s about sth** estar indeciso or dudar ante algo; **could you ~ the baby this afternoon?** ¿podrías cuidar al niño esta tarde?; **could you ~ my bags for a few minutes?** ¿me cuidas las bolsas un momento?; **"~ the step"** "cuidado con el escalón"; **~ you don't fall** ten cuidado, no te vayas a caer; **I don't ~** me es igual; **do you ~ if I open the window? — no, I don't ~** ¿le importa que abra la ventana? — no, no me importa; **~ you, ...** te advierto que ...; **never ~!** ¡es igual!, ¡no importa!; (*don't worry*) ¡no te preocupes!

minder ['maɪndə'] *n* guardaespaldas

mindful ['maɪndful] *adj*: **~ of** consciente de

mindless ['maɪndlɪs] *adj* (*violence, crime*) sin sentido; (*work*) de autómata

mine [maɪn] *pron* (el) mío/(la) mía *etc*; **a friend of ~** un(a) amigo(-a) mío(-mía) ▷ *adj*: **this book is ~** este libro es mío ▷ *n* mina ▷ *vt* (*coal*) extraer; (*ship, beach*) minar

minefield ['maɪnfiːld] *n* campo de minas

miner ['maɪnə'] *n* minero(-a)

mineral ['mɪnərəl] *adj* mineral ▷ *n* mineral; **minerals** *npl* (*Brit: soft drinks*) refrescos con gas

mineral water *n* agua mineral

mingle ['mɪŋgl] *vi*: **to ~ with** mezclarse con

mini ... [mɪnɪ] *pref* mini..., micro...

miniature ['mɪnətʃə'] *adj* (en) miniatura ▷ *n* miniatura

minibus ['mɪnɪbʌs] *n* microbús

minicab ['mɪnɪkæb] *n* taxi (*que sólo puede pedirse por teléfono*)

MiniDisc® *n* MiniDisc

minim ['mɪnɪm] *n* (*Brit Mus*) blanca

minimal ['mɪnɪml] *adj* mínimo

minimalist ['mɪnɪməlɪst] *adj, n* minimalista

minimize ['mɪnɪmaɪz] *vt* minimizar

minimum ['mɪnɪməm] *n* (*pl* **minima**) ['mɪnɪmə] mínimo ▷ *adj* mínimo; **to reduce sth to a ~** reducir algo al mínimo; **~ wage** salario mínimo

minimum lending rate (MLR) *n* tipo de interés mínimo

mining ['maɪnɪŋ] *n* minería ▷ *adj* minero

mini-series ['mɪnɪsɪəriːz] *n* serie de pocos capítulos, miniserie

miniskirt ['mɪnɪskəːt] *n* minifalda

minister ['mɪnɪstə'] *n* (*Brit Pol*) ministro(-a); (*Rel*) pastor ▷ *vi*: **to ~ to** atender a

ministerial [mɪnɪs'tɪərɪəl] *adj* (*Brit Pol*) ministerial

ministry ['mɪnɪstrɪ] *n* (*Brit Pol*) ministerio; (*Rel*) sacerdocio; **M~ of Defence** Ministerio de Defensa

mink [mɪŋk] *n* visón

minor ['maɪnə'] *adj* (*unimportant*) secundario; (*Mus*) menor ▷ *n* (*Law*) menor de edad

Minorca [mɪ'nɔːkə] *n* Menorca

minority [maɪ'nɔrɪtɪ] *n* minoría; **to be in a ~** estar en or ser minoría

mint [mɪnt] *n* (*plant*) menta, hierbabuena; (*sweet*) caramelo de menta ▷ *vt* (*coin*) acuñar; **the (Royal) M~** (*US*): **the (US) M~** la Casa de la Moneda; **in ~ condition** en perfecto estado

minus ['maɪnəs] *n* (*also*: **minus sign**) signo menos ▷ *prep* menos

minuscule ['mɪnəskjuːl] *adj* minúsculo

minute *n* ['mɪnɪt] minuto; (*fig*) momento; **minutes** *npl* (*of meeting*) actas ▷ *adj* [maɪ'njuːt] diminuto; (*search*) minucioso; **it is 5 ~s past 3** son las 3 y 5 (minutos); **at the last ~** a última hora; **wait a ~!** ¡espera un momento!; **up to the ~** de última hora; **in ~ detail** con todo detalle; **her flat is ~** su apartamento es minúsculo

minutiae [mɪ'njuːʃiiː] *npl* minucias

miracle ['mɪrəkl] *n* milagro

miraculous [mɪ'rækjuləs] *adj* milagroso

mirage ['mɪrɑːʒ] *n* espejismo

mirror ['mɪrə'] *n* espejo; (*in car*) retrovisor ▷ *vt* reflejar

mirth [mə:θ] *n* alegría; (*laughter*) risa, risas

misadventure [mɪsəd'ventʃə'] *n* desventura; **death by ~** muerte accidental

misapprehension ['mɪsæprɪ'henʃən] *n* equivocación

misappropriate [mɪsə'prəuprieit] *vt* (*funds*) malversar

misbehave [mɪsbɪ'heɪv] *vi* portarse mal

misbehaviour, (*US*) **misbehavior** [mɪsbɪ'heɪvjə'] *n* mala conducta

misc. *abbr* = **miscellaneous**

miscalculate [mɪs'kælkjuleit] *vt* calcular mal

miscalculation [mɪskælkju'leɪʃən] *n* error (de cálculo)

miscarriage ['mɪskærɪdʒ] *n* (*Med*) aborto (no provocado); **~ of justice** error judicial

miscarry [mɪs'kærɪ] *vi* (*Med*) abortar (de forma natural); (*fail: plans*) fracasar, malograrse

miscellaneous [mɪsɪ'leɪnɪəs] *adj* varios(-as), diversos(-as); **~ expenses** gastos diversos

mischief ['mɪstʃɪf] n (naughtiness) travesura;
(harm) mal, daño; (maliciousness) malicia
mischievous ['mɪstʃɪvəs] adj travieso; dañino;
(playful) malicioso
misconception ['mɪskən'sɛpʃən] n concepto
erróneo; equivocación
misconduct [mɪs'kɔndʌkt] n mala conducta;
professional ~ falta profesional
misconstrue [mɪskən'struː] vt interpretar mal
misdemeanour, (US) **misdemeanor**
[mɪsdɪ'miːnəʳ] n delito, ofensa
misdirect [mɪsdɪ'rɛkt] vt (person) informar mal;
(letter) poner señas incorrectas en
miser ['maɪzəʳ] n avaro(-a)
miserable ['mɪzərəbl] adj (unhappy) triste,
desgraciado; (wretched) miserable; **to feel** ~
sentirse triste
miserly ['maɪzəlɪ] adj avariento, tacaño
misery ['mɪzərɪ] n (unhappiness) tristeza;
(wretchedness) miseria, desdicha
misfire [mɪs'faɪəʳ] vi fallar
misfit ['mɪsfɪt] n (person) inadaptado(-a)
misfortune [mɪs'fɔːtʃən] n desgracia
misgiving(s) [mɪs'ɡɪvɪŋ(z)] n(pl) (mistrust)
recelo; (apprehension) presentimiento; **to have
misgiving(s) about sth** tener dudas sobre algo
misguided [mɪs'ɡaɪdɪd] adj equivocado
mishandle [mɪs'hændl] vt (treat roughly)
maltratar; (mismanage) manejar mal
mishap ['mɪshæp] n desgracia, contratiempo
misinform [mɪsɪn'fɔːm] vt informar mal
misinterpret [mɪsɪn'təːprɪt] vt interpretar mal
misjudge [mɪs'dʒʌdʒ] vt juzgar mal
mislay [mɪs'leɪ] vt (irreg: like **lay**) extraviar, perder
mislead [mɪs'liːd] vt (irreg: like **lead**) llevar a
conclusiones erróneas; (deliberately) engañar
misleading [mɪs'liːdɪŋ] adj engañoso
mismanage [mɪs'mænɪdʒ] vt administrar mal
mismanagement [mɪs'mænɪdʒmənt] n mala
administración
misnomer [mɪs'nəuməʳ] n término inapropiado
or equivocado
misogynist [mɪ'sɔdʒɪnɪst] n misógino
misplace [mɪs'pleɪs] vt (lose) extraviar; **~d** (trust
etc) inmerecido
misprint ['mɪsprɪnt] n errata, error de imprenta
mispronounce [mɪsprə'nauns] vt pronunciar
mal
misquote ['mɪs'kwəut] vt citar incorrectamente
misread [mɪs'riːd] vt (irreg: like **read**) leer mal
misrepresent [mɪsrɛprɪ'zɛnt] vt falsificar
Miss [mɪs] n Señorita; **Dear ~ Smith** Estimada
Señorita Smith
miss [mɪs] vt (train etc) perder; (shot) errar, fallar;
(appointment, class) faltar a; (escape, avoid) evitar;
(notice loss of: money etc) notar la falta de, echar
en falta; (regret the absence of): **I ~ him** le echo de
menos ▷ vi fallar ▷ n (shot) tiro fallido; **hurry
or you'll ~ the bus** date prisa o perderás el
autobús; **he ~ed the target** no dio en el blanco;
the bus just ~ed the wall faltó poco para que el
autobús se estrelle contra el muro; **you're ~ing**

the point no has entendido la idea; **it's too
good an opportunity to ~** es una oportunidad
demasiado buena para dejarla pasar; **you've
~ed a page** te has saltado una página
▶ **miss out** vt (Brit) omitir
▶ **miss out on** vt fus (fun, party, opportunity)
perderse
misshapen [mɪs'ʃeɪpən] adj deforme
missile ['mɪsaɪl] n (Aviat) misil; (object thrown)
proyectil
missing ['mɪsɪŋ] adj (pupil) ausente, que falta;
(thing) perdido; (Mil) desaparecido; **to be ~** faltar;
~ **person** desaparecido(-a)
mission ['mɪʃən] n misión; **on a ~ for sb** en una
misión para algn
missionary ['mɪʃənrɪ] n misionero(-a)
misspell [mɪs'spɛl] vt (irreg: like **spell**) escribir mal
misspent ['mɪs'spɛnt] adj: **his ~ youth** su
juventud disipada
mist [mɪst] n (light) neblina; (heavy) niebla; (at
sea) bruma ▷ vi (also: **mist over**, **mist up**: weather)
nublarse; (Brit: windows) empañarse
mistake [mɪs'teɪk] n error ▷ vt (irreg: like **take**)
entender mal; **there must be some ~** debe de
haber algún error; **a spelling ~** una falta de
ortografía; **by ~** por equivocación; **to make a ~**
(get mixed up) equivocarse; (in writing, calculating
etc) cometer un error; **I'm sorry, I made a ~**
lo siento, me equivoqué; **he makes a lot of
~s when he speaks English** comete muchos
errores cuando habla inglés; **to ~ A for B**
confundir A con B
mistaken [mɪs'teɪkən] pp of **mistake** ▷ adj (idea
etc) equivocado; **to be ~** equivocarse, engañarse;
~ **identity** identificación errónea
mister ['mɪstəʳ] n (col) señor; see **Mr**
mistletoe ['mɪsltəu] n muérdago
mistook [mɪs'tuk] pt of **mistake**
mistreat [mɪs'triːt] vt maltratar, tratar mal
mistress ['mɪstrɪs] n (lover) amante; (of house)
señora (de la casa); (Brit: in primary school)
maestra; (in secondary school) profesora; see **Mrs**
mistrust [mɪs'trʌst] vt desconfiar de ▷ n: ~ **(of)**
desconfianza (de)
misty ['mɪstɪ] adj nebuloso, brumoso; (day) de
niebla; (glasses) empañado
misunderstand [mɪsʌndə'stænd] vt, vi (irreg: like
understand) entender mal
misunderstanding [mɪsʌndə'stændɪŋ] n
malentendido
misuse n mal uso; (of power) abuso ▷ vt abusar
de; (funds) malversar
mitigate ['mɪtɪɡeɪt] vt mitigar; **mitigating
circumstances** circunstancias atenuantes
mitigation [mɪtɪ'ɡeɪʃən] n mitigación, alivio
mitt(en) ['mɪt(n)] n manopla
mix [mɪks] vt (gen) mezclar; (combine) unir
▷ vi mezclarse ▷ n mezcla; **to ~ sth with sth**
mezclar algo con algo; ~ **the flour with the
sugar** mezcle la harina con el azúcar; **to ~
business with pleasure** combinar los negocios
con el placer; **I like ~ing with all sorts of**

people me gusta tratar con todo tipo de gente;
he doesn't ~ much no se relaciona mucho;
the film is a ~ of science fiction and comedy
la película es una mezcla de ciencia ficción y
comedia; **cake ~** preparado para pastel
▸ **mix in** vt (eggs etc) añadir
▸ **mix up** vt mezclar; (confuse) confundir; **he ~ed
up their names** confundió sus nombres; **the
travel agent ~ed up the bookings** la agencia de
viajes confundió las reservas; **I'm getting ~ed
up** me estoy confundiendo; **to be ~ed up in sth**
estar metido en algo
mixed [mɪkst] adj (assorted) variado, surtido;
(school, marriage etc) mixto
mixed grill n (Brit) parrillada mixta
mixed-up [mɪkst'ʌp] adj (confused) confuso,
revuelto
mixer ['mɪksə'] n (for food) batidora; (person): **he's
a good ~** tiene don de gentes
mixer tap n (grifo) monomando
mixture ['mɪkstʃə'] n mezcla
mix-up ['mɪksʌp] n confusión
MLR n abbr (Brit) = **minimum lending rate**
mm abbr (= millimetre) mm.

moan [məun] n gemido ▸ vi gemir; (col:
complain): **to ~ (about)** quejarse (de)
moat [məut] n foso
mob [mɔb] n multitud; (pej): **the ~** el populacho
▸ vt acosar
mobile ['məubaɪl] adj móvil ▸ n móvil
mobile home n caravana
mobile phone n teléfono móvil
mobility [məu'bɪlɪtɪ] n movilidad; **~ of labour** or
(US) **labor** movilidad de la mano de obra
mock [mɔk] vt (make ridiculous) ridiculizar; (laugh
at) burlarse de ▸ adj fingido
mockery ['mɔkərɪ] n burla; **to make a ~ of**
desprestigiar
mock-up ['mɔkʌp] n maqueta
mod cons ['mɔd'kɔnz] npl abbr = **modern
conveniences**; see **convenience**
mode [məud] n modo; (of transport) medio;
(Comput) modo, modalidad
model ['mɔdl] n (gen) modelo; (Arch) maqueta;
(person: for fashion, Art) modelo ▸ adj modelo ▸ vt
modelar ▸ vi ser modelo; **~ railway** ferrocarril
de juguete; **to ~ clothes** pasar modelos, ser
modelo; **to ~ on** crear a imitación de
modem ['məudəm] n módem
moderate adj, n moderado(-a) ▸ vi moderarse,
calmarse ▸ vt moderar
moderator ['mɔdəreɪtə'] n (mediator)
moderador(a)
modern ['mɔdən] adj moderno; **~ languages**
lenguas modernas
modernize ['mɔdənaɪz] vt modernizar
modest ['mɔdɪst] adj modesto
modesty ['mɔdɪstɪ] n modestia
modicum ['mɔdɪkəm] n: **a ~ of** un mínimo de
modification [mɔdɪfɪ'keɪʃən] n modificación; **to
make ~s** hacer cambios or modificaciones
modify ['mɔdɪfaɪ] vt modificar

module ['mɔdjuːl] n (unit, component, Space)
módulo
mogul ['məugəl] n (fig) magnate
mohair ['məuhɛə'] n mohair
moist [mɔɪst] adj húmedo
moisten ['mɔɪsn] vt humedecer
moisture ['mɔɪstʃə'] n humedad
moisturize ['mɔɪstʃəraɪz] vt (skin) hidratar
moisturizer ['mɔɪstʃəraɪzə'] n crema hidratante
molar ['məulə'] n muela
molasses [məu'læsɪz] n melaza
mold [məuld] n, vt (US) = **mould**
Moldavia [mɔl'deɪvɪə], **Moldova** [mɔl'dəuvə] n
Moldavia, Moldova
mole [məul] n (animal) topo; (spot) lunar
molecule ['mɔlɪkjuːl] n molécula
molest [məu'lɛst] vt importunar; (sexually)
abordar con propósitos deshonestos
mollycoddle ['mɔlɪkɔdl] vt mimar
Molotov cocktail ['mɔlətɔf-] n cóctel Molotov
molt [məult] vi (US) = **moult**
molten ['məultən] adj fundido; (lava) líquido
mom [mɔm] n (US) = **mum**
moment ['məumənt] n momento; **at** or **for the ~**
de momento, por el momento, por ahora; **in a ~**
dentro de un momento; **just a ~!** ¡un momento!;
any ~ now de un momento a otro
momentary ['məuməntərɪ] adj momentáneo
momentous [məu'mɛntəs] adj trascendental,
importante
momentum [məu'mɛntəm] n momento; (fig)
ímpetu; **to gather ~** cobrar velocidad; (fig)
cobrar fuerza
mommy ['mɔmɪ] n (US) = **mummy**
Monaco ['mɔnəkəu] n Mónaco
monarch ['mɔnək] n monarca
monarchy ['mɔnəkɪ] n monarquía
monastery ['mɔnəstərɪ] n monasterio
Monday ['mʌndɪ] n lunes
monetary ['mʌnɪtərɪ] adj monetario
money ['mʌnɪ] n dinero, plata (LAm); **to make
~** ganar dinero; **I've got no ~ left** no me queda
dinero
money order n giro
money-spinner ['mʌnɪspɪnə'] n (col: person, idea,
business) filón
mongrel ['mʌngrəl] n (dog) perro cruzado
monitor ['mɔnɪtə'] n monitor ▸ vt controlar;
(foreign station) escuchar
monk [mʌnk] n monje
monkey ['mʌnkɪ] n mono
monkey nut n (Brit) cacahuete, maní (LAm),
cacahuate (Méx)
monkey wrench n llave inglesa
monogamous [mə'nɔgəməs] adj monógamo
monologue ['mɔnəlɔg] n monólogo
monopolize [mə'nɔpəlaɪz] vt monopolizar
monopoly [mə'nɔpəlɪ] n monopolio;
Monopolies and Mergers Commission (Brit)
comisión reguladora de monopolios y fusiones
monosyllable ['mɔnəsɪləbl] n monosílabo
monotone ['mɔnətəun] n voz (or tono)

monocorde

monotonous [mə'nɔtənəs] *adj* monótono

monotony [mə'nɔtənɪ] *n* monotonía

monoxide [mə'nɔksaɪd] *n*: **carbon ~** monóxido de carbono

monseigneur [mɔnsɛn'jəː^r], **monsignor** [mɔn'siːnjə^r] *n* monseñor

monsoon [mɔn'suːn] *n* monzón

monster ['mɔnstə^r] *n* monstruo

monstrosity [mɔns'trɔsɪtɪ] *n* monstruosidad

monstrous ['mɔnstrəs] *adj* (*huge*) enorme; (*atrocious*) monstruoso

month [mʌnθ] *n* mes; **300 dollars a ~** 300 dólares al mes; **every ~** cada mes

monthly ['mʌnθlɪ] *adj* mensual ▷ *adv* mensualmente ▷ *n* (*magazine*) revista, mensual; **twice ~** dos veces al mes; **~ instalment** mensualidad

monument ['mɔnjumənt] *n* monumento

moo [muː] *vi* mugir

mood [muːd] *n* humor; **to be in a good/bad ~** estar de buen/mal humor

moody ['muːdɪ] *adj* (*variable*) de humor variable; (*sullen*) malhumorado

moon [muːn] *n* luna

moonlight ['muːnlaɪt] *n* luz de la luna ▷ *vi* hacer pluriempleo

moonlighting ['muːnlaɪtɪŋ] *n* pluriempleo

moonlit ['muːnlɪt] *adj*: **a ~ night** una noche de luna

Moor [muə^r] *n* moro(-a)

moor [muə^r] *n* páramo ▷ *vt* (*ship*) amarrar ▷ *vi* echar las amarras

moorings ['muərɪŋz] *npl* (*chains*) amarras; (*place*) amarradero

Moorish ['muərɪʃ] *adj* moro; (*architecture*) árabe

moorland ['muələnd] *n* páramo, brezal

moose [muːs] *n* (*pl inv*) alce

mop [mɔp] *n* fregona; (*of hair*) greñas ▷ *vt* fregar
▶ **mop up** *vt* limpiar

mope [məup] *vi* estar deprimido
▶ **mope about, mope around** *vi* andar abatido

moped ['məuped] *n* ciclomotor

moral ['mɔrl] *adj* moral ▷ *n* moraleja; **morals** *npl* moralidad, moral

morale [mɔ'raːl] *n* moral

morality [mə'rælɪtɪ] *n* moralidad

moralize ['mɔrəlaɪz] *vi*: **to ~ (about)** moralizar (sobre)

morally ['mɔrəlɪ] *adv* moralmente

moral victory *n* victoria moral

morass [mə'ræs] *n* pantano

morbid ['mɔːbɪd] *adj* morboso; (*Med*) mórbido

more [mɔː^r] *adj* **1** (*greater in number etc*) más; **~ people/work than before** más gente/trabajo que antes

2 (*additional*) más; **do you want (some) ~ tea?** ¿quieres más té?; **is there any ~ wine?** ¿queda vino?; **it'll take a few ~ weeks** tardará unas semanas más; **it's 2 kms ~ to the house** faltan 2 kms para la casa; **~ time/letters than we expected** más tiempo del que/más cartas de las

que esperábamos; **I have no ~ money, I don't have any ~ money** (ya) no tengo más dinero
▷ *pron* (*greater amount, additional amount*) más; **~ than 10** más de 10; **it cost ~ than the other one/than we expected** costó más que el otro/más de lo que esperábamos; **is there any ~?** ¿hay más?; **I want ~** quiero más; **and what's ~ ...** y además ...; **much ~** mucho(-a) más; **many ~** muchos(-as) más(-a)
▷ *adv* más; **~ dangerous/easily (than)** más peligroso/fácilmente (que); **~ and ~ expensive** cada vez más caro; **~ or less** más o menos; **~ than ever** más que nunca; **she doesn't live here any ~** ya no vive aquí

moreover [mɔː'rəuvə^r] *adv* además, por otra parte

morgue [mɔːg] *n* depósito de cadáveres

MORI ['mɔːrɪ] *n abbr* (*Brit*) = **Market and Opinion Research Institute**

Mormon ['mɔːmən] *n* mormón(-ona)

morning ['mɔːnɪŋ] *n* (*gen*) mañana; (*early morning*) madrugada; **in the ~** por la mañana; **7 o'clock in the ~** las 7 de la mañana; **this ~** esta mañana; **tomorrow ~** mañana por la mañana; **on Saturday ~** el sábado por la mañana; **the ~ papers** los periódicos de la mañana

morning-after pill ['mɔːnɪŋ'ɑːftə-] *n* píldora del día después

morning sickness *n* (*Med*) náuseas del embarazo

Moroccan [mə'rɔkən] *adj*, *n* marroquí

Morocco [mə'rɔkəu] *n* Marruecos

moron ['mɔːrɔn] *n* imbécil

morphine ['mɔːfiːn] *n* morfina

Morse [mɔːs] *n* (*also*: **Morse code**) (alfabeto) morse

morsel ['mɔːsl] *n* (*of food*) bocado

mortal ['mɔːtl] *adj*, *n* mortal

mortality [mɔː'tælɪtɪ] *n* mortalidad

mortar ['mɔːtə^r] *n* argamasa; (*implement*) mortero

mortgage ['mɔːgɪdʒ] *n* hipoteca ▷ *vt* hipotecar; **to take out a ~** sacar una hipoteca

mortgage company *n* (*US*) ≈ banco hipotecario

mortise (lock) ['mɔːtɪs-] *n* cerradura de muesca

mortuary ['mɔːtjuərɪ] *n* depósito de cadáveres

mosaic [məu'zeɪɪk] *n* mosaico

Moscow ['mɔskəu] *n* Moscú

Moslem ['mɔzləm] *adj*, *n* = **Muslim**

mosque [mɔsk] *n* mezquita

mosquito [mɔs'kiːtəu] (**-es**) *n* mosquito

moss [mɔs] *n* musgo

most [məust] *adj* la mayor parte de, la mayoría de ▷ *pron* la mayor parte, la mayoría ▷ *adv* el más; (*very*) muy; **~ people go out on Friday nights** la mayoría de la gente sale los viernes por la noche; **~ of the time** la mayor parte del tiempo; **I did ~ of the work alone** hice la mayor parte del trabajo solo; **~ of them have cars** la mayoría tienen coches; **the thing she feared ~** lo que más temía; **the ~, he's the one who talks the ~** es el que más habla; **the ~ expensive restaurant** el restaurante más caro; **he won**

the **~ votes** fue el que sacó más votos; **at the (very) ~** a lo sumo, como máximo; **2 hours at the ~** 2 horas como mucho; **to make the ~ of sth** aprovechar algo al máximo; **he made the ~ of his holiday** aprovechó sus vacaciones al máximo; **a ~ interesting book** (frm) un libro interesantísimo

mostly ['məʊstlɪ] adv en su mayor parte, principalmente

MOT n abbr (Brit) = **Ministry of Transport; the ~ (test)** ≈ la ITV

motel [məʊ'tɛl] n motel

moth [mɔθ] n mariposa nocturna; (clothes moth) polilla

mothball ['mɔθbɔːl] n bola de naftalina

mother ['mʌðəʳ] n madre ▷ adj materno ▷ vt (care for) cuidar (como una madre)

motherhood ['mʌðəhʊd] n maternidad

mother-in-law ['mʌðərɪnlɔː] n suegra

motherly ['mʌðəlɪ] adj maternal

mother-of-pearl ['mʌðərəv'pɜːl] n nácar

mother-to-be ['mʌðətə'biː] n futura madre

mother tongue n lengua materna

motif [məʊ'tiːf] n motivo; (theme) tema

motion ['məʊʃən] n movimiento; (gesture) ademán, señal; (at meeting) moción; (Brit: also: **bowel motion**) evacuación intestinal ▷ vt, vi: **to ~ (to) sb to do sth** hacer señas a algn para que haga algo; **to be in ~** (vehicle) estar en movimiento; **to set in ~** poner en marcha; **to go through the ~s of doing sth** (fig) hacer algo mecánicamente or sin convicción

motionless ['məʊʃənlɪs] adj inmóvil

motion picture n película

motivate ['məʊtɪveɪt] vt motivar

motivated ['məʊtɪveɪtɪd] adj motivado

motivation [məʊtɪ'veɪʃən] n motivación

motive ['məʊtɪv] n motivo; **from the best ~s** con las mejores intenciones

motley ['mɔtlɪ] adj variopinto

motor ['məʊtəʳ] n motor; (Brit: col: vehicle) coche, carro (LAm), automóvil, auto (CS) ▷ adj motor

motorbike ['məʊtəbaɪk] n moto

motorboat ['məʊtəbəʊt] n lancha motora

motorcar ['məʊtəkɑːʳ] n (Brit) coche, carro (LAm), automóvil, auto (CS)

motorcycle ['məʊtəsaɪkl] n motocicleta

motorcycle racing n motociclismo

motorcyclist ['məʊtəsaɪklɪst] n motociclista

motoring ['məʊtərɪŋ] n (Brit) automovilismo ▷ adj (accident, offence) de tráfico or tránsito

motorist ['məʊtərɪst] n conductor(a), automovilista

motor racing n (Brit) carreras de coches, automovilismo

motorway ['məʊtəweɪ] n (Brit) autopista

mottled ['mɔtld] adj moteado

motto ['mɔtəʊ] (pl **-es**) n lema; (watchword) consigna

mould, (US) mold [məʊld] n molde; (mildew) moho ▷ vt moldear; (fig) formar

mo(u)ldy ['məʊldɪ] adj enmohecido

moult, (US) molt [məʊlt] vi mudar la piel; (bird) mudar las plumas

mound [maʊnd] n montón m, montículo

mount [maʊnt] n monte; (horse) montura; (for jewel etc) engarce; (for picture) marco ▷ vt montar en, subir a; (stairs) subir; (exhibition) montar; (attack) lanzar; (stamp) pegar, fijar; (picture) enmarcar ▷ vi (also: **mount up**) subirse, montarse

mountain ['maʊntɪn] n montaña ▷ cpd de montaña; **to make a ~ out of a molehill** hacer una montaña de un grano de arena

mountain bike n bicicleta de montaña

mountaineer [maʊntɪ'nɪəʳ] n montañero(-a), alpinista, andinista (LAm)

mountaineering [maʊntɪ'nɪərɪŋ] n montañismo, alpinismo, andinismo (LAm)

mountainous ['maʊntɪnəs] adj montañoso

mountain rescue team n equipo de rescate de montaña

mountainside ['maʊntɪnsaɪd] n ladera de la montaña

mourn [mɔːn] vt llorar, lamentar ▷ vi: **to ~ for** llorar la muerte de, lamentarse por

mourner ['mɔːnəʳ] n doliente

mournful ['mɔːnfʊl] adj triste, lúgubre

mourning ['mɔːnɪŋ] n luto ▷ cpd (dress) de luto; **in ~** de luto

mouse [maʊs] (pl **mice**) n (also Comput) ratón

mouse mat, mouse pad n (Comput) alfombrilla, almohadilla

mousetrap ['maʊstræp] n ratonera

moussaka [mu'sɑːkə] n moussaka

mousse [muːs] n (Culin) mousse; (for hair) espuma (moldeadora)

moustache [məs'tɑːʃ], (US) **mustache** ['mʌstæʃ] n bigote

mousy ['maʊsɪ] adj (person) tímido; (hair) pardusco

mouth [maʊθ] (pl **-s**) n boca; (of river) desembocadura

mouthful ['maʊθfʊl] n bocado

mouth organ n armónica

mouthpiece ['maʊθpiːs] n (of instrument) boquilla; (Tel) micrófono; (spokesman) portavoz

mouthwash ['maʊθwɔʃ] n enjuague bucal

mouth-watering ['maʊθwɔːtərɪŋ] adj apetitoso

movable ['muːvəbl] adj movible

move [muːv] n (movement) movimiento; (course of action) paso; (in game) jugada; (: turn to play) turno; (change of house) mudanza ▷ vt mover; (emotionally) conmover; (Pol: resolution etc) proponer ▷ vi (gen) moverse; (traffic) circular; (Brit: also: **move house**) trasladarse, mudarse; **that was a good ~!** ¡ese fue un paso bien dado!; **it's your ~** te toca jugar; **our ~ from Oxford to Luton** nuestra mudanza de Oxford a Luton; **to get a ~ on** darse prisa; **he can't ~ his arm** no puede mover el brazo; **could you ~ your stuff please?** ¿podrías quitar tus cosas de aquí, por favor?; **to ~ sb to do sth** mover a algn a hacer algo; **to be ~d** estar conmovido; **I was very ~d**

by the film la película me conmovió mucho;
to ~ house mudarse de casa; **don't ~!** ¡no te
muevas!; **the car was moving very slowly**
el coche avanzaba muy lentamente; **we're
moving in July** nos mudamos en julio
▸ **move about** *or* **around** *vi* moverse; (*travel*)
viajar
▸ **move along** *vi* (*stop loitering*) circular; (*along seat
etc*) correrse
▸ **move away** *vi* (*leave*) marcharse
▸ **move back** *vi* (*return*) volver
▸ **move down** *vt* (*demote*) degradar
▸ **move forward** *vi* avanzar ▷ *vt* adelantar
▸ **move in** *vi* (*to a house*) instalarse; **when are
the new tenants moving in?** ¿cuándo vienen
los nuevos inquilinos?
▸ **move off** *vi* ponerse en camino
▸ **move on** *vi* seguir viaje ▷ *vt* (*onlookers*) hacer
circular
▸ **move out** *vi* (*of house*) mudarse
▸ **move over** *vi* hacerse a un lado, correrse;
could you ~ over a bit, please? ¿te podrías
correr un poco, por favor?
▸ **move up** *vi* subir; (*employee*) ser ascendido;
(*make room*) hacerse a un lado, correrse ▷ *vt* subir;
(*employee*) ascender
movement ['mu:vmənt] *n* movimiento; (*Tech*)
mecanismo; (*Med*) evacuación
movie ['mu:vɪ] *n* película; **to go to the ~s** ir al
cine
movie camera *n* cámara cinematográfica
moving ['mu:vɪŋ] *adj* (*emotional*) conmovedor(a);
(*that moves*) móvil; (*instigating*) motor(a)
mow [məʊ] (*pt* **-ed**, *pp* **-ed** *or* **-n**) *vt* (*grass*) cortar;
(*corn: also:* **mow down**) segar; (*shoot*) acribillar
mower ['məʊər] *n* (*also:* **lawnmower**) cortacésped
MP *n abbr* (= *Military Police*) PM; (*Brit*) = **Member of
Parliament**
MP3 ['ɛmpiːθriː] *n* MP3
MP3 player *n* reproductor (de) MP3
mpg *n abbr* (= *miles per gallon*) millas por galón
mph *abbr* = **miles per hour** (*60 mph = 96 km/h*)
Mr, Mr. ['mɪstər] *n*: **Mr Smith** (el) Sr. Smith
Mrs, Mrs. ['mɪsɪz] *n*: **~ Smith** (la) Sra. de Smith
Ms, Ms. [mɪz] *n* (*Miss or Mrs*) *abreviatura con la que se
evita hacer expreso el estado civil de una mujer*
MSc *abbr* = **Master of Science**; *see* **master's
degree**
MSP *n abbr* (*Brit*) = **Member of the Scottish
Parliament**
Mt *abbr* (*Geo*: = *mount*) m.
much [mʌtʃ] *adj* mucho ▷ *adv, n, pron* mucho;
(*before pp*) muy; **I feel ~ better now** ahora me
siento mucho mejor; **I haven't got ~ money**
no tengo mucho dinero; **have you got a lot of
luggage? — no, not ~** ¿tienes mucho equipaje?
— no, no mucho; **it's not ~** no es mucho; **what's
on TV? — not ~** ¿qué ponen en la tele? — nada
especial; **how ~?** ¿cuánto?; **how ~ time have
you got?** ¿cuánto tiempo tienes?; **how ~ is it?**
¿cuánto es?, ¿cuánto cuesta?; **very ~** mucho; **I
enjoyed myself very ~** me divertí mucho; **I**

like it very ~ me gusta mucho; **thank you
very ~** muchas gracias, muy agradecido; **too ~**
demasiado(-a); **that's too ~!** ¡eso es demasiado!;
they give us too ~ homework nos ponen
demasiados deberes; **so ~** tanto(-a); **I like it so ~**
me gusta tanto; **I didn't think it would cost so
~** no pensé que costaría tanto; **I've never seen
so ~ rain** nunca había visto tanta lluvia; **as ~ as**
tanto como; **however ~ he tries** por mucho que
se esfuerce
muck [mʌk] *n* (*dirt*) suciedad; (*fig*) porquería
▸ **muck about** *or* **around** *vi* (*col*) perder el tiempo;
(*enjoy o.s.*) entretenerse; (*tinker*) manosear
▸ **muck in** *vi* (*col*) arrimar el hombro
▸ **muck out** *vt* (*stable*) limpiar
▸ **muck up** *vt* (*col: dirty*) ensuciar; (*: spoil*) echar a
perder; (*: ruin*) estropear
mucky ['mʌkɪ] *adj* (*dirty*) sucio
mucus ['mjuːkəs] *n* mucosidad, moco
mud [mʌd] *n* barro, lodo
muddle ['mʌdl] *n* desorden, confusión; (*mix-up*)
embrollo, lío ▷ *vt* (*also:* **muddle up**) embrollar,
confundir
▸ **muddle along, muddle on** *vi* arreglárselas de
alguna manera
▸ **muddle through** *vi* salir del paso
muddy ['mʌdɪ] *adj* fangoso, cubierto de lodo
mudguard ['mʌdɡaːd] *n* guardabarros
muesli ['mjuːzlɪ] *n* muesli
muffin ['mʌfɪn] *n* bollo
muffle ['mʌfl] *vt* (*sound*) amortiguar; (*against cold*)
abrigar
muffled ['mʌfld] *adj* sordo, apagado
muffler ['mʌflər] *n* (*scarf*) bufanda; (*US Aut*)
silenciador; (*on motorbike*) silenciador, mofle
mug [mʌɡ] *n* (*cup*) taza alta; (*for beer*) jarra; (*col:
face*) jeta; (*: fool*) bobo ▷ *vt* (*assault*) atracar; **it's a
~'s game** es cosa de bobos
▸ **mug up** *vt* (*col: also:* **mug up on**) empollar
mugger ['mʌɡər] *n* atracador(a)
mugging ['mʌɡɪŋ] *n* atraco callejero
muggins ['mʌɡɪnz] *nsg* (*col*) tonto(-a) el bote
muggy ['mʌɡɪ] *adj* bochornoso
mule [mjuːl] *n* mula
mull [mʌl]: **to ~ over** *vt* meditar sobre
multicoloured, (*US*) **multicolored** ['mʌltɪkʌləd]
adj multicolor
multi-level [mʌltɪ'lɛvl] *adj* (*US*) = **multi-storey**
multinational [mʌltɪ'næʃənl] *n* multinacional
▷ *adj* multinacional
multiple ['mʌltɪpl] *adj* múltiple ▷ *n* múltiplo;
(*Brit: also:* **multiple store**) (cadena de) grandes
almacenes
multiple choice *n* examen de tipo test
multiple sclerosis [-sklɪ'rəʊsɪs] *n* esclerosis
múltiple
multiplex ['mʌltɪplɛks] *n* (*also:* **multiplex
cinema**) multicines
multiplication [mʌltɪplɪ'keɪʃən] *n*
multiplicación
multiply ['mʌltɪplaɪ] *vt* multiplicar ▷ *vi*
multiplicarse

multistorey [mʌltɪˈstɔːrɪ] adj (Brit: building, car park) de muchos pisos
multitude [ˈmʌltɪtjuːd] n multitud
mum [mʌm] n (Brit) mamá ▷ adj: **to keep ~ (about sth)** no decir ni mu (de algo)
mumble [ˈmʌmbl] vt decir entre dientes ▷ vi hablar entre dientes, musitar
mummy [ˈmʌmɪ] n (Brit: mother) mamá; (embalmed) momia
mumps [mʌmps] n paperas
munch [mʌntʃ] vt, vi mascar
mundane [mʌnˈdeɪn] adj mundano
municipal [mjuːˈnɪsɪpl] adj municipal
munitions [mjuːˈnɪʃənz] npl municiones
mural [ˈmjuərl] n (pintura) mural
murder [ˈmɜːdər] n asesinato; (in law) homicidio ▷ vt asesinar, matar; **to commit ~** cometer un asesinato or homicidio
murderer [ˈmɜːdərər] n asesino
murderous [ˈmɜːdərəs] adj homicida
murky [ˈmɜːkɪ] adj (water, past) turbio; (room) sombrío
murmur [ˈmɜːmər] n murmullo ▷ vt, vi murmurar; **heart ~** soplo cardíaco
muscle [ˈmʌsl] n músculo
▷ **muscle in** vi entrometerse
muscular [ˈmʌskjulər] adj muscular; (person) musculoso
muscular dystrophy n distrofia muscular
muse [mjuːz] vi meditar ▷ n musa
museum [mjuːˈzɪəm] n museo
mushroom [ˈmʌʃrum] n (gen) seta, hongo; (small) champiñón ▷ vi (fig) crecer de la noche a la mañana
music [ˈmjuːzɪk] n música
musical [ˈmjuːzɪkl] adj melodioso; (person) musical ▷ n (show) (comedia) musical
musical instrument n instrumento musical
music centre n equipo de música
musician [mjuːˈzɪʃən] n músico(-a)
Muslim [ˈmʌzlɪm] adj, n musulmán(-ana)
muslin [ˈmʌzlɪn] n muselina
mussel [ˈmʌsl] n mejillón
must [mʌst] aux vb (obligation): **I ~ do it** debo hacerlo, tengo que hacerlo; **I really ~ go now**

de verdad que me tengo que ir ya; **you ~ come again next year** tienes que volver el año que viene; **you ~n't forget to send her a card** no te vayas a olvidar de mandarle una tarjeta; (probability): **he ~ be there by now** ya debe (de) estar allí; **there ~ be some problem** debe de haber algún problema; **you ~ be tired** debes de estar cansada ▷ n: **it's a ~** es imprescindible
mustache [ˈmʌstæʃ] n (US) = moustache
mustard [ˈmʌstəd] n mostaza
muster [ˈmʌstər] vt juntar, reunir; (also: **muster up**) reunir; (: courage) armarse de
mustn't [ˈmʌsnt] = must not
mutant [ˈmjuːtənt] adj, n mutante
mutate [mjuːˈteɪt] vi sufrir mutación, transformarse
mute [mjuːt] adj, n mudo(-a)
muted [ˈmjuːtɪd] adj (noise) sordo; (criticism) callado
mutilate [ˈmjuːtɪleɪt] vt mutilar
mutiny [ˈmjuːtɪnɪ] n motín ▷ vi amotinarse
mutter [ˈmʌtər] vt, vi murmurar
mutton [ˈmʌtn] n (carne de) cordero
mutual [ˈmjuːtʃuəl] adj mutuo; (friend) común
mutually [ˈmjuːtʃuəlɪ] adv mutuamente
Muzak® [ˈmjuːzæk] n hilo musical
muzzle [ˈmʌzl] n hocico; (protective device) bozal; (of gun) boca ▷ vt amordazar; (dog) poner un bozal a
MW abbr (= medium wave) onda media
my [maɪ] adj mi(s); **my house/brother/sisters** mi casa/hermano/mis hermanas; **I've washed my hair/cut my finger** me he lavado el pelo/cortado un dedo; **is this my pen or yours?** ¿este bolígrafo es mío o tuyo?
Myanmar [ˈmaɪænmɑːr] n Myanmar
myself [maɪˈsɛlf] pron (reflexive) me; (emphatic) yo mismo; (after prep) mí (mismo); see also **oneself**
mysterious [mɪsˈtɪərɪəs] adj misterioso
mystery [ˈmɪstərɪ] n misterio
mystify [ˈmɪstɪfaɪ] vt (perplex) dejar perplejo; (disconcert) desconcertar
myth [mɪθ] n mito
mythical [ˈmɪθɪkl] adj mítico
mythology [mɪˈθɔlədʒɪ] n mitología

Nn

N, n [ɛn] n (*letter*) N, n; **N for Nellie**, (US) **N for Nan** N de Navarra

N *abbr* (= *North*) N

n/a *abbr* (= *not applicable*) no interesa; (*Comm etc*) = **no account**

nab [næb] *vt* (*col: grab*) coger (*Esp*), agarrar (*LAm*); (*: catch out*) pillar

NAFTA ['næftə] n *abbr* (= *North Atlantic Free Trade Agreement*) TLC

nag [næg] n (*pej: horse*) rocín ▷ *vt* (*scold*) regañar; (*annoy*) fastidiar

nagging ['nægɪŋ] *adj* (*doubt*) persistente; (*pain*) continuo ▷ n quejas

nail [neɪl] n (*human*) uña; (*metal*) clavo ▷ *vt* clavar; (*fig: catch*) coger (*Esp*), pillar; **to pay cash on the ~** pagar a tocateja; **to ~ sb down to a date/price** hacer que algn se comprometa a una fecha/un precio

nailbrush ['neɪlbrʌʃ] n cepillo para las uñas

nailfile ['neɪlfaɪl] n lima para las uñas

nail polish n esmalte or laca para las uñas

nail polish remover n quitaesmalte

nail scissors *npl* tijeras para las uñas

nail varnish n (*Brit*) = **nail polish**

naïve [naɪˈiːv] *adj* ingenuo

naked ['neɪkɪd] *adj* (*nude*) desnudo; (*flame*) expuesto al aire; **with the ~ eye** a simple vista

name [neɪm] n (*gen*) nombre; (*surname*) apellido; (*reputation*) fama, renombre ▷ *vt* (*child*) poner nombre a; (*appoint*) nombrar; **by ~** de nombre; **in the ~ of** en nombre de; **what's your ~?** ¿cómo se llama usted?; **my ~ is Peter** me llamo Peter; **to give one's ~ and address** dar sus señas; **to take sb's ~ and address** apuntar las señas de algn; **to make a ~ for o.s** hacerse famoso; **to get (o.s.) a bad ~** forjarse una mala reputación

nameless ['neɪmlɪs] *adj* anónimo, sin nombre

namely ['neɪmlɪ] *adv* a saber

namesake ['neɪmseɪk] n tocayo(-a)

nan bread [naːn-] n pan indio sin apenas levadura

nanny ['nænɪ] n niñera

nap [næp] n (*sleep*) sueñecito, siesta; **they were caught ~ping** les pilló desprevenidos

nape [neɪp] n: **~ of the neck** nuca, cogote

napkin ['næpkɪn] n (*also:* **table napkin**) servilleta

nappy ['næpɪ] n (*Brit*) pañal

nappy rash n prurito

narcissus [naːˈsɪsəs] (*pl* **narcissi**) n narciso

narcotic [naːˈkɒtɪk] *adj, n* narcótico

narrate [nəˈreɪt] *vt* narrar, contar

narrative ['nærətɪv] n narrativa ▷ *adj* narrativo

narrator [nəˈreɪtəʳ] n narrador(a)

narrow ['nærəʊ] *adj* estrecho; (*resources, means*) escaso ▷ *vi* estrecharse; (*diminish*) reducirse ▷ *vt*: **to ~ sth down** reducir algo; **to have a ~ escape** escaparse por los pelos

narrowly ['nærəlɪ] *adv* (*miss*) por poco

narrow-minded [nærəʊˈmaɪndɪd] *adj* de miras estrechas

NASA n *abbr* (US: = *National Aeronautics and Space Administration*) NASA

nasal ['neɪzl] *adj* nasal

nasty ['naːstɪ] *adj* (*remark*) feo; (*person*) antipático; (*revolting: taste, smell*) asqueroso; (*wound, disease etc*) peligroso, grave; **to turn ~** (*situation*) ponerse feo; (*weather*) empeorar; (*person*) ponerse negro

nation ['neɪʃən] n nación

national ['næʃənl] *adj* nacional ▷ n súbdito(-a)

national anthem n himno nacional

National Curriculum n (*Brit*) plan general de estudios (*en Inglaterra y Gales*)

national debt n deuda pública

national dress n traje típico del país

National Guard n (*US*) Guardia Nacional

National Health Service (NHS) n (*Brit*) servicio nacional de sanidad, ≈ INSALUD (*Esp*)

National Insurance n (*Brit*) seguro social nacional, ≈ Seguridad Social

nationalism ['næʃnəlɪzəm] n nacionalismo

nationalist ['næʃnəlɪst] *adj, n* nacionalista

nationality [næʃəˈnælɪtɪ] n nacionalidad

nationalization [næʃnəlaɪˈzeɪʃən] n nacionalización

nationalize ['næʃnəlaɪz] *vt* nacionalizar; **~d industry** industria nacionalizada

nationally ['næʃnəlɪ] *adv* (*nationwide*) a escala nacional; (*as a nation*) como nación

national service n (*Mil*) servicio militar

National Trust n (*Brit*) organización encargada de preservar el patrimonio histórico británico

nationwide ['neɪʃənwaɪd] *adj* a escala nacional

native ['neɪtɪv] n (*local inhabitant*) natural; (*in colonies*) indígena, nativo(-a) ▷ *adj* (*indigenous*) indígena; (*country*) natal; (*innate*) natural, innato; **a ~ of Russia** un(a) natural de Rusia; **~ language** lengua materna; **a ~ speaker of French** un hablante nativo de francés

Native American *adj, n* americano(-a) indígena, amerindio(-a)

Nativity [nə'tɪvɪtɪ] *n*: **the ~** Navidad

nativity play *n* auto del nacimiento

NATO ['neɪtəu] *n abbr* (= *North Atlantic Treaty Organization*) OTAN

natural ['nætʃrəl] *adj* natural; **death from ~ causes** (*Law*) muerte por causas naturales

natural gas *n* gas natural

natural history *n* historia natural

naturalize ['nætʃrəlaɪz] *vt*: **to become ~d** (*person*) naturalizarse; (*plant*) aclimatarse

naturally ['nætʃrəlɪ] *adv* (*speak etc*) naturalmente; (*of course*) desde luego, por supuesto, ¡cómo no! (*LAm*); (*instinctively*) por naturaleza

natural selection *n* selección natural

nature ['neɪtʃəʳ] *n* naturaleza; (*group, sort*) género, clase; (*character*) modo de ser, carácter; **by ~** por naturaleza; **documents of a confidential ~** documentos de tipo confidencial

naught [nɔːt] = **nought**

naughty ['nɔːtɪ] *adj* (*child*) travieso; (*story, film*) picante, escabroso, colorado (*LAm*)

nausea ['nɔːsɪə] *n* náusea

nauseate ['nɔːsɪeɪt] *vt* dar náuseas a; (*fig*) dar asco a

naval ['neɪvl] *adj* naval, de marina

naval officer *n* oficial de marina

nave [neɪv] *n* nave

navel ['neɪvl] *n* ombligo

navigate ['nævɪgeɪt] *vt* (*ship*) gobernar; (*river etc*) navegar por ▷ *vi* navegar; (*Aut*) hacer de copiloto

navigation [nævɪ'geɪʃən] *n* (*action*) navegación; (*science*) náutica

navvy ['nævɪ] *n* (*Brit*) peón caminero

navy ['neɪvɪ] *n* marina de guerra; (*ships*) armada, flota

navy(-blue) ['neɪvɪ('bluː)] *adj* azul marino

Nazi ['nɑːtsɪ] *adj, n* nazi

NB *abbr* (= *nota bene*) nótese

NBA *n abbr* (*US*) = **National Basketball Association; National Boxing Association**

NBC *n abbr* (*US*: = *National Broadcasting Company*) *cadena de televisión*

near [nɪəʳ] *adj* (*place, relation*) cercano; (*time*) próximo ▷ *adv* cerca ▷ *prep* (*also*: **near to**: *space*) cerca de, junto a; (: *time*) cerca de ▷ *vt* acercarse a, aproximarse a; **where's the ~est service station?** ¿dónde está la gasolinera más cercana?; **£25,000 or ~est offer** 25,000 libras o precio a discutir; **in the ~ future** en un futuro cercano; **it's fairly ~** está bastante cerca; **my house is ~ enough to walk** mi casa está muy cerca, se puede ir andando; **~ here/there** cerca de aquí/de allí; **is there a bank ~ here?** ¿hay algún banco por aquí cerca?; **I live ~ Liverpool** vivo cerca de Liverpool; **~ to** cerca de; **it's very ~ to the school** está muy cerca del colegio; **the building is ~ing completion** el edificio está casi terminado

nearby [nɪə'baɪ] *adj* cercano, próximo ▷ *adv* cerca

nearly ['nɪəlɪ] *adv* casi, por poco; **I ~ fell** por poco me caigo; **not ~** ni mucho menos, ni con mucho

near miss *n* (*shot*) tiro casi en el blanco; (*Aviat*) *accidente evitado por muy poco*

nearside ['nɪəsaɪd] *n* (*Aut: right-hand drive*) lado izquierdo; (: *left-hand drive*) lado derecho

near-sighted [nɪə'saɪtɪd] *adj* miope, corto de vista

neat [niːt] *adj* (*place*) ordenado, bien cuidado; (*person*) pulcro; (*plan*) ingenioso; (*spirits*) solo

neatly ['niːtlɪ] *adv* (*tidily*) con esmero; (*skilfully*) ingeniosamente

neatness ['niːtnɪs] *n* (*tidiness*) orden; (*skilfulness*) destreza, habilidad

necessarily ['nɛsɪsrɪlɪ] *adv* necesariamente; **not ~** no necesariamente

necessary ['nɛsɪsrɪ] *adj* necesario, preciso; **he did all that was ~** hizo todo lo necesario; **if ~** si es necesario

necessity [nɪ'sɛsɪtɪ] *n* necesidad; **necessities** *npl* artículos de primera necesidad; **in case of ~** en caso de urgencia

neck [nɛk] *n* (*Anat*) cuello; (*of animal*) pescuezo ▷ *vi* besuquearse; **~ and ~** parejos; **to stick one's ~ out** (*col*) arriesgarse

necklace ['nɛklɪs] *n* collar

neckline ['nɛklaɪn] *n* escote

necktie ['nɛktaɪ] *n* (*US*) corbata

née [neɪ] *adj*: **~ Scott** de soltera Scott

need [niːd] *n* (*necessity*) necesidad; (*lack*) escasez, falta ▷ *vt* (*require*) necesitar; **in case of ~** en caso de necesidad; **there's no ~ to book** no hace falta hacer reserva; **there's no ~ for you to do that** no hace falta que hagas eso; **to be in ~ of, have ~ of** necesitar; **10 will meet my immediate ~s** 10 satisfacerán mis necesidades más apremiantes; **the ~s of industry** las necesidades de la industria; **I ~ a bigger size** necesito una talla más grande; **I ~ to change some money** necesito cambiar dinero; **I ~ to do it** tengo que hacerlo; **you don't ~ to go** no hace falta que vayas; **a signature is ~ed** se requiere una firma

needle ['niːdl] *n* aguja ▷ *vt* (*fig: col*) picar, fastidiar

needless ['niːdlɪs] *adj* innecesario, inútil; **~ to say** huelga decir que

needlework ['niːdlwəːk] *n* (*activity*) costura, labor de aguja

needn't ['niːdnt] = **need not**

needy ['niːdɪ] *adj* necesitado

negative ['nɛgətɪv] *n* (*Phot*) negativo; (*answer*) negativa; (*Ling*) negación ▷ *adj* negativo

negative equity *n situación en la que el valor de la vivienda es menor que el de la hipoteca que pesa sobre ella*

neglect [nɪ'glɛkt] *vt* (*one's duty*) faltar a, no cumplir con; (*child*) descuidar, desatender ▷ *n* (*state*) abandono; (*personal*) dejadez; (*of duty*) incumplimiento; **to ~ to do sth** olvidarse de hacer algo

negligee ['nɛglɪʒeɪ] *n* (*nightdress*) salto de cama

negligence ['nɛglɪdʒəns] n negligencia
negligent ['nɛglɪdʒənt] adj negligente; (casual) descuidado
negligible ['nɛglɪdʒɪbl] adj insignificante, despreciable
negotiable [nɪ'gəʊʃɪəbl] adj (cheque) negociable; **not ~** (cheque) no trasferible
negotiate [nɪ'gəʊʃɪeɪt] vt (treaty, loan) negociar; (obstacle) franquear; (bend in road) tomar ▷ vi: **to ~ (with)** negociar (con); **to ~ with sb for sth** tratar or negociar con algn por algo
negotiating table [nɪ'gəʊʃɪeɪtɪŋ-] n mesa de negociaciones
negotiation [nɪgəʊʃɪ'eɪʃən] n negociación, gestión; **to enter into ~s with sb** entrar en negociaciones con algn
negotiator [nɪ'gəʊʃɪeɪtər] n negociador(a)
Negro ['niːgrəʊ] adj, n negro
neigh [neɪ] n relincho ▷ vi relinchar
neighbour, (US) **neighbor** ['neɪbər] n vecino(-a)
neighbo(u)rhood ['neɪbəhʊd] n (place) vecindad, barrio; (people) vecindario
neighbourhood watch n (Brit: also: **neighbourhood watch scheme**) vigilancia del barrio por los propios vecinos
neighbo(u)ring ['neɪbərɪŋ] adj vecino
neighbo(u)rly ['neɪbəlɪ] adj amigable, sociable
neither ['naɪðər] adj ni ▷ conj: **I didn't move and ~ did John** no me he movido, ni Juan tampoco ▷ pron ninguno; **~ is true** ninguno(-a) de los (las) dos es cierto(-a) ▷ adv: **~ good nor bad** ni bueno ni malo
neologism [nɪ'ɔlədʒɪzəm] n neologismo
neon ['niːɔn] n neón
neon light n lámpara de neón
nephew ['nɛvjuː] n sobrino
nerd [nəːd] n (col) primo(-a)
nerve [nəːv] n (Anat) nervio; (courage) valor; (impudence) descaro, frescura; **a fit of ~s** un ataque de nervios; **to lose one's ~** (self-confidence) perder el valor
nerve centre n (Anat) centro nervioso; (fig) punto neurálgico
nerve-racking ['nəːvrækɪŋ] adj angustioso
nervous ['nəːvəs] adj (anxious, Anat) nervioso; (timid) tímido, miedoso
nervous breakdown n crisis nerviosa
nervous wreck n (col): **to be a ~** estar de los nervios
nervy ['nəːvɪ] adj: **to be ~** estar nervioso
nest [nɛst] n (of bird) nido ▷ vi anidar
nest egg n (fig) ahorros
nestle ['nɛsl] vi: **to ~ down** acurrucarse
net [nɛt] n (gen) red; (fabric) tul ▷ adj (Comm) neto, líquido; (weight, price, salary) neto ▷ vt coger (Esp) or agarrar (LAm) con red; (money: subj: person) cobrar; (: deal, sale) conseguir; (Sport) marcar; **~ of tax** neto; **he earns £10,000 ~ per year** gana 10,000 libras netas por año; **the N~** (Internet) la Red
netball ['nɛtbɔːl] n básquet
net curtain n visillo

Netherlands ['nɛðələndz] npl: **the ~** los Países Bajos
net profit n beneficio neto
nett [nɛt] adj = **net**
netting ['nɛtɪŋ] n red, redes
nettle ['nɛtl] n ortiga
network ['nɛtwəːk] n red ▷ vt (Radio, TV) difundir por la red de emisoras; **local area ~** red local
neurological [njʊərə'lɔdʒɪkl] adj neurológico
neurosis [njʊə'rəʊsɪs] [njʊə'rəʊsɪsiːz] (pl **-ses**) n neurosis
neurotic [njʊə'rɔtɪk] adj, n neurótico(-a)
neuter ['njuːtər] adj (Ling) neutro ▷ vt castrar, capar
neutral ['njuːtrəl] adj (person) neutral; (colour etc, Elec) neutro ▷ n (Aut) punto muerto
neutralize ['njuːtrəlaɪz] vt neutralizar
neutron ['njuːtrɔn] n neutrón
never ['nɛvər] adv nunca, jamás; **I ~ went** no fui nunca; **~ leave valuables in your car** no dejen nunca objetos de valor en el coche; **have you ever been to Argentina? — no, ~** ¿has estado alguna vez en Argentina? — no, nunca; **~ again!** ¡nunca más!; **~, ever do that again!** ¡no vuelvas a hacer eso nunca jamás!; **~ in my life** jamás en la vida; see also **mind**
never-ending [nɛvər'ɛndɪŋ] adj interminable, sin fin
nevertheless [nɛvəðə'lɛs] adv sin embargo, no obstante
new [njuː] adj nuevo; (recent) reciente; **as good as ~** como nuevo; **her ~ boyfriend** su nuevo novio
New Age n Nueva era
newborn ['njuːbɔːn] adj recién nacido
newcomer ['njuːkʌmər] n recién venido or llegado
new-fangled ['njuːfæŋgld] adj (pej) modernísimo
new-found ['njuːfaund] adj (friend) nuevo; (enthusiasm) recién adquirido
newly ['njuːlɪ] adv recién
newly-weds ['njuːlɪwɛdz] npl recién casados
new moon n luna nueva
news [njuːz] n noticias; **a piece of ~** una noticia; **an interesting piece of ~** una noticia interesante; **the ~** (Radio, TV) las noticias, el telediario; **I watch the ~ every evening** veo las noticias todas las noches; **good/bad ~** buenas/malas noticias; **financial ~** noticias financieras; **that's wonderful ~!** ¡qué buena noticia!; **it was nice to have your ~** me dio alegría saber de ti
news agency n agencia de noticias
newsagent ['njuːzeɪdʒənt] n (Brit) vendedor(a) de periódicos
newscaster ['njuːzkaːstər] n presentador(a), locutor(a)
news dealer n (US) = **newsagent**
news flash n noticia de última hora
newsletter ['njuːzlɛtər] n hoja informativa, boletín
newspaper ['njuːzpeɪpər] n periódico, diario;

daily ~ diario; **weekly** ~ periódico semanal
newsprint ['nju:zprɪnt] *n* papel de periódico
newsreader ['nju:zri:dəʳ] *n* = **newscaster**
newsreel ['nju:zri:l] *n* noticiario
newsroom ['nju:zru:m] *n* (Press, Radio, TV) sala de redacción
news stand *n* quiosco *or* puesto de periódicos
newsworthy ['nju:zwə:ðɪ] *adj*: **to be** ~ ser de interés periodístico
newt [nju:t] *n* tritón
new town *n* (Brit) ciudad nueva (construida con subsidios estatales)
New Year *n* Año Nuevo; **Happy** ~! ¡Feliz Año Nuevo!; **to wish sb a happy** ~ desear a algn un feliz año nuevo
New Year's Day *n* Día de Año Nuevo
New Year's Eve *n* Nochevieja
New York [-'jɔ:k] *n* Nueva York
New Zealand [-'zi:lənd] *n* Nueva Zelanda (Esp), Nueva Zelandia (LAm) ▷ *adj* neozelandés(-esa)
New Zealander [-'zi:ləndəʳ] *n* neozelandés(-esa)
next [nɛkst] *adj* (house, room) vecino, de al lado; (meeting) próximo; (page) siguiente ▷ *adv* después; ~ **time** la próxima vez; **the** ~ **time I see you** la próxima vez que te vea; ~ **Saturday** el próximo sábado; ~ **year** el año próximo *or* que viene; ~ **month** el mes que viene *or* entrante; **the week after** ~ no la semana que viene sino la otra; **the** ~ **day** el día siguiente; **"turn to the** ~ **page"** "vuelva a la página siguiente"; ~ **please!** ¡el siguiente, por favor!; **you're** ~ le toca; ~ **to** junto a, al lado de; ~ **to the bank** al lado del banco; ~ **to nothing** casi nada; **what did you do** ~? ¿qué hiciste luego?
next door *adv* en la casa de al lado ▷ *adj* vecino, de al lado; **they live** ~ viven al lado; **the next-door neighbours** los vecinos de al lado
next-of-kin ['nɛkstəv'kɪn] *n* pariente(s) más cercano(s)
NFL *n abbr* (US) = **National Football League**
NHS *n abbr* = **National Health Service**
NI *abbr* = **Northern Ireland**; (Brit) = **National Insurance**
nib [nɪb] *n* plumilla
nibble ['nɪbl] *vt* mordisquear
Nicaragua [nɪkə'rægjuə] *n* Nicaragua
Nicaraguan [nɪkə'rægjuən] *adj, n* nicaragüense, nicaragüeño(-a)
nice [naɪs] *adj* (likeable) simpático, majo; (kind) amable; (pleasant) agradable; (attractive) bonito, mono; (distinction) fino; (taste, smell, meal) rico
nicely ['naɪslɪ] *adv* amablemente; (of health etc) bien; **that will do** ~ perfecto
niceties ['naɪsɪtɪz] *npl* detalles
niche [ni:ʃ] *n* (Arch) nicho, hornacina
nick [nɪk] *n* (wound) rasguño; (cut, indentation) mella, muesca ▷ *vt* (cut) cortar; (col) birlar, mangar; (: arrest) pillar; **in the** ~ **of time** justo a tiempo; **in good** ~ en buen estado; **to** ~ **o.s** cortarse
nickel ['nɪkl] *n* níquel; (US) moneda de 5 centavos
nickname ['nɪkneɪm] *n* apodo, mote ▷ *vt* apodar

nicotine ['nɪkəti:n] *n* nicotina
nicotine patch *n* parche de nicotina
niece [ni:s] *n* sobrina
Nigeria [naɪ'dʒɪərɪə] *n* Nigeria
niggling ['nɪglɪŋ] *adj* (detail: trifling) nimio, insignificante; (annoying) molesto; (doubt, pain) constante
night [naɪt] *n* (gen) noche; (evening) tarde; **last** ~ anoche; **we went to a party last** ~ anoche fuimos a una fiesta; **the** ~ **before last** anteanoche, antes de ayer por la noche; **at** ~, **by** ~ de noche, por la noche; **in the** ~, **during the** ~ durante la noche, por la noche; **good** ~! ¡buenas noches!
nightcap ['naɪtkæp] *n* (drink) bebida que se toma antes de acostarse
night club *n* club nocturno, discoteca
nightdress ['naɪtdrɛs] *n* (Brit) camisón
nightfall ['naɪtfɔ:l] *n* anochecer
nightgown ['naɪtgaun], **nightie** ['naɪtɪ] (Brit) *n* = **nightdress**
nightingale ['naɪtɪŋgeɪl] *n* ruiseñor
night life *n* vida nocturna
nightly ['naɪtlɪ] *adj* de todas las noches ▷ *adv* todas las noches, cada noche
nightmare ['naɪtmɛəʳ] *n* pesadilla
night porter *n* guardián nocturno
night school *n* clase(s) nocturna(s)
night shift *n* turno nocturno *or* de noche
night-time ['naɪttaɪm] *n* noche
night watchman *n* vigilante nocturno, sereno
nil [nɪl] *n* (Brit Sport) cero, nada
Nile [naɪl] *n*: **the** ~ el Nilo
nimble ['nɪmbl] *adj* (agile) ágil, ligero; (skilful) diestro
nine [naɪn] *num* nueve
nineteen ['naɪn'ti:n] *num* diecinueve
nineteenth [naɪn'ti:nθ] *num* decimonoveno, decimonono
ninety ['naɪntɪ] *num* noventa
ninth [naɪnθ] *num* noveno
nip [nɪp] *vt* (pinch) pellizcar; (bite) morder ▷ *vi* (Brit col): **to** ~ **out/down/up** salir/bajar/subir un momento ▷ *n* (drink) trago
nipple ['nɪpl] *n* (Anat) pezón; (of bottle) tetilla; (Tech) boquilla, manguito
nippy ['nɪpɪ] *adj* (Brit: person) rápido; (taste) picante; **it's a very** ~ **car** es un coche muy potente para el tamaño que tiene
nit [nɪt] *n* (of louse) liendre; (col: idiot) imbécil
nitrogen ['naɪtrədʒən] *n* nitrógeno
NM, N.Mex. *abbr* (US) = **New Mexico**
no [nəu] (pl noes) *adv* (opposite of "yes") no; **are you coming?** — **no (I'm not)** ¿vienes? — no; **would you like some more?** — **no thank you** ¿quieres más? — no gracias
▷ *adj* (not any): **I have no money/time/books** no tengo dinero/tiempo/libros; **there's no hot water** no hay agua caliente; **I've got no idea** no tengo ni idea; **I have no questions** no tengo ninguna pregunta; **no other man would have done it** ningún otro lo hubiera hecho; **"no**

entry" "prohibido el paso"; **"no smoking"** "prohibido fumar"; **no way!** ¡ni hablar!
▷ *n* no

no. *abbr* (= *number*) nº, núm.
Nobel prize [nəu'bɛl-] *n* premio Nobel
nobility [nəu'bɪlɪtɪ] *n* nobleza
noble ['nəubl] *adj* (*person*) noble; (*title*) de nobleza
nobody ['nəubədɪ] *pron* nadie
no-claims bonus ['nəukleɪmz-] *n* bonificación por carencia de reclamaciones
nod [nɔd] *vi* saludar con la cabeza; (*in agreement*) asentir con la cabeza ▷ *vt*: **to ~ one's head** inclinar la cabeza ▷ *n* inclinación de cabeza; **they ~ded their agreement** asintieron con la cabeza
  ▶ **nod off** *vi* cabecear
no-fly zone [nəu'flaɪ-] *n* zona de exclusión aérea
noise [nɔɪz] *n* ruido; (*din*) escándalo, estrépito
noisy ['nɔɪzɪ] *adj* (*gen*) ruidoso; (*child*) escandaloso
nominal ['nɔmɪnl] *adj* nominal
nominate ['nɔmɪneɪt] *vt* (*propose*) proponer; (*appoint*) nombrar
nomination [nɔmɪ'neɪʃən] *n* propuesta; nombramiento
nominee [nɔmɪ'niː] *n* candidato(-a)
non... [nɔn] *pref* no, des..., in...
nonalcoholic [nɔnælkə'hɔlɪk] *adj* sin alcohol
noncommittal ['nɔnkə'mɪtl] *adj* (*reserved*) reservado; (*uncommitted*) evasivo
nondescript ['nɔndɪskrɪpt] *adj* anodino, soso
none [nʌn] *pron* ninguno(-a) ▷ *adv* de ninguna manera; **how many sisters have you got? — ~** ¿cuántas hermanas tienes? — ninguna; **~ of you** ninguno de vosotros; **~ of my friends wanted to come** ninguno de mis amigos quiso venir; **I have ~** no tengo ninguno(-a); **I've ~ left** no me queda ninguno(-a); **there are ~ left** no queda ninguno(-a); **there's ~ left** no queda nada; **~ at all** (*not one*) ni uno; **he's ~ the worse for it** no le ha perjudicado
nonentity [nɔ'nɛntɪtɪ] *n* cero a la izquierda, nulidad
nonetheless [nʌnðə'lɛs] *adv* sin embargo, no obstante, aún así
non-event [nɔnɪ'vɛnt] *n* acontecimiento sin importancia; **it was a ~** no pasó absolutamente nada
nonexistent [nɔnɪg'zɪstənt] *adj* inexistente
nonfiction [nɔn'fɪkʃən] *n* no ficción
no-no ['nəunəu] *n* (*col*): **it's a ~** de eso ni hablar
no-nonsense [nəu'nɔnsəns] *adj* sensato
nonplussed [nɔn'plʌst] *adj* perplejo
nonsense ['nɔnsəns] *n* tonterías, disparates; **~!** ¡qué tonterías!; **it is ~ to say that ...** es absurdo decir que ...
nonsensical [nɔn'sɛnsɪkl] *adj* disparatado, absurdo
nonsmoker ['nɔn'sməukəʳ] *n* no fumador(a)
nonstarter [nɔn'stɑːtəʳ] *n*: **it's a ~** no tiene futuro
nonstick ['nɔn'stɪk] *adj* antiadherente
nonstop ['nɔn'stɔp] *adj* continuo; (*Rail*) directo

▷ *adv* sin parar
noodles ['nuːdlz] *npl* tallarines
nook [nuk] *n* rincón; **~s and crannies** escondrijos
noon [nuːn] *n* mediodía
no-one ['nəuwʌn] *pron* = **nobody**
noose [nuːs] *n* lazo corredizo
nor [nɔːʳ] *conj* = **neither** ▷ *adv see* **neither**
norm [nɔːm] *n* norma
normal ['nɔːml] *adj* normal; **to return to ~** volver a la normalidad
normality [nɔː'mælɪtɪ] *n* normalidad
normally ['nɔːməlɪ] *adv* normalmente
Normandy ['nɔːməndɪ] *n* Normandía
north [nɔːθ] *n* norte ▷ *adj* del norte ▷ *adv* al *or* hacia el norte
North Africa *n* África del Norte
North America *n* América del Norte
North American *adj*, *n* norteamericano(-a)
north-east [nɔːθ'iːst] *n* nor(d)este
northerly ['nɔːðəlɪ] *adj* (*point, direction*) hacia el norte, septentrional; (*wind*) del norte
northern ['nɔːðən] *adj* norteño, del norte
Northern Ireland *n* Irlanda del Norte
North Pole *n*: **the ~** el Polo Norte
North Sea *n*: **the ~** el Mar del Norte
North Sea oil *n* petróleo del Mar del Norte
northward(s) ['nɔːθwəd(z)] *adv* hacia el norte
north-west [nɔːθ'wɛst] *n* noroeste
Norway ['nɔːweɪ] *n* Noruega
Norwegian [nɔː'wiːdʒən] *adj* noruego ▷ *n* noruego(-a); (*Ling*) noruego
nos. *abbr* (= *numbers*) núms.
nose [nəuz] *n* (*Anat*) nariz; (*Zool*) hocico; (*sense of smell*) olfato ▷ *vi* (*also*: **nose one's way**) avanzar con cautela; **to pay through the ~ (for sth)** (*col*) pagar un dineral (por algo)
  ▶ **nose about, nose around** *vi* curiosear
nosebleed ['nəuzbliːd] *n* hemorragia nasal
nose-dive ['nəuzdaɪv] *n* picado vertical
nosey ['nəuzɪ] *adj* curioso, fisgón(-ona)
nostalgia [nɔs'tældʒɪə] *n* nostalgia
nostril ['nɔstrɪl] *n* ventana *or* orificio de la nariz
nosy ['nəuzɪ] *adj* = **nosey**
not [nɔt] *adv* no; **I'm ~ sure** no estoy seguro; **are you coming or ~?** ¿vienes o no?; **did you like it? — ~ really** ¿te gustó? — no mucho; **~ at all**, **he's ~ at all selfish** no es nada egoísta; **I don't mind at all** no me importa en absoluto; **thank you very much — ~ at all** muchas gracias — de nada; **~ that...** no es que...; **it's too late, isn't it?** es demasiado tarde, ¿verdad?; **~ yet** todavía no; **they haven't arrived yet** todavía no han llegado; **~ now** ahora no; **why ~?** ¿por qué no?; **I hope ~** espero que no
notable ['nəutəbl] *adj* notable
notably ['nəutəblɪ] *adv* especialmente; (*in particular*) sobre todo
notary ['nəutərɪ] *n* (*also*: **notary public**) notario(-a)
notation [nəu'teɪʃən] *n* notación
notch [nɔtʃ] *n* muesca, corte

▶ **notch up** vt (score, victory) apuntarse

note [nəut] n (Mus, record, letter) nota; (banknote) billete; (tone) tono ▷ vt (observe) notar, observar; (write down) apuntar, anotar; **delivery ~** nota de entrega; **to compare ~s** (fig) cambiar impresiones; **of ~** conocido, destacado; **to take ~s** tomar apuntes; **to take ~ of** (notice) prestar atención a; **just a quick ~ to let you know that** ... sólo unas líneas para informarte que ...

notebook ['nəutbuk] n libreta, cuaderno; (for shorthand) libreta

noted ['nəutɪd] adj célebre, conocido

notepad ['nəutpæd] n bloc

notepaper ['nəutpeɪpə] n papel para cartas

noteworthy ['nəutwə:ðɪ] adj notable, digno de atención

nothing ['nʌθɪŋ] n nada; (zero) cero; **what's wrong? — ~** ¿qué pasa? — nada; **what are you doing tonight? — ~ special** ¿qué haces esta noche? — nada especial; **~ will happen** no pasará nada; **he does ~** no hace nada; **he does ~ but sleep** no hace nada más que dormir; **there's ~ to do** no hay nada que hacer; **~ new** nada nuevo; **for ~** (free) gratis; (in vain) en balde; **~ at all** nada en absoluto

notice ['nəutɪs] n (announcement) anuncio; (physical object) letrero; (dismissal) despido; (resignation) dimisión; (review: of play etc) reseña ▷ vt (perceive) notar; (realize) darse cuenta de; **there's a ~ on the board about the trip** hay un aviso en el tablón sobre el viaje; **there was a ~ outside the house** había un letrero fuera de la casa; **to take ~ of** hacer caso de, prestar atención a; **don't take any ~ of him!** ¡no le hagas caso!; **at short ~** con poca antelación; **without ~** sin previo aviso; **advance ~** previo aviso; **a warning ~** un aviso; **until further ~** hasta nuevo aviso; **to give sb ~ of sth** avisar a algn de algo; **to give ~, hand in one's ~** dimitir, renunciar; **it has come to my ~ that** ... he llegado a saber que ...; **to escape** or **avoid ~** pasar inadvertido; **he won't ~ the mistake** no se dará cuenta del error

noticeable ['nəutɪsəbl] adj evidente, obvio

notice board n (Brit) tablón de anuncios

notification [nəutɪfɪ'keɪʃən] n aviso; (announcement) anuncio

notify ['nəutɪfaɪ] vt: **to ~ sb (of sth)** comunicar (algo) a algn

notion ['nəuʃən] n noción, concepto; (opinion) opinión

notions ['nəuʃənz] npl (US) mercería

notoriety [nəutə'raɪətɪ] n notoriedad, mala fama

notorious [nəu'tɔːrɪəs] adj tristemente célebre; (criminal) muy conocido

notwithstanding [nɔtwɪθ'stændɪŋ] adv no obstante, sin embargo; **~ this** a pesar de esto

nougat ['nuːgaː] n turrón

nought [nɔːt] n cero

noun [naun] n nombre, sustantivo

nourish ['nʌrɪʃ] vt nutrir, alimentar; (fig) fomentar, nutrir

nourishing ['nʌrɪʃɪŋ] adj nutritivo, rico

nourishment ['nʌrɪʃmənt] n alimento, sustento

novel ['nɔvl] n novela ▷ adj (new) nuevo, original; (unexpected) insólito

novelist ['nɔvəlɪst] n novelista

novelty ['nɔvəltɪ] n novedad

November [nəu'vɛmbə] n noviembre

novice ['nɔvɪs] n principiante, novato(-a); (Rel) novicio(-a)

now [nau] adv (at the present time) ahora; (these days) actualmente, hoy día ▷ conj: **~ (that)** ya que, ahora que; **right ~** ahora mismo; **by ~** ya; **it should be ready by ~** ya debería estar listo; **just ~, I'll do it just ~** ahora mismo lo hago; **I'm rather busy just ~** en este momento estoy muy ocupado; **I did it just ~** lo acabo de hacer; **~ and then, ~ and again** de vez en cuando; **from ~ on** de ahora en adelante; **between ~ and Monday** entre hoy y el lunes; **in 3 days from ~** de hoy en 3 días; **that's all for ~** eso es todo por ahora

nowadays ['nauədeɪz] adv hoy (en) día, actualmente

nowhere ['nəuwɛə] adv (direction) a ninguna parte; (location) en ninguna parte; **~ else** en or a ninguna otra parte

no-win situation [nəu'wɪn-] n: **I'm in a ~** haga lo que haga, llevo las de perder

nozzle ['nɔzl] n boquilla

NP n abbr = **notary public**

nth [ɛnθ] adj: **for the ~ time** (col) por enésima vez

nuclear ['njuːklɪə] adj nuclear

nuclear family n familia nuclear

nuclear-free zone ['njuːklɪə'friː-] n zona desnuclearizada

nucleus ['njuːklɪəs] (pl **nuclei**) n núcleo

nude [njuːd] adj, n desnudo(-a); **in the ~** desnudo

nudge [nʌdʒ] vt dar un codazo a

nudist ['njuːdɪst] n nudista

nudity ['njuːdɪtɪ] n desnudez

nuisance ['njuːsns] n molestia, fastidio; (person) pesado, latoso; **what a ~!** ¡qué lata!

null [nʌl] adj: **~ and void** nulo y sin efecto

numb [nʌm] adj entumecido; (fig) insensible ▷ vt quitar la sensación a, entumecer, entorpecer; **to be ~ with cold** estar entumecido de frío; **~ with fear** paralizado de miedo; **~ with grief** paralizado de dolor

number ['nʌmbə] n número; (numeral) número, cifra ▷ vt (pages etc) numerar, poner número a; (amount to) sumar, ascender a; **they live at ~ 5** viven en el número 5; **reference ~** número de referencia; **telephone ~** número de teléfono; **what's your (telephone) ~?** ¿cuál es tu teléfono?; **wrong ~** (Tel) número equivocado; **you've got the wrong ~** se ha equivocado de número; **opposite ~** (person) homólogo(-a); **a ~ of** varios, algunos; **a large ~ of people** un gran número de gente; **they were 10 in ~** eran 10; **to be ~ed among** figurar entre

number plate n (Brit) matrícula, placa

Number Ten n (Brit: 10 Downing Street) residencia del primer ministro; see also **Downing Street**

numbskull ['nʌmskʌl] n (col) papanatas
numeral ['njuːmərəl] n número, cifra
numerate ['njuːmərɪt] adj competente en
aritmética
numerical [njuːˈmɛrɪkl] adj numérico
numerous ['njuːmərəs] adj numerosos, muchos
nun [nʌn] n monja, religiosa
nunnery ['nʌnərɪ] n convento de monjas
nurse [nəːs] n enfermero(-a); (nanny) niñera ▷ vt
(patient) cuidar, atender; (baby: Brit) mecer; (: US)
criar, amamantar; **male ~** enfermero
nursery ['nəːsərɪ] n (institution) guardería
infantil; (room) cuarto de los niños; (for plants)
criadero, semillero
nursery rhyme n canción infantil
nursery school n escuela de preescolar
nursery slope n (Brit Ski) cuesta para
principiantes
nursing ['nəːsɪŋ] n (profession) profesión de
enfermera; (care) asistencia, cuidado ▷ adj
(mother) lactante
nursing home n clínica de reposo
nurture ['nəːtʃəʳ] vt (child, plant) alimentar, nutrir
nut [nʌt] n (Tech) tuerca; (Bot) nuez ▷ adj
(chocolate etc) con nueces; **~s** (Culin) frutos secos
nutcrackers ['nʌtkrækəz] npl cascanueces
nutmeg ['nʌtmɛg] n nuez moscada
nutrition [njuːˈtrɪʃən] n nutrición, alimentación
nutritionist [njuːˈtrɪʃənɪst] n dietista
nutritious [njuːˈtrɪʃəs] adj nutritivo
nuts [nʌts] adj (col) chiflado
nutshell ['nʌtʃɛl] n cáscara de nuez; **in a ~** en
resumidas cuentas
nutty ['nʌtɪ] adj (flavour) a frutos secos; (col:
foolish) chalado
NY abbr (US) = **New York**
nylon ['naɪlɔn] n nylon, nilón ▷ adj de nylon or
nilón

Oo

O, o [əʊ] (*letter*) O, o; **O for Oliver**, (*US*) **O for Oboe** O de Oviedo

oak [əʊk] *n* roble ▷ *adj* de roble

OAP *abbr* = **old-age pensioner**

oar [ɔːʳ] *n* remo; **to put** *or* **shove one's ~ in** (*fig col*) entrometerse

oasis [əʊ'eɪsɪs] [əʊ'eɪsiːz] (*pl* **oases**) *n* oasis

oath [əʊθ] *n* juramento; (*swear word*) palabrota; **on** (*Brit*) *or* **under ~** bajo juramento

oatmeal ['əʊtmiːl] *n* harina de avena

oats [əʊts] *npl* avena

OBE *n abbr* (*Brit*: = *Order of the British Empire*) título ceremonial

obedience [ə'biːdɪəns] *n* obediencia; **in ~ to** de acuerdo con

obedient [ə'biːdɪənt] *adj* obediente

obese [əʊ'biːs] *adj* obeso

obey [ə'beɪ] *vt* obedecer; (*instructions*) cumplir

obituary [ə'bɪtjʊərɪ] *n* necrología

object *n* (*gen*) objeto; (*purpose*) objeto, propósito; (*Ling*) objeto, complemento ▷ *vi*: **to ~ to** (*attitude*) protestar contra; (*proposal*) oponerse a; **expense is no ~** no importan los gastos; **I ~!** ¡protesto!; **to ~ that** objetar que

objection [əb'dʒɛkʃən] *n* objeción; **I have no ~ to ...** no tengo inconveniente en que ....

objectionable [əb'dʒɛkʃənəbl] *adj* (*gen*) desagradable; (*conduct*) censurable

objective [əb'dʒɛktɪv] *adj*, *n* objetivo

obligation [ɔblɪ'geɪʃən] *n* obligación; (*debt*) deber; **"without ~"** "sin compromiso"; **to be under an ~ to sb/to do sth** estar comprometido con algn/a hacer algo

oblige [ə'blaɪdʒ] *vt* (*do a favour for*) complacer, hacer un favor a; **to ~ sb to do sth** obligar a algn a hacer algo; **to be ~d to sb for sth** estarle agradecido a algn por algo; **anything to ~!** (*col*) todo sea por complacerte

obliging [ə'blaɪdʒɪŋ] *adj* servicial, atento

oblique [ə'bliːk] *adj* oblicuo; (*allusion*) indirecto ▷ *n* (*Typ*) barra

obliterate [ə'blɪtəreɪt] *vt* arrasar; (*memory*) borrar

oblivion [ə'blɪvɪən] *n* olvido

oblivious [ə'blɪvɪəs] *adj*: **~ of** inconsciente de

oblong ['ɔblɔŋ] *adj* rectangular ▷ *n* rectángulo

obnoxious [əb'nɔkʃəs] *adj* odioso, detestable; (*smell*) nauseabundo

oboe ['əʊbəʊ] *n* oboe

obscene [əb'siːn] *adj* obsceno

obscenity [əb'sɛnɪtɪ] *n* obscenidad

obscure [əb'skjʊəʳ] *adj* oscuro ▷ *vt* oscurecer; (*hide: sun*) ocultar

obscurity [əb'skjʊərɪtɪ] *n* oscuridad; (*obscure point*) punto oscuro; **to rise from ~** salir de la nada

observant [əb'zɜːvnt] *adj* observador(a)

observation [ɔbzə'veɪʃən] *n* (*also Med*) observación; (*by police etc*) vigilancia

observatory [əb'zɜːvətrɪ] *n* observatorio

observe [əb'zɜːv] *vt* (*gen*) observar; (*rule*) cumplir

observer [əb'zɜːvəʳ] *n* observador(a)

obsess [əb'sɛs] *vt* obsesionar; **to be ~ed by** *or* **with sb/sth** estar obsesionado con algn/algo

obsession [əb'sɛʃən] *n* obsesión

obsessive [əb'sɛsɪv] *adj* obsesivo

obsolescence [ɔbsə'lɛsns] *n* obsolescencia

obsolete ['ɔbsəliːt] *adj* obsoleto

obstacle ['ɔbstəkl] *n* obstáculo; (*nuisance*) estorbo

obstacle race *n* carrera de obstáculos

obstetrician [ɔbstə'trɪʃən] *n* obstetra

obstinate ['ɔbstɪnɪt] *adj* terco, obstinado; (*determined*) tenaz

obstruct [əb'strʌkt] *vt* (*block*) obstruir; (*hinder*) estorbar, obstaculizar

obstruction [əb'strʌkʃən] *n* obstrucción; estorbo, obstáculo

obtain [əb'teɪn] *vt* (*get*) obtener; (*achieve*) conseguir; **to ~ sth (for o.s.)** conseguir *or* adquirir algo

obtainable [əb'teɪnəbl] *adj* asequible

obtuse [əb'tjuːs] *adj* obtuso

obvious ['ɔbvɪəs] *adj* (*clear*) obvio, evidente; (*unsubtle*) poco sutil; **it's ~ that ...** está claro que ..., es evidente que ...

obviously ['ɔbvɪəslɪ] *adv* obviamente, evidentemente; **~ not!** ¡por supuesto que no!; **he was ~ not drunk** era evidente que no estaba borracho; **he was not ~ drunk** no se le notaba que estaba borracho

occasion [ə'keɪʒən] *n* oportunidad, ocasión; (*event*) acontecimiento ▷ *vt* ocasionar, causar; **on that ~** esa vez, en aquella ocasión; **to rise to the ~** ponerse a la altura de las circunstancias

occasional [ə'keɪʒənl] *adj* poco frecuente,

ocasional

occasionally [ə'keɪʒənlɪ] *adv* de vez en cuando; **very ~** muy de tarde en tarde, en muy contadas ocasiones

occult [ɔ'kʌlt] *adj* (*gen*) oculto

occupant ['ɔkjupənt] *n* (*of house*) inquilino(-a); (*of boat, car*) ocupante

occupation [ɔkju'peɪʃən] *n* (*of house*) tenencia; (*job*) trabajo; (*calling*) oficio

occupational hazard *n* gajes del oficio

occupier ['ɔkjupaɪər] *n* inquilino(-a)

occupy ['ɔkjupaɪ] *vt* (*seat, post, time*) ocupar; (*house*) habitar; **to ~ o.s. with** *or* **by doing** (*as job*) dedicarse a hacer; (*to pass time*) entretenerse haciendo; **to be occupied with sth/in doing sth** estar ocupado con algo/haciendo algo

occur [ə'kəːr] *vi* ocurrir, suceder; **to ~ to sb** ocurrírsele a algn

occurrence [ə'kʌrəns] *n* suceso

ocean ['əuʃən] *n* océano; **~s of** (*col*) la mar de

ocean-going ['əuʃəngəuɪŋ] *adj* de alta mar

o'clock [ə'klɔk] *adv*: **it is 5 o'clock** son las 5

OCR *n abbr* = **optical character recognition/reader**

octane ['ɔkteɪn] *n* octano; **high ~ petrol** *or* (*US*) **gas** gasolina de alto octanaje

octave ['ɔktɪv] *n* octava

October [ɔk'təubər] *n* octubre

octopus ['ɔktəpəs] *n* pulpo

odd [ɔd] *adj* (*strange*) extraño, raro; (*number*) impar; (*left over*) sobrante, suelto; **60-~** 60 y pico; **at ~ times** de vez en cuando; **to be the ~ one out** estar de más; **if you have the ~ minute** si tienes unos minutos libres; *see also* **odds**

oddity ['ɔdɪtɪ] *n* rareza; (*person*) excéntrico(-a)

odd-job man [ɔd'dʒɔb-] *n* hombre que hace chapuzas

odd jobs *npl* chapuzas

oddly ['ɔdlɪ] *adv* extrañamente

oddments ['ɔdmənts] *npl* (*Brit Comm*) restos

odds [ɔdz] *npl* (*in betting*) puntos de ventaja; **it makes no ~** da lo mismo; **at ~** reñidos(-as); **to succeed against all the ~** tener éxito contra todo pronóstico; **~ and ends** cachivaches

odds-on [ɔdz'ɔn] *adj* (*col*): **the ~ favourite** el máximo favorito; **it's ~ he'll come** seguro que viene

odometer [ɔ'dɔmɪtər] *n* (*US*) cuentakilómetros

odour, (*US*) **odor** ['əudər] *n* olor; (*perfume*) perfume

oesophagus, (*US*) **esophagus** [iː'sɔfəgəs] *n* esófago

oestrogen, (*US*) **estrogen** ['iːstrədʒən] *n* estrógeno

of [ɔv, əv] *prep* **1** (*gen*) de; **the wheels of the car** las ruedas del coche; **a friend of ours** un amigo nuestro; **a boy of 10** un chico de 10 años; **that was kind of you** eso fue muy amable de tu parte **2** (*expressing quantity, amount, dates etc*) de; **a kilo of flour** un kilo de harina; **there were 3 of them** había 3; **3 of us went** 3 de nosotros fuimos; **the 5th of July** el 5 de julio; **a quarter of 4** (*US*) las 4

menos cuarto **3** (*from, out of*) de; **made of wood** (hecho) de madera

off [ɔf] *adj, adv* (*engine, light*) apagado; (*tap*) cerrado; (*Brit: food: bad*) pasado, malo; (: *milk*) cortado; (*cancelled*) suspendido; (*removed*): **the lid was ~** no estaba puesta la tapadera ▷ *prep* de; **all the lights are ~** todas las luces están apagadas; **are you sure the tap is ~?** ¿seguro que el grifo está cerrado?; **the match is ~** el partido se ha suspendido; **to be ~** (*leave*) irse, marcharse; **I must be ~** tengo que irme; **I'm ~ me voy**; **to be ~ sick** estar enfermo *or* de baja; **a day ~** un día libre; **she took a day ~ work to go to the wedding** se tomó un día libre para ir a la boda; **I've got tomorrow ~** mañana tengo el día libre; **she's ~ school today** hoy no ha ido al colegio; **to have an ~ day** tener un mal día; **he had his coat ~** se había quitado el abrigo; **10% ~** (*Comm*) (con el) 10% de descuento; **it's a long way ~** está muy lejos; **5 km ~ (the road)** a 5 km (de la carretera); **~ the coast** frente a la costa; **I'm ~ meat** (*no longer eat/like it*) paso de la carne; **on the ~ chance** por si acaso; **~ and on, on and ~** de vez en cuando; **to be well/badly ~** andar bien/mal de dinero; **I'm afraid the chicken is ~** (*finished*) desgraciadamente ya no queda pollo; **that's a bit ~, isn't it?** (*fig, col*) ¡eso no se hace!

offal ['ɔfl] *n* (*Brit Culin*) menudillos, asaduras

off-colour ['ɔf'kʌlər] *adj* (*Brit: ill*) indispuesto; **to feel ~** sentirse *or* estar mal

offence, (*US*) **offense** [ə'fɛns] *n* (*crime*) delito; (*insult*) ofensa; **to take ~ at** ofenderse por; **to commit an ~** cometer un delito

offend [ə'fɛnd] *vt* (*person*) ofender ▷ *vi*: **to ~ against** (*law, rule*) infringir

offender [ə'fɛndər] *n* delincuente; (*against regulations*) infractor(a)

offense [ə'fɛns] *n* (*US*) = **offence**

offensive [ə'fɛnsɪv] *adj* ofensivo; (*smell etc*) repugnante ▷ *n* (*Mil*) ofensiva

offer ['ɔfər] *n* (*gen*) oferta, ofrecimiento; (*proposal*) propuesta ▷ *vt* ofrecer; **"on ~"** (*Comm*) "en oferta"; **to make an ~ for sth** hacer una oferta por algo; **to ~ sth to sb, ~ sb sth** ofrecer algo a algn; **to ~ to do sth** ofrecerse a hacer algo

offering ['ɔfərɪŋ] *n* (*Rel*) ofrenda

offertory ['ɔfətrɪ] *n* (*Rel*) ofertorio

offhand [ɔf'hænd] *adj* informal; (*brusque*) desconsiderado ▷ *adv* de improviso, sin pensarlo; **I can't tell you ~** no te lo puedo decir así de improviso *or* (*LAm*) así nomás

office ['ɔfɪs] *n* (*place*) oficina; (*room*) despacho; (*position*) cargo, oficio; **doctor's ~** (*US*) consultorio; **to take ~** entrar en funciones; **through his good ~s** gracias a sus buenos oficios; **O~ of Fair Trading** (*Brit*) oficina que regula normas comerciales

office automation *n* ofimática, buromática

office block, (*US*) **office building** *n* bloque de oficinas

office hours *npl* horas de oficina; (*US Med*) horas

de consulta

officer ['ɔfɪsə^r] n (Mil etc) oficial; (of organization) director(a); (also: **police officer**) agente de policía

office work n trabajo de oficina

office worker n oficinista

official [ə'fɪʃl] adj (authorized) oficial, autorizado; (strike) oficial ▷ n funcionario(-a)

officialdom [ə'fɪʃldəm] n burocracia

officiate [ə'fɪʃieɪt] vi (Rel) oficiar; **to ~ as Mayor** ejercer las funciones de alcalde; **to ~ at a marriage** celebrar una boda

officious [ə'fɪʃəs] adj oficioso

offing ['ɔfɪŋ] n: **in the ~** (fig) en perspectiva

off-licence ['ɔflaɪsns] n (Brit: shop) tienda de bebidas alcohólicas

off line adj, adv (Comput) fuera de línea; (switched off) desconectado

off-load ['ɔfləud] vt descargar, desembarcar

off-peak ['ɔf'piːk] adj (holiday) de temporada baja; (electricity) de banda económica

off-putting ['ɔfputɪŋ] adj (Brit: person) poco amable, difícil; (behaviour) chocante

off-season ['ɔf'siːzn] adj, adv fuera de temporada

offset ['ɔfsɛt] vt (irreg: like **set**); (counteract) contrarrestar, compensar ▷ n (also: **offset printing**) offset

offshoot ['ɔfʃuːt] n (Bot) vástago; (fig) ramificación

offshore [ɔf'ʃɔː^r] adj (breeze, island) costero; (fishing) de bajura; **~ oilfield** campo petrolífero submarino

offside ['ɔf'saɪd] n (Aut: with right-hand drive) lado derecho; (: with left-hand drive) lado izquierdo ▷ adj (Sport) fuera de juego; (Aut) del lado derecho; del lado izquierdo

offspring ['ɔfsprɪŋ] n descendencia

offstage [ɔf'steɪdʒ] adv entre bastidores

off-the-cuff [ɔfðə'kʌf] adj espontáneo

off-the-peg [ɔfðə'pɛg], (US) **off-the-rack** [ɔfðə'ræk] adv confeccionado

off-the-record ['ɔfðə'rɛkɔːd] adj extraoficial, confidencial ▷ adv extraoficialmente, confidencialmente

off-white ['ɔfwaɪt] adj blanco grisáceo

often ['ɔfn] adv a menudo, con frecuencia, seguido (LAm); **how ~ do you go?** ¿cada cuánto vas?

ogle ['əugl] vt comerse con los ojos a

oh [əu] excl ¡ah!

oil [ɔɪl] n aceite; (petroleum) petróleo ▷ vt (machine) engrasar; **fried in ~** frito en aceite

oilcan ['ɔɪlkæn] n lata de aceite

oilfield ['ɔɪlfiːld] n campo petrolífero

oil filter n (Aut) filtro de aceite

oil painting n pintura al óleo

oil refinery n refinería de petróleo

oil rig n torre de perforación

oilskins ['ɔɪlskɪnz] npl impermeable, chubasquero

oil tanker n petrolero

oil well n pozo (de petróleo)

oily ['ɔɪlɪ] adj aceitoso; (food) grasiento

ointment ['ɔɪntmənt] n ungüento

O.K, okay [əu'keɪ] excl O.K., ¡está bien!, ¡vale! ▷ adj bien ▷ n: **to give sth one's okay** dar el visto bueno a or aprobar algo ▷ vt dar el visto bueno a; **it's okay with** or **by me** estoy de acuerdo, me parece bien, are you okay for money? ¿andas or vas bien de dinero?

old [əuld] adj viejo; (former) antiguo; **an ~ house** una casa vieja; **~ people** los ancianos; **how ~ are you?** ¿cuántos años tienes?, ¿qué edad tienes?; **how ~ is the baby?** ¿cuánto tiempo tiene el bebé?; **he's 10 years ~** tiene 10 años; **a 20-year-~ woman** una mujer de 20 años; **~er brother** hermano mayor; **she's 2 years ~er than me** es 2 años mayor que yo; **I'm the ~est in the family** soy el mayor de la familia; **any~thing will do** sirve cualquier cosa; **my ~ English teacher** mi antiguo profesor de inglés

old age n vejez

old-age pension ['əuldeɪdʒ-] n (Brit) jubilación, pensión

old-age pensioner ['əuldeɪdʒ-] n (Brit) jubilado(-a)

old-fashioned ['əuld'fæʃənd] adj anticuado, pasado de moda

olive ['ɔlɪv] n (fruit) aceituna; (tree) olivo ▷ adj (also: **olive-green**) verde oliva

olive oil n aceite de oliva

Olympic [əu'lɪmpɪk] adj olímpico; **the ~ Games, the ~s** npl las Olimpíadas

omelet(te) ['ɔmlɪt] n tortilla, tortilla de huevo (LAm)

omen ['əumən] n presagio

ominous ['ɔmɪnəs] adj de mal agüero, amenazador(a)

omission [əu'mɪʃən] n omisión; (error) descuido

omit [əu'mɪt] vt omitir; (by mistake) olvidar, descuidar; **to ~ to do sth** olvidarse or dejar de hacer algo

on [ɔn] prep **1** (indicating position) en; sobre; **on the wall** en la pared; **it's on the table** está sobre or en la mesa; **on the left** a la izquierda; **I haven't got any money on me** no llevo dinero encima

2 (indicating means, method, condition etc): **on foot** a pie; **it's about 10 minutes on foot** está a unos 10 minutos andando; **on the train/plane** (go) en tren/avión; (be) en el tren/el avión; **on the radio/television** por or en la radio/televisión; **on the telephone** al teléfono; **to be on drugs** drogarse; (Med) estar a tratamiento; **she was on antibiotics for a week** estuvo una semana tomando antibióticos; **to be on holiday/business** estar de vacaciones/en viaje de negocios; **we're on irregular verbs** estamos con los verbos irregulares

3 (referring to time): **on Friday** el viernes; **on Fridays** los viernes; **on June 20th** el 20 de junio; **a week on Friday** del viernes en una semana; **on arrival** al llegar; **on seeing this** al ver esto

4 (about, concerning) sobre, acerca de; **a book on physics** un libro de or sobre física

5 (at the expense of): **this round's on me** esta

ronda la pago yo, invito yo a esta ronda; **the coffee is on the house** al café invita la casa
6 (*earning*): **he's on £16,000 a year** gana 16 mil libras al año
▷ *adv* **1** (*referring to dress*): **to have one's coat on** tener *or* llevar el abrigo puesto; **she put her gloves on** se puso los guantes
2 (*referring to covering*): **"screw the lid on tightly"** "cerrar bien la tapa"
3 (*further, continuously*): **to walk/run** *etc* **on** seguir caminando/corriendo *etc*; **from that day on** desde aquel día; **it was well on in the evening** estaba ya entrada la tarde
4 (*in phrases*): **I'm on to something** creo haber encontrado algo; **my father's always on at me to get a job** (*col*) mi padre siempre me está dando la lata para que me ponga a trabajar; **what is he on about?** ¿de qué está hablando?
▷ *adj* **1** (*functioning, in operation: machine, radio, TV, light*) encendido(-a) (*Esp*), prendido(-a) (*LAm*); (: *tap*) abierto(-a); (: *brakes*) echado(-a), puesto(-a); **I think I left the light on** me parece que he dejado la luz encendida; **is the dishwasher on?** ¿está en marcha el lavavajillas?; **is the meeting still on?** (*in progress*) ¿todavía continúa la reunión?; (*not cancelled*) ¿va a haber reunión al fin?; **there's a good film on at the cinema** ponen una buena película en el cine
2 (*in phrases*): **that's not on!** (*col: not possible*) ¡eso ni hablar!; (: *not acceptable*) ¡eso no se hace!; **I've got a lot on this weekend** tengo mucho que hacer este fin de semana; *see also* **go; put; turn** *etc*

once [wʌns] *adv* una vez; (*formerly*) antiguamente ▷ *conj* una vez que; **at ~** en seguida, inmediatamente; (*simultaneously*) a la vez; **~ a week** una vez a la semana; **~ more** otra vez; **~ in a while** de vez en cuando; **~ and for all** de una vez por todas; **~ upon a time** érase una vez; **I knew him ~** le conocía hace tiempo; **I've been to Italy ~ before** ya he estado una vez en Italia; **~ he had left/it was done** una vez que se había marchado/se hizo

oncoming ['ɔnkʌmɪŋ] *adj* (*traffic*) que viene de frente

one [wʌn] *num* un(o)/una; **~ hundred and fifty** ciento cincuenta; **~ by ~** uno a uno; **it's ~ (o'clock)** es la una
▷ *adj* **1** (*sole*) único; **the ~ book which ...** el único libro que ...; **the ~ man who ...** el único que ...
2 (*same*) mismo(-a); **they came in the ~ car** vinieron en un solo coche
▷ *pron* **1**: **this ~** éste (ésta); **that ~** ése (ésa); (*more remote*) aquél (aquélla); **I've already got (a red) ~** ya tengo uno(-a) (rojo(-a)); **~ by ~** uno(-a) por uno(-a); **to be ~ up on sb** llevar ventaja a algn; **to be at ~ (with sb)** estar completamente de acuerdo (con algn)
2: **~ another** (*us*) nos; (*you*) os (*Esp*); (*you: polite, them*) se; **do you two ever see ~ another?** ¿os veis alguna vez? (*Esp*), ¿se ven alguna vez?; **the two boys didn't dare look at ~ another** los dos chicos no se atrevieron a mirarse (el uno

al otro); **they all kissed ~ another** se besaron unos a otros
3 (*impers*): **~ never knows** nunca se sabe; **to cut ~'s finger** cortarse el dedo; **~ needs to eat** hay que comer

one-day excursion ['wʌndeɪ-] *n* (*US*) billete de ida y vuelta en un día

one-man ['wʌn'mæn] *adj* (*business*) individual

one-man band *n* hombre-orquesta

one-off [wʌn'ɔf] *n* (*Brit col: object*) artículo único; (: *event*) caso especial

one-parent family ['wʌnpɛərənt-] *n* familia monoparental

oneself [wʌn'sɛlf] *pron* uno mismo; (*after prep, also emphatic*) sí (mismo(-a)); **to do sth by ~** hacer algo solo *or* por sí solo

one-sided [wʌn'saɪdɪd] *adj* (*argument*) parcial; (*decision, view*) unilateral; (*game, contest*) desigual

one-to-one ['wʌntəwʌn] *adj* (*relationship*) individualizado

one-upmanship [wʌn'ʌpmənʃɪp] *n*: **the art of ~** el arte de quedar siempre por encima

one-way ['wʌnweɪ] *adj* (*street, traffic*) de dirección única; (*ticket*) sencillo

ongoing ['ɔngəʊɪŋ] *adj* continuo

onion ['ʌnjən] *n* cebolla

on line *adj, adv* (*Comput*) en línea; (*switched on*) conectado

onlooker ['ɔnlʊkəʳ] *n* espectador(a)

only ['əʊnlɪ] *adv* solamente, sólo, nomás (*LAm*)
▷ *adj* único ▷ *conj* solamente que, pero; **how much was it? — ~ £10** ¿cuánto valía? — sólo 10 libras; **it's ~ a game!** ¡es sólo un juego!; **not ~ ... but also...** no sólo ... sino también...; **I'd be ~ too pleased to help** encantado de ayudarles; **I saw her ~ yesterday** la vi ayer mismo; **an ~ child** un hijo único; **Monday is the ~ day I'm free** el lunes es el único día que tengo libre; **I would come, ~ I'm very busy** iría, sólo que estoy muy atareado; **I'd like the same sweater, ~ in black** quería el mismo jersey, pero en negro

ono *abbr* = **or nearest offer**; (*in classified ads*) abierto ofertas

onset ['ɔnsɛt] *n* comienzo

onshore ['ɔnʃɔːʳ] *adj* (*wind*) que sopla del mar hacia la tierra

onslaught ['ɔnslɔːt] *n* ataque, embestida

onto ['ɔntu] *prep* = **on to**

onus ['əʊnəs] *n* responsabilidad; **the ~ is upon him to prove it** le incumbe a él demostrarlo

onward(s) ['ɔnwəd(z)] *adv* (*move*) (hacia) adelante

oops [ups] *excl* (*also*: **oops-a-daisy!**) ¡huy!

ooze [uːz] *vi* rezumar

opaque [əu'peɪk] *adj* opaco

OPEC ['əupɛk] *n abbr* (= *Organization of Petroleum-Exporting Countries*) OPEP

open ['əupn] *adj* abierto; (*car*) descubierto; (*road, view*) despejado; (*meeting*) público; (*admiration*) manifiesto ▷ *vt* abrir ▷ *vi* (*flower, eyes, door, debate*) abrirse; (*book etc: commence*) comenzar; **in the ~ (air)** al aire libre; **~ verdict** veredicto inconcluso

~ ticket billete sin fecha; **~ ground** (*among trees*) claro; (*waste ground*) solar; **to have an ~ mind** (**on sth**) estar sin decidirse aún (sobre algo); **the shop's ~ on Sunday mornings** la tienda está abierta los domingos por la mañana; **are you ~ tomorrow?** ¿abre mañana?; **to ~ a bank account** abrir una cuenta en el banco; **can I ~ the window?** ¿puedo abrir la ventana?; **what time do the shops ~?** ¿a qué hora abren las tiendas?; **the door ~s automatically** la puerta se abre automáticamente

▶ **open on to** *vt fus* (*subj: room, door*) dar a
▶ **open out** *vt* abrir ▷ *vi* (*person*) abrirse
▶ **open up** *vt* abrir; (*blocked road*) despejar ▷ *vi* abrirse

open day *n* (*Brit*) jornada de puertas abiertas *or* acceso público

opening ['əupnɪŋ] *n* abertura; (*beginning*) comienzo; (*opportunity*) oportunidad; (*job*) puesto vacante, vacante

open learning *n* enseñanza flexible a tiempo parcial

openly ['əupnlɪ] *adv* abiertamente

open-minded [əupn'maɪndɪd] *adj* de amplias miras, sin prejuicios

open-necked ['əupnnɛkt] *adj* sin corbata

open-plan ['əupn'plæn] *adj* sin tabiques, de plan abierto

open prison *n* centro penitenciario de régimen abierto

Open University *n* (*Brit*) ≈ Universidad Nacional de Enseñanza a Distancia, UNED

opera ['ɔpərə] *n* ópera

opera house *n* teatro de la ópera

opera singer *n* cantante de ópera

operate ['ɔpəreɪt] *vt* (*machine*) hacer funcionar; (*company*) dirigir ▷ *vi* funcionar; (*drug*) actuar; **to ~ on sb** (*Med*) operar a algn

operatic [ɔpə'rætɪk] *adj* de ópera

operating room *n* (*US*) quirófano, sala de operaciones

operating table *n* mesa de operaciones

operating theatre *n* quirófano, sala de operaciones

operation [ɔpə'reɪʃən] *n* (*gen*) operación; (*of machine*) funcionamiento; **to be in ~** estar funcionando *or* en funcionamiento; **to have an ~** (*Med*) ser operado; **to have an ~ for** operarse de; **the company's ~s during the year** las actividades de la compañía durante el año

operative ['ɔpərətɪv] *adj* (*measure*) en vigor; **the ~ word** la palabra clave

operator ['ɔpəreɪtər] *n* (*of machine*) operario(-a); (*Tel*) operador(a), telefonista

opinion [ə'pɪnjən] *n* (*gen*) opinión; **in my ~** en mi opinión, a mi juicio; **to seek a second ~** pedir una segunda opinión

opinionated [ə'pɪnjənetɪd] *adj* testarudo

opinion poll *n* encuesta, sondeo

opponent [ə'pəunənt] *n* adversario(-a), contrincante

opportune ['ɔpətjuːn] *adj* oportuno

opportunity [ɔpə'tjuːnɪtɪ] *n* oportunidad,

chance (*LAm*); **to take the ~ to do** *or* **of doing** aprovechar la ocasión para hacer

oppose [ə'pəuz] *vt* oponerse a; **to be ~d to sth** oponerse a algo; **as ~d to** en vez de; (*unlike*) a diferencia de

opposing [ə'pəuzɪŋ] *adj* (*side*) opuesto, contrario

opposite ['ɔpəzɪt] *adj* opuesto, contrario; (*house etc*) de enfrente ▷ *adv* en frente ▷ *prep* en frente de, frente a ▷ *n* lo contrario; **the ~ sex** el otro sexo, el sexo opuesto

opposite number *n* (*Brit*) homólogo(-a)

opposition [ɔpə'zɪʃən] *n* oposición

oppress [ə'pres] *vt* oprimir

oppression [ə'preʃən] *n* opresión

oppressive [ə'presɪv] *adj* opresivo

opt [ɔpt] *vi*: **to ~ for** optar por; **to ~ to do** optar por hacer; **to ~ out** (*of NHS etc*) salirse

optical ['ɔptɪkl] *adj* óptico

optical character recognition/reader (OCR) *n* reconocimiento/lector óptico de caracteres

optician [ɔp'tɪʃən] *n* óptico

optimism ['ɔptɪmɪzəm] *n* optimismo

optimist ['ɔptɪmɪst] *n* optimista

optimistic [ɔptɪ'mɪstɪk] *adj* optimista

optimum ['ɔptɪməm] *adj* óptimo

option ['ɔpʃən] *n* opción; **to keep one's ~s open** (*fig*) mantener las opciones abiertas; **I have no ~** no tengo más *or* otro remedio

optional ['ɔpʃənl] *adj* opcional; (*course*) optativo; **~ extras** opciones extras

or [ɔːr] *conj* o; (*before o, ho*) u; (*with negative*) ni; **would you like tea or coffee?** ¿quieres té o café?; **six or eight** seis u ocho; **men or women** mujeres u hombres; **or else** si no; **let me go or I'll scream!** ¡suélteme, o me pongo a gritar!; **hurry up or you'll miss the bus** date prisa, que vas a perder el autobús; **he hasn't seen or heard anything** no ha visto ni oído nada; **I don't eat meat or fish** no como carne ni pescado

oral ['ɔːrəl] *adj* oral ▷ *n* examen oral

orange ['ɔrɪndʒ] *n* (*fruit*) naranja ▷ *adj* (*de color*) naranja

orator ['ɔrətər] *n* orador(a)

orbit ['ɔːbɪt] *n* órbita ▷ *vt, vi* orbitar; **to be in/go into ~ (round)** estar en/entrar en órbita (alrededor de)

orbital ['ɔːbɪtl] *n* (*also:* **orbital motorway**) autopista de circunvalación

orchard ['ɔːtʃəd] *n* huerto; **apple ~** manzanar, manzanal

orchestra ['ɔːkɪstrə] *n* orquesta; (*US: seating*) platea

orchid ['ɔːkɪd] *n* orquídea

ordain [ɔː'deɪn] *vt* (*Rel*) ordenar

ordeal [ɔː'diːl] *n* experiencia terrible

order ['ɔːdər] *n* (*arrangement*) orden; (*command*) orden; (*type, kind*) clase; (*state*) estado; (*Comm*) pedido, encargo ▷ *vt* (*also:* **put in order**) ordenar, poner en orden; (*Comm*) encargar, pedir; (*command*) mandar, ordenar; **in ~** (*gen*) en orden; (*document*) en regla; **in alphabetical ~** por orden

alfabético; **in (working)** ~ en funcionamiento;
a machine in working ~ una máquina en
funcionamiento; **to be out of** ~ *(machine, toilets)*
estar estropeado *or (LAm)* descompuesto; **"out
of ~"** "no funciona"; **to obey an** ~ obedecer una
orden; **we are under ~s to do it** tenemos orden
de hacerlo; **in** ~ **to** para; **he does it in** ~ **to earn
money** lo hace para ganar dinero; **in** ~ **that**
para que; **on** ~ *(Comm)* pedido; **to be on** ~ estar
pedido; **to place an** ~ **for sth with sb** hacer
un pedido de algo a algn; **made to** ~ hecho a la
medida; **his income is of the** ~ **of £24,000 per
year** sus ingresos son del orden de 24 mil libras
al año; **to the** ~ **of** *(Banking)* a la orden de; **a
point of** ~ una cuestión de procedimiento; **to** ~
sb to do sth mandar a algn hacer algo
▶ **order about** *vt* dar órdenes a; **she was fed up
with being ~ed about** estaba harta de que le
dieran órdenes
order form *n* hoja de pedido
orderly ['ɔːdəlɪ] *n (Mil)* ordenanza; *(Med)* auxiliar
(de hospital) ▷ *adj* ordenado
ordinary ['ɔːdnrɪ] *adj* corriente, normal; *(pej)*
común y corriente; **out of the** ~ fuera de lo
común, extraordinario
ordinary degree *n (Brit)* diploma
ordination [ɔːdɪ'neɪʃən] *n* ordenación
Ordnance Survey *n (Brit) servicio oficial de
topografía y cartografía*
ore [ɔːʳ] *n* mineral
organ ['ɔːgən] *n* órgano
organic [ɔː'gænɪk] *adj* orgánico; *(vegetables,
produce)* biológico
organism ['ɔːgənɪzəm] *n* organismo
organist ['ɔːgənɪst] *n* organista
organization [ɔːgənaɪ'zeɪʃən] *n* organización
organize ['ɔːgənaɪz] *vt* organizar; **to get ~d**
organizarse
organized crime *n* crimen organizado
organizer ['ɔːgənaɪzəʳ] *n* organizador(-a)
orgasm ['ɔːgæzəm] *n* orgasmo
Orient ['ɔːrɪənt] *n* Oriente
oriental [ɔːrɪ'entl] *adj* oriental
origin ['ɔrɪdʒɪn] *n* origen; *(point of departure)*
procedencia
original [ə'rɪdʒɪnl] *adj* original; *(first)* primero;
(earlier) primitivo ▷ *n* original
originality [ərɪdʒɪ'nælɪtɪ] *n* originalidad
originally [ə'rɪdʒɪnəlɪ] *adv (at first)* al principio;
(with originality) con originalidad
originate [ə'rɪdʒɪneɪt] *vi*: **to** ~ **from**, ~ **in** surgir
de, tener su origen en
Orkneys ['ɔːknɪz] *npl*: **the** ~ *(also:* **the Orkney
Islands)** las Orcadas
ornament ['ɔːnəmənt] *n* adorno
ornamental [ɔːnə'mentl] *adj* decorativo, de
adorno
ornate [ɔː'neɪt] *adj* recargado
ornithology [ɔːnɪ'θɔlədʒɪ] *n* ornitología
orphan ['ɔːfn] *n* huérfano(-a) ▷ *vt*: **to be ~ed**
quedar huérfano(-a)
orphanage ['ɔːfənɪdʒ] *n* orfanato

orthodox ['ɔːθədɔks] *adj* ortodoxo
orthopaedic, *(US)* **orthopedic** [ɔːθə'piːdɪk] *adj*
ortopédico
Oscar ['ɔskəʳ] *n* óscar
ostensible [ɔs'tɛnsɪbl] *adj* aparente
ostensibly [ɔs'tɛnsɪblɪ] *adv* aparentemente
ostentatious [ɔstɛn'teɪʃəs] *adj* pretencioso,
aparatoso; *(person)* ostentativo
osteopath ['ɔstɪəpæθ] *n* osteópata
ostracize ['ɔstrəsaɪz] *vt* hacer el vacío a
ostrich ['ɔstrɪtʃ] *n* avestruz
other ['ʌðəʳ] *adj* otro ▷ *pron*: **the ~s** *(other people)*
los otros (las otras), los demás (las demás) ▷ *adv*
~ **than** *(apart from)* aparte de; **the** ~ **one** el otro (la
otra); **the** ~ **day** el otro día; **on the** ~ **side of the
street** al otro lado de la calle; **some** ~ **people
have still to arrive** quedan por llegar otros;
some actor or ~ un actor cualquiera
otherwise ['ʌðəwaɪz] *adv, conj* de otra manera;
(not) si no; **an** ~ **good piece of work** un trabajo
que, quitando eso, es bueno
OTT *abbr (col)* = **over the top;** *see* **top**
otter ['ɔtəʳ] *n* nutria
ouch [autʃ] *excl* ¡ay!
ought [ɔːt] *(pt* ~) *aux vb*: **I** ~ **to do it** debería
hacerlo; **you** ~ **not to do that** no deberías
hacer eso; **you** ~ **to have warned me** me
deberías haber avisado; **he** ~ **to have known**
debía saberlo; **this** ~ **to have been corrected**
esto debiera de haberse corregido; **he** ~ **to win**
(probability) debiera ganar; **you** ~ **to go and see** it
vale la pena ir a verlo
ounce [auns] *n* onza *(28.35g)*
our ['auəʳ] *adj* nuestro; *see also* **my**
ours ['auəz] *pron* (el) nuestro/(la) nuestra *etc; see
also* **mine**
ourselves [auə'sɛlvz] *pron pl (reflexive, after prep)*
nosotros; *(emphatic)* nosotros mismos; **we did
it (all) by** ~ lo hicimos nosotros solos; *see also*
oneself
oust [aust] *vt* desalojar
out [aut] *adv (outside)* fuera, afuera; *(not at home)*
fuera (de casa) ▷ *adj (light, fire)* apagado; *(on strike)*
en huelga; *(eliminated)* eliminado ▷ *vt*: **to** ~ **sb**
revelar públicamente la homosexualidad de
algn; **it's cold** ~ fuera hace frío; **he's** ~ *(absent)*
no está, ha salido; **she's** ~ **for the afternoon**
no estará en toda la tarde; **a night** ~ **with my
friends** una noche por ahí con mis amigos; **to
be** ~ **in one's calculations** equivocarse en sus
cálculos; **to run** ~ **(of the house)** salir corriendo
(de la casa); ~ **loud** en alta voz; ~ **of** *prep (outside)*
fuera de; *(because of: anger etc)* por; **he lives** ~ **of
town** vive fuera de la ciudad; **3 kilometres** ~
of town a 3 kilómetros de la ciudad; **to take
sth** ~ **of your pocket** sacar algo del bolsillo; **to
look** ~ **of the window** mirar por la ventana; ~
of curiosity por curiosidad; **to drink** ~ **of a cup**
beber de una taza; **made** ~ **of wood** de madera; ~
of petrol sin gasolina; **we're** ~ **of milk** se nos
acabado la leche; **"~ of order"** "no funciona";
it's ~ **of stock** *(Comm)* está agotado; **in 9 cases**

~ of 10 en 9 de cada 10 casos; **to be ~ and about again** estar repuesto y levantado; **the journey ~** el viaje de ida; **the boat was 10 km ~** el barco estaba a 10 kilómetros de la costa; **before the week was ~** antes del fin de la semana; **he's ~ for all he can get** busca sus propios fines, anda detrás de lo suyo; **all the lights are ~** todas las luces están apagadas; **that's it, Liverpool are ~** ya está, Liverpool queda eliminado; **the film is now ~ on video** la película ya ha salido en vídeo

out-and-out ['autəndaut] *adj* (*liar, thief etc*) redomado, empedernido

outback ['autbæk] *n* interior

outboard ['autbɔːd] *adj*: **~ motor** (motor) fuera borda

outbound ['autbaund] *adj*: **~ from/for** con salida de/hacia

outbreak ['autbreɪk] *n* (*of war*) comienzo; (*of disease*) epidemia; (*of violence etc*) ola

outburst ['autbəːst] *n* explosión, arranque

outcast ['autkɑːst] *n* paria

outcome ['autkʌm] *n* resultado

outcrop ['autkrɔp] *n* (*of rock*) afloramiento

outcry ['autkraɪ] *n* protestas

outdated [aut'deɪtɪd] *adj* anticuado

outdo [aut'duː] *vt* (*irreg: like* do) superar

outdoor [aut'dɔːʳ] *adj* al aire libre

outdoors [aut'dɔːz] *adv* al aire libre

outer ['autəʳ] *adj* exterior, externo

outer space *n* espacio exterior

outfit ['autfɪt] *n* equipo; (*clothes*) traje; (*col: organization*) grupo, organización

outgoing ['autgəuɪŋ] *adj* (*president, tenant*) saliente; (*means of transport*) que sale; (*character*) extrovertido

outgoings ['autgəuɪŋz] *npl* (*Brit*) gastos

outgrow [aut'grəu] *vt* (*irreg: like* grow); **he has ~n his clothes** su ropa le queda pequeña ya

outhouse ['authaus] *n* dependencia

outing ['autɪŋ] *n* excursión, paseo

outlandish [aut'lændɪʃ] *adj* estrafalario

outlaw ['autlɔː] *n* proscrito(-a) ▷ *vt* (*person*) declarar fuera de la ley; (*practice*) declarar ilegal

outlay ['autleɪ] *n* inversión

outlet ['autlɛt] *n* salida; (*of pipe*) desagüe; (*US Elec*) toma de corriente; (*for emotion*) desahogo; (*also:* **retail outlet**) punto de venta

outline ['autlaɪn] *n* (*shape*) contorno, perfil; **in ~** (*fig*) a grandes rasgos

outlive [aut'lɪv] *vt* sobrevivir a

outlook ['autluk] *n* perspectiva; (*opinion*) punto de vista

outlying ['autlaɪɪŋ] *adj* remoto, aislado

outmoded [aut'məudɪd] *adj* anticuado, pasado de moda

outnumber [aut'nʌmbəʳ] *vt* exceder *or* superar en número

out-of-date [autəv'deɪt] *adj* (*passport*) caducado, vencido; (*theory, idea*) anticuado; (*clothes, customs*) pasado de moda

out-of-the-way [autəvðə'weɪ] *adj* (*remote*) apartado; (*unusual*) poco común *or* corriente

outpatient ['autpeɪʃənt] *n* paciente externo(-a)

outpost ['autpəust] *n* puesto avanzado

output ['autput] *n* (volumen de) producción, rendimiento; (*Comput*) salida ▷ *vt* (*Comput: to power*) imprimir

outrage ['autreɪdʒ] *n* (*scandal*) escándalo; (*atrocity*) atrocidad ▷ *vt* ultrajar

outrageous [aut'reɪdʒəs] *adj* (*clothes*) extravagante; (*behaviour*) escandaloso

outright *adv* (*win*) de manera absoluta; (*be killed*) en el acto; (*ask*) abiertamente; (*completely*) completamente ▷ *adj* completo; (*winner*) absoluto; (*refusal*) rotundo

outset ['autsɛt] *n* principio

outside [aut'saɪd] *n* exterior ▷ *adj* exterior, externo ▷ *adv* fuera, afuera (*LAm*) ▷ *prep* fuera de; (*beyond*) más allá de; **the ~ of the house** el exterior de la casa; **at the ~** (*fig*) a lo sumo; **the ~ walls** las paredes exteriores; **an ~ chance** una posibilidad remota; **~ left/right** (*esp Football*) extremo izquierdo/derecho; **it's very cold ~** hace mucho frío fuera; **~ the school** fuera del colegio

outside lane *n* (*Aut*) carril de adelantamiento

outside line *n* (*Tel*) línea (exterior)

outsider [aut'saɪdəʳ] *n* (*stranger*) forastero(-a)

outsize ['autsaɪz] *adj* (*clothes*) de talla grande

outskirts ['autskəːts] *npl* alrededores, afueras

outspoken [aut'spəukən] *adj* muy franco

outstanding [aut'stændɪŋ] *adj* excepcional, destacado; (*unfinished*) pendiente

outstay [aut'steɪ] *vt*: **to ~ one's welcome** quedarse más de la cuenta

outstretched [aut'strɛtʃt] *adj* (*arm*) extendido

outstrip [aut'strɪp] *vt* (*competitors, demand, also fig*) dejar atrás, aventajar

out-tray ['auttreɪ] *n* bandeja de salida

outward ['autwəd] *adj* (*sign, appearances*) externo; (*journey*) de ida

outwardly ['autwədlɪ] *adv* por fuera

outweigh [aut'weɪ] *vt* pesar más que

outwit [aut'wɪt] *vt* ser más listo que

oval ['əuvl] *adj* ovalado ▷ *n* óvalo

ovary ['əuvərɪ] *n* ovario

ovation [əu'veɪʃən] *n* ovación

oven ['ʌvn] *n* horno

ovenproof ['ʌvnpruːf] *adj* refractario, resistente al horno

over ['əuvəʳ] *adv* encima, por encima ▷ *adj* (*finished*) terminado; (*surplus*) de sobra; (*excessively*) demasiado ▷ *prep* (por) encima de; (*above*) sobre; (*on the other side of*) al otro lado de; (*more than*) más de; (*during*) durante; (*about, concerning*): **they fell out ~ money** riñeron por una cuestión de dinero; **~ here** (por) aquí; **~ there** (por) allí *or* allá; **all ~** (*everywhere*) por todas partes; **~ and ~ (again)** una y otra vez; **~ and above** además de; **to ask sb ~** invitar a algn a casa; **to bend ~** inclinarse; **now ~ to our Paris correspondent** damos la palabra a nuestro corresponsal de París; **the world ~** en todo el mundo, en el mundo entero; **all ~ Scotland** en toda Escocia;

I'll be happy when the exams are ~ estaré feliz cuando se hayan terminado los exámenes; **she's not ~ intelligent** no es muy lista que digamos; **there's a mirror ~ the washbasin** encima del lavabo hay un espejo; **the ball went ~ the wall** la pelota pasó por encima de la pared; **I spilled coffee ~ my shirt** me manché la camisa de café; **a bridge ~ the Thames** un puente sobre el Támesis; **the shop is ~ the road** la tienda está al otro lado de la calle; **it's ~ 20 kilos** pesa más de 20 kilos; **the temperature was ~ 30 degrees** la temperatura superaba los 30 grados; **~ the holidays** durante las vacaciones; **~ Christmas** durante las Navidades

overall adj (length) total; (study) de conjunto ▷ adv en conjunto ▷ n (Brit) guardapolvo; **overalls** npl mono, overol (LAm)

overall majority n mayoría absoluta

overanxious [əʊvər'æŋkʃəs] adj demasiado preocupado or ansioso

overawe [əʊvər'ɔː] vt intimidar

overbalance [əʊvə'bæləns] vi perder el equilibrio

overbearing [əʊvə'bɛərɪŋ] adj autoritario, imperioso

overboard ['əʊvəbɔːd] adv (Naut) por la borda; **to go ~ for sth** (fig) enloquecer por algo

overbook [əʊvə'bʊk] vt sobrereservar, reservar con exceso

overcast ['əʊvəkɑːst] adj encapotado

overcharge [əʊvə'tʃɑːdʒ] vt: **to ~ sb** cobrar un precio excesivo a algn

overcoat ['əʊvəkəʊt] n abrigo

overcome [əʊvə'kʌm] vt (irreg: like come); (gen) vencer; (difficulty) superar; **she was quite ~ by the occasion** la ocasión le conmovió mucho

overconfident [əʊvə'kɔnfɪdənt] adj demasiado confiado

overcrowded [əʊvə'kraʊdɪd] adj atestado de gente; (city, country) superpoblado

overdo [əʊvə'duː] vt (irreg: like do) exagerar; (overcook) cocer demasiado; **to ~ it, ~ things** (work too hard) trabajar demasiado

overdose ['əʊvədəʊs] n sobredosis

overdraft ['əʊvədrɑːft] n saldo deudor

overdrawn [əʊvə'drɔːn] adj (account) en descubierto

overdrive ['əʊvədraɪv] n (Aut) sobremarcha, superdirecta

overdue [əʊvə'djuː] adj retrasado; (recognition) tardío; (bill) vencido y no pagado; **that change was long ~** ese cambio tenía que haberse hecho hace tiempo

overemphasis [əʊvər'ɛmfəsɪs] n: **to put an ~ on** poner énfasis excesivo en

overestimate [əʊvər'ɛstɪmeɪt] vt sobreestimar

overexcited [əʊvərɪk'saɪtɪd] adj sobreexcitado

overflow vi desbordarse ▷ n (excess) exceso; (of river) desbordamiento; (also: **overflow pipe**) (cañería de) desagüe

overgrown [əʊvə'grəʊn] adj (garden) cubierto de hierba; **he's just an ~ schoolboy** es un niño en grande

overhaul vt revisar, repasar ▷ n revisión

overhead adv por arriba or encima ▷ adj (cable) aéreo; (railway) elevado, aéreo ▷ n (US) = **overheads**

overheads ['əʊvəhɛdz] npl (Brit) gastos generales

overhear [əʊvə'hɪər] vt (irreg: like hear) oír por casualidad

overheat [əʊvə'hiːt] vi (engine) recalentarse

overjoyed [əʊvə'dʒɔɪd] adj encantado, lleno de alegría

overkill ['əʊvəkɪl] n (Mil) capacidad excesiva de destrucción; (fig) exceso

overland ['əʊvəlænd] adj, adv por tierra

overlap vi superponerse ▷ n superposición

overleaf [əʊvə'liːf] adv al dorso

overload [əʊvə'ləʊd] vt sobrecargar

overlook [əʊvə'lʊk] vt (have view of) dar a, tener vistas a; (miss) pasar por alto; (forgive) hacer la vista gorda a

overnight adv durante la noche; (fig) de la noche a la mañana ▷ adj de noche; **to stay ~** pasar la noche

overpass ['əʊvəpɑːs] n (US) paso elevado or a desnivel

overpay [əʊvə'peɪ] vt: **to ~ sb by £50** pagar 50 libras de más a algn

overplay [əʊvə'pleɪ] vt exagerar; **to ~ one's hand** desmedirse

overpower [əʊvə'paʊər] vt dominar; (fig) embargar

overpowering [əʊvə'paʊərɪŋ] adj (heat) agobiante; (smell) penetrante

overrate [əʊvə'reɪt] vt sobrevalorar

override [əʊvə'raɪd] vt (irreg: like ride); (order, objection) no hacer caso de

overriding [əʊvə'raɪdɪŋ] adj predominante

overrule [əʊvə'ruːl] vt (decision) anular; (claim) denegar

overrun [əʊvə'rʌn] vt (irreg: like run); (Mil: country) invadir; (time limit) rebasar, exceder ▷ vi rebasar el límite previsto; **the town is ~ with tourists** el pueblo está inundado de turistas

overseas [əʊvə'siːz] adv en ultramar; (abroad) en el extranjero ▷ adj (trade) exterior; (visitor) extranjero

oversee [əʊvə'siː] vt supervisar

overshadow [əʊvə'ʃædəʊ] vt (fig) eclipsar

oversight ['əʊvəsaɪt] n descuido; **due to an ~** a causa de un descuido or una equivocación

oversleep [əʊvə'sliːp] vi (irreg: like sleep) dormir más de la cuenta, no despertarse a tiempo

overspend [əʊvə'spɛnd] vi gastar más de la cuenta; **we have overspent by 5 dollars** hemos excedido el presupuesto en 5 dólares

overstate [əʊvə'steɪt] vt exagerar

overstay [əʊvə'steɪ] vt: **to ~ one's time** or **welcome** quedarse más de lo conveniente

overstep [əʊvə'stɛp] vt: **to ~ the mark** or **the limits** pasarse de la raya

overt [əʊ'vɜːt] adj abierto

overtake [əʊvə'teɪk] vt (irreg: like take)

sobrepasar; (Brit Aut) adelantar

verthrow [əuvə'θrəu] vt (irreg: like **throw**); (government) derrocar

vertime ['əuvətaɪm] n horas extraordinarias; **to do** or **work** ~ hacer or trabajar horas extraordinarias or extras

vertone ['əuvətəun] n (fig) tono

verture ['əuvətʃuə^r] n (Mus) obertura; (fig) propuesta

verturn [əuvə'tə:n] vt, vi volcar

verview ['əuvəvju:] n visión de conjunto

verweight [əuvə'weɪt] adj demasiado gordo or pesado

verwhelm [əuvə'wɛlm] vt aplastar

verwhelming [əuvə'wɛlmɪŋ] adj (victory, defeat) arrollador(a); (desire) irresistible; **one's ~ impression is of heat** lo que más impresiona es el calor

verwork [əuvə'wə:k] n trabajo excesivo ▷ vt hacer trabajar demasiado ▷ vi trabajar demasiado

verwrought [əuvə'rɔ:t] adj sobreexcitado

we [əu] vt deber; **to ~ sb sth, ~ sth to sb** deber algo a algn

wing to ['əuɪŋtu:] prep debido a, por causa de

wl [aul] n (long-eared owl) búho, tecolote (CAm,

Méx); (barn owl) lechuza

own [əun] vt tener, poseer ▷ vi: **to ~ to sth/to having done sth** confesar or reconocer algo/ haber hecho algo ▷ adj propio; **this is my ~ recipe** ésta es mi propia receta; **a room of my ~** mi propia habitación; **to get one's ~ back** tomarse la revancha; **on one's ~** solo, a solas; **can I have it for my (very) ~?** ¿puedo quedarme con él?; **to come into one's ~** llegar a realizarse ▷ **own up** vi confesar; **to ~ up to sth** confesar algo

owner ['əunə^r] n dueño(-a)

ownership ['əunəʃɪp] n posesión; **it's under new ~** está bajo nueva dirección

own goal n (Sport) autogol; **to score an ~** marcar un gol en propia puerta, marcar un autogol

ox [ɔks] (pl **oxen**) n buey

Oxbridge ['ɔksbrɪdʒ] n universidades de Oxford y Cambridge

oxide ['ɔksaɪd] n óxido

oxtail ['ɔksteɪl] n: **~ soup** sopa de rabo de buey

oxygen ['ɔksɪdʒən] n oxígeno

oxygen mask n máscara de oxígeno

oyster ['ɔɪstə^r] n ostra

oz. abbr = **ounce(s)**

ozone ['əuzəun] n ozono; **~ layer** capa de ozono

Pp

P, p [piː] n (letter) P, p; **P for Peter** P de París
p abbr (= page) pág.; (Brit) = **penny; pence**
PA n abbr = **personal assistant; public address
system** ▷ abbr (US) = **Pennsylvania**
pa [paː] n (col) papá
pace [peɪs] n paso; (rhythm) ritmo ▷ vi: **to ~
up and down** pasearse de un lado a otro; **to
keep ~ with** llevar el mismo paso que; (events)
mantenerse a la altura de or al corriente de; **to
set the ~** (running) marcar el paso; (fig) marcar
la pauta; **to put sb through his ~s** (fig) poner a
algn a prueba
pacemaker ['peɪsmeɪkəʳ] n (Med) marcapasos
pacific [pə'sɪfɪk] adj pacífico ▷ n: **the P~ (Ocean)**
el (Océano) Pacífico
pacifier ['pæsɪfaɪəʳ] n (US: dummy) chupete
pacifist ['pæsɪfɪst] n pacifista
pack [pæk] n (packet) paquete; (Comm) embalaje;
(of hounds) jauría; (of wolves) manada; (of thieves
etc) banda; (of cards) baraja; (bundle) fardo;
(US: of cigarettes) paquete, cajetilla ▷ vt (wrap)
empaquetar; (fill) llenar; (in suitcase etc) meter,
poner; (cram) llenar, atestar; (fig: meeting etc)
llenar de partidarios; (Comput) comprimir; **to
~ (one's bags)** hacer las maletas; **I've already
~ed my case** ya he hecho mi maleta; **to ~ sb off**
despachar a algn; **the place was ~ed** el local
estaba (lleno) hasta los topes; **to send sb ~ing**
(col) echar a algn con cajas destempladas
▶ **pack in** vi (break down: watch, car) estropearse
▷ vt (col) dejar; **~ it in!** ¡para!, ¡basta ya!
▶ **pack up** vi (col: machine) estropearse; (person)
irse ▷ vt (belongings, clothes) recoger; (goods,
presents) empaquetar, envolver
package ['pækɪdʒ] n paquete; (bulky) bulto; (also:
package deal) acuerdo global ▷ vt (Comm: goods)
envasar, embalar
package holiday n viaje organizado (con todo
incluido)
package tour n viaje organizado
packed lunch [pækt-] n almuerzo frío
packet ['pækɪt] n paquete
packing ['pækɪŋ] n embalaje
packing case n cajón de embalaje
pact [pækt] n pacto
pad [pæd] n (of paper) bloc; (cushion) cojinete;
(launching pad) plataforma (de lanzamiento); (col:

flat) casa ▷ vt rellenar
padded cell ['pædɪd-] n celda acolchada
padding ['pædɪŋ] n relleno; (fig) paja
paddle ['pædl] n (oar) canalete, pala; (US: for table
tennis) pala ▷ vt remar ▷ vi (with feet) chapotear
paddle steamer n vapor de ruedas
paddling pool ['pædlɪŋ-] n (Brit) piscina para
niños
paddock ['pædək] n (field) potrero
paddy field ['pædɪ-] n arrozal
padlock ['pædlɔk] n candado ▷ vt cerrar con
candado
paediatrician, (US) **pediatrician** [piːdɪə'trɪʃən]
n pediatra
paediatrics, (US) **pediatrics** [piːdɪ'ætrɪks] n
pediatría
paedophile, (US) **pedophile** ['piːdəufaɪl] adj de
pedófilos ▷ n pedófilo(-a)
pagan ['peɪgən] adj, n pagano(-a)
page [peɪdʒ] n página; (also: **page boy**) paje ▷ vt
(in hotel etc) llamar por altavoz a
pageant ['pædʒənt] n (procession) desfile; (show)
espectáculo
pageantry ['pædʒəntrɪ] n pompa
pager ['peɪdʒəʳ] n busca
pagination [pædʒɪ'neɪʃən] n paginación
paid [peɪd] pt, pp of **pay** ▷ adj (work) remunerado;
(official) asalariado; **to put ~ to** (Brit) acabar con
paid-up ['peɪdʌp], (US) **paid-in** ['peɪdɪn] adj
(member) con sus cuotas pagadas or al día; (share)
liberado; **~ capital** capital desembolsado
pail [peɪl] n cubo, balde
pain [peɪn] n dolor; **to be in ~** sufrir; **on ~ of
death** so or bajo pena de muerte; see also **pains**
pained [peɪnd] adj (expression) afligido
painful ['peɪnful] adj doloroso; (difficult) penoso;
(disagreeable) desagradable
painfully ['peɪnfəlɪ] adv (fig: very) terriblemente
painkiller ['peɪnkɪləʳ] n analgésico
painless ['peɪnlɪs] adj sin dolor; (method) fácil
pains [peɪnz] npl (efforts) esfuerzos; **to take ~ to
do sth** tomarse trabajo en hacer algo
painstaking ['peɪnzteɪkɪŋ] adj (person)
concienzudo, esmerado
paint [peɪnt] n pintura ▷ vt pintar; **a tin of ~** un
bote de pintura; **to ~ the door blue** pintar la
puerta de azul

paintbrush ['peɪntbrʌʃ] n (artist's) pincel; (decorator's) brocha

painter ['peɪntər] n pintor(a)

painting ['peɪntɪŋ] n pintura

paintwork ['peɪntwəːk] n pintura

pair [peər] n (of shoes, gloves etc) par; (of people) pareja; **a ~ of scissors** unas tijeras; **a ~ of trousers** unos pantalones, un pantalón
▸ **pair off** vi: **to ~ off (with sb)** hacer pareja (con algn)

pajamas [pɪ'dʒɑːməz] npl (US) pijama, piyama (LAm)

Pakistan [pɑːkɪ'stɑːn] n Paquistán

Pakistani [pɑːkɪ'stɑːnɪ] adj, n paquistaní

pal [pæl] n (col) amiguete(-a), colega

palace ['pæləs] n palacio

palatable ['pælɪtəbl] adj sabroso; (acceptable) aceptable

palate ['pælɪt] n paladar

pale [peɪl] adj (gen) pálido; (colour) claro ▸ n: **to be beyond the ~** pasarse de la raya ▸ vi palidecer; **to grow** or **turn ~** palidecer; **to ~ into insignificance (beside)** no poderse comparar (con)

Palestine ['pælɪstaɪn] n Palestina

Palestinian [pælɪs'tɪnɪən] adj, n palestino

palette ['pælɪt] n paleta

pall [pɔːl] n (of smoke) cortina ▸ vi cansar

pallet ['pælɪt] n (for goods) pallet

pallid ['pælɪd] adj pálido

palm [pɑːm] n (Anat) palma; (also: **palm tree**) palmera, palma ▸ vt: **to ~ sth off on sb** (Brit col) endosarle algo a algn

Palm Sunday n Domingo de Ramos

palpable ['pælpəbl] adj palpable

paltry ['pɔːltrɪ] adj (amount etc) miserable

pamper ['pæmpər] vt mimar

pamphlet ['pæmflət] n folleto; (political: handed out in street) panfleto

pan [pæn] n (also: **saucepan**) cacerola, cazuela, olla; (also: **frying pan**) sartén; (of lavatory) taza ▸ vi (Cine) tomar panorámicas; **to ~ for gold** cribar oro

pan- [pæn] pref pan-

Panama ['pænəmɑː] n Panamá

Panama Canal n el Canal de Panamá

pancake ['pænkeɪk] n crepe, panqueque (LAm)

pancreas ['pæŋkrɪəs] n páncreas

panda ['pændə] n panda

panda car n (Brit) coche de la policía

pandemonium [pændɪ'məunɪəm] n (mess) caos; (noise): **there was ~** se armó un tremendo jaleo

pander ['pændər] vi: **to ~ to** complacer a

p & p abbr (Brit: = postage and packing) gastos de envío

pane [peɪn] n cristal

panel ['pænl] n (of wood) panel; (of cloth) paño; (Radio, TV) panel de invitados

panelling, (US) **paneling** ['pænəlɪŋ] n paneles

pang [pæŋ] n: **~s of conscience** remordimientos; **~s of hunger** dolores del hambre

panic ['pænɪk] n pánico ▸ vi dejarse llevar por el pánico

panic buying [-baɪɪŋ] n compras masivas por miedo a futura escasez

panicky ['pænɪkɪ] adj (person) asustadizo

panic-stricken ['pænɪkstrɪkən] adj preso del pánico

panorama [pænə'rɑːmə] n panorama

pansy ['pænzɪ] n (Bot) pensamiento; (col: pej) maricón

pant [pænt] vi jadear

panther ['pænθər] n pantera

panties ['pæntɪz] npl bragas (Esp), calzones (LAm), bombachas (CS)

pantihose ['pæntɪhəuz] n (US) medias, panties

panto ['pæntəu] n (Brit col) = **pantomime**

pantomime ['pæntəmaɪm] n (Brit) representación musical navideña

pantry ['pæntrɪ] n despensa

pants [pænts] n (Brit: underwear: woman's) bragas (Esp), calzones (LAm), bombachas (CS); (: man's) calzoncillos; (US: trousers) pantalones

paparazzi [pæpə'rætsɪ] npl paparazzi

paper ['peɪpər] n papel; (also: **newspaper**) periódico, diario; (study, article) artículo; (exam) examen ▸ adj de papel ▸ vt empapelar; (identity) **~s** npl papeles, documentos; **a piece of ~** un papel; **to put sth down on ~** poner algo por escrito

paperback ['peɪpəbæk] n libro de bolsillo

paper bag n bolsa de papel

paper clip n clip

paper hankie n pañuelo de papel

paper shop n (Brit) tienda de periódicos

paperweight ['peɪpəweɪt] n pisapapeles

paperwork ['peɪpəwəːk] n trabajo administrativo; (pej) papeleo

par [pɑːr] n par; (Golf) par ▸ adj a la par; **to be on a ~ with** estar a la par con; **at ~** a la par; **to be above/below ~** estar sobre/bajo par; **to feel under ~** sentirse en baja forma

parable ['pærəbl] n parábola

parachute ['pærəʃuːt] n paracaídas ▸ vi lanzarse en paracaídas

parade [pə'reɪd] n desfile ▸ vt (gen) recorrer, desfilar por; (show off) hacer alarde de ▸ vi desfilar; (Mil) pasar revista

paradise ['pærədaɪs] n paraíso

paradox ['pærədɔks] n paradoja

paradoxically [pærə'dɔksɪklɪ] adv paradójicamente

paraffin ['pærəfɪn] n (Brit): **~ (oil)** parafina

paragon ['pærəgən] n modelo

paragraph ['pærəgrɑːf] n párrafo, acápite (LAm); **new ~** punto y aparte, punto acápite (LAm)

Paraguay ['pærəgwaɪ] n Paraguay

Paraguayan [pærə'gwaɪən] adj, n paraguayo(-a), paraguayano(-a)

parallel ['pærəlɛl] adj: **~ (with/to)** en paralelo (con/a); (fig) semejante (a) ▸ n (line) paralela; (fig, Geo) paralelo

paralysis [pə'rælɪsɪs] n parálisis

paralytic [pærə'lıtık] adj paralítico
paralyze ['pærəlaız] vt paralizar
paramedic [pærə'mɛdık] n auxiliar sanitario(-a)
parameter [pə'ræmıtəʳ] n parámetro
paramilitary [pærə'mılıtərı] adj (organization, operations) paramilitar
paramount ['pærəmaunt] adj: of ~ importance de suma importancia
paranoia [pærə'nɔıə] n paranoia
paranoid ['pærənɔıd] adj paranoico
paranormal [pærə'nɔːml] adj paranormal
paraphernalia [pærəfə'neılıə] n parafernalia
paraphrase ['pærəfreız] vt parafrasear
parasite ['pærəsaıt] n parásito(-a)
parasol ['pærəsɔl] n sombrilla, quitasol
paratrooper ['pærətruːpəʳ] n paracaidista
parcel ['pɑːsl] n paquete ▷ vt (also: parcel up) empaquetar, embalar; to be part and ~ of ser parte integrante de
  ▶ **parcel out** vt parcelar, repartir
parcel bomb n paquete bomba
parcel post n servicio de paquetes postales
parch [pɑːtʃ] vt secar, resecar
parched [pɑːtʃt] adj (person) muerto de sed
parchment ['pɑːtʃmənt] n pergamino
pardon ['pɑːdn] n perdón; (Law) indulto ▷ vt perdonar; indultar; ~ me!, I beg your ~! ¡perdone usted!; (I beg your) ~? (US): ~ me? ¿cómo (dice)?
parent ['pɛərənt] n: ~s npl padres
parentage ['pɛərəntıdʒ] n familia, linaje; of unknown ~ de padres desconocidos
parenthesis [pə'rɛnθısıs] (pl **parentheses**) n paréntesis; in parentheses entre paréntesis
Paris ['pærıs] n París
parish ['pærıʃ] n parroquia
parishioner [pə'rıʃənəʳ] n feligrés(-esa)
Parisian [pə'rızıən] adj, n parisino(-a), parisiense
parity ['pærıtı] n paridad, igualdad
park [pɑːk] n parque, jardín público ▷ vt, vi estacionar, aparcar (Esp)
parking ['pɑːkıŋ] n estacionamiento, aparcamiento (Esp); "no ~" "prohibido estacionarse or aparcar"
parking lot n (US) parking, aparcamiento (Esp), playa de estacionamiento (LAm)
parking meter n parquímetro
parking place n sitio para estacionar, aparcamiento (Esp)
parking ticket n multa de estacionamiento
Parkinson's ['pɑːkınsənz] n (also: **Parkinson's disease**) (enfermedad de) Parkinson
parlance ['pɑːləns] n lenguaje; in common/ modern ~ en lenguaje corriente/moderno
parliament ['pɑːləmənt] n parlamento; (Spanish) las Cortes
parliamentary [pɑːlə'mɛntərı] adj parlamentario
parlour, (US) **parlor** ['pɑːləʳ] n salón, living (LAm)
Parmesan [pɑːmı'zæn] n (also: **Parmesan cheese**) queso parmesano
parochial [pə'rəukıəl] adj parroquial; (pej) de

miras estrechas
parody ['pærədı] n parodia ▷ vt parodiar
parole [pə'rəul] n: on ~ en libertad condicional
parrot ['pærət] n loro, papagayo
parry ['pærı] vt parar
parsley ['pɑːslı] n perejil
parsnip ['pɑːsnıp] n chirivía
parson ['pɑːsn] n cura
part [pɑːt] n (gen, Mus) parte; (bit) trozo; (of machine) pieza; (Theat etc) papel; (of serial) entrega; (US: in hair) raya ▷ adv = **partly** ▷ vt separar; (break) partir ▷ vi (people) separarse; (roads) bifurcarse; (crowd) apartarse; (break) romperse; the first ~ of the play was boring la primera parte de la obra fue aburrida; she had a small ~ in the film tenía un pequeño papel en la película; spare ~s (Auto) piezas de repuesto; to take ~ in participar or tomar parte en; to take sb's ~ tomar partido por algn; for my ~ por mi parte; for the most ~ en su mayor parte; (people) en su mayoría; for the better ~ of the day durante la mayor parte del día; ~ of speech (Ling) categoría gramatical, parte de la oración; to take sth in good/bad ~ aceptar algo bien/tomarse algo a mal
  ▶ **part with** vt fus ceder, entregar; (money) pagar; (get rid of) deshacerse de; I hate to ~ with this lamp me fastidia tener que desprenderme de esta lámpara
part exchange n (Brit): in ~ como parte del pago
partial ['pɑːʃl] adj parcial; to be ~ to (like) ser aficionado a
participate [pɑː'tısıpeıt] vi: to ~ in participar en
participation [pɑːtısı'peıʃən] n participación
participle ['pɑːtısıpl] n participio
particle ['pɑːtıkl] n partícula; (of dust) mota; (fig) pizca
particular [pə'tıkjuləʳ] adj (special) particular; (concrete) concreto; (given) determinado; (detailed) detallado, minucioso; (fussy) quisquilloso, exigente; particulars npl (information) datos, detalles; (details) pormenores; in ~ en particular; to be very ~ about ser muy exigente en cuanto a; I'm not ~ me es or da igual
particularly [pə'tıkjuləlı] adv especialmente, en particular
parting ['pɑːtıŋ] n (act of) separación; (farewell) despedida; (Brit: in hair) raya ▷ adj de despedida; ~ shot (fig) golpe final
partisan [pɑːtı'zæn] adj partidista ▷ n partidario(-a); (fighter) partisano(-a)
partition [pɑː'tıʃən] n (Pol) división; (wall) tabique ▷ vt dividir; dividir con tabique
partly ['pɑːtlı] adv en parte
partner ['pɑːtnəʳ] n (Comm) socio(-a); (Sport, at dance) pareja; (spouse) cónyuge; (friend etc) compañero(-a) ▷ vt acompañar
partnership ['pɑːtnəʃıp] n (gen) asociación; (Comm) sociedad; to go into ~ (with), form a ~ (with) asociarse (con)
partridge ['pɑːtrıdʒ] n perdiz
part-time ['pɑːt'taım] adj, adv a tiempo parcial

party ['pɑ:tɪ] n (Pol) partido; (celebration) fiesta; (group) grupo; (Law) parte, interesado ▷ adj (Pol) de partido; (dress etc) de fiesta, de gala; **to have** or **give** or **throw a** ~ organizar una fiesta; **dinner** ~ cena; **to be a ~ to a crime** ser cómplice de un crimen

party line n (Pol) línea política del partido; (Tel) línea compartida

party political broadcast n ≈ espacio electoral

pass [pɑ:s] vt (time, object) pasar; (place) pasar por; (exam, law, motion) aprobar; (overtake, surpass) rebasar ▷ vi pasar; (Scol) aprobar ▷ n (permit) permiso, pase; (membership card) carnet; (in mountains) puerto; (Sport) pase; (Scol: also: **pass mark**) aprobado; **could you ~ me the salt, please?** ¿me pasas la sal, por favor?; **to ~ sth through sth** pasar algo por algo; **to ~ the time of day with sb** pasar el rato con algn; **we were ~ed by a huge lorry** nos adelantó un camión enorme; **the time has ~ed quickly** el tiempo ha pasado rápido; **did you ~?** ¿has aprobado?; **a bus ~** un abono para el autobús; **things have come to a pretty ~!** ¡hasta dónde hemos llegado!; **to make a ~ at sb** (col) insinuársele a algn
▸ **pass away** vi fallecer
▸ **pass by** vi pasar ▷ vt (ignore) pasar por alto
▸ **pass down** vt (customs, inheritance) pasar, transmitir
▸ **pass for** vt fus pasar por; **she could ~ for 25** se podría creer que sólo tiene 25 años
▸ **pass on** vi (die) fallecer, morir ▷ vt (hand on): **to ~ on (to)** transmitir (a); (cold, illness) pegar (a); (benefits) dar (a); (price rises) pasar (a)
▸ **pass out** vi desmayarse; (Mil) graduarse
▸ **pass over** vi (die) fallecer ▷ vt omitir, pasar por alto
▸ **pass up** vt (opportunity) dejar pasar, no aprovechar

passable ['pɑ:səbl] adj (road) transitable; (tolerable) pasable

passage ['pæsɪdʒ] n pasillo; (act of passing) tránsito; (fare, in book) pasaje; (by boat) travesía

passenger ['pæsɪndʒəʳ] n pasajero(-a), viajero(-a)

passer-by [pɑ:sə'baɪ] n transeúnte

passing ['pɑ:sɪŋ] adj (fleeting) pasajero; **in ~** de paso

passing place n (Aut) apartadero

passion ['pæʃən] n pasión

passionate ['pæʃənɪt] adj apasionado

passion fruit n fruta de la pasión, granadilla

passion play n drama de la Pasión

passive ['pæsɪv] adj (also Ling) pasivo

passive smoking n efectos del tabaco en fumadores pasivos

Passover ['pɑ:səʊvəʳ] n Pascua (de los judíos)

passport ['pɑ:spɔ:t] n pasaporte

passport control n control de pasaporte

password ['pɑ:swɜ:d] n (also Comput) contraseña

past [pɑ:st] prep (further than) más allá de; (later than) después de ▷ adj pasado; (president etc) antiguo ▷ n (time) pasado; (of person) antecedentes; **the school is 100 metres ~ the traffic lights** el colegio está a unos 100 metros pasado el semáforo; **quarter/half ~ 4** las 4 y cuarto/media; **he's ~ 40** tiene más de 40 años; **it's ~ midnight** es pasada la medianoche; **I'm ~ caring** ya no me importa; **to be ~ it** (col: person) estar acabado; **for the ~ few/3 days** durante los últimos días/últimos 3 días; **this ~ year has been very difficult** este año pasado ha sido muy difícil; **to run ~** pasar corriendo por; **to go ~** pasar; **the bus went ~ without stopping** el autobús pasó sin parar; **I try not to think of the ~** intento no pensar en el pasado; **in the ~** en el pasado, antes; **this was common in the ~** antiguamente esto era normal

pasta ['pæstə] n pasta

paste [peɪst] n (gen) pasta; (glue) engrudo ▷ vt (stick) pegar; (glue) engomar; **tomato ~** tomate concentrado

pasteurized ['pæstəraɪzd] adj pasteurizado

pastille ['pæstl] n pastilla

pastime ['pɑ:staɪm] n pasatiempo

pastry ['peɪstrɪ] n (dough) pasta; (cake) pastel

pasture ['pɑ:stʃəʳ] n (grass) pasto

pasty n ['pæstɪ] empanada ▷ adj ['peɪstɪ] pastoso; (complexion) pálido

pat [pæt] vt dar una palmadita a; (dog etc) acariciar ▷ n (of butter) porción ▷ adv: **he knows it (off)** ~ se lo sabe de memoria or al dedillo; **to give sb/o.s. a ~ on the back** (fig) felicitar a algn/felicitarse

patch [pætʃ] n (of material) parche; (mended part) remiendo; (of land) terreno; (Comput) ajuste ▷ vt (clothes) remendar; **(to go through) a bad ~** (pasar por) una mala racha
▸ **patch up** vt (mend temporarily) reparar; **to ~ up a quarrel** hacer las paces

patchy ['pætʃɪ] adj desigual

pâté ['pæteɪ] n paté

patent ['peɪtnt] n patente ▷ vt patentar ▷ adj patente, evidente

patent leather n charol

paternal [pə'tɜ:nl] adj paternal; (relation) paterno

paternity [pə'tɜ:nɪtɪ] n paternidad

path [pɑ:θ] n camino, sendero; (trail, track) pista; (of missile) trayectoria

pathetic [pə'θetɪk] adj (pitiful) penoso, patético; (very bad) malísimo; (moving) conmovedor(a)

pathological [pæθə'lɔdʒɪkəl] adj patológico

pathologist [pə'θɔlədʒɪst] n patólogo(-a)

pathos ['peɪθɔs] n patetismo

pathway ['pɑ:θweɪ] n sendero, vereda

patience ['peɪʃns] n paciencia; (Brit Cards) solitario; **to lose one's ~** perder la paciencia

patient ['peɪʃnt] n paciente ▷ adj paciente, sufrido; **to be ~ with sb** tener paciencia con algn

patio ['pætɪəʊ] n patio

patriot ['peɪtrɪət] n patriota

patriotic [pætrɪ'ɔtɪk] adj patriótico

patriotism ['pætrɪətɪzəm] n patriotismo

patrol [pə'trəʊl] n patrulla ▷ vt patrullar por; **to**

be on ~ patrullar, estar de patrulla
patrol car *n* coche patrulla
patrolman [pə'trəulmən] *n* (US) policía
patron ['peɪtrən] *n* (*in shop*) cliente; (*of charity*)
patrocinador(a); **~ of the arts** mecenas
patronize ['pætrənaɪz] *vt* (*shop*) ser cliente de;
(*look down on*) tratar con condescendencia a
patron saint *n* santo(-a) patrón(-ona)
patter ['pætə'] *n* golpeteo; (*sales talk*) labia ▷ *vi*
(*rain*) tamborilear
pattern ['pætən] *n* (*Sewing*) patrón; (*design*)
dibujo; (*behaviour, events*) esquema; **~ of events**
curso de los hechos; **behaviour ~s** modelos de
comportamiento
paunch [pɔ:ntʃ] *n* panza, barriga
pauper ['pɔ:pə'] *n* pobre
pause [pɔ:z] *n* pausa; (*interval*) intervalo ▷ *vi*
hacer una pausa; **to ~ for breath** detenerse para
tomar aliento
pave [peɪv] *vt* pavimentar; **to ~ the way for**
preparar el terreno para
pavement ['peɪvmənt] *n* (*Brit*) acera, vereda (*CS*),
andén (*CAm, Col*), banqueta (*Méx*); (US) calzada,
pavimento
pavilion [pə'vɪlɪən] *n* pabellón; (*Sport*) vestuarios
paving ['peɪvɪŋ] *n* pavimento
paving stone *n* losa
paw [pɔ:] *n* pata; (*claw*) garra ▷ *vt* (*animal*) tocar
con la pata; (*pej: touch*) tocar, manosear
pawn [pɔ:n] *n* (*Chess*) peón; (*fig*) instrumento ▷ *vt*
empeñar
pawnbroker ['pɔ:nbrəukə'] *n* prestamista
pawnshop ['pɔ:nʃɔp] *n* casa de empeños
pay [peɪ] *n* paga; (*wage etc*) sueldo, salario ▷ *vb*
(*pt, pp* **paid**) ▷ *vt* pagar; (*respect*) ofrecer ▷ *vi*
pagar; (*be profitable*) rendir, compensar, ser
rentable; **a ~ rise** un aumento de sueldo; **to be
in sb's ~** estar al servicio de algn; **to ~ attention
(to)** prestar atención (a); **to ~ sb a visit** ir a ver a
algn; **Paul paid us a visit last night** Paul vino a
vernos anoche; **I paid £5 for that record** pagué
5 libras por ese disco; **how much did you ~ for
it?** ¿cuánto pagaste por él?; **can I ~ by cheque?**
¿puedo pagar con cheque?; **to ~ money into an
account** ingresar dinero en una cuenta; **to ~
one's way** (*contribute one's share*) pagar su parte;
(*remain solvent: company*) ser solvente; **does your
current account ~ interest?** ¿le rinde intereses
su cuenta corriente?; **to ~ dividends** (*Comm*)
pagar dividendos; (*fig*) compensar; **it won't ~
you to do that** no te merece la pena hacer eso;
to put paid to (*plan, person*) acabar con
▶ **pay back** *vt* (*money*) devolver, reembolsar;
(*person*) pagar; **I'll ~ you back tomorrow**
mañana te devuelvo el dinero; **I'll ~ you back
for this!** ¡me las vas a pagar!
▶ **pay for** *vt fus* pagar; **I paid for my ticket**
pagué el billete
▶ **pay in** *vt* ingresar
▶ **pay off** *vt* liquidar; (*person*) pagar; (*debts*)
liquidar, saldar; (*creditor*) cancelar, redimir;
(*workers*) despedir; (*mortgage*) cancelar, redimir

▷ *vi* (*scheme, decision*) dar resultado; **to ~ sth off in
instalments** pagar algo a plazos
▶ **pay out** *vt* (*rope*) ir dando; (*money*) gastar,
desembolsar
▶ **pay up** *vt* pagar
payable ['peɪəbl] *adj* pagadero; **to make a
cheque ~ to sb** extender un cheque a favor de
algn
pay award *n* aumento de sueldo
PAYE *n abbr* (*Brit*: = *pay as you earn*) sistema de retención
fiscal en la fuente de ingresos
payee [peɪ'i:] *n* portador(a)
pay envelope *n* (US) = **pay packet**
payment ['peɪmənt] *n* pago; **advance ~** (*part sum*)
anticipo, adelanto; (*total sum*) saldo; **monthly
~** mensualidad; **deferred ~, ~ by instalments**
pago a plazos *or* diferido; **on ~ of £5** mediante
pago de *or* pagando 5 libras; **in ~ for** (*goods, sum
owed*) en pago de
pay packet *n* (*Brit*) sobre (de la paga)
pay-phone ['peɪfəun] *n* teléfono público
payroll ['peɪrəul] *n* nómina; **to be on a firm's ~**
estar en la nómina de una compañía
pay slip *n* hoja del sueldo
PC *n abbr* (= *personal computer*) PC, OP; (*Brit*) = **police
constable** ▷ *adj abbr* = **politically correct**
pc *abbr* = **per cent; postcard**
PDA *n abbr* (= *personal digital assistant*) agenda
electrónica
PE *n abbr* (= *physical education*) ed. física ▷ *abbr*
(*Canada*) = **Prince Edward Island**
pea [pi:] *n* guisante (*Esp*), arveja (*LAm*), chícharo
(*Méx*)
peace [pi:s] *n* paz; (*calm*) paz, tranquilidad; **to
be at ~ with sb/sth** estar en paz con algn/algo;
to keep the ~ (*policeman*) mantener el orden;
(*citizen*) guardar el orden
peaceful ['pi:sful] *adj* (*gentle*) pacífico; (*calm*)
tranquilo, sosegado
peacekeeping ['pi:ski:pɪŋ] *adj* de pacificación
▷ *n* pacificación
peacekeeping force *n* fuerza de pacificación
peach [pi:tʃ] *n* melocotón (*Esp*), durazno (*LAm*)
peacock ['pi:kɔk] *n* pavo real
peak [pi:k] *n* (*of mountain: top*) cumbre, cima;
(: *point*) pico; (*of cap*) visera; (*fig*) cumbre
peak hours *npl*, **peak period** *n* horas punta
peak rate *n* tarifa máxima
peal [pi:l] *n* repique; **~ of laughter** carcajada
peanut ['pi:nʌt] *n* cacahuete, maní (*LAm*),
cacahuate (*Méx*)
pear [pɛə'] *n* pera
pearl [pə:l] *n* perla
peasant ['pɛznt] *n* campesino(-a)
peat [pi:t] *n* turba
pebble ['pɛbl] *n* guijarro
peck [pɛk] *vt* (*also*: **peck at**) picotear; (*food*) comer
sin ganas ▷ *n* picotazo; (*kiss*) besito
pecking order *n* orden de jerarquía
peckish ['pɛkɪʃ] *adj* (*Brit col*): **I feel ~** tengo ganas
de picar algo
peculiar [pɪ'kju:lɪə'] *adj* (*odd*) extraño, raro;

(*typical*) propio, característico; (*particular: importance, qualities*) particular; ~ **to** propio de

pedal ['pɛdl] *n* pedal ▷ *vi* pedalear

pedantic [pɪ'dæntɪk] *adj* pedante

peddle ['pɛdl] *vt* (*goods*) ir vendiendo *or* vender de puerta en puerta; (*drugs*) traficar con; (*gossip*) divulgar

peddler ['pɛdlər] *n* vendedor(a) ambulante

pedestal ['pɛdəstl] *n* pedestal

pedestrian [pɪ'dɛstrɪən] *n* peatón ▷ *adj* pedestre

pedestrian crossing *n* (*Brit*) paso de peatones

pedestrian precinct *n* zona reservada para peatones

pediatrics [piːdɪ'ætrɪks] *n* (*US*) = **paediatrics**

pedigree ['pɛdɪgriː] *n* genealogía; (*of animal*) pedigrí ▷ *cpd* (*animal*) de raza, de casta

pee [piː] *vi* (*col*) mear

peek [piːk] *vi* mirar a hurtadillas; (*Comput*) inspeccionar

peel [piːl] *n* piel; (*of orange, lemon*) cáscara; (*: removed*) peladuras ▷ *vt* pelar ▷ *vi* (*paint etc*) desconcharse; (*wallpaper*) despegarse, desprenderse

▶ **peel back** *vt* pelar

peep [piːp] *n* (*Brit: look*) mirada furtiva; (*sound*) pío ▷ *vi* (*Brit: look*) mirar rápidamente; (*: furtively*) mirar furtivamente; (*sound*) piar

▶ **peep out** *vi* asomar la cabeza

peephole ['piːphəul] *n* mirilla

peer [pɪər] *vi*: **to ~ at** escudriñar ▷ *n* (*noble*) par; (*equal*) igual

peerage ['pɪərɪdʒ] *n* nobleza

peeved [piːvd] *adj* enojado

peg [pɛg] *n* clavija; (*for coat etc*) gancho, colgador; (*Brit: also*: **clothes peg**) pinza; (*tent peg*) estaca ▷ *vt* (*clothes*) tender; (*groundsheet*) fijar con estacas; (*fig: wages, prices*) fijar

pejorative [pɪ'dʒɔrətɪv] *adj* peyorativo

pekinese [piːkɪ'niːz] *n* pequinés(-esa)

pelican ['pɛlɪkən] *n* pelícano

pelican crossing *n* (*Brit Aut*) paso de peatones señalizado

pellet ['pɛlɪt] *n* bolita; (*bullet*) perdigón

pelt [pɛlt] *vt*: **to ~ sb with sth** arrojarle algo a algn ▷ *vi* (*rain: also*: **pelt down**) llover a cántaros ▷ *n* pellejo

pelvis ['pɛlvɪs] *n* pelvis

pen [pɛn] *n* (*ballpoint pen*) bolígrafo; (*fountain pen*) pluma; (*for sheep*) redil; (*US col: prison*) cárcel, chirona; **to put ~ to paper** tomar la pluma

penal ['piːnl] *adj* penal; **~ servitude** trabajos forzados

penalize ['piːnəlaɪz] *vt* (*punish*) castigar; (*Sport*) sancionar, penalizar

penalty ['pɛnltɪ] *n* (*gen*) pena; (*fine*) multa; (*Sport*) sanción; **~ (kick)** (*Football*) penalty, penal (*LAm*)

penalty area *n* (*Brit Sport*) área de castigo

penalty shoot-out [-'ʃuːtaut] *n* (*Football*) tanda de penaltis

penance ['pɛnəns] *n* penitencia

pence [pɛns] *pl of* **penny**

penchant ['pã:ʃã:ŋ] *n* predilección, inclinación

pencil ['pɛnsl] *n* lápiz, lapicero (*LAm*) ▷ *vt* (*also*: **pencil in**) escribir con lápiz

pencil case *n* estuche

pencil sharpener *n* sacapuntas

pendant ['pɛndnt] *n* pendiente

pending ['pɛndɪŋ] *prep* antes de ▷ *adj* pendiente; **~ the arrival of ...** hasta que llegue ..., hasta llegar ...

pendulum ['pɛndjuləm] *n* péndulo

penetrate ['pɛnɪtreɪt] *vt* penetrar

penetration [pɛnɪ'treɪʃən] *n* penetración

penfriend ['pɛnfrɛnd] *n* (*Brit*) amigo(-a) por correspondencia

penguin ['pɛŋgwɪn] *n* pingüino

penicillin [pɛnɪ'sɪlɪn] *n* penicilina

peninsula [pə'nɪnsjulə] *n* península

penis ['piːnɪs] *n* pene

penitence ['pɛnɪtns] *n* penitencia

penitentiary [pɛnɪ'tɛnʃərɪ] *n* (*US*) cárcel, presidio

penknife ['pɛnnaɪf] *n* navaja

pen name *n* seudónimo

pennant ['pɛnənt] *n* banderola; banderín

penniless ['pɛnɪlɪs] *adj* sin dinero

Pennines ['pɛnaɪnz] *npl* (*Montes*) Peninos

penny ['pɛnɪ] (*pl* **pennies** *or* (*Brit*) **pence**) (*Brit*) *n* penique; (*US*) centavo

penpal ['pɛnpæl] *n* amigo(-a) por correspondencia

penpusher ['pɛnpuʃər] *n* (*pej*) chupatintas

pension ['pɛnʃən] *n* (*allowance, state payment*) pensión; (*old-age*) jubilación

▶ **pension off** *vt* jubilar

pensioner ['pɛnʃənər] *n* (*Brit*) jubilado(-a)

pension fund *n* fondo de pensiones

pensive ['pɛnsɪv] *adj* pensativo; (*withdrawn*) preocupado

pentagon ['pɛntəgən] *n* pentágono; **the P~** (*US Pol*) el Pentágono

Pentecost ['pɛntɪkɔst] *n* Pentecostés

penthouse ['pɛnthaus] *n* ático (de lujo)

pent-up ['pɛntʌp] *adj* (*feelings*) reprimido

penultimate [pɛ'nʌltɪmət] *adj* penúltimo

people ['piːpl] *npl* gente; (*citizens*) pueblo, ciudadanos ▷ *n* (*nation, race*) pueblo, nación ▷ *vt* poblar; **a lot of ~** mucha gente; **6 ~ 6** personas; **several ~ came** vinieron varias personas; **~ say that ...** dice la gente que ..., dicen que ...; **how many ~ are there in your family?** ¿cuántos sois en tu familia?; **old/young ~** los ancianos/jóvenes; **Spanish ~** los españoles; **~ at large** la gente en general; **a man of the ~** un hombre del pueblo

pep [pɛp] *n* (*col*) energía

▶ **pep up** *vt* animar

pepper ['pɛpər] *n* (*spice*) pimienta; (*vegetable*) pimiento, ají (*LAm*), chile (*LAm*) ▷ *vt* (*fig*) salpicar

peppermint ['pɛpəmɪnt] *n* menta; (*sweet*) pastilla de menta

pepperoni [pɛpə'rəunɪ] *n* ≈ salchichón picante

peptalk ['pɛptɔːk] *n* (*col*): **to give sb a ~** darle a algn una inyección de ánimo

per [pəːʳ] *prep* por; **~ day/person** por día/persona; **as ~ your instructions** de acuerdo con sus instrucciones

per capita *adj, adv* per cápita

perceive [pə'siːv] *vt* percibir; *(realize)* darse cuenta de

per cent, *(US)* **percent** [pə'sɛnt] *n* por ciento; **a 20 ~ discount** un descuento del 20 por ciento

percentage [pə'sɛntɪdʒ] *n* porcentaje; **to get a ~ on all sales** percibir un tanto por ciento sobre todas las ventas; **on a ~ basis** a porcentaje

percentage point *n* punto (porcentual)

perception [pə'sɛpʃən] *n* percepción; *(insight)* perspicacia

perceptive [pə'sɛptɪv] *adj* perspicaz

perch [pəːtʃ] *n (fish)* perca; *(for bird)* percha ▷ *vi* posarse

percolate ['pəːkəleɪt] *vt (coffee)* filtrar ▷ *vi (coffee, fig)* filtrarse

percolator ['pəːkəleɪtəʳ] *n* cafetera de filtro

percussion [pə'kʌʃən] *n* percusión

perennial [pə'rɛnɪəl] *adj* perenne

perfect *adj* perfecto ▷ *n (also:* **perfect tense)** perfecto ▷ *vt* perfeccionar; **he's a ~ stranger to me** no le conozco de nada, me es completamente desconocido

perfection [pə'fɛkʃən] *n* perfección

perfectly ['pəːfɪktlɪ] *adv* perfectamente; **I'm ~ happy with the situation** estoy muy contento con la situación; **you know ~ well** lo sabes muy bien *or* perfectamente

perforate ['pəːfəreɪt] *vt* perforar

perforation [pəːfə'reɪʃən] *n* perforación

perform [pə'fɔːm] *vt (carry out)* realizar, llevar a cabo; *(Theat)* representar; *(piece of music)* interpretar ▷ *vi (Theat)* actuar; *(Tech)* funcionar

performance [pə'fɔːməns] *n (of task)* realización; *(of a play)* representación; *(of player etc)* actuación; *(of engine)* rendimiento; *(of car)* prestaciones; *(of function)* desempeño; **the team put up a good ~** el equipo se defendió bien

performer [pə'fɔːməʳ] *n (actor)* actor, actriz; *(Mus)* intérprete

performing arts *npl* **the ~** las artes teatrales

perfume ['pəːfjuːm] *n* perfume

perfunctory [pə'fʌŋktərɪ] *adj* superficial

perhaps [pə'hæps] *adv* quizá(s), tal vez; **~ so/not** puede que sí/no

peril ['pɛrɪl] *n* peligro, riesgo

perilous ['pɛrɪləs] *adj* peligroso

perimeter [pə'rɪmɪtəʳ] *n* perímetro

period ['pɪərɪəd] *n* período, periodo; *(History)* época; *(Scol)* clase; *(full stop)* punto; *(Med)* regla, periodo; *(US Sport)* tiempo ▷ *adj (costume, furniture)* de época; **for a ~ of three weeks** durante (un período de) tres semanas; **the holiday ~** el período de vacaciones

periodical [pɪərɪ'ɔdɪkl] *adj* periódico ▷ *n* revista, publicación periódica

period pains *npl* dolores de la regla *or* de la menstruación

peripheral [pə'rɪfərəl] *adj* periférico ▷ *n (Comput)* periférico, unidad periférica

periphery [pə'rɪfərɪ] *n* periferia

perish ['pɛrɪʃ] *vi* perecer; *(decay)* echarse a perder

perishable ['pɛrɪʃəbl] *adj* perecedero

perjure ['pəːdʒəʳ] *vt:* **to ~ o.s** perjurar

perjury ['pəːdʒərɪ] *n (Law)* perjurio

perk [pəːk] *n* beneficio, extra

▶ **perk up** *vi (cheer up)* animarse

perky ['pəːkɪ] *adj* alegre, animado

perm [pəːm] *n* permanente ▷ *vt:* **to have one's hair ~ed** hacerse una permanente

permanent ['pəːmənənt] *adj* permanente; *(job, position)* fijo; *(dye, ink)* indeleble; **~ address** domicilio permanente; **I'm not ~ here** no estoy fijo aquí

permeate ['pəːmɪeɪt] *vi* penetrar, trascender ▷ *vt* penetrar, trascender a

permissible [pə'mɪsɪbl] *adj* permisible, lícito

permission [pə'mɪʃən] *n* permiso; **to give sb ~ to do sth** autorizar a algn para que haga algo; **with your ~** con su permiso

permissive [pə'mɪsɪv] *adj* permisivo

permit *n* permiso, licencia; *(entrance pass)* pase ▷ *vt* [pə'mɪt] permitir; *(accept)* tolerar ▷ *vi:* **weather ~ting** si el tiempo lo permite; **fishing ~** permiso de pesca; **building/export ~** licencia *or* permiso de construcción/exportación

perpendicular [pəːpən'dɪkjuləʳ] *adj* perpendicular

perpetual [pə'pɛtjuəl] *adj* perpetuo

perplex [pə'plɛks] *vt* dejar perplejo

perplexed [pə'plɛkst] *adj* perplejo, confuso

persecute ['pəːsɪkjuːt] *vt (pursue)* perseguir; *(harass)* acosar

persecution [pəːsɪ'kjuːʃən] *n* persecución

perseverance [pəːsɪ'vɪərəns] *n* perseverancia

persevere [pəːsɪ'vɪəʳ] *vi* perseverar

Persia ['pəːʃə] *n* Persia

Persian ['pəːʃən] *adj, n* persa ▷ *n:* **the ~ Gulf** el Golfo Pérsico

persist [pə'sɪst] *vi* persistir; **to ~ in doing sth** empeñarse en hacer algo

persistence [pə'sɪstəns] *n* empeño

persistent [pə'sɪstənt] *adj (lateness, rain)* persistente; *(determined)* porfiado; *(continuing)* constante; **~ offender** *(Law)* multirreincidente

person ['pəːsn] *n* persona; **in ~** en persona; **on** *or* **about one's ~** *(weapon, money)* encima; **a ~ to ~ call** *(Tel)* una llamada (de) persona a persona

personal ['pəːsnl] *adj* personal, individual; *(visit)* en persona; *(Brit Tel)* persona a persona

personal assistant (PA) *n* ayudante personal

personal column *n* anuncios personales

personal computer (PC) *n* ordenador *m* personal

personal identification number (PIN) *n (Comput, Banking)* número personal de identificación

personality [pəːsə'nælɪtɪ] *n* personalidad

personal loan *n* préstamo personal

personally ['pəːsnəlɪ] *adv* personalmente

personal organizer *n* agenda (profesional);

(*electronic*) organizador personal
personal property *n* bienes muebles
personal stereo *n* Walkman®
personify [pəˈsɔnɪfaɪ] *vt* encarnar, personificar
personnel [pəːsəˈnɛl] *n* personal
personnel department *n* departamento de personal
personnel manager *n* jefe de personal
perspective [pəˈspɛktɪv] *n* perspectiva; **to get sth into ~** ver algo en perspectiva *or* como es
Perspex® [ˈpəːspɛks] *n* (*Brit*) vidrio acrílico, plexiglás®
perspiration [pəːspɪˈreɪʃən] *n* transpiración, sudor
perspire [pəˈspaɪəʳ] *vi* transpirar, sudar
persuade [pəˈsweɪd] *vt*: **to ~ sb to do sth** persuadir a algn para que haga algo; **to ~ sb of sth/that** persuadir *or* convencer a algn de algo/de que; **I am ~d that** ... estoy convencido de que ...
persuasion [pəˈsweɪʒən] *n* persuasión; (*persuasiveness*) persuasiva; (*creed*) creencia
persuasive [pəˈsweɪsɪv] *adj* persuasivo
pertaining [pəːˈteɪnɪŋ]: **~ to** *prep* relacionado con
pertinent [ˈpəːtɪnənt] *adj* pertinente, a propósito
perturb [pəˈtəːb] *vt* perturbar
Peru [pəˈruː] *n* el Perú
peruse [pəˈruːz] *vt* (*examine*) leer con detención, examinar; (*glance at*) mirar por encima
Peruvian [pəˈruːvɪən] *adj*, *n* peruano(-a)
pervade [pəˈveɪd] *vt* impregnar; (*influence, ideas*) extenderse por
perverse [pəˈvəːs] *adj* perverso; (*stubborn*) terco; (*wayward*) travieso
perversion [pəˈvəːʃən] *n* perversión
pervert *n* pervertido(-a) ▷ *vt* pervertir
pessimism [ˈpɛsɪmɪzəm] *n* pesimismo
pessimist [ˈpɛsɪmɪst] *n* pesimista
pessimistic [pɛsɪˈmɪstɪk] *adj* pesimista
pest [pɛst] *n* (*insect*) insecto nocivo; (*fig*) lata, molestia; **pests** *npl* plaga
pester [ˈpɛstəʳ] *vt* molestar, acosar
pesticide [ˈpɛstɪsaɪd] *n* pesticida
pet [pɛt] *n* animal doméstico; (*favourite*) favorito(-a) ▷ *vt* acariciar ▷ *vi* (*col*) besuquearse ▷ *cpd*: **my ~ aversion** mi manía
petal [ˈpɛtl] *n* pétalo
peter [ˈpiːtəʳ]: **to ~ out** *vi* agotarse, acabarse
petite [pəˈtiːt] *adj* menuda, chiquita
petition [pəˈtɪʃən] *n* petición ▷ *vt* presentar una petición a ▷ *vi*: **to ~ for divorce** pedir el divorcio
petrified [ˈpɛtrɪfaɪd] *adj* (*fig*) pasmado, horrorizado
petrol [ˈpɛtrəl] (*Brit*) *n* gasolina; (*for lighter*) bencina; **two/four-star ~** gasolina normal/súper
petrol bomb *n* cóctel Molotov
petrol can *n* bidón de gasolina
petroleum [pəˈtrəulɪəm] *n* petróleo
petrol pump *n* (*Brit*: *in car*) bomba de gasolina; (*in garage*) surtidor de gasolina
petrol station *n* (*Brit*) gasolinera

petrol tank *n* (*Brit*) depósito (de gasolina)
petticoat [ˈpɛtɪkəut] *n* combinación, enagua(s) (*LAm*)
petty [ˈpɛtɪ] *adj* (*mean*) mezquino; (*unimportant*) insignificante
petty cash *n* dinero para gastos menores
petty officer *n* contramaestre
petulant [ˈpɛtjulənt] *adj* malhumorado
pew [pjuː] *n* banco
pewter [ˈpjuːtəʳ] *n* peltre
PG *n abbr* (*Cine*) = **parental guidance**
pH *n abbr* (= *pH value*) pH
phantom [ˈfæntəm] *n* fantasma
pharmacist [ˈfɑːməsɪst] *n* farmacéutico(-a)
pharmacy [ˈfɑːməsɪ] *n* (*US*) farmacia
phase [feɪz] *n* fase ▷ *vt*: **to ~ sth in/out** introducir/retirar algo por etapas; **~d withdrawal** retirada progresiva
PhD *abbr* = **Doctor of Philosophy**
pheasant [ˈfɛznt] *n* faisán
phenomenal [fɪˈnɔmɪnl] *adj* fenomenal, extraordinario
phenomenon [fəˈnɔmɪnən] (*pl* **phenomena**) *n* fenómeno
Philippines [ˈfɪlɪpiːnz] *npl*: **the ~** (las Islas) Filipinas
philosopher [fɪˈlɔsəfəʳ] *n* filósofo(-a)
philosophical [fɪləˈsɔfɪkl] *adj* filosófico
philosophy [fɪˈlɔsəfɪ] *n* filosofía
phobia [ˈfəubjə] *n* fobia
phone [fəun] *n* teléfono ▷ *vt* telefonear, llamar por teléfono; **to be on the ~** tener teléfono; (*be calling*) estar hablando por teléfono
  ▶ **phone back** *vt*, *vi* volver a llamar
  ▶ **phone up** *vt*, *vi* llamar por teléfono
phone book *n* guía telefónica
phone box, phone booth *n* cabina telefónica
phone call *n* llamada (telefónica)
phonecard [ˈfəunkɑːd] *n* tarjeta telefónica
phone-in [ˈfəunɪn] *n* (*Brit Radio, TV*) *programa de radio or televisión con las líneas abiertas al público*
phone tapping [-tæpɪŋ] *n* escuchas telefónicas
phonetics [fəˈnɛtɪks] *n* fonética
phon(e)y [ˈfəunɪ] *adj* falso ▷ *n* (*person*) farsante
photo [ˈfəutəu] *n* foto
photocall [ˈfəutəukɔːl] *n* sesión fotográfica para la prensa
photocopier [ˈfəutəukɔpɪəʳ] *n* fotocopiadora
photocopy [ˈfəutəukɔpɪ] *n* fotocopia ▷ *vt* fotocopiar
Photofit® [ˈfəutəufɪt] *n* (*also*: **Photofit picture**) retrato robot
photograph [ˈfəutəgræf] *n* fotografía ▷ *vt* fotografiar; **to take a ~ of sb** sacar una foto de algn
photographer [fəˈtɔgrəfəʳ] *n* fotógrafo
photography [fəˈtɔgrəfɪ] *n* fotografía
photo opportunity *n* *oportunidad de salir en la foto*
phrase [freɪz] *n* frase ▷ *vt* (*letter*) expresar, redactar
phrase book *n* libro de frases
physical [ˈfɪzɪkl] *adj* físico; **~ examination**

reconocimiento médico; **~ exercises** ejercicios físicos

physical education n educación física

physically ['fɪsɪklɪ] adv físicamente

physician [fɪ'zɪʃən] n médico(-a)

physicist ['fɪzɪsɪst] n físico(-a)

physics ['fɪzɪks] n física

physiotherapy [fɪzɪəu'θerəpɪ] n fisioterapia

physique [fɪ'ziːk] n físico

pianist ['pɪənɪst] n pianista

piano [pɪ'ænəu] n piano

pick [pɪk] n (tool: also: **pick-axe**) pico, piqueta ▷ vt (select) elegir, escoger; (gather: fruit, flowers) coger (Esp), recoger (LAm); (lock) abrir con ganzúa; (scab, spot) rascar ▷ vi: **to ~ and choose** ser muy exigente; **take your ~** escoja lo que quiera; **the ~ of** lo mejor de; **I ~ed the biggest piece** elegí el trozo más grande; **I've been ~ed for the team** me han seleccionado para el equipo; **to ~ one's nose/teeth** hurgarse las narices/escarbarse los dientes; **to ~ pockets** ratear, ser carterista; **to ~ one's way through** andar a tientas, abrirse camino; **to ~ a fight/quarrel with sb** buscar pelea/camorra con algn; **to ~ sb's brains** aprovecharse de los conocimientos de algn
  ▸ **pick at** vt fus: **to ~ at one's food** comer con poco apetito
  ▸ **pick off** vt (kill) matar de un tiro
  ▸ **pick on** vt fus (person) meterse con; **she's always ~ing on me** siempre se está metiendo conmigo
  ▸ **pick out** vt escoger; (distinguish) identificar; **I like them all — it's difficult to ~ one out** todos me gustan, es difícil escoger uno
  ▸ **pick up** vi (improve: sales) ir mejor; (: patient) reponerse; (: Finance) recobrarse ▷ vt (from floor) recoger; (buy) comprar; (find) encontrar; (learn) aprender; (Radio, TV, Tel) captar; **could you help me - up the toys?** ¿me ayudas a recoger los juguetes?; **we'll come to the airport to ~ you up** iremos a recogerte al aeropuerto; **I ~ed up some Spanish during my holiday** aprendí un poco de español en las vacaciones; **to ~ up speed** acelerarse; **to ~ o.s. up** levantarse; **to ~ up where one left off** reempezar algo donde lo había dejado

pickaxe, (US) **pickax** ['pɪkæks] n pico, zapapico

picket ['pɪkɪt] n (in strike) piquete ▷ vt hacer un piquete en, piquetear; **to be on ~ duty** estar de piquete

pickle ['pɪkl] n (also: **pickles**: as condiment) escabeche; (fig: mess) apuro ▷ vt conservar en escabeche; (in vinegar) conservar en vinagre; **in a ~** en un lío, en apuros

pickpocket ['pɪkpɔkɪt] n carterista

pickup ['pɪkʌp] n (Brit: on record player) brazo; (small truck: also: **pickup truck, pickup van**) furgoneta

picnic ['pɪknɪk] n picnic, merienda ▷ vi merendar en el campo

picture ['pɪktʃər] n cuadro; (painting) pintura; (drawing) dibujo; (photograph) fotografía; (film) película; (TV) imagen ▷ vt (paint) pintar; **a ~ by**

Picasso un cuadro de Picasso; **a ~ of his wife** un retrato de su mujer; **children's books have lots of ~s** los libros para niños tienen muchas ilustraciones; **my ~ was in the paper** mi foto salió en el periódico; **to draw a ~ of sth** dibujar algo; **to paint a ~ of sth** pintar algo; **to take a ~ of sb/sth** hacer or sacar una foto a algn/de algo; **the garden is a ~ in June** el jardín es una preciosidad en junio; **the overall ~** la impresión general; **to put sb in the ~** poner a algn al corriente or al tanto; **we get a good ~ here** (TV) captamos bien la imagen aquí; **the ~s** (Brit) el cine; **shall we go to the ~s?** ¿vamos al cine?; **to ~ sth to o.s.** imaginarse algo

picture book n libro de dibujos

picture messaging n (envío de) mensajes con imágenes

picturesque [pɪktʃə'resk] adj pintoresco

pie [paɪ] n (of meat etc: large) pastel; (: small) empanada; (sweet) tarta

piece [piːs] n pedazo, trozo; (of cake) trozo; (Draughts etc) ficha; (Chess, part of a set) pieza; (item): **a ~ of furniture/advice/news** un mueble/un consejo/una noticia ▷ vt: **to ~ together** juntar; (Tech) armar; **a ~ of plaster fell from the roof** un pedazo de yeso se cayó del tejado; **a small ~, please** un trocito, por favor; **to take sth to ~s** desmontar; **a 10p ~** una moneda de 10 peniques; **a 500-~ jigsaw** un puzzle de 500 piezas; **a 6-~ band** un conjunto de 6 (músicos); **in one ~** (object) de una sola pieza; **we got back all in one ~** llegamos sanos y salvos; **~ by ~** pieza por or a pieza; **to say one's ~** decir su parecer

piecemeal ['piːsmiːl] adv poco a poco

piecework ['piːswəːk] n trabajo a destajo

pie chart n gráfico de sectores or de tarta

pier [pɪər] n muelle, embarcadero

pierce [pɪəs] vt penetrar en, perforar; **to have one's ears ~d** hacerse los agujeros de las orejas

pig [pɪg] n cerdo, puerco, chancho (LAm); (person: greedy) tragón(-ona), comilón(-ona); (: nasty) cerdo(-a)

pigeon ['pɪdʒən] n paloma; (as food) pichón

pigeonhole ['pɪdʒənhəul] n casilla

piggy bank ['pɪgɪbæŋk] n hucha (en forma de cerdito)

piglet ['pɪglɪt] n cerdito, cochinillo

pigmentation [pɪgmən'teɪʃən] n pigmentación

pigmy ['pɪgmɪ] n = **pygmy**

pigskin ['pɪgskɪn] n piel de cerdo

pigsty ['pɪgstaɪ] n pocilga

pigtail ['pɪgteɪl] n (girl's) trenza; (Chinese, Taur) coleta

pike [paɪk] n (spear) pica; (fish) lucio

pilchard ['pɪltʃəd] n sardina

pile [paɪl] n (heap) montón; (of carpet) pelo; (vb: also: **pile up**) ▷ vt amontonar; (fig) acumular ▷ vi amontonarse; **in a ~** en un montón; **to ~ into** (car) meterse en
  ▸ **pile on** vt: **to ~ it on** (col) exagerar

piles [paɪlz] npl (Med) almorranas, hemorroides

pile-up ['paɪlʌp] n (Aut) accidente múltiple

pilfering ['pɪlfərɪŋ] n ratería
pilgrim ['pɪlgrɪm] n peregrino(-a); **the P~ Fathers** or **P~s** los primeros colonos norteamericanos; see also **Thanksgiving (Day)**
pilgrimage ['pɪlgrɪmɪdʒ] n peregrinación, romería
pill [pɪl] n píldora; **the ~** la píldora; **to be on the ~** tomar la píldora (anticonceptiva)
pillage ['pɪlɪdʒ] vt pillar, saquear
pillar ['pɪlər] n pilar, columna
pillar box n (Brit) buzón
pillion ['pɪljən] n (of motorcycle) asiento trasero; **to ride ~** ir en el asiento trasero
pillow ['pɪləu] n almohada
pillowcase ['pɪləukeɪs], **pillowslip** ['pɪləuslɪp] n funda (de almohada)
pilot ['paɪlət] n piloto ▷ adj (scheme etc) piloto ▷ vt pilotar; (fig) guiar, conducir
pilot light n piloto
pimp [pɪmp] n chulo, cafiche (LAm)
pimple ['pɪmpl] n grano
PIN n abbr (= personal identification number) NPI
pin [pɪn] n alfiler; (Elec: of plug) clavija; (Tech) perno; (: wooden) clavija; (drawing pin) chincheta; (in grenade) percutor ▷ vt prender con (alfiler); sujetar con perno; **~s and needles** hormigueo; **to ~ sth on sb** (fig) cargar a algn con la culpa de algo
▶ **pin down** vt (fig): **there's something strange here, but I can't quite ~ it down** aquí hay algo raro pero no puedo precisar qué es; **to ~ sb down** hacer que algn concrete
pinafore ['pɪnəfɔːr] n delantal
pinball ['pɪnbɔːl] n (also: **pinball machine**) millón, fliper
pincers ['pɪnsəz] npl pinzas, tenazas
pinch [pɪntʃ] n pellizco; (of salt etc) pizca ▷ vt pellizcar; (col: steal) birlar ▷ vi (shoe) apretar; **at a ~** en caso de apuro; **to feel the ~** (fig) pasar apuros or estrecheces
pincushion ['pɪnkuʃən] n acerico
pine [paɪn] n (also: **pine tree**) pino ▷ vi: **to ~ for** suspirar por
▶ **pine away** vi morirse de pena
pineapple ['paɪnæpl] n piña, ananá(s) (LAm)
ping [pɪŋ] n (noise) sonido agudo
Ping-Pong® ['pɪŋpɔn] n pingpong
pink [pɪŋk] adj (de color) rosa ▷ n (colour) rosa; (Bot) clavel
pinpoint ['pɪnpɔɪnt] vt precisar
pint [paɪnt] n pinta (Brit = 0,57 l; US = 0,47 l); (Brit col: of beer) pinta de cerveza, ≈ jarra (Esp)
pin-up ['pɪnʌp] n (picture) fotografía de mujer u hombre medio desnudos; **~ (girl)** ≈ chica de calendario
pioneer [paɪə'nɪər] n pionero(-a) ▷ vt promover
pious ['paɪəs] adj piadoso, devoto
pip [pɪp] n (seed) pepita; **the ~s** (Brit Tel) la señal
pipe [paɪp] n tubería, cañería; (for smoking) pipa, cachimba (LAm), cachimbo (LAm) ▷ vt conducir en cañerías; **(bag)pipes** npl gaita
▶ **pipe down** vi (col) callarse
pipe cleaner n limpiapipas

pipe dream n sueño imposible
pipeline ['paɪplaɪn] n tubería, cañería; (for oil) oleoducto; (for natural gas) gaseoducto; **it is in the ~** (fig) está en trámite
piper ['paɪpər] n (gen) flautista; (with bagpipes) gaitero(-a)
piping ['paɪpɪŋ] adv: **to be ~ hot** estar calentito
pique [piːk] n pique, resentimiento
pirate ['paɪərət] n pirata ▷ vt (record, video, book) hacer una copia pirata de
Pisces ['paɪsiːz] n Piscis
piss [pɪs] vi (col) mear
pissed [pɪst] adj (col!: drunk) mamado
pistol ['pɪstl] n pistola
piston ['pɪstən] n pistón, émbolo
pit [pɪt] n hoyo; (also: **coal pit**) mina; (in garage) foso de inspección; (also: **orchestra pit**) foso de la orquesta; (quarry) cantera ▷ vt (subj: chickenpox) picar; (: rust) comer; **to ~ A against B** oponer A a B; **pits** npl (Aut) box; **~ted with** (chickenpox) picado de
pitch [pɪtʃ] n (throw) lanzamiento; (Mus) tono; (Brit Sport) campo, terreno; (tar) brea; (in market etc) puesto; (fig: degree) nivel, grado ▷ vt (throw) arrojar, lanzar ▷ vi (fall) caer(se); (Naut) cabecear; **a football ~** un campo de fútbol; **I can't keep working at this ~** no puedo seguir trabajando a este ritmo; **at its (highest) ~** en su punto máximo; **his anger reached such a ~ that ...** su ira or cólera llegó a tal extremo que ...; **to ~ a tent** montar una tienda (de campaña); **to ~ one's aspirations too high** tener ambiciones desmesuradas
pitch-black ['pɪtʃ'blæk] adj negro como boca de lobo
pitched battle [pɪtʃt-] n batalla campal
piteous ['pɪtɪəs] adj lastimoso
pitfall ['pɪtfɔːl] n riesgo
pith [pɪθ] n (of orange) piel blanca; (fig) meollo
pithy ['pɪθɪ] adj jugoso
pitiful ['pɪtɪful] adj (touching) lastimoso, conmovedor(a); (contemptible) lamentable
pitiless ['pɪtɪlɪs] adj despiadado, implacable
pittance ['pɪtns] n miseria
pity ['pɪtɪ] n (compassion) compasión, piedad; (shame) lástima ▷ vt compadecer(se de); **to have** or **take ~ on sb** compadecerse de algn; **what a ~!** ¡qué pena!; **it is a ~ that you can't come** ¡qué pena que no puedas venir!
pivot ['pɪvət] n eje ▷ vi: **to ~ on** girar sobre; (fig) depender de
pixel ['pɪksl] n (Comput) pixel, punto
pizza ['piːtsə] n pizza
placard ['plækɑːd] n (in march etc) pancarta
placate [plə'keɪt] vt apaciguar
place [pleɪs] n lugar, sitio; (rank) rango; (seat) plaza, asiento; (post) puesto; (in street names) plaza; (home): **at/to his ~** en/a su casa ▷ vt (object) poner, colocar; (identify) reconocer; (find a post for) dar un puesto a, colocar; (goods) vender; **it's a quiet ~** es un lugar tranquilo; **a parking ~** un sitio para estacionar; **from ~ to**

~ de un sitio a or para otro; **book your ~ for the trip now** reserve ya su plaza para el viaje; **a university ~** una plaza en la universidad; **to take ~** tener lugar; **out of ~** (not suitable) fuera de lugar; **Britain won third ~ in the games** Gran Bretaña consiguió el tercer puesto en los juegos; **in the first ~** (fig: first of all) en primer lugar; **to change ~s with sb** cambiarse de sitio con algn; **all over the ~** por todas partes; **he's going ~s** (fig, col) llegará lejos; **I feel rather out of ~ here** me encuentro algo desplazado; **to put sb in his ~** (fig) poner a algn en su lugar; **it is not my ~ to do it** no me incumbe a mí hacerlo; **he ~d his hand on hers** colocó su mano sobre la de ella; **to ~ an order with sb (for)** hacer un pedido a algn (de); **I can't ~ him** no le recuerdo; **to be ~d** (in race, exam) colocarse; **we are better ~d than a month ago** estamos en mejor posición que hace un mes

placid ['plæsɪd] adj apacible, plácido

plagiarism ['pleɪdʒərɪzm] n plagio

plague [pleɪg] n plaga; (Med) peste ▷ vt (fig) acosar, atormentar; **to ~ sb with questions** acribillar a algn a preguntas

plaice [pleɪs] n (pl inv) platija

plaid [plæd] n (material) tela de cuadros

plain [pleɪn] adj (clear) claro, evidente; (simple) sencillo; (frank) franco, abierto; (not handsome/beautiful) poco atractivo; (pure) natural, puro ▷ adv claramente ▷ n llano, llanura; **to make sth ~ to sb** dejar algo en claro a algn; **it was ~ to see** era obvio; **a ~ white blouse** una blusa blanca sencilla; **a ~ tie** (not patterned) una corbata lisa; **in ~ clothes** (police) vestido de paisano

plain chocolate n chocolate oscuro or amargo

plainly ['pleɪnlɪ] adv claramente, evidentemente; (frankly) francamente

plaintiff ['pleɪntɪf] n demandante

plaintive ['pleɪntɪv] adj (cry, voice) lastimero, quejumbroso; (look) que da lástima

plait [plæt] n trenza ▷ vt trenzar

plan [plæn] n (scheme) plan, proyecto; (drawing) plano ▷ vt (think) pensar; (prepare) proyectar, planear; (intend) pensar, tener la intención de ▷ vi hacer proyectos; **have you any ~s for today?** ¿piensas hacer algo hoy?; **what are your ~s for the holidays?** ¿qué planes tienes para las vacaciones?; **to make ~s** hacer planes; **everything went according to ~** todo fue según lo previsto; **a ~ of the campsite** un plano del camping; **we're ~ning a trip to France** estamos planeando hacer un viaje a Francia; **~ your revision carefully** tienes que planificar bien el repaso; **to ~ to do** pensar hacer, tener la intención de hacer; **I'm ~ning to get a job in the holidays** tengo la intención de encontrar un trabajo para las vacaciones; **how long do you ~ to stay?** ¿cuánto tiempo piensas quedarte?; **to ~ for** planear, proyectar

▸ **plan out** vt planear detalladamente

plane [pleɪn] n (Aviat) avión; (tree) plátano; (tool)

cepillo; (Math) plano

planet ['plænɪt] n planeta

plank [plæŋk] n tabla

planner ['plænər] n planificador(a); (chart) diagrama de planificación; **town ~** urbanista

planning ['plænɪŋ] n (Pol, Econ) planificación; **family ~** planificación familiar

planning permission n licencia de obras

plant [plɑːnt] n planta; (machinery) maquinaria; (factory) fábrica ▷ vt plantar; (field) sembrar; (bomb) colocar

plantation [plæn'teɪʃən] n plantación; (estate) hacienda

plant pot n maceta, tiesto

plaque [plæk] n placa

plasma ['plæzmə] n plasma

plaster ['plɑːstər] n (for walls) yeso; (also: **plaster of Paris**) yeso mate; (Med: for broken leg etc) escayola; (Brit: also: **sticking plaster**) tirita (Esp), curita (LAm) ▷ vt enyesar; (cover): **to ~ with** llenar or cubrir de; **to be ~ed with mud** estar cubierto de barro

plastered ['plɑːstəd] adj (col) borracho

plastic ['plæstɪk] n plástico ▷ adj de plástico

plastic bag n bolsa de plástico

plastic bullet n bala de goma

plastic explosive n goma 2®

plasticine® ['plæstɪsiːn] n (Brit) plastilina®

plastic surgery n cirujía plástica

plate [pleɪt] n (dish) plato; (metal, in book) lámina; (Phot, on door) placa; (Aut: number plate) matrícula

plateau ['plætəu] (pl -s or -x) n meseta, altiplanicie

plate glass n vidrio or cristal cilindrado

platform ['plætfɔːm] n (Rail) andén; (stage) plataforma; (at meeting) tribuna; (Pol) programa (electoral); **the train leaves from ~ 7** el tren sale del andén número 7

platinum ['plætɪnəm] n platino

platter ['plætər] n fuente

plausible ['plɔːzɪbl] adj verosímil; (person) convincente

play [pleɪ] n (gen) juego; (Theat) obra ▷ vt (tennis, football, cards) jugar a; (instrument) tocar; (Theat) representar; (: part) hacer el papel de; (fig) desempeñar ▷ vi jugar; (frolic) juguetear; **to bring** or **call into ~** poner en juego; **a ~ by Shakespeare** una obra de Shakespeare; **to put on a ~** montar una obra; **the children were ~ing a game in the garden** los niños estaban jugando en el jardín; **can you ~ pool?** ¿sabes jugar al billar americano?; **Spain will ~ Scotland next month** España juega contra Escocia el mes que viene; **I ~ the guitar** toco la guitarra; **what sort of music do they ~?** ¿qué clase de música tocan?; **she's always ~ing that record** siempre está poniendo ese disco; **I would love to ~ Cleopatra** me encantaría hacer de Cleopatra; **to ~ safe** ir a lo seguro; **to ~ a trick on sb** gastar una broma a algn; **they're ~ing at soldiers** están jugando a (los) soldados; **to ~ for time** (fig) tratar de ganar tiempo; **to ~ into sb's**

hands (fig) hacerle el juego a algn; **a smile ~ed on his lips** una sonrisa le bailaba en los labios
▶ **play about, play around** vi (person) hacer el tonto; **to ~ about** or **around with** (fiddle with) juguetear con; (idea) darle vueltas a
▶ **play along** vi: **to ~ along with** seguirle el juego a ▷ vt: **to ~ sb along** (fig) jugar con algn
▶ **play back** vt poner
▶ **play down** vt quitar importancia a; **he tried to ~ down his illness** trató de quitarle importancia a su enfermedad
▶ **play on** vt fus (sb's feelings, credulity) aprovecharse de; **to ~ on sb's nerves** atacarle los nervios a algn
▶ **play up** vi (cause trouble: children) dar guerra; **the engine's ~ing up again** el motor está haciendo de las suyas otra vez

playact ['pleɪækt] vi (fig) hacer comedia or teatro

playboy ['pleɪbɔɪ] n playboy

player ['pleɪə^r] n jugador(a); (Theat) actor, actriz; (Mus) músico(-a)

playful ['pleɪful] adj juguetón(-ona)

playground ['pleɪgraund] n (in school) patio de recreo

playgroup ['pleɪgru:p] n jardín de infancia

playing card ['pleɪɪŋ-] n naipe, carta

playing field n campo de deportes

playmaker ['pleɪmeɪkə^r] n (Sport) jugador encargado de facilitar buenas jugadas a sus compañeros

playmate ['pleɪmeɪt] n compañero(-a) de juego

play-off ['pleɪɔf] n (Sport) (partido de) desempate

playpen ['pleɪpɛn] n corral

plaything ['pleɪθɪŋ] n juguete

playtime ['pleɪtaɪm] n (Scol) (hora de) recreo

playwright ['pleɪraɪt] n dramaturgo(-a)

plc abbr (= public limited company) S.A.

plea [pli:] n (request) súplica, petición; (excuse) pretexto, disculpa; (Law) alegato, defensa

plea bargaining (Law) acuerdo entre fiscal y defensor para agilizar los trámites judiciales

plead [pli:d] vt (Law): **to ~ sb's case** defender a algn; (give as excuse) poner como pretexto ▷ vi (Law) declararse; (beg): **to ~ with sb** suplicar or rogar a algn; **to ~ guilty/not guilty** (defendant) declararse culpable/inocente; **to ~ for sth** (beg for) suplicar algo

pleasant ['plɛznt] adj agradable

pleasantries ['plɛzntrɪz] npl (polite remarks) cortesías; **to exchange ~** conversar amablemente

please [pli:z] vt (give pleasure to) dar gusto a, agradar ▷ vi (think fit): **do as you ~** haz lo que quieras or lo que te dé la gana; **to ~ o.s.** hacer lo que le parezca; **~ yourself!** ¡haz lo que quieras!, ¡como quieras!; **two coffees, ~** dos cafés, por favor; **can we have the bill ~?** ¿nos puede traer la cuenta?; **~ come in** pase; **~!** ¡por favor!; **~ don't cry!** ¡no llores! te lo ruego; **would you ~ be quiet?** ¿quieres hacer el favor de callarte?

pleased [pli:zd] adj (happy) alegre, contento; (satisfied): **~ (with)** satisfecho (de); **~ to meet you** (col) ¡encantado!, ¡tanto or mucho gusto!;

to be ~ (about sth) alegrarse (de algo); **we are ~ to inform you that ...** tenemos el gusto de comunicarle que ...

pleasing ['pli:zɪŋ] adj agradable, grato

pleasure ['plɛʒə^r] n placer, gusto; (will) voluntad ▷ cpd de recreo; **"it's a ~"** "el gusto es mío"; **it's a ~ to see him** da gusto verle; **I have much ~ in informing you that ...** tengo el gran placer de comunicarles que ...; **with ~** con mucho or todo gusto; **is this trip for business or ~?** ¿este viaje es de negocios o de placer?

pleasure cruise n crucero de placer

pleat [pli:t] n pliegue

pleb [plɛb] n: **the ~s** la gente baja, la plebe

plebiscite ['plɛbɪsɪt] n plebiscito

plectrum ['plɛktrəm] n plectro

pledge [plɛdʒ] n (object) prenda; (promise) promesa, voto ▷ vt (pawn) empeñar; (promise) prometer; **to ~ support for sb** prometer su apoyo a algn; **to ~ sb to secrecy** hacer jurar a algn que guardará el secreto

plentiful ['plɛntɪful] adj copioso, abundante

plenty ['plɛntɪ] n abundancia; **~ of** mucho(s)(-a(s)); **we've got ~ of time to get there** tenemos tiempo de sobra para llegar

pleurisy ['pluərɪsɪ] n pleuresía

pliable ['plaɪəbl] adj flexible

pliers ['plaɪəz] npl alicates, tenazas

plight [plaɪt] n condición or situación difícil

plimsolls ['plɪmsəlz] npl (Brit) zapatillas de tenis

plinth [plɪnθ] n plinto

plod [plɒd] vi caminar con paso pesado; (fig) trabajar laboriosamente

plonk [plɒŋk] (col) n (Brit: wine) vino peleón ▷ vt: **to ~ sth down** dejar caer algo

plot [plɒt] n (scheme) complot, conjura; (of story, play) argumento; (of land) terreno, parcela ▷ vt (mark out) trazar; (conspire) tramar, urdir ▷ vi conspirar; **a vegetable ~** un cuadro de hortalizas

plough, (US) **plow** [plau] n arado ▷ vt (earth) arar
▶ **plough back** vt (Comm) reinvertir
▶ **plough through** vt fus (crowd) abrirse paso a la fuerza por

ploughman ['plaumən] n: **~'s lunch** pan con queso y cebolla

plow [plau] (US) = **plough**

ploy [plɔɪ] n truco, estratagema

pluck [plʌk] vt (fruit) coger (Esp), recoger (LAm); (musical instrument) puntear; (bird) desplumar ▷ n valor, ánimo; **to ~ up courage** hacer de tripas corazón; **to ~ one's eyebrows** depilarse las cejas

plucky ['plʌkɪ] adj valiente

plug [plʌg] n tapón; (Elec) enchufe, clavija; (Aut: also: **spark(ing) plug**) bujía ▷ vt (hole) tapar; (col: advertise) dar publicidad a; **to give sb/sth a ~** dar publicidad a algn/algo; **to ~ a lead into a socket** enchufar un hilo en una toma
▶ **plug in** vt, vi (Elec) enchufar

plum [plʌm] n (fruit) ciruela; (also: **plum job**) chollo

plumb [plʌm] adj vertical ▷ n plomo ▷ adv

(*exactly*) exactamente, en punto ▷ *vt* sondar; (*fig*) sondear

▸ **plumb in** *vt* (*washing machine*) conectar
plumber ['plʌmə^r] *n* fontanero(-a), plomero(-a) (*LAm*)
plumbing ['plʌmɪŋ] *n* (*trade*) fontanería, plomería (*LAm*); (*piping*) cañerías
plummet ['plʌmɪt] *vi*: **to ~ (down)** caer a plomo
plump [plʌmp] *adj* rechoncho, rollizo ▷ *vt*: **to ~ sth (down) on** dejar caer algo en

▸ **plump for** *vt fus* (*col: choose*) optar por
▸ **plump up** *vt* ahuecar
plunder ['plʌndə^r] *n* pillaje; (*loot*) botín ▷ *vt* saquear, pillar
plunge [plʌndʒ] *n* zambullida ▷ *vt* sumergir, hundir ▷ *vi* (*fall*) caer; (*dive*) saltar; (*person*) arrojarse; (*sink*) hundirse; **to take the ~** lanzarse; **to ~ a room into darkness** sumir una habitación en la oscuridad
plunger ['plʌndʒə^r] *n* émbolo; (*for drain*) desatascador
plunging ['plʌndʒɪŋ] *adj* (*neckline*) escotado
pluperfect [pluː'pəːfɪkt] *n* pluscuamperfecto
plural ['pluərl] *n* plural
plus [plʌs] *n* (*also*: **plus sign**) signo más; (*fig*) punto a favor ▷ *adj*: **a ~ factor** (*fig*) un factor a favor ▷ *prep* más, y, además de; **ten/twenty ~** más de diez/veinte
plush [plʌʃ] *adj* de felpa
ply [plaɪ] *vt* (*a trade*) ejercer ▷ *vi* (*ship*) ir y venir; (*for hire*) ofrecerse (para alquilar); **3 ~** (*wool*) de 3 cabos; **to ~ sb with drink** no dejar de ofrecer copas a algn
plywood ['plaɪwud] *n* madera contrachapada
PM *n abbr* (*Brit*) = **Prime Minister**
pneumatic [njuː'mætɪk] *adj* neumático
pneumatic drill *n* taladradora neumática
pneumonia [njuː'məunɪə] *n* pulmonía, neumonía
PO *n abbr* (= *Post Office*) Correos; (*Naut*) = **petty officer**
po *abbr* = **postal order**
poach [pəutʃ] *vt* (*cook*) escalfar; (*steal*) cazar/pescar en vedado ▷ *vi* cazar/pescar en vedado
poached [pəutʃt] *adj* (*egg*) escalfado
poacher ['pəutʃə^r] *n* cazador(a) furtivo(-a)
PO Box *n abbr* = **Post Office Box**
pocket ['pɔkɪt] *n* bolsillo; (*of air,: Geo, fig*) bolsa; (*Billiards*) tronera ▷ *vt* meter en el bolsillo; (*steal*) embolsarse; (*Billiards*) entronerar; **breast ~** bolsillo de pecho; **~ of resistance** foco de resistencia; **~ of warm air** bolsa de aire caliente; **to be out of ~** salir perdiendo; **to be £5 in/out of ~** salir ganando/perdiendo 5 libras
pocketbook ['pɔkɪtbuk] *n* (*US: wallet*) cartera; (: *handbag*) bolso
pocket knife *n* navaja
pocket money *n* asignación
pod [pɔd] *n* vaina
podgy ['pɔdʒɪ] *adj* gordinflón(-ona)
podiatrist [pɔ'diːətrɪst] *n* (*US*) podólogo(-a)
podium ['pəudɪəm] *n* podio

poem ['pəuɪm] *n* poema
poet ['pəuɪt] *n* poeta
poetic [pəu'ɛtɪk] *adj* poético
poet laureate [-'lɔːrɪɪt] *n* poeta laureado
poetry ['pəuɪtrɪ] *n* poesía
poignant ['pɔɪnjənt] *adj* conmovedor(a)
point [pɔɪnt] *n* punto; (*tip*) punta; (*purpose*) fin, propósito; (*use*) utilidad; (*significant part*) lo esencial; (*place*) punto, lugar; (*Brit Elec: also*: **power point**) toma de corriente, enchufe; (*also*: **decimal point**): **2 ~ 3 (2.3)** 2 coma 3 (2,3) ▷ *vt* (*gun etc*): **to ~ sth at sb** apuntar con algo a algn ▷ *vi* señalar con el dedo; **points** *npl* (*Aut*) contactos; (*Rail*) agujas; **a ~ on the horizon** un punto en el horizonte; **they scored 5 ~s** sacaron 5 puntos; **a pencil with a sharp ~** un lápiz con la punta afilada; **to be on the ~ of doing sth** estar a punto de hacer algo; **they were on the ~ of finding it** estaban a punto de encontrarlo; **at that ~, we decided to leave** en aquel momento decidimos marcharnos; **there's no ~** no tiene sentido; **there's no ~ in waiting** no tiene sentido esperar; **what's the ~?** ¿para qué?; **what's the ~ of leaving so early?** ¿para qué salir tan pronto?; **to come to the ~** ir al meollo; **when it comes to the ~** a la hora de la verdad; **to get the ~** comprender; **sorry, I don't get the ~** perdona, pero no lo entiendo; **that's the whole ~!** ¡de eso se trata!; **to be beside the ~** no venir al caso; **that's not the ~** eso no tiene nada que ver; **to make a ~ of doing sth** poner empeño en hacer algo; **he made some interesting ~s** hizo algunos comentarios de interés; **you've got a ~ there!**, **that's a good ~!** ¡tienes razón!; **punctuality isn't my strong ~** la puntualidad no es mi fuerte; **~ of order** cuestión de procedimiento; **in ~ of fact** en realidad; **a ~ of view** un punto de vista; **~ of departure** (*also fig*) punto de partida; **~ of sale** (*Comm*) punto de venta; **~-of-sale advertising** publicidad en el punto de venta; **the train stops at Carlisle and all ~s south** el tren para en Carlisle, y en todas las estaciones al sur; **don't ~!** ¡no señales con el dedo!; **to ~ at sb** señalar a algn con el dedo

▸ **point out** *vt* señalar; **the guide ~ed out the Alhambra to us** el guía nos señaló la Alhambra; **I should ~ out that...** me gustaría indicar que...
▸ **point to** *vt fus* indicar con el dedo; (*fig*) indicar, señalar
point-blank ['pɔɪnt'blæŋk] *adv* (*also*: **at point-blank range**) a quemarropa
pointed ['pɔɪntɪd] *adj* (*shape*) puntiagudo, afilado; (*remark*) intencionado
pointer ['pɔɪntə^r] *n* (*stick*) puntero; (*needle*) aguja, indicador; (*clue*) indicación, pista; (*advice*) consejo
pointless ['pɔɪntlɪs] *adj* sin sentido
point of view *n* punto de vista
poise [pɔɪz] *n* (*of head, body*) porte; (*calmness*) aplomo

poison ['pɔɪzn] n veneno ▷ vt envenenar
poisonous ['pɔɪznəs] adj venenoso; (fumes etc)
tóxico; (fig: ideas, literature) pernicioso; (: rumours,
individual) nefasto
poke [pəuk] vt (fire) hurgar, atizar; (jab with finger,
stick etc) dar; (Comput) almacenar; (put): **to ~ sth
in(to)** introducir algo en ▷ n (jab) empujoncito;
(with elbow) codazo; **to ~ one's head out of the
window** asomar la cabeza por la ventana; **to ~
fun at sb** ridiculizar a algn; **to give the fire a ~**
atizar el fuego
▸ **poke about** vi fisgonear
poker ['pəukə'] n atizador; (Cards) póker
poky ['pəukɪ] adj estrecho
Poland ['pəulənd] n Polonia
polar ['pəulə'] adj polar
polar bear n oso polar
polarize ['pəuləraɪz] vt polarizar
Pole [pəul] n polaco(-a)
pole [pəul] n palo; (Geo) polo; (Tel) poste;
(flagpole) asta; (tent pole) mástil
poleaxe ['pəulæks] vt (fig) desnucar
pole bean n (US) judía trepadora
pole star n estrella polar
pole vault n salto con pértiga
police [pə'liːs] n policía ▷ vt (streets, city, frontier)
vigilar
police car n coche-patrulla
police constable n (Brit) guardia, policía
police department n (US) policía
police force n cuerpo de policía
policeman [pə'liːsmən] n guardia, policía,
agente (LAm)
police officer n guardia, policía
police station n comisaría
policewoman [pə'liːswumən] n mujer policía
policy ['pɔlɪsɪ] n política; (also: **insurance policy**)
póliza; (of newspaper, company) política; **it is our
~ to do that** tenemos por norma hacer eso; **to
take out a ~** sacar una póliza, hacerse un seguro
polio ['pəulɪəu] n polio
Polish ['pəulɪʃ] adj, n polaco
polish ['pɔlɪʃ] n (for shoes) betún; (for floor) cera (de
lustrar); (for nails) esmalte; (shine) brillo, lustre;
(fig: refinement) refinamiento ▷ vt (shoes) limpiar;
(make shiny) pulir, sacar brillo a; (fig: improve)
perfeccionar, refinar
▸ **polish off** vt (work) terminar; (food) despachar
▸ **polish up** vt (shoes, furniture etc) limpiar, sacar
brillo a; (fig: language) perfeccionar
polished ['pɔlɪʃt] adj (fig: person) refinado
polite [pə'laɪt] adj cortés, atento; (formal)
correcto; **it's not ~ to do that** es de mala
educación hacer eso
politeness [pə'laɪtnɪs] n cortesía
political [pə'lɪtɪkl] adj político
politically [pə'lɪtɪkəlɪ] adv políticamente
politically correct adj políticamente correcto
politician [pɔlɪ'tɪʃən] n político(-a)
politics ['pɔlɪtɪks] n política
poll [pəul] n (votes) votación, votos; (also: **opinion
poll**) sondeo, encuesta ▷ vt (votes) obtener; (in

opinion poll) encuestar; **to go to the ~s** (voters)
votar; (government) acudir a las urnas
pollen ['pɔlən] n polen
pollen count n índice de polen
polling booth ['pəulɪŋ] n cabina de votar
polling day n día de elecciones
polling station n centro electoral
pollster ['pəulstə'] n (person) encuestador(a);
(organization) empresa de encuestas or sondeos
poll tax n (Brit, formerly) contribución municipal
(no progresiva)
pollutant [pə'luːtənt] n (agente) contaminante
pollute [pə'luːt] vt contaminar
pollution [pə'luːʃən] n contaminación, polución
polo ['pəuləu] n (sport) polo
polo-neck ['pəuləunɛk] adj de cuello vuelto ▷ n
(sweater) suéter de cuello vuelto
poly bag ['pɔlɪ-] n (Brit col) bolsa de plástico
polyester [pɔlɪ'ɛstə'] n poliéster
polygraph ['pɔlɪɡrɑːf] n polígrafo
polystyrene [pɔlɪ'staɪriːn] n poliestireno
polytechnic [pɔlɪ'tɛknɪk] n escuela politécnica
polythene ['pɔlɪθiːn] n (Brit) polietileno
polythene bag n bolsa de plástico
polyurethane [pɔlɪ'juərɪθeɪn] n poliuretano
pomegranate ['pɔmɪɡrænɪt] n granada
pomp [pɔmp] n pompa
pompous ['pɔmpəs] adj pomposo; (person)
presumido
pond [pɔnd] n (natural) charca; (artificial)
estanque
ponder ['pɔndə'] vt meditar
ponderous ['pɔndərəs] adj pesado
pong [pɔŋ] n (Brit col) peste ▷ vi (Brit col) apestar
pontiff ['pɔntɪf] n pontífice
pony ['pəunɪ] n poney, potro
ponytail ['pəunɪteɪl] n coleta, cola de caballo
pony trekking [-'trɛkɪŋ] n (Brit) excursión a
caballo
poodle ['puːdl] n caniche
pooh-pooh [puː'puː] vt desdeñar
pool [puːl] n (natural) charca; (pond) estanque;
(also: **swimming pool**) piscina, alberca (CAm,
Méx), pileta (RP); (billiards) billar americano;
(Comm: consortium) consorcio; (: US: monopoly
trust) trust ▷ vt juntar; **typing ~** servicio de
mecanografía; (football) **~s** npl quinielas
poor [puə'] adj pobre; (bad) malo ▷ npl: **the ~** los
pobres
poorly ['puəlɪ] adj mal, enfermo
pop [pɔp] n ¡pum!; (sound) ruido seco; (Mus)
(música) pop; (US col: father) papá; (col: drink)
gaseosa ▷ vt (burst) hacer reventar ▷ vi reventar;
(cork) saltar; **she ~ped her head out (of the
window)** sacó de repente la cabeza (por la
ventana)
▸ **pop in** vi entrar un momento
▸ **pop out** vi salir un momento
▸ **pop up** vi aparecer inesperadamente
pop concert n concierto pop
popcorn ['pɔpkɔːn] n palomitas (de maíz)
pope [pəup] n papa

poplar ['pɒplər] n álamo
popper ['pɒpər] n corchete, botón automático
poppy ['pɒpɪ] n amapola; see also **Remembrance Sunday**
Popsicle® ['pɒpsɪkl] n (US) polo
popular ['pɒpjulər] adj popular; **a ~ song** una canción popular; **to be ~ (with)** (person) caer bien (a); (decision) ser popular (entre)
popularity [pɒpju'lærɪtɪ] n popularidad
population [pɒpju'leɪʃən] n población
porcelain ['pɔ:slɪn] n porcelana
porch [pɔ:tʃ] n pórtico, entrada
porcupine ['pɔ:kjupaɪn] n puerco espín
pore [pɔ:r] n poro ▷ vi: **to ~ over** enfrascarse en
pork [pɔ:k] n (carne de) cerdo or chancho (LAm)
porn [pɔ:n] adj, n (col) porno
pornographic [pɔ:nə'græfɪk] adj pornográfico
pornography [pɔ:'nɔgrəfɪ] n pornografía
porpoise ['pɔ:pəs] n marsopa
porridge ['pɒrɪdʒ] n gachas de avena
port [pɔ:t] n (harbour) puerto; (Naut: left side) babor; (wine) oporto; (Comput) puerta, puerto, port; **~ of call** puerto de escala
portable ['pɔ:təbl] adj portátil
porter ['pɔ:tər] n (for luggage) maletero; (doorkeeper) portero(-a), conserje; (US Rail) mozo de los coches-cama
portfolio [pɔ:t'fəuliəu] n (case, of artist) cartera, carpeta; (Pol, Finance) cartera
porthole ['pɔ:θəul] n portilla
portion ['pɔ:ʃən] n porción; (helping) ración
portly ['pɔ:tlɪ] adj corpulento
portrait ['pɔ:treɪt] n retrato
portray [pɔ:'treɪ] vt retratar; (in writing) representar
portrayal [pɔ:'treɪəl] n representación
Portugal ['pɔ:tjugl] n Portugal
Portuguese [pɔ:tju'gi:z] adj portugués(-esa) ▷ n (pl inv) portugués(-esa); (Ling) portugués
pose [pəuz] n postura, actitud; (pej) afectación, pose ▷ vi posar; (pretend): **to ~ as** hacerse pasar por ▷ vt (question) plantear; **to strike a ~** tomar or adoptar una pose or actitud
poser ['pəuzər] n problema /pregunta difícil; (person) = **poseur**
poseur [pəu'zə:r] n presumido(-a), persona afectada
posh [pɒʃ] adj (col) elegante, de lujo ▷ adv (col): **to talk ~** hablar con acento afectado
position [pə'zɪʃən] n posición; (job) puesto ▷ vt colocar; **to be in a ~ to do sth** estar en condiciones de hacer algo
positive ['pɒzɪtɪv] adj positivo; (certain) seguro; (definite) definitivo; **we look forward to a ~ reply** (Comm) esperamos que pueda darnos una respuesta en firme; **he's a ~ nuisance** es un auténtico pelmazo; **~ cash flow** (Comm) flujo positivo de efectivo
posse ['pɒsɪ] n (US) pelotón
possess [pə'zes] vt poseer; **whatever can have ~ed you?** ¿cómo se te ocurrió?
possessed [pə'zest] adj poseso, poseído; **like one**

~ como un poseído
possession [pə'zeʃən] n posesión; **to take ~ of sth** tomar posesión de algo
possessive [pə'zesɪv] adj posesivo
possessiveness [pə'zesɪvnɪs] n posesividad
possibility [pɒsɪ'bɪlɪtɪ] n posibilidad; **he's a ~ for the part** es uno de los posibles para el papel
possible ['pɒsɪbl] adj posible; **as big as ~** lo más grande posible; **it is ~ to do it** es posible hacerlo; **as far as ~** en la medida de lo posible; **a ~ candidate** un(a) posible candidato(-a)
possibly ['pɒsɪblɪ] adv (perhaps) posiblemente, tal vez; **I cannot ~ come** me es imposible venir; **could you ~ ...?** ¿podrías ...?
post [pəust] n (Brit: letters, delivery) correo; (job, situation) puesto; (trading post) factoría; (pole) poste ▷ vt (Brit: send by post) mandar por correo; (: put in mailbox) echar al correo; (Mil) apostar; (bills) fijar, pegar; (Brit: appoint): **to ~ to** destinar a; **by ~** por correo; **by return of ~** a vuelta de correo; **to keep sb ~ed** tener a algn al corriente
post... [pəust] pref post..., pos...; **post 1950** pos(t) 1950
postage ['pəustɪdʒ] n porte, franqueo
postage stamp n sello (de correo)
postal ['pəustl] adj postal, de correos
postal order n giro postal
postbox ['pəustbɒks] n (Brit) buzón
postcard ['pəustkɑ:d] nf (tarjeta) postal
postcode ['pəustkəud] n (Brit) código postal
poster ['pəustər] n cartel, afiche (LAm)
poste restante [pəust'restɔ̃nt] n (Brit) lista de correos
posterior [pɒs'tɪərɪər] n (col) trasero
posterity [pɒs'terɪtɪ] n posteridad
postgraduate ['pəust'grædjuɪt] n posgraduado(-a)
posthumous ['pɒstjuməs] adj póstumo
postman ['pəustmən] n cartero
postmark ['pəustmɑ:k] n matasellos
post-mortem [pəust'mɔ:təm] n autopsia
post office n (building) (oficina de) correos; (organization): **the Post Office** Administración General de Correos
Post Office Box (PO Box) n apartado postal, casilla de correos (LAm)
postpone [pəs'pəun] vt aplazar, postergar (LAm)
postponement [pəs'pəunmənt] n aplazamiento
posture ['pɒstʃər] n postura, actitud
postwar [pəust'wɔ:r] adj de la posguerra
posy ['pəuzɪ] n ramillete (de flores)
pot [pɒt] n (for cooking) olla; (for flowers) tiesto, maceta; (for jam) tarro, pote (LAm); (piece of pottery) cacharro; (col: marijuana) costo ▷ vt (plant) poner en tiesto or maceta; (conserve) conservar (en tarros); **~s of** (col) montones de; **to go to ~** (col: work, performance) irse al traste
potato [pə'teɪtəu] (pl **-es**) n patata, papa (LAm)
potato crisps, (US) **potato chips** npl patatas or papas (LAm)
potato peeler n pelapatatas
potent ['pəutnt] adj potente, poderoso; (drink)

fuerte

potential [pə'tɛnʃl] *adj* potencial, posible ▷ *n* potencial; **to have** ~ prometer

pothole ['pɔthəul] *n* (*in road*) bache; (*Brit: underground*) gruta

potholing ['pɔthəulɪŋ] *n* (*Brit*): **to go** ~ dedicarse a la espeleología

potion ['pəuʃən] *n* poción, pócima

potluck [pɔt'lʌk] *n*: **to take** ~ conformarse con lo que haya

potted ['pɔtɪd] *adj* (*food*) en conserva; (*plant*) en tiesto or maceta; (*fig: shortened*) resumido

potter ['pɔtər] *n* alfarero(-a) ▷ *vi*: **to** ~ **around**, ~ **about** entretenerse haciendo cosillas; **~'s wheel** torno de alfarero; **to** ~ **round the house** estar en casa haciendo cosillas

pottery ['pɔtərɪ] *n* cerámica, alfarería; **a piece of** ~ un objeto de cerámica

potty ['pɔtɪ] *adj* (*col: mad*) chiflado ▷ *n* orinal de niño

pouch [pautʃ] *n* (*Zool*) bolsa; (*for tobacco*) petaca

poultry ['pəultrɪ] *n* aves de corral; (*dead*) pollos

pounce [pauns] *vi*: **to** ~ **on** precipitarse sobre ▷ *n* salto, ataque

pound [paund] *n* libra; (*for dogs*) perrera; (*for cars*) depósito ▷ *vt* (*beat*) golpear; (*crush*) machacar ▷ *vi* (*beat*) dar golpes; **half a** ~ media libra; **a 5** ~ **note** un billete de 5 libras

pour [pɔːr] *vt* echar; (*tea*) servir ▷ *vi* correr, fluir; (*rain*) llover a cántaros

▶ **pour away, pour off** *vt* vaciar, verter

▶ **pour in** *vi* (*people*) entrar en tropel; **to come ~ing in** (*water*) entrar a raudales; (*letters*) llegar a montones; (*cars, people*) llegar en tropel

▶ **pour out** *vi* (*people*) salir en tropel ▷ *vt* (*drink*) echar, servir

pouring ['pɔːrɪŋ] *adj*: ~ **rain** lluvia torrencial

pout [paut] *vi* hacer pucheros

poverty ['pɔvətɪ] *n* pobreza, miseria; (*fig*) falta, escasez

poverty line *n*: **below the** ~ por debajo del umbral de pobreza

poverty-stricken ['pɔvətɪstrɪkn] *adj* necesitado

POW *n abbr* = **prisoner of war**

powder ['paudər] *n* polvo; (*face powder*) polvos; (*gun powder*) pólvora ▷ *vt* empolvar; **to** ~ **one's face** ponerse polvos; **to** ~ **one's nose** empolvarse la nariz, ponerse polvos; (*euphemism*) ir al baño

powder compact *n* polvera

powdered milk ['paudəd-] *n* leche en polvo

powder keg *n* (*fig*) polvorín

powder puff *n* borla (para empolvarse)

powder room *n* aseos

power ['pauər] *n* poder; (*strength*) fuerza; (*nation*) potencia; (*drive*) empuje; (*Tech*) potencia; (*Elec*) energía ▷ *vt* impulsar; **to be in** ~ (*Pol*) estar en el poder; **to do all in one's** ~ **to help sb** hacer todo lo posible por ayudar a algn; **the world ~s** las potencias mundiales; **the ~'s off** (*Elec*) se ha ido la corriente; **nuclear/solar** ~ la energía nuclear/solar

power cut *n* (*Brit*) apagón

powered ['pauəd] *adj*: ~ **by** impulsado por; **nuclear-~ submarine** submarino nuclear

power failure *n* = **power cut**

powerful ['pauəful] *adj* poderoso; (*engine*) potente; (*strong*) fuerte; (*play, speech*) conmovedor(a)

powerless ['pauəlɪs] *adj* impotente, ineficaz

power of attorney *n* poder, procuración

power point *n* (*Brit*) enchufe

power station *n* central eléctrica

pp *abbr* (= *per procurationem: by proxy*) p.p.

PPS *abbr* (= *post postscriptum*) posdata adicional; (*Brit*: = *Parliamentary Private Secretary*) *ayudante de un ministro*

PR *n abbr* = **proportional representation**; (= *public relations*) relaciones públicas ▷ *abbr* (*US*) = **Puerto Rico**

practical ['præktɪkl] *adj* práctico

practicality [præktɪ'kælɪtɪ] *n* (*of situation etc*) aspecto práctico

practical joke *n* broma pesada

practically ['præktɪklɪ] *adv* (*almost*) casi, prácticamente

practice ['præktɪs] *n* (*habit*) costumbre; (*exercise*) práctica; (*training*) adiestramiento; (*Med*) clientela ▷ *vt, vi* (*US*) = **practise**; **in** ~ (*in reality*) en la práctica; **out of** ~ desentrenado; **to put sth into** ~ poner algo en práctica; **it's common** ~ es bastante corriente; **target** ~ práctica de tiro; **he has a small** ~ (*doctor*) tiene pocos pacientes; **to set up in** ~ **as** establecerse como

practise, (*US*) **practice** ['præktɪs] *vt* (*carry out*) practicar; (*profession*) ejercer; (*train at*) practicar ▷ *vi* ejercer; (*train*) practicar

practising, (*US*) **practicing** ['præktɪsɪŋ] *adj* (*Christian etc*) practicante; (*lawyer*) que ejerce; (*homosexual*) activo

practitioner [præk'tɪʃənər] *n* practicante; (*Med*) médico(-a)

pragmatic [præg'mætɪk] *adj* pragmático

prairie ['prɛərɪ] *n* (*US*) pampa

praise [preɪz] *n* alabanza(s), elogio(s)

praiseworthy ['preɪswə:ðɪ] *adj* loable

pram [præm] *n* (*Brit*) cochecito de niño

prance [prɑːns] *vi* (*horse*) hacer cabriolas

prank [præŋk] *n* travesura

prat [præt] *n* (*Brit col*) imbécil

prawn [prɔːn] *n* gamba

pray [preɪ] *vi* rezar; **to** ~ **for forgiveness** pedir perdón

prayer [prɛər] *n* oración, rezo; (*entreaty*) ruego, súplica

preach [priːtʃ] *vi* predicar

preacher ['priːtʃər] *n* predicador(a); (*US: minister*) pastor(a)

prearrange [priːə'reɪndʒ] *vt* organizar or acordar de antemano

precarious [prɪ'kɛərɪəs] *adj* precario

precaution [prɪ'kɔːʃən] *n* precaución

precede [prɪ'siːd] *vt, vi* preceder

precedent ['prɛsɪdənt] *n* precedente; **to establish** or **set a** ~ sentar un precedente

precinct ['pri:sɪŋkt] n recinto; (US: district)
distrito, barrio; **precincts** npl recinto;
pedestrian ~ (Brit) zona peatonal; **shopping ~**
(Brit) centro comercial

precious ['prɛʃəs] adj precioso; (treasured)
querido; (stylized) afectado ▷ adv (col): **~ little/
few** muy poco/pocos; **your ~ dog** (ironic) tu
querido perro

precipitate adj (hasty) precipitado ▷ vt precipitar

precise [prɪ'saɪs] adj preciso, exacto; (person)
escrupuloso

precisely [prɪ'saɪslɪ] adv exactamente,
precisamente

precision [prɪ'sɪʒən] n precisión

preclude [prɪ'klu:d] vt excluir

precocious [prɪ'kəuʃəs] adj precoz

precondition [pri:kən'dɪʃən] n condición previa

predator ['prɛdətəʳ] n depredador

predecessor ['pri:dɪsesəʳ] n antecesor(a)

predestination [pri:dɛstɪ'neɪʃən] n
predestinación

predicament [prɪ'dɪkəmənt] n apuro

predict [prɪ'dɪkt] vt predecir, pronosticar

predictable [prɪ'dɪktəbl] adj previsible

prediction [prɪ'dɪkʃən] n pronóstico, predicción

predominant [prɪ'dɔmɪnənt] adj predominante

predominantly [prɪ'dɔmɪnəntlɪ] adv en su
mayoría

pre-eminent [pri:'ɛmɪnənt] adj preeminente

pre-empt [pri:'ɛmt] vt (Brit) adelantarse a

preen [pri:n] vt: **to ~ itself** (bird) limpiarse las
plumas; **to ~ o.s.** pavonearse

prefab ['pri:fæb] n casa prefabricada

preface ['prɛfəs] n prefacio

prefect ['pri:fɛkt] n (Brit: in school) monitor(a)

prefer [prɪ'fə:ʳ] vt preferir; (Law: charges, complaint)
presentar; (: action) entablar; **to ~ coffee to tea**
preferir el café al té

preferable ['prɛfrəbl] adj preferible

preferably ['prɛfrəblɪ] adv preferentemente,
más bien

preference ['prɛfrəns] n preferencia; **in ~ to sth**
antes que algo

preferential [prɛfə'rɛnʃəl] adj preferente

prefix ['pri:fɪks] n prefijo

pregnancy ['prɛgnənsɪ] n embarazo

pregnancy test n prueba del embarazo

pregnant ['prɛgnənt] adj embarazada; **3
months ~** embarazada de 3 meses; **~ with
meaning** cargado de significado

prehistoric ['pri:hɪs'tɔrɪk] adj prehistórico

prejudge [pri:'dʒʌdʒ] vt prejuzgar

prejudice ['prɛdʒudɪs] n (bias) prejuicio; (harm)
perjuicio ▷ vt (bias) predisponer; (harm)
perjudicar; **to ~ sb in favour of/against** (bias)
predisponer a algn a favor de/en contra de

prejudiced ['prɛdʒudɪst] adj (person)
predispuesto; (view) parcial, interesado; **to be ~
against sb/sth** estar predispuesto en contra de
algn/algo

preliminary [prɪ'lɪmɪnərɪ] adj preliminar

prelude ['prɛlju:d] n preludio

premarital ['pri:'mærɪtl] adj prematrimonial,
premarital

premature ['prɛmətʃuəʳ] adj (arrival etc)
prematuro; **you are being a little ~** te has
adelantado

premeditation [pri:mɛdɪ'teɪʃən] n
premeditación

premier ['prɛmɪəʳ] adj primero, principal ▷ n
(Pol) primer(a) ministro(-a)

première ['prɛmɪɛəʳ] n estreno

premise ['prɛmɪs] n premisa

premises ['prɛmɪsɪs] npl local; **on the ~** en el
lugar mismo; **business ~** locales comerciales

premium ['pri:mɪəm] n prima; **to be at a ~** estar
muy solicitado; **to sell at a ~** (shares) vender caro

premium bond n (Brit) bono del estado que participa
en una lotería nacional

premonition [prɛmə'nɪʃən] n presentimiento

preoccupied [pri:'ɔkjupaɪd] adj (worried)
preocupado; (absorbed) ensimismado

prep [prɛp] adj abbr: **~ school = preparatory
school** ▷ n abbr (Scol: = preparation) deberes

prepaid [pri:'peɪd] adj porte pagado; **~ envelope**
sobre de porte pagado

preparation [prɛpə'reɪʃən] n preparación;
preparations npl preparativos; **in ~ for sth** en
preparación para algo

preparatory [prɪ'pærətərɪ] adj preparatorio,
preliminar; **~ to sth/to doing sth** como
preparación para algo/para hacer algo

preparatory school n (Brit) colegio privado de
enseñanza primaria; (US) colegio privado de enseñanza
secundaria; see also **public school**

prepare [prɪ'pɛəʳ] vt preparar, disponer ▷ vi:
to ~ for prepararse or disponerse para; (make
preparations) hacer preparativos para

prepared [prɪ'pɛəd] adj (willing): **to be ~ to help
sb** estar dispuesto a ayudar a algn

preposition [prɛpə'zɪʃən] n preposición

preposterous [prɪ'pɔstərəs] adj absurdo, ridículo

prerequisite [pri:'rɛkwɪzɪt] n requisito previo

prescribe [prɪ'skraɪb] vt prescribir; (Med) recetar
~d books (Brit Scol) libros del curso

prescription [prɪ'skrɪpʃən] n (Med) receta; **to
make up** or (US) **fill a ~** preparar una receta;
only available on ~ se vende solamente con
receta (médica)

presence ['prɛzns] n presencia; (attendance)
asistencia

presence of mind n aplomo

present adj (in attendance) presente; (current)
actual ▷ n (gift) regalo; (actuality) actualidad,
presente ▷ vt (introduce) presentar; (expound)
exponer; (give) presentar, dar, ofrecer; (Theat)
representar; **to be ~ at** asistir a, estar presente
en; **he wasn't ~ at the meeting** no estuvo
presente en la reunión; **those ~** los presentes;
the ~ situation la situación actual; **the ~ tense**
el presente; **to give sb a ~** regalar algo a algn;
he gave me a lovely ~ me hizo un precioso
regalo; **to live in the ~** vivir el presente; **at ~**
actualmente; **for the ~** por el momento; **up to**

the ~ hasta el momento presente; **to ~ sb with
sth** entregar algo a algn; **the Mayor ~ed the
winner with a medal** el alcalde le entregó una
medalla al vencedor; **to ~ o.s. for an interview**
presentarse a una entrevista; **may I ~ Miss
Clark** permítame presentarle or le presento a
la Srta Clark; **he agreed to ~ the show** aceptó
presentar el espectáculo

presentation [prɛzn'teɪʃən] n presentación;
(*gift*) obsequio; (*of case*) exposición; (*Theat*)
representación; **on ~ of the voucher** al
presentar el vale

present-day ['prɛzntdeɪ] adj actual

presenter [prɪ'zɛntəʳ] n (*Radio, TV*) locutor(a)

presently ['prɛzntlɪ] adv (*soon*) dentro de poco;
(*US: now*) ahora

preservation [prɛzə'veɪʃən] n conservación

preservative [prɪ'zə:vətɪv] n conservante

preserve [prɪ'zə:v] vt (*keep safe*) preservar,
proteger; (*maintain*) mantener; (*food*) conservar;
(*in salt*) salar ▷ n (*for game*) coto, vedado; (*often pl*:
jam) confitura

presidency ['prɛzɪdənsɪ] n presidencia

president ['prɛzɪdənt] n presidente; (*US: of
company*) director(a)

presidential [prɛzɪ'dɛnʃl] adj presidencial

press [prɛs] n (*tool, machine, newspapers*) prensa;
(*printer's*) imprenta; (*of hand*) apretón ▷ vt (*push*)
empujar; (*squeeze*) apretar; (*grapes*) pisar; (*clothes:
iron*) planchar; (*pressure*) presionar; (*doorbell*)
apretar, pulsar, tocar; (*insist*): **to ~ sth on sb**
insistir en que algn acepte algo ▷ vi (*squeeze*)
apretar; (*pressurize*) ejercer presión; **to go to
~** (*newspaper*) entrar en prensa; **to be in the ~**
(*being printed*) estar en prensa; (*in the newspapers*)
aparecer en la prensa; **the story appeared in
the ~ last week** la historia salió en la prensa la
semana pasada; **don't ~ too hard!** ¡no aprietes
muy fuerte!; **he ~ed the accelerator** pisó
el acelerador; **we are ~ed for time** tenemos
poco tiempo; **to ~ sb to do** or **into doing sth**
(*urge, entreat*) presionar a algn para que haga
algo; **to ~ sb for an answer** insistir a algn para
que conteste; **to ~ charges against sb** (*Law*)
demandar a algn

▶ **press ahead** vi seguir adelante

▶ **press on** vi avanzar; (*hurry*) apretar el paso

press agency n agencia de prensa

press conference n rueda de prensa

pressing ['prɛsɪŋ] adj apremiante

press officer n jefe(-a) de prensa

press release n comunicado de prensa

press stud n (*Brit*) botón de presión

press-up ['prɛsʌp] n (*Brit*) flexión

pressure ['prɛʃəʳ] n (*urgency*) apremio,
urgencia; (*influence*) influencia; **high/low ~**
alta/baja presión; **to put ~ on sb** presionar a
algn, hacer presión sobre algn; **to be under
~** estar presionado; **she was under ~ from
the management** estaba presionada por la
dirección; **he's been under a lot of ~ recently**
últimamente ha estado muy agobiado

pressure cooker n olla a presión

pressure gauge n manómetro

pressure group n grupo de presión

pressurized ['prɛʃəraɪzd] adj (*container*) a presión

prestige [prɛs'ti:ʒ] n prestigio

prestigious [prɛs'tɪdʒəs] adj prestigioso

presumably [prɪ'zju:məblɪ] adv es de suponer
que, cabe presumir que; **~ he did it** es de
suponer que lo hizo él

presume [prɪ'zju:m] vt suponer, presumir; **to ~
to do** (*dare*) atreverse a hacer

presumption [prɪ'zʌmpʃən] n suposición;
(*pretension*) presunción

presuppose [pri:sə'pəuz] vt presuponer

pretence, (*US*) **pretense** [prɪ'tɛns] n (*claim*)
pretensión; (*pretext*) pretexto; (*make-believe*)
fingimiento; **on** or **under the ~ of doing sth**
bajo or con el pretexto de hacer algo; **she is
devoid of all ~** no es pretenciosa

pretend [prɪ'tɛnd] vt (*feign*) fingir ▷ vi (*feign*)
fingir; (*claim*): **to ~ to sth** pretender a algo

pretense [prɪ'tɛns] n (*US*) = **pretence**

pretension [prɪ'tɛnʃən] n (*claim*) pretensión; **to
have no ~s to** sth/to being sth no engañarse en
cuanto a algo/a ser algo

pretext ['pri:tɛkst] n pretexto; **on** or **under the ~
of doing sth** con el pretexto de hacer algo

pretty ['prɪtɪ] adj (*gen*) bonito, lindo (*LAm*) ▷ adv
bastante

prevail [prɪ'veɪl] vi (*gain mastery*) prevalecer; (*be
current*) predominar; (*persuade*): **to ~ (up)on sb to
do sth** persuadir a algn para que haga algo

prevailing [prɪ'veɪlɪŋ] adj (*dominant*)
predominante

prevalent ['prɛvələnt] adj (*dominant*) dominante;
(*widespread*) extendido; (*fashionable*) de moda

prevent [prɪ'vɛnt] vt: **to ~ sb from doing sth**
impedir a algn hacer algo

preventative [prɪ'vɛntətɪv] adj preventivo

prevention [prɪ'vɛnʃən] n prevención

preventive [prɪ'vɛntɪv] adj preventivo

preview ['pri:vju:] n (*of film*) preestreno

previous ['pri:vɪəs] adj previo, anterior; **he
has no ~ experience in that field** no tiene
experiencia previa en ese campo; **I have a ~
engagement** tengo un compromiso anterior

previously ['pri:vɪəslɪ] adv antes

prewar [pri:'wɔːʳ] adj antes de la guerra

prey [preɪ] n presa ▷ vi: **to ~ on** vivir a costa
de; (*feed on*) alimentarse de; **it was ~ing on his
mind** le obsesionaba

price [praɪs] n precio; (*Betting: odds*) puntos de
ventaja ▷ vt (*goods*) fijar el precio de; **to go up**
or **rise in ~** subir de precio; **to come down in
~** bajar de precio; **what is the ~ of ...?** ¿qué
precio tiene ...?; **to put a ~ on sth** poner precio
a algo; **what ~ his promises now?** ¿para qué
sirven ahora sus promesas?; **he regained his
freedom, but at a ~** recobró su libertad, pero le
había costado caro; **to be ~d out of the market**
(*article*) no encontrar comprador por ese precio;
(*nation*) no ser competitivo

priceless ['praislis] *adj* que no tiene precio; (*col: amusing*) divertidísimo
price list *n* tarifa
pricey ['praisi] *adj* (*Brit col*) caro
prick [prik] *n* pinchazo; (*with pin*) alfilerazo; (*sting*) picadura ▷ *vt* pinchar; picar; **to ~ up one's ears** aguzar el oído
prickle ['prikl] *n* (*sensation*) picor; (*Bot*) espina; (*Zool*) púa
prickly ['prikli] *adj* espinoso; (*fig: person*) enojadizo
prickly heat *n* sarpullido causado por exceso de calor
pride [praid] *n* orgullo; (*pej*) soberbia ▷ *vt*: **to ~ o.s. on** enorgullecerse de; **to take (a) ~ in** enorgullecerse de; **her ~ and joy** su orgullo; **to have ~ of place** tener prioridad
priest [pri:st] *n* sacerdote
priesthood ['pri:sthud] *n* (*practice*) sacerdocio; (*priests*) clero
prim [prim] *adj* (*demure*) remilgado; (*prudish*) gazmoño
primal ['praiməl] *adj* original; (*important*) principal
primarily ['praimərili] *adv* (*above all*) ante todo, primordialmente
primary ['praiməri] *adj* primario; (*first in importance*) principal ▷ *n* (*US: also*: **primary election**) (elección) primaria
primary school *n* (*Brit*) escuela primaria
primate *n* ['praimit] (*Rel*) primado ▷ *n* ['praimeit] (*Zool*) primate
prime [praim] *adj* primero, principal; (*basic*) fundamental; (*excellent*) selecto, de primera clase ▷ *n*: **in the ~ of life** en la flor de la vida ▷ *vt* (*gun, pump*) cebar; (*fig*) preparar
Prime Minister (PM) *n* primer(a) ministro(-a); *see also* **Downing Street**
primer ['praimə'] *n* (*book*) texto elemental; (*paint*) capa preparatoria
primeval [prai'mi:vəl] *adj* primitivo
primitive ['primitiv] *adj* primitivo; (*crude*) rudimentario; (*uncivilized*) inculto
primrose ['primrəuz] *n* primavera, prímula
primus (stove)® ['praiməs-] *n* (*Brit*) hornillo de camping
prince [prins] *n* príncipe
princess [prin'ses] *n* princesa
principal ['prinsipl] *adj* principal ▷ *n* director(a); (*in play*) protagonista principal; (*Comm*) capital, principal; *see also* **pantomime**
principle ['prinsipl] *n* principio; **in ~** en principio; **on ~** por principio
print [print] *n* (*impression*) marca, impresión; huella; (*letters*) letra de molde; (*fabric*) estampado; (*Art*) grabado; (*Phot*) impresión ▷ *vt* (*gen*) imprimir; (*write in capitals*) escribir en letras de molde; **out of ~** agotado
▶ **print out** *vt* (*Comput*) imprimir
printed matter *n* impresos
printer ['printə'] *n* (*person*) impresor(a); (*machine*) impresora

printing ['printiŋ] *n* (*art*) imprenta; (*act*) impresión; (*quantity*) tirada
printout ['printaut] *n* (*Comput*) printout
prior ['praiə'] *adj* anterior, previo ▷ *n* prior; **~ to doing** antes de *or* hasta hacer; **without ~ notice** sin previo aviso; **to have a ~ claim to sth** tener prioridad en algo
priority [prai'ɔriti] *n* prioridad; **to have** *or* **take ~ over sth** tener prioridad sobre algo
prise, (*US*) **prize** [praiz] *vt*: **to ~ open** abrir con palanca
prism ['prizəm] *n* prisma
prison ['prizn] *n* cárcel, prisión ▷ *cpd* carcelario
prisoner ['priznə'] *n* (*in prison*) preso(-a); (*under arrest*) detenido(-a); (*in dock*) acusado(-a); **the ~ at the bar** el (la) acusado(-a); **to take sb ~** hacer *or* tomar prisionero a algn
prisoner of war *n* prisionero(-a) *or* preso(-a) de guerra
pristine ['pristi:n] *adj* pristino
privacy ['privəsi] *n* (*seclusion*) soledad; (*intimacy*) intimidad; **in the strictest ~** con el mayor secreto
private ['praivit] *adj* (*personal*) particular; (*confidential*) secreto, confidencial; (*intimate*) privado, íntimo; (*sitting etc*) a puerta cerrada ▷ *n* soldado raso; **"~"** (*on envelope*) "confidencial"; (*on door*) "privado"; **in ~** en privado; **in (his) ~ life** en su vida privada; **to be in ~ practice** tener consulta particular
private enterprise *n* la empresa privada
private eye *n* detective privado(-a)
private limited company *n* (*Brit*) sociedad de responsabilidad limitada
private property *n* propiedad privada
private school *n* colegio privado
privatize ['praivitaiz] *vt* privatizar
privet ['privit] *n* alheña
privilege ['privilidʒ] *n* privilegio; (*prerogative*) prerrogativa
privy ['privi] *adj*: **to be ~ to** estar enterado de
Privy Council *n* consejo privado (de la Corona)
prize [praiz] *n* premio ▷ *adj* (*first class*) de primera clase ▷ *vt* apreciar, estimar; (*US*) = **prise**
prize-giving ['praizgiviŋ] *n* distribución de premios
prizewinner ['praizwinə'] *n* premiado(-a)
pro [prəu] *n* (*Sport*) profesional; **the ~s and cons** los pros y los contras
pro- [prəu] *pref* (*in favour of*) pro, en pro de; **~Soviet** pro-soviético
proactive [prəu'æktiv] *adj*: **to be ~** impulsar la actividad
probability [prɔbə'biliti] *n* probabilidad; **in all ~ he won't turn up** lo más probable es que no aparezca
probable ['prɔbəbl] *adj* probable; **it is ~/hardly ~ that** es probable/poco probable que
probably ['prɔbəbli] *adv* probablemente
probation [prə'beiʃən] *n*: **on ~** (*employee*) a prueba;

(*Law*) en libertad condicional
probation officer *n* *persona a cargo de los presos en libertad condicional*
probe [prəub] *n* (*Med, Space*) sonda; (*enquiry*) investigación ▷ *vt* sondar; (*investigate*) investigar
problem ['prɒbləm] *n* problema; **what's the ~?** ¿cuál es el problema?, ¿qué pasa?; **no ~!** ¡por supuesto!; **to have ~s with the car** tener problemas con el coche
problematic(al) [prɒblə'mætɪk(l)] *adj* problemático
procedure [prə'si:dʒəʳ] *n* procedimiento; (*bureaucratic*) trámites; **cashing a cheque is a simple ~** cobrar un cheque es un trámite sencillo
proceed [prə'si:d] *vi* proceder, (*continue*): **to ~ (with)** continuar (con); **to ~ against sb** (*Law*) proceder contra algn; **I am not sure how to ~** no sé cómo proceder; *see also* **proceeds**
proceedings [prə'si:dɪŋz] *npl* acto, actos; (*Law*) proceso; (*meeting*) función; (*records*) actas
proceeds ['prəusi:dz] *npl* ganancias, ingresos
process ['prəusɛs] *n* proceso; (*method*) sistema; (*proceeding*) procedimiento ▷ *vt* tratar, elaborar ▷ *vi* [prə'sɛs] (*Brit: formal: go in procession*) desfilar; **the peace ~** el proceso de paz; **in ~** en curso; **we are in the ~ of moving to …** estamos en vías de mudarnos a …; **we're in the ~ of painting the kitchen** ahora mismo estamos pintando la cocina
processing ['prəusɛsɪŋ] *n* elaboración
procession [prə'sɛʃən] *n* desfile; **funeral ~** cortejo fúnebre
proclaim [prə'kleɪm] *vt* proclamar; (*announce*) anunciar
procrastinate [prəu'kræstɪneɪt] *vi* demorarse
procreation [prəukrɪ'eɪʃən] *n* procreación
Procurator Fiscal ['prɔkjureɪtə-] *n* (*Scottish*) fiscal
procure [prə'kjuəʳ] *vt* conseguir, obtener
prod [prɒd] *vt* (*push*) empujar; (*with elbow*) dar un codazo a ▷ *n* empujoncito; codazo
prodigal ['prɒdɪgl] *adj* pródigo
prodigious [prə'dɪdʒəs] *adj* prodigioso
prodigy ['prɒdɪdʒɪ] *n* prodigio
produce *n* (*Agr*) productos agrícolas ▷ *vt* producir; (*yield*) rendir; (*bring*) sacar; (*show*) presentar, mostrar; (*proof of identity*) enseñar, presentar; (*Theat*) presentar, poner en escena; (*offspring*) dar a luz
producer [prə'dju:səʳ] *n* (*Theat*) director(a); (*Agr, Cine*) productor(a)
product ['prɒdʌkt] *n* producto
production [prə'dʌkʃən] *n* (*act*) producción; (*Theat*) representación, montaje; **to put into ~** lanzar a la producción
production line *n* línea de producción
productive [prə'dʌktɪv] *adj* productivo
productivity [prɒdʌk'tɪvɪtɪ] *n* productividad
Prof. [prɒf] *abbr* (= *professor*) Prof.
profane [prə'feɪn] *adj* profano
profess [prə'fɛs] *vt* profesar; **I do not ~ to be an**

expert no pretendo ser experto
profession [prə'fɛʃən] *n* profesión
professional [prə'fɛʃnl] *n* profesional ▷ *adj* profesional; (*by profession*) de profesión; **to take ~ advice** buscar un consejo profesional
professor [prə'fɛsəʳ] *n* (*Brit*) catedrático(-a); (*US: teacher*) profesor(a)
proficiency [prə'fɪʃənsɪ] *n* capacidad, habilidad
proficient [prə'fɪʃənt] *adj* experto, hábil
profile ['prəufaɪl] *n* perfil; **to keep a high/low ~** tratar de llamar la atención/pasar inadvertido
profit ['prɒfɪt] *n* (*Comm*) ganancia; (*fig*) provecho ▷ *vi*: **to ~ by** *or* **from** aprovechar *or* sacar provecho de; **~ and loss account** cuenta de ganancias y pérdidas; **with ~s endowment assurance** seguro dotal con beneficios; **to sell sth at a ~** vender algo con ganancia
profitability [prɒfɪtə'bɪlɪtɪ] *n* rentabilidad
profitable ['prɒfɪtəbl] *adj* (*Econ*) rentable; (*beneficial*) provechoso, útil
profound [prə'faund] *adj* profundo
profusely [prə'fju:slɪ] *adv* profusamente
programme, (*US*) **program** ['prəugræm] *n* programa ▷ *vt* programar
program(m)er ['prəugræməʳ] *n* programador(a)
program(m)ing ['prəugræmɪŋ] *n* programación
progress *n* progreso; (*development*) desarrollo ▷ *vi* progresar, avanzar; desarrollarse; **in ~** (*meeting, work etc*) en curso; **as the match ~ed** a medida que avanzaba el partido
progression [prə'grɛʃən] *n* progresión
progressive [prə'grɛsɪv] *adj* progresivo; (*person*) progresista
prohibit [prə'hɪbɪt] *vt* prohibir; **to ~ sb from doing sth** prohibir a algn hacer algo; **"smoking ~ed"** "prohibido fumar"
prohibition [prəuɪ'bɪʃən] *n* (*US*) prohibicionismo
project *n* proyecto; (*Scol, Univ: research*) trabajo, proyecto ▷ *vt* proyectar ▷ *vi* (*stick out*) salir, sobresalir
projection [prə'dʒɛkʃən] *n* proyección; (*overhang*) saliente
projector [prə'dʒɛktəʳ] *n* proyector
proletariat [prəulɪ'tɛərɪət] *n* proletariado
prolific [prə'lɪfɪk] *adj* prolífico
prologue, (*US*) **prolog** ['prəulɒg] *n* prólogo
prolong [prə'lɒŋ] *vt* prolongar, extender
prom [prɒm] *n abbr* (*Brit*) = **promenade**; **promenade concert** ▷ *n* (*US: ball*) baile de gala
promenade [prɒmə'nɑ:d] *n* (*by sea*) paseo marítimo ▷ *vi* (*stroll*) pasearse
promenade concert *n* concierto (*en que parte del público permanece de pie*); *see also* **prom**
prominence ['prɒmɪnəns] *n* (*fig*) importancia
prominent ['prɒmɪnənt] *adj* (*standing out*) saliente; (*important*) eminente, importante; **he is ~ in the field of …** destaca en el campo de …
promiscuity [prɒmɪs'kju:ɪtɪ] *n* promiscuidad
promiscuous [prə'mɪskjuəs] *adj* (*sexually*) promiscuo
promise ['prɒmɪs] *n* promesa ▷ *vt, vi* prometer;

to make sb a ~ prometer algo a algn; **a young man of ~** un joven con futuro; **to ~ (sb) to do sth** prometer (a algn) hacer algo; **to ~ well** ser muy prometedor

promising ['prɒmɪsɪŋ] *adj* prometedor(a)

promote [prə'məut] *vt* promover; (*new product*) dar publicidad a, lanzar; (*Mil*) ascender; **the team was ~d to the second division** (*Brit Football*) el equipo ascendió a la segunda división

promoter [prə'məutə'] *n* (*of sporting event*) promotor(a); (*of company, business*) patrocinador(a)

promotion [prə'məuʃən] *n* (*gen*) promoción; (*Mil*) ascenso

prompt [prɒmpt] *adj* pronto ⊳ *adv*: **at 6 o'clock ~** a las 6 en punto ⊳ *n* (*Comput*) aviso, guía ⊳ *vt* (*urge*) mover, incitar; (*Theat*) apuntar; **to be ~ to do sth** no tardar en hacer algo; **they're very ~** (*punctual*) son muy puntuales; **to ~ sb to do sth** instar a algn a hacer algo

promptly ['prɒmptlɪ] *adv* (*punctually*) puntualmente; (*rapidly*) rápidamente

prone [prəun] *adj* (*lying*) postrado; **~ to** propenso a

prong [prɒŋ] *n* diente, punta

pronoun ['prəunaun] *n* pronombre

pronounce [prə'nauns] *vt* pronunciar; (*declare*) declarar ⊳ *vi*: **to ~ (up)on** pronunciarse sobre; **they ~d him unfit to plead** le declararon incapaz de defenderse

pronunciation [prənʌnsɪ'eɪʃən] *n* pronunciación

proof [pru:f] *n* prueba; **70° ~** graduación del 70 por 100 ⊳ *adj*: **~ against** a prueba de ⊳ *vt* (*tent, anorak*) impermeabilizar

proofreader ['pru:fri:də'] *n* corrector(a) de pruebas

prop [prɒp] *n* apoyo; (*fig*) sostén ⊳ *vt* (*also*: **prop up**) apoyar; (*lean*): **to ~ sth against** apoyar algo contra

propaganda [prɒpə'gændə] *n* propaganda

propel [prə'pɛl] *vt* impulsar, propulsar

propeller [prə'pɛlə'] *n* hélice

propensity [prə'pɛnsɪtɪ] *n* propensión

proper ['prɒpə'] *adj* (*suited, right*) propio; (*exact*) justo; (*apt*) apropiado, conveniente; (*timely*) oportuno; (*seemly*) correcto, decente; (*authentic*) verdadero; (*col: real*) auténtico; **to go through the ~ channels** (*Admin*) ir por la vía oficial

properly ['prɒpəlɪ] *adv* (*adequately*) correctamente; (*decently*) decentemente

proper noun *n* nombre propio

property ['prɒpətɪ] *n* propiedad; (*estate*) finca; **lost ~** objetos perdidos; **personal ~** bienes muebles

prophecy ['prɒfɪsɪ] *n* profecía

prophesy ['prɒfɪsaɪ] *vt* profetizar; (*fig*) predecir

prophet ['prɒfɪt] *n* profeta

proportion [prə'pɔːʃən] *n* proporción; (*share*) parte; **to be in/out of ~ to** *or* **with sth** estar en/no guardar proporción con algo; **to see sth in ~** (*fig*) ver algo en su justa medida

proportional [prə'pɔːʃənl] *adj* proporcional

proportional representation (PR) *n* (*Pol*) representación proporcional

proposal [prə'pəuzl] *n* propuesta; (*offer of marriage*) oferta de matrimonio; (*plan*) proyecto; (*suggestion*) sugerencia

propose [prə'pəuz] *vt* proponer; (*have in mind*): **to ~ sth/to do** *or* **doing sth** proponer algo/proponerse hacer algo ⊳ *vi* declararse

proposer [prə'pəuzə'] *n* (*of motion*) proponente

proposition [prɒpə'zɪʃən] *n* propuesta, proposición; **to make sb a ~** proponer algo a algn

proprietor [prə'praɪətə'] *n* propietario(-a), dueño(-a)

propriety [prə'praɪətɪ] *n* decoro

pro rata [prəu'rɑːtə] *adv* a prorrata

prose [prəuz] *n* prosa; (*Scol*) traducción inversa

prosecute ['prɒsɪkjuːt] *vt* (*Law*) procesar; **"trespassers will be ~d"** (*Law*) "se procesará a los intrusos"

prosecution [prɒsɪ'kjuːʃən] *n* proceso, causa; (*accusing side*) acusación

prosecutor ['prɒsɪkjuːtə'] *n* acusador(a); (*also*: **public prosecutor**) fiscal

prospect *n* (*chance*) posibilidad; (*outlook*) perspectiva; (*hope*) esperanza ⊳ *vt* explorar ⊳ *vi* buscar; **prospects** *npl* (*for work etc*) perspectivas; **to be faced with the ~ of ...** tener que enfrentarse a la posibilidad de que ...; **we were faced with the ~ of leaving early** se nos planteó la posibilidad de marcharnos pronto; **there is every ~ of an early victory** hay buenas perspectivas de una pronta victoria

prospecting [prə'spɛktɪŋ] *n* prospección

prospective [prə'spɛktɪv] *adj* (*possible*) probable, eventual; (*certain*) futuro; (*buyer*) presunto; (*legislation, son-in-law*) futuro

prospectus [prə'spɛktəs] *n* prospecto

prosper ['prɒspə'] *vi* prosperar

prosperity [prɒ'spɛrɪtɪ] *n* prosperidad

prosperous ['prɒspərəs] *adj* próspero

prostate ['prɒsteɪt] *n* (*also*: **prostate gland**) próstata

prostitute ['prɒstɪtjuːt] *n* prostituta; **male ~** prostituto

prostitution [prɒstɪ'tjuːʃən] *n* prostitución

prostrate *adj* postrado; (*fig*) abatido ⊳ *vt*: **to ~ o.s.** postrarse

protagonist [prə'tægənɪst] *n* protagonista

protect [prə'tɛkt] *vt* proteger

protection [prə'tɛkʃən] *n* protección; **to be under sb's ~** estar amparado por algn

protective [prə'tɛktɪv] *adj* protector(a); **~ custody** (*Law*) detención preventiva

protégé ['prəutɛʒeɪ] *n* protegido(-a)

protein ['prəutiːn] *n* proteína

protest *n* protesta ⊳ *vi* protestar ⊳ *vt* (*affirm*) afirmar, declarar; **to do sth under ~** hacer algo bajo protesta; **to ~ against/about** protestar en contra de/por

Protestant ['prɒtɪstənt] *adj, n* protestante

protester, protestor [prə'tɛstə'] *n* (*in*

demonstration) manifestante

protocol ['prəutəkɔl] *n* protocolo

prototype ['prəutətaɪp] *n* prototipo

protracted [prə'træktɪd] *adj* prolongado

protrude [prə'truːd] *vi* salir, sobresalir

proud [praud] *adj* orgulloso; (*pej*) soberbio, altanero ▷ *adv*: **to do sb ~** tratar a algn a cuerpo de rey; **to do o.s. ~** no privarse de nada; **to be ~ to do sth** estar orgulloso de hacer algo

prove [pruːv] *vt* probar; (*verify*) comprobar; (*show*) demostrar ▷ *vi*: **to ~ correct** resultar correcto; **to ~ o.s.** ponerse a prueba; **he was ~d right in the end** al final se vio que tenía razón

proverb ['prɔvəːb] *n* refrán

provide [prə'vaɪd] *vt* proporcionar, dar; **to ~ sb with sth** proveer a algn de algo; **to be ~d with** ser provisto de

▶ **provide for** *vt fus* (*person*) mantener a; (*problem etc*) tener en cuenta

provided [prə'vaɪdɪd] *conj*: **~ (that)** con tal de que, a condición de que

providing [prə'vaɪdɪŋ] *conj* a condición de que, con tal de que

province ['prɔvɪns] *n* provincia; (*fig*) esfera

provincial [prə'vɪnʃəl] *adj* provincial; (*pej*) provinciano

provision [prə'vɪʒən] *n* provisión; (*supply*) suministro, abastecimiento; **provisions** *npl* provisiones, víveres; **to make ~ for** (*one's family, future*) atender las necesidades de

provisional [prə'vɪʒənl] *adj* provisional, provisorio (*LAm*); (*temporary*) interino ▷ *n*: **P~** (*Irish Pol*) Provisional (*miembro de la tendencia activista del IRA*)

provisional driving licence *n* (*Brit Aut*) carnet de conducir provisional; *see also* **L-plates**

proviso [prə'vaɪzəu] *n* condición, estipulación; **with the ~ that** a condición de que

provocation [prɔvə'keɪʃən] *n* provocación

provocative [prə'vɔkətɪv] *adj* provocativo

provoke [prə'vəuk] *vt* (*arouse*) provocar, incitar; (*cause*) causar, producir; (*anger*) enojar; **to ~ sb to sth/to do** *or* **into doing sth** provocar a algn a algo/a hacer algo

provost ['prɔvəst] *n* (*Brit: of university*) rector(a); (*Scottish*) alcalde(esa)

prow [prau] *n* proa

prowess ['prauɪs] *n* (*skill*) destreza, habilidad; (*courage*) valor; **his ~ as a footballer** (*skill*) su habilidad como futbolista

prowl [praul] *vi* (*also:* **prowl about, prowl around**) merodear ▷ *n*: **on the ~** de merodeo, merodeando

prowler ['praulə^r] *n* merodeador(a)

proximity [prɔk'sɪmɪtɪ] *n* proximidad

proxy ['prɔksɪ] *n* poder; (*person*) apoderado(-a); **by ~** por poderes

prudent ['pruːdnt] *adj* prudente

prune [pruːn] *n* ciruela pasa ▷ *vt* podar

pry [praɪ] *vi*: **to ~ into** entrometerse en

PS *abbr* (= *postscript*) P.D.

psalm [sɑːm] *n* salmo

PSBR *n abbr* (*Brit*: = *public sector borrowing requirement*) endeudamiento público

pseudo ... [sjuː'dəu] *pref* seudo...

pseudonym ['sjuːdənɪm] *n* seudónimo

PSV *n abbr* (*Brit*) = **public service vehicle**

psyche ['saɪkɪ] *n* psique

psychiatric [saɪkɪ'ætrɪk] *adj* psiquiátrico

psychiatrist [saɪ'kaɪətrɪst] *n* psiquiatra

psychiatry [saɪ'kaɪətrɪ] *n* psiquiatría

psychic ['saɪkɪk] *adj* (*also:* **psychical**) psíquico

psychoanalysis [saɪkəuə'nælɪsɪs] (*pl* **psychoanalyses**) *n* psicoanálisis

psychoanalyst [saɪkəu'ænəlɪst] *n* psicoanalista

psychological [saɪkə'lɔdʒɪkl] *adj* psicológico

psychologist [saɪ'kɔlədʒɪst] *n* psicólogo(-a)

psychology [saɪ'kɔlədʒɪ] *n* psicología

psychopath ['saɪkəupæθ] *n* psicópata

psychosis [saɪ'kəusɪs] (*pl* **psychoses**) *n* psicosis

psychotherapy [saɪkəu'θerəpɪ] *n* psicoterapia

PT *n abbr* (*Brit*: = *Physical Training*) Ed. Fís.

pt *abbr* = **pint(s); point(s)**

PTA *n abbr* (*Brit*: = *Parent-Teacher Association*) ≈ Asociación de Padres de Alumnos

PTO *abbr* (= *please turn over*) sigue

pub [pʌb] *n abbr* (= *public house*) pub, bar

pub crawl *n* (*col*): **to go on a ~** ir a recorrer bares

puberty ['pjuːbətɪ] *n* pubertad

public ['pʌblɪk] *adj, n* público; **in ~** en público; **to make sth ~** revelar *or* hacer público algo; **to be ~ knowledge** ser del dominio público; **to go ~** (*Comm*) proceder a la venta pública de acciones

public address system (PA) *n* megafonía, sistema de altavoces

publican ['pʌblɪkən] *n* dueño(-a) *or* encargado(-a) de un bar

publication [pʌblɪ'keɪʃən] *n* publicación

public company *n* sociedad anónima

public convenience *n* (*Brit*) aseos públicos, sanitarios (*LAm*)

public holiday *n* día de fiesta, (día) feriado (*LAm*)

public house *n* (*Brit*) bar, pub

publicity [pʌb'lɪsɪtɪ] *n* publicidad

publicize ['pʌblɪsaɪz] *vt* publicitar; (*advertise*) hacer propaganda para

public limited company (plc) *n* sociedad anónima (S.A.)

public opinion *n* opinión pública

public relations (PR) *n* relaciones públicas

public relations officer *n* encargado(-a) de relaciones públicas

public school *n* (*Brit*) colegio privado; (*US*) instituto

public sector *n* sector público

public service vehicle (PSV) *n* vehículo de servicio público

public-spirited [pʌblɪk'spɪrɪtɪd] *adj* cívico

public transport, (*US*) **public transportation** *n* transporte público

public utility *n* servicio público

publish ['pʌblɪʃ] *vt* publicar

publisher ['pʌblɪʃə^r] *n* (*person*) editor(a); (*firm*) editorial

publishing ['pʌblɪʃɪŋ] n (*industry*) industria del libro

puck [pʌk] n (*Ice Hockey*) puck

pucker ['pʌkəʳ] vt (*pleat*) arrugar; (*brow etc*) fruncir

pudding ['pudɪŋ] n pudín; (*Brit: sweet*) postre; **black ~** morcilla; **rice ~** arroz con leche

puddle ['pʌdl] n charco

puerile ['pjuəraɪl] adj pueril

Puerto Rican ['pwɜːtəuˈriːkən] adj, n puertorriqueño(-a)

Puerto Rico [-'riːkəu] n Puerto Rico

puff [pʌf] n soplo; (*of smoke*) bocanada; (*of breathing, engine*) resoplido; (*powder puff*) borla ▷ vt: **to ~ one's pipe** dar chupadas a la pipa; (*also:* **puff out**: *sails, cheeks*) hinchar, inflar ▷ vi (*gen*) soplar; (*pant*) jadear

puffed [pʌft] adj (*col: out of breath*) sin aliento

puffin ['pʌfɪn] n frailecillo

puff pastry, (US) **puff paste** n hojaldre

puffy ['pʌfɪ] adj hinchado

pull [pul] n (*tug*): **to give sth a ~** dar un tirón a algo; (*fig: advantage*) ventaja; (: *influence*) influencia ▷ vt tirar de, jalar (*LAm*); (*haul*) tirar, jalar (*LAm*), arrastrar; (*strain*): **to ~ a muscle** sufrir un tirón ▷ vi tirar, jalar (*LAm*); **she ~ed my hair** me tiró del pelo; **to ~ to pieces** hacer pedazos; **to ~ one's punches** andarse con bromas; **to ~ one's weight** hacer su parte; **to ~ o.s. together** tranquilizarse; **to ~ sb's leg** tomar el pelo a algn; **to ~ strings (for sb)** enchufar (a algn); **he ~ed the trigger** apretó el gatillo; **~ as hard as you can** tira con todas tus fuerzas

▶ **pull about** vt (*handle roughly: object*) manosear; (: *person*) maltratar

▶ **pull apart** vt (*take apart*) desmontar

▶ **pull down** vt (*house*) derribar, echar abajo; **the old school was ~ed down last year** el año pasado echaron abajo la vieja escuela

▶ **pull in** vi (*Aut: at the kerb*) parar (junto a la acera); (*Rail*) llegar

▶ **pull off** vt (*deal etc*) cerrar

▶ **pull out** vi irse, marcharse; (*Aut: from kerb*) salir ▷ vt tirar, sacar, arrancar; **the car ~ed out to overtake** el coche se echó a un lado para adelantar; **she ~ed out of the tournament** se retiró del torneo; **to ~ a tooth out** sacar una muela

▶ **pull over** vi (*Aut*) hacerse a un lado

▶ **pull round, pull through** vi salvarse; (*Med*) recobrar la salud, recuperarse; **they think he'll ~ through** creen que se recuperará

▶ **pull up** vi (*stop*) parar ▷ vt (*uproot*) arrancar, desarraigar; (*stop*) parar; **a black car ~ed up beside me** un coche negro paró a mi lado

pulley ['pulɪ] n polea

pull-out ['pulaut] n suplemento ▷ cpd (*pages, magazine*) separable

pullover ['puləuvəʳ] n jersey, suéter

pulp [pʌlp] n (*of fruit*) pulpa; (*for paper*) pasta; (*pej:*

also: **pulp magazines** *etc*) prensa amarilla; **to reduce sth to ~** hacer algo papilla

pulpit ['pulpɪt] n púlpito

pulsate [pʌl'seɪt] vi pulsar, latir

pulse [pʌls] n (*Anat*) pulso; (*of music, engine*) pulsación; (*Bot*) legumbre; **to feel** *or* **take sb's ~** tomar el pulso a algn

pulverize ['pʌlvəraɪz] vt pulverizar; (*fig*) hacer polvo

puma ['pjuːmə] n puma

pump [pʌmp] n bomba; (*shoe*) zapatilla de tenis ▷ vt sacar con una bomba; (*fig: col*) (son)sacar; **to ~ sb for information** (son)sacarle información a algn

▶ **pump up** vt inflar

pumpkin ['pʌmpkɪn] n calabaza

pun [pʌn] n juego de palabras

punch [pʌntʃ] n (*blow*) golpe, puñetazo; (*tool*) punzón; (*for paper*) perforadora; (*for tickets*) taladro; (*drink*) ponche ▷ vt (*hit*): **to ~ sb/sth** dar un puñetazo *or* golpear a algn/algo; (*make a hole in*) punzar; perforar

punch line n (*of joke*) remate

punch-up ['pʌntʃʌp] n (*Brit col*) riña

punctual ['pʌŋktjuəl] adj puntual

punctuality [pʌŋktjuˈælɪtɪ] n puntualidad

punctuate ['pʌŋktjueɪt] vt puntuar; (*fig*) interrumpir

punctuation [pʌŋktjuˈeɪʃən] n puntuación

punctuation mark n signo de puntuación

puncture ['pʌŋktʃəʳ] (*Brit*) n pinchazo ▷ vt pinchar; **to have a ~** tener un pinchazo

pundit ['pʌndɪt] n experto(-a)

pungent ['pʌndʒənt] adj acre

punish ['pʌnɪʃ] vt castigar; **to ~ sb for sth/for doing sth** castigar a algn por algo/por haber hecho algo

punishment ['pʌnɪʃmənt] n castigo; (*fig, col*): **to take a lot of ~** (*boxer*) recibir una paliza; (*car*) ser maltratado

punk [pʌŋk] n (*also:* **punk rocker**) punki; (*also:* **punk rock**) música punk; (*US col: hoodlum*) matón

punt [pʌnt] n (*boat*) batea; (*Ireland*) libra irlandesa ▷ vi (*bet*) apostar

punter ['pʌntəʳ] n (*gambler*) jugador(a)

puny ['pjuːnɪ] adj enclenque

pup [pʌp] n cachorro

pupil ['pjuːpl] n alumno(-a); (*of eye*) pupila

puppet ['pʌpɪt] n títere

puppy ['pʌpɪ] n cachorro, perrito

purchase ['pɜːtʃɪs] n compra; (*grip*) agarre, asidero ▷ vt comprar

purchaser ['pɜːtʃɪsəʳ] n comprador(a)

pure ['pjuəʳ] adj puro; **a ~ wool jumper** un jersey de pura lana; **it's laziness, ~ and simple** es pura vagancia

purée ['pjuəreɪ] n puré

purely ['pjuəlɪ] adv puramente

purgatory ['pɜːgətərɪ] n purgatorio

purge [pɜːdʒ] n (*Med, Pol*) purga ▷ vt purgar

purify ['pjuərɪfaɪ] vt purificar, depurar

purist ['pjuərɪst] n purista

puritan ['pjuərɪtən] *n* puritano(-a)
purity ['pjuərɪtɪ] *n* pureza
purple ['pə:pl] *adj* morado
purport [pə:'pɔ:t] *vi*: **to ~ to be/do** dar a entender que es/hace
purpose ['pə:pəs] *n* propósito; **on ~** a propósito, adrede; **to no ~** para nada, en vano; **for teaching ~s** con fines pedagógicos; **for the ~s of this meeting** para los fines de esta reunión
purposeful ['pə:pəsful] *adj* resuelto, determinado
purr [pə:ʳ] *n* ronroneo ▷ *vi* ronronear
purse [pə:s] *n* monedero; (US: *handbag*) bolso ▷ *vt* fruncir
purser ['pə:səʳ] *n* (*Naut*) comisario(-a)
pursue [pə'sju:] *vt* seguir; (*harass*) perseguir; (*profession*) ejercer; (*pleasures*) buscar; (*inquiry, matter*) seguir
pursuit [pə'sju:t] *n* (*chase*) caza; (*of pleasure etc*) busca; (*occupation*) actividad; **in (the) ~ of sth** en busca de algo
pus [pʌs] *n* pus
push [puʃ] *n* empujón; (*Mil*) ataque; (*drive*) empuje ▷ *vt* empujar; (*button*) apretar; (*promote*) promover; (*fig: press, advance: views*) fomentar; (*thrust*): **to ~ sth into** meter algo a la fuerza en ▷ *vi* empujar; (*fig*) hacer esfuerzos; **to give sb a ~** dar un empujón a algn; **at a ~** (*col*) a duras penas; **she's ~ing 50** (*col*) raya en los 50; **to be ~ed for time/money** andar justo de tiempo/escaso de dinero; **to ~ a door open/shut** abrir/cerrar una puerta empujándola; **to ~ drugs** pasar droga; **don't ~ your luck!** ¡no tientes a la suerte!; **"~"** (*on door*) "empujar"; (*on bell*) "pulse"; **don't ~!** ¡no empujes!; **to ~ for** (*better pay, conditions*) reivindicar
▶ **push around** *vt* dar órdenes a; **he likes ~ing people around** le gusta dar órdenes a la gente
▶ **push aside** *vt* apartar con la mano
▶ **push in** *vi* colarse
▶ **push off** *vi* (*col*) largarse; **~ off!** ¡lárgate!
▶ **push on** *vi* (*continue*) seguir adelante
▶ **push through** *vt* despachar; **I ~ed my way through** me abrí camino a empujones
▶ **push up** *vt* (*total, prices*) hacer subir
pushchair ['puʃtʃeəʳ] *n* (Brit) silla de niño
pusher ['puʃəʳ] *n* (*drug pusher*) traficante de drogas
pushover ['puʃəuvəʳ] *n* (*col*): **it's a ~** está tirado
push-up ['puʃʌp] *n* (US) flexión
pushy ['puʃɪ] *adj* (*pej*) agresivo
puss [pus], **pussy(-cat)** ['pusɪ(kæt)] *n* minino
put [put] (*pt, pp ~*) *vt* (*place*) poner, colocar; (*put into*) meter; (*express, say*) expresar; (*a question*) hacer; (*estimate*) calcular; (*cause to be*): **to ~ sb in a good/bad mood** poner a algn de buen/mal humor; **where shall I ~ my things?** ¿dónde pongo mis cosas?; **don't forget to ~ your name on the paper** no te olvides de poner tu nombre en la hoja; **to ~ a lot of time into sth** dedicar mucho tiempo a algo; **to ~ money on a horse** apostar dinero en un caballo; **to ~ money into a company** invertir dinero en una compañía; **to ~**

sb to a lot of trouble causar mucha molestia a algn; **we ~ the children to bed** acostamos a los niños; **how shall I ~ it?** ¿cómo puedo explicarlo or decirlo?; **I ~ it to you that ...** le sugiero que ...; **to stay ~** no moverse
▶ **put about** *vi* (*Naut*) virar ▷ *vt* (*rumour*) hacer correr
▶ **put across** *vt* (*ideas etc*) comunicar; **he finds it hard to ~ his ideas across** le cuesta comunicar sus ideas
▶ **put aside** *vt* (*lay down: book etc*) dejar *or* poner a un lado; (*save*) ahorrar; (*in shop*) apartar; **can you ~ this aside for me till tomorrow?** ¿me lo puede apartar hasta mañana?
▶ **put away** *vt* (*store*) guardar; (*in prison*) encerrar; **can you ~ the dishes away, please?** ¿guardas los platos?; **I hope they ~ him away for a long time** espero que lo encierren por muchos años
▶ **put back** *vt* (*replace*) poner en su sitio; (*postpone*) posponer; (*set back: watch, clock*) retrasar; **~ it back when you've finished with it** ponlo en su sitio cuando hayas terminado; **the meeting has been ~ back till 2 o'clock** la reunión ha sido aplazada hasta las 2; **this will ~ us back 10 years** esto nos retrasará 10 años
▶ **put by** *vt* (*money*) guardar
▶ **put down** *vt* (*on ground*) poner en el suelo; (*animal*) sacrificar; (*in writing*) apuntar; (*suppress: revolt etc*) sofocar; (*attribute*) atribuir; **~ it down!** ¡déjalo!; **we had to have our dog ~ down** tuvimos que sacrificar a nuestro perro; **I've ~ down a few ideas** he apuntado algunas ideas; **~ me down for £15** apúntame por 15 libras; **~ it down on my account** (*Comm*) póngalo en mi cuenta; **to ~ the phone down** colgar
▶ **put forward** *vt* (*ideas*) presentar, proponer; (*date, clock*) adelantar
▶ **put in** *vt* (*application, complaint*) presentar; (*install*) poner; **he has ~ in a lot of work on this project** ha dedicado mucho trabajo a este proyecto
▶ **put in for** *vt fus* (*job*) solicitar; (*promotion*) pedir; **I've ~ in for a new job** he solicitado otro empleo
▶ **put off** *vt* (*postpone*) aplazar; (*discourage*) desanimar, quitar las ganas a; (*light, TV*) apagar; (*distract*) distraer; **I keep ~ting it off** no hago más que aplazarlo; **stop ~ting me off!** ¡deja ya de distraerme!
▶ **put on** *vt* (*clothes, lipstick etc*) ponerse; (*tape, record*) poner; (*light etc*) encender; (*brake*) echar; (*assume: accent, manner*) afectar, fingir; (*airs*) adoptar, darse; (*play etc*) poner en escena; (*concert, exhibition etc*) montar; (*extra bus, train etc*) poner; (*col: kid, have on: esp US*) tomar el pelo a; (*inform, indicate*): **to ~ sb on to sb/sth** informar a algn de algn/algo; **I ~ my coat on** me puse el abrigo; **~ on some music** pon algo de música; **shall I ~ the heater on?** ¿enciendo el radiador?; **she's not ill: she's just ~ting it on** no está enferma: es puro teatro; **to ~ on weight** engordar
▶ **put out** *vt* (*fire, light*) apagar; (*one's hand*)

alargar; (*news, rumour*) hacer circular; (*tongue etc*) sacar; (*person: inconvenience*) molestar, fastidiar; (*dislocate: shoulder, vertebra, knee*) dislocar(se) ▷ *vi* (*Naut*): **to ~ out to sea** hacerse a la mar; **to ~ out from Plymouth** salir de Plymouth; **he's a bit ~ out that nobody came** le sentó mal que no viniera nadie

▸ **put through** *vt* (*call*) poner; **~ me through to Miss Blair** póngame *or* comuníqueme (*LAm*) con la Señorita Blair; **I'm ~ting you through** le pongo

▸ **put together** *vt* unir, reunir; (*assemble: furniture*) armar, montar; (*meal*) preparar

▸ **put up** *vt* (*raise*) levantar, alzar; (*hang*) colgar; (*build*) construir; (*increase*) aumentar; (*accommodate*) alojar; (*incite*): **to ~ sb up to doing sth** instar *or* incitar a algn a hacer algo; **I'll ~ it up on my wall** lo colgaré en la pared; **they've ~ up the price** han subido el precio; **my friend will ~ me up for the night** me quedaré a dormir en casa de mi amigo; **to ~ sth up for sale** poner algo a la venta; **we ~ up our tent in a field** montamos la tienda en un prado

▸ **put upon** *vt fus*: **to be ~ upon** (*imposed upon*) dejarse explotar

▸ **put up with** *vt fus* aguantar; **I'm not going to ~ up with it any longer** no pienso aguantarlo

más

putt [pʌt] *vt* hacer un putt ▷ *n* putt, golpe corto

putter ['pʌtəʳ] *n* putter

putting green ['pʌtɪŋ-] *n* green, minigolf

putty ['pʌtɪ] *n* masilla

put-up ['pʌtʌp] *adj*: **~ job** (*Brit*) estafa

puzzle ['pʌzl] *n* (*riddle*) acertijo; (*jigsaw*) rompecabezas; (*also*: **crossword puzzle**) crucigrama; (*mystery*) misterio ▷ *vt* dejar perplejo, confundir ▷ *vi*: **to ~ about** quebrar la cabeza por; **to ~ over** (*sb's actions*) quebrarse la cabeza por; (*mystery, problem*) devanarse los sesos sobre; **to be ~d about sth** no llegar a entender algo

puzzling ['pʌzlɪŋ] *adj* (*question*) misterioso, extraño; (*attitude, set of instructions*) extraño

PVC *n abbr* (= *polyvinyl chloride*) P.V.C.

pygmy ['pɪgmɪ] *n* pigmeo(-a)

pyjamas, (*US*) **pajamas** [pɪ'dʒɑːməz] *npl* pijama, piyama (*LAm*); **a pair of ~** un pijama

pylon ['paɪlən] *n* torre de conducción eléctrica

pyramid ['pɪrəmɪd] *n* pirámide

Pyrenean [pɪrə'niːən] *adj* pirenaico

Pyrenees [pɪrə'niːz] *npl*: **the ~** los Pirineos

Pyrex® ['paɪreks] *n* pírex ▷ *cpd*: **~ casserole** cazuela de pírex

python ['paɪθən] *n* pitón

Qq

Q, q [kjuː] *n (letter)* Q, q; **Q for Queen** Q de Quebec

QC *n abbr (Brit: = Queen's Counsel) título concedido a determinados abogados*

QED *abbr (= quod erat demonstrandum)* Q.E.D.

qty *abbr (= quantity)* ctdad

quack [kwæk] *n (of duck)* graznido; *(pej: doctor)* curandero(-a), matasanos ▷ *vi* graznar

quad [kwɔd] *abbr* = **quadrangle; quadruple; quadruplet**

quadrangle ['kwɔdræŋgl] *n (Brit: courtyard: abbr)*: **quad** patio

quadruple [kwɔ'druːpl] *vt, vi* cuadruplicar

quadruplet [kwɔ'druːplɪt] *n* cuatrillizo

quagmire ['kwægmaɪə'] *n* lodazal, cenegal

quail [kweɪl] *n (bird)* codorniz ▷ *vi* amedrentarse

quaint [kweɪnt] *adj* extraño; *(picturesque)* pintoresco

quake [kweɪk] *vi* temblar ▷ *n abbr* = **earthquake**

qualification [kwɔlɪfɪ'keɪʃən] *n (reservation)* reserva; *(modification)* modificación; *(act)* calificación; *(paper qualification)* título; **what are your ~s?** ¿qué títulos tienes?

qualified ['kwɔlɪfaɪd] *adj (trained)* cualificado; *(fit)* capacitado; *(limited)* limitado; *(professionally)* titulado; **~ for/to do sth** capacitado para/para hacer algo; **he's not ~ for the job** no está capacitado para ese trabajo; **it was a ~ success** fue un éxito relativo

qualify ['kwɔlɪfaɪ] *vt (Ling)* calificar a; *(capacitate)* capacitar; *(modify: statement, remark)* matizar ▷ *vi (Sport)* clasificarse; **to ~ (as)** calificarse (de), graduarse (en), recibirse (de) *(LAm)*; **to ~ (for)** reunir los requisitos (para); **to ~ as an engineer** sacar el título de ingeniero; **our team didn't ~ for the finals** nuestro equipo no se clasificó para la final

quality ['kwɔlɪtɪ] *n* calidad; *(moral)* cualidad; **of good/poor ~** de buena *or* alta/poca calidad

quality of life *n* calidad de vida

quality press *n* prensa seria

qualm [kwɑːm] *n* escrúpulo; **to have ~s about sth** sentir escrúpulos por algo

quandary ['kwɔndrɪ] *n:* **to be in a ~** verse en un dilema

quango ['kwæŋgəu] *n abbr (Brit: = quasi-autonomous non-governmental organization) organismo* *semi-autónomo de subvención estatal*

quantifiable [kwɔntɪ'faɪəbl] *adj* cuantificable

quantity ['kwɔntɪtɪ] *n* cantidad; **in ~** en grandes cantidades

quantity surveyor *n* aparejador(a)

quantum leap ['kwɔntəm-] *n (fig)* avance espectacular

quarantine ['kwɔrntiːn] *n* cuarentena

quarrel ['kwɔrl] *n* riña, pelea ▷ *vi* reñir, pelearse; **to have a ~ with sb** reñir *or* pelearse con algn; **I can't ~ with that** no le veo pegas

quarrelsome ['kwɔrəlsəm] *adj* pendenciero

quarry ['kwɔrɪ] *n (for stone)* cantera; *(animal)* presa

quart [kwɔːt] *n cuarto de galón, = 1,136 l*

quarter ['kwɔːtə'] *n* cuarto, cuarta parte; *(of year)* trimestre; *(district)* barrio; *(US, Canada: 25 cents)* cuarto de dólar ▷ *vt* dividir en cuartos; *(Mil: lodge)* alojar; **quarters** *npl (barracks)* cuartel; *(living quarters)* alojamiento; **a ~ of an hour** un cuarto de hora; **to pay by the ~** pagar trimestralmente *or* cada 3 meses; **it's a ~ to** *or* (US) **of 3** son las 3 menos cuarto; **it's a ~ past** *or* (US) **after 3** son las 3 y cuarto; **from all ~s** de todas partes; **at close ~s** de cerca

quarterback ['kwɔːtəbæk] *n (US: football)* mariscal de campo

quarter final *n* cuarto de final

quarterly ['kwɔːtəlɪ] *adj* trimestral ▷ *adv* cada 3 meses, trimestralmente

quartet(te) [kwɔː'tɛt] *n* cuarteto

quartz [kwɔːts] *n* cuarzo

quash [kwɔʃ] *vt (verdict)* anular, invalidar

quaver ['kweɪvə'] *n (Brit Mus)* corchea ▷ *vi* temblar

quay [kiː] *n (also: quayside)* muelle

queasy ['kwiːzɪ] *adj:* **to feel ~** tener náuseas

queen [kwiːn] *n* reina; *(Cards etc)* dama

queen mother *n* reina madre

queer [kwɪə'] *adj (odd)* raro, extraño ▷ *n (pej: col)* marica

quell [kwɛl] *vt* calmar; *(put down)* sofocar

quench [kwɛntʃ] *vt (flames)* apagar; **to ~ one's thirst** apagar la sed

querulous ['kwɛruləs] *adj (person, voice)* quejumbroso

query ['kwɪərɪ] *n (question)* pregunta; *(doubt)* duda

▷ *vt* preguntar; (*disagree with, dispute*) no estar conforme con, dudar de

quest [kwɛst] *n* busca, búsqueda

question ['kwɛstʃən] *n* pregunta; (*matter*) asunto, cuestión ▷ *vt* (*doubt*) dudar de; (*interrogate: suspect*) interrogar; (: *exam candidate, interviewee*) hacer preguntas a; **to ask sb a ~, put a ~ to sb** hacerle una pregunta a algn; **can I ask a ~?** ¿puedo hacer una pregunta?; **the ~ is ...** el asunto es ...; **it's just a ~ of ...** tan sólo es cuestión de ...; **at the time in ~** a la hora en cuestión; **to bring** *or* **call sth into ~** poner algo en (tela de) duda; **beyond ~** fuera de toda duda; **it's out of the ~** es imposible, ni hablar; **he was ~ed by the police** lo interrogó la policía

questionable ['kwɛstʃənəbl] *adj* discutible; (*doubtful*) dudoso

question mark *n* punto de interrogación

questionnaire [kwɛstʃə'nɛəʳ] *n* cuestionario

queue [kju:] (*Brit*) *n* cola ▷ *vi* hacer cola; **to jump the ~** colarse

quibble ['kwɪbl] *vi* andarse con sutilezas

quick [kwɪk] *adj* rápido; (*temper*) vivo; (*agile*) ágil; (*mind*) listo; (*eye*) agudo; (*ear*) fino ▷ *n*: **cut to the ~** (*fig*) herido en lo más vivo; **a ~ lunch** un almuerzo rápido; **it's ~er by train** se va más rápido en tren; **she's a ~ learner** aprende rápido; **be ~!** ¡date prisa!; **~, phone the police!** ¡rápido, llama a la policía!; **to be ~ to act** obrar con prontitud; **she was ~ to see that** se dio cuenta de eso en seguida

quicken ['kwɪkən] *vt* apresurar ▷ *vi* apresurarse, darse prisa

quick fix *n* (*pej*) parche

quickly ['kwɪklɪ] *adv* rápidamente, de prisa; **we must act ~** tenemos que actuar cuanto antes

quicksand ['kwɪksænd] *n* arenas movedizas

quick-witted [kwɪk'wɪtɪd] *adj* listo, despabilado

quid [kwɪd] *n* (*pl inv*: *Brit col*) libra

quiet ['kwaɪət] *adj* (*not busy: day*) tranquilo; (*silent*) callado; (*reserved*) reservado; (*discreet*) discreto; (*not noisy: engine*) silencioso ▷ *n* tranquilidad ▷ *vt, vi* (*US*) = **quieten**; **keep ~!** ¡cállate!, ¡silencio!; **business is ~ at this time of year** hay poco movimiento en esta época

quieten ['kwaɪətn] (*also*: **quieten down**) *vi* (*grow calm*) calmarse; (*grow silent*) callarse ▷ *vt* calmar; hacer callar

quietly ['kwaɪətlɪ] *adv* tranquilamente; (*silently*) silenciosamente

quietness ['kwaɪətnɪs] *n* (*silence*) silencio; (*calm*) tranquilidad

quilt [kwɪlt] *n* (*Brit*) edredón

quin [kwɪn] *n abbr* = **quintuplet**

quintuplet [kwɪn'tju:plɪt] *n* quintillizo

quip [kwɪp] *n* ocurrencia ▷ *vi* decir con ironía

quirk [kwəːk] *n* peculiaridad; **by some ~ of fate** por algún capricho del destino

quit [kwɪt] (*pt, pp ~* or *-ted*) *vt* dejar, abandonar; (*premises*) desocupar; (*Comput*) abandonar ▷ *vi* (*give up*) renunciar; (*go away*) irse; (*resign*) dimitir; **~ stalling!** (*US col*) ¡déjate de evasivas!

quite [kwaɪt] *adv* (*rather*) bastante; (*entirely*) completamente, totalmente; **~ new** bastante nuevo; **she's ~ pretty** es bastante guapa; **I ~ liked the film, but it was too long** la película me gustó bastante, pero fue demasiado larga; **how was the film? — ~ good** ¿qué tal la película? — no está mal; **it's ~ different** es totalmente distinto; **it's ~ clear that this plan won't work** está clarísimo que este plan no va a funcionar; **that's not ~ right** eso no está del todo bien; **I'm not ~ sure** no estoy del todo seguro; **it's not ~ the same** no es exactamente lo mismo; **I ~ agree with you** estoy totalmente de acuerdo contigo; **~ (so)!** ¡así es!, ¡exactamente!; **it was ~ a shock** fue todo un susto; **~ a lot** bastante; **I've been there ~ a lot** he estado allí bastante; **~ a lot of money** bastante dinero; **it costs ~ a lot to go abroad** es bastante caro ir al extranjero; **there were ~ a few people there** había bastante gente allí; **~ a few of them** un buen número de ellos; **not ~ as many as last time** no tantos como la última vez

quits [kwɪts] *adj*: **~ (with)** en paz (con); **let's call it ~** quedamos en paz

quiver ['kwɪvəʳ] *vi* estremecerse ▷ *n* (*for arrows*) carcaj

quiz [kwɪz] *n* (*game*) concurso; (: *TV, Radio*) programa-concurso; (*questioning*) interrogatorio ▷ *vt* interrogar

quizzical ['kwɪzɪkl] *adj* burlón(-ona)

quorum ['kwɔːrəm] *n* quórum

quota ['kwəʊtə] *n* cuota

quotation [kwəʊ'teɪʃən] *n* cita; (*estimate*) presupuesto

quotation marks *npl* comillas

quote [kwəʊt] *n* cita ▷ *vt* (*sentence*) citar; (*Comm: sum, figure*) cotizar ▷ *vi*: **to ~ from** citar de; **quotes** *npl* (*inverted commas*) comillas; **in ~s** entre comillas; **the figure ~d for the repairs** el presupuesto dado para las reparaciones; **~ ... un~** (*in dictation*) comillas iniciales ... finales

quotient ['kwəʊʃənt] *n* cociente

qv *n abbr* (= *quod vide: which see*) q.v.

Rr

R, r [ɑːʳ] *n* (*letter*) R, r; **R for Robert**, (US) **R for Roger** R de Ramón

R *abbr* (= *right*) dcha.; (= *river*) R.; (= *Réaumur (scale)*) R; (*US Cine*: = *restricted*) *sólo mayores*; (*US Pol*) = **republican**; (*Brit*) = **Rex**; (= *Regina*) R.

rabbi ['ræbaɪ] *n* rabino

rabbit ['ræbɪt] *n* conejo ▷ *vi*: **to ~ (on)** (*Brit col*) hablar sin ton ni son

rabbit hutch *n* conejera

rabble ['ræbl] *n* (*pej*) chusma, populacho

rabies ['reɪbiːz] *n* rabia

RAC *n abbr* (*Brit*: = *Royal Automobile Club*) ≈ RACE (*Esp*)

race [reɪs] *n* carrera; (*species*) raza ▷ *vt* (*horse*) hacer correr; (*person*) competir contra; (*engine*) acelerar ▷ *vi* (*compete*) competir; (*run*) correr; (*pulse*) latir a ritmo acelerado ▷ *vt* echarle una carrera a; **the arms ~** la carrera armamentista; **the human ~** el género humano; **~ relations** las relaciones interraciales; **we ~d to get there on time** corrimos para llegar allí a tiempo; **he ~d across the road** cruzó corriendo la carretera; **to ~ in/out** entrar/salir corriendo; **I'll ~ you!** ¡te echo una carrera!

race car *n* (US) = **racing car**

race car driver *n* (US) = **racing driver**

racecourse ['reɪskɔːs] *n* hipódromo

racehorse ['reɪshɔːs] *n* caballo de carreras

racetrack ['reɪstræk] *n* hipódromo; (*for cars*) circuito de carreras

racial ['reɪʃl] *adj* racial

racing ['reɪsɪŋ] *n* carreras

racing car *n* (*Brit*) coche de carreras

racing driver *n* (*Brit*) corredor(a) de coches

racism ['reɪsɪzəm] *n* racismo

racist ['reɪsɪst] *adj*, *n* racista

rack [ræk] *n* (*also*: **luggage rack**) rejilla (portaequipajes); (*shelf*) estante; (*also*: **roof rack**) baca; (*clothes rack*) perchero ▷ *vt* (*cause pain to*) atormentar; **to go to ~ and ruin** venirse abajo; **to ~ one's brains** devanarse los sesos
▷ **rack up** *vt* conseguir, ganar

racket ['rækɪt] *n* (*for tennis*) raqueta; (*noise*) ruido, estrépito; (*swindle*) estafa, timo

racquet ['rækɪt] *n* raqueta

racy ['reɪsɪ] *adj* picante, subido

radar ['reɪdɑːʳ] *n* radar

radial ['reɪdɪəl] *adj* (*tyre*: *also*: **radial-ply**) radial

radiant ['reɪdɪənt] *adj* brillante, resplandeciente

radiate ['reɪdɪeɪt] *vt* (*heat*) radiar, irradiar ▷ *vi* (*lines*) extenderse

radiation [reɪdɪ'eɪʃən] *n* radiación

radiator ['reɪdɪeɪtəʳ] *n* (*Aut*) radiador

radical ['rædɪkl] *adj* radical

radii ['reɪdɪaɪ] *npl of* **radius**

radio ['reɪdɪəu] *n* radio ▷ *vi*: **to ~ to sb** mandar un mensaje por radio a algn ▷ *vt* (*information*) radiar, transmitir por radio; (*one's position*) indicar por radio; (*person*) llamar por radio; **on the ~** en or por la radio

radioactive [reɪdɪəu'æktɪv] *adj* radi(o)activo

radioactivity [reɪdɪəuæk'tɪvɪtɪ] *n* radi(o)actividad

radio station *n* emisora

radio taxi *n* radio taxi

radiotherapy ['reɪdɪəuθεrəpɪ] *n* radioterapia

radish ['rædɪʃ] *n* rábano

radium ['reɪdɪəm] *n* radio

radius ['reɪdɪəs] (*pl* **radii**) *n* radio; **within a ~ of 50 miles** en un radio de 50 millas

RAF *n abbr see* **Royal Air Force**

raffle ['ræfl] *n* rifa, sorteo ▷ *vt* (*object*) rifar

raft [rɑːft] *n* (*craft*) balsa; (*also*: **life raft**) balsa salvavidas

rafter ['rɑːftəʳ] *n* viga

rag [ræg] *n* (*piece of cloth*) trapo; (*torn cloth*) harapo; (*pej*: *newspaper*) periodicucho; (*for charity*) *actividades estudiantiles benéficas* ▷ *vt* (*Brit*) tomar el pelo a; **rags** *npl* harapos; **in ~s** en harapos, hecho jirones

rag doll *n* muñeca de trapo

rage [reɪdʒ] *n* (*fury*) rabia, furor ▷ *vi* (*person*) rabiar, estar furioso; (*storm*) bramar; **to fly into a ~** montar en cólera; **it's all the ~** es lo último

ragged ['rægɪd] *adj* (*edge*) desigual, mellado; (*cuff*) roto; (*appearance*) andrajoso, harapiento; **~ left/right** (*text*) margen izquierdo/derecho irregular

raid [reɪd] *n* (*Mil*) incursión; (*criminal*) asalto; (*by police*) redada, allanamiento (*LAm*) ▷ *vt* invadir, atacar; asaltar

rail [reɪl] *n* (*on stair*) barandilla, pasamanos; (*on bridge*) pretil; (*of balcony, ship*) barandilla; (*for train*) riel, carril; **rails** npl vía; **by ~** por ferrocarril, en tren

railcard ['reɪlkɑːd] n (Brit) tarjeta para obtener descuentos en el tren; **Young Person's ~** = Tarjeta joven (Esp)

railing(s) ['reɪlɪŋz] n(pl) verja

railway ['reɪlweɪ], (US) **railroad** ['reɪlrəud] n ferrocarril, vía férrea

railway line n (Brit) línea (de ferrocarril)

railwayman ['reɪlweɪmən] n (Brit) ferroviario

railway station n (Brit) estación de ferrocarril

rain [reɪn] n lluvia ▷ vi llover; **in the ~** bajo la lluvia; **it's ~ing** llueve, está lloviendo; **it's ~ing cats and dogs** está lloviendo a cántaros or a mares

rainbow ['reɪnbəu] n arco iris

raincoat ['reɪnkəut] n impermeable

raindrop ['reɪndrɔp] n gota de lluvia

rainfall ['reɪnfɔːl] n lluvia

rainforest ['reɪnfɔrɪst] n selva tropical

rainstorm ['reɪnstɔːm] n temporal (de lluvia)

rainwater ['reɪnwɔːtəʳ] n agua de lluvia

rainy ['reɪnɪ] adj lluvioso

raise [reɪz] n aumento ▷ vt (lift) levantar; (build) erigir, edificar; (increase) aumentar; (doubts) suscitar; (a question) plantear; (cattle, family) criar; (crop) cultivar; (army) reclutar; (funds) recaudar; (loan) obtener; (end: embargo) levantar; **to ~ one's hand** levantar la mano; **to ~ one's voice** alzar la voz; **to ~ one's glass to sb/sth** brindar por algn/ algo; **to ~ a laugh/a smile** provocar risa/una sonrisa; **to ~ sb's hopes** dar esperanzas a algn; **to ~ money** recaudar fondos

raisin ['reɪzn] n pasa de Corinto

rake [reɪk] n (tool) rastrillo; (person) libertino ▷ vt (garden) rastrillar; (fire) hurgar; (with machine gun) barrer

▶ **rake in, rake together** vt sacar

rally ['rælɪ] n reunión; (Pol) mitin; (Aut) rallye; (Tennis) peloteo ▷ vt reunir ▷ vi reunirse; (sick person, Stock Exchange) recuperarse

▶ **rally round** vt fus (fig) dar apoyo a

RAM [ræm] n abbr (= random access memory) RAM

ram [ræm] n carnero; (Tech) pisón ▷ vt (crash into) dar contra, chocar con; (tread down) apisonar

ramble ['ræmbl] n caminata, excursión en el campo ▷ vi (pej: also: **ramble on**) divagar

rambler ['ræmbləʳ] n excursionista, (Bot) trepadora

rambling ['ræmblɪŋ] adj (speech) inconexo; (Bot) trepador(a); (house) laberíntico

ramp [ræmp] n rampa; **on/off ~** n (US Aut) vía de acceso/salida; **"~"** (Aut) "rampa"

rampage [ræm'peɪdʒ] n: **to be on the ~** desmandarse

rampant ['ræmpənt] adj (disease etc): **to be ~** estar muy extendido

rampart ['ræmpɑːt] n terraplén; (wall) muralla

ram raid vt atracar (rompiendo el escaparate etc con un coche)

ramshackle ['ræmʃækl] adj destartalado

ran [ræn] pt of **run**

ranch [rɑːntʃ] n (US) hacienda, estancia

rancher ['rɑːntʃəʳ] n ganadero

rancid ['rænsɪd] adj rancio

rancour, (US) **rancor** ['ræŋkəʳ] n rencor

random ['rændəm] adj fortuito, sin orden; (Comput, Math) aleatorio ▷ n: **at ~** al azar

random access n (Comput) acceso aleatorio

randy ['rændɪ] adj (Brit col) cachondo, caliente

rang [ræŋ] pt of **ring**

range [reɪndʒ] n (of missile) alcance; (of voice) registro; (series) serie; (of products) surtido; (Mil: also: **shooting range**) campo de tiro; (also: **kitchen range**) fogón ▷ vt (place) colocar; (arrange) arreglar ▷ vi: **to ~ over** (wander) recorrer; (extend) extenderse por; **a ~ of mountains, a mountain ~** una cadena de montañas, una cordillera; **within (firing) ~** a tiro; **there's a wide ~ of colours** hay una amplia gama de colores; **do you have anything else in this price ~?** ¿tiene algo más de esta gama de precios?; **it's out of my price ~** está fuera de mis posibilidades; **intermediate-/short-~ missile** proyectil de medio/corto alcance; **to ~ from... to...** oscilar entre ... y...; **~d left/right** (text) alineado a la izquierda/derecha

ranger [reɪndʒəʳ] n guardabosques

rank [ræŋk] n (row) fila; (Mil) rango; (status) categoría; (Brit: also: **taxi rank**) parada ▷ vi: **to ~ among** figurar entre ▷ adj (stinking) fétido, rancio; (hypocrisy, injustice etc) manifiesto; **the ~ and file** (fig) las bases; **to close ~s** (Mil) cerrar filas; (fig) hacer un frente común; **~ outsider** participante sin probabilidades de vencer; **I ~ him 6th** yo le pongo en sexto lugar

rankle ['ræŋkl] vi (insult) doler

ransack ['rænsæk] vt (search) registrar; (plunder) saquear

ransom ['rænsəm] n rescate; **to hold sb to ~** (fig) poner a algn entre la espada y la pared

rant [rænt] vi despotricar

rap [ræp] vt golpear, dar un golpecito en

rape [reɪp] n violación; (Bot) colza ▷ vt violar

rape(seed) oil ['reɪp(siːd)-] n aceite de colza

rapid ['ræpɪd] adj rápido

rapidly ['ræpɪdlɪ] adv rápidamente

rapids ['ræpɪdz] npl (Geo) rápidos

rapist ['reɪpɪst] n violador

rapport [ræ'pɔːʳ] n entendimiento

rapture ['ræptʃəʳ] n éxtasis

rapturous ['ræptʃərəs] adj extático; (applause) entusiasta

rare [reəʳ] adj raro, poco común; (Culin: steak) poco hecho; **it is ~ to find that ...** es raro descubrir que ...

rarely ['reəlɪ] adv rara vez, pocas veces

raring ['reərɪŋ] adj: **to be ~ to go** (col) tener muchas ganas de empezar

rascal ['rɑːskl] n pillo(-a), pícaro(-a)

rash [ræʃ] adj imprudente, precipitado ▷ n (Med) salpullido, erupción (cutánea); **to come out in a ~** salir salpullidos

rasher ['ræʃəʳ] n loncha

raspberry ['rɑːzbərɪ] n frambuesa

rasping ['rɑːspɪŋ] adj: **a ~ noise** un ruido áspero

rat [ræt] n rata

ratchet ['rætʃɪt] n (Tech) trinquete

rate [reɪt] n (ratio) razón; (price) precio; (: of hotel) tarifa; (of interest) tipo, tasa; (speed) velocidad ▷ vt (value) tasar; (estimate) estimar ▷ vi: **to ~ as** ser considerado como; **rates** npl (Brit) impuesto municipal; (fees) tarifa; **failure ~** porcentaje de fallos; **birth ~** tasa de natalidad; **pulse ~** pulsaciones por minuto; **bank ~** tipo or tasa de interés bancario; **~s of pay** sueldos; **at a ~ of 60 kph** a una velocidad de 60 kph; **~ of growth** ritmo de crecimiento; **~ of return** (Comm) tasa de rendimiento; **at any ~** en todo caso; **to ~ sb/ sth highly** tener a algn/algo en alta estima

rateable value ['reɪtəbl-] n (Brit) valor impuesto

ratepayer ['reɪtpeɪə'] n (Brit) contribuyente

rather ['rɑːðə'] adv (somewhat) algo, un poco; (quite) bastante; **it's ~ expensive** es algo caro; (too much) es demasiado caro; **there's ~ a lot** hay bastante; **I would** or **I'd ~ stay in tonight** preferiría no salir esta noche; **I'd ~ not** prefiero que no; **I'd ~ he didn't come to the party** preferiría que no viniera a la fiesta; **~ than ...** en lugar de ...; **I ~ think he won't come** me inclino a creer que no vendrá; **or ~** (more accurately) o mejor dicho

ratify ['rætɪfaɪ] vt ratificar

rating ['reɪtɪŋ] n (valuation) tasación; (standing) posición; (Brit Naut: sailor) marinero; **ratings** npl (Radio, TV) clasificación

ratio ['reɪʃɪəu] n razón; **in the ~ of 100 to 1** a razón de or en la proporción de 100 a 1

ration ['ræʃən] n ración ▷ vt racionar; **rations** npl víveres

rational ['ræʃnl] adj racional; (solution, reasoning) lógico, razonable; (person) cuerdo, sensato

rationale [ræʃə'nɑːl] n razón fundamental

rationalize ['ræʃnəlaɪz] vt (reorganize: industry) racionalizar

rationally ['ræʃnəlɪ] adv racionalmente; (logically) lógicamente

ratpack ['rætpæk] n (Brit col) periodistas que persiguen a los famosos

rat race n lucha incesante por la supervivencia

rattle ['rætl] n golpeteo; (of train etc) traqueteo; (object: of baby) sonaja, sonajero; (: of sports fan) matraca ▷ vi sonar, golpear; traquetear; (small objects) castañetear ▷ vt hacer sonar agitando; (col: disconcert) poner nervioso a

rattlesnake ['rætlsneɪk] n serpiente de cascabel

ratty ['rætɪ] adj (col) furioso; **to get ~** mosquearse

raucous ['rɔːkəs] adj estridente, ronco

raunchy ['rɔːntʃɪ] adj (col) lascivo

ravage ['rævɪdʒ] vt hacer estragos en, destrozar; **ravages** npl estragos

rave [reɪv] vi (in anger) encolerizarse; (with enthusiasm) entusiasmarse; (Med) delirar, desvariar ▷ cpd: **~ review** reseña entusiasta; **a ~ (party)** macrofiesta con música máquina; **~ music** música máquina

raven ['reɪvən] n cuervo

ravenous ['rævənəs] adj: **to be ~** tener un hambre canina

ravine [rə'viːn] n barranco

raving ['reɪvɪŋ] adj: **~ lunatic** loco de atar

ravioli [rævɪ'əulɪ] n ravioles, ravioli

ravish ['rævɪʃ] vt (charm) encantar, embelesar; (rape) violar

ravishing ['rævɪʃɪŋ] adj encantador(a)

raw [rɔː] adj (uncooked) crudo; (not processed) bruto; (sore) vivo; (inexperienced) novato, inexperto

raw deal n (col: bad deal) mala pasada or jugada; (: harsh treatment) injusticia

raw material n materia prima

ray [reɪ] n rayo; **~ of hope** (rayo de) esperanza

raze [reɪz] vt (also: **raze to the ground**) arrasar, asolar

razor ['reɪzə'] n (open) navaja; (safety razor) máquina de afeitar, rastrillo (Méx)

razor blade n hoja de afeitar

RC abbr = **Roman Catholic**

Rd abbr = **road**

RE n abbr (Brit) = **religious education**; (Brit Mil) = **Royal Engineers**

re [riː] prep con referencia a

reach [riːtʃ] n alcance; (Boxing) envergadura; (of river etc) extensión entre dos recodos ▷ vt alcanzar, llegar a; (achieve: goal, target) lograr ▷ vi extenderse; (stretch out hand: also: **reach down, reach over**: also: **reach across** etc) alargar la mano; **within ~** al alcance (de la mano); **within easy ~ of** a poca distancia de; **out of ~** fuera del alcance; **we hope to ~ the final** esperamos llegar a la final; **eventually they ~ed a decision** finalmente llegaron a una decisión; **can I ~ you at your hotel?** ¿puedo localizarte en tu hotel?; **to ~ sb by phone** comunicarse con algn por teléfono; **how can I ~ you?** ¿cómo puedo ponerme en contacto contigo?; **to ~ out for sth** alargar or tender la mano para tomar algo

react [riː'ækt] vi reaccionar

reaction [riː'ækʃən] n reacción

reactionary [riː'ækʃənrɪ] adj, n reaccionario(-a)

reactor [riː'æktə'] n reactor

read [riːd] (pt, pp -) vi leer ▷ vt leer; (understand) entender; (study) estudiar; **to take sth as ~** (fig) dar algo por sentado; **to ~ between the lines** leer entre líneas

▶ **read out** vt leer en alta voz

▶ **read over** vt repasar

▶ **read through** vt (quickly) leer rápidamente, echar un vistazo a; (thoroughly) leer con cuidado or detenidamente

▶ **read up** vt, **read up on** vt fus documentarse sobre

readable ['riːdəbl] adj (writing) legible; (book) que merece la pena leer

reader ['riːdə'] n lector(a); (book) libro de lecturas; (Brit: at university) profesor(a)

readership ['riːdəʃɪp] n (of paper etc) número de lectores

readily ['redɪlɪ] adv (willingly) de buena gana;

(*easily*) fácilmente; (*quickly*) en seguida

readiness ['rɛdɪnɪs] *n* buena voluntad; (*preparedness*) preparación; **in ~** (*prepared*) listo, preparado

reading ['ri:dɪŋ] *n* lectura; (*understanding*) comprensión; (*on instrument*) indicación

readjustment [ri:ə'dʒʌstmənt] *n* reajuste

ready ['rɛdɪ] *adj* listo, preparado; (*willing*) dispuesto; (*available*) disponible ▷ *n*: **at the ~** (*Mil*) listo para tirar; **~ for use** listo para usar; **to be ~ to do sth** estar listo para hacer algo; **to get ~** *vi* prepararse ▷ *vt* preparar

ready-made ['rɛdɪ'meɪd] *adj* confeccionado

ready money *n* dinero contante

ready-to-wear ['rɛdɪtə'wɛəʳ] *adj* confeccionado

reaffirm [ri:ə'fə:m] *vt* reafirmar

real [rɪəl] *adj* (*true*) verdadero; (*not fake: leather, diamond*) auténtico; **the ~ reason** el verdadero motivo; **it was a ~ nightmare** fue una verdadera pesadilla; **in ~ terms** en términos reales; **in ~ life** en la vida real, en la realidad

real ale *n* cerveza elaborada tradicionalmente

real estate *n* bienes raíces

realism ['rɪəlɪzəm] *n* (*also Art*) realismo

realist ['rɪəlɪst] *n* realista

realistic [rɪə'lɪstɪk] *adj* realista

realistically [rɪə'lɪstɪklɪ] *adv* de modo realista

reality [ri:'ælɪtɪ] *n* realidad; **in ~** en realidad

realization [rɪəlaɪ'zeɪʃən] *n* comprensión; (*of a project*; *Comm*: *of assets*) realización

realize ['rɪəlaɪz] *vt* (*understand*) darse cuenta de; (*a project*; *Comm*: *asset*) realizar; **I ~ that ...** comprendo *or* entiendo que ...

really ['rɪəlɪ] *adv* (*very*): **she's ~ nice** es muy simpática; **it's ~ ugly** es feo de verdad; (*genuinely*): **do you ~ think so?** ¿tú crees?; **do you want to go? — not ~** ¿quieres ir? — la verdad es que no ▷ *excl*: **~?** ¿de veras?, ¿de verdad?

realm [rɛlm] *n* reino; (*fig*) esfera

Realtor® ['rɪəltɔːʳ] *n* (*US*) corredor(a) de bienes raíces

reap [ri:p] *vt* segar; (*fig*) cosechar, recoger

reappear [ri:ə'pɪəʳ] *vi* reaparecer

reappraisal [ri:ə'preɪzl] *n* revaluación

rear [rɪəʳ] *adj* trasero ▷ *n* parte trasera ▷ *vt* (*cattle, family*) criar ▷ *vi* (*also*: **rear up**: *animal*) encabritarse

rearguard ['rɪəgɑːd] *n* retaguardia

rearrange [ri:ə'reɪndʒ] *vt* ordenar *or* arreglar de nuevo

rear-view ['rɪəvjuː]: **~ mirror** *n* (*Aut*) espejo retrovisor

reason ['ri:zn] *n* razón ▷ *vi*: **to ~ with sb** tratar de que algn entre en razón; **there's no ~ to think that ...** no hay razón para pensar que ...; **the ~ for/why** la causa de/la razón por la cual; **that was the main ~ I went** fui mayormente por eso; **for security ~s** por motivos de seguridad; **she claims with good ~ that she's underpaid** dice con razón que está mal pagada; **all the more ~ why you should not sell it** razón de más para que no lo vendas; **it stands to ~ that ...** es lógico

que ...

reasonable ['ri:znəbl] *adj* razonable; (*sensible*) sensato

reasonably ['ri:znəblɪ] *adv* razonablemente; **a ~ accurate report** un informe bastante exacto

reasoning ['ri:znɪŋ] *n* razonamiento, argumentos

reassurance [ri:ə'ʃuərəns] *n* consuelo

reassure [ri:ə'ʃuəʳ] *vt* tranquilizar; **to ~ sb that** tranquilizar a algn asegurándole que

rebate ['ri:beɪt] *n* (*on product*) rebaja; (*on tax etc*) desgravación; (*repayment*) reembolso

rebel *n* rebelde ▷ *vi* rebelarse, sublevarse

rebellion [rɪ'bɛljən] *n* rebelión, sublevación

rebellious [rɪ'bɛljəs] *adj* rebelde; (*child*) revoltoso

rebirth [rɪ'bə:θ] *n* renacimiento

rebound *vi* (*ball*) rebotar ▷ *n* rebote

rebuff [rɪ'bʌf] *n* desaire, rechazo ▷ *vt* rechazar

rebuild [rɪ'bɪld] *vt* (*irreg: like* **build**) reconstruir

rebuke [rɪ'bju:k] *n* reprimenda ▷ *vt* reprender

rebut [rɪ'bʌt] *vt* rebatir

recall [rɪ'kɔ:l] *vt* (*remember*) recordar; (*ambassador etc*) retirar; (*Comput*) volver a llamar ▷ *n* recuerdo

recant [rɪ'kænt] *vi* retractarse

recap ['ri:kæp] *vt, vi* recapitular

recd., rec'd *abbr* (= *received*) rbdo

recede [rɪ'si:d] *vi* retroceder

receding [rɪ'si:dɪŋ] *adj* (*forehead, chin*) hundido; **~ hairline** entradas

receipt [rɪ'si:t] *n* (*document*) recibo; (*act of receiving*) recepción; **receipts** *npl* (*Comm*) ingresos; **to acknowledge ~ of** acusar recibo de; **we are in ~ of ...** obra en nuestro poder ...

receive [rɪ'si:v] *vt* recibir; (*guest*) acoger; (*wound*) sufrir; **"~d with thanks"** (*Comm*) "recibí"

Received Pronunciation [rɪ'si:vd-] *n see* **RP**

receiver [rɪ'si:vəʳ] *n* (*Tel*) auricular; (*Radio*) receptor; (*of stolen goods*) perista; (*Law*) administrador jurídico

receivership [rɪ'si:vəʃɪp] *n*: **to go into ~** entrar en liquidación

recent ['ri:snt] *adj* reciente; **in ~ years** en los últimos años

recently ['ri:sntlɪ] *adv* recientemente, recién (*LAm*); **~ arrived** recién llegado; **until ~** hasta hace poco

receptacle [rɪ'sɛptɪkl] *n* receptáculo

reception [rɪ'sɛpʃən] *n* (*in building, office etc*) recepción; (*welcome*) acogida

reception desk *n* recepción

receptionist [rɪ'sɛpʃənɪst] *n* recepcionista

recess [rɪ'sɛs] *n* (*in room*) hueco; (*for bed*) nicho; (*secret place*) escondrijo; (*Pol etc: holiday*) período vacacional; (*US Law: short break*) descanso; (*Scol: esp US*) recreo

recession [rɪ'sɛʃən] *n* recesión, depresión

recharge [ri:'tʃɑːdʒ] *vt* (*battery*) recargar

recipe ['rɛsɪpɪ] *n* receta

recipient [rɪ'sɪpɪənt] *n* recibidor(a); (*of letter*) destinatario(-a)

reciprocate [rɪ'sɪprəkeɪt] *vt* devolver, corresponder a ▷ *vi* corresponder

recital [rɪ'saɪtl] n (Mus) recital

recitation [rɛsɪ'teɪʃən] n (of poetry) recitado; (of complaints etc) enumeración, relación

recite [rɪ'saɪt] vt (poem) recitar; (complaints etc) enumerar

reckless ['rɛkləs] adj temerario, imprudente; (speed) peligroso

reckon ['rɛkən] vt (count) contar; (consider) considerar ▷ vi: **to ~ without sb/sth** dejar de contar con algn/algo; **he is somebody to be ~ed with** no se le puede descartar; **I ~ that ...** me parece que ..., creo que ...
  ▶ **reckon on** vt fus contar con

reckoning ['rɛkənɪŋ] n (calculation) cálculo

reclaim [rɪ'kleɪm] vt (land) recuperar; (: from sea) rescatar; (demand back) reclamar

recline [rɪ'klaɪn] vi reclinarse

reclining [rɪ'klaɪnɪŋ] adj (seat) reclinable

recluse [rɪ'kluːs] n recluso(-a)

recognition [rɛkəg'nɪʃən] n reconocimiento; **transformed beyond ~** irreconocible; **in ~ of** en reconocimiento de

recognize [rɛkəg'naɪz] vt reconocer, conocer; **to ~ (by/as)** reconocer (por/como)

recoil [rɪ'kɔɪl] vi (person): **to ~ from doing sth** retraerse de hacer algo ▷ n (of gun) retroceso

recollect [rɛkə'lɛkt] vt recordar, acordarse de

recollection [rɛkə'lɛkʃən] n recuerdo; **to the best of my ~** que yo recuerde

recommend [rɛkə'mɛnd] vt recomendar; **she has a lot to ~ her** tiene mucho a su favor

recommendation [rɛkəmɛn'deɪʃən] n recomendación

recommended retail price (RRP) n (Brit) precio (recomendado) de venta al público

reconcile ['rɛkənsaɪl] vt (two people) reconciliar; (two facts) conciliar; **to ~ o.s. to sth** resignarse or conformarse a algo

reconciliation [rɛkənsɪlɪ'eɪʃən] n reconciliación

recondition [riːkən'dɪʃən] vt (machine) reparar, reponer

reconditioned [riːkən'dɪʃənd] adj renovado, reparado

reconnoitre, (US) **reconnoiter** [rɛkə'nɔɪtəʳ] vt, vi (Mil) reconocer

reconsider [riːkən'sɪdəʳ] vt repensar

reconstruct [riːkən'strʌkt] vt reconstruir

reconvene [riːkən'viːn] vt volver a convocar ▷ vi volver a reunirse

record n (Mus) disco; (of meeting etc) relación; (register) registro, partida; (file) archivo; (also: **police** or **criminal record**) antecedentes penales; (written) expediente; (Sport) récord; (Comput) registro ▷ vt (set down, also Comput) registrar; (relate) hacer constar; (Mus: song etc) grabar; **there is no ~ of your booking** no tenemos constancia de su reserva; **public ~s** archivos nacionales; **he is on ~ as saying that ...** hay pruebas de que ha dicho públicamente que ...; **Spain's excellent ~** el excelente historial de España; **off the ~** adj no oficial ▷ adv confidencialmente; **he's got a criminal ~** tiene

antecedentes penales; **the world ~** el récord mundial; **in ~ time** en un tiempo récord

record card n (in file) ficha

recorded delivery letter [rɪ'kɔːdɪd-] n (Brit Post) carta de entrega con acuse de recibo

recorder [rɪ'kɔːdəʳ] n (Mus) flauta de pico; (Tech) contador

record holder n (Sport) actual poseedor(a) del récord

recording [rɪ'kɔːdɪŋ] n (Mus) grabación

recording studio n estudio de grabación

record library n discoteca

record player n tocadiscos

recount [rɪ'kaunt] vt contar

re-count n (Pol: of votes) segundo escrutinio, recuento ▷ vt volver a contar

recoup [rɪ'kuːp] vt: **to ~ one's losses** recuperar las pérdidas

recourse [rɪ'kɔːs] n recurso; **to have ~ to** recurrir a

recover [rɪ'kʌvəʳ] vt recuperar; (rescue) rescatar ▷ vi recuperarse

recovery [rɪ'kʌvərɪ] n recuperación; rescate; (Med): **to make a ~** restablecerse

recreate [riːkrɪ'eɪt] vt recrear

recreation [rɛkrɪ'eɪʃən] n recreación; (amusement) recreo

recreational [rɛkrɪ'eɪʃənl] adj de recreo

recreational drug n droga recreativa

recrimination [rɪkrɪmɪ'neɪʃən] n recriminación

recruit [rɪ'kruːt] n recluta ▷ vt reclutar; (staff) contratar

recruitment [rɪ'kruːtmənt] n reclutamiento

rectangle ['rɛktæŋgl] n rectángulo

rectangular [rɛk'tæŋgjuləʳ] adj rectangular

rectify ['rɛktɪfaɪ] vt rectificar

rector ['rɛktəʳ] n (Rel) párroco; (Scol) rector(a)

rectum ['rɛktəm] n (Anat) recto

recuperate [rɪ'kuːpəreɪt] vi reponerse, restablecerse

recur [rɪ'kəːʳ] vi repetirse; (pain, illness) producirse de nuevo

recurrence [rɪ'kərns] n repetición

recurrent [rɪ'kərnt] adj repetido

recyclable [riː'saɪkləbl] adj reciclable

recycle [riː'saɪkl] vt reciclar

red [rɛd] n rojo ▷ adj rojo; **to be in the ~** (account) estar en números rojos; (business) tener un saldo negativo; **to give sb the ~ carpet treatment** recibir a algn con todos los honores

red alert n alerta roja

red-blooded ['rɛd'blʌdɪd] adj (col) viril

Red Cross n Cruz Roja

redcurrant ['rɛdkʌrənt] n grosella

redden ['rɛdn] vt enrojecer ▷ vi enrojecerse

reddish ['rɛdɪʃ] adj (hair) rojizo

redecorate [riː'dɛkəreɪt] pintar de nuevo; volver a decorar

redeem [rɪ'diːm] vt (sth in pawn) desempeñar; (fig, also Rel) rescatar

redeeming [rɪ'diːmɪŋ] adj: **~ feature** punto

bueno *or* favorable

redefine [riːdɪˈfaɪn] *vt* redefinir

redemption [rɪˈdɛmpʃən] *n* (*Rel*) redención; **to be past** *or* **beyond ~** no tener remedio

redeploy [riːdɪˈplɔɪ] *vt* (*resources*) disponer de nuevo

redeployment [riːdɪˈplɔɪmənt] *n* redistribución

red-handed [rɛdˈhændɪd] *adj*: **he was caught ~** le pillaron con las manos en la masa

redhead [ˈrɛdhɛd] *n* pelirrojo(-a)

red herring *n* (*fig*) pista falsa

red-hot [rɛdˈhɔt] *adj* candente

redirect [riːdaɪˈrɛkt] *vt* (*mail*) reexpedir

rediscover [riːdɪsˈkʌvəˈ] *vt* redescubrir

redistribute [riːdɪsˈtrɪbjuːt] *vt* redistribuir, hacer una nueva distribución de

red light *n*: **to go through** *or* **jump a ~** (*Aut*) saltarse un semáforo

red-light district *n* barrio chino, zona de tolerancia

red meat *n* carne roja

redo [riːˈduː] *vt* (*irreg: like* **do**) rehacer

redolent [ˈrɛdələnt] *adj*: **~ of** (*smell*) con fragancia a; **to be ~ of** (*fig*) evocar

redouble [riːˈdʌbl] *vt*: **to ~ one's efforts** redoblar los esfuerzos

redraft [riːˈdrɑːft] *vt* volver a redactar

redress [rɪˈdrɛs] *n* reparación ▷ *vt* reparar, corregir; **to ~ the balance** restablecer el equilibrio

Red Sea *n*: **the ~** el mar Rojo

redskin [ˈrɛdskɪn] *n* piel roja

red tape *n* (*fig*) trámites, papeleo (*col*)

reduce [rɪˈdjuːs] *vt* reducir; (*lower*) rebajar; **to ~ sth by/to** reducir algo en/a; **to ~ sb to silence/despair/tears** hacer callar/desesperarse/llorar a algn; **"~ speed now"** (*Aut*) "reduzca la velocidad"

reduced [rɪˈdjuːst] *adj* (*decreased*) reducido, rebajado; **at a ~ price** con rebaja *or* descuento; **"greatly ~ prices"** "grandes rebajas"

reduction [rɪˈdʌkʃən] *n* reducción; (*of price*) rebaja; (*discount*) descuento

redundancy [rɪˈdʌndənsɪ] *n* despido; (*unemployment*) desempleo; **voluntary ~** baja voluntaria

redundant [rɪˈdʌndənt] *adj* (*Brit: worker*) parado, sin trabajo; (*detail, object*) superfluo; **to be made ~** quedar(se) sin trabajo, perder el empleo

reed [riːd] *n* (*Bot*) junco, caña; (*Mus*) lengüeta

re-educate [riːˈɛdjukeɪt] *vt* reeducar

reef [riːf] *n* (*at sea*) arrecife

reek [riːk] *vi*: **to ~ (of)** oler *or* apestar (a)

reel [riːl] *n* carrete, bobina; (*of film*) rollo ▷ *vt* (*Tech*) devanar; (*also:* **reel in**) sacar ▷ *vi* (*sway*) tambalear(se); **my head is ~ing** me da vueltas la cabeza

▶ **reel off** *vt* recitar de memoria

ref [rɛf] *n abbr* (*col*) **= referee**

ref. *abbr* (*Comm*: **= with** *reference to*) Ref

refectory [rɪˈfɛktərɪ] *n* comedor

refer [rɪˈfəːˈ] *vt* (*send*) remitir; (*ascribe*) referir a,

relacionar con ▷ *vi*: **to ~ to** (*allude to*) referirse a, aludir a; (*apply to*) relacionarse con; (*consult*) remitirse a; **he ~red me to the manager** me envió al gerente

referee [rɛfəˈriː] *n* árbitro; (*Brit: for job application*) avalista ▷ *vt* (*match*) arbitrar en

reference [ˈrɛfrəns] *n* (*mention, in book*) referencia; (*sending*) remisión; (*relevance*) relación; (*for job application: letter*) carta de recomendación; **with ~ to** con referencia a; (*Comm: in letter*) me remito a

reference book *n* libro de consulta

reference library *n* biblioteca de consulta

referendum [rɛfəˈrɛndəm] (*pl* **referenda**) *n* referéndum

referral [rɪˈfəːrəl] *n* remisión

refill *vt* rellenar ▷ *n* repuesto, recambio

refine [rɪˈfaɪn] *vt* (*sugar, oil*) refinar

refined [rɪˈfaɪnd] *adj* (*person, taste*) refinado, culto

refinement [rɪˈfaɪnmənt] *n* (*of person*) cultura, educación

refinery [rɪˈfaɪnərɪ] *n* refinería

refit (*Naut*) *n* [ˈriːfɪt] reparación ▷ *vt* [riːˈfɪt] reparar

reflect [rɪˈflɛkt] *vt* (*light, image*) reflejar ▷ *vi* (*think*) reflexionar, pensar; **it ~s badly/well on him** le perjudica/le hace honor

reflection [rɪˈflɛkʃən] *n* (*act*) reflexión; (*image*) reflejo; (*discredit*) crítica; **on ~** pensándolo bien

reflector [rɪˈflɛktəˈ] *n* (*Aut*) catafaros; (*telescope*) reflector

reflex [ˈriːflɛks] *adj, n* reflejo

reflexive [rɪˈflɛksɪv] *adj* (*Ling*) reflexivo

reform [rɪˈfɔːm] *n* reforma ▷ *vt* reformar

reformat [riːˈfɔːmæt] *vt* (*Comput*) recomponer

Reformation [rɛfəˈmeɪʃən] *n*: **the ~** la Reforma

reformatory [rɪˈfɔːmətərɪ] *n* (*US*) reformatorio

refrain [rɪˈfreɪn] *vi*: **to ~ from doing** abstenerse de hacer ▷ *n* (*Mus etc*) estribillo

refresh [rɪˈfrɛʃ] *vt* refrescar

refresher course *n* (*Brit*) curso de repaso

refreshing [rɪˈfrɛʃɪŋ] *adj* (*drink*) refrescante; (*sleep*) reparador; (*change etc*) estimulante; (*idea, point of view*) estimulante, interesante

refreshments [rɪˈfrɛʃmənts] *npl* (*drinks*) refrescos

refrigeration [rɪfrɪdʒəˈreɪʃən] *n* refrigeración

refrigerator [rɪˈfrɪdʒəreɪtəˈ] *n* frigorífico, refrigeradora (*LAm*), heladera (*LAm*)

refuel [riːˈfjuəl] *vi* repostar (combustible)

refuge [ˈrɛfjuːdʒ] *n* refugio, asilo; **to take ~ in** refugiarse en

refugee [rɛfjuˈdʒiː] *n* refugiado(-a)

refugee camp *n* campamento para refugiados

refund *n* reembolso ▷ *vt* devolver, reembolsar

refurbish [riːˈfəːbɪʃ] *vt* restaurar, renovar

refusal [rɪˈfjuːzəl] *n* negativa; **first ~** primera opción; **to have first ~ on sth** tener la primera opción a algo

refuse *n* basura ▷ *vt* (*reject*) rehusar; (*say no to*) negarse a ▷ *vi* negarse; (*horse*) rehusar; **to ~ to do sth** negarse a *or* rehusar hacer algo

refuse collection [ˈrɛfjuːs-] *n* recogida de

basuras

regain [rɪ'geɪn] vt recobrar, recuperar

regal ['ri:gl] adj regio, real

regard [rɪ'gɑ:d] n (gaze) mirada; (aspect) respecto; (esteem) respeto, consideración ▷ vt (consider) considerar; (look at) mirar; **to give one's ~s to** saludar de su parte a; **"(kind) ~s"** "muy atentamente"; **"with kindest ~s"** "con muchos recuerdos"; **~s to María, please give my ~s to María** recuerdos a María, dele recuerdos a María de mi parte; **as ~s, with ~ to** con respecto a, en cuanto a; **they ~ed it as unfair** lo consideraron injusto

regarding [rɪ'gɑ:dɪŋ] prep con respecto a, en cuanto a

regardless [rɪ'gɑ:dlɪs] adv a pesar de todo; **~ of** sin reparar en

regatta [rɪ'gætə] n regata

reggae ['rɛgeɪ] n reggae

régime [reɪ'ʒi:m] n régimen

regiment n ['rɛdʒɪmənt] regimiento ▷ vt ['rɛdʒɪmɛnt] reglamentar

regimental [rɛdʒɪ'mɛntl] adj militar

region ['ri:dʒən] n región; **in the ~ of** (fig) alrededor de

regional ['ri:dʒənl] adj regional

register ['rɛdʒɪstə'] n registro ▷ vt registrar; (birth) declarar; (letter) certificar; (subj: instrument) marcar, indicar ▷ vi (at hotel) registrarse; (sign on) inscribirse; (make impression) producir impresión; **to ~ a protest** presentar una queja; **to ~ for a course** matricularse or inscribirse en un curso

registered ['rɛdʒɪstəd] adj (design) registrado; (Brit: letter) certificado; (student) matriculado; (voter) registrado

registered trademark n marca registrada

registrar ['rɛdʒɪstrɑ:'] n secretario(-a) (del registro civil)

registration [rɛdʒɪs'treɪʃən] n (act) declaración; (Aut: also: **registration number**) matrícula

registry ['rɛdʒɪstrɪ] n registro

registry office n (Brit) registro civil; **to get married in a** ~ casarse por lo civil

regret [rɪ'grɛt] n sentimiento, pesar; (remorse) remordimiento ▷ vt sentir, lamentar; (repent of) arrepentirse de; **we ~ to inform you that ...** sentimos informarle que ...

regretfully [rɪ'grɛtfəlɪ] adv con pesar, sentidamente

regular ['rɛgjulə'] adj regular; (soldier) profesional; (col: intensive) verdadero; (listener, reader) asiduo, habitual ▷ n (client etc) cliente(-a) habitual

regularity [rɛgju'lærɪtɪ] n regularidad

regularly ['rɛgjuləlɪ] adv con regularidad

regulate ['rɛgjuleɪt] vt (gen) controlar; (Tech) regular, ajustar

regulation [rɛgju'leɪʃən] n (rule) regla, reglamento; (adjustment) regulación

rehabilitate [ri:ə'bɪlɪteɪt] vt rehabilitar

rehabilitation ['ri:əbɪlɪ'teɪʃən] n rehabilitación

rehash [ri:'hæʃ] vt (col) hacer un refrito de

rehearsal [rɪ'hə:səl] n ensayo; **dress ~** ensayo general or final

rehearse [rɪ'hə:s] vt ensayar

rehouse [ri:'hauz] vt dar nueva vivienda a

reign [reɪn] n reinado; (fig) predominio ▷ vi reinar; (fig) imperar

reigning ['reɪnɪŋ] adj (monarch) reinante, actual; (predominant) imperante

reimburse [ri:ɪm'bə:s] vt reembolsar

rein [reɪn] n (for horse) rienda; **to give sb free ~** dar rienda suelta a algn

reincarnation [ri:ɪnkɑ:'neɪʃən] n reencarnación

reindeer ['reɪndɪə'] n (pl inv) reno

reinforce [ri:ɪn'fɔ:s] vt reforzar

reinforced concrete [ri:ɪn'fɔ:st-] n hormigón armado

reinforcement [ri:ɪn'fɔ:smənt] n (action) refuerzo; **reinforcements** npl (Mil) refuerzos

reinstate [ri:ɪn'steɪt] vt (worker) reintegrar (a su puesto)

reiterate [ri:'ɪtəreɪt] vt reiterar, repetir

reject n (thing) desecho ▷ vt rechazar; (proposition, offer etc) descartar

rejection [rɪ'dʒɛkʃən] n rechazo

rejoice [rɪ'dʒɔɪs] vi: **to ~ at** or **over** regocijarse or alegrarse de

rejuvenate [rɪ'dʒu:vəneɪt] vt rejuvenecer

relapse [rɪ'læps] n (Med) recaída; (into crime) reincidencia

relate [rɪ'leɪt] vt (tell) contar, relatar; (connect) relacionar ▷ vi relacionarse; **to ~ to** (connect) relacionarse or tener que ver con

related [rɪ'leɪtɪd] adj afín; (person) emparentado; **~ to** con referencia a, relacionado con

relating [rɪ'leɪtɪŋ]: **~ to** prep referente a

relation [rɪ'leɪʃən] n (person) pariente; (link) relación; **in ~ to** en relación con, en lo que se refiere a; **to bear a ~ to** guardar relación con; **diplomatic/international ~s** relaciones diplomáticas/internacionales

relationship [rɪ'leɪʃənʃɪp] n relación; (personal) relaciones; (also: **family relationship**) parentesco

relative ['rɛlətɪv] n pariente, familiar ▷ adj relativo

relatively ['rɛlətɪvlɪ] adv (fairly, rather) relativamente

relax [rɪ'læks] vi descansar; (quieten down) relajarse ▷ vt relajar; (grip) aflojar; **~!** (calm down) ¡tranquilo!

relaxation [ri:læk'seɪʃən] n (rest) descanso; (easing) relajación, relajamiento; (amusement) recreo; (entertainment) diversión

relaxed [rɪ'lækst] adj relajado; (tranquil) tranquilo

relaxing [rɪ'læksɪŋ] adj relajante

relay n (race) carrera de relevos ▷ vt (Radio, TV, pass on) retransmitir

release [rɪ'li:s] n (of prisoner, hostage) puesta en libertad; (of gas etc) escape; (of film) estreno; (of record, video) puesta en venta ▷ vt (prisoner) poner en libertad; (film) estrenar; (book) publicar; (record, video) sacar a la venta; (piece of *news*) difundir; (*gas etc*) despedir, arrojar; (*free: from wreckage etc*) liberar; (*Tech: catch, spring etc*) desenganchar; (*let go*) soltar, aflojar; **the band's latest** ~ el último trabajo del grupo

relegate ['rɛləgeɪt] *vt* relegar; (*Sport*): **to be ~d to** bajar a

relent [rɪ'lɛnt] *vi* ceder, ablandarse; (*let up*) descansar

relentless [rɪ'lɛntlɪs] *adj* implacable

relevance ['rɛləvəns] *n* relación

relevant ['rɛləvənt] *adj* (*fact*) pertinente; ~ **to** relacionado con

reliability [rɪlaɪə'bɪlɪtɪ] *n* fiabilidad; seguridad; veracidad

reliable [rɪ'laɪəbl] *adj* (*person, firm*) de confianza, de fiar; (*method, machine*) seguro; (*source*) fidedigno

reliably [rɪ'laɪəblɪ] *adv*: **to be ~ informed that** ... saber de fuente fidedigna que ....

reliance [rɪ'laɪəns] *n*: ~ **(on)** dependencia (de)

relic ['rɛlɪk] *n* (*Rel*) reliquia; (*of the past*) vestigio

relief [rɪ'liːf] *n* (*from pain, anxiety*) alivio, desahogo; (*help, supplies*) socorro, ayuda; (*Art, Geo*) relieve; **by way of light** ~ a modo de diversión

relieve [rɪ'liːv] *vt* (*pain, patient*) aliviar; (*bring help to*) ayudar, socorrer; (*burden*) aligerar; (*take over from: gen*) sustituir a; (*: guard*) relevar; **to ~ sb of sth** quitar algo a algn; **to ~ sb of his command** (*Mil*) relevar a algn de su mando; **to ~ o.s.** hacer sus necesidades; **I am ~d to hear you are better** me alivia saber que estás *or* te encuentras mejor

religion [rɪ'lɪdʒən] *n* religión

religious [rɪ'lɪdʒəs] *adj* religioso

religious education *n* educación religiosa

relinquish [rɪ'lɪŋkwɪʃ] *vt* abandonar; (*plan, habit*) renunciar a

relish ['rɛlɪʃ] *n* (*Culin*) salsa; (*enjoyment*) entusiasmo; (*flavour*) sabor, gusto ▷ *vt* (*food, challenge etc*) saborear; **to ~ doing** gozar haciendo

relive [riː'lɪv] *vt* vivir de nuevo, volver a vivir

relocate [riː:ləu'keɪt] *vt* trasladar ▷ *vi* trasladarse

reluctance [rɪ'lʌktəns] *n* desgana, renuencia

reluctant [rɪ'lʌktənt] *adj* reacio; **to be ~ to do sth** resistirse a hacer algo

reluctantly [rɪ'lʌktəntlɪ] *adv* de mala gana

rely [rɪ'laɪ]: **to ~ on** *vt fus* confiar en, fiarse de; (*be dependent on*) depender de; **you can ~ on my discretion** puedes contar con mi discreción

remain [rɪ'meɪn] *vi* (*survive*) quedar; (*be left*) sobrar; (*continue*) quedar(se), permanecer; **to ~ silent** permanecer callado; **I ~, yours faithfully** (*in letters*) le saluda atentamente

remainder [rɪ'meɪndər] *n* resto

remaining [rɪ'meɪnɪŋ] *adj* sobrante

remains [rɪ'meɪnz] *npl* restos

remand [rɪ'mɑːnd] *n*: **on ~** detenido (bajo custodia) ▷ *vt*: **to ~ in custody** mantener bajo custodia

remand home *n* (*Brit*) reformatorio

remark [rɪ'mɑːk] *n* comentario ▷ *vt* comentar; **to ~ on sth** hacer observaciones sobre algo

remarkable [rɪ'mɑːkəbl] *adj* notable; (*outstanding*) extraordinario

remedial [rɪ'miːdɪəl] *adj*: ~ **education** educación de los niños atrasados

remedy ['rɛmədɪ] *n* remedio ▷ *vt* remediar, curar

remember [rɪ'mɛmbər] *vt* acordarse, recordar ▷ *vt* acordarse de, recordar; (*bear in mind*) tener presente; **I don't ~** no me acuerdo, no recuerdo; **don't you ~ me?** ¿no se acuerda usted de mí?, ¿no me recuerda?; **I ~ seeing it, I ~ having seen it** recuerdo haberlo visto; **she ~ed to do it** se acordó de hacerlo; ~ **your passport!** ¡no te olvides del pasaporte!; ~ **me to your wife and children!** ¡déle recuerdos a su familia!

remembrance [rɪ'mɛmbrəns] *n* (*memory, souvenir*) recuerdo; **in ~ of** en conmemoración de

remind [rɪ'maɪnd] *vt*: **to ~ sb to do sth** recordar a algn que haga algo; **to ~ sb of sth** recordar algo a algn; **she ~s me of her mother** me recuerda a su madre; **that ~s me!** ¡a propósito!

reminder [rɪ'maɪndər] *n* notificación; (*memento*) recuerdo

reminisce [rɛmɪ'nɪs] *vi* recordar (viejas historias)

reminiscent [rɛmɪ'nɪsnt] *adj*: **to be ~ of sth** recordar algo

remiss [rɪ'mɪs] *adj* descuidado; **it was ~ of me** fue un descuido de mi parte

remission [rɪ'mɪʃən] *n* remisión; (*of sentence*) reducción de la pena

remit [rɪ'mɪt] *vt* (*send: money*) remitir, enviar

remittance [rɪ'mɪtns] *n* remesa, envío

remnant ['rɛmnənt] *n* resto; (*of cloth*) retal, retazo; **remnants** *npl* (*Comm*) restos de serie

remorse [rɪ'mɔːs] *n* remordimientos

remorseful [rɪ'mɔːsful] *adj* arrepentido

remorseless [rɪ'mɔːslɪs] *adj* (*fig*) implacable, inexorable

remote [rɪ'məut] *adj* remoto; (*distant*) lejano; (*person*) distante; **there is a ~ possibility that** ... hay una posibilidad remota de que ....

remote control *n* mando a distancia

remotely [rɪ'məutlɪ] *adv* remotamente; (*slightly*) levemente

remould ['riːməuld] *n* (*Brit: tyre*) neumático *or* llanta (*LAm*) recauchutado(-a)

removable [rɪ'muːvəbl] *adj* (*detachable*) separable

removal [rɪ'muːvəl] *n* (*taking away*) (el) quitar; (*Brit: from house*) mudanza; (*from office: dismissal*) destitución; (*Med*) extirpación

removal van *n* (*Brit*) camión de mudanzas

remove [rɪ'muːv] *vt* quitar; (*employee*) destituir; (*name: from list*) tachar, borrar; (*doubt*) disipar; (*Tech*) retirar, separar; (*Med*) extirpar; **first cousin once ~d** (*parent's cousin*) tío(-a) segundo(-a); (*cousin's child*) sobrino(-a) segundo(-a)

remuneration [rɪmjuː:nə'reɪʃən] *n* remuneración

Renaissance [rɪ'neɪsɔ̃ns] *n*: **the ~** el

Renacimiento

rename [riː'neɪm] vt poner nuevo nombre a

render ['rɛndəʳ] vt (thanks) dar; (aid) proporcionar; (honour) dar, conceder; (assistance) dar, prestar; (make) dejar; **the accident ~ed him blind** el accidente lo dejó ciego, volver algo

rendering ['rɛndərɪŋ] n (Mus etc) interpretación

rendez-vous ['rɒndɪvuː] n cita ▷ vi reunirse, encontrarse; (spaceship) efectuar una reunión espacial

rendition [rɛn'dɪʃən] n (Mus) interpretación

renew [rɪ'njuː] vt renovar; (resume) reanudar; (extend date) prorrogar; (negotiations) volver a

renewable [rɪ'njuːəbl] adj renovable; **~ energy**, **~s** energías renovables

renewal [rɪ'njuːəl] n renovación; reanudación; prórroga

renounce [rɪ'nauns] vt renunciar a; (right, inheritance) renunciar

renovate ['rɛnəveɪt] vt renovar

renovation [rɛnə'veɪʃən] n renovación

renown [rɪ'naun] n renombre

renowned [rɪ'naund] adj renombrado

rent [rɛnt] n alquiler; (for house) arriendo, renta ▷ vt (also: **rent out**) alquilar

rental ['rɛntl] n (for television, car) alquiler

rent boy n (Brit col) chapero

reopen [riː'əupən] vt volver a abrir, reabrir

reorder [riː'ɔːdəʳ] vt volver a pedir, repetir el pedido de; (rearrange) volver a ordenar or arreglar

reorganization [riːɔːgənaɪ'zeɪʃən] n reorganización

reorganize [riː'ɔːgənaɪz] vt reorganizar

rep [rɛp] n abbr (Comm) = **representative**; (Theat) = **repertory**

Rep. abbr (US Pol) = **representative**; **republican**

repair [rɪ'pɛəʳ] n reparación, arreglo; (patch) remiendo ▷ vt reparar, arreglar; **in good/bad ~** en buen/mal estado; **under ~** en obras

repair kit n caja de herramientas

repatriate [riː'pætrɪeɪt] vt repatriar

repay [riː'peɪ] vt (irreg: like **pay**); (money) devolver, reembolsar; (person) pagar; (debt) liquidar; (sb's efforts) devolver, corresponder a

repayment [riː'peɪmənt] n reembolso, devolución; (sum of money) recompensa

repeal [rɪ'piːl] n revocación ▷ vt revocar

repeat [rɪ'piːt] n (Radio, TV) reposición ▷ vt repetir ▷ vi repetirse

repeatedly [rɪ'piːtɪdlɪ] adv repetidas veces

repel [rɪ'pɛl] vt repugnar

repellent [rɪ'pɛlənt] adj repugnante ▷ n: **insect ~** crema/loción anti-insectos

repent [rɪ'pɛnt] vi: **to ~ (of)** arrepentirse (de)

repentance [rɪ'pɛntəns] n arrepentimiento

repercussion [riːpə'kʌʃən] n (consequence) repercusión; **to have ~s** repercutir

repertoire ['rɛpətwɑːʳ] n repertorio

repertory ['rɛpətərɪ] n (also: **repertory theatre**) teatro de repertorio

repertory company n compañía de repertorio

repetition [rɛpɪ'tɪʃən] n repetición

repetitive [rɪ'pɛtɪtɪv] adj (movement, work) repetitivo, reiterativo; (speech) lleno de repeticiones

rephrase [riː'freɪz] vt decir or formular de otro modo

replace [rɪ'pleɪs] vt (put back) devolver a su sitio; (take the place of) reemplazar, sustituir

replacement [rɪ'pleɪsmənt] n reemplazo; (act) reposición; (thing) recambio; (person) suplente

replay ['riːpleɪ] n (Sport) partido de desempate; (TV: playback) repetición

replenish [rɪ'plɛnɪʃ] vt (tank etc) rellenar; (stock etc) reponer; (with fuel) repostar

replica ['rɛplɪkə] n réplica, reproducción

reply [rɪ'plaɪ] n respuesta, contestación ▷ vi contestar, responder; **in ~** en respuesta; **there's no ~** (Tel) no contestan

reply coupon n cupón-respuesta

report [rɪ'pɔːt] n informe; (Press: also: **news report**) reportaje; (Brit: also: **school report**) informe escolar; (of gun) detonación ▷ vt informar sobre; (Press etc) hacer un reportaje sobre; (notify: accident, culprit) denunciar ▷ vi (make a report) presentar un informe; (present o.s.): **to ~ (to sb)** presentarse (ante algn); **annual ~** (Comm) informe anual; **I got a good ~ this term** he sacado buenas notas este trimestre; **I ~ed the theft to the police** di parte del robo a la policía; **to ~ on** hacer un informe sobre; **it is ~ed from Berlin that ...** se informa desde Berlín que ...; **I'll ~ back as soon as I hear anything** en cuanto tenga noticias, te lo haré saber

report card n (US, Scottish) cartilla escolar

reportedly [rɪ'pɔːtɪdlɪ] adv según se dice, según se informa

reporter [rɪ'pɔːtəʳ] n (Press) periodista, reportero(-a); (Radio, TV) locutor(a)

repose [rɪ'pəuz] n: **in ~** (face, mouth) en reposo

repossession order [riːpə'zɛʃən-] n orden de devolución de la vivienda por el impago de la hipoteca

represent [rɛprɪ'zɛnt] vt representar; (Comm) ser agente de

representation [rɛprɪzɛn'teɪʃən] n representación; (petition) petición; **representations** npl (protest) quejas

representative [rɛprɪ'zɛntətɪv] n (US Pol) representante, diputado(-a); (Comm) representante ▷ adj: **~ (of)** representativo (de)

repress [rɪ'prɛs] vt reprimir

repression [rɪ'prɛʃən] n represión

reprieve [rɪ'priːv] n (Law) indulto; (fig) alivio ▷ vt indultar; (fig) salvar

reprimand ['rɛprɪmɑːnd] n reprimenda ▷ vt reprender

reprint n reimpresión ▷ vt reimprimir

reprisal [rɪ'praɪzl] n represalia; **to take ~s** tomar represalias

reproach [rɪ'prəutʃ] n reproche ▷ vt: **to ~ sb with sth** reprochar algo a algn; **beyond ~** intachable

reproachful [rɪ'prəutʃful] adj de reproche, de acusación

reproduce [riːprə'djuːs] vt reproducir ▷ vi

reproducirse
reproduction [riːprə'dʌkʃən] n reproducción
reproof [rɪ'pruːf] n reproche
reptile ['reptaɪl] n reptil
republic [rɪ'pʌblɪk] n república
republican [rɪ'pʌblɪkən] adj, n republicano(-a)
repudiate [rɪ'pjuːdɪeɪt] vt (accusation) rechazar; (obligation) negarse a reconocer
repugnant [rɪ'pʌgnənt] adj repugnante
repulsive [rɪ'pʌlsɪv] adj repulsivo
reputable ['repjutəbl] adj (make etc) de renombre
reputation [repju'teɪʃən] n reputación; **he has a ~ for being awkward** tiene fama de difícil
repute [rɪ'pjuːt] n reputación, fama
reputed [rɪ'pjuːtɪd] adj supuesto; **to be ~ to be rich/intelligent** etc tener fama de rico/inteligente etc
reputedly [rɪ'pjuːtɪdlɪ] adv según dicen or se dice
request [rɪ'kwest] n solicitud, petición ▷ vt: **to ~ sth of** or **from sb** solicitar algo a algn; **at the ~ of** a petición de; **"you are ~ed not to smoke"** "se ruega no fumar"
request stop n (Brit) parada discrecional
requiem ['rekwɪəm] n réquiem
require [rɪ'kwaɪəʳ] vt (need: person) necesitar, tener necesidad de; (: thing, situation) exigir, requerir; (want: demand) insistir en que; **to ~ sb to do sth/sth of sb** exigir que algn haga algo; **what qualifications are ~d?** ¿qué títulos se requieren?; **~d by law** requerido por la ley
requirement [rɪ'kwaɪəmənt] n requisito; (need) necesidad
requisite ['rekwɪzɪt] n requisito ▷ adj necesario, requerido
requisition [rekwɪ'zɪʃən] n solicitud; (Mil) requisa ▷ vt (Mil) requisar
reroute [riːˈruːt] vt desviar
rescue ['reskjuː] n rescate ▷ vt rescatar; **to come/go to sb's ~** ir en auxilio de uno, socorrer a algn; **to ~ from** librar de
rescue party n equipo de salvamento
rescuer ['reskjuəʳ] n salvador(a)
research [rɪ'səːtʃ] n investigaciones ▷ vt investigar; **a piece of ~** un trabajo de investigación; **to ~ (into sth)** investigar (algo)
research and development (R & D) n investigación y desarrollo
researcher [rɪ'səːtʃəʳ] n investigador(a)
resemblance [rɪ'zembləns] n parecido; **to bear a strong ~ to** parecerse mucho a
resemble [rɪ'zembl] vt parecerse a
resent [rɪ'zent] vt resentirse por, ofenderse por; **he ~s my being here** le molesta que esté aquí
resentful [rɪ'zentful] adj resentido
resentment [rɪ'zentmənt] n resentimiento
reservation [rezə'veɪʃən] n reserva; (Brit: also: **central reservation**) mediana; **with ~s** con reservas
reservation desk n (US: in hotel) recepción
reserve [rɪ'zəːv] n reserva; (Sport) suplente ▷ vt (seats etc) reservar; **reserves** npl (Mil) reserva; **in ~** en reserva

reserved [rɪ'zəːvd] adj reservado
reservoir ['rezəvwɑːʳ] n (artificial lake) embalse, represa; (small) depósito
reset [riːˈset] vt (Comput) reinicializar
reshape [riːˈʃeɪp] vt (policy) reformar, rehacer
reshuffle [riːˈʃʌfl] n: **Cabinet ~** (Pol) remodelación del gabinete
reside [rɪ'zaɪd] vi residir
residence ['rezɪdəns] n residencia; (formal: home) domicilio; (length of stay) permanencia; **in ~** (doctor) residente; **to take up ~** instalarse
residence permit n (Brit) permiso de residencia
resident ['rezɪdənt] n vecino(-a); (in hotel) huésped(a) ▷ adj residente; (population) permanente
residential [rezɪ'denʃəl] adj residencial
residue ['rezɪdjuː] n resto, residuo
resign [rɪ'zaɪn] vt (gen) renunciar a ▷ vi: **to ~ (from)** dimitir (de), renunciar (a); **to ~ o.s. to** (endure) resignarse a
resignation [rezɪg'neɪʃən] n dimisión; (state of mind) resignación; **to tender one's ~** presentar la dimisión
resigned [rɪ'zaɪnd] adj resignado
resilience [rɪ'zɪlɪəns] n (of material) elasticidad; (of person) resistencia
resilient [rɪ'zɪlɪənt] adj (person) resistente
resin ['rezɪn] n resina
resist [rɪ'zɪst] vt resistirse a; (temptation, damage) resistir
resistance [rɪ'zɪstəns] n resistencia
resistant [rɪ'zɪstənt] adj: **~ (to)** resistente (a)
resolute ['rezəluːt] adj resuelto
resolution [rezə'luːʃən] n (gen) resolución; (purpose) propósito; (Comput) definición; **to make a ~** tomar una resolución
resolve [rɪ'zɔlv] n (determination) resolución; (purpose) propósito ▷ vt resolver ▷ vi resolverse; **to ~ to do** resolver hacer
resolved [rɪ'zɔlvd] adj resuelto
resort [rɪ'zɔːt] n (town) centro turístico; (recourse) recurso ▷ vi: **to ~ to** recurrir a; **in the last ~** como último recurso; **seaside ~** playa, estación balnearia; **winter sports ~** centro de deportes de invierno
resound [rɪ'zaund] vi: **to ~ (with)** resonar (con)
resounding [rɪ'zaundɪŋ] adj sonoro; (fig) clamoroso
resource [rɪ'sɔːs] n recurso; **resources** npl recursos; **natural ~s** recursos naturales; **to leave sb to his/her own ~s** (fig) abandonar a algn/a a sus propios recursos
resourceful [rɪ'sɔːsful] adj ingenioso
respect [rɪs'pekt] n (consideration) respeto; (relation) respecto ▷ vt respetar; **respects** npl recuerdos, saludos; **with ~ to** con respecto a; **in this ~** en cuanto a eso; **to have** or **show ~ for** tener or mostrar respeto a; **out of ~ for** por respeto a; **in some ~s** en algunos aspectos; **with due ~ I still think you're wrong** con el respeto debido, sigo creyendo que está equivocado
respectable [rɪs'pektəbl] adj respetable; (quite

big: amount etc) apreciable; (*passable*) tolerable; (*quite good: player, result etc*) bastante bueno

respected [rɪs'pɛktɪd] *adj* respetado, estimado

respectful [rɪs'pɛktful] *adj* respetuoso

respective [rɪs'pɛktɪv] *adj* respectivo

respiration [rɛspɪ'reɪʃən] *n* respiración

respite ['rɛspaɪt] *n* respiro; (*Law*) prórroga

resplendent [rɪs'plɛndənt] *adj* resplandeciente

respond [rɪs'pɔnd] *vi* responder; (*react*) reaccionar

response [rɪs'pɔns] *n* respuesta; (*reaction*) reacción; **in ~ to** como respuesta a

responsibility [rɪspɔnsɪ'bɪlɪtɪ] *n* responsabilidad; **to take ~ for sth/sb** admitir responsabilidad por algo/algn

responsible [rɪs'pɔnsɪbl] *adj* (*liable*): **~ (for)** responsable (de); (*character*) serio, formal; (*job*) de responsabilidad; **to be ~ to sb (for sth)** ser responsable ante algn (de algo)

responsive [rɪs'pɔnsɪv] *adj* sensible

rest [rɛst] *n* descanso; (*Mus*) pausa, silencio; (*support*) apoyo; (*remainder*) resto ▷ *vi* descansar; (*be supported*): **to ~ on** apoyarse en ▷ *vt* (*eyes, feet*) descansar; (*lean*): **to ~ sth on/against** apoyar algo en *or* sobre/contra; **to have a ~** descansar; **to set sb's mind at ~** tranquilizar a algn; **to be at ~** (*not moving*) estar en reposo; **the ~ of the money** el resto del dinero; **the ~ of them** (*people, objects*) los demás; **it ~s with him** depende de él; **~ assured that …** tenga por seguro que …; **to ~ one's eyes** *or* **gaze on** fijar la mirada en

restaurant ['rɛstərɔŋ] *n* restaurante

restaurant car *n* (*Brit*) coche-comedor

restful ['rɛstful] *adj* descansado, tranquilo

restitution [rɛstɪ'tjuːʃən] *n*: **to make ~ to sb for sth** restituir algo a algn; (*paying*) indemnizar a algn por algo

restive ['rɛstɪv] *adj* inquieto

restless ['rɛstlɪs] *adj* inquieto; **to get ~** impacientarse

restoration [rɛstə'reɪʃən] *n* restauración; (*giving back*) devolución, restitución

restore [rɪ'stɔːr] *vt* (*building*) restaurar; (*stolen item*) devolver, restituir; (*health*) restablecer

restrain [rɪs'treɪn] *vt* (*feeling*) contener, refrenar; (*person*): **to ~ (from doing)** disuadir (de hacer)

restrained [rɪs'treɪnd] *adj* (*style*) reservado

restraint [rɪs'treɪnt] *n* (*restriction*) freno, control; (*of style*) reserva; **wage ~** control de los salarios

restrict [rɪs'trɪkt] *vt* restringir, limitar

restriction [rɪs'trɪkʃən] *n* restricción, limitación

rest room *n* (*US*) aseos

restructure [riː'strʌktʃər] *vt* reestructurar

result [rɪ'zʌlt] *n* resultado ▷ *vi*: **to ~ in** terminar en, tener por resultado; **as a ~ of** a *or* como consecuencia de; **to ~ (from)** resultar (de)

resume [rɪ'zjuːm] *vt* (*work, journey*) reanudar; (*sum up*) resumir ▷ *vi* (*meeting*) continuar

résumé ['reɪzjuːmeɪ] *n* (*summary*) resumen; (*US: curriculum vitae*) currículum

resumption [rɪ'zʌmpʃən] *n* reanudación

resurgence [rɪ'səːdʒəns] *n* resurgimiento

resurrection [rɛzə'rɛkʃən] *n* resurrección

resuscitate [rɪ'sʌsɪteɪt] *vt* (*Med*) resucitar

retail ['riːteɪl] *n* venta al por menor ▷ *cpd* al por menor ▷ *vt* vender al por menor *or* al detalle ▷ *vi*: **to ~ at** (*Comm*) tener precio de venta al público de

retailer ['riːteɪlər] *n* minorista, detallista

retail price *n* precio de venta al público, precio al detalle *or* al por menor

retain [rɪ'teɪn] *vt* (*keep*) retener, conservar; (*employ*) contratar

retainer [rɪ'teɪnər] *n* (*servant*) criado; (*fee*) anticipo

retaliate [rɪ'tælɪeɪt] *vi*: **to ~ (against)** tomar represalias (contra)

retaliation [rɪtælɪ'eɪʃən] *n* represalias; **in ~ for** como represalia por

retarded [rɪ'tɑːdɪd] *adj* retrasado

retch [rɛtʃ] *vi* darle a algn arcadas

retentive [rɪ'tɛntɪv] *adj* (*memory*) retentivo

reticence ['rɛtɪsns] *n* reticencia, reserva

retina ['rɛtɪnə] *n* retina

retire [rɪ'taɪər] *vi* (*give up work*) jubilarse; (*withdraw*) retirarse; (*go to bed*) acostarse

retired [rɪ'taɪəd] *adj* (*person*) jubilado

retirement [rɪ'taɪəmənt] *n* jubilación; **early ~** jubilación anticipada

retiring [rɪ'taɪərɪŋ] *adj* (*departing: chairman*) saliente; (*shy*) retraído

retort [rɪ'tɔːt] *n* (*reply*) réplica ▷ *vi* replicar

retrace [riː'treɪs] *vt*: **to ~ one's steps** volver sobre sus pasos, desandar lo andado

retract [rɪ'trækt] *vt* (*statement*) retirar; (*claws*) retraer; (*undercarriage, aerial*) replegar ▷ *vi* retractarse

retrain [riː'treɪn] *vt* reciclar

retread ['riːtrɛd] *n* neumático *or* llanta (*LAm*) recauchutado(-a)

retreat [rɪ'triːt] *n* (*place*) retiro; (*Mil*) retirada ▷ *vi* retirarse; (*flood*) bajar; **to beat a hasty ~** (*fig*) retirarse en desbandada

retrial ['riːtraɪəl] *n* nuevo proceso

retribution [rɛtrɪ'bjuːʃən] *n* desquite

retrieval [rɪ'triːvəl] *n* recuperación; **information ~** recuperación de datos

retrieve [rɪ'triːv] *vt* recobrar; (*situation, honour*) salvar; (*Comput*) recuperar; (*error*) reparar

retriever [rɪ'triːvər] *n* perro cobrador

retrospect ['rɛtrəspɛkt] *n*: **in ~** retrospectivamente

retrospective [rɛtrə'spɛktɪv] *adj* retrospectivo; (*law*) retroactivo ▷ *n* exposición retrospectiva

return [rɪ'təːn] *n* (*going or coming back*) vuelta, regreso; (*Brit: also*: **return ticket**) billete de ida y vuelta; (*of sth stolen etc*) devolución; (*recompense*) recompensa; (*Finance: from land, shares*) ganancia, ingresos; (*Comm: of merchandise*) devolución ▷ *cpd* (*journey*) de regreso; (*Brit: ticket*) de ida y vuelta; (*match*) de vuelta ▷ *vi* (*person etc: come or go back*) volver, regresar; (*symptoms etc*) reaparecer ▷ *vt* (*thing borrowed*) devolver; (*favour, love etc*) corresponder a; (*Law: verdict*) pronunciar; (*Pol: candidate*) elegir; **returns** *npl* (*Comm*) ingresos;

tax ~ declaración de la renta; **in** ~ **(for)** a cambio (de); **by** ~ **of post** a vuelta de correo; **many happy ~s (of the day)!** ¡feliz cumpleaños!
returning officer [rɪ'tə:nɪŋ-] n (Brit Pol) escrutador(a)
reunion [ri:'ju:nɪən] n reencuentro
reunite [ri:ju:'naɪt] vt reunir; (reconcile) reconciliar
rev [rεv] n abbr (Aut: = revolution) revolución ▷ vt (also: **rev up**) acelerar
revaluation [ri:vælju:'eɪʃən] n revalorización
revamp [ri:'væmp] vt renovar
Rev(d). abbr (= reverend) R., Rvdo.
reveal [rɪ'vi:l] vt (make known) revelar
revealing [rɪ'vi:lɪŋ] adj revelador(a)
reveille [rɪ'vælɪ] n (Mil) diana
revel ['rεvl] vi: **to** ~ **in sth/in doing sth** gozar de algo/haciendo algo
revelation [rεvə'leɪʃən] n revelación
revelry ['rεvlrɪ] n jarana, juerga
revenge [rɪ'vεndʒ] n venganza; (in sport) revancha; **to take** ~ **on** vengarse de; **to get one's** ~ **(for sth)** vengarse (de algo)
revenue ['rεvənju:] n ingresos, rentas
reverberate [rɪ'və:bəreɪt] vi (sound) resonar, retumbar
reverence ['rεvərəns] n reverencia
Reverend ['rεvərənd] adj (in titles): **the** ~ **John Smith** (Anglican) el Reverendo John Smith; (Catholic) el Padre John Smith; (Protestant) el Pastor John Smith
reverent ['rεvərənt] adj reverente
reverie ['rεvərɪ] n ensueño
reversal [rɪ'və:sl] n (of order) inversión; (of policy) cambio de rumbo; (of decision) revocación
reverse [rɪ'və:s] n (opposite) contrario; (back: of cloth) revés; (: of coin) reverso; (: of paper) dorso; (Aut: also: **reverse gear**) marcha atrás ▷ adj (order) inverso; (direction) contrario ▷ vt (decision, Aut) dar marcha atrás a; (position, function) invertir ▷ vi (Brit Aut) poner en marcha atrás; **in** ~ **order** en orden inverso; **the** ~ lo contrario; **to go into** ~ dar marcha atrás
reverse-charge call [rɪ'və:stʃɑ:dʒ-] n (Brit) llamada a cobro revertido
reversing lights [rɪ'və:sɪŋ-] npl (Brit Aut) luces de marcha atrás
revert [rɪ'və:t] vi: **to** ~ **to** volver or revertir a
review [rɪ'vju:] n (magazine, Mil) revista; (of book, film) reseña; (US: examination) repaso, examen ▷ vt repasar, examinar; (Mil) pasar revista a; (book, film) reseñar; **to come under** ~ ser examinado
reviewer [rɪ'vju:ər] n crítico(-a)
revile [rɪ'vaɪl] vt injuriar, vilipendiar
revise [rɪ'vaɪz] vt (manuscript) corregir; (opinion) modificar; (Brit: study: subject) repasar; (look over) revisar; **~d edition** edición corregida
revision [rɪ'vɪʒən] n corrección; modificación; (of subject) repaso; (revised version) revisión
revitalize [ri:'vaɪtəlaɪz] vt revivificar
revival [rɪ'vaɪvəl] n (recovery) reanimación; (Pol)

resurgimiento; (of interest) renacimiento; (Theat) reestreno; (of faith) despertar
revive [rɪ'vaɪv] vt resucitar; (custom) restablecer; (hope, courage) reanimar; (play) reestrenar ▷ vi (person) volver en sí; (from tiredness) reponerse; (business) reactivarse
revoke [rɪ'vəuk] vt revocar
revolt [rɪ'vəult] n rebelión ▷ vi rebelarse, sublevarse ▷ vt dar asco a, repugnar; **to** ~ **(against sb/sth)** rebelarse (contra algn/algo)
revolting [rɪ'vəultɪŋ] adj asqueroso, repugnante
revolution [rεvə'lu:ʃən] n revolución
revolutionary [rεvə'lu:ʃənrɪ] adj, n revolucionario(-a)
revolutionize [rεvə'lu:ʃənaɪz] vt revolucionar
revolve [rɪ'vɔlv] vi dar vueltas, girar
revolver [rɪ'vɔlvər] n revólver
revolving [rɪ'vɔlvɪŋ] adj (chair, door etc) giratorio
revue [rɪ'vju:] n (Theat) revista
revulsion [rɪ'vʌlʃən] n asco, repugnancia
reward [rɪ'wɔ:d] n premio, recompensa ▷ vt: **to** ~ **(for)** recompensar or premiar (por)
rewarding [rɪ'wɔ:dɪŋ] adj (fig) gratificante; **financially** ~ económicamente provechoso
rewind [ri:'waɪnd] vt (watch) dar cuerda a; (wool etc) devanar
rewire [ri:'waɪər] vt (house) renovar la instalación eléctrica de
reword [ri:'wə:d] vt expresar en otras palabras
rewrite [ri:'raɪt] vt (irreg: like **write**) reescribir
Rh abbr (= rhesus) Rh
rheumatism ['ru:mətɪzəm] n reumatismo, reúma
rheumatoid arthritis ['ru:mətɔɪd-] n reúma articular
Rhine [raɪn] n: **the** ~ el (río) Rin
rhinoceros [raɪ'nɔsərəs] n rinoceronte
Rhone [rəun] n: **the** ~ el (río) Ródano
rhubarb ['ru:bɑ:b] n ruibarbo
rhyme [raɪm] n rima; (verse) poesía ▷ vi: **to** ~ **(with)** rimar (con); **without** ~ **or reason** sin ton ni son
rhythm ['rɪðm] n ritmo
rhythmic(al) ['rɪðmɪk(l)] adj rítmico
rhythm method n método (de) Ogino
RI n abbr (Brit: = religious instruction) ed. religiosa ▷ abbr (US) = **Rhode Island**
rib [rɪb] n (Anat) costilla ▷ vt (mock) tomar el pelo a
ribbon ['rɪbən] n cinta; **in ~s** (torn) hecho trizas
rice [raɪs] n arroz
rice pudding n arroz con leche
rich [rɪtʃ] adj rico; (soil) fértil; (food) pesado; (: sweet) empalagoso; **the rich** npl los ricos; **riches** npl riqueza; **to be** ~ **in sth** abundar en algo
rickets ['rɪkɪts] n raquitismo
rickety ['rɪkɪtɪ] adj (old) desvencijado; (shaky) tambaleante
rickshaw ['rɪkʃɔ:] n carro de culí
rid [rɪd] (pt, pp ~) vt: **to** ~ **sb of sth** librar a algn de algo; **to get** ~ **of** deshacerse or desembarazarse

de
iddance ['rɪdns] n: **good ~!** ¡y adiós muy buenas!
iddle ['rɪdl] n (conundrum) acertijo; (mystery)
enigma, misterio ▷ vt: **to be ~d with** ser lleno or
plagado de
ide [raɪd] n paseo; (distance covered) viaje,
recorrido ▷ vb (pt **rode**, pp **ridden**) ▷ vi (on horse:
as sport) montar; (go somewhere: on horse, bicycle)
dar un paseo, pasearse; (journey: on bicycle, motor
cycle, bus) viajar ▷ vt (a horse) montar a; (distance)
viajar; **to ~ a bicycle** andar en bicicleta; **to ~ at
anchor** (Naut) estar fondeado; **can you ~ a bike?**
¿sabes montar en bici(cleta)?; **to go for a ~** dar
un paseo; **to take sb for a ~** (fig) tomar el pelo
a algn
▶ **ride out** vt: **to ~ out the storm** (fig) capear el
temporal
ider ['raɪdər] n (on horse) jinete; (on bicycle)
ciclista; (on motorcycle) motociclista
idge [rɪdʒ] n (of hill) cresta; (of roof) caballete;
(wrinkle) arruga
idicule ['rɪdɪkjuːl] n irrisión, burla ▷ vt poner en
ridículo a, burlarse de; **to hold sth/sb up to ~**
poner algo/a algn en ridículo
idiculous [rɪ'dɪkjuləs] adj ridículo
iding ['raɪdɪŋ] n equitación; **I like ~** me gusta
montar a caballo
iding school n escuela de equitación
ife [raɪf] adj: **to be ~** ser muy común; **to be ~
with** abundar en
iffraff ['rɪfræf] n chusma, gentuza
ifle ['raɪfl] n rifle, fusil ▷ vt saquear
▶ **rifle through** vt fus saquear
ifle range n campo de tiro; (at fair) tiro al blanco
ift [rɪft] n (fig: between friends) desavenencia; (: in
party) escisión
ig [rɪg] n (also: **oil rig**: on land) torre de
perforación; (: at sea) plataforma petrolera ▷ vt
(election etc) amañar los resultados de
▶ **rig out** vt (Brit) ataviar
▶ **rig up** vt improvisar
igging ['rɪgɪŋ] n (Naut) aparejo
ight [raɪt] adj (true, correct) correcto, exacto;
(suitable) indicado, debido; (proper) apropiado,
propio; (just) justo; (morally good) bueno; (not
left) derecho ▷ n (title, claim) derecho; (not left)
derecha ▷ adv (correctly) bien, correctamente;
(straight) derecho, directamente; (not on the left) a
la derecha; (to the right) hacia la derecha ▷ vt (put
straight) enderezar ▷ excl ¡bueno!, ¡está bien!; **to
be ~** (person) tener razón; (statement, opinion) ser
verdad; **that's ~!** ¡es verdad!; **to get sth ~** acertar
en algo; **you did the ~ thing** hiciste bien; **let's
get it ~ this time!** ¡a ver si esta vez nos sale
bien!; **to put a mistake ~** corregir un error;
the ~ time la hora exacta; (fig) el momento
oportuno; **we're on the ~ train** estamos en el
tren adecuado; **it's not ~ to behave like that**
no está bien comportarse así; **by ~s** en justicia;
~ and wrong el bien y el mal; **you've got no ~ to
do that** no tienes derecho de hacer eso; **film ~s**
derechos de la película; **on the ~** a la derecha; **to**

be in the ~ tener razón; **~ now** ahora mismo; **~
before/after** inmediatamente antes/después; **~
in the middle** exactamente en el centro; **~ away**
en seguida; **to go ~ to the end of sth** llegar
hasta el final de algo; **~, who's next?** bueno,
¿quién sigue?; **all ~!** ¡vale!; **I'm/I feel all ~ now**
ya estoy bien
right angle n ángulo recto
righteous ['raɪtʃəs] adj justo, honrado; (anger)
justificado
rightful ['raɪtful] adj (heir) legítimo
right-handed [raɪt'hændɪd] adj (person) que usa
la mano derecha
right-hand man n brazo derecho
right-hand side n derecha
rightly ['raɪtlɪ] adv correctamente, debidamente;
(with reason) con razón; **if I remember ~** si
recuerdo bien
right of way n (on path etc) derecho de paso; (Aut)
prioridad de paso
right-wing [raɪt'wɪŋ] adj (Pol) de derechas,
derechista
rigid ['rɪdʒɪd] adj rígido; (person, ideas) inflexible
rigidly ['rɪdʒɪdlɪ] adv rígidamente; (inflexibly)
inflexiblemente
rigmarole ['rɪgmərəul] n galimatías
rigor mortis ['rɪgə'mɔːtɪs] n rigidez cadavérica
rigorous ['rɪgərəs] adj riguroso
rile [raɪl] vt irritar
rim [rɪm] n borde; (of spectacles) montura, aro; (of
wheel) llanta
rind [raɪnd] n (of bacon, cheese) corteza; (of lemon
etc) cáscara
ring [rɪŋ] n (of metal) aro; (on finger) anillo; (of
people) corro; (of objects) círculo; (gang) banda; (for
boxing) cuadrilátero; (of circus) pista; (bull ring)
ruedo, plaza; (sound of bell) toque; (telephone call)
llamada ▷ vb (pt **rang**, pp **rung**) ▷ vi (on telephone)
llamar por teléfono; (large bell) repicar; (also: **ring
out**: voice, words) sonar; (ears) zumbar ▷ vt (Brit
Tel: also: **ring up**) llamar; (bell etc) hacer sonar;
(doorbell) tocar; **to stand in a ~** formar un círculo;
there was a ~ at the door se oyó el timbre de
la puerta; **that has the ~ of truth about it** eso
suena a verdad; **to give sb a ~** (Brit Tel) llamar
por teléfono a algn, dar un telefonazo a algn;
the phone's ~ing el teléfono está sonando; **the
name doesn't ~ a bell (with me)** el nombre no
me suena; **to ~ sb (up)** llamar a algn
▶ **ring back** vt, vi (Tel: return call) devolver la
llamada; (call again) volver a llamar
▶ **ring off** vi (Brit Tel) colgar, cortar la
comunicación
ring binder n carpeta de anillas
ringing ['rɪŋɪŋ] n (of bell) toque, tañido; (louder, of
large bell) repique; (in ears) zumbido
ringing tone n (Tel) tono de llamada
ringleader ['rɪŋliːdər] n (of gang) cabecilla
ringlets ['rɪŋlɪts] npl tirabuzones, bucles
ring road n (Brit) carretera periférica or de
circunvalación
rink [rɪŋk] n (also: **ice rink**) pista de hielo; (for

roller-skating) pista de patinaje

rinse [rɪns] *n* (*of dishes*) enjuague; (*of clothes*) aclarado; (*of hair*) reflejo ▷ *vt* enjuagar; aclarar; dar reflejos a

riot ['raɪət] *n* motín, disturbio ▷ *vi* amotinarse; **to run ~** desmandarse

riot gear *n* uniforme antidisturbios

riotous ['raɪətəs] *adj* alborotado; (*party*) bullicioso; (*uncontrolled*) desenfrenado

riot police *n* policía antidisturbios

RIP *abbr* (= *rest in peace*) q.e.p.d.

rip [rɪp] *n* rasgón, desgarrón ▷ *vt* rasgar, desgarrar ▷ *vi* rasgarse

▶ **rip up** *vt* hacer pedazos

ripcord ['rɪpkɔːd] *n* cabo de desgarre

ripe [raɪp] *adj* (*fruit*) maduro

ripen ['raɪpən] *vt, vi* madurar

rip-off ['rɪpɔf] *n* (*col*): **it's a ~!** ¡es una estafa!, ¡es un timo!

ripple ['rɪpl] *n* onda, rizo; (*sound*) murmullo ▷ *vi* rizarse ▷ *vt* rizar

rise [raɪz] *n* (*slope*) cuesta, pendiente; (*hill*) altura; (*increase: in wages: Brit*) aumento; (: *in prices, temperature*) subida, alza; (*fig: to power etc*) ascenso; (: *ascendancy*) auge ▷ *vi* (*pt* **rose**, *pp* **-n**) [rəuz, 'rɪzn] (*gen*) elevarse; (*prices*) subir; (*waters*) crecer; (*river*) nacer; (*sun*) salir; (*person: from bed etc*) levantarse; (*also*: **rise up**: *rebel*) sublevarse; (*in rank*) ascender; **a sudden ~ in temperature** una repentina subida de las temperaturas; **~ to power** ascenso al poder; **to give ~ to** dar lugar *or* origen a; **to ~ to the occasion** ponerse a la altura de las circunstancias

rising ['raɪzɪŋ] *adj* (*increasing: number*) creciente; (: *prices*) en aumento *or* alza; (*tide*) creciente; (*sun, moon*) naciente ▷ *n* (*uprising*) sublevación

rising star *n* (*fig*) figura en alza

risk [rɪsk] *n* riesgo, peligro ▷ *vt* (*gen*) arriesgar; (*dare*) atreverse a; **to take** *or* **run the ~ of doing** correr el riesgo de hacer; **at ~** en peligro; **at one's own ~** bajo su propia responsabilidad; **fire/health/security ~** peligro de incendio/para la salud/para la seguridad

risky ['rɪskɪ] *adj* arriesgado, peligroso

risqué ['riːskeɪ] *adj* (*joke*) subido de color

rissole ['rɪsəul] *n* croqueta

rite [raɪt] *n* rito; **last ~s** últimos sacramentos

ritual ['rɪtjuəl] *adj* ritual ▷ *n* ritual, rito

rival ['raɪvl] *n* rival; (*in business*) competidor(a) ▷ *adj* rival, opuesto ▷ *vt* competir con

rivalry ['raɪvlrɪ] *n* rivalidad, competencia

river ['rɪvəʳ] *n* río ▷ *cpd* (*port, traffic*) de río, del río; **up/down ~** río arriba/abajo

riverbank ['rɪvəbæŋk] *n* orilla (del río)

rivet ['rɪvɪt] *n* roblón, remache ▷ *vt* remachar; (*fig*) fascinar

riveting ['rɪvɪtɪŋ] *adj* (*fig*) fascinante

Riviera [rɪvɪ'eərə] *n*: **the (French) ~** la Costa Azul, la Riviera (francesa); **the Italian ~** la Riviera italiana

road [rəud] *n* (*gen*) camino; (*motorway etc*) carretera; (*in town*) calle; **major/minor ~**

carretera general/secundaria; **main ~** carretera, **it takes 4 hours by ~** se tarda 4 horas por carretera; **on the ~ to success** camino del éxito

roadblock ['rəudblɔk] *n* barricada, control, retén (*LAm*)

roadhog ['rəudhɔg] *n* loco(-a) del volante

road map *n* mapa de carreteras

road rage *n* conducta agresiva de los conductores

road safety *n* seguridad vial

roadside ['rəudsaɪd] *n* borde (del camino) ▷ *cpd* al lado de la carretera; **by the ~** al borde del camino

roadsign ['rəudsaɪn] *n* señal de tráfico

roadway ['rəudweɪ] *n* calzada

roadworks ['rəudwəːks] *npl* obras

roadworthy ['rəudwəːðɪ] *adj* (*car*) en buen estado para circular

roam [rəum] *vi* vagar ▷ *vt* vagar por

roar [rɔːʳ] *n* (*of animal*) rugido, bramido; (*of crowd*) clamor, rugido; (*of vehicle, storm*) estruendo; (*of laughter*) carcajada ▷ *vi* rugir, bramar; hacer estruendo; **to ~ with laughter** reírse a carcajadas

roast [rəust] *n* carne asada, asado ▷ *vt* (*meat*) asar; (*coffee*) tostar

roast beef *n* rosbif

roasting ['rəustɪŋ] *n*: **to give sb a ~** (*col*) echar una buena bronca a algn

rob [rɔb] *vt* robar; **to ~ sb of sth** robar algo a algn; (*fig: deprive*) quitar algo a algn

robber ['rɔbəʳ] *n* ladrón(-ona)

robbery ['rɔbərɪ] *n* robo

robe [rəub] *n* (*for ceremony etc*) toga; (*also*: **bath robe**) bata

robin ['rɔbɪn] *n* petirrojo

robot ['rəubɔt] *n* robot

robust [rəu'bʌst] *adj* robusto, fuerte

rock [rɔk] *n* (*gen*) roca; (*boulder*) peña, peñasco; (*Brit: sweet*) = pirulí ▷ *vt* (*swing gently*) mecer; (*shake*) sacudir ▷ *vi* mecerse, balancearse; sacudirse; **on the ~s** (*drink*) con hielo; **their marriage is on the ~s** su matrimonio se está yendo a pique; **to ~ the boat** (*fig*) crear problemas

rock-bottom ['rɔk'bɔtəm] *adj* (*fig*) por los suelos; **to reach** *or* **touch ~** (*price*) estar por los suelos; (*person*) tocar fondo

rockery ['rɔkərɪ] *n* cuadro alpino

rocket ['rɔkɪt] *n* cohete ▷ *vi* (*prices*) dispararse, ponerse por las nubes

rocking chair ['rɔkɪŋ-] *n* mecedora

rocking horse *n* caballo de balancín

rocky ['rɔkɪ] *adj* (*gen*) rocoso; (*unsteady: table*) inestable

rod [rɔd] *n* vara, varilla; (*Tech*) barra; (*also*: **fishing rod**) caña

rode [rəud] *pt of* **ride**

rodent ['rəudnt] *n* roedor

rodeo ['rəudɪəu] *n* rodeo

roe [rəu] *n* (*species: also*: **roe deer**) corzo; (*of fish*): **hard/soft ~** hueva/lecha

rogue [rəug] *n* pícaro, pillo

role [rəul] *n* papel, rol
role-model ['rəulmɔdl] *n* modelo a imitar
role play *n* (*also:* **role playing**) juego de papeles
or roles
roll [rəul] *n* rollo; (*of bank notes*) fajo; (*also:* **bread roll**) panecillo; (*register*) lista, nómina; (*sound: of drums etc*) redoble; (*movement: of ship*) balanceo
▷ *vt* hacer rodar; (*also:* **roll up:** *string*) enrollar;
(*: sleeves*) arremangar; (*cigarette*) liar; (*also:* **roll out:** *pastry*) extender con el rodillo ▷ *vi* (*gen*)
rodar; (*drum*) redoblar; (*in walking*) bambolearse;
(*ship*) balancearse; **~ of film** carrete de fotos;
cheese ~ panecillo de queso
▶ **roll about, roll around** *vi* (*person*) revolcarse
▶ **roll by** *vi* (*time*) pasar
▶ **roll in** *vi* (*mail, cash*) entrar a raudales
▶ **roll over** *vi* dar una vuelta
▶ **roll up** *vi* (*col: arrive*) presentarse, aparecer ▷ *vt*
(*carpet, cloth, map*) arrollar; (*sleeves*) arremangar;
to ~ o.s. up into a ball acurrucarse, hacerse un
ovillo
roll call *n:* **to take a ~** pasar lista
roller ['rəulə'] *n* rodillo; (*wheel*) rueda
roller coaster *n* montaña rusa
roller skates *npl* patines de rueda
rolling ['rəulɪŋ] *adj* (*landscape*) ondulado
rolling pin *n* rodillo (de cocina)
rolling stock *n* (*Rail*) material rodante
ROM [rɔm] *n abbr* (= *read only memory*) (memoria)
ROM
Roman ['rəumən] *adj, n* romano(-a)
Roman Catholic *adj, n* católico(-a) (romano(-a))
romance [rə'mæns] *n* (*love affair*) amor, idilio;
(*charm*) lo romántico; (*novel*) novela de amor
Romania [ru:'meɪnɪə] *n* = **Rumania**
Romanian [ru:'meɪnɪən] *adj, n* = **Rumanian**
Roman numeral *n* número romano
romantic [rə'mæntɪk] *adj* romántico
Rome [rəum] *n* Roma
romp [rɔmp] *n* retozo, jugueteo ▷ *vi* (*also:* **romp about**) juguetear; **to ~ home** (*horse*) ganar
fácilmente
rompers ['rɔmpəz] *npl* pelele
roof [ru:f] *n* (*gen*) techo; (*of house*) tejado ▷ *vt*
techar, poner techo a; **~ of the mouth** paladar
roofing ['ru:fɪŋ] *n* techumbre
roof rack *n* (*Aut*) baca
rook [ruk] *n* (*bird*) graja; (*Chess*) torre
rookie ['rukɪ] *n* (*col*) novato(-a); (*Mil*) chivo
room [ru:m] *n* (*in house*) cuarto, habitación,
pieza (*esp LAm*); (*also:* **bedroom**) dormitorio; (*in school etc*) sala; (*space*) sitio; **rooms** *npl* (*lodging*)
alojamiento; **"~s to let"** (*US*): **"~s for rent"**
"se alquilan pisos *or* cuartos"; **single/double
~** habitación individual/doble *or* para dos
personas; **is there ~ for this?** ¿cabe esto?; **to
make ~ for sb** hacer sitio para algn; **there is ~
for improvement** podría mejorarse
rooming house ['ru:mɪŋ-] *n* (*US*) pensión
roommate ['ru:mmeɪt] *n* compañero(-a) de
cuarto
room service *n* servicio de habitaciones

roomy ['ru:mɪ] *adj* espacioso
roost [ru:st] *n* percha ▷ *vi* pasar la noche
rooster ['ru:stə'] *n* gallo
root [ru:t] *n* (*Bot, Math*) raíz ▷ *vi* (*plant, belief*)
arraigar(se); **to take ~** (*plant*) echar raíces; (*idea*)
arraigar(se); **the ~ of the problem is that ...** la
raíz del problema es que ...
▶ **root about** *vi* (*fig*) rebuscar
▶ **root for** *vt fus* apoyar a
▶ **root out** *vt* desarraigar
root beer *n* (*US*) *refresco sin alcohol de extractos de
hierbas*
rope [rəup] *n* cuerda; (*Naut*) cable ▷ *vt* (*box*) atar
or amarrar con (una) cuerda; (*climbers: also:* **rope
together**) encordarse; **to ~ sb in** (*fig*) persuadir a
algn a tomar parte; **to know the ~s** (*fig*) conocer
los trucos (del oficio)
ropey ['rəupɪ] *adj* (*col*) chungo
rosary ['rəuzərɪ] *n* rosario
rose [rəuz] *pt of* **rise** ▷ *n* rosa; (*also:* **rosebush**)
rosal; (*on watering can*) roseta ▷ *adj* color de rosa
rosé ['rəuzeɪ] *n* vino rosado, clarete
rosebud ['rəuzbʌd] *n* capullo de rosa
rosebush ['rəuzbuʃ] *n* rosal
rosemary ['rəuzmərɪ] *n* romero
rosette [rəu'zɛt] *n* rosetón
roster ['rɔstə'] *n:* **duty ~** lista de tareas
rostrum ['rɔstrəm] *n* tribuna
rosy ['rəuzɪ] *adj* rosado, sonrosado; **the future
looks ~** el futuro parece prometedor
rot [rɔt] *n* (*decay*) putrefacción, podredumbre;
(*fig: pej*) tonterías ▷ *vt* pudrir, corromper ▷ *vi*
pudrirse, corromperse; **it has ~ted** está podrido;
to stop the ~ (*fig*) poner fin a las pérdidas
rota ['rəutə] *n* lista (de tareas)
rotary ['rəutərɪ] *adj* rotativo
rotate [rəu'teɪt] *vt* (*revolve*) hacer girar, dar
vueltas a; (*change round: crops*) cultivar en
rotación; (*: jobs*) alternar ▷ *vi* (*revolve*) girar, dar
vueltas
rotating [rəu'teɪtɪŋ] *adj* (*movement*) rotativo
rote [rəut] *n:* **by ~** de memoria
rotor ['rəutə'] *n* rotor
rotten ['rɔtn] *adj* (*decayed*) podrido; (*: wood*)
carcomido; (*fig*) corrompido; (*col: bad*) pésimo;
to feel ~ (*ill*) sentirse fatal; **~ to the core**
completamente podrido
rotund [rəu'tʌnd] *adj* rotundo
rough [rʌf] *adj* (*skin, surface*) áspero; (*terrain*)
accidentado; (*road*) desigual; (*voice*) bronco;
(*person, manner: coarse*) tosco, grosero; (*weather*)
borrascoso; (*treatment*) brutal; (*sea*) embravecido;
(*cloth*) basto; (*plan*) preliminar; (*guess*)
aproximado; (*violent*) violento ▷ *n* (*Golf*): **in
the ~** en las hierbas altas ▷ *vt:* **to ~ it** vivir sin
comodidades ▷ *adv:* **to sleep ~** (*Brit*) pasar la
noche al raso; **the sea is ~ today** el mar está
agitado hoy; **to have a ~ time (of it)** pasar una
mala racha; **it's a ~ area** (*dangerous*) es una zona
peligrosa; **~ estimate** cálculo aproximado; **I've
got a ~ idea** tengo una idea aproximada; **to feel
~** sentirse mal

roughage ['rʌfɪdʒ] n fibra(s), forraje
rough-and-ready ['rʌfən'redɪ] adj improvisado, tosco
rough copy, rough draft n borrador
roughly ['rʌflɪ] adv (handle) torpemente; (make) toscamente; (approximately) aproximadamente; ~ **speaking** más o menos
roughness ['rʌfnɪs] n aspereza; tosquedad; brutalidad
roulette [ru:'lɛt] n ruleta
Roumania [ru:'meɪnɪə] n = **Rumania**
round [raund] adj redondo ▷ n círculo; (of policeman) ronda; (of milkman) recorrido; (of doctor) visitas; (game: of cards, in competition) partida; (of ammunition) cartucho; (Boxing) asalto; (of talks) ronda ▷ vt (corner) doblar ▷ prep alrededor de ▷ adv: **all** ~ por todos lados; **the long way** ~ por el camino menos directo; **all the year** ~ durante todo el año; **to ask sb** ~ invitar a algn a casa; **to go the** ~**s** (story) divulgarse; **a** ~ **of applause** una salva de aplausos; **a** ~ **of drinks/sandwiches** una ronda de bebidas/bocadillos; **I think it's my** ~ creo que me toca pagar; **a** ~ **of toast** (Brit) una tostada; **a** ~ **of golf** una vuelta de golf; **the daily** ~ la rutina cotidiana; **I'll be** ~ **at 6 o'clock** llegaré a eso de las 6; **she arrived** ~ **(about) noon** llegó alrededor del mediodía; **it costs** ~ **about £100** cuesta alrededor de 100 libras esterlinas; ~ **about 8 o'clock** hacia las 8; ~ **the clock** adv las 24 horas; **to go** ~ **to sb's (house)** ir a casa de algn; **to go** ~ **the back** pasar por atrás; **to go** ~ **a house/museum** visitar una casa/un museo; **enough to go** ~ bastante (para todos); **to have a look** ~ echar un vistazo; **in** ~ **figures** en números redondos; **she wore a scarf** ~ **her neck** levaba una bufanda alrededor del cuello; **he lives** ~ **here** vive aquí cerca; **it's just** ~ **the corner** (fig) está a la vuelta de la esquina
▶ **round off** vt (speech etc) acabar, poner término a
▶ **round up** vt (cattle) acorralar; (people) reunir; (prices) redondear
roundabout ['raundəbaut] n (Brit: Aut) glorieta, rotonda; (: at fair) tiovivo ▷ adj (route, means) indirecto
rounders ['raundəz] n (Brit: game) juego similar al béisbol
roundly ['raundlɪ] adv (fig) rotundamente
round-shouldered ['raund'ʃəuldəd] adj cargado de espaldas
round trip n viaje de ida y vuelta
roundup ['raundʌp] n rodeo; (of criminals) redada; **a** ~ **of the latest news** un resumen de las últimas noticias
rouse [rauz] vt (wake up) despertar; (stir up) suscitar
rousing ['rauzɪŋ] adj (applause) caluroso; (speech) conmovedor(a)
rout [raut] n (Mil) derrota; (flight) desbandada ▷ vt derrotar
route [ru:t] n ruta, camino; (of bus) recorrido; (of shipping) rumbo, derrota; **the best** ~ **to London** el mejor camino or la mejor ruta para ir a

Londres; **en** ~ **from ... to** en el viaje de ... a; **en** ~ **for** rumbo a, con destino en
route map n (Brit: for journey) mapa de carreteras
routine [ru:'ti:n] adj (work) rutinario ▷ n rutina; (Theat) número; (Comput) rutina; ~ **procedure** trámite rutinario
row [rəu] n (line) fila, hilera; (Knitting) vuelta [rau] (noise) escándalo; (dispute) bronca, pelea; (fuss) jaleo; (scolding) reprimenda ▷ vi (in boat) remar [rau] reñir(se) ▷ vt (boat) conducir remando; **4 days in a** ~ 4 días seguidos; **to make a** ~ armar un lío; **to have a** ~ pelearse, reñir
rowboat ['rəubəut] n (US) bote de remos
rowdy ['raudɪ] adj (person: noisy) ruidoso; (: quarrelsome) pendenciero; (occasion) alborotado ▷ n pendenciero
rowing ['rəuɪŋ] n remo
rowing boat n (Brit) bote or barco de remos
royal ['rɔɪəl] adj real
Royal Academy (of Arts) n (Brit) la Real Academia de Bellas Artes
Royal Air Force (RAF) n Fuerzas Aéreas Británicas
royalist ['rɔɪəlɪst] adj, n monárquico(-a)
Royal Navy (RN) n (Brit) Marina Británica
royalty ['rɔɪəltɪ] n (royal persons) (miembros de la) familia real; (payment to author) derechos de autor
RP n abbr = **Received Pronunciation**
rpm abbr (= revs per minute) r.p.m.
RSPB n abbr (Brit) = **Royal Society for the Protection of Birds**
RSPCA n abbr (Brit) = **Royal Society for the Prevention of Cruelty to Animals**
RTA n abbr (= road traffic accident) accidente de carretera
Rt. Hon. abbr (Brit: = Right Honourable) tratamiento honorífico de diputado
Rt. Rev. abbr (= Right Reverend) Rvdo.
rub [rʌb] vt (gen) frotar; (hard) restregar ▷ n (gen) frotamiento; (touch) roce; **to** ~ **sb up** or (US) ~ **sb the wrong way** sacar de quicio a algn
▶ **rub down** vt (body) secar frotando; (horse) almohazar
▶ **rub in** vt (ointment) frotar
▶ **rub off** vt borrarse ▷ vi quitarse (frotando); **to** ~ **off on sb** influir en algn, pegársele a algn
▶ **rub out** vt borrar ▷ vi borrarse
rubber ['rʌbər] n caucho, goma; (Brit: eraser) goma de borrar
rubber band n goma, gomita
rubber bullet n bala de goma
rubber plant n ficus
rubber ring n (for swimming) flotador
rubbish ['rʌbɪʃ] (Brit) n (from household) basura; (waste) desperdicios; (fig: pej) tonterías; (trash) basura, porquería ▷ vt (col) poner por los suelos; **what you've just said is** ~ lo que acabas de decir es una tontería
rubbish bin n cubo or tacho (CS) or bote (Méx) de la basura
rubbish dump n (in town) vertedero, basurero
rubble ['rʌbl] n escombros

ruby ['ruːbɪ] n rubí

RUC n abbr (= Royal Ulster Constabulary) fuerza de policía en Irlanda del Norte

rucksack ['rʌksæk] n mochila

ruddy ['rʌdɪ] adj (face) rubicundo; (col: damned) condenado

rude [ruːd] adj (impolite: person) grosero, maleducado; (: word, manners) rudo, grosero; (indecent) indecente; **to be ~ to sb** ser grosero con algn

rudimentary [ruːdɪ'mɛntərɪ] adj rudimentario

rue [ruː] vt arrepentirse de

rueful ['ruːful] adj arrepentido

ruffian ['rʌfɪən] n matón, criminal

ruffle ['rʌfl] vt (hair) despeinar; (clothes) arrugar; (fig: person) agitar

rug [rʌg] n alfombra; (Brit: for knees) manta

rugby ['rʌgbɪ] n (also: **rugby football**) rugby

rugged ['rʌgɪd] adj (landscape) accidentado; (features) robusto

rugger ['rʌgəʳ] n (Brit col) rugby

ruin ['ruːɪn] n ruina ▷ vt arruinar; (spoil) estropear; **ruins** npl ruinas, restos; **in ~s** en ruinas

rule [ruːl] n (norm) norma, costumbre; (regulation, ruler) regla; (government) dominio; (dominion etc) ▷ vt (country, person) gobernar; (decide) disponer; (draw: line) trazar; (draw lines on: paper) reglar ▷ vi gobernar; (Law) fallar; **it's against the ~s** está prohibido; **as a ~** por regla general, generalmente; **by ~ of thumb** por experiencia; **majority ~** (Pol) gobierno mayoritario; **to ~ against/in favour of/on** fallar en contra de/a favor de/sobre; **to ~ that ...** (umpire, judge) fallar que ...

▸ **rule out** vt excluir

ruled [ruːld] adj (paper) rayado

ruler ['ruːləʳ] n (sovereign) soberano; (for measuring) regla

ruling ['ruːlɪŋ] adj (party) gobernante; (class) dirigente ▷ n (Law) fallo, decisión

rum [rʌm] n ron

Rumania [ruː'meɪnɪə] n Rumanía

Rumanian [ruː'meɪnɪən] adj, n rumano(-a)

rumble ['rʌmbl] n ruido sordo; (of thunder) redoble ▷ vi retumbar, hacer un ruido sordo; (stomach, pipe) sonar

rummage ['rʌmɪdʒ] vi revolverlo todo

rumour, (US) **rumor** ['ruːməʳ] n rumor ▷ vt: **it is ~ed that ...** se rumorea que ..; **~ has it that ...** corre la voz de que ...

rump [rʌmp] n (of animal) ancas, grupa

rump steak n filete de lomo

rumpus ['rʌmpəs] n (col) lío, jaleo; (quarrel) pelea, riña; **to kick up a ~** armar un follón or armar bronca

run [rʌn] n (Sport) carrera; (outing) paseo, excursión; (distance travelled) trayecto; (series) serie; (Theat) temporada; (Ski) pista; (in tights, stockings) carrera ▷ vb (pt **ran**, pp **~**) ▷ vt (operate: business) dirigir; (: competition, course) organizar;

(: hotel, house) administrar, llevar; (Comput: program) ejecutar; (to pass: hand) pasar; (bath): **to ~ a bath** llenar la bañera ▷ vi (gen) correr; (work: machine) funcionar, marchar; (bus, train: operate) circular, ir; (: travel) ir; (: continue: play) seguir en cartel; (: contract) ser válido; (flow: river, bath) fluir; (colours, washing) desteñirse; (in election) ser candidato; **to go for a ~** ir a correr; **to make a ~ for it** echar(se) a correr, escapar(se), huir; **to have the ~ of sb's house** tener el libre uso de la casa de algn; **a ~ of luck** una racha de suerte; **there was a ~ on** (meat, tickets) hubo mucha demanda de; **in the long ~** a la larga; **on the ~** en fuga; **I ran five kilometres** corrí cinco kilómetros; **I'll ~ you to the station** te llevaré a la estación en coche; **to ~ a risk** correr un riesgo; **to ~ errands** hacer recados; **it's very cheap to ~** es muy económico; **to be ~ off one's feet** estar ocupadísimo; **to ~ for the bus** correr tras el autobús; **we shall have to ~ for it** tendremos que escapar; **the train ~s between Gatwick and Victoria** el tren circula entre Gatwick y Victoria; **the bus ~s every 20 minutes** el autobús pasa cada 20 minutos; **the buses stop ~ning at midnight** los autobuses dejan de funcionar a medianoche; **to ~ on petrol/on diesel/off batteries** funcionar con gasolina/gasoil/baterías; **my salary won't ~ to a car** mi sueldo no me da para comprarme un coche; **don't leave the tap ~ning** no dejen el grifo abierto

▸ **run about, run around** vi (children) correr por todos lados

▸ **run across** vt fus (find) dar or topar con

▸ **run away** vi huir

▸ **run down** vi (clock) pararse ▷ vt (reduce: production) ir reduciendo; (factory) restringir la producción de; (Aut) atropellar; (criticize) criticar; **to be ~ down** (person: tired) encontrarse agotado

▸ **run in** vt (Brit: car) rodar

▸ **run into** vt fus (meet: person, trouble) tropezar con; (collide with) chocar contra; **the car ran into the lamppost** el coche chocó contra el farol; **to ~ into debt** contraer deudas, endeudarse

▸ **run off** vt (water) dejar correr ▷ vi huir corriendo

▸ **run out** vi (person) salir corriendo; (liquid) irse; (lease) caducar, vencer; (money) acabarse; **time is ~ning out** queda poco tiempo

▸ **run out of** vt fus quedarse sin; **we ran out of money** nos quedamos sin dinero; **I've ~ out of petrol** se me acabó la gasolina

▸ **run over** vt (Aut) atropellar ▷ vt fus (revise) repasar; **to get ~ over** ser atropellado

▸ **run through** vt fus (instructions) repasar

▸ **run up** vt (debt) incurrir en; **to ~ up against** (difficulties) tropezar con

run-around ['rʌnəraund] n: **to give sb the ~** traer a algn al retortero

runaway ['rʌnəweɪ] adj (horse) desbocado; (truck) sin frenos; (person) fugitivo

rung [rʌŋ] pp of **ring** ▷ n (of ladder) escalón,

peldaño

run-in ['rʌnɪn] n (col) altercado

runner ['rʌnə'] n (in race: person) corredor(a); (: horse) caballo; (on sledge) patín; (wheel) ruedecilla

runner bean n (Brit) judía verde (Esp), habichuela (LAm), ejote (CAm, Méx), chaucha (RP)

runner-up [rʌnər'ʌp] n subcampeón(-ona)

running ['rʌnɪŋ] n (sport) atletismo; (race) carrera ▷ adj (costs, water) corriente; (commentary) en directo; **to be in/out of the ~ for sth** tener/no tener posibilidades de ganar algo; **6 days ~** 6 días seguidos

running costs npl (of business) gastos corrientes; (of car) gastos de mantenimiento

runny ['rʌnɪ] adj derretido

run-of-the-mill ['rʌnəvðə'mɪl] adj común y corriente

runt [rʌnt] n (also pej) enano

run-up ['rʌnʌp] n: ~ **to** (election etc) período previo a

runway ['rʌnweɪ] n (Aviat) pista (de aterrizaje)

rupee [ru:'pi:] n rupia

rupture ['rʌptʃə'] n (Med) hernia ▷ vt: **to ~ o.s** causarse una hernia

rural ['ruərl] adj rural

rush [rʌʃ] n ímpetu; (hurry) prisa, apuro (LAm); (Comm) demanda repentina; (Bot) junco; (current) corriente fuerte, ráfaga ▷ vt apresurar; (work) hacer de prisa; (attack: town etc) asaltar ▷ vi correr, precipitarse; **gold ~** fiebre del oro; **we've had a ~ of orders** ha habido una gran demanda; **I'm in a ~ (to do)** tengo prisa or apuro (LAm) (por hacer); **is there any ~ for this?** ¿te corre prisa esto?; **to ~ sth off** hacer algo de prisa y corriendo
▶ **rush through** vt fus (meal) comer de prisa; (book) leer de prisa; (work) hacer de prisa; (town) atravesar a toda velocidad; (Comm: order) despachar rápidamente

rush hour n horas punta

rusk [rʌsk] n bizcocho tostado

Russia ['rʌʃə] n Rusia

Russian ['rʌʃən] adj ruso ▷ n ruso(-a); (Ling) ruso

rust [rʌst] n herrumbre, moho ▷ vi oxidarse

rustic ['rʌstɪk] adj rústico

rustle ['rʌsl] vi susurrar ▷ vt (paper) hacer crujir; (US: cattle) hurtar, robar

rustproof ['rʌstpru:f] adj inoxidable

rusty ['rʌstɪ] adj oxidado

rut [rʌt] n surco; (Zool) celo; **to be in a ~** ser esclavo de la rutina

ruthless ['ru:θlɪs] adj despiadado

rye [raɪ] n centeno

rye bread n pan de centeno

Ss

, s Es *n* (*letter*) S, s; **S for Sugar** S de sábado

A *n abbr* = **South Africa; South America**

abbath ['sæbəθ] *n* domingo; (*Jewish*) sábado

abotage ['sæbətɑːʒ] *n* sabotaje ▷ *vt* sabotear

accharin(e) ['sækərɪn] *n* sacarina

achet ['sæʃeɪ] *n* sobrecito

ack [sæk] *n* (*bag*) saco, costal ▷ *vt* (*dismiss*) despedir, echar; (*plunder*) saquear; **to get the ~** ser despedido; **to give sb the ~** despedir *or* echar a algn

acking ['sækɪŋ] *n* (*material*) arpillera

acrament ['sækrəmənt] *n* sacramento

acred ['seɪkrɪd] *adj* sagrado, santo

acrifice ['sækrɪfaɪs] *n* sacrificio ▷ *vt* sacrificar; **to make ~s (for sb)** sacrificarse (por algn)

acrilege ['sækrɪlɪdʒ] *n* sacrilegio

ad [sæd] *adj* (*unhappy*) triste; (*deplorable*) lamentable

addle ['sædl] *n* silla (de montar); (*of cycle*) sillín ▷ *vt* (*horse*) ensillar; **to ~ sb with sth** (*col: task, bill, name*) cargar a algn con algo; (*responsibility*) gravar a algn con algo; **to be ~d with sth** (*col*) quedar cargado con algo

addlebag ['sædlbæg] *n* alforja

adist ['seɪdɪst] *n* sádico(-a)

adistic [sə'dɪstɪk] *adj* sádico

adly ['sædlɪ] *adv* tristemente; (*regrettably*) desgraciadamente; **~ lacking (in)** muy deficiente (en)

adness ['sædnɪs] *n* tristeza

ae *abbr* (Brit: = *stamped addressed envelope*) sobre con las propias señas de uno y con sello

afari [sə'fɑːrɪ] *n* safari

afe [seɪf] *adj* (*out of danger*) a salvo, fuera de peligro; (*not dangerous, sure*) seguro; (*unharmed*) ileso ▷ *n* caja de caudales, caja fuerte; **you're ~ now** ya estás a salvo; **to feel ~** sentirse seguro; **is the water ~ to drink?** ¿es agua potable?; **don't worry, it's perfectly ~** no te preocupes, no tiene el menor peligro; **~ and sound** sano y salvo; **(just) to be on the ~ side** para mayor seguridad; **~ journey!** ¡buen viaje!; **it is ~ to say that ...** se puede decir con confianza que ...

afe-conduct [seɪf'kɔndʌkt] *n* salvoconducto

afe-deposit ['seɪfdɪpɔzɪt] *n* (*vault*) cámara acorazada; (*box*) caja de seguridad *or* de caudales

afeguard ['seɪfgɑːd] *n* protección, garantía ▷ *vt* proteger, defender

safe haven *n* refugio

safekeeping ['seɪf'kiːpɪŋ] *n* custodia

safely ['seɪflɪ] *adv* seguramente, con seguridad; (*without mishap*) sin peligro; **I can ~ say** puedo decir *or* afirmar con toda seguridad

safe sex *n* sexo seguro *or* sin riesgo

safety ['seɪftɪ] *n* seguridad ▷ *cpd* de seguridad; **road ~** seguridad en carretera; **~ first!** ¡precaución!

safety belt *n* cinturón (de seguridad)

safety catch *n* seguro

safety pin *n* imperdible, seguro (LAm)

safety valve *n* válvula de seguridad *or* de escape

sag [sæg] *vi* aflojarse

saga ['sɑːgə] *n* (*History*) saga; (*fig*) epopeya

sage [seɪdʒ] *n* (*herb*) salvia; (*man*) sabio

Sagittarius [sædʒɪ'tɛərɪəs] *n* Sagitario

Sahara [sə'hɑːrə] *n*: **the ~ (Desert)** el Sáhara

said [sɛd] *pt, pp of* **say**

sail [seɪl] *n* (*on boat*) vela ▷ *vt* (*boat*) gobernar ▷ *vi* (*travel: ship*) navegar; (*passenger*) pasear en barco; (*set off: also*: **to set sail**) zarpar; **to go for a ~** dar un paseo en barco; **they ~ed into Copenhagen** arribaron a Copenhague

▷ **sail through** *vt fus* (*exam*) aprobar fácilmente

sailboat ['seɪlbəut] *n* (US) velero, barco de vela

sailing ['seɪlɪŋ] *n* (*Sport*) balandrismo; **to go ~** salir en balandro

sailing ship *n* barco de vela

sailor ['seɪləʳ] *n* marinero, marino

saint [seɪnt] *n* santo; **S~ John** San Juan

sake [seɪk] *n*: **for the ~ of** por; **for the ~ of argument** digamos, es un decir; **art for art's ~** el arte por el arte

salad ['sæləd] *n* ensalada; **tomato ~** ensalada de tomate

salad bowl *n* ensaladera

salad cream *n* (Brit) mayonesa

salad dressing *n* aliño

salami [sə'lɑːmɪ] *n* salami, salchichón

salary ['sælərɪ] *n* sueldo

sale [seɪl] *n* venta; (*at reduced prices*) liquidación, saldo; **"for ~"** "se vende"; **on ~** en venta; **on ~ or return** (*goods*) venta por reposición; **closing-down** *or* (US) **liquidation ~** liquidación; **~ and lease back** venta y arrendamiento al vendedor

saleroom ['seɪlruːm] n sala de subastas
sales assistant n (Brit) dependiente(-a)
sales clerk n (US) dependiente(-a)
sales conference n conferencia de ventas
sales figures npl cifras de ventas
sales force n personal de ventas
salesman ['seɪlzmən] n vendedor; (in shop) dependiente; (representative) viajante
saleswoman ['seɪlzwumən] n vendedora; (in shop) dependienta; (representative) viajante
saliva [sə'laɪvə] n saliva
sallow ['sæləu] adj cetrino
sally forth, sally out vi salir, ponerse en marcha
salmon ['sæmən] n (pl inv) salmón
saloon [sə'luːn] n (US) bar, taberna; (Brit Aut) (coche de) turismo; (ship's lounge) cámara, salón
salt [sɔːlt] n sal ▷ vt salar; (put salt on) poner sal en; **an old ~** un lobo de mar
▸ **salt away** vt (col: money) ahorrar
salt cellar n salero
saltwater ['sɔːlt'wɔːtə'] adj (fish etc) de agua salada, de mar
salty ['sɔːltɪ] adj salado
salute [sə'luːt] n saludo; (of guns) salva ▷ vt saludar
salvage ['sælvɪdʒ] n (saving) salvamento, recuperación; (things saved) objetos salvados ▷ vt salvar
salvation [sæl'veɪʃən] n salvación
Salvation Army n Ejército de Salvación
Samaritan [sə'mærɪtən] n: **to call the ~s** llamar al teléfono de la esperanza
same [seɪm] adj mismo ▷ pron: **the ~** el mismo (la misma); **the ~ book as** el mismo libro que; **on the ~ day** el mismo día; **at the ~ time** (at the same moment) al mismo tiempo; (yet) sin embargo; **it's not the ~** no es lo mismo; **they're exactly the ~** son exactamente iguales; **the house is still the ~** la casa sigue igual; **all or just the ~** sin embargo, aun así; **they're one and the ~** (person) son la misma persona; (thing) son iguales; **to do the ~ (as sb)** hacer lo mismo (que otro); **and the ~ to you!** ¡igualmente!; **~ here!** ¡yo también!; **the ~ again** (in bar etc) otro igual
sample ['sɑːmpl] n muestra ▷ vt (food, wine) probar; **to take a ~** tomar una muestra; **free ~** muestra gratuita
sanatorium [sænə'tɔːrɪəm] (pl -ria) [-rɪə] n (Brit) sanatorio
sanctimonious [sæŋktɪ'məunɪəs] adj santurrón(-ona)
sanction ['sæŋkʃən] n sanción ▷ vt sancionar; **to impose economic ~s on** or **against** imponer sanciones económicas a or contra
sanctity ['sæŋktɪtɪ] n (gen) santidad; (inviolability) inviolabilidad
sanctuary ['sæŋktjuərɪ] n (gen) santuario; (refuge) asilo, refugio
sand [sænd] n arena; (beach) playa ▷ vt (also: **sand down**: wood etc) lijar

sandal ['sændl] n sandalia
sandbag ['sændbæg] n saco de arena
sandbox ['sændbɒks] n (US) = **sandpit**
sandcastle ['sændkɑːsl] n castillo de arena
sand dune n duna
sandpaper ['sændpeɪpə'] n papel de lija
sandpit ['sændpɪt] n cajón de arena
sandstone ['sændstəun] n piedra arenisca
sandstorm ['sændstɔːm] n tormenta de arena
sandwich ['sændwɪtʃ] n bocadillo (Esp), sandwich (LAm) ▷ vt (also: **sandwich in**) intercalar; **to be ~ed between** estar apretujado entre; **cheese/ham ~** sandwich de queso/jamón
sandy ['sændɪ] adj arenoso; (colour) rojizo
sane [seɪn] adj cuerdo, sensato
sang [sæŋ] pt of **sing**
sanitary ['sænɪtərɪ] adj (system, arrangements) sanitario; (clean) higiénico
sanitary towel, (US) **sanitary napkin** n paño higiénico, compresa
sanitation [sænɪ'teɪʃən] n (in house) servicios higiénicos; (in town) servicio de desinfección
sanitation department n (US) departamento de limpieza y recogida de basuras
sanity ['sænɪtɪ] n cordura; (of judgment) sensatez
sank [sæŋk] pt of **sink**
Santa Claus [sæntə'klɔːz] n San Nicolás, Papá Noel
sap [sæp] n (of plants) savia ▷ vt (strength) minar, agotar
sapling ['sæplɪŋ] n árbol nuevo or joven
sapphire ['sæfaɪə'] n zafiro
sarcasm ['sɑːkæzm] n sarcasmo
sarcastic [sɑː'kæstɪk] adj sarcástico; **to be ~** ser sarcástico
sardine [sɑː'diːn] n sardina
Sardinia [sɑː'dɪnɪə] n Cerdeña
SARS [sɑːz] n abbr (= severe acute respiratory syndrome) neumonía asiática, SARS
SAS n abbr (Brit Mil: = Special Air Service) cuerpo del ejército británico encargado de misiones clandestinas
sash [sæʃ] n faja
sat [sæt] pt, pp of **sit**
Satan ['seɪtn] n Satanás
satchel ['sætʃl] n bolsa; (child's) cartera, mochila (LAm)
satellite ['sætəlaɪt] n satélite
satellite television n televisión por satélite
satin ['sætɪn] n raso ▷ adj de raso; **with a ~ finish** satinado
satire ['sætaɪə'] n sátira
satisfaction [sætɪs'fækʃən] n satisfacción; **it gives me great ~** es para mí una gran satisfacción; **has it been done to your ~?** ¿se ha hecho a su satisfacción?
satisfactory [sætɪs'fæktərɪ] adj satisfactorio
satisfied ['sætɪsfaɪd] adj satisfecho; **to be ~ (with sth)** estar satisfecho (de algo)
satisfy ['sætɪsfaɪ] vt satisfacer; (pay) liquidar; (convince) convencer; **to ~ the requirements** llenar los requisitos; **to ~ sb that** convencer a algn de que; **to ~ o.s. of sth** convencerse de algo

satisfying ['sætɪsfaɪɪŋ] *adj* satisfactorio
satsuma [sæt'su:mə] *n* satsuma
saturated fat [sætʃəreɪtɪd-] *n* grasa saturada
saturation [sætʃə'reɪʃən] *n* saturación
saturday ['sætədɪ] *n* sábado
sauce [sɔ:s] *n* salsa; (*sweet*) crema
saucepan ['sɔ:spən] *n* cacerola, olla
saucer ['sɔ:sə^r] *n* platillo
saucy ['sɔ:sɪ] *adj* fresco, descarado
Saudi Arabia ['saudɪ-] *n* Arabia Saudí *or* Saudita
Saudi (Arabian) ['saudɪ-] *adj*, *n* saudí, saudita
sauna ['sɔ:nə] *n* sauna
saunter ['sɔ:ntə^r] *vi* deambular
sausage ['sɔsɪdʒ] *n* salchicha; (*salami etc*) salchichón
sausage roll *n* empanadilla
savage ['sævɪdʒ] *adj* (*cruel*, *fierce*) feroz, furioso; (*primitive*) salvaje ▷ *n* salvaje ▷ *vt* embestir
save [seɪv] *vt* (*rescue*) salvar, rescatar; (*money*, *time*) ahorrar; (*put by*) guardar; (*Comput*) salvar (y guardar); (*avoid: trouble*) evitar ▷ *vi* (*also*: **save up**) ahorrar ▷ *n* (*Sport*) parada ▷ *prep* salvo, excepto; **I've ~d £50 already** ya llevo ahorradas 50 libras; **it ~d us time** nos ahorró tiempo; **we went in a taxi to ~ time** para ganar tiempo fuimos en taxi; **I ~d you a piece of cake** te he guardado un trozo de tarta; **I ~d the file onto a diskette** guardé el archivo en un disquete; **to ~ face** salvar las apariencias; **God ~ the Queen!** ¡Dios guarde a la Reina!, ¡Viva la Reina!
saving ['seɪvɪŋ] *n* (*on price etc*) economía ▷ *adj*: **the ~ grace of** el único mérito de; **savings** *npl* ahorros; **to make ~s** economizar
savings account *n* cuenta de ahorros
savings bank *n* caja de ahorros
saviour, (*US*) **savior** ['seɪvjə^r] *n* salvador(a)
savour, (*US*) **savor** ['seɪvə^r] *n* sabor, gusto ▷ *vt* saborear
savo(u)ry ['seɪvərɪ] *adj* sabroso; (*dish: not sweet*) salado
saw [sɔ:] *pt of* **see** ▷ *n* (*tool*) sierra ▷ *vt* (*pt* **-ed**, *pp* **-ed** *or* **-n**) [sɔ:n] serrar; **to ~ sth up** (a)serrar algo
sawdust ['sɔ:dʌst] *n* (a)serrín
sawmill ['sɔ:mɪl] *n* aserradero
sawn-off ['sɔ:nɔf], (*US*) **sawed-off** ['sɔ:dɔf] *adj*: **~ shotgun** escopeta de cañones recortados
saxophone ['sæksəfəun] *n* saxófono
say [seɪ] *n*: **to have one's ~** expresar su opinión; **to have a** *or* **some ~ in sth** tener voz y voto en algo ▷ *vt*, *vi* (*pt*, *pp* **said**) decir; **to ~ yes/no** decir que sí/no; **my watch ~s 3 o'clock** mi reloj marca las tres; **could you ~ that again?** ¿podrías repetir eso?; **that is to ~** es decir; **that goes without ~ing** ni que decir tiene; **she said (that) I was to give you this** me pidió que te diera esto; **I should ~ it's worth about £100** yo diría que vale unas 100 libras; **~ after me** repite lo que yo diga; **shall we ~ Tuesday?** ¿quedamos, por ejemplo, el martes?; **that doesn't ~ much for him** eso no dice nada a su favor; **when all is said and done** al fin y al cabo, a fin de cuentas; **there is something** *or* **a lot to be said for it** hay

algo *or* mucho que decir a su favor
saying ['seɪɪŋ] *n* dicho, refrán
say-so ['seɪsəu] *n* (*col*) autorización
scab [skæb] *n* costra; (*pej*) esquirol(a)
scaffold ['skæfəld] *n* (*for execution*) cadalso
scaffolding ['skæfəldɪŋ] *n* andamio, andamiaje
scald [skɔ:ld] *n* escaldadura ▷ *vt* escaldar
scale [skeɪl] *n* (*gen*, *Mus*) escala; (*of fish*) escama; (*of salaries, fees etc*) escalafón ▷ *vt* (*mountain*) escalar; (*tree*) trepar; **scales** *npl* (*small*) balanza; (*large*) báscula; **on a large ~** a gran escala; **~ of charges** tarifa, lista de precios; **pay ~** escala salarial; **to draw sth to ~** dibujar algo a una escala
  ▷ **scale down** *vt* reducir
scallop ['skɔləp] *n* (*Zool*) venera
scalp [skælp] *n* cabellera ▷ *vt* escalpar
scalpel ['skælpl] *n* bisturí
scam [skæm] *n* (*col*) estafa, timo
scamper ['skæmpə^r] *vi*: **to ~ away**, **~ off** escabullirse
scampi ['skæmpɪ] *npl* gambas
scan [skæn] *vt* (*examine*) escudriñar; (*glance at quickly*) dar un vistazo a; (*TV*, *Radar*) explorar, registrar ▷ *n* (*Med*) examen ultrasónico
scandal ['skændl] *n* escándalo; (*gossip*) chismes
scandalize ['skændəlaɪz] *vt* escandalizar
scandalous ['skændələs] *adj* escandaloso
Scandinavia [skændɪ'neɪvɪə] *n* Escandinavia
Scandinavian [skændɪ'neɪvɪən] *adj*, *n* escandinavo(-a)
scanner ['skænə^r] *n* (*Radar*, *Med*, *Comput*) escáner
scant [skænt] *adj* escaso
scanty ['skæntɪ] *adj* (*meal*) insuficiente; (*clothes*) ligero
scapegoat ['skeɪpgəut] *n* cabeza de turco, chivo expiatorio
scar [ska:] *n* cicatriz ▷ *vt* marcar con una cicatriz ▷ *vi* cicatrizarse
scarce [skeəs] *adj* escaso
scarcely ['skeəslɪ] *adv* apenas; **~ anybody** casi nadie; **I can ~ believe it** casi no puedo creerlo
scare [skeə^r] *n* susto, sobresalto; (*panic*) pánico ▷ *vt* asustar, espantar; **to ~ sb stiff** dar a algn un susto de muerte; **bomb ~** amenaza de bomba
  ▷ **scare away**, **scare off** *vt* espantar, ahuyentar
scarecrow ['skeəkrəu] *n* espantapájaros
scared [skeəd] *adj*: **to be ~** asustarse, estar asustado
scarf (*pl* **scarves**) [ska:f, ska:vz] *n* (*long*) bufanda; (*square*) pañuelo
scarlet ['ska:lɪt] *adj* escarlata
scarlet fever *n* escarlatina
scarper ['ska:pə^r] *vi* (*Brit col*) largarse
scarves [ska:vz] *npl of* **scarf**
scary ['skeərɪ] *adj* (*col*) de miedo; **it's ~** da miedo
scathing ['skeɪðɪŋ] *adj* mordaz; **to be ~ about sth** criticar algo duramente
scatter ['skætə^r] *vt* (*spread*) esparcir, desparramar; (*put to flight*) dispersar ▷ *vi* desparramarse; dispersarse
scatterbrained ['skætəbreɪnd] *adj* ligero de cascos

scavenge ['skævɪndʒ] *vi*: **to ~ (for)** *(person)* revolver entre la basura (para encontrar); **to ~ for food** nutrirse de carroña

scavenger ['skævɪndʒəʳ] *n* *(person)* mendigo/a que rebusca en la basura; *(Zool: animal)* animal de carroña; *(: bird)* ave de carroña

scenario [sɪ'nɑːrɪəu] *n* *(Theat)* argumento; *(Cine)* guión; *(fig)* escenario

scene [siːn] *n* *(Theat, fig etc)* escena; *(of crime, accident)* escenario; *(sight, view)* vista, perspectiva; *(fuss)* escándalo; **the political ~ in Spain** el panorama político español; **behind the ~s** *(also fig)* entre bastidores; **to appear** *or* **come on the ~** *(also fig)* aparecer, presentarse; **to make a ~** *(col: fuss)* armar un escándalo

scenery ['siːnərɪ] *n* *(Theat)* decorado; *(landscape)* paisaje

scenic ['siːnɪk] *adj* *(picturesque)* pintoresco

scent [sɛnt] *n* perfume, olor; *(fig: track)* rastro, pista; *(sense of smell)* olfato ▷ *vt* perfumar; *(suspect)* presentir; **to put** *or* **throw sb off the ~** *(fig)* despistar a algn

sceptic, (US) **skeptic** ['skɛptɪk] *n* escéptico(-a)

sceptical, (US) **skeptical** ['skɛptɪkl] *adj* escéptico

schedule ['ʃɛdjuːl, US 'skɛdjuːl] *n* *(of trains)* horario; *(of events)* programa; *(list)* lista ▷ *vt* *(timetable)* establecer el horario de; *(list)* catalogar; *(visit)* fijar la hora de; **on ~** a la hora, sin retraso; **to be ahead of/behind ~** estar adelantado/retrasado; **we are working to a very tight ~** tenemos un programa de trabajo muy apretado; **a busy ~** una agenda muy apretada; **everything went according to ~** todo salió según lo previsto; **the meeting is ~d for 7** *or* **to begin at 7** la reunión está fijada para las 7

scheduled ['ʃɛdjuːld, US 'skɛdjuːld] *adj* *(date, time)* fijado; *(visit, event, bus, train)* programado; *(stop)* previsto; **~ flight** vuelo regular

scheme [skiːm] *n* *(plan)* plan, proyecto; *(method)* esquema; *(plot)* intriga; *(trick)* ardid; *(arrangement)* disposición; *(pension scheme etc)* sistema ▷ *vt* proyectar ▷ *vi* *(plan)* hacer proyectos; *(intrigue)* intrigar; **colour ~** combinación de colores

scheming ['skiːmɪŋ] *adj* intrigante

schism ['skɪzəm] *n* cisma

schizophrenia [skɪtsə'friːnɪə] *n* esquizofrenia

schizophrenic [skɪtsə'frɛnɪk] *adj* esquizofrénico

scholar ['skɔləʳ] *n* *(pupil)* alumno(-a), estudiante; *(learned person)* sabio(-a), erudito(-a)

scholarly ['skɔləlɪ] *adj* erudito

scholarship ['skɔləʃɪp] *n* erudición; *(grant)* beca

school [skuːl] *n* *(gen)* escuela, colegio; *(in university)* facultad; *(of fish)* banco ▷ *vt* *(animal)* amaestrar; **to be at** *or* **go to ~** ir al colegio *or* a la escuela

school age *n* edad escolar

schoolbook ['skuːlbuk] *n* libro de texto

schoolboy ['skuːlbɔɪ] *n* alumno

schoolchild ['skuːltʃaɪld] *(pl* **-children**) *n* alumno(-a)

schoolgirl ['skuːlɡəːl] *n* alumna

schooling ['skuːlɪŋ] *n* enseñanza

school-leaver ['skuːlliːvəʳ] *n* (Brit) joven que ha terminado la educación secundaria

schoolmaster ['skuːlmɑːstəʳ] *n* *(primary)* maestro; *(secondary)* profesor

schoolmistress ['skuːlmɪstrɪs] *n* *(primary)* maestra; *(secondary)* profesora

schoolteacher ['skuːltiːtʃəʳ] *n* *(primary)* maestro(-a); *(secondary)* profesor(a)

schoolyard ['skuːljɑːd] *n* (US) patio del colegio

sciatica [saɪ'ætɪkə] *n* ciática

science ['saɪəns] *n* ciencia; **the ~s** las ciencias

science fiction *n* ciencia-ficción

scientific [saɪən'tɪfɪk] *adj* científico

scientist ['saɪəntɪst] *n* científico(-a)

sci-fi ['saɪfaɪ] *n abbr* (col) = **science fiction**

Scilly Isles ['sɪlɪ-], **Scillies** ['sɪlɪz] *npl*: **the ~** las Islas Sorlingas

scissors ['sɪzəz] *npl* tijeras; **a pair of ~** unas tijeras

scoff [skɔf] *vt* (Brit col: eat) engullir ▷ *vi*: **to ~ (at)** *(mock)* mofarse (de)

scold [skəuld] *vt* regañar

scone [skɔn] *n* pastel de pan

scoop [skuːp] *n* cucharón; *(for flour etc)* pala; *(Press)* exclusiva ▷ *vt* *(Comm: market)* adelantarse a; *(: profit)* sacar; *(Comm, Press: competitors)* adelantarse a
  ▸ **scoop out** *vt* excavar
  ▸ **scoop up** *vt* recoger

scooter ['skuːtəʳ] *n* *(motor cycle)* Vespa®; *(toy)* patinete

scope [skəup] *n* *(of plan, undertaking)* ámbito; *(reach)* alcance; *(of person)* competencia; *(opportunity)* libertad (de acción); **there is plenty of ~ for improvement** hay bastante campo par efectuar mejoras

scorch [skɔːtʃ] *vt* *(clothes)* chamuscar; *(earth, grass* quemar, secar

scorching ['skɔːtʃɪŋ] *adj* abrasador(a)

score [skɔːʳ] *n* *(points etc)* puntuación; *(Mus)* partitura; *(reckoning)* cuenta; *(twenty)* veintena ▷ *vt* *(goal)* marcar; *(point)* anotarse; *(mark, cut)* rayar ▷ *vi* marcar un tanto; *(Football)* marcar un gol; *(keep score)* llevar la cuenta; **to keep (the) ~** llevar la cuenta; **what's the ~?** ¿cómo van?; **the final ~ was 3 nil** el resultado fue de 3 a cero; **to have an old ~ to settle with sb** *(fig)* tener cuentas pendientes con algn; **on that ~** en lo que se refiere a eso; **~s of people** *(fig)* muchísim gente, cantidad de gente; **to ~ 6 out of 10** obtener una puntuación de 6 sobre 10
  ▸ **score out** *vt* tachar

scoreboard ['skɔːbɔːd] *n* marcador

scoreline ['skɔːlaɪn] *n* (Sport) resultado final

scorn [skɔːn] *n* desprecio ▷ *vt* despreciar

Scorpio ['skɔːpɪəu] *n* Escorpión

scorpion ['skɔːpɪən] *n* alacrán, escorpión

Scot [skɔt] *n* escocés(-esa)

Scotch [skɔtʃ] *n* whisky escocés

scotch [skɔtʃ] *vt* *(rumour)* desmentir; *(plan)* frustrar

scot-free [skɔt'fri:] *adv*: **to get off ~** (*unpunished*) salir impune; (*unhurt*) salir ileso

Scotland ['skɔtlənd] *n* Escocia

Scots [skɔts] *adj* escocés(-esa)

Scotsman ['skɔtsmən] *n* escocés

Scotswoman ['skɔtswumən] *n* escocesa

Scottish ['skɔtɪʃ] *adj* escocés(-esa); **the ~ National Party** partido político independista escocés; **the ~ Parliament** el Parlamento escocés

scoundrel ['skaundrəl] *n* canalla, sinvergüenza

scour ['skauəʳ] *vt* (*clean*) fregar, estregar; (*search*) recorrer, registrar

scourge [skə:dʒ] *n* azote

scout [skaut] *n* (*Mil, also:* **boy scout**) explorador
  ▶ **scout around** *vi* reconocer el terreno

scowl [skaul] *vi* fruncir el ceño; **to ~ at sb** mirar con ceño a algn

scrabble ['skræbl] *vi* (*claw*): **to ~ (at)** arañar ▷ *n*: **S~®** Intelect®; **to ~ about for sth** revolver todo buscando algo

scram [skræm] *vi* (*col*) largarse

scramble ['skræmbl] *n* (*climb*) subida (difícil); (*struggle*) pelea ▷ *vi*: **to ~ out/through** salir/ abrirse paso con dificultad; **to ~ for** pelear por

scrambled eggs ['skræmbld-] *npl* huevos revueltos

scrap [skræp] *n* (*bit*) pedacito; (*fig*) pizca; (*fight*) riña, bronca; (*also:* **scrap iron**) chatarra, hierro viejo ▷ *vt* (*discard*) desechar, descartar ▷ *vi* reñir, armar (una) bronca; **scraps** *npl* (*waste*) sobras, desperdicios; **to sell sth for ~** vender algo como chatarra

scrapbook ['skræpbuk] *n* álbum de recortes

scrap dealer *n* chatarrero(-a)

scrape [skreɪp] *n* (*fig*) lío, apuro ▷ *vt* raspar; (*skin etc*) rasguñar; (*scrape against*) rozar
  ▶ **scrape through** *vi* (*succeed*) salvarse por los pelos; (*exam*) aprobar por los pelos

scrap heap *n* (*fig*): **on the ~** desperdiciado; **to throw sth on the ~** desechar *or* descartar algo

scrap merchant *n* (*Brit*) chatarrero(-a)

scrap paper *n* pedazos de papel

scrap yard *n* depósito de chatarra; (*for cars*) cementerio de coches

scratch [skrætʃ] *n* rasguño; (*from claw*) arañazo ▷ *adj*: **~ team** equipo improvisado ▷ *vt* (*record*) rayar; (*with claw, nail*) rasguñar, arañar; (*Comput*) borrar ▷ *vi* rascarse; **to start from ~** partir de cero; **to be up to ~** cumplir con los requisitos

scrawl [skrɔ:l] *n* garabatos ▷ *vt* hacer garabatos

scrawny ['skrɔ:nɪ] *adj* (*person, neck*) flaco

scream [skri:m] *n* chillido ▷ *vi* chillar; **it was a ~** (*fig, col*) fue para morirse de risa *or* muy divertido; **he's a ~** (*fig, col*) es muy divertido *or* de lo más gracioso; **to ~ at sb (to do sth)** gritarle a algn (para que haga algo)

screech [skri:tʃ] *vi* chirriar

screen [skri:n] *n* (*Cine, TV*) pantalla; (*movable*) biombo; (*wall*) tabique; (*also:* **windscreen**) parabrisas ▷ *vt* (*conceal*) tapar; (*from the wind etc*) proteger; (*film*) proyectar; (*fig: person: for security*) investigar; (: *for illness*) hacer una exploración a

screenful ['skri:nful] *n* pantalla

screening ['skri:nɪŋ] *n* (*of film*) proyección; (*for security*) investigación; (*Med*) exploración

screenplay ['skri:npleɪ] *n* guión

screen saver [-seɪvəʳ] *n* salvapantallas

screw [skru:] *n* tornillo; (*propeller*) hélice ▷ *vt* atornillar; **to ~ sth to the wall** fijar algo a la pared con tornillos
  ▶ **screw up** *vt* (*paper, material etc*) arrugar; (*col: ruin*) fastidiar; **to ~ up one's eyes** arrugar el entrecejo; **to ~ up one's face** torcer *or* arrugar la cara

screwdriver ['skru:draɪvəʳ] *n* destornillador

screwed-up ['skru:d'ʌp] *adj* (*col*): **she's totally ~** está trastornada

scribble ['skrɪbl] *n* garabatos ▷ *vt* escribir con prisa; **to ~ sth down** garabatear algo

script [skrɪpt] *n* (*Cine etc*) guión; (*writing*) escritura, letra

Scripture ['skrɪptʃəʳ] *n* Sagrada Escritura

scroll [skrəul] *n* rollo ▷ *vt* (*Comput*) desplazar

scrotum ['skrəutəm] *n* escroto

scrounge [skraundʒ] (*col*) *vt*: **to ~ sth off** *or* **from sb** gorronear algo a algn ▷ *vi*: **to ~ on sb** vivir a costa de algn

scrounger ['skraundʒəʳ] *n* gorrón(-ona)

scrub [skrʌb] *n* (*clean*) fregado; (*land*) maleza ▷ *vt* fregar, restregar; (*reject*) cancelar, anular

scruff [skrʌf] *n*: **by the ~ of the neck** por el pescuezo

scruffy ['skrʌfɪ] *adj* desaliñado, desaseado

scrum(mage) ['skrʌm(mɪdʒ)] *n* (*Rugby*) melée

scruple ['skru:pl] *n* escrúpulo; **to have no ~s about doing sth** no tener reparos en *or* escrúpulos para hacer algo

scrupulous ['skru:pjuləs] *adj* escrupuloso

scrutinize ['skru:tɪnaɪz] *vt* escudriñar; (*votes*) escrutar

scrutiny ['skru:tɪnɪ] *n* escrutinio, examen; **under the ~ of sb** bajo la mirada *or* el escrutinio de algn

scuba diving *n* buceo con escafandra autónoma

scuff [skʌf] *vt* (*shoes, floor*) rayar

scuffle ['skʌfl] *n* refriega

scullery ['skʌlərɪ] *n* trascocina

sculptor ['skʌlptəʳ] *n* escultor(a)

sculpture ['skʌlptʃəʳ] *n* escultura

scum [skʌm] *n* (*on liquid*) espuma; (*pej: people*) escoria

scupper ['skʌpəʳ] *vt* (*Brit: boat*) hundir; (: *fig: plans etc*) acabar con

scurrilous ['skʌrɪləs] *adj* difamatorio, calumnioso

scurry ['skʌrɪ] *vi*: **to ~ off** escabullirse

scuttle ['skʌtl] *n* (*also:* **coal scuttle**) cubo, carbonera ▷ *vt* (*ship*) barrenar ▷ *vi* (*scamper*): **to ~ away, ~ off** escabullirse

scythe [saɪð] *n* guadaña

sea [si:] *n* mar; **by ~** (*travel*) en barco; **on the ~** (*boat*) en el mar; (*town*) junto al mar; **to be all at ~** (*fig*) estar despistado; **out to** *or* **at ~** en alta mar; **to go by ~** ir en barco; **heavy** *or* **rough**

~s marejada; **by** or **beside the ~** (*holiday*) en la playa; (*village*) a orillas del mar; **a ~ of faces** una multitud de caras

sea bed *n* fondo del mar

seaboard ['siːbɔːd] *n* litoral

seafood ['siːfuːd] *n* mariscos

sea front *n* (*beach*) playa; (*prom*) paseo marítimo

seagoing ['siːgəʊɪŋ] *adj* (*ship*) de alta mar

seagull ['siːgʌl] *n* gaviota

seal [siːl] *n* (*animal*) foca; (*stamp*) sello ▷ *vt* (*close*) cerrar; (*: with seal*) sellar; (*decide: sb's fate*) decidir; (*: bargain*) cerrar; **~ of approval** sello de aprobación

▸ **seal off** *vt* obturar

sea level *n* nivel del mar

sea lion *n* león marino

seam [siːm] *n* costura; (*of metal*) juntura; (*of coal*) veta, filón; **the hall was bursting at the ~s** la sala rebosaba de gente

seaman ['siːmən] *n* marinero

seance ['seɪɒns] *n* sesión de espiritismo

seaplane ['siːpleɪn] *n* hidroavión

search [səːtʃ] *n* (*for person, thing*) busca, búsqueda; (*of drawer, pockets*) registro; (*inspection*) reconocimiento ▷ *vt* (*look in*) buscar en; (*examine*) examinar; (*person, place*) registrar; (*Comput*) buscar ▷ *vi*: **to ~ for** buscar; **in ~ of** en busca de; **"~ and replace"** (*Comput*) "buscar y reemplazar"

▸ **search through** *vt fus* registrar

search engine *n* buscador

searching ['səːtʃɪŋ] *adj* (*question*) penetrante

searchlight ['səːtʃlaɪt] *n* reflector

search party *n* equipo de salvamento

search warrant *n* mandamiento judicial

seashore ['siːʃɔːʳ] *n* playa, orilla del mar; **on the ~** a la orilla del mar

seasick ['siːsɪk] *adj* mareado; **to be ~** marearse

seaside ['siːsaɪd] *n* playa, orilla del mar; **to go to the ~** ir a la playa

seaside resort *n* playa

season ['siːzn] *n* (*of year*) estación; (*sporting etc*) temporada; (*gen*) época, período ▷ *vt* (*food*) sazonar; **to be in/out of ~** estar en sazón/fuera de temporada; **the busy ~** (*for hotels etc*) la temporada alta; **the open ~** (*Hunting*) la temporada de caza or de pesca

seasonal ['siːznl] *adj* estacional

seasoned ['siːznd] *adj* (*wood*) curado; (*fig: worker, actor*) experimentado; (*troops*) curtido; **~ campaigner** veterano(-a)

seasoning ['siːznɪŋ] *n* condimento

season ticket *n* abono

seat [siːt] *n* (*in bus, train: place*) asiento; (*chair*) silla; (*Parliament*) escaño; (*buttocks*) trasero; (*centre: of government etc*) sede ▷ *vt* sentar; (*have room for*) tener cabida para; **are there any ~s left?** ¿quedan plazas?; **to take one's ~** sentarse, tomar asiento; **to be ~ed** estar sentado, sentarse

seat belt *n* cinturón de seguridad

sea water *n* agua del mar

seaweed ['siːwiːd] *n* alga marina

seaworthy ['siːwəːðɪ] *adj* en condiciones de navegar

sec. *abbr* = **second(s)**

secluded [sɪ'kluːdɪd] *adj* retirado

seclusion [sɪ'kluːʒən] *n* retiro

second *adj* segundo ▷ *adv* (*in race etc*) en segundo lugar ▷ *n* (*gen*) segundo; (*Aut: also:* **second gear**) segunda; (*Comm*) artículo con algún desperfecto; (*Brit Scol: degree*) título universitario de segunda clase ▷ *vt* (*motion*) apoyar; (*employee*) trasladar temporalmente; **~ floor** (*Brit*) segundo piso; (*US*) primer piso; **Charles the S~** Carlos Segundo; **to ask for a ~ opinion** (*Med*) pedir una segunda opinión; **to have ~ thoughts** cambiar de opinión; **on ~ thoughts** or (*US*) **~ thought** pensándolo bien; **~ mortgage** segunda hipoteca; **the ~ of March** el dos de marzo; **to come ~** llegar en segundo lugar; **it'll only take a ~** es un segundo nada más; **just a ~!** ¡un momento!

secondary ['sɛkəndərɪ] *adj* secundario

secondary education *n* enseñanza secundaria

secondary school *n* escuela secundaria

second-class ['sɛkənd'klɑːs] *adj* de segunda clase ▷ *adv*: **to send sth ~** enviar algo por correo de segunda clase; **to travel ~** viajar en segunda; **~ citizen** ciudadano(-a) de segunda (clase)

second cousin *n* primo(-a) segundo(-a)

second-guess ['sɛkənd'gɛs] *vt* (*evaluate*) juzgar (a posteriori); (*anticipate*): **to ~ sth/sb** (intentar) adivinar algo/lo que va a hacer algn

secondhand ['sɛkənd'hænd] *adj* de segunda mano, usado ▷ *adv*: **to buy sth ~** comprar algo de segunda mano; **to hear sth ~** oír algo indirectamente

second hand *n* (*on clock*) segundero

secondly ['sɛkəndlɪ] *adv* en segundo lugar

secondment [sɪ'kɔndmənt] *n* (*Brit*) traslado temporal

second-rate ['sɛkənd'reɪt] *adj* de segunda categoría

secrecy ['siːkrəsɪ] *n* secreto

secret ['siːkrɪt] *adj, n* secreto; **in ~** *adv* en secreto; **to keep sth ~ (from sb)** ocultarle algo (a algn); **to make no ~ of sth** no ocultar algo

secret agent *n* agente secreto(-a), espía

secretary ['sɛkrətərɪ] *n* secretario(-a); **S~ of State** (*Brit Pol*) Ministro (con cartera)

secretary-general ['sɛkrətərɪ'dʒɛnərl] *n* secretario(-a) general

secrete [sɪ'kriːt] *vt* (*Med, Anat, Bio*) secretar; (*hide*) ocultar, esconder

secretive ['siːkrətɪv] *adj* reservado, sigiloso

secretly ['siːkrɪtlɪ] *adv* en secreto

secret police *n* policía secreta

secret service *n* servicio secreto

sect [sɛkt] *n* secta

sectarian [sɛk'tɛərɪən] *adj* sectario

section ['sɛkʃən] *n* sección; (*part*) parte; (*of document*) artículo; (*of opinion*) sector; **business ~** (*Press*) sección de economía

sector ['sɛktəʳ] *n* (*gen, Comput*) sector

secular ['sɛkjuləʳ] *adj* secular, seglar
secure [sɪ'kjuəʳ] *adj* (*free from anxiety*) seguro;
(*firmly fixed*) firme, fijo ▷ *vt* (*fix*) asegurar,
afianzar; (*get*) conseguir; (*Comm: loan*)
garantizar; **to make sth ~** afianzar algo; **to ~
sth for sb** conseguir algo para algn
security [sɪ'kjuərɪtɪ] *n* seguridad; (*for loan*)
fianza; (: *object*) prenda; **securities** *npl* (*Comm*)
valores, títulos; **~ of tenure** tenencia asegurada;
to increase/tighten ~ aumentar/estrechar las
medidas de seguridad; **job ~** seguridad en el
empleo
Security Council *n*: **the ~** el Consejo de
Seguridad
security forces *npl* fuerzas de seguridad
security guard *n* guardia de seguridad
secy. *abbr* (= *secretary*) Srio(-a)
sedan [sɪ'dæn] *n* (*US Aut*) sedán
sedate [sɪ'deɪt] *adj* tranquilo ▷ *vt* administrar
sedantes a, sedar
sedation [sɪ'deɪʃən] *n* (*Med*) sedación; **to be
under ~** estar bajo sedación
sedative ['sɛdɪtɪv] *n* sedante, calmante
sediment ['sɛdɪmənt] *n* sedimento
seduce [sɪ'djuːs] *vt* (*gen*) seducir
seduction [sɪ'dʌkʃən] *n* seducción
seductive [sɪ'dʌktɪv] *adj* seductor(-a)
see [siː] (*pt* **saw**, *pp* **-n**) *vt* (*gen*) ver; (*understand*)
ver, comprender; (*look at*) mirar ▷ *vi* ver ▷ *n*
sede; **I can't ~** no veo nada; **there was nobody
to be ~n** no se veía a nadie; **let me ~** (*show me*)
a ver; (*let me think*) vamos a ver; **to ~ sb to the
door** acompañar a algn a la puerta; **to ~ that**
(*ensure*) asegurarse de que; **~ you!** ¡hasta luego!;
~ you soon/later/tomorrow! ¡hasta pronto/
luego/mañana!; **as far as I can ~** por lo visto
or por lo que veo; **to go and ~ sb** ir a ver a algn;
you need to ~ a doctor tienes que ir a ver a un
médico; **~ for yourself** compruébalo tú mismo;
I don't know what she ~s in him no sé qué le
encuentra
  ▶ **see about** *vt fus* atender a, encargarse de
  ▶ **see off** *vt* despedir
  ▶ **see through** *vt fus* calar ▷ *vt* llevar a cabo
  ▶ **see to** *vt fus* atender a, encargarse de
seed [siːd] *n* semilla; (*in fruit*) pepita; (*fig*)
germen; (*Tennis*) preseleccionado(-a); **to go to ~**
(*plant*) granar; (*fig*) descuidarse
seedling ['siːdlɪŋ] *n* planta de semillero
seedy ['siːdɪ] *adj* (*person*) desaseado; (*place*)
sórdido
seeing ['siːɪŋ] *conj*: **~ (that)** visto que, en vista
de que
seek [siːk] (*pt*, *pp* **sought**) *vt* (*gen*) buscar; (*post*)
solicitar; **to ~ advice/help from sb** pedir
consejos/solicitar ayuda a algn
  ▶ **seek out** *vt* (*person*) buscar
seem [siːm] *vi* parecer; **there ~s to be ...** parece
que hay ...; **it ~s (that) ...** parece que ...; **what ~s
to be the trouble?** ¿qué pasa?; **I did what ~ed
best** hice lo que parecía mejor
seemingly ['siːmɪŋlɪ] *adv* aparentemente, según

parece
seen [siːn] *pp of* **see**
seep [siːp] *vi* filtrarse
seesaw ['siːsɔː] *n* balancín, subibaja
seethe [siːð] *vi* hervir; **to ~ with anger**
enfurecerse
see-through ['siːθruː] *adj* transparente
segment ['sɛgmənt] *n* segmento
segregate ['sɛgrɪgeɪt] *vt* segregar
seize [siːz] *vt* (*grasp*) agarrar, asir; (*take possession
of*) apoderarse de; (: *territory*) apoderarse de;
(*opportunity*) aprovecharse de
  ▶ **seize up** *vi* (*Tech*) agarrotarse
  ▶ **seize (up)on** *vt fus* valerse de
seizure ['siːʒəʳ] *n* (*Med*) ataque; (*Law*) incautación
seldom ['sɛldəm] *adv* rara vez
select [sɪ'lɛkt] *adj* selecto, escogido; (*hotel,
restaurant, clubs*) exclusivo ▷ *vt* escoger, elegir;
(*Sport*) seleccionar; **a ~ few** una minoría selecta
selection [sɪ'lɛkʃən] *n* selección, elección;
(*Comm*) surtido
self [sɛlf] *n* (*pl* **selves**) [sɛlvz] uno mismo ▷ *pref*
auto ...; **the ~** el yo
self-appointed [sɛlfə'pɔɪntɪd] *adj*
autonombrado
self-assurance [sɛlfə'ʃuərəns] *n* confianza en
sí mismo
self-assured [sɛlfə'ʃuəd] *adj* seguro de sí mismo
self-catering [sɛlf'keɪtərɪŋ] *adj* (*Brit*) sin
pensión *or* servicio de comida; **~ apartment**
apartamento con cocina propia
self-centred, (*US*) **self-centered** [sɛlf'sɛntəd]
adj egocéntrico
self-confessed [sɛlfkən'fɛst] *adj* (*alcoholic etc*)
confeso
self-confidence [sɛlf'kɔnfɪdns] *n* confianza en
sí mismo
self-confident [sɛlf'kɔnfɪdnt] *adj* seguro de sí
(mismo), lleno de confianza en sí mismo
self-conscious [sɛlf'kɔnʃəs] *adj* cohibido
self-contained [sɛlfkən'teɪnd] *adj* (*gen*)
independiente; (*Brit: flat*) con entrada particular
self-control [sɛlfkən'trəul] *n* autodominio
self-defence, (*US*) **self-defense** [sɛlfdɪ'fɛns] *n*
defensa propia
self-discipline [sɛlf'dɪsɪplɪn] *n* autodisciplina
self-employed [sɛlfɪm'plɔɪd] *adj* que trabaja por
cuenta propia, autónomo
self-esteem [sɛlfɪ'stiːm] *n* amor propio
self-evident [sɛlf'ɛvɪdnt] *adj* patente
self-explanatory [sɛlfɪks'plænətərɪ] *adj* que no
necesita explicación
self-governing [sɛlf'gʌvənɪŋ] *adj* autónomo
self-help ['sɛlf'hɛlp] *n* autosuficiencia, ayuda
propia
self-indulgent [sɛlfɪn'dʌldʒənt] *adj* indulgente
consigo mismo
self-inflicted [sɛlfɪn'flɪktɪd] *adj* infligido a sí
mismo
self-interest [sɛlf'ɪntrɪst] *n* egoísmo
selfish ['sɛlfɪʃ] *adj* egoísta
selfishness ['sɛlfɪʃnɪs] *n* egoísmo

selfless ['sɛlflɪs] adj desinteresado

self-pity [sɛlf'pɪtɪ] n lástima de sí mismo

self-portrait [sɛlf'pɔːtreɪt] n autorretrato

self-possessed [sɛlfpə'zɛst] adj sereno, dueño de sí mismo

self-preservation ['sɛlfprɛzə'veɪʃən] n propia conservación

self-respect [sɛlfrɪ'spɛkt] n amor propio

self-righteous [sɛlf'raɪtʃəs] adj santurrón(-ona)

self-sacrifice [sɛlf'sækrɪfaɪs] n abnegación

self-same [sɛlfseɪm] adj mismo, mismísimo

self-satisfied [sɛlf'sætɪsfaɪd] adj satisfecho de sí mismo

self-service [sɛlf'səːvɪs] adj de autoservicio

self-sufficient [sɛlfsə'fɪʃənt] adj autosuficiente

self-tanning adj autobronceador(a)

self-taught [sɛlf'tɔːt] adj autodidacta

sell [sɛl] (pt, pp **sold**) vt vender ▷ vi venderse; **he sold it to me** me lo vendió; **to ~ sb an idea** (fig) convencer a algn de una idea; **to ~ at** or **for £10** venderse a 10 libras
  ▶ **sell off** vt liquidar
  ▶ **sell out** vi (tickets, goods) agotarse; (fig) transigir, transar (LAm) ▷ vt agotar las existencias de, venderlo todo; **to ~ out (to sb/sth)** (Comm) vender su negocio (a algn/algo); **the tickets are all sold out** las entradas están agotadas
  ▶ **sell up** vi (Comm) liquidarse

sell-by date ['sɛlbaɪ-] n fecha de caducidad

seller ['sɛləʳ] n vendedor(a); **~'s market** mercado de demanda

selling price ['sɛlɪŋ-] n precio de venta

Sellotape® ['sɛləuteɪp] n (Brit) cinta adhesiva, celo, scotch®

sellout ['sɛlaut] n traición; **it was a ~** (Theat etc) fue un éxito de taquilla

selves [sɛlvz] npl of **self**

semblance ['sɛmbləns] n apariencia

semen ['siːmən] n semen

semester [sɪ'mɛstəʳ] n (US) semestre

semi ['sɛmɪ] n = **semidetached house**

semicircle ['sɛmɪsəːkl] n semicírculo

semicolon [sɛmɪ'kəulən] n punto y coma

semiconductor [sɛmɪkən'dʌktəʳ] n semiconductor

semidetached (house) [sɛmɪdɪ'tætʃt-] n casa adosada

semi-final [sɛmɪ'faɪnl] n semi-final

seminar ['sɛmɪnɑːʳ] n seminario

seminary ['sɛmɪnərɪ] n (Rel) seminario

semiskilled ['sɛmɪskɪld] adj (work, worker) semicualificado

semi-skimmed adj semidesnatado

Sen., sen. abbr = **senator; senior**

senate ['sɛnɪt] n senado; see also **Congress**

senator ['sɛnɪtəʳ] n senador(a)

send [sɛnd] (pt, pp **sent**) vt mandar, enviar; **to ~ by post** mandar por correo; **to ~ sb for sth** mandar a algn a buscar algo; **to ~ word that ...** avisar or mandar aviso de que ...; **she ~s (you) her love** te manda or envía cariñosos recuerdos;

to ~ sb to sleep/into fits of laughter dormir/ hacer reír a algn; **to ~ sb flying** echar a algn; **to ~ sth flying** tirar algo
  ▶ **send away** vt (letter, goods) despachar
  ▶ **send away for** vt fus pedir
  ▶ **send back** vt devolver
  ▶ **send for** vt fus mandar traer; (by post) escribir pidiendo
  ▶ **send in** vt (report, application, resignation) mandar
  ▶ **send off** vt (goods) despachar; (Brit Sport: player) expulsar; **he was sent off** lo expulsaron
  ▶ **send off for** vt fus (by post) escribir pidiendo
  ▶ **send on** vt (letter) mandar, expedir; (luggage etc: in advance) facturar
  ▶ **send out** vt (invitation) mandar; (emit: light, heat) emitir, difundir; (signal) emitir
  ▶ **send out for** vt fus pedir por teléfono; **let's ~ out for a pizza** vamos a pedir una pizza por teléfono
  ▶ **send round** vt (letter, document etc) hacer circular
  ▶ **send up** vt (person, price) hacer subir; (Brit: parody) parodiar

sender ['sɛndəʳ] n remitente

send-off ['sɛndɔf] n: **a good ~** una buena despedida

send-up ['sɛndʌp] n (col) parodia, sátira

senile ['siːnaɪl] adj senil

senior ['siːnɪəʳ] adj (older) mayor, más viejo; (: on staff) más antiguo; (of higher rank) superior ▷ n mayor; **P. Jones ~** = P. Jones padre

senior citizen n persona de la tercera edad

senior high school n (US) ≈ instituto de enseñanza media; see also **high school**

seniority [siːnɪ'ɔrɪtɪ] n antigüedad; (in rank) rango superior

sensation [sɛn'seɪʃən] n (physical feeling, impression) sensación

sensational [sɛn'seɪʃənl] adj sensacional

sense [sɛns] n (faculty, meaning) sentido; (feeling) sensación; (good sense) sentido común, juicio ▷ vt sentir, percibir; **the five ~s** los cinco sentidos; **a keen ~ of smell** un olfato finísimo; **~ of humour** sentido del humor; **it makes ~** tiene sentido; **there is no ~ in (doing) that** no tiene sentido (hacer) eso; **use your common ~!** ¡usa el sentido común!; **to come to one's ~s** (regain consciousness) volver en sí, recobrar el sentido; **to take leave of one's ~s** perder el juicio

senseless ['sɛnslɪs] adj estúpido, insensato; (unconscious) sin conocimiento

sensibility [sɛnsɪ'bɪlɪtɪ] n sensibilidad; **sensibilities** npl delicadeza

sensible ['sɛnsɪbl] adj sensato; (reasonable) razonable, lógico

sensibly ['sɛnsɪblɪ] adv sensatamente; razonablemente, de modo lógico

sensitive ['sɛnsɪtɪv] adj sensible; (touchy) susceptible; **he is very ~ about it** es muy susceptible acerca de eso

sensitivity [sɛnsɪ'tɪvɪtɪ] n sensibilidad; susceptibilidad

sensual ['sɛnsjuəl] *adj* sensual
sensuous ['sɛnsjuəs] *adj* sensual
sent [sɛnt] *pt, pp of* **send**
sentence ['sɛntəns] *n* (*Ling*) frase, oración; (*Law*) sentencia, fallo ▷ *vt*: **to ~ sb to death/to 5 years** condenar a algn a muerte/a 5 años de cárcel; **to pass ~ on sb** (*also fig*) sentenciar *or* condenar a algn
sentiment ['sɛntɪmənt] *n* sentimiento; (*opinion*) opinión
sentimental [sɛntɪ'mɛntl] *adj* sentimental
sentry ['sɛntrɪ] *n* centinela
separate *adj* separado; (*distinct*) distinto ▷ *vt* separar; (*part*) dividir ▷ *vi* separarse; **~ from** separado *or* distinto de; **under ~ cover** (*Comm*) por separado; **to ~ into** dividir *or* separar en; **he is ~d from his wife, but not divorced** está separado de su mujer, pero no (está) divorciado
separately ['sɛprɪtlɪ] *adv* por separado
separates ['sɛprɪts] *npl* (*clothes*) coordinados
separation [sɛpə'reɪʃən] *n* separación
September [sɛp'tɛmbəʳ] *n* se(p)tiembre
septic ['sɛptɪk] *adj* séptico; **to go ~** ponerse séptico
septic tank *n* fosa séptica
sequel ['si:kwl] *n* consecuencia, resultado; (*of story*) continuación
sequence ['si:kwəns] *n* sucesión, serie; (*Cine*) secuencia; **in ~** en orden *or* serie
sequin ['si:kwɪn] *n* lentejuela
Serb [sə:b] *adj, n* = **Serbian**
Serbia ['sə:bɪə] *n* Serbia
Serbian ['sə:bɪən] *adj* serbio ▷ *n* serbio(-a); (*Ling*) serbio
serenade [sɛrə'neɪd] *n* serenata ▷ *vt* dar serenata a
serene [sɪ'ri:n] *adj* sereno, tranquilo
sergeant ['sɑ:dʒənt] *n* sargento
serial ['sɪərɪəl] *n* novela por entregas; (*TV*) telenovela
serial killer *n* asesino(-a) múltiple
serial number *n* número de serie
series ['sɪəri:z] *n* (*pl inv*) serie
serious ['sɪərɪəs] *adj* serio; (*grave*) grave; **are you ~ (about it)?** ¿lo dices en serio?
seriously ['sɪərɪəslɪ] *adv* en serio; (*ill, wounded etc*) gravemente; (*col: extremely*) de verdad; **to take sth/sb ~** tomar algo/a algn en serio; **he's ~ rich** es una pasada de rico
sermon ['sə:mən] *n* sermón
serpent ['sə:pənt] *n* serpiente
serrated [sɪ'reɪtɪd] *adj* serrado, dentellado
serum ['sɪərəm] *n* suero
servant ['sə:vənt] *n* (*gen*) servidor(a); (*house servant*) criado(-a)
serve [sə:v] *vt* servir; (*customer*) atender; (*train*) tener parada en; (*apprenticeship*) hacer; (*prison term*) cumplir ▷ *vi* (*servant, soldier etc*) servir; (*Tennis*) sacar ▷ *n* (*Tennis*) servicio, saque; **dinner is ~d** la cena está servida; **it ~s him right** se lo merece, se lo tiene merecido; **to ~ a summons on sb** entregar una citación a algn; **it ~s my**

purpose me sirve para lo que quiero; **are you being ~d?** ¿le atienden?; **the power station ~s the entire region** la central eléctrica abastece a toda la región; **to ~ time** cumplir condena; **to ~ as/for/to do** servir de/para/para hacer; **to ~ on a committee/a jury** ser miembro de una comisión/un jurado
▶ **serve out, serve up** *vt* (*food*) servir
service ['sə:vɪs] *n* (*gen*) servicio; (*Rel: Catholic*) misa; (: *other*) oficio (religioso); (*Aut*) mantenimiento; (*of dishes*) juego ▷ *vt* (*car, washing machine*) mantener; (: *repair*) reparar; **the Services** las fuerzas armadas; **~ is included** el servicio está incluido; **the essential ~s** los servicios esenciales; **medical/social ~s** servicios médicos/sociales; **the armed ~s** las fuerzas armadas; **the postal ~** el servicio de correos; **a bus ~** una línea de autobús; **the train ~ to London** los trenes a Londres; **to be of ~ to sb** ser útil a algn; **funeral ~** exequias; **to hold a ~** celebrar un oficio religioso; **the car needs a ~** al coche le hace falta una revisión
serviceable ['sə:vɪsəbl] *adj* servible, utilizable
service charge *n* (*Brit*) servicio; **there's no ~** el servicio va incluido
serviceman ['sə:vɪsmən] *n* militar
service station *n* estación de servicio
serviette [sə:vɪ'ɛt] *n* (*Brit*) servilleta
session ['sɛʃən] *n* (*sitting*) sesión; **to be in ~** estar en sesión
set [sɛt] *n* juego; (*Radio*) aparato; (*TV*) televisor; (*of utensils*) batería; (*of cutlery*) cubierto; (*of books*) colección; (*Tennis*) set; (*group of people*) grupo; (*Cine*) plató; (*Theat*) decorado; (*Hairdressing*) marcado ▷ *adj* (*fixed*) fijo; (*ready*) listo; (*resolved*) resuelto, decidido ▷ *vb* (*pt, pp ~*) ▷ *vt* (*place*) poner, colocar; (*fix*) fijar; (*adjust*) ajustar, arreglar; (*decide: rules etc*) establecer, decidir; (*assign: task*) asignar; (: *homework*) poner ▷ *vi* (*sun*) ponerse; (*jam, jelly*) cuajarse; (*concrete*) fraguar; **a ~ of false teeth** una dentadura postiza; **a ~ of dining-room furniture** muebles de comedor; **the sofa and chairs are only sold as a ~** el sofá y los sillones no se venden por separado; **~ in one's ways** con costumbres arraigadas; **a ~ phrase** una frase hecha; **to be all ~ to do sth** estar listo para hacer algo; **to be ~ on doing sth** estar empeñado en hacer algo; **a novel ~ in Valencia** una novela ambientada en Valencia; **to ~ to music** poner música a; **to ~ on fire** incendiar, prender fuego a; **to ~ free** poner en libertad; **to ~ sth going** poner algo en marcha; **to ~ sail** zarpar, hacerse a la mar; **to ~ the table** poner la mesa; **I ~ the alarm for 7 o'clock** puse el despertador a las 7; **the world record was ~ last year** el récord mundial se estableció el año pasado
▶ **set about** *vt fus*: **to ~ about doing sth** ponerse a hacer algo
▶ **set aside** *vt* poner aparte, dejar de lado
▶ **set back** *vt* (*progress*) retrasar; **this has ~ us back some years** esto nos ha retrasado varios

años; **a house ~ back from the road** una casa apartada de la carretera

▶ **set down** vt (bus, train) dejar; (record) poner por escrito

▶ **set in** vi (infection) declararse; (complications) comenzar; **the rain has ~ in for the day** parece que va a llover todo el día

▶ **set off** vi salir, partir; **we ~ off for London at 9 o'clock** salimos para Londres a las 9 ▷ vt (bomb) hacer estallar; (cause to start) poner en marcha; (show up well) hacer resaltar

▶ **set out** vi: **to ~ out to do sth** proponerse hacer algo ▷ vt (arrange) disponer; (state) exponer; **to ~ out (from/for)** salir (de/para)

▶ **set up** vt (organization) establecer

setback ['sɛtbæk] n (hitch) revés, contratiempo; (in health) recaída

set menu n menú

set phrase n frase hecha

settee [sɛ'tiː] n sofá

setting ['sɛtɪŋ] n (scenery) marco; (of jewel) engaste, montadura

settle ['sɛtl] vt (argument, matter) resolver; (pay: bill, accounts) pagar, liquidar; (colonize: land) colonizar; (Med: calm) calmar, sosegar ▷ vi (dust etc) depositarse; (weather) estabilizarse; (also: **settle down**) instalarse; (calm down) tranquilizarse; **to ~ for sth** convenir en aceptar algo; **to ~ on sth** decidirse por algo; **that's ~d then** bueno, está arreglado; **to ~ one's stomach** asentar el estómago

▶ **settle in** vi instalarse

▶ **settle up** vi: **to ~ up with sb** ajustar cuentas con algn

settlement ['sɛtlmənt] n (payment) liquidación; (agreement) acuerdo, convenio; (village etc) poblado; **in ~ of our account** (Comm) en pago or liquidación de nuestra cuenta

settler ['sɛtlər] n colono(-a), colonizador(a)

setup ['sɛtʌp] n sistema

seven ['sɛvn] num siete

seventeen [sɛvn'tiːn] num diecisiete

seventh ['sɛvnθ] adj séptimo

seventy ['sɛvntɪ] num setenta

sever ['sɛvər] vt cortar; (relations) romper

several ['sɛvərl] adj, pron varios(-as), algunos(-as); **~ of us** varios de nosotros; **~ times** varias veces

severance ['sɛvərəns] n (of relations) ruptura

severance pay n indemnización por despido

severe [sɪ'vɪər] adj severo; (serious) grave; (hard) duro; (pain) intenso

severity [sɪ'vɛrɪtɪ] n severidad; gravedad; intensidad

Seville [sə'vɪl] n Sevilla

sew [səu] (pt **-ed**, pp **-n**) vt, vi coser

▶ **sew up** vt coser

sewage ['suːɪdʒ] n (effluence) aguas residuales; (system) alcantarillado

sewage works n estación depuradora (de aguas residuales)

sewer ['suːər] n alcantarilla, cloaca

sewing ['səuɪŋ] n costura

sewing machine n máquina de coser

sewn [səun] pp of **sew**

sex [sɛks] n sexo; **the opposite ~** el sexo opuesto; **to have ~ with sb** tener relaciones (sexuales) con algn

sex appeal n sex-appeal, gancho

sex education n educación sexual

sexist ['sɛksɪst] adj, n sexista

sex life n vida sexual

sex object n objeto sexual

sexual ['sɛksjuəl] adj sexual; **~ assault** atentado contra el pudor; **~ harassment** acoso sexual; **~ intercourse** relaciones sexuales

sexy ['sɛksɪ] adj sexy

shabby ['ʃæbɪ] adj (person) desharrapado; (clothes) raído, gastado

shack [ʃæk] n choza, chabola

shackles ['ʃæklz] npl grillos, grilletes

shade [ʃeɪd] n sombra; (for lamp) pantalla; (for eyes) visera; (of colour) tono, tonalidad; (US: window shade) persiana ▷ vt dar sombra a; **shades** npl (US: sunglasses) gafas de sol; **in the ~** a la sombra; (small quantity): **a ~ of** un poquito de; **a ~ smaller** un poquito más pequeño

shadow ['ʃædəu] n sombra ▷ vt (follow) seguir y vigilar; **without or beyond a ~ of doubt** sin lugar a dudas

shadow cabinet n (Brit Pol) gobierno en la oposición

shadowy ['ʃædəuɪ] adj oscuro; (dim) indistinto

shady ['ʃeɪdɪ] adj sombreado; (fig: dishonest) sospechoso; (deal) turbio

shaft [ʃɑːft] n (of arrow, spear) astil; (Aut, Tech) eje, árbol; (of mine) pozo; (of lift) hueco, caja; (of light) rayo; **ventilator ~** chimenea de ventilación

shaggy ['ʃægɪ] adj peludo

shake [ʃeɪk] (pt **shook**, pp **-n**) ['ʃeɪkn] vt sacudir; (building) hacer temblar; (perturb) inquietar, perturbar; (weaken) debilitar; (alarm) trastornar ▷ vi estremecerse; (tremble) temblar ▷ n (movement) sacudida; **"~ well before use"** "agítese bien antes de usarse"; **to ~ one's head** (in refusal) negar con la cabeza; (in dismay) mover or menear la cabeza, incrédulo; **to ~ hands with sb** estrechar la mano a algn; **they shook hands** se dieron la mano; **he was shaking with cold** temblaba de frío; **to ~ in one's shoes** (fig) temblar de miedo

▶ **shake off** vt sacudirse; (fig) deshacerse de

▶ **shake up** vt agitar

shake-up ['ʃeɪkʌp] n reorganización

shaky ['ʃeɪkɪ] adj (unstable) inestable, poco firme; (trembling) tembloroso; (health) delicado; (memory) defectuoso; (person: from illness) temblando; (premise etc) incierto

shall [ʃæl] aux vb: **I ~ go** iré

shallot [ʃə'lɒt] n (Brit) cebollita, chalote

shallow ['ʃæləu] adj poco profundo; (fig) superficial

sham [ʃæm] n fraude, engaño ▷ adj falso, fingido ▷ vt fingir, simular

shambles ['ʃæmblz] n desorden, confusión; **the economy is (in) a complete ~** la economía está en un estado desastroso

shame [ʃeɪm] n vergüenza; (pity) lástima, pena ▷ vt avergonzar; **it is a ~ that/to do** es una lástima or pena que/hacer; **what a ~!** ¡qué lástima or pena!; **to put sth/sb to ~** (fig) ridiculizar algo/a algn

shamefaced ['ʃeɪmfeɪst] adj avergonzado

shameful ['ʃeɪmful] adj vergonzoso

shameless ['ʃeɪmlɪs] adj descarado

shampoo [ʃæm'puː] n champú ▷ vt lavar con champú

shampoo and set n lavado y marcado

shamrock ['ʃæmrɔk] n trébol

shandy ['ʃændɪ], (US) **shandygaff** ['ʃændɪgæf] n clara, cerveza con gaseosa

shan't [ʃɑːnt] = **shall not**

shanty town ['ʃæntɪ-] n barrio de chabolas

shape [ʃeɪp] n forma ▷ vt formar, dar forma a; (clay) modelar; (stone) labrar; (sb's ideas) formar; (sb's life) determinar ▷ vi (also: **shape up**: events) desarrollarse; (person) formarse; **to take ~** tomar forma; **to get o.s. into** ~ ponerse en forma or en condiciones; **in the ~ of a heart** en forma de corazón; **I can't bear gardening in any ~ or form** no aguanto la jardinería de ningún modo

shapeless ['ʃeɪplɪs] adj informe, sin forma definida

shapely ['ʃeɪplɪ] adj bien formado or proporcionado

share [ʃɛəʳ] n (part) parte, porción; (contribution) cuota; (Comm) acción ▷ vt dividir; (fig: have in common) compartir ▷ vi: **to ~ in** participar en; **to have a ~ in the profits** tener una proporción de las ganancias; **he has a 50% ~ in a new business venture** tiene una participación del 50% en un nuevo negocio; **to ~ a room with sb** compartir habitación con algn; **to ~ out (among or between)** repartir (entre)

share certificate n certificado or título de una acción

shareholder ['ʃɛəhəuldəʳ] n (Brit) accionista

share issue n emisión de acciones

shark [ʃɑːk] n tiburón

sharp [ʃɑːp] adj (razor, knife) afilado; (point) puntiagudo; (outline) definido; (pain) intenso; (Mus) desafinado; (contrast) marcado; (voice) agudo; (curve, bend) cerrado; (person: quick-witted) avispado; (: dishonest) poco escrupuloso ▷ n (Mus) sostenido ▷ adv: **at 2 o'clock ~** a las 2 en punto; **to be ~ with sb** hablar a algn de forma brusca y tajante; **turn ~ left** tuerce del todo a la izquierda

sharpen ['ʃɑːpn] vt afilar; (pencil) sacar punta a; (fig) agudizar

sharpener ['ʃɑːpnəʳ] n (gen) afilador; (pencil sharpener) sacapuntas

sharp-eyed [ʃɑːp'aɪd] adj de vista aguda

sharply ['ʃɑːplɪ] adv (abruptly) bruscamente; (clearly) claramente; (harshly) severamente

shatter ['ʃætəʳ] vt hacer añicos or pedazos; (fig:

ruin) destruir, acabar con ▷ vi hacerse añicos

shattered ['ʃætəd] adj (grief-stricken) destrozado, deshecho; (exhausted) agotado, hecho polvo

shave [ʃeɪv] vt afeitar, rasurar ▷ vi afeitarse ▷ n: **to have a ~** afeitarse

shaver ['ʃeɪvəʳ] n (also: **electric shaver**) máquina de afeitar (eléctrica)

shaving ['ʃeɪvɪŋ] n (action) afeitado; **shavings** npl (of wood etc) virutas

shaving brush n brocha (de afeitar)

shaving cream n crema (de afeitar)

shawl [ʃɔːl] n chal

she [ʃiː] pron ella; **there ~ is** allí está; **~-cat** gata

sheaf [ʃiːf] **sheaves**) n (of corn) gavilla; (of arrows) haz; (of papers) fajo

shear [ʃɪəʳ] vt (pt, pp **-ed** or **shorn**) (sheep) esquilar, trasquilar

▶ **shear off** vi romperse

shears ['ʃɪəz] npl (for hedge) tijeras de jardín

sheath [ʃiːθ] n vaina; (contraceptive) preservativo

shed [ʃed] n cobertizo; (Industry, Rail) nave ▷ vt (pt, pp **-**) (skin) mudar; (tears) derramar; **to ~ light on** (problem, mystery) aclarar, arrojar luz sobre

she'd [ʃiːd] = **she had**; **she would**

sheen [ʃiːn] n brillo, lustre

sheep [ʃiːp] n (pl inv) oveja

sheepdog ['ʃiːpdɔg] n perro pastor

sheepish ['ʃiːpɪʃ] adj tímido, vergonzoso

sheepskin ['ʃiːpskɪn] n piel de carnero

sheer [ʃɪəʳ] adj (utter) puro, completo; (steep) escarpado; (material) diáfano ▷ adv verticalmente; **by ~ chance** de pura casualidad

sheet [ʃiːt] n (on bed) sábana; (of paper) hoja; (of glass, metal) lámina

sheik(h) [ʃeɪk] n jeque

shelf [ʃelf] **shelves**) n estante

shelf life n (Comm) periodo de conservación antes de la venta

shell [ʃel] n (on beach) concha, caracol (LAm); (of egg, nut etc) cáscara; (explosive) proyectil, obús; (of building) armazón ▷ vt (peas) desenvainar; (Mil) bombardear

▶ **shell out** vi (col): **to ~ out (for)** soltar el dinero (para), desembolsar (para)

she'll [ʃiːl] = **she will**; **she shall**

shellfish ['ʃelfɪʃ] n (pl inv) crustáceo; (pl: as food) mariscos

shellsuit ['ʃelsuːt] n chándal (de tactel®)

shelter ['ʃeltəʳ] n abrigo, refugio ▷ vt (aid) amparar, proteger; (give lodging to) abrigar; (hide) esconder ▷ vi abrigarse, refugiarse; **to take ~ (from)** refugiarse or asilarse (de); **bus ~** parada de autobús cubierta

sheltered ['ʃeltəd] adj (life) protegido; (spot) abrigado

shelve [ʃelv] vt (fig) dar carpetazo a

shelves [ʃelvz] npl of **shelf**

shepherd ['ʃepəd] n pastor ▷ vt (guide) guiar, conducir

shepherd's pie n pastel de carne y puré de patatas

sheriff ['ʃerɪf] n (US) sheriff

sherry ['ʃerɪ] n jerez

she's [ʃiːz] = **she is**; **she has**

Shetland ['ʃetlənd] n (also: **the Shetlands, the Shetland Isles**) las Islas Shetland

Shetland pony n pony de Shetland

shield [ʃiːld] n escudo; (Tech) blindaje ▷ vt: **to ~ (from)** proteger (de)

shift [ʃɪft] n (change) cambio; (at work) turno ▷ vt trasladar; (remove) quitar ▷ vi moverse; (change place) cambiar de sitio; **the wind has ~ed to the south** el viento ha virado al sur; **a ~ in demand** (Comm) un desplazamiento de la demanda

shift work n (Brit) trabajo por turnos; **to do ~** trabajar por turnos

shifty ['ʃɪftɪ] adj tramposo; (eyes) furtivo

Shiite ['ʃiːaɪt] adj, n shiíta

shilling ['ʃɪlɪŋ] n (Brit) chelín

shilly-shally ['ʃɪlɪʃælɪ] vi titubear, vacilar

shimmer ['ʃɪmə^r] n reflejo trémulo ▷ vi relucir

shin [ʃɪn] n espinilla ▷ vi: **to ~ down/up a tree** bajar de/trepar un árbol

shine [ʃaɪn] (pt, pp **shone**) n brillo, lustre ▷ vi brillar, relucir ▷ vt (shoes) lustrar, sacar brillo a; **to ~ a torch on sth** dirigir una linterna hacia algo

shingle ['ʃɪŋgl] n (on beach) guijarras

shingles ['ʃɪŋglz] n (Med) herpes

shiny ['ʃaɪnɪ] adj brillante, lustroso

ship [ʃɪp] n buque, barco ▷ vt (goods) embarcar; (oars) desarmar; (send) transportar or enviar por vía marítima; **on board ~** a bordo

shipbuilding ['ʃɪpbɪldɪŋ] n construcción naval

shipment ['ʃɪpmənt] n (act) embarque; (goods) envío

shipper ['ʃɪpə^r] n compañía naviera

shipping ['ʃɪpɪŋ] n (act) embarque; (traffic) buques

shipwreck ['ʃɪprɛk] n naufragio ▷ vt: **to be ~ed** naufragar

shipyard ['ʃɪpjɑːd] n astillero

shire ['ʃaɪə^r] n (Brit) condado

shirk [ʃəːk] vt eludir, esquivar; (obligations) faltar a

shirt [ʃəːt] n camisa; **in ~ sleeves** en mangas de camisa

shirty ['ʃəːtɪ] adj (Brit col): **to be ~** estar de malas pulgas

shit [ʃɪt] (col!) n mierda; (nonsense) chorradas; **to be a ~** ser un cabrón ▷ excl ¡mierda!; **tough ~!** ¡te jodes!

shiver ['ʃɪvə^r] vi temblar, estremecerse; (with cold) tiritar

shoal [ʃəul] n (of fish) banco

shock [ʃɔk] n (impact) choque; (Elec) descarga (eléctrica); (emotional) conmoción; (start) sobresalto, susto; (Med) postración nerviosa ▷ vt dar un susto a; (offend) escandalizar; **to get a ~** (Elec) sentir una sacudida eléctrica; **to give sb a ~** dar un susto a algn; **to be suffering from ~** padecer una postración nerviosa; **it came as a ~ to hear that ...** me (etc) asombró descubrir que ...

shock absorber [-əbsɔːbə^r] n amortiguador

shocking ['ʃɔkɪŋ] adj (awful: weather, handwriting) espantoso, horrible; (improper) escandaloso; (result) inesperado

shock wave n onda expansiva or de choque

shod [ʃɔd] pt, pp of **shoe** ▷ adj calzado

shoddy ['ʃɔdɪ] adj de pacotilla

shoe [ʃuː] n zapato; (for horse) herradura; (brake shoe) zapata ▷ vt (pt, pp **shod**) (horse) herrar

shoelace ['ʃuːleɪs] n cordón, agujeta (Méx), pasador (Perú)

shoe polish n betún

shoeshop ['ʃuːʃɔp] n zapatería

shoestring ['ʃuːstrɪŋ] n (shoelace) cordón; (fig): **on a ~** con muy poco dinero, a lo barato

shone [ʃɔn] pt, pp of **shine**

shoo [ʃuː] excl ¡fuera!; (to animals) ¡zape! ▷ vt (also: **shoo away, shoo off**) ahuyentar

shook [ʃuk] pt of **shake**

shoot [ʃuːt] n (on branch, seedling) retoño, vástago; (shooting party) cacería; (competition) concurso de tiro; (preserve) coto de caza ▷ vb (pt, pp **shot**) ▷ vt disparar; (kill) matar a tiros; (execute) fusilar; (Cine: film, scene) rodar, filmar ▷ vi (with gun) disparar; (Football) chutar; **he shot himself with a revolver** se pegó un tiro con un revólver; **he was shot dead by the police** murió de un disparo de la policía; **don't ~!** ¡no disparen!; **to ~ at goal** tirar a gol; **to ~ at sb** disparar a algn; **to ~ past** pasar como un rayo; **to ~ in/out** vi entrar corriendo/salir disparado

▶ **shoot down** vt (plane) derribar

▶ **shoot up** vi (prices) dispararse

shooting ['ʃuːtɪŋ] n (shots) tiros, tiroteo; (Hunting) caza con escopeta; (act: murder) asesinato (a tiros); (Cine) rodaje

shooting star n estrella fugaz

shop [ʃɔp] n tienda; (workshop) taller ▷ vi (also: **go shopping**) ir de compras; **to talk ~** (fig) hablar del trabajo; **repair ~** taller de reparaciones

▶ **shop around** vi comparar precios

shopaholic ['ʃɔpə'hɔlɪk] n (col) adicto(-a) a las compras

shop assistant n (Brit) dependiente(-a)

shop floor n (Brit fig) taller, fábrica

shopkeeper ['ʃɔpkiːpə^r] n (Brit) tendero(-a)

shoplift ['ʃɔplɪft] vi robar en las tiendas

shoplifter ['ʃɔplɪftə^r] n ratero(-a)

shoplifting ['ʃɔplɪftɪŋ] n ratería, robo (en las tiendas)

shopper ['ʃɔpə^r] n comprador(a)

shopping ['ʃɔpɪŋ] n (goods) compras

shopping bag n bolsa (de compras)

shopping centre, (US) **shopping center** n centro comercial

shopping mall n centro comercial

shop steward n (Brit Industry) enlace sindical

shop window n escaparate, vidriera (LAm)

shore [ʃɔː^r] n (of sea, lake) orilla ▷ vt: **to ~ (up)** reforzar; **on ~** en tierra

shorn [ʃɔːn] pp of **shear**

short [ʃɔːt] adj (not long) corto; (in time) breve, de corta duración; (person) bajo; (curt) brusco, seco ▷ vi (Elec) ponerse en cortocircuito ▷ n (*also*: **short film**) cortometraje; (**a pair of**) **~s** (*unos*) pantalones cortos; **to be ~ of sth** estar falto de algo; **in ~** en pocas palabras; **a ~ time ago** hace poco (tiempo); **a ~ break** un pequeño descanso; **at ~ notice** con poco tiempo de antelación; **in the ~ term** a corto plazo; **to be in ~ supply** escasear, haber escasez de; **I'm ~ of time** me falta tiempo; **~ of doing ...** a menos que hagamos *etc* ...; **everything ~ of ...** todo menos ...; **it is ~ for** es la forma abreviada de; **to cut ~** (*speech, visit*) interrumpir, terminar inesperadamente; **to fall ~ of** no alcanzar; **to run ~ of sth** acabársele algo; **to stop ~** parar en seco; **to stop ~ of** detenerse antes de

shortage ['ʃɔːtɪdʒ] *n* escasez, falta

shortbread ['ʃɔːtbred] *n pasta de mantequilla*

short-change [ʃɔːt'tʃeɪndʒ] *vt*: **to ~ sb** no dar el cambio completo a algn

short-circuit [ʃɔːt'səːkɪt] *n* cortocircuito ▷ *vt* poner en cortocircuito ▷ *vi* ponerse, en cortocircuito

shortcoming ['ʃɔːtkʌmɪŋ] *n* defecto, deficiencia

short(crust) pastry ['ʃɔːt(krʌst)-] *n* (*Brit*) pasta quebradiza

shortcut ['ʃɔːtkʌt] *n* atajo

shorten ['ʃɔːtn] *vt* acortar; (*visit*) interrumpir

shortfall ['ʃɔːtfɔːl] *n* déficit, deficiencia

shorthand ['ʃɔːthænd] *n* (*Brit*) taquigrafía; **to take sth down in ~** taquigrafiar algo

shorthand typist *n* (*Brit*) taquimecanógrafo(-a)

short list *n* (*Brit: for job*) lista de candidatos pre-seleccionados

short-lived ['ʃɔːt'lɪvd] *adj* efímero

shortly ['ʃɔːtlɪ] *adv* en breve, dentro de poco

short-sighted [ʃɔːt'saɪtɪd] *adj* (*Brit*) miope, corto de vista; (*fig*) imprudente

short-staffed [ʃɔːt'stɑːft] *adj* falto de personal

short story *n* cuento

short-tempered [ʃɔːt'tempəd] *adj* enojadizo

short-term ['ʃɔːttəːm] *adj* (*effect*) a corto plazo

short wave *n* (*Radio*) onda corta

shot [ʃɔt] *pt, pp of* **shoot** ▷ *n* (*sound*) tiro, disparo; (*person*) tirador(a); (*try*) tentativa; (*injection*) inyección; (*Phot*) toma, fotografía; (*shotgun pellets*) perdigones; **to fire a ~ at sb/sth** tirar *or* disparar contra algn/algo; **to have a ~ at (doing) sth** probar suerte con algo; **like a ~** (*without any delay*) como un rayo; **a big ~** (*col*) un pez gordo; **to get ~ of sth/sb** (*col*) deshacerse de algo/algn, quitarse algo/a algn de encima

shotgun ['ʃɔtgʌn] *n* escopeta

should [ʃud] *aux vb*: **I ~ go now** debo irme ahora; **you ~ take more exercise** deberías hacer más ejercicio; **I ~ have told you before** tendría que habértelo dicho antes; **he ~ be there now** debe de haber llegado (ya); **I ~ go if I were you** yo en tu lugar me iría; **I ~ like to** me gustaría; **~ he phone ...** si llamara ..., en caso de que llamase ...; **I ~ be so lucky!** ¡ojalá!

shoulder ['ʃəuldə^r] *n* hombro; (*Brit: of road*): **hard ~** arcén ▷ *vt* (*fig*) cargar con; **to look over one's ~** mirar hacia atrás; **to rub ~s with sb** (*fig*)

codearse con algn; **to give sb the cold ~** (*fig*) dar de lado a algn

shoulder blade *n* omóplato

shoulder bag *n* bolso de bandolera

shoulder strap *n* tirante

shouldn't ['ʃudnt] = **should not**

shout [ʃaut] *n* grito ▷ *vt* gritar ▷ *vi* gritar, dar voces

▶ **shout down** *vt* hundir a gritos

shouting ['ʃautɪŋ] *n* griterío

shouting match *n* (*col*) discusión a voz en grito

shove [ʃʌv] *n* empujón ▷ *vt* empujar; (*col: put*): **to ~ sth in** meter algo a empellones; **he ~d me out of the way** me quitó de en medio de un empujón

▶ **shove off** *vi* (*Naut*) alejarse del muelle; (*fig: col*) largarse

shovel ['ʃʌvl] *n* pala; (*mechanical*) excavadora ▷ *vt* mover con pala

show [ʃəu] *n* (*of emotion*) demostración; (*semblance*) apariencia; (*Comm, Tech: exhibition*) exhibición, exposición; (*Theat*) función, espectáculo; (*organization*) negocio, empresa ▷ *vb* (*pt* **-ed**, *pp* **-n**) ▷ *vt* mostrar, enseñar; (*courage etc*) mostrar, manifestar; (*exhibit*) exponer; (*film*) proyectar ▷ *vi* mostrarse; (*appear*) aparecer; **on ~** (*exhibits etc*) expuesto; **to be on ~** estar expuesto; **it's just for ~** es sólo para impresionar; **to ask for a ~ of hands** pedir una votación a mano alzada; **who's running the ~ here?** ¿quién manda aquí?; **to ~ a profit/loss** (*Comm*) arrojar un saldo positivo/negativo); **I have nothing to ~ for it** no saqué ningún provecho (de ello); **to ~ sb to his seat/to the door** acompañar a algn a su asiento/a la puerta; **as ~n in the illustration** como se ve en el grabado; **it just goes to ~ that ...** queda demostrado que ...; **it doesn't ~** no se ve *or* nota

▶ **show in** *vt* (*person*) hacer pasar

▶ **show off** *vi* (*pej*) presumir ▷ *vt* (*display*) lucir; (*pej*) hacer alarde de

▶ **show out** *vt*: **to ~ sb out** acompañar a algn a la puerta

▶ **show up** *vi* (*stand out*) destacar; (*col: turn up*) presentarse ▷ *vt* descubrir; (*unmask*) desenmascarar; (*embarrass*) dejar en ridículo

showbiz ['ʃəubɪz] *n* (*col*) = **show business**

show business *n* el mundo del espectáculo

showdown ['ʃəudaun] *n* crisis, momento decisivo

shower ['ʃauə^r] *n* (*rain*) chaparrón, chubasco; (*of stones etc*) lluvia; (*also*: **shower bath**) ducha ▷ *vi* llover ▷ *vt*: **to ~ sb with sth** colmar a algn de algo; **to have** *or* **take a ~** ducharse

showery ['ʃauərɪ] *adj* (*weather*) lluvioso

showing ['ʃəuɪŋ] *n* (*of film*) proyección

show jumping *n* hípica

shown [ʃəun] *pp of* **show**

show-off ['ʃəuɔf] *n* (*col: person*) fantasmón(-ona)

showpiece ['ʃəupiːs] *n* (*of exhibition etc*) objeto más valioso, joya; **that hospital is a ~** ese hospital es un modelo del género

showroom ['ʃəuru:m] n sala de muestras
show trial n juicio propagandístico
shrank [ʃræŋk] pt of **shrink**
shrapnel ['ʃræpnl] n metralla
shred [ʃred] n (gen pl) triza, jirón; (fig: of truth, evidence) pizca, chispa ▷ vt hacer trizas; (documents) triturar; (Culin) desmenuzar
shredder ['ʃredə'] n (vegetable shredder) picadora; (document shredder) trituradora (de papel)
shrewd [ʃru:d] adj astuto
shriek [ʃri:k] n chillido ▷ vt, vi chillar
shrill [ʃril] adj agudo, estridente
shrimp [ʃrimp] n camarón
shrine [ʃrain] n santuario, sepulcro
shrink [ʃrɪŋk] (pt **shrank**, pp **shrunk**) vi encogerse; (be reduced) reducirse ▷ vt encoger; **to ~ from (doing) sth** no atreverse a hacer algo
▸ **shrink away** vi retroceder, retirarse
shrinkage ['ʃrɪŋkɪdʒ] n encogimiento; reducción; (Comm: in shops) pérdidas
shrink-wrap ['ʃrɪŋkræp] vt empaquetar en envase termorretráctil
shrivel ['ʃrivl] (also: **shrivel up**) vt (dry) secar; (crease) arrugar ▷ vi secarse; arrugarse
shroud [ʃraud] n sudario ▷ vt: **~ed in mystery** envuelto en el misterio
Shrove Tuesday ['ʃrəuv-] n martes de carnaval
shrub [ʃrʌb] n arbusto
shrubbery ['ʃrʌbəri] n arbustos
shrug [ʃrʌg] n encogimiento de hombros ▷ vt, vi: **to ~ (one's shoulders)** encogerse de hombros
▸ **shrug off** vt negar importancia a; (cold, illness) deshacerse de
shrunk [ʃrʌŋk] pp of **shrink**
shrunken ['ʃrʌŋkn] adj encogido
shudder ['ʃʌdə'] n estremecimiento, escalofrío ▷ vi estremecerse
shuffle ['ʃʌfl] vt (cards) barajar; **to ~ (one's feet)** arrastrar los pies
shun [ʃʌn] vt rehuir, esquivar
shunt [ʃʌnt] vt (Rail) maniobrar
shut [ʃʌt] (pt, pp **~**) vt cerrar ▷ vi cerrarse
▸ **shut down** vt, vi cerrar; (machine) parar
▸ **shut off** vt (stop: power, water supply etc) interrumpir, cortar; (engine) parar
▸ **shut out** vt (person) excluir, dejar fuera; (noise, cold) no dejar entrar; (block: view) tapar; (memory) tratar de olvidar
▸ **shut up** vi (col: keep quiet) callarse ▷ vt (close) cerrar; (silence) callar
shutter ['ʃʌtə'] n contraventana; (Phot) obturador
shuttle ['ʃʌtl] n lanzadera; (also: **shuttle service**: Aviat) puente aéreo ▷ vi (vehicle, person) ir y venir ▷ vt (passengers) transportar, trasladar
shuttlecock ['ʃʌtlkɔk] n volante
shy [ʃai] adj tímido ▷ vi: **to ~ away from doing sth** (fig) rehusar hacer algo; **to be ~ of doing sth** esquivar hacer algo
Siberia [sai'biəriə] n Siberia
sibling ['sɪblɪŋ] n (formal) hermano(-a)
Sicily ['sɪsɪli] n Sicilia

sick [sik] adj (ill) enfermo; (nauseated) mareado; (humour) morboso; **to be ~** (Brit) vomitar; **to feel ~** estar mareado; **to be ~ of** (fig) estar harto de; **a ~ person** un(a) enfermo(-a); **to be (off) ~** estar ausente por enfermedad; **to fall** or **take ~** ponerse enfermo
sickbag ['sikbæg] n bolsa para el mareo
sick bay n enfermería
sick building syndrome n enfermedad causada por falta de ventilación y luz natural en un edificio
sicken ['sikn] vt dar asco a ▷ vi enfermar; **to be ~ing for** (cold, flu etc) mostrar síntomas de
sickening ['siknɪŋ] adj (fig) asqueroso
sickle ['sikl] n hoz
sick leave n baja por enfermedad
sickly ['sikli] adj enfermizo; (taste) empalagoso
sickness ['siknis] n enfermedad, mal; (vomiting) náuseas
sick pay n prestación por enfermedad pagada por la empresa
side [said] n (gen) lado; (face, surface) cara; (of paper, record, tape) cara; (slice of bread) rebanada; (of body) costado; (of animal) ijar, ijada; (of hill) ladera; (of lake) orilla; (of road) borde; (part) lado; (aspect) aspecto; (team: Sport) equipo; (: Pol etc) partido ▷ adj (door, entrance) lateral ▷ vi: **to ~ with sb** ponerse de parte de algn; **by the ~ of** al lado de; **~ by ~** juntos(-as); **from all ~s** de todos lados; **to take ~s (with)** tomar partido (por); **I'm on your ~** yo estoy de tu parte; **~ of beef** flanco de vaca; **the right/wrong ~** el derecho/revés; **he was driving on the wrong ~ of the road** iba por el lado contrario de la carretera; **from ~ to ~** de un lado a otro
sideboard ['saidbɔ:d] n aparador
sideboards ['saidbɔ:dz], (Brit) **sideburns** ['saidbə:nz] npl patillas
side effect n efecto secundario
sidelight ['saidlait] n (Aut) luz lateral
sideline ['saidlain] n (Sport) línea lateral; (fig) empleo suplementario
sidelong ['saidlɔŋ] adj de soslayo; **to give a ~ glance at sth** mirar algo de reojo
sidesaddle ['saidsædl] adv a la amazona
side show n (stall) caseta; (fig) atracción secundaria
sidestep ['saidstep] vt (question) eludir; (problem) esquivar ▷ vi (Boxing etc) dar un quiebro
side street n calle lateral
sidetrack ['saidtræk] vt (fig) desviar (de su propósito)
sidewalk ['saidwɔ:k] n (US) acera, vereda (CS), andén (CAm, Col), banqueta (Méx)
sideways ['saidweiz] adv de lado
siding ['saidɪŋ] n (Rail) apartadero, vía muerta
sidle ['saidl] vi: **to ~ up (to)** acercarse furtivamente (a)
siege [si:dʒ] n cerco, sitio; **to lay ~ to** cercar, sitiar
sieve [siv] n colador ▷ vt cribar
sift [sift] vt cribar ▷ vi: **to ~ through** pasar por una criba; (information) analizar cuidadosamente

sigh [saɪ] *n* suspiro ▷ *vi* suspirar

sight [saɪt] *n* (*faculty*) vista; (*spectacle*) espectáculo; (*on gun*) mira, alza ▷ *vt* ver, divisar; **in** ~ a la vista; **out of** ~ fuera de (la) vista; **keep out of** ~! ¡que no te vean!; **at** ~ a la vista; **at first** ~ a primera vista; **to lose** ~ **of sth/sb** perder algo/a algn de vista; **to catch** ~ **of sth/sb** divisar algo/a algn; **I know her by** ~ la conozco de vista; **to set one's** ~**s on (doing) sth** aspirar a *or* ambicionar (hacer) algo; **the** ~**s** las atracciones turísticas; **to see the** ~**s of London** hacer turismo por Londres

sightseeing ['saɪtsi:ɪŋ] *n* excursionismo, turismo; **to go** ~ visitar monumentos

sign [saɪn] *n* (*with hand*) señal, seña; (*trace*) huella, rastro; (*notice*) letrero; (*written*) signo; (*road sign*) indicador; (: *with instructions*) señal de tráfico ▷ *vt* firmar; **as a** ~ **of** en señal de; **it's a good/bad** ~ es buena/mala señal; **there's no** ~ **of improvement** no hay señales de mejoría; **plus/minus** ~ signo de más/de menos; **what** ~ **are you?** ¿de qué signo eres?; **to** ~ **one's name** firmar

▶ **sign away** *vt* (*rights etc*) ceder

▶ **sign off** *vi* (*Radio, TV*) cerrar el programa

▶ **sign on** *vi* (*Mil*) alistarse; (*as unemployed*) apuntarse al paro; (*employee*) firmar un contrato ▷ *vt* (*Mil*) alistar; (*employee*) contratar; **to** ~ **on for a course** matricularse en un curso

▶ **sign out** *vi* firmar el registro (al salir)

▶ **sign over** *vt*: **to** ~ **sth over to sb** traspasar algo a algn

▶ **sign up** *vi* (*Mil*) alistarse ▷ *vt* (*employee, player*) contratar

signal ['sɪgnl] *n* señal ▷ *vi* (*Aut*) señalizar ▷ *vt* (*person*) hacer señas a; (*message*) transmitir; **the engaged** ~ (*Tel*) la señal de comunicando; **the** ~ **is very weak** (*TV*) no captamos bien el canal; **to** ~ **a left/right turn** (*Aut*) indicar que se va a doblar a la izquierda/derecha; **to** ~ **to sb (to do sth)** hacer señas a algn (para que haga algo)

signalman ['sɪgnlmən] *n* (*Rail*) guardavía

signature ['sɪgnətʃəʳ] *n* firma

signature tune *n* sintonía

signet ring ['sɪgnət-] *n* (anillo de) sello

significance [sɪg'nɪfɪkəns] *n* significado; (*importance*) trascendencia; **that is of no** ~ eso no tiene importancia

significant [sɪg'nɪfɪkənt] *adj* significativo; trascendente; **it is** ~ **that** ... es significativo que ...

sign language *n* mímica, lenguaje por *or* de señas

signpost ['saɪnpəust] *n* indicador

silence ['saɪlns] *n* silencio ▷ *vt* hacer callar; (*guns*) reducir al silencio

silencer ['saɪlnsəʳ] *n* (*on gun, Brit Aut*) silenciador

silent ['saɪlnt] *adj* (*gen*) silencioso; (*not speaking*) callado; (*film*) mudo; **to keep** *or* **remain** ~ guardar silencio

silent partner *n* (*Comm*) socio(-a) comanditario(-a)

silhouette [sɪlu:'ɛt] *n* silueta; ~**d against** destacado sobre *or* contra

silicon ['sɪlɪkən] *n* silicio

silicon chip *n* chip, plaqueta de silicio

silicone ['sɪlɪkəun] *n* silicona

silk [sɪlk] *n* seda ▷ *cpd* de seda

silky ['sɪlkɪ] *adj* sedoso

silly ['sɪlɪ] *adj* (*person*) tonto; (*idea*) absurdo; **to do sth** ~ hacer una tontería

silt [sɪlt] *n* sedimento

silver ['sɪlvəʳ] *n* plata; (*money*) moneda suelta ▷ *adj* de plata

silver paper, (*Brit*) **silver foil** *n* papel de plata

silver-plated [sɪlvə'pleɪtɪd] *adj* plateado

silversmith ['sɪlvəsmɪθ] *n* platero(-a)

silvery ['sɪlvrɪ] *adj* plateado

similar ['sɪmɪləʳ] *adj*: ~ **to** parecido *or* semejante a

similarity [sɪmɪ'lærɪtɪ] *n* parecido, semejanza

similarly ['sɪmɪləlɪ] *adv* del mismo modo; (*in a similar way*) de manera parecida; (*equally*) igualmente

simile ['sɪmɪlɪ] *n* símil

simmer ['sɪməʳ] *vi* hervir a fuego lento

▶ **simmer down** *vi* (*fig, col*) calmarse, tranquilizarse

simple ['sɪmpl] *adj* (*easy*) sencillo; (*foolish, Comm*) simple; **the** ~ **truth** la pura verdad

simplicity [sɪm'plɪsɪtɪ] *n* sencillez; (*foolishness*) ingenuidad

simplify ['sɪmplɪfaɪ] *vt* simplificar

simply ['sɪmplɪ] *adv* (*in a simple way: live, talk*) sencillamente; (*just, merely*) sólo

simulate ['sɪmjuleɪt] *vt* simular

simultaneous [sɪməl'teɪnɪəs] *adj* simultáneo

sin [sɪn] *n* pecado ▷ *vi* pecar

since [sɪns] *adv* desde entonces ▷ *prep* desde ▷ *conj* (*time*) desde que; (*because*) ya que, puesto que; **I haven't seen him** ~ desde entonces no lo he vuelto a ver; ~ **then** desde entonces; ~ **Monday** desde el lunes; (**ever**) ~ **I arrived** desde que llegué; **it's a few years** ~ **I've seen them** hace varios años que no los veo

sincere [sɪn'sɪəʳ] *adj* sincero

sincerely [sɪn'sɪəlɪ] *adv* sinceramente; **yours** ~ (*in letters*) le saluda atentamente; ~ **yours** (*US: in letters*) le saluda atentamente

sincerity [sɪn'sɛrɪtɪ] *n* sinceridad

sinew ['sɪnju:] *n* tendón

sinful ['sɪnful] *adj* (*thought*) pecaminoso; (*person*) pecador(a)

sing [sɪŋ] (*pt* **sang**, *pp* **sung**) *vt* cantar ▷ *vi* (*gen*) cantar; (*bird*) trinar; (*ears*) zumbar

singe [sɪndʒ] *vt* chamuscar

singer ['sɪŋəʳ] *n* cantante

singing ['sɪŋɪŋ] *n* (*of person, bird*) canto; (*songs*) canciones; (*in the ears*) zumbido; (*of kettle*) silbido

single ['sɪŋgl] *adj* único, solo; (*unmarried*) soltero; (*not double*) individual, sencillo ▷ *n* (*Brit: also*: **single ticket**) billete de ida; (*record*) sencillo, single; **singles** *npl* (*Tennis*) individuales; **every** ~ **day** todos los días (sin excepción); **not a** ~ **one was left** no quedaba ni uno; **she hadn't said a**

~ **word** no había dicho una sola palabra; **not a**
~ **thing** nada de nada; **a** ~ **mother** una madre
soltera; **a** ~ **bed** una cama individual; **the**
women's ~**s** (*Tennis*) los individuales femeninos
▶ **single out** vt (*choose*) escoger; (*point out*)
singularizar
single-breasted [sɪŋgl'brɛstɪd] *adj* (*jacket, suit*)
recto, sin cruzar
Single European Market *n*: **the** ~ el Mercado
Único Europeo
single file *n*: **in** ~ en fila de uno
single-handed [sɪŋgl'hændɪd] *adv* sin ayuda
single-minded [sɪŋgl'maɪndɪd] *adj* resuelto,
firme
single parent *n* (*mother*) madre soltera;
(*father*) padre soltero; **a** ~ **family** una familia
monoparental
single room *n* habitación individual
singly ['sɪŋglɪ] *adv* uno por uno
singular ['sɪŋgjʊləʳ] *adj* singular, extraordinario;
(*odd*) extraño; (*Ling*) singular ▷ *n* (*Ling*) singular;
in the feminine ~ en femenino singular
sinister ['sɪnɪstəʳ] *adj* siniestro
sink [sɪŋk] *n* (*in kitchen*) fregadero, pileta (*RP*);
(*in bathroom*) lavabo, pileta (*RP*) ▷ *vb* (*pt* **sank**,
pp **sunk**) ▷ *vt* (*ship*) hundir, echar a pique;
(*foundations*) excavar; (*piles etc*): **to** ~ **sth into**
hundir algo en ▷ *vi* (*gen*) hundirse; **he sank into**
a chair/the mud se dejó caer en una silla/se
hundió en el barro; **the shares** *or* **share prices**
have sunk to 3 dollars las acciones han bajado
a 3 dólares
▶ **sink in** vi (*fig*) penetrar, calar; **the news took**
a long time to ~ **in** la noticia tardó mucho en
hacer mella en él (*or* mí *etc*)
sinner ['sɪnəʳ] *n* pecador(a)
sinus ['saɪnəs] *n* (*Anat*) seno
sip [sɪp] *n* sorbo ▷ *vt* sorber, beber a sorbitos
siphon ['saɪfən] *n* sifón ▷ *vt* (*also*: **siphon off**:
funds) desviar
sir [səːʳ] *n* señor; **S~ John Smith** el Señor John
Smith; **yes** ~ sí, señor; **Dear S~** (*in letter*) Muy
señor mío, Estimado Señor; **Dear S~s** Muy
señores nuestros, Estimados Señores
siren ['saɪərn] *n* sirena
sirloin ['səːlɔɪn] *n* solomillo; ~ **steak** filete de
solomillo
sissy ['sɪsɪ] *n* (*col*) marica
sister ['sɪstəʳ] *n* hermana; (*Brit: nurse*) enfermera
jefe
sister-in-law ['sɪstərɪnlɔː] *n* cuñada
sit [sɪt] (*pt, pp* **sat**) *vi* sentarse; (*be sitting*) estar
sentado; (*assembly*) reunirse; (*dress etc*) caer,
sentar ▷ *vt* (*exam*) presentarse a; **that jacket**
~**s well** esa chaqueta sienta bien; **to** ~ **on a**
committee ser miembro de una comisión *or* un
comité
▶ **sit about, sit around** vi holgazanear
▶ **sit back** vi (*in seat*) recostarse
▶ **sit down** vi sentarse; **to be ~ting down** estar
sentado
▶ **sit in on** vt fus: **to** ~ **in on a discussion** asistir a

una discusión
▶ **sit up** vi incorporarse; (*not go to bed*) no
acostarse
sitcom ['sɪtkɔm] *n abbr* (= *situation comedy*)
telecomedia
site [saɪt] *n* sitio; (*also*: **building site**) solar ▷ *vt*
situar
sit-in ['sɪtɪn] *n* (*demonstration*) sentada
sitting ['sɪtɪŋ] *n* (*of assembly etc*) sesión; (*in canteen*)
turno
sitting room *n* sala de estar
situated ['sɪtjʊeɪtɪd] *adj* situado, ubicado (*LAm*)
situation [sɪtjuˈeɪʃən] *n* situación; **"~s vacant"**
(*Brit*) "ofertas de trabajo"
situation comedy *n* (*TV, Radio*) serie cómica,
comedia de situación
six [sɪks] *num* seis
sixteen [sɪks'tiːn] *num* dieciséis
sixth [sɪksθ] *adj* sexto; **the upper/lower** ~ (*Scol*)
el séptimo/sexto año
sixty ['sɪkstɪ] *num* sesenta
size [saɪz] *n* (*gen*) tamaño; (*extent*) extensión; (*of*
clothing) talla; (*of shoes*) número; **I take** ~ **5 shoes**
calzo el número cinco; **I take** ~ **14** mi talla es la
42; **I'd like the small/large** ~ (*of soap powder etc*)
quisiera el tamaño pequeño/grande
▶ **size up** vt formarse una idea de
sizeable ['saɪzəbl] *adj* importante, considerable
sizzle ['sɪzl] *vi* crepitar
skate [skeɪt] *n* patín; (*fish: pl inv*) raya ▷ *vi* patinar
▶ **skate over, skate round** vt fus (*problem, issue*)
pasar por alto
skateboard ['skeɪtbɔːd] *n* monopatín
skater ['skeɪtəʳ] *n* patinador(a)
skating ['skeɪtɪŋ] *n* patinaje; **figure** ~ patinaje
artístico
skating rink *n* pista de patinaje
skeleton ['skɛlɪtn] *n* esqueleto; (*Tech*) armazón;
(*outline*) esquema
skeleton staff *n* personal reducido
skeptic *etc* ['skɛptɪk] (*US*) = **sceptic** *etc*
sketch [skɛtʃ] *n* (*drawing*) dibujo; (*outline*) esbozo,
bosquejo; (*Theat*) pieza corta ▷ *vt* dibujar;
esbozar
sketch book *n* bloc de dibujo
sketchy ['skɛtʃɪ] *adj* incompleto
skewer ['skjuːəʳ] *n* broqueta
ski [skiː] *n* esquí ▷ *vi* esquiar
ski boot *n* bota de esquí
skid [skɪd] *n* patinazo ▷ *vi* patinar; **to go into a** ~
comenzar a patinar
skier ['skiːəʳ] *n* esquiador(a)
skiing ['skiːɪŋ] *n* esquí; **to go** ~ practicar el esquí,
(ir a) esquiar
ski jump *n* pista para salto de esquí
skilful, (*US*) **skillful** ['skɪlful] *adj* diestro, experto
ski lift *n* telesilla, telesquí
skill [skɪl] *n* destreza, pericia; (*technique*) arte,
técnica; **there's a certain** ~ **to doing it** se
necesita cierta habilidad para hacerlo
skilled [skɪld] *adj* hábil, diestro; (*worker*)
cualificado

skillful etc ['skɪlful] (US) = **skilful** etc

skim [skɪm] vt (milk) desnatar; (glide over) rozar, rasar ▷ vi: **to ~ through** (book) hojear

skimmed milk [skɪmd-] n leche desnatada or descremada

skimp [skɪmp] vt (work) chapucear; (cloth etc) escatimar; **to ~ on** (material etc) economizar; (work) escatimar

skimpy ['skɪmpɪ] adj (meagre) escaso; (skirt) muy corto

skin [skɪn] n (gen) piel; (complexion) cutis; (of fruit, vegetable) piel, cáscara; (crust: on pudding, paint) nata ▷ vt (fruit etc) pelar; (animal) despellejar; **wet** or **soaked to the ~** calado hasta los huesos

skin cancer n cáncer de piel

skin-deep ['skɪn'di:p] adj superficial

skin diving n buceo

skinhead ['skɪnhɛd] n cabeza rapada, skin(head)

skinny ['skɪnɪ] adj flaco, magro

skintight ['skɪntaɪt] adj (dress etc) muy ajustado

skip [skɪp] n brinco, salto; (container) contenedor ▷ vi brincar; (with rope) saltar a la comba ▷ vt (pass over) omitir, saltar

ski pants npl pantalones de esquí

ski pole n bastón de esquiar

skipper ['skɪpəʳ] n (Naut, Sport) capitán

skipping rope ['skɪpɪŋ-] n (Brit) comba, cuerda (de saltar)

skirmish ['skə:mɪʃ] n escaramuza

skirt [skə:t] n falda, pollera (And, CS) ▷ vt (surround) ceñir, rodear; (go round) ladear

skirting board ['skə:tɪŋ-] n (Brit) rodapié

ski suit n traje de esquiar

skittle ['skɪtl] n bolo; **~s** (game) boliche

skive [skaɪv] vi (Brit col) gandulear

skulk [skʌlk] vi esconderse

skull [skʌl] n calavera; (Anat) cráneo

skunk [skʌŋk] n mofeta

sky [skaɪ] n cielo; **to praise sb to the skies** poner a algn por las nubes

skydiving ['skaɪdaɪvɪŋ] n paracaidismo acrobático

sky-high ['skaɪ'haɪ] adj (col) por las nubes ▷ adv (throw) muy alto; **prices have gone ~** (col) los precios están por las nubes

skylight ['skaɪlaɪt] n tragaluz, claraboya

skyline ['skaɪlaɪn] n (horizon) horizonte; (of city) perfil

skyscraper ['skaɪskreɪpəʳ] n rascacielos

slab [slæb] n (stone) bloque; (of wood) tabla, plancha; (flat) losa; (of cake) trozo; (of meat, cheese) tajada, trozo

slack [slæk] adj (loose) flojo; (slow) de poca actividad; (careless) descuidado; (Comm: market) poco activo; (: demand) débil; (period) bajo; **business is ~** hay poco movimiento en el negocio

slacken ['slækn] (also: **slacken off**) vi aflojarse ▷ vt aflojar; (speed) disminuir

slag [slæg] n escoria, escombros

slag heap n escorial, escombrera

slain [sleɪn] pp of **slay**

slam [slæm] vt (door) cerrar de golpe; (throw) arrojar (violentamente); (criticize) vapulear, vituperar ▷ vi cerrarse de golpe

slander ['slɑ:ndəʳ] n calumnia, difamación ▷ vt calumniar, difamar

slang [slæŋ] n argot; (jargon) jerga

slanging match ['slæŋɪŋ-] n (Brit col) bronca gorda

slant [slɑ:nt] n sesgo, inclinación; (fig) punto de vista; **to get a new ~ on sth** obtener un nuevo punto de vista sobre algo

slanted ['slɑ:ntɪd], **slanting** ['slɑ:ntɪŋ] adj inclinado

slap [slæp] n palmada; (in face) bofetada ▷ vt dar una palmada/bofetada a ▷ adv (directly) de lleno

slapdash ['slæpdæʃ] adj chapucero

slapstick ['slæpstɪk] n: **~ comedy** comedia de payasadas

slap-up ['slæpʌp] adj: **a ~ meal** (Brit) un banquetazo, una comilona

slash [slæʃ] vt acuchillar; (fig: prices) quemar

slat [slæt] n (of wood, plastic) tablilla, listón

slate [sleɪt] n pizarra ▷ vt (Brit: fig: criticize) vapulear

slaughter ['slɔ:təʳ] n (of animals) matanza; (of people) carnicería ▷ vt matar

slaughterhouse ['slɔ:təhaus] n matadero

slave [sleɪv] n esclavo(-a) ▷ vi (also: **slave away**) trabajar como un negro; **to ~ (away) at sth** trabajar como un negro en algo

slave driver n (col, pej) tirano(-a)

slavery ['sleɪvərɪ] n esclavitud

slavish ['sleɪvɪʃ] adj (devotion) de esclavo; (imitation) servil

slay [sleɪ] (pt **slew**, pp **slain**) vt (literary) matar

sleazy ['sli:zɪ] adj (fig: place) sórdido

sledge [slɛdʒ], (US) **sled** [slɛd] n trineo

sledgehammer ['slɛdʒhæməʳ] n mazo

sleek [sli:k] adj (shiny) lustroso

sleep [sli:p] n sueño ▷ vi dormir ▷ vb (pt, pp **slept**) ▷ vt: **we can ~ 4** podemos alojar a 4, tenemos cabida para 4; **to go to ~** dormirse; **to have a good night's ~** dormir toda la noche; **to put to ~** (patient) dormir; (animal: euphemism: kill) sacrificar; **to ~ lightly** tener el sueño ligero; **to ~ with sb** (euphemism) acostarse con algn
   ▶ **sleep in** vi (oversleep) quedarse dormido

sleeper ['sli:pəʳ] n (person) durmiente; (Brit Rail: on track) traviesa; (: train) coche-cama

sleeping bag ['sli:pɪŋ-] n saco de dormir

sleeping car n coche-cama

sleeping partner n (Comm) socio(-a) comanditario(-a)

sleeping pill n somnífero

sleepless ['sli:plɪs] adj: **a ~ night** una noche en blanco

sleepover ['sli:pəuvəʳ] n: **we're having a ~ at Jo's** nos vamos a quedar a dormir en casa de Jo

sleepwalk ['sli:pwɔ:k] vi caminar dormido; (habitually) ser sonámbulo

sleepwalker ['sli:pwɔ:kəʳ] n sonámbulo(-a)

sleepy ['sli:pɪ] adj soñoliento; **to be** or **feel ~**

tener sueño
sleet [sli:t] n aguanieve
sleeve [sli:v] n manga; (Tech) manguito; (of record) funda
sleigh [sleɪ] n trineo
sleight [slaɪt] n: ~ **of hand** prestidigitación
slender ['slɛndə'] adj delgado; (means) escaso
slept [slɛpt] pt, pp of **sleep**
slew [slu:] vi (veer) torcerse ▷ pt of **slay**
slice [slaɪs] n (of meat) tajada; (of bread) rebanada; (of lemon) rodaja; (utensil) paleta ▷ vt cortar, tajar; rebanar; **~d bread** pan de molde
slick [slɪk] adj (skilful) hábil, diestro ▷ n (also: **oil slick**) capa de aceite
slid [slɪd] pt, pp of **slide**
slide [slaɪd] n (in playground) tobogán; (Phot) diapositiva; (microscope slide) portaobjetos, plaquilla de vidrio; (Brit: also: **hair slide**) pasador ▷ vb (pt, pp **slid**) ▷ vt correr, deslizar ▷ vi (slip) resbalarse; (glide) deslizarse; **to let things ~** (fig) dejar que ruede la bola
sliding ['slaɪdɪŋ] adj (door) corredizo; **~ roof** (Aut) techo de corredera
sliding scale n escala móvil
slight [slaɪt] adj (slim) delgado; (frail) delicado; (pain etc) leve; (trifling) insignificante; (small) pequeño ▷ n desaire ▷ vt (offend) ofender, desairar; **a ~ improvement** una ligera mejora; **not in the ~est** en absoluto; **there's not the ~est possibility** no hay la menor or más mínima posibilidad
slightly ['slaɪtlɪ] adv ligeramente, un poco; **~ built** delgado
slim [slɪm] adj delgado, esbelto ▷ vi adelgazar
slime [slaɪm] n limo, cieno
slimming ['slɪmɪŋ] n adelgazamiento ▷ adj (diet, pills) adelgazante
slimy ['slaɪmɪ] adj limoso; (covered with mud) fangoso; (also fig: person) adulón, zalamero
sling [slɪŋ] n (Med) cabestrillo; (weapon) honda ▷ vt (pt, pp **slung**) tirar, arrojar; **to have one's arm in a ~** llevar el brazo en cabestrillo
slip [slɪp] n (slide) resbalón; (mistake) descuido; (underskirt) combinación; (of paper) papelito ▷ vt (slide) deslizar ▷ vi (slide) deslizarse; (stumble) resbalar; (decline) decaer; (move smoothly): **to ~ into/out of** (room etc) colarse en/salirse de; **to let a chance ~ by** dejar escapar la oportunidad; **to ~ sth on/off** ponerse/quitarse algo; **to ~ on a jumper** ponerse un jersey or un suéter; **it ~ped from her hand** se la cayó de la mano; **he ~ped on the ice** resbaló en el hielo; **to give sb the ~** dar esquinazo a algn; **wages ~** (Brit) hoja del sueldo; **a ~ of the tongue** un lapsus
▸ **slip away** vi escabullirse
▸ **slip in** vt meter ▷ vi meterse, colarse
▸ **slip out** vi (go out) salir (un momento)
▸ **slip up** vi (make a mistake) equivocarse
slipped disc [slɪpt-] n vértebra dislocada
slipper ['slɪpə'] n zapatilla, pantufla
slippery ['slɪpərɪ] adj resbaladizo
slip road n (Brit) carretera de acceso

slipshod ['slɪpʃɔd] adj descuidado, chapucero
slip-up ['slɪpʌp] n (error) desliz
slipway ['slɪpweɪ] n grada, gradas
slit [slɪt] n raja; (cut) corte ▷ vt (pt, pp **-**) rajar, cortar; **to ~ sb's throat** cortarle el pescuezo a algn
slither ['slɪðə'] vi deslizarse
sliver ['slɪvə'] n (of glass, wood) astilla; (of cheese, sausage) lonja, loncha
slob [slɔb] n (col) patán(-ana), palurdo(-a)
slog [slɔg] (Brit) vi sudar tinta ▷ n: **it was a ~** costó trabajo (hacerlo)
slogan ['sləugən] n eslogan, lema
slop [slɔp] vi (also: **slop over**) derramarse, desbordarse ▷ vt derramar, verter
slope [sləup] n (up) cuesta, pendiente; (down) declive; (side of mountain) falda, vertiente ▷ vi: **to ~ down** estar en declive; **to ~ up** subir (en pendiente)
sloping ['sləupɪŋ] adj en pendiente; en declive
sloppy ['slɔpɪ] adj (work) descuidado; (appearance) desaliñado
slot [slɔt] n ranura; (fig: in timetable) hueco; (Radio, TV) espacio ▷ vt: **to ~ into** encajar en
sloth [sləuθ] n (vice) pereza; (Zool) oso perezoso
slot machine n (Brit: vending machine) máquina expendedora; (for gambling) máquina tragaperras
slouch [slautʃ] vi: **to ~ about, ~ around** (laze) gandulear
Slovak ['sləuvæk] adj eslovaco ▷ n eslovaco(-a); (Ling) eslovaco; **the ~ Republic** Eslovaquia
Slovakia [sləu'vækɪə] n Eslovaquia
Slovakian [sləu'vækɪən] adj, n = **Slovak**
Slovene [sləu'vi:n] adj esloveno ▷ n esloveno(-a); (Ling) esloveno
Slovenia [sləu'vi:nɪə] n Eslovenia
slovenly ['slʌvənlɪ] adj (dirty) desaliñado, desaseado; (careless) descuidado
slow [sləu] adj lento; (watch): **to be ~** estar atrasado ▷ adv lentamente, despacio ▷ vt (also: **slow down, slow up**) retardar; (engine, machine) reducir la marcha de ▷ vi (also: **slow down, slow up**) ir más despacio; **"~"** (road sign) "disminuir la velocidad"; **at a ~ speed** a una velocidad lenta; **the ~ lane** el carril derecho; **business is ~** (Comm) hay poca actividad; **my watch is 20 minutes ~** mi reloj lleva 20 minutos de retraso; **he's a bit ~** (unintelligent) es un poco lento; **bake for 2 hours in a ~ oven** cocer or asar 2 horas en el horno a fuego lento; **to be ~ to act/decide** tardar en obrar/decidir; **to go ~** (driver) conducir despacio; (in industrial dispute) trabajar a ritmo lento
slowly ['sləulɪ] adv lentamente, despacio; **to drive ~** conducir despacio; **~ but surely** lento pero seguro
slow motion n: **in ~** a cámara lenta
sludge [slʌdʒ] n lodo, fango
slug [slʌg] n babosa; (bullet) posta
sluggish ['slʌgɪʃ] adj (slow) lento; (lazy) perezoso; (business, market, sales) inactivo
sluice [slu:s] n (gate) esclusa; (channel) canal ▷ vt:

to ~ down or **out** regar

slum [slʌm] n (area) barrios bajos; (house) casucha

slump [slʌmp] n (economic) depresión ▷ vi hundirse; **the ~ in the price of copper** la baja repentina del precio del cobre; **he was ~ed over the wheel** se había desplomado encima del volante

slung [slʌŋ] pt, pp of **sling**

slur [sləːʳ] n calumnia ▷ vt calumniar, difamar; (word) pronunciar mal; **to cast a ~ on sb** manchar la reputación de algn, difamar a algn

slurp [sləːp] vt, vi sorber ruidosamente

slurred [sləːd] adj (pronunciation) poco claro

slush [slʌʃ] n nieve a medio derretir

slush fund n fondos para sobornar

slut [slʌt] n marrana

sly [slaɪ] adj (clever) astuto; (nasty) malicioso

smack [smæk] n (slap) manotada; (blow) golpe ▷ vt dar una manotada a; golpear con la mano ▷ vi: **to ~ of** saber a, oler a ▷ adv: **it fell ~ in the middle** (col) cayó justo en medio

small [smɔːl] adj pequeño, chico (LAm); (in height) bajo, chaparro (LAm); (letter) en minúscula ▷ n: **~ of the back** región lumbar; **~ shopkeeper** pequeño(-a) comerciante; **to get** or **grow ~er** (stain, town) empequeñecer; (debt, organization, numbers) reducir, disminuir; **to make ~er** (amount, income) reducir; (garden, object, garment) achicar

small ads npl (Brit) anuncios por palabras

small business n pequeño negocio; **~es** la pequeña empresa

small change n suelto, cambio

smallholder ['smɔːlhəuldəʳ] n (Brit) granjero(-a), parcelero(-a)

small hours npl: **in the ~** a altas horas de la noche

smallpox ['smɔːlpɔks] n viruela

small talk n cháchara

smarmy ['smɑːmɪ] adj (Brit pej) pelotillero (fam)

smart [smɑːt] adj elegante; (clever) listo, inteligente; (quick) rápido, vivo; (weapon) inteligente ▷ vi escocer, picar; **the ~ set** la gente de buen tono; **to look ~** estar elegante; **my eyes are ~ing** me pican los ojos

smartcard ['smɑːtkɑːd] n tarjeta inteligente

smash [smæʃ] n (also: **smash-up**) choque; (sound) estrépito ▷ vt (break) hacer pedazos; (car etc) estrellar; (Sport: record) batir ▷ vi hacerse pedazos; (against wall etc) estrellarse

▶ **smash up** vt (car) hacer pedazos; (room) destrozar

smashing ['smæʃɪŋ] adj (col) cojonudo

smattering ['smætərɪŋ] n: **a ~ of Spanish** algo de español

smear [smɪəʳ] n mancha; (Med) frotis (cervical); (insult) calumnia ▷ vt untar; (fig) calumniar, difamar; **his hands were ~ed with oil/ink** tenía las manos manchadas de aceite/tinta

smear campaign n campaña de calumnias

smell [smɛl] n olor; (sense) olfato ▷ vb (pt, pp **smelt** or **-ed**) ▷ vt, vi oler; **it ~s good/of garlic** huele bien/a ajo

smelly ['smɛlɪ] adj maloliente

smile [smaɪl] n sonrisa ▷ vi sonreír

smirk [sməːk] n sonrisa falsa or afectada

smock [smɔk] n blusón; (children's) babi; (US: overall) guardapolvo, bata

smog [smɔg] n smog

smoke [sməuk] n humo ▷ vi fumar; (chimney) echar humo ▷ vt (cigarettes) fumar; **to go up in ~** (house etc) quemarse; (fig) quedar en agua de borrajas; **do you ~?** ¿fumas?

smoked [sməukt] adj (bacon, glass) ahumado

smokeless fuel ['sməuklɪs-] n combustible sin humo

smoker ['sməukəʳ] n (person) fumador(a); (Rail) coche de fumadores

smoke screen n cortina de humo

smoking ['sməukɪŋ] n: **"no ~"** "prohibido fumar"; **he's given up ~** ha dejado de fumar

smoky ['sməukɪ] adj (room) lleno de humo

smolder ['sməuldəʳ] vi (US) = **smoulder**

smooth [smuːð] adj liso; (sea) tranquilo; (flavour, movement) suave; (person: pej) meloso ▷ vt alisar; (also: **smooth out**: creases) alisar; (difficulties) allanar

▶ **smooth over** vt: **to ~ things over** (fig) limar las asperezas

smother ['smʌðəʳ] vt sofocar; (repress) contener

smoulder, (US) **smolder** ['sməuldəʳ] vi arder sin llama

SMS n abbr (= short message service) (servicio) SMS

SMS message n (mensaje) SMS

smudge [smʌdʒ] n mancha ▷ vt manchar

smug [smʌg] adj engreído

smuggle ['smʌgl] vt pasar de contrabando; **to ~ in/out** (goods etc) meter/sacar de contrabando

smuggler ['smʌgləʳ] n contrabandista

smuggling ['smʌglɪŋ] n contrabando

smutty ['smʌtɪ] adj (fig) verde, obsceno

snack [snæk] n bocado, tentempié; **to have a ~** tomar un bocado

snack bar n cafetería

snag [snæg] n problema; **to run into** or **hit a ~** encontrar inconvenientes, dar con un obstáculo

snail [sneɪl] n caracol

snake [sneɪk] n (gen) serpiente; (harmless) culebra; (poisonous) víbora

snap [snæp] n (sound) chasquido; golpe seco; (photograph) foto ▷ adj (decision) instantáneo ▷ vt (fingers etc) castañetear; (break) partir, quebrar; (photograph) tomar una foto de ▷ vi (break) partirse, quebrarse; (fig: person) contestar bruscamente; **to ~ (at sb)** (person) hablar con brusquedad (a algn); (dog) intentar morder (a algn); **to ~ shut** cerrarse de golpe; **to ~ one's fingers at sth/sb** (fig) burlarse de algo/uno; **a cold ~** (of weather) una ola de frío

▶ **snap off** vi (break) partirse

▶ **snap up** vt agarrar

snappy ['snæpɪ] adj (col: answer) instantáneo; (slogan) conciso; **make it ~!** (hurry up) ¡date prisa!

snapshot ['snæpʃɔt] n foto (instantánea)

snare [snɛər] n trampa ▷ vt cazar con trampa; (fig) engañar

snarl [snɑːl] n gruñido ▷ vi gruñir; **to get ~ed up** (wool, plans) enmarañarse, enredarse; (traffic) quedar atascado

snatch [snætʃ] n (fig) robo; **~es of** trocitos de ▷ vt (snatch away) arrebatar; (grasp) coger (Esp), agarrar; **~es of conversation** fragmentos de conversación; **to ~ a sandwich** comer un bocadillo a prisa; **to ~ some sleep** buscar tiempo para dormir; **don't ~!** ¡no me lo quites!
▸ **snatch up** vt agarrar

snazzy ['snæzɪ] adj (col) guapo

sneak [sniːk] vi: **to ~ in/out** entrar/salir a hurtadillas ▷ vt: **to ~ a look at sth** mirar algo de reojo ▷ n (fam) soplón(-ona)

sneakers ['sniːkəz] npl (US) zapatos de lona, zapatillas

sneer [snɪər] n sonrisa de desprecio ▷ vi sonreír con desprecio; **to ~ at sth/sb** burlarse or mofarse de algo/uno

sneeze [sniːz] n estornudo ▷ vi estornudar

sniff [snɪf] vi sorber (por la nariz) ▷ vt husmear, oler; (glue, drug) esnifar
▸ **sniff at** vt fus: **it's not to be ~ed at** no es de despreciar

sniffer dog ['snɪfə-] n (for drugs) perro antidroga; (for explosives) perro antiexplosivos

snigger ['snɪgər] n risa disimulada ▷ vi reírse con disimulo

snip [snɪp] n (piece) recorte; (bargain) ganga ▷ vt tijeretear

sniper ['snaɪpər] n francotirador(a)

snippet ['snɪpɪt] n retazo

snivelling, (US) **sniveling** ['snɪvlɪŋ] adj llorón(-ona)

snob [snɒb] n (e)snob

snobbery ['snɒbərɪ] n (e)snobismo

snobbish ['snɒbɪʃ] adj (e)snob

snog [snɒg] vi (Brit col) besuquearse, morrear; **to ~ sb** besuquear a algn

snooker ['snuːkər] n snooker

snoop [snuːp] vi: **to ~ about** fisgonear

snooty ['snuːtɪ] adj (e)snob

snooze [snuːz] n siesta ▷ vi echar una siesta

snore [snɔːr] vi roncar ▷ n ronquido

snorkel ['snɔːkl] n tubo de respiración

snort [snɔːt] n bufido ▷ vi bufar ▷ vt (col: drugs) esnifar

snout [snaʊt] n hocico, morro

snow [snəʊ] n nieve ▷ vi nevar ▷ vt: **to be ~ed under with work** estar agobiado de trabajo

snowball ['snəʊbɔːl] n bola de nieve ▷ vi ir aumentándose

snowbound ['snəʊbaʊnd] adj bloqueado por la nieve

snowdrift ['snəʊdrɪft] n ventisquero

snowdrop ['snəʊdrɒp] n campanilla

snowfall ['snəʊfɔːl] n nevada

snowflake ['snəʊfleɪk] n copo de nieve

snowman ['snəʊmæn] n figura de nieve

snowplough, (US) **snowplow** ['snəʊplaʊ] n quitanieves

snowshoe ['snəʊʃuː] n raqueta (de nieve)

snowstorm ['snəʊstɔːm] n tormenta de nieve, nevasca

snowy ['snəʊɪ] adj de (mucha) nieve

SNP n abbr (Brit Pol) = **Scottish National Party**

snub [snʌb] vt: **to ~ sb** desairar a algn ▷ n desaire, repulsa

snub-nosed [snʌb'nəʊzd] adj chato

snuff [snʌf] n rapé ▷ vt (also: **snuff out**: candle) apagar

snug [snʌg] adj (cosy) cómodo; (fitted) ajustado

snuggle ['snʌgl] vi: **to ~ down in bed** hacerse un ovillo or acurrucarse en la cama; **to ~ up to sb** acurrucarse junto a algn

so [səʊ] adv **1** (thus, likewise) así, de este modo; **if so** de ser así; **that's not so** no es así; **I like swimming — so do I** a mí me gusta nadar — a mí también; **I've got work to do — so has Paul** tengo trabajo que hacer — Paul también; **it's 5 o'clock — so it is!** son las 5 — ¡pues es verdad!; **I hope/think so** espero/creo que sí; **so far** hasta ahora; (in past) hasta este momento; **so to speak** por decirlo así

2 (in comparisons etc: to such a degree) tan; **so quickly (that)** tan rápido (que); **so big (that)** tan grande (que); **she's not so clever as her brother** no es tan lista como su hermano; **it was so heavy!** ¡pesaba tanto!; **we were so worried** estábamos preocupadísimos

3: **so much** adj tanto(-a)
▷ adv tanto; **I love you so much** te quiero tanto; **she's got so much energy** tiene tanta energía; **so many** tantos(-as)

4 (phrases): **10 or so** unos 10, 10 o así; **so long!** (col: goodbye) ¡hasta luego!; **she didn't so much as send me a birthday card** no me mandó ni una tarjeta siquiera por mi cumpleaños; **so (what?)** (col) ¿y qué?
▷ conj **1** (expressing purpose): **so as to do** para hacer; **so (that)** para que; **we hurried so (that) we wouldn't be late** nos dimos prisa para no llegar tarde

2 (expressing result) así que; **the shop was closed, so I went home** la tienda estaba cerrada, así que me fui a casa; **so you see, I could have gone** así que ya ves, (yo) podría haber ido; **so that's the reason!** ¡así que es por eso or por eso es!; **so, have you always lived in London?** así que, ¿siempre has vivido en Londres?

soak [səʊk] vt (drench) empapar; (put in water) remojar ▷ vi remojarse, estar a remojo
▸ **soak in** vi penetrar
▸ **soak up** vt absorber

so-and-so ['səʊənsəʊ] n (somebody) fulano(-a) de tal

soap [səʊp] n jabón

soapbox ['səʊpbɒks] n tribuna improvisada

soapflakes ['səʊpfleɪks] npl jabón en escamas

soap opera n (TV) telenovela; (Radio) radionovela

soap powder n jabón en polvo

soapy ['səupɪ] *adj* jabonoso

soar [sɔːʳ] *vi* (*on wings*) remontarse; (*building etc*) elevarse; (*price*) subir vertiginosamente; (*morale*) elevarse

sob [sɔb] *n* sollozo ▷ *vi* sollozar

sober ['səubəʳ] *adj* (*moderate*) moderado; (*serious*) serio; (*not drunk*) sobrio; (*colour, style*) discreto
  ▶ **sober up** *vi* pasársele a algn la borrachera

sob story *n* (*col, pej*) dramón

so-called ['səu'kɔːld] *adj* presunto, supuesto

soccer ['sɔkəʳ] *n* fútbol

sociable ['səuʃəbl] *adj* sociable

social ['səuʃl] *adj* social ▷ *n* velada, fiesta

social club *n* club

socialism ['səuʃəlɪzəm] *n* socialismo

socialist ['səuʃəlɪst] *adj, n* socialista

socialize ['səuʃəlaɪz] *vi* hacer vida social; **to ~ with** (*colleagues*) salir con

social life *n* vida social

social science(s) *n*(*pl*) ciencias sociales

social security *n* seguridad social

social services *npl* servicios sociales

social work *n* asistencia social

social worker *n* asistente(-a) social

society [sə'saɪətɪ] *n* sociedad; (*club*) asociación; (*also:* **high society**) buena sociedad ▷ *cpd* (*party, column*) social, de sociedad

sociologist [səusɪ'ɔlədʒɪst] *n* sociólogo(-a)

sociology [səusɪ'ɔlədʒɪ] *n* sociología

sock [sɔk] *n* calcetín, media (*LAm*); **to pull one's ~s up** (*fig*) hacer esfuerzos, despabilarse

socket ['sɔkɪt] *n* (*Elec*) enchufe

sod [sɔd] *n* (*of earth*) césped; (*col!*) cabrón(-ona) (*!*) ▷ *excl*: **~ off!** (*col!*) ¡vete a la porra!

soda ['səudə] *n* (*Chem*) sosa; (*also:* **soda water**) soda; (*US: also:* **soda pop**) gaseosa

sodden ['sɔdn] *adj* empapado

sodium ['səudɪəm] *n* sodio

sodium chloride *n* cloruro sódico *or* de sodio

sofa ['səufə] *n* sofá

soft [sɔft] *adj* (*teacher, parent*) blando; (*gentle, not loud*) suave; (*stupid*) bobo

soft drink *n* bebida no alcohólica

soften ['sɔfn] *vt* ablandar; suavizar ▷ *vi* ablandarse; suavizarse

softener ['sɔfnəʳ] *n* suavizante

softly ['sɔftlɪ] *adv* suavemente; (*gently*) delicadamente, con delicadeza

softness ['sɔftnɪs] *n* blandura; suavidad

software ['sɔftwɛəʳ] *n* (*Comput*) software

soggy ['sɔgɪ] *adj* empapado

soil [sɔɪl] *n* (*earth*) tierra, suelo ▷ *vt* ensuciar

solace ['sɔlɪs] *n* consuelo

solar ['səuləʳ] *adj* solar

solarium [sə'lɛərɪəm] (*pl* **solaria**) *n* solario

solar panel *n* panel solar

solar power *n* energía solar

solar system *n* sistema solar

sold [səuld] *pt, pp* of **sell**

solder ['səuldəʳ] *vt* soldar ▷ *n* soldadura

soldier ['səuldʒəʳ] *n* (*gen*) soldado; (*army man*) militar ▷ *vi*: **to ~ on** seguir adelante; **toy ~**

soldadito de plomo

sold out *adj* (*Comm*) agotado

sole [səul] *n* (*of foot*) planta; (*of shoe*) suela; (*fish: pl inv*) lenguado ▷ *adj* único; **the ~ reason** la única razón

solemn ['sɔləm] *adj* solemne

sole trader *n* (*Comm*) comerciante exclusivo(-a)

solicit [sə'lɪsɪt] *vt* (*request*) solicitar ▷ *vi* (*prostitute*) abordar clientes

solicitor [sə'lɪsɪtəʳ] *n* abogado(-a); *see also* **barrister**

solid ['sɔlɪd] *adj* sólido; (*gold etc*) macizo; (*line*) continuo; (*vote*) unánime ▷ *n* sólido; **we waited 2 ~ hours** esperamos 2 horas enteras; **to be on ~ ground** estar en tierra firme; (*fig*) estar seguro

solidarity [sɔlɪ'dærɪtɪ] *n* solidaridad

solid fuel *n* combustible sólido

solitaire [sɔlɪ'tɛəʳ] *n* (*game, gem*) solitario

solitary ['sɔlɪtərɪ] *adj* solitario, solo; (*isolated*) apartado, aislado; (*only*) único

solitary confinement *n* incomunicación; **to be in ~** estar incomunicado

solitude ['sɔlɪtjuːd] *n* soledad

solo ['səuləu] *n* solo

soloist ['səuləuɪst] *n* solista

solstice ['sɔlstɪs] *n* solsticio

soluble ['sɔljubl] *adj* soluble

solution [sə'luːʃən] *n* solución

solve [sɔlv] *vt* resolver, solucionar

solvency ['sɔlvənsɪ] *n* (*Comm*) solvencia

solvent ['sɔlvənt] *adj* (*Comm*) solvente ▷ *n* (*Chem*) solvente

solvent abuse *n* uso indebido de disolventes

Somaliland [sə'mɑːlɪlænd] *n* Somaliland

sombre, (*US*) **somber** ['sɔmbəʳ] *adj* sombrío

some [sʌm] *adj* **1** (*a certain amount or number of*): **~ tea/water/biscuits** té/agua/(unas) galletas; **have ~ tea** tómese un té; **there's ~ milk in the fridge** hay leche en el frigo; **there were ~ people outside** había algunas personas fuera; **I've got ~ money, but not much** tengo algo de dinero, pero no mucho
  2 (*certain: in contrasts*) algunos(-as); **~ people say that …** hay quien dice que …; **~ films were excellent, but most were mediocre** hubo películas excelentes, pero la mayoría fueron mediocres
  3 (*unspecified*): **~ woman was asking for you** una mujer estuvo preguntando por ti; **~ day** algún día; **~ day next week** un día de la semana que viene; **he was asking for ~ book (or other)** pedía no sé qué libro; **in ~ way or other** de alguna que otra manera
  4 (*considerable amount of*) bastante; **~ days ago** hace unos cuantos días; **after ~ time** pasado algún tiempo; **at ~ length** con mucho detalle
  5 (*col: intensive*): **that was ~ party!** ¡menuda fiesta!
  ▷ *pron* **1** (*a certain number*): **I've got ~** (*books etc*) tengo algunos(-as)
  2 (*a certain amount*) algo; **I've got ~** (*money, milk*) tengo algo; **would you like ~?** (*coffee etc*) ¿quiere

un poco?; (books etc) ¿quiere alguno?; **could I have ~ of that cheese?** ¿me puede dar un poco de ese queso?; **I've read ~ of the book** he leído parte del libro
▷ adv: **~ 10 people** unas 10 personas, una decena de personas

somebody ['sʌmbədɪ] pron alguien; **~ or other** alguien

someday ['sʌmdeɪ] adv algún día

somehow ['sʌmhau] adv de alguna manera; (for some reason) por una u otra razón

someone ['sʌmwʌn] pron = **somebody**

someplace ['sʌmpleɪs] adv (US) = **somewhere**

somersault ['sʌməsɔːlt] n (deliberate) salto mortal; (accidental) vuelco ▷ vi dar un salto mortal; dar vuelcos

something ['sʌmθɪŋ] pron algo ▷ adv: **he's ~ like me** es un poco como yo; **it cost £100, or ~ like that** costó 100 libras, o algo así; **~ to do** algo que hacer; **wear ~ warm** ponte algo que abrigue; **his name is Peter or ~** se llama Peter o algo por el estilo; **it's ~ of a problem** es bastante problemático

sometime ['sʌmtaɪm] adv (in future) algún día, en algún momento; **~ last month** durante el mes pasado; **I'll finish it ~** lo terminaré un día de éstos

sometimes ['sʌmtaɪmz] adv a veces

somewhat ['sʌmwɔt] adv algo

somewhere ['sʌmwɛəʳ] adv (be) en alguna parte; (go) a alguna parte; **~ else** (be) en otra parte; (go) a otra parte

son [sʌn] n hijo

sonar ['səunɑːʳ] n sonar

song [sɔŋ] n canción

songwriter ['sɔŋraɪtəʳ] n compositor(a) de canciones

sonic ['sɔnɪk] adj (boom) sónico

son-in-law ['sʌnɪnlɔː] n yerno

sonnet ['sɔnɪt] n soneto

sonny ['sʌnɪ] n (col) hijo

soon [suːn] adv pronto, dentro de poco; **~ afterwards** poco después; **very/quite ~** muy/bastante pronto; **how ~ can you be ready?** ¿cuánto tardas en prepararte?; **it's too ~ to tell** es demasiado pronto para saber; **see you ~!** ¡hasta pronto!; see also **as**

sooner ['suːnəʳ] adv (time) antes, más temprano; **I would ~ do that** preferiría hacer eso; **~ or later** tarde o temprano; **no ~ said than done** dicho y hecho; **the ~ the better** cuanto antes mejor; **no ~ had we left than ...** apenas nos habíamos marchado cuando ...

soot [sut] n hollín

soothe [suːð] vt tranquilizar; (pain) aliviar

sophisticated [sə'fɪstɪkeɪtɪd] adj sofisticado

sophomore ['sɔfəmɔːʳ] n (US) estudiante de segundo año

sopping ['sɔpɪŋ] adj: **~ (wet)** empapado

soppy ['sɔpɪ] adj (pej) bobo, tonto

soprano [sə'prɑːnəu] n soprano

sorbet ['sɔːbeɪ] n sorbete

sorcerer ['sɔːsərəʳ] n hechicero

sordid ['sɔːdɪd] adj (place etc) sórdido; (motive etc) mezquino

sore [sɔːʳ] adj (painful) doloroso, que duele; (offended) resentido ▷ n llaga; **~ throat** dolor de garganta; **my eyes are ~, I have ~ eyes** me duelen los ojos; **it's a ~ point** es un asunto delicado or espinoso

sorely adv: **I am ~ tempted to (do it)** estoy muy tentado a (hacerlo)

sorrow ['sɔrəu] n pena, dolor

sorry ['sɔrɪ] adj (regretful) arrepentido; (condition, excuse) lastimoso; (sight, failure) triste; **~!** ¡perdón!, ¡perdone!; **~?** ¿cómo?; **I'm (very) ~** lo siento (mucho); **I'm ~ I'm late** siento llegar tarde; **to be ~ about sth** lamentar algo; **I'm ~ about the noise** perdón por el ruido; **I feel ~ for him** me da lástima or pena; **I'm ~ to hear that ...** siento saber que ...; **you'll be ~!** ¡te arrepentirás!

sort [sɔːt] n clase, género, tipo; (make: of coffee, car etc) marca ▷ vt (also: **sort out**: papers) clasificar; (: problems) arreglar, solucionar; (Comput) clasificar; **what ~ do you want?** (make) ¿qué marca quieres?; **what ~ of car?** ¿qué tipo de coche?; **all ~s of ...** todo tipo de ...; **I shall do nothing of the ~** no pienso hacer nada parecido; **it's ~ of awkward** (col) es bastante difícil; **~ out all your books** ordena todos tus libros

sorting office ['sɔːtɪŋ-] n oficina de clasificación del correo

SOS n SOS

so-so ['səusəu] adv regular, así así

soufflé ['suːfleɪ] n suflé

sought [sɔːt] pt, pp of **seek**

soul [səul] n alma; **God rest his ~** Dios le reciba en su seno or en su gloria; **I didn't see a ~** no vi a nadie; **the poor ~ had nowhere to sleep** el pobre no tenía dónde dormir

soulful ['səulful] adj lleno de sentimiento

sound [saund] adj (healthy) sano; (safe, not damaged) en buen estado; (valid: argument, policy, claim) válido; (: move) acertado; (dependable: person) de fiar; (sensible) sensato, razonable ▷ adv: **~ asleep** profundamente dormido ▷ n (noise) sonido, ruido; (Geo) estrecho ▷ vt (alarm) sonar; (also: **sound out**: opinions) consultar, sondear ▷ vi sonar, resonar; (fig: seem) parecer; **to be of ~ mind** estar en su sano juicio; **he gave me some ~ advice** me dio un buen consejo; **don't make a ~!** ¡no hagas ruido!; **the ~ of footsteps** el ruido de pasos; **at the speed of ~** a la velocidad del sonido; **can I turn the ~ down?** ¿puedo bajar el volumen?; **I don't like the ~ of it** no me gusta nada; **that ~s interesting** eso suena interesante; **it ~s like French** suena a francés; **that ~s like a good idea** eso me parece buena idea; **it ~s as if ...** parece que ...
▷ **sound off** vi (col): **to ~ off (about)** (give one's opinions) despotricar (contra)

sound barrier n barrera del sonido

sound bite n cita jugosa

sound effects npl efectos sonoros

soundly ['saundlɪ] *adv* (*sleep*) profundamente; (*beat*) completamente
soundproof ['saundpru:f] *adj* insonorizado
sound system *n* equipo de sonido
soundtrack ['saundtræk] *n* (*of film*) banda sonora
soup [su:p] *n* (*thick*) sopa; (*thin*) caldo; **in the ~** (*fig*) en apuros
soup plate *n* plato sopero
soupspoon ['su:pspu:n] *n* cuchara sopera
sour ['sauə'] *adj* agrio; (*milk*) cortado; **it's just ~ grapes!** (*fig*) ¡pura envidia!, ¡están verdes!; **to go** *or* **turn ~** (*milk*) cortarse; (*wine*) agriarse; (*fig: relationship*) agriarse; (: *plans*) irse a pique
source [sɔ:s] *n* fuente; **I have it from a reliable ~ that** ... sé de fuente fidedigna que ....
south [sauθ] *n* sur ▷ *adj* del sur ▷ *adv* al sur, hacia el sur; **(to the) ~ of** al sur de; **the S~ of France** el Sur de Francia; **to travel ~** viajar hacia el sur
South Africa *n* Sudáfrica
South African *adj, n* sudafricano(-a)
South America *n* América del Sur, Sudamérica
South American *adj, n* sudamericano(-a)
south-east [sauθ'i:st] *n* sudeste ▷ *adj* (*counties etc*) (del) sudeste
southerly ['sʌðəlɪ] *adj* sur; (*from the south*) del sur
southern ['sʌðən] *adj* del sur, meridional; **the ~ hemisphere** el hemisferio sur
South Pole *n* Polo Sur
South Vietnam *n* Vietnam del Sur
southward(s) ['sauθwəd(z)] *adv* hacia el sur
south-west [sauθ'wɛst] *n* suroeste
souvenir [su:və'nɪə'] *n* recuerdo
sovereign ['sɔvrɪn] *adj, n* soberano(-a)
soviet ['səuvɪət] *adj* soviético
sow [sau] *n* cerda, puerca ▷ *vt* [səu] (*pt* -**ed**, *pp* -**n**) [səun] (*gen*) sembrar; (*spread*) esparcir
soya ['sɔɪə], (*US*) **soy** [sɔɪ] *n* soja
soy(a) bean *n* semilla de soja
soy(a) sauce *n* salsa de soja
sozzled ['sɔzld] *adj* (*Brit col*) mamado
spa [spa:] *n* balneario
space [speɪs] *n* espacio; (*room*) sitio ▷ *vt* (*also*: **space out**) espaciar; **to clear a ~ for sth** hacer sitio para algo; **in a confined ~** en un espacio restringido; **in a short ~ of time** en poco *or* un corto espacio de tiempo; **(with)in the ~ of an hour/three generations** en el espacio de una hora/tres generaciones
spacecraft ['speɪskra:ft] *n* nave espacial, astronave
spaceman ['speɪsmæn] *n* astronauta, cosmonauta
spaceship ['speɪsʃɪp] *n* = **spacecraft**
spacesuit ['speɪssu:t] *n* traje espacial
spacewoman ['speɪswumən] *n* astronauta, cosmonauta
spacing ['speɪsɪŋ] *n* espacio
spacious ['speɪʃəs] *adj* amplio
spade [speɪd] *n* (*tool*) pala; **spades** *npl* (*Cards: British*) picas; (*Spanish*) espadas
spaghetti [spə'gɛtɪ] *n* espaguetis

Spain [speɪn] *n* España
spam [spæm] *n* (*junk e-mail*) correa basura, spam
span [spæn] *n* (*of bird, plane*) envergadura; (*of hand*) palmo; (*of arch*) luz; (*in time*) lapso ▷ *vt* extenderse sobre, cruzar; (*fig*) abarcar
Spaniard ['spænjəd] *n* español(a)
spaniel ['spænjəl] *n* perro de aguas
Spanish ['spænɪʃ] *adj* español(a) ▷ *n* (*Ling*) español, castellano; **the Spanish** *npl* (*people*) los españoles; **~ omelette** tortilla española *or* de patata
spank [spæŋk] *vt* zurrar, dar unos azotes a
spanner ['spænə'] *n* (*Brit*) llave inglesa
spar [spa:'] *n* palo, verga ▷ *vi* (*Boxing*) entrenarse (en el boxeo)
spare [spɛə'] *adj* de reserva; (*surplus*) sobrante, de más ▷ *n* (*part*) pieza de repuesto ▷ *vt* (*do without*) pasarse sin; (*afford to give*) tener de sobra; (*refrain from hurting*) perdonar; (*details etc*) ahorrar; **have you got a ~ pencil?** ¿tienes un lápiz de sobra?; **~ room** cuarto de los huéspedes; **there are 2 going** ~ sobran *or* quedan 2; **I've lost my key — have you got a ~?** he perdido la llave — ¿tienes una de sobra?; **to ~ no expense** no escatimar gastos; **can you ~ (me) £10?** ¿puedes prestarme *or* darme 10 libras?; **can you ~ the time?** ¿tienes tiempo?; **to ~ (surplus)** sobrante, de sobra; **I've a few minutes to ~** tengo unos minutos libres; **there is no time to ~** no hay tiempo que perder; **we arrived with time to ~** llegamos con tiempo de sobra
spare part *n* pieza de repuesto
spare time *n* ratos de ocio, tiempo libre
spare wheel *n* (*Aut*) rueda de recambio
sparing ['spɛərɪŋ] *adj*: **to be ~ with** ser parco en
sparingly ['spɛərɪŋlɪ] *adv* escasamente
spark [spa:k] *n* chispa; (*fig*) chispazo
spark(ing) plug ['spa:k(ɪŋ)-] *n* bujía
sparkle ['spa:kl] *n* centelleo, destello ▷ *vi* centellear; (*shine*) relucir, brillar
sparkler ['spa:klə'] *n* bengala
sparkling ['spa:klɪŋ] *adj* centelleante; (*wine*) espumoso
sparring partner ['spa:rɪŋ-] *n* sparring; (*fig*) contrincante
sparrow ['spærəu] *n* gorrión
sparse [spa:s] *adj* esparcido, escaso
spartan ['spa:tən] *adj* (*fig*) espartano
spasm ['spæzəm] *n* (*Med*) espasmo; (*fig*) arranque, ataque
spasmodic [spæz'mɔdɪk] *adj* espasmódico
spastic ['spæstɪk] *n* espástico(-a)
spat [spæt] *pt, pp of* **spit** ▷ *n* (*US*) riña
spate [speɪt] *n* (*fig*): **~ of** torrente de; **in ~** (*river*) crecido
spatter ['spætə'] *vt*: **to ~ with** salpicar de
spawn [spɔ:n] *vt* (*pej*) engendrar ▷ *vi* desovar, frezar ▷ *n* huevas
speak [spi:k] (*pt* **spoke**, *pp* **spoken**) *vt* (*language*) hablar; (*truth*) decir ▷ *vi* hablar; (*make a speech*) intervenir; **to ~ one's mind** hablar claro *or* con franqueza; **to ~ to sb/of** *or* **about sth** hablar con

algn/de or sobre algo; **to ~ at a conference/in a debate** hablar en un congreso/un debate; **he has no money to ~ of** no tiene mucho dinero que digamos; **~ing!** ¡al habla!; **~ up!** ¡habla más alto!

▶ **speak for** vt fus: **to ~ for sb** hablar por or en nombre de algn; **that picture is already spoken for** (in shop) ese cuadro está reservado

speaker ['spi:kə^r] n (in public) orador(a); (also: **loudspeaker**) altavoz (also Comput); (for stereo etc) altavoz, bafle; (Pol): **the S~** (Brit) el Presidente de la Cámara de los Comunes; (US) el Presidente del Congreso; **are you a Welsh ~?** ¿habla Ud galés?

spear [spɪə^r] n lanza; (for fishing) arpón ▷ vt alancear; arponear

spearhead ['spɪəhɛd] vt (attack etc) encabezar ▷ n punta de lanza, vanguardia

spec [spɛk] n (col): **on ~** por si acaso; **to buy on ~** arriesgarse a comprar

special ['spɛʃl] adj especial; (edition etc) extraordinario; (delivery) urgente ▷ n (train) tren especial; **nothing ~** nada de particular, nada extraordinario

special effects npl (Cine) efectos especiales

specialist ['spɛʃəlɪst] n especialista; **a heart ~** (Med) un(a) especialista del corazón

speciality [spɛʃɪ'ælɪtɪ], (US) **specialty** ['spɛʃəltɪ] n especialidad

specialize ['spɛʃəlaɪz] vi: **to ~ (in)** especializarse (en)

specially ['spɛʃlɪ] adv especialmente

specialty ['spɛʃəltɪ] n (US) = **speciality**

species ['spi:ʃi:z] n especie

specific [spə'sɪfɪk] adj específico

specifically [spə'sɪfɪklɪ] adv (explicitly: state, warn) específicamente, expresamente; (especially: design, intend) especialmente

specification [spɛsɪfɪ'keɪʃən] n especificación; **specifications** npl (plan) presupuesto; (of car, machine) descripción técnica; (for building) plan detallado

specimen ['spɛsɪmən] n ejemplar; (Med: of urine) espécimen; (: of blood) muestra

speck [spɛk] n grano, mota

speckled ['spɛkld] adj moteado

specs [spɛks] npl (col) gafas (Esp), anteojos

spectacle ['spɛktəkl] n espectáculo

spectacles ['spɛktəklz] npl (Brit) gafas (Esp), anteojos

spectacular [spɛk'tækjulə^r] adj espectacular; (success) impresionante

spectator [spɛk'teɪtə^r] n espectador(a)

spectator sport n deporte espectáculo

spectrum ['spɛktrəm] n (pl **spectra**) n espectro

speculate ['spɛkjuleɪt] vi especular; (try to guess): **to ~ about** especular sobre

speculation [spɛkju'leɪʃən] n especulación

sped [spɛd] pt, pp of **speed**

speech [spi:tʃ] n (faculty) habla; (formal talk) discurso; (words) palabras; (manner of speaking) forma de hablar; (language) idioma, lenguaje

speechless ['spi:tʃlɪs] adj mudo, estupefacto

speed [spi:d] n (also Aut, Tech: gear) velocidad; (haste) prisa; (promptness) rapidez ▷ vi (pt, pp **sped**) (Aut: exceed speed limit) conducir con exceso de velocidad; **at full** or **top ~** a máxima velocidad; **at a ~ of 70 km/h** a una velocidad de 70 km por hora; **at ~** a gran velocidad; **5-gearbox** una caja de cambios de 5 velocidades; **shorthand/typing ~** rapidez en taquigrafía/ mecanografía; **the years sped by** los años pasaron volando

▶ **speed up** vi acelerarse ▷ vt acelerar

speedboat ['spi:dbəut] n lancha motora

speedily ['spi:dɪlɪ] adv rápido, rápidamente

speeding ['spi:dɪŋ] n (Aut) exceso de velocidad

speed limit n límite de velocidad, velocidad máxima

speedometer [spɪ'dɔmɪtə^r] n velocímetro

speed trap n (Aut) control de velocidades

speedway ['spi:dweɪ] n (Sport) pista de carrera

speedy ['spi:dɪ] adj (fast) veloz, rápido; (prompt) pronto

spell [spɛl] n (also: **magic spell**) encanto, hechizo; (period of time) rato, período; (turn) turno ▷ vt (pt, pp **spelt** or **-ed**) [spɛlt, spɛld] (also: **spell out**) deletrear; (fig) anunciar, presagiar; **to cast a ~ on sb** hechizar a algn; **he can't ~** no sabe escribir bien, comete faltas de ortografía; **can you ~ it for me?** ¿cómo se deletrea or se escribe?; **how do you ~ your name?** ¿cómo se escribe tu nombre?

spellbound ['spɛlbaund] adj embelesado, hechizado

spelling ['spɛlɪŋ] n ortografía

spelling mistake n falta de ortografía

spelt [spɛlt] pt, pp of **spell**

spend [spɛnd] (pt, pp **spent**) vt (money) gastar; (time) pasar; (life) dedicar; **he spent a month in France** pasó un mes en Francia; **to ~ time/ money/effort on sth** gastar tiempo/dinero/ energías en algo

spending money n dinero para gastos

spendthrift ['spɛndθrɪft] n derrochador(a), manirroto(-a)

spent [spɛnt] pt, pp of **spend** ▷ adj (cartridge, bullets, match) usado

sperm [spə:m] n esperma

sperm bank n banco de esperma

spew [spju:] vt vomitar, arrojar

sphere [sfɪə^r] n esfera

spice [spaɪs] n especia ▷ vt especiar

spicy ['spaɪsɪ] adj picante

spick-and-span ['spɪkən'spæn] adj impecable

spider ['spaɪdə^r] n araña

spider's web n telaraña

spiel [ʃpi:l] n (col) rollo

spike [spaɪk] n (point) punta; (Zool) pincho, púa; (Bot) espiga; (Elec) pico parásito ▷ vt: **to ~ a quote** cancelar una cita; **spikes** npl (Sport) zapatillas con clavos

spill [spɪl] (pt, pp **spilt** or **-ed**) [spɪlt, spɪld] vt derramar, verter; (blood) derramar ▷ vi derramarse; **to ~ the beans** (col) descubrir el

pastel
▶ **spill out** vi derramarse, desparramarse
▶ **spill over** vi desbordarse
spillage ['spɪlɪdʒ] n (event) derrame; (substance) vertidos
spin [spɪn] n (revolution of wheel) vuelta, revolución; (Aviat) barrena; (trip in car) paseo (en coche) ▷ vb (pt, pp **spun**) ▷ vt (wool etc) hilar; (wheel) girar ▷ vi girar, dar vueltas; **the car spun out of control** el coche se descontroló y empezó a dar vueltas
▶ **spin out** vt alargar, prolongar
spina bifida ['spaɪnə'bɪfɪdə] n espina bífida
spinach ['spɪnɪtʃ] n espinacas
spinal ['spaɪnl] adj espinal
spinal cord n médula espinal
spindly ['spɪndlɪ] adj (leg) zanquivano
spin doctor n (col) informador(a) parcial al servicio de un partido político
spin-dryer [spɪn'draɪər] n (Brit) secadora centrífuga
spine [spaɪn] n espinazo, columna vertebral; (thorn) espina
spineless ['spaɪnlɪs] adj (fig) débil, flojo
spinning ['spɪnɪŋ] n (of thread) hilado; (art) hilandería
spinning top n peonza
spinning wheel n rueca, torno de hilar
spin-off ['spɪnɔf] n derivado, producto secundario
spinster ['spɪnstər] n soltera; (pej) solterona
spiral ['spaɪərl] n espiral ▷ adj en espiral ▷ vi (prices) dispararse; **the inflationary ~** la espiral inflacionaria
spiral staircase n escalera de caracol
spire ['spaɪər] n aguja, chapitel
spirit ['spɪrɪt] n (soul) alma; (ghost) fantasma; (attitude) espíritu; (courage) valor, ánimo; **spirits** npl (drink) alcohol, bebidas alcohólicas; **in good ~s** alegre, de buen ánimo; **Holy S~** Espíritu Santo; **community ~, public ~** civismo
spirited ['spɪrɪtɪd] adj enérgico, vigoroso
spirit level n nivel de aire
spiritual ['spɪrɪtjuəl] adj espiritual ▷ n (also: Negro spiritual) canción religiosa, espiritual
spiritualism ['spɪrɪtjuəlɪzəm] n espiritualismo
spit [spɪt] n (for roasting) asador, espetón; (spittle) esputo, escupitajo; (saliva) saliva ▷ vi (pt, pp **spat**) escupir; (sound) chisporrotear
spite [spaɪt] n rencor, ojeriza ▷ vt fastidiar; **in ~ of** a pesar de, pese a
spiteful ['spaɪtful] adj rencoroso, malévolo
spittle ['spɪtl] n saliva, baba
splash [splæʃ] n (sound) chapoteo; (of colour) mancha ▷ vt salpicar de ▷ vi (also: **splash about**) chapotear; **to ~ paint on the floor** manchar el suelo de pintura
spleen [spliːn] n (Anat) bazo
splendid ['splɛndɪd] adj espléndido
splint [splɪnt] n tablilla
splinter ['splɪntər] n astilla ▷ vi astillarse, hacer astillas

split [splɪt] n hendedura, raja; (fig) división; (Pol) escisión ▷ vb (pt, pp **-**) ▷ vt partir, rajar; (party) dividir; (work, profits) repartir ▷ vi (divide) dividirse, escindirse; **to ~ sth down the middle** (also fig) dividir algo en dos; **to ~ the difference** partir la diferencia
▶ **split up** vi (couple) separarse, romper; (meeting) acabarse
split personality n doble personalidad
splits [splɪts] n: **to do the ~** hacer el spagat
split second n fracción de segundo
splutter ['splʌtər] vi chisporrotear; (person) balbucear
spoil [spɔɪl] (pt, pp **-t** or **-ed**) [spɔɪlt, spɔɪld] vt (damage) dañar; (ruin) estropear, echar a perder; (child) mimar, consentir; (ballot paper) invalidar ▷ vi: **to be ~ing for a fight** estar con ganas de lucha, andar con ganas de pelea
spoiled [spɔɪld] adj (US: food: bad) pasado, malo; (milk) cortado
spoils [spɔɪlz] npl despojo, botín
spoilsport ['spɔɪlspɔːt] n aguafiestas
spoilt [spɔɪlt] pt, pp of **spoil** ▷ adj (child) mimado, consentido; (ballot paper) invalidado
spoke [spəuk] pt of **speak** ▷ n rayo, radio
spoken ['spəukn] pp of **speak**
spokesman ['spəuksmən] n portavoz, vocero (LAm)
spokesperson ['spəukspəːsn] n portavoz, vocero(-a) (LAm)
spokeswoman ['spəukswumən] n portavoz, vocera (LAm)
sponge [spʌndʒ] n esponja; (Culin: also: **sponge cake**) bizcocho ▷ vt (wash) lavar con esponja ▷ vi: **to ~ on** or (US) **off sb** vivir a costa de algn
sponge bag n (Brit) neceser
sponsor ['spɔnsər] n (Radio, TV) patrocinador(a); (for membership) padrino (madrina); (Comm) fiador(a), avalador(a) ▷ vt patrocinar; apadrinar; (parliamentary bill) apoyar, respaldar; (idea etc) presentar, promover; **I ~ed him at 3p a mile** (in fund-raising race) me apunté para darle 3 peniques la milla
sponsorship ['spɔnsəʃɪp] n patrocinio
spontaneous [spɔn'teɪnɪəs] adj espontáneo
spooky ['spuːkɪ] adj (col: place, atmosphere) espeluznante, horripilante
spool [spuːl] n carrete; (of sewing machine) canilla
spoon [spuːn] n cuchara
spoon-feed ['spuːnfiːd] vt dar de comer con cuchara a; (fig) dárselo todo mascado a
spoonful ['spuːnful] n cucharada
sporadic [spə'rædɪk] adj esporádico
sport [spɔːt] n deporte; (person) buen(a) perdedor(a); (amusement) juego, diversión; **indoor/outdoor ~s** deportes en sala cubierta/al aire libre; **to say sth in ~** decir algo en broma
sporting ['spɔːtɪŋ] adj deportivo; **to give sb a ~ chance** darle a algn su oportunidad
sports car n coche sport
sports ground n campo de deportes, centro deportivo

sports jacket, (US) **sport jacket** n chaqueta deportiva

sportsman ['spɔːtsmən] n deportista

sportsmanship ['spɔːtsmənʃip] n deportividad

sportswear ['spɔːtsweə'] n ropa de deporte

sportswoman ['spɔːtswumən] n deportista

sporty ['spɔːtɪ] adj deportivo

spot [spɔt] n sitio, lugar; (dot: on pattern) lunar; (stain, mark) mancha; (pimple) grano; (also: **advertising spot**) spot; (small amount): **a ~ of** un poquito de ▷ vt (notice) notar, observar ▷ adj (Comm) inmediatamente efectivo; **on the ~** en el acto, acto seguido; (in difficulty) en un aprieto; **to do sth on the ~** hacer algo en el acto; **to put sb on the ~** poner a algn en un apuro; **a red dress with white ~s** un vestido rojo con lunares blancos; **he's covered in ~s** está lleno de granos; **I ~ted a mistake** noté un error

spot check n reconocimiento rápido

spotless ['spɔtlis] adj (clean) inmaculado; (reputation) intachable

spotlight ['spɔtlait] n foco, reflector; (Aut) faro auxiliar

spot-on [spɔt'ɔn] adj (Brit col) exacto

spotted ['spɔtid] adj (pattern) de puntos

spotty ['spɔti] adj (face) con granos

spouse [spaus] n cónyuge

spout [spaut] n (of jug) pico; (pipe) caño ▷ vi chorrear

sprain [sprein] n torcedura, esguince ▷ vt: **to ~ one's ankle** torcerse el tobillo

sprang [spræŋ] pt of **spring**

sprawl [sprɔːl] vi tumbarse ▷ n: **urban ~** crecimiento urbano descontrolado; **to send sb ~ing** tirar a algn al suelo

spray [sprei] n rociada; (of sea) espuma; (container) atomizador; (of paint) pistola rociadora; (of flowers) ramita ▷ vt rociar; (crops) regar ▷ cpd (deodorant) en atomizador

spread [sprɛd] n (extent) extensión; (propagation: of disease, fire) propagación; (: of idea) diseminación; (col: food) comilona; (Press, Typ: two pages) plana ▷ vb (pt, pp ~) ▷ vt (tablecloth, map, glue) extender; (news, information) divulgar; (rumour) hacer correr, difundir; (butter) untar; (wings, sails) desplegar; (scatter) esparcir ▷ vi (in space) extenderse; (news, fire, disease) propagarse; (information) difundirse; (butter) untarse; (scatter) esparcirse; **middle-age ~** gordura de la mediana edad; **cheese ~** queso para untar; **chocolate ~** crema de chocolate; **~ the top of the cake with whipped cream** unte la parte superior de la tarta con nata montada; **repayments will be ~ over 18 months** los pagos se harán a lo largo de 18 meses
  ▶ **spread out** vi (disperse: people) dispersarse; (extend: city, liquid) extenderse ▷ vt (tablecloth, map etc) desplegar

spread-eagled ['sprɛdi:gld] adj: **to be ~** estar despatarrado

spreadsheet ['sprɛdʃi:t] n (Comput) hoja de cálculo

spree [spriː] n: **to go on a ~** ir de juerga or farra (LAm)

sprightly ['spraitlɪ] adj vivo, enérgico

spring [spriŋ] n (season) primavera; (leap) salto, brinco; (of water) fuente; (coiled metal) resorte, manantial; (bounciness) elasticidad ▷ vb (pt **sprang**, pp **sprung**) ▷ vi (arise) brotar, nacer; (leap) saltar, brincar ▷ vt: **to ~ a leak** (pipe etc) empezar a hacer agua; **he sprang the news on me** de repente me soltó la noticia; **in (the) ~** en (la) primavera; **to walk with a ~ in one's step** andar dando saltos or brincos; **to ~ into action** lanzarse a la acción
  ▶ **spring up** vi (problem) surgir

springboard ['spriŋbɔːd] n trampolín

spring-clean [spriŋ'kliːn] n (also: **spring-cleaning**) limpieza general

spring onion n cebolleta

spring roll n rollito de primavera

springtime ['spriŋtaim] n primavera

sprinkle ['spriŋkl] vt (pour) rociar; **to ~ water on**, **~ with water** rociar or salpicar de agua

sprinkler ['spriŋklə'] n (for lawn) aspersor; (to put out fire) aparato de rociadura automática

sprint [sprint] n (e)sprint ▷ vi (gen) correr a toda velocidad; (Sport) esprintar; **the 200 metres ~** el (e)sprint de 200 metros

sprinter ['sprintə'] n velocista

spritzer ['spritsə'] n vino blanco con soda

sprout [spraut] vi brotar, retoñar ▷ n: **(Brussels) ~s** npl coles de Bruselas

spruce [spruːs] n (Bot) pícea ▷ adj aseado, pulcro
  ▶ **spruce up** vt (tidy) arreglar, acicalar; (smarten up: room etc) ordenar; **to ~ o.s. up** arreglarse

sprung [sprʌŋ] pp of **spring**

spry [sprai] adj ágil, activo

spun [spʌn] pt, pp of **spin**

spur [spəː'] n espuela; (fig) estímulo, aguijón ▷ vt (also: **spur on**) estimular, incitar; **on the ~ of the moment** de improviso

spurious ['spjuəriəs] adj falso

spurn [spəːn] vt desdeñar, rechazar

spurt [spəːt] n chorro; (of energy) arrebato ▷ vi chorrear; **to put in or on a ~** (runner) acelerar; (fig: in work etc) hacer un gran esfuerzo

spy [spai] n espía ▷ vi: **to ~ on** espiar a ▷ vt (see) divisar, lograr ver ▷ cpd (film, story) de espionaje

spying ['spaiiŋ] n espionaje

Sq. abbr (in address: = Square) Plza

sq. abbr (Math etc) = **square**

squabble ['skwɔbl] n riña, pelea ▷ vi reñir, pelear

squad [skwɔd] n (Mil) pelotón; (Police) brigada; (Sport) equipo; **flying ~** (Police) brigada móvil

squaddie ['skwɔdi] n (Mil: col) chivo

squadron ['skwɔdrn] n (Mil) escuadrón; (Aviat, Naut) escuadra

squalid ['skwɔlid] adj miserable

squall [skwɔːl] n (storm) chubasco; (wind) ráfaga

squalor ['skwɔlə'] n miseria

squander ['skwɔndə'] vt (money) derrochar, despilfarrar; (chances) desperdiciar

square [skwɛə'] n cuadro; (in town) plaza; (US:

block of houses) manzana, cuadra (LAm) ▷ adj cuadrado ▷ vt (arrange) arreglar; (Math) cuadrar; (reconcile): **can you ~ it with your conscience?** ¿cómo se justifica ante sí mismo? ▷ vi cuadrar, conformarse; **all ~ igual(es); a ~ meal** una comida decente; **2 metres ~** 2 metros por 2; **1 ~ metre** un metro cuadrado; **to get one's accounts ~** dejar las cuentas claras; **I'll ~ it with him** (col) yo lo arreglo con él; **we're back to ~ one** (fig) hemos vuelto al punto de partida
▶ **square up** vi (settle): **to ~ up (with sb)** ajustar cuentas (con algn)
squarely ['skwɛəlɪ] adv (fully) de lleno; (honestly, fairly) honradamente, justamente
square root n raíz cuadrada
squash [skwɔʃ] n (vegetable) calabaza; (Sport) squash; (Brit: drink): **lemon/orange ~** zumo (Esp) or jugo (LAm) de limón/naranja ▷ vt aplastar
squat [skwɔt] adj achaparrado ▷ vi agacharse, sentarse en cuclillas; (in property) ocupar un inmueble ilegalmente
squatter ['skwɔtəʳ] n ocupante ilegal, okupa
squawk [skwɔːk] vi graznar
squeak [skwiːk] vi (hinge, wheel) chirriar, rechinar; (shoe, wood) crujir ▷ n (of hinge, wheel etc) chirrido, rechinamiento; (of shoes) crujir; (of mouse etc) chillido
squeaky ['skwiːkɪ] adj que cruje; **to be ~ clean** (fig) ser superhonrado
squeal [skwiːl] vi chillar, dar gritos agudos
squeamish ['skwiːmɪʃ] adj delicado, remilgado
squeeze [skwiːz] n presión; (of hand) apretón; (Comm: credit squeeze) restricción ▷ vt (lemon etc) exprimir; (hand, arm) apretar; **a ~ of lemon** unas gotas de limón; **to ~ past/under sth** colarse al lado de/por debajo de algo
▶ **squeeze out** vt exprimir; (fig) excluir
▶ **squeeze through** vi abrirse paso con esfuerzos
squelch [skwɛltʃ] vi chapotear
squid [skwɪd] n calamar
squiggle ['skwɪgl] n garabato
squint [skwɪnt] vi entrecerrar los ojos ▷ n (Med) estrabismo; **to ~ at sth** mirar algo entornando los ojos
squirm [skwəːm] vi retorcerse, revolverse
squirrel ['skwɪrəl] n ardilla
squirt [skwəːt] vi salir a chorros
Sr abbr = **senior; sister** (Rel)
SS abbr (= steamship) M.V
St abbr (= saint) Sto.(-a); (= street) c/
stab [stæb] n (with knife etc) puñalada; (of pain) pinchazo; **to have a ~ at (doing) sth** (col) probar (a hacer) algo ▷ vt apuñalar; **to ~ sb to death** matar a algn a puñaladas
stable ['steɪbl] adj estable ▷ n cuadra, caballeriza; **riding ~s** escuela hípica
stack [stæk] n montón, pila; (col) mar ▷ vt amontonar, apilar; **there's ~s of time to finish it** hay cantidad de tiempo para acabarlo
stadium ['steɪdɪəm] n estadio
staff [stɑːf] n (work force) personal, plantilla; (Brit Scol: also: **teaching staff**) cuerpo docente; (stick)

bastón ▷ vt proveer de personal; **to be ~ed by Asians/women** tener una plantilla asiática/femenina
stag [stæg] n ciervo, venado; (Brit Stock Exchange) especulador con nuevas emisiones
stage [steɪdʒ] n (Theat) escenario; (platform) plataforma; (point) etapa ▷ vt (play) poner en escena, representar; (organize) montar, organizar; (fig: perform: recovery etc) efectuar; **the ~** el escenario, el teatro; **to come on ~** (band) salir al escenario; **in ~s** por etapas; **in the early/final ~s** en las primeras/últimas etapas; **to go through a difficult ~** pasar una fase or etapa mala; **at this ~ in the negotiations** a estas alturas de las negociaciones
stagecoach ['steɪdʒkəʊtʃ] n diligencia
stage manager n director(a) de escena
stagger ['stægəʳ] vi tambalear ▷ vt (amaze) asombrar; (hours, holidays) escalonar
staggering ['stægərɪŋ] adj (amazing) asombroso, pasmoso
stagnant ['stægnənt] adj estancado
stagnate [stæg'neɪt] vi estancarse; (fig: economy, mind) quedarse estancado
stag night, stag party n despedida de soltero
staid [steɪd] adj (clothes) serio, formal
stain [steɪn] n mancha; (colouring) tintura ▷ vt manchar; (wood) teñir
stained glass window [steɪnd-] n vidriera de colores
stainless ['steɪnlɪs] adj (steel) inoxidable
stain remover n quitamanchas
stair [stɛəʳ] n (step) peldaño, escalón; **stairs** npl escaleras
staircase ['stɛəkeɪs], **stairway** ['stɛəweɪ] n escalera
stake [steɪk] n estaca, poste; (Betting) apuesta ▷ vt (bet) apostar; (also: **stake out**: area) cercar con estacas; **to be at ~** estar en juego; **to have a ~ in sth** tener interés en algo; **to ~ a claim to (sth)** presentar reclamación por or reclamar (algo)
stalactite ['stæləktaɪt] n estalactita
stalagmite ['stæləgmaɪt] n estalagmita
stale [steɪl] adj (bread) duro; (food) pasado
stalemate ['steɪlmeɪt] n tablas; **to reach ~** (fig) estancarse, alcanzar un punto muerto
stalk [stɔːk] n tallo, caña ▷ vt acechar, cazar al acecho; **to ~ off** irse airado
stall [stɔːl] n (in market) puesto; (in stable) casilla (de establo) ▷ vt (Aut) parar, calar ▷ vi (Aut) pararse, calarse; (fig) buscar evasivas; **stalls** npl (Brit: in cinema, theatre) butacas; **a newspaper ~** un quiosco (de periódicos); **a flower ~** un puesto de flores
stallion ['stælɪən] n semental, garañón
stalwart ['stɔːlwət] n partidario(-a) incondicional
stamina ['stæmɪnə] n resistencia
stammer ['stæməʳ] n tartamudeo, balbuceo ▷ vi tartamudear, balbucir
stamp [stæmp] n sello, estampilla (LAm); (mark, also fig) marca, huella; (on document) timbre

▷ vi (also: **stamp one's foot**) patear ▷ vt patear, golpear con el pie; (letter) poner sellos en; (with rubber stamp) marcar con sello; **~ed addressed envelope (sae)** sobre sellado con las señas propias
▶ **stamp out** vt (fire) apagar con el pie; (crime, opposition) acabar con
stamp album n álbum para sellos
stamp collecting n filatelia
stampede [stæmˈpiːd] n (of cattle) estampida
stance [stæns] n postura
stand [stænd] n (attitude) posición, postura; (for taxis) parada; (music stand) atril; (Sport) tribuna; (at exhibition) stand ▷ vb (pt, pp **stood**) ▷ vi (be) estar, encontrarse; (be on foot) estar de pie; (rise) levantarse, ponerse de pie; (remain) quedar en pie ▷ vt (place) poner, colocar; (tolerate, withstand) aguantar, soportar; **stands** npl: **the ~s** la tribuna; **to make a ~** resistir; (fig) mantener una postura firme; **to take a ~ on an issue** adoptar una actitud hacia una cuestión; **to ~ for parliament** (Brit) presentarse (como candidato) a las elecciones; **nothing ~s in our way** nada nos lo impide; **to ~ still** quedarse inmóvil; **to let sth ~ as it is** dejar algo como está; **as things ~** tal como están las cosas; **to ~ sb a drink/meal** invitar a algn a una copa/a comer; **the company will have to ~ the loss** la empresa tendrá que hacer frente a las pérdidas; **I can't ~ him** no le aguanto, no le puedo ver; **to ~ guard** or **watch** (Mil) hacer guardia
▶ **stand aside** vi apartarse, mantenerse aparte
▶ **stand by** vi (be ready) estar listo ▷ vt fus (opinion) mantener; (person) apoyar
▶ **stand down** vi (withdraw) ceder el puesto; (Mil, Law) retirarse
▶ **stand for** vt fus (signify) significar; (tolerate) admitir, permitir; **I won't ~ for that** eso no lo admito
▶ **stand in for** vt fus sustituir
▶ **stand out** vi (be prominent) destacarse
▶ **stand up** vi (rise) levantarse, ponerse de pie, pararse (LAm); (be on foot) estar de pie
▶ **stand up for** vt fus defender
▶ **stand up to** vt fus hacer frente a
standard [ˈstændəd] n patrón, norma; (flag) estandarte ▷ adj (size etc) normal, corriente, estándar; **standards** npl (morals) valores morales; **the gold ~** (Comm) el patrón oro; **high/ low ~ de alto/bajo nivel; **below** or **not up to ~** (work) de calidad inferior; **to be** or **come up to ~** satisfacer los requisitos; **to apply a double ~** aplicar un doble criterio
standardize [ˈstændədaɪz] vt estandarizar
standard lamp n (Brit) lámpara de pie
standard of living n nivel de vida
stand-by [ˈstændbaɪ] n (alert) alerta, aviso; (also: **stand-by ticket** (Theat) entrada reducida de última hora; (: Aviat) billete standby; **to be on ~** estar preparado; (doctor) estar listo para acudir; (Aviat) estar en la lista de espera
stand-by ticket n (Aviat) (billete) standby

stand-in [ˈstændɪn] n suplente; (Cine) doble
standing [ˈstændɪŋ] adj (upright) derecho; (on foot) de pie, en pie; (permanent: committee) permanente; (: rule) fijo; (: army) permanente, regular; (grievance) constante, viejo ▷ n reputación; (duration): **of 6 months' ~** que lleva 6 meses; **of many years' ~** que lleva muchos años; **he was given a ~ ovation** le dieron una calurosa ovación de pie; **~ joke** motivo constante de broma; **a man of some ~** un hombre de cierta posición or categoría
standing order n (Brit: at bank) giro bancario; **~s** npl (Mil) reglamento general
standing room n sitio para estar de pie
stand-off [ˈstændɔf] n (esp US: stalemate) punto muerto
stand-offish [stændˈɔfɪʃ] adj distante
standpoint [ˈstændpɔɪnt] n punto de vista
standstill [ˈstændstɪl] n: **at a ~** paralizado, en un punto muerto; **to come to a ~** pararse, quedar paralizado
stank [stæŋk] pt of **stink**
staple [ˈsteɪpl] n (for papers) grapa; (product) producto or artículo de primeva necesidad ▷ adj (crop, industry, food etc) básico ▷ vt grapar
stapler [ˈsteɪplə'] n grapadora
star [stɑː'] n estrella; (celebrity) estrella, astro ▷ vi: **to ~ in** ser la estrella de; **four-~ hotel** hotel de cuatro estrellas; **4-~ petrol** gasolina extra
starboard [ˈstɑːbəd] n estribor
starch [stɑːtʃ] n almidón
stardom [ˈstɑːdəm] n estrellato
stare [stɛə'] n mirada fija ▷ vi: **to ~ at** mirar fijo
starfish [ˈstɑːfɪʃ] n estrella de mar
stark [stɑːk] adj (bleak) severo, escueto; (simplicity, colour) austero; (reality, truth) puro; (poverty) absoluto ▷ adv: **~ naked** en cueros
starkers [ˈstɑːkəz] adj (Brit col): **to be ~** estar en cueros
starling [ˈstɑːlɪŋ] n estornino
starry [ˈstɑːrɪ] adj estrellado
starry-eyed [stɑːrɪˈaɪd] adj (gullible, innocent) inocentón(-ona), ingenuo; (idealistic) idealista; (from wonder) asombrado; (from love) enamoradísimo
Stars and Stripes npl: **the ~** las barras y las estrellas, la bandera de EEUU
star sign n signo del zodíaco
start [stɑːt] n (beginning) principio, comienzo; (departure) salida; (sudden movement) sobresalto; (advantage) ventaja ▷ vt empezar, comenzar; (cause) causar; (found: business, newspaper) establecer, fundar; (engine) poner en marcha; (car, engine) arrancar, poner en marcha ▷ vi (begin) comenzar, empezar; (with fright) asustarse, sobresaltarse; (train etc) salir; **at the ~** al principio; **from the ~** desde el principio; **for a ~** en primer lugar; **to make an early ~** ponerse en camino temprano; **shall we make a ~ on the washing-up?** ¿nos ponemos a fregar los platos?; **to give sb a ~** dar un susto a algn; **the thieves had 3 hours' ~** los ladrones llevaban 3 horas de

ventaja; **to ~ a fire** provocar un incendio; **to ~ doing** or **to do sth** empezar a hacer algo; **the car wouldn't ~** el coche no arrancaba; **to ~ (off) with ...** (firstly) para empezar; (at the beginning) al principio
▸ **start off** vi empezar, comenzar; (leave) salir, ponerse en camino
▸ **start over** vi (US) volver a empezar
▸ **start up** vi comenzar; (car, engine) arrancar, ponerse en marcha ▷ vt comenzar; (car) arrancar, poner en marcha
starter ['stɑːtəʳ] n (Aut) botón de arranque; (Sport: official) juez de salida; (: runner) corredor(a); (Brit Culin) entrada
starting point ['stɑːtɪŋ-] n punto de partida
startle ['stɑːtl] vt asustar, sobresaltar
startling ['stɑːtlɪŋ] adj alarmante
starvation [stɑːˈveɪʃən] n hambre, hambruna (LAm); (Med) inanición
starve [stɑːv] vi pasar hambre; (to death) morir de hambre ▷ vt hacer pasar hambre; (fig) privar; **I'm starving** estoy muerto de hambre
stash [stæʃ] vt: **to ~ sth away** (col) poner algo a buen recaudo
state [steɪt] n estado; (pomp): **in ~** con mucha ceremonia ▷ vt (say, declare) afirmar; (a case) presentar, exponer; **~ of emergency** estado de excepción or emergencia; **~ of mind** estado de ánimo; **to lie in ~** (corpse) estar de cuerpo presente; **to be in a ~** estar agitado
State Department n (US) Ministerio de Asuntos Exteriores
stately ['steɪtlɪ] adj majestuoso, imponente
statement ['steɪtmənt] n afirmación; (Law) declaración; (Comm) estado; **official ~** informe oficial; **~ of account, bank ~** estado de cuenta
States [steɪts] npl: **the ~** los Estados Unidos
state school n escuela or colegio estatal
statesman ['steɪtsmən] n estadista
static ['stætɪk] n (Radio) parásitos ▷ adj estático
station ['steɪʃən] n (gen) estación; (place) puesto, sitio; (Radio) emisora; (rank) posición social ▷ vt colocar, situar; (Mil) apostar; **action ~s!** ¡a los puestos de combate!; **to be ~ed in** (Mil) estar estacionado en
stationary ['steɪʃnərɪ] adj estacionario, fijo
stationer ['steɪʃənəʳ] n papelero(-a)
stationer's (shop) n (Brit) papelería
stationery ['steɪʃənərɪ] n (writing paper) papel de escribir; (writing materials) artículos de escritorio
station master n (Rail) jefe de estación
station wagon n (US) coche familiar con ranchera
statistic [stəˈtɪstɪk] n estadística
statistics [stəˈtɪstɪks] n (science) estadística
statue ['stætjuː] n estatua
stature ['stætʃəʳ] n estatura; (fig) talla
status ['steɪtəs] n condición, estado; (reputation) reputación, estatus; **the ~ quo** el statu quo
status symbol n símbolo de prestigio
statute ['stætjuːt] n estatuto, ley
statutory ['stætjutrɪ] adj estatutario; **~ meeting** junta ordinaria

staunch [stɔːntʃ] adj leal, incondicional ▷ vt (flow, blood) restañar
stave [steɪv] vt: **to ~ off** (attack) rechazar; (threat) evitar
stay [steɪ] n (period of time) estancia; (Law): **~ of execution** aplazamiento de una sentencia ▷ vi (remain) quedar(se); (as guest) alojarse; **to ~ the night/5 days** pasar la noche/estar or quedarse 5 días; **where are you ~ing?** ¿dónde te alojas?; **to ~ with friends** quedarse en casa de unos amigos; **we ~ed in Belgium for a few days** pasamos unos días en Bélgica; **to ~ put** seguir en el mismo sitio
▸ **stay behind** vi quedar atrás
▸ **stay in** vi (at home) quedarse en casa
▸ **stay on** vi quedarse
▸ **stay out** vi (of house) no volver a casa; (strikers) no volver al trabajo
▸ **stay up** vi (at night) velar, quedarse levantado; **we ~ed up till midnight** nos quedamos levantados hasta las doce
staying power ['steɪɪŋ-] n resistencia, aguante
STD n abbr (Brit: = subscriber trunk dialling) servicio de conferencias automáticas; (= sexually transmitted disease) ETS
stead [stɛd] n: **in sb's ~** en lugar de algn; **to stand sb in good ~** ser muy útil a algn
steadfast ['stɛdfɑːst] adj firme, resuelto
steadily ['stɛdɪlɪ] adv (firmly) firmemente; (unceasingly) sin parar; (fixedly) fijamente; (walk) normalmente; (drive) a velocidad constante
steady ['stɛdɪ] adj (fixed) firme, fijo; (regular) regular; (boyfriend etc) formal, fijo; (person, character) sensato, juicioso ▷ vt (hold) mantener firme; (stabilize) estabilizar; (nerves) calmar; **to ~ o.s. on** or **against sth** afirmarse en algo
steak [steɪk] n (gen) filete; (beef) bistec
steal [stiːl] (pt **stole**, pp **stolen**) vt, vi robar
▸ **steal away, steal off** vi marcharse furtivamente, escabullirse
stealth [stɛlθ] n: **by ~** a escondidas, sigilosamente
stealthy ['stɛlθɪ] adj cauteloso, sigiloso
steam [stiːm] n vapor; (mist) vaho, humo ▷ vt (Culin) cocer al vapor ▷ vi echar vapor; (ship): **to ~ along** avanzar, ir avanzando; **under one's own ~** (fig) por sus propios medios or propias fuerzas; **to run out of ~** (fig: person) quedar(se) agotado, quemarse; **to let off ~** (fig) desahogarse
▸ **steam up** vi (window) empañarse; **to get ~ed up about sth** (fig) ponerse negro por algo
steam engine n máquina de vapor
steamer ['stiːməʳ] n (buque de) vapor; (Culin) recipiente para cocinar al vapor
steamroller ['stiːmrəuləʳ] n apisonadora
steamship ['stiːmʃɪp] n = **steamer**
steamy ['stiːmɪ] adj (room) lleno de vapor; (window) empañado
steel [stiːl] n acero ▷ adj de acero
steelworks ['stiːlwəːks] n acería, fundición de acero

steep [sti:p] adj escarpado, abrupto; (stair) empinado; (price) exorbitante, excesivo ▷ vt empapar, remojar

steeple ['sti:pl] n aguja, campanario

steeplejack ['sti:pldʒæk] n reparador(a) de chimeneas or de campanarios

steer [stɪəʳ] vt (car) conducir (Esp), manejar (LAm); (person) dirigir, guiar ▷ vi conducir; **to ~ clear of sb/sth** (fig) esquivar a algn/evadir algo

steering ['stɪərɪŋ] n (Aut) dirección

steering wheel n volante

stem [stɛm] n (of plant) tallo; (of glass) pie; (of pipe) cañón ▷ vt detener; (blood) restañar
  ▶ **stem from** vt fus ser consecuencia de

stench [stɛntʃ] n hedor

stencil ['stɛnsl] n (typed) cliché, clisé; (lettering) plantilla ▷ vt hacer un cliché de

stenographer [stɛˈnɔgrəfəʳ] n (US) taquígrafo(-a)

step [stɛp] n paso; (sound) paso, pisada; (stair) peldaño, escalón ▷ vi dar un paso; **steps** npl (Brit) = **stepladder**; **to take a ~ forward** dar un paso adelante; **~ by ~** paso a paso; (fig) poco a poco; **to keep in ~ (with)** llevar el paso (de); (fig) llevar el paso (de), estar de acuerdo (con); **to be in/out of ~ with** estar acorde con/estar en disonancia con; **to take ~s to solve a problem** tomar medidas para resolver un problema; **to ~ forward** dar un paso adelante; **~ this way, please** pase por aquí, por favor
  ▶ **step aside** vi hacerse a un lado
  ▶ **step back** vi retroceder
  ▶ **step down** vi (fig) retirarse
  ▶ **step in** vi entrar; (fig) intervenir
  ▶ **step off** vt fus bajar de
  ▶ **step on** vt fus pisar
  ▶ **step over** vt fus pasar por encima de
  ▶ **step up** vt (increase) aumentar

step aerobics npl step

stepbrother ['stɛpbrʌðəʳ] n hermanastro

stepdaughter ['stɛpdɔ:təʳ] n hijastra

stepfather ['stɛpfɑ:ðəʳ] n padrastro

stepladder ['stɛplædəʳ] n escalera doble or de tijera

stepmother ['stɛpmʌðəʳ] n madrastra

stepping stone ['stɛpɪŋ-] n pasadera

stepsister ['stɛpsɪstəʳ] n hermanastra

stepson ['stɛpsʌn] n hijastro

stereo ['stɛrɪəu] n estéreo ▷ adj (also: **stereophonic**) estéreo, estereofónico; **in ~** en estéreo

stereotype ['stɪərɪətaɪp] n estereotipo ▷ vt estereotipar

sterile ['stɛraɪl] adj estéril

sterilization [stɛrɪlaɪˈzeɪʃən] n esterilización

sterilize ['stɛrɪlaɪz] vt esterilizar

sterling ['stə:lɪŋ] adj (silver) de ley ▷ n (Econ) libras esterlinas; **a pound ~** una libra esterlina; **he is of ~ character** tiene un carácter excelente

stern [stə:n] adj severo, austero ▷ n (Naut) popa

steroid ['stɪərɔɪd] n esteroide

stethoscope ['stɛθəskəup] n estetoscopio

stew [stju:] n cocido, estofado, guisado (LAm) ▷ vt, vi estofar, guisar; (fruit) cocer; **~ed fruit** compota de fruta

steward ['stju:əd] n (Brit: gen) camarero; (shop steward) enlace sindical

stewardess ['stju:ədəs] n azafata

stewardship ['stju:ədʃɪp] n tutela

St. Ex. abbr = **stock exchange**

stg abbr (= sterling) ester

stick [stɪk] n palo; (as weapon) porra; (walking stick) bastón ▷ vb (pt, pp **stuck**) ▷ vt (glue) pegar; (col: put) meter; (: tolerate) aguantar, soportar ▷ vi pegarse; (come to a stop) quedarse parado; (get jammed: door, lift) atascarse; **to get hold of the wrong end of the ~** entender al revés; **I can't ~ it any longer** ya no lo aguanto más; **to ~ to** (word, principles) atenerse a, ser fiel a; (promise) cumplir; **it stuck in my mind** se me quedó grabado; **to ~ sth into** clavar or hincar algo en
  ▶ **stick around** vi (col) quedarse
  ▶ **stick out** vi sobresalir ▷ vt sacar; **she stuck out her tongue** sacó la lengua; **to ~ it out** (col) aguantar
  ▶ **stick up** vi sobresalir
  ▶ **stick up for** vt fus defender

sticker ['stɪkəʳ] n (label) etiqueta adhesiva; (with slogan) pegatina

sticking plaster ['stɪkɪŋ-] n (Brit) esparadrapo

sticking point n (fig) punto de fricción

stickler ['stɪkləʳ] n: **to be a ~ for** insistir mucho en

stick-up ['stɪkʌp] n asalto, atraco

sticky ['stɪkɪ] adj pegajoso; (label) adhesivo; (fig) difícil

stiff [stɪf] adj rígido, tieso; (hard) duro; (difficult) difícil; (person) inflexible; (price) exorbitante; **to have a ~ neck/back** tener tortícolis/dolor de espalda; **the door's ~** la puerta está atrancada

stiffen ['stɪfn] vt hacer más rígido; (limb) entumecer ▷ vi endurecerse; (grow stronger) fortalecerse

stifle ['staɪfl] vt ahogar, sofocar

stigma ['stɪgmə] pl (pl -**s** or -**ta**) [stɪgˈmɑ:tə] ▷ n estigma

stile [staɪl] n escalera (para pasar una cerca)

stiletto [stɪˈlɛtəu] n (Brit: also: **stiletto heel**) tacón de aguja

still [stɪl] adj inmóvil, quieto; (orange juice etc) sin gas ▷ adv (up to this time) todavía; (even) aún; (nonetheless) sin embargo, aun así ▷ n (Cine) foto fija; **he stood ~** se quedó quieto; **keep ~!** ¡estate quieto!, ¡no te muevas!; **he ~ hasn't arrived** todavía no ha llegado; **do you ~ live in Glasgow?** ¿sigues viviendo en Glasgow?; **better ~** mejor aún; **she knows I don't like it, but she ~ does it** sabe que no me gusta, pero aun así lo hace; **~, it's the thought that counts** en fin, la intención es lo que cuenta

stillborn ['stɪlbɔ:n] adj nacido muerto

still life n naturaleza muerta

stilt [stɪlt] n zanco; (pile) pilar, soporte

stilted ['stɪltɪd] adj afectado, artificial

stimulant ['stɪmjulənt] n estimulante
stimulate ['stɪmjuleɪt] vt estimular
stimulating ['stɪmjuleɪtɪŋ] adj estimulante
stimulation [stɪmju'leɪʃən] n estímulo
stimulus ['stɪmjuləs] (pl **stimuli**) ['stɪmjulaɪ] n estímulo, incentivo
sting [stɪŋ] n (wound) picadura; (pain) escozor, picazón; (organ) aguijón; (col: confidence trick) timo ▷ vb (pt, pp **stung**) ▷ vt picar ▷ vi picar, escocer; **my eyes are ~ing** me pican or escuecen los ojos
stingy ['stɪndʒɪ] adj tacaño
stink [stɪŋk] n hedor, tufo ▷ vi (pt **stank**, pp **stunk**) heder, apestar
stinking ['stɪŋkɪŋ] adj hediondo, fétido; (fig: col) horrible
stint [stɪnt] n tarea, destajo; **to do one's ~ at sth** hacer su parte (de algo), hacer lo que corresponde (de algo) ▷ vi: **to ~ on** escatimar
stir [stə:ʳ] n (fig: agitation) conmoción ▷ vt (tea etc) remover; (fire) atizar; (move) agitar; (fig: emotions) conmover ▷ vi moverse; **to give sth a ~** remover algo; **to cause a ~** causar conmoción or sensación
▶ **stir up** vt excitar; (trouble) fomentar
stir-fry ['stə:fraɪ] vt sofreír removiendo ▷ n plato preparado sofriendo y removiendo los ingredientes
stirrup ['stɪrəp] n estribo
stitch [stɪtʃ] n (Sewing) puntada; (Knitting) punto; (Med) punto (de sutura); (pain) punzada ▷ vt coser; (Med) suturar
stoat [stəut] n armiño
stock [stɔk] n (Comm: reserves) existencias, stock; (: selection) surtido; (Agr) ganado, ganadería; (Culin) caldo; (fig: lineage) estirpe, cepa; (Finance) capital; (: shares) acciones; (Rail: rolling stock) material rodante ▷ adj (Comm: goods, size) normal, de serie; (fig: reply etc) clásico, trillado; (: greeting) acostumbrado ▷ vt (have in stock) tener existencias de; (supply) proveer, abastecer; (sell) vender; **stocks** npl (History: as punishment) cepo; **in ~** en existencia or almacén; **to have sth in ~** tener existencias de algo; **out of ~** agotado; **to take ~ of** (fig) considerar, examinar; **~s and shares** acciones y valores; **government ~** papel del Estado; **~s of ammunition** reservas de munición
▶ **stock up with** vt fus abastecerse de
stockbroker ['stɔkbrəukəʳ] n agente or corredor(a) de bolsa
stock cube n pastilla or cubito de caldo
stock exchange n bolsa
stocking ['stɔkɪŋ] n media
stock market n bolsa (de valores)
stock phrase n vieja frase
stockpile ['stɔkpaɪl] n reserva ▷ vt acumular, almacenar
stockroom ['stɔkru:m] n almacén, depósito
stocktaking ['stɔkteɪkɪŋ] n (Brit Comm) inventario, balance
stocky ['stɔkɪ] adj (strong) robusto; (short) achaparrado
stodgy ['stɔdʒɪ] adj indigesto, pesado

stoke [stəuk] vt atizar
stole [stəul] pt of **steal** ▷ n estola
stolen ['stəuln] pp of **steal**
stolid ['stɔlɪd] adj (person) imperturbable, impasible
stomach ['stʌmək] n (Anat) estómago; (belly) vientre ▷ vt tragar, aguantar
stomach ache n dolor de estómago
stone [stəun] n piedra; (in fruit) hueso; (Brit: weight) = 6,35 kg ▷ adj de piedra ▷ vt apedrear; **within a ~'s throw of the station** a tiro de piedra or a dos pasos de la estación
stone-cold ['stəun'kəuld] adj helado
stone-deaf ['stəun'dɛf] adj sordo como una tapia
stonewall [stəun'wɔ:l] vi alargar la cosa innecesariamente ▷ vt dar largas a
stonework ['stəunwə:k] n (art) cantería
stood [stud] pt, pp of **stand**
stooge [stu:dʒ] n (col) hombre de paja
stool [stu:l] n taburete
stoop [stu:p] vi (also: **have a stoop**) ser cargado de espaldas; (bend) inclinarse, encorvarse; **to ~ to (doing) sth** rebajarse a (hacer) algo
stop [stɔp] n parada, alto; (in punctuation) punto ▷ vt parar, detener; (break off) suspender; (block) tapar, cerrar; (prevent) impedir; (also: **put a stop to**) poner término a, acabar con ▷ vi pararse, detenerse; (end) acabarse; **bus ~** parada de autobús; **this is my ~** yo me bajo aquí; **to ~ doing sth** dejar de hacer algo; **to ~ sb (from) doing sth** impedir que algn haga algo; **the bus doesn't ~ there** el autobús no para allí; **to ~ dead** pararse en seco; **I think the rain's going to ~** creo que va a dejar de llover; **this has got to ~!** ¡esto se tiene que acabar!; **~ it!** ¡basta ya!, ¡párate!
▶ **stop by** vt fus pasar por
▶ **stop off** vi interrumpir el viaje
▶ **stop up** vt (hole) tapar
stopgap ['stɔpgæp] n interino; (person) sustituto(-a); (measure) medida provisional ▷ cpd (situation) provisional
stopover ['stɔpəuvəʳ] n parada intermedia; (Aviat) escala
stoppage ['stɔpɪdʒ] n (strike) paro; (temporary stop) interrupción; (of pay) suspensión; (blockage) obstrucción
stopper ['stɔpəʳ] n tapón
stop press n noticias de última hora
stopwatch ['stɔpwɔtʃ] n cronómetro
storage ['stɔ:rɪdʒ] n almacenaje; (Comput) almacenamiento
storage heater n acumulador de calor
store [stɔ:ʳ] n (stock) provisión; (depot, Brit: large shop) almacén; (US) tienda; (reserve) reserva, repuesto ▷ vt (gen, Comput) almacenar; (keep) guardar; (in filing system) archivar; **stores** npl víveres; **who knows what is in ~ for us** quién sabe lo que nos espera; **to set great/little ~ by sth** dar mucha/poca importancia a algo, valorar mucho/poco algo
▶ **store up** vt acumular

storeroom ['stɔ:ru:m] n despensa
storey, (US) **story** ['stɔ:rɪ] n piso
stork [stɔ:k] n cigüeña
storm [stɔ:m] n tormenta; (wind) vendaval; (fig)
tempestad ▷ vi (fig) rabiar ▷ vt tomar por asalto,
asaltar; **to take a town by ~** (Mil) tomar una
ciudad por asalto
stormy ['stɔ:mɪ] adj tempestuoso
story ['stɔ:rɪ] n historia; (Press) artículo; (joke)
cuento, chiste; (plot) argumento; (lie) cuento;
(US) = **storey**
storybook ['stɔ:rɪbuk] n libro de cuentos
stout [staut] adj (strong) sólido; (fat) gordo,
corpulento ▷ n cerveza negra
stove [stəuv] n (for cooking) cocina; (for heating)
estufa; **gas/electric ~** cocina de gas/eléctrica
stow [stəu] vt meter, poner; (Naut) estibar
stowaway ['stəuəweɪ] n polizón(-ona)
straddle ['strædl] vt montar a horcajadas
straggle ['strægl] vi (wander) vagar en desorden;
(lag behind) rezagarse
straight [streɪt] adj (not wavy, curly etc: line)
recto; (: hair) liso; (direct) recto, derecho; (plain,
uncomplicated) sencillo; (frank) franco, directo;
(in order) en orden; (continuous) continuo; (Theat:
part, play) serio; (person: conventional) recto,
convencional; (: heterosexual) heterosexual ▷ adv
derecho, directamente; (drink) solo; **to put** or
get sth ~ (clear) dejar algo en claro; **10 ~ wins**
10 victorias seguidas; **to be (all) ~** (tidy) estar
en orden; (clarified) estar claro; **I went ~ home**
(me) fui directamente a casa; **I'll come ~ back**
vuelvo enseguida; **keep ~ on** siga todo recto; **he
looked ~ at me** me miró directamente a los ojos;
~ away, ~ off (at once) en seguida
straighten ['streɪtn] vt (also: **straighten out**)
enderezar, poner derecho; **to ~ things out** poner
las cosas en orden
straight-faced [streɪt'feɪst] adj serio ▷ adv sin
mostrar emoción, impávido
straightforward [streɪt'fɔ:wəd] adj (simple)
sencillo; (honest) sincero
strain [streɪn] n (gen) tensión; (Tech) esfuerzo;
(Med) distensión, torcedura; (breed) raza; (lineage)
linaje; (of virus) variedad ▷ vt (back etc) distender,
torcerse; (tire) cansar; (stretch) estirar; (filter)
filtrar; (meaning) tergiversar ▷ vi esforzarse;
strains npl (Mus) son; **she's under a lot of ~** está
bajo mucha tensión
strained [streɪnd] adj (muscle) torcido; (laugh)
forzado; (relations) tenso
strainer ['streɪnər] n colador
strait [streɪt] n (Geo) estrecho; **to be in dire ~s**
(fig) estar en un gran aprieto
straitjacket ['streɪtdʒækɪt] n camisa de fuerza
strait-laced [streɪt'leɪst] adj mojigato, gazmoño
strand [strænd] n (of thread) hebra; (of rope)
ramal; **a ~ of hair** un pelo
stranded ['strændɪd] adj (person) colgado
strange [streɪndʒ] adj (not known) desconocido;
(odd) extraño, raro
stranger ['streɪndʒər] n desconocido(-a); (from

another area) forastero(-a); **I'm a ~ here** no soy
de aquí
strangle ['stræŋgl] vt estrangular
stranglehold ['stræŋglhəuld] n (fig) dominio
completo
strap [stræp] n correa; (of slip, dress) tirante ▷ vt
atar con correa
strapped [stræpt] adj: **to be ~ for cash** (col)
andar mal de dinero
strapping ['stræpɪŋ] adj robusto, fornido
strategic [strə'ti:dʒɪk] adj estratégico
strategy ['strætɪdʒɪ] n estrategia
straw [strɔ:] n paja; (drinking straw) caña, pajita;
that's the last ~! ¡eso es el colmo!
strawberry ['strɔ:bərɪ] n fresa, frutilla (CS)
stray [streɪ] adj (animal) extraviado; (bullet)
perdido; (scattered) disperso ▷ vi extraviarse,
perderse; (wander: walker) vagar, ir sin rumbo fijo;
(: speaker) desvariar
streak [stri:k] n raya; (fig: of madness etc) vena
▷ vt rayar ▷ vi: **to ~ past** pasar como un rayo; **to
have ~s in one's hair** tener vetas en el pelo; **a
winning/losing ~** una racha de buena/mala
suerte
streaker ['stri:kər] n corredor(a) desnudo(-a)
stream [stri:m] n riachuelo, arroyo; (jet) chorro;
(flow) corriente; (of people) oleada ▷ vt (Scol)
dividir en grupos por habilidad ▷ vi correr,
fluir; **to ~ in/out** (people) entrar/salir en tropel;
against the ~ a contracorriente; **on ~** (new power
plant etc) en funcionamiento
streamer ['stri:mər] n serpentina
streamline ['stri:mlaɪn] vt aerodinamizar; (fig)
racionalizar
streamlined ['stri:mlaɪnd] adj aerodinámico
street [stri:t] n calle ▷ adj callejero; **the back ~s**
las callejuelas; **to be on the ~s** (homeless) estar
sin vivienda; (as prostitute) hacer la calle
streetcar ['stri:tkɑ:] n (US) tranvía
street lamp n farol
street plan n plano callejero
streetwise ['stri:twaɪz] adj (col) pícaro
strength [strɛŋθ] n fuerza; (of girder, knot etc)
resistencia; (of chemical solution) potencia; (of
wine) graduación de alcohol; **on the ~ of** a base
de, en base a; **to be at full/be below ~** tener/no
tener completo el cupo
strengthen ['strɛŋθn] vt fortalecer, reforzar
strenuous ['strɛnjuəs] adj (tough) arduo,
(energetic) enérgico; (opposition) firme, tenaz;
(efforts) intensivo
stress [strɛs] n (force, pressure) presión; (mental
strain) estrés, tensión; (accent, emphasis) énfasis,
acento; (Ling, Poetry) acento; (Tech) tensión, carga
▷ vt subrayar, recalcar; **to be under ~** estar
estresado; **to lay great ~ on sth** hacer hincapié
en algo
stretch [strɛtʃ] n (of sand etc) trecho; (of road)
tramo; (of time) período, tiempo ▷ vi estirarse;
(extend): **to ~ to** or **as far as** extenderse hasta;
(be enough: money, food): **to ~ to** alcanzar para, dar
de sí para ▷ vt extender, estirar; (make demands

of) exigir el máximo esfuerzo a; **to ~ one's legs** estirar las piernas

▸ **stretch out** *vi* tenderse ▷ *vt* (*arm etc*) extender; (*spread*) estirar

stretcher ['strɛtʃəʳ] *n* camilla

strewn [struːn] *adj*: **~ with** cubierto *or* sembrado de

stricken ['strɪkən] *adj* (*person*) herido; (*city, industry etc*) condenado; **~ with** (*arthritis, disease*) afligido por; **grief-~** destrozado por el dolor

strict [strɪkt] *adj* (*order, rule etc*) estricto; (*discipline, ban*) severo; **in ~ confidence** en la más absoluta confianza

stride [straɪd] *n* zancada, tranco ▷ *vi* (*pt* **strode**, *pp* **stridden**) [strəud, 'strɪdn] dar zancadas, andar a trancos; **to take in one's ~** (*fig: changes etc*) tomar con calma

strife [straɪf] *n* lucha

strike [straɪk] *n* (*industrial action*) huelga; (*of oil etc*) descubrimiento; (*attack*) ataque; (*Sport*) golpe ▷ *vb* (*pt, pp* **struck**) ▷ *vt* golpear, pegar; (*oil etc*) descubrir; (*obstacle*) topar con; (*produce: coin, medal*) acuñar; (: *agreement, deal*) concertar ▷ *vi* (*workers*) declarar la huelga; (*attack: Mil etc*) atacar; (*clock*) dar la hora; **to be on ~** (*workers*) estar en huelga; **to call a ~** declarar una huelga; **to go on** *or* **come out on ~** ponerse *or* declararse en huelga; **to ~ a match** encender una cerilla; **to ~ a balance** (*fig*) encontrar un equilibrio; **to ~ a bargain** cerrar un trato; **the clock struck 9 o'clock** el reloj dio las 9

▸ **strike back** *vi* (*Mil*) contraatacar; (*fig*) devolver el golpe

▸ **strike down** *vt* derribar

▸ **strike off** *vt* (*from list*) tachar; (*doctor etc*) suspender

▸ **strike out** *vt* borrar, tachar

▸ **strike up** *vt* (*Mus*) empezar a tocar; (*conversation*) entablar; (*friendship*) trabar

striker ['straɪkəʳ] *n* huelguista; (*Sport*) delantero

striking ['straɪkɪŋ] *adj* (*colour*) llamativo; (*obvious*) notorio

Strimmer® ['strɪməʳ] *n* cortacéspedes (*especial para los bordes*)

string [strɪŋ] *n* (*gen*) cuerda; (*row*) hilera; (*Comput*) cadena ▷ *vt* (*pt, pp* **strung**); **to ~ together** ensartar; **to ~ out** extenderse; **the strings** *npl* (*Mus*) los instrumentos de cuerda; **to pull ~s** (*fig*) mover palancas; **to get a job by pulling ~s** conseguir un trabajo por enchufe; **with no ~s attached** (*fig*) sin compromiso

string bean *n* judía verde (*Esp*), habichuela (*LAm*), ejote (*CAm, Méx*), chaucha (*RP*)

string(ed) instrument [strɪŋ(d)-] *n* (*Mus*) instrumento de cuerda

stringent ['strɪndʒənt] *adj* riguroso, severo

strip [strɪp] *n* tira; (*of land*) franja; (*of metal*) cinta, lámina ▷ *vt* desnudar; (*also:* **strip down**: *machine*) desmontar ▷ *vi* desnudarse

strip cartoon *n* tira cómica, historieta (*LAm*)

stripe [straɪp] *n* raya; (*Mil*) galón; **white with green ~s** blanco con rayas verdes

striped [straɪpt] *adj* a rayas, rayado

strip lighting *n* alumbrado fluorescente

stripper ['strɪpəʳ] *n* artista de striptease

strip-search ['strɪpsəːtʃ] *vt*: **to ~ sb** desnudar y registrar a algn

strive [straɪv] (*pt* **strove**, *pp* **-n**) [strəuv, 'strɪvn] *vi*: **to ~ to do sth** esforzarse *or* luchar por hacer algo

strode [strəud] *pt of* **stride**

stroke [strəuk] *n* (*blow*) golpe; (*Med*) apoplejía; (*caress*) caricia; (*of pen*) trazo; (*Swimming: style*) estilo; (*of piston*) carrera ▷ *vt* acariciar; **at a ~** de golpe; **a ~ of luck** un golpe de suerte; **two-~ engine** motor de dos tiempos

stroll [strəul] *n* paseo, vuelta ▷ *vi* dar un paseo *or* una vuelta; **to go for a ~, have** *or* **take a ~** dar un paseo

stroller ['strəuləʳ] *n* (*US: pushchair*) cochecito

strong [strɔŋ] *adj* fuerte; (*bleach, acid*) concentrado ▷ *adv*: **to be going ~** (*company*) marchar bien; (*person*) conservarse bien; **they are 50 ~** son 50

stronghold ['strɔŋhəuld] *n* fortaleza; (*fig*) baluarte

strongly ['strɔŋlɪ] *adv* fuertemente, con fuerza; (*believe*) firmemente; **to feel ~ about sth** tener una opinión firme sobre algo

strongroom ['strɔŋruːm] *n* cámara acorazada

stroppy ['strɔpɪ] *adj* (*Brit col*) borde; **to get ~** ponerse borde

strove [strəuv] *pt of* **strive**

struck [strʌk] *pt, pp of* **strike**

structural ['strʌktʃərəl] *adj* estructural

structure ['strʌktʃəʳ] *n* estructura; (*building*) construcción

struggle ['strʌgl] *n* lucha ▷ *vi* luchar; **to have a ~ to do sth** esforzarse por hacer algo

strum [strʌm] *vt* (*guitar*) rasguear

strung [strʌŋ] *pt, pp of* **string**

strut [strʌt] *n* puntal ▷ *vi* pavonearse

stub [stʌb] *n* (*of ticket etc*) matriz; (*of cigarette*) colilla ▷ *vt*: **to ~ one's toe on sth** dar con el dedo del pie contra algo

▸ **stub out** *vt* (*cigarette*) apagar

stubble ['stʌbl] *n* rastrojo; (*on chin*) barba (*incipiente*)

stubborn ['stʌbən] *adj* terco, testarudo

stuck [stʌk] *pt, pp of* **stick** ▷ *adj* (*jammed*) atascado

stuck-up [stʌk'ʌp] *adj* engreído, presumido

stud [stʌd] *n* (*shirt stud*) corchete; (*of boot*) taco; (*of horses*) caballeriza; (*also:* **stud horse**) caballo semental ▷ *vt* (*fig*): **~ded with** salpicado de

student ['stjuːdənt] *n* estudiante ▷ *adj* estudiantil; **a law/medical ~** un(a) estudiante de derecho/medicina

student driver *n* (*US Aut*) aprendiz(a) de conductor

students' union *n* (*Brit: association*) sindicato de estudiantes; (: *building*) centro de estudiantes

studio ['stjuːdɪəu] *n* estudio; (*artist's*) taller

studious ['stjuːdɪəs] *adj* estudioso; (*studied*) calculado

studiously ['stjuːdɪəslɪ] *adv* (*carefully*) con esmero

study ['stʌdɪ] n estudio ▷ vt estudiar; (examine) examinar, investigar ▷ vi estudiar; **to make a ~ of sth** realizar una investigación de algo; **to ~ for an exam** preparar un examen

stuff [stʌf] n materia; (cloth) tela; (substance) material, sustancia; (things, belongings) cosas ▷ vt llenar; (Culin) rellenar; (animal: for exhibition) disecar; **my nose is ~ed up** tengo la nariz tapada; **~ed toy** juguete or muñeco de trapo

stuffing ['stʌfɪŋ] n relleno

stuffy ['stʌfɪ] adj (room) mal ventilado; (person) de miras estrechas

stumble ['stʌmbl] vi tropezar, dar un traspié
▸ **stumble across** vt fus (fig) tropezar con

stumbling block ['stʌmblɪŋ-] n tropiezo, obstáculo

stump [stʌmp] n (of tree) tocón; (of limb) muñón ▷ vt: **to be ~ed** quedarse perplejo; **to be ~ed for an answer** quedarse sin saber qué contestar

stun [stʌn] vt aturdir

stung [stʌŋ] pt, pp de **sting**

stunk [stʌŋk] pp de **stink**

stunning ['stʌnɪŋ] adj (fig) pasmoso

stunt [stʌnt] n (Aviat) vuelo acrobático; (publicity stunt) truco publicitario

stunted ['stʌntɪd] adj enano, achaparrado

stuntman ['stʌntmæn] n especialista

stupendous [stju:'pɛndəs] adj estupendo, asombroso

stupid ['stju:pɪd] adj estúpido, tonto

stupidity [stju:'pɪdɪtɪ] n estupidez

sturdy ['stə:dɪ] adj robusto, fuerte

stutter ['stʌtəʳ] n tartamudeo ▷ vi tartamudear

sty [staɪ] n (for pigs) pocilga

stye [staɪ] n (Med) orzuelo

style [staɪl] n estilo; (fashion) moda; (of dress etc) hechura; (hair style) corte; **in the latest ~** en el último modelo

stylish ['staɪlɪʃ] adj elegante, a la moda

stylist ['staɪlɪst] n (hair stylist) peluquero(-a)

stylus ['staɪləs] (pl **styli** or **-es**) ['staɪlaɪ] n (of record player) aguja

suave [swɑ:v] adj cortés, fino

sub [sʌb] n abbr = **submarine; subscription**

sub... [sʌb] pref sub...

subconscious [sʌb'kɔnʃəs] adj subconsciente ▷ n subconsciente

subcontinent [sʌb'kɔntɪnənt] n: **the Indian ~** el subcontinente (de la India)

subcontract n ['sʌb'kɔntrækt] subcontrato ▷ vt ['sʌbkən'trækt] subcontratar

subcontractor ['sʌbkən'træktəʳ] n subcontratista

subdue [səb'dju:] vt sojuzgar; (passions) dominar

subdued [səb'dju:d] adj (light) tenue; (person) sumiso, manso

subject n súbdito; (Scol) tema, materia ▷ vt: **to ~ sb to sth** someter a algn a algo ▷ adj: **to be ~ to** (law) estar sujeto a; **~ to confirmation in writing** sujeto a confirmación por escrito; **to change the ~** cambiar de tema

subjective [səb'dʒɛktɪv] adj subjetivo

subject matter n materia; (content) contenido

subjunctive [səb'dʒʌŋktɪv] adj, n subjuntivo

sublet [sʌb'lɛt] vt, vi subarrendar, realquilar

submarine [sʌbmə'ri:n] n submarino

submerge [səb'mə:dʒ] vt sumergir; (flood) inundar ▷ vi sumergirse

submission [səb'mɪʃən] n sumisión; (to committee etc) ponencia

submissive [səb'mɪsɪv] adj sumiso

submit [səb'mɪt] vt someter; (proposal, claim) presentar ▷ vi someterse; **I ~ that ...** me permito sugerir que ...

subnormal [sʌb'nɔ:məl] adj subnormal

subordinate [sə'bɔ:dɪnət] adj, n subordinado(-a)

subpoena [səb'pi:nə] (Law) n citación ▷ vt citar

subscribe [səb'skraɪb] vi suscribir; **to ~ to** (fund) suscribir, aprobar; (opinion) estar de acuerdo con; (newspaper) suscribirse a

subscriber [səb'skraɪbəʳ] n (to periodical) suscriptor(a); (to telephone) abonado(-a)

subscription [səb'skrɪpʃən] n (to club) abono; (to magazine) suscripción; **to take out a ~ to** suscribirse a

subsequent ['sʌbsɪkwənt] adj subsiguiente, posterior; **~ to** posterior a

subsequently ['sʌbsɪkwəntlɪ] adv posteriormente, más tarde

subside [səb'saɪd] vi hundirse; (flood) bajar; (wind) amainar

subsidence [səb'saɪdns] n hundimiento; (in road) socavón

subsidiarity [səbsɪdɪ'ærɪtɪ] n (Pol) subsidiariedad

subsidiary [səb'sɪdɪərɪ] n sucursal, filial ▷ adj (Univ: subject) secundario

subsidize ['sʌbsɪdaɪz] vt subvencionar

subsidy ['sʌbsɪdɪ] n subvención

subsistence [səb'sɪstəns] n subsistencia

substance ['sʌbstəns] n sustancia; (fig) esencia; **to lack ~** (argument) ser poco convincente; (accusation) no tener fundamento; (film, book) tener poca profundidad

substance abuse n uso indebido de sustancias tóxicas

substantial [səb'stænʃl] adj sustancial, sustancioso; (fig) importante

substantially [səb'stænʃəlɪ] adv sustancialmente; **~ bigger** bastante más grande

substantiate [səb'stænʃɪeɪt] vt comprobar

substitute ['sʌbstɪtju:t] n (person) suplente; (thing) sustituto ▷ vt: **to ~ A for B** sustituir B por A, reemplazar A por B

substitution [sʌbstɪ'tju:ʃən] n sustitución

subterranean [sʌbtə'reɪnɪən] adj subterráneo

subtitle ['sʌbtaɪtl] n subtítulo

subtle ['sʌtl] adj sutil

subtlety ['sʌtltɪ] n sutileza

subtotal [sʌb'təutl] n subtotal

subtract [səb'trækt] vt restar; sustraer

subtraction [səb'trækʃən] n resta; sustracción

suburb ['sʌbə:b] n barrio residencial; **the ~s** las afueras (de la ciudad)

suburban [sə'bə:bən] *adj* suburbano; *(train etc)* de cercanías

suburbia [sə'bə:bɪə] *n* barrios residenciales

subversive [səb'və:sɪv] *adj* subversivo

subway ['sʌbweɪ] *n (Brit)* paso subterráneo *or* inferior; *(US)* metro

succeed [sək'si:d] *vi (person)* tener éxito; *(plan)* salir bien ▷ *vt* suceder a; **to ~ in doing** lograr hacer

succeeding [sək'si:dɪŋ] *adj (following)* sucesivo; **~ generations** generaciones futuras

success [sək'sɛs] *n* éxito; *(gain)* triunfo

successful [sək'sɛsful] *adj (venture)* de éxito, exitoso *(esp LAm)*; **to be ~ (in doing)** lograr (hacer)

successfully [sək'sɛsfulɪ] *adv* con éxito

succession [sək'sɛfən] *n (series)* sucesión, serie; *(descendants)* descendencia; **in ~** sucesivamente

successive [sək'sɛsɪv] *adj* sucesivo, consecutivo; **on 3 ~ days** tres días seguidos

successor [sək'sɛsəʳ] *n* sucesor(a)

succinct [sək'sɪŋkt] *adj* sucinto

succulent ['sʌkjulənt] *adj* suculento ▷ *n (Bot)*: **~s** plantas carnosas

succumb [sə'kʌm] *vi* sucumbir

such [sʌtʃ] *adj* tal, semejante; *(of that kind)*: **~ a book** tal libro; **~ books** tales libros; *(so much)*: **~ courage** tanto valor ▷ *adv* tan; **~ a long trip** un viaje tan largo; **~ a lot of** tanto; **it's ~ a long time since we saw each other** hace tanto tiempo que no nos vemos; **~ a long time ago** hace tantísimo tiempo; **~ as** *(like)* tal como; **a noise ~ as to ...** un ruido tal que ...; **the pain was ~ that ...** el dolor era tal que ...; **~ books as I have** cuantos libros tengo; **I wouldn't dream of doing ~ a thing** no se me ocurriría hacer tal cosa; **I said no ~ thing** no dije tal cosa; **there's no ~ thing** eso no existe; **there's no ~ thing as the yeti** el yeti no existe; **as ~** *adv*: **she's not an expert as ~** no es una experta propiamente dicha

such-and-such ['sʌtʃənsʌtʃ] *adj* tal o cual

suchlike ['sʌtʃlaɪk] *pron (col)*: **and ~** y cosas por el estilo

suck [sʌk] *vt* chupar; *(bottle)* sorber; *(breast)* mamar; *(pump, machine)* aspirar

sucker ['sʌkəʳ] *n (Bot)* serpollo; *(Zool)* ventosa; *(col)* bobo, primo

suction ['sʌkʃən] *n* succión

sudden ['sʌdn] *adj (rapid)* repentino, súbito; *(unexpected)* imprevisto; **all of a ~** de repente

sudden-death [sʌdn'dɛθ] *n (also: **sudden-death play off**)* desempate instantáneo, muerte súbita

suddenly ['sʌdnlɪ] *adv* de repente

suds [sʌdz] *npl* espuma de jabón

sue [su:] *vt* demandar; **to ~ (for)** demandar (por); **to ~ for divorce** solicitar *or* pedir el divorcio; **to ~ for damages** demandar por daños y perjuicios

suede [sweɪd] *n* ante, gamuza *(LAm)*

suet ['suɪt] *n* sebo

suffer ['sʌfəʳ] *vt* sufrir, padecer; *(tolerate)* aguantar, soportar; *(undergo: loss, setback)*

experimentar ▷ *vi* sufrir, padecer; **to ~ from** sufrir, tener; **to ~ from the effects of alcohol/a fall** sufrir los efectos del alcohol/ resentirse de una caída

sufferer ['sʌfərəʳ] *n* víctima; *(Med)*: **~ from** enfermo(-a) de

suffering ['sʌfərɪŋ] *n (hardship, deprivation)* sufrimiento; *(pain)* dolor

suffice [sə'faɪs] *vi* bastar, ser suficiente

sufficient [sə'fɪʃənt] *adj* suficiente, bastante

sufficiently [sə'fɪʃəntlɪ] *adv* suficientemente, bastante

suffix ['sʌfɪks] *n* sufijo

suffocate ['sʌfəkeɪt] *vi* ahogarse, asfixiarse

sugar ['ʃugəʳ] *n* azúcar ▷ *vt* echar azúcar a, azucarar

sugar beet *n* remolacha

sugar cane *n* caña de azúcar

suggest [sə'dʒɛst] *vt* sugerir; *(recommend)* aconsejar; **what do you ~ I do?** ¿qué sugieres que haga?; **this ~s that ...** esto hace pensar que ...

suggestion [sə'dʒɛstʃən] *n* sugerencia; **there's no ~ of ...** no hay indicación *or* evidencia de ...

suicide ['suɪsaɪd] *n* suicidio; *(person)* suicida; **to commit ~** suicidarse

suicide bombing *n* atentado suicida

suit [su:t] *n (man's)* traje; *(woman's)* traje de chaqueta; *(Law)* pleito; *(Cards)* palo ▷ *vt* convenir; *(clothes)* sentar bien a, ir bien a; *(adapt)*: **to ~ sth to** adaptar *or* ajustar algo a; **to be ~ed to sth** *(suitable for)* ser apto para algo; **well ~ed** *(couple)* hechos el uno para el otro; **to bring a ~ against sb** entablar demanda contra algn; **to follow ~** *(Cards)* seguir el palo; *(fig)* seguir el ejemplo (de algn); **that ~s me** me va bien

suitable ['su:təbl] *adj* conveniente; *(apt)* indicado

suitably ['su:təblɪ] *adv* convenientemente; *(appropriately)* en forma debida

suitcase ['su:tkeɪs] *n* maleta, petaca *(Méx)*, valija *(RP)*

suite [swi:t] *n (of rooms, Mus)* suite; *(furniture)*: **bedroom/dining room ~** (juego de) dormitorio/ comedor; **a three-piece ~** un tresillo

suitor ['su:təʳ] *n* pretendiente

sulfur ['sʌlfəʳ] *n (US)* = **sulphur**

sulk [sʌlk] *vi* estar de mal humor

sulky ['sʌlkɪ] *adj* malhumorado

sullen ['sʌlən] *adj* hosco, malhumorado

sulphur, *(US)* **sulfur** ['sʌlfəʳ] *n* azufre

sultana [sʌl'tɑ:nə] *n (fruit)* pasa de Esmirna

sultry ['sʌltrɪ] *adj (weather)* bochornoso; *(seductive)* seductor(a)

sum [sʌm] *n* suma; *(total)* total
  ▷ **sum up** *vt* resumir; *(evaluate rapidly)* evaluar ▷ *vi* hacer un resumen

summarize ['sʌməraɪz] *vt* resumir

summary ['sʌmərɪ] *n* resumen ▷ *adj (justice)* sumario

summer ['sʌməʳ] *n* verano ▷ *adj* de verano; **in (the) ~** en (el) verano

summerhouse ['sʌməhaus] n (in garden) cenador, glorieta
summertime ['sʌmətaɪm] n (season) verano
summer time n (by clock) hora de verano
summit ['sʌmɪt] n cima, cumbre
summit (conference) n (conferencia) cumbre
summon ['sʌmən] vt (person) llamar; (meeting) convocar; **to ~ a witness** citar a un testigo
▶ **summon up** vt (courage) armarse de
summons ['sʌmənz] n llamamiento, llamada
▷ vt citar, emplazar; **to serve a ~ on sb** citar a algn ante el juicio
sumo ['su:məu] n (also: **sumo wrestling**) sumo
sump [sʌmp] n (Brit Aut) cárter
sun [sʌn] n sol; **they have everything under the ~** no les falta nada, tienen de todo
sunbathe ['sʌnbeɪð] vi tomar el sol
sunbed ['sʌnbed] n cama solar
sunburn ['sʌnbə:n] n (painful) quemadura del sol; (tan) bronceado
sunburnt ['sʌnbə:nt], **sunburned** ['sʌnbə:nd] adj (tanned) bronceado; (painfully) quemado por el sol
Sunday ['sʌndɪ] n domingo
Sunday paper n (periódico) dominical
Sunday school n catequesis
sundial ['sʌndaɪəl] n reloj de sol
sundown ['sʌndaun] n anochecer, puesta de sol
sundries ['sʌndrɪz] npl géneros diversos
sundry ['sʌndrɪ] adj varios, diversos; **all and ~** todos sin excepción
sunflower ['sʌnflauəʳ] n girasol
sung [sʌŋ] pp of **sing**
sunglasses ['sʌnglɑ:sɪz] npl gafas de sol
sunk [sʌŋk] pp of **sink**
sunlight ['sʌnlaɪt] n luz del sol
sunlit ['sʌnlɪt] adj iluminado por el sol
sunny ['sʌnɪ] adj soleado; (day) de sol; (fig) alegre; **it is ~** hace sol
sunrise ['sʌnraɪz] n salida del sol
sun roof n (Aut) techo corredizo or solar; (on building) azotea, terraza
sunscreen ['sʌnskri:n] n protector solar
sunset ['sʌnset] n puesta del sol
sunshade ['sʌnʃeɪd] n (over table) sombrilla
sunshine ['sʌnʃaɪn] n sol
sunstroke ['sʌnstrəuk] n insolación
suntan ['sʌntæn] n bronceado
suntanned ['sʌntænd] adj bronceado
suntan oil n aceite bronceador
super ['su:pəʳ] adj (col) bárbaro
superannuation [su:pərænju'eɪʃən] n jubilación, pensión
superb [su:'pə:b] adj magnífico, espléndido
Super Bowl n (US Sport) super copa de fútbol americano
supercilious [su:pə'sɪlɪəs] adj (disdainful) desdeñoso; (haughty) altanero
superconductor [su:pəkən'dʌktəʳ] n superconductor
superficial [su:pə'fɪʃəl] adj superficial
superfluous [su'pə:fluəs] adj superfluo, de sobra
superglue ['su:pəglu:] n cola de contacto, supercola
superhighway ['su:pəhaɪweɪ] n (US) superautopista; **the information ~** la superautopista de la información
superimpose ['su:pərɪm'pəuz] vt sobreponer
superintendent [su:pərɪn'tɛndənt] n director(a); (police superintendent) subjefe(-a)
superior [su'pɪərɪəʳ] adj superior; (smug: person) altivo, desdeñoso; (: smile, air) de suficiencia; (: remark) desdeñoso ▷ n superior; **Mother S~** (Rel) madre superiora
superiority [supɪərɪ'ɔrɪtɪ] n superioridad; desdén
superlative [su'pə:lətɪv] adj, n superlativo
superman ['su:pəmæn] n superhombre
supermarket ['su:pəmɑ:kɪt] n supermercado
supermodel ['su:pəmɔdl] n top model, supermodelo
supernatural [su:pə'nætʃərəl] adj sobrenatural
supernova [su:pə'nəuvə] n supernova
superpower ['su:pəpauəʳ] n (Pol) superpotencia
supersede [su:pə'si:d] vt suplantar
supersonic ['su:pə'sɔnɪk] adj supersónico
superstar ['su:pəstɑːʳ] n superestrella ▷ adj de superestrella
superstition [su:pə'stɪʃən] n superstición
superstitious [su:pə'stɪʃəs] adj supersticioso
superstore ['su:pəstɔːʳ] n (Brit) hipermercado
supervise ['su:pəvaɪz] vt supervisar
supervision [su:pə'vɪʒən] n supervisión
supervisor [su:pəvaɪzəʳ] n (gen, Univ) supervisor(a)
supine ['su:paɪn] adj supino
supper ['sʌpəʳ] n cena; **to have ~** cenar
supple ['sʌpl] adj flexible
supplement n suplemento ▷ vt suplir
supplementary [sʌplɪ'mɛntərɪ] adj suplementario
supplementary benefit n (Brit) subsidio adicional de la seguridad social
supplier [sə'plaɪəʳ] n suministrador(a); (Comm) distribuidor(a)
supply [sə'plaɪ] vt (provide) suministrar; (information) facilitar; (fill: need, want) suplir, satisfacer; (equip): **to ~ (with)** proveer (de) ▷ n provisión; (of gas, water etc) suministro ▷ adj (Brit: teacher etc) suplente; **supplies** npl (food) víveres, (Mil) pertrechos; **office supplies** materiales para oficina; **to be in short ~** escasear, haber escasez de; **the electricity/water/gas ~** el suministro de electricidad/agua/gas; **~ and demand** la oferta y la demanda
support [sə'pɔːt] n (moral, financial etc) apoyo; (Tech) soporte ▷ vt apoyar; (financially) mantener; (uphold) sostener; (Sport: team) seguir, ser hincha de; **they stopped work in ~ (of)** pararon de trabajar en apoyo (de); **to ~ o.s** (financially) ganarse la vida; **what team do you ~?** ¿de qué equipo eres?
supporter [sə'pɔːtəʳ] n (Pol etc) partidario(-a); (Sport) aficionado(-a); (Football) hincha
supporting [sə'pɔːtɪŋ] adj (wall) de apoyo; ~

role papel secundario; ~ **actor/actress** actor secundario (actriz secundaria)

supportive [sə'pɔːtɪv] *adj* de apoyo; **I have a ~ family/wife** mi familia/mujer me apoya

suppose [sə'pəuz] *vt, vi* suponer; (*imagine*) imaginarse; **to be ~d to do sth** deber hacer algo; **I don't ~ she'll come** no creo que venga; **he's ~d to be an expert** se le supone un experto

supposedly [sə'pəuzɪdlɪ] *adv* según cabe suponer

supposing [sə'pəuzɪŋ] *conj* en caso de que; **always ~ (that) he comes** suponiendo que venga

suppress [sə'prɛs] *vt* suprimir; (*yawn*) ahogar

supreme [su'priːm] *adj* supremo

Supreme Court *n* (US) Tribunal Supremo, Corte Suprema

supremo [su'priːməu] *n* autoridad máxima

surcharge ['sɜːtʃɑːdʒ] *n* sobretasa, recargo

sure [ʃuə^r] *adj* seguro; (*definite, convinced*) cierto; (*aim*) certero ▷ *adv*: **that ~ is pretty, that's ~ pretty** (US) ¡qué bonito es!; **are you ~?** ¿estás seguro?; **to be ~ of sth** estar seguro de algo; **to be ~ of o.s.** estar seguro de sí mismo; **to make ~ of sth/that** asegurarse de algo/asegurar que; **I'm not ~ how/why/when** no estoy seguro de cómo/por qué/cuándo; **~!** (*of course*) ¡claro!, ¡por supuesto!; **~ enough** efectivamente

sure-fire ['ʃuəfaɪə^r] *adj* (*col*) infalible

surely ['ʃuəlɪ] *adv* (*certainly*) seguramente; **~ you don't mean that!** ¡no lo dices en serio!

surety ['ʃuərətɪ] *n* fianza; (*person*) fiador(a); **to go** *or* **stand ~ for sb** ser fiador de algn, salir garante por algn

surf [sɜːf] *n* olas ▷ *vt*: **to ~ the Net** navegar por Internet

surface ['sɜːfɪs] *n* superficie ▷ *vt* (*road*) revestir ▷ *vi* salir a la superficie ▷ *cpd* (Mil, Naut) de (la) superficie; **on the ~ it seems that ...** (*fig*) a primera vista parece que ...

surface mail *n* vía terrestre

surfboard ['sɜːfbɔːd] *n* plancha (de surf)

surfeit ['sɜːfɪt] *n*: **a ~ of** un exceso de

surfer ['sɜːfə^r] *n* súrfer

surfing ['sɜːfɪŋ] *n* surf

surge [sɜːdʒ] *n* oleada, oleaje; (Elec) sobretensión transitoria ▷ *vi* avanzar a tropel; **to ~ forward** avanzar rápidamente

surgeon ['sɜːdʒən] *n* cirujano(-a)

surgery ['sɜːdʒərɪ] *n* cirugía; (Brit: *room*) consultorio; (: Pol) horas en las que los electores pueden *reunirse personalmente con su diputado*; **to undergo ~** operarse; *see also* **constituency**

surgical ['sɜːdʒɪkl] *adj* quirúrgico

surgical spirit *n* (Brit) alcohol

surly ['sɜːlɪ] *adj* hosco, malhumorado

surname ['sɜːneɪm] *n* apellido

surplus ['sɜːpləs] *n* excedente; (Comm) superávit ▷ *adj* (Comm) excedente, sobrante; **to have a ~ of sth** tener un excedente de algo; **it is ~ to our requirements** nos sobra; **~ stock** saldos

surprise [sə'praɪz] *n* sorpresa ▷ *vt* sorprender; **to take sb by ~** coger a algn desprevenido *or* por sorpresa, sorprender a algn; (Mil: *town, fort*) atacar por sorpresa

surprising [sə'praɪzɪŋ] *adj* sorprendente

surprisingly [sə'praɪzɪŋlɪ] *adv* (*easy, helpful*) de modo sorprendente; **(somewhat) ~, he agreed** para sorpresa de todos, aceptó

surrealism [sə'rɪəlɪzəm] *n* surrealismo

surrender [sə'rɛndə^r] *n* rendición, entrega ▷ *vi* rendirse, entregarse ▷ *vt* (*claim, right*) renunciar

surreptitious [sʌrəp'tɪʃəs] *adj* subrepticio

surrogate ['sʌrəgɪt] *n* (Brit: *substitute*) sustituto(-a) ▷ *adj* (*substance, material*) sucedáneo

surrogate mother *n* madre de alquiler

surround [sə'raund] *vt* rodear, circundar; (Mil *etc*) cercar

surrounding [sə'raundɪŋ] *adj* circundante

surroundings [sə'raundɪŋz] *npl* alrededores, cercanías

surveillance [sɜː'veɪləns] *n* vigilancia

survey *n* inspección reconocimiento; (*inquiry*) encuesta; (*comprehensive view: of situation etc*) vista de conjunto ▷ *vt* examinar, inspeccionar; (*Surveying: building*) inspeccionar; (: *land*) hacer un reconocimiento de, reconocer; (*look at*) mirar, contemplar; (*make inquiries about*) hacer una encuesta de; **to carry out a ~ of** inspeccionar, examinar

surveyor [sə'veɪə^r] *n* (Brit: *of building*) perito; (*of land*) agrimensor(a)

survival [sə'vaɪvl] *n* supervivencia

survive [sə'vaɪv] *vi* sobrevivir; (*custom etc*) perdurar ▷ *vt* sobrevivir a

survivor [sə'vaɪvə^r] *n* superviviente

susceptible [sə'sɛptəbl] *adj* (*easily influenced*) influenciable; (*to disease, illness*): **~ to** propenso a

suspect *adj, n* sospechoso(-a) ▷ *vt* sospechar

suspected [səs'pɛktɪd] *adj* presunto; **to have a ~ fracture** tener una posible fractura

suspend [səs'pɛnd] *vt* suspender

suspended animation [səs'pɛndəd-] *n*: **in a state of ~** en (estado de) hibernación

suspended sentence *n* (Law) libertad condicional

suspender belt [səs'pɛndə^r-] *n* (Brit) liguero, portaligas (LAm)

suspenders [səs'pɛndəz] *npl* (Brit) ligas; (US) tirantes

suspense [səs'pɛns] *n* incertidumbre, duda; (*in film etc*) suspense

suspension [səs'pɛnʃən] *n* (*gen, Aut*) suspensión; (*of driving licence*) privación

suspension bridge *n* puente colgante

suspicion [səs'pɪʃən] *n* sospecha; (*distrust*) recelo; (*trace*) traza; **to be under ~** estar bajo sospecha; **arrested on ~ of murder** detenido bajo sospecha de asesinato

suspicious [səs'pɪʃəs] *adj* (*suspecting*) receloso; (*causing suspicion*) sospechoso; **to be ~ of** *or* **about sb/sth** tener sospechas de algn/algo

sustain [səs'teɪn] *vt* sostener, apoyar; (*suffer*) sufrir, padecer

sustainable [səs'teɪnəbl] *adj* sostenible

sustainable development n desarrollo
sostenible

sustained [səs'teɪnd] adj (effort) sostenido

sustenance ['sʌstɪnəns] n sustento

swab [swɔb] n (Med) algodón, frotis ▷ vt (Naut:
also: **swab down**) limpiar, fregar

swagger ['swægə'] vi pavonearse

swallow ['swɔləu] n (bird) golondrina; (of food)
bocado; (of drink) trago ▷ vt tragar
▶ **swallow up** vt (savings etc) consumir

swam [swæm] pt of **swim**

swamp [swɔmp] n pantano, ciénaga ▷ vt
abrumar, agobiar

swan [swɔn] n cisne

swap [swɔp] n canje, trueque ▷ vt: **to ~ (for)**
canjear (por)

swarm [swɔ:m] n (of bees) enjambre; (fig)
multitud ▷ vi (fig) hormiguear, pulular

swarthy ['swɔ:ðɪ] adj moreno

swastika ['swɔstɪkə] n esvástica, cruz gamada

swat [swɔt] vt aplastar ▷ n (also: **fly swat**)
matamoscas

sway [sweɪ] vi mecerse, balancearse ▷ vt
(influence) mover, influir en ▷ n (rule, power):
~ (over) dominio (sobre); **to hold ~ over sb**
dominar a algn, mantener el dominio sobre
algn

swear [sweə'] (pt **swore**, pp **sworn**) vi jurar; (with
swearwords) decir tacos ▷ vt: **to ~ an oath** prestar
juramento, jurar; **to ~ to sth** declarar algo bajo
juramento
▶ **swear in** vt tomar juramento(-a) (a)

swearword ['sweəwɔ:d] n taco, palabrota

sweat [swet] n sudor ▷ vi sudar

sweatband ['swetbænd] n (Sport: on head) banda;
(: on wrist) muñequera

sweater ['swetə'] n suéter

sweatshirt ['swetʃə:t] n sudadera

sweaty ['swetɪ] adj sudoroso

Swede [swi:d] n sueco(-a)

swede [swi:d] n (Brit) nabo

Sweden ['swi:dn] n Suecia

Swedish ['swi:dɪʃ] adj, n (Ling) sueco

sweep [swi:p] n (act) barrida; (of arm) manotazo;
(curve) curva, alcance; (also: **chimney sweep**)
deshollinador(a) ▷ vb (pt, pp **swept**) ▷ vt barrer;
(disease, fashion) recorrer ▷ vi barrer
▶ **sweep away** vt barrer; (rub out) borrar
▶ **sweep past** vi pasar rápidamente; (brush by)
rozar
▶ **sweep up** vi barrer

sweeper ['swi:pə'] n (person) barrendero(-a);
(machine) barredora; (Football) líbero, libre

sweeping ['swi:pɪŋ] adj (gesture) dramático;
(generalized) generalizado; (changes, reforms)
radical

sweet [swi:t] n (candy) dulce, caramelo; (Brit:
pudding) postre ▷ adj dulce; (sugary) azucarado;
(charming: person) encantador(a); (: smile, character)
dulce, amable, agradable ▷ adv: **to smell/taste**
~ oler/saber dulce

sweet and sour adj agridulce

sweetcorn ['swi:tkɔ:n] n maíz (dulce), elote
(CAm, Méx), choclo (CS)

sweeten ['swi:tn] vt (person) endulzar; (add sugar
to) poner azúcar a

sweetener ['swi:tnə'] n (Culin) edulcorante

sweetheart ['swi:thɑ:t] n amor, novio(-a); (in
speech) amor, cariño

sweetness ['swi:tnɪs] n (gen) dulzura

sweet pea n guisante de olor

sweetshop ['swi:tʃɔp] n (Brit) confitería,
bombonería

swell [swel] n (of sea) marejada, oleaje ▷ adj (US:
col: excellent) estupendo, fenomenal ▷ vb (pt
-ed, pp **swollen** or **-ed**) ▷ vt hinchar, inflar ▷ vi
hincharse, inflarse

swelling ['swelɪŋ] n (Med) hinchazón

sweltering ['sweltərɪŋ] adj sofocante, de mucho
calor

swept [swept] pt, pp of **sweep**

swerve [swə:v] n regate; (in car) desvío brusco
▷ vi desviarse bruscamente

swift [swɪft] n (bird) vencejo ▷ adj rápido, veloz

swig [swɪg] n (col: drink) trago

swill [swɪl] n bazofia ▷ vt (also: **swill out, swill**
down) lavar, limpiar con agua

swim [swɪm] n: **to go for a ~** ir a nadar or a
bañarse ▷ vb (pt **swam**, pp **swum**) ▷ vi nadar;
(head, room) dar vueltas ▷ vt pasar a nado; **to go**
~ming ir a nadar; **to ~ a length** nadar or hacer
un largo

swimmer ['swɪmə'] n nadador(a)

swimming ['swɪmɪŋ] n natación

swimming cap n gorro de baño

swimming costume n traje de baño, bañador
(Esp), malla (CS)

swimmingly ['swɪmɪŋlɪ] adv: **to go ~** (wonderfully)
ir como una seda or sobre ruedas

swimming pool n piscina, alberca (CAm, Méx),
pileta (RP)

swimming trunks npl traje de baño, bañador
(Esp)

swimsuit ['swɪmsu:t] n = **swimming costume**

swindle ['swɪndl] n estafa ▷ vt estafar

swine [swaɪn] n (pl inv) cerdo, puerco; (col!)
canalla (!)

swing [swɪŋ] n (in playground) columpio;
(movement) balanceo, vaivén; (change of direction)
viraje; (rhythm) ritmo; (Pol: in votes etc): **there**
has been a ~ towards/away from Labour ha
habido un viraje en favor/en contra del Partido
Laborista ▷ vb (pt, pp **swung**) ▷ vt balancear; (on
a swing) columpiar; (also: **swing round**) voltear,
girar ▷ vi balancearse; (on a swing) columpiarse;
(hang) colgar; (also: **swing round**) dar media
vuelta; **a ~ to the left** un movimiento hacia
la izquierda; **to be in full ~** estar en plena
marcha; **to get into the ~ of things** meterse
en situación; **he was ~ing his bag back and**
forth balanceaba la bolsa de un lado al otro;
Roy swung his legs off the couch con un
movimiento rápido, Roy quitó las piernas del
sofá; **he was ~ing on a rope** se balanceaba

colgado de una cuerda; **a large key swung from his belt** le colgaba una gran llave del cinturón; **the canoe suddenly swung round** de repente la canoa dio un viraje; **the road ~s south** la carretera gira hacia el sur

swing bridge n puente giratorio

swing door, (US) **swinging door** ['swɪŋɪŋ-] n puerta giratoria

swingeing ['swɪndʒɪŋ] adj (Brit) abrumador(a)

swipe [swaɪp] n golpe fuerte ▷ vt (hit) golpear fuerte; (col: steal) guindar; (credit card etc) pasar

swirl [swə:l] vi arremolinarse

swish [swɪʃ] n (sound: of whip) chasquido; (: of skirts) frufrú; (: of grass) crujido ▷ adj (col: smart) elegante ▷ vi chasquear

Swiss [swɪs] adj, n (pl inv) suizo(-a)

switch [swɪtʃ] n (for light, radio etc) interruptor; (change) cambio ▷ vt (change) cambiar de; (invert: also: **switch round**, **switch over**) intercambiar
▶ **switch off** vt apagar; (engine) parar
▶ **switch on** vt (Aut: ignition) encender, prender (LAm); (engine, machine) arrancar; (water supply) conectar

switchboard ['swɪtʃbɔ:d] n (Tel) centralita (de teléfonos) (Esp), conmutador (LAm)

Switzerland ['swɪtsələnd] n Suiza

swivel ['swɪvl] vi (also: **swivel round**) girar

swollen ['swəulən] pp of **swell**

swoon [swu:n] vi desmayarse

swoop [swu:p] n (by police etc) redada; (of bird etc) descenso en picado, calada ▷ vi (also: **swoop down**) caer en picado

swop [swɔp] = **swap**

sword [sɔ:d] n espada

swordfish ['sɔ:dfɪʃ] n pez espada

swore [swɔːʳ] pt of **swear**

sworn [swɔ:n] pp of **swear**

swot [swɔt] (Brit) vt, vi empollar ▷ n empollón(-ona)

swum [swʌm] pp of **swim**

swung [swʌŋ] pt, pp of **swing**

syllable ['sɪləbl] n sílaba

syllabus ['sɪləbəs] n programa de estudios; **on the ~** en el programa de estudios

symbol ['sɪmbl] n símbolo

symbolic(al) [sɪmˈbɔlɪk(l)] adj simbólico; **to be**

symbolic(al) of sth simbolizar algo

symbolism ['sɪmbəlɪzəm] n simbolismo

symbolize ['sɪmbəlaɪz] vt simbolizar

symmetrical [sɪˈmɛtrɪkl] adj simétrico

symmetry ['sɪmɪtrɪ] n simetría

sympathetic [sɪmpəˈθɛtɪk] adj compasivo; (understanding) comprensivo; **to be ~ to a cause** (well-disposed) apoyar una causa; **to be ~ towards** (person) ser comprensivo con

sympathize ['sɪmpəθaɪz] vi: **to ~ with sb** compadecerse de algn; (understand) comprender a algn

sympathizer ['sɪmpəθaɪzəʳ] n (Pol) simpatizante

sympathy ['sɪmpəθɪ] n (pity) compasión; (understanding) comprensión; **a letter of ~** un pésame; **with our deepest ~** nuestro más sentido pésame

symphony ['sɪmfənɪ] n sinfonía

symposium [sɪmˈpəuzɪəm] n simposio

symptom ['sɪmptəm] n síntoma, indicio

synagogue ['sɪnəgɔg] n sinagoga

sync [sɪŋk] n (col): **to be in/out of ~ (with)** ir/no ir al mismo ritmo (que); (fig: people) conectar/no conectar con

synchronized swimming ['sɪŋkrənaɪzd-] n natación sincronizada

syndicate ['sɪndɪkɪt] n (gen) sindicato; (Press) agencia (de noticias)

syndrome ['sɪndrəum] n síndrome

synonym ['sɪnənɪm] n sinónimo

synopsis [sɪˈnɔpsɪs] (pl **synopses**) [sɪˈnɔpsi:z] n sinopsis

syntax ['sɪntæks] n sintaxis

synthetic [sɪnˈθɛtɪk] adj, n sintético

syphilis ['sɪfɪlɪs] n sífilis

syphon ['saɪfən] = **siphon**

Syria ['sɪrɪə] n Siria

syringe [sɪˈrɪndʒ] n jeringa

syrup ['sɪrəp] n jarabe, almíbar

system ['sɪstəm] n sistema; (Anat) organismo; **it was quite a shock to his ~** fue un golpe para él

systematic [sɪstəˈmætɪk] adj sistemático; metódico

system disk n (Comput) disco del sistema

systems analyst n analista de sistemas

Tt

T, t [ti:] *n* (*letter*) T, t; **T for Tommy** T de
Tarragona

TA *n abbr* (*Brit*) = **Territorial Army**

ta [tɑ:] *excl* (*Brit: col*) ¡gracias!

tab [tæb] *n abbr* = **tabulator** ▷ *n* lengüeta; (*label*)
etiqueta; **to keep ~s on** (*fig*) vigilar

tabby ['tæbɪ] *n* (*also:* **tabby cat**) gato atigrado

tabernacle ['tæbənækl] *n* tabernáculo

table ['teɪbl] *n* mesa; (*chart: of statistics etc*) cuadro,
tabla ▷ *vt* (*Brit: motion etc*) presentar; **to lay** *or*
set the ~ poner la mesa; **to clear the ~** quitar
or levantar la mesa; **league ~** (*Football, Rugby*)
clasificación del campeonato; **~ of contents**
índice de materias

tablecloth ['teɪblklɔθ] *n* mantel

table d'hôte [tɑ:bl'dəut] *n* menú

table lamp *n* lámpara de mesa

tablemat ['teɪblmæt] *n* salvamanteles,
posaplatos

tablespoon ['teɪblspu:n] *n* cuchara grande; (*also:*
tablespoonful: *as measurement*) cucharada

tablet ['tæblɪt] *n* (*Med*) pastilla, comprimido; (*for
writing*) bloc; (*of stone*) lápida; **~ of soap** pastilla
de jabón

table tennis *n* ping-pong, tenis de mesa

table wine *n* vino de mesa

tabloid ['tæblɔɪd] *n* (*newspaper*) periódico popular
sensacionalista

taboo [tə'bu:] *adj, n* tabú

tabulate ['tæbjuleɪt] *vt* disponer en tablas

tabulator ['tæbjuleɪtəʳ] *n* tabulador

tachograph ['tækəgrɑ:f] *n* tacógrafo

tacit ['tæsɪt] *adj* tácito

tack [tæk] *n* (*nail*) tachuela; (*stitch*) hilván;
(*Naut*) bordada ▷ *vt* (*nail*) clavar con tachuelas;
(*stitch*) hilvanar ▷ *vi* virar; **to ~ sth on to (the
end of) sth** (*of letter, book*) añadir algo a(l final
de) algo

tackle ['tækl] *n* (*gear*) equipo; (*fishing tackle, for
lifting*) aparejo; (*Football*) entrada, tackle; (*Rugby*)
placaje ▷ *vt* (*difficulty*) enfrentarse a, abordar;
(*grapple with*) agarrar; (*Football*) entrar a; (*Rugby*)
placar

tacky ['tækɪ] *adj* pegajoso; (*fam*) hortera

tact [tækt] *n* tacto, discreción

tactful ['tæktful] *adj* discreto, diplomático; **to be
~** tener tacto, actuar discretamente

tactical ['tæktɪkl] *adj* táctico

tactical voting *n* voto útil

tactician [tæk'tɪʃən] *n* táctico(-a)

tactics ['tæktɪks] *n, npl* táctica

tactless ['tæktlɪs] *adj* indiscreto

tadpole ['tædpəul] *n* renacuajo

taffy ['tæfɪ] *n* (*US*) melcocha

tag [tæg] *n* (*label*) etiqueta; **price/name ~**
etiqueta del precio/con el nombre
▶ **tag along** *vi:* **to ~ along with sb** engancharse
a algn

tail [teɪl] *n* cola; (*Zool*) rabo; (*of shirt, coat*) faldón
▷ *vt* (*follow*) vigilar a; **heads or ~s** cara o cruz; **to
turn ~** volver la espalda
▶ **tail away, tail off** *vi* (*in size, quality etc*) ir
disminuyendo

tailback ['teɪlbæk] *n* (*Brit Aut*) cola

tail end *n* cola, parte final

tailgate ['teɪlgeɪt] *n* (*Aut*) puerta trasera

tailor ['teɪləʳ] *n* sastre ▷ *vt:* **to ~ sth (to)**
confeccionar algo a medida (para); **~'s (shop)**
sastrería

tailoring ['teɪlərɪŋ] *n* (*cut*) corte; (*craft*) sastrería

tailor-made ['teɪlə'meɪd] *adj* (*also fig*) hecho a (la)
medida

tailwind ['teɪlwɪnd] *n* viento de cola

tainted ['teɪntɪd] *adj* (*water, air*) contaminado;
(*fig*) manchado

Tajikistan [tɑ:dʒɪkɪ'stɑ:n] *n* Tayikistán

take [teɪk] (*pt* **took,** *pp* **-n**) *vt* tomar; (*grab*) coger
(*Esp*), agarrar (*LAm*); (*gain: prize*) ganar; (*require:
effort, courage*) exigir; (*support weight of*) aguantar;
(*hold: passengers etc*) tener cabida para; (*accompany,
bring, carry*) llevar; (*exam*) presentarse a; (*conduct:
meeting*) presidir; (*put up with*) soportar; (*accept*)
aceptar ▷ *vi* (*fire*) prender; (*dye*) coger (*Esp*),
agarrar, tomar ▷ *n* (*Cine*) toma; **to ~ sth from**
(*drawer etc*) sacar algo de; (*person*) coger algo a
(*Esp*); **he took a plate out of the cupboard**
sacó un plato del armario; **to ~ sb's hand** tomar
de la mano a algn; **it ~s a lot of courage** exige
gran valor; **it ~s a lot of money to do that** hace
falta mucho dinero para hacer eso; **don't forget
to ~ your camera** no te olvides de llevarte la
cámara; **I only took Russian for one year** sólo
estudié ruso un año; **have you ~n your driving
test yet?** ¿ya has hecho el examen de conducir?;

he can't ~ **being criticized** no soporta que le critiquen; **we ~ credit cards** aceptamos tarjetas de crédito; **to ~ notes** tomar apuntes; **do you ~ sugar?** ¿tomas azúcar?; **~ the first on the left** toma la primera a la izquierda; **I took him for a doctor** le tenía por médico; **it won't ~ long** durará poco; **it will ~ at least 5 litres** tiene cabida por lo menos para 5 litros; **to be ~n ill** ponerse enfermo; **to be ~n with sb/sth** (*attracted*) tomarle cariño a algn/tomarle gusto a algo; **I ~ it that …** supongo que …
▸ **take after** *vt fus* parecerse a
▸ **take apart** *vt* desmontar
▸ **take away** *vt* (*remove*) quitar; (*carry off*) llevar; **hot meals to ~ away** platos calientes para llevar ▷ *vi*: **to ~ away from** quitar mérito a
▸ **take back** *vt* (*return*) devolver; (*one's words*) retractar; **I ~ it all back!** ¡retiro lo dicho!
▸ **take down** *vt* (*building*) derribar; (*dismantle: scaffolding*) desmantelar; (*write down: message etc*) apuntar, tomar nota de; **she took down the painting** quitó el cuadro
▸ **take in** *vt* (*Brit: deceive*) engañar; (*understand*) entender; (*include*) abarcar; (*lodger*) acoger, recibir; (*orphan, stray dog*) recoger; (*Sewing*) achicar; **they were ~n in by his story** se dejaron engañar por la historia que les contó
▸ **take off** *vi* (*Aviat*) despegar, decolar (*LAm*) ▷ *vt* (*remove*) quitar; (*imitate*) imitar, remedar; **~ your coat off** quítate el abrigo
▸ **take on** *vt* (*work*) emprender; (*employee*) contratar; (*opponent*) desafiar
▸ **take out** *vt* sacar; (*remove*) quitar; **he opened his wallet and took out some money** abrió la cartera y sacó dinero; **he took her out to the theatre** la invitó al teatro; **don't ~ it out on me!** ¡no te desquites conmigo!
▸ **take over** *vt* (*business*) tomar posesión de; **he took over the running of the company** se hizo cargo del control de la empresa ▷ *vi*: **to ~ over from sb** (*replace*) reemplazar a algn; (*in shift work*) relevar a algn
▸ **take to** *vt fus* (*person*) coger cariño a (*Esp*), encariñarse con (*LAm*); (*activity*) aficionarse a; **to ~ to doing sth** aficionarse a hacer algo
▸ **take up** *vt* (*dress etc*) acortar; (*occupy: time, space*) ocupar; (*engage in: hobby etc*) dedicarse a; (*absorb: liquids*) absorber; (*accept: offer, challenge*) aceptar ▷ *vi*: **to ~ up with sb** hacerse amigo de algn
▸ **take upon** *vt*: **to ~ it upon o.s. to do sth** encargarse de hacer algo
takeaway ['teɪkəweɪ] *adj* (*Brit: food*) para llevar
taken ['teɪkən] *pp of* **take**
takeoff ['teɪkɔf] *n* (*Aviat*) despegue, decolaje (*LAm*)
takeover ['teɪkəuvə^r] *n* (*Comm*) absorción
takeover bid *n* oferta pública de adquisición
takings ['teɪkɪŋz] *npl* (*Comm*) ingresos
talc [tælk] *n* (*also*: **talcum powder**) talco
tale [teɪl] *n* (*story*) cuento; (*account*) relación; **to tell ~s** (*fig*) contar chismes
talent ['tælnt] *n* talento

talented ['tæləntɪd] *adj* talentoso, de talento
talisman ['tælɪzmən] *n* talismán
talk [tɔːk] *n* charla; (*gossip*) habladurías, chismes; (*conversation*) conversación ▷ *vi* (*speak*) hablar; (*chatter*) charlar ▷ *vt*: **to ~ sb into doing sth** convencer a algn para que haga algo; **to ~ sb out of doing sth** disuadir a algn de que haga algo; **talks** *npl* (*Pol etc*) conversaciones; **I had a ~ with my Mum about it** hablé sobre eso con mi madre; **to give a ~** dar una charla o conferencia; **it's just ~** (*gossip*) son sólo habladurías; (*hot air*) es pura palabrería; **to ~ about** hablar de; **to ~ to sb** hablar con algn; **to ~ to o.s.** hablar consigo mismo; **~ing of films, have you seen …?** hablando de películas, ¿has visto …?; **to ~ shop** hablar del trabajo
▸ **talk over** *vt* discutir; **to ~ sth over with sb** discutir algo con algn
talkative ['tɔːkətɪv] *adj* hablador(a)
talking point ['tɔːkɪŋ-] *n* tema de conversación
talking-to ['tɔːkɪŋtuː] *n*: **to give sb a good ~** echar una buena bronca a algn
talk show *n* programa magazine
tall [tɔːl] *adj* alto; (*tree*) grande; **to be 6 feet ~** = medir 1 metro 80, tener 1 metro 80 de alto; **how ~ are you?** ¿cuánto mides?
tall story *n* cuento chino
tally ['tælɪ] *n* cuenta ▷ *vi*: **to ~ (with)** concordar (con), cuadrar (con); **to keep a ~ of sth** llevar la cuenta de algo
talon ['tælən] *n* garra
tambourine [tæmbə'riːn] *n* pandereta
tame [teɪm] *adj* (*mild*) manso; (*tamed*) domesticado; (*fig: story, style, person*) soso, anodino
tamper ['tæmpə^r] *vi*: **to ~ with** (*lock etc*) intentar forzar; (*papers*) falsificar
tampon ['tæmpən] *n* tampón
tan [tæn] *n* (*also*: **suntan**) bronceado ▷ *vt* broncear ▷ *vi* ponerse moreno ▷ *adj* (*colour*) marrón; **to get a ~** broncearse, ponerse moreno
tang [tæŋ] *n* sabor fuerte
tangent ['tændʒənt] *n* (*Math*) tangente; **to go off at a ~** (*fig*) salirse por la tangente
tangerine [tændʒə'riːn] *n* mandarina
tangible ['tændʒəbl] *adj* tangible; **~ assets** bienes tangibles
tangle ['tæŋgl] *n* enredo; **to get in(to) a ~** enredarse
tank [tæŋk] *n* (*water tank*) depósito, tanque; (*for fish*) acuario; (*Mil*) tanque
tanker ['tæŋkə^r] *n* (*ship*) petrolero; (*truck*) camión cisterna
tannoy® ['tænɔɪ] *n*: **over the ~** por el altavoz
tantalizing ['tæntəlaɪzɪŋ] *adj* tentador(a)
tantamount ['tæntəmaunt] *adj*: **~ to** equivalente a
tantrum ['tæntrəm] *n* rabieta; **to throw a ~** coger una rabieta
tap [tæp] *n* (*Brit: on sink etc*) grifo, canilla (*LAm*); (*gentle blow*) golpecito; (*gas tap*) llave ▷ *vt* (*table etc*) tamborilear; (*shoulder etc*) dar palmaditas en; (*resources*) utilizar, explotar; (*telephone conversation*)

intervenir, pinchar; **on ~** (*fig: resources*) a mano;
beer on ~ cerveza de barril
tap-dancing ['tæpdɑ:nsɪŋ] *n* claqué
tape [teɪp] *n* cinta; (*also:* **magnetic tape**) cinta
magnética; (*sticky tape*) cinta adhesiva ▷ *vt*
(*record*) grabar (en cinta); **on ~** (*song etc*) grabado
(en cinta)
tape deck *n* pletina
tape measure *n* cinta métrica, metro
taper ['teɪpə'] *n* cirio ▷ *vi* afilarse
tape recorder *n* grabadora
tapestry ['tæpɪstrɪ] *n* (*object*) tapiz; (*art*) tapicería
tar [tɑ:'] *n* alquitrán, brea; **low/middle ~
cigarettes** cigarrillos con contenido bajo/medio
de alquitrán
target ['tɑ:gɪt] *n* (*gen*) blanco; **to be on ~** (*project*)
seguir el curso previsto
tariff ['tærɪf] *n* tarifa
tarmac ['tɑ:mæk] *n* (*Brit: on road*) alquitranado;
(*Aviat*) pista (de aterrizaje)
tarnish ['tɑ:nɪʃ] *vt* deslustrar
tarot ['tærəʊ] *n* tarot
tarpaulin [tɑ:'pɔ:lɪn] *n* alquitranado
tarragon ['tærəgən] *n* estragón
tart [tɑ:t] *n* (*Culin*) tarta; (*Brit col: pej: woman*)
fulana ▷ *adj* (*flavour*) agrio, ácido
▸ **tart up** *vt* (*room, building*) dar tono a
tartan ['tɑ:tn] *n* tartán ▷ *adj* de tartán
tartar ['tɑ:tə'] *n* (*on teeth*) sarro
tartar sauce *n* salsa tártara
task [tɑ:sk] *n* tarea; **to take to ~** reprender
task force *n* (*Mil, Police*) grupo de operaciones
tassel ['tæsl] *n* borla
taste [teɪst] *n* sabor, gusto; (*also:* **aftertaste**)
dejo; (*sip*) sorbo; (*fig: glimpse, idea*) muestra, idea
▷ *vt* probar ▷ *vi:* **to ~ of** *or* **like** (*fish etc*) saber a;
you can ~ the garlic (in it) se nota el sabor a ajo;
can I have a ~ of this wine? ¿puedo probar este
vino?; **to have a ~ for sth** ser aficionado a algo;
in good/bad ~ de buen/mal gusto; **to be in bad**
or **poor ~** ser de mal gusto
tasteful ['teɪstful] *adj* de buen gusto
tasteless ['teɪstlɪs] *adj* (*food*) soso; (*remark*) de
mal gusto
tasty ['teɪstɪ] *adj* sabroso, rico
ta-ta ['tæ'tɑ:] *interj* (*Brit col*) hasta luego, adiós
tatters ['tætəz] *npl:* **in ~** (*also:* **tattered**) hecho
jirones
tattoo [tə'tu:] *n* tatuaje; (*spectacle*) espectáculo
militar ▷ *vt* tatuar
tatty ['tætɪ] *adj* (*Brit col*) cochambroso
taught [tɔ:t] *pt, pp of* **teach**
taunt [tɔ:nt] *n* pulla ▷ *vt* lanzar pullas a
Taurus ['tɔ:rəs] *n* Tauro
taut [tɔ:t] *adj* tirante, tenso
tax [tæks] *n* impuesto ▷ *vt* gravar (con un
impuesto); (*fig: test*) poner a prueba; (: *patience*)
agotar; **before/after ~** impuestos excluidos/
incluidos; **free of ~** libre de impuestos
taxable ['tæksəbl] *adj* (*income*) imponible, sujeto
a impuestos
taxation [tæk'seɪʃən] *n* impuestos; **system of ~**

sistema tributario
tax avoidance *n* evasión de impuestos
tax disc *n* (*Brit Aut*) pegatina del impuesto de
circulación
tax evasion *n* evasión fiscal
tax-free ['tæksfri:] *adj* libre de impuestos
taxi ['tæksɪ] *n* taxi ▷ *vi* (*Aviat*) rodar por la pista
taxi driver *n* taxista
taxi rank, (*Brit*) **taxi stand** *n* parada de taxis
tax payer *n* contribuyente
tax rebate *n* devolución de impuestos,
reembolso fiscal
tax relief *n* desgravación fiscal
tax return *n* declaración de la renta
TB *n abbr* = **tuberculosis**
tbc *abbr* (= *to be confirmed*) por confirmar
TD *n abbr* (*US*) = **Treasury Department**; (: *Football*)
= **touchdown**
tea [ti:] *n* té; (*Brit: snack*) ≈ merienda; **high ~** (*Brit*)
≈ merienda-cena
tea bag *n* bolsita de té
tea break *n* (*Brit*) descanso para el té
teach [ti:tʃ] (*pt, pp* **taught**) *vt:* **to ~ sb sth, ~ sth to
sb** enseñar algo a algn ▷ *vi* enseñar; (*be a teacher*)
ser profesor(a); **it taught him a lesson** (eso) le
sirvió de escarmiento
teacher ['ti:tʃə'] *n* (*in secondary school*) profesor(a);
(*in primary school*) maestro(-a); **Spanish ~**
profesor(a) de español
teaching ['ti:tʃɪŋ] *n* enseñanza
tea cosy *n* cubretetera
teacup ['ti:kʌp] *n* taza de té
teak [ti:k] *n* (*madera de*) teca
team [ti:m] *n* equipo; (*of animals*) pareja
▸ **team up** *vi* asociarse
teamwork ['ti:mwə:k] *n* trabajo en equipo
teapot ['ti:pɔt] *n* tetera
tear [tɛə'] *n* rasgón, desgarrón [tɪə'] lágrima ▷ *vb*
[tɛə'] (*pt* **tore**, *pp* **torn**) [tɔ:', tɔ:n] ▷ *vt* romper,
rasgar ▷ *vi* rasgarse; **in ~s** llorando; **to burst
into ~s** deshacerse en lágrimas; **to ~ to pieces**
or **to bits** *or* **to shreds** (*also fig*) hacer pedazos,
destrozar
▸ **tear along** *vi* (*rush*) precipitarse
▸ **tear apart** *vt* (*also fig*) hacer pedazos
▸ **tear away** *vt:* **to ~ o.s. away (from sth)**
alejarse (de algo)
▸ **tear out** *vt* (*sheet of paper, cheque*) arrancar
▸ **tear up** *vt* (*sheet of paper etc*) romper
tearful ['tɪəful] *adj* lloroso
tear gas ['tɪə-] *n* gas lacrimógeno
tearoom ['ti:ru:m] *n* salón de té
tease [ti:z] *n* bromista ▷ *vt* tomar el pelo a
tea set *n* servicio de té
teaspoon ['ti:spu:n] *n* cucharita; (*also:
teaspoonful: as measurement*) cucharadita
teat [ti:t] *n* (*of bottle*) boquilla, tetilla
teatime ['ti:taɪm] *n* hora del té
tea towel *n* (*Brit*) paño de cocina
technical ['tɛknɪkl] *adj* técnico
technical college *n* centro de formación
profesional

technicality [tɛknɪ'kælɪtɪ] n detalle técnico; **on a legal ~** por una cuestión formal

technically ['tɛknɪklɪ] adv técnicamente

technician [tɛk'nɪʃn] n técnico(-a)

technique [tɛk'niːk] n técnica

technological [tɛknə'lɒdʒɪkl] adj tecnológico

technology [tɛk'nɒlədʒɪ] n tecnología

teddy (bear) ['tɛdɪ-] n osito de peluche

tedious ['tiːdɪəs] adj pesado, aburrido

tee [tiː] n (Golf) tee

teem [tiːm] vi: **to ~ with** rebosar de; **it is ~ing (with rain)** llueve a mares

teenage ['tiːneɪdʒ] adj (fashions etc) juvenil

teenager ['tiːneɪdʒəʳ] n adolescente, quinceañero(-a)

teens [tiːnz] npl: **to be in one's ~** ser adolescente

tee-shirt ['tiːʃəːt] n = **T-shirt**

teeter ['tiːtəʳ] vi balancearse

teeth [tiːθ] npl of **tooth**

teethe [tiːð] vi echar los dientes

teething ring ['tiːðɪŋ-] n mordedor

teething troubles npl (fig) dificultades iniciales

teetotal ['tiː'təutl] adj (person) abstemio

TEFL ['tɛfl] n abbr = **Teaching of English as a Foreign Language**; **~ qualification** título para la enseñanza del inglés como lengua extranjera

tel. abbr (= telephone) tel

teleconferencing ['tɛlɪkɒnfərənsɪŋ] n teleconferencias

telegram ['tɛlɪgræm] n telegrama

telegraph ['tɛlɪgrɑːf] n telégrafo

telegraph pole n poste telegráfico

telepathic [tɛlɪ'pæθɪk] adj telepático

telephone ['tɛlɪfəun] n teléfono ▷ vt llamar por teléfono, telefonear; **to be on the ~** (subscriber) tener teléfono; (be speaking) estar hablando por teléfono

telephone booth, (Brit) **telephone box** n cabina telefónica

telephone call n llamada telefónica

telephone directory n guía telefónica

telephone number n número de teléfono

telephonist [tə'lɛfənɪst] n (Brit) telefonista

telesales ['tɛlɪseɪlz] npl televentas

telescope ['tɛlɪskəup] n telescopio

Teletext® ['tɛlɪtɛkst] n teletexto

telethon ['tɛlɪθɒn] n telemaratón, maratón televisivo (con fines benéficos)

television ['tɛlɪvɪʒən] n televisión; **to watch ~** mirar or ver la televisión

television licence n impuesto por uso de televisor

television set n televisor

teleworker ['tɛlɪwɜːkəʳ] n teletrabajador(a)

teleworking ['tɛlɪwɜːkɪŋ] n teletrabajo

telex ['tɛlɛks] n télex

tell [tɛl] (pt, pp **told**) vt decir; (relate: story) contar; (distinguish): **to ~ sth from** distinguir algo de ▷ vi: **to ~ of sth** hablar de algo; **did you ~ your mother?** ¿se lo has dicho a tu madre?; **I told him I was going on holiday** le dije que me iba de vacaciones; **to ~ sb to do sth** decir a algn

que haga algo; **to ~ sb about sth** contar algo a algn; **to ~ the time** dar or decir la hora; **can you ~ me the time?** ¿me puedes decir la hora?; **to ~ lies** decir mentiras; **(I) ~ you what ...** fíjate ...; **I couldn't ~ them apart, I couldn't ~ the difference between them** no podía distinguirlos; **who can ~?** ¿quién sabe?; **you can ~ he's not serious** se nota que no se lo toma en serio; **that would be ~ing!** (fam) ¡es un secreto!

▶ **tell off** vt: **to ~ sb off** regañar a algn

▶ **tell on** vt fus: **to ~ on sb** (fam: sneak on) chivarse de algn; **the strain is beginning to ~ on him** (affect) la tensión está empezando a afectarle

teller ['tɛləʳ] n (in bank) cajero(-a)

telling ['tɛlɪŋ] adj (remark, detail) revelador(a)

telltale ['tɛlteɪl] adj (sign) indicador(a)

telly ['tɛlɪ] n (Brit col) tele

temp [tɛmp] n abbr (Brit: = temporary office worker) empleado(-a) eventual ▷ vi trabajar como empleado(-a) eventual

temper ['tɛmpəʳ] n (mood) humor; (bad temper) (mal) genio; (fit of anger) ira; (of child) rabieta ▷ vt (moderate) moderar; **to be in a ~** estar furioso; **to lose one's ~** enfadarse, enojarse (LAm); **to keep one's ~** contenerse, no alterarse

temperament ['tɛmprəmənt] n (nature) temperamento

temperamental [tɛmprə'mɛntl] adj temperamental

temperate ['tɛmprət] adj moderado; (climate) templado

temperature ['tɛmprətʃəʳ] n temperatura; **to have** or **run a ~** tener fiebre

template ['tɛmplɪt] n plantilla

temple ['tɛmpl] n (building) templo; (Anat) sien

temporary ['tɛmpərərɪ] adj provisional, temporal; (passing) transitorio; (worker) eventual; **~ teacher** maestro(-a) interino(-a)

tempt [tɛmpt] vt tentar; **to ~ sb into doing sth** tentar or inducir a algn a hacer algo; **to be ~ed to do sth** (person) sentirse tentado de hacer algo

temptation [tɛmp'teɪʃən] n tentación

ten [tɛn] num diez; **~s of thousands** decenas de miles

tenacity [tə'næsɪtɪ] n tenacidad

tenancy ['tɛnənsɪ] n alquiler

tenant ['tɛnənt] n (rent-payer) inquilino(-a); (occupant) habitante

tend [tɛnd] vt (sick etc) cuidar, atender; (cattle, machine) vigilar, cuidar ▷ vi: **to ~ to do sth** tener tendencia a hacer algo

tendency ['tɛndənsɪ] n tendencia

tender ['tɛndəʳ] adj tierno, blando; (delicate) delicado; (sore) sensible; (affectionate) tierno, cariñoso ▷ n (Comm: offer) oferta; (money): **legal ~** moneda de curso legal ▷ vt ofrecer; **to put in a ~ (for)** hacer una oferta (para); **to put work out to ~** ofrecer un trabajo a contrata; **to ~ one's resignation** presentar la dimisión

tenement ['tɛnəmənt] n casa or bloque de pisos or vecinos (LAm)

tenet ['tɛnət] n principio

tenner ['tɛnə^r] n (billete de) diez libras
tennis ['tɛnɪs] n tenis
tennis ball n pelota de tenis
tennis court n cancha de tenis
tennis player n tenista
tennis racket n raqueta de tenis
tennis shoes npl zapatillas de tenis
tenor ['tɛnə^r] n (Mus) tenor
tenpin bowling ['tɛnpɪn-] n bolos
tense [tɛns] adj tenso; (stretched) tirante; (stiff) rígido, tieso; (person) nervioso ▷ n (Ling) tiempo ▷ vt (tighten: muscles) tensar
tension ['tɛnʃən] n tensión
tent [tɛnt] n tienda (de campaña), carpa (LAm)
tentative ['tɛntətɪv] adj (person) indeciso; (provisional) provisional
tenterhooks ['tɛntəhuks] npl: **on** ~ sobre ascuas
tenth [tɛnθ] adj décimo
tent peg n clavija, estaca
tent pole n mástil
tenuous ['tɛnjuəs] adj tenue
tenure ['tɛnjuə^r] n posesión, tenencia; **to have** ~ tener posesión or título de propiedad
tepid ['tɛpɪd] adj tibio
term [tə:m] n (limit) límite; (Comm) plazo; (word) término; (period) período; (Scol) trimestre ▷ vt llamar, calificar de; **terms** npl (conditions) condiciones; (Comm) precio, tarifa; **in the short/long** ~ a corto/largo plazo; **during his** ~ **of office** bajo su mandato; **to be on good** ~**s with sb** llevarse bien con algn; **to come to** ~**s with** (problem) aceptar; **in** ~**s of ...** en cuanto a ..., en términos de ...
terminal ['tə:mɪnl] adj terminal ▷ n (Elec) borne; (Comput) terminal; (also: **air terminal**) terminal; (Brit: also: **coach terminal**) (estación) terminal
terminate ['tə:mɪneɪt] vt poner término a; (pregnancy) interrumpir ▷ vi: **to ~ in** acabar en
terminology [tə:mɪ'nɔlədʒɪ] n terminología
terminus ['tə:mɪnəs] n término, (estación) terminal
termite ['tə:maɪt] n termita, comején
term paper n (US Univ) trabajo escrito trimestral or semestral
terrace ['tɛrəs] n terraza; (Brit: row of houses) hilera de casas adosadas; **the** ~**s** (Brit Sport) las gradas
terraced ['tɛrəst] adj (garden) escalonado; (house) adosado
terracotta ['tɛrə'kɔtə] n terracota
terrain [tɛ'reɪn] n terreno
terrible ['tɛrɪbl] adj terrible, horrible; (fam) malísimo
terribly ['tɛrɪblɪ] adv terriblemente; (very badly) malísimamente
terrier ['tɛrɪə^r] n terrier
terrific [tə'rɪfɪk] adj fantástico, fenomenal, macanudo (LAm); (wonderful) maravilloso
terrify ['tɛrɪfaɪ] vt aterrorizar; **to be terrified** estar aterrado or aterrorizado
territory ['tɛrɪtərɪ] n territorio
terror ['tɛrə^r] n terror

terror attack n atentado (terrorista)
terrorism ['tɛrərɪzəm] n terrorismo
terrorist ['tɛrərɪst] n terrorista
terrorize ['tɛrəraɪz] vt aterrorizar
terse [tə:s] adj (style) conciso; (reply) brusc
TESL [tɛsl] n abbr = **Teaching of English as a Second Language**
test [tɛst] n (trial, check) prueba, ensayo; (: of goods in factory) control; (of courage etc, Chem, Med) prueba; (of blood, urine) análisis; (exam) examen, test; (also: **driving test**) examen de conducir ▷ vt probar, poner a prueba; (Med) examinar; (: blood) analizar; **a spelling** ~ una prueba de ortografía; **an eye** ~ un examen de la vista; **to put sth to the** ~ someter algo a prueba; **he ~ed us on the new vocabulary** nos hizo una prueba del vocabulario nuevo; **to** ~ **sth for sth** analizar algo en busca de algo; **she was ~ed for drugs** le hicieron la prueba antidoping; **to** ~ **something out** probar algo
testament ['tɛstəmənt] n testamento; **the Old/New T**~ el Antiguo/Nuevo Testamento
testicle ['tɛstɪkl] n testículo
testify ['tɛstɪfaɪ] vi (Law) prestar declaración; **to** ~ **to sth** atestiguar algo
testimony ['tɛstɪmənɪ] n (Law) testimonio, declaración
test match n partido internacional
testosterone [tɛs'tɔstərəun] n testosterona
test pilot n piloto de pruebas
test tube n probeta
tetanus ['tɛtənəs] n tétano
tether ['tɛðə^r] vt atar (con una cuerda) ▷ n: **to be at the end of one's** ~ no aguantar más
text [tɛkst] n texto ▷ vt: **to** ~ **sb** enviar un mensaje (de texto) or un SMS a algn
textbook ['tɛkstbuk] n libro de texto
textiles ['tɛkstaɪlz] npl tejidos
text message n mensaje de texto, SMS
text messaging n (envío de) mensajes de texto, (envío de) SMS
textual ['tɛkstjuəl] adj del texto, textual
texture ['tɛkstʃə^r] n textura
Thames [tɛmz] n: **the** ~ el (río) Támesis
than [ðæn, ðən] conj que; (with numerals): **more** ~ **10/once** más de 10/una vez; **she's taller** ~ **me** es más alta que yo; **I have more/less** ~ **you** tengo más/menos que tú; **it is better to phone** ~ **to write** es mejor llamar por teléfono que escribir; **no sooner did he leave** ~ **the phone rang** en cuanto se marchó, sonó el teléfono
thank [θæŋk] vt dar las gracias a, agradecer; ~ **you (very much)** muchas gracias; ~ **heavens,** ~ **God!** ¡gracias a Dios!, ¡menos mal!
thankful ['θæŋkful] adj: ~ **for** agradecido por
thankless ['θæŋklɪs] adj ingrato
thanks [θæŋks] npl gracias ▷ excl ¡gracias!; ~ **to** prep gracias a
Thanksgiving (Day) ['θæŋksgɪvɪŋ-] n día de Acción de Gracias
that [ðæt] (pl those) adj (demonstrative) ese(-a); (pl) esos(-as); (more remote) aquel (aquella); (pl)

aquellos(-as); **leave those books on the table** deja esos libros sobre la mesa; ~ **one** ése (ésa); (more remote) aquél (aquélla); ~ **one over there** ése (ésa) de ahí; aquél (aquélla) de allí ▷ pron **1** (demonstrative) ése(-a); (pl) ésos(-as); (neuter) eso; (more remote) aquél (aquélla); (pl) aquéllos(-as); (neuter) aquello; **what's ~?** ¿qué es eso (or aquello)?; **who's ~?** ¿quién es?; (when pointing etc) ¿quién es ése/a?; **is ~ you?** ¿eres tú?; **will you eat all ~?** ¿vas a comer todo eso?; **~'s my house** ésa es mi casa; **~'s what he said** eso es lo que dijo; **~ is (to say)** es decir; **at** or **with ~ she …** en eso, ella …; **do it like ~** hazlo así

2 (relative: subject, object) que; (with preposition) (el (la)) que, el (la) cual; **the book (~) I read** el libro que leí; **the books ~ are in the library** los libros que están en la biblioteca; **all (~) I have** todo lo que tengo; **the box (~) I put it in** la caja en la que or donde lo puse; **the people (~) I spoke to** la gente con la que hablé; **not ~ I know of** que yo sepa, no

3 (relative: of time) que; **the day (~) he came** el día (en) que vino ▷ conj que; **he thought ~ I was ill** creyó que yo estaba enfermo ▷ adv (demonstrative): **I can't work ~ much** no puedo trabajar tanto; **I didn't realize it was ~ bad** no creí que fuera tan malo; **~ high** así de alto

thatched [θætʃt] adj (roof) de paja; **~ cottage** casita con tejado de paja

thaw [θɔː] n deshielo ▷ vi (ice) derretirse; (food) descongelarse ▷ vt (food) descongelar

the [ðiː, ðə] def art **1** (gen) el; (fˇ) la; (pl) los; (fpl) las; (NB = el immediately before feminine noun beginning with stressed (h)a; a+el = al; de+el = del): **~ boy/girl** el chico/la chica; **~ books/flowers** los libros/las flores; **to ~ postman/from ~ drawer** al cartero/del cajón; **I haven't ~ time/money** no tengo tiempo/dinero; **one euro to ~ dollar** un euro por dólar; **paid by ~ hour** pagado por hora

2 (+ adj to form noun) los; lo; **~ rich and ~ poor** los ricos y los pobres; **to attempt ~ impossible** intentar lo imposible

3 (in titles, surnames): **Elizabeth ~ First** Isabel Primera; **Peter ~ Great** Pedro el Grande; **do you know ~ Smiths?** ¿conoce a los Smith?

4 (in comparisons): **~ more he works ~ more he earns** cuanto más trabaja más gana

theatre, (US) **theater** ['θɪətər] n teatro

theatre-goer, (US) **theater-goer** ['θɪətəgəuər] n aficionado(-a) al teatro

theatrical [θɪˈætrɪkl] adj teatral

theft [θeft] n robo

their [ðɛər] adj su

theirs [ðɛəz] pron (el) suyo/(la) suya etc; see also **my**; **mine**

them [ðɛm, ðəm] pron (direct) los(-las); (indirect) les; (stressed, after prep) ellos(-ellas); **I see ~** los veo; **both of ~** ambos(-as), los(-las) dos; **give me a few of ~** dame algunos(-as); see also **me**

theme [θiːm] n tema

theme park n parque temático

theme song n tema (musical)

themselves [ðəmˈsɛlvz] pl pron (subject) ellos mismos(-ellas mismas); (complement) se; (after prep) sí (mismos(-as)); see also **oneself**

then [ðɛn] adv (at that time) entonces; (in those days) en aquella época; (next) después; (later) luego, después; (and also) además ▷ conj (therefore) en ese caso, entonces ▷ adj: **the ~ president** el entonces presidente; **from ~ on** desde entonces; **until ~** hasta entonces; **by ~ it was too late** para entonces ya era demasiado tarde; **and ~ what?** y luego, ¿qué?; **now and ~ de vez en cuando; what do you want me to do, ~?** ¿entonces, qué quiere que haga?; **my pen's run out — use a pencil ~!** se me ha acabado el bolígrafo — ¡pues usa un lápiz!

theologian [θɪəˈləudʒən] n teólogo(-a)

theology [θɪˈɔlədʒɪ] n teología

theoretical [θɪəˈrɛtɪkl] adj teórico

theorize ['θɪəraɪz] vi teorizar

theory ['θɪərɪ] n teoría

therapeutic(al) [θɛrəˈpjuːtɪk(l)] adj terapéutico

therapist ['θɛrəpɪst] n terapeuta

therapy ['θɛrəpɪ] n terapia

there ['ðɛər] adv **1**: **~ is, ~ are** hay; **~ is no-one here** no hay nadie aquí; **~ is no bread left** no queda pan; **~ has been an accident** ha habido un accidente

2 (referring to place) ahí; (distant) allí; **it's ~** está ahí; **put it in/on/up/down** ~ ponlo ahí dentro/encima/arriba/abajo; **I want that book ~** quiero ese libro de ahí; **~ he is!** ¡ahí está!; **~'s the bus** ahí or ya viene el autobús; **back/down ~** allí atrás/abajo; **over ~, through ~** por allí

3: **~, ~** (esp to child) ¡venga, venga!

thereabouts ['ðɛərəˈbauts] adv por ahí

thereafter [ðɛərˈɑːftər] adv después

thereby ['ðɛəbaɪ] adv así, de ese modo

therefore ['ðɛəfɔːr] adv por lo tanto

there's [ðɛəz] = **there is**; **there has**

thereupon [ðɛərəˈpɔn] adv en eso, en seguida

thermal ['θəːml] adj termal

thermometer [θəˈmɔmɪtər] n termómetro

Thermos® ['θəːməs] n (also: **Thermos flask**) termo

thermostat ['θəːməustæt] n termostato

thesaurus [θɪˈsɔːrəs] n tesoro, diccionario de sinónimos

these [ðiːz] pl adj estos(-as) ▷ pl pron éstos(-as)

thesis ['θiːsɪs] (pl **theses**) ['θiːsiːz] n tesis; see also **doctorate**

they [ðeɪ] pl pron ellos(-ellas); **~ say that …** (it is said that) se dice que …

they'd [ðeɪd] = **they had**; **they would**

they'll [ðeɪl] = **they shall**; **they will**

they're [ðeər] = **they are**

they've [ðeɪv] = **they have**

thick [θɪk] adj (wall, slice) grueso; (dense: liquid, smoke etc) espeso; (vegetation, beard) tupido; (stupid) torpe ▷ n: **in the ~ of the battle** en lo más reñido de la batalla; **it's 20 cm ~** tiene 20 cm de espesor

thicken ['θɪkn] *vi* espesarse ▷ *vt* (*sauce etc*) espesar

thicket ['θɪkɪt] *n* espesura

thickness ['θɪknɪs] *n* espesor, grueso

thickset [θɪk'sɛt] *adj* fornido

thickskinned [θɪk'skɪnd] *adj* (*fig*) insensible

thief [θiːf] (*pl* **thieves**) [θiːvz] *n* ladrón(-ona)

thigh [θaɪ] *n* muslo

thimble ['θɪmbl] *n* dedal

thin [θɪn] *adj* delgado; (*wall, layer*) fino; (*watery*) aguado; (*light*) tenue; (*hair*) escaso; (*fog*) ligero; (*crowd*) disperso ▷ *vt*: **to ~ (down)** (*sauce, paint*) diluir ▷ *vi* (*fog*) aclararse; (*also*: **thin out**: *crowd*) dispersarse; **his hair is ~ning** se está quedando calvo

thing [θɪŋ] *n* cosa; (*object*) objeto, artículo; (*contraption*) chisme; (*mania*) manía; **things** *npl* (*belongings*) cosas; **the best ~ would be to ...** lo mejor sería ...; **the main ~ is ...** lo principal es ...; **first ~ (in the morning)** a primera hora (de la mañana); **last ~ (at night)** a última hora (de la noche); **the ~ is ...** lo que pasa es que ...; **how are ~s?** ¿qué tal van las cosas?; **she's got a ~ about mice** le dan no sé qué los ratones; **poor ~!** ¡pobre!, ¡pobrecito(-a)!

think [θɪŋk] (*pt, pp* **thought**) *vi* pensar ▷ *vt* pensar, creer; (*imagine*) imaginar; **what did you ~ of it?** ¿qué te parece?; **to ~ about sth/sb** pensar en algo/algn; **I'll ~ about it** lo pensaré; **~ carefully before you reply** piénsalo bien antes de responder; **to ~ of doing sth** pensar en hacer algo; **I ~ so** creo que sí; **I don't ~ so** creo que no; **I ~ you're wrong** creo que estás equivocado; **~ again!** ¡piénsalo bien!; **to ~ aloud** pensar en voz alta; **to ~ well of sb** tener buen concepto de algn; **~ what life would be like without cars** imagínate cómo sería la vida sin coches

▶ **think out** *vt* (*plan*) elaborar, tramar; (*solution*) encontrar

▶ **think over** *vt* reflexionar sobre, meditar; **I'll ~ it over** lo pensaré; **I'd like to ~ things over** me gustaría pensármelo

▶ **think through** *vt* pensar bien

▶ **think up** *vt* imaginar

think tank *n* grupo de expertos

thinly ['θɪnlɪ] *adv* (*cut*) en lonchas finas; (*spread*) en una capa fina

third [θəːd] *adj* (*before nmsg*) tercer, tercero ▷ *n* tercero(-a); (*fraction*) tercio; (*Brit Scol: degree*) título universitario de tercera clase

thirdly ['θəːdlɪ] *adv* en tercer lugar

third party insurance *n* (*Brit*) seguro a terceros

third-rate ['θəːd'reɪt] *adj* de poca calidad

Third World *n*: **the ~** el Tercer Mundo tercermundista

thirst [θəːst] *n* sed

thirsty ['θəːstɪ] *adj* (*person*) sediento; **to be ~** tener sed

thirteen [θəː'tiːn] *num* trece

thirteenth [θəː'tiːnθ] *adj* decimotercero ▷ *n* (*in series*) decimotercero(-a); (*fraction*) decimotercio

thirtieth ['θəːtɪəθ] *adj* trigésimo ▷ *n* (*in series*) trigésimo(-a); (*fraction*) treintavo

thirty ['θəːtɪ] *num* treinta

this [ðɪs] (*pl* **these**) *adj* (*demonstrative*) este(-a); (*pl*) estos(-as); (*neuter*) esto; **~ man/woman** este hombre/esta mujer; **these children/flowers** estos chicos/estas flores; **~ way** por aquí; **~ time last year** hoy hace un año; **~ one (here)** éste(-a), esto (de aquí)

▷ *pron* (*demonstrative*) éste(-a); (*pl*) éstos(-as); (*neuter*) esto; **who is ~?** ¿quién es éste(-ésta)?; **what is ~?** ¿qué es esto?; **~ is where I live** aquí vivo; **~ is what he said** esto es lo que dijo; **~ is Mr Brown** (*in introductions*) le presento al Sr. Brown; (*in photo*) éste es el Sr. Brown; (*on telephone*) habla el Sr. Brown; **they were talking of ~ and that** hablaban de esto y lo otro

▷ *adv* (*demonstrative*): **~ high/long** así de alto/largo; **~ far** hasta aquí

thistle ['θɪsl] *n* cardo

thorn [θɔːn] *n* espina

thorough ['θʌrə] *adj* (*search*) minucioso; (*knowledge*) profundo; (*research*) a fondo

thoroughbred ['θʌrəbrɛd] *adj* (*horse*) de pura sangre

thoroughfare ['θʌrəfɛəʳ] *n* calle; **"no ~"** "prohibido el paso"

thoroughly ['θʌrəlɪ] *adv* minuciosamente; a fondo

those [ðəuz] *pl pron* ésos (ésas); (*more remote*) aquéllos(-as) ▷ *pl adj* esos (esas); aquellos(-as)

though [ðəu] *conj* aunque ▷ *adv* sin embargo, aún así; **even ~** aunque; **it's not so easy, ~** sin embargo no es tan fácil

thought [θɔːt] *pt, pp of* **think** ▷ *n* pensamiento; (*opinion*) opinión; (*intention*) intención; **to give sth some ~** pensar algo detenidamente; **after much ~** después de pensarlo bien; **I've just had a ~** se me acaba de ocurrir una idea; **he kept his ~s to himself** no le dijo a nadie lo que pensaba; **it was a nice ~, thank you** fue muy amable de tu parte, gracias

thoughtful ['θɔːtful] *adj* pensativo; (*considerate*) atento

thoughtless ['θɔːtlɪs] *adj* desconsiderado

thousand ['θauzənd] *num* mil; **two ~** dos mil; **~s of** miles de

thousandth ['θauzəntθ] *num* milésimo

thrash [θræʃ] *vt* dar una paliza a

▶ **thrash about** *vi* revolverse

▶ **thrash out** *vt* discutir a fondo

thread [θrɛd] *n* hilo; (*of screw*) rosca ▷ *vt* (*needle*) enhebrar

threadbare ['θrɛdbɛəʳ] *adj* raído

threat [θrɛt] *n* amenaza; **to be under ~ of** estar amenazado de

threaten ['θrɛtn] *vi* amenazar ▷ *vt*: **to ~ sb with sth/to do** amenazar a algn con algo/con hacer

three [θriː] *num* tres

three-dimensional [θriːdɪ'mɛnʃənl] *adj* tridimensional

threefold ['θriːfəuld] *adv*: **to increase ~** triplicar

three-piece ['θriːpiːs]: **~ suit** n traje de tres piezas; **~ suite** n tresillo

three-ply [θriːˈplaɪ] adj (wood) de tres capas; (wool) triple

three-quarter [θriːˈkwɔːtər] adj: **~ length sleeves** mangas tres cuartos

three-quarters [θriːˈkwɔːtəz] npl tres cuartas partes; **~ full** tres cuartas partes lleno

thresh [θrɛʃ] vt (Agr) trillar

threshold ['θrɛʃhəuld] n umbral; **to be on the ~ of** (fig) estar al borde de

threw [θruː] pt of **throw**

thrift [θrɪft] n economía

thrifty ['θrɪftɪ] adj económico

thrill [θrɪl] n (excitement) emoción ▷ vt emocionar; **to be ~ed** (with gift etc) estar encantado

thriller ['θrɪlər] n película/novela de suspense

thrilling ['θrɪlɪŋ] adj emocionante

thrive [θraɪv] (pt **-d, throve**, pp **-d, -n**) [θrəuv, 'θrɪvn] vi (grow) crecer; (do well) prosperar

thriving ['θraɪvɪŋ] adj próspero

throat [θrəut] n garganta; **I have a sore ~** me duele la garganta

throb [θrɒb] n (of heart) latido; (of engine) vibración ▷ vi latir; vibrar; (with pain) dar punzadas; **my head is ~bing** la cabeza me da punzadas

throes [θrəuz] npl: **in the ~ of** en medio de

thrombosis [θrɒmˈbəusɪs] n trombosis

throne [θrəun] n trono

throng [θrɒŋ] n multitud, muchedumbre ▷ vt, vi apiñarse, agolparse

throttle ['θrɒtl] n (Aut) acelerador ▷ vt estrangular

through [θruː] prep a través de, por; (time) durante; (by means of) por medio de, mediante; (owing to) gracias a ▷ adj (ticket, train) directo ▷ adv completamente; de parte a parte; de principio a fin; **to look ~ a telescope** mirar a través de un telescopio; **I know her ~ my sister** la conozco a través de mi hermana; **the thief got in ~ the kitchen window** el ladrón entró por la ventana de la cocina; **to walk ~ the woods** pasear por el bosque; **to go ~ a tunnel** atravesar un túnel; **to go ~ sb's papers** mirar entre los papeles de algn; **I saw him ~ the crowd** lo vi entre la multitud; **I am halfway ~ the book** voy por la mitad del libro; **all ~ the night** durante toda la noche; **(from) Monday ~ Friday** (US) de lunes a viernes; **he went straight ~ to the dining room** pasó directamente al comedor; **from May ~ to September** desde mayo hasta septiembre; **the soldiers didn't let us ~** los soldados no nos dejaron pasar; **it's frozen ~** está completamente helado; **the nail went right ~** el clavo penetró de parte a parte; **the window was dirty and I couldn't see ~** la ventana estaba sucia y no podía ver nada; **to put sb ~ to sb** (Tel) poner or pasar a algn con algn; **to be ~** (Tel) tener comunicación; (have finished) haber terminado; **"no ~ road"** (Brit) "calle sin salida"

throughout [θruːˈaut] prep (place) por todas partes de, por todo; (time) durante todo ▷ adv por or en todas partes

throve [θrəuv] pt of **thrive**

throw [θrəu] n tiro; (Sport) lanzamiento ▷ vt (pt **threw**, pp **-n**) tirar, echar; (Sport) lanzar; (rider) derribar; (fig) desconcertar; **he threw the ball to me** me tiró la pelota; **to ~ a party** dar una fiesta

▸ **throw about, throw around** vt (litter etc) tirar, esparcir

▸ **throw away** vt (rubbish) tirar, botar (LAm); (chance) desperdiciar

▸ **throw off** vt deshacerse de

▸ **throw open** vt (doors, windows) abrir de par en par; (competition, race) abrir a todos

▸ **throw out** vt (rubbish) tirar, botar (LAm); (person) echar

▸ **throw together** vt (clothes) amontonar; (meal) preparar a la carrera

▸ **throw up** vi vomitar, devolver

throwaway ['θrəuəweɪ] adj para tirar, desechable

throw-in ['θrəuɪn] n (Sport) saque de banda

thrown [θrəun] pp of **throw**

thru [θruː] (US) = **through**

thrush [θrʌʃ] n zorzal, tordo; (Med) candiasis

thrust [θrʌst] n (Tech) empuje ▷ vt (pt, pp **-**) empujar; (push in) introducir

thud [θʌd] n golpe sordo

thug [θʌg] n gamberro(-a)

thumb [θʌm] n (Anat) pulgar ▷ vt: **to ~ a lift** hacer dedo; **to give sth/sb the ~s up/down** aprobar/desaprobar algo/a algn

▸ **thumb through** vt fus (book) hojear

thumbtack ['θʌmtæk] n (US) chincheta, chinche

thump [θʌmp] n golpe; (sound) ruido seco or sordo ▷ vt, vi golpear

thunder ['θʌndər] n trueno; (of applause etc) estruendo ▷ vi tronar; (train etc): **to ~ past** pasar como un trueno

thunderbolt ['θʌndəbəult] n rayo

thunderclap ['θʌndəklæp] n trueno

thunderstorm ['θʌndəstɔːm] n tormenta

thundery ['θʌndərɪ] adj tormentoso

Thursday ['θəːzdɪ] n jueves; see also **Tuesday**

thus [ðʌs] adv así, de este modo

thwart [θwɔːt] vt frustrar

thyme [taɪm] n tomillo

tiara [tɪˈɑːrə] n tiara, diadema

tick [tɪk] n (sound: of clock) tictac; (mark) señal (de visto bueno), palomita (LAm); (Zool) garrapata; (Brit col): **in a ~** en un instante; (Brit col: credit): **to buy sth on ~** comprar algo a crédito ▷ vi hacer tictac ▷ vt marcar, señalar; **to put a ~ against sth** poner una señal en algo

▸ **tick off** vt marcar; (person) reñir

▸ **tick over** vi (Brit: engine) girar en marcha lenta; (: fig) ir tirando

ticket ['tɪkɪt] n billete, tíquet, boleto (LAm); (for cinema etc) entrada, boleto (LAm); (in shop: on goods) etiqueta; (for library) tarjeta; (US Pol) lista (de candidatos); **to get a parking ~** (Aut) ser multado por estacionamiento ilegal

ticket collector n revisor(a)

ticket office n (Theat) taquilla, boletería (LAm); (Rail) despacho de billetes or boletos (LAm)

tickle ['tɪkl] n: **to give sb a ~** hacer cosquillas a algn ▷ vt hacer cosquillas a

ticklish ['tɪklɪʃ] adj (which tickles: blanket) que pica; (: cough) irritante; **to be ~** tener cosquillas

tidal ['taɪdl] adj de marea

tidal wave n maremoto

tidbit ['tɪdbɪt] (US) = **titbit**

tiddlywinks ['tɪdlɪwɪŋks] n juego de la pulga

tide [taɪd] n marea; (fig: of events) curso, marcha ▷ vt: **to ~ sb over (until)** sacar a algn del apuro (hasta); **high/low ~** marea alta/baja

tidy ['taɪdɪ] adj (room) ordenado; (drawing, work) limpio; (person) (bien) arreglado; (: in character) metódico; (mind) claro, metódico ▷ vt (also: **tidy up**) ordenar, poner en orden

tie [taɪ] n (string etc) atadura; (Brit: necktie) corbata; (fig: link) vínculo, lazo; (Sport: draw) empate ▷ vt atar ▷ vi (Sport) empatar; **family ~s** obligaciones familiares; **cup ~** (Sport: match) partido de copa; **to ~ sth in a bow** hacer un lazo con algo; **to ~ a knot in sth** hacer un nudo en algo; **they ~d 3** all empataron a 3

▶ **tie down** vt (with rope) sujetar, amarrar (LAm); (fig) atar; **he felt ~d down by the relationship** se sentía atado por la relación; **to ~ sb down to** (commit) obligar a algn a

▶ **tie in** vi: **to ~ in (with)** (correspond) concordar (con)

▶ **tie on** vt (Brit: label etc) atar

▶ **tie up** vt (dog, shoelaces, person) atar; (parcel) envolver; (boat) amarrar; (arrangements) concluir; **to be ~d up** (busy) estar ocupado

tier [tɪəʳ] n grada; (of cake) piso

tiger ['taɪɡəʳ] n tigre

tight [taɪt] adj (rope) tirante; (clothes: close-fitting) ceñido, ajustado; (too small) estrecho, apretado; (budget) ajustado; (programme) apretado; (col: drunk) borracho ▷ adv (squeeze) muy fuerte; (shut) herméticamente; **money was ~** estábamos bastante escasos de dinero; **to be packed ~** (suitcase) estar completamente lleno; (people) estar apretados; **everybody hold ~!** ¡agárrense bien!

tighten ['taɪtn] vt (rope) tensar, estirar; (screw) apretar ▷ vi estirarse; apretarse

tight-fisted [taɪt'fɪstɪd] adj tacaño

tight-lipped ['taɪt'lɪpt] adj: **to be ~** (silent) rehusar hablar; (angry) apretar los labios

tightly ['taɪtlɪ] adv (grasp) muy fuerte

tightrope ['taɪtrəup] n cuerda floja

tights [taɪts] npl (Brit) medias, panties

tile [taɪl] n (on roof) teja; (on floor) baldosa; (on wall) azulejo ▷ vt (floor) poner baldosas en; (wall) alicatar

tiled [taɪld] adj (floor) embaldosado; (wall, bathroom) alicatado; (roof) con tejas

till [tɪl] n caja (registradora) ▷ vt (land) cultivar ▷ prep, conj = **until**

tiller ['tɪləʳ] n (Naut) caña del timón

tilt [tɪlt] vt inclinar ▷ vi inclinarse ▷ n (slope) inclinación; **to wear one's hat at a ~** llevar el sombrero echado a un lado or terciado; **(at) full ~** a toda velocidad or carrera

timber ['tɪmbəʳ] n (material) madera; (trees) árboles

time [taɪm] n tiempo; (epoch: often pl) época; (by clock) hora; (moment) momento; (occasion) vez; (Mus) compás ▷ vt calcular or medir el tiempo de; (race) cronometrar; (remark etc) elegir el momento para; **a long ~** mucho tiempo; **for the ~ being** de momento, por ahora; **in ~** (soon enough) a tiempo; (after some time) con el tiempo; (Mus) al compás; **we arrived in ~ for lunch** llegamos a tiempo para el almuerzo; **just in ~** justo a tiempo; **in a week's ~** dentro de una semana; **in no ~** en un abrir y cerrar de ojos; **any ~** cuando sea; **on ~** a la hora; **to be 30 minutes behind/ahead of ~** llevar media hora de retraso/adelanto; **to take one's ~** tomárselo con calma; **he'll do it in his own ~** (without being hurried) lo hará sin prisa; (out of working hours) lo hará en su tiempo libre; **by the ~ he arrived** cuando llegó; **what ~ is it?** ¿qué hora es?; **what ~ do you make it?** ¿qué hora es or tiene?; **what ~ do you get up?** ¿a qué hora te levantas?; **it was 2 o'clock, Spanish ~** eran las 2, hora española; **to be behind the ~s** estar atrasado; **this isn't a good ~ to ask him** éste no es buen momento para preguntarle; **come and see us any ~** ven a vernos cuando quieras; **how many ~s?** ¿cuánta veces?; **4 at a ~** 4 a la vez; **to carry 3 boxes at a ~** llevar 3 cajas a la vez; **at ~s** a veces, a ratos; **~ after ~, ~ and again** repetidas veces, una y otra vez; **from ~ to ~** de vez en cuando; **5 ~s 5** 5 por 5; **to keep ~** llevar el ritmo or el compás; **to have a good ~** pasarlo bien, divertirse; **to ~ sth well/badly** elegir un buen/mal momento para algo; **the bomb was ~d to explode 5 minutes later** la bomba estaba programada para explotar 5 minutos más tarde

time bomb n bomba de relojería

time frame n plazo

time lag n desfase

timeless ['taɪmlɪs] adj eterno

timely ['taɪmlɪ] adj oportuno

time off n tiempo libre

timer ['taɪməʳ] n (timer switch) interruptor; (in kitchen, Tech) temporizador

time scale n escala de tiempo

time switch n (Brit) interruptor (horario)

timetable ['taɪmteɪbl] n horario; (programme of events etc) programa

time zone n huso horario

timid ['tɪmɪd] adj tímido

timing ['taɪmɪŋ] n (Sport) cronometraje; **the ~ of his resignation** el momento que eligió para dimitir

timpani ['tɪmpənɪ] npl tímpanos

tin [tɪn] n estaño; (also: **tin plate**) hojalata; (Brit: can) lata

tinfoil ['tɪnfɔɪl] n papel de estaño

tinge [tɪndʒ] n matiz ▷ vt: **~d with** teñido de

tingle ['tɪŋgl] n hormigueo ▷ vi (cheeks, skin: from cold) sentir comezón; (: from bad circulation) sentir hormigueo

tinker ['tɪŋkər] n calderero(-a); (gipsy) gitano(-a)
  ► **tinker with** vt fus jugar con, tocar

tinkle ['tɪŋkl] vi tintinear

tinned [tɪnd] adj (Brit: food) en lata, en conserva

tinnitus ['tɪnɪtəs] n (Med) acufeno

tin opener [-əupnər] n (Brit) abrelatas

tinsel ['tɪnsl] n oropel

tint [tɪnt] n matiz; (for hair) tinte ▷ vt (hair) teñir

tinted ['tɪntɪd] adj (hair) teñido; (glass, spectacles) ahumado

tiny ['taɪnɪ] adj minúsculo, pequeñito

tip [tɪp] n (end) punta; (gratuity) propina; (Brit: for rubbish) vertedero; (advice) consejo ▷ vt (waiter) dar una propina a; (tilt) inclinar; (empty: also: **tip out**) vaciar, echar; (predict: winner) pronosticar; (: horse) recomendar; **he ~ped out the contents of the box** volcó el contenido de la caja
  ► **tip off** vt avisar, poner sobreaviso a
  ► **tip over** vt volcar ▷ vi volcarse

tip-off ['tɪpɔf] n (hint) advertencia

tipped [tɪpt] adj (Brit: cigarette) con filtro

Tipp-Ex® ['tɪpeks] n Tipp-Ex®

tipster ['tɪpstər] n (Racing) pronosticador(a)

tipsy ['tɪpsɪ] adj alegre, achispado

tiptoe ['tɪptəu] n (Brit): **on ~** de puntillas

tiptop ['tɪptɔp] adj: **in ~ condition** en perfectas condiciones

tirade [taɪ'reɪd] n diatriba

tire ['taɪər] n (US) = **tyre** ▷ vt cansar ▷ vi (gen) cansarse; (become bored) aburrirse
  ► **tire out** vt agotar, rendir

tired ['taɪəd] adj cansado; **to be ~ of sth** estar harto de algo; **to be/feel/look ~** estar/sentirse/parecer cansado

tireless ['taɪəlɪs] adj incansable

tiresome ['taɪəsəm] adj aburrido

tiring ['taɪrɪŋ] adj cansado

tissue ['tɪʃuː] n tejido; (paper handkerchief) pañuelo de papel, kleenex®

tissue paper n papel de seda

tit [tɪt] n (bird) herrerillo común; **to give ~ for tat** dar ojo por ojo

titbit ['tɪtbɪt], (US) **tidbit** ['tɪdbɪt] n (food) golosina; (news) pedazo

title ['taɪtl] n título; (Law: right): **~ (to)** derecho (a)

title deed n (Law) título de propiedad

title role n papel principal

titter ['tɪtər] vi reírse entre dientes

TM abbr (= trademark) marca de fábrica; = **transcendental meditation**

to [tuː, tə] prep 1 (direction) a; **to go to France/ London/school/the station** ir a Francia/ Londres/al colegio/a la estación; **to go to Claude's/the doctor's** ir a casa de Claude/al médico; **the road to Edinburgh** la carretera de Edimburgo; **to the left/right** a la izquierda/ derecha

2 (as far as) hasta, a; **from here to London** de aquí a or hasta Londres; **to count to 10** contar hasta 10; **from 40 to 50 people** entre 40 y 50 personas

3 (with expressions of time): **a quarter/twenty to 5** las 5 menos cuarto/veinte

4 (for, of): **the key to the front door** la llave de la puerta principal; **she is secretary to the director** es la secretaria del director; **a letter to his wife** una carta a or para su mujer

5 (expressing indirect object) a; **to give sth to sb** darle algo a algn; **give it to me** dámelo; **to talk to sb** hablar con algn; **to be a danger to sb** ser un peligro para algn; **to carry out repairs to sth** hacer reparaciones en algo

6 (in relation to): **3 goals to 2** 3 goles a 2; **30 miles to the gallon** = 9,4 litros a los cien (kilómetros); **8 apples to the kilo** 8 manzanas por kilo

7 (purpose, result): **to come to sb's aid** venir en auxilio or ayuda de algn; **to sentence sb to death** condenar a algn a muerte; **to my great surprise** con gran sorpresa mía

▷ with vb 1 (simple infin): **to go/eat** ir/comer

2 (following another vb; see also relevant vb): **to want/try/start to do** querer/intentar/empezar a hacer

3 (with vb omitted): **I don't want to** no quiero

4 (purpose, result) para; **I did it to help you** lo hice para ayudarte; **he came to see you** vino a verte

5 (equivalent to relative clause): **I have things to do** tengo cosas que hacer; **the main thing is to try** lo principal es intentarlo

6 (after adj etc): **ready to go** listo para irse; **too old to ...** demasiado viejo (como) para ...

▷ adv: **pull/push the door to** cerrar la de/empujar la puerta; **to go to and fro** ir y venir

toad [təud] n sapo

toadstool ['təudstuːl] n seta venenosa

toast [təust] n (Culin: also: **piece of toast**) tostada; (drink, speech) brindis ▷ vt (Culin) tostar; (drink to) brindar

toaster ['təustər] n tostador

tobacco [tə'bækəu] n tabaco

tobacconist [tə'bækənɪst] n estanquero(-a), tabaquero(-a) (LAm); **~'s (shop)** (Brit) estanco, tabaquería (LAm)

toboggan [tə'bɔgən] n tobogán

today [tə'deɪ] adv, n (also fig) hoy; **what day is it ~?** ¿qué día es hoy?; **what date is it ~?** ¿a qué fecha estamos hoy?; **~ is the 4th of March** hoy es el 4 de marzo; **~'s paper** el periódico de hoy; **a fortnight ~** de hoy en 15 días, dentro de 15 días

toddler ['tɔdlər] n niño(-a) (que empieza a andar)

toe [təu] n dedo (del pie); (of shoe) punta ▷ vt: **to ~ the line** (fig) acatar las normas; **big/little ~** dedo gordo/pequeño del pie

TOEFL n abbr = **Test(ing) of English as a Foreign Language**

toenail ['təuneɪl] n uña del pie

toffee ['tɔfɪ] n caramelo

toffee apple n (Brit) manzana de caramelo

tofu ['təufuː] n tofu

toga ['təugə] n toga
together [tə'gɛðə'] adv juntos; (at same time) al mismo tiempo, a la vez; **~ with** prep junto con
toil [tɔɪl] n trabajo duro, labor ▷ vi esforzarse
toilet ['tɔɪlət] n (Brit: lavatory) servicios, wáter (Esp), baño (LAm) ▷ cpd (bag, soap etc) de aseo; **to go to the ~** ir al baño; see also **toilets**
toilet paper n papel higiénico
toiletries ['tɔɪlətrɪz] npl artículos de aseo; (make-up etc) artículos de tocador
toilet roll n rollo de papel higiénico
toilets ['tɔɪləts] npl (Brit) servicios
toilet water n (agua de) colonia
token ['təukən] n (sign) señal, muestra; (souvenir) recuerdo; (voucher) vale; (disc) ficha ▷ cpd (fee, strike) nominal, simbólico; **book/record ~** (Brit) vale para comprar libros/discos; **by the same ~** (fig) por la misma razón
tokenism ['təukənɪzəm] n (Pol) política simbólica or de fachada
told [təuld] pt, pp of **tell**
tolerable ['tɔlərəbl] adj (bearable) soportable; (fairly good) pasable
tolerance ['tɔlərns] n (also Tech) tolerancia
tolerant ['tɔlərnt] adj: **~ of** tolerante con
tolerate ['tɔləreɪt] vt tolerar
toll [təul] n (of casualties) número de víctimas; (tax, charge) peaje ▷ vi (bell) doblar
toll bridge n puente de peaje
tomato [tə'mɑːtəu] (pl -es) n tomate, jitomate (Méx)
tomb [tuːm] n tumba
tomboy ['tɔmbɔɪ] n marimacho
tombstone ['tuːmstəun] n lápida
tomcat ['tɔmkæt] n gato
tomorrow [tə'mɔrəu] adv, n (also fig) mañana; **the day after ~** pasado mañana; **~ morning** mañana por la mañana; **a week ~** de mañana en ocho (días)
ton [tʌn] n (Brit = 1.016 kg, US: also: **short ton:** = 907,18 kg) tonelada; **~s of** (col) montones de
tone [təun] n tono ▷ vi armonizar; **dialling ~** (Tel) señal para marcar
  ▶ **tone down** vt (criticism) suavizar; (colour) atenuar
  ▶ **tone up** vt (muscles) tonificar
tone-deaf [təun'dɛf] adj sin oído musical
tongs [tɔŋz] npl (for coal) tenazas; (for hair) tenacillas
tongue [tʌŋ] n lengua; **~ in cheek** adv en plan de broma
tongue-tied ['tʌŋtaɪd] adj (fig) mudo
tongue-twister ['tʌŋtwɪstə'] n trabalenguas
tonic ['tɔnɪk] n (Med) tónico; (Mus) tónica; (also: **tonic water**) (agua) tónica
tonight [tə'naɪt] adv, n esta noche; **I'll see you ~** nos vemos esta noche
tonsil ['tɔnsl] n amígdala; **to have one's ~s out** sacarse las amígdalas or anginas
tonsillitis [tɔnsɪ'laɪtɪs] n amigdalitis; **to have ~** tener amigdalitis
too [tuː] adv (excessively) demasiado; (very) muy;

(also) también; **it's ~ sweet** está demasiado dulce; **I'm not ~ sure about that** no estoy muy seguro de eso; **I went ~** yo también fui; **~ much** adv, adj demasiado; **~ many** adj demasiados(-as); **~ bad!** ¡mala suerte!
took [tuk] pt of **take**
tool [tuːl] n herramienta
tool box n caja de herramientas
toot [tuːt] n (of horn) bocinazo; (of whistle) silbido ▷ vi (with car horn) tocar la bocina
tooth [tuːθ] (pl teeth) n (Anat, Tech) diente; (molar) muela; **to clean one's teeth** lavarse los dientes; **to have a ~ out** sacarse una muela; **by the skin of one's teeth** por un pelo
toothache ['tuːθeɪk] n dolor de muelas
toothbrush ['tuːθbrʌʃ] n cepillo de dientes
toothpaste ['tuːθpeɪst] n pasta de dientes
toothpick ['tuːθpɪk] n palillo
top [tɔp] n (of mountain) cumbre, cima; (of head) coronilla; (of ladder) (lo) alto; (of cupboard, table) superficie; (lid: of box, jar) tapa; (: of bottle) tapón; (of list, table, queue, page) cabeza; (toy) peonza; (Dress: blouse) blusa; (: T-shirt) camiseta; (: of pyjamas) chaqueta ▷ adj de arriba; (in rank) principal, primero; (best) mejor ▷ vt (exceed) exceder; (be first in) encabezar; **on ~ of** sobre, encima de; **there's a surcharge on ~ of that** hay un recargo, además; **from ~ to bottom** de pies a cabeza; **I searched the house from ~ to bottom** busqué en la casa de arriba abajo; **the ~ of the milk** la nata; **a bikini ~** la parte de arriba del bikini; **at the ~ of the stairs** en lo alto de la escalera; **at the ~ of the street** al final de la calle; **at the ~ of one's voice** (fig) a voz en grito; **over the ~** (col) excesivo, desmesurado; **to go over the ~** pasarse; **it's on the ~ shelf** está en la estantería de arriba; **the ~ floor** el último piso; **the ~ layer of skin** la capa superior de la piel; **at ~ speed** a máxima velocidad; **a ~ surgeon** uno de los mejores cirujanos; **a ~ model** una top model; **a ~ hotel** un hotel de primera; **he always gets ~ marks in French** siempre saca excelentes notas en francés
  ▶ **top up**, (US) **top off** vt volver a llenar
top-class ['tɔp'klɑːs] adj de primera clase
top floor n último piso
top hat n sombrero de copa
top-heavy [tɔp'hɛvɪ] adj (object) con más peso en la parte superior
topic ['tɔpɪk] n tema
topical ['tɔpɪkl] adj actual
topless ['tɔplɪs] adj (bather etc) topless
top-level ['tɔplɛvl] adj (talks) al más alto nivel
topmost ['tɔpməust] adj más alto
top-notch ['tɔp'nɔtʃ] adj (col) de primerísima categoría
topple ['tɔpl] vt volcar, derribar ▷ vi caerse
top-secret ['tɔp'siːkrɪt] adj de alto secreto
topsy-turvy ['tɔpsɪ'təːvɪ] adj, adv patas arriba
top-up loan n (Brit) préstamo complementario
torch [tɔːtʃ] n antorcha; (Brit: electric) linterna
tore [tɔː'] pt of **tear**

torment *n* tormento ▷ *vt* atormentar; (*fig: annoy*) fastidiar

torn [tɔːn] *pp of* **tear**

tornado [tɔːˈneɪdəu] **-es**) *n* tornado

torpedo [tɔːˈpiːdəu] **-es**) *n* torpedo

torrent [ˈtɔrnt] *n* torrente

torrid [ˈtɔrɪd] *adj* tórrido; (*fig*) apasionado

torso [ˈtɔːsəu] *n* torso

tortoise [ˈtɔːtəs] *n* tortuga

torture [ˈtɔːtʃə^r] *n* tortura ▷ *vt* torturar; (*fig*) atormentar

Tory [ˈtɔːrɪ] *adj, n* (*Brit Pol*) conservador(a)

toss [tɔs] *vt* tirar, echar; (*head*) sacudir ▷ *n* (*movement: of head etc*) sacudida; (*of coin*) tirada, echada (*LAm*); **to ~ a coin** echar a cara o cruz; **to ~ up for sth** jugar algo a cara o cruz; **to ~ and turn** (*in bed*) dar vueltas (en la cama); **to win/ lose the ~** (*also Sport*) ganar/perder (a cara o cruz)

tot [tɔt] *n* (*Brit: drink*) copita; (*child*) nene(-a)

▶ **tot up** *vt* sumar

total [ˈtəutl] *adj* total, entero ▷ *n* total, suma ▷ *vt* (*add up*) sumar; (*amount to*) ascender a; **grand ~** cantidad total; (*cost*) importe total; **in ~** en total, en suma

totality [təuˈtælɪtɪ] *n* totalidad

totally [ˈtəutəlɪ] *adv* totalmente

totter [ˈtɔtə^r] *vi* tambalearse

touch [tʌtʃ] *n* (*sense*) tacto; (*contact*) contacto; (*Football*) fuera de juego ▷ *vt* tocar; (*emotionally*) conmover; **a ~ of** (*fig*) una pizca *or* un poquito de; **to get/keep in ~ with sb** ponerse/mantenerse en contacto con algn; **keep in ~!** (*write*) ¡escribe de vez en cuando!; (*phone*) ¡llama de vez en cuando!; **I'll be in ~** le llamaré/escribiré; **to lose ~** (*friends*) perder contacto; **to be out of ~ with events** no estar al corriente (de los acontecimientos); **the personal ~** el toque personal; **to put the finishing ~es to sth** dar el último toque a algo; **no artist in the country can ~ him** no hay artista en todo el país que le iguale

▶ **touch on** *vt fus* (*topic*) aludir (brevemente) a

▶ **touch up** *vt* (*paint*) retocar

touch-and-go [ˈtʌtʃənˈgəu] *adj* arriesgado

touchdown [ˈtʌtʃdaun] *n* aterrizaje; (*US Football*) ensayo

touched [tʌtʃt] *adj* conmovido; (*col*) chiflado

touching [ˈtʌtʃɪŋ] *adj* conmovedor(a)

touchline [ˈtʌtʃlaɪn] *n* (*Sport*) línea de banda

touch-sensitive [ˈtʌtʃˈsɛnsɪtɪv] *adj* sensible al tacto

touchy [ˈtʌtʃɪ] *adj* (*person*) quisquilloso

tough [tʌf] *adj* (*meat*) duro; (*journey*) penoso; (*task, problem, situation*) difícil; (*resistant*) resistente; (*person*) fuerte; (: *pej*) bruto ▷ *n* (*gangster etc*) gorila; **they got ~ with the workers** se pusieron muy duros con los trabajadores

toughen [ˈtʌfn] *vt* endurecer

toupée [ˈtuːpeɪ] *n* peluquín

tour [ˈtuə^r] *n* viaje; (*also:* **package tour**) viaje con todo incluido; (*of town, museum*) visita ▷ *vt* viajar por; **to go on a ~ of** (*region, country*) ir de viaje

por; (*museum, castle*) visitar; **to go on ~** partir *or* ir de gira

tourism [ˈtuərɪzm] *n* turismo

tourist [ˈtuərɪst] *n* turista ▷ *cpd* turístico; **the ~ trade** el turismo

tourist class *n* (*Aviat*) clase turista

tourist office *n* oficina de turismo

tournament [ˈtuənəmənt] *n* torneo

tousled [ˈtauzld] *adj* (*hair*) despeinado

tout [taut] *vi*: **to ~ for business** solicitar clientes ▷ *n*: **ticket ~** revendedor(a)

tow [təu] *n*: **to give sb a ~** (*Aut*) remolcar a algn ▷ *vt* remolcar; **"on** *or* (*US*) **in ~"** (*Aut*) "a remolque"

toward(s) [təˈwɔːd(z)] *prep* hacia; (*of purpose*) para; **he came toward(s) me** vino hacia mí; **toward(s) the end of the year** hacia finales de año; **toward(s) noon** alrededor de mediodía; **to feel friendly toward(s) sb** sentir amistad hacia algn; **his attitude toward(s)** ... su actitud para con *or* respecto a *or* hacia ...; **we're saving toward(s) our holiday** ahorramos dinero para nuestras vacaciones

towel [ˈtauəl] *n* toalla; **to throw in the ~** (*fig*) darse por vencido, renunciar

towelling [ˈtauəlɪŋ] *n* (*fabric*) felpa

towel rail, (*US*) **towel rack** *n* toallero

tower [ˈtauə^r] *n* torre; (*also Comput*) ▷ *vi* (*building, mountain*) elevarse; **to ~ above** *or* **over sth/sb** dominar algo/destacarse sobre algn

tower block *n* (*Brit*) bloque de pisos

towering [ˈtauərɪŋ] *adj* muy alto, imponente

town [taun] *n* ciudad; **to go to ~** ir a la ciudad; (*fig*) tirar la casa por la ventana; **in the ~** en la ciudad; **to be out of ~** estar fuera de la ciudad

town centre *n* centro de la ciudad

town council *n* Ayuntamiento, consejo municipal

town hall *n* ayuntamiento

townie [ˈtaunɪ] *n* (*Brit col*) persona de la ciudad

town plan *n* plano de la ciudad

town planning *n* urbanismo

township [ˈtaunʃɪp] *n* municipio habitado sólo por negros en Sudáfrica

towrope [ˈtəurəup] *n* cable de remolque

tow truck *n* (*US*) camión grúa

toxic [ˈtɔksɪk] *adj* tóxico

toxin [ˈtɔksɪn] *n* toxina

toy [tɔɪ] *n* juguete

▶ **toy with** *vt fus* jugar con; (*idea*) acariciar

trace [treɪs] *n* rastro ▷ *vt* (*draw*) trazar, delinear; (*locate*) encontrar; **there was no ~ of it** no había ningún indicio de ello

tracing paper [ˈtreɪsɪŋ-] *n* papel de calco

track [træk] *n* (*mark*) huella, pista; (*path: gen*) camino, senda; (: *of bullet etc*) trayectoria; (: *of suspect, animal*) pista, rastro; (*Rail*) vía; (*Comput, Sport*) pista; (*on record*) canción ▷ *vt* seguir la pista de; **to keep ~ of** mantenerse al tanto de, seguir; **a 4-~ tape** una cinta de 4 pistas; **the first ~ on the record/tape** la primera canción en el disco/la cinta; **to be on the right ~** (*fig*) ir por

buen camino
▶ **track down** vt (person) localizar
track meet n (US) concurso de carreras y saltos
track record n: **to have a good ~** (fig) tener un buen historial
tracksuit ['træksu:t] n chandal
tract [trækt] n (Geo) región; (pamphlet) folleto
traction ['trækʃən] n (Aut: power) tracción; **in ~** (Med) en tracción
tractor ['træktər] n tractor
trade [treɪd] n comercio, negocio; (skill, job) oficio, empleo; (industry) industria ▷ vi negociar, comerciar; **foreign ~** comercio exterior
▶ **trade in** vt ofrecer como parte del pago
Trade Descriptions Act n (Brit) ley sobre descripciones comerciales
trade fair n feria de muestras
trade-in ['treɪdɪn] adj: **~ price/value** precio/valor de un artículo usado que se descuenta del precio de otro nuevo
trademark ['treɪdmɑːk] n marca de fábrica
trade name n marca registrada
trade-off n: **a ~ (between)** un equilibrio (entre)
trader ['treɪdər] n comerciante
trade secret n secreto profesional
tradesman ['treɪdzmən] n (shopkeeper) comerciante
trade union n sindicato
trade unionist [-'juːnjənɪst] n sindicalista
tradition [trə'dɪʃən] n tradición
traditional [trə'dɪʃənl] adj tradicional
traffic ['træfɪk] n (gen, Aut) tráfico, circulación, tránsito ▷ vi: **to ~ in** (pej: liquor, drugs) traficar en; **air ~** tráfico aéreo
traffic calming [-'kɑːmɪŋ] n reducción de la velocidad de la circulación
traffic circle n (US) glorieta de tráfico
traffic island n refugio, isleta
traffic jam n embotellamiento, atasco
traffic lights npl semáforo
traffic warden n guardia de tráfico
tragedy ['trædʒədɪ] n tragedia
tragic ['trædʒɪk] adj trágico
trail [treɪl] n (tracks) rastro, pista; (path) camino, sendero; (dust, smoke) estela ▷ vt (drag) arrastrar; (follow) seguir la pista de; (follow closely) vigilar ▷ vi arrastrarse; **to be on sb's ~** seguir la pista de algn
▶ **trail away, trail off** vi (sound) desvanecerse; (interest, voice) desaparecer
▶ **trail behind** vi quedar a la zaga
trailer ['treɪlər] n (Aut) remolque; (caravan) caravana; (Cine) trailer, avance
train [treɪn] n tren; (of dress) cola; (series): **~ of events** curso de los acontecimientos ▷ vt (educate) formar; (teach skills to) adiestrar; (sportsman) entrenar; (dog) amaestrar; (point: gun etc): **to ~ on** apuntar a ▷ vi (Sport) entrenarse; (be educated, learn a skill) formarse; **to go by ~** ir en tren; **one's ~ of thought** el razonamiento de algn; **to ~ sb to do sth** enseñar a algn a hacer algo
trained [treɪnd] adj (worker) cualificado; (animal) amaestrado
trainee [treɪ'niː] n trabajador(a) en prácticas ▷ cpd: **he's a ~ teacher** (primary) es estudiante de magisterio; (secondary) está haciendo las prácticas del I.C.E.
trainer ['treɪnər] n (Sport) entrenador(a); (of animals) domador(a); **trainers** npl (shoes) zapatillas (de deporte)
training ['treɪnɪŋ] n formación; entrenamiento; **to be in ~** (Sport) estar entrenando; (: fit) estar en forma
training college n (gen) colegio de formación profesional; (for teachers) escuela normal
traipse [treɪps] vi andar penosamente
trait [treɪt] n rasgo
traitor ['treɪtər] n traidor(a)
tram [træm] n (Brit: also: **tramcar**) tranvía
tramp [træmp] n (person) vagabundo(-a); (col: offensive: woman) puta ▷ vi andar con pasos pesados
trample ['træmpl] vt: **to ~ (underfoot)** pisotear
trampoline ['træmpəliːn] n trampolín
trance [trɑːns] n trance; **to go into a ~** entrar en trance
tranquil ['træŋkwɪl] adj tranquilo
tranquillizer, (US) **tranquilizer** ['træŋkwɪlaɪzər] n (Med) tranquilizante
transact [træn'zækt] vt (business) tramitar
transaction [træn'zækʃən] n transacción, operación; **cash ~s** transacciones al contado
transatlantic ['trænzət'læntɪk] adj transatlántico
transcend [træn'sɛnd] vt rebasar
transcendental [trænsɛn'dɛntl] adj: **~ meditation** meditación transcendental
transcribe [træn'skraɪb] vt transcribir, copiar
transcript ['trænskrɪpt] n copia
transcription [træn'skrɪpʃən] n transcripción
transfer n transferencia; (Sport) traspaso; (picture, design) calcomanía ▷ vt trasladar, pasar; **to ~ the charges** (Brit Tel) llamar a cobro revertido; **by bank ~** por transferencia bancaria or giro bancario; **to ~ money from one account to another** transferir dinero de una cuenta a otra; **to ~ sth to sb's name** transferir algo al nombre de algn
transform [træns'fɔːm] vt transformar
transformation [trænsfə'meɪʃən] n transformación
transfusion [træns'fjuːʒən] n transfusión
transient ['trænzɪənt] adj transitorio
transistor [træn'zɪstər] n (Elec) transistor
transit ['trænzɪt] n: **in ~** en tránsito
transition [træn'zɪʃən] n transición
transition period n período de transición
transitive ['trænzɪtɪv] adj (Ling) transitivo
translate [trænz'leɪt] vt: **to ~ (from/into)** traducir (de/a)
translation [trænz'leɪʃən] n traducción
translator [trænz'leɪtər] n traductor(a)
transmission [trænz'mɪʃən] n transmisión
transmit [trænz'mɪt] vt transmitir

transmitter [trænz'mɪtər] n transmisor; (station) emisora

transparency [træns'pɛərnsɪ] n (Brit Phot) diapositiva

transparent [træns'pærnt] adj transparente

transpire [træns'paɪər] vi (turn out) resultar (ser); (happen) ocurrir, suceder; (become known): **it finally ~d that ...** por fin se supo que ...

transplant vt transplantar ▷ n (Med) transplante; **to have a heart ~** hacerse un transplante de corazón

transport n transporte ▷ vt transportar; **public ~** transporte público

transportation [trænspɔː'teɪʃən] n transporte; (of prisoners) deportación

transport café n (Brit) bar-restaurante de carretera

transsexual [trænz'sɛksjuəl] adj, n transexual

transvestite [trænz'vɛstaɪt] n travesti

trap [træp] n (snare, trick) trampa; (carriage) cabriolé ▷ vt coger (Esp) or agarrar (LAm) en una trampa; (immobilize) bloquear; (jam) atascar; **to set** or **lay a ~ (for sb)** poner(le) una trampa (a algn); **to ~ one's finger in the door** pillarse el dedo en la puerta

trap door n escotilla

trapeze [trə'piːz] n trapecio

trappings ['træpɪŋz] npl adornos

trash [træʃ] n basura; (nonsense) tonterías

trash can n (US) cubo, cubo or tacho (CS) or bote (Méx) de la basura

trashy ['træʃɪ] adj (col) chungo

trauma ['trɔːmə] n trauma

traumatic [trɔː'mætɪk] adj (Psych, fig) traumático

travel ['trævl] n viaje ▷ vi viajar ▷ vt (distance) recorrer; **this wine doesn't ~ well** este vino pierde con los viajes

travel agency n agencia de viajes

travel agent n agente de viajes

traveller, (US) **traveler** ['trævlər] n viajero(-a); (Comm) viajante

traveller's cheque, (US) **traveler's check** n cheque de viaje

travelling, (US) **traveling** ['trævlɪŋ] n los viajes, el viajar ▷ adj (circus, exhibition) ambulante ▷ cpd (bag, clock) de viaje

travel sickness n mareo

travesty ['trævəstɪ] n parodia

trawler ['trɔːlər] n pesquero de arrastre

tray [treɪ] n (for carrying) bandeja; (on desk) cajón

treacherous ['trɛtʃərəs] adj traidor(a); **road conditions are ~** el estado de las carreteras es peligroso

treachery ['trɛtʃərɪ] n traición

treacle ['triːkl] n (Brit) melaza

tread [trɛd] n paso, pisada; (of tyre) banda de rodadura ▷ vi (pt **trod**, pp **trodden**) pisar
▷ **tread on** vt fus pisar

treason ['triːzn] n traición

treasure ['trɛʒər] n tesoro ▷ vt (value) apreciar, valorar

treasurer ['trɛʒərər] n tesorero(-a)

treasury ['trɛʒərɪ] n: **the T~** (US): **the T~ Department** ≈ el Ministerio de Economía y de Hacienda

treat [triːt] n (present) regalo; (pleasure) placer ▷ vt tratar; (consider) considerar; **to give sb a ~** hacer un regalo a algn; **to ~ sb to sth** invitar a algn a algo; **to ~ sth as a joke** tomar algo a broma

treatise ['triːtɪz] n tratado

treatment ['triːtmənt] n tratamiento; **to have ~ for sth** recibir tratamiento por algo

treaty ['triːtɪ] n tratado

treble ['trɛbl] adj triple ▷ vt triplicar ▷ vi triplicarse

treble clef n (Mus) clave de sol

tree [triː] n árbol

trek [trɛk] n (long journey) expedición; (tiring walk) caminata

trellis ['trɛlɪs] n enrejado

tremble ['trɛmbl] vi temblar

tremendous [trɪ'mɛndəs] adj tremendo; (enormous) enorme; (excellent) estupendo

tremor ['trɛmər] n temblor; (also: **earth tremor**) temblor de tierra

trench [trɛntʃ] n zanja; (Mil) trinchera

trend [trɛnd] n (tendency) tendencia; (of events) curso; (fashion) moda; **~ towards/away from sth** tendencia hacia/en contra de algo; **to set the ~** marcar la pauta

trendy ['trɛndɪ] adj de moda

trepidation [trɛpɪ'deɪʃən] n inquietud

trespass ['trɛspəs] vi: **to ~ on** entrar sin permiso en; **"no ~ing"** "prohibido el paso"

trestle ['trɛsl] n caballete

trial ['traɪəl] n (Law) juicio, proceso; (test: of machine etc) prueba; (hardship) desgracia; **trials** npl (Athletics, of horses) pruebas; **to bring sb to ~ (for a crime)** llevar a algn a juicio (por un delito); **~ by jury** juicio ante jurado; **to be sent for ~** ser remitido al tribunal; **by ~ and error** a fuerza de probar

triangle ['traɪæŋgl] n (Math, Mus) triángulo

triathlon [traɪ'æθlən] n triatlón

tribe [traɪb] n tribu

tribesman ['traɪbzmən] n miembro de una tribu

tribunal [traɪ'bjuːnl] n tribunal

tributary ['trɪbjutərɪ] n (river) afluente

tribute ['trɪbjuːt] n homenaje, tributo; **to pay ~ to** rendir homenaje a

trice [traɪs] n: **in a ~** en un santiamén

trick [trɪk] n trampa; (conjuring trick, deceit) truco; (joke) broma; (Cards) baza ▷ vt engañar; **it's a ~ of the light** es una ilusión óptica; **to play a ~ on sb** gastar una broma a algn; **that should do the ~** eso servirá; **to ~ sb out of sth** quitarle algo a algn con engaños; **to ~ sb into doing sth** hacer que algn haga algo con engaños

trickery ['trɪkərɪ] n engaño

trickle ['trɪkl] n (of water etc) hilo ▷ vi gotear

tricky ['trɪkɪ] adj difícil; (problem) delicado

tricycle ['traɪsɪkl] n triciclo

tried [traɪd] adj probado

trifle ['traɪfl] n bagatela; (Culin) dulce de bizcocho,

gelatina, fruta y natillas ▷ *adv*: **a ~ long** un pelín largo ▷ *vi*: **to ~ with** jugar con

trifling ['traɪflɪŋ] *adj* insignificante

trigger ['trɪgə^r] *n* (*of gun*) gatillo
▶ **trigger off** *vt* desencadenar

trilogy ['trɪlədʒɪ] *n* trilogía

trim [trɪm] *adj* (*elegant*) aseado; (*house, garden*) en buen estado; (*figure*): **to be ~** tener buen talle ▷ *n* (*haircut etc*) recorte ▷ *vt* (*neaten*) arreglar; (*cut*) recortar; (*decorate*) adornar; (*Naut: a sail*) orientar; **to keep in (good) ~** mantener en buen estado

trimmings ['trɪmɪŋz] *npl* (*extras*) accesorios; (*cuttings*) recortes

Trinity ['trɪnɪtɪ] *n*: **the ~** la Trinidad

trinket ['trɪŋkɪt] *n* chuchería, baratija

trio ['triːəu] *n* trío

trip [trɪp] *n* viaje; (*excursion*) excursión; (*stumble*) traspié ▷ *vi* (*stumble*) tropezar; (*go lightly*) andar a paso ligero; **on a ~** de viaje
▶ **trip over** *vt fus* tropezar con
▶ **trip up** *vi* tropezar, caerse ▷ *vt* hacer tropezar *or* caer

tripe [traɪp] *n* (*Culin*) callos; (*pej: rubbish*) bobadas

triple ['trɪpl] *adj* triple ▷ *adv*: **~ the distance/the speed** 3 veces la distancia/la velocidad

triple jump *n* triple salto

triplets ['trɪplɪts] *npl* trillizos(-as)

triplicate ['trɪplɪkət] *n*: **in ~** por triplicado

tripod ['traɪpɔd] *n* trípode

tripwire ['trɪpwaɪə^r] *n* cable de trampa

trite [traɪt] *adj* trillado

triumph ['traɪʌmf] *n* triunfo ▷ *vi*: **to ~ (over)** vencer

trivia ['trɪvɪə] *npl* trivialidades

trivial ['trɪvɪəl] *adj* insignificante, trivial

trod [trɔd] *pt of* **tread**

trodden ['trɔdn] *pp of* **tread**

trolley ['trɔlɪ] *n* carrito; (*in hospital*) camilla

trombone [trɔm'bəun] *n* trombón

troop [truːp] *n* grupo, banda; *see also* **troops**
▶ **troop in** *vi* entrar en tropel
▶ **troop out** *vi* salir en tropel

troops [truːps] *npl* tropas

trophy ['trəufɪ] *n* trofeo

tropic ['trɔpɪk] *n* trópico; **the ~s** los trópicos, la zona tropical; **T~ of Cancer/Capricorn** trópico de Cáncer/Capricornio

tropical ['trɔpɪkl] *adj* tropical

trot [trɔt] *n* trote ▷ *vi* trotar; **on the ~** (*Brit fig*) seguidos(-as)
▶ **trot out** *vt* (*excuse, reason*) volver a usar; (*names, facts*) sacar a relucir

trouble ['trʌbl] *n* problema, dificultad; (*worry*) preocupación; (*bother, effort*) molestia, esfuerzo; (*unrest*) inquietud; (*with machine etc*) fallo, avería; (*Med*): **stomach ~** problemas gástricos ▷ *vt* molestar; (*worry*) preocupar, inquietar ▷ *vi*: **to ~ to do sth** molestarse en hacer algo; **troubles** *npl* (*Pol etc*) conflictos; **to be in ~** estar en un apuro; (*for doing wrong*) tener problemas; **to have ~ doing sth** tener dificultad en *or* para hacer algo; **to go to the ~ of doing sth** tomarse la

molestia de hacer algo; **don't worry, it's no ~** no te preocupes, no importa; **to take a lot of ~ over something** poner mucho cuidado en algo; **what's the ~?** ¿qué pasa?; **the ~ is ...** el problema es ..., lo que pasa es ...; **please don't ~ yourself** por favor no se moleste

troubled ['trʌbld] *adj* (*person*) preocupado; (*epoch, life*) agitado

troublemaker ['trʌblmeɪkə^r] *n* agitador(a)

troubleshooter ['trʌblʃuːtə^r] *n* (*in conflict*) mediador(a)

troublesome ['trʌblsəm] *adj* molesto, inoportuno

troubling ['trʌblɪŋ] *adj* (*thought*) preocupante; **these are ~ times** son malos tiempos

trough [trɔf] *n* (*also*: **drinking trough**) abrevadero; (*also*: **feeding trough**) comedero

trounce [trauns] *vt* dar una paliza a

troupe [truːp] *n* grupo

trousers ['trauzəz] *npl* pantalones; **short ~** pantalones cortos

trouser suit *n* traje pantalón

trout [traut] *n* (*pl inv*) trucha

trowel ['trauəl] *n* paleta

truant ['truənt] *n*: **to play ~** (*Brit*) hacer novillos

truce [truːs] *n* tregua

truck [trʌk] *n* (*US*) camión; (*Rail*) vagón

trucker ['trʌkə^r] *n* (*esp US*) camionero(-a)

truck farm *n* (*US*) huerto de hortalizas

trudge [trʌdʒ] *vi* caminar penosamente

true [truː] *adj* verdadero; (*accurate*) exacto; (*genuine*) auténtico; (*faithful*) fiel; (*wheel*) centrado; (*wall*) a plomo; (*beam*) alineado; **~ to life** verídico; **to come ~** realizarse, cumplirse

truffle ['trʌfl] *n* trufa

truly ['truːlɪ] *adv* realmente; (*faithfully*) fielmente; **yours ~** (*in letter-writing*) atentamente

trump [trʌmp] *n* (*Cards*) triunfo; **to turn up ~s** (*fig*) salir *or* resultar bien

trumped-up ['trʌmptʌp] *adj* inventado

trumpet ['trʌmpɪt] *n* trompeta

truncheon ['trʌntʃən] *n* (*Brit*) porra

trundle ['trʌndl] *vt, vi*: **to ~ along** rodar haciendo ruido

trunk [trʌŋk] *n* (*of tree, person*) tronco; (*of elephant*) trompa; (*case*) baúl; (*US Aut*) maletero, cajuela (*Méx*), baúl (*CS*); *see also* **trunks**

trunks [trʌŋks] *npl* (*also*: **swimming trunks**) traje de baño, bañador (*Esp*)

truss [trʌs] *n* (*Med*) braguero ▷ *vt*: **to ~ (up)** atar

trust [trʌst] *n* confianza; (*Comm*) trust; (*Law*) fideicomiso ▷ *vt* (*rely on*) tener confianza en; (*entrust*): **to ~ sth to sb** confiar algo a algn; (*hope*): **to ~ (that)** esperar (que); **in ~** en fideicomiso; **you'll have to take it on ~** tienes que aceptarlo a ojos cerrados

trusted ['trʌstɪd] *adj* de confianza, fiable, de fiar

trustee [trʌs'tiː] *n* (*Law*) fideicomisario

trustful ['trʌstful] *adj* confiado

trustworthy ['trʌstwəːðɪ] *adj* digno de confianza, fiable, de fiar

truth [truːθ] (*pl -s*) [truːðz] *n* verdad

truthful ['truːθfəl] *adj* (*person*) sincero; (*account*) fidedigno

try [traɪ] *n* tentativa, intento; (*Rugby*) ensayo ▷ *vt* (*Law*) juzgar, procesar; (*test: sth new*) probar, someter a prueba; (*attempt*) intentar; (*strain: patience*) hacer perder ▷ *vi* probar; **to give sth a ~** intentar hacer algo; **it's worth a ~** vale la pena intentarlo; **have a ~!** ¡inténtalo!; **would you like to ~ some?** ¿quieres probar un poco?; **to ~ one's (very) best** *or* **hardest** poner todo su empeño, esmerarse; **to ~ to do sth** intentar hacer algo; **to ~ again** volver a intentar

▸ **try on** *vt* (*clothes*) probarse

▸ **try out** *vt* probar, poner a prueba

trying ['traɪɪŋ] *adj* cansado; (*person*) pesado

T-shirt ['tiːʃəːt] *n* camiseta

T-square ['tiːskwɛəʳ] *n* regla en T

tub [tʌb] *n* cubo (*Esp*), balde (*LAm*); (*bath*) bañera, tina (*LAm*)

tubby ['tʌbɪ] *adj* regordete

tube [tjuːb] *n* tubo; (*Brit: underground*) metro; (*US col: television*) tele

tuberculosis [tjubəːkjuˈləʊsɪs] *n* tuberculosis

TUC *n abbr* (*Brit: = Trades Union Congress*) federación nacional de sindicatos

tuck [tʌk] *n* (*Sewing*) pliegue ▷ *vt* (*put*) poner

▸ **tuck away** *vt* esconder

▸ **tuck in** *vt* meter; (*child*) arropar ▷ *vi* (*eat*) comer con apetito

▸ **tuck up** *vt* (*child*) arropar

tuck shop *n* (*Scol*) tienda de golosinas

Tuesday ['tjuːzdɪ] *n* martes; **on ~** el martes; **on ~s** los martes; **every ~** todos los martes; **every other ~** cada dos martes, un martes sí y otro no; **last/next ~** el martes pasado/próximo; **a week/ fortnight on ~, ~ week/fortnight** del martes en 8/15 días, del martes en una semana/dos semanas

tuft [tʌft] *n* mechón; (*of grass etc*) manojo

tug [tʌg] *n* (*ship*) remolcador ▷ *vt* remolcar

tug-of-love [tʌgəvˈlʌv] *n*: **~ children** hijos envueltos en el litigio de los padres por su custodia

tug-of-war [tʌgəvˈwɔːʳ] *n* juego de la cuerda

tuition [tjuːˈɪʃən] *n* (*Brit*) enseñanza; (: *private tuition*) clases particulares; (*US: school fees*) matrícula

tulip ['tjuːlɪp] *n* tulipán

tumble ['tʌmbl] *n* (*fall*) caída ▷ *vi* caerse, tropezar; **to ~ to sth** (*col*) caer en la cuenta de algo

tumbledown ['tʌmbldaʊn] *adj* ruinoso

tumble dryer *n* (*Brit*) secadora

tumbler ['tʌmbləʳ] *n* vaso

tummy ['tʌmɪ] *n* (*col*) barriga, vientre

tumour, (*US*) **tumor** ['tjuːməʳ] *n* tumor

tuna ['tjuːnə] *n* (*pl inv: also:* **tuna fish**) atún

tune [tjuːn] *n* (*melody*) melodía ▷ *vt* (*Mus*) afinar; (*Radio, TV, Aut*) sintonizar; **to be in/out of ~** (*instrument*) estar afinado/desafinado; (*singer*) afinar/desafinar; **to be in/out of ~ with** (*fig*) armonizar/desentonar con; **to the ~ of** (*fig: amount*) por (la) cantidad de

▸ **tune in** *vi* (*Radio, TV*): **to ~ in (to)** sintonizar (con)

▸ **tune up** *vi* (*musician*) afinar (su instrumento)

tuneful ['tjuːnful] *adj* melodioso

tuner ['tjuːnəʳ] *n* (*radio set*) sintonizador; **piano ~** afinador(a) de pianos

tunic ['tjuːnɪk] *n* túnica

Tunisia [tjuːˈnɪzɪə] *n* Túnez

tunnel ['tʌnl] *n* túnel; (*in mine*) galería ▷ *vi* construir un túnel/una galería

tunnel vision *n* (*Med*) visión periférica restringida; (*fig*) estrechez de miras

turbo ['təːbəʊ] *n* turbo

turbulence ['təːbjuləns] *n* (*Aviat*) turbulencia

tureen [təˈriːn] *n* sopera

turf [təːf] *n* césped; (*clod*) tepe ▷ *vt* cubrir con césped

▸ **turf out** *vt* (*col*) echar a la calle

turgid ['təːdʒɪd] *adj* (*prose*) pesado

Turk [təːk] *n* turco(-a)

Turkey ['təːkɪ] *n* Turquía

turkey ['təːkɪ] *n* pavo

Turkish ['təːkɪʃ] *adj* turco ▷ *n* (*Ling*) turco

turmoil ['təːmɔɪl] *n* desorden, alboroto

turn [təːn] *n* turno; (*in road*) curva; (*Theat*) número; (*Med*) ataque ▷ *vt* girar, volver, voltear (*LAm*); (*collar, steak*) dar la vuelta a; (*shape: wood, metal*) tornear; (*change*): **to ~ sth into** convertir algo en ▷ *vi* volver, voltearse (*LAm*); (*person: look back*) volverse; (*reverse direction*) dar la vuelta, voltear (*LAm*); (*milk*) cortarse; (*change*) cambiar; (*become*) ponerse; **a good ~** un favor; **it gave me quite a ~** me dio un susto; **"no left ~"** (*Aut*) "prohibido girar a la izquierda"; **it's your ~** te toca a ti; **in ~** por turnos; **to take ~s** turnarse; **at the ~ of the year/century** a fin de año/a finales de siglo; **to take a ~ for the worse** (*situation, patient*) empeorar; **they ~ed him against us** le pusieron en contra nuestra; **the car ~ed the corner** el coche dobló la esquina; **to ~ left** (*Aut*) torcer *or* girar a la izquierda; **to ~ into sth** (*become*) convertirse *or* transformarse en algo; **to ~ awkward/nasty** (*person*) ponerse difícil/ antipático; **the weather ~ed cold** empezó a hacer frío

▸ **turn away** *vi* apartar la vista ▷ *vt* (*reject: person, business*) rechazar

▸ **turn back** *vi* volverse atrás

▸ **turn down** *vt* (*refuse: offer etc*) rechazar; (*reduce: heating, volume etc*) bajar; (*fold*) doblar

▸ **turn in** *vi* (*col: go to bed*) acostarse ▷ *vt* (*fold*) doblar hacia dentro

▸ **turn off** *vi* (*from road*) desviarse ▷ *vt* (*light, radio etc*) apagar; (*engine*) parar; (*tap*) cerrar

▸ **turn on** *vt* (*light, radio etc*) encender, prender (*LAm*); (*engine*) poner en marcha; (*tap*) abrir

▸ **turn out** *vt* (*light, gas*) apagar; (*produce: goods, novel etc*) producir ▷ *vi* (*attend: troops*) presentarse; (: *doctor*) atender; **it ~ed out to be a mistake** resultó ser un error; **it ~ed out that she was right** resultó que ella tenía razón

▸ **turn over** *vi* (*person*) volverse ▷ *vt* (*mattress, card*)

dar la vuelta a; (*page*) volver

▶**turn round** *vi* (*person*) volverse, darse la espalda; (*car*) dar la vuelta; (*rotate*) girar ▷ *vt* dar la vuelta a

▶**turn to** *vt fus*: **to ~ to sb** acudir a algn; **she has no-one to ~ to** no tiene a quién recurrir

▶**turn up** *vi* (*person*) llegar, presentarse; (*lost object*) aparecer ▷ *vt* (*radio*) subir, poner más alto; (*heat, gas*) poner más fuerte

turning ['tə:nɪŋ] *n* (*side road*) bocacalle; (*bend*) curva; **the first ~ on the right** la primera bocacalle a la derecha

turning point *n* (*fig*) momento decisivo

turnip ['tə:nɪp] *n* nabo

turnout ['tə:naut] *n* asistencia, número de asistentes, público

turnover ['tə:nəuvəʳ] *n* (*Comm: amount of money*) facturación; (*of goods*;) movimiento; **there is a rapid ~ in staff** hay mucho movimiento de personal

turnpike ['tə:npaɪk] *n* (*US*) autopista de peaje

turnstile ['tə:nstaɪl] *n* torniquete

turntable ['tə:nteɪbl] *n* plato

turn-up ['tə:nʌp] *n* (*Brit: on trousers*) vuelta

turpentine ['tə:pəntaɪn] *n* (*also*: **turps**) trementina

turquoise ['tə:kwɔɪz] *n* (*stone*) turquesa ▷ *adj* color turquesa

turret ['tʌrɪt] *n* torreón

turtle ['tə:tl] *n* tortuga (marina)

turtleneck (sweater) ['tə:tlnɛk-] *n* (jersey de) cuello cisne

tusk [tʌsk] *n* colmillo

tussle ['tʌsl] *n* lucha, pelea

tutor ['tju:təʳ] *n* profesor(a)

tutorial [tju:'tɔ:rɪəl] *n* (*Scol*) seminario

tuxedo [tʌk'si:dəu] *n* (*US*) smóking, esmoquin

TV [ti:'vi:] *n abbr* (= *television*) televisión

TV dinner *n* cena precocinada

TV licence *n* licencia que se paga por el uso del televisor, destinada a financiar la BBC

twang [twæŋ] *n* (*of instrument*) tañido; (*of voice*) timbre nasal

tweed [twi:d] *n* tweed

tweezers ['twi:zəz] *npl* pinzas (de depilar)

twelfth [twɛlfθ] *num* duodécimo

twelve [twɛlv] *num* doce; **at ~ o'clock** (*midday*) a mediodía; (*midnight*) a medianoche

twentieth ['twɛntɪɪθ] *num* vigésimo

twenty ['twɛntɪ] *num* veinte

twerp [twə:p] *n* (*col*) idiota

twice [twaɪs] *adv* dos veces; **~ as much** dos veces más, el doble; **she is ~ your age** ella te dobla edad; **~ a week** dos veces a la *or* por semana

twiddle ['twɪdl] *vt, vi*: **to ~ (with) sth** dar vueltas a algo; **to ~ one's thumbs** (*fig*) estar de brazos cruzados

twig [twɪg] *n* ramita ▷ *vi* (*col*) caer en la cuenta

twilight ['twaɪlaɪt] *n* crepúsculo; (*morning*)

madrugada; **in the ~** en la media luz

twin [twɪn] *adj, n* gemelo(-a) ▷ *vt* hermanar

twin(-bedded) room ['twɪn('bɛdɪd)-] *n* habitación con dos camas

twine [twaɪn] *n* bramante ▷ *vi* (*plant*) enroscarse

twinge [twɪndʒ] *n* (*of pain*) punzada; (*of conscience*) remordimiento

twinkle ['twɪŋkl] *n* centelleo ▷ *vi* centellear; (*eyes*) parpadear

twin town *n* ciudad hermanada *or* gemela

twirl [twə:l] *n* giro ▷ *vt* dar vueltas a ▷ *vi* piruetear

twist [twɪst] *n* (*action*) torsión; (*in road, coil*) vuelta; (*in wire, flex*) doblez; (*in story*) giro ▷ *vt* torcer, retorcer; (*roll around*) enrollar; (*fig*) deformar ▷ *vi* serpentear; **to ~ one's ankle/wrist** (*Med*) torcerse el tobillo/la muñeca

twisted ['twɪstɪd] *adj* (*wire, rope*) trenzado, enroscado; (*ankle, wrist*) torcido; (*fig: logic, mind*) retorcido

twit [twɪt] *n* (*col*) tonto

twitch [twɪtʃ] *n* sacudida; (*nervous*) tic nervioso ▷ *vi* moverse nerviosamente

two [tu:] *num* dos; **~ by ~, in ~s** de dos en dos; **to put ~ and ~ together** (*fig*) atar cabos

two-bit [tu:'bɪt] *adj* (*esp US: col, pej*) de poca monta, de tres al cuarto

two-door [tu:'dɔ:ʳ] *adj* (*Aut*) de dos puertas

two-faced [tu:'feɪst] *adj* (*pej: person*) falso, hipócrita

twofold ['tu:fəuld] *adv*: **to increase ~** duplicarse ▷ *adj* (*increase*) doble; (*reply*) en dos partes

two-piece [tu:'pi:s] *n* (*also*: **two-piece suit**) traje de dos piezas; (*also*: **two-piece swimsuit**) dos piezas, bikini

twosome ['tu:səm] *n* (*people*) pareja

two-way [tu:'weɪ] *adj*: **~ traffic** circulación de dos sentidos; **~ radio** radio emisora y receptora

tycoon [taɪ'ku:n] *n*: **(business) ~** magnate

type [taɪp] *n* (*category*) tipo, género; (*model*) modelo; (*Typ*) tipo, letra ▷ *vt* (*letter etc*) escribir a máquina; **what ~ do you want?** ¿qué tipo quieres?; **in bold/italic ~** en negrita/cursiva

type-cast ['taɪpka:st] *adj* (*actor*) encasillado

typeface ['taɪpfeɪs] *n* tipo de letra

typescript ['taɪpskrɪpt] *n* texto mecanografiado

typesetter ['taɪpsɛtəʳ] *n* cajista

typewriter ['taɪpraɪtəʳ] *n* máquina de escribir

typewritten ['taɪprɪtn] *adj* mecanografiado

typhoid ['taɪfɔɪd] *n* (*fiebre*) tifoidea

typhoon [taɪ'fu:n] *n* tifón

typhus ['taɪfəs] *n* tifus

typical ['tɪpɪkl] *adj* típico

typing ['taɪpɪŋ] *n* mecanografía

typist ['taɪpɪst] *n* mecanógrafo(-a)

tyrant ['taɪərənt] *n* tirano(-a)

tyre, (*US*) **tire** ['taɪəʳ] *n* neumático, llanta (*LAm*)

tyre pressure *n* presión de los neumáticos

Uu

U, u [ju:] *n* (*letter*) U, u; **U for Uncle** U de Uruguay
U *n abbr* (*Brit: Cine:* = *universal*) todos los públicos
U-bend ['ju:bend] *n* (*Aut, in pipe*) recodo
ubiquitous [ju:'bɪkwɪtəs] *adj* omnipresente, ubicuo
udder ['ʌdəʳ] *n* ubre
UEFA [ju:'eɪfə] *n abbr* (= *Union of European Football Associations*) U.E.F.A.
UFO ['ju:fəʊ] *n abbr* (= *unidentified flying object*) OVNI
Uganda [ju:'gændə] *n* Uganda
UGC *n abbr* (*Brit:* = *University Grants Committee*) entidad gubernamental que controla las finanzas de las universidades
ugh [ə:h] *excl* ¡uf!
ugly ['ʌglɪ] *adj* feo; (*dangerous*) peligroso
UHF *abbr* (= *ultra-high frequency*) UHF
UHT *adj abbr* = **ultra heat treated; ~ milk** leche uperizada
UK *n abbr* (= *United Kingdom*) Reino Unido, R.U.
Ukraine [ju:'kreɪn] *n* Ucrania
ulcer ['ʌlsəʳ] *n* úlcera; **mouth ~** úlcera bucal
Ulster ['ʌlstəʳ] *n* Ulster
ulterior [ʌl'tɪərɪəʳ] *adj* ulterior; **~ motive** segundas intenciones
ultimate ['ʌltɪmət] *adj* último, final; (*greatest*) mayor ▷ *n:* **the ~ in luxury** el colmo del lujo
ultimately ['ʌltɪmətlɪ] *adv* (*in the end*) por último, al final; (*basically*) a fin de cuentas
ultimatum [ʌltɪ'meɪtəm] (*pl* **-s** or **ultimata**) [ʌltɪ'meɪtə] *n* ultimátum
ultrasound ['ʌltrəsaʊnd] *n* (*Med*) ultrasonido
ultraviolet ['ʌltrə'vaɪəlɪt] *adj* ultravioleta
umbilical cord [ʌmbɪ'laɪkl-] *n* cordón umbilical
umbrella [ʌm'brɛlə] *n* paraguas; **under the ~ of** (*fig*) bajo la protección de
umlaut ['umlaʊt] *n* diéresis
umpire ['ʌmpaɪəʳ] *n* árbitro ▷ *vt* arbitrar
umpteen [ʌmp'ti:n] *num* tropecientos
UN *n abbr* (= *United Nations*) ONU
unable [ʌn'eɪbl] *adj:* **to be ~ to do sth** no poder hacer algo; (*not know how to*) ser incapaz de hacer algo, no saber hacer algo
unacceptable [ʌnək'sɛptəbl] *adj* (*proposal, behaviour, price*) inaceptable; **it's ~ that** no se puede aceptar que
unaccompanied [ʌnə'kʌmpənɪd] *adj* no acompañado; (*singing*) sin acompañamiento

unaccountably [ʌnə'kaʊntəblɪ] *adv* inexplicablemente
unaccustomed [ʌnə'kʌstəmd] *adj:* **to be ~ to** no estar acostumbrado a
unanimous [ju:'nænɪməs] *adj* unánime
unanimously [ju:'nænɪməslɪ] *adv* unánimemente
unarmed [ʌn'ɑ:md] *adj* (*person*) desarmado; (*combat*) sin armas
unashamed [ʌnə'ʃeɪmd] *adj* desvergonzado
unassuming [ʌnə'sju:mɪŋ] *adj* modesto, sin pretensiones
unattached [ʌnə'tætʃt] *adj* (*person*) soltero; (*part etc*) suelto
unattended [ʌnə'tɛndɪd] *adj* (*car, luggage*) sin atender
unattractive [ʌnə'træktɪv] *adj* poco atractivo
unauthorized [ʌn'ɔ:θəraɪzd] *adj* no autorizado
unavailable [ʌnə'veɪləbl] *adj* (*article, room, book*) no disponible; (*person*) ocupado
unavoidable [ʌnə'vɔɪdəbl] *adj* inevitable
unaware [ʌnə'wɛəʳ] *adj:* **to be ~ of** ignorar
unawares [ʌnə'wɛəz] *adv* de improviso
unbalanced [ʌn'bælənst] *adj* desequilibrado; (*mentally*) trastornado
unbearable [ʌn'bɛərəbl] *adj* insoportable
unbeatable [ʌn'bi:təbl] *adj* (*gen*) invencible; (*price*) inmejorable
unbeaten [ʌn'bi:tn] *adj* (*team*) imbatido; (*army*) invicto; (*record*) no batido
unbeknown(st) [ʌnbɪ'nəʊn(st)] *adv:* **unbeknown(st) to me** sin saberlo yo
unbelievable [ʌnbɪ'li:vəbl] *adj* increíble
unbend [ʌn'bend] (*irreg: like* **bend**) *vi* (*fig: person*) relajarse ▷ *vt* (*wire*) enderezar
unbias(s)ed [ʌn'baɪəst] *adj* imparcial
unborn [ʌn'bɔ:n] *adj* que va a nacer
unbreakable [ʌn'breɪkəbl] *adj* irrompible
unbroken [ʌn'brəʊkən] *adj* (*seal*) intacto; (*series*) continuo, ininterrumpido; (*record*) no batido; (*spirit*) indómito
unbutton [ʌn'bʌtn] *vt* desabrochar
uncalled-for [ʌn'kɔ:ldfɔ:ʳ] *adj* gratuito, inmerecido
uncanny [ʌn'kænɪ] *adj* extraño, extraordinario
unceasing [ʌn'si:sɪŋ] *adj* incesante
unceremonious ['ʌnsɛrɪ'məʊnɪəs] *adj* (*abrupt,*

rude) brusco, hosco

uncertain [ʌnˈsɜːtn] *adj* incierto; (*indecisive*) indeciso; **it's ~ whether** no se sabe si; **in no ~ terms** sin dejar lugar a dudas

uncertainty [ʌnˈsɜːtntɪ] *n* incertidumbre

unchanged [ʌnˈtʃeɪndʒd] *adj* sin cambiar *or* alterar

unchecked [ʌnˈtʃɛkt] *adj* desenfrenado

uncivilized [ʌnˈsɪvɪlaɪzd] *adj* (*gen*) inculto, poco civilizado; (*fig: behaviour etc*) bárbaro

uncle [ˈʌŋkl] *n* tío

unclear [ʌnˈklɪər] *adj* poco claro; **I'm still ~ about what I'm supposed to do** todavía no tengo muy claro lo que tengo que hacer

uncomfortable [ʌnˈkʌmfətəbl] *adj* incómodo; (*uneasy*) inquieto

uncommon [ʌnˈkɔmən] *adj* poco común, raro

uncompromising [ʌnˈkɔmprəmaɪzɪŋ] *adj* intransigente

unconcerned [ʌnkənˈsɜːnd] *adj* indiferente; **to be ~ about** ser indiferente a, no preocuparse de

unconditional [ʌnkənˈdɪʃənl] *adj* incondicional

unconnected [ʌnkəˈnɛktɪd] *adj* (*unrelated*): **to be ~ with** no estar relacionado con

unconscious [ʌnˈkɔnʃəs] *adj* sin sentido; (*unaware*) inconsciente ▷ *n*: **the ~** el inconsciente; **to knock sb ~** dejar a algn sin sentido

unconsciously [ʌnˈkɔnʃəslɪ] *adv* inconscientemente

unconstitutional [ʌnkɔnstɪˈtjuːʃənl] *adj* anti-constitucional

uncontrollable [ʌnkənˈtrəuləbl] *adj* (*temper*) indomable; (*laughter*) incontenible

unconventional [ʌnkənˈvɛnʃənl] *adj* poco convencional

unconvinced [ʌnkənˈvɪnst] *adj*: **to be** *or* **remain ~** seguir sin convencerse

uncouth [ʌnˈkuːθ] *adj* grosero, inculto

uncover [ʌnˈkʌvər] *vt* (*gen*) descubrir; (*take lid off*) destapar

undecided [ʌndɪˈsaɪdɪd] *adj* (*character*) indeciso; (*question*) no resuelto, pendiente

under [ˈʌndər] *prep* debajo de; (*less than*) menos de; (*according to*) según, de acuerdo con ▷ *adv* debajo, abajo; **~ there** ahí debajo; **the tunnel goes ~ the Channel** el túnel pasa por debajo del Canal; **~ construction** en construcción; en obras; **~ the circumstances** dadas las circunstancias; **in ~ 2 hours** en menos de dos horas; **children ~ 10** niños menores de 10 años; **~ anaesthetic** bajo los efectos de la anestesia; **~ discussion** en discusión, sobre el tapete

under-age [ʌndərˈeɪdʒ] *adj* menor de edad

undercarriage [ˈʌndəkærɪdʒ] *n* (*Brit Aviat*) tren de aterrizaje

undercharge [ʌndəˈtʃɑːdʒ] *vt* cobrar de menos

underclass [ˈʌndəklɑːs] *n* clase marginada

undercoat [ˈʌndəkəut] *n* (*paint*) primera mano

undercover [ʌndəˈkʌvər] *adj* clandestino

undercurrent [ˈʌndəkʌrnt] *n* corriente submarina; (*fig*) tendencia oculta

undercut [ˈʌndəkʌt] *vt* (*irreg: like* **cut**) vender más barato que; fijar un precio más barato que

underdog [ˈʌndədɔg] *n* desvalido(-a)

underdone [ʌndəˈdʌn] *adj* (*Culin*) poco hecho

underestimate [ʌndərˈɛstɪmeɪt] *vt* subestimar

underfed [ʌndəˈfɛd] *adj* subalimentado

underfoot [ʌndəˈfut] *adv*: **it's wet ~** el suelo está mojado

undergo [ʌndəˈgəu] *vt* (*irreg: like* **go**) sufrir; (*treatment*) recibir, someterse a; **the car is ~ing repairs** están reparando el coche

undergraduate [ˈʌndəˈgrædjuət] *n* estudiante ▷ *cpd*: **~ courses** cursos de licenciatura

underground [ˈʌndəgraund] *n* (*Brit: railway*) metro; (*Pol*) movimiento clandestino ▷ *adj* subterráneo

undergrowth [ˈʌndəgrəuθ] *n* maleza

underhand(ed) [ʌndəˈhænd(ɪd)] *adj* (*fig*) poco limpio

underlie [ʌndəˈlaɪ] *vt* (*irreg: like* **lie**); (*fig*) ser la razón fundamental de; **the underlying cause** la causa fundamental

underline [ʌndəˈlaɪn] *vt* subrayar

underling [ˈʌndəlɪŋ] *n* (*pej*) subalterno(-a)

undermine [ʌndəˈmaɪn] *vt* socavar, minar

underneath [ʌndəˈniːθ] *adv* debajo ▷ *prep* debajo de, bajo

underpaid [ʌndəˈpeɪd] *adj* mal pagado

underpants [ˈʌndəpænts] *npl* calzoncillos

underpass [ˈʌndəpɑːs] *n* (*Brit*) paso subterráneo

underprivileged [ʌndəˈprɪvɪlɪdʒd] *adj* desvalido

underrate [ʌndəˈreɪt] *vt* infravalorar, subestimar

underscore [ˈʌndəskɔːr] *vt* subrayar, sostener

undershirt [ˈʌndəʃəːt] *n* (*US*) camiseta

undershorts [ˈʌndəʃɔːts] *npl* (*US*) calzoncillos

underside [ˈʌndəsaɪd] *n* parte inferior, revés

undersigned [ˈʌndəsaɪnd] *adj*, *n*: **the ~** el/la *etc* abajo firmante

underskirt [ˈʌndəskəːt] *n* (*Brit*) enaguas

understand [ʌndəˈstænd] (*irreg: like* **stand**) *vt*, *vi* entender, comprender; (*assume*) tener entendido; **to make o.s. understood** hacerse entender; **I ~ you have been absent** tengo entendido que (usted) ha estado ausente

understandable [ʌndəˈstændəbl] *adj* comprensible

understanding [ʌndəˈstændɪŋ] *adj* comprensivo ▷ *n* comprensión, entendimiento; (*agreement*) acuerdo; **to come to an ~ with sb** llegar a un acuerdo con algn; **on the ~ that** a condición de que

understate [ʌndəˈsteɪt] *vt* minimizar

understatement [ʌndəˈsteɪtmənt] *n* subestimación; (*modesty*) modestia (excesiva); **to say it was good is quite an ~** decir que estuvo bien es quedarse corto

understood [ʌndəˈstud] *pt*, *pp of* **understand** ▷ *adj* entendido; (*implied*): **it is ~ that** se sobreentiende que

understudy [ˈʌndəstʌdɪ] *n* suplente

undertake [ʌndəˈteɪk] (*irreg: like* **take**) *vt*

emprender; **to ~ to do sth** comprometerse a
hacer algo

undertaker ['ʌndəteɪkəʳ] n director(a) de
pompas fúnebres

undertaking ['ʌndəteɪkɪŋ] n empresa; (promise)
promesa

undertone ['ʌndətəun] n (of criticism)
connotación; (low voice): **in an ~** en voz baja

underwater [ʌndə'wɔ:təʳ] adv bajo el agua ▷ adj
submarino

underwear ['ʌndəwɛəʳ] n ropa interior or íntima
(LAm)

underworld ['ʌndəwə:ld] n (of crime) hampa,
inframundo

underwrite [ʌndə'raɪt] (irreg: like **write**) vt (Comm)
suscribir; (Insurance) asegurar (contra riesgos)

underwriter ['ʌndəraɪtəʳ] n (Insurance)
asegurador(a)

undesirable [ʌndɪ'zaɪərəbl] adj indeseable

undies ['ʌndɪz] npl (col) paños menores

undiluted [ʌndaɪ'lu:tɪd] adj (concentrated)
concentrado

undiplomatic [ʌndɪplə'mætɪk] adj poco
diplomático

undisciplined [ʌn'dɪsɪplɪnd] adj indisciplinado

undisputed [ʌndɪ'spju:tɪd] adj incontestable

undivided [ʌndɪ'vaɪdɪd] adj: **I want your ~
attention** quiero su completa atención

undo [ʌn'du:] vt (irreg: like **do**) deshacer

undoing [ʌn'du:ɪŋ] n ruina, perdición

undone [ʌn'dʌn] pp of **undo** ▷ adj: **to come ~**
(clothes) desabrocharse; (parcel) desatarse

undoubted [ʌn'dautɪd] adj indudable

undoubtedly [ʌn'dautɪdlɪ] adv indudablemente,
sin duda

undress [ʌn'drɛs] vi desnudarse, desvestirse (esp
LAm)

undue [ʌn'dju:] adj indebido, excesivo

undulating ['ʌndjuleɪtɪŋ] adj ondulante

unduly [ʌn'dju:lɪ] adv excesivamente,
demasiado

undying [ʌn'daɪɪŋ] adj eterno

unearth [ʌn'ə:θ] vt desenterrar

unearthly [ʌn'ə:θlɪ] adj: **~ hour** (col) hora
intempestiva

unease [ʌn'i:z] n malestar

uneasy [ʌn'i:zɪ] adj intranquilo; (worried)
preocupado; **to feel ~ about doing sth** sentirse
incómodo con la idea de hacer algo

uneconomic(al) ['ʌni:kə'nɔmɪk(l)] adj no
económico

uneducated [ʌn'ɛdjukeɪtɪd] adj ignorante,
inculto

unemployed [ʌnɪm'plɔɪd] adj parado, sin
trabajo ▷ npl: **the ~** los parados

unemployment [ʌnɪm'plɔɪmənt] n paro,
desempleo, cesantía (LAm)

unemployment benefit n (Brit) subsidio de
desempleo or paro

unending [ʌn'ɛndɪŋ] adj interminable

unenviable [ʌn'ɛnvɪəbl] adj poco envidiable

unerring [ʌn'ə:rɪŋ] adj infalible

uneven [ʌn'i:vn] adj desigual; (road etc) con
baches

uneventful [ʌnɪ'vɛntful] adj sin incidentes

unexpected [ʌnɪk'spɛktɪd] adj inesperado

unexpectedly [ʌnɪk'spɛktɪdlɪ] adv
inesperadamente

unexplained [ʌnɪks'pleɪnd] adj inexplicado

unfailing [ʌn'feɪlɪŋ] adj (support) indefectible;
(energy) inagotable

unfair [ʌn'fɛəʳ] adj: **~ (to sb)** injusto (con algn);
it's ~ that ... es injusto que ..., no es justo que ...

unfaithful [ʌn'feɪθful] adj infiel

unfamiliar [ʌnfə'mɪlɪəʳ] adj extraño,
desconocido; **to be ~ with sth** desconocer or
ignorar algo

unfashionable [ʌn'fæʃnəbl] adj (clothes) pasado
or fuera de moda; (district) poco elegante

unfasten [ʌn'fɑ:sn] vt desatar

unfavourable, (US) **unfavorable** [ʌn'feɪvərəbl]
adj desfavorable

unfeeling [ʌn'fi:lɪŋ] adj insensible

unfinished [ʌn'fɪnɪʃt] adj inacabado, sin
terminar

unfit [ʌn'fɪt] adj en baja forma; (incompetent)
incapaz; **~ for work** no apto para trabajar

unfold [ʌn'fəuld] vt desdoblar; (fig) revelar ▷ vi
abrirse; revelarse

unforeseen ['ʌnfɔ:'si:n] adj imprevisto

unforgettable [ʌnfə'gɛtəbl] adj inolvidable

unforgivable [ʌnfə'gɪvəbl] adj imperdonable

unfortunate [ʌn'fɔ:tʃnət] adj desgraciado; (event,
remark) inoportuno

unfortunately [ʌn'fɔ:tʃnətlɪ] adv
desgraciadamente, por desgracia

unfounded [ʌn'faundɪd] adj infundado

unfriendly [ʌn'frɛndlɪ] adj antipático

unfurl [ʌn'fə:l] vt desplegar

ungainly [ʌn'geɪnlɪ] adj (walk) desgarbado

ungodly [ʌn'gɔdlɪ] adj: **at an ~ hour** a una hora
intempestiva

ungrateful [ʌn'greɪtful] adj ingrato

unhappiness [ʌn'hæpɪnɪs] n tristeza

unhappy [ʌn'hæpɪ] adj (sad) triste; (unfortunate)
desgraciado; (childhood) infeliz; **~ with**
(arrangements etc) poco contento con, descontento
de

unharmed [ʌn'hɑ:md] adj (person) ileso

UNHCR n abbr (= United Nations High Comm[...] for
Refugees) ACNUR

unhealthy [ʌn'hɛlθɪ] adj (gen) malsano,
insalubre; (person) enfermizo; (interest) morboso

unheard-of [ʌn'hə:dɔv] adj inaudito, sin
precedente

unholy [ʌn'həulɪ] adj: **an ~ alliance** una alianza
nefasta; **he returned at an ~ hour** volvió a una
hora intempestiva

unhurt [ʌn'hə:t] adj ileso

unhygienic [ʌnhaɪ'dʒi:nɪk] adj antihigiénico

UNICEF ['ju:nɪsɛf] n abbr (= United Nations
International Children's Emergency Fund) UNICEF

unidentified [ʌnaɪ'dɛntɪfaɪd] adj no
identificado; **~ flying object (UFO)** objeto

volante no identificado

uniform ['ju:nɪfɔ:m] n uniforme ▷ adj uniforme

uniformity [ju:nɪ'fɔ:mɪtɪ] n uniformidad

unify ['ju:nɪfaɪ] vt unificar, unir

uninhabited [ʌnɪn'hæbɪtɪd] adj desierto; (country) despoblado; (house) deshabitado, desocupado

uninspiring [ʌnɪn'spaɪərɪŋ] adj anodino

unintentional [ʌnɪn'tɛnʃənəl] adj involuntario

union ['ju:njən] n unión; (also: **trade union**) sindicato ▷ cpd sindical; **the U~** (US) la Unión

Union Jack n bandera del Reino Unido

unique [ju:'ni:k] adj único

unison [ju:nɪsn] n: **in ~** en armonía

unit ['ju:nɪt] n unidad; (team, squad) grupo; **kitchen ~** módulo de cocina; **production ~** taller de fabricación; **sink ~** fregadero

unite [ju:'naɪt] vt unir ▷ vi unirse

united [ju:'naɪtɪd] adj unido

United Kingdom (UK) n Reino Unido

United Nations (Organization) (UN, UNO) n Naciones Unidas

United States (of America) (US, USA) n Estados Unidos (de América)

unit trust n (Brit) bono fiduciario

unity ['ju:nɪtɪ] n unidad

Univ. abbr = **university**

universal [ju:nɪ'və:sl] adj universal

universe ['ju:nɪvə:s] n universo

university [ju:nɪ'və:sɪtɪ] n universidad ▷ cpd (student, professor, education, degree) universitario; (year) académico; **to be at/go to ~** estudiar en/ir a la universidad

unjust [ʌn'dʒʌst] adj injusto

unkempt [ʌn'kɛmpt] adj descuidado; (hair) despeinado

unkind [ʌn'kaɪnd] adj poco amable; (comment etc) cruel

unknown [ʌn'nəun] adj desconocido ▷ adv: **~ to me** sin saberlo yo; **~ quantity** (Math, fig) incógnita

unlawful [ʌn'lɔ:ful] adj ilegal, ilícito

unleaded [ʌn'lɛdɪd] n (also: **unleaded petrol**) gasolina sin plomo

unleash [ʌn'li:ʃ] vt desatar

unless [ʌn'lɛs] conj a menos que; **~ he comes** a menos que venga; **~ otherwise stated** salvo indicación contraria; **~ I am mistaken** si no mi equivoco

unlike [ʌn'laɪk] adj distinto ▷ prep a diferencia de

unlikely [ʌn'laɪklɪ] adj improbable

unlimited [ʌn'lɪmɪtɪd] adj ilimitado; **~ liability** responsabilidad ilimitada

unlisted [ʌn'lɪstɪd] adj (US Tel) que no figura en la guía; **~ company** empresa sin cotización en bolsa

unload [ʌn'ləud] vt descargar

unlock [ʌn'lɔk] vt abrir (con llave)

unlucky [ʌn'lʌkɪ] adj desgraciado; (object, number) que da mala suerte; **to be ~** (person) tener mala suerte

unmarked [ʌn'mɑːkt] adj (unstained) sin mancha;

~ police car vehículo policial camuflado

unmarried [ʌn'mærɪd] adj soltero

unmistakable [ʌnmɪs'teɪkəbl] adj inconfundible

unmitigated [ʌn'mɪtɪgeɪtɪd] adj rematado, absoluto

unnamed [ʌn'neɪmd] adj (nameless) sin nombre; (anonymous) anónimo

unnatural [ʌn'nætʃrəl] adj (gen) antinatural; (manner) afectado; (habit) perverso

unnecessary [ʌn'nɛsəsərɪ] adj innecesario, inútil

unnerve [ʌn'nə:v] vt (accident) poner nervioso; (hostile attitude) acobardar; (long wait, interview) intimidar

unnoticed [ʌn'nəutɪst] adj: **to go** or **pass ~** pasar desapercibido

UNO ['ju:nəu] n abbr (= United Nations Organization) ONU

unobtainable [ʌnəb'teɪnəbl] adj inasequible; (Tel) inexistente

unobtrusive [ʌnəb'tru:sɪv] adj discreto

unofficial [ʌnə'fɪʃl] adj no oficial; **~ strike** huelga no oficial

unorthodox [ʌn'ɔ:θədɔks] adj poco ortodoxo

unpack [ʌn'pæk] vi deshacer las maletas, desempacar (LAm)

unpaid [ʌn'peɪd] adj (bill, debt) sin pagar, impagado; (Comm) pendiente; (holiday) sin sueldo; (work) sin pago, voluntario

unpalatable [ʌn'pælətəbl] adj (truth) desagradable

unparalleled [ʌn'pærəleld] adj (unequalled) sin par; (unique) sin precedentes

unpleasant [ʌn'plɛznt] adj (disagreeable) desagradable; (person, manner) antipático

unplug [ʌn'plʌg] vt desenchufar, desconectar

unpopular [ʌn'pɔpjuləʳ] adj poco popular; **to be ~ with sb** (person, law) no ser popular con algn; **to make o.s. ~ (with)** hacerse impopular (con)

unprecedented [ʌn'prɛsɪdəntɪd] adj sin precedentes

unpredictable [ʌnprɪ'dɪktəbl] adj imprevisible

unprofessional [ʌnprə'fɛʃənl] adj poco profesional; **~ conduct** negligencia

UNPROFOR ['ʌnprəufɔ:ʳ] n abbr (= United Nations Protection Force) FORPRONU, Unprofor

unprotected ['ʌnprə'tɛktɪd] adj (sex) sin protección

unpunished [ʌn'pʌnɪʃt] adj: **to go ~** quedar sin castigo, salir impune

unqualified [ʌn'kwɔlɪfaɪd] adj sin título, no cualificado; (success) total, incondicional

unquestionably [ʌn'kwɛstʃənəblɪ] adv indiscutiblemente

unravel [ʌn'rævl] vt desenmarañar

unreal [ʌn'rɪəl] adj irreal

unrealistic [ʌnrɪə'lɪstɪk] adj poco realista

unreasonable [ʌn'ri:znəbl] adj irrazonable; **to make ~ demands on sb** hacer demandas excesivas a algn

unrecognizable [ʌn'rɛkəgnaɪzəbl] adj

irreconocible

unrelated [ˌʌnrɪˈleɪtɪd] *adj* sin relación; *(family)* no emparentado

unrelenting [ˌʌnrɪˈlentɪŋ] *adj* implacable

unreliable [ˌʌnrɪˈlaɪəbl] *adj (person)* informal; *(machine)* poco fiable

unremitting [ˌʌnrɪˈmɪtɪŋ] *adj* incesante

unrepeatable [ˌʌnrɪˈpiːtəbl] *adj* irrepetible

unrepentant [ˌʌnrɪˈpentənt] *adj (smoker, sinner)* impenitente; **to be ~ about sth** no arrepentirse de algo

unreservedly [ˌʌnrɪˈzɜːvɪdlɪ] *adv* sin reserva

unrest [ʌnˈrest] *n* inquietud, malestar; *(Pol)* disturbios

unripe [ʌnˈraɪp] *adj* verde, inmaduro

unrivalled, *(US)* **unrivaled** [ʌnˈraɪvəld] *adj* incomparable, sin par

unroll [ʌnˈrəul] *vt* desenrollar

unruly [ʌnˈruːlɪ] *adj* indisciplinado

unsafe [ʌnˈseɪf] *adj (journey)* peligroso; *(car etc)* inseguro; *(method)* arriesgado; **~ to drink/eat** no apto para el consumo humano

unsaid [ʌnˈsed] *adj*: **to leave sth ~** dejar algo sin decir

unsatisfactory [ˈʌnsætɪsˈfæktərɪ] *adj* poco satisfactorio

unsavoury, *(US)* **unsavory** [ʌnˈseɪvərɪ] *adj (fig)* repugnante

unscathed [ʌnˈskeɪðd] *adj* ileso

unscrew [ʌnˈskruː] *vt* destornillar

unscrupulous [ʌnˈskruːpjuləs] *adj* sin escrúpulos

unseat [ʌnˈsiːt] *vt (rider)* hacer caerse de la silla a; *(fig: official)* hacer perder su escaño a

unseeded [ʌnˈsiːdɪd] *adj (Sport)* no preseleccionado

unseen [ʌnˈsiːn] *adj (person, danger)* oculto

unselfish [ʌnˈselfɪʃ] *adj* generoso, poco egoísta; *(act)* desinteresado

unsettled [ʌnˈsetld] *adj* inquieto; *(situation)* inestable; *(weather)* variable

unsettling [ʌnˈsetlɪŋ] *adj* perturbador(a), inquietante

unshaven [ʌnˈʃeɪvn] *adj* sin afeitar

unsightly [ʌnˈsaɪtlɪ] *adj* desagradable

unskilled [ʌnˈskɪld] *adj*: **~ workers** mano de obra no cualificada

unspeakable [ʌnˈspiːkəbl] *adj* indecible; *(awful)* incalificable

unstable [ʌnˈsteɪbl] *adj* inestable

unsteady [ʌnˈstedɪ] *adj* inestable

unstuck [ʌnˈstʌk] *adj*: **to come ~** despegarse; *(fig)* fracasar

unsubscribe [ˌʌnsəbˈskraɪb] *vi (Internet)* borrarse

unsuccessful [ˌʌnsəkˈsesful] *adj (attempt)* infructuoso; *(writer, proposal)* sin éxito; **to be ~** *(in attempting sth)* no tener éxito, fracasar

unsuitable [ʌnˈsuːtəbl] *adj* inconveniente, inapropiado; *(time)* inoportuno

unsung [ˈʌnsʌŋ] *adj*: **an ~ hero** un héroe desconocido

unsure [ʌnˈʃuəʳ] *adj* inseguro, poco seguro; **to be**

~ of o.s. estar poco seguro de sí mismo

unsuspecting [ˌʌnsəˈspektɪŋ] *adj* confiado

unsympathetic [ˌʌnsɪmpəˈθetɪk] *adj (attitude)* poco comprensivo; *(person)* sin compasión; **~ (to)** indiferente (a)

untapped [ʌnˈtæpt] *adj (resources)* sin explotar

unthinkable [ʌnˈθɪŋkəbl] *adj* inconcebible, impensable

untidy [ʌnˈtaɪdɪ] *adj (room)* desordenado, en desorden; *(appearance)* desaliñado

untie [ʌnˈtaɪ] *vt* desatar

until [ənˈtɪl] *prep* hasta ▷ *conj* hasta que; **~ now** hasta ahora; **~ then** hasta entonces; **from morning ~ night** de la mañana a la noche; **~ he comes** hasta que venga

untimely [ʌnˈtaɪmlɪ] *adj* inoportuno; *(death)* prematuro

untold [ʌnˈtəuld] *adj (story)* nunca contado; *(suffering)* indecible; *(wealth)* incalculable

untoward [ˌʌntəˈwɔːd] *adj (behaviour)* impropio; *(event)* adverso

untrue [ʌnˈtruː] *adj (statement)* falso

unused [ʌnˈjuːzd] *adj* sin usar, nuevo; **to be ~ to (doing) sth** no estar acostumbrado a (hacer) algo

unusual [ʌnˈjuːʒuəl] *adj* insólito, poco común

unveil [ʌnˈveɪl] *vt (statue)* descubrir

unwanted [ʌnˈwɒntɪd] *adj (person, effect)* no deseado

unwelcome [ʌnˈwelkəm] *adj (at a bad time)* inoportuno, molesto; **to feel ~** sentirse incómodo

unwell [ʌnˈwel] *adj*: **to feel ~** estar indispuesto, sentirse mal

unwieldy [ʌnˈwiːldɪ] *adj* difícil de manejar

unwilling [ʌnˈwɪlɪŋ] *adj*: **to be ~ to do sth** estar poco dispuesto a hacer algo

unwillingly [ʌnˈwɪlɪŋlɪ] *adv* de mala gana

unwind [ʌnˈwaɪnd] *(irreg: like* **wind***) vt* desenvolver ▷ *vi (relax)* relajarse

unwise [ʌnˈwaɪz] *adj* imprudente

unwitting [ʌnˈwɪtɪŋ] *adj* inconsciente

unworkable [ʌnˈwəːkəbl] *adj (plan)* impracticable

unworthy [ʌnˈwəːðɪ] *adj* indigno; **to be ~ of sth/ to do sth** ser indigno de algo/de hacer algo

unwrap [ʌnˈræp] *vt* deshacer

unwritten [ʌnˈrɪtn] *adj (agreement)* tácito; *(rules, law)* no escrito

up [ʌp] *prep*: **to go/be up sth** bir/estar subido en algo; **he went up the sta s/the hill** subió las escaleras/la colina; **we w lked/climbed up the hill** subimos la colina; **they live further up the street** viven más arriba en la calle; **go up that road and turn left** sigue por esa calle y gira a la izquierda

▷ *adv* **1** *(upwards, higher)* más arriba; **up in the mountains** en lo alto (de la montaña); **put it a bit higher up** ponlo un poco más arriba *or* alto; **to stop halfway up** pararse a la mitad del camino *or* de la subida; **up there** ahí *or* allí arriba; **up above** en lo alto, por encima, arriba;

"this side up" "este lado hacia arriba"; **to live/ go up North** vivir en el norte/ir al norte
2: to be up (*out of bed*) estar levantado; (*prices, level*) haber subido; (*building*) estar construido; (*tent*) estar montado; (*curtains, paper etc*) estar puesto; **we were up at 6** a las 6 estábamos levantados; **he's not up yet** todavía no se ha levantado; **time's up** se acabó el tiempo; **when the year was up** al terminarse el año; **he's well up in** or **on politics** (Brit: *knowledgeable*) está muy al día en política; **what's up?** (*wrong*) ¿qué pasa?; **what's up with him?** ¿qué le pasa?; **prices are up on last year** los precios han subido desde el año pasado
3: up to (*as far as*) hasta; **to count up to 50** contar hasta 50; **up to now** hasta ahora or la fecha
4: to be up to (*depending on*): **it's up to you** depende de ti; **he's not up to it** (*job, task etc*) no es capaz de hacerlo; **I don't feel up to it** no me encuentro con ánimos para ello; **his work is not up to the required standard** su trabajo no da la talla; (col: *be doing*): **what is he up to?** ¿qué estará tramando?
▷ *vi* (col): **she upped and left** se levantó y se marchó
▷ *vt* (col: *price*) subir
▷ *n*: **ups and downs** altibajos
up-and-coming [ʌpənd'kʌmɪŋ] *adj* prometedor(a)
upbringing ['ʌpbrɪŋɪŋ] *n* educación
upcoming ['ʌpkʌmɪŋ] *adj* próximo
update [ʌp'deɪt] *vt* poner al día
upfront [ʌp'frʌnt] *adj* claro, directo ▷ *adv* a las claras; (*pay*) por adelantado; **to be ~ about sth** admitir algo claramente
upgrade [ʌp'greɪd] *vt* ascender; (*Comput*) modernizar
upheaval [ʌp'hiːvl] *n* trastornos; (*Pol*) agitación
uphill [ʌp'hɪl] *adj* cuesta arriba; (*fig: task*) penoso, difícil ▷ *adv*: **to go ~** ir cuesta arriba
uphold [ʌp'həʊld] (*irreg: like* **hold**) *vt* sostener
upholstery [ʌp'həʊlstərɪ] *n* tapicería
upkeep ['ʌpkiːp] *n* mantenimiento
upon [ə'pɒn] *prep* sobre
upper ['ʌpəʳ] *adj* superior, de arriba ▷ *n* (*of shoe: also:* **uppers**) pala
upper-class [ʌpə'klɑːs] *adj* (*district, people, accent*) de clase alta; (*attitude*) altivo
uppercut ['ʌpəkʌt] *n* uppercut, gancho a la cara
upper hand *n*: **to have the ~** tener la sartén por el mango
uppermost ['ʌpəməʊst] *adj* el más alto; **what was ~ in my mind** lo que me preocupaba más
upright ['ʌpraɪt] *adj* vertical; (*fig*) honrado
uprising ['ʌpraɪzɪŋ] *n* sublevación
uproar ['ʌprɔːʳ] *n* tumulto, escándalo
uproarious [ʌp'rɔːrɪəs] *adj* escandaloso; (*hilarious*) graciosísimo; (*exceptional*) espectacular
uproot [ʌp'ruːt] *vt* desarraigar
upset *n* (*to plan etc*) revés, contratiempo; (*Med*) trastorno ▷ *vt* (*irreg: like* **set**); (*glass etc*) volcar;

(*spill*) derramar; (*plan*) alterar; (*person: distress*) afectar; (: *hurt, make sad*) disgustar; (: *offend*) ofender ▷ *adj* (*distressed*) alterado; (*hurt, sad*) disgustado; (*offended*) ofendido; (*annoyed*) molesto; (*stomach*) revuelto; **to have a stomach ~** or **an ~ stomach** tener el estómago revuelto; **to get ~** (*distressed*) alterarse; (*hurt*) disgustarse; (*offended*) ofenderse; (*annoyed*) enfadarse; **don't ~ yourself** no te disgustes; (*don't get angry*) no te enfades
upsetting [ʌp'sɛtɪŋ] *adj* (*worrying*) inquietante; (*offending*) ofensivo; (*annoying*) molesto
upshot ['ʌpʃɒt] *n* resultado
upside-down ['ʌpsaɪd'daʊn] *adv* al revés
upstage [ʌp'steɪdʒ] *vt* robar protagonismo a
upstairs [ʌp'stɛəz] *adv* arriba ▷ *adj* (*room*) de arriba ▷ *n* el piso superior
upstart ['ʌpstɑːt] *n* advenedizo
upstream [ʌp'striːm] *adv* río arriba
uptake ['ʌpteɪk] *n*: **he is quick/slow on the ~** es muy listo/torpe
uptight [ʌp'taɪt] *adj* tenso, nervioso
up-to-date [ʌptə'deɪt] *adj* moderno, actual; **to bring sb ~ (on sth)** poner a algn al corriente/ tanto (de algo)
upturn ['ʌptəːn] *n* (*in luck*) mejora; (*Comm: in market*) resurgimiento económico; (: *in value of currency*) aumento
upward ['ʌpwəd] *adj* ascendente
upwardly-mobile ['ʌpwədlɪ'məʊbaɪl] *adj*: **to be ~** mejorar socialmente
upward(s) ['ʌpwəd(z)] *adv* hacia arriba
uranium [juə'reɪnɪəm] *n* uranio
Uranus [juə'reɪnəs] *n* (*Astro*) Urano
urban ['əːbən] *adj* urbano
urbane [əː'beɪn] *adj* cortés, urbano
urchin ['əːtʃɪn] *n* pilluelo, golfillo
Urdu ['uəduː] *n* urdu
urge [əːdʒ] *n* (*force*) impulso; (*desire*) deseo ▷ *vt*: **to ~ sb to do sth** animar a algn a hacer algo
▶ **urge on** *vt* animar
urgency ['əːdʒənsɪ] *n* urgencia
urgent ['əːdʒənt] *adj* (*earnest, persistent: plea*) insistente; (: *tone*) urgente
urinal [juə'raɪnl] *n* (*building*) urinario; (*vessel*) orinal
urinate ['juərɪneɪt] *vi* orinar
urine ['juərɪn] *n* orina
urn [əːn] *n* urna; (*also:* **tea urn**) tetera (grande)
Uruguay ['juərəgwaɪ] *n* el Uruguay
Uruguayan [juərə'gwaɪən] *adj, n* uruguayo(-a)
US *n abbr* (= *United States*) EE.UU.
us [ʌs] *pron* nos; (*after prep*) nosotros(-as); (col: *me*): **give us a kiss** dame un beso; *see also* **me**
USA *n abbr see* **United States of America**; (*Mil*) = **United States Army**
usable ['juːzəbl] *adj* utilizable
usage ['juːzɪdʒ] *n* (*Ling*) uso; (*utilization*) utilización
use *n* uso, empleo; (*usefulness*) utilidad ▷ *vt* usar, emplear; **"directions for ~"** "modo de empleo"; **in ~** en uso; **out of ~** en desuso; **to**

be of ~ servir; **ready for** ~ listo (para usar); **to make** ~ **of sth** aprovecharse *or* servirse de algo; **it's no** ~ *(pointless)* es inútil; *(not useful)* no sirve; **it's no** ~, **I can't do it** no hay manera, no puedo hacerlo; **can I** ~ **your phone?** ¿puedo usar tu teléfono?; **what's this** ~**d for?** ¿para qué sirve esto?; **to be** ~**d to** estar acostumbrado a *(Esp)*, acostumbrar; **to get** ~**d to** acostumbrarse a; **she** ~**d to do it** (ella) solía *or* acostumbraba hacerlo; **I didn't** ~ **to like maths, but now** ... antes no me gustaban las matemáticas, pero ahora ...
▸ **use up** *vt* agotar
used [ju:zd] *adj (car)* usado
useful ['ju:sful] *adj* útil; **to come in** ~ ser útil
usefulness ['ju:sfəlnɪs] *n* utilidad
useless ['ju:slɪs] *adj* inútil; *(unusable: object)* inservible
user ['ju:zər] *n* usuario(-a); *(of petrol, gas etc)* consumidor(a)
user-friendly ['ju:zə'frɛndlɪ] *adj (Comput)* fácil de utilizar
usher ['ʌʃər] *n (at wedding)* ujier; *(in cinema etc)* acomodador ▸ *vt*: **to** ~ **sb in** *(into room)* hacer pasar a algn; **it** ~**ed in a new era** *(fig)* inició una nueva era
usherette [ʌʃə'rɛt] *n (in cinema)* acomodadora
USSR *n abbr*: **the (former)** ~ la (antigua) U.R.S.S.
usu. *abbr* = **usually**
usual ['ju:ʒuəl] *adj* normal, corriente; **as** ~ como de costumbre, como siempre
usually ['ju:ʒuəlɪ] *adv* normalmente
utensil [ju:'tɛnsl] *n* utensilio; **kitchen** ~**s** batería de cocina
uterus ['ju:tərəs] *n* útero
utility [ju:'tɪlɪtɪ] *n* utilidad
utility room *n* trascocina
utmost ['ʌtməust] *adj* mayor ▸ *n*: **to do one's** ~ hacer todo lo posible; **it is of the** ~ **importance that** ... es de la mayor importancia que ...
utter ['ʌtər] *adj* total, completo ▸ *vt* pronunciar, proferir
utterance ['ʌtərns] *n* palabras, declaración
utterly ['ʌtəlɪ] *adv* completamente, totalmente
U-turn ['ju:'tə:n] *n* cambio de sentido; *(fig)* giro de 180 grados
Uzbekistan [ʌzbɛkɪ'sta:n] *n* Uzbekistán

Vv

V, v [vi:] (letter) V, v; **V for Victor** V de Valencia

v. abbr (= verse) vers.°; (= vide: see) V, vid., vide; (= versus) vs.; = **volt**

vac [væk] n abbr (Brit col) = **vacation**

vacancy ['veɪkənsɪ] n (Brit: job) vacante; (room) cuarto libro; **have you any vacancies?** ¿tiene or hay alguna habitación or algún cuarto libre?

vacant ['veɪkənt] adj desocupado, libre; (expression) distraído

vacant lot n (US) solar

vacate [vəˈkeɪt] vt (house) desocupar; (job) dejar (vacante)

vacation [vəˈkeɪʃən] n vacaciones; **on ~** de vacaciones; **to take a ~** (esp US) tomarse unas vacaciones

vaccinate ['væksɪneɪt] vt vacunar

vaccination [væksɪˈneɪʃən] n vacunación

vaccine ['væksiːn] n vacuna

vacuum ['vækjum] n vacío

vacuum cleaner n aspiradora

vacuum-packed ['vækjum'pækt] adj envasado al vacío

vagina [vəˈdʒaɪnə] n vagina

vagrant ['veɪgrənt] n vagabundo(-a)

vague [veɪg] adj vago; (blurred: memory) borroso; (uncertain) incierto, impreciso; (person) distraído; **I haven't the ~st idea** no tengo la más remota idea

vaguely ['veɪglɪ] adv vagamente

vain [veɪn] adj (conceited) presumido; (useless) vano, inútil; **in ~** en vano

vainly ['veɪnlɪ] adv (to no effect) en vano; (conceitedly) vanidosamente

valentine ['væləntaɪn] n (also: **valentine card**) tarjeta del Día de los Enamorados

valiant ['væljənt] adj valiente

valid ['vælɪd] adj válido; (ticket) valedero; (law) vigente

valley ['vælɪ] n valle

valour, (US) **valor** ['vælər] n valor, valentía

valuable ['væljuəbl] adj (jewel) de valor; (time) valioso; **valuables** npl objetos de valor

valuation [væljuˈeɪʃən] n tasación, valuación

value ['væljuː] n valor; (importance) importancia ▷ vt (fix price of) tasar, valorar; (esteem) apreciar; **values** npl (moral) valores morales; **to lose (in) ~** (currency) bajar; (property) desvalorizarse; **to gain**

(in) ~ (currency) subir; (property) valorizarse; **you get good ~ (for money) in that shop** la relación calidad-precio es muy buena en esa tienda; **to be of great ~ to sb** ser de gran valor para algn; **it is ~d at £8** está valorado en ocho libras

value added tax (VAT) n (Brit) impuesto sobre el valor añadido or agregado (LAm)

valued ['væljuːd] adj (appreciated) apreciado

valve [vælv] n (Anat, Tech) válvula

vampire ['væmpaɪər] n vampiro

van [væn] n (Aut) furgoneta, camioneta (LAm); (Brit Rail) furgón (de equipajes)

V and A n abbr (Brit) = **Victoria and Albert Museum**

vandal ['vændl] n vándalo(-a)

vandalism ['vændəlɪzəm] n vandalismo

vandalize ['vændəlaɪz] vt dañar, destruir, destrozar

vanguard ['vængɑːd] n vanguardia

vanilla [vəˈnɪlə] n vainilla

vanish ['vænɪʃ] vi desaparecer, esfumarse

vanity ['vænɪtɪ] n vanidad

vantage point ['vɑːntɪdʒ-] n posición ventajosa

vapour, (US) **vapor** ['veɪpər] n vapor; (on breath, window) vaho

variable ['vɛərɪəbl] adj, n variable

variance ['vɛərɪəns] n: **to be at ~ (with)** estar en desacuerdo (con), no cuadrar (con)

variant ['vɛərɪənt] n variante

variation [vɛərɪˈeɪʃən] n variación

varicose ['værɪkəus] adj: **~ veins** varices

varied ['vɛərɪd] adj variado

variety [vəˈraɪətɪ] n variedad, diversidad; (quantity) surtido; **for a ~ of reasons** por varias or diversas razones

variety show n espectáculo de variedades

various ['vɛərɪəs] adj varios(-as), diversos(-as); **at ~ times** (different) en distintos momentos; (several) varias veces

varnish ['vɑːnɪʃ] n (gen) barniz; (nail varnish) esmalte ▷ vt (gen) barnizar; (nails) pintar (con esmalte)

vary ['vɛərɪ] vt variar; (change) cambiar ▷ vi variar; (disagree) discrepar; **to ~ with** or **according to** variar según or de acuerdo con

vase [vɑːz] n florero

vasectomy [vəˈsɛktəmɪ] n vasectomía

Vaseline® ['væsɪli:n] n vaselina®

vast [vɑːst] adj enorme; (success) abrumador(a), arrollador(a)

vastly ['vɑːstlɪ] adv enormemente

VAT [væt] n abbr (Brit: = value added tax) IVA

vat [væt] n tina, tinaja

Vatican ['vætɪkən] n: **the ~** el Vaticano

vatman ['vætmæn] n (Brit col) inspector or recaudador del IVA; **"how to avoid the~"** "cómo evitar pagar el IVA"

vault [vɔːlt] n (of roof) bóveda; (tomb) tumba; (in bank) cámara acorazada ▷ vt (also: **vault over**) saltar (por encima de)

vaunted ['vɔːntɪd] adj: **much ~** cacareado

VCR n abbr = **video cassette recorder**

VD n abbr = **venereal disease**

VDU n abbr = **visual display unit**

veal [viːl] n ternera

veer [vɪə^r] vi (ship) virar

veg. [vɛdʒ] n abbr (Brit col) = **vegetable(s)**

vegan ['viːgən] n vegetariano(-a) estricto(-a)

vegeburger, veggieburger ['vɛdʒɪbə:gə^r] n hamburguesa vegetal

vegetable ['vɛdʒtəbl] n (Bot) vegetal; (edible plant) legumbre, hortaliza ▷ adj vegetal; **vegetables** npl (cooked) verduras

vegetarian [vɛdʒɪ'tɛərɪən] adj, n vegetariano(-a)

vegetation [vɛdʒɪ'teɪʃən] n vegetación

vegetative ['vɛdʒɪtətɪv] adj vegetativo; (Bot) vegetal

vehement ['viːɪmənt] adj vehemente, apasionado; (dislike, hatred) violento

vehicle ['viːɪkl] n vehículo; (fig) vehículo, medio

veil [veɪl] n velo ▷ vt velar; **under a ~ of secrecy** (fig) en el mayor secreto

veiled [veɪld] adj (also fig) disimulado, velado

vein [veɪn] n vena; (of ore etc) veta

Velcro® ['vɛlkrəu] n velcro®

velour [və'luə^r] n velvetón

velvet ['vɛlvɪt] n terciopelo ▷ adj aterciopelado

vending machine ['vɛndɪŋ-] n máquina expendedora, expendedor

veneer [və'nɪə^r] n chapa, enchapado; (fig) barniz

venereal disease (VD) [vɪ'nɪərɪəl-] n enfermedad venérea

Venetian blind [vɪ'niːʃən-] n persiana

Venezuela [vɛnɛ'zweɪlə] n Venezuela

Venezuelan [vɛnɛ'zweɪlən] adj, n venezolano(-a)

vengeance ['vɛndʒəns] n venganza; **with a ~** (fig) con creces

venison ['vɛnɪsn] n carne de venado

venom ['vɛnəm] n veneno

venomous ['vɛnəməs] adj venenoso

vent [vɛnt] n (opening) abertura; (air hole) respiradero; (in wall) rejilla (de ventilación) ▷ vt (fig: feelings) desahogar

ventilation [vɛntɪ'leɪʃən] n ventilación

ventilator ['vɛntɪleɪtə^r] n ventilador

ventriloquist [vɛn'trɪləkwɪst] n ventrílocuo(-a)

venture ['vɛntʃə^r] n empresa ▷ vt arriesgar; (opinion) ofrecer ▷ vi arriesgarse, lanzarse; **a business ~** una empresa comercial; **to ~ to do**

sth aventurarse a hacer algo

venue ['vɛnjuː] n (meeting place) lugar de reunión; (for concert) local

Venus ['viːnəs] n (Astro) Venus

veranda(h) [və'rændə] n terraza; (with glass) galería

verb [və:b] n verbo

verbal ['və:bl] adj verbal

verbatim [və:'beɪtɪm] adj, adv al pie de la letra, palabra por palabra

verdict ['və:dɪkt] n veredicto, fallo; (fig: opinion) opinión, juicio; **~ of guilty/not guilty** veredicto de culpabilidad/inocencia

verge [və:dʒ] n (Brit) borde; **to be on the ~ of doing sth** estar a punto de hacer algo
▷ **verge on** vt fus rayar en

verify ['vɛrɪfaɪ] vt comprobar, verificar; (Comput) verificar; (prove the truth of) confirmar

vermin ['və:mɪn] npl (animals) bichos; (insects, fig) sabandijas

vermouth ['və:məθ] n vermut

versatile ['və:sətaɪl] adj (person) polifacético; (machine, tool etc) versátil

verse [və:s] n versos, poesía; (stanza) estrofa; (in bible) versículo; **in ~** en verso

version ['və:ʃən] n versión

versus ['və:səs] prep contra

vertical ['və:tɪkl] adj vertical

vertigo ['və:tɪgəu] n vértigo; **to suffer from ~** tener vértigo

verve [və:v] n brío

very ['vɛrɪ] adv muy ▷ adj mismo; **~ well/little** muy bien/poco; **~ high frequency** (Radio) frecuencia muy alta; **not ~ interesting** no demasiado interesante; **it's ~ cold** hace mucho frío; **~ much** muchísimo; **the ~ last** el último (de todos); **at the ~ least** al menos; **we were thinking the ~ same thing** estábamos pensando exactamente lo mismo; **in this ~ house** en esta misma casa; **the ~ book which ...** el mismo libro que ...; **the ~ thought (of it) alarms me** con sólo pensarlo me entra miedo; **the ~ idea!** ¡cómo se te ocurre!

vessel ['vɛsl] n (Anat) vaso; (ship) barco; (container) vasija

vest [vɛst] n (Brit) camiseta; (US: waistcoat) chaleco

vested interests ['vɛstɪd-] npl (Comm) intereses creados

vet [vɛt] n abbr = **veterinary surgeon** ▷ vt revisar; **to ~ sb for a job** someter a investigación a algn para un trabajo

veteran ['vɛtərn] n veterano(-a) ▷ adj: **she is a ~ campaigner for ...** es una veterana de la campaña de ...

veterinarian [vɛtrɪ'nɛərɪən] n (US) = **veterinary surgeon**

veterinary surgeon n (Brit) veterinario(-a)

veto ['viːtəu] n (pl **-es**) veto ▷ vt prohibir, vedar; **to put a ~ on** vetar

vetting ['vɛtɪŋ] n: **positive ~** investigación gubernamental de los futuros altos cargos de la

Administración

vex [vɛks] *vt* (*irritate*) fastidiar; (*make impatient*) impacientar

vexed [vɛkst] *adj* (*question*) controvertido

VG *n abbr* (*Brit Scol etc*: = *very good*) S (= *sobresaliente*)

VHF *abbr* (= *very high frequency*) VHF

via ['vaɪə] *prep* por, por vía de

viable ['vaɪəbl] *adj* viable

vial ['vaɪəl] *n* frasco pequeño

vibes [vaɪbz] *npl* (*col*): **I got good/bad ~** me dio buen/mal rollo

vibrate [vaɪ'breɪt] *vi* vibrar

vibration [vaɪ'breɪʃən] *n* vibración

vicar ['vɪkəʳ] *n* párroco

vicarage ['vɪkərɪdʒ] *n* parroquia

vicarious [vɪ'kɛərɪəs] *adj* indirecto; (*responsibility*) delegado

vice [vaɪs] *n* (*evil*) vicio; (*Tech*) torno de banco

vice- [vaɪs] *pref* vice...

vice versa ['vaɪsɪ'vəːsə] *adv* viceversa

vicinity [vɪ'sɪnɪtɪ] *n* (*area*) vecindad; (*nearness*) proximidad; **in the ~ (of)** cercano (a)

vicious ['vɪʃəs] *adj* (*remark*) malicioso; (*blow*) brutal; **a ~ circle** un círculo vicioso

victim ['vɪktɪm] *n* víctima; **to be the ~ of** ser víctima de

victimize ['vɪktɪmaɪz] *vt* (*strikers etc*) tomar represalias contra

victor ['vɪktəʳ] *n* vencedor(a)

Victorian [vɪk'tɔːrɪən] *adj* victoriano

victorious [vɪk'tɔːrɪəs] *adj* vencedor(a)

victory ['vɪktərɪ] *n* victoria; **to win a ~ over sb** obtener una victoria sobre algn

video ['vɪdɪəu] *cpd* de vídeo ▷ *n* vídeo ▷ *vt* grabar (en vídeo)

video camera *n* videocámara, cámara de vídeo

video cassette *n* videocassette

video (cassette) recorder *n* vídeo, videocassette

video game *n* videojuego

videophone ['vɪdɪəufəun] *n* videoteléfono, videófono

video tape *n* cinta de vídeo

vie [vaɪ] *vi*: **to ~ with** competir con

Vienna [vɪ'ɛnə] *n* Viena

Vietnam, Viet Nam [vjɛt'næm] *n* Vietnam

Vietnamese [vjɛtnə'miːz] *adj* vietnamita ▷ *n* (*pl inv*) vietnamita; (*Ling*) vietnamita

view [vjuː] *n* vista; (*landscape*) paisaje; (*opinion*) opinión, criterio ▷ *vt* (*look at*) mirar; (*examine*) examinar; **there's an amazing ~** la vista es magnífica; **he stood up to get a better ~** se puso de pie para ver mejor; **on ~** (*in museum etc*) expuesto; **in full ~ of sb** a la vista de algn; **to be within ~ (of sth)** estar a la vista (de algo); **an overall ~ of the situation** una visión de conjunto de la situación; **in ~ of the fact that** en vista de que; **in my ~** en mi opinión; **to take** *or* **hold the ~ that ...** opinar *or* pensar que ...; **with a ~ to doing sth** con miras *or* vistas a hacer algo

viewer ['vjuːəʳ] *n* (*small projector*) visionadora; (*TV*) televidente, telespectador(a)

viewfinder ['vjuːfaɪndəʳ] *n* visor de imagen

viewpoint ['vjuːpɔɪnt] *n* punto de vista

vigil ['vɪdʒɪl] *n* vigilia; **to keep ~** velar

vigilante [vɪdʒɪ'læntɪ] *n* vecino/a que se toma la justicia por su mano

vigorous ['vɪgərəs] *adj* enérgico, vigoroso

vile [vaɪl] *adj* (*action*) vil, infame; (*smell*) repugnante

villa ['vɪlə] *n* (*country house*) casa de campo; (*suburban house*) chalet

village ['vɪlɪdʒ] *n* aldea

villager ['vɪlɪdʒəʳ] *n* aldeano(-a)

villain ['vɪlən] *n* (*scoundrel*) malvado(-a); (*criminal*) maleante; *see also* **pantomime**

vinaigrette [vɪneɪ'grɛt] *n* vinagreta

vindicate ['vɪndɪkeɪt] *vt* vindicar, justificar

vindictive [vɪn'dɪktɪv] *adj* vengativo

vine [vaɪn] *n* vid

vinegar ['vɪnɪgəʳ] *n* vinagre

vineyard ['vɪnjɑːd] *n* viña, viñedo

vintage ['vɪntɪdʒ] *n* (*year*) vendimia, cosecha; **the 1970 ~** la cosecha de 1970

vintage car *n* coche antiguo *or* de época

vintage wine *n* vino añejo

vinyl ['vaɪnl] *n* vinilo

viola [vɪ'əulə] *n* (*Mus*) viola

violate ['vaɪəleɪt] *vt* violar

violence ['vaɪələns] *n* violencia; **acts of ~** actos de violencia

violent ['vaɪələnt] *adj* (*gen*) violento; (*pain*) intenso; **a ~ dislike of sb/sth** una profunda antipatía *or* manía a algn/algo

violet ['vaɪələt] *adj* violado, violeta ▷ *n* (*plant*) violeta

violin [vaɪə'lɪn] *n* violín

violinist [vaɪə'lɪnɪst] *n* violinista

VIP *n abbr* (= *very important person*) VIP

virgin ['vəːdʒɪn] *n, adj* virgen; **the Blessed V~** la Santísima Virgen

virginity [vəː'dʒɪnɪtɪ] *n* virginidad

Virgo ['vəːgəu] *n* Virgo

virile ['vɪraɪl] *adj* viril

virtual ['vəːtjuəl] *adj* virtual

virtually ['vəːtjuːlɪ] *adv* (*almost*) prácticamente, virtualmente; **it is ~ impossible** es prácticamente imposible

virtual reality *n* realidad virtual

virtue ['vəːtjuː] *n* virtud; **by ~ of** en virtud de

virtuosity [vəːtju'ɔsɪtɪ] *n* virtuosismo

virtuous ['vəːtjuəs] *adj* virtuoso

virus ['vaɪərəs] *n* virus

visa ['viːzə] *n* visado, visa (*LAm*)

visibility [vɪzɪ'bɪlɪtɪ] *n* visibilidad

visible ['vɪzəbl] *adj* visible; **~ exports/imports** exportaciones/importaciones visibles

vision ['vɪʒən] *n* (*sight*) vista; (*foresight, in dream*) visión

visit ['vɪzɪt] *n* visita ▷ *vt* (*person*) visitar, hacer una visita a; (*place*) ir a, (ir a) conocer; **to pay a ~ to** (*person*) visitar a; **on a private/official ~** en visita privada/oficial

visiting hours ['vɪzɪtɪŋ-] *npl* (*in hospital etc*) horas de visita

visitor ['vɪzɪtəʳ] *n* (*gen*) visitante; (*to one's house*) visita; (*tourist*) turista; (*tripper*) excursionista; **to have -s** (*at home*) tener visita

visitors' book *n* libro de visitas

visor ['vaɪzəʳ] *n* visera

vista ['vɪstə] *n* vista, panorama

visual ['vɪzjuəl] *adj* visual

visual aid *n* medio visual

visual arts *npl* artes plásticas

visual display unit (VDU) *n* unidad *f* de despliegue visual, monitor *m*

visualize ['vɪzjuəlaɪz] *vt* imaginarse; (*foresee*) prever

vital ['vaɪtl] *adj* (*essential*) esencial, imprescindible; (*crucial*) crítico; (*person*) enérgico, vivo; (*of life*) vital; **of - importance (to sb/sth)** de suma importancia (para algn/algo)

vitality [vaɪ'tælɪtɪ] *n* energía, vitalidad

vitally ['vaɪtəlɪ] *adv*: **- important** de suma importancia

vital statistics *npl* (*of population*) estadísticas demográficas; (*col: woman's*) medidas (corporales)

vitamin ['vɪtəmɪn] *n* vitamina

vitamin pill *n* pastilla de vitaminas

viva ['vaɪvə] *n* (*also*: **viva voce**) examen oral

vivacious [vɪ'veɪʃəs] *adj* vivaz, alegre

vivid ['vɪvɪd] *adj* (*account*) gráfico; (*light*) intenso; (*imagination*) vivo

vividly ['vɪvɪdlɪ] *adv* (*describe*) gráficamente; (*remember*) como si fuera hoy

viz *abbr* (= *videlicet: namely*) v.gr.

V-neck ['viː:nɛk] *n* cuello de pico

vocabulary [vəu'kæbjulərɪ] *n* vocabulario

vocal ['vəukl] *adj* vocal; (*articulate*) elocuente

vocal cords *npl* cuerdas vocales

vocalist ['vəukəlɪst] *n* cantante

vocation [vəu'keɪʃən] *n* vocación

vocational [vəu'keɪʃənl] *adj* vocacional; **- guidance** orientación profesional; **- training** formación profesional

vociferous [və'sɪfərəs] *adj* vociferante

vodka ['vɒdkə] *n* vodka

vogue [vəug] *n* boga, moda; **to be in -**, **be the -** estar de moda *or* en boga

voice [vɔɪs] *n* voz ▷ *vt* (*opinion*) expresar; **in a loud/soft -** en voz alta/baja; **to give - to** expresar

voice mail *n* (*Tel*) buzón de voz

voice-over ['vɔɪsəuvəʳ] *n* voz en off

void [vɔɪd] *n* vacío; (*hole*) hueco ▷ *adj* (*invalid*) nulo, inválido; (*empty*): **- of** carente *or* desprovisto de

vol. *abbr* (= *volume*) t.

volatile ['vɒlətaɪl] *adj* volátil; (*Comput: memory*) no permanente

volcano [vɒl'keɪnəu] (*pl* **-es**) *n* volcán

volition [və'lɪʃən] *n*: **of one's own -** por su propia voluntad

volley ['vɒlɪ] *n* (*of gunfire*) descarga; (*of stones etc*) lluvia; (*Tennis etc*) volea

volleyball ['vɒlɪbɔ:l] *n* voleibol, balonvolea

volt [vəult] *n* voltio

voltage ['vəultɪdʒ] *n* voltaje; **high/low -** alto/ bajo voltaje, alta/baja tensión

volume ['vɒlju:m] *n* (*of tank*) volumen; (*book*) tomo; **volumes** *npl* (*great quantities*) cantidad; **- one/two** (*of book*) tomo primero/segundo; **his expression spoke -s** su expresión (lo) decía todo

voluntarily ['vɒləntrɪlɪ] *adv* libremente, voluntariamente

voluntary ['vɒləntərɪ] *adj* voluntario, espontáneo

volunteer [vɒlən'tɪəʳ] *n* voluntario(-a) ▷ *vi* ofrecerse (de voluntario); **to - to do** ofrecerse a hacer

vomit ['vɒmɪt] *n* vómito ▷ *vt, vi* vomitar

voracious [və'reɪʃəs] *adj* voraz; (*reader*) ávido

vote [vəut] *n* voto; (*votes cast*) votación; (*right to vote*) derecho a votar; (*franchise*) sufragio ▷ *vt* (*chairman*) elegir ▷ *vi* votar, ir a votar; **to put sth to the -**, **to take a - on sth** someter algo a votación; **- for** *or* **in favour of/against** voto a favor de/en contra de; **- of thanks** voto de gracias; **to pass a - of confidence/no confidence** aprobar un voto de confianza/de censura; **he was -d secretary** fue elegido secretario por votación; **to - Labour** votar por *or* a los laboristas; **to - to do sth** votar por hacer algo; **who did you - for?** ¿a quién votaste?

voter ['vəutəʳ] *n* votante

voting ['vəutɪŋ] *n* votación

vouch [vautʃ]: **to - for** *vt fus* garantizar, responder de

voucher ['vautʃəʳ] *n* (*for meal, petrol*) vale; **luncheon/travel -** vale de comida/de viaje

vow [vau] *n* voto ▷ *vi* hacer voto; **to take** *or* **make a - to do sth** jurar hacer algo, comprometerse a hacer algo

vowel ['vauəl] *n* vocal

voyage ['vɔɪɪdʒ] *n* (*journey*) viaje

voyeur [vwɑː'jəːʳ] *n* voyeur, mirón(-ona)

vs *abbr* (= *versus*) vs.

VSO *n abbr* (*Brit*: = *Voluntary Service Overseas*) organización que envía jóvenes voluntarios a trabajar y enseñar en los países del Tercer Mundo

vulgar ['vʌlgəʳ] *adj* (*rude*) ordinario, grosero; (*in bad taste*) de mal gusto

vulnerable ['vʌlnərəbl] *adj* vulnerable

vulture ['vʌltʃəʳ] *n* buitre, gallinazo (*LAm*)

Ww

W, w ['dʌblju:] *n* (*letter*) W, w; **W for William** W de Washington

wad [wɔd] *n* (*of cotton wool, paper*) bolita; (*of banknotes etc*) fajo

waddle ['wɔdl] *vi* andar como un pato

wade [weɪd] *vi*: **to ~ through** (*water*) caminar por; (*fig: a book*) leer con dificultad

wafer ['weɪfəʳ] *n* (*biscuit*) barquillo; (*Rel*) oblea; (: *consecrated*) hostia; (*Comput*) oblea, microplaqueta

waffle ['wɔfl] *n* (*Culin*) gofre ▷ *vi* meter el rollo

waft [wɔft] *vt* llevar por el aire ▷ *vi* flotar

wag [wæg] *vt* menear, agitar ▷ *vi* moverse, menearse; **the dog ~ged its tail** el perro meneó la cola

wage [weɪdʒ] *n* (*also*: **wages**) sueldo, salario ▷ *vt*: **to ~ war** hacer la guerra; **a day's ~** el sueldo de un día

wage earner *n* asalariado(-a)

wage packet *n* sobre de la paga

wager ['weɪdʒəʳ] *n* apuesta ▷ *vt* apostar

waggle ['wægl] *vt* menear, mover

wag(g)on ['wægən] *n* (*horse-drawn*) carro; (*Brit Rail*) vagón

wail [weɪl] *n* gemido ▷ *vi* gemir

waist [weɪst] *n* cintura, talle

waistcoat ['weɪstkəut] *n* (*Brit*) chaleco

waistline ['weɪstlaɪn] *n* talle

wait [weɪt] *n* espera; (*interval*) pausa ▷ *vi* esperar; **to lie in ~ for** acechar a; **to ~ for** esperar (a); **to keep sb ~ing** hacer esperar a algn; **I can't ~ to** (*fig*) estoy deseando; **I can't ~ for the holidays** estoy deseando que lleguen las vacaciones; **~ a moment!** ¡un momento!, ¡un momentito!; **"repairs while you ~"** "reparaciones en el acto"
  ▶ **wait behind** *vi* quedarse
  ▶ **wait on** *vt fus* servir a
  ▶ **wait up** *vi* esperar levantado

waiter ['weɪtəʳ] *n* camarero

waiting ['weɪtɪŋ] *n*: **"no ~"** (*Brit Aut*) "prohibido estacionarse"

waiting list *n* lista de espera

waiting room *n* sala de espera

waitress ['weɪtrɪs] *n* camarera

waive [weɪv] *vt* suspender

wake [weɪk] *vb* (*pt* **woke** *or* **-d**, *pp* **woken** *or* **-d**) ▷ *vt* (*also*: **wake up**) despertar ▷ *vi* (*also*: **wake up**) despertarse ▷ *n* (*for dead person*) velatorio; (*Naut*) estela; **to ~ up to sth** (*fig*) darse cuenta de algo; **in the ~ of** tras, después de; **to follow in sb's ~** (*fig*) seguir las huellas de algn

waken ['weɪkn] *vt, vi* = **wake**

Wales [weɪlz] *n* País de Gales

walk [wɔ:k] *n* (*stroll*) paseo; (*hike*) excursión a pie, caminata; (*gait*) paso, andar ▷ *vi* andar, caminar; (*go on foot*) ir a pie; (*for pleasure, exercise*) pasearse ▷ *vt* (*distance*) recorrer a pie, andar; (*dog*) (sacar a) pasear; **to go for a ~** ir a dar un paseo; **10 minutes' ~ from here** a 10 minutos de aquí andando; **people from all ~s of life** gente de todas las esferas; **to ~ in one's sleep** ser sonámbulo(-a); **we ~ed 10 kilometres** anduvimos 10 kilómetros; **I'll ~ you home** te acompañaré a casa
  ▶ **walk out** *vi* (*go out*) salir; (*as protest*) marcharse, salirse; (*strike*) declararse en huelga; **to ~ out on sb** abandonar a algn

walkabout ['wɔ:kəbaut] *n*: **to go (on a) ~** darse un baño de multitudes

walker ['wɔ:kəʳ] *n* (*person*) paseante, caminante

walkie-talkie ['wɔ:kɪ'tɔ:kɪ] *n* walkie-talkie

walking ['wɔ:kɪŋ] *n* (el) andar; **it's within ~ distance** se puede ir andando *or* a pie

walking shoes *npl* zapatos para andar

walking stick *n* bastón

Walkman® ['wɔ:kmən] *n* walkman®

walkout ['wɔ:kaut] *n* (*of workers*) huelga

walkover ['wɔ:kəuvəʳ] *n* (*col*) pan comido

walkway ['wɔ:kweɪ] *n* paseo

wall [wɔ:l] *n* pared; (*exterior*) muro; (*city wall etc*) muralla; **to go to the ~** (*fig: firm etc*) quebrar, ir a la bancarrota
  ▶ **wall in** *vt* (*garden etc*) cercar con una tapia

walled [wɔ:ld] *adj* (*city*) amurallado; (*garden*) con tapia

wallet ['wɔlɪt] *n* cartera, billetera (*esp LAm*)

wallflower ['wɔ:lflauəʳ] *n* alhelí; **to be a ~** (*fig*) comer pavo

wallop ['wɔləp] *vt* (*col*) zurrar

wallow ['wɔləu] *vi* revolcarse; **to ~ in one's grief** sumirse en su pena

wallpaper ['wɔ:lpeɪpəʳ] *n* papel pintado

wally ['wɔlɪ] *n* (*col*) majadero(-a)

walnut ['wɔ:lnʌt] *n* nuez; (*tree*) nogal

walrus ['wɔːlrəs] (*pl* - *or* -**es**) *n* morsa

waltz [wɔːlts] *n* vals ▷ *vi* bailar el vals

wan [wɔn] *adj* pálido

wand [wɔnd] *n* (*also:* **magic wand**) varita (mágica)

wander ['wɔndəʳ] *vi* (*person*) vagar; deambular; (*thoughts*) divagar ▷ *vt* recorrer, vagar por

wane [weɪn] *vi* menguar

wangle ['wæŋgl] (*Brit col*) *vt:* **to** ~ **sth** agenciarse *or* conseguir algo ▷ *n* chanchullo

want [wɔnt] *vt* (*wish for*) querer, desear; (*need*) necesitar; (*lack*) carecer de ▷ *n* (*poverty*) pobreza; (*lack*): **for** ~ **of** por falta de; **wants** *npl* (*needs*) necesidades; **to** ~ **to do** querer hacer; **to** ~ **sb to do sth** querer que algn haga algo; **you're** ~**ed on the phone** te llaman al teléfono; **"cook** ~**ed"** "se necesita cocinero(-a)"; **to be in** ~ estar necesitado

wanting ['wɔntɪŋ] *adj:* **to be** ~ **(in)** estar falto (de); **to be found** ~ no estar a la altura de las circunstancias

wanton ['wɔntn] *adj* (*playful*) juguetón(-ona); (*licentious*) lascivo

war [wɔːʳ] *n* guerra; **to make** ~ hacer la guerra; **the First/Second World W~** la primera/ segunda guerra mundial

ward [wɔːd] *n* (*in hospital*) sala; (*Pol*) distrito electoral; (*Law: child*) pupilo(-a)

  ▷ **ward off** *vt* desviar, parar; (*attack*) rechazar

warden ['wɔːdn] *n* (*Brit: of institution*) director(a); (*of park, game reserve*) guardián(-ana); (*Brit: also:* **traffic warden**) guardia

warder ['wɔːdəʳ] *n* (*Brit*) guardián(-ana), carcelero(-a)

wardrobe ['wɔːdrəub] *n* armario, guardarropa, ropero, clóset/closet (*LAm*)

warehouse ['wɛəhaus] *n* almacén, depósito

wares [wɛəz] *npl* mercancías

warfare ['wɔːfɛəʳ] *n* guerra

warhead ['wɔːhɛd] *n* cabeza armada; **nuclear** ~**s** cabezas nucleares

warily ['wɛərɪlɪ] *adv* con cautela, cautelosamente

warm [wɔːm] *adj* caliente; (*person, greeting, heart*) afectuoso, cariñoso; (*supporter*) entusiasta; (*thanks, congratulations, apologies*) efusivo; (*clothes etc*) que abriga; (*welcome, day*) caluroso; **it's** ~ hace calor; **I'm** ~ tengo calor; **to keep sth** ~ mantener algo caliente

  ▷ **warm up** *vi* (*room*) calentarse; (*person*) entrar en calor; (*athlete*) hacer ejercicios de calentamiento; (*discussion*) acalorarse ▷ *vt* calentar

war memorial *n* monumento a los caídos

warm-hearted [wɔːm'hɑːtɪd] *adj* afectuoso

warmly ['wɔːmlɪ] *adv* afectuosamente

warmth [wɔːmθ] *n* calor

warm-up ['wɔːmʌp] *n* (*Sport*) ejercicios de calentamiento

warn [wɔːn] *vt* avisar, advertir; **to** ~ **sb not to do sth** *or* **against doing sth** aconsejar a algn que no haga algo

warning ['wɔːnɪŋ] *n* aviso, advertencia; **gale** ~ (*Meteorology*) aviso de vendaval; **without (any)** ~

sin aviso *or* avisar

warning light *n* luz de advertencia

warning triangle *n* (*Aut*) triángulo señalizador

warp [wɔːp] *vi* (*wood*) combarse

warrant ['wɔrnt] *n* (*Law: to arrest*) orden de detención; (*: to search*) mandamiento de registro ▷ *vt* (*justify, merit*) merecer

warranty ['wɔrəntɪ] *n* garantía; **under** ~ (*Comm*) bajo garantía

warren ['wɔrən] *n* (*of rabbits*) madriguera; (*fig*) laberinto

warrior ['wɔrɪəʳ] *n* guerrero(-a)

Warsaw ['wɔːsɔː] *n* Varsovia

warship ['wɔːʃɪp] *n* buque *or* barco de guerra

wart [wɔːt] *n* verruga

wartime ['wɔːtaɪm] *n:* **in** ~ en tiempos de guerra, en la guerra

wary ['wɛərɪ] *adj* cauteloso; **to be** ~ **about** *or* **of doing sth** tener cuidado con hacer algo

was [wɔz] *pt of* **be**

wash [wɔʃ] *vt* lavar; (*sweep, carry: sea etc*) llevar ▷ *vi* lavarse ▷ *n* (*clothes etc*) lavado; (*bath*) baño; (*of ship*) estela; **he was** ~**ed overboard** fue arrastrado del barco por las olas; **to háve a** ~ lavarse

  ▶ **wash away** *vt* (*stain*) quitar lavando; (*river etc*) llevarse; (*fig*) limpiar

  ▶ **wash down** *vt* lavar

  ▶ **wash off** *vt* quitar lavando

  ▶ **wash up** *vi* (*Brit*) fregar los platos; (*US: have a wash*) lavarse

washable ['wɔʃəbl] *adj* lavable

washbasin ['wɔʃbeɪsn], (*US*) **washbowl** ['wɔʃbəul] *n* lavabo

washcloth ['wɔʃklɔθ] *n* (*US*) manopla

washer ['wɔʃəʳ] *n* (*Tech*) arandela

washing ['wɔʃɪŋ] *n* (*dirty*) ropa sucia; (*clean*) colada

washing machine *n* lavadora

washing powder *n* (*Brit*) detergente (en polvo)

washing-up [wɔʃɪŋ'ʌp] *n* fregado; (*dishes*) platos (para fregar); **to do the** ~ fregar los platos

washing-up liquid *n* lavavajillas

wash-out ['wɔʃaut] *n* (*col*) fracaso

washroom ['wɔʃrum] *n* servicios

wasn't ['wɔznt] = **was not**

wasp [wɔsp] *n* avispa

wastage ['weɪstɪdʒ] *n* desgaste; (*loss*) pérdida; **natural** ~ desgaste natural

waste [weɪst] *n* derroche, despilfarro; (*misuse*) desgaste; (*of time*) pérdida; (*food*) sobras; (*rubbish*) basura, desperdicios ▷ *adj* (*material*) de desecho; (*left over*) sobrante; (*energy, heat*) desperdiciado; (*land, ground: in city*) sin construir; (*: in country*) baldío ▷ *vt* (*money*) malgastar, derrochar; (*time*) perder; (*food, opportunity*) desperdiciar; **wastes** *npl* (*area of land*) tierras baldías; **it's such a** ~! ¡qué desperdicio!; **it's a** ~ **of money** es tirar el dinero; **nuclear** ~ residuos radioactivos; **to go to** ~ desperdiciarse; **to lay** ~ devastar, arrasar; **to** ~ **time** perder el tiempo

  ▶ **waste away** *vi* consumirse

wastebasket ['weɪstbɑːskɪt] n (esp US) =
wastepaper basket

waste disposal (unit) n (Brit) triturador de
basura

wasteful ['weɪstful] adj derrochador(a); (process)
antieconómico

waste ground n (Brit) terreno baldío

wastepaper basket ['weɪstpeɪpə-] n papelera

waste pipe n tubo de desagüe

waster ['weɪstəʳ] n (col) gandul

watch [wɒtʃ] n reloj; (vigil) vigilia; (vigilance)
vigilancia; (Mil: guard) centinela; (Naut: spell
of duty) guardia ▷ vt (look at) mirar, observar;
(: match, programme, TV) ver; (spy on, guard) vigilar;
(be careful of) cuidar, tener cuidado de ▷ vi ver,
mirar; (keep guard) montar guardia; **to keep a
close ~ on sth/sb** vigilar algo/a algn de cerca; ~
how you drive/what you're doing ten cuidado
al conducir/con lo que haces
▸ **watch out** vi cuidarse, tener cuidado; ~ **out!**
¡cuidado!

watchdog ['wɒtʃdɒg] n perro guardián; (fig)
organismo de control

watchful ['wɒtʃful] adj vigilante, sobre aviso

watchmaker ['wɒtʃmeɪkəʳ] n relojero(-a)

watchman ['wɒtʃmən] n guardián; (also:
night watchman) sereno, vigilante; (in factory)
vigilante nocturno

watch strap n pulsera (de reloj)

watchword ['wɒtʃwəːd] n consigna, contraseña

water ['wɔːtəʳ] n agua ▷ vt (plant) regar ▷ vi (eyes)
llorar; **I'd like a drink of ~** quisiera un vaso de
agua; **in British ~s** en aguas británicas; **to pass
~** orinar; **his mouth ~ed** se le hizo la boca agua
▸ **water down** vt (milk etc) aguar

watercolour, (US) **watercolor** ['wɔːtəkʌləʳ] n
acuarela

watercress ['wɔːtəkres] n berro

waterfall ['wɔːtəfɔːl] n cascada, salto de agua

water heater n calentador de agua

watering can ['wɔːtərɪŋ-] n regadera

water lily n nenúfar

waterline ['wɔːtəlaɪn] n (Naut) línea de flotación

waterlogged ['wɔːtəlɒgd] adj (boat) anegado;
(ground) inundado

water main n cañería del agua

watermark ['wɔːtəmɑːk] n (on paper) filigrana

watermelon ['wɔːtəmelən] n sandía

waterproof ['wɔːtəpruːf] adj impermeable

watershed ['wɔːtəʃed] n (Geo) cuenca; (fig)
momento crítico

water-skiing ['wɔːtəskiːɪŋ] n esquí acuático

water tank n depósito de agua

watertight ['wɔːtətaɪt] adj hermético

waterway ['wɔːtəweɪ] n vía fluvial or navegable

waterworks ['wɔːtəwəːks] npl central
depuradora

watery ['wɔːtərɪ] adj (colour) desvaído; (coffee)
aguado; (eyes) lloroso

watt [wɒt] n vatio

wave [weɪv] n ola; (of hand) señal con la mano;
(Radio, in hair) onda; (fig: of enthusiasm, strikes)

oleada ▷ vi agitar la mano; (flag) ondear ▷ vt
(handkerchief, gun) agitar; **short/medium/long ~**
(Radio) onda corta/media/larga; **the new ~** (Cine,
Mus) la nueva ola; **to ~ to sb** (say hello) saludar
a algn con la mano; **to ~ goodbye to sb** decir
adiós a algn con la mano; **he ~d us over to his
table** nos hizo señas (con la mano) para que nos
acercásemos a su mesa
▸ **wave aside, wave away** vt (person): **to ~ sb
aside** apartar a algn con la mano; (fig: suggestion,
objection) rechazar; (doubts) desechar

wavelength ['weɪvleŋθ] n longitud de onda

waver ['weɪvəʳ] vi oscilar; (confidence) disminuir;
(faith) flaquear

wavy ['weɪvɪ] adj ondulado

wax [wæks] n cera ▷ vt encerar ▷ vi (moon) crecer

waxworks ['wækswəːks] npl museo de cera

way [weɪ] n camino; (distance) trayecto,
recorrido; (direction) dirección, sentido; (manner)
modo, manera; (habit) costumbre; **I don't know
the ~** no sé el camino; **do you know the ~ to the
hotel?** ¿sabes cómo llegar al hotel?; **which ~ is
it?** ¿por dónde es?; **the supermarket is this ~** el
supermercado es por aquí; **on the ~** (en route) en
(el) camino; (expected) en camino; **to be on one's
~** estar en camino; **you pass it on your ~ home**
está de camino a tu casa; **the ~ back** el camino
de vuelta; **to lose one's ~** perderse, extraviarse;
to make ~ (for sb/sth) dejar paso (a algn/algo);
(fig) abrir camino (a algn/algo); **to be in the ~**
bloquear el camino; (fig) estorbar; **the village
is rather out of the ~** el pueblo está un poco
apartado or retirado; **to keep out of sb's ~**
esquivar a algn; **to go out of one's ~ to do sth**
desvivirse por hacer algo; **by the ~** a propósito;
by ~ of (via) pasando por; (as a sort of) como, a
modo de; **"~ in"** (Brit) "entrada"; **"~ out"** (Brit)
"salida"; **"give ~"** (Brit Aut) "ceda el paso"; **it's a
long ~ away** está muy lejos; **she looked at me
in a strange ~** me miró de manera extraña; **this
book tells you the right ~ to do it** este libro
explica cómo hay que hacerlo; **you're doing it
the wrong ~** lo estás haciendo mal; **put it the
right ~ up** ponlo boca arriba; **to be the wrong
~ round** estar del or al revés; **a ~ of life** un estilo
de vida; **to get one's own ~** salirse con la suya;
he's in a bad ~ está grave; **in a ~** en cierto modo
or sentido; **no ~!** (col) ¡ni pensarlo!; **to be under ~**
(work, project) estar en marcha

waylay [weɪ'leɪ] vt (irreg: like **lay**) atacar

wayward ['weɪwəd] adj díscolo, caprichoso

WC ['dʌblju'siː] n abbr (Brit: = water closet) váter

we [wiː] pl pron nosotros(-as); **we understand**
(nosotros) entendemos; **here we are** aquí
estamos

weak [wiːk] adj débil, flojo; (tea, coffee) flojo,
aguado; **to grow ~(er)** debilitarse

weaken ['wiːkən] vi debilitarse; (give way) ceder
▷ vt debilitar

weakling ['wiːklɪŋ] n debilucho(-a)

weakness ['wiːknɪs] n debilidad; (fault) punto
débil

wealth [wɛlθ] n (money, resources) riqueza; (of details) abundancia

wealthy ['wɛlθɪ] adj rico

wean [wiːn] vt destetar

weapon ['wɛpən] n arma; **~s of mass destruction** armas de destrucción masiva

wear [wɛəʳ] n (use) uso; (deterioration through use) desgaste; (clothing): **children's ~** ropa de niños; **evening ~** (man's) traje de etiqueta; (woman's) traje de noche ▷ vb (pt **wore**, pp **worn**) ▷ vt (clothes, beard) llevar; (shoes) calzar; (look, smile) tener; (damage: through use) gastar, usar ▷ vi (last) durar; (rub through etc) desgastarse; **she was ~ing black** iba vestida de negro; **to ~ a hole in sth** hacer un agujero en algo

▶ **wear away** vt gastar ▷ vi desgastarse
▶ **wear down** vt gastar; (strength) agotar
▶ **wear off** vi (pain, excitement etc) pasar, desaparecer
▶ **wear out** vt desgastar; (person) agotar

wear and tear n desgaste

weary ['wɪərɪ] adj (tired) cansado; (dispirited) abatido ▷ vt cansar ▷ vi: **to ~ of** cansarse de, aburrirse de

weasel ['wiːzl] n (Zool) comadreja

weather ['wɛðəʳ] n tiempo ▷ vt (storm, crisis) hacer frente a; **under the ~** (fig: ill) mal, pachucho; **what's the ~ like?** ¿qué tiempo hace?, ¿cómo hace?

weather-beaten ['wɛðəbiːtn] adj curtido

weathercock ['wɛðəkɔk] n veleta

weather forecast n boletín meteorológico

weatherman ['wɛðəmæn] n hombre del tiempo

weather vane n = **weathercock**

weave [wiːv] (pt **wove**, pp **woven**) vt (cloth) tejer; (fig) entretejer ▷ vi (fig) (pt, pp **-d**) (move in and out) zigzaguear

weaver ['wiːvəʳ] n tejedor(a)

web [wɛb] n (of spider) telaraña; (on foot) membrana; (network) red; **the (World Wide) W~** el or la Web

web page n: (**página**) **web**

website ['wɛbsaɪt] n sitio web

wed [wɛd] vt (pt, pp **-ded**) casar ▷ n: **the newly-~s** los recién casados

we'd [wiːd] = **we had; we would**

wedding ['wɛdɪŋ] n boda, casamiento

wedding anniversary n aniversario de boda; **silver/golden ~** bodas de plata/de oro

wedding day n día de la boda

wedding dress n traje de novia

wedding present n regalo de boda

wedding ring n alianza

wedge [wɛdʒ] n (of wood etc) cuña; (of cake) trozo ▷ vt acuñar; (push) apretar

Wednesday ['wɛdnzdɪ] n miércoles; see also **Tuesday**

wee [wiː] adj (Scottish) pequeñito

weed [wiːd] n mala hierba, maleza ▷ vt escardar, desherbar

▶ **weed out** vt eliminar

weedkiller ['wiːdkɪləʳ] n herbicida

weedy ['wiːdɪ] adj (person) debilucho

week [wiːk] n semana; **a ~ today** de hoy en ocho días; **Tuesday ~, a ~ on Tuesday** del martes en una semana; **once/twice a ~** una vez/dos veces a la semana; **this ~** esta semana; **in 2 ~s' time** dentro de 2 semanas; **every other ~** cada 2 semanas

weekday ['wiːkdeɪ] n día laborable; **on ~s** entre semana, en días laborables

weekend [wiːkˈɛnd] n fin de semana

weekly ['wiːklɪ] adv semanalmente, cada semana ▷ adj semanal ▷ n semanario; **~ newspaper** semanario

weep (pt, pp [wiːp] **wept**) vi, vt llorar; (Med: wound etc) supurar

weeping willow ['wiːpɪŋ-] n sauce llorón

weepy ['wiːpɪ] n (col: film) película lacrimógena; (: story) historia lacrimógena

weigh [weɪ] vt, vi pesar; **to ~ anchor** levar anclas; **to ~ the pros and cons** pesar los pros y los contras

▶ **weigh down** vt sobrecargar; (fig: with worry) agobiar
▶ **weigh out** vt (goods) pesar
▶ **weigh up** vt pesar

weight [weɪt] n peso; (on scale) pesa; **to lose/put on ~** adelgazar/engordar; **~s and measures** pesas y medidas

weighting ['weɪtɪŋ] n (allowance): (**London**) **~** dietas (por residir en Londres)

weight lifter [-lɪftəʳ] n levantador(a) de pesas

weight training n musculación (con pesas)

weighty ['weɪtɪ] adj pesado

weir [wɪəʳ] n presa

weird [wɪəd] adj raro, extraño

weirdo ['wɪədəu] n (col) tío(-a) raro(-a)

welcome ['wɛlkəm] adj bienvenido ▷ n bienvenida ▷ vt dar la bienvenida a; (be glad of) alegrarse de; **to make sb ~** recibir or acoger bien a algn; **thank you — you're ~** gracias — de nada; **you're ~ to try** puede intentar cuando quiera; **we ~ this step** celebramos esta medida

weld [wɛld] n soldadura ▷ vt soldar

welfare ['wɛlfɛəʳ] n bienestar; (social aid) asistencia social; **W~** (US) subsidio de paro; **to look after sb's ~** cuidar del bienestar de algn

welfare state n estado del bienestar

welfare work n asistencia social

well [wɛl] n pozo ▷ adv bien ▷ adj: **to be ~** estar bien (de salud) ▷ excl ¡vaya!, ¡bueno!; **to do ~** (business) ir bien; **I did ~ in my exams** me han salido bien los exámenes; **they are doing ~ now** les va bien ahora; **~ done!** ¡bien hecho!; **I don't feel ~** no me encuentro or siento bien; **get ~ soon!** ¡que te mejores pronto!; **to think ~ of sb** pensar bien de algn; **~, as I was saying** ... bueno, como decía ...; **it's enormous! ~, quite big anyway** ¡es enorme! bueno, digamos que bastante grande; **as ~** (in addition) además, también; **as ~ as** además de; **you might as ~ tell me** más vale que me lo digas; **it would be as ~ to ask** más valdría preguntar

▶ **well up** vi brotar
we'll [wi:l] = **we will; we shall**
well-behaved ['wɛlbɪ'heɪvd] adj: **to be ~** portarse bien
well-being ['wɛl'bi:ɪŋ] n bienestar
well-built ['wɛl'bɪlt] adj (person) fornido
well-deserved ['wɛldɪ'zə:vd] adj merecido
well-dressed ['wɛl'drɛst] adj bien vestido
well-heeled ['wɛl'hi:ld] adj (col: wealthy) rico
wellingtons ['wɛlɪŋtənz] npl (also: **Wellington boots**) botas de goma
well-known ['wɛl'nəʊn] adj (person) conocido
well-mannered ['wɛl'mænəd] adj educado
well-meaning ['wɛl'mi:nɪŋ] adj bienintencionado
well-off ['wɛl'ɔf] adj acomodado
well-read ['wɛl'rɛd] adj culto
well-to-do ['wɛltə'du:] adj acomodado
well-wisher ['wɛlwɪʃəʳ] n admirador(a)
Welsh [wɛlʃ] adj galés(-esa) ▷ n (Ling) galés; **the Welsh** npl los galeses; **the ~ Assembly** el Parlamento galés
Welshman ['wɛlʃmən] n galés
Welsh rarebit [-'rɛəbɪt] n pan con queso tostado
Welshwoman ['wɛlʃwumən] n galesa
went [wɛnt] pt of **go**
wept [wɛpt] pt, pp of **weep**
were [wə:ʳ] pt of **be**
we're [wɪəʳ] = **we are**
weren't [wə:nt] = **were not**
west [wɛst] n oeste ▷ adj occidental, del oeste ▷ adv al or hacia el oeste; **the W~** Occidente
West Country n: **the ~** el suroeste de Inglaterra
westerly ['wɛstəlɪ] adj (wind) del oeste
western ['wɛstən] adj occidental ▷ n (Cine) película del oeste
westerner ['wɛstənəʳ] n (Pol) occidental
West German (formerly) adj de Alemania Occidental ▷ n alemán(-ana) (de Alemania Occidental)
West Germany n (formerly) Alemania Occidental
West Indian adj, n antillano(-a)
West Indies [-'ɪndɪz] npl: **the ~** las Antillas
Westminster ['wɛstmɪnstəʳ] n el parlamento británico, Westminster
westward(s) ['wɛstwəd(z)] adv hacia el oeste
wet [wɛt] adj (damp) húmedo; (wet through) mojado; (rainy) lluvioso ▷ vt (pt, pp or or **-ted**) **to ~ one's pants** or **o.s.** mearse; **to get ~** mojarse; **"~ paint"** "recién pintado"
wet blanket n: **to be a ~** (fig) ser un(-una) aguafiestas
wet suit n traje de buzo
we've [wi:v] = **we have**
whack [wæk] vt dar un buen golpe a
whale [weɪl] n (Zool) ballena
whaling ['weɪlɪŋ] n pesca de ballenas
wharf [wɔ:f] (pl **wharves** [wɔ:vz]) n muelle
what [wɔt] adj **1** (in direct/indirect questions) qué; **~ size is he?** ¿qué talla usa?; **~ colour/shape is it?** ¿de qué color/forma es?; **~ books do you need?** ¿qué libros necesitas?

2 (in exclamations): **~ a mess!** ¡qué desastre!; **~ a fool I am!** ¡qué tonto soy!
▷ pron **1** (interrogative) qué; **~ are you doing?** ¿qué haces or estás haciendo?; **~ is happening?** ¿qué pasa or está pasando?; **~ is it called?** ¿cómo se llama?; **~ about me?** ¿y yo qué?; **~ about doing ...?** ¿qué tal si hacemos ...?; **~ is his address?** ¿cuáles son sus señas?; **~ will it cost?** ¿cuánto costará?

2 (relative) lo que; **I saw ~ you did/was on the table** vi lo que hiciste/había en la mesa; **~ I want is a cup of tea** lo que quiero es una taza de té; **I don't know ~ to do** no sé qué hacer; **tell me ~ you're thinking about** dime en qué estás pensando

3 (reported questions): **she asked me ~ I wanted** me preguntó qué quería
▷ excl (disbelieving) ¡cómo!; (what did you say?) ¿cómo?; **~, no coffee!** ¡que no hay café!
whatever [wɔt'ɛvəʳ] adj: **~ book you choose** cualquier libro que elijas ▷ pron: **do ~ is necessary** haga lo que sea necesario; **no reason ~** ninguna razón en absoluto; **nothing ~** nada en absoluto; **~ it costs** cueste lo que cueste
wheat [wi:t] n trigo
wheedle ['wi:dl] vt: **to ~ sb into doing sth** engatusar a algn para que haga algo; **to ~ sth out of sb** sonsacar algo a algn
wheel [wi:l] n rueda; (Aut: also: **steering wheel**) volante; (Naut) timón ▷ vt (pram etc) empujar ▷ vi (also: **wheel round**) dar la vuelta, girar; **four-~ drive** tracción en las cuatro ruedas; **front-/rear-~ drive** tracción delantera/trasera
wheelbarrow ['wi:lbærəu] n carretilla
wheelchair ['wi:ltʃɛəʳ] n silla de ruedas
wheel clamp n (Aut) cepo
wheelie-bin ['wi:lɪbɪn] n (Brit) contenedor de basura
wheeze [wi:z] vi resollar
wheezy ['wi:zɪ] adj silbante
when [wɛn] adv cuando; **~ did it happen?** ¿cuándo ocurrió?; **I know ~ it happened** sé cuándo ocurrió
▷ conj **1** (at, during, after the time that) cuando; **be careful ~ you cross the road** ten cuidado al cruzar la calle; **that was ~ I needed you** entonces era cuando te necesitaba; **I'll buy you a car ~ you're 18** te compraré un coche cuando cumplas 18 años

2 (on, at which): **on the day ~ I met him** el día en qué le conocí

3 (whereas) cuando; **you said I was wrong ~ in fact I was right** dijiste que no tenía razón, cuando en realidad sí la tenía
whenever [wɛn'ɛvəʳ] conj cuando; (every time) cada vez que; **I go ~ I can** voy siempre or todas las veces que puedo
where [wɛəʳ] adv dónde ▷ conj donde; **this is ~** aquí es donde; **~ possible** donde sea posible; **~ are you from?** ¿de dónde es usted?
whereabouts ['wɛərəbauts] adv dónde ▷ n: **nobody knows his ~** nadie conoce su paradero

whereas [wɛərˈæz] *conj* mientras

whereby [wɛəˈbaɪ] *adv* mediante el(-la) cual *etc*

whereupon [wɛərəˈpɒn] *conj* con lo cual, después de lo cual

wherever [wɛərˈɛvəʳ] *adv* dondequiera que; (*interrogative*) dónde; **sit ~ you like** siéntese donde quiera

wherewithal [ˈwɛərwɪðɔːl] *n* recursos; **the ~ (to do sth)** los medios económicos (para hacer algo)

whet [wɛt] *vt* estimular; (*appetite*) abrir

whether [ˈwɛðəʳ] *conj* si; **I don't know ~ to accept or not** no sé si aceptar o no; **~ you go or not** vayas o no vayas

which [wɪtʃ] *adj* **1** (*interrogative*: direct, indirect) qué; **~ picture(s) do you want?** ¿qué cuadro(s) quieres?; **~ one?** ¿cuál?; **~ one of you?** ¿cuál de vosotros?; **tell me ~ one you want** dime cuál (es el que) quieres

2: **in ~ case** en cuyo caso; **we got there at 8 p.m., by ~ time the cinema was full** llegamos allí a las 8, cuando el cine estaba lleno
▷ *pron* **1** (*interrogative*) cuál; **I don't mind ~** el(-la) que sea; **~ do you want?** ¿cuál quieres?

2 (*relative*: replacing noun) que; (: replacing clause) lo que; (: after preposition) (el(-la)) que, el(-la) cual; **the apple ~ you ate/~ is on the table** la manzana que comiste/que está en la mesa; **the chair on ~ you are sitting** la silla en la que estás sentado; **he didn't believe it, ~ upset me** no se lo creyó, lo cual or lo que me disgustó; **after ~** después de lo cual

whichever [wɪtʃˈɛvəʳ] *adj*: **take ~ book you prefer** coja el libro que prefiera; **~ book you take** cualquier libro que coja

whiff [wɪf] *n* bocanada; **to catch a ~ of sth** oler algo

while [waɪl] *n* rato, momento ▷ *conj* (*during the time that*) mientras; (*whereas*) mientras que; (*although*) aunque ▷ *vt*: **to ~ away the time** pasar el rato; **after a ~** después de un rato; **a ~ ago** hace un momento; **for a ~** durante algún tiempo; **in a ~** dentro de poco; **all the ~** todo el tiempo; **we'll make it worth your ~** te compensaremos generosamente; **you hold the torch ~ I look inside** aguanta la linterna mientras yo miro por dentro; **~ you are away** mientras estés fuera; **Isobel is very dynamic, ~ Kay is more laid-back** Isabel es muy dinámica, mientras que Kay es más tranquila

whim [wɪm] *n* capricho

whimper [ˈwɪmpəʳ] *n* (*weeping*) lloriqueo; (*moan*) quejido ▷ *vi* lloriquear; quejarse

whimsical [ˈwɪmzɪkl] *adj* (*person*) caprichoso

whine [waɪn] *n* (*of pain*) gemido; (*of engine*) zumbido ▷ *vi* gemir; zumbar

whip [wɪp] *n* látigo; (*Brit Pol*) *diputado encargado de la disciplina del partido en el parlamento* ▷ *vt* azotar; (*snatch*) arrebatar; (*US Culin*) batir

▸ **whip up** *vt* (*cream etc*) batir (rápidamente); (*col: meal*) preparar rápidamente; (: *stir up: support, feeling*) avivar

whipped cream [wɪpt-] *n* nata montada

whip-round [ˈwɪpraund] *n* (*Brit*) colecta

whirl [wəːl] *n* remolino ▷ *vt* hacer girar, dar vueltas a ▷ *vi* (*dancers*) girar, dar vueltas; (*leaves, dust, water etc*) arremolinarse

whirlpool [ˈwəːlpuːl] *n* remolino

whirlwind [ˈwəːlwɪnd] *n* torbellino

whirr [wəːʳ] *vi* zumbar

whisk [wɪsk] *n* (*Brit Culin*) batidor ▷ *vt* (*Brit Culin*) batir; **to ~ sb away** or **off** llevarse volando a algn

whiskers [ˈwɪskəz] *npl* (*of animal*) bigotes; (*of man*) patillas

whisky, (*US, Ireland*) **whiskey** [ˈwɪskɪ] *n* whisky

whisper [ˈwɪspəʳ] *n* cuchicheo; (*rumour*) rumor; (*fig*) susurro, murmullo ▷ *vi* cuchichear, hablar bajo; (*fig*) susurrar ▷ *vt* decir en voz muy baja; **to ~ sth to sb** decirle algo al oído a algn

whistle [ˈwɪsl] *n* (*sound*) silbido; (*object*) silbato ▷ *vi* silbar; **to ~ a tune** silbar una melodía

white [waɪt] *adj* blanco; (*pale*) pálido ▷ *n* blanco; (*of egg*) clara; **to turn** or **go ~** (*person*) palidecer, ponerse blanco; (*hair*) encanecer; **the ~s** (*washing*) la ropa blanca; **tennis ~s** ropa de tenis

white coffee *n* (*Brit*) café con leche

white-collar worker [ˈwaɪtkɒlə-] *n* oficinista

white elephant *n* (*fig*) maula

white lie *n* mentirijilla

white paper *n* (*Pol*) libro blanco

whitewash [ˈwaɪtwɒʃ] *n* (*paint*) cal, jalbegue ▷ *vt* encalar, blanquear; (*fig*) encubrir

whiting [ˈwaɪtɪŋ] *n* (*pl inv: fish*) pescadilla

Whitsun [ˈwɪtsn] *n* (*Brit*) Pentecostés

whittle [ˈwɪtl] *vt*: **to ~ away, ~ down** ir reduciendo

whizz [wɪz] *vi*: **to ~ past** or **by** pasar a toda velocidad

whizz kid *n* (*col*) prodigio(-a)

WHO *n abbr* (= World Health Organization) OMS

who [huː] *pron* **1** (*interrogative*) quién; **~ is it?, ~'s there?** ¿quién es?; **~ are you looking for?** ¿a quién buscas?; **I told her ~ I was** le dije quién era yo

2 (*relative*) que; **the man/woman ~ spoke to me** el hombre/la mujer que habló conmigo; **those ~ can swim** los que saben or sepan nadar

whodun(n)it [huːˈdʌnɪt] *n* (*col*) novela policíaca

whoever [huːˈɛvəʳ] *pron*: **~ finds it** cualquiera or quienquiera que lo encuentre; **ask ~ you like** pregunta a quien quieras; **~ he marries** se case con quien se case

whole [həul] *adj* (*complete*) todo, entero; (*not broken*) intacto ▷ *n* (*total*) total; (*sum*) conjunto; **~ villages were destroyed** pueblos enteros fueron destruídos; **2 ~ days** 2 días enteros; **the ~ (of the) town** toda la ciudad, la ciudad entera; **on the ~, as a ~** en general

wholehearted [həulˈhɑːtɪd] *adj* (*support, approval*) total; (*sympathy*) todo

wholemeal [ˈhəulmiːl] *adj* (*Brit: flour, bread*) integral

wholesale [ˈhəulseɪl] *n* venta al por mayor ▷ *adj* al por mayor; (*destruction*) sistemático

wholesaler [ˈhəulseɪləʳ] *n* mayorista

wholesome ['həulsəm] *adj* sano

wholewheat ['həulwiːt] *adj* = **wholemeal**

wholly ['həulɪ] *adv* totalmente, enteramente

whom [huːm] *pron* **1** (*interrogative*): ~ **did you see?** ¿a quién viste?; **to** ~ **did you give it?** ¿a quién se lo diste?; **tell me from** ~ **you received it** dígame de quién lo recibiste

2 (*relative*) que; **to** ~ a quien(es), **of** ~ de quien(es), del/de la que; **the man** ~ **I saw** el hombre qui vi; **the man to** ~ **I wrote** el hombre a quien escribí; **the lady about** ~ **I was talking** la señora de (la) que hablaba; **the lady with** ~ **I was talking** la señora con quien *or* (la) que hablaba

whooping cough ['huːpɪŋ-] *n* tos ferina

whoops [wuːps] *excl* (*also*: **whoops-a-daisy!**) ¡huy!

whore [hɔːʳ] *n* (*col*: *pej*) puta

whose [huːz] *adj* **1** (*possessive*: *interrogative*) de quién; ~ **book is this?**, ~ **is this book?** ¿de quién es este libro?; ~ **pencil have you taken?** ¿de quién es el lápiz que has cogido?; ~ **daughter are you?** ¿de quién eres hija?

2 (*possessive*: *relative*) cuyo(-a); (*pl*) cuyos(-as); **the man** ~ **son they rescued** el hombre cuyo hijo rescataron; **the girl** ~ **sister he was speaking to** la chica con cuya hermana estaba hablando; **those** ~ **passports I have** aquellas personas cuyos pasaportes tengo; **the woman** ~ **car was stolen** la mujer a quien le robaron el coche ▷ *pron* de quién; ~ **is this?** ¿de quién es esto?; **I know** ~ **it is** sé de quién es

why [waɪ] *adv* por qué; ~ **not?** ¿por qué no?; ~ **not do it now?** ¿por qué no lo haces (*or* hacemos) ahora?

▷ *conj*: **I wonder** ~ **he said that** me pregunto por qué dijo eso; **that's not** ~ **I'm here** no es por eso (por lo) que estoy aquí; **the reason** ~ la razón por la que

▷ *excl* (*expressing surprise, shock, annoyance*) ¡hombre!, ¡vaya!; (*explaining*): ~, **it's you!** ¡hombre, eres tú!; ~, **that's impossible** ¡pero si eso es imposible!

whyever [waɪˈevəʳ] *adv* por qué

wicked ['wɪkɪd] *adj* malvado, cruel

wicket ['wɪkɪt] *n* (*Cricket*) palos

wide [waɪd] *adj* ancho; (*area, knowledge*) vasto, grande; (*choice*) grande ▷ *adv*: **to open** ~ abrir de par en par; **to shoot** ~ errar el tiro; **it is 3 metres** ~ tiene 3 metros de ancho; **how** ~ **is the room?** ¿cómo es de ancha la habitación?

wide-angle lens ['waɪdæŋgl-] *n* (objetivo) gran angular

wide-awake [waɪdəˈweɪk] *adj* bien despierto

widely ['waɪdlɪ] *adv* (*differing*) muy; **it is** ~ **believed that …** existe la creencia generalizada de que …; **to be** ~ **read** (*author*) ser muy leído; (*reader*) haber leído mucho

widen ['waɪdn] *vt* ensanchar

wide open *adj* abierto de par en par

widespread ['waɪdsprɛd] *adj* (*belief etc*) extendido, general

widow ['wɪdəu] *n* viuda

widowed ['wɪdəud] *adj* viudo

widower ['wɪdəuəʳ] *n* viudo

width [wɪdθ] *n* anchura; (*of cloth*) ancho; **it's 7 metres in** ~ tiene 7 metros de ancho

wield [wiːld] *vt* (*sword*) manejar; (*power*) ejercer

wife [waɪf] (*pl* **wives**) [waɪvz] *n* mujer, esposa

wig [wɪg] *n* peluca

wiggle ['wɪgl] *vt* menear ▷ *vi* menearse

wild [waɪld] *adj* (*animal*) salvaje; (*plant*) silvestre; (*rough*) furioso, violento; (*idea*) descabellado; (*col*: *angry*) furioso ▷ *n*: **the** ~ la naturaleza; **wilds** *npl* regiones salvajes, tierras vírgenes; **to be** ~ **about** (*enthusiastic*) estar *or* andar loco por; **in its** ~ **state** en estado salvaje

wild card *n* (*Comput*) comodín

wildcat ['waɪldkæt] *n* gato montés

wilderness ['wɪldənɪs] *n* desierto; (*jungle*) jungla

wildfire ['waɪldfaɪəʳ] *n*: **to spread like** ~ correr como un reguero de pólvora

wild-goose chase [waɪldˈguːs-] *n* (*fig*) búsqueda inútil

wildlife ['waɪldlaɪf] *n* fauna

wildly ['waɪldlɪ] *adv* (*roughly*) violentamente; (*foolishly*) locamente; (*rashly*) descabelladamente

wilful, (*US*) **willful** ['wɪlful] *adj* (*action*) deliberado; (*obstinate*) testarudo

will [wɪl] *aux vb* **1** (*forming future tense*): **I** ~ **finish it tomorrow** lo terminaré *or* voy a terminar mañana; **I** ~ **have finished it by tomorrow** lo habré terminado para mañana; ~ **you do it?** ¿lo harás? — **yes I** ~/**no I won't** sí/no; **you won't lose it,** ~ **you?** no lo vayas a perder *or* no lo perderás ¿verdad?

2 (*in conjectures, predictions*): **he** ~ *or* **he'll be there by now** ya habrá llegado, ya debe (de) haber llegado; **that** ~ **be the postman** será el cartero, debe ser el cartero

3 (*in commands, requests, offers*): ~ **you be quiet!** ¿quieres callarte?; ~ **you help me?** ¿quieres ayudarme?; ~ **you have a cup of tea?** ¿te apetece un té?; **I won't put up with it!** ¡no lo soporto!

4 (*habits, persistence*): **the car won't start** el coche no arranca; **accidents** ~ **happen** son cosas que pasan

▷ *vt* (*pt, pp* -**ed**); **to** ~ **sb to do sth** desear que algn haga algo; **he** ~**ed himself to go on** con gran fuerza de voluntad, continuó

▷ *n* **1** (*desire*) voluntad; **against sb's** ~ contra la voluntad de algn; **he did it of his own free** ~ lo hizo por su propia voluntad

2 (*Law*) testamento; **to make a** *or* **one's** ~ hacer su testamento

willing ['wɪlɪŋ] *adj* (*with goodwill*) de buena voluntad; complaciente; **he's** ~ **to do it** está dispuesto a hacerlo; **to show** ~ mostrarse dispuesto

willingly ['wɪlɪŋlɪ] *adv* con mucho gusto

willingness ['wɪlɪŋnɪs] *n* buena voluntad

willow ['wɪləu] *n* sauce

willpower ['wɪlpauəʳ] *n* fuerza de voluntad

willy-nilly [wɪlɪˈnɪlɪ] *adv* quiérase o no

wilt [wɪlt] *vi* marchitarse

wily ['waɪlɪ] *adj* astuto

wimp [wɪmp] n (col) enclenque; (character) calzonazos

win [wɪn] n (in sports etc) victoria, triunfo ▷ vb (pt, pp **won**) ▷ vt ganar; (obtain: contract etc) conseguir, lograr ▷ vi ganar
  ▶ **win over**
  ▶ **win round** (Brit) vt convencer a

wince [wɪns] vi encogerse

winch [wɪntʃ] n torno

wind, n wɪnd] n viento; (Med) gases; (breath) aliento, vb waɪnd] (pt, pp **wound**) [waund] ▷ vt (rope, wire) enrollar; (wrap) envolver; (clock, toy) dar cuerda a [wɪnd] (take breath away from) (pt, pp ed) dejar sin aliento a ▷ vi (road, river) serpentear; **into** or **against the ~** contra el viento; **to get ~ of sth** enterarse de algo; **to break ~** ventosear; **a ~ instrument** un instrumento de viento
  ▶ **wind down** vt (car window) bajar; (fig: production, business) disminuir
  ▶ **wind up** vt (clock) dar cuerda a; (debate) concluir, terminar

windfall ['wɪndfɔːl] n golpe de suerte

winding ['waɪndɪŋ] adj (road) tortuoso

wind instrument n (Mus) instrumento de viento

windmill ['wɪndmɪl] n molino de viento

window ['wɪndəu] n ventana; (in car, train) ventana; (in shop etc) escaparate, vitrina (LAm), vidriera (LAm); (Comput) ventana

window box n jardinera (de ventana)

window cleaner n (person) limpiacristales

window ledge n alféizar, repisa

window pane n cristal

window-shopping [wɪndəu'ʃɔpɪŋ] n: **to go ~** ir a ver or mirar escaparates

windowsill ['wɪndəusɪl] n alféizar, repisa

windpipe ['wɪndpaɪp] n tráquea

wind power n energía eólica

windscreen ['wɪndskriːn], (US) **windshield** ['wɪndʃiːld] n parabrisas

windscreen washer, (US) **windshield washer** n lavaparabrisas

windscreen wiper, windshield wiper [-'waɪpə'] (US) n limpiaparabrisas

windsurfing ['wɪndsəːfɪŋ] n windsurf

windswept ['wɪndswɛpt] adj azotado por el viento

windy ['wɪndɪ] adj de mucho viento; **it's ~** hace viento

wine [waɪn] n vino ▷ vt: **to ~ and dine sb** agasajar or festejar a algn

wine bar n bar especializado en vinos

wine cellar n bodega

wine glass n copa (de o para vino)

wine list n lista de vinos

wine waiter n escanciador

wing [wɪŋ] n ala; (Brit Aut) aleta; **wings** npl (Theat) bastidores

winger ['wɪŋə'] n (Sport) extremo

wink [wɪŋk] n guiño; (blink) pestañeo ▷ vi guiñar; (blink) pestañear; (light etc) parpadear

winner ['wɪnə'] n ganador(a)

winning ['wɪnɪŋ] adj (team) ganador(a); (goal) decisivo; (charming) encantador(a)

winnings ['wɪnɪŋz] npl ganancias

winter ['wɪntə'] n invierno ▷ vi invernar

winter sports npl deportes de invierno

wintry ['wɪntrɪ] adj invernal

wipe [waɪp] n: **to give sth a ~** pasar un trapo sobre algo ▷ vt limpiar; **to ~ one's nose** limpiarse la nariz
  ▶ **wipe off** vt limpiar con un trapo
  ▶ **wipe out** vt (debt) liquidar; (memory) borrar; (destroy) destruir
  ▶ **wipe up** vt limpiar

wire ['waɪə'] n alambre; (Elec) cable (eléctrico); (Tel) telegrama ▷ vt (house) poner la instalación eléctrica en; (also: **wire up**) conectar

wireless ['waɪəlɪs] n (Brit) radio

wire service n (US) agencia de noticias

wiring ['waɪərɪŋ] n instalación eléctrica

wiry ['waɪərɪ] adj enjuto y fuerte

wisdom ['wɪzdəm] n sabiduría, saber; (good sense) cordura

wisdom tooth n muela del juicio

wise [waɪz] adj sabio; (sensible) juicioso; **I'm none the ~r** sigo sin entender
  ▶ **wise up** vi (col): **to ~ up (to sth)** enterarse (de algo)

wisecrack ['waɪzkræk] n broma

wish [wɪʃ] n (desire) deseo ▷ vt desear; (want) querer ▷ vi: **to ~ for** desear; **to ~ to do sth** querer hacer algo; **to make a ~** pedir un deseo; **best ~es** (on birthday etc) felicidades; **with best ~es** (in letter) saludos, recuerdos; **to ~ sb goodbye** despedirse de algn; **to ~ sb happy birthday** desear a algn un feliz cumpleaños; **he ~ed me well** me deseó mucha suerte; **to ~ sth on sb** imponer algo a algn; **to ~ sb to do sth** querer que algn haga algo; **I ~ you were here!** ¡ojalá estuvieras aquí!; **I ~ you'd told me!** ¡me lo podrías haber dicho!

wishbone ['wɪʃbəun] n espoleta (de la que tiran dos personas quien se quede con el hueso más largo pide un deseo)

wishful ['wɪʃful] adj: **it's ~ thinking** eso es hacerse ilusiones

wistful ['wɪstful] adj pensativo; (nostalgic) nostálgico

wit [wɪt] n (wittiness) ingenio, gracia; (intelligence: also: **wits**) inteligencia; (person) chistoso(-a); **to have** or **keep one's ~s about one** no perder la cabeza

witch [wɪtʃ] n bruja

witchcraft ['wɪtʃkrɑːft] n brujería

with [wɪð, wɪθ] prep **1** (accompanying, in the company of) con; **I was ~ him** estaba con él; **we stayed ~ friends** nos quedamos en casa de unos amigos
2 (descriptive, indicating manner etc) con; de; **a room ~ a view** una habitación con vistas; **the man ~ the grey hat/blue eyes** el hombre del sombrero gris/de los ojos azules; **red ~ anger** rojo de ira; **to shake ~ fear** temblar de miedo; **to fill sth ~ water** llenar algo de agua
3: I'm ~ you/I'm not ~ you (understand) ya te

entiendo/no te entiendo; **I'm not really ~ it
today** no doy pie con bola hoy
withdraw [wɪðˈdrɔː] (*irreg: like* **draw**) *vt* retirar
▷ *vi* retirarse; (*go back on promise*) retractarse; **to
~ money (from the bank)** retirar fondos (del
banco); **to ~ into o.s.** ensimismarse
withdrawal [wɪðˈdrɔːəl] *n* retirada
withdrawal symptoms *npl* síndrome de
abstinencia
withdrawn [wɪðˈdrɔːn] *adj* (*person*) reservado,
introvertido ▷ *pp of* **withdraw**
wither [ˈwɪðəʳ] *vi* marchitarse
withhold [wɪðˈhəʊld] *vt* (*irreg: like* **hold**); (*money*)
retener; (*decision*) aplazar; (*permission*) negar;
(*information*) ocultar
within [wɪðˈɪn] *prep* dentro de ▷ *adv* dentro; **~
reach** al alcance de la mano; **the shops are ~
easy reach** las tiendas están cerca; **~ sight of** a
la vista de; **~ an hour from now** dentro de una
hora; **~ the week** antes de que acabe la semana;
the police arrived ~ minutes la policía llegó a
los pocos minutos; **to be ~ the law** atenerse a la
legalidad
without [wɪðˈaʊt] *prep* sin; **to go** *or* **do ~ sth**
prescindir de algo; **~ anybody knowing** sin
saberlo nadie
withstand [wɪðˈstænd] *vt* (*irreg: like* **stand**)
resistir a
witness [ˈwɪtnɪs] *n* (*person*) testigo; (*evidence*)
testimonio ▷ *vt* (*event*) presenciar, ser testigo
de; (*document*) atestiguar la veracidad de; **~
for the prosecution/defence** testigo de
cargo/descargo; **to ~ to** (*having seen*) **sth** dar
testimonio de (haber visto) algo
witness box, (US) **witness stand** *n* tribuna de
los testigos
witticism [ˈwɪtɪsɪzm] *n* dicho ingenioso
witty [ˈwɪtɪ] *adj* ingenioso
wives [waɪvz] *npl of* **wife**
wizard [ˈwɪzəd] *n* hechicero
wk *abbr* = **week**
wobble [ˈwɒbl] *vi* tambalearse
woe [wəʊ] *n* desgracia
woeful [ˈwəʊful] *adj* (*bad*) lamentable; (*sad*)
apesadumbrado
wok [wɒk] *n* wok
woke [wəʊk] *pt of* **wake**
woken [ˈwəʊkn] *pp of* **wake**
wolf [wʊlf] (*pl* **wolves**) [wʊlvz] *n* lobo
woman [ˈwʊmən] (*pl* **women**) [ˈwɪmɪn] *n* mujer;
young ~ (mujer) joven; **women's page** (*Press*)
sección de la mujer
womanly [ˈwʊmənlɪ] *adj* femenino
womb [wuːm] *n* (*Anat*) matriz, útero
women [ˈwɪmɪn] *npl of* **woman**
Women's (Liberation) Movement *n* (*also*:
women's lib) Movimiento de liberación de la
mujer
won [wʌn] *pt, pp of* **win**
wonder [ˈwʌndəʳ] *n* maravilla, prodigio; (*feeling*)
asombro ▷ *vi*: **to ~ whether** preguntarse si; **to ~
at** asombrarse de; **to ~ about** pensar sobre *or* en;

it's no ~ that no es de extrañar que
wonderful [ˈwʌndəful] *adj* maravilloso
wonky [ˈwɒŋkɪ] *adj* (Brit col: *unsteady*) poco seguro,
cojo; (: *broken down*) estropeado
wont [wɒnt] *n*: **as is his/her ~** como tiene por
costumbre
won't [wəʊnt] = **will not**
woo [wuː] *vt* (*woman*) cortejar
wood [wʊd] *n* (*timber*) madera; (*forest*) bosque
▷ *cpd* de madera
wood carving *n* tallado en madera
wooded [ˈwʊdɪd] *adj* arbolado
wooden [ˈwʊdn] *adj* de madera; (*fig*) inexpresivo
woodpecker [ˈwʊdpɛkəʳ] *n* pájaro carpintero
woodwind [ˈwʊdwɪnd] *n* (*Mus*) instrumentos de
viento de madera
woodwork [ˈwʊdwəːk] *n* carpintería
woodworm [ˈwʊdwəːm] *n* carcoma
wool [wʊl] *n* lana; **knitting ~** lana (de hacer
punto); **to pull the ~ over sb's eyes** (*fig*) dar a
algn gato por liebre
woollen, (US) **woolen** [ˈwʊlən] *adj* de lana ▷ *n*:
~s géneros de lana
woolly, (US) **wooly** [ˈwʊlɪ] *adj* de lana; (*fig*: *ideas*)
confuso
woozy [ˈwuːzɪ] *adj* (*col*) mareado
word [wəːd] *n* palabra; (*news*) noticia; (*promise*)
palabra (de honor) ▷ *vt* redactar; **~ for ~**
palabra por palabra; **what's the ~ for "pen" in
Spanish?** ¿cómo se dice "pen" en español?; **to
put sth into ~s** expresar algo en palabras; **to
have a ~ with sb** hablar (dos palabras) con algn;
in other ~s en otras palabras; **to break/keep
one's ~** faltar a la palabra/cumplir la promesa;
to leave ~ (with/for sb) that … dejar recado
(con/para algn) de que …; **to have ~s with sb**
(*quarrel with*) discutir *or* reñir con algn; **the ~s**
(*lyrics*) la letra
wording [ˈwəːdɪŋ] *n* redacción
word-of-mouth [wəːdəvˈmaʊθ] *n*: **by** *or*
through ~ de palabra, por el boca a boca
word processing *n* procesamiento *or*
tratamiento de textos
word processor [-ˈprəʊsɛsəʳ] *n* procesador de
textos
wore [wɔːʳ] *pt of* **wear**
work [wəːk] *n* trabajo; (*job*) empleo, trabajo; (*Art,
Lit*) obra ▷ *vi* trabajar; (*mechanism*) funcionar,
marchar; (*medicine*) ser eficaz, surtir efecto
▷ *vt* (*shape*) trabajar; (*stone etc*) tallar; (*mine etc*)
explotar; (*machine*) manejar, hacer funcionar;
(*cause*) producir; **to go to ~** ir a trabajar *or* al
trabajo; **to be at ~ (on sth)** (*working*) estar
trabajando (en algo); **he's at ~ until 5** (*in office
etc*) está en el trabajo hasta las 5; **I'm off ~ for a
week** tengo una semana de permiso; **to set to
~, start ~** ponerse a trabajar; **to be out of ~** estar
parado, no tener trabajo; **his life's ~** el trabajo
de su vida; **to ~ hard** trabajar mucho *or* duro; **to
~ rule** (*Industry*) hacer una huelga de celo; **the
heating isn't ~ing** la calefacción no funciona;
my plan ~ed perfectly mi plan funcionó a la

perfección; **to ~ loose** (*part*) desprenderse; (*knot*) aflojarse; *see also* **works**

▸ **work off** *vt*: **to ~ off one's feelings** desahogarse

▸ **work on** *vt fus* trabajar en, dedicarse a; (*principle*) basarse en; **he's ~ing on the car** está reparando el coche

▸ **work out** *vi* (*plans etc*) salir bien, funcionar; (*Sport*) hacer ejercicios ▷ *vt* (*problem*) resolver; (*plan*) elaborar; **it ~s out at £100** asciende a 100 libras; **I ~ed it out in my head** lo calculé en mi cabeza; **I just couldn't ~ it out** (*understand*) no lograba entenderlo

▸ **work up** *vi*: **he ~ed his way up in the company** ascendió en la compañía mediante sus propios esfuerzos

workable ['wə:kəbl] *adj* (*solution*) práctico, factible

workaholic [wə:kə'hɔlɪk] *n* adicto(-a) al trabajo

worked up [wə:kt-] *adj*: **to get ~** excitarse

worker ['wə:kəʳ] *n* trabajador(a), obrero(-a); **office ~** oficinista

work force *n* mano de obra

working class ['wə:kɪŋ-] *n* clase obrera ▷ *adj*: **working-class** obrero

working order *n*: **in ~** en funcionamiento

workload ['wə:kləud] *n* cantidad de trabajo

workman ['wə:kmən] *n* obrero

workmanship ['wə:kmənʃɪp] *n* (*art*) hechura; (*skill*) habilidad

workmate ['wə:kmeɪt] *n* compañero(-a) de trabajo

workout ['wə:kaut] *n* (*Sport*) sesión de ejercicios

works [wə:ks] *nsg* (*Brit: factory*) fábrica ▷ *npl* (*of clock, machine*) mecanismo

worksheet ['wə:kʃi:t] *n* (*Comput*) hoja de trabajo

workshop ['wə:kʃɔp] *n* taller

work station *n* estación de trabajo

worktop ['wə:ktɔp] *n* encimera

work-to-rule ['wə:ktə'ru:l] *n* (*Brit*) huelga de celo

world [wə:ld] *n* mundo ▷ *cpd* (*champion*) del mundo; (*power, war*) mundial; **all over the ~** por todo el mundo, en el mundo entero; **the business ~** el mundo de los negocios; **what in the ~ is he doing?** ¿qué diablos está haciendo?; **to think the ~ of sb** (*fig*) tener un concepto muy alto de algn; **to do sb a ~ of good** sentar muy bien a algn; **W~ War One/Two** la primera/ segunda Guerra Mundial

World Cup *n* (*Football*): **the ~** el Mundial, los Mundiales

worldly ['wə:ldlɪ] *adj* mundano

World Series *n*: **the ~** (*US Baseball*) el campeonato nacional de béisbol de EEUU

World Service *n* *see* **BBC**

world-wide ['wə:ldwaɪd] *adj* mundial, universal

worm [wə:m] *n* gusano; (*earthworm*) lombriz

worn [wɔ:n] *pp of* **wear** ▷ *adj* usado

worn-out ['wɔ:naut] *adj* (*object*) gastado; (*person*) rendido, agotado

worried ['wʌrɪd] *adj* preocupado; **to be ~ about sth** estar preocupado por algo

worry ['wʌrɪ] *n* preocupación ▷ *vt* preocupar, inquietar ▷ *vi* preocuparse; **to ~ about** *or* **over sth/sb** preocuparse por algo/algn

worrying ['wʌrɪɪŋ] *adj* inquietante

worse [wə:s] *adj, adv* peor ▷ *n* el peor, lo peor; **a change for the ~** un empeoramiento; **so much the ~ for you** tanto peor para ti; **he is none the ~ for it** se ha quedado tan fresco *or* tan tranquilo; **to get ~**, **to grow ~** empeorar

worsen ['wə:sn] *vt, vi* empeorar

worse off *adj* (*fig*): **you'll be ~ this way** de esta forma estarás peor que antes

worship ['wə:ʃɪp] *n* (*organized worship*) culto; (*act*) adoración ▷ *vt* adorar; **Your W~** (*Brit: to mayor*) su Ilustrísima; (*: to judge*) su señoría

worst [wə:st] *adj* (el/la) peor ▷ *adv* peor ▷ *n* lo peor; **at ~** en el peor de los casos; **to come off ~** llevar la peor parte; **if the ~ comes to the ~** en el peor de los casos

worth [wə:θ] *n* valor ▷ *adj*: **to be ~** valer; **how much is it ~?** ¿cuánto vale?; **it's ~ it** vale *or* merece la pena; **to be ~ one's while** (**to do**) merecer la pena (hacer); **it's not ~ the trouble** no vale *or* merece la pena

worthless ['wə:θlɪs] *adj* sin valor; (*useless*) inútil

worthwhile ['wə:θwaɪl] *adj* (*activity*) que merece la pena; (*cause*) loable

worthy ['wə:ðɪ] *adj* (*person*) respetable; (*motive*) honesto; **~ of** digno de

would [wud] *aux vb* **1** (*conditional tense*): **if you asked him he ~ do it** si se lo pidieras, lo haría; **if you had asked him he ~ have done it** si se lo hubieras pedido, lo habría *or* hubiera hecho

2 (*in offers, invitations, requests*): **~ you like a biscuit?** ¿quieres una galleta?; (*formal*) ¿querría una galleta?; **~ you ask him to come in?** ¿quiere hacerle pasar?; **~ you open the window please?** ¿quiere *or* podría abrir la ventana, por favor?

3 (*in indirect speech*): **I said I ~ do it** dije que lo haría

4 (*emphatic*): **it WOULD have to snow today!** ¡tenía que nevar precisamente hoy!

5 (*insistence*): **she ~n't behave** no quiso comportarse bien

6 (*conjecture*): **it ~ have been midnight** sería medianoche; **so it ~ seem** parece ser que sí

7 (*indicating habit*): **he ~ go there on Mondays** iba allí los lunes

would-be ['wudbi:] *adj* (*pej*) presunto

wouldn't ['wudnt] = **would not**

wound [waund] *pt, pp of* **wind** ▷ *n* [wu:nd] herida ▷ *vt* [wu:nd] herir

wove [wəuv] *pt of* **weave**

woven ['wəuvən] *pp of* **weave**

WP *n abbr* = **word processing; word processor**

WPC *n abbr* (*Brit*) = **woman police constable**

wpm *abbr* (= *words per minute*) p.p.m.

wrap [ræp] *n* (*stole*) chal ▷ *vt* (*also*: **wrap up**) envolver; **under ~s** (*fig: plan, scheme*) oculto, tapado

wrapper ['ræpəʳ] *n* (*Brit: of book*) sobrecubierta;

(*on chocolate etc*) envoltura
wrapping paper ['ræpɪŋ-] *n* papel de envolver
wrath [rɔθ] *n* cólera
wreak [ri:k] *vt* (*destruction*) causar; **to ~ havoc
(on)** hacer *or* causar estragos (en); **to ~
vengeance (on)** vengarse (en)
wreath [ri:θ] (*pl* **-s**) [ri:ðz] *n* (*funeral wreath*)
corona; (*of flowers*) guirnalda
wreck [rɛk] *n* (*ship: destruction*) naufragio;
(*: remains*) restos del barco; (*pej: person*) ruina ▷ *vt*
destrozar; **to be ~ed** (*Naut*) naufragar
wreckage ['rɛkɪdʒ] *n* (*remains*) restos; (*of building*)
escombros
wren [rɛn] *n* (*Zool*) reyezuelo
wrench [rɛntʃ] *n* (*Tech*) llave inglesa; (*tug*) tirón
▷ *vt* arrancar; **to ~ sth from sb** arrebatar algo
violentamente a algn
wrestle ['rɛsl] *vi*: **to ~ (with sb)** luchar (con *or*
contra algn)
wrestler ['rɛslə'] *n* luchador(a) (de lucha libre)
wrestling ['rɛslɪŋ] *n* lucha libre
wretched ['rɛtʃɪd] *adj* miserable
wriggle ['rɪgl] *vi* serpentear
wring [rɪŋ] (*pt, pp* **wrung**) [rʌŋ] *vt* torcer, retorcer;
(*wet clothes*) escurrir; (*fig*): **to ~ sth out of sb**
sacar algo por la fuerza a algn
wrinkle ['rɪŋkl] *n* arruga ▷ *vt* arrugar ▷ *vi*
arrugarse
wrist [rɪst] *n* muñeca
wrist watch *n* reloj de pulsera
writ [rɪt] *n* mandato judicial; **to serve a ~ on sb**
notificar un mandato judicial a algn
write [raɪt] (*pt* **wrote**, *pp* **written**) *vt, vi* escribir;
to ~ sb a letter escribir una carta a algn
▸ **write away** *vi*: **to ~ away for** (*information, goods*)
pedir por escrito *or* carta
▸ **write down** *vt* (*note down*) apuntar, anotar; **can
you ~ it down for me, please?** ¿me lo puedes
anotar, por favor?
▸ **write off** *vt* (*debt*) borrar (como incobrable);
(*fig*) desechar por inútil; (*smash up: car*) destrozar
▸ **write out** *vt* escribir

▸ **write up** *vt* redactar
write-off ['raɪtɔf] *n* siniestro total; **the car is a ~**
el coche es pura chatarra
writer ['raɪtə'] *n* escritor(a)
writhe [raɪð] *vi* retorcerse
writing ['raɪtɪŋ] *n* escritura; (*handwriting*) letra;
(*of author*) obras; **in ~** por escrito; **to put sth in ~**
poner algo por escrito; **in my own ~** escrito por
mí; *see also* **writings**
writing paper *n* papel de escribir
writings *npl* obras
written ['rɪtn] *pp of* **write**
wrong [rɔŋ] *adj* (*wicked*) malo; (*unfair*) injusto;
(*incorrect*) equivocado, incorrecto; (*not suitable*)
inoportuno, inconveniente ▷ *adv* mal ▷ *n* mal;
(*injustice*) injusticia ▷ *vt* ser injusto con; (*hurt*)
agraviar; **the ~ answer** la respuesta incorrecta;
to be ~ (*person*) equivocarse; **it's ~ to steal,
stealing is ~** es mal robar; **you are ~ to do it**
haces mal en hacerlo; **you are ~ about that**
en eso estás equivocado; **what's ~?** ¿qué pasa?;
what's ~ with the car? ¿qué le pasa al coche?;
there's nothing ~ no pasa nada; **you have the
~ number** (*Tel*) se ha equivocado de número;
you've done it ~ lo has hecho mal; **to go ~**
(*person*) equivocarse; (*plan*) salir mal; (*machine*)
estropearse; **to be in the ~** no tener razón;
(*guilty*) tener la culpa
wrongdoer ['rɔŋduə'] *n* malhechor(a)
wrong-foot [rɔŋ'fut] *vt* (*Sport*) hacer perder el
equilibrio a; (*fig*) poner en un aprieto a
wrongful ['rɔŋful] *adj* injusto; **~ dismissal**
(*Industry*) despido improcedente
wrongly ['rɔŋlɪ] *adv* (*answer, do, count*)
incorrectamente; (*treat*) injustamente
wrote [rəut] *pt of* **write**
wrought [rɔ:t] *adj*: **~ iron** hierro forjado
wrung [rʌŋ] *pt, pp of* **wring**
WRVS *n abbr* (*Brit:* = *Women's Royal Voluntary Service*)
cuerpo de voluntarias al servicio de la comunidad
wry [raɪ] *adj* irónico
wt. *abbr* = **weight**

Xx

X, x [eks] *n* (*letter*) X, x; (*Brit Cine: formerly*) no apto para menores de 18 años; **X for Xmas** X de Xiquena; **if you earn X dollars a year** si ganas X dólares al año

X-certificate [ˈɛkssəˈtɪfɪkɪt] *adj* (*Brit: film: formerly*) no apto para menores de 18 años

Xerox® [ˈzɪərɔks] *n* (*also:* **Xerox machine**) fotocopiadora; (*photocopy*) fotocopia ▷ *vt* fotocopiar

XL *abbr* = **extra large**

Xmas [ˈɛksməs] *n abbr* = **Christmas**

X-rated [ˈeksˈreɪtɪd] *adj* (*US: film*) no apto para menores de 18 años

X-ray [ɛksˈreɪ] *n* radiografía; **X-rays** *npl* rayos X ▷ *vt* radiografiar

xylophone [ˈzaɪləfəun] *n* xilófono

Y, y [waɪ] n (letter) Y, y; **Y for Yellow**, (US) **Y for Yoke** Y de Yegua

yacht [jɔt] n yate

yachting ['jɔtɪŋ] n (sport) balandrismo

yachtsman ['jɔtsmən] n balandrista

Yank [jæŋk], **Yankee** ['jæŋkɪ] n (pej) yanqui

yank [jæŋk] vt tirar de, jalar de (LAm) ▷ n tirón

yap [jæp] vi (dog) aullar

yard [jɑːd] n patio; (US: garden) jardín; (measure) yarda; **builder's ~** almacén

yardstick ['jɑːdstɪk] n (fig) criterio, norma

yarn [jɑːn] n hilo; (tale) cuento (chino), historia

yawn [jɔːn] n bostezo ▷ vi bostezar

yawning ['jɔːnɪŋ] adj (gap) muy abierto

yd. abbr (= yard) yda

yeah [jɛə] adv (col) sí

year [jɪəʳ] n año; (Scol, Univ) curso; **this ~** este año; **last ~** el año pasado; **~ in, ~ out** año tras año; **a** or **per ~** al año; **to be 8 ~s old** tener 8 años; **she's 3 ~s old** tiene 3 años; **an eight-~-old child** un niño de ocho años (de edad); **she's in the fifth ~** está en quinto

yearly ['jɪəlɪ] adj anual ▷ adv anualmente, cada año; **twice ~** dos veces al año

yearn [jəːn] vi: **to ~ for sth** añorar algo, suspirar por algo

yeast [jiːst] n levadura

yell [jɛl] n grito, alarido ▷ vi gritar

yellow ['jɛləu] adj, n amarillo

Yellow Pages® npl páginas amarillas

yelp [jɛlp] n aullido ▷ vi aullar

yeoman ['jəumən] n: **Y~ of the Guard** alabardero de la Casa Real

yes [jɛs] adv, n sí; **to say/answer ~** decir/ contestar que sí; **to say ~ (to)** decir que sí (a), conformarse (con)

yesterday ['jɛstədɪ] adv, n ayer; **~ morning/ evening** ayer por la mañana/tarde; **all day ~** todo el día de ayer; **the day before ~** antes de ayer, anteayer

yet [jɛt] adv todavía ▷ conj sin embargo, a pesar de todo; **it is not finished ~** todavía no está acabado; **have you finished ~?** ¿has terminado ya?; **the best ~** el/la mejor hasta ahora; **as ~** hasta ahora, todavía; **there's no news as ~** todavía no se tienen noticias; **~ again** de nuevo

yew [juː] n tejo

Y-fronts® ['waɪfrʌnts] npl (Brit) calzoncillos, eslip tradicional

yield [jiːld] n producción; (Agr) cosecha; (Comm) rendimiento ▷ vt producir, dar; (profit) rendir ▷ vi rendirse, ceder; (US Aut) ceder el paso; **a ~ of 5%** un rédito del 5 por ciento

YMCA n abbr (= Young Men's Christian Association) Asociación de Jóvenes Cristianos

yob(bo) ['jɔb(bəu)] n (Brit col) gamberro

yoga ['jəugə] n yoga

yog(h)ourt, yog(h)urt ['jəugət] n yogur

yoke [jəuk] n (of oxen) yunta; (on shoulders) balancín; (fig) yugo ▷ vt (also: **yoke together**: oxen) uncir

yolk [jəuk] n yema (de huevo)

yonder ['jɔndəʳ] adv allá (a lo lejos)

yonks [jɔŋks] npl (col): **I haven't seen him for ~** hace siglos que no lo veo

you [juː] pron **1** (subject: familiar: ['familjar]) tú, vos (CAm, CS); (pl) vosotros(-as) (Esp), ustedes (LAm); (polite) usted; (pl) ustedes; **~ are very kind** eres/es etc muy amable; **~ French enjoy your food** a vosotros (or ustedes) los franceses os (or les) gusta la comida; **~ and I will go** iremos tú y yo

2 (object: direct: familiar) te; (pl) os (Esp), les (LAm); (polite) lo or le; (pl) los or les; (f) la; (pl) las; **I know ~** te/le etc conozco

3 (object: indirect: familiar) te; (pl) os (Esp), les (LAm); (polite) le; (pl) les; **I gave the letter to ~ yesterday** te/os etc di la carta ayer

4 (stressed): **I told YOU to do it** te dije a ti que lo hicieras, es a ti a quien dije que lo hicieras; see also **3, 5**

5 (after prep: NB: con +ti = contigo: familiar) ti; (pl) vosotros(-as) (Esp), ustedes (LAm); (: polite) usted; (pl) ustedes; **it's for ~** es para ti/vosotros etc

6 (comparisons: familiar) tú; (pl) vosotros(-as) (Esp), ustedes (LAm); (: polite) usted; (pl) ustedes; **she's younger than ~** es más joven que tú/vosotros etc

7 (impersonal: one): **fresh air does ~ good** el aire puro (te) hace bien; **~ never know** nunca se sabe; **~ can't do that!** ¡eso no se hace!

you'd [juːd] = **you had; you would**

you'll [juːl] = **you will; you shall**

young [jʌŋ] adj joven ▷ npl (of animal) cría; (people): **the ~** (young people) los jóvenes, la juventud; **a ~ man/lady** un(a) joven; **he's ~er**

than me es menor que yo; **he's 2 years ~er than
me** es dos años más joven que yo, tiene dos años
menos que yo; **my ~er brother** mi hermano
menor *or* pequeño; **the ~er generation** la nueva
generación

youngster ['jʌŋstə'] *n* joven

your [jɔː'] *adj* tu; (*pl*) vuestro (*Esp*), su (*Am*);
(*formal*) su; **~ house** tu *etc* casa; *see also* **my**

you're [juə'] = **you are**

yours [jɔːz] *pron* tuyo; (*pl*) vuestro (*Esp*), suyo
(*LAm*); (*formal*) suyo; **a friend of ~** un amigo tuyo
etc; *see also* **faithfully; mine; sincerely**

yourself [jɔː'sɛlf] *pron* (*reflexive*) tú mismo;
(*complement*) te; (*after prep*) tí (mismo); (*formal*)
usted mismo; (: *complement*) se; (: *after prep*) sí
(mismo); **you ~ told me** me lo dijiste tú mismo;
(all) by ~ sin ayuda de nadie, solo; *see also* **oneself**

yourselves [jɔː'sɛlvz] *pl pron* vosotros mismos
(*Esp*), ustedes mismos (*LAm*); (*after prep*) vosotros
(mismos) (*Esp*), ustedes (mismos) (*LAm*); (*formal*)
ustedes (mismos); (: *complement*) se; (: *after prep*)
sí mismos

youth [ju:θ] *n* juventud; (*young man*) (*pl* **-s**) [ju:ðz]
joven; **in my ~** en mi juventud

youth club *n* club juvenil

youthful ['ju:θful] *adj* juvenil

youth hostel *n* albergue juvenil

you've [ju:v] = **you have**

yr *abbr* (= *year*) a.

Yugoslav ['ju:gəuslɑːv] *adj, n* yugoslavo(-a)

Yugoslavia [ju:gəu'slɑːvɪə] *n* Yugoslavia

yuppie ['jʌpɪ] (*col*) *adj, n* yuppie

YWCA *n abbr* (= *Young Women's Christian Association*)
Asociación de Jóvenes Cristianas

Zz

Z, z [zɛd, US zi:] n (letter) Z, z; **Z for Zebra** Z de
  Zaragoza
zany ['zeɪnɪ] adj estrafalario
zap [zæp] vt (Comput) borrar
zeal [zi:l] n celo, entusiasmo
zebra ['zi:brə] n cebra
zebra crossing n (Brit) paso de peatones
zero ['zɪərəu] n cero; **5 degrees below** ~ 5 grados
  bajo cero
zest [zɛst] n entusiasmo; ~ **for living** brío
zigzag ['zɪgzæg] n zigzag ▷ vi zigzaguear
Zimbabwe [zɪm'bɑ:bwɪ] n Zimbabwe
Zimmer® ['zɪmə'] n (also: **Zimmer frame**)
  andador, andaderas
zinc [zɪŋk] n cinc, zinc
zip [zɪp] n (also: **zip fastener**, (US) **zipper**)
  cremallera, cierre relámpago (LAm); (energy)
energía, vigor ▷ vt (also: **zip up**) cerrar la
  cremallera de ▷ vi: **to** ~ **along to the shops** ir de
  compras volando
zip code n (US) código postal
zodiac ['zəudɪæk] n zodíaco
zombie ['zɔmbɪ] n zombi
zone [zəun] n zona
zonked [zɔŋkt] adj (col) hecho polvo
zoo [zu:] n zoo, (parque) zoológico
zoologist [zu'ɔlədʒɪst] n zoólogo(-a)
zoology [zu:'ɔlədʒɪ] n zoología
zoom [zu:m] vi: **to** ~ **past** pasar zumbando; **to** ~
  in (on sth/sb) (Phot, Cine) enfocar (algo/a algn)
  con el zoom
zoom lens n zoom
zucchini [zu:'ki:nɪ] (pl - or -**s**) (US) calabacín,
  zapallito (CS), calabacita (Méx)